WRITING SAMPLES

Writing samples in this book show you representative types of writing about literature—from initial notes to a revised, final research paper. Reading these samples along with their commentary should help you understand what is expected when your instructor asks you to write about the literature you are reading.

CRITICAL APPROACHES

This short guide to important critical approaches b
professional critics and theorists employ when the)

THE NORTON INTRODUCTION TO LITERATURE

TWELFTH EDITION

THE NORTON INTRODUCTION TO LITERATURE

TWELFTH EDITION

KELLY J. MAYS

UNIVERSITY OF NEVADA, LAS VEGAS

 W. W. NORTON & COMPANY New York, London

W. W. Norton & Company has been independent since its founding in 1923, when William Warder Norton and Mary D. Herter Norton first published lectures delivered at the People's Institute, the adult education division of New York City's Cooper Union. The firm soon expanded its program beyond the Institute, publishing books by celebrated academics from America and abroad. By mid-century, the two major pillars of Norton's publishing program—trade books and college texts—were firmly established. In the 1950s, the Norton family transferred control of the company to its employees, and today—with a staff of four hundred and a comparable number of trade, college, and professional titles published each year—W. W. Norton & Company stands as the largest and oldest publishing house owned wholly by its employees.

Editor: Spencer Richardson-Jones
Project Editor: Christine D'Antonio
Editorial Assistant: Rachel Taylor
Associate Editor: Emily Stuart
Manuscript Editor: Jude Grant
Managing Editor, College: Marian Johnson
Managing Editor, College Digital Media: Kim Yi
Production Manager: Ashley Horna
Media Editor: Carly Fraser Doria
Assistant Media Editor: Cara Folkman
Media Editorial Assistant: Ava Bramson
Marketing Manager, Literature: Kimberly Bowers
Design Director: Rubina Yeh
Book Designer: Jo Anne Metsch
Photo Editor: Evan Luberger
Photo Research: Julie Tesser
Permissions Manager: Megan Schindel
Permissions Clearer: Margaret Gorenstein
Composition: Westchester Book Group
Manufacturing: LSC Communications

Printed in the United States of America

The Library of Congress has cataloged an earlier edition as follows:
Library of Congress Cataloging-in-Publication Data
Names: Mays, Kelly J., editor.
Title: The Norton introduction to literature / [edited by] Kelly J. Mays.
Description: Twelfth edition. | New York : W. W. Norton & Company, 2016. |
Includes bibliographical references and index.
Identifiers: LCCN 2016000571 | ISBN 9780393938913 (hardcover)
Subjects: LCSH: Literature—Collections.
Classification: LCC PN6014 .N67 2016b | DDC 808.8—dc23 LC record available at http://lccn.loc.gov/2016000571

This edition: **ISBN 978-0-393-62356-7**

W. W. Norton & Company, Inc., 500 Fifth Avenue, New York, NY 10110

www.wwnorton.com

W. W. Norton & Company Ltd., 15 Carlisle Street, London W1D 3BS

3 4 5 6 7 8 9 0

Contents

Fiction

Drama

Preface for Instructors

Like its predecessors, this Twelfth Edition of *The Norton Introduction to Literature* offers in a single volume a complete course in reading literature and writing about it. A teaching anthology focused on the actual tasks, challenges, and questions typically faced by students and instructors, *The Norton Introduction to Literature* offers practical advice to help students transform their first impressions of literary works into fruitful discussions and meaningful critical essays, and it helps students and instructors together tackle the complex questions at the heart of literary study.

The Norton Introduction to Literature has been revised with an eye to providing a book that is as flexible and as useful as possible—adaptable to many different teaching styles and individual preferences—and that also conveys the excitement at the heart of literature itself.

FEATURES OF *THE NORTON INTRODUCTION TO LITERATURE*

Although this Twelfth Edition contains much that is new or refashioned, the essential features of the text have remained consistent over many editions:

Diverse selections with broad appeal

Because readings are the central component of any literature class, my most important task has been to select a rich array of appealing and challenging literary works. Among the 68 stories, 325 poems, and 15 plays in *The Norton Introduction to Literature*, readers will find selections by well-established and emerging voices alike, representing a broad range of times, places, cultural perspectives, and styles. The readings are excitingly diverse in terms of subject and style as well as authorship and national origin. In selecting and presenting literary texts, my top priorities continue to be quality as well as pedagogical relevance and usefulness. I have integrated the new with the old and the experimental with the canonical, believing that contrast and variety help students recognize and respond to the unique features of any literary work. In this way, I aim to help students and instructors alike approach the unfamiliar by way of the familiar (and vice versa).

Helpful and unobtrusive editorial matter

As always, the instructional material before and after each selection avoids dictating any particular interpretation or response, instead highlighting essential terms and concepts in order to make the literature that follows more accessible to student readers. Questions and writing suggestions help readers apply general concepts to specific readings in order to develop, articulate, refine, and defend their own responses. As in all Norton anthologies, I have annotated the works with a light hand, seeking to be informative but not interpretive.

An introduction to the study of literature

To introduce students to fiction, poetry, and drama is to open up a complex field of study with a long history. The Introduction addresses many of the questions that students may have about the nature of literature as well as the practice of literary criticism. By exploring some of the most compelling reasons for reading and writing about literature, much of the mystery about matters of method is cleared away, and I provide motivated students with a sense of the issues and opportunities that lie ahead as they study literature. As in earlier editions, I continue to encourage student fascination with particular authors and their careers, expanding upon the featured "Authors on Their Work" boxes as well as single-author chapters and albums.

Thoughtful guidance for writing about literature

The Twelfth Edition integrates opportunities for student writing at each step of the course, highlighting the mastery of skills for students at every level. "Reading, Responding, Writing" sections at the beginning of each genre unit, including a thoroughly revised opener to the poetry unit, offer students concrete advice about how to transform careful reading into productive and insightful writing. Sample questions for each work or about each element (e.g., "Questions about Character") provide exercises for answering these questions or for applying new concepts to particular works, and examples of student writing demonstrate how a student's notes on a story or poem may be developed into a response paper or an organized critical argument. New essays bring the total number of examples of student writing to seventeen.

The constructive, step-by-step approach to the writing process is thoroughly demonstrated in several chapters called "Writing about Literature." As in the chapters introducing concepts and literary selections, the first steps presented in the writing section are simple and straightforward, outlining the basic formal elements common to essays—thesis, structure, and so on. Following these steps encourages students to approach the essay both as a distinctive genre with its own elements and as an accessible form of writing with a clear purpose. From here, I walk students through the writing process: how to choose a topic, gather evidence, and develop an argument; the methods of writing a research essay; and the mechanics of effective quotation and responsible citation and documentation. New, up-to-date material on using the Internet for research has been included. Also featured is a sample research paper that has been annotated to call attention to important features of good student writing.

Even more resources for student writers are available at the free student website, LitWeb, described below.

A comprehensive approach to the contexts of literature

The Twelfth Edition not only offers expanded resources for interpreting and writing about literature, but it also extends the perspectives from which students can view particular authors and works. One of the greatest strengths of *The Norton Introduction to Literature* has been its exploration of the relation between literary texts and a variety of contexts. For several editions, "Author's Work" and "Critical Contexts" chapters have served as mini-casebooks that contain a wealth of material for in-depth, context-focused reading and writing assignments. Recent editions have also been supplemented with "Cultural Contexts" chapters that explore a cultural moment or setting.

In the Twelfth Edition I have revised and expanded the current context chapters and added an entirely new chapter on Tim O'Brien's seminal story, "The Things They Carried." Other revised context chapters include an updated chapter on Adrienne Rich, featuring work from her final collection of poetry and essays published shortly before her death, and re-edited excerpts from scholarly essays in the chapter on Sophocles's *Antigone*, as well as general revision and updates throughout each context chapter.

The "Critical Approaches" section provides an overview of contemporary critical theory and its terminology and is useful as an introduction, a refresher, or a preparation for further exploration.

A sensible and teachable organization

The accessible format of *The Norton Introduction to Literature*, which has worked so well for teachers and students for many editions, remains the same. Each genre is approached in three logical steps. Fiction, for example, is introduced by "Fiction: Reading, Responding, Writing," which treats the purpose and nature of fiction, the reading experience, and the steps one takes to begin writing about fiction. This feature is followed by the six-chapter section called "Understanding the Text," which concentrates on the genre's key elements. The third section, "Exploring Contexts" suggests ways to embrace a work of literature by considering various literary, temporal, and cultural contexts. "Reading More Fiction," the final component in the Fiction section, is a reservoir of additional readings for independent study or a different approach. The Poetry and Drama sections, in turn, follow exactly the same organizational format as Fiction.

The book's arrangement allows movement from narrower to broader frameworks, from simpler to more complex questions and issues, and mirrors the way people read—wanting to learn more as they experience more. At the same time, no chapter or section depends on any other, so that individual teachers can pick and choose which chapters or sections to assign and in what order.

Deep representation of select authors

The Norton Introduction to Literature offers a range of opportunities for in-depth study of noted authors. Author's Work chapters on Flannery O'Connor, Adrienne Rich, William Blake, and William Shakespeare in the "Exploring Contexts" sections substantively engage with multiple works by each author, allowing students to make substantive connections between works from different phases of an author's career. In addition, "albums" of multiple works by Emily Dickinson, W. B. Yeats, Pat Mora, and, new to this edition, Kevin Young allow students to explore on their own a larger sampling of each poet's work. Other chapters, such as the "Cultural and Historical Contexts" chapters, explore the historical milieu of such works as Susan Glaspell's "Jury of Her Peers," Charlotte Perkins Gilman's "The Yellow Wallpaper," and Kate Chopin's "Story of An Hour," as well as Lorraine Hansberry's *A Raisin in the Sun*. "Critical Contexts" chapters in each genre section, including Tim O'Brien's "The Things They Carried," Sylvia Plath's "Daddy," and Sophocles's *Antigone*, encourage students to delve deeper into each author's work after they have sampled the rich and varied tradition of commentary that each author has inspired.

NEW TO THE TWELFTH EDITION

Fifty-one new selections

There are nine new stories, forty new poems, and two new plays in this Twelfth Edition of *The Norton Introduction to Literature*. You will find new selections from popular and canonical writers such as Tim O'Brien, August Wilson, Toni Cade Bambara, Philip Larkin, Lucille Clifton, Langston Hughes, William Blake, Yusef Komunyakaa, Christina Rossetti, John Milton, Ray Bradbury, Sharon Olds, and Walt Whitman, as well as works by exciting newer authors such as Junot Díaz, Kevin Young, Patricia Lockwood, William Gibson, Jennifer Egan, Charlie Smith, Todd Boss, Adrienne Su, Quiara Alegría Hudes, Zadie Smith, Kim Addonizio, U. A. Fanthorpe, and C. K. Wiliams.

Significantly improved writing pedagogy

Recent editions *The Norton Introduction to Literature* greatly expanded and improved the resources for student writers, including thorough introductions to each genre in "Reading, Responding, Writing," broadened online materials, and new student essays. For the Twelfth Edition, the chapters on Writing about Literature have been completely revised to be much more focused on the essentials moves of writing and interpretation, as well as much more coverage on the kinds of writing students are most frequently assigned. In addition, four new samples of student writing for different kinds of assignments have been added to the book, bringing the total number of such samples to eighteen. More generally, throughout the Twelfth Edition I have thoroughly revised the writing prompts and suggestions.

A new Critical Context chapter on Tim O'Brien's "The Things They Carried"

"The Things They Carried" is among the most widely taught works in introductory literature courses, and, in order to offer a compelling exploration of this story in anthology, a new Critical Context chapter has been built around it. This new chapter offers a incisive, array of scholarly essays on diverse topics related to O'Brien's work, and will help spur lively classroom discussion and encourage engaging student writing.

New and revised thematic "albums"

Recognizing that many courses build their reading lists around resonant topics or themes, I have expanded in this Twelfth Edition several topic-oriented clusters of stories and poems. A new album of short stories, "The Future," features new and classic works of science fiction by Ray Bradbury, Zadie Smith, William Gibson, and Jennifer Egan. In the poetry section, two new albums—"Response, Reinterpretation, Remixing," an exploration of how poems respond and reinvent themes found in other poems and other art forms, and a new single-author album on the work of poet Kevin Young, highlighting works from his acclaimed volume *Book of Hours*—join albums on topics such as "Cross-Cultural Encounters," "Monsters," "Exploring Gender," and "The Sonnet." These albums provide students and instructors with ample opportunity to approach their reading (and the course) through a comparison of varied treatments of a common topic, setting, or subgenre.

STUDENT RESOURCES

LitWeb (digital.wwnorton.com/litweb)

Improved and expanded, this free resource offers tools that help students read and write about literature with skill and understanding:

- New Pause & Practice exercises expand on the "Writing about Literature" chapters and offer additional opportunities to practice effective writing. Seven exercises, each tied to a specific writing skill, test students on what they know, provide instruction both text and video for different learning styles, assess students on what they've learned, and give them an opportunity to apply newly strengthened skills.
- In-depth workshops feature fifty-five often-taught works from the text, all rooted in the guidance given in the "Reading, Responding, Writing" chapters. These workshops have been updated an expanded for the 12th edition and include rich embedded media to show students how literature connects with the world around them.
- Self-grading multiple-choice quizzes on sixty of the most widely taught works offer instant feedback designed to hone students' close-reading skills

INSTRUCTOR RESOURCES

Instructor's Manual

This thorough guide offers in-depth discussions of nearly all the works in the anthology as well as teaching suggestions and tips for the writing-intensive literature course.

Coursepacks for learning management systems

Available for all major learning management systems (including Blackboard, Angel, Moodle), this free and customizable resource makes the features of LitWeb and plus the Writing about Literature video series and other material available to instructors within the online framework of their choice.

Teaching Poetry: A Handbook of Exercises for Large and Small Classes (Allan J. Gedalof, University of Western Ontario)

This practical handbook offers a wide variety of innovative in-class exercises to enliven classroom discussion of poetry. Each of these flexible teaching exercises includes straightforward step-by-step guidelines and suggestions for variation.

Play DVDs

DVDs of most of the plays in the anthology are available to qualified adopters.

To obtain instructional resources, please contact your local Norton representative.

ACKNOWLEDGMENTS

In working on this book, I have been guided by teachers and students in my own and other English departments who have used this textbook and responded with comments and suggestions. Thanks to such capable help, I am hopeful that this book will continue to offer a solid and stimulating introduction to the experience of literature.

This project continually reminds me why I follow the vocation of teaching literature, which after all is a communal rather than a solitary calling. Since its inception, *The Norton Introduction to Literature* has been very much a collaborative effort. I am grateful for the opportunity to carry on the work begun by the late Carl Bain and Jerome Beaty, whose student I will always be. And I am equally indebted to my wonderful colleagues Paul Hunter and Alison Booth. Their wisdom and intelligence have had a profound effect on me, and their stamp will endure on this and all future editions of this book. I am thankful to Alison especially for the erudition, savvy, grace, and humor she brought to our partnership.

Thanks also to Jason Snart, of the College of Dupage, for his work preparing the online resources for students. As more and more instructors have integrated online materials into their teaching, users of this book have benefited from his experienced insight into teaching writing and literature, as well as his thoughtful development of exercises, quizzes, videos and more. I would also like to thank Carly Fraser Doria, emedia editor for the Twelfth Edition, as well as Kimberly Bowers, marketing manager for both the Eleventh and Twelfth Editions.

In putting together the Twelfth Edition, I have accrued many debts to friends and colleagues and to users of the Eleventh Edition who reached out to point out its mistakes, as well as successes. I am grateful for their generosity and insight, as I also am that of my wise and patient editor, Spencer Richardson-Jones. But I am also peculiarly aware this edition of more enduring and personal debts as well, which I hope it's not entirely out of place to honor here—to my mother, Lola Mays, who died in the very midst of this book's making, and to both my sister, Nelda Mays, and my husband and in-house editor, Hugh Jackson, without whom I'm not sure I would have made it through that loss, this book, or anything else. To them, much love, much thanks.

The Norton Introduction to Literature continues to thrive because so many teachers and students generously take the time to provide valuable feedback and suggestions. Thank you to all who have done so. This book is equally your making.

At the beginning of planning for the Twelfth Edition, my editors at Norton solicited the guidance of hundreds of instructors via in-depth reviews and a Web-hosted survey. The response was impressive, bordering on overwhelming; it was also immensely helpful. Thank you to those provided extensive written commentary: Julianne Altenbernd (Cypress College), Troy Appling (Florida Gateway College), Christina Bisirri (Seminole State College), Jill Channing (Mitchell Community College), Thomas Chester (Ivy Tech), Marcelle Cohen (Valencia College), Patricia Glanville (State College of Florida), Julie Gibson (Greenville Tech), Christina Grant (St. Charles Community College), Lauren Hahn (City Colleges of Chicago), Zachary Hyde (Valencia College), Brenda Jernigan (Methodist University), Mary Anne Keefer (Lord Fairfax Community College), Shari Koopman (Valencia College), Jessica Rabin (Anne Arundel Community College), Angela Rasmussen (Spokane Community College), Britnee Shandor (Lanier Technical College), Heidi Sheridan (Ocean County College), Jeff Tix (Wharton Jr. College), Bente Videbaek (Stony Brook University), Patrice Willaims (Northwest Florida State College), and Connie Youngblood (Blinn College).

Thanks also to everyone who responded to the survey online:

Sue Abbotson (Rhode Island College), Emory Abbott (Georgia Perimeter College), Mary Adams (Lincoln College-Normal), Julie Altenbernd (Cypress College), Troy Appling (Florida Gateway College), Marilyn Judith Atlas (Ohio University), Unoma Azuah (Lane College), Diann Baecker (Virginia State University), Aaron Barrell (Everett Community College), Craig Barrette (Brescia University), John Bell (American River College), Monica Berlin (Knox College), Mary Anne Bernal (San Antonio College), Jolan Bishop (Southeastern Community College), Randall Blankenship (Valencia College), Margaret Boas (Anne Arundel Community College), Andrew Bodenrader (Manhattanville College), James Borton (Coastal Carolina University), Ethel Bowden (Central Maine Community College), Amy Braziller (Red Rocks Community College), Jason Brown (Herkimer County Community College), Alissa Burger (SUNY Delhi), Michael Burns (Spokane Community College), Ryan Campbell (Front Range Community College), Anna Cancelli (Coastal Carolina Community College), Vanessa Canete-Jurado (Binghamton University), Rebecca Cash (SUNY Adirondack), Kevin Cavanaugh (Dutchess Community College), Emily Chamison (Georgia College & State University), Jill Channing (Mitchell Community College), Thomas Chester (Ivy Tech), Ann Clark (Jefferson Community College), Thomas Coakley (Mount Aloysius College), Susan Cole (Albert Magnus College), Tera Joy Cole (Idaho State University), Vicki Collins (University of South Carolina Aiken), Jonathan Cook (Durham Technical Community College), Beth Copeland (Methodist University), Bill Corby (Berkshire Community College), James Crowley (Bridgewater State University), Diane D'Amico (Allegheny College), Susan Dauer (Valencia College), Emily Dial-Driver (Rogers State

University), Lorraine DiCicco (University of Western Ontario), Christina Devlin (Montgomery College), Jess Domanico (Point University), William Donovan (Idaho State University), Bonnie Dowd (Montclair State University), Douglas Dowland (Ohio Northern University), Justine Dymond (Springfield College), Jason Evans (Prairie State College), Richard Farias (San Antonio College), Karen Feldman (Seminole State College), V. Ferretti (Westmoreland County Community College), Bradley Fest (University of Pittsburgh), Glynn-Ellen Fisichelli (Nassau Community College), Colleen Flanagan (Seminole State College of Florida), Michael Flynn (University of North Dakota), Matthew Fullerty (Chowan University), Robert Galin (University of New Mexico at Gallup), Margaret Gardineer (Felician College), Jan Geyer (Hudson Valley Community College), Seamus Gibbons (Bergen Community College), Eva Gold (Southeastern Louisiana University), Melissa Green (Ohio University Chillicothe), Frank Gruber (Bergen Community College), Lauren Hahn (City Colleges of Chicago), Rob Hale (Western Kentucky University), Nada Halloway (Manhattanville College), Melody Hargraves (St. Johns River State College), Elizabeth Harlan (Northern Virginia Community College), Stephanie Harzewski (University of New Hampshire), Lance Hawvermale (Ranger College), Catherine Heath (Victoria College), Beth Heim de Bera (Rochester Community and Technical College), Natalie Hewitt (Hope International University), Melissa Hoban (Blinn College), Charles Hood (Antelope Valley College), Trish Hopkins (Community College of Vermont), Spring Hyde (Lincoln College), Tammy Jabin (Chemeketa Community College), Kim Jacobs-Beck (University of Cincinnati Clermont College), Brenda Jerrigan (Methodist University), Kathy Johnson (SUNY Cobleskill), Darlene Johnston (Ohio Northern University), Kimberly Kaczorowski (University of Utah), Maryellen Keefe (SUNY Maritime College), Mary Anne Keefer (Lord Fairfax Community College), Caroline Kelley (Bergen Community College), Tim Kelley (Northwest-Shoals Community College), Mary Catherine Killany (Robert Morris University), Amy Kolker (Black Hawk College), Beth Kolp (Dutchess Community College), Shari Koopman (Valencia College), Jill Kronstadt (Montgomery College), Liz Langemak (La Salle University), Audrey Lapointe (Cuyamaca College), Dawn Lattin (Idaho State University), Richard Lee (Elon University), Nancy Lee-Jones (Endicott College), Sharon Levy (Northampton Community College), Erika Lin (George Mason University), Clare Little (Embry-Riddle Aeronautical University), Paulette Longmore (Essex County College), Carol Luther (Pellissippi State Community College), Sean McAuley (North Georgia Technical College), Sheila McAvey (Becker College), Kelli McBride (Seminole State College), Jim McWilliams (Dickinson State University), Vickie Melograno (Atlantic Cape Community College), Agnetta Mendoza (Nashville State Community College), David Merchant (Louisiana Tech University), Edith Miller (Angelina College), Benjamin Mitchell (Georgia College & State University), James Norman (Bridgewater State University), Angelia Northrip-Rivera (Missouri State University), James Obertino (University of Central Missouri), Elaine Ostry (SUNY Plattsburg), Michelle Paulsen (Victoria College), Russell Perkin (Saint Mary's University), Katherine Perry (Georgia Perimeter College), Thomas Pfister (Idaho State University), Gemmicka Piper (University of Iowa), Michael Podolny (Onondaga Community College), Wanda Pothier-Hill (Mt. Wachusett Community College), Gregg Pratt (SUNY Adirondack, Wilton Campus), Jonathan Purkiss (Pulaski Technical College), Jessica Rabin (Anne Arundel Community College), Elizabeth Rambo (Campbell University), Angela Rasmussen (Spokane Community College), Rhonda Ray (East Stroudsburg University), Janet Red Feather (Normandale Community College), Joan Reeves (Northeast Alabama Community College), Matthias Regan (North Central College), Elizabeth Rescher (Richard Bland College), Stephanie Roberts (Georgia Military College), Paul Robichaud (Albert Magnus College), Nancy Roche (University of Utah), Mary Rohrer-Dann (Pennsylvania State University), Michael Rottnick (Ellsworth Community College), Scott Rudd (Monroe Community College), Ernest Rufleth (Louisiana Tech University), Frank Rusciano (Rider University), Michael Sarabia (University of Iowa), Susan Scheckel (Stony Brook University), Lori Schroeder (Knox College), Britnee Shandor (Lanier Technical College), Jolie Sheffer (Bowling Green State University), Olympia Sibley, (Blinn College), Christine Sizemore (Spelman College), Chris Small (New Hampshire Technical Institute), Katherine Smit (Housatonic Community College), Whitney Smith (Miami University), Jason Snart (College of Dupage), John Snider (Montana State University- Northern), Shannon Stewart (Costal Carolina University), Susan St. Peters (Riverside City College), Michael Stubbs (Idaho State University), Patrice Suggs (Craven Community College), Joseph Sullivan (Marietta College), Heidi L. Sura (Kirtland Community College), David Susman (York County Community College), Fred Svoboda (University of Michigan), Taryne Taylor (University of Iowa), Nancy Thompson (Community College of Vermont), Rita Treutel (University of Alabama at Birmingham), Keja Valens (Salem State University), Diana Vecchio (Widener University), Bente Videbaek (Stony Brook University), Donna Waldron (Campbell University), Kent Walker (Brock University), Brandi Wallace (Wallace Community College), Valerie Wallace (City Colleges of Chicago), Maureen Walters (Vance-Granville Community College), Megan Walsh (St. Bonaventure University), Kimberly Ward (Campbell University), Catherine Welter (University of New Hampshire), Jeff Westover (Boise State University), Kathy Whitaker (East Georgia State College), Bruce Wigutow (Farmingdale State College), Jessica Wilkie (Monroe Community College), Leigh Williams (Dutchess Community College), Jenny Williams (Spartanburg Community College), Patrice Williams (Northwest Florida State College), Gregory Wilson (St. John's University), Mark WIlson (Southwestern Oregon Community College), Rita Wisdom (Tarrant County College), Martha Witt (William Paterson University), Robert Wiznura (Grant MacEwan University), Jarrell Wright (University of Pittsburgh), Kelly Yacobucci (SUNY Cobleskill), Kidane Yohannes (Burlington County College), Brian Yost (Texas A&M University), Connie Youngblood (Blinn College), Susan Youngs (Southern New Hampshire University), and Jason Ziebart (Central Carolina Community College).

Introduction

In the opening chapters of Charles Dickens's novel *Hard Times* (1854), the aptly named Thomas Gradgrind warns the teachers and pupils at his "model" school to avoid using their imaginations. "Teach these boys and girls nothing but Facts. Facts alone are wanted in life," exclaims Mr. Gradgrind. To press his point, Mr. Gradgrind asks "girl number twenty," Sissy Jupe, the daughter of a circus performer, to define a horse. When she cannot, Gradgrind turns to Bitzer, a pale, spiritless boy who "looked as though, if he were cut, he would bleed white." A "model" student of this "model" school, Bitzer gives exactly the kind of definition to satisfy Mr. Gradgrind:

> Quadruped. Graminivorous. Forty teeth, namely, twenty-four grinders, four eye-teeth, and twelve incisive. Sheds coat in spring; in marshy countries, sheds hoofs.

Anyone who has any sense of what a horse is rebels against Bitzer's lifeless picture of that animal and against the "Gradgrind" view of reality. As these first scenes of *Hard Times* lead us to expect, in the course of the novel the fact-grinding Mr. Gradgrind learns that human beings cannot live on facts alone; that it is dangerous to stunt the faculties of imagination and feeling; that, in the words of one of the novel's more lovable characters, "People must be amused." Through the downfall of an exaggerated enemy of the imagination, Dickens reminds us why we like and even *need* to read literature.

WHAT IS LITERATURE?

But what is literature? Before you opened this book, you probably could guess that it would contain the sorts of stories, poems, and plays you have encountered in English classes or in the literature section of a library or bookstore. But why are some written works called *literature* whereas others are not? And who gets to decide? *The American Heritage Dictionary of the English Language* offers a number of definitions for the word *literature*, one of which is "imaginative or creative writing, especially of recognized artistic value." In this book, we adopt a version of that definition by focusing on fictional stories, poems, and plays—the three major kinds (or **genres**) of "imaginative or creative writing" that form the heart of literature as it has been taught in schools and universities for over a century. Many of the works we have chosen to include are already ones "of recognized artistic value" and thus belong to what scholars call the **canon**, a select, if much-debated and ever-evolving, list of the most highly and widely esteemed works. Though quite a few of the literary texts we include are simply too new to have earned that status, they, too, have already drawn praise, and some have even generated controversy.

Certainly it helps to bear in mind what others have thought of a literary work. Yet one of this book's primary goals is to get you to think for yourself, as well as communicate with others, about what "imaginative writing" and "artistic value" are or might be and thus about what counts as literature. What makes a story or poem different from an essay, a newspaper editorial, or a technical manual? For that matter, what makes a published, canonical story like Herman Melville's BARTLEBY, THE SCRIVENER both like and unlike the sorts of stories we tell each other every day? What about so-called *oral literature*, such as the fables and folktales that circulated by word of mouth for hundreds of years before they were ever written down? Or published works such as comic strips and graphic novels that rely little, if at all, on the written word? Or Harlequin romances, television shows, and the stories you collaborate in making when you play a video game? Likewise, how is Shakespeare's poem MY MISTRESS'S EYES ARE NOTHING LIKE THE SUN both like and unlike a verse you might find in a Hallmark card or even a jingle in a mouthwash commercial?

Today, literature departments offer courses in many of these forms of expression, expanding the realm of literature far beyond the limits of the dictionary definition. An essay, a song lyric, a screenplay, a supermarket romance, a novel by Toni Morrison or William Faulkner, and a poem by Walt Whitman or Emily Dickinson—each may be read and interpreted in *literary ways* that yield insight and pleasure. What makes the literary way of reading different from pragmatic reading is, as scholar Louise Rosenblatt explains, that it does not focus "on what will remain [. . .] *after* the reading—the information to be acquired, the logical solution to a problem, the actions to be carried out," but rather on "what happens

during [. . .] reading." The difference between pragmatic and literary reading, in other words, resembles the difference between a journey that is only about reaching a destination and one that is just as much about fully experiencing the ride.

In the pages of this book, you will find cartoons, an excerpt from a graphic novel, song lyrics, folktales, and stories and plays that have spawned movies. Through this inclusiveness, we do not intend to suggest that there are no distinctions among these various forms of expression or between a good story, poem, or play and a bad one; rather, we want to get you thinking, talking, and writing both about what the key differences and similarities among these forms are and what makes one work a better example of its genre than another. Sharpening your skills at these peculiarly intensive and responsive sorts of reading and interpretation is a primary purpose of this book and of most literature courses.

Another goal of inclusiveness is simply to remind you that literature doesn't just belong in a textbook or a classroom, even if textbooks and classrooms are essential means for expanding your knowledge of the literary terrain and of the concepts and techniques essential to thoroughly enjoying and understanding a broad range of literary forms. You may or may not be the kind of person who always takes a novel when you go to the beach or secretly writes a poem about your experience when you get back home. You may or may not have taken a literature course (or courses) before. Yet you already have a good deal of literary experience and even expertise, as well as much more to discover about literature. A major aim of this book is to make you more conscious of how and to what end you might use the tools you already possess and to add many new ones to your tool belt.

WHAT DOES LITERATURE DO?

One quality that may well differentiate stories, poems, and plays from other kinds of writing is that they help us move beyond and probe beneath abstractions by giving us concrete, vivid particulars. Rather than talking *about* things, they bring them to life for us by *representing* experience, and so they *become* an experience for us—one that engages our emotions, our imagination, and all of our senses, as well as our intellects. As the British poet and critic Matthew Arnold put it more than a century ago, "The interpretations of science do not give us this intimate sense of objects as the interpretations of poetry give it; they appeal to a limited faculty, and not to the whole man. It is not Linnaeus [. . .] who gives us the true sense of animals, or water, or plants, who seizes their secret for us, who makes us participate in their life; it is Shakespeare [. . .] Wordsworth [. . .] Keats."

To test Arnold's theory, compare the *American Heritage Dictionary*'s rather dry definition of *literature* with the following poem, in which John Keats describes his first encounter with a specific literary work—George Chapman's translation of the *Iliad* and the *Odyssey*, two **epics** by the ancient Greek poet Homer.

JOHN KEATS

On First Looking into Chapman's Homer[1]

Much have I traveled in the realms of gold,
And many goodly states and kingdoms seen;
Round many western islands have I been
Which bards in fealty to Apollo[2] hold.
Oft of one wide expanse had I been told
That deep-browed Homer ruled as his demesne;
Yet did I never breathe its pure serene[3]
Till I heard Chapman speak out loud and bold:
Then felt I like some watcher of the skies
When a new planet swims into his ken;[4]
Or like stout Cortez[5] when with eagle eyes
He stared at the Pacific—and all his men
Looked at each other with a wild surmise—
Silent, upon a peak in Darien.

1816

Keats makes us *see* literature as a "wide expanse" by greatly developing this **metaphor** and complementing it with **similes** likening reading to the sighting of a "new planet" and the first glimpse of an undiscovered ocean. More important, he shows us what literature means and why it matters by allowing us to share with him the subjective experience of reading and the complex sensations it inspires—the dizzying exhilaration of discovery; the sense of power, accomplishment, and pride that comes of achieving something difficult; the wonder we feel in those rare moments when a much-anticipated experience turns out to be even greater than we had imagined it would be.

It isn't the definitions of words alone that bring this experience to life for us as we read Keats's poem, but also their sensual qualities—the way the words look, sound, and even feel in our mouths because of the particular way they are put together on the page. The sensation of excitement—of a racing heart and mind—is reproduced *in* us as we read the poem. For example, notice how the lines in the middle run into each other, but then Keats forces us to slow down at the poem's end—stopped short by that dash and comma in the poem's final lines, just as Cortez and his men are when they reach the edge of the known world and peer into what lies beyond.

WHAT ARE THE GENRES OF LITERATURE?

The conversation that is literature, as well as the conversation about literature, invites all comers, requiring neither a visa nor a special license of any kind. Yet literary studies, like all disciplines, has developed its own terminology and its own

1. George Chapman's were among the most famous Renaissance translations of Homer; he completed his *Iliad* in 1611, his *Odyssey* in 1616. Keats wrote the sonnet after being led to Chapman by a former teacher and reading the *Iliad* all night long.

2. Greek god of poetry and music. *Fealty*: literally, the loyalty owed by a vassal to his feudal lord.

3. Atmosphere.

4. Range of vision; awareness.

5. Actually, Balboa; he first viewed the Pacific from Darien, in Panama.

systems of classification. Helping you understand and effectively use both is a major focus of this book; especially important terms appear in bold throughout and are defined in a glossary at the back.

Some essential literary terms are common, everyday words used in a special way in the conversation about literature. A case in point, perhaps, is the term *literary criticism*, as well as the closely related term *literary critic*. Despite the usual connotations of the word *criticism*, literary criticism is called *criticism* not because it is negative or corrective but rather because those who write criticism ask searching, analytical, "critical" questions about the works they read. Literary criticism is both the process of interpreting and commenting on literature and the result of that process. If you write an essay on the play *Hamlet*, the poetry of John Keats, or the development of the short story in the 1990s, you engage in literary criticism, and by writing the essay, you've become a literary critic.

Similarly, when we classify works of literature, we use terms that may be familiar to you but have specific meanings in a literary context. All academic disciplines have systems of classification, or taxonomies, as well as jargon. Biologists, for example, classify all organisms into a series of ever-smaller, more specific categories: *kingdom*, *phylum* or *division*, *class*, *order*, *family*, *genus*, and *species*. Classification and comparison are just as essential in the study of literature. We expect a poem to work in a certain way, for example, when we know from the outset that it *is* a poem and not, say, a factual news report or a short story. And—whether consciously or not—we compare it, as we read, to other poems we've read in the past. If we know, further, that the poem was first published in eighteenth-century Japan, we expect it to work differently from one that appeared in the latest *New Yorker*. Indeed, we often choose what to read, just as we choose what movie to see, based on the "class" or "order" of book or movie we like or what we are in the mood for that day—horror or comedy, action or science fiction.

As these examples suggest, we generally tend to categorize literary works in two ways: (1) on the basis of contextual factors, especially historical and cultural context—that is, when, by whom, and where it was produced (as in *nineteenth-century literature*, *the literature of the Harlem Renaissance*, *American literature*, or *African American literature*)—and (2) on the basis of formal textual features. For the latter type of classification, the one we focus on in this book, the key term is *genre*, which simply means, as the *Oxford English Dictionary* tells us, "A particular style or category of works of art; esp. a type of literary work characterized by a particular form, style, or purpose."

Applied rigorously, *genre* refers to the largest categories around which this book is organized—**fiction**, **poetry**, and **drama** (as well as **nonfiction** prose). The word *subgenre* applies to smaller divisions within a genre, and the word *kind* to divisions within a subgenre. *Subgenres* of fiction include the **novel**, the **novella**, and the **short story**. *Kinds* of novels, in turn, include things like the **bildungsroman** or the epistolary novel. Similarly, important subgenres of nonfiction include the essay, as well as **biography** and autobiography; a memoir is a particular kind of autobiography, and so on.

However, the terms of literary criticism are not so fixed or so consistently, rigorously used as biologists' are. You will often see the word *genre* applied both much more narrowly—referring to the novel, for example, or even to a kind of novel such as the epistolary novel or the historical novel.

The way we classify a work depends on which aspects of its form or style we concentrate on, and categories may overlap. When we divide fiction, for example, into the subgenres novel, novella, and short story, we take the length of the works as the salient aspect. (Novels are much longer than short stories.) But other fictional subgenres—detective fiction, **gothic fiction**, **historical fiction**, science fiction, and even **romance**—are based on the types of **plots**, **characters**, **settings**, and so on that are customarily featured in these works. These latter categories may include works from all the other, length-based categories. There are, after all, gothic novels (think Stephenie Meyer), as well as gothic short stories (think Edgar Allan Poe).

A few genres even cut across the boundaries dividing poetry, fiction, drama, and nonfiction. A prime example is **satire**—any literary work (whether poem, play, fiction, or nonfiction) "in which prevailing vices and follies are held up to ridicule" (*Oxford English Dictionary*). Examples of satire include poems such as Alexander Pope's *Dunciad* (1728); plays, movies, and television shows, from Molière's *Tartuffe* (1664) to Stanley Kubrick's *Dr. Strangelove* (1964) to *South Park* and *The Daily Show*; works of fiction like Jonathan Swift's *Gulliver's Travels* (1726) and Voltaire's *Candide* (1759); and works of nonfiction such as Swift's "A Modest Proposal" (1729) and Ambrose Bierce's *The Devil's Dictionary* (1906). Three other major genres that cross the borders between fiction, poetry, drama, and nonfiction are **parody**, **pastoral**, and romance.

Individual works can thus belong simultaneously to multiple generic categories or observe some **conventions** of a genre without being an example of that genre in any simple or straightforward way. The Old English poem *Beowulf* is an **epic** and, because it's written in verse, a poem. Yet because (like all epics) it narrates a story, it is also a work of fiction in the more general sense of that term.

Given this complexity, the system of literary genres can be puzzling, especially to the uninitiated. Used well, however, classification schemes are among the most essential and effective tools we use to understand and enjoy just about everything, including literature.

WHY READ LITERATURE?

Because there has never been and never will be absolute, lasting agreement about where exactly the boundaries between one literary genre and another should be drawn or even about what counts as literature at all, it might be more useful from the outset to focus on *why* we look at particular forms of expression.

Over the ages, people have sometimes dismissed *all* literature or at least certain genres as a luxury, a frivolous pastime, even a sinful indulgence. Plato famously banned poetry from his ideal republic on the grounds that it tells beautiful lies that "feed and water our passions" rather than our reason. Thousands of years later, the influential eighteenth-century philosopher Jeremy Bentham decried the "magic art" of literature as doing a good deal of "mischief" by "stimulating our passions" and "exciting our prejudices." One of Bentham's contemporaries—a minister—blamed the rise of immorality, irreligion, and even prostitution on the increasing popularity of that particular brand of literature called the novel.

Today, many Americans express their sense of literature's insignificance by simply not reading it: The 2004 government report *Reading at Risk* indicates that less than half of U.S. adults read imaginative literature, with the sharpest declines occurring among the youngest age groups. Even if they very much enjoy reading on their own, many contemporary U.S. college students nonetheless hesitate to study or major in literature for fear that their degree won't provide them with marketable credentials, knowledge, or skills.

Yet the enormous success of *The Hunger Games* trilogy and the proliferation of reading groups are only two of many signs that millions of people continue to find both reading literature and discussing it with others to be enjoyable, meaningful, even essential activities. English thrives as a major at most colleges and universities, almost all of which require undergraduates majoring in other areas to take at least one course in literature. (Perhaps that's why you are reading this book!) Schools of medicine, law, and business are today *more* likely to require their students to take literature courses than they were in past decades, and they continue to welcome literature majors as applicants, as do many corporations. So why do so many people read and study literature, and why do schools encourage and even require students to do so? Even if we know what literature is, what does it *do* for us? What is its value?

There are, of course, as many answers to such questions as there are readers. For centuries, a standard answer has been simply that imaginative literature provides a unique brand of "instruction and delight." John Keats's ON LOOKING INTO CHAPMAN'S HOMER illustrates some of the many forms such delight can take. Some kinds of imaginative writing offer us the delight of immediate escape, but imaginative writing that is more difficult to read and understand than a Harry Potter or Twilight novel offers escape of a different and potentially more instructive sort, liberating us from the confines of our own time, place, and social milieu, as well as our habitual ways of thinking, feeling, and looking at the world. In this way, a story, poem, or play can satisfy our desire for broader experience—including the sorts of experience we might be unable or unwilling to endure in real life. We can learn what it might be like to grow up on a Canadian fox farm or to clean ashtrays in the Singapore airport. We can travel back into the past, experiencing war from the perspective of a soldier watching his comrade die or of prisoners suffering in a Nazi labor camp. We can journey into the future or into universes governed by entirely different rules than our own. Perhaps we yearn for such knowledge because we can best come to understand our own identities and outlooks by leaping over the boundaries that separate us from other selves and worlds.

Keats's friend and fellow poet Percy Bysshe Shelley argued that literature increases a person's ability to make such leaps, to "imagine intensely and comprehensively" and "put himself in the place of another and of many othe[r]" people in order "to be greatly good." Shelley meant "good" in a moral sense, reasoning that the ability both to accurately imagine and to truly *feel* the human consequences of our actions is the key to ethical behavior. But universities and professional schools today also define this "good" in distinctly pragmatic ways. In virtually any career you choose, you will need to interact positively and productively with both coworkers and clients, and in today's increasingly globalized world, you will need to learn to deal effectively and empathetically with people vastly different from yourself. At the very least, literature written by people from various backgrounds and depicting various places, times, experiences, and feelings will give you some understanding of how others' lives and worldviews may differ from your own—or how they may be very much the same.

Similarly, our rapidly changing world and economy require intellectual flexibility, adaptability, and ingenuity, making ever more essential the human knowledge, general skills, and habits of mind developed through the study of literature. Literature explores issues and questions relevant in any walk of life. Yet rather than offering us neat or comforting solutions and answers, literature enables us to experience difficult situations and human conundrums in all their complexity and to look at them from various points of view. In so doing, it invites us sometimes to question conventional thinking and sometimes to see its wisdom, even as it helps us imagine altogether new possibilities.

Finally, literature awakens us to the richness and complexity of language—our primary tool for engaging with, understanding, and shaping the world around us. As we read more and more, seeing how different writers use language to help us feel their joy, pain, love, rage, or laughter, we begin to recognize the vast range of possibilities for self-expression. Writing and discussion in turn give us invaluable practice in discovering, expressing, and defending our own nuanced, often contradictory thoughts about both literature and life. The study of literature enhances our command of language and our sensitivity to its effects and meanings in every form or medium, providing interpretation and communication skills especially crucial in our information age. By learning to appreciate and articulate what the language of a story, poem, a play, or an essay does to us and by considering how it affects others, we also learn much about what we can do with language.

What We Do with Literature: Three Tips

1. *Take a literary work on its own terms.* Adjust to the work; don't make the work adjust to you. Be prepared to hear things you do not want to hear. Not all works are about your ideas, nor will they always present emotions you want to feel. But be tolerant and listen to the work first; later you can explore the ways you do or don't agree with it.
2. *Assume there is a reason for everything.* Writers do make mistakes, but when a work shows some degree of verbal control it is usually safest to assume that the writer chose each word carefully; if the choice seems peculiar, you may be missing something. Try to account for everything in a work, see what kind of sense you can make of it, and figure out a coherent pattern that explains the text as it stands.
3. *Remember that literary texts exist in time, and times change.* Not only the meanings of words, but whole ways of looking at the universe vary in different ages. Consciousness of time works two ways: Your knowledge of history provides a context for reading the work, and the work may modify your notion of a particular age.

WHY STUDY LITERATURE?

You may already feel the power and pleasure to be gained from a sustained encounter with challenging reading. Then why not simply enjoy it in solitude, on your own free time? Why take a course in literature? Literary study, like all disciplines, has developed its own terminology and its own techniques. Some knowledge and understanding of both can greatly enhance our personal appreciation of literature and our conversations with others about it. Literature also has a context and a history, and learning something about them can make all the difference in the amount and kind of pleasure and insight you derive from literature. By reading and discussing different genres of literature, as well as works from varied times and places, you may well come to appreciate and even love works that you might never have discovered or chosen to read on your own or that you might have disliked or misunderstood if you did.

Most important, writing about works of literature and discussing them with your teachers and other students will give you practice in analyzing literature in greater depth and in considering alternative views of both the works themselves and the situations and problems the works explore. A clear understanding of the aims and designs of a story, poem, or play never falls like a bolt from the blue. Instead, it emerges from a process that involves trying to put into words *how* and *why* this work had such an effect on you and, just as important, responding to what others say or write about it. Literature itself is a vast, ongoing, ever-evolving conversation in which we most fully participate when we enter into actual conversation with others.

As you engage in this conversation, you will notice that interpretation is always variable, always open to discussion. A great diversity of interpretations might suggest that the discussion is pointless. On the contrary, that's when the discussion gets most interesting. Because there is no single, straight, paved road to an understanding of a literary text, you can explore a variety of blazed trails and less-traveled paths. In sharing your own interpretations, tested against your peers' responses and guided by your instructor's or other critics' expertise, you will hone your skills at both interpretation and communication. After the intricate and interactive process of interpretation, you will find that the work has changed when you read it again. What we do with literature alters what it does to us.

FICTION

James Baldwin

FICTION
Reading, Responding, Writing

Stories are a part of daily life in every culture. Stories are what we tell when we return from vacation or survive an accident or illness. They help us make sense of growing up or growing old, of a hurricane or a war, of the country and world we live in. In conversations, a story may be invited by the listener ("What did you do last night?") or initiated by the teller ("Guess what I saw when I was driving home!"). We assume such stories are true, or at least that they are meant to describe an experience honestly. Of course, many of the stories we encounter daily, from jokes to online games to television sitcoms to novels and films, are intended to be **fiction**—that is, stories or narratives about imaginary persons and events. Every story, however, whether a news story, sworn testimony, idle gossip, or a fairy tale, is always a version of events told from a particular perspective (or several), and it may be incomplete, biased, or just plain made up. As we listen to others' stories, we keep alert to the details, which make the stories rich and entertaining. But we also need to spend considerable time and energy making sure that we accurately interpret what we hear: We ask ourselves who is telling the story, why the story is being told, and whether we have all the information we need to understand it fully.

Even newspaper articles, which are supposed to tell true stories—the facts of what actually happened—may be open to such interpretation. Take as an example the following article, which appeared in the *New York Times* on January 1, 1920:

> **_ACCUSED WIFE KILLS HER ALLEGED LOVER_**
>
> **_Cumberland (Md.) Woman Becomes Desperate When Her Husband Orders Her from Home._**
>
> *Special to The New York Times.*
>
> CUMBERLAND, Md., Dec. 31.–Accused by her husband of unfaithfulness, Mrs. Kate Uhl, aged 25, this morning stabbed to death Bryan Pownall, who she alleged was the cause of the estrangement with her husband, Mervin Uhl.
>
> Mrs. Uhl, who is the mother of three children, denies her husband's charge of misconduct with Pownall, asserting that the latter forced his attentions on her by main physical strength against her will.
>
> The stabbing this morning came as a dramatic sequel to the woman's dilemma after she had been ordered to leave her home. Mrs. Uhl summoned Pownall after her husband had gone to work this morning, and according to her story begged him to tell her husband that she, Mrs. Uhl, was not to blame. This Pownall refused to do, but again tried to make love to her, Mrs. Uhl said. When Pownall sought to kiss her Mrs. Uhl seized a thin-bladed butcher knife and stabbed the man to the heart, she admitted.

The report's appearance in a reliable newspaper; its identification of date, location, and other information; and the legalistic adjectives "accused" and "alleged" suggest that it strives to be accurate and objective. But given the distance between us and the events described here, it's also easy to imagine this chain of events being recounted in a play, murder mystery, Hollywood film, or televised trial. In other words, this news story is still fundamentally a *story.* Note that certain points of view are better represented than others and certain details are highlighted, as might be the case in a novel or short story. The news item is based almost entirely on what Kate Uhl asserts, and even the subtitle, "Woman Becomes Desperate," plays up the "dramatic sequel to the woman's dilemma." We don't know what Mervin Uhl said when he allegedly accused his wife and turned her out of the house, and Bryan Pownall, the murdered man, never had a chance to defend himself. Presumably, the article reports accurately the husband's accusation of adultery and the wife's accusation of rape, but we have no way of knowing whose accusations are true.

Our everyday interpretation of the stories we hear from various sources—including other people, television, newspapers, and advertisements—has much in common with the interpretation of short stories such as those in this anthology. In fact, you'll probably discover that the processes of reading, responding to, and writing about stories are already somewhat familiar to you. Most readers already know, for instance, that they should pay close attention to seemingly trivial details; they should ask questions and find out more about any matters of fact that seem mysterious, odd, or unclear. Most readers are well aware that words can have several meanings and that there are alternative ways to tell a story. How would someone else have told the story? What are the storyteller's perspective and motives? What is the context of the tale—for instance, when is it supposed to have taken place and what was the occasion of telling it? These and other questions from our experience of everyday storytelling are equally relevant in reading fiction. Similarly, we can usually tell in reading a story or hearing it whether it is supposed to make us laugh, shock us, or provoke some other response.

TELLING STORIES: INTERPRETATION

Everyone has a unique story to tell. In fact, many stories are about this difference or divergence among people's interpretations of reality. A number of the stories in this anthology explore issues of storytelling and interpretation.

Consider a well-known tale, "The Blind Men and the Elephant," a Buddhist story over two thousand years old. Like other stories that have been transmitted orally, this one exists in many versions. Here's one way of telling it:

The Elephant in the Village of the Blind

Once there was a village high in the mountains in which everyone was born blind. One day a traveler arrived from far away with many fine things to sell and many tales to tell. The villagers asked, "How did you travel so far and so high carrying so much?" The traveler said, "On my elephant." "What is an elephant?" the villagers asked, having never even heard of such an animal in their remote mountain village. "See for yourself," the traveler replied.

The elders of the village were a little afraid of the strange-smelling creature that took up so much space in the middle of the village square. They could hear it breathing and munching on hay, and feel its slow, swaying movements disturbing the air around them. First one elder reached out and felt its flapping ear. "An elephant is soft but tough, and flexible, like a leather fan." Another grasped its back leg. "An elephant is a rough, hairy pillar." An old woman took hold of a tusk and gasped, "An elephant is a cool, smooth staff." A young girl seized the tail and declared, "An elephant is a fringed rope." A boy took hold of the trunk and announced, "An elephant is a water pipe." Soon others were stroking its sides, which were furrowed like a dry plowed field, and others determined that its head was an overturned washing tub attached to the water pipe.

At first each villager argued with the others on the definition of the elephant, as the traveler watched in silence. Two elders were about to come to blows about a fan that could not possibly be a pillar. Meanwhile the elephant patiently enjoyed the investigations as the cries of curiosity and angry debate mixed in the afternoon sun. Soon someone suggested that a list could be made of all the parts: the elephant had four pillars, one tub, two fans, a water pipe, and two staffs, and was covered in tough, hairy leather or dried mud. Four young mothers, sitting on a bench and comparing impressions, realized that the elephant was in fact an enormous, gentle ox with a stretched nose. The traveler agreed, adding only that it was also a powerful draft horse and that if they bought some of his wares for a good price he would be sure to come that way again in the new year.

• • •

The different versions of such a tale, like the different descriptions of the elephant, alter its meaning. Changing any aspect of the story will inevitably change how it works and what it means to the listener or reader. For example, most versions of this story feature not an entire village of blind people (as this version does), but a small group of blind men who claim to be wiser than their sighted neighbors. These blind men quarrel endlessly because none of them can see; none can put together all the evidence of all their senses or all the elephant's various parts to create a whole. Such traditional versions of the story criticize people who are too proud of what they think they know; these versions imply that sighted people would know better what an elephant is. However, other versions of the tale, like the one above, are set in an imaginary "country" of the blind. This setting changes the emphasis of the story from the errors of a few blind wise men to the value and the insufficiency of *any* one person's perspective. For though it's clear that the various members of the community in this version will never agree entirely on one interpretation of (or story about) the elephant, they do not let themselves get bogged down in endless dispute. Instead they compare and combine their various stories and "readings" in order to form a more satisfying, holistic understanding of the wonder in their midst. Similarly, listening to others' different interpretations of stories, based on their different perspectives, can enhance your experience of a work of literature and your skill in responding to new works.

Just as stories vary depending on who is telling them, so their meaning varies depending on who is responding to them. In the elephant story, the villagers pay attention to what the tail or the ear feels like, and then they draw on comparisons to what they already know. But ultimately, the individual interpretations of the elephant depend on what previous experiences each villager brings to bear (of pillars, water pipes, oxen, and dried mud, for example), and also on where (quite literally) he or she stands in relation to the elephant. In the same way, readers participate in re-creating a story as they interpret it. When you read a story for the first time, your response will be informed by other stories you have heard and read as well as your expectations for this kind of story. To grapple with what is new in any story, start by observing one part at a time and gradually trying to understand how those parts work together to form a whole. As you make sense of each new piece of the picture, you adjust your expectations about what is yet to come. When you have read and grasped it as fully as possible, you may share your interpretation with other readers, discussing different ways of seeing the story. Finally, you might express your reflective understanding in writing—in a sense, telling *your* story about the work.

Questions about the Elements of Fiction

- Expectations: What do you expect?
  - from the title? from the first sentence or paragraph?
  - after the first events or interactions of characters?
  - as the **conflict** is resolved?
- What happens in the story? (See ch. 1.)
  - Do the characters or the situation change from the beginning to the end?
  - Can you summarize the **plot**? Is it a recognizable kind or **genre** of story?
- How is the story narrated? (See ch. 2.)
  - Is the **narrator** identified as a character?
  - Is it narrated in the past or present tense?
  - Is it narrated in the first, second, or third person?
  - Do you know what every character is thinking, or only some characters, or none?
- Who are the **characters**? (See ch. 3.)
  - Who is the **protagonist**(s) (hero, heroine)?
  - Who is the **antagonist**(s) (villain, opponent, obstacle)?
  - Who are the other characters? What is their role in the story?
  - Do your expectations change with those of the characters, or do you know more or less than each of the characters?
- What is the **setting** of the story? (See ch. 4.)
  - When does the story take place?
  - Where does it take place?
  - Does the story move from one setting to another? Does it move in one direction only or back and forth in time and place?
- What do you notice about how the story is written?
  - What is the **style** of the prose? Are the sentences and the vocabulary simple or complex?
  - Are there any **images**, **figures of speech** or **symbols**? (See ch. 5.)
  - What is the **tone** or mood? Does the reader feel sad, amused, worried, curious?
- What does the story mean? Can you express its **theme** or themes? (See ch. 6.)
  - Answers to these big questions may be found in many instances in your answers to the previous questions. The story's meaning or theme depends on all its features.

READING AND RESPONDING TO FICTION

When imaginary events are acted out onstage or onscreen, our experience of those events is that of being a witness to them. In contrast, prose fiction, whether oral or written, is relayed to us by someone. Reading it is more like hearing what happened after the fact than witnessing it before our very eyes. The teller, or **narrator**, of fiction addresses a listener or reader, often referred to as the audience. How much or how little we know about the characters and what they say or do depends on what a narrator tells us.

You should read a story attentively, just as you would listen attentively to someone telling a story out loud. This means limiting distractions and interruptions; you should take a break from social networking and obtrusive music. Literary prose, as well as poetry, works with the sounds as well as meanings of words, just as film works with music and sound as well as images. Be prepared to mark up the text and to make notes.

While reading and writing, you should always have a good college-level dictionary on hand so that you can look up any unfamiliar terms. In the era of the Internet it's especially easy to learn more about any word or concept, and doing so can help enrich your reading and writing. Another excellent resource is the *Oxford English Dictionary*, available in the reference section of most academic libraries or on their websites, which reveals the wide range of meanings words have had over time. Words in English always have a long story to tell because over the centuries so many languages have contributed to our current vocabulary. It's not uncommon for meanings to overlap or even reverse themselves.

The following short short story is a contemporary work. As in THE ELEPHANT IN THE VILLAGE OF THE BLIND, this narrator gives us a minimal amount of information, merely observing the characters' different perceptions and interpretations of things they see during a cross-country car trip. As you read the story, pay attention to your expectations, drawing on your personal experience as well as such clues as the title; the characters' opinions, behavior, and speech; specifics of setting (time and place); and any repetitions or changes. When and how does the story begin to challenge and change your initial expectations? You can use the questions above to guide your reading of any story and help you focus on some of its important features.

LINDA BREWER
20/20

By the time they reached Indiana, Bill realized that Ruthie, his driving companion, was incapable of theoretical debate. She drove okay, she went halves on gas, etc., but she refused to argue. She didn't seem to know how. Bill was used to East Coast women who disputed everything he said, every step of the way. Ruthie stuck to simple observation, like "Look, cows." He chalked it up to the fact that she was from rural Ohio and thrilled to death to be anywhere else.

She didn't mind driving into the setting sun. The third evening out, Bill rested his eyes while she cruised along making the occasional announcement.

"Indian paintbrush. A golden eagle."

Miles later he frowned. There was no Indian paintbrush, that he knew of, near Chicago.

The next evening, driving, Ruthie said, "I never thought I'd see a Bigfoot in 5
real life." Bill turned and looked at the side of the road streaming innocently out behind them. Two red spots winked back—reflectors nailed to a tree stump.

"Ruthie, I'll drive," he said. She stopped the car and they changed places in the light of the evening star.

"I'm so glad I got to come with you," Ruthie said. Her eyes were big, blue, and capable of seeing wonderful sights. A white buffalo near Fargo. A UFO above Twin Falls. A handsome genius in the person of Bill himself. This last vision came to her in Spokane and Bill decided to let it ride.

1996

• • •

SAMPLE WRITING: ANNOTATION AND NOTES ON "20/20"

Now re-read the story, along with the brief note one reader made in the margins, based on the questions in the box on page 15. The reader then expanded these annotations into longer, more detailed notes. These notes could be organized and expanded into a response paper on the story. Some of your insights might even form the basis for a longer essay on one of the elements of the story.

Like "20/20 hindsight" or perfect vision? Also like the way Bill and Ruthie go 50/50 on the trip, and see things in two different ways.

20/20

By the time they reached Indiana, Bill realized that Ruthie, his driving companion, was incapable of theoretical debate. She drove okay, she went halves on gas, etc., but she refused to argue. She didn't seem to know how. Bill was used to East Coast women who disputed everything he said, every step of the way. Ruthie stuck to simple observation, like "Look, cows." He chalked it up to the fact that she was from rural Ohio and thrilled to death to be anywhere else.

Bill's doubts about Ruthie. Is he reliable? Does she "refuse" or not "know how" to argue? What's her view of him?

Bill's keeping score; maybe Ruthie's nicer, or has better eyesight. She notices things.

She didn't mind driving into the setting sun. The third evening out, Bill rested his eyes while she cruised along making the occasional announcement.

"Indian paintbrush. A golden eagle."

Miles later he frowned. There was no Indian paintbrush, that he knew of, near Chicago.

The next evening, driving, Ruthie said, "I never thought I'd see a Bigfoot in real life." Bill turned and looked at the side of the road streaming innocently out behind them. Two red spots winked back—reflectors nailed to a tree stump.

"Ruthie, I'll drive," he said. She stopped the car and they changed places in the light of the evening star.

"I'm so glad I got to come with you," Ruthie said. Her eyes were big, blue, and capable of seeing wonderful sights. A white buffalo near Fargo. A UFO above Twin Falls. A handsome genius in the person of Bill himself. This last vision came to her in Spokane and Bill decided to let it ride.

Repetition, like folk tale: 2n[d] sunset drive, 3rd time she speak[s]. Not muc[h] dialogue in stor[y]

Bill's only speec[h]. Turning point: Bi[ll] sees something h[e] doesn't alread[y] kno[w]

Repetition, like joke, in 3 thing[s] Ruthie see[s]

Story begins an[d] ends in the middl[e] of things: "By th[at] time," "let it ride"

Initial Impressions

Plot: begins in the middle of action, on a journey. *Narration*: past tense, third person. *Setting*: Indiana is a middling, unromantic place.

Paragraph 1

Narration and Character: Bill's judgments of Ruthie show that he prides himself on arguing about abstract ideas; that he thinks Ruthie must be stupid; that they didn't know each other well and aren't suited for a long trip together. Bill is from the unfriendly East Coast; Ruthie, from easygoing, dull "rural Ohio." *Style*: The casual language—"okay" and "etc."—sounds like Bill's voice, but he's not the narrator. The vague "etc." hints that Bill isn't really curious about her. The observation of cows sounds funny, childlike, even stupid. But why does he have to "chalk it up" or keep score?

Paragraph 2

Plot and Character: This is the first specific time given in the story, the "third evening": Ruthie surprises the reader and Bill with more than dull "observation."

Paragraph 4

Style, Character, Setting, and Tone: Dozing in the speeding car, Bill is too late to check out what she says. He frowns (he doesn't argue) because the plant and the bird can't be seen in the Midwest. Brewer uses a series of place names to indicate the route of the car. There's humor in Ruthie's habit of pointing out bizarre sights.

Paragraph 5

Character and Setting: Bigfoot is a legendary monster living in Western forests. Is Ruthie's imagination getting the better of Bill's logic? "Innocently" personifies the road, and the reflectors on the stump wink like the monster; Bill is finally looking (though in hindsight). The scenery seems to be playing a joke on him.

Paragraph 6

Plot and Character: Here the characters change places. He wants to drive (is she hallucinating?), but it's as if she has won. The narration (which has been relying on Bill's voice and perspective) for the first time notices a romantic detail of scenery that Ruthie doesn't point out (the evening star).

Paragraph 7

Character and Theme: Bill begins to see Ruthie and what she is capable of. What they see *is* the journey these characters take toward falling in love, in the West where things become unreal. *Style*: The long "o" sounds and images in "A white buffalo near Fargo. A UFO above Twin Falls" (along with the words Ohio, Chicago, and Spokane) give a feeling for the wildness (notice the Indian place names). The outcome of the story is that they *go far* to Fargo, see double and fall in love at Twin Falls—see and imagine wonderful things in each other. They end up with perfectly matched vision.

READING AND RESPONDING TO GRAPHIC FICTION

You may approach any kind of narrative with the same kinds of questions that have been applied to 20/20. Try it on the following chapter of Marjane Satrapi's *Persepolis*. This best-selling graphic novel, or graphic memoir, originally written in French and now a successful film, relates Satrapi's own experience as a girl in Iran through her artwork and words. *Persepolis* begins with a portrait of ten-year-old Satrapi, wearing a black veil, in 1980. The Islamic leaders of Iran had recently imposed religious law, including mandatory head coverings for schoolgirls. On September 22, 1980, Iraq invaded Iran, beginning a conflict that lasted until 1988, greatly affecting Satrapi's childhood in Tehran (once known as Persepolis). The Iran-Iraq War was a precursor of the Persian Gulf War of 1990–91 and the Iraq War, or Second Gulf War, that began in 2003.

This excerpt resembles an illustrated short story, though it is closely based on actual events. How do the images contribute to expectations, narration (here, telling and showing), characterization, plot, setting, style, and themes? Read (and view) with these questions in mind and a pencil in hand. Annotating or taking notes will guide you to a more reflective response.

MARJANE SATRAPI
(b. 1969)

The Shabbat

As the granddaughter of Nasreddine Shah, the last Quadjar emperor of Iran, Iranian-born Marjane Satrapi is a princess by birth and a self-declared pacifist by inclination. Only ten years old at the time of the 1979 Islamist revolution, she was reportedly expelled at age fourteen from her French-language school after hitting a principal who demanded she stop wearing jewelry. Fearing for her safety, Satrapi's secularist parents sent her to Vienna, Austria, where she would remain until age eighteen, when she returned to Iran to attend college. After a brief marriage ended in divorce, Satrapi moved to France in 1994, where her graphic memoir, *Persepolis,* was published to great acclaim in 2000. Subsequently translated into numerous languages, it appeared in the United States as *Persepolis: The Story of a Childhood* (2003) and *Persepolis 2: The Story of a Return* (2004). A 2007 animated movie version was nominated for an Academy Award in 2008. Satrapi's other works are *Embroideries* (2005), which explores Iranian women's views of sex and love through a conversation among Satrapi's female relatives; *Chicken with Plums* (2006), which tells the story of both the 1953 CIA-backed Iranian coup d'état and the last days of Satrapi's great-uncle, a musician who committed suicide; and several children's books.

THE SHABBAT

TO KEEP US FROM FORGETTING THAT WE WERE AT WAR, IRAQ OPTED FOR A NEW STRATEGY...
I HEARD THEY'RE GOING TO USE BALLISTIC MISSILES AGAINST US.
WHAT ARE YOU SAYING? WE'RE NOT AT WAR WITH THE SOVIET UNION. I DON'T BELIEVE THE IRAQIS HAVE WEAPONS LIKE THAT.

FROM THE IRAQI BORDER TO TEHRAN IT'S THOUSANDS OF MILES. MISSILES THAT CAN GO THAT FAR COST A FORTUNE!
WELL, THAT'S WHAT THE RUMORS SAY!
WE IRANIANS ARE OLYMPIC CHAMPIONS WHEN IT COMES TO GOSSIP.

SHE'S RIGHT. WE LOVE TO EXAGGERATE.

YOU SEEM TO HAVE THE OPPOSITE SYMPTOM.
WHY DO YOU SAY THAT?

EVEN WHEN YOU SEE SOMETHING WITH YOUR OWN EYES, YOU NEED CONFIRMATION FROM THE BBC.
MY NATURAL OPTIMISM JUST LEADS ME TO BE SKEPTICAL.

Shabbat: sabbath (Hebrew).

MOM'S PESSIMISM SOON WON OUT OVER DAD'S OPTIMISM. IT TURNED OUT THAT THE IRAQIS DID HAVE MISSILES. THEY WERE CALLED "SCUDS" AND TEHRAN BECAME THEIR TARGET.

WHEN THE SIRENS WENT ON, IT MEANT WE HAD THREE MINUTES TO KNOW IF THE END HAD COME.
WE'RE NOT GOING TO THE BASEMENT?
IT WOULDN'T MAKE ANY DIFFERENCE!!

CONSIDERING THE DAMAGE THEY DO, WHETHER WE'RE IN THE BASEMENT OR ON THE ROOF, IT'S THE SAME THING.

THE THREE MINUTES SEEMED LIKE THREE DAYS. FOR THE FIRST TIME, I REALIZED JUST HOW MUCH DANGER WE WERE IN.

BOOM!!

I DON'T WANT TO DIE!
YOU WON'T DEAR. I PROMISE YOU!

NOW THAT TEHRAN WAS UNDER ATTACK, MANY FLED. THE CITY WAS DESERTED. AS FOR US, WE STAYED. NOT JUST OUT OF FATALISM. IF THERE WAS TO BE A FUTURE, IN MY PARENTS' EYES, THAT FUTURE WAS LINKED TO MY FRENCH EDUCATION. AND TEHRAN WAS THE ONLY PLACE I COULD GET IT.

SOME PEOPLE, MORE CIRCUMSPECT, TOOK SHELTER IN THE BASEMENTS OF BIG HOTELS, WELL-KNOWN FOR THEIR SAFETY. APPARENTLY, THEIR REINFORCED CONCRETE STRUCTURES WERE BOMBPROOF.

ONE EXAMPLE WAS OUR NEIGHBORS, THE BABA-LEVYS. THEY WERE AMONG THE FEW JEWISH FAMILIES THAT HAD STAYED AFTER THE REVOLUTION. MR. BABA-LEVY SAID THEIR ANCESTORS HAD COME THREE THOUSAND YEARS AGO, AND IRAN WAS THEIR HOME.

...THEIR DAUGHTER NEDA WAS A QUIET GIRL WHO DIDN'T PLAY MUCH, BUT WE WOULD TALK ABOUT ROMANCE FROM TIME TO TIME.

...ONE DAY A BLOND PRINCE WITH BLUE EYES WILL COME AND TAKE ME TO HIS CASTLE...
OH YEAH! ME TOO!
SO LIFE WENT ON...

The Shah: the shah, or king, of Iran was deposed in 1979, the beginning of what was soon known as the Islamic Revolution under the leadership of Ayatollah Ruholla Khomeini (1900–89). An ayatollah is a high-ranking cleric in the Shia branch of Islam to which most Iranians adhere.

FASTER! PLEASE HURRY...

A CROWD HAD GATHERED IN FRONT OF MY STREET! THE BOMB HAD HIT MY STREET!

MA'AM, WHICH BUILDING WAS HIT?
APPARENTLY, IT EXPLODED AT THE END OF THE STREET.

MY BUILDING AND THE BABA-LEVY'S WERE AT THE END OF THE STREET.
LET ME THROUGH.

ONE CHANCE IN TWO THAT IT WAS OUR BUILDING.
PLEASE, LET ME THROUGH.

YOU CAN'T GO BEYOND THIS POINT!
...I LIVE HERE...
AND HE LET ME THROUGH.

I DIDN'T WANT TO LOOK UP. I LOOKED AT MY TREMBLING LEGS. I COULDN'T GO FORWARD, LIKE IN A NIGHTMARE.
LET THEM BE ALIVE. LET THEM BE ALIVE. LET THEM...

MARJI

MARJI!
MOM!

YOU'RE ALL RIGHT? DAD'S ALL RIGHT? GRANDMA'S ALL RIGHT?
EVERYONE'S OK. I WAS THE ONLY ONE HOME.

OH, MOM.
...

YOU KNOW THE TAPE I PUT ON THE WINDOWS? IT WORKED PERFECTLY. ALL THE WINDOWS ARE BROKEN, BUT THERE'S NOT A PIECE OF BROKEN GLASS IN THE HOUSE!

I COULD TELL THAT MY MOTHER WAS TRYING TO CHANGE THE SUBJECT.

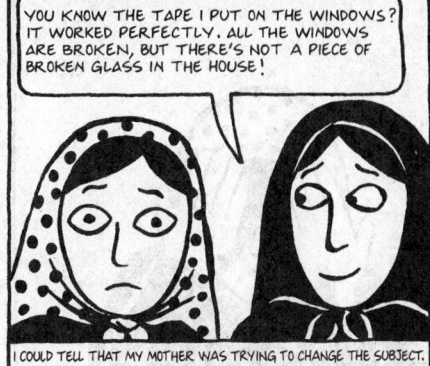

WHEN WE WALKED PAST THE BABA-LEVY'S HOUSE, WHICH WAS COMPLETELY DESTROYED, I COULD FEEL THAT SHE WAS DISCREETLY PULLING ME AWAY. SOMETHING TOLD ME THAT THE BABA-LEVYS HAD BEEN AT HOME. SOMETHING CAUGHT MY ATTENTION.

I SAW A TURQUOISE BRACELET. IT WAS NEDA'S. HER AUNT HAD GIVEN IT TO HER FOR HER FOURTEENTH BIRTHDAY...

THE BRACELET WAS STILL ATTACHED TO...
I DON'T KNOW WHAT...

NO SCREAM IN THE WORLD COULD HAVE RELIEVED MY SUFFERING AND MY ANGER.

2000

KEY CONCEPTS

As you read, respond to, and write about fiction, some key terms and concepts may be useful in comparing or distinguishing different kinds of stories. Stories may be oral rather than written down, and they may be of different lengths. They may be based on true stories or completely invented. They may be written in verse rather than prose, or they may be created in media other than the printed page.

STORY AND NARRATIVE

Generally speaking, a *story* is a short account of an incident or series of incidents, whether actual or invented. The word is often used to refer to an entertaining tale of imaginary people and events, but it is also used in phrases like "the *story* of my life"—suggesting a true account. The term **narrative** is especially useful as a general concept for the substance rather than the form of what is told about persons and their actions. A story or a tale is usually short, whereas a narrative may be of any length from a sentence to a series of novels and beyond.

Narratives in Daily Life

Narrative plays an important role in our lives beyond the telling of fictional stories. Consider the following:

- Today, sociologists and historians may collect *personal narratives* to present an account of society and everyday life in a certain time or place.
- Since the 1990s, the practice of *narrative medicine* has spread as an improved technique of diagnosis and treatment that takes into account the patient's point of view.
- There is a movement to encourage *mediation* rather than litigation in divorce cases. A mediator may collaborate with the couple in arriving at a shared perspective on the divorce; in a sense, they try to agree on the story of their marriage and how it ended.
- Some countries have attempted to recover from the trauma of genocidal ethnic conflict through *official hearings of testimony* by victims as well as defendants. South Africa's Truth and Reconciliation Commission is an example of this use of stories.

ORAL NARRATIVE AND TALES

We tend to think of stories in their written form, but many of the stories that we now regard as among the world's greatest, such as Homer's *Iliad* and the Old English epic *Beowulf,* were sung or recited by generations of storytellers before being written down. Just as rumors change shape as they circulate, oral stories tend to be more fluid than printed stories. Traditionally oral **tales** such as fairy tales or folktales may endure for a very long time yet take different forms in various countries and eras. And it's often difficult or impossible to trace such a story back to a single "author" or creator. In a sense, then, an oral story is the creation of a whole community or communities, just as oral storytelling tends to be a more communal event than reading.

Certain recognizable signals set a story or tale apart from common speech and encourage us to pay a different kind of attention. Children know that a story is beginning when they hear or read "Once upon a time . . . ," and traditional oral storytellers have formal ways to set up a tale, such as *Su-num-twee* ("listen to me"), as Spokane storytellers say. "And they lived happily ever after," or simply "The End," may similarly indicate when the story is over. Such conventions have been adapted since the invention of printing and the spread of literacy.

FICTION AND NONFICTION

The word *fiction* comes from the Latin root *fingere* 'to fashion or form.' The earliest definitions concern the act of making something artificial to imitate something else. In the past two centuries, *fiction* has become more narrowly defined as "prose narrative about imaginary people and events," the main meaning of the word as we use it in this anthology.

Genres of Prose Fiction by Length

A **novel** is a work of prose fiction of about forty thousand words or more. The form arose in the seventeenth and early eighteenth centuries as prose romances and adventure tales began to adopt techniques of history and travel narrative as well as memoir, letters, and biography.

A **novella** is a work of prose fiction of about seventeen thousand to forty thousand words. The novella form was especially favored between about 1850 and 1950, largely because it can be more tightly controlled and concentrated than a long novel, while focusing on the inner workings of a character.

A **short story** is broadly defined as anywhere between one thousand and twenty thousand words. One expectation of a short story is that it may be read in a single sitting. The modern short story developed in the mid-nineteenth century, in part because of the growing popularity of magazines.

A **short short story**, sometimes called "flash fiction" or "micro-fiction," is generally not much longer than one thousand words and sometimes much shorter. There have always been very short fictions, including parables and fables, but the short short story is an invention of recent decades.

In contrast with fiction, **nonfiction** usually refers to *factual* prose narrative. Some major nonfiction genres are history, biography, and autobiography. In film, documentaries and "biopics," or biographical feature films, similarly attempt to represent real people, places, and events. The boundary between fiction and non-fiction is often blurred today, as it was centuries ago. So-called true crime novels such as Truman Capote's *In Cold Blood* (1966) and novelized biographies such as Colm Tóibín's *The Master* (2004), about the life of the novelist Henry James, use the techniques of fiction writing to narrate actual events. Graphic novels, with a format derived from comic books, have become an increasingly popular medium for memoirs. (Two examples are Art Spiegelman's *Maus* [1986, 1991] and Marjane Satrapi's *Persepolis.*) Some Hollywood movies and TV shows dramatize real people in everyday situations or contexts, or real events such as the assassination of President John F. Kennedy. In contrast, **historical fiction**, developed by Sir Walter Scott around 1815, comprises prose narratives that present history in imaginative ways. Such works of prose fiction adhere closely to the facts of history and actual lives, just as many "true" life stories are more or less fictionalized.

• • •

The fiction chapters in this volume present a collection of prose works—mostly short stories—almost all of which were printed within the author's lifetime. Even as you read the short prose fiction in this book, bear in mind the many ways we encounter stories or narrative in everyday life, and consider the almost limitless variety of forms that fiction may take.

WRITING ABOUT FICTION

During your first reading of any story, you may want to read without stopping to address each of the questions on page 15. After you have read the whole piece once, re-read it carefully, using the questions as a guide. It's always interesting to compare your initial reactions with your later ones. In fact, a paper may focus on comparing the expectations of readers (and characters) at the beginning of a story to their later conclusions. Responses to fiction may come in unpredictable order, so feel free to address the questions as they arise. Looking at how the story is told and what happens to which characters may lead to observations on expectations or setting. Consideration of setting and style can help explain the personalities, actions, mood, and effect of the story, which can lead to well-informed ideas about the meaning of the whole. But any one of the questions, pursued further, can serve as the focus of more formal writing.

Following this chapter are three written responses to Raymond Carver's short story CATHEDRAL. First, read the story and make notes on any features that you find interesting, important, or confusing. Then look at the notes and response paper by Wesley Rupton and the essay by Bethany Qualls, which show two different ways of writing about "Cathedral."

RAYMOND CARVER (1938–88)

Cathedral

Born in the logging town of Clatskanie, Oregon, to a working-class family, Raymond Carver married at nineteen and had two children by the time he was twenty-one. Despite these early responsibilities and a lifelong struggle with alcoholism, Carver published his first story in 1961 and graduated from Humboldt State College in 1963. He published his first book, *Near Klamath*, a collection of poems, in 1968 and thereafter supported himself with visiting lectureships at the University of California at Berkeley, Syracuse University, and the Iowa Writer's Workshop, among other institutions. Described by the *New York Times* as "surely the most influential writer of American short stories in the second half of the twentieth century"; credited by others with "reviving what was once thought of as a dying literary form"; and compared to such literary luminaries as Ernest Hemingway, Stephen Crane, and Anton Chekhov, Carver often portrays characters whom one reviewer describes as living, much as Carver long did, "on the edge: of poverty, alcoholic self-destruction, loneliness." The author himself labeled them the sort of "good people," "doing the best they could," who "filled" America. Dubbed a "minimalist" due to his spare style and low-key plots, Carver himself suffered an early death, of lung cancer, at age fifty. His major short-story collections include *Will You Please Be Quiet, Please?* (1976), *What We Talk about When We Talk about Love* (1983), and the posthumously published *Call if You Need Me* (2001).

This blind man, an old friend of my wife's, he was on his way to spend the night. His wife had died. So he was visiting the dead wife's relatives in Connecticut. He called my wife from his in-laws'. Arrangements were made. He would come by train, a five-hour trip, and my wife would meet him at the station. She hadn't seen him since she worked for him one summer in Seattle ten years ago. But she and the blind man had kept in touch. They made tapes and mailed them back and forth. I wasn't enthusiastic about his visit. He was no one I knew. And his being blind bothered me. My idea of blindness came from the movies. In the movies, the blind moved slowly and never laughed. Sometimes they were led by seeing-eye dogs. A blind man in my house was not something I looked forward to.

That summer in Seattle she had needed a job. She didn't have any money. The man she was going to marry at the end of the summer was in officers' training school. He didn't have any money, either. But she was in love with the guy, and he was in love with her, etc. She'd seen something in the paper: HELP WANTED—*Reading to Blind Man*, and a telephone number. She phoned and went over, was hired on the spot. She'd worked with this blind man all summer.

She read stuff to him, case studies, reports, that sort of thing. She helped him organize his little office in the county social-service department. They'd become good friends, my wife and the blind man. How do I know these things? She told me. And she told me something else. On her last day in the office, the blind man asked if he could touch her face. She agreed to this. She told me he touched his fingers to every part of her face, her nose—even her neck! She never forgot it. She even tried to write a poem about it. She was always trying to write a poem. She wrote a poem or two every year, usually after something really important had happened to her.

When we first started going out together, she showed me the poem. In the poem, she recalled his fingers and the way they had moved around over her face. In the poem, she talked about what she had felt at the time, about what went through her mind when the blind man touched her nose and lips. I can remember I didn't think much of the poem. Of course, I didn't tell her that. Maybe I just don't understand poetry. I admit it's not the first thing I reach for when I pick up something to read.

Anyway, this man who'd first enjoyed her favors, the officer-to-be, he'd been her childhood sweetheart. So okay. I'm saying that at the end of the summer she let the blind man run his hands over her face, said goodbye to him, married her childhood etc., who was now a commissioned officer, and she moved away from Seattle. But they'd kept in touch, she and the blind man. She made the first contact after a year or so. She called him up one night from an Air Force base in Alabama. She wanted to talk. They talked. He asked her to send him a tape and tell him about her life. She did this. She sent the tape. On the tape, she told the blind man about her husband and about their life together in the military. She told the blind man she loved her husband but she didn't like it where they lived and she didn't like it that he was a part of the military-industrial thing. She told the blind man she'd written a poem and he was in it. She told him that she was writing a poem about what it was like to be an Air Force officer's wife. The poem wasn't finished yet. She was still writing it. The blind man made a tape. He sent her the tape. She made a tape. This went on for years. My wife's officer was posted to one base and then another. She sent tapes from Moody AFB, McGuire, McConnell, and finally Travis, near Sacramento, where one night she got to feeling lonely and cut off from people she kept losing in that moving-around life. She got to feeling she couldn't go it another step. She went in and swallowed all the pills and capsules in the medicine chest and washed them down with a bottle of gin. Then she got into a hot bath and passed out.

But instead of dying, she got sick. She threw up. Her officer—why should 5
he have a name? he was the childhood sweetheart, and what more does he want?—came home from somewhere, found her, and called the ambulance. In time, she put it all on a tape and sent the tape to the blind man. Over the years, she put all kinds of stuff on tapes and sent the tapes off lickety-split. Next to writing a poem every year, I think it was her chief means of recreation. On one tape, she told the blind man she'd decided to live away from her officer for a time. On another tape, she told him about her divorce. She and I began going out, and of course she told her blind man about it. She told him every-

thing, or so it seemed to me. Once she asked me if I'd like to hear the latest tape from the blind man. This was a year ago. I was on the tape, she said. So I said okay, I'd listen to it. I got us drinks and we settled down in the living room. We made ready to listen. First she inserted the tape into the player and adjusted a couple of dials. Then she pushed a lever. The tape squeaked and someone began to talk in this loud voice. She lowered the volume. After a few minutes of harmless chitchat, I heard my own name in the mouth of this stranger, this blind man I didn't even know! And then this: "From all you've said about him, I can only conclude—" But we were interrupted, a knock at the door, something, and we didn't ever get back to the tape. Maybe it was just as well. I'd heard all I wanted to.

Now this same blind man was coming to sleep in my house.

"Maybe I could take him bowling," I said to my wife. She was at the draining board doing scalloped potatoes. She put down the knife she was using and turned around.

"If you love me," she said, "you can do this for me. If you don't love me, okay. But if you had a friend, any friend, and the friend came to visit, I'd make him feel comfortable." She wiped her hands with the dish towel.

"I don't have any blind friends," I said.

10 "You don't have *any* friends," she said. "Period. Besides," she said, "goddamn it, his wife's just died! Don't you understand that? The man's lost his wife!"

I didn't answer. She'd told me a little about the blind man's wife. Her name was Beulah. Beulah! That's a name for a colored woman.

"Was his wife a Negro?" I asked.

"Are you crazy?" my wife said. "Have you just flipped or something?" She picked up a potato. I saw it hit the floor, then roll under the stove. "What's wrong with you?" she said. "Are you drunk?"

"I'm just asking," I said.

15 Right then my wife filled me in with more detail than I cared to know. I made a drink and sat at the kitchen table to listen. Pieces of the story began to fall into place.

Beulah had gone to work for the blind man the summer after my wife had stopped working for him. Pretty soon Beulah and the blind man had themselves a church wedding. It was a little wedding—who'd want to go to such a wedding in the first place?—just the two of them, plus the minister and the minister's wife. But it was a church wedding just the same. It was what Beulah had wanted, he'd said. But even then Beulah must have been carrying the cancer in her glands. After they had been inseparable for eight years—my wife's word, *inseparable*—Beulah's health went into a rapid decline. She died in a Seattle hospital room, the blind man sitting beside the bed and holding on to her hand. They'd married, lived and worked together, slept together—had sex, sure—and then the blind man had to bury her. All this without his having ever seen what the goddamned woman looked like. It was beyond my understanding. Hearing this, I felt sorry for the blind man for a little bit. And then I found myself thinking what a pitiful life this woman must have led. Imagine a woman who could never see herself as she was seen in the eyes of her loved one. A woman who could go on day after day and never receive the smallest compliment from her beloved. A woman whose husband could never read the expression on her face, be it misery or something better. Someone who could wear makeup or not—what difference to him? She could, if she wanted, wear green eye-shadow around one eye, a straight pin in her nostril, yellow slacks and purple shoes, no matter. And then to slip off into death, the blind man's hand on her hand, his blind eyes streaming tears—I'm imagining now—her last thought maybe this: that he never even knew what she looked like, and she on an express to the grave. Robert was left with a small insurance policy and half of a twenty-peso Mexican coin. The other half of the coin went into the box with her. Pathetic.

So when the time rolled around, my wife went to the depot to pick him up. With nothing to do but wait—sure, I blamed him for that—I was having a drink and watching the TV when I heard the car pull into the drive. I got up from the sofa with my drink and went to the window to have a look.

I saw my wife laughing as she parked the car. I saw her get out of the car and shut the door. She was still wearing a smile. Just amazing. She went around to the other side of the car to where the blind man was already starting to get out. This blind man, feature this, he was wearing a full beard! A beard on a blind man! Too much, I say. The blind man reached into the back seat and dragged out a suitcase. My wife took his arm, shut the car door, and, talking all the way, moved him down the drive and then up the steps to the front porch. I turned off the TV. I finished my drink, rinsed the glass, dried my hands. Then I went to the door.

My wife said, "I want you to meet Robert. Robert, this is my husband. I've told you all about him." She was beaming. She had this blind man by his coat sleeve.

The blind man let go of his suitcase and up came his hand. 20

I took it. He squeezed hard, held my hand, and then he let it go.

"I feel like we've already met," he boomed.

"Likewise," I said. I didn't know what else to say. Then I said, "Welcome. I've heard a lot about you." We began to move then, a little group, from the porch into the living room, my wife guiding him by the arm. The blind man was carrying his suitcase in his other hand. My wife said things like, "To your left here, Robert. That's right. Now watch it, there's a chair. That's it. Sit down right here. This is the sofa. We just bought this sofa two weeks ago."

I started to say something about the old sofa. I'd liked that old sofa. But I didn't say anything. Then I wanted to say something else, small-talk, about the scenic ride along the Hudson. How going *to* New York, you should sit on the right-hand side of the train, and coming *from* New York, the left-hand side.

"Did you have a good train ride?" I said. "Which side of the train did you sit 25
on, by the way?"

"What a question, which side!" my wife said. "What's it matter which side?" she said.

"I just asked," I said.

"Right side," the blind man said. "I hadn't been on a train in nearly forty years. Not since I was a kid. With my folks. That's been a long time. I'd nearly forgotten the sensation. I have winter in my beard now," he said. "So I've been told, anyway. Do I look distinguished, my dear?" the blind man said to my wife.

"You look distinguished, Robert," she said. "Robert," she said. "Robert, it's just so good to see you."

30 My wife finally took her eyes off the blind man and looked at me. I had the feeling she didn't like what she saw. I shrugged.

I've never met, or personally known, anyone who was blind. This blind man was late forties, a heavy-set, balding man with stooped shoulders, as if he carried a great weight there. He wore brown slacks, brown shoes, a light-brown shirt, a tie, a sports coat. Spiffy. He also had this full beard. But he didn't use a cane and he didn't wear dark glasses. I'd always thought dark glasses were a must for the blind. Fact was, I wished he had a pair. At first glance, his eyes looked like anyone else's eyes. But if you looked close, there was something different about them. Too much white in the iris, for one thing, and the pupils seemed to move around in the sockets without his knowing it or being able to stop it. Creepy. As I stared at his face, I saw the left pupil turn in toward his nose while the other made an effort to keep in one place. But it was only an effort, for that eye was on the roam without his knowing it or wanting it to be.

I said, "Let me get you a drink. What's your pleasure? We have a little of everything. It's one of our pastimes."

"Bub, I'm a Scotch man myself," he said fast enough in this big voice.

"Right," I said. Bub! "Sure you are. I knew it."

35 He let his fingers touch his suitcase, which was sitting alongside the sofa. He was taking his bearings. I didn't blame him for that.

"I'll move that up to your room," my wife said.

"No, that's fine," the blind man said loudly. "It can go up when I go up."

"A little water with the Scotch?" I said.

"Very little," he said.

40 "I knew it," I said.

He said, "Just a tad. The Irish actor, Barry Fitzgerald? I'm like that fellow. When I drink water, Fitzgerald said, I drink water. When I drink whiskey, I drink whiskey." My wife laughed. The blind man brought his hand up under his beard. He lifted his beard slowly and let it drop.

I did the drinks, three big glasses of Scotch with a splash of water in each. Then we made ourselves comfortable and talked about Robert's travels. First the long flight from the West Coast to Connecticut, we covered that. Then from Connecticut up here by train. We had another drink concerning that leg of the trip.

I remembered having read somewhere that the blind didn't smoke because, as speculation had it, they couldn't see the smoke they exhaled. I thought I knew that much and that much only about blind people. But this blind man smoked his cigarette down to the nubbin and then lit another one. This blind man filled his ashtray and my wife emptied it.

When we sat down at the table for dinner, we had another drink. My wife heaped Robert's plate with cube steak, scalloped potatoes, green beans. I buttered him up two slices of bread. I said, "Here's bread and butter for you." I swallowed some of my drink. "Now let us pray," I said, and the blind man lowered his head. My wife looked at me, her mouth agape. "Pray the phone won't ring and the food doesn't get cold," I said.

45 We dug in. We ate everything there was to eat on the table. We ate like there was no tomorrow. We didn't talk. We ate. We scarfed. We grazed that table. We

were into serious eating. The blind man had right away located his foods, he knew just where everything was on his plate. I watched with admiration as he used his knife and fork on the meat. He'd cut two pieces of meat, fork the meat into his mouth, and then go all out for the scalloped potatoes, the beans next, and then he'd tear off a hunk of buttered bread and eat that. He'd follow this up with a big drink of milk. It didn't seem to bother him to use his fingers once in a while, either.

We finished everything, including half a strawberry pie. For a few moments, we sat as if stunned. Sweat beaded on our faces. Finally, we got up from the table and left the dirty plates. We didn't look back. We took ourselves into the living room and sank into our places again. Robert and my wife sat on the sofa. I took the big chair. We had us two or three more drinks while they talked about the major things that had come to pass for them in the past ten years. For the most part, I just listened. Now and then I joined in. I didn't want him to think I'd left the room, and I didn't want her to think I was feeling left out. They talked of things that had happened to them—to them!—these past ten years. I waited in vain to hear my name on my wife's sweet lips: "And then my dear husband came into my life"—something like that. But I heard nothing of the sort. More talk of Robert. Robert had done a little of everything, it seemed, a regular blind jack-of-all-trades. But most recently he and his wife had had an Amway distributorship, from which, I gathered, they'd earned their living, such as it was. The blind man was also a ham radio operator. He talked in his loud voice about conversations he'd had with fellow operators in Guam, in the Philippines, in Alaska, and even in Tahiti. He said he'd have a lot of friends there if he ever wanted to go visit those places. From time to time, he'd turn his blind face toward me, put his hand under his beard, ask me something. How long had I been in my present position? (Three years.) Did I like my work? (I didn't.) Was I going to stay with it? (What were the options?) Finally, when I thought he was beginning to run down, I got up and turned on the TV.

My wife looked at me with irritation. She was heading toward a boil. Then she looked at the blind man and said, "Robert, do you have a TV?"

The blind man said, "My dear, I have two TVs. I have a color set and a black-and-white thing, an old relic. It's funny, but if I turn the TV on, and I'm always turning it on, I turn on the color set. It's funny, don't you think?"

I didn't know what to say to that. I had absolutely nothing to say to that. No opinion. So I watched the news program and tried to listen to what the announcer was saying.

"This is a color TV," the blind man said. "Don't ask me how, but I can tell." 50

"We traded up a while ago," I said.

The blind man had another taste of his drink. He lifted his beard, sniffed it, and let it fall. He leaned forward on the sofa. He positioned his ashtray on the coffee table, then put the lighter to his cigarette. He leaned back on the sofa and crossed his legs at the ankles.

My wife covered her mouth, and then she yawned. She stretched. She said, "I think I'll go upstairs and put on my robe. I think I'll change into something else. Robert, you make yourself comfortable," she said.

"I'm comfortable," the blind man said.

55 "I want you to feel comfortable in this house," she said.

"I am comfortable," the blind man said.

After she'd left the room, he and I listened to the weather report and then to the sports roundup. By that time, she'd been gone so long I didn't know if she was going to come back. I thought she might have gone to bed. I wished she'd come back downstairs. I didn't want to be left alone with a blind man. I asked him if he wanted another drink, and he said sure. Then I asked if he wanted to smoke some dope with me. I said I'd just rolled a number. I hadn't, but I planned to do so in about two shakes.

"I'll try some with you," he said.

"Damn right," I said. "That's the stuff."

60 I got our drinks and sat down on the sofa with him. Then I rolled us two fat numbers. I lit one and passed it. I brought it to his fingers. He took it and inhaled.

"Hold it as long as you can," I said. I could tell he didn't know the first thing.

My wife came back downstairs wearing her pink robe and her pink slippers.

"What do I smell?" she said.

"We thought we'd have us some cannabis," I said.

65 My wife gave me a savage look. Then she looked at the blind man and said, "Robert, I didn't know you smoked."

He said, "I do now, my dear. There's a first time for everything. But I don't feel anything yet."

"This stuff is pretty mellow," I said. "This stuff is mild. It's dope you can reason with," I said. "It doesn't mess you up."

"Not much it doesn't, bub," he said, and laughed.

My wife sat on the sofa between the blind man and me. I passed her the number. She took it and toked and then passed it back to me. "Which way is this going?" she said. Then she said, "I shouldn't be smoking this. I can hardly keep my eyes open as it is. That dinner did me in. I shouldn't have eaten so much."

70 "It was the strawberry pie," the blind man said. "That's what did it," he said, and he laughed his big laugh. Then he shook his head.

"There's more strawberry pie," I said.

"Do you want some more, Robert?" my wife said.

"Maybe in a little while," he said.

We gave our attention to the TV. My wife yawned again. She said, "Your bed is made up when you feel like going to bed, Robert. I know you must have had a long day. When you're ready to go to bed, say so." She pulled his arm. "Robert?"

75 He came to and said, "I've had a real nice time. This beats tapes, doesn't it?"

I said, "Coming at you," and I put the number between his fingers. He inhaled, held the smoke, and then let it go. It was like he'd been doing it since he was nine years old.

"Thanks, bub," he said. "But I think this is all for me. I think I'm beginning to feel it," he said. He held the burning roach out for my wife.

"Same here," she said. "Ditto. Me, too." She took the roach and passed it to me. "I may just sit here for a while between you two guys with my eyes closed.

But don't let me bother you, okay? Either one of you. If it bothers you, say so. Otherwise, I may just sit here with my eyes closed until you're ready to go to bed," she said. "Your bed's made up, Robert, when you're ready. It's right next to our room at the top of the stairs. We'll show you up when you're ready. You wake me up now, you guys, if I fall asleep." She said that and then she closed her eyes and went to sleep.

The news program ended. I got up and changed the channel. I sat back down on the sofa. I wished my wife hadn't pooped out. Her head lay across the back of the sofa, her mouth open. She'd turned so that her robe had slipped away from her legs, exposing a juicy thigh. I reached to draw her robe back over her, and it was then that I glanced at the blind man. What the hell! I flipped the robe open again.

"You say when you want some strawberry pie," I said. 80

"I will," he said.

I said, "Are you tired? Do you want me to take you up to your bed? Are you ready to hit the hay?"

"Not yet," he said. "No, I'll stay up with you, bub. If that's all right. I'll stay up until you're ready to turn in. We haven't had a chance to talk. Know what I mean? I feel like me and her monopolized the evening." He lifted his beard and he let it fall. He picked up his cigarettes and his lighter.

"That's all right," I said. Then I said, "I'm glad for the company."

And I guess I was. Every night I smoked dope and stayed up as long as I 85
could before I fell asleep. My wife and I hardly ever went to bed at the same time. When I did go to sleep, I had these dreams. Sometimes I'd wake up from one of them, my heart going crazy.

Something about the church and the Middle Ages was on the TV. Not your run-of-the-mill TV fare. I wanted to watch something else. I turned to the other channels. But there was nothing on them, either. So I turned back to the first channel and apologized.

"Bub, it's all right," the blind man said. "It's fine with me. Whatever you want to watch is okay. I'm always learning something. Learning never ends. It won't hurt me to learn something tonight. I got ears," he said.

We didn't say anything for a time. He was leaning forward with his head turned at me, his right ear aimed in the direction of the set. Very disconcerting. Now and then his eyelids drooped and then they snapped open again. Now and then he put his fingers into his beard and tugged, like he was thinking about something he was hearing on the television.

On the screen, a group of men wearing cowls was being set upon and tormented by men dressed in skeleton costumes and men dressed as devils. The men dressed as devils wore devil masks, horns, and long tails. This pageant was part of a procession. The Englishman who was narrating the thing said it took place in Spain once a year. I tried to explain to the blind man what was happening.

"Skeletons," he said. "I know about skeletons," he said, and he nodded. 90

The TV showed this one cathedral. Then there was a long, slow look at another one. Finally, the picture switched to the famous one in Paris, with its flying buttresses and its spires reaching up to the clouds. The camera pulled away to show the whole of the cathedral rising above the skyline.

There were times when the Englishman who was telling the thing would shut up, would simply let the camera move around over the cathedrals. Or else the camera would tour the countryside, men in fields walking behind oxen. I waited as long as I could. Then I felt I had to say something. I said, "They're showing the outside of this cathedral now. Gargoyles. Little statues carved to look like monsters. Now I guess they're in Italy. Yeah, they're in Italy. There's paintings on the walls of this one church."

"Are those fresco paintings, bub?" he asked, and he sipped from his drink.

I reached for my glass. But it was empty. I tried to remember what I could remember. "You're asking me are those frescoes?" I said. "That's a good question. I don't know."

95 The camera moved to a cathedral outside Lisbon. The differences in the Portuguese cathedral compared with the French and Italian were not that great. But they were there. Mostly the interior stuff. Then something occurred to me, and I said, "Something has occurred to me. Do you have any idea what a cathedral is? What they look like, that is? Do you follow me? If somebody says cathedral to you, do you have any notion what they're talking about? Do you know the difference between that and a Baptist church, say?"

He let the smoke dribble from his mouth. "I know they took hundreds of workers fifty or a hundred years to build," he said. "I just heard the man say that, of course. I know generations of the same families worked on a cathedral. I heard him say that, too. The men who began their life's work on them, they never lived to see the completion of their work. In that wise, bub, they're no different from the rest of us, right?" He laughed. Then his eyelids drooped again. His head nodded. He seemed to be snoozing. Maybe he was imagining himself in Portugal. The TV was showing another cathedral now. This one was in Germany. The Englishman's voice droned on. "Cathedrals," the blind man said. He sat up and rolled his head back and forth. "If you want the truth, bub, that's about all I know. What I just said. What I heard him say. But maybe you could describe one to me? I wish you'd do it. I'd like that. If you want to know, I really don't have a good idea."

I stared hard at the shot of the cathedral on the TV. How could I even begin to describe it? But say my life depended on it. Say my life was being threatened by an insane guy who said I had to do it or else.

I stared some more at the cathedral before the picture flipped off into the countryside. There was no use. I turned to the blind man and said, "To begin with, they're very tall." I was looking around the room for clues. "They reach way up. Up and up. Toward the sky. They're so big, some of them, they have to have these supports. To help hold them up, so to speak. These supports are called buttresses. They remind me of viaducts, for some reason. But maybe you don't know viaducts, either? Sometimes the cathedrals have devils and such carved into the front. Sometimes lords and ladies. Don't ask me why this is," I said.

He was nodding. The whole upper part of his body seemed to be moving back and forth.

"I'm not doing so good, am I?" I said. 100

He stopped nodding and leaned forward on the edge of the sofa. As he listened to me, he was running his fingers through his beard. I wasn't getting through to him, I could see that. But he waited for me to go on just the same. He nodded, like he was trying to encourage me. I tried to think what else to say. "They're really big," I said. "They're massive. They're built of stone. Marble, too, sometimes. In those olden days, when they built cathedrals, men wanted to be close to God. In those olden days, God was an important part of everyone's life. You could tell this from their cathedral-building. I'm sorry," I said, "but it looks like that's the best I can do for you. I'm just no good at it."

"That's all right, bub," the blind man said. "Hey, listen. I hope you don't mind my asking you. Can I ask you something? Let me ask you a simple question, yes or no. I'm just curious and there's no offense. You're my host. But let me ask if you are in any way religious? You don't mind my asking?"

I shook my head. He couldn't see that, though. A wink is the same as a nod to a blind man. "I guess I don't believe in it. In anything. Sometimes it's hard. You know what I'm saying?"

"Sure, I do," he said.

"Right," I said. 105

The Englishman was still holding forth. My wife sighed in her sleep. She drew a long breath and went on with her sleeping.

"You'll have to forgive me," I said. "But I can't tell you what a cathedral looks like. It just isn't in me to do it. I can't do any more than I've done."

The blind man sat very still, his head down, as he listened to me.

I said, "The truth is, cathedrals don't mean anything special to me. Nothing. Cathedrals. They're something to look at on late-night TV. That's all they are."

It was then that the blind man cleared his throat. He brought something up. 110
He took a handkerchief from his back pocket. Then he said, "I get it, bub. It's okay. It happens. Don't worry about it," he said. "Hey, listen to me. Will you do me a favor? I got an idea. Why don't you find us some heavy paper? And a pen. We'll do something. We'll draw one together. Get us a pen and some heavy paper. Go on, bub, get the stuff," he said.

So I went upstairs. My legs felt like they didn't have any strength in them. They felt like they did after I'd done some running. In my wife's room, I looked around. I found some ballpoints in a little basket on her table. And then I tried to think where to look for the kind of paper he was talking about.

Downstairs, in the kitchen, I found a shopping bag with onion skins in the bottom of the bag. I emptied the bag and shook it. I brought it into the living room and sat down with it near his legs. I moved some things, smoothed the wrinkles from the bag, spread it out on the coffee table.

The blind man got down from the sofa and sat next to me on the carpet.

He ran his fingers over the paper. He went up and down the sides of the paper. The edges, even the edges. He fingered the corners.

"All right," he said. "All right, let's do her." 115

He found my hand, the hand with the pen. He closed his hand over my hand. "Go ahead, bub, draw," he said. "Draw. You'll see. I'll follow along with you. It'll be okay. Just begin now like I'm telling you. You'll see. Draw," the blind man said.

So I began. First I drew a box that looked like a house. It could have been the house I lived in. Then I put a roof on it. At either end of the roof, I drew spires. Crazy.

"Swell," he said. "Terrific. You're doing fine," he said. "Never thought anything like this could happen in your lifetime, did you, bub? Well, it's a strange life, we all know that. Go on now. Keep it up."

I put in windows with arches. I drew flying buttresses. I hung great doors. I couldn't stop. The TV station went off the air. I put down the pen and closed and opened my fingers. The blind man felt around over the paper. He moved the tips of his fingers over the paper, all over what I had drawn, and he nodded.

120 "Doing fine," the blind man said.

I took up the pen again, and he found my hand. I kept at it. I'm no artist. But I kept drawing just the same.

My wife opened up her eyes and gazed at us. She sat up on the sofa, her robe hanging open. She said, "What are you doing? Tell me, I want to know."

I didn't answer her.

The blind man said, "We're drawing a cathedral. Me and him are working on it. Press hard," he said to me. "That's right. That's good," he said. "Sure. You got it, bub. I can tell. You didn't think you could. But you can, can't you? You're cooking with gas now. You know what I'm saying? We're going to really have us something here in a minute. How's the old arm?" he said. "Put some people in there now. What's a cathedral without people?"

125 My wife said, "What's going on? Robert, what are you doing? What's going on?"

"It's all right," he said to her. "Close your eyes now," the blind man said to me.

I did it. I closed them just like he said.

"Are they closed?" he said. "Don't fudge."

"They're closed," I said.

130 "Keep them that way," he said. He said, "Don't stop now. Draw."

So we kept on with it. His fingers rode my fingers as my hand went over the paper. It was like nothing else in my life up to now.

Then he said, "I think that's it. I think you got it," he said. "Take a look. What do you think?"

But I had my eyes closed. I thought I'd keep them that way for a little longer. I thought it was something I ought to do.

"Well?" he said. "Are you looking?"

135 My eyes were still closed. I was in my house. I knew that. But I didn't feel like I was inside anything.

"It's really something," I said.

1983

SAMPLE WRITING: READING NOTES

Wesley Rupton wrote the notes below with the "Questions about the Elements of Fiction" in mind (p. 15). As you read these notes, compare them to the notes you took as you read CATHEDRAL. Do Rupton's notes reveal anything to you that you didn't notice while reading the story? Did you notice anything he did not, or do you disagree with any of his interpretations?

Notes on Raymond Carver's "Cathedral"

What do you expect?

- Title: The first words are "this blind man," and those words keep being repeated. Why not call it "The Blind Man" or "The Blind Man's Visit"?
- The threatening things the husband says made me expect that he would attack the blind man. I thought the wife might leave her husband for the blind man, who has been nicer to her.
- When they talk about going up to bed, and the wife goes to "get comfortable" and then falls asleep, I thought there was a hint about sex.

What happens in the story?

- Not that much. It is a story about one evening in which a husband and wife and their guest drink, have dinner, talk, and then watch TV.
- These people have probably drunk two bottles of hard liquor (how many drinks?) before, during, and after a meal. And then they smoke marijuana.
- In the final scene, the two men try to describe and draw cathedrals that are on the TV show. Why cathedrals? Though it connects with the title.
- The husband seems to have a different attitude at the end: He likes Robert and seems excited about the experience "like nothing else in my life up to now."

How is the story narrated?

- It's told in first person and past tense. The husband is the narrator. We never get inside another character's thoughts. He seems to be telling someone about the incident, first saying the blind man was coming, and then filling in the background about his wife and the blind man, and then telling what happens after the guest arrives.

- The narrator describes people and scenes and summarizes the past; there is dialogue.
- It doesn't have episodes or chapters, but there are two gaps on the page, before paragraph 57 and before paragraph 88. Maybe time passes here.

Who are the characters?

- Three main characters: husband, wife, and blind man (the blind man's own wife has just died, and the wife divorced her first husband). I don't think we ever know the husband's or wife's names. The blind man, Robert, calls him "bub," like "buddy." They seem to be white, middle-class Americans. The wife is lonely and looking for meaning. The blind man seems sensitive, and he cares about the poetry and tapes.
- The husband is sort of acting out, though mostly in his own mind. Asking "Was his wife a Negro?" sounds like he wants to make fun of black or blind people. His wife asks, "Are you drunk?" and says that he has no friends; I thought he's an unhappy man who gets drunk and acts "crazy" a lot and that she doesn't really expect him to be that nice.
- It sounds like these people have plenty of food and things, but aren't very happy. They all sound smart, but the narrator is ignorant, and he has no religion. All three characters have some bad or nervous habits (alcohol, cigarettes, drugs; insomnia; suicide attempt; divorce).

What is the setting and time of the story?

- Mostly in the house the evening the blind man arrives. But after the intro there's a kind of flashback to the summer in Seattle ten years ago (par. 2). The story about the visit starts again in paragraph 6, and then the wife tells the husband more about the blind man's marriage—another flashback in paragraph 16. In paragraph 17, "the time rolled around" to the story's main event. After that, it's chronological.
- We don't know the name of the town, but it seems to be on the U.S. East Coast (five hours by train from Connecticut [par. 1]). It can't be too long ago or too recent either: They mention trains, audiotapes, color TV, no Internet. No one seems worried about food or health the way they might be today.
- I noticed that travel came up in the story. Part of what drives the wife crazy about her first husband is moving around to different military bases (par. 4). In paragraph 46, Robert tells us about his contact with ham radio operators in places he would like to visit (Guam, Alaska). The TV show takes Robert and the narrator on a tour of France, Italy, and Portugal.

What do you notice about how the story is written?

- The narrator is irritating. He repeats words a lot. He uses stereotypes. He seems to be informally talking to someone, as if he can't get over it. But then he sometimes uses exaggerated or bored-sounding phrases: "this man who'd first enjoyed her favors," "So okay. I'm saying . . . married her childhood etc." (par. 4). His style is almost funny.

- Things he repeats: Paragraphs 2 and 3: "She told me" (3 times), "he could touch her face . . . he touched his fingers to every part of her face . . ." (and later "touched her nose" and "they'd kept in touch"). "She even tried to write a poem . . . always trying to write a poem" (and 4 more times "poem"). The words "talk," "tape," "told" are also repeated.

What does the story mean? Can you express its theme or themes?

- The way the narrator learns to get along with the blind man must be important. The narrator is disgusted by blind people at first, and at the end he closes his eyes on purpose.
- I think it makes a difference that the two men imagine and try to draw a cathedral, not a flower or an airplane. It's something made by human beings, and it's religious. As they mention, the builders of cathedrals don't live to see them finished, but the buildings last for centuries. It's not like the narrator is saved or becomes a great guy, but he gets past whatever he's afraid of at night, and he seems inspired for a little while. I don't know why the wife has to be left out of this, but probably the husband couldn't open up if he was worrying about how close she is to Robert.

SAMPLE WRITING: RESPONSE PAPER

A response paper may use a less formal organization and style than a longer, more formal essay, but it should not just be a summary or description of the work. Indeed, a response paper could be a step on the way to a longer essay. You need not form a single thesis or argument, but you should try to develop your ideas and feelings about the story through your writing. The point is to get your thoughts in writing without worrying too much about form and style.

Almost everything in the following response paper comes directly from the notes above, but notice how the writer has combined observations, adding a few direct quotations or details from the text to support claims about the story's effects and meaning. For ease of reference, we have altered the citations in this paper to refer to paragraph numbers. Unless your instructor indicates otherwise, however, you should always follow convention by instead citing page numbers when writing about fiction.

Rupton 1

Wesley Rupton
Professor Suarez
English 170
6 January 2017

Response Paper on Raymond Carver's "Cathedral"

Not much happens in Raymond Carver's short story "Cathedral," and at first I wondered what it was about and why it was called "Cathedral." The narrator, the unnamed husband, seems to be telling someone about the evening that Robert, a blind friend of his wife, came to stay at their house, not long after Robert's own wife has died. After the narrator fills us in about his wife's first marriage and her relationship with the blind man, he describes what the three characters do that evening: they drink a lot of alcohol, eat a huge dinner that leaves them "stunned" (par. 46), smoke marijuana, and after the wife falls asleep the two men watch TV. A show about cathedrals leads the husband to try to describe what a cathedral looks like, and then the men try to draw one together. The husband seems to have a different attitude at the end: he likes Robert and seems excited about an experience "like nothing else in my life up to now" (par. 131).

The husband's way of telling the story is definitely important. He is sort of funny, but also irritating. As he makes jokes about stereotypes, you start to

Rupton 2

dislike or distrust him. When he hears about Robert's wife, Beulah, he asks, "Was his wife a Negro?" (par. 12) just because her name sounds like a black woman's name to him. In three paragraphs, he flashes back to the time ten years ago when his wife was the blind man's assistant and the blind man

> asked if he could touch her face. . . . She told me he touched his fingers to every part of her face. . . . She even tried to write a poem about it. . . .
> . . . In the poem, she recalled his fingers . . . over her face. In the poem, she talked about what she had felt . . . when the blind man touched her nose and lips. (pars. 2-3)

The narrator seems to be going over and over the same creepy idea of a man feeling his wife's face. It seems to disgust him that his wife and the blind man communicated or expressed themselves, perhaps because he seems incapable of doing so. When his wife asks, "Are you drunk?" and says that he has no friends, I got a feeling that the husband is an unhappy man who gets drunk and acts "crazy" a lot and that his wife doesn't really expect him to be very nice (pars. 8-13). He's going to make fun of their guest (asking a blind man to go bowling). The husband is sort of acting out, though he's mostly rude in his own mind.

There's nothing heroic or dramatic or even unusual about these people (except that one is blind). The events take place in a house somewhere in an American suburb and not too long ago. Other than the quantity of alcohol and drugs they consume, these people don't do anything unusual, though the blind man seems strange to the narrator. The ordinary setting and plot make the idea of something as grand and old as a European cathedral come as a surprise at the end of the story. I wondered if part of the point is that they desperately want to get out of a trap they're in. I noticed that travel came up in the story. Part of what drove the wife crazy with her first husband was moving around to different military bases (par. 4). In paragraph 46, Robert tells us about his contact with ham radio operators in places he would like to visit (Guam, Alaska). The TV show takes Robert and the narrator on a tour of France, Italy, and Portugal.

The way the narrator changes from disliking the blind man to getting along with him must be important to the meaning of the story. After the wife goes up to "get comfortable," suggesting that they might go to bed, the story focuses on the two men. Later she falls asleep on the sofa between them, and the narrator decides not to cover up her leg where her robe has fallen open, as if he has stopped being jealous. At this point the narrator decides he is "glad for the company" of his guest (par. 84). The cooperation between the two men is the turning point. The narrator is disgusted by blind people at first, and at the end he closes his eyes on purpose. The two men try to imagine something and build something together, and Robert is coaching the narrator. Robert says, "let's do her," and then says, "*You're* doing fine" (pars. 115, 118; emphasis added). I think it makes a difference that they imagine and draw a cathedral, not a flower or a cow

Rupton 3

or an airplane. It's something made by human beings, and it's religious. I don't think the men are converted to believing in God at the end, but this narrow-minded guy gets past whatever he's afraid of at night and finds some sort of inspiring feeling. I don't know why the wife has to be left out, but probably the husband couldn't open up if he was worrying about how close she is to Robert.

The ideas of communicating or being in touch and travel seem connected to me. I think that the husband tries to tell this story about the cathedral the way his wife tried to write a poem. The narrator has had an exciting experience that gets him in touch with something beyond his small house. After drawing the cathedral, the narrator says that he "didn't feel like I was inside anything" (par. 135). Though I still didn't like the narrator, I felt more sympathy, and I thought the story showed that even this hostile person could open up.

Rupton 4

Work Cited

Carver, Raymond. "Cathedral." *The Norton Introduction to Literature*, edited by Kelly J. Mays, 12th ed., W. W. Norton, 2017, pp. 32-42.

SAMPLE WRITING: ESSAY

Bethany Qualls wrote the following first draft of an essay analyzing character and narration in Carver's CATHEDRAL. Read this paper as you would one of your peers' papers, looking for opportunities for the writer to improve her presentation. Is the tone consistently appropriate for academic writing? Does the essay maintain its focus? Does it demonstrate a steady progression of well-supported arguments that build toward a strong, well-earned conclusion? Is there any redundant or otherwise unnecessary material? Are there ideas that need to be developed further? For a critique and revision of this essay's conclusion, see ch. 32, "The Literature Essay," in the Writing about Literature section of this book.

(For ease of reference, we have altered the citations in this essay to refer to paragraph numbers. Unless your instructor indicates otherwise, however, you should always follow convention by instead citing page numbers when writing about fiction. For more on citation, please refer to ch. 34.)

Qualls 1

Bethany Qualls
Professor Netherton
English 301
16 January 2017

A Narrator's Blindness in Raymond Carver's "Cathedral"

A reader in search of an exciting plot will be pretty disappointed by Raymond Carver's "Cathedral" because the truth is nothing much happens. A suburban husband and wife receive a visit from her former boss, who is blind. After the wife falls asleep, the two men watch a TV program about cathedrals and eventually try to draw one. Along the way the three characters down a few cocktails and smoke a little pot. But that's about as far as the action goes. Instead of focusing on plot, then, the story really asks us to focus on the characters, especially the husband who narrates the story. Through his words even more than his actions, the narrator unwittingly shows us why nothing much happens to him by continually demonstrating his utter inability to connect with others or to understand himself.

The narrator's isolation is most evident in the distanced way he introduces his own story and the people in it. He does not name the other characters or himself, referring to them only by using labels such as "this blind man," "his wife," "my wife" (par. 1), and "the man [my wife] was going to marry" (par. 2). Even after the narrator's wife starts referring to their visitor as "Robert," the narrator keeps calling him "the blind man." These labels distance him from the other characters and also leave readers with very little connection to them.

At least three times the narrator notices that this habit of not naming or really acknowledging people is significant. Referring to his wife's "officer," he

Qualls 2

asks, "why should he have a name? he was the childhood sweetheart, and what more does he want?" (par. 5). Moments later he describes how freaked out he was when he listened to a tape the blind man had sent his wife and "heard [his] own name in the mouth of this . . . blind man [he] didn't even know!" (par. 5). Yet once the blind man arrives and begins to talk with the wife, the narrator finds himself "wait[ing] in vain to hear [his] name on [his] wife's sweet lips" and disappointed to hear "nothing of the sort" (par. 46). Simply using someone's name suggests an intimacy that the narrator avoids and yet secretly yearns for.

Also reinforcing the narrator's isolation and dissatisfaction with it are the awkward euphemisms and clichés he uses, which emphasize how disconnected he is from his own feelings and how uncomfortable he is with other people's. Referring to his wife's first husband, the narrator says it was he "who'd first enjoyed her favors" (par. 4), an antiquated expression even in 1983, the year the story was published. Such language reinforces our sense that the narrator cannot speak in language that is meaningful or heartfelt, especially when he tries to talk about emotions. He describes his wife's feelings for her first husband, for example, by using generic language and then just trailing off entirely: "she was in love with the guy, and he was in love with her, etc." (par. 2). When he refers to the blind man and his wife as "inseparable," he points out that this is, in fact, his "wife's word," not one that he's come up with (par. 16). And even when he admits that he would like to hear his wife talk about him (par. 46), he speaks in language that seems to come from books or movies rather than the heart.

Once the visit actually begins, the narrator's interactions and conversations with the other characters are even more awkward. His discomfort with the very idea of the visit is obvious to his wife and to the reader. As he says in his usual deadpan manner, "I wasn't enthusiastic about his visit" (par. 1). During the visit he sits silent when his wife and Robert are talking and then answers Robert's questions about his life and feelings with the shortest possible phrases: "How long had I been in my present position? (Three years.) Did I like my work? (I didn't.)" (par. 46). Finally, he tries to escape even that much involvement by simply turning on the TV and tuning Robert out.

Despite Robert's best attempt to make a connection with the narrator, the narrator resorts to a label again, saying that he "didn't want to be left alone with a blind man" (par. 57). Robert, merely "a blind man," remains a category, not a person, and the narrator can initially relate to Robert only by invoking the stereotypes about that category that he has learned "from the movies" (par. 1). He confides to the reader that he believes that blind people always wear dark glasses, that they never smoke (par. 43), and that a beard on a blind man is "too much" (par. 18). It follows that the narrator is amazed about the connection his wife and Robert have because he is unable to see Robert as a person like any other. "Who'd want to go to such a wedding in the first place?" (par. 16), he asks rhetorically about Robert's wedding to his wife, Beulah.

Misconceptions continue as the narrator assumes Beulah would "never receive the smallest compliment from her beloved," since the compliments he is

Qualls 3

thinking about are physical ones (par. 16). Interestingly, when faced with a name that is specific (Beulah), the narrator immediately assumes that he knows what the person with that name must be like ("a colored woman," par. 11), even though she is not in the room or known to him. Words fail or mislead the narrator in both directions, as he's using them and as he hears them.

There is hope for the narrator at the end as he gains some empathy and forges a bond with Robert over the drawing of a cathedral. That process seems to begin when the narrator admits to himself, the reader, and Robert that he is "glad for [Robert's] company" (par. 84) and, for the first time, comes close to disclosing the literally nightmarish loneliness of his life. It culminates in a moment of physical and emotional intimacy that the narrator admits is "like nothing else in my life up to now" (par. 131)—a moment in which discomfort with the very idea of blindness gives way to an attempt to actually experience blindness from the inside. Because the narrator has used words to distance himself from the world, it seems fitting that all this happens only when the narrator *stops* using words. They have a tendency to blind him.

However, even at the very end it isn't clear just whether or how the narrator has really changed. He does not completely interact with Robert but has to be prodded into action by him. By choosing to keep his eyes closed, he not only temporarily experiences blindness but also shuts out the rest of the world, since he "didn't feel like [he] was inside anything" (par. 135). Perhaps most important, he remains unable to describe his experience meaningfully, making it difficult for readers to decide whether or not he has really changed. For example, he says, "It was like nothing else in my life up to now" (par. 131), but he doesn't explain why this is true. Is it because he is doing something for someone else? Because he is thinking about the world from another's perspective? Because he feels connected to Robert? Because he is drawing a picture while probably drunk and high? There is no way of knowing.

It's possible that not feeling "inside anything" (par. 135) could be a feeling of freedom from his own habits of guardedness and insensitivity, his emotional "blindness." But even with this final hope for connection, for the majority of the story the narrator is a closed, judgmental man who isolates himself and cannot connect with others. The narrator's view of the world is one filled with misconceptions that the visit from Robert starts to slowly change, yet it is not clear what those changes are, how far they will go, or whether they will last.

Qualls 4

Work Cited

Carver, Raymond. "Cathedral." *The Norton Introduction to Literature*, edited by Kelly J. Mays, 12th ed., W. W. Norton, 2017, pp. 32-42.

Telling Stories

AN ALBUM

Is it human nature or human culture? Is it hardwired in our brains or inspired by our need to live with others in a community? Whatever the cause, people tell stories in every known society. Professional and amateur storytellers, as well as scholars in the humanities and sciences, have been paying more attention to the phenomenon of stories or narrative in recent decades. Online forums and organizations around the world are dedicated to a revival of oral storytelling, rather like the twentieth-century revival of folk music. Educators, religious leaders, therapists, and organizers of programs for the young or the needy have turned to various publications and programs for guidance on how the techniques of storytelling might benefit their clients.

Stories are part of our everyday lives, and everyone has stories to tell. Perhaps you have heard the life stories broadcast every week on National Public Radio's *Morning Edition* in conjunction with the StoryCorps project, which allows ordinary Americans to record their own interviews with friends or family (often in a traveling "studio" van) and have their recordings archived in the Library of Congress. Most likely you are familiar with blogs, *Facebook*, *Twitter*, *YouTube* videos, and other means of producing or sharing some version of yourself, some aspect of your experience or your life.

Authors of short fiction have often reflected on the irresistible appeal of stories by making storytelling part of the plot or action *within* their fiction. We include here three stories that do just that. As you read the stories, think about what each implies about how stories and storytelling work and what they can do for us. When and why do we both tell stories and listen to those of others? What do we derive from the act of telling or listening, as well as from the story itself? What makes a story compelling, worth listening to or even writing down? How might the sorts of choices we make in telling a story resemble those a fiction writer makes in writing one? As listeners or readers, how are our expectations of a story and our responses to it shaped by our knowledge of or assumptions about its teller? In what different ways might stories, whether oral or written, be "true"?

SHERMAN ALEXIE
(b. 1966)
Flight Patterns

Sherman Alexie grew up with his four siblings on a reservation near Spokane, Washington, an experience he once described as the "origin" of "everything I do now, writing and otherwise." After attending high school in nearby Reardan, where he was the only Native American other than the school mascot, he earned a BA in American Studies from Washington State University and soon after published the first of over twelve collections of poetry, *The Business of Fancydancing* (1991). Named a *New York Times* Notable Book of the Year, it also earned high praise from the *New York Times Book Review,* which hailed its twenty-six-year-old author as "one of the major lyric voices of our time." Yet Alexie is perhaps better understood as an accomplished storyteller in verse and prose. His first collection of fiction, *The Lone Ranger and Tonto Fistfight in Heaven* (1993), received a PEN/Hemingway Award for Best First Book, which Alexie followed up over fifteen years later with a PEN/Faulkner Award for his fourth collection, *War Dances* (2010). In between have come novels—including *Reservation Blues* (1995), *Flight* (2007), and the National Book Award–winning young adult novel *The Absolutely True Diary of a Part-Time Indian* (2009)—as well as radio scripts and screenplays: *Smoke Signals* (1998) was featured at the Sundance Film Festival. A sometime stand-up comedian and four-time champion of the World Heavyweight Poetry Slam, he lives in Seattle, Washington, with his wife and two sons.

At 5:05 A.M., Patsy Cline fell loudly to pieces on William's clock radio.[1] He hit the snooze button, silencing lonesome Patsy, and dozed for fifteen more minutes before Donna Fargo bragged about being the happiest girl in the whole USA. William wondered what had ever happened to Donna Fargo,[2] whose birth name was the infinitely more interesting Yvonne Vaughn, and wondered *why* he knew Donna Fargo's birth name. Ah, he was the bemused and slightly embarrassed owner of a twenty-first-century American mind. His intellect was a big comfy couch stuffed with sacred and profane trivia. He knew the names of all nine of Elizabeth Taylor's husbands and could quote from memory the entire Declaration of Independence. William knew Donna Fargo's birth name because he *wanted* to know her birth name. He wanted to know all of the great big and tiny little American details. He didn't want to choose between Ernie Hemingway and the Spokane tribal elders, between Mia Hamm and Crazy Horse, between *The Heart Is a Lonely Hunter* and Chief Dan George. William wanted all of it. Hunger was his crime. As for dear Miss Fargo, William figured she probably played the Indian casino circuit along with the Righteous Brothers, Smokey Robinson, Eddie Money, Pat Benatar, RATT, REO Speedwagon, and

1. Reference to country music singer Patsy Cline's recording of "I Fall to Pieces" (1961).
2. American singer (b. 1949) best known for her recording of "Happiest Girl in the Whole U.S.A." (1972).

dozens of other formerly famous rock- and country-music stars. Many of the Indian casino acts were bad, and most of the rest were pure nostalgic entertainment, but a small number made beautiful and timeless music. William knew the genius Merle Haggard played thirty or forty Indian casinos every year, so long live Haggard and long live tribal economic sovereignty. Who cares about fishing and hunting rights? Who cares about uranium mines and nuclear-waste-dump sites on sacred land? Who cares about the recovery of tribal languages? Give me Freddy Fender singing "Before the Next Teardrop Falls" in English and Spanish to 206 Spokane Indians, William thought, and I will be a happy man.

But William wasn't happy this morning. He'd slept poorly—he always slept poorly—and wondered again if his insomnia was a physical or a mental condition. His doctor had offered him sleeping-pill prescriptions, but William declined for philosophical reasons. He was an Indian who didn't smoke or drink or eat processed sugar. He lifted weights three days a week, ran every day, and competed in four triathlons a year. A two-mile swim, a 150-mile bike ride, and a full marathon. A triathlon was a religious quest. If Saint Francis were still around, he'd be a triathlete. Another exaggeration! Theological hyperbole! Rabid self-justification! Diagnostically speaking, William was an obsessive-compulsive workaholic who was afraid of pills. So he suffered sleepless nights and constant daytime fatigue.

This morning, awake and not awake, William turned down the radio, changing Yvonne Vaughn's celebratory anthem into whispered blues, and rolled off the couch onto his hands and knees. His back and legs were sore because he'd slept on the living room couch so the alarm wouldn't disturb his wife and daughter upstairs. Still on his hands and knees, William stretched his spine, using the twelve basic exercises he'd learned from Dr. Adams, that master practitioner of white middle-class chiropractic voodoo. This was all part of William's regular morning ceremony. Other people find God in ornate ritual, but William called out to Geronimo, Jesus Christ, Saint Therese, Buddha, Allah, Billie Holiday, Simon Ortiz, Abe Lincoln, Bessie Smith, Howard Hughes, Leslie Marmon Silko, Joan of Arc and Joan of Collins, John Woo, Wilma Mankiller, and Karl and Groucho Marx while he pumped out fifty push-ups and fifty abdominal crunches. William wasn't particularly religious; he was generally religious. Finished with his morning calisthenics, William showered in the basement, suffering the water that was always too cold down there, and threaded his long black hair into two tight braids—the indigenous businessman's tonsorial special—and dressed in his best travel suit, a navy three-button pinstripe he'd ordered online. He'd worried about the fit, but his tailor was a magician and had only mildly chastised William for such an impulsive purchase. After knotting his blue paisley tie, purchased in person and on sale, William walked upstairs in bare feet and kissed his wife, Marie, good-bye.

"Cancel your flight," she said. "And come back to bed."

"You're supposed to be asleep," he said. 5

She was a small and dark woman who seemed to be smaller and darker at that time of the morning. Her long black hair had once again defeated its braids, but she didn't care. She sometimes went two or three days without brushing it. William was obsessive about his mane, tying and retying his ponytail, knotting and reknotting his braids, experimenting with this shampoo and that conditioner. He greased down his cowlicks (inherited from a cowlicked father and grandfather) with shiny pomade, but Marie's hair was always unkempt, wild, and renegade. William's hair hung around the fort, but Marie's rode on the warpath! She constantly pulled stray strands out of her mouth. William loved her for it. During sex, they spent as much time readjusting her hair as they did readjusting positions. Such were the erotic dangers of loving a Spokane Indian woman.

"Take off your clothes and get in bed," Marie pleaded now.

"I can't do that," William said. "They're counting on me."

"Oh, the plane will be filled with salesmen. Let some other salesman sell what you're selling."

10 "Your breath stinks."

"So do my feet, my pits, and my butt, but you still love me. Come back to bed, and I'll make it worth your while."

William kissed Marie, reached beneath her pajama top, and squeezed her breasts. He thought about reaching inside her pajama bottoms. She wrapped her arms and legs around him and tried to wrestle him into bed. Oh, God, he wanted to climb into bed and make love. He wanted to fornicate, to sex, to breed, to screw, to make the beast with two backs. *Oh, sweetheart, be my little synonym*! He wanted her to be both subject and object. Perhaps it was wrong (and unavoidable) to objectify female strangers, but shouldn't every husband seek to objectify his wife at least once a day? William loved and respected his wife, and delighted in her intelligence, humor, and kindness, but he also loved to watch her lovely ass when she walked, and stare down the front of her loose shirts when she leaned over, and grab her breasts at wildly inappropriate times—during dinner parties and piano recitals and uncontrolled intersections, for instance. He constantly made passes at her, not necessarily expecting to be successful, but to remind her he still desired her and was excited by the thought of her. She was his passive and active.

"Come on," she said. "If you stay home, I'll make you Scooby."

He laughed at the inside joke, created one night while he tried to give her sexual directions and was so aroused that he sounded exactly like Scooby-Doo.

15 "Stay home, stay home, stay home," she chanted and wrapped herself tighter around him. He was supporting all of her weight, holding her two feet off the bed.

"I'm not strong enough to do this," he said.

"Baby, baby, I'll make you strong," she sang, and it sounded like she was writing a Top 40 hit in the Brill Building, circa 1962. How could he leave a woman who sang like that? He hated to leave, but he loved his work. He was a man, and men needed to work. More sexism! More masculine tunnel vision! More need for gender-sensitivity workshops! He pulled away from her, dropping her back onto the bed, and stepped away.

"Willy Loman," she said, "you must pay attention to me."[3]

"I love you," he said, but she'd already fallen back to sleep—a narcoleptic gift William envied—and he wondered if she would dream about a man who never left her, about some unemployed agoraphobic Indian warrior who liked to cook and wash dishes.

20 William tiptoed into his daughter's bedroom, expecting to hear her light snore, but she was awake and sitting up in bed, and looked so magical and

3. Protagonist of Arthur Miller's play *Death of a Salesman* (1949); Willy's wife, Linda, says of her husband, "Attention, attention must finally be paid to such a person."

androgynous with her huge brown eyes and crew-cut hair. She'd wanted to completely shave her head: *I don't want long hair, I don't want short hair, I don't want hair at all, and I don't want to be a girl or a boy, I want to be a yellow and orange leaf some little kid picks up and pastes in his scrapbook.*

"Daddy," she said.

"Grace," he said. "You should be asleep. You have school today."

"I know," she said. "But I wanted to see you before you left."

"Okay," said William as he kissed her forehead, nose, and chin. "You've seen me. Now go back to sleep. I love you and I'm going to miss you."

She fiercely hugged him.

"Oh," he said. "You're such a lovely, lovely girl."

Preternaturally serious, she took his face in her eyes and studied his eyes. Morally examined by a kindergartner!

"Daddy," she said. "Go be silly for those people far away."

She cried as William left her room. Already quite sure he was only an adequate husband, he wondered, as he often did, if he was a bad father. During these mornings, he felt generic and violent, like some caveman leaving the fire to hunt animals in the cold and dark. Maybe his hands were smooth and clean, but they felt bloody.

Downstairs, he put on his socks and shoes and overcoat and listened for his daughter's crying, but she was quiet, having inherited her mother's gift for instant sleep. She had probably fallen back into one of her odd little dreams. While he was gone, she often drew pictures of those dreams, coloring the sky green and the grass blue—everything backward and wrong—and had once sketched a man in a suit crashing an airplane into the bright yellow sun. Ah, the rage, fear, and loneliness of a five-year-old, simple and true! She'd been especially afraid since September 11 of the previous year[4] and constantly quizzed William about what he would do if terrorists hijacked his plane.

"I'd tell them I was your father," he'd said to her before he left for his last business trip. "And they'd stop being bad."

"You're lying," she'd said. "I'm not supposed to listen to liars. If you lie to me, I can't love you."

He couldn't argue with her logic. Maybe she was the most logical person on the planet. Maybe she should be illegally elected president of the United States.

William understood her fear of flying and of his flight. He was afraid of flying, too, but not of terrorists. After the horrible violence of September 11, he figured hijacking was no longer a useful weapon in the terrorist arsenal. These days, a terrorist armed with a box cutter would be torn to pieces by all of the coach-class passengers and fed to the first-class upgrades. However, no matter how much he tried to laugh his fear away, William always scanned the airports and airplanes for little brown guys who reeked of fundamentalism. That meant William was equally afraid of Osama bin Laden and Jerry Falwell wearing the last vestiges of a summer tan. William himself was a little brown guy, so the other travelers were always sniffing around him, but he smelled only of Dove soap, Mennen deodorant, and sarcasm. Still, he understood why people were afraid of him, a brown-skinned man with dark hair and eyes. If Norwegian

4. That is, September 11, 2001, when hijacked planes were flown into the World Trade Center in New York and into the Pentagon in Washington, D.C., killing thousands.

terrorists had exploded the World Trade Center, then blue-eyed blondes would be viewed with more suspicion. Or so he hoped.

35 Locking the front door behind him, William stepped away from his house, carried his garment bag and briefcase onto the front porch, and waited for his taxi to arrive. It was a cold and foggy October morning. William could smell the saltwater of Elliott Bay and the freshwater of Lake Washington. Surrounded by gray water and gray fog and gray skies and gray mountains and a gray sun, he'd lived with his family in Seattle for three years and loved it. He couldn't imagine living anywhere else, with any other wife or child, in any other time.

William was tired and happy and romantic and exaggerating the size of his familial devotion so he could justify his departure, so he could survive his departure. He did sometimes think about other women and other possible lives with them. He wondered how his life would have been different if he'd married a white woman and fathered half-white children who grew up to complain and brag about their biracial identities: *Oh, the only box they have for me is Other! I'm not going to check any box! I'm not the Other! I am Tiger Woods!* But William most often fantasized about being single and free to travel as often as he wished—maybe two million miles a year—and how much he'd enjoy the benefits of being a platinum frequent flier. Maybe he'd have one-night stands with a long series of traveling saleswomen, all of them thousands of miles away from husbands and children who kept looking up "feminism" in the dictionary. William knew that was yet another sexist thought. In this capitalistic and democratic culture, talented women should also enjoy the freedom to emotionally and physically abandon their families. After all, talented and educated men have been doing it for generations. Let freedom ring!

Marie had left her job as a corporate accountant to be a full-time mother to Grace. William loved his wife for making the decision, and he tried to do his share of the housework, but he suspected he was an old-fashioned bastard who wanted his wife to stay at home and wait, wait, wait for him.

Marie was always waiting for William to call, to come home, to leave messages saying he was getting on the plane, getting off the plane, checking in to the hotel, going to sleep, waking up, heading for the meeting, catching an earlier or later flight home. He spent one third of his life trying to sleep in uncomfortable beds and one third of his life trying to stay awake in airports. He traveled with thousands of other capitalistic foot soldiers, mostly men but increasing numbers of women, and stayed in the same Ramadas, Holiday Inns, and Radissons. He ate the same room-service meals and ran the same exercise-room treadmills and watched the same pay-per-view porn and stared out the windows at the same strange and lonely cityscapes. Sure, he was an enrolled member of the Spokane Indian tribe, but he was also a fully recognized member of the notebook-computer tribe and the security-checkpoint tribe and the rental-car tribe and the hotel-shuttle-bus tribe and the cell-phone-roaming-charge tribe.

William traveled so often, the Seattle-based flight attendants knew him by first name.

40 At five minutes to six, the Orange Top taxi pulled into the driveway. The driver, a short and thin black man, stepped out of the cab and waved. William rushed down the stairs and across the pavement. He wanted to get away from the house before he changed his mind about leaving.

"Is that everything, sir?" asked the taxi driver, his accent a colonial cocktail of American English, formal British, and French sibilants added to a base of what must have been North African.

"Yes, it is, sir," said William, self-consciously trying to erase any class differences between them. In Spain the previous summer, an elderly porter had cursed at William when he insisted on carrying his own bags into the hotel. "Perhaps there is something wrong with the caste system, sir," the hotel concierge had explained to William. "But all of us, we want to do our jobs, and we want to do them well."

William didn't want to insult anybody; he wanted the world to be a fair and decent place. At least that was what he wanted to want. More than anything, he wanted to stay home with his fair and decent family. He supposed he wanted the world to be fairer and more decent to his family. We are special, he thought, though he suspected they were just one more family on this block of neighbors, in this city of neighbors, in this country of neighbors, in a world of neighbors. He looked back at his house, at the windows behind which slept his beloved wife and daughter. When he traveled, he had nightmares about strangers breaking into the house and killing and raping Marie and Grace. In other nightmares, he arrived home in time to save his family by beating the intruders and chasing them away. During longer business trips, William's nightmares became more violent as the days and nights passed. If he was gone over a week, he dreamed about mutilating the rapists and eating them alive while his wife and daughter cheered for him.

"Let me take your bags, sir," said the taxi driver.

"What?" asked William, momentarily confused.

"Your bags, sir."

William handed him the briefcase but held on to the heavier garment bag. A stupid compromise, thought William, but it's too late to change it now. God, I'm supposed to be some electric aboriginal warrior, but I'm really a wimpy liberal pacifist. *Dear Lord, how much longer should I mourn the death of Jerry Garcia?*[5]

The taxi driver tried to take the garment bag from William.

"I've got this one," said William, then added, "I've got it, sir."

The taxi driver hesitated, shrugged, opened the trunk, and set the briefcase inside. William laid the garment bag next to his briefcase. The taxi driver shut the trunk and walked around to open William's door.

"No, sir," said William as he awkwardly stepped in front of the taxi driver, opened the door, and took a seat. "I've got it."

"I'm sorry, sir," said the taxi driver and hurried around to the driver's seat. This strange American was making him uncomfortable, and he wanted to get behind the wheel and drive. Driving comforted him.

"To the airport, sir?" asked the taxi driver as he started the meter.

"Yes," said William. "United Airlines."

"Very good, sir."

In silence, they drove along Martin Luther King Jr. Way, the bisector of an African American neighborhood that was rapidly gentrifying. William and his family were Native American gentry! They were the very first Indian family to

5. Guitarist (1942–95) for the Grateful Dead, a rock group noted for its live concerts and fiercely devoted fans.

ever move into a neighborhood and bring up the property values! That was one of William's favorite jokes, self-deprecating and politely racist. White folks could laugh at a joke like that and not feel guilty. But how guilty could white people feel in Seattle? Seattle might be the only city in the country where white people lived comfortably on a street named after Martin Luther King, Jr.

No matter where he lived, William always felt uncomfortable, so he enjoyed other people's discomfort. These days, in the airports, he loved to watch white people enduring random security checks. It was a perverse thrill, to be sure, but William couldn't help himself. He knew those white folks wanted to scream and rage: *Do I look like a terrorist?* And he knew the security officers, most often low-paid brown folks, wanted to scream back: *Define terror, you Anglo bastard!* William figured he'd been pulled over for pat-down searches about 75 percent of the time. Random, my ass! But that was okay! William might have wanted to irritate other people, but he didn't want to scare them. He wanted his fellow travelers to know exactly who and what he was: *I am a Native American and therefore have ten thousand more reasons to terrorize the U.S. than any of those Taliban jerk-offs, but I have chosen instead to become a civic American citizen, so all of you white folks should be celebrating my kindness and moral decency and awesome ability to forgive*! Maybe William should have worn beaded vests when he traveled. Maybe he should have brought a hand drum and sang "Way, ya, way, ya, hey." Maybe he should have thrown casino chips into the crowd.

The taxi driver turned west on Cherry, drove twenty blocks into downtown, took the entrance ramp onto I-5, and headed south for the airport. The freeway was moderately busy for that time of morning.

"Where are you going, sir?" asked the taxi driver.

60 "I've got business in Chicago," William said. He didn't really want to talk. He needed to meditate in silence. He needed to put his fear of flying inside an imaginary safe deposit box and lock it away. We all have our ceremonies, thought William, our personal narratives. He'd always needed to meditate in the taxi on the way to the airport. Immediately upon arrival at the departure gate, he'd listen to a tape he'd made of rock stars who died in plane crashes. Buddy Holly, Otis Redding, Stevie Ray, "Oh Donna," "Chantilly Lace," "(Sittin' on) The Dock of the Bay." William figured God would never kill a man who listened to such a morbid collection of music. Too easy a target, and plus, God could never justify killing a planeful of innocents to punish one minor sinner.

"What do you do, sir?" asked the taxi driver.

"You know, I'm not sure," said William and laughed. It was true. He worked for a think tank and sold ideas about how to improve other ideas. Two years ago, his company had made a few hundred thousand dollars by designing and selling the idea of a better shopping cart. The CGI prototype was amazing. It looked like a mobile walk-in closet. But it had yet to be manufactured and probably never would be.

"You wear a good suit," said the taxi driver, not sure why William was laughing. "You must be a businessman, no? You must make lots of money."

"I do okay."

65 "Your house is big and beautiful."

"Yes, I suppose it is."

"You are a family man, yes?"

"I have a wife and daughter."

"Are they beautiful?"

William was pleasantly surprised to be asked such a question. "Yes," he said. "Their names are Marie and Grace. They're very beautiful. I love them very much."

"You must miss them when you travel."

"I miss them so much I go crazy," said William. "I start thinking I'm going to disappear, you know, just vanish, if I'm not home. Sometimes I worry their love is the only thing that makes me human, you know? I think if they stopped loving me, I might burn up, spontaneously combust, and turn into little pieces of oxygen and hydrogen and carbon. Do you know what I'm saying?"

"Yes sir, I understand love can be so large."

William wondered why he was being honest and poetic with a taxi driver. There is emotional safety in anonymity, he thought.

"I have a wife and three sons," said the driver. "But they live in Ethiopia with my mother and father. I have not seen any of them for many years."

For the first time, William looked closely at the driver. He was clear-eyed and handsome, strong of shoulder and arm, maybe fifty years old, maybe older. A thick scar ran from his right ear down his neck and beneath his collar. A black man with a violent history, William thought and immediately reprimanded himself for racially profiling the driver: *Excuse me, sir, but I pulled you over because your scar doesn't belong in this neighborhood.*

"I still think of my children as children," the driver said. "But they are men now. Taller and stronger than me. They are older now than I was when I last saw them."

William did the math and wondered how this driver could function with such fatherly pain. "I bet you can't wait to go home and see them again," he said, following the official handbook of the frightened American male: *When confronted with the mysterious, you can defend yourself by speaking in obvious generalities.*

"I cannot go home," said the taxi driver, "and I fear I will never see them again."

William didn't want to be having this conversation. He wondered if his silence would silence the taxi driver. But it was too late for that.

"What are you?" the driver asked.

"What do you mean?"

"I mean, you are not white, your skin, it is dark like mine."

"Not as dark as yours."

"No," said the driver and laughed. "Not so dark, but too dark to be white. What are you? Are you Jewish?"

Because they were so often Muslim, taxi drivers all over the world had often asked William if he was Jewish. William was always being confused for something else. He was ambiguously ethnic, living somewhere in the darker section of the Great American Crayola Box, but he was more beige than brown, more mauve than sienna.

"Why do you want to know if I'm Jewish?" William asked.

"Oh, I'm sorry, sir, if I offended you. I am not anti-Semitic. I love all of my brothers and sisters. Jews, Catholics, Buddhists, even the atheists, I love them all. Like you Americans sing, 'Joy to the world and Jeremiah Bullfrog!'"[6]

6. Made famous by the band Three Dog Night, the song "Joy to the World" begins, "Jeremiah was a bullfrog."

The taxi driver laughed again, and William laughed with him.

90 "I'm Indian," William said.

"From India?"

"No, not jewel-on-the-forehead Indian," said William. "I'm a bows-and-arrows Indian."

"Oh, you mean ten little, nine little, eight little Indians?"

"Yeah, sort of," said William. "I'm that kind of Indian, but much smarter. I'm a Spokane Indian. We're salmon people."

95 "In England, they call you Red Indians."

"You've been to England?"

"Yes, I studied physics at Oxford."

"Wow," said William, wondering if this man was a liar.

"You are surprised by this, I imagine. Perhaps you think I'm a liar?"

100 William covered his mouth with one hand. He smiled this way when he was embarrassed.

"Aha, you do think I'm lying. You ask yourself questions about me. How could a physicist drive a taxi? Well, in the United States, I am a cabdriver, but in Ethiopia, I was a jet-fighter pilot."

By coincidence or magic, or as a coincidence that could willfully be interpreted as magic, they drove past Boeing Field at that exact moment.

"Ah, you see," said the taxi driver, "I can fly any of those planes. The prop planes, the jet planes, even the very large passenger planes. I can also fly the experimental ones that don't fly. But I could make them fly because I am the best pilot in the world. Do you believe me?"

"I don't know," said William, very doubtful of this man but fascinated as well. If he was a liar, then he was a magnificent liar.

105 On both sides of the freeway, blue-collared men and women drove trucks and forklifts, unloaded trains, trucks, and ships, built computers, televisions, and airplanes. Seattle was a city of industry, of hard work, of calluses on the palms of hands. So many men and women working so hard. William worried that his job—his selling of the purely theoretical—wasn't a real job at all. He didn't build anything. He couldn't walk into department and grocery stores and buy what he'd created, manufactured, and shipped. William's life was measured by imaginary numbers: the binary code of computer languages, the amount of money in his bank accounts, the interest rate on his mortgage, and the rise and fall of the stock market. He invested much of his money in socially responsible funds. Imagine that! Imagine choosing to trust your money with companies that supposedly made their millions through ethical means. Imagine the breathtaking privilege of such a choice. All right, so maybe this was an old story for white men. For most of American history, who else but a white man could endure the existential crisis of economic success? But this story was original and aboriginal for William. For thousands of years, Spokane Indians had lived subsistence lives, using every last part of the salmon and deer because they'd die without every last part, but William only ordered salmon from menus and saw deer on television. Maybe he romanticized the primal—for thousands of years, Indians also died of ear infections—but William wanted his comfortable and safe life to contain more *wilderness.*

"Sir, forgive me for saying this," the taxi driver said, "but you do not look like the Red Indians I have seen before."

"I know," William said. "People usually think I'm a longhaired Mexican."

"What do you say to them when they think such a thing?"

"*No habla español. Indio de Norteamericanos.*"

"People think I'm black American. They always want to hip-hop rap to me. 'Are you East Coast or West Coast?' they ask me, and I tell them I am Ivory Coast."

"How have things been since September eleventh?"

"Ah, a good question, sir. It's been interesting. Because people think I'm black, they don't see me as a terrorist, only as a crackhead addict on welfare. So I am a victim of only one misguided idea about who I am."

"We're all trapped by other people's ideas, aren't we?"

"I suppose that is true, sir. How has it been for you?"

"It's all backward," William said. "A few days after it happened, I was walking out of my gym downtown, and this big phallic pickup pulled up in front of me in the crosswalk. Yeah, this big truck with big phallic tires and a big phallic flagpole and a big phallic flag flying, and the big phallic symbol inside leaned out of his window and yelled at me, 'Go back to your own country!'"

"Oh, that is sad and funny," the taxi driver said.

"Yeah," William said. "And it wasn't so much a hate crime as it was a crime of irony, right? And I was laughing so hard, the truck was halfway down the block before I could get breath enough to yell back, 'You first!'"

William and the taxi driver laughed and laughed together. Two dark men laughing at dark jokes.

"I had to fly on the first day you could fly," William said. "And I was flying into Baltimore, you know, and D.C. and Baltimore are pretty much the same damn town, so it was like flying into Ground Zero, you know?"

"It must have been terrifying."

"It was, it was. I was sitting in the plane here in Seattle, getting ready to take off, and I started looking around for suspicious brown guys. I was scared of little brown guys. So was everybody else. We were all afraid of the same things. I started looking around for big white guys because I figured they'd be undercover cops, right?"

"Imagine wanting to be surrounded by white cops!"

"Exactly! I didn't want to see some pacifist, vegan, whole-wheat, free-range, organic, progressive, gray-ponytail, communist, liberal, draft-dodging, NPR-listening wimp! What are they going to do if somebody tries to hijack the plane? Throw a Birkenstock at him? Offer him some pot?"

"Marijuana might actually stop the violence everywhere in the world," the taxi driver said.

"You're right," William said. "But on that plane, I was hoping for about twenty-five NRA-loving, gun-nut, serial-killing, psychopathic, Ollie North,[7]

7. Oliver North (b. 1943), an ex–marine officer, now author and political commentator, first became famous for his involvement in a secret weapons-for-hostages deal with the Iranian government.

Norman Schwarzkopf,[8] right-wing, Agent Orange, post-traumatic-stress-disorder, CIA, FBI, automatic-weapon, smart-bomb, laser-sighting bastards!"

"You wouldn't want to invite them for dinner," the taxi driver said. "But you want them to protect your children, am I correct?"

"Yes, but it doesn't make sense. None of it makes sense. It's all contradictions."

"The contradictions are the story, yes?"

"Yes."

130 "I have a story about contradictions," said the taxi driver. "Because you are a Red Indian, I think you will understand my pain."

"*Su-num-twee,*" said William.

"What is that? What did you say?"

"*Su-num-twee.* It's Spokane. My language."

"What does it mean?"

135 "Listen to me."

"Ah, yes, that's good. *Su-num-twee, su-num-twee.* So, what is your name?"

"William."

The taxi driver sat high and straight in his seat, like he was going to say something important. "William, my name is Fekadu. I am Oromo and Muslim, and I come from Addis Ababa in Ethiopia, and I want you to *su-num-twee.*"

There was nothing more important than a person's name and the names of his clan, tribe, city, religion, and country. By the social rules of his tribe, William should have reciprocated and officially identified himself. He should have been polite and generous. He was expected to live by so many rules, he sometimes felt like he was living inside an indigenous version of an Edith Wharton[9] novel.

140 "Mr. William," asked Fekadu, "do you want to hear my story? Do you want to *su-num-twee*?"

"Yes, I do, sure, yes, please," said William. He was lying. He was twenty minutes away from the airport and so close to departure.

"I was not born into an important family," said Fekadu. "But my father worked for an important family. And this important family worked for the family of Emperor Haile Selassie.[1] He was a great and good and kind and terrible man, and he loved his country and killed many of his people. Have you heard of him?"

"No, I'm sorry, I haven't."

"He was magical. Ruled our country for forty-three years. Imagine that! We Ethiopians are strong. White people have never conquered us. We won every war we fought against white people. For all of our history, our emperors have been strong, and Selassie was the strongest. There has never been a man capable of such love and destruction."

145 "You fought against him?"

Fekadu breathed in so deeply that William recognized it as a religious moment, as the first act of a ceremony, and with the second act, an exhalation, the ceremony truly began.

8. Norman Schwarzkopf (1934–2012), celebrated commander in chief of U.S. forces in Operation Desert Shield (1990).

9. American novelist (1862–1937) known for her sophisticated depictions of upper-class mores.

1. Haile Selassie (1892–1975), emperor of Ethiopia from 1930 to 1936 and again from 1941 to 1974, when he was overthrown in a violent military coup.

"No," Fekadu said. "I was a smart child. A genius. A prodigy. It was Selassie who sent me to Oxford. And there I studied physics and learned the math and art of flight. I came back home and flew jets for Selassie's army."

"Did you fly in wars?" William asked.

"Ask me what you really want to ask me, William. You want to know if I was a killer, no?"

150 William had a vision of his wife and daughter huddling terrified in their Seattle basement while military jets screamed overhead. It happened every August when the U.S. Navy Blue Angels came to entertain the masses with their aerial acrobatics.

"Do you want to know if I was a killer?" asked Fekadu. "Ask me if I was a killer."

William wanted to know the terrible answer without asking the terrible question.

"Will you not ask me what I am?" asked Fekadu.

"I can't."

155 "I dropped bombs on my own people."

In the sky above them, William counted four, five, six jets flying in holding patterns while awaiting permission to land.

"For three years, I killed my own people," said Fekadu. "And then, on the third of June in 1974, I could not do it anymore. I kissed my wife and sons goodbye that morning, and I kissed my mother and father, and I lied to them and told them I would be back that evening. They had no idea where I was going. But I went to the base, got into my plane, and flew away."

"You defected?" William asked. How could a man steal a fighter plane? Was that possible? And if possible, how much courage would it take to commit such a crime? William was quite sure he could never be that courageous.

"Yes, I defected," said Fekadu. "I flew my plane to France and was almost shot down when I violated their airspace, but they let me land, and they arrested me, and soon enough, they gave me asylum. I came to Seattle five years ago, and I think I will live here the rest of my days."

160 Fekadu took the next exit. They were two minutes away from the airport. William was surprised to discover that he didn't want this journey to end so soon. He wondered if he should invite Fekadu for coffee and a sandwich, for a slice of pie, for brotherhood. William wanted to hear more of this man's stories and learn from them, whether they were true or not. Perhaps it didn't matter if any one man's stories were true. Fekadu's autobiography might have been completely fabricated, but William was convinced that somewhere in the world, somewhere in Africa or the United States, a man, a jet pilot, wanted to fly away from the war he was supposed to fight. There must be hundreds, maybe thousands, of such men, and how many were courageous enough to fly away? If Fekadu wasn't describing his own true pain and loneliness, then he might have been accidentally describing the pain of a real and lonely man.

"What about your family?" asked William, because he didn't know what else to ask and because he was thinking of his wife and daughter. "Weren't they in danger? Wouldn't Selassie want to hurt them?"

"I could only pray Selassie would leave them be. He had always been good to me, but he saw me as impulsive, so I hoped he would know my family had nothing to do with my flight. I was a coward for staying and a coward for leaving. But none of it mattered, because Selassie was overthrown a few weeks after I defected."

"A coup?"

"Yes, the Derg[2] deposed him, and they slaughtered all of their enemies and their enemies' families. They suffocated Selassie with a pillow the next year. And now I could never return to Ethiopia because Selassie's people would always want to kill me for my betrayal and the Derg would always want to kill me for being Selassie's soldier. Every night and day, I worry that any of them might harm my family. I want to go there and defend them. I want to bring them here. They can sleep on my floor! But even now, after democracy has almost come to Ethiopia, I cannot go back. There is too much history and pain, and I am too afraid."

"How long has it been since you've talked to your family?"

"We write letters to each other, and sometimes we receive them. They sent me photos once, but they never arrived for me to see. And for two days, I waited by the telephone because they were going to call, but it never rang."

Fekadu pulled the taxi to a slow stop at the airport curb. "We are here, sir," he said. "United Airlines."

William didn't know how this ceremony was supposed to end. He felt small and powerless against the collected history. "What am I supposed to do now?" he asked.

"Sir, you must pay me thirty-eight dollars for this ride," said Fekadu and laughed. "Plus a very good tip."

"How much is good?"

"You see, sometimes I send cash to my family. I wrap it up and try to hide it inside the envelope. I know it gets stolen, but I hope some of it gets through to my family. I hope they buy themselves gifts from me. I hope."

"You pray for this?"

"Yes, William, I pray for this. And I pray for your safety on your trip, and I pray for the safety of your wife and daughter while you are gone."

"Pop the trunk, I'll get my own bags," said William as he gave sixty dollars to Fekadu, exited the taxi, took his luggage out of the trunk, and slammed it shut. Then William walked over to the passenger-side window, leaned in, and studied Fekadu's face and the terrible scar on his neck.

"Where did you get that?" William asked.

Fekadu ran a finger along the old wound. "Ah," he said. "You must think I got this flying in a war. But no, I got this in a taxicab wreck. William, I am a much better jet pilot than a car driver."

Fekadu laughed loudly and joyously. William wondered how this poor man could be capable of such happiness, however temporary it was.

"Your stories," said William. "I want to believe you."

"Then believe me," said Fekadu.

Unsure, afraid, William stepped back.

2. Brutal military junta that overthrew Haile Selassie in 1974 and ruled Ethiopia until the Derg ("Committee") was itself toppled in 1991.

"Good-bye, William American," Fekadu said and drove away.

Standing at curbside, William couldn't breathe well. He wondered if he was dying. Of course he was dying, a flawed mortal dying day by day, but he felt like he might fall over from a heart attack or stroke right there on the sidewalk. He left his bags and ran inside the terminal. Let a luggage porter think his bags were dangerous! Let a security guard x-ray the bags and find mysterious shapes! Let a bomb-squad cowboy explode the bags as precaution! Let an airport manager shut down the airport and search every possible traveler! Let the FAA president order every airplane to land! Let the American skies be empty of everything with wings! Let the birds stop flying! Let the very air go still and cold! William didn't care. He ran through the terminal, searching for an available pay phone, a landline, something true and connected to the ground, and he finally found one and dropped two quarters into the slot and dialed his home number, and it rang and rang and rang and rang, and William worried that his wife and daughter were harmed, were lying dead on the floor, but then Marie answered.

"Hello, William," she said.

"I'm here," he said.

2003

QUESTIONS

1. William tells himself a variety of stories to cope with his feelings. How do these stories relate to his dialogue with the taxi driver and the stories the driver tells?
2. The taxi driver asks William, "The contradictions are the story, yes?" (par. 128). What might this indicate about Sherman Alexie's conception of the reality behind a good story?
3. At the end of FLIGHT PATTERNS, does William fully believe Fekadu's story? Does it matter to William whether or not Fekadu's story is factual?

GRACE PALEY (1922–2007)

A Conversation with My Father

Born to Russian immigrants in the Bronx, New York, Grace Paley attended Hunter College and New York University but never finished college because she was too busy reading and writing poetry before she turned to fiction. Her short stories, first published in *The Little Disturbances of Man: Stories of Men and Women at Love* (1959), *Enormous Changes at the Last Minute* (1974), and *Later the Same Day* (1985), are assembled in *The Collected Stories* (1994); her poetry, in *Begin Again: Collected Poems* (2000); and her essays, reviews, and lectures, in *Just as I Thought* (1998). In 1987, she was awarded a Senior Fellowship by the National Endowment for the Arts, in recognition of her lifetime contribution to literature. In 1988, she was named the first New York State Author. Always politically engaged, she was an outspoken critic of the Vietnam War and a lifelong antinuclear activist and feminist.

My father is eighty-six years old and in bed. His heart, that bloody motor, is equally old and will not do certain jobs any more. It still floods his head with brainy light. But it won't let his legs carry the weight of his body around the house. Despite my metaphors, this muscle failure is not due to his old heart, he says, but to a potassium shortage. Sitting on one pillow, leaning on three, he offers last-minute advice and makes a request.

"I would like you to write a simple story just once more," he says, "the kind de Maupassant wrote, or Chekhov, the kind you used to write. Just recognizable people and then write down what happened to them next."

I say, "Yes, why not? That's possible." I want to please him, though I don't remember writing that way. I *would* like to try to tell such a story, if he means the kind that begins: "There was a woman . . ." followed by plot, the absolute line between two points which I've always despised. Not for literary reasons, but because it takes all hope away. Everyone, real or invented, deserves the open destiny of life.

Finally I thought of a story that had been happening for a couple of years right across the street. I wrote it down, then read it aloud. "Pa," I said, "how about this? Do you mean something like this?"

5 Once in my time there was a woman and she had a son. They lived nicely, in a small apartment in Manhattan. This boy at about fifteen became a junkie, which is not unusual in our neighborhood. In order to maintain her close friendship with him, she became a junkie too. She said it was part of the youth culture, with which she felt very much at home. After a while, for a number of reasons, the boy gave it all up and left the city and his mother in disgust. Hopeless and alone, she grieved. We all visit her.

"O.K., Pa, that's it," I said, "an unadorned and miserable tale."

"But that's not what I mean," my father said. "You misunderstood me on purpose. You know there's a lot more to it. You know that. You left everything out. Turgenev[1] wouldn't do that. Chekhov wouldn't do that. There are in fact Russian writers you never heard of, you don't have an inkling of, as good as anyone, who can write a plain ordinary story, who would not leave out what you have left out. I object not to facts but to people sitting in trees talking senselessly, voices from who knows where . . ."

"Forget that one, Pa, what have I left out now? In this one?"

"Her looks, for instance."

10 "Oh. Quite handsome, I think. Yes."

"Her hair?"

"Dark, with heavy braids, as though she were a girl or a foreigner."

"What were her parents like, her stock? That she became such a person. It's interesting, you know."

"From out of town. Professional people. The first to be divorced in their county. How's that? Enough?" I asked.

15 "With you, it's all a joke," he said. "What about the boy's father. Why didn't you mention him? Who was he? Or was the boy born out of wedlock?"

1. Ivan Sergeyevich Turgenev (1818–83); his best-known novel, *Fathers and Sons*, deals with the conflict between generations.

"Yes," I said. "He was born out of wedlock."

"For Godsakes, doesn't anyone in your stories get married? Doesn't anyone have the time to run down to City Hall before they jump into bed?"

"No," I said. "In real life, yes. But in my stories, no."

"Why do you answer me like that?"

"Oh, Pa, this is a simple story about a smart woman who came to N.Y.C. full 20
of interest love trust excitement very up to date, and about her son, what a hard time she had in this world. Married or not, it's of small consequence."

"It is of great consequence," he said.

"O.K.," I said.

"O.K. O.K. yourself," he said, "but listen. I believe you that she's good-looking, but I don't think she was so smart."

"That's true," I said. "Actually that's the trouble with stories. People start out fantastic. You think they're extraordinary, but it turns out as the work goes along, they're just average with a good education. Sometimes the other way around, the person's a kind of dumb innocent, but he outwits you and you can't even think of an ending good enough."

"What do you do then?" he asked. He had been a doctor for a couple of 25
decades and then an artist for a couple of decades and he's still interested in details, craft, technique.

"Well, you just have to let the story lie around till some agreement can be reached between you and the stubborn hero."

"Aren't you talking silly, now?" he asked. "Start again," he said. "It so happens I'm not going out this evening. Tell the story again. See what you can do this time."

"O.K.," I said. "But it's not a five-minute job." Second attempt:

> Once, across the street from us, there was a fine handsome woman, our neighbor. She had a son whom she loved because she'd known him since birth (in helpless chubby infancy, and in the wrestling, hugging ages, seven to ten, as well as earlier and later). This boy, when he fell into the fist of adolescence, became a junkie. He was not a hopeless one. He was in fact hopeful, an ideologue and successful converter. With his busy brilliance, he wrote persuasive articles for his high-school newspaper. Seeking a wider audience, using important connections, he drummed into Lower Manhattan newsstand distribution a periodical called *Oh! Golden Horse!*[2]
>
> In order to keep him from feeling guilty (because guilt is the stony heart of 30
> nine tenths of all clinically diagnosed cancers in America today, she said), and because she had always believed in giving bad habits room at home where one could keep an eye on them, she too became a junkie. Her kitchen was famous for a while—a center for intellectual addicts who knew what they were doing. A few felt artistic like Coleridge[3] and others were scientific and revolutionary like Leary.[4] Although she was often high herself, certain good mothering reflexes remained, and she saw to it that there was lots of orange juice around and honey and milk and vitamin pills. However, she never cooked

2. *Horse* is slang for heroin.

3. Samuel Taylor Coleridge (1772–1834), English Romantic poet, claimed that his poem "Kubla Khan" recorded what he remembered of a dream stimulated by opium.

4. Timothy Leary (1920–96), American psychologist, promoted the use of psychedelic drugs.

anything but chili, and that no more than once a week. She explained, when we talked to her, seriously, with neighborly concern, that it was her part in the youth culture and she would rather be with the young, it was an honor, than with her own generation.

One week, while nodding through an Antonioni[5] film, this boy was severely jabbed by the elbow of a stern and proselytizing girl, sitting beside him. She offered immediate apricots and nuts for his sugar level, spoke to him sharply, and took him home.

She had heard of him and his work and she herself published, edited, and wrote a competitive journal called *Man Does Live By Bread Alone.* In the organic heat of her continuous presence he could not help but become interested once more in his muscles, his arteries, and nerve connections. In fact he began to love them, treasure them, praise them with funny little songs in *Man Does Live . . .*

the fingers of my flesh transcend
my transcendental soul
the tightness in my shoulders end
my teeth have made me whole

To the mouth of his head (that glory of will and determination) he brought hard apples, nuts, wheat germ, and soybean oil. He said to his old friends, From now on, I guess I'll keep my wits about me. I'm going on the natch. He said he was about to begin a spiritual deep-breathing journey. How about you too, Mom? he asked kindly.

His conversion was so radiant, splendid, that neighborhood kids his age began to say that he had never been a real addict at all, only a journalist along for the smell of the story. The mother tried several times to give up what had become without her son and his friends a lonely habit. This effort only brought it to supportable levels. The boy and his girl took their electronic mimeograph and moved to the bushy edge of another borough. They were very strict. They said they would not see her again until she had been off drugs for sixty days.

At home alone in the evening, weeping, the mother read and reread the seven issues of *Oh! Golden Horse!* They seemed to her as truthful as ever. We often crossed the street to visit and console. But if we mentioned any of our children who were at college or in the hospital or dropouts at home, she would cry out, My baby! My baby! and burst into terrible, face-scarring, time-consuming tears. The End.

First my father was silent, then he said, "Number One: You have a nice sense of humor. Number Two: I see you can't tell a plain story. So don't waste time." Then he said sadly, "Number Three: I suppose that means she was alone, she was left like that, his mother. Alone. Probably sick?"

I said, "Yes."

"Poor woman. Poor girl, to be born in a time of fools, to live among fools. The end. The end. You were right to put that down. The end."

5. Michelangelo Antonioni (1912–2007), Italian film director (*Blow-Up*, *Zabriskie Point*). *Nodding*: a slang term referring to the narcotic effect of heroin.

I didn't want to argue, but I had to say, "Well, it is not necessarily the end, Pa."

"Yes," he said, "what a tragedy. The end of a person." 40

"No, Pa," I begged him. "It doesn't have to be. She's only about forty. She could be a hundred different things in this world as time goes on. A teacher or a social worker. An ex-junkie! Sometimes it's better than having a master's in education."

"Jokes," he said. "As a writer that's your main trouble. You don't want to recognize it. Tragedy! Plain tragedy! Historical tragedy! No hope. The end."

"Oh, Pa," I said. "She could change."

"In your own life, too, you have to look it in the face." He took a couple of nitroglycerin.[6] "Turn to five," he said, pointing to the dial on the oxygen tank. He inserted the tubes into his nostrils and breathed deep. He closed his eyes and said, "No."

I had promised the family to always let him have the last word when arguing, 45
but in this case I had a different responsibility. That woman lives across the street. She's my knowledge and my invention. I'm sorry for her. I'm not going to leave her there in that house crying. (Actually neither would Life, which unlike me has no pity.)

Therefore: She did change. Of course her son never came home again. But right now, she's the receptionist in a storefront community clinic in the East Village. Most of the customers are young people, some old friends. The head doctor said to her, "If we only had three people in this clinic with your experiences . . ."

"The doctor said that?" My father took the oxygen tubes out of his nostrils and said, "Jokes. Jokes again."

"No, Pa, it could really happen that way, it's a funny world nowadays."

"No," he said. "Truth first. She will slide back. A person must have character. She does not."

"No, Pa," I said. "That's it. She's got a job. Forget it. She's in that storefront 50
working."

"How long will it be?" he asked. "Tragedy! You too. When will you look it in the face?"

1974

QUESTIONS

1. What different ideas about stories and storytelling do the narrator and her father seem to have in A CONVERSATION WITH MY FATHER? What might account for their different attitudes?
2. In what ways is the narrator's second version of her story an improvement over the first? Why does her father still reject the story?
3. Why does the narrator's father object so strongly to the jokes in the stories, even though he compliments her "nice sense of humor" (par. 36)? Are jokes out of place in a story about someone facing death?

6. Medicine for certain heart conditions.

AUTHORS ON THEIR WORK
GRACE PALEY (1922–2007)

From "Conversation with Grace Paley" (1980)*

I have lots of pages that I'll never turn into a story. [. . . They] are just a paragraph of nice writing, or something like that [. . .] It's not that they're not *worth* working with, but nothing in that paragraph gives me that feeling which is one of the impetuses of all storytelling: "I want to tell you a story—I want to tell you something."

• • •

[. . . E]verybody tells stories, and we all tell stories all day long. I've told about seven or eight today myself. And we are storytellers—I mean, we're keeping the record of this life on this place, on earth, you know—all the time. And often you tell a story and somebody says to you, "Gee, that's a good story," and you think to yourself, "Well, it certainly is a good story—it must be good—I've told it about six times." But then you don't write it. And you don't write it because you've told it so many times. And also because in writing there has to be [. . .] some of the joy of mystery. [. . .] There's a way I have of thinking about what you write, really *write*—you write what you *don't* know about what you know.

• • •

I don't really intend to be funny. [. . .] I have a story [. . .] "Conversation with My Father," in which my father keeps telling me: "All you do is tell jokes." And it was true [. . .] this was one of the things that he would always kind of bug me about. He'd say, "Okay, yeah, more jokes, you think that's funny, right?" And I'd say, "No, I didn't say it was funny. If people laugh, I can't help it—I didn't say it was funny."

*"Conversation with Grace Paley." Interview by Leonard Michaels. *Threepenny Review,* no. 3, Autumn 1980, pp. 4–6. *JSTOR,* www.jstor.org/stable/4382967.

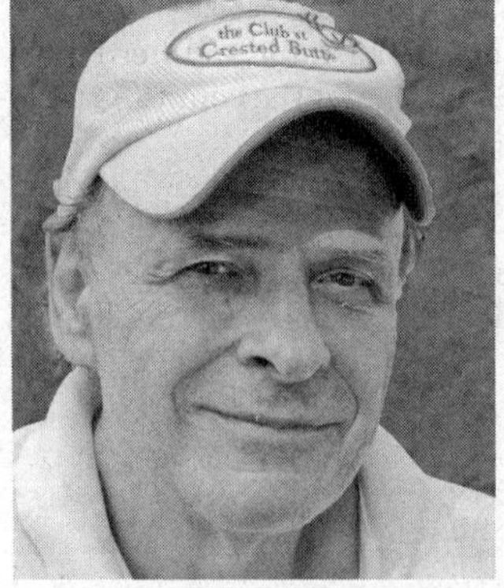

TIM O'BRIEN
(b. 1946)
The Lives of the Dead

The son of an insurance salesman who was also a World War II veteran and of an elementary-school teacher who had served, during the war, as a WAVE (navy-speak for Women Accepted for Volunteer Emergency Service), William Timothy (Tim) O'Brien grew up in Worthington, Minnesota, a place he has suggested one might find a sketch of "[i]f you look in a dictionary under the word 'boring.'" After a childhood spent playing Little League and "reading books like [. . .] *Huckleberry Finn* and *Tom Sawyer*," as well as "crap [. . .] like *The Hardy Boys*," O'Brien headed to college in 1964, just as the Vietnam War was escalating. In 1968, he was welcomed home, political science degree in hand, by a draft notice. Opposed to the war, O'Brien seriously considered evading service by heading to nearby Canada, only to decide that he simply "couldn't do it." Four months later he was an infantryman in Vietnam on a thirteen-month tour of duty. Returning home, in 1970, with a Bronze Star and a Purple Heart, O'Brien began work on a Harvard PhD (in government) that he would never finish and, with his hybrid memoir/novel *If I Die in a Combat Zone, Box Me Up and Ship Me Home* (1973), launched his career. Though he has published several other novels, O'Brien is primarily known for three books—*If I Die . . .*, the National Book Award–winning novel *Going after Cacciato* (1978), and the short-story collection *The Things They Carried* (1990). A finalist for both the Pulitzer Prize and the National Book Critics Circle Award, the latter book opens with "The Things They Carried" and closes with "The Lives of the Dead."

But this too is true: stories can save us. I'm forty-three years old, and a writer now, and even still, right here, I keep dreaming Linda alive. And Ted Lavender, too, and Kiowa, and Curt Lemon, and a slim young man I killed, and an old man sprawled beside a pigpen, and several others whose bodies I once lifted and dumped into a truck. They're all dead. But in a story, which is a kind of dreaming, the dead sometimes smile and sit up and return to the world.

Start here: a body without a name. On an afternoon in 1969 the platoon took sniper fire from a filthy little village along the South China Sea.[1] It lasted only a minute or two, and nobody was hurt, but even so Lieutenant Jimmy Cross got on the radio and ordered up an air strike. For the next half hour we watched the place burn. It was a cool bright morning, like early autumn, and the jets were glossy black against the sky. When it ended, we formed into a loose line and swept east through the village. It was all wreckage. I remember the smell of burnt straw; I remember broken fences and torn-up trees and heaps of stone and brick and pottery. The place was deserted—no people, no animals—and the only confirmed kill was an old man who lay face-up near a pigpen at the center of the village. His right arm was gone. At his face there were already many flies and gnats.

Dave Jensen went over and shook the old man's hand. "How-dee-doo," he said.

One by one the others did it too. They didn't disturb the body, they just grabbed the old man's hand and offered a few words and moved away.

Rat Kiley bent over the corpse. "Gimme five," he said. "A real honor." 5

"Pleased as punch," said Henry Dobbins.

I was brand-new to the war. It was my fourth day; I hadn't yet developed a sense of humor. Right away, as if I'd swallowed something, I felt a moist sickness rise up in my throat. I sat down beside the pigpen, closed my eyes, put my head between my knees.

After a moment Dave Jensen touched my shoulder.

1. Part of the Pacific Ocean enclosed by China and Taiwan (to the north), the Philippines (to the east), and Vietnam (to the west). This story takes place in Vietnam during the Vietnam War (c. 1954–75).

"Be polite now," he said. "Go introduce yourself. Nothing to be afraid about, just a nice old man. Show a little respect for your elders."

10 "No way."

"Maybe it's too real for you?"

"That's right," I said. "Way too real."

Jensen kept after me, but I didn't go near the body. I didn't even look at it except by accident. For the rest of the day there was still that sickness inside me, but it wasn't the old man's corpse so much, it was that awesome act of greeting the dead. At one point, I remember, they sat the body up against a fence. They crossed his legs and talked to him. "The guest of honor," Mitchell Sanders said, and he placed a can of orange slices in the old man's lap. "Vitamin C," he said gently. "A guy's health, that's the most important thing."

They proposed toasts. They lifted their canteens and drank to the old man's family and ancestors, his many grandchildren, his newfound life after death. It was more than mockery. There was a formality to it, like a funeral without the sadness.

15 Dave Jensen flicked his eyes at me.

"Hey. O'Brien," he said, "you got a toast in mind? Never too late for manners."

I found things to do with my hands. I looked away and tried not to think.

Late in the afternoon, just before dusk, Kiowa came up and asked if he could sit at my foxhole for a minute. He offered me a Christmas cookie from a batch his father had sent him. It was February now, but the cookies tasted fine.

For a few moments Kiowa watched the sky.

20 "You did a good thing today," he said. "That shaking hands crap, it isn't decent. The guys'll hassle you for a while—especially Jensen—but just keep saying no. Should've done it myself. Takes guts, I know that."

"It wasn't guts. I was scared."

Kiowa shrugged. "Same difference."

"No. I couldn't *do* it. A mental block or something . . . I don't know, just creepy."

"Well, you're new here. You'll get used to it." He paused for a second, studying the green and red sprinkles on a cookie. "Today—I guess this was your first look at a real body?"

25 I shook my head. All day long I'd been picturing Linda's face, the way she smiled.

"It sounds funny," I said, "but that poor old man, he reminds me of . . . I mean, there's this girl I used to know. I took her to the movies once. My first date."

Kiowa looked at me for a long while. Then he leaned back and smiled.

"Man," he said, "that's a bad date."

Linda was nine then, as I was, but we were in love. And it was real. When I write about her now, three decades later, it's tempting to dismiss it as a crush, an infatuation of childhood, but I know for a fact that what we felt for each other was as deep and rich as love can ever get. It had all the shadings and complexities of mature adult love, and maybe more, because there were not yet words for it, and because it was not yet fixed to comparisons or chronologies or the ways by which adults measure such things.

30 I just loved her.

She had poise and great dignity. Her eyes, I remember, were deep brown like her hair, and she was slender and very quiet and fragile-looking.

Even then, at nine years old, I wanted to live inside her body. I wanted to melt into her bones—*that* kind of love.

And so in the spring of 1956, when we were in the fourth grade, I took her out on the first real date of my life—a double date, actually, with my mother and father. Though I can't remember the exact sequence, my mother had somehow arranged it with Linda's parents, and on that damp spring night my dad did the driving while Linda and I sat in the back seat and stared out opposite windows, both of us trying to pretend it was nothing special. For me, though, it was very special. Down inside I had important things to tell her, big profound things, but I couldn't make any words come out. I had trouble breathing. Now and then I'd glance over at her, thinking how beautiful she was: her white skin and those dark brown eyes and the way she always smiled at the world—always, it seemed—as if her face had been designed that way. The smile never went away. That night, I remember, she wore a new red cap, which seemed to me very stylish and sophisticated, very unusual. It was a stocking cap, basically, except the tapered part at the top seemed extra long, almost too long, like a tail growing out of the back of her head. It made me think of the caps that Santa's elves wear, the same shape and color, the same fuzzy white tassel at the tip.

Sitting there in the back seat, I wanted to find some way to let her know how I felt, a compliment of some sort, but all I could manage was a stupid comment about the cap. "Jeez," I must've said, "what a *cap*."

Linda smiled at the window—she knew what I meant—but my mother turned and gave me a hard look. It surprised me. It was as if I'd brought up some horrible secret.

For the rest of the ride I kept my mouth shut. We parked in front of the Ben Franklin store[2] and walked up Main Street toward the State Theater. My parents went first, side by side, and then Linda in her new red cap, and then me tailing along ten or twenty steps behind. I was nine years old; I didn't yet have the gift for small talk. Now and then my mother glanced back, making little motions with her hand to speed me up.

At the ticket booth, I remember, Linda stood off to one side. I moved over to the concession area, studying the candy, and both of us were very careful to avoid the awkwardness of eye contact. Which was how we knew about being in love. It was pure knowing. Neither of us, I suppose, would've thought to use that word, love, but by the fact of not looking at each other, and not talking, we understood with a clarity beyond language that we were sharing something huge and permanent.

Behind me, in the theater, I heard cartoon music.

"Hey, step it up," I said. I almost had the courage to look at her. "You want popcorn or *what*?"

The thing about a story is that you dream it as you tell it, hoping that others might then dream along with you, and in this way memory and imagination and language

2. Discount store common in small towns throughout the United States since the 1920s.

combine to make spirits in the head. There is the illusion of aliveness. In Vietnam, for instance, Ted Lavender had a habit of popping four or five tranquilizers every morning. It was his way of coping, just dealing with the realities, and the drugs helped to ease him through the days. I remember how peaceful his eyes were. Even in bad situations he had a soft, dreamy expression on his face, which was what he wanted, a kind of escape. "How's the war today?" somebody would ask, and Ted Lavender would give a little smile to the sky and say, "Mellow—a nice smooth war today." And then in April he was shot in the head outside the village of Than Khe. Kiowa and I and a couple of others were ordered to prepare his body for the dustoff.[3] I remember squatting down, not wanting to look but then looking. Lavender's left cheekbone was gone. There was a swollen blackness around his eye. Quickly, trying not to feel anything, we went through the kid's pockets. I remember wishing I had gloves. It wasn't the blood I hated; it was the deadness. We put his personal effects in a plastic bag and tied the bag to his arm. We stripped off the canteens and ammo, all the heavy stuff, and wrapped him up in his own poncho and carried him out to a dry paddy and laid him down.

For a while nobody said much. Then Mitchell Sanders laughed and looked over at the green plastic poncho.

"Hey, Lavender," he said, "how's the war today?"

There was a short quiet.

"Mellow," somebody said.

"Well, that's good," Sanders murmured, "that's real, real good. Stay cool now."

"Hey, no sweat, I'm mellow."

"Just ease on back, then. Don't need no pills. We got this incredible chopper on call, this once in a lifetime mind-trip."

"Oh, yeah—mellow!"

Mitchell Sanders smiled. "There it is, my man, this chopper gonna take you up high and cool. Gonna relax you. Gonna alter your whole perspective on this sorry, sorry shit."

We could almost see Ted Lavender's dreamy blue eyes. We could almost hear him.

"Roger that," somebody said. "I'm ready to fly."

There was the sound of the wind, the sound of birds and the quiet afternoon, which was the world we were in.

That's what a story does. The bodies are animated. You make the dead talk. They sometimes say things like, "Roger that." Or they say, "Timmy, stop crying," which is what Linda said to me after she was dead.

Even now I can see her walking down the aisle of the old State Theater in Worthington, Minnesota.[4] I can see her face in profile beside me, the cheeks softly lighted by coming attractions.

The movie that night was *The Man Who Never Was*.[5] I remember the plot clearly, or at least the premise, because the main character was a corpse. That

3. Medical evacuation helicopter, perhaps an acronym for Dedicated Unhesitating Service to Our Fighting Forces.

4. Small town near the South Dakota border where author Tim O'Brien grew up.

5. Film (1956) based on real events that occurred during World War II.

fact alone, I know, deeply impressed me. It was a World War Two film: the Allies[6] devise a scheme to mislead Germany about the site of the upcoming landings in Europe. They get their hands on a body—a British soldier, I believe; they dress him up in an officer's uniform, plant fake documents in his pockets, then dump him in the sea and let the currents wash him onto a Nazi beach. The Germans find the documents; the deception wins the war. Even now, I can remember the awful splash as that corpse fell into the sea. I remember glancing over at Linda, thinking it might be too much for her, but in the dim gray light she seemed to be smiling at the screen. There were little crinkles at her eyes, her lips open and gently curving at the corners. I couldn't understand it. There was nothing to smile at. Once or twice, in fact, I had to close my eyes, but it didn't help much. Even then I kept seeing the soldier's body tumbling toward the water, splashing down hard, how inert and heavy it was, how completely dead.

It was a relief when the movie finally ended.

Afterward, we drove out to the Dairy Queen at the edge of town. The night had a quilted, weighted-down quality, as if somehow burdened, and all around us the Minnesota prairies reached out in long repetitive waves of corn and soybeans, everything flat, everything the same. I remember eating ice cream in the back seat of the Buick, and a long blank drive in the dark, and then pulling up in front of Linda's house. Things must've been said, but it's all gone now except for a few last images. I remember walking her to the front door. I remember the brass porch light with its fierce yellow glow, my own feet, the juniper bushes along the front steps, the wet grass, Linda close beside me. We were in love. Nine years old, yes, but it was real love, and now we were alone on those front steps. Finally we looked at each other.

"Bye," I said.

Linda nodded and said, "Bye."

Over the next few weeks Linda wore her new red cap to school every day. She 60
never took it off, not even in the classroom, and so it was inevitable that she took some teasing about it. Most of it came from a kid named Nick Veenhof. Out on the playground, during recess, Nick would creep up behind her and make a grab for the cap, almost yanking it off, then scampering away. It went on like that for weeks: the girls giggling, the guys egging him on. Naturally I wanted to do something about it, but it just wasn't possible. I had my reputation to think about. I had my pride. And there was also the problem of Nick Veenhof. So I stood off to the side, just a spectator, wishing I could do things I couldn't do. I watched Linda clamp down the cap with the palm of her hand, holding it there, smiling over in Nick's direction as if none of it really mattered.

For me, though, it did matter. It still does. I should've stepped in; fourth grade is no excuse. Besides, it doesn't get easier with time, and twelve years later, when Vietnam presented much harder choices, some practice at being brave might've helped a little.

Also, too, I might've stopped what happened next. Maybe not, but at least it's possible.

Most of the details I've forgotten, or maybe blocked out, but I know it was an afternoon in late spring, and we were taking a spelling test, and halfway into

6. Coalition of nations including France, Great Britain, and the United States.

the test Nick Veenhof held up his hand and asked to use the pencil sharpener. Right away a couple of kids laughed. No doubt he'd broken the pencil on purpose, but it wasn't something you could prove, and so the teacher nodded and told him to hustle it up. Which was a mistake. Out of nowhere Nick developed a terrible limp. He moved in slow motion, dragging himself up to the pencil sharpener and carefully slipping in his pencil and then grinding away forever. At the time, I suppose, it was funny. But on the way back to his seat Nick took a short detour. He squeezed between two desks, turned sharply right, and moved up the aisle toward Linda.

I saw him grin at one of his pals. In a way, I already knew what was coming. As he passed Linda's desk, he dropped the pencil and squatted down to get it. When he came up, his left hand slipped behind her back. There was a half-second hesitation. Maybe he was trying to stop himself; maybe then, just briefly, he felt some small approximation of guilt. But it wasn't enough. He took hold of the white tassel, stood up, and gently lifted off her cap.

Somebody must've laughed. I remember a short, tinny echo. I remember Nick Veenhof trying to smile. Somewhere behind me, a girl said, "Uh," or a sound like that.

Linda didn't move.

Even now, when I think back on it, I can still see the glossy whiteness of her scalp. She wasn't bald. Not quite. Not completely. There were some tufts of hair, little patches of grayish brown fuzz. But what I saw then, and keep seeing now, is all that whiteness. A smooth, pale, translucent white. I could see the bones and veins; I could see the exact structure of her skull. There was a large Band-Aid at the back of her head, a row of black stitches, a piece of gauze taped above her left ear.

Nick Veenhof took a step backward. He was still smiling, but the smile was doing strange things.

The whole time Linda stared straight ahead, her eyes locked on the blackboard, her hands loosely folded at her lap. She didn't say anything. After a time, though, she turned and looked at me across the room. It lasted only a moment, but I had the feeling that a whole conversation was happening between us. *Well?* she was saying, and I was saying, *Sure, okay.*

Later on, she cried for a while. The teacher helped her put the cap back on, then we finished the spelling test and did some fingerpainting, and after school that day Nick Veenhof and I walked her home.

It's now 1990. I'm forty-three years old, which would've seemed impossible to a fourth grader, and yet when I look at photographs of myself as I was in 1956, I realize that in the important ways I haven't changed at all. I was Timmy then; now I'm Tim. But the essence remains the same. I'm not fooled by the baggy pants or the crew cut or the happy smile—I know my own eyes—and there is no doubt that the Timmy smiling at the camera is the Tim I am now. Inside the body, or beyond the body, there is something absolute and unchanging. The human life is all one thing, like a blade tracing loops on ice: a little kid, a twenty-three-year-old infantry sergeant, a middle-aged writer knowing guilt and sorrow.

And as a writer now, I want to save Linda's life. Not her body—her life.

She died, of course. Nine years old and she died. It was a brain tumor. She lived through the summer and into the first part of September, and then she was dead.

But in a story I can steal her soul. I can revive, at least briefly, that which is 75
absolute and unchanging. In a story, miracles can happen. Linda can smile and sit up. She can reach out, touch my wrist, and say, "Timmy, stop crying.

I needed that kind of miracle. At some point I had come to understand that Linda was sick, maybe even dying, but I loved her and just couldn't accept it. In the middle of the summer, I remember, my mother tried to explain to me about brain tumors. Now and then, she said, bad things start growing inside us. Sometimes you can cut them out and other times you can't, and for Linda it was one of the times when you can't.

I thought about it for several days. "All right," I finally said. "So will she get better now?"

"Well, no," my mother said, "I don't think so." She stared at a spot behind my shoulder. "Sometimes people don't ever get better. They die sometimes."

I shook my head.

"Not Linda," I said. 80

But on a September afternoon, during noon recess, Nick Veenhof came up to me on the school playground. "Your girlfriend," he said, "she kicked the bucket."

At first I didn't understand.

"She's dead," he said. "My mom told me at lunch-time. No lie, she actually kicked the goddang *bucket*."

All I could do was nod. Somehow it didn't quite register. I turned away, glanced down at my hands for a second, then walked home without telling anyone.

It was a little after one o'clock, I remember, and the house was empty. 85

I drank some chocolate milk and then lay down on the sofa in the living room, not really sad, just floating, trying to imagine what it was to be dead. Nothing much came to me. I remember closing my eyes and whispering her name, almost begging, trying to make her come back. "Linda," I said, "please." And then I concentrated. I willed her alive. It was a dream, I suppose, or a daydream, but I made it happen. I saw her coming down the middle of Main Street, all alone. It was nearly dark and the street was deserted, no cars or people, and Linda wore a pink dress and shiny black shoes. I remember sitting down on the curb to watch. All her hair had grown back. The scars and stitches were gone. In the dream, if that's what it was, she was playing a game of some sort, laughing and running up the empty street, kicking a big aluminum water bucket.

Right then I started to cry. After a moment Linda stopped and carried her water bucket over to the curb and asked why I was so sad.

"Well, God," I said, "you're dead."

Linda nodded at me. She was standing under a yellow streetlight. A nine-year-old girl, just a kid, and yet there was something ageless in her eyes—not a child, not an adult—just a bright ongoing everness, that same pinprick of absolute lasting light that I see today in my own eyes as Timmy smiles at Tim from the graying photographs of that time.

"Dead," I said. 90

Linda smiled. It was a secret smile, as if she knew things nobody could ever know, and she reached out and touched my wrist and said, "Timmy, stop crying. It doesn't *matter*."

In Vietnam, too, we had ways of making the dead seem not quite so dead. Shaking hands, that was one way. By slighting death, by acting, we pretended it was not the terrible thing it was. By our language, which was both hard and wistful, we transformed the bodies into piles of waste. Thus, when someone got killed, as Curt Lemon did, his body was not really a body, but rather one small bit of waste in the midst of a much wider wastage. I learned that words make a difference. It's easier to cope with a kicked bucket than a corpse; if it isn't human, it doesn't matter much if it's dead. And so a VC nurse, fried by napalm,[7] was a crispy critter. A Vietnamese baby, which lay nearby, was a roasted peanut. "Just a crunchie munchie," Rat Kiley said as he stepped over the body.

We kept the dead alive with stories. When Ted Lavender was shot in the head, the men talked about how they'd never seen him so mellow, how tranquil he was, how it wasn't the bullet but the tranquilizers that blew his mind. He wasn't dead, just laid-back. There were Christians among us, like Kiowa, who believed in the New Testament stories of life after death. Other stories were passed down like legends from old-timer to newcomer. Mostly, though, we had to make up our own. Often they were exaggerated, or blatant lies, but it was a way of bringing body and soul back together, or a way of making new bodies for the souls to inhabit. There was a story, for instance, about how Curt Lemon had gone trick-or-treating on Halloween. A dark, spooky night, and so Lemon put on a ghost mask and painted up his body all different colors and crept across a paddy to a sleeping village—almost stark naked, the story went, just boots and balls and an M-16—and in the dark Lemon went from hootch to hootch[8]—ringing doorbells, he called it—and a few hours later, when he slipped back into the perimeter, he had a whole sackful of goodies to share with his pals: candles and joss sticks[9] and a pair of black pajamas and statuettes of the smiling Buddha. That was the story, anyway. Other versions were much more elaborate, full of descriptions and scraps of dialogue. Rat Kiley liked to spice it up with extra details: "See, what happens is, it's like four in the morning, and Lemon sneaks into a hootch with that weird ghost mask on. Everybody's asleep, right? So he wakes up this cute little mama-san.[1] Tickles her foot. 'Hey, Mama-san,' he goes, real soft like. Hey, Mama-san—trick or treat!' Should've seen her face. About freaks. I mean, there's this buck naked ghost standing there, and he's got this M-16 up against her ear and he whispers, 'Hey, Mama-san, trick or fuckin' treat!' Then he takes off her pj's. Strips her right down. Sticks the pajamas in his sack and tucks her into bed and heads for the next hootch."

Pausing a moment. Rat Kiley would grin and shake his head. "Honest to God," he'd murmur. "Trick or treat. Lemon—there's one class act."

To listen to the story, especially as Rat Kiley told it, you'd never know that Curt Lemon was dead. He was still out there in the dark, naked and painted

7. Flammable jelly used in incendiary bombs. *VC*: Viet Cong (military acronym/slang), short for Viet Nam Cong Sam, meaning "Vietnamese Communists," the guerrilla force that fought, with the support of the North Vietnamese Army, against both South Vietnam and the United States during the Vietnam War.

8. Hut or small dwelling (slang).

9. Incense sticks.

1. In East Asia, a woman in authority; in Japanese, *san* is an honorific suffix, a title (not unlike "Mr." or "Mrs.") added to names and proper nouns to indicate respect.

up, trick-or-treating, sliding from hootch to hootch in that crazy white ghost mask. But he was dead.

In September, the day after Linda died, I asked my father to take me down to Benson's Funeral Home to view the body. I was a fifth grader then; I was curious. On the drive downtown my father kept his eyes straight ahead. At one point, I remember, he made a scratchy sound in his throat. It took him a long time to light up a cigarette.

"Timmy," he said, "you're sure about this?"

I nodded at him. Down inside, of course. I wasn't sure, and yet I had to see her one more time. What I needed, I suppose, was some sort of final confirmation, something to carry with me after she was gone.

When we parked in front of the funeral home, my father turned and looked at me. "If this bothers you," he said, "just say the word. We'll make a quick getaway. Fair enough?"

"Okay," I said. 100

"Or if you start to feel sick or anything—"

"I *won't*," I told him.

Inside, the first thing I noticed was the smell, thick and sweet, like something sprayed out of a can. The viewing room was empty except for Linda and my father and me. I felt a rush of panic as we walked up the aisle. The smell made me dizzy. I tried to fight it off, slowing down a little, taking short, shallow breaths through my mouth. But at the same time I felt a funny excitement. Anticipation, in a way—that same awkward feeling as when I'd walked up the sidewalk to ring her doorbell on our first date. I wanted to impress her. I wanted something to happen between us, a secret signal of some sort. The room was dimly lighted, almost dark, but at the far end of the aisle Linda's white casket was illuminated by a row of spotlights up in the ceiling. Everything was quiet. My father put his hand on my shoulder, whispered something, and backed off. After a moment I edged forward a few steps, pushing up on my toes for a better look.

It didn't seem real. A mistake, I thought. The girl lying in the white casket wasn't Linda. There was a resemblance, maybe, but where Linda had always been very slender and fragile-looking, almost skinny, the body in that casket was fat and swollen. For a second I wondered if somebody had made a terrible blunder. A technical mistake: pumped her too full of formaldehyde or embalming fluid or whatever they used. Her arms and face were bloated. The skin at her cheeks was stretched out tight like the rubber skin on a balloon just before it pops open. Even her fingers seemed puffy. I turned and glanced behind me, where my father stood, thinking that maybe it was a joke—hoping it was a joke—almost believing that Linda would jump out from behind one of the curtains and laugh and yell out my name.

But she didn't. The room was silent. When I looked back at the casket, I felt 105
dizzy again. In my heart, I'm sure, I knew this was Linda, but even so I couldn't find much to recognize. I tried to pretend she was taking a nap, her hands folded at her stomach, just sleeping away the afternoon. Except she didn't *look* asleep. She looked dead. She looked heavy and totally dead.

I remember closing my eyes. After a while my father stepped up beside me.

"Come on now," he said. "Let's go get some ice cream."

In the months after Ted Lavender died, there were many other bodies. I never shook hands—not that—but one afternoon I climbed a tree and threw down what was left of Curt Lemon. I watched my friend Kiowa sink into the muck along the Song Tra Bong. And in early July, after a battle in the mountains, I was assigned to a six-man detail to police up the enemy KIAs.[2] There were twenty-seven bodies altogether, and parts of several others. The dead were everywhere. Some lay in piles. Some lay alone. One, I remember, seemed to kneel. Another was bent from the waist over a small boulder, the top of his head on the ground, his arms rigid, the eyes squinting in concentration as if he were about to perform a handstand or somersault. It was my worst day at the war. For three hours we carried the bodies down the mountain to a clearing alongside a narrow dirt road. We had lunch there, then a truck pulled up, and we worked in two-man teams to load the truck. I remember swinging the bodies up. Mitchell Sanders took a man's feet, I took the arms, and we counted to three, working up momentum, and then we tossed the body high and watched it bounce and come to rest among the other bodies. The dead had been dead for more than a day. They were all badly bloated. Their clothing was stretched tight like sausage skins, and when we picked them up, some made sharp burping sounds as the gases were released. They were heavy. Their feet were bluish green and cold. The smell was terrible. At one point Mitchell Sanders looked at me and said, "Hey, man, I just realized something."

"What?"

He wiped his eyes and spoke very quietly, as if awed by his own wisdom.

"Death sucks," he said.

Lying in bed at night, I made up elaborate stories to bring Linda alive in my sleep. I invented my own dreams. It sounds impossible, I know, but I did it. I'd picture somebody's birthday party—a crowded room, I'd think, and a big chocolate cake with pink candles—and then soon I'd be dreaming it, and after a while Linda would show up, as I knew she would, and in the dream we'd look at each other and not talk much, because we were shy, but then later I'd walk her home and we'd sit on her front steps and stare at the dark and just be together.

She'd say amazing things sometimes. "Once you're alive," she'd say, "you can't ever be dead."

Or she'd say: "Do I *look* dead?"

It was a kind of self-hypnosis. Partly willpower, partly faith, which is how stories arrive.

But back then it felt like a miracle. My dreams had become a secret meeting place, and in the weeks after she died I couldn't wait to fall asleep at night. I began going to bed earlier and earlier, sometimes even in bright daylight. My mother, I remember, finally asked about it at breakfast one morning. "Timmy, what's *wrong*?" she said, but all I could do was shrug and say, "Nothing. I just need sleep, that's all." I didn't dare tell the truth. It was embarrassing, I suppose, but it was also a precious secret, like a magic trick, where if I tried to explain it, or even talk about it, the thrill and mystery would be gone. I didn't want to lose Linda.

2. Killed in action (military acronym/slang).

She was dead. I understood that. After all, I'd seen her body. And yet even as a nine-year-old I had begun to practice the magic of stories. Some I just dreamed up. Others I wrote down—the scenes and dialogue. And at nighttime I'd slide into sleep knowing that Linda would be there waiting for me. Once, I remember, we went ice skating late at night, tracing loops and circles under yellow floodlights. Later we sat by a wood stove in the warming house, all alone, and after a while I asked her what it was like to be dead. Apparently Linda thought it was a silly question. She smiled and said, "Do I *look* dead?"

I told her no, she looked terrific. I waited a moment, then asked again, and Linda made a soft little sigh. I could smell our wool mittens drying on the stove.

For a few seconds she was quiet.

"Well, right now," she said, "I'm *not* dead. But when I am, it's like . . . I don't 120
know. I guess it's like being inside a book that nobody's reading."

"A book?" I said.

"An old one. It's up on a library shelf, so you're safe and everything, but the book hasn't been checked out for a long, long time. All you can do is wait. Just hope somebody'll pick it up and start reading."

Linda smiled at me.

"Anyhow, it's not so bad," she said. "I mean, when you're dead, you just have to be yourself." She stood up and put on her red stocking cap. "This is stupid. Let's go skate some more."

So I followed her down to the frozen pond. It was late, and nobody else was 125
there, and we held hands and skated almost all night under the yellow lights.

And then it becomes 1990. I'm forty-three years old, and a writer now, still dreaming Linda alive in exactly the same way. She's not the embodied Linda; she's mostly made up, with a new identity and a new name, like the man who never was. Her real name doesn't matter. She was nine years old. I loved her and then she died. And yet right here, in the spell of memory and imagination, I can still see her as if through ice, as if I'm gazing into some other world, a place where there are no brain tumors and no funeral homes, where there are no bodies at all. I can see Kiowa, too, and Ted Lavender and Curt Lemon, and sometimes I can even see Timmy skating with Linda under the yellow floodlights. I'm young and happy. I'll never die. I'm skimming across the surface of my own history, moving fast, riding the melt beneath the blades, doing loops and spins, and when I take a high leap into the dark and come down thirty years later, I realize it is as Tim trying to save Timmy's life with a story.

1986, 1990

QUESTIONS

1. This story begins, "But this too is true: stories can save us" (par. 1). In what different ways does that prove true in this story? Why "but"?
2. In terms of the story's exploration of the relationship between fact and fiction, life and stories, how might it matter that the story's narrator is called Tim O'Brien? that the movie Linda and Timmy see is *The Man Who Never Was*?
3. What do Nick Veenhof and the incident with Linda's red cap contribute to the story? How would the story work differently, and how might its meaning change without this character or incident?

SUGGESTIONS FOR WRITING

1. Citing examples from one or more of the stories in this album, write an essay discussing the effects of storytelling on the actions, attitudes, and/or relationships of the characters.
2. Write an essay comparing what A CONVERSATION WITH MY FATHER and THE LIVES OF THE DEAD suggest about the relationship between death and stories. Might the various characters within each story (and especially Paley's) express different views? If so, which, if any, does each story seem to embrace?
3. Write a response paper or essay comparing an experience you've had either telling or hearing a personally revealing story to the experience of Fekadu or William in FLIGHT PATTERNS. What might the depiction of this character's experience now help you see or understand about your own? Conversely, how might your experience shape your response to theirs?

Understanding the Text

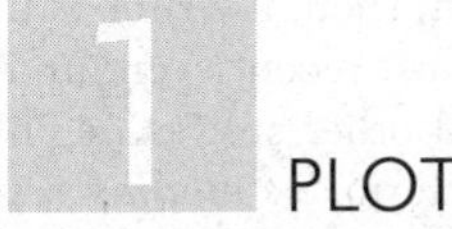

1 PLOT

At its most basic, every story is an attempt to answer the question *What happened?* In some cases, this question is easy to answer. J. R. R. Tolkien's *The Lord of the Rings* trilogy (1954–55) is full of battles, chases, and other heart-stopping dramatic action; Mark Twain's *Adventures of Huckleberry Finn* (1884) relates Huck and Jim's adventures as they travel down the Mississippi River. Yet if we ask what happens in other works of fiction, our initial answer might well be, "Not much." In one of the most pivotal scenes in Henry James's novel *The Portrait of a Lady* (1881), for example, a woman enters a room, sees a man sitting down and a woman standing up, and beats a hasty retreat. Not terribly exciting stuff, it would seem. Yet this event ends up radically transforming the lives of just about everyone in the novel. "On very tiny pivots do human lives turn" would thus seem to be one common message—or **theme**—of fiction.

All fiction, regardless of its subject matter, should make us ask, *What will happen next?* and *How will all this turn out?* And responsive readers of fiction will often pause to answer those questions, trying to articulate just what their expectations are and how the story has shaped them. But great fiction and responsive readers are often just as interested in questions about *why* things happen and about *how* the characters' lives are affected as a result. These *how* and *why* questions are likely to be answered very differently by different readers of the very same fictional work; as a result, such questions will often generate powerful essays, whereas mainly factual questions about what happens in the work usually won't.

PLOT VERSUS ACTION, SEQUENCE, AND SUBPLOT

The term **plot** is sometimes used to refer to the events recounted in a fictional work. But in this book we instead use the term **action** in this way, reserving the term *plot* for the way the author sequences and paces the events so as to shape our response and interpretation.

The difference between action and plot resembles the difference between ancient chronicles that merely list the events of a king's reign in chronological order and more modern histories that make a meaningful sequence out of those events. As the British novelist and critic E. M. Forster put it, "The king died and then the queen died" is not a plot, for it has not been "tampered with." "The queen died after the king died" describes the same events, but the order in which they are reported has been changed. The reader of the first sentence focuses on the king first, the reader of the second on the queen. The second sentence, moreover, subtly encourages us to speculate about *why* things happened, not just *what* happened and *when*: Did the queen die *because* her husband did? If so, was her death the result of her grief? Or was she murdered by a rival who saw the king's death as the perfect opportunity to get rid of her, too? Though our two sentences describe the same action, each has quite a different focus, emphasis, effect, and meaning thanks to its *sequencing*—the precise order in which events are related.

Like chronicles, many fictional works do relate events in chronological order, starting with the earliest and ending with the latest. Folktales, for example, have this sort of plot. But fiction writers have other choices; events need not be recounted in the particular order in which they happened. Quite often, then, a writer will choose to mix things up, perhaps opening a story with the most recent event and then moving backward to show us all that led up to it. Still other stories begin somewhere in the middle of the action or, to use the Latin term, ***in medias res*** (literally, "in the middle of things"). In such plots, events that occurred before the story's opening are sometimes presented in **flashbacks**. Conversely, a story might jump forward in time to recount a later **episode** or event in a **flashforward**. **Foreshadowing** occurs when an author merely gives subtle clues or hints about what will happen later in the story.

Though we often talk about *the* plot of a fictional work, however, keep in mind that some works, especially longer ones, have two or more. A plot that receives significantly less time and attention than another is called a **subplot**.

PACE

In life, we sometimes have little choice about how long a particular event lasts. If you want a driver's license, you may have to spend a boring hour or two at the motor vehicle office. And much as you might prefer to relax and enjoy your lunch, occasionally you have to scarf it down in the ten minutes it takes you to drive to campus.

One of the pleasures of turning experiences into a story, however, is that doing so gives a writer more power over them. In addition to choosing the order in which to recount events, the writer can also decide how much time and attention to devote to each. *Pacing*, or the duration of particular episodes—especially relative to each other and to the time they would have taken in real life—is a vital tool of storytellers and another important factor to consider in analyzing plots. In all fiction, pace as much as sequence determines focus and emphasis, effect and meaning. And though it can be very helpful to differentiate between "fast-paced" and "slow-paced" fiction, all effective stories contain both faster and slower bits. When an author slows down to home in on a particular moment and scene, often introduced by a phrase such as "Later that evening . . ." or "The day before Maggie fell down . . . ," we call this a **discriminated occasion**. For example, the first paragraph of Linda Brewer's 20/20 quickly and generally refers to events that occur over three days. Then Brewer suddenly slows down, pinpointing an incident that takes place on "[t]he third evening out. . . ." That episode consumes four paragraphs of the story, even though the action described in those paragraphs accounts for only a few minutes of Bill and Ruthie's time. Next the story devotes two more paragraphs to an incident that occurs "[t]he next evening." In the last paragraph, Brewer speeds up again, telling us about the series of "wonderful sights" Ruthie sees between Indiana and Spokane, Washington.

CONFLICTS

Whatever their sequence and pace, all plots hinge on at least one **conflict**—some sort of struggle—and its resolution. Conflicts may be *external* or *internal.* External conflicts arise between characters and something or someone outside themselves. Adventure stories and films often present this sort of conflict in its purest form, keeping us poised on the edge of our seats as James Bond struggles to outwit and outfight an arch-villain intent on world domination or destruction. Yet external conflicts can also be much subtler, pitting an individual against nature or fate, against a social force such as racism or poverty, or against another person or group of people with a different way of looking at things (as in "20/20"). The cartoon below presents an external conflict of the latter type and one you may well see quite differently than the cartoonist does.

Internal conflicts occur when a character struggles to reconcile two competing desires, needs, or duties, or two parts or aspects of himself: His head, for instance, might tell him to do one thing, his heart another. Often, a conflict is simultaneously external and internal, as in the following brief folktale, in which a woman seems to struggle simultaneously with nature, with mortality, with God, and with her desire to hold on to someone she loves versus her need to let go.

JACOB AND WILHELM GRIMM

The Shroud

There was once a mother who had a little boy of seven years old, who was so handsome and lovable that no one could look at him without liking him, and she herself worshipped him above everything in the world. Now it so happened that he suddenly became ill, and God took him to himself; and for this the mother could not be comforted, and wept both day and night. But soon afterwards, when the child had been buried, it appeared by night in the places where it had sat and played during its life, and if the mother wept, it wept also, and, when morning came, it disappeared. As, however, the mother would not stop crying, it came one night, in the little white shroud in which it had been laid in its coffin, and with its wreath of flowers round its head, and stood on the bed at her feet, and said, "Oh, mother, do stop crying, or I shall never fall asleep in my coffin, for my shroud will not dry because of all thy tears which fall upon it." The mother was afraid when she heard that, and wept no more. The next night the child came again, and held a little light in its hand, and said, "Look, mother, my shroud is nearly dry, and I can rest in my grave." Then the mother gave her sorrow into God's keeping, and bore it quietly and patiently, and the child came no more, but slept in its little bed beneath the earth.

1812

• • •

THE FIVE PARTS OF PLOT

Even compact and simple plots, like that of THE SHROUD, have the same five parts or phases as lengthy and complex plots: (1) exposition, (2) rising action, (3) climax or turning point, (4) falling action, and (5) conclusion or resolution. The following diagram, named Freytag's pyramid after the nineteenth-century German scholar Gustav Freytag, maps out a typical plot structure:

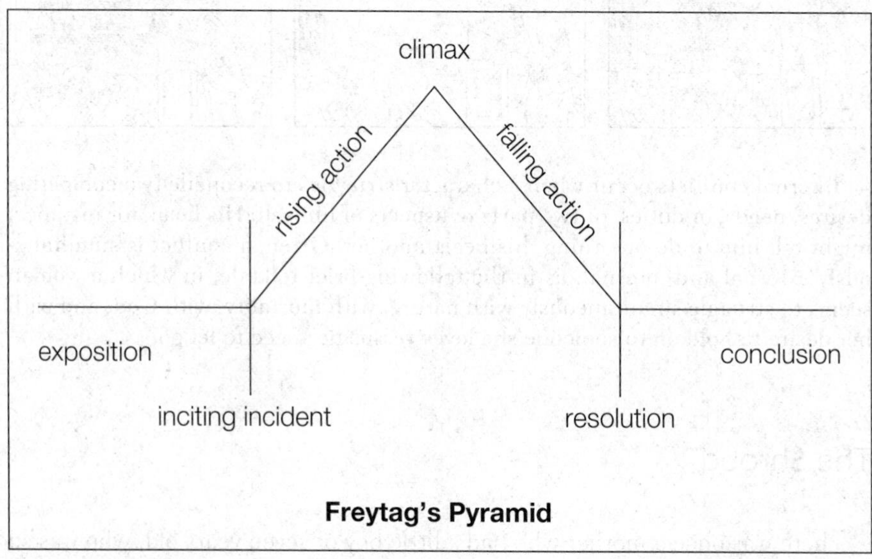

Freytag's Pyramid

Exposition

The first part of the plot, called the **exposition**, introduces the characters, their situations, and, usually, a time and place, giving us all the basic information we need to understand what is to come. In longer works of fiction, exposition may go on for paragraphs or even pages, and some exposition may well be deferred until later phases of the plot. But in our examples, the exposition is all up-front and brief: Trudeau's first panel shows us a teacher (or at least his words), a group of students, and a classroom; the Grimms' first sentence introduces a mother, her young son, and the powerful love she feels for him.

Exposition usually reveals some source or seed of potential conflict in the initial situation, of which the characters may be as yet unaware. In Trudeau's cartoon, the contrast between the talkative teacher, who expects "independent thought" from those in his class, and the silent, scribbling students suggests a conflict in the making. So, too, does the Grimms' statement that the mother "worshipped" her boy "above everything" else in a world in which nothing and no one lasts forever.

Rising Action

By suggesting a conflict, exposition may blend into the second phase of the plot, the **rising action**, which begins with an **inciting incident** or *destabilizing event*—that is, some action that destabilizes the initial situation and incites open conflict, as does the death of the little boy in the second sentence of the folktale. Typically, what keeps the action rising is a **complication**, an event that introduces a new conflict or intensifies an existing one. This happens in the third sentence of "The Shroud," when the mother begins to see her little boy every night, although he is dead and buried.

Climax or Turning Point

The plot's **climax** or **turning point** is the moment of greatest emotional intensity. (Notice the way boldface lettering appears and exclamation points replace question marks in the second-to-last panel of the *Doonesbury* strip.) The climax is also the moment when the outcome of the plot and the fate of the characters are decided. (A climax thus tends to be a literally *pivotal* incident that "turns things around," or involves, in Aristotle's words, "the change from one state of things [. . .] to its opposite.") THE SHROUD reaches its climax when the mother stops crying after her little boy tells her that her grief is what keeps him from sleeping and that peaceful sleep is what he craves.

Here, as in many plots, the turning point involves a discovery or new insight or even an **epiphany**, a sudden revelation of truth inspired by a seemingly trivial event. As a result, turning points often involve internal or psychological events, even if they are prompted by, and lead to, external action. In "The Shroud," for instance, the mother's new insight results in different behavior: She "wept no more."

Sometimes, though, critics differentiate between the story's climax and the **crisis** that precedes and precipitates it. In "The Shroud," for example, these critics would describe the crisis as the moment when the son confronts the mother with information that implicitly requires her to make a choice, the climax as the moment when she makes it. This distinction might be especially helpful when you grapple with longer works of fiction in which much more time and action intervenes between the crisis and the climax.

Falling Action

The **falling action** brings a release of emotional tension and moves us toward the resolution of the conflict or conflicts. This release occurs in "The Shroud" when the boy speaks for the second and last time, assuring his mother that her more peaceful demeanor is giving him peace as well.

In some works of fiction, resolution is achieved through an utterly unexpected twist, as in "Meanwhile, unknown to our hero, the marines were just on the other side of the hill," or "Susan rolled over in bed and realized the whole thing had been just a dream." Such a device is sometimes called a **deus ex machina**. (This Latin term literally means "god out of a machine" and derives from the ancient theatrical practice of using a machine to lower onto the stage a god who solves the problems of the human characters.)

Conclusion

Finally, just as a plot begins with a situation that is later destabilized, so its **conclusion** presents us with a new and at least somewhat stable situation—one that gives a sense of closure because the conflict or conflicts have been resolved, if only temporarily and not necessarily in the way we or the characters had expected. In "The Shroud," that resolution comes in the last sentence, in which the mother bears her grief "quietly and patiently" and the child quietly sleeps his last sleep. The final *Doonesbury* panel presents us with a situation that is essentially the reverse of the one with which the strip begins—with the teacher silently slumped over his podium, his students suddenly talking to each other instead of scribbling down his words. Many plots instead end with a situation that outwardly looks almost identical to the one with which they began. But thanks to all that has happened between the story's beginning and its end, the final "steady state" at which the characters arrive can never be exactly the same as the one in which they started. A key question to ask at the end of a work of fiction is precisely why, as well as how, things are different.

Some fictional works may also include a final section called an **epilogue**, which ties up loose ends left dangling in the conclusion proper, updates us on what has happened to the characters since their conflicts were resolved, and/or provides some sort of commentary on the story's larger significance. (An epilogue is thus a little like this paragraph, which comes after we have concluded our discussion of the five phases of plot but still feel that there is one more term to deal with.)

A Note on *Dénouement*

In discussions of plot, you will very often encounter the French word **dénouement** (literally, "untying," as of a knot). In this anthology, however, we generally try to avoid using *dénouement* because it can be, and often is, used in three different, potentially contradictory ways—as a synonym for *falling action*; as a synonym for *conclusion* or *resolution*; and even as a label for a certain kind of epilogue.

Plot Summary: An Example and an Exercise

Although any good **plot summary** should be a relatively brief recounting (or *synopsis*) of what happens in a work of fiction, it need not necessarily tell what happens in the same order that the work itself does. As a result, many a plot summary is in fact more like an action summary in the sense that we define the terms *action* and *plot* in this book. But unless you have a good reason for reordering events, it is generally a good idea to follow the plot. The following plot summary of Raymond Carver's CATHEDRAL does just that:

> The narrator is annoyed to learn that his wife's old friend Robert, a blind man who once employed her as a reader, is coming to visit the couple. The wife has corresponded with her friend for years via cassette tapes, describing the details of her early marriage, divorce, and remarriage to her husband, the narrator. Uncomfortable with the prospect of having a blind person in his home, the narrator is surprised by Robert's appearance and behavior: his booming voice and full beard are not what he expected, and he eats, drinks, and smokes marijuana with relish. After dinner the three watch television. After the narrator's wife has fallen asleep, a program about cathedrals begins. The narrator asks Robert if he knows what cathedrals look like or represent, and Robert, admitting that he does not, asks the narrator to draw one. With Robert's hand lying on top of his own, the narrator traces roofs, spires, arches, and even people. Eventually Robert instructs the narrator to close his eyes and continue drawing. The narrator reports that this experience was like nothing else in my life up to now. (From "Raymond Carver: 'Cathedral,'" *Characters in Twentieth Century Literature,* Book Two [Gale Research, 1995].)

Now try this yourself: Choose any of the stories in this anthology and write a one-paragraph plot summary. Then, in a paragraph or two, reflect on your choices about which details to include, which to omit, and how to order them (especially if you've deviated from the plot). What does your summary imply about the story's focus, meaning, and significance? Now repeat the exercise, summarizing the story in a different way and then reflecting on the significance and effect of the changes you've made.

Alternatively, try the same exercise with a friend who has also read the story: Each of you should write your own summary; then exchange them and (separately or together) write a few paragraphs comparing your summaries and reflecting on the significance of the similarities and differences.

COMMON PLOT TYPES

If most plots are essentially variations on the same five-part pattern, some plots have even more features in common. As you think back over the fiction you have read and the movies you have seen (not to mention the video games you have played), you might be surprised to discover just how many of their plots involve a quest—a character or characters' journey to find something or someone that seems, at least at first, of tremendous material or spiritual value. Traditionally, that requires a literal journey, the challenge being not only to find and acquire the object but also to return home with it. Such quests occur often in folktales and are a **convention** of chivalric **romance** and **epic**, in which the questing heroes are often men of high rank sent on their quests by someone with even greater power—a god, a wizard, a prophet, a king. And many works of modern fiction—from James Joyce's ARABY to Tolkien's *Lord of the Rings* to William Gibson's science-fiction classic *Neuromancer* (1984)—depend for their full effect on our knowledge of the conventions of traditional quest plots.

Many fictional works both ancient and modern also (or instead) follow patterns derived from the two most important and ancient forms (or subgenres) of drama—**tragedy** and **comedy**. Tragic plots, on the one hand, trace a downward movement centering on a character's fall from fortune into misfortune and isolation; they end unhappily, often with death. Comedic plots, on the other hand, tend to end happily, often with marriage or some other act of social integration and celebration.

• • •

As you read the stories in this chapter, or any other work of fiction, think about what sets each one apart when it comes to plot; how each uses variations on common plot conventions; how each generates, fulfills, and often frustrates our expectations about the action to come; and how each uses sequence, pace, and other techniques to endow action with both emotional charge and meaning. When it comes to action and plot, every good story holds its own surprises and offers a unique answer to the nagging question *What happened?*

Questions about Plot

- Read the first few paragraphs and then stop. What potential for conflict do you see here? What do you expect to happen in the rest of the story?
- What is the inciting incident or destabilizing event? How and why does this event destabilize the initial situation?
- How would you describe the conflict that ultimately develops? To what extent is it external, internal, or both? What, if any, complications or secondary conflicts arise?
- Where, when, how, and why does the story defy your expectations about what will happen next? What in this story—and in your experience of other stories—created these expectations?
- What is the climax or turning point? Why and how so?
- How is the conflict resolved? How and why might this resolution fulfill or defy your expectations? How and why is the situation at the end of the story different from what it was at the beginning?
- Looking back at the story as a whole, what seems especially significant and effective about its plot, especially in terms of the sequence and pace of the action?
- Does this plot follow any common plot pattern? Is there, for example, a quest of any kind? Or does this plot follow a tragic or comedic pattern?

JAMES BALDWIN (1924–87)

Sonny's Blues

For much of his life, James Baldwin was a leading literary spokesman for civil rights and racial equality in America. Born in New York City but long a resident of France, he first attracted critical attention with two extraordinary novels, *Go Tell It on the Mountain* (1953), which draws on his past as a teenage preacher in the Fireside Pentecostal Church, and *Giovanni's Room* (1956), which deals with the anguish of being black and homosexual in a largely white and heterosexual society. Other works include the novels *Another Country* (1962) and *If Beale Street Could Talk* (1974), the play *Blues for Mr. Charlie* (1964), and a story collection, *Going to Meet the Man* (1965). Baldwin is perhaps best remembered as a perceptive and eloquent essayist, the author of *Notes of a Native Son* (1955), *Nobody Knows My Name* (1961), *The Fire Next Time* (1963), *No Name in the Street* (1972), and *The Price of a Ticket* (1985).

I read about it in the paper, in the subway, on my way to work. I read it, and I couldn't believe it, and I read it again. Then perhaps I just stared at it, at the newsprint spelling out his name, spelling out the story. I stared at it in the swinging lights of the subway car, and in the faces and bodies of the people, and in my own face, trapped in the darkness which roared outside.

It was not to be believed and I kept telling myself that, as I walked from the subway station to the high school. And at the same time I couldn't doubt it. I was scared, scared for Sonny. He became real to me again. A great block of ice got settled in my belly and kept melting there slowly all day long, while I taught my classes algebra. It was a special kind of ice. It kept melting, sending trickles of ice water all up and down my veins, but it never got less. Sometimes it hardened and seemed to expand until I felt my guts were going to come spilling out or that I was going to choke or scream. This would always be at a moment when I was remembering some specific thing Sonny had once said or done.

When he was about as old as the boys in my classes his face had been bright and open, there was a lot of copper in it; and he'd had wonderfully direct brown eyes, and great gentleness and privacy. I wondered what he looked like now. He had been picked up, the evening before, in a raid on an apartment downtown, for peddling and using heroin.

I couldn't believe it: but what I mean by that is that I couldn't find any room for it anywhere inside me. I had kept it outside me for a long time. I hadn't wanted to know. I had had suspicions, but I didn't name them, I kept putting them away. I told myself that Sonny was wild, but he wasn't crazy. And he'd always been a good boy, he hadn't ever turned hard or evil or disrespectful, the way kids can, so quick, so quick, especially in Harlem. I didn't want to believe that I'd ever see my brother going down, coming to nothing, all that light in his face gone out, in the condition I'd already seen so many others. Yet it had happened and here I was, talking about algebra to a lot of boys who might, every one of them for all I knew, be popping off needles every time they went to the head.[1] Maybe it did more for them than algebra could.

5 I was sure that the first time Sonny had ever had horse,[2] he couldn't have been much older than these boys were now. These boys, now, were living as we'd been living then, they were growing up with a rush and their heads bumped abruptly against the low ceiling of their actual possibilities. They were filled with rage. All they really knew were two darknesses, the darkness of their lives, which was now closing in on them, and the darkness of the movies, which had blinded them to that other darkness, and in which they now, vindictively, dreamed, at once more together than they were at any other time, and more alone.

When the last bell rang, the last class ended, I let out my breath. It seemed I'd been holding it for all that time. My clothes were wet—I may have looked as though I'd been sitting in a steam bath, all dressed up, all afternoon. I sat alone in the classroom a long time. I listened to the boys outside, downstairs, shouting and cursing and laughing. Their laughter struck me for perhaps the first time. It was not the joyous laughter which—God knows why—one associates with children. It was mocking and insular, its intent was to denigrate. It was disenchanted, and in this, also, lay the authority of their curses. Perhaps I was listening to them because I was thinking about my brother and in them I heard my brother. And myself.

One boy was whistling a tune, at once very complicated and very simple, it seemed to be pouring out of him as though he were a bird, and it sounded very cool and moving through all that harsh, bright air, only just holding its own through all those other sounds.

I stood up and walked over to the window and looked down into the courtyard. It was the beginning of the spring and the sap was rising in the boys. A teacher passed through them every now and again, quickly, as though he or she couldn't wait to get out of that courtyard, to get those boys out of their sight and off their minds. I started collecting my stuff. I thought I'd better get home and talk to Isabel.

The courtyard was almost deserted by the time I got downstairs. I saw this boy standing in the shadow of a doorway, looking just like Sonny. I almost called his name. Then I saw that it wasn't Sonny, but somebody we used to know, a boy from around our block. He'd been Sonny's friend. He'd never been mine, having been too young for me, and, anyway, I'd never liked him. And now, even though he was a grown-up man, he still hung around that block, still spent hours on the street corners, was always high and raggy. I used to run into him from time to time and he'd often work around to asking me for a quarter or fifty cents. He always had some real good excuse, too, and I always gave it to him. I don't know why.

10 But now, abruptly, I hated him. I couldn't stand the way he looked at me, partly like a dog, partly like a cunning child. I wanted to ask him what the hell he was doing in the school courtyard.

1. Lavatory.

2. Heroin.

He sort of shuffled over to me, and he said, "I see you got the papers. So you already know about it."

"You mean about Sonny? Yes, I already know about it. How come they didn't get you?"

He grinned. It made him repulsive and it also brought to mind what he'd looked like as a kid. "I wasn't there. I stay away from them people."

"Good for you." I offered him a cigarette and I watched him through the smoke. "You come all the way down here just to tell me about Sonny?"

"That's right." He was sort of shaking his head and his eyes looked strange, as though they were about to cross. The bright sun deadened his damp dark brown skin and it made his eyes look yellow and showed up the dirt in his kinked hair. He smelled funky. I moved a little away from him and I said, "Well, thanks. But I already know about it and I got to get home."

"I'll walk you a little ways," he said. We started walking. There were a couple of kids still loitering in the courtyard and one of them said goodnight to me and looked strangely at the boy beside me.

"What're you going to do?" he asked me. "I mean, about Sonny?"

"Look. I haven't seen Sonny for over a year, I'm not sure I'm going to do anything. Anyway, what the hell *can* I do?"

"That's right," he said quickly, "ain't nothing you can do. Can't much help old Sonny no more, I guess."

It was what I was thinking and so it seemed to me he had no right to say it.

"I'm surprised at Sonny, though," he went on—he had a funny way of talking, he looked straight ahead as though he were talking to himself—"I thought Sonny was a smart boy, I thought he was too smart to get hung."

"I guess he thought so too," I said sharply, "and that's how he got hung. And how about you? You're pretty goddamn smart, I bet."

Then he looked directly at me, just for a minute. "I ain't smart," he said. "If I was smart, I'd have reached for a pistol a long time ago."

"Look. Don't tell *me* your sad story, if it was up to me, I'd give you one." Then I felt guilty—guilty, probably, for never having supposed that the poor bastard *had* a story of his own, much less a sad one, and I asked, quickly, "What's going to happen to him now?"

He didn't answer this. He was off by himself some place.

"Funny thing," he said, and from his tone we might have been discussing the quickest way to get to Brooklyn, "when I saw the papers this morning, the first thing I asked myself was if I had anything to do with it. I felt sort of responsible."

I began to listen more carefully. The subway station was on the corner, just before us, and I stopped. He stopped, too. We were in front of a bar and he ducked slightly, peering in, but whoever he was looking for didn't seem to be there. The juke box was blasting away with something black and bouncy and I half watched the barmaid as she danced her way from the juke box to her place behind the bar. And I watched her face as she laughingly responded to something someone said to her, still keeping time to the music. When she smiled one saw the little girl, one sensed the doomed, still-struggling woman beneath the battered face of the semi-whore.

"I never *give* Sonny nothing," the boy said finally, "but a long time ago I come to school high and Sonny asked me how it felt." He paused, I couldn't bear to watch him, I watched the barmaid, and I listened to the music which seemed to be causing the pavement to shake. "I told him it felt great." The music stopped, the barmaid paused and watched the juke box until the music began again. "It did."

All this was carrying me some place I didn't want to go. I certainly didn't want to know how it felt. It filled everything, the people, the houses, the music, the dark, quicksilver barmaid, with menace; and this menace was their reality.

30 "What's going to happen to him now?" I asked again.

"They'll send him away some place and they'll try to cure him." He shook his head. "Maybe he'll even think he's kicked the habit. Then they'll let him loose"—he gestured, throwing his cigarette into the gutter. "That's all."

"What do you mean, that's *all*?"

But I knew what he meant.

"I *mean*, that's *all*." He turned his head and looked at me, pulling down the corners of his mouth. "Don't you know what I mean?" he asked, softly.

35 "How the hell *would* I know what you mean?" I almost whispered it, I don't know why.

"That's right," he said to the air, "how would *he* know what I mean?" He turned toward me again, patient and calm, and yet I somehow felt him shaking, shaking as though he were going to fall apart. I felt that ice in my guts again, the dread I'd felt all afternoon; and again I watched the barmaid, moving about the bar, washing glasses, and singing. "Listen. They'll let him out and then it'll just start all over again. That's what I mean."

"You mean—they'll let him out. And then he'll just start working his way back in again. You mean he'll never kick the habit. Is that what you mean?"

"That's right," he said, cheerfully. "*You* see what I mean."

"Tell me," I said at last, "why does he want to die? He must want to die, he's killing himself, why does he want to die?"

40 He looked at me in surprise. He licked his lips. "He don't want to die. He wants to live. Don't nobody want to die, ever."

Then I wanted to ask him—too many things. He could not have answered, or if he had, I could not have borne the answers. I started walking. "Well, I guess it's none of my business."

"It's going to be rough on old Sonny," he said. We reached the subway station. "This is your station?" he asked. I nodded. I took one step down. "Damn!" he said, suddenly. I looked up at him. He grinned again. "Damn it if I didn't leave all my money home. You ain't got a dollar on you, have you? Just for a couple of days, is all."

All at once something inside gave and threatened to come pouring out of me. I didn't hate him any more. I felt that in another moment I'd start crying like a child.

"Sure," I said. "Don't sweat." I looked in my wallet and didn't have a dollar, I only had a five. "Here," I said. "That hold you?"

45 He didn't look at it—he didn't want to look at it. A terrible, closed look came over his face, as though he were keeping the number on the bill a secret from him and me. "Thanks," he said, and now he was dying to see me go. "Don't worry about Sonny. Maybe I'll write him or something."

"Sure," I said. "You do that. So long."

"Be seeing you," he said. I went on down the steps.

And I didn't write Sonny or send him anything for a long time. When I finally did, it was just after my little girl died, and he wrote me back a letter which made me feel like a bastard.

Here's what he said:

Dear brother, 50

You don't know how much I needed to hear from you. I wanted to write you many a time but I dug how much I must have hurt you and so I didn't write. But now I feel like a man who's been trying to climb up out of some deep, real deep and funky hole and just saw the sun up there, outside. I got to get outside.

I can't tell you much about how I got here. I mean I don't know how to tell you. I guess I was afraid of something or I was trying to escape from something and you know I have never been very strong in the head (smile). I'm glad Mama and Daddy are dead and can't see what's happened to their son and I swear if I'd known what I was doing I would never have hurt you so, you and a lot of other fine people who were nice to me and who believed in me.

I don't want you to think it had anything to do with me being a musician. It's more than that. Or maybe less than that. I can't get anything straight in my head down here and I try not to think about what's going to happen to me when I get outside again. Sometime I think I'm going to flip and *never* get outside and sometime I think I'll come straight back. I tell you one thing, though, I'd rather blow my brains out than go through this again. But that's what they all say, so they tell me. If I tell you when I'm coming to New York and if you could meet me, I sure would appreciate it. Give my love to Isabel and the kids and I was sure sorry to hear about little Gracie. I wish I could be like Mama and say the Lord's will be done, but I don't know it seems to me that trouble is the one thing that never does get stopped and I don't know what good it does to blame it on the Lord. But maybe it does some good if you believe it.

Your brother,
Sonny

Then I kept in constant touch with him and I sent him whatever I could and I went to meet him when he came back to New York. When I saw him many things I thought I had forgotten came flooding back to me. This was because I had begun, finally, to wonder about Sonny, about the life that Sonny lived inside. This life, whatever it was, had made him older and thinner and it had deepened the distant stillness in which he had always moved. He looked very unlike my baby brother. Yet, when he smiled, when we shook hands, the baby brother I'd never known looked out from the depths of his private life, like an animal waiting to be coaxed into the light.

"How you been keeping?" he asked me.

"All right. And you?" 55

"Just fine." He was smiling all over his face. "It's good to see you again."

"It's good to see you."

The seven years' difference in our ages lay between us like a chasm: I wondered if these years would ever operate between us as a bridge. I was remembering, and it made it hard to catch my breath, that I had been there when he was born; and I had heard the first words he had ever spoken. When he started to walk, he walked from our mother straight to me. I caught him just before he fell when he took the first steps he ever took in this world.

"How's Isabel?"

"Just fine. She's dying to see you."

"And the boys?"

"They're fine, too. They're anxious to see their uncle."

"Oh, come on. You know they don't remember me."

"Are you kidding? Of course they remember you."

He grinned again. We got into a taxi. We had a lot to say to each other, far too much to know how to begin.

As the taxi began to move, I asked, "You still want to go to India?"

He laughed. "You still remember that. Hell, no. This place is Indian enough for me."

"It used to belong to them," I said.

And he laughed again. "They damn sure knew what they were doing when they got rid of it."

Years ago, when he was around fourteen, he'd been all hipped on the idea of going to India. He read books about people sitting on rocks, naked, in all kinds of weather, but mostly bad, naturally, and walking barefoot through hot coals and arriving at wisdom. I used to say that it sounded to me as though they were getting away from wisdom as fast as they could. I think he sort of looked down on me for that.

"Do you mind," he asked, "if we have the driver drive alongside the park? On the west side—I haven't seen the city in so long."

"Of course not," I said. I was afraid that I might sound as though I were humoring him, but I hoped he wouldn't take it that way.

So we drove along, between the green of the park and the stony, lifeless elegance of hotels and apartment buildings, toward the vivid, killing streets of our childhood. These streets hadn't changed, though housing projects jutted up out of them now like rocks in the middle of a boiling sea. Most of the houses in which we had grown up had vanished, as had the stores from which we had stolen, the basements in which we had first tried sex, the rooftops from which we had hurled tin cans and bricks. But houses exactly like the houses of our past yet dominated the landscape, boys exactly like the boys we once had been found themselves smothering in these houses, came down into the streets for light and air and found themselves encircled by disaster. Some escaped the trap, most didn't. Those who got out always left something of themselves behind, as some animals amputate a leg and leave it in the trap. It might be said, perhaps, that I had escaped, after all, I was a school teacher; or that Sonny had, he hadn't lived in Harlem for years. Yet, as the cab moved uptown through streets which seemed, with a rush, to darken with dark people, and as I covertly studied Sonny's face, it came to me that what we both were seeking through our separate cab windows was that part of ourselves which had been left behind. It's always at the hour of trouble and confrontation that the missing member aches.

We hit 110th Street and started rolling up Lenox Avenue. And I'd known this avenue all my life, but it seemed to me again, as it had seemed on the day I'd first heard about Sonny's trouble, filled with a hidden menace which was its very breath of life.

"We almost there," said Sonny. 75

"Almost." We were both too nervous to say anything more.

We live in a housing project. It hasn't been up long. A few days after it was up it seemed uninhabitably new, now, of course, it's already rundown. It looks like a parody of the good, clean, faceless life—God knows the people who live in it do their best to make it a parody. The beat-looking grass lying around isn't enough to make their lives green, the hedges will never hold out the streets, and they know it. The big windows fool no one, they aren't big enough to make space out of no space. They don't bother with the windows, they watch the TV screen instead. The playground is most popular with the children who don't play at jacks, or skip rope, or roller skate, or swing, and they can be found in it after dark. We moved in partly because it's not too far from where I teach, and partly for the kids; but it's really just like the houses in which Sonny and I grew up. The same things happen, they'll have the same things to remember. The moment Sonny and I started into the house I had the feeling that I was simply bringing him back into the danger he had almost died trying to escape.

Sonny has never been talkative. So I don't know why I was sure he'd be dying to talk to me when supper was over the first night. Everything went fine, the oldest boy remembered him, and the youngest boy liked him, and Sonny had remembered to bring something for each of them; and Isabel, who is really much nicer than I am, more open and giving, had gone to a lot of trouble about dinner and was genuinely glad to see him. And she's always been able to tease Sonny in a way that I haven't. It was nice to see her face so vivid again and to hear her laugh and watch her make Sonny laugh. She wasn't, or, anyway, she didn't seem to be, at all uneasy or embarrassed. She chatted as though there were no subject which had to be avoided and she got Sonny past his first, faint stiffness. And thank God she was there, for I was filled with that icy dread again. Everything I did seemed awkward to me, and everything I said sounded freighted with hidden meaning. I was trying to remember everything I'd heard about dope addiction and I couldn't help watching Sonny for signs. I wasn't doing it out of malice. I was trying to find out something about my brother. I was dying to hear him tell me he was safe.

"Safe!" my father grunted, whenever Mama suggested trying to move to a neighborhood which might be safer for children. "Safe, hell! Ain't no place safe for kids, nor nobody."

He always went on like this, but he wasn't, ever, really as bad as he sounded, 80
not even on weekends, when he got drunk. As a matter of fact, he was always on the lookout for "something a little better," but he died before he found it. He died suddenly, during a drunken weekend in the middle of the war, when Sonny was fifteen. He and Sonny hadn't ever got on too well. And this was partly because Sonny was the apple of his father's eye. It was because he loved Sonny so much and was frightened for him, that he was always fighting with him. It doesn't do any good to fight with Sonny. Sonny just moves back, inside himself, where he can't be reached. But the principal reason that they never hit it off is

that they were so much alike. Daddy was big and rough and loud-talking, just the opposite of Sonny, but they both had—that same privacy.

Mama tried to tell me something about this, just after Daddy died. I was home on leave from the army.

This was the last time I ever saw my mother alive. Just the same, this picture gets all mixed up in my mind with pictures I had of her when she was younger. The way I always see her is the way she used to be on a Sunday afternoon, say, when the old folks were talking after the big Sunday dinner. I always see her wearing pale blue. She'd be sitting on the sofa. And my father would be sitting in the easy chair, not far from her. And the living room would be full of church folks and relatives. There they sit, in chairs all around the living room, and the night is creeping up outside, but nobody knows it yet. You can see the darkness growing against the windowpanes and you hear the street noises every now and again, or maybe the jangling beat of a tambourine from one of the churches close by, but it's real quiet in the room. For a moment nobody's talking, but every face looks darkening, like the sky outside. And my mother rocks a little from the waist, and my father's eyes are closed. Everyone is looking at something a child can't see. For a minute they've forgotten the children. Maybe a kid is lying on the rug, half asleep. Maybe somebody's got a kid in his lap and is absent-mindedly stroking the kid's head. Maybe there's a kid, quiet and big-eyed, curled up in a big chair in the corner. The silence, the darkness coming, and the darkness in the faces frighten the child obscurely. He hopes that the hand which strokes his forehead will never stop—will never die. He hopes that there will never come a time when the old folks won't be sitting around the living room, talking about where they've come from, and what they've seen, and what's happened to them and their kinfolk.

But something deep and watchful in the child knows that this is bound to end, is already ending. In a moment someone will get up and turn on the light. Then the old folks will remember the children and they won't talk any more that day. And when light fills the room, the child is filled with darkness. He knows that every time this happens he's moved just a little closer to that darkness outside. The darkness outside is what the old folks have been talking about. It's what they've come from. It's what they endure. The child knows that they won't talk any more because if he knows too much about what's happened to *them,* he'll know too much too soon, about what's going to happen to *him.*

The last time I talked to my mother, I remember I was restless. I wanted to get out and see Isabel. We weren't married then and we had a lot to straighten out between us.

85 There Mama sat, in black, by the window. She was humming an old church song, *Lord, you brought me from a long ways off.* Sonny was out somewhere. Mama kept watching the streets.

"I don't know," she said, "if I'll ever see you again, after you go off from here. But I hope you'll remember the things I tried to teach you."

"Don't talk like that," I said, and smiled. "You'll be here a long time yet."

She smiled, too, but she said nothing. She was quiet for a long time. And I said, "Mama, don't you worry about nothing. I'll be writing all the time, and you be getting the checks. . . ."

"I want to talk to you about your brother," she said, suddenly. "If anything happens to me he ain't going to have nobody to look out for him."

90 "Mama," I said, "ain't nothing going to happen to you *or* Sonny. Sonny's all right. He's a good boy and he's got good sense."

"It ain't a question of his being a good boy," Mama said, "nor of his having good sense. It ain't only the bad ones, nor yet the dumb ones that gets sucked under." She stopped, looking at me. "Your Daddy once had a brother," she said, and she smiled in a way that made me feel she was in pain. "You didn't never know that, did you?"

"No," I said, "I never knew that," and I watched her face.

"Oh, yes," she said, "your Daddy had a brother." She looked out of the window again. "I know you never saw your Daddy cry. But *I* did—many a time, through all these years."

I asked her, "What happened to his brother? How come nobody's ever talked about him?"

95 This was the first time I ever saw my mother look old.

"His brother got killed," she said, "when he was just a little younger than you are now. I knew him. He was a fine boy. He was maybe a little full of the devil, but he didn't mean nobody no harm."

Then she stopped and the room was silent, exactly as it had sometimes been on those Sunday afternoons. Mama kept looking out into the streets.

"He used to have a job in the mill," she said, "and, like all young folks, he just liked to perform on Saturday nights. Saturday nights, him and your father would drift around to different places, go to dances and things like that, or just sit around with people they knew, and your father's brother would sing, he had a fine voice, and play along with himself on his guitar. Well, this particular Saturday night, him and your father was coming home from some place, and they were both a little drunk and there was a moon that night, it was bright like day. Your father's brother was feeling kind of good, and he was whistling to himself, and he had his guitar slung over his shoulder. They was coming down a hill and beneath them was a road that turned off from the highway. Well, your father's brother, being always kind of frisky, decided to run down this hill, and he did, with that guitar banging and clanging behind him, and he ran across the road, and he was making water behind a tree. And your father was sort of amused at him and he was still coming down the hill, kind of slow. Then he heard a car motor and that same minute his brother stepped from behind the tree, into the road, in the moonlight. And he started to cross the road. And your father started to run down the hill, he says he don't know why. This car was full of white men. They was all drunk, and when they seen your father's brother they let out a great whoop and holler and they aimed the car straight at him. They was having fun, they just wanted to scare him, the way they do sometimes, you know. But they was drunk. And I guess the boy, being drunk, too, and scared, kind of lost his head. By the time he jumped it was too late. Your father says he heard his brother scream when the car rolled over him, and he heard the wood of that guitar when it give, and he heard them strings go flying, and he heard them white men shouting, and the car kept on a-going and it ain't stopped till this day. And, time your father got down the hill, his brother weren't nothing but blood and pulp."

Tears were gleaming on my mother's face. There wasn't anything I could say.

100 "He never mentioned it," she said, "because I never let him mention it before you children. Your Daddy was like a crazy man that night and for many a night

thereafter. He says he never in his life seen anything as dark as that road after the lights of that car had gone away. Weren't nothing, weren't nobody on that road, just your Daddy and his brother and that busted guitar. Oh, yes. Your Daddy never did really get right again. Till the day he died he weren't sure but that every white man he saw was the man that killed his brother."

She stopped and took out her handkerchief and dried her eyes and looked at me.

"I ain't telling you all this," she said, "to make you scared or bitter or to make you hate nobody. I'm telling you this because you got a brother. And the world ain't changed."

I guess I didn't want to believe this. I guess she saw this in my face. She turned away from me, toward the window again, searching those streets.

"But I praise my Redeemer," she said at last, "that He called your Daddy home before me. I ain't saying it to throw no flowers at myself, but, I declare, it keeps me from feeling too cast down to know I helped your father get safely through this world. Your father always acted like he was the roughest, strongest man on earth. And everybody took him to be like that. But if he hadn't had me there—to see his tears!"

She was crying again. Still, I couldn't move. I said, "Lord, Lord, Mama, I didn't know it was like that."

"Oh, honey," she said, "there's a lot that you don't know. But you are going to find out." She stood up from the window and came over to me. "You got to hold on to your brother," she said, "and don't let him fall, no matter what it looks like is happening to him and no matter how evil you gets with him. You going to be evil with him many a time. But don't you forget what I told you, you hear?"

"I won't forget," I said. "Don't you worry, I won't forget. I won't let nothing happen to Sonny."

My mother smiled as though she was amused at something she saw in my face. Then, "You may not be able to stop nothing from happening. But you got to let him know you's *there*."

Two days later I was married, and then I was gone. And I had a lot of things on my mind and I pretty well forgot my promise to Mama until I got shipped home on a special furlough for her funeral.

And, after the funeral, with just Sonny and me alone in the empty kitchen, I tried to find out something about him.

"What do you want to do?" I asked him.

"I'm going to be a musician," he said.

For he had graduated, in the time I had been away, from dancing to the juke box to finding out who was playing what, and what they were doing with it, and he had bought himself a set of drums.

"You mean, you want to be a drummer?" I somehow had the feeling that being a drummer might be all right for other people but not for my brother Sonny.

"I don't think," he said, looking at me very gravely, "that I'll ever be a good drummer. But I think I can play a piano."

I frowned. I'd never played the role of the oldest brother quite so seriously before, had scarcely ever, in fact, *asked* Sonny a damn thing. I sensed myself in the presence of something I didn't really know how to handle, didn't understand. So I made my frown a little deeper as I asked: "What kind of musician do you want to be?"

He grinned. "How many kinds do you think there are?"

"Be *serious*," I said.

He laughed, throwing his head back, and then looked at me. "I *am* serious."

"Well, then, for Christ's sake, stop kidding around and answer a serious 120
question. I mean, do you want to be a concert pianist, you want to play classical music and all that, or—or what?" Long before I finished he was laughing again. "For Christ's *sake*, Sonny!"

He sobered, but with difficulty. "I'm sorry. But you sound so—*scared*!" and he was off again.

"Well, you may think it's funny now, baby, but it's not going to be so funny when you have to make your living at it, let me tell you *that*." I was furious because I knew he was laughing at me and I didn't know why.

"No," he said, very sober now, and afraid, perhaps, that he'd hurt me, "I don't want to be a classical pianist. That isn't what interests me. I mean"—he paused, looking hard at me, as though his eyes would help me to understand, and then gestured helplessly, as though perhaps his hand would help—"I mean, I'll have a lot of studying to do, and I'll have to study *everything*, but, I mean, I want to play *with*—jazz musicians." He stopped. "I want to play jazz," he said.

Well, the word had never before sounded as heavy, as real, as it sounded that afternoon in Sonny's mouth. I just looked at him and I was probably frowning a real frown by this time. I simply couldn't see why on earth he'd want to spend his time hanging around nightclubs, clowning around on bandstands, while people pushed each other around a dance floor. It seemed—beneath him, somehow. I had never thought about it before, had never been forced to, but I suppose I had always put jazz musicians in a class with what Daddy called "good-time people."

"Are you *serious*?" 125

"Hell, *yes*, I'm serious."

He looked more helpless than ever, and annoyed, and deeply hurt.

I suggested, helpfully: "You mean—like Louis Armstrong?"[3]

His face closed as though I'd struck him. "No. I'm not talking about none of that old-time, down-home crap."

"Well, look, Sonny, I'm sorry, don't get mad. I just don't altogether get it, 130
that's all. Name somebody—you know, a jazz musician you admire."

"Bird."

"Who?"

"Bird! Charlie Parker![4] Don't they teach you nothing in the goddamn army?"

I lit a cigarette. I was surprised and then a little amused to discover that I was trembling. "I've been out of touch," I said. "You'll have to be patient with me. Now. Who's this Parker character?"

3. New Orleans–born trumpeter and singer (1901–71); by the 1950s, his music would have seemed old-fashioned to a jazz aficionado.

4. Charlie ("Bird") Parker (1920–55), brilliant saxophonist and jazz innovator; working in New York in the mid-1940s, he developed, with Dizzy Gillespie and others, the style of jazz called "bebop." He was a narcotics addict.

135 "He's just one of the greatest jazz musicians alive," said Sonny, sullenly, his hands in his pockets, his back to me. "Maybe *the* greatest," he added, bitterly, "that's probably why *you* never heard of him."

"All right," I said, "I'm ignorant. I'm sorry. I'll go out and buy all the cat's records right away, all right?"

"It don't," said Sonny, with dignity, "make any difference to me. I don't care what you listen to. Don't do me no favors."

I was beginning to realize that I'd never seen him so upset before. With another part of my mind I was thinking that this would probably turn out to be one of those things kids go through and that I shouldn't make it seem important by pushing it too hard. Still, I didn't think it would do any harm to ask: "Doesn't all this take a lot of time? Can you make a living at it?"

He turned back to me and half leaned, half sat, on the kitchen table. "Everything takes time," he said, "and—well, yes, sure, I can make a living at it. But what I don't seem to be able to make you understand is that it's the only thing I want to do."

140 "Well, Sonny," I said gently, "you know people can't always do exactly what they *want* to do—"

"*No,* I don't know that," said Sonny, surprising me. "I think people *ought* to do what they want to do, what else are they alive for?"

"You getting to be a big boy," I said desperately, "it's time you started thinking about your future."

"I'm thinking about my future," said Sonny, grimly. "I think about it all the time."

I gave up. I decided, if he didn't change his mind, that we could always talk about it later. "In the meantime," I said, "you got to finish school." We had already decided that he'd have to move in with Isabel and her folks. I knew this wasn't the ideal arrangement because Isabel's folks are inclined to be dicty[5] and they hadn't especially wanted Isabel to marry me. But I didn't know what else to do. "And we have to get you fixed up at Isabel's."

145 There was a long silence. He moved from the kitchen table to the window. "That's a terrible idea. You know it yourself."

"Do you have a *better* idea?"

He just walked up and down the kitchen for a minute. He was as tall as I was. He had started to shave. I suddenly had the feeling that I didn't know him at all.

He stopped at the kitchen table and picked up my cigarettes. Looking at me with a kind of mocking, amused defiance, he put one between his lips. "You mind?"

"You smoking already?"

150 He lit the cigarette and nodded, watching me through the smoke. "I just wanted to see if I'd have the courage to smoke in front of you." He grinned and blew a great cloud of smoke to the ceiling. "It was easy." He looked at my face. "Come on, now. I bet you was smoking at my age, tell the truth."

I didn't say anything but the truth was on my face, and he laughed. But now there was something very strained in his laugh. "Sure. And I bet that ain't all you was doing."

5. Snobbish, bossy.

He was frightening me a little. "Cut the crap," I said. "We already decided that you was going to go and live at Isabel's. Now what's got into you all of a sudden?"

"*You* decided it," he pointed out. "*I* didn't decide nothing." He stopped in front of me, leaning against the stove, arms loosely folded. "Look, brother. I don't want to stay in Harlem no more, I really don't." He was very earnest. He looked at me, then over toward the kitchen window. There was something in his eyes I'd never seen before, some thoughtfulness, some worry all his own. He rubbed the muscle of one arm. "It's time I was getting out of here."

"Where do you want to *go*, Sonny?"

155 "I want to join the army. Or the navy, I don't care. If I say I'm old enough, they'll believe me."

Then I got mad. It was because I was so scared. "You must be crazy. You goddamn fool, what the hell do you want to go and join the *army* for?"

"I just told you. To get out of Harlem."

"Sonny, you haven't even finished *school*. And if you really want to be a musician, how do you expect to study if you're in the *army*?"

He looked at me, trapped, and in anguish. "There's ways. I might be able to work out some kind of deal. Anyway, I'll have the G.I. Bill when I come out."

160 "*If* you come out." We stared at each other. "Sonny, please. Be reasonable. I know the setup is far from perfect. But we got to do the best we can."

"I ain't learning nothing in school," he said. "Even when I go." He turned away from me and opened the window and threw his cigarette out into the narrow alley. I watched his back. "At least, I ain't learning nothing you'd want me to learn." He slammed the window so hard I thought the glass would fly out, and turned back to me. "And I'm sick of the stink of these garbage cans!"

"Sonny," I said, "I know how you feel. But if you don't finish school now, you're going to be sorry later that you didn't." I grabbed him by the shoulders. "And you only got another year. It ain't so bad. And I'll come back and I swear I'll help you do *whatever* you want to do. Just try to put up with it till I come back. Will you please do that? For me?"

He didn't answer and he wouldn't look at me.

"Sonny. You hear me?"

165 He pulled away. "I hear you. But you never hear anything *I* say."

I didn't know what to say to that. He looked out of the window and then back at me. "OK," he said, and sighed. "I'll try."

Then I said, trying to cheer him up a little, "They got a piano at Isabel's. You can practice on it."

And as a matter of fact, it did cheer him up for a minute. "That's right," he said to himself. "I forgot that." His face relaxed a little. But the worry, the thoughtfulness, played on it still, the way shadows play on a face which is staring into the fire.

But I thought I'd never hear the end of that piano. At first, Isabel would write me, saying how nice it was that Sonny was so serious about his music and how, as soon as he came in from school, or wherever he had been when he was supposed to be at school, he went straight to that piano and stayed there until suppertime. And, after supper, he went back to that piano and stayed there until everybody went to bed. He was at the piano all day Saturday and all day Sunday. Then he bought a record player and started playing records. He'd play one record over and over again, all day long sometimes, and he'd improvise along with it on the piano. Or he'd play one section of the record, one chord, one change, one progression, then he'd do it on the piano. Then back to the record. Then back to the piano.

Well, I really don't know how they stood it. Isabel finally confessed that it wasn't like living with a person at all, it was like living with sound. And the sound didn't make any sense to her, didn't make any sense to any of them—naturally. They began, in a way, to be afflicted by this presence that was living in their home. It was as though Sonny were some sort of god, or monster. He moved in an atmosphere which wasn't like theirs at all. They fed him and he ate, he washed himself, he walked in and out of their door; he certainly wasn't nasty or unpleasant or rude, Sonny isn't any of those things; but it was as though he were all wrapped up in some cloud, some fire, some vision all his own; and there wasn't any way to reach him.

At the same time, he wasn't really a man yet, he was still a child, and they had to watch out for him in all kinds of ways. They certainly couldn't throw him out. Neither did they dare to make a great scene about that piano because even they dimly sensed, as I sensed, from so many thousands of miles away, that Sonny was at that piano playing for his life.

But he hadn't been going to school. One day a letter came from the school board and Isabel's mother got it—there had, apparently, been other letters but Sonny had torn them up. This day, when Sonny came in, Isabel's mother showed him the letter and asked where he'd been spending his time. And she finally got it out of him that he'd been down in Greenwich Village, with musicians and other characters, in a white girl's apartment. And this scared her and she started to scream at him and what came up, once she began—though she denies it to this day—was what sacrifices they were making to give Sonny a decent home and how little he appreciated it.

Sonny didn't play the piano that day. By evening, Isabel's mother had calmed down but then there was the old man to deal with, and Isabel herself. Isabel says she did her best to be calm but she broke down and started crying. She says she just watched Sonny's face. She could tell, by watching him, what was happening with him. And what was happening was that they penetrated his cloud, they had reached him. Even if their fingers had been a thousand times more gentle than human fingers ever are, he could hardly help feeling that they had stripped him naked and were spitting on that nakedness. For he also had to see that his presence, that music, which was life or death to him, had been torture for them and that they had endured it, not at all for his sake, but only for mine. And Sonny couldn't take that. He can take it a little better today than he could then but he's still not very good at it and, frankly, I don't know anybody who is.

The silence of the next few days must have been louder than the sound of all the music ever played since time began. One morning, before she went to work, Isabel was in his room for something and she suddenly realized that all of his records were gone. And she knew for certain that he was gone. And he was. He went as far as the navy would carry him. He finally sent me a postcard from some place in Greece and that was the first I knew that Sonny was still alive. I didn't see him any more until we were both back in New York and the war had long been over.

He was a man by then, of course, but I wasn't willing to see it. He came by 175
the house from time to time, but we fought almost every time we met. I didn't like the way he carried himself, loose and dreamlike all the time, and I didn't like his friends, and his music seemed to be merely an excuse for the life he led. It sounded just that weird and disordered.

Then we had a fight, a pretty awful fight, and I didn't see him for months. By and by I looked him up, where he was living, in a furnished room in the Village, and I tried to make it up. But there were lots of other people in the room and Sonny just lay on his bed, and he wouldn't come downstairs with me, and he treated these other people as though they were his family and I weren't. So I got mad and then he got mad, and then I told him that he might just as well be dead as live the way he was living. Then he stood up and he told me not to worry about him any more in life, that he *was* dead as far as I was concerned. Then he pushed me to the door and the other people looked on as though nothing were happening, and he slammed the door behind me. I stood in the hallway, staring at the door. I heard somebody laugh in the room and then the tears came to my eyes. I started down the steps, whistling to keep from crying, I kept whistling to myself, *You going to need me, baby, one of these cold, rainy days.*

I read about Sonny's trouble in the spring. Little Grace died in the fall. She was a beautiful little girl. But she only lived a little over two years. She died of polio and she suffered. She had a slight fever for a couple of days, but it didn't seem like anything and we just kept her in bed. And we would certainly have called the doctor, but the fever dropped, she seemed to be all right. So we thought it had just been a cold. Then, one day, she was up, playing, Isabel was in the kitchen fixing lunch for the two boys when they'd come in from school, and she heard Grace fall down in the living room. When you have a lot of children you don't always start running when one of them falls, unless they start screaming or something. And, this time, Gracie was quiet. Yet, Isabel says that when she heard that *thump* and then that silence, something happened to her to make her afraid. And she ran to the living room and there was little Grace on the floor, all twisted up, and the reason she hadn't screamed was that she couldn't get her breath. And when she did scream, it was the worst sound, Isabel says, that she'd ever heard in all her life, and she still hears it sometimes in her dreams. Isabel will sometimes wake me up with a low, moaning, strangling sound and I have to be quick to awaken her and hold her to me and where Isabel is weeping against me seems a mortal wound.

I think I may have written Sonny the very day that little Grace was buried. I was sitting in the living room in the dark, by myself, and I suddenly thought of Sonny. My trouble made his real.

One Saturday afternoon, when Sonny had been living with us, or anyway, been in our house, for nearly two weeks, I found myself wandering aimlessly about the living room, drinking from a can of beer, and trying to work up courage to search Sonny's room. He was out, he was usually out whenever I was home, and Isabel had taken the children to see their grandparents. Suddenly I was standing still in front of the living room window, watching Seventh Avenue. The idea of searching Sonny's room made me still. I scarcely dared to admit to myself what I'd be searching for. I didn't know what I'd do if I found it. Or if I didn't.

On the sidewalk across from me, near the entrance to a barbecue joint, some people were holding an old-fashioned revival meeting. The barbecue cook, wearing a dirty white apron, his conked[6] hair reddish and metallic in the pale sun, and a cigarette between his lips, stood in the doorway, watching them. Kids and older people paused in their errands and stood there, along with some older men and a couple of very tough-looking women who watched everything that happened on the avenue, as though they owned it, or were maybe owned by it. Well, they were watching this, too. The revival was being carried on by three sisters in black, and a brother. All they had were their voices and their Bibles and a tambourine. The brother was testifying[7] and while he testified two of the sisters stood together, seeming to say, amen, and the third sister walked around with the tambourine outstretched and a couple of people dropped coins into it. Then the brother's testimony ended and the sister who had been taking up the collection dumped the coins into her palm and transferred them to the pocket of her long black robe. Then she raised both hands, striking the tambourine against the air, and then against one hand, and she started to sing. And the two other sisters and the brother joined in.

It was strange, suddenly, to watch, though I had been seeing these meetings all my life. So, of course, had everybody else down there. Yet, they paused and watched and listened and I stood still at the window. "*'Tis the old ship of Zion,*" they sang, and the sister with the tambourine kept a steady, jangling beat, "*it has rescued many a thousand!*" Not a soul under the sound of their voices was hearing this song for the first time, not one of them had been rescued. Nor had they seen much in the way of rescue work being done around them. Neither did they especially believe in the holiness of the three sisters and the brother, they knew too much about them, knew where they lived, and how. The woman with the tambourine, whose voice dominated the air, whose face was bright with joy, was divided by very little from the woman who stood watching her, a cigarette between her heavy, chapped lips, her hair a cuckoo's nest, her face scarred and swollen from many beatings, and her black eyes glittering like coal. Perhaps they both knew this, which was why, when, as rarely, they addressed each other, they addressed each other as Sister. As the singing filled the air the watching, listening faces underwent a change, the eyes focusing on something within; the music seemed to soothe a poison out of them; and time seemed, nearly, to fall away from the sullen, belligerent, battered faces, as though they were fleeing back to their first condition, while dreaming of their last. The barbecue cook half shook his head and smiled, and dropped his cigarette and disappeared into his joint. A man fumbled in his pockets for change and stood holding it in his hand impatiently, as though he had just remembered a pressing appointment further up the avenue. He looked furious. Then I saw Sonny, standing on the edge of the crowd. He was carrying a wide, flat notebook with a green cover, and it made him look, from where I was standing, almost like a schoolboy. The coppery sun brought out the copper in his skin, he was very faintly smiling, standing very still. Then the singing stopped, the tambourine turned into a collection plate again. The furious man dropped in his coins and vanished, so did

6. Processed: straightened and greased.
7. Publicly professing belief.

a couple of the women, and Sonny dropped some change in the plate, looking directly at the woman with a little smile. He started across the avenue, toward the house. He has a slow, loping walk, something like the way Harlem hipsters walk, only he's imposed on this his own half-beat. I had never really noticed it before.

I stayed at the window, both relieved and apprehensive. As Sonny disappeared from my sight, they began singing again. And they were still singing when his key turned in the lock.

"Hey," he said.

"Hey, yourself. You want some beer?"

"No. Well, maybe." But he came up to the window and stood beside me, looking out. "What a warm voice," he said.

They were singing *If I could only hear my mother pray again!*

"Yes," I said, "and she can sure beat that tambourine."

"But what a terrible song," he said, and laughed. He dropped his notebook on the sofa and disappeared into the kitchen. "Where's Isabel and the kids?"

"I think they went to see their grandparents. You hungry?"

"No." He came back into the living room with his can of beer. "You want to come some place with me tonight?"

I sensed, I don't know how, that I couldn't possibly say no. "Sure. Where?"

He sat down on the sofa and picked up his notebook and started leafing through it. "I'm going to sit in with some fellows in a joint in the Village."

"You mean, you're going to play, tonight?"

"That's right." He took a swallow of his beer and moved back to the window. He gave me a sidelong look. "If you can stand it."

"I'll try," I said.

He smiled to himself and we both watched as the meeting across the way broke up. The three sisters and the brother, heads bowed, were singing *God be with you till we meet again.* The faces around them were very quiet. Then the song ended. The small crowd dispersed. We watched the three women and the lone man walk slowly up the avenue.

"When she was singing before," said Sonny, abruptly, "her voice reminded me for a minute of what heroin feels like sometimes—when it's in your veins. It makes you feel sort of warm and cool at the same time. And distant. And—and sure." He sipped his beer, very deliberately not looking at me. I watched his face. "It makes you feel—in control. Sometimes you've got to have that feeling."

"Do you?" I sat down slowly in the easy chair.

"Sometimes." He went to the sofa and picked up his notebook again. "Some people do."

"In order," I asked, "to play?" And my voice was very ugly, full of contempt and anger.

"Well"—he looked at me with great, troubled eyes, as though, in fact, he hoped his eyes would tell me things he could never otherwise say—"they *think* so. And *if* they think so—!"

"And what do *you* think?" I asked.

He sat on the sofa and put his can of beer on the floor. "I don't know," he said, and I couldn't be sure if he were answering my question or pursuing his thoughts. His face didn't tell me. "It's not so much to *play.* It's to *stand* it, to be able to make it at all. On any level." He frowned and smiled: "In order to keep from shaking to pieces."

"But these friends of yours," I said, "they seem to shake themselves to pieces pretty goddamn fast."

205 "Maybe." He played with the notebook. And something told me that I should curb my tongue, that Sonny was doing his best to talk, that I should listen. "But of course you only know the ones that've gone to pieces. Some don't—or at least they haven't *yet* and that's just about all *any* of us can say." He paused. "And then there are some who just live, really, in hell, and they know it and they see what's happening and they go right on. I don't know." He sighed, dropped the notebook, folded his arms. "Some guys, you can tell from the way they play, they on something *all* the time. And you can see that, well, it makes something real for them. But of course," he picked up his beer from the floor and sipped it and put the can down again, "they *want* to, too, you've got to see that. Even some of them that say they don't—*some*, not all."

"And what about you?" I asked—I couldn't help it. "What about you? Do *you* want to?"

He stood up and walked to the window and I remained silent for a long time. Then he sighed. "Me," he said. Then: "While I was downstairs before, on my way here, listening to that woman sing, it struck me all of a sudden how much suffering she must have had to go through—to sing like that. It's *repulsive* to think you have to suffer that much."

I said: "But there's no way not to suffer—is there, Sonny?"

"I believe not," he said and smiled, "but that's never stopped anyone from trying." He looked at me. "Has it?" I realized, with this mocking look, that there stood between us, forever, beyond the power of time or forgiveness, the fact that I had held silence—so long!—when he had needed human speech to help him. He turned back to the window. "No, there's no way not to suffer. But you try all kinds of ways to keep from drowning in it, to keep on top of it, and to make it seem—well, like *you*. Like you did something, all right, and now you're suffering for it. You know?" I said nothing. "Well you know," he said, impatiently, "why *do* people suffer? Maybe it's better to do something to give it a reason, *any* reason."

210 "But we just agreed," I said, "that there's no way not to suffer. Isn't it better, then, just to—take it?"

"But nobody just takes it," Sonny cried, "that's what I'm telling you! *Everybody* tries not to. You're just hung up on the *way* some people try—it's not *your* way!"

The hair on my face began to itch, my face felt wet. "That's not true," I said, "that's not true. I don't give a damn what other people do, I don't even care how they suffer. I just care how *you* suffer." And he looked at me. "Please believe me," I said, "I don't want to see you—die—trying not to suffer."

"I won't," he said flatly, "die trying not to suffer. At least, not any faster than anybody else."

"But there's no need," I said, trying to laugh, "is there? in killing yourself."

215 I wanted to say more, but I couldn't. I wanted to talk about will power and how life could be—well, beautiful. I wanted to say that it was all within; but was it? or, rather, wasn't that exactly the trouble? And I wanted to promise that I would never fail him again. But it would all have sounded—empty words and lies.

So I made the promise to myself and prayed that I would keep it.

"It's terrible sometimes, inside," he said, "that's what's the trouble. You walk these streets, black and funky and cold, and there's not really a living ass to talk to, and there's nothing shaking, and there's no way of getting it out—that storm inside. You can't talk it and you can't make love with it, and when you finally try to get with it and play it, you realize *nobody's* listening. So *you've* got to listen. You got to find a way to listen."

And then he walked away from the window and sat on the sofa again, as though all the wind had suddenly been knocked out of him. "Sometimes you'll do *anything* to play, even cut your mother's throat." He laughed and looked at me. "Or your brother's." Then he sobered. "Or your own." Then: "Don't worry. I'm all right now and I think I'll *be* all right. But I can't forget—where I've been. I don't mean just the physical place I've been, I mean where I've *been*. And *what* I've been."

"What have you been, Sonny?" I asked.

He smiled—but sat sideways on the sofa, his elbow resting on the back, his fingers playing with his mouth and chin, not looking at me. "I've been something I didn't recognize, didn't know I could be. Didn't know anybody could be." He stopped, looking inward, looking helplessly young, looking old. "I'm not talking about it now because I feel *guilty* or anything like that—maybe it would be better if I did, I don't know. Anyway, I can't really talk about it. Not to you, not to anybody," and now he turned and faced me. "Sometimes, you know, and it was actually when I was most *out* of the world, I felt that I was in it, that I was *with* it, really, and I could play or I didn't really have to *play*, it just came out of me, it was there. And I don't know how I played, thinking about it now, but I know I did awful things, those times, sometimes, to people. Or it wasn't that I *did* anything to them—it was that they weren't real." He picked up the beer can; it was empty; he rolled it between his palms: "And other times—well, I needed a fix, I needed to find a place to lean, I needed to clear a space to *listen*—and I couldn't find it, and I—went crazy, I did terrible things to *me*, I was terrible *for* me." He began pressing the beer can between his hands, I watched the metal begin to give. It glittered, as he played with it like a knife, and I was afraid he would cut himself, but I said nothing. "Oh well. I can never tell you. I was all by myself at the bottom of something, stinking and sweating and crying and shaking, and I smelled it, you know? *my* stink, and I thought I'd die if I couldn't get away from it and yet, all the same, I knew that everything I was doing was just locking me in with it. And I didn't know," he paused, still flattening the beer can, "I didn't know, I still *don't* know, something kept telling me that maybe it was good to smell your own stink, but I didn't think that *that* was what I'd been trying to do—and—who can stand it?" and he abruptly dropped the ruined beer can, looking at me with a small, still smile, and then rose, walking to the window as though it were the lodestone rock. I watched his face, he watched the avenue. "I couldn't tell you when Mama died—but the reason I wanted to leave Harlem so bad was to get away from drugs. And then, when I ran away, that's what I was running from—really. When I came back, nothing had changed, *I* hadn't changed, I was just—older." And he stopped, drumming with his fingers on the windowpane. The sun had vanished, soon darkness would fall. I watched his face. "It can come again," he said, almost as though speaking to himself. Then he turned to me. "It can come again," he repeated. "I just want you to know that."

"All right," I said, at last. "So it can come again. All right."

He smiled, but the smile was sorrowful. "I had to try to tell you," he said.

"Yes," I said. "I understand that."

"You're my brother," he said, looking straight at me, and not smiling at all.

"Yes," I repeated, "yes. I understand that."

He turned back to the window, looking out. "All that hatred down there," he said, "all that hatred and misery and love. It's a wonder it doesn't blow the avenue apart."

We went to the only nightclub on a short, dark street, downtown. We squeezed through the narrow, chattering, jampacked bar to the entrance of the big room, where the bandstand was. And we stood there for a moment, for the lights were very dim in this room and we couldn't see. Then, "Hello, boy," said the voice and an enormous black man, much older than Sonny or myself, erupted out of all that atmospheric lighting and put an arm around Sonny's shoulder. "I been sitting right here," he said, "waiting for you."

He had a big voice, too, and heads in the darkness turned toward us.

Sonny grinned and pulled a little away, and said, "Creole, this is my brother. I told you about him."

Creole shook my hand. "I'm glad to meet you, son," he said, and it was clear that he was glad to meet me *there*, for Sonny's sake. And he smiled, "You got a real musician in *your* family," and he took his arm from Sonny's shoulder and slapped him, lightly, affectionately, with the back of his hand.

"Well. Now I've heard it all," said a voice behind us. This was another musician, and a friend of Sonny's, a coal-black, cheerful-looking man, built close to the ground. He immediately began confiding to me, at the top of his lungs, the most terrible things about Sonny, his teeth gleaming like a lighthouse and his laugh coming up out of him like the beginning of an earthquake. And it turned out that everyone at the bar knew Sonny, or almost everyone; some were musicians, working there, or nearby, or not working, some were simply hangers-on, and some were there to hear Sonny play. I was introduced to all of them and they were all very polite to me. Yet, it was clear that, for them, I was only Sonny's brother. Here, I was in Sonny's world. Or, rather: his kingdom. Here, it was not even a question that his veins bore royal blood.

They were going to play soon and Creole installed me, by myself, at a table in a dark corner. Then I watched them, Creole, and the little black man, and Sonny, and the others, while they horsed around, standing just below the bandstand. The light from the bandstand spilled just a little short of them and, watching them laughing and gesturing and moving about, I had the feeling that they, nevertheless, were being most careful not to step into that circle of light too suddenly; that if they moved into the light too suddenly, without thinking, they would perish in flame. Then, while I watched, one of them, the small black man, moved into the light and crossed the bandstand and started fooling around with his drums. Then—being funny and being, also, extremely ceremonious—Creole took Sonny by the arm and led him to the piano. A woman's voice called Sonny's name and a few hands started clapping. And Sonny, also being funny and being ceremonious, and so touched, I think, that he could have cried, but neither hiding it nor showing it, riding it like a man, grinned, and put both hands to his heart and bowed from the waist.

Creole then went to the bass fiddle and a lean, very bright-skinned brown man jumped up on the bandstand and picked up his horn. So there they were, and the atmosphere on the bandstand and in the room began to change and tighten. Someone stepped up to the microphone and announced them. Then there were all kinds of murmurs. Some people at the bar shushed others. The waitress ran around, frantically getting in the last orders, guys and chicks got closer to each other, and the lights on the bandstand, on the quartet, turned to a kind of indigo. Then they all looked different there. Creole looked about him for the last time, as though he were making certain that all his chickens were in the coop, and then he—jumped and struck the fiddle. And there they were.

All I know about music is that not many people ever really hear it. And even then, on the rare occasions when something opens within, and the music enters, what we mainly hear, or hear corroborated, are personal, private, vanishing evocations. But the man who creates the music is hearing something else, is dealing with the roar rising from the void and imposing order on it as it hits the air. What is evoked in him, then, is of another order, more terrible because it has no words, and triumphant, too, for that same reason. And his triumph, when he triumphs, is ours. I just watched Sonny's face. His face was troubled, he was working hard, but he wasn't with it. And I had the feeling that, in a way, everyone on the bandstand was waiting for him, both waiting for him and pushing him along. But as I began to watch Creole, I realized that it was Creole who held them all back. He had them on a short rein. Up there, keeping the beat with his whole body, wailing on the fiddle, with his eyes half closed, he was listening to everything, but he was listening to Sonny. He was having a dialogue with Sonny. He wanted Sonny to leave the shoreline and strike out for the deep water. He was Sonny's witness that deep water and drowning were not the same thing—he had been there, and he knew. And he wanted Sonny to know. He was waiting for Sonny to do the things on the keys which would let Creole know that Sonny was in the water.

235 And, while Creole listened, Sonny moved, deep within, exactly like someone in torment. I had never before thought of how awful the relationship must be between the musician and his instrument. He has to fill it, this instrument, with the breath of life, his own. He has to make it do what he wants it to do. And a piano is just a piano. It's made out of so much wood and wires and little hammers and big ones, and ivory. While there's only so much you can do with it, the only way to find this out is to try; to try and make it do everything.

And Sonny hadn't been near a piano for over a year. And he wasn't on much better terms with his life, not the life that stretched before him now. He and the piano stammered, started one way, got scared, stopped; started another way, panicked, marked time, started again; then seemed to have found a direction, panicked again, got stuck. And the face I saw on Sonny I'd never seen before. Everything had been burned out of it, and, at the same time, things usually hidden were being burned in, by the fire and fury of the battle which was occurring in him up there.

Yet, watching Creole's face as they neared the end of the first set, I had the feeling that something had happened, something I hadn't heard. Then they finished, there was scattered applause, and then, without an instant's warning, Creole started into something else, it was almost sardonic, it was *Am I Blue*.[8] And, as though he commanded, Sonny began to play. Something began to happen. And Creole let out the reins. The dry, low, black man said something awful on the drums, Creole answered, and the drums talked back. Then the horn insisted, sweet and high, slightly detached perhaps, and Creole listened, commenting now and then, dry, and driving, beautiful and calm and old. Then they all came together again, and Sonny was part of the family again. I could tell this from his face. He seemed to have found, right there beneath his fingers, a damn brand-new piano. It seemed that he couldn't get over it. Then, for a while, just being happy with Sonny, they seemed to be agreeing with him that brand-new pianos certainly were a gas.

Then Creole stepped forward to remind them that what they were playing was the blues. He hit something in all of them, he hit something in me, myself, and the music tightened and deepened, apprehension began to beat the air. Creole began to tell us what the blues were all about. They were not about anything very new. He and his boys up there were keeping it new, at the risk of ruin, destruction, madness, and death, in order to find new ways to make us listen. For, while the tale of how we suffer, and how we are delighted, and how we may triumph is never new, it always must be heard. There isn't any other tale to tell, it's the only light we've got in all this darkness.

And this tale, according to that face, that body, those strong hands on those strings, has another aspect in every country, and a new depth in every generation. Listen, Creole seemed to be saying, listen. Now these are Sonny's blues. He made the little black man on the drums know it, and the bright, brown man on the horn. Creole wasn't trying any longer to get Sonny in the water. He was wishing him Godspeed. Then he stepped back, very slowly, filling the air with the immense suggestion that Sonny speak for himself.

240 Then they all gathered around Sonny and Sonny played. Every now and again one of them seemed to say, amen. Sonny's fingers filled the air with life, his life. But that life contained so many others. And Sonny went all the way back, he really began with the spare, flat statement of the opening phrase of the song. Then he began to make it his. It was very beautiful because it wasn't hurried and it was no longer a lament. I seemed to hear with what burning he had made it his, and what burning we had yet to make it ours, how we could cease lamenting. Freedom lurked around us and I understood, at last, that he could help us to be free if we would listen, that he would never be free until we did. Yet, there was no battle in his face now, I heard what he had gone through, and would continue to go through until he came to rest in earth. He had made it his: that long line, of which we knew only Mama and Daddy. And he was giving it back, as everything must be given back, so that, passing through death, it can live forever. I saw my mother's face again, and felt, for the first time, how the stones of the road she had walked on must have bruised her feet. I saw the moonlit road where my father's brother died. And it brought something else back to me, and carried me past it, I saw my little girl again and felt Isabel's tears again, and I felt my own tears begin to rise. And I was yet aware that this

8. A favorite jazz standard, brilliantly recorded by Billie Holiday.

was only a moment, that the world waited outside, as hungry as a tiger, and that trouble stretched above us, longer than the sky.

Then it was over. Creole and Sonny let out their breath, both soaking wet, and grinning. There was a lot of applause and some of it was real. In the dark, the girl came by and I asked her to take drinks to the bandstand. There was a long pause, while they talked up there in the indigo light and after awhile I saw the girl put a Scotch and milk on top of the piano for Sonny. He didn't seem to notice it, but just before they started playing again, he sipped from it and looked toward me, and nodded. Then he put it back on top of the piano. For me, then, as they began to play again, it glowed and shook above my brother's head like the very cup of trembling.[9]

1957

QUESTIONS

1. SONNY'S BLUES begins *in medias res.* What does Baldwin achieve by beginning the story as he does? How does the order in which events are related later in the story affect your experience of reading it and interpreting its meaning?
2. What external conflict(s) is (or are) depicted in the story? What internal conflict(s)? How are they resolved?
3. James Baldwin famously avowed that "[i]t is only in his music [. . .] that the Negro in America has been able to tell his story," and music of various kinds features prominently in SONNY'S BLUES. Note all the times when music is mentioned, as well as all the varieties of music. What story seems to be told both *through* and *about* music in SONNY'S BLUES?

EDITH WHARTON (1862–1937)

Roman Fever[1]

Edith Jones was born into a distinguished New York family. Educated by private tutors and governesses, she published a book of her poems privately but did not begin to write for a public audience until after her marriage, to Edward Wharton, in 1885. The author of more than fifty volumes of poetry, essays, fiction, travelogues, and criticism, she was the first woman to receive an honorary doctorate from Yale University, in 1923. Although she immigrated to France in 1907 (and later was awarded the Legion of Honor for her philanthropic work during World War I), she continued to write about the New England of her youth in novels such as the popular

9. See Isaiah 51.17, 22–23: "Awake, awake, stand up, O Jerusalem, which hast drunk at the hand of the Lord the cup of his fury; thou hast drunken the dregs of the cup of trembling, and wrung them out. [. . .] Behold, I have taken out of thine hand the cup of trembling, even the dregs of the cup of my fury; thou shalt no more drink it again: But I will put it into the hand of them that afflict thee [. . .]."

1. Type of malaria once thought to be caused by the alternating hot and cool temperatures of the Roman climate. Anglo-American tourists traditionally feared exposure to it at certain times and seasons.

Ethan Frome (1911), *The House of Mirth* (1905), and the Pulitzer Prize–winning *The Age of Innocence* (1920). Primarily remembered as a novelist, Wharton nonetheless ranks as one of America's greatest short-story writers, publishing almost ninety between 1891 and 1937. Though many offer the realistic dissections of upper-class life for which she is most famous, she also excelled at what one of her narrators calls the ghost story that "isn't exactly a ghost-story," including those published in the posthumous collection *Ghosts* (1937).

I

From the table at which they had been lunching two American ladies of ripe but well-cared-for middle age moved across the lofty terrace of the Roman restaurant and, leaning on its parapet, looked first at each other, and then down on the outspread glories of the Palatine[2] and the Forum,[3] with the same expression of vague but benevolent approval.

As they leaned there a girlish voice echoed up gaily from the stairs leading to the court below. "Well, come along, then," it cried, not to them but to an invisible companion, "and let's leave the young things to their knitting"; and a voice as fresh laughed back: "Oh, look here, Babs, not actually *knitting*—" "Well, I mean figuratively," rejoined the first. "After all, we haven't left our poor parents much else to do . . ." and at that point the turn of the stairs engulfed the dialogue.

The two ladies looked at each other again, this time with a tinge of smiling embarrassment, and the smaller and paler one shook her head and colored slightly.

"Barbara!" she murmured, sending an unheard rebuke after the mocking voice in the stairway.

5 The other lady, who was fuller, and higher in color, with a small determined nose supported by vigorous black eyebrows, gave a good-humored laugh. "That's what our daughters think of us!"

Her companion replied by a deprecating gesture. "Not of us individually. We must remember that. It's just the collective modern idea of Mothers. And you see—" Half guiltily she drew from her handsomely mounted black hand-bag a twist of crimson silk run through by two fine knitting needles. "One never knows," she murmured. "The new system has certainly given us a good deal of time to kill; and sometimes I get tired just looking—even at this." Her gesture was now addressed to the stupendous scene at their feet.

The dark lady laughed again, and they both relapsed upon the view, contemplating it in silence, with a sort of diffused serenity which might have been borrowed from the spring effulgence of the Roman skies. The luncheon-hour was long past, and the two had their end of the vast terrace to themselves. At its opposite extremity a few groups, detained by a lingering look at the outspread city, were gathering up guide-books and fumbling for tips. The last of them scattered, and the two ladies were alone on the air-washed height.

2. One of the seven hills on which the oldest part of Rome was built.
3. Central plaza of ancient Rome.

"Well, I don't see why we shouldn't just stay here," said Mrs. Slade, the lady of the high color and energetic brows. Two derelict basket-chairs stood near, and she pushed them into the angle of the parapet, and settled herself in one, her gaze upon the Palatine. "After all, it's still the most beautiful view in the world."

"It always will be, to me," assented her friend Mrs. Ansley, with so slight a stress on the "me" that Mrs. Slade, though she noticed it, wondered if it were not merely accidental, like the random underlinings of old-fashioned letter-writers.

10 "Grace Ansley was always old-fashioned," she thought; and added aloud, with a retrospective smile: "It's a view we've both been familiar with for a good many years. When we first met here we were younger than our girls are now. You remember?"

"Oh, yes, I remember," murmured Mrs. Ansley, with the same undefinable stress—"There's that head-waiter wondering," she interpolated. She was evidently far less sure than her companion of herself and of her rights in the world.

"I'll cure him of wondering," said Mrs. Slade, stretching her hand toward a bag as discreetly opulent-looking as Mrs. Ansley's. Signing to the head-waiter, she explained that she and her friend were old lovers of Rome, and would like to spend the end of the afternoon looking down on the view—that is, if it did not disturb the service? The headwaiter, bowing over her gratuity, assured her that the ladies were most welcome, and would be still more so if they would condescend to remain for dinner. A full moon night, they would remember . . .

Mrs. Slade's black brows drew together, as though references to the moon were out-of-place and even unwelcome. But she smiled away her frown as the head-waiter retreated. "Well, why not? We might do worse. There's no knowing, I suppose, when the girls will be back. Do you even know back from *where*? I don't!"

Mrs. Ansley again colored slightly. "I think those young Italian aviators we met at the Embassy invited them to fly to Tarquinia[4] for tea. I suppose they'll want to wait and fly back by moonlight."

15 "Moonlight—moonlight! What a part it still plays. Do you suppose they're as sentimental as we were?"

"I've come to the conclusion that I don't in the least know what they are," said Mrs. Ansley. "And perhaps we didn't know much more about each other."

"No; perhaps we didn't."

Her friend gave her a shy glance. "I never should have supposed you were sentimental, Alida."

"Well, perhaps I wasn't." Mrs. Slade drew her lids together in retrospect; and for a few moments the two ladies, who had been intimate since childhood, reflected how little they knew each other. Each one, of course, had a label ready to attach to the other's name; Mrs. Delphin Slade, for instance, would have told herself, or any one who asked her, that Mrs. Horace Ansley, twenty-five years ago, had been exquisitely lovely—no, you wouldn't believe it, would you? . . . though, of course, still charming, distinguished . . . Well, as a girl she had been exquisite; far more beautiful than her daughter Barbara, though certainly Babs,

4. Now Corneto, Italy, an ancient Etruscan city, ninety kilometers from Rome, the site of well-preserved underground tombs with vivid wall paintings.

according to the new standards at any rate, was more effective—had more *edge*, as they say. Funny where she got it, with those two nullities as parents. Yes; Horace Ansley was—well, just the duplicate of his wife. Museum specimens of old New York. Good-looking, irreproachable, exemplary. Mrs. Slade and Mrs. Ansley had lived opposite each other—actually as well as figuratively—for years. When the drawing-room curtains in No. 20 East 73rd Street were renewed, No. 23, across the way, was always aware of it. And of all the movings, buyings, travels, anniversaries, illnesses—the tame chronicle of an estimable pair. Little of it escaped Mrs. Slade. But she had grown bored with it by the time her husband made his big *coup* in Wall Street, and when they bought in upper Park Avenue had already begun to think: "I'd rather live opposite a speak-easy[5] for a change; at least one might see it raided." The idea of seeing Grace raided was so amusing that (before the move) she launched it at a woman's lunch. It made a hit, and went the rounds—she sometimes wondered if it had crossed the street, and reached Mrs. Ansley. She hoped not, but didn't much mind. Those were the days when respectability was at a discount, and it did the irreproachable no harm to laugh at them a little.

A few years later, and not many months apart, both ladies lost their husbands. There was an appropriate exchange of wreaths and condolences, and a brief renewal of intimacy in the half-shadow of their mourning; and now, after another interval, they had run across each other in Rome, at the same hotel, each of them the modest appendage of a salient daughter. The similarity of their lot had again drawn them together, lending itself to mild jokes, and the mutual confession that, if in old days it must have been tiring to "keep up" with daughters, it was now, at times, a little dull not to.

No doubt, Mrs. Slade reflected, she felt her unemployment more than poor Grace ever would. It was a big drop from being the wife of Delphin Slade to being his widow. She had always regarded herself (with a certain conjugal pride) as his equal in social gifts, as contributing her full share to the making of the exceptional couple they were: but the difference after his death was irremediable. As the wife of the famous corporation lawyer, always with an international case or two on hand, every day brought its exciting and unexpected obligation: the impromptu entertaining of eminent colleagues from abroad, the hurried dashes on legal business to London, Paris or Rome, where the entertaining was so handsomely reciprocated; the amusement of hearing in her wake: "What, that handsome woman with the good clothes and the eyes is Mrs. Slade—*the* Slade's wife? Really? Generally the wives of celebrities are such frumps."

Yes; being *the* Slade's widow was a dullish business after that. In living up to such a husband all her faculties had been engaged; now she had only her daughter to live up to, for the son who seemed to have inherited his father's gifts had died suddenly in boyhood. She had fought through that agony because her husband was there, to be helped and to help; now, after the father's death, the thought of the boy had become unbearable. There was nothing left but to mother her daughter; and dear Jenny was such a perfect daughter that she needed no excessive mothering. "Now with Babs Ansley I don't know that I *should* be so quiet," Mrs. Slade sometimes half-enviously reflected; but Jenny, who was younger

5. Illegal tavern during the period of Prohibition (1919–31) in the United States.

than her brilliant friend, was that rare accident, an extremely pretty girl who somehow made youth and prettiness seem as safe as their absence. It was all perplexing—and to Mrs. Slade a little boring. She wished that Jenny would fall in love—with the wrong man, even; that she might have to be watched, out-manoeuvred, rescued. And instead, it was Jenny who watched her mother, kept her out of draughts, made sure that she had taken her tonic . . .

Mrs. Ansley was much less articulate than her friend, and her mental portrait of Mrs. Slade was slighter, and drawn with fainter touches. "Alida Slade's awfully brilliant; but not as brilliant as she thinks," would have summed it up; though she would have added, for the enlightenment of strangers, that Mrs. Slade had been an extremely dashing girl; much more so than her daughter, who was pretty, of course, and clever in a way, but had none of her mother's—well, "vividness," someone had once called it. Mrs. Ansley would take up current words like this, and cite them in quotation marks, as unheard-of audacities. No; Jenny was not like her mother. Sometimes Mrs. Ansley thought Alida Slade was disappointed; on the whole she had had a sad life. Full of failures and mistakes; Mrs. Ansley had always been rather sorry for her . . .

So these two ladies visualized each other, each through the wrong end of her little telescope.

II

For a long time they continued to sit side by side without speaking. It seemed as though, to both, there was a relief in laying down their somewhat futile activities in the presence of the vast Memento Mori[6] which faced them. Mrs. Slade sat quite still, her eyes fixed on the golden slope of the Palace of the Caesars,[7] and after a while Mrs. Ansley ceased to fidget with her bag, and she too sank into meditation. Like many intimate friends, the two ladies had never before had occasion to be silent together, and Mrs. Ansley was slightly embarrassed by what seemed, after so many years, a new stage in their intimacy, and one with which she did not yet know how to deal.

Suddenly the air was full of that deep clangor of bells which periodically covers Rome with a roof of silver. Mrs. Slade glanced at her wrist-watch. "Five o'clock already," she said, as though surprised.

Mrs. Ansley suggested interrogatively: "There's bridge at the Embassy at five." For a long time Mrs. Slade did not answer. She appeared to be lost in contemplation, and Mrs. Ansley thought the remark had escaped her. But after a while she said, as if speaking out of a dream: "Bridge, did you say? Not unless you want to . . . But I don't think I will, you know."

"Oh, no," Mrs. Ansley hastened to assure her. "I don't care to at all. It's so lovely here; and so full of old memories, as you say." She settled herself in her chair, and almost furtively drew forth her knitting. Mrs. Slade took sideway note of this activity, but her own beautifully cared-for hands remained motionless on her knee.

"I was just thinking," she said slowly, "what different things Rome stands for to each generation of travellers. To our grandmothers, Roman fever; to our

6. Reminder of human mortality; literally, "Remember that you must die" (Latin).
7. The palace of the Roman emperors is on the Palatine hill.

mothers, sentimental dangers—how we used to be guarded!—to our daughters, no more dangers than the middle of Main Street. They don't know it—but how much they're missing!"

30 The long golden light was beginning to pale, and Mrs. Ansley lifted her knitting a little closer to her eyes. "Yes; how we were guarded!"

"I always used to think," Mrs. Slade continued, "that our mothers had a much more difficult job than our grandmothers. When Roman fever stalked the streets it must have been comparatively easy to gather in the girls at the danger hour; but when you and I were young, with such beauty calling us, and the spice of disobedience thrown in, and no worse risk than catching cold during the cool hour after sunset, the mothers used to be put to it to keep us in—didn't they?"

She turned again toward Mrs. Ansley, but the latter had reached a delicate point in her knitting. "One, two, three—slip two; yes, they must have been," she assented, without looking up.

Mrs. Slade's eyes rested on her with a deepened attention. "She can knit—in the face of *this*! How like her . . ."

Mrs. Slade leaned back, brooding, her eyes ranging from the ruins which faced her to the long green hollow of the Forum, the fading glow of the church fronts beyond it, and the outlying immensity of the Colosseum.[8] Suddenly she thought: "It's all very well to say that our girls have done away with sentiment and moonlight. But if Babs Ansley isn't out to catch that young aviator—the one who's a Marchese—then I don't know anything. And Jenny has no chance beside her. I know that too. I wonder if that's why Grace Ansley likes the two girls to go everywhere together? My poor Jenny as a foil—I" Mrs. Slade gave a hardly audible laugh, and at the sound Mrs. Ansley dropped her knitting.

35 "Yes—?"

"I—oh, nothing. I was only thinking how your Babs carries everything before her. That Campolieri boy is one of the best matches in Rome. Don't look so innocent, my dear—you know he is. And I was wondering, ever so respectfully, you understand . . . wondering how two such exemplary characters as you and Horace had managed to produce anything quite so dynamic." Mrs. Slade laughed again, with a touch of asperity.

Mrs. Ansley's hands lay inert across her needles. She looked straight out at the great accumulated wreckage of passion and splendor at her feet. But her small profile was almost expressionless. At length she said: "I think you overrate Babs, my dear."

Mrs. Slade's tone grew easier. "No; I don't. I appreciate her. And perhaps envy you. Oh, my girl's perfect; if I were a chronic invalid I'd—well, I think I'd rather be in Jenny's hands. There must be times . . . but there! I always wanted a brilliant daughter . . . and never quite understood why I got an angel instead."

Mrs. Ansley echoed her laugh in a faint murmur. "Babs is an angel too."

40 "Of course—of course! But she's got rainbow wings. Well, they're wandering by the sea with their young men; and here we sit . . . and it all brings back the past a little too acutely."

Mrs. Ansley had resumed her knitting. One might almost have imagined (if one had known her less well, Mrs. Slade reflected) that, for her also, too many

8. Great Roman amphitheater built in the first century CE, site of lavish spectacles featuring wild animals and mortal combat.

memories rose from the lengthening shadows of those august ruins. But no; she was simply absorbed in her work. What was there for her to worry about? She knew that Babs would almost certainly come back engaged to the extremely eligible Campolieri. "And she'll sell the New York house, and settle down near them in Rome, and never be in their way . . . she's much too tactful. But she'll have an excellent cook, and just the right people in for bridge and cocktails . . . and a perfectly peaceful old age among her grandchildren."

Mrs. Slade broke off this prophetic flight with a recoil of self-disgust. There was no one of whom she had less right to think unkindly than of Grace Ansley. Would she never cure herself of envying her? Perhaps she had begun too long ago.

She stood up and leaned against the parapet, filling her troubled eyes with the tranquillizing magic of the hour. But instead of tranquillizing her the sight seemed to increase her exasperation. Her gaze turned toward the Colosseum. Already its golden flank was drowned in purple shadow, and above it the sky curved crystal clear, without light or color. It was the moment when afternoon and evening hang balanced in mid-heaven.

Mrs. Slade turned back and laid her hand on her friend's arm. The gesture was so abrupt that Mrs. Ansley looked up, startled.

"The sun's set. You're not afraid, my dear?" 45

"Afraid—?"

"Of Roman fever or pneumonia? I remember how ill you were that winter. As a girl you had a very delicate throat, hadn't you?"

"Oh, we're all right up here. Down below, in the Forum, it does get deathly cold, all of a sudden . . . but not here."

"Ah, of course you know because you had to be so careful." Mrs. Slade turned back to the parapet. She thought: "I must make one more effort not to hate her." Aloud she said, "Whenever I look at the Forum from up here, I remember that story about a great-aunt of yours, wasn't she? A dreadfully wicked great-aunt?"

"Oh, yes; Great-aunt Harriet. The one who was supposed to have sent her 50
young sister out to the Forum after sunset to gather a nightblooming flower for her album. All our great-aunts and grandmothers used to have albums of dried flowers."

Mrs. Slade nodded. "But she really sent her because they were in love with the same man—"

"Well, that was the family tradition. They said Aunt Harriet confessed it years afterward. At any rate, the poor little sister caught the fever and died. Mother used to frighten us with the story when we were children."

"And you frightened *me* with it, that winter when you and I were here as girls. The winter I was engaged to Delphin."

Mrs. Ansley gave a faint laugh. "Oh, did I? Really frightened you? I don't believe you're easily frightened."

"Not often; but I was then. I was easily frightened because I was too happy. 55
I wonder if you know what that means?"

"I—yes . . ." Mrs. Ansley faltered.

"Well, I suppose that was why the story of your wicked aunt made such an impression on me. And I thought: 'There's no more Roman fever, but the Forum is deathly cold after sunset—especially after a hot day. And the Colosseum's even colder and damper.'"

"The Colosseum—?"

"Yes. It wasn't easy to get in, after the gates were locked for the night. Far from easy. Still, in those days it could be managed; it *was* managed, often. Lovers met there who couldn't meet elsewhere. You knew that?"

"I—I daresay. I don't remember."

"You don't remember? You don't remember going to visit some ruins or other one evening, just after dark, and catching a bad chill? You were supposed to have gone to see the moon rise. People always said that expedition was what caused your illness."

There was a moment's silence; then Mrs. Ansley rejoined: "Did they? It was all so long ago."

"Yes. And you got well again—so it didn't matter. But I suppose it struck your friends—the reason given for your illness, I mean—because everybody knew you were so prudent on account of your throat, and your mother took such care of you . . . You *had* been out late sight-seeing, hadn't you, that night?"

"Perhaps I had. The most prudent girls aren't always prudent. What made you think of it now?"

Mrs. Slade seemed to have no answer ready. But after a moment she broke out: "Because I simply can't bear it any longer—!"

Mrs. Ansley lifted her head quickly. Her eyes were wide and very pale. "Can't bear what?"

"Why—your not knowing that I've always known why you went."

"Why I went—?"

"Yes. You think I'm bluffing, don't you? Well, you went to meet the man I was engaged to—and I can repeat every word of the letter that took you there."

While Mrs. Slade spoke Mrs. Ansley had risen unsteadily to her feet. Her bag, her knitting and gloves, slid in a panic-stricken heap to the ground. She looked at Mrs. Slade as though she were looking at a ghost.

"No, no—don't," she faltered out.

"Why not? Listen, if you don't believe me. 'My one darling, things can't go on like this. I must see you alone. Come to the Colosseum immediately after dark tomorrow. There will be somebody to let you in. No one whom you need fear will suspect'—but perhaps you've forgotten what the letter said?"

Mrs. Ansley met the challenge with an unexpected composure. Steadying herself against the chair she looked at her friend, and replied: "No; I know it by heart too."

"And the signature? 'Only *your* D.S.' Was that it? I'm right, am I? That was the letter that took you out that evening after dark?"

Mrs. Ansley was still looking at her. It seemed to Mrs. Slade that a slow struggle was going on behind the voluntarily controlled mask of her small quiet face. "I shouldn't have thought she had herself so well in hand," Mrs. Slade reflected, almost resentfully. But at this moment Mrs. Ansley spoke. "I don't know how you knew. I burnt that letter at once."

"Yes; you would, naturally—you're so prudent!" The sneer was open now. "And if you burnt the letter you're wondering how on earth I know what was in it. That's it, isn't it?"

Mrs. Slade waited, but Mrs. Ansley did not speak.

"Well, my dear, I know what was in that letter because I wrote it!"

"You wrote it?"

"Yes."

The two women stood for a minute staring at each other in the last golden light. Then Mrs. Ansley dropped back into her chair. "Oh," she murmured, and covered her face with her hands.

Mrs. Slade waited nervously for another word or movement. None came, and at length she broke out. "I horrify you."

Mrs. Ansley's hands dropped to her knee. The face they uncovered was streaked with tears. "I wasn't thinking of you. I was thinking—it was the only letter I ever had from him!"

"And I wrote it. Yes; I wrote it! But I was the girl he was engaged to. Did you happen to remember that?"

Mrs. Ansley's head drooped again. "I'm not trying to excuse myself . . . I remembered . . ."

"And still you went?"

"Still I went."

Mrs. Slade stood looking down on the small bowed figure at her side. The flame of her wrath had already sunk, and she wondered why she had ever thought there would be any satisfaction in inflicting so purposeless a wound on her friend. But she had to justify herself.

"You do understand? I'd found out—and I hated you, hated you. I knew you were in love with Delphin—and I was afraid; afraid of you, of your quiet ways, your sweetness . . . your . . . well, I wanted you out of the way, that's all. Just for a few weeks; just till I was sure of him. So in a blind fury I wrote that letter . . . I don't know why I'm telling you now."

"I suppose," said Mrs. Ansley slowly, "it's because you've always gone on hating me."

"Perhaps. Or because I wanted to get the whole thing off my mind." She paused. "I'm glad you destroyed the letter. Of course I never thought you'd die."

Mrs. Ansley relapsed into silence, and Mrs. Slade, leaning above her, was conscious of a strange sense of isolation, of being cut off from the warm current of human communion. "You think me a monster!"

"I don't know . . . It was the only letter I had, and you say he didn't write it?"

"Ah, how you care for him, still!"

"I cared for that memory," said Mrs. Ansley.

Mrs. Slade continued to look down on her. She seemed physically reduced by the blow—as if, when she got up, the wind might scatter her like a puff of dust. Mrs. Slade's jealousy suddenly leapt up again at the sight. All these years the woman had been living on that letter. How she must have loved him, to treasure the mere memory of its ashes! The letter of the man her friend was engaged to. Wasn't it she who was the monster?

"You tried your best to get him away from me, didn't you? But you failed; and I kept him. That's all."

"Yes. That's all."

"I wish now I hadn't told you. I'd no idea you'd feel about it as you do; I thought you'd be amused. It all happened so long ago, as you say; and you must do me the justice to remember that I had no reason to think you'd ever taken it seriously. How could I, when you were married to Horace Ansley two months afterward? As soon as you could get out of bed your mother rushed you off to Florence and married you. People were rather surprised—they wondered at its being done so quickly; but I thought I knew. I had an idea you did it out of *pique*—to be able to say you'd got ahead of Delphin and me. Girls have such silly reasons for doing the most serious things. And your marrying so soon convinced me that you'd never really cared."

100 "Yes. I suppose it would," Mrs. Ansley assented.

The clear heaven overhead was emptied of all its gold. Dusk spread over it, abruptly darkening the Seven Hills. Here and there lights began to twinkle through the foliage at their feet. Steps were coming and going on the deserted terrace—waiters looking out of the doorway at the head of the stairs, then reappearing with trays and napkins and flasks of wine. Tables were moved, chairs straightened. A feeble string of electric lights flickered out. Some vases of faded flowers were carried away, and brought back replenished. A stout lady in a dust-coat suddenly appeared, asking in broken Italian if any one had seen the elastic band which held together her tattered Baedeker.[9] She poked with her stick under the table at which she had lunched, the waiters assisting.

The corner where Mrs. Slade and Mrs. Ansley sat was still shadowy and deserted. For a long time neither of them spoke. At length Mrs. Slade began again: "I suppose I did it as a sort of joke—"

"A joke?"

"Well, girls are ferocious sometimes, you know. Girls in love especially. And I remember laughing to myself all that evening at the idea that you were waiting around there in the dark, dodging out of sight, listening for every sound, trying to get in—. Of course I was upset when I heard you were so ill afterward."

105 Mrs. Ansley had not moved for a long time. But now she turned slowly toward her companion. "But I didn't wait. He'd arranged everything. He was there. We were let in at once," she said.

Mrs. Slade sprang up from her leaning position. "Delphin there? They let you in?—Ah, now you're lying!" she burst out with violence.

Mrs. Ansley's voice grew clearer, and full of surprise. "But of course he was there. Naturally he came—"

"Came? How did he know he'd find you there? You must be raving!"

Mrs. Ansley hesitated, as though reflecting. "But I answered the letter. I told him I'd be there. So he came."

110 Mrs. Slade flung her hands up to her face. "Oh, God—you answered! I never thought of your answering . . ."

"It's odd you never thought of it, if you wrote the letter."

"Yes. I was blind with rage."

Mrs. Ansley rose, and drew her fur scarf about her. "It is cold here. We'd better go . . . I'm sorry for you," she said, as she clasped the fur about her throat.

The unexpected words sent a pang through Mrs. Slade. "Yes; we'd better go." She gathered up her bag and cloak. "I don't know why you should be sorry for me," she muttered.

9. Any one of the very popular tourist guidebooks published by German publisher Karl Baedeker (founded 1827).

Mrs. Ansley stood looking away from her toward the dusky secret mass of the Colosseum. "Well—because I didn't have to wait that night." 115

Mrs. Slade gave an unquiet laugh. "Yes; I was beaten there. But I oughtn't to begrudge it to you, I suppose. At the end of all these years. After all, I had everything; I had him for twenty-five years. And you had nothing but that one letter that he didn't write."

Mrs. Ansley was again silent. At length she turned toward the door of the terrace. She took a step, and turned back, facing her companion.

"I had Barbara," she said, and began to move ahead of Mrs. Slade toward the stairway.

1936

QUESTIONS

1. What are the first hints of submerged conflict between Mrs. Slade and Mrs. Ansley? What details in part 1 bring out the differences in their personalities and their lives? How has their relationship changed by the end, and how do the last six paragraphs of the story show the change?
2. Discuss how dramatic irony plays out in ROMAN FEVER. What is the full story that neither Mrs. Slade nor Mrs. Ansley knows? What prompts the two ladies to reveal what they know to each other?
3. In part 2, Mrs. Slade remembers how earlier generations tried to protect their daughters in Rome. What are the similarities and differences between the older women's memories and the daughters' current experiences of courtship in Italy?

JOYCE CAROL OATES (b. 1938)

Where Are You Going, Where Have You Been?

A remarkably, even uniquely, prolific writer of short stories, poems, novels, and nonfiction, Joyce Carol Oates was born in Lockport, New York. Daughter of a tool-and-die designer and his wife, she submitted her first novel to a publisher at fifteen and a few years later became the first person in her family to graduate from high school, later earning a BA from Syracuse University (1960) and an MA from the University of Wisconsin (1961). The recipient of countless awards, including a National Book Award for the novel *them* (1969), an O. Henry Special Award for Continuing Achievement (1970, 1986), a Pushchart Prize (1976), and at least four lifetime achievement awards, Oates taught for over thirty-five years at Princeton University, retiring in 2014. Her recent novels include *Little Bird of Heaven* (2009), *Mudwoman* (2012), *Daddy Love* and *The Accursed* (2013), and *Carthage* (2014). A new short-story collection, *High Crime Area: Tales of Darkness and Dread*, came out in 2012, one year after her memoir *A Widow's Story*.

For Bob Dylan

Her name was Connie. She was fifteen and she had a quick, nervous giggling habit of craning her neck to glance into mirrors or checking other people's faces to make sure her own was all right. Her mother, who noticed everything and knew everything and who hadn't much reason any longer to look at her own face, always scolded Connie about it. "Stop gawking at yourself. Who are you? You think you're so pretty?" she would say. Connie would raise her eyebrows at these familiar old complaints and look right through her mother, into a shadowy vision of herself as she was right at that moment: she knew she was pretty and that was everything. Her mother had been pretty once too, if you could believe those old snapshots in the album, but now her looks were gone and that was why she was always after Connie.

"Why don't you keep your room clean like your sister? How've you got your hair fixed—what the hell stinks? Hair spray? You don't see your sister using that junk."

Her sister, June, was twenty-four and still lived at home. She was a secretary in the high school Connie attended, and if that wasn't bad enough—with her in the same building—she was so plain and chunky and steady that Connie had to hear her praised all the time by her mother and her mother's sisters. June did this, June did that, she saved money and helped clean the house and cooked and Connie couldn't do a thing, her mind was all filled with trashy daydreams. Their father was away at work most of the time and when he came home he wanted supper and he read the newspaper at supper and after supper he went to bed. He didn't bother talking much to them, but around his bent head Connie's mother kept picking at her until Connie wished her mother was dead and she herself was dead and it was all over. "She makes me want to throw up sometimes," she complained to her friends. She had a high, breathless, amused voice that made everything she said sound a little forced, whether it was sincere or not.

There was one good thing: June went places with girl friends of hers, girls who were just as plain and steady as she, and so when Connie wanted to do that her mother had no objections. The father of Connie's best girl friend drove the girls the three miles to town and left them at a shopping plaza so they could walk through the stores or go to a movie, and when he came to pick them up again at eleven he never bothered to ask what they had done.

5 They must have been familiar sights, walking around the shopping plaza in their shorts and flat ballerina slippers that always scuffed on the sidewalk, with charm bracelets jingling on their thin wrists; they would lean together to whisper and laugh secretly if someone passed who amused or interested them. Connie had long dark blond hair that drew anyone's eye to it, and she wore part of it pulled up on her head and puffed out and the rest of it she let fall down her back. She wore a pullover jersey top that looked one way when she was at home and another way when she was away from home. Everything about her had two sides to it, one for home and one for anywhere that was not home: her walk, which could be childlike and bobbing, or languid enough to make anyone think she was hearing music in her head; her mouth, which was pale and smirking most of the time, but bright and pink on these evenings out; her laugh, which was cynical and drawling at home—"Ha, ha, very funny,"—but high-pitched and nervous anywhere else, like the jingling of the charms on her bracelet.

Sometimes they did go shopping or to a movie, but sometimes they went across the highway, ducking fast across the busy road, to a drive-in restaurant where older kids hung out. The restaurant was shaped like a big bottle, though squatter than a real bottle, and on its cap was a revolving figure of a grinning boy holding a hamburger aloft. One night in midsummer they ran across, breathless with daring, and right away someone leaned out a car window and invited them over, but it was just a boy from high school they didn't like. It made them feel good to be able to ignore him. They went up through the maze of parked and cruising cars to the bright-lit, fly-infested restaurant, their faces pleased and expectant as if they were entering a sacred building that loomed up out of the night to give them what haven and blessing they yearned for. They sat at the counter and crossed their legs at the ankles, their thin shoulders rigid with excitement, and listened to the music that made everything so good: the music was always in the background, like music at a church service; it was something to depend upon.

A boy named Eddie came in to talk with them. He sat backward on his stool, turning himself jerkily around in semicircles and then stopping and turning back again, and after a while he asked Connie if she would like something to eat. She said she would so she tapped her friend's arm on her way out—her friend pulled her face up into a brave, droll look—and Connie said she would meet her at eleven across the way. "I just hate to leave her like that," Connie said earnestly, but the boy said that she wouldn't be alone for long. So they went out to his car, and on the way Connie couldn't help but let her eyes wander over the windshields and faces all around her, her face gleaming with a joy that had nothing to do with Eddie or even this place; it might have been the music. She drew her shoulders up and sucked in her breath with the pure pleasure of being alive, and just at that moment she happened to glance at a face just a few feet away from hers. It was a boy with shaggy black hair, in a convertible jalopy[1] painted gold. He stared at her and then his lips widened into a grin. Connie slit her eyes at him and turned away, but she couldn't help glancing back and there he was, still watching her. He wagged a finger and laughed and said, "Gonna get you, baby," and Connie turned away again without Eddie noticing anything.

She spent three hours with him, at the restaurant where they ate hamburgers and drank Cokes in wax cups that were always sweating, and then down an alley a mile or so away, and when he left her off at five to eleven only the movie house was still open at the plaza. Her girl friend was there, talking with a boy. When Connie came up, the two girls smiled at each other and Connie said, "How was the movie?" and the girl said, "*You* should know." They rode off with the girl's father, sleepy and pleased, and Connie couldn't help but look back at the darkened shopping plaza with its big empty parking lot and its signs that were faded and ghostly now, and over at the drive-in restaurant where cars were still circling tirelessly. She couldn't hear the music at this distance.

Next morning June asked her how the movie was and Connie said, "So-so."

She and that girl and occasionally another girl went out several times a week, 10
and the rest of the time Connie spent around the house—it was summer vacation—getting in her mother's way and thinking, dreaming about the boys she met. But all the boys fell back and dissolved into a single face that was not even a

1. Older car, often in poor condition.

face but an idea, a feeling, mixed up with the urgent insistent pounding of the music and the humid night air of July. Connie's mother kept dragging her back to the daylight by finding things for her to do or saying suddenly, "What's this about the Pettinger girl?"

And Connie would say nervously, "Oh, her. That dope." She always drew thick clear lines between herself and such girls, and her mother was simple and kind enough to believe it. Her mother was so simple, Connie thought, that it was maybe cruel to fool her so much. Her mother went scuffling around the house in old bedroom slippers and complained over the telephone to one sister about the other, then the other called up and the two of them complained about the third one. If June's name was mentioned her mother's tone was approving, and if Connie's name was mentioned it was disapproving. This did not really mean she disliked Connie, and actually Connie thought that her mother preferred her to June just because she was prettier, but the two of them kept up a pretense of exasperation, a sense that they were tugging and struggling over something of little value to either of them. Sometimes, over coffee, they were almost friends, but something would come up—some vexation that was like a fly buzzing suddenly around their heads—and their faces went hard with contempt.

One Sunday Connie got up at eleven—none of them bothered with church—and washed her hair so that it could dry all day long in the sun. Her parents and sister were going to a barbecue at an aunt's house and Connie said no, she wasn't interested, rolling her eyes to let her mother know just what she thought of it. "Stay home alone then," her mother said sharply. Connie sat out back in a lawn chair and watched them drive away, her father quiet and bald, hunched around so that he could back the car out, her mother with a look that was still angry and not at all softened through the windshield, and in the backseat poor old June, all dressed up as if she didn't know what a barbecue was, with all the running yelling kids and the flies. Connie sat with her eyes closed in the sun, dreaming and dazed with the warmth about her as if this were a kind of love, the caresses of love, and her mind slipped over onto thoughts of the boy she had been with the night before and how nice he had been, how sweet it always was, not the way someone like June would suppose but sweet, gentle, the way it was in movies and promised in songs; and when she opened her eyes she hardly knew where she was, the backyard ran off into weeds and a fencelike line of trees and behind it the sky was perfectly blue and still. The asbestos "ranch house"[2] that was now three years old startled her—it looked small. She shook her head as if to get awake.

It was too hot. She went inside the house and turned on the radio to drown out the quiet. She sat on the edge of her bed, barefoot, and listened for an hour and a half to a program called *XYZ Sunday Jamboree*, record after record of hard, fast, shrieking songs she sang along with, interspersed by exclamations from "Bobby King": "An' look here, you girls at Napoleon's—Son and Charley want you to pay real close attention to this song coming up!"

And Connie paid close attention herself, bathed in a glow of slow-pulsed joy that seemed to rise mysteriously out of the music itself and lay languidly about the airless little room, breathed in and breathed out with each gentle rise and fall of her chest.

2. Style of long, one-story houses common in suburban neighborhoods built between the 1940s and 1980s. *Asbestos*: fireproof building material once used in roofs and siding, but now known to be toxic.

15 After a while she heard a car coming up the drive. She sat up at once, startled, because it couldn't be her father so soon. The gravel kept crunching all the way in from the road—the driveway was long—and Connie ran to the window. It was a car she didn't know. It was an open jalopy, painted a bright gold that caught the sunlight opaquely. Her heart began to pound and her fingers snatched at her hair, checking it, and she whispered, "Christ, Christ," wondering how she looked. The car came to a stop at the side door and the horn sounded four short taps, as if this were a signal Connie knew.

She went into the kitchen and approached the door slowly, then hung out the screen door, her bare toes curling down off the step. There were two boys in the car and now she recognized the driver: he had shaggy, shabby black hair that looked crazy as a wig and he was grinning at her.

"I ain't late, am I?" he said.

"Who the hell do you think you are?" Connie said.

"Toldja I'd be out, didn't I?"

20 "I don't even know who you are."

She spoke sullenly, careful to show no interest or pleasure, and he spoke in a fast, bright monotone. Connie looked past him to the other boy, taking her time. He had fair brown hair, with a lock that fell onto his forehead. His sideburns gave him a fierce, embarrassed look, but so far he hadn't even bothered to glance at her. Both boys wore sunglasses. The driver's glasses were metallic and mirrored everything in miniature.

"You wanta come for a ride?" he said.

Connie smirked and let her hair fall loose over one shoulder.

"Don'tcha like my car? New paint job," he said. "Hey."

25 "What?"

"You're cute."

She pretended to fidget, chasing flies away from the door.

"Don'tcha believe me, or what?" he said.

"Look, I don't even know who you are," Connie said in disgust.

30 "Hey, Ellie's got a radio, see. Mine broke down." He lifted his friend's arm and showed her the little transistor radio the boy was holding, and now Connie began to hear the music. It was the same program that was playing inside the house.

"Bobby King?" she said.

"I listen to him all the time. I think he's great."

"He's kind of great," Connie said reluctantly.

"Listen, that guy's *great*. He knows where the action is."

35 Connie blushed a little, because the glasses made it impossible for her to see just what this boy was looking at. She couldn't decide if she liked him or if he was a jerk, and so she dawdled in the doorway and wouldn't come down or go back inside. She said, "What's all that stuff painted on your car?"

"Can'tcha read it?" He opened the door very carefully, as if he were afraid it might fall off. He slid out just as carefully, planting his feet firmly on the ground, the tiny metallic world in his glasses slowing down like gelatine hardening, and in the midst of it Connie's bright-green blouse. "This here is my name, to begin with," he said. ARNOLD FRIEND was written in tarlike black letters on the side, with a drawing of a round, grinning face that reminded Connie of a pumpkin, except it wore sunglasses. "I wanta introduce myself. I'm Arnold Friend and that's my real name and I'm gonna be your friend, honey, and inside the car's Ellie

Oscar, he's kinda shy." Ellie brought his transistor radio up to his shoulder and balanced it there. "Now, these numbers are a secret code, honey," Arnold Friend explained. He read off the numbers 33, 19, 17 and raised his eyebrows at her to see what she thought of that, but she didn't think much of it. The left rear fender had been smashed and around it was written, on the gleaming gold background: DONE BY CRAZY WOMAN DRIVER. Connie had to laugh at that. Arnold Friend was pleased at her laughter and looked up at her. "Around the other side's a lot more—you wanta come and see them?"

"No."

"Why not?"

"Why should I?"

40 "Don'tcha wanta see what's on the car? Don'tcha wanta go for a ride?"

"I don't know."

"Why not?"

"I got things to do."

"Like what?"

45 "Things."

He laughed as if she had said something funny. He slapped his thighs. He was standing in a strange way, leaning back against the car as if he were balancing himself. He wasn't tall, only an inch or so taller than she would be if she came down to him. Connie liked the way he was dressed, which was the way all of them dressed: tight faded jeans stuffed into black, scuffed boots, a belt that pulled his waist in and showed how lean he was, and a white pullover shirt that was a little soiled and showed the hard small muscles of his arms and shoulders. He looked as if he probably did hard work, lifting and carrying things. Even his neck looked muscular. And his face was a familiar face, somehow; the jaw and chin and cheeks slightly darkened because he hadn't shaved for a day or two, and the nose long and hawklike, sniffing as if she was a treat he was going to gobble up and it was all a joke.

"Connie, you ain't telling the truth. This is your day set aside for a ride with me and you know it," he said, still laughing. The way he straightened and recovered from his fit of laughing showed that it had been all fake.

"How do you know what my name is?" she said suspiciously.

"It's Connie."

50 "Maybe and maybe not."

"I know my Connie," he said, wagging his finger. Now she remembered him even better, back at the restaurant, and her cheeks warmed at the thought of how she had sucked in her breath just at the moment she passed him—how she must have looked to him. And he had remembered her. "Ellie and I come out here especially for you," he said. "Ellie can sit in back. How about it?"

"Where?"

"Where what?"

"Where're we going?"

55 He looked at her. He took off the sunglasses and she saw how pale the skin around his eyes was, like holes that were not in shadow but instead in light. His eyes were like chips of broken glass that catch the light in an amiable way. He smiled. It was as if the idea of going for a ride somewhere, to someplace, was a new idea to him.

"Just for a ride, Connie sweetheart."

"I never said my name was Connie," she said.

"But I know what it is. I know your name and all about you, lots of things," Arnold Friend said. He had not moved yet but stood still leaning back against the side of his jalopy. "I took a special interest in you, such a pretty girl, and found out all about you—like I know your parents and sister are gone somewheres and I know where and how long they're going to be gone, and I know who you were with last night, and your best girl friend's name is Betty. Right?"

He spoke in a simple lilting voice, exactly as if he was reciting the words to a song. His smile assured her that everything was fine. In the car Ellie turned up the volume on his radio and did not bother to look around at them.

"Ellie can sit in the backseat," Arnold Friend said. He indicated his friend 60
with a casual jerk of his chin, as if Ellie did not count and she should not bother with him.

"How'd you find out all that stuff?" Connie said.

"Listen: Betty Schultz and Tony Fitch and Jimmy Pettinger and Nancy Pettinger," he said in a chant. "Raymond Stanley and Bob Hutter—"

"Do you know all those kids?"

"I know everybody."

"Look, you're kidding. You're not from around here." 65

"Sure."

"But—how come we never saw you before?"

"Sure you saw me before," he said. He looked down at his boots, as if he was a little offended. "You just don't remember."

"I guess I'd remember you," Connie said.

"Yeah?" He looked up at this, beaming. He was pleased. He began to mark time 70
with the music from Ellie's radio, tapping his fists lightly together. Connie looked away from his smile to the car, which was painted so bright it almost hurt her eyes to look at it. She looked at that name, ARNOLD FRIEND. And up at the front fender was an expression that was familiar—MAN THE FLYING SAUCERS. It was an expression kids had used the year before but didn't use this year. She looked at it for a while as if the words meant something to her that she did not yet know.

"What're you thinking about? Huh?" Arnold Friend demanded. "Not worried about your hair blowing around in the car, are you?"

"No."

"Think I maybe can't drive good?"

"How do I know?"

"You're a hard girl to handle. How come?" he said. "Don't you know I'm your 75
friend? Didn't you see me put my sign in the air when you walked by?"

"What sign?"

"My sign." And he drew an *X* in the air, leaning out toward her. They were maybe ten feet apart. After his hand fell back to his side the *X* was still in the air, almost visible. Connie let the screen door close and stood perfectly still inside it, listening to the music from her radio and the boy's blend together. She stared at Arnold Friend. He stood there so stiffly relaxed, pretending to be relaxed, with one hand idly on the door handle as if he was keeping himself up that way and had no intention of ever moving again. She recognized most things about him, the tight jeans that showed his thighs and buttocks and the greasy leather boots and the tight shirt, and even that slippery friendly smile of his, that sleepy dreamy smile that all the boys used to get across ideas they didn't want to put into words. She recognized all this and also the singsong way he talked, slightly mocking, kidding, but serious and a little melancholy, and she recognized the way he tapped one fist against the other in homage to the perpetual music behind him. But all these things did not come together.

She said suddenly, "Hey, how old are you?"

His smile faded. She could see then that he wasn't a kid, he was much older—thirty, maybe more. At this knowledge her heart began to pound faster.

80 "That's a crazy thing to ask. Can'tcha see I'm your own age?"

"Like hell you are."

"Or maybe a coupla years older. I'm eighteen."

"Eighteen?" she said doubtfully.

He grinned to reassure her and lines appeared at the corners of his mouth. His teeth were big and white. He grinned so broadly his eyes became slits and she saw how thick the lashes were, thick and black as if painted with a black tar-like material. Then, abruptly, he seemed to become embarrassed and looked over his shoulder at Ellie. "*Him*, he's crazy," he said. "Ain't he a riot? He's a nut, a real character." Ellie was still listening to the music. His sunglasses told nothing about what he was thinking. He wore a bright-orange shirt unbuttoned halfway to show his chest, which was a pale, bluish chest and not muscular like Arnold Friend's. His shirt collar was turned up all around and the very tips of the collar pointed out past his chin as if they were protecting him. He was pressing the transistor radio up against his ear and sat there in a kind of daze, right in the sun.

85 "He's kinda strange," Connie said.

"Hey, she says you're kinda strange! Kinda strange!" Arnold Friend cried. He pounded on the car to get Ellie's attention. Ellie turned for the first time and Connie saw with shock that he wasn't a kid either—he had a fair, hairless face, cheeks reddened slightly as if the veins grew too close to the surface of his skin, the face of a forty-year-old baby. Connie felt a wave of dizziness rise in her at this sight and she stared at him as if waiting for something to change the shock of the moment, make it all right again. Ellie's lips kept shaping words, mumbling along with the words blasting in his ear.

"Maybe you two better go away," Connie said faintly.

"What? How come?" Arnold Friend cried. "We come out here to take you for a ride. It's Sunday." He had the voice of the man on the radio now. It was the same voice, Connie thought. "Don'tcha know it's Sunday all day? And honey, no matter who you were with last night, today you're with Arnold Friend and don't you forget it! Maybe you better step out here," he said, and this last was in a different voice. It was a little flatter, as if the heat was finally getting to him.

"No. I got things to do."

90 "Hey."

"You two better leave."

"We ain't leaving until you come with us."

"Like hell I am—"

"Connie, don't fool around with me. I mean—I mean, don't fool *around*," he said, shaking his head. He laughed incredulously. He placed his sunglasses on top of his head, carefully, as if he was indeed wearing a wig, and brought the stems down behind his ears. Connie stared at him, another wave of dizziness and fear rising in her so that for a moment he wasn't even in focus but was just a blur standing there against his gold car, and she had the idea that he had driven up the driveway all right but had come from nowhere before that and belonged nowhere and that everything about him and even about the music that was so familiar to her was only half real.

"If my father comes and sees you—" 95

"He ain't coming. He's at a barbecue."

"How do you know that?"

"Aunt Tillie's. Right now they're—uh—they're drinking. Sitting around," he said vaguely, squinting as if he was staring all the way to town and over to Aunt Tillie's backyard. Then the vision seemed to get clear and he nodded energetically. "Yeah. Sitting around. There's your sister in a blue dress, huh? And high heels, the poor sad bitch—nothing like you, sweetheart! And your mother's helping some fat woman with the corn, they're cleaning the corn—husking the corn—"

"What fat woman?" Connie cried.

"How do I know what fat woman, I don't know every goddamn fat woman in 100
the world!" Arnold Friend laughed.

"Oh, that's Mrs. Hornsby. . . . Who invited her?" Connie said. She felt a little light-headed. Her breath was coming quickly.

"She's too fat. I don't like them fat. I like them the way you are, honey," he said, smiling sleepily at her. They stared at each other for a while through the screen door. He said softly, "Now, what you're going to do is this: you're going to come out that door. You're going to sit up front with me and Ellie's going to sit in the back, the hell with Ellie, right? This isn't Ellie's date. You're my date. I'm your lover, honey."

"What? You're crazy—"

"Yes. I'm your lover. You don't know what that is but you will," he said. "I know that too. I know all about you. But look: it's real nice and you couldn't ask for nobody better than me, or more polite. I always keep my word. I'll tell you how it is, I'm always nice at first, the first time. I'll hold you so tight you won't think you have to try to get away or pretend anything because you'll know you can't. And I'll come inside you where it's all secret and you'll know you can't. And I'll come inside you where it's all secret and you'll give in to me and you'll love me—"

"Shut up! You're crazy!" Connie said. She backed away from the door. She 105
put her hands up against her ears as if she'd heard something terrible, something not meant for her. "People don't talk like that, you're crazy," she muttered. Her heart was almost too big now for her chest and its pumping made sweat break out all over her. She looked out to see Arnold Friend pause and then take a step toward the porch, lurching. He almost fell. But, like a clever drunken man, he managed to catch his balance. He wobbled in his high boots and grabbed hold of one of the porch posts.

"Honey?" he said. "You still listening?"

"Get the hell out of here!"

"Be nice, honey. Listen."

"I'm going to call the police—"

He wobbled again and out of the side of his mouth came a fast spat curse, an 110
aside not meant for her to hear. But even this "Christ!" sounded forced. Then he

began to smile again. She watched this smile come, awkward as if he was smiling from inside a mask. His whole face was a mask, she thought wildly, tanned down to his throat but then running out as if he had plastered makeup on his face but had forgotten about his throat.

"Honey—? Listen, here's how it is. I always tell the truth and I promise you this: I ain't coming in that house after you."

"You better not! I'm going to call the police if you—if you don't—"

"Honey," he said, talking right through her voice, "honey. I'm not coming in there but you are coming out here. You know why?"

She was panting. The kitchen looked like a place she had never seen before, some room she had run inside but that wasn't good enough, wasn't going to help her. The kitchen window had never had a curtain, after three years, and there were dishes in the sink for her to do—probably—and if you ran your hand across the table you'd probably feel something sticky there.

115 "You listening, honey? Hey?"

"—going to call the police—"

"Soon as you touch the phone I don't need to keep my promise and can come inside. You won't want that."

She rushed forward and tried to lock the door. Her fingers were shaking. "But why lock it," Arnold Friend said gently, talking right into her face. "It's just a screen door. It's just nothing." One of his boots was at a strange angle, as if his foot wasn't in it. It pointed out to the left, bent at the ankle. "I mean, anybody can break through a screen door and glass and wood and iron or anything else if he needs to, anybody at all, and specially Arnold Friend. If the place got lit up with a fire, honey, you'd come runnin' our into my arms, right into my arms an' safe at home—like you knew I was your lover and'd stopped fooling around. I don't mind a nice shy girl but I don't like no fooling around." Part of those words were spoken with a slight rhythmic lilt, and Connie somehow recognized them—the echo of a song from last year, about a girl rushing into her boyfriend's arms and coming home again—

Connie stood barefoot on the linoleum floor, staring at him. "What do you want?" she whispered.

120 "I want you," he said.

"What?"

"Seen you that night and thought, that's the one, yes sir. I never needed to look anymore."

"But my father's coming back. He's coming to get me. I had to wash my hair first—" She spoke in a dry, rapid voice, hardly raising it for him to hear.

"No, your daddy is not coming and yes, you had to wash your hair and you washed it for me. It's nice and shining and all for me. I thank you, sweetheart," he said with a mock bow, but again he almost lost his balance. He had to bend and adjust his boots. Evidently his feet did not go all the way down; the boots must have been stuffed with something so that he would seem taller. Connie stared out at him and behind him at Ellie in the car, who seemed to be looking off toward Connie's right, into nothing. Then Ellie said, pulling the words out of the air one after another as if he were just discovering them, "You want me to pull out the phone?"

125 "Shut your mouth and keep it shut," Arnold Friend said, his face red from bending over or maybe from embarrassment because Connie had seen his boots. "This ain't none of your business."

"What—what are you doing? What do you want?" Connie said. "If I call the police they'll get you, they'll arrest you—"

"Promise was not to come in unless you touch that phone, and I'll keep that promise," he said. He resumed his erect position and tried to force his shoulders back. He sounded like a hero in a movie, declaring something important. But he spoke too loudly and it was as if he was speaking to someone behind Connie. "I ain't made plans for coming in that house where I don't belong but just for you to come out to me, the way you should. Don't you know who I am?"

"You're crazy," she whispered. She backed away from the door but did not want to go into another part of the house, as if this would give him permission to come through the door. "What do you . . . you're crazy, you . . ."

"Huh? What're you saying, honey?"

Her eyes darted everywhere in the kitchen. She could not remember what it 130
was, this room.

"This is how it is, honey: you come out and we'll drive away, have a nice ride. But if you don't come out we're gonna wait till your people come home and then they're all going to get it."

"You want that telephone pulled out?" Ellie said. He held the radio away from his ear and grimaced, as if without the radio the air was too much for him.

"I toldja shut up, Ellie," Arnold Friend said, "you're deaf, get a hearing aid, right? Fix yourself up. This little girl's no trouble and's gonna be nice to me, so Ellie keep to yourself, this ain't your date—right? Don't hem in on me, don't hog, don't crush, don't bird dog, don't trail me," he said in a rapid, meaningless voice, as if he were running through all the expressions he'd learned but was no longer sure which of them was in style, then rushing on to new ones, making them up with his eyes closed. "Don't crawl under my fence, don't squeeze in my chipmunk hole, don't sniff my glue, suck my Popsicle, keep your own greasy fingers on yourself!" He shaded his eyes and peered in at Connie, who was backed against the kitchen table. "Don't mind him, honey, he's just a creep. He's a dope. Right? I'm the boy for you and like I said, you come out here nice like a lady and give me your hand, and nobody else gets hurt, I mean, your nice old bald-headed daddy and your mummy and your sister in her high heels. Because listen: why bring them in this?"

"Leave me alone," Connie whispered.

"Hey, you know that old woman down the road, the one with the chickens 135
and stuff—you know her?"

"She's dead!"

"Dead? What? You know her?" Arnold Friend said.

"She's dead—"

"Don't you like her?"

"She's dead—she's—she isn't here anymore—" 140

"But don't you like her, I mean, you got something against her? Some grudge or something?" Then his voice dipped as if he was conscious of a rudeness. He touched the sunglasses perched up on top of his head as if to make sure they were still there. "Now, you be a good girl."

"What are you going to do?"

"Just two things, or maybe three," Arnold Friend said. "But I promise it won't last long and you'll like me the way you get to like people you're close to. You will. It's all over for you here, so come on out. You don't want your people in any trouble, do you?"

She turned and bumped against a chair or something, hurting her leg, but she ran into the back room and picked up the telephone. Something roared in her ear, a tiny roaring, and she was so sick with fear that she could do nothing but listen to it—the telephone was clammy and very heavy and her fingers groped down to the dial but were too weak to touch it. She began to scream into the phone, into the roaring. She cried out, she cried for her mother, she felt her breath start jerking back and forth in her lungs as if it was something Arnold Friend was stabbing her with again and again with no tenderness. A noisy sorrowful wailing rose all about her and she was locked inside it the way she was locked inside this house.

145 After a while she could hear again. She was sitting on the floor with her wet back against the wall.

Arnold Friend was saying from the door, "That's a good girl. Put the phone back."

She kicked the phone away from her.

"No, honey. Pick it up. Put it back right."

She picked it up and put it back. The dial tone stopped.

150 "That's a good girl. Now, you come outside."

She was hollow with what had been fear but what was now just an emptiness. All that screaming had blasted it out of her. She sat, one leg cramped under her, and deep inside her brain was something like a pin-point of light that kept going and would not let her relax. She thought, I'm not going to see my mother again. She thought, I'm not going to sleep in my bed again. Her bright-green blouse was all wet.

Arnold Friend said, in a gentle-loud voice that was like a stage voice, "The place where you came from ain't there anymore, and where you had in mind to go is canceled out. This place you are now—inside your daddy's house—is nothing but a cardboard box I can knock down anytime. You know that and always did know it. You hear me?"

She thought, *I have got to think. I have got to know what to do.*

"We'll go out to a nice field, out in the country here where it smells so nice and it's sunny," Arnold Friend said. "I'll have my arms tight around you so you won't need to try to get away and I'll show you what love is like, what it does. The hell with this house! It looks solid all right," he said. He ran his fingernail down the screen and the noise did not make Connie shiver, as it would have the day before. "Now, put your hand on your heart, honey. Feel that? That feels solid too but we know better. Be nice to me, be sweet like you can because what else is there for a girl like you but to be sweet and pretty and give in?—and get away before her people get back?"

155 She felt her pounding heart. Her hand seemed to enclose it. She thought for the first time in her life that it was nothing that was hers, that belonged to her, but just a pounding, living thing inside this body that wasn't really hers either.

"You don't want them to get hurt," Arnold Friend went on. "Now, get up, honey. Get up all by yourself."

She stood.

"Now, turn this way. That's right. Come over here to me.—Ellie, put that away, didn't I tell you? You dope. You miserable creepy dope," Arnold Friend said.

His words were not angry but only part of an incantation. The incantation was kindly. "Now, come out through the kitchen to me, honey, and let's see a smile, try it, you're a brave, sweet little girl and now they're eating corn and hot dogs cooked to bursting over an outdoor fire, and they don't know one thing about you and never did and honey, you're better than them because not a one of them would have done this for you."

Connie felt the linoleum under her feet; it was cool. She brushed her hair back out of her eyes. Arnold Friend let go of the post tentatively and opened his arms for her, his elbows pointing in toward each other and his wrists limp, to show that this was an embarrassed embrace and a little mocking, he didn't want to make her self-conscious.

She put out her hand against the screen. She watched herself push the door 160
slowly open as if she was back safe somewhere in the other doorway, watching this body and this head of long hair moving out into the sunlight where Arnold Friend waited.

"My sweet little blue-eyed girl," he said in a half-sung sigh that had nothing to do with her brown eyes but was taken up just the same by the vast sunlit reaches of the land behind him and on all sides of him—so much land that Connie had never seen before and did not recognize except to know that she was going to it.

1966

QUESTIONS

1. At what specific points in the story do your expectations about "where you are going" change? Why and how so? How might these shifts in your expectations relate to Connie's?
2. To what extent is the major conflict in Oates's story external (between Connie and Arnold, Connie and her family, Connie and her milieu)? To what extent is it internal (within Connie herself)? Why might she act as she does at the story's end? What happens next, or does it matter?
3. Both Connie and Arnold Friend more than once suggest that he is, or should be, familiar to her. Aside from the fact she has seen him at least once before, why and how does he seem familiar? Why might that familiarity be significant, or how might it shape your sense of who Arnold is or what he might represent in the story?

AUTHORS ON THEIR WORK

JOYCE CAROL OATES (b. 1938)

From "'Where Are You Going, Where Have You Been?' and *Smooth Talk*: Short Story into Film" (1986)*

Some years ago in the American Southwest there surfaced a tabloid psychopath known as "The Pied Piper of Tucson." I have forgotten his name, but his specialty was the seduction and occasional murder of teen-aged girls. He may or may not have had actual accomplices, but his bizarre activities were known among a circle of teenagers in the Tucson area; for some reason they kept his secret, deliberately did not inform parents or police. (316)

It was not after all the mass murderer himself who intrigued me, but the disturbing fact that a number of teenagers—from "good" families—aided and abetted his crimes. This is the sort of thing authorities and responsible citizens invariably call "inexplicable" because they can't find explanations for it. *They* would not have fallen under this maniac's spell, after all.

An early draft [. . .] had the rather too explicit title "Death and the Maiden." It was cast in a mode of fiction to which I am still partial—indeed, every third or fourth story of mine is probably in this mode—"realistic allegory," it might be called. It is Hawthornean, romantic, shading into parable. Like the medieval German engraving from which my title was taken, the story was minutely detailed yet clearly an allegory of the fatal attractions of death (or the devil). An innocent young girl is seduced by way of her own vanity; she mistakes death for erotic romance of a particularly American/trashy sort.

In subsequent drafts the story changed its tone, its focus, its language, its title. It became "Where Are You Going, Where Have You Been?" Written at a time when the author was intrigued by the music of Bob Dylan, particularly the hauntingly elegiac song "It's All Over Now, Baby Blue," it was dedicated to Bob Dylan. The charismatic mass murderer drops into the background and his innocent victim, a fifteen-year-old moves into the foreground. She becomes the true protagonist of the tale [. . .]. (317–18)

*"'Where Are You Going, Where Have You Been?' and *Smooth Talk*: Short Story into Film." *(Woman) Writer: Occasions and Opportunities*, Dutton, 1988, pp. 316–21.

SUGGESTIONS FOR WRITING

1. Write an essay comparing the way any two of the stories in this chapter handle the traditional elements of plot: exposition, rising action, climax, falling action, conclusion. Consider especially how plot elements contribute to the overall artistic effect.
2. Many stories depict events out of chronological order. For example, SONNY'S BLUES makes liberal use of flashbacks. Select any story from this anthology, and write an essay discussing the significance of sequence.
3. Re-read ROMAN FEVER and record the instances when the story prompts you to form expectations that may or may not be borne out by the events to follow. Write an essay in which you analyze the way Wharton has rearranged the chronology of events in order to build suspense and stimulate reader engagement with the text.
4. Write an essay comparing Connie's encounter with Arnold Friend in Oates's WHERE ARE YOU GOING, WHERE HAVE YOU BEEN? to that between the Grandmother and the Misfit in Flannery O'Connor's A GOOD MAN IS HARD TO FIND.
5. Write an essay that explores the central conflict in any one of the stories in this chapter. What is the nature of the conflict? When, where, and how does it develop or become more complicated as the story unfolds? How is it resolved at the end of the story? Why and how is that resolution satisfying?

SAMPLE WRITING: RESEARCH ESSAY

The following essay demonstrates one way to write about plot. In it, student writer Ann Warren analyzes William Faulkner's A ROSE FOR EMILY. Focusing on the sequencing of the action and the story's division into numbered parts or sections, she illuminates both the story's tragic plot pattern and its similarities to one particular and particularly famous tragedy—William Shakespeare's HAMLET. Because Warren draws on the arguments of other literary critics to develop her own, her paper is also a critical-contexts research essay. (To learn more about this type of essay, see ch. 36.)

Warren 1

Ann Warren
Mr. Jeffreys
ENG 3011: The Short Story
15 March 2017

The Tragic Plot of "A Rose for Emily"

In "The Structure of 'A Rose for Emily,'" Floyd C. Watkins says that "[i]f analyses in periodicals and inclusion in anthologies are a dependable criterion for a short story," then this Faulkner story is "not only his best story, but also one of the best written by any modern American writer" (46). The amount of attention the story has gotten does not seem surprising. It's definitely the only story I've ever read about someone who sleeps with the dead body of a man she poisoned! A lot of criticism on the story focuses on figuring out why Emily does it, how we should feel about her and what she does, and what we're supposed to take away from the story. In terms of how we should feel about her, there are two opposite points of view. On one side, Cleanth Brooks and Robert Penn Warren declare she's a tragic hero, and her "refusal to accept the herd values carries with it a dignity and courage" that are admirable (28). On the other side, T. J. Stafford says that Miss Emily's actions are simply "abnormal, degenerate, and meaningless" and "unworthy of [. . .] pride" (87).

As far as I know, only Floyd Watkins has paid attention to how the plot is structured. His article shows it is important that Faulkner "divided the story into five parts and based them on incidents of isolation and intrusion" (46). Because the one part that doesn't include incidents like this is the middle one (pt. 3),

Warren 2

it helps give the story "a perfect symmetry" and shows "the indomitableness of the decadent Southern aristocrat" (46, 47). While I think Watkins's argument is good, I also think he and other writers have missed something about the five-part structure and the third part that shows that Miss Emily is a tragic hero. Specifically, she's like Hamlet.

As Watkins says, parts 1, 2, 4 and 5 of the story show how "adherents of the new order in the town" invade her house (46). In part 1, Miss Emily dies, and the neighbors come to the funeral and to look in her house. Then we hear about how earlier the "deputation" from the Board of Aldermen of a younger "generation" came to tell her she had to pay taxes that an earlier generation (specifically, Colonel Sartoris) had told her she never had to pay (10). Part 2 also has two invasions. Four men from the Board of Aldermen spread lime to try to get rid of the smell at Miss Emily's house. Then, after Miss Emily's father's death (which is actually earlier in time), people from the town come in to "offer condolence and aid" and then "to persuade her to let them dispose of the body" (12). As Watkins writes, part 4 "contains two forced entrances" by a minister and then Miss Emily's relatives, who are trying to make her break up with Homer Barron (46). Then in part 5 everyone comes to Miss Emily's house for the funeral and then to force open the room upstairs that no one except her has been in for forty years.

Part 3 is different. Watkins says, "The inviolability of Miss Emily's isolation is maintained in the central division, part three, in which no outsider enters her home. Her triumph is further revealed in this part when she buys the arsenic without telling what she plans to use it for" (47). But there's more to it than that. It's not just that no one "enters her home"; it's that she *leaves it for the first time in the story!* In fact, we hear about her leaving it twice just like people invade her home twice in other sections. First Homer Barron arrives in town, and the neighbors "began to see him and Miss Emily on Sunday afternoons driving in the yellow-wheeled buggy" (12). Then she buys the poison to kill Homer, and we know she goes to the drugstore to do that because the narrator says, "she opened the package *at home"* later (13; emphasis added).

At first, I thought that this was the only section where we see Miss Emily go out, but then I noticed that in the next section the narrator says she "had been to the jeweler's" and "bought a complete outfit of men's clothing" (14). Still, part 3 is the real turning point because it's the only time where she has the chance for love and a real life of her own (the first time or reason she leaves the house) and where she reacts to losing that chance by buying rat poison to kill Homer with.

Before and after this, the story is more about everybody else doing things to Emily, even in a way trying to kill her or at least to kill her chance of having any real life of her own, if only by judging and talking about her all the time. Even the moments when she seems strong are more about her not doing or saying things, saying "no" to other people, and just holing up in her house and not letting people in, just like her father started all this by not letting in the young men she might have married. As the narrator says it in part 2, she "vanquished" (11) the tax deputation in part I just by the fact that "[s]he did not ask them to sit" and "just stood in the door and listened quietly" (10). In part 2, she just "sat . . . motionless as . . . an idol" inside her house while the "four men slunk about the house like burglars" (11). Then when her father dies she won't let people in and just "told them that her father was not dead" for three days before "she broke down" (12). In part 4, she "did not appear on the streets" and "closed" the door of her house "for good" after opening it up for Homer and then some painting students (because she needed the money) (15). In part 5, again, she's dead (like in the first part) and can't do anything.

But she still surprises and even "vanquishes" them in this last part—because of the active thing she did in part 3 by going out of the house to buy the poison. In that section she takes things into her own hands. Having gone out with Homer, it's like if she can't keep going out with him (literally!), she'll make sure he can't go out either. It's after that (in time and in the story) that she stops going out at all, but at least she has made sure that she is not the only one buried in that "tomb" of a house from then on (16). The thing she does might be "abnormal" and "degenerate." I'm not saying it is right, but it doesn't seem "meaningless" either (Stafford 87). It's like she is literally backed into a corner. She doesn't have any money, just that house, which is what she retreats to and takes Homer home with her. Part 3 is the turning point where Emily takes the action that decides what happens at the end.

How Faulkner mixes up the chronology to divide the story into five parts makes the plot and story even more perfect (and difficult to explain!). In addition to everything else, this makes the story like a tragedy like *Hamlet,* which also has five acts and the turning point in the third. Other plays besides *Hamlet* have five acts, and their turning points also might come in the third act, but there are other connections to *Hamlet.* First, what happens in act 3 of *Hamlet* is that Hamlet kills Polonius when he hides behind a curtain to spy on Hamlet and his mother. Hamlet doesn't mean to kill Polonius (he thinks it's the king hiding), but he does mean to kill someone, as Miss Emily apparently gets ready to do in the third part of her story.

Also, Hamlet calls Polonius "a rat" after he kills him (3.4.26), which Polonius is. He may not be a little brown furry animal, but he is "a contemptible person" and an "informer" ("Rat," def. 2). In "A Rose for Emily," Homer is also "a sneaky, contemptible person," though not exactly "an informer," for seeing what Miss Emily's life is like and taking her out of it (literally!) and then just dumping her. (Also, he sneaks into her house at night, which seems to be when he dies, even though it's not the main character he's hiding from like in *Hamlet.*) Homer is also called a "rat," but indirectly because of the way his murder is mistaken for a rat's three times: Judge Stevens says that the smell at the house is "probably just a snake or a rat" that the servant "killed in the yard" when it's really Homer that was killed in the house by Miss Emily (11), and when Miss Emily goes to

Warren 4

the druggist for poison, he says to her it's "For rats" and then writes it on the box she sees when she gets home (13).

Noticing these details made me see deeper similarities in the characters and conflicts of Emily and Hamlet. Both spend a lot of time not doing much very active, both are being watched by other people, and both are seen by those people as crazy and maybe they even plan to be seen as crazy (at least Hamlet). What's more important is that both of them become murderers, if not crazy, because they are haunted by their fathers. In *Hamlet,* there is an actual ghost. "A Rose for Emily" has a symbolic or psychological ghost. Her father is like a ghost in the story because his death is mentioned so many times:[1] "the death of her father" (9), "her father's death" (11, 12), "her father died" (12). He is like a ghost in her actual house because "[o]n a tarnished gilt easel before the fireplace stood a crayon portrait of Miss Emily's father" (9). This portrait is first shown in the first section (like the ghost appears in the first act of *Hamlet*). And the story is also organized so that all the other quotations about Emily's father's death above are in the first three parts, and the last two parts don't say anything about her father until in the last one where she's dead and "the crayon face of her father mus[es] profoundly above the bier" (15). The picture being in the first and last sections is another kind of "symmetry," and it might be more evidence that the third part is a turning point and that in a way Homer's ghost replaces her father's once she's killed him.

Maybe she even kills Homer because of her father. The narrator, author, and critics strongly blame him. The narrator says, "her father had driven away" "all the young men" and "robbed her" (12) and "thwarted her woman's life so many times" and was "too virulent and too furious to die" (14). Faulkner said so when someone asked him why he wrote the story:

> In this case there was the young girl with a young girl's normal aspirations to find love and then a husband and a family, who was brow-beaten and kept down by her father, a selfish man who didn't want her to leave home because he wanted a housekeeper, and it was a natural instinct . . . —you can't repress it—you can mash it down but it comes up somewhere else and very likely in a tragic form, and that was simply another manifestation of man's injustice to man. . . . ("Comments" 22)

Ray B. West, Jr., says, "She does not resist change completely . . . until she has known two separate betrayals, the first by her father (traditional decorum)" (36). William Van O'Connor writes, "The severity of Miss Emily's father was the cause of her frustrations and her retreat" (45). Irving Malin argues, "Emily's attachment to the will of the father—it is said that he had driven all the young men away—has stunted her growth" (48).

These writers don't associate Miss Emily and Hamlet. But I think all this still supports the view that Miss Emily is like a tragic hero and especially like Hamlet. The two characters are obviously not exactly alike, and Faulkner didn't necessarily intend the comparison. But Hamlet is the most famous tragic hero, and I do think that Faulkner meant to portray Miss Emily as a tragic hero,

Warren 5

someone we pity even if we don't like her (he says he might not have) or even if she is sort of perversely happy. Faulkner even says above that her "normal aspirations to find love" come out in "a *tragic* form" because of how she's made to "mash them down." The plot is one thing Faulkner uses to make the story and Miss Emily tragic.

Warren 6

Note

1. In his recent article, Thomas Klein backs me up when he says that Faulkner "described 'A Rose for Emily' as a 'ghost story,' " but the only "candidates" for the ghost position that he mentions are Miss Emily, Homer, Tobe, and the "pervasive, shape-shifting, haunting" "voice of the town" that narrates the story (231).

Warren 7

Works Cited

Brooks, Cleanth, and Robert Penn Warren. "An Interpretation of 'A Rose for Emily.'" Inge, pp. 25-29.

Faulkner, William. "Comments on 'A Rose for Emily.'" Inge, pp. 20-22.

---. "A Rose for Emily." Inge, pp. 9-16.

Inge, M. Thomas, editor. *William Faulkner: A Rose for Emily.* Merrill, 1970. Merrill Literary Casebook Series.

Klein, Thomas. "The Ghostly Voice of Gossip in Faulkner's 'A Rose for Emily.'" *The Explicator,* vol. 65, no. 4, 2007, pp. 299-32.

Malin, Irving. "Miss Emily's Perversion." Inge, pp. 48-49.

O'Connor, William Van. "History in 'A Rose for Emily.'" Inge, pp. 44-45.

"Rat." *Merriam-Webster's Collegiate Dictionary*, 11th ed., 2003.

Shakespeare, William. *Hamlet.* Washington Square, 1992.

Stafford, T. J. "Tobe's Significance in 'A Rose for Emily.'" Inge, pp. 87-89.

Watkins, Floyd C. "The Structure of 'A Rose for Emily.'" Inge, pp. 46-47.

West, Ray B., Jr. "Faulkner's 'A Rose for Emily.'" Inge, pp. 36-37.

Initiation Stories

AN ALBUM

It may be true that most people's lives mainly consist of the "middle"—a long, stable passage of adult years—instead of the promising start, the turning point or crisis, the eventual catastrophe or triumph. Nevertheless, a great deal of fiction (as well as movies, television, and other media) focuses on the more momentous changes that we associate with youth. This album features a common kind of short fiction, the **initiation story**, also known as the coming-of-age story—the story of what happens as we define ourselves and set our own course toward the future. The short story, which often focuses on a brief, momentous occasion, is a form well suited to telling this sort of story.

Across cultures, social groups have various initiation rites to mark the *coming of age* of their youths—from "sweet sixteen" parties, bar and bat mitzvahs, debutante balls, and the *quinceañera*, to the laws that permit twenty-one-year-olds to inherit property and buy alcohol. These practices may feature prominently in stories that explore the transformation from childhood to adulthood, but such fiction doesn't have to include an obvious initiation rite like a fraternity hazing or a birthday party.

Initiation stories usually have common characteristics related to the "plot" of growing up. They always feature at least one young person, a child, an adolescent, or a young adult, who undergoes some sort of transformation. This character learns a significant truth about the world, society, people, or himself or herself. The nature of this knowledge differs widely in such stories, as does the character's response, but the plot of the story must culminate in a change of status or awareness that is more adult. The protagonist may struggle to find a place in society, but more often the challenge is to adjust his or her ideals to actual circumstances. Initiation stories may zoom in on such moments as when a child loses the protection of adults, a teenager sees a fellow creature die, or a young person faced with rejection or disappointment is suddenly made aware of a separate, lonely identity and an unknown future. Sometimes newfound freedom can lead to a joyful, if frightening, sense of possibility. At other times, the response of the young protagonist may be disbelief, denial, or retreat from the truth. Often the reader can only guess how the character will adapt to the hard-won, still-confusing knowledge gained in the experience.

Naturally there are countless such stories to tell, from the tragic to the euphoric and everything in between. Innumerable novels, films, and television shows—J. D. Salinger's *The Catcher in the Rye* (1951), *Ferris Bueller's Day Off* (1986), *Twilight* (2008), to name a few—center on the trials and adventures of teens, often with pain, whimsy, humor, embarrassment, nostalgia, sympathy, and insight. Here we offer a variety of initiation stories that have some common features as well as very different visions of initiation. Which characters undergo initiation in each of these stories? What general or specific social conditions is each character initiated into, and how does each respond? Is there something about the passage of time and growing up that is both necessary and cruel? Can you recognize common elements in this selection of stories? in your own experience?

TONI CADE BAMBARA (1939–95)

The Lesson

Born in New York City, Toni Cade Bambara grew up in Harlem and Bedford-Stuyvesant, two of New York's poorest neighborhoods. She began writing as a child and took her last name from a signature on a sketchbook she found in a trunk belonging to her great-grandmother. (The Bambara are a people of northwest Africa.) After graduating from Queens College, she wrote fiction in "the predawn in-betweens" while studying for her MA at the City College of New York and working at a variety of jobs: dancer, social worker, recreation director, psychiatric counselor, college English teacher, literary critic, and film producer. Bambara began to publish her stories in 1962. Her fiction includes two collections of stories, *Gorilla, My Love* (1972) and *The Sea Birds Are Still Alive* (1977), as well as two novels, *The Salt Eaters* (1980) and *If Blessing Comes* (1987). Bambara also edited two anthologies, *The Black Woman* (1970) and *Stories for Black Folks* (1971).

Back in the days when everyone was old and stupid or young and foolish and me and Sugar were the only ones just right, this lady moved on our block with nappy[1] hair and proper speech and no makeup. And quite naturally we laughed at her, laughed the way we did at the junk man who went about his business like he was some big-time president and his sorry-ass horse his secretary. And we kinda hated her too, hated the way we did the winos who cluttered up our parks and pissed on our handball walls and stank up our hallways and stairs so you couldn't halfway play hide-and-seek without a goddamn gas mask. Miss Moore was her name. The only woman on the block with no first name. And she was black as hell, cept for her feet, which were fish-white and spooky. And she was always planning these boring-ass things for us to do, us being my cousin, mostly, who lived on the block cause we all moved North the same time and to the same apartment then spread out gradual to breathe. And our parents would yank our heads into some kinda shape and crisp up our clothes so we'd be presentable for travel with Miss Moore, who always looked like she was going to church, though she never did. Which is just one of the things the grown-ups talked about when they talked behind her back like a dog. But when she came calling with some sachet she'd sewed up or some gingerbread she'd made or some book, why then they'd all be too embarrassed to turn her down and we'd get handed over all spruced up. She'd been to college and said it was only right that she should take responsibility for the young ones' education, and she not even related by marriage or blood. So they'd go for it. Specially Aunt Gretchen. She was the main gofer in the family. You got some ole dumb shit foolishness you want somebody to go for, you send for Aunt

1. Untreated and unstraightened, naturally curly or coiled.

Gretchen. She been screwed into the go-along for so long, it's a blood-deep natural thing with her. Which is how she got saddled with me and Sugar and Junior in the first place while our mothers were in a la-de-da apartment up the block having a good ole time.

So this one day Miss Moore rounds us all up at the mailbox and it's puredee hot and she's knockin herself out about arithmetic. And school suppose to let up in summer I heard, but she don't never let up. And the starch in my pinafore scratching the shit outta me and I'm really hating this nappy-head bitch and her goddamn college degree. I'd much rather go to the pool or to the show where it's cool. So me and Sugar leaning on the mailbox being surly, which is a Miss Moore word. And Flyboy checking out what everybody brought for lunch. And Fat Butt already wasting his peanut-butter-and-jelly sandwich like the pig he is. And Junebug punchin on Q.T.'s arm for potato chips. And Rosie Giraffe shifting from one hip to the other waiting for somebody to step on her foot or ask her if she from Georgia so she can kick ass, preferably Mercedes'. And Miss Moore asking us do we know what money is, like we a bunch of retards. I mean real money, she say, like it's only poker chips or monopoly papers we lay on the grocer. So right away I'm tired of this and say so. And would much rather snatch Sugar and go to the Sunset and terrorize the West Indian kids and take their hair ribbons and their money too. And Miss Moore files that remark away for next week's lesson on brotherhood, I can tell. And finally I say we oughta get to the subway cause it's cooler and besides we might meet some cute boys. Sugar done swiped her mama's lipstick, so we ready.

So we heading down the street and she's boring us silly about what things cost and what our parents make and how much goes for rent and how money ain't divided up right in this country. And then she gets to the part about we all poor and live in the slums, which I don't feature. And I'm ready to speak on that, but she steps out in the street and hails two cabs just like that. Then she hustles half the crew in with her and hands me a five-dollar bill and tells me to calculate 10 percent tip for the driver. And we're off. Me and Sugar and Junebug and Flyboy hangin out the window and hollering to everybody, putting lipstick on each other cause Flyboy a faggot anyway, and making farts with our sweaty armpits. But I'm mostly trying to figure how to spend this money. But they all fascinated with the meter ticking and Junebug starts laying bets as to how much it'll read when Flyboy can't hold his breath no more. Then Sugar lays bets as to how much it'll be when we get there. So I'm stuck. Don't nobody want to go for my plan, which is to jump out at the next light and run off to the first bar-b-que we can find. Then the driver tells us to get the hell out cause we there already. And the meter reads eighty-five cents. And I'm stalling to figure out the tip and Sugar say give him a dime. And I decide he don't need it bad as I do, so later for him. But then he tries to take off with Junebug foot still in the door so we talk about his mama something ferocious. Then we check out that we on Fifth Avenue[2] and everybody dressed up in stockings. One lady in a fur coat, hot as it is. White folks crazy.

"This is the place," Miss Moore say, presenting it to us in the voice she uses at the museum. "Let's look in the windows before we go in."

2. Major Manhattan street famous for its expensive, exclusive shops.

"Can we steal?" Sugar asks very serious like she's getting the ground rules squared away before she plays. "I beg your pardon," say Miss Moore, and we fall out. So she leads us around the windows of the toy store and me and Sugar screamin, "This is mine, that's mine, I gotta have that, that was made for me, I was born for that," till Big Butt drowns us out.

"Hey, I'm goin to buy that there."

"That there? You don't even know what it is, stupid."

"I do so," he say punchin on Rosie Giraffe. "It's a microscope."

"Whatcha gonna do with a microscope, fool?"

"Look at things."

"Like what, Ronald?" ask Miss Moore. And Big Butt ain't got the first notion. So here go Miss Moore gabbing about the thousands of bacteria in a drop of water and the somethinorother in a speck of blood and the million and one living things in the air around us is invisible to the naked eye. And what she say that for? Junebug go to town on that "naked" and we rolling. Then Miss Moore ask what it cost. So we all jam into the window smudgin it up and the price tag say $300. So then she ask how long'd take for Big Butt and Junebug to save up their allowances. "Too long," I say. "Yeh," adds Sugar, "outgrown it by that time." And Miss Moore say no, you never outgrow learning instruments. "Why, even medical students and interns and," blah, blah, blah. And we ready to choke Big Butt for bringing it up in the first damn place.

"This here costs four hundred eighty dollars," say Rosie Giraffe. So we pile up all over her to see what she pointin out. My eyes tell me it's a chunk of glass cracked with something heavy, and different-color inks dripped into the splits, then the whole thing put into a oven or something. But for $480 it don't make sense.

"That's a paperweight made of semi-precious stones fused together under tremendous pressure," she explains slowly, with her hands doing the mining and all the factory work.

"So what's a paperweight?" asks Rosie Giraffe.

"To weigh paper with, dumbbell," say Flyboy, the wise man from the East.[3]

"Not exactly," say Miss Moore, which is what she say when you warm or way off too. "It's to weigh paper down so it won't scatter and make your desk untidy." So right away me and Sugar curtsy to each other and then to Mercedes who is more the tidy type.

"We don't keep paper on top of the desk in my class," say Junebug, figuring Miss Moore crazy or lyin one.

"At home, then," she say. "Don't you have a calendar and a pencil case and a blotter[4] and a letter-opener on your desk at home where you do your homework?" And she know damn well what our homes look like cause she nosys around in them every chance she gets.

"I don't even have a desk," say Junebug. "Do we?"

"No. And I don't get no homework neither," say Big Butt.

"And I don't even have a home," say Flyboy like he do at school to keep the white folks off his back and sorry for him. Send this poor kid to camp posters, is his specialty.

3. Allusion to the biblical story of the three wise men who traveled from the East to visit the newborn Christ.

4. Framed sheet or pad of paper designed to protect a desktop from excess ink.

“I do,” says Mercedes. “I have a box of stationery on my desk and a picture of my cat. My godmother bought the stationery and the desk. There’s a big rose on each sheet and the envelopes smell like roses.”

“Who wants to know about your smelly-ass stationery,” say Rosie Giraffe fore I can get my two cents in.

“It’s important to have a work area all your own so that . . .”

“Will you look at this sailboat, please,” say Flyboy, cuttin her off and pointin 25
to the thing like it was his. So once again we tumble all over each other to gaze at this magnificent thing in the toy store which is just big enough to maybe sail two kittens across the pond if you strap them to the posts tight. We all start reciting the price tag like we in assembly. “Handcrafted sailboat of fiberglass at one thousand one hundred ninety-five dollars.”

“Unbelievable,” I hear myself say and am really stunned. I read it again for myself just in case the group recitation put me in a trance. Same thing. For some reason this pisses me off. We look at Miss Moore and she lookin at us, waiting for I dunno what.

“Who’d pay all that when you can buy a sailboat set for a quarter at Pop’s, a tube of glue for a dime, and a ball of string for eight cents? “It must have a motor and a whole lot else besides,” I say. “My sailboat cost me about fifty cents.”

“But will it take water?” say Mercedes with her smart ass.

“Took mine to Alley Pond Park once,” say Flyboy. “String broke, Lost it. Pity.”

“Sailed mine in Central Park and it keeled over and sank. Had to ask my 30
father for another dollar.”

“And you got the strap,” laugh Big Butt. “The jerk didn’t even have a string on it. My old man wailed on his behind.”

Little Q.T. was staring hard at the sailboat and you could see he wanted it bad. But he too little and somebody’d just take it from him. So what the hell. “This boat for kids, Miss Moore?”

“Parents silly to buy something like that just to get all broke up,” say Rosie Giraffe.

“That much money it should last forever,” I figure.

“My father’d buy it for me if I wanted it.” 35

“Your father, my ass,” say Rosie Giraffe getting a chance to finally push Mercedes.

“Must be rich people shop here,” say Q.T.

“You are a very bright boy,” say Flyboy. “What was your first clue?” And he rap him on the head with the back of his knuckles, since Q.T. the only one he could get away with. Though Q.T. liable to come up behind you years later and get his licks in when you half expect it.

“What I want to know is,” I says to Miss Moore though I never talk to her, I wouldn’t give the bitch that satisfaction, “is how much a real boat costs? I figure a thousand’d get you a yacht any day.”

“Why don’t you check that out,” she says, “and report back to the group?” 40
Which really pains my ass. If you gonna mess up a perfectly good swim day least you could do is have some answers. “Let’s go in,” she say like she got something up her sleeve. Only she don’t lead the way. So me and Sugar turn the corner to where the entrance is, but when we get there I kinda hang back. Not that I’m scared, what’s there to be afraid of, just a toy store. But I feel funny, shame. But what I got to be shamed about? Got as much right to go in as anybody. But somehow I can’t

seem to get hold of the door, so I step away for Sugar to lead. But she hangs back too. And I look at her and she looks at me and this is ridiculous. I mean, damn, I have never ever been shy about doing nothing or going nowhere. But then Mercedes steps up and then Rosie Giraffe and Big Butt crowd in behind and shove, and next thing we all stuffed into the doorway with only Mercedes squeezing past us, smoothing out her jumper and walking right down the aisle. Then the rest of us tumble in like a glued-together jigsaw done all wrong. And people lookin at us. And it's like the time me and Sugar crashed into the Catholic church on a dare. But once we got in there and everything so hushed and holy and the candles and the bowin and the handkerchiefs on all the drooping heads, I just couldn't go through with the plan. Which was for me to run up to the altar and do a tap dance while Sugar played the nose flute and messed around in the holy water. And Sugar kept givin me the elbow. Then later teased me so bad I tied her up in the shower and turned it on and locked her in. And she'd be there till this day if Aunt Gretchen hadn't finally figured I was lyin about the boarder[5] takin a shower.

Same thing in the store. We all walkin on tiptoe and hardly touchin the games and puzzles and things. And I watched Miss Moore who is steady watchin us like she waitin for a sign. Like Mama Drewery watches the sky and sniffs the air and takes note of just how much slant is in the bird formation. Then me and Sugar bump smack into each other, so busy gazing at the toys, 'specially the sailboat. But we don't laugh and go into our fat-lady bump-stomach routine. We just stare at that price tag. Then Sugar run a finger over the whole boat. And I'm jealous and want to hit her. Maybe not her, but I sure want to punch somebody in the mouth.

"Watcha bring us here for, Miss Moore?"

"You sound angry, Sylvia. Are you mad about something?" Givin me one of them grins like she tellin a grown-up joke that never turns out to be funny. And she's lookin very closely at me like maybe she plannin to do my portrait from memory. I'm mad, but I won't give her that satisfaction. So I slouch around the store bein very bored and say, "Let's go."

Me and Sugar at the back of the train watchin the tracks whizzin by large then small then gettin gobbled up in the dark. I'm thinkin about this tricky toy I saw in the store. A clown that somersaults on a bar then does chin-ups just cause you yank lightly at his leg. Cost $35. I could see me askin my mother for a $35 birthday clown. "You wanna who that costs what?" she'd say, cocking her head to the side to get a better view of the hole in my head. Thirty-five dollars could buy new bunk beds for Junior and Gretchen's boy. Thirty-five dollars and the whole household could go visit Granddaddy Nelson in the country. Thirty-five dollars would pay for the rent and the piano bill too. Who are these people that spend that much for performing clowns and $1,000 for toy sailboats? What kinda work they do and how they live and how come we ain't in on it? Where we are is who we are, Miss Moore always pointin out. But it don't necessarily have to be that way, she always adds then waits for somebody to say that poor people have to wake up and demand their share of the pie and don't none of us know what kind of pie she talkin about in the first damn place. But she ain't so smart cause I still got her four dollars from the taxi and she sure ain't gettin it. Messin up my day with this shit. Sugar nudges me in my pocket and winks.

5. Tenant in another person's house.

Miss Moore lines us up in front of the mailbox where we started from, seem 45
like years ago, and I got a headache for thinkin so hard. And we lean all over each other so we can hold up under the draggy-ass lecture she always finishes us off with at the end before we thank her for borin us to tears. But she just looks at us like she readin tea leaves. Finally she say, "Well, what did you think of F.A.O. Schwarz?"[6]

Rosie Giraffe mumbles, "White folks crazy."

"I'd like to go there again when I get my birthday money," says Mercedes, and we shove her out the pack so she has to lean on the mailbox by herself.

"I'd like a shower. Tiring day," say Flyboy.

Then Sugar surprises me by sayin, "You know, Miss Moore, I don't think all of us here put together eat in a year what that sailboat costs." And Miss Moore lights up like somebody goosed her. "And?" she say, urging Sugar on. Only I'm standin on her foot so she don't continue.

"Imagine for a minute what kind of society it is in which some people can spend 50
on a toy what it would cost to feed a family of six or seven. What do you think?"

"I think," say Sugar pushing me off her feet like she never done before, cause I whip her ass in a minute, "that this is not much of a democracy if you ask me. Equal chance to pursue happiness means an equal crack at the dough, don't it?" Miss Moore is besides herself and I am disgusted with Sugar's treachery. So I stand on her foot one more time to see if she'll shove me. She shuts up, and Miss Moore looks at me, sorrowfully I'm thinkin. And somethin weird is goin on, I can feel it in my chest.

"Anybody else learn anything today?" lookin dead at me.

I walk away and Sugar has to run to catch up and don't even seem to notice when I shrug her arm off my shoulder.

"Well, we got four dollars anyway," she says.

"Uh hunh." 55

"We could go to Hascombs and get half a chocolate layer and then go to the Sunset and still have plenty money for potato chips and ice-cream sodas."

"Uh hunh."

"Race you to Hascombs," she say.

We start down the block and she gets ahead which is O.K. by me cause I'm goin to the West End and then over to the Drive to think this day through. She can run if she want to and even run faster. But ain't nobody gonna beat me at nuthin.

1972

QUESTIONS

1. How does Sylvia feel about Miss Moore, and why? How do you know? Do her feelings change over the course of the story?
2. What lesson does Miss Moore seem to want the children to learn? What lesson does Sylvia seem to learn?
3. In terms of these lessons and THE LESSON as a whole, what might be interesting and significant about the fact that the children visit a toy store? about each of the three specific and expensive items they encounter there?

6. Manhattan toy store (founded 1862), one of the world's largest and oldest, known for its expensive, one-of-a-kind offerings.

AUTHORS ON THEIR WORK

TONI CADE BAMBARA (1939–95)

From "How She Came By Her Name" (1996)*

I went to the library and read a bunch of [short-story] collections and noticed that the voice was consistent, but it was a boring and monotonous voice. Oh, your voice is supposed to be consistent in a collection, I figured. Then I pulled out a lot of stories that had a young protagonist-narrator because that voice is kind of consistent—a young, tough, compassionate girl.

The book [*Gorilla, My Love*] came out, and I never dreamed that such a big fuss would be made. "Oh, *Gorilla, My Love,* what a radical use of dialect! What a bold, political angle on linguistics!" At first I felt like a fraud. It didn't have anything to do with a political stance. I just thought people lived and moved around in this particular language system. It is also the language system I tend to remember childhood in. This is the language many of us speak. It just seemed polite to handle the characters in this mode.

*"How She Came by Her Name: An Interview with Louis Massiah." *Deep Sightings and Rescue Missions: Fiction, Essays, and Conversations*, edited by Toni Morrison, Pantheon Books, 1996, pp. 201–45.

ALICE MUNRO

(b. 1931)

Boys and Girls

Described by novelist Jonathan Franzen as having "a strong claim to being the best fiction writer now working in North America" and by the committee that awarded her the 2013 Nobel Prize for Literature as a "master of the contemporary short story," Alice Munro today enjoys an enviably high reputation. That was long in coming and unexpected for a girl raised during the Great Depression and World War II, on a farm in southwestern Ontario—that unglamorous terrain she has since so vividly memorialized in her fiction. She began publishing stories while attending the University of Western Ontario. But when her two-year scholarship ran out, she left the university, married James Munro, and moved first to Vancouver and then to Victoria, where the couple raised three daughters. Though her stories appeared sporadically during the 1950s, it was not until 1968 that then-thirty-eight-year-old Munro published her first book and with it won the first of multiple Governor General's Awards, Canada's highest literary prize. Divorced and remarried, Munro returned to Ontario and began regularly publishing collections including *Something I've Been Meaning to Tell You* (1974), *The Progress of Love* (1986), *Open Secrets* (1994), the Booker Prize–winning *View from Castle Rock* (2006), and *Dear Life* (2012). One reason Munro has not achieved the wide fame many believe she merits is her focus on short fiction: The one work she published as a novel, *Lives of Girls and Women* (1971), is in fact a series of interlinked stories.

My father was a fox farmer. That is, he raised silver foxes, in pens; and in the fall and early winter, when their fur was prime, he killed them and skinned them and sold their pelts to the Hudson's Bay Company or the Montreal Fur Traders. These companies supplied us with heroic calendars to hang, one on each side of the kitchen door. Against a background of cold blue sky and black pine forests and treacherous northern rivers, plumed adventurers planted the flags of England or of France; magnificent savages bent their backs to the portage.

For several weeks before Christmas, my father worked after supper in the cellar of our house. The cellar was white-washed, and lit by a hundred-watt bulb over the worktable. My brother Laird and I sat on the top step and watched. My father removed the pelt inside-out from the body of the fox, which looked surprisingly small, mean and rat-like, deprived of its arrogant weight of fur. The naked, slippery bodies were collected in a sack and buried at the dump. One time the hired man, Henry Bailey, had taken a swipe at me with this sack, saying, "Christmas present!" My mother thought that was not funny. In fact she disliked the whole pelting operation—that was what the killing, skinning, and preparation of the furs was called—and wished it did not have to take place in the house. There was the smell. After the pelt had been stretched inside-out on a long board my father scraped away delicately, removing the little clotted webs of blood vessels, the bubbles of fat; the smell of blood and animal fat, with the strong primitive odour of the fox itself, penetrated all parts of the house. I found it reassuringly seasonal, like the smell of oranges and pine needles.

Henry Bailey suffered from bronchial troubles. He would cough and cough until his narrow face turned scarlet, and his light blue, derisive eyes filled up with tears; then he took the lid off the stove, and, standing well back, shot out a great clot of phlegm—hsss—straight into the heart of the flames. We admired him for this performance and for his ability to make his stomach growl at will, and for his laughter, which was full of high whistlings and gurglings and involved the whole faulty machinery of his chest. It was sometimes hard to tell what he was laughing at, and always possible that it might be us.

After we had been sent to bed we could still smell fox and still hear Henry's laugh, but these things, reminders of the warm, safe, brightly lit downstairs world, seemed lost and diminished, floating on the stale cold air upstairs. We were afraid at night in the winter. We were not afraid of *outside* though this was the time of year when snowdrifts curled around our house like sleeping whales and the wind harassed us all night, coming up from the buried fields, the frozen swamp, with its old bugbear chorus of threats and misery. We were afraid of *inside*, the room where we slept. At this time the upstairs of our house was not finished. A brick chimney went up one wall. In the middle of the floor was a square hole, with a wooden railing around it; that was where the stairs came up. On the other side of the stairwell were the things that nobody had any use for any more—a soldiery roll of linoleum, standing on end, a wicker baby carriage, a fern basket, china jugs and basins with cracks in them, a picture of the Battle of Balaclava,[1] very sad to look at. I had told Laird, as soon as he was old enough to understand such things, that bats and skeletons lived over there; whenever a man escaped from the county jail, twenty miles away, I imagined that he had somehow let himself in the window and was hiding behind the linoleum. But we had rules to keep us safe. When the light was on, we were safe as long as we did not step off the square of worn carpet which defined our bedroom-space; when the light was off no place was safe but the beds themselves. I had to turn out the light kneeling on the end of my bed, and stretching as far as I could to reach the cord.

5 In the dark we lay on our beds, our narrow life rafts, and fixed our eyes on the faint light coming up the stairwell, and sang songs. Laird sang "Jingle Bells," which he would sing any time, whether it was Christmas or not, and I sang "Danny Boy." I loved the sound of my own voice, frail and supplicating, rising in the dark. We could make out the tall frosted shapes of the windows now, gloomy and white. When I came to the part, *When I am dead, as dead I well may be*—a fit of shivering caused not by the cold sheets but by pleasurable emotion almost silenced me. *You'll kneel and say, an Ave there above me*—What was an Ave? Every day I forgot to find out.

Laird went straight from singing to sleep. I could hear his long, satisfied, bubbly breaths. Now for the time that remained to me, the most perfectly private and perhaps the best time of the whole day, I arranged myself tightly under the covers and went on with one of the stories I was telling myself from night to night. These stories were about myself, when I had grown a little older; they took place in a world that was recognizably mine, yet one that presented opportunities for courage, boldness and self-sacrifice, as mine never did. I rescued people from a bombed building (it discouraged me that the real war[2] had gone on so far away from Jubilee). I shot two rabid wolves who were menacing the schoolyard (the teachers cowered terrified at my back). I rode a fine horse spiritedly down the main street of Jubilee, acknowledging the townspeople's gratitude for some yet-to-be-worked-out piece of heroism (nobody ever rode a horse there, except King Billy in the Orangemen's Day[3] parade). There was always riding and shooting in these stories, though I had only been on a horse twice—bareback because we did not own a saddle—and the second time I had slid right around and dropped under the horse's feet; it had stepped placidly over me. I really was learning to shoot, but I could not hit anything yet, not even tin cans on fence posts.

Alive, the foxes inhabited a world my father made for them. It was surrounded by a high guard fence, like a medieval town, with a gate that was padlocked at night. Along the streets of this town were ranged large, sturdy pens. Each of them had a real door that a man could go through, a wooden ramp along the wire, for the foxes to run up and down on, and a kennel—something like a clothes chest with airholes—where they slept and stayed in winter and had their

1. Indecisive Crimean War battle fought on October 25, 1854, famous for the Charge of the Light Brigade.

2. World War II (1939–45).

3. The Orange Society is an Irish Protestant group named after William of Orange, who, as King William III of England, defeated the Catholic James II. The society sponsors an annual procession on July 12 to commemorate the victory of William III at the Battle of the Boyne (1690).

young. There were feeding and watering dishes attached to the wire in such a way that they could be emptied and cleaned from the outside. The dishes were made of old tin cans, and the ramps and kennels of odds and ends of old lumber. Everything was tidy and ingenious; my father was tirelessly inventive and his favourite book in the world was *Robinson Crusoe*.[4] He had fitted a tin drum on a wheelbarrow, for bringing water down to the pens. This was my job in summer, when the foxes had to have water twice a day. Between nine and ten o'clock in the morning, and again after supper, I filled the drum at the pump and trundled it down through the barnyard to the pens, where I parked it, and filled my watering can and went along the streets. Laird came too, with his little cream and green gardening can, filled too full and knocking against his legs and slopping water on his canvas shoes. I had the real watering can, my father's, though I could only carry it three-quarters full.

The foxes all had names, which were printed on a tin plate and hung beside their doors. They were not named when they were born, but when they survived the first year's pelting and were added to the breeding stock. Those my father had named were called names like Prince, Bob, Wally and Betty. Those I had named were called Star or Turk, or Maureen or Diana. Laird named one Maud after a hired girl we had when he was little, one Harold after a boy at school, and one Mexico, he did not say why.

Naming them did not make pets out of them, or anything like it. Nobody but my father ever went into the pens, and he had twice had blood-poisoning from bites. When I was bringing them their water they prowled up and down on the paths they had made inside their pens, barking seldom—they saved that for nighttime, when they might get up a chorus of community frenzy—but always watching me, their eyes burning, clear gold, in their pointed, malevolent faces. They were beautiful for their delicate legs and heavy, aristocratic tails and the bright fur sprinkled on dark down their backs—which gave them their name—but especially for their faces, drawn exquisitely sharp in pure hostility, and their golden eyes.

10 Besides carrying water I helped my father when he cut the long grass, and the lamb's quarter and flowering money-musk, that grew between the pens. He cut with the scythe and I raked into piles. Then he took a pitchfork and threw freshcut grass all over the top of the pens, to keep the foxes cooler and shade their coats, which were browned by too much sun. My father did not talk to me unless it was about the job we were doing. In this he was quite different from my mother, who, if she was feeling cheerful, would tell me all sorts of things—the name of a dog she had had when she was a little girl, the names of boys she had gone out with later on when she was grown up, and what certain dresses of hers had looked like—she could not imagine now what had become of them. Whatever thoughts and stories my father had were private, and I was shy of him and would never ask him questions. Nevertheless I worked willingly under his eyes, and with a feeling of pride. One time a feed salesman came down into the pens to talk to him and my father said, "Like to have you meet my new hired man." I turned away and raked furiously, red in the face with pleasure.

"Could of fooled me," said the salesman. "I thought it was only a girl."

4. Novel (1719) by Daniel Defoe about a man shipwrecked on a desert island; it goes into great detail about the ingenious contraptions he fashions from simple materials.

After the grass was cut, it seemed suddenly much later in the year. I walked on stubble in the earlier evening, aware of the reddening skies, the entering silences, of fall. When I wheeled the tank out of the gate and put the padlock on, it was almost dark. One night at this time I saw my mother and father standing talking on the little rise of ground we called the gangway, in front of the barn. My father had just come from the meathouse; he had his stiff bloody apron on, and a pail of cut-up meat in his hand.

It was an odd thing to see my mother down at the barn. She did not often come out of the house unless it was to do something—hang out the wash or dig potatoes in the garden. She looked out of place, with her bare lumpy legs, not touched by the sun, her apron still on and damp across the stomach from the supper dishes. Her hair was tied up in a kerchief, wisps of it falling out. She would tie her hair up like this in the morning, saying she did not have time to do it properly, and it would stay tied up all day. It was true, too; she really did not have time. These days our back porch was piled with baskets of peaches and grapes and pears, bought in town, and onions and tomatoes and cucumbers grown at home, all waiting to be made into jelly and jam and preserves, pickles and chili sauce. In the kitchen there was a fire in the stove all day, jars clinked in boiling water, sometimes a cheesecloth bag was strung on a pole between two chairs, straining blue-black grape pulp for jelly. I was given jobs to do and I would sit at the table peeling peaches that had been soaked in the hot water, or cutting up onions, my eyes smarting and streaming. As soon as I was done I ran out of the house, trying to get out of earshot before my mother thought of what she wanted me to do next. I hated the hot dark kitchen in summer, the green blinds and the flypapers, the same old oilcloth table and wavy mirror and bumpy linoleum. My mother was too tired and preoccupied to talk to me, she had no heart to tell about the Normal School Graduation Dance; sweat trickled over her face and she was always counting under her breath, pointing at jars, dumping cups of sugar. It seemed to me that work in the house was endless, dreary and peculiarly depressing; work done out of doors, and in my father's service, was ritualistically important.

I wheeled the tank up to the barn, where it was kept, and I heard my mother saying, "Wait till Laird gets a little bigger, then you'll have a real help."

15 What my father said I did not hear. I was pleased by the way he stood listening, politely as he would to a salesman or a stranger, but with an air of wanting to get on with his real work. I felt my mother had no business down here and I wanted him to feel the same way. What did she mean about Laird? He was no help to anybody. Where was he now? Swinging himself sick on the swing, going around in circles, or trying to catch caterpillars. He never once stayed with me till I was finished.

"And then I can use her more in the house," I heard my mother say. She had a dead-quiet, regretful way of talking about me that always made me uneasy. "I just get my back turned and she runs off. It's not like I had a girl in the family at all."

I went and sat on a feed bag in the corner of the barn, not wanting to appear when this conversation was going on. My mother, I felt, was not to be trusted. She was kinder than my father and more easily fooled, but you could not depend on her, and the real reasons for the things she said and did were not to be known. She loved me, and she sat up late at night making a dress of the difficult style I wanted, for me to wear when school started, but she was also my enemy. She was always plotting. She was plotting now to get me to stay in the house more, although she knew I hated it (*because* she knew I hated it) and keep me from working for my father. It seemed to me she would do this simply out of perversity, and to try her power. It did not occur to me that she could be lonely, or jealous. No grown-up could be; they were too fortunate. I sat and kicked my heels monotonously against a feed bag, raising dust, and did not come out till she was gone.

At any rate, I did not expect my father to pay any attention to what she said. Who could imagine Laird doing my work—Laird remembering the padlock and cleaning out the watering-dishes with a leaf on the end of a stick, or even wheeling the tank without it tumbling over? It showed how little my mother knew about the way things really were.

I have forgotten to say what the foxes were fed. My father's bloody apron reminded me. They were fed horsemeat. At this time most farmers still kept horses, and when a horse got too old to work, or broke a leg or got down and would not get up, as they sometimes did, the owner would call my father, and he and Henry went out to the farm in the truck. Usually they shot and butchered the horse there, paying the farmer from five to twelve dollars. If they had already too much meat on hand, they would bring the horse back alive, and keep it for a few days or weeks in our stable, until the meat was needed. After the war the farmers were buying tractors and gradually getting rid of horses altogether, so it sometimes happened that we got a good healthy horse, that there was just no use for any more. If this happened in the winter we might keep the horse in our stable till spring, for we had plenty of hay and if there was a lot of snow—and the plow did not always get our road cleared—it was convenient to be able to go to town with a horse and cutter.[5]

The winter I was eleven years old we had two horses in the stable. We did 20
not know what names they had had before, so we called them Mack and Flora. Mack was an old black workhorse, sooty and indifferent. Flora was a sorrel mare, a driver. We took them both out in the cutter. Mack was slow and easy to handle. Flora was given to fits of violent alarm, veering at cars and even at other horses, but we loved her speed and high-stepping, her general air of gallantry and abandon. On Saturdays we went down to the stable and as soon as we opened the door on its cosy, animal-smelling darkness Flora threw up her head, rolled her eyes, whinnied despairingly and pulled herself through a crisis of nerves on the spot. It was not safe to go into her stall; she would kick.

This winter also I began to hear a great deal more on the theme my mother had sounded when she had been talking in front of the barn. I no longer felt safe. It seemed that in the minds of the people around me there was a steady undercurrent of thought, not to be deflected, on this one subject. The word *girl* had formerly seemed to me innocent and unburdened, like the world *child*; now it appeared that it was no such thing. A girl was not, as I had supposed, simply what I was; it was what I had to become. It was a definition, always touched with emphasis, with reproach and disappointment. Also it was a joke on me. Once Laird and I were fighting, and for the first time ever I had to use all my strength against him; even so, he caught and pinned my arm for a moment, really hurting

5. Small, light sleigh.

me. Henry saw this, and laughed, saying, "Oh, that there Laird's gonna show you, one of these days!" Laird was getting a lot bigger. But I was getting bigger too.

My grandmother came to stay with us for a few weeks and I heard other things. "Girls don't slam doors like that." "Girls keep their knees together when they sit down." And worse still, when I asked some questions, "That's none of girls' business." I continued to slam the doors and sit as awkwardly as possible, thinking that by such measures I kept myself free.

When spring came, the horses were let out in the barnyard. Mack stood against the barn wall trying to scratch his neck and haunches, but Flora trotted up and down and reared at the fences, clattering her hooves against the rails. Snow drifts dwindled quickly, revealing the hard grey and brown earth, the familiar rise and fall of the ground, plain and bare after the fantastic landscape of winter. There was a great feeling of opening-out, of release. We just wore rubbers now, over our shoes; our feet felt ridiculously light. One Saturday we went out to the stable and found all the doors open, letting in the unaccustomed sunlight and fresh air. Henry was there, just idling around looking at his collection of calendars which were tacked up behind the stalls in a part of the stable my mother had probably never seen.

"Come to say goodbye to your old friend Mack?" Henry said. "Here, you give him a taste of oats." He poured some oats into Laird's cupped hands and Laird went to feed Mack. Mack's teeth were in bad shape. He ate very slowly, patiently shifting the oats around in his mouth, trying to find a stump of a molar to grind it on. "Poor old Mack," said Henry mournfully. "When a horse's teeth's gone, he's gone. That's about the way."

"Are you going to shoot him today?" I said. Mack and Flora had been in the stable so long I had almost forgotten they were going to be shot.

Henry didn't answer me. Instead he started to sing in a high, trembly, mocking-sorrowful voice, *Oh, there's no more work, for poor Uncle Ned, he's gone where the good darkies go.*[6] Mack's thick, blackish tongue worked diligently at Laird's hand. I went out before the song was ended and sat down on the gangway.

I had never seen them shoot a horse, but I knew where it was done. Last summer Laird and I had come upon a horse's entrails before they were buried. We had thought it was a big black snake, coiled up in the sun. That was around in the field that ran up beside the barn. I thought that if we went inside the barn, and found a wide crack or knothole to look through we would be able to see them do it. It was not something I wanted to see; just the same, if a thing really happened, it was better to see it, and know.

My father came down from the house, carrying the gun.

"What are you doing here?" he said.

"Nothing."

"Go on up and play around the house."

He sent Laird out of the stable. I said to Laird, "Do you want to see them shoot Mack?" and without waiting for an answer led him around to the front door of the barn, opened it carefully, and went in. "Be quiet or they'll hear us," I said. We could hear Henry and my father talking in the stable, then the heavy, shuffling steps of Mack being backed out of his stall.

6. Lines from the Stephen Foster (1826–64) song "Old Uncle Ned."

In the loft it was cold and dark. Thin, crisscrossed beams of sunlight fell through the cracks. The hay was low. It was a rolling country, hills and hollows, slipping under our feet. About four feet up was a beam going around the walls. We piled hay up in one corner and I boosted Laird up and hoisted myself. The beam was not very wide; we crept along it with our hands flat on the barn walls. There were plenty of knotholes, and I found one that gave me the view I wanted—a corner of the barnyard, the gate, part of the field. Laird did not have a knothole and began to complain.

I showed him a widened crack between two boards. "Be quiet and wait. If they hear you you'll get us in trouble."

My father came in sight carrying the gun. Henry was leading Mack by the 35
halter. He dropped it and took out his cigarette papers and tobacco; he rolled cigarettes for my father and himself. While this was going on Mack nosed around in the old, dead grass along the fence. Then my father opened the gate and they took Mack through. Henry led Mack way from the path to a patch of ground and they talked together, not loud enough for us to hear. Mack again began searching for a mouthful of fresh grass, which was not to be found. My father walked away in a straight line, and stopped short at a distance which seemed to suit him. Henry was walking away from Mack too, but sideways, still negligently holding on to the halter. My father raised the gun and Mack looked up as if he had noticed something and my father shot him.

Mack did not collapse at once but swayed, lurched sideways and fell, first on his side; then he rolled over on his back and, amazingly, kicked his legs for a few seconds in the air. At this Henry laughed, as if Mack had done a trick for him. Laird, who had drawn a long, groaning breath of surprise when the shot was fired, said out loud, "He's not dead." And it seemed to me it might be true. But his legs stopped, he rolled on his side again, his muscles quivered and sank. The two men walked over and looked at him in a businesslike way; they bent down and examined his forehead where the bullet had gone in, and now I saw his blood on the brown grass.

"Now they just skin him and cut him up," I said. "Let's go." My legs were a little shaky and I jumped gratefully down into the hay. "Now you've seen how they shoot a horse," I said in a congratulatory way, as if I had seen it many times before. "Let's see if any barn cat's had kittens in the hay." Laird jumped. He seemed young and obedient again. Suddenly I remembered how, when he was little, I had brought him into the barn and told him to climb the ladder to the top beam. That was in the spring, too, when the hay was low. I had done it out of a need for excitement, a desire for something to happen so that I could tell about it. He was wearing a little bulky brown and white checked coat, made down from one of mine. He went all the way up, just as I told him, and sat down on the top beam with the hay far below him on one side, and the barn floor and some old machinery on the other. Then I ran screaming to my father, "Laird's up on the top beam!" My father came, my mother came, my father went up the ladder talking very quietly and brought Laird down under his arm, at which my mother leaned against the ladder and began to cry. They said to me, "Why weren't you watching him?" but nobody ever knew the truth. Laird did not know enough to tell. But whenever I saw the brown and white checked coat hanging in the closet, or at the bottom of the rag bag, which was where it ended up, I felt a weight in my stomach, the sadness of unexorcized guilt.

I looked at Laird who did not even remember this, and I did not like the look on this thin, winter-pale face. His expression was not frightened or upset, but remote, concentrating. "Listen," I said, in an unusually bright and friendly voice, "you aren't going to tell, are you?"

"No," he said absently.

40 "Promise."

"Promise," he said. I grabbed the hand behind his back to make sure he was not crossing his fingers. Even so, he might have a nightmare; it might come out that way. I decided I had better work hard to get all thoughts of what he had seen out of his mind—which, it seemed to me, could not hold very many things at a time. I got some money I had saved and that afternoon we went into Jubilee and saw a show, with Judy Canova,[7] at which we both laughed a great deal. After that I thought it would be all right.

Two weeks later I knew they were going to shoot Flora. I knew from the night before, when I heard my mother ask if the hay was holding out all right, and my father said, "Well, after to-morrow there'll just be the cow, and we should be able to put her out to grass in another week." So I knew it was Flora's turn in the morning.

This time I didn't think of watching it. That was something to see just one time. I had not thought about it very often since, but sometimes when I was busy, working at school, or standing in front of the mirror combing my hair and wondering if I would be pretty when I grew up, the whole scene would flash into my mind: I would see the easy, practised way my father raised the gun, and hear Henry laughing when Mack kicked his legs in the air. I did not have any great feeling of horror and opposition, such as a city child might have had; I was too used to seeing the death of animals as a necessity by which we lived. Yet I felt a little ashamed, and there was a new wariness, a sense of holding-off, in my attitude to my father and his work.

It was a fine day, and we were going around the yard picking up tree branches that had been torn off in winter storms. This was something we had been told to do, and also we wanted to use them to make a teepee. We heard Flora whinny, and then my father's voice and Henry's shouting, and we ran down to the barnyard to see what was going on.

45 The stable door was open. Henry had just brought Flora out, and she had broken away from him. She was running free in the barnyard, from one end to the other. We climbed up on the fence. It was exciting to see her running, whinnying, going up on her hind legs, prancing and threatening like a horse in a Western movie, an unbroken ranch horse, though she was just an old driver, an old sorrel mare. My father and Henry ran after her and tried to grab the dangling halter. They tried to work her into a corner, and they had almost succeeded when she made a run between them, wild-eyed, and disappeared around the corner of the barn. We heard the rails clatter down as she got over the fence, and Henry yelled, "She's into the field now!"

That meant she was in the long L-shaped field that ran up by the house. If she got around the center, heading towards the lane, the gate was open; the truck had been driven into the field this morning. My father shouted to me, because I was on the other side of the fence, nearest the lane, "Go shut the gate!"

7. American comedian (1913–83) best known for her yodeling in hillbilly movies of the 1940s.

I could run very fast. I ran across the garden, past the tree where our swing was hung, and jumped across a ditch into the lane. There was the open gate. She had not got out, I could not see her up on the road; she must have run to the other end of the field. The gate was heavy. I lifted it out of the gravel and carried it across the roadway. I had it half-way across when she came in sight, galloping straight towards me. There was just time to get the chain on. Laird came scrambling through the ditch to help me.

Instead of shutting the gate, I opened it as wide as I could. I did not make any decision to do this, it was just what I did. Flora never slowed down; she galloped straight past me, and Laird jumped up and down, yelling, "Shut it, shut it!" even after it was too late. My father and Henry appeared in the field a moment too late to see what I had done. They only saw Flora heading for the township road. They would think I had not got there in time.

They did not waste any time asking about it. They went back to the barn and got the gun and the knives they used, and put these in the truck; then they turned the truck around and came bouncing up the field toward us. Laird called to them, "Let me go too, let me go too!" and Henry stopped the truck and they took him in. I shut the gate after they were all gone.

50 I supposed Laird would tell. I wondered what would happen to me. I had never disobeyed my father before, and I could not understand why I had done it. Flora would not really get away. They would catch up with her in the truck. Or if they did not catch her this morning somebody would see her and telephone us this afternoon or tomorrow. There was no wild country here for her to run to, only farms. What was more, my father had paid for her, we needed the meat to feed the foxes, we needed the foxes to make our living. All I had done was make more work for my father who worked hard enough already. And when my father found out about it he was not going to trust me any more, he would know that I was not entirely on his side. I was on Flora's side, and that made me no use to anybody, not even to her. Just the same, I did not regret it; when she came running at me and I held the gate open, that was the only thing I could do.

I went back to the house, and my mother said, "What's all the commotion?" I told her that Flora had kicked down the fence and got away. "Your poor father," she said, "now he'll have to go chasing over the countryside. Well, there isn't any use planning dinner before one." She put up the ironing board. I wanted to tell her, but thought better of it and went upstairs and sat on my bed.

Lately I had been trying to make my part of the room fancy, spreading the bed with old lace curtains, and fixing myself a dressing-table with some leftovers of cretonne for a skirt. I planned to put up some kind of barricade between my bed and Laird's, to keep my section separate from his. In the sunlight, the lace curtains were just dusty rags. We did not sing at night any more. One night when I was singing Laird said, "You sound silly," and I went right on but the next night I did not start. There was not so much need to anyway, we were no longer afraid. We knew it was just old furniture over there, old jumble and confusion. We did not keep to the rules. I still stayed awake after Laird was asleep and told myself stories, but even in these stories something different was happening, mysterious alterations took place. A story might start off in the old way, with a spectacular danger, a fire or wild animals, and for a while I might rescue people; then things would change around, and instead, somebody would be rescuing me. It might be a boy from our class at school, or even Mr. Campbell, our teacher, who tickled girls under the arms. And at this point the story concerned itself at great length with what I looked like—how long my hair was, and what kind of dress I had on; by the time I had these details worked out the real excitement of the story was lost.

It was later than one o'clock when the truck came back. The tarpaulin was over the back, which meant there was meat in it. My mother had to heat dinner up all over again. Henry and my father had changed from their bloody overalls into ordinary working overalls in the barn, and they washed their arms and necks and faces at the sink, and splashed water on their hair and combed it. Laird lifted his arm to show off a streak of blood. "We shot old Flora," he said, "and cut her up in fifty pieces."

"Well I don't want to hear about it," my mother said. "And don't come to my table like that."

My father made him go and wash the blood off.

We sat down and my father said grace and Henry pasted his chewing-gum on the end of his fork, the way he always did; when he took it off he would have us admire the pattern. We began to pass the bowls of steaming, overcooked vegetables. Laird looked across the table at me and said proudly, distinctly, "Anyway it was her fault Flora got away."

"What?" my father said.

"She could of shut the gate and she didn't. She just open' it up and Flora run out."

"Is that right?" my father said.

Everybody at the table was looking at me. I nodded, swallowing food with great difficulty. To my shame, tears flooded my eyes.

My father made a curt sound of disgust. "What did you do that for?"

I did not answer. I put down my fork and waited to be sent from the table, still not looking up.

But this did not happen. For some time nobody said anything, then Laird said matter-of-factly, "She's crying."

"Never mind," my father said. He spoke with resignation, even good humour, the words which absolved and dismissed me for good. "She's only a girl," he said.

I didn't protest that, even in my heart. Maybe it was true.

1968

QUESTIONS

1. Since there is only one girl character (the narrator) and one boy character (the narrator's younger brother) in BOYS AND GIRLS, why do you think Alice Munro uses plural words in the title?
2. Find the two occurrences of the phrase "only a girl." Why and how does the meaning of the phrase change in each case?
3. Why does the narrator choose not to shut the gate on Flora? What role does this act play in her initiation?

JOHN UPDIKE
(1932–2009)

A & P[1]

The man *The Oxford Encyclopedia of American Literature* dubs "perhaps America's most versatile, prolific, and distinguished man of letters of the second half of the twentieth century" spent the early years of his life in Reading and rural Shillington, Pennsylvania. John Updike went on to study English literature at Harvard, where he also contributed cartoons and articles to the famous *Lampoon*. Marrying a Radcliffe fine-arts student in 1953, Updike the next year graduated summa cum laude and sold both his first poem and his first story to the *New Yorker*, whose staff he joined in 1955. Though he would continue to contribute essays, poems, and fiction to the *New Yorker* for the rest of his life, in 1957 Updike moved with his young family from Manhattan to rural Massachusetts. In the two years following the move, he published both his first book, a collection of poems (1958), and his first novel (1959). Updike went on to publish some twenty-one novels, thirteen short-story collections, seven volumes of poetry (including *Collected Poems, 1953–1993* [1993]), as well as seven collections of essays, a play, and a memoir. He is best known for the tetralogy tracing the life of high-school basketball star turned car salesman Harry C. Rabbit Angstrom. Begun with *Rabbit, Run* in 1960, the series of novels includes *Rabbit Is Rich* (1981) and *Rabbit at Rest* (1990), both of which were awarded Pulitzer Prizes.

In walks these three girls in nothing but bathing suits. I'm in the third check-out slot, with my back to the door, so I don't see them until they're over by the bread. The one that caught my eye first was the one in the plaid green two-piece. She was a chunky kid, with a good tan and a sweet broad soft-looking can with those two crescents of white just under it, where the sun never seems to hit, at the top of the backs of her legs. I stood there with my hand on a box of HiHo crackers trying to remember if I rang it up or not. I ring it up again and the customer starts giving me hell. She's one of these cash-register-watchers, a witch about fifty with rouge on her cheekbones and no eyebrows, and I know it made her day to trip me up. She'd been watching cash registers for fifty years and probably never seen a mistake before.

By the time I got her feathers smoothed and her goodies into a bag—she gives me a little snort in passing, if she'd been born at the right time they would have burned her over in Salem[2]—by the time I get her on her way the girls had circled around the bread and were coming back, without a pushcart, back my

1. The Great Atlantic and Pacific Tea Company, so named in 1859, became by the 1930s the leading national chain of supermarkets. The A&P Corporation today has more than 300 stores under various names.

2. The store is located not far from Salem, Massachusetts, where in 1692 nineteen women and men were hanged after being convicted of witchcraft.

way along the counters, in the aisle between the checkouts and the Special bins. They didn't even have shoes on. There was this chunky one, with the two-piece—it was bright green and the seams on the bra were still sharp and her belly was still pretty pale so I guessed she just got it (the suit)—there was this one, with one of those chubby berry-faces, the lips all bunched together under her nose, this one, and a tall one, with black hair that hadn't quite frizzed right, and one of these sunburns right across under the eyes, and a chin that was too long—you know, the kind of girl other girls think is very "striking" and "attractive" but never quite makes it, as they very well know, which is why they like her so much—and then the third one, that wasn't quite so tall. She was the queen. She kind of led them, the other two peeking around and making their shoulders round. She didn't look around, not this queen, she just walked straight on slowly, on these long white prima-donna legs. She came down a little hard on her heels, as if she didn't walk in her bare feet that much, putting down her heels and then letting the weight move along to her toes as if she was testing the floor with every step, putting a little deliberate extra action into it. You never know for sure how girls' minds work (do you really think it's a mind in there or just a little buzz like a bee in a glass jar?) but you got the idea she had talked the other two into coming in here with her, and now she was showing them how to do it, walk slow and hold yourself straight.

She had on a kind of dirty-pink—beige maybe, I don't know—bathing suit with a little nubble all over it and, what got me, the straps were down. They were off her shoulders looped loose around the cool tops of her arms, and I guess as a result the suit had slipped a little on her, so all around the top of the cloth there was this shining rim. If it hadn't been there you wouldn't have known there could have been anything whiter than those shoulders. With the straps pushed off, there was nothing between the top of the suit and the top of her head except just *her*, this clean bare plane of the top of her chest down from the shoulder bones like a dented sheet of metal tilted in the light. I mean, it was more than pretty.

She had sort of oaky hair that the sun and salt had bleached, done up in a bun that was unravelling, and a kind of prim face. Walking into the A & P with your straps down, I suppose it's the only kind of face you *can* have. She held her head so high her neck, coming up out of those white shoulders, looked kind of stretched, but I didn't mind. The longer her neck was, the more of her there was.

5 She must have felt in the corner of her eye me and over my shoulder Stokesie in the second slot watching, but she didn't tip. Not this queen. She kept her eyes moving across the racks, and stopped, and turned so slow it made my stomach rub the inside of my apron, and buzzed to the other two, who kind of huddled against her for relief, and then they all three of them went up the cat-and-dog-food-breakfast-cereal-macaroni-rice-raisins-seasonings-spreads-spaghetti-soft-drinks-crackers-and-cookies aisle. From the third slot I look straight up this aisle to the meat counter, and I watched them all the way. The fat one with the tan sort of fumbled with the cookies, but on second thought she put the package back. The sheep pushing their carts down the aisle—the girls were walking against the usual traffic (not that we have one-way signs or anything)—were pretty hilarious. You could see them, when Queenie's white shoulders dawned on them, kind of jerk, or hop, or hiccup, but their eyes snapped back to their own baskets and on they pushed. I bet you could set off dynamite in an A & P and the people would by and large keep reaching and checking oatmeal off their lists and

muttering "Let me see, there was a third thing, began with A, asparagus, no, ah, yes, applesauce!" or whatever it is they do mutter. But there was no doubt, this jiggled them. A few houseslaves in pin curlers even looked around after pushing their carts past to make sure what they had seen was correct.

You know, it's one thing to have a girl in a bathing suit down on the beach, where what with the glare nobody can look at each other much anyway, and another thing in the cool of the A & P, under the fluorescent lights, against all those stacked packages, with her feet paddling along naked over our checkerboard green-and-cream rubber-tile floor.

"Oh Daddy," Stokesie said beside me. "I feel so faint."

"Darling," I said. "Hold me tight." Stokesie's married, with two babies chalked up on his fuselage already, but as far as I can tell that's the only difference. He's twenty-two, and I was nineteen this April.

"Is it done?" he asks, the responsible married man finding his voice. I forgot to say he thinks he's going to be manager some sunny day, maybe in 1990 when it's called the Great Alexandrov and Petrooshki Tea Company or something.

What he meant was, our town is five miles from a beach, with a big summer 10
colony out on the Point, but we're right in the middle of town, and the women generally put on a shirt or shorts or something before they get out of the car into the street. And anyway these are usually women with six children and varicose veins mapping their legs and nobody, including them, could care less. As I say, we're right in the middle of town, and if you stand at our front doors you can see two banks and the Congregational church and the newspaper store and three real-estate offices and about twenty-seven old freeloaders tearing up Central Street because the sewer broke again. It's not as if we're on the Cape; we're north of Boston and there's people in this town haven't seen the ocean for twenty years.

The girls had reached the meat counter and were asking McMahon something. He pointed, they pointed, and they shuffled out of sight behind a pyramid of Diet Delight peaches. All that was left for us to see was old McMahon patting his mouth and looking after them sizing up their joints. Poor kids, I began to feel sorry for them, they couldn't help it.

• • •

Now here comes the sad part of the story, at least my family says it's sad, but I don't think it's so sad myself. The store's pretty empty, it being Thursday afternoon, so there was nothing much to do except lean on the register and wait for the girls to show up again. The whole store was like a pinball machine and I didn't know which tunnel they'd come out of. After a while they come around out of the far aisle, around the light bulbs, records at discount of the Caribbean Six or Tony Martin Sings[3] or some such gunk you wonder they waste the wax on, sixpacks of candy bars, and plastic toys done up in cellophane that fall apart when a kid looks at them anyway. Around they come, Queenie still leading the way, and holding a little gray jar in her hand. Slots Three through Seven are unmanned and I could see her wondering between Stokes and me, but Stokesie with his usual luck draws an old party in baggy gray pants who stumbles up with

3. Typical titles of record albums at the time of the story (1962). Tony Martin (1913–2012), a popular singer and actor, was featured on radio and television in the 1940s and 1950s.

four giant cans of pineapple juice (what do these bums *do* with all that pineapple juice? I've often asked myself) so the girls come to me. Queenie puts down the jar and I take it into my fingers icy cold. Kingfish Fancy Herring Snacks in Pure Sour Cream: 49¢. Now her hands are empty, not a ring or a bracelet, bare as God made them, and I wonder where the money's coming from. Still with that prim look she lifts a folded dollar bill out of the hollow at the center of her nubbled pink top. The jar went heavy in my hand. Really, I thought that was so cute.

Then everybody's luck begins to run out. Lengel comes in from haggling with a truck full of cabbages on the lot and is about to scuttle into that door marked MANAGER behind which he hides all day when the girls touch his eye. Lengel's pretty dreary, teaches Sunday school and the rest, but he doesn't miss that much. He comes over and says, "Girls, this isn't the beach."

Queenie blushes, though maybe it's just a brush of sunburn I was noticing for the first time, now that she was so close. "My mother asked me to pick up a jar of herring snacks." Her voice kind of startled me, the way voices do when you see the people first, coming out so flat and dumb yet kind of tony, too, the way it ticked over "pick up" and "snacks." All of a sudden I slid right down her voice into her living room. Her father and the other men were standing around in ice-cream coats and bow ties and the women were in sandals picking up herring snacks on toothpicks off a big glass plate and they were all holding drinks the color of water with olives and sprigs of mint in them. When my parents have somebody over they get lemonade and if it's a real racy affair Schlitz in tall glasses with "They'll Do It Every Time" cartoons stencilled on.[4]

15 "That's all right," Lengel said. "But this isn't the beach." His repeating this struck me as funny, as if it had just occurred to him, and he had been thinking all these years the A & P was a great big dune and he was the head lifeguard. He didn't like my smiling—as I say he doesn't miss much—but he concentrates on giving the girls that sad Sunday-school-superintendent stare.

Queenie's blush is no sunburn now, and the plump one in plaid, that I liked better from the back—a really sweet can—pipes up, "We weren't doing any shopping. We just came in for the one thing."

"That makes no difference," Lengel tells her, and I could see from the way his eyes went that he hadn't noticed she was wearing a two-piece before. "We want you decently dressed when you come in here."

"We *are* decent," Queenie says suddenly, her lower lip pushing, getting sore now that she remembers her place, a place from which the crowd that runs the A & P must look pretty crummy. Fancy Herring Snacks flashed in her very blue eyes.

"Girls, I don't want to argue with you. After this come in here with your shoulders covered. It's our policy." He turns his back. That's policy for you. Policy is what the kingpins want. What the others want is juvenile delinquency.

20 All this while, the customers had been showing up with their carts but, you know, sheep, seeing a scene, they had all bunched up on Stokesie, who shook open a paper bag as gently as peeling a peach, not wanting to miss a word. I could feel in the silence everybody getting nervous, most of all Lengel, who asks me, "Sammy, have you rung up their purchase?"

4. Schlitz is an inexpensive brand of beer. The cheap glasses are decorated with a popular saying derived from a syndicated series of single-panel cartoons printed between 1929 and 2008.

I thought and said "No" but it wasn't about that I was thinking. I go through the punches, 4, 9, GROC, TOT—it's more complicated than you think, and after you do it often enough, it begins to make a little song, that you hear words to, in my case "Hello (*bing*) there, you (*gung*) hap-py *pee*-pul (*splat*)!"—the *splat* being the drawer flying out. I uncrease the bill, tenderly as you may imagine, it just having come from between the two smoothest scoops of vanilla I had ever known were there, and pass a half and a penny into her narrow pink palm, and nestle the herrings in a bag and twist its neck and hand it over, all the time thinking.

The girls, and who'd blame them, are in a hurry to get out, so I say "I quit" to Lengel quick enough for them to hear, hoping they'll stop and watch me, their unsuspected hero. They keep right on going, into the electric eye; the door flies open and they flicker across the lot to their car, Queenie and Plaid and Big Tall Goony-Goony (not that as raw material she was so bad), leaving me with Lengel and a kink in his eyebrow.

"Did you say something, Sammy?"

"I said I quit."

"I thought you did." 25

"You didn't have to embarrass them."

"It was they who were embarrassing us."

I started to say something that came out "Fiddle-de-doo." It's a saying of my grandmother's, and I know she would have been pleased.

"I don't think you know what you're saying," Lengel said.

"I know you don't," I said. "But I do." I pull the bow at the back of my apron 30
and start shrugging it off my shoulders. A couple customers that had been heading for my slot begin to knock against each other, like scared pigs in a chute.

Lengel sighs and begins to look very patient and old and gray. He's been a friend of my parents for years. "Sammy, you don't want to do this to your Mom and Dad," he tells me. It's true, I don't. But it seems to me that once you begin a gesture it's fatal not to go through with it. I fold the apron, "Sammy" stitched in red on the pocket, and put it on the counter, and drop the bow tie on top of it. The bow tie is theirs, if you've ever wondered. "You'll feel this for the rest of your life," Lengel says, and I know that's true, too, but remembering how he made that pretty girl blush makes me so scrunchy inside I punch the No Sale tab and the machine whirs "pee-pul" and the drawer splats out. One advantage to this scene taking place in summer, I can follow this up with a clean exit, there's no fumbling around getting your coat and galoshes, I just saunter into the electric eye in my white shirt that my mother ironed the night before, and the door heaves itself open, and outside the sunshine is skating around on the asphalt.

I look around for my girls, but they're gone, of course. There wasn't anybody but some young married screaming with her children about some candy they didn't get by the door of a powder-blue Falcon station wagon. Looking back in the big windows, over the bags of peat moss and aluminum lawn furniture stacked on the pavement, I could see Lengel in my place in the slot, checking the sheep through. His face was dark gray and his back stiff, as if he'd just had an injection of iron, and my stomach kind of fell as I felt how hard the world was going to be to me hereafter.

1962

QUESTIONS

1. The narrator of A & P announces the turning point or climax of the action, "the sad part of the story" (par. 12), adding, "[t]hen everybody's luck begins to run out" (par. 13). Is the climax of the story as significant as this sounds? Does the tone of Sammy's telling of the story match the events?
2. This brief incident at the grocery store involves both younger and older females and males, married or not. Compare the male employees and female customers of different ages and status. How does Sammy's view of these people suggest the theme of growing up or predict the options in life of the various people?
3. How does the setting of the story shape the initiation and its meaning? How do details about the merchandise or space contribute to the story?

AUTHORS ON THEIR WORK
JOHN UPDIKE (1932–2009)

From "An Interview with John Updike" (1995)*

There is always some ambiguity or some room for various responses to a story. But I certainly see him [Sammy] as a typical, well-intentioned American male trying to find his way in the society and full of good impulses. I think that he quit his job on a good impulse. [. . .] A kind of feminist protest, in a way, is what he does here. Who knows what his adult life will bring, but I think for the moment he's a boy who's tried to reach out of his immediate environment toward something bigger and better.

*"An Interview with John Updike." Interview by Donald M. Murray, directed by Bruce Schwartz (1995), posted by Murray. *Spike*, 2001.

SUGGESTIONS FOR WRITING

1. Initiation stories often concern a choice to abandon or join a family, group, or community. Write an essay in which you examine the choices made by one or more of the main characters in these stories. How do such choices shape the plot of each story or the changes characters go through?
2. A child, teenager, or adult will have different perspectives on the same situations, and initiation stories often dramatically reveal such differences in the way characters and narrators respond. Write an essay on the way the narrator's age affects your understanding of the "initiation" in one of the stories in this album.
3. Traditional cultures like that of the Masai people of East Africa have highly ritualized methods of inducting young people into adulthood. Might developed Western societies also be said to have ritual forms of initiation? Drawing evidence from at least two stories in this album, write an essay exploring how young people in modern Western societies are initiated into adulthood.
4. Choose a story from any other chapter of this book and write an essay explaining why it should be considered an initiation story.
5. Using any story in this album as a model, write a first-person narrative of an actual or fictional initiation into adulthood.

2 NARRATION AND POINT OF VIEW

When we read fiction, our sense of who is telling us the story is as important as what happens. Unlike drama, in which events are acted out in front of us, fiction is always mediated or represented to us by someone else, a **narrator**. Often a reader is very aware of the **voice** of a narrator telling the story, as if the words are being spoken aloud. Commonly, stories also reveal a distinct angle of vision or perspective from which the characters, events, and other aspects are viewed. Just as the verbal quality of narration is called the voice, the visual angle is called the **focus**. Focus acts much as a camera does, choosing the direction of our gaze, the framework in which we see things. Both voice and focus are generally considered together in the term **point of view**. To understand how a story is narrated, you need to recognize both voice and focus. These in turn shape what we know and care about as the plot unfolds, and they determine how close we feel to each character.

A story is said to be from a character's point of view, or a character is said to be a focal or focalizing character, if for the most part the action centers on that character, as if we see with that character's eyes or we watch that character closely. But the effects of narration certainly involve more than attaching a video camera to a character's head or tracking wherever the character moves. What about the spoken and unspoken words? In some stories, the narrator is a character, and we may feel as if we are overhearing his or her thoughts, whereas in other stories the narrator takes a very distant or critical view of the characters. At times a narrator seems more like a disembodied, unidentified voice. Prose fiction has many ways to convey speech and thought, so it is important to consider voice as well as focus when we try to understand the narration of a story.

Besides focus and voice, point of view encompasses more general matters of value. A story's narrator may explicitly endorse or subtly support whatever a certain character values, knows, or seeks, even when the character is absent or silent or unaware. Other narrators may treat characters and their interests with far more detachment. At the same time, the **style** and **tone** of the narrator's voice—from echoing the characters' feelings to mocking their pretentious speech or thoughts to stating their actions in formal diction—may convey clues that a character or a narrator's perspective is limited. Such discrepancies or gaps between vision and voice, intentions and understandings, or expectations and outcomes generate **irony**.

Sometimes the point of view shifts over the course of a narrative. Or the style of narration itself may even change dramatically from one section to another. Bram Stoker's novel *Dracula* (1897), for example, is variously narrated through characters' journals and letters, as well as newspaper articles.

The point of view varies according to the narrator's position in the story and the grammatical person (for example, first or third) the narrative voice assumes.

These elements determine who is telling the story, whom it is about, and what information the reader has access to.

TYPES OF NARRATION

Third-Person Narration

A *third-person narrator* tells an unidentified listener or reader what happened, referring to all characters using the pronouns *he*, *she*, or *they*. Third-person narration is virtually always external, meaning that the narrator is not a character in the story and does not participate in its action. Even so, different types of third-person narration—omniscient, limited, and objective—provide the reader with various amounts and kinds of information about the characters.

An *omniscient* or *unlimited narrator* has access to the thoughts, perceptions, and experiences of more than one character (often of several), though such narrators usually focus selectively on a few important characters. A *limited narrator* is an external, third-person narrator who tells the story from a distinct point of view, usually that of a single character, revealing that character's thoughts and relating the action from his or her perspective. This focal character is also known as a **central consciousness**. Sometimes a limited narrator will reveal the thoughts and feelings of a small number of the characters in order to enhance the story told about the central consciousness. (Jane Austen's novel *Emma* [1815] includes a few episodes from Mr. Knightley's point of view to show what he thinks about Emma Woodhouse, the focal character, and her relationships.) Finally, an *objective narrator* does not explicitly report the characters' thoughts and feelings but may obliquely suggest them through the characters' speech and actions. Stories with objective narrators consist mostly of dialogue interspersed with minimal description.

First-Person Narration

Instead of using third-person narration, an author might choose to tell a story from the point of view of a *first-person narrator*. Most common is first-person singular narration, in which the narrator uses the pronoun *I*. The narrator may be a major or minor character within the story and therefore is an *internal narrator*. Notice that the first-person narrator may be telling a story mainly about someone else or about his or her own experience. Sometimes the first-person narrator addresses an **auditor**, a listener within the fiction whose possible reaction is part of the story.

One kind of narrator that is especially effective at producing irony is the *unreliable narrator*. First-person narrators may unintentionally reveal their flaws as they try to impress. Or narrators may make claims that other characters or the audience know to be false or distorted. Some fictions are narrated by villains, insane people, fools, liars, or hypocrites. When we resist a narrator's point of view and judge his or her flaws or misperceptions, we call that narrator unreliable. This does not mean that you should dismiss everything such a narrator says, but you should be on the alert for ironies.

Less common is the first-person plural, where the narrator uses the pronoun *we*. The plural may be used effectively to express the shared perspective of a community, particularly one that is isolated, unusually close-knit, or highly regulated. Elizabeth Gaskell's classic short novel *Cranford* (1853) is a good example. The narrator is a young woman who visits a community of genteel widows and spinsters in the English village of Cranford and describes their customs. At one point, a visitor arrives, Lady Glenmire, and all of Cranford society is in awe of her aristocratic rank and title. At an evening party, "We were all very silent at first. We were thinking what we could talk about, that should be high enough to interest My Lady. There had been a rise in the price of sugar, which, as preserving-time was near, was a piece of intelligence to all our housekeeping hearts, and would have been the natural topic if Lady Glenmire had not been by. But we were not sure if the Peerage ate preserves" (that is, whether aristocrats ate fruit jam). The high price of sugar doesn't seem "high enough" in another sense for a high-ranked guest to talk about.

The narrator of Cranford does refer to herself as "I" and sometimes addresses the reader as "you." The narrative perspective and voice is rather similar in Kazuo Ishiguro's *Never Let Me Go* (2005), a novel that also portrays an isolated group that follows regulated customs. At a boarding school, a student, Polly, suddenly questions one of the rules: "*We* all went silent. Miss Lucy [the teacher] didn't often get cross, but when she did, *you* certainly knew about it, and we thought for a second Polly was for it [would be punished]. But then we saw Miss Lucy wasn't angry, just deep in thought. *I* remember feeling furious at Polly for so stupidly breaking the unwritten rule, but at the same time, being terribly excited about what answer Miss Lucy might give" (emphasis added). Ishiguro's narrator, like Gaskell's, resorts to different narrative perspectives and voices to represent the experience of both a community and an individual in it.

Second-Person Narration

Like narrators who refer to themselves as "we" throughout a work of fiction, *second-person narrators* who consistently speak to *you* are unusual. This technique has the effect of turning the reader into a character in the story. Jay McInerney, for example, in his novel *Bright Lights, Big City* (1984) employs the second-person voice, creating an effect similar to conversational anecdotes. But second-person narratives can instead sound much like instructional manuals or "how-to" books or like parents or other elders speaking to children.

TENSE

Along with the grammatical "person," the verb tense used has an effect on the narration of a story. Since narrative is so wrapped up in memory, most stories rely on the past tense. In contemporary fiction, however, the present tense is also frequently used. The present tense can lend an impression of immediacy, of frequent repetition, or of a dreamlike or magical state in which time seems suspended. An author might also use the present tense to create a conversational tone. Rarely, for a strange prophetic outlook, a narrator may even use the future tense, predicting what *will* happen.

NARRATOR VERSUS IMPLIED AUTHOR

As you discover how a story is being narrated, by whom, and from what point of view, how should you respond to the shifting points of view, tones of voice, and hints of critical distance or irony toward characters? Who is really shaping the story, and how do you know what is intended? Readers may answer the question

"Who is telling this story?" with the name of the author. It is more accurate and practical, however, to distinguish between the narrator who presents the story and the flesh-and-blood author who wrote it, even when the two are hard to tell apart. If you are writing an essay about a short story, you do not need to research the biography of the author or find letters or interviews in which the author comments on the writing process or the intended themes of the work. This sort of biographical information may enrich your study of the story (it can be a good critical approach), but it is not *necessary* to an understanding of the text. And yet if you only consider the narrator when you interpret a story, you may find it difficult to account for the effects of distance and irony that come from a narrator's or a character's limitations. Many critics rely on the concept of the *implied author*, not to be confused with either the flesh-and-blood person who wrote the work or the narrator who relates the words to us. Most of the time, when we ask questions about the "author" of a work, we are asking about its implied author, the perspective and values that govern the whole work, including the narrator.

Why not ignore the idea of the narrator or the implied author? What's wrong with writing an essay about *Great Expectations* (1860–61) in which you refer only to the author, Charles Dickens? After all, his name is on the title page, and we know that Pip's coming-of-age story has some autobiographical aspects. Yet from the first sentence of the novel it is clear that someone besides Charles Dickens is telling the story: Pip, the first-person narrator. "My father's family name being Pirrip, and my Christian name Philip, my infant tongue could make of both names nothing longer or more explicit than Pip. So, I called myself Pip, and came to be called Pip." The reader sympathizes with Pip, the focal character-narrator, as an abused child, but he is also flawed and makes mistakes, as Pip himself realizes when he has grown up and tells the story of his own life. The reader understands Pip's errors through the subtle guidance of the implied author who created the narrator and shaped the plot and other characters. How useful or accurate would it be to attribute Pip's character and experience to the real Charles Dickens? The facts of the flesh-and-blood author's life and his actual personality differ widely from the novel's character, which in turn may differ from what Charles Dickens himself consciously intended. Hence the value of referring to a narrator and an implied author of a work of fiction. In critical essays, these concepts help us discover what even the most detailed biography might never pin down: Who in fact was Charles Dickens, and what did he actually intend in *Great Expectations*?

Reading a story, we know that it consists of words on a page, but we imagine the narrator speaking to us, giving shape, focus, and voice to a particular history. At the same time, we recognize that the reader should not take the narrator's words as absolute truth, but rather as effects shaped by an implied author. The concept of the implied author helps keep the particulars of the real author's (naturally imperfect) personality and life out of the picture. But it also reminds us to distinguish between the act of writing the work and the imaginary utterance of "telling" the story: The narrator is *neither* the real nor the implied author.

Questions about Narration and Point of View

- Does the narrator speak in the first, second, or third person?
- Is the story narrated in the past or present tense? Does the verb tense affect your reading of it in any way?
- Does the narrator use a distinctive vocabulary, style, and tone, or is the language more standard and neutral?
- Is the narrator identified as a character, and if so, how much does he or she participate in the action?
- Does the narrator ever seem to speak to the reader directly (addressing "you") or explicitly state opinions or values?
- Do you know what every character is thinking, or only some characters, or none?
- Does the narrative voice or focus shift during the story or remain consistent?
- Do the narrator, the characters, and the reader all perceive matters in the same way, or are there differences in levels of understanding?

* * *

Because our responses to a work of fiction are largely guided by the designs and values implied in a certain way of telling the story, questions about narration and point of view can often lead to good essay topics. You might start by considering any other choices the implied author might have made and how these would change your reading of the story. As you read the stories in this chapter, imagine different voices and visions, different narrative techniques, in order to assess the specific effects of the particular types of narration and point of view. How would each story's meaning and effects change if its narrative voice or focus were different? Can you show the reader of your essay how the specific narration and point of view of a story contribute to its significant effects?

EDGAR ALLAN POE
(1809–49)

The Cask of Amontillado

Orphaned before he was three, Edgar Poe was adopted by John Allan, a wealthy Richmond businessman. Poe received his early schooling in Richmond and in England before a brief, unsuccessful stint at the University of Virginia. After serving for two years in the army, he was appointed to West Point in 1830 but expelled within the year for cutting classes. Living in Baltimore with his grandmother, aunt, and cousin Virginia (whom he married in 1835, when she was thirteen), Poe eked out a precarious living as an editor; his keen-edged reviews earned him numerous literary enemies. His two-volume *Tales of the Grotesque and Arabesque* received little critical attention when published in 1839, but his poem "The Raven"

(1845) made him a literary celebrity. After his wife's death of tuberculosis in 1847, Poe, already an alcoholic, became increasingly erratic; two years later he died mysteriously in Baltimore.

The thousand injuries of Fortunato I had borne as I best could, but when he ventured upon insult I vowed revenge. You, who so well know the nature of my soul, will not suppose, however, that I gave utterance to a threat. *At length* I would be avenged; this was a point definitively settled—but the very definitiveness with which it was resolved precluded the idea of risk. I must not only punish but punish with impunity. A wrong is unredressed when retribution overtakes its redresser. It is equally unredressed when the avenger fails to make himself felt as such to him who has done the wrong.

It must be understood that neither by word nor deed had I given Fortunato cause to doubt my good will. I continued, as was my wont, to smile in his face, and he did not perceive that my smile *now* was at the thought of his immolation.

He had a weak point—this Fortunato—although in other regards he was a man to be respected and even feared. He prided himself upon his connoisseurship in wine. Few Italians have the true virtuoso spirit. For the most part their enthusiasm is adopted to suit the time and opportunity, to practice imposture upon the British and Austrian *millionaires*. In painting and gemmary, Fortunato, like his countrymen, was a quack, but in the matter of old wines he was sincere. In this respect I did not differ from him materially;—I was skilful in the Italian vintages myself, and bought largely whenever I could.

It was about dusk, one evening during the supreme madness of the carnival season, that I encountered my friend. He accosted me with excessive warmth, for he had been drinking much. The man wore motley. He had on a tight-fitting parti-striped dress,[1] and his head was surmounted by the conical cap and bells. I was so pleased to see him that I should never have done wringing his hand.

5 I said to him—"My dear Fortunato, you are luckily met. How remarkably well you are looking to-day. But I have received a pipe[2] of what passes for Amontillado, and I have my doubts."

"How?" said he. "Amontillado? A pipe? Impossible! And in the middle of the carnival!"

"I have my doubts," I replied; "and I was silly enough to pay the full Amontillado price without consulting you in the matter. You were not to be found, and I was fearful of losing a bargain."

"Amontillado!"

"I have my doubts."

10 "Amontillado!"

"And I must satisfy them."

"Amontillado!"

1. Fortunato wears a jester's costume (i.e., motley), not a woman's dress.

2. Large cask.

"As you are engaged, I am on my way to Luchresi. If any one has a critical turn it is he. He will tell me——"

"Luchresi cannot tell Amontillado from Sherry."

"And yet some fools will have it that his taste is a match for your own."

"Come, let us go."

"Whither?"

"To your vaults."

"My friend, no; I will not impose upon your good nature. I perceive you have an engagement. Luchresi——"

"I have no engagement;—come."

"My friend, no. It is not the engagement, but the severe cold with which I perceive you are afflicted. The vaults are insufferably damp. They are encrusted with nitre."[3]

"Let us go, nevertheless. The cold is merely nothing. Amontillado! You have been imposed upon. And as for Luchresi, he cannot distinguish Sherry from Amontillado."

Thus speaking, Fortunato possessed himself of my arm; and putting on a mask of black silk and drawing a *roquelaire*[4] closely about my person, I suffered him to hurry me to my palazzo.

There were no attendants at home; they had absconded to make merry in honour of the time. I had told them that I should not return until the morning, and had given them explicit orders not to stir from the house. These orders were sufficient, I well knew, to insure their immediate disappearance, one and all, as soon as my back was turned.

I took from their sconces two flambeaux,[5] and giving one to Fortunato, bowed him through several suites of rooms to the archway that led into the vaults. I passed down a long and winding staircase, requesting him to be cautious as he followed. We came at length to the foot of the descent, and stood together upon the damp ground of the catacombs of the Montresors.

The gait of my friend was unsteady, and the bells upon his cap jingled as he strode.

"The pipe," said he.

"It is farther on," said I; "but observe the white web-work which gleams from these cavern walls."

He turned towards me, and looked into my eyes with two filmy orbs that distilled the rheum of intoxication.

"Nitre?" he asked, at length.

"Nitre," I replied. "How long have you had that cough?"

"Ugh! ugh! ugh!—ugh! ugh! ugh!—ugh! ugh! ugh!—ugh! ugh! ugh!—ugh! ugh! ugh!"

My poor friend found it impossible to reply for many minutes.

"It is nothing," he said, at last.

3. Potassium nitrate (saltpeter), a white mineral often found on the walls of damp caves and used in gunpowder.

4. Man's heavy, knee-length cloak.

5. That is, two torches from their wall brackets.

"Come," I said, with decision, "we will go back; your health is precious. You are rich, respected, admired, beloved; you are happy, as once I was. You are a man to be missed. For me it is no matter. We will go back; you will be ill, and I cannot be responsible. Besides, there is Luchresi——"

"Enough," he said; "the cough is a mere nothing; it will not kill me. I shall not die of a cough."

"True—true," I replied; "and, indeed, I had no intention of alarming you unnecessarily—but you should use all proper caution. A draught of this Medoc[6] will defend us from the damps."

Here I knocked off the neck of a bottle which I drew from a long row of its fellows that lay upon the mould.

"Drink," I said, presenting him the wine.

He raised it to his lips with a leer. He paused and nodded to me familiarly, while his bells jingled.

"I drink," he said, "to the buried that repose around us."

"And I to your long life."

He again took my arm, and we proceeded.

"These vaults," he said, "are extensive."

"The Montresors," I replied, "were a great and numerous family."

"I forget your arms."

"A huge human foot d'or,[7] in a field azure; the foot crushes a serpent rampant whose fangs are imbedded in the heel."

"And the motto?"

"*Nemo me impune lacessit.*"[8]

"Good!" he said.

The wine sparkled in his eyes and the bells jingled. My own fancy grew warm with the Medoc. We had passed through long walls of piled skeletons, with casks and puncheons[9] intermingling, into the inmost recesses of the catacombs. I paused again, and this time I made bold to seize Fortunato by an arm above the elbow.

"The nitre!" I said; "see, it increases. It hangs like moss upon the vaults. We are below the river's bed. The drops of moisture trickle among the bones. Come, we will go back ere it is too late. Your cough——"

"It is nothing," he said; "let us go on. But first, another draught of the Medoc."

I broke and reached him a flaçon of De Grâve. He emptied it at a breath. His eyes flashed with a fierce light. He laughed and threw the bottle upwards with a gesticulation I did not understand.

I looked at him in surprise. He repeated the movement—a grotesque one.

"You do not comprehend?" he said.

"Not I," I replied.

"Then you are not of the brotherhood."

"How?"

6. Like De Grâve (below), a French wine.
7. Of gold.
8. No one provokes me with impunity (Latin).
9. Large casks.

"You are not of the masons."[1]

"Yes, yes," I said; "yes, yes."

"You? Impossible! A mason?"

"A mason," I replied.

"A sign," he said, "a sign."

"It is this," I answered, producing from beneath the folds of my *roquelaire* a trowel.

"You jest," he exclaimed, recoiling a few paces. "But let us proceed to the Amontillado."

"Be it so," I said, replacing the tool beneath the cloak and again offering him my arm. He leaned upon it heavily. We continued our route in search of the Amontillado. We passed through a range of low arches, descended, passed on, and descending again, arrived at a deep crypt, in which the foulness of the air caused our flambeaux rather to glow than flame.

At the most remote end of the crypt there appeared another less spacious. Its walls had been lined with human remains, piled to the vault overhead, in the fashion of the great catacombs of Paris. Three sides of this interior crypt were still ornamented in this manner. From the fourth side the bones had been thrown down, and lay promiscuously upon the earth, forming at one point a mound of some size. Within the wall thus exposed by the displacing of the bones, we perceived a still interior crypt or recess, in depth about four feet, in width three, in height six or seven. It seemed to have been constructed for no especial use within itself, but formed merely the interval between two of the colossal supports of the roof of the catacombs, and was backed by one of their circumscribing walls of solid granite.

It was in vain that Fortunato, uplifting his dull torch, endeavoured to pry into the depth of the recess. Its termination the feeble light did not enable us to see.

"Proceed," I said; "herein is the Amontillado. As for Luchresi——"

"He is an ignoramus," interrupted my friend, as he stepped unsteadily forward, while I followed immediately at his heels. In an instant he had reached the extremity of the niche, and finding his progress arrested by the rock, stood stupidly bewildered. A moment more and I had fettered him to the granite. In its surface were two iron staples, distant from each other about two feet, horizontally. From one of these depended a short chain, from the other a padlock. Throwing the links about his waist, it was but the work of a few seconds to secure it. He was too much astounded to resist. Withdrawing the key I stepped back from the recess.

"Pass your hand," I said, "over the wall; you cannot help feeling the nitre. Indeed, it is *very* damp. Once more let me *implore* you to return. No? Then I must positively leave you. But I will first render you all the little attentions in my power."

"The Amontillado!" ejaculated my friend, not yet recovered from his astonishment.

1. Masons or Freemasons, an international secret society condemned by the Catholic Church. Montresor means by *mason* one who builds with stone, brick, etc.

"True," I replied; "the Amontillado."

75 As I said these words I busied myself among the pile of bones of which I have before spoken. Throwing them aside, I soon uncovered a quantity of building stone and mortar. With these materials and with the aid of my trowel, I began vigorously to wall up the entrance of the niche.

I had scarcely laid the first tier of the masonry when I discovered that the intoxication of Fortunato had in great measure worn off. The earliest indication I had of this was a low moaning cry from the depth of the recess. It was *not* the cry of a drunken man. There was then a long and obstinate silence. I laid the second tier, and the third, and the fourth; and then I heard the furious vibration of the chain. The noise lasted for several minutes, during which, that I might hearken to it with the more satisfaction, I ceased my labours and sat down upon the bones. When at last the clanking subsided, I resumed the trowel, and finished without interruption the fifth, the sixth, and the seventh tier. The wall was now nearly upon a level with my breast. I again paused, and holding the flambeaux over the mason-work, threw a few feeble rays upon the figure within.

A succession of loud and shrill screams, bursting suddenly from the throat of the chained form, seemed to thrust me violently back. For a brief moment I hesitated, I trembled. Unsheathing my rapier, I began to grope with it about the recess; but the thought of an instant reassured me. I placed my hand upon the solid fabric of the catacombs and felt satisfied. I reapproached the wall. I replied to the yells of him who clamoured. I re-echoed, I aided, I surpassed them in volume and in strength. I did this, and the clamourer grew still.

It was now midnight, and my task was drawing to a close. I had completed the eighth, the ninth and the tenth tier. I had finished a portion of the last and the eleventh; there remained but a single stone to be fitted and plastered in. I struggled with its weight; I placed it partially in its destined position. But now there came from out the niche a low laugh that erected the hairs upon my head. It was succeeded by a sad voice, which I had difficulty in recognizing as that of the noble Fortunato. The voice said—

"Ha! ha! ha!—he! he! he!—a very good joke, indeed—an excellent jest. We will have many a rich laugh about it at the palazzo—he! he! he!—over our wine—he! he! he!"

80 "The Amontillado!" I said.

"He! he! he!—he! he! he!—yes, the Amontillado. But is it not getting late? Will not they be awaiting us at the palazzo—the Lady Fortunato and the rest? Let us be gone."

"Yes," I said, "let us be gone."

"For the love of God, Montresor!"

"Yes," I said, "for the love of God!"

85 But to these words I hearkened in vain for a reply. I grew impatient. I called aloud—

"Fortunato!"

No answer. I called again—

"Fortunato!"

No answer still. I thrust a torch through the remaining aperture and let it fall within. There came forth in return only a jingling of the bells. My heart grew sick; it was the dampness of the catacombs that made it so. I hastened to make an end of my labour. I forced the last stone into its position; I plastered it up. Against the new masonry I re-erected the old rampart of bones. For the half of a century no mortal has disturbed them. *In pace requiescat!*[2]

1846

QUESTIONS

1. What can the reader infer about Montresor's social position and character from hints in the text? What evidence does the text provide that Montresor is an unreliable narrator?
2. Who is the auditor, the "You," addressed in the first paragraph of THE CASK OF AMONTILLADO? When is the story being told? Why is it being told? How does your knowledge of the auditor and the occasion influence the effect the story has on you?
3. What devices does Poe use to create and heighten the suspense in the story? Is the outcome ever in doubt?

JAMAICA KINCAID (b. 1949)

Girl

Raised in poverty by her homemaker mother and carpenter stepfather on the small Caribbean island of Antigua, Elaine Potter Richardson was sent to the United States to earn her own living at age seventeen, much like the protagonists of her first novels, *Annie John* (1983) and *Lucy* (1990). Working as an au pair and receptionist, she earned her high-school equivalency degree and studied photography at the New School for Social Research in New York and, briefly, Franconia College in New Hampshire. Returning to New York, she took the name of a character in a George Bernard Shaw play, at least in part out of resentment toward her mother, with whom she had once been very close. After a short stint as a freelance journalist, Kincaid worked as a regular contributor to the *New Yorker* from 1976 until 1995, in 1979 marrying its editor's son, composer Allen Shawn, with whom she would eventually move to Bennington, Vermont and raise two children. "Girl," her first published story, appeared in the *New Yorker* in 1978 and was later republished in her first collection, *At the Bottom of the River* (1983). Subsequent novels include *The Autobiography of My Mother* (1996), paradoxically the least autobiographical of her books; *Mr. Potter* (2002), a fictionalized account of her efforts to understand the biological father she never knew; and *See Now Then* (2013). Kincaid's equally impressive nonfiction includes *My Brother* (1997), a memoir inspired by her youngest brother's death from AIDS, and *A Small Place* (1988), an essay exploring the profound economic and psychological impact of Antigua's dependence on tourism. Divorced in 2002, Kincaid is currently Professor of African and African American Studies in Residence at Harvard.

2. May he rest in peace (Latin).

Wash the white clothes on Monday and put them on the stone heap; wash the color clothes on Tuesday and put them on the clothesline to dry; don't walk barehead in the hot sun; cook pumpkin fritters in very hot sweet oil; soak your little cloths right after you take them off; when buying cotton to make yourself a nice blouse, be sure that it doesn't have gum on it, because that way it won't hold up well after a wash; soak salt fish overnight before you cook it; is it true that you sing benna[1] in Sunday school?; always eat your food in such a way that it won't turn someone else's stomach; on Sundays try to walk like a lady and not like the slut you are so bent on becoming; don't sing benna in Sunday school; you mustn't speak to wharf-rat boys, not even to give directions; don't eat fruits on the street—flies will follow you; *but I don't sing benna on Sundays at all and never in Sunday school*; this is how to sew on a button; this is how to make a buttonhole for the button you have just sewed on; this is how to hem a dress when you see the hem coming down and so to prevent yourself from looking like the slut I know you are so bent on becoming; this is how you iron your father's khaki shirt so that it doesn't have a crease; this is how you iron your father's khaki pants so that they don't have a crease; this is how you grow okra—far from the house, because okra tree harbors red ants; when you are growing dasheen, make sure it gets plenty of water or else it makes your throat itch when you are eating it; this is how you sweep a corner; this is how you sweep a whole house; this is how you sweep a yard; this is how you smile to someone you don't like too much; this is how you smile to someone you don't like at all; this is how you smile to someone you like completely; this is how you set a table for tea; this is how you set a table for dinner; this is how you set a table for dinner with an important guest; this is how you set a table for lunch; this is how you set a table for breakfast; this is how to behave in the presence of men who don't know you very well, and this way they won't recognize immediately the slut I have warned you against becoming; be sure to wash every day, even if it is with your own spit; don't squat down to play marbles—you are not a boy, you know; don't pick people's flowers—you might catch something; don't throw stones at blackbirds, because it might not be a blackbird at all; this is how to make a bread pudding; this is how to make doukona;[2] this is how to make pepper pot; this is how to make a good medicine for a cold; this is how to make a good medicine to throw away a child before it even becomes a child; this is how to catch a fish; this is how to throw back a fish you don't like, and that way something bad won't fall on you; this is how to bully a man; this is how a man bullies you; this is how to love a man, and if this doesn't work there are other ways, and if they don't work don't feel too bad about giving up; this is how to spit up in the air if you feel like it, and this is how to move quick so that it doesn't fall on you; this is how to make ends meet; always squeeze bread to make sure it's fresh; *but what if the baker won't let me feel the bread?*; you mean to say that after all you are really going to be the kind of woman who the baker won't let near the bread?

1983

1. Caribbean folk-music style.
2. Spicy pudding, often made from plantain and wrapped in a plantain or banana leaf.

QUESTIONS

1. Describe the focus, or focalization, in GIRL. Do we see what one person sees or observe one person in particular? Describe the voice of the narrator in GIRL. Who is the "you"? How do the focus and voice contribute to the reader's response to the story?
2. Look closely at the indications of time in the story. What actions take place at certain times? Does any event or action happen only once? Is there a plot in GIRL? If so, how would you summarize it?
3. The instructions in GIRL have different qualities, as if they come from different people or have different purposes. Why are two phrases in italics? Can you pick out the phrases that are more positive from the girl's point of view? Are there some that seem humorous or ironic?

GEORGE SAUNDERS
(b. 1958)
Puppy

When he described early-twentieth-century American novelist Thomas Wolfe as "broken-hearted [. . .] emotional, and in love with the world," George Saunders might have been talking about himself. A MacArthur "genius grant" recipient, Saunders is often compared to Kurt Vonnegut for his extraordinary ability to capture life's tragedy while simultaneously making readers laugh. Saunders's fiction includes intricately plotted social satires set in bizarre worlds. *The Brief and Frightening Reign of Phil* (2005), for instance, takes place in Inner and Outer Horner, the former a place "so small that only one Inner Hornerite at a time could fit inside." For all its fantastical, humorous elements, however, his work often concerns a very down-to-earth issue: compassion and the lack thereof.

Born in Amarillo, Texas, Saunders recalls that his first story, written when he was in third grade, depicted "a third-grade kid [. . .] who, in the face of an extreme manpower shortage, gets drafted by the Marines and goes to fight in WWII." Despite such precocious beginnings, Saunders took a circuitous path to his career as a writer, earning a degree in geophysical engineering from the Colorado School of Mines (1981) and working as everything from a slaughterhouse knuckle-puller in Texas to an oil-exploration crewman in Sumatra before entering the creative-writing program at Syracuse University (MA, 1988), where he now teaches. This diverse experience informs the short stories, novellas, and essays collected in *Civil Warland in Bad Decline* (1996), *Pastoralia* (2000), *In Persuasion Nation* (2006), *The Braindead Megaphone* (2007) and *Tenth of December* (2013).

Twice already Marie had pointed out the brilliance of the autumnal sun on the perfect field of corn, because the brilliance of the autumnal sun on the perfect field of corn put her in mind of a haunted house—not a haunted house she had ever actually seen but the mythical one that sometimes appeared in her mind (with adjacent graveyard and cat on a fence) whenever she saw the brilliance of the autumnal sun on the perfect etc. etc., and she wanted to make sure that, if the kids had a corresponding mythical haunted house that appeared in their minds whenever they saw the brilliance of the etc. etc., it would come up now, so that they could all experience it together, like friends, like college friends on a road trip, sans pot, ha ha ha!

But no. When she, a third time, said, "Wow, guys, check that out," Abbie said, "O.K., Mom, we get it, it's corn," and Josh said, "Not now, Mom, I'm Leavening my Loaves," which was fine with her; she had no problem with that, Noble Baker being preferable to Bra Stuffer, the game he'd asked for.

Well, who could say? Maybe they didn't even have any mythical vignettes in their heads. Or maybe the mythical vignettes they had in their heads were totally different from the ones she had in her head. Which was the beauty of it, because, after all, they were their own little people! You were just a caretaker. They didn't have to feel what *you* felt; they just had to be supported in feeling what *they* felt.

Still, wow, that cornfield was such a classic.

5 "Whenever I see a field like that, guys?" she said. "I somehow think of a haunted house!"

"Slicing Knife! Slicing Knife!" Josh shouted. "You nimrod machine! I chose that!"

Speaking of Halloween, she remembered last year, when their cornstalk column had tipped their shopping cart over. Gosh, how they'd laughed at that! Oh, family laughter was golden; she'd had none of that in her childhood, Dad being so dour and Mom so ashamed. If Mom and Dad's cart had tipped, Dad would have given the cart a despairing kick and Mom would have stridden purposefully away to reapply her lipstick, distancing herself from Dad, while she, Marie, would have nervously taken that horrid plastic Army man she'd named Brady into her mouth.

Well, in this family laughter was encouraged! Last night, when Josh had goosed her with his GameBoy, she'd shot a spray of toothpaste across the mirror and they'd all cracked up, rolling around on the floor with Goochie, and Josh had said, such nostalgia in his voice, "Mom, remember when Goochie was a puppy?" Which was when Abbie had burst into tears, because, being only five, she had no memory of Goochie as a puppy.

Hence this Family Mission. And as far as Robert? Oh, God bless Robert! There was a man. He would have no problem whatsoever with this Family Mission. She loved the way he had of saying "Ho HO!" whenever she brought home something new and unexpected.

10 "Ho HO!" Robert had said, coming home to find the iguana. "Ho HO!" he had said, coming home to find the ferret trying to get into the iguana cage. "We appear to be the happy operators of a menagerie!"

She loved him for his playfulness—you could bring home a hippo you'd put on a credit card (both the ferret and the iguana had gone on credit cards) and he'd just say "Ho HO!" and ask what the creature ate and what hours it slept and what the heck they were going to name the little bugger.

In the back seat, Josh made the *git-git-git* sound he always made when his Baker was in Baking Mode, trying to get his Loaves into the oven while fighting off various Hungry Denizens, such as a Fox with a distended stomach; such as a fey Robin that would improbably carry the Loaf away, speared on its beak, whenever it had succeeded in dropping a Clonking Rock on your Baker—all of which Marie had learned over the summer by studying the Noble Baker manual while Josh was asleep.

And it had helped, it really had. Josh was less withdrawn lately, and when she came up behind him now while he was playing and said, like, "Wow, honey, I didn't know you could do Pumpernickel," or "Sweetie, try Serrated Blade, it cuts quicker. Try it while doing Latch the Window," he would reach back with his non-controlling hand and swat at her affectionately, and yesterday they'd shared a good laugh when he'd accidentally knocked off her glasses.

So her mother could go right ahead and claim that she was spoiling the kids. These were not spoiled kids. These were *well-loved* kids. At least she'd never left one of them standing in a blizzard for two hours after a junior-high dance. At least she'd never drunkenly snapped at one of them, "I hardly consider you college material." At least she'd never locked one of them in a closet (a closet!) while entertaining a literal ditchdigger in the parlor.

Oh, God, what a beautiful world! The autumn colors, that glinting river, that lead-colored cloud pointing down like a rounded arrow at that half-remodelled McDonald's standing above I-90 like a castle.

This time would be different, she was sure of it. The kids would care for this pet themselves, since a puppy wasn't scaly and didn't bite. ("Ho HO!" Robert had said the first time the iguana bit him. "I see you have an opinion on the matter!")

Thank you, Lord, she thought, as the Lexus flew through the cornfield. You have given me so much: struggles and the strength to overcome them; grace, and new chances every day to spread that grace around. And in her mind she sang out, as she sometimes did when feeling that the world was good and she had at last found her place in it, "Ho HO, ho HO!"

Callie pulled back the blind.

Yes. Awesome. It was still solved so *perfect*.

There was plenty for him to do back there. A yard could be a whole world, like her yard when she was a kid had been a whole world. From the three holes in her wood fence she'd been able to see Exxon (Hole One) and Accident Corner (Hole Two), and Hole Three was actually two holes that if you lined them up right your eyes would do this weird crossing thing and you could play Oh My God I Am So High by staggering away with your eyes crossed, going "Peace, man, peace."

When Bo got older, it would be different. Then he'd need his freedom. But now he just needed not to get killed. Once they found him way over on Testament. And that was across I-90. How had he crossed I-90? She knew how. Darted. That's how he crossed streets. Once a total stranger called them from Hightown Plaza. Even Dr. Brile had said it: "Callie, this boy is going to end up dead if you don't get this under control. Is he taking the medication?"

Well, sometimes he was and sometimes he wasn't. The meds made him grind his teeth and his fist would suddenly pound down. He'd broken plates that way, and once a glass tabletop and got four stitches in his wrist.

Today he didn't need the medication because he was safe in the yard, because she'd fixed it so *perfect*.

He was out there practicing pitching by filling his Yankees helmet with pebbles and winging them at the tree.

25 He looked up and saw her and did the thing where he blew a kiss.

Sweet little man.

Now all she had to worry about was the pup. She hoped the lady who'd called would actually show up. It was a nice pup. White, with brown around one eye. Cute. If the lady showed up, she'd definitely want it. And if she took it Jimmy was off the hook. He'd hated doing it that time with the kittens. But if no one took the pup he'd do it. He'd have to. Because his feeling was, when you said you were going to do a thing and didn't do it, that was how kids got into drugs. Plus, he'd been raised on a farm, or near a farm anyways, and anybody raised on a farm knew that you had to do what you had to do in terms of sick animals or extra animals—the pup being not sick, just extra.

That time with the kittens, Jessi and Mollie had called him a murderer, getting Bo all worked up, and Jimmy had yelled, "Look, you kids, I was raised on a farm and you got to do what you got to do!" Then he'd cried in bed, saying how the kittens had mewed in the bag all the way to the pond, and how he wished he'd never been raised on a farm, and she'd almost said, "You mean near a farm" (his dad had run a car wash outside Cortland[1]), but sometimes when she got too smart-assed he would do this hard pinching thing on her arm while waltzing her around the bedroom, as if the place where he was pinching were like her handle, going, "I'm not sure I totally heard what you just said to me."

So, that time after the kittens, she'd only said, "Oh, honey, you did what you had to do."

30 And he'd said, "I guess I did, but it's sure not easy raising kids the right way."

And then, because she hadn't made his life harder by being a smart-ass, they had lain there making plans, like why not sell this place and move to Arizona and buy a car wash, why not buy the kids "Hooked on Phonics," why not plant tomatoes, and then they'd got to wrestling around and (she had no idea why she remembered this) he had done this thing of, while holding her close, bursting this sudden laugh/despair snort into her hair, like a sneeze, or like he was about to start crying.

Which had made her feel special, him trusting her with that.

So what she would love, for tonight? Was getting the pup sold, putting the kids to bed early, and then, Jimmy seeing her as all organized in terms of the pup, they could mess around and afterward lie there making plans, and he could do that laugh/snort thing in her hair again.

Why that laugh/snort meant so much to her she had no freaking idea. It was just one of the weird things about the Wonder That Was Her, ha ha ha.

35 Outside, Bo hopped to his feet, suddenly curious, because (here we go) the lady who'd called had just pulled up?

Yep, and in a nice car, too, which meant too bad she'd put "Cheap" in the ad.

Abbie squealed, "I love it, Mommy, I want it!," as the puppy looked up dimly from its shoebox and the lady of the house went trudging away and one-two-three-four plucked up four *dog turds* from the rug.

1. City in upstate New York, between Binghamton and Syracuse.

Well, now, what a super field trip for the kids, Marie thought, ha ha (the filth, the mildew smell, the dry aquarium holding the single encyclopedia volume, the pasta pot on the bookshelf with an inflatable candy cane inexplicably sticking out of it), and although some might have been disgusted (by the spare tire *on the dining-room table*, by the way the glum mother dog, the presumed in-house pooper, was dragging its rear over the pile of clothing in the corner, in a sitting position, splay-legged, a moronic look of pleasure on her face), Marie realized (resisting the urge to rush to the sink and wash her hands, in part because the sink had *a basketball in it*) that what this really was was deeply sad.

Please do not touch anything, please do not touch, she said to Josh and Abbie, but just in her head, wanting to give the children a chance to observe her being democratic and accepting, and afterward they could all wash up at the half-remodelled McDonald's, as long as they just please please kept their hands out of their mouths, and God forbid they should rub their eyes.

The phone rang, and the lady of the house plodded into the kitchen, placing 40
the daintily held, paper-towel-wrapped turds *on the counter*.

"Mommy, I want it," Abbie said.

"I will definitely walk him like twice a day," Josh said.

"Don't say 'like,'" Marie said.

"I will definitely walk him twice a day," Josh said.

O.K., then, all right, they would adopt a white-trash dog. Ha ha. They could 45
name it Zeke, buy it a little corncob pipe and a straw hat. She imagined the puppy, having crapped on the rug, looking up at her, going, *Cain't hep it*. But no. Had she come from a perfect place? Everything was transmutable. She imagined the puppy grown up, entertaining some friends, speaking to them in a British accent: *My family of origin was, um, rather not, shall we say, of the most respectable* . . .

Ha ha, wow, the mind was amazing, always cranking out these—

Marie stepped to the window and, anthropologically pulling the blind aside, was shocked, so shocked that she dropped the blind and shook her head, as if trying to wake herself, shocked to see a young boy, just a few years younger than Josh, harnessed and chained to a tree, via some sort of doohickey by which—she pulled the blind back again, sure she could not have seen what she thought she had—

When the boy ran, the chain spooled out. He was running now, looking back at her, showing off. When he reached the end of the chain, it jerked and he dropped as if shot.

He rose to a sitting position, railed against the chain, whipped it back and forth, crawled to a bowl of water, and, lifting it to his lips, took a drink: a drink *from a dog's bowl*.

Josh joined her at the window. She let him look. He should know that the 50
world was not all lessons and iguanas and Nintendo. It was also this muddy simple boy tethered like an animal.

She remembered coming out of the closet to find her mother's scattered lingerie and the ditchdigger's metal hanger full of orange flags. She remembered waiting outside the junior high in the bitter cold, the snow falling harder, as she counted over and over to two hundred, promising herself each time that when she reached two hundred she would begin the long walk back—

God, she would have killed for just one righteous adult to confront her mother, shake her, and say, "You idiot, this is your child, your child you're—"

"So what were you guys thinking of naming him?" the woman said, coming out of the kitchen.

The cruelty and ignorance just radiated from her fat face, with its little smear of lipstick.

55 "I'm afraid we won't be taking him after all," Marie said coldly.

Such an uproar from Abbie! But Josh—she would have to praise him later, maybe buy him the Italian Loaves Expansion Pak—hissed something to Abbie, and then they were moving out through the trashed kitchen (past some kind of *crankshaft* on a cookie sheet, past a partial red pepper afloat *in a can of green paint*) while the lady of the house scuttled after them, saying, wait, wait, they could have it for free, please take it—she really wanted them to have it.

No, Marie said, it would not be possible for them to take it at this time, her feeling being that one really shouldn't possess something if one wasn't up to properly caring for it.

"Oh," the woman said, slumping in the doorway, the scrambling pup on one shoulder.

Out in the Lexus, Abbie began to cry softly, saying, "Really, that was the perfect pup for me."

60 And it was a nice pup, but Marie was not going to contribute to a situation like this in even the smallest way.

Simply was not going to do it.

The boy came to the fence. If only she could have said to him, with a single look, *Life will not necessarily always be like this. Your life could suddenly blossom into something wonderful. It can happen. It happened to me.*

But secret looks, looks that conveyed a world of meaning with their subtle blah blah blah—that was all bullshit. What was not bullshit was a call to Child Welfare, where she knew Linda Berling, a very no-nonsense lady who would snatch this poor kid away so fast it would make that fat mother's thick head spin.

Callie shouted, "Bo, back in a sec!," and, swiping the corn out of the way with her non-pup arm, walked until there was nothing but corn and sky.

65 It was so small it didn't move when she set it down, just sniffed and tumped over.

Well, what did it matter, drowned in a bag or starved in the corn? This way Jimmy wouldn't have to do it. He had enough to worry about. The boy she'd first met with hair to his waist was now this old man shrunk with worry. As far as the money, she had sixty hidden away. She'd give him twenty of that and go, "The people who bought the pup were super-nice."

Don't look back, don't look back, she said in her head as she raced away through the corn.

Then she was walking along Teallback Road like a sportwalker, like some lady who walked every night to get slim, except that she was nowhere near slim, she knew that, and she also knew that when sportwalking you did not wear jeans and unlaced hiking boots. Ha ha! She wasn't stupid. She just made bad choices. She remembered Sister Carol saying, "Callie, you are bright enough but you incline toward that which does not benefit you." *Yep, well, Sister, you got that right*, she said to the nun in her mind. But what the hell. What the heck. When things got easier moneywise, she'd get some decent tennis shoes and start walking and get slim. And start night school. Slimmer. Maybe medical technology. She was never going to be really slim. But Jimmy liked her the way she was, and she liked him the way he was, which maybe that's what love was, liking someone how he was and doing things to help him get even better.

Like right now she was helping Jimmy by making his life easier by killing something so he—no. All she was doing was walking, walking away from—

Pushing the words *killing puppy* out of her head, she put in her head the 70
words *beautiful sunny day wow I'm loving this beautiful sunny day so much*—

What had she just said? That had been good. *Love was liking someone how he was and doing things to help him get better.*

Like Bo wasn't perfect, but she loved him how he was and tried to help him get better. If they could keep him safe, maybe he'd mellow out as he got older. If he mellowed out, maybe he could someday have a family. Like there he was now in the yard, sitting quietly, looking at flowers. Tapping with his bat, happy enough. He looked up, waved the bat at her, gave her that smile. Yesterday he'd been stuck in the house, all miserable. He'd ended the day screaming in bed, so frustrated. Today he was looking at flowers. Who was it that thought up that idea, the idea that had made today better than yesterday? Who loved him enough to think that up? Who loved him more than anyone else in the world loved him?

Her.

She did.

2007

QUESTIONS

1. At what point in Puppy do you begin to realize that Saunders's third-person narrator might be speaking *like* or using the voice of his two main characters—first Marie, then Callie, and so on? How is your initial response and attitude to the characters different than it would be if one or both of these characters actually narrated the story (in the first-person) or if the third-person narrator's voice were consistent throughout the story? What are the most distinctive features of each voice, and what do they tell us about the characters?
2. How does each of the subsequent shifts in both focus and voice affect the way you interpret and feel about the characters and their situations? What is the effect of Saunders's choice to end the story with Callie's point of view?
3. What is the effect of the way the narrator refers to real consumer products by using their brand names (Game Boy) and discusses (in some detail) entirely fictional ones like the games "Noble Baker" and "Bra Stuffer"? What do these details contribute to the story, especially in terms of our attitudes toward the various characters and their world (or our own)?

AUTHORS ON THEIR WORK

GEORGE SAUNDERS (b. 1958)

From "'Knowable in the Smallest Fragment': An Interview with George Saunders" (n.d.)*

MV: While your short stories always have interesting plots [. . .] it's the voices of these stories [. . .] that make them so memorable. In fact, when I remember your stories, I remember the voices: the rhythms, the repetition, the idiosyncratic logic, the corporate-babble, the exuberance, the wisecracks. Can you talk a bit about the importance of voice in your fiction, and how you come to discover the voices of your characters?

GS: Basically, I work at voice through constant anal-retentive revising. The criteria is basically ear-driven—I keep changing it until it sounds right and it surprises me in some way. I think it has something to do with a thing we did in Chicago back when I was a kid, this constant mimicking of other people, invented people, famous people. [. . .] And then of course voice and plot get all tangled up—a certain plot point is interesting, or attainable, or believable, in and only in a certain voice. The belief of the reader is engaged with the voice. [. . .] So it's all tied up together somehow. A character whose voice expresses limited intelligence, for example, we are more likely to believe him getting duped by somebody. That sort of thing.

*"'Knowable in the Smallest Fragment': An Interview with George Saunders." Interview by Matthew Vollmer. *GutCult*, vol. 1, no. 2, 2003, gutcult.com/litjourn2/html/GS1.html.

3 CHARACTER

Robert Buss, *Dickens' Dream* (1870)

In the unfinished watercolor *Dickens' Dream*, the nineteenth-century writer peacefully dozes while above and around him float ghostly images of the hundreds of characters that people his novels and, apparently, his dreams. This image captures the undeniable fact that characters loom large in the experience of fiction, for both its writers and its readers. Speaking for the former, Elie Wiesel describes a novelist like himself as practically possessed by characters who "force the writer to tell their stories" because "they want to get out." As readers of fiction, we care about *what* happens and *how* mainly because it happens *to* someone. Indeed, without a "someone," it is unlikely that anything would happen at all.

It is also often a "someone," or the *who* of a story, that sticks with us long after we have forgotten the details of what, where, and how. In this way, characters sometimes seem to take on a life of their own, to float free of the texts where we first encounter them, and even to haunt us. You may know almost nothing about Charles Dickens, but you probably have a vivid sense of his characters Ebenezer Scrooge and Tiny Tim from *A Christmas Carol* (1843).

A **character** is any personage in a literary work who acts, appears, or is referred to as playing a part. Though *personage* usually means a human being, it doesn't have to. Whole genres or subgenres of fiction are distinguished, in part, by the specific kinds of nonhuman characters they conventionally feature, whether alien species and intelligent machines (as in science fiction), animals (as in fables), or elves and monsters (as in traditional fairy tales and modern fantasy). All characters must have at least some human qualities, however, such as the ability to think, to feel pain, or to fall in love.

Evidence to Consider in Analyzing a Character: A Checklist

- the character's name
- the character's physical appearance
- objects and places associated with the character
- the character's actions
- the character's thoughts and speech, including
  - content (what he or she thinks or says)
  - timing (when he or she thinks or says it)
  - phrasing (how he or she thinks or says it)
- other characters' thoughts about the character
- other characters' comments to and about the character
- the narrator's comments about the character

HEROES AND VILLAINS VERSUS PROTAGONISTS AND ANTAGONISTS

A common term for the character with the leading male role is **hero**, the "good guy," who opposes the **villain**, or "bad guy." The leading female character is the **heroine**. Heroes and heroines are usually larger than life, stronger or better than most human beings, sometimes almost godlike. They are characters that a text encourages us to admire and even to emulate, so that the words *hero* and *heroine* can also be applied to especially admirable characters who do not play leading roles.

In most modern fiction, however, the leading character is much more ordinary, not so clearly or simply a "good guy." For that reason, it is usually more appropriate to use the older and more neutral terms *protagonist* and *antagonist* for the leading character and his or her opponent. These terms do not imply either the presence or the absence of outstanding virtue or vice.

The claim that a particular character either is or is not heroic might well make a good thesis for an essay, whereas the claim that he is or is not the protagonist generally won't. You might argue, for instance, that Montresor (in Poe's THE CASK OF AMONTILLADO) or Ebenezer Scrooge (in Dickens's *A Christmas Carol*) is a hero, but most readers would agree that each is his story's protagonist. Like most rules, however, this one admits of exceptions. Some stories do leave open to debate the question of which character most deserves to be called the *protagonist*. In SONNY'S BLUES, for example, Sonny and his brother are equally central.

Controversial in a different way is a particular type of protagonist known as an **antihero**. Found mainly in fiction written since around 1850, an antihero, as the name implies, possesses traits that make him or her the opposite of a traditional hero. An antihero may be difficult to like or admire. One early and influential example of an antihero is the narrator-protagonist of Fyodor Dostoevsky's 1864 Russian-language novella *Notes from the Underground*—a man utterly paralyzed by his own hypersensitivity. More familiar and recent examples are Homer and Bart Simpson.

It would be a mistake to see the quality of a work of fiction as dependent on whether we find its characters likable or admirable, just as it would be wrong to assume that an author's outlook or values are the same as those of the protagonist. Often, the characters we initially find least likable or admirable may ultimately move and teach us the most.

MAJOR VERSUS MINOR CHARACTERS

The *major* or *main characters* are those we see more of over time; we learn more about them, and we think of them as more complex and, frequently, as more "realistic" than the *minor characters*, the figures who fill out the story. These major characters can grow and change, too, sometimes defying our expectations.

Yet even though minor characters are less prominent and may seem less complex, they are ultimately just as indispensable to a story as major characters. Minor characters often play a key role in shaping our interpretations of, and attitudes toward, the major characters, and also in precipitating the changes that major characters undergo. For example, a minor character might function as a **foil**—a character that helps by way of contrast to reveal the unique qualities of another (especially main) character.

Questions about minor characters can lead to good essay topics precisely because such characters' significance to a story is not immediately apparent. Rather, we often have to probe the details of the story to formulate a persuasive interpretation of their roles.

FLAT VERSUS ROUND AND STATIC VERSUS DYNAMIC CHARACTERS

Characters that act from varied, often conflicting motives, impulses, and desires, and who seem to have psychological complexity, are said to be *round characters*; they can "surprise convincingly," as one critic puts it. Simple, one-dimensional characters that behave and speak in predictable or repetitive (if sometimes odd) ways are called *flat*. Sometimes characters seem round to us because our impression of them evolves as a story unfolds. Other times, the characters themselves—not just our impression of them—change as a result of events that occur in the story. A character that changes is *dynamic*; one that doesn't is *static*. Roundness and dynamism tend to go together. But the two qualities are distinct, and one does not require the other: Not all round characters are dynamic; not all dynamic characters are round.

Terms like *flat* and *round* or *dynamic* and *static* are useful so long as we do not let them harden into value judgments. Because flat characters are less complex than round ones, it is easy to assume they are artistically inferior; however, we need only to think of the characters of Charles Dickens, many of whom are flat, to realize that this is not always the case. A truly original flat character with only one or two very distinctive traits or behavioral or verbal tics will often prove more memorable than a round one. Unrealistic as such characters might seem, in real life you probably know at least one or two people who can always be counted on to say or do pretty much the same thing every time you see them. Exaggeration can provide insight, as well as humor. Dickens's large gallery of lovable flat characters includes a middle-aged man who constantly pulls himself up by his own hair and an old one who must continually be "fluffed up" by others because he tends to slide right out of his chair. *South Park*'s Kenny is little more than a hooded orange snowsuit and a habit of dying in ever more outrageous ways only to come back to life over and over again.

STOCK CHARACTERS AND ARCHETYPES

Flat characters who represent a familiar, frequently recurring type—the dumb blond, the mad scientist, the inept sidekick, the plain yet ever-sympathetic best friend—are called *stock characters* because they seem to be pulled out of a stock-room of familiar, prefabricated figures. Characters that recur in the myths and literature of many different ages and cultures are instead called **archetypes**, though this term also applies to recurring elements other than characters (such as actions or symbols). One archetypal character is the trickster figure that appears in the guise of Brer Rabbit in the Uncle Remus stories, the spider Anansi in certain African and Afro-Caribbean folktales, the coyote in Native American folklore, and, perhaps, Bugs Bunny. Another such character is the **scapegoat**.

READING CHARACTER IN FICTION AND LIFE

On the one hand, we get to know characters in a work of fiction and try to understand them much as we do people in real life. We observe what they own and wear, what they look like and where they live, how they carry themselves and what expressions flit across their faces, how they behave in various situations, what they say and how they say it, what they don't say, what others say about them, and how others act in their presence. Drawing on all that evidence and on our own past experience of both literature and life, we try to deduce characters' motives and desires, their values and beliefs, their strengths and weaknesses—in short, to figure out what makes them tick and how they might react if circumstances changed. In our daily lives, being able to "read" other people in this way is a vital skill, one that we may well hone by reading fiction. The skills of observation and interpretation, the enlarged experience and capacity for empathy, that we develop in reading fiction can help us better navigate our real world.

On the other hand, however, fictional characters are not real people; they are imaginary personages crafted by authors. Fiction offers us a more orderly and expansive world than the one we inhabit every day—one in which each person, gesture, and word is a meaningful part of a coherent, purposeful design—one in which our responses to people are guided by a narrator and, ultimately, an author; one in which we can sometimes crawl inside other people's heads and know their thoughts; one in which we can get to know murderers and ministers, monsters and miracle workers—the sorts of people (or personages) we might be afraid, unwilling, or simply unable to meet or spend time with in real life.

In other words, fictional characters are the products not of nature, chance, or God, but of careful, deliberate **characterization**—the art and technique of representing fictional personages. In analyzing character, we thus need to consider not only who a character is and what precisely are his or her most important traits, motivations, and values, but also precisely how the text shapes our interpretation of, and degree of sympathy or admiration for, the character; what function the character serves in the narrative; and what the character might represent.

This last issue is important because all characters, no matter how individualized and idiosyncratic, ultimately become meaningful to us only if they represent something beyond the story, something bigger than themselves—a type of person, a particular set of values or way of looking at the world, a human tendency, a demographic group. When you set out to write about a character, consider how the story would be different without the character and what the author says or shows us through the character.

Direct and Indirect Characterization: An Example and an Exercise

The following conversation appears in the pages of a well-known nineteenth-century novel. Even without being familiar with this novel, you should be able to discern a great deal about the two characters that converse in this scene simply by carefully attending to what each says and how each says it. As you will see, one of the things that differentiates the two speakers is that they hold conflicting views of "character" itself:

> "In what order you keep these rooms, Mrs Fairfax!" said I. "No dust, no canvas coverings: except that the air feels chilly, one would think they were inhabited daily."
>
> "Why, Miss Eyre, though Mr Rochester's visits here are rare, they are always sudden and unexpected; and as I observed that it put him out to find everything swathed up, and to have a bustle of arrangement on his arrival, I thought it best to keep the rooms in readiness."
>
> "Is Mr Rochester an exacting, fastidious sort of man?"
>
> "Not particularly so; but he has a gentleman's tastes and habits, and he expects to have things managed in conformity to them."
>
> "Do you like him? Is he generally liked?"
>
> "O yes; the family have always been respected here. Almost all the land in this neighbourhood, as far as you can see, has belonged to the Rochesters time out of mind."
>
> "Well, but leaving his land out of the question, do you like him? Is he liked for himself?"
>
> "I have no cause to do otherwise than like him; and I believe he is considered a just and liberal landlord by his tenants: but he has never lived much amongst them."

(continued on next page)

(continued)

"But has he no peculiarities? What, in short, is his character?"

"Oh! his character is unimpeachable, I suppose. He is rather peculiar, perhaps: he has travelled a great deal, and seen a great deal of the world, I should think. I daresay he is clever: but I never had much conversation with him."

"In what way is he peculiar?"

"I don't know—it is not easy to describe—nothing striking, but you feel it when he speaks to you: you cannot be always sure whether he is in jest or earnest, whether he is pleased or the contrary; you don't thoroughly understand him, in short—at least, I don't: but it is of no consequence, he is a very good master."

- What facts about the two speakers can you glean from this conversation? What do you infer about their individual outlooks, personalities, and values?
- What different definitions of the word *character* emerge here? How would you describe each speaker's view of what matters most in the assessment of character?

This scene—from Charlotte Brontë's *Jane Eyre* (1847)—demonstrates the first of the two major methods of presenting character—*indirect characterization* or showing (as opposed to *direct characterization* or telling). In this passage Brontë simply *shows* us what Jane (the narrator) and Mrs. Fairfax say and invites us to infer from their words who each character is (including the absent Mr. Rochester), how each looks at the world, and what each cares about.

Sometimes, however, authors present characters more directly, having narrators *tell* us what makes a character tick and what we are to think of him or her. Charlotte Brontë engages in both direct and indirect characterization in the paragraph of *Jane Eyre* that immediately follows the passage above. Here, Jane (the narrator) tells the reader precisely what she thinks this conversation reveals about Mrs. Fairfax, even as she reveals more about herself in the process:

This was all the account I got from Mrs Fairfax of her employer and mine. There are people who seem to have no notion of sketching a character, or observing and describing salient points, either in persons or things: the good lady evidently belonged to this class; my queries puzzled, but did not draw her out. Mr Rochester was Mr Rochester in her eyes; a gentleman, a landed proprietor—nothing more: she inquired and searched no further, and evidently wondered at my wish to gain a more definite notion of his identity.

- How does Jane's interpretation of Mrs. Fairfax compare to yours?
- How and why might this paragraph corroborate or complicate your view of Jane herself?

Characters, Conventions, and Beliefs

Just as fiction and the characters that inhabit it operate by somewhat different rules than do the real world and real people, so the rules that govern particular fictional worlds and their characters differ from one another. As the critic James Wood argues,

> our hunger for the particular depth or reality level of a character is tutored by each writer, and adapts to the internal conventions of each book. This is how we can read W. G. Sebald one day and Virginia Woolf or Philip Roth the next, and not demand that each resemble the other. [. . . Works of fiction] tend to fail not when the characters are not vivid or "deep" enough, but when the [work] in question has failed to teach us how to adapt to its conventions, has failed to manage a specific hunger for its own characters, its own reality level.

Works of fiction in various subgenres differ widely in how they handle characterization. Were a folktale, for example, to depict more than a few, mainly flat, archetypal characters; to make us privy to its characters' thoughts; or to offer up detailed descriptions of their physiques and wardrobes, it would cease both to be a folktale and to yield the particular sorts of pleasures and insights that only a folktale can. By the same token, readers of a folktale miss out on its pleasures and insights if they expect the wrong things of its characters and modes of characterization.

But even within the same fictional subgenre, the treatment of character varies over time and across cultures. Such variations sometimes reflect profound differences in the way people understand human nature. Individuals and cultures hold conflicting views of what produces personality, whether innate factors such as genes, environmental factors such as upbringing, supernatural forces, unconscious impulses or drives, or a combination of some or all of these. Views differ as well as to whether character is simply an unchanging given or something that can change through experience, conversion, or an act of will. Some works of fiction tackle such issues head on. But many others—especially from cultures or eras different from our own—may raise these questions for us simply because their modes of characterization imply an understanding of the self different from the one we take for granted.

We can thus learn a lot about our own values, prejudices, and beliefs by reading a wide array of fiction. Similarly, we learn from encountering a wide array of fictional characters, including those whose values, beliefs, and ways of life are vastly different from our own.

• • •

The stories in this chapter differ widely in terms of the number and types of characters they depict and the techniques they use to depict them. In their pages, you will meet a range of diverse individuals—some complex and compelling, some utterly ordinary—struggling to make sense of the people around them just as you work to make sense of them and, through them, yourself.

Questions about Character

- Who is the protagonist, or might there be more than one? Why and how so? Which other characters, if any, are main or major characters? Which are minor characters?
- What are the protagonist's most distinctive traits, and what is most distinctive about his or her outlook and values? What motivates the character? What is it about the character that creates internal and/or external conflict?
- Which textual details and moments reveal most about this character? Which are most surprising or might complicate your interpretation of this character? How is your view of the character affected by what you *don't* know about him or her?
- What are the roles of other characters? Which, if any, functions as an antagonist? Which, if any, serves as a foil? Why and how so? How would the story as a whole (not just its action or plot) be different if any of these characters disappeared? What points might the author be raising or illustrating through each character?
- Which of the characters, or which aspects of the characters, does the text encourage us to sympathize with or to admire? to view negatively? Why and how so?
- Does your view of any character change over the course of the story, or do any of the characters themselves change? If so, when, how, and why?
- Does characterization tend to be indirect or direct in the story? What kinds of information do and don't we get about the characters, and how does the story tend to give us that information?

WILLIAM FAULKNER
(1897–1962)

Barn Burning

A native of Oxford, Mississippi, William Faulkner left high school without graduating, joined the Royal Canadian Air Force in 1918, and in the mid-1920s lived briefly in New Orleans, where he was encouraged as a writer by Sherwood Anderson. He then spent a few miserable months as a clerk in a New York bookstore, published a collection of poems, *The Marble Faun*, in 1924, and took a long walking tour of Europe in 1925 before returning to Mississippi. With the publication of *Sartoris* in 1929, Faulkner began a cycle of works, featuring recurrent characters and set in fictional Yoknapatawpha County, including *The Sound and the Fury* (1929), *As I Lay Dying* (1930), *Light in August* (1932), *Absalom, Absalom!* (1936), *The Hamlet* (1940), and *Go Down, Moses* (1942). He spent time in Hollywood, writing screenplays for *The Big Sleep* and other films, and lived his last years in Charlottesville, Virginia. Faulkner received the Nobel Prize for Literature in 1950.

The store in which the Justice of the Peace's court was sitting smelled of cheese. The boy, crouched on his nail keg at the back of the crowded room, knew he smelled cheese, and more: from where he sat he could see the ranked shelves close-packed with the solid, squat, dynamic shapes of tin cans whose labels his stomach read, not from the lettering which meant nothing to his mind but from the scarlet devils and the silver curve of fish—this, the cheese which he knew he smelled and the hermetic meat which his intestines believed he smelled coming in intermittent gusts momentary and brief between the other constant one, the smell and sense just a little of fear because mostly of despair and grief, the old fierce pull of blood. He could not see the table where the Justice sat and before which his father and his father's enemy (*our enemy* he thought in that despair; *ourn! mine and hisn both! He's my father!*) stood, but he could hear them, the two of them that is, because his father had said no word yet:

"But what proof have you, Mr. Harris?"

"I told you. The hog got into my corn. I caught it up and sent it back to him. He had no fence that would hold it. I told him so, warned him. The next time I put the hog in my pen. When he came to get it I gave him enough wire to patch up his pen. The next time I put the hog up and kept it. I rode down to his house and saw the wire I gave him still rolled on to the spool in his yard. I told him he could have the hog when he paid me a dollar pound fee. That evening a nigger came with the dollar and got the hog. He was a strange nigger. He said, 'He say to tell you wood and hay kin burn.' I said, 'What?' 'That whut he say to tell you,' the nigger said. 'Wood and hay kin burn.' That night my barn burned. I got the stock out but I lost the barn."

"Where is the nigger? Have you got him?"

"He was a strange nigger, I tell you. I don't know what became of him." 5

"But that's not proof. Don't you see that's not proof?"

"Get that boy up here. He knows." For a moment the boy thought too that the man meant his older brother until Harris said, "Not him. The little one. The boy," and, crouching, small for his age, small and wiry like his father, in patched and faded jeans even too small for him, with straight, uncombed, brown hair and eyes gray and wild as storm scud, he saw the men between himself and the table part and become a lane of grim faces, at the end of which he saw the Justice, a shabby, collarless, graying man in spectacles, beckoning him. He felt no floor under his bare feet; he seemed to walk beneath the palpable weight of the grim turning faces. His father, stiff in his black Sunday coat donned not for the trial but for the moving, did not even look at him. *He aims for me to lie,* he thought, again with that frantic grief and despair. *And I will have to do hit.*

"What's your name, boy?" the Justice said.

"Colonel Sartoris Snopes," the boy whispered.

"Hey?" the Justice said. "Talk louder. Colonel Sartoris? I reckon anybody 10
named for Colonel Sartoris in this country can't help but tell the truth, can they?" The boy said nothing. *Enemy! Enemy!* he thought; for a moment he could not even see, could not see that the Justice's face was kindly nor discern that his voice was troubled when he spoke to the man named Harris: "Do you want me to question this boy?" But he could hear, and during those subsequent long seconds while there was absolutely no sound in the crowded little room save that of quiet and intent breathing it was as if he had swung outward at the end of a

grape vine, over a ravine, and at the top of the swing had been caught in a prolonged instant of mesmerized gravity, weightless in time.

"No!" Harris said violently, explosively. "Damnation! Send him out of here!" Now time, the fluid world, rushed beneath him again, the voices coming to him again through the smell of cheese and sealed meat, the fear and despair and the old grief of blood:

"This case is closed. I can't find against you, Snopes, but I can give you advice. Leave this country and don't come back to it."

His father spoke for the first time, his voice cold and harsh, level, without emphasis: "I aim to. I don't figure to stay in a country among people who . . ." he said something unprintable and vile, addressed to no one.

"That'll do," the Justice said. "Take your wagon and get out of this country before dark. Case dismissed."

15 His father turned, and he followed the stiff black coat, the wiry figure walking a little stiffly from where a Confederate provost's man's[1] musket ball had taken him in the heel on a stolen horse thirty years ago, followed the two backs now, since his older brother had appeared from somewhere in the crowd, no taller than the father but thicker, chewing tobacco steadily, between the two lines of grim-faced men and out of the store and across the worn gallery and down the sagging steps and among the dogs and half-grown boys in the mild May dust, where as he passed a voice hissed:

"Barn burner!"

Again he could not see, whirling; there was a face in a red haze, moonlike, bigger than the full moon, the owner of it half again his size, he leaping in the red haze toward the face, feeling no blow, feeling no shock when his head struck the earth, scrabbling up and leaping again, feeling no blow this time either and tasting no blood, scrabbling up to see the other boy in full flight and himself already leaping into pursuit as his father's hand jerked him back, the harsh, cold voice speaking above him: "Go get in the wagon."

It stood in a grove of locusts and mulberries across the road. His two hulking sisters in their Sunday dresses and his mother and her sister in calico and sunbonnets were already in it, sitting on and among the sorry residue of the dozen and more movings which even the boy could remember—the battered stove, the broken beds and chairs, the clock inlaid with mother-of-pearl, which would not run, stopped at some fourteen minutes past two o'clock of a dead and forgotten day and time, which had been his mother's dowry. She was crying, though when she saw him she drew her sleeve across her face and began to descend from the wagon. "Get back," the father said.

"He's hurt. I got to get some water and wash his . . ."

20 "Get back in the wagon," his father said. He got in too, over the tail-gate. His father mounted to the seat where the older brother already sat and struck the gaunt mules two savage blows with the peeled willow, but without heat. It was not even sadistic; it was exactly that same quality which in later years would cause his descendants to overrun the engine before putting a motor car into motion, striking and reining back in the same movement. The wagon went on, the store with its quiet crowd of grimly watching men dropped behind; a curve

1. Military policeman's.

in the road hid it. *Forever* he thought. *Maybe he's done satisfied now, now that he has* . . . stopping himself, not to say it aloud even to himself. His mother's hand touched his shoulder.

"Does hit hurt?" she said.

"Naw," he said. "Hit don't hurt. Lemme be."

"Can't you wipe some of the blood off before hit dries?"

"I'll wash to-night," he said. "Lemme be, I tell you."

The wagon went on. He did not know where they were going. None of them ever did or ever asked, because it was always somewhere, always a house of sorts waiting for them a day or two days or even three days away. Likely his father had already arranged to make a crop on another farm before he . . . Again he had to stop himself. He (the father) always did. There was something about his wolf-like independence and even courage when the advantage was at least neutral which impressed strangers, as if they got from his latent ravening ferocity not so much a sense of dependability as a feeling that his ferocious conviction in the rightness of his own actions would be of advantage to all whose interest lay with his.

That night they camped, in a grove of oaks and beeches where a spring ran. The nights were still cool and they had a fire against it, of a rail lifted from a nearby fence and cut into lengths—a small fire, neat, niggard almost, a shrewd fire; such fires were his father's habit and custom always, even in freezing weather. Older, the boy might have remarked this and wondered why not a big one; why should not a man who had not only seen the waste and extravagance of war, but who had in his blood an inherent voracious prodigality with material not his own, have burned everything in sight? Then he might have gone a step farther and thought that that was the reason: that niggard blaze was the living fruit of nights passed during those four years in the woods hiding from all men, blue or gray,[2] with his strings of horses (captured horses, he called them). And older still, he might have divined the true reason: that the element of fire spoke to some deep mainspring of his father's being, as the element of steel or of powder spoke to other men, as the one weapon for the preservation of integrity, else breath were not worth the breathing, and hence to be regarded with respect and used with discretion.

But he did not think this now and he had seen those same niggard blazes all his life. He merely ate his supper beside it and was already half asleep over his iron plate when his father called him, and once more he followed the stiff back, the stiff and ruthless limp, up the slope and on to the starlit road where, turning, he could see his father against the stars but without face or depth—a shape black, flat, and bloodless as though cut from tin in the iron folds of the frockcoat which had not been made for him, the voice harsh like tin and without heat like tin:

"You were fixing to tell them. You would have told him." He didn't answer. His father struck him with the flat of his hand on the side of the head, hard but without heat, exactly as he had struck the two mules at the store, exactly as he would strike either of them with any stick in order to kill a horse fly, his voice still without heat or anger: "You're getting to be a man. You got to learn. You got to learn to stick to your own blood or you ain't going to have any blood to stick to you. Do

2. Colors of Union and Confederate Civil War (1861–65) uniforms, respectively.

you think either of them, any man there this morning, would? Don't you know all they wanted was a chance to get at me because they knew I had them beat? Eh?" Later, twenty years later, he was to tell himself, "If I had said they wanted only truth, justice, he would have hit me again." But now he said nothing. He was not crying. He just stood there. "Answer me," his father said.

"Yes," he whispered. His father turned.

"Get on to bed. We'll be there tomorrow."

Tomorrow they were there. In the early afternoon the wagon stopped before a paintless two-room house identical almost with the dozen others it had stopped before even in the boy's ten years, and again, as on the other dozen occasions, his mother and aunt got down and began to unload the wagon, although his two sisters and his father and brother had not moved.

"Likely hit ain't fitten for hawgs," one of the sisters said.

"Nevertheless, fit it will and you'll hog it and like it," his father said. "Get out of them chairs and help your Ma unload."

The two sisters got down, big, bovine, in a flutter of cheap ribbons; one of them drew from the jumbled wagon bed a battered lantern, the other a worn broom. His father handed the reins to the older son and began to climb stiffly over the wheel. "When they get unloaded, take the team to the barn and feed them." Then he said, and at first the boy thought he was still speaking to his brother: "Come with me."

"Me?" he said.

"Yes," his father said. "You."

"Abner," his mother said. His father paused and looked back—the harsh level stare beneath the shaggy, graying, irascible brows.

"I reckon I'll have a word with the man that aims to begin to-morrow owning me body and soul for the next eight months."

They went back up the road. A week ago—or before last night, that is—he would have asked where they were going, but not now. His father had struck him before last night but never before had he paused afterward to explain why; it was as if the blow and the following calm, outrageous voice still rang, repercussed, divulging nothing to him save the terrible handicap of being young, the light weight of his few years, just heavy enough to prevent his soaring free of the world as it seemed to be ordered but not heavy enough to keep him footed solid in it, to resist it and try to change the course of its events.

Presently he could see the grove of oaks and cedars and the other flowering trees and shrubs, where the house would be, though not the house yet. They walked beside a fence massed with honeysuckle and Cherokee roses and came to a gate swinging open between two brick pillars, and now, beyond a sweep of drive, he saw the house for the first time and at that instant he forgot his father and the terror and despair both, and even when he remembered his father again (who had not stopped) the terror and despair did not return. Because, for all the twelve movings, they had sojourned until now in a poor country, a land of small farms and fields and houses, and he had never seen a house like this before. *Hit's big as a courthouse* he thought quietly, with a surge of peace and joy whose reason he could not have thought into words, being too young for that: *They are safe from him. People whose lives are a part of this peace and dignity are beyond his touch, he no more to them than a buzzing wasp: capable of stinging for a little moment but that's all; the spell of this peace and dignity rendering even the barns and stable and cribs which belong to it impervious to the puny flames he might contrive* . . . this, the peace and joy, ebbing for an instant as he looked again at the stiff black back, the stiff and implacable limp of the figure which was not dwarfed by the house, for the reason that it had never looked big anywhere and which now, against the serene columned backdrop, had more than ever that impervious quality of something cut ruthlessly from tin, depthless, as though, sidewise to the sun, it would cast no shadow. Watching him, the boy remarked the absolutely undeviating course which his father held and saw the stiff foot come squarely down in a pile of fresh droppings where a horse had stood in the drive and which his father could have avoided by a simple change of stride. But it ebbed only for a moment, though he could not have thought this into words either, walking on in the spell of the house, which he could even want but without envy, without sorrow, certainly never with that ravening and jealous rage which unknown to him walked in the ironlike black coat before him: *Maybe he will feel it too. Maybe it will even change him now from what maybe he couldn't help but be.*

They crossed the portico. Now he could hear his father's stiff foot as it came down on the boards with clocklike finality, a sound out of all proportion to the displacement of the body it bore and which was not dwarfed either by the white door before it, as though it had attained to a sort of vicious and ravening minimum not to be dwarfed by anything—the flat, wide, black hat, the formal coat of broadcloth which had once been black but which had now that friction-glazed greenish cast of the bodies of old house flies, the lifted sleeve which was too large, the lifted hand like a curled claw. The door opened so promptly that the boy knew the Negro must have been watching them all the time, an old man with neat grizzled hair, in a linen jacket, who stood barring the door with his body, saying, "Wipe yo foots, white man, fo you come in here. Major ain't home nohow."

"Get out of my way, nigger," his father said, without heat too, flinging the door back and the Negro also and entering, his hat still on his head. And now the boy saw the prints of the stiff foot on the doorjamb and saw them appear on the pale rug behind the machinelike deliberation of the foot which seemed to bear (or transmit) twice the weight which the body compassed. The Negro was shouting "Miss Lula! Miss Lula!" somewhere behind them, then the boy, deluged as though by a warm wave by a suave turn of carpeted stair and a pendant glitter of chandeliers and a mute gleam of gold frames, heard the swift feet and saw her too, a lady—perhaps he had never seen her like before either—in a gray, smooth gown with lace at the throat and an apron tied at the waist and the sleeves turned back, wiping cake or biscuit dough from her hands with a towel as she came up the hall, looking not at his father at all but at the tracks on the blond rug with an expression of incredulous amazement.

"I tried," the Negro cried. "I tole him to . . ."

"Will you please go away?" she said in a shaking voice. "Major de Spain is not at home. Will you please go away?"

His father had not spoken again. He did not speak again. He did not even 45
look at her. He just stood stiff in the center of the rug, in his hat, the shaggy iron-gray brows twitching slightly above the pebble-colored eyes as he appeared

to examine the house with brief deliberation. Then with the same deliberation he turned; the boy watched him pivot on the good leg and saw the stiff foot drag round the arc of the turning, leaving a final long and fading smear. His father never looked at it, he never once looked down at the rug. The Negro held the door. It closed behind them, upon the hysteric and indistinguishable woman-wail. His father stopped at the top of the steps and scraped his boot clean on the edge of it. At the gate he stopped again. He stood for a moment, planted stiffly on the stiff foot, looking back at the house. "Pretty and white, ain't it?" he said. "That's sweat. Nigger sweat. Maybe it ain't white enough yet to suit him. Maybe he wants to mix some white sweat with it."

Two hours later the boy was chopping wood behind the house within which his mother and aunt and the two sisters (the mother and aunt, not the two girls, he knew that; even at this distance and muffled by walls the flat loud voices of the two girls emanated an incorrigible idle inertia) were setting up the stove to prepare a meal, when he heard the hooves and saw the linen-clad man on a fine sorrel mare, whom he recognized even before he saw the rolled rug in front of the Negro youth following on a fat bay carriage horse—a suffused, angry face vanishing, still at full gallop, beyond the corner of the house where his father and brother were sitting in the two tilted chairs; and a moment later, almost before he could have put the axe down, he heard the hooves again and watched the sorrel mare go back out of the yard, already galloping again. Then his father began to shout one of the sisters' names, who presently emerged backward from the kitchen door dragging the rolled rug along the ground by one end while the other sister walked behind it.

"If you ain't going to tote, go on and set up the wash pot," the first said.

"You, Sarty!" the second shouted. "Set up the wash pot!" His father appeared at the door, framed against that shabbiness, as he had been against that other bland perfection, impervious to either, the mother's anxious face at his shoulder.

"Go on," the father said. "Pick it up." The two sisters stooped, broad, lethargic; stooping, they presented an incredible expanse of pale cloth and a flutter of tawdry ribbons.

"If I thought enough of a rug to have to git hit all the way from France I wouldn't keep hit where folks coming in would have to tromp on hit," the first said. They raised the rug.

"Abner," the mother said. "Let me do it."

"You go back and git dinner," his father said. "I'll tend to this."

From the woodpile through the rest of the afternoon the boy watched them, the rug spread flat in the dust beside the bubbling wash-pot, the two sisters stooping over it with that profound and lethargic reluctance, while the father stood over them in turn, implacable and grim, driving them though never raising his voice again. He could smell the harsh homemade lye they were using; he saw his mother come to the door once and look toward them with an expression not anxious now but very like despair; he saw his father turn, and he fell to with the axe and saw from the corner of his eye his father raise from the ground a flattish fragment of field stone and examine it and return to the pot, and this time his mother actually spoke: "Abner. Abner. Please don't. Please, Abner."

Then he was done too. It was dusk; the whippoorwills had already begun. He could smell coffee from the room where they would presently eat the cold food remaining from the mid-afternoon meal, though when he entered the house he realized they were having coffee again probably because there was a fire on the hearth, before which the rug now lay spread over the backs of the two chairs. The tracks of his father's foot were gone. Where they had been were now long, water-cloudy scoriations resembling the sporadic course of a Lilliputian mowing machine.

It still hung there while they ate the cold food and then went to bed, scattered 55
without order or claim up and down the two rooms, his mother in one bed, where his father would later lie, the older brother in the other, himself, the aunt, and the two sisters on pallets on the floor. But his father was not in bed yet. The last thing the boy remembered was the depthless, harsh silhouette of the hat and coat bending over the rug and it seemed to him that he had not even closed his eyes when the silhouette was standing over him, the fire almost dead behind it, the stiff foot prodding him awake. "Catch up the mule," his father said.

When he returned with the mule his father was standing in the black door, the rolled rug over his shoulder. "Ain't you going to ride?" he said.

"No. Give me your foot."

He bent his knee into his father's hand, the wiry, surprising power flowed smoothly, rising, he rising with it, on to the mule's bare back (they had owned a saddle once; the boy could remember it though not when or where) and with the same effortlessness his father swung the rug up in front of him. Now in the starlight they retraced the afternoon's path, up the dusty road rife with honeysuckle, through the gate and up the black tunnel of the drive to the lightless house, where he sat on the mule and felt the rough warp of the rug drag across his thighs and vanish.

"Don't you want me to help?" he whispered. His father did not answer and now he heard again that stiff foot striking the hollow portico with that wooden and clocklike deliberation, that outrageous overstatement of the weight it carried. The rug, hunched, not flung (the boy could tell that even in the darkness) from his father's shoulder struck the angle of wall and floor with a sound unbelievably loud, thunderous, then the foot again, unhurried and enormous; a light came on in the house and the boy sat, tense, breathing steadily and quietly and just a little fast, though the foot itself did not increase its beat at all, descending the steps now; now the boy could see him.

"Don't you want to ride now?" he whispered. "We kin both ride now," the 60
light within the house altering now, flaring up and sinking. *He's coming down the stairs now,* he thought. He had already ridden the mule up beside the horse block; presently his father was up behind him and he doubled the reins over and slashed the mule across the neck, but before the animal could begin to trot the hard, thin arm came round him, the hard, knotted hand jerking the mule back to a walk.

In the first red rays of the sun they were in the lot, putting plow gear on the mules. This time the sorrel mare was in the lot before he heard it at all, the rider collarless and even bareheaded, trembling, speaking in a shaking voice as the woman in the house had done, his father merely looking up once before stooping again to the hame he was buckling, so that the man on the mare spoke to his stooping back:

"You must realize you have ruined that rug. Wasn't there anybody here, any of your women . . ." he ceased, shaking, the boy watching him, the older brother leaning now in the stable door, chewing, blinking slowly and steadily at nothing apparently. "It cost a hundred dollars. But you never had a hundred dollars. You never will. So I'm going to charge you twenty bushels of corn against your crop. I'll add it in your contract and when you come to the commissary you can sign it. That won't keep Mrs. de Spain quiet but maybe it will teach you to wipe your feet off before you enter her house again."

Then he was gone. The boy looked at his father, who still had not spoken or even looked up again, who was now adjusting the logger-head in the hame.

"Pap," he said. His father looked at him—the inscrutable face, the shaggy brows beneath which the gray eyes glinted coldly. Suddenly the boy went toward him, fast, stopping as suddenly. "You done the best you could!" he cried. "If he wanted hit done different why didn't he wait and tell you how? He won't git no twenty bushels! He won't git none! We'll gether hit and hide hit! I kin watch . . ."

65 "Did you put the cutter back in that straight stock like I told you?"

"No, sir," he said.

"Then go do it."

That was Wednesday. During the rest of that week he worked steadily, at what was within his scope and some which was beyond it, with an industry that did not need to be driven nor even commanded twice; he had this from his mother, with the difference that some at least of what he did he liked to do, such as splitting wood with the half-size axe which his mother and aunt had earned, or saved money somehow, to present him with at Christmas. In company with the two older women (and on one afternoon, even one of the sisters), he built pens for the shoat and the cow which were a part of his father's contract with the landlord, and one afternoon, his father being absent, gone somewhere on one of the mules, he went to the field.

They were running a middle buster[3] now, his brother holding the plow straight while he handled the reins, and walking beside the straining mule, the rich black soil shearing cool and damp against his bare ankles, he thought *Maybe this is the end of it. Maybe even that twenty bushels that seems hard to have to pay for just a rug will be a cheap price for him to stop forever and always from being what he used to be;* thinking, dreaming now, so that his brother had to speak sharply to him to mind the mule: *Maybe he even won't collect the twenty bushels. Maybe it will all add up and balance and vanish—corn, rug, fire; the terror and grief, the being pulled two ways like between two teams of horses—gone, done with for ever and ever.*

70 Then it was Saturday; he looked up from beneath the mule he was harnessing and saw his father in the black coat and hat. "Not that," his father said. "The wagon gear." And then, two hours later, sitting in the wagon bed behind his father and brother on the seat, the wagon accomplished a final curve, and he saw the weathered paintless store with its tattered tobacco- and patent-medicine posters and the tethered wagons and saddle animals below the gallery. He mounted the gnawed steps behind his father and brother, and there again was the lane of quiet, watching faces for the three of them to walk through. He saw the man in spectacles sitting at the plank table and he did not need to be told this was a Justice of the Peace; he sent one glare of fierce, exultant, partisan defiance at the man in collar and cravat now, whom he had seen but twice before in his life,

3. Double moldboard plow that throws a ridge of earth both ways.

and that on a galloping horse, who now wore on his face an expression not of rage but of amazed unbelief which the boy could not have known was at the incredible circumstance of being sued by one of his own tenants, and came and stood against his father and cried at the Justice: "He ain't done it! He ain't burnt . . ."

"Go back to the wagon," his father said.

"Burnt?" the Justice said. "Do I understand this rug was burned too?"

"Does anybody here claim it was?" his father said. "Go back to the wagon." But he did not, he merely retreated to the rear of the room, crowded as that other had been, but not to sit down this time, instead, to stand pressing among the motionless bodies, listening to the voices:

"And you claim twenty bushels of corn is too high for the damage you did to the rug?"

"He brought the rug to me and said he wanted the tracks washed out of it. I 75
washed the tracks out and took the rug back to him."

"But you didn't carry the rug back to him in the same condition it was in before you made the tracks on it."

His father did not answer, and now for perhaps half a minute there was no sound at all save that of breathing, the faint, steady suspiration of complete and intent listening.

"You decline to answer that, Mr. Snopes?" Again his father did not answer. "I'm going to find against you, Mr. Snopes. I'm going to find that you were responsible for the injury to Major de Spain's rug and hold you liable for it. But twenty bushels of corn seems a little high for a man in your circumstances to have to pay. Major de Spain claims it cost a hundred dollars. October corn will be worth about fifty cents. I figure that if Major de Spain can stand a ninety-five dollar loss on something he paid cash for, you can stand a five-dollar loss you haven't earned yet. I hold you in damages to Major de Spain to the amount of ten bushels of corn over and above your contract with him, to be paid to him out of your crop at gathering time. Court adjourned."

It had taken no time hardly, the morning was but half begun. He thought they would return home and perhaps back to the field, since they were late, far behind all other farmers. But instead his father passed on behind the wagon, merely indicating with his hand for the older brother to follow with it, and crossed the road toward the blacksmith shop opposite, pressing on after his father, overtaking him, speaking, whispering up at the harsh, calm face beneath the weathered hat: "He won't git no ten bushels neither. He won't git one. We'll . . ." until his father glanced for an instant down at him, the face absolutely calm, the grizzled eyebrows tangled above the cold eyes, the voice almost pleasant, almost gentle:

"You think so? Well, we'll wait till October anyway." 80

The matter of the wagon—the setting of a spoke or two and the tightening of the tires—did not take long either, the business of the tires accomplished by driving the wagon into the spring branch behind the shop and letting it stand there, the mules nuzzling into the water from time to time, and the boy on the seat with the idle reins, looking up the slope and through the sooty tunnel of the shed where the slow hammer rang and where his father sat on an upended cypress bolt, easily, either talking or listening, still sitting there when the boy brought the dripping wagon up out of the branch and halted it before the door.

"Take them on to the shade and hitch," his father said. He did so and returned. His father and the smith and a third man squatting on his heels inside the door were talking, about crops and animals; the boy, squatting too in the ammoniac dust and hoof-parings and scales of rust, heard his father tell a long and unhurried story out of the time before the birth of the older brother even when he had been a professional horsetrader. And then his father came up beside him where he stood before a tattered last year's circus poster on the other side of the store, gazing rapt and quiet at the scarlet horses, the incredible poisings and convolutions of tulle and tights and the painted leers of comedians, and said, "It's time to eat."

But not at home. Squatting beside his brother against the front wall, he watched his father emerge from the store and produce from a paper sack a segment of cheese and divide it carefully and deliberately into three with his pocket knife and produce crackers from the same sack. They all three squatted on the gallery and ate, slowly, without talking; then in the store again, they drank from a tin dipper tepid water smelling of the cedar bucket and of living beech trees. And still they did not go home. It was a horse lot this time, a tall rail fence upon and along which men stood and sat and out of which one by one horses were led, to be walked and trotted and then cantered back and forth along the road while the slow swapping and buying went on and the sun began to slant westward, they—the three of them—watching and listening, the older brother with his muddy eyes and his steady, inevitable tobacco, the father commenting now and then on certain of the animals, to no one in particular.

It was after sundown when they reached home. They ate supper by lamplight, then, sitting on the doorstep, the boy watched the night fully accomplish, listening to the whippoorwills and the frogs, when he heard his mother's voice: "Abner! No! No! Oh, God. Oh, God. Abner!" and he rose, whirled, and saw the altered light through the door where a candle stub now burned in a bottle neck on the table and his father, still in the hat and coat, at once formal and burlesque as though dressed carefully for some shabby and ceremonial violence, emptying the reservoir of the lamp back into the five-gallon kerosene can from which it had been filled, while the mother tugged at his arm until he shifted the lamp to the other hand and flung her back, not savagely or viciously, just hard, into the wall, her hands flung out against the wall for balance, her mouth open and in her face the same quality of hopeless despair as had been in her voice. Then his father saw him standing in the door.

85 "Go to the barn and get that can of oil we were oiling the wagon with," he said. The boy did not move. Then he could speak.

"What . . ." he cried. "What are you . . ."

"Go get that oil," his father said. "Go."

Then he was moving, running, outside the house, toward the stable: this the old habit, the old blood which he had not been permitted to choose for himself, which had been bequeathed him willy nilly and which had run for so long (and who knew where, battening on what of outrage and savagery and lust) before it came to him. *I could keep on,* he thought. *I could run on and on and never look back, never need to see his face again. Only I can't. I can't,* the rusted can in his hand now, the liquid sploshing in it as he ran back to the house and into it, into the sound of his mother's weeping in the next room, and handed the can to his father.

"Ain't you going to even send a nigger?" he cried. "At least you sent a nigger before!"

This time his father didn't strike him. The hand came even faster than the blow had, the same hand which had set the can on the table with almost excruciating care flashing from the can toward him too quick for him to follow it, gripping him by the back of his shirt and on to tiptoe before he had seen it quit the can, the face stooping at him in breathless and frozen ferocity, the cold, dead voice speaking over him to the older brother, who leaned against the table, chewing with that steady, curious, sidewise motion of cows: 90

"Empty the can into the big one and go on. I'll catch up with you."

"Better tie him up to the bedpost," the brother said.

"Do like I told you," the father said. Then the boy was moving, his bunched shirt and the hard, bony hand between his shoulder-blades, his toes just touching the floor, across the room and into the other one, past the sisters sitting with spread heavy thighs in the two chairs over the cold hearth, and to where his mother and aunt sat side by side on the bed, the aunt's arms about his mother's shoulders.

"Hold him," the father said. The aunt made a startled movement. "Not you," the father said. "Lennie. Take hold of him. I want to see you do it." His mother took him by the wrist. "You'll hold him better than that. If he gets loose don't you know what he is going to do? He will go up yonder." He jerked his head toward the road. "Maybe I'd better tie him."

"I'll hold him," his mother whispered. 95

"See you do then." Then his father was gone, the stiff foot heavy and measured upon the boards, ceasing at last.

Then he began to struggle. His mother caught him in both arms, he jerking and wrenching at them. He would be stronger in the end, he knew that. But he had no time to wait for it. "Lemme go!" he cried. "I don't want to have to hit you!"

"Let him go!" the aunt said. "If he don't go, before God, I am going up there myself!"

"Don't you see I can't?" his mother cried. "Sarty! Sarty! No! No! Help me, Lizzie!"

Then he was free. His aunt grasped at him but it was too late. He whirled, running, his mother stumbled forward on to her knees behind him, crying to the nearer sister: "Catch him, Net! Catch him!" But that was too late too, the sister (the sisters were twins, born at the same time, yet either of them now gave the impression of being, encompassing as much living meat and volume and weight as any other two of the family) not yet having begun to rise from the chair, her head, face, alone merely turned, presenting to him in the flying instant an astonishing expanse of young female features untroubled by any surprise even, wearing only an expression of bovine interest. Then he was out of the room, out of the house, in the mild dust of the starlit road and the heavy rifeness of honeysuckle, the pale ribbon unspooling with terrific slowness under his running feet, reaching the gate at last and turning in, running, his heart and lungs drumming, on up the drive toward the lighted house, the lighted door. He 100 did not knock, he burst in, sobbing for breath, incapable for the moment of speech; he saw the astonished face of the Negro in the linen jacket without knowing when the Negro had appeared.

"De Spain!" he cried, panted. "Where's . . ." then he saw the white man too emerging from a white door down the hall. "Barn!" he cried. "Barn!"

"What?" the white man said. "Barn?"

"Yes!" the boy cried. "Barn!"

"Catch him!" the white man shouted.

But it was too late this time too. The Negro grasped his shirt, but the entire sleeve, rotten with washing, carried away, and he was out that door too and in the drive again, and had actually never ceased to run even while he was screaming into the white man's face.

Behind him the white man was shouting, "My horse! Fetch my horse!" and he thought for an instant of cutting across the park and climbing the fence into the road, but he did not know the park nor how high the vine-massed fence might be and he dared not risk it. So he ran on down the drive, blood and breath roaring; presently he was in the road again though he could not see it. He could not hear either: the galloping mare was almost upon him before he heard her, and even then he held his course, as if the very urgency of his wild grief and need must in a moment more find his wings, waiting until the ultimate instant to hurl himself aside and into the weed-choked roadside ditch as the horse thundered past and on, for an instant in furious silhouette against the stars, the tranquil early summer night sky which, even before the shape of the horse and rider vanished, stained abruptly and violently upward: a long, swirling roar incredible and soundless, blotting the stars, and he springing up and into the road again, running again, knowing it was too late yet still running even after he heard the shot and, an instant later, two shots, pausing now without knowing he had ceased to run, crying "Pap! Pap!", running again before he knew he had begun to run, stumbling, tripping over something and scrabbling up again without ceasing to run, looking backward over his shoulder at the glare as he got up, running on among the invisible trees, panting, sobbing, "Father! Father!"

At midnight he was sitting on the crest of a hill. He did not know it was midnight and he did not know how far he had come. But there was no glare behind him now and he sat now, his back toward what he had called home for four days anyhow, his face toward the dark woods which he would enter when breath was strong again, small, shaking steadily in the chill darkness, hugging himself into the remainder of his thin, rotten shirt, the grief and despair now no longer terror and fear but just grief and despair. *Father. My father,* he thought. "He was brave!" he cried suddenly, aloud but not loud, no more than a whisper: "He was! He was in the war! He was in Colonel Sartoris' cav'ry!" not knowing that his father had gone to that war a private in the fine old European sense, wearing no uniform, admitting the authority of and giving fidelity to no man or army or flag, going to war as Malbrouck[4] himself did: for booty—it meant nothing and less than nothing to him if it were enemy booty or his own.

4. John Churchill, the first duke of Marlborough (1650–1722), an English general whose name became distorted as Malbrough and Malbrouch in English and French popular songs celebrating his exploits.

The slow constellations wheeled on. It would be dawn and then sun-up after a while and he would be hungry. But that would be to-morrow and now he was only cold, and walking would cure that. His breathing was easier now and he decided to get up and go on, and then he found that he had been asleep because he knew it was almost dawn, the night almost over. He could tell that from the whippoorwills. They were everywhere now among the dark trees below him, constant and inflectioned and ceaseless, so that, as the instant for giving over to the day birds drew nearer and nearer, there was no interval at all between them. He got up. He was a little stiff, but walking would cure that too as it would the cold, and soon there would be the sun. He went on down the hill, toward the dark woods within which the liquid silver voices of the birds called unceasing—the rapid and urgent beating of the urgent and quiring heart of the late spring night. He did not look back.

1939

QUESTIONS

1. At one point in Barn Burning, Sarty thinks that "*maybe*" his father "*couldn't help but be*" what he is (par. 40). What *is* Abner Snopes? What desires, motives, values, and views—especially of justice—seem to drive and explain him? What does the story imply about how and why he has become the man he is? What might be admirable, as well as abhorrent, about him? How does the narrative point of view shape your understanding of, and attitude toward, Abner?
2. How is Sarty characterized? How is this characterization affected by the multiple flashforwards in the story and by the way Sarty's thoughts are presented? Does Sarty change over the course of the story? How and why does he change or not change?
3. What do each of the minor characters contribute to the story, especially Sarty's mother, sisters, and older brother?

TONI MORRISON
(b. 1931)

Recitatif[1]

Born in Lorain, Ohio, a steel town on the shores of Lake Erie, Chloe Anthony Wofford was the first member of her family to go to college, graduating from Howard University in 1953 and earning an MA from Cornell. She taught at both Texas Southern University and at Howard before becoming an editor at Random House, where she worked for nearly twenty years. In such novels as *The Bluest Eye* (1969), *Sula* (1973), *Song of Solomon* (1977), *Beloved* (1987), and *Paradise* (1998), Morrison traces the problems and possibilities faced by black Americans struggling with slavery and its aftermath in the United States. More recent work includes her eighth novel, *Love* (2003); two picture books for children co-authored with her son, Slade—*The Bog Box* (1999) and *Book of Mean People* (2002); a book for young adults, *Remember:*

1. In classical music such as opera, a vocal passage that is sung in a speechlike manner.

The Journey to School Integration (2004); and *What Moves at the Margin: Selected Nonfiction* (2008). In 1993, Morrison became the first African American author to win the Nobel Prize for Literature.

My mother danced all night and Roberta's was sick. That's why we were taken to St. Bonny's. People want to put their arms around you when you tell them you were in a shelter, but it really wasn't bad. No big long room with one hundred beds like Bellevue.[2] There were four to a room, and when Roberta and me came, there was a shortage of state kids, so we were the only ones assigned to 406 and could go from bed to bed if we wanted to. And we wanted to, too. We changed beds every night and for the whole four months we were there we never picked one out as our own permanent bed.

It didn't start out that way. The minute I walked in and the Big Bozo introduced us, I got sick to my stomach. It was one thing to be taken out of your own bed early in the morning—it was something else to be stuck in a strange place with a girl from a whole other race. And Mary, that's my mother, she was right. Every now and then she would stop dancing long enough to tell me something important and one of the things she said was that they never washed their hair and they smelled funny. Roberta sure did. Smell funny, I mean. So when the Big Bozo (nobody ever called her Mrs. Itkin, just like nobody ever said St. Bonaventure)—when she said, "Twyla, this is Roberta. Roberta, this is Twyla. Make each other welcome." I said, "My mother won't like you putting me in here."

"Good," said Bozo. "Maybe then she'll come and take you home."

How's that for mean? If Roberta had laughed I would have killed her, but she didn't. She just walked over to the window and stood with her back to us.

5 "Turn around," said the Bozo. "Don't be rude. Now Twyla. Roberta. When you hear a loud buzzer, that's the call for dinner. Come down to the first floor. Any fights and no movie." And then, just to make sure we knew what we would be missing, *"The Wizard of Oz."*

Roberta must have thought I meant that my mother would be mad about my being put in the shelter. Not about rooming with her, because as soon as Bozo left she came over to me and said, "Is your mother sick too?"

"No," I said. "She just likes to dance all night."

"Oh," she nodded her head and I liked the way she understood things so fast. So for the moment it didn't matter that we looked like salt and pepper standing there and that's what the other kids called us sometimes. We were eight years old and got F's all the time. Me because I couldn't remember what I read or what the teacher said. And Roberta because she couldn't read at all and didn't even listen to the teacher. She wasn't good at anything except jacks, at which she was a killer: pow scoop pow scoop pow scoop.

We didn't like each other all that much at first, but nobody else wanted to play with us because we weren't real orphans with beautiful dead parents in the sky. We were dumped. Even the New York City Puerto Ricans and the upstate Indians ignored us. All kinds of kids were in there, black ones, white ones, even

2. Large New York City hospital best known for its psychiatric wards.

two Koreans. The food was good, though. At least I thought so. Roberta hated it and left whole pieces of things on her plate: Spam, Salisbury steak—even jello with fruit cocktail in it, and she didn't care if I ate what she wouldn't. Mary's idea of supper was popcorn and a can of Yoo-Hoo. Hot mashed potatoes and two weenies was like Thanksgiving for me.

10 It really wasn't bad, St. Bonny's. The big girls on the second floor pushed us around now and then. But that was all. They wore lipstick and eyebrow pencil and wobbled their knees while they watched TV. Fifteen, sixteen, even, some of them were. They were put-out girls, scared runaways most of them. Poor little girls who fought their uncles off but looked tough to us, and mean. God did they look mean. The staff tried to keep them separate from the younger children, but sometimes they caught us watching them in the orchard where they played radios and danced with each other. They'd light out after us and pull our hair or twist our arms. We were scared of them, Roberta and me, but neither of us wanted the other one to know it. So we got a good list of dirty names we could shout back when we ran from them through the orchard. I used to dream a lot and almost always the orchard was there. Two acres, four maybe, of these little apple trees. Hundreds of them. Empty and crooked like beggar women when I first came to St. Bonny's but fat with flowers when I left. I don't know why I dreamt about that orchard so much. Nothing really happened there. Nothing all that important, I mean. Just the big girls dancing and playing the radio. Roberta and me watching. Maggie fell down there once. The kitchen woman with legs like parentheses. And the big girls laughed at her. We should have helped her up, I know, but we were scared of those girls with lipstick and eyebrow pencil. Maggie couldn't talk. The kids said she had her tongue cut out, but I think she was just born that way: mute. She was old and sandy-colored and she worked in the kitchen. I don't know if she was nice or not. I just remember her legs like parentheses and how she rocked when she walked. She worked from early in the morning till two o'clock, and if she was late, if she had too much cleaning and didn't get out till two-fifteen or so, she'd cut through the orchard so she wouldn't miss her bus and have to wait another hour. She wore this really stupid little hat—a kid's hat with ear flaps—and she wasn't much taller than we were. A really awful little hat. Even for a mute, it was dumb—dressing like a kid and never saying anything at all.

"But what about if somebody tries to kill her?" I used to wonder about that. "Or what if she wants to cry? Can she cry?"

"Sure," Roberta said. "But just tears. No sounds come out."

"She can't scream?"

"Nope. Nothing."

15 "Can she hear?"

"I guess."

"Let's call her," I said. And we did.

"Dummy! Dummy!" She never turned her head.

"Bow legs! Bow legs!" Nothing. She just rocked on, the chin straps of her baby-boy hat swaying from side to side. I think we were wrong. I think she could hear and didn't let on. And it shames me even now to think there was somebody in there after all who heard us call her those names and couldn't tell on us.

20 We got along all right, Roberta and me. Changed beds every night, got F's in civics and communication skills and gym. The Bozo was disappointed in us, she said. Out of 130 of us state cases, 90 were under twelve. Almost all were real orphans with beautiful dead parents in the sky. We were the only ones dumped and the only ones with F's in three classes including gym. So we got along—what with her leaving whole pieces of things on her plate and being nice about not asking questions.

I think it was the day before Maggie fell down that we found out our mothers were coming to visit us on the same Sunday. We had been at the shelter twenty-eight days (Roberta twenty-eight and a half) and this was their first visit with us. Our mothers would come at ten o'clock in time for chapel, then lunch with us in the teachers' lounge. I thought if my dancing mother met her sick mother it might be good for her. And Roberta thought her sick mother would get a big bang out of a dancing one. We got excited about it and curled each other's hair. After breakfast we sat on the bed watching the road from the window. Roberta's socks were still wet. She washed them the night before and put them on the radiator to dry. They hadn't, but she put them on anyway because their tops were so pretty—scalloped in pink. Each of us had a purple construction-paper basket that we had made in craft class. Mine had a yellow crayon rabbit on it. Roberta's had eggs with wiggly lines of color. Inside were cellophane grass and just the jelly beans because I'd eaten the two marshmallow eggs they gave us. The Big Bozo came herself to get us. Smiling she told us we looked very nice and to come downstairs. We were so surprised by the smile we'd never seen before, neither of us moved.

"Don't you want to see your mommies?"

I stood up first and spilled the jelly beans all over the floor. Bozo's smile disappeared while we scrambled to get the candy up off the floor and put it back in the grass.

She escorted us downstairs to the first floor, where the other girls were lining up to file into the chapel. A bunch of grown-ups stood to one side. Viewers mostly. The old biddies who wanted servants and the fags who wanted company looking for children they might want to adopt. Once in a while a grandmother. Almost never anybody young or anybody whose face wouldn't scare you in the night. Because if any of the real orphans had young relatives they wouldn't be real orphans. I saw Mary right away. She had on those green slacks I hated and hated even more now because didn't she know we were going to chapel? And that fur jacket with the pocket linings so ripped she had to pull to get her hands out of them. But her face was pretty—like always, and she smiled and waved like she was the little girl looking for her mother—not me.

25 I walked slowly, trying not to drop the jelly beans and hoping the paper handle would hold. I had to use my last Chiclet because by the time I finished cutting everything out, all the Elmer's was gone. I am left-handed and the scissors never worked for me. It didn't matter, though; I might just as well have chewed the gum. Mary dropped to her knees and grabbed me, mashing the basket, the jelly beans, and the grass into her ratty fur jacket.

"Twyla, baby. Twyla, baby!"

I could have killed her. Already I heard the big girls in the orchard the next time saying, "Twyyyyyla, baby!" But I couldn't stay mad at Mary while she was smiling and hugging me and smelling of Lady Esther dusting powder. I wanted to stay buried in her fur all day.

To tell the truth I forgot about Roberta. Mary and I got in line for the traipse into chapel and I was feeling proud because she looked so beautiful even in those ugly green slacks that made her behind stick out. A pretty mother on earth is better than a beautiful dead one in the sky even if she did leave you all alone to go dancing.

I felt a tap on my shoulder, turned, and saw Roberta smiling. I smiled back, but not too much lest somebody think this visit was the biggest thing that ever happened in my life. Then Roberta said, "Mother, I want you to meet my roommate, Twyla. And that's Twyla's mother."

30 I looked up it seemed for miles. She was big. Bigger than any man and on her chest was the biggest cross I'd ever seen. I swear it was six inches long each way. And in the crook of her arm was the biggest Bible ever made.

Mary, simple-minded as ever, grinned and tried to yank her hand out of the pocket with the raggedy lining—to shake hands, I guess. Roberta's mother looked down at me and then looked down at Mary too. She didn't say anything, just grabbed Roberta with her Bible-free hand and stepped out of line, walking quickly to the rear of it. Mary was still grinning because she's not too swift when it comes to what's really going on. Then this light bulb goes off in her head and she says "That bitch!" really loud and us almost in the chapel now. Organ music whining; the Bonny Angels singing sweetly. Everybody in the world turned around to look. And Mary would have kept it up—kept calling names if I hadn't squeezed her hand as hard as I could. That helped a little, but she still twitched and crossed and uncrossed her legs all through service. Even groaned a couple of times. Why did I think she would come there and act right? Slacks. No hat like the grandmothers and viewers, and groaning all the while. When we stood for hymns she kept her mouth shut. Wouldn't even look at the words on the page. She actually reached in her purse for a mirror to check her lipstick. All I could think of was that she really needed to be killed. The sermon lasted a year, and I knew the real orphans were looking smug again.

We were supposed to have lunch in the teachers' lounge, but Mary didn't bring anything, so we picked fur and cellophane grass off the mashed jelly beans and ate them. I could have killed her. I sneaked a look at Roberta. Her mother had brought chicken legs and ham sandwiches and oranges and a whole box of chocolate-covered grahams. Roberta drank milk from a thermos while her mother read the Bible to her.

Things are not right. The wrong food is always with the wrong people. Maybe that's why I got into waitress work later—to match up the right people with the right food. Roberta just let those chicken legs sit there, but she did bring a stack of grahams up to me later when the visit was over. I think she was sorry that her mother would not shake my mother's hand. And I liked that and I liked the fact that she didn't say a word about Mary groaning all the way through the service and not bringing any lunch.

Roberta left in May when the apple trees were heavy and white. On her last day we went to the orchard to watch the big girls smoke and dance by the radio. It didn't matter that they said, "Twyyyyyla, baby." We sat on the ground and breathed. Lady Esther. Apple blossoms. I still go soft when I smell one or the other. Roberta was going home. The big cross and the big Bible was coming to get her and she seemed sort of glad and sort of not. I thought I would die in that room of four beds without her and I knew Bozo had plans to move some other dumped kid in there with me. Roberta promised to write every day, which was really sweet of her because she couldn't read a lick so how could she write anybody. I would have drawn pictures and sent them to her but she never gave me her address. Little by little she faded. Her wet socks with the pink scalloped tops and her big serious-looking eyes—that's all I could catch when I tried to bring her to mind.

I was working behind the counter at the Howard Johnson's on the Thruway just before the Kingston exit. Not a bad job. Kind of a long ride from Newburgh,[3] but okay once I got there. Mine was the second night shift—eleven to seven. Very light until a Greyhound checked in for breakfast around six-thirty. At that hour the sun was all the way clear of the hills behind the restaurant. The place looked better at night—more like shelter—but I loved it when the sun broke in, even if it did show all the cracks in the vinyl and the speckled floor looked dirty no matter what the mop boy did.

It was August and a bus crowd was just unloading. They would stand around a long while: going to the john, and looking at gifts and junk-for-sale machines, reluctant to sit down so soon. Even to eat. I was trying to fill the coffee pots and get them all situated on the electric burners when I saw her. She was sitting in a booth smoking a cigarette with two guys smothered in head and facial hair. Her own hair was so big and wild I could hardly see her face. But the eyes. I would know them anywhere. She had on a powder-blue halter and shorts outfit and earrings the size of bracelets. Talk about lipstick and eyebrow pencil. She made the big girls look like nuns. I couldn't get off the counter until seven o'clock, but I kept watching the booth in case they got up to leave before that. My replacement was on time for a change, so I counted and stacked my receipts as fast as I could and signed off. I walked over to the booth, smiling and wondering if she would remember me. Or even if she wanted to remember me. Maybe she didn't want to be reminded of St. Bonny's or to have anybody know she was ever there. I know I never talked about it to anybody.

I put my hands in my apron pockets and leaned against the back of the booth facing them.

"Roberta? Roberta Fisk?"

She looked up. "Yeah?"

"Twyla."

She squinted for a second and then said, "Wow."

"Remember me?"

"Sure. Hey. Wow."

"It's been a while," I said, and gave a smile to the two hairy guys.

"Yeah. Wow. You work here?"

"Yeah," I said. "I live in Newburgh."

"Newburgh? No kidding?" She laughed then a private laugh that included the guys but only the guys, and they laughed with her. What could I do but laugh too and wonder why I was standing there with my knees showing out from

3. City on the Hudson River north of New York City.

under that uniform. Without looking I could see the blue and white triangle on my head, my hair shapeless in a net, my ankles thick in white oxfords. Nothing could have been less sheer than my stockings. There was this silence that came down right after I laughed. A silence it was her turn to fill up. With introductions, maybe, to her boyfriends or an invitation to sit down and have a Coke. Instead she lit a cigarette off the one she'd just finished and said, "We're on our way to the Coast. He's got an appointment with Hendrix." She gestured casually toward the boy next to her.

"Hendrix? Fantastic," I said. "Really fantastic. What's she doing now?"

Roberta coughed on her cigarette and the two guys rolled their eyes up at the ceiling.

"Hendrix. Jimi Hendrix, asshole. He's only the biggest—Oh, wow. Forget it." 50

I was dismissed without anyone saying goodbye, so I thought I would do it for her.

"How's your mother?" I asked. Her grin cracked her whole face. She swallowed. "Fine," she said. "How's yours?"

"Pretty as a picture," I said and turned away. The backs of my knees were damp. Howard Johnson's really was a dump in the sunlight.

James is as comfortable as a house slipper. He liked my cooking and I liked his big loud family. They have lived in Newburgh all of their lives and talk about it the way people do who have always known a home. His grandmother is a porch swing older than his father and when they talk about streets and avenues and buildings they call them names they no longer have. They still call the A & P[4] Rico's because it stands on property once a mom and pop store owned by Mr. Rico. And they call the new community college Town Hall because it once was. My mother-in-law puts up jelly and cucumbers and buys butter wrapped in cloth from a dairy. James and his father talk about fishing and baseball and I can see them all together on the Hudson in a raggedy skiff. Half the population of Newburgh is on welfare now, but to my husband's family it was still some upstate paradise of a time long past. A time of ice houses and vegetable wagons, coal furnaces and children weeding gardens. When our son was born my mother-in-law gave me the crib blanket that had been hers.

But the town they remembered had changed. Something quick was in the 55
air. Magnificent old houses, so ruined they had become shelter for squatters and rent risks, were bought and renovated. Smart IBM[5] people moved out of their suburbs back into the city and put shutters up and herb gardens in their backyards. A brochure came in the mail announcing the opening of a Food Emporium. Gourmet food it said—and listed items the rich IBM crowd would want. It was located in a new mall at the edge of town and I drove out to shop there one day—just to see. It was late in June. After the tulips were gone and the Queen Elizabeth roses were open everywhere. I trailed my cart along the aisle tossing in smoked oysters and Robert's sauce and things I knew would sit in my cupboard for years. Only when I found some Klondike ice cream bars did

4. Supermarket, part of a chain originally known as the Great Atlantic and Pacific Tea Company.

5. The International Business Machine Corporation, which had its executive headquarters in Poughkeepsie, New York.

I feel less guilty about spending James's fireman's salary so foolishly. My father-in-law ate them with the same gusto little Joseph did.

Waiting in the check-out line I heard a voice say, "Twyla!"

The classical music piped over the aisles had affected me and the woman leaning toward me was dressed to kill. Diamonds on her hand, a smart white summer dress. "I'm Mrs. Benson," I said.

"Ho. Ho. The Big Bozo," she sang.

For a split second I didn't know what she was talking about. She had a bunch of asparagus and two cartons of fancy water.

"Roberta!"

"Right."

"For heaven's sake. Roberta."

"You look great," she said.

"So do you. Where are you? Here? In Newburgh?"

"Yes. Over in Annandale."

I was opening my mouth to say more when the cashier called my attention to her empty counter.

"Meet you outside." Roberta pointed her finger and went into the express line.

I placed the groceries and kept myself from glancing around to check Roberta's progress. I remembered Howard Johnson's and looking for a chance to speak only to be greeted with a stingy "wow." But she was waiting for me and her huge hair was sleek now, smooth around a small, nicely shaped head. Shoes, dress, everything lovely and summery and rich. I was dying to know what happened to her, how she got from Jimi Hendrix to Annandale, a neighborhood full of doctors and IBM executives. Easy, I thought. Everything is so easy for them. They think they own the world.

"How long," I asked her. "How long have you been here?"

"A year. I got married to a man who lives here. And you, you're married too, right? Benson, you said."

"Yeah. James Benson."

"And is he nice?"

"Oh, is he nice?"

"Well, is he?" Roberta's eyes were steady as though she really meant the question and wanted an answer.

"He's wonderful, Roberta. Wonderful."

"So you're happy."

"Very."

"That's good," she said and nodded her head. "I always hoped you'd be happy. Any kids? I know you have kids."

"One. A boy. How about you?"

"Four."

"Four?"

She laughed. "Step kids. He's a widower."

"Oh."

"Got a minute? Let's have a coffee."

I thought about the Klondikes melting and the inconvenience of going all the way to my car and putting the bags in the trunk. Served me right for buying all that stuff I didn't need. Roberta was ahead of me.

"Put them in my car. It's right here."

And then I saw the dark blue limousine.

"You married a Chinaman?"

"No," she laughed. "He's the driver."

"Oh, my. If the Big Bozo could see you now." 90

We both giggled. Really giggled. Suddenly, in just a pulse beat, twenty years disappeared and all of it came rushing back. The big girls (whom we called gar girls—Roberta's misheard word for the evil stone faces described in a civics class) there dancing in the orchard, the ploppy mashed potatoes, the double weenies, the Spam with pineapple. We went into the coffee shop holding on to one another and I tried to think why we were glad to see each other this time and not before. Once, twelve years ago, we passed like strangers. A black girl and a white girl meeting in a Howard Johnson's on the road and having nothing to say. One in a blue and white triangle waitress hat—the other on her way to see Hendrix. Now we were behaving like sisters separated for much too long. Those four short months were nothing in time. Maybe it was the thing itself. Just being there, together. Two little girls who knew what nobody else in the world knew—how not to ask questions. How to believe what had to be believed. There was politeness in that reluctance and generosity as well. Is your mother sick too? No, she dances all night. Oh—and an understanding nod.

We sat in a booth by the window and fell into recollection like veterans.

"Did you ever learn to read?"

"Watch." She picked up the menu. "Special of the day. Cream of corn soup. Entrées. Two dots and a wriggly line. Quiche. Chef salad, scallops . . ."

I was laughing and applauding when the waitress came up. 95

"Remember the Easter baskets?"

"And how we tried to *introduce* them?"

"Your mother with that cross like two telephone poles."

"And yours with those tight slacks."

We laughed so loudly heads turned and made the laughter harder to suppress. 100

"What happened to the Jimi Hendrix date?"

Roberta made a blow-out sound with her lips.

"When he died I thought about you."

"Oh, you heard about him finally?"

"Finally. Come on, I was a small-town country waitress." 105

"And I was a small-town country dropout. God, were we wild. I still don't know how I got out of there alive."

"But you did."

"I did. I really did. Now I'm Mrs. Kenneth Norton."

"Sounds like a mouthful."

"It is." 110

"Servants and all?"

Roberta held up two fingers.

"Ow! What does he do?"

"Computers and stuff. What do I know?"

"I don't remember a hell of a lot from those days, but Lord, St. Bonny's is as clear as daylight. Remember Maggie? The day she fell down and those gar girls laughed at her?" 115

Roberta looked up from her salad and stared at me. "Maggie didn't fall," she said.

"Yes, she did. You remember."

"No, Twyla. They knocked her down. Those girls pushed her down and tore her clothes. In the orchard."

"I don't—that's not what happened."

"Sure it is. In the orchard. Remember how scared we were?"

"Wait a minute. I don't remember any of that."

"And Bozo was fired."

"You're crazy. She was there when I left. You left before me."

"I went back. You weren't there when they fired Bozo."

"What?"

"Twice. Once for a year when I was about ten, another for two months when I was fourteen. That's when I ran away."

"You ran away from St. Bonny's?"

"I had to. What do you want? Me dancing in that orchard?"

"Are you sure about Maggie?"

"Of course I'm sure. You've blocked it, Twyla. It happened. Those girls had behavior problems, you know."

"Didn't they, though. But why can't I remember the Maggie thing?"

"Believe me. It happened. And we were there."

"Who did you room with when you went back?" I asked her as if I would know her. The Maggie thing was troubling me.

"Creeps. They tickled themselves in the night."

My ears were itching and I wanted to go home suddenly. This was all very well but she couldn't just comb her hair, wash her face and pretend everything was hunky-dory. After the Howard Johnson's snub. And no apology. Nothing.

"Were you on dope or what that time at Howard Johnson's?" I tried to make my voice sound friendlier than I felt.

"Maybe, a little. I never did drugs much. Why?"

"I don't know; you acted sort of like you didn't want to know me then."

"Oh, Twyla, you know how it was in those days: black—white. You know how everything was."

But I didn't know. I thought it was just the opposite. Busloads of blacks and whites came into Howard Johnson's together. They roamed together then: students, musicians, lovers, protesters. You got to see everything at Howard Johnson's and blacks were very friendly with whites in those days. But sitting there with nothing on my plate but two hard tomato wedges wondering about the melting Klondikes it seemed childish remembering the slight. We went to her car, and with the help of the driver, got my stuff into my station wagon.

"We'll keep in touch this time," she said.

"Sure," I said. "Sure. Give me a call."

"I will," she said, and then just as I was sliding behind the wheel, she leaned into the window. "By the way. Your mother. Did she ever stop dancing?"

I shook my head. "No. Never."

Roberta nodded.

"And yours? Did she ever get well?"

She smiled a tiny sad smile. "No. She never did. Look, call me, okay?"

"Okay," I said, but I knew I wouldn't. Roberta had messed up my past somehow with that business about Maggie. I wouldn't forget a thing like that. Would I?

Strife came to us that fall. At least that's what the paper called it. Strife. Racial strife. The word made me think of a bird—a big shrieking bird out of 1,000,000,000 B.C. Flapping its wings and cawing. Its eye with no lid always bearing down on you. All day it screeched and at night it slept on the rooftops. It woke you in the morning and from the *Today* show to the eleven o'clock news it kept you an awful company. I couldn't figure it out from one day to the next. I knew I was supposed to feel something strong, but I didn't know what, and James wasn't any help. Joseph was on the list of kids to be transferred from the junior high school to another one at some far-out-of-the-way place and I thought it was a good thing until I heard it was a bad thing. I mean I didn't know. All the schools seemed dumps to me, and the fact that one was nicer looking didn't hold much weight. But the papers were full of it and then the kids began to get jumpy. In August, mind you. Schools weren't even open yet. I thought Joseph might be frightened to go over there, but he didn't seem scared so I forgot about it, until I found myself driving along Hudson Street out there by the school they were trying to integrate and saw a line of women marching. And who do you suppose was in line, big as life, holding a sign in front of her bigger than her mother's cross? MOTHERS HAVE RIGHTS TOO! it said.

I drove on, and then changed my mind. I circled the block, slowed down, and honked my horn.

Roberta looked over and when she saw me she waved. I didn't wave back, but I didn't move either. She handed her sign to another woman and came over to where I was parked.

"Hi."

"What are you doing?"

"Picketing. What's it look like?"

"What for?"

"What do you mean, 'What for?' They want to take my kids and send them out of the neighborhood. They don't want to go."

"So what if they go to another school? My boy's being bussed too, and I don't mind. Why should you?"

"It's not about us, Twyla. Me and you. It's about our kids."

"What's more *us* than that?"

"Well, it is a free country."

"Not yet, but it will be."

"What the hell does that mean? I'm not doing anything to you."

"You really think that?"

"I know it."

"I wonder what made me think you were different."

"I wonder what made me think you were different."

"Look at them," I said. "Just look. Who do they think they are? Swarming all over the place like they own it. And now they think they can decide where my child goes to school. Look at them, Roberta. They're Bozos."

Roberta turned around and looked at the women. Almost all of them were standing still now, waiting. Some were even edging toward us. Roberta looked at me out of some refrigerator behind her eyes. "No, they're not. They're just mothers."

"And what am I? Swiss cheese?"

170 "I used to curl your hair."

"I hated your hands in my hair."

The women were moving. Our faces looked mean to them of course and they looked as though they could not wait to throw themselves in front of a police car, or better yet, into my car and drag me away by my ankles. Now they surrounded my car and gently, gently began to rock it. I swayed back and forth like a sideways yo-yo. Automatically I reached for Roberta, like the old days in the orchard when they saw us watching them and we had to get out of there, and if one of us fell the other pulled her up and if one of us was caught the other stayed to kick and scratch, and neither would leave the other behind. My arm shot out of the car window but no receiving hand was there. Roberta was looking at me sway from side to side in the car and her face was still. My purse slid from the car seat down under the dashboard. The four policemen who had been drinking Tab in their car finally got the message and strolled over, forcing their way through the women. Quietly, firmly they spoke. "Okay, ladies. Back in line or off the streets."

Some of them went away willingly; others had to be urged away from the car doors and the hood. Roberta didn't move. She was looking steadily at me. I was fumbling to turn on the ignition, which wouldn't catch because the gearshift was still in drive. The seats of the car were a mess because the swaying had thrown my grocery coupons all over it and my purse was sprawled on the floor.

"Maybe I am different now, Twyla. But you're not. You're the same little state kid who kicked a poor old black lady when she was down on the ground. You kicked a black lady and you have the nerve to call me a bigot."

175 The coupons were everywhere and the guts of my purse were bunched under the dashboard. What was she saying? Black? Maggie wasn't black.

"She wasn't black," I said.

"Like hell she wasn't, and you kicked her. We both did. You kicked a black lady who couldn't even scream."

"Liar!"

"You're the liar! Why don't you just go on home and leave us alone, huh?"

180 She turned away and I skidded away from the curb.

The next morning I went into the garage and cut the side out of the carton our portable TV had come in. It wasn't nearly big enough, but after a while I had a decent sign: red spray-painted letters on a white background—AND SO DO CHILDREN ****. I meant just to go down to the school and tack it up somewhere so those cows on the picket line across the street could see it, but when I got there, some ten or so others had already assembled—protesting the cows across the street. Police permits and everything. I got in line and we strutted in time on our side while Roberta's group strutted on theirs. That first day we were all dignified, pretending the other side didn't exist. The second day there was name calling and finger gestures. But that was about all. People changed signs from time to time, but Roberta never did and neither did I. Actually my sign didn't make sense without Roberta's. "And so do children what?" one of the women on my side asked me. Have rights, I said, as though it was obvious.

Roberta didn't acknowledge my presence in any way and I got to thinking maybe she didn't know I was there. I began to pace myself in the line, jostling people one minute and lagging behind the next, so Roberta and I could reach the end of our respective lines at the same time and there would be a moment in our turn when we would face each other. Still, I couldn't tell whether she saw me and knew my sign was for her. The next day I went early before we were scheduled to assemble. I waited until she got there before I exposed my new creation. As soon as she hoisted her MOTHERS HAVE RIGHTS TOO I began to wave my new one, which said, HOW WOULD YOU KNOW? I know she saw that one, but I had gotten addicted now. My signs got crazier each day, and the women on my side decided that I was a kook. They couldn't make heads or tails out of my brilliant screaming posters.

I brought a painted sign in queenly red with huge black letters that said, IS YOUR MOTHER WELL? Roberta took her lunch break and didn't come back for the rest of the day or any day after. Two days later I stopped going too and couldn't have been missed because nobody understood my signs anyway.

It was a nasty six weeks. Classes were suspended and Joseph didn't go to anybody's school until October. The children—everybody's children—soon got bored with that extended vacation they thought was going to be so great. They looked at TV until their eyes flattened. I spent a couple of mornings tutoring my son, as the other mothers said we should. Twice I opened a text from last year that he had never turned in. Twice he yawned in my face. Other mothers organized living room sessions so the kids would keep up. None of the kids could concentrate so they drifted back to *The Price Is Right* and *The Brady Bunch*.[6] When the school finally opened there were fights once or twice and some sirens roared through the streets every once in a while. There were a lot of photographers from Albany. And just when ABC was about to send up a news crew, the kids settled down like nothing in the world had happened. Joseph hung my HOW WOULD YOU KNOW? sign in his bedroom. I don't know what became of AND SO DO CHILDREN ****. I think my father-in-law cleaned some fish on it. He was always puttering around in our garage. Each of his five children lived in Newburgh and he acted as though he had five extra homes.

I couldn't help looking for Roberta when Joseph graduated from high school, but I didn't see her. It didn't trouble me much what she had said to me in the car. I mean the kicking part. I know I didn't do that, I couldn't do that. But I was puzzled by her telling me Maggie was black. When I thought about it I actually couldn't be certain. She wasn't pitch-black, I knew, or I would have remembered that. What I remember was the kiddie hat, and the semicircle legs. I tried to reassure myself about the race thing for a long time until it dawned on me that the truth was already there, and Roberta knew it. I didn't kick her; I didn't join in with the gar girls and kick that lady, but I sure did want to. We watched and never tried to help her and never called for help. Maggie was my dancing mother. Deaf, I thought, and dumb. Nobody inside. Nobody who would hear you if you cried in the night. Nobody who could tell you anything important that you could use. Rocking, dancing, swaying as she walked. And when

6. Television sitcom popular in the 1970s. *The Price Is Right*: television game show popular in the 1970s.

the gar girls pushed her down, and started roughhousing, I knew she wouldn't scream, couldn't—just like me—and I was glad about that.

We decided not to have a tree, because Christmas would be at my mother-in-law's house, so why have a tree at both places? Joseph was at SUNY New Paltz and we had to economize, we said. But at the last minute, I changed my mind. Nothing could be that bad. So I rushed around town looking for a tree, something small but wide. By the time I found a place, it was snowing and very late. I dawdled like it was the most important purchase in the world and the tree man was fed up with me. Finally I chose one and had it tied onto the trunk of the car. I drove away slowly because the sand trucks were not out yet and the streets could be murder at the beginning of a snowfall. Downtown the streets were wide and rather empty except for a cluster of people coming out of the Newburgh Hotel. The one hotel in town that wasn't built out of cardboard and Plexiglas. A party, probably. The men huddled in the snow were dressed in tails and the women had on furs. Shiny things glittered from underneath their coats. It made me tired to look at them. Tired, tired, tired. On the next corner was a small diner with loops and loops of paper bells in the window. I stopped the car and went in. Just for a cup of coffee and twenty minutes of peace before I went home and tried to finish everything before Christmas Eve.

"Twyla?"

There she was. In a silvery evening gown and dark fur coat. A man and another woman were with her, the man fumbling for change to put in the cigarette machine. The woman was humming and tapping on the counter with her fingernails. They all looked a little bit drunk.

"Well. It's you."

190 "How are you?"

I shrugged. "Pretty good. Frazzled. Christmas and all."

"Regular?" called the woman from the counter.

"Fine," Roberta called back and then, "Wait for me in the car."

She slipped into the booth beside me. "I have to tell you something, Twyla. I made up my mind if I ever saw you again, I'd tell you."

195 "I'd just as soon not hear anything, Roberta. It doesn't matter now, anyway."

"No," she said. "Not about that."

"Don't be long," said the woman. She carried two regulars to go and the man peeled his cigarette pack as they left.

"It's about St. Bonny's and Maggie."

"Oh, please."

200 "Listen to me. I really did think she was black. I didn't make that up. I really thought so. But now I can't be sure. I just remember her as old, so old. And because she couldn't talk—well, you know, I thought she was crazy. She'd been brought up in an institution like my mother was and like I thought I would be too. And you were right. We didn't kick her. It was the gar girls. Only them. But, well, I wanted to. I really wanted them to hurt her. I said we did it, too. You and me, but that's not true. And I don't want you to carry that around. It was just that I wanted to do it so bad that day—wanting to is doing it."

Her eyes were watery from the drinks she'd had, I guess. I know it's that way with me. One glass of wine and I start bawling over the littlest thing.

"We were kids, Roberta."

"Yeah. Yeah. I know, just kids."

"Eight."

"Eight."

"And lonely."

"Scared, too."

She wiped her cheeks with the heel of her hand and smiled. "Well, that's all I wanted to say."

I nodded and couldn't think of any way to fill the silence that went from the diner past the paper bells on out into the snow. It was heavy now. I thought I'd better wait for the sand trucks before starting home.

"Thanks, Roberta."

"Sure."

"Did I tell you? My mother, she never did stop dancing."

"Yes. You told me. And mine, she never got well." Roberta lifted her hands from the tabletop and covered her face with her palms. When she took them away she really was crying. "Oh shit, Twyla. Shit, shit, shit. What the hell happened to Maggie?"

1983

QUESTIONS

1. At the end of RECITATIF, how do Twyla's and Roberta's explorations of the "truth" of what they had seen at St. Bonny's many years earlier affect your sense of the "truth" of later episodes in the story? Is either Twyla or Roberta more reliable than the other?
2. At what point in the story do you first begin to make assumptions about the race and class of the two main characters, Twyla and Roberta? Why? Do you change your mind later in the story? When and why so—or not? What is the significance of Morrison's choice both to withhold information about the characters' race and class and to have Twyla narrate the story?
3. How does the relationship between Twyla and Roberta evolve over the course of the story?

AUTHORS ON THEIR WORK

TONI MORRISON (b. 1931)

From "Toni Morrison: The Art of Fiction CXXXIV" (1993)*

MORRISON: Faulkner in *Absalom, Absalom!* spends the entire book tracing race, and you can't find it. No one can see it, even the character who *is* black can't see it. [. . .] Do you know how hard it is to withhold that kind of information but hinting, pointing all of the time? And then to reveal it in order to say that it is *not* the point anyway? It is technically just astonishing. As a reader you have been forced to hunt for a drop of black blood that means everything and nothing. The insanity of racism.

• • •

MORRISON: [. . .] I wrote a story entitled "Recitatif," in which there are two little girls in an orphanage, one white and one black. But the reader doesn't know which is white and which is black. I use class codes, but no racial codes.

INTERVIEWER: Is this meant to confuse the reader?

MORRISON: Well, yes. But to provoke and enlighten. I did that as a lark. What was exciting was to be forced as a writer not to be lazy and rely on obvious codes. Soon as I say, "Black woman . . ." I can rest on or provoke predictable responses, but if I leave it out then I have to talk about her in a complicated way—as a person.

*"Toni Morrison: The Art of Fiction CXXXIV." Interview by Elisa Schappell with Claudia Brodsky Lacour. *The Paris Review*, no. 128, Fall 1993, www.theparisreview.org/interviews/1888/the-art-of-fiction-no-134-toni-morrison.

DAVID FOSTER WALLACE (1962–2008)

Good People

Born in Ithaca, New York, to a philosophy professor and an English teacher, David Foster Wallace has been dubbed an "outrageously gifted novelist" and "the genius of his generation," as well as a "recovering smart aleck" and "a decent, decent man." A philosophy and English major at Amherst College, he contemplated a career in math before—at age twenty-four—earning an MFA from the University of Arizona and publishing his first novel, *The Broom of the System* (1987). His subsequent work includes short-story collections like *Brief Interviews with Hideous Men* (1999) and *Oblivion* (2006), as well as wide-ranging nonfiction, some of which appears in *A Supposedly Fun Thing I'll Never Do Again* (1997) and *Consider the Lobster and Other Essays* (2006). At over a thousand pages and with almost four hundred footnotes, his most famous novel, *Infinite Jest* (1996), intertwines several narratives set in a near-future in which years are named by their corporate sponsors ("Year of the Whopper") and New England is a giant toxic-waste dump. Included on *Time*'s list of the hundred best novels published since 1923, it also helped earn Wallace a MacArthur "genius grant."

Wallace described his own goal as "morally passionate, passionately moral fiction" that might help readers "become less alone inside." Though admired as much for its humor as its bulk and complexity, his fiction often dwells on what he called "an ineluctable part of being a human"—"suffering." Though Wallace long battled depression, his 2008 suicide shocked and saddened fans and fellow writers around the world. The story "Good People," first published in 2007, ultimately became part of *The Pale King* (2011), the unfinished novel he left behind.

They were up on a picnic table at that park by the lake, by the edge of the lake, with part of a downed tree in the shallows half hidden by the bank. Lane A. Dean, Jr., and his girlfriend, both in bluejeans and button-up shirts. They sat up on the table's top portion and had their shoes on the bench part that people sat on to picnic or fellowship together in carefree times. They'd gone to different high schools but the same junior college, where they had met in campus ministries. It was springtime, and the park's grass was very green and the air suffused with honeysuckle and lilacs both, which was almost too much. There were bees, and the angle of the sun made the water of the shallows look dark. There had been more storms that week, with some downed trees and the sound of chainsaws all up and down his parents' street. Their postures on the picnic table were both the same forward kind with their shoulders rounded and elbows on their knees. In this position the girl rocked slightly and once put her face in her hands, but she was not crying. Lane was very still and immobile and looking past the bank at the downed tree in the shallows and its ball of exposed roots going all directions and the tree's cloud of branches all half in the water. The only other individual nearby was a dozen spaced tables away, by himself, standing upright. Looking at the torn-up hole in the ground there where the tree had gone over. It was still early yet and all the shadows wheeling right and shortening. The girl wore a thin old checked cotton shirt with pearl-colored snaps with the long sleeves down and always smelled very good and clean, like someone you could trust and care about even if you weren't in love. Lane Dean had liked the smell of her right away. His mother called her *down to earth* and liked her, thought she was good people, you could tell—she made this evident in little ways. The shallows lapped from different directions at the tree as if almost teething on it. Sometimes when alone and thinking or struggling to turn a matter over to Jesus Christ in prayer, he would find himself putting his fist in his palm and turning it slightly as if still playing and pounding his glove to stay sharp and alert in center. He did not do this now; it would be cruel and indecent to do this now. The older individual stood beside his picnic table—he was at it but not sitting—and looked also out of place in a suit coat or jacket and the kind of men's hat Lane's grandfather wore in photos as a young insurance man. He appeared to be looking across the lake. If he moved, Lane didn't see it. He looked more like a picture than a man. There were not any ducks in view.

One thing Lane Dean did was reassure her again that he'd go with her and be there with her. It was one of the few safe or decent things he could really say. The second time he said it again now she shook her head and laughed in an unhappy way that was more just air out her nose. Her real laugh was different. Where he'd be was the waiting room, she said. That he'd be thinking about her and feeling bad for her, she knew, but he couldn't be in there with her. This was so obviously true that he felt like a ninny that he'd kept on about it and now knew what she had thought every time he went and said it—it hadn't brought her comfort or eased the burden at all. The worse he felt, the stiller he sat. The whole thing felt balanced on a knife or wire; if he moved to put his arm up or touch her the whole thing could tip over. He hated himself for sitting so frozen. He could almost visualize himself tiptoeing past something explosive. A big stupid-looking tiptoe, like in a cartoon. The whole last black week had been this way and it was wrong. He knew it was wrong, knew something was required of him that was not this terrible frozen care and caution, but he pretended to himself he did not know what it was that was required. He pretended it had no name. He pretended that not saying aloud what he knew to be right and true was for her sake, was for the sake of her needs and feelings. He also worked dock and routing at UPS, on top of school, but had traded to get the day off after they'd decided together. Two days before, he had awakened very early and tried to pray but could not. He was freezing more and more solid, he felt like, but he had not thought of his father or the blank frozenness of his father, even in church, which had once filled him with such pity. This was the truth. Lane Dean, Jr., felt sun on one arm as he pictured in his mind an image of himself on a train, waving mechanically to something that got smaller and smaller as the train pulled away. His father and his mother's father had the same birthday, a Cancer. Sheri's hair was colored an almost corn blond, very clean, the skin through her central part pink in the sunlight. They'd sat here long enough that only their right side was shaded now. He could look at her head, but not at her. Different parts of him felt unconnected to each other. She was smarter than him and they both knew it. It wasn't just school—Lane Dean was in accounting and business and did all right; he was hanging in there. She was a year older, twenty, but it was also more—she had always seemed to Lane to be on good terms with her life in a way that age could not account for. His mother had put it that she *knew what it is she wanted*, which was nursing and not an easy program at Peoria Junior College, and plus she worked hostessing at the Embers and had bought her own car. She was serious in a way Lane liked. She had a cousin that died when she was thirteen, fourteen, that she'd loved and been close with. She only talked about it that once. He liked her smell and her downy arms and the way she exclaimed when something made her laugh. He had liked just being with her and talking to her. She was serious in her faith and values in a way that Lane had liked and now, sitting here with her on the table, found himself afraid of. This was an awful thing. He was starting to believe that he might not be serious in his faith. He might be somewhat of a hypocrite, like the Assyrians in Isaiah,[1] which would be a far graver sin than the appointment—he had decided he believed this. He was desperate to be good people, to still be able to feel he was good. He rarely before now had thought of damnation and Hell—that part of it didn't speak to his spirit—and in worship services he more just tuned himself out and tolerated Hell when it came up, the same way you tolerate the job you've got to have to save up for what it is you want. Her tennis shoes had little things doodled on them from sitting in her class lectures. She stayed looking down like that. Little notes or reading assignments in Bic in her neat round hand on the rubber elements around the sneaker's rim. Lane A. Dean, looking now at her inclined head's side's barrettes in the shape of blue ladybugs. The appointment was for afternoon, but when the doorbell had rung so early and his mother'd called to him up the stairs, he had known, and a terrible kind of blankness had commenced falling through him.

1. Perhaps a reference to Isaiah 36, in which the Assyrians promise to save the kingdom of Judah if its king will trust and surrender to them rather than relying on God. Later chapters describe Assyria's fall as punishment for their hubris.

He told her that he did not know what to do. That he knew if he was the salesman of it and forced it upon her that was awful and wrong. But he was trying to understand—they'd prayed on it and talked it through from every different angle. Lane said how sorry she knew he was, and that if he was wrong in believing they'd truly decided together when they decided to make the appointment she should please tell him, because he thought he knew how she must have felt as it got closer and closer and how she must be so scared, but that what he couldn't tell was if it was more than that. He was totally still except for moving his mouth, it felt like. She did not reply. That if they needed to pray on it more and talk it through, then he was here, he was ready, he said. The appointment could get moved back; if she just said the word they could call and push it back to take more time to be sure in the decision. It was still so early in it—they both knew that, he said. This was true, that he felt this way, and yet he also knew he was also trying to say things that would get her to open up and say enough back that he could see her and read her heart and know what to say to get her to go through with it. He knew this without admitting to himself that this was what he wanted, for it would make him a hypocrite and liar. He knew, in some locked-up little part of him, why it was that he'd gone to no one to open up and seek their life counsel, not Pastor Steve or the prayer partners at campus ministries, not his UPS friends or the spiritual counselling available through his parents' old church. But he did not know why Sheri herself had not gone to Pastor Steve—he could not read her heart. She was blank and hidden. He so fervently wished it never happened. He felt like he knew now why it was a true sin and not just a leftover rule from past society. He felt like he had been brought low by it and humbled and now did believe that the rules were there for a reason. That the rules were concerned with him personally, as an individual. He promised God he had learned his lesson. But what if that, too, was a hollow promise, from a hypocrite who repented only after, who promised submission but really only wanted a reprieve? He might not even know his own heart or be able to read and know himself. He kept thinking also of 1 Timothy and the hypocrite therein who *disputeth over words.*[2] He felt a terrible inner resistance but could not feel what it was that it resisted. This was the truth. All the different angles and ways they had come at the decision together did not ever include it—the word—for had he once said it, avowed that he did love her, loved Sheri Fisher, then it all would have been transformed. It would not be a different stance or angle, but a difference in the very thing they were praying and deciding on together. Sometimes they had prayed together over the phone, in a kind of half code in case anybody accidentally picked up the extension. She continued to sit as if thinking, in the pose of thinking, like that one statue. They were right up next to each other on the table. He was looking over past her at the tree in the water. But he could not say he did: it was not true.

But neither did he ever open up and tell her straight out he did not love her. This might be his *lie by omission.* This might be the frozen resistance—were he to look right at her and tell her he didn't, she would keep the appointment and

2. See 1 Timothy 6.3–4: "If any man teach otherwise, and consent not to wholesome words, *even* the words of our Lord Jesus Christ, and to the doctrine which is according to godliness; He is proud, knowing nothing, but doting about questions and strifes of words, whereof cometh envy, strife, railings, evil surmisings."

go. He knew this. Something in him, though, some terrible weakness or lack of values, could not tell her. It felt like a muscle he did not have. He didn't know why; he just could not do it, or even pray to do it. She believed he was good, serious in his values. Part of him seemed willing to more or less just about lie to someone with that kind of faith and trust, and what did that make him? How could such a type of individual even pray? What it really felt like was a taste of the reality of what might be meant by Hell. Lane Dean had never believed in Hell as a lake of fire or a loving God consigning folks to a burning lake of fire—he knew in his heart this was not true. What he believed in was a living God of compassion and love and the possibility of a personal relationship with Jesus Christ through whom this love was enacted in human time. But sitting here beside this girl as unknown to him now as outer space, waiting for whatever she might say to unfreeze him, now he felt like he could see the edge or outline of what a real vision of Hell might be. It was of two great and terrible armies within himself, opposed and facing each other, silent. There would be battle but no victor. Or never a battle—the armies would stay like that, motionless, looking across at each other, and seeing therein something so different and alien from themselves that they could not understand, could not hear each other's speech as even words or read anything from what their face looked like, frozen like that, opposed and uncomprehending, for all human time. Two-hearted, a hypocrite to yourself either way.

5 When he moved his head, a part of the lake further out flashed with sun—the water up close wasn't black now, and you could see into the shallows and see that all the water was moving but gently, this way and that—and in this same way he besought to return to himself as Sheri moved her leg and started to turn beside him. He could see the man in the suit and gray hat standing motionless now at the lake's rim, holding something under one arm and looking across at the opposite side where a row of little forms on camp chairs sat in a way that meant they had lines in the water for crappie—which mostly only your blacks from the East Side ever did—and the little white shape at the row's end a Styrofoam creel. In his moment or time at the lake now just to come, Lane Dean first felt he could take this all in whole: everything seemed distinctly lit, for the circle of the pin oak's shade had rotated off all the way, and they sat now in sun with their shadow a two-headed thing in the grass before them. He was looking or gazing again at where the downed tree's branches seemed to all bend so sharply just under the shallows' surface when he was given to know that through all this frozen silence he'd despised he had, in truth, been praying, or some little part of his heart he could not hear had, for he was answered now with a type of vision, what he would later call within his own mind a vision or *moment of grace*. He was not a hypocrite, just broken and split off like all men. Later on, he believed that what happened was he'd had a moment of almost seeing them both as Jesus saw them—as blind but groping, wanting to please God despite their inborn fallen nature. For in that same given moment he saw, quick as light, into Sheri's heart, and was made to know what would occur here as she finished turning to him and the man in the hat watched the fishing and the downed elm shed cells into the water. This down-to-earth girl that smelled good and wanted to be a nurse would take and hold one of his hands in both of hers to unfreeze him and make him look at her, and she would say that she cannot do it. That

she is sorry she did not know this sooner, that she hadn't meant to lie—she agreed because she'd wanted to believe that she could, but she cannot. That she will carry this and have it; she has to. With her gaze clear and steady. That all night last night she prayed and searched inside herself and decided this is what love commands of her. That Lane should please please sweetie let her finish. That listen—this is her own decision and obliges him to nothing. That she knows he does not love her, not that way, has known it all this time, and that it's all right. That it is as it is and it's all right. She will carry this, and have it, and love it and make no claim on Lane except his good wishes and respecting what she has to do. That she releases him, all claim, and hopes he finishes up at P.J.C. and does so good in his life and has all joy and good things. Her voice will be clear and steady, and she will be lying, for Lane has been given to read her heart. To see through her. One of the opposite side's blacks raises his arm in what may be greeting, or waving off a bee. There is a mower cutting grass someplace off behind them. It will be a terrible, last-ditch gamble born out of the desperation in Sheri Fisher's soul, the knowledge that she can neither do this thing today nor carry a child alone and shame her family. Her values blocked the way either way, Lane could see, and she has no other options or choice—this lie is not a sin. Galatians 4:16, *Have I then become your enemy?*[3] She is gambling that he is good. There on the table, neither frozen nor yet moving, Lane Dean, Jr., sees all this, and is moved with pity, and also with something more, something without any name he knows, that is given to him in the form of a question that never once in all the long week's thinking and division had even so much as occurred—why is he so sure he doesn't love her? Why is one kind of love any different? What if he has no earthly idea what love is? What would even Jesus do? For it was just now he felt her two small strong soft hands on his, to turn him. What if he was just afraid, if the truth was no more than this, and if what to pray for was not even love but simple courage, to meet both her eyes as she says it and trust his heart?

2007

QUESTIONS

1. How would you summarize or characterize Lane Dean, Jr.'s conflicts, both internal and external? How does his faith intensify or even create those conflicts and help him resolve them?
2. How is your interpretation of Lane Dean, Jr.'s character and conflicts shaped by all that the story withholds from us, including dialogue; Sheri's point of view or thoughts; explicit information about the nature of Sheri's "appointment" or of the "it" he "wished [. . .] never happened" (par. 3); a description of what actually happens at the end rather than Lane Dean's "vision" of what would happen and/or his later "belie[f]" about what happened?
3. What different definitions of "good people" or of a "good person" are implied here, or how might Lane Dean, Jr.'s understanding of what it means to be "good people"

3. "Am I therefore become your enemy, because I tell you the truth?" (Gal. 4.16). Earlier in this letter, Paul exhorts the Galatians to understand that when they "knew not God," they inevitably served "them which by nature are no gods," but now that they know God such "bondage" is instead a choice. At the same time, he reminds them that he is, like them, fallible, and that despite that "temptation which was in my flesh ye despised [me] not, nor rejected."

change over the course of the story? What part does the idea of hypocrisy play in those definitions?

ALISSA NUTTING
(b. 1981)
Model's Assistant

Born in rural Michigan and raised in Florida, Alissa Nutting describes herself as, for better or worse, irresistibly drawn to writing, calling her chosen career "kind of like an insane asylum that I checked myself into voluntarily: I can choose to leave any time, but I never will." Nutting earned her MFA at the University of Alabama (2008) and her PhD at the University of Nevada–Las Vegas (2011). Even before graduation, however, Nutting won the 2010 Starcherone Prize for Innovative Fiction for *Unclean Jobs for Women and Girls*, a collection featuring stories ranging from "Model's Assistant" and "Knife Thrower" to "Corpse Smoker" and "Dinner." As these titles suggest, Nutting's work is marked by a darkly satirical edge and a dash of the provocative and even surreal. Her stories and essays have appeared in venues ranging from the modern fairy-tale anthology *My Mother She Killed Me, My Father He Ate Me* (2010) to the *New York Times* online Anxiety column and *O: The Oprah Magazine*. Dubbed "Most Controversial Book of Summer 2013" by both *Cosmopolitan* and the British *Guardian*, Nutting's first novel, *Tampa* (2013), shares with "Model's Assistant" a concern with our contemporary tendency to, in her words, "treat beauty as a currency."

My best friend Garla is a model from somewhere Swedishy; if you try to pin down where, like what town, or if actually Sweden, she just yells, "Vodka," or if she's in a better mood, "Vodka, you know?" which seems like she's maybe saying she's Russian, but really she just wants to drink. Garla hates particulars, and is actually able to avoid them because where she *actually* lives is model-land. I wish I lived in model-land, too, but the closest I can come to that is hanging out with Garla, which is like going on vacation to a model-land timeshare.

We met at a party in Chelsea[1] that I pond-skipped to. I definitely wasn't invited. I'd gone with a real friend to a not-so-hot party, and then left with her friend to go to a better party where I met someone new who took me to a quite hot party. It was there that I made out with the photographer who took me to the party of Garla. She wasn't hosting it but she was present, and anywhere Garla goes is Garla's party.

I think the only reason I ever saw Garla again was because I was drunk enough to tell her the truth. She was trying on bizarre clothes—there was a shroud that

1. Name of fashionable neighborhoods in both New York City and London.

looked fiercely spacelike yet medical, like a gown one might wear to get a pap smear on Mars. Then Garla put on a dress whose pleating created the suggestion of a displaced goiter somewhere to the left of her neck and she sashayed towards me. I was holding my head onto my body, carefully and by the window, so that its breeze might sober me up enough to walk to the end of the room where I might then become sober enough to walk to the toilet and land on the floor. There, hopefully, the pressure from my cheek against my cell phone could call someone who knew me and liked me and wanted to get me a cab and make sure this night was not where my life's journey would end. But for all I knew it was, and when I saw Garla I held on to my head just a little bit tighter, because she appeared to be strutting over to grab it and rip it off.

"You," she said, and I straightened up grammar-school style. I puked in my mouth but absolutely did not open my lips and let it fall on the floor. "Do you like this?" She did a turn that was so beautiful and practiced and impossible but to Garla was something that accidentally slipped out of her like a tiny fart.

"It makes you look like you're pregnant in the back," I said, and used the nose of my beer bottle to itch the middle of my back where the seam of her dress magically globed out. She scowled and pranced off. I assumed she was offended until she brought over a silver-plated bowl filled with the car keys of various guests.

"Use for vomit," she said, and then, "have phone," and slipped a miniature crystallized computer-wallet into my purse. I think at that point two large, gray wolfhounds walked up to either side of her and the three of them then headed towards the kitchen. "You love dogs and have a tendency to hallucinate them," I told myself as I stumbled towards the bathroom. Various refined guests were staring at me with horror as I pawed around Helen Keller-style,[2] groping everything in sight to stabilize my journey into a small room housing cold linoleum and a sink. "Why am I always the nerd at the party?" I thought. "I am in my thirties and by now I should at least know how to pretend."

The thing about bathrooms in parties is they don't always stay bathrooms; they start out as such but then become make-out rooms or coke rooms or shower-bubble-madness rooms. When I burst through the door holding my abdomen, a slight and waify couple seemed to be using it as a get-to know-one-another room; they were drinking very red wine, sitting on the side of the bathtub and giggling, drawing simple pictures with fingertips of wine onto the white tile. The "braap'" sound I made while becoming sick intrigued them a little bit. They were children nearly, perhaps nineteen. I could feel them looking at me with something real and concentrated. I don't think it was pity as much as curiosity; they seemed to wonder very much what it might be like to be so uncomposed. "I don't get when people use puking in art," said the boy, and the girl said, "Well it's not like *that*, when they do," meaning not like me but like Garla throwing up pink paint onto a teal ceramic raccoon.

"I need a cab," I mumbled, and the boy was sympathetic but firm.

"I won't touch you," he told me.

"Of course not," I said, "Heavens no. Just call one and I'll get myself down to the door.

2. Author and political activist (1880–1968), who was both blind and deaf from early childhood.

It took a great while to do this. At some point I wondered if I should try to find Garla and give her the phone back, but then I saw a great flash and there she was, the camera's light bouncing off her translucent thigh, her foot inside the host's tropical aquarium. Everyone wanted a shot of her leather bondage shoe surrounded by fake coral: people were holding up cell phones and professional equipment and thin digital cameras, "Tickle fish," Garla was saying to everyone, and there was simply no way I could have that amount of attention suddenly focus over to my own body, even if I was waving a phone that belonged to the darling of their affections. I was like a turd inside someone who'd accidentally swallowed an engagement ring: I was nothing, yet I carried something uniquely special.

I fell easily down the stairs and by the time I was able to stand, to my great surprise, a cab had come. "Thank you," I called up to the beautiful children in the bathroom, but it was a gurgle and I knew they weren't listening.

I kept the phone on my desk for several days wondering what to do about it. There was something wrong with the phone; it didn't ring. Garla's phone would ring, wouldn't it?

It didn't ring until the fourth day.

"Hi Womun." It was Garla. I began explaining how I'd meant to give it back, etc., but she stopped me quite quickly, "It your phone for me. I call you with it," she said, to which I could've said a lot of things, like how I already have a phone, or that I was very afraid of getting killed for this jewel-phone, should someone see me talking on it in my neighborhood, because I don't have a lot of money and neither does anyone else who lives here, but oftentimes people badly need money, for personal reasons, and desperate times/desperate measures.

"I get you for fashion show," she said, "tonight at the seven-thirty."

Out of some type of pride I wanted to make sure that she didn't mean *I* would be in the fashion show, that it wasn't an ironic thing where the beautiful each try to snag themselves an ugly, and whoever snags the ugliest ugly and dresses it up is the winner. "You mean go watch one with you?" I asked, and she said "Ha," then lit a cigarette and said, "Ha. Ha. I mean this," and told me where to meet her.

Since that night my life has changed in a myriad of ways. I'm still no one, unless I am with Garla, and then I become with *Garla*, a new and exciting identity that makes nearly everything possible, except being a model myself. And except being someone when I am not with Garla.

At the oxygen bar, Garla gives my face three firm slaps on the cheek. She is always taking grandmotherly liberties such as these. "Put you in special coffin," she says, which is a term of endearment on her part but I don't know what it means exactly. I like to think that it's a sort of Snow White reference, that I'm dear to her in some way that entails it would be pleasant for her to have me on her nightstand forever asleep in a glass box.[3] Though I guess it could also mean she wants to say goodnight and close me inside an iron maiden.[4]

3. In most versions of the folktale, after Snow White eats an apple poisoned by the jealous queen and falls asleep, she is put in a glass box by the dwarves who have twice saved her life.

4. Torture device consisting of a hollow statue or coffin shaped like a woman and lined with spikes that impale the enclosed victim.

Garla is sitting in front of a laptop with a solar charger plugged into it, although it is raining outside and we are in a darkened room. Garla doesn't have opinions on things; she's not really the pro or con type. Right now she is into global warming because she knows that global warming is chic. Things are either chic or they aren't, and if they're chic then they're for Garla. "The web won't come," Garla says.

"Solar charger," I point out. "There's no sun."

"Global warming," Garla says. She will often randomly say the media titles of controversial topics, such as "Crisis in Darfur,"[5] then take a drink and be silent for a few more hours.

A woman wearing a unisex hemp robe enters with two tanks and two breathing masks, hooking Garla in first. With the mask on Garla appears to be a pilot from the future, possibly a computer-generated one. Her perfect skin looks like a plasma screen.

"I love your accent," the smocked woman says. "Where are you from?"

"Vodka, you know?" says Garla, and the woman's eyes frown; perhaps she has just Botoxed[6] because I can tell she really wants to frown but her eyes simply flutter a little.

"Could she get a glass of vodka," I translate, and the woman mentions that alcohol is not usually consumed during the treatment. She is already on the way to get it, though, and when she returns there's also a glass for me.

It gets a little overwhelming in the mask when the pure oxygen starts to hit us at the same time as the vodka. Garla takes my hand. I don't know if I'm attracted to her or if she's just beautiful. I think it's the latter because she doesn't say much, and what she does say doesn't make much sense. But people don't have to talk a lot or make sense for others to love them. Just look at dogs and babies.

"Cloud of vodka!" Garla screams. I decide she wants another glass because I want another glass, so I hold two fingers up at the woman in hemp while pointing down to our melted ice. *Garla,* I think, *you are a magic swan with Tourette's.*[7] My fingers stay in an upright "peace" position; with our masks I imagine that Garla and I are on some kind of extreme rollercoaster that goes into the stratosphere, and we're passing the camera that takes a picture for us to buy at the end, and I am saying, "This is me and Garla. Peace."

She has made me the best-dressed party nerd of all time. Once, she put these chain-link pants on me and I couldn't move, not even like a robot. Garla—wearing six-inch stiletto heels—actually picked me up, carried me up the stairs to the party, and planted me by yet another fish tank, either so I'd have something to watch or because she knew that at some point, a part of her body would be posing inside of it and she very much wanted for me to be there to say, "Now Garla has to go home" when it started to get boring for her.

5. Between 2003 and 2010, hundreds of thousands died and millions were displaced due to conflict in the Darfur region of southwest Sudan, in northern Africa, inspiring a Save Darfur campaign championed by actor George Clooney and other celebrities.

6. That is, been injected with Botox, a chemical that reduces the appearance of wrinkles by paralyzing facial muscles.

7. Neurological disorder causing tics and uncontrollable verbal outbursts.

30 There was never a conversation where Garla hired me to be her assistant. I just started speaking up when it made sense to, like when people asked if they could cut her arm a tiny bit with a sword in order to drink a drop of it off the blade's tip and she answered them with "Special coffin," in a very tiny voice. "We have to go, Garla," I used to say, but I soon learned that "Garla has to go" is a better way to phrase it, because then it seems like it's entirely out of her control and she doesn't have a choice. Garla does not like choices.

Tonight we go to another fashion show. Garla's walking in it so I wait backstage in the chair where her makeup was done, and at several points people inquire as to why I'm there. Very few actually want me to leave; they're just genuinely trying to understand.

Afterwards we go to the home of a fellow model where I watch Garla drink herself into a deep sea. She is a metronomical[8] drinker. I can count the glasses she drinks per hour, like a time signature, and know exactly how drunk she is at any given moment. With me it's the opposite; the drunk is that mystery wedding guest who may show up early, late, or not at all. By four a.m. Garla is lying on an island countertop in the kitchen. Some guy has dumped a miniature Buddhist sand garden[9] out on her abdomen, and he's swirling the sand around over her stomach with a tiny bamboo rake. Her head is not on the counter; it's flipped back like a Pez dispenser, and I walk over and we have this intoxicated moment.

"I know you're more," my drunken eyes say. They say this in a breathy, hesitant manner that insists it has taken a lot of time for them to work up the courage to say such a thing, without words nonetheless.

"Yes," answer Garla's eyes, and like all of Garla's answers it is a mysterious pearl whose full value I begin to appraise immediately. I walk over to her and lift her head up with my hands so it is level with the counter, holding it. I look down at her like a surgeon.

35 "Some type of sausage," Garla says; she likes the cured meats.

It is hard not to drop her head, not to toss it away like a shell that seemed of greater worth from a distance, beneath the water.

• • •

I keep wondering if Garla will ask me to quit my regular job copyediting and join her full-time in model-land. Her agency is very good to her, but I know she needs me, or at least could really use me, more than she does, which leads me to wonder two things: Does Garla have others like Me? If so, how many Mes are there? Does she really need Me at all? The thing about Garla is that it's always okay for Garla. No matter what happens, Garla will be okay. I just speed the okayness up a little bit for her so that okay is sure to happen in real time.

Although my life has so many more great things in it now than before I met Garla, I'm still beginning to feel used. And—how can I deny this—I want more of Garla. She is a rare substance, if only because of the role and power she has

8. That is, like a metronome, a device that marks time by ticking at precise intervals, allowing musicians to keep the meter indicated by the notation known as a *time signature*.

9. Space decorated with sand, rocks, and other natural materials in lines or patterns to create the meditative environment prized by Zen Buddhists.

in our society and not anything she holds innately. Rare substances make people feel selfish and greedy, and Garla is no exception. Neither am I.

I am also getting a little sick of my special Garla-phone, but it's really expensive and the only thing Garla will call me on. I got rid of my other phone and now have only the phone Garla gave me, perhaps because I know she intended it to only be used when she called me, and this is a small rebellion on my part. Garla doesn't pick up on rebellions though, big or small. She has no need for them.

I decide to ask if I can be her paid assistant, because she probably will not say yes or no, and I can just interpret it as yes. If anything, by quitting my job and hanging out with her more I will get additional goodies I can eBay, and Garla's schwag pays several times more than my current employer.

I strike when we are in the back of a town car on the way to a designer's private shoot. Garla is stretched out on my lap with her muss of blond hair hanging down over my knees. Her hair is softer than my shaved legs.

"Garla," I say, "I'm going to quit my job and be your assistant. You don't have to pay me hardly anything. I don't make very much as it is." There's a pause and she hands up a tiny golden comb to me, I presume for me to begin brushing her hair with. I also presume this means "yes," is a quid pro quo gesture. I call my boss right then on the Garla-phone and quit as loudly as I can without seeming hostile, just to try to burn the event a little deeper into the ether of Garla's memory.

The shoot goes well. Afterwards I take her glasses of chilled vodka that look like refreshing water and we have a look at the pictures, which are beautiful. We leave with giant bags of expensive clothing that we didn't pay or ask for.

I am feeling more visible by the second. Perhaps, I think, I should move into Garla's apartment. That way I'd always be there to do whatever she needed, and there wouldn't be all the Garla-phone calls in the middle of the night; she could just yell or do a special grunt. Although Garla never needs to yell. Everyone is already paying attention.

Except the next morning, she doesn't answer my calls, and she doesn't call me. This goes on for another week and a half. I sulk like a real model. I don't eat and I drink lots of vodka and I cut my own hair in the bathroom with dull scissors and then regret it, and the next morning I think about going to a really expensive salon and having it fixed except I don't have the money for that, especially now that I have no job. For that, I need Garla.

This is the root of my pain. I had convinced myself that she needed me, when really, anyone could and would do what I did: follow around a gorgeous person and get gifts and call outrages by name for what they are. How did I lend any type of panache to that role? Looking in the mirror at my botched home haircut, I realize that my new expensive clothes still look nerdy because they don't fit me right. They never will.

When the Garla-phone finally lights up and makes its synthetic music, it's like an air-raid siren. I'm paralyzed with fear but angst-ridden from loneliness and desperation. "Where have you been?" I scream. "We agreed I'd be your assistant. I quit my job! I haven't seen you for like ten days!"

"Vodka head," Garla explains. I want to pretend like nothing is wrong. "I'm not a bad assistant. I'm a good assistant, which means I need to be where you are, and help you with things."

"Later, a party," she says. I can hear happy screams in the background and their shrillness stabs into me. I know those screams belong to completely impractical people, and I hate them for it. "When?" I ask, "How do I get there?"

50 I stop by a nearby bar to have a few drinks alone before going up to the party. It feels good to sulk over a glass in public. How could I have let my guard down so badly? Before Garla, I had been all-guard. Before Garla, I would've seen Garla coming. My pre-Garla life suddenly seems like an amazing thing; I hadn't even known what I was missing. As I walk out of the bar and look up near the balcony I'm headed to, I can actually see Garla. It makes me feel creepy but I stand there and watch for a while anyway, until the two of us seem like strangers. Under the streetlamp and despite our distance, I notice her bone structure dazzle in the candlelight.

Compared to her, I am like a sandwich. I am completely inhuman and benign. I try to remember a sandwich I'd eaten in the fourth grade and cannot. I can't even really remember one I'd eaten a month ago. We all must be like fourth-grade sandwiches to Garla.

It's not until I get inside the suite and look around that I realize it's the same residence where I first met Garla. This makes my hands and feet sweat rapidly; the line is suddenly becoming a circle.

But circles are infinite too. It's not just lines that go on forever.

As the night moves on, it's like going back in time. When I enter, Garla gives me a soft embrace and kisses my cheek, but I want restitution. I quit my job and had the week from hell, and she isn't going to flash a quick smile and reenter my life. Maybe I'm replaceable, but I don't have to be happy about it.

55 I take my old seat by the window and start rapidly boozing. The lights change colors in ways that suggest I'm going too fast, and that is the speed I want to go. It's a rush, like skydiving. I keep giving Garla a scowl that says, "Hey, you. I'm not holding on. See my empty hands."

She's rubbing pieces of chocolate over her lips like Chap Stick and men are helplessly pulled to her side of the room. Garla's face is a centrifuge that separates the confident from the weak and the jealous, and I have been spun away.

Stumbling to the bathroom, I get out my jeweled Garla-phone. Part of me wants to put it into the toilet, or at least try to see if it will fit through the hole in the bottom of the bowl. I want to puke on it but it is so shiny that with its jeweled crystals and my drunken compound fly-eye vision, I couldn't aim if I wanted to. Instead the puke falls into the water and the phone falls on the ground, and when I'm finished and my cheek hits the floor the phone looks like a store of riches behind the plunger. I grab the phone and open it, kind of bumping it around, hoping it will call a friend who will come pick me up.

But it's Garla's phone, so it calls Garla. I hang up but a few minutes later she's standing over me in an Amazonian[1] manner, one leg on either side of my body. "Put you in tiny coffin," she says, rolling out some toilet paper and batting it against my wet cheek.

"I wish you would."

1. In Greek mythology the Amazons were a group of powerful female warriors.

She doesn't appreciate my display of self-pity. I watch her toss her martini 60
glass out the window onto the patio where it breaks. "You go home and rest doctor-television."

After she leaves, a bodyguard enters and picks me up with a disgusted look, like he's emptying a full bedpan. He helps me into the taxi. Motoring away, I watch the colored streaks of Garla on the patio upstairs.

With panic I check my purse to make sure I still have it: the Garla-phone, the jewel. The cursed treasure that brought distress alongside fortune. Glistening in my lap it is too beautiful to be trusted. As the cab nears my apartment, I have the urge to leave the phone behind on the seat for someone else to find and answer. But I won't. Instead I'll go home and wait for her to call me and turn me into something special for however long she wants, and this time I won't forget to be grateful.

2010

QUESTIONS

1. What might we learn about the narrator by the style, as well as content, of her narration?
2. What attracts the narrator to Garla and vice versa?
3. Is the narrator's conflict external, internal, or both? Why doesn't she abandon the phone at the story's end?

SUGGESTIONS FOR WRITING

1. Choose any story in this anthology in which a character changes because of the events that occur in the story. Write an essay exploring exactly how, when, and why the character changes.
2. Choose any story in this chapter and write an essay analyzing its handling of character and methods of characterization. Do the story's characters tend to be more flat or round, static or dynamic, highly individualized or nearly indistinguishable? Is indirect or direct characterization more important? How important is each type of evidence listed on the checklist that appears earlier in this chapter? Why and how is this treatment of character appropriate to the story?
3. Imagine that you are a lawyer with the job of defending Abner Snopes. He is undoubtedly guilty of the crime of burning Major de Spain's barn, but how might you persuade the court that he deserves leniency? Write an essay in which you lay out your argument to a jury, making sure both to support your claims with facts from the story and to anticipate the portrayal of Abner Snopes's character and behavior that the prosecution will likely put forward.
4. Write an essay comparing how the adult lives and personalities of the two central characters in Recitatif are shaped by their experience in the orphanage. Why and how is this experience so traumatic? How does each character understand and cope with this experience over time? In these terms, how are Twyla and Roberta both similar and different, and what role does Maggie play in their efforts to come to terms with their past?
5. Write an essay exploring how plotting—especially sequence and pace—and narration—including focus, voice, tense, and (biblical) allusion—contribute to the characterization of Lane Dean, Jr., in Good People.

Monsters

AN ALBUM

I used to wonder why he looked familiar
Then I realized it was a mirror.
Oh, and now it is plain to see,
The whole time the monster was me.

—GNARLS BARKLEY, "THE BOOGIE MONSTER"

The world's oldest work of fiction is a story about monsters. Known as *The Epic of Gilgamesh*, it depicts the unlikely friendship between the wise but ruthless king of Uruk (in modern Iraq) and his opposite, Enkidu. A hairy (and, by some accounts, horned and hooved) creature of the forest who runs naked with the animals, knowing "nothing of land or peoples" until he is taught how to speak, eat, and clothe himself like a man, Enkidu clearly counts as a *monster* in the term's most literal sense—"a mythical creature which is part animal and part human, or combines elements of two or more animal forms, and is frequently of great size and ferocious appearance" (*Oxford English Dictionary*). Yet Enkidu ultimately accompanies Gilgamesh deep into the Cedar Forest in order to slay its far more monstrous guardian—the dreaded, fire-breathing giant Humbaba the Terrible. Even before that, Enkidu stops Gilgamesh from exercising his "right" to be the first to enjoy the sexual favors of every newly married bride in his kingdom—precisely the sort of behavior that makes the king seem, at least to his people, the real *monster* in that term's more figurative or moral sense—"A person [. . .] exhibiting such extreme cruelty or wickedness as to appear inhuman." Like many of the greatest "monster stories" to come, the world's oldest provokes us to ponder just who "the monster" truly is and whether it just might be us.

Though human beings and their stories have obviously changed enormously in the thousands of years since someone etched *Gilgamesh* onto clay tablets, one thing that hasn't changed is their fascination with creatures who cross borders we like to consider stable and impermeable—between human and animal, civilized and savage, good and evil, even life and death. Strange as it may seem, Stephenie Meyer's Edward Cullen and Jacob Black, J. K. Rowling's Professor Lupin and J. R. R. Tolkien's hobbits and dragon, even Disney's Beast, are as much Enkidu and Humbaba's descendants as are *Beowulf*'s Grendel, Bram Stoker's Dracula, and Robert Louis Stevenson's Mr. Hyde. If one of fiction's basic goals is simply to help us imagine what it is like either to be, or to cope with, someone who appears utterly different from ourselves, the "monster" may well be the ultimate fictional character. As outsiders, outcasts, and sometimes **scapegoats**, such characters have also, at least since Mary Shelley's *Frankenstein* (1818), served as a means through which authors explore a variety of specific social prejudices, norms, and forms of exclusion and oppression. Often, they do so by allowing us to perceive the world from the point of view of the monster itself—precisely that point of view with which conventional horror fiction and film often have little sympathy.

Though different, all of the stories in this album do precisely that, taking us into a deliberately fantastic world in order to give us new insight into our own. As you read them, think about how each story depicts its protagonist's peculiar character and situation. In what different senses is and is not each of these characters a "monster"? To what real people and situations do the stories encourage us to compare their fantastical ones? Or how might they help us to better understand our own distinctly human way of experiencing the world, ourselves, even time itself, by imagining an utterly alien way?

MARGARET ATWOOD (b. 1939)

Lusus Naturae[1]

Margaret Atwood spent her first eleven years in sparsely populated areas of northern Ontario and Quebec, where her father worked as an entomologist—an upbringing that may help explain her enduring concern with humanity's often-destructive relationship with the natural world. Educated at the University of Toronto and Harvard, the woman now widely regarded as Canada's preeminent woman of letters published her first poem at nineteen and the first of numerous poetry collections, *Double Persephone,* three years later. An equally gifted short-story writer who counts Edgar Allan Poe among her early inspirations, Atwood is best known for her novels. Translated into over thirty languages and often, like her poetry, exploring the unique experiences and perspectives of women, past, present, and future, her novels include straightforwardly realistic narratives like *The Edible Woman* (1969) and *Bodily Harm* (1982), at least one modernized fairy tale (*The Robber Bride* [1993]), multilayered historical fictions such as *Alias Grace* (1996) and the Booker Prize–winning *The Blind Assassin* (2000), and the futuristic dystopias Atwood herself prefers to call "speculative" rather than "science fiction"—*Oryx and Crake* (2003), *The Year of the Flood* (2009), *MaddAdam* (2013), and *The Handmaid's Tale* (1986), which inspired both a Danish opera and a Hollywood movie.

What could be done with me, what should be done with me? These were the same question. The possibilities were limited. The family discussed them all, lugubriously, endlessly, as they sat around the kitchen table at night, with the shutters closed, eating their dry whiskery sausages and their potato soup. If I was in one of my lucid phases I would sit with them, entering into the conversation as best I could while searching out the chunks of potato in my bowl. If not, I'd be off in the darkest corner, mewing to myself and listening to the twittering voices nobody else could hear.

1. Freak of nature (Latin).

"She was such a lovely baby," my mother would say. "There was nothing wrong with her." It saddened her to have given birth to an item such as myself: it was like a reproach, a judgment. What had she done wrong?

"Maybe it's a curse," said my grandmother. She was as dry and whiskery as the sausages, but in her it was natural because of her age.

"She was fine for years," said my father. "It was after that case of measles, when she was seven. After that."

"Who would curse us?" said my mother. 5

My grandmother scowled. She had a long list of candidates. Even so, there was no one she could single out. Our family had always been respected, and even liked, more or less. It still was. It still would be, if something could be done about me. Before I leaked out, so to say.

"The doctor says it's a disease," said my father. He liked to claim he was a rational man. He took the newspapers. It was he who insisted that I learn to read, and he'd persisted in his encouragement, despite everything. I no longer nestled into the crook of his arm, however. He sat me on the other side of the table. Though this enforced distance pained me, I could see his point.

"Then why didn't he give us some medicine?" said my mother. My grandmother snorted. She had her own ideas, which involved puffballs and stump water. Once she'd held my head under the water in which the dirty clothes were soaking, praying while she did it. That was to eject the demon she was convinced had flown in through my mouth and was lodged near my breastbone. My mother said she had the best of intentions, at heart.

Feed her bread, the doctor had said. *She'll want a lot of bread. That, and potatoes. She'll want to drink blood. Chicken blood will do, or the blood of a cow. Don't let her have too much.* He told us the name of the disease, which had some Ps and Rs in it and meant nothing to us.[2] He'd only seen a case like me once before, he'd said, looking at my yellow eyes, my pink teeth, my red fingernails, the long dark hair that was sprouting on my chest and arms. He wanted to take me away to the city, so other doctors could look at me, but my family refused. "She's a lusus naturae," he'd said.

"What does that mean?" said my grandmother. 10

"Freak of nature," the doctor said. He was from far away: we'd summoned him. Our own doctor would have spread rumors. "It's Latin. Like a monster." He thought I couldn't hear, because I was mewing. "It's nobody's fault."

"She's a human being," said my father. He paid the doctor a lot of money to go away to his foreign parts and never come back.

"Why did God do this to us?" said my mother.

"Curse or disease, it doesn't matter," said my older sister. "Either way, no one will marry me if they find out." I nodded my head: true enough. She was a pretty girl, and we weren't poor, we were almost gentry. Without me, her coast would be clear.

2. Porphyria, a group of usually incurable genetic disorders disrupting the body's production of hemoglobin (the protein that makes blood red); symptoms of the disease's more acute forms include insomnia, hallucinations, light sensitivity, excess body hair, reddish teeth, painful skin conditions, even disfigurement. Such symptoms, as well as certain blood-related treatments, have led some to propose porphyria as an inspiration for vampire legends, though such theories have been repeatedly debunked.

15 In the daytimes I stayed shut up in my darkened room: I was getting beyond a joke. That was fine with me, because I couldn't stand sunlight. At night, sleepless, I would roam the house, listening to the snores of the others, their yelps of nightmare. The cat kept me company. He was the only living creature who wanted to be close to me. I smelled of blood, old dried-up blood: perhaps that was why he shadowed me, why he would climb up onto me and start licking.

They'd told the neighbors I had a wasting illness, a fever, a delirium. The neighbors sent eggs and cabbages; from time to time they visited, to scrounge for news, but they weren't eager to see me: whatever it was might be catching.

It was decided that I should die. That way I would not stand in the way of my sister, I would not loom over her like a fate. "Better one happy than both miserable," said my grandmother, who had taken to sticking garlic cloves around my door frame. I agreed to this plan, as I wanted to be helpful.

The priest was bribed; in addition to that, we appealed to his sense of compassion. Everyone likes to think they are doing good while at the same time pocketing a bag of cash, and our priest was no exception. He told me God had chosen me as a special girl, a sort of bride, you might say. He said I was called on to make sacrifices. He said my sufferings would purify my soul. He said I was lucky, because I would stay innocent all my life, no man would want to pollute me, and then I would go straight to Heaven.

He told the neighbors I had died in a saintly manner. I was put on display in a very deep coffin in a very dark room, in a white dress with a lot of white veiling over me, fitting for a virgin and useful in concealing my whiskers. I lay there for two days, though of course I could walk around at night. I held my breath when anyone entered. They tiptoed, they spoke in whispers, they didn't come close, they were still afraid of my disease. To my mother they said I looked just like an angel.

20 My mother sat in the kitchen and cried as if I really had died; even my sister managed to look glum. My father wore his black suit. My grandmother baked. Everyone stuffed themselves. On the third day they filled the coffin with damp straw and carted it off to the cemetery and buried it, with prayers and a modest headstone, and three months later my sister got married. She was driven to the church in a coach, a first in our family. My coffin was a rung on her ladder.

Now that I was dead, I was freer. No one but my mother was allowed into my room, my former room as they called it. They told the neighbors they were keeping it as a shrine to my memory. They hung a picture of me on the door, a picture made when I still looked human. I didn't know what I looked like now. I avoided mirrors.

In the dimness I read Pushkin,[3] and Lord Byron, and the poetry of John Keats. I learned about blighted love, and defiance, and the sweetness of death. I found these thoughts comforting. My mother would bring me my potatoes and bread, and my cup of blood, and take away the chamber pot. Once she used to

3. Russian poet (1799–1837) associated, like Lord Byron and John Keats, with the Romantic movement; his verse-novel *Eugene Onegin* (1825–32) describes the ill-fated romance of a young aristocrat, who travels the world out of both boredom with high society and guilt over killing his friend in a duel.

brush my hair, before it came out in handfuls; she'd been in the habit of hugging me and weeping; but she was past that now. She came and went as quickly as she could. However she tried to hide it, she resented me, of course. There's only so long you can feel sorry for a person before you come to feel that their affliction is an act of malice committed by them against you.

At night I had the run of the house, and then the run of the yard, and after that the run of the forest. I no longer had to worry about getting in the way of other people and their futures. As for me, I had no future. I had only a present, a present that changed—it seemed to me—along with the moon. If it weren't for the fits, and the hours of pain, and the twittering of the voices I couldn't understand, I might have said I was happy.

My grandmother died, then my father. The cat became elderly. My mother sank further into despair. "My poor girl," she would say, though I was no longer exactly a girl. "Who will take care of you when I'm gone?"

There was only one answer to that: it would have to be me. I began to explore the limits of my power. I found I had a great deal more of it when unseen than when seen, and most of all when partly seen. I frightened two children in the woods, on purpose: I showed them my pink teeth, my hairy face, my red fingernails, I mewed at them, and they ran away screaming. Soon people avoided our end of the forest. I peered into a window at night, and caused hysterics in a young woman. "A thing! I saw a thing!" she sobbed. I was a thing, then. I considered this. In what way is a thing not a person?

A stranger made an offer to buy our farm. My mother wanted to sell and move in with my sister and her gentry husband and her healthy growing family, whose portraits had just been painted; she could no longer manage; but how could she leave me?

"Do it," I told her. By now my voice was a sort of growl. "I'll vacate my room. There's a place I can stay." She was grateful, poor soul. She had an attachment to me, as if to a hangnail, a wart: I was hers. But she was glad to be rid of me. She'd done enough duty for a lifetime.

During the packing-up and the sale of our furniture I spent the days inside a hayrick. It was sufficient, but it would not do for winter. Once the new people had moved in, it was no trouble to get rid of them. I knew the house better than they did, its entrances, its exits. I could make my way around it in the dark. I became an apparition, then another one; I was a red-nailed hand touching a face in the moonlight; I was the sound of a rusted hinge that I made despite myself. They took to their heels, and branded our place as haunted. Then I had it to myself.

I lived on stolen potatoes dug by moonlight, on eggs filched from henhouses. Once in a while I'd purloin a hen—I'd drink the blood first. There were guard dogs, but though they howled at me, they never attacked: they didn't know what I was. Inside our house, I tried a mirror. They say dead people can't see their own reflections, and it was true; I could not see myself. I saw something, but that something was not myself: it looked nothing like the innocent, pretty girl I knew myself to be, at heart.

But now things are coming to an end. I've become too visible.

This is how it happened.

I was picking blackberries in the dusk, at the verge where the meadow met the trees, and I saw two people approaching, from opposite sides. One was a young man, the other a girl. His clothing was better than hers. He had shoes.

The two of them looked furtive. I knew that look—the glances over the shoulder, the stops and starts—as I was unusually furtive myself. I crouched in the brambles to watch. They met, they twined together, they fell to the ground. Mewing noises came from them, growls, little screams. Perhaps they were having fits, both of them at once. Perhaps they were—oh, at last!—beings like myself. I crept closer to see better. They did not look like me—they were not hairy, for instance, except on their heads, and I could tell this because they had shed most of their clothing—but then, it had taken me some time to grow into what I was. They must be in the preliminary stages, I thought. They know they are changing, they have sought out each other for the company, and to share their fits.

They appeared to derive pleasure from their flailings about, even if they occasionally bit each other. I knew how that could happen. What a consolation it would be to me if I, too, could join in! Through the years I had hardened myself to loneliness; now I found that hardness dissolving. Still, I was too timorous to approach them.

One evening the young man fell asleep. The girl covered him with his cast-off shirt and kissed him on the forehead. Then she walked carefully away.

I detached myself from the brambles and came softly toward him. There he was, asleep in an oval of crushed grass, as if laid out on a platter. I'm sorry to say I lost control. I laid my red-nailed hands on him. I bit him on the neck. Was it lust or hunger? How could I tell the difference? He woke up, he saw my pink teeth, my yellow eyes; he saw my black dress fluttering; he saw me running away. He saw where.

He told the others in the village, and they began to speculate. They dug up my coffin and found it empty, and feared the worst. Now they're marching toward this house, in the dusk, with long stakes, with torches. My sister is among them, and her husband, and the young man I kissed. I meant it to be a kiss.

What can I say to them, how can I explain myself? When demons are required someone will always be found to supply the part, and whether you step forward or are pushed is all the same in the end. "I am a human being," I could say. But what proof do I have of that? "I am a lusus naturae! Take me to the city! I should be studied!" No hope there. I'm afraid it's bad news for the cat. Whatever they do to me, they'll do to him as well.

I am of a forgiving temperament, I know they have the best of intentions at heart. I've put on my white burial dress, my white veil, as befits a virgin. One must have a sense of occasion. The twittering voices are very loud: it's time for me to take flight. I'll fall from the burning rooftop like a comet, I'll blaze like a bonfire. They'll have to say many charms over my ashes, to make sure I'm really dead this time. After a while I'll become an upside-down saint; my finger bones will be sold as dark relics. I'll be a legend, by then.

Perhaps in Heaven I'll look like an angel. Or perhaps the angels will look like me. What a surprise that will be, for everyone else! It's something to look forward to.

2004

QUESTIONS

1. How and why does the protagonist's attitude toward her own situation change over the course of the story? How and why does she paradoxically become more alive and powerful after she "dies" and as she becomes more and more "invisible"?
2. Why does she nonetheless choose to make herself "visible" at the story's conclusion (par. 30)? What new insight might this episode provide into both her character and situation, on the one hand, and "normal" human behavior, on the other? How, for example, might the conclusion complicate the idea that the story is exclusively about illness or disability and our attitudes toward it?
3. What conflicts does the protagonist's condition create for the story's other characters? How do they each understand that condition? How might the story encourage us to view their attitudes and behaviors?

KAREN RUSSELL
(b. 1981)
St. Lucy's Home for Girls Raised by Wolves

Karen Russell's first novel, *Swamplandia!* (2011), details the lives of a family of alligator wrestlers in what she calls "the most bizarre place" on Earth—her childhood home of South Florida. After leaving Florida, Russell attended Northwestern University and toyed with the idea of becoming a veterinarian. Deciding that "loving animals and removing deflated basketballs from the intestinal tracts of animals are two very different skill sets," she instead turned to writing, earning an MFA from Columbia University. Just twenty-six when she published her first short-story collection, *St. Lucy's Home for Girls Raised by Wolves* (2006), Russell is almost as renowned for her youth as for her remarkable fiction; both ensured her inclusion on *New York Magazine*'s list of twenty-seven impressive New Yorkers under the age of twenty-six (2005), *Granta*'s Best Young American Novelists (2007), the National Book Foundation's "5 Under 35" (2009), and the *New Yorker*'s "20 under 40" (2010). Since winning a 2013 MacArthur Foundation "genius grant," Russell has published *Vampires in the Lemon Grove: Stories* (2013) and *Sleep Donation: A Novella* (2014). Often blending realism with the totally outlandish, her work has been compared to "slipstream," a genre-bending form of fiction with roots in magical realism. Russell herself, however, often cites "George Saunders's sad/funny ratio" and his work's "deep humility" as her inspirations.

> Stage 1: The initial period is one in which everything is new, exciting, and interesting for your students. It is fun for your students to explore their new environment.
>
> —From *The Jesuit Handbook on Lycanthropic Culture Shock*

At first, our pack was all hair and snarl and floor-thumping joy. We forgot the barked cautions of our mothers and fathers, all the promises we'd made to be civilized and ladylike, couth and kempt. We tore through the austere rooms, overturning dresser drawers, pawing through the neat piles of the Stage 3 girls' starched underwear, smashing lightbulbs with our bare fists. Things felt less foreign in the dark. The dim bedroom was windowless and odorless. We remedied this by spraying exuberant yellow streams all over the bunks. We jumped from bunk to bunk, spraying. We nosed each other midair, our bodies buckling in kinetic laughter. The nuns watched us from the corner of the bedroom, their tiny faces pinched with displeasure.

"Ay caramba," Sister Maria de la Guardia sighed. *"Que barbaridad!"*[1] She made the Sign of the Cross. Sister Maria came to St. Lucy's from a halfway home in Copacabana. In Copacabana, the girls are fat and languid and eat pink slivers of guava right out of your hand. Even at Stage 1, their pelts are silky, sunbleached to near invisibility. Our pack was hirsute and sinewy and mostly brunette. We had terrible posture. We went knuckling along the wooden floor on the calloused pads of our fists, baring row after row of tiny, wood-rotted teeth. Sister Josephine sucked in her breath. She removed a yellow wheel of floss from under her robes, looping it like a miniature lasso.

"The girls at our facility are *backwoods*,'" Sister Josephine whispered to Sister Maria de la Guardia with a beatific smile. "You must be patient with them." I clamped down on her ankle, straining to close my jaws around the woolly XXL sock. Sister Josephine tasted like sweat and freckles. She smelled easy to kill.

We'd arrived at St. Lucy's that morning, part of a pack fifteen-strong. We were accompanied by a mousy, nervous-smelling social worker; the baby-faced deacon; Bartholomew, the blue wolfhound; and four burly woodsmen. The deacon handed out some stale cupcakes and said a quick prayer. Then he led us through the woods. We ran past the wild apiary, past the felled oaks, until we could see the white steeple of St. Lucy's rising out of the forest. We stopped short at the edge of a muddy lake. Then the deacon took our brothers. Bartholomew helped him to herd the boys up the ramp of a small ferry. We girls ran along the shore, tearing at our new jumpers in a plaid agitation. Our brothers stood on the deck, looking small and confused.

5 Our mothers and fathers were werewolves. They lived an outsider's existence in caves at the edge of the forest, threatened by frost and pitchforks. They had been ostracized by the local farmers for eating their silled fruit pies and terrorizing the heifers. They had ostracized the local wolves by having sometimes-thumbs, and regrets, and human children. (Their condition skips a generation.) Our pack grew up in a green purgatory. We couldn't keep up with the purebred wolves, but we never stopped crawling. We spoke a slab-tongued pidgin[2] in the cave, inflected with frequent howls. Our parents wanted something better for us; they wanted us to get braces, use towels, be fully bilingual. When the nuns showed up, our parents couldn't refuse their offer. The nuns, they said, would make us naturalized citizens of human society. We would go to St. Lucy's to study a better culture. We didn't know at the time that our parents were sending us away for good. Neither did they.

1. What barbarity (Spanish). *Ay Caramba*: good grief (Spanish).
2. Simplified speech used for communication between speakers of different languages.

That first afternoon, the nuns gave us free rein of the grounds. Everything was new, exciting, and interesting. A low granite wall surrounded St. Lucy's, the blue woods humming for miles behind it. There was a stone fountain full of delectable birds. There was a statue of St. Lucy.[3] Her marble skin was colder than our mother's nose, her pupil-less eyes rolled heavenward. Doomed squirrels gamboled around her stony toes. Our diminished pack threw back our heads in a celebratory howl—an exultant and terrible noise, even without a chorus of wolf brothers in the background. There were holes everywhere!

We supplemented these holes by digging some of our own. We interred sticks, and our itchy new jumpers, and the bones of the friendly, unfortunate squirrels. Our noses ached beneath an invisible assault. Everything was smudged with a human odor: baking bread, petrol, the nuns' faint woman-smell sweating out beneath a dark perfume of tallow and incense. We smelled one another, too, with the same astounded fascination. Our own scent had become foreign in this strange place.

We had just sprawled out in the sun for an afternoon nap, yawning into the warm dirt, when the nuns reappeared. They conferred in the shadow of the juniper tree, whispering and pointing. Then they started towards us. The oldest sister had spent the past hour twitching in her sleep, dreaming of fatty and infirm elk. (The pack used to dream the same dreams back then, as naturally as we drank the same water and slept on the same red scree.[4]) When our oldest sister saw the nuns approaching, she instinctively bristled. It was an improvised bristle, given her new, human limitations. She took clumps of her scraggly, nut-brown hair and held it straight out from her head.

Sister Maria gave her a brave smile.

"And what is your name?" she asked. 10

The oldest sister howled something awful and inarticulable, a distillate of hurt and panic, half-forgotten hunts and eclipsed moons. Sister Maria nodded and scribbled on a yellow legal pad. She slapped on a name tag: HELLO, MY NAME IS ________! "Jeanette it is."

The rest of the pack ran in a loose, uncertain circle, torn between our instinct to help her and our new fear. We sensed some subtler danger afoot, written in a language we didn't understand.

Our littlest sister had the quickest reflexes. She used her hands to flatten her ears to the side of her head. She backed towards the far corner of the garden, snarling in the most menacing register that an eight-year-old wolf-girl can muster. Then she ran. It took them two hours to pin her down and tag her: HELLO, MY NAME IS MIRABELLA!

"Stage 1," Sister Maria sighed, taking careful aim with her tranquilizer dart. "It can be a little overstimulating."

> Stage 2: After a time, your students realize that they must work to adjust to the new culture. This work may be stressful and students may experience a strong sense of dislocation. They may miss certain foods. They may spend a

3. Patron saint of the blind, St. Lucy (283–304) either took out her own eyes or was blinded by others, according to legend, defending her vow to remain a virgin and dedicate her life and fortune to God rather than marry a pagan.
4. Loose stones or rocky debris.

lot of time daydreaming during this period. Many students feel isolated, irritated, bewildered, depressed, or generally uncomfortable.

15 Those were the days when we dreamed of rivers and meat. The full-moon nights were the worst! Worse than cold toilet seats and boiled tomatoes, worse than trying to will our tongues to curl around our false new names. We would snarl at one another for no reason. I remember how disorienting it was to look down and see two square-toed shoes instead of my own four feet. Keep your mouth shut, I repeated during our walking drills, staring straight ahead. Keep your shoes on your feet. Mouth shut, shoes on feet. Do not chew on your new penny loafers. Do not. I stumbled around in a daze, my mouth black with shoe polish. The whole pack was irritated, bewildered, depressed. We were all uncomfortable, and between languages. We had never wanted to run away so badly in our lives; but who did we have to run back to? Only the curled black grimace of the mother. Only the father, holding his tawny head between his paws. Could we betray our parents by going back to them? After they'd given us the choicest part of the woodchuck, loved us at our hairless worst, nosed us across the ice floes and abandoned us at St. Lucy's for our own betterment?

Physically, we were all easily capable of clearing the low stone walls. Sister Josephine left the wooden gates wide open. They unslatted the windows at night so that long fingers of moonlight beckoned us from the woods. But we knew we couldn't return to the woods; not till we were civilized, not if we didn't want to break the mother's heart. It all felt like a sly, human taunt.

It was impossible to make the blank, chilly bedroom feel like home. In the beginning, we drank gallons of bathwater as part of a collaborative effort to mark our territory. We puddled up the yellow carpet of old newspapers. But later, when we returned to the bedroom, we were dismayed to find all trace of the pack musk had vanished. Someone was coming in and erasing us. We sprayed and sprayed every morning; and every night, we returned to the same ammonia eradication. We couldn't make our scent stick here; it made us feel invisible. Eventually we gave up. Still, the pack seemed to be adjusting on the same timetable. The advanced girls could already alternate between two speeds: "slouch" and "amble." Almost everybody was fully bipedal.

Almost.

The pack was worried about Mirabella.

20 Mirabella would rip foamy chunks out of the church pews and replace them with ham bones and girl dander. She loved to roam the grounds wagging her invisible tail. (We all had a hard time giving that up. When we got excited, we would fall to the ground and start pumping our backsides. Back in those days we could pump at rabbity velocities. *Que horror!* Sister Maria frowned, looking more than a little jealous.) We'd give her scolding pinches. "Mirabella," we hissed, imitating the nuns. "No." Mirabella cocked her ears at us, hurt and confused.

Still, some things remained the same. The main commandment of wolf life is Know Your Place, and that translated perfectly. Being around other humans had awakened a slavish-dog affection in us. An abasing, belly-to-the-ground desire to please. As soon as we realized that someone higher up in the food chain was watching us, we wanted only to be pleasing in their sight. Mouth shut, I repeated, shoes on feet. But if Mirabella had this latent instinct, the nuns couldn't figure out how to activate it. She'd go bounding around, gleefully spraying on their gilded statue of St. Lucy, mad-scratching at the virulent fleas that survived all of their powders and baths. At Sister Maria's tearful insistence, she'd stand upright for roll call, her knobby, oddly muscled legs quivering from the effort. Then she'd collapse right back to the ground with an ecstatic *oomph!* She was still loping around on all fours (which the nuns had taught us to see looked unnatural and ridiculous—we could barely believe it now, the shame of it, that we used to locomote like that!), her fists blue-white from the strain. As if she were holding a secret tight to the ground. Sister Maria de la Guardia would sigh every time she saw her. "*Caramba!*" She'd sit down with Mirabella and pry her fingers apart. "You see?" she'd say softly, again and again. "What are you holding on to? Nothing, little one. Nothing."

Then she would sing out the standard chorus, "Why can't you be more like your sister Jeanette?"

The pack hated Jeanette. She was the most successful of us, the one furthest removed from her origins. Her real name was GWARR!, but she wouldn't respond to this anymore. Jeanette spiffed her penny loafers until her very shoes seemed to gloat. (Linguists have since traced the colloquial origins of "goody two-shoes" back to our facilities.) She could even growl out a demonic-sounding precursor to "Pleased to meet you." She'd delicately extend her former paws to visitors, wearing white kid gloves.

"Our little wolf, disguised in sheep's clothing!" Sister Ignatius liked to joke with the visiting deacons, and Jeanette would surprise everyone by laughing along with them, a harsh, inhuman, barking sound. Her hearing was still twig-snap sharp. Jeanette was the first among us to apologize; to drink apple juice out of a sippy cup; to quit eyeballing the cleric's jugular in a disconcerting fashion. She curled her lips back into a cousin of a smile as the traveling barber cut her pelt into bangs. Then she swept her coarse black curls under the rug. When we entered a room, our nostrils flared beneath the new odors: onion and bleach, candle wax, the turnipy smell of unwashed bodies. Not Jeanette. Jeanette smiled and pretended like she couldn't smell a thing.

I was one of the good girls. Not great and not terrible, solidly middle of the pack. But I had an ear for languages, and I could read before I could adequately wash myself. I probably could have vied with Jeanette for the number-one spot, but I'd seen what happened if you gave in to your natural aptitudes. This wasn't like the woods, where you had to be your fastest and your strongest and your bravest self. Different sorts of calculations were required to survive at the home.

The pack hated Jeanette, but we hated Mirabella more. We began to avoid her, but sometimes she'd surprise us, curled up beneath the beds or gnawing on a scapula in the garden. It was scary to be ambushed by your sister. I'd bristle and growl, the way that I'd begun to snarl at my own reflection as if it were a stranger.

"Whatever will become of Mirabella?" we asked, gulping back our own fear. We'd heard rumors about former wolf-girls who never adapted to their new culture. It was assumed that they were returned to our native country, the vanishing woods. We liked to speculate about this before bedtime, scaring ourselves with stories of catastrophic bliss. It was the disgrace, the failure that we all guiltily hoped for in our hard beds. Twitching with the shadow question: *Whatever will become of me?*

We spent a lot of time daydreaming during this period. Even Jeanette. Sometimes I'd see her looking out at the woods in a vacant way. If you interrupted her in the midst of one of these reveries, she would lunge at you with an elder-sister ferocity, momentarily forgetting her human catechism. We liked her better then, startled back into being foamy old Jeanette.

In school, they showed us the St. Francis of Assisi[5] slide show, again and again. Then the nuns would give us bags of bread. They never announced these things as a test; it was only much later that I realized that we were under constant examination. "Go feed the ducks," they urged us. "Go practice compassion for all God's creatures." *Don't pair me with Mirabella,* I prayed, *anybody but Mirabella.* "Claudette"—Sister Josephine beamed—"why don't you and Mirabella take some pumpernickel down to the ducks?"

"Ohhkaaythankyou," I said. (It took me a long time to say anything; first I had to translate it in my head from the Wolf.) It wasn't fair. They knew Mirabella couldn't make bread balls yet. She couldn't even undo the twist tie of the bag. She was sure to eat the birds; Mirabella didn't even try to curb her desire to kill things—and then who would get blamed for the dark spots of duck blood on our Peter Pan collars? Who would get penalized with negative Skill Points? Exactly.

As soon as we were beyond the wooden gates, I snatched the bread away from Mirabella and ran off to the duck pond on my own. Mirabella gave chase, nipping at my heels. She thought it was a game. "Stop it," I growled. I ran faster, but it was Stage 2 and I was still unsteady on my two feet. I fell sideways into a leaf pile, and then all I could see was my sister's blurry form, bounding towards me. In a moment, she was on top of me, barking the old word for tug-of-war. When she tried to steal the bread out of my hands, I whirled around and snarled at her, pushing my ears back from my head. I bit her shoulder, once, twice, the only language she would respond to. I used my new motor skills. I threw dirt, I threw stones. "Get away!" I screamed, long after she had made a cringing retreat into the shadows of the purple saplings. "Get away, get away!"

Much later, they found Mirabella wading in the shallows of a distant river, trying to strangle a mallard with her rosary beads. I was at the lake; I'd been sitting there for hours. Hunched in the long cattails, my yellow eyes flashing, shoving ragged hunks of bread into my mouth.

I don't know what they did to Mirabella. Me they separated from my sisters. They made me watch another slide show. This one showed images of former wolf-girls, the ones who had failed to be rehabilitated. Long-haired, sad-eyed women, limping after their former wolf packs in white tennis shoes and pleated culottes. A wolf-girl bank teller, her makeup smeared in oily rainbows, eating a raw steak on the deposit slips while her colleagues looked on in disgust. Our parents. The final slide was a bolded sentence in St. Lucy's prim script: DO YOU WANT TO END UP SHUNNED BY BOTH SPECIES?

After that, I spent less time with Mirabella. One night she came to me, holding her hand out. She was covered with splinters, keening a high, whining noise through her nostrils. Of course I understood what she wanted; I wasn't that far

5. In one of many legends illustrating his special relationship with animals, St. Francis (1181–1226) first talks a village out of killing a wolf that has been attacking them and convinces the wolf to stop killing; the villagers then make a pet of the wolf.

removed from our language (even though I was reading at a fifth-grade level, halfway into Jack London's *The Son of the Wolf.*)[6]

"Lick your own wounds," I said, not unkindly. It was what the nuns had 35
instructed us to say; wound licking was not something you did in polite company. Etiquette was so confounding in this country. Still, looking at Mirabella—her fists balled together like small, white porcupines, her brows knitted in animal confusion—I felt a throb of compassion. *How can people live like they do?* I wondered. Then I congratulated myself. This was a Stage 3 thought.

> Stage 3: It is common that students who start living in a new and different culture come to a point where they reject the host culture and withdraw into themselves. During this period, they make generalizations about the host culture and wonder how the people can live like they do. Your students may feel that their own culture's lifestyle and customs are far superior to those of the host country.

The nuns were worried about Mirabella, too. To correct a failing, you must first be aware of it as a failing. And there was Mirabella, shucking her plaid jumper in full view of the visiting cardinal. Mirabella, battling a raccoon under the dinner table while the rest of us took dainty bites of peas and borscht. Mirabella, doing belly flops into compost.

"You have to pull your weight around here," we overheard Sister Josephine saying one night. We paused below the vestry window and peered inside.

"Does Mirabella try to earn Skill Points by shelling walnuts and polishing Saint-in-the-Box? No. Does Mirabella even know how to say the word *walnut*? Has she learned how to say anything besides a sinful 'HraaaHA!' as she commits frottage[7] against the organ pipes? No."

There was a long silence.

"Something must be done," Sister Ignatius said firmly. The other nuns nod- 40
ded, a sea of thin, colorless lips and kettle-black brows. "Something must be done," they intoned. That ominously passive construction; a something so awful that nobody wanted to assume responsibility for it.

I could have warned her. If we were back home, and Mirabella had come under attack by territorial beavers or snow-blind bears, I would have warned her. But the truth is that by Stage 3 I wanted her gone. Mirabella's inability to adapt was taking a visible toll. Her teeth were ground down to nubbins; her hair was falling out. She hated the spongy, long-dead foods we were served, and it showed—her ribs were poking through her uniform. Her bright eyes had dulled to a sour whiskey color. But you couldn't show Mirabella the slightest kindness anymore—she'd never leave you alone! You'd have to sit across from her at meals, shoving her away as she begged for your scraps. I slept fitfully during that period, unable to forget that Mirabella was living under my bed, gnawing on my loafers.

It was during Stage 3 that we met our first purebred girls. These were girls raised in captivity, volunteers from St. Lucy's School for Girls. The apple-cheeked

6. **Short story (1900) about a white settler in the Yukon whose determination to marry an indigenous woman over the objections of her people results in the death of two tribesmen.**

7. **Rubbing against a person or object for sexual stimulation.**

fourth-grade class came to tutor us in playing. They had long golden braids or short, severe bobs. They had frilly-duvet names like Felicity and Beulah; and pert, bunny noses; and terrified smiles. We grinned back at them with genuine ferocity. It made us nervous to meet new humans. There were so many things that we could do wrong! And the rules here were different depending on which humans we were with: dancing or no dancing, checkers playing or no checkers playing, pumping or no pumping.

The purebred girls played checkers with us.

"These girl-girls sure is dumb," my sister Lavash panted to me between games. "I win it again! Five to none."

45 She was right. The purebred girls were making mistakes on purpose, in order to give us an advantage. "King me," I growled, out of turn. *"I say king me!"* and Felicity meekly complied. Beulah pretended not to mind when we got frustrated with the oblique, fussy movement from square to square and shredded the board to ribbons. I felt sorry for them. I wondered what it would be like to be bred in captivity, and always homesick for a dimly sensed forest, the trees you've never seen.

Jeanette was learning how to dance. On Holy Thursday, she mastered a rudimentary form of the Charleston. *"Brava!"* The nuns clapped. *"Brava!"*

Every Friday, the girls who had learned how to ride a bicycle celebrated by going on chaperoned trips into town. The purebred girls sold seven hundred rolls of gift-wrap paper and used the proceeds to buy us a yellow fleet of bicycles built for two. We'd ride the bicycles uphill, a sanctioned pumping, a grim-faced nun pedaling behind each one of us. "Congratulations!" the nuns would huff. "Being human is like riding this bicycle. Once you've learned how, you'll never forget." Mirabella would run after the bicycles, growling out our old names. HWRAA! GWARR! TRRRRRRR! We pedaled faster.

At this point, we'd had six weeks of lessons, and still nobody could do the Sausalito but Jeanette. The nuns decided we needed an inducement to dance. They announced that we would celebrate our successful rehabilitations with a Debutante Ball. There would be brothers, ferried over from the Home for Man-Boys Raised by Wolves. There would be a photographer from the *Gazette Sophisticate.* There would be a three-piece jazz band from West Toowoomba, and root beer in tiny plastic cups. The brothers! We'd almost forgotten about them. Our invisible tails went limp. I should have been excited; instead, I felt a low mad anger at the nuns. They knew we weren't ready to dance with the brothers; we weren't even ready to talk to them. Things had been so much simpler in the woods. That night I waited until my sisters were asleep. Then I slunk into the closet and practiced the Sausalito two-step in secret, a private mass of twitch and foam. Mouth shut—shoes on feet! Mouth shut—shoes on feet! Mouthshutmouthshut . . .

One night I came back early from the closet and stumbled on Jeanette. She was sitting in a patch of moonlight on the windowsill, reading from one of her library books. (She was the first of us to sign for her library card, too.) Her cheeks looked dewy.

50 "Why you cry?" I asked her, instinctively reaching over to lick Jeanette's cheek and catching myself in the nick of time.

Jeanette blew her nose into a nearby curtain. (Even her mistakes annoyed us—they were always so well intentioned.) She sniffled and pointed to a line in her book: "The lake-water was reinventing the forest and the white moon above it, and wolves lapped up the cold reflection of the sky." But none of the pack besides me could read yet, and I wasn't ready to claim a common language with Jeanette.

The following day, Jeanette golfed. The nuns set up a miniature putt-putt course in the garden. Sister Maria dug four sandtraps and got old Walter, the groundskeeper, to make a windmill out of a lawn mower engine. The eighteenth hole was what they called a "doozy," a minuscule crack in St. Lucy's marble dress. Jeanette got a hole in one.

On Sundays, the pretending felt almost as natural as nature. The chapel was our favorite place. Long before we could understand what the priest was saying, the music instructed us in how to feel. The choir director—aggressively perfumed Mrs. Valuchi, gold necklaces like pineapple rings around her neck—taught us more than the nuns ever did. She showed us how to pattern the old hunger into arias. Clouds moved behind the frosted oculus of the nave, glass shadows that reminded me of my mother. The mother, I'd think, struggling to conjure up a picture. A black shadow, running behind the watery screen of pines.

We sang at the chapel annexed to the home every morning. We understood that this was the humans' moon, the place for howling beyond purpose. Not for mating, not for hunting, not for fighting, not for anything but the sound itself. And we'd howl along with the choir, hurling every pitted thing within us at the stained glass. "Sotto voce."[8] The nuns would frown. But you could tell that they were pleased.

> Stage 4: As a more thorough understanding of the host culture is acquired, your students will begin to feel more comfortable in their new environment. Your students feel more at home, and their self-confidence grows. Everything begins to make sense.

"Hey, Claudette," Jeanette growled to me on the day before the ball. "Have 55
you noticed that everything's beginning to make sense?"

Before I could answer, Mirabella sprang out of the hall closet and snapped through Jeanette's homework binder. Pages and pages of words swirled around the stone corridor, like dead leaves off trees.

"What about you, Mirabella?" Jeanette asked politely, stooping to pick up her erasers. She was the only one of us who would still talk to Mirabella; she was high enough in the rankings that she could afford to talk to the scruggliest wolf-girl. "Has everything begun to make more sense, Mirabella?"

Mirabella let out a whimper. She scratched at us and scratched at us, raking her nails along our shins so hard that she drew blood. Then she rolled belly-up on the cold stone floor, squirming on a bed of spelling-bee worksheets. Above us, small pearls of light dotted the high, tinted window.

Jeanette frowned. "You are a late bloomer, Mirabella! Usually, everything's begun to make more sense by Month Twelve at the latest." I noticed that she stumbled on the word *bloomer.* HraaaHA! Jeanette could never fully shake our accent. She'd talk like that her whole life, I thought with a gloomy satisfaction, each word winced out like an apology for itself.

8. In a low voice (Italian).

60 "Claudette, help me," she yelped. Mirabella had closed her jaws around Jeanette's bald ankle and was dragging her towards the closet. "Please. Help me to mop up Mirabella's mess."

I ignored her and continued down the hall. I had only four more hours to perfect the Sausalito. I was worried only about myself. By that stage, I was no longer certain of how the pack felt about anything.

At seven o'clock on the dot, Sister Ignatius blew her whistle and frog-marched us into the ball. The nuns had transformed the rectory into a very scary place. Purple and silver balloons started popping all around us. Black streamers swooped down from the eaves and got stuck in our hair like bats. A full yellow moon smirked outside the window. We were greeted by blasts of a saxophone, and fizzy pink drinks, and the brothers.

The brothers didn't smell like our brothers anymore. They smelled like pomade and cold, sterile sweat. They looked like little boys. Someone had washed behind their ears and made them wear suspendered dungarees. Kyle used to be a blustery alpha male, BTWWWR!, chewing through rattlesnakes, spooking badgers, snatching a live trout out of a grizzly's mouth. He stood by the punch bowl, looking pained and out of place.

"My stars!" I growled. "What lovely weather we've been having!"

65 "Yeees," Kyle growled back. "It is beginning to look a lot like Christmas." All around the room, boys and girls raised by wolves were having the same conversation. Actually, it had been an unseasonably warm and brown winter, and just that morning a freak hailstorm had sent Sister Josephina to an early grave. But we had only gotten up to Unit 7: Party Dialogue; we hadn't yet learned the vocabulary for Unit 12: How to Tactfully Acknowledge Disaster. Instead, we wore pink party hats and sucked olives on little sticks, inured to our own strangeness.

The nuns swept our hair back into high, bouffant hairstyles. This made us look more girlish and less inclined to eat people, the way that squirrels are saved from looking like rodents by their poofy tails. I was wearing a white organdy dress with orange polka dots. Jeanette was wearing a mauve organdy dress with blue polka dots. Linette was wearing a red organdy dress with white polka dots. Mirabella was in a dark corner, wearing a muzzle. Her party culottes were duct-taped to her knees. The nuns had tied little bows on the muzzle to make it more festive. Even so, the jazz band from West Toowoomba kept glancing nervously her way.

"You smell astoooounding!" Kyle was saying, accidentally stretching the diphthong into a howl and then blushing. "I mean—"

"Yes, I know what it is that you mean," I snapped. (That's probably a little narrative embellishment on my part; it must have been months before I could really "snap" out words.) I didn't smell astounding. I had rubbed a pumpkin muffin all over my body earlier that morning to mask my natural, feral scent. Now I smelled like a purebred girl, easy to kill. I narrowed my eyes at Kyle and flattened my ears, something I hadn't done for months. Kyle looked panicked, trying to remember the words that would make me act like a girl again. I felt hot, oily tears squeezing out of the red corners of my eyes. *Shoesonfeet!* I barked at myself. I tried again. "My! What lovely weather—"

The jazz band struck up a tune.

70 "The time has come to do the Sausalito," Sister Maria announced, beaming into the microphone. "Every sister grab a brother!" She switched on Walter's

industrial flashlight, struggling beneath its weight, and aimed the beam in the center of the room.

Uh-oh. I tried to skulk off into Mirabella's corner, but Kyle pushed me into the spotlight. "No," I moaned through my teeth, "noooooo." All of a sudden the only thing my body could remember how to do was pump and pump. In a flash of white-hot light, my months at St. Lucy's had vanished, and I was just a terrified animal again. As if of their own accord, my feet started to wiggle out of my shoes. *Mouth shut,* I gasped, staring down at my naked toes, *mouthshutmouthshut.*

"Ahem. The time has come," Sister Maria coughed, "to do the Sausalito." She paused. "The Sausalito," she added helpfully, "does not in any way resemble the thing that you are doing."

Beads of sweat stood out on my forehead. I could feel my jaws gaping open, my tongue lolling out of the left side of my mouth. What were the steps? I looked frantically for Jeanette; she would help me, she would tell me what to do.

Jeanette was sitting in the corner, sipping punch through a long straw and watching me pant. I locked eyes with her, pleading with the mute intensity that I had used to beg her for weasel bones in the forest. "What are the steps?" I mouthed.

"The steps!"

"The steps?" Then Jeanette gave me a wide, true wolf smile. For an instant, she looked just like our mother. "Not for you," she mouthed back.

I threw my head back, a howl clawing its way up my throat. I was about to lose all my Skill Points, I was about to fail my Adaptive Dancing test. But before the air could burst from my lungs, the wind got knocked out of me. *Oomph!* I fell to the ground, my skirt falling softly over my head. Mirabella had intercepted my eye-cry for help. She'd chewed through her restraints and tackled me from behind, barking at unseen cougars, trying to shield me with her tiny body. *"Caramba!"* Sister Maria squealed, dropping the flashlight. The music ground to a halt. And I have never loved someone so much, before or since, as I loved my littlest sister at that moment. I wanted to roll over and lick her ears, I wanted to kill a dozen spotted fawns and let her eat first.

But everybody was watching; everybody was waiting to see what I would do. "I wasn't talking to you," I grunted from underneath her. "I didn't want your help. Now you have ruined the Sausalito! You have ruined the ball!" I said more loudly, hoping the nuns would hear how much my enunciation had improved.

"You have ruined it!" my sisters panted, circling around us, eager to close ranks. "Mirabella has ruined it!" Every girl was wild-eyed and itching under her polka dots, punch froth dribbling down her chin. The pack had been waiting for this moment for some time. "Mirabella cannot adapt! Back to the woods, back to the woods!"

The band from West Toowoomba had quietly packed their instruments into black suitcases and were sneaking out the back. The boys had fled back towards the lake, bow ties spinning, snapping suspenders in their haste. Mirabella was still snarling in the center of it all, trying to figure out where the danger was so that she could defend me against it. The nuns exchanged glances.

In the morning, Mirabella was gone. We checked under all the beds. I pretended to be surprised. I'd known she would have to be expelled the minute I felt her weight on my back. Walter came and told me this in secret after the ball, "So you can say yer good-byes." I didn't want to face Mirabella. Instead, I packed a tin lunch pail for her: two jelly sandwiches on saltine crackers, a chloroformed squirrel, a gilt-edged placard of St. Bolio. I left it for her with Sister Ignatius, with a little note: "Best wishes!" I told myself I'd done everything I could.

"Hooray!" the pack crowed. "Something has been done!"

We raced outside into the bright sunlight, knowing full well that our sister had been turned loose, that we'd never find her. A low roar rippled through us and surged up and up, disappearing into the trees. I listened for an answering howl from Mirabella, heart thumping—what if she heard us and came back? But there was nothing.

We graduated from St. Lucy's shortly thereafter. As far as I can recollect, that was our last communal howl.

> Stage 5: At this point your students are able to interact effectively in the new cultural environment. They find it easy to move between the two cultures.

85 One Sunday, near the end of my time at St. Lucy's, the sisters gave me a special pass to go visit the parents. The woodsman had to accompany me; I couldn't remember how to find the way back on my own. I wore my best dress and brought along some prosciutto and dill pickles in a picnic basket. We crunched through the fall leaves in silence, and every step made me sadder. "I'll wait out here," the woodsman said, leaning on a blue elm and lighting a cigarette.

The cave looked so much smaller than I remembered it. I had to duck my head to enter. Everybody was eating when I walked in. They all looked up from the bull moose at the same time, my aunts and uncles, my sloe-eyed, lolling cousins, the parents. My uncle dropped a thighbone from his mouth. My littlest brother, a cross-eyed wolf-boy who has since been successfully rehabilitated and is now a dour, balding children's book author, started whining in terror. My mother recoiled from me, as if I was a stranger. TRRR? She sniffed me for a long moment. Then she sank her teeth into my ankle, looking proud and sad. After all the tail wagging and perfunctory barking had died down, the parents sat back on their hind legs. They stared up at me expectantly, panting in the cool gray envelope of the cave, waiting for a display of what I had learned.

"So," I said, telling my first human lie. "I'm home."

2006

QUESTIONS

1. How and why does the protagonist change over the course of the story? How might those changes be reflected in the way she shifts, as a narrator, between first-person plural and singular?
2. At one point in the story, the narrator remarks, "This wasn't like the woods, where you had to be your fastest and your strongest and your bravest self. Different sorts of calculations were required to survive [. . .]" (par. 25). What do you think she means? How might this comment help us to understand both her later behavior and the roles that Jeanette and Mirabella play in her life and in the story?
3. To what extent do you think this story is simply about growing up, making the transition from childhood to adulthood? about schooling or education? about the experience of those who are bilingual or even bicultural? What might the story suggest

about the difficulties of those experiences? their benefits and costs? In these terms, what role is played by the quotations from the (fictional) *Jesuit Handbook on Lycanthropic Culture Shock*?

JORGE LUIS BORGES (1899–1986)

The House of Asterion[1]

Widely considered Latin America's foremost author, Jorge Luis Borges was born and raised in Buenos Aires, Argentina. The son of a lawyer and would-be writer who also taught in an English school, the young Borges reportedly learned to speak English before Spanish and read avidly and widely; his early favorites included *The Adventures of Huckleberry Finn, The Arabian Nights*, and the novels of H. G. Wells and Charles Dickens. While traveling in Europe, his family was trapped in Geneva at the outbreak of World War I, and Borges attended the Collège de Genève, where he added French, German, and Latin to his linguistic arsenal. He then spent two years in Spain, where he wrote his first poems, before returning to Argentina in 1921. Despite his persistent, outspoken opposition to the military dictatorship of Juan Perón, Borges became the director of Argentina's national library in 1955. The very same year, Borges lost his long battle against encroaching blindness; ordered by doctors never to read or write again, he abandoned fiction for poetry for the last thirty years of his life, taking comfort in the example of the great blind poets Homer and Milton. Though he thus began and ended his writing life as a poet, Borges—who never wrote a novel—is best known as both a writer of short *ficciones* ("fictions"), a label he preferred to *cuentos* ("stories"), and as a pioneer of magical realism.

And the queen gave birth to a son named Asterion.

APOLLODORUS,[2] *Library*, III:I

I know that I am accused of arrogance and perhaps of misanthropy, and perhaps even of madness. These accusations (which I shall punish in due time) are ludicrous. It is true that I never leave my house, but it is also true that its doors (whose number is infinite[3]) stand open night and day to men and also to animals. Anyone who wishes to enter may do so. Here, no womanly splendors, no palatial ostentation shall be found, but only calm and solitude. Here shall be found a house like none other on the face of the earth. (Those who say

1. Translated by Andrew Hurley.
2. Greek scholar (d. after 120 BCE); a librarian at the renowned library in Alexandria, Egypt, and author of works on history, philosophy, mythology, and geography. Though long attributed to him, the influential compendium of Greek myths known as *The Library* was in fact composed long after his death.
3. The original reads "fourteen," but there is more than enough cause to conclude that when spoken by Asterion that number stands for "infinite" [Borges's note].

there is a similar house in Egypt speak lies.) Even my detractors admit that *there is not a single piece of furniture in the house*. Another absurd tale is that I, Asterion, am a prisoner. Need I repeat that the door stands open? Need I add that there is no lock? Furthermore, one afternoon I did go out into the streets; if I returned before nightfall, I did so because of the terrible dread inspired in me by the faces of the people—colorless faces, as flat as the palm of one's hand. The sun had already gone down, but the helpless cry of a babe and the crude supplications of the masses were signs that I had been recognized. The people prayed, fled, fell prostrate before me; some climbed up onto the stylobate[4] of the temple of the Axes, others gathered stones. One, I believe, hid in the sea. Not for nothing was my mother a queen; I cannot mix with commoners, even if my modesty should wish it.

The fact is, I am unique. I am not interested in what a man can publish abroad to other men; like the philosopher, I think that nothing can be communicated by the art of writing. Vexatious and trivial minutiæ find no refuge in my spirit, which has been formed for greatness; I have never grasped for long the difference between one letter and another. A certain generous impatience has prevented me from learning to read. Sometimes I regret that, because the nights and the days are long.

Of course I do not lack for distractions. Sometimes I run like a charging ram through the halls of stone until I tumble dizzily to the ground; sometimes I crouch in the shadow of a wellhead or at a corner in one of the corridors and pretend I am being hunted. There are rooftops from which I can hurl myself until I am bloody. I can pretend anytime I like that I am asleep, and lie with my eyes closed and my breathing heavy. (Sometimes I actually fall asleep; sometimes by the time I open my eyes, the color of the day has changed.) But of all the games, the one I like best is pretending that there is another Asterion. I pretend that he has come to visit me, and I show him around the house. Bowing majestically, I say to him: *Now let us return to our previous intersection* or *Let us go this way, now, out into another courtyard* or *I knew that you would like this rain gutter* or *Now you will see a cistern that has filled with sand* or *Now you will see how the cellar forks.* Sometimes I make a mistake and the two of us have a good laugh over it.

It is not just these games I have thought up—I have also thought a great deal about the house. Each part of the house occurs many times; any particular place is another place. There is not one wellhead, one courtyard, one drinking trough, one manger; there are fourteen [an infinite number of] mangers, drinking troughs, courtyards, wellheads. The house is as big as the world—or rather, it *is* the world. Nevertheless, by making my way through every single courtyard with its wellhead and every single dusty gallery of gray stone, I have come out onto the street and seen the temple of the Axes and the sea. That sight, I did not understand until a night vision revealed to me that there are also fourteen [an infinite number of] seas and temples. Everything exists many times, fourteen times, but there are two things in the world that apparently exist but once—on high, the intricate sun, and below, Asterion. Perhaps I have created the stars and the sun and this huge house, and no longer remember it.

4. In classical architecture, the base or pavement supporting a row of columns.

5 Every nine years, nine men come into the house so that I can free them from all evil.[5] I hear their footsteps or their voices far away in the galleries of stone, and I run joyously to find them. The ceremony lasts but a few minutes. One after another, they fall, without my ever having to bloody my hands. Where they fall, they remain, and their bodies help distinguish one gallery from the others. I do not know how many there have been, but I do know that one of them predicted as he died that someday my redeemer would come. Since then, there has been no pain for me in solitude, because I know that my redeemer lives, and in the end he will rise and stand above the dust.[6] If my ear could hear every sound in the world, I would hear his footsteps. I hope he takes me to a place with fewer galleries and fewer doors. What will my redeemer be like, I wonder. Will he be bull or man? Could he possibly be a bull with the face of a man? Or will he be like me?

The morning sun shimmered on the bronze sword. Now there was not a trace of blood left on it.

"Can you believe it, Ariadne?" said Theseus. "The Minotaur[7] scarcely defended itself."

For Maria Mosquera Eastman

1949

QUESTIONS

1. In reading or re-reading the story, when and how might you start to suspect or know that its narrator is the mythical Minotaur and/or that its setting is a labyrinth or maze?
2. What is the effect and significance of point of view in the story? of the title and epigraph, especially the fact that both use the name Asterion rather than Minotaur?
3. What various things might the labyrinth and the Minotaur symbolize in the story? In these terms, what might be the significance of the biblical allusions? the narrator's insistence that he is not "a prisoner" (par. 1)?

5. Possibly, an echo of the Lord's Prayer, which ends, "And lead us not into temptation, but deliver us from evil: For thine is the kingdom, and the power, and the glory, for ever. Amen" (Matt. 6.13).

6. Compare Job 19.25–26: "For I know that my redeemer liveth, and that he shall stand at the latter day upon the earth: / And though after my skin worms destroy this body, yet in my flesh shall I see God"; "But ye should say, Why persecute we him [. . .] / Be ye afraid of the sword: for wrath bringeth the punishments of the sword, that ye may know there is a judgment."

7. Literally, the bull of Minos, also called Asterion or Asterius, meaning "the starry one" (Greek); in classical mythology, the creature born of the union between Queen Pasiphae of Crete (wife of King Minos and daughter of the sun god and a sea nymph) and a white bull sent by the sea god, Poseidon. To quote *The Library* from which Borges takes his epigraph, "Asterius, who was called the Minotaur," "had the face of a bull, but the rest of him was human; and Minos, in compliance with certain oracles, shut him up and guarded him in the Labyrinth" made by the great Athenian artificer Daedalus. By Minos's order, every year or every nine years Athens had to send seven young men and seven young women to be devoured by the Minotaur. Eventually, however, the Athenian hero Theseus volunteers to go and—with the help of a thread given to him by Minos and Pasiphaë's daughter (and thus also Asterion's half sister), Ariadne—succeeds in killing Asterion and escaping the labyrinth.

AUTHORS ON THEIR WORK
JORGE LUIS BORGES (1899–1986)

From "An Interview with Jorge Luis Borges" (1970)*

A[NSWER:] [. . .] when people tell me that they're down-to-earth and they tell me that I should be down-to-earth and think of reality, I wonder why a dream or an idea should be less real than this table for example, or why Macbeth should be less real than today's newspaper. I cannot quite understand this. [. . .] I'm not sure I have to define myself. I'd rather go on wondering and puzzling about things, for I find that very enjoyable.

Q[UESTION:] That reminds me of the image of the labyrinth that recurs throughout your work.

A[NSWER:] Yes, it keeps cropping up all the time. It's the most obvious symbol of feeling puzzled and baffled, isn't it? It came to me through an engraving when I was a boy, an engraving of the seven wonders of the world, and there was one of the labyrinth. [. . .] I thought that if I looked into it, if I peered into it very closely, perhaps I might make out the minotaur at the center. Somehow I was rather frightened of that engraving [. . .]. I was afraid of the minotaur coming out. (317)

• • •

[G. K.] Chesterton said, "What a man is really afraid of is a maze without a center." I suppose he was thinking of a godless universe, but I was thinking of the labyrinth without a minotaur, I mean, if anything is terrible, it is terrible because it is meaningless. (318)

[. . . I]f there's no minotaur, then the whole thing's incredible. You have a monstrous building built round a monster, and that in a sense is logical. But if there is no monster, then the whole thing is senseless, and that would be the case for the universe, for all we know. (318)

*"An Interview with Jorge Luis Borges." Interview by L. S. Dembo. *Contemporary Literature*, vol. 11, no. 3, Summer 1970, pp. 315–23. *JSTOR*, www.jstor.org/stable/1207790.

SUGGESTIONS FOR WRITING

1. Which of the monsters in these stories do you identify with most? least? Write an informal paper reflecting on your responses to at least two of these characters and the way those responses are shaped both by specifics in the story and by your personal experience.
2. Write a response paper or essay reflecting on the use of humor in at least one of the stories in this album. What kinds of humor do you see in the story? How does humor shape your response to the story and its characters?
3. Write an essay comparing how any two characters in these stories understand and cope (or not) with their deviation from the human norm and what each gains or loses as a result.

4. Write an essay comparing the conflicts experienced by the families in Lusus Naturae and St. Lucy's Home for Girls Raised by Wolves. Though we might not approve of the way some or all of these characters ultimately choose to resolve those conflicts, how and why might the stories encourage us to view these characters at least somewhat sympathetically?
5. Like Maggie in Toni Morrison's Recitatif, both the protagonist of Atwood's Lusus Naturae and Mirabella, in St. Lucy's Home for Girls Raised by Wolves, could be described as ***scapegoats*** (another archetype), which simply means a person or group of people whom a community harshly punishes, casts out, or even kills in the hope of preserving its own unity, purity, and strength. Why are these characters singled out? What do the other characters in each story hope to gain by treating the "monsters" as they do? Write an essay in which you explore what at least one of these stories suggests about whom we tend to treat as scapegoats, when and why we do so, and what the consequences tend to be.
6. In the library or on the Internet, research traditional representations (literary and/or visual) of the Minotaur myth, as well as some authoritative interpretations of it. Then write an essay in which you draw on these sources and on Borges's story to explore how it reworks and perhaps comments on these traditions.

4 SETTING

If plot and action are the way fictional works answer the question *What happened?* and characters are the *who*, **setting** is the *where* and *when*. All action in fiction, as in the real world, takes place in a context or setting—a time and place and a social environment or milieu.

TEMPORAL AND PHYSICAL, GENERAL AND PARTICULAR SETTING

The **time**—a work's *temporal setting* or *plot time*—can be roughly the same as that in which the work was written (its *author time*); or it can be much later, as in most science fiction; or much earlier, as in most **historical fiction**. Especially in short stories, which tend not to cover as much time or space as novels do, time may be very restricted, involving only a few hours or even minutes. Yet even in short stories, the action may span years or even decades.

Similarly, the place—a work's *geographical* or *physical setting*—might be limited to a single locale, or it might encompass several disparate ones. Those places might be common and ordinary, unique and extraordinary, or fantastic and even impossible according to the laws of our world (as in modern **fantasy** or **magic realism**).

Even when a story's action takes place in multiple times and places, we still sometimes refer to its *setting* (singular). By this, we indicate what we might call the entire story's *general setting*—the year(s) and the region, country, or even world in which the story unfolds and which often provides a historical and cultural context for the action. The general setting of Margaret Mitchell's historical novel *Gone with the Wind* (1936), for instance, is the Civil War–era South. But this novel, like many, has numerous *particular settings*; it opens, for instance, on an April morning on the porch of a north Georgia mansion called Tara, where Scarlett O'Hara flirts with two beaus and ignores their talk of a possible war to come. To fully appreciate the nature and role of setting, we thus need to consider the specific time of day and year as well as the specific locales in which the action unfolds.

Some stories merely offer hints about setting; others describe setting in great sensory detail. Especially in the latter case, we might be tempted to skim through what seems like mere "scenery" or "background information" to find out what happens next or how things turn out. But in good fiction, setting always functions as an integral part of the whole.

FUNCTIONS OF SETTING

Fiction often relies on setting to establish mood, situation, and character. The first sentence of Edgar Allan Poe's short story "The Fall of the House of Usher" (1839), for example, quickly sets the tone:

> During the whole of a dull, dark, and soundless day in the autumn of the year, when the clouds hung oppressively low in the heavens, I had been passing alone, on horseback, through a singularly dreary tract of country; and at length found myself, as the shades of the evening drew on, within view of the melancholy House of Usher.

This sentence aims to instill in the reader the same fear, "melancholy," and "sense of insufferable gloom" the narrator feels. With it, Poe prepares the reader emotionally, as well as mentally, for the sad and eerie tale that is about to unfold. He also generates suspense and certain expectations about just what might happen, as well as empathy with the narrator-protagonist.

Here, as in other fiction, specific details prove crucial to setting's emotional effect and meaning precisely because, as Poe's narrator himself observes,

> there *are* combinations of very simple natural objects which have the power of thus affecting us [. . .]. It was possible, I reflected, that a mere different arrangement of the particulars of the scene, of the details of the picture, would be sufficient to modify [. . .] its [. . .] impression.

In addition to creating such emotional impressions, setting can reveal or even shape a character's personality, outlook, and values; it can occasionally be an actor in the plot; and it often prompts characters' actions. (Who might you become and what might you do if you lived in the isolated, gloomy House of Usher?) Descriptions of setting may even (as in the first boxed example below) suggest a key **conflict** or **theme**. To gloss over descriptions of setting would thus mean not only missing much of the pleasure fiction affords but also potentially misreading its meanings. Setting is one of the many ways we learn about characters and the chief means by which characters and plots take on a larger historical, social, or even universal significance.

VAGUE AND VIVID SETTINGS

Not all stories, of course, rely so heavily on setting as Poe's does. In some individual works and in some subgenres, the general time, place, or both may be so vague as to seem, at first glance, unimportant. Many folktales and fairy tales take place in **archetypal** settings: "A long time ago," in "the forest" or "a village" or "a cottage," "in a land far, far away." By offering little, if any, specific information about their settings—neither locating the "forest" or "village" or faraway land in a place we can find on a map or a time we can locate on a calendar or clock, nor describing it in any detail—these works implicitly urge us to see the conflicts and aspects of human experience they depict (death, grief, a mother's relationship to her child, the danger and incomprehensibility of the unknown) as timeless and universal. Here, the very lack of attention to setting paradoxically turns out to be all-important.

At the opposite extreme are works and subgenres of fiction in which setting generates the conflicts, defines the characters, and gives the story purpose and meaning—so much so that there would be little, if any, story left if all the details about setting were removed or the characters and plot were somehow transported to a different time, place, and social milieu. Without their settings, what would remain of historical novels like *Gone with the Wind* or Nathaniel Hawthorne's *The Scarlet Letter* (1850)? An even more extreme example is Italo Calvino's fantasy novel *Invisible Cities*, which consists almost entirely of a series of descriptions of impossible, yet often hauntingly beautiful places like the following one.

ITALO CALVINO
From *Invisible Cities*

What makes Argia different from other cities is that it has earth instead of air. The streets are completely filled with dirt, clay packs the rooms to the ceiling, on every stair another stairway is set in negative, over the roofs of the houses hang layers of rocky terrain like skies with clouds. We do not know if the inhabitants can move about the city, widening the worm tunnels and the crevices where roots twist: the dampness destroys people's bodies and they have scant strength; everyone is better off remaining still, prone; anyway, it is dark.

From up here, nothing of Argia can be seen; some say, "It's down below there," and we can only believe them. The place is deserted. At night, putting your ear to the ground, you can sometimes hear a door slam.

1972

• • •

Most fiction, of course, occupies a middle ground between the extremes of Calvino's novel or historical fiction (with their highly particularized settings) versus folklore (with its generic, archetypal setting). Though all fiction may ultimately deal with some types of people, aspects of human experience, and conflicts that can crop up in some form or fashion anywhere or any time, much fiction also draws our attention to the way people, their experience, and their conflicts are twisted into a particular "form and fashion" by specific contexts.

Analyzing Descriptions of Setting: An Example and an Exercise

The novel *Gone with the Wind*, like the movie, opens on the front porch of Tara, where a carefree Scarlett O'Hara flirts with the Tarleton twins and studiously ignores the first rumors of war. Then the narrator pulls back to show us, with great detail, both the time of year and the landscape in which that porch is situated. After you read the following description, write a paragraph or two that draws on details from the passage to explain the feelings and impressions it conjures up, the functions it might serve at the beginning of the novel, and the way it achieves its effects. How, for example, might this description **foreshadow** and even help explain subsequent events? Why else might the novel need all this detail?

Spring had come early that year, with warm quick rains and sudden frothing of pink peach blossoms and dogwood dappling with white stars the dark river swamp and far-off hills. Already the plowing was nearly finished, and the bloody glory of the sunset colored the fresh-cut furrows of red Georgia clay to even redder hues. The moist hungry earth, waiting upturned for the cotton seeds, showed pinkish on the sandy tops of furrows, vermilion and scarlet and maroon where shadows lay along the sides of the trenches. The whitewashed brick plantation house seemed an island set in a wild red sea, a sea of spiraling, curving, crescent billows petrified suddenly at the moment when the pink-tipped waves were breaking into surf. For here were no long, straight furrows, such as could be seen in the yellow clay fields of the flat middle Georgia country or in the lush black earth of the coastal plantations. The rolling foothill country of north Georgia was plowed in a million curves to keep the rich earth from washing down into the river bottoms.

It was a savagely red land, blood-colored after rains, brick dust in droughts, the best cotton land in the world. It was a pleasant land of white houses, peaceful plowed fields and sluggish yellow rivers, but a land of contrasts, of bright sun glare and densest shade. The plantation clearings and miles of cotton fields smiled up to a warm sun, placid, complacent. At their edges rose the virgin forests, dark and cool even in the hottest noons, mysterious, a little sinister, the soughing pines seem to wait with an age-old patience, to threaten with soft sighs: "Be careful! Be careful! We had you once. We can take you back again."

TRADITIONAL EXPECTATIONS OF TIME AND PLACE

The effects and meanings evoked by setting depend on our traditional associations with, and often unconscious assumptions about, particular times, places, and even such factors as weather conditions—autumn, evening, a deserted country road, a house grand enough to have a name, a sky full of low and lowering clouds (to refer back to the Poe example).

Traditional associations derive, in part, from literature and myth, and some are culturally specific. (To someone unfamiliar with the Old Testament, an apple orchard would simply be an apple orchard, without any suggestion of evil or sin. Likewise, to someone who knows little about the U.S. Civil War, a big white house in the middle of a cotton field might seem like nothing more than a very beautiful place full of lucky, wealthy, happy people.) These associations also come from our learning, our experience, our own specific social and historical context, and even our primal instincts and physical condition as human beings. Almost all of us are more vulnerable in the dark and in inclement weather. And people do behave differently and expect different things to happen in different times and places—on a Saturday versus a Sunday versus a Monday, during spring break versus midsemester or midweek, at a posh beach resort we are just visiting versus the grocery store in our own neighborhood, and so on.

Often, however, authors draw on such associations precisely in order to reverse and question them. John Updike has said that he was initially inspired to write A & P because a suburban grocery store seemed just the sort of mundane place no reader would expect either heroism or a story to take place. ("Why don't you ever read a story set in an A & P?" he reportedly asked his wife.) By reversing expectations in this way, stories not only deepen their emotional effect but also encourage us to rethink our assumptions about particular times and places and the people who inhabit them.

This early scene from *Gone with the Wind* (1939) takes place on the porch of a mansion in Georgia, just before the start of the Civil War.

Connecting Setting, Point of View, and Character: An Example and an Exercise

For the purpose of analysis, we distinguish setting from other elements such as character, plot, point of view, and language. Perhaps paradoxically, we need to do so precisely in order to understand how these elements work together. The following passage from Alice Randall's controversial novel *The Wind Done Gone* (2002), for example, paints a dramatically different picture of the antebellum South than do earlier novels and films like *Gone with the Wind*, in part because it looks at that time and place from a very different point of view.

After you read the passage, write a paragraph or two about how its effect and meaning are shaped by point of view and **figurative language** or **imagery**. What might the passage tell us about Randall's narrator? How does the passage encourage us to rethink traditional views of the antebellum South?

Alternatively, compare this passage to the one from Mitchell's *Gone with the Wind* in this chapter's first "Example and Exercise," focusing on how each passage differently depicts the same time and place and how each passage's effect and meaning derive from its point of view and from its distinctive use of somewhat similar language and images.

> Mammy worked from can't-see in the morning to can't-see at night, in that great whitewashed wide-columned house surrounded by curvy furrowed fields. The mud, the dirt, was so red, when you looked at the cotton blooming in a field it brought to mind a sleeping gown after childbirth—all soft white cotton and blood.
>
> If it was mine to be able to paint pictures, if I possessed the gift of painting, I would paint a cotton gown balled up and thrown into a corner waiting to be washed, and I would call it "Georgia."

Setting is key to each of the stories gathered in this chapter. The settings in these stories range from the United States to Russia and China; from the late-nineteenth century to the late-twentieth; from coastal resorts to crowded, cosmopolitan cities. The stories take place in just about every season and all kinds of weather, but regardless of the specific setting each paints a revealing portrait of a time and place. Just as our own memories of important experiences include complex impressions of when and where they occurred—the weather, the shape of the room, the music that was playing, even the fashions or the events in the news back then—so stories rely on setting to evoke emotion and generate meaning.

Questions about Setting

General Setting

- What is the general temporal and geographical setting of this work of fiction? How do you know?
- How important does the general setting seem to be? In what ways is it important? What about the plot and characters would remain the same if they were magically transported to a different setting? What wouldn't? For example, how does the setting
  - create or shape conflict?
  - affect characters' personalities, outlooks, and actions?
  - shape our impressions of who the characters are and what they represent?
  - establish mood?

Particular Settings

- Does all the action occur in one time and place, or in more than one? If the latter, what are those times and places?
- What patterns do you notice regarding where and when things happen? Which characters are associated with each setting? How do different characters

(continued on next page)

(continued)

relate to the same setting? When, how, and why do characters move from one setting to another? Are there significant deviations from these patterns?

- Are particular settings described in detail, or merely sketched? If the former, what seems significant about the details? How might they establish mood, reveal character, and affect individual characters and their interactions with one another?

ANTON CHEKHOV
(1860–1904)
The Lady with the Dog[1]

The grandson of an emancipated serf, Anton Chekhov was born in the Russian town of Taganrog. In 1875, his father, a grocer facing bankruptcy and imprisonment, fled to Moscow, and soon the rest of the family lost their house to a former friend and lodger, a situation that Chekhov would revisit in his play *The Cherry Orchard* (1904). In 1884, Chekhov received his MD from the University of Moscow. He purchased an estate near Moscow in the early 1890s and became both an industrious landowner and doctor to the local peasants. After contributing stories to magazines and journals throughout the 1880s, he began writing for the stage in 1887, the same year he published his first collection of fiction. Chekhov himself once declared that fiction is "a lawful wife, but the Stage is a noisy, flashy, and insolent mistress." Forced by tuberculosis to winter on the coast after 1897, Chekhov married the actress Olga Knipper in 1901, but the couple had no children.

I

It was said that a new person had appeared on the sea-front: a lady with a little dog. Dmitri Dmitritch Gurov, who had by then been a fortnight at Yalta,[2] and so was fairly at home there, had begun to take an interest in new arrivals. Sitting in Verney's pavilion, he saw, walking on the sea-front, a fair-haired young lady of medium height, wearing a *béret*; a white Pomeranian dog was running behind her.

And afterwards he met her in the public gardens and in the square several times a day. She was walking alone, always wearing the same *béret*, and always with the same white dog; no one knew who she was, and every one called her simply "the lady with the dog."

1. Translated by Constance Garnett.
2. Russian city on the Black Sea; a resort.

"If she is here alone without a husband or friends, it wouldn't be amiss to make her acquaintance," Gurov reflected.

He was under forty, but he had a daughter already twelve years old, and two sons at school. He had been married young, when he was a student in his second year, and by now his wife seemed half as old again as he. She was a tall, erect woman with dark eyebrows, staid and dignified, and, as she said of herself, intellectual. She read a great deal, used phonetic spelling, called her husband, not Dmitri, but Dimitri, and he secretly considered her unintelligent, narrow, inelegant, was afraid of her, and did not like to be at home. He had begun being unfaithful to her long ago—had been unfaithful to her often, and, probably on that account, almost always spoke ill of women, and when they were talked about in his presence, used to call them "the lower race."

It seemed to him that he had been so schooled by bitter experience that he 5
might call them what he liked, and yet he could not get on for two days together without "the lower race." In the society of men he was bored and not himself, with them he was cold and uncommunicative; but when he was in the company of women he felt free, and knew what to say to them and how to behave; and he was at ease with them even when he was silent. In his appearance, in his character, in his whole nature, there was something attractive and elusive which allured women and disposed them in his favour; he knew that, and some force seemed to draw him, too, to them.

Experience often repeated, truly bitter experience, had taught him long ago that with decent people, especially Moscow people—always slow to move and irresolute—every intimacy, which at first so agreeably diversifies life and appears a light and charming adventure, inevitably grows into a regular problem of extreme intricacy, and in the long run the situation becomes unbearable. But at every fresh meeting with an interesting woman this experience seemed to slip out of his memory, and he was eager for life, and everything seemed simple and amusing.

One evening he was dining in the gardens, and the lady in the *béret* came up slowly to take the next table. Her expression, her gait, her dress, and the way she did her hair told him that she was a lady, that she was married, that she was in Yalta for the first time and alone, and that she was dull there. . . . The stories told of the immorality in such places as Yalta are to a great extent untrue; he despised them, and knew that such stories were for the most part made up by persons who would themselves have been glad to sin if they had been able; but when the lady sat down at the next table three paces from him, he remembered these tales of easy conquests, of trips to the mountains, and the tempting thought of a swift, fleeting love affair, a romance with an unknown woman, whose name he did not know, suddenly took possession of him.

He beckoned coaxingly to the Pomeranian, and when the dog came up to him he shook his finger at it. The Pomeranian growled: Gurov shook his finger at it again.

The lady looked at him and at once dropped her eyes.

"He doesn't bite," she said, and blushed. 10

"May I give him a bone?" he asked; and when she nodded he asked courteously, "Have you been long in Yalta?"

"Five days."

"And I have already dragged out a fortnight here."

There was a brief silence.

15 "Time goes fast, and yet it is so dull here!" she said, not looking at him.

"That's only the fashion to say it is dull here. A provincial will live in Belyov or Zhidra and not be dull, and when he comes here it's 'Oh, the dulness! Oh, the dust!' One would think he came from Grenada."[3]

She laughed. Then both continued eating in silence, like strangers, but after dinner they walked side by side; and there sprang up between them the light jesting conversation of people who are free and satisfied, to whom it does not matter where they go or what they talk about. They walked and talked of the strange light on the sea: the water was of a soft warm lilac hue, and there was a golden streak from the moon upon it. They talked of how sultry it was after a hot day. Gurov told her that he came from Moscow, that he had taken his degree in Arts, but had a post in a bank; that he had trained as an opera-singer, but had given it up, that he owned two houses in Moscow. . . . And from her he learnt that she had grown up in Petersburg, but had lived in S— since her marriage two years before, that she was staying another month in Yalta, and that her husband, who needed a holiday too, might perhaps come and fetch her. She was not sure whether her husband had a post in a Crown Department or under the Provincial Council[4]—and was amused by her own ignorance. And Gurov learnt, too, that she was called Anna Sergeyevna.

Afterwards he thought about her in his room at the hotel—thought she would certainly meet him next day; it would be sure to happen. As he got into bed he thought how lately she had been a girl at school, doing lessons like his own daughter; he recalled the diffidence, the angularity, that was still manifest in her laugh and her manner of talking with a stranger. This must have been the first time in her life she had been alone in surroundings in which she was followed, looked at, and spoken to merely from a secret motive which she could hardly fail to guess. He recalled her slender, delicate neck, her lovely grey eyes.

"There's something pathetic about her, anyway," he thought, and fell asleep.

II

20 A week had passed since they had made acquaintance. It was a holiday. It was sultry indoors, while in the street the wind whirled the dust round and round, and blew people's hats off. It was a thirsty day, and Gurov often went into the pavilion, and pressed Anna Sergeyevna to have syrup and water or an ice. One did not know what to do with oneself.

In the evening when the wind had dropped a little, they went out on the groyne to see the steamer come in. There were a great many people walking about the harbour; they had gathered to welcome some one, bringing bouquets. And two peculiarities of a well-dressed Yalta crowd were very conspicuous: the elderly ladies were dressed like young ones, and there were great numbers of generals.

Owing to the roughness of the sea, the steamer arrived late, after the sun had set, and it was a long time turning about before it reached the groyne.

3. Romantic city in southern Spain.

4. That is, a post in a national department, appointed by the czar, or a post in an elective local council.

Anna Sergeyevna looked through her lorgnette at the steamer and the passengers as though looking for acquaintances, and when she turned to Gurov her eyes were shining. She talked a great deal and asked disconnected questions, forgetting next moment what she had asked; then she dropped her lorgnette in the crush.

The festive crowd began to disperse; it was too dark to see people's faces. The wind had completely dropped, but Gurov and Anna Sergeyevna still stood as though waiting to see some one else come from the steamer. Anna Sergeyevna was silent now, and sniffed the flowers without looking at Gurov.

"The weather is better this evening," he said. "Where shall we go now? Shall we drive somewhere?"

She made no answer.

Then he looked at her intently, and all at once put his arm round her and kissed her on the lips, and breathed in the moisture and the fragrance of the flowers; and he immediately looked round him, anxiously wondering whether any one had seen them.

"Let us go to your hotel," he said softly. And both walked quickly.

The room was close and smelt of the scent she had bought at the Japanese shop. Gurov looked at her and thought: "What different people one meets in the world!" From the past he preserved memories of careless, good-natured women, who loved cheerfully and were grateful to him for the happiness he gave them, however brief it might be; and of women like his wife who loved without any genuine feeling, with superfluous phrases, affectedly, hysterically, with an expression that suggested that it was not love nor passion, but something more significant; and of two or three others, very beautiful, cold women, on whose faces he had caught a glimpse of a rapacious expression—an obstinate desire to snatch from life more than it could give, and these were capricious, unreflecting, domineering, unintelligent women not in their first youth, and when Gurov grew cold to them their beauty excited his hatred, and the lace on their linen seemed to him like scales.

But in this case there was still the diffidence, the angularity of inexperienced youth, an awkward feeling; and there was a sense of consternation as though some one had suddenly knocked at the door. The attitude of Anna Sergeyevna—"the lady with the dog"—to what had happened was somehow peculiar, very grave, as though it were her fall—so it seemed, and it was strange and inappropriate. Her face dropped and faded, and on both sides of it her long hair hung down mournfully; she mused in a dejected attitude like "the woman who was a sinner" in an old-fashioned picture.

"It's wrong," she said. "You will be the first to despise me now."

There was a water-melon on the table. Gurov cut himself a slice and began eating it without haste. There followed at least half an hour of silence.

Anna Sergeyevna was touching; there was about her the purity of a good, simple woman who had seen little of life. The solitary candle burning on the table threw a faint light on her face, yet it was clear that she was very unhappy.

"How could I despise you?" asked Gurov. "You don't know what you are saying."

"God forgive me," she said, and her eyes filled with tears. "It's awful."

"You seem to feel you need to be forgiven."

"Forgiven? No. I am a bad, low woman; I despise myself and don't attempt to justify myself. It's not my husband but myself I have deceived. And not only just now; I have been deceiving myself for a long time. My husband may be a good, honest man, but he is a flunkey! I don't know what he does there, what his work is, but I know he is a flunkey! I was twenty when I was married to him. I have been tormented by curiosity; I wanted something better. 'There must be a different sort of life,' I said to myself. I wanted to live! To live, to live! . . . I was fired by curiosity . . . you don't understand it, but, I swear to God, I could not control myself; something happened to me: I could not be restrained. I told my husband I was ill, and came here. . . . And here I have been walking about as though I were dazed, like a mad creature; . . . and now I have become a vulgar, contemptible woman whom any one may despise."

Gurov felt bored already, listening to her. He was irritated by the naïve tone, by this remorse, so unexpected and inopportune; but for the tears in her eyes, he might have thought she was jesting or playing a part.

"I don't understand," he said softly. "What is it you want?"

She hid her face on his breast and pressed close to him.

"Believe me, believe me, I beseech you . . ." she said. "I love a pure, honest life, and sin is loathsome to me. I don't know what I am doing. Simple people say: 'The Evil One has beguiled me.' And I may say of myself now that the Evil One has beguiled me."

"Hush, hush! . . ." he muttered.

He looked at her fixed, scared eyes, kissed her, talked softly and affectionately, and by degrees she was comforted, and her gaiety returned; they both began laughing.

Afterwards when they went out there was not a soul on the sea-front. The town with its cypresses had quite a deathlike air, but the sea still broke noisily on the shore; a single barge was rocking on the waves, and a lantern was blinking sleepily on it.

They found a cab and drove to Oreanda.

"I found out your surname in the hall just now: it was written on the board—Von Diderits," said Gurov. "Is your husband a German?"

"No; I believe his grandfather was a German, but he is an Orthodox Russian himself."

At Oreanda they sat on a seat not far from the church, looked down at the sea, and were silent. Yalta was hardly visible through the morning mist; white clouds stood motionless on the mountain-tops. The leaves did not stir on the trees, grasshoppers chirruped, and the monotonous hollow sound of the sea rising up from below, spoke of the peace, of the eternal sleep awaiting us. So it must have sounded when there was no Yalta, no Oreanda here; so it sounds now, and it will sound as indifferently and monotonously when we are all no more. And in this constancy, in this complete indifference to the life and death of each of us, there lies hid, perhaps, a pledge of our eternal salvation, of the unceasing movement of life upon earth, of unceasing progress towards perfection. Sitting beside a young woman who in the dawn seemed so lovely, soothed and spellbound in these magical surroundings—the sea, mountains, clouds, the open sky—Gurov thought how in reality everything is beautiful in this world when one reflects: everything except what we think or do ourselves when we forget our human dignity and the higher aims of our existence.

A man walked up to them—probably a keeper—looked at them and walked away. And this detail seemed mysterious and beautiful, too. They saw a steamer come from Theodosia, with its lights out in the glow of dawn.

"There is dew on the grass," said Anna Sergeyevna, after a silence.

"Yes. It's time to go home." 50

They went back to the town.

Then they met every day at twelve o'clock on the sea-front, lunched and dined together, went for walks, admired the sea. She complained that she slept badly, that her heart throbbed violently; asked the same questions, troubled now by jealousy and now by the fear that he did not respect her sufficiently. And often in the square or gardens, when there was no one near them, he suddenly drew her to him and kissed her passionately. Complete idleness, these kisses in broad daylight while he looked round in dread of some one's seeing them, the heat, the smell of the sea, and the continual passing to and fro before him of idle, well-dressed, well-fed people, made a new man of him; he told Anna Sergeyevna how beautiful she was, how fascinating. He was impatiently passionate, he would not move a step away from her, while she was often pensive and continually urged him to confess that he did not respect her, did not love her in the least, and thought of her as nothing but a common woman. Rather late almost every evening they drove somewhere out of town, to Oreanda or to the waterfall; and the expedition was always a success, the scenery invariably impressed them as grand and beautiful.

They were expecting her husband to come, but a letter came from him, saying that there was something wrong with his eyes, and he entreated his wife to come home as quickly as possible. Anna Sergeyevna made haste to go.

"It's a good thing I am going away," she said to Gurov. "It's the finger of destiny!"

She went by coach and he went with her. They were driving the whole day. 55
When she had got into a compartment of the express, and when the second bell had rung, she said:

"Let me look at you once more . . . look at you once again. That's right."

She did not shed tears, but was so sad that she seemed ill, and her face was quivering.

"I shall remember you . . . think of you," she said. "God be with you; be happy. Don't remember evil against me. We are parting forever—it must be so, for we ought never to have met. Well, God be with you."

The train moved off rapidly, its lights soon vanished from sight, and a minute later there was no sound of it, as though everything had conspired together to end as quickly as possible that sweet delirium, that madness. Left alone on the platform, and gazing into the dark distance, Gurov listened to the chirrup of the grasshoppers and the hum of the telegraph wires, feeling as though he had only just waked up. And he thought, musing, that there had been another episode or adventure in his life, and it, too, was at an end, and nothing was left of it but a memory. . . . He was moved, sad, and conscious of a slight remorse. This young woman whom he would never meet again had not been happy with him; he was genuinely warm and affectionate with her, but yet in his manner, his tone, and his caresses there had been a shade of light irony, the coarse condescension of a happy man who was, besides, almost twice her age. All the time she had called him kind, exceptional, lofty; obviously he had seemed to her different from what he really was, so he had unintentionally deceived her. . . .

Here at the station was already a scent of autumn; it was a cold evening.

"It's time for me to go north," thought Gurov as he left the platform. "High time!"

III

At home in Moscow everything was in its winter routine; the stoves were heated, and in the morning it was still dark when the children were having breakfast and getting ready for school, and the nurse would light the lamp for a short time. The frosts had begun already. When the first snow has fallen, on the first day of sledge-driving it is pleasant to see the white earth, the white roofs, to draw soft, delicious breath, and the season brings back the days of one's youth. The old limes and birches, white with hoar-frost, have a good-natured expression; they are nearer to one's heart than cypresses and palms, and near them one doesn't want to be thinking of the sea and the mountains.

Gurov was Moscow born; he arrived in Moscow on a fine frosty day, and when he put on his fur coat and warm gloves, and walked along Petrovka, and when on Saturday evening he heard the ringing of the bells, his recent trip and the places he had seen lost all charm for him. Little by little he became absorbed in Moscow life, greedily read three newspapers a day, and declared he did not read the Moscow papers on principle! He already felt a longing to go to restaurants, clubs, dinner-parties, anniversary celebrations, and he felt flattered at entertaining distinguished lawyers and artists, and at playing cards with a professor at the doctors' club. He could already eat a whole plateful of salt fish and cabbage. . . .

In another month, he fancied, the image of Anna Sergeyevna would be shrouded in a mist in his memory, and only from time to time would visit him in his dreams with a touching smile as others did. But more than a month passed, real winter had come, and everything was still clear in his memory as though he had parted with Anna Sergeyevna only the day before. And his memories glowed more and more vividly. When in the evening stillness he heard from his study the voices of his children, preparing their lessons, or when he listened to a song or the organ at the restaurant, or the storm howled in the chimney, suddenly everything would rise up in his memory: what had happened on the groyne, and the early morning with the mist on the mountains, and the steamer coming from Theodosia, and the kisses. He would pace a long time about his room, remembering it all and smiling; then his memories passed into dreams, and in his fancy the past was mingled with what was to come. Anna Sergeyevna did not visit him in dreams, but followed him about everywhere like a shadow and haunted him. When he shut his eyes he saw her as though she were living before him, and she seemed to him lovelier, younger, tenderer than she was; and he imagined himself finer than he had been in Yalta. In the evenings she peeped out at him from the bookcase, from the fireplace, from the corner—he heard her breathing, the caressing rustle of her dress. In the street he watched the women, looking for some one like her.

He was tormented by an intense desire to confide his memories to some one. 65
But in his home it was impossible to talk of his love, and he had no one outside; he could not talk to his tenants nor to any one at the bank. And what had he to talk of? Had he been in love, then? Had there been anything beautiful, poetical, or edifying or simply interesting in his relations with Anna Sergeyevna? And there was nothing for him but to talk vaguely of love, of woman, and no one guessed what it meant; only his wife twitched her black eyebrows, and said: "The part of a lady-killer does not suit you at all, Dimitri."

One evening, coming out of the doctors' club with an official with whom he had been playing cards, he could not resist saying:

"If only you knew what a fascinating woman I made the acquaintance of in Yalta!"

The official got into his sledge and was driving away, but turned suddenly and shouted:

"Dmitri Dmitritch!"

"What?" 70

"You were right this evening: the sturgeon was a bit too strong!"

These words, so ordinary, for some reason moved Gurov to indignation, and struck him as degrading and unclean. What savage manners, what people! What senseless nights, what uninteresting, uneventful days! The rage for card-playing, the gluttony, the drunkenness, the continual talk always about the same thing. Useless pursuits and conversations always about the same things absorb the better part of one's time, the better part of one's strength, and in the end there is left a life grovelling and curtailed, worthless and trivial, and there is no escaping or getting away from it—just as though one were in a madhouse or a prison.

Gurov did not sleep all night, and was filled with indignation. And he had a headache all next day. And the next night he slept badly; he sat up in bed, thinking, or paced up and down his room. He was sick of his children, sick of the bank; he had no desire to go anywhere or to talk of anything.

In the holidays in December he prepared for a journey, and told his wife he was going to Petersburg to do something in the interests of a young friend—and he set off for S—. What for? He did not very well know himself. He wanted to see Anna Sergeyevna and to talk with her—to arrange a meeting, if possible.

He reached S— in the morning, and took the best room at the hotel, in which 75
the floor was covered with grey army cloth, and on the table was an inkstand, grey with dust and adorned with a figure on horseback, with its hat in its hand and its head broken off. The hotel porter gave him the necessary information; Von Diderits lived in a house of his own in Old Gontcharny Street—it was not far from the hotel: he was rich and lived in good style, and had his own horses; every one in the town knew him. The porter pronounced the name "Dridirits."

Gurov went without haste to Old Gontcharny Street and found the house. Just opposite the house stretched a long grey fence adorned with nails.

"One would run away from a fence like that," thought Gurov, looking from the fence to the windows of the house and back again.

He considered: to-day was a holiday, and the husband would probably be at home. And in any case it would be tactless to go into the house and upset her. If he were to send her a note it might fall into her husband's hands, and then it might ruin everything. The best thing was to trust to chance. And he kept walking up and down the street by the fence, waiting for the chance. He saw a beggar go in at the gate and dogs fly at him; then an hour later he heard a piano, and the sounds were faint and indistinct. Probably it was Anna Sergeyevna playing. The front door suddenly opened, and an old woman came out, followed by the familiar white Pomeranian. Gurov was on the point of calling to the dog, but his heart began beating violently, and in his excitement he could not remember the dog's name.

He walked up and down, and loathed the grey fence more and more, and by now he thought irritably that Anna Sergeyevna had forgotten him, and was perhaps already amusing herself with some one else, and that that was very natural in a young woman who had nothing to look at from morning till night but that confounded fence. He went back to his hotel room and sat for a long while on the sofa, not knowing what to do, then he had dinner and a long nap.

80 "How stupid and worrying it is!" he thought when he woke and looked at the dark windows: it was already evening. "Here I've had a good sleep for some reason. What shall I do in the night?"

He sat on the bed, which was covered by a cheap grey blanket, such as one sees in hospitals, and he taunted himself in his vexation:

"So much for the lady with the dog . . . so much for the adventure. . . . You're in a nice fix. . . ."

That morning at the station a poster in large letters had caught his eye. "The Geisha"[5] was to be performed for the first time. He thought of this and went to the theatre.

"It's quite possible she may go to the first performance," he thought.

85 The theatre was full. As in all provincial theatres, there was a fog above the chandelier, the gallery was noisy and restless; in the front row the local dandies were standing up before the beginning of the performance, with their hands behind them; in the Governor's box the Governor's daughter, wearing a boa, was sitting in the front seat, while the Governor himself lurked modestly behind the curtain with only his hands visible; the orchestra was a long time tuning up; the stage curtain swayed. All the time the audience were coming in and taking their seats Gurov looked at them eagerly.

Anna Sergeyevna, too, came in. She sat down in the third row, and when Gurov looked at her his heart contracted, and he understood clearly that for him there was in the whole world no creature so near, so precious, and so important to him; she, this little woman, in no way remarkable, lost in a provincial crowd, with a vulgar lorgnette in her hand, filled his whole life now, was his sorrow and his joy, the one happiness that he now desired for himself, and to the sounds of the inferior orchestra, of the wretched provincial violins, he thought how lovely she was. He thought and dreamed.

A young man with small side-whiskers, tall and stooping, came in with Anna Sergeyevna and sat down beside her; he bent his head at every step and seemed to be continually bowing. Most likely this was the husband whom at Yalta, in a rush of bitter feeling, she had called a flunkey. And there really was in his long figure, his side-whiskers, and the small bald patch on his head, something of

5. Operetta by Sidney Jones (1861–1946) that toured eastern Europe in 1898–99.

the flunkey's obsequiousness; his smile was sugary, and in his buttonhole there was some badge of distinction like the number on a waiter.

During the first interval the husband went away to smoke; she remained alone in her stall. Gurov, who was sitting in the stalls, too, went up to her and said in a trembling voice, with a forced smile:

"Good-evening."

90 She glanced at him and turned pale, then glanced again with horror, unable to believe her eyes, and tightly gripped the fan and the lorgnette in her hands, evidently struggling with herself not to faint. Both were silent. She was sitting, he was standing, frightened by her confusion and not venturing to sit down beside her. The violins and the flute began tuning up. He felt suddenly frightened; it seemed as though all the people in the boxes were looking at them. She got up and went quickly to the door; he followed her, and both walked senselessly along passages, and up and down stairs, and figures in legal, scholastic, and civil service uniforms, all wearing badges, flitted before their eyes. They caught glimpses of ladies, of fur coats hanging on pegs; the draughts blew on them, bringing a smell of stale tobacco. And Gurov, whose heart was beating violently, thought:

"Oh, heavens! Why are these people here and this orchestra! . . ."

And at that instant he recalled how when he had seen Anna Sergeyevna off at the station he had thought that everything was over and they would never meet again. But how far they were still from the end!

On the narrow, gloomy staircase over which was written "To the Amphitheatre," she stopped.

"How you have frightened me!" she said, breathing hard, still pale and overwhelmed. "Oh, how you have frightened me! I am half dead. Why have you come? Why?"

95 "But do understand, Anna, do understand . . ." he said hastily in a low voice. "I entreat you to understand. . . ."

She looked at him with dread, with entreaty, with love; she looked at him intently, to keep his features more distinctly in her memory.

"I am so unhappy," she went on, not heeding him. "I have thought of nothing but you all the time; I live only in the thought of you. And I wanted to forget, to forget you; but why, oh, why, have you come?"

On the landing above them two schoolboys were smoking and looking down, but that was nothing to Gurov; he drew Anna Sergeyevna to him, and began kissing her face, her cheeks, and her hands.

"What are you doing, what are you doing!" she cried in horror, pushing him away. "We are mad. Go away to-day; go away at once. . . . I beseech you by all that is sacred, I implore you. . . . There are people coming this way!"

100 Some one was coming up the stairs.

"You must go away," Anna Sergeyevna went on in a whisper. "Do you hear, Dmitri Dmitritch? I will come and see you in Moscow. I have never been happy; I am miserable now, and I never, never shall be happy, never! Don't make me suffer still more! I swear I'll come to Moscow. But now let us part. My precious, good, dear one, we must part!"

She pressed his hand and began rapidly going downstairs, looking round at him, and from her eyes he could see that she really was unhappy. Gurov stood for a little while, listened, then, when all sound had died away, he found his coat and left the theatre.

IV

And Anna Sergeyevna began coming to see him in Moscow. Once in two or three months she left S—, telling her husband that she was going to consult a doctor about an internal complaint—and her husband believed her, and did not believe her. In Moscow she stayed at the Slaviansky Bazaar hotel, and at once sent a man in a red cap to Gurov. Gurov went to see her, and no one in Moscow knew of it.

Once he was going to see her in this way on a winter morning (the messenger had come the evening before when he was out). With him walked his daughter, whom he wanted to take to school: it was on the way. Snow was falling in big wet flakes.

"It's three degrees above freezing-point, and yet it is snowing," said Gurov to his daughter. "The thaw is only on the surface of the earth; there is quite a different temperature at a greater height in the atmosphere."

"And why are there no thunderstorms in the winter, father?"

He explained that, too. He talked, thinking all the while that he was going to see *her*, and no living soul knew of it, and probably never would know. He had two lives: one, open, seen and known by all who cared to know, full of relative truth and of relative falsehood, exactly like the lives of his friends and acquaintances; and another life running its course in secret. And through some strange, perhaps accidental, conjunction of circumstances, everything that was essential, of interest and of value to him, everything in which he was sincere and did not deceive himself, everything that made the kernel of his life, was hidden from other people; and all that was false in him, the sheath in which he hid himself to conceal the truth—such, for instance, as his work in the bank, his discussions at the club, his "lower race," his presence with his wife at anniversary festivities—all that was open. And he judged of others by himself, not believing in what he saw, and always believing that every man had his real, most interesting life under the cover of secrecy and under the cover of night. All personal life rested on secrecy, and possibly it was partly on that account that civilised man was so nervously anxious that personal privacy should be respected.

After leaving his daughter at school, Gurov went on to the Slaviansky Bazaar. He took off his fur coat below, went upstairs, and softly knocked at the door. Anna Sergeyevna, wearing his favourite grey dress, exhausted by the journey and the suspense, had been expecting him since the evening before. She was pale; she looked at him, and did not smile, and he had hardly come in when she fell on his breast. Their kiss was slow and prolonged, as though they had not met for two years.

"Well, how are you getting on there?" he asked. "What news?"

"Wait; I'll tell you directly. . . . I can't talk."

She could not speak; she was crying. She turned away from him, and pressed her handkerchief to her eyes.

"Let her have her cry out. I'll sit down and wait," he thought, and he sat down in an arm-chair.

Then he rang and asked for tea to be brought him, and while he drank his tea she remained standing at the window with her back to him. She was crying from emotion, from the miserable consciousness that their life was so hard for them; they could only meet in secret, hiding themselves from people, like thieves! Was not their life shattered?

"Come, do stop!" he said.

It was evident to him that this love of theirs would not soon be over, that he 115
could not see the end of it. Anna Sergeyevna grew more and more attached to him. She adored him, and it was unthinkable to say to her that it was bound to have an end some day; besides, she would not have believed it!

He went up to her and took her by the shoulders to say something affectionate and cheering, and at that moment he saw himself in the looking-glass.

His hair was already beginning to turn grey. And it seemed strange to him that he had grown so much older, so much plainer during the last few years. The shoulders on which his hands rested were warm and quivering. He felt compassion for this life, still so warm and lovely, but probably already not far from beginning to fade and wither like his own. Why did she love him so much? He always seemed to women different from what he was, and they loved in him not himself, but the man created by their imagination, whom they had been eagerly seeking all their lives; and afterwards, when they noticed their mistake, they loved him all the same. And not one of them had been happy with him. Time passed, he had made their acquaintance, got on with them, parted, but he had never once loved; it was anything you like, but not love.

And only now when his head was grey he had fallen properly, really in love—for the first time in his life.

Anna Sergeyevna and he loved each other like people very close and akin, like husband and wife, like tender friends; it seemed to them that fate itself had meant them for one another, and they could not understand why he had a wife and she a husband; and it was as though they were a pair of birds of passage, caught and forced to live in different cages. They forgave each other for what they were ashamed of in their past, they forgave everything in the present, and felt that this love of theirs had changed them both.

In moments of depression in the past he had comforted himself with any 120
arguments that came into his mind, but now he no longer cared for arguments; he felt profound compassion, he wanted to be sincere and tender. . . .

"Don't cry, my darling," he said. "You've had your cry; that's enough. . . . Let us talk now, let us think of some plan."

Then they spent a long while taking counsel together, talked of how to avoid the necessity for secrecy, for deception, for living in different towns and not seeing each other for long at a time. How could they be free from this intolerable bondage?

"How? How?" he asked, clutching his head. "How?"

And it seemed as though in a little while the solution would be found, and then a new and splendid life would begin; and it was clear to both of them that they had still a long, long road before them, and that the most complicated and difficult part of it was only just beginning.

1899

QUESTIONS

1. **When Gurov and Anna take their first walk together, they discuss "the strange light of the sea: the water was of a soft warm lilac hue, and there was a golden streak**

from the moon upon it" (par. 17). Why do you think Chekhov waits until this moment to provide descriptive details of the story's setting in Yalta?

2. How do the weather and season described in each section relate to the action in that section?
3. What is Gurov's attitude toward his affair with Anna at the outset? What is Anna's attitude? What are some indications that both Gurov and Anna are unprepared for the relationship that develops between them?

AMY TAN

(b. 1952)

A Pair of Tickets

Amy Tan was born in Oakland, California, just two and a half years after her parents immigrated from China. She received her MA in linguistics from San Jose State University and has worked on programs for disabled children and as a freelance writer. In 1987, at age thirty-five, she visited China for the first time—"As soon as my feet touched China, I became Chinese"—and returned to write her first book, *The Joy Luck Club* (1989), a novel composed of stories told by four Chinese immigrant women and their American-born daughters. Tan has written more novels—including *The Kitchen God's Wife* (1991), *The Hundred Secret Senses* (1995), *The Bonesetter's Daughter* (2000), and *Saving Fish from Drowning* (2006)—and has coauthored two children's books. Her first book of nonfiction, *The Opposite of Fate: A Book of Musings* (2003), explores lucky accidents, choice, and memory. Tan is also a backup singer for Rock Bottom Remainders, a rock band made up of fellow writers, including Stephen King and Dave Barry; they make appearances at benefits that support literacy programs for children.

The minute our train leaves the Hong Kong border and enters Shenzhen, China, I feel different. I can feel the skin on my forehead tingling, my blood rushing through a new course, my bones aching with a familiar old pain. And I think, My mother was right. I am becoming Chinese.

"Cannot be helped," my mother said when I was fifteen and had vigorously denied that I had any Chinese whatsoever below my skin. I was a sophomore at Galileo High in San Francisco, and all my Caucasian friends agreed: I was about as Chinese as they were. But my mother had studied at a famous nursing school in Shanghai, and she said she knew all about genetics. So there was no doubt in her mind, whether I agreed or not: Once you are born Chinese, you cannot help but feel and think Chinese.

"Someday you will see," said my mother. "It's in your blood, waiting to be let go."

And when she said this, I saw myself transforming like a werewolf, a mutant tag of DNA suddenly triggered, replicating itself insidiously into a *syndrome*, a cluster of telltale Chinese behaviors, all those things my mother did to embarrass me—haggling with store owners, pecking her mouth with a toothpick in public, being color-blind to the fact that lemon yellow and pale pink are not good combinations for winter clothes.

But today I realize I've never really known what it means to be Chinese. I am 5
thirty-six years old. My mother is dead and I am on a train, carrying with me her dreams of coming home. I am going to China.

We are going to Guangzhou, my seventy-two-year-old father, Canning Woo, and I, where we will visit his aunt, whom he has not seen since he was ten years old. And I don't know whether it's the prospect of seeing his aunt or if it's because he's back in China, but now he looks like he's a young boy, so innocent and happy I want to button his sweater and pat his head. We are sitting across from each other, separated by a little table with two cold cups of tea. For the first time I can ever remember, my father has tears in his eyes, and all he is seeing out the train window is a sectioned field of yellow, green, and brown, a narrow canal flanking the tracks, low rising hills, and three people in blue jackets riding an ox-driven cart on this early October morning. And I can't help myself. I also have misty eyes, as if I had seen this a long, long time ago, and had almost forgotten.

In less than three hours, we will be in Guangzhou, which my guidebook tells me is how one properly refers to Canton these days. It seems all the cities I have heard of, except Shanghai, have changed their spellings. I think they are saying China has changed in other ways as well. Chungking is Chongqing. And Kweilin is Guilin. I have looked these names up, because after we see my father's aunt in Guangzhou, we will catch a plane to Shanghai, where I will meet my two half-sisters for the first time.

They are my mother's twin daughters from her first marriage, little babies she was forced to abandon on a road as she was fleeing Kweilin for Chungking in 1944. That was all my mother had told me about these daughters, so they had remained babies in my mind, all these years, sitting on the side of a road, listening to bombs whistling in the distance while sucking their patient red thumbs.

And it was only this year that someone found them and wrote with this joyful news. A letter came from Shanghai, addressed to my mother. When I first heard about this, that they were alive, I imagined my identical sisters transforming from little babies into six-year-old girls. In my mind, they were seated next to each other at a table, taking turns with the fountain pen. One would write a neat row of characters: *Dearest Mama. We are alive.* She would brush back her wispy bangs and hand the other sister the pen, and she would write: *Come get us. Please hurry.*

Of course they could not know that my mother had died three months 10
before, suddenly, when a blood vessel in her brain burst. One minute she was talking to my father, complaining about the tenants upstairs, scheming how to evict them under the pretense that relatives from China were moving in. The next minute she was holding her head, her eyes squeezed shut, groping for the sofa, and then crumpling softly to the floor with fluttering hands.

So my father had been the first one to open the letter, a long letter it turned out. And they did call her Mama. They said they always revered her as their true mother. They kept a framed picture of her. They told her about their life, from the time my mother last saw them on the road leaving Kweilin to when they were finally found.

And the letter had broken my father's heart so much—these daughters calling my mother from another life he never knew—that he gave the letter to my mother's old friend Auntie Lindo and asked her to write back and tell my sisters, in the gentlest way possible, that my mother was dead.

But instead Auntie Lindo took the letter to the Joy Luck Club and discussed with Auntie Ying and Auntie An-mei what should be done, because they had known for many years about my mother's search for her twin daughters, her endless hope. Auntie Lindo and the others cried over this double tragedy, of losing my mother three months before, and now again. And so they couldn't help but think of some miracle, some possible way of reviving her from the dead, so my mother could fulfill her dream.

So this is what they wrote to my sisters in Shanghai: "Dearest Daughters, I too have never forgotten you in my memory or in my heart. I never gave up hope that we would see each other again in a joyous reunion. I am only sorry it has been too long. I want to tell you everything about my life since I last saw you. I want to tell you this when our family comes to see you in China. . . ." They signed it with my mother's name.

15 It wasn't until all this had been done that they first told me about my sisters, the letter they received, the one they wrote back.

"They'll think she's coming, then," I murmured. And I had imagined my sisters now being ten or eleven, jumping up and down, holding hands, their pigtails bouncing, excited that their mother—*their* mother—was coming, whereas my mother was dead.

"How can you say she is not coming in a letter?" said Auntie Lindo. "She is their mother. She is your mother. You must be the one to tell them. All these years, they have been dreaming of her." And I thought she was right.

But then I started dreaming, too, of my mother and my sisters and how it would be if I arrived in Shanghai. All these years, while they waited to be found, I had lived with my mother and then had lost her. I imagined seeing my sisters at the airport. They would be standing on their tiptoes, looking anxiously, scanning from one dark head to another as we got off the plane. And I would recognize them instantly, their faces with the identical worried look.

"*Jyejye, Jyejye.* Sister, Sister. We are here," I saw myself saying in my poor version of Chinese.

20 "Where is Mama?" they would say, and look around, still smiling, two flushed and eager faces. "Is she hiding?" And this would have been like my mother, to stand behind just a bit, to tease a little and make people's patience pull a little on their hearts. I would shake my head and tell my sisters she was not hiding.

"Oh, that must be Mama, no?" one of my sisters would whisper excitedly, pointing to another small woman completely engulfed in a tower of presents. And that, too, would have been like my mother, to bring mountains of gifts, food, and toys for children—all bought on sale—shunning thanks, saying the gifts were nothing, and later turning the labels over to show my sisters, "Calvin Klein, 100% wool."

I imagined myself starting to say, "Sisters, I am sorry, I have come alone . . ." and before I could tell them—they could see it in my face—they were wailing, pulling their hair, their lips twisted in pain, as they ran away from me. And then I saw myself getting back on the plane and coming home.

After I had dreamed this scene many times—watching their despair turn from horror into anger—I begged Auntie Lindo to write another letter. And at first she refused.

"How can I say she is dead? I cannot write this," said Auntie Lindo with a stubborn look.

"But it's cruel to have them believe she's coming on the plane," I said. "When they see it's just me, they'll hate me."

"Hate you? Cannot be." She was scowling. "You are their own sister, their only family."

"You don't understand," I protested.

"What I don't understand?" she said.

And I whispered, "They'll think I'm responsible, that she died because I didn't appreciate her."

And Auntie Lindo looked satisfied and sad at the same time, as if this were true and I had finally realized it. She sat down for an hour, and when she stood up she handed me a two-page letter. She had tears in her eyes. I realized that the very thing I had feared, she had done. So even if she had written the news of my mother's death in English, I wouldn't have had the heart to read it.

"Thank you," I whispered.

The landscape has become gray, filled with low flat cement buildings, old factories, and then tracks and more tracks filled with trains like ours passing by in the opposite direction. I see platforms crowded with people wearing drab Western clothes, with spots of bright colors: little children wearing pink and yellow, red and peach. And there are soldiers in olive green and red, and old ladies in gray tops and pants that stop mid-calf. We are in Guangzhou.

Before the train even comes to a stop, people are bringing down their belongings from above their seats. For a moment there is a dangerous shower of heavy suitcases laden with gifts to relatives, half-broken boxes wrapped in miles of string to keep the contents from spilling out, plastic bags filled with yarn and vegetables and packages of dried mushrooms, and camera cases. And then we are caught in a stream of people rushing, shoving, pushing us along, until we find ourselves in one of a dozen lines waiting to go through customs. I feel as if I were getting on a number 30 Stockton bus in San Francisco. I am in China, I remind myself. And somehow the crowds don't bother me. It feels right. I start pushing too.

I take out the declaration forms and my passport. "Woo," it says at the top, and below that, "June May," who was born in "California, U.S.A.," in 1951. I wonder if the customs people will question whether I'm the same person as in the passport photo. In this picture, my chin-length hair is swept back and artfully styled. I am wearing false eyelashes, eye shadow, and lip liner. My cheeks are hollowed out by bronze blusher. But I had not expected the heat in October. And now my hair hangs limp with the humidity. I wear no makeup; in Hong Kong my mascara had melted into dark circles and everything else had felt like layers of grease. So today my face is plain, unadorned except for a thin mist of shiny sweat on my forehead and nose.

Even without makeup, I could never pass for true Chinese. I stand five-foot-six, and my head pokes above the crowd so that I am eye level only with other tourists. My mother once told me my height came from my grandfather, who was a northerner, and may have even had some Mongol blood. "This is what your grandmother once told me," explained my mother. "But now it is too late to ask her. They are all dead, your grandparents, your uncles, and their wives and children, all killed in the war, when a bomb fell on our house. So many generations in one instant."

She had said this so matter-of-factly that I thought she had long since gotten over any grief she had. And then I wondered how she knew they were all dead.

"Maybe they left the house before the bomb fell," I suggested.

"No," said my mother. "Our whole family is gone. It is just you and I."

"But how do you know? Some of them could have escaped."

"Cannot be," said my mother, this time almost angrily. And then her frown was washed over by a puzzled blank look, and she began to talk as if she were trying to remember where she had misplaced something. "I went back to that house. I kept looking up to where the house used to be. And it wasn't a house, just the sky. And below, underneath my feet, were four stories of burnt bricks and wood, all the life of our house. Then off to the side I saw things blown into the yard, nothing valuable. There was a bed someone used to sleep in, really just a metal frame twisted up at one corner. And a book, I don't know what kind, because every page had turned black. And I saw a teacup which was unbroken but filled with ashes. And then I found my doll, with her hands and legs broken, her hair burned off. . . . When I was a little girl, I had cried for that doll, seeing it all alone in the store window, and my mother had bought it for me. It was an American doll with yellow hair. It could turn its legs and arms. The eyes moved up and down. And when I married and left my family home, I gave the doll to my youngest niece, because she was like me. She cried if that doll was not with her always. Do you see? If she was in the house with that doll, her parents were there, and so everybody was there, waiting together, because that's how our family was."

The woman in the customs booth stares at my documents, then glances at me briefly, and with two quick movements stamps everything and sternly nods me along. And soon my father and I find ourselves in a large area filled with thousands of people and suitcases. I feel lost and my father looks helpless.

"Excuse me," I say to a man who looks like an American. "Can you tell me where I can get a taxi?" He mumbles something that sounds Swedish or Dutch.

"Syau Yen! Syau Yen!" I hear a piercing voice shout from behind me. An old woman in a yellow knit beret is holding up a pink plastic bag filled with wrapped trinkets. I guess she is trying to sell us something. But my father is staring down at this tiny sparrow of a woman, squinting into her eyes. And then his eyes widen, his face opens up and he smiles like a pleased little boy.

"Aiyi! Aiyi!"—Auntie Auntie!—he says softly.

"Syau Yen!" coos my great-aunt. I think it's funny she has just called my father "Little Wild Goose." It must be his baby milk name, the name used to discourage ghosts from stealing children.

They clasp each other's hands—they do not hug—and hold on like this, taking turns saying, "Look at you! You are so old. Look how old you've become!" They are both crying openly, laughing at the same time, and I bite my lip, trying not to cry. I'm afraid to feel their joy. Because I am thinking how different our arrival in Shanghai will be tomorrow, how awkward it will feel.

Now Aiyi beams and points to a Polaroid picture of my father. My father had wisely sent pictures when he wrote and said we were coming. See how smart she was, she seems to intone as she compares the picture to my father. In the letter, my father had said we would call her from the hotel once we arrived, so this is a surprise, that they've come to meet us. I wonder if my sisters will be at the airport.

It is only then that I remember the camera. I had meant to take a picture of my father and his aunt the moment they met. It's not too late.

"Here, stand together over here," I say, holding up the Polaroid. The camera flashes and I hand them the snapshot. Aiyi and my father still stand close together, each of them holding a corner of the picture, watching as their images begin to form. They are almost reverentially quiet. Aiyi is only five years older than my father, which makes her around seventy-seven. But she looks ancient, shrunken, a mummified relic. Her thin hair is pure white, her teeth are brown with decay. So much for stories of Chinese women looking young forever, I think to myself.

50 Now Aiyi is crooning to me: *"Jandale."* So big already. She looks up at me, at my full height, and then peers into her pink plastic bag—her gifts to us, I have figured out—as if she is wondering what she will give to me, now that I am so old and big. And then she grabs my elbow with her sharp pincerlike grasp and turns me around. A man and a woman in their fifties are shaking hands with my father, everybody smiling and saying, "Ah! Ah!" They are Aiyi's oldest son and his wife, and standing next to them are four other people, around my age, and a little girl who's around ten. The introductions go by so fast, all I know is that one of them is Aiyi's grandson, with his wife, and the other is her granddaughter, with her husband. And the little girl is Lili, Aiyi's great-granddaughter.

Aiyi and my father speak the Mandarin dialect from their childhood, but the rest of the family speaks only the Cantonese of their village. I understand only Mandarin but can't speak it that well. So Aiyi and my father gossip unrestrained in Mandarin, exchanging news about people from their old village. And they stop only occasionally to talk to the rest of us, sometimes in Cantonese, sometimes in English.

"Oh, it is as I suspected," says my father, turning to me. "He died last summer." And I already understood this. I just don't know who this person, Li Gong, is. I feel as if I were in the United Nations and the translators had run amok.

"Hello," I say to the little girl. "My name is Jing-mei." But the little girl squirms to look away, causing her parents to laugh with embarrassment. I try to think of Cantonese words I can say to her, stuff I learned from friends in Chinatown, but all I can think of are swear words, terms for bodily functions, and short phrases like "tastes good," "tastes like garbage," and "she's really ugly." And then I have another plan: I hold up the Polaroid camera, beckoning Lili with my finger. She immediately jumps forward, places one hand on her hip in the manner of a fashion model, juts out her chest, and flashes me a toothy smile. As soon as I take the picture she is standing next to me, jumping and giggling every few seconds as she watches herself appear on the greenish film.

By the time we hail taxis for the ride to the hotel, Lili is holding tight onto my hand, pulling me along.

55 In the taxi, Aiyi talks nonstop, so I have no chance to ask her about the different sights we are passing by.

"You wrote and said you would come only for one day," says Aiyi to my father in an agitated tone. "One day! How can you see your family in one day! Toishan is many hours' drive from Guangzhou. And this idea to call us when you arrive. This is nonsense. We have no telephone."

My heart races a little. I wonder if Auntie Lindo told my sisters we would call from the hotel in Shanghai?

Aiyi continues to scold my father. "I was so beside myself, ask my son, almost turned heaven and earth upside down trying to think of a way! So we decided the best was for us to take the bus from Toishan and come into Guangzhou—meet you right from the start."

And now I am holding my breath as the taxi driver dodges between trucks and buses, honking his horn constantly. We seem to be on some sort of long freeway overpass, like a bridge above the city. I can see row after row of apartments, each floor cluttered with laundry hanging out to dry on the balcony. We pass a public bus, with people jammed in so tight their faces are nearly wedged against the window. Then I see the skyline of what must be downtown Guangzhou. From a distance, it looks like a major American city, with highrises and construction going on everywhere. As we slow down in the more congested part of the city, I see scores of little shops, dark inside, lined with counters and shelves. And then there is a building, its front laced with scaffolding made of bamboo poles held together with plastic strips. Men and women are standing on narrow platforms, scraping the sides, working without safety straps or helmets. Oh, would OSHA[1] have a field day here, I think.

60 Aiyi's shrill voice rises up again: "So it is a shame you can't see our village, our house. My sons have been quite successful, selling our vegetables in the free market. We had enough these last few years to build a big house, three stories, all of new brick, big enough for our whole family and then some. And every year, the money is even better. You Americans aren't the only ones who know how to get rich!"

The taxi stops and I assume we've arrived, but then I peer out at what looks like a grander version of the Hyatt Regency. "This is communist China?" I wonder out loud. And then I shake my head toward my father. "This must be the wrong hotel." I quickly pull out our itinerary, travel tickets, and reservations. I had explicitly instructed my travel agent to choose something inexpensive, in the thirty-to-forty-dollar range. I'm sure of this. And there it says on our itinerary: Garden Hotel, Huanshi Dong Lu. Well, our travel agent had better be prepared to eat the extra, that's all I have to say.

The hotel is magnificent. A bellboy complete with uniform and sharp-creased cap jumps forward and begins to carry our bags into the lobby. Inside, the hotel looks like an orgy of shopping arcades and restaurants all encased in granite and glass. And rather than be impressed, I am worried about the

1. The Occupational Safety and Health Administration, a division of the U.S. Department of Labor.

expense, as well as the appearance it must give Aiyi, that we rich Americans cannot be without our luxuries even for one night.

But when I step up to the reservation desk, ready to haggle over this booking mistake, it is confirmed. Our rooms are prepaid, thirty-four dollars each. I feel sheepish, and Aiyi and the others seem delighted by our temporary surroundings. Lili is looking wide-eyed at an arcade filled with video games.

Our whole family crowds into one elevator, and the bellboy waves, saying he will meet us on the eighteenth floor. As soon as the elevator door shuts, everybody becomes very quiet, and when the door finally opens again, everybody talks at once in what sounds like relieved voices. I have the feeling Aiyi and the others have never been on such a long elevator ride.

Our rooms are next to each other and are identical. The rugs, drapes, bed- 65
spreads are all in shades of taupe. There's a color television with remote-control panels built into the lamp table between the two twin beds. The bathroom has marble walls and floors. I find a built-in wet bar with a small refrigerator stocked with Heineken beer, Coke Classic, and Seven-Up, mini-bottles of Johnnie Walker Red, Bacardi rum, and Smirnoff vodka, and packets of M & M's, honey-roasted cashews, and Cadbury chocolate bars. And again I say out loud, "This is communist China?"

My father comes into my room. "They decided we should just stay here and visit," he says, shrugging his shoulders. "They say, Less trouble that way. More time to talk."

"What about dinner?" I ask. I have been envisioning my first real Chinese feast for many days already, a big banquet with one of those soups steaming out of a carved winter melon, chicken wrapped in clay, Peking duck, the works.

My father walks over and picks up a room service book next to a *Travel & Leisure* magazine. He flips through the pages quickly and then points to the menu. "This is what they want," says my father.

So it's decided. We are going to dine tonight in our rooms, with our family, sharing hamburgers, french fries, and apple pie à la mode.

Aiyi and her family are browsing the shops while we clean up. After a hot ride 70
on the train, I'm eager for a shower and cooler clothes.

The hotel has provided little packets of shampoo which, upon opening, I discover is the consistency and color of hoisin sauce.[2] This is more like it, I think. This is China. And I rub some in my damp hair.

Standing in the shower, I realize this is the first time I've been by myself in what seems like days. But instead of feeling relieved, I feel forlorn. I think about what my mother said, about activating my genes and becoming Chinese. And I wonder what she meant.

Right after my mother died, I asked myself a lot of things, things that couldn't be answered, to force myself to grieve more. It seemed as if I wanted to sustain my grief, to assure myself that I had cared deeply enough.

But now I ask the questions mostly because I want to know the answers. What was that pork stuff she used to make that had the texture of sawdust?

2. Sweet brownish-red sauce made from soybeans, sugar, water, spices, garlic, and chili.

What were the names of the uncles who died in Shanghai? What had she dreamt all these years about her other daughters? All the times when she got mad at me, was she really thinking about them? Did she wish I were they? Did she regret that I wasn't?

75 At one o'clock in the morning, I awake to tapping sounds on the window. I must have dozed off and now I feel my body uncramping itself. I'm sitting on the floor, leaning against one of the twin beds. Lili is lying next to me. The others are asleep, too, sprawled out on the beds and floor. Aiyi is seated at a little table, looking very sleepy. And my father is staring out the window, tapping his fingers on the glass. The last time I listened my father was telling Aiyi about his life since he last saw her. How he had gone to Yenching University, later got a post with a newspaper in Chungking, met my mother there, a young widow. How they later fled together to Shanghai to try to find my mother's family house, but there was nothing there. And then they traveled eventually to Canton and then to Hong Kong, then Haiphong and finally to San Francisco. . . .

"Suyuan didn't tell me she was trying all these years to find her daughters," he is now saying in a quiet voice. "Naturally, I did not discuss her daughters with her. I thought she was ashamed she had left them behind."

"Where did she leave them?" asks Aiyi. "How were they found?"

I am wide awake now. Although I have heard parts of this story from my mother's friends.

"It happened when the Japanese took over Kweilin," says my father.

80 "Japanese in Kweilin?" says Aiyi. "That was never the case. Couldn't be. The Japanese never came to Kweilin."

"Yes, that is what the newspapers reported. I know this because I was working for the news bureau at the time. The Kuomintang[3] often told us what we could say and could not say. But we knew the Japanese had come into Kwangsi Province. We had sources who told us how they had captured the Wuchang-Canton railway. How they were coming overland, making very fast progress, marching toward the provincial capital."

Aiyi looks astonished. "If people did not know this, how could Suyuan know the Japanese were coming?"

"An officer of the Kuomintang secretly warned her," explains my father. "Suyuan's husband also was an officer and everybody knew that officers and their families would be the first to be killed. So she gathered a few possessions and, in the middle of the night, she picked up her daughters and fled on foot. The babies were not even one year old."

"How could she give up those babies!" sighs Aiyi. "Twin girls. We have never had such luck in our family." And then she yawns again.

85 "What were they named?" she asks. I listen carefully. I had been planning on using just the familiar "Sister" to address them both. But now I want to know how to pronounce their names.

3. National People's Party, led by Generalissimo Chiang Kai-shek (1887–1975), which fought successfully against the Japanese occupation before being defeated militarily in 1949 by the Chinese Communist Party, led by Mao Zedong (1893–1976).

"They have their father's surname, Wang," says my father. "And their given names are Chwun Yu and Chwun Hwa."

"What do the names mean?" I ask.

"Ah." My father draws imaginary characters on the window. "One means 'Spring Rain,' the other 'Spring Flower,'" he explains in English, "because they born in the spring, and of course rain come before flower, same order these girls are born. Your mother like a poet, don't you think?"

I nod my head. I see Aiyi nod her head forward, too. But it falls forward and stays there. She is breathing deeply, noisily. She is asleep.

"And what does Ma's name mean?" I whisper. 90

"'Suyuan,'" he says, writing more invisible characters on the glass. "The way she write it in Chinese, it mean 'Long-Cherished Wish.' Quite a fancy name, not so ordinary like flower name. See this first character, it mean something like 'Forever Never Forgotten.' But there is another way to write 'Suyuan.' Sound exactly the same, but the meaning is opposite." His finger creates the brush-strokes of another character. "The first part look the same: 'Never Forgotten.' But the last part add to first part make the whole word mean 'Long-Held Grudge.' Your mother get angry with me, I tell her her name should be Grudge."

My father is looking at me, moist-eyed. "See, I pretty clever, too, hah?"

I nod, wishing I could find some way to comfort him. "And what about my name," I ask, "what does 'Jing-mei' mean?"

"Your name also special," he says. I wonder if any name in Chinese is not something special. "'Jing' like excellent *jing.* Not just good, it's something pure, essential, the best quality. *Jing* is good leftover stuff when you take impurities out of something like gold, or rice, or salt. So what is left—just pure essence. And 'Mei,' this is common *mei,* as in *meimei,* 'younger sister.'"

I think about this. My mother's long-cherished wish. Me, the younger sister 95 who was supposed to be the essence of the others. I feed myself with the old grief, wondering how disappointed my mother must have been. Tiny Aiyi stirs suddenly, her head rolls and then falls back, her mouth opens as if to answer my question. She grunts in her sleep, tucking her body more closely into the chair.

"So why did she abandon those babies on the road?" I need to know, because now I feel abandoned too.

"Long time I wondered this myself," says my father. "But then I read that letter from her daughters in Shanghai now, and I talk to Auntie Lindo, all the others. And then I knew. No shame in what she done. None."

"What happened?"

"Your mother running away—" begins my father.

"No, tell me in Chinese," I interrupt. "Really, I can understand." 100

He begins to talk, still standing at the window, looking into the night.

After fleeing Kweilin, your mother walked for several days trying to find a main road. Her thought was to catch a ride on a truck or wagon, to catch enough rides until she reached Chungking, where her husband was stationed.

She had sewn money and jewelry into the lining of her dress, enough, she thought, to barter rides all the way. If I am lucky, she thought, I will not have to trade the heavy gold bracelet and jade ring. These were things from her mother, your grandmother.

By the third day, she had traded nothing. The roads were filled with people, everybody running and begging for rides from passing trucks. The trucks rushed by, afraid to stop. So your mother found no rides, only the start of dysentery pains in her stomach.

105 Her shoulders ached from the two babies swinging from scarf slings. Blisters grew on the palms from holding two leather suitcases. And then the blisters burst and began to bleed. After a while, she left the suitcases behind, keeping only the food and a few clothes. And later she also dropped the bags of wheat flour and rice and kept walking like this for many miles, singing songs to her little girls, until she was delirious with pain and fever.

Finally, there was not one more step left in her body. She didn't have the strength to carry those babies any farther. She slumped to the ground. She knew she would die of her sickness, or perhaps from thirst, from starvation, or from the Japanese, who she was sure were marching right behind her.

She took the babies out of the slings and sat them on the side of the road, then lay down next to them. You babies are so good, she said, so quiet. They smiled back, reaching their chubby hands for her, wanting to be picked up again. And then she knew she could not bear to watch her babies die with her.

She saw a family with three young children in a cart going by. "Take my babies, I beg you," she cried to them. But they stared back with empty eyes and never stopped.

She saw another person pass and called out again. This time a man turned around, and he had such a terrible expression—your mother said it looked like death itself—she shivered and looked away.

110 When the road grew quiet, she tore open the lining of her dress, and stuffed jewelry under the shirt of one baby and money under the other. She reached into her pocket and drew out the photos of her family, the picture of her father and mother, the picture of herself and her husband on their wedding day. And she wrote on the back of each the names of the babies and this same message: "Please care for these babies with the money and valuables provided. When it is safe to come, if you bring them to Shanghai, 9 Weichang Lu, the Li family will be glad to give you a generous reward. Li Suyuan and Wang Fuchi."

And then she touched each baby's cheek and told her not to cry. She would go down the road to find them some food and would be back. And without looking back, she walked down the road, stumbling and crying, thinking only of this one last hope, that her daughters would be found by a kindhearted person who would care for them. She would not allow herself to imagine anything else.

She did not remember how far she walked, which direction she went, when she fainted, or how she was found. When she awoke, she was in the back of a bouncing truck with several other sick people, all moaning. And she began to scream, thinking she was now on a journey to Buddhist hell. But the face of an American missionary lady bent over her and smiled, talking to her in a soothing language she did not understand. And yet she could somehow understand. She had been saved for no good reason, and it was now too late to go back and save her babies.

When she arrived in Chungking, she learned her husband had died two weeks before. She told me later she laughed when the officers told her this news, she was so delirious with madness and disease. To come so far, to lose so much and to find nothing.

I met her in a hospital. She was lying on a cot, hardly able to move, her dysentery had drained her so thin. I had come in for my foot, my missing toe, which was cut off by a piece of falling rubble. She was talking to herself, mumbling.

115 "Look at these clothes," she said, and I saw she had on a rather unusual dress for wartime. It was silk satin, quite dirty, but there was no doubt it was a beautiful dress.

"Look at this face," she said, and I saw her dusty face and hollow cheeks, her eyes shining black. "Do you see my foolish hope?"

"I thought I had lost everything, except these two things," she murmured. "And I wondered which I would lose next. Clothes or hope? Hope or clothes?"

"But now, see here, look what is happening," she said, laughing, as if all her prayers had been answered. And she was pulling hair out of her head as easily as one lifts new wheat from wet soil.

It was an old peasant woman who found them. "How could I resist?" the peasant woman later told your sisters when they were older. They were still sitting obediently near where your mother had left them, looking like little fairy queens waiting for their sedan to arrive.

120 The woman, Mei Ching, and her husband, Mei Han, lived in a stone cave. There were thousands of hidden caves like that in and around Kweilin so secret that the people remained hidden even after the war ended. The Meis would come out of their cave every few days and forage for food supplies left on the road, and sometimes they would see something that they both agreed was a tragedy to leave behind. So one day they took back to their cave a delicately painted set of rice bowls, another day a little footstool with a velvet cushion and two new wedding blankets. And once, it was your sisters.

They were pious people, Muslims, who believed the twin babies were a sign of double luck, and they were sure of this when, later in the evening, they discovered how valuable the babies were. She and her husband had never seen rings and bracelets like those. And while they admired the pictures, knowing the babies came from a good family, neither of them could read or write. It was not until many months later that Mei Ching found someone who could read the writing on the back. By then, she loved these baby girls like her own.

In 1952 Mei Han, the husband, died. The twins were already eight years old, and Mei Ching now decided it was time to find your sisters' true family.

She showed the girls the picture of their mother and told them they had been born into a great family and she would take them back to see their true mother and grandparents. Mei Ching told them about the reward, but she swore she would refuse it. She loved these girls so much, she only wanted them to have what they were entitled to—a better life, a fine house, educated ways. Maybe the family would let her stay on as the girls' amah.[4] Yes, she was certain they would insist.

Of course, when she found the place at 9 Weichang Lu, in the old French Concession, it was something completely different. It was the site of a factory building, recently constructed, and none of the workers knew what had become of the family whose house had burned down on that spot.

4. Maidservant or nurse.

125 Mei Ching could not have known, of course, that your mother and I, her new husband, had already returned to that same place in 1945 in hopes of finding both her family and her daughters.

Your mother and I stayed in China until 1947. We went to many different cities—back to Kweilin, to Changsha, as far south as Kunming. She was always looking out of one corner of her eye for twin babies, then little girls. Later we went to Hong Kong, and when we finally left in 1949 for the United States, I think she was even looking for them on the boat. But when we arrived, she no longer talked about them. I thought, At last, they have died in her heart.

When letters could be openly exchanged between China and the United States, she wrote immediately to old friends in Shanghai and Kweilin. I did not know she did this. Auntie Lindo told me. But of course, by then, all the street names had changed. Some people had died, others had moved away. So it took many years to find a contact. And when she did find an old schoolmate's address and wrote asking her to look for her daughters, her friend wrote back and said this was impossible, like looking for a needle on the bottom of the ocean. How did she know her daughters were in Shanghai and not somewhere else in China? The friend, of course, did not ask, How do you know your daughters are still alive?

So her schoolmate did not look. Finding babies lost during the war was a matter of foolish imagination, and she had no time for that.

But every year, your mother wrote to different people. And this last year, I think she got a big idea in her head, to go to China and find them herself. I remember she told me, "Canning, we should go, before it is too late, before we are too old." And I told her we were already too old, it was already too late.

130 I just thought she wanted to be a tourist! I didn't know she wanted to go and look for her daughters. So when I said it was too late, that must have put a terrible thought in her head that her daughters might be dead. And I think this possibility grew bigger and bigger in her head, until it killed her.

Maybe it was your mother's dead spirit who guided her Shanghai schoolmate to find her daughters. Because after your mother died, the schoolmate saw your sisters, by chance, while shopping for shoes at the Number One Department Store on Nanjing Dong Road. She said it was like a dream, seeing these two women who looked so much alike, moving down the stairs together. There was something about their facial expressions that reminded the schoolmate of your mother.

She quickly walked over to them and called their names, which of course, they did not recognize at first, because Mei Ching had changed their names. But your mother's friend was so sure, she persisted. "Are you not Wang Chwun Yu and Wang Chwun Hwa?" she asked them. And then these double-image women became very excited, because they remembered the names written on the back of an old photo, a photo of a young man and woman they still honored, as their much-loved first parents, who had died and become spirit ghosts still roaming the earth looking for them.

At the airport, I am exhausted. I could not sleep last night. Aiyi had followed me into my room at three in the morning, and she instantly fell asleep on one of the twin beds, snoring with the might of a lumberjack. I lay awake thinking about my mother's story, realizing how much I have never known about her, grieving that my sisters and I had both lost her.

And now at the airport, after shaking hands with everybody, waving good-bye, I think about all the different ways we leave people in this world. Cheerily waving good-bye to some at airports, knowing we'll never see each other again. Leaving others on the side of the road, hoping that we will. Finding my mother in my father's story and saying good-bye before I have a chance to know her better.

Aiyi smiles at me as we wait for our gate to be called. She is so old. I put one 135
arm around her and one arm around Lili. They are the same size, it seems. And then it's time. As we wave good-bye one more time and enter the waiting area, I get the sense I am going from one funeral to another. In my hand I'm clutching a pair of tickets to Shanghai. In two hours we'll be there.

The plane takes off. I close my eyes. How can I describe to them in my broken Chinese about our mother's life? Where should I begin?

"Wake up, we're here," says my father. And I awake with my heart pounding in my throat. I look out the window and we're already on the runway. It's gray outside.

And now I'm walking down the steps of the plane, onto the tarmac and toward the building. If only, I think, if only my mother had lived long enough to be the one walking toward them. I am so nervous I cannot even feel my feet. I am just moving somehow.

Somebody shouts, "She's arrived!" And then I see her. Her short hair. Her small body. And that same look on her face. She has the back of her hand pressed hard against her mouth. She is crying as though she had gone through a terrible ordeal and were happy it is over.

And I know it's not my mother, yet it is the same look she had when I was five 140
and had disappeared all afternoon, for such a long time, that she was convinced I was dead. And when I miraculously appeared, sleepy-eyed, crawling from underneath my bed, she wept and laughed, biting the back of her hand to make sure it was true.

And now I see her again, two of her, waving, and in one hand there is a photo, the Polaroid I sent them. As soon as I get beyond the gate, we run toward each other, all three of us embracing, all hesitations and expectations forgotten.

"Mama, Mama," we all murmur, as if she is among us.

My sisters look at me, proudly. *"Meimei jandale,"* says one sister proudly to the other. "Little Sister has grown up." I look at their faces again and I see no trace of my mother in them. Yet they still look familiar. And now I also see what part of me is Chinese. It is so obvious. It is my family. It is in our blood. After all these years, it can finally be let go.

My sisters and I stand, arms around each other, laughing and wiping the tears from each other's eyes. The flash of the Polaroid goes off and my father hands me the snapshot. My sisters and I watch quietly together, eager to see what develops.

The gray-green surface changes to the bright colors of our three images, 145
sharpening and deepening all at once. And although we don't speak, I know we

all see it: Together we look like our mother. Her same eyes, her same mouth, open in surprise to see, at last, her long-cherished wish.

1989

QUESTIONS

1. Why is the opening scene of A PAIR OF TICKETS—the train journey from Hong Kong to Guangzhou—an appropriate setting for June May's remark that she is "becoming Chinese" (par. 1)?
2. When June May arrives in Guangzhou, what are some details that seem familiar to her, and what are some that seem exotic? Why is she so preoccupied with comparing China to America?
3. June May says that she "could never pass for true Chinese" (par. 35), yet by the end of the story she has discovered "what part of [her] is Chinese" (par. 143). How does the meaning of "Chinese" evolve throughout the story?

JUDITH ORTIZ COFER
(1952–2016)
Volar[1]

Born in Hormigueros, Puerto Rico, Judith Ortiz Cofer just two years later moved with her family, first to New Jersey and later to Georgia, experiences that would inspire much of her later fiction and poetry. "How can you inject passion and purpose into your work if it has no roots?" she wrote, avowing that her own roots include a long line of women storytellers who "infected" her at a very early age with the desire to tell stories both on and off the page. After earning an MA at Florida Atlantic University (1977), Ortiz Cofer returned to Georgia, where she was an emeritus professor at the University of Georgia. Among her numerous publications are the novels *The Line of the Sun* (1989), in which a young girl relates the history of her ne'er-do-well uncle's emigration from Puerto Rico, *The Meaning of Consuelo* (2003), and *Call Me Maria* (2006); the poetry collection *A Love Story Beginning in Spanish* (2005); and *The Latin Deli* (1993) and *The Year of Our Revolution* (1998), two collections that seamlessly interweave fiction, nonfiction, and poetry, thereby demonstrating, in Ortiz Cofer's words, "the need to put things together in a holistic way."

At twelve I was an avid consumer of comic books—*Supergirl* being my favorite. I spent my allowance of a quarter a day on two twelve-cent comic books or a double issue for twenty-five. I had a stack of *Legion of Super Heroes* and *Supergirl* comic books in my bedroom closet that was as tall as I am. I had a recurring dream in those days: that I had long blond hair and could fly. In my

1. To fly (Spanish).

dream I climbed the stairs to the top of our apartment building as myself, but as I went up each flight, changes would be taking place. Step by step I would fill out: My legs would grow long, my arms harden into steel, and my hair would magically go straight and turn a golden color. Of course I would add the bonus of breasts, but not too large; Supergirl had to be aerodynamic. Sleek and hard as a supersonic missile. Once on the roof, my parents safely asleep in their beds, I would get on tiptoe, arms outstretched in the position for flight, and jump out my fifty-story-high window into the black lake of the sky. From up there, over the rooftops, I could see everything, even beyond the few blocks of our barrio;[2] with my X-ray vision I could look inside the homes of people who interested me. Once I saw our landlord, whom I knew my parents feared, sitting in a treasure-room dressed in an ermine coat and a large gold crown. He sat on the floor counting his dollar bills. I played a trick on him. Going up to his building's chimney, I blew a little puff of my superbreath into his fireplace, scattering his stacks of money so that he had to start counting all over again. I could more or less program my Supergirl dreams in those days by focusing on the object of my current obsession. This way I "saw" into the private lives of my neighbors, my teachers, and in the last days of my childish fantasy and the beginning of adolescence, into the secret room of the boys I liked. In the mornings I'd wake up in my tiny bedroom with the incongruous—at least in our tiny apartment—white "princess" furniture my mother had chosen for me, and find myself back in my body: my tight curls still clinging to my head, skinny arms and legs and flat chest unchanged.

In the kitchen my mother and father would be talking softly over a café con leche.[3] She would come "wake me" exactly forty-five minutes after they had gotten up. It was their time together at the beginning of each day and even at an early age I could feel their disappointment if I interrupted them by getting up too early. So I would stay in my bed recalling my dreams of flight, perhaps planning my next flight. In the kitchen they would be discussing events in the barrio. Actually, he would be carrying that part of the conversation; when it was her turn to speak she would, more often than not, try shifting the topic toward her desire to see her *familia* on the Island: *How about a vacation in Puerto Rico together this year, Querido?*[4] *We could rent a car, go to the beach. We could . . .* And he would answer patiently, gently, *Mi amor,*[5] *do you know how much it would cost for all of us to fly there? It is not possible for me to take the time off . . . Mi vida,*[6] *please understand. . . .* And I knew that soon she would rise from the table. Not abruptly. She would light a cigarette and look out the kitchen window. The view was of a dismal alley that was littered with refuse thrown from windows. The space was too narrow for anyone larger than a skinny child to enter safely, so it was never cleaned. My mother would check the time on the clock over her sink, the one with a prayer for patience and grace written in Spanish. A birthday gift. She would see that it was time to wake me. She'd sigh

2. Spanish-speaking neighborhood or district in the United States or any district in a Spanish-speaking country.
3. Coffee with milk (Spanish).
4. Beloved, dear (Spanish).
5. My love (Spanish).
6. My life (Spanish).

deeply and say the same thing the view from her kitchen window always inspired her to say: *Ay, si yo pudiera volar.*[7]

1993

7. Oh, if only I could fly (Spanish).

QUESTIONS

1. VOLAR seems simultaneously vague about its general setting and much more detailed about its particular setting, at least when it comes to place (versus time). How does this combination of vagueness and specificity shape your response to the story and your sense of whom and what it is about?
2. What does the story suggest about how the characters have been shaped by their environment? about how they feel about it, and why?
3. What is the effect of the way Spanish is used both in the title and throughout the story itself? What might these uses of Spanish add to our understanding of the setting, the characters, and their conflicts?

SUGGESTIONS FOR WRITING

1. Write an essay in which you compare the use of setting in any two stories in this book. You might compare the re-creation of two similar settings, such as landscapes far from home, foreign cities, or stifling suburbs; or you might contrast the treatment of different kinds of settings. Be sure to consider not only the authors' descriptive techniques but also the way the authors use setting to shape plot, point of view, and character.
2. In A PAIR OF TICKETS, Amy Tan provides detailed descriptions of June May's journeys to Guangzhou and Shanghai. In his account of his wife's escape from Kweilin, June May's father says little about the landscape. Write an essay in which you compare the two very different storytelling techniques used in this story.
3. In at least two of the stories in this chapter, a place encountered for the first time by a traveler is described with great vividness: the city of Guangzhou in A PAIR OF TICKETS and the city of Yalta in THE LADY WITH THE DOG. Citing examples from these stories, write an essay in which you discuss the effect of new surroundings on our perceptions, emotions, and memories.
4. Choose any story in this chapter and write an essay that explores how the story both draws on and also encourages us to rethink our ideas about a particular place and time and social milieu, perhaps (but not necessarily) by showing us characters who themselves either come to see a setting differently or refuse to do so.
5. Whereas THE LADY WITH THE DOG and A PAIR OF TICKETS each cover a relatively long period of time and take us to a variety of places, the much shorter VOLAR has a more circumscribed setting. Write a response paper or essay exploring how these factors enhance our sense of the characters' conflicts and even the story's theme.
6. Write a story in which a newcomer brings a fresh perspective to a familiar setting.

SAMPLE WRITING: ESSAY

In the following essay, student writer Steven Matview explores the role of setting in Anton Chekhov's The Lady with the Dog. Read the essay responsively and critically, taking time to consider the details Steven chooses to highlight and the way he interprets them. Does he manage to build a convincing and thorough argument about the role of setting in "The Lady with the Dog"? What other details from the story might deserve a place in this argument? In particular, notice how Steven concentrates on temporal setting (the seasons) while commenting only briefly on spatial setting and on the interconnections between time and space in the story. If Steven were your classmate, what three things would you suggest he most needs to do in order to improve the essay in revision? (For ease of reference, we have altered the citations in this paper to refer to paragraph numbers. Unless your instructor indicates otherwise, however, you should always follow convention by instead citing page numbers when writing about fiction.)

Matview 1

Steven Matview
Professor Anne Stevens
English 298
6 March 2017

How Setting Reflects Emotions in Anton Chekhov's "The Lady with the Dog"

Setting is important to Chekhov's "The Lady with the Dog." But wait, isn't setting important to all stories? Not necessarily. In many stories, like Hemingway's "Hills like White Elephants," the plot could be happening anywhere, and it would not matter. But in "The Lady with the Dog" the setting plays an important role in the story, in particular to Dmitri, who is the main character and who experiences the most growth throughout. He goes from being a man at forty who is full of youthful energy and thinks he has been loved by many women to an old man who realizes that he is just experiencing love for the first time. During the course of the narrative, the setting Chekhov maps out shows the progression of Dmitri's affair with Anna Sergeyevna, Dmitri's state of mind, and the changes that Dmitri undergoes. The setting in this story is just as important as any character.

Matview 2

In fact, I would argue that the setting is the single most important component of the story.

Dmitri's relationship with the lady with the dog has its ups and downs, which are reflected in the seasons and the descriptions of weather. He makes this apparent when he says, "The weather is better this evening" (par. 24). Their lives are better when they are together in the summer. This is the time Dmitri and Anna meet and start their courtship. Both are married, and both have spent so much time forcing themselves to love their partners that they do not recognize real love when they feel it. Dmitri initially only wants a fling and doesn't even learn or use Anna's name, referring to her only as "the lady with the dog." There isn't any stress yet, and the two can be just happy with things the way they are. They go on dates and spend time together in Anna's hotel room. Dmitri starts to think of her as "Anna Sergeyevna—'the lady with the dog'" (par. 29), showing a shift within the relationship. He shows he's started to think of this as more of a relationship by using her full name but doesn't completely switch, as he adds in that epithet "lady with the dog." He is trying to resist because he is still married. Dmitri feels young and alive and thinks back to all the women he has made happy in his life.

Another aspect of the setting are the places described in the story, which relate to things the characters feel or know on a subconscious level. At the start of the story, Dmitri is staying at a seaside resort in Yalta. We know that a resort is an impersonal place, where someone can reinvent themselves or get away from the things they don't like about home. Dmitri reinvents his idea about what love is while getting away from a wife he does not care for. Dmitri meets Anna for the first time "in the public gardens" (par. 2). A garden is a place of growth, reflecting the soon-to-be growth of their relationship, as well as the growth Dmitri will experience as a person. They then go on a date, and we become privy to a metaphor describing Dmitri's marriage and how things will go with Anna: "Owing to the roughness of the sea, the steamer arrived late, after the sun had set, and it was a long time turning about before it reached the groyne" (par. 22). The steamer is Dmitri, the sea is his life, and the groyne, a device designed to disrupt the flow of water, is Anna. It took Dmitri longer to find true love, and he has gone through a rough time in a boring marriage, and now there is someone to break that up. This is when Dmitri starts to feel love for Anna, though he does not realize it is love because it is so different from what he has known in the past.

Things change as soon as the next season approaches. The first challenges that arise in the courtship of Dmitri and Anna come when the season begins to change from summer to autumn. Dmitri mentions here that "it was a cold evening" (par. 60), the first time cold is mentioned in the present (before it was only used to describe the unhappy places Anna and Dmitri were escaping from) and a stark contrast to his comment about the weather earlier in the story. Things are starting to get worse for the relationship. Word gets to Anna that she must travel back to her home to be with her husband, who has

Matview 3

fallen ill. Dmitri finds that he does not want to let Anna go, that the fling he wanted has turned into something much more. Dmitri thinks that he was "warm and affectionate with [Anna]" (par. 59), terms associated with summer weather. But, with autumn approaching, Dmitri decides that they were not really in love. This is because the feeling he has does not resemble the forced love he has always experienced with his wife and mistresses, but it is brought up as the object of his "warm feelings" leaves and is replaced with the "cold night."

Change of place goes hand in hand with a change of seasons and weather here. And we are told shortly before Anna leaves that "Yalta was hardly visible through the morning mist; white clouds stood motionless on the mountain-tops" (par. 47). The mist covering Yalta is like the uncertainty that lies in their future as the summer is winding down. Neither can see clearly what will come from their summer tryst when the time comes to separate. White is a color that is often associated with purity, and Dmitri is experiencing a pure, true kind of love for the first time, but he also has obstacles to overcome that are represented by the mountains.

Dmitri thinks he will get over Anna quickly now that she's gone, but winter brings him even more hardships. The most difficult time the couple face comes in the season of winter. Winter is a cold season often affiliated with sadness and the absence of hope. We find out that "[t]he frosts had begun already" (par. 62), meaning the bad times have already started, and we join Dmitri after he's already been back in Moscow for a short time. In Moscow Dmitri has not stopped thinking of Anna Sergeyevna, who is only referred to by her full name now. Referring to her as "Anna Sergeyevna" instead of "the lady with the dog" is a subtle way of letting us know that Dmitri is thinking of her as more than a fling that has gone by, as we saw earlier that he only called her "the lady with the dog" when he didn't have feelings for her. They are separated by cities and by circumstance, and it seems the relationship might be over. In winter all the plants die, and Dmitri and Anna, whose relationship first blossomed in a garden, seem to have a dead relationship. We find out that "more than a month passed" and that "real winter had come" (par. 64), real winter representing the increasing feelings of separation anxiety Dmitri is suffering from.

We get more visual descriptions in Moscow and Anna's unnamed city relating to the characters' thoughts. After Anna leaves and Dmitri returns to his home in Moscow, we find out that he wants to escape to "restaurants, clubs, dinner-parties, [and] anniversary celebrations" (par. 63), showing us that Dmitri is feeling repressed at home compared to the freedom he had at the resort. After confiding in a local his problems, Dmitri thinks, "there is no escaping or getting away from it—just as though one were in a madhouse or a prison" (par. 72). A madhouse and a prison are two places that no one wants to be. Both places are where you are kept from loved ones. But they are also places you are put in when you have done something wrong, a hint that Dmitri feels he's made mistakes in the past, done his time, and now wants to be free to be with Anna.

Matview 4

Dmitri then decides to go to Anna's city, which is left unnamed in the story. This reflects that it is really Dmitri's journey. Dmitri has a hard time reaching Anna at first, as she is tucked away in the house she shares with her husband. When Dmitri finally does confront Anna she does not initially seem happy to see him. Dmitri confronts Anna at a performance of the play *The Geisha*. The opera and the opera house it is performed in have many qualities that suggest Dmitri's emotional state. The opera house is described as having "a fog above the chandelier," and its "gallery was noisy and restless" (par. 85). Dmitri has lots of noisy thoughts in his head as he approaches Anna with uncertainty. As Dmitri approaches Anna the musicians begin tuning their instruments. They are getting ready for the big performance, as Dmitri is getting ready to renew his relationship with Anna. Anna at first appears to be unhappy and takes Dmitri down a path of winding corridors and then up and down a "narrow, gloomy staircase" (par. 93). The outlook seems gloomy for Dmitri, but she does agree to see him again and proceeds to profess her love for him.

At the end of winter, with spring fast approaching, things between Dmitri and Anna begin to show slight improvement over early winter. The weather is described as being "three degrees above freezing-point, and yet it is snowing" (par. 105). Things are getting better for Dmitri, who knows now that Anna loves him and wants to be with him, but it's not all great yet as both are still married and forced to keep their relationship a secret. The open-air setting of the gardens that their relationship started in is replaced by a hotel room, giving the final scene a claustrophobic feel as Anna wonders how they can be together. At the end of the story the couple is still trying to find a way to make their relationship work when we are told, "it seemed as though in a little while the solution would be found" (par. 124). Winter is ending, and spring, a season of growth, new beginnings, and love, is on the horizon. From this we might deduce that the couple will make it, at least into the spring.

But will they? The fact that the story ends with the couple in a "gray area" is fitting because gray, a color associated with ambiguity (shades of gray compared to a black-and-white situation; a "gray area"), in fact appears often in the story. Dmitri is in a situation that involves a lot of moral ambiguity. During the course of the narrative he ends up in love with a married woman while he himself is also married. They begin existing in this gray area where we as readers begin to wonder if what they are doing is really wrong, since they are committing adultery. Anna's eyes are gray, reminding us that Dmitri is entering into a moral gray area whenever he is engaging in this relationship. When Dmitri goes to find Anna and resume their relationship in her home town, he stays at a hotel room whose "floor was covered with grey army cloth" (par. 75) and where there is gray dust and a gray blanket. He enters another gray area when he wants to do what his heart says is right by reuniting with Anna, but doing so is committing more adultery.

But I feel that the recurring gray colors also imply something besides ambiguity—the sadness and lack of excitement that Dmitri has always had in

Matview 5

his life thanks to his unhappy marriage and that he might, paradoxically, have come to expect or even need. We can see this when he refers to his hotel in Anna's city as "the best room at the hotel" (par. 75), but filled with items of gray, or when Anna is "wearing his favourite grey dress" (par. 108). The hotel room and Anna are both things that are great or that he adores, but they have that tinge of sadness, represented by the gray, that he needs.

Looking back over the story, we as readers can come to our own conclusions about whether or not Dmitri and Anna stay together. From looking at the progression of the weather we see that in the summer things are good, in fall bad situations arise, winter is the worst time, and the dawn of spring shows slight hope. Following this progression, I believe that when spring finally hits they will be able to come up with a plan to stay a couple. Dmitri and Anna would be happy. We would see Dmitri and Anna figuring out a way to make their relationship public and no longer to be confined to enclosed hiding places. The real question then would be whether the gray would fade out of Dmitri's life after he finds a happiness with Anna that will last past the following summer or whether the cycle is just doomed to repeat itself, as summer eventually turns into winter and the brightest of colors and emotions fade into gray.

Matview 6

Work Cited

Chekhov, Anton. "The Lady with the Dog." *The Norton Introduction to Literature*, edited by Kelly J. Mays, 12th ed., W. W. Norton, 2017, pp. 268-79.

ACADEMY
Academy

The Future

AN ALBUM

I don't try to describe the future. I try to prevent it.
—RAY BRADBURY

When we say that many fictional subgenres are defined partly or even primarily by the settings they conventionally feature, what we usually have in mind is *where* the action takes place—in a forest, cottage, or village (as in most **folktales**) or in a dark, decaying, and actually or apparently haunted medieval castle or abbey (as in early **gothic fiction**). In a few cases, however, *where* turns out to be infinitely less important than *when*. The most obvious such case is historical fiction—by strict definition, fiction set in a time previous to its author's birth. If writers of such fiction might be said to comment on their present by revisiting a moment from the actual past, writers of what some literary scholars call *future fiction* do the opposite: They show us something important about our present by imagining one or more possible futures.

But what of that amorphous, much-debated thing called *science fiction* or, more familiarly, *sf*? Though definitions of sf are as abundant and varied as planets visited in *Star Trek*, few of those definitions *require* a future setting. The *Oxford English Dictionary*, for example, describes sf as fiction "featur[ing] hypothetical scientific or technological advances, the existence of alien life, space or time travel, etc., especially"—but not exclusively—"such fictions set in the future, or an imagined alternative universe." Insisting even less on particularities of setting, one early (1958) essay on the genre defines it as "a form of literature which crosses the frontiers of knowledge using imagination, intuition or logic to guide it," but relying, when it "goes beyond known facts," on "deductions" that are "feasible or at least not in obvious conflict with accepted [scientific] theories." Though much future fiction falls into the category of sf and vice versa, in other words, the two aren't precisely the same. Mary Shelley's two novels, *Frankenstein* (1818) and *The Last Man* (1826), for instance, are today widely considered early examples of sf, despite the fact that only the latter depicts the future and that both appeared over a hundred years before "pulp" magazine editor Hugo Gernsback first popularized the actual term *science fiction*.

Either way, fictional futures are ultimately as numerous and varied as there are writers to imagine them. Yet they often work in interestingly similar ways. For one thing, many are based on the principle of extrapolation—essentially, an educated guess about the unknown (in this case, the future) based on observations of the known (the present). Such fiction, in other words, invites us into a world that reflects its author's sense of where we might be headed *if* we continue on the path we're already on. For another thing, fictional futures have, over time, tended to swing between one of two extremes: Either they are models of perfection or *utopias*, like the world imagined in the sixteenth-century book by Sir Thomas More from which that word derives, or they are the very opposite—*dystopias*. Whatever particular shape they take, however, "imaginary futures are necessarily," as sf author

William Gibson puts it, "about the moment in which they are written," even if the very best of them continue to be meaningful long after that particular moment is past.

In this album, you'll find four very different sf stories written at different moments in time, ranging from the 1950s to the 2010s. What are the key characteristics of the future each describes? What might each imply about how that future came to be? Which describe their particular future mainly or only, in Bradbury's words, "to prevent it"?

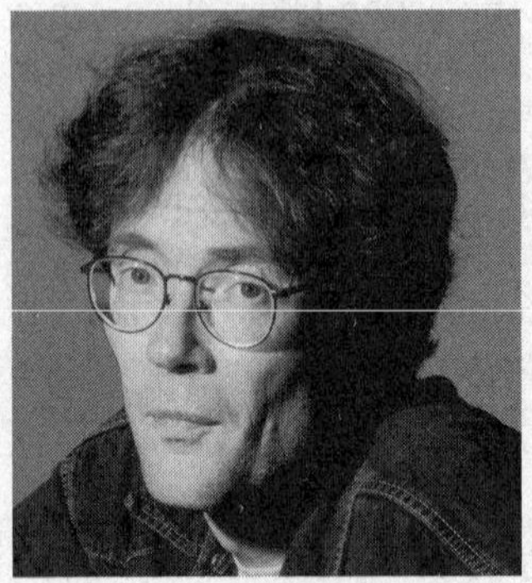

WILLIAM GIBSON
(b. 1948)
The Gernsback Continuum[1]

Widely hailed as the father of "cyberpunk" science fiction, the inventor of the term *cyberspace,* and one of the first fiction writers to make the "hacker" a hero, William Gibson was born in South Carolina but raised (from age six) in a small town in southwestern Virginia, where he and his mother moved after his contractor father's untimely death. An only child, Gibson today credits this experience of "trauma" and "exile" with turning him both on to science fiction and into "the sort of introverted, hyper-bookish boy you'll find in the biographies of most American science fiction writers." Gibson rocketed to fame thanks to his novel *Neuromancer* (1984), the first work ever to win all three of science fiction's top prizes (the Nebula, Hugo, and Philip K. Dick awards). In addition to the two other novels in the "Sprawl" or "Cyberspace" trilogy—*Count Zero* (1986) and *Mona Lisa Overdrive* (1988)—Gibson's publications include *Burning Chrome* (1986); *The Difference Engine* (1990), a novel coauthored with Bruce Sterling; the "Bridge" and "Blue Ant" trilogies (1993–99, 2003–10); and *Distrust the Particular Flavor* (2012), a collection of essays and articles.

Mercifully, the whole thing is starting to fade, to become an episode. When I do still catch the odd glimpse, it's peripheral; mere fragments of mad-doctor chrome, confining themselves to the corner of the eye. There was that flying-wing liner[2] over San Francisco last week, but it was almost translucent. And the shark-fin roadsters[3] have gotten scarcer, and freeways discreetly

1. Like a spectrum, a whole characterized as a collection or sequence of slightly varying elements or states. *Gernsback*: between the late 1920s and early 1950s, Hugo Gernsback (1884–1967) founded and edited a series of science-fiction magazines, starting with the world's first, *Amazing Stories*.

2. A large tailless passenger aircraft with a flattened appearance created by the way the wings flow seamlessly into the body.

3. Open-top two-seater automobile with a sharklike tail fin, a futuristic design popular in the 1950s and 1960s.

avoid unfolding themselves into the gleaming eighty-lane monsters I was forced to drive last month in my rented Toyota. And I know that none of it will follow me to New York; my vision is narrowing to a single wavelength of probability. I've worked hard for that. Television helped a lot.

I suppose it started in London, in that bogus Greek taverna in Battersea Park Road, with lunch on Cohen's corporate tab. Dead steam-table food and it took them thirty minutes to find an ice bucket for the retsina.[4] Cohen works for Barris-Watford, who publish big, trendy "trade" paperbacks: illustrated histories of the neon sign, the pinball machine, the windup toys of Occupied Japan.[5] I'd gone over to shoot a series of shoe ads; California girls with tanned legs and frisky Day-Glo jogging shoes had capered for me down the escalators of St. John's Wood and across the platforms of Tooting Bec.[6] A lean and hungry young agency had decided that the mystery of London Transport would sell waffle-tread nylon runners.[7] They decide; I shoot. And Cohen, whom I knew vaguely from the old days in New York, had invited me to lunch the day before I was due out of Heathrow.[8] He brought along a very fashionably dressed young woman named Dialta Downes, who was virtually chinless and evidently a noted pop-art historian. In retrospect, I see her walking in beside Cohen under a floating neon sign that flashes **THIS WAY LIES MADNESS** in huge sans-serif[9] capitals.

Cohen introduced us and explained that Dialta was the prime mover behind the latest Barris-Watford project, an illustrated history of what she called "American Streamlined Moderne." Cohen called it "raygun Gothic." Their working title was *The Airstream Futuropolis: The Tomorrow That Never Was.*

There's a British obsession with the more baroque elements of American pop culture, something like the weird cowboys-and-Indians fetish of the West Germans or the aberrant French hunger for old Jerry Lewis[1] films. In Dialta Downes this manifested itself in a mania for a uniquely American form of architecture that most Americans are scarcely aware of. At first I wasn't sure what she was talking about, but gradually it began to dawn on me. I found myself remembering Sunday morning television in the Fifties.

Sometimes they'd run old eroded newsreels as filler on the local station. 5
You'd sit there with a peanut butter sandwich and a glass of milk, and a static-ridden Hollywood baritone would tell you that there was A Flying Car in Your Future. And three Detroit engineers would putter around with this big old Nash[2]

4. Strong resin-flavored Greek wine.

5. After its defeat in World War II, Japan was occupied for almost ten years (1945–52) by the Allied powers, led by the United States and Great Britain.

6. Subway station in Tooting, South London. *St. John's Wood*: affluent neighborhood in northwest London.

7. Running shoes or sneakers (British). *London Transport*: public and brand name of the government body overseeing all public transportation in London, including the subway, buses, etc.

8. Major London airport.

9. Plain typeface, often used for headlines, in which letters are not embellished with decorative line strokes.

1. American comedian (b. 1926) featured in many popular 1950s films.

2. Car produced in the United States between 1916 and 1957.

with wings, and you'd see it rumbling furiously down some deserted Michigan runway. You never actually saw it take off, but it flew away to Dialta Downes's never-never land, true home of a generation of completely uninhibited technophiles. She was talking about those odds and ends of "futuristic" Thirties and Forties architecture you pass daily in American cities without noticing; the movie marquees ribbed to radiate some mysterious energy, the dime stores faced with fluted aluminum, the chrome-tube chairs gathering dust in the lobbies of transient hotels. She saw these things as segments of a dreamworld, abandoned in the uncaring present; she wanted me to photograph them for her.

The Thirties had seen the first generation of American industrial designers; until the Thirties, all pencil sharpeners had looked like pencil sharpeners—your basic Victorian[3] mechanism, perhaps with a curlicue of decorative trim. After the advent of the designers, some pencil sharpeners looked as though they'd been put together in wind tunnels. For the most part, the change was only skin-deep; under the streamlined chrome shell, you'd find the same Victorian mechanism. Which made a certain kind of sense, because the most successful American designers had been recruited from the ranks of Broadway theater designers. It was all a stage set, a series of elaborate props for playing at living in the future.

Over coffee, Cohen produced a fat manila envelope full of glossies. I saw the winged statues that guard the Hoover Dam,[4] forty-foot concrete hood ornaments leaning steadfastly into an imaginary hurricane. I saw a dozen shots of Frank Lloyd Wright's Johnson's Wax Building, juxtaposed with the covers of old *Amazing Stories* pulps, by an artist named Frank R. Paul;[5] the employees of Johnson's Wax must have felt as though they were walking into one of Paul's spray-paint pulp utopias. Wright's building looked as though it had been designed for people who wore white togas and Lucite sandals. I hesitated over one sketch of a particularly grandiose prop-driven airliner, all wing, like a fat symmetrical boomerang with windows in unlikely places. Labeled arrows indicated the locations of the grand ballroom and two squash courts. It was dated 1936.

"This thing couldn't have flown . . . ?" I looked at Dialta Downes.

"Oh, no, quite impossible, even with those twelve giant props; but they loved the look, don't you see? New York to London in less than two days, first-class

3. Dating from the reign of Queen Victoria of England (1837–1901).

4. On the Nevada-Arizona border, completed 1936; according to their creator, the "Winged Figures of the Republic," the iconic (bronze, not concrete) statues alluded to here represent "the immutable calm of intellectual resolution, and the enormous power of trained physical strength, equally enthroned in placid triumph of scientific accomplishment."

5. American illustrator (1884–1963) renowned for his work for popular science-fiction magazines including *Amazing Stories* (founded by Hugo Gernsback in 1926); popular, sensational publications, of whatever genre, are sometimes referred to as *pulps* because of the cheap paper on which they were printed. *Frank Lloyd Wright's Johnson's Wax Building*: Wisconsin headquarters of the company (founded 1886) now known as S. C. Johnson & Son; designed by famed modern architect Frank Lloyd Wright (1867–1959).

dining rooms, private cabins, sun decks, dancing to jazz in the evening . . . The designers were populists, you see; they were trying to give the public what it wanted. What the public wanted was the future."

I'd been in Burbank[6] for three days, trying to suffuse a really dull-looking rocker 10
with charisma, when I got the package from Cohen. It is possible to photograph what isn't there; it's damned hard to do, and consequently a very marketable talent. While I'm not bad at it, I'm not exactly the best, either, and this poor guy strained my Nikon's credibility. I got out, depressed because I do like to do a good job, but not totally depressed, because I did make sure I'd gotten the check for the job, and I decided to restore myself with the sublime artiness of the Barris-Watford assignment. Cohen had sent me some books on Thirties design, more photos of streamlined buildings, and a list of Dialta Downes's fifty favorite examples of the style in California.

Architectural photography can involve a lot of waiting; the building becomes a kind of sundial, while you wait for a shadow to crawl away from a detail you want, or for the mass and balance of the structure to reveal itself in a certain way. While I was waiting, I thought myself in Dialta Downes's America. When I isolated a few of the factory buildings on the ground glass of the Hasselblad,[7] they came across with a kind of sinister totalitarian dignity, like the stadiums Albert Speer[8] built for Hitler. But the rest of it was relentlessly tacky: ephemeral stuff extruded by the collective American subconscious of the Thirties, tending mostly to survive along depressing strips lined with dusty motels, mattress wholesalers, and small used-car lots. I went for the gas stations in a big way.

During the high point of the Downes Age, they put Ming the Merciless[9] in charge of designing California gas stations. Favoring the architecture of his native Mongo, he cruised up and down the coast erecting raygun emplacements in white stucco. Lots of them featured superfluous central towers ringed with those strange radiator flanges that were a signature motif of the style, and made them look as though they might generate potent bursts of raw technological enthusiasm, if you could only find the switch that turned them on. I shot one in San Jose an hour before the bulldozers arrived and drove right through the structural truth of plaster and lathing and cheap concrete.

"Think of it," Dialta Downes had said, "as a kind of alternate America: a 1980 that never happened. An architecture of broken dreams."

6. City just north of Los Angeles, California; Walt Disney and Warner Brothers are two of many media companies headquartered there.

7. High-quality camera made by the Swedish Hasselblad company. *Ground glass*: viewer inserted in the back of a camera for help with focusing and composing.

8. Chief architect (1905–81) and minister of armaments and war production in Nazi Germany; one of his projects was a monumental 400,000-seat stadium begun in 1937 but never completed.

9. Evil tyrant, from the planet Mongo, featured in *Flash Gordon*, a science-fiction comic strip and film series of the 1930s.

And that was my frame of mind as I made the stations of her convoluted socioarchitectural cross[1] in my red Toyota—as I gradually tuned in to her image of a shadowy America-that-wasn't, of Coca-Cola plants like beached submarines, and fifth-run movie houses like the temples of some lost sect that had worshiped blue mirrors and geometry. And as I moved among these secret ruins, I found myself wondering what the inhabitants of that lost future would think of the world I lived in. The Thirties dreamed white marble and slipstream chrome, immortal crystal and burnished bronze, but the rockets on the covers of the Gernsback pulps had fallen on London in the dead of night, screaming. After the war,[2] everyone had a car—no wings for it—and the promised superhighway to drive it down, so that the sky itself darkened, and the fumes ate the marble and pitted the miracle crystal. . . .

And one day, on the outskirts of Bolinas,[3] when I was setting up to shoot a particularly lavish example of Ming's martial architecture, I penetrated a fine membrane, a membrane of probability. . . .

Every so gently, I went over the Edge—

And looked up to see a twelve-engined thing like a bloated boomerang, all wing, thrumming its way east with an elephantine grace, so low that I could count the rivets in its dull silver skin, and hear—maybe—the echo of jazz.

I took it to Kihn.

Merv Kihn, free-lance journalist with an extensive line in Texas pterodactyls, redneck UFO contactees, bush-league Loch Ness monsters, and the Top Ten conspiracy theories in the loonier reaches of the American mass mind.

"It's good," said Kihn, polishing his yellow Polaroid shooting glasses on the hem of his Hawaiian shirt, "but it's not *mental*; lacks the true quill."

"But I saw it, Mervyn." We were seated poolside in brilliant Arizona sunlight. He was in Tucson waiting for a group of retired Las Vegas civil servants whose leader received messages from Them on her microwave oven. I'd driven all night and was feeling it.

"Of course you did. Of course you saw it. You've read my stuff; haven't you grasped my blanket solution to the UFO problem? It's simple, plain and country simple: people"—he settled the glasses carefully on his long hawk nose and fixed me with his best basilisk glare—"*see* . . . things. People see these things. Nothing's there, but people *see* them anyway. Because they need to, probably. You've read Jung,[4] you should know the score. . . . In your case, it's so obvious: You admit you were thinking about this crackpot architecture, having fantasies. . . . Look, I'm sure you've taken your share of drugs, right? How many people survived the Sixties in California without having the odd hallucination? All those nights when you discovered that whole armies of Disney technicians

1. The term *stations of the cross* refers both to a series of images or statues, especially in a church, depicting the chief scenes of Christ's final suffering and death and to an act of religious devotion that involves meditating or praying at each station.

2. World War II (1939–45); between September 1940 and May 1941, London was bombed some seventy-one times.

3. Coastal community in Northern California, just north of San Francisco.

4. Carl Jung (1875–1961), Swiss psychiatrist who posited the concept of the *collective unconscious*, a reservoir of memories, impulses, and images (or *archetypes*) that all humans or at least those of a particular culture share in common without being consciously aware of.

had been employed to weave animated holograms of Egyptian hieroglyphs into the fabric of your jeans, say, or the times when—"

"But it wasn't like that."

"Of course not. It wasn't like that at all; it was 'in a setting of clear reality,' right? Everything normal, and then there's the monster, the mandala,[5] the neon cigar. In your case, a giant Tom Swift[6] airplane. It happens *all the time*. You aren't even crazy. You know that, don't you?" He fished a beer out of the battered foam cooler beside his deck chair.

"Last week I was in Virginia. Grayson County. I interviewed a sixteen-year-old girl who'd been assaulted by a *bar hade*."

"A what?"

"A bear head. The severed head of a bear. This *bar hade*, see, was floating around on its own little flying saucer, looked kind of like the hubcaps on cousin Wayne's vintage Caddy. Had red, glowing eyes like two cigar stubs and telescoping chrome antennas poking up behind its ears." He burped.

"It assaulted her? How?"

"You don't want to know; you're obviously impressionable. 'It was cold'"—he lapsed into his bad southern accent—"'and metallic.' It made electronic noises. Now that is the real thing, the straight goods from the mass unconscious, friend; that little girl is a witch. There's just no place for her to function in this society. She'd have seen the devil, if she hadn't been brought up on *The Bionic Man* and all those *Star Trek* reruns.[7] She is clued into the main vein. And she knows that it happened to her. I got out ten minutes before the heavy UFO boys showed up with the polygraph."

I must have looked pained, because he set his beer down carefully beside the cooler and sat up.

"If you want a classier explanation, I'd say you saw a semiotic ghost. All these contactee stories, for instance, are framed in a kind of sci-fi imagery that permeates our culture. I could buy aliens, but not aliens that look like Fifties' comic art. They're semiotic[8] phantoms, bits of deep cultural imagery that have split off and taken on a life of their own, like the Jules Verne[9] airships that those old Kansas farmers were always seeing. But you saw a different kind of ghost, that's all. That plane was part of the mass unconscious, once. You picked up on that, somehow. The important thing is not to worry about it."

I did worry about it, though.

Kihn combed his thinning blond hair and went off to hear what They had had to say over the radar range lately, and I drew the curtains in my room and lay down in air-conditioned darkness to worry about it. I was still worrying about it when I woke up. Kihn had left a note on my door; he was flying up north in a

5. Literally, "sacred circle" (Sanskrit); in Hinduism and Buddhism, as well as Jungian therapy, a circular figure representing the universe and used as an aid to meditation.

6. Protagonist of a series of young-adult science-fiction and adventure novels that debuted in 1910.

7. The original series aired from 1966 to 1969. *The Bionic Man*: Actually, *The Six Million Dollar Man*, a popular 1970s American television series about a former astronaut turned secret agent outfitted with bionic implants.

8. Of or relating to signs and symbols, systems of meaning making.

9. French author (1828–1905) often hailed as a father of science fiction thanks to novels such as *Journey to the Center of the Earth* (1864) and *Twenty Thousand Leagues Under the Sea* (1870).

chartered plane to check out a cattle-mutilation rumor ("muties," he called them; another of his journalistic specialties).

I had a meal, showered, took a crumbling diet pill that had been kicking around in the bottom of my shaving kit for three years, and headed back to Los Angeles.

35 The speed limited my vision to the tunnel of the Toyota's headlights. The body could drive, I told myself, while the mind maintained. Maintained and stayed away from the weird peripheral window dressing of amphetamine and exhaustion, the spectral, luminous vegetation that grows out of the corners of the mind's eye along late-night highways. But the mind had its own ideas, and Kihn's opinion of what I was already thinking of as my "sighting" rattled endlessly, through my head in a tight, lopsided orbit. Semiotic ghosts. Fragments of the Mass Dream, whirling past in the wind of my passage. Somehow this feedback-loop aggravated the diet pill, and the speed-vegetation along the road began to assume the colors of infrared satellite images, glowing shreds blown apart in the Toyota's slipstream.

I pulled over, then, and a half-dozen aluminum beer cans winked goodnight as I killed the headlights. I wondered what time it was in London, and tried to imagine Dialta Downes having breakfast in her Hampstead flat,[1] surrounded by streamlined chrome figurines and books on American culture.

Desert nights in that country are enormous; the moon is closer. I watched the moon for a long time and decided that Kihn was right. The main thing was not to worry. All across the continent, daily, people who were more normal than I'd ever aspired to be saw giant birds, Bigfeet, flying oil refineries; they kept Kihn busy and solvent. Why should I be upset by a glimpse of the 1930s pop imagination loose over Bolinas? I decided to go to sleep, with nothing worse to worry about than rattlesnakes and cannibal hippies, safe amid the friendly roadside garbage of my own familiar continuum. In the morning I'd drive down to Nogales[2] and photograph the old brothels, something I'd intended to do for years. The diet pill had given up.

The light woke me, and then the voices.

The light came from somewhere behind me and threw shifting shadows inside the car. The voices were calm, indistinct, male and female, engaged in conversation.

40 My neck was stiff and my eyeballs felt gritty in their sockets. My leg had gone to sleep, pressed against the steering wheel. I fumbled for my glasses in the pocket of my work shirt and finally got them on.

Then I looked behind me and saw the city.

The books on Thirties' design were in the trunk; one of them contained sketches of an idealized city that drew on *Metropolis* and *Things to Come*,[3] but squared everything, soaring up through an architect's perfect clouds to zeppe-

1. Apartment (British). *Hampstead*: London neighborhood known for its artsy, intellectual atmosphere.

2. One or both of the two adjacent cities of that name lying on either side of the Arizona-Mexico border.

3. British science-fiction film (1936) conceived by H. G. Wells (1866–1946) about a decades-long world war that begins in 1940 and the utopia that—by the twenty-first century—replaces the civilization that war destroys. *Metropolis*: German silent science-fiction film (1927) about a vast future city of towering high-rises occupied by the wealthy and powered by machines operated by laborers who must live and toil below ground.

lin docks and mad neon spires. That city was a scale model of the one that rose behind me. Spire stood on spire in gleaming ziggurat steps that climbed to a central golden temple tower ringed with the crazy radiator flanges of the Mongo gas stations. You could hide the Empire State Building[4] in the smallest of those towers. Roads of crystal soared between the spires, crossed and recrossed by smooth silver shapes like beads of running mercury. The air was thick with ships: giant wing-liners, little darting silver things (sometimes one of the quicksilver shapes from the sky bridges rose gracefully into the air and flew up to join the dance), mile-long blimps, hovering dragonfly things that were gyrocopters . . .

I closed my eyes tight and swung around in the seat. When I opened them, I willed myself to see the mileage meter, the pale road dust on the black plastic dashboard, the overflowing ashtray.

"Amphetamine psychosis," I said. I opened my eyes. The dash was still there, the dust, the crushed filtertips. Very carefully, without moving my head, I turned the headlights on.

And saw them.

They were blond. They were standing beside their car, an aluminum avocado with a central shark-fin rudder jutting up from its spine and smooth black tires like a child's toy. He had his arm around her waist and was gesturing toward the city. They were both in white: loose clothing, bare legs, spotless white sun shoes. Neither of them seemed aware of the beams of my headlights. He was saying something wise and strong, and she was nodding, and suddenly I was frightened, frightened in an entirely different way. Sanity had ceased to be an issue; I knew, somehow, that the city behind me was Tucson—a dream Tucson thrown up out of the collective yearning of an era. That it was real, entirely real. But the couple in front of me lived in it, and they frightened me.

They were the children of Dialta Downes's '80-that-wasn't; they were Heirs to the Dream. They were white, blond, and they probably had blue eyes. They were American. Dialta had said that the Future had come to America first, but had finally passed it by. But not here, in the heart of the Dream. Here, we'd gone on and on, in a dream logic that knew nothing of pollution, the finite bounds of fossil fuel, or foreign wars it was possible to lose. They were smug, happy, and utterly content with themselves and their world. And in the Dream, it was *their* world.

Behind me, the illuminated city: Searchlights swept the sky for the sheer joy of it. I imagined them thronging the plazas of white marble, orderly and alert, their bright eyes shining with enthusiasm for their floodlit avenues and silver cars.

It had all the sinister fruitiness of Hitler Youth[5] propaganda.

I put the car in gear and drove forward slowly, until the bumper was within three feet of them. They still hadn't seen me. I rolled the window down and listened to what the man was saying. His words were bright and hollow as the pitch in some Chamber of Commerce brochure, and I knew that he believed in them absolutely.

4. Iconic Manhattan skyscraper heralded as the world's tallest building when completed in 1931.

5. Youth organization of the German Nazi Party, founded in the 1920s; membership became compulsory for those over seventeen in 1939; two years later, the age was lowered to ten. Key to Hitler's plan to create an Aryan master race, it emphasized both physical training and ideological indoctrination.

"John," I heard the woman say, "we've forgotten to take our food pills." She clicked two bright wafers from a thing on her belt and passed one to him. I backed onto the highway and headed for Los Angeles, wincing and shaking my head.

I phoned Kihn from a gas station. A new one, in bad Spanish Modern. He was back from his expedition and didn't seem to mind the call.

"Yeah, that is a weird one. Did you try to get any pictures? Not that they ever come out, but it adds an interesting *frisson*[6] to your story, not having the pictures turn out. . . ."

But what should I do?

"Watch lots of television, particularly game shows and soaps. Go to porn movies. Ever see *Nazi Love Motel*? They've got it on cable, here. Really awful. Just what you need."

What was he talking about?

"Quit yelling and listen to me. I'm letting you in on a trade secret: Really bad media can exorcise your semiotic ghosts. If it keeps the saucer people off my back, it can keep these Art Deco[7] futuroids off yours. Try it. What have you got to lose?"

Then he begged off, pleading an early-morning date with the Elect.

"The who?"

"These oldsters from Vegas; the ones with the microwaves."

I considered putting a collect call through to London, getting Cohen at Barris-Watford and telling him his photographer was checked out for a protracted season in the Twilight Zone.[8] In the end, I let a machine mix me a really impossible cup of black coffee and climbed back into the Toyota for the haul to Los Angeles.

Los Angeles was a bad idea, and I spent two weeks there. It was prime Downes country; too much of the Dream there, and too many fragments of the Dream waiting to snare me. I nearly wrecked the car on a stretch of overpass near Disneyland, when the road fanned out like an origami trick and left me swerving through a dozen minilanes of whizzing chrome teardrops with shark fins. Even worse, Hollywood was full of people who looked too much like the couple I'd seen in Arizona. I hired an Italian director who was making ends meet doing darkroom work and installing patio decks around swimming pools until his ship came in; he made prints of all the negatives I'd accumulated on the Downes job. I didn't want to look at the stuff myself. It didn't seem to bother Leonardo, though, and when he was finished I checked the prints, riffling through them like a deck of cards, sealed them up, and sent them air freight to London. Then I took a taxi to a theater that was showing *Nazi Love Motel*, and kept my eyes shut all the way.

Cohen's congratulatory wire was forwarded to me in San Francisco a week later. Dialta had loved the pictures. He admired the way I'd "really gotten into it," and looked forward to working with me again. That afternoon I spotted a

6. Sudden, brief, shiver-inducing thrill.

7. Popular, self-consciously modern design style of the 1920s and 1930s featuring bold outlines, geometric forms, and the use of cutting-edge materials such as plastic.

8. Literally, an in-between space or one outside ordinary legal or ethical limits; figuratively, a fantastic or illusory world; also the title of a popular American television series (1959–64) featuring unrelated stories usually involving a bizarre, often macabre premise or ending with an unexpected twist.

flying wing over Castro Street,[9] but there was something tenuous about it, as though it were only half there. I rushed into the nearest newsstand and gathered up as much as I could find on the petroleum crisis[1] and the nuclear energy hazard.[2] I'd just decided to buy a plane ticket for New York.

"Hell of a world we live in, huh?" The proprietor was a thin black man with bad teeth and an obvious wig. I nodded, fishing in my jeans for change, anxious to find a park bench where I could submerge myself in hard evidence of the human near-dystopia we live in. "But it could be worse, huh?"

"That's right," I said, "or even worse, it could be perfect."

He watched me as I headed down the street with my little bundle of condensed catastrophe.

1981

QUESTIONS

1. What exactly is Merv Kihn's explanation for what happens to the narrator in Bolinas? How might the rest of the story either validate or complicate his explanation?
2. Why and how might it matter that the story begins in England but takes place mainly in the American West? that the conversation with which the story ends takes place on Castro Street in San Francisco?
3. In addition to making evocative use of setting, what might THE GERNSBACK CONTINUUM have to say *about* setting or about the worlds created in and by fiction (among other things)?

AUTHORS ON THEIR WORK

WILLIAM GIBSON (b. 1948)

From "Maximus Clarke Talks with William Gibson about His 'Speculative Novels of Last Wednesday'" (2010)*

WG [WILLIAM GIBSON]: [. . .] I forget who it was [. . .] who said something to the effect that people make a terribly big deal about the future, but when we get there, it's just as shabby and small as the present.

MC [INTERVIEWER MAXIMUS CLARKE]: And I think what you did early on that grabbed a lot of people's attention was to refract the future through that lens—to make the future not shiny—to make it just sort of a place. It was the overturning of the utopian "raygun gothic" future, as you satirized it in "The Gernsback Continuum," and its replacement with something that felt more like a real place. I don't know whether you thought of that story as a kind of manifesto for what you wanted to do, but it feels retrospectively like one.

9. Main thoroughfare of one of the oldest and most famous gay neighborhoods in the United States.

1. Throughout the 1970s, the United States faced a series of "energy" or "oil crises" caused by unprecedentedly high demand, increasing reliance on imported oil, and various actions taken by oil-producing nations motivated, in part, by anger over U.S. actions in the Middle East.

2. A partial meltdown at Pennsylvania's Three Mile Island nuclear plant on March 28, 1979, crystallized the concerns of a growing national antinuclear movement.

WG: It was, to some extent. [. . .] Actually, how the story came to be written is that I was writing little bits and pieces of non-fiction for fanzines and little amateur science fiction magazines. Someone had given me a book called *The Streamlined Decade,* which was a sort of paperbound coffee table book of Art Moderne design. And I wrote a review of it, comparing it to Hugo Gernsback's universe, and submitted it to one of these little magazines. And they rejected it.

• • •

When I started writing it as a story, I didn't particularly expect that it would work.

Then as I proceeded with it, it was building momentum, and actually working, in spite of this unlikely pile of socio-artistic analysis that I was building it with. And the bricolage aspect of it really impressed me. I thought, "Hmm, that's the way to do this! I thought I just had to sit here and make stuff up, but actually I can import material, and build things out of it, and somehow the thing takes on a life of its own."

*"Maximus Clarke Talks with William Gibson about His 'Speculative Novels of Last Wednesday.'" Interview by Maximus Clarke. *Maud Newton,* 22 Sept. 2010, maudnewton.com/blog/maximus-clarke-talks-with-william-gibson-about-his-speculative-novels-of-last-wednesday/.

RAY BRADBURY (1920–2012)

The Veldt[1]

The only writer ever to receive a National Medal of Arts (2004) and to have both a lunar crater (1971) and a Mars rover landing site (2012) named in his honor, Ray Bradbury was born and raised mostly in Waukegan, Illinois, until 1934, when the Great Depression took his family to Los Angeles. Here he began publishing short stories in the "pulp" magazines that had first introduced him (at age eight) to science fiction. After winning his first O. Henry Award for "The Lake" (1942), Bradbury left off selling newspapers to become a full-time writer. He never looked back. Arguably the twentieth century's most widely read science-fiction/fantasy writer and the first to attract a mainstream audience, Bradbury is perhaps most famous for two books. More a collection of interlinked stories than a novel, *The Martian Chronicles* (1950) imagines the colonization of Mars circa 1999–2026, focusing on the ways in which the human colonists both interact with the planet's gentle, shape-shifting, telepathic inhabitants and project their own desires and cultural values onto their new home. The novel *Fahrenheit 451* (1953) features what novelist Kingsley Amis hailed as "the most skilfully drawn of all science fiction's conformist hells"—a future in which reading is outlawed and firemen are tasked with burning books. In addition to other novels, including *Something Wicked This Way Comes* (1962) and *Farewell Summer* (2006), Bradbury wrote for both stage and screen, even featuring in

1. Area of grassy land with scattered trees and shrubs, especially in southern (sub-Saharan) Africa.

his own television series, *The Ray Bradbury Theater*, from 1985 to 1992. First and foremost, however, Bradbury was a short-story writer; *The Stories of Ray Bradbury* (1980) and *Ray Bradbury Stories, Volume 2* (2009) gather some of his best.

George, I wish you'd look at the nursery."

"What's wrong with it?"

"I don't know."

"Well, then."

"I just want you to look at it, is all, or call a psychologist in to look at it." 5

"What would a psychologist want with a nursery?"

"You know very well what he'd want." His wife paused in the middle of the kitchen and watched the stove busy humming to itself, making supper for four.

"It's just that the nursery is different now than it was."

"All right, let's have a look."

They walked down the hall of their soundproofed, Happylife Home, which had cost them thirty thousand dollars installed, this house which clothed and fed and rocked them to sleep and played and sang and was good to them. Their approach sensitized a switch somewhere and the nursery light flicked on when they came within ten feet of it. Similarly, behind them, in the halls, lights went on and off as they left them behind, with a soft automaticity. 10

"Well," said George Hadley.

They stood on the thatched floor of the nursery. It was forty feet across by forty feet long and thirty feet high; it had cost half again as much as the rest of the house. "But nothing's too good for our children," George had said.

The nursery was silent. It was empty as a jungle glade at hot high noon. The walls were blank and two dimensional. Now, as George and Lydia Hadley stood in the center of the room, the walls began to purr and recede into crystalline distance, it seemed, and presently an African veldt appeared, in three dimensions; on all sides, in colors reproduced to the final pebble and bit of straw. The ceiling above them became a deep sky with a hot yellow sun.

George Hadley felt the perspiration start on his brow.

"Let's get out of the sun," he said. "This is a little too real. But I don't see anything wrong." 15

"Wait a moment, you'll see," said his wife.

Now the hidden odorophonics were beginning to blow a wind of odor at the two people in the middle of the baked veldtland. The hot straw smell of lion grass, the cool green smell of the hidden water hole, the great rusty smell of animals, the smell of dust like a red paprika in the hot air. And now the sounds: the thump of distant antelope feet on grassy sod, the papery rustling of vultures. A shadow passed through the sky. The shadow flickered on George Hadley's upturned, sweating face.

"Filthy creatures," he heard his wife say.

"The vultures."

"You see, there are the lions, far over, that way. Now they're on their way to the water hole. They've just been eating," said Lydia. "I don't know what." 20

"Some animal." George Hadley put his hand up to shield off the burning light from his squinted eyes. "A zebra or a baby giraffe, maybe."

"Are you sure?" His wife sounded peculiarly tense.

"No, it's a little late to be sure," he said, amused. "Nothing over there I can see but cleaned bone, and the vultures dropping for what's left."

"Did you hear that scream?" she asked.

"No."

"About a minute ago?"

"Sorry, no."

The lions were coming. And again George Hadley was filled with admiration for the mechanical genius who had conceived this room. A miracle of efficiency selling for an absurdly low price. Every home should have one. Oh, occasionally they frightened you with their clinical accuracy, they startled you, gave you a twinge, but most of the time what fun for everyone, not only your own son and daughter, but for yourself when you felt like a quick jaunt to a foreign land, a quick change of scenery. Well, here it was!

And here were the lions now, fifteen feet away, so real, so feverishly and startlingly real that you could feel the prickling fur on your hand, and your mouth was stuffed with the dusty upholstery smell of their heated pelts, and the yellow of them was in your eyes like the yellow of an exquisite French tapestry, the yellows of lions and summer grass, and the sound of the matted lion lungs exhaling on the silent noontide, and the smell of meat from the panting, dripping mouths.

The lions stood looking at George and Lydia Hadley with terrible green-yellow eyes.

"Watch out!" screamed Lydia.

The lions came running at them.

Lydia bolted and ran. Instinctively, George sprang after her. Outside, in the hall, with the door slammed, he was laughing and she was crying, and they both stood appalled at the other's reaction.

"George!"

"Lydia! Oh, my dear poor sweet Lydia!"

"They almost got us!"

"Walls, Lydia, remember; crystal walls, that's all they are. Oh, they look real, I must admit—Africa in your parlor—but it's all dimensional superreactionary, supersensitive color film and mental tape film behind glass screens. It's all odorophonics and sonics, Lydia. Here's my handkerchief."

"I'm afraid." She came to him and put her body against him and cried steadily. "Did you see? Did you *feel*? It's too real."

"Now, Lydia . . ."

"You've got to tell Wendy and Peter[2] not to read any more on Africa."

"Of course—of course." He patted her.

"Promise?"

"Sure."

"And lock the nursery for a few days until I get my nerves settled."

"You know how difficult Peter is about that. When I punished him a month ago by locking the nursery for even a few hours—the tantrum he threw! And Wendy too. They *live* for the nursery."

2. The children in Bradbury's story bear the same names as characters featured in the work of English author J. M. Barrie (1860–1937), including his play *Peter Pan, or the Boy Who Wouldn't Grow Up* (1904).

"It's got to be locked, that's all there is to it."

"All right." Reluctantly he locked the huge door. "You've been working too hard. You need a rest."

"I don't know—I don't know," she said, blowing her nose, sitting down in a chair that immediately began to rock and comfort her. "Maybe I don't have enough to do. Maybe I have time to think too much. Why don't we shut the whole house off for a few days and take a vacation?"

"You mean you want to fry my eggs for me?"

"Yes." She nodded.

"And darn my socks?"

"Yes." A frantic, watery-eyed nodding.

"And sweep the house?"

"Yes, yes—oh, yes!"

"But I thought that's why we bought this house, so we wouldn't have to do anything?"

"That's just it. I feel like I don't belong here. The house is wife and mother now and nursemaid. Can I compete with an African veldt? Can I give a bath and scrub the children as efficiently or quickly as the automatic scrub bath can? I can not. And it isn't just me. It's you. You've been awfully nervous lately."

"I suppose I have been smoking too much."

"You look as if you didn't know what to do with yourself in this house, either. You smoke a little more every morning and drink a little more every afternoon and need a little more sedative every night. You're beginning to feel unnecessary too."

"Am I?" He paused and tried to feel into himself to see what was really there.

"Oh, George!" She looked beyond him, at the nursery door. "Those lions can't get out of there, can they?"

He looked at the door and saw it tremble as if something had jumped against it from the other side.

"Of course not," he said.

At dinner they ate alone, for Wendy and Peter were at a special plastic carnival across town and had televised home to say they'd be late, to go ahead eating. So George Hadley, bemused, sat watching the dining-room table produce warm dishes of food from its mechanical interior.

"We forgot the ketchup," he said.

"Sorry," said a small voice within the table, and ketchup appeared.

As for the nursery, thought George Hadley, it won't hurt for the children to be locked out of it awhile. Too much of anything isn't good for anyone. And it was clearly indicated that the children had been spending a little too much time on Africa. That sun. He could feel it on his neck, still, like a hot paw. And the lions. And the smell of blood. Remarkable how the nursery caught the telepathic emanations of the children's minds and created life to fill their every desire. The children thought lions, and there were lions. The children thought zebras, and there were zebras. Sun—sun. Giraffes—giraffes. Death and death.

That last. He chewed tastelessly on the meat that the table had cut for him. Death thoughts. They were awfully young, Wendy and Peter, for death thoughts. Or, no, you were never too young, really. Long before you knew what death was you were wishing it on someone else. When you were two years old you were shooting people with cap pistols.

But this—the long, hot African veldt—the awful death in the jaws of a lion. And repeated again and again.

"Where are you going?"

He didn't answer Lydia. Preoccupied, he let the lights glow softly on ahead of him, extinguished behind him as he padded to the nursery door. He listened against it. Far away, a lion roared.

He unlocked the door and opened it. Just before he stepped inside, he heard a faraway scream. And then another roar from the lions, which subsided quickly.

He stepped into Africa. How many times in the last year had he opened this door and found Wonderland, Alice, the Mock Turtle, or Aladdin and his Magical Lamp, or Jack Pumpkinhead of Oz, or Dr. Doolittle, or the cow jumping over a very real-appearing moon[3]—all the delightful contraptions of a make-believe world. How often had he seen Pegasus[4] flying in the sky ceiling, or seen fountains of red fireworks, or heard angel voices singing. But now, this yellow hot Africa, this bake oven with murder in the heat. Perhaps Lydia was right. Perhaps they needed a little vacation from the fantasy which was growing a bit too real for ten-year-old children. It was all right to exercise one's mind with gymnastic[5] fantasies, but when the lively child mind settled on *one* pattern . . . ? It seemed that, at a distance, for the past month, he had heard lions roaring, and smelled their strong odor seeping as far away as his study door. But, being busy, he had paid it no attention.

George Hadley stood on the African grassland alone. The lions looked up from their feeding, watching him. The only flaw to the illusion was the open door through which he could see his wife, far down the dark hall, like a framed picture, eating her dinner abstractedly.

"Go away," he said to the lions.

They did not go.

He knew the principle of the room exactly. You sent out your thoughts. Whatever you thought would appear.

"Let's have Aladdin and his lamp," he snapped.

The veldtland remained; the lions remained.

"Come on, room! I demand Aladdin!" he said.

Nothing happened. The lions mumbled in their baked pelts.

"Aladdin!"

He went back to dinner. "The fool room's out of order," he said. "It won't respond."

"Or—"

"Or what?"

"Or it *can't* respond," said Lydia, "because the children have thought about Africa and lions and killing so many days that the room's in a rut."

"Could be."

"Or Peter's set it to remain that way."

"*Set* it?"

3. Places and characters from famous works of children's literature, including Lewis Carroll's *Alice's Adventures in Wonderland* (1865); the Middle Eastern folktale "Aladdin and the Magic [or Wonderful] Lamp," about a young orphan and the genie of the lamp who grants his wishes; L. Frank Baum's novels, beginning with *The Marvelous Land of Oz* (1904); Hugh Long's "Doctor Doolittle" series (1920–52); and the nursery rhyme "Hey Diddle Diddle."

4. Flying horse of Greek myth.

5. Athletic.

"He may have got into the machinery and fixed something."

"Peter doesn't know machinery."

"He's a wise one for ten. That I.Q. of his—"

"Nevertheless—"

"Hello, Mom. Hello, Dad."

The Hadleys turned. Wendy and Peter were coming in the front door, cheeks like peppermint candy, eyes like bright blue agate marbles, a smell of ozone on their jumpers from their trip in the helicopter.

"You're just in time for supper," said both parents.

"We're full of strawberry ice cream and hot dogs," said the children, holding hands. "But we'll sit and watch."

"Yes, come tell us about the nursery," said George Hadley.

The brother and sister blinked at him and then at each other. "Nursery?"

"All about Africa and everything," said the father with false joviality.

"I don't understand," said Peter.

"Your mother and I were just traveling through Africa with rod and reel; Tom Swift[6] and his Electric Lion," said George Hadley.

"There's no Africa in the nursery," said Peter simply.

"Oh, come now, Peter. We know better."

"I don't remember any Africa," said Peter to Wendy. "Do you?"

"No."

"Run see and come tell."

She obeyed.

"Wendy, come back here!" said George Hadley, but she was gone. The house lights followed her like a flock of fireflies. Too late, he realized he had forgotten to lock the nursery door after his last inspection.

"Wendy'll look and come tell us," said Peter.

"She doesn't have to tell *me*. I've seen it."

"I'm sure you're mistaken, Father."

"I'm not, Peter. Come along now."

But Wendy was back. "It's not Africa," she said breathlessly.

"We'll see about this," said George Hadley, and they all walked down the hall together and opened the nursery door.

There was a green, lovely forest, a lovely river, a purple mountain, high voices singing, and Rima,[7] lovely and mysterious, lurking in the trees with colorful flights of butterflies, like animated bouquets, lingering on her long hair. The African veldtland was gone. The lions were gone. Only Rima was here now, singing a song so beautiful that it brought tears to your eyes.

George Hadley looked in at the changed scene. "Go to bed," he said to the children.

They opened their mouths.

"You heard me," he said.

6. Hero of a series of books launched in 1910 and relating adventures made possible by his ingenious inventions.

7. South American forest-dwelling heroine of W. H. Hudson's *Green Mansions: A Romance of the Tropical Forest* (1904).

They went off to the air closet, where a wind sucked them like brown leaves up the flue to their slumber rooms.

George Hadley walked through the singing glade and picked up something that lay in the corner near where the lions had been. He walked slowly back to his wife.

"What is that?" she asked.

"An old wallet of mine," he said.

He showed it to her. The smell of hot grass was on it and the smell of a lion. There were drops of saliva on it, it had been chewed, and there were blood smears on both sides.

He closed the nursery door and locked it, tight.

In the middle of the night he was still awake and he knew his wife was awake. "Do you think Wendy changed it?" she said at last, in the dark room.

"Of course."

"Made it from a veldt into a forest and put Rima there instead of lions?"

"Yes."

"Why?"

"I don't know. But it's staying locked until I find out."

"How did your wallet get there?"

"I don't know anything," he said, "except that I'm beginning to be sorry we bought that room for the children. If children are neurotic at all, a room like that—"

"It's supposed to help them work off their neuroses in a healthful way."

"I'm starting to wonder." He stared at the ceiling.

"We've given the children everything they ever wanted. Is this our reward—secrecy, disobedience?"

"Who was it said, 'Children are carpets, they should be stepped on occasionally'? We've never lifted a hand. They're insufferable—let's admit it. They come and go when they like; they treat us as if *we* were offspring. They're spoiled and we're spoiled."

"They've been acting funny ever since you forbade them to take the rocket to New York a few months ago."

"They're not old enough to do that alone, I explained."

"Nevertheless, I've noticed they've been decidedly cool toward us since."

"I think I'll have David McClean come tomorrow morning to have a look at Africa."

"But it's not Africa now, it's Green Mansions country and Rima."

"I have a feeling it'll be Africa again before then."

A moment later they heard the screams.

Two screams. Two people screaming from downstairs. And then a roar of lions.

"Wendy and Peter aren't in their rooms," said his wife.

He lay in his bed with his beating heart. "No," he said. "They've broken into the nursery."

"Those screams—they sound familiar."

"Do they?"

"Yes, awfully."

And although their beds tried very hard, the two adults couldn't be rocked to sleep for another hour. A smell of cats was in the night air.

"Father?" said Peter.

"Yes."

Peter looked at his shoes. He never looked at his father any more, nor at his mother. "You aren't going to lock up the nursery for good, are you?"

"That all depends."

"On what?" snapped Peter.

"On you and your sister. If you intersperse this Africa with a little variety—oh, Sweden perhaps, or Denmark or China—"

"I thought we were free to play as we wished."

"You are, within reasonable bounds."

"What's wrong with Africa, Father?"

"Oh, so now you admit you have been conjuring up Africa, do you?"

"I wouldn't want the nursery locked up," said Peter coldly. "Ever."

"Matter of fact, we're thinking of turning the whole house off for about a month. Live sort of a carefree one-for-all existence."

"That sounds dreadful! Would I have to tie my own shoes instead of letting the shoe tier do it? And brush my own teeth and comb my hair and give myself a bath?"

"It would be fun for a change, don't you think?"

"No, it would be horrid. I didn't like it when you took out the picture painter last month."

"That's because I wanted you to learn to paint all by yourself, son."

"I don't want to do anything but look and listen and smell; what else *is* there to do?"

"All right, go play in Africa."

"Will you shut off the house sometime soon?"

"We're considering it."

"I don't think you'd better consider it any more, Father."

"I won't have any threats from my son!"

"Very well." And Peter strolled off to the nursery.

"Am I on time?" said David McClean.

"Breakfast?" asked George Hadley.

"Thanks, had some. What's the trouble?"

"David, you're a psychologist."

"I should hope so."

"Well, then, have a look at our nursery. You saw it a year ago when you dropped by; did you notice anything peculiar about it then?"

"Can't say I did; the usual violences, a tendency toward a slight paranoia here or there, usual in children because they feel persecuted by parents constantly, but, oh, really nothing."

They walked down the hall. "I locked the nursery up," explained the father, "and the children broke back into it during the night. I let them stay so they could form the patterns for you to see."

There was a terrible screaming from the nursery.

"There it is," said George Hadley. "See what you make of it."

They walked in on the children without rapping.

The screams had faded. The lions were feeding.

"Run outside a moment, children," said George Hadley. "No, don't change the mental combination. Leave the walls as they are. Get!"

With the children gone, the two men stood studying the lions clustered at a distance, eating with great relish whatever it was they had caught.

"I wish I knew what it was," said George Hadley. "Sometimes I can almost see. Do you think if I brought high-powered binoculars here and—"

David McClean laughed dryly. "Hardly." He turned to study all four walls. "How long has this been going on?"

"A little over a month."

"It certainly doesn't *feel* good."

"I want facts, not feelings."

"My dear George, a psychologist never saw a fact in his life. He only hears about feelings; vague things. This doesn't feel good, I tell you. Trust my hunches and my instincts. I have a nose for something bad. This is very bad. My advice to you is to have the whole damn room torn down and your children brought to me every day during the next year for treatment."

"Is it that bad?"

"I'm afraid so. One of the original uses of these nurseries was so that we could study the patterns left on the walls by the child's mind, study at our leisure, and help the child. In this case, however, the room has become a channel toward—destructive thoughts, instead of a release away from them."

"Didn't you sense this before?"

"I sensed only that you had spoiled your children more than most. And now you're letting them down in some way. What way?"

"I wouldn't let them go to New York."

"What else?"

"I've taken a few machines from the house and threatened them, a month ago, with closing up the nursery unless they did their homework. I did close it for a few days to show I meant business."

"Ah, ha!"

"Does that mean anything?"

"Everything. Where before they had a Santa Claus now they have a Scrooge.[8] Children prefer Santas. You've let this room and this house replace you and your wife in your children's affections. This room is their mother and father, far more important in their lives than their real parents. And now you come along and want to shut it off. No wonder there's hatred here. You can feel it coming out of the sky. Feel that sun. George, you'll have to change your life. Like too many others, you've built it around creature comforts. Why, you'd starve tomorrow if something went wrong in your kitchen. You wouldn't know how to tap an egg. Nevertheless, turn everything off. Start new. It'll take time. But we'll make good children out of bad in a year, wait and see."

"But won't the shock be too much for the children, shutting the room up abruptly, for good?"

"I don't want them going any deeper into this, that's all."

The lions were finished with their red feast.

The lions were standing on the edge of the clearing watching the two men.

8. Stingy, hard-hearted protagonist of Charles Dickens's *A Christmas Carol* (1843).

"Now *I'm* feeling persecuted," said McClean. "Let's get out of here. I never have cared for these damned rooms. Make me nervous."

"The lions look real, don't they?" said George Hadley. "I don't suppose there's any way—"

"What?"

"—that they could *become* real?"

"Not that I know."

"Some flaw in the machinery, a tampering or something?"

"No."

They went to the door.

"I don't imagine the room will like being turned off," said the father.

"Nothing ever likes to die—even a room."

"I wonder if it hates me for wanting to switch it off?"

"Paranoia is thick around here today," said David McClean. "You can follow it like a spoor. Hello." He bent and picked up a bloody scarf. "This yours?"

"No." George Hadley's face was rigid. "It belongs to Lydia."

They went to the fuse box together and threw the switch that killed the nursery.

The two children were in hysterics. They screamed and pranced and threw things. They yelled and sobbed and swore and jumped at the furniture.

"You can't do that to the nursery, you can't!"

"Now, children."

The children flung themselves onto a couch, weeping.

"George," said Lydia Hadley, "turn on the nursery, just for a few moments. You can't be so abrupt."

"No."

"You can't be so cruel."

"Lydia, it's off, and it stays off. And the whole damn house dies as of here and now. The more I see of the mess we've put ourselves in, the more it sickens me. We've been contemplating our mechanical, electronic navels for too long. My God, how we need a breath of honest air!"

And he marched about the house turning off the voice clocks, the stoves, the heaters, the shoe shiners, the shoe lacers, the body scrubbers and swabbers and massagers, and every other machine he could put his hand to.

The house was full of dead bodies, it seemed. It felt like a mechanical cemetery. So silent. None of the humming hidden energy of machines waiting to function at the tap of a button.

"Don't let them do it!" wailed Peter at the ceiling, as if he was talking to the house, the nursery. "Don't let Father kill everything." He turned to his father. "Oh, I hate you!"

"Insults won't get you anywhere."

"I wish you were dead!"

"We were, for a long while. Now we're going to really start living. Instead of being handled and massaged, we're going to *live*."

Wendy was still crying and Peter joined her again. "Just a moment, just one moment, just another moment of nursery," they wailed.

"Oh, George," said the wife, "it can't hurt."

"All right—all right, if they'll only just shut up. One minute, mind you, and then off forever."

"Daddy, Daddy, Daddy!" sang the children, smiling with wet faces.

"And then we're going on a vacation. David McClean is coming back in half an hour to help us move out and get to the airport. I'm going to dress. You turn the nursery on for a minute, Lydia, just a minute, mind you."

And the three of them went babbling off while he let himself be vacuumed upstairs through the air flue and set about dressing himself. A minute later Lydia appeared.

"I'll be glad when we get away," she sighed.

"Did you leave them in the nursery?"

"I wanted to dress too. Oh, that horrid Africa. What can they see in it?"

"Well, in five minutes we'll be on our way to Iowa. Lord, how did we ever get in this house? What prompted us to buy a nightmare?"

"Pride, money, foolishness."

"I think we'd better get downstairs before those kids get engrossed with those damned beasts again."

Just then they heard the children calling, "Daddy, Mommy, come quick—quick!"

They went downstairs in the air flue and ran down the hall. The children were nowhere in sight. "Wendy? Peter!"

They ran into the nursery. The veldtland was empty save for the lions waiting, looking at them. "Peter, Wendy?"

The door slammed.

"Wendy, Peter!"

George Hadley and his wife whirled and ran back to the door.

"Open the door!" cried George Hadley, trying the knob. "Why, they've locked it from the outside! Peter!" He beat at the door. "Open up!"

He heard Peter's voice outside, against the door.

"Don't let them switch off the nursery and the house," he was saying.

Mr. and Mrs. George Hadley beat at the door. "Now, don't be ridiculous, children. It's time to go. Mr. McClean'll be here in a minute and . . ."

And then they heard the sounds.

The lions on three sides of them, in the yellow veldt grass, padding through the dry straw, rumbling and roaring in their throats.

The lions.

Mr. Hadley looked at his wife and they turned and looked back at the beasts edging slowly forward, crouching, tails stiff.

Mr. and Mrs. Hadley screamed.

And suddenly they realized why those other screams had sounded familiar.

"Well, here I am," said David McClean in the nursery doorway. "Oh, hello." He stared at the two children seated in the center of the open glade eating a little picnic lunch. Beyond them was the water hole and the yellow veldtland; above was the hot sun. He began to perspire. "Where are your father and mother?"

The children looked up and smiled. "Oh, they'll be here directly."

"Good, we must get going." At a distance Mr. McClean saw the lions fighting and clawing and then quieting down to feed in silence under the shady trees.

He squinted at the lions with his hand up to his eyes.

Now the lions were done feeding. They moved to the water hole to drink.

A shadow flickered over Mr. McClean's hot face. Many shadows flickered. The vultures were dropping down the blazing sky.

"A cup of tea?" asked Wendy in the silence.

1951

QUESTIONS

1. Only George and Lydia Hadley appear in the story's first part: How are they and their lives characterized? How does each parent view their Happylife Home and especially the nursery? What might account for the differences in their views at this stage?
2. How and why do those views, especially George's, evolve over the course of the story?
3. As the story makes clear, the nursery could have turned into any setting either Peter and Wendy or their creator, Ray Bradbury, chose. How might the choice of an African veldt affect the story's characterization of the children and the relationship between parents and children? How might it affect the story's theme?

AUTHORS ON THEIR WORK

RAY BRADBURY (1920–2012)

From "Tangent Online Presents: An Interview with Ray Bradbury" (1976)*

BRADBURY: [. . .] You write stories of murder because we want to kill people. It's the reverse of love and this is part of the dichotomy, or paradox, of being human. Unless we can accept the fact that we have love-hate relationships quite often, our friends, our lovers, our mothers and fathers—then we'll never be human. If we try to deny the darkness in our souls then we'll become completely dark. [. . .] The Greek philosophies teach us that we are a combination of dark and light, good and evil, and murderer and savior, hmm? And until we know this completely about ourselves we cannot love well, and we cannot forgive ourselves.

[. . .] Any child, at some time or another, has had thoughts of murdering their mother and father . . . like my story "The Veldt." Every child who reads this, where lions come out of the walls of the room, in order to devour the parents, all the kids go "Whoopee! Hurray! I know that." [. . . W]e've *all* wanted to kill—in that moment of love—the person that we love. It's part of the human mechanism. *Why* the mechanism works the way it does is a mystery to us; we can't expect anything too perfect.

TANGENT: A lot of people feel there is too much violence on TV today. How do you feel about this?

BRADBURY: [. . .] There is a kind of violence at times that is so inordinate that it is *sick*. [. . .] So, we can't even talk about it.

But ordinary violence, which comes in a way of comparing good and evil, helps exorcize those spirits within ourselves which need to be exorcized. [. . .O]ur arts must help us to free the violence that is in our soul. Now, I don't know what all of the rules of the game are, but if our movies and our televisions don't have a certain amount of this we will become a society bound *completely* by laws, so the anarchy that rages within us on occasion will burst out and be ten times worse. So, if we need these steam valves to let some of this out of us occasionally—and we have to look at this very carefully—to find the right proportion for our children, and for ourselves. Somehow we've got to find the right proportion if we want to build a society that allows itself to vent its rages, so that we don't have to go outside the law for it.

*"Tangent Online Presents: An Interview with Ray Bradbury." 1976. Interview by Robert Jacobs, Dave Truesdale, and Bob Wayne. *Tangent*, 9 June 2012, www.tangentonline.com/interviews-columnsmenu-166/1864-classic-ray-bradbury-interview.

ZADIE SMITH (b. 1975)

Meet the President!

Sadie Smith grew up in North London, a self-described "working-class kid" who lived in public housing until she was eight and enjoyed a "black and white and mixed" life like that "of millions of people throughout the world." Part of a "big and boisterous" family headed by a Jamaican-born Rastafarian who earned a social-work degree in her thirties and a much older, "short white" World War II veteran who left school at twelve, Smith attended public school, read voraciously, took tap-dancing lessons, changed her name to "Zadie" (at fourteen), and dreamed of some day appearing in Hollywood musicals. Both of her younger brothers eventually did become entertainers. But Smith instead attended Cambridge, publishing short stories and penning her first novel. A multi-award-winning international best seller about two multicultural families in North London, *White Teeth* (2000) made Smith, at age twenty-two, a critics' darling, a household name, and what some called a "drop-dead cool" "poster girl for the new Britain." Committed to "taking risks," Smith has since produced a remarkably diverse body of work. Though she is best known for her novels—*The Autograph Man* (2002), *On Beauty* (2005), and *NW* (2012)—Smith's nonfiction, some of which is collected in *Changing My Mind* (2009), ranges from interviews with Jay-Z to meditations on the work of Franz Kafka. Her equally varied short stories include the BBC National Short Story Award finalist "Miss Adele Amidst the Corsets" (2014), about an aging transgender New Yorker. Mostly a New Yorker herself these days and a married mother of two, Smith teaches creative writing at NYU but spends her summers in North London; here, she says, "my life returns to its previous state"—"complication" and "chaos."

"What you got there, then?"

The boy didn't hear the question. He stood at the end of a ruined pier, believing himself quite alone. But now he registered the presence at his back, and turned.

"What you got there?"

A very old person, a woman, stood before him, gripping the narrow shoulder of a girl child. Both of them local, typically stunted, dim: they stared up at him stupidly. The boy turned again to the sea. All week long he had been hoping for a clear day to try out the new technology—not new to the world, but new to the boy—and now at last here was a break in the rain. Gray sky met gray sea. Not ideal, but sufficient. Ideally he would be standing on a cairn in Scotland or some other tropical spot, experiencing backlit clarity. Ideally he would be—

"Is it one of them what you see through?"

A hand, lousy with blue veins, reached out for the light encircling the boy's head, as if it were a substantial thing, to be grasped like the handle of a mug.

"Ooh, look at the green, Aggie. That shows you it's on."

The boy was ready to play. He touched the node on his finger to the node at his temple, raising the volume.

"Course, he'd have to be somebody, Aggs, cos they don't give 'em to nobody"—the boy felt the shocking touch of a hand on his own flesh. "Are you somebody, then?"

She had shuffled around until she stood square in front of him, unavoidable. Hair as white as paper. A long, shapeless black dress, made of some kind of cloth, and what appeared to be a pair of actual glasses. Forty-nine years old, type O, a likelihood of ovarian cancer, some ancient debt infraction—nothing more. A blank, more or less. Same went for the girl: never left the country, eighty-five-per-cent chance of macular degeneration,[1] an uncle on the database, long ago located, eliminated. She would be nine in two days. Melinda Durham and Agatha Hanwell. They shared no more DNA than strangers.

"Can you see us?" The old woman let go of her charge and waved her hands wildly. The tips of her fingers barely reached the top of the boy's head. "Are we in it? What are we?"

The boy, unused to proximity, took a single step forward. Farther he could not go. Beyond was the ocean; above, a mess of weather, clouds closing in on blue wherever blue tried to assert itself. A dozen or so craft darted up and down, diving low like seabirds after a fish, and no bigger than seabirds, skimming the dirty foam, then returning to the heavens, directed by unseen hands. On his first day here the boy had trailed his father on an inspection tour to meet those hands: intent young men at their monitors, over whose shoulders the boy's father leaned, as he sometimes leaned over the boy to insure he ate breakfast.

"What d'you call one of them there?"

The boy tucked his shirt in all round: "AG 12."

The old woman snorted as a mark of satisfaction, but did not leave.

He tried looking the females directly in their dull brown eyes. It was what his mother would have done, a kindly woman with a great mass of waist-length flame-colored hair, famed for her patience with locals. But his mother was long dead, he had never known her, he was losing what little light the day afforded. He blinked twice, said, "Hand to hand." Then, having a change of heart: "Weaponry." He looked down at his torso, to which he now attached a quantity of guns.

"You carry on, lad," the old woman said. "We won't get in your way. He can see it all, duck," she told the girl, who paid her no mind. "Got something in his hands—or thinks he does."

1. Degenerative eye disease that destroys the central part of the retina, or "macula."

She took a packet of tobacco from a deep pocket in the front of her garment and began to roll a cigarette, using the girl as a shield from the wind.

"Them clouds, dark as bulls. Racing, racing. They always win." To illustrate, she tried turning Aggie's eyes to the sky, lifting the child's chin with a finger, but the girl would only gawk stubbornly at the woman's elbow. "They'll dump on us before we even get there. If you didn't have to, I wouldn't go, Aggie, no chance, not in this. It's for you I do it. I've been wet and wet and wet. All my life. And I bet he's looking at blazing suns and people in their what-have-yous and all-togethers! Int yer? Course you are! And who'd blame you?" She laughed so loud the boy heard her. And then the child—who did not laugh, whose pale face, with its triangle chin and enormous, fair-lashed eyes, seemed capable only of astonishment—pulled at his actual leg, forcing him to mute for a moment and listen to her question.

20 "Well, I'm Bill Peek," he replied, and felt very silly, like somebody in an old movie.

"Bill Peek!" the old woman cried. "Oh, but we've had Peeks in Anglia[2] a long time. You'll find a Peek or two or three down in Sutton Hoo.[3] Bill Peek! You from round here, Bill Peek?"

His grandparents? Very possibly. Local and English—or his great-grandparents. His hair and eyes and skin and name suggested it. But it was not a topic likely to engage his father, and the boy himself had never felt any need or desire to pursue it. He was simply global, accompanying his father on his inspections, though usually to livelier spots than this. What a sodden dump it was! Just as everyone had warned him it would be. The only people left in England were the ones who couldn't leave.

"From round here, are you? Or maybe a Norfolk[4] one? He looks like a Norfolk one, Aggs, wouldn't you say?"

Bill Peek raised his eyes to the encampment on the hill, pretending to follow with great interest those dozen circling, diving craft, as if he, uniquely, as the child of personnel, had nothing to fear from them. But the woman was occupied with her fag[5] and the girl only sang "Bill Peek, Bill Peek, Bill Peek" to herself, and smiled sadly at her own turned-in feet. They were too local even to understand the implied threat. He jumped off the pier onto the deserted beach. It was low tide—it seemed you could walk to Holland. He focussed upon the thousands of tiny spirals on the sand, like miniature turds stretching out to the horizon.

25 Felixstowe, England. A Norman[6] village; later, briefly, a resort, made popular by the German royal family; much fishing, once upon a time. A hundred years earlier, almost to the very month, a quaint flood had killed only forty-eight people. Over the years, the place had been serially flooded, mostly abandoned. Now the sad little town had retreated three miles inland and up a hill. Pop.: 850. The boy blinked twice more; he did not care much for history. He narrowed his attention to a single turd. *Arenicola marina.* Sandworms. Lugworms. These were its coiled castings. Castings? But here he found his interest fading once again.

2. Originally, the medieval Latin name for England; today, one name for one of its easternmost and thus partly coastal regions.

3. Located in East Anglia and one of England's most famous archaeological sites; the wealth of Anglo-Saxon artifacts discovered here includes an entire seventh-century ship.

4. County in East Anglia.

5. Cigarette (British slang).

6. Peoples of Normandy, in northern France, who invaded and conquered England in 1066.

He touched his temple and said, "Blood Head 4." Then: "Washington." It was his first time at this level. Another world began to construct itself around Bill Peek, a shining city on a hill.

"Poor little thing," Melinda Durham said. She sat on the pier, legs dangling, and pulled the girl into her lap. "Demented with grief she is. We're going to a laying out. Aggie's sister is laid out today. Her last and only relation. Course, the cold truth is, Aggie's sister weren't much better than trash, and a laying out's a sight too good for her—she'd be better off laid out on this beach here and left for the gulls. But I ain't going for *her.* I do it for Aggie. Aggie knows why. Aggie's been a great help to me what with one thing and another."

While he waited, as incidental music played, the boy idly checked a message from his father: at what time could he be expected back at the encampment? *At what time could he be expected.* This was a pleasing development, being an inquiry rather than an order. He would be fifteen in May, almost a man! A man who could let another man know when he could be expected, and let him know in his own sweet time, when he had the inclination. He performed some rudimentary stretches and bounced up and down on the balls of his feet.

"Maud, that was her name. And she was born under the same steeple she'll be buried under. Twelve years old. But so whorish—" Melinda covered Aggie's ears, and the girl leaned into the gesture, having mistaken it for affection. "So whorish she looked like a crone. If you lived round here, Bill Peek, you'd've *known* Maud, if you understand me correctly. You would've known Maud right up to the Biblical and beyond. Terrible. But Aggie's cut from quite different sod, thank goodness!" Aggie was released and patted on the head. "And she's no one left, so here I am, muggins here, taking her to a laying out when I've a million other stones to be lifted off the pile."

The boy placed a number of grenades about his person. In each chapter of the Pathways Global Institute (in Paris, New York, Shanghai, Nairobi, Jerusalem, Tokyo), the boy had enjoyed debating with friends the question of whether it was better to augment around the "facts on the ground," incorporating whatever was at hand ("flagging," it was called, the pleasure being the unpredictability), or to choose spots where there were barely any facts to work around. The boy was of the latter sensibility. He wanted to augment in clean, blank places, where he was free to fully extend, unhindered. He looked down the beach as the oil streaks in the sand were overlaid now with a gleaming pavement, lined on either side by the National Guard, saluting him. It was three miles to the White House. He picked out a large pair of breasts to wear, for reasons of his own, and a long, scaled tail, for purposes of strangulation.

"Oh, fuck a duck—you wouldn't do me an awful favor and keep an eye on Aggie just a minute, would you?—I've left my rosary! I can't go to no laying out without it. It's more than my soul's worth. Oh, Aggie, how did you ever let me leave without it? She's a good girl, but she's thoughtless sometimes—her sister were thoughtless, too. Bill Peek, you will keep an eye on her, won't you? I won't be a moment. We're shacked up just on that hill by the old Martello[7] tower. Eight minutes I'll be. No more. Would you do that for me, Bill Peek?"

7. Small, round forts first built throughout southeast England during the early nineteenth century, mainly to defend against a possible French invasion.

Bill Peek nodded his head, once rightward, twice leftward. Knives shot out of his wrists and splayed beautifully like the fronds of a fern.

It was perhaps twenty minutes later, as he approached the pile of rubble—pounded by enemy craft—that had once been the Monument, that young Bill Peek felt again a presence at his back and turned and found Aggie Hanwell with her fist in her mouth, tears streaming, jaw working up and down in an agonized fashion. He couldn't hear her over the explosions. Reluctantly, he paused.

"She ain't come back."

"Excuse me?"

"She went but she ain't come back!"

"Who?" he asked, but then scrolled back until he found it. "M. Durham?"

The girl gave him that same astonished look.

"My Melly," she said. "She promised to take me but she went and she ain't come back!"

The boy swiftly located M. Durham—as much an expedience as an act of charity—and experienced the novelty of sharing the information with the girl, in the only way she appeared able to receive it. "She's two miles away," he said, with his own mouth. "Heading north."

Aggie Hanwell sat down on her bum in the wet sand. She rolled something in her hand. The boy looked at it and learned that it was a periwinkle—a snail of the sea! He recoiled, disliking those things which crawled and slithered upon the earth. But this one proved broken, with only a pearlescent nothing inside it.

"So it was all a lie," Aggie said, throwing her head back dramatically to consider the sky. "Plus one of them's got my number. I've done nothing wrong but still Melly's gone and left me and one of them thing's been following me, since the pier—even before that."

"If you've done nothing wrong," Bill Peek said, solemnly parroting his father, "you've nothing to worry about. It's a precise business." He had been raised to despair of the type of people who spread misinformation about the Program. Yet along with his new maturity had come fresh insight into the complexities of his father's world. For didn't those with bad intent on occasion happen to stand beside the good, the innocent, or the underaged? And in those circumstances could precision be entirely guaranteed? "Anyway, they don't track children. Don't you understand anything?"

Hearing this, the girl laughed—a bitter and cynical cackle, at odds with her pale little face—and Bill Peek made the mistake of being, for a moment, rather impressed. But she was only imitating her elders, as he was imitating his.

"Go home," he said.

Instead she set about burrowing her feet into the wet sand.

"Everyone's got a good angel and a bad angel," she explained. "And if it's a bad angel that picks you out"—she pointed to a craft swooping low—"there's no escaping it. You're done for."

He listened in wonderment. Of course he'd always known there were people who thought in this way—there was a module you did on them in sixth grade—but he had never met anyone who really harbored what his anthrosoc teacher, Mr. Lin, called "animist beliefs."[8]

8. "Animism" involves the attribution of life and consciousness to inanimate objects.

The girl sighed, scooped up more handfuls of sand, and added them to the two mounds she had made on top of her feet, patting them down, encasing herself up to the ankles. Meanwhile all around her Bill Peek's scene of fabulous chaos was frozen—a Minotaur[9] sat in the lap of stony Abe Lincoln and a dozen carefully planted I.E.D.s awaited detonation. He was impatient to return.

"Must advance," he said, pointing down the long stretch of beach, but she held up her hands, she wanted pulling up. He pulled. Standing, she clung to him, hugging his knees. He felt her face damp against his leg.

"Oh, it's awful bad luck to miss a laying out! Melly's the one knew where to go. She's got the whole town up here," she said, tapping her temple, making the boy smile. "Memoried. No one knows town like Melly. She'll say, 'This used to be here, but they knocked it down,' or, 'There was a pub here with a mark on the wall where the water rose.' She's memoried every corner. She's my friend."

"Some friend!" the boy remarked. He succeeded in unpeeling the girl from his body, and strode on down the beach, firefighting a gang of Russian commandoes as they parachuted into view. Alongside him a scurrying shape ran; sometimes a dog, sometimes a droid, sometimes a huddle of rats. Her voice rose out of it.

"Can I see?"

Bill Peek disembowelled a fawn to his left. "Do you have an Augmentor?"

"No."

"Do you have a complementary system?"

"No."

He knew he was being cruel—but she was ruining his concentration. He stopped running and split the visuals, the better to stare her down.

"Any system?"

"No."

"Therefore no. No, you can't."

Her nose was pink, a drop of moisture hung from it. She had an innocence that practically begged to be corrupted. Bill Peek could think of more than a few Pathways boys of his acquaintance who wouldn't hesitate to take her under the next boardwalk and put a finger inside her. And the rest. As the son of personnel, however, Bill Peck was held to a different standard.

"Jimmy Kane had one—he was a fella of Maud's, her main fella. He flew in and then he flew out—you never knew when he'd be flying in again. He was a captain in the Army. He had an old one of them . . . but said it still worked. He said it made her nicer to look at when they were doing it. He was from nowhere, too."

"Nowhere?"

"Like you."

Not for the first time the boy was struck by the great human mysteries of this world. He was almost fifteen, almost a man, and the great human mysteries of this world were striking him with satisfying regularity, as was correct for his stage of development. (From the Pathways Global Institute prospectus: "As our students reach tenth grade they begin to gain insight into the great human mysteries of this world, and a special sympathy for locals, the poor, ideologues, and

9. In Greek myth, the monster—part bull, part human—imprisoned in the labyrinth of King Minos, where he fed on the young men and women sent to him in tribute.

all those who have chosen to limit their own human capital in ways that it can be difficult at times for us to comprehend.") From the age of six months, when he was first enrolled in the school, he had hit every mark that Pathways expected of its pupils—walking, talking, divesting, monetizing,[1] programming, augmenting—and so it was all the more shocking to find himself face-to-face with an almost nine-year-old so absolutely blind, so lost, so developmentally debased.

"*This*"—he indicated Felixstowe, from the beach with its turd castings and broken piers, to the empty-shell buildings and useless flood walls, up to the hill where his father hoped to expect him—"is nowhere. If you can't move, you're no one from nowhere. 'Capital must flow.'" (This last was the motto of his school, though she needn't know that.) "Now, if you're asking me where I was born, the event of my birth occurred in Bangkok,[2] but wherever I was born I would remain a member of the Incipio Security Group, which employs my father—and within which I have the highest clearance." He was surprised by the extent of the pleasure this final, outright lie gave him. It was like telling a story, but in a completely new way—a story that could not be verified or checked, and which only total innocence would accept. Only someone with no access of any kind. Never before had he met someone like this, who could move only in tiny local spirals, a turd on a beach.

Moved, the boy bent down suddenly and touched the girl gently on her face. As he did so he had a hunch that he probably looked like the first prophet of some monotheistic[3] religion, bestowing his blessing on a recent convert, and, upon re-watching the moment and finding this was so, he sent it out, both to Mr. Lin and to his fellow Pathways boys, for peer review. It would surely count toward completion of Module 19, which emphasized empathy for the dispossessed.

"Where is it you want to go, my child?"

She lit up with gratitude, her little hand gripped his, the last of her tears rolling into her mouth and down her neck. "St. Jude's!"[4] she cried. She kept talking as he replayed the moment to himself and added a small note of explanatory context for Mr. Lin, before he refocussed on her stream of prattle: "And I'll say goodbye to her. And I'll kiss her on her face and nose. Whatever they said about her she was my own sister and I loved her and she's going to a better place—I don't care if she's stone cold in that church, I'll hold her!"

70 "Not a church," the boy corrected. "14 Ware Street, built 1950, originally domestic property, situated on a floodplain, condemned for safety. Site of 'St. Jude's'—local, outlier congregation. Has no official status."

"St. Jude's is where she'll be laid out," she said and squeezed his hand. "And I'll kiss her no matter how cold she is."

The boy shook his head and sighed.

1. Like *divesting*, primarily a banking/investment term. To "monetize" something is to turn it into money, as when a debt is purchased so as to increase the supply of ready money. To "divest" is to shed something or to dispossess someone else of it.

2. Capital of Thailand.

3. Having one god.

4. Named for the patron saint of desperate and lost causes.

"We're going in the same direction. Just follow me. No speaking." He put his finger to his lips, and she tucked her chin into her neck meekly, seeming to understand. Re-starting, he flagged her effectively, transforming little Aggie Hanwell into his sidekick, his familiar,[5] a sleek reddish fox. He was impressed by the perfect visual reconstruction of the original animal, apparently once common in this part of the world. Re-named Mystus, she provided cover for his left flank and mutely admired Bill Peek as he took the traitor Vice-President hostage and dragged him down the Mall[6] with a knife to his neck.

After a spell they came to the end of the beach. Here the sand shaded into pebbles and then a rocky cove, and barnacles held on furiously where so much else had been washed away. Above their heads, the craft were finishing their sallies and had clustered like bees, moving as one back to the landing bay at the encampment. Bill Peek and his familiar were also nearing the end of their journey, moments away from kicking in the door to the Oval Office, where—if all went well—they would meet the President and be thanked for their efforts. But at the threshold, unaccountably, Bill Peek's mind began to wander. Despite the many friends around the world watching (there was a certain amount of kudos granted to any boy who successfully met the President in good, if not record, time, on his first run-through), he found himself pausing to stroke Mystus and worry about whether his father would revoke his AG after this trip. It had been a bribe and a sop in the first place—it was unregistered. Bill had wanted to stay on at the Tokyo campus for the whole summer, and then move to Norway, before tsunami season, for a pleasant fall. His father had wanted him by his side, here, in the damp, unlit graylands. An AG 12 was the compromise. But these later models were security risks, easily hacked, and the children of personnel were not meant to carry hackable devices. That's how much my father loves me, Bill Peek thought hopefully, that's how much he wants me around.

Previously the boy had believed that the greatest testament to love was the 75
guarantee—which he had had all his life—of total personal security. He could count on one hand the amount of times he'd met a local; radicals were entirely unknown to him; he had never travelled by any mode of transport that held more than four people. But now, almost adult, he had a new thought, saw the matter from a fresh perspective, which he hoped would impress Mr. Lin with its age-appropriate intersectionality.[7] He rested against the Oval Office door and sent his thought to the whole Pathways family: "Daring to risk personal security can be a sign of love, too." Feeling inspired, he split the visual in order to pause and once more appreciate the human mysteries of this world slash how far he'd come.

He found that he was resting on a slimy rock, his fingers tangled in the unclean hair follicles of Agatha Hanwell. She saw him looking at her. She said, "Are we there yet?" The full weight of her innocence emboldened him. They were five minutes from Ware Street. Wasn't that all the time he needed? No

5. Attendant spirit usually embodied in an animal; in folklore, a cat often serves as a witch's familiar.
6. National park in downtown Washington, D.C., stretching from the Lincoln Memorial to the U.S. Capitol, with the Washington Monument at its center.
7. Study of how different forces intersect with each other.

matter what lay beyond that door, it would be dispatched by Bill Peek, brutally, beautifully; he would step forward, into his destiny. He would meet the President! He would shake the President's hand.

"Follow me."

She was quick on the rocks, perhaps even a little quicker than he, moving on all fours like an animal. They took a right, a left, and Bill Peek slit many throats. The blood ran down the walls of the Oval Office and stained the Presidential seal and at the open windows a crowd of cheering, anonymous well-wishers pressed in. At which point Mystus strayed from him and rubbed herself along their bodies, and was stroked and petted in turn.

"So many people come to see your Maud. Does the soul good."

"How are you, Aggie, love? Bearing up?"

"They took her from the sky. Boom! 'Public depravity.' I mean, I ask you!"

"Come here, Aggs, give us a hug."

"Who's that with her?"

"Look, that's the little sis. Saw it all. Poor little thing."

"She's in the back room, child. You go straight through. You've more right than anybody."

All Bill Peek knew is that many bodies were lying on the ground and a space was being made for him to approach. He stepped forward like a king. The President saluted him. The two men shook hands. But the light was failing, and then failed again; the celebrations were lost in infuriating darkness. . . . The boy touched his temple, hot with rage: a low-ceilinged parlor came into view, with its filthy window, further shaded by a ragged net curtain, the whole musty hovel lit by candles. He couldn't even extend an arm—there were people everywhere, local, offensive to the nose, to all other senses. He tried to locate Agatha Hanwell, but her precise coördinates were of no use here; she was packed deep into this crowd—he could no more get to her than to the moon. A fat man put a hand on his shoulder and asked, "You in the right place, boy?" A distressing female with few teeth said, "Leave him be." Bill Peek felt himself being pushed forward, deeper into the darkness. A song was being sung, by human voices, and though each individual sang softly, when placed side by side like this, like rows of wheat in the wind, they formed a weird unity, heavy and light at the same time. "*Because I do not hope to turn again . . . Because I do not hope . . .* "[8] In one voice, like a great beast moaning. A single craft carrying the right hardware could take out the lot of them, but they seemed to have no fear of that. Swaying, singing.

Bill Peek touched his sweaty temple and tried to focus on a long message from his father—something about a successful inspection and Mexico in the morning—but he was being pushed by many hands, ever forward, until he reached the back wall where a long box, made of the kind of wood you saw washed up on the beach, sat on a simple table, with candles all around it. The singing grew ever louder. Still, as he passed through their number, it seemed that no man or woman among them sang above a whisper. Then, cutting across it all like a stick through the sand, a child's voice wailed, an acute, high-pitched sound, such as a small animal makes when, out of sheer boredom, you break its

8. First lines of T. S. Eliot's long poem *Ash Wednesday* (1930); published after his conversion to Anglicanism, it traces the speaker's struggle to embrace faith in both God and the possibility of human salvation.

leg. Onward they pushed him; he saw it all perfectly clearly in the candlelight—the people in black, weeping, and Aggie on her knees by the table, and inside the driftwood box the lifeless body of a real girl, the first object of its kind that young Bill Peek had ever seen. Her hair was red and set in large, infantile curls, her skin very white, and her eyes wide open and green. A slight smile revealed the gaps in her teeth, and suggested secret knowledge, the kind of smile he had seen before on the successful sons of powerful men with full clearance—the boys who never lose. Yet none of it struck him quite as much as the sensation that there was someone or something else in that grim room, both unseen and present, and coming for him as much as for anybody.

2013

QUESTIONS

1. What are the most important characteristics—social, environmental or ecological, and technological—of the future Smith imagines in MEET THE PRESIDENT!? What might the story imply about how this future came to be?
2. What might be the significance and effect of Smith's choice of geographical setting? of the characters' references to real places in, and real features of, that setting? How are characters characterized, in part, by their relationship to (this) place?
3. How would you describe what happens to Bill Peek over the course of the story? Does he change or learn something new? How and why so, or not?

JENNIFER EGAN
(b. 1962)
Black Box[1]

Best known for *A Visit from the Goon Squad*, the 2010 book that earned both the Pulitzer Prize and the National Book Critics Circle Award for Fiction, Jennifer Egan was born in Chicago and grew up in San Francisco, where she lived with her mother after her parents' divorce. After graduating with a BA in English from the University of Pennsylvania (while dating Apple cofounder Steve Jobs), Egan spent two years at Cambridge University and then traveled widely across Europe and Asia, living mainly out of her backpack and gathering the experiences that would ultimately inform her early work—the novels *Invisible Circus* (1995), *Look at Me* (2001), and *The Keep* (2006), as well as the collection *Emerald City and Other Stories* (1993, 1996). Egan is no stranger to genre-bending forms of narrative experimentation: Simultaneously a novel and a series of interlinked short stories set in times ranging from the 1970s to the near-future, *A Visit from the Goon Squad* includes one chapter/story composed entirely of PowerPoint slides; "Black Box," which features a character from *Goon Squad*, was originally conceived and published as a series of tweets.

1. Broadly, any complicated electronic device with a hidden internal mechanism mysterious to its user; narrowly, a device for recording in-flight data and cockpit conversations on airplanes, designed to survive a crash and to help investigators determine its cause.

1

People rarely look the way you expect them to, even when you've seen pictures.

The first thirty seconds in a person's presence are the most important.

If you're having trouble perceiving and projecting, focus on projecting.

Necessary ingredients for a successful projection: giggles; bare legs; shyness.

5 The goal is to be both irresistible and invisible.

When you succeed, a certain sharpness will go out of his eyes.

2

Some powerful men actually call their beauties "Beauty."

Counter to reputation, there is a deep camaraderie among beauties.

If your Designated Mate is widely feared, the beauties at the house party where you've gone undercover to meet him will be especially kind.

10 Kindness feels good, even when it's based on a false notion of your identity and purpose.

3

Posing as a beauty means not reading what you would like to read on a rocky shore in the South of France.

Sunlight on bare skin can be as nourishing as food.

Even a powerful man will be briefly self-conscious when he first disrobes to his bathing suit.

It is technically impossible for a man to look better in a Speedo than in swim trunks.

If you love someone with dark skin, white skin looks drained of something vital. 15

4

When you know that a person is violent and ruthless, you will see violent ruthlessness in such basic things as his swim stroke.

"What are you doing?" from your Designated Mate amid choppy waves after he has followed you into the sea may or may not betray suspicion.

Your reply—"Swimming"—may or may not be perceived as sarcasm.

"Shall we swim together toward those rocks?" may or may not be a question.

"All that way?" will, if spoken correctly, sound ingenuous. 20

"We'll have privacy there" may sound unexpectedly ominous.

5

A hundred feet of blue-black Mediterranean will allow you ample time to deliver a strong self-lecture.

At such moments, it may be useful to explicitly recall your training:

"You will be infiltrating the lives of criminals.

"You will be in constant danger. 25

"Some of you will not survive, but those who do will be heroes.

"A few of you will save lives and even change the course of history.

"We ask of you an impossible combination of traits: ironclad scruples and a willingness to violate them;

"An abiding love for your country and a willingness to consort with individuals who are working actively to destroy it;

30 "The instincts and intuition of experts, and the blank records and true freshness of ingénues.

"You will each perform this service only once, after which you will return to your lives.

"We cannot promise that your lives will be exactly the same when you go back to them."

6

Eagerness and pliability can be expressed even in the way you climb from the sea onto chalky yellow rocks.

"You're a very fast swimmer," uttered by a man who is still submerged, may not be intended as praise.

35 Giggling is sometimes better than answering.

"You are a lovely girl" may be meant straightforwardly.

Ditto "I want to fuck you now."

"Well? What do you think about that?" suggests a preference for direct verbal responses over giggling.

"I like it" must be uttered with enough gusto to compensate for a lack of declarative color.

"You don't sound sure" indicates 40
insufficient gusto.

"I'm *not* sure" is acceptable only when followed, coyly, with "You'll have to convince me."

Throwing back your head and closing your eyes allows you to give the appearance of sexual readiness while concealing revulsion.

7

Being alone with a violent and ruthless man, surrounded by water, can make the shore seem very far away.

You may feel solidarity, at such a time, with the beauties just visible there in their bright bikinis.

You may appreciate, at such a 45
time, why you aren't being paid for this work.

Your voluntary service is the highest form of patriotism.

Remind yourself that you aren't being paid when he climbs out of the water and lumbers toward you.

Remind yourself that you aren't being paid when he leads you behind a boulder and pulls you onto his lap.

The Dissociation Technique is like a parachute—you must pull the cord at the correct time.

Too soon, and you may hinder 50
your ability to function at a crucial moment;

Too late, and you will be lodged too deeply inside the action to wriggle free.

You will be tempted to pull the cord when he surrounds you with arms whose bulky strength reminds you, fleetingly, of your husband's.

You will be tempted to pull it when you feel him start to move against you from below.

You will be tempted to pull it when his smell envelops you: metallic, like a warm hand clutching pennies.

The directive "Relax" suggests that your discomfort is palpable.

"No one can see us" suggests that your discomfort has been understood as fear of physical exposure.

"Relax, relax," uttered in rhythmic, throaty tones, suggests that your discomfort is not unwelcome.

8

Begin the Dissociation Technique only when physical violation is imminent.

Close your eyes and slowly count backward from ten.

With each number, imagine yourself rising out of your body and moving one step farther away from it.

By eight, you should be hovering just outside your skin.

By five, you should be floating a foot or two above your body, feeling only vague anxiety over what is about to happen to it.

By three, you should feel fully detached from your physical self.

By two, your body should be able to act and react without your participation.

By one, your mind should drift so free that you lose track of what is happening below.

White clouds spin and curl.

A blue sky is as depthless as the sea.

The sound of waves against rocks existed millennia before there were creatures who could hear it.

Spurs and gashes of stone narrate a violence that the earth itself has long forgotten.

Your mind will rejoin your body when it is safe to do so.

9

Return to your body carefully, as if you were reëntering your home after a hurricane.

Resist the impulse to reconstruct what has just happened.

Focus instead on gauging your Designated Mate's reaction to the new intimacy between you.

In some men, intimacy will prompt a more callous, indifferent attitude.

In others, intimacy may awaken problematic curiosity about you.

"Where did you learn to swim like that?," uttered lazily, while supine, with two fingers in your hair, indicates curiosity.

Tell the truth without precision.

"I grew up near a lake" is both true and vague.

"Where was the lake?" conveys dissatisfaction with your vagueness.

"Columbia County,[2] New York" suggests precision while avoiding it.

"Manhattan?" betrays unfamiliarity with the geography of New York State.

2. Located in eastern New York State, roughly 130 miles north of the borough of Manhattan in New York City.

Never contradict your Designated Mate.

"Where did you grow up?," asked of a man who has just asked you the same thing, is known as "mirroring."

Mirror your Designated Mate's attitudes, interests, desires, and tastes.

Your goal is to become part of his atmosphere: a source of comfort and ease.

Only then will he drop his guard when you are near.

Only then will he have significant conversations within your earshot.

Only then will he leave his possessions in a porous and unattended state.

Only then can you begin to gather information systematically.

10

"Come. Let's go back," uttered brusquely, suggests that your Designated Mate has no more wish to talk about himself than you do.

Avoid the temptation to analyze his moods and whims.

Salt water has a cleansing effect.

11

You will see knowledge of your new intimacy with your Designated Mate in the eyes of every beauty on shore.

"We saved lunch for you" may or may not be an allusion to the reason for your absence.

Cold fish is unappealing, even when served in a good lemon sauce.

Be friendly to other beauties, but not solicitous.

When you are in conversation with a beauty, it is essential that you be perceived as no more or less than she is.

Be truthful about every aspect of your life except marriage (if any).

If married, say that you and your spouse have divorced, to give an impression of unfettered freedom.

"Oh, that's sad!" suggests that the beauty you're chatting with would like to marry.

12

If your Designated Mate abruptly veers toward the villa, follow him.

Taking his hand and smiling congenially can create a sense of low-key accompaniment.

An abstracted smile in return, as if he'd forgotten who you are, may be a sign of pressing concerns.

The concerns of your Designated Mate are your concerns.

The room assigned to a powerful man will be more lavish than the one you slept in while awaiting his arrival.

Never look for hidden cameras: the fact that you're looking will give you away.

Determine whether your Designated Mate seeks physical intimacy; if not, feign the wish for a nap.

Your pretense of sleep will allow him to feel that he is alone.

Curling up under bedclothes, even those belonging to an enemy subject, may be soothing.

110 You're more likely to hear his handset vibrate if your eyes are closed.

13

A door sliding open signals his wish to take the call on the balcony.

Your Designated Mate's important conversations will take place outdoors.

If you are within earshot of his conversation, record it.

Since beauties carry neither pocketbooks nor timepieces, you cannot credibly transport recording devices.

115 A microphone has been implanted just beyond the first turn of your right ear canal.

Activate the microphone by pressing the triangle of cartilage across your ear opening.

You will hear a faint whine as recording begins.

In extreme quiet, or to a person whose head is adjacent to yours, this whine may be audible.

Should the whine be detected, swat your ear as if to deflect a mosquito, hitting the on/off cartilage to deactivate the mike.

120 You need not identify or comprehend the language your subject is using.

Your job is proximity; if you are near your Designated Mate, recording his private speech, you are succeeding.

Profanity sounds the same in every language.

An angry subject will guard his words less carefully.

14

If your subject is angry, you may leave your camouflage position and move as close to him as possible to improve recording quality.

You may feel afraid as you do this. 125

Your pounding heartbeat will not be recorded.

If your Designated Mate is standing on a balcony, hover in the doorway just behind him.

If he pivots and discovers you, pretend that you were on the verge of approaching him.

Anger usually trumps suspicion.

If your subject brushes past you 130
and storms out of the room, slamming the door, you have eluded detection.

15

If your Designated Mate leaves your company a second time, don't follow him again.

Deactivate your ear mike and resume your "nap."

A moment of repose may be a good time to reassure your loved ones.

Nuanced communication is too easily monitored by the enemy.

Your Subcutaneous Pulse System 135
issues pings so generic that detection would reveal neither source nor intent.

A button is embedded behind the inside ligament of your right knee (if right-handed).

Depress twice to indicate to loved ones that you are well and thinking of them.

You may send this signal only once each day.

A continuous depression of the button indicates an emergency.

You will debate, each day, the best time to send your signal.

You will reflect on the fact that your husband, coming from a culture of tribal allegiance, understands and applauds your patriotism.

You will reflect on the enclosed and joyful life that the two of you have shared since graduate school.

You will reflect on the fact that America is your husband's chosen country, and that he loves it.

You will reflect on the fact that your husband's rise to prominence would have been unimaginable in any other nation.

You will reflect on your joint conviction that your service had to be undertaken before you had children.

You will reflect on the fact that you are thirty-three, and have spent your professional life fomenting musical trends.

You will reflect on the fact that you must return home the same person you were when you left.

You will reflect on the fact that you've been guaranteed you will *not* be the same person.

You will reflect on the fact that you had stopped being that person even before leaving.

You will reflect on the fact that too much reflection is pointless.

You will reflect on the fact that these "instructions" are becoming less and less instructive.

Your Field Instructions, stored in a chip beneath your hairline, will serve as both a mission log and a guide for others undertaking this work.

Pressing your left thumb (if right-handed) against your left middle fingertip begins recording.

For clearest results, mentally speak the thought, as if talking to yourself.

Always filter your observations and experience through the lens of their didactic value.

Your training is ongoing; you must learn from each step you take.

When your mission is complete, you may view the results of the download before adding your Field Instructions to your mission file.

Where stray or personal thoughts have intruded, you may delete them.

16

Pretend sleep can lead to actual sleep.

Sleep is restorative in almost every circumstance.

The sound of showering likely indicates the return of your Designated Mate.

As a beauty, you will be expected to return to your room and change clothes often; a fresh appearance at mealtimes is essential.

The goal is to be a lovely, innocuous, evolving surprise.

A crisp white sundress against tanned skin is widely viewed as attractive.

Avoid overbright colors; they are attention-seeking and hinder camouflage.

White is not technically speaking, a bright color.

White is, nevertheless, bright.

Gold spike-heeled sandals may compromise your ability to run or jump, but they look good on tanned feet.

Thirty-three is still young enough to register as "young."

170 Registering as "young" is especially welcome to those who may not register as "young" much longer.

If your Designated Mate leads you to dinner with an arm at your waist, assume that your attire change was successful.

17

When men begin serious talk, beauties are left to themselves.

"How long have you been divorced?" suggests the wish to resume a prior conversation.

"A few months," when untrue, should be uttered without eye contact.

175 "What was he like, your husband?" may be answered honestly.

"From Africa. Kenya" will satisfy your wish to talk about your husband.

"Black?," with eyebrows raised, may indicate racism.

"Yes. Black," in measured tones, should deliver a gentle reprimand.

"How black?" suggests that it did not.

180 "Very black" is somewhat less gentle, especially when accompanied by a pointed stare.

"Nice" hints at personal experience.

"Yes. It is nice" contradicts one's alleged divorce. "Was nice" is a reasonable correction.

"But not nice enough?" with laughter, indicates friendly intimacy. Especially when followed by "Or too nice!"

18

House-party hosts are universally eager to make guests eat.

For most beauties, the lure of food is a hazard; as a beauty of limited tenure, you may eat what you want. 185

Squab[3] can be consumed by ripping the bird apart with your hands and sucking the meat from the bones.

A stunned expression reveals that your host expected the use of utensils.

A host who caters to violent guests will understand implicitly the need for discretion.

The adjacency of your host's chair to your own may presage a confidence.

If your job is to appear simple-minded, a confidence may mean that you have failed. 190

Everyone should brush his teeth before dinner.

Turning your ear toward your host's mouth will prevent you from having to smell the breath coming from it.

Ears must be kept clean at all times.

If your host warns you that your Designated Mate may pose an immediate danger to you, assume that your Designated Mate has left the room.

3. Young domestic pigeon, a delicacy typically served whole.

19

Going to the rest room is the most efficient means of self-jettisoning.

Never betray urgency, not even in an empty hallway.

If you have no idea in which direction your Designated Mate has gone, hold still.

If you find yourself hovering beside a pair of glass doors, you may open them and step outside.

Nights in the South of France are a strange, dark, piercing blue.

A bright moon can astonish, no matter how many times you have seen it.

If you were a child who loved the moon, looking at the moon will forever remind you of childhood.

Fatherless girls may invest the moon with a certain paternal promise.

Everyone has a father.

A vague story like "Your father died before you were born" may satisfy a curious child for an unlikely number of years.

The truth of your paternity, discovered in adulthood, will make the lie seem retroactively ludicrous.

Publicists occasionally have flings with their movie-star clients.

Discovering that you are a movie star's daughter is not necessarily a comfort.

It is especially not a comfort when the star in question has seven other children from three different marriages.

Discovering that you are a movie star's daughter may prompt you to watch upward of sixty movies, dating from the beginning of his career.

You may think, watching said movies, You don't know about me, but I am here.

You may think, watching said movies, I'm invisible to you, but I am here.

A sudden reconfiguration of your past can change the fit and feel of your adulthood.

It may cleave you, irreparably, from the mother whose single goal has been your happiness.

If your husband has transformed greatly in his own life, he will understand your transformation.

Avoid excessive self-reflection; your job is to look out, not in.

20

"There you are," whispered from behind by your Designated Mate, suggests that he has been looking for you.

Holding still can sometimes prove more effective than actively searching.

"Come," uttered softly, may communicate a renewed wish for intimate contact.

The moon's calm face can make you feel, in advance, that you are understood and forgiven.

The sea is audible against the rocks well before you see it.

Even at night, the Mediterranean is more blue than black.

If you wish to avoid physical intimacy, the sight of a speedboat will bring relief, despite the myriad new problems it presents.

If no words are exchanged between your Designated Mate and the speedboat's captain, their meeting was likely prearranged.

A man known for his cruelty may still show great care in guiding his beauty into a rocking speedboat.

225 He may interpret her hesitation to board as a fear of falling in.

Resist the impulse to ask where you are going.

Try, when anxious, to summon up a goofy giggle.

Locate your Personal Calming Source and use it.

If your Personal Calming Source is the moon, be grateful that it is dark and that the moon is especially bright.

230 Reflect on the many reasons you can't yet die:

You need to see your husband.

You need to have children.

You need to tell the movie star that he has an eighth child, and that she is a hero.

21

The moon may appear to move, but really it is you who are moving.

235 At high velocity, a speedboat slams along the tops of waves.

Fear and excitement are sometimes indistinguishable.

When the captain of a boat adjusts his course in response to commands from your Designated Mate, he may not know where he is taking you.

If your Designated Mate keeps looking up, he's probably using the stars for navigation.

The Mediterranean is vast enough to have once seemed infinite.

A beauty should require no more context than the presence of her Designated Mate. 240

A beauty must appear to enjoy any journey he initiates.

Simulate said enjoyment by putting an affectionate arm around him and nestling your head close to his.

A beauty whose head is aligned with her Designated Mate's can share in his navigation and thus calculate the route.

At night, far from shore, stars pulse with a strength that is impossible to conceive of in the proximity of light.

Your whereabouts will never be a mystery; you will be visible at all times as a dot of light on the screens of those watching over you. 245

You are one of hundreds, each a potential hero.

Technology has afforded ordinary people a chance to glow in the cosmos of human achievement.

Your lack of espionage and language training is what makes your record clean and neutral.

You are an ordinary person undertaking an extraordinary task.

You need not be remarkable for your credentials or skill sets, only for your bravery and equilibrium. 250

Knowing that you are one of hundreds shouldn't feel belittling.

In the new heroism, the goal is to merge with something larger than yourself.

In the new heroism, the goal is to throw off generations of self-involvement.

In the new heroism, the goal is to renounce the American fixation with being seen and recognized.

In the new heroism, the goal is to dig beneath your shiny persona.

You'll be surprised by what lies under it: a rich, deep crawl space of possibilities.

Some liken this discovery to a dream in which a familiar home acquires new wings and rooms.

The power of individual magnetism is nothing against the power of combined selfless effort.

You may accomplish astonishing personal feats, but citizen agents rarely seek individual credit.

They liken the need for personal glory to cigarette addiction: a habit that feels life-sustaining even as it kills you.

Childish attention-seeking is usually satisfied at the expense of real power.

An enemy of the state could not have connived a better way to declaw and distract us.

Now our notorious narcissism is our camouflage.

Knowing your latitude and longitude is not the same as knowing where you are.

A new remote and unfamiliar place can make the prior remote and unfamiliar place seem like home.

Imagining yourself as a dot of light on a screen is oddly reassuring.

Because your husband is a visionary in the realm of national security, he occasionally has access to that screen.

If it calms you to imagine your husband tracking your dot of light, then imagine it.

Do not however, close your eyes while ascending a rocky path in darkness.

At Latitude X, Longitude Y, the flora is dry and crumbles under your feet.

A voice overhead suggests that your arrival was expected and observed.

An empty shore is not necessarily unpatrolled.

The best patrols are imperceptible.

22

After a juddering ride of several hours, you may not notice at first that the boat is approaching ashore.

A single lighted structure stands out strongly on a deserted coastline.

Silence after a roaring motor is a sound of its own.

The speedboat's immediate departure signals that you won't be making a return trip anytime soon.

23

A formal handshake between your new host and your Designated Mate implies that this is their first meeting.

A formal handshake followed by a complex and stylized hand gesture implies a shared allegiance.

So does the immediate use of a language you don't recognize.

In certain rich, powerful men, physical slightness will seem a source of strength.

The failure of your new host to acknowledge you may indicate that women do not register in his field of vision.

Being invisible means that you won't be closely watched.

Your job is to be forgotten yet still present.

A white, sparkling villa amid so much scrabbly darkness will appear miragelike.

A man to whom women are invisible may still have many beauties in his domain.

These neglected beauties will vie for his scant attention.

Among neglected beauties, there is often an alpha beauty who assumes leadership.

As you enter the house, her cool scrutiny will ripple through the other beauties and surround you.

The sensation will remind you of going as a child with your mother to visit families with two parents and multiple children.

At first, the knot of unfamiliar kids would seem impenetrable.

You would wish, keenly, that you had a sibling who could be your ally.

Feeling at the mercy of those around you prompted a seismic internal response.

The will to dominate was deeper than yourself.

You were never childish, even as a child.

Your unchildishness is something your husband has always loved in you.

Once the new children were under your control, it was crushing to leave their midst.

24

A small table and chairs carved into a spindly clifftop promontory are doubtless designed for private conversation.

If your Designated Mate brings you with him to this place, it may mean that he feels less than perfectly at ease with your new host.

When your new host dismisses his own alpha beauty, important business may be under way.

An alpha[4] beauty will not tolerate her own exclusion if another beauty is included.

If your new host makes a motion of dismissal at you, look to your Designated Mate.

Take orders from no one but your Designated Mate.

If your Designated Mate keeps an arm around you in the face of your new host's dismissal, you have become the object of a power play.

If your new host moves close to your face and speaks directly into it, he is likely testing your ignorance of his language.

If your Designated Mate stiffens beside you, your new host's words are probably offensive.

When you become an object of contention, try to neutralize the conflict.

A giggle and a look of incomprehension are a beauty's most reliable tools.

If the men relax into their chairs, neutralization has been successful.

Your new host has insulted you and, by extension, your Designated Mate.

4. First or lead, most powerful or dominant.

Your Designated Mate has prevailed in his claim that you're too harmless to bother sending away.

Congratulate yourself on preserving your adjacency and activate your ear mike.

25

In the presence of business conversation, project an utter lack of interest or curiosity.

Notice where you are at all times.

On a high, narrow promontory at Latitude X, Longitude Y, the ocean and heavens shimmer in all directions.

There will be moments in your mission, perhaps very few, when you'll sense the imminence of critical information.

It may come in the form of a rush of joy.

This joy may arise from your discovery that the moon, hard and radiant, is still aloft.

It may arise from the knowledge that, when your task is complete, you will return to the husband you adore.

It may arise from the extremity of the natural beauty around you, and the recognition that you are alive in this moment.

It may arise from your knowledge that you have accomplished every goal you've set for yourself since childhood.

It may arise from the knowledge that at long last you've found a goal worthy of your considerable energies.

It may arise from the knowledge that, by accomplishing this goal, you'll have helped to perpetuate American life as you know it.

A wave of joy can make it difficult to sit still.

Beware of internal states—positive or negative—that obscure what is happening around you.

When two subjects begin making sketches, concrete planning may have commenced.

The camera implanted in your left eye is operated by pressing your left tear duct.

In poor light, a flash may be activated by pressing the outside tip of your left eyebrow.

When using the flash, always cover your non-camera eye to shield it from temporary blindness occasioned by the flash.

Never deploy flash photography in the presence of other people.

26

Springing from your seat with a gasp and peering toward the house will focus the attention of others in that direction.

Having heard something inaudible to others puts you in an immediate position of authority.

"What? What did you hear?," uttered close to your face by your Designated Mate, means that your diversion was successful.

Wait until their eagerness to know verges on anger, evidenced by the shaking of your shoulders.

Then tell them, faintly, "I heard screaming."

Men with a history of violence live in fear of retribution.

Your new host will be the first to depart in the direction of alleged screaming.

Your Designated Mate's glance toward the dock, far below, may reveal that his interests are not fully aligned with your new host's.

His attention to his handset may portend that your diversion has run amok, undermining the transaction you meant to capture.

340 Among the violent, there is always a plan for escape.

27

It is reasonable to hope that a backlit screen will distract its user from a camera flash at some slight distance.

Move close to the sketches you wish to photograph, allowing them to fill your field of vision.

Hold very still.

A flash is far more dramatic in total darkness.

345 An epithet in another language, followed by "What the fuck was that?," means you overestimated your Designated Mate's, handset absorption.

A bright, throbbing total blindness means that you neglected to cover your non-camera eye.

Distance yourself from agency in the flash by crying out, truthfully, "I can't see!"

It is hard to safely navigate a clifftop promontory at high speed while blind.

It is hard to defer said navigation when your Designated Mate is forcefully yanking your hand.

A distant buzz presages an 350
approaching speedboat.

Cooler air and a downward slope indicate that you are now below the cliff's edge.

Trying to negotiate a crumbling wooded path in a state of blindness (and heels) will soon lead to tripping and collapsing.

Receding downhill footfalls indicate that you've overtaxed your limited value to your Designated Mate.

A sense of helpless disorientation may prevent you from doing much more than sitting there in the dirt.

28

Variegation in the textures around 355
you is a first sign that your temporary blindness has begun to fade.

Temporary blindness sharpens one's appreciation for not being blind.

In the aftermath of blindness, the accretion of objects around you may have an almost sensual quality.

A boat departing at high speed will send a vibration trembling up through the soil.

The knowledge that you are alone, without your Designated Mate, will settle upon you slowly and coldly.

Each new phase of aloneness 360
reveals that you were previously less alone than you thought.

This more profound isolation may register, at first, as paralysis.

If it soothes you to lie back in the dirt, then lie back.

The moon shines everywhere.

The moon can seem as expressive as a face.

Human beings are fiercely, primordially resilient.

In uneasy times, draw on the resilience you carry inside you.

Recall that the mythical feats you loved to read about as a child are puny beside the accomplishments of human beings on earth.

29

The presence of another person can be sensed, even when not directly perceived.

The discovery of another person at close range, when you thought you were alone, may occasion fear.

Leaping from a supine into a standing posture will induce a head rush.

"I see you. Come out" must be uttered calmly, from the Readiness Position.

If you show fear, make sure that it isn't the fear you actually feel.

When you've expected a man, the appearance of a woman may be shocking.

Despite all that you know and are, you may experience that shock as a relief.

"Why are you here?," uttered by your new host's alpha beauty, is likely hostile.

Respond to abstract questions on the most literal level: "He left without me."

"Bastard," muttered bitterly, suggests familiarity with the phenomenon of being left behind.

Sympathy from an unexpected source can prompt a swell of emotion.

Measure the potential liability of shedding tears before you let them fall.

The perfumed arm of a beauty may pour strength and hope directly into your skin.

30

A lavish clifftop villa may look even more miragelike on a second approach.

Sustaining an atmosphere of luxury in a remote place requires an enormous amount of money.

So does coördinated violence.

Your job is to follow money to its source.

A powerful man whose associate has fled the premises after a false alarm is unlikely to be cheerful.

The reappearance of the vanished associate's stranded beauty will likely startle him.

Astonishment is satisfying to witness on any face.

"Where the fuck did he go?" is remarkably easy to decipher, even in a language you don't recognize.

A shrug is comprehensible to everyone.

An alpha beauty's complete indifference to the consternation of her mate may mean that he's easily moved to consternation.

It may also mean that he's not her mate.

As a beauty, you will sometimes be expected to change hands.

Generally, you will pass from the hands of a less powerful man to those of a more powerful man.

Greater proximity to the source of money and control is progress.

395 Your job is identical regardless of whose hands you are in.

If your vulnerability and helplessness have drawn the interest of an enemy subject, accentuate them.

Scraped and dirty legs may accentuate your vulnerability to the point of disgust.

They might get you a hot shower, though.

31

Homes of the violent rich have excellent first-aid cabinets.

400 If, after tending to your scrapes, you are shown to a bathing area with a stone-encrusted waterfall, assume you won't be alone for long.

The fact that a man has ignored and then insulted you does not mean that he won't want to fuck you.

Slim, powerful men often move with catlike swiftness.

Begin your countdown early—as he lowers himself into the tub.

By the time he seizes your arm, you should be at five.

405 By the time your forehead is jammed against a rock, you should perceive your body only vaguely, from above.

32

If you feel, on returning to your body, that much time has passed, don't dwell on how much.

If your limbs are sore and your forehead scraped and raw, don't dwell on why.

When you emerge from a warm, churning bath where you've spent an indeterminate period of time, expect to feel shaky and weak.

Remind yourself that you are receiving no payment, in currency or kind, for this or any act you have engaged in.

These acts are forms of sacrifice. 410

An abundance of diaphanous bathrobes suggests that the occupants of this bathroom are often female.

A soiled and tattered white sundress can seem oddly precious when it's all you have.

Keep with you the things that matter—you won't come back for them later.

The stationing of a male attendant outside the bathroom means that you haven't been forgotten.

If he shows you to a tiny room 415
containing a very large bed, your utility to your new host may not have been exhausted.

A tray containing a meat pie, grapes, and a pitcher of water suggests that visits such as yours are routine.

At times, you may wish to avoid the moon.

At times, the moon may appear like a surveillance device, tracking your movements.

The ability to sleep in stressful conditions is essential to this work.

Sleep whenever you can safely do so.

33

Your abrupt awakening may feel like a reaction to a sound.

In moments of extreme solitude, you may believe you've heard your name.

We reassure ourselves by summoning, in our dreams, those we love and miss.

Having awakened to find them absent, we may be left with a sense of having spoken with them.

Even the most secure houses achieve, in deep night, a state of relative unconsciousness.

A beauty in a diaphanous lavender bathrobe can go anywhere, as long as she appears to be delivering herself to someone.

34

A universal principle of home construction makes it possible to guess which door will lead to the master bedroom.

Linen closets, with doors closed, can resemble master bedrooms.

So can bathrooms.

Bare feet are virtually soundless on a stone floor.

Even a slim, catlike man may snore.

When trespassing in a sleeping man's bedroom, go straight to his bed, as if you were seeking him out.

An alpha beauty who has appeared to have no tie to your new host may turn out to be his intimate, after all.

Their sleeping entanglement may contradict everything you have witnessed between them.

A small crib near the bed may indicate the presence of a baby.

Avoid indulging your own amazement; it wastes time.

Master bedrooms in lavish homes often divide into "his" and "hers" areas.

A beauty's closet is unmistakable, like a quiver of bright arrows.

The closet of a slight, catlike man will usually be compact.

Having penetrated a man's personal space; immediately seek out his Sweet Spot.

The Sweet Spot is where he empties his pockets at the end of the day and stores the essentials he needs to begin the next.

The Sweet Spot of a secretive, catlike man will most often be inside a cupboard or a drawer.

When you find it, consider using a Data Surge to capture the contents of his handset.

A Data Surge must be deployed with extreme caution, and only if you feel confident of an exceptional yield.

The quantity of information captured will require an enormous amount of manpower to tease apart.

Its transmission will register on any monitoring device.

We can guarantee its effectiveness only once.

35

Reach between your right fourth and pinky toes (if right-handed) and remove the Data Plug from your Universal Port.

Attached to the plug is a cable with a connection pin at one end for insertion into the handset's data port.

Sit on the floor, away from sharp surfaces, and brace your back against a wall.

A red ribbon has been tucked inside your Universal Port; enclose this in one of your palms.

Spread apart your toes and gently reinsert the plug, now fused to your subject's handset, into your Universal Port.

You will feel the surge as the data flood your body.

The surge may contain feeling, memory, heat, cold, longing, pain, even joy.

Although the data are alien, the memories dislodged will be your own:

Peeling an orange for your husband in bed on a Sunday, sunlight splashing the sheets;

The smoky earthen smell of the fur of your childhood cat;

The flavor of the peppermints your mother kept for you inside her desk.

The impact of a Data Surge may prompt unconsciousness or short-term memory loss.

The purpose of the red ribbon is to orient you; if you awaken to find yourself clutching one, look to your foot.

When your body is quiet, unplug the handset and return it to its original location.

36

A Data Surge leaves a ringing in your ears that may obscure the sound of another person's arrival.

A face that brought you relief once may trigger relief a second time.

When an alpha beauty accosts you at high volume in an unfamiliar language, it may mean she's too sleepy to remember who you are.

It may also mean she's calling someone else.

Beauty status will not excuse, for another beauty, your appearance where you are not supposed to be.

Should you be perceived as an enemy, prepare to defend yourself at the first sign of physical encroachment.

Your new host lunging at you, shouting. "What the fuck are you doing?," constitutes physical encroachment.

Thrust your elbow upward into the tender socket underneath his jaw, sending him backward onto the floor.

The wails of a newborn will lure its mother away from almost anything, including the physical travails of her mate.

A man disabled by an elbow blow will have little reaction to infant cries.

37

At the revelation of martial-arts expertise, a man who has perceived you as merely a beauty will recalculate your identity and purpose.

Watch his eyes: he'll be measuring the distance to his nearest firearm.

An immediate exit is advisable.

A slim, catlike man may well rebound before a hasty exit can be made.

Obstructing the path of a violent man to his firearm will nearly always result in another encroachment.

Kicking him in the foreneck, even barefoot, will temporarily occlude his windpipe.

The alpha beauty of a violent man will know where his firearm is kept, and how to use it.

A woman holding a gun and a baby no longer qualifies as a beauty.

No beauty is really a beauty.

Disabling a gun holder is likely to hurt the baby she is holding, too.

When self-preservation requires that you harm the innocent, we can provide no more than guidelines.

As Americans, we value human rights above all else and cannot sanction their violation.

When someone threatens our human rights, however, a wider leeway becomes necessary.

Follow your instincts while bearing in mind that we must, and will, hew to our principles.

A woman holding a thrashing baby in one arm may have trouble aiming a firearm with the other.

Bullets do actually whistle in an enclosed space.

If a person has shot at you and missed, incapacitate her before she can fire again.

We are most reluctant to hurt those who remind us of ourselves.

38

A lag time exists between getting shot and knowing that you have been shot.

Assuming there is no artery involvement, wounds to the upper limbs are preferable.

Bony, tendony body parts bleed less, but are harder to reconstruct if shattered.

The right shoulder is a bony, tendony part.

When shots have been fired in a powerful man's home, you have minutes, if not seconds, before the arrival of security.

Your physical person is our Black Box; without it, we have no record of what has happened on your mission.

It is imperative that you remove yourself from enemy possession.

When you find yourself cornered and outnumbered, you may unleash, as a last resort, your Primal Roar.

The Primal Roar is the human equivalent of an explosion, a sound that combines screaming, shrieking, and howling.

The Roar must be accompanied by facial contortions and frenetic body movement, suggesting a feral,[5] unhinged state.

The Primal Roar must transform you from a beauty into a monster.

The goal is to horrify your opponent the way trusted figures, turned evil, are horrifying in movies and in nightmares.

Deploy your camera flash repeatedly while Roaring.

5. Wild, undomesticated.

When approached by a howling, spasmodic, flashing monster, most women holding newborns will step aside.

Discontinue Roaring the instant you're free from immediate danger.

Those stampeding to the aid of a powerful man will barely notice a dishevelled beauty they pass in a hallway.

If you're lucky, this will buy you time to flee his house.

Resume your beauty role while running: smooth your hair and cover your bleeding wound with the sundress scrunched in your pocket.

The fact that you can't hear alarms doesn't mean you haven't set them off.

39

After violence in a closed room, cool night air will have a clarifying effect.

Get to the bottom of a hill any way you can, including sliding and rolling.

In residences of the violent rich, there will be at least one guard at each port of egress.[6]

In deep night, if you are extremely lucky (and quiet), that guard will be asleep.

Assume, as well as you can, the air of a beauty larkishly gambolling.[7]

If running barefoot onto a dock transports you back to your childhood, pain may be making you hallucinate.

Lying with girlfriends on a still-warm dock in upstate New York, watching shooting stars, is a sensation you remember after many years.

Hindsight creates the illusion that your life has led you inevitably to the present moment.

It's easier to believe in a foregone conclusion than to accept that our lives are governed by chance.

Showing up for a robotics course by accident, because of a classroom mixup, is chance.

Finding an empty seat beside a boy with very dark skin and beautiful hands is chance.

When someone has become essential to you, you will marvel that you could have lain on a warm dock and not have known him yet.

Expect reimmersion in your old life to be difficult.

Experience leaves a mark, regardless of the reasons and principles behind it.

What our citizen agents most often require is simply for time to pass.

Our counsellors are available around the clock for the first two weeks of your reimmersion and during business hours thereafter.

We ask that you allow our Therapeutic Agents, rather than those in the general population, to address your needs.

Secrecy is the basis of what we do, and we require your extreme discretion.

6. Exit.

7. Lively running or jumping. *Larkishly*: happily and mischievously, like a lark.

40

Even preternatural swimming strength cannot propel you across a blue-black sea.

Staring with yearning ferocity from the end of a dock cannot propel you across a blue-black sea.

When your body has been granted exceptional powers, it is jarring to encounter a gulf between your desires and your abilities.

For millennia, engineers have empowered human beings to accomplish mythical feats.

Your husband is an engineer.

Children raised among wild animals learn to detect irregular movements in their landscape.

That particular awareness, coupled with scientific genius, has made your husband a national-security hero.

Intimacy with another human can allow you to scrutinize your surroundings as he would.

Along a rocky, moonlit shore, the irregular movement is the one that is lurching in time with the water beneath an overhang of brush.

A speedboat has most likely been hidden by your new host as a means of emergency escape.

The key will be inside it.

41

Slither between branches and board the boat; untie it and lower its motor into the water.

Be grateful for the lakes in upstate New York where you learned to pilot motorboats.

Fluff up your hair with your functional arm and essay a wide, carefree smile.

A smile is like a shield; it freezes your face into a mask of muscle that you can hide behind.

A smile is like a door that is both open and closed.

Turn the key and gun the motor once before aiming into the blue-black sea and jamming the accelerator.

Wave and giggle loudly at the stunned, sleepy guard.

Steer in a zigzag motion until you are out of gunshot range.

42

The exultation of escape will be followed almost immediately by a crushing onslaught of pain.

The house, its occupants, even the gunshots will seem like phantoms beside this clanging immediacy.

If the pain makes thought impossible, concentrate solely on navigation.

Only in specific Geographic Hotspots can we intervene.

While navigating toward a Hotspot, indicate an emergency by pressing the button behind your knee for sixty continuous seconds.

You must remain conscious.

If it helps, imagine yourself in the arms of your husband.

If it helps, imagine yourself in your apartment, where his grandfather's hunting knife is displayed inside a Plexiglas box.

If it helps, imagine harvesting the small tomatoes you grow on your fire escape in summer.

If it helps, imagine that the contents of the Data Surge will help thwart an attack in which thousands of American lives would have been lost.

Even without enhancements, you can pilot a boat in a semi-conscious state.

Human beings are superhuman.

Let the moon and the stars direct you.

43

When you reach the approximate location of a Hotspot, cut the engine.

You will be in total darkness, in total silence.

If you wish, you may lie down at the bottom of the boat.

The fact that you feel like you're dying doesn't mean that you will die.

Remember that, should you die, your body will yield a crucial trove of information.

Remember that, should you die, your Field Instructions will provide a record of your mission and lessons for those who follow.

Remember that, should you die, you will have triumphed merely by delivering your physical person into our hands.

The boat's movement on the sea will remind you of a cradle.

You'll recall your mother rocking you in her arms when you were a baby.

You'll recall that she has always loved you fiercely and entirely.

You'll discover that you have forgiven her.

You'll understand that she concealed your paternity out of faith that her own inexhaustible love would be enough.

The wish to tell your mother that you forgive her is yet another reason you must make it home alive.

You will not be able to wait, but you will have to wait.

We can't tell you in advance what direction relief will come from.

We can only reassure you that we have never yet failed to recover a citizen agent, dead or alive, who managed to reach a Hotspot.

44

Hotspots are not hot.

Even a warm night turns frigid at the bottom of a wet boat.

The stars are always there, scattered and blinking.

Looking up at the sky from below can feel like floating, suspended, and looking down.

The universe will seem to hang beneath you in its milky glittering mystery.

Only when you notice a woman like yourself, crumpled and bleeding at the bottom of a boat, will you realize what has happened.

You've deployed the Dissociation Technique without meaning to.

There is no harm in this.

Released from pain, you can waft free in the night sky.

Released from pain, you can enact the fantasy of flying that you nurtured as a child.

Keep your body in view at all times; if your mind loses track of your body, it may be hard—even impossible—to reunite the two.

As you waft free in the night sky, you may notice a steady rhythmic churning in the gusting wind.

Helicopter noise is inherently menacing.

A helicopter without lights is like a mixture of bat, bird, and monstrous insect.

Resist the urge to flee this apparition; it has come to save you.

45

Know that in returning to your body you are consenting to be racked, once again, by physical pain.

Know that in returning to your body you are consenting to undertake a jarring reimmersion into an altered life.

Some citizen agents have chosen not to return.

They have left their bodies behind, and now they shimmer sublimely in the heavens.

In the new heroism, the goal is to transcend individual life, with its petty pains and loves, in favor of the dazzling collective.

You may picture the pulsing stars as the heroic spirits of former agent beauties.

You may imagine Heaven as a vast screen crowded with their dots of light.

46

If you wish to return to your body, it is essential that you reach it before the helicopter does.

If it helps, count backward.

By eight, you should be close enough to see your bare and dirty feet.

By five, you should be close enough to see the bloody dress wrapped around your shoulder.

By three, you should be close enough to see the dimples you were praised for as a child.

By two, you should hear the shallow bleating of your breath.

47

Having returned to your body, witness the chopper's slow, throbbing descent.

It may appear to be the instrument of a purely mechanical realm.

It may look as if it had come to wipe you out.

It may be hard to believe that there are human beings inside it.

You won't know for sure until you see them crouching above you, their faces taut with hope, ready to jump.

2012

QUESTIONS

1. In addition to unfolding in tweetable (140-character-long) segments, Black Box is presented as a sort of manual- or rulebook-in-progress narrated (like many such books) in the second person. How might each of these two distinct aspects of narration affect the story's tone and your responses both to the story and to its protagonist? How might each shape the way the story handles each of the traditional elements of plot—exposition, rising action, and so on?
2. Narrated via a relatively new technology, Egan's story is arguably also *about* technology (among other things). What technologies, real and imagined, appear in the story? What—through them—might the story suggest about how such technologies—including *Twitter*—are changing or might change us?
3. How does the story define "the new heroism"? What makes it "new"? What makes it necessary? What conflicts does that version of heroism create for the narrator? How is that conflict resolved? To what extent does and/or doesn't the narrator become a "new hero"?

AUTHORS ON THEIR WORK

JENNIFER EGAN (b. 1962)

From "Coming Soon: Jennifer Egan's 'Black Box'" (2012)*

Several of my long-standing fictional interests converged in the writing of "Black Box." One involves fiction that takes the form of lists; stories that appear to be told inadvertently, using a narrator's notes to him or herself. My working title for this story was "Lessons Learned," and my hope was to tell a story whose shape would emerge from the lessons the narrator derived from each step in the action, rather than from descriptions of the action itself. Another long-term goal of mine has been to take a character from a naturalistic story and travel with her into a different genre. [. . .] I wondered whether I could do [that] with a character from my novel "A Visit From the Goon Squad." [. . .] I'd also been wondering about how to write fiction whose structure would lend itself to serialization on Twitter. This is not a new idea, of course, but it's a rich one—because of the intimacy of reaching people through their phones, and because of the odd poetry that can happen in a hundred and forty characters. I found myself imagining a series of terse mental dispatches from a female spy of the future, working undercover by the Mediterranean Sea. I wrote these bulletins by hand in a Japanese notebook that had eight rectangles on each page. The story was originally nearly twice its present length; it took me a year, on and off, to control and calibrate the material into what is now "Black Box."

*"Coming Soon: Jennifer Egan's 'Black Box.'" *The New Yorker Blog*, 23 May 2012, www.newyorker.com/books/page-turner/coming-soon-jennifer-egans-black-box.

SUGGESTIONS FOR WRITING

1. Write a response paper or essay reflecting on the ways in which THE VELDT, MEET THE PRESIDENT!, or BLACK BOX engage in extrapolation. What developments or trends of the early 1950s or the 2010s does the story comment on by imagining the specific future it does?
2. Write an essay exploring what THE GERNSBACK CONTINUUM might suggest about the nature and social role of science fiction. Alternatively, draw on the definitions in this album or on other definitions you discover on your own, as well as evidence from the story, to explore just whether and why either THE GERNSBACK CONTINUUM or Jennifer Egan's BLACK BOX should count as science fiction.
3. Write an essay comparing what at least two stories in this album suggest about technology's effects on human relationships. If one of your stories is Jennifer Egan's BLACK BOX, be sure to consider *Twitter*—the medium via which the story was originally published.
4. Write an essay comparing the role of setting in two stories in this album. What is the effect, for example, of Bradbury's choice to focus exclusively on the Hadley home in THE VELDT and to ignore the world outside its borders? of Smith's choice to set her story in one very specific and partly real place? of the numerous, specific places in which the action of THE GERNSBACK CONTINUUM unfolds?

5 SYMBOL AND FIGURATIVE LANGUAGE

A symbol is something that represents something else. Sometimes a symbol resembles or closely relates to what it represents, but often the association is arbitrary or subtle. Even so, through common usage, many symbols are instantly understood by almost everyone in a particular group. Although we rarely think of them as such, the letters of the English alphabet are themselves symbols, representing different sounds. We simply learn to recognize them, however, without thinking about whether there is any resemblance between what the symbols look like and what they represent. In other languages, one character may stand for an object or concept, such as the Chinese characters for "fire." Yet some symbols do help us by resembling what they stand for, such as the symbol for a fire alarm.

Similarly, abstractions may be represented by symbols that resemble things that are associated with them:

Although the smiley face can simply mean "Smile!" its meanings when used as an "emoticon" in e-mails and text messages range from "I like this" to "Just joking." The skull and crossbones symbol is used on warning labels to indicate that the contents are poisonous, but it has also been associated with death, cemeteries, and pirates.

Other symbols are more arbitrary, having no literal connection with what they represent. Octagons and the color red have little to do with stopping a car, but most Americans, even if they are too young to drive, understand what a stop sign means. Such symbols, though not based on resemblances, elicit an unconscious and reflexive response from us. The meaning of a symbol is not always so concrete and practical, however. The U.S. national flag is an arbitrary symbol, having no direct resemblance to what it represents, but most people recognize its primary significance; the "stars and stripes" undoubtedly stands for the United States. Nevertheless, the flag differs from a traffic sign in that the flag evokes much more varied, complex, and even conflicting responses.

LITERARY SYMBOLISM

A **symbol** usually conveys an abstraction or cluster of abstractions, from the ideal to the imperceptible or the irrational, in a more concrete form. A symbol in a work of literature compares or puts together two things that are in some ways dissimilar. But literary symbolism rarely comes down to a simple equation of one thing to another. Unlike an arbitrary symbol such as a letter or traffic sign, a symbol in literature usually carries richer and more varied meanings, as does a flag or a religious image. And because of its significance, a symbol usually appears or is hinted at numerous times throughout the work. In reading literature, it may be challenging to recognize symbols, and readers may have good reasons to disagree about their interpretation, since literary works often incorporate symbolism for which there is no single "correct" interpretation. No one would say that reading a short story should be like a treasure hunt for some shiny symbol that clearly reveals all the hidden meanings; the complexity remains and requires further exploration even when we have recognized a symbol's significance at some level. A literary symbol may be understood as an extended figure of speech that rewards further interpretation. (For one fiction-writer's views of how literary symbolism works, see the excerpt from Flannery O'Connor's THE NATURE AND AIM OF FICTION.)

Traditional Symbols and Archetypes

Some symbols have been in use by many people for a long time (in which case they are known as *traditional symbols*); a white dove, for example, is a traditional symbol of peace and love. A rose can be a symbol of godly love, of romantic desire, of female beauty, of mortality (because the flower wilts), or of hidden cruelty (because it has thorns). The snake has traditionally been a symbol of evil, but in Rudyard Kipling's *The Jungle Book* (1894), the python Ka, while frightening, is on the side of law and order. A few symbolic character types, plots, objects, or settings—for example, the trickster, the quest, the garden—have become so pervasive and have recurred in so many cultures that they are considered **archetypes** (literary elements that recur in the literature and myths of multiple cultures). Fire, water, a flower, or a tree can all be considered archetypes because numerous cultures use them symbolically, often within their system of religion or myth. Literary symbolism frequently borrows from the symbols and archetypes associated with religion or myth.

Allegory and Myth

A common literary form, especially in works written by and for religious believers, is the **allegory**, which may be regarded as an "extended" symbol or series of symbols that encompasses a whole work. In an allegory, concrete things and abstract concepts may be associated with each other across a narrative that consistently maintains at least two distinct levels of meaning. Because allegories set up series of correspondences, they usually help the reader translate these correspondences through the use of names that readily function as labels, often with obvious moral implications. In *The Pilgrim's Progress* (1678), probably the most famous prose allegory in English, the central character is named Christian; he was born in the City of Destruction and sets out for the Celestial City, passes through the Slough of Despond and Vanity Fair, meets men named Pliable and Obstinate, and so on. The point of an allegory is not to make us hunt for disguised meanings, so it is no defect if an allegory's intended meaning is clear. Instead, the purpose is to let us enjoy an invented world where everything is especially meaningful and everything corresponds to something else according to a moral or otherwise "correct" plan.

When an entire story is allegorical or symbolic, it is sometimes called a **myth**. *Myth* originally referred to a story of communal origin that provided an explanation or religious interpretation of humanity, nature, the universe, or the relations among them. Sometimes we apply the term *myth* to stories associated with religions we do not believe in, and sometimes to literature that seeks to express experiences or truths that transcend any one location, culture, or time.

FIGURES OF SPEECH

Figures of speech, or **figurative language**, are similar to symbols in that they supplement or replace literal meaning, often by creating imaginative connections between our ideas and our senses. Sometimes referred to as *tropes* (literally, "turnings"), figures of speech could be described as *bending* the usual meaning of language and *shaping* our response to a work. Whether or not they have anything to do with spatial forms or "figures," or whether they rely on vision, such tropes contribute to what are called the **images** or **imagery** of a story. Many figures of speech are known by the Latin or Greek names used in classical Greek and Roman **rhetoric**, the art and science of speech and persuasion.

Just as you can enjoy gymnastics or diving events during the Olympics without knowing the names of the specific twists and turns, you can enjoy the figurative language in a story without identifying each figure of speech. Yet for the purposes of interpreting and writing about literature, it is important to learn some basic terms and distinctions so that you have access to a shared and economical language for describing your responses and the techniques that trigger them. The box below defines some of the most frequently encountered figures of speech.

Key Figures of Speech

allegory an extended association, often sustained in every element (character, plot, setting, etc.) and throughout an entire work, between two levels of meaning, usually literal and abstract. In *Animal Farm* (1945), for example, George Orwell uses an uprising of barnyard animals as an allegory for the Bolshevik revolution in Russia.

allusion a reference, usually brief, to another text or some person or entity external to the work. Examples may range from a direct quotation of the Bible to the mention of a famous name.

irony a meaning or outcome contrary to what is expected; in *verbal irony*, a speaker or narrator says one thing and means the reverse. When the intended meaning is harshly critical or mocking, it is called *sarcasm*. If a teenager says, "I just love it when my mom lectures me," she may well be using irony.

metaphor a representation of one thing as if it were something else, without a verbal signal such as *like* or *as*. When Scout, in *To Kill a Mockingbird* (1960), remarks that she "inched sluggishly along the treadmill of the Maycomb County school system," she doesn't indicate what literally happened at school. She figuratively suggests how it felt by implicitly comparing the experience to being on a treadmill.

metonymy using the name of one thing to refer to another thing associated with it. The common phrase *red tape* is a metonym for excessive paperwork and procedure that slows down an official transaction, based on the fact that papers used to be tied up with red tape.

oxymoron a combination of contradictory or opposite ideas, qualities, or entities, as in *wise fool*.

personification sometimes called *anthropomorphism*, attributing human qualities to objects or animals. In THE OPEN BOAT, Stephen Crane personifies the birds who "sat comfortably in groups" and looked at the men with "unblinking scrutiny." He pushes personification to comic extreme in the shipwrecked men's thoughts: "If this old ninny-woman, Fate, cannot do better than this [. . .] she is an old hen who knows not her intention." Here, "hen" is a metaphor for a silly woman, who in turn personifies the idea of destiny or fate.

simile a representation of one thing as if it were something else, with an explicit verbal signal such as *like* or *as*. In *To Kill a Mockingbird*, Scout describes a teacher who "looked and smelled like a peppermint drop" and bored students "wriggling like a bucket of Catawba worms."

symbol a person, place, object, or image that represents more than its literal meaning. A symbol is more than a passing comparison (such as a simile); instead, as in allegory, its meaning usually relates to most details and themes of the work. Unlike allegory, a symbol usually associates more than two entities or ideas and may be obscure or ambiguous in its meaning. Short stories (or poems) may refer to their central symbolic figure in the title, as in CATHEDRAL.

synecdoche a form of metonymy (or name substitution) in which the part represents the whole (a *sail* refers to a ship).

INTERPRETING SYMBOLISM AND FIGURATIVE LANGUAGE

The context of an entire story or poem or play can guide you in deciding how far to push your own "translation" of a figure of speech or whether a metaphor has the deeper significance of a symbol. It is best to read the entire story and note all of the figures of speech or imagery before you examine one as a symbol. Often, a symbol is a focal point in a story, a single object or situation that draws the attention of one or more characters.

In F. Scott Fitzgerald's *The Great Gatsby* (1925), for example, a faded billboard featuring a pair of bespectacled eyes takes on a central and multilayered significance, though there is no longstanding tradition of symbolic meaning for billboards or spectacles. Although the billboard is a purely realistic detail of setting (one can easily imagine seeing something like it along any highway today), it comes to function as a symbol, too, only because of the number of times and specific ways it is discussed by the narrator and characters. When one character, George Wilson, looks up at the looming eyes and remarks, "God sees everything," it becomes pretty clear what the billboard symbolizes to him. Yet when another character immediately reminds Wilson that what he sees is only "an advertisement," we are forced to consider both what Wilson's interpretation might tell us about him and with what alternative or additional meanings the rest of the novel might invest this object. The symbol remains ambiguous and complex.

Effective symbols and figurative language cannot be extracted from the story they serve, but they can leave a lasting image of what the story is about. With guidance and practice, identifying and interpreting literary symbolism and other figurative language will begin to feel almost as familiar to you as reading the letter symbols on a page, though the meanings may be subtle, ambiguous, and far-reaching rather than straightforward.

Responding to Symbolism: Some Guidelines

- Read the story carefully, noting any details that seem to have exceptional significance, such as names, repeated actions or statements, recurring references to objects, peculiar places, allusions, or other figures of speech.
- Using your list of such possibly symbolic details, look back through the story to find the passages that feature these details. Are any of the passages connected to each other in a pattern? Do any of these interconnected details suggest themes?
- Note any symbols or images that you recognize from mythology, religion, or any other literature, art, or popular culture. Look again at the way the story presents such material. What are the signals that the fire is more than a fire, the tree is more than a tree, the ring is more than a ring? If the story invents its own symbol, find any words in the story that show how the characters see something meaningful in it.
- Once you have found a symbol—an aspect of the story that is a figure of speech, trope, image, or connection between literal and nonliteral; is extended beyond a few sentences; is more complicated than an allegory's one-to-one translation; and may be interpreted in multiple ways—review every aspect of the story, on the literal level, that relates to this symbol.
- As you write about the symbol or symbolism in a story, consider your claims about its meaning. Try not to narrow down the possible meanings of either the symbol or the story, but at the same time don't make overly grand claims

for their ability to reveal the meaning of life. When in doubt, refer back to the story and its characterization, plot, and setting.

- Remember to cite specific passages that will help your reader understand the symbol's significance. Your reader may suspect that you are reading too much into it or miscasting its meanings, so this evidence is crucial to explaining your interpretation and persuading your reader that it is reasonable.

NATHANIEL HAWTHORNE
(1804–64)

The Birth-Mark

Nathaniel Hawthorne was born in Salem, Massachusetts, a descendant of Puritan immigrants. Educated at Bowdoin College, he was agonizingly slow in winning recognition for his work and supported himself from time to time in government service—working in the customhouses of Boston and Salem and serving as the U.S. consul in Liverpool. His early collections of stories, *Twice-Told Tales* (1837) and *Mosses from an Old Manse* (1846), did not sell well, and it was not until the publication of his most famous novel, *The Scarlet Letter* (1850), that his fame spread beyond a discerning few. His other novels include *The House of the Seven Gables* (1851) and *The Blithedale Romance* (1852). Burdened by a deep sense of guilt for his family's role in the notorious Salem witchcraft trials over a century before he was born (one ancestor had been a judge), Hawthorne used fiction as a means of exploring the moral dimensions of sin and the human soul.

In the latter part of the last century[1] there lived a man of science, an eminent proficient in every branch of natural philosophy,[2] who not long before our story opens had made experience of a spiritual affinity more attractive than any chemical one. He had left his laboratory to the care of an assistant, cleared his fine countenance from the furnace-smoke, washed the stain of acids from his fingers, and persuaded a beautiful woman to become his wife. In those days, when the comparatively recent discovery of electricity and other kindred mysteries of Nature seemed to open paths into the region of miracle, it was not unusual for the love of science to rival the love of woman in its depth and absorbing energy. The higher intellect, the imagination, the spirit, and even the heart might all find their congenial aliment in pursuits which, as some of their ardent votaries believed, would ascend from one step of powerful intelligence

1. That is, the eighteenth century; this story was first published in 1843.
2. The body of knowledge we now call science.

to another, until the philosopher should lay his hand on the secret of creative force and perhaps make new worlds for himself. We know not whether Aylmer possessed this degree of faith in man's ultimate control over nature. He had devoted himself, however, too unreservedly to scientific studies ever to be weakened from them by any second passion. His love for his young wife might prove the stronger of the two; but it could only be by intertwining itself with his love of science and uniting the strength of the latter to his own.

Such a union accordingly took place, and was attended with truly remarkable consequences and a deeply impressive moral. One day, very soon after their marriage, Aylmer sat gazing at his wife with a trouble in his countenance that grew stronger until he spoke.

"Georgiana," said he, "has it never occurred to you that the mark upon your cheek might be removed?"

"No, indeed," said she, smiling; but, perceiving the seriousness of his manner, she blushed deeply. "To tell you the truth, it has been so often called a charm, that I was simple enough to imagine it might be so."

5 "Ah, upon another face perhaps it might," replied her husband; "but never on yours. No, dearest Georgiana, you came so nearly perfect from the hand of Nature, that this slightest possible defect, which we hesitate whether to term a defect or a beauty, shocks me, as being the visible mark of earthly imperfection."

"Shocks you, my husband!" cried Georgiana, deeply hurt; at first reddening with momentary anger, but then bursting into tears. "Then why did you take me from my mother's side? You cannot love what shocks you!"

To explain this conversation, it must be mentioned that in the center of Georgiana's left cheek there was a singular mark, deeply interwoven, as it were, with the texture and substance of her face. In the usual state of her complexion—a healthy though delicate bloom—the mark wore a tint of deeper crimson, which imperfectly defined its shape amid the surrounding rosiness. When she blushed it gradually became more indistinct, and finally vanished amid the triumphant rush of blood that bathed the whole cheek with its brilliant glow. But if any shifting motion caused her to turn pale there was the mark again, a crimson stain upon the snow, in what Aylmer sometimes deemed an almost fearful distinctness. Its shape bore not a little similarity to the human hand, though of the smallest pygmy size. Georgiana's lovers were wont to say that some fairy at her birth-hour had laid her tiny hand upon the infant's cheek, and left this impress there in token of the magic endowments that were to give her such sway over all hearts. Many a desperate swain would have risked life for the privilege of pressing his lips to the mysterious hand. It must not be concealed, however, that the impression wrought by this fairy sign-manual varied exceedingly according to the difference of temperament in the beholders. Some fastidious persons—but they were exclusively of her own sex—affirmed that the bloody hand, as they chose to call it, quite destroyed the effect of Georgiana's beauty and rendered her countenance even hideous. But it would be as reasonable to say that one of those small blue stains which sometimes occur in the purest statuary marble would convert the Eve of Powers[3] to a monster. Masculine

3. Hiram Powers (1805–73), American sculptor and friend of Hawthorne, produced noted marble statues, including *Eve Tempted* and *Eve Disconsolate*.

observers, if the birthmark did not heighten their admiration, contented themselves with wishing it away, that the world might possess one living specimen of ideal loveliness without the semblance of a flaw. After his marriage—for he thought little or nothing of the matter before—Aylmer discovered that this was the case with himself.

Had she been less beautiful—if Envy's self could have found aught else to sneer at—he might have felt his affection heightened by the prettiness of this mimic hand, now vaguely portrayed, now lost, now stealing forth again and glimmering to and fro with every pulse of emotion that throbbed within her heart; but, seeing her otherwise so perfect, he found this one defect grow more and more intolerable with every moment of their united lives. It was the fatal flaw of humanity which Nature, in one shape or another, stamps ineffaceably on all her productions, either to imply that they are temporary and finite, or that their perfection must be wrought by toil and pain. The crimson hand expressed the ineludible gripe in which mortality clutches the highest and purest of earthly mould, degrading them into kindred with the lowest, and even with the very brutes, like whom their visible frames return to dust. In this manner, selecting it as the symbol of his wife's liability to sin, sorrow, decay, and death, Aylmer's somber imagination was not long in rendering the birthmark a frightful object, causing him more trouble and horror than ever Georgiana's beauty, whether of soul or sense, had given him delight.

At all the seasons which should have been their happiest he invariably, and without intending it, nay, in spite of a purpose to the contrary, reverted to this one disastrous topic. Trifling as it at first appeared, it so connected itself with innumerable trains of thought and modes of feeling that it became the central point of all. With the morning twilight Aylmer opened his eyes upon his wife's face and recognized the symbol of imperfection; and when they sat together at the evening hearth his eyes wandered stealthily to her cheek, and beheld, flickering with the blaze of the wood-fire, the spectral hand that wrote mortality where he would fain[4] have worshipped. Georgiana soon learned to shudder at his gaze. It needed but a glance with the peculiar expression that his face often wore to change the roses of her cheek into a death-like paleness, amid which the crimson hand was brought strongly out, like a bas relief of ruby on the whitest marble.

Late one night, when the lights were growing dim so as hardly to betray the 10
stain on the poor wife's cheek, she herself, for the first time, voluntarily took up the subject.

"Do you remember, my dear Aylmer," said she, with a feeble attempt at a smile, "have you any recollection, of a dream last night about this odious hand?"

"None! none whatever!" replied Aylmer, starting; but then he added, in a dry, cold tone, affected for the sake of concealing the real depth of his emotion, "I might well dream of it; for, before I fell asleep, it had taken a pretty firm hold of my fancy."

"And you did dream of it?" continued Georgiana, hastily; for she dreaded lest a gush of tears should interrupt what she had to say. "A terrible dream! I wonder that you can forget it. Is it possible to forget this one expression?—'It is in her

4. Eagerly, preferably.

heart now; we must have it out!' Reflect, my husband; for by all means I would have you recall that dream."

The mind is in a sad state when Sleep, the all-involving, cannot confine her specters within the dim region of her sway, but suffers them to break forth, affrighting this actual life with secrets that perchance belong to a deeper one. Aylmer now remembered his dream. He had fancied himself with his servant Aminadab attempting an operation for the removal of the birth-mark; but the deeper went the knife, the deeper sank the hand, until at length its tiny grasp appeared to have caught hold of Georgiana's heart; whence, however, her husband was inexorably resolved to cut or wrench it away.

15 When the dream had shaped itself perfectly in his memory, Aylmer sat in his wife's presence with a guilty feeling. Truth often finds its way to the mind close muffled in robes of sleep, and then speaks with uncompromising directness of matters in regard to which we practice an unconscious self-deception during our waking moments. Until now he had not been aware of the tyrannizing influence acquired by one idea over his mind, and of the lengths which he might find in his heart to go for the sake of giving himself peace.

"Aylmer," resumed Georgiana, solemnly, "I know not what may be the cost to both of us to rid me of this fatal birth-mark. Perhaps its removal may cause cureless deformity; or it may be the stain goes as deep as life itself. Again: do we know that there is a possibility, on any terms, of unclasping the firm gripe of this little hand which was laid upon me before I came into the world?"

"Dearest Georgiana, I have spent much thought upon the subject," hastily interrupted Aylmer. "I am convinced of the perfect practicability of its removal."

"If there be the remotest possibility of it," continued Georgiana, "let the attempt be made, at whatever risk. Danger is nothing to me; for life, while this hateful mark makes me the object of your horror and disgust—life is a burden which I would fling down with joy. Either remove this dreadful hand, or take my wretched life! You have deep science. All the world bears witness of it. You have achieved great wonders. Cannot you remove this little, little mark, which I cover with the tips of two small fingers? Is this beyond your power, for the sake of your own peace, and to save your poor wife from madness?"

"Noblest, dearest, tenderest wife," cried Aylmer, rapturously, "doubt not my power. I have already given this matter the deepest thought—thought which might almost have enlightened me to create a being less perfect than yourself. Georgiana, you have led me deeper than ever into the heart of science. I feel myself fully competent to render this dear cheek as faultless as its fellow; and then, most beloved, what will be my triumph when I shall have corrected what Nature left imperfect in her fairest work! Even Pygmalion,[5] when his sculptured woman assumed life, felt not greater ecstasy than mine will be."

20 "It is resolved, then," said Georgiana, faintly smiling. "And, Aylmer, spare me not, though you should find the birth-mark take refuge in my heart at last."

Her husband tenderly kissed her cheek—her right cheek—not that which bore the impress of the crimson hand.

5. Pygmalion was a legendary artist of Cyprus who fell in love with the statue he made of a beautiful woman; in Ovid's *Metamorphoses*, she comes to life.

The next day Aylmer apprised his wife of a plan that he had formed whereby he might have opportunity for the intense thought and constant watchfulness which the proposed operation would require; while Georgiana, likewise, would enjoy the perfect repose essential to its success. They were to seclude themselves in the extensive apartments occupied by Aylmer as a laboratory, and where, during his toilsome youth, he had made discoveries in the elemental powers of Nature that had roused the admiration of all the learned societies in Europe. Seated calmly in this laboratory, the pale philosopher had investigated the secrets of the highest cloud-region and of the profoundest mines; he had satisfied himself of the causes that kindled and kept alive the fires of the volcano; and had explained the mystery of fountains, and how it is that they gush forth, some so bright and pure, and others with such rich medicinal virtues, from the dark bosom of the earth. Here, too, at an earlier period, he had studied the wonders of the human frame, and attempted to fathom the very process by which Nature assimilates all her precious influences from earth and air, and from the spiritual world, to create and foster man, her masterpiece. The latter pursuit, however, Aylmer had long laid aside in unwilling recognition of the truth—against which all seekers sooner or later stumble—that our great creative Mother, while she amuses us with apparently working in the broadest sunshine, is yet severely careful to keep her own secrets, and, in spite of her pretended openness, shows us nothing but results. She permits us, indeed, to mar, but seldom to mend, and, like a jealous patentee, on no account to make. Now, however, Aylmer resumed these half-forgotten investigations; not, of course, with such hopes or wishes as first suggested them; but because they involved much physiological truth and lay in the path of his proposed scheme for the treatment of Georgiana.

As he led her over the threshold of the laboratory Georgiana was cold and tremulous. Aylmer looked cheerfully into her face, with intent to reassure her, but was so startled with the intense glow of the birth-mark upon the whiteness of her cheek that he could not restrain a strong convulsive shudder. His wife fainted.

"Aminadab! Aminadab!" shouted Aylmer, stamping violently on the floor.

Forthwith there issued from an inner apartment a man of low stature, but bulky frame, with shaggy hair hanging about his visage, which was grimed with the vapors of the furnace. This personage had been Aylmer's underworker during his whole scientific career, and was admirably fitted for that office by his great mechanical readiness, and the skill with which, while incapable of comprehending a single principle, he executed all the details of his master's experiments. With his vast strength, his shaggy hair, his smoky aspect, and the indescribable earthiness that incrusted him, he seemed to represent man's physical nature; while Aylmer's slender figure, and pale, intellectual face, were no less apt a type of the spiritual element.

"Throw open the door of the boudoir, Aminadab," said Aylmer, "and burn a pastil."[6]

"Yes, master," answered Aminadab, looking intently at the lifeless form of Georgiana; and then he muttered to himself. "If she were my wife, I'd never part with that birth-mark."

6. Pastille, a lozenge or tablet of medicinal incense.

When Georgiana recovered consciousness she found herself breathing an atmosphere of penetrating fragrance, the gentle potency of which had recalled her from her death-like faintness. The scene around her looked like enchantment. Aylmer had converted those smoky, dingy, somber rooms, where he had spent his brightest years in recondite pursuits, into a series of beautiful apartments not unfit to be the secluded abode of a lovely woman. The walls were hung with gorgeous curtains, which imparted the combination of grandeur and grace that no other species of adornment can achieve; and, as they fell from the ceiling to the floor, their rich and ponderous folds, concealing all angles and straight lines, appeared to shut in the scene from infinite space. For aught Georgiana knew, it might be a pavilion among the clouds. And Aylmer, excluding the sunshine, which would have interfered with his chemical processes, had supplied its place with perfumed lamps, emitting flames of various hue, but all uniting in a soft, impurpled radiance. He now knelt by his wife's side, watching her earnestly, but without alarm; for he was confident in his science, and felt that he could draw a magic circle round her within which no evil might intrude.

"Where am I? Ah, I remember," said Georgiana, faintly; and she placed her hand over her cheek to hide the terrible mark from her husband's eyes.

"Fear not, dearest!" exclaimed he. "Do not shrink from me! Believe me, Georgiana, I even rejoice in this single imperfection, since it will be such a rapture to remove it."

"O, spare me!" sadly replied his wife. "Pray do not look at it again. I never can forget that convulsive shudder."

In order to soothe Georgiana, and, as it were, to release her mind from the burden of actual things, Aylmer now put in practice some of the light and playful secrets which science had taught him among its profounder lore. Airy figures, absolutely bodiless ideas, and forms of unsubstantial beauty came and danced before her, imprinting their momentary footsteps on beams of light. Though she had some indistinct idea of the method of these optical phenomena, still the illusion was almost perfect enough to warrant the belief that her husband possessed say over the spiritual world. Then again, when she felt a wish to look forth from her seclusion, immediately, as if her thoughts were answered, the procession of external existence flitted across a screen. The scenery and the figures of actual life were perfectly represented but with that bewitching yet indescribable difference which always makes a picture, an image, or a shadow so much more attractive than the original. When wearied of this, Aylmer bade her cast her eyes upon a vessel containing a quantity of earth. She did so, with little interest at first; but was soon startled to perceive the germ of a plant shooting upward from the soil. Then came the slender stalk; the leaves gradually unfolded themselves; and amid them was a perfect and lovely flower.

"It is magical!" cried Georgiana. "I dare not touch it."

"Nay, pluck it," answered Aylmer—"pluck it, and inhale its brief perfume while you may. The flower will wither in a few moments and leave nothing save its brown seed vessels; but thence may be perpetuated a race as ephemeral as itself."

But Georgiana had no sooner touched the flower than the whole plant suffered a blight, its leaves turning coal-black as if by the agency of fire.

"There was too powerful a stimulus," said Aylmer, thoughtfully.

To make up for this abortive experiment, he proposed to take her portrait by a scientific process of his own invention. It was to be affected by rays of light striking upon a polished plate of metal. Georgiana assented; but, on looking at the result, was affrighted to find the features of the portrait blurred and indefinable; while the minute figure of a hand appeared where the cheek should have been. Aylmer snatched the metallic plate and threw it into a jar of corrosive acid.

Soon, however, he forgot these mortifying failures. In the intervals of study and chemical experiment he came to her flushed and exhausted, but seemed invigorated by her presence, and spoke in glowing language of the resources of his art. He gave a history of the long dynasty of the alchemists, who spent so many ages in quest of the universal solvent by which the golden principle might be elicited from all things vile and base.[7] Aylmer appeared to believe that, by the plainest scientific logic, it was altogether within the limits of possibility to discover this long-sought medium. "But," he added, "a philosopher who should go deep enough to acquire the power would attain too lofty a wisdom to stoop to the exercise of it." Not less singular were his opinions in regard to the elixir vitae.[8] He more than intimated that it was at his option to concoct a liquid that should prolong life for years, perhaps interminably; but that it would produce a discord in Nature which all the world, and chiefly the quaffer of the immortal nostrum, would find cause to curse.

"Aylmer, are you in earnest?" asked Georgiana, looking at him with amazement and fear. "It is terrible to possess such power, or even to dream of possessing it."

"O, do not tremble, my love," said her husband. "I would not wrong either you or myself by working such inharmonious effects upon our lives; but I would have you consider how trifling, in comparison, is the skill requisite to remove this little hand."

At the mention of the birth-mark, Georgiana, as usual, shrank as if a red-hot iron had touched her cheek.

Again Aylmer applied himself to his labors. She could hear his voice in the distant furnace-room giving directions to Aminadab, whose harsh, uncouth, misshapen tones were audible in response, more like the grunt or growl of a brute than human speech. After hours of absence, Aylmer reappeared and proposed that she should now examine his cabinet of chemical products and natural treasures of the earth. Among the former he showed her a small vial, in which, he remarked, was contained a gentle yet most powerful fragrance, capable of impregnating all the breezes that blow across a kingdom. They were of inestimable value, the contents of that little vial; and, as he said so, he threw some of the perfume into the air and filled the room with piercing and invigorating delight.

"And what is this?" asked Georgiana, pointing to a small crystal globe containing a gold-colored liquid. "It is so beautiful to the eye that I could imagine it the elixir of life."

"In one sense it is," replied Aylmer; "or rather, the elixir of immortality. It is the most precious poison that ever was concocted in this world. By its aid I could apportion the lifetime of any mortal at whom you might point your finger.

7. Before the advent of modern chemistry, alchemists studied the properties of matter in a search for spiritual essences and the secret of transforming base metals into gold.

8. Literally, the drink or potion of life (Latin), imagined to give immortality.

The strength of the dose would determine whether he were to linger out years, or drop dead in the midst of a breath. No king on his guarded throne could keep his life if I, in my private station, should deem that the welfare of millions justified me in depriving him of it."

"Why do you keep such a terrific drug?" inquired Georgiana, in horror.

"Do not mistrust me, dearest," said her husband, smiling; "its virtuous potency is yet greater than its harmful one. But see! here is a powerful cosmetic. With a few drops of this in a vase of water, freckles may be washed away as easily as the hands are cleansed. A stronger infusion would take the blood out of the cheek, and leave the rosiest beauty a pale ghost."

"Is it with this lotion that you intend to bathe my cheek?" asked Georgiana, anxiously.

"O no," hastily replied her husband; "this is merely superficial. Your case demands a remedy that shall go deeper."

In his interviews with Georgiana, Aylmer generally made minute inquiries as to her sensations, and whether the confinement of the rooms and the temperature of the atmosphere agreed with her. These questions had such a particular drift that Georgiana began to conjecture that she was already subjected to certain physical influences, either breathed in with the fragrant air or taken with her food. She fancied likewise, but it might be altogether fancy, that there was a stirring up of her system—a strange, indefinite sensation creeping through her veins, and tingling, half painfully, half pleasurably, at her heart. Still, whenever she dared to look into the mirror, there she beheld herself pale as a white rose and with the crimson birth-mark stamped upon her cheek. Not even Aylmer now hated it so much as she.

To dispel the tedium of the hours which her husband found it necessary to devote to the processes of combination and analysis, Georgiana turned over the volumes of his scientific library. In many dark old tomes she met with chapters full of romance and poetry. They were the works of the philosophers of the Middle Ages, such as Albertus Magnus, Cornelius Agrippa, Paracelsus, and the famous friar who created the prophetic Brazen Head.[9] All these antique naturalists stood in advance of their centuries, yet were imbued with some of their credulity, and therefore were believed, and perhaps imagined themselves to have acquired from the investigation of Nature a power above Nature, and from physics a sway over the spiritual world. Hardly less curious and imaginative were the early volumes of the Transactions of the Royal Society,[1] in which the members, knowing little of the limits of natural possibility, were continually recording wonders or proposing methods whereby wonders might be wrought.

But, to Georgiana, the most engrossing volume was a large folio from her husband's own hand, in which he had recorded every experiment of his scientific career, its original aim, the methods adopted for its development, and its final success or failure, with the circumstances to which either event was attributable.

9. The Brazen Head, a brass bust of a man, was supposed to be able to answer any question; the "famous friar" is Roger Bacon (c. 1214–94), an English natural philosopher, as scientists were then called. Albertus Magnus (1193/1206–80), Agrippa (1496–1535), and Paracelsus (1493–1541) were all European experimenters reputed to have near-magical powers in alchemy or astrology.

1. *The Philosophical Transactions of the Royal Society* is the oldest scientific journal in English, published since 1665.

The book, in truth, was both the history and emblem of his ardent, ambitious, imaginative, yet practical and laborious life. He handled physical details as if there were nothing beyond them; yet spiritualized them all, and redeemed himself from materialism by his strong and eager aspiration towards the infinite. In his grasp the veriest clod of earth assumed a soul. Georgiana, as she read, reverenced Aylmer and loved him more profoundly than ever, but with a less entire dependence on his judgment than heretofore. Much as he had accomplished, she could not but observe that his most splendid successes were almost invariably failures, if compared with the ideal at which he aimed. His brightest diamonds were the merest pebbles, and felt to be so by himself, in comparison with the inestimable gems which lay hidden beyond his reach. The volume, rich with achievements that had won renown for its author, was yet as melancholy a record as ever mortal hand had penned. It was the sad confession and continual exemplification of the shortcomings of the composite man, the spirit burdened with clay and working in matter, and of the despair that assails the higher nature at finding itself so miserably thwarted by the earthly part. Perhaps every man of genius, in whatever sphere, might recognize the image of his own experience in Aylmer's journal.

So deeply did these reflections affect Georgiana that she laid her face upon the open volume and burst into tears. In this situation she was found by her husband.

"It is dangerous to read in a sorcerer's books," said he with a smile, though his countenance was uneasy and displeased. "Georgiana, there are pages in that volume which I can scarcely glance over and keep my senses. Take heed lest it prove as detrimental to you."

"It has made me worship you more than ever," said she.

55 "Ah, wait for this one success," rejoined he, "then worship me if you will. I shall deem myself hardly unworthy of it. But come, I have sought you for the luxury of your voice. Sing to me, dearest."

So she poured out the liquid music of her voice to quench the thirst of his spirit. He then took his leave with a boyish exuberance of gayety, assuring her that her seclusion would endure but a little longer, and that the result was already certain. Scarcely had he departed when Georgiana felt irresistibly impelled to follow him. She had forgotten to inform Aylmer of a symptom which for two or three hours past had begun to excite her attention. It was a sensation in the fatal birth-mark, not painful, but which induced a restlessness throughout her system. Hastening after her husband, she intruded for the first time into the laboratory.

The first thing that struck her eye was the furnace, that hot and feverish worker, with the intense glow of its fire, which by the quantities of soot clustered above it seemed to have been burning for ages. There was a distilling-apparatus in full operation. Around the room were retorts, tubes, cylinders, crucibles, and other apparatus of chemical research. An electrical machine stood ready for immediate use. The atmosphere felt oppressively close, and was tainted with gaseous odors which had been tormented forth by the processes of science. The severe and homely simplicity of the apartment, with its naked walls and brick pavement, looked strange, accustomed as Georgiana had become to the fantastic elegance of her boudoir. But what chiefly, indeed almost solely, drew her attention, was the aspect of Aylmer himself.

He was pale as death, anxious and absorbed, and hung over the furnace as if it depended upon his utmost watchfulness whether the liquid which it was distilling should be the draught of immortal happiness or misery. How different from the sanguine and joyous mien that he had assumed for Georgiana's encouragement!

"Carefully now, Aminadab; carefully, thou human machine; carefully, thou man of clay," muttered Aylmer, more to himself than his assistant. "Now, if there be a thought too much or too little, it is all over."

"Ho! ho!" mumbled Aminadab. "Look, master! look!"

Aylmer raised his eyes hastily, and at first reddened, then grew paler than ever, on beholding Georgiana. He rushed towards her and seized her arm with a gripe that left the print of his fingers upon it.

"Why do you come hither? Have you no trust in your husband?" cried he, impetuously. "Would you throw the blight of that fatal birth-mark over my labors? It is not well done. Go, prying woman! go!"

"Nay, Aylmer," said Georgiana with the firmness of which she possessed no stinted endowment, "it is not you that have a right to complain. You mistrust your wife; you have concealed the anxiety with which you watch the development of this experiment. Think not so unworthily of me, my husband. Tell me all the risk we run, and fear not that I shall shrink; for my share in it is far less than your own."

"No, no, Georgiana!" said Aylmer, impatiently; "it must not be."

"I submit," replied she, calmly. "And, Aylmer, I shall quaff whatever draught you bring me; but it will be on the same principle that would induce me to take a dose of poison if offered by your hand."

"My noble wife," said Aylmer, deeply moved, "I knew not the height and depth of your nature until now. Nothing shall be concealed. Know, then, that this crimson hand, superficial as it seems, has clutched its grasp into your being with a strength of which I had no previous conception. I have already administered agents powerful enough to do aught except to change your entire physical system. Only one thing remains to be tried. If that fail us we are ruined."

"Why did you hesitate to tell me this?" asked she.

"Because, Georgiana," said Aylmer, in a low voice, "there is danger."

"Danger? There is but one danger—that this horrible stigma shall be left upon my cheek!" cried Georgiana. "Remove it, remove it, whatever be the cost, or we shall both go mad!"

"Heaven knows your words are too true," said Aylmer, sadly. "And now, dearest, return to your boudoir. In a little while all will be tested."

He conducted her back and took leave of her with a solemn tenderness which spoke far more than his words how much was now at stake. After his departure Georgiana became rapt in musings. She considered the character of Aylmer, and did it completer justice than at any previous moment. Her heart exulted, while it trembled, at his honorable love—so pure and lofty that it would accept nothing less than perfection, nor miserably make itself contented with an earthlier nature than he had dreamed of. She felt how much more precious was such a sentiment than that meaner kind which would have borne with the imperfection for her sake, and have been guilty of treason to holy love by degrading its perfect idea to the level of the actual; and with her whole spirit she prayed that, for a single moment, she might satisfy his highest and deepest conception. Longer than one moment she well knew it could not be; for his spirit was ever on the march, ever ascending, and each instant required something that was beyond the scope of the instant before.

The sound of her husband's footsteps aroused her. He bore a crystal goblet containing a liquor colorless as water, but bright enough to be the draught of immortality. Aylmer was pale; but it seemed rather the consequence of a highly wrought state of mind and tension of spirit than of fear or doubt.

"The concoction of the draught has been perfect," said he, in answer to Georgiana's look. "Unless all my science have deceived me, it cannot fail."

"Save on your account, my dearest Aylmer," observed his wife, "I might wish to put off this birth-mark of mortality by relinquishing mortality itself in preference to any other mode. Life is but a sad possession to those who have attained precisely the degree of moral advancement at which I stand. Were I weaker and blinder, it might be happiness. Were I stronger, it might be endured hopefully. But, being what I find myself, methinks I am of all mortals the most fit to die."

"You are fit for heaven without tasting death!" replied her husband. "But why do we speak of dying? The draught cannot fail. Behold its effect upon this plant."

On the window-seat there stood a geranium diseased with yellow blotches, which had overspread all its leaves. Aylmer poured a small quantity of the liquid upon the soil in which it grew. In a little time, when the roots of the plant had taken up the moisture, the unsightly blotches began to be extinguished in a living verdure.

"There needed no proof," said Georgiana, quietly. "Give me the goblet. I joyfully stake all upon your word."

"Drink, then, thou lofty creature!" exclaimed Aylmer, with fervid admiration. "There is no taint of imperfection on thy spirit. Thy sensible frame, too, shall soon be all perfect."

She quaffed the liquid and returned the goblet to his hand.

"It is grateful," said she, with a placid smile. "Methinks it is like water from a heavenly fountain; for it contains I know not what of unobtrusive fragrance and deliciousness. It allays a feverish thirst that had parched me for many days. Now, dearest, let me sleep. My earthly senses are closing over my spirit like the leaves around the heart of a rose at sunset."

She spoke the last words with a gentle reluctance, as if it required almost more energy than she could command to pronounce the faint and lingering syllables. Scarcely had they loitered through her lips ere she was lost in slumber. Aylmer sat by her side, watching her aspect with the emotions proper to a man, the whole value of whose existence was involved in the process now to be tested. Mingled with this mood, however, was the philosophic investigation characteristic of the man of science. Not the minutest symptom escaped him. A heightened flush of the cheek, a slight irregularity of breath, a quiver of the eyelid, a hardly perceptible tremor through the frame—such were the details which, as the moments passed, he wrote down in his folio volume. Intense thought had set its stamp upon every previous page of that volume; but the thoughts of years were all concentrated upon the last.

While thus employed, he failed not to gaze often at the fatal hand, and not without a shudder. Yet once, by a strange and unaccountable impulse, he pressed it with his lips. His spirit recoiled, however, in the very act; and Georgiana, out of the midst of her deep sleep, moved uneasily and murmured, as if in remonstrance. Again Aylmer resumed his watch. Nor was it without avail. The crimson hand, which at first had been strongly visible upon the marble paleness of Georgiana's cheek, now grew more faintly outlined. She remained not less pale than ever; but the birth-mark, with every breath that came and went, lost somewhat of its former distinctness. Its presence had been awful; its departure was more awful still. Watch the stain of the rainbow fading out of the sky, and you will know how that mysterious symbol passed away.

"By Heaven! it is wellnigh gone!" said Aylmer to himself, in almost irrepressible ecstasy. "I can scarcely trace it now. Success! success! And now it is like the faintest rose-color. The lightest flush of blood across her cheek would overcome it. But she is so pale!"

He drew aside the window-curtain and suffered the light of natural day to fall into the room and rest upon her cheek. At the same time he heard a gross, hoarse chuckle, which he had long known as his servant Aminadab's expression of delight.

85 "Ah, clod! ah, earthly mass!" cried Aylmer, laughing in a sort of frenzy, "you have served me well! Matter and spirit—earth and heaven—have both done their part in this! Laugh, thing of the senses! You have earned the right to laugh."

These exclamations broke Georgiana's sleep. She slowly unclosed her eyes and gazed into the mirror which her husband had arranged for that purpose. A faint smile flitted over her lips when she recognized how barely perceptible was now that crimson hand which had once blazed forth with such disastrous brilliancy as to scare away all their happiness. But then her eyes sought Aylmer's face with a trouble and anxiety that he could by no means account for.

"My poor Aylmer!" murmured she.

"Poor? Nay, richest, happiest, most favored!" exclaimed he. "My peerless bride, it is successful! You are perfect!"

"My poor Aylmer," she repeated, with a more than human tenderness, "you have aimed loftily; you have done nobly. Do not repent that, with so high and pure a feeling, you have rejected the best the earth could offer. Aylmer, dearest Aylmer, I am dying!"

90 Alas! it was too true! The fatal hand had grappled with the mystery of life, and was the bond by which an angelic spirit kept itself in union with a mortal frame. As the last crimson tint of the birth-mark—that sole token of human imperfection—faded from her cheek, the parting breath of the now perfect woman passed into the atmosphere, and her soul, lingering a moment near her husband, took its heavenward flight. Then a hoarse, chuckling laugh was heard again! Thus ever does the gross fatality of earth exult in its invariable triumph over the immortal essence which, in this dim sphere of half-development, demands the completeness of a higher state. Yet, had Aylmer reached a profounder wisdom, he need not thus have flung away the happiness which would have woven his mortal life of the self-same texture with the celestial. The momentary circumstance was too strong for him; he failed to look beyond the shadowy scope of time, and, living once for all in eternity, to find the perfect future in the present.

1843

QUESTIONS

1. What difference would it make if the mark on Georgiana's cheek were shaped like a fish, a heart, or an irregular oval? Why (and when) does the mark appear redder or more visible or faint? If the birthmark is explicitly a "symbol of imperfection" (par. 9), what *kinds* of imperfection does it represent?
2. Aylmer says to his wife, "Even Pygmalion, when his sculptured woman assumed life, felt not greater ecstasy than mine will be" (par. 19). How does this literary allusion to the myth of Pygmalion enhance the meaning of THE BIRTH-MARK? Is this allusion ironic, given what happens to Alymer's project to make his wife perfect?
3. Look closely at the settings of the story, from the laboratory to the boudoir. Note the similes, metaphors, and other figures of speech that help characterize these places. How do these different patterns of imagery contribute to the symbolism of the story? to an allegorical reading of the story?

A. S. BYATT
(b. 1936)

The Thing in the Forest

The oldest of four children (and half sister of novelist Margaret Drabble), Antonia Susan Byatt was born in Sheffield, England; graduated from Newnham College, Cambridge; and worked toward a doctorate in English literature at Bryn Mawr College in Pennsylvania and at Oxford University. In the early 1960s Byatt began teaching at the University of London and published her first novel, *The Shadow of the Sun* (1964). By far the most successful of the numerous works that followed is *Possession: A Romance* (1990), the Booker Prize–winning best seller that inspired a 1996 film starring Gwyneth Paltrow. Interweaving the story of the unlikely romance between two Victorian poets reminiscent of Christina Rossetti and Robert Browning, on the one hand, with the tale of the two modern academics who uncover it, on the other, along with poems and tales ostensibly written by its protagonists, *Possession* is simultaneously a fascinating blend of literary genres—from detective and historical fiction to romance, fairy tale, and dramatic monologue—and a reflection *on* literature—how we use it to make sense of and thus "possess" our present and our past and why it often takes "possession" of us. In this, it resembles other Byatt novels such as *The Children's Book* (2009), the novellas in *Angels and Insects* (1992), and many of her short stories. Made a Dame Commander of the British Empire in 1999, Dame Byatt is also a distinguished literary critic who has written books on novelist Iris Murdoch, poets William Wordsworth and Samuel Taylor Coleridge, as well as *Portraits in Fiction* (2001), a collection of biographical essays.

There were once two little girls who saw, or believed they saw, a thing in a forest. The two little girls were evacuees, who had been sent away from the city by train with a large number of other children.[1] They all had their names attached to their coats with safety pins, and they carried little bags or satchels, and the regulation gas mask. They wore knitted scarves and bonnets or caps, and many had knitted gloves attached to long tapes that ran along their sleeves, inside their coats, and over their shoulders and out, so that they could leave their ten woollen fingers dangling, like a spare pair of hands, like a scarecrow. They all had bare legs and scuffed shoes and wrinkled socks. Most had wounds on their knees in varying stages of freshness and scabbiness. They were at the age when children fall often and their knees were unprotected. With their suitcases, some of which were almost too big to carry, and their other impedimenta, a doll, a toy car, a comic, they were like a disorderly dwarf regiment, stomping along the platform.

The two little girls had not met before, and made friends on the train. They shared a square of chocolate, and took alternate bites at an apple. Their names were Penny and Primrose. Penny was thin and dark and taller, possibly older, than Primrose, who was plump and blond and curly. Primrose had bitten nails, and a velvet collar on her dressy green coat. Penny had a bloodless transparent paleness, a touch of blue in her fine lips. Neither of them knew where they were going, nor how long the journey might take. They did not even know why they were going, since neither of their mothers had quite known how to explain the danger to them. How do you say to your child, I am sending you away, because enemy bombs may fall out of the sky, but I myself am staying here, in what I believe may be daily danger of burning, being buried alive, gas, and ultimately perhaps a gray army rolling in on tanks over the suburbs? So the mothers (who did not resemble each other at all) behaved alike, and explained nothing—it was easier. Their daughters, they knew, were little girls, who would not be able to understand or imagine.

The girls discussed whether it was a sort of holiday or a sort of punishment, or a bit of both. Both had the idea that these were all perhaps not very good children, possibly being sent away for that reason. They were pleased to be able to define each other as "nice." They would stick together, they agreed.

The train crawled sluggishly farther and farther away from the city and their homes. It was not a clean train—the upholstery of their carriage had the dank smell of unwashed trousers, and the gusts of hot steam rolling backward past their windows were full of specks of flimsy ash, and sharp grit, and occasionally fiery sparks that pricked face and fingers like hot needles if you opened the window. It was very noisy, too, whenever it picked up a little speed. The windowpanes were both grimy and misted up. The train stopped frequently, and when it stopped they used their gloves to wipe rounds, through which they peered out at flooded fields, furrowed hillsides, and tiny stations whose names were carefully blacked out, whose platforms were empty of life.

5 The children did not know that the namelessness was meant to baffle or delude an invading army. They felt—they did not think it out, but somewhere inside them the idea sprouted—that the erasure was because of them, because

1. The story takes place during the Blitz—that is, during the period (1940–41) when British cities were frequently bombed by German warplanes. Many children were evacuated from cities to safer locations in the countryside.

they were not meant to know where they were going or, like Hansel and Gretel, to find the way back. They did not speak to each other of this anxiety, but began the kind of conversation children have about things they really dislike, things that upset, or disgust, or frighten them. Semolina pudding with its grainy texture, mushy peas, fat on roast meat. Having your head held roughly back over the basin to have your hair washed, with cold water running down inside your liberty bodice. Gangs in playgrounds. They felt the pressure of all the other alien children in all the other carriages as a potential gang. They shared another square of chocolate, and licked their fingers, and looked out at a great white goose flapping its wings beside an inky pond.

The sky grew dark gray and in the end the train halted. The children got out, and lined up in a crocodile,[2] and were led to a mud-colored bus. Penny and Primrose managed to get a seat together, although it was over the wheel, and both of them began to feel sick as the bus bumped along snaking country lanes, under whipping branches, with torn strips of thin cloud streaming across a full moon.

They were billeted in a mansion commandeered from its owner. The children were told they were there temporarily, until families were found to take them. Penny and Primrose held hands, and said to each other that it would be wizard if they could go to the same family, because at least they would have each other. They didn't say anything to the rather tired-looking ladies who were ordering them about, because, with the cunning of little children, they knew that requests were most often counterproductive—adults liked saying no. They imagined possible families into which they might be thrust. They did not discuss what they imagined, as these pictures, like the black station signs, were too frightening, and words might make some horror solid, in some magical way. Penny, who was a reading child, imagined Victorian dark pillars of severity, like Jane Eyre's Mr. Brocklehurst, or David Copperfield's Mr. Murdstone. Primrose imagined—she didn't know why—a fat woman with a white cap and round red arms who smiled nicely but made the children wear sacking aprons and scrub the steps and the stove. "It's like we were orphans," she said to Penny. "But we're not." Penny said, "If we manage to stick together. . . ."

The great house had a double flight of imposing stairs to its front door, and carved griffins and unicorns on its balustrade. There was no lighting, because of the blackout. All the windows were shuttered. The children trudged up the staircase in their crocodile, and were given supper (Irish stew and rice pudding with a dollop of blood-red jam) before going to bed in long makeshift dormitories, where once servants had slept. They had camp beds (military issue) and gray shoddy blankets. Penny and Primrose got beds together but couldn't get a corner. They queued[3] to brush their teeth in a tiny washroom, and both suffered (again without speaking) suffocating anxiety about what would happen if they wanted to pee in the middle of the night. They also suffered from a fear that in the dark the other children would start laughing and rushing and teasing, and turn themselves into a gang. But that did not happen. Everyone was tired and anxious and orphaned. An uneasy silence, a drift of perturbed

2. Group of people lined up two by two.
3. Lined up.

sleep, came over them all. The only sounds—from all parts of the great dormitory, it seemed—were suppressed snuffles and sobs, from faces pressed into thin pillows.

When daylight came, things seemed, as they mostly do, brighter and better. The children were given breakfast in a large vaulted room, at trestle tables, porridge made with water, and a dab of the red jam, heavy cups of strong tea. Then they were told they could go out and play until lunchtime. Children in those days—wherever they came from—were not closely watched, were allowed to come and go freely, and those evacuated children were not herded into any kind of holding pen or transit camp. They were told they should be back for lunch at twelve-thirty, by which time those in charge hoped to have sorted out their provisional future lives. It was not known how they would know when it was twelve-thirty, but it was expected that—despite the fact that few of them had wristwatches—they would know how to keep an eye on the time. It was what they were used to.

Penny and Primrose went out together, in their respectable coats and laced shoes, onto the terrace. The terrace appeared to them to be vast. It was covered with a fine layer of damp gravel, stained here and there bright green, or invaded by mosses. Beyond it was a stone balustrade, with a staircase leading down to a lawn. Across the lawn was a sculpted yew hedge. In the middle of the hedge was a wicket gate, and beyond the gate were trees. A forest, the little girls said to themselves.

"Let's go into the forest," said Penny, as though the sentence were required of her.

Primrose hesitated. Most of the other children were running up and down the terrace. Some boys were kicking a ball on the grass.

"O.K.," said Primrose. "We needn't go far."

"No. I've never been in a forest."

"Nor me."

"We ought to look at it, while we've got the opportunity," said Penny.

There was a very small child—one of the smallest—whose name, she told everyone, was Alys. With a "y," she told those who could spell, and those who couldn't, which surely included herself. She was barely out of nappies.[4] She was quite extraordinarily pretty, pink and white, with large pale-blue eyes, and sparse little golden curls all over her head and neck, through which her pink skin could be seen. Nobody seemed to be in charge of her, no elder brother or sister. She had not quite managed to wash the tearstains from her dimpled cheeks.

She had made several attempts to attach herself to Penny and Primrose. They did not want her. They were excited about meeting and liking each other. She said now, "I'm coming, too, into the forest."

"No, you aren't," said Primrose.

"You are too little, you must stay here," said Penny.

"You'll get lost," said Primrose.

"You won't get lost. I'll come with you," said the little creature, with an engaging smile, made for loving parents and grandparents.

4. Diapers.

"We don't want you, you see," said Primrose.

"It's for your own good," said Penny.

Alys went on smiling hopefully, the smile becoming more of a mask.

"It will be all right," said Alys.

"Run," said Primrose.

They ran; they ran down the steps and across the lawn, and through the gate, into the forest. They didn't look back. They were long-legged little girls. The trees were silent round them, holding out their branches to the sun.

Primrose touched the warm skin of the nearest saplings, taking off her gloves to feel the cracks and knots. Penny looked into the thick of the forest. There was undergrowth—a mat of brambles and bracken. There were no obvious paths. Dark and light came and went, inviting and mysterious, as the wind pushed clouds across the face of the sun.

"We have to be careful not to get lost," she said. "In stories, people make marks on tree trunks, or unroll a thread, or leave a trail of white pebbles—to find their way back."

"We needn't go out of sight of the gate," said Primrose. "We could just explore a little bit."

They set off, very slowly. They went on tiptoe, making their own narrow passages through the undergrowth, which sometimes came as high as their thin shoulders. They were urban, and unaccustomed to silence. Then they began to hear small sounds. The chatter and repeated lilt and alarm of invisible birds, high up, further in. Rustling in dry leaves. Slitherings, dry coughs, sharp cracks. They went on, pointing out to each other creepers draped with glistening berries, crimson, black, and emerald, little crops of toadstools, some scarlet, some ghostly pale, some a dead-flesh purple, some like tiny parasols—and some like pieces of meat protruding from tree trunks. They met blackberries, but didn't pick them, in case in this place they were dangerous or deceptive. They admired from a safe distance the stiff upright fruiting rods of the lords-and-ladies,[5] packed with fat red berries.

Did they hear it first or smell it? Both sound and scent were at first infinitesimal and dispersed. They gave the strange impression of moving in—in waves—from the whole perimeter of the forest. Both increased very slowly in intensity, and both were mixed, a sound and a smell fabricated of many disparate sounds and smells. A crunching, a crackling, a crushing, a heavy thumping, combining with threshing and thrashing, and added to that a gulping, heaving, boiling, bursting, steaming sound, full of bubbles and farts, piffs and explosions, swallowings and wallowings. The smell was worse, and more aggressive, than the sound. It was a liquid smell of putrefaction, the smell of maggoty things at the bottom of untended dustbins, blocked drains, mixed with the smell of bad eggs, and of rotten carpets and ancient polluted bedding. The ordinary forest smells and sounds were extinguished. The two little girls looked at each other, and took each other's hand. Speechlessly and instinctively, they crouched down behind a fallen tree trunk, and trembled, as the thing came into view.

5. Wild arum, a flowering perennial common to southern Britain.

Its head appeared to form, or first become visible in the distance, between the trees. Its face—which was triangular—appeared like a rubbery or fleshy mask over a shapeless sprouting bulb of a head, like a monstrous turnip. Its color was the color of flayed flesh, pitted with wormholes, and its expression was neither wrath nor greed but pure misery. Its most defined feature was a vast mouth, pulled down and down at the corners, tight with a kind of pain. Its lips were thin, and raised, like welts from whip-strokes. It had blind, opaque white eyes, fringed with fleshy lashes and brows like the feelers of sea anemones. Its face was close to the ground and moved toward the children between its forearms, which were squat, thick, powerful, and akimbo, like a cross between a washer-woman's and a primeval dragon's. The flesh on these forearms was glistening and mottled.

The rest of its very large body appeared to be glued together, like still wet papier-mâché, or the carapace of stones and straws and twigs worn by caddis flies underwater. It had a tubular shape, as a turd has a tubular shape, a provisional amalgam. It was made of rank meat, and decaying vegetation, but it also trailed veils and prostheses of man-made materials, bits of wire netting, foul dishcloths, wire-wool full of pan scrubbings, rusty nuts and bolts. It had feeble stubs and stumps of very slender legs, growing out of it at all angles, wavering and rippling like the suckered feet of a caterpillar or the squirming fringe of a centipede. On and on it came, bending and crushing whatever lay in its path, including bushes, though not substantial trees, which it wound between, awkwardly. The little girls observed, with horrified fascination, that when it met a sharp stone, or a narrow tree trunk, it allowed itself to be sliced through, flowed sluggishly round in two or three smaller worms, convulsed, and reunited. Its progress was apparently very painful, for it moaned and whined among its other burblings and belchings. They thought it could not see, or certainly could not see clearly. It and its stench passed within a few feet of their tree trunk, humping along, leaving behind it a trail of bloody slime and dead foliage.

Its end was flat and blunt, almost transparent, like some earthworms.

When it had gone, Penny and Primrose, kneeling on the moss and dead leaves, put their arms about each other, and hugged each other, shaking with dry sobs. Then they stood up, still silent, and stared together, hand in hand, at the trail of obliteration and destruction, which wound out of the forest and into it again. They went back, hand in hand, without looking behind them, afraid that the wicket gate, the lawn, the stone steps, the balustrade, the terrace, and the great house would be transmogrified, or simply not there. But the boys were still playing football on the lawn, a group of girls were skipping and singing shrilly on the gravel. They let go each other's hand, and went back in.

They did not speak to each other again.

The next day, they were separated and placed with strange families. Their stay in these families—Primrose was in a dairy farm, Penny was in a parsonage—did not in fact last very long, though then the time seemed slow motion and endless. Later, Primrose remembered the sound of milk spurting in the pail, and Penny remembered the empty corsets of the Vicar's wife, hanging bony on the line. They remembered dandelion clocks, but you can remember those from anywhere, any time. They remembered the thing they had seen in the forest, on the contrary, in the way you remember those very few dreams—almost all nightmares—that have the quality of life itself. (Though what are dreams if not life itself?) They remembered too solid flesh, too precise a stink, a rattle and a soughing that thrilled the nerves and the cartilage of their growing ears. In the memory, as in such a dream, they felt, I cannot get out, this is a real thing in a real place.

They returned from evacuation, like many evacuees, so early that they then 40
lived through wartime in the city, bombardment, blitz, unearthly light and roaring, changed landscapes, holes in their world where the newly dead had been. Both lost their fathers. Primrose's father was in the Army, and was killed, very late in the war, on a crowded troop carrier sunk in the Far East. Penny's father, a much older man, was in the Auxiliary Fire Service, and died in a sheet of flame in the East India Docks on the Thames, pumping evaporating water from a puny coil of hose. They found it hard, after the war, to remember these different men. The claspers of memory could not grip the drowned and the burned. Primrose saw an inane grin under a khaki cap, because her mother had a snapshot. Penny thought she remembered her father, already gray-headed, brushing ash off his boots and trouser cuffs as he put on his tin hat to go out. She thought she remembered a quaver of fear in his tired face, and the muscles composing themselves into resolution. It was not much what either of them remembered.

After the war, their fates were still similar and dissimilar. Penny's widowed mother embraced grief, closed her face and her curtains. Primrose's mother married one of the many admirers she had had before the ship went down, gave birth to another five children, and developed varicose veins and a smoker's cough. She dyed her blond hair with peroxide when it faded. Both Primrose and Penny were only children who now, because of the war, lived in amputated or unreal families. Penny was a good student and in due course went to university, where she chose to study developmental psychology. Primrose had little education. She was always being kept off school to look after the others. She, too, dyed her blond curls with peroxide when they turned mousy and faded. She got fat as Penny got thin. Neither of them married. Penny became a child psychologist, working with the abused, the displaced, the disturbed. Primrose did this and that. She was a barmaid. She worked in a shop. She went to help at various church crèches and Salvation Army gatherings, and discovered she had a talent for storytelling. She became Aunty Primrose, with her own repertoire. She was employed to tell tales to kindergartens and entertain at children's parties. She was much in demand at Halloween, and had her own circle of bright-colored plastic chairs in a local shopping mall, where she kept an eye on the children of burdened women, keeping them safe, offering them just a frisson of fear and terror, which made them wriggle with pleasure.

The house in the country aged differently. During this period of time—while the little girls became women—it was handed over to the nation, which turned it into a living museum. Guided tours took place in it, at regulated times. During these tours, the ballroom and intimate drawing rooms were fenced off with crimson twisted ropes on little brass one-eyed pedestals. The bored and the curious peered in at four-poster beds and pink silk fauteuils,[6] at silver-framed

6. Armchairs.

photographs of wartime royalty, and crackling crazing[7] Renaissance and Enlightenment portraits. In the room where the evacuees had eaten their rationed meals, the history of the house was displayed, on posters, in glass cases, with helpful notices and opened copies of old diaries and records. There was no mention of the evacuees, whose presence appeared to have been too brief to have left any trace.

The two women met in this room on an autumn day in 1984. They had come with a group, walking in a chattering crocodile behind a guide. They prowled around the room, each alone with herself, in opposite directions, each without acknowledging the other's presence. Their mothers had died that spring, within a week of each other, though this coincidence was unknown to them. It had made both of them think of taking a holiday, and both had chosen that part of the world. Penny was wearing a charcoal trouser suit and a black velvet hat. Primrose wore a floral knit long jacket over a shell-pink cashmere sweater, over a rustling long skirt with an elastic waist, in a mustard-colored tapestry print. Her hips and bosom were bulky. Both of them, at the same moment, leaned over an image in a medieval-looking illustrated book. Primrose thought it was a very old book. Penny assumed it was nineteenth-century mock-medieval. It showed a knight, on foot, in a forest, lifting his sword to slay something. The knight shone on the rounded slope of the page, in the light, which caught the gilding on his helmet and sword belt. It was not possible to see what was being slain. This was because, both in the tangled vegetation of the image and in the way the book was displayed in the case, the enemy, or victim, was in shadows.

Neither of them could read the ancient (or pseudo-ancient) black letter of the text beside the illustration. There was a typed description, under the book. They had to lean forward to read it, and to see what was worming its way into, or out of, the deep spine of the book, and that was how each came to see the other's face, close up, in the glass, which was both transparent and reflective. Their transparent reflected faces lost detail—cracked lipstick, pouches, fine lines of wrinkles—and looked both younger and grayer, less substantial. And that is how they came to recognize each other, as they might not have done, plump face to bony face. They breathed each other's names—Penny, Primrose—and their breath misted the glass, obscuring the knight and his opponent. I could have died, I could have wet my knickers, said Penny and Primrose afterward to each other, and both experienced this still moment as pure, dangerous shock. They read the caption, which was about the Loathly Worm, which, tradition held, had infested the countryside and had been killed more than once by scions of that house—Sir Lionel, Sir Boris, Sir Guillem. The Worm, the typewriter had tapped out, was an English worm, not a European dragon, and, like most such worms, was wingless. In some sightings it was reported as having vestigial legs, hands, or feet. In others it was limbless. It had, in monstrous form, the capacity of common or garden worms to sprout new heads or trunks if it was divided, so that two worms, or more, replaced one. This was why it had been killed so often, yet reappeared. It had been reported travelling with a slithering pack of young ones, but these may have been only revitalized segments.

7. Sealed with varnish that, with age, has cracked in patterns.

45 Being English, they thought of tea. There was a tearoom in the great house, in a converted stable at the back. There they stood silently side by side, clutching floral plastic trays spread with briar roses, and purchased scones, superior raspberry jam in tiny jam jars, little plastic tubs of clotted cream. "You couldn't get cream or real jam in the war," said Primrose as they found a corner table. She said wartime rationing had made her permanently greedy, and thin Penny agreed it had—clotted cream was still a treat.

They watched each other warily, offering bland snippets of autobiography in politely hushed voices. Primrose thought Penny looked gaunt, and Penny thought Primrose looked raddled.[8] They established the skein of coincidences—dead fathers, unmarried status, child-caring professions, recently dead mothers. Circling like beaters,[9] they approached the covert thing in the forest. They discussed the great house, politely. Primrose admired the quality of the carpets. Penny said it was nice to see the old pictures back on the wall. Primrose said, Funny really, that there was all that history, but no sign that they, the children, that was, had ever been there. Funny, said Penny, that they should meet each other next to that book, with that picture. "Creepy," said Primrose in a light, light cobweb voice, not looking at Penny. "We saw that thing. When we went in the forest."

"Yes, we did," said Penny. "We saw it."

"Did you ever wonder," asked Primrose, "if we really saw it?"

"Never for a moment," said Penny. "That is, I don't know what it was, but I've always been quite sure we saw it."

50 "Does it change—do you remember all of it?"

"It was a horrible thing, and yes, I remember all of it, there isn't a bit of it I can manage to forget. Though I forget all sorts of things," said Penny, in a thin voice, a vanishing voice.

"And have you ever told anyone of it, spoken of it?" asked Primrose more urgently, leaning forward.

"No," said Penny. She had not. She said, "Who would believe it?"

"That's what I thought," said Primrose. "I didn't speak. But it stuck in my mind like a tapeworm in your gut. I think it did me no good."

55 "It did me no good either," said Penny. "No good at all. I've thought about it," she said to the aging woman opposite, whose face quivered under her dyed goldilocks. "I think, I think there are things that are real—more real than we are—but mostly we don't cross their paths, or they don't cross ours. Maybe at very bad times we get into their world, or notice what they are doing in ours."

Primrose nodded energetically. She looked as though sharing was solace, and Penny, to whom it was not solace, grimaced with pain.

"Sometimes I think that thing finished me off," Penny said to Primrose, a child's voice rising in a woman's gullet, arousing a little girl's scared smile, which wasn't a smile on Primrose's face.

Primrose said, "It did finish her off, that little one, didn't it? She got into its path, didn't she? And when it had gone by—she wasn't anywhere," said Primrose. "That was how it was?"

"Nobody ever asked where she was or looked for her," said Penny.

8. Frazzled.

9. Hunters who beat the bushes to drive out game.

"I wondered if we'd made her up," said Primrose. "But I didn't, we didn't."

"Her name was Alys."

"With a 'y.'"

There had been a mess, a disgusting mess, they remembered, but no particular sign of anything that might have been, or been part of, or belonged to, a persistent little girl called Alys.

Primrose shrugged voluptuously, let out a gale of a sigh, and rearranged her flesh in her clothes.

"Well, we know we're not mad, anyway," she said. "We've got into a mystery, but we didn't make it up. It wasn't a delusion. So it was good we met, because now we needn't be afraid we're mad, need we—we can get on with things, so to speak?"

They arranged to have dinner together the following evening. They were staying in different bed-and-breakfasts and neither of them thought of exchanging addresses. They agreed on a restaurant in the market square of the local town—Seraphina's Hot Pot—and a time, seven-thirty. They did not even discuss spending the next day together. Primrose went on a local bus tour. Penny took a long solitary walk. The weather was gray, spitting fine rain. Both arrived at their lodgings with headaches, and both made tea with the tea bags and kettle provided in their rooms. They sat on their beds. Penny's had a quilt with blowsy cabbage roses. Primrose's had a black-and-white checked gingham duvet. They turned on their televisions, watched the same game show, listened to the inordinate jolly laughter.

Seven-thirty came and went, and neither woman moved. Both, indistinctly, imagined the other waiting at a table, watching a door open and shut. Neither moved. What could they have said, they asked themselves, but only perfunctorily.

The next day, Penny thought about the wood, put on her walking shoes, and set off obliquely in the opposite direction. Primrose sat over her breakfast, which was English and ample. The wood, the real and imagined wood—both before and after she had entered it with Penny—had always been simultaneously a source of attraction and of discomfort, shading into terror. Without speaking to herself a sentence in her head—"I shall go there"—Primrose decided. And she went straight there, full of warm food, arriving as the morning brightened with the first busload of tourists, and giving them the slip, to take the path they had once taken, across the lawn and through the wicket gate.

The wood was much the same, but denser and more inviting in its new greenness. Primrose's body decided to set off in a rather different direction from the one the little girls had taken. New bracken was uncoiling with snaky force. Yesterday's rain still glittered on limp new hazel leaves and threads of gossamer. Small feathered throats above her whistled and trilled with enchanting territorial aggression and male self-assertion, which were to Primrose simply the chorus. She found a mossy bank, with posies of primroses, which she recognized and took vaguely as a good sign, a personal sign. She was better at flowers than birds, because there had been Flower Fairies in the school bookshelves when she was little, with the flowers painted accurately, accompanied by truly pretty human creatures, all children, clothed in the blues and golds, russets and purples of the flowers and fruits. Here she saw and recognized them, windflower and bryony, self-heal and dead nettle, and had—despite where she was—a lovely lapping sense of invisible, just invisible life swarming in the leaves and along the twigs.

She stopped. She did not like the sound of her own toiling breath. She was 70
not very fit. She saw, then, a whisking in the bracken, a twirl of fur, thin and flaming, quivering on a tree trunk. She saw a squirrel, a red squirrel, watching her from a bough. She had to sit down, as she remembered her mother. She sat on a hummock of grass, rather heavily. She remembered them all, Nutkin and Moldywarp, Brock and Sleepy Dormouse, Natty Newt and Ferdy Frog. Her mother hadn't told stories and hadn't opened gates into imaginary worlds. But she had been good with her fingers. Every Christmas during the war, when toys, and indeed materials, were not to be had, Primrose had woken to find in her stocking a new stuffed creature, made from fur fabric, with button eyes and horny claws. There had been an artistry to them. The stuffed squirrel was the essence of squirrel, the fox was watchful, the newt was slithery. They did not wear anthropomorphic jackets or caps, which made it easier to invest them with imaginary natures. She believed in Father Christmas, and the discovery that her mother had made the toys, the vanishing of magic, had been a breathtaking blow. She could not be grateful for the skill and the imagination, so uncharacteristic of her flirtatious mother. The creatures continued to accumulate. A spider, a Bambi. She told herself stories at night about a girlwoman, an enchantress in a fairy wood, loved and protected by an army of wise and gentle animals. She slept banked in by stuffed creatures, as the house in the blitz was banked in by inadequate sandbags.

Primrose registered the red squirrel as disappointing—stringier and more ratlike than its plump gray city cousins. But she knew it was special, and when it took off from branch to branch, flicking its extended tail like a sail, gripping with its tiny hands, she set out to follow it. It would take her to the center, she thought. It could easily have leaped out of sight, she thought, but it didn't. She pushed through brambles into denser, greener shadows. Juices stained her skirts and skin. She began to tell herself a story about staunch Primrose, not giving up, making her way to "the center." Her childhood stories had all been in the third person. "She was not afraid." "She faced up to the wild beasts. They cowered." She laddered her tights and muddied her shoes and breathed heavier. The squirrel stopped to clean its face. She crushed bluebells and saw the sinister hoods of arum lilies.

She had no idea how far she had come, but she decided that the clearing where she found herself was the center. The squirrel had stopped, and was running up and down a single tree. There was a mossy mound that could have had a thronelike aspect, if you were being imaginative. So she sat on it. "She came to the center and sat on the mossy chair."

Now what?

She had not forgotten what they had seen, the blank miserable face, the powerful claws, the raggle-taggle train of accumulated decay. She had come neither to look for it nor to confront it, but she had come because it was there. She had known all her life that she, Primrose, had really been in a magic forest. She knew that the forest was the source of terror. She had never frightened the littluns she entertained, with tales of lost children in forests. She frightened them with slimy things that came up the plughole, or swarmed out of the U-bend in the lavatory, and were dispatched by bravery and magic. But the woods in her tales bred glamour. They were places where you used words like "spangles" and "sequins" for real dewdrops on real dock leaves. Primrose knew that glamour and the thing they had seen, brilliance and the ashen stink, came from the same place. She made both things safe for the littluns by restricting them to pantomime flats and sweet illustrations. She didn't look at what she knew, better not, but she did know she knew, she recognized confusedly.

Now what?

She sat on the moss, and a voice in her head said, "I want to go home." And she heard herself give a bitter, entirely grownup little laugh, for what was home? What did she know about home?

Where she lived was above a Chinese takeaway. She had a dangerous cupboard-corner she cooked in, a bed, a clothes-rail, an armchair deformed by generations of bottoms. She thought of this place in faded browns and beiges, seen through drifting coils of Chinese cooking steam, scented with stewing pork and a bubbling chicken broth. Home was not real, as all the sturdy twigs and roots in the wood were real. The stuffed animals were piled on the bed and the carpet, their fur rubbed, their pristine stare gone from their scratched eyes. She thought about what one thought was real, sitting there on the moss throne at the center. When Mum had come in, snivelling, to say Dad was dead, Primrose herself had been preoccupied with whether pudding would be tapioca or semolina, whether there would be jam, and, subsequently, how ugly Mum's dripping nose was, how she looked as though she were putting it on.[1] She remembered the semolina and the rather nasty blackberry jam, the taste and the texture, to this day. So was that real, was that home?

She had later invented a picture of a cloudy aquamarine sea under a gold sun, in which a huge fountain of white curling water rose from a foundering ship. It was very beautiful but not real. She could not remember Dad. She could remember the Thing in the Forest, and she could remember Alys. The fact that the mossy tump had lovely colors—crimson and emerald—didn't mean she didn't remember the Thing. She remembered what Penny had said about "things that are more real than we are." She had met one. Here at the center, the spout of water was more real than the semolina, because she was where such things reign. The word she found was "reign." She had understood something, and did not know what she had understood. She wanted badly to go home, and she wanted never to move. The light was lovely in the leaves. The squirrel flirted its tail and suddenly set off again, springing into the branches. The woman lumbered to her feet and licked the bramble scratches on the back of her hands.

Penny walked very steadily, keeping to hedgerows and field-edge paths. She remembered the Thing. She remembered it clearly and daily. But she walked away, noticing and not noticing that her path was deflected by field forms and the lay of the land into a snaking sickle shape. As the day wore on, she settled into her stride and lifted her eyes. When she saw the wood on the horizon, she

1. Pretending.

knew it was the wood, although she was seeing it from an unfamiliar aspect, from where it appeared to be perched on a conical hillock, ridged as though it had been grasped and squeezed by coils of strength. It was almost dusk. She mounted the slope, and went in over a suddenly discovered stile.[2]

Once inside, she moved cautiously. She stood stock-still, and snuffed the air 80
for the remembered rottenness: she listened to the sounds of the trees and the creatures. She smelled rottenness, but it was normal rottenness, leaves and stems mulching back into earth. She heard sounds. Not birdsong, for it was too late in the day, but the odd raucous warning croak. She heard her own heartbeat in the thickening brown air.

It was no use looking for familiar tree trunks or tussocks. They had had a lifetime, her lifetime, to alter out of recognition.

She began to think she discerned dark tunnels in the undergrowth, where something might have rolled and slid. Mashed seedlings, broken twigs and fronds, none of it very recent. There were things caught in the thorns, flimsy colorless shreds of damp wool or fur. She peered down the tunnels and noted where the scrapings hung thickest. She forced herself to go into the dark, stooping, occasionally crawling on hands and knees. The silence was heavy. She found threadworms of knitting wool, unravelled dishcloth cotton, clinging newsprint. She found odd sausage-shaped tubes of membrane, containing fragments of hair and bone and other inanimate stuffs. They were like monstrous owl pellets, or the gut-shaped hairballs vomited by cats. Penny went forward, putting aside briars and tough stems with careful fingers. It had been here, but how long ago?

Quite suddenly, she came out at a place she remembered. The clearing was larger, the tree trunks were thicker, but the great log behind which they had hidden still lay there. The place was almost the ghost of a camp. The trees round about were hung with pennants and streamers, like the scorched, hacked, threadbare banners in the chapel of the great house, with their brown stains of earth or blood. It had been here, it had never gone away.

Penny moved slowly and dreamily round, looking for things. She found a mock-tortoiseshell hairslide, and a shoe button with a metal shank. She found a bird skeleton, quite fresh, bashed flat. She found ambivalent shards and several teeth, of varying sizes and shapes. She found—spread around, half hidden by roots, stained green but glinting white—a collection of small bones, finger bones, tiny toes, a rib, and finally what might be a brainpan and brow. She thought of putting them in her knapsack, and then thought she could not. She was not an anatomist. The tiny bones might have been badger or fox.

She sat down, with her back against the fallen trunk. She thought, Now I am 85
watching myself as you do in a safe dream, but then, when I saw it, it was one of those dreams where you are inside and cannot get out. Except that it wasn't a dream.

It was the encounter with the Thing that had led her to deal professionally in dreams. Something that resembled unreality had lumbered into reality, and she had seen it. She had been the reading child, but after the sight of the Thing she had not been able to inhabit the customary and charming unreality of books.

2. Set of steps for climbing over a fence or hedge.

She had become good at studying what could not be seen. She took an interest in the dead, who inhabited real history. She was drawn to the invisible forces that moved in molecules and caused them to coagulate or dissipate. She had become a psychotherapist "to be useful." That was not quite accurate. The corner of the blanket that covered the unthinkable had been turned back enough for her to catch sight of it. She was in its world. It was not by accident that she had come to specialize in severely autistic children, children who twittered, or banged, or stared, who sat damp and absent on Penny's official lap and told her no dreams. The world they knew was a real world. Often Penny thought it was the real world, from which even their desperate parents were at least partly shielded. Somebody had to occupy themselves with the hopeless. Penny felt she could.

All the leaves of the forest began slowly to quaver and then to clatter. Far away, there was the sound of something heavy, and sluggish, stirring. Penny sat very still and expectant. She heard the old blind rumble, she sniffed the old stink. It came from no direction; it was all around; as though the Thing encompassed the wood, or as though it travelled in multiple fragments, as it was described in the old text. It was dark now. What was visible had no distinct color, only shades of ink and elephant.

Now, thought Penny, and just as suddenly as it had begun the turmoil ceased. It was as though the Thing had turned away; she could feel the tremble of the wood recede and become still. Quite rapidly, over the treetops, a huge disk of white gold mounted and hung. Penny remembered her father, standing in the cold light of the full moon, and saying wryly that the bombers would not come tonight, they were safe under a cloudless full moon. He had vanished in an oven of red-yellow roaring, Penny had guessed, or been told, or imagined. Her mother had sent her away before allowing the fireman to speak, who had come with the news. She had been a creep-mouse on stairs and in cubbyholes, trying to overhear what was being imparted. Her mother didn't, or couldn't, want her company. She caught odd phrases of talk—"nothing really to identify," "absolutely no doubt." He had been a tired, gentle man with ash in his trouser turnups. There had been a funeral. Penny remembered thinking there was nothing, or next to nothing, in the coffin his fellow-firemen shouldered. It went up so lightly. It was so easy to set down on the crematorium slab.

They had been living behind the blackout anyway, but her mother went on living behind drawn curtains long after the war was over.

The moon had released the wood, it seemed. Penny stood up and brushed leaf mold off her clothes. She had been ready for it, and it had not come. She felt disappointed. But she accepted her release and found her way back to the fields and her village along liquid trails of moonlight.

The two women took the same train back to the city, but did not encounter each other until they got out. The passengers scurried and shuffled toward the exit, mostly heads down. Both women remembered how they had set out in the wartime dark, with their twig legs and gas masks. Both raised their heads as they neared the barrier, not in hope of being met, for they would not be, but automatically, to calculate where to go and what to do. They saw each other's faces in the cavernous gloom, two pale, recognizable rounds, far enough apart for speech, and even greetings, to be awkward. In the dimness, they were reduced to similarity—dark eyeholes, set mouth. For a moment or two, they stood and simply stared. On that first occasion the station vault had been full of curling steam, and the air gritty with ash. Now the blunt-nosed sleek diesel they had left was blue and gold under a layer of grime. They saw each other through the black imagined veil that grief or pain or despair hangs over the visible world. Each saw the other's face and thought of the unforgettable misery of the face they had seen in the forest. Each thought that the other was the witness, who made the thing certainly real, who prevented her from slipping into the comfort of believing she had imagined it or made it up. So they stared at each other, blankly, without acknowledgment, then picked up their baggage, and turned away into the crowd.

Penny found that the black veil had somehow become part of her vision. She thought constantly about faces, her father's, her mother's, Primrose's face, the hopeful little girl, the woman staring up at her from the glass case, staring at her conspiratorially over the clotted cream. The blond infant Alys, an ingratiating sweet smile. The half-human face of the Thing. She tried to remember that face completely, and suffered over the detail of the dreadful droop of its mouth, the exact inanity of its blind squinnying.[3] Present faces were blank disks, shadowed moons. Her patients came and went. She was increasingly unable to distinguish one from another. The face of the Thing hung in her brain, jealously soliciting her attention, distracting her from dailiness. She had gone back to its place, and had not seen it. She needed to see it. Why she needed it was because it was more real than she was. She would go and face it. What else was there, she asked herself, and answered herself, nothing.

So she made her way back, sitting alone in the train as the fields streaked past, drowsing through a century-long night under the cabbage quilt in the B. and B. This time, she went in the old way, from the house, through the garden gate; she found the old trail quickly, her sharp eye picked up the trace of its detritus, and soon enough she was back in the clearing, where her cairn of tiny bones by the tree trunk was undisturbed. She gave a little sigh, dropped to her knees, and then sat with her back to the rotting wood and silently called the Thing. Almost immediately, she sensed its perturbation, saw the trouble in the branches, heard the lumbering, smelled its ancient smell. It was a grayish, unremarkable day. She closed her eyes briefly as the noise and movement grew stronger. When it came, she would look it in the face, she would see what it was. She clasped her hands loosely in her lap. Her nerves relaxed. Her blood slowed. She was ready.

Primrose was in the shopping mall, putting out her circle of rainbow-colored plastic chairs. She creaked as she bent over them. It was pouring with rain outside, but the mall was enclosed like a crystal palace in a casing of glass. The floor under the rainbow chairs was gleaming dappled marble. They were in front of a dimpling fountain, with lights shining up through the greenish water, making golden rings round the polished pebbles and wishing coins that lay there. The little children collected round her: their mothers kissed them goodbye, told them to be good and quiet and listen to the nice lady. They had little

3. Squinting.

transparent plastic cups of shining orange juice, and each had a biscuit in silver foil. They were all colors—black skin, brown skin, pink skin, freckled skin, pink jacket, yellow jacket, purple hood, scarlet hood. Some grinned and some whimpered, some wriggled, some were still. Primrose sat on the edge of the fountain. She had decided what to do. She smiled her best, most comfortable smile, and adjusted her golden locks. Listen to me, she told them, and I'll tell you something amazing, a story that's never been told before.

95 There were once two little girls who saw, or believed they saw, a thing in a forest. . . .

2000

QUESTIONS

1. Traditional fairy tales often rely on symbolic objects, actions, settings, or characters. How is THE THING IN THE FOREST like a fairy tale in this respect? How is it different? Are there figures of speech in this story that you would argue are not symbolic?
2. Is the "Loathly Worm" (par. 44) supernatural, imaginary, or real? Notice the description of its appearances. Can you identify different *kinds* of literal or physical traits that people see in it? Can you identify three or more concepts, feelings, or historical conditions that it might represent? Is it personified? Does it resemble other monsters in literature, art, or media?
3. Are "Penny" and "Primrose" allegorical names? How do the differences between the characters add to the symbolic meaning of the Thing? How do their different actions in the story help reveal its meanings?

EDWIDGE DANTICAT
(b. 1969)

A Wall of Fire Rising

When she was twelve, Edwidge Danticat moved from Port-au-Prince, Haiti, to Brooklyn, New York, where her parents had relocated eight years before. Having grown up speaking only French and Creole, Danticat published her first writing in English at age fourteen, a newspaper article about her immigration to the United States that developed into her first novel, *Breath, Eyes, Memory* (1994). Danticat received a degree in French literature from Barnard College and an MFA from Brown University. *Krik? Krak!* (1991), a collection of short stories, was nominated for the National Book Award. Her second novel, *The Farming of Bones* (1998), is based on the 1937 massacre of Haitians at the border of the Dominican Republic. In 2002, Danticat published *After the Dance: A Walk through Carnival in Jacmel, Haiti*, an account of her travels. More recent publications include *The Dew Breaker* (2004), a collection of stories that examines the life of a Haitian torturer; *Brother, I'm Dying* (2007), winner of the National Book Critics Circle Award for Autobiography; the essay collection *Create Dangerously: The Immigrant Artist at Work* (2010); and the novel *Claire of the Sea Light* (2013).

"Listen to what happened today," Guy said as he barged through the rattling door of his tiny shack.

His wife, Lili, was squatting in the middle of their one-room home, spreading cornmeal mush on banana leaves for their supper.

"Listen to what happened to *me* today!" Guy's seven-year-old son—Little Guy—dashed from a corner and grabbed his father's hand. The boy dropped his composition notebook as he leaped to his father, nearly stepping into the corn mush and herring that his mother had set out in a trio of half gourds on the clay floor.

"Our boy is in a play." Lili quickly robbed Little Guy of the honor of telling his father the news.

"A play?" Guy affectionately stroked the boy's hair. 5

The boy had such tiny corkscrew curls that no amount of brushing could ever make them all look like a single entity. The other boys at the Lycée Jean-Jacques[1] called him "pepper head" because each separate kinky strand was coiled into a tight tiny ball that looked like small peppercorns.

"When is this play?" Guy asked both the boy and his wife. "Are we going to have to buy new clothes for this?"

Lili got up from the floor and inclined her face towards her husband's in order to receive her nightly peck on the cheek.

"What role do you have in the play?" Guy asked, slowly rubbing the tip of his nails across the boy's scalp. His fingers made a soft grating noise with each invisible circle drawn around the perimeters of the boy's head. Guy's fingers finally landed inside the boy's ears, forcing the boy to giggle until he almost gave himself the hiccups.

"Tell me, what is your part in the play?" Guy asked again, pulling his fingers away from his son's ear. 10

"I am Boukman," the boy huffed out, as though there was some laughter caught in his throat.

"Show Papy your lines," Lili told the boy as she arranged the three open gourds on a piece of plywood raised like a table on two bricks, in the middle of the room. "My love, Boukman is the hero of the play."

The boy went back to the corner where he had been studying and pulled out a thick book carefully covered in brown paper.

"You're going to spend a lifetime learning those." Guy took the book from the boy's hand and flipped through the pages quickly. He had to strain his eyes to see the words by the light of an old kerosene lamp, which that night—like all others—flickered as though it was burning its very last wick.

"All these words seem so long and heavy," Guy said. "You think you can do this, son?" 15

"He has one very good speech," Lili said. "Page forty, remember, son?"

The boy took back the book from his father. His face was crimped in an of-course-I-remember look as he searched for page forty.

1. Haiti is French speaking; Little Guy attends a *lycée* (school) named after Jean-Jacques Dessalines (1758–1806), the founder of independent Haiti. A former slave, Dessalines was declared emperor Jacques I in 1804.

"Bouk-man," Guy struggled with the letters of the slave revolutionary's name as he looked over his son's shoulders. "I see some very hard words here, son."

"He already knows his speech," Lili told her husband.

"Does he now?" asked Guy.

"We've been at it all afternoon," Lili said. "Why don't you go on and recite that speech for your father?"

The boy tipped his head towards the rusting tin on the roof as he prepared to recite his lines.

Lili wiped her hands on an old apron tied around her waist and stopped to listen.

"Remember what you are," Lili said, "a great rebel leader. Remember, it is the revolution."

"Do we want him to be all of that?" Guy asked.

"He is Boukman," Lili said. "What is the only thing on your mind now, Boukman?"

"Supper," Guy whispered, enviously eyeing the food cooling off in the middle of the room. He and the boy looked at each other and began to snicker.

"Tell us the other thing that is on your mind," Lili said, joining in their laughter.

"Freedom!" shouted the boy, as he quickly slipped into his role.

"Louder!" urged Lili.

"Freedom is on my mind!" yelled the boy.

"Why don't you start, son?" said Guy. "If you don't, we'll never get to that other thing that we have on our minds."

The boy closed his eyes and took a deep breath. At first, his lips parted but nothing came out. Lili pushed her head forward as though she were holding her breath. Then like the last burst of lightning out of clearing sky, the boy began.

"A wall of fire is rising and in the ashes, I see the bones of my people. Not only those people whose dark hollow faces I see daily in the fields, but all those souls who have gone ahead to haunt my dreams. At night I relive once more the last caresses from the hand of a loving father, a valiant love, a beloved friend."[2]

It was obvious that this was a speech written by a European man, who gave to the slave revolutionary Boukman the kind of European phrasing that might have sent the real Boukman turning in his grave. However, the speech made Lili and Guy stand on the tips of their toes from great pride. As their applause thundered in the small space of their shack that night, they felt as though for a moment they had been given the rare pleasure of hearing the voice of one of the forefathers of Haitian independence in the forced baritone of their only child. The experience left them both with a strange feeling that they could not explain. It left the hair on the back of their necks standing on end. It left them feeling much more love than they ever knew that they could add to their feeling for their son.

2. On the night of August 22, 1791, slaves led by a slave foreman named Boukman (who was secretly a voodoo high priest) built a "wall of fire" that destroyed many plantations in the north of the French colony of Saint-Domingue, marking the beginning of a mass slave revolt that would lead, fourteen years later, to the establishment of independent Haiti.

"Bravo," Lili cheered, pressing her son into the folds of her apron. "Long live Boukman and long live my boy."

"Long live our supper," Guy said, quickly batting his eyelashes to keep tears from rolling down his face.

The boy kept his eyes on his book as they ate their supper that night. Usually Guy and Lili would not have allowed that, but this was a special occasion. They watched proudly as the boy muttered his lines between swallows of cornmeal.

The boy was still mumbling the same words as the three of them used the last of the rainwater trapped in old gasoline containers and sugarcane pulp from the nearby sugarcane mill to scrub the gourds that they had eaten from.

When things were really bad for the family, they boiled clean sugarcane pulp to make what Lili called her special sweet water tea. It was supposed to suppress gas and kill the vermin in the stomach that made poor children hungry. That and a pinch of salt under the tongue could usually quench hunger until Guy found a day's work or Lili could manage to buy spices on credit and then peddle them for a profit at the marketplace.

That night, anyway, things were good. Everyone had eaten enough to put all their hunger vermin to sleep.

The boy was sitting in front of the shack on an old plastic bucket turned upside down, straining his eyes to find the words on the page. Sometimes when there was no kerosene for the lamp, the boy would have to go sit by the side of the road and study under the street lamps with the rest of the neighborhood children. Tonight, at least, they had a bit of their own light.

Guy bent down by a small clump of old mushrooms near the boy's feet, trying to get a better look at the plant. He emptied the last drops of rainwater from a gasoline container on the mushroom, wetting the bulging toes sticking out of his sons' sandals, which were already coming apart around his endlessly growing feet.

Guy tried to pluck some of the mushrooms, which were being pushed into the dust as though they wanted to grow beneath the ground as roots. He took one of the mushrooms in his hand, running his smallest finger over the round bulb. He clipped the stem and buried the top in a thick strand of his wife's hair.

The mushroom looked like a dried insect in Lili's hair.

"It sure makes you look special," Guy said, teasing her.

"Thank you so much," Lili said, tapping her husband's arm. "It's nice to know that I deserve these much more than roses."

Taking his wife's hand, Guy said, "Let's go to the sugar mill."

"Can I study my lines there?" the boy asked.

"You know them well enough already," Guy said.

"I need many repetitions," the boy said.

Their feet sounded as though they were playing a wet wind instrument as they slipped in and out of the puddles between the shacks in the shantytown. Near the sugar mill was a large television screen in an iron grill cage that the government had installed so that the shantytown dwellers could watch the state-sponsored news at eight o'clock every night. After the news, a gendarme[3] would

3. Policeman or guard (French).

come and turn off the television set, taking home the key. On most nights, the people stayed at the site long after this gendarme had gone and told stories to one another beneath the big blank screen. They made bonfires with dried sticks, corn husks, and paper, cursing the authorities under their breath.

There was a crowd already gathering for the nightly news event. The sugar mill workers sat in the front row in chairs or on old buckets.

Lili and Guy passed the group, clinging to their son so that in his childhood naïveté he wouldn't accidentally glance at the wrong person and be called an insolent child. They didn't like the ambiance of the nightly news watch. They spared themselves trouble by going instead to the sugar mill, where in the past year they had discovered their own wonder.

55 Everyone knew that the family who owned the sugar mill were eccentric "Arabs," Haitians of Lebanese or Palestinian descent whose family had been in the country for generations. The Assad family had a son who, it seems, was into all manner of odd things, the most recent of which was a hot-air balloon, which he had brought to Haiti from America and occasionally flew over the shanty-town skies.

As they approached the fence surrounding the field where the large wicker basket and deflated balloon rested on the ground, Guy let go of the hands of both his wife and the boy.

Lili walked on slowly with her son. For the last few weeks, she had been feeling as though Guy was lost to her each time he reached this point, twelve feet away from the balloon. As Guy pushed his hand through the barbed wire, she could tell from the look on his face that he was thinking of sitting inside the square basket while the smooth rainbow surface of the balloon itself floated above his head. During the day, when the field was open, Guy would walk up to the basket, staring at it with the same kind of longing that most men display when they admire very pretty girls.

Lili and the boy stood watching from a distance as Guy tried to push his hand deeper, beyond the chain link fence that separated him from the balloon. He reached into his pants pocket and pulled out a small pocketknife, sharpening the edges on the metal surface of the fence. When his wife and child moved closer, he put the knife back in his pocket, letting his fingers slide across his son's tightly coiled curls.

"I wager you I can make this thing fly," Guy said.

60 "Why do you think you can do that?" Lili asked.

"I know it," Guy replied.

He followed her as she circled the sugar mill, leading to their favorite spot under a watch light. Little Guy lagged faithfully behind them. From this distance, the hot-air balloon looked like an odd spaceship.

Lili stretched her body out in the knee-high grass in the field. Guy reached over and tried to touch her between her legs.

"You're not one to worry, Lili," he said. "You're not afraid of the frogs, lizards, or snakes that could be hiding in this grass?"

65 "I am here with my husband," she said. "You are here to protect me if anything happens."

Guy reached into his shirt pocket and pulled out a lighter and a crumpled piece of paper. He lit the paper until it burned to an ashy film. The burning paper floated in the night breeze for a while, landing in fragments on the grass.

"Did you see that, Lili?" Guy asked with a flame in his eyes brighter than the lighter's. "Did you see how the paper floated when it was burned? This is how that balloon flies."

"What did you mean by saying that you could make it fly?" Lili asked.

"You already know all my secrets," Guy said as the boy came charging towards them.

"Papa, could you play *Lago* with me?" the boy asked.

Lili lay peacefully on the grass as her son and husband played hide-and-seek. Guy kept hiding and his son kept finding him as each time Guy made it easier for the boy.

"We rest now." Guy was becoming breathless.

The stars were circling the peaks of the mountains, dipping into the cane fields belonging to the sugar mill. As Guy caught his breath, the boy raced around the fence, running as fast as he could to purposely make himself dizzy.

"Listen to what happened today," Guy whispered softly in Lili's ear.

"I heard you say that when you walked in the house tonight," Lili said. "With the boy's play, I forgot to ask you."

The boy sneaked up behind them, his face lit up, though his brain was spinning. He wrapped his arms around both their necks.

"We will go back home soon," Lili said.

"Can I recite my lines?" asked the boy.

"We have heard them," Guy said. "Don't tire your lips."

The boy mumbled something under his breath. Guy grabbed his ear and twirled it until it was a tiny ball in his hand. The boy's face contorted with agony as Guy made him kneel in the deep grass in punishment.

Lili looked tortured as she watched the boy squirming in the grass, obviously terrified of the crickets, lizards, and small snakes that might be there.

"Perhaps we should take him home to bed," she said.

"He will never learn," Guy said, "if I say one thing and you say another."

Guy got up and angrily started walking home. Lili walked over, took her son's hand, and raised him from his knees.

"You know you must not mumble," she said.

"I was saying my lines," the boy said.

"Next time say them loud," Lili said, "so he knows what is coming out of your mouth."

That night Lili could hear her son muttering his lines as he tucked himself in his corner of the room and drifted off to sleep. The boy still had the book with his monologue in it clasped under his arm as he slept.

Guy stayed outside in front of the shack as Lili undressed for bed. She loosened the ribbon that held the old light blue cotton skirt around her waist and let it drop past her knees. She grabbed half a lemon that she kept in the corner by the folded mat that she and Guy unrolled to sleep on every night. Lili let her blouse drop to the floor as she smoothed the lemon over her ashen legs.

Guy came in just at that moment and saw her bare chest by the light of the smaller castor oil lamp that they used for the later hours of the night. Her skin had coarsened a bit over the years, he thought. Her breasts now drooped from having nursed their son for two years after he was born. It was now easier for him to imagine their son's lips around those breasts than to imagine his anywhere near them.

He turned his face away as she fumbled for her nightgown. He helped her open the mat, tucking the blanket edges underneath.

Fully clothed, Guy dropped onto the mat next to her. He laid his head on her chest, rubbing the spiky edges of his hair against her nipples.

"What was it that happened today?" Lili asked, running her fingers along Guy's hairline, an angular hairline, almost like a triangle, in the middle of his forehead. She nearly didn't marry him because it was said that people with angular hairlines often have very troubled lives.

"I got a few hours' work for tomorrow at the sugar mill," Guy said. "That's what happened today."

"It was such a long time coming," Lili said.

It was almost six months since the last time Guy had gotten work there. The jobs at the sugar mill were few and far between. The people who had them never left, or when they did they would pass the job on to another family member who was already waiting on line.

Guy did not seem overjoyed about the one day's work.

"I wish I had paid more attention when you came in with the news," Lili said. "I was just so happy about the boy."

"I was born in the shadow of that sugar mill," Guy said. "Probably the first thing my mother gave me to drink as a baby was some sweet water tea from the pulp of the sugarcane. If anyone deserves to work there, I should."

"What will you be doing for your day's work?"

"Would you really like to know?"

"There is never any shame in honest work," she said.

"They want me to scrub the latrines."

"It's honest work," Lili said, trying to console him.

"I am still number seventy-eight on the permanent hire list," he said. "I was thinking of putting the boy on the list now, so maybe by the time he becomes a man he can be up for a job."

Lili's body jerked forward, rising straight up in the air. Guy's head dropped with a loud thump onto the mat.

"I don't want him on that list," she said. "For a young boy to be on any list like that might influence his destiny. I don't want him on the list."

"Look at me," Guy said. "If my father had worked there, if he had me on the list, don't you think I would be working?"

"If you have any regard for me," she said, "you will not put him on the list."

She groped for her husband's chest in the dark and laid her head on it. She could hear his heart beating loudly as though it were pumping double, triple its normal rate.

"You won't put the boy on any lists, will you?" she implored.

"Please, Lili, no more about the boy. He will not go on the list."

"Thank you."

"Tonight I was looking at that balloon in the yard behind the sugar mill," he said. "I have been watching it real close."

"I know." 115

"I have seen the man who owns it," he said. "I've seen him get in it and put it in the sky and go up there like it was some kind of kite and he was the kite master. I see the men who run after it trying to figure out where it will land. Once I was there and I was one of those men who were running and I actually guessed correctly. I picked a spot in the sugarcane fields. I picked the spot from a distance and it actually landed there."

"Let me say something to you, Guy—"

"Pretend that this is the time of miracles and we believed in them. I watched the owner for a long time, and I think I can fly that balloon. The first time I saw him do it, it looked like a miracle, but the more and more I saw it, the more ordinary it became."

"You're probably intelligent enough to do it," she said.

"I am intelligent enough to do it. You're right to say that I can." 120

"Don't you think about hurting yourself?"

"Think like this. Can't you see yourself up there? Up in the clouds somewhere like some kind of bird?"

"If God wanted people to fly, he would have given us wings on our backs."

"You're right, Lili, you're right. But look what he gave us instead. He gave us reasons to want to fly. He gave us the air, the birds, our son."

"I don't understand you," she said. 125

"Our son, your son, you do not want him cleaning latrines."

"He can do other things."

"Me too. I can do other things too."

A loud scream came from the corner where the boy was sleeping. Lili and Guy rushed to him and tried to wake him. The boy was trembling when he opened his eyes.

"What is the matter?" Guy asked. 130

"I cannot remember my lines," the boy said.

Lili tried to string together what she could remember of her son's lines. The words slowly came back to the boy. By the time he fell back to sleep, it was almost dawn.

The light was slowly coming up behind the trees. Lili could hear the whispers of the market women, their hisses and swearing as their sandals dug into the sharp-edged rocks on the road.

She turned her back to her husband as she slipped out of her nightgown, quickly putting on her day clothes.

"Imagine this," Guy said from the mat on the floor. "I have never really seen your entire body in broad daylight." 135

Lili shut the door behind her, making her way out to the yard. The empty gasoline containers rested easily on her head as she walked a few miles to the public water fountains. It was harder to keep them steady when the containers were full. The water splashed all over her blouse and rippled down her back.

The sky was blue as it was most mornings, a dark indigo-shaded turquoise that would get lighter when the sun was fully risen.

Guy and the boy were standing in the yard waiting for her when she got back.

"You did not get much sleep, my handsome boy," she said, running her wet fingers over the boy's face.

140 "He'll be late for school if we do not go right now," Guy said. "I want to drop him off before I start work."

"Do we remember our lines this morning?" Lili asked, tucking the boy's shirt down deep into his short pants.

"We just recited them," Guy said. "Even I know them now."

Lili watched them walk down the footpath, her eyes following them until they disappeared.

As soon as they were out of sight, she poured the water she had fetched into a large calabash, letting it stand beside the house.

145 She went back into the room and slipped into a dry blouse. It was never too early to start looking around, to scrape together that night's meal.

"Listen to what happened again today," Lili said when Guy walked through the door that afternoon.

Guy blotted his face with a dust rag as he prepared to hear the news. After the day he'd had at the factory, he wanted to sit under a tree and have a leisurely smoke, but he did not want to set a bad example for his son by indulging his very small pleasures.

"You tell him, son," Lili urged the boy, who was quietly sitting in a corner, reading.

"I've got more lines," the boy announced, springing up to his feet. "Papy, do you want to hear them?"

150 "They are giving him more things to say in the play," Lili explained, "because he did such a good job memorizing so fast."

"My compliments, son. Do you have your new lines memorized too?" Guy asked.

"Why don't you recite your new lines for your father?" Lili said.

The boy walked to the middle of the room and prepared to recite. He cleared his throat, raising his eyes towards the ceiling.

"There is so much sadness in the faces of my people. I have called on their gods, now I call on our gods. I call on our young. I call on our old. I call on our mighty and the weak. I call on everyone and anyone so that we shall all let out one piercing cry that we may either live freely or we should die."

155 "I see your new lines have as much drama as the old ones," Guy said. He wiped a tear away, walked over to the chair, and took the boy in his arms. He pressed the boy's body against his chest before lowering him to the ground.

"Your new lines are wonderful, son. They're every bit as affecting as the old." He tapped the boy's shoulder and walked out of the house.

"What's the matter with Papy?" the boy asked as the door slammed shut behind Guy.

"His heart hurts," Lili said.

After supper, Lili took her son to the field where she knew her husband would be. While the boy ran around, she found her husband sitting in his favorite spot behind the sugar mill.

"Nothing, Lili," he said. "Ask me nothing about this day that I have had." 160

She sat down on the grass next to him, for once feeling the sharp edges of the grass blades against her ankles.

"You're really good with that boy," he said, drawing circles with his smallest finger on her elbow. "You will make a performer of him. I know you will. You can see the best in that whole situation. It's because you have those stars in your eyes. That's the first thing I noticed about you when I met you. It was your eyes, Lili, so dark and deep. They drew me like danger draws a fool."

He turned over on the grass so that he was staring directly at the moon up in the sky. She could tell that he was also watching the hot-air balloon behind the sugar mill fence out of the corner of his eye.

"Sometimes I know you want to believe in me," he said. "I know you're wishing things for me. You want me to work at the mill. You want me to get a pretty house for us. I know you want these things too, but mostly you want me to feel like a man. That's why you're not one to worry about, Lili. I know you can take things as they come."

"I don't like it when you talk this way," she said. 165

"Listen to this, Lili. I want to tell you a secret. Sometimes, I just want to take that big balloon and ride it up in the air. I'd like to sail off somewhere and keep floating until I got to a really nice place with a nice plot of land where I could be something new. I'd build my own house, keep my own garden. Just *be* something new."

"I want you to stay away from there."

"I know you don't think I should take it. That can't keep me from wanting."

"You could be injured. Do you ever think about that?"

"Don't you ever want to be something new?" 170

"I don't like it," she said.

"Please don't get angry with me," he said, his voice straining almost like the boy's.

"If you were to take that balloon and fly away, would you take me and the boy?"

"First you don't want me to take it and now you want to go?"

"I just want to know that when you dream, me and the boy, we're always in your dreams." 175

He leaned his head on her shoulders and drifted off to sleep. Her back ached as she sat there with his face pressed against her collar bone. He drooled and the saliva dripped down to her breasts, soaking her frayed polyester bra. She listened to the crickets while watching her son play, muttering his lines to himself as he went in a circle around the field. The moon was glowing above their heads. Winking at them, as Guy liked to say, on its way to brighter shores.

Opening his eyes, Guy asked her, "How do you think a man is judged after he's gone?"

How did he expect her to answer something like that?

"People don't eat riches," she said. "They eat what it can buy."

"What does that mean, Lili? Don't talk to me in parables. Talk to me honestly." 180

"A man is judged by his deeds," she said. "The boy never goes to bed hungry. For as long as he's been with us, he's always been fed."

Just as if he had heard himself mentioned, the boy came dashing from the other side of the field, crashing in a heap on top of his parents.

"My new lines," he said. "I have forgotten my new lines."

"Is this how you will be the day of this play, son?" Guy asked. "When people give you big responsibilities, you have to try to live up to them."

The boy had relearned his new lines by the time they went to bed.

That night, Guy watched his wife very closely as she undressed for bed.

"I would like to be the one to rub that piece of lemon on your knees tonight," he said.

She handed him the half lemon, then raised her skirt above her knees.

Her body began to tremble as he rubbed his fingers over her skin.

"You know that question I asked you before," he said, "how a man is remembered after he's gone? I know the answer now. I know because I remember my father, who was a very poor struggling man all his life. I remember him as a man that I would never want to be."

Lili got up with the break of dawn the next day. The light came up quickly above the trees. Lili greeted some of the market women as they walked together to the public water fountain.

On her way back, the sun had already melted a few gray clouds. She found the boy standing alone in the yard with a terrified expression on his face, the old withered mushrooms uprooted at his feet. He ran up to meet her, nearly knocking her off balance.

"What happened?" she asked. "Have you forgotten your lines?"

The boy was breathing so heavily that his lips could not form a single word.

"What is it?" Lili asked, almost shaking him with anxiety.

"It's Papa," he said finally, raising a stiff finger in the air.

The boy covered his face as his mother looked up at the sky. A rainbow-colored balloon was floating aimlessly above their heads.

"It's Papa," the boy said. "He is in it."

She wanted to look down at her son and tell him that it wasn't his father, but she immediately recognized the spindly arms, in a bright flowered shirt that she had made, gripping the cables.

From the field behind the sugar mill a group of workers were watching the balloon floating in the air. Many were clapping and cheering, calling out Guy's name. A few of the women were waving their head rags at the sky, shouting, "Go! Beautiful, go!"

Lili edged her way to the front of the crowd. Everyone was waiting, watching the balloon drift higher up into the clouds.

"He seems to be right over our heads," said the factory foreman, a short slender mulatto with large buckteeth.

Just then, Lili noticed young Assad, his thick black hair sticking to the beads of sweat on his forehead. His face had the crumpled expression of disrupted sleep.

"He's further away than he seems," said young Assad. "I still don't understand. How did he get up there? You need a whole crew to fly these things."

"I don't know," the foreman said. "One of my workers just came in saying 205
there was a man flying above the factory."

"But how the hell did he start it?" Young Assad was perplexed.

"He just did it," the foreman said.

"Look, he's trying to get out!" someone hollered.

A chorus of screams broke out among the workers.

The boy was looking up, trying to see if his father was really trying to jump 210
out of the balloon. Guy was climbing over the side of the basket. Lili pressed her son's face into her skirt.

Within seconds, Guy was in the air hurtling down towards the crowd. Lili held her breath as she watched him fall. He crashed not far from where Lili and the boy were standing, his blood immediately soaking the landing spot.

The balloon kept floating free, drifting on its way to brighter shores. Young Assad rushed towards the body. He dropped to his knees and checked the wrist for a pulse, then dropped the arm back to the ground.

"It's over!" The foreman ordered the workers back to work.

Lili tried to keep her son's head pressed against her skirt as she moved closer to the body. The boy yanked himself away and raced to the edge of the field where his father's body was lying on the grass. He reached the body as young Assad still knelt examining the corpse. Lili rushed after him.

"He is mine," she said to young Assad. "He is my family. He belongs to me." 215

Young Assad got up and raised his head to search the sky for his aimless balloon, trying to guess where it would land. He took one last glance at Guy's bloody corpse, then raced to his car and sped away.

The foreman and another worker carried a cot and blanket from the factory.

Little Guy was breathing quickly as he looked at his father's body on the ground. While the foreman draped a sheet over Guy's corpse, his son began to recite the lines from his play.

"A wall of fire is rising and in the ashes, I see the bones of my people. Not only those people whose dark hollow faces I see daily in the fields, but all those souls who have gone ahead to haunt my dreams. At night I relive once more the last caresses from the hand of a loving father, a valiant love, a beloved friend."

"Let me look at him one last time," Lili said, pulling back the sheet. 220

She leaned in very close to get a better look at Guy's face. There was little left of that countenance that she had loved so much. Those lips that curled when he was teasing her. That large flat nose that felt like a feather when rubbed against hers. And those eyes, those night-colored eyes. Though clouded with blood, Guy's eyes were still bulging open. Lili was searching for some kind of sign—a blink, a smile, a wink—something that would remind her of the man that she had married.

"His eyes aren't closed," the foreman said to Lili. "Do you want to close them, or should I?"

The boy continued reciting his lines, his voice rising to a man's grieving roar. He kept his eyes closed, his fists balled at his side as he continued with his newest lines.

"There is so much sadness in the faces of my people. I have called on their gods, now I call on our gods. I call on our young. I call on our old. I call on our mighty and the weak. I call on everyone and anyone so that we shall all let out one piercing cry that we may either live freely or we should die."

225 "Do you want to close the eyes?" the foreman repeated impatiently.

"No, leave them open," Lili said. "My husband, he likes to look at the sky."

1991

QUESTIONS

1. What do you think the hot-air balloon symbolizes to Assad, its owner? to Guy? to the implied author?
2. The title of the story alludes to a speech that Little Guy must memorize for a school play about Haiti's history. The lines of the speech are rich in figurative language, including metaphors: "*A wall of fire is rising and in the ashes, I see the bones of my people*" (par. 34). How do the title's allusion and other aspects of the story confirm that the speech's image of "a wall of fire" is symbolic?
3. What do you think happens at the end of A Wall of Fire Rising? Is Guy's plunge to the earth a deliberate suicide or an accident? What are some symbolic interpretations of both possibilities?

SUGGESTIONS FOR WRITING

1. Choose any story in this chapter, read it thoroughly, and follow the guidelines for responding to symbolism that appear earlier in this chapter. Write an essay in which you explore the various meanings of the story's major symbol and the way these emerge over the course of the story.
2. In The Birth-Mark, Aylmer the scientist is portrayed as "spiritual" and "intellectual," in contrast with his crudely physical laboratory assistant, Aminadab (par. 25). Write an essay in which you argue that the allegory of Aylmer's terrible experiment on his wife refers not only to a man's desire for immortal beauty but also to his desire for control of everything physical, including the laborer.
3. Write an essay in which you compare the way symbolism works in The Birth-Mark and A Wall of Fire Rising. For example, what is the effect and significance of both the magical atmosphere of Hawthorne's story and the way its characters explicitly refer to particular objects as symbols? How might symbolism work differently in Danticat's story because of its realistic, contemporary setting and plot and the fact that its characters don't explicitly refer to anything as a symbol?
4. To what extent are characters aware of the symbolism in a story? Do characters accept the symbolism as objective and real, even if what happens seems magical or impossible? Write an essay focused on characters' different ways of responding to or believing in a symbol or symbolism in one or two stories. For instance, in The Thing in the Forest, Primrose says, "We've got into a mystery, but we didn't make it up" (par. 65). What else in the story confirms that their memories are more than illusion? How do the two women respond differently after they meet again? You might raise similar questions concerning The Birth-Mark and compare the characters' awareness and response to the respective symbols in Byatt's and Hawthorne's stories.

SAMPLE WRITING: COMPARATIVE ESSAY

The essay below compares two stories by exploring the role symbolism plays in each. As you read the essay, try to identify the specific strategies and techniques this student writer uses to create one coherent argument out of observations about two quite different literary texts. (For ease of reference, we have altered the citations in this essay to refer to paragraph numbers. Unless your instructor indicates otherwise, however, you should always follow convention by instead citing page numbers when writing about fiction.)

Collins 1

Charles Collins
Dr. Mays
English 298
15 March 2017

Symbolism in "The Birth-Mark" and "The Thing in the Forest"

In "The Birth-Mark" by Nathaniel Hawthorne and A. S. Byatt's "The Thing in the Forest," the symbols of the birthmark and the Thing move the plots of the stories. Characters in both stories are compelled by these objects to act, though in different ways. In "The Birth-Mark," the main character, Aylmer, views his wife's birthmark as a flaw in her beauty, as well as a symbol of human imperfection, and tries to remove it. In "The Thing in the Forest," the protagonists, Penny and Primrose, react to the Thing both as a real thing and as a symbol. The characters' interpretation of these things is what creates conflict, and the stories are both shaped by the symbolic meanings that the characters ascribe to those things.

In "The Birth-Mark," Aylmer, a "natural philosopher," becomes obsessed with a birthmark in the shape of a small hand on his wife's face. The plot of the story concerns his attempt to remove the mark, which results in the death of Georgiana, his wife. The reader finds out in the very beginning that Aylmer views Georgiana's birthmark as more than a mere birthmark. In fact, it is because he views the mark as symbolic that he becomes obsessed with it. He makes his thoughts clear when he says to his wife, in response to her stating that other people have found her birthmark attractive, "No, dearest Georgiana, you came so nearly perfect from the hand of Nature, that this slightest possible defect, which we hesitate whether to term a defect or a beauty, shocks me, as being the visible mark of earthly imperfection" (par. 5). Aylmer sees his wife as nearly perfect, so when he sees something that does not seem consistent with his idea of beauty, he is disturbed by it and begins to view it as having a greater meaning. The narrator later clarifies this point by saying, "In this manner, selecting it as the symbol of his wife's liability to sin, sorrow, decay, and death, Aylmer's somber imagination was not long in rendering the birthmark a frightful object, causing him more trouble and horror than ever Georgiana's beauty, whether of soul or sense, had given him delight" (par. 8). Here the story explicitly states that Aylmer sees his wife's birthmark as more than a physical feature; to him, it is a symbol of all of the imperfect things about humans.

Though the narrator suggests that "[w]e know not whether Aylmer possessed this degree of faith in man's ultimate control over nature," such that "the philosopher should lay his hand upon on the secret of creative force and perhaps make new worlds for himself" (par. 1), Aylmer's actions throughout the story suggest that he does believe this. Once Aylmer sees the birthmark as a "frightful object," he becomes intent upon removing it. The birthmark to him symbolizes human imperfection, and so it is a challenge to him to conquer that imperfection and control the "defect" that Nature placed upon his wife. It is only because he views the birthmark as a symbol that it comes to have this level of control over him and to motivate his actions and thus the plot of the story.

Unfortunately for Aylmer, he does not realize the cost of getting rid of the birthmark. He succeeds in his plan, but by succeeding he ends up killing his wife. What he sees as a symbol of imperfection the reader can see as a symbol of life. In Aylmer's dream the birthmark is tied to Georgiana's heart, and he must remove her heart to remove the birthmark. Georgiana's heart and her birthmark are actually symbolic of the human spark of life that keeps her alive. Perhaps part of this spark involves imperfection, or perhaps it is "a charm," but either way Georgiana cannot live without it. Aminadab seems to understand this and remarks to himself that "[i]f she were my wife, I'd never part with that birth-mark" (par. 27).

However, both Aylmer and Georgiana are so horrified by what the birthmark represents that they are willing to take incredible risks to get rid of it. Georgiana even acknowledges that removing the birthmark might kill her, but says, "Danger is nothing to me; for life, while this hateful mark makes me the object of your horror and disgust . . . is a burden which I would fling down with joy" (par. 18). Because Aylmer and Georgiana view the birthmark as a mark of human imperfection, they are willing to try to remove it, so much so that Aylmer fails to see how the birthmark is tied to Georgiana's life and that Georgiana is willing to lose her life to be rid of it. Aylmer misinterprets the birthmark, thinking that it represents imperfection instead of life, and so he ends up losing his perfect wife.

Collins 3

The symbolism in "The Birth-Mark" is fairly straightforward. The characters openly acknowledge the power of the symbol, and the narrator of the story clearly states what meaning Aylmer finds in it. In "The Thing in the Forest" what the Thing represents is not as clear. Penny and Primrose, the story's main characters, do not view the Thing as symbolic, as Aylmer does the birthmark. Neither the narrator nor the characters directly say why the Thing is important to Penny and Primrose or even whether the Thing they see in the forest is the monster, the Loathly Worm, that they later read about in the book at the mansion. Instead of viewing the Thing as a symbol, Penny and Primrose view the Thing as real and physical. Penny says, "I think, I think there are things that are real—more real than we are—but mostly we don't cross their paths, or they don't cross ours" (par. 55). When Primrose returns to the forest she also realizes that the Thing is real, even more real than her everyday life at home. Penny and Primrose comfort each other by acknowledging that the Thing really exists, that they saw it, and that it "finished off" Alys. But despite their assertions that the Thing exists, they do not say what it is. Primrose says to Penny, "We've got into a mystery, but we didn't make it up. It wasn't a delusion" (par. 65). Though they reassure one another that the Thing is real, they recognize that what they saw is more mysterious than the mythical Loathly Worm.

Though they do not define the Thing, it motivates Penny and Primrose to act just as the birthmark causes Aylmer to act. However, each girl responds in a different way. On the one hand, Primrose, who makes her living telling fantastic stories to children, "had never frightened the littluns she entertained, with tales of lost children in the forest" (par. 74). Primrose has avoided the Thing by entering a world of fairy tales where she speaks of the forest in unrealistic terms. After going to the forest and realizing "[s]he had understood something, and did not know what she had understood" (par. 78), she is able to continue with her life by finally telling the story of their encounter with the Thing as a fairy tale to children. She makes the Thing unreal and is therefore able live with it.

Penny, on the other hand, tries to study the Thing because "[s]omething that resembled unreality had lumbered into reality, and she had seen it" (par. 86). After seeing the Thing, she becomes uninterested in fiction, like the stories Primrose told or like the novels she read as a child, and instead becomes a child psychologist who tries to scientifically study children who see things that are "more real." Upon the death of her mother and her visit to the mansion and the forest, Penny feels compelled to confront the Thing, refusing to take it as a symbol. She goes into the forest to seek out the Thing, but it does not come to her. As time passes, she begins to see the darkness of the thing all around her, and so she goes back to the forest once again to confront the Thing, where presumably it "finishes her off," as there is no account of her life after the encounter. When Penny goes to see the Thing for the final time, "she would look it in the face, she would see what it was. She clasped her hands loosely in her lap. Her nerves relaxed. Her blood slowed. She was ready" (par. 93). Penny treats

Collins 4

the Thing as real, and so there are real consequences for her. Though the story does not state so explicitly, presumably the Thing kills Penny as it did Alys.

Though the characters in the story do not state what the Thing represents, the story suggests that it is a symbol of suffering and death, among other things. The women's visits to the Thing correspond with the deaths of their parents. The first time the girls see the Thing is during the bombing of London during World War II, shortly before their fathers die. When they go to the mansion the second time, it is shortly after the deaths of their mothers. When the adult Primrose goes into the forest, instead of seeing the worm, she recognizes that the memory of her mother telling her about her father's death was "real," like the Thing. The Thing also looks and smells like something that has died, like "liquid . . . putrefaction" and "maggoty things at the bottom of untended dustbins" (par. 33), something that is decomposing. Furthermore, the characters believe that the Thing got Alys, that is, that she died. All of this suggests that the Thing is a symbol for death and that the story is about how different people handle death.

While symbolism is present in both "The Birth-Mark" and "The Thing in the Forest," it is handled in different ways. In "The Birth-Mark," on the one hand, Aylmer consistently views the birthmark as a symbol. He is obsessed with the birthmark because of what he thinks it represents. He has little concern for the birthmark as a physical, real thing. Penny and Primrose, on the other hand, are initially worried about the Thing as something real and physical. Penny never views the Thing as a symbol, but instead views it as a real thing, a monster, and presumably at the end of the story she faces it, and it kills her. Primrose, however, understands that the Thing is real, but chooses to make it a part of a fairy tale and thereby deals with it as a type of symbol, even though she does not understand what the Thing is a symbol of. By choosing to tell a story about the Thing, she makes it unreal, and it does not harm her. In both stories, the power given to symbolism or its rejection is what motivates the actions of the characters and determines the consequences they suffer.

Collins 5

Works Cited

Byatt, A. S. "The Thing in the Forest." Mays, pp. 377-92.

Hawthorne, Nathaniel. "The Birth-Mark." Mays, pp. 365-76.

Mays, Kelly J., editor. *The Norton Introduction to Literature.* 12th ed., W. W. Norton, 2017.

6 THEME

At some point, a responsive reader of any story or novel will inevitably ask, *Why does it all matter? What does it all mean? What's the point?* When we ask what a text means, we are inquiring, at least in part, about its **theme**—a general idea or insight conveyed by the work in its entirety. Theme is certainly not the only way fiction matters nor the only thing we take away from our experience of reading it. Nor is theme fiction's *point* in the sense of its sole "objective" or "purpose." Yet theme is a fictional work's *point* in the sense of its "essential meaning" (or meanings). And our experience of any work isn't complete unless we grapple with the question of its theme.

On rare occasions, we might not have to grapple hard or look far: A very few texts, such as **fables** and certain fairy tales and folktales, explicitly state their themes. To succeed, however, even these works must ultimately "earn" their themes, bringing a raw statement to life through their characters, plot, setting, symbols, and narration. The following fable, by Aesop, succinctly makes its point through a brief dialogue.

AESOP

The Two Crabs

One fine day two crabs came out from their home to take a stroll on the sand. "Child," said the mother, "you are walking very ungracefully. You should accustom yourself to walking straight forward without twisting from side to side."

"Pray, mother," said the young one, "do but set the example yourself, and I will follow you."

"EXAMPLE IS THE BEST PRECEPT."

• • •

In most works, however, all the elements work together to imply an unstated theme that usually requires re-reading to decipher. Even the most careful and responsive readers will likely disagree about just what the theme is or how best to state it. And each statement of a given theme will imply a slightly different view of what matters most and why.

THEME(S): SINGULAR OR PLURAL?

In practice, readers disagree about the precise meaning of the term *theme.* One source of disagreement hinges on the question of whether any single work of fiction can convey more than one theme. On one side of the debate are those who use the word *theme* to refer only to the central or main idea of a work. On the other are those who use the term, as we generally do in this book, to refer to any idea a work conveys. While the former readers tend to talk about *the* theme, the latter instead refer to *a* theme in order to stress that each theme is only one of many. Regardless of whether we call all of the ideas expressed in a work *themes* or instead refer to some of them as *subthemes,* the essential points on which all agree are that a single literary work often expresses multiple ideas and that at least one of those ideas is likely to be more central or overarching and inclusive than others.

THE TWO CRABS demonstrates that even the most simple and straightforward of stories can convey more than one idea. This fable's stated theme, "Example is the best precept," emerges only because the little crab "back-talks" to its mother, implicitly suggesting another theme: that children are sometimes wiser than their parents or even that we sometimes learn by questioning, rather than blindly following, authority. The fact that crabs naturally "twist from side to side"—that no crab *can* walk straight—certainly adds **irony** to the fable, but might it also imply yet another theme?

BE SPECIFIC: THEME AS IDEA VERSUS TOPIC OR SUBJECT

Often, you will see the term *theme* used very loosely to refer to a topic or subject captured in a noun phrase—"the wisdom of youth," "loss of innocence," "the dangers of perfectionism"—or even a single noun—"loss," "youth," "grief," or "prejudice." Identifying such topics—especially those specific enough to require a noun phrase rather than a simple noun—can be a useful first step on the way to figuring out a particular story's themes and also to grouping stories together for the purpose of comparison.

For now, though, we urge you to consider this merely a first step on the path to interpreting a story. The truth is, we haven't yet said anything very insightful, revealing, or debatable about the meaning of an individual story until we articulate the idea it expresses *about* a topic such as love, prejudice, or grief. To state a theme in this much more restricted and helpful sense you will need at least one complete sentence. Note, however, that a complete sentence is still not necessarily a statement of theme. For example, an online student essay begins with the less than scintillating sentence, "In Nathaniel Hawthorne's 'The Birthmark' the reader finds several themes—guilt, evil, love and alienation." One reason this sentence is both unexciting and unhelpful is that—despite its specific list of topics—we could in fact substitute for THE BIRTH-MARK almost any other story in this book. (Try it yourself.) Notice how much more interesting things get, however, when we instead articulate the story's particular insight about just one of these very general topics: "Nathaniel Hawthorne's 'The Birth-Mark' shows us that we too often destroy the very thing we love by trying to turn the good into the perfect."

DON'T BE TOO SPECIFIC: THEME AS *GENERAL* IDEA

Though a theme is specific in the sense that it is a complete idea or statement rather than a topic, it is nonetheless a *general* idea rather than one that describes the characters, plot, or settings unique to one story. Theme is a general insight illustrated *through* these elements rather than an insight *about* any of them. Look again at the statement above—"Nathaniel Hawthorne's 'The Birth-Mark' shows us that we too often destroy the very thing we love by trying to turn the good into the perfect." Now compare this statement with one such as this: "In Nathaniel Hawthorne's 'The Birth-Mark,' the scientist Aylmer kills his wife because he can't tolerate imperfection." Though both statements are valid, only the first of them is truly a statement of theme—of what the story shows us about love through Aylmer rather than what it suggests about Aylmer himself.

THEME VERSUS MORAL

In some cases, a theme may take the form of a **moral**—a rule of conduct or maxim for living. But most themes are instead general observations and insights about how humans actually *do* behave, or about how life, the world, or some particular corner of it actually *is*, rather than moral imperatives about how people *should* behave or how life *should* ideally be. As one contemporary critic puts it, a responsive reader should thus "ask not *What does this story teach?* but *What does this story reveal?*" By the same token, we're usually on safer and more fertile ground if we phrase a theme as a statement rather than as a command. Hawthorne's "The Birth-Mark," for example, certainly demonstrates the dangers of arrogantly seeking a perfection that isn't natural or human. As a result, we might well be tempted to reduce its theme to a moral such as "Accept imperfection," "Avoid arrogance," or "Don't mess with Mother Nature." None of these statements is wholly inappropriate to the story. Yet each of them seems to underestimate the story's complexity and especially its implicit emphasis on all that humanity gains, as well as loses, in the search for perfection. As a result, a better statement of the story's theme might be "Paradoxically, both our drive for perfection and our inevitable imperfection together make us human."

* * *

As you decipher and discuss the themes of the stories that follow, keep in mind that to identify a theme is not to "close the case" but rather to begin a more searching investigation of the details that make each story vivid and unique. Theme is an abstraction from the story; the story and its details do not disappear or lose significance once distilled into theme, nor could you reconstruct a story merely from a statement of its theme. Indeed, theme and story are fused, inseparable. Or, as Flannery O'Connor puts it, "You tell a story because a statement [alone] would be inadequate" (see ch. 8, p. 599). Often difficult to put into words, themes are nonetheless the essential common ground that helps you care about a story and relate it to your own life—even though it seems to be about lives and experiences very different from your own.

Tips for Identifying Themes

Because theme emerges from a work in its entirety and from all the other elements working together, there is no "one-size-fits-all" method for identifying theme. Here, however, are some things to look for and consider as you read and re-read the work.

TIP	EXAMPLE
1. Pay attention to the title. A title will seldom spell out in full a work's main theme, but some titles do suggest a central topic or topics or a clue to theme. Probe the rest of the story to see what, if any, insights about that topic it ultimately seems to offer.	What might Bharati Mukherjee's "The Management of Grief," suggest about whether and how grief can be "managed"?
2. List any recurring phrases and words, especially those for abstract concepts (e.g., love, honor). Certain concrete terms (especially if noted in the title) may likewise provide clues; objects of value or potency might attract significant attention in the text (an heirloom, a weapon, a tree in a garden). Then probe the story to see how and where else it might implicitly deal with that concept or entity and what, if any, conclusions the story proposes.	Versions of the word *blind* occur six times in the relatively short first paragraph of Raymond Carver's "Cathedral," and the word recurs throughout the story. What different kinds of blindness does the story depict? What truth or insight about blindness might it ultimately offer?
3. Identify any statements that the characters or narrator(s) make about a general concept, issue, or topic such as human nature, the natural world, and so on. Look, too, for statements that potentially have a general meaning or application beyond the story, even if they refer to a specific situation in it. Then consider whether and how the story as a whole corroborates, overturns, or complicates any one such view or statement.	In A. S. Byatt's "The Thing in the Forest," one of the two protagonists observes, "I think there are things that are real—more real than we are—but mostly we don't cross their paths, or they don't cross ours. Maybe at very bad times we get into their world, or notice what they are doing in ours" (par. 55). How does the rest of the story both flesh out what these "things" might be and either corroborate or complicate this character's generalization about them?
4. If a character changes over the course of the story, articulate the truth or insight that he or she seems to discover. Then consider whether and how the story as a whole corroborates or complicates that insight.	The end of "The Thing in the Forest" implies that one of its protagonists has come to believe that even the most fantastic stories have an important function in real life. What is that function? Does the story as a whole confirm her conclusions?

TIP	EXAMPLE
5. Identify a conflict depicted in the work and state it in general terms or turn it into a general question, leaving out any reference to specific characters, situations, and so on. Then think about the insight or theme that might be implied by the way the conflict is resolved.	Through Sarty, William Faulkner's "Barn Burning" raises the question of how we should reconcile loyalty to our family with our own individual sense of right and wrong. In the end, the story implies that following our own moral code can sometimes be the more painful, as well as the more noble, option.

STEPHEN CRANE
(1871–1900)
The Open Boat

One of fourteen children, Stephen Crane and his family moved frequently before settling, after his father's death in 1880, in Asbury Park, New Jersey. Crane sporadically attended various preparatory schools and colleges without excelling at much besides baseball. Determined to be a journalist, he left school for the last time in 1891 and began contributing pieces to New York newspapers. His city experiences led him to write *Maggie: A Girl of the Streets*, a realist social-reform novel published in 1893 at his own expense. His next novel, *The Red Badge of Courage* (1895), presented a stark picture of the Civil War and brought him widespread fame; many of his stories were published in the collections *The Open Boat and Other Tales of Adventure* (1898) and *The Monster and Other Stories* (1899). Crane served as a foreign correspondent, reporting on conflicts in Cuba and Greece, and lived his last years abroad, dying of tuberculosis at the age of twenty-eight.

A Tale Intended to Be after the Fact:[1] Being the Experience of Four Men from the Sunk Steamer Commodore

I

None of them knew the color of the sky. Their eyes glanced level and were fastened upon the waves that swept toward them. These waves were of the hue of slate, save for the tops, which were of foaming white, and all of the men knew the colors of the sea. The horizon narrowed and widened, and dipped and rose,

1. Crane had an experience very like the one here re-created in fiction. His autobiographical account of his adventure at sea was published in the *New York Press* on January 7, 1897.

and at all times its edge was jagged with waves that seemed thrust up in points like rocks.

Many a man ought to have a bathtub larger than the boat which here rode upon the sea. These waves were most wrongfully and barbarously abrupt and tall, and each froth-top was a problem in small-boat navigation.

The cook squatted in the bottom, and looked with both eyes at the six inches of gunwale which separated him from the ocean. His sleeves were rolled over his fat forearms, and the two flaps of his unbuttoned vest dangled as he bent to bail out the boat. Often he said, "Gawd! that was a narrow clip." As he remarked it he invariably gazed eastward over the broken sea.

The oiler, steering with one of the two oars in the boat, sometimes raised himself suddenly to keep clear of water that swirled in over the stern. It was a thin little oar, and it seemed often ready to snap.

5 The correspondent, pulling at the other oar, watched the waves and wondered why he was there.

The injured captain, lying in the bow, was at this time buried in that profound dejection and indifference which comes, temporarily at least, to even the bravest and most enduring when, willy-nilly, the firm fails, the army loses, the ship goes down. The mind of the master of a vessel is rooted deep in the timbers of her, though he command for a day or a decade; and this captain had on him the stern impression of a scene in the grays of dawn of seven turned faces, and later a stump of a topmast with a white ball on it, that slashed to and fro at the waves, went low and lower, and down. Thereafter there was something strange in his voice. Although steady, it was deep with mourning, and of a quality beyond oration or tears.

"Keep'er a little more south, Billie," said he.

"A little more south, sir," said the oiler in the stern.

A seat in his boat was not unlike a seat upon a bucking broncho, and by the same token a broncho is not much smaller. The craft pranced and reared and plunged like an animal. As each wave came, and she rose for it, she seemed like a horse making at a fence outrageously high. The manner of her scramble over these walls of water is a mystic thing, and, moreover, at the top of them were ordinarily these problems in white water, the foam racing down from the summit of each wave requiring a new leap, and a leap from the air. Then, after scornfully bumping a crest, she would slide and race and splash down a long incline, and arrive bobbing and nodding in front of the next menace.

10 A singular disadvantage of the sea lies in the fact that after successfully surmounting one wave you discover that there is another behind it just as important and just as nervously anxious to do something effective in the way of swamping boats. In a ten-foot dinghy one can get an idea of the resources of the sea in the line of waves that is not probable to the average experience, which is never at sea in a dinghy. As each slaty wall of water approached, it shut all else from the view of the men in the boat, and it was not difficult to imagine that this particular wave was the final outburst of the ocean, the last effort of the grim water. There was a terrible grace in the move of the waves, and they came in silence, save for the snarling of the crests.

In the wan light the faces of the men must have been gray. Their eyes must have glinted in strange ways as they gazed steadily astern. Viewed from a balcony, the whole thing would, doubtless, have been weirdly picturesque. But the men in the boat had no time to see it, and if they had had leisure, there were other things to occupy their minds. The sun swung steadily up the sky, and they knew it was broad day because the color of the sea changed from slate to emerald-green streaked with amber lights, and the foam was like tumbling snow. The process of the breaking day was unknown to them. They were aware only of this effect upon the color of the waves that rolled toward them.

In disjointed sentences the cook and the correspondent argued as to the difference between a life-saving station and a house of refuge. The cook had said: "There's a house of refuge just north of the Mosquito Inlet Light, and as soon as they see us they'll come off in their boat and pick us up."

"As soon as who see us?" said the correspondent.

"The crew," said the cook.

"Houses of refuge don't have crews," said the correspondent. "As I understand them, they are only places where clothes and grub are stored for the benefit of shipwrecked people. They don't carry crews."

"Oh, yes, they do," said the cook.

"No, they don't," said the correspondent.

"Well, we're not there yet, anyhow," said the oiler, in the stern.

"Well," said the cook, "perhaps it's not a house of refuge that I'm thinking of as being near Mosquito Inlet Light; perhaps it's a life-saving station."

"We're not there yet," said the oiler in the stern.

II

As the boat bounced from the top of each wave the wind tore through the hair of the hatless men, and as the craft plopped her stern down again the spray slashed past them. The crest of each of these waves was a hill, from the top of which the men surveyed for a moment a broad tumultuous expanse, shining and wind-riven. It was probably splendid, it was probably glorious, this play of the free sea, wild with lights of emerald and white and amber.

"Bully good thing it's an on-shore wind," said the cook. "If not, where would we be? Wouldn't have a show."

"That's right," said the correspondent.

The busy oiler nodded his assent.

Then the captain, in the bow, chuckled in a way that expressed humor, contempt, tragedy, all in one. "Do you think we've got much of a show now, boys?" said he.

Whereupon the three were silent, save for a trifle of hemming and hawing. To express any particular optimism at this time they felt to be childish and stupid, but they all doubtless possessed this sense of the situation in their minds. A young man thinks doggedly at such times. On the other hand, the ethics of their condition was decidedly against any open suggestion of hopelessness. So they were silent.

"Oh, well," said the captain, soothing his children, "we'll get ashore all right."

But there was that in his tone which made them think; so the oiler quoth, "Yes! if this wind holds."

The cook was bailing. "Yes! if we don't catch hell in the surf."

30 Canton-flannel[2] gulls flew near and far. Sometimes they sat down on the sea, near patches of brown seaweed that rolled over the waves with a movement like carpets on a line in a gale. The birds sat comfortably in groups, and they were envied by some in the dinghy, for the wrath of the sea was no more to them than it was to a covey of prairie chickens a thousand miles inland. Often they came very close and stared at the men with black bead-like eyes. At these times they were uncanny and sinister in their unblinking scrutiny, and the men hooted angrily at them, telling them to be gone. One came, and evidently decided to alight on the top of the captain's head. The bird flew parallel to the boat and did not circle, but made short sidelong jumps in the air in chicken fashion. His black eyes were wistfully fixed upon the captain's head. "Ugly brute," said the oiler to the bird. "You look as if you were made with a jackknife." The cook and the correspondent swore darkly at the creature. The captain naturally wished to knock it away with the end of the heavy painter,[3] but he did not dare do it, because anything resembling an emphatic gesture would have capsized this freighted boat; and so, with his open hand, the captain gently and carefully waved the gull away. After it had been discouraged from the pursuit the captain breathed easier on account of his hair, and others breathed easier because the bird struck their minds at this time as being somehow gruesome and ominous.

In the meantime the oiler and the correspondent rowed; and also they rowed. They sat together in the same seat, and each rowed an oar. Then the oiler took both oars; then the correspondent took both oars, then the oiler; then the correspondent. They rowed and they rowed. The very ticklish part of the business was when the time came for the reclining one in the stern to take his turn at the oars. By the very last star of truth, it is easier to steal eggs from under a hen than it was to change seats in the dinghy. First the man in the stern slid his hand along the thwart and moved with care, as if he were of Sèvres.[4] Then the man in the rowing-seat slid his hand along the other thwart. It was all done with the most extraordinary care. As the two sidled past each other, the whole party kept watchful eyes on the coming wave, and the captain cried: "Look out, now! Steady, there!"

The brown mats of seaweed that appeared from time to time were like islands, bits of earth. They were travelling, apparently, neither one way nor the other. They were, to all intents, stationary. They informed the men in the boat that it was making progress slowly toward the land.

The captain, rearing cautiously in the bow after the dinghy soared on a great swell, said that he had seen the lighthouse at Mosquito Inlet. Presently the cook remarked that he had seen it. The correspondent was at the oars then, and for some reason he too wished to look at the lighthouse; but his back was toward the far shore, and the waves were important, and for some time he could not seize an opportunity to turn his head. But at last there came a wave more gentle than the others, and when at the crest of it he swiftly scoured the western horizon.

2. Plain-weave cotton fabric.

3. Mooring rope attached to the bow of a boat.

4. Type of fine china.

"See it?" said the captain.

"No," said the correspondent, slowly; "I didn't see anything." 35

"Look again," said the captain. He pointed. "It's exactly in that direction."

At the top of another wave the correspondent did as he was bid, and this time his eyes chanced on a small, still thing on the edge of the swaying horizon. It was precisely like the point of a pin. It took an anxious eye to find a lighthouse so tiny.

"Think we'll make it, Captain?"

"If this wind holds and the boat don't swamp, we can't do much else," said the captain.

The little boat, lifted by each towering sea and splashed viciously by the crests, 40
made progress that in the absence of seaweed was not apparent to those in her. She seemed just a wee thing wallowing, miraculously top up, at the mercy of five oceans. Occasionally a great spread of water, like white flames, swarmed into her.

"Bail her, cook," said the captain, serenely.

"All right, Captain," said the cheerful cook.

III

It would be difficult to describe the subtle brotherhood of men that was here established on the seas. No one said that it was so. No one mentioned it. But it dwelt in the boat, and each man felt it warm him. They were a captain, an oiler, a cook, and a correspondent, and they were friends—friends in a more curiously iron-bound degree than may be common. The hurt captain, lying against the water jar in the bow, spoke always in a low voice and calmly; but he could never command a more ready and swiftly obedient crew than the motley three of the dinghy. It was more than a mere recognition of what was best for the common safety. There was surely in it a quality that was personal and heart-felt. And after this devotion to the commander of the boat, there was this comradeship, that the correspondent, for instance, who had been taught to be cynical of men, knew even at the time was the best experience of his life. But no one said that it was so. No one mentioned it.

"I wish we had a sail," remarked the captain. "We might try my overcoat on the end of an oar, and give you two boys a chance to rest." So the cook and the correspondent held the mast and spread wide the overcoat; the oiler steered; and the little boat made good way with her new rig. Sometimes the oiler had to scull sharply to keep a sea from breaking into the boat, but otherwise sailing was a success.

Meanwhile the lighthouse had been growing slowly larger. It had now almost 45
assumed color, and appeared like a little gray shadow on the sky. The man at the oars could not be prevented from turning his head rather often to try for a glimpse of this little gray shadow.

At last, from the top of each wave, the men in the tossing boat could see land. Even as the lighthouse was an upright shadow on the sky, this land seemed but a long black shadow on the sea. It certainly was thinner than paper. "We must be about opposite New Smyrna,"[5] said the cook, who had coasted

5. Town on the Florida coast.

this shore often in schooners. "Captain, by the way, I believe they abandoned that life-saving station there about a year ago."

"Did they?" said the captain.

The wind slowly died away. The cook and the correspondent were not now obliged to slave in order to hold high the oar. But the waves continued their old impetuous swooping at the dinghy, and the little craft, no longer underway, struggled woundily over them. The oiler or the correspondent took the oars again.

Shipwrecks are *apropos* of nothing. If men could only train for them and have them occur when the men had reached pink condition, there would be less drowning at sea. Of the four in the dinghy none had slept any time worth mentioning for two days and two nights previous to embarking in the dinghy, and in the excitement of clambering about the deck of a foundering ship they had also forgotten to eat heartily.

For these reasons, and for others, neither the oiler nor the correspondent was fond of rowing at this time. The correspondent wondered ingenuously how in the name of all that was sane could there be people who thought it amusing to row a boat. It was not an amusement; it was a diabolical punishment, and even a genius of mental aberrations could never conclude that it was anything but a horror to the muscles and a crime against the back. He mentioned to the boat in general how the amusement of rowing struck him, and the weary-faced oiler smiled in full sympathy. Previously to the foundering, by the way, the oiler had worked a double watch in the engine-room of the ship.

"Take her easy, now, boys," said the captain. "Don't spend yourselves. If we have to run a surf you'll need all your strength, because we'll sure have to swim for it. Take your time."

Slowly the land arose from the sea. From a black line it became a line of black and a line of white—trees and sand. Finally the captain said that he could make out a house on the shore. "That's the house of refuge, sure," said the cook. "They'll see us before long, and come out after us."

The distant lighthouse reared high. "The keeper ought to be able to make us out now, if he's looking through a glass," said the captain. "He'll notify the life-saving people."

"None of those other boats could have got ashore to give word of the wreck," said the oiler, in a low voice, "else the life-boat would be out hunting us."

Slowly and beautifully the land loomed out of the sea. The wind came again. It had veered from the northeast to the southeast. Finally a new sound struck the ears of the men in the boat. It was the low thunder of the surf on the shore. "We'll never be able to make the lighthouse now," said the captain. "Swing her head a little more north, Billie."

"A little more north, sir," said the oiler.

Whereupon the little boat turned her nose once more down the wind, and all but the oarsman watched the shore grow. Under the influence of this expansion doubt and direful apprehension were leaving the minds of the men. The management of the boat was still most absorbing, but it could not prevent a quiet cheerfulness. In an hour, perhaps, they would be ashore.

Their backbones had become thoroughly used to balancing in the boat, and they now rode this wild colt of a dinghy like circus men. The correspondent thought that he had been drenched to the skin, but happening to feel in the top pocket of his coat, he found therein eight cigars. Four of them were soaked with sea-water; four were perfectly scatheless. After a search, somebody produced three dry matches; and thereupon the four waifs rode impudently in their little boat and, with an assurance of an impending rescue shining in their eyes, puffed at the big cigars, and judged well and ill of all men. Everybody took a drink of water.

IV

"Cook," remarked the captain, "there don't seem to be any signs of life about your house of refuge."

"No," replied the cook. "Funny they don't see us!" 60

A broad stretch of lowly coast lay before the eyes of the men. It was of low dunes topped with dark vegetation. The roar of the surf was plain, and sometimes they could see the white lip of a wave as it spun up the beach. A tiny house was blocked out black upon the sky. Southward, the slim lighthouse lifted its little gray length.

Tide, wind, and waves were swinging the dinghy northward. "Funny they don't see us," said the men.

The surf's roar was here dulled, but its tone was nevertheless thunderous and mighty. As the boat swam over the great rollers the men sat listening to this roar. "We'll swamp sure," said everybody.

It is fair to say here that there was not a life-saving station within twenty miles in either direction; but the men did not know this fact, and in consequence they made dark and opprobrious remarks concerning the eyesight of the nation's life-savers. Four scowling men sat in the dinghy and surpassed records in the invention of epithets.

"Funny they don't see us." 65

The light-heartedness of a former time had completely faded. To their sharpened minds it was easy to conjure pictures of all kinds of incompetency and blindness and, indeed, cowardice. There was the shore of the populous land, and it was bitter and bitter to them that from it came no sign.

"Well," said the captain, ultimately, "I suppose we'll have to make a try for ourselves. If we stay out here too long, we'll none of us have strength left to swim after the boat swamps."

And so the oiler, who was at the oars, turned the boat straight for the shore. There was a sudden tightening of muscles. There was some thinking.

"If we don't all get ashore," said the captain—"if we don't all get ashore, I suppose you fellows know where to send news of my finish?"

They then briefly exchanged some addresses and admonitions. As for the 70
reflections of the men, there was a great deal of rage in them. Perchance they might be formulated thus: "If I am going to be drowned—if I am going to be drowned—if I am going to be drowned, why, in the name of the seven mad gods who rule the sea, was I allowed to come thus far and contemplate sand and trees? Was I brought here merely to have my nose dragged away as I was about to nibble the sacred cheese of life? It is preposterous. If this old ninny-woman, Fate, cannot do better than this, she should be deprived of the management of men's fortunes. She is an old hen who knows not her intention. If she has

decided to drown me, why did she not do it in the beginning and save me all this trouble? The whole affair is absurd. . . . But no; she cannot mean to drown me. She dare not drown me. She cannot drown me. Not after all this work." Afterward the man might have had an impulse to shake his fist at the clouds. "Just you drown me, now, and then hear what I call you!"

The billows that came at this time were more formidable. They seemed always just about to break and roll over the little boat in a turmoil of foam. There was a preparatory and long growl in the speech of them. No mind unused to the sea would have concluded that the dinghy could ascend these sheer heights in time. The shore was still afar. The oiler was a wily surfman. "Boys," he said, swiftly, "she won't live three minutes more, and we're too far out to swim. Shall I take her to sea again, Captain?"

"Yes; go ahead!" said the captain.

This oiler, by a series of quick miracles and fast and steady oarsmanship, turned the boat in the middle of the surf and took her safely to sea again.

There was a considerable silence as the boat bumped over the furrowed sea to deeper water. Then somebody in gloom spoke: "Well, anyhow, they must have seen us from the shore by now."

75 The gulls went in slanting flight up the wind toward the gray, desolate east. A squall, marked by dingy clouds and clouds brick-red, like smoke from a burning building, appeared from the southeast.

"What do you think of those life-saving people? Ain't they peaches?"

"Funny they haven't seen us."

"Maybe they think we're out here for sport! Maybe they think we're fishin'. Maybe they think we're damned fools."

It was a long afternoon. A changed tide tried to force them southward, but wind and wave said northward. Far ahead, where coast-line, sea, and sky formed their mighty angle, there were little dots which seemed to indicate a city on the shore.

80 "St. Augustine."

The captain shook his head. "Too near Mosquito Inlet."

And the oiler rowed, and then the correspondent rowed; then the oiler rowed. It was a weary business. The human back can become the seat of more aches and pains than are registered in books for the composite anatomy of a regiment. It is a limited area, but it can become the theatre of innumerable muscular conflicts, tangles, wrenches, knots, and other comforts.

"Did you ever like to row, Billie?" asked the correspondent.

"No," said the oiler. "Hang it."

85 When one exchanged the rowing-seat for a place in the bottom of the boat, he suffered a bodily depression that caused him to be careless of everything save an obligation to wiggle one finger. There was cold sea-water swashing to and fro in the boat, and he lay in it. His head, pillowed on a thwart, was within an inch of the swirl of a wave-crest, and sometimes a particularly obstreperous sea came inboard and drenched him once more. But these matters did not annoy him. It is almost certain that if the boat had capsized he would have tumbled comfortably out upon the ocean as if he felt sure that it was a great soft mattress.

"Look! There's a man on the shore!"

"There? See 'im? See 'im?"

"Yes, sure! He's walking along."

"Now he's stopped. Look! He's facing us!"

"He's waving at us!"

"So he is! By thunder!"

"Ah, now we're all right! Now we're all right! There'll be a boat out here for us in half an hour."

"He's going on. He's running. He's going up to that house there."

The remote beach seemed lower than the sea, and it required a searching glance to discern the little black figure. The captain saw a floating stick, and they rowed to it. A bath towel was by some weird chance in the boat, and, tying this on the stick, the captain waved it. The oarsman did not dare turn his head, so he was obliged to ask questions.

"What's he doing now?"

"He's standing still again. He's looking, I think. . . . There he goes again—toward the house. . . . Now he's stopped again."

"Is he waving at us?"

"No, not now; he was, though."

"Look! There comes another man!"

"He's running."

"Look at him go, would you!"

"Why, he's on a bicycle. Now he's met the other man. They're both waving at us. Look!"

"There comes something up the beach."

"What the devil is that thing?"

"Why, it looks like a boat."

"Why, certainly, it's a boat."

"No; it's on wheels."

"Yes, so it is. Well, that must be the life-boat. They drag them along shore on a wagon."

"That's the life-boat, sure."

"No, by God, it's—it's an omnibus."

"I tell you it's a life-boat."

"It is not! It's an omnibus. I can see it plain. See? One of these big hotel omnibuses."

"By thunder, you're right. It's an omnibus, sure as fate. What do you suppose they are doing with an omnibus? Maybe they are going around collecting the life-crew, hey?"

"That's it, likely. Look! There's a fellow waving a little black flag. He's standing on the steps of the omnibus. There comes those other two fellows. Now they're all talking together. Look at the fellow with the flag. Maybe he ain't waving it!"

"That ain't a flag, is it? That's his coat. Why, certainly, that's his coat."

"So it is: it's his coat. He's taken it off and is waving it around his head. But would you look at him swing it!"

"Oh, say, there isn't any life-saving station there. That's just a winter-resort."

"What's that idiot with the coat mean? What's he signaling, anyhow?"

"It looks as if he were trying to tell us to go north. There must be a life-saving station up there."

"No; he thinks we're fishing. Just giving us a merry hand. See? Ah, there, Willie!"

"Well, I wish I could make something out of those signals. What do you suppose he means?"

"He don't mean anything; he's just playing."

"Well, if he'd just signal us to try the surf again, or to go to sea and wait, or go north, or go south, or go to hell, there would be some reason in it. But look at him! He just stands there and keeps his coat revolving like a wheel. The ass!"

"There come more people."

"Now there's quite a mob. Look! Isn't that a boat?"

"Where? Oh, I see where you mean. No, that's no boat."

"That fellow is still waving his coat."

"He must think we like to see him to do that. Why don't he quit? It don't mean anything."

"I don't know. I think he is trying to make us go north. It must be that there's a life-saving station there somewhere."

"Say, he ain't tired yet. Look at 'im wave!"

"Wonder how long he can keep that up. He's been revolving his coat ever since he caught sight of us. He's an idiot. Why aren't they getting men to bring a boat out? A fishing boat—one of those big yawls—could come out here all right. Why don't he do something?"

"Oh, it's all right now."

"They'll have a boat out here for us in less than no time, now that they've seen us."

A faint yellow tone came into the sky over the low land. The shadows on the sea slowly deepened. The wind bore coldness with it, and the men began to shiver.

"Holy smoke!" said one, allowing his voice to express his impious mood, "if we keep on monkeying out here! If we've got to flounder out here all night!"

"Oh, we'll never have to stay here all night! Don't you worry. They've seen us now, and it won't be long before they'll come chasing out after us."

The shore grew dusky. The man waving a coat blended gradually into this gloom, and it swallowed in the same manner the omnibus and the group of people. The spray, when it dashed uproariously over the side, made the voyagers shrink and swear like men who were being branded.

"I'd like to catch the chump who waved the coat. I feel like socking him one, just for luck."

"Why? What did he do?"

"Oh, nothing, but then he seemed so damned cheerful."

In the meantime the oiler rowed, and then the correspondent rowed, and then the oiler rowed. Gray-faced and bowed forward, they mechanically, turn by turn, plied the leaden oars. The form of the lighthouse had vanished from the southern horizon, but finally a pale star appeared, just lifting from the sea. The streaked saffron in the west passed before the all-merging darkness, and the sea to the east was black. The land had vanished, and was expressed only by the low and drear thunder of the surf.

"If I am going to be drowned—if I am going to be drowned—if I am going to be drowned, why, in the name of the seven mad gods who rule the sea, was I allowed to come thus far and contemplate sand and trees? Was I brought here merely to have my nose dragged away as I was about to nibble the sacred cheese of life?"

The patient captain, drooped over the water-jar, was sometimes obliged to speak to the oarsman.

"Keep her head up! Keep her head up!"

"Keep her head up, sir." The voices were weary and low. 145

This was surely a quiet evening. All save the oarsman lay heavily and listlessly in the boat's bottom. As for him, his eyes were just capable of noting the tall black waves that swept forward in a most sinister silence, save for an occasional subdued growl of a crest.

The cook's head was on a thwart, and he looked without interest at the water under his nose. He was deep in other scenes. Finally he spoke. "Billie," he murmured, dreamfully, "what kind of pie do you like best?"

V

"Pie!" said the oiler and the correspondent, agitatedly. "Don't talk about those things, blast you!"

"Well," said the cook, "I was just thinking about ham sandwiches, and ——"

A night on the sea in an open boat is a long night. As darkness settled finally, 150
the shine of the light, lifting from the sea in the south, changed to full gold. On the northern horizon a new light appeared, a small bluish gleam on the edge of the waters. These two lights were the furniture of the world. Otherwise there was nothing but waves.

Two men huddled in the stern, and distances were so magnificent in the dinghy that the rower was enabled to keep his feet partly warm by thrusting them under his companions. Their legs indeed extended far under the rowing-seat until they touched the feet of the captain forward. Sometimes, despite the efforts of the tired oarsman, a wave came piling into the boat, an icy wave of the night, and the chilling water soaked them anew. They would twist their bodies for a moment and groan, and sleep the dead sleep once more, while the water in the boat gurgled about them as the craft rocked.

The plan of the oiler and the correspondent was for one to row until he lost the ability, and then arouse the other from his sea-water couch in the bottom of the boat.

The oiler plied the oars until his head drooped forward and the overpowering sleep blinded him; and he rowed yet afterward. Then he touched a man in the bottom of the boat, and called his name. "Will you spell me for a little while?" he said meekly.

"Sure, Billie," said the correspondent, awaking and dragging himself to a sitting position. They exchanged places carefully, and the oiler, cuddling down in the sea-water at the cook's side, seemed to go to sleep instantly.

The particular violence of the sea had ceased. The waves came without 155
snarling. The obligation of the man at the oars was to keep the boat headed so that the tilt of the rollers would not capsize her, and to preserve her from filling when the crests rushed past. The black waves were silent and hard to be seen in the darkness. Often one was almost upon the boat before the oarsman was aware.

In a low voice the correspondent addressed the captain. He was not sure that the captain was awake, although this iron man seemed to be always awake. "Captain, shall I keep her making for that light north, sir?"

The same steady voice answered him. "Yes. Keep it about two points off the port bow."

The cook had tied a life-belt around himself in order to get even the warmth which this clumsy cork contrivance could donate, and he seemed almost stove-like when a rower, whose teeth invariably chattered wildly as soon as he ceased his labor, dropped down to sleep.

The correspondent, as he rowed, looked down at the two men sleeping underfoot. The cook's arm was around the oiler's shoulders, and, with their fragmentary clothing and haggard faces, they were the babes of the sea—a grotesque rendering of the old babes in the wood.

160 Later he must have grown stupid at his work, for suddenly there was a growling of water, and a crest came with a roar and a swash into the boat, and it was a wonder that it did not set the cook afloat in his life-belt. The cook continued to sleep, but the oiler sat up, blinking his eyes and shaking with the new cold.

"Oh, I'm awful sorry, Billie," said the correspondent, contritely.

"That's all right, old boy," said the oiler, and lay down again and was asleep.

Presently it seemed that even the captain dozed, and the correspondent thought that he was the one man afloat on all the ocean. The wind had a voice as it came over the waves, and it was sadder than the end.

There was a long, loud swishing astern of the boat, and a gleaming trail of phosphorescence, like blue flame, was furrowed on the black waters. It might have been made by a monstrous knife.

165 Then there came a stillness, while the correspondent breathed with open mouth and looked at the sea.

Suddenly there was another swish and another long flash of bluish light, and this time it was alongside the boat, and might almost have been reached with an oar. The correspondent saw an enormous fin speed like a shadow through the water, hurling the crystalline spray and leaving the long glowing trail.

The correspondent looked over his shoulder at the captain. His face was hidden, and he seemed to be asleep. He looked at the babes of the sea. They certainly were asleep. So, being bereft of sympathy, he leaned a little way to one side and swore softly into the sea.

But the thing did not then leave the vicinity of the boat. Ahead or astern, on one side or the other, at intervals long or short, fled the long sparkling streak, and there was to be heard the *whirroo* of the dark fin. The speed and power of the thing was greatly to be admired. It cut the water like a gigantic and keen projectile.

The presence of this biding thing did not affect the man with the same horror that it would if he had been a picnicker. He simply looked at the sea dully and swore in an undertone.

170 Nevertheless, it is true that he did not wish to be alone with the thing. He wished one of his companions to awake by chance and keep him company with it. But the captain hung motionless over the water-jar and the oiler and the cook in the bottom of the boat were plunged in slumber.

VI

"If I am going to be drowned—if I am going to be drowned—if I am going to be drowned, why, in the name of the seven mad gods who rule the sea, was I allowed to come thus far and contemplate sand and trees?"

During this dismal night, it may be remarked that a man would conclude that it was really the intention of the seven mad gods to drown him, despite the abominable injustice of it. For it was certainly an abominable injustice to drown a man who had worked so hard, so hard. The man felt it would be a crime most unnatural. Other people had drowned at sea since galleys swarmed with painted sails, but still——

When it occurs to a man that nature does not regard him as important, and that she feels she would not maim the universe by disposing of him, he at first wishes to throw bricks at the temple, and he hates deeply the fact that there are no bricks and no temples. Any visible expression of nature would surely be pelleted with his jeers.

Then, if there be no tangible thing to hoot, he feels, perhaps, the desire to confront a personification and indulge in pleas, bowed to one knee, and with hands supplicant, saying, "Yes, but I love myself."

A high cold star on a winter's night is the word he feels that she says to him. Thereafter he knows the pathos of his situation.

The men in the dinghy had not discussed these matters, but each had, no doubt, reflected upon them in silence and according to his mind. There was seldom any expression upon their faces save the general one of complete weariness. Speech was devoted to the business of the boat.

To chime the notes of his emotions, a verse mysteriously entered the correspondent's head. He had even forgotten that he had forgotten this verse, but it suddenly was in his mind.

> A soldier of the Legion lay dying in Algiers;
> There was lack of woman's nursing, there was dearth of woman's tears;
> But a comrade stood beside him, and he took the comrade's hand,
> And he said, "I never more shall see my own, my native land."[6]

In his childhood the correspondent had been made acquainted with the fact that a soldier of the Legion lay dying in Algiers, but he had never regarded it as important. Myriads of his schoolfellows had informed him of the soldier's plight, but the dinning had naturally ended by making him perfectly indifferent. He had never considered it his affair that a soldier of the Legion lay dying in Algiers, nor had it appeared to him as a matter for sorrow. It was less to him than the breaking of a pencil's point.

Now, however, it quaintly came to him as a human, living thing. It was no longer merely a picture of a few throes in the breast of a poet, meanwhile drinking tea and warming his feet at the grate; it was an actuality—stern, mournful, and fine.

The correspondent plainly saw the soldier. He lay on the sand with his feet out straight and still. While his pale left hand was upon his chest in an attempt

6. From "Bingen on the Rhine," by Caroline Norton (1808–77).

to thwart the going of his life, the blood came between his fingers. In the far Algerian distance, a city of low square forms was set against a sky that was faint with the last sunset hues. The correspondent, plying the oars and dreaming of the slow and slower movements of the lips of the soldier, was moved by a profound and perfectly impersonal comprehension. He was sorry for the soldier of the Legion who lay dying in Algiers.

180 The thing which had followed the boat and waited had evidently grown bored at the delay. There was no longer to be heard the slash of the cutwater, and there was no longer the flame of the long trail. The light in the north still glimmered, but it was apparently no nearer to the boat. Sometimes the boom of the surf rang in the correspondent's ears, and he turned the craft seaward then and rowed harder. Southward, some one had evidently built a watch-fire on the beach. It was too low and too far to be seen, but it made a shimmering, roseate reflection upon the bluff in back of it, and this could be discerned from the boat. The wind came stronger, and sometimes a wave suddenly raged out like a mountain-cat, and there was to be seen the sheen and sparkle of a broken crest.

The captain, in the bow, moved on his water-jar and sat erect. "Pretty long night," he observed to the correspondent. He looked at the shore. "Those life-saving people take their time."

"Did you see that shark playing around?"

"Yes, I saw him. He was a big fellow, all right."

"Wish I had known you were awake."

185 Later the correspondent spoke into the bottom of the boat. "Billie!" There was a slow and gradual disentanglement. "Billie, will you spell me?"

"Sure," said the oiler.

As soon as the correspondent touched the cold, comfortable seawater in the bottom of the boat and had huddled close to the cook's life-belt he was deep in sleep, despite the fact that his teeth played all the popular airs. This sleep was so good to him that it was but a moment before he heard a voice call his name in a tone that demonstrated the last stages of exhaustion. "Will you spell me?"

"Sure, Billie."

The light in the north had mysteriously vanished, but the correspondent took his course from the wide-awake captain.

190 Later in the night they took the boat farther out to sea, and the captain directed the cook to take one oar at the stern and keep the boat facing the seas. He was to call out if he should hear the thunder of the surf. This plan enabled the oiler and the correspondent to get respite together. "We'll give those boys a chance to get into shape again," said the captain. They curled down and, after a few preliminary chatterings and trembles, slept once more the dead sleep. Neither knew they had bequeathed to the cook the company of another shark, or perhaps the same shark.

As the boat caroused on the waves, spray occasionally bumped over the side and gave them a fresh soaking, but this had no power to break their repose. The ominous slash of the wind and the water affected them as it would have affected mummies.

"Boys," said the cook, with the notes of every reluctance in his voice, "she's drifted in pretty close. I guess one of you had better take her to sea again." The correspondent, aroused, heard the crash of the toppled crests.

As he was rowing, the captain gave him some whiskey-and-water, and this steadied the chills out of him. "If I ever get ashore and anybody shows me even a photograph of an oar——"

At last there was a short conversation.

"Billie! . . . Billie, will you spell me?" 195

"Sure," said the oiler.

VII

When the correspondent again opened his eyes, the sea and the sky were each of the gray hue of the dawning. Later, carmine and gold was painted upon the waters. The morning appeared finally, in its splendor, with a sky of pure blue, and the sunlight flamed on the tips of the waves.

On the distant dunes were set many little black cottages, and a tall white windmill reared above them. No man, nor dog, nor bicycle appeared on the beach. The cottages might have formed a deserted village.

The voyagers scanned the shore. A conference was held in the boat. "Well," said the captain, "if no help is coming, we might better try a run through the surf right away. If we stay out here much longer we will be too weak to do anything for ourselves at all." The others silently acquiesced in this reasoning. The boat was headed for the beach. The correspondent wondered if none ever ascended the tall wind-tower,[7] and if then they never looked seaward. This tower was a giant, standing with its back to the plight of the ants. It represented in a degree, to the correspondent, the serenity of nature amid the struggles of the individual—nature in the wind, and nature in the vision of men. She did not seem cruel to him then, nor beneficent, nor treacherous, nor wise. But she was indifferent, flatly indifferent. It is, perhaps, plausible that a man in this situation, impressed with the unconcern of the universe, should see the innumerable flaws of his life, and have them taste wickedly in his mind, and wish for another chance. A distinction between right and wrong seems absurdly clear to him, then, in this new ignorance of the grave-edge, and he understands that if he were given another opportunity he would mend his conduct and his words, and be better and brighter during an introduction or at a tea.

"Now, boys," said the captain, "she is going to swamp sure. All we can do is 200
to work her in as far as possible, and then when she swamps, pile out and scramble for the beach. Keep cool now, and don't jump until she swamps sure."

The oiler took the oars. Over his shoulders he scanned the surf. "Captain," he said, "I think I'd better bring her about and keep her head-on to the seas and back her in."

"All right, Billie," said the captain. "Back her in." The oiler swung the boat then, and, seated in the stern, the cook and the correspondent were obliged to look over their shoulders to contemplate the lonely and indifferent shore.

The monstrous inshore rollers heaved the boat high until the men were again enabled to see the white sheets of water scudding up the slanted beach. "We won't get in very close," said the captain. Each time a man could wrest his attention from the rollers, he turned his glance toward the shore, and in the expression of the eyes during this contemplation there was a singular quality. The

7. Watchtower for observing weather.

correspondent, observing the others, knew that they were not afraid, but the full meaning of their glances was shrouded.

As for himself, he was too tired to grapple fundamentally with the fact. He tried to coerce his mind into thinking of it, but the mind was dominated at this time by the muscles, and the muscles said they did not care. It merely occurred to him that if he should drown it would be a shame.

205 There were no hurried words, no pallor, no plain agitation. The men simply looked at the shore. "Now, remember to get well clear of the boat when you jump," said the captain.

Seaward the crest of a roller suddenly fell with a thunderous crash, and the long white comber came roaring down upon the boat.

"Steady now," said the captain. The men were silent. They turned their eyes from the shore to the comber and waited. The boat slid up the incline, leaped at the furious top, bounced over it, and swung down the long back of the wave. Some water had been shipped, and the cook bailed it out.

But the next crest crashed also. The tumbling, boiling flood of white water caught the boat and whirled it almost perpendicular. Water swarmed in from all sides. The correspondent had his hands on the gunwale at this time, and when the water entered at that place he swiftly withdrew his fingers, as if he objected to wetting them.

The little boat, drunken with this weight of water, reeled and snuggled deeper into the sea.

210 "Bail her out, cook! Bail her out!" said the captain.

"All right, Captain," said the cook.

"Now, boys, the next one will do for us sure," said the oiler. "Mind to jump clear of the boat."

The third wave moved forward, huge, furious, implacable. It fairly swallowed the dinghy, and almost simultaneously the men tumbled into the sea. A piece of life-belt had lain in the bottom of the boat, and as the correspondent went overboard he held this to his chest with his left hand.

The January water was icy, and reflected immediately that it was colder than he had expected to find it off the coast of Florida. This appeared to his dazed mind as a fact important enough to be noted at the time. The coldness of the water was sad; it was tragic. This fact was somehow mixed and confused with his opinion of his own situation, so that it seemed almost a proper reason for tears. The water was cold.

215 When he came to the surface he was conscious of little but the noisy water. Afterward he saw his companions in the sea. The oiler was ahead in the race. He was swimming strongly and rapidly. Off to the correspondent's left, the cook's great white and corked back bulged out of the water, and in the rear the captain was hanging with his one good hand to the keel of the overturned dinghy.

There is a certain immovable quality to a shore, and the correspondent wondered at it amid the confusion of the sea.

It seemed also very attractive; but the correspondent knew that it was a long journey, and he paddled leisurely. The piece of life-preserver lay under him, and sometimes he whirled down the incline of a wave as if he were on a hand-sled.

But finally he arrived at a place in the sea where travel was beset with difficulty. He did not pause swimming to inquire what manner of current had caught him, but there his progress ceased. The shore was set before him like a bit of scenery on a stage, and he looked at it and understood with his eyes each detail of it.

As the cook passed, much farther to the left, the captain was calling to him, "Turn over on your back, cook! Turn over on your back and use the oar."

"All right, sir." The cook turned on his back, and, paddling with an oar, went 220
ahead as if he were a canoe.

Presently the boat also passed to the left of the correspondent, with the captain clinging with one hand to the keel. He would have appeared like a man raising himself to look over a board fence if it were not for the extraordinary gymnastics of the boat. The correspondent marvelled that the captain could still hold to it.

They passed on nearer to shore—the oiler, the cook, the captain—and following them went the water-jar, bouncing gaily over the seas.

The correspondent remained in the grip of this strange new enemy, a current. The shore, with its white slope of sand and its green bluff topped with little silent cottages, was spread like a picture before him. It was very near to him then, but he was impressed as one who, in a gallery, looks at a scene from Brittany or Algiers.

He thought: "I am going to drown? Can it be possible? Can it be possible? Can it be possible?" Perhaps an individual must consider his own death to be the final phenomenon of nature.

But later a wave perhaps whirled him out of this small deadly current, for he 225
found suddenly that he could again make progress toward the shore. Later still he was aware that the captain, clinging with one hand to the keel of the dinghy, had his face turned away from the shore and toward him, and was calling his name. "Come to the boat! Come to the boat!"

In his struggle to reach the captain and the boat, he reflected that when one gets properly wearied drowning must really be a comfortable arrangement—a cessation of hostilities accompanied by a large degree of relief; and he was glad of it, for the main thing in his mind for some moments had been horror of the temporary agony; he did not wish to be hurt.

Presently he saw a man running along the shore. He was undressing with most remarkable speed. Coat, trousers, shirt, everything flew magically off him.

"Come to the boat!" called the captain.

"All right, Captain." As the correspondent paddled, he saw the captain let himself down to bottom and leave the boat. Then the correspondent performed his one little marvel of the voyage. A large wave caught him and flung him with ease and supreme speed completely over the boat and far beyond it. It struck him even then as an event in gymnastics and a true miracle of the sea. An overturned boat in the surf is not a plaything to a swimming man.

The correspondent arrived in water that reached only to his waist, but his 230
condition did not enable him to stand for more than a moment. Each wave knocked him into a heap, and the undertow pulled at him.

Then he saw the man who had been running and undressing, and undressing and running, come bounding into the water. He dragged ashore the cook, and then waded toward the captain; but the captain waved him away and sent him to the correspondent. He was naked—naked as a tree in winter; but a halo was about his head, and he shone like a saint. He gave a strong pull, and a long drag, and a bully heave at the correspondent's hand. The correspondent, schooled in the minor formulae, said, "Thanks, old man." But suddenly the man cried, "What's that?" He pointed a swift finger. The correspondent said, "Go."

In the shallows, face downward, lay the oiler. His forehead touched sand that was periodically, between each wave, clear of the sea.

The correspondent did not know all that transpired afterward. When he achieved safe ground he fell, striking the sand with each particular part of his body. It was as if he had dropped from a roof, but the thud was grateful to him.

It seems that instantly the beach was populated with men with blankets, clothes, and flasks, and women with coffee-pots and all the remedies sacred to their minds. The welcome of the land to the men from the sea was warm and generous; but a still and dripping shape was carried slowly up the beach, and the land's welcome for it could only be the different and sinister hospitality of the grave.

When it came night, the white waves paced to and fro in the moonlight, and the wind brought the sound of the great sea's voice to the men on the shore, and they felt that they could then be interpreters.

1898

QUESTIONS

1. When do you become aware that your view of events in THE OPEN BOAT is limited to things seen and heard by the four men in the boat? In what specific ways is that important to the story's effect? Where does the story's perspective "expand" to include larger reflections and generalizations? How are they justified by the narrative point of view?
2. Examine paragraphs 3–6; then differentiate the four men as fully as you can. What distinguishing features help you keep them straight as the narrative proceeds? What facts are provided later about each of the men? In which of the men do you become most interested as the story develops?
3. Which, if any, of the following seem like apt statements of the story's theme, and why? Which, if any, seems most central?

   a. All human beings are ultimately the same in that we are all equally powerless against nature.
   b. As the novelist George Eliot once said, "Character is destiny."
   c. In the face of disaster, people tend to become selfless, forgetting their differences and bonding together.
   d. Our individual fates are ultimately determined by forces beyond our control.
   e. We can never know the full truth; all we have is our own limited individual perspective.
   f. Pride is man's downfall.

GABRIEL GARCÍA MÁRQUEZ (1928–2014)

A Very Old Man with Enormous Wings: A Tale for Children[1]

Born in Aracataca, Colombia, a remote town near the Caribbean coast, Gabriel García Márquez studied law at the University of Bogotá and then worked as a journalist in Latin America, Europe, and the United States. In 1967, he took up permanent residence in Barcelona, Spain. His first published book, *Leaf Storm* (1955), set in the fictional small town of Macondo, is based on the myths and legends of his childhood home. His most famous novel, *One Hundred Years of Solitude* (1967), fuses magic, reality, fable, and fantasy to present six generations of one Macondo family, a microcosm of many of the social, political, and economic problems of Latin America. Among his many works are *The Autumn of the Patriarch* (1975), *Chronicle of a Death Foretold* (1981), *Love in the Time of Cholera* (1987), *Of Love and Other Demons* (1994), and *Living to Tell the Tale* (2003), a three-volume set of memoirs. Márquez won the Nobel Prize for Literature in 1982.

On the third day of rain they had killed so many crabs inside the house that Pelayo had to cross his drenched courtyard and throw them into the sea, because the newborn child had a temperature all night and they thought it was due to the stench. The world had been sad since Tuesday. Sea and sky were a single ashgray thing and the sands of the beach, which on March nights glimmered like powdered light, had become a stew of mud and rotten shellfish. The light was so weak at noon that when Pelayo was coming back to the house after throwing away the crabs, it was hard for him to see what it was that was moving and groaning in the rear of the courtyard. He had to go very close to see that it was an old man, a very old man, lying face down in the mud, who, in spite of his tremendous efforts, couldn't get up, impeded by his enormous wings.

Frightened by that nightmare, Pelayo ran to get Elisenda, his wife, who was putting compresses on the sick child, and he took her to the rear of the courtyard. They both looked at the fallen body with mute stupor. He was dressed like a ragpicker.[2] There were only a few faded hairs left on his bald skull and very few teeth in his mouth, and his pitiful condition of a drenched great-grandfather had taken away any sense of grandeur he might have had. His huge buzzard wings, dirty and half-plucked, were forever entangled in the mud. They looked at him so long and so closely that Pelayo and Elisenda very soon overcame their surprise and in the end found him familiar. Then they dared speak to him, and he answered in an incomprehensible dialect with a strong sailor's voice. That was how they skipped over the inconvenience of the wings and quite intelligently

1. Translated by Gregory Rabassa.
2. Someone who earns a living by collecting rags and other refuse.

concluded that he was a lonely castaway from some foreign ship wrecked by the storm. And yet, they called in a neighbor woman who knew everything about life and death to see him, and all she needed was one look to show them their mistake.

"He's an angel," she told them. "He must have been coming for the child, but the poor fellow is so old that the rain knocked him down."

On the following day everyone knew that a flesh-and-blood angel was held captive in Pelayo's house. Against the judgment of the wise neighbor woman, for whom angels in those times were the fugitive survivors of a celestial conspiracy, they did not have the heart to club him to death. Pelayo watched over him all afternoon from the kitchen, armed with his bailiff's[3] club, and before going to bed he dragged him out of the mud and locked him up with the hens in the wire chicken coop. In the middle of the night, when the rain stopped, Pelayo and Elisenda were still killing crabs. A short time afterward the child woke up without a fever and with a desire to eat. Then they felt magnanimous and decided to put the angel on a raft with fresh water and provisions for three days and leave him to his fate on the high seas. But when they went out into the courtyard with the first light of dawn, they found the whole neighborhood in front of the chicken coop having fun with the angel, without the slightest reverence, tossing him things to eat through the openings in the wire as if he weren't a supernatural creature but a circus animal.

5 Father Gonzaga arrived before seven o'clock, alarmed at the strange news. By that time onlookers less frivolous than those at dawn had already arrived and they were making all kinds of conjectures concerning the captive's future. The simplest among them thought that he should be named mayor of the world. Others of sterner mind felt that he should be promoted to the rank of five-star general in order to win all wars. Some visionaries hoped that he could be put to stud in order to implant on earth a race of winged wise men who could take charge of the universe. But Father Gonzaga, before becoming a priest, had been a robust woodcutter. Standing by the wire, he reviewed his catechism in an instant and asked them to open the door so that he could take a close look at that pitiful man who looked more like a huge decrepit hen among the fascinated chickens. He was lying in a corner drying his open wings in the sunlight among the fruit peels and breakfast leftovers that the early risers had thrown him. Alien to the impertinences of the world, he only lifted his antiquarian eyes and murmured something in his dialect when Father Gonzaga went into the chicken coop and said good morning to him in Latin. The parish priest had his first suspicion of an imposter when he saw that he did not understand the language of God or know how to greet His ministers. Then he noticed that seen close up he was much too human: he had an unbearable smell of the outdoors, the back side of his wings was strewn with parasites and his main feathers had been mistreated by terrestrial winds, and nothing about him measured up to the proud dignity of angels. Then he came out of the chicken coop and in a brief sermon warned the curious against the risks of being ingenuous. He reminded them that the devil had the bad habit of making use of carnival tricks in order to confuse the unwary. He argued that if wings were not the essential element in determining the differ-

3. Local government official, usually one employed to make arrests and serve warrants.

ence between a hawk and an airplane, they were even less so in the recognition of angels. Nevertheless, he promised to write a letter to his bishop so that the latter would write to his primate[4] so that the latter would write to the Supreme Pontiff in order to get the final verdict from the highest courts.

His prudence fell on sterile hearts. The news of the captive angel spread with such rapidity that after a few hours the courtyard had the bustle of a marketplace and they had to call in troops with fixed bayonets to disperse the mob that was about to knock the house down. Elisenda, her spine all twisted from sweeping up so much marketplace trash, then got the idea of fencing in the yard and charging five cents admission to see the angel.

The curious came from far away. A traveling carnival arrived with a flying acrobat who buzzed over the crowd several times, but no one paid any attention to him because his wings were not those of an angel but, rather, those of a sidereal[5] bat. The most unfortunate invalids on earth came in search of health: a poor woman who since childhood had been counting her heartbeats and had run out of numbers; a Portuguese man who couldn't sleep because the noise of the stars disturbed him; a sleepwalker who got up at night to undo the things he had done while awake; and many others with less serious ailments. In the midst of that shipwreck disorder that made the earth tremble, Pelayo and Elisenda were happy with fatigue, for in less than a week they had crammed their rooms with money and the line of pilgrims waiting their turn to enter still reached beyond the horizon.

The angel was the only one who took no part in his own act. He spent his time trying to get comfortable in his borrowed nest, befuddled by the hellish heat of the oil lamps and sacramental candles that had been placed along the wire. At first they tried to make him eat some mothballs, which, according to the wisdom of the wise neighbor woman, were the food prescribed for angels. But he turned them down, just as he turned down the papal lunches[6] that the penitents brought him, and they never found out whether it was because he was an angel or because he was an old man that in the end he ate nothing but eggplant mush. His only supernatural virtue seemed to be patience. Especially during the first days, when the hens pecked at him, searching for the stellar parasites that proliferated in his wings, and the cripples pulled out feathers to touch their defective parts with, and even the most merciful threw stones at him, trying to get him to rise so they could see him standing. The only time they succeeded in arousing him was when they burned his side with an iron for branding steers, for he had been motionless for so many hours that they thought he was dead. He awoke with a start, ranting in his hermetic language and with tears in his eyes, and he flapped his wings a couple of times, which brought on a whirlwind of chicken dung and lunar dust and a gale of panic that did not seem to be of this world. Although many thought that his reaction had been one not of rage but of pain, from then on they were careful not to annoy him, because the majority understood that his passivity was not that of a hero taking his ease but that of a cataclysm in repose.

4. Highest bishop of a given state.
5. Of, or relating to, the stars.
6. Expensive, elaborately prepared meals.

Father Gonzaga held back the crowd's frivolity with formulas of maidservant inspiration while awaiting the arrival of a final judgment on the nature of the captive. But the mail from Rome showed no sense of urgency. They spent their time finding out if the prisoner had a navel, if his dialect had any connection with Aramaic, how many times he could fit on the head of a pin, or whether he wasn't just a Norwegian with wings. Those meager letters might have come and gone until the end of time if a providential event had not put an end to the priest's tribulations.

It so happened that during those days, among so many other carnival attractions, there arrived in town the traveling show of the woman who had been changed into a spider for having disobeyed her parents. The admission to see her was not only less than the admission to see the angel, but people were permitted to ask her all manner of questions about her absurd state and to examine her up and down so that no one would ever doubt the truth of her horror. She was a frightful tarantula the size of a ram and with the head of a sad maiden. What was most heart-rending, however, was not her outlandish shape but the sincere affliction with which she recounted the details of her misfortune. While still practically a child she had sneaked out of her parents' house to go to a dance, and while she was coming back through the woods after having danced all night without permission, a fearful thunderclap rent the sky in two and through the crack came the lightning bolt of brimstone that changed her into a spider. Her only nourishment came from the meatballs that charitable souls chose to toss into her mouth. A spectacle like that, full of so much human truth and with such a fearful lesson, was bound to defeat without even trying that of a haughty angel who scarcely deigned to look at mortals. Besides, the few miracles attributed to the angel showed a certain mental disorder, like the blind man who didn't recover his sight but grew three new teeth, or the paralytic who didn't get to walk but almost won the lottery, and the leper whose sores sprouted sunflowers. Those consolation miracles, which were more like mocking fun, had already ruined the angel's reputation when the woman who had been changed into a spider finally crushed him completely. That was how Father Gonzaga was cured forever of his insomnia and Pelayo's courtyard went back to being as empty as during the time it had rained for three days and crabs walked through the bedrooms.

The owners of the house had no reason to lament. With the money they saved they built a two-story mansion with balconies and gardens and high netting so that crabs wouldn't get in during the winter, and with iron bars on the windows so that angels wouldn't get in. Pelayo also set up a rabbit warren close to town and gave up his job as bailiff for good, and Elisenda bought some satin pumps with high heels and many dresses of iridescent silk, the kind worn on Sunday by the most desirable women in those times. The chicken coop was the only thing that didn't receive any attention. If they washed it down with creolin[7] and burned tears of myrrh inside it every so often, it was not in homage to the angel but to drive away the dungheap stench that still hung everywhere like a ghost and was turning the new house into an old one. At first, when the child learned to walk, they were careful that he not get too close to the chicken coop.

7. Disinfectant.

But then they began to lose their fears and got used to the smell, and before the child got his second teeth he'd gone inside the chicken coop to play, where the wires were falling apart. The angel was no less standoffish with him than with other mortals, but he tolerated the most ingenious infamies with the patience of a dog who had no illusions. They both came down with chicken pox at the same time. The doctor who took care of the child couldn't resist the temptation to listen to the angel's heart, and he found so much whistling in the heart and so many sounds in his kidneys that it seemed impossible for him to be alive. What surprised him most, however, was the logic of his wings. They seemed so natural on that completely human organism that he couldn't understand why other men didn't have them too.

When the child began school it had been some time since the sun and rain had caused the collapse of the chicken coop. The angel went dragging himself about here and there like a stray dying man. They would drive him out of the bedroom with a broom and a moment later find him in the kitchen. He seemed to be in so many places at the same time that they grew to think that he'd been duplicated, that he was reproducing himself all through the house, and the exasperated and unhinged Elisenda shouted that it was awful living in that hell full of angels. He could scarcely eat and his antiquarian eyes had also become so foggy that he went about bumping into posts. All he had left were the bare cannulae of his last feathers. Pelayo threw a blanket over him and extended him the charity of letting him sleep in the shed, and only then did they notice that he had a temperature at night, and was delirious with the tongue twisters of an old Norwegian. That was one of the few times they became alarmed, for they thought he was going to die and not even the wise neighbor woman had been able to tell them what to do with dead angels.

And yet he not only survived his worst winter, but seemed improved with the first sunny days. He remained motionless for several days in the farthest corner of the courtyard, where no one would see him, and at the beginning of December some large, stiff feathers began to grow on his wings, the feathers of a scarecrow, which looked more like another misfortune of decrepitude. But he must have known the reason for those changes, for he was quite careful that no one should notice them, that no one should hear the sea chanteys that he sometimes sang under the stars. One morning Elisenda was cutting some bunches of onions for lunch when a wind that seemed to come from the high seas blew into the kitchen. Then she went to the window and caught the angel in his first attempts at flight. They were so clumsy that his fingernails opened a furrow in the vegetable patch and he was on the point of knocking the shed down with the ungainly flapping that slipped on the light and couldn't get a grip on the air. But he did manage to gain altitude. Elisenda let out a sigh of relief, for herself and for him, when she saw him pass over the last houses, holding himself up in some way with the risky flapping of a senile vulture. She kept watching him even when she was through cutting the onions and she kept on watching until it was no longer possible for her to see him, because then he was no longer an annoyance in her life but an imaginary dot on the horizon of the sea.

1968

QUESTIONS

1. The subtitle of this story is "A Tale for Children." Why and how does this seem like an apt description? an inapt or ironic one?
2. How do the various characters interpret the winged man? How do they arrive at their interpretations? What might their interpretations reveal about them? about people and/or the process of interpretation in general?
3. Why do so many people at first come to see the winged man and later stop doing so? Why is Elisenda so relieved when he finally flies away? What insights into human behavior might be revealed here? Might any constitute a theme?

YASUNARI KAWABATA
(1899–1972)
The Grasshopper and the Bell Cricket[1]

Born in Osaka, Japan, to a prosperous family, Yasunari Kawabata graduated from Tokyo Imperial University in 1924 and had his first literary success with the semiautobiographical novella *The Izu Dancer* (1926). He cofounded the journal *Contemporary Literature* in support of the Neosensualist movement, which had much in common with the European literary movements of Dadaism, Expressionism, and Cubism. His best-known works include *Snow Country* (1937), *Thousand Cranes* (1952), *The Sound of the Mountain* (1954), *The Lake* (1955), *The Sleeping Beauty* (1960), *The Old Capital* (1962), and the collection *Palm-of-the-Hand Stories* (translated in 1988). Kawabata was awarded the Nobel Prize for Literature in 1968. After long suffering from poor health, he committed suicide in 1972.

Walking along the tile-roofed wall of the university, I turned aside and approached the upper school. Behind the white board fence of the school playground, from a dusky clump of bushes under the black cherry trees, an insect's voice could be heard. Walking more slowly and listening to that voice, and furthermore reluctant to part with it, I turned right so as not to leave the playground behind. When I turned to the left, the fence gave way to an embankment planted with orange trees. At the corner, I exclaimed with surprise. My eyes gleaming at what they saw up ahead, I hurried forward with short steps.

At the base of the embankment was a bobbing cluster of beautiful varicolored lanterns, such as one might see at a festival in a remote country village. Without going any farther, I knew that it was a group of children on an insect chase among the bushes of the embankment. There were about twenty lanterns. Not only were there crimson, pink, indigo, green, purple, and yellow lanterns, but one lantern glowed with five colors at once. There were even some little red store-bought lanterns. But most of the lanterns were beautiful square

1. Translated by Lane Dunlop.

ones which the children had made themselves with love and care. The bobbing lanterns, the coming together of children on this lonely slope—surely it was a scene from a fairy tale?

One of the neighborhood children had heard an insect sing on this slope one night. Buying a red lantern, he had come back the next night to find the insect. The night after that, there was another child. This new child could not buy a lantern. Cutting out the back and front of a small carton and papering it, he placed a candle on the bottom and fastened a string to the top. The number of children grew to five, and then to seven. They learned how to color the paper that they stretched over the windows of the cutout cartons, and to draw pictures on it. Then these wise child-artists, cutting out round, three-cornered, and lozenge leaf shapes in the cartons, coloring each little window a different color, with circles and diamonds, red and green, made a single and whole decorative pattern. The child with the red lantern discarded it as a tasteless object that could be bought at a store. The child who had made his own lantern threw it away because the design was too simple. The pattern of light that one had had in hand the night before was unsatisfying the morning after. Each day, with cardboard, paper, brush, scissors, penknife, and glue, the children made new lanterns out of their hearts and minds. Look at my lantern! Be the most unusually beautiful! And each night, they had gone out on their insect hunts. These were the twenty children and their beautiful lanterns that I now saw before me.

Wide-eyed, I loitered near them. Not only did the square lanterns have old-fashioned patterns and flower shapes, but the names of the children who had made them were cut out in squared letters of the syllabary. Different from the painted-over red lanterns, others (made of thick cutout cardboard) had their designs drawn onto the paper windows, so that the candle's light seemed to emanate from the form and color of the design itself. The lanterns brought out the shadows of the bushes like dark light. The children crouched eagerly on the slope wherever they heard an insect's voice.

"Does anyone want a grasshopper?" A boy, who had been peering into a bush 5
about thirty feet away from the other children, suddenly straightened up and
shouted.

"Yes! Give it to me!" Six or seven children came running up. Crowding behind the boy who had found the grasshopper, they peered into the bush. Brushing away their outstretched hands and spreading out his arms, the boy stood as if guarding the bush where the insect was. Waving the lantern in his right hand, he called again to the other children.

"Does anyone want a grasshopper? A grasshopper!"

"I do! I do!" Four or five more children came running up. It seemed you could not catch a more precious insect than a grasshopper. The boy called out a third time.

"Doesn't anyone want a grasshopper?"

Two or three more children came over. 10

"Yes. I want it."

It was a girl, who just now had come up behind the boy who'd discovered the insect. Lightly turning his body, the boy gracefully bent forward. Shifting the lantern to his left hand, he reached his right hand into the bush.

"It's a grasshopper."

"Yes. I'd like to have it."

15 The boy quickly stood up. As if to say "Here!" he thrust out his fist that held the insect at the girl. She, slipping her left wrist under the string of her lantern, enclosed the boy's fist with both hands. The boy quietly opened his fist. The insect was transferred to between the girl's thumb and index finger.

"Oh! It's not a grasshopper. It's a bell cricket." The girl's eyes shone as she looked at the small brown insect.

"It's a bell cricket! It's a bell cricket!" The children echoed in an envious chorus.

"It's a bell cricket. It's a bell cricket."

Glancing with her bright intelligent eyes at the boy who had given her the cricket, the girl opened the little insect cage hanging at her side and released the cricket in it.

20 "It's a bell cricket."

"Oh, it's a bell cricket," the boy who'd captured it muttered. Holding up the insect cage close to his eyes, he looked inside it. By the light of his beautiful many colored lantern, also held up at eye level, he glanced at the girl's face.

Oh, I thought. I felt slightly jealous of the boy, and sheepish. How silly of me not to have understood his actions until now! Then I caught my breath in surprise. Look! It was something on the girl's breast which neither the boy who had given her the cricket, nor she who had accepted it, nor the children who were looking at them noticed.

In the faint greenish light that fell on the girl's breast, wasn't the name "Fujio" clearly discernible? The boy's lantern, which he held up alongside the girl's insect cage, inscribed his name, cut out in the green papered aperture, onto her white cotton kimono. The girl's lantern, which dangled loosely from her wrist, did not project its pattern so clearly, but still one could make out, in a trembling patch of red on the boy's waist, the name "Kiyoko." This chance interplay of red and green—if it was chance or play—neither Fujio nor Kiyoko knew about.

Even if they remembered forever that Fujio had given her the cricket and that Kiyoko had accepted it, not even in dreams would Fujio ever know that his name had been written in green on Kiyoko's breast or that Kiyoko's name had been inscribed in red on his waist, nor would Kiyoko ever know that Fujio's name had been inscribed in green on her breast or that her own name had been written in red on Fujio's waist.

25 Fujio! Even when you have become a young man, laugh with pleasure at a girl's delight when, told that it's a grasshopper, she is given a bell cricket; laugh with affection at a girl's chagrin when, told that it's a bell cricket, she is given a grasshopper.

Even if you have the wit to look by yourself in a bush away from the other children, there are not many bell crickets in the world. Probably you will find a girl like a grasshopper whom you think is a bell cricket.

And finally, to your clouded, wounded heart, even a true bell cricket will seem like a grasshopper. Should that day come, when it seems to you that the world is only full of grasshoppers, I will think it a pity that you have no way to remember tonight's play of light, when your name was written in green by your beautiful lantern on a girl's breast.

1988

QUESTIONS

1. Who might the narrator of this story be? What clues are provided in the story?
2. What might the grasshopper and the bell cricket each come to symbolize in the story?
3. Might the final three paragraphs of this story come close to stating its theme(s)? How would you state the theme(s)?

JUNOT DÍAZ
(b. 1968)

Wildwood

Aptly described by one British newspaper as "a truly all-American writer" and by himself as "African diasporic, migrant, Caribbean, Dominican, Jersey boy," MIT professor and MacArthur Foundation "genius grant" winner Junot Díaz lived in the Dominican Republic until age six, when he and the rest of his family joined his father in the United States. While his mother worked on a factory assembly line and his father, a former military policeman, drove a forklift, Díaz and his four siblings navigated life in what he calls a "very black, very Puerto Rican and very poor" New Jersey neighborhood. Díaz supported himself through college, earning a BA in English from Rutgers and a Cornell MFA. A year after graduating, Díaz published *Drown* (1996), a collection of interrelated short stories. A decade later, his novel, *The Brief Wondrous Life of Oscar Wao* (2007), won numerous prizes, including both a National Book Critics Circle Award and a Pulitzer. *Oscar Wao* is a tale of a lovelorn and utterly lovable "ghetto nerd," who dreams of becoming the next J. R. R. Tolkien and three generations of his Dominican American family. Díaz published a second short-story collection, *This Is How you Lose Her* (2012), and cofounded the pioneering Voices of Our Nations Arts Foundation to nurture the work of writers of color. "Wildwood," published almost simultaneously as both a short story and a chapter of *Oscar Wao,* is something of a departure for Díaz thanks to its female narrator-protagonist. But it is characteristic in its creation of an entirely new fictional language to capture the unique voices, experiences, and outlooks of its funny, complicated, thoroughly all-American cast of characters.

It's never the changes we want that change everything.

This is how it all starts: with your mother calling you into the bathroom. You will remember what you were doing at that precise moment for the rest of your life: you were reading "Watership Down"[1] and the bucks and their does were making the dash for the raft and you didn't want to stop reading, the book had to go back to your brother tomorrow, but then she called you again, louder, her I'm-not-fucking-around voice, and you mumbled irritably, Sí, señora.

1. Richard Adams's classic novel (1972) about the adventures of a community of English rabbits who, inspired by the prophetic vision of one of their youngest and smallest members, must flee their doomed warren and create a new home.

She is standing in front of the medicine-cabinet mirror, naked from the waist up, her bra slung about her hips like a torn sail, the scar on her back as vast and inconsolable as the sea. You want to return to your book, to pretend you didn't hear her, but it is too late. Her eyes meet yours, the same big smoky eyes you will have in the future. Ven acá,[2] she commands. She is frowning at something on one of her breasts.

Your mother's breasts are immensities. One of the wonders of the world. The only ones you've seen that are bigger are in nudie magazines or on really fat ladies. They're forty-two triple Ds and the aureoles are as big as saucers and black as pitch and at their edges are fierce hairs that sometimes she plucks and sometimes she doesn't. These breasts have always embarrassed you and when you walk in public with her you are conscious of them. After her face and her hair, her tetas are what she is most proud of. Your father could never get enough of them, she always brags. But given the fact that he ran off on her after their third year of marriage it seemed in the end that he could.

5 You dread conversations with your mother. These one-sided dressing-downs. You figure that she has called you in to give you another earful about your diet. Your mom's convinced that if you only eat more plátanos you will suddenly acquire her extraordinary train-wrecking secondary sex characteristics. Even at that age you are nothing if not your mother's daughter. You are twelve years old and already as tall as her, a long slender-necked ibis of a girl. You have her straight hair, which makes you look more Hindu than Dominican, and a behind that the boys haven't been able to stop talking about since the fifth grade and whose appeal you do not yet understand. You have her complexion, too, which means you are dark as night. But for all your similarities the tides of inheritance have yet to reach your chest. You have only the slightest hint of breasts: from most angles you're flat as a board and you're thinking she's going to order you to stop wearing bras again because they're suffocating your potential breasts, discouraging them from popping out. You're ready to argue with her to the death, because you're as possessive of your bras as you are of the pads you now buy yourself.

But no, she doesn't say a word about eating more plátanos. Instead, she takes your right hand and guides you. Your mom is rough in all things, but this time she is gentle. You did not think her capable of it.

Do you feel that? she asks in her too familiar raspy voice.

At first all you feel is the density of the tissue and the heat of her, like a bread that never stopped rising. She kneads your fingers into her. You're as close as you've ever been and your breathing is what you hear.

Don't you feel that?

10 She turns toward you. Coño, muchacha,[3] stop looking at me and feel.

So you close your eyes and your fingers are pushing down and you're thinking of Helen Keller[4] and how when you were little you wanted to be her except more nunnish and then suddenly you do feel something. A knot just beneath her skin, tight and secretive as a plot. And at that moment, for reasons you will never quite

2. Come here (Spanish).

3. Damn, girl (Dominican Spanish).

4. Famously blind and deaf American author, activist, and lecturer (1880–1968).

understand, you are overcome by the feeling, the premonition, that something in your life is about to change. You become light-headed and you can feel a throbbing in your blood, a rhythm, a drum. Bright lights zoom through you like photon torpedoes, like comets. You don't know how or why you know this thing, but that you know it cannot be doubted. It is exhilarating. For as long as you've been alive you've had bruja[5] ways; even your mother will not begrudge you that much. Hija de Liborio, she called you after you picked your tía's[6] winning numbers for her and when you guessed correctly how old to the day she'd been when she left home for the U.S. (a fact she'd never told anyone). You assumed Liborio was a relative. That was before Santo Domingo, before you knew about the Great Power of God.

I feel it, you say, too loudly. Lo siento.[7]

And like that, everything changes. Before the winter is out the doctors remove that breast you were kneading and its partner, along with the auxiliary lymph nodes. Because of the operations, your mother will have trouble lifting her arms over her head for the rest of her life. Her hair begins to fall out and one day she pulls it all out herself and puts it in a plastic bag. You change, too. Not right away, but it happens. And it's in that bathroom that it all begins. That you begin.

A punk chick. That's what I became. A Siouxsie and the Banshees-loving[8] punk chick. The Puerto Rican kids on the block couldn't stop laughing when they saw my hair; they called me Blacula. And the morenos,[9] they didn't know what to say; they just called me devil-bitch. Yo, devil-bitch, yo, *yo!* My tía Rubelka thought it was some kind of mental illness. Hija, she said while frying pastelitos, maybe you need *help.* But my mother was the worst. It's the last straw, she screamed. The. Last. Straw. But it always was with her. Mornings when I came downstairs she'd be in the kitchen making her coffee in la greca and listening to Radio WADO[1] and when she saw me and my hair she'd get mad all over again, as if during the night she'd forgotten who I was.

My mother was one of the tallest women in Paterson[2] and her anger was just 15
as tall. It pincered you in its long arms, and if you showed any weakness you were finished. Que muchacha tan fea,[3] she said in disgust, splashing the rest of her coffee in the sink. Fea had become my name. It was nothing new, to tell the truth. She'd been saying stuff like that all our lives. My mother would never win any awards, believe me. You could call her an absentee parent: if she wasn't at work she was sleeping and when she wasn't sleeping all she did was scream and hit. As kids, me and Oscar were more scared of our mother than we were of the

5. Witch (Spanish).

6. Aunt's (Spanish). *Hija de Liborio*: literally, child of Liborio (Spanish), an allusion to Olivorio Liborio Mateo (1876–1922), a peasant farmer turned messianic faith healer regarded by his followers as an incarnation of Christ; remnants of his once-powerful Liborista movement still survive.

7. I feel it (Spanish).

8. English rock band (1976–96) created and fronted by Siouxsie Sioux, hailed by the London *Times* as inventing "a form of post-punk discord [. . .] as influential as it was underrated."

9. Literally, browns (Spanish), a term for people with dark skin.

1. Spanish-language news and talk station owned by Univision. *La greca*: Italian-style aluminum stovetop espresso pot (Spanish).

2. New Jersey city in the New York Metropolitan area, home to many Hispanic and Middle Eastern immigrants.

3. What an ugly girl (Spanish).

dark or el cuco.[4] She would hit us anywhere, in front of anyone, always free with the chanclas and the correa,[5] but now with her cancer there wasn't much she could do anymore. The last time she tried to whale on me it was because of my hair, but instead of cringing or running I punched her hand. It was a reflex more than anything, but once it happened I knew I couldn't take it back, not ever, and so I just kept my fist clenched, waiting for whatever came next, for her to attack me with her teeth like she had this one lady in the Pathmark.[6] But she just stood there shaking, in her stupid wig and her stupid bata,[7] with two huge foam prostheses in her bra, the smell of burning wig all around us. I almost felt sorry for her. This is how you treat your mother? she cried. And if I could I would have broken the entire length of my life across her face, but instead I screamed back, And this is how you treat your daughter?

Things had been bad between us all year. How could they not have been? She was my Old World Dominican mother who had come alone to the United States and I was her only daughter, the one she had raised up herself with the help of nobody, which meant it was her duty to keep me crushed under her heel. I was fourteen and desperate for my own patch of world that had nothing to do with her. I wanted the life that I used to see when I watched "Big Blue Marble"[8] as a kid, the life that drove me to make pen pals and to borrow atlases from school. The life that existed beyond Paterson, beyond my family, beyond Spanish. And as soon as she became sick I saw my chance and I'm not going to pretend or apologize; I saw my chance and eventually I took it.

If you didn't grow up like I did then you don't know and if you don't know it's probably better you don't judge. You don't know the hold our mothers have on us, even the ones that are never around—*especially* the ones that are never around. What it's like to be the perfect Dominican daughter, which is just a nice way of saying a perfect Dominican slave. You don't know what it's like to grow up with a mother who never said anything that wasn't negative, who was always suspicious, always tearing you down and splitting your dreams straight down the seams. On TV and in books mothers talk to daughters, about life, about themselves, but on Main Street in Paterson mothers say not a word unless it's to hurt you. When my first pen pal, Tomoko, stopped writing me after three letters my mother was the one who said, You think someone's going to lose life writing to you? Of course I cried; I was eight and I had already planned that Tomoko and her family would adopt me. My mother, of course, saw clean into the marrow of those dreams and laughed. I wouldn't write to you, either, she said.

She was that kind of mother: who makes you doubt yourself, who would wipe you out if you let her. But I'm not going to pretend, either. For a long time I let her say what she wanted about me and, what was worse, for a long time I believed her. I was a fea, I was a worthless, I was an idiota. From ages two to thirteen I believed her and because I believed her I was the perfect hija. I was the one cooking, cleaning, doing the wash, buying groceries, writing letters to

4. Mythical ghost-monster, a sort of Spanish-language "boogie-man."

5. Belt (Spanish). *Chanclas*: flip-flops (Spanish).

6. Grocery store, part of a chain owned (as A&P is) by the Great Atlantic and Pacific Tea Company.

7. Bathrobe (Spanish).

8. American television series for children (1974–83); featuring stories about children around the world, the show sponsored an international pen-pal club.

the bank to explain why a house payment was going to be late, translating. I had the best grades in my class. I never caused trouble, even when the morenas used to come after me with scissors because of my straight straight hair. I stayed at home and made sure my little brother Oscar was fed and everything ran right while she was at work. I raised him and I raised me. I was the one. You're my hija, she said, that's what you're supposed to be doing. When that thing happened to me when I was eight and I finally told her what our neighbor had done she told me to shut my mouth and stop crying and I did exactly that, I shut my mouth and clenched my legs and my mind and within a year I couldn't have told you what he looked like or even his name. All you do is complain, she said to me, but you have no idea what life really is. Sí, señora.

When she told me that I could go on my sixth-grade sleepaway to Bear Mountain[9] and I bought a backpack with my own paper-route money and wrote Bobby Santos notes because he was promising to break into my cabin and kiss me in front of everyone I believed her and when on the morning of the trip she announced that I wasn't going and I said, But you promised, and she said, Muchacha del diablo,[1] I promised you nothing, I didn't throw my backpack at her or pull out my hair, and when it was Laura Saenz who ended up kissing Bobby Santos, not me, I didn't say anything, either. I just lay in my room with stupid Bear-Bear and sang under my breath, imagining where I would run away to when I grew up. To Japan maybe, where I would track down Tomoko, or to Austria, where my singing would inspire a remake of "The Sound of Music."

All my favorite books from that period were about runaways—"Watership 20
Down," "The Incredible Journey," "My Side of the Mountain"[2]—and when Bon Jovi's "Runaway"[3] came out I imagined it was me they were singing about. No one had any idea. I was the tallest, dorkiest girl in school, the one who dressed up as Wonder Woman[4] every Halloween, the one who never said a word. People saw me in my glasses and my hand-me-down clothes and could not have imagined what I was capable of. And then when I was twelve I got that feeling, the scary witchy one, and before I knew it my mother was sick and the wildness that had been in me all along, that I had tried to tamp down with chores and with homework and with promises that once I reached college I would be able to do whatever I pleased, burst out. I couldn't help it. I tried to keep it down, but it just flooded through all my quiet spaces. It was a message more than a feeling, a message that tolled like a bell: Change, change, change.

It didn't happen overnight. Yes the wildness was in me, yes it kept my heart beating fast all the long day, yes it danced around me while I walked down the street, yes it let me look boys straight in the face when they stared at me, yes it turned my laugh from a cough into a wild fever, but I was still scared. How

9. New York state park, located in the mountains along the Hudson River.

1. Devil girl (Spanish).

2. 1959 novel about the adventures of a twelve-year-old boy who flees his family's cramped New York City apartment and learns to survive on his own in the Catskill Mountains. *The Incredible Journey*: novel (1961) and, later, a Disney movie (1963) about a bull terrier, a Siamese cat, and a Labrador retriever who trek through the Canadian wilderness in search of their human masters.

3. Earliest hit record by the rock band formed in New Jersey in 1983.

4. Fictional superhero featured in DC Comics since the 1940s and in an American television series (1975–79).

could I not be? I was my mother's daughter. Her hold on me was stronger than love. And then one day I was walking home with Karen Cepeda, who at that time was my friend. Karen did the goth thing really well; she had spiky Robert Smith[5] hair and wore all black and had the skin color of a ghost. Walking with her in Paterson was like walking with the bearded lady. Everybody would stare and it was the scariest thing and that was, I guess, why I did it.

We were walking down Main and being glared at by everybody and out of nowhere I said, Karen, I want you to cut my hair. As soon as I said it I knew. The feeling in my blood, the rattle, came over me again. Karen raised her eyebrow: What about your mother? You see, it wasn't just me—everybody was scared of Belicia de León.

Fuck her, I said.

Karen looked at me like I was being stupid—I never cursed, but that was something else that was about to change. The next day we locked ourselves in her bathroom while downstairs her father and uncles were bellowing at some soccer game. Well, how do you want it? she asked. I looked at the girl in the mirror for a long time. All I knew was that I didn't want to see her ever again. I put the clippers in Karen's hand, turned them on, and guided her hand until it was all gone.

So now you're punk? Karen asked uncertainly.

Yes, I said.

The next day my mother threw the wig at me. You're going to wear this. You're going to wear it every day. And if I see you without it on I'm going to kill you!

I didn't say a word. I held the wig over the burner.

Don't do it, she said as the burner clicked. Don't you dare—

It went up in a flash, like gasoline, like a stupid hope, and if I hadn't thrown it in the sink it would have taken my hand. The smell was horrible, like all the chemicals from all the factories in Elizabeth.[6]

That was when she slapped at me, when I struck her hand and she snatched it back, like I was the fire.

Of course everyone thought I was the worst daughter ever. My tía and our neighbors kept saying, Hija, she's your mother, she's dying, but I wouldn't listen. When I hit her hand, a door opened. And I wasn't about to turn my back on it.

But God how we fought! Sick or not, dying or not, my mother wasn't going to go down easy. She wasn't una pendeja.[7] I'd seen her slap grown men, push white police officers onto their asses, curse a whole group of bochincheras.[8] She had raised me and my brother by herself, she had worked three jobs until she could buy this house we lived in, she had survived being abandoned by my father, she had come from Santo Domingo all by herself, and as a young girl she'd been beaten, set on

5. Former Siouxsie and the Banshees guitarist (b. 1959) and (since 1976) lead singer-songwriter of the English rock band the Cure.

6. Elizabeth, New Jersey is home to a major oil refinery consistently ranked as among the nation's worst polluters.

7. Dumbass, fool, pushover, or coward (Spanish).

8. Gossips (Spanish).

fire, left for dead. (This last part she didn't tell me, my tía Rubelka did, in a whisper, Your mother almost died, she almost died, and when I asked my mother about it at dinner she took my dinner and gave it to my brother.) That was my mother and there was no way she was going to let me go without killing me first. Figurín de mierda, she called me. You think you're someone, but you ain't nada.[9]

She dug hard, looking for my seams, wanting me to tear like always, but I didn't, I wasn't going to. It was that feeling I had that my life was waiting for me on the other side that made me fearless. When she threw away my Smiths and Sisters of Mercy posters—aquí yo no quiero maricones[1]—I bought replacements. When she threatened to rip up my new clothes I started keeping them in my locker and at Karen's house. When she told me that I had to quit my job at the Greek diner I explained to my boss that my mother was starting to lose it because of her chemo, and when she called to say I couldn't work there anymore he just handed me the phone and stared out at his customers in embarrassment. When she changed the locks on me—I had started staying out late, going to the Limelight because even though I was fourteen I looked twenty-five—I would knock on Oscar's window and he would let me in, scared because the next day my mother would run around the house screaming, Who the hell let that hija de la gran puta[2] in the house? Who? Who? And Oscar would be at the breakfast table stammering, I don't know, Mami, I don't.

Her rage filled the house, like flat stale smoke. It got into everything, into our hair and our food, like the fallout they told us about in school that would one day drift down soft as snow. My brother didn't know what to do. He stayed in his room, though sometimes he would lamely try to ask me what was going on. Nothing. You can tell me, Lola, he said, and I could only laugh. You need to lose weight, I told him.

In those final weeks I knew better than to go near my mother. Most of the time she just looked at me with the stink eye, but sometimes without warning she would grab me by my throat and hang on until I pried her fingers off. She didn't bother talking to me unless it was to make death threats: When you grow up you'll meet me in a dark alley when you least expect it and then I'll kill you and nobody will know I did it! Gloating as she said this.

You're crazy, I told her.

You don't call me crazy, she said, and then she sat down panting.

It was bad, but no one expected what came next. So obvious when you think about it.

All my life I'd been swearing that one day I would just disappear.

And one day I did.

I ran off, dique,[3] because of a boy.

9. Nothing (Spanish). *Figurín de mierda*: literally, perhaps something like figure made of crap; figuratively, a phony, something that only looks refined (Spanish).

1. I don't want to have those fags here (Spanish). *Smiths and Sisters of Mercy*: influential British alternative rock bands of the 1980s, fronted by highly literary singer-songwriter Morrissey (who once described himself as "humasexual") and Andrew Eldritch.

2. Daughter of a bitch (Spanish).

3. Supposedly or so they say (Dominican Spanish).

What can I really tell you about him? He was like all boys: beautiful and callow and, like an insect, he couldn't sit still. Un blanquito[4] with long hairy legs who I met one night at the Limelight.

His name was Aldo.

He was nineteen and lived down at the Jersey Shore with his seventy-four-year-old father. In the back of his Oldsmobile on University I pulled my leather skirt up and my fishnet stockings down and the smell of me was everywhere. I didn't let him go all the way, but still. The spring of my sophomore year we wrote and called each other at least once a day. I even drove down with Karen to visit him in Wildwood[5] (she had a license, I didn't). He lived and worked near the boardwalk, one of three guys who operated the bumper cars, the only one without tattoos. You should stay, he told me that night while Karen walked ahead of us on the beach. Where would I live? I asked, and he smiled. With me. Don't lie, I said, but he looked out at the surf. I want you to come, he said seriously.

He asked me three times. I counted, I know.

That summer my brother announced that he was going to dedicate his life to designing role-playing games, and my mother was trying to keep a second job for the first time since her operation. It wasn't working out. She was coming home exhausted, and since I wasn't helping, nothing around the house was getting done. Some weekends my tía Rubelka would help out with the cooking and cleaning and would lecture us both, but she had her own family to look after, so most of the time we were on our own. Come, he said on the phone. And then in August Karen left for Slippery Rock.[6] She had graduated from high school a year early. If I don't see Paterson again it will be too soon, she said before she left. Five days later, school started. I cut class six times in the first two weeks. I just couldn't do school anymore. Something inside wouldn't let me. It didn't help that I was reading "The Fountainhead" and had decided that I was Dominique and Aldo was Roark.[7] And finally what we'd all been waiting for happened. My mother announced at dinner, quietly, I want you both to listen to me: the doctor is running more tests on me.

Oscar looked like he was going to cry. He put his head down. And my reaction? I looked at her and said, Could you please pass the salt?

These days I don't blame her for smacking me across my face, but right then it was all I needed. We jumped on each other and the table fell and the sancocho[8] spilled all over the floor and Oscar just stood in the corner bellowing, Stop it, stop it, stop it!

Hija de tu maldita madre![9] she shrieked. And I said, This time I hope you die from it.

4. Little white boy (Spanish).

5. Beachfront community on the Jersey shore; the town's population surges from around 5,000 in the off-season to over 200,000 in season.

6. University in Pennsylvania about fifty miles north of Pittsburgh.

7. Influential and controversial best seller (1943) by Ayn Rand; a celebration of individualism, it chronicles young architect Howard Roark's struggles to achieve success without compromising, even with the equally headstrong architect's daughter (Dominique Francon) with whom he eventually falls in love.

8. Thick soup or stew common in South America and the Caribbean.

9. Child of a motherfucker, considered one of the worst possible insults in Dominican Spanish.

For a couple of days the house was a war zone, and then on Friday she let me out of my room and I was allowed to sit next to her on the sofa and watch novelas with her. She was waiting for her blood work to come back, but you would never have known her life was in the balance. She watched the TV like it was the only thing that mattered, and whenever one of the characters did something underhanded she would start waving her arms: Someone has to stop her! Can't they see what that puta[1] is up to?

I hate you, I said very quietly, but she didn't hear.

Go get me some water, she said. Put an ice cube in it.

That was the last thing I did for her. The next morning I was on the bus bound for the shore. One bag, two hundred dollars in tips, Tío[2] Rudolfo's old knife, and the only picture my mother had of my father, which she had hidden under her bed (she was in the picture, too, but I pretended not to notice). I was so scared. I couldn't stop shaking. The whole ride down I was expecting the sky to split open and my mother to reach down and shake me. But it didn't happen. Nobody but the man across the aisle noticed me. You're really beautiful, he said. Like a girl I once knew.

I didn't write them a note. That's how much I hated them. Her.

That night while Aldo and I lay in his sweltering kitty-litter-infested room I told him: I want you to do it to me.

He started unbuttoning my pants. Are you sure?

Definitely, I said grimly.

He had a long thin dick that hurt like hell, but the whole time I just said, Oh yes, Aldo, yes, because that was what I imagined you were supposed to say while you were losing your virginity to some boy you thought you loved.

It was like the stupidest thing I ever did. I was miserable. And so bored. But of course I wouldn't admit it. I had run away, so I was happy! Happy!

Aldo had neglected to mention, all those times he asked me to live with him, that his father hated him like I hated my mother. Aldo, Sr., had been in the Second World War and he'd never forgiven the "Japs" for all the friends he had lost. My dad's so full of shit, Aldo said. He never left Fort Dix.[3] I don't think his father said nine words to me the whole time I lived with them. He was one mean viejito[4] and even had a padlock on the refrigerator. Stay the hell out of it, he told me. We couldn't even get ice cubes out.

Aldo and his dad lived in one of the cheapest little bungalows on New Jersey Avenue, and me and Aldo slept in a room where his father kept the litter box for his two cats, and at night we would move it out into the hallway, but he always woke up before us and put it back in the room: I told you to leave my crap alone! Which is funny when you think about it. But it wasn't funny then. I got a job selling French fries on the boardwalk and between the hot oil and the cat piss I couldn't smell anything else. On my days off I would drink with Aldo or I would sit in the sand dressed in all black and try to write in my journal, which I was

1. Whore (Spanish).
2. Uncle (Spanish).
3. U.S. military post just south of Trenton, New Jersey.
4. Old man (Spanish).

sure would form the foundation for a utopian society after we blew ourselves into radioactive kibble. Sometimes boys would walk up to me and throw lines at me like, Who fuckin' died? They would sit down next to me in the sand. You a good-looking girl, you should be in a bikini. Why, so you can rape me? Jesus Christ, one of them said, jumping to his feet. What the hell is wrong with you?

To this day I don't know how I lasted. At the beginning of October I was laid off from the French-fry palace; by then most of the boardwalk was closed up and I had nothing to do except hang out at the public library, which was even smaller than my high-school one. Aldo had moved on to working with his dad at his garage, which only made them more pissed off at each other and by extension more pissed off at me. When they got home they would drink Schlitz[5] and complain about the Phillies. I guess I should count myself lucky that they didn't decide to bury the hatchet by gangbanging me. I stayed out as much as I could and waited for the feeling to come back to me, to tell me what I should do next, but I was bone dry, bereft, no visions whatsoever. I started to think that maybe it was like in the books: as soon as I lost my virginity I lost my power. I got really mad at Aldo after that. You're a drunk, I told him. And an idiot. So what, he shot back. Your pussy smells. Then stay out of it! I will!

But of course I was happy! Happy! I kept waiting to run into my family posting flyers of me on the boardwalk—my mom, the tallest blackest chestiest thing in sight, Oscar looking like the Brown Blob, my tía Rubelka, maybe even my tío if they could get him off the heroin long enough—but the closest I came to any of that was some flyers someone had put up for a lost cat. That's white people for you. They lose a cat and it's an all-points bulletin, but we Dominicans lose a daughter and we might not even cancel our appointment at the salon.

65 By November I was so finished. I would sit there with Aldo and his putrid father and the old shows would come on the TV, the ones me and my brother used to watch when we were kids, "Three's Company," "What's Happening!!," "The Jeffersons,"[6] and my disappointment would grind against some organ that was very soft and tender. It was starting to get cold, too, and wind just walked right into the bungalow and got under your blankets or jumped in the shower with you. It was awful. I kept having these stupid visions of my brother trying to cook for himself. Don't ask me why. I was the one who cooked for us. The only thing Oscar knew how to make was grilled cheese. I imagined him thin as a reed, wandering around the kitchen, opening cabinets forlornly. I even started dreaming about my mother, except in my dreams she was young, my age, and it was because of those dreams that I realized something obvious: she had run away, too, and that was why we were all in the United States.

I put away the photo of her and my father, but the dreams didn't stop. I guess when a person is with you they're only with you when they're with you, but when they're gone, when they're really gone, they're with you forever.

5. Notoriously cheap American beer.

6. Like *Three's Company* (1977–84) and *What's Happening!!* (1976–79), a popular American sitcom (1975–85). Where *What's Happening!!* focuses on three working-class African American teens in Los Angeles, both *The Jeffersons* and *Three's Company* focus partly on the conflicts and humor arising from particular living arrangements: the former features a newly affluent African American family who have moved from working-class Queens into a luxurious Manhattan high-rise; in the latter, which has an all-Caucasian cast, two young women can maintain their apartment only by convincing their landlord that their male roommate is gay.

And then at the end of November Aldo, my wonderful boyfriend, decided to be cute. I knew he was getting unhappy with us, but I didn't know exactly how bad it was until one night he had his friends over. His father had gone to Atlantic City[7] and they were all drinking and smoking and telling dumb jokes and suddenly Aldo says, Do you know what Pontiac stands for? Poor Old Nigger Thinks It's A Cadillac. Who was he looking at when he told his punch line? He was looking straight at me.

That night he wanted me but I pushed his hand away. Don't touch me.

Don't get sore, he said, putting my hand on his cock. It wasn't nothing.

And then he laughed.

So what did I do a couple days later—a really dumb thing. I called home. The first time no one answered. The second time it was Oscar. The de León residence, how may I direct your call? That was my brother for you. This is why everybody in the world hated his guts.

It's me, dumb-ass.

Lola. He was so quiet and then I realized he was crying. Where *are* you?

You don't want to know. I switched ears, trying to keep my voice casual. How is everybody?

Lola, Mami's going to *kill* you.

Dumb-ass, could you keep your voice down. Mami isn't home, is she?

She's working.

What a surprise, I said. Mami working. On the last minute of the last hour of the last day my mother would be at work. She would be at work when the missiles were in the air.

I guess I must have missed him real bad or I just wanted to see somebody who knew anything about me, or the cat piss had damaged my common sense, because I gave him the address of a coffee shop on the boardwalk and told him to bring my clothes and some of my books.

Bring me money, too.

He paused. I don't know where Mami keeps it.

You know, Mister. Just bring it.

How much? he asked timidly.

All of it.

That's a lot of money, Lola.

Just bring me the money, Oscar.

O.K., O.K. He inhaled deeply. Will you at least tell me if you're O.K. or not?

I'm O.K., I said, and that was the only point in the conversation where I almost cried. I kept quiet until I could speak again and then I asked him how he was going to get down here without our mother finding out.

You know me, he said weakly. I might be a dork, but I'm a resourceful dork.

I should have known not to trust anybody whose favorite books as a child were Encyclopedia Brown.[8] But I wasn't really thinking; I was so looking forward to seeing him.

7. Somewhat rundown New Jersey beach town renowned for its casinos.

8. Fictional series (1963–present) about the adventures of bookish boy detective Leroy ("Encyclopedia") Brown.

By then I had this plan. I was going to convince my brother to run away with me. My plan was that we would go to Dublin. I had met a bunch of Irish guys on the boardwalk and they had sold me on their country. I would become a backup singer for U2[9] and both Bono and the drummer would fall in love with me, and Oscar could become the Dominican James Joyce.[1] I really believed it would happen, too. That's how deluded I was by then.

The next day I walked into the coffee shop, looking brand-new, and he was there, with the bag. Oscar, I said, laughing. You're so fat!

I know, he said, ashamed. I was worried about you.

We embraced for like an hour and then he started crying. Lola, I'm sorry.

It's O.K., I said, and that's when I looked up and saw my mother and my tía Rubelka and my tío Rudolfo boiling out of the kitchen.

Oscar! I screamed, but it was too late. My mother already had me in her hands. She looked so thin and worn, almost like a hag, but she was holding on to me like I was her last nickel, and underneath her red wig her green eyes were *furious*. I noticed, absently, that she had dressed up for the occasion. That was typical. Muchacha del diablo, she shrieked. I managed to haul her out of the coffee shop and when she pulled back her hand to smack me I broke free. I ran for it. Behind me I could feel her sprawling, hitting the curb hard with a crack, but I wasn't looking back. No—I was running. In elementary school, whenever we had field day I was always the fastest girl in my grade, took home all the ribbons; they said it wasn't fair, because I was so big, but I didn't care. I could even have beaten the boys if I'd wanted to, so there was no way my sick mother, my messed-up tíos, and my fat brother were going to catch me. I was going to run as fast as my long legs could carry me. I was going to run down the boardwalk, past Aldo's miserable house, out of Wildwood, out of New Jersey, and I wasn't going to stop. I was going to *fly*.

Anyway, that's how it *should* have worked out. But I looked back. I couldn't help it. It's not like I didn't know my Bible, all the pillars-of-salt stuff,[2] but when you're someone's daughter that she raised by herself with no help from nobody habits die hard. I just wanted to make sure my mom hadn't broken her arm or smashed open her skull. I mean, really, who the hell wants to kill her own mother by accident? That's the only reason I glanced back. She was sprawled on the ground, her wig had fallen out of reach, her poor bald head out in the day like something private and shameful, and she was bawling like a lost calf, Hija, hija! And there I was wanting to run off into my future. It was right then that I needed that feeling to guide me, but it wasn't anywhere in sight. Only me. In the end I didn't have the ovaries. She was on the ground, bald as a baby, crying, probably a month away from dying, and here I was, her one and only daughter. And there was nothing I could do about it. So I walked back and when I

9. Wildly successful Irish rock band formed in Dublin in 1976 by, among others, frontman Bono, guitarist The Edge, and drummer Larry Mullen, Jr.

1. Celebrated Dublin-born author (1882–1941) of books including the short-story collection *Dubliners* (1914).

2. In the book of Genesis, Lot and his wife flee the iniquitous Sodom at the behest of angels who warn them not to look back lest they share in that city's well-earned destruction; when Lot's wife ignores the warning, she turns into a pillar of salt.

reached down to help her she clamped on to me with both hands. That was when I realized she hadn't been crying at all. She'd been faking! Her smile was like a lion's.

Ya te tengo,[3] she said, jumping triumphantly to her feet. Te tengo.

And that is how I ended up in Santo Domingo.[4] I guess my mother thought it would be harder for me to run away from an island where I knew no one, and in a way she was right. I'm into my sixth month here and these days I'm just trying to be philosophical about the whole thing. I wasn't like that at first, but in the end I had to let it go. It was like the fight between the egg and the rock, my abuela[5] said. No winning.

I'm actually going to school, not that it's going to count when I return to Paterson, but it keeps me busy and out of trouble and around people my own age. You don't need to be around us viejos all day, Abuela says. I have mixed feelings about the school. For one thing, it's improved my Spanish a lot. It's a private school, a Carol Morgan[6] wanna-be filled with people my tío Carlos Moya calls los hijos de mami y papi.[7] And then there's me. If you think it was tough being a goth in Paterson, try being a Dominican york in one of those private schools back in D.R. You will never meet bitchier girls in your whole life. They whisper about me to death. Someone else would have had a nervous breakdown, but after Wildwood I'm not so brittle. I don't let it get to me.

And the irony of all ironies? I'm on our school's track team. I joined because my friend Rosio, the scholarship girl from Los Mina,[8] told me I could win a spot on the team on the length of my legs alone. Those are the pins of a winner, she prophesied. Well, she must have known something I didn't, because I'm now our school's top runner in the four hundred metres and under. That I have talent at this simple thing never ceases to amaze me. Karen would pass out if she could see me running sprints out behind my school while Coach Cortés screams at us, first in Spanish and then in Catalán. Breathe, breathe, *breathe!* I've got like no fat left on me and the musculature of my legs impresses everyone, even me. I can't wear shorts anymore without causing traffic jams, and the other day when my abuela accidentally locked us out of the house she turned to me in frustration and said, Hija, just kick the door open. That pushed a laugh out of both of us.

So much has changed these last months, in my head, my heart. Rosio has me dressing up like a real Dominican girl. She's the one who fixes my hair and helps me with my makeup, and sometimes when I see myself in mirrors I don't even know who I am anymore. Not that I'm unhappy or anything. Even if I found a hot-air balloon that would whisk me straight to U2's house I'm not sure I would take it. (I'm still not talking to my traitor brother, though.) The truth is

3. Now I've got you (Spanish).
4. Capital city (founded 1496) of the Dominican Republic, which, along with the Republic of Haiti, occupies Hispaniola Island.
5. Grandmother (Spanish).
6. Prestigious English-language school in Santo Domingo, founded in 1933 by U.S. missionaries Carol and Barney Morgan.
7. Spoiled kids, something like "Daddy's girls" and "Mommy's boys" (Spanish).
8. Neighborhood in Santo Domingo.

I'm even thinking of staying one more year. Abuela doesn't want me ever to leave—I'll miss you, she says so simply it can't be anything but true—and my mom has told me I can stay if I want to but that I would be welcome at home, too. Tía Rubelka tells me she's hanging tough, my mother, that she's back to two jobs. They sent me a picture of the whole family and Abuela framed it and I can't look at it without misting up. My mother's not wearing her fakies in it; she looks so thin I don't even recognize her.

Just know that I would die for you, she told me the last time we talked. And before I could say anything she hung up.

But that's not what I wanted to tell you. It's about that crazy feeling that started this whole mess, the bruja feeling that comes singing out of my bones, that takes hold of me the way blood seizes cotton. The feeling that tells me that everything in my life is about to change. It's come back. Just the other day I woke up from all these dreams and it was there, pulsing inside of me. I imagine this is what it feels like to have a child in you. At first I was scared, because I thought it was telling me to run away again, but every time I looked around our house, every time I saw my abuela the feeling got stronger, so I knew this was something different.

I was dating a boy by then, a sweet morenito[9] by the name of Max Sánchez, who I had met in Los Mina while visiting Rosio. He's short, but his smile and his snappy dressing make up for a lot. Because I'm from Nueba Yol[1] he talks about how rich he's going to become and I try to explain to him that I don't care about that, but he looks at me like I'm crazy. I'm going to get a white Mercedes-Benz, he says. Tú verás.[2] But it's the job he has that I love best, that got me and him started. In Santo Domingo two or three theatres often share the same set of reels for a movie, so when the first theatre finishes with the first reel they put it in Max's hands and he rides his motorcycle like crazy to make it to the second theatre and then he drives back, waits, picks up the second reel, and so on. If he's held up or gets into an accident the first reel will end and there will be no second reel and the people in the audience will throw bottles. So far he's been blessed, he tells me while kissing his San Miguel[3] medal. Because of me, he brags, one movie becomes three. I'm the man who puts together the pictures. Max is not from la clase alta,[4] as my abuela would describe it, and if any of the stuck-up bitches in school saw us they would just about die, but I'm fond of him. He holds open doors, he calls me his morena; when he's feeling brave he touches my arm gently and then pulls back.

Anyway I thought maybe the feeling was about Max, and so one day I let him take me to one of the love motels. He was so excited he almost fell off the bed, and the first thing he wanted was to look at my ass. I never knew my big ass could be such a star attraction, but he kissed it, four, five times, gave me goose

9. Literally, *moreno* (brown) plus *-ito* (a diminutive suffix) equals "little brown" (Spanish), that is, a little brown-skinned boy.

1. New York City (Spanish).

2. You'll see (Spanish).

3. St. Michael (Spanish), leader of God's army and angel of death, who ensures the redeemed soul's safe passage to heaven.

4. The upper class (Spanish).

bumps with his breath, and pronounced it a tesoro. When we were done and he was in the bathroom washing himself I stood in front of the mirror naked and looked at my culo for the first time. A tesoro,[5] I repeated. A treasure.

Well? Rosio asked at school. And I nodded once, quickly, and she grabbed me and laughed and all the girls I hated turned to look, but what could they do? Happiness, when it comes, is stronger than all the jerk girls in Santo Domingo combined.

But I was still confused. Because the feeling, it just kept getting stronger and stronger, wouldn't let me sleep, wouldn't give me any peace. I started losing races, which was something I never did.

You ain't so great, are you, gringa,[6] the girls on the other teams hissed at me, and I could only hang my head. Coach Cortés was so unhappy he just locked himself in his car and wouldn't say anything to any of us.

The whole thing was driving me crazy, and then one night I came home from being out with Max. He had taken me for a walk along the Malecón[7]—he never had money for anything else—and we had watched the bats zigzagging over the palms and an old ship head into the distance. While I stretched my hamstrings, he talked quietly about moving to the U.S. My abuela was waiting for me at the living-room table. Even though she still wears black to mourn the husband she lost when she was young she's one of the most handsome women I've ever known. We have the same jagged lightning-bolt part, and when I saw her at the airport, the first time in ten years, I didn't want to admit it but I knew that things were going to be O.K. between us. She stood like she was her own best thing[8] and when she saw me she said, Hija, I have waited for you since the day you left. And then she hugged me and kissed me and said, I'm your abuela, but you can call me La Inca.[9]

Standing over her that night, her part like a crack in her hair, I felt a surge of tenderness. I put my arms around her and that was when I noticed that she was looking at photos. Old photos, the kind I'd never seen in my house. Photos of my mother when she was young, before she had her breasts. She was even skinnier than me! I picked the smallest photo up. Mami was standing in front of a bakery. Even with an apron on she looked potent, like someone who was going to be someone.

She was very guapa, I said casually.

Abuela snorted. Guapa soy yo. Your mother was a diosa. But so cabeza dura. When she was your age we never got along. She was cabeza dura and I was . . . exigente.[1] You and her are more alike than you think.

5. Treasure (Spanish). *Culo*: ass (Spanish).

6. English-speaking foreigner (Spanish).

7. Santo Domingo's world-famous oceanfront promenade.

8. Perhaps an allusion to Toni Morrison's novel *Beloved* (1987), in which a man works to convince his lover, a mother grieving for her children, that she, not they, is her "own best thing." In interviews, Díaz has referred to his "relationship with" Morrison's work as "the most sustained love of mine, the one that's carried me through all these years."

9. The Incan (Spanish), a noble, member, or follower of the Indian peoples who established, in what is now Peru, pre-Columbia America's largest empire (c. thirteenth century through 1572).

1. Demanding. *Guapa soy yo*: I am pretty or attractive. *Diosa*: goddess. *Cabeza dura*: hard-headed (all Spanish).

I know she ran away. From you. From Santo Domingo.

115 La Inca stared at me, incredulous. Your mother didn't run away. We had to *send* her away. To keep her from being murdered. To keep us all from being murdered. She didn't listen and she fell in love with the wrong man. She didn't listen. Jesu Cristo, hija—

She was about to say something more and then she stopped.

And that's when it hit with the force of a hurricane. The *feeling.* My abuela was sitting there, forlorn, trying to cobble together the right words, and I could not move or breathe. I felt like I always did in the last seconds of a race, when I was sure that I was going to explode. She was about to say something and I was waiting for whatever she was going to give me. I was waiting to begin.

2007

QUESTIONS

1. WILDWOOD begins with Lola's observation that "[i]t's never the changes we want that change everything." How and why exactly does Lola change over the course of the story?
2. WILDWOOD ends with Lola's remark, "I was waiting to begin." Why do you think the story ends with reference to a beginning, or how does this line shape the way you understand the nature and significance of the changes Lola has undergone up to this point, as well as the story's ultimate theme(s)?
3. How do Díaz's specific ways of intermixing Spanish and English, as well as his frequent allusions (literary, musical, televisual, and biblical), help to flesh out the story's central conflicts and/or theme(s)?

SUGGESTIONS FOR WRITING

1. Choose any story in this chapter and write an essay exploring how character, point of view, setting, symbolism, or any recurring word or phrase contributes to the development of theme. Be sure to state that theme in a sentence.
2. Sometimes the theme in a work of literature can be expressed as a strong, clear statement: "A always follows from B," or "An X can never be a Y." More often, though, especially in modern literature, authors offer subtler, often ambiguous themes that deliberately undermine our faith in simple absolutes: "A doesn't necessarily always follow B," or "There are times when an X can be a Y." Write an essay in which you argue that one of the stories in this chapter has an "always" or "never" kind of theme, and contrast it to the more indeterminate theme of another story. Alternatively, use your essay to explain why we might be both tempted and wrong to see one of these stories as having an "always" or "never" theme. What is the overly simplistic version of the theme, and what is the more complex one?
3. Write an essay exploring how theme is developed through the juxtaposition of realistic detail and fantastic elements in A VERY OLD MAN WITH ENORMOUS WINGS, especially (but not exclusively) in the description of the winged man himself.
4. Though the main theme of WILDWOOD may well be a universal one (an insight that applies to all or most people), its major characters are all contemporary working-class Domican Americans. Write an essay exploring how the story characterizes

their life and how this characterization shapes the story's theme, perhaps giving the story a culturally and historically specific, as well as universal, resonance and relevance.

5. Write an essay comparing the way Stephen Crane's THE OPEN BOAT and Nathaniel Hawthorne's THE BIRTH-MARK portray the relationship between human beings and nature. What is similar and different about the nature-related themes of the two stories?
6. Write your own fable, perhaps reworking or modernizing one by Aesop. Be sure both to state the theme and to make sure it is demonstrated in the fable itself.

McDowell's
No1
Celebration

Cross-Cultural Encounters

AN ALBUM

Few of us in today's increasingly wired world either inhabit or trace our roots to a single culture. Rather, most of us live across cultures and identify with multiple "tribes," habitually performing rituals both ancient and modern—whether we recognize them as such or not. When Native American author Sherman Alexie describes himself as "just as influenced" by sitcoms as by "pow-wows," he might well be speaking for most of us. Whether or not we choose to watch television, see Hollywood movies, eat at McDonald's, or post to *Facebook*, few, if any, of us can avoid being heavily influenced by these phenomena or participating in the shared culture they help constitute. Yet like Alexie, each of us has a slightly different relationship to that common culture, depending in part upon where we, our parents, and even our grandparents grew up; what languages we speak or read; what faiths we follow.

Increased mobility, globalization, and the Internet have done as much to exaggerate or at least to enhance awareness of cultural diversity as they have to erode it. They also ensure that all of us have to navigate cultural differences—to communicate and in one way or another work with people whose experiences, habits, worldviews, and values differ dramatically from our own. Such cross-cultural encounters—whether they occur between people or within a single person—can be exhilarating and enlightening, as well as difficult and painful. Paradoxically, it is often only by encountering a foreign culture that we come to appreciate what is specific, special, even foreign and funny, about our own, or even to recognize it as our own. As a character in Nobel Prize–winning author Wole Soyinka's 1975 play *Death and the King's Horseman* remarks, he didn't understand what he "took" from his Nigerian homeland until he left for another country: "But I found out over there. I am grateful . . . for that. And I will never give it up."

Like many authors studied in English literature classes today, Soyinka hails neither from England nor from America, but from a former British colony, Nigeria—a reminder that English is today a world language and a world literature, thanks in part to imperialism and the far from equitable cross-cultural encounters it entailed, as well as the rich hybrid cultures, literatures, and languages it created. One of the most exciting literary developments of the past half-century has been the emergence of so-called *postcolonial literature*—that is, works written either by those raised in former colonies (like Soyinka or Salman Rushdie) or by their children and grandchildren (like Jhumpa Lahiri), who may never have even visited their "cultural homelands." Not surprisingly, that literature often investigates the varied ways in which cultures intersect and clash today, as well as the ways in which today's world has been shaped by the cultural confrontations of yesterday.

By exploring such issues, postcolonial literature may help us to navigate our own distinctly modern world. But it also builds on a tradition stretching from literature's very beginnings to today's popular culture. What else, after all, are Homer's *Odyssey*, Shakespeare's *The Tempest*, and even, perhaps, the Christian Bible about, if not cross-cultural encounters? Conversely, how many contemporary movies can you think of that are essentially what Hollywood calls "fish-out-of-water" stories about cultural difference? (Have you ever seen *E.T.* or *Borat*?)

Such stories can be comic as well as tragic and everything in between, just as the conclusions they reach vary widely. The stories in this album vividly demonstrate that range of tone and theme. In each of them, characters find themselves in the position of translator, forced to interpret one language or culture to another, and in the process learning much about those cultures and themselves. Just what do each of these characters learn, and what might their stories reveal about the way culture and environment shape us—both linking us to, and dividing us from, others? What might the stories suggest about when and why cross-cultural communication or translation fails? How do the stories define the costs and benefits of literally and figuratively learning a new language, journeying outside our familiar world, even seeing ourselves and our own culture as others do? When and how might cultural belonging and identity become a matter of choice? And when it does, why do people seem to make the choices they do? Which stories envision the clash or choice of cultures as one between "ancient" and "modern" traditions? How do they envision the strengths and weaknesses of each?

BHARATI MUKHERJEE
(b. 1940)
The Management of Grief

Bharati Mukherjee grew up in Calcutta, India, in what she calls an "extraordinarily close-knit" and wealthy Hindu family of which her highly educated chemist father was "the benevolent patriarch." Moving with her family among Calcutta, London, and Switzerland, Mukherjee attended mainly English-language private schools, both Protestant and Catholic. Armed with a University of Calcutta BA and an MA in English and Ancient Indian Culture from the University of Baroda, in western India, she moved to the United States in 1961, earning both an MFA in creative writing and a PhD in English and comparative literature at the University of Iowa. There, too, she met and married Canadian Clark Blaise, abandoning her plan to return to India and let her father choose her spouse. Teaching at various Canadian and U.S. universities, the couple cowrote two works of nonfiction—*Days and Nights in Calcutta* (1977), which chronicles a 1972 visit to India, and *The Sorrow and the Terror* (1987), a carefully researched account of a 1985 Air India terrorist bombing that killed 329 and also inspired "The Management of Grief." Though Mukherjee had previously published novels, beginning with *The Tiger's Daughter* (1971), and one short-story collection (*Darkness* [1985]), *Days and Nights* remained her most highly acclaimed book until *The Middleman and Other Stories* won the National Book Critics Circle Award in 1988. Since then, in novels such as *Jasmine* (1989), *The Holder of the World* (1993), *The Tree Bride* (2004), and *Miss New India* (2011), Mukherjee has continued to explore the "extreme transformations" wrought by immigration—on individuals, families, and the texture of both American and Indian life and identity.

A woman I don't know is boiling tea the Indian way in my kitchen. There are a lot of women I don't know in my kitchen, whispering, and moving tactfully. They open doors, rummage through the pantry, and try not to ask me where things are kept. They remind me of when my sons were small, on Mother's Day or when Vikram and I were tired, and they would make big, sloppy omelets. I would lie in bed pretending I didn't hear them.

Dr. Sharma, the treasurer of the Indo-Canada Society, pulls me into the hallway. He wants to know if I am worried about money. His wife, who has just come up from the basement with a tray of empty cups and glasses, scolds him. "Don't bother Mrs. Bhave with mundane details." She looks so monstrously pregnant her baby must be days overdue. I tell her she shouldn't be carrying heavy things. "Shaila," she says, smiling, "this is the fifth." Then she grabs a teenager by his shirttails. He slips his Walkman[1] off his head. He has to be one of her four children, they have the same domed and dented foreheads. "What's the official word now?" she demands. The boy slips the headphones back on. "They're acting evasive, Ma. They're saying it could be an accident or a terrorist bomb."

All morning, the boys have been muttering, Sikh Bomb, Sikh Bomb.[2] The men, not using the word, bow their heads in agreement. Mrs. Sharma touches her forehead at such a word. At least they've stopped talking about space debris and Russian lasers.

Two radios are going in the dining room. They are tuned to different stations. Someone must have brought the radios down from my boys' bedrooms. I haven't gone into their rooms since Kusum came running across the front lawn in her bathrobe. She looked so funny, I was laughing when I opened the door.

The big TV in the den is being whizzed through American networks and 5
cable channels.

"Damn!" some man swears bitterly. "How can these preachers carry on like nothing's happened?" I want to tell him we're not that important. You look at the audience, and at the preacher in his blue robe with his beautiful white hair, the potted palm trees under a blue sky, and you know they care about nothing.

The phone rings and rings. Dr. Sharma's taken charge. "We're with her," he keeps saying. "Yes, yes, the doctor has given calming pills. Yes, yes, pills are having necessary effect." I wonder if pills alone explain this calm. Not peace, just a deadening quiet. I was always controlled, but never repressed. Sound can reach me, but my body is tensed, ready to scream. I hear their voices all around me. I hear my boys and Vikram cry, "Mommy, Shaila!" and their screams insulate me, like headphones.

1. Handheld audiocassette or CD player.

2. Sikhs are adherents of Sikhism, a religion founded c. 1500; Sikhs constitute a substantial minority of India's population.

The woman boiling water tells her story again and again. "I got the news first. My cousin called from Halifax before six A.M., can you imagine? He'd gotten up for prayers and his son was studying for medical exams and he heard on a rock channel that something had happened to a plane. They said first it had disappeared from the radar, like a giant eraser just reached out. His father called me, so I said to him, what do you mean, 'something bad'? You mean a hijacking? And he said, *behn*,[3] there is no confirmation of anything yet, but check with your neighbors because a lot of them must be on that plane. So I called poor Kusum straightaway. I knew Kusum's husband and daughter were booked to go yesterday."

Kusum lives across the street from me. She and Satish had moved in less than a month ago. They said they needed a bigger place. All these people, the Sharmas and friends from the Indo-Canada Society had been there for the housewarming. Satish and Kusum made homemade tandoori on their big gas grill and even the white neighbors piled their plates high with that luridly red, charred, juicy chicken. Their younger daughter had danced, and even our boys had broken away from the Stanley Cup telecast to put in a reluctant appearance. Everyone took pictures for their albums and for the community newspapers—another of our families had made it big in Toronto—and now I wonder how many of those happy faces are gone. "Why does God give us so much if all along He intends to take it away?" Kusum asks me.

10 I nod. We sit on carpeted stairs, holding hands like children. "I never once told him that I loved him," I say. I was too much the well brought up woman. I was so well brought up I never felt comfortable calling my husband by his first name.

"It's all right," Kusum says. "He knew. My husband knew. They felt it. Modern young girls have to say it because what they feel is fake."

Kusum's daughter, Pam, runs in with an overnight case. Pam's in her McDonald's uniform. "Mummy! You have to get dressed!" Panic makes her cranky. "A reporter's on his way here."

"Why?"

"You want to talk to him in your bathrobe?" She starts to brush her mother's long hair. She's the daughter who's always in trouble. She dates Canadian boys and hangs out in the mall, shopping for tight sweaters. The younger one, the goody-goody one according to Pam, the one with a voice so sweet that when she sang *bhajans*[4] for Ethiopian relief even a frugal man like my husband wrote out a hundred dollar check, *she* was on that plane. *She* was going to spend July and August with grandparents because Pam wouldn't go. Pam said she'd rather waitress at McDonald's. "If it's a choice between Bombay and Wonderland,[5] I'm picking Wonderland," she'd said.

15 "Leave me alone," Kusum yells. "You know what I want to do? If I didn't have to look after you now, I'd hang myself."

3. Sister.
4. Hymns.
5. Toronto amusement park.

Pam's young face goes blotchy with pain. "Thanks," she says, "don't let me stop you."

"Hush," pregnant Mrs. Sharma scolds Pam. "Leave your mother alone. Mr. Sharma will tackle the reporters and fill out the forms. He'll say what has to be said."

Pam stands her ground. "You think I don't know what Mummy's thinking? *Why her?* that's what. That's sick! Mummy wishes my little sister were alive and I were dead."

Kusum's hand in mine is trembly hot. We continue to sit on the stairs.

She calls before she arrives, wondering if there's anything I need. Her name is Judith Templeton and she's an appointee of the provincial government. "Multiculturalism?" I ask, and she says, "partially," but that her mandate is bigger. "I've been told you knew many of the people on the flight," she says. "Perhaps if you'd agree to help us reach the others . . . ?"

She gives me time at least to put on tea water and pick up the mess in the front room. I have a few *samosas*[6] from Kusum's housewarming that I could fry up, but then I think, why prolong this visit?

Judith Templeton is much younger than she sounded. She wears a blue suit with a white blouse and a polka dot tie. Her blond hair is cut short, her only jewelry is pearl drop earrings. Her briefcase is new and expensive looking, a gleaming cordovan leather. She sits with it across her lap. When she looks out the front windows onto the street, her contact lenses seem to float in front of her light blue eyes.

"What sort of help do you want from me?" I ask. She has refused the tea, out of politeness, but I insist, along with some slightly stale biscuits.[7]

"I have no experience," she admits. "That is, I have an MSW[8] and I've worked in liaison with accident victims, but I mean I have no experience with a tragedy of this scale—"

"Who could?" I ask.

"—and with the complications of culture, language, and customs. Someone mentioned that Mrs. Bhave is a pillar—because you've taken it more calmly."

At this, perhaps, I frown, for she reaches forward, almost to take my hand. "I hope you understand my meaning, Mrs. Bhave. There are hundreds of people in Metro[9] directly affected, like you, and some of them speak no English. There are some widows who've never handled money or gone on a bus, and there are old parents who still haven't eaten or gone outside their bedrooms. Some houses and apartments have been looted. Some wives are still hysterical. Some husbands are in shock and profound depression. We want to help, but our hands are tied in so many ways. We have to distribute money to some people, and there are legal documents—these things can be done. We have interpreters, but we don't always have the human touch, or maybe the right human touch. We don't want to make mistakes, Mrs. Bhave, and that's why we'd like to ask you to help us."

6. Fried turnovers filled with finely chopped meat or vegetables.

7. Cookies.

8. Master's degree in social work.

9. That is, the municipality of metropolitan Toronto.

"More mistakes, you mean," I say.

"Police matters are not in my hands," she answers.

30 "Nothing I can do will make any difference," I say. "We must all grieve in our own way."

"But you are coping very well. All the people said, Mrs. Bhave is the strongest person of all. Perhaps if the others could see you, talk with you, it would help them."

"By the standards of the people you call hysterical, I am behaving very oddly and very badly, Miss Templeton." I want to say to her, *I wish I could scream, starve, walk into Lake Ontario, jump from a bridge.* "They would not see me as a model. I do not see myself as a model."

I am a freak. No one who has ever known me would think of me reacting this way. This terrible calm will not go away.

She asks me if she may call again, after I get back from a long trip that we all must make. "Of course," I say. "Feel free to call, anytime."

35 Four days later, I find Kusum squatting on a rock overlooking a bay in Ireland. It isn't a big rock, but it juts sharply out over water. This is as close as we'll ever get to them. June breezes balloon out her sari and unpin her knee-length hair. She has the bewildered look of a sea creature whom the tides have stranded.

It's been one hundred hours since Kusum came stumbling and screaming across my lawn. Waiting around the hospital, we've heard many stories. The police, the diplomats, they tell us things thinking that we're strong, that knowledge is helpful to the grieving, and maybe it is. Some, I know, prefer ignorance, or their own versions. The plane broke into two, they say. Unconsciousness was instantaneous. No one suffered. My boys must have just finished their breakfasts. They loved eating on planes, they loved the smallness of plates, knives, and forks. Last year they saved the airline salt and pepper shakers. Half an hour more and they would have made it to Heathrow.[1]

Kusum says that we can't escape our fate. She says that all those people—our husbands, my boys, her girl with the nightingale voice, all those Hindus, Christians, Sikhs, Muslims, Parsis, and atheists on that plane—were fated to die together off this beautiful bay. She learned this from a swami[2] in Toronto.

I have my Valium.

Six of us "relatives"—two widows and four widowers—choose to spend the day today by the waters instead of sitting in a hospital room and scanning photographs of the dead. That's what they call us now: relatives. I've looked through twenty-seven photos in two days. They're very kind to us, the Irish are very understanding. Sometimes understanding means freeing a tourist bus for this trip to the bay, so we can pretend to spy our loved ones through the glassiness of waves or in sunspeckled cloud shapes.

40 I could die here, too, and be content.

"What is that, out there?" She's standing and flapping her hands and for a moment I see a head shape bobbing in the waves. She's standing in the water, I, on the boulder. The tide is low, and a round, black, headsized rock has just risen

1. Major London airport.
2. Hindu religious teacher.

from the waves. She returns, her sari end dripping and ruined and her face is a twisted remnant of hope, the way mine was a hundred hours ago, still laughing but inwardly knowing that nothing but the ultimate tragedy could bring two women together at six o'clock on a Sunday morning. I watch her face sag into blankness.

"That water felt warm, Shaila," she says at length.

"You can't," I say. "We have to wait for our turn to come."

I haven't eaten in four days, haven't brushed my teeth.

"I know," she says. "I tell myself I have no right to grieve. They are in a better 45
place than we are. My swami says I should be thrilled for them. My swami says depression is a sign of our selfishness."

Maybe I'm selfish. Selfishly I break away from Kusum and run, sandals slapping against stones, to the water's edge. What if my boys aren't lying pinned under the debris? What if they aren't stuck a mile below that innocent blue chop? What if, given the strong currents. . . .

Now I've ruined my sari, one of my best. Kusum has joined me, knee-deep in water that feels to me like a swimming pool. I could settle in the water, and my husband would take my hand and the boys would slap water in my face just to see me scream.

"Do you remember what good swimmers my boys were, Kusum?"

"I saw the medals," she says.

One of the widowers, Dr. Ranganathan from Montreal, walks out to us, 50
carrying his shoes in one hand. He's an electrical engineer. Someone at the hotel mentioned his work is famous around the world, something about the place where physics and electricity come together. He has lost a huge family, something indescribable. "With some luck," Dr. Ranganathan suggests to me, "a good swimmer could make it safely to some island. It is quite possible that there may be many, many microscopic islets scattered around."

"You're not just saying that?" I tell Dr. Ranganathan about Vinod, my elder son. Last year he took diving as well.

"It's a parent's duty to hope," he says. "It is foolish to rule out possibilities that have not been tested. I myself have not surrendered hope."

Kusum is sobbing once again. "Dear lady," he says, laying his free hand on her arm, and she calms down.

"Vinod is how old?" he asks me. He's very careful, as we all are. *Is*, not was.

"Fourteen. Yesterday he was fourteen. His father and uncle were going to 55
take him down to the Taj and give him a big birthday party. I couldn't go with them because I couldn't get two weeks off from my stupid job in June." I process bills for a travel agent. June is a big travel month.

Dr. Ranganathan whips the pockets of his suit jacket inside out. Squashed roses, in darkening shades of pink, float on the water. He tore the roses off creepers in somebody's garden. He didn't ask anyone if he could pluck the roses, but now there's been an article about it in the local papers. When you see an Indian person, it says, please give him or her flowers.

"A strong youth of fourteen," he says, "can very likely pull to safety a younger one."

My sons, though four years apart, were very close. Vinod wouldn't let Mithun drown. *Electrical engineering*, I think, foolishly perhaps: this man knows important secrets of the universe, things closed to me. Relief spins me light-headed. No wonder my boys' photographs haven't turned up in the gallery of photos of the recovered dead. "Such pretty roses," I say.

"My wife loved pink roses. Every Friday I had to bring a bunch home. I used to say, why? After twenty-odd years of marriage you're still needing proof positive of my love?" He has identified his wife and three of his children. Then others from Montreal, the lucky ones, intact families with no survivors. He chuckles as he wades back to shore. Then he swings around to ask me a question. "Mrs. Bhave, you are wanting to throw in some roses for your loved ones? I have two big ones left."

60 But I have other things to float: Vinod's pocket calculator; a half-painted model B-52 for my Mithun. They'd want them on their island. And for my husband? For him I let fall into the calm, glassy waters a poem I wrote in the hospital yesterday. Finally he'll know my feelings for him.

"Don't tumble, the rocks are slippery," Dr. Ranganathan cautions. He holds out a hand for me to grab.

Then it's time to get back on the bus, time to rush back to our waiting posts on hospital benches.

Kusum is one of the lucky ones. The lucky ones flew here, identified in multiplicate their loved ones, then will fly to India with the bodies for proper ceremonies. Satish is one of the few males who surfaced. The photos of faces we saw on the walls in an office at Heathrow and here in the hospital are mostly of women. Women have more body fat, a nun said to me matter-of-factly. They float better. Today I was stopped by a young sailor on the street. He had loaded bodies, he'd gone into the water when—he checks my face for signs of strength—when the sharks were first spotted. I don't blush, and he breaks down. "It's all right," I say. "Thank you." I had heard about the sharks from Dr. Ranganathan. In his orderly mind, science brings understanding, it holds no terror. It is the shark's duty. For every deer there is a hunter, for every fish a fisherman.

The Irish are not shy; they rush to me and give me hugs and some are crying. I cannot imagine reactions like that on the streets of Toronto. Just strangers, and I am touched. Some carry flowers with them and give them to any Indian they see.

65 After lunch, a policeman I have gotten to know quite well catches hold of me. He says he thinks he has a match for Vinod. I explain what a good swimmer Vinod is.

"You want me with you when you look at photos?" Dr. Ranganathan walks ahead of me into the picture gallery. In these matters, he is a scientist, and I am grateful. It is a new perspective. "They have performed miracles," he says. "We are indebted to them."

The first day or two the policemen showed us relatives only one picture at a time; now they're in a hurry, they're eager to lay out the possibles, and even the probables.

The face on the photo is of a boy much like Vinod; the same intelligent eyes, the same thick brows dipping into a V. But this boy's features, even his cheeks, are puffier, wider, mushier.

"No." My gaze is pulled by other pictures. There are five other boys who look like Vinod.

The nun assigned to console me rubs the first picture with a fingertip. "When 70
they've been in the water for a while, love, they look a little heavier." The bones under the skin are broken, they said on the first day—try to adjust your memories. It's important.

"It's not him. I'm his mother. I'd know."

"I know this one!" Dr. Ranganathan cries out suddenly from the back of the gallery. "And this one!" I think he senses that I don't want to find my boys. "They are the Kutty brothers. They were also from Montreal." I don't mean to be crying. On the contrary, I am ecstatic. My suitcase in the hotel is packed heavy with dry clothes for my boys.

The policeman starts to cry. "I am so sorry, I am so sorry, ma'am. I really thought we had a match."

With the nun ahead of us and the policeman behind, we, the unlucky ones without our children's bodies, file out of the makeshift gallery.

From Ireland most of us go on to India. Kusum and I take the same direct flight 75
to Bombay, so I can help her clear customs quickly. But we have to argue with a man in uniform. He has large boils on his face. The boils swell and glow with sweat as we argue with him. He wants Kusum to wait in line and he refuses to take authority because his boss is on a tea break. But Kusum won't let her coffins out of sight, and I shan't desert her though I know that my parents, elderly and diabetic, must be waiting in a stuffy car in a scorching lot.

"You bastard!" I scream at the man with the popping boils. Other passengers press closer. "You think we're smuggling contraband in those coffins!"

Once upon a time we were well brought up women; we were dutiful wives who kept our heads veiled, our voices shy and sweet.

In India, I become, once again, an only child of rich, ailing parents. Old friends of the family come to pay their respects. Some are Sikh, and inwardly, involuntarily, I cringe. My parents are progressive people; they do not blame communities for a few individuals.

In Canada it is a different story now.

"Stay longer," my mother pleads. "Canada is a cold place. Why would you 80
want to be all by yourself?" I stay.

Three months pass. Then another.

"Vikram wouldn't have wanted you to give up things!" they protest. They call my husband by the name he was born with. In Toronto he'd changed to Vik so the men he worked with at his office would find his name as easy as Rod or Chris. "You know, the dead aren't cut off from us!"

My grandmother, the spoiled daughter of a rich *zamindar*,[3] shaved her head with rusty razor blades when she was widowed at sixteen. My grandfather died of childhood diabetes when he was nineteen, and she saw herself as the harbinger of bad luck. My mother grew up without parents, raised indifferently by an uncle, while her true mother slept in a hut behind the main estate house and took her food with the servants. She grew up a rationalist. My parents abhor mindless mortification.

3. Landowner.

The zamindar's daughter kept stubborn faith in Vedic[4] rituals; my parents rebelled. I am trapped between two modes of knowledge. At thirty-six, I am too old to start over and too young to give up. Like my husband's spirit, I flutter between worlds.

85 Courting aphasia,[5] we travel. We travel with our phalanx of servants and poor relatives. To hill stations and to beach resorts. We play contract bridge in dusty gymkhana clubs. We ride stubby ponies up crumbly mountain trails. At tea dances, we let ourselves be twirled twice round the ballroom. We hit the holy spots we hadn't made time for before. In Varanasi, Kalighat, Rishikesh, Hardwar, astrologers and palmists seek me out and for a fee offer me cosmic consolations.

Already the widowers among us are being shown new bride candidates. They cannot resist the call of custom, the authority of their parents and older brothers. They must marry; it is the duty of a man to look after a wife. The new wives will be young widows with children, destitute but of good family. They will make loving wives, but the men will shun them. I've had calls from the men over crackling Indian telephone lines. "Save me," they say, these substantial, educated, successful men of forty. "My parents are arranging a marriage for me." In a month they will have buried one family and returned to Canada with a new bride and partial family.

I am comparatively lucky. No one here thinks of arranging a husband for an unlucky widow.

Then, on the third day of the sixth month into this odyssey, in an abandoned temple in a tiny Himalayan village, as I make my offering of flowers and sweetmeats to the god of a tribe of animists, my husband descends to me. He is squatting next to a scrawny *sadhu*[6] in moth-eaten robes. Vikram wears the vanilla suit he wore the last time I hugged him. The *sadhu* tosses petals on a butter-fed flame, reciting Sanskrit mantras and sweeps his face of flies. My husband takes my hands in his.

You're beautiful, he starts. Then, *What are you doing here?*

90 *Shall I stay?* I ask. He only smiles, but already the image is fading. *You must finish alone what we started together.* No seaweed wreathes his mouth. He speaks too fast just as he used to when we were an envied family in our pink split-level. He is gone.

In the windowless altar room, smoky with joss sticks and clarified butter lamps, a sweaty hand gropes for my blouse. I do not shriek. The *sadhu* arranges his robe. The lamps hiss and sputter out.

When we come out of the temple, my mother says, "Did you feel something weird in there?"

My mother has no patience with ghosts, prophetic dreams, holy men, and cults.

"No," I lie. "Nothing."

95 But she knows that she's lost me. She knows that in days I shall be leaving.

4. Of or relating to the Vedas, Hinduism's most ancient and authoritative texts.

5. Loss of the ability to articulate ideas or comprehend language.

6. Hindu holy man.

Kusum's put her house up for sale. She wants to live in an ashram[7] in Hardwar. Moving to Hardwar was her swami's idea. Her swami runs two ashrams, the one in Hardwar and another here in Toronto.

"Don't run away," I tell her.

"I'm not running away," she says. "I'm pursuing inner peace. You think you or that Ranganathan fellow are better off?"

Pam's left for California. She wants to do some modelling, she says. She says when she comes into her share of the insurance money she'll open a yoga-cum-aerobics studio in Hollywood. She sends me postcards so naughty I daren't leave them on the coffee table. Her mother has withdrawn from her and the world.

The rest of us don't lose touch, that's the point. Talk is all we have, says Dr. Ranganathan, who has also resisted his relatives and returned to Montreal and to his job, alone. He says, whom better to talk with than other relatives? We've been melted down and recast as a new tribe.

100 He calls me twice a week from Montreal. Every Wednesday night and every Saturday afternoon. He is changing jobs, going to Ottawa. But Ottawa is over a hundred miles away, and he is forced to drive two hundred and twenty miles a day. He can't bring himself to sell his house. The house is a temple, he says; the king-sized bed in the master bedroom is a shrine. He sleeps on a folding cot. A devotee.

There are still some hysterical relatives. Judith Templeton's list of those needing help and those who've "accepted" is in nearly perfect balance. Acceptance means you speak of your family in the past tense and you make active plans for moving ahead with your life. There are courses at Seneca and Ryerson[8] we could be taking. Her gleaming leather briefcase is full of college catalogues and lists of cultural societies that need our help. She has done impressive work, I tell her.

"In the textbooks on grief management," she replies—I am her confidante, I realize, one of the few whose grief has not sprung bizarre obsessions—"there are stages to pass through: rejection, depression, acceptance, reconstruction." She has compiled a chart and finds that six months after the tragedy, none of us still reject reality, but only a handful are reconstructing. "Depressed Acceptance" is the plateau we've reached. Remarriage is a major step in reconstruction (though she's a little surprised, even shocked, over *how* quickly some of the men have taken on new families). Selling one's house and changing jobs and cities is healthy.

How do I tell Judith Templeton that my family surrounds me, and that like creatures in epics, they've changed shapes? She sees me as calm and accepting but worries that I have no job, no career. My closest friends are worse off than I. I cannot tell her my days, even my nights, are thrilling.

She asks me to help with families she can't reach at all. An elderly couple in Agincourt whose sons were killed just weeks after they had brought their

7. Residence of a Hindu religious community and its particular leader or guru.

8. Seneca College of Applied Arts and Technology, in Willowdale; Ryerson Polytechnical Institute, Toronto.

parents over from a village in Punjab. From their names, I know they are Sikh. Judith Templeton and a translator have visited them twice with offers of money for air fare to Ireland, with bank forms, power-of-attorney forms, but they have refused to sign, or to leave their tiny apartment. Their sons' money is frozen in the bank. Their sons' investment apartments have been trashed by tenants, the furnishings sold off. The parents fear that anything they sign or any money they receive will end the company's or the country's obligations to them. They fear they are selling their sons for two airline tickets to a place they've never seen.

105 The high-rise apartment is a tower of Indians and West Indians, with a sprinkling of Orientals. The nearest bus stop kiosk is lined with women in saris. Boys practice cricket in the parking lot. Inside the building, even I wince a bit from the ferocity of onion fumes, the distinctive and immediate Indianness of frying *ghee*,[9] but Judith Templeton maintains a steady flow of information. These poor old people are in imminent danger of losing their place and all their services.

I say to her, "They are Sikh. They will not open up to a Hindu woman." And what I want to add is, as much as I try not to, I stiffen now at the sight of beards and turbans. I remember a time when we all trusted each other in this new country, it was only the new country we worried about.

The two rooms are dark and stuffy. The lights are off, and an oil lamp sputters on the coffee table. The bent old lady has let us in, and her husband is wrapping a white turban over his oiled, hip-length hair. She immediately goes to the kitchen, and I hear the most familiar sound of an Indian home, tap water hitting and filling a teapot.

They have not paid their utility bills, out of fear and the inability to write a check. The telephone is gone; electricity and gas and water are soon to follow. They have told Judith their sons will provide. They are good boys, and they have always earned and looked after their parents.

We converse a bit in Hindi. They do not ask about the crash and I wonder if I should bring it up. If they think I am here merely as a translator, then they may feel insulted. There are thousands of Punjabi-speakers, Sikhs, in Toronto to do a better job. And so I say to the old lady, "I too have lost my sons, and my husband, in the crash."

110 Her eyes immediately fill with tears. The man mutters a few words which sound like a blessing. "God provides and God takes away," he says.

I want to say, but only men destroy and give back nothing. "My boys and my husband are not coming back," I say. "We have to understand that."

Now the old woman responds. "But who is to say? Man alone does not decide these things." To this her husband adds his agreement.

Judith asks about the bank papers, the release forms. With a stroke of the pen, they will have a provincial trustee to pay their bills, invest their money, send them a monthly pension.

"Do you know this woman?" I ask them.

115 The man raises his hand from the table, turns it over and seems to regard each finger separately before he answers. "This young lady is always coming here, we make tea for her and she leaves papers for us to sign." His eyes scan

9. Clarified butter.

a pile of papers in the corner of the room. "Soon we will be out of tea, then will she go away?"

The old lady adds, "I have asked my neighbors and no one else gets *angrezi*[1] visitors. What have we done?"

"It's her job," I try to explain. "The government is worried. Soon you will have no place to stay, no lights, no gas, no water."

"Government will get its money. Tell her not to worry, we are honorable people."

I try to explain the government wishes to give money, not take. He raises his hand. "Let them take," he says. "We are accustomed to that. That is no problem."

"We are strong people," says the wife. "Tell her that." 120

"Who needs all this machinery?" demands the husband. "It is unhealthy, the bright lights, the cold air on a hot day, the cold food, the four gas rings. God will provide, not government."

"When our boys return," the mother says. Her husband sucks his teeth. "Enough talk," he says.

Judith breaks in. "Have you convinced them?" The snaps on her cordovan briefcase go off like firecrackers in that quiet apartment. She lays the sheaf of legal papers on the coffee table. "If they can't write their names, an X will do—I've told them that."

Now the old lady has shuffled to the kitchen and soon emerges with a pot of tea and two cups. "I think my bladder will go first on a job like this," Judith says to me, smiling. "If only there was some way of reaching them. Please thank her for the tea. Tell her she's very kind."

I nod in Judith's direction and tell them in Hindi, "She thanks you for the 125
tea. She thinks you are being very hospitable but she doesn't have the slightest idea what it means."

I want to say, humor her. I want to say, my boys and my husband are with me too, more than ever. I look in the old man's eyes and I can read his stubborn, peasant's message: *I have protected this woman as best I can. She is the only person I have left. Give to me or take from me what you will, but I will not sign for it. I will not pretend that I accept.*

In the car, Judith says, "You see what I'm up against? I'm sure they're lovely people, but their stubbornness and ignorance are driving me crazy. They think signing a paper is signing their sons' death warrants, don't they?"

I am looking out the window. I want to say, *In our culture, it is a parent's duty to hope.*

"Now Shaila, this next woman is a real mess. She cries day and night, and she refuses all medical help. We may have to—"

"—Let me out at the subway," I say. 130

"I beg your pardon?" I can feel those blue eyes staring at me.

It would not be like her to disobey. She merely disapproves, and slows at a corner to let me out. Her voice is plaintive. "Is there anything I said? Anything I did?"

1. English, Anglo.

I could answer her suddenly in a dozen ways, but I choose not to. "Shaila? Let's talk about it," I hear, then slam the door.

A wife and mother begins her new life in a new country, and that life is cut short. Yet her husband tells her: Complete what we have started. We, who stayed out of politics and came halfway around the world to avoid religious and political feuding have been the first in the New World to die from it. I no longer know what we started, nor how to complete it. I write letters to the editors of local papers and to members of Parliament. Now at least they admit it was a bomb. One MP[2] answers back, with sympathy, but with a challenge. You want to make a difference? Work on a campaign. Work on mine. Politicize the Indian voter.

My husband's old lawyer helps me set up a trust. Vikram was a saver and a careful investor. He had saved the boys' boarding school and college fees. I sell the pink house at four times what we paid for it and take a small apartment downtown. I am looking for a charity to support.

We are deep in the Toronto winter, gray skies, icy pavements. I stay indoors, watching television. I have tried to assess my situation, how best to live my life, to complete what we began so many years ago. Kusum has written me from Hardwar that her life is now serene. She has seen Satish and has heard her daughter sing again. Kusum was on a pilgrimage, passing through a village when she heard a young girl's voice, singing one of her daughter's favorite *bhajans*. She followed the music through the squalor of a Himalayan village, to a hut where a young girl, an exact replica of her daughter, was fanning coals under the kitchen fire. When she appeared, the girl cried out, "Ma!" and ran away. What did I think of that?

I think I can only envy her.

Pam didn't make it to California, but writes me from Vancouver. She works in a department store, giving make-up hints to Indian and Oriental girls. Dr. Ranganathan has given up his commute, given up his house and job, and accepted an academic position in Texas where no one knows his story and he has vowed not to tell it. He calls me now once a week.

I wait, I listen, and I pray, but Vikram has not returned to me. The voices and the shapes and the nights filled with visions ended abruptly several weeks ago. I take it as a sign.

One rare, beautiful, sunny day last week, returning from a small errand on Yonge Street, I was walking through the park from the subway to my apartment. I live equidistant from the Ontario Houses of Parliament and the University of Toronto. The day was not cold, but something in the bare trees caught my attention. I looked up from the gravel, into the branches and the clear blue sky beyond. I thought I heard the rustling of larger forms, and I waited a moment for voices. Nothing.

"What?" I asked.

Then as I stood in the path looking north to Queen's Park and west to the university, I heard the voices of my family one last time. *Your time has come,* they said. *Go, be brave.*

2. Member of Parliament.

I do not know where this voyage I have begun will end. I do not know which direction I will take. I dropped the package on a park bench and started walking.

1988

QUESTIONS

1. How would you characterize Shaila Bhave's central conflict? In what ways might it resemble that of any grieving wife and mother? of any victim of terrorism? How is it created or exacerbated by her particular cultural location and situation?
2. Why does Shaila choose to return to Canada? What exactly does she seem to be choosing at the story's end? How do her choices compare to those of other characters in the story? What is the thematic significance of those choices?
3. How does Shaila's work with Judith affect her and the story's themes?

AUTHORS ON THEIR WORK

BHARATI MUKHERJEE (b. 1940)

From "Author Interviews: Bharati Mukherjee Runs the West Coast Offense" (2002)*

MUKHERJEE: My husband, Clark Blaise, and I wrote a nonfiction book [*The Sorrow and the Terror* (1987)] about the terrorist bombing of an Air India jet that took off from Toronto on its way to Bombay with 329 people on board, 90 percent of whom were Canadians of Indian origin. The bad guys were Canadians, but Sikh, militant [. . .] in politics. It was the bloodiest terrorist incident until WTC [World Trade Center].

[. . .] The book was a nonfiction bestseller in Canada. We were under death threat for two years. When I sat down to write *The Middleman and Other Stories* [1988] as a collection of stories about diaspora, "The Management of Grief" came out in one sitting. It was a very sad story to write.

I would have been on that plane if I hadn't left Canada for the U.S. five years before—that's the plane we used to take to India, the first one after school closing. I lost a friend on that flight.

DAVE: Having created two products from one body of research, [. . .] how do you account for the[ir] life spans being so different?

MUKHERJEE: [. . .] Yes, they've long forgotten the nonfiction book, [. . .] but the story lives on.

The persuasive power of fiction was heartening. [. . .] The story of individual families or individual victims lived on and spoke to people in ways that the statement of facts didn't.

*"Author Interviews: Bharati Mukherjee Runs the West Coast Offense." Interview by Dave Welch. *PowellsBooks Blog*, 4 April 2002, www.powells.com/post/interviews/bharati-mukherjee-runs-the-west-coast-offense.

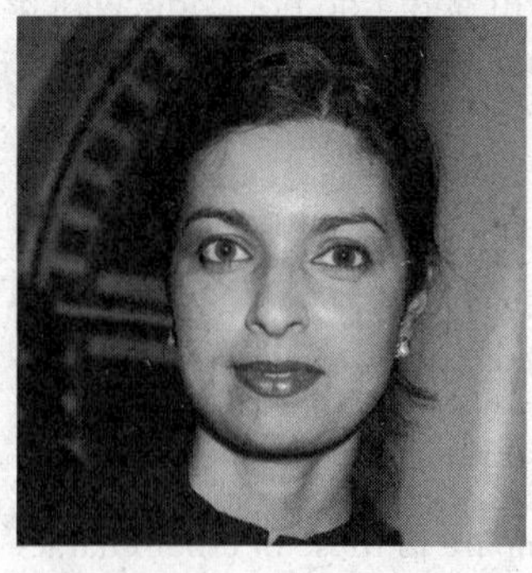

JHUMPA LAHIRI
(b. 1967)

Interpreter of Maladies

Born in London and raised in Rhode Island, Jhumpa Lahiri is the daughter of Bengali parents; much of her fiction addresses the difficulty of reconciling an Indian heritage with life in the United States. Lahiri earned a BA from Barnard College and several degrees from Boston University: an MA in English, an MFA in creative writing, an MA in comparative studies in literature and the arts, and a PhD in Renaissance studies. She has published many stories in well-known periodicals such as the *New Yorker* and won the 2000 Pulitzer Prize for her first collection, *Interpreter of Maladies* (1999), a best seller that has been translated into twenty-nine languages. Her second collection, *Unaccustomed Earth* (2008), debuted at the top of the *New York Times* best-seller list. Lahiri is also the author of two novels: *The Namesake* (2003) was made into a film in 2006; *The Lowland* (2013) was short-listed for both the Man Booker Prize and the National Book Award.

At the tea stall Mr. and Mrs. Das bickered about who should take Tina to the toilet. Eventually Mrs. Das relented when Mr. Das pointed out that he had given the girl her bath the night before. In the rearview mirror Mr. Kapasi watched as Mrs. Das emerged slowly from his bulky white Ambassador, dragging her shaved, largely bare legs across the back seat. She did not hold the little girl's hand as they walked to the rest room.

They were on their way to see the Sun Temple at Konarak.[1] It was a dry, bright Saturday, the mid-July heat tempered by a steady ocean breeze, ideal weather for sightseeing. Ordinarily Mr. Kapasi would not have stopped so soon along the way, but less than five minutes after he'd picked up the family that morning in front of Hotel Sandy Villa, the little girl had complained. The first thing Mr. Kapasi had noticed when he saw Mr. and Mrs. Das, standing with their children under the portico of the hotel, was that they were very young, perhaps not even thirty. In addition to Tina they had two boys, Ronny and Bobby, who appeared very close in age and had teeth covered in a network of flashing silver wires. The family looked Indian but dressed as foreigners did, the children in stiff, brightly colored clothing and caps with translucent visors. Mr. Kapasi was accustomed to foreign tourists; he was assigned to them regularly because he could speak English. Yesterday he had driven an elderly couple from Scotland, both with spotted faces and fluffy white hair so thin it exposed their sunburnt scalps. In comparison, the tanned, youthful faces of Mr. and Mrs.

1. In paragraphs 91–98, the story provides an accurate history and description of the Sun Temple at Konark (or Konarak), still a pilgrimage as well as tourist site near the east coast in the Orissa region of India. According to legend, the temple was built because Samba, son of Lord Krishna, was cured of leprosy by Surya, the sun god.

Das were all the more striking. When he'd introduced himself, Mr. Kapasi had pressed his palms together in greeting, but Mr. Das squeezed hands like an American so that Mr. Kapasi felt it in his elbow. Mrs. Das, for her part, had flexed one side of her mouth, smiling dutifully at Mr. Kapasi, without displaying any interest in him.

As they waited at the tea stall, Ronny, who looked like the older of the two boys, clambered suddenly out of the back seat, intrigued by a goat tied to a stake in the ground.

"Don't touch it," Mr. Das said. He glanced up from his paperback tour book, which said "INDIA" in yellow letters and looked as if it had been published abroad. His voice, somehow tentative and a little shrill, sounded as though it had not yet settled into maturity.

"I want to give it a piece of gum," the boy called back as he trotted ahead. 5

Mr. Das stepped out of the car and stretched his legs by squatting briefly to the ground. A clean-shaven man, he looked exactly like a magnified version of Ronny. He had a sapphire blue visor, and was dressed in shorts, sneakers, and a T-shirt. The camera slung around his neck, with an impressive telephoto lens and numerous buttons and markings, was the only complicated thing he wore. He frowned, watching as Ronny rushed toward the goat, but appeared to have no intention of intervening. "Bobby, make sure that your brother doesn't do anything stupid."

"I don't feel like it," Bobby said, not moving. He was sitting in the front seat beside Mr. Kapasi, studying a picture of the elephant god taped to the glove compartment.

"No need to worry," Mr. Kapasi said. "They are quite tame." Mr. Kapasi was forty-six years old, with receding hair that had gone completely silver, but his butterscotch complexion and his unlined brow, which he treated in spare moments to dabs of lotus-oil balm, made it easy to imagine what he must have looked like at an earlier age. He wore gray trousers and a matching jacket-style shirt, tapered at the waist, with short sleeves and a large pointed collar, made of a thin but durable synthetic material. He had specified both the cut and the fabric to his tailor—it was his preferred uniform for giving tours because it did not get crushed during his long hours behind the wheel. Through the windshield he watched as Ronny circled around the goat, touched it quickly on its side, then trotted back to the car.

"You left India as a child?" Mr. Kapasi asked when Mr. Das had settled once again into the passenger seat.

"Oh, Mina and I were both born in America," Mr. Das announced with an 10
air of sudden confidence. "Born and raised. Our parents live here now, in Assansol.[2] They retired. We visit them every couple years." He turned to watch as the little girl ran toward the car, the wide purple bows of her sundress flopping on her narrow brown shoulders. She was holding to her chest a doll with yellow hair that looked as if it had been chopped, as a punitive measure, with a pair of dull scissors. "This is Tina's first trip to India, isn't it, Tina?"

"I don't have to go to the bathroom anymore," Tina announced.

2. Or Asonsol, a city in northeastern India, not far from Calcutta and about three hundred miles from Puri, the coastal city in Orissa that the Das family is visiting. Puri is both a tourist resort and a Hindu holy city, said to be dominated by the forces of both the gods and humanity.

"Where's Mina?" Mr. Das asked.

Mr. Kapasi found it strange that Mr. Das should refer to his wife by her first name when speaking to the little girl. Tina pointed to where Mrs. Das was purchasing something from one of the shirtless men who worked at the tea stall. Mr. Kapasi heard one of the shirtless men sing a phrase from a popular Hindi love song as Mrs. Das walked back to the car, but she did not appear to understand the words of the song, for she did not express irritation, or embarrassment, or react in any other way to the man's declarations.

He observed her. She wore a red-and-white-checkered skirt that stopped above her knees, slip-on shoes with a square wooden heel, and a close-fitting blouse styled like a man's undershirt. The blouse was decorated at chest-level with a calico appliqué in the shape of a strawberry. She was a short woman, with small hands like paws, her frosty pink fingernails painted to match her lips, and was slightly plump in her figure. Her hair, shorn only a little longer than her husband's, was parted far to one side. She was wearing large dark brown sunglasses with a pinkish tint to them, and carried a big straw bag, almost as big as her torso, shaped like a bowl, with a water bottle poking out of it. She walked slowly, carrying some puffed rice tossed with peanuts and chili peppers in a large packet made from newspapers. Mr. Kapasi turned to Mr. Das.

15 "Where in America do you live?"

"New Brunswick, New Jersey."

"Next to New York?"

"Exactly. I teach middle school there."

"What subject?"

20 "Science. In fact, every year I take my students on a trip to the Museum of Natural History in New York City. In a way we have a lot in common, you could say, you and I. How long have you been a tour guide, Mr. Kapasi?"

"Five years."

Mrs. Das reached the car. "How long's the trip?" she asked, shutting the door.

"About two and a half hours," Mr. Kapasi replied.

At this Mrs. Das gave an impatient sigh, as if she had been traveling her whole life without pause. She fanned herself with a folded Bombay film magazine written in English.

25 "I thought that the Sun Temple is only eighteen miles north of Puri," Mr. Das said, tapping on the tour book.

"The roads to Konarak are poor. Actually it is a distance of fifty-two miles," Mr. Kapasi explained.

Mr. Das nodded, readjusting the camera strap where it had begun to chafe the back of his neck.

Before starting the ignition, Mr. Kapasi reached back to make sure the crank-like locks on the inside of each of the back doors were secured. As soon as the car began to move the little girl began to play with the lock on her side, clicking it with some effort forward and backward, but Mrs. Das said nothing to stop her. She sat a bit slouched at one end of the back seat, not offering her puffed rice to anyone. Ronny and Tina sat on either side of her, both snapping bright green gum.

"Look," Bobby said as the car began to gather speed. He pointed with his finger to the tall trees that lined the road. "Look."

30 "Monkeys!" Ronny shrieked. "Wow!"

They were seated in groups along the branches, with shining black faces, silver bodies, horizontal eyebrows, and crested heads. Their long gray tails dangled like a series of ropes among the leaves. A few scratched themselves with black leathery hands, or swung their feet, staring as the car passed.

"We call them the hanuman," Mr. Kapasi said. "They are quite common in the area."

As soon as he spoke, one of the monkeys leaped into the middle of the road, causing Mr. Kapasi to brake suddenly. Another bounced onto the hood of the car, then sprang away. Mr. Kapasi beeped his horn. The children began to get excited, sucking in their breath and covering their faces partly with their hands. They had never seen monkeys outside of a zoo, Mr. Das explained. He asked Mr. Kapasi to stop the car so that he could take a picture.

While Mr. Das adjusted his telephoto lens, Mrs. Das reached into her straw bag and pulled out a bottle of colorless nail polish, which she proceeded to stroke on the tip of her index finger.

The little girl stuck out a hand. "Mine too. Mommy, do mine too."

"Leave me alone," Mrs. Das said, blowing on her nail and turning her body slightly. "You're making me mess up."

The little girl occupied herself by buttoning and unbuttoning a pinafore on the doll's plastic body.

"All set," Mr. Das said, replacing the lens cap.

The car rattled considerably as it raced along the dusty road, causing them all to pop up from their seats every now and then, but Mrs. Das continued to polish her nails. Mr. Kapasi eased up on the accelerator, hoping to produce a smoother ride. When he reached for the gearshift the boy in front accommodated him by swinging his hairless knees out of the way. Mr. Kapasi noted that this boy was slightly paler than the other children. "Daddy, why is the driver sitting on the wrong side in this car, too?" the boy asked.

"They all do that here, dummy," Ronny said.

"Don't call your brother a dummy," Mr. Das said. He turned to Mr. Kapasi. "In America, you know . . . it confuses them."

"Oh yes, I am well aware," Mr. Kapasi said. As delicately as he could, he shifted gears again, accelerating as they approached a hill in the road. "I see it on *Dallas*, the steering wheels are on the left-hand side."

"What's *Dallas*?" Tina asked, banging her now naked doll on the seat behind Mr. Kapasi.

"It went off the air," Mr. Das explained. "It's a television show."[3]

They were all like siblings, Mr. Kapasi thought as they passed a row of date trees. Mr. and Mrs. Das behaved like an older brother and sister, not parents. It seemed that they were in charge of the children only for the day; it was hard to believe they were regularly responsible for anything other than themselves. Mr. Das tapped on his lens cap, and his tour book, dragging his thumbnail occasionally across the pages so that they made a scraping sound. Mrs. Das continued to polish her nails. She had still not removed her sunglasses. Every now and then Tina renewed her plea that she wanted her nails done, too, and so at one

3. Reruns of this American television show (1978–91) featuring the rich, dysfunctional Ewing family of Dallas continue worldwide.

point Mrs. Das flicked a drop of polish on the little girl's finger before depositing the bottle back inside her straw bag.

"Isn't this an air-conditioned car?" she asked, still blowing on her hand. The window on Tina's side was broken and could not be rolled down.

"Quit complaining," Mr. Das said. "It isn't so hot."

"I told you to get a car with air-conditioning," Mrs. Das continued. "Why do you do this, Raj, just to save a few stupid rupees. What are you saving us, fifty cents?"

Their accents sounded just like the ones Mr. Kapasi heard on American television programs, though not like the ones on *Dallas*.

"Doesn't it get tiresome, Mr. Kapasi, showing people the same thing every day?" Mr. Das asked, rolling down his own window all the way. "Hey, do you mind stopping the car. I just want to get a shot of this guy."

Mr. Kapasi pulled over to the side of the road as Mr. Das took a picture of a barefoot man, his head wrapped in a dirty turban, seated on top of a cart of grain sacks pulled by a pair of bullocks. Both the man and the bullocks were emaciated. In the back seat Mrs. Das gazed out another window, at the sky, where nearly transparent clouds passed quickly in front of one another.

"I look forward to it, actually," Mr. Kapasi said as they continued on their way. "The Sun Temple is one of my favorite places. In that way it is a reward for me. I give tours on Fridays and Saturdays only. I have another job during the week."

"Oh? Where?" Mr. Das asked.

"I work in a doctor's office."

"You're a doctor?"

"I am not a doctor. I work with one. As an interpreter."

"What does a doctor need an interpreter for?"

"He has a number of Gujarati patients. My father was Gujarati, but many people do not speak Gujarati in this area,[4] including the doctor. And so the doctor asked me to work in his office, interpreting what the patients say."

"Interesting. I've never heard of anything like that," Mr. Das said.

Mr. Kapasi shrugged. "It is a job like any other."

"But so romantic," Mrs. Das said dreamily, breaking her extended silence. She lifted her pinkish brown sunglasses and arranged them on top of her head like a tiara. For the first time, her eyes met Mr. Kapasi's in the rearview mirror: pale, a bit small, their gaze fixed but drowsy.

Mr. Das craned to look at her. "What's so romantic about it?"

"I don't know. Something." She shrugged, knitting her brows together for an instant. "Would you like a piece of gum, Mr. Kapasi?" she asked brightly. She reached into her straw bag and handed him a small square wrapped in green-and-white-striped paper. As soon as Mr. Kapasi put the gum in his mouth a thick sweet liquid burst onto his tongue.

"Tell us more about your job, Mr. Kapasi," Mrs. Das said.

"What would you like to know, madame?"

4. Gujarat is a northwestern region of India, on the Arabian Sea. Mr. Kapasi speaks several of India's disparate regional languages—those of Bengal and Orissa, near where he lives, and Gujarati, from the opposite coast—along with the more widespread Hindi and English.

"I don't know," she shrugged, munching on some puffed rice and licking the mustard oil from the corners of her mouth. "Tell us a typical situation." She settled back in her seat, her head tilted in a patch of sun, and closed her eyes. "I want to picture what happens."

"Very well. The other day a man came in with a pain in his throat."

"Did he smoke cigarettes?"

"No. It was very curious. He complained that he felt as if there were long pieces of straw stuck in his throat. When I told the doctor he was able to prescribe the proper medication."

"That's so neat."

"Yes," Mr. Kapasi agreed after some hesitation.

"So these patients are totally dependent on you," Mrs. Das said. She spoke slowly, as if she were thinking aloud. "In a way, more dependent on you than the doctor."

"How do you mean? How could it be?"

"Well, for example, you could tell the doctor that the pain felt like a burning, not straw. The patient would never know what you had told the doctor, and the doctor wouldn't know that you had told the wrong thing. It's a big responsibility."

"Yes, a big responsibility you have there, Mr. Kapasi," Mr. Das agreed.

Mr. Kapasi had never thought of his job in such complimentary terms. To him it was a thankless occupation. He found nothing noble in interpreting people's maladies, assiduously translating the symptoms of so many swollen bones, countless cramps of bellies and bowels, spots on people's palms that changed color, shape, or size. The doctor, nearly half his age, had an affinity for bell-bottom trousers and made humorless jokes about the Congress party.[5] Together they worked in a stale little infirmary where Mr. Kapasi's smartly tailored clothes clung to him in the heat, in spite of the blackened blades of a ceiling fan churning over their heads.

The job was a sign of his failings. In his youth he'd been a devoted scholar of foreign languages, the owner of an impressive collection of dictionaries. He had dreamed of being an interpreter for diplomats and dignitaries, resolving conflicts between people and nations, settling disputes of which he alone could understand both sides. He was a self-educated man. In a series of notebooks, in the evenings before his parents settled his marriage, he had listed the common etymologies of words, and at one point in his life he was confident that he could converse, if given the opportunity, in English, French, Russian, Portuguese, and Italian, not to mention Hindi, Bengali, Orissi, and Gujarati. Now only a handful of European phrases remained in his memory, scattered words for things like saucers and chairs. English was the only non-Indian language he spoke fluently anymore. Mr. Kapasi knew it was not a remarkable talent. Sometimes he feared that his children knew better English than he did, just from watching television. Still, it came in handy for the tours.

5. The Indian National Congress party, founded in 1885, led the movement for independence from Britain (gained in 1947) through the successive leadership of Mohandas Gandhi (1869–1948) and Jawaharlal Nehru (1889–1964). The party divided and subdivided, but a faction once led by Indira Gandhi (1917–84) dominated through the 1980s and much of the 1990s, despite being constantly accused of corruption and the use of violent tactics.

He had taken the job as an interpreter after his first son, at the age of seven, contracted typhoid—that was how he had first made the acquaintance of the doctor. At the time Mr. Kapasi had been teaching English in a grammar school, and he bartered his skills as an interpreter to pay the increasingly exorbitant medical bills. In the end the boy had died one evening in his mother's arms, his limbs burning with fever, but then there was the funeral to pay for, and the other children who were born soon enough, and the newer, bigger house, and the good schools and tutors, and the fine shoes and the television, and the countless other ways he tried to console his wife and to keep her from crying in her sleep, and so when the doctor offered to pay him twice as much as he earned at the grammar school, he accepted. Mr. Kapasi knew that his wife had little regard for his career as an interpreter. He knew it reminded her of the son she'd lost, and that she resented the other lives he helped, in his own small way, to save. If ever she referred to his position, she used the phrase "doctor's assistant," as if the process of interpretation were equal to taking someone's temperature, or changing a bedpan. She never asked him about the patients who came to the doctor's office, or said that his job was a big responsibility.

For this reason it flattered Mr. Kapasi that Mrs. Das was so intrigued by his job. Unlike his wife, she had reminded him of its intellectual challenges. She had also used the word "romantic." She did not behave in a romantic way toward her husband, and yet she had used the word to describe him. He wondered if Mr. and Mrs. Das were a bad match, just as he and his wife were. Perhaps they, too, had little in common apart from three children and a decade of their lives. The signs he recognized from his own marriage were there—the bickering, the indifference, the protracted silences. Her sudden interest in him, an interest she did not express in either her husband or her children, was mildly intoxicating. When Mr. Kapasi thought once again about how she had said "romantic," the feeling of intoxication grew.

80 He began to check his reflection in the rearview mirror as he drove, feeling grateful that he had chosen the gray suit that morning and not the brown one, which tended to sag a little in the knees. From time to time he glanced through the mirror at Mrs. Das. In addition to glancing at her face he glanced at the strawberry between her breasts, and the golden brown hollow in her throat. He decided to tell Mrs. Das about another patient, and another: the young woman who had complained of a sensation of raindrops in her spine, the gentleman whose birthmark had begun to sprout hairs. Mrs. Das listened attentively, stroking her hair with a small plastic brush that resembled an oval bed of nails, asking more questions, for yet another example. The children were quiet, intent on spotting more monkeys in the trees, and Mr. Das was absorbed by his tour book, so it seemed like a private conversation between Mr. Kapasi and Mrs. Das. In this manner the next half hour passed, and when they stopped for lunch at a roadside restaurant that sold fritters and omelette sandwiches, usually something Mr. Kapasi looked forward to on his tours so that he could sit in peace and enjoy some hot tea, he was disappointed. As the Das family settled together under a magenta umbrella fringed with white and orange tassels, and placed their orders with one of the waiters who marched about in tricornered caps, Mr. Kapasi reluctantly headed toward a neighboring table.

"Mr. Kapasi, wait. There's room here," Mrs. Das called out. She gathered Tina onto her lap, insisting that he accompany them. And so, together, they had bottled mango juice and sandwiches and plates of onions and potatoes deep-fried in graham-flour batter. After finishing two omelette sandwiches Mr. Das took more pictures of the group as they ate.

"How much longer?" he asked Mr. Kapasi as he paused to load a new roll of film in the camera.

"About half an hour more."

By now the children had gotten up from the table to look at more monkeys perched in a nearby tree, so there was a considerable space between Mrs. Das and Mr. Kapasi. Mr. Das placed the camera to his face and squeezed one eye shut, his tongue exposed at one corner of his mouth. "This looks funny. Mina, you need to lean in closer to Mr. Kapasi."

She did. He could smell a scent on her skin, like a mixture of whiskey and 85
rosewater. He worried suddenly that she could smell his perspiration, which he knew had collected beneath the synthetic material of his shirt. He polished off his mango juice in one gulp and smoothed his silver hair with his hands. A bit of the juice dripped onto his chin. He wondered if Mrs. Das had noticed.

She had not. "What's your address, Mr. Kapasi?" she inquired, fishing for something inside her straw bag.

"You would like my address?"

"So we can send you copies," she said. "Of the pictures." She handed him a scrap of paper which she had hastily ripped from a page of her film magazine. The blank portion was limited, for the narrow strip was crowded by lines of text and a tiny picture of a hero and heroine embracing under a eucalyptus tree.

The paper curled as Mr. Kapasi wrote his address in clear, careful letters. She would write to him, asking about his days interpreting at the doctor's office, and he would respond eloquently, choosing only the most entertaining anecdotes, ones that would make her laugh out loud as she read them in her house in New Jersey. In time she would reveal the disappointment of her marriage, and he his. In this way their friendship would grow, and flourish. He would possess a picture of the two of them, eating fried onions under a magenta umbrella, which he would keep, he decided, safely tucked between the pages of his Russian grammar. As his mind raced, Mr. Kapasi experienced a mild and pleasant shock. It was similar to a feeling he used to experience long ago when, after months of translating with the aid of a dictionary, he would finally read a passage from a French novel, or an Italian sonnet, and understand the words, one after another, unencumbered by his own efforts. In those moments Mr. Kapasi used to believe that all was right with the world, that all struggles were rewarded, that all of life's mistakes made sense in the end. The promise that he would hear from Mrs. Das now filled him with the same belief.

When he finished writing his address Mr. Kapasi handed her the paper, but 90
as soon as he did so he worried that he had either misspelled his name, or accidentally reversed the numbers of his postal code. He dreaded the possibility of a lost letter, the photograph never reaching him, hovering somewhere in Orissa, close but ultimately unattainable. He thought of asking for the slip of paper again, just to make sure he had written his address accurately, but Mrs. Das had already dropped it into the jumble of her bag.

They reached Konarak at two-thirty. The temple, made of sandstone, was a massive pyramid-like structure in the shape of a chariot. It was dedicated to the great master of life, the sun, which struck three sides of the edifice as it made its journey each day across the sky. Twenty-four giant wheels were carved on the north and south sides of the plinth. The whole thing was drawn by a team of seven horses, speeding as if through the heavens. As they approached, Mr. Kapasi explained that the temple had been built between A.D. 1243 and 1255, with the efforts of twelve hundred artisans, by the great ruler of the Ganga dynasty, King Narasimhadeva the First, to commemorate his victory against the Muslim army.

"It says the temple occupies about a hundred and seventy acres of land," Mr. Das said, reading from his book.

"It's like a desert," Ronny said, his eyes wandering across the sand that stretched on all sides beyond the temple.

"The Chandrabhaga River once flowed one mile north of here. It is dry now," Mr. Kapasi said, turning off the engine.

They got out and walked toward the temple, posing first for pictures by the pair of lions that flanked the steps. Mr. Kapasi led them next to one of the wheels of the chariot, higher than any human being, nine feet in diameter.

"'The wheels are supposed to symbolize the wheel of life,'" Mr. Das read. "'They depict the cycle of creation, preservation, and achievement of realization.' Cool." He turned the page of his book. "'Each wheel is divided into eight thick and thin spokes, dividing the day into eight equal parts. The rims are carved with designs of birds and animals, whereas the medallions in the spokes are carved with women in luxurious poses, largely erotic in nature.'"

What he referred to were the countless friezes of entwined naked bodies, making love in various positions, women clinging to the necks of men, their knees wrapped eternally around their lovers' thighs. In addition to these were assorted scenes from daily life, of hunting and trading, of deer being killed with bows and arrows and marching warriors holding swords in their hands.

It was no longer possible to enter the temple, for it had filled with rubble years ago, but they admired the exterior, as did all the tourists Mr. Kapasi brought there, slowly strolling along each of its sides. Mr. Das trailed behind, taking pictures. The children ran ahead, pointing to figures of naked people, intrigued in particular by the Nagamithunas, the half-human, half-serpentine couples who were said, Mr. Kapasi told them, to live in the deepest waters of the sea. Mr. Kapasi was pleased that they liked the temple, pleased especially that it appealed to Mrs. Das. She stopped every three or four paces, staring silently at the carved lovers, and the processions of elephants, and the topless female musicians beating on two-sided drums.

Though Mr. Kapasi had been to the temple countless times, it occurred to him, as he, too, gazed at the topless women, that he had never seen his own wife fully naked. Even when they had made love she kept the panels of her blouse hooked together, the string of her petticoat knotted around her waist. He had never admired the backs of his wife's legs the way he now admired those of Mrs. Das, walking as if for his benefit alone. He had, of course, seen plenty of bare limbs before, belonging to the American and European ladies who took his tours. But Mrs. Das was different. Unlike the other women, who had an interest only in the temple, and kept their noses buried in a guidebook, or their eyes behind the lens of a camera, Mrs. Das had taken an interest in him.

Mr. Kapasi was anxious to be alone with her, to continue their private con- 100
versation, yet he felt nervous to walk at her side. She was lost behind her sunglasses, ignoring her husband's requests that she pose for another picture, walking past her children as if they were strangers. Worried that he might disturb her, Mr. Kapasi walked ahead, to admire, as he always did, the three life-sized bronze avatars of Surya, the sun god, each emerging from its own niche on the temple facade to greet the sun at dawn, noon, and evening. They wore elaborate headdresses, their languid, elongated eyes closed, their bare chests draped with carved chains and amulets. Hibiscus petals, offerings from previous visitors, were strewn at their gray-green feet. The last statue, on the northern wall of the temple, was Mr. Kapasi's favorite. This Surya had a tired expression, weary after a hard day of work, sitting astride a horse with folded legs. Even his horse's eyes were drowsy. Around his body were smaller sculptures of women in pairs, their hips thrust to one side.

"Who's that?" Mrs. Das asked. He was startled to see that she was standing beside him.

"He is the Astachala-Surya," Mr. Kapasi said. "The setting sun."

"So in a couple of hours the sun will set right here?" She slipped a foot out of one of her square-heeled shoes, rubbed her toes on the back of her other leg.

"That is correct."

She raised her sunglasses for a moment, then put them back on again. "Neat." 105

Mr. Kapasi was not certain exactly what the word suggested, but he had a feeling it was a favorable response. He hoped that Mrs. Das had understood Surya's beauty, his power. Perhaps they would discuss it further in their letters. He would explain things to her, things about India, and she would explain things to him about America. In its own way this correspondence would fulfill his dream, of serving as an interpreter between nations. He looked at her straw bag, delighted that his address lay nestled among its contents. When he pictured her so many thousands of miles away he plummeted, so much so that he had an overwhelming urge to wrap his arms around her, to freeze with her, even for an instant, in an embrace witnessed by his favorite Surya. But Mrs. Das had already started walking.

"When do you return to America?" he asked, trying to sound placid.

"In ten days."

He calculated: A week to settle in, a week to develop the pictures, a few days to compose her letter, two weeks to get to India by air. According to his schedule, allowing room for delays, he would hear from Mrs. Das in approximately six weeks' time.

The family was silent as Mr. Kapasi drove them back, a little past four-thirty, to 110
Hotel Sandy Villa. The children had bought miniature granite versions of the chariot's wheels at a souvenir stand, and they turned them round in their hands. Mr. Das continued to read his book. Mrs. Das untangled Tina's hair with her brush and divided it into two little ponytails.

Mr. Kapasi was beginning to dread the thought of dropping them off. He was not prepared to begin his six-week wait to hear from Mrs. Das. As he stole glances at her in the rearview mirror, wrapping elastic bands around Tina's hair, he wondered how he might make the tour last a little longer. Ordinarily he sped back to Puri using a shortcut, eager to return home, scrub his feet and hands with sandalwood soap, and enjoy the evening newspaper and a cup of tea that his wife would serve him in silence. The thought of that silence, something to which he'd long been resigned, now oppressed him. It was then that he suggested visiting the hills at Udayagiri and Khandagiri, where a number of monastic dwellings were hewn out of the ground, facing one another across a defile. It was some miles away, but well worth seeing, Mr. Kapasi told them.

"Oh yeah, there's something mentioned about it in this book," Mr. Das said. "Built by a Jain king or something."[6]

"Shall we go then?" Mr. Kapasi asked. He paused at a turn in the road. "It's to the left."

Mr. Das turned to look at Mrs. Das. Both of them shrugged.

"Left, left," the children chanted.

Mr. Kapasi turned the wheel, almost delirious with relief. He did not know what he would do or say to Mrs. Das once they arrived at the hills. Perhaps he would tell her what a pleasing smile she had. Perhaps he would compliment her strawberry shirt, which he found irresistibly becoming. Perhaps, when Mr. Das was busy taking a picture, he would take her hand.

He did not have to worry. When they got to the hills, divided by a steep path thick with trees, Mrs. Das refused to get out of the car. All along the path, dozens of monkeys were seated on stones, as well as on the branches of the trees. Their hind legs were stretched out in front and raised to shoulder level, their arms resting on their knees.

"My legs are tired," she said, sinking low in her seat. "I'll stay here."

"Why did you have to wear those stupid shoes?" Mr. Das said. "You won't be in the pictures."

"Pretend I'm there."

"But we could use one of these pictures for our Christmas card this year. We didn't get one of all five of us at the Sun Temple. Mr. Kapasi could take it."

"I'm not coming. Anyway, those monkeys give me the creeps."

"But they're harmless," Mr. Das said. He turned to Mr. Kapasi. "Aren't they?"

"They are more hungry than dangerous," Mr. Kapasi said. "Do not provoke them with food, and they will not bother you."

Mr. Das headed up the defile with the children, the boys at his side, the little girl on his shoulders. Mr. Kapasi watched as they crossed paths with a Japanese man and woman, the only other tourists there, who paused for a final photograph, then stepped into a nearby car and drove away. As the car disappeared out of view some of the monkeys called out, emitting soft whooping sounds, and then walked on their flat black hands and feet up the path. At one point a group of them formed a little ring around Mr. Das and the children. Tina screamed in delight. Ronny ran in circles around his father. Bobby bent down and picked up

6. This site is not a major tourist attraction; "giri" means mountain. Jainism, one of the several main religions of India, is an atheist sect that emerged from Hinduism around 580 BCE, at about the same time as Buddhism.

a fat stick on the ground. When he extended it, one of the monkeys approached him and snatched it, then briefly beat the ground.

"I'll join them," Mr. Kapasi said, unlocking the door on his side. "There is much to explain about the caves."

"No. Stay a minute," Mrs. Das said. She got out of the back seat and slipped in beside Mr. Kapasi. "Raj has his dumb book anyway." Together, through the windshield, Mrs. Das and Mr. Kapasi watched as Bobby and the monkey passed the stick back and forth between them.

"A brave little boy," Mr. Kapasi commented.

"It's not so surprising," Mrs. Das said.

"No?"

"He's not his."

"I beg your pardon?"

"Raj's. He's not Raj's son."

Mr. Kapasi felt a prickle on his skin. He reached into his shirt pocket for the small tin of lotus-oil balm he carried with him at all times, and applied it to three spots on his forehead. He knew that Mrs. Das was watching him, but he did not turn to face her. Instead he watched as the figures of Mr. Das and the children grew smaller, climbing up the steep path, pausing every now and then for a picture, surrounded by a growing number of monkeys.

"Are you surprised?" The way she put it made him choose his words with care.

"It's not the type of thing one assumes," Mr. Kapasi replied slowly. He put the tin of lotus-oil balm back in his pocket.

"No, of course not. And no one knows, of course. No one at all. I've kept it a secret for eight whole years." She looked at Mr. Kapasi, tilting her chin as if to gain a fresh perspective. "But now I've told you."

Mr. Kapasi nodded. He felt suddenly parched, and his forehead was warm and slightly numb from the balm. He considered asking Mrs. Das for a sip of water, then decided against it.

"We met when we were very young," she said. She reached into her straw bag in search of something, then pulled out a packet of puffed rice. "Want some?"

"No, thank you."

She put a fistful in her mouth, sank into the seat a little, and looked away from Mr. Kapasi, out the window on her side of the car. "We married when we were still in college. We were in high school when he proposed. We went to the same college, of course. Back then we couldn't stand the thought of being separated, not for a day, not for a minute. Our parents were best friends who lived in the same town. My entire life I saw him every weekend, either at our house or theirs. We were sent upstairs to play together while our parents joked about our marriage. Imagine! They never caught us at anything, though in a way I think it was all more or less a setup. The things we did those Friday and Saturday nights, while our parents sat downstairs drinking tea . . . I could tell you stories, Mr. Kapasi."

As a result of spending all her time in college with Raj, she continued, she did not make many close friends. There was no one to confide in about him at the end of a difficult day, or to share a passing thought or a worry. Her parents now lived on the other side of the world, but she had never been very close to them, anyway. After marrying so young she was overwhelmed by it all, having a child so quickly, and nursing, and warming up bottles of milk and testing their temperature against her wrist while Raj was at work, dressed in sweaters and corduroy pants, teaching his students about rocks and dinosaurs. Raj never looked cross or harried, or plump as she had become after the first baby.

Always tired, she declined invitations from her one or two college girlfriends, to have lunch or shop in Manhattan. Eventually the friends stopped calling her, so that she was left at home all day with the baby, surrounded by toys that made her trip when she walked or wince when she sat, always cross and tired. Only occasionally did they go out after Ronny was born, and even more rarely did they entertain. Raj didn't mind; he looked forward to coming home from teaching and watching television and bouncing Ronny on his knee. She had been outraged when Raj told her that a Punjabi friend,[7] someone whom she had once met but did not remember, would be staying with them for a week for some job interviews in the New Brunswick area.

Bobby was conceived in the afternoon, on a sofa littered with rubber teething toys, after the friend learned that a London pharmaceutical company had hired him, while Ronny cried to be freed from his playpen. She made no protest when the friend touched the small of her back as she was about to make a pot of coffee, then pulled her against his crisp navy suit. He made love to her swiftly, in silence, with an expertise she had never known, without the meaningful expressions and smiles Raj always insisted on afterward. The next day Raj drove the friend to JFK.[8] He was married now, to a Punjabi girl, and they lived in London still, and every year they exchanged Christmas cards with Raj and Mina, each couple tucking photos of their families into the envelopes. He did not know that he was Bobby's father. He never would.

"I beg your pardon, Mrs. Das, but why have you told me this information?" Mr. Kapasi asked when she had finally finished speaking, and had turned to face him once again.

"For God's sake, stop calling me Mrs. Das. I'm twenty-eight. You probably have children my age."

"Not quite." It disturbed Mr. Kapasi to learn that she thought of him as a parent. The feeling he had had toward her, that had made him check his reflection in the rearview mirror as they drove, evaporated a little.

"I told you because of your talents." She put the packet of puffed rice back into her bag without folding over the top.

"I don't understand," Mr. Kapasi said.

"Don't you see? For eight years I haven't been able to express this to anybody, not to friends, certainly not to Raj. He doesn't even suspect it. He thinks I'm still in love with him. Well, don't you have anything to say?"

"About what?"

"About what I've just told you. About my secret, and about how terrible it makes me feel. I feel terrible looking at my children, and at Raj, always terrible. I have terrible urges, Mr. Kapasi, to throw things away. One day I had the urge to throw everything I own out of the window, the television, the children, everything. Don't you think it's unhealthy?"

7. Person from the Punjab, a northern region of India, near Pakistan.

8. John F. Kennedy International Airport, in New York City.

He was silent.

"Mr. Kapasi, don't you have anything to say? I thought that was your job."

"My job is to give tours, Mrs. Das."

"Not that. Your other job. As an interpreter."

"But we do not face a language barrier. What need is there for an interpreter?"

"That's not what I mean. I would never have told you otherwise. Don't you realize what it means for me to tell you?"

"What does it mean?"

"It means that I'm tired of feeling so terrible all the time. Eight years, Mr. Kapasi, I've been in pain eight years. I was hoping you could help me feel better, say the right thing. Suggest some kind of remedy."

He looked at her, in her red plaid skirt and strawberry T-shirt, a woman not yet thirty, who loved neither her husband nor her children, who had already fallen out of love with life. Her confession depressed him, depressed him all the more when he thought of Mr. Das at the top of the path, Tina clinging to his shoulders, taking pictures of ancient monastic cells cut into the hills to show his students in America, unsuspecting and unaware that one of his sons was not his own. Mr. Kapasi felt insulted that Mrs. Das should ask him to interpret her common, trivial little secret. She did not resemble the patients in the doctor's office, those who came glassy-eyed and desperate, unable to sleep or breathe or urinate with ease, unable, above all, to give words to their pains. Still, Mr. Kapasi believed it was his duty to assist Mrs. Das. Perhaps he ought to tell her to confess the truth to Mr. Das. He would explain that honesty was the best policy. Honesty, surely, would help her feel better, as she'd put it. Perhaps he would offer to preside over the discussion, as a mediator. He decided to begin with the most obvious question, to get to the heart of the matter, and so he asked, "Is it really pain you feel, Mrs. Das, or is it guilt?"

She turned to him and glared, mustard oil thick on her frosty pink lips. She opened her mouth to say something, but as she glared at Mr. Kapasi some certain knowledge seemed to pass before her eyes, and she stopped. It crushed him; he knew at that moment that he was not even important enough to be properly insulted. She opened the car door and began walking up the path, wobbling a little on her square wooden heels, reaching into her straw bag to eat handfuls of puffed rice. It fell through her fingers, leaving a zigzagging trail, causing a monkey to leap down from a tree and devour the little white grains. In search of more, the monkey began to follow Mrs. Das. Others joined him, so that she was soon being followed by about half a dozen of them, their velvety tails dragging behind.

Mr. Kapasi stepped out of the car. He wanted to holler, to alert her in some way, but he worried that if she knew they were behind her, she would grow nervous. Perhaps she would lose her balance. Perhaps they would pull at her bag or her hair. He began to jog up the path, taking a fallen branch in his hand to scare away the monkeys. Mrs. Das continued walking, oblivious, trailing grains of puffed rice. Near the top of the incline, before a group of cells fronted by a row of squat stone pillars, Mr. Das was kneeling on the ground, focusing the lens of his camera. The children stood under the arcade, now hiding, now emerging from view.

"Wait for me," Mrs. Das called out. "I'm coming."

165 Tina jumped up and down. "Here comes Mommy!"

"Great," Mr. Das said without looking up. "Just in time. We'll get Mr. Kapasi to take a picture of the five of us."

Mr. Kapasi quickened his pace, waving his branch so that the monkeys scampered away, distracted, in another direction.

"Where's Bobby?" Mrs. Das asked when she stopped.

Mr. Das looked up from the camera. "I don't know. Ronny, where's Bobby?"

170 Ronny shrugged. "I thought he was right here."

"Where is he?" Mrs. Das repeated sharply. "What's wrong with all of you?"

They began calling his name, wandering up and down the path a bit. Because they were calling, they did not initially hear the boy's screams. When they found him, a little farther down the path under a tree, he was surrounded by a group of monkeys, over a dozen of them, pulling at his T-shirt with their long black fingers. The puffed rice Mrs. Das had spilled was scattered at his feet, raked over by the monkeys' hands. The boy was silent, his body frozen, swift tears running down his startled face. His bare legs were dusty and red with welts from where one of the monkeys struck him repeatedly with the stick he had given to it earlier.

"Daddy, the monkey's hurting Bobby," Tina said.

Mr. Das wiped his palms on the front of his shorts. In his nervousness he accidentally pressed the shutter on his camera; the whirring noise of the advancing film excited the monkeys, and the one with the stick began to beat Bobby more intently. "What are we supposed to do? What if they start attacking?"

175 "Mr. Kapasi," Mrs. Das shrieked, noticing him standing to one side. "Do something, for God's sake, do something!"

Mr. Kapasi took his branch and shooed them away, hissing at the ones that remained, stomping his feet to scare them. The animals retreated slowly, with a measured gait, obedient but unintimidated. Mr. Kapasi gathered Bobby in his arms and brought him back to where his parents and siblings were standing. As he carried him he was tempted to whisper a secret into the boy's ear. But Bobby was stunned, and shivering with fright, his legs bleeding slightly where the stick had broken the skin. When Mr. Kapasi delivered him to his parents, Mr. Das brushed some dirt off the boy's T-shirt and put the visor on him the right way. Mrs. Das reached into her straw bag to find a bandage which she taped over the cut on his knee. Ronny offered his brother a fresh piece of gum. "He's fine. Just a little scared, right, Bobby?" Mr. Das said, patting the top of his head.

"God, let's get out of here," Mrs. Das said. She folded her arms across the strawberry on her chest. "This place gives me the creeps."

"Yeah. Back to the hotel, definitely," Mr. Das agreed.

"Poor Bobby," Mrs. Das said. "Come here a second. Let Mommy fix your hair." Again she reached into her straw bag, this time for her hairbrush, and began to run it around the edges of the translucent visor. When she whipped out the hairbrush, the slip of paper with Mr. Kapasi's address on it fluttered away in the wind. No one but Mr. Kapasi noticed. He watched as it rose, carried higher and higher by the breeze, into the trees where the monkeys now sat, solemnly observing the scene below. Mr. Kapasi observed it too, knowing that this was the picture of the Das family he would preserve forever in his mind.

1999

QUESTIONS

1. How does it matter—to Mr. Kapasi and this story—that the Das family both are and aren't "foreign" (par. 2)?
2. How might his encounter with the Das family alter Mr. Kapasi's sense of what it means to be Indian? Why is it important that this encounter has as its background a visit to ancient Indian religious shrines?
3. What is the thematic significance of the secret that Mrs. Das reveals to Mr. Kapasi? What is its relationship to the rest of the story and to aspects of human behavior that transcend culture and upbringing?

AUTHORS ON THEIR WORK
JHUMPA LAHIRI (b. 1967)

From "Interviews: Jhumpa Lahiri" (2008)*

[INTERVIEWER:] One thing that fascinates me about your previous stories is the way you view the marriages of people in your parents' generation. [. . .] Was that a fascination for you growing up: *What is going on with my folks?* And do you think it was especially interesting to you because you were growing up in [London, in] a culture different from the one in which they grew up [in India]?

[LAHIRI:] I don't know why, but the older I get the more interested I get in my parents' marriage. [. . .] I do think it's a question that has preoccupied me in all the books I've written. My parents had an arranged marriage, as did so many other people when I was growing up. My father came and had a life in the United States one way and my mother had a different one, and I was very aware of those things. I continue to wonder about it, and I will continue to write about it.

* * *

From "Interview with Jhumpa Lahiri" (2003)**

[INTERVIEWER: Lahiri's 2003 novel] *The Namesake* deals with Indian immigrants in the United States as well as their children. What, in your opinion, distinguishes the experiences of the former from the latter?

[LAHIRI:] In a sense, very little. The question of identity is always a difficult one, but especially so for those who are culturally displaced, as immigrants are, or those who grow up in two worlds simultaneously, as is the case for their children. The older I get, the more I am aware that I have somehow inherited a sense of exile from my parents, even though in many ways I am so much more American than they are. In fact, it is still very hard to think of myself as an American. (This is of course complicated by the fact that I was born in London.) I think that for immigrants, the challenges of exile, the loneliness, the constant sense of alienation, the knowledge of and longing for a lost world, are more explicit and distressing than for their children. On the other hand, the problem for the children of immigrants—those with strong ties to their country of origin—is that they feel neither one thing nor the other. This has been my experience, in any case. For example, I never know how to answer the question "Where are you from?" If I say I'm from Rhode Island, people are seldom satisfied. They want to know more, based on things such as my name, my appearance, etc. Alternatively, if I say I'm from India, a place where I was not born and have never lived, this is also inaccurate. It bothers me less now. But it bothered me growing up, the feeling that there was no single place to which I fully belonged.

[. . . INTERVIEWER:] You write frequently from the male point of view. Why?

[LAHIRI:] In the beginning I think it was mainly curiosity. I have no brothers, and growing up, men generally seemed like mysterious creatures to me. Except for an early story I wrote in college, the first thing I wrote from the male point of view was the story "This Blessed House," in *Interpreter of Maladies*. It was an exhilarating and liberating thing to do, so much so that I wrote three stories in a row, all from the male perspective. It's a challenge, as well. I always have to ask myself, would a man think this? do this?

*"Interviews: Jhumpa Lahiri." Interview by Isaac Chotiner. *The Atlantic Monthly*, 2008, www.theatlantic.com/magazine/archive/2008/04/jhumpa-lahiri/306725/.

**"Interview with Jhumpa Lahiri." *Readers Read*, Nov. 2003, www.writerswrite.com/books/interview-with-jhumpa-lahiri-110120031.

DAVID SEDARIS
(b. 1956)

Jesus Shaves

Dubbed by some "the funniest writer alive," David Sedaris uses his own life and the absurdities of the everyday as fodder for stories that often blur the line between fiction and nonfiction. Juxtaposing the highbrow with the lowbrow, they treat everything from his fleeting interests in crystal meth and bee-sized suits of armor to his brother's basement barbecue-sauce business. Sedaris was raised in the suburbs of Raleigh, North Carolina, after his Greek American family moved there from New York. Openly gay, Sedaris points to his inability to play jazz guitar as the source of his father's disappointment—"Fortunately there were six of us [. . .] it was easy to get lost in the crowd." After graduating from the School of the Art Institute of Chicago, he worked a series of now-well-documented menial jobs in New York City and Chicago before radio host Ira Glass discovered him at a Chicago nightclub, reading from his diary. "Santaland Diaries," which recounts his adventures as a department-store elf, was later featured on National Public Radio, making Sedaris an overnight sensation. Author of multiple *New York Times* best sellers, including *Me Talk Pretty One Day* (2000), *Dress Your Family in Corduroy and Denim* (2004), *When You Are Engulfed in Flames* (2008), and *Let's Explore Diabetes with Owls* (2013), as well as *Squirrel Seeks Chipmunk* (2010), "a collection of fables without morals," Sedaris has also collaborated with his sister, actress-comedian Amy Sedaris, on a number of plays, including *Incident at Cobbler's Knob* (1997) and *The Book of Liz* (2002). As renowned for his voice and comic timing as for his writing, Sedaris draws sellout crowds on his worldwide reading tours.

"And what does one do on the fourteenth of July? Does one celebrate Bastille Day?"

It was my second month of French class, and the teacher was leading us in an exercise designed to promote the use of *one*, our latest personal pronoun.

"Might one sing on Bastille Day?" she asked. "Might one dance in the street? Somebody give me an answer."

Printed in our textbooks was a list of major holidays alongside a scattered arrangement of photos depicting French people in the act of celebration. The object was to match the holiday with the corresponding picture. It was simple enough but seemed an exercise better suited to the use of the word *they*. I didn't know about the rest of the class, but when Bastille Day eventually rolled around, I planned to stay home and clean my oven.

5 Normally, when working from the book, it was my habit to tune out my fellow students and scout ahead, concentrating on the question I'd calculated might fall to me, but this afternoon, we were veering from the usual format. Questions were answered on a volunteer basis, and I was able to sit back, confident that the same few students would do the talking. Today's discussion was dominated by an Italian nanny, two chatty Poles, and a pouty, plump Moroccan woman who had grown up speaking French and had enrolled in the class to improve her spelling.[1] She'd covered these lessons back in the third grade and took every opportunity to demonstrate her superiority. A question would be asked and she'd give the answer, behaving as though this were a game show and, if quick enough, she might go home with a tropical vacation or a side-by-side refrigerator-freezer. By the end of her first day, she'd raised her hand so many times, her shoulder had given out. Now she just leaned back in her seat and shouted the answers, her bronzed arms folded across her chest like some great grammar genie.

We finished discussing Bastille Day, and the teacher moved on to Easter, which was represented in our textbook by a black-and-white photograph of a chocolate bell lying upon a bed of palm fronds.

"And what does one do on Easter? Would anyone like to tell us?"

The Italian nanny was attempting to answer the question when the Moroccan student interrupted, shouting, "Excuse me, but what's an Easter?"

Despite her having grown up in a Muslim country, it seemed she might have heard it mentioned once or twice, but no. "I mean it," she said. "I have no idea what you people are talking about."

10 The teacher then called upon the rest of us to explain.

1. France controlled most of Morocco between 1912 and 1956; as a result, though Arabic is now the country's official language, French is still widely taught and serves as the primary language of business and government.

The Poles led the charge to the best of their ability. "It is," said one, "a party for the little boy of God who call his self Jesus and . . . oh, shit."

She faltered, and her fellow countryman came to her aid.

"He call his self Jesus, and then he be die one day on two . . . morsels of . . . lumber."

The rest of the class jumped in, offering bits of information that would have given the pope an aneurysm.

"He die one day, and then he go above of my head to live with your father."

"He weared the long hair, and after he died, the first day he come back here for to say hello to the peoples."

"He nice, the Jesus."

"He make the good things, and on the Easter we be sad because somebody makes him dead today."

Part of the problem had to do with grammar. Simple nouns such as *cross* and *resurrection* were beyond our grasp, let alone such complicated reflexive phrases as "To give of yourself your only begotten son." Faced with the challenge of explaining the cornerstone of Christianity, we did what any self-respecting group of people might do. We talked about food instead.

"Easter is a party for to eat of the lamb," the Italian nanny explained. "One, too, may eat of the chocolate."

"And who brings the chocolate?" the teacher asked.

I knew the word, and so I raised my hand, saying, "The Rabbit of Easter. He bring of the chocolate."

My classmates reacted as though I'd attributed the delivery to the Antichrist. They were mortified.

"A rabbit?" The teacher, assuming I'd used the wrong word, positioned her index fingers on top of her head, wiggling them as though they were ears. "You mean one of these? A rabbit rabbit?"

"Well, sure," I said. "He come in the night when one sleep on a bed. With a hand he have the basket and foods."

The teacher sadly shook her head, as if this explained everything that was wrong with my country. "No, no," she said. "Here in France the chocolate is brought by the big bell that flies in from Rome."[2]

I called for a time-out. "But how do the bell know where you live?"

"Well," she said, "how does a rabbit?"

It was a decent point, but at least a rabbit has eyes. That's a start. Rabbits move from place to place, while most bells can only go back and forth—and they can't even do that on their own power. On top of that, the Easter Bunny has character; he's someone you'd like to meet and shake hands with. A bell has all the personality of a cast-iron skillet. It's like saying that come Christmas, a magic dustpan flies in from the North Pole, led by eight flying cinder blocks. Who wants to stay up all night so they can see a bell? And why fly one in from Rome when they've got more bells than they know what to do with right here in Paris? That's the most implausible aspect of the whole story, as there's no way

2. In remembrance of Jesus's death, bells across France are customarily silenced from the Thursday before Good Friday until Easter morning; children are encouraged to believe that the bells fly to Rome to visit the pope, returning with gifts.

the bells of France would allow a foreign worker to fly in and take their jobs. That Roman bell would be lucky to get work cleaning up after a French bell's dog—and even then he'd need papers. It just didn't add up.

Nothing we said was of any help to the Moroccan student. A dead man with long hair supposedly living with her father, a leg of lamb served with palm fronds and chocolate. Confused and disgusted, she shrugged her massive shoulders and turned her attention back to the comic book she kept hidden beneath her binder. I wondered then if, without the language barrier, my classmates and I could have done a better job making sense of Christianity, an idea that sounds pretty far-fetched to begin with. 30

In communicating any religious belief, the operative word is *faith*, a concept illustrated by our very presence in that classroom. Why bother struggling with the grammar lessons of a six-year-old if each of us didn't believe that, against all reason, we might eventually improve? If I could hope to one day carry on a fluent conversation, it was a relatively short leap to believing that a rabbit might visit my home in the middle of the night, leaving behind a handful of chocolate kisses and a carton of menthol cigarettes. So why stop there? If I could believe in myself, why not give other improbabilities the benefit of the doubt? I accepted the idea that an omniscient God had cast me in his own image and that he watched over me and guided me from one place to the next. The virgin birth, the resurrection, and the countless miracles—my heart expanded to encompass all the wonders and possibilities of the universe.

A bell, though, that's fucked up.

2000

QUESTIONS

1. How might it be thematically significant that the class exercise focuses on use of the pronoun *one*?
2. At one point, the narrator claims that grammar is "[p]art of the problem" (par. 19). How does grammar contribute to the humor of JESUS SHAVES? to its theme?
3. What "lesson" does the narrator seem to draw from this class exercise? In these terms, what might be significant, as well as funny, about the story's last sentence?

SUGGESTIONS FOR WRITING

1. Write a response paper comparing your reactions to JESUS SHAVES, on the one hand, and to either THE MANAGEMENT OF GRIEF or INTERPRETER OF MALADIES, on the other. How does your personal relationship to the various cultural traditions depicted in the two stories, especially those of each protagonist, affect your response?
2. In THE MANAGEMENT OF GRIEF, Shaila describes herself as "trapped between two modes of knowledge" (par. 84). Write an essay exploring whether and how this claim holds true both for Shaila and for a character in any other story in this album. What "two [or more] modes of knowledge" inform the characters' thinking and behavior, and how so? In what ways is each character "trapped" and in what ways liberated or even empowered by that situation?
3. Write an essay exploring how THE MANAGEMENT OF GRIEF and INTERPRETER OF MALADIES characterize what the former story calls "the New World" versus the Old (par. 134). According to these stories, what is distinctive about the life and people of North America and about the values or worldview of those who live there? What seems to be most and least attractive about them? How do the two

stories ultimately differ (or not) in their attitudes toward North America and North Americans?

4. Compare how any two stories in this album treat the issue of linguistic and cultural interpretation and translation. What does each story imply about when, how, and why such translation works or fails, and about what those who act as interpreters or translators might learn from doing so? How does narration contribute to each story's articulation of its theme?
5. Write an essay exploring how any other story, poem, or play in this anthology depicts a cross-cultural encounter and what its major conclusion about that (or its theme) seems to be, perhaps comparing this work to one of the stories in this album.

7 THE LONGER WORK

In terms of all the elements—plot, narration and point of view, character, setting, symbol, and theme—longer works of fiction are built out of the same components as shorter ones and invite similar interpretive strategies. So what are the differences? Definitions of the short story and novel—and in between them, the novella—tend to focus wholly on length. Most critics today define a **short story** as a work of prose fiction up to approximately 15,000–20,000 words, a **novella** as one of about 15,000–50,000 words, and a **novel** as one of at least 40,000 words. (These approximate and overlapping lengths indicate that individual works may be placed in different genre categories by different critics.) Yet the size of fiction matters in part because size affects fiction's substance and scope as well as how we read and experience it. Shorter fiction, not unlike lyric poetry, depends on compression and implication (*showing* versus *telling*), whereas longer fiction permits extended development and greater detail. One modern critic, Mark Shorer, describes shorter fiction, especially the modern short story, as an "art of moral revelation," longer fiction, especially the novel, as an "art of moral evolution." Champions of the novella have praised its combination of the "revelation" or intensity of the short story with the "evolution" or extension of the novel.

Perhaps the most important differences between short and long fiction have to do with the way we read them. Edgar Allan Poe, one of the first and best writers of the modern short story, attributed the "unity of effort or impression" in "the brief tale" to the fact that it may be read "at one sitting." Yet as Thomas A. Gullason insists, the spare economy of a story and its reliance on implying rather than fully explaining or developing its elements means that we *need* to read a story more than once: "like the diamond, the short story throws off glints of meanings" only captured through careful reading and re-reading. The reading of longer works of fiction, in contrast, tends to be a prolonged and often interrupted process. We likely read most novels only once, over several days or weeks. Our attention to them may be just as concentrated, and their implications may be just as brilliant as those of short fiction, but the scope and effects are on a different scale.

How can you apply your reading skills to novellas like the two in this chapter, Herman Melville's Bartleby, the Scrivener and Franz Kafka's The Metamorphosis? It helps to review some of the history and the characteristics of longer fiction—not only the familiar elements but also the conventions of the genre and its modes of representing human experience. Some of the literary context offered in this chapter concerns concepts such as comedy, tragedy, and realism that are relevant to many forms and genres of literature, not just fiction, but these concepts help put the special achievements of these novellas in perspective.

A BRIEF HISTORY OF THE NOVEL

Before the eighteenth century, longer fiction would usually take the form of **epic** or **romance**, whether in verse or prose. Shorter narratives, referred to in Spanish as *novelas*, or in Italian as *novellas*, usually ranged less widely in space and time, and presented more-common characters in less magical or supernatural circumstances than found in epic or romance. Forerunners of the modern novel, such as Boccaccio's *Decameron*, were interconnected prose *novellas* (what we would call tales or stories) with contemporary setting and characters of middling or low rank. Miguel de Cervantes's *Don Quixote* (Spain, 1605, 1615) is often identified as the first novel, though both the tales that are told by characters within *Don Quixote* and the work as a whole were referred to in Spanish as *novelas*. The protagonist is an elderly gentleman who ignores the realities of his contemporary surroundings to embark on madly idealistic quests, believing he is a knight-errant like the protagonists of the countless romances he has read. Thus *Don Quixote* is sometimes called a "mock romance" or "anti-romance."

As longer prose narratives began to be published in book form, they drew on the resources of other kinds of literature, particularly those that purported to offer a true picture of the world abroad as well as familiar social life at home, including journalism, histories, travels, biography, and letters. (Tellingly, the word *novel* also means "new" and is related to the word *news*.) The earliest novels in English were influenced by Italian, Spanish, and French models of prose romance, epic, novellas, and travel memoirs. Many early novels were *epistolary*, as if reprinting a series of letters (or *epistles*) written by real people in contemporary society. In addition to drawing on the models of nonfiction prose, novels adapted the plot structures of drama. Novels often followed the conventions of **comedy** (with its happy ending in success or marriage), rather than **tragedy** (with its ultimate destruction of a noble or admirable protagonist), though some novellas and novels since the mid-nineteenth century follow the five-act structure of tragic drama. One of the popular comedic forms of fiction has been the **bildungsroman**—from the German terms for "shaping" or "portrait" and novel—modeled on Johan Wolfgang von Goethe's *Wilhelm Meister's Apprenticeship* (1795–96). In a bildungsroman—an "education" or "development" novel—the protagonist overcomes adversity to attain social standing, vocation, and marriage; classics in English include Charlotte Brontë's *Jane Eyre* (1847) and Charles Dickens's *David Copperfield* (1850).

A prevalent mode for novels since the mid-nineteenth century has been **realism**. Realist fiction of any length has certain characteristics:

1. settings correspond in detail with historical or contemporary time and space, with facts and conditions known;
2. the main characters are complex, individualized, and often working-class or middle-class; and
3. the plot is explicable and probable—the sorts of things that could happen to ordinary people in the real world.

Yet the supernatural and imaginative aspects of romance, epic, and folktales retain their influence, and novels, novellas, and stories often gain effects by bending some of the rules of the reader's realm of possibility. By the 1790s, **gothic** novels were widely popular, with their special effects of horror and terror. More-recent novelists have continued to exploit the more uncanny or imaginative possibilities of gothic and romance genres, along with **fantasy** and science fiction. Thus today, in fiction of various lengths as in film and television, we still encounter the different aims of representing everyday experience versus traveling into the past, the future, or imaginary or exotic societies and worlds.

In the United States today, the novel is so popular and ubiquitous that the words *novel* and *book* sometimes seem to be taken as synonyms. The label *graphic novel* is routinely used as a blanket term for any book-length "comic," whether it is nonfiction or a collection of shorter pieces. And despite its name, Oprah's Book Club has over the years featured far more novels than any other kind of book.

THE NOVELLA

If the novel is a relatively new genre that has absorbed the traits of many other genres and has come to dominate literature today, the novella (in the English meaning of the term) is newer still, and less common. Mid-length fiction (between 15,000 and 50,000 words) came into favor around 1880 and afterward, as novels began to be published in one volume and shorter fiction became more popular in mass-circulation magazines. Modern fiction writers like Henry James (1843–1916) and Joseph Conrad (1857–1924) favored the scale of the novella as right for their intended effects: It combines the focus on significant detail and the controlled structure of the short story with room to develop complex characters, more than one setting, and more complex plots.

A novella may:

- have a more complex **plot** than a short story (and even a **subplot**), involving more discriminated occasions and episodes;
- feature more **characters** and give more of them an individualized, dynamic treatment—that is, it may have more round characters than a short story;
- cover more time and space, having more numerous and more thoroughly described **settings** than a short story; and
- include more description, summary, or commentary on characters, circumstances, or **themes** than a short story, which usually must dramatize one main event.

A novella has scope to give readers a sense of a **central consciousness**'s isolation or alienation, as in James Joyce's THE DEAD. Instead of limiting itself to one main character or the events of one evening, a novella can describe weeks or months in which a group of people are tested in their response to an outsider or in which an unusual or artistic personality pushes the limits of what is socially acceptable. A novella allows for a transformation of outlook from beginning to end, but with the momentum of a play, opera, or ballet rather than the episodic journey of a novel.

Often the outcome of a modern novella is bleak. In fact, a remarkable number of classic novellas are tragedies. Henry James's *Daisy Miller* (1878), Kate Chopin's *The Awakening* (1899), and Nella Larsen's *Quicksand* (1928) are all realist novellas that are also tragedies in which society proves too strong for an exceptional woman. But some novellas end without dooming the main character, and the novella's length gives writers sufficient space to vary the mood of even the most somber piece by including humorous scenes or curious observations.

In responding to longer fiction, as always when interpreting a literary work, you should ask what effect the form, including the length, has on the meaning. As you read the two novellas in this chapter, ask yourself: What would have to be eliminated to convert these novellas into short stories? What could be added to *Bartleby, the Scrivener* or *The Metamorphosis* to lengthen them into novels? What precisely might be improved, marred, or lost by either shrinking or expanding each narrative? For example, how does length affect characterization in Melville's or Kafka's work? How does the portrayal of everyday modern life and people affect our response to the extraordinary action in these novellas? What aspects of the characterization or plot cannot be explained by the standards of fact and reality that we—and some characters in the novellas—live by? Are these novellas tragedies?

HERMAN MELVILLE
(1819–91)

Bartleby, the Scrivener: A Story of Wall Street

When his father died in debt, twelve-year-old Herman Melville's life of privilege became one of struggle. At eighteen, he left his native New York to teach in a backwoods Massachusetts school, then trained as a surveyor; finding no work, he became a sailor in 1839. After five years in the South Seas, he wrote *Typee* (1846) and *Omoo* (1847), sensationalized and wildly popular accounts of his voyages. They proved the pinnacle of Melville's career in his lifetime, however; *Mardi* (1849) was judged too abstruse, the travel narratives *Redburn* (1849) and *White-Jacket* (1850) too listless. Melville's magnum opus, *Moby Dick* (1851), was alternately shunned and condemned. His later novels—*Pierre* (1852), *Israel Potter* (1853), and *The Confidence-Man* (1856)—as well as his poetry collection *Battle-Pieces* (1866) were all but ignored. Melville's reputation as one of the giants of American literature was established only after his death; the novella *Billy Budd, Sailor* (not published until 1924), like *Moby Dick*, is judged a masterpiece.

I am a rather elderly man. The nature of my avocations for the last thirty years has brought me into more than ordinary contact with what would seem an interesting and somewhat singular set of men, of whom as yet nothing that I know of has ever been written:—I mean the law-copyists or scriveners. I have known very many of them, professionally and privately, and if I pleased, could relate div-ers histories, at which good-natured gentlemen might smile, and sentimental souls might weep. But I waive the biographies of all other scriveners for a few passages in the life of Bartleby, who was a scrivener the strangest I ever saw or heard of. While of other law-copyists I might write the complete life, of Bartleby nothing of that sort can be done. I believe that no materials exist for a full and satisfactory biography of this man. It is an irreparable loss to literature. Bartleby was one of those beings of whom nothing is ascertainable, except from the original sources, and in his case those are very small. What my own astonished eyes saw of Bartleby, *that* is all I know of him, except, indeed, one vague report which will appear in the sequel.[1]

Ere introducing the scrivener, as he first appeared to me, it is fit I make some mention of myself, my *employées*, my business, my chambers, and general surroundings; because some such description is indispensable to an adequate understanding of the chief character about to be presented.

Imprimis:[2] I am a man who, from his youth upwards, has been filled with a profound conviction that the easiest way of life is the best. Hence, though I belong to a profession proverbially energetic and nervous, even to turbulence, at times, yet nothing of that sort have I ever suffered to invade my peace. I am one of those unambitious lawyers who never addresses a jury, or in any way draws down public applause; but in the cool tranquillity of a snug retreat, do a snug business among rich men's bonds and mortgages and title-deeds. All who know me, consider me an eminently *safe* man. The late John Jacob Astor,[3] a personage little given to poetic enthusiasm, had no hesitation in pronouncing my first grand point to be prudence; my next, method. I do not speak it in vanity, but simply record the fact, that I was not unemployed in my profession by the late John Jacob Astor; a name which, I admit, I love to repeat, for it hath a rounded and orbicular sound to it, and rings like unto bullion. I will freely add that I was not insensible to the late John Jacob Astor's good opinion.

Some time prior to the period at which this little history begins, my avocations had been largely increased. The good old office, now extinct in the State of New York, of a Master in Chancery[4] had been conferred upon me. It was not a very arduous office, but very pleasantly remunerative. I seldom lose my temper; much more seldom indulge in dangerous indignation at wrongs and outrages; but I must be permitted to be rash here and declare, that I consider the sudden and violent abrogation of the office of Master in Chancery, by the new Constitution, as a—premature act; inasmuch as I had counted upon a life-lease of the profits, whereas I only received those of a few short years. But this is by the way.

My chambers were up stairs at No. —— Wall Street. At one end they looked 5
upon the white wall of the interior of a spacious skylight shaft, penetrating the building from top to bottom. This view might have been considered rather tame than otherwise, deficient in what landscape painters call "life." But if so, the view from the other end of my chambers offered, at least, a contrast, if nothing more. In that direction my windows commanded an unobstructed view of a lofty brick

1. That is, in the following story.
2. In the first place.
3. New York fur merchant and landowner (1763–1848) who died the richest man in the United States.
4. A court of chancery can temper the law, applying "dictates of conscience" or "the principles of natural justice"; the office of Master was abolished in 1847.

wall, black by age and everlasting shade; which wall required no spyglass to bring out its lurking beauties, but for the benefit of all near-sighted spectators, was pushed up to within ten feet of my window panes. Owing to the great height of the surrounding buildings, and my chambers being on the second floor, the interval between this wall and mine not a little resembled a huge square cistern.

At the period just preceding the advent of Bartleby, I had two persons as copyists in my employment, and a promising lad as an office-boy. First, Turkey; second, Nippers, third, Ginger Nut. These may seem names the like of which are not usually found in the Directory.[5] In truth they were nicknames, mutually conferred upon each other by my three clerks, and were deemed expressive of their respective persons or characters. Turkey was a short, pursy[6] Englishman of about my own age, that is, somewhere not far from sixty. In the morning, one might say, his face was of a fine florid hue, but after twelve o'clock, meridian—his dinner hour—it blazed like a grate full of Christmas coals; and continued blazing—but, as it were, with a gradual wane—till 6 o'clock, P.M. or thereabouts, after which I saw no more of the proprietor of the face, which gaining its meridian with the sun, seemed to set with it, to rise, culminate, and decline the following day, with the like regularity and undiminished glory. There are many singular coincidences I have known in the course of my life, not the least among which was the fact, that exactly when Turkey displayed his fullest beams from his red and radiant countenance, just then, too, at that critical moment, began the daily period when I considered his business capacities as seriously disturbed for the remainder of the twenty-four hours. Not that he was absolutely idle, or averse to business then; far from it. The difficulty was, he was apt to be altogether too energetic. There was a strange, inflamed, flurried, flighty recklessness of activity about him. He would be incautious in dipping his pen into his inkstand. All his blots upon my documents were dropped there after twelve o'clock, meridian. Indeed, not only would he be reckless and sadly given to making blots in the afternoon, but some days he went further, and was rather noisy. At such times, too, his face flamed with augmented blazonry, as if cannel coal had been heaped on anthracite.[7] He made an unpleasant racket with his chair; spilled his sand-box; in mending his pens, impatiently split them all to pieces, and threw them on the floor in a sudden passion; stood up and leaned over his table, boxing his papers about in a most indecorous manner, very sad to behold in an elderly man like him. Nevertheless, as he was in many ways a most valuable person to me, and all the time before twelve o'clock, meridian, was the quickest, steadiest creature too, accomplishing a great deal of work in a style not easy to be matched—for these reasons, I was willing to overlook his eccentricities, though indeed, occasionally, I remonstrated with him. I did this very gently, however, because, though the civilest, nay, the blandest and most reverential of men in the morning, yet in the afternoon he was disposed, upon provocation, to be slightly rash with his tongue, in fact, insolent. Now, valuing his morning services as I did, and resolved not to lose them; yet, at the same time made uncomfortable by his inflamed ways after twelve o'clock; and being a man of peace, unwilling by my admonitions to call forth unseemly retorts from him; I took upon me, one Saturday noon (he was always worse on Satur-

5. Post Office Directory.

6. Fat, short-winded.

7. Fast, bright-burning coal heaped on slow-burning, barely glowing coal.

days), to hint to him, very kindly, that perhaps now that he was growing old, it might be well to abridge his labors; in short, he need not come to my chambers after twelve o'clock, but, dinner over, had best go home to his lodgings and rest himself till tea-time. But no; he insisted upon his afternoon devotions. His countenance became intolerably fervid, as he oratorically assured me—gesticulating with a long ruler at the other end of the room—that if his services in the morning were useful, how indispensable, then, in the afternoon?

"With submission, sir," said Turkey on this occasion, "I consider myself your right-hand man. In the morning I but marshal and deploy my columns; but in the afternoon I put myself at their head, and gallantly charge the foe, thus!"—and he made a violent thrust with the ruler.

"But the blots, Turkey," intimated I.

"True,—but, with submission, sir, behold these hairs! I am getting old. Surely, sir, a blot or two of a warm afternoon is not to be severely urged against gray hairs. Old age—even if it blot the page—is honorable. With submission, sir, we *both* are getting old."

This appeal to my fellow-feeling was hardly to be resisted. At all events, I saw that go he would not. So I made up my mind to let him stay, resolving, nevertheless, to see to it, that during the afternoon he had to do with my less important papers.

Nippers, the second on my list, was a whiskered, sallow, and, upon the whole, rather piratical-looking young man of about five and twenty. I always deemed him the victim of two evil powers—ambition and indigestion. The ambition was evinced by a certain impatience of the duties of a mere copyist, an unwarrantable usurpation of strictly professional affairs, such as the original drawing up of legal documents. The indigestion seemed betokened in an occasional nervous testiness and grinning irritability, causing the teeth to audibly grind together over mistakes committed in copying; unnecessary maledictions, hissed, rather than spoken, in the heat of business; and especially by a continual discontent with the height of the table where he worked. Though of a very ingenious mechanical turn, Nippers could never get this table to suit him. He put chips under it, blocks of various sorts, bits of pasteboard, and at last went so far as to attempt an exquisite adjustment by final pieces of folded blotting-paper. But no invention would answer. If, for the sake of easing his back, he brought the table lid at a sharp angle well up towards his chin, and wrote there like a man using the steep roof of a Dutch house for his desk:—then he declared that it stopped the circulation in his arms. If now he lowered the table to his waistbands, and stooped over it in writing, then there was a sore aching in his back. In short, the truth of the matter was, Nippers knew not what he wanted. Or, if he wanted any thing, it was to be rid of a scrivener's table altogether. Among the manifestations of his diseased ambition was a fondness he had for receiving visits from certain ambiguous-looking fellows in seedy coats, whom he called his clients. Indeed I was aware that not only was he, at times, considerable of a ward-politician, but he occasionally did a little business at the Justices' courts, and was not unknown on the steps of the Tombs.[8] I have good reason to believe, however, that one individual who called upon him at my chambers, and who, with a grand air, he insisted was his client, was no other than a dun,[9] and the alleged title-

8. Prison in New York City.
9. Bill collector.

deed, a bill. But with all his failings, and the annoyances he caused me, Nippers, like his compatriot Turkey, was a very useful man to me; wrote a neat, swift hand; and, when he chose, was not deficient in a gentlemanly sort of deportment. Added to this, he always dressed in a gentlemanly sort of way: and so, incidentally, reflected credit upon my chambers. Whereas with respect to Turkey, I had much ado to keep him from being a reproach to me. His clothes were apt to look oily and smell of eating-houses. He wore his pantaloons very loose and baggy in summer. His coats were execrable; his hat not to be handled. But while the hat was a thing of indifference to me, inasmuch as his natural civility and deference, as a dependent Englishman, always led him to doff it the moment he entered the room, yet his coat was another matter. Concerning his coats, I reasoned with him; but with no effect. The truth was, I suppose, that a man with so small an income, could not afford to sport such a lustrous face and a lustrous coat at one and the same time. As Nippers once observed, Turkey's money went chiefly for red ink. One winter day I presented Turkey with a highly-respectable looking coat of my own, a padded gray coat, of a most comfortable warmth, and which buttoned straight up from the knee to the neck. I thought Turkey would appreciate the favor, and abate his rashness and obstreperousness of afternoons. But no. I verily believe that buttoning himself up in so downy and blanket-like a coat had a pernicious effect upon him; upon the same principle that too much oats are bad for horses. In fact, precisely as a rash, restive horse is said to feel his oats, so Turkey felt his coat. It made him insolent. He was a man whom prosperity harmed.

Though concerning the self-indulgent habits of Turkey I had my own private surmises, yet touching Nippers I was well persuaded that whatever might be his faults in other respects, he was, at least, a temperate young man. But indeed, nature herself seemed to have been his vintner,[1] and at his birth charged him so thoroughly with an irritable, brandy-like disposition, that all subsequent potations were needless. When I consider how, amid the stillness of my chambers, Nippers would sometimes impatiently rise from his seat, and stooping over his table, spread his arms wide apart, seize the whole desk, and move it, and jerk it, with a grim, grinding motion on the floor, as if the table were a perverse voluntary agent, intent on thwarting and vexing him; I plainly perceive that for Nippers, brandy and water were altogether superfluous.

It was fortunate for me that, owing to its peculiar cause—indigestion—the irritability and consequent nervousness of Nippers, were mainly observable in the morning, while in the afternoon he was comparatively mild. So that Turkey's paroxysms only coming on about twelve o'clock, I never had to do with their eccentricities at one time. Their fits relieved each other like guards. When Nippers' was on, Turkey's was off; and *vice versa*. This was a good natural arrangement under the circumstances.

Ginger Nut, the third on my list, was a lad some twelve years old. His father was a carman,[2] ambitious of seeing his son on the bench instead of a cart, before he died. So he sent him to my office as student at law, errand boy, and cleaner and sweeper, at the rate of one dollar a week. He had a little desk to himself, but

1. Wine seller.
2. Driver of wagon or cart that hauls goods.

he did not use it much. Upon inspection, the drawer exhibited a great array of the shells of various sorts of nuts. Indeed, to this quick-witted youth the whole noble science of the law was contained in a nutshell. Not the least among the employments of Ginger Nut, as well as one which he discharged with the most alacrity, was his duty as cake and apple purveyor for Turkey and Nippers. Copying law papers being proverbially a dry, husky sort of business, my two scriveners were fain to moisten their mouths very often with Spitzenbergs[3] to be had at the numerous stalls nigh the Custom House and Post Office. Also, they sent Ginger Nut very frequently for that peculiar cake—small, flat, round, and very spicy—after which he had been named by them. Of a cold morning when business was but dull, Turkey would gobble up scores of these cakes, as if they were mere wafers—indeed they sell them at the rate of six or eight for a penny—the scrape of his pen blending with the crunching of the crisp particles in his mouth. Of all the fiery afternoon blunders and flurried rashnesses of Turkey, was his once moistening a ginger-cake between his lips, and clapping it on to a mortgage for a seal. I came within an ace of dismissing him then. But he mollified me by making an oriental bow, and saying—"With submission, sir, it was generous of me to find you in[4] stationery on my own account."

Now my original business—that of a conveyancer and title hunter,[5] and drawer-up of recondite documents of all sorts—was considerably increased by receiving the master's office. There was now great work for scriveners. Not only must I push the clerks already with me, but I must have additional help. In answer to my advertisement, a motionless young man one morning stood upon my office threshold, the door being open, for it was summer. I can see that figure now—pallidly neat, pitiably respectable, incurably forlorn! It was Bartleby.

After a few words touching his qualifications, I engaged him, glad to have among my corps of copyists a man of so singularly sedate an aspect, which I thought might operate beneficially upon the flighty temper of Turkey, and the fiery one of Nippers.

I should have stated before that ground glass folding-doors divided my premises into two parts, one of which was occupied by my scriveners, the other by myself. According to my humor I threw open these doors, or closed them. I resolved to assign Bartleby a corner by the folding-doors, but on my side of them, so as to have this quiet man within easy call, in case any trifling thing was to be done. I placed his desk close up to a small side-window in that part of the room, a window which originally had afforded a lateral view of certain grimy backyards and bricks, but which, owing to subsequent erections, commanded at present no view at all, though it gave some light. Within three feet of the panes was a wall, and the light came down from far above, between two lofty buildings, as from a very small opening in a dome. Still further to a satisfactory arrangement, I procured a high green folding screen, which might entirely isolate Bartleby from my sight, though not remove him from my voice. And thus, in a manner, privacy and society were conjoined.

3. Red-and-yellow American apple.

4. Supply you with.

5. Lawyer who draws up deeds for transferring property, and one who searches out legal control of title deeds.

At first Bartleby did an extraordinary quantity of writing. As if long famishing for something to copy, he seemed to gorge himself on my documents. There was no pause for digestion. He ran a day and night line, copying by sunlight and by candlelight. I should have been quite delighted with his application, had he been cheerfully industrious. But he wrote on silently, palely, mechanically.

It is, of course, an indispensable part of a scrivener's business to verify the accuracy of his copy, word by word. Where there are two or more scriveners in an office, they assist each other in this examination, one reading from the copy, the other holding the original. It is a very dull, wearisome, and lethargic affair. I can readily imagine that to some sanguine temperaments it would be altogether intolerable. For example, I cannot credit that the mettlesome poet Byron would have contentedly sat down with Bartleby to examine a law document of, say, five hundred pages, closely written in a crimpy hand.

Now and then, in the haste of business, it had been my habit to assist in comparing some brief document myself, calling Turkey or Nippers for this purpose. One object I had in placing Bartleby so handy to me behind the screen, was to avail myself of his services on such trivial occasions. It was on the third day, I think, of his being with me, and before any necessity had arisen for having his own writing examined, that, being much hurried to complete a small affair I had in hand, I abruptly called to Bartleby. In my haste and natural expectancy of instant compliance, I sat with my head bent over the original on my desk, and my right hand sideways, and somewhat nervously extended with the copy, so that immediately upon emerging from his retreat, Bartleby might snatch it and proceed to business without the least delay.

In this very attitude did I sit when I called to him, rapidly stating what it was I wanted him to do—namely, to examine a small paper with me. Imagine my surprise, nay, my consternation, when without moving from his privacy, Bartleby, in a singularly mild, firm voice, replied, "I would prefer not to."

I sat awhile in perfect silence, rallying my stunned faculties. Immediately it occurred to me that my ears had deceived me, or Bartleby had entirely misunderstood my meaning. I repeated my request in the clearest tone I could assume. But in quite as clear a one came the previous reply, "I would prefer not to."

"Prefer not to," echoed I, rising in high excitement, and crossing the room with a stride. "What do you mean? Are you moon-struck?[6] I want you to help me compare this sheet here—take it," and I thrust it towards him.

"I would prefer not to," said he.

I looked at him steadfastly. His face was leanly composed; his gray eye dimly calm. Not a wrinkle of agitation rippled him. Had there been the least uneasiness, anger, impatience or impertinence in his manner; in other words, had there been anything ordinarily human about him, doubtless I should have violently dismissed him from the premises. But as it was, I should have as soon thought of turning my pale plaster-of-paris bust of Cicero[7] out-of-doors. I stood gazing at him awhile, as he went on with his own writing, and then reseated myself at my desk. This is very strange, thought I. What had one best do? But my business hurried me. I

6. Crazy.

7. Marcus Tullius Cicero (106–43 BCE), pro-republican Roman statesman, barrister, writer, and orator.

concluded to forget the matter for the present, reserving it for my future leisure. So calling Nippers from the other room, the paper was speedily examined.

A few days after this, Bartleby concluded four lengthy documents, being quadruplicates of a week's testimony taken before me in my High Court of Chancery. It became necessary to examine them. It was an important suit, and great accuracy was imperative. Having all things arranged I called Turkey, Nippers and Ginger Nut from the next room, meaning to place the four copies in the hands of my four clerks, while I should read from the original. Accordingly Turkey, Nippers and Ginger Nut had taken their seats in a row, each with his document in hand, when I called to Bartleby to join this interesting group.

"Bartleby! quick, I am waiting."

I heard a slow scrape of his chair legs on the uncarpeted floor, and soon he appeared standing at the entrance of his hermitage.

"What is wanted?" said he mildly.

"The copies, the copies," said I hurriedly. "We are going to examine them. There"—and I held towards him the fourth quadruplicate.

"I would prefer not to," he said, and gently disappeared behind the screen.

For a few moments I was turned into a pillar of salt,[8] standing at the head of my seated column of clerks. Recovering myself, I advanced towards the screen, and demanded the reason for such extraordinary conduct.

"*Why* do you refuse?"

"I would prefer not to."

With any other man I should have flown outright into a dreadful passion, scorned all further words, and thrust him ignominiously from my presence. But there was something about Bartleby that not only strangely disarmed me, but in a wonderful manner touched and disconcerted me. I began to reason with him.

"These are your own copies we are about to examine. It is labor saving to you, because one examination will answer for your four papers. It is common usage. Every copyist is bound to help examine his copy. Is it not so? Will you not speak? Answer!"

"I prefer not to," he replied in a flute-like tone. It seemed to me that while I had been addressing him, he carefully revolved every statement that I made; fully comprehended the meaning; could not gainsay the irresistible conclusion; but, at the same time, some paramount consideration prevailed with him to reply as he did.

"You are decided, then, not to comply with my request—a request made according to common usage and common sense?"

He briefly gave me to understand that on that point my judgment was sound. Yes: his decision was irreversible.

It is not seldom the case that when a man is browbeaten in some unprecedented and violently unreasonable way, he begins to stagger in his own plainest faith. He begins, as it were, vaguely to surmise that, wonderful as it may be, all the justice and all the reason is on the other side. Accordingly, if any disinterested persons are present, he turns to them for some reinforcement for his own faltering mind.

8. Struck dumb; in Genesis 19.26, Lot's wife, defying God's command, "looked back from behind him, and she became a pillar of salt."

"Turkey," said I, "what do you think of this? Am I not right?"

"With submission, sir," said Turkey, with his blandest tone, "I think that you are."

"Nippers," said I, "what do *you* think of it?"

"I think I should kick him out of the office."

(The reader of nice perceptions will here perceive that, it being morning, Turkey's answer is couched in polite and tranquil terms, but Nippers replies in ill-tempered ones. Or, to repeat a previous sentence, Nippers's ugly mood was on duty, and Turkey's off.)

"Ginger Nut," said I, willing to enlist the smallest suffrage[9] in my behalf, "what do *you* think of it?"

"I think, sir, he's a little *luny*," replied Ginger Nut, with a grin.

"You hear what they say," said I, turning towards the screen, "come forth and do your duty."

But he vouchsafed no reply. I pondered a moment in sore perplexity. But once more business hurried me. I determined again to postpone the consideration of this dilemma to my future leisure. With a little trouble we made out to examine the papers without Bartleby, though at every page or two, Turkey deferentially dropped his opinion that this proceeding was quite out of the common; while Nippers, twitching in his chair with a dyspeptic nervousness, ground out between his set teeth occasional hissing maledictions against the stubborn oaf behind the screen. And for his (Nippers's) part, this was the first and the last time he would do another man's business without pay.

Meanwhile Bartleby sat in his hermitage, oblivious to everything but his own peculiar business there.

Some days passed, the scrivener being employed upon another lengthy work. His late remarkable conduct led me to regard his ways narrowly. I observed that he never went to dinner; indeed that he never went anywhere. As yet I had never of my personal knowledge known him to be outside of my office. He was a perpetual sentry in the corner. At about eleven o'clock though, in the morning, I noticed that Ginger Nut would advance toward the opening in Bartleby's screen, as if silently beckoned thither by a gesture invisible to me where I sat. The boy would then leave the office jingling a few pence, and reappear with a handful of ginger-nuts which he delivered in the hermitage, receiving two of the cakes for his trouble.

He lives, then, on ginger-nuts, thought I; never eats a dinner, properly speaking; he must be a vegetarian then; but no; he never eats even vegetables, he eats nothing but ginger-nuts. My mind then ran on in reveries concerning the probable effects upon the human constitution of living entirely on ginger-nuts. Ginger-nuts are so called because they contain ginger as one of their peculiar constituents, and the final flavoring one. Now what was ginger? A hot, spicy thing. Was Bartleby hot and spicy? Not at all. Ginger, then, had no effect upon Bartleby. Probably he preferred it should have none.

Nothing so aggravates an earnest person as a passive resistance. If the individual so resisted be of a not inhumane temper, and the resisting one perfectly harmless in his passivity; then, in the better moods of the former, he

9. Favorable vote.

will endeavor charitably to construe to his imagination what proves impossible to be solved by his judgment. Even so, for the most part, I regarded Bartleby and his ways. Poor fellow! thought I, he means no mischief; it is plain he intends no insolence; his aspect sufficiently evinces that his eccentricities are involuntary. He is useful to me. I can get along with him. If I turn him away, the chances are he will fall in with some less indulgent employer, and then he will be rudely treated, and perhaps driven forth miserably to starve. Yes. Here I can cheaply purchase a delicious self-approval. To befriend Bartleby; to humor him in his strange wilfulness, will cost me little or nothing, while I lay up in my soul what will eventually prove a sweet morsel for my conscience. But this mood was not invariable with me. The passiveness of Bartleby sometimes irritated me. I felt strangely goaded on to encounter him in new opposition, to elicit some angry spark from him answerable to my own. But indeed I might as well have essayed to strike fire with my knuckles against a bit of Windsor soap.[1] But one afternoon the evil impulse in me mastered me, and the following little scene ensued:

"Bartleby," said I, "when those papers are all copied, I will compare them with you."

"I would prefer not to." 55

"How? Surely you do not mean to persist in that mulish vagary?"

No answer.

I threw open the folding-doors near by, and turning upon Turkey and Nippers, exclaimed in an excited manner—

"He says, a second time, he won't examine his papers. What do you think of it, Turkey?"

It was afternoon, be it remembered. Turkey sat glowing like a brass boiler, 60 his bald head steaming, his hands reeling among his blotted papers.

"Think of it?" roared Turkey; "I think I'll just step behind his screen, and black his eyes for him!"

So saying, Turkey rose to his feet and threw his arms into a pugilistic position. He was hurrying away to make good his promise, when I detained him, alarmed at the effect of incautiously rousing Turkey's combativeness after dinner.

"Sit down, Turkey," said I, "and hear what Nippers has to say. What do you think of it, Nippers? Would I not be justified in immediately dismissing Bartleby?"

"Excuse me, that is for you to decide, sir. I think his conduct quite unusual, and indeed unjust, as regards Turkey and myself. But it may only be a passing whim."

"Ah," exclaimed I, "you have strangely changed your mind then—you speak 65 very gently of him now."

"All beer," cried Turkey; "gentleness is effects of beer—Nippers and I dined together today. You see how gentle *I* am, sir. Shall I go and black his eyes?"

"You refer to Bartleby, I suppose. No, not today, Turkey," I replied; "pray, put up your fists."

1. Scented soap, usually brown.

I closed the doors, and again advanced towards Bartleby. I felt additional incentives tempting me to my fate. I burned to be rebelled against again. I remembered that Bartleby never left the office.

"Bartleby," said I, "Ginger Nut is away; just step round to the Post Office, won't you? (it was but a three minutes' walk,) and see if there is anything for me."

"I would prefer not to."

"You *will* not?"

"I *prefer* not."

I staggered to my desk, and sat there in a deep study. My blind inveteracy returned. Was there any other thing in which I could procure myself to be ignominiously repulsed by this lean, penniless wight?—my hired clerk? What added thing is there, perfectly reasonable, that he will be sure to refuse to do?

"Bartleby!"

No answer.

"Bartleby," in a louder tone.

No answer.

"Bartleby," I roared.

Like a very ghost, agreeably to the laws of magical invocation, at the third summons, he appeared at the entrance of his hermitage.

"Go to the next room, and tell Nippers to come to me."

"I prefer not to," he respectfully and slowly said, and mildly disappeared.

"Very good, Bartleby," said I, in a quiet sort of serenely severe self-possessed tone, intimating the unalterable purpose of some terrible retribution very close at hand. At the moment I half intended something of the kind. But upon the whole, as it was drawing towards my dinner-hour, I thought it best to put on my hat and walk home for the day, suffering much from perplexity and distress of mind.

Shall I acknowledge it? The conclusion of this whole business was, that it soon became a fixed fact of my chambers, that a pale young scrivener, by the name of Bartleby, had a desk there; that he copied for me at the usual rate of four cents a folio (one hundred words); but he was permanently exempt from examining the work done by him, that duty being transferred to Turkey and Nippers, one of compliment doubtless to their superior acuteness; moreover, said Bartleby was never on any account to be dispatched on the most trivial errand of any sort; and that even if entreated to take upon him such a matter, it was generally understood that he would prefer not to—in other words, that he would refuse point-blank.

As days passed on, I became considerably reconciled to Bartleby. His steadiness, his freedom from all dissipation, his incessant industry (except when he chose to throw himself into a standing revery behind his screen), his great stillness, his unalterableness of demeanor under all circumstances, made him a valuable acquisition. One prime thing was this,—*he was always there*;—first in the morning, continually through the day, and the last at night. I had a singular confidence in his honesty. I felt my most precious papers perfectly safe in his hands. Sometimes to be sure I could not, for the very soul of me, avoid falling into sudden spasmodic passions with him. For it was exceeding difficult to bear in mind all the time those strange peculiarities, privileges, and unheard of exemptions, forming the tacit stipulations on Bartleby's part under which he remained in my office. Now and then, in the eagerness of dispatching pressing business, I would inadvertently summon Bartleby, in a short, rapid tone, to put his finger, say, on the incipient tie of a bit of red tape with which I was about compressing some papers. Of course, from behind the screen the usual answer, "I prefer not to," was sure to come; and then, how could a human creature with the common infirmities of our nature, refrain from bitterly exclaiming upon such perverseness—such unreasonableness? However, every added repulse of this sort which I received only tended to lessen the probability of my repeating the inadvertence.

Here it must be said, that according to the custom of most legal gentlemen 85
occupying chambers in densely-populated law buildings, there were several keys to my door. One was kept by a woman residing in the attic, which person weekly scrubbed and daily swept and dusted my apartments. Another was kept by Turkey for convenience sake. The third I sometimes carried in my own pocket. The fourth I knew not who had.

Now, one Sunday morning I happened to go to Trinity Church, to hear a celebrated preacher, and finding myself rather early on the ground, I thought I would walk round to my chambers for a while. Luckily I had my key with me; but upon applying it to the lock, I found it resisted by something inserted from the inside. Quite surprised, I called out; when to my consternation a key was turned from within; and thrusting his lean visage at me, and holding the door ajar, the apparition of Bartleby appeared, in his shirt sleeves, and otherwise in a strangely tattered dishabille, saying quietly that he was sorry, but he was deeply engaged just then, and—preferred not admitting me at present. In a brief word or two, he moreover added, that perhaps I had better walk round the block two or three times, and by that time he would probably have concluded his affairs.

Now, the utterly unsurmised appearance of Bartleby, tenanting my law-chambers of a Sunday morning, with his cadaverously gentlemanly *nonchalance*, yet withal firm and self-possessed, had such a strange effect upon me, that incontinently I slunk away from my own door, and did as desired. But not without sundry twinges of impotent rebellion against the mild effrontery of this unaccountable scrivener. Indeed, it was his wonderful mildness, chiefly, which not only disarmed me, but unmanned me, as it were. For I consider that one, for the time, is sort of unmanned when he tranquilly permits his hired clerk to dictate to him, and order him away from his own premises. Furthermore, I was full of uneasiness as to what Bartleby could possibly be doing in my office in his shirt sleeves, and in an otherwise dismantled condition of a Sunday morning. Was anything amiss going on? Nay, that was out of the question. It was not to be thought of for a moment that Bartleby was an immoral person. But what could he be doing there?—copying? Nay again, whatever might be his eccentricities, Bartleby was an eminently decorous person. He would be the last man to sit down to his desk in any state approaching to nudity. Besides, it was Sunday; and there was something about Bartleby that forbade the supposition that he would by any secular occupation violate the proprieties of the day.

Nevertheless, my mind was not pacified; and full of a restless curiosity, at last I returned to the door. Without hindrance I inserted my key, opened it, and entered. Bartleby was not to be seen. I looked round anxiously, peeped behind his screen; but it was very plain that he was gone. Upon more closely examining the place, I surmised that for an indefinite period Bartleby must have ate, dressed, and slept in my office, and that too without plate, mirror, or bed. The cushioned seat of a ricketty old sofa in one corner bore the faint impress of a lean, reclining form. Rolled away under his desk, I found a blanket under the empty grate, a blacking box[2] and brush; on a chair, a tin basin, with soap and a ragged towel; in a newspaper a few crumbs of ginger-nuts and a morsel of cheese. Yes, thought I, it is evident enough that Bartleby has been making his home here, keeping bachelor's hall all by himself. Immediately then the thought came sweeping across me, What miserable friendlessness and loneliness are here revealed! His poverty is great; but his solitude, how horrible! Think of it. Of a Sunday, Wall Street is deserted as Petra;[3] and every night of every day it is an emptiness. This building too, which of weekdays hums with industry and life, at nightfall echoes with sheer vacancy, and all through Sunday is forlorn. And here Bartleby makes his home; sole spectator of a solitude which he has seen all populous—a sort of innocent and transformed Marius brooding among the ruins of Carthage![4]

For the first time in my life a feeling of overpowering stinging melancholy seized me. Before, I had never experienced aught but a not-unpleasing sadness. The bond of a common humanity now drew me irresistibly to gloom. A fraternal melancholy! For both I and Bartleby were sons of Adam. I remembered the bright silks and sparkling faces I had seen that day, in gala trim, swan-like sailing down the Mississippi of Broadway; and I contrasted them with the pallid copyist, and thought to myself, Ah, happiness courts the light, so we deem the world is gay; but misery hides aloof, so we deem that misery there is none. These sad fancyings—chimeras, doubtless, of a sick and silly brain—led on to other and more special thoughts, concerning the eccentricities of Bartleby. Presentiments of strange discoveries hovered round me. The scrivener's pale form appeared to me laid out, among uncaring strangers, in its shivering winding sheet.

90 Suddenly I was attracted by Bartleby's closed desk, the key in open sight left in the lock.

I mean no mischief, seek the gratification of no heartless curiosity, thought I; besides, the desk is mine, and its contents too, so I will make bold to look within. Everything was methodically arranged, the papers smoothly placed. The pigeonholes were deep, and removing the files of documents, I groped into their recesses. Presently I felt something there, and dragged it out. It was an old bandanna handkerchief, heavy and knotted. I opened it, and saw it was a savings' bank.

I now recalled all the quiet mysteries which I had noted in the man. I remembered that he never spoke but to answer; that though at intervals he had considerable time to himself, yet I had never seen him reading—no, not even a newspaper; that for long periods he would stand looking out, at his pale window

2. Box of black shoe polish.

3. Once a flourishing Middle Eastern trade center, long in ruins.

4. Gaius (or Caius) Marius (157–86 BCE), Roman consul and general, expelled from Rome in 88 BCE by Sulla; when an officer of Sextilius, the governor, forbade him to land in Africa, Marius replied, "Go tell him that you have seen Caius Marius sitting in exile among the ruins of Carthage," applying the example of the fortune of that city to the change of his own condition. The image was so common that a few years after "Bartleby," Dickens apologizes for using it: "like that lumbering Marius among the ruins of Carthage, who has sat heavy on a thousand millions of similes" ("The Calais Night-Mail," in *The Uncommercial Traveler*).

behind the screen, upon the dead brick wall; I was quite sure he never visited any refectory or eating house; while his pale face clearly indicated that he never drank beer like Turkey, or tea and coffee even, like other men; that he never went anywhere in particular that I could learn; never went out for a walk, unless indeed that was the case at present; that he had declined telling who he was, or whence he came, or whether he had any relatives in the world; that though so thin and pale, he never complained of ill health. And more than all, I remembered a certain unconscious air of pallid—how shall I call it?—of pallid haughtiness, say, or rather an austere reserve about him, which had positively awed me into my tame compliance with his eccentricities, when I had feared to ask him to do the slightest incidental thing for me, even though I might know, from his long-continued motionlessness, that behind his screen he must be standing in one of those dead-wall reveries of his.

Revolving all these things, and coupling them with the recently discovered fact that he made my office his constant abiding place and home, and not forgetful of his morbid moodiness; revolving all these things, a prudential feeling began to steal over me. My first emotions had been those of pure melancholy and sincerest pity; but just in proportion as the forlornness of Bartleby grew and grew to my imagination, did that same melancholy merge into fear, that pity into repulsion. So true it is, and so terrible too, that up to a certain point the thought or sight of misery enlists our best affections; but, in certain special cases, beyond that point it does not. They err who would assert that invariably this is owing to the inherent selfishness of the human heart. It rather proceeds from a certain hopelessness of remedying excessive and organic ill. To a sensitive being, pity is not seldom pain. And when at last it is perceived that such pity cannot lead to effectual succor, common sense bids the soul be rid of it. What I saw that morning persuaded me that the scrivener was the victim of innate and incurable disorder. I might give alms to his body; but his body did not pain him; it was his soul that suffered, and his soul I could not reach.

I did not accomplish the purpose of going to Trinity Church that morning. Somehow, the things I had seen disqualified me for the time from churchgoing. I walked homeward, thinking what I would do with Bartleby. Finally, I resolved upon this;—I would put certain calm questions to him the next morning, touching his history, &c., and if he declined to answer them openly and unreservedly (and I supposed he would prefer not), then to give him a twenty-dollar bill over and above whatever I might owe him, and tell him his services were no longer required; but that if in any other way I could assist him, I would be happy to do so, especially if he desired to return to his native place, wherever that might be, I would willingly help to defray the expenses. Moreover, if, after reaching home, he found himself at any time in want of aid, a letter from him would be sure of a reply.

The next morning came. 95

"Bartleby," said I, gently calling to him behind his screen.

No reply.

"Bartleby," said I, in a still gentler tone, "come here; I am not going to ask you to do anything you would prefer not to do—I simply wish to speak to you."

Upon this he noiselessly slid into view.

"Will you tell me, Bartleby, where you were born?" 100

"I would prefer not to."

"Will you tell me *anything* about yourself?"

"I would prefer not to."

"But what reasonable objection can you have to speak to me? I feel friendly towards you."

He did not look at me while I spoke, but kept his glance fixed upon my bust of Cicero, which as I then sat, was directly behind me, some six inches above my head.

"What is your answer, Bartleby?" said I, after waiting a considerable time for a reply, during which his countenance remained immovable, only there was the faintest conceivable tremor of the white attenuated mouth.

"At present I prefer to give no answer," he said, and retired into his hermitage.

It was rather weak in me I confess, but his manner on this occasion nettled me. Not only did there seem to lurk in it a certain calm disdain, but his perverseness seemed ungrateful, considering the undeniable good usage and indulgence he had received from me.

Again I sat ruminating what I should do. Mortified as I was at his behavior, and resolved as I had been to dismiss him when I entered my office, nevertheless I strangely felt something superstitious knocking at my heart, and forbidding me to carry out my purpose, and denouncing me for a villain if I dared to breathe one bitter word against this forlornest of mankind. At last, familiarly drawing my chair behind his screen, I sat down and said: "Bartleby, never mind then about revealing your history; but let me entreat you, as a friend, to comply as far as may be with the usages of this office. Say now you will help to examine papers tomorrow or next day: in short, say now that in a day or two you will begin to be a little reasonable:—say so, Bartleby."

"At present I would prefer not to be a little reasonable," was his mildly cadaverous reply.

Just then the folding-doors opened, and Nippers approached. He seemed suffering from an unusually bad night's rest, induced by severer indigestion than common. He overheard those final words of Bartleby.

"*Prefer not*, eh?" gritted Nippers—"I'd *prefer* him, if I were you, sir," addressing me—"I'd *prefer* him; I'd give him preferences, the stubborn mule! What is it, sir, pray, that he *prefers* not to do now?"

Bartleby moved not a limb.

"Mr. Nippers," said I, "I'd prefer that you would withdraw for the present."

Somehow, of late I had got into the way of involuntarily using this word "prefer" upon all sorts of not exactly suitable occasions. And I trembled to think that my contact with the scrivener had already and seriously affected me in a mental way. And what further and deeper aberration might it not yet produce? This apprehension had not been without efficacy in determining me to summary means.

As Nippers, looking very sour and sulky, was departing, Turkey blandly and deferentially approached.

"With submission, sir," said he, "yesterday I was thinking about Bartleby here, and I think that if he would but prefer to take a quart of good ale every day, it would do much towards mending him and enabling him to assist in examining his papers."

"So you have got the word too," said I, slightly excited.

"With submission, what word, sir?" asked Turkey, respectfully crowding himself into the contracted space behind the screen, and by so doing making me jostle the scrivener. "What word, sir?"

"I would prefer to be left alone here," said Bartleby, as if offended at being mobbed in his privacy.

"*That's* the word, Turkey," said I—"*that's* it."

"Oh, *prefer*? oh yes—queer word. I never use it myself. But, sir, as I was saying, if he would but prefer—"

"Turkey," interrupted I, "you will please withdraw."

"Oh certainly, sir, if you prefer that I should."

As he opened the folding-door to retire, Nippers at his desk caught a glimpse of me, and asked whether I would prefer to have a certain paper copied on blue paper or white. He did not in the least roguishly accent the word *prefer*. It was plain that it involuntarily rolled from his tongue. I thought to myself, surely I must get rid of a demented man, who already has in some degree turned the tongues, if not the heads of myself and clerks. But I thought it prudent not to break the dismission at once.

The next day I noticed that Bartleby did nothing but stand at his window in his dead-wall revery. Upon asking him why he did not write, he said that he had decided upon doing no more writing.

"Why, how now? what next?" exclaimed I, "do no more writing?"

"No more."

"And what is the reason?"

"Do you not see the reason for yourself," he indifferently replied.

I looked steadfastly at him, and perceived that his eyes looked dull and glazed. Instantly it occurred to me, that his unexampled diligence in copying by his dim window for the first few weeks of his stay with me might have temporarily impaired his vision.

I was touched. I said something in condolence with him. I hinted that of course he did wisely in abstaining from writing for a while; and urged him to embrace that opportunity of taking wholesome exercise in the open air. This, however, he did not do. A few days after this, my other clerks being absent, and being in a great hurry to dispatch certain letters by the mail, I thought that, having nothing else earthly to do, Bartleby would surely be less inflexible than usual, and carry these letters to the post office. But he blankly declined. So, much to my inconvenience, I went myself.

Still added days went by. Whether Bartleby's eyes improved or not, I could not say. To all appearance, I thought they did. But when I asked him if they did, he vouchsafed no answer. At all events, he would do no copying. At last, in reply to my urgings, he informed me that he had permanently given up copying.

"What!" exclaimed I; "suppose your eyes should get entirely well—better than ever before—would you not copy then?"

"I have given up copying," he answered, and slid aside.

He remained, as ever, a fixture in my chamber. Nay—if that were possible—he became still more of a fixture than before. What was to be done? He would do nothing in the office: why should he stay there? In plain fact, he had now become a millstone[5] to me, not only useless as a necklace, but afflictive to bear. Yet I was sorry for him. I speak less than truth when I say that, on his own account, he occasioned me uneasiness. If he would but have named a single relative or friend, I would instantly have written, and urged their taking the poor fellow away to some convenient retreat. But he seemed alone, absolutely alone in the universe. A bit of wreck in the mid-Atlantic. At length, necessities connected with my business tyrannized over all other considerations. Decently as I could, I told Bartleby that in six days' time he must unconditionally leave the office. I warned him to take measures, in the interval, for procuring some other abode. I offered to assist him in this endeavor, if he himself would but take the first step towards a removal. "And when you finally quit me, Bartleby," added I, "I shall see that you go not away entirely unprovided. Six days from this hour, remember."

At the expiration of that period, I peeped behind the screen, and lo! Bartleby was there.

I buttoned up my coat, balanced myself; advanced slowly towards him, touched his shoulder, and said, "The time has come; you must quit this place; I am sorry for you; here is money; but you must go."

"I would prefer not," he replied, with his back still towards me.

"You *must*."

He remained silent.

Now I had an unbounded confidence in this man's common honesty. He had frequently restored to me sixpences and shillings[6] carelessly dropped upon the floor, for I am apt to be very reckless in such shirt-button affairs. The proceeding then which followed will not be deemed extraordinary.

"Bartleby," said I, "I owe you twelve dollars on account; here are thirty-two; the odd twenty are yours.—Will you take it?" and I handed the bills towards him.

But he made no motion.

"I will leave them here then," putting them under a weight on the table. Then taking my hat and cane and going to the door I tranquilly turned and added—"After you have removed your things from these offices, Bartleby, you will of course lock the door—since everyone is now gone for the day but you—and if you please, slip your key underneath the mat, so that I may have it in the morning. I shall not see you again; so good-bye to you. If hereafter in your new place of abode I can be of any service to you, do not fail to advise me by letter. Good-bye, Bartleby, and fare you well."

But he answered not a word; like the last column of some ruined temple, he remained standing mute and solitary in the middle of the otherwise deserted room.

As I walked home in a pensive mood, my vanity got the better of my pity. I could not but highly plume myself on my masterly management in getting rid of Bartleby. Masterly I call it, and such it must appear to any dispassionate thinker. The beauty of my procedure seemed to consist in its perfect quietness. There was no vulgar bullying, no bravado of any sort, no choleric hectoring, and strid-

5. Heavy stone for grinding grain. See Matthew 18.6: "But whoso shall offend one of these little ones which believe in me, it were better for him that a millstone were hanged about his neck, and that he were drowned in the depth of the sea."
6. Coins.

ing to and fro across the apartment, jerking out vehement commands for Bartleby to bundle himself off with his beggarly traps.[7] Nothing of the kind. Without loudly bidding Bartleby depart—as an inferior genius might have done—I *assumed* the ground that depart he must; and upon that assumption built all I had to say. The more I thought over my procedure, the more I was charmed with it. Nevertheless, next morning, upon awakening, I had my doubts,—I had somehow slept off the fumes of vanity. One of the coolest and wisest hours a man has is just after he awakes in the morning. My procedure seemed as sagacious as ever,—but only in theory. How it would prove in practice—there was the rub. It was truly a beautiful thought to have assumed Bartleby's departure; but, after all, that assumption was simply my own, and none of Bartleby's. The great point was, not whether I had assumed that he would quit me, but whether he would prefer so to do. He was more a man of preferences than assumptions.

After breakfast, I walked downtown, arguing the probabilities *pro* and *con*. One moment I thought it would prove a miserable failure, and Bartleby would be found all alive at my office as usual; the next moment it seemed certain that I should see his chair empty. And so I kept veering about. At the corner of Broadway and Canal Street, I saw quite an excited group of people standing in earnest conversation.

"I'll take odds he doesn't," said a voice as I passed.

"Doesn't go?—done!" said I, "put up your money." 150

I was instinctively putting my hand in my pocket to produce my own, when I remembered that this was an election day. The words I had overheard bore no reference to Bartleby, but to the success or non-success of some candidate for the mayoralty. In my intent frame of mind, I had, as it were, imagined that all Broadway shared in my excitement, and were debating the same question with me. I passed on, very thankful that the uproar of the street screened my momentary absent-mindedness.

As I had intended, I was earlier than usual at my office door. I stood listening for a moment. All was still. He must be gone. I tried the knob. The door was locked. Yes, my procedure had worked to a charm; he indeed must be vanished. Yet a certain melancholy mixed with this: I was almost sorry for my brilliant success. I was fumbling under the door mat for the key, which Bartleby was to have left there for me, when accidentally my knee knocked against a panel, producing a summoning sound, and in response a voice came to me from within—"Not yet; I am occupied."

It was Bartleby.

I was thunderstruck. For an instant I stood like the man who, pipe in mouth, was killed one cloudless afternoon long ago in Virginia, by summer lightning; at his own warm open window he was killed, and remained leaning out there upon the dreamy afternoon, till some one touched him, when he fell.

"Not gone!" I murmured at last. But again obeying that wondrous ascendancy which the inscrutable scrivener had over me, and from which ascendency, for all my chafing, I could not completely escape, I slowly went downstairs and out into the street, and while walking round the block, considered what I should next do in this unheard-of perplexity. Turn the man out by an actual 155

7. Personal belongings, luggage.

thrusting I could not; to drive him away by calling him hard names would not do; calling in the police was an unpleasant idea; and yet, permit him to enjoy his cadaverous triumph over me,—this too I could not think of. What was to be done? or, if nothing could be done, was there anything further that I could *assume* in the matter? Yes, as before I had prospectively assumed that Bartleby would depart, so now I might retrospectively assume that departed he was. In the legitimate carrying out of this assumption, I might enter my office in a great hurry, and pretending not to see Bartleby at all, walk straight against him as if he were air. Such a proceeding would in a singular degree have the appearance of a home-thrust.[8] It was hardly possible that Bartleby could withstand such an application of the doctrine of assumptions. But upon second thoughts the success of the plan seemed rather dubious. I resolved to argue the matter over with him again.

"Bartleby," said I, entering the office, with a quietly severe expression, "I am seriously displeased. I am pained, Bartleby. I had thought better of you. I had imagined you of such a gentlemanly organization, that in any delicate dilemma a slight hint would suffice—in short, an assumption. But it appears I am deceived. Why," I added, unaffectedly starting, "you have not even touched that money yet," pointing to it, just where I had left it the evening previous.

He answered nothing.

"Will you, or will you not, quit me?" I now demanded in a sudden passion, advancing close to him.

"I would prefer *not* to quit you," he replied, gently emphasizing the *not*.

160 "What earthly right have you to stay here? Do you pay any rent? Do you pay my taxes? Or is this property yours?"

He answered nothing.

"Are you ready to go on and write now? Are your eyes recovered? Could you copy a small paper for me this morning? or help examine a few lines? or step round to the post office? In a word, will you do anything at all, to give a coloring to your refusal to depart the premises?"

He silently retired into his hermitage.

I was now in such a state of nervous resentment that I thought it but prudent to check myself at present from further demonstrations. Bartleby and I were alone. I remembered the tragedy of the unfortunate Adams and the still more unfortunate Colt in the solitary office of the latter;[9] and how poor Colt, being dreadfully incensed by Adams, and imprudently permitting himself to get wildly excited, was at unawares hurried into his fatal act—an act which certainly no man could possibly deplore more than the actor himself. Often it had occurred to me in my ponderings upon the subject, that had that altercation taken place in the public street, or at a private residence, it would not have terminated as it did. It was the circumstance of being alone in a solitary office, up stairs, of a building entirely unhallowed by humanizing domestic associations—an uncarpeted office, doubtless, of a dusty, haggard sort of appearance;—this it must have been, which greatly helped to enhance the irritable desperation of the hapless Colt.

8. In fencing, a successful thrust to the opponent's body.

9. In 1841, John C. Colt, brother of the famous gunmaker, unintentionally killed Samuel Adams, a printer, when he hit him on the head during a fight.

165 But when this old Adam[1] of resentment rose in me and tempted me concerning Bartleby, I grappled him and threw him. How? Why, simply by recalling the divine injunction: "A new commandment[2] give I unto you, that ye love one another." Yes, this it was that saved me. Aside from higher considerations, charity often operates as a vastly wise and prudent principle—a great safeguard to its possessor. Men have committed murder for jealousy's sake, and anger's sake, and hatred's sake, and selfishness' sake, and spiritual pride's sake; but no man that ever I heard of, ever committed a diabolical murder for sweet charity's sake. Mere self-interest, then, if no better motive can be enlisted, should, especially with high-tempered men, prompt all beings to charity and philanthropy. At any rate, upon the occasion in question, I strove to drown my exasperated feelings towards the scrivener by benevolently construing his conduct. Poor fellow, poor fellow! thought I, he don't mean anything; and besides, he has seen hard times, and ought to be indulged.

I endeavored also immediately to occupy myself, and at the same time to comfort my despondency. I tried to fancy that in the course of the morning, at such time as might prove agreeable to him, Bartleby, of his own free accord, would emerge from his hermitage, and take up some decided line of march in the direction of the door. But no. Half-past twelve o'clock came; Turkey began to glow in the face, overturn his inkstand, and become generally obstreperous; Nippers abated down into quietude and courtesy; Ginger Nut munched his noon apple; and Bartleby remained standing at his window in one of his profoundest dead-wall reveries. Will it be credited? Ought I to acknowledge it? That afternoon I left the office without saying one further word to him.

Some days now passed, during which, at leisure intervals I looked a little into "Edwards on the Will," and "Priestley on Necessity."[3] Under the circumstances, those books induced a salutary feeling. Gradually I slid into the persuasion that these troubles of mine touching the scrivener, had been all predestinated from eternity, and Bartleby was billeted upon me for some mysterious purpose of an all-wise Providence, which it was not for a mere mortal like me to fathom. Yes, Bartleby, stay there behind your screen, thought I; I shall persecute you no more; you are harmless and noiseless as any of these old chairs; in short, I never feel so private as when I know you are here. At least I see it, I feel it; I penetrate to the predestinated purpose of my life. I am content. Others may have loftier parts to enact; but my mission in this world, Bartleby, is to furnish you with office-room for such period as you may see fit to remain.

I believe that this wise and blessed frame of mind would have continued with me, had it not been for the unsolicited and uncharitable remarks obtruded

1. Sinful element in human nature; see, e.g., "Invocation of Blessing on the Child" in the Book of Common Prayer: "Grant that the old Adam in this child may be so buried, that the new man may be raised up in him." Christ is sometimes called the "new Adam."

2. In John 13.34, where, however, the phrasing is "I give unto [. . .]"

3. Jonathan Edwards (1703–58), New England Calvinist theologian and revivalist, in *The Freedom of the Will* (1754), argued that human beings are not in fact free, for though they choose according to the way they see things, that way is predetermined (by biography, environment, and character), and they act out of personality rather than by will. Joseph Priestley (1733–1804), dissenting preacher, scientist, grammarian, and philosopher, argued in *The Doctrine of Philosophical Necessity* (1777) that free will is theologically objectionable, metaphysically incomprehensible, and morally undesirable.

upon me by my professional friends who visited the rooms. But thus it often is, that the constant friction of illiberal minds wears out at last the best resolves of the more generous. Though to be sure, when I reflected upon it, it was not strange that people entering my office should be struck by the peculiar aspect of the unaccountable Bartleby, and so be tempted to throw out some sinister observations concerning him. Sometimes an attorney having business with me, and calling at my office, and finding no one but the scrivener there, would undertake to obtain some sort of precise information from him touching my whereabouts; but without heeding his idle talk, Bartleby would remain standing immovable in the middle of the room. So after contemplating him in that position for a time, the attorney would depart, no wiser than he came.

Also, when a Reference[4] was going on, and the room full of lawyers and witnesses and business was driving fast; some deeply occupied legal gentleman present, seeing Bartleby wholly unemployed, would request him to run round to his (the legal gentleman's) office and fetch some papers for him. Thereupon, Bartleby would tranquilly decline, and yet remain idle as before. Then the lawyer would give a great stare, and turn to me. And what could I say? At last I was made aware that all through the circle of my professional acquaintance, a whisper of wonder was running round, having reference to the strange creature I kept at my office. This worried me very much. And as the idea came upon me of his possibly turning out a long-lived man, and keep occupying my chambers, and denying my authority; and perplexing my visitors; and scandalizing my professional reputation; and casting a general gloom over the premises; keeping soul and body together to the last upon his savings (for doubtless he spent but half a dime a day), and in the end perhaps outlive me, and claim possession of my office by right of his perpetual occupancy: as all these dark anticipations crowded upon me more and more, and my friends continually intruded their relentless remarks upon the apparition in my room; a great change was wrought in me. I resolved to gather all my faculties together, and forever rid me of this intolerable incubus.[5]

170 Ere revolving any complicated project, however, adapted to this end, I first simply suggested to Bartleby the propriety of his permanent departure. In a calm and serious tone, I commended the idea to his careful and mature consideration. But having taken three days to meditate upon it, he apprised me that his original determination remained the same; in short, that he still preferred to abide with me.

What shall I do? I now said to myself, buttoning up my coat to the last button. What shall I do? what ought I to do? what does conscience say I *should* do with this man, or rather ghost. Rid myself of him, I must; go, he shall. But how? You will not thrust him, the poor, pale, passive mortal,—you will not thrust such a helpless creature out of your door? you will not dishonor yourself by such cruelty? No, I will not, I cannot do that. Rather would I let him live and die here, and then mason up his remains in the wall. What then will you do? For all your coaxing, he will not budge. Bribes he leaves under your own paperweight on your table; in short, it is quite plain that he prefers to cling to you.

4. Consultation or committee meeting.
5. Evil spirit.

Then something severe, something unusual must be done. What! surely you will not have him collared by a constable, and commit his innocent pallor to the common jail? And upon what ground could you procure such a thing to be done?—a vagrant, is he? What! he a vagrant, a wanderer, who refuses to budge? It is because he will *not* be a vagrant, then, that you seek to count him *as* a vagrant. That is too absurd. No visible means of support: there I have him. Wrong again: for indubitably he *does* support himself, and that is the only unanswerable proof that any man can show of his possessing the means so to do. No more then. Since he will not quit me, I must quit him. I will change my offices; I will move elsewhere; and give him fair notice, that if I find him on my new premises I will then proceed against him as a common trespasser.

Acting accordingly, next day I thus addressed him: "I find these chambers too far from the City Hall; the air is unwholesome. In a word, I propose to remove my offices next week, and shall no longer require your services. I tell you this now, in order that you may seek another place."

He made no reply, and nothing more was said.

On the appointed day I engaged carts and men, proceeded to my chambers, 175
and having but little furniture, everything was removed in a few hours. Throughout, the scrivener remained standing behind the screen, which I directed to be removed the last thing. It was withdrawn; and being folded up like a huge folio, left him the motionless occupant of a naked room. I stood in the entry watching him a moment, while something from within me upbraided me.

I re-entered, with my hand in my pocket—and—and my heart in my mouth.

"Good-bye, Bartleby; I am going—good-bye, and God some way bless you; and take that," slipping something in his hand. But it dropped upon the floor, and then,—strange to say—I tore myself from him whom I had so longed to be rid of.

Established in my new quarters, for a day or two I kept the door locked, and started at every footfall in the passages. When I returned to my rooms after any little absence, I would pause at the threshold for an instant, and attentively listen, ere applying my key. But these fears were needless. Bartleby never came nigh me.

I thought all was going well, when a perturbed-looking stranger visited me, inquiring whether I was the person who had recently occupied rooms at No. —— Wall Street.

Full of forebodings, I replied that I was. 180

"Then sir," said the stranger, who proved a lawyer, "you are responsible for the man you left there. He refuses to do any copying; he refuses to do anything; he says he prefers not to; and he refuses to quit the premises."

"I am very sorry, sir," said I, with assumed tranquillity, but an inward tremor, "but, really, the man you allude to is nothing to me—he is no relation or apprentice of mine, that you should hold me responsible for him."

"In mercy's name, who is he?"

"I certainly cannot inform you. I know nothing about him. Formerly I employed him as a copyist; but he has done nothing for me now for some time past."

"I shall settle him then,—good morning, sir." 185

Several days passed, and I heard nothing more; and though I often felt a charitable prompting to call at the place and see poor Bartleby, yet a certain squeamishness of I know not what withheld me.

All is over with him, by this time, thought I at last, when through another week no further intelligence reached me. But coming to my room the day after, I found several persons waiting at my door in a high state of nervous excitement.

"That's the man—here he comes," cried the foremost one, whom I recognized as the lawyer who had previously called upon me alone.

"You must take him away, sir, at once," cried a portly person among them, advancing upon me, and whom I knew to be the landlord of No. —— Wall Street. "These gentlemen, my tenants, cannot stand it any longer; Mr. B——" pointing to the lawyer, "has turned him out of his room, and he now persists in haunting the building generally, sitting upon the banisters of the stairs by day, and sleeping in the entry by night. Everybody is concerned; clients are leaving the offices; some fears are entertained of a mob; something you must do, and that without delay."

Aghast at this torrent, I fell back before it, and would fain have locked myself in my new quarters. In vain I persisted that Bartleby was nothing to me—no more than to anyone else. In vain:—I was the last person known to have anything to do with him, and they held me to the terrible account. Fearful then of being exposed in the papers (as one person present obscurely threatened) I considered the matter, and at length said, that if the lawyer would give me a confidential interview with the scrivener, in his (the lawyer's) own room, I would that afternoon strive my best to rid them of the nuisance they complained of.

Going upstairs to my old haunt, there was Bartleby silently sitting upon the banister at the landing.

"What are you doing here, Bartleby?" said I.

"Sitting upon the banister," he mildly replied.

I motioned him into the lawyer's room, who then left us.

"Bartleby," said I, "are you aware that you are the cause of great tribulation to me, by persisting in occupying the entry after being dismissed from the office?"

No answer.

"Now one of two things must take place. Either you must do something, or something must be done to you. Now what sort of business would you like to engage in? Would you like to re-engage in copying for someone?"

"No; I would prefer not to make any change."

"Would you like a clerkship in a drygoods store?"

"There is too much confinement about that. No, I would not like a clerkship; but I am not particular."

"Too much confinement," I cried, "why you keep yourself confined all the time!"

"I would prefer not to take a clerkship," he rejoined, as if to settle that little item at once.

"How would a bartender's business suit you? There is no trying of the eyesight in that."

"I would not like it at all; though, as I said before, I am not particular."

His unwonted wordiness inspirited me. I returned to the charge.

"Well then, would you like to travel through the country collecting bills for the merchants? That would improve your health."

"No, I would prefer to be doing something else."

"How then would going as a companion to Europe, to entertain some young gentleman with your conversation,—how would that suit you?"

"Not at all. It does not strike me that there is anything definite about that. I like to be stationary. But I am not particular."

"Stationary you shall be then," I cried, now losing all patience, and for the 210
first time in all my exasperating connection with him fairly flying into a passion. "If you do not go away from these premises before night, I shall feel bound—indeed I *am* bound—to—to—to quit the premises myself!" I rather absurdly concluded, knowing not with what possible threat to try to frighten his immobility into compliance. Despairing of all further efforts, I was precipitately leaving him, when a final thought occurred to me—one which had not been wholly unindulged before.

"Bartleby," said I, in the kindest tone I could assume under such exciting circumstances, "will you go home with me now—not to my office, but my dwelling—and remain there till we can conclude upon some convenient arrangement for you at our leisure? Come, let us start now, right away."

"No: at present I would prefer not to make any change at all."

I answered nothing; but effectually dodging everyone by the suddenness and rapidity of my flight, rushed from the building, ran up Wall Street toward Broadway, and jumping into the first omnibus was soon removed from pursuit. As soon as tranquillity returned I distinctly perceived that I had now done all that I possibly could, both in respect to the demands of the landlord and his tenants, and with regard to my own desire and sense of duty, to benefit Bartleby, and shield him from rude persecution. I now strove to be entirely carefree and quiescent; and my conscience justified me in the attempt; though indeed it was not so successful as I could have wished. So fearful was I of being again hunted out by the incensed landlord and his exasperated tenants, that, surrendering my business to Nippers, for a few days I drove about the upper part of the town and through the suburbs, in my rockaway;[6] crossed over to Jersey City and Hoboken, and paid fugitive visits to Manhattanville and Astoria. In fact I almost lived in my rockaway for the time.

When again I entered my office, lo, a note from the landlord lay upon the desk. I opened it with trembling hands. It informed me that the writer had sent to the police, and had Bartleby removed to the Tombs as a vagrant. Moreover, since I knew more about him than anyone else, he wished me to appear at that place, and make a suitable statement of the facts. These tidings had a conflicting effect upon me. At first I was indignant; but at last almost approved. The landlord's energetic, summary disposition had led him to adopt a procedure which I do not think I would have decided upon myself; and yet as a last resort, under such peculiar circumstances, it seemed the only plan.

As I afterwards learned, the poor scrivener, when told that he must be con- 215
ducted to the Tombs, offered not the slightest obstacle, but in his pale unmoving way, silently acquiesced.

Some of the compassionate and curious bystanders joined the party; and headed by one of the constables arm in arm with Bartleby, the silent procession filed its way through all the noise, and heat, and joy of the roaring thoroughfares at noon.

The same day I received the note I went to the Tombs, or to speak more properly, the Halls of Justice. Seeking the right officer, I stated the purpose of my call, and was informed that the individual I described was indeed within. I then assured the functionary that Bartleby was a perfectly honest man, and greatly to be compassionated, however unaccountably eccentric. I narrated all I

6. Light, four-wheeled carriage.

knew, and closed by suggesting the idea of letting him remain in as indulgent confinement as possible till something less harsh might be done—though indeed I hardly knew what. At all events, if nothing else could be decided upon, the alms-house must receive him. I then begged to have an interview.

Being under no disgraceful charge, and quite serene and harmless in all his ways, they had permitted him freely to wander about the prison, and especially in the inclosed grass-platted yards thereof. And so I found him there, standing all alone in the quietest of the yards, his face towards a high wall, while all around, from the narrow slits of the jail windows, I thought I saw peering out upon him the eyes of murderers and thieves.

"Bartleby!"

"I know you," he said, without looking round,—"and I want nothing to say to you."

"It was not I that brought you here, Bartleby," said I, keenly pained at his implied suspicion. "And to you, this should not be so vile a place. Nothing reproachful attaches to you by being here. And see, it is not so sad a place as one might think. Look, there is the sky, and here is the grass."

"I know where I am," he replied, but would say nothing more, and so I left him.

As I entered the corridor again, a broad meat-like man, in an apron, accosted me, and jerking his thumb over his shoulder said—"Is that your friend?"

"Yes."

"Does he want to starve? If he does, let him live on the prison fare, that's all."

"Who are you?" asked I, not knowing what to make of such an unofficially-speaking person in such a place.

"I am the grub-man. Such gentlemen as have friends here, hire me to provide them with something good to eat."

"Is this so?" said I, turning to the turnkey.

He said it was.

"Well then," said I, slipping some silver into the grub-man's hands (for so they called him). "I want you to give particular attention to my friend there; let him have the best dinner you can get. And you must be as polite to him as possible."

"Introduce me, will you?" said the grub-man, looking at me with an expression which seemed to say he was all impatience for an opportunity to give a specimen of his breeding.

Thinking it would prove of benefit to the scrivener, I acquiesced; and asking the grub-man his name, went up with him to Bartleby.

"Bartleby, this is Mr. Cutlets; you will find him very useful to you."

"Your sarvant, sir, your sarvant," said the grub-man, making a low salutation behind his apron. "Hope you find it pleasant here, sir;—spacious grounds—cool apartments, sir—hope you'll stay with us some time—try to make it agreeable. May Mrs. Cutlets and I have the pleasure of your company to dinner, sir, in Mrs. Cutlets' private room?"

"I prefer not to dine today," said Bartleby, turning away. "It would disagree with me; I am unused to dinners." So saying he slowly moved to the other side of the inclosure, and took up a position fronting the dead-wall.

"How's this?" said the grub-man, addressing me with a stare of astonishment. "He's odd, ain't he?"

"I think he is a little deranged," said I, sadly.

"Deranged? deranged is it? Well now, upon my word, I thought that friend of yourn was a gentleman forger; they are always pale and genteel-like, them forgers. I can't help pity 'em—can't help it, sir. Did you know Monroe Edwards?"[7] he added touchingly, and paused. Then laying his hand pityingly on my shoulder, sighed, "he died of consumption at Sing Sing. So you weren't acquainted with Monroe?"

"No, I was never socially acquainted with any forgers. But I cannot stop longer. Look to my friend yonder. You will not lose by it. I will see you again."

Some few days after this, I again obtained admission to the Tombs, and went through the corridors in quest of Bartleby; but without finding him.

"I saw him coming from his cell not long ago," said a turnkey, "may be he's gone to loiter in the yards."

So I went in that direction.

"Are you looking for the silent man?" said another turnkey passing me. "Yonder he lies—sleeping in the yard there. 'Tis not twenty minutes since I saw him lie down."

The yard was entirely quiet. It was not accessible to the common prisoners. The surrounding walls, of amazing thickness, kept off all sounds behind them. The Egyptian character of the masonry weighed upon me with its gloom. But a soft imprisoned turf grew under foot. The heart of the eternal pyramids, it seemed, wherein, by some strange magic, through the clefts, grass seed, dropped by birds, had sprung.

Strangely huddled at the base of the wall, his knees drawn up, and lying on his side, his head touching the cold stones, I saw the wasted Bartleby. But nothing stirred. I paused; then went close up to him; stooped over, and saw that his dim eyes were open; otherwise he seemed profoundly sleeping. Something prompted me to touch him. I felt his hand, when a tingling shiver ran up my arm and down my spine to my feet.

The round face of the grub-man peered upon me now. "His dinner is ready. Won't he dine today, either? Or does he live without dining?"

"Lives without dining," said I, and closed the eyes.

"Eh!—He's asleep, ain't he?"

"With kings and counsellors,"[8] murmured I.

There would seem little need for proceeding further in this history. Imagination will readily supply the meager recital of poor Bartleby's interment. But ere parting with the reader, let me say, that if this little narrative has sufficiently interested him, to awaken curiosity as to who Bartleby was, and what manner of life he led prior to the present narrator's making his acquaintance, I can only reply, that in such curiosity I fully share, but am wholly unable to gratify it. Yet here I hardly know whether I should divulge one little item of rumor, which came to my ear a few months after the scrivener's decease. Upon what basis it rested, I could never ascertain; and hence, how true it is I cannot now tell. But inasmuch as this vague report has not been without a certain strange suggestive interest to me, however sad, it may prove the same with some others; and so I

7. Famously flamboyant swindler and forger (1808–47) who died in Sing Sing prison, north of New York City.

8. That is, dead. See Job 3.13–14: "[T]hen had I been at rest, With kings and counsellors of the earth, which built desolate places for themselves."

will briefly mention it. The report was this: that Bartleby had been a subordinate clerk in the Dead Letter Office at Washington, from which he had been suddenly removed by a change in the administration. When I think over this rumor, I cannot adequately express the emotions which seize me. Dead letters! does it not sound like dead men? Conceive a man by nature and misfortune prone to a pallid hopelessness, can any business seem more fitted to heighten it than that of continually handling these dead letters, and assorting them for the flames? For by the cartload they are annually burned. Sometimes from out the folded paper the pale clerk takes a ring:—the finger it was meant for, perhaps, molders in the grave; a banknote sent in swiftest charity:—he whom it would relieve, nor eats nor hungers any more; pardon for those who died despairing; hope for those who died unhoping; good tidings for those who died stifled by unrelieved calamities. On errands of life, these letters speed to death.

Ah Bartleby! Ah humanity!

1853

QUESTIONS

1. By the end of BARTLEBY, THE SCRIVENER, what does the reader know for certain about Bartleby? Why do you think Melville provides so little explicit information about this character?
2. The narrator tells us that his clerks' nicknames are "expressive of their respective persons or characters," but he explains only Turkey's nickname in this regard. How would you explain the appropriateness of Nipper's nickname? of Ginger Nut's?
3. One of the few words Bartleby utters is *prefer*, and the other characters find themselves using this "queer word." What can we learn about Bartleby and the others by the ways in which they use the word *prefer*?

FRANZ KAFKA
(1883–1924)
The Metamorphosis[1]

Born into a middle-class Jewish family in Prague, Franz Kafka earned a doctorate in law from the German University in that city and held an inconspicuous position in the civil service for many years. Emotionally and physically ill for the last seven or eight years of his short life, he died of tuberculosis in Vienna, never having married (though he was twice engaged to the same woman and lived with an actress in Berlin for some time before he died) and not having published his three major novels, *The Trial* (1925), *The Castle* (1926), and *Amerika* (1927). Indeed, he ordered his friend Max Brod to destroy them and other works he had left in manuscript. Fortunately, Brod did not; and not long after Kafka's death, his sometimes-dreamlike, sometimes-nightmarish work became known and admired all over the world. His stories in English translation are collected in *The Great Wall of China* (1933), *The Penal Colony* (1948), and *The Complete Stories* (1976).

1. Translated from the original German by Susan Bernofsky.

I

When Gregor Samsa woke one morning from troubled dreams, he found himself transformed right there in his bed into some sort of monstrous insect. He was lying on his back—which was hard, like a carapace—and when he raised his head a little he saw his curved brown belly segmented by rigid arches atop which the blanket, already slipping, was just barely managing to cling. His many legs, pitifully thin compared to the rest of him, waved helplessly before his eyes.

"What in the world has happened to me?" he thought. It was no dream. His room, a proper human room, if admittedly rather too small, lay peacefully between the four familiar walls. Above the table, where an unpacked collection of cloth samples was arranged (Samsa was a traveling salesman), hung the picture he had recently clipped from a glossy magazine and placed in an attractive gilt frame. This picture showed a lady in a fur hat and fur boa who sat erect, holding out to the viewer a heavy fur muff in which her entire forearm had vanished.

Gregor's gaze then shifted to the window, where the bleak weather—raindrops could be heard striking the metal sill—made him feel quite melancholy. "What if I just go back to sleep for a little while and forget all this foolishness," he thought, but this proved utterly impossible, for it was his habit to sleep on his right side, and in his present state he was unable to assume this position. No matter how forcefully he thrust himself onto his side, he kept rolling back. Perhaps a hundred times he attempted it, closing his eyes so as not to have to see those struggling legs, and relented only when he began to feel a faint dull ache in his side, unlike anything he'd ever felt before.

"Good Lord," he thought, "what an exhausting profession I've chosen. Day in and day out on the road. Work like this is far more unsettling than business conducted at home, and then I have the agony of traveling itself to contend with: worrying about train connections, the irregular, unpalatable meals, and human intercourse that is constantly changing, never developing the least constancy or warmth. Devil take it all!" He felt a faint itch high up on his belly; still on his back, he laboriously edged himself over to the bedpost so he could raise his head more easily; identified the site of the itch: a cluster of tiny white dots he was unable to judge; and wanted to probe the spot with a leg, but drew it back again at once, for the touch sent cold shivers rippling through him.

He slid back into his earlier position. "All this early rising," he thought, "it's 5
enough to make one soft in the head. Human beings need their sleep. Other traveling salesmen live like harem girls. When I go back to the boardinghouse, for example, to copy out the morning's commissions: why, these gentlemen may still be sitting at breakfast. I'd like to see my boss's face if I tried that some time; he'd can me on the spot. Although who knows, maybe that would be the best thing for me. If I didn't have to hold back for my parents' sake, I'd have given notice long ago—I'd have marched right up to him and given him a piece of my mind. He'd have fallen right off his desk! And what an odd custom that is: perching high up atop one's elevated desk and from this considerable height addressing one's employee down below, especially as the latter is obliged to stand quite close because his boss is hard of hearing. Well, all hope is not yet lost; as soon as I've saved up enough money to pay back what my parents owe him—another

five or six years ought to be enough—I'll most definitely do just that. This will be the great parting of ways. For the time being, though, I've got to get up, my train leaves at five."

And he glanced over at the alarm clock ticking away atop the wardrobe. "Heavenly Father!" he thought. It was half past six, and the clock's hands kept shifting calmly forward, in fact the half-hour had already passed, it was getting on toward six forty-five. Could the alarm have failed to ring? Even from the bed one could see it was properly set for four o'clock; it must have rung. Yes, but was it possible to sleep tranquilly through this furniture-shaking racket? Well, his sleep hadn't been exactly tranquil, but no doubt that's why it had been so sound. But what should he do now? The next train was at seven o'clock; to catch it, he would have to rush like a madman, and his sample case wasn't even packed yet, and he himself felt far from agile or alert. And even if he managed to catch this train, his boss was certain to unleash a thunderstorm of invective upon his head, for the clerk who met the five o'clock train had no doubt long since reported Gregor's absence. This clerk was the boss's underling, a creature devoid of backbone and wit. What if he called in sick? But that would be mortifying and also suspicious, since Gregor had never once been ill in all his five years of service. No doubt his boss would come calling with the company doctor, would reproach Gregor's parents for their son's laziness, silencing all objections by referring them to this doctor, in whose opinion there existed only healthy individuals unwilling to work. And would the doctor be so terribly wrong in this instance? Aside from a mild drowsiness that was certainly superfluous after so many hours of sleep, Gregor felt perfectly fine; in fact, he was ravenous.

While he was considering these matters with the greatest possible speed, yet still without managing to make up his mind to leave the bed (the clock was just striking a quarter to seven), a timid knock came at the door at the head of his bed. "Gregor," the voice called—it was his mother—"it's a quarter to seven. Didn't you want to catch your train?" That gentle voice! Gregor flinched when he heard his own in response: it was unmistakably his old voice, but now it had been infiltrated as if from below by a tortured peeping sound that was impossible to suppress—leaving each word intact, comprehensible, but only for an instant before so completely annihilating it as it continued to reverberate that a person could not tell for sure whether his ears were deceiving him. Gregor had meant to give a proper response explaining everything, but under the circumstances he limited himself to saying, "Yes, thank you, Mother, I'm just getting up." Because of the wooden door, the change in Gregor's voice appeared not to be noticeable from the other side, for his mother was reassured by his response and shuffled off. But their brief conversation had alerted the other family members that Gregor was unexpectedly still at home, and already his father was knocking at one of the room's side doors, softly, but with his fist: "Gregor, Gregor," he called. "What's the problem?" And after a short while he repeated his question in a deeper register: "Gregor! Gregor!" Meanwhile, at the other side door came his sister's faint lament: "Gregor? Are you unwell? Do you need anything?" "Just a second," Gregor answered in both directions at once, making an effort, by enunciating as clearly as possible and inserting long pauses between the individual words, to remove anything conspicuous from his voice. And in fact his father returned to his breakfast, but his sister whispered: "Gregor, open the door, I implore you." But Gregor had no intention of opening the door; he praised the cautious habit he had acquired while traveling of locking all his doors at night, even at home.

First he would get up calmly and undisturbed, he would get dressed and above all have breakfast, and only then would he consider his next steps, for all these supine contemplations, he suddenly realized, would yield no useful results. He recalled often having felt mild aches and pains in bed, caused perhaps by lying in an awkward position, and this pain had then proven to be a figment of his imagination the moment he got up; he was curious to see how this morning's imaginings would gradually fade. The change in his voice was nothing more than the harbinger of a proper head cold, an occupational hazard among traveling salesmen; this he doubted not in the least.

It was simple enough to rid himself of the blanket; he needed only puff himself up a bit, and it fell right off. But the rest proved difficult, not least because he was so exceedingly wide. He would have needed arms and hands to prop himself up; but instead all he had were these many little legs, variously in motion, that he was unable to control. If he tried to bend one leg, it would be the first to straighten; and when he finally succeeded in getting one leg to do his bidding, all the others went flailing about in an unnerving frenzy. "Enough of this lying about uselessly in bed," Gregor said to himself.

At first he tried to maneuver the lower part of his body out of the bed, but 10
this lower part—which, by the way, he had not yet seen and couldn't properly imagine—proved too unwieldy; it all went so slowly; and when at last, half-mad with impatience, he thrust himself recklessly forward with all his strength, it was in the wrong direction, and he slammed against the lower bedpost; the throbbing pain he felt instructed him that for now at least the lower part of his body was perhaps the most sensitive.

So he decided to try leading instead with his upper body and carefully twisted his head toward the edge of the bed. This was easily accomplished, and in the end, despite his width and weight, the mass of his body slowly followed the turning of his head. But once his head was dangling in midair outside the bed, he was afraid to keep shifting forward like this, since if eventually he had to let himself fall in this position, it would be practically a miracle if his head escaped injury. And right now he had to keep his wits about him at all costs, even if it meant staying where he was.

But when, sighing after redoubled efforts, he found himself lying there as before, watching his little legs engaged in their struggles, perhaps more flailingly now, and seeing no possible way to bring calm or order to this chaos, he told himself once more that he could not possibly remain lying here any longer and that the most sensible thing would be to sacrifice anything and everything as long as there remained even the slightest hope of liberating himself from the bed. Simultaneously, though, he continued to remind himself that calm consideration—indeed, the calmest consideration—was far preferable to resolutions seized on in despair. At such moments he fixed his eyes as sharply as possible on the window, but regrettably the view of the morning fog, which veiled even the far side of the narrow street, offered little by way of optimism and good spirits. "Seven o'clock already," he said to himself as the clock struck once more, "already seven and still such dense fog." And for a little while he lay there quietly, his breathing shallow, in the expectation, perhaps, that this perfect silence might possibly restore the real and ordinary state of things.

Then he said to himself: "Before it strikes a quarter past seven, I must absolutely have gotten myself completely out of bed. Besides, by then someone will have come from the office to inquire after me, as the office opens before seven." And he now set himself to rocking his body out of the bed as evenly as possible along his entire length. If he allowed himself to fall from the bed like this, his head—which he intended to lift up cleanly as he fell—would in all likelihood remain unharmed. His back seemed to be hard; surely it would sustain no damage as he fell to the rug. His greatest concern was what to do about the loud crash that would clearly result, no doubt calling forth not terror perhaps but certainly alarm behind each door. Nonetheless it would have to be ventured.

By the time Gregor was already protruding halfway out of bed—this new method was more a game than a struggle, all he had to do was keep rocking sideways a little at a time—it occurred to him how simple things would be if only someone came to his aid. Two strong individuals—he was thinking of his father and the maidservant—would suffice; all they'd have to do was slip their arms beneath his curved back to scoop him out of bed, then crouch down with their burden and wait patiently for him to flip himself over onto the floor, where he hoped those tiny legs of his would take on some meaning. But even aside from the fact that the doors were locked, should he really call for help? Despite his distress, he couldn't help smiling at the thought.

15 Already he'd reached the point where the vigorous rocking motion was making it almost impossible for him to keep his balance, and soon he would have to make up his mind and take the plunge, for a quarter after seven was only five minutes away—when the front doorbell rang. "It's someone from the office," he said to himself and nearly froze while his little legs went on scrabbling all the more frenetically. For a moment all was still. "They won't answer," Gregor said to himself, caught up in some deluded hope. But then of course, as always, the maid strode resolutely to the door and opened it.

Gregor needed only hear the visitor's first words of greeting to know who it was: the general manager himself. Why oh why was Gregor condemned to serve in a firm where even the most negligible falling short was enough to arouse the greatest possible suspicion? Was every last one of the firm's employees a scoundrel, was there not a single loyal, devoted soul among them who would be driven mad by pangs of conscience should he fail to make the best possible use of even just a few morning hours for his employer's benefit, such that his guilt would render him virtually incapable of rising from his bed? Would it really not have sufficed to send an apprentice to inquire—if indeed such inquiries were necessary at all—did the general manager have to come in person, and was it necessary to demonstrate to the entire innocent family that the investigation of this suspicious matter could be entrusted only to the general manager's sharp intellect? And more because of the agitation aroused in Gregor by this train of thought than because of some proper resolution on his part, he swung himself out of bed with all his might. There was a loud thud, you couldn't really call it a crash. The rug cushioned the impact a little, and since his back was more elastic than he'd thought, the resulting sound was muffled and not so obvious. But he hadn't managed to hold his head up carefully enough and had bumped it;

he turned it this way and that, pressing it against the rug in his vexation and pain.

"Something just fell in there," the general manager now said in the room on the left. Gregor tried to imagine whether anything like what he was now experiencing could ever befall the general manager; the possibility must certainly be admitted. But as if brusquely dismissing the question, the manager now took a few purposeful steps in the next room, making his patent leather boots creak. From the room on the right came the whisper of Gregor's sister informing him: "Gregor, the general manager is here." "I know," Gregor murmured; but he didn't dare raise his voice high enough for his sister to hear.

"Gregor," his father now said from the room on the left, "the general manager has come to inquire why you failed to depart by the early train. We don't know what to tell him. Besides, he'd like to have a word with you in person. So please open the door. I'm sure he'll be kind enough not to take offense at the untidiness of your room." "Good morning, Herr[2] Samsa," the general manager now cried out in a friendly tone. "He isn't well," Gregor's mother said to the general manager while his father was still having his say beside the door, "not well at all, take my word for it, sir. Why else would Gregor miss his train! The office is the only thing that boy ever thinks of. It really bothers me that he never goes out in the evening; he's been back in the city an entire week now, but he's spent every last evening at home. He just sits at the table with us, quietly reading the newspaper, or else studies the timetables. Even just doing woodworking projects seems to entertain him. He carved a little picture frame, for example, did it in two or three evenings with his fretsaw; you'll be amazed how pretty it is; it's hanging there in his room; you'll see it in a minute when Gregor opens the door. Oh, and I'm so glad you paid us a visit, sir; on our own we'd never have managed to persuade Gregor to open up; he's so stubborn; and surely he isn't well, even though he denied it this morning." "Be . . . right . . . there," Gregor said, not moving, so as not to miss a single word of their conversation. "No other explanation, madam, is conceivable to me," the general manager said. "Let us hope it is nothing grave. Though on the other hand I would note that, as businessmen—fortunately or unfortunately, as one will—we are very often obliged to suppress indispositions out of consideration for the firm." "So are you ready to let the general manager in?" Gregor's impatient father asked, knocking again at the door. "No," Gregor responded. In the left-hand room horrified silence, while in the room on the right Gregor's sister began to sob.

Why didn't his sister go to join the others? She must have just gotten out of bed and not yet begun to dress. And why was she crying? Because he wasn't getting up and opening his door to the general manager, because he was in danger of losing his position, and because his boss would then start hounding his parents once more over their ancient debt? For the time being, all such worries were assuredly unnecessary. Gregor was still here, and abandoning his family was the farthest thing from his thoughts. At the moment, to be sure, he was lying on the rug, and no one familiar with his current state would seriously expect him to let the general manager in. But surely he wouldn't be sent packing just like that because of so trivial an act of discourtesy, for which it would be simple

2. Mr. (German).

enough to find an appropriate excuse later on. And it seemed to Gregor it would be far more sensible to just leave him in peace rather than disturbing him with all this weeping and cajoling. But the others were distressed by the uncertainty of it all; their behavior was understandable.

20 "Herr Samsa," the general manager now called out, raising his voice. "What has come over you? You barricade yourself in your room, you reply to queries only with yes and no, you cause your parents onerous, unnecessary worries, and you are neglecting—let me permit myself to note—your professional responsibilities in a truly unprecedented manner. I speak here in the name of your parents as well as your employer and in all seriousness must ask you for a clear and immediate explanation. I am astonished, utterly astonished. I have always known you as a calm, sensible person, and now it seems you've begun to permit yourself the most whimsical extravagances. To be sure, the boss did suggest one possible explanation for your absence this morning—it concerns the cash payments recently entrusted to your care—and truthfully, I all but gave him my word of honor that this explanation could not be correct. But confronted here with your incomprehensible obstinacy, I find myself losing any desire I might have had to come to your defense. And your position is anything but secure. It was originally my intention to discuss all this with you in a private conversation, but since you compel me to waste my time here, I do not know why your esteemed parents should not hear of it as well. In short: your productivity of late has been highly unsatisfactory; admittedly this is not the best season for drumming up business, we do acknowledge this; but a season in which no business at all is drummed up is something that does not, and indeed may not exist, Herr Samsa."

"But sir," Gregor cried out, beside himself and forgetting all else in his agitation, "I shall open the door at once, this very instant. A slight indisposition, a fit of dizziness kept me from getting up. Even now I'm still in bed. But already I am feeling very much refreshed. Here, I'm getting up. Just a moment's patience! It's a bit more difficult than I thought. But already I'm feeling quite fine. How odd, the way such a thing can suddenly come over one. Yesterday evening I felt perfectly all right, my parents can attest to this, or rather: I did in fact feel a mild foreboding yesterday evening already. Surely it was noticeable to anyone looking at me. Why didn't I send word to the office? But we always just assume we'll be able to overcome these illnesses without staying home. Sir! Do be gentle with my parents. The allegations you make are unfounded, and no one has ever mentioned anything of the sort to me. Perhaps you haven't yet looked over the most recent commissions I sent in. In any case, I'll be back on the road in time for the eight o'clock train; these additional hours of rest have fortified me. Please do not allow me to detain you any longer, sir; I shall be at the office myself in no time; do be so good as to say I'm on my way and give my regards to the boss."

And while Gregor was hastily blurting out all of this, scarcely knowing what he said, he edged closer to the wardrobe with minimal effort, no doubt thanks to the practice he had already acquired while still in bed, and now he did his best to haul himself upright. Indeed, he really did want to open the door, to show himself and speak with the general manager; he was eager to learn what the others, who were so anxious to see him, would say when they finally laid eyes on him. If they recoiled in horror, Gregor could surrender all responsibility and rest easy. But if they accepted it all calmly, that meant he too had no reason to get himself worked up, and if he hurried, he could still make it to the station by eight. At first he couldn't get a grip on the wardrobe's smooth surface, but finally he gave a great heave and found himself standing upright; he no longer paid any heed to the pain in his lower body, ache as it might. Now he let himself drop against the back of a nearby chair, clinging to its edges with his little legs. And having thus attained control over himself, he fell silent, for now he could listen to the general manager.

"Did you understand a single word?" the manager was asking Gregor's parents. "Surely he isn't trying to make fools of us?" "For heaven's sake," Gregor's mother cried, already weeping, "he might be gravely ill, and here we are tormenting him. Grete! Grete!" she cried out. "Mother?" Gregor's sister called from the other side. They were communicating through Gregor's room. "You must go for the doctor at once. Gregor is ill. Quick, fetch the doctor. Did you hear him speaking just now?" "That was an animal's voice," the general manager said, speaking in noticeably subdued tones compared to the cries of Gregor's mother. "Anna! Anna!" the father shouted into the kitchen through the vestibule, clapping his hands. "Run and fetch a locksmith, hurry!" And already the two girls were racing through the vestibule, their skirts rustling (how had Gregor's sister possibly gotten dressed so quickly?), and flung open the front door. There was no sound of the door closing again; no doubt they had left it standing open, as one sees with apartments in which a great calamity has occurred.

But Gregor was far less troubled now. Even though the others were no longer able to understand his words—though they had seemed to him clear enough, clearer than in the past, perhaps because his ear had grown accustomed to their sound—they were now convinced that things were not right with him and were prepared to offer help. The confidence and conviction with which these first arrangements had been made comforted him. He felt drawn once more into the circle of humankind and was expecting both the doctor and the locksmith—without properly differentiating between the two—to perform magnificent, astounding feats. So as to have as intelligible a voice as possible for the crucial discussions that lay ahead, he cleared his throat a little, making an effort to do this as discreetly as possible, since even this sound might differ from human throat-clearing, which he no longer trusted himself to judge. In the next room, meanwhile, all was quiet. Perhaps his parents sat whispering at the table with the general manager, or perhaps all of them were leaning against the door, listening.

Gregor slowly pushed himself over to the door using the armchair, then let go 25
and allowed himself to fall against the door, propping himself upright—the pads of his little legs turned out to be slightly sticky—and there he rested briefly from his exertions. Then he set about turning the key in the lock using his mouth. Unfortunately it seemed he had no real teeth—so how was he supposed to grasp the key?—but his jaws turned out to be surprisingly strong; and with their help he actually succeeded in causing the key to move, paying no heed to the fact that he was no doubt injuring himself in the process, for a brown fluid ran out of his mouth and down the key, dripping onto the floor. "Listen to that," the general manager said in the next room, "he's turning the key in the lock." Gregor found these words most encouraging; but all of them should have been cheering him on, including his father and mother: "Come on, Gregor!" they

should have shouted, "just keep at it, keep working on that lock!" And now, imagining all of them following his efforts with great suspense, he bit down on the key uncomprehendingly, with all the force he could muster. With each revolution of the key, he danced about the lock, holding himself upright using only his mouth and, as needed, either clinging to the key or using the entire weight of his body to press it down. The brighter sound of the lock finally springing open positively revived him. Sighing in relief, he said to himself: "I guess I didn't need the locksmith after all," and he laid his head upon the handle of the door to press it open.

But he remained hidden from view as the door swung toward him, even after it was wide open. To be seen, he had to work his way slowly around one of the wings of the double door, a delicate operation if he wanted to avoid plopping down awkwardly on his back before he'd even entered the room. He was still occupied with this difficult maneuver and had no leisure to attend to anything else when he heard the general manager utter a loud "Oh!"—it sounded like wind howling—and now he saw him too, saw how the general manager, who was standing closest to the door, pressed his hand to his open mouth, slowly retreating, as though being driven back by an invisible, steady force. Gregor's mother—who despite the general manager's presence stood with her hair still undone from the night, wildly bristling—first looked over at his father, her hands clasped, then took two steps in Gregor's direction before falling down in the midst of all her billowing skirts, her face vanishing completely where it sank to her bosom. Gregor's father clenched his fist with a hostile grimace, as if he intended to thrust Gregor back into his room, then glanced uncertainly about the living room, shaded his eyes with his hands, and wept until his mighty chest shook.

Gregor made no move to enter the room, instead he leaned from the inside against the wing of the door that was bolted fast, so that only half his body and the head inclined sideways above it could be seen as he peered across at the others. Meanwhile it had grown much lighter out; on the far side of the street, a section of the infinitely long, dark gray building opposite—a hospital—came into view with its regular windows punched into the facade; rain was still falling, but only in large drops that were separately visible and seemed to have been hurled one by one to the ground. An inordinate number of breakfast dishes crowded the table, for Gregor's father considered breakfast the most important meal of the day and would drag it out for hours reading various newspapers. Straight ahead, on the opposite wall, hung a photograph of Gregor from his time in the military, showing him as a second lieutenant whose carefree smile as he rested his hand on his dagger commanded respect for his bearing and his uniform. The door to the vestibule was open, and since the front door was open as well, one could see all the way out to the landing and the head of the stairs leading down.

"Well," Gregor said, quite conscious of the fact that he was the only one who had retained his composure, "I shall get dressed at once, pack up my samples and be on my way. As for the rest of you, are you prepared to let me do so? You can see, sir"—he said, addressing the general manager—"I am not obstinate, nor a shirker; traveling is burdensome, but without it I could not live. Where are you going now, sir? To the office? Yes? Will you report all these things truthfully? A person can be incapable of working at the moment, but this is precisely the right time to recall his earlier accomplishments and consider that he will later, once the hindrance has been overcome, work all the more industriously and with greater focus. I am so dreadfully indebted to the boss, surely you're aware of this. On the other hand, I have my parents and sister to think of. Truly I'm in a bind, but I shall work my way out of it. Don't make things more difficult for me than they already are. Take my side at the office! No one loves us drummers, I know. Everyone thinks the salesmen rake in a king's ransom while enjoying life's pleasures. And there's never any particular cause to reconsider this prejudice. But you, sir, have a far better grasp of the general circumstances than the rest of the staff, better even—if I may speak confidentially—than the boss himself, who in his role as businessman can easily err in his opinion to an employee's disadvantage. And you no doubt know quite well that a drummer, who spends almost the entire year away from the office, can easily become the victim of gossip, happenstance and groundless complaints against which he cannot possibly defend himself, as he usually never even learns of them, or only when he has completed one of his journeys, exhausted, and then back at home is forced to observe the dire physical effects of causes that can no longer be identified. Please, sir, do not leave without saying something to show you agree with me at least to some small extent!"

But the general manager had already turned away as soon as Gregor began to speak, and merely glanced back at him over a hunched shoulder, his mouth contorted. And during Gregor's speech he did not stand still for a moment but instead continued to retreat—not letting Gregor out of his sight—in the direction of the door, but only gradually, as though it were secretly prohibited to exit this room. Already he was in the vestibule, and to judge by the abrupt motion with which he withdrew his foot from the living room for the last time, one might have supposed he'd just burned it. Having reached the vestibule, however, he stretched out his right hand, gesturing broadly in the direction of the stairs, as if some all but supernatural salvation awaited him there.

Gregor realized he could not possibly allow the general manager to depart in 30
his present frame of mind if his own position at the firm was not to be put in the gravest jeopardy. His parents didn't fully comprehend his situation: over these long years they had formed the conviction that Gregor was provided for in this office for life, and besides they were so preoccupied with their present worries that they were bereft of all foresight. But Gregor had this foresight. The general manager would have to be detained, reasoned with, convinced and finally won over; after all, Gregor's future and that of his family depended on it. If only his sister were here! She was clever; she had already begun to weep while Gregor was still lying quietly on his back. And surely the general manager, ever the ladies' man, would have let himself be assuaged by her; she would have closed the front door of the apartment and talked him out of his fear in the vestibule. But his sister was not there, so Gregor himself would have to act. And without stopping to consider that he was not yet familiar with his current abilities with respect to locomotion, nor even taking into account the fact that this last speech of his had quite possibly—indeed probably—eluded comprehension, he let go of the door; forced his way through the opening; meant to walk over to where the general manager, already out on the landing, was foolishly clutching at the banister with both hands; but right away, groping in vain for something to

catch hold of, he fell with a faint shriek upon his many little legs. No sooner had this occurred than he felt—for the first time all morning—a sense of physical well-being; his legs had solid ground beneath them; they obeyed his will perfectly, as he noted to his delight; they even strove to bear him wherever he wished; and already it seemed to him he would soon be delivered from all his sufferings. But as he lay there on the floor directly in front of his mother and not far from her, swaying with mobility held in check, she suddenly leapt up—rapt as she had appeared within her own contemplations—leapt high up into the air, her arms thrust wide, fingers spread, crying out: "Help me, for God's sake, help!" her head cocked at an angle, as if to see Gregor better, but then, contradicting this, she senselessly retreated; but she had forgotten the table set for breakfast just behind her; sat down hurriedly upon it as soon as she reached it, as if absentmindedly; and didn't seem to notice that the big overturned coffeepot beside her was pouring a thick stream of coffee on the rug.

"Mother, Mother," Gregor said softly, gazing up at her. For a moment he had forgotten all about the general manager; on the other hand, he could not restrain himself, when he beheld this flowing coffee, from snapping his jaws several times. At this, the mother gave another shriek and fled from the table into the arms of Gregor's father as he rushed to her aid. But Gregor had no time for his parents now; the general manager was already on the stairs; his chin propped on the banister, he looked back on the scene one last time. Gregor was just preparing to dash after him to be sure of catching up with him; but the manager must have sensed something, for he leapt down several steps at once and vanished; and the cry of horror he gave as he fled resounded through the stairwell. Unfortunately the manager's flight now appeared to utterly discombobulate Gregor's father, who up till then had been relatively composed, for instead of running after the manager himself or at least not hindering Gregor in his own pursuit, he seized the manager's walking stick in one hand—it had been left lying on an armchair along with his overcoat and hat—with the other took up a large newspaper from the table, and set about driving Gregor back into his room with a great stamping of feet, brandishing both newspaper and stick. All Gregor's entreaties were in vain, nor were they even understood, for as submissively as he might swivel his head, his father only stamped his feet all the more ferociously. Across the room, his mother had flung open a window despite the chilly weather, and, leaning out, she pressed her face into her hands far outside the window frame. Between street and stairwell, a powerful draft arose, the window curtains flew into the air, the newspapers on the table rustled, and a few pages scudded across the floor. Inexorably Gregor's father drove him backward, uttering hissing sounds like a wild man. But Gregor had no practice at all in reverse locomotion, and his progress was very slow. If only he'd been permitted to turn around, he'd have been back in his room at once, but he was afraid of provoking his father's fury with this time-consuming maneuver, and at any moment a fatal blow from the stick in his father's hand might come crashing down on his back or head. In the end, though, he had no alternative: horrified, he realized he was incapable of controlling his direction; and so he began, with constant anxious glances back at his father, to turn around as quickly as he could, which in fact was rather slowly. Perhaps his father discerned his good intentions, for he did not hinder him in this operation but instead even guided his rotation here and there from a distance, using the tip of his stick. If only his father were not making that unbearable hissing noise! It made Gregor lose his head completely. He had already turned almost all the way around when—still with this hissing in his ear—he became confused and started turning back in the wrong direction. But when finally he succeeded in positioning his head in front of the doorway, it turned out that his body was too wide to fit through the opening. And of course in his father's current state it could not possibly have occurred to him to open the door's other wing to create an adequate passage. He was fixated on the notion that Gregor must disappear into his room as quickly as possible. Never would he have tolerated the complicated preparations necessary for Gregor to prop himself up so as possibly to pass through the door in an upright position. Instead, as though there were no obstacle at all, he now drove Gregor before him, raising a great din: what Gregor heard at his back no longer resembled the voice of merely a single father; it was do or die, and Gregor thrust himself—come what would—into the doorway. One side of his body tilted up, rising at an angle as he pressed forward, scraping his one flank raw and leaving ugly stains behind on the white door, and soon he was wedged tight, unable to move on his own; on one side, his little legs dangled trembling in midair, while on the other they were crushed painfully beneath him—then his father administered a powerful shove from behind, a genuinely liberating thrust that sent him flying, bleeding profusely, into the far reaches of his room. The door was banged shut with the stick, and then at last all was still.

II

Only as dusk was falling did Gregor wake from his heavy, faintlike sleep. He probably wouldn't have slept much longer even without a disturbance, for he felt sufficiently rested and restored, but it seemed to him he had been woken by a fleeting step and the careful shutting of the door to the vestibule. The pallid gleam of the electric streetlamps touched the ceiling here and there and the upper edges of the furniture, but down where Gregor lay, all was dark. Slowly, groping awkwardly with his feelers, which he was only now learning to appreciate, he dragged himself toward the door, wanting to see what had happened. His left side felt like one long unpleasantly contracting scar, and he was forced to limp outright on his two rows of legs. One of these diminutive legs, incidentally, had suffered grievous injuries in the course of the morning's events—it was almost miraculous only one had been injured—and now trailed lifelessly behind him.

Not until he reached the door did he realize what in fact had lured him there: it was the smell of something edible. There stood a bowl filled with sweet milk in which little pieces of white bread were floating. He almost laughed with delight, for his hunger was now even more powerful than in the morning, and right away he dunked his head in the milk almost up to his eyes. But he quickly drew it out again in disappointment; it wasn't just that eating was difficult thanks to his tender left side—and he couldn't eat at all without his entire body becoming gaspingly involved—but beyond that: even though milk had always been his favorite drink, which is no doubt why his sister had brought him some, now it didn't taste good to him at all, indeed it was almost with revulsion that he turned away from the bowl and crept back to the center of the room.

In the living room, as Gregor saw through the crack, the gas had been lit, but while usually at this hour his father liked to read aloud from the afternoon paper to Gregor's mother and sometimes his sister as well in a dramatic voice, now there was not a sound to be heard. Well, perhaps this customary reading aloud that his sister had often told and written him about had recently fallen out of practice. But even in the other rooms everything was so still, even though the apartment was surely not empty. "What a quiet life my family has been leading," Gregor said to himself, and as he gazed fixedly into the darkness before him, he felt great pride at having been able to give his parents and sister a life like this in such a beautiful apartment. But what if all this tranquility, all this prosperity and contentment were now coming to a horrific end? So as not to get lost in such contemplations, Gregor set himself in motion, crawling back and forth across the room.

Once in the course of this long evening one of the side doors was opened a tiny crack and then quickly shut again, and once the other one; someone must have felt an urge to enter and then been overcome by misgivings. Gregor now stationed himself just in front of the living room door, determined to somehow coax the hesitant visitor inside or at least find out who it was; but the door did not open again, and Gregor waited in vain. Before, when all the doors were locked, everyone kept trying to come in, and now that he had opened the one door and the others had apparently been opened during the day, no one came, and the keys were sticking in their locks from the outside.

It was late at night by the time the light in the living room went out, and now it was easy to ascertain that Gregor's parents and sister had remained awake all this time, for all three of them could clearly be heard departing on tiptoe. Now it was unlikely anyone would come into Gregor's room before morning; so he had plenty of time to ponder how best to reorder his life. But this high open room in which he was forced to lie flat on the floor distressed him, without his being able to determine the cause—after all, it was his room, which he had been living in for five years now—and with a half-unconscious motion, and not without a twinge of shame, he scurried beneath the settee, where even though his back was a bit cramped and he could no longer raise his head, he at once felt right at home, his only regret being that his body was too wide across to be accommodated entirely beneath this piece of furniture.

Here he remained the entire night, which he spent by turns dozing—though he was woken again and again by his hunger—and mulling over his worries and indistinct hopes, which however all led to the conclusion that, for the time being, he should behave calmly and, by employing patience and the utmost consideration, assist his family in enduring the inconveniences his current state inevitably forced him to impose on them.

Early the next morning already, so early it was almost still night, Gregor had the opportunity to test the strength of these resolutions he had made, for from the vestibule his sister, almost completely clothed, opened his door and cast an anxious glance into the room. She didn't immediately spot him, but when she noticed him beneath the settee—well, goodness, he had to be somewhere, it's not as if he might have flown away—the sight so alarmed her that, unable to control herself, she slammed the door from the outside. But as if regretting this conduct, she opened it again at once and came in, walking on tiptoe as though she were entering the room of a gravely ill patient or even a stranger. Gregor, having slid his head to just beneath the edge of the settee, observed her. Would she see that he had left the milk standing, and not because of a lack of hunger, and would she bring him some other food more to his liking? If she failed to do so of her own accord, he would sooner starve than call this to her attention, though in fact he felt a nearly monstrous urge to scoot out from beneath the settee, throw himself at his sister's feet, and beg her for something good to eat. But his sister immediately remarked with surprise that the bowl was still full, with just a little of its milk spilled on the floor around it, and she picked it up right away—not with her bare hands, to be sure, but with a rag—and carried it out of the room. Gregor was exceptionally curious to see what she would bring in its stead and mulled over various possibilities. But never would he have been able to predict what his sister in her kindness proceeded to do. To gauge his tastes, she brought him an entire assortment of foodstuffs, all spread out on an old newspaper. There were old, half-rotten vegetables; bones from the family supper the night before caked in a congealed white sauce; a few raisins and almonds; a piece of cheese Gregor had declared inedible two days before; a dry piece of bread; a slice of buttered bread; and a slice of bread with butter and salt. In addition, she placed beside this feast the bowl that apparently had been reserved for Gregor once and for all; it was now filled with water. And out of delicacy, since she knew Gregor would not eat in front of her, she quickly withdrew and even turned the key in the lock so that Gregor would understand he could make himself at home. Gregor's little legs whirred as he now went to take his meal. His wounds, incidentally, seemed to have healed entirely in the meantime, for he no longer felt the least impairment; this was astonishing, for more than a month ago he had cut his finger just a tiny bit with a knife, and this wound had still been painful enough just the day before yesterday. "Might I be less fastidious than before?" he thought, already sucking greedily at the cheese, to which he'd found himself immediately, inexorably drawn, more than to any of the other items. Quickly, his eyes shedding tears of gratification, he devoured in swift succession: the cheese, the vegetables, and the sauce; the fresh food, by contrast, did not taste good to him, in fact he could not even stand the smell of it and so dragged the things he wished to eat a little to one side. He had long since finished everything and was just lying indolently where he was when his sister slowly turned the key in the lock as a signal for him to withdraw. At once he gave a start, though he'd been on the point of nodding off, and he hurried back under the settee. But it cost him a great deal of willpower to remain there even for the short period of time his sister spent in the room, for the hearty meal he'd enjoyed had caused his abdomen to swell, and he could scarcely breathe in his confinement. In between little attacks of suffocation, he peered out with slightly bulging eyes as his sister, oblivious, used a broom to sweep up not only the remains of his meal but also the food he hadn't even touched, as if these items too were no longer fit for consumption, then she hastily dumped everything in a bucket that she covered with a wooden lid before carrying it all out of the room again. She had scarcely turned her back when Gregor hauled himself out from under the settee, stretching and puffing up his body.

This was how Gregor now received his food each day, once in the morning, when his parents and the maid were still asleep, and the second time after everyone had eaten lunch, for his parents would always nap a little afterward, and his sister would send the maid out on some errand or other. Surely they didn't want Gregor to starve either, but perhaps it would have been too much for them to experience his meals through more than hearsay, or perhaps his sister wanted to spare them even this modest sorrow, for Lord knows they were suffering enough.

40 Gregor never learned on what pretext the doctor and locksmith had been sent away that first morning, for since he himself could not be understood, it occurred to no one, not even his sister, that he could understand the others, so when his sister came to his room, he had to be content merely with hearing the sighs she heaved now and then and her words of supplication addressed to the saints. Only later, when she had started to grow accustomed to all of this—though of course it was impossible to become fully accustomed to circumstances like these—would Gregor sometimes catch a remark that was meant in a friendly way or could be interpreted as such. "He tucked right in today," she would say when Gregor had found the food she left him particularly tasty, while in the opposite case, which gradually began to occur more and more often, she was in the habit of saying almost mournfully: "This time he didn't touch a thing."

But while no news reached Gregor directly, he sometimes was able to overhear this and that from the rooms to either side of his, and whenever he heard voices, he would immediately run over to the door in question and press his entire body against it. Especially in the early days there was rarely a conversation that did not somehow, if only indirectly, refer to him. For two days, every mealtime was spent deliberating how the family should now comport itself; but even between meals this same discussion continued, for at least two members of the household were present at all times, since apparently no one wanted to remain at home alone, and of course leaving the apartment unattended was out of the question. What's more, the maid had fallen on her knees before Gregor's mother that very first day—it was not entirely clear what and how much she knew of what had occurred—begging to be released from the family's service, and when she took her leave a quarter of an hour later, she tearfully thanked them for dismissing her, as though this were the greatest benefaction she had experienced at their hands, and without anyone asking this of her, she swore a solemn oath never to reveal anything at all to anyone.

Now Gregor's sister was forced to do the cooking in concert with his mother; to be sure, not much effort was involved, as no one did much eating. Again and again Gregor would hear one of them pressing the others to eat—always in vain, and never with any other response than "Thank you, I've had all I want," or similar words. Perhaps they didn't drink anything either. Often Gregor's sister would ask her father if he wouldn't like a beer, affectionately offering to fetch it herself, and when he did not respond, she would say, wishing to relieve him of all scruples, that she could send the porter's wife for it as well, but then the father would utter a great "No," and no one spoke of it any longer.

Already in the course of the first day, Gregor's father explained the family's finances and prospects not only to Gregor's mother but to his sister as well. Now and then he would get up from the table and, from his small Wertheim safe, which he had salvaged when his business collapsed five years before, extract some receipt or memorandum book. One could hear him opening the complicated lock and then bolting it shut again after removing the desired item. These explanations on his father's part included the first bits of heartening news Gregor had heard since his captivity began. He had been under the impression that his father had retained nothing at all of his former firm's holdings, or at least his father had never said anything to the contrary, and admittedly Gregor himself had never asked him about this. At the time, his only concern had been to do everything in his power to let the family forget, as quickly as possible, the mercantile catastrophe that had plunged all of them into a state of utter hopelessness. And so he had set to work with particular zeal and risen almost overnight from petty clerk to salesman, in which capacity of course he had a quite different earning potential, and his professional accomplishments, in the form of commissions, were immediately transformed into cash that could be plunked down on the table at home, before the eyes of his astonished, delighted family. Those had been lovely times, and never since had they been repeated, at least not with such glory, although Gregor later earned so much money that he was in a position to cover the expenses for the entire family, which he then did. All had grown accustomed to this arrangement, not just the family but Gregor as well: they gratefully accepted the money, and he was happy to provide it, but the exchange no longer felt particularly warm. Only Gregor's sister had remained close to him all this time, and it was his secret plan to send her off to study at the Conservatory next year (unlike Gregor, she dearly loved music and could play the violin quite movingly), despite the considerable costs this would no doubt entail, money that could surely be brought in by other means. Often during the brief periods of time Gregor spent in town, the Conservatory would come up in his conversations with his sister, but only ever as a lovely dream whose realization was unthinkable, and their parents did not like to hear it mentioned even in this innocuous way; but Gregor was thinking the matter over with great determination and intended to make a formal announcement on Christmas Eve.

Thoughts like these, utterly futile in his current state, passed through his head as he stood pressed against the door, eavesdropping. Sometimes general exhaustion made it impossible for him to go on listening, and he would carelessly let his head bump against the door, but then he would immediately hold his head still again, for even the faint sound this produced had been heard in the next room, causing everyone to fall silent. "I wonder what he's getting up to now," his father would say after a while, apparently facing the door, and only then would the interrupted conversation resume.

Gregor now learned, and learned quite well (his father tended to repeat him- 45
self in his explanations, in part because it had been so long since he'd last concerned himself with such matters, in part because Gregor's mother did not always understand everything the first time), that despite all their misfortunes, a small nest egg—really only a tiny one—still remained to them from before, and had even grown a little thanks to the untouched interest that had accumulated meanwhile. In addition, the money Gregor had brought home each month—he only ever kept a few gulden[3] for himself—had not yet been entirely used up and had grown into a small capital. Behind his door, Gregor nodded eagerly, delighted at this unexpected prudence and thrift. To be sure, he might have

3. Currency of the Austro-Hungarian empire.

used this surplus to pay off more of his father's debts with his boss, and the day on which he would have been able to divest himself of his post would no longer have been nearly so far off, but as things stood, his father's arrangements were no doubt for the best.

Now this money was by no means sufficient to allow the family to live off the interest or anything of that sort; it might possibly have been enough to sustain the family for a year, two at most, but that's all there was. So in fact it was the kind of sum one really shouldn't touch, one to be set aside in case of emergency; the money to live on would have to be earned. Gregor's father was admittedly in good health, but he was old and hadn't worked in a full five years, and in any case he was supposed to avoid overtaxing himself; in those five years—the first holiday in his strenuous and yet unsuccessful life—he had put on a lot of weight and now lumbered as he walked. And was Gregor's old mother now supposed to hold down a job, despite her asthma and the fact that it was already an exertion for her to cross from one end of the apartment to the other, for which reason she spent every second day gasping for breath on the sofa beside the open window? And was his sister to go out working, this child of seventeen whose lifestyle no one would begrudge her: dressing nicely, sleeping late, helping out around the house, taking part in a few modest entertainments, and above all, playing the violin? Whenever the family came to speak of the necessity of someone earning money, Gregor would let go of the door and throw himself down upon the cool leather sofa beside it, burning with shame and sorrow.

Often he would lie there the entire long night, not sleeping for a moment, just scrabbling for hours against the leather. Or, not shunning the great effort it cost him to push an armchair over to the window, he would climb up the sill and, propped in the armchair, lean against the window, apparently lost in some sort of reverie of how liberating he'd always found it to gaze outside. For in truth he saw even the objects that were quite near at hand less and less clearly as the days progressed; the hospital across the way whose all too constant sight he had earlier reviled was now no longer even visible to him, and if he had not known perfectly well that he was a resident of Charlottenstrasse,[4] a quiet but perfectly urban street, he might have imagined he was gazing out his window onto a desert in which the gray sky and the gray earth were indistinguishably conjoined. His attentive sister only had to see the armchair standing beside the window twice before she started pushing it back to its place there each time she tidied his room; indeed she even began leaving the window's inner sash open.

If only Gregor had been able to speak to his sister and thank her for all she was compelled to do for him, he would have found her ministrations easier to bear; as it was, he suffered beneath them. His sister, to be sure, did all she could to obscure the awkwardness of the situation, and the more time passed, the better she succeeded, of course, but Gregor came to see it all more and more clearly. Even the way she made her entrance jangled his nerves. The moment she came in, without even pausing to shut the door—although she always took such pains to shield the others from the sight of Gregor's room—she would race straightaway to the window and fling it open with hasty hands as though she were on the point of suffocating, then remain standing there, however cold it might be, gulping in the air. All this racing and racket was inflicted on Gregor

4. Charlotte Street (German).

twice a day; he would be trembling beneath the settee, painfully aware that she would no doubt have willingly spared him this disruption if it were possible for her to endure being in the same room as Gregor with the window closed.

Once—it must have been a month since Gregor's metamorphosis, so there was no particular call for his sister to be startled by his appearance—she came into his room a little earlier than usual and discovered him, motionless and propped upright as if for horrific effect, gazing out the window. Gregor would not have found it surprising if she had chosen not to enter, since his position prevented her from opening the window right away, but she didn't just not enter: she started in alarm and shut the door; a stranger might have thought Gregor had been lying in wait, meaning to bite her. Gregor naturally went and hid himself away beneath the settee, but he had to wait there until noon before his sister returned, and she seemed far more agitated than usual. From this he understood that his appearance was still unbearable to her and would remain so, and that she no doubt had to struggle to force herself not to run away at the sight of even the small part of his body that protruded from beneath the settee. In order to spare her even this sight, one day he carried the bedsheet over to the settee on his back—this labor cost him four hours—and arranged it in such a way that he was now completely covered, so that his sister would not be able to see him even if she bent down. If she considered the sheet unnecessary, she could have removed it, since it was clear enough that it could not possibly be considered a pleasure for Gregor to shut himself off so completely, but she left the sheet where it was, and Gregor even thought he glimpsed a grateful look when at one point he carefully lifted the sheet just a little with his head to see how his sister liked the new arrangement.

During the first fortnight, Gregor's parents could not bring themselves to enter his room, and often he heard them expressing their heartfelt appreciation of his sister's labors, whereas earlier they had often been annoyed with her, since she had seemed to them a rather useless girl. But now both of them, father and mother alike, would often be waiting just outside Gregor's door while his sister tidied up his room, and as soon as she emerged, she had to give a full report on what things looked like in the room, what Gregor had eaten, how he had behaved this time, and whether perhaps any modest improvement could be seen. His mother, incidentally, had wanted to visit him relatively soon, but his father and sister held her back, appealing at first to her sense of reason as Gregor listened attentively, wholeheartedly approving. Later, though, she had to be held back by force, and when she then cried out: "Let me go to Gregor, he is my unhappy son! Can't you understand that I must go to him?" then Gregor thought it would perhaps be good for his mother to visit him, not every day of course, but perhaps once a week; after all, she had a far better grasp of things than his sister, who despite her courage was still a child and, when it came right down to it, had perhaps only taken on this difficult task out of childish frivolity.

Gregor's wish to see his mother was soon fulfilled. During the day, Gregor avoided showing himself at the window, if only out of consideration for his parents, but there wasn't much crawling he could do in the few square meters of space the floor provided, lying still was already difficult for him to endure during the night, eating had soon ceased to give him even the slightest pleasure, and so to divert himself he took up the habit of crawling back and forth across the walls and ceiling. He particularly liked hanging from the ceiling high above the room; it was completely different from lying on the floor; one could breathe more freely there; a gentle swaying motion rocked the body; and in the almost happy absentmindedness Gregor experienced, it might happen, to his own astonishment, that he would let go and crash to the floor. But now, of course, he had his body far better under control than before, and even as great a fall as this did him no harm. His sister immediately noticed the new entertainment Gregor had devised for himself—his peregrinations left behind sticky trails here and there—and she got it into her head to make it possible for Gregor to range as widely as possible by removing the furniture that impeded his movement, above all the wardrobe and desk. But she wasn't able to do so on her own; she didn't dare ask her father for help; the maid most certainly would not have helped her, for this girl of sixteen or so, though she had courageously remained in the household after the departure of the former cook, had at the same time requested the privilege of keeping the kitchen locked at all times and only opening the door upon particular request; and so the sister had no choice but to summon her mother one day when her father was out. The mother arrived with exclamations of feverish joy but fell silent at the door to Gregor's room. At first, of course, Gregor's sister checked to confirm that all in the room was as it should be; only then did she allow her mother to enter. With the utmost haste, Gregor had tugged the sheet down lower and in looser folds so that it really did look as if a bedsheet just happened to have been tossed over the settee. He also refrained from peering out from beneath the sheet this time; for the moment, he would resign himself to not seeing his mother and just be glad she had come. "It's all right, come in, you won't see him," Gregor's sister said, apparently leading her mother by the hand. Gregor now heard the sounds of these two weak women grappling with this in fact quite heavy old wardrobe, with his sister laying claim to the bulk of the work, not listening to the admonitions of her mother, who was afraid she would overtax herself. It took a very long time. After perhaps a quarter of an hour's labor, Gregor's mother said they should leave the wardrobe where it was after all; in the first place, it was too heavy—they would not finish before Gregor's father came home, and by leaving the wardrobe in the middle of the room, they would prevent Gregor from moving around at all—and secondly, it wasn't even clear they were doing him a favor by taking away the furniture. To her, it seemed the opposite was true: the sight of the empty wall positively oppressed her heart; and why should Gregor not experience this same sentiment, since after all he was long accustomed to having this furniture around him—wouldn't he feel abandoned in an emptied-out room? "And is it not as if," his mother concluded in a low voice—in fact, she had been whispering all along, as though she wished to avoid letting Gregor, whose exact whereabouts she did not know, hear so much as the sound of her voice, for she was convinced he could not understand her words—"and is it not as if by removing the furniture we would be showing that we are giving up all hope of a cure and are ruthlessly abandoning him to his own devices? I think it would be best if we try to keep the room in precisely the same state it was in before, so that when Gregor returns to us he will find everything unchanged, which will make it that much easier for him to forget all that has happened in the meantime."

Hearing his mother's words, Gregor realized that the absence of all direct human address, combined with the monotony of life in his family's midst, must have muddled his understanding over the course of these two months, for he could not otherwise explain to himself how he could seriously have wished to have his room emptied out. Did he really want to have this warm room, comfortably furnished with family heirlooms, transformed into a cave or den—in which, to be sure, he would be able to crawl about unhindered in every direction, but at the price of simultaneously swiftly and completely forgetting his human past? He was already on the verge of forgetting, and only his mother's voice, which he had gone so long now without hearing, had shaken him awake. Nothing should be removed; everything must remain; he was unwilling to forego the good influence this furniture had on his condition; and if the furniture got in the way of his practicing this mindless crawling about, this was by no means to his detriment, in fact, it was a great advantage.

Unfortunately his sister was of a different opinion; she had developed the habit—not entirely without cause, to be sure—of presenting herself as the holder of particular expertise when discussing Gregor with her parents, and so now too her mother's counsel was reason enough for her to insist on the removal not only of the wardrobe and desk, as she had originally been intending, but of every last bit of the room's furnishings, with the exception of the indispensable settee. Naturally, it was not simply childish defiance and the hard-won self-assurance she had so unexpectedly acquired in recent weeks that dictated this demand; she had, in fact, observed that Gregor needed a great deal of space to crawl around in, while as far as anyone could see, he made no use whatever of the furniture. But perhaps the fanciful imagination of a girl of her age played a role as well, a sensibility always seeking its own gratification, and one which Grete now allowed to persuade her to render Gregor's situation even more horrific than before, so as to be able to do even more for him than she had hitherto. For a room in which Gregor held sole dominion over empty walls was a place where no one other than Grete would ever dare to set foot.

And so she held fast to her resolve despite the protests of her mother, who appeared troubled to the point of indecision even by the room in its present state; she soon fell silent and helped Gregor's sister remove the wardrobe as best she could. Well, the wardrobe was something Gregor could do without if need be, but the desk would certainly have to stay. And no sooner had the women left the room with the cabinet, groaning as they pressed against its weight, than Gregor poked out his head from beneath the settee to see how he might, cautiously and as considerately as possible, intervene. But unfortunately his mother was the first to return while Grete was still in the next room, clasping the wardrobe in her arms and tipping it back and forth on her own—without, of course, moving it from the spot. But Gregor's mother was unaccustomed to his appearance, it might have made her ill to catch a glimpse of him, and so Gregor in alarm withdrew as fast as he could to the far end of the settee, but it was too late to prevent the front edge of the bedsheet from stirring a little. This was enough to attract his mother's notice. Startled, she froze for a moment, then went back to where Grete was.

Although Gregor kept telling himself that nothing extraordinary was hap- 55
pening, just a few sticks of furniture being shifted about, he was soon forced to admit that all this coming and going on the part of the women, their little exclamations, the furniture scraping against the floor, had the combined effect of a

tumultuous hubbub intensifying all around him, and no matter how tightly he drew his head and legs in and pressed his body against the floor, he soon was forced to consider that he would not be able to endure this much longer. They were clearing out his room; taking from him all that was dear to him; they had already borne away the cabinet in which lay his fretsaw and other tools; and now they were prying loose the desk that had dug itself firmly into the floorboards, this desk at which he had written his homework assignments as a student at the commercial academy, and as a secondary and even primary school pupil—truly there was no time left to explore the good intentions of these two women, whose existence, by the way, he had almost forgotten, for their exhaustion was now making them labor in silence, and one heard only their heavy footsteps.

And so he burst out of hiding—the women in the next room were just leaning on the desk to catch their breath—changing direction four times as he raced about, for he really didn't know what to save first, but then his eyes lit on the picture of the lady clad all in furs, conspicuous now on the otherwise empty wall, and quickly he made his way up to it and pressed himself against the glass, which adhered to him, pleasantly cool against his hot belly. At least this picture, which Gregor's body now covered up completely, was absolutely certain not to be taken away from him. He swiveled his head toward the living room door to observe the women as they returned.

They hadn't permitted themselves much rest at all and were already on their way back; Grete had slung one arm about her mother and was nearly carrying her. "So what should we take next?" Grete said, looking around. Then her eyes met those of Gregor where he clung to the wall. It was no doubt only because of her mother's presence that she kept her composure; bowing her face toward her mother to prevent her from glancing about, she said—hastily and trembling, to be sure—"Let's go back to the living room for a moment, shall we?" Grete's intentions were perfectly clear to Gregor: she meant to bring their mother to safety and then chase him from the wall. Well, let her try! He sat there on his picture and would not give it up. He'd sooner leap right in her face.

But Grete's words succeeded in unsettling her mother even more: taking one step to the side, she saw the huge brown blotch on the flowered wallpaper, and before she was even able to realize that what she saw there was Gregor, she cried out in a hoarse, shrieking voice, "Oh God, oh God!" and fell back upon the settee, her arms spread wide as though she were giving up everything, and lay there without moving. "Gregor!" his sister shouted, raising her fist with a threatening glower. It was the first time she had addressed him directly since his metamorphosis. She ran into the next room to fetch some sort of essence that could be used to awaken her mother from her faint; Gregor wanted to help as well—there would be time enough to save the picture later—but he stuck fast to the glass and had to tear himself away by force; he too then ran into the next room as if he might offer his sister advice of some sort, like in the old days; but then could only stand idly behind her as she rummaged among various little bottles, and scared her out of her wits when she turned around; one bottle flew to the floor and shattered; a shard of glass scratched Gregor's face, and some sort of corrosive medicine engulfed him; without further delay, Grete took up as many bottles as she could hold and ran with them to her mother, slamming the door behind her with her foot. Gregor was now cut off from his mother, who was possibly on the brink of death, for which he himself was to blame; he could not open the door if he didn't want to drive away his sister, who had to stay there with his mother; there was nothing for him to do but wait; and tormented by his worries and self-reproach, he began to crawl about, crawling over everything, walls, furniture, the ceiling, and finally in his despair, as the entire room began to spin around him, he fell smack in the middle of the big table.

A short while passed. Gregor lay there, spent, and around him all was still, possibly a good sign. Then the bell rang. The maid was naturally locked up in her kitchen and so Grete had to open the door. Their father was back. "What happened?" were his first words; the look on Grete's face had no doubt revealed all. Grete's voice as she responded was muffled, apparently she was pressing her face against his chest: "Mother fainted, but she's better already. Gregor has broken out." "That's just what I expected," the father said. "I kept telling you, but you women refused to listen." To Gregor it was clear his father had misinterpreted Grete's all too brief pronouncement to assume him guilty of some act of violence. So it behooved Gregor to try to pacify his father, as he was lacking both the time and means to enlighten him. With this in mind, he fled to the door of his room and pressed himself against it, so that the moment his father came into the living room from the vestibule he would see that Gregor had every intention of returning at once to his room, that it was unnecessary to drive him back inside, and that one had merely to open the door, and he would disappear at once.

But his father was in no mood to take note of subtleties. "Ah!" he exclaimed 60
upon entering, in a tone of voice suggesting he was at once furious and glad. Gregor pulled his head back from the door and turned it toward his father. He had truly not expected to see his father looking as he looked now standing before him; though to be sure the novelty of crawling about had distracted him recently from paying as much attention as before to the goings-on in the rest of the apartment, and really he ought to have been prepared to find a changed set of circumstances. Even so, even so: was this still his father? The same man who used to lie wearily entombed in his bed when Gregor set off on a business trip; who would greet him on the evening of his return sitting in an armchair in his nightshirt; who, incapable of rising, would merely raise his arms to signify his delight, and on the rare walks they still shared, a few Sundays each year and on major holidays, would trudge between Gregor and his mother, who themselves were already walking rather slowly, moving even a bit slower than they, bundled up in his old overcoat, always with his gingerly advancing cane and almost invariably coming to a halt and collecting his companions around him whenever he had something to say? Now he was standing properly erect; dressed in a smart blue uniform with gold buttons of the sort worn by porters in banking establishments; above the jacket's tall, stiff collar his powerful double chin unfurled; beneath bushy eyebrows, his black eyes peered out acutely and attentively; his once disheveled white hair had been painstakingly combed and parted until it gleamed. He tossed his cap, to which a gold monogram was affixed, probably that of a bank, across the entire room in a wide arc to land on the settee, then advanced grim-faced upon Gregor with the tips of his long uniform jacket flung back and his hands in his trouser pockets. He himself probably had no idea what he intended to do; at any rate, he raised up each foot

unusually high, and Gregor marveled at the gigantic dimensions of his boot-soles. But he did not lose any time over them, having learned on the very first day of his new life that his father considered only the utmost severity appropriate for him. And so he fled from his father, hesitating whenever his father stopped short, and then rushing forward again as soon as he stirred. They circled the room several times in this manner without anything decisive occurring, and indeed, given the slow speed at which this interaction was taking place, without its even having the appearance of a chase. For this reason Gregor remained at floor level for the time being, especially as he feared his father might consider it particular wickedness on his part if he were to take refuge on the walls or ceiling. To be sure, he was forced to realize he would not be able to keep up even this pace for long, since each time his father took a step, he himself had to execute any number of motions. A shortness of breath began to set in—even in his earlier life his lungs had been none too reliable. As he now lurched along, reserving all his strength for this continued flight, his eyes barely open (and not thinking, in his stupefaction, that there might be other ways of saving himself than running across the floor, indeed he had almost forgotten he also had the walls at his disposal, though here, to be sure, they were obstructed by delicately carved furniture full of jagged, pointy edges), all at once something flew to the rug beside him, casually flung, and rolled across his path. It was an apple; and already a second one came flying after it; in horror, Gregor stopped in his tracks; there was no point continuing to run now that his father had decided to bombard him. He had filled his pockets from the fruit bowl on the sideboard and now was tossing apple after apple in Gregor's direction, for the moment not even bothering to take particular aim. The petite red apples rolled around the floor as if electrified, knocking into each other. One lightly lobbed apple grazed Gregor's back and slid off again harmlessly. But it was immediately followed by another that embedded itself in his back. Gregor tried to drag himself forward, as if this sudden shocking pain might vanish with a change of place; but he felt nailed to the spot and collapsed there, his legs splaying out, all his senses in a state of utter bewilderment. He caught only a last glimpse of the door to his room flying open, his shrieking sister, and his mother running out of the room before her wearing only a chemise, for his sister had undressed the unconscious woman to let her breathe more freely, then he saw his mother rush to his father's side, her unfastened skirts slipping one by one from about her waist as she ran, saw her stumble across these skirts as she threw herself at his father and, embracing him, in perfect union with him—but now Gregor's vision began to fail him—she clasped her hands at the back of his father's head and pleaded with him to spare Gregor's life.

III

The grievous wound Gregor had received, which plagued him for over a month—the apple remained lodged there in his flesh, a visible memento, since no one dared to remove it—seemed to have reminded even his father that Gregor, despite his current lamentable, repulsive form, was a member of the family who should not be treated like an enemy, for family duty dictated that the others swallow down the disgust he aroused in them and show him tolerance, only tolerance.

And even though this wound cost Gregor some of his mobility, probably for good, and for the time being he required many, many minutes to hobble across his room like an old invalid—crawling up the walls was out of the question now—he was compensated for this worsening of his condition by what seemed to him a perfectly adequate substitute: as evening approached, the door to the living room, on which he would start keeping a sharp eye an hour or two beforehand, would always be opened so as to permit him, lying in his own dark room and invisible from the living room, to watch the entire family sitting at the brightly lit table and listen to their conversations now, as it were, in an officially sanctioned capacity and thus quite differently than before.

To be sure, these were no longer the animated conversations of earlier times that Gregor used to think back on with a certain longing from various cramped hotel rooms when it was time to throw himself, exhausted, into the damp bedding. Now everything was fairly quiet. Gregor's father would fall asleep in his armchair soon after supper; his mother and sister would admonish one another to silence; his mother, bent far over beneath the light, would be sewing ladies' underthings for a dress shop; his sister, who had taken a job as a salesgirl, was studying stenography and French in the evenings so as possibly to move to a better position later on. Sometimes Gregor's father would wake up and, as if unaware he had been sleeping, would say to Gregor's mother: "How long you've been sewing again today!" and then go right back to sleep, which would prompt Gregor's mother and sister to exchange weary smiles.

In a peculiar form of stubbornness, Gregor's father refused to take off his porter's uniform even at home; and while his nightshirt hung uselessly on its hook, he would slumber where he sat, fully clothed, as though he remained ready for service at all times and even here was awaiting his supervisor's call. As a result, his uniform, which had not been new to start with, soon forfeited much of its cleanliness, despite the care lavished on it by mother and sister, and Gregor would sometimes gaze for an entire evening at this stain-covered jacket resplendent with gold buttons, always highly polished, in which the old man slept in considerable discomfort but nonetheless soundly.

The moment the clock struck ten, Gregor's mother would attempt to rouse 65
his father with a few hushed words and then persuade him to go to bed, for he would get no proper sleep sitting here, and sleep was something Gregor's father—who had to report for duty at six in the morning—desperately needed. But in keeping with the stubbornness that had taken hold of him when he started working as a porter, he always insisted on continuing to sit there at the table, even though he kept falling asleep, and then it was only with the greatest effort that he could be persuaded to exchange armchair for bed. Gregor's mother and sister could persist in their little admonishments as doggedly as they liked; for a quarter of an hour, he would just shake his head slowly, his eyes closed, without getting up. Gregor's mother would pluck at his sleeve, whispering cajoling words in his ear, and his sister would set aside her studies to come to her mother's aid, but to no avail. Gregor's father only settled deeper into his armchair. Only when the women gripped him beneath the arms would he open his eyes, looking by turns at mother and sister and saying: "What sort of life is this? Is this the peace and quiet of my old age?" Then, supported by the two women,

he would rise, laboriously, as though he himself were receiving the brunt of this burden, and allow the women to escort him to the doorway, where he would shoo them away and continue on his own, while Gregor's mother hastily threw down her sewing and his sister her pen so they could run after him to offer further assistance. The household was ever further reduced; the maid was now let go after all; a bony giant of a charwoman with white hair flapping about her head came by in the morning and evening to perform the heaviest labors; everything else was handled by Gregor's mother along with all her sewing. It even came to pass that several pieces of jewelry that had been in the family—jewels Gregor's mother and sister had delighted in wearing at entertainments and festivities—were sold, as Gregor would learn in the evening when the price each piece had brought would be discussed. But their greatest lament was always that they were unable to leave this apartment, which was far too large for their current circumstances, since no one could imagine how Gregor might be moved. But Gregor understood that it was not only out of consideration for him that a move was being ruled out, since he could easily enough have been transported in a crate of appropriate size with a few air holes; the main thing keeping the family from moving to a new apartment was their complete sense of hopelessness and the thought that they had been struck with a misfortune such as no one else in their entire circle of relations and friends had ever experienced. They were fulfilling to the utmost the demands the world makes on the poor: Gregor's father fetched breakfast for the petty employees at the bank, his mother sacrificed herself for the underclothes of strangers, his sister ran back and forth behind the shop counter at her customers' behest, but this was all the strength they had. And the wound in Gregor's back would begin to ache anew when mother and sister, having brought his father to bed, would now return and, leaving their work where it lay, huddle close beside one another pressing their cheeks together; when Gregor's mother, gesturing toward his room, would say: "Shut the door now, Grete"; and when Gregor was left in the dark again while next door the two women intermingled their tears or else sat there tearless, staring down at the table.

Gregor spent his nights and days almost entirely without sleeping. Sometimes he thought about taking the family's affairs in hand again, just as he used to, the next time his door was opened; once more his boss and the general manager would appear before his mind's eye after all this time, the clerks and apprentices, the dull-witted hired man, two or three friends from other firms, a chambermaid from a provincial hotel (a sweet, fleeting specter), the shopgirl from a haberdashery whom he had courted earnestly but too slowly—all of these now appeared to him, interspersed with strangers or people already forgotten, but instead of coming to his aid and that of his family, every last one of them was unapproachable, and he was glad when they disappeared. At other times he would be not at all in a frame of mind to look after his family; instead he was filled with rage at how poorly he was attended to, and although he could not imagine anything he would have liked to eat, he plotted how he might gain access to the pantry so as to help himself to what—despite his total absence of hunger—was his due. Without bothering to consider how she might give Gregor particular pleasure, his sister would quickly thrust some randomly chosen foodstuff into his room with her foot on her way to work in the morning or at midday, only to sweep it out again at night with a quick swipe of the broom, paying no heed if the food had been only barely nibbled at or—as was most often the case now—not touched at all. Setting Gregor's room to rights, a task she now saved for the evenings, could not possibly have been done any more perfunctorily. Great streaks of dirt extended across the walls, with balls of dust and rubbish lying scattered about. At first when Gregor's sister came into his room he would position himself in corners particularly indicative of this problem—to reproach her, as it were, by his presence there. But he could just as well have spent entire weeks sitting there without any improvement on his sister's part; after all, she saw the dirt as plainly as he did, but had made up her mind to leave it be. At the same time, with a sensitivity that was new in her, one that had now taken hold of the family as a whole, she was on her guard to make sure the task of tidying Gregor's room was reserved for her. Once Gregor's mother had subjected his room to a thorough scrubbing, which she accomplished only after using up several buckets of water—admittedly, all this moisture was itself an affront to Gregor, who lay stretched out, bitter and immobile, upon the settee—but his mother did not escape punishment. For no sooner had his sister remarked the change in Gregor's room that evening than she ran into the living room, grievously insulted, and ignoring her mother's imploringly raised hands, set to weeping so violently that her parents—naturally her father was startled out of his chair—at first stood by helpless and astonished; until they too began to stir; on the right, Gregor's father reproached his mother for not having left the cleaning of Gregor's room to his sister; while on the left he shouted at Gregor's sister, threatening that she would never again be permitted to clean Gregor's room; while his mother attempted to drag his father, now so agitated he hardly recognized himself, into the bedroom; Gregor's sister, shaking with sobs, pummeled the table with her tiny fists; and Gregor hissed loudly in fury because it had occurred to no one to shut the door of his room to spare him this sight and commotion.

But even if Gregor's sister, who was exhausted by her professional work, had wearied of caring for Gregor as she'd previously done, there was absolutely no need for his mother to fill her shoes, and Gregor needn't have suffered neglect. For now the charwoman was here. This old widow—who had seen and survived the worst in her long life with the help of her sturdy bones—felt no particular repugnance toward Gregor. Without being at all inquisitive, she had once chanced to open the door to his room and, seeing Gregor, who had begun to run back and forth although no one was chasing him, she stood there staring in astonishment, her hands clasped across her lap. Ever since, she never failed to open the door a crack for a moment every morning and evening to look in on him. At the beginning she would call him over to her, saying things that were probably intended to sound friendly, like "Hey, over here, you old dung beetle!" or "Just look at the old dung beetle!" Thus addressed, Gregor gave no reply but instead remained where he was, immobile, as if the door had never been opened. If only this charwoman, instead of being allowed to disturb him uselessly at whim, had been given instructions to clean his room daily! Once, early in the morning—a heavy rain, perhaps already a portent of the coming spring, was beating against the windowpanes—Gregor became so infuriated when the charwoman started up again with her quips that he turned on her as if to attack, if admittedly slowly and decrepitly. But instead of being frightened, the charwoman just picked up a chair that was standing beside the door and held it high in the air; and as she stood there, her mouth gaping wide, her intention was clear: not to close her mouth again until the chair in her hand had come crashing down upon Gregor's back. "Aha, so that's as far as it goes?" she asked as Gregor turned around again, and she placed the chair calmly back in its corner.

Gregor now ate almost nothing at all. Only if he happened by chance to wander past the food that had been prepared for him might he playfully take a bite of something into his mouth, where he would hold it for hours and then usually spit it out again later. At first he thought it was his sorrow at the state of his room that prevented him from eating, but in fact he had resigned himself very quickly to the changes there. Everyone had gotten into the habit of using his room to store things there was no space for in other parts of the apartment, and now there were many such things, since one room of the apartment had been rented out to three lodgers. These solemn gentlemen—all three of them were bearded, as Gregor once noted, peering through the crack of the door—were scrupulously intent on having everything tidy, not just in their room but also, since they were now paying rent here, in the entire household, particularly the kitchen. They could not bear the presence of unnecessary, much less dirty items. Moreover, they had brought most of their own furnishings with them. For this reason, many things had become superfluous, things that could not be sold but were still too valuable to throw out. All of this found its way into Gregor's room. As did the ash box and the garbage pail from the kitchen. The charwoman, always in a great hurry, would simply fling any unserviceable item into Gregor's room; mercifully, Gregor generally saw only the object in question and the hand that held it. The charwoman may have intended at some point, when she had occasion or a free minute, to come collect these things, or else throw all of them out at once, but as it was they remained wherever they first landed, except when Gregor made his way through the refuse, stirring it around—at first out of necessity, since there was no room left for him to crawl about, but later with ever-increasing pleasure, though after these wanderings, which left him mortally exhausted and sad, he would spend hours without moving.

Since the lodgers sometimes also took their supper at home in the shared living room, the living room door remained shut on some evenings, but Gregor was happy to forgo having the door open; in fact, even when it was open, he sometimes failed to take advantage of it and instead, unbeknownst to his family, would remain lying in the darkest corner of his room. Once, however, the charwoman had left the door to the living room slightly ajar, and ajar it remained even when the lodgers came in that evening and struck a light. They sat down at the head of the table where in earlier times Gregor had sat with his father and mother, unfolded the napkins and took up their knives and forks. At once Gregor's mother appeared in the doorway with a serving dish filled with meat, and right behind her came his sister bearing a plate piled high with potatoes. A heavy vapor rose from the steaming food. The lodgers bent over the dishes that had been placed before them, as though wishing to inspect them before beginning their meal, and in fact the one who sat in the middle and appeared to be an authority figure to the other two cut off a piece of meat right there on the platter to check whether it was tender enough and didn't have to be sent back to the kitchen. He was satisfied, and Gregor's mother and sister, who had been watching nervously, now smiled with relief.

The family members themselves ate in the kitchen. Nonetheless Gregor's 70
father visited the living room on his way to the kitchen and with a single bow, cap in hand, took a tour around the table. The lodgers all rose from their seats and mumbled into their beards. Left alone again, they ate in almost perfect silence. It struck Gregor as peculiar that amid all the various sounds of this meal, one could also make out their champing teeth, as if to demonstrate to Gregor that a person needs teeth to eat and that even the most splendid jaws, if toothless, can accomplish nothing at all. "I'm hungry," Gregor said sorrowfully to himself, "but not for these things. Just look how these lodgers take their nourishment while I am wasting away!"

On this very evening—Gregor couldn't remember having heard the violin once in all this time—the sound of it was heard coming from the kitchen. The lodgers had already finished their evening meal, the one in the middle had pulled out a newspaper, giving each of the others a page, and now the three of them were reading, leaning back in their chairs and smoking. When the violin began to play, their interest was piqued, they got up from their chairs and tiptoed over to the doorway leading to the vestibule, where they stood in a tight cluster. The sounds of this activity must have traveled to the kitchen, for Gregor's father now called out: "Are the gentlemen disturbed by this playing? It can be silenced at once." "On the contrary," said the one in the middle, "would the young lady care to join us and play here in the living room, where it is much more comfortable and pleasant?" "Why, of course," Gregor's father exclaimed, as though he were the violinist. The gentlemen went back into the room and waited. Soon Gregor's father arrived with the music stand, his mother with the sheet music and his sister with the violin. His sister calmly prepared to play; his parents, who never rented out rooms in earlier days and therefore were treating these lodgers with exaggerated deference, did not even dare to sit in their own armchairs; his father leaned against the door, his right hand tucked between two buttons of his closed livery jacket; his mother, meanwhile, was offered an armchair by one of the lodgers, and since she left the chair where he had happened to place it, she sat off to one side in a corner.

Gregor's sister began to play; on either side, his father and mother attentively followed each movement of her hands. Attracted by her playing, Gregor had ventured a bit farther than usual and was already sticking his head into the living room. It scarcely surprised him that he had become so inconsiderate of the others; earlier on, his considerateness had been a source of pride. And he had all the more reason to keep himself hidden away now: thanks to the dust that lay everywhere in his room and would swirl up at the slightest motion, he too was covered in dust; he dragged around threads, hair and food scraps clinging to his back and sides; his general indifference was far too great now for him to keep up with a habit he'd once practiced several times a day: flipping over so as to scrub his back against the rug. And despite his condition, he did not hesitate now to continue his advance a little way out onto the immaculate floor of the living room.

To be sure, no one paid him the slightest heed. The family was completely absorbed in the violin playing; the lodgers, on the other hand, having at first positioned themselves, hands in their trouser pockets, much too close behind his sister's music stand, so that they could all look at the sheet music, which surely must have distracted her, soon withdrew to the window, conversing in an undertone, and remained there, anxiously observed by Gregor's father. It appeared more than clear they had been disappointed in their expectation of hearing beautiful or entertaining violin music and now, tired of the whole performance, were continuing to tolerate this disturbance of their peace only out of politeness. Particularly the way in which all of them were blowing the smoke of their cigars high into the air from their noses and mouths suggested extreme agitation. And yet his sister's playing was so lovely. Her face was tilted to one side; searchingly, sadly, her eyes followed the lines of notes. Gregor crept a bit farther forward and ducked his head down close to the floor so as perhaps to catch her eye. Was he a beast, that music so moved him? He felt as if he were being shown the way to that unknown nourishment he craved. He was determined to creep all the way up to his sister, to pluck at her skirt and in this way indicate to her that she should come to his room with her violin, for no one here was rewarding her playing as he meant to reward her. He would not allow her to leave his room ever again, at least as long as he was alive; his horrific figure would, for the first time ever, be useful to him; he would be at all the doors of his room at once, growling at his attackers; but his sister should remain with him not by force but of her own free will; she should sit beside him on the settee, bend down, the better to hear, and he would confess to her that he'd had the firm intention of sending her to the Conservatory and that if the disaster had not disrupted his plans, he would have made a general announcement last Christmas—Christmas had passed now, hadn't it?—without letting himself be swayed by objections of any sort. After this declaration, his sister would be moved to the point of tears, and Gregor would raise himself to the height of her armpit and kiss her throat, which, now that she went to the office every day, she wore free of ribbon or collar.

"Herr Samsa!" the gentleman in the middle shouted at Gregor's father, and without wasting a single word, pointed his finger at Gregor, who was slowly advancing. The violin fell silent, the middle lodger at first just smiled and shook his head, turning toward his friends, then looked again at Gregor. Gregor's father apparently found the task of driving Gregor back into his room less urgent than that of calming the lodgers, despite the fact that they did not appear particularly worked up and seemed to be finding Gregor more entertaining than the music. He hurried over to them and tried with outspread arms to herd them back into their room, at the same time using his body to shield Gregor from their view. And now they did in fact become a little angry, though it was no longer clear whether this was on account of Gregor's father's behavior or the realization dawning on them that without their knowledge they had been sharing their home with a roommate of this sort. They demanded explanations of Gregor's father; now it was their turn to throw their arms into the air; they plucked uneasily at their beards and only slowly withdrew in the direction of their room. Meanwhile Gregor's sister, who had been standing there at a loss since her playing had been so unexpectedly interrupted—she still held violin and bow in her carelessly dangling hands, looking over at the notes as though she were continuing to play—all at once pulled herself together, laid her instrument in the lap of her mother, who still sat there in her armchair, her lungs heaving as she fought for breath, and ran into the next room, toward which the lodgers were now moving somewhat more quickly as Gregor's father urged them on. One saw how, beneath his sister's practiced hands, the beds' blankets and pillows flew into the air and into orderliness. Even before the lodgers reached the room, she had finished making up the beds and slipped out. Gregor's father appeared to be once more so firmly in the grip of his own stubbornness that he forgot the basic respect that, after all, he owed his tenants. He kept up his pressing and urging until, already standing in the doorway, the middle lodger thunderously stamped his foot, causing Gregor's father to stop short. "I hereby declare," he said, raising his hand and seeking out Gregor's mother and sister too as he glanced about, "that in consideration of the reprehensible circumstances prevailing in this apartment and family"—and here he spat on the floor without forethought—"I give notice on my room effective immediately. It goes without saying that I will not pay a penny for the days I have spent here; on the contrary, I shall consider whether or not to pursue you with—please believe me—easily justifiable claims." He fell silent and went on looking straight before him expectantly. And indeed his two friends at once chimed in with the words, "We too give notice effective immediately." Hereupon he seized the door handle and with a great crash slammed the door.

Gregor's father staggered to his armchair with groping hands and let himself 75
fall into it; it looked as though he was stretching out for his customary evening nap, but the violent nodding of his anchorless head showed that he was absolutely not sleeping. Gregor had gone on lying quietly on the spot where the lodgers had espied him. His disappointment at the failure of his plan and perhaps also the weakness caused by starvation rendered him incapable of moving. With a certain definitiveness he sensed, terrified, that everything was about to collapse all around him, and so he waited. Not even the violin startled him when it fell from his mother's lap beneath her trembling fingers, giving off a note that echoed in the air.

"Dear parents," his sister said, striking the table by way of preamble, "things cannot go on like this. Even if you two perhaps do not realize it, I most certainly do. I am unwilling to utter my brother's name before this creature, and therefore will say only: we have to try to get rid of it. We have done everything humanly possible to care for it and show it tolerance, I don't think anyone would reproach us on this account."

"She is right a thousand times over," Gregor's father murmured under his breath. His mother, still incapable of breathing freely, began to cough dully into her lifted hand, a lunatic expression in her eyes.

Gregor's sister hurried over to her mother and held her forehead. Her words seemed to have given her father an idea, for he now sat up straight, playing with his uniform cap between the plates left behind on the table from the lodgers' supper and glancing over from time to time at a quiet Gregor.

"We have to try to get rid of it," his sister said, addressing her words exclusively to Gregor's father this time, for his mother was coughing too hard to hear anything. "It'll be the death of you two, I can see it now. When people have to work as hard as all of us have been doing, it just isn't possible to endure these endless torments at home. I cannot bear it anymore either." And she burst into sobs, weeping so forcefully that her tears flowed down upon her mother's face, from which the girl wiped them with a mechanical gesture.

80 "Child," her father said sympathetically and with noticeable compassion, "but what can we do?"

Gregor's sister just shrugged her shoulders as a sign of the helplessness that had come over her while she was weeping, in contrast to the confidence she'd displayed a moment before.

"If he understood us," Gregor's father said, half-questioning; his sister, still caught up in her weeping, shook one hand vehemently as a sign of how unthinkable she found this.

"If he understood us," his father repeated, closing his eyes to absorb her conviction that this was utterly out of the question, "then it might be possible to come to an agreement with him. But as things stand—"

"It has to go," Gregor's sister cried out, "that's the only way, Father. You just have to try to let go of the notion that this thing is Gregor. The real disaster is that we believed this for so long. But how could it be Gregor? If it were Gregor, it would have realized a long time ago that it just isn't possible for human beings to live beside such a creature, and it would have gone away on its own. We still would have been lacking a brother but we would have been able to go on living and honoring his memory. But now we have this beast tormenting us; it drives away our lodgers and apparently intends to take over the entire apartment and have us sleep in the gutter. Just look, Father," she suddenly shrieked, "he's starting again!" And in a fright that Gregor found bewildering, she now went so far as to leave her mother behind, launching herself from her chair as if she would rather sacrifice her mother than remain in Gregor's proximity, and ran to take cover behind her father who, agitated by the way she was carrying on, rose from his own chair and half-raised his arms as if to shield her.

85 But Gregor was far from wanting to frighten anyone, above all his sister. All he'd done was start to turn around to make his way back to his room, and admittedly this operation would have been hard not to notice, since in his current injured state he was obliged to use his head to help with this difficult maneuver; he kept raising it up and then thumping it against the floor. Pausing, he glanced around. His good intentions seemed to have been recognized; it had been only a momentary fright. Now all of them gazed at him sadly and in silence. His mother lay in her armchair, her extended legs pressed together, barely able to keep her eyes open in her exhaustion; his father and sister sat side by side, and his sister had draped one hand across her father's neck.

"Perhaps I'll be allowed to turn around now," Gregor thought and resumed his labors. He could not entirely suppress the wheezing this exertion produced, and now and then he had to rest. Otherwise no one was harassing him, he had been left to attend to matters on his own. When he had completed this rotation, he immediately made straight for the door to his room. He was astonished at how great a distance separated him from his destination, and he didn't understand how, weak as he was, he had been able to traverse the same distance just a little while before almost without noticing. Steadfastly concentrating only on crawling as quickly as possible, he scarcely paid any heed to the fact that not a word, not a cry came from his family to disturb him. Only when he was already in the doorway did he turn his head—not all the way around, as he felt his neck growing stiff, but even so he was able to see that all was unchanged behind him, except that his sister had risen to her feet. The last thing he saw was a glimpse of his mother, who had now fallen entirely asleep.

No sooner was he in his room again than the door was hastily pressed shut, locked and bolted. The sudden commotion at his back gave him such a frightful start that his little legs gave way beneath him. It was his sister who had hurried thus. She had already been standing there upright and waiting, then pounced so lightfootedly Gregor didn't hear her approach, and she cried out, "Finally!" to her parents as she turned the key in the lock.

"And now?" Gregor wondered, looking around in the dark. He soon made the discovery that he was no longer capable of moving at all. He wasn't surprised at this; on the contrary, it struck him as unnatural that he had actually until now been able to support himself on those thin little legs. As for the rest, he felt relatively at ease. Admittedly his entire body was racked with pain, but it seemed to him as if it was gradually becoming weaker and weaker and in the end would fade away altogether. Already he could scarcely feel the rotting apple in his back, nor the inflamed area surrounding it, both now enveloped in soft dust. He thought back on his family with tenderness and love. His opinion that he must by all means disappear was possibly even more emphatic than that of his sister. He remained in this state of empty, peaceful reflection until the clock-tower struck the third hour of morning. He watched as everything began to lighten outside his window. Then his head sank all the way to the floor without volition and from his nostrils his last breath faintly streamed.

When the charwoman arrived early the next morning, slamming the doors so loudly in her strength and haste—often as she'd been asked to avoid this—that sleep was out of the question anywhere in the apartment after her arrival, her usual cursory visit to Gregor's room revealed at first nothing out of the ordinary. She thought he was lying there so motionless on purpose, feigning indignation; she considered him perfectly capable of rational thought. Since she happened to be holding the long broom in her hand, she tried tickling Gregor with it from the doorway. When even this had no effect, she grew vexed and began to poke Gregor a little, and only when she had actually shifted him from the spot where he lay with no resistance at all were her suspicions roused. When soon thereafter the facts of the matter became clear to her, she gawked in surprise, gave a low whistle, then without further delay flung open the door of the bedroom and in a loud voice shouted into the darkness: "Come have a look, it's gone and croaked—just lying there, dead as a doornail!"

The Samsa couple shot upright in their marital bed and first had to struggle 90
to recover from their shock at the charwoman's conduct before they were able to grasp her words. But then Herr and Frau[5] Samsa hurriedly got out of bed, one on either side, Herr Samsa threw the blanket about his shoulders while Frau Samsa emerged wearing only her nightdress; in this state, they entered Gregor's room. Meanwhile the door to the living room, where Grete had been sleeping since the lodgers' arrival, had opened as well; she was fully dressed, as though she had not slept at all, as even the pallor of her cheeks seemed to prove. "Dead?" Frau Samsa asked, looking questioningly up at the charwoman, although she

5. Mrs. (German).

herself was free to investigate and, indeed, could see how things stood even without investigation. "I should say so," the charwoman said, and by way of proof, pushed Gregor's corpse quite some way to the side with her broom. Frau Samsa made a gesture as though she wanted to hold back the broom but didn't. "Well," Herr Samsa said, "now we can thank God." He crossed himself, and the three women followed his example. Grete, who did not take her eyes off the corpse for a moment, said: "Just look how skinny he was. He went such a long time without eating anything at all. All the food that went into his room would come out again just as before." And indeed Gregor's body was completely flat and dry, which hadn't really been noticeable until now when he was no longer raised up on those little legs and nothing else remained to distract the gaze.

"Grete, come sit with us for a bit," Frau Samsa said with a melancholy smile, and Grete, glancing back at the corpse, followed her parents into their bedroom. The charwoman shut the door and opened the window wide. Despite the early morning, the crisp air was already tempered by a certain mildness: after all, it was already the end of March.

The three lodgers now emerged from their room and looked about in astonishment for their breakfast; they had been forgotten. "Where's breakfast?" the one in the middle asked the charwoman peevishly. But she just put a finger to her lips and then quickly, without a word, beckoned the lodgers into Gregor's room. They did as she bade them and with their hands in the pockets of their slightly threadbare little jackets, they surrounded Gregor's corpse in the room that had meanwhile become quite bright.

Then the bedroom door opened, and Herr Samsa appeared wearing his livery, with his wife on one arm, his daughter on the other. All three looked as if they'd been weeping; Grete kept pressing her face against her father's arm.

"Leave my home at once!" Herr Samsa said, pointing at the door without letting go of the womenfolk. "What do you mean?" the gentleman in the middle inquired, dumbfounded, and gave a saccharine smile. The two others held their hands at their backs and kept rubbing them together uninterruptedly, as if in gleeful expectation of a fight that was certain to be decided in their favor. "I mean exactly what I say," Herr Samsa replied, now advancing on the lodger flanked by his two companions. The lodger just stood there at first, looking at the ground, as if things were just rearranging themselves in his head into a new order. "So we'll be leaving," he said then, looking up at Herr Samsa as if this new humility that had suddenly come over him required him to petition for the approval of even this decision. Herr Samsa merely nodded curtly in his direction a few times, goggle-eyed. At this, the gentleman did, in fact, make haste to stride back out to the vestibule, where his two friends had been listening attentively for some moments, their hands at rest, and now they practically hopped and skipped in their hurry to follow, as if worried Herr Samsa might somehow precede them into the vestibule, cutting off their line of communication with their leader.

In the vestibule, all three of them took their hats from the coat rack, withdrew their walking sticks from the cane stand, made a silent bow and left the apartment. Displaying what soon proved to be an utterly unfounded mistrustfulness, Herr Samsa stepped out onto the landing with the two women; leaning against the banister, they watched as the three gentlemen descended the long staircase, moving slowly but at a steady pace and disappearing on each floor at a certain bend of the stairwell only to appear again a few moments later; the farther down they went, the more the Samsa family's interest in them faded, and when a butcher's apprentice came toward and then passed them on his way up, proudly bearing his tray upon his head, Herr Samsa and the women abandoned the banister, and all of them returned, seemingly relieved, to their apartment.

They decided to spend the day resting and to go out for a stroll; they had not only earned this respite from their work, but were desperately in need of it. And so they all sat down at the table and wrote three letters of excuse: Herr Samsa to his supervisor, Frau Samsa to her employer, and Grete to her superior. While they were writing, the charwoman came in to say she was leaving, as her morning's work was completed. The three scribes at first merely nodded without looking up, and only when the charwoman failed to go on her way did they glance up in annoyance. "Well?" Herr Samsa asked. The charwoman stood smiling in the doorway as if she had some splendid good fortune to announce to the family but would not do so until she was properly questioned. The nearly vertical little ostrich feathers on her hat, which had annoyed Herr Samsa for as long as she had been in the family's service, bobbed gently in all directions. "So what is it you want?" she was asked now by Frau Samsa, the member of the family for whom the charwoman still had the most respect. "Well," the charwoman replied, her own good-natured laughter making it impossible at first for her to go on speaking, "there's no need for you to go worrying about how to get rid of that mess in there. It's already taken care of." Frau Samsa and Grete bent down over their letters as if they meant to go on writing; Herr Samsa, who saw that the charwoman was about to start describing everything in detail, summarily silenced her with an outstretched hand. And since she was not permitted to say what she wished, she suddenly remembered the great hurry she was in, and so with an insulted air she cried, "So long, everyone," turned wildly on her heel, and with the most excruciating slamming of doors left the apartment.

"Tonight she'll be let go," Herr Samsa said, but received an answer neither from his wife nor his daughter, for the charwoman seemed to have disturbed the equanimity they had only just attained. They rose from their seats, went to the window, and remained there with their arms about each other. Herr Samsa turned in his chair to look at them and observed them quietly for a little while. Then he cried out: "So come here already. Let these old matters rest. And show a little consideration for me as well." At once the women obeyed, hurried over to him, caressed him and quickly finished their letters.

Then all three of them left the apartment together, something they had not done for months, and took the electric tram all the way to the open countryside at the edge of town. The car in which they sat all alone was entirely suffused with warm sunlight. Cozily leaning back in their seats, they discussed their future prospects, and on closer investigation it appeared that these prospects were not bad at all, for all three of their positions—something they had never before properly discussed—were in fact quite advantageous and above all offered promising opportunities for advancement. The greatest immediate improvement in their situation, of course, would be easily achieved by moving to a new apartment; they now wished to take a smaller and cheaper but more convenient and above all more practical flat than their current one, which had been picked out for them by Gregor. As they were conversing in this way, Herr and Frau Samsa were struck almost as one while observing their daughter, who was growing ever more vivacious, by the thought that despite all the torments that had made her cheeks grow pale, she had recently blossomed into a beautiful, voluptuous girl. Growing quieter now and communicating with one another almost unconsciously by an exchange of glances, they thought about how it would soon be time to find her a good husband. And when they arrived at their destination, it seemed to them almost a confirmation of their new dreams and good intentions when their daughter swiftly sprang to her feet and stretched her young body.

1915

QUESTIONS

1. What characteristics of THE METAMORPHOSIS are specific to its being a novella? What would likely be sacrificed in the narrative had Kafka opted for the short-story form, particularly in terms of plot and character development? Would the meaning have been different? How so?
2. How does Kafka use Gregor's metamorphosis into an insect as a metaphor? What does he seem to be suggesting about the human condition by using this particular image?
3. What are the practical implications of Gregor's transformation for the Samsa family? What negative effects does it have on the family? What positive effects?
4. What is the significance of Gregor's loss of appetite for food over the course of the novella? What does he become more "hungry" for, and how do his actions prior to his death signify this growing need?
5. How are alienation and isolation—prevailing themes of modernist fiction—exemplified in THE METAMORPHOSIS? In what ways does Gregor's room become symbolic of his alienation? How does the treatment of the room by others both illustrate and exacerbate Gregor's isolation?
6. How does time work in the story? How is it symbolized? Does your understanding of the passing of time change throughout the novella?

SUGGESTIONS FOR WRITING

1. Write an essay analyzing the character of Bartleby the scrivener. Is Bartleby a flat or a fully rounded character? Does his character change or remain static? Is he best understood as a realistic character or as a type or representative of an idea? How do the narrator and the focused time and action of this novella affect the characterization of Bartleby?
2. A short story about Bartleby would be simpler and more comic because the situation is so incongruous: an employee who refuses to work. In a shorter story, both Bartleby and the narrator might be flat characters like the other office workers, Turkey, Nippers, and Ginger Nut. Write an essay in which you argue that the novella allows room for the narrator's gradual change of perspective on Bartleby, noting comments and responses that add complexity or roundness to the employer as well as Bartleby, for instance, "Poor fellow! thought I, he means no mischief. [. . .] I can get along with him" (par. 53).
3. Though Gregor Samsa's bodily transformation into a "monstrous insect" is *the* prevailing metamorphosis in the novella, other changes also occur, both for Gregor and his family. Write an essay in which you follow the transformations in the novella, supporting the thesis that a short novel or novella is the appropriate scope for such altera-

tions in more than one character over a certain period of time. Could the full effect have been achieved in a short story? What would be diminished in a longer novel?

4. Write an essay in which you trace the development of Gregor's consciousness in the story. How does he first react to his transformation? What are his initial preoccupations in section I? How does his attitude toward his condition develop, and how are his preoccupations different by the novella's conclusion?
5. Of the various relationships explored in the story, the one between Gregor and his sister, Grete, stands out as particularly complex. Write an essay in which you evaluate the dynamics of this relationship, especially the role reversals and emotional shifts that take place, using evidence from the text. Do these characters genuinely care about each other? How do they show their care or lack thereof? How does this relationship highlight the themes of the narrative as a whole? How does the scope of a novella allow Kafka to reveal changing attitudes in more than one character while maintaining focus on one problem?
6. Although THE METAMORPHOSIS and BARTLEBY, THE SCRIVENER are realist novellas in many respects, they both depend on a central character's improbable difference from the society around him. Write an essay in which you compare and contrast the alienation or isolation of Gregor Samsa and Bartleby in their respective narratives. Be sure to take into account narration and point of view.

Exploring Contexts

8 THE AUTHOR'S WORK AS CONTEXT: FLANNERY O'CONNOR

As soon as we read more than one work by an author, we begin to recognize similar qualities in the works, as if we are getting to know a personality. Each story, poem, or play is part of the author's entire body of work, or **oeuvre**. Though the voice and vision may vary from work to work, there will be continuities across the oeuvre. The concerns and assumptions that permeate an author's oeuvre do more than relate the individual works to one another; they also serve as the author's trademark. We read each new work by the same author with certain expectations about setting, characterization, style, tone, and other elements.

Unless a work of literature is anonymous or ancient, it is relatively easy to find out about the person who wrote it. In this book we provide short biographies of writers, and numerous sources in libraries and online can add detail and complexity to your first impressions of an author. Curiosity about a writer may lead you not only to biographies but also to other things the author wrote, including essays, letters, diaries, and memoirs—anything that promises insight into the experience, the worldview, and the process that helped produce the work.

In this chapter we will look closely at the work of the American fiction writer Flannery O'Connor (1925–64), focusing on three stories: the title stories of both her first collection, *A Good Man Is Hard to Find* (1955), and her last, *Everything That Rises Must Converge* (published posthumously in 1965), as well as Good Country People, which appeared in the first collection. O'Connor's career was short, hampered by her struggles with lupus, but her accomplishments were considerable: She died at thirty-nine, having published some thirty-one stories and two novels, as well as numerous essays and reviews.

Flannery O'Connor

O'Connor's settings are most often in the American South, rural or urban, and her characters most often Southerners, white or black. Consequently, her subject is often what she called "the race business." O'Connor has a keen eye for realistic detail and for the truth that lies beneath the surface of language and self-image. Her means of uncovering this truth is often violence that shocks the reader and, usually, the characters themselves. Though O'Connor was a deeply religious and serious writer, her stories are replete with irony and wit and are sometimes downright funny. Indeed, as you will see, she is not above mixing comedy and horror or using comic pratfalls to achieve serious (even tragic) ends. As with many other powerful writers, it is not difficult to recognize a story by Flannery O'Connor.

In the rest of this chapter, we first offer general guidance on biographical approaches to authors and their works. Then we discuss more fully some terms and concepts that you have encountered in earlier chapters, but that are especially useful in reading and responding to multiple works by the same author: the distinctions among types of narration as well as matters of tone, style, and imagery. To round out the picture of Flannery O'Connor and to provide material you might use for a critical essay, the chapter concludes with passages from O'Connor's essays and letters and samples of biographical criticism.

BIOGRAPHICAL APPROACHES TO LITERATURE

An author's works always relate in some way to his or her life, though not necessarily offering a direct account of actual experience. A biographical approach to interpretation not only brings us closer to the person behind the work but also gives us a stronger sense of the work's origins. Even a few biographical facts about the author can help guide our expectations about the work and place its **themes** in perspective.

Before you write about any work, it is always a good idea to find out when and where an author lived and wrote, just as you would notice the **setting** (the time and place) within the work. Any essay on a work of literature may include carefully cited information or evidence about the author's life, career, and views. For example, it may be useful to know that Franz Kafka (1883–1924) was a well-educated Jewish civil servant who wrote in German while living in Prague and Vienna. His fiction, then, should not be read as if it were written yesterday in a suburb of Los Angeles. And it *may* be read, in part, as a response to the mixture of assimilation and exile that many Eastern European Jews experienced at the turn of the twentieth century.

Be aware, however, that the biographical approach has some limitations and drawbacks. In a short essay on one or more works by a single author, it is usually better to focus on the works themselves. But even if you are writing a longer paper, knowing a great deal about the author's life and personality or about the author's stated intentions can bias you for or against the author's work regardless of its merits, or lead to irrelevant or reductive interpretations. On the one hand, learning negative details about an author's life—that he or she held objectionable political views, was addicted to alcohol or drugs, or abused spouses and friends—may adversely color the way you feel about the work. On the other hand, a reader may view his or her favorite writers as heroes, glamorizing their failings and confusing interest in a personality with response to the text.

More importantly, you should always be careful not to misread the fictional work as factual autobiography or to treat features of the work as direct results of some biographical cause. Such cause-and-effect biographical critiques ignore other explanations and interpretations. Any literary work that spoke exclusively about or to one individual's personal experience (rather than being informed by it) would likely not be worth reading. Finally, when you read essays, reviews, and criticism in which writers reflect on their own work, it is tempting to take such comments as the final word about the work. But anyone who has ever tried to write knows that the result can have unintended effects on other people. Literary writing opens itself up to multiple interpretations, and any evidence of a writer's conscious intentions shouldn't close down the interpretive process.

It is possible to avoid these pitfalls and take a moderate approach to biographical criticism, however. After all, the text didn't pop into existence in a vacuum; a real human being in a specific historical time and place did write it. Knowing more about the context in which a work was created—including the circumstances and vision of the author who created it—can lead you to deeper understanding and appreciation.

IMPLIED AUTHOR OR NARRATOR

Chapter 2 introduced key concepts about narrators that will help you in reading Flannery O'Connor's stories. A GOOD MAN IS HARD TO FIND, GOOD COUNTRY PEOPLE, and EVERYTHING THAT RISES MUST CONVERGE, like the rest of O'Connor's stories, are narrated in the third person. Yet these narrators are not the same in every story.

Each narrator adopts a slightly different position toward the focal character. Immediately this difference indicates that Flannery O'Connor, who wrote all of the stories, is *not* the fictional teller or narrator of them. Did the real Flannery O'Connor share the voice and perspective of any of her narrators? What did the real O'Connor hope to teach her readers? We have only a few of her statements to go on; the actual author is inaccessible to us. These gaps in what a reader can access or know have inspired the concept of the *implied author*. This concept helps us to avoid reading the story as the writer's direct personal communication, allows for the variety of stories by one writer, and reminds us not only that the narrator of a story is *not* the author of it but also that we aren't talking about the flesh-and-blood person who wrote other works as well. When writing your critical essays, be sure to identify the narrator (as a character or not) and to distinguish the narrator from the author.

STYLE AND TONE

Exploring multiple works by the same author immediately gives you a broader view of the way that author writes. Each author has certain tendencies of **style**, which includes **figures of speech** and **imagery**. A writer's style also includes **diction** or word choice—whether *formal* or *informal* (think *implement* versus *tool*, or *coiffure* versus *hairdo*), whether ornate, standard, colloquial, dialect, or slang. The diction of many of the stories in this book is somewhat informal, particularly those narrated in the first person. An author may highlight the regional or dialect differences of a narrator's language, just as Flannery O'Connor filters the everyday Southern speech patterns of her characters through an articulate, perceptive narrator with correct diction.

In O'Connor's fiction, such distinctions between the diction and syntax of the characters and of the narrator contribute to the **tone** of her work, or the attitude of the implied author and the narrator toward the characters and events, an element somewhat analogous to tone of voice. When what is being said and how it is said (tone) are in harmony, it is difficult to separate one from the other; when there seems to be a discrepancy, we have a number of terms to describe the difference. If the language seems exaggerated, we call it **overstatement**, or *hyperbole*. Sometimes it will be the narrator, sometimes a character, who uses language so intensive or exaggerated that we must read it at a discount, as it were, and judge the speaker's accuracy or honesty in the process. The opposite of overstatement is **understatement**, or **litotes**.

O'Connor's work is also characterized by **irony**. When a word or expression carries not only its literal meaning but a different meaning for the speaker as well, we have an example of *verbal irony*. For example, the phrase "good country people" accumulates ironies when Hulga, a character who has groaned at the idea, uses it herself. As you read O'Connor's stories, look out also for nonverbal forms of irony. The most common form is *situational irony*, which occurs when a character holds a position or has an expectation that is reversed or fulfilled in an unexpected way. A form of situational irony known as *dramatic irony* occurs when a gap opens between what a character believes or expects and what the reader or audience knows. This gap may be revealed when a character says something that has unintended alternative meanings to a better-informed listener or that later becomes true in an unintended way. Dramatic irony also may be sustained throughout an entire work by an unreliable first-person narrator, who perceives or tries to "spin" his or her circumstances in a distorted way. All three types of irony occur throughout O'Connor's stories. Rather than demeaning her characters, O'Connor's ironic treatment testifies to her keen observation of the limits of all human awareness and of the way people tend to rationalize and misconstrue their situations and their own characters.

The distinctive Southern voices of the dialogue in an O'Connor story and the vivid setting and imagery are hallmarks of this author's style. But even more, we know an O'Connor story by the dryly humorous distance her narrators maintain from all characters, the often-violent harm characters do to one another, the belated revelation that destroys a character's pride in knowing more than others—the commandment, in a sense, to awaken before we meet eternal damnation.

THREE STORIES BY FLANNERY O'CONNOR

FLANNERY O'CONNOR
A Good Man Is Hard to Find

The grandmother didn't want to go to Florida. She wanted to visit some of her connections in east Tennessee and she was seizing at every chance to change Bailey's mind. Bailey was the son she lived with, her only boy. He was sitting on the edge of his chair at the table, bent over the orange sports section of the *Journal*. "Now look here, Bailey," she said, "see here, read this," and she stood with one hand on her thin hip and the other rattling the newspaper at his bald head. "Here this fellow that calls himself The Misfit is aloose from the Federal Pen and headed toward Florida and you read here what it says he did to these people. Just you read it. I wouldn't take my children in any direction with a criminal like that aloose in it. I couldn't answer to my conscience if I did."

Bailey didn't look up from his reading so she wheeled around then and faced the children's mother, a young woman in slacks, whose face was as broad and innocent as a cabbage and was tied around with a green head-kerchief that had two points on the top like a rabbit's ears. She was sitting on the sofa, feeding the baby his apricots out of a jar. "The children have been to Florida before," the old lady said. "You all ought to take them somewhere else for a change so they would see different parts of the world and be broad. They never have been to east Tennessee."

The children's mother didn't seem to hear her but the eight-year-old boy, John Wesley, a stocky child with glasses, said, "If you don't want to go to Florida, why dontcha stay at home?" He and the little girl, June Star, were reading the funny papers on the floor.

"She wouldn't stay at home to be queen for a day," June Star said without raising her yellow head.

5 "Yes and what would you do if this fellow, The Misfit, caught you?" the grandmother asked.

"I'd smack his face," John Wesley said.

"She wouldn't stay at home for a million bucks," June Star said. "Afraid she'd miss something. She has to go everywhere we go."

"All right, Miss," the grandmother said. "Just remember that the next time you want me to curl your hair."

June Star said her hair was naturally curly.

10 The next morning the grandmother was the first one in the car, ready to go. She had her big black valise that looked like the head of a hippopotamus in one corner, and underneath it she was hiding a basket with Pitty Sing,[1] the cat, in it. She didn't intend for the cat to be left alone in the house for three days because he would miss her too much and she was afraid he might brush against one of the gas burners and accidentally asphyxiate himself. Her son, Bailey, didn't like to arrive at a motel with a cat.

She sat in the middle of the back seat with John Wesley and June Star on either side of her. Bailey and the children's mother and the baby sat in front and they left Atlanta at eight forty-five with the mileage on the car at 55890. The grandmother wrote this down because she thought it would be interesting to say how many miles they had been when they got back. It took them twenty minutes to reach the outskirts of the city.

The old lady settled herself comfortably, removing her white cotton gloves and putting them up with her purse on the shelf in front of the back window. The children's mother still had on slacks and still had her head tied up in a green kerchief, but the grandmother had on a navy blue straw sailor hat with a bunch of white violets on the brim and a navy blue dress with a small white dot in the print. Her collars and cuffs were white organdy trimmed with lace and at her neckline she had pinned a purple spray of cloth violets containing a sachet. In case of an accident, anyone seeing her dead on the highway would know at once that she was a lady.

1. Named after Pitti-Sing, one of the "three little maids from school" in Gilbert and Sullivan's operetta *The Mikado* (1885).

She said she thought it was going to be a good day for driving, neither too hot nor too cold, and she cautioned Bailey that the speed limit was fifty-five miles an hour and that the patrolmen hid themselves behind billboards and small clumps of trees and sped out after you before you had a chance to slow down. She pointed out interesting details of the scenery: Stone Mountain; the blue granite that in some places came up to both sides of the highway; the brilliant red clay banks slightly streaked with purple; and the various crops that made rows of green lace-work on the ground. The trees were full of silver-white sunlight and the meanest of them sparkled. The children were reading comic magazines and their mother had gone back to sleep.

"Let's go through Georgia fast so we won't have to look at it much," John Wesley said.

15 "If I were a little boy," said the grandmother, "I wouldn't talk about my native state that way. Tennessee has the mountains and Georgia has the hills."

"Tennessee is just a hillbilly dumping ground," John Wesley said, "and Georgia is a lousy state too."

"You said it," June Star said.

"In my time," said the grandmother, folding her thin veined fingers, "children were more respectful of their native states and their parents and everything else. People did right then. Oh look at the cute little pickaninny!" she said and pointed to a Negro child standing in the door of a shack. "Wouldn't that make a picture, now?" she asked and they all turned and looked at the little Negro out of the back window. He waved.

"He didn't have any britches on," June Star said.

20 "He probably didn't have any," the grandmother explained. "Little niggers in the country don't have things like we do. If I could paint, I'd paint that picture," she said.

The children exchanged comic books.

The grandmother offered to hold the baby and the children's mother passed him over the front seat to her. She set him on her knee and bounced him and told him about the things they were passing. She rolled her eyes and screwed up her mouth and stuck her leathery thin face into his smooth bland one. Occasionally he gave her a faraway smile. They passed a large cotton field with five or six graves fenced in the middle of it, like a small island. "Look at the graveyard!" the grandmother said, pointing it out. "That was the old family burying ground. That belonged to the plantation."

"Where's the plantation?" John Wesley asked.

"Gone with the Wind,"[2] said the grandmother. "Ha. Ha."

25 When the children finished all the comic books they had brought, they opened the lunch and ate it. The grandmother ate a peanut butter sandwich and an olive and would not let the children throw the box and the paper napkins out the window. When there was nothing else to do they played a game by choosing a cloud and making the other two guess what shape it suggested. John Wesley took one the shape of a cow and June Star guessed a cow and John Wesley

2. Title of an immensely popular novel, published in 1936, by Margaret Mitchell (1900–49); the novel depicts a large, prosperous Southern plantation, Tara, that is destroyed by Northern troops in the American Civil War.

said, no, an automobile, and June Star said he didn't play fair, and they began to slap each other over the grandmother.

The grandmother said she would tell them a story if they would keep quiet. When she told a story, she rolled her eyes and waved her head and was very dramatic. She said once when she was a maiden lady she had been courted by a Mr. Edgar Atkins Teagarden from Jasper, Georgia. She said he was a very good-looking man and a gentleman and that he brought her a watermelon every Saturday afternoon with his initials cut in it, E. A. T. Well, one Saturday, she said, Mr. Teagarden brought the watermelon and there was nobody at home and he left it on the front porch and returned in his buggy to Jasper, but she never got the watermelon, she said, because a nigger boy ate it when he saw the initials, E. A. T.! This story tickled John Wesley's funny bone and he giggled and giggled but June Star didn't think it was any good. She said she wouldn't marry a man that just brought her a watermelon on Saturday. The grandmother said she would have done well to marry Mr. Teagarden because he was a gentleman and had bought Coca-Cola stock when it first came out and that he had died only a few years ago, a very wealthy man.

They stopped at The Tower for barbecued sandwiches. The Tower was a part stucco and part wood filling station and dance hall set in a clearing outside of Timothy. A fat man named Red Sammy Butts ran it and there were signs stuck here and there on the building and for miles up and down the highway saying, TRY RED SAMMY'S FAMOUS BARBECUE. NONE LIKE FAMOUS RED SAMMY'S! RED SAM! THE FAT BOY WITH THE HAPPY LAUGH! A VETERAN! RED SAMMY'S YOUR MAN!

Red Sammy was lying on the bare ground outside The Tower with his head under a truck while a gray monkey about a foot high, chained to a small chinaberry tree, chattered nearby. The monkey sprang back into the tree and got on the highest limb as soon as he saw the children jump out of the car and run toward him.

Inside, The Tower was a long dark room with a counter at one end and tables at the other and dancing space in the middle. They all sat down at a board table next to the nickelodeon[3] and Red Sam's wife, a tall burnt-brown woman with hair and eyes lighter than her skin, came and took their order. The children's mother put a dime in the machine and played "The Tennessee Waltz," and the grandmother said that tune always made her want to dance. She asked Bailey if he would like to dance but he only glared at her. He didn't have a naturally sunny disposition like she did and trips made him nervous. The grandmother's brown eyes were very bright. She swayed her head from side to side and pretended she was dancing in her chair. June Star said play something she could tap to so the children's mother put in another dime and played a fast number and June Star stepped out onto the dance floor and did her tap routine.

30 "Ain't she cute?" Red Sam's wife said, leaning over the counter. "Would you like to come be my little girl?"

"No I certainly wouldn't," June Star said. "I wouldn't live in a broken-down place like this for a million bucks!" and she ran back to the table.

"Ain't she cute?" the woman repeated, stretching her mouth politely.

3. Jukebox.

"Aren't you ashamed?" hissed the grandmother.

Red Sam came in and told his wife to quit lounging on the counter and hurry up with these people's order. His khaki trousers reached just to his hip bones and his stomach hung over them like a sack of meal swaying under his shirt. He came over and sat down at a table nearby and let out a combination sigh and yodel. "You can't win," he said. "You can't win," and he wiped his sweating red face off with a gray handkerchief. "These days you don't know who to trust," he said. "Ain't that the truth?"

"People are certainly not nice like they used to be," said the grandmother. 35

"Two fellers come in here last week," Red Sammy said, "driving a Chrysler. It was a old beat-up car but it was a good one and these boys looked all right to me. Said they worked at the mill and you know I let them fellers charge the gas they bought? Now why did I do that?"

"Because you're a good man!" the grandmother said at once.

"Yes'm, I suppose so," Red Sam said as if he were struck with this answer.

His wife brought the orders, carrying the five plates all at once without a tray, two in each hand and one balanced on her arm. "It isn't a soul in this green world of God's that you can trust," she said. "And I don't count nobody out of that, not nobody," she repeated, looking at Red Sammy.

"Did you read about that criminal, The Misfit, that's escaped?" asked the 40
grandmother.

"I wouldn't be a bit surprised if he didn't attact this place right here," said the woman. "If he hears about it being here, I wouldn't be none surprised to see him. If he hears it's two cent in the cash register, I wouldn't be a tall surprised if he . . ."

"That'll do," Red Sam said. "Go bring these people their Co'-Colas," and the woman went off to get the rest of the order.

"A good man is hard to find," Red Sammy said. "Everything is getting terrible. I remember the day you could go off and leave your screen door unlatched. Not no more."

He and the grandmother discussed better times. The old lady said that in her opinion Europe was entirely to blame for the way things were now. She said the way Europe acted you would think we were made of money and Red Sam said it was no use talking about it, she was exactly right. The children ran outside into the white sunlight and looked at the monkey in the lacy chinaberry tree. He was busy catching fleas on himself and biting each one carefully between his teeth as if it were a delicacy.

They drove off again into the hot afternoon. The grandmother took cat naps 45
and woke up every few minutes with her own snoring. Outside of Toombsboro she woke up and recalled an old plantation that she had visited in this neighborhood once when she was a young lady. She said the house had six white columns across the front and that there was an avenue of oaks leading up to it and two little wooden trellis arbors on either side in front where you sat down with your suitor after a stroll in the garden. She recalled exactly which road to turn off to get to it. She knew that Bailey would not be willing to lose any time looking at an old house, but the more she talked about it, the more she wanted to see it once again and find out if the little twin arbors were still standing. "There was a secret panel in this house," she said craftily, not telling the truth but wishing

that she were, "and the story went that all the family silver was hidden in it when Sherman came through but it was never found . . ."

"Hey!" John Wesley said. "Let's go see it! We'll find it! We'll poke all the woodwork and find it! Who lives there? Where do you turn off at? Hey Pop, can't we turn off there?"

"We never have seen a house with a secret panel!" June Star shrieked. "Let's go to the house with the secret panel! Hey Pop, can't we go see the house with the secret panel!"

"It's not far from here, I know," the grandmother said. "It wouldn't take over twenty minutes."

Bailey was looking straight ahead. His jaw was as rigid as a horseshoe. "No," he said.

50 The children began to yell and scream that they wanted to see the house with the secret panel. John Wesley kicked the back of the front seat and June Star hung over her mother's shoulder and whined desperately into her ear that they never had any fun even on their vacation, that they could never do what THEY wanted to do. The baby began to scream and John Wesley kicked the back of the seat so hard that his father could feel the blows in his kidney.

"All right!" he shouted and drew the car to a stop at the side of the road. "Will you all shut up? Will you all just shut up for one second? If you don't shut up, we won't go anywhere."

"It would be very educational for them," the grandmother murmured.

"All right," Bailey said, "but get this: this is the only time we're going to stop for anything like this. This is the one and only time."

"The dirt road that you have to turn down is about a mile back," the grandmother directed. "I marked it when we passed."

55 "A dirt road," Bailey groaned.

After they had turned around and were headed toward the dirt road, the grandmother recalled other points about the house, the beautiful glass over the front doorway and the candle-lamp in the hall. John Wesley said that the secret panel was probably in the fireplace.

"You can't go inside this house," Bailey said. "You don't know who lives there."

"While you all talk to the people in front, I'll run around behind and get in a window," John Wesley suggested.

"We'll all stay in the car," his mother said.

60 They turned onto the dirt road and the car raced roughly along in a swirl of pink dust. The grandmother recalled the times when there were no paved roads and thirty miles was a day's journey. The dirt road was hilly and there were sudden washes in it and sharp curves on dangerous embankments. All at once they would be on a hill, looking down over the blue tops of trees for miles around, then the next minute, they would be in a red depression with the dust-coated trees looking down on them.

"This place had better turn up in a minute," Bailey said, "or I'm going to turn around."

The road looked as if no one had traveled on it in months.

"It's not much farther," the grandmother said and just as she said it, a horrible thought came to her. The thought was so embarrassing that she turned red in the face and her eyes dilated and her feet jumped up, upsetting her valise in the corner. The instant the valise moved, the newspaper top she had over the basket under it rose with a snarl and Pitty Sing, the cat, sprang onto Bailey's shoulder.

The children were thrown to the floor and their mother, clutching the baby, out the door onto the ground; the old lady was thrown into the front seat. The car turned over once and landed right-side-up in a gulch off the side of the road. Bailey remained in the driver's seat with the cat—gray-striped with a broad white face and an orange nose—clinging to his neck like a caterpillar.

As soon as the children saw they could move their arms and legs, they scram- 65
bled out of the car, shouting, "We've had an ACCIDENT!" The grandmother was curled up under the dashboard, hoping she was injured so that Bailey's wrath would not come down on her all at once. The horrible thought she had had before the accident was that the house she had remembered so vividly was not in Georgia but in Tennessee.

Bailey removed the cat from his neck with both hands and flung it out the window against the side of a pine tree. Then he got out of the car and started looking for the children's mother. She was sitting against the side of the red gutted ditch, holding the screaming baby, but she only had a cut down her face and a broken shoulder. "We've had an ACCIDENT!" the children screamed in a frenzy of delight.

"But nobody's killed," June Star said with disappointment as the grandmother limped out of the car, her hat still pinned to her head but the broken front brim standing up at a jaunty angle and the violet spray hanging off the side. They all sat down in the ditch, except the children, to recover from the shock. They were all shaking.

"Maybe a car will come along," said the children's mother hoarsely.

"I believe I have injured an organ," said the grandmother, pressing her side, but no one answered her. Bailey's teeth were clattering. He had on a yellow sport shirt with bright blue parrots designed in it and his face was as yellow as the shirt. The grandmother decided that she would not mention that the house was in Tennessee.

The road was about ten feet above and they could see only the tops of the 70
trees on the other side of it. Behind the ditch they were sitting in there were more woods, tall and dark and deep. In a few minutes they saw a car some distance away on top of a hill, coming slowly as if the occupants were watching them. The grandmother stood up and waved both arms dramatically to attract their attention. The car continued to come on slowly, disappeared around a bend and appeared again, moving even slower, on top of the hill they had gone over. It was a big black battered hearselike automobile. There were three men in it.

It came to a stop just over them and for some minutes, the driver looked down with a steady expressionless gaze to where they were sitting, and didn't speak. Then he turned his head and muttered something to the other two and they got out. One was a fat boy in black trousers and a red sweat shirt with a silver stallion embossed on the front of it. He moved around on the right side of them and stood staring, his mouth partly open in a kind of loose grin. The other had on khaki pants and a blue striped coat and a gray hat pulled down very low, hiding most of his face. He came around slowly on the left side. Neither spoke.

The driver got out of the car and stood by the side of it, looking down at them. He was an older man than the other two. His hair was just beginning to gray and he wore silver-rimmed spectacles that gave him a scholarly look. He had a long creased face and didn't have on any shirt or undershirt. He had on blue jeans that were too tight for him and was holding a black hat and a gun. The two boys also had guns.

"We've had an ACCIDENT!" the children screamed.

The grandmother had the peculiar feeling that the bespectacled man was someone she knew. His face was as familiar to her as if she had known him all her life but she could not recall who he was. He moved away from the car and began to come down the embankment, placing his feet carefully so that he wouldn't slip. He had on tan and white shoes and no socks, and his ankles were red and thin. "Good afternoon," he said. "I see you all had you a little spill."

"We turned over twice!" said the grandmother.

"Oncet," he corrected. "We seen it happen. Try their car and see will it run, Hiram," he said quietly to the boy with the gray hat.

"What you got that gun for?" John Wesley asked. "Whatcha gonna do with that gun?"

"Lady," the man said to the children's mother, "would you mind calling them children to sit down by you? Children make me nervous. I want all you all to sit down right together there where you're at."

"What are you telling US what to do for?" June Star asked.

Behind them the line of woods gaped like a dark open mouth. "Come here," said their mother.

"Look here now," Bailey began suddenly, "we're in a predicament! We're in . . ."

The grandmother shrieked. She scrambled to her feet and stood staring. "You're The Misfit!" she said. "I recognized you at once!"

"Yes'm," the man said, smiling slightly as if he were pleased in spite of himself to be known, "but it would have been better for all of you, lady, if you hadn't of reckernized me."

Bailey turned his head sharply and said something to his mother that shocked even the children. The old lady began to cry and The Misfit reddened.

"Lady," he said, "don't you get upset. Sometimes a man says things he don't mean. I don't reckon he meant to talk to you thataway."

"You wouldn't shoot a lady, would you?" the grandmother said and removed a clean handkerchief from her cuff and began to slap at her eyes with it.

The Misfit pointed the toe of his shoe into the ground and made a little hole and then covered it up again. "I would hate to have to," he said.

"Listen," the grandmother almost screamed, "I know you're a good man. You don't look a bit like you have common blood. I know you must come from nice people!"

"Yes mam," he said, "finest people in the world." When he smiled he showed a row of strong white teeth. "God never made a finer woman than my mother and my daddy's heart was pure gold," he said. The boy with the red sweat shirt had come around behind them and was standing with his gun at his hip. The Misfit squatted down on the ground. "Watch them children, Bobby Lee," he said. "You know they make me nervous." He looked at the six of them huddled together in front of him and he seemed to be embarrassed as if he couldn't think of anything to say. "Ain't a cloud in the sky," he remarked, looking up at it. "Don't see no sun but don't see no cloud neither."

"Yes, it's a beautiful day," said the grandmother. "Listen," she said, "you 90
shouldn't call yourself The Misfit because I know you're a good man at heart. I can just look at you and tell."

"Hush!" Bailey yelled. "Hush! Everybody shut up and let me handle this!" He was squatting in the position of a runner about to sprint forward but he didn't move.

"I pre-chate that, lady," The Misfit said and drew a little circle in the ground with the butt of his gun.

"It'll take a half a hour to fix this here car," Hiram called, looking over the raised hood of it.

"Well, first you and Bobby Lee get him and that little boy to step over yonder with you," The Misfit said, pointing to Bailey and John Wesley. "The boys want to ast you something," he said to Bailey. "Would you mind stepping back in them woods there with them?"

"Listen," Bailey began, "we're in a terrible predicament! Nobody realizes 95
what this is," and his voice cracked. His eyes were as blue and intense as the parrots in his shirt and he remained perfectly still.

The grandmother reached up to adjust her hat brim as if she were going to the woods with him but it came off in her hand. She stood staring at it and after a second she let it fall on the ground. Hiram pulled Bailey up by the arm as if he were assisting an old man. John Wesley caught hold of his father's hand and Bobby Lee followed. They went off toward the woods and just as they reached the dark edge, Bailey turned and supporting himself against a gray naked pine trunk, he shouted, "I'll be back in a minute, Mamma, wait on me!"

"Come back this instant!" his mother shrilled but they all disappeared into the woods.

"Bailey Boy!" the grandmother called in a tragic voice but she found she was looking at The Misfit squatting on the ground in front of her. "I just know you're a good man," she said desperately. "You're not a bit common!"

"Nome, I ain't a good man," The Misfit said after a second as if he had considered her statement carefully, "but I ain't the worst in the world neither. My daddy said I was a different breed of dog from my brothers and sisters. 'You know,' Daddy said, 'it's some that can live their whole life out without asking about it and it's others has to know why it is, and this boy is one of the latters. He's going to be into everything!'" He put on his black hat and looked up suddenly and then away deep into the woods as if he were embarrassed again. "I'm sorry I don't have on a shirt before you ladies," he said, hunching his shoulders slightly. "We buried our clothes that we had on when we escaped and we're just making do until we can get better. We borrowed these from some folks we met," he explained.

"That's perfectly all right," the grandmother said. "Maybe Bailey has an extra 100
shirt in his suitcase."

"I'll look and see terrectly," The Misfit said.

"Where are they taking him?" the children's mother screamed.

"Daddy was a card himself," The Misfit said. "You couldn't put anything over on him. He never got in trouble with the Authorities though. Just had the knack of handling them."

"You could be honest too if you'd only try," said the grandmother. "Think how wonderful it would be to settle down and live a comfortable life and not have to think about somebody chasing you all the time."

105 The Misfit kept scratching in the ground with the butt of his gun as if he were thinking about it. "Yes'm, somebody is always after you," he murmured.

The grandmother noticed how thin his shoulder blades were just behind his hat because she was standing up looking down on him. "Do you ever pray?" she asked.

He shook his head. All she saw was the black hat wiggle between his shoulder blades. "Nome," he said.

There was a pistol shot from the woods, followed closely by another. Then silence. The old lady's head jerked around. She could hear the wind move through the tree tops like a long satisfied insuck of breath. "Bailey Boy!" she called.

"I was a gospel singer for a while," The Misfit said. "I been most everything. Been in the arm service, both land and sea, at home and abroad, been twict married, been an undertaker, been with the railroads, plowed Mother Earth, been in a tornado, seen a man burnt alive oncet," and looked up at the children's mother and the little girl who were sitting close together, their faces white and their eyes glassy; "I even seen a woman flogged," he said.

110 "Pray, pray," the grandmother began, "pray, pray. . . ."

"I never was a bad boy that I remember of," The Misfit said in an almost dreamy voice, "but somewheres along the line I done something wrong and got sent to the penitentiary. I was buried alive," and he looked up and held her attention to him by a steady stare.

"That's when you should have started to pray," she said. "What did you do to get sent to the penitentiary that first time?"

"Turn to the right, it was a wall," The Misfit said, looking up again at the cloudless sky. "Turn to the left, it was a wall. Look up it was a ceiling, look down it was a floor. I forgot what I done, lady. I set there and set there, trying to remember what it was I done and I ain't recalled it to this day. Oncet in a while, I would think it was coming to me, but it never come."

"Maybe they put you in by mistake," the old lady said vaguely.

115 "Nome," he said. "It wasn't no mistake. They had the papers on me."

"You must have stolen something," she said.

The Misfit sneered slightly. "Nobody had nothing I wanted," he said. "It was a head-doctor at the penitentiary said what I had done was kill my daddy but I known that for a lie. My daddy died in nineteen ought nineteen of the epidemic flu and I never had a thing to do with it. He was buried in the Mount Hopewell Baptist churchyard and you can go there and see for yourself."

"If you would pray," the old lady said, "Jesus would help you."

"That's right," The Misfit said.

120 "Well then, why don't you pray?" she asked trembling with delight suddenly.

"I don't want no hep," he said. "I'm doing all right by myself."

Bobby Lee and Hiram came ambling back from the woods. Bobby Lee was dragging a yellow shirt with bright blue parrots in it.

"Thow me that shirt, Bobby Lee," The Misfit said. The shirt came flying at him and landed on his shoulder and he put it on. The grandmother couldn't name what the shirt reminded her of. "No, lady," The Misfit said while he was buttoning it up, "I found out the crime don't matter. You can do one thing or you can do another, kill a man or take a tire off his car, because sooner or later you're going to forget what it was you done and just be punished for it."

The children's mother had begun to make heaving noises as if she couldn't get her breath. "Lady," he asked, "would you and that little girl like to step off yonder with Bobby Lee and Hiram and join your husband?"

"Yes, thank you," the mother said faintly. Her left arm dangled helplessly and 125
she was holding the baby, who had gone to sleep, in the other. "Hep that lady up, Hiram," The Misfit said as she struggled to climb out of the ditch, "and Bobby Lee, you hold onto that little girl's hand."

"I don't want to hold hands with him," June Star said. "He reminds me of a pig."

The fat boy blushed and laughed and caught her by the arm and pulled her off into the woods after Hiram and her mother.

Alone with The Misfit, the grandmother found that she had lost her voice. There was not a cloud in the sky nor any sun. There was nothing around her but woods. She wanted to tell him that he must pray. She opened and closed her mouth several times before anything came out. Finally she found herself saying, "Jesus, Jesus," meaning, Jesus will help you, but the way she was saying it, it sounded as if she might be cursing.

"Yes'm," The Misfit said as if he agreed. "Jesus thown everything off balance. It was the same case with Him as with me except He hadn't committed any crime and they could prove I had committed one because they had the papers on me. Of course," he said, "they never shown me my papers. That's why I sign myself now. I said long ago, you get you a signature and sign everything you do and keep a copy of it. Then you'll know what you done and you can hold up the crime to the punishment and see do they match and in the end you'll have something to prove you ain't been treated right. I call myself The Misfit," he said, "because I can't make what all I done wrong fit what all I gone through in punishment."

There was a piercing scream from the woods, followed closely by a pistol 130
report. "Does it seem right to you, lady, that one is punished a heap and another ain't punished at all?"

"Jesus!" the old lady cried. "You've got good blood! I know you wouldn't shoot a lady! I know you come from nice people! Pray! Jesus, you ought not to shoot a lady. I'll give you all the money I've got!"

"Lady," The Misfit said, looking beyond her far into the woods, "there never was a body that give the undertaker a tip."

There were two more pistol reports and the grandmother raised her head like a parched old turkey hen crying for water and called, "Bailey Boy, Bailey Boy!" as if her heart would break.

"Jesus was the only One that ever raised the dead." The Misfit continued, "and He shouldn't have done it. He thown everything off balance. If He did what He said, then it's nothing for you to do but thow away everything and follow Him, and if He didn't, then it's nothing for you to do but enjoy the few minutes you got left the best way you can—by killing somebody or burning down his house or doing some other meanness to him. No pleasure but meanness," he said and his voice had become almost a snarl.

135 "Maybe He didn't raise the dead," the old lady mumbled, not knowing what she was saying and feeling so dizzy that she sank down in the ditch with her legs twisted under her.

"I wasn't there so I can't say He didn't," The Misfit said. "I wisht I had of been there," he said, hitting the ground with his fist. "It ain't right I wasn't there because if I had of been there I would of known. Listen lady," he said in a high voice, "if I had of been there I would of known and I wouldn't be like I am now." His voice seemed about to crack and the grandmother's head cleared for an instant. She saw the man's face twisted close to her own as if he were going to cry and she murmured, "Why you're one of my babies. You're one of my own children!" She reached out and touched him on the shoulder. The Misfit sprang back as if a snake had bitten him and shot her three times through the chest. Then he put his gun down on the ground and took off his glasses and began to clean them.

Hiram and Bobby Lee returned from the woods and stood over the ditch, looking down at the grandmother who half sat and half lay in a puddle of blood with her legs crossed under her like a child's and her face smiling up at the cloudless sky.

Without his glasses, The Misfit's eyes were red-rimmed and pale and defenseless-looking. "Take her off and thow her where you thown the others," he said, picking up the cat that was rubbing itself against his leg.

"She was a talker, wasn't she?" Bobby Lee said, sliding down the ditch with a yodel.

140 "She would of been a good woman," The Misfit said, "if it had been somebody there to shoot her every minute of her life."

"Some fun!" Bobby Lee said.

"Shut up, Bobby Lee," The Misfit said. "It's no real pleasure in life."

1953

FLANNERY O'CONNOR

Good Country People

Besides the neutral expression that she wore when she was alone, Mrs. Freeman had two others, forward and reverse, that she used for all her human dealings. Her forward expression was steady and driving like the advance of a heavy truck. Her eyes never swerved to left or right but turned as the story turned as if they followed a yellow line down the center of it. She seldom used the other expression because it was not often necessary for her to retract a statement, but when she did, her face came to a complete stop, there was an almost imperceptible movement of her black eyes, during which they seemed to be receding, and then the observer would see that Mrs. Freeman, though she might stand there as real as several grain sacks thrown on top of each other, was no longer there in spirit. As for getting anything across to her when this was the case, Mrs. Hopewell had given it up. She might talk her head off. Mrs. Freeman could never be brought to admit herself wrong on any point. She would stand there and if she could be brought to say anything, it was something like, "Well, I wouldn't of said it was and I wouldn't of said it wasn't," or letting her gaze range over the top kitchen shelf where there was an assortment of dusty bottles, she might remark, "I see you ain't ate many of them figs you put up last summer."

They carried on their most important business in the kitchen at breakfast. Every morning Mrs. Hopewell got up at seven o'clock and lit her gas heater and Joy's. Joy was her daughter, a large blonde girl who had an artificial leg. Mrs. Hopewell thought of her as a child though she was thirty-two years old and highly educated. Joy would get up while her mother was eating and lumber into the bathroom and slam the door, and before long, Mrs. Freeman would arrive at the back door. Joy would hear her mother call, "Come on in," and then they would talk for a while in low voices that were indistinguishable in the bathroom. By the time Joy came in, they had usually finished the weather report and were on one or the other of Mrs. Freeman's daughters, Glynese or Carramae, Joy called them Glycerin and Caramel. Glynese, a redhead, was eighteen and had many admirers; Carramae, a blonde, was only fifteen but already married and pregnant. She could not keep anything on her stomach. Every morning Mrs. Freeman told Mrs. Hopewell how many times she had vomited since the last report.

Mrs. Hopewell liked to tell people that Glynese and Carramae were two of the finest girls she knew and that Mrs. Freeman was a *lady* and that she was never ashamed to take her anywhere or introduce her to anybody they might meet. Then she would tell how she had happened to hire the Freemans in the first place and how they were a godsend to her and how she had had them four years. The reason for her keeping them so long was that they were not trash. They were good country people. She had telephoned the man whose name they had given as a reference and he had told her that Mr. Freeman was a good farmer but that his wife was the nosiest woman ever to walk the earth. "She's got to be into everything," the man said. "If she don't get there before the dust settles, you can bet she's dead, that's all. She'll want to know all your business. I can stand him real good," he had said, "but me nor my wife neither could have stood that woman one more minute on this place." That had put Mrs. Hopewell off for a few days.

She had hired them in the end because there were no other applicants but she had made up her mind beforehand exactly how she would handle the woman. Since she was the type who had to be into everything, then, Mrs. Hopewell had decided, she would not only let her be into everything, she would *see to it* that she was into everything—she would give her the responsibility of everything, she would put her in charge. Mrs. Hopewell had no bad qualities of her own but she was able to use other people's in such a constructive way that she never felt the lack. She had hired the Freemans and she had kept them four years.

5 Nothing is perfect. This was one of Mrs. Hopewell's favorite sayings. Another was: that is life! And still another, the most important, was: well, other people have their opinions too. She would make these statements, usually at the table, in a tone of gentle insistence as if no one held them but her, and the large hulking Joy, whose constant outrage had obliterated every expression from her face, would stare just a little to the side of her, her eyes icy blue, with the look of someone who has achieved blindness by an act of will and means to keep it.

When Mrs. Hopewell said to Mrs. Freeman that life was like that, Mrs. Freeman would say, "I always said so myself." Nothing had been arrived at by anyone that had not first been arrived at by her. She was quicker than Mr. Freeman. When Mrs. Hopewell said to her after they had been on the place a while, "You know, you're the wheel behind the wheel," and winked, Mrs. Freeman had said, "I know it. I've always been quick. It's some that are quicker than others."

"Everybody is different," Mrs. Hopewell said.

"Yes, most people is," Mrs. Freeman said.

"It takes all kinds to make the world."

10 "I always said it did myself."

The girl was used to this kind of dialogue for breakfast and more of it for dinner; sometimes they had it for supper too. When they had no guest they ate in the kitchen because that was easier. Mrs. Freeman always managed to arrive at some point during the meal and to watch them finish it. She would stand in the doorway if it were summer but in the winter she would stand with one elbow on top of the refrigerator and look down on them, or she would stand by the gas heater, lifting the back of her skirt slightly. Occasionally she would stand against the wall and roll her head from side to side. At no time was she in any hurry to leave. All this was very trying on Mrs. Hopewell but she was a woman of great patience. She realized that nothing is perfect and that in the Freemans she had good country people and that if, in this day and age, you get good country people, you had better hang onto them.

She had had plenty of experience with trash. Before the Freemans she had averaged one tenant family a year. The wives of these farmers were not the kind you would want to be around you for very long. Mrs. Hopewell, who had divorced her husband long ago, needed someone to walk over the fields with her; and when Joy had to be impressed for these services, her remarks were usually so ugly and her face so glum that Mrs. Hopewell would say, "If you can't come pleasantly, I don't want you at all," to which the girl, standing square and rigid-shouldered with her neck thrust slightly forward, would reply, "If you want me, here I am—LIKE I AM."

Mrs. Hopewell excused this attitude because of the leg (which had been shot off in a hunting accident when Joy was ten). It was hard for Mrs. Hopewell to realize that her child was thirty-two now and that for more than twenty years she had had only one leg. She thought of her still as a child because it tore her heart to think instead of the poor stout girl in her thirties who had never danced a step or had any *normal* good times. Her name was really Joy but as soon as she was twenty-one and away from home, she had had it legally changed. Mrs. Hopewell was certain that she had thought and thought until she had hit upon the ugliest name in any language. Then she had gone and had the beautiful name, Joy, changed without telling her mother until after she had done it. Her legal name was Hulga.

When Mrs. Hopewell thought the name, Hulga, she thought of the broad blank hull of a battleship. She would not use it. She continued to call her Joy to which the girl responded but in a purely mechanical way.

15 Hulga had learned to tolerate Mrs. Freeman who saved her from taking walks with her mother. Even Glynese and Carramae were useful when they

occupied attention that might otherwise have been directed at her. At first she had thought she could not stand Mrs. Freeman for she had found that it was not possible to be rude to her. Mrs. Freeman would take on strange resentments and for days together she would be sullen but the source of her displeasure was always obscure; a direct attack, a positive leer, blatant ugliness to her face—these never touched her. And without warning one day, she began calling her Hulga.

She did not call her that in front of Mrs. Hopewell who would have been incensed but when she and the girl happened to be out of the house together, she would say something and add the name Hulga to the end of it, and the big spectacled Joy-Hulga would scowl and redden as if her privacy had been intruded upon. She considered the name her personal affair. She had arrived at it first purely on the basis of its ugly sound and then the full genius of its fitness had struck her. She had a vision of the name working like the ugly sweating Vulcan who stayed in the furnace and to whom, presumably, the goddess had to come when called. She saw it as the name of her highest creative act. One of her major triumphs was that her mother had not been able to turn her dust into Joy, but the greater one was that she had been able to turn it herself into Hulga. However, Mrs. Freeman's relish for using the name only irritated her. It was as if Mrs. Freeman's beady steel-pointed eyes had penetrated far enough behind her face to reach some secret fact. Something about her seemed to fascinate Mrs. Freeman and then one day Hulga realized that it was the artificial leg. Mrs. Freeman had a special fondness for the details of secret infections, hidden deformities, assaults upon children. Of diseases, she preferred the lingering or incurable. Hulga had heard Mrs. Hopewell give her the details of the hunting accident, how the leg had been literally blasted off, how she had never lost consciousness. Mrs. Freeman could listen to it any time as if it had happened an hour ago.

When Hulga stumped into the kitchen in the morning (she could walk without making the awful noise but she made it—Mrs. Hopewell was certain—because it was ugly-sounding), she glanced at them and did not speak. Mrs. Hopewell would be in her red kimono with her hair tied around her head in rags. She would be sitting at the table, finishing her breakfast and Mrs. Freeman would be hanging by her elbow outward from the refrigerator, looking down at the table. Hulga always put her eggs on the stove to boil and then stood over them with her arms folded, and Mrs. Hopewell would look at her—a kind of indirect gaze divided between her and Mrs. Freeman—and would think that if she would only keep herself up a little, she wouldn't be so bad looking. There was nothing wrong with her face that a pleasant expression wouldn't help. Mrs. Hopewell said that people who looked on the bright side of things would be beautiful even if they were not.

Whenever she looked at Joy this way, she could not help but feel that it would have been better if the child had not taken the Ph.D. It had certainly not brought her out any and now that she had it, there was no more excuse for her to go to school again. Mrs. Hopewell thought it was nice for girls to go to school to have a good time but Joy had "gone through." Anyhow, she would not have been strong enough to go again. The doctors had told Mrs. Hopewell that with the best of care, Joy might see forty-five. She had a weak heart. Joy had made it plain that if it had not been for this condition, she would be far from these red hills[1] and good country people. She would be in a university lecturing to people who knew what she was talking about. And Mrs. Hopewell could very well picture her there, looking like a scarecrow and lecturing to more of the same. Here she went about all day in a six-year-old skirt and a yellow sweat shirt with a faded cowboy on a horse embossed on it. She thought this was funny; Mrs. Hopewell thought it was idiotic and showed simply that she was still a child. She was brilliant but she didn't have a grain of sense. It seemed to Mrs. Hopewell that every year she grew less like other people and more like herself—bloated, rude, and squint-eyed. And she said such strange things! To her own mother she had said—without warning, without excuse, standing up in the middle of a meal with her face purple and her mouth half full—"Woman! do you ever look inside? Do you ever look inside and see what you are *not*? God!" she had cried sinking down again and staring at her plate, "Malebranche[2] was right: we are not our own light. We are not our own light!" Mrs. Hopewell had no idea to this day what brought that on. She had only made the remark, hoping Joy would take it in, that a smile never hurt anyone.

The girl had taken the Ph.D. in philosophy and this left Mrs. Hopewell at a complete loss. You could say, "My daughter is a nurse," or "My daughter is a schoolteacher," or even, "My daughter is a chemical engineer." You could not say, "My daughter is a philosopher." That was something that had ended with the Greeks and Romans. All day Joy sat on her neck in a deep chair, reading. Sometimes she went for walks but she didn't like dogs or cats or birds or flowers or nature or nice young men. She looked at nice young men as if she could smell their stupidity.

20 One day Mrs. Hopewell had picked up one of the books the girl had just put down and opening it at random, she read, "Science, on the other hand, has to assert its soberness and seriousness afresh and declare that it is concerned solely with what-is. Nothing—how can it be for science anything but a horror and a phantasm? If science is right, then one thing stands firm: science wishes to know nothing of nothing. Such is after all the strictly scientific approach to Nothing. We know it by wishing to know nothing of Nothing."[3] These words had been underlined with a blue pencil and they worked on Mrs. Hopewell like some evil incantation in gibberish. She shut the book quickly and went out of the room as if she were having a chill.

This morning when the girl came in, Mrs. Freeman was on Carramae. "She thrown up four times after supper," she said, "and was up twict in the night after three o'clock. Yesterday she didn't do nothing but ramble in the bureau drawer. All she did. Stand up there and see what she could run up on."

"She's got to eat," Mrs. Hopewell muttered, sipping her coffee, while she watched Joy's back at the stove. She was wondering what the child had said to

1. Like many of O'Connor's stories, this one is set in rural Georgia, in a hilly landscape of red soil similar to the surroundings of O'Connor's mother's farm, Andalusia, near Milledgeville, Georgia.
2. Nicolas Malebranche (1638–1715), renowned philosopher and author of *The Search after Truth*, expressing his skepticism about the human capacity to know one's own mind or the world except through God. Here, Hulga rephrases Malebranche's quotation from St. Augustine to the effect that we are not our own "light."
3. Passage from German philosopher Martin Heidegger's (1889–1976) inaugural lecture (1929) at the University of Freiburg, "What Is Metaphysics?"

the Bible salesman. She could not imagine what kind of a conversation she could possibly have had with him.

He was a tall gaunt hatless youth who had called yesterday to sell them a Bible. He had appeared at the door, carrying a large black suitcase that weighted him so heavily on one side that he had to brace himself against the door facing. He seemed on the point of collapse but he said in a cheerful voice, "Good morning, Mrs. Cedars!" and set the suitcase down on the mat. He was not a bad-looking young man though he had on a bright blue suit and yellow socks that were not pulled up far enough. He had prominent face bones and a streak of sticky-looking brown hair falling across his forehead.

"I'm Mrs. Hopewell," she said.

25 "Oh!" he said, pretending to look puzzled but with his eyes sparkling, "I saw it said 'The Cedars' on the mailbox so I thought you was Mrs. Cedars!" and he burst out in a pleasant laugh. He picked up the satchel and under cover of a pant, he fell forward into her hall. It was rather as if the suitcase had moved first, jerking him after it. "Mrs. Hopewell!" he said and grabbed her hand. "I hope you are well!" and he laughed again and then all at once his face sobered completely. He paused and gave her a straight earnest look and said, "Lady, I've come to speak of serious things."

"Well, come in," she muttered, none too pleased because her dinner was almost ready. He came into the parlor and sat down on the edge of a straight chair and put the suitcase between his feet and glanced around the room as if he were sizing her up by it. Her silver gleamed on the two sideboards; she decided he had never been in a room as elegant as this.

"Mrs. Hopewell," he began, using her name in a way that sounded almost intimate, "I know you believe in Chrustian service."

"Well yes," she murmured.

"I know," he said and paused, looking very wise with his head cocked on one side, "that you're a good woman. Friends have told me."

30 Mrs. Hopewell never liked to be taken for a fool. "What are you selling?" she asked.

"Bibles," the young man said and his eye raced around the room before he added, "I see you have no family Bible in your parlor, I see that is the one lack you got!"

Mrs. Hopewell could not say, "My daughter is an atheist and won't let me keep the Bible in the parlor." She said, stiffening slightly, "I keep my Bible by my bedside." This was not the truth. It was in the attic somewhere.

"Lady," he said, "the word of God ought to be in the parlor."

"Well, I think that's a matter of taste," she began. "I think. . . ."

35 "Lady," he said, "for a Chrustian, the word of God ought to be in every room in the house besides in his heart. I know you're a Chrustian because I can see it in every line of your face."

She stood up and said, "Well, young man, I don't want to buy a Bible and I smell my dinner burning."

He didn't get up. He began to twist his hands and looking down at them, he said softly, "Well lady, I'll tell you the truth—not many people want to buy one nowadays and besides, I know I'm real simple. I don't know how to say a thing but to say it. I'm just a country boy." He glanced up into her unfriendly face. "People like you don't like to fool with country people like me!"

"Why!" she cried, "good country people are the salt of the earth! Besides, we all have different ways of doing, it takes all kinds to make the world go 'round. That's life!"

"You said a mouthful," he said.

"Why, I think there aren't enough good country people in the world!" she said, stirred. "I think that's what's wrong with it!"

His face had brightened. "I didn't inraduce myself," he said. "I'm Manley Pointer from out in the country around Willohobie, not even from a place, just from near a place."

"You wait a minute," she said. "I have to see about my dinner." She went out to the kitchen and found Joy standing near the door where she had been listening.

"Get rid of the salt of the earth," she said, "and let's eat."

Mrs. Hopewell gave her a pained look and turned the heat down under the vegetables. "*I* can't be rude to anybody," she murmured and went back into the parlor.

He had opened the suitcase and was sitting with a Bible on each knee.

"You might as well put those up," she told him. "I don't want one."

"I appreciate your honesty," he said. "You don't see any more real honest people unless you go way out in the country."

"I know," she said, "real genuine folks!" Through the crack in the door she heard a groan.

"I guess a lot of boys come telling you they're working their way through college," he said, "but I'm not going to tell you that. Somehow," he said, "I don't want to go to college. I want to devote my life to Chrustian service. See," he said, lowering his voice, "I got this heart condition. I may not live long. When you know it's something wrong with you and you may not live long, well then, lady . . ." He paused, with his mouth open, and stared at her.

He and Joy had the same condition! She knew that her eyes were filling with tears but she collected herself quickly and murmured, "Won't you stay for dinner? We'd love to have you!" and was sorry the instant she heard herself say it.

"Yes mam," he said in an abashed voice, "I would sher love to do that!"

Joy had given him one look on being introduced to him and then throughout the meal had not glanced at him again. He had addressed several remarks to her, which she had pretended not to hear. Mrs. Hopewell could not understand deliberate rudeness, although she lived with it, and she felt she had always to overflow with hospitality to make up for Joy's lack of courtesy. She urged him to talk about himself and he did. He said he was the seventh child of twelve and that his father had been crushed under a tree when he himself was eight year old. He had been crushed very badly, in fact, almost cut in two and was practically not recognizable. His mother had got along the best she could by hard working and she had always seen that her children went to Sunday School and that they read the Bible every evening. He was now nineteen year old and he had been selling Bibles for four months. In that time he had sold seventy-seven Bibles and had the promise of two more sales. He wanted to become a missionary because he thought that was the way you could do most for people. "He who losest his life shall find it," he said simply and he was so sincere, so genuine and earnest that Mrs. Hopewell would not for the world have smiled. He prevented his peas from sliding onto the table by blocking them with a piece of bread which he later cleaned his plate with. She could see Joy observing sidewise how he handled his knife and fork and she saw too that every few minutes, the boy would dart a keen appraising glance at the girl as if he were trying to attract her attention.

After dinner Joy cleared the dishes off the table and disappeared and Mrs. Hopewell was left to talk with him. He told her again about his childhood and his father's accident and about various things that had happened to him. Every five minutes or so she would stifle a yawn. He sat for two hours until finally she told him she must go because she had an appointment in town. He packed his Bibles and thanked her and prepared to leave, but in the doorway he stopped and wrung her hand and said that not on any of his trips had he met a lady as nice as her and he asked if he could come again. She had said she would always be happy to see him.

Joy had been standing in the road, apparently looking at something in the distance, when he came down the steps toward her, bent to the side with his heavy valise. He stopped where she was standing and confronted her directly. Mrs. Hopewell could not hear what he said but she trembled to think what Joy would say to him. She could see that after a minute Joy said something and that then the boy began to speak again, making an excited gesture with his free hand. After a minute Joy said something else at which the boy began to speak once more. Then to her amazement, Mrs. Hopewell saw the two of them walk off together, toward the gate. Joy had walked all the way to the gate with him and Mrs. Hopewell could not imagine what they had said to each other, and she had not yet dared to ask.

Mrs. Freeman was insisting upon her attention. She had moved from the 55
refrigerator to the heater so that Mrs. Hopewell had to turn and face her in order to seem to be listening. "Glynese gone out with Harvey Hill again last night," she said. "She had this sty."

"Hill," Mrs. Hopewell said absently, "is that the one who works in the garage?"

"Nome,[4] he's the one that goes to chiropracter school," Mrs. Freeman said. "She had this sty. Been had it two days. So she says when he brought her in the other night he says, 'Lemme get rid of that sty for you,' and she says, 'How?' and he says, 'You just lay yourself down acrost the seat of that car and I'll show you.' So she done it and he popped her neck. Kept on a-popping it several times until she made him quit. This morning," Mrs. Freeman said, "she ain't got no sty. She ain't got no traces of a sty."

"I never heard of that before," Mrs. Hopewell said.

"He ast her to marry him before the Ordinary,"[5] Mrs. Freeman went on, "and she told him she wasn't going to be married in no *office*."

"Well, Glynese is a fine girl," Mrs. Hopewell said. "Glynese and Carramae 60
are both fine girls."

"Carramae said when her and Lyman was married Lyman said it sure felt sacred to him. She said he said he wouldn't take five hundred dollars for being married by a preacher."

4. Contraction of "No, ma'am."
5. That is, a legal official, in the local county courthouse.

"How much would he take?" the girl asked from the stove.

"He said he wouldn't take five hundred dollars," Mrs. Freeman repeated.

"Well we all have work to do," Mrs. Hopewell said.

65 "Lyman said it just felt more sacred to him," Mrs. Freeman said. "The doctor wants Carramae to eat prunes. Says instead of medicine. Says them cramps is coming from pressure. You know where I think it is?"

"She'll be better in a few weeks," Mrs. Hopewell said.

"In the tube,"[6] Mrs. Freeman said. "Else she wouldn't be as sick as she is."

Hulga had cracked her two eggs into a saucer and was bringing them to the table along with a cup of coffee that she had filled too full. She sat down carefully and began to eat, meaning to keep Mrs. Freeman there by questions if for any reason she showed an inclination to leave. She could perceive her mother's eye on her. The first round-about question would be about the Bible salesman and she did not wish to bring it on. "How did he pop her neck?" she asked.

Mrs. Freeman went into a description of how he had popped her neck. She said he owned a '55 Mercury but that Glynese said she would rather marry a man with only a '36 Plymouth who would be married by a preacher. The girl asked what if he had a '32 Plymouth and Mrs. Freeman said what Glynese had said was a '36 Plymouth.

70 Mrs. Hopewell said there were not many girls with Glynese's common sense. She said what she admired in those girls was their common sense. She said that reminded her that they had had a nice visitor yesterday, a young man selling Bibles. "Lord," she said, "he bored me to death but he was so sincere and genuine I couldn't be rude to him. He was just good country people, you know," she said, "—just the salt of the earth."

"I seen him walk up," Mrs. Freeman said, "and then later—I seen him walk off," and Hulga could feel the slight shift in her voice, the slight insinuation, that he had not walked off alone, had he? Her face remained expressionless but the color rose into her neck and she seemed to swallow it down with the next spoonful of egg. Mrs. Freeman was looking at her as if they had a secret together.

"Well, it takes all kinds of people to make the world go 'round," Mrs. Hopewell said. "It's very good we aren't all alike."

"Some people are more alike than others," Mrs. Freeman said.

Hulga got up and stumped, with about twice the noise that was necessary, into her room and locked the door. She was to meet the Bible salesman at ten o'clock at the gate. She had thought about it half the night. She had started thinking of it as a great joke and then she had begun to see profound implications in it. She had lain in bed imagining dialogues for them that were insane on the surface but that reached below to depths that no Bible salesman would be aware of. Their conversation yesterday had been of this kind.

75 He had stopped in front of her and had simply stood there. His face was bony and sweaty and bright, with a little pointed nose in the center of it, and his look was different from what it had been at the dinner table. He was gazing at her with open curiosity, with fascination, like a child watching a new fantastic ani-

6. That is, an ectopic or tubal pregnancy outside the uterus, a life-threatening condition for both mother and baby.

mal at the zoo, and he was breathing as if he had run a great distance to reach her. His gaze seemed somehow familiar but she could not think where she had been regarded with it before. For almost a minute he didn't say anything. Then on what seemed an insuck of breath, he whispered, "You ever ate a chicken that was two days old?"

The girl looked at him stonily. He might have just put this question up for consideration at the meeting of a philosophical association. "Yes," she presently replied as if she had considered it from all angles.

"It must have been mighty small!" he said triumphantly and shook all over with little nervous giggles, getting very red in the face, and subsiding finally into his gaze of complete admiration, while the girl's expression remained exactly the same.

"How old are you?" he asked softly.

She waited some time before she answered. Then in a flat voice she said, "Seventeen."

His smiles came in succession like waves breaking on the surface of a little lake. "I see you got a wooden leg," he said. "I think you're brave. I think you're real sweet."

The girl stood blank and solid and silent.

"Walk to the gate with me," he said. "You're a brave sweet little thing and I liked you the minute I seen you walk in the door."

Hulga began to move forward.

"What's your name?" he asked, smiling down on the top of her head.

"Hulga," she said.

"Hulga," he murmured, "Hulga. Hulga. I never heard of anybody name Hulga before. You're shy, aren't you, Hulga?" he asked.

She nodded, watching his large red hand on the handle of the giant valise.

"I like girls that wear glasses," he said. "I think a lot. I'm not like these people that a serious thought don't ever enter their heads. It's because I may die."

"I may die too," she said suddenly and looked up at him. His eyes were very small and brown, glittering feverishly.

"Listen," he said, "don't you think some people was meant to meet on account of what all they got in common and all? Like they both think serious thoughts and all?" He shifted the valise to his other hand so that the hand nearest her was free. He caught hold of her elbow and shook it a little. "I don't work on Saturday," he said. "I like to walk in the woods and see what Mother Nature is wearing. O'er the hills and far away. Pic-nics and things. Couldn't we go on a pic-nic tomorrow? Say yes, Hulga," he said and gave her a dying look as if he felt his insides about to drop out of him. He had even seemed to sway slightly toward her.

During the night she had imagined that she seduced him. She imagined that the two of them walked on the place until they came to the storage barn beyond the two back fields and there, she imagined, that things came to such a pass that she very easily seduced him and that then, of course, she had to reckon with his remorse. True genius can get an idea across even to an inferior mind. She imagined that she took his remorse in hand and changed it into a deeper understanding of life. She took all his shame away and turned it into something useful.

She set off for the gate at exactly ten o'clock, escaping without drawing Mrs. Hopewell's attention. She didn't take anything to eat, forgetting that food is usually taken on a picnic. She wore a pair of slacks and a dirty white shirt, and as an afterthought, she had put some Vapex[7] on the collar of it since she did not own any perfume. When she reached the gate no one was there.

She looked up and down the empty highway and had the furious feeling that she had been tricked, that he had only meant to make her walk to the gate after the idea of him. Then suddenly he stood up, very tall, from behind a bush on the opposite embankment. Smiling, he lifted his hat which was new and wide-brimmed. He had not worn it yesterday and she wondered if he had bought it for the occasion. It was toast-colored with a red and white band around it and was slightly too large for him. He stepped from behind the bush still carrying the black valise. He had on the same suit and the same yellow socks sucked down in his shoes from walking. He crossed the highway and said, "I knew you'd come!"

The girl wondered acidly how he had known this. She pointed to the valise and asked, "Why did you bring your Bibles?"

95 He took her elbow, smiling down on her as if he could not stop. "You can never tell when you'll need the word of God, Hulga," he said. She had a moment in which she doubted that this was actually happening and then they began to climb the embankment. They went down into the pasture toward the woods. The boy walked lightly by her side, bouncing on his toes. The valise did not seem to be heavy today; he even swung it. They crossed half the pasture without saying anything and then, putting his hand easily on the small of her back, he asked softly, "Where does your wooden leg join on?"

She turned an ugly red and glared at him and for an instant the boy looked abashed. "I didn't mean you no harm," he said. "I only meant you're so brave and all. I guess God takes care of you."

"No," she said, looking forward and walking fast, "I don't even believe in God."

At this he stopped and whistled. "No!" he exclaimed as if he were too astonished to say anything else.

She walked on and in a second he was bouncing at her side, fanning with his hat. "That's very unusual for a girl," he remarked, watching her out of the corner of his eye. When they reached the edge of the wood, he put his hand on her back again and drew her against him without a word and kissed her heavily.

100 The kiss, which had more pressure than feeling behind it, produced that extra surge of adrenaline in the girl that enables one to carry a packed trunk out of a burning house, but in her, the power went at once to the brain. Even before he released her, her mind, clear and detached and ironic anyway, was regarding him from a great distance, with amusement but with pity. She had never been kissed before and she was pleased to discover that it was an unexceptional experience and all a matter of the mind's control. Some people might enjoy drain water if they were told it was vodka. When the boy, looking expectant but uncertain, pushed her gently away, she turned and walked on, saying nothing as if such business, for her, were common enough.

7. Brand of nasal decongestant.

He came along panting at her side, trying to help her when he saw a root that she might trip over. He caught and held back the long swaying blades of thorn vine until she had passed beyond them. She led the way and he came breathing heavily behind her. Then they came out on a sunlit hillside, sloping softly into another one a little smaller. Beyond, they could see the rusted top of the old barn where the extra hay was stored.

The hill was sprinkled with small pink weeds. "Then you ain't saved?" he asked suddenly, stopping.

The girl smiled. It was the first time she had smiled at him at all. "In my economy," she said, "I'm saved and you are damned but I told you I didn't believe in God."

Nothing seemed to destroy the boy's look of admiration. He gazed at her now as if the fantastic animal at the zoo had put its paw through the bars and given him a loving poke. She thought he looked as if he wanted to kiss her again and she walked on before he had the chance.

"Ain't there somewheres we can sit down sometime?" he murmured, his 105
voice softening toward the end of the sentence.

"In that barn," she said.

They made for it rapidly as if it might slide away like a train. It was a large two-story barn, cool and dark inside. The boy pointed up the ladder that led into the loft and said, "It's too bad we can't go up there."

"Why can't we?" she asked.

"Yer leg," he said reverently.

The girl gave him a contemptuous look and putting both hands on the ladder, 110
she climbed it while he stood below, apparently awestruck. She pulled herself expertly through the opening and then looked down at him and said, "Well, come on if you're coming," and he began to climb the ladder, awkwardly bringing the suitcase with him.

"We won't need the Bible," she observed.

"You never can tell," he said, panting. After he had got into the loft, he was a few seconds catching his breath. She had sat down in a pile of straw. A wide sheath of sunlight, filled with dust particles, slanted over her. She lay back against a bale, her face turned away, looking out the front opening of the barn where hay was thrown from a wagon into the loft. The two pink-speckled hillsides lay back against a dark ridge of woods. The sky was cloudless and cold blue. The boy dropped down by her side and put one arm under her and the other over her and began methodically kissing her face, making little noises like a fish. He did not remove his hat but it was pushed far enough back not to interfere. When her glasses got in his way, he took them off of her and slipped them into his pocket.

The girl at first did not return any of the kisses but presently she began to and after she had put several on his cheek, she reached his lips and remained there, kissing him again and again as if she were trying to draw all the breath out of him. His breath was clear and sweet like a child's and the kisses were sticky like a child's. He mumbled about loving her and about knowing when he first seen her that he loved her, but the mumbling was like the sleepy fretting of a child being put to sleep by his mother. Her mind, throughout this, never stopped or lost itself for a second to her feelings. "You ain't said you loved me none," he whispered finally, pulling back from her. "You got to say that."

She looked away from him off into the hollow sky and then down at a black ridge and then down farther into what appeared to be two green swelling lakes. She didn't realize he had taken her glasses but this landscape could not seem exceptional to her for she seldom paid any close attention to her surroundings.

"You got to say it," he repeated. "You got to say you love me."

She was always careful how she committed herself. "In a sense," she began, "if you use the word loosely, you might say that. But it's not a word I use. I don't have illusions. I'm one of those people who see *through* to nothing."

The boy was frowning. "You got to say it. I said it and you got to say it," he said.

The girl looked at him almost tenderly. "You poor baby," she murmured. "It's just as well you don't understand," and she pulled him by the neck, face-down, against her. "We are all damned," she said, "but some of us have taken off our blindfolds and see that there's nothing to see. It's a kind of salvation."

The boy's astonished eyes looked blankly through the ends of her hair. "Okay," he almost whined, "but do you love me or don'tcher?"

"Yes," she said and added, "in a sense. But I must tell you something. There mustn't be anything dishonest between us." She lifted his head and looked him in the eye. "I am thirty years old," she said. "I have a number of degrees."

The boy's look was irritated but dogged. "I don't care," he said. "I don't care a thing about what all you done. I just want to know if you love me or don'tcher?" and he caught her to him and wildly planted her face with kisses until she said, "Yes, yes."

"Okay then," he said, letting her go. "Prove it."

She smiled, looking dreamily out on the shifty landscape. She had seduced him without even making up her mind to try. "How?" she asked, feeling that he should be delayed a little.

He leaned over and put his lips to her ear. "Show me where your wooden leg joins on," he whispered.

The girl uttered a sharp little cry and her face instantly drained of color. The obscenity of the suggestion was not what shocked her. As a child she had sometimes been subject to feelings of shame but education had removed the last traces of that as a good surgeon scrapes for cancer; she would no more have felt it over what he was asking than she would have believed in his Bible. But she was as sensitive about the artificial leg as a peacock about his tail. No one ever touched it but her. She took care of it as someone else would his soul, in private and almost with her own eyes turned away. "No," she said.

"I known it," he muttered, sitting up. "You're just playing me for a sucker."

"Oh no no!" she cried. "It joins on at the knee. Only at the knee. Why do you want to see it?"

The boy gave her a long penetrating look. "Because," he said, "it's what makes you different. You ain't like anybody else."

She sat staring at him. There was nothing about her face or her round freezing-blue eyes to indicate that this had moved her; but she felt as if her heart had stopped and left her mind to pump her blood. She decided that for the first time in her life she was face to face with real innocence. This boy, with an instinct that came from beyond wisdom, had touched the truth about her. When after a minute, she said in a hoarse high voice, "All right," it was like surrendering to him completely. It was like losing her own life and finding it again, miraculously, in his.

Very gently he began to roll the slack leg up. The artificial limb, in a white 130
sock and brown flat shoe, was bound in a heavy material like canvas and ended in an ugly jointure where it was attached to the stump. The boy's face and his voice were entirely reverent as he uncovered it and said, "Now show me how to take it off and on."

She took it off for him and put it back on again and then he took it off himself, handling it as tenderly as if it were a real one. "See!" he said with a delighted child's face. "Now I can do it myself!"

"Put it back on," she said. She was thinking that she would run away with him and that every night he would take the leg off and every morning put it back on again. "Put it back on," she said.

"Not yet," he murmured, setting it on its foot out of her reach. "Leave it off for a while. You got me instead."

She gave a little cry of alarm but he pushed her down and began to kiss her again. Without the leg she felt entirely dependent on him. Her brain seemed to have stopped thinking altogether and to be about some other function that it was not very good at. Different expressions raced back and forth over her face. Every now and then the boy, his eyes like two steel spikes, would glance behind him where the leg stood. Finally she pushed him off and said, "Put it back on me now."

"Wait," he said. He leaned the other way and pulled the valise toward him 135
and opened it. It had a pale blue spotted lining and there were only two Bibles in it. He took one of these out and opened the cover of it. It was hollow and contained a pocket flask of whiskey, a pack of cards, and a small blue box with printing on it. He laid these out in front of her one at a time in an evenly-spaced row, like one presenting offerings at the shrine of a goddess. He put the blue box in her hand. THIS PRODUCT TO BE USED ONLY FOR THE PREVENTION OF DISEASE, she read, and dropped it. The boy was unscrewing the top of the flask. He stopped and pointed, with a smile, to the deck of cards. It was not an ordinary deck but one with an obscene picture on the back of each card. "Take a swig," he said, offering her the bottle first. He held it in front of her, but like one mesmerized, she did not move.

Her voice when she spoke had an almost pleading sound. "Aren't you," she murmured, "aren't you just good country people?"

The boy cocked his head. He looked as if he were just beginning to understand that she might be trying to insult him. "Yeah," he said, curling his lip slightly, "but it ain't held me back none. I'm as good as you any day in the week."

"Give me my leg," she said.

He pushed it farther away with his foot. "Come on now, let's begin to have us a good time," he said coaxingly. "We ain't got to know one another good yet."

"Give me my leg!" she screamed and tried to lunge for it but he pushed her 140
down easily.

"What's the matter with you all of a sudden?" he asked, frowning as he screwed the top on the flask and put it quickly back inside the Bible. "You just a while ago said you didn't believe in nothing. I thought you was some girl!"

Her face was almost purple. "You're a Christian!" she hissed. "You're a fine Christian! You're just like them all—say one thing and do another. You're a perfect Christian, you're . . ."

The boy's mouth was set angrily. "I hope you don't think," he said in a lofty indignant tone, "that I believe in that crap! I may sell Bibles but I know which end is up and I wasn't born yesterday and I know where I'm going!"

"Give me my leg!" she screeched. He jumped up so quickly that she barely saw him sweep the cards and the blue box into the Bible and throw the Bible into the valise. She saw him grab the leg and then she saw it for an instant slanted forlornly across the inside of the suitcase with a Bible at either side of its opposite ends. He slammed the lid shut and snatched up the valise and swung it down the hole and then stepped through himself.

145 When all of him had passed but his head, he turned and regarded her with a look that no longer had any admiration in it. "I've gotten a lot of interesting things," he said. "One time I got a woman's glass eye this way. And you needn't to think you'll catch me because Pointer ain't really my name. I use a different name at every house I call at and don't stay nowhere long. And I'll tell you another thing, Hulga," he said, using the name as if he didn't think much of it, "you ain't so smart. I been believing in nothing ever since I was born!" and then the toast-colored hat disappeared down the hole and the girl was left, sitting on the straw in the dusty sunlight. When she turned her churning face toward the opening, she saw his blue figure struggling successfully over the green speckled lake.

Mrs. Hopewell and Mrs. Freeman, who were in the back pasture, digging up onions, saw him emerge a little later from the woods and head across the meadow toward the highway. "Why, that looks like that nice dull young man that tried to sell me a Bible yesterday," Mrs. Hopewell said, squinting. "He must have been selling them to the Negroes back in there. He was so simple," she said, "but I guess the world would be better off if we were all that simple."

Mrs. Freeman's gaze drove forward and just touched him before he disappeared under the hill. Then she returned her attention to the evil-smelling onion shoot she was lifting from the ground. "Some can't be that simple," she said. "I know I never could."

1955

FLANNERY O'CONNOR

Everything That Rises Must Converge

Her doctor had told Julian's mother that she must lose twenty pounds on account of her blood pressure, so on Wednesday nights Julian had to take her downtown on the bus for a reducing class at the Y. The reducing class was designed for working girls over fifty, who weighed from 165 to 200 pounds. His mother was one of the slimmer ones, but she said ladies did not tell their age or weight. She would not ride the buses by herself at night since they had been integrated, and because the reducing class was one of her few pleasures, necessary for her health, and *free*, she said Julian could at least put himself out to take her, considering all she did for him. Julian did not like to consider all she did for him, but every Wednesday night he braced himself and took her.

She was almost ready to go, standing before the hall mirror, putting on her hat, while he, his hands behind him, appeared pinned to the door frame, waiting like Saint Sebastian for the arrows to begin piercing him.[1] The hat was new and had cost her seven dollars and a half. She kept saying, "Maybe I shouldn't have paid that for it. No, I shouldn't have. I'll take it off and return it tomorrow. I shouldn't have bought it."

Julian raised his eyes to heaven. "Yes, you should have bought it," he said. "Put it on and let's go." It was a hideous hat. A purple velvet flap came down on one side of it and stood up on the other; the rest of it was green and looked like a cushion with the stuffing out. He decided it was less comical than jaunty and pathetic. Everything that gave her pleasure was small and depressed him.

She lifted the hat one more time and set it down slowly on top of her head. Two wings of gray hair protruded on either side of her florid face, but her eyes, sky-blue, were as innocent and untouched by experience as they must have been when she was ten. Were it not that she was a widow who had struggled fiercely to feed and clothe and put him through school and who was supporting him still, "until he got on his feet," she might have been a little girl that he had to take to town.

5 "It's all right, it's all right," he said. "Let's go." He opened the door himself and started down the walk to get her going. The sky was a dying violet and the houses stood out darkly against it, bulbous liver-colored monstrosities of a uniform ugliness though no two were alike. Since this had been a fashionable neighborhood forty years ago, his mother persisted in thinking they did well to have an apartment in it. Each house had a narrow collar of dirt around it in which sat, usually, a grubby child. Julian walked with his hands in his pockets, his head down and thrust forward and his eyes glazed with the determination to make himself completely numb during the time he would be sacrificed to her pleasure.

The door closed and he turned to find the dumpy figure, surmounted by the atrocious hat, coming toward him. "Well," she said, "you only live once and paying a little more for it, I at least won't meet myself coming and going."

"Some day I'll start making money," Julian said gloomily—he knew he never would—"and you can have one of those jokes whenever you take the fit." But first they would move. He visualized a place where the nearest neighbors would be three miles away on either side.

"I think you're doing fine," she said, drawing on her gloves. "You've only been out of school a year. Rome wasn't built in a day."

She was one of the few members of the Y reducing class who arrived in hat and gloves and who had a son who had been to college. "It takes time," she said, "and the world is in such a mess. This hat looked better on me than any of the others, though when she brought it out I said, 'Take that thing back. I wouldn't have it on my head,' and she said, 'Now wait till you see it on,' and when she put

1. Discovered to be a Christian, Sebastian, Roman commander in Milan, was tied to a tree, shot with arrows, and left for dead. (He recovered, but when he reasserted his faith he was clubbed to death.)

it on me, I said, 'We-ull,' and she said, 'If you ask me, that hat does something for you and you do something for the hat, and besides,' she said, 'with that hat, you won't meet yourself coming and going.'"

10 Julian thought he could have stood his lot better if she had been selfish, if she had been an old hag who drank and screamed at him. He walked along, saturated in depression, as if in the midst of his martyrdom he had lost his faith. Catching sight of his long, hopeless, irritated face, she stopped suddenly with a grief-stricken look, and pulled back on his arm. "Wait on me," she said. "I'm going back to the house and take this thing off and tomorrow I'm going to return it. I was out of my head. I can pay the gas bill with that seven-fifty."

He caught her arm in a vicious grip. "You are not going to take it back," he said. "I like it."

"Well," she said, "I don't think I ought . . ."

"Shut up and enjoy it," he muttered, more depressed than ever.

"With the world in the mess it's in," she said, "it's a wonder we can enjoy anything. I tell you, the bottom rail is on the top."

15 Julian sighed.

"Of course," she said, "if you know who you are, you can go anywhere." She said this every time he took her to the reducing class. "Most of them in it are not our kind of people," she said, "but I can be gracious to anybody. I know who I am."

"They don't give a damn for your graciousness," Julian said savagely. "Knowing who you are is good for one generation only. You haven't the foggiest idea where you stand now or who you are."

She stopped and allowed her eyes to flash at him. "I most certainly do know who I am," she said, "and if you don't know who you are, I'm ashamed of you."

"Oh hell," Julian said.

20 "Your great-grandfather was a former governor of this state," she said. "Your grandfather was a prosperous land-owner. Your grandmother was a Godhigh."

"Will you look around you," he said tensely, "and see where you are now?" and he swept his arm jerkily out to indicate the neighborhood, which the growing darkness at least made less dingy.

"You remain what you are," she said. "Your great-grandfather had a plantation and two hundred slaves."

"There are no more slaves," he said irritably.

"They were better off when they were," she said. He groaned to see that she was off on that topic. She rolled onto it every few days like a train on an open track. He knew every stop, every junction, every swamp along the way, and knew the exact point at which her conclusion would roll majestically into the station: "It's ridiculous. It's simply not realistic. They should rise, yes, but on their own side of the fence."

25 "Let's skip it," Julian said.

"The ones I feel sorry for," she said, "are the ones that are half white. They're tragic."

"Will you skip it?"

"Suppose we were half white. We would certainly have mixed feelings."

"I have mixed feelings now," he groaned.

30 "Well let's talk about something pleasant," she said. "I remember going to Grandpa's when I was a little girl. Then the house had double stairways that

went up to what was really the second floor—all the cooking was done on the first. I used to like to stay down in the kitchen on account of the way the walls smelled. I would sit with my nose pressed against the plaster and take deep breaths. Actually the place belonged to the Godhighs but your grandfather Chestny paid the mortgage and saved it for them. They were in reduced circumstances," she said, "but reduced or not, they never forgot who they were."

"Doubtless that decayed mansion reminded them," Julian muttered. He never spoke of it without contempt or thought of it without longing. He had seen it once when he was a child before it had been sold. The double stairways had rotted and been torn down. Negroes were living in it. But it remained in his mind as his mother had known it. It appeared in his dreams regularly. He would stand on the wide porch, listening to the rustle of oak leaves, then wander through the high-ceilinged hall into the parlor that opened onto it and gaze at the worn rugs and faded draperies. It occurred to him that it was he, not she, who could have appreciated it. He preferred its threadbare elegance to anything he could name and it was because of it that all the neighborhoods they had lived in had been a torment to him—whereas she had hardly known the difference. She called her insensitivity "being adjustable."

"And I remember the old darky who was my nurse, Caroline. There was no better person in the world. I've always had a great respect for my colored friends," she said. "I'd do anything in the world for them and they'd . . ."

"Will you for God's sake get off that subject?" Julian said. When he got on a bus by himself, he made it a point to sit down beside a Negro, in reparation as it were for his mother's sins.

"You're mighty touchy tonight," she said. "Do you feel all right?"

"Yes I feel all right," he said. "Now lay off." 35

She pursed her lips. "Well, you certainly are in a vile humor," she observed. "I just won't speak to you at all."

They had reached the bus stop. There was no bus in sight and Julian, his hands still jammed in his pockets and his head thrust forward, scowled down the empty street. The frustration of having to wait on the bus as well as ride on it began to creep up his neck like a hot hand. The presence of his mother was borne in upon him as she gave a pained sigh. He looked at her bleakly. She was holding herself very erect under the preposterous hat, wearing it like a banner of her imaginary dignity. There was in him an evil urge to break her spirit. He suddenly unloosened his tie and pulled it off and put it in his pocket.

She stiffened. "Why must you look like *that* when you take me to town?" she said. "Why must you deliberately embarrass me?"

"If you'll never learn where you are," he said, "you can at least learn where I am."

"You look like a—thug," she said. 40

"Then I must be one," he murmured.

"I'll just go home," she said. "I will not bother you. If you can't do a little thing like that for me . . ."

Rolling his eyes upward, he put his tie back on. "Restored to my class," he muttered. He thrust his face toward her and hissed, "True culture is in the mind, the *mind*," he said, and tapped his head, "the mind."

"It's in the heart," she said, "and in how you do things and how you do things is because of who you *are*."

"Nobody in the damn bus cares who you are."

"I care who I am," she said icily.

The lighted bus appeared on top of the next hill and as it approached, they moved out into the street to meet it. He put his hand under her elbow and hoisted her up on the creaking step. She entered with a little smile, as if she were going into a drawing room where everyone had been waiting for her. While he put in the tokens, she sat down on one of the broad front seats for three which faced the aisle. A thin woman with protruding teeth and long yellow hair was sitting on the end of it. His mother moved up beside her and left room for Julian beside herself. He sat down and looked at the floor across the aisle where a pair of thin feet in red and white canvas sandals were planted.

His mother immediately began a general conversation meant to attract anyone who felt like talking. "Can it get any hotter?" she said and removed from her purse a folding fan, black with a Japanese scene on it, which she began to flutter before her.

"I reckon it might could," the woman with the protruding teeth said, "but I know for a fact my apartment couldn't get no hotter."

"It must get the afternoon sun," his mother said. She sat forward and looked up and down the bus. It was half filled. Everybody was white. "I see we have the bus to ourselves," she said. Julian cringed.

"For a change," said the woman across the aisle, the owner of the red and white canvas sandals. "I come on one the other day and they were thick as fleas—up front and all through."

"The world is in a mess everywhere," his mother said. "I don't know how we've let it get in this fix."

"What gets my goat is all those boys from good families stealing automobile tires," the woman with the protruding teeth said. "I told my boy, I said you may not be rich but you been raised right and if I ever catch you in any such mess, they can send you on to the reformatory. Be exactly where you belong."

"Training tells," his mother said. "Is your boy in high school?"

"Ninth grade," the woman said.

"My son just finished college last year. He wants to write but he's selling typewriters until he gets started," his mother said.

The woman leaned forward and peered at Julian. He threw her such a malevolent look that she subsided against the seat. On the floor across the aisle there was an abandoned newspaper. He got up and got it and opened it out in front of him. His mother discreetly continued the conversation in a lower tone but the woman across the aisle said in a loud voice, "Well that's nice. Selling typewriters is close to writing. He can go right from one to the other."

"I tell him," his mother said, "that Rome wasn't built in a day."

Behind the newspaper Julian was withdrawing into the inner compartment of his mind where he spent most of his time. This was a kind of mental bubble in which he established himself when he could not bear to be a part of what was going on around him. From it he could see out and judge but in it he was safe from any kind of penetration from without. It was the only place where he felt free of the general idiocy of his fellows. His mother had never entered it but from it he could see her with absolute clarity.

60 The old lady was clever enough and he thought that if she had started from any of the right premises, more might have been expected of her. She lived according to the laws of her own fantasy world, outside of which he had never seen her set foot. The law of it was to sacrifice herself for him after she had first created the necessity to do so by making a mess of things. If he had permitted her sacrifices, it was only because her lack of foresight had made them necessary. All of her life had been a struggle to act like a Chestny without the Chestny goods, and to give him everything she thought a Chestny ought to have; but since, said she, it was fun to struggle, why complain? And when you had won, as she had won, what fun to look back on the hard times! He could not forgive her that she had enjoyed the struggle and that she thought *she* had won.

What she meant when she said she had won was that she had brought him up successfully and had sent him to college and that he had turned out so well—good looking (her teeth had gone unfilled so that his could be straightened), intelligent (he realized he was too intelligent to be a success), and with a future ahead of him (there was of course no future ahead of him). She excused his gloominess on the grounds that he was still growing up and his radical ideas on his lack of practical experience. She said he didn't yet know a thing about "life," that he hadn't even entered the real world—when already he was as disenchanted with it as a man of fifty.

The further irony of all this was that in spite of her, he had turned out so well. In spite of going to only a third-rate college, he had, on his own initiative, come out with a first-rate education; in spite of growing up dominated by a small mind, he had ended up with a large one; in spite of all her foolish views, he was free of prejudice and unafraid to face facts. Most miraculous of all, instead of being blinded by love for her as she was for him, he had cut himself emotionally free of her and could see her with complete objectivity. He was not dominated by his mother.

The bus stopped with a sudden jerk and shook him from his meditation. A woman from the back lurched forward with little steps and barely escaped falling in his newspaper as she righted herself. She got off and a large Negro got on. Julian kept his paper lowered to watch. It gave him a certain satisfaction to see injustice in daily operation. It confirmed his view that with a few exceptions there was no one worth knowing within a radius of three hundred miles. The Negro was well dressed and carried a briefcase. He looked around and then sat down on the other end of the seat where the woman with the red and white canvas sandals was sitting. He immediately unfolded a newspaper and obscured himself behind it. Julian's mother's elbow at once prodded insistently into his ribs. "Now you see why I won't ride on these buses by myself," she whispered.

The woman with the red and white canvas sandals had risen at the same time the Negro sat down and had gone further back in the bus and taken the seat of the woman who had got off. His mother leaned forward and cast her an approving look.

65 Julian rose, crossed the aisle, and sat down in the place of the woman with the canvas sandals. From this position, he looked serenely across at his mother. Her face had turned an angry red. He stared at her, making his eyes the eyes of

a stranger. He felt his tension suddenly lift as if he had openly declared war on her.

He would have liked to get in conversation with the Negro and to talk with him about art or politics or any subject that would be above the comprehension of those around them, but the man remained entrenched behind his paper. He was either ignoring the change of seating or had never noticed it. There was no way for Julian to convey his sympathy.

His mother kept her eyes fixed reproachfully on his face. The woman with the protruding teeth was looking at him avidly as if he were a type of monster new to her.

"Do you have a light?" he asked the Negro.

Without looking away from his paper, the man reached in his pocket and handed him a packet of matches.

70 "Thanks," Julian said. For a moment he held the matches foolishly. A NO SMOKING sign looked down upon him from over the door. This alone would not have deterred him; he had no cigarettes. He had quit smoking some months before because he could not afford it. "Sorry," he muttered and handed back the matches. The Negro lowered the paper and gave him an annoyed look. He took the matches and raised the paper again.

His mother continued to gaze at him but she did not take advantage of his momentary discomfort. Her eyes retained their battered look. Her face seemed to be unnaturally red, as if her blood pressure had risen. Julian allowed no glimmer of sympathy to show on his face. Having got the advantage, he wanted desperately to keep it and carry it through. He would have liked to teach her a lesson that would last her a while, but there seemed no way to continue the point. The Negro refused to come out from behind his paper.

Julian folded his arms and looked stolidly before him, facing her but as if he did not see her, as if he had ceased to recognize her existence. He visualized a scene in which, the bus having reached their stop, he would remain in his seat and when she said, "Aren't you going to get off?" he would look at her as a stranger who had rashly addressed him. The corner they got off on was usually deserted, but it was well lighted and it would not hurt her to walk by herself the four blocks to the Y. He decided to wait until the time came and then decide whether or not he would let her get off by herself. He would have to be at the Y at ten to bring her back, but he could leave her wondering if he was going to show up. There was no reason for her to think she could always depend on him.

He retired again into the high-ceilinged room sparsely settled with large pieces of antique furniture. His soul expanded momentarily but then he became aware of his mother across from him and the vision shriveled. He studied her coldly. Her feet in little pumps dangled like a child's and did not quite reach the floor. She was training on him an exaggerated look of reproach. He felt completely detached from her. At that moment he could with pleasure have slapped her as he would have slapped a particularly obnoxious child in his charge.

He began to imagine various unlikely ways by which he could teach her a lesson. He might make friends with some distinguished Negro professor or lawyer and bring him home to spend the evening. He would be entirely justified but her blood pressure would rise to 300. He could not push her to the extent of making her have a stroke, and moreover, he had never been successful at making any Negro friends. He had tried to strike up an acquaintance on the bus with some of the better types, with ones that looked like professors or ministers or lawyers. One morning he had sat down next to a distinguished-looking dark brown man who had answered his questions with a sonorous solemnity but who had turned out to be an undertaker. Another day he had sat down beside a cigar-smoking Negro with a diamond ring on his finger, but after a few stilted pleasantries, the Negro had rung the buzzer and risen, slipping two lottery tickets into Julian's hand as he climbed over him to leave.

He imagined his mother lying desperately ill and his being able to secure 75
only a Negro doctor for her. He toyed with that idea for a few minutes and then dropped it for a momentary vision of himself participating as a sympathizer in a sit-in demonstration. This was possible but he did not linger with it. Instead, he approached the ultimate horror. He brought home a beautiful suspiciously Negroid woman. Prepare yourself, he said. There is nothing you can do about it. This is the woman I've chosen. She's intelligent, dignified, even good, and she's suffered and she hasn't thought it *fun*. Now persecute us, go ahead and persecute us. Drive her out of here, but remember, you're driving me too. His eyes were narrowed and through the indignation he had generated, he saw his mother across the aisle, purple-faced, shrunken to the dwarf-like proportions of her moral nature, sitting like a mummy beneath the ridiculous banner of her hat.

He was tilted out of his fantasy again as the bus stopped. The door opened with a sucking hiss and out of the dark a large, gaily dressed, sullen-looking colored woman got on with a little boy. The child, who might have been four, had on a short plaid suit and a Tyrolean hat with a blue feather in it. Julian hoped that he would sit down beside him and that the woman would push in beside his mother. He could think of no better arrangement.

As she waited for her tokens, the woman was surveying the seating possibilities—he hoped with the idea of sitting where she was least wanted. There was something familiar-looking about her but Julian could not place what it was. She was a giant of a woman. Her face was set not only to meet opposition but to seek it out. The downward tilt of her large lower lip was like a warning sign: DON'T TAMPER WITH ME. Her bulging figure was encased in a green crepe dress and her feet overflowed in red shoes. She had on a hideous hat. A purple velvet flap came down on one side of it and stood up on the other; the rest of it was green and looked like a cushion with the stuffing out. She carried a mammoth red pocketbook that bulged throughout as if it were stuffed with rocks.

To Julian's disappointment, the little boy climbed up on the empty seat beside his mother. His mother lumped all children, black and white, into the common category, "cute," and she thought little Negroes were on the whole cuter than little white children. She smiled at the little boy as he climbed on the seat.

Meanwhile the woman was bearing down upon the empty seat beside Julian. To his annoyance, she squeezed herself into it. He saw his mother's face change as the woman settled herself next to him and he realized with satisfaction that this was more objectionable to her than it was to him. Her face seemed almost gray and there was a look of dull recognition in her eyes, as if suddenly she had sickened at some awful confrontation. Julian saw that it was because she and the woman had, in a sense, swapped sons. Though his mother would not realize the symbolic significance of this, she would feel it. His amusement showed plainly on his face.

80 The woman next to him muttered something unintelligible to herself. He was conscious of a kind of bristling next to him, a muted growling like that of an angry cat. He could not see anything but the red pocketbook upright on the bulging green thighs. He visualized the woman as she had stood waiting for her tokens—the ponderous figure, rising from the red shoes upward over the solid hips, the mammoth bosom, the haughty face, to the green and purple hat.

His eyes widened.

The vision of the two hats, identical, broke upon him with the radiance of a brilliant sunrise. His face was suddenly lit with joy. He could not believe that Fate had thrust upon his mother such a lesson. He gave a loud chuckle so that she would look at him and see that he saw. She turned her eyes on him slowly. The blue in them seemed to have turned a bruised purple. For a moment he had an uncomfortable sense of her innocence, but it lasted only a second before principle rescued him. Justice entitled him to laugh. His grin hardened until it said to her as plainly as if he were saying aloud: Your punishment exactly fits your pettiness. This should teach you a permanent lesson.

Her eyes shifted to the woman. She seemed unable to bear looking at him and to find the woman preferable. He became conscious again of the bristling presence at his side. The woman was rumbling like a volcano about to become active. His mother's mouth began to twitch slightly at one corner. With a sinking heart, he saw incipient signs of recovery on her face and realized that this was going to strike her suddenly as funny and was going to be no lesson at all. She kept her eyes on the woman and an amused smile came over her face as if the woman were a monkey that had stolen her hat. The little Negro was looking up at her with large fascinated eyes. He had been trying to attract her attention for some time.

"Carver!" the woman said suddenly. "Come heah!"

85 When he saw that the spotlight was on him at last, Carver drew his feet up and turned himself toward Julian's mother and giggled.

"Carver!" the woman said. "You heah me? Come heah!"

Carver slid down from the seat but remained squatting with his back against the base of it, his head turned slyly around toward Julian's mother, who was smiling at him. The woman reached a hand across the aisle and snatched him to her. He righted himself and hung backwards on her knees, grinning at Julian's mother.

"Isn't he cute?" Julian's mother said to the woman with the protruding teeth.

"I reckon he is," the woman said without conviction.

The Negress yanked him upright but he eased out of her grip and shot across the aisle and scrambled, giggling wildly, onto the seat beside his love.

90 "I think he likes me," Julian's mother said, and smiled at the woman. It was the smile she used when she was being particularly gracious to an inferior. Julian saw everything was lost. The lesson had rolled off her like rain on a roof.

The woman stood up and yanked the little boy off the seat as if she were snatching him from contagion. Julian could feel the rage in her at having no weapon like his mother's smile. She gave the child a sharp slap across his leg.

He howled once and then thrust his head into her stomach and kicked his feet against her shins. "Behave," she said vehemently.

The bus stopped and the Negro who had been reading the newspaper got off. The woman moved over and set the little boy down with a thump between herself and Julian. She held him firmly by the knee. In a moment he put his hands in front of his face and peeped at Julian's mother through his fingers.

"I see yooooooo!" she said and put her hand in front of her face and peeped at him.

The woman slapped his hand down. "Quit yo' foolishness," she said, "before I knock the living Jesus out of you!"

Julian was thankful that the next stop was theirs. He reached up and pulled 95
the cord. The woman reached up and pulled it at the same time. Oh my God, he thought. He had the terrible intuition that when they got off the bus together, his mother would open her purse and give the little boy a nickel. The gesture would be as natural to her as breathing. The bus stopped and the woman got up and lunged to the front, dragging the child, who wished to stay on, after her. Julian and his mother got up and followed. As they neared the door, Julian tried to relieve her of her pocketbook.

"No," she murmured, "I want to give the little boy a nickel."

"No!" Julian hissed. "No!"

She smiled down at the child and opened her bag. The bus door opened and the woman picked him up by the arm and descended with him, hanging at her hip. Once in the street she set him down and shook him.

Julian's mother had to close her purse while she got down the bus step but as soon as her feet were on the ground, she opened it again and began to rummage inside. "I can't find but a penny," she whispered, "but it looks like a new one."

"Don't do it!" Julian said fiercely between his teeth. There was a streetlight 100
on the corner and she hurried to get under it so that she could better see into her pocketbook. The woman was heading off rapidly down the street with the child still hanging backward on her hand.

"Oh little boy!" Julian's mother called and took a few quick steps and caught up with them just beyond the lamppost. "Here's a bright new penny for you," and she held out the coin, which shone bronze in the dim light.

The huge woman turned and for a moment stood, her shoulders lifted and her face frozen with frustrated rage, and stared at Julian's mother. Then all at once she seemed to explode like a piece of machinery that had been given one ounce of pressure too much. Julian saw the black fist swing out with the red pocketbook. He shut his eyes and cringed as he heard the woman shout, "He don't take nobody's pennies!" When he opened his eyes, the woman was disappearing down the street with the little boy staring wide-eyed over her shoulder. Julian's mother was sitting on the sidewalk.

"I told you not to do that," Julian said angrily. "I told you not to do that!"

He stood over her for a minute, gritting his teeth. Her legs were stretched out in front of her and her hat was on her lap. He squatted down and looked her in the face. It was totally expressionless. "You got exactly what you deserved," he said. "Now get up."

105 He picked up her pocketbook and put what had fallen out back in it. He picked the hat up off her lap. The penny caught his eye on the sidewalk and he picked that up and let it drop before her eyes into the purse. Then he stood up and leaned over and held his hands out to pull her up. She remained immobile. He sighed. Rising above them on either side were black apartment buildings, marked with irregular rectangles of light. At the end of the block a man came out of a door and walked off in the opposite direction. "All right," he said, "suppose somebody happens by and wants to know why you're sitting on the sidewalk?"

She took the hand and, breathing hard, pulled heavily up on it and then stood for a moment, swaying slightly as if the spots of light in the darkness were circling around her. Her eyes, shadowed and confused, finally settled on his face. He did not try to conceal his irritation. "I hope this teaches you a lesson," he said. She leaned forward and her eyes raked his face. She seemed trying to determine his identity. Then, as if she found nothing familiar about him, she started off with a headlong movement in the wrong direction.

"Aren't you going on to the Y?" he asked.

"Home," she muttered.

"Well, are we walking?"

110 For answer she kept going. Julian followed along, his hands behind him. He saw no reason to let the lesson she had had go without backing it up with an explanation of its meaning. She might as well be made to understand what had happened to her. "Don't think that was just an uppity Negro woman," he said. "That was the whole colored race which will no longer take your condescending pennies. That was your black double. She can wear the same hat as you, and to be sure," he added gratuitously (because he thought it was funny), "it looked better on her than it did on you. What all this means," he said, "is that the old world is gone. The old manners are obsolete and your graciousness is not worth a damn." He thought bitterly of the house that had been lost for him. "You aren't who you think you are," he said.

She continued to plow ahead, paying no attention to him. Her hair had come undone on one side. She dropped her pocketbook and took no notice. He stooped and picked it up and handed it to her but she did not take it.

"You needn't act as if the world had come to an end," he said, "because it hasn't. From now on you've got to live in a new world and face a few realities for a change. Buck up," he said, "it won't kill you."

She was breathing fast.

"Let's wait on the bus," he said.

115 "Home," she said thickly.

"I hate to see you behave like this," he said. "Just like a child. I should be able to expect more of you." He decided to stop where he was and make her stop and wait for a bus. "I'm not going any farther," he said stopping. "We're going on the bus."

She continued to go on as if she had not heard him. He took a few steps and caught her arm and stopped her. He looked into her face and caught his breath. He was looking into a face he had never seen before. "Tell Grandpa to come get me," she said.

He stared, stricken.

"Tell Caroline to come get me," she said.

Stunned, he let her go and she lurched forward again, walking as if one leg 120
were shorter than the other. A tide of darkness seemed to be sweeping her from him. "Mother!" he cried. "Darling, sweetheart, wait!" Crumpling, she fell to the pavement. He dashed forward and fell at her side, crying, "Mamma, Mamma!" He turned her over. Her face was fiercely distorted. One eye, large and staring, moved slightly to the left as if it had become unmoored. The other remained fixed on him, raked his face again, found nothing and closed.

"Wait here, wait here!" he cried and jumped up and began to run for help toward a cluster of lights he saw in the distance ahead of him. "Help, help!" he shouted, but his voice was thin, scarcely a thread of sound. The lights drifted farther away the faster he ran and his feet moved numbly as if they carried him nowhere. The tide of darkness seemed to sweep him back to her, postponing from moment to moment his entry into the world of guilt and sorrow.

1961

Passages from Flannery O'Connor's *Essays and Letters*

ESSAYS

From "The Fiction Writer and His Country" (1957)

[. . . W]hen I look at stories I have written I find that they are, for the most part, about people who are poor, who are afflicted in both mind and body, who have little—or at best a distorted—sense of spiritual purpose, and whose actions do not apparently give the reader a great assurance of the joy of life.

Yet how is this? For I am no disbeliever in spiritual purpose and no vague believer. I see from the standpoint of Christian orthodoxy. This means that for me the meaning of life is centered in our Redemption by Christ and what I see in the world I see in its relation to that. [. . .]

Some may blame preoccupation with the grotesque on the fact that here we have a Southern writer and that this is just the type of imagination that Southern life fosters. [. . .] I find it hard to believe that what is observable behavior in one section can be entirely without parallel in another. At least, of late, Southern writers have had the opportunity of pointing out that none of us invented Elvis Presley and that that youth is himself probably less an occasion for concern than his popularity, which is not restricted to the Southern part of the country.

* * *

When you can assume that your audience holds the same beliefs you do, you can relax a little and use more normal means of talking to it; when you have to assume that it does not, then you have to make your vision apparent by shock—to the hard of hearing you shout, and for the almost-blind you draw large and startling figures.

From "The Nature and Aim of Fiction"[1] (posthumously published in 1969)

The beginning of human knowledge is through the senses, and the fiction writer begins where human perception begins. He appeals through the senses, and you cannot appeal to the senses with abstractions.

* * *

Now the word *symbol* scares a good many people off, just as the word *art* does. They seem to feel that a symbol is some mysterious thing put in arbitrarily by the writer to frighten the common reader [. . .]. They seem to think that it is a way of saying something that you aren't actually saying, and so [. . .] they approach it as if it were a problem in algebra. Find *x*. And when they do find or think they find this abstraction, *x*, then they go off with an elaborate sense of satisfaction and the notion that they have "understood" the story. [. . .]

I think for the fiction writer himself, symbols are something he uses simply as a matter of course. You might say that these are details that, while having their essential place in the literal level of the story, operate in depth as well as on the surface, increasing the story in every direction.

O'Connor alongside self-portrait with peacock

From "Writing Short Stories" (posthumously published in 1969)

Nothing essential to the main experience can be left out of a short story. All the action has to be satisfactorily accounted for in terms of motivation, and there has to be a beginning, a middle, and an end, though not necessarily in that order.

* * *

People talk about the theme of a story as if the theme were like the string that a sack of chicken feed is tied with. They think that if you can pick out the theme, the way you pick the right thread in the chicken-feed sack, you can rip the story open and feed the chickens. But this is not the way meaning works in fiction.

When you can state the theme of a story, when you can separate it from the story itself, then you can be sure the story is not a very good one. The meaning of a story has to be embodied in it, has to be made concrete in it. A story is a way to say something that can't be said any other way, and it takes every word in the

1. These selections and those that follow are composites, edited from O'Connor manuscripts by Sally and Robert Fitzgerald and published in *Mystery and Manners: Occasional Prose*. Farrar, Straus & Giroux, 1969.

story to say what the meaning is. You tell a story because a statement would be inadequate.

* * *

An idiom characterizes a society, and when you ignore the idiom, you are very likely ignoring the whole social fabric that could make a meaningful character. You can't cut characters off from their society and say much about them as individuals. You can't say anything meaningful about the mystery of a personality unless you put that personality in a believable and significant social context.

From "On Her Own Work" (posthumously published in 1969)

I often ask myself what makes a story work, and what makes it hold up as a story, and I have decided that it is probably some action, some gesture of a character that is unlike any other in the story, one which indicates where the real heart of the story lies. This would have to be an action or a gesture which was both totally right and totally unexpected; it would have to be one that was both in character and beyond character; it would have to suggest both the world and eternity. The action or gesture I'm talking about would have to be on the anagogical level, that is, the level which has to do with the Divine life and our participation in it. It would be a gesture that transcended any neat allegory that might have been intended or any pat moral categories a reader could make. It would be a gesture which somehow made contact with mystery.

* * *

[. . . I]n my own stories I have found that violence is strangely capable of returning my characters to reality and preparing them to accept their moment of grace.

* * *

We hear many complaints about the prevalence of violence in modern fiction, and it is always assumed that this violence is a bad thing and meant to be an end in itself. With the serious writer, violence is never an end in itself. It is the extreme situation that best reveals what we are essentially.

From "Novelist and Believer" (written 1963; posthumously published in 1969)

Great fiction [. . .] is not simply an imitation of feeling. The good novelist not only finds a symbol for feeling, he finds a symbol and a way of lodging it which tells the intelligent reader whether this feeling is adequate or inadequate, whether it is moral or immoral, whether it is good or evil. And his theology, even in its most remote reaches, will have a direct bearing on this.

* * *

The artist penetrates the concrete world in order to find at its depths the image of its source, the image of ultimate reality. This in no way hinders his perception of evil but rather sharpens it, for only when the natural world is seen as good does evil become intelligible as a destructive force and a necessary result of our freedom.

LETTERS[1]

To Louise and Tom Gossett,[2] 10 April 1961
I have just read a review of my book [*The Violent Bear It Away*], long and damming [*sic*], which says it don't give us hope and courage and that all novels should give us hope and courage. I think if the novel is to give us virtue the selection of hope and courage is rather arbitrary—why not charity, peace, patience, joy, benignity, long-suffering and fear of the Lord? Or faith? The fact of the matter is that the modern mind opposes courage to faith. It also demands that the novel provide us with gifts that only religion can give. I don't think the novel can offend against the truth, but I think its truths are more particular than general. But this is a large subject and I ain't no aesthetician.

To Roslyn Barnes,[3] 17 June 1961
Can you tell me if the statement: "everything that rises must converge" is a true proposition in physics? I can easily see its moral, historical and evolutionary significance, but I want to know if it is also a correct physical statement.

To John Hawkes,[4] 28 November 1961
You haven't convinced me that I write with the Devil's will or belong in the romantic tradition and I'm prepared to argue some more with you on this if I can remember where we left off at. I think the reason we can't agree on this is because there is a difference in our two devils. My Devil has a name, a history and a definite plan. His name is Lucifer, he's a fallen angel, his sin is pride, and his aim is the destruction of the Divine plan. Now I judge that your Devil is co-equal to God, not his creature: that pride is his virtue not his sin; and that his aim is not to destroy the Divine plan because there isn't any Divine plan to destroy. My Devil is objective and yours is subjective. You say one becomes "evil" when one leaves the herd. I say that depends entirely on what the herd is doing.

To "A," 9 December 1961
Some friends of mine in Texas wrote me that a friend of theirs went into a bookstore looking for a paperback copy of *A Good Man*. The clerk said, "We

1. None of the letters below is reproduced in full; each is an excerpt.
2. The Drs. Gossett were literary scholars; Thomas (1916–2005), a professor of English, was suspended from his position at Wesleyan College, in Macon, Georgia, for supporting racial integration. His best-known book is *Race: The History of an Idea in America* (1963, 1997).
3. Roslyn Barnes began a long correspondence and friendship with O'Connor while a student at O'Connor's alma mater, Georgia State College for Women (now Georgia State College and University) in Milledgeville.
4. American novelist and short-story writer (1925–98).

don't have that one but we have another by that author, called *The Bear That Ran Away With It*."[5] I foresee the trouble I am going to have with "Everything That Rises Must Converge"—"Every Rabbit That Rises Is a Sage."

To "A," 1 September 1963

The topical is poison. I got away with it in "Everything That Rises" but only because I say a plague on everybody's house as far as the race business goes.

CRITICAL EXCERPTS

Mary Gordon

From Flannery's Kiss (2004)[1]

I have been asked to speak at an academic conference devoted to Flannery O'Connor. It is taking place in her home town, Milledgeville, Georgia. I arrive in the middle of a session. One of the speakers is a young Jesuit. He talks about some letters of Flannery O'Connor's that were not included in Sally Fitzgerald's collection.[2] They were written in 1955, to a young Danish man who was a book salesman for her publisher, Harcourt Brace. The Jesuit reads the letters. They are girlish. If there are not triple exclamation points, there should be. She tells the Dane how much she enjoys his company. "If you were here we could talk for about a million years," she says. The Jesuit tracks the Dane down in Denmark. He is now an old man, but he remembers the encounter with Flannery vividly. He tells the Jesuit that he enjoyed Flannery's companionship very much and that one day when he'd taken her for a drive in the country, it occurs to him that she is a woman, and that she would like him to kiss her. When he does kiss her, the experience horrifies him. He says that Flannery did not know how to kiss. Whereas when he had kissed other women they had offered him soft lips, Flannery presented him with teeth. He remembered that she was chronically ill and he felt like he was kissing a skull. Worried that she was in love with him, he returned quite soon to Denmark. Six months later, he wrote her that he was engaged to be married. Flannery sat down upon receiving the letter and within a matter of days completed her story, "Good Country People," which is about a Bible salesman who is a fetishist of prosthetic devices and who steals a girl's wooden leg when she thinks she is seducing him. Flannery sends the story to the Dane and tells him not to think it's about him, even though the fetishist, whose name is Manley Pointer, is a Bible salesman and the Dane is a book salesman.

In a letter to a friend, Flannery says that the character she most identifies with is the girl whose wooden leg is stolen.

* * *

5. The actual title of O'Connor's 1960 novel is *The Violent Bear It Away*.

1. Mary Gordon. "Flannery's Kiss." *Michigan Quarterly Review*, no. 43, Summer 2004, pp. 328–49. Unless otherwise indicated, all footnotes have been added by the editor.

2. All citations from Flannery O'Connor's letters are from *Flannery O'Connor: The Habit of Being: Letters Selected and with an Introduction by Sally Fitzgerald* (NY: Farrar, Straus, Giroux, 1979) [Gordon's note].

Flannery O'Connor represents two images of the artist, both of which suggest that the way I have lived my life means I cannot be a real artist.[3] The Catholic and the Romantic, both insisting on the inferiority of human connectedness, the superiority of artistic isolation. Among the least acceptable of human connections for the artist: the connection to one's children. When Faulkner's daughter complained that he didn't pay attention to her, he replied, "Whoever heard of Shakespeare's daughter?" Even Virginia Woolf only spoke of Shakespeare's sister.[4] Until very recently, no important woman writer has had children. I am the mother of a daughter and a son.

For a variety of reasons then, Flannery has for many years caused me to feel unworthy. She has for many years caused me to feel ashamed. And in revenge, the words come to me unbidden, "No one would say I don't know how to kiss."

* * *

Miraculously, Flannery got herself out of Milledgeville, a town that was once the state capital of Georgia, a town noted for its prison and its mental hospital, a town of fewer than ten thousand people not any of whom, perhaps, really understood her, to the Writers' Workshop at the University of Iowa. Having graduated from Iowa, she went to the writers' colony Yaddo, in Saratoga Springs, briefly to New York, and then to live with Sally and Robert Fitzgerald in their house in Connecticut. But then she became ill; she was diagnosed with lupus, the disease that had killed her father. She resigned herself to the life of an invalid. She resigned herself to being taken care of by her mother.

Andalusia, which is pronounced AnduLOOZia, not AndaluTHEEa, is a dairy farm on a gently sloping tract of land. The line of trees which finds its way into so many of O'Connor's stories is visible from the front porch, screened in, with many rockers, looking as if they belonged more properly on the front porch of a small hotel. Just inside the front door, your eye falls on a velvet rope, cordoning something off. It is Flannery's bedroom. I ask the curator if I can go behind the velvet ropes and he says no.

I have rarely seen a more uncomfortable room. Her bed is single, dark wooden, monastic. The desk is near the bed, so she could get to it easily in the days when walking was difficult for her. The bedspread and the drapes are a heavy ungiving blue. There is a black and white picture of the Sacred Heart, books in bookcases, some knickknacks on the mantle which I cannot see from the doorway across which the velvet rope stretches. Propped against the wall are Flannery's crutches, cruel-looking steel devices with semicircles where her arms might rest. The most famous picture of Flannery O'Connor catches her standing on the porch, leaning on her crutches. One of her peacocks stands beside her, a little to her left, on a lower porch step.

* * *

3. Gordon (b. 1949) is a novelist and memoirist, as well as a literary critic.
4. In her famous 1929 lecture/essay *A Room of One's Own*, Woolf imagines what might have happened had Shakespeare had a sister who yearned to be a writer.

If Flannery had not been ill, would she have traveled? Met new people, had experiences that would have changed the quality of her work? She says in one of her letters: "I have never been anywhere but sick. In a sense sickness is a place, more instructive than a long trip to Europe, and it's always a place where there's no company, where nobody can follow. . . . The surface hereabouts has always been very flat. I come from a family where the only emotion respectable to show is irritation. In some this tendency produces hives, in others literature, in me both."

If she had traveled, if she had met new people, if she had been able to give and receive more affection (which she gives and receives in her letters, written from the house that she never leaves), would her work have changed?

Do we want that work changed?

* * *

She would deny that her stories are loveless. She would say that the love of God scalds, it does not comfort. Let us take her on her own terms. In her stories there is very little comfort. But there is also very little kindness from the author to her characters. And after reading her for a while, I become impatient at the partialness of her vision. At what is left out. Love. I can see the mocking spelling she might use for the word love. She might spell it *looove*. Or *lurv*.

* * *

O'Connor does not allow her characters to feel the pain of loss. They are denied the experience of grieving. I have often wondered if people are more comfortable with violence than with grief: violence is sharp, clear, bounded; grief can be eternal; it percolates and permutates. Its path is gradual and slow. It's the kind of thing that, as an artist, O'Connor can't do. [. . .] Her stories, as she says, are romances, in the tradition of Hawthorne. She is interested in the climactic moment, not in the consequences of the climax. She is interested in redemption, but not in forgiveness. Consider the vast tonal difference in the two words: *redemption* and *forgiveness*. Consider the differences in temperature. [. . .] In Catholic sacramentology, sins can only be forgiven in the sacrament if the sinner asks forgiveness. As we all go on sinning, we must constantly be forgiven. Indeed re-forgiven. Redemption took place once in history; forgiveness must be relived.

* * *

In trying to understand my feelings about Flannery O'Connor, the best I can say is that I often do not like Flannery O'Connor, but I can't get over loving her. The woman and the work. I go back and back to her. The reason for that is something she would despise. I am drawn not only to Flannery O'Connor the writer, but to Flannery O'Connor the woman. The woman who lived the life I refused and was grateful not to have to live. But who lived it with purity and gallantry. With singleness of heart. With bravery and good humor. She is the good Catholic I can never be. And yet she made me feel there was a place for me, or for the likes of me.

Ann E. Reuman

From Revolting Fictions: Flannery O'Connor's Letter to Her Mother (1993)[1]

In her letters, O'Connor sketches the portrait of Regina Cline O'Connor, who, though slight in build, possessed a commanding presence. Proud of her patrician family and immensely self-assured, Regina was more Cline than O'Connor, conscious of lineage, propriety, and appearance. [. . .] With proud reverence for the past, she hosted at the Cline House visitors who made the annual garden club pilgrimage to notable, historic homes in the community. When walking through the town center, she would be recognized for her social prominence before her daughter would be remembered for her nationally acclaimed literature. And, as manager of her house and affairs, she expected unquestioning observance of her rules, with gratitude for her generosity. [. . .] Attentive to appearances, Mrs. O'Connor checked extensions of herself—her house, her daughter—as she checked herself. She displayed the Cline family portraits in her parlor, proud of their visible claim to an honorable heritage; [. . .] she tried to show her daughter to advantage, spotlighting her public awards and curtaining her less glamorous habits. Writing to the Fitzgeralds about her recent receipt of the Kenyon Fellowship awarded on the basis of her work on *Wise Blood* (her first novel, dedicated to her mother), O'Connor comments, "My mamma [sic] is getting a big bang out of notifying all the kin who didn't like the book that the Rockerfeller [sic] Foundation, etc. etc.—this very casual like on the back of Christmas cards. Money talks, she says, and the name Rockerfeller don't hurt a bit" (*Habit* 49). And in a later note regarding a television play of one of her stories, she remarks, "My mother has been collecting congratulations . . . all week like eggs in a basket" (207).

Yet, while she praised what was already publicly acclaimed, O'Connor's mother worked just as hard to repress the socially unacceptable in her daughter's writing and behavior, urging O'Connor not to publish near the reading populace of Milledgeville a story which she found objectionable from the local standpoint; clearly expressing her disapproval of Flannery's tendency to "make a spectacle" of herself by wearing adolescent clothes into her thirties; and tersely reminding her daughter that her language was a reflection on herself. As O'Connor reports in one of her letters in a seemingly offhand way, her mother once said, "You talk just like a nigger and someday you are going to be away from home and do it and people are going to wonder WHERE YOU CAME FROM" (148; O'Connor's emphasis).

Clearly, under the surface of controlled and witty letters in which Mrs. O'Connor appears to be as Sally Fitzgerald sees her, "relished and admired, joked with and about, altogether clearly loved" (Fitzgerald x) by her daughter, O'Connor hints at a darker and more complicated portrait. [. . .] Punctuating her letters with refrains of "You can't get ahead of mother" and "My parent is back at large," O'Connor hints at a domineering, invasive, and aloof mother whose presence "never contribute[d] to [O'Connor's] articulateness" (195).

O'Connor's self-portrait is equally complex. [. . .] She used distortion to great effect in her work, though [. . .] O'Connor most often in her letters refers to

1. Ann E. Reuman. "Revolting Fictions: Flannery O'Connor's Letter to Her Mother." *Papers on Language and Literature*, vol. 29, no. 2, 1993, pp. 197–214. The essay's bibliography has been edited.

herself comically and with an outside observer's eye. [. . .] Frequently in reference to the proofs she received of photographs to be pasted on jacket backs, she caricatured herself as being "all teeth and spectacles" (454), looking alternately "like a refugee from deep thought" (33) or like she "had just bitten [her] grandmother and this was one of [her] few pleasures" (31). [. . .]

[. . .] O'Connor's recurrent bouts with lupus [. . .] redirected her course, first sending her back to Milledgeville for medical tests and ultimately returning her to her mother's home. [. . .] O'Connor found little escape from her mother's presence while living under the same roof. Bottled up by Southern codes of silence and Catholic respect for elders, and aggravated by dependence on her mother without hope of change in her status, O'Connor's adolescent resentment carried into adulthood, building in intensity and exploding into her fiction.

Clearly there is a change in tone, characterization, and focus in O'Connor's stories written after 1951 when she was forced to live with her mother and move to Andalusia. In her earlier works, O'Connor deals primarily with Georgia folks, often displaced by a move to the city, usually struggling against personal fears to assert themselves or gain affection. [. . .] In each of these stories, though the character has a fearful glimpse of his or her vulnerability and impotence, the action is minimal, the tone is subdued, and the focus is primarily on an individual protagonist. The shift from passive and personal experience to explosive interaction, from humility and withdrawal to angry and violent revelation, from timid attempts to win love to fierce refusal of it, marks an abrupt redirection in O'Connor's writing after her return home, as if to dramatize her mother's crippling influence on her life.

• • •

Like the literal-minded mother in [O'Connor's short story] "The Enduring Chill" who wishes her son would go out and do work—real work, not writing—and who urges him to write something good like *Gone With the Wind*, Mrs. O'Connor, an inveterate subscriber to *Reader's Digest*, does not seem to appreciate her daughter's brand of writing. O'Connor's confession to a fellow writer tells much:

> The other day [my mother] asked me why I didn't try to write something that people liked instead of the kind of thing I do write. Do you think, she said, that you are really using the talent God gave you when you don't write something that a lot, a LOT, of people like? This always leaves me shaking and speechless, raises my blood pressure 140 degrees, etc. All I can ever say is, if you have to ask, you'll never know. (*Habit* 326)

• • •

O'Connor may have written her stories for her mother, hiding the "letter to her parent" in her text, eager to have her mother find her private revelation yet protecting her from public embarrassment. As O'Connor suggested in several letters, her mother was her primary and most trying reader, preferring O'Connor's painting (which she felt she could understand) to her writing, and constantly falling asleep on her books.

• • •

Where relative passivity and emotional suicide fail to register with her mother, O'Connor lodges her discontent in more violent, boldly stroked stories, filled with troops of Flannerys and Reginas in a wild assortment of shapes, sizes, ages, and sexes, but always quite recognizable versions of the original pair. In "The Comforts of Home" and "Everything That Rises Must Converge," effeminate sons bristle against overpowering mothers.

• • •

[. . . I]n "Everything That Rises Must Converge," Julian Chestny, a thirty-year-old unappreciated writer, strikes out indirectly at his mother's ignorance, bigotry, and oppressive expectation of gratitude. In the portrait of the mother, O'Connor once again draws from material in her own life. [. . .]

[. . .] Unable either to communicate with his mother or break the tie that binds him, Julian—much like O'Connor in her fiction—retreats into his fantasy world. [. . .] Stating in one of her letters her annoyance with her mother's repeated "assault" on her bedroom, which she periodically would invade and clean, installing revolting curtains and changing her rug—an experience which O'Connor tellingly claimed made her feel "like she was being sawed in two without ether" (*Habit* 158–59)—O'Connor suggests that her "fiction," expressive of herself and unviolated by her mother's penchant for "tidiness," is the only "room" which she can preserve intact.

• • •

The recurrence in O'Connor's later fiction of these intolerable parents and murderous children struggling for articulation and dominance suggests an intense and urgent need expressible only in violent action—and in fiction. In one letter, O'Connor herself remarks, "Most of the violences carried to their logical conclusions in the stories manage to be warded off in fact here [at the dairy farm]—*though most of them exist in potentiality*" (198; emphasis added). [. . .]

That O'Connor saw herself in her fiction is clear. As she wrote to one correspondent, "My heroine already is, and is Hulga . . . a projection of myself into this kind of tragic comic action" (106).

• • •

[. . . I]n its portrayal of a world without love, "Good Country People" touches the core of O'Connor's own life. As she wrote in an early letter, "Everything funny I have written is more terrible than it is funny, or only funny because it is terrible, or only terrible because it is funny" (*Habit* 105).

WORKS CITED

Fitzgerald, Sally. Introduction. In O'Connor, *The Habit of Being.*

O'Connor, Flannery. *The Habit of Being: Letters.* Ed. Sally Fitzgerald. New York: Farrar, Straus & Giroux, 1979.

Eileen Pollack

From Flannery O'Connor and the New Criticism: A Response to Mark McGurl (2007)[1]

To writers who teach to earn their living, Flannery O'Connor has long represented the benefits that accrue to writers who refuse to teach (or, in O'Connor's case, are prevented from doing so by illness). Her continued exposure to irritating Southern matrons and Jesus-haunted back-woods preachers kept her fiction gritty and eccentric in ways that might have been impossible if she had remained in the academy.

However, as Mark McGurl so ably demonstrates, studying for two years at Iowa was enough to influence O'Connor's fiction for the rest of her life. Although legend would have it that she arrived in Iowa City fully formed as a writer,[2] then sat quietly in the back of her workshops except for the "occasional amused and shy smile at something absurd" (as Robert Giroux tells us in his introduction to the collected stories) (viii), McGurl wisely points out that the New Critical approach O'Connor absorbed from studying with Robert Penn Warren and reading the textbook/anthology he authored with Cleanth Brooks is evident in everything she ever published.[3]

* * *

For O'Connor, the advice that she write what she know took the form of setting her stories in rural Georgia and centering each story on the thematic question of what it might take to get a sinner to recognize the central mysteries of Christianity. Her problem as an artist was how to write about such a theme for an audience composed largely of nonbelievers. Preaching or moralizing about her characters' sins would have been not only inartistic but ineffective. The advice that she show rather than tell was particularly well suited to her thematic concerns as a Christian because it would allow her to bring alive for her readers the spiritual struggles of characters unlike themselves, creating on the page the power of unfamiliar sacraments such as baptism and/or the operation of grace in the material world.[4]

In addition, she believed that the divine (the thematic, the expository, that which must be told) is immanent in the concrete details of the material world (that which can be shown). Just as the spirit is made flesh in the Word, just as

1. Eileen Pollack. "Flannery O'Connor and the New Criticism." *American Literary History*, no. 19, 2007, pp. 546–56. Pollack's essay is a response to another essay in the same journal issue: Mark McGurl's "Understanding Iowa: Flannery O'Connor, B.A., M.F.A." Unless otherwise indicated, all footnotes have been added by the editor.
2. O'Connor graduated with an MA degree from the prestigious Iowa Writers' Workshop at the University of Iowa in 1947 [editor's note].
3. Novelist Robert Penn Warren (1905–89) and critic Cleanth Brooks (1906–94) collaborated on an influential series of essays and textbooks that helped lay the foundations for what came to be known as the New Criticism, which urged the importance of "close reading" and rejected the use of biography and secondary sources in literary studies.
4. See O'Connor, *Mystery*, 162 [Pollack's note].

God assumed the body of a man and suffered as humans suffered, so too the grand themes of Christianity can be embodied in the physical particulars of a flawed character's very human struggles against the devil. The fiction writer, O'Connor tells us in "The Teaching of Literature," "is concerned with mystery that is lived. He's concerned with ultimate mystery as we find it embodied in the concrete world of sense experience" (*Mystery* 125).

In the same way, O'Connor's obsessive use of the effaced third-person narrator was a choice that came not from her time at Iowa or a mindless adherence to some stricture laid down by Brooks and Warren but rather from the demands imposed by the Southern setting of her work, her thematic concerns as a believing Christian, and her friendship with the novelist Caroline Gordon.[5] [. . .] It is clear from O'Connor's letters that she sent nearly everything she ever wrote to Gordon for editing and that Gordon scolded her every time she lapsed from strict adherence to this limited third-person point of view.[6]

[. . .] O'Connor could not use first-person narrators because those narrators would have spoken in a thick rural Southern dialect that few readers would have understood or had the patience to decipher, just as Engel[7] could not understand O'Connor's speech when she showed up in his office to try to worm her way into his workshop. [. . .] O'Connor chose to rely on narrators who spoke standard English, allowing her characters to speak dialect only in limited and easily digestible doses in dialogue.

* * *

O'Connor endowed her narrators with perfect diction in accordance with Gordon's dictum that allowing the narrator to slip into dialect lowers the tone of a story and saps it of the tension that might otherwise have accrued from the subtle conflict between the cultures represented by the two ways of speaking.

* * *

We have seen, then, that O'Connor chose to show rather than tell and used limited third-person narrators because this style and this technique suited her particular needs as a Southerner and a Christian rather than because she was slavishly adhering to some New Critical creed she picked up at Iowa.

* * *

As she wrote in a letter to Betty Hester ("A") in September 1955, "I understand that something of oneself gets through and often something that one is not conscious of. Also to have sympathy for any character, you have to put a good deal of yourself into him." [. . . The artist must] make sure that those elements of

5. American novelist Caroline Ferguson Gordon (1895–1981); like O'Connor, she was best known for her short stories and her Roman Catholicism.
6. See O'Connor, *Habit*, 69, 95, 157, 260, 295 [Pollack's note].
7. American writer Paul Engel (1908–91), O'Connor's teacher at the Iowa Writers' Workshop.

the author's personality "that don't bear on the subject at hand are excluded. Everything has to be subordinated to a whole which is not you" (*Habit* 105).

WORKS CITED

O'Connor, Flannery. *The Complete Stories*. New York: Farrar, Straus, Giroux, 1973.

———. *The Habit of Being: Letters of Flannery O'Connor*. Ed. Sally Fitzgerald. New York: Farrar, Straus, Giroux, 1979.

———. *Mystery and Manners*. Ed. Sally Fitzgerald and Robert Fitzgerald. New York: Farrar, Straus, Giroux, 1970.

SUGGESTIONS FOR WRITING

1. Flannery O'Connor wrote that "the beginning of human knowledge is through the senses, and the fiction writer begins where human perception begins." Citing examples from the O'Connor stories and the nonfiction passages in this chapter, write an essay exploring O'Connor's use of imagery, including figurative language (metaphor, simile, symbol) and references to vision or other senses. Are the senses trustworthy? How does the physical world portrayed through this imagery affect other elements of the story or stories (characterization, plot, theme, etc.)?
2. Flannery O'Connor wrote that "in my own stories I have found that violence is strangely capable of returning my characters to reality and preparing them to accept their moment of grace" and that violence "is the extreme situation that best reveals what we are essentially." Write an essay analyzing the three stories by O'Connor in this chapter in light of these statements about violence. What "moments of grace" do you see? Can you assess what O'Connor considers the essence of humanity ("what we are")?
3. Jean W. Cash's biography *Flannery O'Connor: A Life* provides details about O'Connor's experience at Georgia State College for Women in the 1940s, when she was planning to be a cartoonist and contributed cartoons as well as writings to the school's publications. Write an essay in which you use this biographical information as an insight into one or more of O'Connor's stories. For instance, identify two or three scenes in a story and analyze their effect as primarily physical comedy or visual effect similar to that in cartoons.
4. Write an essay interpreting some aspect of one of O'Connor's stories in light of information about O'Connor's life. Be sure to cite Flannery O'Connor's own words from her letters and essays excerpted in this chapter, from the critical essays, or from other sources. What does the biographical context help explain? What qualities or aspects of the story does your biographical approach *not* account for?
5. Choose two of the stories in this chapter and write an essay comparing the way they are narrated (see the excerpt from Pollack's essay above). Pay close attention to passages in which the narrator relates the voice, vision, thoughts, or perspective of a focal character. How does the treatment of each character contribute to tone, irony, or other effects of the story?
6. After making your own list of what all three stories in this chapter have in common, write a short story in the Flannery O'Connor manner. Are you able to make it a little humorous without being too absurd? violent or shocking without being too cruel? unsettling but not disgusting? Is your story at all autobiographical?
7. Choose any story in this book (perhaps your favorite) and read at least one other story by the same writer. Write an essay comparing the stories, focusing on a specific element or aspect of them. Judging by these stories, what seems most distinctive about this author's work or worldview?

9 THE AUTHOR'S WORK AS CONTEXT: JAMES JOYCE'S *DUBLINERS*

Today, a good short story, like a popular song, will likely appear in four different forms over time:

- The story appears in a periodical, whether a general-interest, large-circulation venue like *Atlantic Monthly* or the *San Francisco Chronicle*, or a smaller, more specialized one such as filmmaker Francis Ford Coppola's *Zoetrope: All Story*. (Similarly, a song—let's take Radiohead's "Lucky" as an example—might be released as a single.)
- The story becomes part of a short-story collection—a book that collects multiple, often related stories by the same author (just as a song will turn up on an album, as "Lucky" did on Radiohead's 1997 *OK Computer*). Alternatively, the story might be transformed into a chapter in a novel.
- With a little luck, the story might be chosen for inclusion in an anthology of works by many authors, whether a textbook like the one you are reading right now or a book such as *Best American Short Stories of 2015*. (The musical equivalent would be a compilation album such as *Help: A Charity Project for the Children of Bosnia* [1995] or *Six Feet Under: Everything Ends, Vol. 2* [2005], both of which included "Lucky.")
- Finally, often years later, the story might make its way into the author's "collected" or "selected" works. (The musical parallel would be a greatest hits or remix album such as Radiohead's 2008 *The Best of Radiohead*—again including "Lucky.")

This is not the place to pursue all the ways that music reaches its audience today, though the analogy between story and song is thought-provoking. The same recording of a song on the radio, in a random mix or playlist, or in a crowded room will get different levels of your attention and may move you in different ways. Similarly, a short story changes when it appears in different formats or venues. Sometimes the change is literal if the author decides to revise the story at one of these stages, just as a singer or band might do a remix, live, or acoustic version of a song. But even if a writer or publisher doesn't alter a word or move a comma, the story changes nonetheless simply because each of these different publishing contexts subtly alters the work's effect on its audience. Whether you are reading a story or listening to a song, then, it's worth paying attention to how its effects and meanings are shaped and reshaped by the different contexts in which you and other audiences encounter it.

For example, long before Annie Proulx's short story "Brokeback Mountain" was turned into a major motion picture, it first appeared in the *New Yorker*, a magazine aimed at affluent, well-educated, mainly urban readers. In the *New Yorker*,

Proulx's story was broken up by a poem by Marie Howe and cartoons depicting businessmen swilling martinis and precocious children using words like *juvenilia*; it was sandwiched between articles on the writer Truman Capote and the PBS cooking-show host Julia Child, as well as ads for Salvador Dali prints, Steinway pianos, goose-down robes, and exclusive vacation destinations ("RENT YOUR OWN IRISH CASTLE"). In such a context, the story's gritty Western setting, its sheep-tending protagonists, their hardscrabble, often violent way of life, and their rural speech stand out as strange and exotic, if not crude. Such factors may well have been more jarring to *New Yorker* readers than the sexual relationship between two men that has since become the most controversial aspect of "Brokeback Mountain."

Yet if you pick up Proulx's *Close Range: Wyoming Stories* and read it from front to back, you encounter "Brokeback Mountain" only after making your way through ten other stories that depict the same general geographical and social environment. Here, the protagonists, Jack and Ennis, suddenly seem right at home amid a cast of characters consisting of what one reviewer dubs "hardpan ranchers, battered cowpokes and bull riders, bar girls and bar brawlers" whose "lives are a futile uphill struggle" to "wres[t] a living out of a land as poor as it is beautiful." Because reading all these stories makes this milieu more familiar, the collection gives readers both a clearer picture of Jack and Ennis as individuals (rather than types living in a remote land) and a deeper understanding of all that the word *it* might mean when Ennis says, "If you can't fix it, you got to stand it."

THE SHORT-STORY SEQUENCE OR CYCLE

All works written by a single author have something in common, as the stories by Flannery O'Connor in chapter 8 demonstrate. But the stories a writer publishes together in a single collection usually have even more in common, becoming interrelated parts of a larger work sometimes labeled a *short-story* **sequence** or *cycle*. At the very least, the stories in such a collection are usually written during roughly the same period of an author's life and thus provide a window into one phase in the author's biography and career.

At the opposite extreme, a short-story cycle might—like Tim O'Brien's *The Things They Carried* (1990)—closely resemble a novel, its stories all depicting the same characters and general setting, the action of one story taking up where the last leaves off. Like Proulx's *Close Range*, however, most modern short-story collections fall somewhere in between these two extremes: Their stories feature similar characters, settings, situations, plots, conflicts, imagery, and other stylistic features, without being overtly related to each other. The reader is invited to trace connections and make comparisons. Each of the stories works fine on its own and is thus a complete, self-contained "work" in its own right. But the stories also work together to form a single, larger work that is somehow more than the sum of its parts.

As a result, some authors feel that any one story in a sequence or cycle can never be all that it was meant to be unless it is read in the context of the whole. Such a cycle "suffers from being broken up or crowded in with other books," in the words of short-story writer Frank O'Connor, because cycles "should be read by themselves, as unities." We could liken the experience of reading one part of a carefully constructed story collection to downloading only one or two music tracks from a CD or listening to the tracks in a different order than the artist intended, practices that famed Clash guitarist Mick Jones compares to "buying the *Mona Lisa* and only buying the eyeball because that was the bit you liked. [. . .] It's not going to ultimately be the complete experience that [the artist] had in mind." Jhumpa Lahiri, author of the short-story cycle *The Interpreter of Maladies* (the title story of which appears in this anthology), uses a different metaphor:

> [Readers] think of [a short-story collection] as a chocolate box, an assorted thing. You present it, and readers can say, I like that one, that was my favorite, I like the orange cream. Whereas with a novel I think they regard it more as a thing of substance, an entrée, if you will; they don't pick it apart in terms of the mashed potato part of it and the peas and the meat part, it's all this thing in concert.

All things considered, Lahiri's gustatory metaphor is probably more apt than Mick Jones's more extreme one. Reading a single short story from a collection usually does much less violence to the work than cutting out the eyeball of Leonardo's famous painting. But both Jones and Lahiri have a point: A story does work and signify differently when we read it in isolation or in the context of stories by various authors than it does when we read it in the context of the collection or cycle of which it is a part. And the order in which stories appear in a cycle or collection also affects the way we read and respond to them.

JAMES JOYCE'S *DUBLINERS*

James Joyce at age 22 (1904)

At the risk of presenting you with the eyeball from the *Mona Lisa*, this chapter invites you to sample three stories from one of the most famous and influential short-story collections in the English language. First begun in 1904, when its author was only 22, and completed in 1907, James Joyce's *Dubliners* wasn't published in its entirety until ten years later, largely because of publishers' concerns about potential lawsuits. Yet from the beginning it was conceived by Joyce not just as a coherent collection but also and specifically as a very deliberately ordered "series" or sequence of what he called "epiclets" (that is, mini-**epics**).

As the book's title makes clear, the most obvious element that unifies its stories is their setting—Dublin, Ireland, in the late nineteenth and early twentieth century, the hometown Joyce permanently left behind while writing the book. But the title and the stories focus on the people as much as the place—Dublin*ers*, not just Dublin. And Joyce himself insisted in his letters that the book's fifteen stories fell into four groups, each corresponding to a particular aspect or phase of Dubliners' lives—childhood, adolescence, mature life, and public life.

New Irish Books

Ready or to appear shortly

DUBLINERS. By J. Joyce. Crown 8vo, cloth. 3s. 6d. net (*24th Nov.*)

A book of studies of Dublin life, which, although detached, is by no means a mere collection of sketches, but has a very distinct unity. Never before has this side of Dublin life been presented in quite so real a manner. The author's style at once removes the book from the category of ordinary fiction and makes it the piece of literature that will no doubt win the same recognition from discerning critics as did his book of poems published a few years ago, of which Mr. Arthur Symons wrote: " . . . so singularly good, so fine and delicate, and yet so full of music and suggestion, that I can hardly choose among them . . . to do such tiny evanescent things . . . is to evoke, not only roses in mid-winter, but the very dew on the roses. Sometimes we are reminded of Elizabethan, more often of Jacobean lyrics."

MAUNSEL & CO., LIMITED
96 Middle Abbey Street, Dublin.

Advertisement for an edition of *Dubliners* that never appeared

The three stories we include here represent three of those four groups and phases. The **initiation story** "Araby" is the third story in *Dubliners* and the last of its three stories of childhood. It is immediately followed—both in this chapter and in *Dubliners*—by "Eveline," the first of three stories of adolescence. "The Dead" is the final story of both the entire collection and its stories of public life, as well as the last short story Joyce ever wrote. In fact, however, "The Dead" is not short, especially in comparison with the fourteen stories that precede it, and its length has ensured that it is sometimes classed as a **novella** rather than a short story. Joyce's main pursuit in the years after he completed *Dubliners* was the writing of novels—*A Portrait of the Artist as a Young Man* (1916), *Ulysses* (1922), and *Finnegans Wake* (1939).

A wealth of useful material about *Dubliners* and about Joyce's life and career appears at the end of this chapter, including a timeline of major events both in Joyce's life and in what Joyce called the very "curious history" of his only short-story collection; excerpts from Joyce's early essays and from "Gas from a Burner," a farcical poem Joyce wrote from the point of view of the printer and publisher who initially agreed, but later refused, to bring out the book; and part of a scholarly essay on *Dubliners* that incorporates very suggestive comments about the collection made by Joyce in letters we cannot reproduce here.

Questions about Short-Story Collections

1. What is the overall **tone** of these stories? Does it change across the stories—and if so, how? How might the order of the stories affect the overall tone of the collection?
2. How would you describe the stories' **protagonists**? What characteristics do the protagonists share? In these terms, do you see any development across the stories?
3. How would you describe the other **characters** whom the protagonists encounter? Are there similar types, or characters who perform similar functions (as **foils** or **antagonists**, for example)? Again, is there a pattern of development here? For instance, do certain types of characters appear in early stories, but not in later ones?
4. What problems and **conflicts** do the protagonists typically face? How are the conflicts resolved? In both the nature of the conflicts and their resolution, do you see any development across the stories, and what is the effect and significance of their order?
5. What similarities do you see in the stories' **action** and **plots**? What typically happens in these stories? How do they tend to begin and end? Are there similarities in the way events are ordered? (For example, do the stories begin ***in medias res*** or make use of **flashbacks**?)
6. How would you characterize the **setting** of these stories? How detailed is the description of setting, and what is its significance and role in the stories?
7. What patterns do you see in the **narration** of these stories? Does the narrative strategy or **point of view** change or evolve across the stories? If so, how?
8. Do the stories make use of **symbols**? Are there recurring symbols?
9. What are the most distinctive features of the **style** of these stories and the language used in them (diction, syntax, and so on)? Do the same or similar **images** recur in the various stories?
10. Thinking of the stories as a unit, what is or are its major **theme(s)**? How does each story contribute to the articulation of the theme(s)? In these terms, what is the effect and significance of the order of the stories?

THREE STORIES BY JAMES JOYCE

JAMES JOYCE

Araby

North Richmond Street, being blind,[1] was a quiet street except at the hour when the Christian Brothers' School set the boys free. An uninhabited house of two storeys stood at the blind end, detached from its neighbours in a square ground. The other houses of the street, conscious of decent lives within them, gazed at one another with brown imperturbable faces.

The former tenant of our house, a priest, had died in the back drawing-room. Air, musty from having been long enclosed, hung in all the rooms, and the waste room behind the kitchen was littered with old useless papers. Among

1. That is, a dead-end street.

these I found a few paper-covered books, the pages of which were curled and damp: *The Abbot*, by Walter Scott, *The Devout Communicant* and *The Memoirs of Vidocq*.[2] I liked the last best because its leaves were yellow. The wild garden behind the house contained a central apple-tree and a few straggling bushes under one of which I found the late tenant's rusty bicycle-pump. He had been a very charitable priest; in his will he had left all his money to institutions and the furniture of his house to his sister.

When the short days of winter came dusk fell before we had well eaten our dinners. When we met in the street the houses had grown sombre. The space of sky above us was the colour of ever-changing violet and towards it the lamps of the street lifted their feeble lanterns. The cold air stung us and we played till our bodies glowed. Our shouts echoed in the silent street. The career of our play brought us through the dark muddy lanes behind the houses where we ran the gantlet of the rough tribes from the cottages, to the back doors of the dark dripping gardens where odours arose from the ashpits,[3] to the dark odorous stables where a coachman smoothed and combed the horse or shook music from the buckled harness. When we returned to the street light from the kitchen windows had filled the areas. If my uncle was seen turning the corner we hid in the shadow until we had seen him safely housed. Or if Mangan's sister came out on the doorstep to call her brother in to his tea we watched her from our shadow peer up and down the street. We waited to see whether she would remain or go in and, if she remained, we left our shadow and walked up to Mangan's steps resignedly. She was waiting for us, her figure defined by the light from the half-opened door. Her brother always teased her before he obeyed and I stood by the railings looking at her. Her dress swung as she moved her body and the soft rope of her hair tossed from side to side.

Every morning I lay on the floor in the front parlour watching her door. The blind was pulled down to within an inch of the sash so that I could not be seen. When she came out on the doorstep my heart leaped. I ran to the hall, seized my books and followed her. I kept her brown figure always in my eye and, when we came near the point at which our ways diverged, I quickened my pace and passed her. This happened morning after morning. I had never spoken to her, except for a few casual words, and yet her name was like a summons to all my foolish blood.

5 Her image accompanied me even in places the most hostile to romance. On Saturday evenings when my aunt went marketing I had to go to carry some of the parcels. We walked through the flaring streets, jostled by drunken men and bargaining women, amid the curses of labourers, the shrill litanies of shop-boys who stood on guard by the barrels of pigs' cheeks, the nasal chanting of street-singers, who sang a *come-all-you* about O'Donovan Rossa,[4] or a ballad about the troubles in our native land. These noises converged in a single sensation of life for me: I

2. The "memoirs" were probably *not* written by François Vidocq (1775–1857), a French criminal who became chief of detectives and who died poor and disgraced for his part in a crime that he solved; the 1820 novel by Sir Walter Scott (1771–1834) is a romance about the Catholic Mary, Queen of Scots (1542–87), who was beheaded; *The Devout Communicant: or Pious Meditations and Aspirations for the Three Days Before and Three Days after Receiving the Holy Eucharist* (1813) is a Catholic religious tract.
3. Where fireplace ashes and other household refuse were dumped.
4. Jeremiah O'Donovan (1831–1915) was a militant Irish nationalist who fought on despite terms in prison and banishment. *Come-all-you*: a song, of which there were many, that began "Come, all you Irishmen."

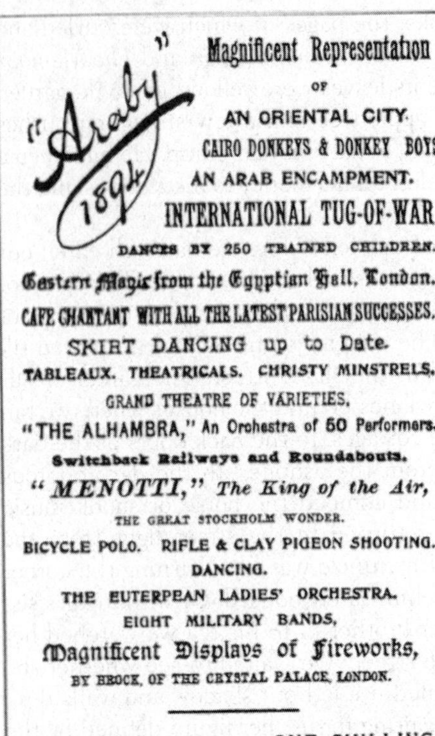

imagined that I bore my chalice safely through a throng of foes. Her name sprang to my lips at moments in strange prayers and praises which I myself did not understand. My eyes were often full of tears (I could not tell why) and at times a flood from my heart seemed to pour itself out into my bosom. I thought little of the future. I did not know whether I would ever speak to her or not or, if I spoke to her, how I could tell her of my confused adoration. But my body was like a harp and her words and gestures were like fingers running upon the wires.

"Araby" 1894
Magnificent Representation
OF
AN ORIENTAL CITY.
CAIRO DONKEYS & DONKEY BOYS
AN ARAB ENCAMPMENT.
INTERNATIONAL TUG-OF-WAR
DANCES BY 250 TRAINED CHILDREN.
Eastern Magic from the Egyptian Hall, London.
CAFE CHANTANT WITH ALL THE LATEST PARISIAN SUCCESSES.
SKIRT DANCING up to Date.
TABLEAUX. THEATRICALS. CHRISTY MINSTRELS.
GRAND THEATRE OF VARIETIES.
"THE ALHAMBRA," An Orchestra of 50 Performers.
Switchback Railways and Roundabouts.
"MENOTTI," The King of the Air,
THE GREAT STOCKHOLM WONDER.
BICYCLE POLO. RIFLE & CLAY PIGEON SHOOTING.
DANCING.
THE EUTERPEAN LADIES' ORCHESTRA.
EIGHT MILITARY BANDS.
Magnificent Displays of Fireworks,
BY BROCK, OF THE CRYSTAL PALACE, LONDON.
ADMISSION • • ONE SHILLING

One evening I went into the back drawing-room in which the priest had died. It was a dark rainy evening and there was no sound in the house. Through one of the broken panes I heard the rain impinge upon the earth, the fine incessant needles of water playing in the sodden beds. Some distant lamp or lighted window gleamed below me. I was thankful that I could see so little. All my senses seemed to desire to veil themselves and, feeling that I was about to slip from them, I pressed the palms of my hands together until they trembled, murmuring: *O love! O love!* many times.

At last she spoke to me. When she addressed the first words to me I was so confused that I did not know what to answer. She asked me was I going to *Araby*.[5] I forget whether I answered yes or no. It would be a splendid bazaar, she said; she would love to go.

—And why can't you? I asked.

While she spoke she turned a silver bracelet round and round her wrist. She could not go, she said, because there would be a retreat[6] that week in her convent. Her brother and two other boys were fighting for their caps and I was alone at the railings. She held one of the spikes, bowing her head towards me. The light from the lamp opposite our door caught the white curve of her neck, lit up her hair that rested there and, falling, lit up the hand upon the railing. It fell over one side of her dress and caught the white border of a petticoat, just visible as she stood at ease.

10 —It's well for you, she said.

—If I go, I said, I will bring you something.

5. A charity bazaar billed as a "Grand Oriental Fete," Dublin, May 1894.

6. A period of withdrawal dedicated to prayer and religious study.

What innumerable follies laid waste my waking and sleeping thoughts after that evening! I wished to annihilate the tedious intervening days. I chafed against the work of school. At night in my bedroom and by day in the classroom her image came between me and the page I strove to read. The syllables of the word *Araby* were called to me through the silence in which my soul luxuriated and cast an Eastern enchantment over me. I asked for leave to go to the bazaar on Saturday night. My aunt was surprised and hoped it was not some Freemason[7] affair. I answered few questions in class. I watched my master's face pass from amiability to sternness; he hoped I was not beginning to idle. I could not call my wandering thoughts together. I had hardly any patience with the serious work of life which, now that it stood between me and my desire, seemed to me child's play, ugly monotonous child's play.

On Saturday morning I reminded my uncle that I wished to go to the bazaar in the evening. He was fussing at the hall-stand, looking for the hat-brush, and answered me curtly:

—Yes, boy, I know.

As he was in the hall I could not go into the front parlour and lie at the win- 15
dow. I left the house in bad humour and walked slowly towards the school. The air was pitilessly raw and already my heart misgave me.

When I came home to dinner my uncle had not yet been home. Still it was early. I sat staring at the clock for some time and, when its ticking began to irritate me, I left the room. I mounted the staircase and gained the upper part of the house. The high cold empty gloomy rooms liberated me and I went from room to room singing. From the front window I saw my companions playing below in the street. Their cries reached me weakened and indistinct and, leaning my forehead against the cool glass, I looked over at the dark house where she lived. I may have stood there for an hour, seeing nothing but the brown-clad figure cast by my imagination, touched discreetly by the lamplight at the curved neck, at the hand upon the railings and at the border below the dress.

When I came downstairs again I found Mrs Mercer sitting at the fire. She was an old garrulous woman, a pawnbroker's widow, who collected used stamps for some pious purpose. I had to endure the gossip of the tea-table. The meal was prolonged beyond an hour and still my uncle did not come. Mrs Mercer stood up to go: she was sorry she couldn't wait any longer, but it was after eight o'clock and she did not like to be out late, as the night air was bad for her. When she had gone I began to walk up and down the room, clenching my fists. My aunt said:

—I'm afraid you may put off your bazaar for this night of Our Lord.

At nine o'clock I heard my uncle's latchkey in the halldoor. I heard him talking to himself and heard the hallstand rocking when it had received the weight of his overcoat. I could interpret these signs. When he was midway through his dinner I asked him to give me the money to go to the bazaar. He had forgotten.

—The people are in bed and after their first sleep now, he said. 20

I did not smile. My aunt said to him energetically:

—Can't you give him the money and let him go? You've kept him late enough as it is.

7. Freemasons—members of an influential, secretive, and highly ritualistic fraternal organization—were considered enemies of the Catholics.

My uncle said he was very sorry he had forgotten. He said he believed in the old saying: *All work and no play makes Jack a dull boy.* He asked me where I was going and, when I had told him a second time he asked me did I know *The Arab's Farewell to his Steed.*[8] When I left the kitchen he was about to recite the opening lines of the piece to my aunt.

I held a florin[9] tightly in my hand as I strode down Buckingham Street towards the station. The sight of the streets thronged with buyers and glaring with gas recalled to me the purpose of my journey. I took my seat in a third-class carriage of a deserted train. After an intolerable delay the train moved out of the station slowly. It crept onward among ruinous houses and over the twinkling river. At Westland Row Station a crowd of people pressed to the carriage doors; but the porters moved them back, saying that it was a special train for the bazaar. I remained alone in the bare carriage. In a few minutes the train drew up beside an improvised wooden platform. I passed out on to the road and saw by the lighted dial of a clock that it was ten minutes to ten. In front of me was a large building which displayed the magical name.

I could not find any sixpenny entrance and, fearing that the bazaar would be closed, I passed in quickly through a turnstile, handing a shilling to a weary-looking man. I found myself in a big hall girdled at half its height by a gallery. Nearly all the stalls were closed and the greater part of the hall was in darkness. I recognized a silence like that which pervades a church after a service. I walked into the centre of the bazaar timidly. A few people were gathered about the stalls which were still open. Before a curtain, over which the words *Café Chantant*[1] were written in coloured lamps, two men were counting money on a salver. I listened to the fall of the coins.

Remembering with difficulty why I had come I went over to one of the stalls and examined porcelain vases and flowered tea-sets. At the door of the stall a young lady was talking and laughing with two young gentlemen. I remarked their English accents and listened vaguely to their conversation.

—O, I never said such a thing!

—O, but you did!

—O, but I didn't!

—Didn't she say that?

—Yes. I heard her.

—O, there's a . . . fib!

Observing me the young lady came over and asked me did I wish to buy anything. The tone of her voice was not encouraging; she seemed to have spoken to me out of a sense of duty. I looked humbly at the great jars that stood like eastern guards at either side of the dark entrance to the stall and murmured:

—No, thank you.

The young lady changed the position of one of the vases and went back to the two young men. They began to talk of the same subject. Once or twice the young lady glanced at me over her shoulder.

8. Or *The Arab's Farewell to His Horse*, a sentimental nineteenth-century poem by Caroline Norton. The speaker has sold the horse.

9. A two-shilling piece; thus four times the "sixpenny entrance" fee.

1. Café with music (French).

I lingered before her stall, though I knew my stay was useless, to make my interest in her wares seem the more real. Then I turned away slowly and walked down the middle of the bazaar. I allowed the two pennies to fall against the sixpence in my pocket. I heard a voice call from one end of the gallery that the light was out. The upper part of the hall was now completely dark.

Gazing up into the darkness I saw myself as a creature driven and derided by vanity; and my eyes burned with anguish and anger.

1914

JAMES JOYCE
Eveline

She sat at the window watching the evening invade the avenue. Her head was leaned against the window curtains and in her nostrils was the odour of dusty cretonne.[1] She was tired.

Few people passed. The man out of the last house passed on his way home; she heard his footsteps clacking along the concrete pavement and afterwards crunching on the cinder path before the new red houses. One time there used to be a field there in which they used to play every evening with other people's children. Then a man from Belfast bought the field and built houses in it—not like their little brown houses but bright brick houses with shining roofs. The children of the avenue used to play together in that field—the Devines, the Waters, the Dunns, little Keogh the cripple, she and her brothers and sisters. Ernest, however, never played: he was too grown up. Her father used often to hunt them in out of the field with his blackthorn stick; but usually little Keogh used to keep *nix*[2] and call out when he saw her father coming. Still they seemed to have been rather happy then. Her father was not so bad then; and besides, her mother was alive. That was a long time ago; she and her brothers and sisters were all grown up; her mother was dead. Tizzie Dunn was dead, too, and the Waters had gone back to England. Everything changes. Now she was going to go away like the others, to leave her home.

Home! She looked round the room, reviewing all its familiar objects which she had dusted once a week for so many years, wondering where on earth all the dust came from. Perhaps she would never see again those familiar objects from which she had never dreamed of being divided. And yet during all those years she had never found out the name of the priest whose yellowing photograph hung on the wall above the broken harmonium[3] beside the coloured print of the promises made to Blessed Margaret Mary Alacoque.[4] He had been a school friend of her father. Whenever he showed the photograph to a visitor her father used to pass it with a casual word:

1. Heavy fabric for upholstery and drapery.
2. That is, keep watch.
3. Musical instrument similar to an organ.
4. French nun (1647–90) officially declared "blessed" by the Catholic Church in 1864 and canonized as a saint in 1920. A series of divine visitations that began in her childhood revealed to her Jesus's twelve promises to the faithful, including (1) *I will give them all the graces necessary for their state of life*, (2) *I will establish peace in their families or homes*, and (3) *I will console them in all their troubles*.

—He is in Melbourne[5] now.

5 She had consented to go away, to leave her home. Was that wise? She tried to weigh each side of the question. In her home anyway she had shelter and food; she had those whom she had known all her life about her. Of course she had to work hard both in the house and at business. What would they say of her in the Stores when they found out that she had run away with a fellow? Say she was a fool, perhaps; and her place would be filled up by advertisement. Miss Gavan would be glad. She had always had an edge[6] on her, especially whenever there were people listening.

—Miss Hill, don't you see these ladies are waiting?

—Look lively, Miss Hill, please.

She would not cry many tears at leaving the Stores.

But in her new home, in a distant unknown country, it would not be like that. Then she would be married—she, Eveline. People would treat her with respect then. She would not be treated as her mother had been. Even now, though she was over nineteen, she sometimes felt herself in danger of her father's violence. She knew it was that that had given her the palpitations. When they were growing up he had never gone for her, like he used to go for Harry and Ernest, because she was a girl; but latterly he had begun to threaten her and say what he would do to her only for her dead mother's sake. And now she had nobody to protect her. Ernest was dead and Harry, who was in the church decorating business, was nearly always down somewhere in the country. Besides, the invariable squabble for money on Saturday nights had begun to weary her unspeakably. She always gave her entire wages—seven shillings—and Harry always sent up what he could but the trouble was to get any money from her father. He said she used to squander the money, that she had no head,[7] that he wasn't going to give her his hard-earned money to throw about the streets, and much more, for he was usually fairly bad of a Saturday night. In the end he would give her the money and ask her had she any intention of buying Sunday's dinner. Then she had to rush out as quickly as she could and do her marketing, holding her black leather purse tightly in her hand as she elbowed her way through the crowds and returning home late under her load of provisions. She had hard work to keep the house together and to see that the two young children who had been left to her charge went to school regularly and got their meals regularly. It was hard work—a hard life—but now that she was about to leave it she did not find it a wholly undesirable life.

10 She was about to explore another life with Frank. Frank was very kind, manly, open-hearted. She was to go away with him by the night-boat to be his wife and to live with him in Buenos Ayres[8] where he had a home waiting for her. How well she remembered the first time she had seen him; he was lodging in a house on the main road where she used to visit. It seemed a few weeks ago. He was standing at the gate, his peaked cap pushed back on his head and his hair tumbled forward

5. City in Australia, a British colony and, like the United States, a frequent destination of nineteenth-century Irish immigrants.

6. That is, a hard, sarcastic manner.

7. No common sense or intelligence, especially regarding business matters.

8. Or Buenos Aires, capital and largest city of Argentina, in South America; its Spanish name literally means "good air."

Dublin docks, circa 1890

over a face of bronze. Then they had come to know each other. He used to meet her outside the Stores every evening and see her home. He took her to see *The Bohemian Girl*[9] and she felt elated as she sat in an unaccustomed part of the theatre with him. He was awfully fond of music and sang a little. People knew that they were courting and, when he sang about the lass that loves a sailor,[1] she always felt pleasantly confused. He used to call her Poppens out of fun. First of all it had been an excitement for her to have a fellow and then she had begun to like him. He had tales of distant countries. He had started as a deck boy at a pound a month on a ship of the Allan Line going out to Canada. He told her the names of the ships he had been on and the names of the different services. He had sailed through the Straits of Magellan[2] and he told her stories of the terrible Patagonians.[3] He had fallen on his feet in Buenos Ayres, he said, and had come over to the old country just for a holiday. Of course, her father had found out the affair and had forbidden her to have anything to say to him.

—I know these sailor chaps, he said.

One day he had quarrelled with Frank and after that she had to meet her lover secretly.

The evening deepened in the avenue. The white of two letters in her lap grew indistinct. One was to Harry; the other was to her father. Ernest had been her favourite but she liked Harry too. Her father was becoming old lately, she noticed; he would miss her. Sometimes he could be very nice. Not long before, when she had been laid up for a day, he had read her out a ghost story and made toast for her at the fire. Another day, when their mother was alive, they had all

9. 1843 opera by Dubliner Michael Balfe (1808–70) in which a young noblewoman, kidnapped by Gypsies, falls in love with a nobleman who has taken refuge with the Gypsies, and—after being restored to her father and home—decides to leave home once again to marry her lover.

1. Popular song by Charles Dibdin (1745–1814) about drunken sailors' toasts to their wives and sweethearts. "The Lass That Loved a Sailor" is also the subtitle of *H.M.S. Pinafore*, a well-known 1878 comic operetta by W. S. Gilbert and Arthur Sullivan.

2. Sea passage in South America through which ships can pass between the Atlantic and Pacific oceans.

3. Name given by Ferdinand Magellan (1480–1521) and other early explorers to the supposedly fearsome giants native to southernmost South America.

gone for a picnic to the Hill of Howth.[4] She remembered her father putting on her mother's bonnet to make the children laugh.

Her time was running out but she continued to sit by the window, leaning her head against the window curtain, inhaling the odour of dusty cretonne. Down far in the avenue she could hear a street organ[5] playing. She knew the air. Strange that it should come that very night to remind her of the promise to her mother, her promise to keep the home together as long as she could. She remembered the last night of her mother's illness; she was again in the close dark room at the other side of the hall and outside she heard a melancholy air of Italy. The organ-player had been ordered to go away and given sixpence. She remembered her father strutting back into the sickroom saying:

15 —Damned Italians! coming over here!

As she mused the pitiful vision of her mother's life laid its spell on the very quick of her being—that life of commonplace sacrifices closing in final craziness. She trembled as she heard again her mother's voice saying constantly with foolish insistence:

—Derevaun Seraun! Derevaun Seraun![6]

She stood up in a sudden impulse of terror. Escape! She must escape! Frank would save her. He would give her life, perhaps love, too. But she wanted to live. Why should she be unhappy? She had a right to happiness. Frank would take her in his arms, fold her in his arms. He would save her.

• • •

She stood among the swaying crowd in the station at the North Wall.[7] He held her hand and she knew that he was speaking to her, saying something about the passage over and over again. The station was full of soldiers[8] with brown baggages. Through the wide doors of the sheds she caught a glimpse of the black mass of the boat, lying in beside the quay wall, with illumined portholes. She answered nothing. She felt her cheek pale and cold and, out of a maze of distress, she prayed to God to direct her, to show her what was her duty. The boat blew a long mournful whistle into the mist. If she went, to-morrow she would be on the sea with Frank, steaming towards Buenos Ayres. Their passage had been booked. Could she still draw back after all he had done for her? Her distress awoke a nausea in her body and she kept moving her lips in silent fervent prayer.

20 A bell clanged upon her heart. She felt him seize her hand:

—Come!

All the seas of the world tumbled about her heart. He was drawing her into them: he would drown her. She gripped with both hands at the iron railing.

—Come!

4. The Howth peninsula is just northeast of Dublin; the hill overlooking its harbor is a popular picnic spot.

5. Portable harmonium usually played by professional street musicians, many of whom were Italian immigrants.

6. The meaning of this phrase is unknown, though scholars speculate that the words are either pure nonsense or a garbled version of Gaelic phrases meaning "The end of pleasure is pain" or "The end of song is derangement."

7. Embarkation point for Dublin emigrants.

8. Probably English soldiers stationed in Ireland.

No! No! No! It was impossible. Her hands clutched the iron in frenzy. Amid the seas she sent a cry of anguish!

—Eveline! Evvy! 25

He rushed beyond the barrier and called to her to follow. He was shouted at to go on but he still called to her. She set her white face to him, passive, like a helpless animal. Her eyes gave him no sign of love or farewell or recognition.

1914

JAMES JOYCE
The Dead

Lily, the caretaker's daughter, was literally run off her feet. Hardly had she brought one gentleman into the little pantry behind the office on the ground floor and helped him off with his overcoat than the wheezy hall-door bell clanged again and she had to scamper along the bare hallway to let in another guest. It was well for her she had not to attend to the ladies also. But Miss Kate and Miss Julia had thought of that and had converted the bathroom upstairs into a ladies' dressing-room. Miss Kate and Miss Julia were there, gossiping and laughing and fussing, walking after each other to the head of the stairs, peering down over the banisters and calling down to Lily to ask her who had come.

It was always a great affair, the Misses Morkan's annual dance. Everybody who knew them came to it, members of the family, old friends of the family, the members of Julia's choir, any of Kate's pupils that were grown up enough and even some of Mary Jane's pupils too. Never once had it fallen flat. For years and years it had gone off in splendid style as long as anyone could remember; ever since Kate and Julia, after the death of their brother Pat, had left the house in Stoney Batter and taken Mary Jane, their only niece, to live with them in the dark gaunt house on Usher's Island, the upper part of which they had rented from Mr Fulham, the corn-factor[1] on the ground floor. That was a good thirty years ago if it was a day. Mary Jane, who was then a little girl in short clothes, was now the main prop of the household for she had the organ in Haddington Road. She had been through the Academy[2] and gave a pupils' concert every year in the upper room of the Antient Concert Rooms. Many of her pupils belonged to better-class families on the Kingstown and Dalkey line. Old as they were, her aunts also did their share. Julia, though she was quite grey, was still the leading soprano in Adam and Eve's,[3] and Kate, being too feeble to go about much, gave music lessons to beginners on the old square piano in the back room. Lily, the caretaker's daughter, did housemaid's work for them. Though their life was modest they believed in eating well; the best of everything: diamond-bone sirloins, three-shilling tea[4] and the best bottled stout. But Lily seldom made a mistake in the orders so that she got on

1. Someone who buys and sells grain. *Usher's Island*: Dublin neighborhood, beside the river Liffey.
2. The Royal Academy of Music (founded 1848), Ireland's most prestigious music school. *Haddington Road*: Mary Jane is the organist at St. Mary's Roman Catholic Church on Haddington Road.
3. Nickname of the Franciscan Church of St. Francis of Assisi near Usher's Island.
4. That is, especially expensive tea and cuts of beef.

well with her three mistresses. They were fussy, that was all. But the only thing they would not stand was back answers.

Of course they had good reason to be fussy on such a night. And then it was long after ten o'clock and yet there was no sign of Gabriel and his wife. Besides they were dreadfully afraid that Freddy Malins might turn up screwed.[5] They would not wish for worlds that any of Mary Jane's pupils should see him under the influence; and when he was like that it was sometimes very hard to manage him. Freddy Malins always came late but they wondered what could be keeping Gabriel: and that was what brought them every two minutes to the banisters to ask Lily had Gabriel or Freddy come.

—O, Mr Conroy, said Lily to Gabriel when she opened the door for him, Miss Kate and Miss Julia thought you were never coming. Good-night, Mrs Conroy.

—I'll engage they did, said Gabriel, but they forget that my wife here takes three mortal hours to dress herself.

He stood on the mat, scraping the snow from his goloshes, while Lily led his wife to the foot of the stairs and called out:

—Miss Kate, here's Mrs Conroy.

Kate and Julia came toddling down the dark stairs at once. Both of them kissed Gabriel's wife, said she must be perished alive and asked was Gabriel with her.

—Here I am as right as the mail, Aunt Kate! Go on up. I'll follow, called out Gabriel from the dark.

He continued scraping his feet vigorously while the three women went upstairs, laughing, to the ladies' dressing-room. A light fringe of snow lay like a cape on the shoulders of his overcoat and like toecaps on the toes of his goloshes; and, as the buttons of his overcoat slipped with a squeaking noise through the snow-stiffened frieze, a cold fragrant air from out-of-doors escaped from crevices and folds.

—Is it snowing again, Mr Conroy? asked Lily.

She had preceded him into the pantry to help him off with his overcoat. Gabriel smiled at the three syllables she had given his surname and glanced at her. She was a slim, growing girl, pale in complexion and with hay-coloured hair. The gas in the pantry made her look still paler. Gabriel had known her when she was a child and used to sit on the lowest step nursing a rag doll.

—Yes, Lily, he answered, and I think we're in for a night of it.

He looked up at the pantry ceiling, which was shaking with the stamping and shuffling of feet on the floor above, listened for a moment to the piano and then glanced at the girl, who was folding his overcoat carefully at the end of a shelf.

—Tell me, Lily, he said in a friendly tone, do you still go to school?

—O no, sir, she answered. I'm done schooling this year and more.

—O, then, said Gabriel gaily, I suppose we'll be going to your wedding one of these fine days with your young man, eh?

The girl glanced back at him over her shoulder and said with great bitterness:

—The men that is now is only all palaver[6] and what they can get out of you.

Gabriel coloured as if he felt he had made a mistake and, without looking at her, kicked off his goloshes and flicked actively with his muffler at his patent-leather shoes.

5. Drunk.

6. Flattery, empty talk.

He was a stout tallish young man. The high colour of his cheeks pushed upwards even to his forehead where it scattered itself in a few formless patches of pale red; and on his hairless face there scintillated restlessly the polished lenses and the bright gilt rims of the glasses which screened his delicate and restless eyes. His glossy black hair was parted in the middle and brushed in a long curve behind his ears where it curled slightly beneath the groove left by his hat.

When he had flicked lustre into his shoes he stood up and pulled his waistcoat down more tightly on his plump body. Then he took a coin rapidly from his pocket.

—O Lily, he said, thrusting it into her hands, it's Christmas-time, isn't it? Just . . . here's a little. . . .

He walked rapidly towards the door.

—O no, sir! cried the girl, following him. Really, sir, I wouldn't take it. 25

—Christmas-time! Christmas-time! said Gabriel, almost trotting to the stairs and waving his hand to her in deprecation.

The girl, seeing that he had gained the stairs, called out after him:

—Well, thank you, sir.

He waited outside the drawing-room door until the waltz should finish, listening to the skirts that swept against it and to the shuffling of feet. He was still discomposed by the girl's bitter and sudden retort. It had cast a gloom over him which he tried to dispel by arranging his cuffs and the bows of his tie. Then he took from his waistcoat pocket a little paper and glanced at the headings he had made for his speech. He was undecided about the lines from Robert Browning for he feared they would be above the heads of his hearers. Some quotation that they could recognise from Shakespeare or from the Melodies[7] would be better. The indelicate clacking of the men's heels and the shuffling of their soles reminded him that their grade of culture differed from his. He would only make himself ridiculous by quoting poetry to them which they could not understand. They would think that he was airing his superior education. He would fail with them just as he had failed with the girl in the pantry. He had taken up a wrong tone. His whole speech was a mistake from first to last, an utter failure.

Just then his aunts and his wife came out of the ladies' dressing-room. His 30
aunts were two small plainly dressed old women. Aunt Julia was an inch or so the taller. Her hair, drawn low over the tops of her ears, was grey; and grey also, with darker shadows, was her large flaccid face. Though she was stout in build and stood erect her slow eyes and parted lips gave her the appearance of a woman who did not know where she was or where she was going. Aunt Kate was more vivacious. Her face, healthier than her sister's, was all puckers and creases, like a shrivelled red apple, and her hair, braided in the same old-fashioned way, had not lost its ripe nut colour.

They both kissed Gabriel frankly. He was their favourite nephew, the son of their dead elder sister, Ellen, who had married T. J. Conroy of the Port and Docks.[8]

—Gretta tells me you're not going to take a cab back to Monkstown to-night, Gabriel, said Aunt Kate.

7. *Irish Melodies* (1807–35), a popular collection of poems by Dublin-born writer Thomas Moore (1779–1852). *Robert Browning*: English poet (1812–89) best known for his dramatic monologues.

8. The Dublin Port and Docks Board was the powerful group that regulated shipping activities, managed harbor facilities, and collected customs duties.

—No, said Gabriel, turning to his wife, we had quite enough of that last year, hadn't we? Don't you remember, Aunt Kate, what a cold Gretta got out of it? Cab windows rattling all the way, and the east wind blowing in after we passed Merrion. Very jolly it was. Gretta caught a dreadful cold.

Aunt Kate frowned severely and nodded her head at every word.

—Quite right, Gabriel, quite right, she said. You can't be too careful.

—But as for Gretta there, said Gabriel, she'd walk home in the snow if she were let.

Mrs Conroy laughed.

—Don't mind him, Aunt Kate, she said. He's really an awful bother, what with green shades for Tom's eyes at night and making him do the dumb-bells, and forcing Eva to eat the stirabout.[9] The poor child! And she simply hates the sight of it! . . . O, but you'll never guess what he makes me wear now!

She broke out into a peal of laughter and glanced at her husband, whose admiring and happy eyes had been wandering from her dress to her face and hair. The two aunts laughed heartily too, for Gabriel's solicitude was a standing joke with them.

—Goloshes! said Mrs Conroy. That's the latest. Whenever it's wet underfoot I must put on my goloshes. To-night even he wanted me to put them on, but I wouldn't. The next thing he'll buy me will be a diving suit.

Gabriel laughed nervously and patted his tie reassuringly while Aunt Kate nearly doubled herself, so heartily did she enjoy the joke. The smile soon faded from Aunt Julia's face and her mirthless eyes were directed towards her nephew's face. After a pause she asked:

—And what are goloshes, Gabriel?

—Goloshes, Julia! exclaimed her sister. Goodness me, don't you know what goloshes are? You wear them over your . . . over your boots, Gretta, isn't it?

—Yes, said Mrs Conroy. Guttapercha[1] things. We both have a pair now. Gabriel says everyone wears them on the continent.

—O, on the continent, murmured Aunt Julia, nodding her head slowly.

Gabriel knitted his brows and said, as if he were slightly angered:

—It's nothing very wonderful but Gretta thinks it very funny because she says the word reminds her of Christy Minstrels.[2]

—But tell me, Gabriel, said Aunt Kate, with brisk tact. Of course, you've seen about the room. Gretta was saying . . .

—O, the room is all right, replied Gabriel. I've taken one in the Gresham.

—To be sure, said Aunt Kate, by far the best thing to do. And the children, Gretta, you're not anxious about them?

—O, for one night, said Mrs Conroy. Besides, Bessie will look after them.

—To be sure, said Aunt Kate again. What a comfort it is to have a girl like that, one you can depend on! There's that Lily, I'm sure I don't know what has come over her lately. She's not the girl she was at all.

9. Oatmeal or cornmeal porridge.

1. Tough plastic substance resembling rubber.

2. New York–based theatrical company founded by Edward Christy in the 1840s, which pioneered the blackface minstrel shows that became wildly popular in the mid- to late nineteenth century. These music and comedy shows featured white performers in dark makeup playing stereotypical African American characters. The word *goloshes* may remind Greta of the Christy Minstrels because it sounds like *gollywog*, a doll with exaggerated black features that first appeared in 1895.

Gabriel was about to ask his aunt some questions on this point but she broke off suddenly to gaze after her sister who had wandered down the stairs and was craning her neck over the banisters.

—Now, I ask you, she said, almost testily, where is Julia going? Julia! Julia! Where are you going?

Julia, who had gone halfway down one flight, came back and announced 55
blandly:

—Here's Freddy.

At the same moment a clapping of hands and a final flourish of the pianist told that the waltz had ended. The drawing-room door was opened from within and some couples came out. Aunt Kate drew Gabriel aside hurriedly and whispered into his ear:

—Slip down, Gabriel, like a good fellow and see if he's all right, and don't let him up if he's screwed.[3] I'm sure he's screwed. I'm sure he is.

Gabriel went to the stairs and listened over the banisters. He could hear two persons talking in the pantry. Then he recognised Freddy Malins' laugh. He went down the stairs noisily.

—It's such a relief, said Aunt Kate to Mrs Conroy, that Gabriel is here. I 60
always feel easier in my mind when he's here. . . . Julia, there's Miss Daly and Miss Power will take some refreshment. Thanks for your beautiful waltz, Miss Daly. It made lovely time.

A tall wizen-faced man, with a stiff grizzled moustache and swarthy skin, who was passing out with his partner said:

—And may we have some refreshment, too, Miss Morkan?

—Julia, said Aunt Kate summarily, and here's Mr Browne and Miss Furlong. Take them in, Julia, with Miss Daly and Miss Power.

—I'm the man for the ladies, said Mr Browne, pursing his lips until his moustache bristled and smiling in all his wrinkles. You know, Miss Morkan, the reason they are so fond of me is—

He did not finish his sentence, but, seeing that Aunt Kate was out of earshot, 65
at once led the three young ladies into the back room. The middle of the room was occupied by two square tables placed end to end, and on these Aunt Julia and the caretaker were straightening and smoothing a large cloth. On the sideboard were arrayed dishes and plates, and glasses and bundles of knives and forks and spoons. The top of the closed square piano served also as a sideboard for viands and sweets. At a smaller sideboard in one corner two young men were standing, drinking hop-bitters.[4]

Mr Browne led his charges thither and invited them all, in jest, to some ladies' punch, hot, strong and sweet. As they said they never took anything strong he opened three bottles of lemonade for them. Then he asked one of the young men to move aside, and, taking hold of the decanter, filled out for himself a goodly measure of whisky. The young men eyed him respectfully while he took a trial sip.

—God help me, he said, smiling, it's the doctor's orders.

His wizened face broke into a broader smile, and the three young ladies laughed in musical echo to his pleasantry, swaying their bodies to and fro, with nervous jerks of their shoulders. The boldest said:

3. Drunk.

4. Nonalcoholic drink.

—O, now, Mr Browne, I'm sure the doctor never ordered anything of the kind.

70 Mr Browne took another sip of his whisky and said, with sidling mimicry:

—Well, you see, I'm like the famous Mrs Cassidy, who is reported to have said: *Now, Mary Grimes, if I don't take it, make me take it, for I feel I want it.*

His hot face had leaned forward a little too confidentially and he had assumed a very low Dublin accent so that the young ladies, with one instinct, received his speech in silence. Miss Furlong, who was one of Mary Jane's pupils, asked Miss Daly what was the name of the pretty waltz she had played; and Mr Browne, seeing that he was ignored, turned promptly to the two young men who were more appreciative.

A red-faced young woman, dressed in pansy,[5] came into the room, excitedly clapping her hands and crying:

—Quadrilles! Quadrilles![6]

75 Close on her heels came Aunt Kate, crying:

—Two gentlemen and three ladies, Mary Jane!

—O, here's Mr Bergin and Mr Kerrigan, said Mary Jane. Mr Kerrigan, will you take Miss Power? Miss Furlong, may I get you a partner, Mr Bergin. O, that'll just do now.

—Three ladies, Mary Jane, said Aunt Kate.

The two young gentlemen asked the ladies if they might have the pleasure, and Mary Jane turned to Miss Daly.

80 —O, Miss Daly, you're really awfully good, after playing for the last two dances, but really we're so short of ladies to-night.

—I don't mind in the least, Miss Morkan.

—But I've a nice partner for you, Mr Bartell D'Arcy, the tenor. I'll get him to sing later on. All Dublin is raving about him.

—Lovely voice, lovely voice! said Aunt Kate.

As the piano had twice begun the prelude to the first figure Mary Jane led her recruits quickly from the room. They had hardly gone when Aunt Julia wandered slowly into the room, looking behind her at something.

85 —What is the matter, Julia? asked Aunt Kate anxiously. Who is it?

Julia, who was carrying in a column of table-napkins, turned to her sister and said, simply, as if the question had surprised her:

—It's only Freddy, Kate, and Gabriel with him.

In fact right behind her Gabriel could be seen piloting Freddy Malins across the landing. The latter, a young man of about forty, was of Gabriel's size and build, with very round shoulders. His face was fleshy and pallid, touched with colour only at the thick hanging lobes of his ears and at the wide wings of his nose. He had coarse features, a blunt nose, a convex and receding brow, tumid and protruded lips. His heavy-lidded eyes and the disorder of his scanty hair made him look sleepy. He was laughing heartily in a high key at a story which he had been telling Gabriel on the stairs and at the same time rubbing the knuckles of his left fist backwards and forwards into his left eye.

—Good-evening, Freddy, said Aunt Julia.

5. That is, a dress the color of a pansy—bluish-purple or violet.

6. Elaborate square dance of French origin composed of five different sections or "figures" performed by four couples.

Freddy Malins bade the Misses Morkan good-evening in what seemed an offhand fashion by reason of the habitual catch in his voice and then, seeing that Mr Browne was grinning at him from the sideboard, crossed the room on rather shaky legs and began to repeat in an undertone the story he had just told to Gabriel.

—He's not so bad, is he? said Aunt Kate to Gabriel.

Gabriel's brows were dark but he raised them quickly and answered:

—O no, hardly noticeable.

—Now, isn't he a terrible fellow! she said. And his poor mother made him take the pledge[7] on New Year's Eve. But come on, Gabriel, into the drawing-room.

Before leaving the room with Gabriel she signaled to Mr Browne by frowning and shaking her forefinger in warning to and fro. Mr Browne nodded in answer and, when she had gone, said to Freddy Malins:

—Now, then, Teddy, I'm going to fill you out a good glass of lemonade just to buck you up.

Freddy Malins, who was nearing the climax of his story, waved the offer aside impatiently but Mr Browne, having first called Freddy Malins' attention to a disarray in his dress, filled out and handed him a full glass of lemonade. Freddy Malins' left hand accepted the glass mechanically, his right hand being engaged in the mechanical readjustment of his dress. Mr Browne, whose face was once more wrinkling with mirth, poured out for himself a glass of whisky while Freddy Malins exploded, before he had well reached the climax of his story, in a kink of high-pitched bronchitic laughter and, setting down his untasted and overflowing glass, began to rub the knuckles of his left fist backwards and forwards into his left eye, repeating words of his last phrase as well as his fit of laughter would allow him.

• • •

Gabriel could not listen while Mary Jane was playing her Academy piece, full of runs and difficult passages, to the hushed drawing-room. He liked music but the piece she was playing had no melody for him and he doubted whether it had any melody for the other listeners, though they had begged Mary Jane to play something. Four young men, who had come from the refreshment-room to stand in the doorway at the sound of the piano, had gone away quietly in couples after a few minutes. The only persons who seemed to follow the music were Mary Jane herself, her hands racing along the key-board or lifted from it at the pauses like those of a priestess in momentary imprecation, and Aunt Kate standing at her elbow to turn the page.

Gabriel's eyes, irritated by the floor, which glittered with beeswax under the heavy chandelier, wandered to the wall above the piano. A picture of the balcony scene in *Romeo and Juliet*[8] hung there and beside it was a picture of the two murdered princes in the Tower[9] which Aunt Julia had worked in red, blue

7. Temperance or teetotal pledge, an oath not to drink alcohol.

8. Famous scene of Shakespeare's tragedy (2.2) in which Romeo declares his love to Juliet as she stands on the balcony above him.

9. In 1483, the two young sons of King Edward IV of England died while imprisoned in the Tower of London, their deaths purportedly ordered by their uncle, who became King Richard III the same year.

and brown wools when she was a girl. Probably in the school they had gone to as girls that kind of work had been taught, for one year his mother had worked for him as a birthday present a waistcoat of purple tabinet,[1] with little foxes' heads upon it, lined with brown satin and having round mulberry buttons. It was strange that his mother had had no musical talent though Aunt Kate used to call her the brains carrier of the Morkan family. Both she and Julia had always seemed a little proud of their serious and matronly sister. Her photograph stood before the pierglass.[2] She held an open book on her knees and was pointing out something in it to Constantine who, dressed in a man-o'-war suit,[3] lay at her feet. It was she who had chosen the names for her sons for she was very sensible of the dignity of family life. Thanks to her, Constantine was now senior curate[4] in Balbriggan and, thanks to her, Gabriel himself had taken his degree in the Royal University. A shadow passed over his face as he remembered her sullen opposition to his marriage. Some slighting phrases she had used still rankled in his memory; she had once spoken of Gretta as being country cute[5] and that was not true of Gretta at all. It was Gretta who had nursed her during all her last long illness in their house at Monkstown.

He knew that Mary Jane must be near the end of her piece for she was playing again the opening melody with runs of scales after every bar and while he waited for the end the resentment died down in his heart. The piece ended with a trill of octaves in the treble and a final deep octave in the bass. Great applause greeted Mary Jane as, blushing and rolling up her music nervously, she escaped from the room. The most vigorous clapping came from the four young men in the doorway who had gone away to the refreshment-room at the beginning of the piece but had come back when the piano had stopped.

Lancers[6] were arranged. Gabriel found himself partnered with Miss Ivors. She was a frank-mannered talkative young lady, with a freckled face and prominent brown eyes. She did not wear a low-cut bodice and the large brooch which was fixed in the front of her collar bore on it an Irish device.

When they had taken their places she said abruptly:

—I have a crow to pluck with you.

—With me? said Gabriel.

She nodded her head gravely.

—What is it? asked Gabriel, smiling at her solemn manner.

—Who is G. C.? answered Miss Ivors, turning her eyes upon him.

Gabriel coloured and was about to knit his brows, as if he did not understand, when she said bluntly:

—O, innocent Amy! I have found out that you write for *The Daily Express*. Now, aren't you ashamed of yourself?

1. Damask-like poplin fabric.

2. Large high mirror, especially one designed to be hung between two windows.

3. That is, a sailor suit—a child's outfit designed to look like the uniform worn by a sailor serving on the type of ship known as a man-of-war.

4. Clergyman in charge of a parish or church district.

5. Beginning of a pejorative idiomatic expression that ends "and city clever"; *cute* in this context is an abbreviation of *acute*.

6. Popular form of quadrille that could be danced by more than four couples.

—Why should I be ashamed of myself? asked Gabriel, blinking his eyes and 110
trying to smile.

—Well, I'm ashamed of you, said Miss Ivors frankly. To say you'd write for a rag like that. I didn't think you were a West Briton.[7]

A look of perplexity appeared on Gabriel's face. It was true that he wrote a literary column every Wednesday in *The Daily Express*, for which he was paid fifteen shillings. But that did not make him a West Briton surely. The books he received for review were almost more welcome than the paltry cheque. He loved to feel the covers and turn over the pages of newly printed books. Nearly every day when his teaching in the college was ended he used to wander down the quays to the second-hand booksellers, to Hickey's on Bachelor's Walk, to Webb's or Massey's on Aston's Quay, or to O'Clohissey's in the by-street. He did not know how to meet her charge. He wanted to say that literature was above politics. But they were friends of many years' standing and their careers had been parallel, first at the University and then as teachers: he could not risk a grandiose phrase with her. He continued blinking his eyes and trying to smile and murmured lamely that he saw nothing political in writing reviews of books.

When their turn to cross had come he was still perplexed and inattentive. Miss Ivors promptly took his hand in a warm grasp and said in a soft friendly tone:

—Of course, I was only joking. Come, we cross now.

When they were together again she spoke of the University question[8] and 115
Gabriel felt more at ease. A friend of hers had shown her his review of Browning's poems. That was how she had found out the secret: but she liked the review immensely. Then she said suddenly:

—O, Mr Conroy, will you come for an excursion to the Aran Isles[9] this summer? We're going to stay there a whole month. It will be splendid out in the Atlantic. You ought to come. Mr Clancy is coming, and Mr Kilkelly and Kathleen Kearney. It would be splendid for Gretta too if she'd come. She's from Connacht,[1] isn't she?

—Her people are, said Gabriel shortly.

—But you will come, won't you? said Miss Ivors, laying her warm hand eagerly on his arm.

—The fact is, said Gabriel, I have already arranged to go—

—Go where? asked Miss Ivors. 120

—Well, you know, every year I go for a cycling tour with some fellows and so—

—But where? asked Miss Ivors.

—Well, we usually go to France or Belgium or perhaps Germany, said Gabriel awkwardly.

—And why do you go to France and Belgium, said Miss Ivors, instead of visiting your own land?

7. Irishman so loyal to Britain that he considers Ireland to be merely Britain's westernmost province.

8. Controversy over the organization and character of Irish higher education, primarily regarding both the role of Catholicism and Protestantism and the possible admission of women.

9. Islands off Galway on the west coast of Ireland whose largely Gaelic-speaking inhabitants continued to live in what many in the late nineteenth century regarded as traditional, hence "true" Irish fashion; the islands were made famous by Irish Revivalist J. M. Synge's play *Riders to the Sea* (1901) and his nonfictional *Aran Islands* (1907).

1. Ireland's westernmost province; it includes both the county and city of Galway.

—Well, said Gabriel, it's partly to keep in touch with the languages and partly for a change.

—And haven't you your own language to keep in touch with—Irish? Asked Miss Ivors.

—Well, said Gabriel, if it comes to that, you know, Irish is not my language.

Their neighbours had turned to listen to the cross-examination. Gabriel glanced right and left nervously and tried to keep his good humour under the ordeal which was making a blush invade his forehead.

—And haven't you your own land to visit, continued Miss Ivors, that you know nothing of, your own people, and your own country?

—O, to tell you the truth, retorted Gabriel suddenly, I'm sick of my own country, sick of it!

—Why? Asked Miss Ivors.

Gabriel did not answer for his retort had heated him.

—Why? repeated Miss Ivors.

They had to go visiting together and, as he had not answered her, Miss Ivors said warmly:

—Of course, you've no answer.

Gabriel tried to cover his agitation by taking part in the dance with great energy. He avoided her eyes for he had seen a sour expression on her face. But when they met in the long chain he was surprised to feel his hand firmly pressed. She looked at him from under her brows for a moment quizzically until he smiled. Then, just as the chain was about to start again, she stood on tiptoe and whispered into his ear:

—West Briton!

When the lancers were over Gabriel went away to a remote corner of the room where Freddy Malins' mother was sitting. She was a stout feeble old woman with white hair. Her voice had a catch in it like her son's and she stuttered slightly. She had been told that Freddy had come and that he was nearly all right. Gabriel asked her whether she had had a good crossing. She lived with her married daughter in Glasgow and came to Dublin on a visit once a year. She answered placidly that she had had a beautiful crossing and that the captain had been most attentive to her. She spoke also of the beautiful house her daughter kept in Glasgow, and of all the nice friends they had there. While her tongue rambled on Gabriel tried to banish from his mind all memory of the unpleasant incident with Miss Ivors. Of course the girl or woman, or whatever she was, was an enthusiast but there was a time for all things. Perhaps he ought not to have answered her like that. But she had no right to call him a West Briton before people, even in joke. She had tried to make him ridiculous before people, heckling him and staring at him with her rabbit's eyes.

He saw his wife making her way towards him through the waltzing couples. When she reached him she said into his ear:

—Gabriel, Aunt Kate wants to know won't you carve the goose as usual. Miss Daly will carve the ham and I'll do the pudding.

—All right, said Gabriel.

—She's sending in the younger ones first as soon as this waltz is over so that we'll have the table to ourselves.

—Were you dancing? Asked Gabriel.

—Of course I was. Didn't you see me? What words had you with Molly Ivors?

—No words. Why? Did she say so? 145

—Something like that. I'm trying to get that Mr D'Arcy to sing. He's full of conceit, I think.

—There were no words, said Gabriel moodily, only she wanted me to go for a trip to the west of Ireland and I said I wouldn't.

His wife clasped her hands excitedly and gave a little jump.

—O, do go, Gabriel, she cried. I'd love to see Galway again.

—You can go if you like, said Gabriel coldly. 150

She looked at him for a moment, then turned to Mrs Malins and said:

—There's a nice husband for you, Mrs Malins.

While she was threading her way back across the room Mrs Malins, without adverting to the interruption, went on to tell Gabriel what beautiful places there were in Scotland and beautiful scenery. Her son-in-law brought them every year to the lakes and they used to go fishing. Her son-in-law was a splendid fisher. One day he caught a fish, a beautiful big big fish, and the man in the hotel boiled it for their dinner.

Gabriel hardly heard what she said. Now that supper was coming near he began to think again about his speech and about the quotation. When he saw Freddy Malins coming across the room to visit his mother Gabriel left the chair free for him and retired into the embrasure of the window. The room had already cleared and from the back room came the clatter of plates and knives. Those who still remained in the drawing-room seemed tired of dancing and were conversing quietly in little groups. Gabriel's warm trembling fingers tapped the cold pane of the window. How cool it must be outside! How pleasant it would be to walk out alone, first along by the river and then through the park! The snow would be lying on the branches of the trees and forming a bright cap on the top of the Wellington Monument.[2] How much more pleasant it would be there than at the supper-table!

He ran over the headings of his speech: Irish hospitality, sad memories, the 155
Three Graces, Paris,[3] the quotation from Browning. He repeated to himself a phrase he had written in his review: *One feels that one is listening to a thought-tormented music.* Miss Ivors had praised the review. Was she sincere? Had she really any life of her own behind all her propagandism? There had never been any ill-feeling between them until that night. It unnerved him to think that she would be at the supper-table, looking up at him while he spoke with her critical quizzing eyes. Perhaps she would not be sorry to see him fail in his speech. An

2. Monument in Dublin's Phoenix Park (just to the west of Usher Island) commemorating the achievements of Dublin-born Arthur Wellesley (1769–1852), Duke of Wellington, the Anglo-Irish Protestant and political conservative who defeated Napoleon at Waterloo (1816) and later served as British prime minister (1828–30).

3. Trojan prince of Greek literature and myth who, asked to judge a beauty contest between the three principal Greek goddesses, chooses Aphrodite, who bribes or rewards him with Helen, the human world's most beautiful woman. Because Helen is already married to the King of Sparta, however, her elopement with Paris ultimately causes the war with the Greeks that destroys Troy. *Three Graces*: Aglaia, Thalia, and Euphrosyne, the three goddesses of Greek mythology who personified and bestowed beauty, charm, and grace.

idea came into his mind and gave him courage. He would say, alluding to Aunt Kate and Aunt Julia: *Ladies and Gentlemen, the generation which is now on the wane among us may have had its faults but for my part I think it had certain qualities of hospitality, of humour, of humanity, which the new and very serious and hypereducated generation that is growing up around us seems to me to lack.* Very good: that was one for Miss Ivors. What did he care that his aunts were only two ignorant old women?

A murmur in the room attracted his attention. Mr Browne was advancing from the door, gallantly escorting Aunt Julia, who leaned upon his arm, smiling and hanging her head. An irregular musketry of applause escorted her also as far as the piano and then, as Mary Jane seated herself on the stool, and Aunt Julia, no longer smiling, half turned so as to pitch her voice fairly into the room, gradually ceased. Gabriel recognised the prelude. It was that of an old song of Aunt Julia's—*Arrayed for the Bridal.*[4] Her voice, strong and clear in tone, attacked with great spirit the runs which embellish the air and though she sang very rapidly she did not miss even the smallest of the grace notes. To follow the voice, without looking at the singer's face, was to feel and share the excitement of swift and secure flight. Gabriel applauded loudly with all the others at the close of the song and loud applause was borne in from the invisible supper-table. It sounded so genuine that a little colour struggled into Aunt Julia's face as she bent to replace in the music-stand the old leather-bound song-book that had her initials on the cover. Freddy Malins, who had listened with his head perched sideways to hear her better, was still applauding when everyone else had ceased and talking animatedly to his mother who nodded her head gravely and slowly in acquiescence. At last, when he could clap no more, he stood up suddenly and hurried across the room to Aunt Julia whose hand he seized and held in both his hands, shaking it when words failed him or the catch in his voice proved too much for him.

—I was just telling my mother, he said, I never heard you sing so well, never. No, I never heard your voice so good as it is to-night. Now! Would you believe that now? That's the truth. Upon my word and honour that's the truth. I never heard your voice sound so fresh and so . . . so clear and fresh, never.

Aunt Julia smiled broadly and murmured something about compliments as she released her hand from his grasp. Mr Browne extended his open hand towards her and said to those who were near him in the manner of a showman introducing a prodigy to an audience:

—Miss Julia Morkan, my latest discovery!

He was laughing very heartily at this himself when Freddy Malins turned to him and said:

—Well, Browne, if you're serious you might make a worse discovery. All I can say is I never heard her sing half so well as long as I am coming here. And that's the honest truth.

—Neither did I, said Mr Browne. I think her voice has greatly improved.

Aunt Julia shrugged her shoulders and said with meek pride:

4. Song by George Linley based on an aria in Italian composer Vincenzo Bellini's *I Puritani di Scozia* ("The Puritans of Scotland," 1835), an opera based, in turn, on Scottish writer Sir Walter Scott's novel *Old Mortality* (1816). In the opera, set during the English Civil War, a Puritan father wishes to marry his daughter to another Puritan despite her love for a Royalist; she ultimately wins her father's consent to marry her true love.

—Thirty years ago I hadn't a bad voice as voices go.

—I often told Julia, said Aunt Kate emphatically, that she was simply thrown away in that choir. But she never would be said[5] by me.

She turned as if to appeal to the good sense of the others against a refractory child while Aunt Julia gazed in front of her, a vague smile of reminiscence playing on her face.

—No, continued Aunt Kate, she wouldn't be said or led by anyone, slaving there in that choir night and day, night and day. Six o'clock on Christmas morning! And all for what?

—Well, isn't it for the honour of God, Aunt Kate? asked Mary Jane, twisting round on the piano-stool and smiling.

Aunt Kate turned fiercely on her niece and said:

—I know all about the honour of God, Mary Jane, but I think it's not at all honourable for the pope to turn out the women out of the choirs that have slaved there all their lives and put little whipper-snappers of boys over their heads.[6] I suppose it is for the good of the Church if the pope does it. But it's not just, Mary Jane, and it's not right.

She had worked herself into a passion and would have continued in defence of her sister for it was a sore subject with her but Mary Jane, seeing that all the dancers had come back, intervened pacifically:

—Now, Aunt Kate, you're giving scandal to Mr Browne who is of the other persuasion.[7]

Aunt Kate turned to Mr Browne, who was grinning at this allusion to his religion, and said hastily:

—O, I don't question the pope's being right. I'm only a stupid old woman and I wouldn't presume to do such a thing. But there's such a thing as common everyday politeness and gratitude. And if I were in Julia's place I'd tell that Father Healy straight up to his face . . .

—And besides, Aunt Kate, said Mary Jane, we really are all hungry and when we are hungry we are all very quarrelsome.

—And when we are thirsty we are also quarrelsome, added Mr Browne.

—So that we had better go to supper, said Mary Jane, and finish the discussion afterwards.

On the landing outside the drawing-room Gabriel found his wife and Mary Jane trying to persuade Miss Ivors to stay for supper. But Miss Ivors, who had put on her hat and was buttoning her cloak, would not stay. She did not feel in the least hungry and she had already overstayed her time.

—But only for ten minutes, Molly, said Mrs Conroy. That won't delay you.

—To take a pick itself,[8] said Mary Jane, after all your dancing.

—I really couldn't, said Miss Ivors.

—I am afraid you didn't enjoy yourself at all, said Mary Jane hopelessly.

5. Advised or gainsaid.

6. In 1903, Pope Pius X ordered that women should not be allowed to sing in church choirs because choristers (like priests) perform "a real liturgical office," which women are "incapable of exercising." Their place was to be taken by boys.

7. That is, a Protestant.

8. Bite (of food).

—Ever so much, I assure you, said Miss Ivors, but you really must let me run off now.

—But how can you get home? asked Mrs Conroy.

—O, it's only two steps up the quay.

Gabriel hesitated a moment and said:

—If you will allow me, Miss Ivors, I'll see you home if you really are obliged to go.

But Miss Ivors broke away from them.

—I won't hear of it, she cried. For goodness sake go in to your suppers and don't mind me. I'm quite well able to take care of myself.

—Well, you're the comical girl, Molly, said Mrs Conroy frankly.

—*Beannacht libh,*[9] cried Miss Ivors, with a laugh, as she ran down the staircase.

Mary Jane gazed after her, a moody puzzled expression on her face, while Mrs Conroy leaned over the banisters to listen for the hall-door. Gabriel asked himself was he the cause of her abrupt departure. But she did not seem to be in ill humour: she had gone away laughing. He stared blankly down the staircase.

At that moment Aunt Kate came toddling out of the supper-room, almost wringing her hands in despair.

—Where is Gabriel? she cried. Where on earth is Gabriel? There's everyone waiting in there, stage to let, and nobody to carve the goose!

—Here I am, Aunt Kate! cried Gabriel, with sudden animation, ready to carve a flock of geese, if necessary.

A fat brown goose lay at one end of the table and at the other end, on a bed of creased paper strewn with sprigs of parsley, lay a great ham, stripped of its outer skin and peppered over with crust crumbs, a neat paper frill round its shin and beside this was a round of spiced beef. Between these rival ends ran parallel lines of side-dishes: two little minsters of jelly, red and yellow; a shallow dish full of blocks of blancmange[1] and red jam, a large green leaf-shaped dish with a stalk-shaped handle, on which lay bunches of purple raisins and peeled almonds, a companion dish on which lay a solid rectangle of Smyrna figs, a dish of custard topped with grated nutmeg, a small bowl full of chocolates and sweets wrapped in gold and silver papers and a glass vase in which stood some tall celery stalks. In the centre of the table there stood, as sentries to a fruit-stand which upheld a pyramid of oranges and American apples, two squat old-fashioned decanters of cut glass, one containing port and the other dark sherry. On the closed square piano a pudding in a huge yellow dish lay in waiting and behind it were three squads of bottles of stout and ale and minerals,[2] drawn up according to the colours of their uniforms, the first two black, with brown and red labels, the third and smallest squad white, with transverse green sashes.

Gabriel took his seat boldly at the head of the table and, having looked to the edge of the carver, plunged his fork firmly into the goose. He felt quite at ease

9. Gaelic farewell; literally, "Blessing to ye" or "My blessings go with you."

1. White gelatin dessert or pudding flavored with almonds, vanilla, rum, or brandy.

2. Mineral water.

now for he was an expert carver and liked nothing better than to find himself at the head of a well-laden table.

—Miss Furlong, what shall I send you? he asked. A wing or a slice of the breast?

—Just a small slice of the breast.

—Miss Higgins, what for you?

—O, anything at all, Mr Conroy.

While Gabriel and Miss Daly exchanged plates of goose and plates of ham and spiced beef Lily went from guest to guest with a dish of hot floury potatoes wrapped in a white napkin. This was Mary Jane's idea and she had also suggested apple sauce for the goose but Aunt Kate had said that plain roast goose without apple sauce had always been good enough for her and she hoped she might never eat worse. Mary Jane waited on her pupils and saw that they got the best slices and Aunt Kate and Aunt Julia opened and carried across from the piano bottles of stout and ale for the gentlemen and bottles of minerals for the ladies. There was a great deal of confusion and laughter and noise, the noise of orders and counter-orders, of knives and forks, of corks and glass-stoppers. Gabriel began to carve second helpings as soon as he had finished the first round without serving himself. Everyone protested loudly so that he compromised by taking a long draught of stout for he had found the carving hot work. Mary Jane settled down quietly to her supper but Aunt Kate and Aunt Julia were still toddling round the table, walking on each other's heels, getting in each other's way and giving each other unheeded orders. Mr Browne begged of them to sit down and eat their suppers and so did Gabriel but they said there was time enough so that, at last, Freddy Malins stood up and, capturing Aunt Kate, plumped her down on her chair amid general laughter.

When everyone had been well served Gabriel said, smiling:

—Now, if anyone wants a little more of what vulgar people call stuffing[3] let him or her speak.

A chorus of voices invited him to begin his own supper and Lily came forward with three potatoes which she had reserved for him.

—Very well, said Gabriel amiably, as he took another preparatory draught, kindly forget my existence, ladies and gentlemen, for a few minutes.

He set to his supper and took no part in the conversation with which the table covered Lily's removal of the plates. The subject of talk was the opera company which was then at the Theatre Royal. Mr Bartell D'Arcy, the tenor, a dark-complexioned young man with a smart moustache, praised very highly the leading contralto of the company but Miss Furlong thought she had a rather vulgar style of production. Freddy Malins said there was a negro chieftain singing in the second part of the Gaiety pantomime who had one of the finest tenor voices he had ever heard.

—Have you heard him? he asked Mr Bartell D'Arcy across the table.

—No, answered Mr Bartell D'Arcy carelessly.

—Because, Freddy Malins explained, now I'd be curious to hear your opinion of him. I think he has a grand voice.

3. *Forcemeat* would be the more genteel term.

—It takes Teddy to find out the really good things, said Mr Browne familiarly to the table.

—And why couldn't he have a voice too? asked Freddy Malins sharply. Is it because he's only a black?

Nobody answered this question and Mary Jane led the table back to the legitimate opera. One of her pupils had given her a pass for *Mignon*.[4] Of course it was very fine, she said, but it made her think of poor Georgina Burns.[5] Mr Browne could go back farther still, to the old Italian companies that used to come to Dublin—Tietjens, Ilma de Murzka, Campanini, the great Trebelli, Giuglini, Ravelli, Aramburo.[6] Those were the days, he said, when there was something like singing to be heard in Dublin. He told too of how the top gallery of the old Royal used to be packed night after night, of how one night an Italian tenor had sung five encores to *Let Me Like a Soldier Fall*,[7] introducing a high C every time, and of how the gallery boys would sometimes in their enthusiasm unyoke the horses from the carriage of some great *prima donna* and pull her themselves through the streets to her hotel. Why did they never play the grand old operas now, he asked, *Dinorah*,[8] *Lucrezia Borgia*? Because they could not get the voices to sing them: that was why.

—O, well, said Mr Bartell D'Arcy, I presume there are as good singers to-day as there were then.

—Where are they? asked Mr Browne defiantly.

—In London, Paris, Milan, said Mr Bartell D'Arcy warmly. I suppose Caruso,[9] for example, is quite as good, if not better than any of the men you have mentioned.

—Maybe so, said Mr Browne. But I may tell you I doubt it strongly.

—O, I'd give anything to hear Caruso sing, said Mary Jane.

—For me, said Aunt Kate, who had been picking a bone, there was only one tenor. To please me, I mean. But I suppose none of you ever heard of him.

—Who was he, Miss Morkan? asked Mr Bartell D'Arcy politely.

4. 1886 opera by French composer Ambroise Thomas (1811–96); its heroine is a girl abducted by Gypsies and ultimately revealed to be of noble birth—but only after being tortured by unrequited love, nearly dying in a building set ablaze by the madman who loves her, learning that her own mother died of grief after her disappearance, and finally winning the hand of her true love.

5. Celebrated soprano who debuted in Dublin in the 1878 Theatre Royal production of *The Bohemian Girl* and also appeared in *Mignon*. The Irish baritone to whom she was married apparently died suddenly only months before the Morkans' fictional party.

6. Many of the singers listed here met tragic ends: Ill with cancer, Therese Titjiens collapsed onstage at the end of her final London performance; Ilma di Murska died in poverty after losing her voice, her death inspiring her daughter's suicide; Campanini, too, lost his voice, while Giuglini died shortly after his release from a London mental asylum.

7. Aria sung by the hero of William Vincent Wallace's 1845 opera *Maritana*, after he learns that by marrying the title character he will be allowed to die nobly, "like a soldier," by firing squad.

8. 1859 opera by Giacomo Meyerbeer in which a peasant girl's marriage to a goatherd is frustrated by natural disasters, supernatural forces, and her own madness; *Lucrezia Borgia*: 1833 opera by Gaetano Donizetti about an infamous fifteenth-century Venetian noblewoman; it culminates with Borgia dying of grief after learning that her son is among the six men she has just poisoned.

9. Italian tenor Enrico Caruso (1873–1921), perhaps the most famous singer of the early twentieth century.

—His name, said Aunt Kate, was Parkinson.[1] I heard him when he was in his prime and I think he had then the purest tenor voice that was ever put into a man's throat.

—Strange, said Mr Bartell D'Arcy. I never even heard of him.

—Yes, yes, Miss Morkan is right, said Mr Browne. I remember hearing of old Parkinson but he's too far back for me.

—A beautiful pure sweet mellow English tenor, said Aunt Kate with enthusiasm.

Gabriel having finished, the huge pudding was transferred to the table. The clatter of forks and spoons began again. Gabriel's wife served out spoonfuls of the pudding and passed the plates down the table. Midway down they were held up by Mary Jane, who replenished them with raspberry or orange jelly or with blancmange and jam. The pudding was of Aunt Julia's making and she received praises for it from all quarters. She herself said that it was not quite brown enough.

—Well, I hope, Miss Morkan, said Mr Browne, that I'm brown enough for you because, you know, I'm all brown.

All the gentlemen, except Gabriel, ate some of the pudding out of compliment to Aunt Julia. As Gabriel never ate sweets the celery had been left for him. Freddy Malins also took a stalk of celery and ate it with his pudding. He had been told that celery was a capital thing for the blood and he was just then under doctor's care. Mrs Malins, who had been silent all through the supper, said that her son was going down to Mount Melleray[2] in a week or so. The table then spoke of Mount Melleray, how bracing the air was down there, how hospitable the monks were and how they never asked for a penny-piece from their guests.

—And do you mean to say, asked Mr Browne incredulously, that a chap can go down there and put up there as if it were a hotel and live on the fat of the land and then come away without paying a farthing?

—O, most people give some donation to the monastery when they leave, said Mary Jane.

—I wish we had an institution like that in our Church, said Mr Browne candidly.

He was astonished to hear that the monks never spoke, got up at two in the morning and slept in their coffins. He asked what they did it for.

—That's the rule of the order,[3] said Aunt Kate firmly.

—Yes, but why? asked Mr Browne.

Aunt Kate repeated that it was the rule, that was all. Mr Browne still seemed not to understand. Freddy Malins explained to him, as best he could, that the monks were trying to make up for the sins committed by all the sinners in the outside world. The explanation was not very clear for Mr Browne grinned and said:

1. Perhaps an English-born organist who had a relatively brief career as a singer with a well-known Dublin opera company before becoming a theatrical manager.

2. Cistercian Abbey in southeastern Ireland founded in the 1830s, a refuge for alcoholics in need of rest, cure, and spiritual renewal.

3. Though the rules of the Cistercian monks do not require sleeping in coffins, they are rigorous, mandating a vow of silence and a day that begins with prayers at 2 a.m.

—I like that idea very much but wouldn't a comfortable spring bed do them as well as a coffin?

—The coffin, said Mary Jane, is to remind them of their last end.

As the subject had grown lugubrious it was buried in a silence of the table during which Mrs Malins could be heard saying to her neighbour in an indistinct undertone:

—They are very good men, the monks, very pious men.

The raisins and almonds and figs and apples and oranges and chocolates and sweets were now passed about the table and Aunt Julia invited all the guests to have either port or sherry. At first Mr Bartell D'Arcy refused to take either but one of his neighbours nudged him and whispered something to him upon which he allowed his glass to be filled. Gradually as the last glasses were being filled the conversation ceased. A pause followed, broken only by the noise of the wine and by unsettlings of chairs. The Misses Morkan, all three, looked down at the tablecloth. Someone coughed once or twice and then a few gentlemen patted the table gently as a signal for silence. The silence came and Gabriel pushed back his chair and stood up.

The patting at once grew louder in encouragement and then ceased altogether. Gabriel leaned his ten trembling fingers on the tablecloth and smiled nervously at the company. Meeting a row of upturned faces he raised his eyes to the chandelier. The piano was playing a waltz tune and he could hear the skirts sweeping against the drawing-room door. People, perhaps, were standing in the snow on the quay outside, gazing up at the lighted windows and listening to the waltz music. The air was pure there. In the distance lay the park where the trees were weighted with snow. The Wellington Monument wore a gleaming cap of snow that flashed westward over the white field of Fifteen Acres.

He began:

—Ladies and Gentlemen.

—It has fallen to my lot this evening, as in years past, to perform a very pleasing task but a task for which I am afraid my poor powers as a speaker are all too inadequate.

—No, no! said Mr Browne.

—But, however that may be, I can only ask you to-night to take the will for the deed and to lend me your attention for a few moments while I endeavour to express to you in words what my feelings are on this occasion.

—Ladies and Gentlemen. It is not the first time that we have gathered together under this hospitable roof, around this hospitable board. It is not the first time that we have been the recipients—or perhaps, I had better say, the victims—of the hospitality of certain good ladies.

He made a circle in the air with his arm and paused. Everyone laughed or smiled at Aunt Kate and Aunt Julia and Mary Jane who all turned crimson with pleasure. Gabriel went on more boldly:

—I feel more strongly with every recurring year that our country has no tradition which does it so much honour and which it should guard so jealously as that of its hospitality. It is a tradition that is unique as far as my experience goes (and I have visited not a few places abroad) among the modern nations. Some would say, perhaps, that with us it is rather a failing than anything to be boasted of. But granted even that, it is, to my mind, a princely failing, and one that I trust will long be cultivated among us. Of one thing, at least, I am sure. As long as this one roof shelters the good ladies aforesaid—and I wish from my heart it may do so for many and many a long year to come—the tradition of genuine warm-hearted courteous Irish hospitality, which our forefathers have handed down to us and which we in turn must hand down to our descendants, is still alive among us.

A hearty murmur of assent ran round the table. It shot through Gabriel's mind that Miss Ivors was not there and that she had gone away discourteously: and he said with confidence in himself:

—Ladies and Gentlemen. 250

—A new generation is growing up in our midst, a generation actuated by new ideas and new principles. It is serious and enthusiastic for these new ideas and its enthusiasm, even when it is misdirected, is, I believe, in the main sincere. But we are living in a sceptical and, if I may use the phrase, a thought-tormented age: and sometimes I fear that this new generation, educated or hypereducated as it is, will lack those qualities of humanity, of hospitality, of kindly humour which belonged to an older day. Listening to-night to the names of all those great singers of the past it seemed to me, I must confess, that we were living in a less spacious age. Those days might, without exaggeration, be called spacious days: and if they are gone beyond recall let us hope, at least, that in gatherings such as this we shall still speak of them with pride and affection, still cherish in our hearts the memory of those dead and gone great ones whose fame the world will not willingly let die.[4]

—Hear, hear! said Mr Browne loudly.

—But yet, continued Gabriel, his voice falling into a softer inflection, there are always in gatherings such as this sadder thoughts that will recur to our minds: thoughts of the past, of youth, of changes, of absent faces that we miss here to-night. Our path through life is strewn with many such sad memories: and were we to brood upon them always we could not find the heart to go on bravely with our work among the living. We have all of us living duties and living affections which claim, and rightly claim, our strenuous endeavours.

—Therefore, I will not linger on the past. I will not let any gloomy moralising intrude upon us here to-night. Here we are gathered together for a brief moment from the bustle and rush of our everyday routine. We are met here as friends, in the spirit of good-fellowship, as colleagues, also to a certain extent, in the true spirit of *camaraderie*, and as the guests of—what shall I call them?—the Three Graces of the Dublin musical world.

The table burst into applause and laughter at this sally. Aunt Julia vainly 255
asked each of her neighbours in turn to tell her what Gabriel had said.

—He says we are the Three Graces, Aunt Julia, said Mary Jane.

Aunt Julia did not understand but she looked up, smiling, at Gabriel, who continued in the same vein:

—Ladies and Gentlemen.

—I will not attempt to play to-night the part that Paris played on another occasion. I will not attempt to choose between them. The task would be an invidious one and one beyond my poor powers. For when I view them in turn, whether it be our chief hostess herself, whose good heart, whose too good

4. In *The Reason of Church Government Urg'd against Prelaty* (1641), John Milton expresses the hope that he "might perhaps leave something so written to after times as they should not willingly let it die."

heart, has become a byword with all who know her, or her sister, who seems to be gifted with perennial youth and whose singing must have been a surprise and a revelation to us all to-night, or, last but not least, when I consider our youngest hostess, talented, cheerful, hard-working and the best of nieces, I confess, Ladies and Gentlemen, that I do not know to which of them I should award the prize.

Gabriel glanced down at his aunts and, seeing the large smile on Aunt Julia's face and the tears which had risen to Aunt Kate's eyes, hastened to his close. He raised his glass of port gallantly, while every member of the company fingered a glass expectantly, and said loudly:

—Let us toast them all three together. Let us drink to their health, wealth, long life, happiness and prosperity and may they long continue to hold the proud and self-won position which they hold in their profession and the position of honour and affection which they hold in our hearts.

All the guests stood up, glass in hand, and, turning towards the three seated ladies, sang in unison, with Mr Browne as leader:

For they are jolly gay fellows,
For they are jolly gay fellows,
For they are jolly gay fellows,
Which nobody can deny.

Aunt Kate was making frank use of her handkerchief and even Aunt Julia seemed moved. Freddy Malins beat time with his pudding-fork and the singers turned towards one another, as if in melodious conference, while they sang, with emphasis:

Unless he tells a lie,
Unless he tells a lie.

Then, turning once more towards their hostesses, they sang:

For they are jolly gay fellows,
For they are jolly gay fellows,
For they are jolly gay fellows,
Which nobody can deny.

The acclamation which followed was taken up beyond the door of the supper-room by many of the other guests and renewed time after time, Freddy Malins acting as officer with his fork on high.

• • •

The piercing morning air came into the hall where they were standing so that Aunt Kate said:

—Close the door, somebody. Mrs Malins will get her death of cold.

—Browne is out there, Aunt Kate, said Mary Jane.

—Browne is everywhere, said Aunt Kate, lowering her voice.

Mary Jane laughed at her tone.

—Really, she said archly, he is very attentive.

—He has been laid on here like the gas, said Aunt Kate in the same tone, all during the Christmas.

She laughed herself this time good-humouredly and then added quickly:

—But tell him to come in, Mary Jane, and close the door. I hope to goodness he didn't hear me.

At that moment the hall-door was opened and Mr Browne came in from the doorstep, laughing as if his heart would break. He was dressed in a long green overcoat with mock astrakhan[5] cuffs and collar and wore on his head an oval fur cap. He pointed down the snow-covered quay from where the sound of shrill prolonged whistling was borne in.

—Teddy will have all the cabs in Dublin out, he said.

Gabriel advanced from the little pantry behind the office, struggling into his overcoat and, looking round the hall, said:

—Gretta not down yet?

—She's getting on her things, Gabriel, said Aunt Kate.

—Who's playing up there? asked Gabriel.

—Nobody. They're all gone.

—O no, Aunt Kate, said Mary Jane. Bartell D'Arcy and Miss O'Callaghan aren't gone yet.

—Someone is strumming at the piano, anyhow, said Gabriel.

Mary Jane glanced at Gabriel and Mr Browne and said with a shiver:

—It makes me feel cold to look at you two gentlemen muffled up like that. I wouldn't like to face your journey home at this hour.

—I'd like nothing better this minute, said Mr Browne stoutly, than a rattling fine walk in the country or a fast drive with a good spanking goer between the shafts.

—We used to have a very good horse and trap at home, said Aunt Julia sadly.

—The never-to-be-forgotten Johnny, said Mary Jane, laughing.

Aunt Kate and Gabriel laughed too.

—Why, what was wonderful about Johnny? asked Mr Browne.

—The late lamented Patrick Morkan, our grandfather, that is, explained Gabriel, commonly known in his later years as the old gentleman, was a glue-boiler.[6]

—O, now, Gabriel, said Aunt Kate, laughing, he had a starch mill.

—Well, glue or starch, said Gabriel, the old gentleman had a horse by the name of Johnny. And Johnny used to work in the old gentleman's mill, walking round and round in order to drive the mill. That was all very well; but now comes the tragic part about Johnny. One fine day the old gentleman thought he'd like to drive out with the quality[7] to a military review in the park.

—The Lord have mercy on his soul, said Aunt Kate compassionately.

—Amen, said Gabriel. So the old gentleman, as I said, harnessed Johnny and put on his very best tall hat and his very best stock collar and drove out in grand style from his ancestral mansion somewhere near Back Lane, I think.

Everyone laughed, even Mrs Malins, at Gabriel's manner and Aunt Kate said:

—O now, Gabriel, he didn't live in Back Lane, really. Only the mill was there.

—Out from the mansion of his forefathers, continued Gabriel, he drove with Johnny. And everything went on beautifully until Johnny came in sight of King

5. Expensive fabric made from the wool of newborn lambs from the Russian city of Astrakhan.

6. Glue was made by boiling the hides and hooves of animals, especially old horses.

7. The upper classes.

Billy's[8] statue: and whether he fell in love with the horse King Billy sits on or whether he thought he was back again in the mill, anyhow he began to walk round the statue.

Gabriel paced in a circle round the hall in his goloshes amid the laughter of the others.

—Round and round he went, said Gabriel, and the old gentleman, who was a very pompous old gentleman, was highly indignant. *Go on, sir! What do you mean, sir? Johnny! Johnny! Most extraordinary conduct! Can't understand the horse!*

The peals of laughter which followed Gabriel's imitation of the incident were interrupted by a resounding knock at the hall-door. Mary Jane ran to open it and let in Freddy Malins. Freddy Malins, with his hat well back on his head and his shoulders humped with cold, was puffing and steaming after his exertions.

—I could only get one cab, he said.

—O, we'll find another along the quay, said Gabriel.

—Yes, said Aunt Kate. Better not keep Mrs Malins standing in the draught.

Mrs Malins was helped down the front steps by her son and Mr Browne and, after many manœuvres, hoisted into the cab. Freddy Malins clambered in after her and spent a long time settling her on the seat, Mr Browne helping him with advice. At last she was settled comfortably and Freddy Malins invited Mr Browne into the cab. There was a good deal of confused talk, and then Mr Browne got into the cab. The cabman settled his rug over his knees, and bent down for the address. The confusion grew greater and the cabman was directed differently by Freddy Malins and Mr Browne, each of whom had his head out through a window of the cab. The difficulty was to know where to drop Mr Browne along the route and Aunt Kate, Aunt Julia and Mary Jane helped the discussion from the doorstep with cross-directions and contradictions and abundance of laughter. As for Freddy Malins he was speechless with laughter. He popped his head in and out of the window every moment, to the great danger of his hat, and told his mother how the discussion was progressing till at last Mr Browne shouted to the bewildered cabman above the din of everybody's laughter:

—Do you know Trinity College?[9]

—Yes, sir, said the cabman.

—Well, drive bang up against Trinity College gates, said Mr Browne, and then we'll tell you where to go. You understand now?

—Yes, sir, said the cabman.

—Make like a bird for Trinity College.

—Right, sir, cried the cabman.

The horse was whipped up and the cab rattled off along the quay amid a chorus of laughter and adieus.

8. 1701 equestrian statue, which stands outside the Irish Parliament and commemorates King William III or William of Orange; Parliament chose to put William on the British throne because he was Protestant, and he went on to vanquish Ireland's last kings at the Battle of the Boyne in 1690, which effectively turned Ireland into a British colony.

9. Ireland's oldest and most prestigious university, founded by Queen Elizabeth I in 1592.

Gabriel had not gone to the door with the others. He was in a dark part of the hall gazing up the staircase. A woman was standing near the top of the first flight, in the shadow also. He could not see her face but he could see the terracotta and salmonpink panels of her skirt which the shadow made appear black and white. It was his wife. She was leaning on the banisters, listening to something. Gabriel was surprised at her stillness and strained his ear to listen also. But he could hear little save the noise of laughter and dispute on the front steps, a few chords struck on the piano and a few notes of a man's voice singing.

He stood still in the gloom of the hall, trying to catch the air that the voice was singing and gazing up at his wife. There was grace and mystery in her attitude as if she were a symbol of something. He asked himself what is a woman standing on the stairs in the shadow, listening to distant music, a symbol of. If he were a painter he would paint her in that attitude. Her blue felt hat would show off the bronze of her hair against the darkness and the dark panels of her skirt would show off the light ones. *Distant Music* he would call the picture if he were a painter.

The hall-door was closed; and Aunt Kate, Aunt Julia and Mary Jane came down the hall, still laughing.

—Well, isn't Freddy terrible? said Mary Jane. He's really terrible.

Gabriel said nothing but pointed up the stairs towards where his wife was standing. Now that the hall-door was closed the voice and the piano could be heard more clearly. Gabriel held up his hand for them to be silent. The song seemed to be in the old Irish tonality and the singer seemed uncertain both of his words and of his voice. The voice, made plaintive by distance and by the singer's hoarseness, faintly illuminated the cadence of the air with words expressing grief:

O, the rain falls on my heavy locks
And the dew wets my skin,
My babe lies cold . . .[1]

—O, exclaimed Mary Jane. It's Bartell D'Arcy singing and he wouldn't sing all the night. O, I'll get him to sing a song before he goes.

—O do, Mary Jane, said Aunt Kate.

Mary Jane brushed past the others and ran to the staircase but before she reached it the singing stopped and the piano was closed abruptly.

—O, what a pity! she cried. Is he coming down, Gretta?

Gabriel heard his wife answer yes and saw her come down towards them. A few steps behind her were Mr Bartell D'Arcy and Miss O'Callaghan.

—O, Mr D'Arcy, cried Mary Jane, it's downright mean of you to break off like that when we were all in raptures listening to you.

—I have been at him all the evening, said Miss O'Callaghan, and Mrs Conroy too and he told us he had a dreadful cold and couldn't sing.

—O, Mr D'Arcy, said Aunt Kate, now that was a great fib to tell.

—Can't you see that I'm as hoarse as a crow? said Mr D'Arcy roughly.

1. Tragic old Irish ballad often called *The Lass of Aughrim* (after a small village in County Galway) about a peasant girl either seduced and abandoned by her noble lover (in some versions) or separated from him by the machinations of his mother (in other versions).

He went into the pantry hastily and put on his overcoat. The others, taken aback by his rude speech, could find nothing to say. Aunt Kate wrinkled her brows and made signs to the others to drop the subject. Mr D'Arcy stood swathing his neck carefully and frowning.

—It's the weather, said Aunt Julia, after a pause.

—Yes, everybody has colds, said Aunt Kate readily, everybody.

—They say, said Mary Jane, we haven't had snow like it for thirty years; and I read this morning in the newspapers that the snow is general all over Ireland.

—I love the look of snow, said Aunt Julia sadly.

—So do I, said Miss O'Callaghan. I think Christmas is never really Christmas unless we have the snow on the ground.

—But poor Mr D'Arcy doesn't like the snow, said Aunt Kate, smiling.

Mr D'Arcy came from the pantry, fully swathed and buttoned, and in a repentant tone told them the history of his cold. Everyone gave him advice and said it was a great pity and urged him to be very careful of his throat in the night air. Gabriel watched his wife who did not join in the conversation. She was standing right under the dusty fanlight and the flame of the gas lit up the rich bronze of her hair which he had seen her drying at the fire a few days before. She was in the same attitude and seemed unaware of the talk about her. At last she turned towards them and Gabriel saw that there was colour on her cheeks and that her eyes were shining. A sudden tide of joy went leaping out of his heart.

—Mr D'Arcy, she said, what is the name of that song you were singing?

—It's called *The Lass of Aughrim*, said Mr D'Arcy, but I couldn't remember it properly. Why? Do you know it?

—*The Lass of Aughrim*, she repeated. I couldn't think of the name.

—It's a very nice air, said Mary Jane. I'm sorry you were not in voice to-night.

—Now, Mary Jane, said Aunt Kate, don't annoy Mr D'Arcy. I won't have him annoyed.

Seeing that all were ready to start she shepherded them to the door where good-night was said:

—Well, good-night, Aunt Kate, and thanks for the pleasant evening.

—Good-night, Gabriel. Good-night, Gretta!

—Good-night, Aunt Kate, and thanks ever so much. Good-night, Aunt Julia.

—O, good-night, Gretta, I didn't see you.

—Good-night, Mr D'Arcy. Good-night, Miss O'Callaghan.

—Good-night, Miss Morkan.

—Good-night, again.

—Good-night, all. Safe home.

—Good-night. Good-night.

The morning was still dark. A dull yellow light brooded over the houses and the river; and the sky seemed to be descending. It was slushy underfoot; and only streaks and patches of snow lay on the roofs, on the parapets of the quay and on the area railings. The lamps were still burning redly in the murky air and, across the river, the palace of the Four Courts stood out menacingly against the heavy sky.

She was walking on before him with Mr Bartell D'Arcy, her shoes in a brown parcel tucked under one arm and her hands holding her skirt up from the slush.

She had no longer any grace of attitude but Gabriel's eyes were still bright with happiness. The blood went bounding along his veins; and the thoughts went rioting through his brain, proud, joyful, tender, valorous.

She was walking on before him so lightly and so erect that he longed to run after her noiselessly, catch her by the shoulders and say something foolish and affectionate into her ear. She seemed to him so frail that he longed to defend her against something and then to be alone with her. Moments of their secret life together burst like stars upon his memory. A heliotrope[2] envelope was lying beside his breakfast-cup and he was caressing it with his hand. Birds were twittering in the ivy and the sunny web of the curtain was shimmering along the floor: he could not eat for happiness. They were standing on the crowded platform and he was placing a ticket inside the warm palm of her glove. He was standing with her in the cold, looking in through a grated window at a man making bottles in a roaring furnace. It was very cold. Her face, fragrant in the cold air, was quite close to his; and suddenly she called out to the man at the furnace:

—Is the fire hot, sir?

But the man could not hear her with the noise of the furnace. It was just as well. He might have answered rudely.

A wave of yet more tender joy escaped from his heart and went coursing in warm flood along his arteries. Like the tender fires of stars moments of their life together, that no one knew of or would ever know of, broke upon and illumined his memory. He longed to recall to her those moments, to make her forget the years of their dull existence together and remember only their moments of ecstasy. For the years, he felt, had not quenched his soul or hers. Their children, his writing, her household cares had not quenched all their souls' tender fire. In one letter that he had written to her then he had said: *Why is it that words like these seem to me so dull and cold? Is it because there is no word tender enough to be your name?*

Like distant music these words that he had written years before were borne towards him from the past. He longed to be alone with her. When the others had gone away, when he and she were in their room in the hotel, then they would be alone together. He would call her softly:

—Gretta!

Perhaps she would not hear at once: she would be undressing. Then something in his voice would strike her. She would turn and look at him. . . .

At the corner of Winetavern Street they met a cab. He was glad of its rattling noise as it saved him from conversation. She was looking out of the window and seemed tired. The others spoke only a few words, pointing out some building or street. The horse galloped along wearily under the murky morning sky, dragging his old rattling box after his heels, and Gabriel was again in a cab with her, galloping to catch the boat, galloping to their honeymoon.

As the cab drove across O'Connell Bridge Miss O'Callaghan said:

—They say you never cross O'Connell Bridge without seeing a white horse.

—I see a white man this time, said Gabriel.

—Where? asked Mr Bartell D'Arcy.

2. Shade of purple.

O'Connell Bridge, Dublin, circa 1880

Gabriel pointed to the statue,[3] on which lay patches of snow. Then he nodded familiarly to it and waved his hand.

—Good-night, Dan, he said gaily.

When the cab drew up before the hotel Gabriel jumped out and, in spite of Mr Bartell D'Arcy's protest, paid the driver. He gave the man a shilling over his fare. The man saluted and said:

—A prosperous New Year to you, sir.

—The same to you, said Gabriel cordially.

She leaned for a moment on his arm in getting out of the cab and while standing at the curbstone, bidding the others good-night. She leaned lightly on his arm, as lightly as when she had danced with him a few hours before. He had felt proud and happy then, happy that she was his, proud of her grace and wifely carriage. But now, after the kindling again of so many memories, the first touch of her body, musical and strange and perfumed, sent through him a keen pang of lust. Under cover of her silence he pressed her arm closely to his side; and, as they stood at the hotel door, he felt that they had escaped from their lives and duties, escaped from home and friends and run away together with wild and radiant hearts to a new adventure.

An old man was dozing in a great hooded chair in the hall. He lit a candle in the office and went before them to the stairs. They followed him in silence, their

3. 1882 monument commemorating Irish politician Daniel O'Connell (1775–1847), after whom the most important bridge over the river Liffey (built in 1880) is also named. An early champion of Irish self-rule, O'Connell is widely known as "The Liberator" because of his role in overturning laws prohibiting Catholics from serving in the British Parliament.

feet falling in soft thuds on the thickly carpeted stairs. She mounted the stairs behind the porter, her head bowed in the ascent, her frail shoulders curved as with a burden, her skirt girt tightly about her. He could have flung his arms about her hips and held her still for his arms were trembling with desire to seize her and only the stress of his nails against the palms of his hands held the wild impulse of his body in check. The porter halted on the stairs to settle his guttering candle. They halted too on the steps below him. In the silence Gabriel could hear the falling of the molten wax into the tray and the thumping of his own heart against his ribs.

The porter led them along a corridor and opened a door. Then he set his unstable candle down on a toilet-table and asked at what hour they were to be called in the morning.

—Eight, said Gabriel.

The porter pointed to the tap of the electric-light and began a muttered apology but Gabriel cut him short.

—We don't want any light. We have light enough from the street. And I say, he added, pointing to the candle, you might remove that handsome article, like a good man.

The porter took up his candle again, but slowly for he was surprised by such a novel idea. Then he mumbled good-night and went out. Gabriel shot the lock to.

A ghostly light from the street lamp lay in a long shaft from one window to the door. Gabriel threw his overcoat and hat on a couch and crossed the room towards the window. He looked down into the street in order that his emotion might calm a little. Then he turned and leaned against a chest of drawers with his back to the light. She had taken off her hat and cloak and was standing before a large swinging mirror, unhooking her waist. Gabriel paused for a few moments, watching her, and then said:

—Gretta!

She turned away from the mirror slowly and walked along the shaft of light towards him. Her face looked so serious and weary that the words would not pass Gabriel's lips. No, it was not the moment yet.

—You looked tired, he said.

—I am a little, she answered.

—You don't feel ill or weak?

—No, tired: that's all.

She went on to the window and stood there, looking out. Gabriel waited again and then, fearing that diffidence was about to conquer him, he said abruptly:

—By the way, Gretta!

—What is it?

—You know that poor fellow Malins? he said quickly.

—Yes. What about him?

—Well, poor fellow, he's a decent sort of chap after all, continued Gabriel in a false voice. He gave me back that sovereign[4] I lent him and I didn't expect it really. It's a pity he wouldn't keep away from that Browne, because he's not a bad fellow at heart.

4. Gold coin worth one pound or twenty shillings.

He was trembling now with annoyance. Why did she seem so abstracted? He did not know how he could begin. Was she annoyed, too, about something? If she would only turn to him or come to him of her own accord! To take her as she was would be brutal. No, he must see some ardour in her eyes first. He longed to be master of her strange mood.

390 —When did you lend him the pound? she asked, after a pause.

Gabriel strove to restrain himself from breaking out into brutal language about the sottish Malins and his pound. He longed to cry to her from his soul, to crush her body against his, to overmaster her. But he said:

—O, at Christmas, when he opened that little Christmas-card shop in Henry Street.

He was in such a fever of rage and desire that he did not hear her come from the window. She stood before him for an instant, looking at him strangely. Then, suddenly raising herself on tiptoe and resting her hands lightly on his shoulders, she kissed him.

—You are a very generous person, Gabriel, she said.

395 Gabriel, trembling with delight at her sudden kiss and at the quaintness of her phrase, put his hands on her hair and began smoothing it back, scarcely touching it with his fingers. The washing had made it fine and brilliant. His heart was brimming over with happiness. Just when he was wishing for it she had come to him of her own accord. Perhaps her thoughts had been running with his. Perhaps she had felt the impetuous desire that was in him and then the yielding mood had come upon her. Now that she had fallen to him so easily he wondered why he had been so diffident.

He stood, holding her head between his hands. Then, slipping one arm swiftly about her body and drawing her towards him, he said softly:

—Gretta dear, what are you thinking about?

She did not answer nor yield wholly to his arm. He said again, softly:

—Tell me what it is, Gretta. I think I know what is the matter. Do I know?

400 She did not answer at once. Then she said in an outburst of tears:

—O, I am thinking about that song, *The Lass of Aughrim*.

She broke loose from him and ran to the bed and, throwing her arms across the bed-rail, hid her face. Gabriel stood stock-still for a moment in astonishment and then followed her. As he passed in the way of the cheval-glass[5] he caught sight of himself in full length, his broad, well-filled shirt-front, the face whose expression always puzzled him when he saw it in a mirror and his glimmering gilt-rimmed eyeglasses. He halted a few paces from her and said:

—What about the song? Why does that make you cry?

She raised her head from her arms and dried her eyes with the back of her hand like a child. A kinder note than he had intended went into his voice.

405 —Why, Gretta? he asked.

—I am thinking about a person long ago who used to sing that song.

—And who was the person long ago? asked Gabriel, smiling.

—It was a person I used to know in Galway when I was living with my grandmother, she said.

5. Full-length, frame-mounted, adjustable mirror.

The smile passed away from Gabriel's face. A dull anger began to gather again at the back of his mind and the dull fires of his lust began to glow angrily in his veins.

—Someone you were in love with? he asked ironically.

—It was a young boy I used to know, she answered, named Michael Furey. He used to sing that song, *The Lass of Aughrim.* He was very delicate.

Gabriel was silent. He did not wish her to think that he was interested in this delicate boy.

—I can see him so plainly, she said after a moment. Such eyes as he had: big dark eyes! And such an expression in them—an expression!

—O then, you were in love with him? said Gabriel.

—I used to go out walking with him, she said, when I was in Galway.

A thought flew across Gabriel's mind.

—Perhaps that was why you wanted to go to Galway with that Ivors girl? he said coldly.

She looked at him and asked in surprise:

—What for?

Her eyes made Gabriel feel awkward. He shrugged his shoulders and said:

—How do I know? To see him perhaps.

She looked away from him along the shaft of light towards the window in silence.

—He is dead, she said at length. He died when he was only seventeen. Isn't it a terrible thing to die so young as that?

—What was he? asked Gabriel, still ironically.

—He was in the gasworks,[6] she said.

Gabriel felt humiliated by the failure of his irony and by the evocation of this figure from the dead, a boy in the gasworks. While he had been full of memories of their secret life together, full of tenderness and joy and desire, she had been comparing him in her mind with another. A shameful consciousness of his own person assailed him. He saw himself as a ludicrous figure, acting as a pennyboy[7] for his aunts, a nervous well-meaning sentimentalist, orating to vulgarians and idealising his own clownish lusts, the pitiable fatuous fellow he had caught a glimpse of in the mirror. Instinctively he turned his back more to the light lest she might see the shame that burned upon his forehead.

He tried to keep up his tone of cold interrogation but his voice when he spoke was humble and indifferent.

—I suppose you were in love with this Michael Furey, Gretta, he said.

—I was great with him at that time, she said.

Her voice was veiled and sad. Gabriel, feeling now how vain it would be to try to lead her whither he had purposed, caressed one of her hands and said, also sadly:

—And what did he die of so young, Gretta? Consumption,[8] was it?

—I think he died for me, she answered.

A vague terror seized Gabriel at this answer as if, at that hour when he had hoped to triumph, some impalpable and vindictive being was coming against

6. Factory where gas for heating was manufactured from coal.

7. Cheap entertainer or someone who performs small tasks and errands for very little money.

8. Tuberculosis, a lung disease.

him, gathering forces against him in its vague world. But he shook himself free of it with an effort of reason and continued to caress her hand. He did not question her again for he felt that she would tell him of herself. Her hand was warm and moist: it did not respond to his touch but he continued to caress it just as he had caressed her first letter to him that spring morning.

—It was in the winter, she said, about the beginning of the winter when I was going to leave my grandmother's and come up here to the convent. And he was ill at the time in his lodgings in Galway and wouldn't be let out and his people in Oughterard were written to. He was in decline, they said, or something like that. I never knew rightly.

She paused for a moment and sighed.

—Poor fellow, she said. He was very fond of me and he was such a gentle boy. We used to go out together, walking, you know, Gabriel, like the way they do in the country. He was going to study singing only for his health. He had a very good voice, poor Michael Furey.

—Well; and then? asked Gabriel.

—And then when it came to the time for me to leave Galway and come up to the convent he was much worse and I wouldn't be let see him so I wrote a letter saying I was going up to Dublin and would be back in the summer and hoping he would be better then.

She paused for a moment to get her voice under control and then went on:

—Then the night before I left I was in my grandmother's house in Nuns' Island,[9] packing up, and I heard gravel thrown up against the window. The window was so wet I couldn't see so I ran downstairs as I was and slipped out the back into the garden and there was the poor fellow at the end of the garden, shivering.

—And did you not tell him to go back? asked Gabriel.

—I implored of him to go home at once and told him he would get his death in the rain. But he said he did not want to live. I can see his eyes as well as well! He was standing at the end of the wall where there was a tree.

—And did he go home? asked Gabriel.

—Yes, he went home. And when I was only a week in the convent he died and he was buried in Oughterard where his people came from. O, the day I heard that, that he was dead!

She stopped, choking with sobs, and, overcome by emotion, flung herself face downward on the bed, sobbing in the quilt. Gabriel held her hand for a moment longer, irresolutely, and then, shy of intruding on her grief, let it fall gently and walked quietly to the window.

She was fast asleep.

Gabriel, leaning on his elbow, looked for a few moments unresentfully on her tangled hair and half-open mouth, listening to her deep-drawn breath. So she had had that romance in her life: a man had died for her sake. It hardly pained him now to think how poor a part he, her husband, had played in her life. He watched her while she slept as though he and she had never lived together as man and wife. His curious eyes rested long upon her face and on her hair: and, as he thought of what she must have been then, in that time of her first girlish

9. Semi-island in the river that runs through the city of Galway, somewhat like Dublin's Usher Island.

beauty, a strange friendly pity for her entered his soul. He did not like to say even to himself that her face was no longer beautiful but he knew that it was no longer the face for which Michael Furey had braved death.

Perhaps she had not told him all the story. His eyes moved to the chair over which she had thrown some of her clothes. A petticoat string dangled to the floor. One boot stood upright, its limp upper fallen down: the fellow of it lay upon its side. He wondered at his riot of emotions of an hour before. From what had it proceeded? From his aunt's supper, from his own foolish speech, from the wine and dancing, the merrymaking when saying good-night in the hall, the pleasure of the walk along the river in the snow. Poor Aunt Julia! She, too, would soon be a shade with the shade of Patrick Morkan and his horse. He had caught that haggard look upon her face for a moment when she was singing *Arrayed for the Bridal.* Soon, perhaps, he would be sitting in that same drawing-room, dressed in black, his silk hat on his knees. The blinds would be drawn down and Aunt Kate would be sitting beside him, crying and blowing her nose and telling him how Julia had died. He would cast about in his mind for some words that might console her, and would find only lame and useless ones. Yes, yes: that would happen very soon.

The air of the room chilled his shoulders. He stretched himself cautiously along under the sheets and lay down beside his wife. One by one they were all becoming shades. Better pass boldly into that other world, in the full glory of some passion, than fade and wither dismally with age. He thought of how she who lay beside him had locked in her heart for so many years that image of her lover's eyes when he had told her that he did not wish to live.

Generous tears filled Gabriel's eyes. He had never felt like that himself towards any woman but he knew that such a feeling must be love. The tears gathered more thickly in his eyes and in the partial darkness he imagined he saw the form of a young man standing under a dripping tree. Other forms were near. His soul had approached that region where dwell the vast hosts of the dead. He was conscious of, but could not apprehend, their wayward and flickering existence. His own identity was fading out into a grey impalpable world: the solid world itself which these dead had one time reared and lived in was dissolving and dwindling.

A few light taps upon the pane made him turn to the window. It had begun to snow again. He watched sleepily the flakes, silver and dark, falling obliquely against the lamplight. The time had come for him to set out on his journey westward. Yes, the newspapers were right: snow was general all over Ireland. It was falling on every part of the dark central plain, on the treeless hills, falling softly upon the Bog of Allen and, farther westward, softly falling into the dark mutinous Shannon[1] waves. It was falling, too, upon every part of the lonely churchyard on the hill where Michael Furey lay buried. It lay thickly drifted on the crooked crosses and headstones, on the spears of the little gate, on the barren thorns. His soul swooned slowly as he heard the snow falling faintly through the universe and faintly falling, like the descent of their last end, upon all the living and the dead.

1914

1. The river Shannon is the informal boundary separating the West of Ireland (including Galway) from the rest of the country.

Chronology: James Joyce and Dubliners

1882	February 2	James Augustine Aloysius Joyce is born in a suburb of Dublin, Ireland, first of the ten surviving children of John and Mary Joyce, a pianist.
1888		Joyce enters Clongowes Wood College, a Jesuit boarding school just outside Dublin.
1891	October	The death of beloved but disgraced Irish politician Charles Stewart Parnell inspires Joyce's earliest known literary effort, a poem entitled "Et Tu, Healy" ("And you, Healy," an allusion to Julius Caesar's last words to his assassins).
1893		Joyce enters Belvedere College, a Jesuit day school in Dublin.
1899		Joyce enters University College, Dublin, another Jesuit institution.
1900		Joyce begins a series of prose poems he calls *Epiphanies*.
1902	October	Joyce graduates and begins to introduce himself to Ireland's most important writers, including poet W. B. Yeats.
	December	Joyce moves to Paris, ostensibly to begin medical studies.
1903	April	Joyce returns to Dublin because of his mother's illness; she dies in August. In an August 1904 letter to his future wife, Joyce will avow that his "mind rejects the whole present social order and Christianity—home, the recognised virtues." "How could I like the idea of home?" he asks, explaining that when he saw his mother in her coffin, he "cursed the system which had made her a victim."
1904	January	Joyce writes an essay entitled "A Portrait of the Artist." After its rejection by a magazine, Joyce begins turning it into the autobiographical novel *Stephen Hero*.
	July	The editor of *Irish Homestead* magazine invites Joyce to submit a short story that is "simple, rural?, livemaking?" and won't "shock the readers." In response, Joyce writes "The Sisters," which appears the next month under the pseudonym "Stephen Daedalus."
	September	"Eveline" appears in *Irish Homestead*. In a letter, Joyce avows that "There is no life" in Ireland, "no naturalness or honesty. People live together in the same houses all their lives and at the end they are as far apart as ever."
	October	Joyce leaves for Europe with Nora Barnacle, a hotel employee whom he had met four months earlier. Unable to find work in Zurich, Switzerland, the unmarried couple settles in Pola, Austro-Hungary (now Croatia), where Joyce teaches English at the Berlitz school.
	December	*Irish Homestead* publishes a third Joyce story, and Joyce informs a correspondent that all three stories are part of "a series of [ten] epi-clets" (mini-epics) called *Dubliners*.
1905	July	Nora gives birth to a son.

October Joyce persuades his favorite brother, Stanislaus, to join them in Trieste.

Meanwhile, though *Irish Homestead* rejects a fourth story, Joyce completes a total of ten by the time he writes to English publisher William Heinemann (in September) offering him "a collection of twelve short stories" called *Dubliners*. When Heinemann declines, Joyce sends the manuscript to English publisher Grant Richards (in November). After a contract is signed, more stories are submitted, and the first pages are printed, the book's printer and publisher discover what they believe to be legally actionable material, initiating months of wrangling with Joyce and some changes to the manuscript. (For excerpts from Joyce's correspondence with Richards, see Patrick McCarthy's introduction to *Rejoycing: New Readings of* Dubliners, later in this chapter.)

1906 July Joyce moves his family to Rome, Italy, where he works as a bank clerk and writes two more *Dubliners* stories.

September Grant Richards decides not to publish *Dubliners*.

1907 Joyce's *Chamber Music*, a collection of poems, appears; meanwhile, *Dubliners* is rejected by another English publisher.

Joyce writes the fifteenth and final *Dubliners* story, "The Dead," and turns to his reconceived and retitled novel *A Portrait of the Artist as a Young Man*.

1908 Seven more English publishers reject *Dubliners*. In part because of his father's straitened circumstances, Joyce persuades one of his sisters to join his family in Trieste.

1909 August Joyce visits Dublin, secures a contract with Maunsel and Company for publication of *Dubliners*, and convinces a second sister to move to Trieste.

1910 A fearful Maunsel indefinitely postpones publication of *Dubliners*.

1912 July Joyce makes what will turn out to be his last visit to Dublin and secures a proof of *Dubliners*, which Maunsel now definitely refuses to publish. Joyce writes the satirical poem "Gas from a Burner."

By year's end, at least five other publishers reject *Dubliners*.

1914 January Grant Richards agrees to publish *Dubliners*.

February Thanks to American poet Ezra Pound, *Portrait* begins to appear serially in the London-based *Egoist* magazine.

15 June *Dubliners* appears (almost ten years after publication of "The Sisters"); Joyce begins work on the novel *Ulysses* and a play, *Exiles*.

1915 After the outbreak of World War I and the internment of Stanislaus (in January), Joyce moves his family to Zurich, Switzerland (a neutral country). On the recommendation of Pound and Yeats, Joyce receives a small grant from Britain's Royal Literary Fund and, later, the British Society of Authors.

1916		*A Portrait of the Artist* appears in volume form in New York, followed by the first U.S. edition of *Dubliners*. In August, the British government awards Joyce a Civil List grant.
1917		*Portrait* is published in London by one of Joyce's patrons. Attacked by glaucoma, Joyce has the first of eleven eye surgeries and begins to receive monetary gifts from various sympathetic patrons.
1918	March	The American *Little Review* begins to serialize *Ulysses*.
	May	*Exiles* is published in England and the United States.
1919		*Exiles* is staged for the first time in Munich, Germany; *The Egoist* begins to serialize *Ulysses*.
1920		The New York Society for the Suppression of Vice lodges a complaint of obscenity against the *Little Review* because of *Ulysses*.
1921		The *Ulysses* obscenity trial begins in the United States, ultimately resulting in a guilty verdict and ending its serialization.
1922	February	*Ulysses* is published by Joyce supporters in Paris and London.
1923		Joyce begins work on the novel *Finnegans Wake*, fragments of which will begin to appear in periodicals in April 1924.
1931	July	Concerned about the future of his adult children and first grandchild, Joyce marries Nora Barnacle in London.
	December	Joyce's 82-year-old father dies.
1933		A U.S. judge rules that *Ulysses* is not pornographic, paving the way for an American edition.
1934		The first complete U.S. edition of *Ulysses* appears, and Joyce makes his first visit to the United States.
1939		*Finnegans Wake* is published in England and the United States.
1941	January	Joyce dies in Zurich, Switzerland, following surgery for a perforated ulcer.

Passages from James Joyce's Early Writings

From Drama and Life (1900)

Life indeed nowadays is often a sad bore. Many feel [. . .] that they have been born too late in a world too old, and their wanhope[1] and nerveless unheroism point on ever sternly to a last nothing, a vast futility and meanwhile—a bearing of fardels.[2] Epic savagery is rendered impossible by vigilant policing, chivalry has been killed by the fashion oracles of the boulevards. There is no clank of mail, no halo about gallantry, no hat-sweeping, no roystering! The traditions of

1. Hopelessness, despair.
2. Bundles or burdens.

romance are upheld only in Bohemia.[3] Still I think out of the dreary sameness of existence, a measure of dramatic life may be drawn. Even the most commonplace, the deadest among the living, may play a part in a great drama. It is a sinful foolishness to sigh back for the good old times, to feed the hunger of us with the cold stones they afford. Life we must accept as we see it before our eyes, men and women as we meet them in the real world, not as we apprehend them in the world of faery. The great human comedy in which each has a share, gives limitless scope to the true artist, to-day as yesterday and as in years gone by.

Dublin street scene, circa 1890s

From Ireland, Island of Saints and Sages (1907)

[. . . T]he Irish nation's [present-day] insistence on developing its own culture by itself[1] is not so much the demand of a young nation that wants to make good in the European concert as the demand of a very old nation to renew under new forms the glories of a past civilization.

• • •

Ireland prides itself on being faithful body and soul to its national tradition as well as to the Holy See. The majority of the Irish consider fidelity to these two traditions their cardinal article of faith.

• • •

[. . . W]hen the Irishman is found outside of Ireland in another environment, he very often becomes a respected man. The economic and intellectual conditions that prevail in his own country do not permit the development of individuality. The soul of the country is weakened by centuries of useless struggle and broken treaties, and individual initiative is paralysed by the influence and admonitions of the church, while its body is manacled by the police, the tax office, and the garrison. No one who has any self-respect stays in Ireland, but flees afar as though from a country that has undergone the visitation of an angered Jove.[2]

3. Imaginary place inhabited by artists and writers who pursue an unconventional lifestyle, named for the literal Bohemia, a former kingdom of the Czech Republic.

1. Joyce here alludes to the Irish Revival, a movement to revive traditional Irish culture and language (Gaelic); the Revival was closely associated with, but distinct from, the movement to make Ireland politically independent of Britain.

2. A.k.a. Jupiter, the supreme god of Roman mythology.

Cartoon from 1854

• • •

[. . . I]f Ireland has been able to give all this practical talent to the service of others, it means that there must be something inimical, unpropitious, and despotic in its own present condition, since her sons cannot give their efforts to their own native land.

Because, even today, the flight of the wild geese continues. Every year, Ireland, decimated as she already is, loses 60,000 of her sons. From 1850 to the present day, more than 5,000,000 emigrants have left for America, and every post brings to Ireland their inviting letters to friends and relatives at home. The old men, the corrupt, the children, and the poor stay at home, where the double yoke wears another groove in the tamed neck; and around the death bed where the poor, anaemic, almost lifeless body lies in agony, the rulers give orders and the priests administer last rites.

Is this country destined to resume its ancient position as the Hellas[3] of the north some day? Is the Celtic mind [. . .] destined to enrich the civil conscience with new discoveries and new insights in the future? Or must the Celtic world, [. . .] driven by stronger nations to the edge of the continent, to the outermost islands of Europe, finally be cast into the ocean after a struggle of centuries?

• • •

[. . .] I confess that I do not see what good it does to fulminate against the English tyranny while the Roman tyranny occupies the palace of the soul.

I do not see the purpose of the bitter invectives against the English despoiler, the disdain for the vast Anglo-Saxon civilization, even though it is almost

3. Greece.

entirely a materialistic civilization, nor the empty boasts that the art of miniature in the ancient Irish books, such as the *Book of Kells*[4] [. . .], which date back to a time when England was an uncivilized country, is almost as old as the Chinese, and that Ireland made and exported to Europe its own fabrics for several generations before the first Fleming arrived in London to teach the English how to make bread. If an appeal to the past in this manner were valid, the fellahin[5] of Cairo would have all the right in the world to disdain to act as porters for English tourists. Ancient Ireland is dead just as ancient Egypt is dead. Its death chant has been sung, and on its gravestone has been placed the seal.

From Gas from a Burner (1912)[1]

Ladies and gents, you are here assembled
To hear why earth and heaven trembled
Because of the black and sinister arts
Of an Irish writer in foreign parts.[2]
He sent me a book ten years ago.
I read it a hundred times or so,
Backwards and forwards, down and up,
Through both ends of a telescope.
I printed it all to the very last word
But by the mercy of the Lord
The darkness of my mind was rent
And I saw the writer's foul intent.
But I owe a duty to Ireland:
I hold her honour in my hand,
This lovely land that always sent
Her writers and artists to banishment
And in a spirit of Irish fun
Betrayed her own leaders, one by one.
. . . .
O Ireland my first and only love
Where Christ and Caesar are hand and glove!
O lovely land where the shamrock grows!
(Allow me, ladies, to blow my nose)
To show you for strictures I don't care a button
I printed the poems of Mountainy Mutton[3]
And a play he wrote (you've read it I'm sure)
Where they talk of "bastard," "bugger" and "whore"[4]
. . . .

4. Illuminated manuscript (ca. 800 CE) regarded as a masterwork of Western calligraphy and as one of Ireland's greatest national treasures.

5. Arab peasants or agricultural laborers.

1. The speaker of Joyce's poem is a fictional amalgam of the head of the Dublin publishing company Maunsel and Company and its printer, who first agreed and later refused to print and publish *Dubliners*.

2. At this time, Joyce lived in Trieste, Austria.

3. Joseph Campbell (1879–1944); his collection of poems, *The Mountainy Singer*, was published by Maunsel in 1909.

4. Campbell's play *Judgment*, published by Maunsel in 1912.

I printed folklore from North and South
By Gregory of the Golden Mouth:[5]
I printed poets, sad, silly and solemn:
I printed Patrick What-do-you-Colm:[6]
. . . .
But I draw the line at that bloody fellow,
That was over here dressed in Austrian yellow,
Spouting Italian by the hour
To O'Leary Curtis[7] and John Wyse Power
And writing of Dublin, dirty and dear,
In a manner no blackamoor printer could bear.
Shite and onions! Do you think I'll print
The name of the Wellington Monument,
Sydney Parade and Sandymount tram,
Downes's cakeshop and Williams's jam?[8]
I'm damned if I do—I'm damned to blazes!
Talk about *Irish Names of Places*![9]
It's a wonder to me, upon my soul,
He forgot to mention Curly's Hole.[1]
No, ladies, my press shall have no share in
So gross a libel on Stepmother Erin.
. . . .
Who was it said: Resist not evil?[2]
I'll burn that book, so help me devil.
I'll sing a psalm as I watch it burn
And the ashes I'll keep in a one-handled urn.
I'll penance do with farts and groans
Kneeling upon my marrowbones.
This very next Lent I will unbare
My penitent buttocks to the air
And sobbing beside my printing press
My awful sin I will confess.
My Irish foreman from Bannockburn[3]
Shall dip his right hand in the urn
And sign crisscross with reverent thumb
Memento homo[4] upon my bum.

5. Dramatist and folklorist Lady Augusta Gregory (1852–1932), a major figure in the Irish Literary Revival; Maunsel published her *Kiltartan History Book and The Kiltartan Wonder Book* (1909, 1910).
6. Padraic Colum (1881–1972), a poet associated with the Irish Revival.
7. Dublin journalist, as was John Wyse Power (1859–1926); Power was also a member of the Irish Republican Brotherhood and a founder of the still-extant Gaelic Athletic Association for the Preservation and Cultivation of National Pastimes.
8. One objection to publishing *Dubliners* was the fear that the volume's many references to specific, actual Dublin places and businesses (like the ones listed here) would inspire lawsuits.
9. *The Origin and History of Irish Names and Places* (1869), by Patrick Joyce (no relation).
1. Dublin-area bathing and fishing spot.
2. Jesus says these words in the Sermon on the Mount: "But I say unto you, that ye resist not evil: but whosoever shall smite thee on thy right cheek, turn to him the other also" (Matt. 5.39).
3. Village in Scotland.
4. "Memento, homo, quia pulvis es, et in pulverem reverteris" ("Remember, human, that you are dust, and to dust you will return"); words, adapted from Genesis 3.19, that begin the prayer spoken on Ash Wednesday by priests as they use ashes to mark the sign of the cross on congregants' foreheads.

CRITICAL EXCERPT

Patrick A. McCarthy

From Rejoycing: New Readings of *Dubliners* (1998)[1]

James Joyce began *Dubliners* in 1904 as a short story sequence for [. . . the] agricultural journal *The Irish Homestead*, which published versions of "The Sisters," "Eveline," and "After the Race" before complaints from readers offended by the stories' caustic treatment of Irish life led [the editor] to suspend publication of the stories. By then, however, Joyce was already planning to recast his series of discrete narratives into a book of stories linked by their common concern with Catholic middle-class life in Dublin as well as by various overlapping themes, images, and situations. *Dubliners* was published in 1914, after numerous delays and complicated negotiations with the English publisher Grant Richards (who canceled a 1906 contract but issued a new one eight years later and finally brought out the volume) and with the Dublin firm of Maunsel and Company, whose printer raised objections to the stories both because of their alleged obscenity and because he feared lawsuits by people and businesses named in them.[2] When it was published the book attracted none of the legal actions feared by Joyce's publishers and printers; on the other hand, it received mixed reviews, and its sales were meager, as Joyce noted in a letter to Richards in which he expressed regret that "neither you nor I have gained anything" from the book's publication (*D* 292; *Letters* 2:340–41). For Joyce, the lack of royalties was less disappointing than the fact that the book had done little to stimulate interest in his new projects or to establish him as a major author.

The publication of *Dubliners* thus proved anticlimactic, an event easily overshadowed by the appearance of *A Portrait of the Artist as a Young Man* (serialized in *The Egoist*, 1914–15; first book publication, December 1916) and, far more spectacularly, by the 1922 publication of *Ulysses*, after which Joyce was widely recognized as a central modernist writer—indeed, as one of the most important avant-garde artists of his time. In retrospect, however, 1914 stands out as an important year in the history of the modernist short story and modern fiction in general. Several reasons for the importance of *Dubliners* are suggested by Joyce's own description of his aims and methods in a May 1906 letter to Grant Richards:

> My intention was to write a chapter of the moral history of my country and I chose Dublin for the scene because that city seemed to me the centre of paralysis. I have tried to present it to the indifferent public under four of its aspects: childhood, adolescence, maturity and public life. The stories are

1. From the introduction to *New Readings of* Dubliners, edited by Rosa M. Bollettieri Bosinelli and Harold F. Mosher Jr., UP of Kentucky, 1998, pp. 1–9. Copyright 1998 by The University Press of Kentucky. All notes are McCarthy's; some of his works cited have been omitted.

2. For more detailed accounts of the composition of *Dubliners* (hereafter cited with page numbers as *D*) and the disputes involved in its publication, see Morris Beja 32–39; Richard Ellmann 207–11, 219–22, 231–32, 267, 290–91, 310–11, 313–15, 323–24, 328–38, 348–54; Michael Groden 78–84; Florence L. Walzl 160–64; and "The Evidence of the Letters" (*D* 257–93). See especially "A Curious History" (*D* 289–92). Joyce satirized Maunsel and Company and the Dublin printer John Falconer in his 1912 broadside "Gas from a Burner" (*Critical Writings* 242–45).

> arranged in this order. I have written it for the most part in a style of scrupulous meanness and with the conviction that he is a very bold man who dares to alter in the presentment, still more to deform, whatever he has seen and heard. [*D* 269; *Letters* 2:134]

Here, in capsule form, are Joyce's defenses of the collection on the bases of its subject matter (a critique of Dublin society as "the centre of paralysis"), its comprehensive organization, its "style of scrupulous meanness," and above all its realism and adherence to the truth. Setting himself against "the indifferent public," Joyce implies that by portraying the "paralysis" at the heart of Dublin's public life he will force readers out of their apathy. A similar note appears in a letter to Richards written seven weeks later, in which Joyce argues that "the odour of ashpits and old weeds and offal" emanating from his stories is a necessary part of his depiction of the city and grandly declares that Richard's failure to publish *Dubliners* would "retard the course of civilisation in Ireland by preventing the Irish people from having one good book to look at themselves in [his] nicely polished looking-glass" (*D* 286; *Letters* 1:63–64).

As a contribution to the art of the short story, *Dubliners* is noteworthy for several reasons. Its sparse yet economical style, its use of suggestive details that at times seem to have a symbolic meaning, its refusal of any sort of neat conclusion have all influenced the shape of the modern short story.[3] Equally important is the fact that *Dubliners* is a coherent collection of related stories, a sort of novel with a collective rather than an individual protagonist. A few earlier collections had included stories with common locations, themes, and images [. . .] but *Dubliners* is the most fully realized, and most influential, volume of the kind. Apart from the first few stories that Joyce wrote, all of the *Dubliners* narratives were composed with book publication in mind, and the stories often take on different meanings when read within the context of the collection than they do in isolation. Sometimes the connections between stories are made by small touches, as when Eveline's "holding her black leather purse tightly in her hand as she elbowed her way through the crowds" (*D* 38) ironically undercuts the more romantic version of this image in "Araby," where, as he makes his way through a similar crowd, the narrator imagines himself bearing a "chalice" rather than a purse (*D* 31). Some of the book's forms of repetition are obvious enough—the conclusions of several stories involve darkness, tears, or both [. . .]—while others are more subtle, but they all contribute to the economy of *Dubliners*.

As an example of a significant recurrent element in Joyce's portrayal of Dublin we might cite the emphasis on absence. The theme is introduced on the first page of "The Sisters," whose narrator associates the key word *paralysis* with two other words whose contexts he specifies: "*gnomon* in the Euclid and . . . *simony* in the Catechism" (*D* 9). These three italicized words connect Joyce's themes of passivity (*paralysis*), corruption (*simony*), and absence (*gnomon*).[4] [. . .] Absence,

3. The most thorough examination of Joyce's relationship to earlier short story writers remains that of Marvin Magalaner and Richard M. Kain.

4. "Simony," so called after the example of Simon Magus (see Acts 8.18–19), refers to attempts to buy or sell pardons or other spiritual things; "gnomon," as the term is used in Euclidean geometry, denotes the irregular geometrical figure created by removing a parallelogram from one of the corners of a larger parallelogram. Other meanings of the *gnomon* image have been explored in Joyce criticism, most recently (and interestingly) by David Weir in *Joyce's Art of Mediation* and by Fritz Senn in the essay ["Gnomon Inverted"]

for Joyce, is a kind of presence, exerting pressure on what remains, as we see from the examples of dead people who continue to influence the living: Eveline Hill's mother in "Eveline, [. . .] Michael Furey in "The Dead." Characters who are alive but absent [. . .] play their own parts in the stories, as do any number of missing items. [. . .]

Joyce's original plan for a series of ten stories had been expanded to twelve by the time he sent the manuscript to Richards at the end of 1905, with two more—"Two Gallants" and "A Little Cloud"—following in 1906. Had the book been published as it then stood, a collection of fourteen stories beginning with "The Sisters" and ending with "Grace," it would have been very different from the book we now have: opening with a story of a priest whom the boy associates with simony and concluding with another whose treatment of God as an accountant implies a related corruption of the spiritual realm by materialism, *Dubliners* would have been a more insistently ironical portrayal of Dublin's "paralysis," focusing on the characters' inability to escape or improve their stagnant lives. The addition of "The Dead" in 1907 not only gave the book a very different—a more ambiguous as well as a more symbolic and more stylistically powerful—conclusion; it also balanced Joyce's criticism of Dublin with a display of its hospitality. In other ways as well, the scope of the collection was enlarged by "The Dead," which has a far broader vision of the human condition than any other story in *Dubliners.* That scope is especially evident in the final apocalyptic vision of "all the living and the dead," which is strikingly unlike the abrupt, minimalist conclusions of the earlier stories.

While "The Dead" may be read in isolation, some of its effects are lost if we do not recognize that it was the only story Joyce wrote with the rest of the collection in mind, a fact that led Joyce to incorporate into the story many coda-like echoes of other *Dubliners* stories. [. . .] While recapitulating themes, images, situations, and verbal motifs from earlier *Dubliners* stories, however, "The Dead" also serves as a turning point in Joyce's fiction, for it is the story whose mundane materials are most fully transformed, even redeemed, by their incorporation within its grand human vision.

Just as the stories of *Dubliners* may be read in isolation or as part of the collection, the book may be read by itself or as an integral part of Joyce's major work, which, apart from *Dubliners,* consists primarily of *A Portrait of the Artist as a Young Man* (1916), *Ulysses* (1922), and *Finnegans Wake* (1939). Each book could be regarded as the unique product of a phase in Joyce's career, an experiment in literary form that he never repeated: *Dubliners,* a realistic collection of short stories, was followed by *A Portrait,* an impressionistic novel, based on Joyce's early life, that describes the growth of an artist's imagination; by *Ulysses,* a stylistic and narrational tour de force filled with innumerable allusions and based in part on an analogy between the epic world of *Odyssey* and the modern Dublin traversed by a humane advertising canvasser; and by *Finnegans Wake,* a fantastic dream vision narrated in an obscure but often hilarious punning lan-

---

printed in this volume. For discussions of Joyce's "gnomonics" in terms related to those I have touched on here, see Bernard Benstock's chapter 2 and Phillip F. Herring's argument that the gnomon image "suggests that certain kinds of absence are typical of the whole of Dublin at a significant *time* in its history. . . . In effect, a *gnomon* may be a key synecdoche of absence, part of a political rhetoric of silence within a larger framework of language" (4).

guage. Thus the pattern of Joyce's career is one of incessant internalization, moving from realism toward a concern with the mind and the language through which the mind attempts to come to terms with the world and with itself. At the same time, *Dubliners* gives us fine examples of several important recurrent features of Joyce's work, including its intricate craftsmanship, its careful attention to all aspects of style, its concern with the relationship between individual characters and the cultural and historical environment in which they live, and its exploration of the relationship between art and politics.

WORKS CITED

Beja, Morris. *James Joyce: A Literary Life.* Columbus: Ohio State Univ. Press, 1992.

Benstock, Bernard. *Narrative Con/Texts in* Dubliners. Urbana: Univ. of Illinois Press, 1994.

Ellmann, Richard. *James Joyce.* Rev. ed. New York: Oxford Univ. Press, 1982.

Groden, Michael. "A Textual and Publishing History." In *A Companion to Joyce Studies,* ed. Zack Bowen and James F. Carens, 71–128. Westport, Conn.: Greenwood, 1984.

Herring, Phillip F. *Joyce's Uncertainty Principle.* Princeton, N.J.: Princeton Univ. Press, 1987.

Joyce, James. *The Critical Writings of James Joyce.* Ed. Ellsworth Mason and Richard Ellmann. New York: Viking, 1964.

———. *Dubliners: Text, Criticism, and Notes.* Ed. Robert Scholes and A. Walton Litz. New York: Viking, 1969.

———. *Letters of James Joyce.* Ed. Stuart Gilbert and Richard Ellmann. 3 vols. New York: Viking, 1966.

Magalaner, Marvin, and Richard M. Kain. *Joyce: The Man, the Work, the Reputation.* New York: New York Univ. Press, 1956.

Walzl, Florence L. "*Dubliners.*" In *A Companion to Joyce Studies,* ed. Zack Bowen and James F. Carens, 157–228. Westport, Conn.: Greenwood, 1984.

Weir, David. *Joyce's Art of Mediation.* Ann Arbor: Univ. of Michigan Press, 1996.

SUGGESTIONS FOR WRITING

1. First, read ARABY and write a brief response paper outlining what you see as its two or three most memorable and important elements or aspects. Next, read the story again after reading the stories in the "Initiation Stories" album; then write another brief response paper describing two new things in or about Joyce's story that this reading experience has helped you to see for the first time or in a different way. (That is, how is your interpretion of ARABY different when you read it in the context of other initiation stories?) Finally, read EVELINE and THE DEAD and then reread ARABY one more time; in a final response paper, describe how reading these three stories together has changed your impression and interpretation of ARABY. (That is, how is your interpretation of ARABY different when you read it in the context of other *Dubliners* stories?)
2. In his letters, Joyce identified "paralysis" as the central problem explored in *Dubliners.* Write an essay outlining the various kinds of paralysis that plague the characters in at least two of the stories in this chapter, perhaps drawing on some of the other materials included here, as well as the stories themselves. In these terms, what are the most important similarities and differences among characters and

stories? What might the stories individually and collectively suggest about why Dubliners suffer from this paralysis and whether it might be overcome and how? In these terms, what is the effect or significance of the order of the stories?

3. Literary critic Berni Benstock argues that "Every time-revered precept of the [middle classes] is carefully dismantled in *Dubliners*: that they are hard-working, honest, religious, temperate, and secure." Drawing on evidence from all three stories in this chapter, write an essay exploring the validity of Benstock's claim. In other words, how might some or all of these stories suggest that middle-class Dubliners aren't in fact as "hard-working, honest, religious, temperate, and [or] secure" as they might seem, even to themselves?
4. Benstock also argues that gender plays a vital role in determining the different social and economic fates of the characters in *Dubliners*. Write an essay exploring this or any way that gender matters in these stories. For example, what role do girls and women play in the two stories in which the focal characters and protagonists are male? By instead giving us a female protagonist and point of view, how might EVELINE give us a different perspective on the kind of situations, relationships, and issues explored in the other stories?
5. Drawing on the James Joyce and *Dubliners* chronology in this chapter and on the excerpts from Joyce's early writings, write an essay that explores how at least one Joyce story expresses any of the strong personal feelings or ideas that Joyce articulates in his other writings.
6. Research the history of Joyce's life and career up to the completion of *Dubliners*. Then write an essay exploring how any two stories from the sequence allow Joyce to reflect critically on, or even perhaps come to terms with, what he called—in an August 1904 letter to his future wife—"the actual difficulties of [his own] life."
7. Use online resources to identify any story in this anthology that also appears in a short-story collection to which you have access. Read or reread the story and record your impressions. Then read at least two other stories in the collection and reread the story you started with. In a short essay, explain how and why your impression and interpretation of the story changed after the second reading.
8. Write a short story that depicts an encounter between characters from at least two of the Joyce stories in this chapter. (For instance, what might happen if Eveline met the protagonist of ARABY on her way home from the docks, or if Eveline took a job as maid at the hotel where Gabriel and Gretta Conroy spend the night at the end of THE DEAD? Alternatively, if you imagine that Gabriel Conroy is the grown-up version of the narrator-protagonist of ARABY, what might have happened to him in between to explain how and why he becomes the man he does?)

10 CULTURAL AND HISTORICAL CONTEXTS: WOMEN IN TURN-OF-THE-CENTURY AMERICA

Over the past two hundred years, the meaning of the word *culture* has broadened considerably, from "cultivation" (as in *agriculture*) to "the arts or familiarity with the arts" (*high culture, a cultured person*) to "a whole way of life" (*American culture, African American culture*). The fact that we still use the one word for both "the arts" and "a whole way of life" implies a close, even fundamental relationship between the two. The double implications of "culture" suggest that works of art both reflect and help shape the way we live.

On the one hand, art in a particular time and place takes the form it does because of the larger cultural context—what the nineteenth-century writer William Hazlitt called "the spirit of the age." In other words, authors, like the rest of us, live in particular times and places, and authorial visions, however unique, are inevitably shaped by cultural and historical context.

On the other hand, literature can shape history, too. Testifying to the powerful effect that writers can exercise, one member of the generation born just after World War I noted that Ernest Hemingway's "impact upon us was tremendous"; We could follow him, ape his manner"; "we began unconsciously to [. . .] impose on everything we did and felt the particular emotions [his fiction] aroused in us." Authors sometimes choose to write precisely because they want to affect the way their contemporaries think, feel, and behave. Our understanding of a particular text or of an author's entire body of work often is enhanced if we learn more about that context.

But what happens to either the personal or the universal aspects of a literary work as we focus on its relationship to its cultural and historical context? At its best, the process is one of addition rather than subtraction. Reading a text in light of its context simply gives us a different but complementary perspective to that of reading the text on its own terms. Indeed, what makes the study of literature both exciting and enriching is its multilayered, multidimensional quality: the way that Flannery O'Connor's EVERYTHING THAT RISES MUST CONVERGE, for example, simultaneously embodies its author's personal vision of the association between violence and enlightenment, explores the universal problem of generational conflict, and evaluates the dramatic cultural transformations particular to the American South during the 1950s. The point, then, of reading with an eye toward cultural and historical context is not to foreclose other ways of reading but rather to enrich our experience of the text and, through it, our sense of what is both constant and variable about human experience across ages and cultures.

WOMEN AT THE TURN OF THE CENTURY: AN OVERVIEW

The period between about 1890 and 1920, often referred to as "the turn of the century" or the Progressive Era, saw transformations in many aspects of society in the United States. The nation's rapid industrialization and urbanization, in changing the way people worked and lived, also inspired a number of economic, political, and social reforms. The Progressive Era brought attempts to regulate corporations and improve working conditions through the creation of new government agencies and the passage of labor laws. In the social sphere, reformers sought advances in education, sanitation, and health care. Many of these efforts, perhaps most notably the women's suffrage and temperance movements, were spearheaded by middle-class women, trying to improve their own circumstances and those of women in all socioeconomic classes.

Works of literature written by American women during this period provide valuable insights into the predicaments of married middle-class white women in Progressive-Era America. This chapter examines three classics in the context of women's roles at the turn of the century: Charlotte Perkins Gilman's THE YELLOW WALLPAPER (1892), Kate Chopin's THE STORY OF AN HOUR (1894), and Susan Glaspell's A JURY OF HER PEERS (1917, based on her 1916 play TRIFLES). Without directly commenting on historic developments, these realistic stories about married women in domestic settings reflect changing outlooks. The chapter includes a selective chronology (from the first Women's Rights Convention in 1848 and the birth of Kate Chopin in 1850 to the death of Susan Glaspell in 1948) and a sample of contemporary documents on relevant topics. The list of sources and the writing suggestions point out several possible avenues for interpreting and writing about these stories. But first, we introduce some of the issues women faced at the time: work inside and outside the home; marriage law, domestic violence, and divorce; and the medical treatment of women—all matters that came under scrutiny thanks to Charlotte Perkins Gilman and other women leaders of the time.

In the Progressive Era, it was still the norm for a married white woman to serve as full-time manager of the home and any servants in it: By 1920, only 6.5 percent of married white women in the United States worked outside the home. In contrast, married African American women, who in the post–Civil War South had long been forced to work for minimal pay in the fields or as laundresses or cooks in white households, continued to seek paid work after migrating to Northern cities. Among single women of all races, half worked as paid employees at this time.

Work in the home, for wives or servants, could be very hard. For decades after the Civil War, women of all classes and races produced most of their households' clothing and food, quilts and curtains, and were kept busy tending wood or coal fires, making candles, or tending oil or gas lamps. Water had to be pumped, carried, and heated over fires, and laundry took more than a day's hard labor. It was rare, even among poorer families, for a house to be run without at least part-time hired help.

Toward the end of the nineteenth century, a series of inventions reduced domestic chores, and so domestic service declined. After the 1850s, sewing machines gradually became affordable not only for manufacturers but also for individuals, and the invention of the Mason jar in 1857 enabled families to preserve their homegrown fruits and vegetables for the winter. In 1931, the National

Susan Glaspell at typewriter (Berg Collection, New York Public Library)

Association of Real Estate Boards looked back at changes in the home: A newspaper article, "Home Necessities Once Were Luxury," quotes the association's finding that since the 1870s, "The electric light and the development of the array of electrical appliances did the work of the modern housewife," while bathtubs, once rare, newsworthy luxuries, were now installed in many homes (*New York Times*, 18 January 1931).

Some Innovations in Travel and Communication

- **Train**—first available for passengers in the 1820s, widely used in the United States by the 1890s.
- **Automobile**—mass produced by 1908, though horse-drawn carts and carriages remained in use in many areas through the 1930s.
- **Telegraph**—first developed in the 1830s; transatlantic in 1866; improved in the 1870s; wireless by the 1890s.
- **Telephone**—Alexander Graham Bell's first patent was granted in 1876; hand-crank telephones reached Iowa farms by 1900, with households sharing "party" lines.
- **Typewriter**—available in less expensive models for more businesses from the 1870s onward; women began to work as "typewriters."

A new convenience or labor-saving device, from the automobile to electricity to the telephone, could free a housewife from hours of work and allow her to pursue another occupation, to stay in touch with friends, to develop artistic talents, or to experience the world. The changes spread slowly, however, and were more common in urban areas and well-to-do homes than on farms or in working-class tenements. Social expectations for upper-class women kept many of them idle and dependent on servants.

Middle-class women's usefulness as household producers declined before opportunities for education and meaningful careers opened up. Medicine and law became organized, standardized professions at the turn of the century, for example, but both of these highly paid fields excluded women (and many men). At the same time, medical treatments and legal procedures that responded to any of the dysfunctions of married life tended to directly and indirectly increase men's domination of women. The "rest cure," psychoanalysis, and other medical practices developed by professional men became common ways to treat women suffering from the illnesses and depression that may have resulted in part from their feelings of purposelessness and inactivity. A woman might find her desire to pursue a career diagnosed as an illness; her acts of self-determination or resistance might be prohibited, punished, or judged insane.

Well into the twentieth century, divorce was expensive and difficult and usually resulted in a clouded reputation for the woman (as it did for the divorced Charlotte Stetson before she married George Hougton Gilman). Not until 1900 were some women able to sue successfully for divorce on the grounds of the husband's "mental cruelty"; previously, they would have needed to prove that he was violent or had committed adultery.

WOMEN WRITERS IN A CHANGING WORLD

In the United States and Europe, women's roles were slowly changing, however, thanks to the efforts of reform groups. Both Gilman and Glaspell participated in such efforts, on behalf of women and others, through their work with Heterodoxy, a New York group that advocated women's civil rights and suffrage. Gilman, in testimony before Congress on January 28, 1896, argued that extending the vote to women would "improve the race by improving the women." "You can not have as good a citizen, as good a class of people, where half the people are no part of the Government [. . .]," she argued, "And to debar any part of the race from its development is to carry along with society a dead weight, a part of the organism which is not living organic matter, which is a thing to be carried instead of to help. To give suffrage to this half of the race will develop it as it never has been developed before."[1] Gilman and Glaspell both lived to see U.S. women gain the vote in 1920.

Especially after 1870, women began to gain access to higher education and to demand entrance to careers other than teaching, writing, or the arts. By the beginning of the twentieth century, some women pursued careers in nursing, social work, libraries, fashion, and business, though most were employed in lower-paid positions, as clerical or support staff rather than as managers. Writing had long been a way to earn a living for some educated women, but the spread of newspapers and mass-market magazines from the 1890s onward provided openings for a new kind of worker, the woman journalist.

1. Charlotte Perkins Gilman, testimony before Congress of the National American Woman Suffrage Association Committee on the Judiciary in Washington, DC, January 28, 1896. Originally published in *In This Our World* (Small, Maynard, 1893), pp. 95–100.

Remington typewriter advertisement, 1919

Chopin, Gilman, and Glaspell, needing to earn a living, embraced such opportunities. Susan Glaspell began her journalism career after college, as a reporter in Iowa, and covered a scandalous murder case similar to the one in her story "A Jury of Her Peers." These writers' careers and writings, including the works featured here, reflect both the expanding prospects and continuing limitations on women's lives in this transitional period.

KATE CHOPIN (1850–1904)

The Story of an Hour

Katherine O'Flaherty was born in St. Louis, Missouri, to a Creole-Irish family that enjoyed a high place in society. Her father died when she was four, and Kate was raised by her mother, grandmother, and great-grandmother. Very well read at a young age, she received her formal education at the St. Louis

Academy of the Sacred Heart. In 1870, she married Oscar Chopin, a Louisiana businessman, and lived with him in Natchitoches Parish and New Orleans, where she became a close observer of Creole and Cajun life. Following her husband's sudden death in 1884, she returned to St. Louis, where she raised her six children and began her literary career. In slightly more than a decade she produced a substantial body of work, including the story collections *Bayou Folk* (1894) and *A Night in Acadie* (1897) and the classic novella *The Awakening* (1899), which was greeted with a storm of criticism for its frank treatment of female sexuality.

Knowing that Mrs. Mallard was afflicted with a heart trouble, great care was taken to break to her as gently as possible the news of her husband's death.

It was her sister Josephine who told her, in broken sentences; veiled hints that revealed in half concealing. Her husband's friend Richards was there, too, near her. It was he who had been in the newspaper office when intelligence of the railroad disaster was received, with Brently Mallard's name leading the list of "killed." He had only taken the time to assure himself of its truth by a second telegram, and had hastened to forestall any less careful, less tender friend in bearing the sad message.

She did not hear the story as many women have heard the same, with a paralyzed inability to accept its significance. She wept at once, with sudden, wild abandonment, in her sister's arms. When the storm of grief had spent itself she went away to her room alone. She would have no one follow her.

There stood, facing the open window, a comfortable, roomy armchair. Into this she sank, pressed down by a physical exhaustion that haunted her body and seemed to reach into her soul.

She could see in the open square before her house the tops of trees that were 5
all aquiver with the new spring life. The delicious breath of rain was in the air. In the street below a peddler was crying his wares. The notes of a distant song which some one was singing reached her faintly, and countless sparrows were twittering in the eaves.

There were patches of blue sky showing here and there through the clouds that had met and piled one above the other in the west facing her window.

She sat with her head thrown back upon the cushion of the chair, quite motionless, except when a sob came up into her throat and shook her, as a child who has cried itself to sleep continues to sob in its dreams.

She was young, with a fair, calm face, whose lines bespoke repression and even a certain strength. But now there was a dull stare in her eyes, whose gaze was fixed away off yonder on one of those patches of blue sky. It was not a glance of reflection, but rather indicated a suspension of intelligent thought.

There was something coming to her and she was waiting for it, fearfully. What was it? She did not know; it was too subtle and elusive to name. But she felt it, creeping out of the sky, reaching toward her through the sounds, the scents, the color that filled the air.

10 Now her bosom rose and fell tumultuously. She was beginning to recognize this thing that was approaching to possess her, and she was striving to beat it back with her will—as powerless as her two white slender hands would have been.

When she abandoned herself a little whispered word escaped her slightly parted lips. She said it over and over under her breath: "free, free, free!" The vacant stare and the look of terror that had followed it went from her eyes. They stayed keen and bright. Her pulses beat fast, and the coursing blood warmed and relaxed every inch of her body.

She did not stop to ask if it were or were not a monstrous joy that held her. A clear and exalted perception enabled her to dismiss the suggestion as trivial.

She knew that she would weep again when she saw the kind, tender hands folded in death; the face that had never looked save with love upon her, fixed and gray and dead. But she saw beyond that bitter moment a long procession of years to come that would belong to her absolutely. And she opened and spread her arms out to them in welcome.

There would be no one to live for her during those coming years; she would live for herself. There would be no powerful will bending hers in that blind persistence with which men and women believe they have a right to impose a private will upon a fellow-creature. A kind intention or a cruel intention made the act seem no less a crime as she looked upon it in that brief moment of illumination.

15 And yet she had loved him—sometimes. Often she had not. What did it matter! What could love, the unsolved mystery, count for in face of this possession of self-assertion which she suddenly recognized as the strongest impulse of her being!

"Free! Body and soul free!" she kept whispering.

Josephine was kneeling before the closed door with her lips to the keyhold, imploring for admission. "Louise, open the door! I beg; open the door—you will make yourself ill. What are you doing, Louise? For heaven's sake open the door."

"Go away. I am not making myself ill." No; she was drinking in a very elixir of life through that open window.

Her fancy was running riot along those days ahead of her. Spring days, and summer days, and all sorts of days that would be her own. She breathed a quick prayer that life might be long. It was only yesterday she had thought with a shudder that life might be long.

20 She arose at length and opened the door to her sister's importunities. There was a feverish triumph in her eyes, and she carried herself unwittingly like a goddess of Victory. She clasped her sister's waist, and together they descended the stairs. Richards stood waiting for them at the bottom.

Some one was opening the front door with a latchkey. It was Brently Mallard who entered, a little travel-stained, composedly carrying his grip-sack and umbrella. He had been far from the scene of accident, and did not even know there had been one. He stood amazed at Josephine's piercing cry; at Richards' quick motion to screen him from the view of his wife.

But Richards was too late.

When the doctors came they said she had died of heart disease—of joy that kills.

1894

CHARLOTTE PERKINS GILMAN (1860–1935)

The Yellow Wallpaper

Charlotte Anna Perkins was born in Hartford, Connecticut. After a painful, lonely childhood and several years of supporting herself as a governess, art teacher, and designer of greeting cards, Perkins married the artist Charles Stetson. Following her several extended periods of depression, Charles Stetson put his wife in the care of a doctor who, in her own words, "sent me home with the solemn advice to 'live as domestic a life as [. . .] possible,' to 'have but two hours' intellectual life a day,' and 'never to touch pen, brush, or pencil again' as long as I lived." Three months of this regimen brought her "near the borderline of utter mortal ruin" and inspired her masterpiece, "The Yellow Wallpaper." In 1900, she married George Houghton Gilman, having divorced Stetson in 1892. Her nonfiction works, springing from the early women's movement, include *Women and Economics* (1898) and *Man-Made World* (1911). She also wrote several utopian novels, including *Moving the Mountain* (1911) and *Herland* (1915).

It is very seldom that mere ordinary people like John and myself secure ancestral halls for the summer.

A colonial mansion, a hereditary estate, I would say a haunted house, and reach the height of romantic felicity—but that would be asking too much of fate!

Still I will proudly declare that there is something queer about it.

Else, why should it be let so cheaply? And why have stood so long untenanted?

John laughs at me, of course, but one expects that in marriage. 5

John is practical in the extreme. He has no patience with faith, an intense horror of superstition, and he scoffs openly at any talk of things not to be felt and seen and put down in figures.

John is a physician, and *perhaps*—(I would not say it to a living soul, of course, but this is dead paper and a great relief to my mind—) *perhaps* that is one reason I do not get well faster.

You see he does not believe I am sick!

And what can one do?

If a physician of high standing, and one's own husband, assures friends and 10
relatives that there is really nothing the matter with one but temporary nervous depression—a slight hysterical tendency—what is one to do?

My brother is also a physician, and also of high standing, and he says the same thing.

So I take phosphates or phosphites—whichever it is, and tonics, and journeys, and air, and exercise, and am absolutely forbidden to "work" until I am well again.

Personally, I disagree with their ideas.

Personally, I believe that congenial work, with excitement and change, would do me good.

15 But what is one to do?

I did write for a while in spite of them; but it *does* exhaust me a good deal—having to be so sly about it, or else meet with heavy opposition.

I sometimes fancy that in my condition if I had less opposition and more society and stimulus—but John says the very worst thing I can do is to think about my condition, and I confess it always makes me feel bad.

So I will let it alone and talk about the house.

The most beautiful place! It is quite alone, standing well back from the road, quite three miles from the village. It makes me think of English places that you read about, for there are hedges and walls and gates that lock, and lots of separate little houses for the gardeners and people.

20 There is a *delicious* garden! I never saw such a garden—large and shady, full of box-bordered paths, and lined with long grape-covered arbors with seats under them.

There were greenhouses, too, but they are all broken now.

There was some legal trouble, I believe, something about the heirs and co-heirs; anyhow, the place has been empty for years.

That spoils my ghostliness, I am afraid, but I don't care—there is something strange about the house—I can feel it.

I even said so to John one moonlight evening, but he said what I felt was a *draught*, and shut the window.

25 I get unreasonably angry with John sometimes. I'm sure I never used to be so sensitive. I think it is due to this nervous condition.

But John says if I feel so, I shall neglect proper self-control; so I take pains to control myself—before him, at least, and that makes me very tired.

I don't like our room a bit. I wanted one downstairs that opened on the piazza and had roses all over the window, and such pretty old-fashioned chintz hangings! but John would not hear of it.

He said there was only one window and not room for two beds, and no near room for him if he took another.

He is very careful and loving, and hardly lets me stir without special direction.

30 I have a schedule prescription for each hour in the day; he takes all care from me, and so I feel basely ungrateful not to value it more.

He said we came here solely on my account, that I was to have perfect rest and all the air I could get. "Your exercise depends on your strength, my dear," said he, "and your food somewhat on your appetite; but air you can absorb all the time." So we took the nursery at the top of the house.

It is a big, airy room, the whole floor nearly, with windows that look all ways, and air and sunshine galore. It was nursery first and then playroom and gymnasium, I should judge; for the windows are barred for little children, and there are rings and things in the walls.

The paint and paper look as if a boys' school had used it. It is stripped off—the paper—in great patches all around the head of my bed, about as far as I can reach, and in a great place on the other side of the room low down. I never saw a worse paper in my life.

One of those sprawling flamboyant patterns committing every artistic sin.

It is dull enough to confuse the eye in following, pronounced enough to con- 35
stantly irritate and provoke study, and when you follow the lame uncertain curves for a little distance they suddenly commit suicide—plunge off at outrageous angles, destroy themselves in unheard of contradictions.

The color is repellant, almost revolting; a smouldering unclean yellow, strangely faded by the slow-turning sunlight.

It is a dull yet lurid orange in some places, a sickly sulphur tint in others.

No wonder the children hated it! I should hate it myself if I had to live in this room long.

There comes John, and I must put this away,—he hates to have me write a word.

We have been here two weeks, and I haven't felt like writing before, since that 40
first day.

I am sitting by the window now, up in this atrocious nursery, and there is nothing to hinder my writing as much as I please, save lack of strength.

John is away all day, and even some nights when his cases are serious.

I am glad my case is not serious!

But these nervous troubles are dreadfully depressing.

John does not know how much I really suffer. He knows there is no *reason* to 45
suffer, and that satisfies him.

Of course it is only nervousness. It does weigh on me so not to do my duty in any way!

I mean to be such a help to John, such a real rest and comfort, and here I am a comparative burden already!

Nobody would believe what an effort it is to do what little I am able,—to dress and entertain, and order things.

It is fortunate Mary is so good with the baby. Such a dear baby!

And yet I *cannot* be with him, it makes me so nervous. 50

I suppose John never was nervous in his life. He laughs at me so about this wallpaper!

At first he meant to repaper the room, but afterwards he said that I was letting it get the better of me, and that nothing was worse for a nervous patient than to give way to such fancies.

He said that after the wallpaper was changed it would be the heavy bedstead, and then the barred windows, and then that gate at the head of the stairs, and so on.

"You know the place is doing you good," he said, "and really, dear, I don't care to renovate the house just for a three months' rental."

"Then do let us go downstairs," I said, "there are such pretty rooms there." 55

Then he took me in his arms and called me a blessed little goose, and said he would go down cellar, if I wished, and have it whitewashed into the bargain.

But he is right enough about the beds and windows and things.

It is an airy and comfortable room as any one need wish, and, of course, I would not be so silly as to make him uncomfortable just for a whim.

I'm really getting quite fond of the big room, all but that horrid paper.

Out of one window I can see the garden, those mysterious deep-shaded arbors, the riotous old-fashioned flowers, and bushes and gnarly trees.

Out of another I get a lovely view of the bay and a little private wharf belonging to the estate. There is a beautiful shaded lane that runs down there from the house. I always fancy I see people walking in these numerous paths and arbors, but John has cautioned me not to give way to fancy in the least. He says that with my imaginative power and habit of story-making, a nervous weakness like mine is sure to lead to all manner of excited fancies, and that I ought to use my will and good sense to check the tendency. So I try.

I think sometimes that if I were only well enough to write a little it would relieve the press of ideas and rest me.

But I find I get pretty tired when I try.

It is so discouraging not to have any advice and companionship about my work. When I get really well, John says we will ask Cousin Henry and Julia down for a long visit; but he says he would as soon put fireworks in my pillow-case as to let me have those stimulating people about now.

I wish I could get well faster.

But I must not think about that. This paper looks to me as if it *knew* what a vicious influence it had!

There is a recurrent spot where the pattern lolls like a broken neck and two bulbous eyes stare at you upside down.

I get positively angry with the impertinence of it and the everlastingness. Up and down and sideways they crawl, and those absurd, unblinking eyes are everywhere. There is one place where two breadths didn't match, and the eyes go all up and down the line, one a little higher than the other.

I never saw so much expression in an inanimate thing before, and we all know how much expression they have! I used to lie awake as a child and get more entertainment and terror out of blank walls and plain furniture than most children could find in a toy-store.

I remember what a kindly wink the knobs of our big, old bureau used to have, and there was one chair that always seemed like a strong friend.

I used to feel that if any of the other things looked too fierce I could always hop into that chair and be safe.

The furniture in this room is no worse than inharmonious, however, for we had to bring it all from downstairs. I suppose when this was used as a playroom they had to take the nursery things out, and no wonder! I never saw such ravages as the children have made here.

The wallpaper, as I said before, is torn off in spots, and it sticketh closer than a brother—they must have had perseverance as well as hatred.

Then the floor is scratched and gouged and splintered, the plaster itself is dug out here and there, and this great heavy bed which is all we found in the room, looks as if it had been through the wars.

But I don't mind it a bit—only the paper.

There comes John's sister. Such a dear girl as she is, and so careful of me! I must not let her find me writing.

She is a perfect and enthusiastic housekeeper, and hopes for no better profession. I verily believe she thinks it is the writing which made me sick!

But I can write when she is out, and see her a long way off from these windows.

There is one that commands the road, a lovely shaded winding road, and one that just looks off over the country. A lovely country, too, full of great elms and velvet meadows.

This wallpaper has a kind of sub-pattern in a different shade, a particularly irritating one, for you can only see it in certain lights, and not clearly then.

But in the places where it isn't faded and where the sun is just so—I can see a strange, provoking, formless sort of figure, that seems to skulk about behind that silly and conspicuous front design.

There's sister on the stairs!

Well, the Fourth of July is over! The people are all gone and I am tired out. John thought it might do me good to see a little company, so we just had mother and Nellie and the children down for a week.

Of course I didn't do a thing. Jennie sees to everything now.

But it tired me all the same.

John says if I don't pick up faster he shall send me to Weir Mitchell[1] in the fall.

But I don't want to go there at all. I had a friend who was in his hands once, and she says he is just like John and my brother, only more so!

Besides, it is such an undertaking to go so far.

I don't feel as if it was worth while to turn my hand over for anything, and I'm getting dreadfully fretful and querulous.

I cry at nothing, and cry most of the time.

Of course I don't when John is here, or anybody else, but when I am alone.

And I am alone a good deal just now. John is kept in town very often by serious cases, and Jennie is good and lets me alone when I want her to.

So I walk a little in the garden or down that lovely lane, sit on the porch under the roses, and lie down up here a good deal.

I'm getting really fond of the room in spite of the wallpaper. Perhaps *because* of the wallpaper.

It dwells in my mind so!

I lie here on this great immovable bed—it is nailed down, I believe—and follow that pattern about by the hour. It is as good as gymnastics, I assure you. I start, we'll say, at the bottom, down in the corner over there where it has not been touched, and I determine for the thousandth time that I *will* follow that pointless pattern to some sort of conclusion.

I know a little of the principle of design, and I know this thing was not arranged on any laws of radiation, or alternation, or repetition, or symmetry, or anything else that I ever heard of.

It is repeated, of course, by the breadths, but not otherwise.

Looked at in one way each breadth stands alone, the bloated curves and flourishes—a kind of "debased Romanesque" with *delirium tremens*—go waddling up and down in isolated columns of fatuity.

1. Silas Weir Mitchell (1829–1914), American physician, novelist, and specialist in nerve disorders, popularized the rest cure.

100 But, on the other hand, they connect diagonally, and the sprawling outlines run off in great slanting waves of optic horror, like a lot of wallowing seaweeds in full chase.

The whole thing goes horizontally, too, at least it seems so, and I exhaust myself in trying to distinguish the order of its going in that direction.

They have used a horizontal breadth for a frieze, and that adds wonderfully to the confusion.

There is one end of the room where it is almost intact, and there, when the crosslights fade and the low sun shines directly upon it, I can almost fancy radiation after all,—the interminable grotesque seem to form around a common center and rush off in headlong plunges of equal distraction.

It makes me tired to follow it. I will take a nap I guess.

105 I don't know why I should write this.

I don't want to.

I don't feel able.

And I know John would think it absurd. But I *must* say what I feel and think in some way—it is such a relief!

But the effort is getting to be greater than the relief.

110 Half the time now I am awfully lazy, and lie down ever so much.

John says I mustn't lose my strength, and has me take cod liver oil and lots of tonics and things, to say nothing of ale and wine and rare meat.

Dear John! He loves me very dearly, and hates to have me sick. I tried to have a real earnest reasonable talk with him the other day, and tell him how I wish he would let me go and make a visit to Cousin Henry and Julia.

But he said I wasn't able to go, nor able to stand it after I got there; and I did not make out a very good case for myself, for I was crying before I had finished.

It is getting to be a great effort for me to think straight. Just this nervous weakness I suppose.

115 And dear John gathered me up in his arms, and just carried me upstairs and laid me on the bed, and sat by me and read to me till it tired my head.

He said I was his darling and his comfort and all he had, and that I must take care of myself for his sake, and keep well.

He says no one but myself can help me out of it, that I must use my will and self-control and not let any silly fancies run away with me.

There's one comfort, the baby is well and happy, and does not have to occupy this nursery with the horrid wallpaper.

If we had not used it, that blessed child would have! What a fortunate escape! Why, I wouldn't have a child of mine, an impressionable little thing, live in such a room for worlds.

120 I never thought of it before, but it is lucky that John kept me here after all, I can stand it so much easier than a baby, you see.

Of course I never mention it to them any more—I am too wise,—but I keep watch of it all the same.

There are things in that paper that nobody knows but me, or ever will.

Behind that outside pattern the dim shapes get clearer every day.

It is always the same shape, only very numerous.

And it is like a woman stooping down and creeping about behind that pat- 125
tern. I don't like it a bit. I wonder—I begin to think—I wish John would take me away from here!

It is so hard to talk with John about my case, because he is so wise, and because he loves me so.

But I tried it last night.

It was moonlight. The moon shines in all around just as the sun does.

I hate to see it sometimes, it creeps so slowly, and always comes in by one window or another.

John was asleep and I hated to waken him, so I kept still and watched the 130
moonlight on that undulating wallpaper till I felt creepy.

The faint figure behind seemed to shake the pattern, just as if she wanted to get out.

I got up softly and went to feel and see if the paper *did* move, and when I came back John was awake.

"What is it, little girl?" he said. "Don't go walking about like that—you'll get cold."

I thought it was a good time to talk, so I told him that I really was not gaining here, and that I wished he would take me away.

"Why, darling!" said he, "our lease will be up in three weeks, and I can't see 135
how to leave before.

"The repairs are not done at home, and I cannot possibly leave town just now. Of course if you were in any danger, I could and would, but you really are better, dear, whether you can see it or not. I am a doctor, dear, and I know. You are gaining flesh and color, your appetite is better, I feel really much easier about you."

"I don't weigh a bit more," said I, "nor as much; and my appetite may be better in the evening when you are here, but it is worse in the morning when you are away!"

"Bless her little heart!" said he with a big hug, "she shall be as sick as she pleases! But now let's improve the shining hours by going to sleep, and talk about it in the morning!"

"And you won't go away?" I asked gloomily.

"Why, how can I, dear? It is only three weeks more and then we will take a 140
nice little trip of a few days while Jennie is getting the house ready. Really dear you are better!"

"Better in body perhaps—" I began, and stopped short, for he sat up straight and looked at me with such a stern, reproachful look that I could not say another word.

"My darling," said he, "I beg of you, for my sake and for our child's sake, as well as for your own, that you will never for one instant let that idea enter your mind! There is nothing so dangerous, so fascinating, to a temperament like yours. It is a false and foolish fancy. Can you not trust me as a physician when I tell you so?"

So of course I said no more on that score, and we went to sleep before long. He thought I was asleep first, but I wasn't, and lay there for hours trying to decide whether that front pattern and the back pattern really did move together or separately.

On a pattern like this, by daylight, there is a lack of sequence, a defiance of law, that is a constant irritant to a normal mind.

145 The color is hideous enough, and unreliable enough, and infuriating enough, but the pattern is torturing.

You think you have mastered it, but just as you get well underway in following, it turns a back-somersault and there you are. It slaps you in the face, knocks you down, and tramples upon you. It is like a bad dream.

The outside pattern is a florid arabesque, reminding one of a fungus. If you can imagine a toadstool in joints, an interminable string of toadstools, budding and sprouting in endless convolutions—why, that is something like it.

That is, sometimes!

There is one marked peculiarity about this paper, a thing nobody seems to notice but myself, and that is that it changes as the light changes.

150 When the sun shoots in through the east window—I always watch for that first long, straight ray—it changes so quickly that I never can quite believe it.

That is why I watch it always.

By moonlight—the moon shines in all night when there is a moon—I wouldn't know it was the same paper.

At night in any kind of light, in twilight, candlelight, lamplight, and worst of all by moonlight, it becomes bars! The outside pattern I mean, and the woman behind it is as plain as can be.

I didn't realize for a long time what the thing was that showed behind, that dim sub-pattern, but now I am quite sure it is a woman.

155 By daylight she is subdued, quiet. I fancy it is the pattern that keeps her so still. It is so puzzling. It keeps me quiet by the hour.

I lie down ever so much now. John says it is good for me, and to sleep all I can.

Indeed he started the habit by making me lie down for an hour after each meal.

It is a very bad habit I am convinced, for you see I don't sleep.

And that cultivates deceit, for I don't tell them I'm awake—O no!

160 The fact is I am getting a little afraid of John.

He seems very queer sometimes, and even Jennie has an inexplicable look.

It strikes me occasionally, just as a scientific hypothesis,—that perhaps it is the paper!

I have watched John when he did not know I was looking, and come into the room suddenly on the most innocent excuses, and I've caught him several times *looking at the paper*! And Jennie too. I caught Jennie with her hand on it once.

She didn't know I was in the room, and when I asked her in a quiet, a very quiet voice, with the most restrained manner possible, what she was doing with the paper—she turned around as if she had been caught stealing, and looked quite angry—asked me why I should frighten her so!

165 Then she said that the paper stained everything it touched, that she had found yellow smooches on all my clothes and John's, and she wished we would be more careful!

Did not that sound innocent? But I know she was studying that pattern, and I am determined that nobody shall find it out but myself!

Life is very much more exciting now than it used to be. You see I have something more to expect, to look forward to, to watch. I really do eat better, and am more quiet than I was.

John is so pleased to see me improve! He laughed a little the other day, and said I seemed to be flourishing in spite of my wallpaper.

I turned it off with a laugh. I had no intention of telling him it was *because* of the wallpaper—he would make fun of me. He might even want to take me away.

I don't want to leave now until I have found it out. There is a week more, and I think that will be enough.

I'm feeling ever so much better! I don't sleep much at night, for it is so interesting to watch developments; but I sleep a good deal in the daytime.

In the daytime it is tiresome and perplexing.

There are always new shoots on the fungus, and new shades of yellow all over it. I cannot keep count of them, though I have tried conscientiously.

It is the strangest yellow, that wallpaper! It makes me think of all the yellow things I ever saw—not beautiful ones like buttercups, but old foul, bad yellow things.

But there is something else about that paper—the smell! I noticed it the moment we came into the room, but with so much air and sun it was not bad. Now we have had a week of fog and rain, and whether the windows are open or not, the smell is here.

It creeps all over the house.

I find it hovering in the dining-room, skulking in the parlor, hiding in the hall, lying in wait for me on the stairs.

It gets into my hair.

Even when I go to ride, if I turn my head suddenly and surprise it—there is that smell!

Such a peculiar odor, too! I have spent hours in trying to analyze it, to find what it smelled like.

It is not bad—at first, and very gentle, but quite the subtlest, most enduring odor I ever met.

In this damp weather it is awful, I wake up in the night and find it hanging over me.

It used to disturb me at first. I thought seriously of burning the house—to reach the smell.

But now I am used to it. The only thing I can think of that it is like is the *color* of the paper! A yellow smell.

There is a very funny mark on this wall, low down, near the mopboard. A streak that runs round the room. It goes behind every piece of furniture, except the bed, a long, straight, even *smooch,* as if it had been rubbed over and over.

I wonder how it was done and who did it, and what they did it for. Round and round and round—round and round and round—it makes me dizzy!

I really have discovered something at last.

Through watching so much at night, when it changes so, I have finally found out.

The front pattern *does* move—and no wonder! The woman behind shakes it!

Sometimes I think there are a great many women behind, and sometimes only one, and she crawls around fast, and her crawling shakes it all over.

Then in the very bright spots she keeps still, and in the very shady spots she just takes hold of the bars and shakes them hard.

And she is all the time trying to climb through. But nobody could climb through that pattern—it strangles so; I think that is why it has so many heads.

They get through, and then the pattern strangles them off and turns them upside down, and makes their eyes white!

If those heads were covered or taken off it would not be half so bad.

I think that woman gets out in the daytime!

And I'll tell you why—privately—I've seen her!

I can see her out of every one of my windows!

It is the same woman, I know, for she is always creeping, and most women do not creep by daylight.

I see her in that long shaded lane, creeping up and down. I see her in those dark grape arbors, creeping all around the garden.

I see her on that long road under the trees, creeping along, and when a carriage comes she hides under the blackberry vines.

I don't blame her a bit. It must be very humiliating to be caught creeping by daylight!

I always lock the door when I creep by daylight. I can't do it at night, for I know John would suspect something at once.

And John is so queer now, that I don't want to irritate him. I wish he would take another room! Besides, I don't want anybody to get that woman out at night but myself.

I often wonder if I could see her out of all the windows at once.

But, turn as fast as I can, I can only see out of one at one time.

And though I always see her, she *may* be able to creep faster than I can turn!

I have watched her sometimes away off in the open country, creeping as fast as a cloud shadow in a high wind.

If only that top pattern could be gotten off from the under one! I mean to try it, little by little.

I have found out another funny thing, but I shan't tell it this time! It does not do to trust people too much.

There are only two more days to get this paper off, and I believe John is beginning to notice. I don't like the look in his eyes.

And I heard him ask Jennie a lot of professional questions about me. She had a very good report to give.

She said I slept a good deal in the daytime.

John knows I don't sleep very well at night, for all I'm so quiet!

He asked me all sorts of questions, too, and pretended to be very loving and kind.

As if I couldn't see through him!

Still, I don't wonder he acts so, sleeping under this paper for three months.

It only interests me, but I feel sure John and Jennie are secretly affected by it.

Hurrah! This is the last day, but it is enough. John is to stay in town over night, and won't be out until this evening.

Jennie wanted to sleep with me—the sly thing! but I told her I should undoubtedly rest better for a night all alone.

That was clever, for really I wasn't alone a bit! As soon as it was moonlight and that poor thing began to crawl and shake the pattern, I got up and ran to help her.

I pulled and she shook, I shook and she pulled, and before morning we had peeled off yards of that paper.

A strip about as high as my head and half around the room.

And then when the sun came and that awful pattern began to laugh at me, I declared I would finish it to-day!

We go away to-morrow, and they are moving all my furniture down again to leave things as they were before.

Jennie looked at the wall in amazement, but I told her merrily that I did it out of pure spite at the vicious thing.

She laughed and said she wouldn't mind doing it herself, but I must not get tired.

How she betrayed herself that time!

But I am here, and no person touches this paper but me,—not *alive!*

She tried to get me out of the room—it was too patent! But I said it was so quiet and empty and clean now that I believed I would lie down again and sleep all I could; and not to wake me even for dinner—I would call when I woke.

So now she is gone, and the servants are gone, and the things are gone, and there is nothing left but that great bedstead nailed down, with the canvas mattress we found on it.

We shall sleep downstairs to-night, and take the boat home to-morrow.

I quite enjoy the room, now it is bare again.

How those children did tear about here!

This bedstead is fairly gnawed!

But I must get to work.

I have locked the door and thrown the key down into the front path.

I don't want to go out, and I don't want to have anybody come in, till John comes.

I want to astonish him.

I've got a rope up here that even Jennie did not find. If that woman does get out, and tries to get away, I can tie her!

But I forgot I could not reach far without anything to stand on!

This bed will *not* move!

I tried to lift and push it until I was lame, and then I got so angry I bit off a little piece at one corner—but it hurt my teeth.

Then I peeled off all the paper I could reach standing on the floor. It sticks horribly and the pattern just enjoys it! All those strangled heads and bulbous eyes and waddling fungus growths just shriek with derision!

I am getting angry enough to do something desperate. To jump out of the window would be admirable exercise, but the bars are too strong even to try.

Besides I wouldn't do it. Of course not. I know well enough that a step like that is improper and might be misconstrued.

I don't like to *look* out of the windows even—there are so many of those creeping women, and they creep so fast.

I wonder if they all come out of that wallpaper as I did?

But I am securely fastened now by my well-hidden rope—you don't get *me* out in the road there!

I suppose I shall have to get back behind the pattern when it comes night, and that is hard!

It is so pleasant to be out in this great room and creep around as I please!

I don't want to go outside. I won't, even if Jennie asks me to.

For outside you have to creep on the ground, and everything is green instead of yellow.

But here I can creep smoothly on the floor, and my shoulder just fits in that long smooch around the wall, so I cannot lose my way.

Why there's John at the door!

It is no use, young man, you can't open it!

How he does call and pound!

Now he's crying for an axe.

It would be a shame to break down that beautiful door!

"John dear!" said I in the gentlest voice, "the key is down by the front steps, under a plantain leaf!"

That silenced him for a few moments.

Then he said—very quietly indeed, "Open the door, my darling!"

"I can't," said I. "The key is down by the front door under a plantain leaf!"

And then I said it again, several times, very gently and slowly, and said it so often that he had to go and see, and he got it of course, and came in. He stopped short by the door.

"What is the matter?" he cried. "For God's sake, what are you doing!"

I kept on creeping just the same, but I looked at him over my shoulder.

"I've got out at last," said I, "in spite of you and Jane. And I've pulled off most of the paper, so you can't put me back!"

Now why should that man have fainted? But he did, and right across my path by the wall, so that I had to creep over him every time!

1892

SUSAN GLASPELL (1876–1948)

A Jury of Her Peers

Though today remembered almost exclusively for her masterful one-act play *Trifles* (1916), Susan Glaspell wrote over a dozen plays, fifty short stories, nine novels, and a memoir, in addition to playing a key role in the development of twentieth-century American theater. Born in Davenport, Iowa, she graduated from Drake University in 1899 and spent two years at the *Des Moines Daily News*, where she covered the trial of a fifty-seven-year-old woman accused of murdering her sleeping husband with an axe. When Glaspell's short stories began appearing in magazines, she returned to Davenport. There, she became involved with George Cram Cook, a former English professor, socialist, and married father of two. The two wed in 1913 and moved east, eventually settling in New York's Greenwich Village and in Cape Cod, where they founded the Provincetown Playhouse (later the Playwright's Theater), an extraordinary gathering of freethinking, Left-leaning actors, directors, and playwrights that included Edna St. Vincent Millay and a then-unknown Eugene O'Neill. Between 1916 and 1922, this pioneering group reportedly staged more plays by women than any other contemporary theater; among them were eleven by Glaspell, ranging from realistic dramas such as *Trifles* and satirical comedies like *Woman's Honor* (1918) to her expressionistic *The Verge* (1921). Widowed in 1924, Glaspell ended a brief second marriage in 1931, the same year that her last play, *Alison's House*, won the Pulitzer Prize. Having published her first novel in 1909 and multiple best sellers in the 1920s and 30s, Glaspell spent the last years of her life writing fiction in Provincetown.

When Martha Hale opened the storm door and got a cut of the north wind, she ran back for her big woolen scarf. As she hurriedly wound that round her head her eye made a scandalized sweep of her kitchen. It was no ordinary thing that called her away—it was probably farther from ordinary than anything that had ever happened in Dickson County. But what her eye took in was that her kitchen was in no shape for leaving: her bread all ready for mixing, half the flour sifted and half unsifted.

She hated to see things half done; but she had been at that when the team from town stopped to get Mr. Hale, and then the sheriff came running in to say his wife wished Mrs. Hale would come too—adding, with a grin, that he guessed she was getting scary and wanted another woman along. So she had dropped everything right where it was.

"Martha!" now came her husband's impatient voice. "Don't keep folks waiting out here in the cold."

She again opened the storm door, and this time joined the three men and the one woman waiting for her in the big two-seated buggy.

5 After she had the robes tucked around her she took another look at the woman who sat beside her on the back seat. She had met Mrs. Peters the year before at the county fair, and the thing she remembered about her was that she didn't seem like a sheriff's wife. She was small and thin and didn't have a strong voice. Mrs. Gorman, sheriff's wife before Gorman went out and Peters came in, had a voice that somehow seemed to be backing up the law with every word. But if Mrs. Peters didn't look like a sheriff's wife, Peters made it up in looking like a sheriff. He was to a dot the kind of man who could get himself elected sheriff—a heavy man with a big voice, who was particularly genial with the law-abiding, as if to make it plain that he knew the difference between criminals and non-criminals. And right there it came into Mrs. Hale's mind, with a stab, that this man who was so pleasant and lively with all of them was going to the Wrights' now as a sheriff.

"The country's not very pleasant this time of year," Mrs. Peters at last ventured, as if she felt they ought to be talking as well as the men.

Mrs. Hale scarcely finished her reply, for they had gone up a little hill and could see the Wright place now, and seeing it did not make her feel like talking. It looked very lonesome this cold March morning. It had always been a lonesome-looking place. It was down in a hollow, and the poplar trees around it were lonesome-looking trees. The men were looking at it and talking about what had happened. The county attorney was bending to one side of the buggy, and kept looking steadily at the place as they drew up to it.

"I'm glad you came with me," Mrs. Peters said nervously, as the two women were about to follow the men in through the kitchen door.

Even after she had her foot on the doorstep, her hand on the knob, Martha Hale had a moment of feeling she could not cross that threshold. And the reason it seemed she couldn't cross it now was simply because she hadn't crossed it before. Time and time again it had been in her mind. "I ought to go over and see Minnie Foster"—she still thought of her as Minnie Foster, though for twenty years she had been Mrs. Wright. And then there was always something to do and Minnie Foster would go from her mind. But *now* she could come.

The men went over to the stove. The women stood close together by the door. Young Henderson, the county attorney, turned around and said, "Come up to the fire, ladies."

Mrs. Peters took a step forward, then stopped. "I'm not—cold," she said.

And so the two women stood by the door, at first not even so much as looking around the kitchen.

The men talked for a minute about what a good thing it was the sheriff had sent his deputy out that morning to make a fire for them, and then Sheriff Peters stepped back from the stove, unbuttoned his outer coat, and leaned his hands on the kitchen table in a way that seemed to mark the beginning of official business. "Now, Mr. Hale," he said in a sort of semi-official voice, "before we move things about, you tell Mr. Henderson just what it was you saw when you came here yesterday morning."

The county attorney was looking around the kitchen.

"By the way," he said, "has anything been moved?" He turned to the sheriff. "Are things just as you left them yesterday?"

Peters looked from cupboard to sink; from that to a small worn rocker a little to one side of the kitchen table.

"It's just the same."

"Somebody should have been left here yesterday," said the county attorney.

"Oh—yesterday," returned the sheriff, with a little gesture as of yesterday having been more than he could bear to think of. "When I had to send Frank to Morris Center for that man who went crazy—let me tell you, I had my hands full *yesterday.* I knew you could get back from Omaha by today, George, and as long as I went over everything here myself—"

"Well, Mr. Hale," said the county attorney, in a way of letting what was past and gone go, "tell just what happened when you came here yesterday morning."

Mrs. Hale, still leaning against the door, had that sinking feeling of the mother whose child is about to speak a piece. Lewis often wandered along and got things mixed up in a story. She hoped he would tell this straight and plain, and not say unnecessary things that would just make things harder for Minnie Foster. He didn't begin at once, and she noticed that he looked queer—as if standing in that kitchen and having to tell what he had seen there yesterday morning made him almost sick.

"Yes, Mr. Hale?" the county attorney reminded.

"Harry and I had started to town with a load of potatoes," Mrs. Hale's husband began.

Harry was Mrs. Hale's oldest boy. He wasn't with them now, for the very good reason that those potatoes never got to town yesterday and he was taking them this morning, so he hadn't been home when the sheriff stopped to say he wanted Mr. Hale to come over to the Wright place and tell the county attorney his story there, where he could point it all out. With all Mrs. Hale's other emotions came the fear that maybe Harry wasn't dressed warm enough—they hadn't any of them realized how that north wind did bite.

"We come along this road," Hale was going on, with a motion of his hand to 25
the road over which they had just come, "and as we got in sight of the house I says to Harry, 'I'm goin' to see if I can't get John Wright to take a telephone.' You see," he explained to Henderson, "unless I can get somebody to go in with me they won't come out this branch road except for a price *I* can't pay. I'd spoke to Wright about it once before; but he put me off, saying folks talked too much anyway, and all he asked was peace and quiet—guess you know about how much he talked himself. But I thought maybe if I went to the house and talked about it before his wife, and said all the womenfolks liked the telephones, and that in this lonesome stretch of road it would be a good thing—well, I said to Harry that that was what I was going to say—though I said at the same time that I didn't know as what his wife wanted made much difference to John—"

Now, there he was!—saying things he didn't need to say. Mrs. Hale tried to catch her husband's eye, but fortunately the county attorney interrupted with:

"Let's talk about that a little later, Mr. Hale. I do want to talk about that, but I'm anxious now to get along to just what happened when you got here."

When he began this time, it was very deliberately and carefully:

"I didn't see or hear anything. I knocked at the door. And still it was all quiet inside. I knew they must be up—it was past eight o'clock. So I knocked again, louder, and I thought I heard somebody say 'Come in.' I wasn't sure—I'm not sure yet. But I opened the door—this door," jerking a hand toward the door by which the two women stood, "and there, in that rocker"—pointing to it—"sat Mrs. Wright."

Everyone in the kitchen looked at the rocker. It came into Mrs. Hale's mind 30
that the rocker didn't look in the least like Minnie Foster—the Minnie Foster of twenty years before. It was a dingy red, with wooden rungs up the back, and the middle rung was gone, and the chair sagged to one side.

"How did she—look?" the county attorney was inquiring.

"Well," said Hale, "she looked—queer."

"How do you mean—queer?"

As he asked it he took out a notebook and pencil. Mrs. Hale did not like the sight of that pencil. She kept her eye fixed on her husband, as if to keep him from saying unnecessary things that would go into that notebook and make trouble.

Hale did speak guardedly, as if the pencil had affected him too. 35

"Well, as if she didn't know what she was going to do next. And kind of—done up."

"How did she seem to feel about your coming?"

"Why, I don't think she minded—one way or other. She didn't pay much attention. I said, 'Ho' do, Mrs. Wright? It's cold, ain't it!' And she said, 'Is it?'—and went on pleatin' at her apron.

"Well, I was surprised. She didn't ask me to come up to the stove, or to sit down, but just set there, not even lookin' at me. And so I said: 'I want to see John.'

"And then she—laughed. I guess you would call it a laugh.

"I thought of Harry and the team outside, so I said, a little sharp, 'Can I see John?' 'No,' says she—kind of dull like. 'Ain't he home?' says I. Then she looked at me. 'Yes,' says she, 'he's home.' 'Then why can't I see him?' I asked her, out of patience with her now. 'Cause he's dead,' says she, just as quiet and dull—and fell to pleatin' her apron. 'Dead?' says I, like you do when you can't take in what you've heard.

"She just nodded her head, not getting a bit excited, but rockin' back and forth.

"'Why—where is he?' says I, not knowing *what* to say.

"She just pointed upstairs—like this"—pointing to the room above.

"I got up, with the idea of going up there myself. By this time I—didn't know what to do. I walked from there to here; then I says: 'Why, what did he die of?'

"'He died of a rope around his neck,' says she; and just went on pleatin' at her apron."

Hale stopped speaking, and stood staring at the rocker, as if he were still seeing the woman who had sat there the morning before. Nobody spoke; it was as if everyone were seeing the woman who had sat there the morning before.

"And what did you do then?" the county attorney at last broke the silence.

"I went out and called Harry. I thought I might—need help. I got Harry in, and we went upstairs." His voice fell almost to a whisper. "There he was—lying over the—"

"I think I'd rather have you go into that upstairs," the county attorney interrupted, "where you can point it all out. Just go on now with the rest of the story."

"Well, my first thought was to get that rope off. It looked—"

He stopped, his face twitching.

"But Harry, he went up to him, and he said, 'No, he's dead all right, and we'd better not touch anything.' So we went downstairs.

"She was still sitting the same way. 'Has anybody been notified?' I asked. 'No,' says she, unconcerned.

"'Who did this, Mrs. Wright?' said Harry. He said it business-like, and she stopped pleatin' at her apron. 'I don't know,' she says. 'You don't *know*?' says Harry. 'Weren't you sleepin' in the bed with him?' 'Yes,' says she, 'but I was on the inside.' 'Somebody slipped a rope round his neck and strangled him, and you didn't wake up?' says Harry. 'I didn't wake up,' she said after him.

"We may have looked as if we didn't see how that could be, for after a minute she said, 'I sleep sound.'

"Harry was going to ask her more questions, but I said maybe that weren't our business; maybe we ought to let her tell her story first to the coroner or the sheriff. So Harry went fast as he could over to High Road—the Rivers' place, where there's a telephone."

"And what did she do when she knew you had gone for the coroner?" The attorney got his pencil in his hand all ready for writing.

"She moved from that chair to this one over here"—Hale pointed to a small chair in the corner—"and just sat there with her hands held together and looking down. I got a feeling that I ought to make some conversation, so I said I had come in to see if John wanted to put in a telephone; and at that she started to laugh, and then she stopped and looked at me—scared."

At the sound of a moving pencil the man who was telling the story looked up. 60

"I dunno—maybe it wasn't scared," he hastened; "I wouldn't like to say it was. Soon Harry got back, and then Dr. Lloyd came, and you, Mr. Peters, and so I guess that's all I know that you don't."

He said that last with relief, and moved a little, as if relaxing. Everyone moved a little. The county attorney walked toward the stair door.

"I guess we'll go upstairs first—then out to the barn and around there."

He paused and looked around the kitchen.

"You're convinced there was nothing important here?" he asked the sheriff. 65
"Nothing that would—point to any motive?"

The sheriff too looked all around, as if to reconvince himself.

"Nothing here but kitchen things," he said, with a little laugh for the insignificance of kitchen things.

The county attorney was looking at the cupboard—a peculiar, ungainly structure, half closet and half cupboard, the upper part of it being built in the wall, and the lower part just the old-fashioned kitchen cupboard. As if its queerness attracted him, he got a chair and opened the upper part and looked in. After a moment he drew his hand away sticky.

"Here's a nice mess," he said resentfully.

The two women had drawn nearer, and now the sheriff's wife spoke. 70

"Oh—her fruit," she said, looking to Mrs. Hale for sympathetic understanding. She turned back to the county attorney and explained: "She worried about that when it turned so cold last night. She said the fire would go out and her jars might burst."

Mrs. Peters' husband broke into a laugh.

"Well, can you beat the women! Held for murder, and worrying about her preserves!"

The young attorney set his lips.

"I guess before we're through with her she may have something more serious 75
than preserves to worry about."

"Oh, well," said Mrs. Hale's husband, with good-natured superiority, "women are used to worrying over trifles."

The two women moved a little closer together. Neither of them spoke. The county attorney seemed suddenly to remember his manners—and think of his future.

"And yet," said he, with the gallantry of a young politician, "for all their worries, what would we do without the ladies?"

The women did not speak, did not unbend. He went to the sink and began washing his hands. He turned to wipe them on the roller towel—whirled it for a cleaner place.

"Dirty towels! Not much of a housekeeper, would you say, ladies?" 80

He kicked his foot against some dirty pans under the sink.

"There's a great deal of work to be done on a farm," said Mrs. Hale stiffly.

"To be sure. And yet"—with a little bow to her—"I know there are some Dickson County farmhouses that do not have such roller towels." He gave it a pull to expose its full length again.

"Those towels get dirty awful quick. Men's hands aren't always as clean as they might be."

"Ah, loyal to your sex, I see," he laughed. He stopped and gave her a keen look. "But you and Mrs. Wright were neighbors. I suppose you were friends, too."

Martha Hale shook her head.

"I've seen little enough of her of late years. I've not been in this house—it's more than a year."

"And why was that? You didn't like her?"

"I liked her well enough," she replied with spirit. "Farmers' wives have their hands full, Mr. Henderson. And then"—She looked around the kitchen.

"Yes?" he encouraged.

"It never seemed a very cheerful place," said she, more to herself than to him.

"No," he agreed; "I don't think anyone would call it cheerful. I shouldn't say she had the homemaking instinct."

"Well, I don't know as Wright had, either," she muttered.

"You mean they didn't get on very well?" he was quick to ask.

"No; I don't mean anything," she answered, with decision. As she turned a little away from him, she added: "But I don't think a place would be any the cheerfuler for John Wright's bein' in it."

"I'd like to talk to you about that a little later, Mrs. Hale," he said. "I'm anxious to get the lay of things upstairs now."

He moved toward the stair door, followed by the two men.

"I suppose anything Mrs. Peters does'll be all right?" the sheriff inquired. "She was to take in some clothes for her, you know—and a few little things. We left in such a hurry yesterday."

The county attorney looked at the two women whom they were leaving alone there among the kitchen things.

"Yes—Mrs. Peters," he said, his glance resting on the woman who was not Mrs. Peters, the big farmer woman who stood behind the sheriff's wife. "Of course Mrs. Peters is one of us," he said, in a manner of entrusting responsibility. "And keep your eye out, Mrs. Peters, for anything that might be of use. No telling; you women might come upon a clue to the motive—and that's the thing we need."

Mr. Hale rubbed his face after the fashion of a showman getting ready for a pleasantry.

"But would the women know a clue if they did come upon it?" he said; and, having delivered himself of this, he followed the others through the stair door.

The women stood motionless and silent, listening to the footsteps, first upon the stairs, then in the room above them.

Then, as if releasing herself from something strange, Mrs. Hale began to arrange the dirty pans under the sink, which the county attorney's disdainful push of the foot had deranged.

"I'd hate to have men comin' into my kitchen," she said testily—"snoopin' round and criticizin'."

"Of course it's no more than their duty," said the sheriff's wife, in her manner of timid acquiescence.

"Duty's all right," replied Mrs. Hale bluffly; "but I guess that deputy sheriff that come out to make the fire might have got a little of this on." She gave the roller towel a pull. "Wish I'd thought of that sooner! Seems mean to talk about her for not having things slicked up, when she had to come away in such a hurry."

She looked around the kitchen. Certainly it was not "slicked up." Her eye was held by a bucket of sugar on a low shelf. The cover was off the wooden bucket, and beside it was a paper bag—half full.

Mrs. Hale moved toward it.

"She was putting this in there," she said to herself—slowly. 110

She thought of the flour in her kitchen at home—half sifted, half not sifted. She had been interrupted and had left things half done. What had interrupted Minnie Foster? Why had that work been left half done? She made a move as if to finish it,—unfinished things always bothered her,—and then she glanced around and saw that Mrs. Peters was watching her—and she didn't want Mrs. Peters to get that feeling she had got of work begun and then—for some reason—not finished.

"It's a shame about her fruit," she said, and walked toward the cupboard that the county attorney had opened, and got on the chair, murmuring: "I wonder if it's all gone."

It was a sorry enough looking sight, but "Here's one that's all right," she said at last. She held it toward the light. "This is cherries, too." She looked again. "I declare I believe that's the only one."

With a sigh, she got down from the chair, went to the sink, and wiped off the bottle.

"She'll feel awful bad, after all her hard work in the hot weather. I remember 115
the afternoon I put up my cherries last summer."

She set the bottle on the table, and, with another sigh, started to sit down in the rocker. But she did not sit down. Something kept her from sitting down in that chair. She straightened—stepped back, and, half turned away, stood looking at it, seeing the woman who sat there "pleatin' at her apron."

The thin voice of the sheriff's wife broke in upon her: "I must be getting those things from the front room closet." She opened the door into the other room, started in, stepped back. "You coming with me, Mrs. Hale?" she asked nervously. "You—you could help me get them."

They were soon back—the stark coldness of that shut-up room was not a thing to linger in.

"My!" said Mrs. Peters, dropping the things on the table and hurrying to the stove.

Mrs. Hale stood examining the clothes the woman who was being detained 120
in town had said she wanted.

"Wright was close!" she exclaimed, holding up a shabby black skirt that bore the marks of much making over. "I think maybe that's why she kept so much to herself. I s'pose she felt she couldn't do her part; and then, you don't enjoy things when you feel shabby. She used to wear pretty clothes and be lively—when she was Minnie Foster, one of the town girls, singing in the choir. But that—oh, that was twenty years ago."

With a carefulness in which there was something tender, she folded the shabby clothes and piled them at one corner of the table. She looked at Mrs. Peters, and there was something in the other woman's look that irritated her.

"She don't care," she said to herself. "Much difference it makes to her whether Minnie Foster had pretty clothes when she was a girl."

Then she looked again, and she wasn't so sure; in fact, she hadn't at any time been perfectly sure about Mrs. Peters. She had that shrinking manner, and yet her eyes looked as if they could see a long way into things.

"This all you was to take in?" asked Mrs. Hale.

"No," said the sheriff's wife; "she said she wanted an apron. Funny thing to want," she ventured in her nervous little way, "for there's not much to get you dirty in jail, goodness knows. But I suppose just to make her feel more natural. If you're used to wearing an apron—. She said they were in the bottom drawer of this cupboard. Yes—here they are. And then her little shawl that always hung on the stair door."

She took the small gray shawl from behind the door leading upstairs, and stood a minute looking at it.

Suddenly Mrs. Hale took a quick step toward the other woman.

"Mrs. Peters!"

"Yes, Mrs. Hale?"

"Do you think she—did it?"

A frightened look blurred the other things in Mrs. Peters' eyes.

"Oh, I don't know," she said, in a voice that seemed to shrink away from the subject.

"Well, I don't think she did," affirmed Mrs. Hale stoutly. "Asking for an apron, and her little shawl. Worryin' about her fruit."

"Mr. Peters says—" Footsteps were heard in the room above; she stopped, looked up, then went on in a lowered voice: "Mr. Peters says—it looks bad for her. Mr. Henderson is awful sarcastic in a speech, and he's going to make fun of her saying she didn't—wake up."

For a moment Mrs. Hale had no answer. Then, "Well, I guess John Wright didn't wake up—when they was slippin' that rope under his neck," she muttered.

"No, it's *strange*," breathed Mrs. Peters. "They think it was such a—funny way to kill a man."

She began to laugh; at sound of the laugh, abruptly stopped.

"That's just what Mr. Hale said," said Mrs. Hale, in a resolutely natural voice. "There was a gun in the house. He says that's what he can't understand."

"Mr. Henderson said, coming out, that what was needed for the case was a motive. Something to show anger—or sudden feeling."

"Well, I don't see any signs of anger around here," said Mrs. Hale. "I don't—"

She stopped. It was as if her mind tripped on something. Her eye was caught by a dish towel in the middle of the kitchen table. Slowly she moved toward the table. One half of it was wiped clean, the other half messy. Her eyes made a slow, almost unwilling turn to the bucket of sugar and the half empty bag beside it. Things begun—and not finished.

After a moment she stepped back, and said, in that manner of releasing herself:

"Wonder how they're finding things upstairs? I hope she had it a little more red-up up there. You know,"—she paused, and feeling gathered,—"it seems kind of *sneaking*; locking her up in town and coming out here to get her own house to turn against her!"

"But, Mrs. Hale," said the sheriff's wife, "the law is the law." 145

"I s'pose 'tis," answered Mrs. Hale shortly.

She turned to the stove, saying something about that fire not being much to brag of. She worked with it a minute, and when she straightened up she said aggressively:

"The law is the law—and a bad stove is a bad stove. How'd you like to cook on this?"—pointing with the poker to the broken lining. She opened the oven door and started to express her opinion of the oven; but she was swept into her own thoughts, thinking of what it would mean, year after year, to have that stove to wrestle with. The thought of Minnie Foster trying to bake in that oven—and the thought of her never going over to see Minnie Foster—.

She was startled by hearing Mrs. Peters say: "A person gets discouraged—and loses heart."

The sheriff's wife had looked from the stove to the sink—to the pail of water 150
which had been carried in from outside. The two women stood there silent, above them the footsteps of the men who were looking for evidence against the woman who had worked in that kitchen. That look of seeing into things, of seeing through a thing to something else, was in the eyes of the sheriff's wife now. When Mrs. Hale next spoke to her, it was gently:

"Better loosen up your things, Mrs. Peters. We'll not feel them when we go out."

Mrs. Peters went to the back of the room to hang up the fur tippet she was wearing. A moment later she exclaimed, "Why, she was piecing a quilt," and held up a large sewing basket piled high with quilt pieces.

Mrs. Hale spread some of the blocks on the table.

"It's log-cabin pattern," she said, putting several of them together. "Pretty, isn't it?"

They were so engaged with the quilt that they did not hear the footsteps on 155
the stairs. Just as the stair door opened Mrs. Hale was saying:

"Do you suppose she was going to quilt it or just knot it?"

The sheriff threw up his hands.

"They wonder whether she was going to quilt it or just knot it!"

There was a laugh for the ways of women, a warming of hands over the stove, and then the county attorney said briskly:

"Well, let's go right out to the barn and get that cleared up." 160

"I don't see as there's anything so strange," Mrs. Hale said resentfully, after the outside door had closed on the three men—"our taking up our time with little things while we're waiting for them to get the evidence. I don't see as it's anything to laugh about."

"Of course they've got awful important things on their minds," said the sheriff's wife apologetically.

They returned to an inspection of the blocks for the quilt. Mrs. Hale was looking at the fine, even sewing, and preoccupied with thoughts of the woman who had done that sewing, when she heard the sheriff's wife say, in a queer tone:

"Why, look at this one."

165 She turned to take the block held out to her.

"The sewing," said Mrs. Peters, in a troubled way. "All the rest of them have been so nice and even—but—this one. Why, it looks as if she didn't know what she was about!"

Their eyes met—something flashed to life, passed between them; then, as if with an effort, they seemed to pull away from each other. A moment Mrs. Hale sat there, her hands folded over that sewing which was so unlike all the rest of the sewing. Then she had pulled a knot and drawn the threads.

"Oh, what are you doing, Mrs. Hale?" asked the sheriff's wife, startled.

"Just pulling out a stitch or two that's not sewed very good," said Mrs. Hale mildly.

170 "I don't think we ought to touch things," Mrs. Peters said, a little helplessly.

"I'd just finish up this end," answered Mrs. Hale, still in that mild, matter-of-fact fashion.

She threaded a needle and started to replace bad sewing with good. For a little while she sewed in silence. Then, in that thin, timid voice, she heard:

"Mrs. Hale!"

"Yes, Mrs. Peters?"

175 "What do you suppose she was so—nervous about?"

"Oh, *I* don't know," said Mrs. Hale, as if dismissing a thing not important enough to spend much time on. "I don't know as she was—nervous. I sew awful queer sometimes when I'm just tired."

She cut a thread, and out of the corner of her eye looked up at Mrs. Peters. The small, lean face of the sheriff's wife seemed to have tightened up. Her eyes had that look of peering into something. But the next moment she moved, and said in her thin, indecisive way:

"Well, I must get those clothes wrapped. They may be through sooner than we think. I wonder where I could find a piece of paper—and string."

"In that cupboard, maybe," suggested Mrs. Hale, after a glance around.

180 One piece of the crazy sewing remained unripped. Mrs. Peters' back turned, Martha Hale now scrutinized that piece, compared it with the dainty, accurate sewing of the other blocks. The difference was startling. Holding this block made her feel queer, as if the distracted thoughts of the woman who had perhaps turned to it to try and quiet herself were communicating themselves to her.

Mrs. Peters' voice roused her.

"Here's a birdcage," she said. "Did she have a bird, Mrs. Hale?"

"Why, I don't know whether she did or not." She turned to look at the cage Mrs. Peters was holding up. "I've not been here in so long." She sighed. "There was a man round last year selling canaries cheap—but I don't know as she took one. Maybe she did. She used to sing real pretty herself."

Mrs. Peters looked around the kitchen.

185 "Seems kind of funny to think of a bird here." She half laughed—an attempt to put up a barrier. "But she must have had one—or why would she have a cage? I wonder what happened to it."

"I suppose maybe the cat got it," suggested Mrs. Hale, resuming her sewing.

"No; she didn't have a cat. She's got that feeling some people have about cats—being afraid of them. When they brought her to our house yesterday, my cat got in the room, and she was real upset and asked me to take it out."

"My sister Bessie was like that," laughed Mrs. Hale.

The sheriff's wife did not reply. The silence made Mrs. Hale turn round. Mrs. Peters was examining the birdcage.

"Look at this door," she said slowly. "It's broke. One hinge has been pulled 190
apart."

Mrs. Hale came nearer.

"Looks as if someone must have been—rough with it."

Again their eyes met—startled, questioning, apprehensive. For a moment neither spoke nor stirred. Then Mrs. Hale, turning away, said brusquely:

"If they're going to find any evidence, I wish they'd be about it. I don't like this place."

"But I'm awful glad you came with me, Mrs. Hale." Mrs. Peters put the birdcage 195
on the table and sat down. "It would be lonesome for me—sitting here alone."

"Yes, it would, wouldn't it?" agreed Mrs. Hale, a certain determined naturalness in her voice. She picked up the sewing, but now it dropped in her lap, and she murmured in a different voice: "But I tell you what I *do* wish, Mrs. Peters. I wish I had come over sometimes when she was here. I wish—I had."

"But of course you were awful busy, Mrs. Hale. Your house—and your children."

"I could've come," retorted Mrs. Hale shortly. "I stayed away because it weren't cheerful—and that's why I ought to have come. I"—she looked around—"I've never liked this place. Maybe because it's down in a hollow and you don't see the road. I don't know what it is, but it's a lonesome place, and always was. I wish I had come over to see Minnie Foster sometimes. I can see now—" She did not put it into words.

"Well, you mustn't reproach yourself," counseled Mrs. Peters. "Somehow, we just don't see how it is with other folks till—something comes up."

"Not having children makes less work," mused Mrs. Hale, after a silence, 200
"but it makes a quiet house—and Wright out to work all day—and no company when he did come in. Did you know John Wright, Mrs. Peters?"

"Not to know him. I've seen him in town. They say he was a good man."

"Yes—good," conceded John Wright's neighbor grimly. "He didn't drink, and kept his word as well as most, I guess, and paid his debts. But he was a hard man, Mrs. Peters. Just to pass the time of day with him—." She stopped, shivered a little. "Like a raw wind that gets to the bone." Her eye fell upon the cage on the table before her, and she added, almost bitterly: "I should think she would've wanted a bird!"

Suddenly she leaned forward, looking intently at the cage. "But what do you s'pose went wrong with it?"

"I don't know," returned Mrs. Peters; "unless it got sick and died."

But after she said it she reached over and swung the broken door. Both 205
women watched it as if somehow held by it.

"You didn't know—her?" Mrs. Hale asked, a gentler note in her voice.

"Not till they brought her yesterday," said the sheriff's wife.

"She—come to think of it, she was kind of like a bird herself. Real sweet and pretty, but kind of timid and—fluttery. How—she—did—change."

That held her for a long time. Finally, as if struck with a happy thought and relieved to get back to everyday things, she exclaimed:

"Tell you what, Mrs. Peters, why don't you take the quilt in with you? It might take up her mind."

"Why, I think that's a real nice idea, Mrs. Hale," agreed the sheriff's wife, as if she too were glad to come into the atmosphere of a simple kindness. "There couldn't possibly be any objection to that, could there? Now, just what will I take? I wonder if her patches are in here—and her things."

They turned to the sewing basket.

"Here's some red," said Mrs. Hale, bringing out a roll of cloth. Underneath that was a box. "Here, maybe her scissors are in here—and her things." She held it up. "What a pretty box! I'll warrant that was something she had a long time ago—when she was a girl."

She held it in her hand a moment; then, with a little sigh, opened it.

Instantly her hand went to her nose.

"Why—!"

Mrs. Peters drew nearer—then turned away.

"There's something wrapped up in this piece of silk," faltered Mrs. Hale.

"This isn't her scissors," said Mrs. Peters in a shrinking voice.

Her hand not steady, Mrs. Hale raised the piece of silk. "Oh, Mrs. Peters!" she cried. "It's—"

Mrs. Peters bent closer.

"It's the bird," she whispered.

"But, Mrs. Peters!" cried Mrs. Hale. "*Look* at it! Its neck—look at its neck! It's all—other side *to.*"

She held the box away from her.

The sheriff's wife again bent closer.

"Somebody wrung its neck," said she, in a voice that was slow and deep.

And then again the eyes of the two women met—this time clung together in a look of dawning comprehension, of growing horror. Mrs. Peters looked from the dead bird to the broken door of the cage. Again their eyes met. And just then there was a sound at the outside door.

Mrs. Hale slipped the box under the quilt pieces in the basket, and sank into the chair before it. Mrs. Peters stood holding to the table. The county attorney and the sheriff came in from outside.

"Well, ladies," said the county attorney, as one turning from serious things to little pleasantries, "have you decided whether she was going to quilt it or knot it?"

"We think," began the sheriff's wife in a flurried voice, "that she was going to—knot it."

He was too preoccupied to notice the change that came in her voice on that last.

"Well, that's very interesting, I'm sure," he said tolerantly. He caught sight of the birdcage. "Has the bird flown?"

"We think the cat got it," said Mrs. Hale in a voice curiously even.

He was walking up and down, as if thinking something out.

"Is there a cat?" he asked absently.

Mrs. Hale shot a look up at the sheriff's wife.

"Well, not *now*," said Mrs. Peters. "They're superstitious, you know; they leave." She sank into her chair.

The county attorney did not heed her. "No sign at all of anyone having come in from the outside," he said to Peters, in the manner of continuing an interrupted conversation. "Their own rope. Now let's go upstairs again and go over it, piece by piece. It would have to have been someone who knew just the—"

The stair door closed behind them and their voices were lost.

The two women sat motionless, not looking at each other, but as if peering into something and at the same time holding back. When they spoke now it was as if they were afraid of what they were saying, but as if they could not help saying it.

"She liked the bird," said Martha Hale, low and slowly. "She was going to bury it in that pretty box."

"When I was a girl," said Mrs. Peters, under her breath, "my kitten—there was a boy took a hatchet, and before my eyes—before I could get there—" She covered her face an instant. "If they hadn't held me back I would have"—she caught herself, looked upstairs where footsteps were heard, and finished weakly—"hurt him."

Then they sat without speaking or moving.

"I wonder how it would seem," Mrs. Hale at last began, as if feeling her way over strange ground—"never to have had any children around?" Her eyes made a slow sweep of the kitchen, as if seeing what that kitchen had meant through all the years. "No, Wright wouldn't like the bird," she said after that—"a thing that sang. She used to sing. He killed that too." Her voice tightened.

Mrs. Peters moved uneasily.

"Of course we don't know who killed the bird."

"I knew John Wright," was Mrs. Hale's answer.

"It was an awful thing was done in this house that night, Mrs. Hale," said the sheriff's wife. "Killing a man while he slept—slipping a thing round his neck that choked the life out of him."

Mrs. Hale's hand went out to the birdcage.

"His neck. Choked the life out of him."

"We don't *know* who killed him," whispered Mrs. Peters wildly. "We don't *know*."

Mrs. Hale had not moved. "If there had been years and years of—nothing, then a bird to sing to you, it would be awful—still—after the bird was still."

It was as if something within her not herself had spoken, and it found in Mrs. Peters something she did not know as herself.

"I know what stillness is," she said, in a queer, monotonous voice. "When we homesteaded in Dakota, and my first baby died—after he was two years old—and me with no other then—"

Mrs. Hale stirred.

"How soon do you suppose they'll be through looking for evidence?"

"I know what stillness is," repeated Mrs. Peters, in just that same way. Then she too pulled back. "The law has got to punish crime, Mrs. Hale," she said in her tight little way.

"I wish you'd seen Minnie Foster," was the answer, "when she wore a white dress with blue ribbons, and stood up there in the choir and sang."

The picture of that girl, the fact that she had lived neighbor to that girl for twenty years, and had let her die for lack of life, was suddenly more than she could bear.

"Oh, I *wish* I'd come over here once in a while!" she cried. "That was a crime! That was a crime! Who's going to punish that?"

"We mustn't take on," said Mrs. Peters, with a frightened look toward the stairs.

"I might 'a' *known* she needed help! I tell you, it's *queer,* Mrs. Peters. We live close together, and we live far apart. We all go through the same things—it's all just a different kind of the same thing! If it weren't—why do you and I *understand*? Why do we *know*—what we know this minute?"

She dashed her hand across her eyes. Then, seeing the jar of fruit on the table, she reached for it and choked out:

"If I was you I wouldn't *tell* her her fruit was gone! Tell her it *ain't.* Tell her it's all right—all of it. Here—take this in to prove it to her! She—she may never know whether it was broke or not."

She turned away.

Mrs. Peters reached out for the bottle of fruit as if she were glad to take it—as if touching a familiar thing, having something to do, could keep her from something else. She got up, looked about for something to wrap the fruit in, took a petticoat from the pile of clothes she had brought from the front room, and nervously started winding that round the bottle.

"My!" she began, in a high, false voice, "it's a good thing the men couldn't hear us! Getting all stirred up over a little thing like a—dead canary." She hurried over that. "As if that could have anything to do with—with—My, wouldn't they *laugh*?"

Footsteps were heard on the stairs.

"Maybe they would," muttered Mrs. Hale—"maybe they wouldn't."

"No, Peters," said the county attorney incisively; "it's all perfectly clear, except the reason for doing it. But you know juries when it comes to women. If there was some definite thing—something to show. Something to make a story about. A thing that would connect up with this clumsy way of doing it."

In a covert way Mrs. Hale looked at Mrs. Peters. Mrs. Peters was looking at her. Quickly they looked away from each other. The outer door opened and Mr. Hale came in.

"I've got the team round now," he said. "Pretty cold out there."

"I'm going to stay here awhile by myself," the county attorney suddenly announced. "You can send Frank out for me, can't you?" he asked the sheriff. "I want to go over everything. I'm not satisfied we can't do better."

Again, for one brief moment, the two women's eyes found one another.

The sheriff came up to the table.

"Did you want to see what Mrs. Peters was going to take in?"

The county attorney picked up the apron. He laughed.

"Oh, I guess they're not very dangerous things the ladies have picked out."

Mrs. Hale's hand was on the sewing basket in which the box was concealed. She felt that she ought to take her hand off the basket. She did not seem able to. He picked up one of the quilt blocks which she had piled on to cover the box. Her eyes felt like fire. She had a feeling that if he took up the basket she would snatch it from him.

But he did not take it up. With another little laugh, he turned away, saying:

"No; Mrs. Peters doesn't need supervising. For that matter, a sheriff's wife is married to the law. Ever think of it that way, Mrs. Peters?"

Mrs. Peters was standing beside the table. Mrs. Hale shot a look up at her; but she could not see her face. Mrs. Peters had turned away. When she spoke, her voice was muffled.

"Not—just that way," she said.

"Married to the law!" chuckled Mrs. Peters' husband. He moved toward the door into the front room, and said to the county attorney:

"I just want you to come in here a minute, George. We ought to take a look at these windows."

"Oh—windows," said the county attorney scoffingly.

"We'll be right out, Mr. Hale," said the sheriff to the farmer, who was still waiting by the door.

Hale went to look after the horses. The sheriff followed the county attorney into the other room. Again—for one moment—the two women were alone in that kitchen.

Martha Hale sprang up, her hands tight together, looking at that other woman, with whom it rested. At first she could not see her eyes, for the sheriff's wife had not turned back, since she turned away at that suggestion of being married to the law. But now Mrs. Hale made her turn back. Her eyes made her turn back. Slowly, unwillingly, Mrs. Peters turned her head until her eyes met the eyes of the other woman. There was a moment when they held each other in a steady, burning look in which there was no evasion nor flinching. Then Martha Hale's eyes pointed the way to the basket in which was hidden the thing that would make certain the conviction of the other woman—that woman who was not there and yet who had been there with them all through the hour.

For a moment Mrs. Peters did not move. And then she did it. With a rush forward, she threw back the quilt pieces, got the box, tried to put it in her handbag. It was too big. Desperately she opened it, started to take the bird out. But there she broke—she could not touch the bird. She stood helpless, foolish.

There was the sound of a knob turning in the inner door. Martha Hale snatched the box from the sheriff's wife, and got it in the pocket of her big coat just as the sheriff and the county attorney came back into the kitchen.

"Well, Henry," said the county attorney facetiously, "at least we found out that she was not going to quilt it. She was going to—what is it you call it, ladies?"

Mrs. Hale's hand was against the pocket of her coat.

"We call it—knot it, Mr. Henderson."

1917

Chronology

1848 The First Women's Rights Convention held in Seneca Falls, New York.

1850 Katherine (Kate) O'Flaherty [later Chopin] born in St. Louis. Her father dies in 1855 in a railway accident.

1860 Charlotte Perkins [later Gilman] born in Hartford, Connecticut.

1861–65	American Civil War
1866	American Equal Rights Association founded.
1870	Kate O'Flaherty marries Oscar Chopin of Louisiana.
1874	Women's Christian Temperance Union founded.
1876	Susan Glaspell born in Davenport, Iowa.
1884	Widowed, Kate Chopin moves with her children to St. Louis; publishes first short story in 1889.
	Charlotte Perkins marries fellow artist Walter Stetson.
1888	Charlotte Perkins Stetson separates from her husband and moves with her daughter and mother to California.
1890	Wyoming becomes the first of several western states to grant women the vote; National American Woman Suffrage Association formed.
1892	Charlotte Perkins Stetson publishes "The Yellow Wallpaper" in *New England Magazine*.
1894	Kate Chopin publishes "The Story of an Hour" in *Vogue*.
1898	Charlotte Perkins publishes *Women and Economics*; divorces Stetson.
1899	Chopin publishes *The Awakening*.
1900	Charlotte Perkins marries Charles Houghton Gilman.
	Planned collection of Kate Chopin's stories, *A Vocation and a Voice*, to include "The Story of an Hour"; publisher may have backed off because of controversy over *The Awakening*.
	Susan Glaspell reports on the Hossack murder for the *Des Moines Daily News*: 26 stories by April 11, 1901.
	By now, every state has passed legislation granting married women some control over their property and earnings.
1903	Height of suffragette agitation in Britain (1903–14). Gilman addresses International Congress of Women in Berlin.
1904	Kate Chopin dies.
1909	Gilman begins producing her own magazine, *The Forerunner*.
1910	Glaspell co-founds Heterodoxy, a group of feminist socialists in New York, including Charlotte Perkins Gilman; it lasts through 1920.
1913	Susan Glaspell marries George Cram Cook.
1914–18	World War I
1915	Glaspell and Cook form the Provincetown Players in a theater in an abandoned wharf in Provincetown, Massachusetts.
1916	Glaspell's play *Trifles* first performed at Wharf Theatre.
1917	Russian Revolution. Glaspell's "A Jury of Her Peers" published in *Everyweek*.
1920	Nineteenth Amendment to Constitution grants women the vote.

1929	Stock market crash
1930	Glaspell's full-length play *Alison's House* wins the Pulitzer Prize.
1935	Charlotte Perkins Gilman, with incurable breast cancer, commits suicide.
1939–45	World War II
1948	Susan Glaspell dies in Provincetown, Massachusetts.

CONTEXTUAL EXCERPTS

Charlotte Perkins Gilman

From Similar Cases (1893)[1]

There was once a Neolithic Man,
An enterprising wight,
Who made his chopping implements
Unusually bright.
Unusually clever he,
Unusually brave,
And he drew delightful Mammoths
On the borders of his cave.
To his Neolithic neighbors,
Who were startled and surprised,
Said he, "My friends, in course of time,
We shall be civilized!
We are going to live in cities!
We are going to fight in wars!
We are going to eat three times a day
Without the natural cause!
We are going to turn life upside down
About a thing called gold!
We are going to want the earth, and take
As much as we can hold!
We are going to wear great piles of stuff
Outside our proper skins!
We are going to have diseases!

1. Charlotte Perkins Gilman. "Similar Cases." *In This Our World*, Small, Maynard, 1893, pp. 95–100. Like many at the turn of the century, Charlotte Perkins Stetson, later Gilman, applied Darwin's theory of evolution to society. She advocated *eugenics*—literally "good breeding" or racial improvement—through restricting the reproduction of those considered to be mentally or physically deficient. She believed that traditional domestic relations were retarding human progress. This eugenicist poem spread throughout the newspaper press in 1893 and made "Mrs. Stetson" famous. In the first stanzas, an advanced "Eohippus" (evolutionary ancestor of the horse) predicts that he will evolve into a horse, only to be laughed to scorn by other primitive creatures, and later an ape foretells that he will be a man, encountering similar mockery from his inferior contemporaries. The poem's concluding stanzas appear here.

And Accomplishments!! And Sins!!!"

Then they all rose up in fury
Against their boastful friend,
For prehistoric patience
Cometh quickly to an end.
Said one, "This is chimerical!
Utopian! Absurd!"
Said another, "What a stupid life!
Too dull, upon my word!"
Cried all, "Before such things can come,
You idiotic child,
You must alter Human Nature!"
And they all sat back and smiled.
Thought they, "An answer to that last
It will be hard to find!"
It was a clinching argument
To the Neolithic Mind!

Charlotte Perkins Gilman

From Women and Economics: A Study of the Economic Relation between Men and Women as a Factor in Social Evolution (1898)[1]

In the human species the condition [of women's economic dependence on men] is permanent and general, though there are exceptions, and though the present century is witnessing the beginnings of a great change in this respect. [. . .]

To many this view will not seem clear at first; and the case of working peasant women or females of savage tribes, and the general household industry of women, will be instanced against it. Some careful and honest discrimination is needed to make plain to ourselves the essential facts of the relation, even in these cases. The horse, in his free natural condition, is economically independent. He gets his living by his own exertions, irrespective of any other creature. The horse, in his present condition of slavery, is economically dependent. He gets his living at the hands of his master; and his exertions, though strenuous, bear no direct relation to his living. In fact, the horses who are the best fed and cared for and the horses who are the hardest worked are quite different animals. The horse works, it is true; but what he gets to eat depends on the power and will of his master. His living comes through another. He is economically dependent. So with the hard-worked savage or peasant women. Their labor is the property of another: they work under another will; and what they receive depends not on their labor, but on the power and will of another. They are economically dependent. This is true of the human female both individually and collectively.

1. Charlotte Perkins Stetson. *Women and Economics: A Study of the Economic Relation between Men and Women as a Factor in Social Evolution*. Small, Maynard, 1898.

Barbara Boyd

From Heart and Home Talks: Politics and Milk (1911)[1]

Politics are no longer outside the home. They are very apt to be inside the baby, as Charlotte Perkins Gilman cleverly remarks. And being inside the baby, they certainly become a matter of woman's concerns.

The sphere of politics has changed within the last 50 years. And the sphere of woman's work has changed. Consequently, they are overlapping each other. [. . .]

Politics, in their workings out, have entered the home. Women, in their new fields of labor, have entered domains affected by politics. As a result, women, both in the home and out of it, must take into consideration politics as a factor in their lives.

[. . .] The condition of the milk supplied to all large cities comes under the thumb of politics. Whether it is up to certain healthful requirements or not depends almost altogether upon the laws upon the subject, and upon the inspectors. And both these depend upon politics.

But not only the milk that enters the home and goes inside the baby, but many other things affecting the health of the family depend today upon politics. And so the woman in the home is affected by politics. [. . .] Thus, politics today are her concern, if things that vitally affect the home and family are her concern.

In the field of labor, politics enter with equal importance into her life. The conditions under which she works, the hours of labor, wages even, can all be affected by the ballot box. And she needs to have a voice in saying what all these shall be, if justice is to be done her.

So no longer can women say that politics have nothing to do with her.

Mrs. Arthur Lyttelton

From Women and Their Work (1901)[1]

[. . . A]t present the supply [of servants] is unequal to the demand. This is due to several causes. First, to the fact that many occupations are now open to women which were formerly closed, and that therefore a girl has a choice [. . .]. Then there is the large increase in the number of families who keep servants, for while the larger households have in many cases diminished their establishments, many people who formerly kept no servant now keep one, and those who kept one keep two or more, and consequently the mistresses of the middle class now do less work in the household than was formerly the case. Lastly, there is the fact that in spite of the great rise in the wages of domestic servants, service is looked down upon by the girls of the poorer classes. [. . . T]he "business

1. Barbara Boyd. "Heart and Home Talks: Politics and Milk." *Washington Post*, 11 Sept. 1911.

1. Mrs. Arthur Lyttelton [Kathleen Clive]. *Women and Their Work*. Methuen, 1901. Lyttelton's reference to cooperative kitchens would have been recognized as an idea promoted by Charlotte Perkins Gilman in both her magazine, *Forerunner*, and her internationally influential book *Women and Economics* (1898).

young lady" and the factory girl consider themselves as higher in the social scale than the parlour-maid or the cook.

[. . .] Some [. . .] think that by a system of co-operative kitchens and other labour-saving appliances, we may almost succeed in doing without servants altogether. But probably the best remedy of all would be to raise the whole profession of domestic service. [. . . W]e must begin at the top, and convince women of the upper and middle classes that it is their part to learn to manage households. [. . .] The discomfort and misery and ill-health caused by badly-managed households is incalculable, while, on the other hand, a woman who can manage a household properly [. . .] is fitted for every sort of work outside the home. The administrative gifts, when properly trained, are just those which prove most useful in many kinds of philanthropic and social work.

Rheta Childe Dorr

From What Eight Million Women Want (1910)[1]

Men, ardently, eternally, interested in Woman—one woman at a time—are almost never even faintly interested in women. Strangely, deliberately ignorant of women, they argue that their ignorance is justified by an innate unknowableness of the sex.

I am persuaded that the time is at hand when this sentimental, half contemptuous attitude of half the population towards the other half will have to be abandoned. [. . .]

The Census of 1900 reported nearly six million women in the United States engaged in wage earning outside their homes. Between 1890 and 1900 the number of women in industry increased faster than the number of men in industry. [. . .] Nine million women who have forsaken the traditions of the hearth and are competing with men in the world of paid labor, means that women are rapidly passing from the domestic control of their fathers and their husbands. Surely this is the most important economic fact in the world to-day.

Within the past twenty years no less than nine hundred and fifty-four thousand divorces have been granted in the United States. Two thirds of these divorces were granted to aggrieved wives. In spite [. . .] of tradition and [. . .] social ostracism [. . .] more than six hundred thousand women, in the short space of twenty years, repudiated the burden of uncongenial marriage. Without any doubt this is the most important social fact we have had to face since the slavery question was settled.

[. . .] In half a dozen countries women are already completely enfranchised. In England the opposition is seeking terms of surrender. In the United States the stoutest enemy of the movement acknowledges that woman suffrage is ultimately inevitable. [. . .] Does any one question that this is the most important political fact the modern world has ever faced?

1. Rheta Childe Dorr. *What Eight Million Women Want*. Small, Maynard, 1910. A journalist from Nebraska, Dorr was a follower of Gilman; she praises Gilman's *Women and Economics* (1898) in this book.

The New York Times

From Mrs. Delong Acquitted. She Killed Her Husband, But the Jury Has Set Her Free (1 Dec. 1892)[1]

In October, 1891, Mrs. Delong found her husband with a woman of low character. She remonstrated and a quarrel ensued, which led up to the shooting of her husband. The plea put in by the defense was insanity and self-defense. The evidence was at times quite contradictory, but the story of wrongs and abuse which the defendant had suffered at the hands of her husband [. . .] evidently satisfied the jury that Mrs. Delong acted in self-defense.

• • •

The scene in the courtroom when the verdict was announced was one of great excitement. The prisoner at the bar was sobbing, but when the verdict was given the room was filled with cheers and hurrahs, the clapping of hands, and the stamping of feet. The defendant raised her hands and implored God's blessing upon the jury.

The Washington Post

From The Chances of Divorce (28 Nov. 1909)

If you are married or about to be married, the Government's latest statistics showing the probability of divorce may be of interest. During the twenty-year period from 1887 to 1906 the records of all registered marriages in the United States totaled 12,832,044 and the Courts granted freedom to 820,264 unhappy couples.

From this it is plain to be seen that your chances of divorce are about one in fifteen, so the odds are fairly long that if you are already married or later do marry, death, and not the Divorce Court, will sever your bonds.

Wives who seek freedom will be interested to know that 66.6 per cent of all decrees have been granted to wives, and that alimony has been also allowed in two cases out of every twenty-two.

Divorce is most frequent in the fourth and fifth years of married life. Actors and showmen are the most frequently divorced classes. Commercial travelers come next on the list of guilty. Agricultural laborers are the prize winners for matrimonial constancy. Clergymen are next desirable.

About one third of those divorced remarry, and divorcees enjoy an advantage over widows in this respect, due, as the unfeeling Government ungallantly remarks, to the fact that those who get rid of their husbands by law are usually younger than those who leave his removal to Providence.

1. On December 2, 1900, in Indianola, Iowa, someone killed farmer John Hossack with an axe as he was sleeping in bed beside his wife. Susan Glaspell's reporting and public opinion were largely against Mrs. Hossack, and the first trial ended in a guilty verdict; a retrial ended without a verdict. (Sixteen years after the Hossack murder, Glaspell adapted the case into a play and story, written from a more sympathetic perspective.) At the turn of the century, public opinion about such cases frequently sided with the wife of an abusive husband, as this newspaper account of an earlier murder trial suggests.

Charlotte Perkins Gilman

From Why I Wrote "The Yellow Wall-paper" (1913)[1]

For many years I suffered from a severe and continuous nervous breakdown tending to melancholia—and beyond. During about the third year of this trouble I went, in devout faith and some faint stir of hope, to a noted specialist in nervous diseases, the best known in the country. This wise man put me to bed and applied the rest cure, to which a still good physique responded so promptly that he concluded that there was nothing much the matter with me, and sent me home with solemn advice to "live as domestic a life as possible," to "have but two hours' intelligent life a day," and "never to touch pen, brush or pencil again as long as I lived."

The Washington Post

The Rest Cure (1902)

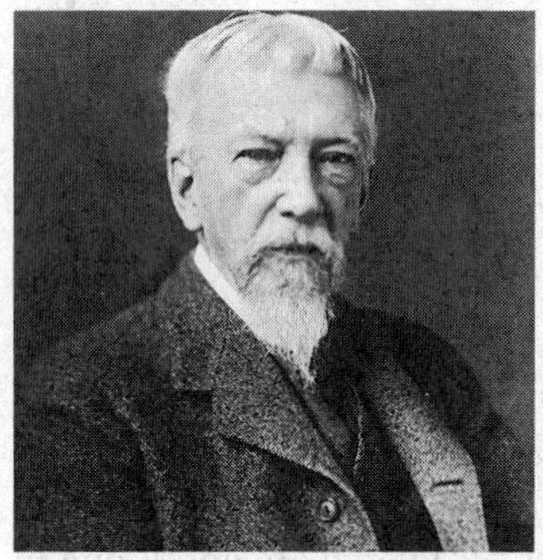

Silas Weir Mitchell, 1829–1914

What makes people tired is not overwork, but overconcentration, overniceness in clinging to one settled rule till the nerves rebel.

What is most needed for recreation is relaxation. In carrying burdens, either mental or physical, there is nothing like "changing hands" often.

Recreation need not always consist of social diversion—of going to the theater or the show. One must vary his routine, if nothing more than to change his position while at work.

Routine kills more Americans than anything else. It brings about depression, despondency, and nervous breakdowns.

These general principles and their application constitute what the doctors call "the rest cure." There's nothing like keeping out of the ruts.

The Washington Post

From Egotism of the Rest Cure (1905)

Many a smart dame spends August at a rest cure, but the woman who would enjoy such a holiday is to be pitied, for the essential point about a rest cure is the egotism of the patient's attitude to herself and those about her. It is signifi-

1. Published in Gilman's magazine *The Forerunner* (Oct. 1913). Gilman suffered postpartum depression after the birth of her daughter. In 1886, she sought treatment by S. Weir Mitchell. Though Gilman repeatedly affirmed that the horrors she described in "The Yellow Wallpaper" had persuaded Weir Mitchell to abandon the "rest cure" treatment, and biographers have tended to repeat this assertion, there is no evidence it was true.

cant that this type of holiday is one very rarely advised in the case of a man or in the case of a real worker.

SUGGESTIONS FOR FURTHER READING

Ben-Zvi, Linda. "'Murder, She Wrote': The Genesis of Susan Glaspell's *Trifles*." *Susan Glaspell: Essays on Her Theater and Fiction*, edited by Linda Ben-Zvi, U of Michigan P, 1995, pp. 19–48.

Bose, Christine E. *Women in 1900*. Temple UP, 2001.

Edelstein, Sari. "Charlotte Perkins Gilman and the Yellow Newspaper." *Legacy*, vol. 24, no. 1, 2007, pp. 72–92.

Griswold, Robert L. "Law, Sex, Cruelty, and Divorce in Victorian America, 1840–1900." Hawes and Nybakken, pp. 145–72.

Hard, William. *The Women of To-Morrow*. Baker, 1911.

Hawes, Joseph M., and Elizabeth I. Nybakken, editors. *Family and Society in American History*. U of Illinois P, 2001.

Hedges, Elaine. "Small Things Reconsidered: 'A Jury of Her Peers.'" *Susan Glaspell: Essays on Her Theater and Fiction*, edited by Linda Ben-Zvi, U of Michigan P, 1995, pp. 49–69.

Karpinski, Joanne B., editor. *Critical Essays on Charlotte Perkins Gilman*. Hall, 1992.

Koloski, Bernard. *Kate Chopin: A Study of the Short Fiction*. Twayne, 1996.

Kleinberg, S. J. *Women in the United States, 1830–1945*. Macmillan, 1999.

Leach, William R. *True Love and Perfect Union: The Feminist Reform of Sex and Society*. Basic Books, 1980.

Llewellyn, K. N. "Behind the Law of Divorce: I." *Columbia Law Review*, vol. 32, no. 8, Dec. 1932, pp. 1281–1308.

Roosevelt, Eleanor [Mrs. Franklin D.]. *It's Up to the Women*. Frederick A. Stokes, 1933.

Smith-Rosenberg, Carroll. *Disorderly Conduct: Visions of Gender in Victorian America*. Alfred A. Knopf, 1985.

SUGGESTIONS FOR WRITING

1. In The Story of an Hour Louise Mallard receives the false report—relayed in two telegrams to a newspaper office and then through her sister—of her husband's death in a railroad accident. Other than these particulars of transportation and communication, the story's simple setting and action might belong to an earlier period. Looking closely at details of the story, write an essay that examines its relation to the historical context of 1894, when it was published. In what respects does the story reflect changes or continuities in family life? Could the same events have happened without the modern means of travel and communication? What role do time or history play in this short incident?
2. The narrator of The Yellow Wallpaper declares, "congenial work [. . .] would do me good. But what is one to do?" (par. 14–15). Notice places in the story where the patient's views or wishes are contradicted, or where she is able to do something to change how she is treated. Write an essay bringing a historical perspective to this story's representation of women's work or ability to act, or "do." The essay might include reference to S. Weir Mitchell's rest cure or other treatments of women's illness in 1880–1920.
3. In A Jury of Her Peers, Mrs. Peters is "married to the law" (in the form of her husband the sheriff, par. 282), whereas Mrs. Hale is married to the farmer who first

discovered the murder. In what ways, including dress, speech and manners, action, and attitude, are the two visiting women alike or different? In what ways do they identify with or distance themselves from the absent wife, Mrs. Wright? How do the men and women take sides separately or together? Is the idea that the murder was provoked a sign of the story's realistic portrayal of marriage around 1900? Write an essay focusing on turn-of-the-century marriage, the law, and alliances as well as differences between men and women ("peers") in this story.

4. The Story of an Hour, A Jury of Her Peers, and The Yellow Wallpaper all take place inside a house, and almost entirely within one room of that house. Entering through a door or gazing out a window may play a significant part in the action. Write an essay in which you focus on domestic space and women's confinement in this period of American society, comparing at least two of these stories.
5. At the end of each of these stories, a husband or wife has collapsed or is dead—a marriage has ended. Write an essay in which you analyze one or more of these three stories as an indirect commentary on turn-of-the-century views of marriage and divorce.
6. Examine the details of the women's housekeeping in A Jury of Her Peers and Trifles, the play by Susan Glaspell, both in the physical setting of the farm kitchen and in the characters' conversations or thoughts. Write an essay on women's work at the turn of the twentieth century as reflected in Glaspell's story and play.
7. Charlotte Perkins Gilman and Barbara Boyd acknowledged that many women were opposed to the idea of changing traditional feminine roles and did not want the vote. Examine sources on the history of the women's movement in the United States—for instance, by consulting the National Women's History Project Web site or printed sources. Write an essay on the ways that women such as the sisters in The Story of an Hour or The Yellow Wallpaper or the more timid Mrs. Peters in A Jury of Her Peers might resist or slow down what Chopin, Gilman, or Glaspell considered to be progress for women. Choose one or two stories and focus on a specific issue such as the idea that women are naturally domestic and subordinate to husbands.
8. For a biographical and historical approach to one of these stories, consult the biography of Chopin, Gilman, or Glaspell in this volume; the entry on this author on *Wikipedia*, the online or print *Dictionary of National Biography,* the online *Literature Resource Center, Literature Online,* or other resources available on the Web or in your library. Compare at least three versions of the author's biography to confirm some of the general facts. Write an essay that interprets the story by this author (The Story of an Hour, The Yellow Wallpaper, or A Jury of Her Peers) in relation both to her life and career and to women's changing roles and conditions as outlined in this chapter.

11 CRITICAL CONTEXTS: TIM O'BRIEN'S "THE THINGS THEY CARRIED"

We have already seen that, although stories may be read as if they stand alone, they are enriched by being situated in authorial, literary, or cultural and historical contexts. Once a work has earned a place in the **canon** of literature, it has already become surrounded by a critical context as well—a conversation among readers that works very much like the conversations about a work that you have in (and beyond) the classroom but that takes place on the page rather than in person and extends over decades rather than hours or days. To write critically about a work of literature is to engage not only the text but also other readers who have written about it. In a critical context essay, the literary text typically functions as your "primary source," published criticism as your "secondary sources."

Reading criticism about a work should not rob you of, or substitute for, your individual response to it any more than discussing it with your friends or classmates does. Rather, in addition to being informative in various ways, reading criticism can help you to clarify and enrich your response and to move from response to argument. After all, we sometimes discover that we have something particular to say or that what we have to say is worth saying only when we learn that someone else has already said something very different—something that we either disagree with or that seems to us to miss "the real point" or at least a point we think shouldn't be missed.

Sometimes entering a critical conversation can seem a daunting prospect, at least at first. What, you might think, can I, a mere student, possibly add? What is left for *anyone* to say about a story about which so much has been said already? The truth, however, is that *all* critics—even the most informed and experienced—must confront a version of these very same questions every time they sit down to write. As important, they—like you—must implicitly answer those questions *in* their writing. When a work has engaged a number of critics, that is, subsequent commentators need not only to acknowledge the previous readings but also, by contradicting or modifying their conclusions, articulate a **motive** for writing—and, more important, for reading—yet another essay on the work. Trying to identify, as you read the work of other and especially more experienced writers, the specific moves, techniques, and strategies that they use to describe and insert themselves into a conversation—to acknowledge and respond to the work of other writers—can give you concrete examples of how to do the very same thing.

The conversation about a work of literature is, in other words, a true conversation, even, at times, a debate. And wherever there is debate there is motive and opportunity—to reconsider both "sides," to take one side or the other, to offer an alternative point of view or one that somehow reconciles seemingly opposed stances, or to simply change the subject. To identify such opportunities, however, you first have to get a handle on how an array of individual arguments fit together as part of *one* conversation. Like any conversation or debate, including the sorts in which you participate every day, a conversation about a literary text tends to circle around a few key issues and questions and, almost inevitably, to ignore or at least slight others. In reading criticism, one of your first tasks is thus to figure out

- what those specific issues and questions are;
- where each of the individual critics stand on them, or what the various "sides" are;
- where, when, and why you find yourself agreeing with their various stances and arguments; and—finally—
- what aspects of the story or ways of looking at it *aren't* brought up at all or at least aren't thoroughly addressed in the conversation that you think should be.

To give you practice at doing just that, this chapter includes both a short story—Vietnam veteran Tim O'Brien's THE THINGS THEY CARRIED—and excerpts from three scholarly essays about it. We've made your job a bit easier by choosing a story at once universally admired and highly controversial, in part because of its subject matter—a war mainly fought not by volunteers but by draftees, the first war the United States ever lost, and one so fiercely, widely, and publicly contested that many feared it might tear the country apart. Focusing on the fortunes and misfortunes of a company of soldiers fighting—as O'Brien himself did—in the jungles of Vietnam in the late 1960s, the story originally debuted in *Esquire* magazine in 1986, eleven years after the Fall of Saigon ended the war the story depicts and only four years before the start of the Gulf War (1990–91), the first of the series of American military engagements that has unfortunately helped to give O'Brien's work—and the controversies over it—ever-new relevance and meaning. Included in *The Best American Short Stories 1987*, "The Things They Carried" became something of an instant classic after its republication in O'Brien's 1990 collection of the same name. So interlinked, in fact, are the twenty-two stories that make up *The Things They Carried*—beginning with the title story and ending with THE LIVES OF THE DEAD—that some commentators refer to the book not as a short-story collection, sequence, or cycle at all but rather as a novel. Whether they categorize "The Things They Carried" as a short story (as we do) or as a novel chapter, however, critics seldom, if ever, analyze it in isolation. Instead, they tend to consider how it works and means in the context of the larger work of which it is a part, of its critical context, and, often, of O'Brien's **oeuvre** or authorial canon as a whole, other literature about the Vietnam War specifically or war literature generally, and/or of the story's historical and cultural contexts (not only the late 1960s, in which it is set, but also the late 1980s, when it was written and published).

We've made your job somewhat easier, too, by handpicking just three essays about the story that directly address—and often vehemently disagree with—one another. And though we have omitted those portions of each essay that deal with stories not included in this anthology, the essays are otherwise reproduced entire. Though this might add to your reading load, it also ensures that you can read and really *use* these essays not only as contributions to the critical conversation about this specific story but also as models of how to engage effectively in a critical conversation about any text or how, that is, to craft compelling arguments about a text by considering its critical context.

Reading critical essays in this light, what you most want to pay attention to is less the content of their various arguments than the formal or rhetorical strategies and techniques writers deploy to insert themselves into the ongoing conversation and to convince you of the worthiness of their contribution to it. The goal is to identify "moves" that you can try out in your own writing. When and how and for what specific purposes, for example, do these writers allude to, paraphrase, summarize, or quote from the arguments of other writers (their own secondary sources)? What specific techniques do they use to signal to you, the reader, when they are referring to or even reproducing the ideas of a source as opposed to their own ideas? What does each writer suggest about why his or her argument is both different from others' and important to the conversation? What, in other words, are their motives? How exactly do these writers work to convince you that they are being fair and balanced in their approach both to the primary source (the literary text) and to their secondary sources (others' arguments about it)?

Just as considering other readers' views of any work of fiction can help you to discover and refine your own, so identifying the specific techniques other writers use to draw on the work of other critics both to make their cases and to convince you the case is worth making will help you discover new ways to do that, too.

TIM O'BRIEN

The Things They Carried

First Lieutenant Jimmy Cross carried letters from a girl named Martha, a junior at Mount Sebastian College in New Jersey. They were not love letters, but Lieutenant Cross was hoping, so he kept them folded in plastic at the bottom of his rucksack. In the late afternoon, after a day's march, he would dig his foxhole, wash his hands under a canteen, unwrap the letters, hold them with the tips of his fingers, and spend the last hour of light pretending. He would imagine romantic camping trips into the White Mountains in New Hampshire. He would sometimes taste the envelope flaps, knowing her tongue had been there. More than anything, he wanted Martha to love him as he loved her, but the letters were mostly chatty, elusive on the matter of love. She was a virgin, he was almost sure. She was an English major at Mount Sebastian, and she wrote beautifully about her professors and roommates and midterm exams, about her respect for Chaucer and her great affection for Virginia Woolf.[1] She often quoted lines of poetry; she never mentioned the war, except to say, Jimmy, take care of yourself. The letters weighed 4 ounces. They were signed Love, Martha, but Lieutenant Cross understood that Love was only a way of signing and did not mean what he sometimes pretended it meant. At dusk, he would carefully return the letters to his rucksack. Slowly, a bit distracted, he would get up and move among his men, checking the perimeter, then at full dark he would return to his hole and watch the night and wonder if Martha was a virgin.

The things they carried were largely determined by necessity. Among the necessities or near-necessities were P-38 can openers, pocket knives, heat tabs,[2] wristwatches, dog tags, mosquito repellent, chewing gum, candy, cigarettes, salt

1. British novelist (1882–1941) and author of *A Room of One's Own* (1929), which explores the difficulties that have inhibited women writers. *Chaucer*: Geoffrey Chaucer (c. 1343–1400), often hailed as the first English poet and the greatest before Shakespeare, author of *The Canterbury Tales*.

2. Flammable tablets used to heat rations. *P-38 can openers*: small can openers developed in 1942 and issued as part of the field rations of U.S. forces between World War II and the 1980s.

tablets, packets of Kool-Aid, lighters, matches, sewing kits, Military Payment Certificates, C rations,[3] and two or three canteens of water. Together, these items weighed between 12 and 18 pounds, depending upon a man's habits or rate of metabolism. Henry Dobbins, who was a big man, carried extra rations; he was especially fond of canned peaches in heavy syrup over pound cake. Dave Jensen, who practiced field hygiene, carried a toothbrush, dental floss, and several hotel-sized bars of soap he'd stolen on R&R[4] in Sydney, Australia. Ted Lavender, who was scared, carried tranquilizers until he was shot in the head outside the village of Than Khe in mid-April. By necessity, and because it was SOP,[5] they all carried steel helmets that weighed 5 pounds including the liner and camouflage cover. They carried the standard fatigue jackets and trousers. Very few carried underwear. On their feet they carried jungle boots—2.1 pounds—and Dave Jensen carried three pairs of socks and a can of Dr. Scholl's foot powder as a precaution against trench foot.[6] Until he was shot, Ted Lavender carried 6 or 7 ounces of premium dope, which for him was a necessity. Mitchell Sanders, the RTO,[7] carried condoms. Norman Bowker carried a diary. Rat Kiley carried comic books. Kiowa, a devout Baptist, carried an illustrated New Testament that had been presented to him by his father, who taught Sunday school in Oklahoma City, Oklahoma. As a hedge against bad times, however, Kiowa also carried his grandmother's distrust of the white man, his grandfather's old hunting hatchet. Necessity dictated. Because the land was mined and booby-trapped, it was SOP for each man to carry a steel-centered, nylon-covered flak jacket, which weighed 6.7 pounds, but which on hot days seemed much heavier. Because you could die so quickly, each man carried at least one large compress bandage, usually in the helmet band for easy access. Because the nights were cold, and because the monsoons were wet, each carried a green plastic poncho that could be used as a raincoat or groundsheet or makeshift tent. With its quilted liner, the poncho weighed almost 2 pounds, but it was worth every ounce. In April, for instance, when Ted Lavender was shot, they used his poncho to wrap him up, then to carry him across the paddy,[8] then to lift him into the chopper that took him away.

They were called legs or grunts.

To carry something was to hump it, as when Lieutenant Jimmy Cross humped his love for Martha up the hills and through the swamps. In its intransitive form,[9] to hump meant to walk, or to march, but it implied burdens far beyond the intransitive.

5 Almost everyone humped photographs. In his wallet, Lieutenant Cross carried two photographs of Martha. The first was a Kodacolor[1] snapshot signed Love, though he knew better. She stood against a brick wall. Her eyes were gray

3. Combat rations, canned meals for use in the field, c. 1940–58. *Military Payment Certificates*: form of currency used to pay U.S. military in some foreign countries from the end of World War II until the late 1970s.

4. Rest and recuperation or relaxation, leave (military acronym/slang).

5. Standard operating procedure (military acronym/slang).

6. Serious medical condition caused by prolonged exposure to damp, cold, unsanitary conditions; so named because of its prevalence among soldiers serving in the trenches of World War I.

7. Radio telephone operator (military acronym/slang).

8. Usually swampy field where rice is grown.

9. That is, when used without a direct object.

1. First color film made by the Eastman Kodak Company c. 1942–63.

and neutral, her lips slightly open as she stared straight-on at the camera. At night, sometimes, Lieutenant Cross wondered who had taken the picture, because he knew she had boyfriends, because he loved her so much, and because he could see the shadow of the picture-taker spreading out against the brick wall. The second photograph had been clipped from the 1968 Mount Sebastian yearbook. It was an action shot—women's volleyball—and Martha was bent horizontal to the floor, reaching, the palms of her hands in sharp focus, the tongue taut, the expression frank and competitive. There was no visible sweat. She wore white gym shorts. Her legs, he thought, were almost certainly the legs of a virgin, dry and without hair, the left knee cocked and carrying her entire weight, which was just over 117 pounds. Lieutenant Cross remembered touching that left knee. A dark theater, he remembered, and the movie was *Bonnie and Clyde*,[2] and Martha wore a tweed skirt, and during the final scene, when he touched her knee, she turned and looked at him in a sad, sober way that made him pull his hand back, but he would always remember the feel of the tweed skirt and the knee beneath it and the sound of the gunfire that killed Bonnie and Clyde, how embarrassing it was, how slow and oppressive. He remembered kissing her good night at the dorm door. Right then, he thought, he should've done something brave. He should've carried her up the stairs to her room and tied her to the bed and touched that left knee all night long. He should've risked it. Whenever he looked at the photographs, he thought of new things he should've done.

What they carried was partly a function of rank, partly of field specialty.

As a first lieutenant and platoon leader, Jimmy Cross carried a compass, maps, code books, binoculars, and a .45-caliber pistol that weighed 2.9 pounds fully loaded. He carried a strobe light and the responsibility for the lives of his men.

As an RTO, Mitchell Sanders carried the PRC-25 radio, a killer, 26 pounds with its battery.

As a medic, Rat Kiley carried a canvas satchel filled with morphine and plasma and malaria tablets and surgical tape and comic books and all the things a medic must carry, including M&M's for especially bad wounds,[3] for a total weight of nearly 18 pounds.

As a big man, therefore a machine gunner, Henry Dobbins carried the M-60, 10
which weighed 23 pounds unloaded, but which was almost always loaded. In addition, Dobbins carried between 10 and 15 pounds of ammunition draped in belts across his chest and shoulders.

As PFCs or Spec 4s,[4] most of them were common grunts and carried the standard M-16 gas-operated assault rifle. The weapon weighed 7.5 pounds unloaded, 8.2 pounds with its full 20-round magazine. Depending on numerous factors, such as topography and psychology, the riflemen carried anywhere from 12 to 20 magazines, usually in cloth bandoliers, adding on another 8.4

2. Oscar-winning film (1967) in which heartthrobs Warren Beatty and Faye Dunaway portray notoriously violent Depression-era outlaws Clyde Barrow (1909–34) and Bonnie Parker (1910–34); in its graphic final scene, shot partly in slow motion, the glamorous couple dies in a hail of machine-gun fire.

3. Medics in Vietnam administered M&M candies as a placebo to those so severely wounded that they wouldn't benefit from any other treatment.

4. Those holding the rank of Specialist Fourth Class, the rank immediately above Private First Class. *PFC*: Private First Class (military acronym/slang), rank between private (PVT) and lance-corporal (LCP).

pounds at minimum, 14 pounds at maximum. When it was available, they also carried M-16 maintenance gear—rods and steel brushes and swabs and tubes of LSA oil[5]—all of which weighed about a pound. Among the grunts, some carried the M-79 grenade launcher, 5.9 pounds unloaded, a reasonably light weapon except for the ammunition, which was heavy. A single round weighed 10 ounces. The typical load was 25 rounds. But Ted Lavender, who was scared, carried 34 rounds when he was shot and killed outside Than Khe, and he went down under an exceptional burden, more than 20 pounds of ammunition, plus the flak jacket and helmet and rations and water and toilet paper and tranquilizers and all the rest, plus the unweighed fear. He was dead weight. There was no twitching or flopping. Kiowa, who saw it happen, said it was like watching a rock fall, or a big sandbag or something—just boom, then down—not like the movies where the dead guy rolls around and does fancy spins and goes ass over teakettle—not like that, Kiowa said, the poor bastard just flat-fuck fell. Boom. Down. Nothing else. It was a bright morning in mid-April. Lieutenant Cross felt the pain. He blamed himself. They stripped off Lavender's canteens and ammo, all the heavy things, and Rat Kiley said the obvious, the guy's dead, and Mitchell Sanders used his radio to report one U.S. KIA[6] and to request a chopper. Then they wrapped Lavender in his poncho. They carried him out to a dry paddy, established security, and sat smoking the dead man's dope until the chopper came. Lieutenant Cross kept to himself. He pictured Martha's smooth young face, thinking he loved her more than anything, more than his men, and now Ted Lavender was dead because he loved her so much and could not stop thinking about her. When the dustoff[7] arrived, they carried Lavender aboard. Afterward they burned Than Khe. They marched until dusk, then dug their holes, and that night Kiowa kept explaining how you had to be there, how fast it was, how the poor guy just dropped like so much concrete. Boom-down, he said. Like cement.

In addition to the three standard weapons—the M-60, M-16 and M-79—they carried whatever presented itself, or whatever seemed appropriate as a means of killing or staying alive. They carried catch-as-catch-can. At various times, in various situations, they carried M-14s and CAR-15s and Swedish Ks and grease guns and captured AK-47s and Chi-Coms and RPGs[8] and Simonov carbines and black market Uzis and .38-caliber Smith & Wesson handguns and 66 mm LAWs and shotguns and silencers and blackjacks[9] and bayonets and C-4 plastic explosives. Lee Strunk carried a slingshot, a weapon of last resort, he called it. Mitchell Sanders carried brass knuckles. Kiowa carried his grandfather's feathered hatchet. Every third or fourth man carried a Claymore antipersonnel mine[1]—3.5 pounds with its firing device. They all carried fragmentation

5. Military acronym/slang for either "lubricant, small arms" or "lubricant, semifluid, automatic [weapons]."
6. Killed in action (military acronym/slang).
7. Medical evacuation helicopter or mission, by some accounts an acronym for Dedicated Unhesitating Service to Our Fighting Forces.
8. Rocket-propelled grenades (military acronym/slang).
9. Leather-covered, often lead-filled clubs with flexible handles. *LAWs*: light antitank or antiarmor weapons (military acronym/slang).

grenades[2]—14 ounces each. They all carried at least one M-18 colored smoke grenade—24 ounces. Some carried CS or tear gas grenades. Some carried white phosphorus grenades. They carried all they could bear, and then some, including a silent awe for the terrible power of the things they carried.

In the first week of April, before Lavender died, Lieutenant Jimmy Cross received a good-luck charm from Martha. It was a simple pebble, an ounce at most. Smooth to the touch, it was a milky white color with flecks of orange and violet, oval-shaped, like a miniature egg. In the accompanying letter, Martha wrote that she had found the pebble on the Jersey shoreline, precisely where the land touched water at high tide, where things came together but also separated. It was this separate-but-together quality, she wrote, that had inspired her to pick up the pebble and to carry it in her breast pocket for several days, where it seemed weightless, and then to send it through the mail, by air, as a token of her truest feelings for him. Lieutenant Cross found this romantic. But he wondered what her truest feelings were, exactly, and what she meant by separate-but-together. He wondered how the tides and waves had come into play on that afternoon along the Jersey shoreline when Martha saw the pebble and bent down to rescue it from geology. He imagined bare feet. Martha was a poet, with the poet's sensibilities, and her feet would be brown and bare, the toenails unpainted, the eyes chilly and somber like the ocean in March, and though it was painful, he wondered who had been with her that afternoon. He imagined a pair of shadows moving along the strip of sand where things came together but also separated. It was phantom jealousy, he knew, but he couldn't help himself. He loved her so much. On the march, through the hot days of early April, he carried the pebble in his mouth, turning it with his tongue, tasting sea salt and moisture. His mind wandered. He had difficulty keeping his attention on the war. On occasion he would yell at his men to spread out the column, to keep their eyes open, but then he would slip away into daydreams, just pretending, walking barefoot along the Jersey shore, with Martha, carrying nothing. He would feel himself rising. Sun and waves and gentle winds, all love and lightness.

What they carried varied by mission.

When a mission took them to the mountains, they carried mosquito netting, 15
machetes, canvas tarps, and extra bug juice.

If a mission seemed especially hazardous, or if it involved a place they knew to be bad, they carried everything they could. In certain heavily mined AOs,[3] where the land was dense with Toe Poppers and Bouncing Betties,[4] they took turns humping a 28-pound mine detector. With its headphones and big sensing plate, the equipment was a stress on the lower back and shoulders, awkward to handle, often useless because of the shrapnel in the earth, but they carried it anyway, partly for safety, partly for the illusion of safety.

1. Remote-control mine that fires steel balls.
2. The most common type of grenade, they fire small projectiles or "fragments."
3. Areas of operation (military acronym/slang).
4. Like *Toe Poppers*, slang for a type of land mine.

On ambush, or other night missions, they carried peculiar little odds and ends. Kiowa always took along his New Testament and a pair of moccasins for silence. Dave Jensen carried night-sight vitamins high in carotene. Lee Strunk carried his slingshot; ammo, he claimed, would never be a problem. Rat Kiley carried brandy and M&M's candy. Until he was shot, Ted Lavender carried the starlight scope,[5] which weighed 6.3 pounds with its aluminum carrying case. Henry Dobbins carried his girlfriend's pantyhose wrapped around his neck as a comforter. They all carried ghosts. When dark come, they would move out single file across the meadows and paddies to their ambush coordinates, where they would quietly set up the Claymores and lie down and spend the night waiting.

Other missions were more complicated and required special equipment. In mid-April, it was their mission to search out and destroy the elaborate tunnel complexes[6] in the Than Khe area south of Chu Lai. To blow the tunnels, they carried one-pound blocks of pentrite high explosives, four blocks to a man, 68 pounds in all. They carried wiring, detonators, and battery-powered clackers.[7] Dave Jensen carried earplugs. Most often, before blowing the tunnels, they were ordered by higher command to search them, which was considered bad news, but by and large they just shrugged and carried out orders. Because he was a big man, Henry Dobbins was excused from tunnel duty. The others would draw numbers. Before Lavender died there were 17 men in the platoon, and whoever drew the number 17 would strip off his gear and crawl in headfirst with a flashlight and Lieutenant Cross's .45-caliber pistol. The rest of them would fan out as security. They would sit down or kneel, not facing the hole, listening to the ground beneath them, imagining cobwebs and ghosts, whatever was down there—the tunnel walls squeezing in—how the flashlight seemed impossibly heavy in the hand and how it was tunnel vision in the very strictest sense, compression in all ways, even time, and how you had to wiggle in—ass and elbows—a swallowed-up feeling—and how you found yourself worrying about odd things: Will your flashlight go dead? Do rats carry rabies? If you screamed, how far would the sound carry? Would your buddies hear it? Would they have the courage to drag you out? In some respects, though not many, the waiting was worse than the tunnel itself. Imagination was a killer.

On April 16, when Lee Strunk drew the number 17, he laughed and muttered something and went down quickly. The morning was hot and very still. Not good, Kiowa said. He looked at the tunnel opening, then out across a dry paddy toward the village of Than Khe. Nothing moved. No clouds or birds or people. As they waited, the men smoked and drank Kool-Aid, not talking much, feeling sympathy for Lee Strunk but also feeling the luck of the draw. You win some, you lose some, said Mitchell Sanders, and sometimes you settle for a rain check. It was a tired line and no one laughed.

20 Henry Dobbins ate a tropical chocolate bar.[8] Ted Lavender popped a tranquilizer and went off to pee.

5. Night-vision device.

6. During the war, a vast system of tunnels was constructed throughout South Vietnam as a stronghold and base for attacks; some contained living areas, storage depots, even hospitals.

7. Handheld firing device for Claymore mines.

8. Candy bar originally developed for the military in World War II, designed to withstand extreme heat.

After five minutes, Lieutenant Jimmy Cross moved to the tunnel, leaned down, and examined the darkness. Trouble, he thought—a cave-in maybe. And then suddenly, without willing it, he was thinking about Martha. The stresses and fractures, the quick collapse, the two of them buried alive under all that weight. Dense, crushing love. Kneeling, watching the hole, he tried to concentrate on Lee Strunk and the war, all the dangers, but his love was too much for him, he felt paralyzed, he wanted to sleep inside her lungs and breathe her blood and be smothered. He wanted her to be a virgin and not a virgin, all at once. He wanted to know her. Intimate secrets: Why poetry? Why so sad? Why that grayness in her eyes? Why so alone? Not lonely, just alone—riding her bike across campus or sitting off by herself in the cafeteria—even dancing, she danced alone—and it was the aloneness that filled him with love. He remembered telling her that one evening. How she nodded and looked away. And how, later, when he kissed her, she received the kiss without returning it, her eyes wide open, not afraid, not a virgin's eyes, just flat and uninvolved.

Lieutenant Cross gazed at the tunnel. But he was not there. He was buried with Martha under the white sand at the Jersey shore. They were pressed together, and the pebble in his mouth was her tongue. He was smiling. Vaguely, he was aware of how quiet the day was, the sullen paddies, yet he could not bring himself to worry about matters of security. He was beyond that. He was just a kid at war, in love. He was twenty-four years old. He couldn't help it.

A few moments later Lee Strunk crawled out of the tunnel. He came up grinning, filthy but alive. Lieutenant Cross nodded and closed his eyes while the others clapped Strunk on the back and made jokes about rising from the dead.

Worms, Rat Kiley said. Right out of the grave. Fuckin' zombie.

The men laughed. They all felt great relief. 25

Spook[9] city, said Mitchell Sanders.

Lee Strunk made a funny ghost sound, a kind of moaning, yet very happy, and right then, when Strunk made that high happy moaning sound, when he went *Ahhooooo*, right then Ted Lavender was shot in the head on his way back from peeing. He lay with his mouth open. The teeth were broken. There was a swollen black bruise under his left eye. The cheekbone was gone. Oh shit, Rat Kiley said, the guy's dead. The guy's dead, he kept saying, which seemed profound—the guy's dead. I mean really.

The things they carried were determined to some extent by superstition. Lieutenant Cross carried his good-luck pebble. Dave Jensen carried a rabbit's foot. Norman Bowker, otherwise a very gentle person, carried a thumb that had been presented to him as a gift by Mitchell Sanders. The thumb was dark brown, rubbery to the touch, and weighed 3 ounces at most. It had been cut from a VC[1] corpse, a boy of fifteen or sixteen. They'd found him at the bottom of an irrigation ditch, badly burned, flies in his mouth and eyes. The boy wore black shorts

9. Ghost, but also used, since the 1940s, as a racial slur, especially with reference to African Americans.

1. Viet Cong (military acronym/slang), short for Viet Nam Cong San, meaning "Vietnamese Communists," the guerrilla force that fought, with the support of the North Vietnamese Army, against both South Vietnam and the United States during the Vietnam War.

and sandals. At the time of his death he had been carrying a pouch of rice, a rifle, and three magazines of ammunition.

You want my opinion, Mitchell Sanders said, there's a definite moral here.

30 He put his hand on the dead boy's wrist. He was quiet for a time, as if counting a pulse, then he patted the stomach, almost affectionately, and used Kiowa's hunting hatchet to remove the thumb.

Henry Dobbins asked what the moral was.

Moral?

You know. *Moral.*

Sanders wrapped the thumb in toilet paper and handed it across to Norman Bowker. There was no blood. Smiling, he kicked the boy's head, watched the flies scatter, and said, Its like with that old TV show—Paladin.[2] Have gun, will travel.

35 Henry Dobbins thought about it.

Yeah, well, he finally said. I don't see no moral.

There it *is*, man.

Fuck off.

They carried USO stationery and pencils and pens. They carried Sterno, safety pins, trip flares, signal flares, spools of wire, razor blades, chewing tobacco, liberated joss sticks and statuettes of the smiling Buddha, candles, grease pencils, *The Stars and Stripes*, fingernail clippers, Psy Ops[3] leaflets, bush hats, bolos, and much more. Twice a week, when the resupply choppers came in, they carried hot chow in green mermite cans[4] and large canvas bags filled with iced beer and soda pop. They carried plastic water containers, each with a 2-gallon capacity. Mitchell Sanders carried a set of starched tiger fatigues[5] for special occasions. Henry Dobbins carried Black Flag insecticide. Dave Jensen carried empty sandbags that could be filled at night for added protection. Lee Strunk carried tanning lotion. Some things they carried in common. Taking turns, they carried the big PRC-77 scrambler radio, which weighed 30 pounds with its battery. They shared the weight of memory. They took up what others could no longer bear. Often, they carried each other, the wounded or weak. They carried infections. They carried chess sets, basketballs, Vietnamese-English dictionaries, insignia of rank, Bronze Stars and Purple Hearts, plastic cards imprinted with the Code of Conduct. They carried diseases, among them malaria and dysentery. They carried lice and ringworm and leeches and paddy algae and various rots and molds. They carried the land itself—Vietnam, the place, the soil—a powdery orange-red dust that covered their boots and fatigues and faces. They carried the sky. The whole atmosphere, they carried it, the humidity, the

2. Gunfighter-protagonist of *Have Gun—Will Travel*, a popular Western television series, 1957–63.

3. Short for psychological operations, military operations designed to affect the state of mind of opposing forces. *USO*: United Service Organizations (acronym), nonprofit organization (founded 1941) providing programs, services, and entertainment to U.S. military personnel and their families. *Sterno*: canned flammable jelly used as portable heat source, usually for cooking. *Trip flares*: devices used to secure an area and detect infiltrators; each consists of a tripwire that sends up a flare when disturbed or "tripped." *Joss sticks*: incense sticks. *Grease pencils*: pencils made of colored grease, usually used for writing on glossy surfaces. *The Stars and Stripes*: newspaper produced by the U.S. Department of Defense since World War II.

4. Insulated aluminum canisters used to transport hot or cold meals to troops in the field.

5. Camouflage uniform designed for jungle combat.

monsoons, the stink of fungus and decay, all of it, they carried gravity. They moved like mules. By daylight they took sniper fire, at night they were mortared, but it was not battle, it was just the endless march, village to village, without purpose, nothing won or lost. They marched for the sake of the march. They plodded along slowly, dumbly, leaning forward against the heat, unthinking, all blood and bone, simple grunts, soldiering with their legs, toiling up the hills and down into the paddies and across the rivers and up again and down, just humping, one step and then the next and then another, but no volition, no will, because it was automatic, it was anatomy, and the war was entirely a matter of posture and carriage, the hump was everything, a kind of inertia, a kind of emptiness, a dullness of desire and intellect and conscience and hope and human sensibility. Their principles were in their feet. Their calculations were biological. They had no sense of strategy or mission. They searched the villages without knowing what to look for, not caring, kicking over jars of rice, frisking children and old men, blowing tunnels, sometimes setting fires and sometimes not, then forming up and moving on to the next village, then other villages, where it would always be the same. They carried their own lives. The pressures were enormous. In the heat of early afternoon, they would remove their helmets and flak jackets, walking bare, which was dangerous but which helped ease the strain. They would often discard things along the route of march. Purely for comfort, they would throw away rations, blow their Claymores and grenades, no matter, because by nightfall the resupply choppers would arrive with more of the same, then a day or two later still more, fresh watermelons and crates of ammunition and sunglasses and woolen sweaters—the resources were stunning—sparklers for the Fourth of July, colored eggs for Easter—it was the great American war chest—the fruits of science, the smokestacks, the canneries, the arsenals at Hartford, the Minnesota forests, the machine shops, the vast fields of corn and wheat—they carried like freight trains; they carried it on their backs and shoulders—and for all the ambiguities of Vietnam, all the mysteries and unknowns, there was at least the single abiding certainty that they would never be at a loss for things to carry.

After the chopper took Lavender away, Lieutenant Jimmy Cross led his men into 40
the village of Than Khe. They burned everything. They shot chickens and dogs, they trashed the village well, they called in artillery and watched the wreckage, then they marched for several hours through the hot afternoon, and then at dusk, while Kiowa explained how Lavender died, Lieutenant Cross found himself trembling.

He tried not to cry. With his entrenching tool, which weighed 5 pounds, he began digging a hole in the earth.

He felt shame. He hated himself. He had loved Martha more than his men, and as a consequence Lavender was now dead, and this was something he would have to carry like a stone in his stomach for the rest of the war.

All he could do was dig. He used his entrenching tool like an ax, slashing, feeling both love and hate, and then later, when it was full dark, he sat at the bottom of his foxhole and wept. It went on for a long while. In part, he was grieving for Ted Lavender, but mostly it was for Martha, and for himself, because she belonged to another world, which was not quite real, and because she was a junior at Mount

Sebastian College in New Jersey, a poet and a virgin and uninvolved, and because he realized she did not love him and never would.

Like cement, Kiowa whispered in the dark. I swear to God—boom, down. Not a word.

45 I've heard this, said Norman Bowker.

A pisser, you know? Still zipping himself up. Zapped while zipping.

All right, fine. That's enough.

Yeah, but you had to see it, the guy just—

I *heard*, man. Cement. So why not shut the fuck *up*?

50 Kiowa shook his head sadly and glanced over at the hole where Lieutenant Jimmy Cross sat watching the night. The air was thick and wet. A warm dense fog had settled over the paddies and there was the stillness that precedes rain.

After a time Kiowa sighed.

One thing for sure, he said. The lieutenant's in some deep hurt. I mean that crying jag—the way he was carrying on—it wasn't fake or anything, it was real heavy-duty hurt. The man cares.

Sure, Norman Bowker said.

Say what you want, the man does care.

55 We all got problems.

Not Lavender.

No, I guess not, Bowker said. Do me a favor, though.

Shut up?

That's a smart Indian. Shut up.

60 Shrugging, Kiowa pulled off his boots. He wanted to say more, just to lighten up his sleep, but instead he opened his New Testament and arranged it beneath his head as a pillow. The fog made things seem hollow and unattached. He tried not to think about Ted Lavender, but then he was thinking how fast it was, no drama, down and dead, and how it was hard to feel anything except surprise. It seemed unchristian. He wished he could find some great sadness, or even anger, but the emotion wasn't there and he couldn't make it happen. Mostly he felt pleased to be alive. He liked the smell of the New Testament under his cheek, the leather and ink and paper and glue, whatever the chemicals were. He liked hearing the sounds of night. Even his fatigue, it felt fine, the stiff muscles and the prickly awareness of his own body, a floating feeling. He enjoyed not being dead. Lying there, Kiowa admired Lieutenant Jimmy Cross's capacity for grief. He wanted to share the man's pain, he wanted to care as Jimmy Cross cared. And yet when he closed his eyes, all he could think was Boom-down, and all he could feel was the pleasure of having his boots off and the fog curling in around him and the damp soil and the Bible smells and the plush comfort of night.

After a moment Norman Bowker sat up in the dark.

What the hell, he said. You want to talk, *talk*. Tell it to me.

Forget it.

No, man, go on. One thing I hate, it's a silent Indian.

For the most part they carried themselves with poise, a kind of dignity. Now and then, however, there were times of panic, when they squealed or wanted to squeal but couldn't, when they twitched and made moaning sounds and covered their heads and said Dear Jesus and flopped around on the earth and fired their weapons blindly and cringed and sobbed and begged for the noise to stop and went wild and made stupid promises to themselves and to God and to their mothers and fathers, hoping not to die. In different ways, it happened to all of them. Afterward, when the firing ended, they would blink and peek up. They would touch their bodies, feeling shame, then quickly hiding it. They would force themselves to stand. As if in slow motion, frame by frame, the world would take on the old logic—absolute silence, then the wind, then sunlight, then voices. It was the burden of being alive. Awkwardly, the men would reassemble themselves, first in private, then in groups, becoming soldiers again. They would repair the leaks in their eyes. They would check for casualties, call in dustoffs, light cigarettes, try to smile, clear their throats and spit and begin cleaning their weapons. After a time someone would shake his head and say, No lie, I almost shit my pants, and someone else would laugh, which meant it was bad, yes, but the guy had obviously not shit his pants, it wasn't that bad, and in any case nobody would ever do such a thing and then go ahead and talk about it. They would squint into the dense, oppressive sunlight. For a few moments, perhaps, they would fall silent, lighting a joint and tracking its passage from man to man, inhaling, holding in the humiliation. Scary stuff, one of them might say. But then someone else would grin or flick his eyebrows and say, Roger-dodger, almost cut me a new asshole, *almost*.

There were numerous such poses. Some carried themselves with a sort of wist- 65
ful resignation, others with pride or stiff soldierly discipline or good humor or macho zeal. They were afraid of dying but they were even more afraid to show it.

They found jokes to tell.

They used a hard vocabulary to contain the terrible softness. *Greased* they'd say. *Offed, lit up, zapped while zipping.* It wasn't cruelty, just stage presence. They were actors. When someone died, it wasn't quite dying, because in a curious way it seemed scripted, and because they had their lines mostly memorized, irony mixed with tragedy, and because they called it by other names, as if to encyst and destroy the reality of death itself. They kicked corpses. They cut off thumbs. They talked grunt lingo. They told stories about Ted Lavender's supply of tranquilizers, how the poor guy didn't feel a thing, how incredibly tranquil he was.

There's a moral here, said Mitchell Sanders.

They were waiting for Lavender's chopper, smoking the dead man's dope. 70

The moral's pretty obvious, Sanders said, and winked. Stay away from drugs. No joke, they'll ruin your day every time.

Cute, said Henry Dobbins.

Mind blower, get it? Talk about wiggy. Nothing left, just blood and brains.

They made themselves laugh.

There it is, they'd say. Over and over—there it is, my friend, there it is—as if 75
the repetition itself were an act of poise, a balance between crazy and almost crazy, knowing without going, there it is, which meant be cool, let it ride, because Oh yeah, man, you can't change what can't be changed, there it is, there it absolutely and positively and fucking well *is*.

They were tough.

They carried all the emotional baggage of men who might die. Grief, terror, love, longing—these were intangibles, but the intangibles had their own mass and specific gravity, they had tangible weight. They carried shameful memories. They carried the common secret of cowardice barely restrained, the instinct to run or freeze or hide, and in many respects this was the heaviest burden of all, for it could never be put down, it required perfect balance and perfect posture. They carried their reputations. They carried the soldier's greatest fear, which was the fear of blushing. Men killed, and died, because they were embarrassed not to. It was what had brought them to the war in the first place, nothing positive, no dreams of glory or honor, just to avoid the blush of dishonor. They died so as not to die of embarrassment. They crawled into tunnels and walked point and advanced under fire. Each morning, despite the unknowns, they made their legs move. They endured. They kept humping. They did not submit to the obvious alternative, which was simply to close the eyes and fall. So easy, really. Go limp and tumble to the ground and let the muscles unwind and not speak and not budge until your buddies picked you up and lifted you into the chopper that would roar and dip its nose and carry you off to the world. A mere matter of falling, yet no one ever fell. It was not courage, exactly; the object was not valor. Rather, they were too frightened to be cowards.

By and large they carried these things inside, maintaining the masks of composure. They sneered at sick call. They spoke bitterly about guys who had found release by shooting off their own toes or fingers. Pussies, they'd say. Candy-asses. It was fierce, mocking talk, with only a trace of envy or awe, but even so the image played itself out behind their eyes.

They imagined the muzzle against flesh. So easy: squeeze the trigger and blow away a toe. They imagined it. They imagined the quick, sweet pain, then the evacuation to Japan, then a hospital with warm beds and cute geisha nurses.

And they dreamed of freedom birds.

At night, on guard, staring into the dark, they were carried away by jumbo jets. They felt the rush of takeoff. Gone! they yelled. And then velocity—wings and engines—a smiling stewardess—but it was more than a plane, it was a real bird, a big sleek silver bird with feathers and talons and high screeching. They were flying. The weights fell off; there was nothing to bear. They laughed and held on tight, feeling the cold slap of wind and altitude, soaring, thinking *It's over, I'm gone!*—they were naked, they were light and free—it was all lightness, bright and fast and buoyant, light as light, a helium buzz in the brain, a giddy bubbling in the lungs as they were taken up over the clouds and the war, beyond duty, beyond gravity and mortification and global entanglements—*Sin loi!*,[6] they yelled. *I'm sorry, motherfuckers, but I'm out of it, I'm goofed, I'm on a space cruise, I'm gone!*—and it was a restful, unencumbered sensation, just riding the light waves, sailing that big silver freedom bird over the mountains and oceans, over America, over the farms and great sleeping cities and cemeteries and highways and the golden arches of McDonald's, it was flight, a kind of fleeing, a kind of falling, falling higher and higher, spinning off the edge of the earth and beyond the sun and through the vast, silent vacuum where there were no burdens and where everything weighed exactly nothing—*Gone!* they screamed. *I'm*

6. Sorry or Excuse me (Vietnamese).

sorry but I'm gone!—and so at night, not quite dreaming, they gave themselves over to lightness, they were carried, they were purely borne.

On the morning after Ted Lavender died, First Lieutenant Jimmy Cross crouched at the bottom of his foxhole and burned Martha's letters. Then he burned the two photographs. There was a steady rain falling, which made it difficult, but he used heat tabs and Sterno to build a small fire, screening it with his body, holding the photographs over the tight blue flame with the tips of his fingers.

He realized it was only a gesture. Stupid, he thought. Sentimental, too, but mostly just stupid.

Lavender was dead. You couldn't burn the blame.

Besides, the letters were in his head. And even now, without photographs, 85
Lieutenant Cross could see Martha playing volleyball in her white gym shorts and yellow T-shirt. He could see her moving in the rain.

When the fire died out, Lieutenant Cross pulled his poncho over his shoulders and ate breakfast from a can.

There was no great mystery, he decided.

In those burned letters Martha had never mentioned the war, except to say, Jimmy, take care of yourself. She wasn't involved. She signed the letters Love, but it wasn't love, and all the fine lines and technicalities did not matter. Virginity was no longer an issue. He hated her. Yes, he did. He hated her. Love, too, but it was a hard, hating kind of love.

The morning came up wet and blurry. Everything seemed part of everything else, the fog and Martha and the deepening rain.

He was a soldier, after all. 90

Half smiling, Lieutenant Jimmy Cross took out his maps. He shook his head hard, as if to clear it, then bent forward and began planning the day's march. In ten minutes, or maybe twenty, he would rouse the men and they would pack up and head west, where the maps showed the country to be green and inviting. They would do what they had always done. The rain might add some weight, but otherwise it would be one more day layered upon all the other days.

He was realistic about it. There was that new hardness in his stomach. He loved her but he hated her.

No more fantasies, he told himself.

Henceforth, when he thought about Martha, it would be only to think that she belonged elsewhere. He would shut down the daydreams. This was not Mount Sebastian, it was another world, where there were no pretty poems or midterm exams, a place where men died because of carelessness and gross stupidity. Kiowa was right. Boom-down, and you were dead, never partly dead.

Briefly, in the rain, Lieutenant Cross saw Martha's gray eyes gazing back at 95
him.

He understood.

It was very sad, he thought. The things men carried inside. The things men did or felt they had to do.

He almost nodded at her, but didn't.

Instead he went back to his maps. He was now determined to perform his duties firmly and without negligence. It wouldn't help Lavender, he knew that, but from this point on he would comport himself as an officer. He would dispose of his good-luck pebble. Swallow it, maybe, or use Lee Strunk's slingshot, or just drop it along the trail. On the march he would impose strict field discipline. He would be careful to send out flank security, to prevent straggling or bunching up, to keep his troops moving at the proper pace and at the proper interval. He would insist on clean weapons. He would confiscate the remainder of Lavender's dope. Later in the day, perhaps, he would call the men together and speak to them plainly. He would accept the blame for what had happened to Ted Lavender. He would be a man about it. He would look them in the eyes, keeping his chin level, and he would issue the new SOPs in a calm, impersonal tone of voice, a lieutenant's voice, leaving no room for argument or discussion. Commencing immediately, he'd tell them, they would no longer abandon equipment along the route of march. They would police up their acts. They would get their shit together, and keep it together, and maintain it neatly and in good working order.

100 He would not tolerate laxity. He would show strength, distancing himself.

Among the men there would be grumbling, of course, and maybe worse, because their days would seem longer and their loads heavier, but Lieutenant Jimmy Cross reminded himself that his obligation was not to be loved but to lead. He would dispense with love; it was not now a factor. And if anyone quarreled or complained, he would simply tighten his lips and arrange his shoulders in the correct command posture. He might give a curt little nod. Or he might not. He might just shrug and say, Carry on, then they would saddle up and form into a column and move out toward the villages west of Than Khe.

1986, 1990

CRITICAL EXCERPTS

Steven Kaplan

From The Undying Uncertainty of the Narrator in Tim O'Brien's *The Things They Carried* (1993)[1]

Before the United States became militarily involved in defending the sovereignty of South Vietnam, it had to, as one historian recently put it, "invent" (Baritz 142–43) the country and the political issues at stake there. The Vietnam War was in many ways a wild and terrible work of fiction written by some dangerous and frightening storytellers. First the United States decided what constituted good and evil, right and wrong, civilized and uncivilized, freedom and oppression for Vietnam, according to American standards; then it traveled the long physical distance to Vietnam and attempted to make its own notions about these things clear to the Vietnamese people—ultimately by brute, technological force. For the U.S. military and government; the Vietnam that they had in effect invented became fact. For the soldiers that the government then sent there,

1. Steven Kaplan. "The Undying Uncertainty of the Narrator in Tim O'Brien's *The Things They Carried.*" *Critique*, vol. 35, no. 1, Fall 1993, pp. 43–52. *Taylor & Francis Online*, doi:10.1080/00111619.1993.9936466. Unless otherwise indicated, all footnotes are Kaplan's. Some of Kaplan's notes and works-cited entries are omitted.

however, the facts that their government had created about who was the enemy, what were the issues, and how the war was to be won were quickly overshadowed by a world of uncertainty. Ultimately, trying to stay alive long enough to return home in one piece was the only thing that made any sense to them. As David Halberstam puts it in his novel, *One Very Hot Day*, the only fact of which an American soldier in Vietnam could be certain was that "yes was no longer yes, no was no longer no, maybe was more certainly maybe" (127). Almost all of the literature on the war, both fictional and nonfictional, makes clear that the only certain thing during the Vietnam War was that nothing was certain. Philip Beidler has pointed out in an impressive study of the literature of that war that "most of the time in Vietnam, there were some things that seemed just too terrible and strange to be true and others that were just too terrible and true to be strange" (4).

The main question that Beidler's study raises is how, in light of the overwhelming ambiguity that characterized the Vietnam experience, could any sense or meaning be derived from what happened and, above all, how could this meaning, if it were found, be conveyed to those who had not experienced the war? The answer Beidler's book offers, as Beidler himself recently said at a conference on writing about the war, is that "words are all we have. In the hands of true artists . . . they may yet preserve us against the darkness" (Lomperis 87). Similarly, for the novelist Tim O'Brien, the language of fiction is the most accurate means for conveying, as Beidler so incisively puts it, "what happened (in Vietnam) . . . what might have happened, what could have happened, what should have happened, and maybe also what can be kept from happening or what can be made to happen" (87). If the experience of Vietnam and its accompanying sense of chaos and confusion can be shown at all, then for Tim O'Brien it will not be in the fictions created by politicians but in the stories told by writers of fiction.

One of Tim O'Brien's most important statements about the inherent problems of understanding and writing about the Vietnam experience appears in a chapter of his novel, *Going After Cacciato*, appropriately titled "The Things They Didn't Know." The novel's protagonist, Paul Berlin, briefly interrupts his fantasy about chasing the deserter Cacciato, who is en route from Vietnam to Paris, to come to terms with the fact that although he is physically in Vietnam and fighting a war, his understanding of where he is and what he is doing there is light-years away. At the center of the chapter is a long catalogue of the things that Berlin and his comrades did not know about Vietnam, and the chapter closes with the statement that what "they" *knew* above all else were the "uncertainties never articulated in war stories" (319). In that chapter Tim O'Brien shows that recognizing and exploring the uncertainties about the war is perhaps the closest one can come to finding anything certain at all. Paul Berlin, in his fantasy about escaping the war and chasing Cacciato to Paris, is in fact attempting to confront and, as far as possible, understand the uncertainties of the Vietnam War through the prism of his imagination. [. . .]

In his most recent work of fiction,[2] *The Things They Carried*, Tim O'Brien takes the act of trying to reveal and understand the uncertainties about the war

2. The reviewers of this book are split on whether to call it a novel or a collection of short stories. In a recent interview, I asked Tim O'Brien what he felt was the most adequate designation. He said that *The Things They Carried* is neither a collection of stories nor a novel: he preferred to call it a work of fiction.

one step further, by looking at it through the imagination. He completely destroys the fine line dividing fact from fiction and tries to show, even more so than in *Cacciato*, that fiction (or the imagined world) can often be truer, especially in the case of Vietnam, than fact. In the first chapter, an almost documentary account of the items referred to in the book's title, O'Brien introduces the reader to some of the things, both imaginary and concrete, emotional and physical, that the average foot soldier had to carry through the jungles of Vietnam. All of the "things" are depicted in a style that is almost scientific in its precision. We are told how much each subject weighs, either psychologically or physically, and, in the case of artillery, we are even told how many ounces each round weighed [. . .].

Even the most insignificant details seem worth mentioning. One main character is not just from Oklahoma City but from "Oklahoma City, Oklahoma" (5), as if mentioning the state somehow makes the location more factual, more certain. More striking than this obsession with even the minutest detail, however, is the academic tone that at times makes the narrative sound like a government report. We find such transitional phrases as "for instance" (5) and "in addition" (7), and whole paragraphs are dominated by sentences that begin with "because" (5). These strengthen our impression that the narrator is striving, above all else, to convince us of the reality, of the concrete certainty, of the things they carried.

In the midst of this factuality and certainty, however, are signals that all the information in this opening chapter will not amount to much: that the certainties are merely there to conceal uncertainties and that the words following the frequent "becauses" do not provide an explanation of anything. We are told in the opening page that the most important thing that First Lieutenant Jimmy Cross carried were some letters from a girl he loved. The narrator [. . .] tells us that the girl did not love Cross, but that he constantly indulged in "hoping" and "pretending" (3) in an effort to turn her love into fact. We are also told "she was a virgin," but this is immediately qualified by the statement that "he was almost sure" of this (3). On the next page, Cross becomes increasingly uncertain as he sits at "night and wonder(s) if Martha was a virgin" (4). Shortly after this, Cross wonders who had taken the pictures he now holds in his hands "because he knew she had boyfriends" (5), but we are never told how he "knew" this. At the end of the chapter, after one of Cross's men has died because Cross was too busy thinking of Martha, Cross sits at the bottom of his foxhole crying, not so much for the member of his platoon who has been killed "but mostly it was for Martha, and for himself, because she belonged to another world, and because she was . . . a poet and a virgin and uninvolved" (17).

This pattern of stating facts and then quickly calling them into question that is typical of Jimmy Cross's thoughts in these opening pages characterizes how the narrator portrays events throughout this book: the facts about an event are given; they then are quickly qualified or called into question; from this uncertainty emerges a new set of facts about the same subject that are again called into question—on and on, without end.

* * *

By giving the reader facts and then calling those facts into question, by telling stories and then saying that those stories happened (147), and then that they did not happen (203), and then that they might have happened (204), O'Brien puts more emphasis in *The Things They Carried* on the question that he first posed in *Going After Cacciato*: how can a work of fiction become paradoxically more real than the events upon which it is based, and how can the confusing experiences of the average soldier in Vietnam be conveyed in such a way that they will acquire at least a momentary sense of certainty.

• • •

When we conceptualize life, we attempt to step outside ourselves and look at who we are. We constantly make new attempts to conceptualize our lives and uncover our true identities because looking at who we might be is as close as we can come to discovering who we actually are. Similarly, representing events in fiction is an attempt to understand them by detaching them from the "real world" and placing them in a world that is being staged. In *The Things They Carried*. Tim O'Brien desperately struggles to make his readers believe that what they are reading is true because he wants them to step outside their everyday reality and participate in the events that he is portraying: he wants us to believe in his stories to the point where we are virtually in the stories so that we might gain a more thorough understanding of, or feeling for, what is being portrayed in them. Representation as O'Brien practices it in this book is not a mimetic act but a "game," as [Wolfgang] Iser calls it in [. . .] "The Play of the Text," a process of acting things out:

> Now since the latter (the text) is fictional, it automatically invokes a convention-governed contract between author and reader indicating that the textual world is to be viewed not as reality but as if it *were* reality. And so whatever is repeated in the text is not meant to denote the world, but merely a world enacted. This may well repeat an identifiable reality, but it contains one all-important difference: what happens within it is relieved of the consequences inherent in the real world referred to. Hence in disclosing itself, fictionality signalizes that everything is only to be taken *as if* it were what it seems to be, to be taken—in other words—as play. (251)

In *The Things They Carried*, representation includes staging what might have happened in Vietnam while simultaneously questioning the accuracy and credibility of the narrative act itself. The reader is thus made fully aware of being made a participant in a game, in a "performative act," and thereby also is asked to become immediately involved in the incredibly frustrating act of trying to make sense of events that resist understanding. The reader is permitted to experience at first hand the uncertainty that characterized being in Vietnam.

• • •

The narrative strategy that O'Brien uses in this book to portray the uncertainty of what happened in Vietnam is not restricted to depicting war, and O'Brien does not limit it to the war alone. He concludes his book with a chapter titled "The Lives of the Dead" in which he moves from his experiences in Vietnam back to when he was nine years old. On the surface, the book's last chapter is about O'Brien's first date, his first love, a girl named Linda who died of a brain tumor a few months after he had taken her to see the movie, *The Man Who Never Was*. What this chapter is really about, however, as its title suggests, is how the dead (which also include people who may never have actually existed) can be given life in a work of fiction. In a story, O'Brien tells us, "memory and imagination and language combine to make spirits in the head. There is the illusion of aliveness" (260). Like the man who never was in the film of that title, the people that never were except in memories and the imagination can become real or alive, if only for a moment, through the act of storytelling.

According to O'Brien, when you tell a story, really tell it, "you objectify your own experience. You separate it from yourself" (178). By doing this you are able to externalize "a swirl of memories that might otherwise have ended in paralysis or worse" (179). However, the storyteller does not just escape from the events and people in a story by placing them on paper; as we have seen, the act of telling a given story is an on-going and never-ending process. By constantly involving and then re-involving the reader in the task of determining what "actually" happened in a given situation, in a story, and by forcing the reader to experience the impossibility of ever knowing with any certainty what actually happened, O'Brien liberates himself from the lonesome responsibility of remembering and trying to understand events. He also creates a community of individuals immersed in the act of experiencing the uncertainty or indeterminacy of all events, regardless of whether they occurred in Vietnam, in a small town in Minnesota (253–273), or somewhere in the reader's own life.

O'Brien thus saves himself, as he puts it in the last sentence of his book, from the fate of his character Norman Bowker who, in a chapter called "Speaking of Courage," kills himself because he cannot find some lasting meaning in the horrible things he experienced in Vietnam. O'Brien saves himself by demonstrating in this book that the most important thing is to be able to recognize and accept that events have no fixed or final meaning and that the only meaning that events can have is one that emerges momentarily and then shifts and changes each time that the events come alive as they are remembered or portrayed.

The character Norman Bowker hangs himself in the locker room of the local YMCA after playing basketball with some friends (181), partially because he has a story locked up inside of himself that he feels he cannot tell because no one would want to hear it. [. . .]

O'Brien, after his war, took on the task "of grabbing people by the shirt and explaining exactly what had happened to me" (179). He explains in *The Things They Carried* that it is impossible to know "exactly what had happened." He wants us to know all of the things he/they/we did not know about Vietnam and will probably never know. He wants us to feel the sense of uncertainty that his character/narrator Tim O'Brien experiences twenty years after the war when he returns to the place where his friend Kiowa sank into a "field of shit" and tries to find "something meaningful and right" (212) to say but ultimately can only say, "well . . . there it is" (212). Each time we, the readers of *The Things They Carried*, return to Vietnam through O'Brien's labyrinth of stories, we become more and more aware that this statement is the closest we probably ever will come to knowing the "real truth," the undying uncertainty of the Vietnam War.

WORKS CITED

Baritz, Loren. *Backfire: A History of How American Culture Led Us into Vietnam and Made Us Fight the Way We Did*. New York: Morrow, 1985.

Beidler, Philip. *American Literature and the Experience of Vietnam*. Athens: U of Georgia P, 1982.

Halberstam, David. *One Very Hot Day*. New York: Houghton, 1967.

Iser, Wolfgang. *Prospecting: From Reader Response to Literary Anthropology*. Baltimore: Johns Hopkins UP, 1989.

Lomperis, Timothy. *"Reading the Wind": The Literature of the Vietnam War: An Interpretative Critique*. Durham: Duke UP, 1989.

O'Brien, Tim. *Going After Cacciato*. New York: Dell, 1978.

———. *The Things They Carried*. Boston: Houghton, 1990.

Lorrie N. Smith

From "The Things Men Do": The Gendered Subtext in Tim O'Brien's *Esquire* Stories (1994)[1]

Tim O'Brien's 1990 book of interlocked stories, *The Things They Carried*, garnered one rave review after another, reinforcing O'Brien's already established position as one of the most important veteran writers of the Vietnam War. The Penguin paperback edition serves up six pages of superlative blurbs like "consummate artistry," "classic," "the best American writer of his generation," "unique," and "master work." A brilliant metafictionist,[2] O'Brien captures the moral and ontological uncertainty experienced by men at war, along with enough visceral realism to "make the stomach believe," as his fictional narrator, Tim O'Brien, puts it. [. . .] Yet, O'Brien—and his reviewers—seem curiously unselfconscious about this book's obsession with and ambivalence about representations of masculinity and femininity, particularly in the five stories originally published during the 1980s in *Esquire*. If this observation is accurate, and if, as one reviewer (Harris) claims, O'Brien's book exposes the nature of all war stories," then we might postulate that "all war stories" are constituted by what Eve Kosofsky Sedgwick calls, in another context, a "drama of gender difference" (6). The book diverts attention from this central play by constructing an elaborate and captivating metafictional surface, but the drama is finally exposed by the sheer exaggeration and aggressiveness of its gendered roles and gendering gestures. "The things" his male characters "carried" to war, it turns out, include plenty of patriarchal baggage. O'Brien purports to tell "true" war stories, but stops short of fully interrogating their ideological underpinnings—either in terms of the binary construction of gender that permeates representations of war in our culture, or in terms of the Vietnam War itself as a political event implicated in

1. Lorrie N. Smith. "'The Things Men Do': The Gendered Subtext in Tim O'Brien's *Esquire* Stories." *Critique*, vol. 36, no. 1, Fall 1994, pp. 16–40. *Taylor & Francis Online*, doi:10.1080/00111619.1994.9935239. Unless otherwise indicated, all footnotes are Smith's. Some of Smith's footnotes and works-cited entries have been omitted.

2. That is, a writer of *metafiction*, fiction that draws attention to its status as fiction in order to explore the nature of fiction and the role of authors and readers [editor's note].

racist, ethnocentric assumptions. Hence, the text offers no challenge to a discourse of war in which apparently innocent American men are tragically wounded and women are objectified, excluded, and silenced. My intent in bringing this subtext to light is not to devalue O'Brien's technical skill or emotional depth, but to account for my own discomfort as a female reader and to position *The Things They Carried* within a larger cultural project to rewrite the Vietnam War from a masculinist and strictly American perspective.

As much about the act of writing as about war itself, O'Brien's book celebrates the reconstructive power of the imagination, which gives shape, substance, and significance to slippery emotion and memory. We might even say that imagination itself—as embodied in the act of storytelling—plays the hero in this book, countering our national propensity for amnesia and offering the hope of personal redemption. O'Brien has often spoken of the imagination as a morally weighted force shaping the narratives and myths we live by. In Timothy Lomperis's *Reading the Wind*, for instance, O'Brien comments, "It's a real thing and I think influences in a major way the kind of real-life decisions we made to go to the war or not to go to the war. Either way, we imagine our futures and then try to step into our own imaginations . . . the purpose of fiction is to explore moral quandaries" (48, 52). In a more recent interview, he claims "exercising the imagination is the main way of finding truth" (Naparsteck 10). Taking his cue from O'Brien, critic Philip Beidler asserts that form, theme, and moral imperative merge in *The Things They Carried*: "It is at once a summation of Tim O'Brien's re-writing of the old dialectic of facts and fictions and a literally exponential prediction of new contexts of vision and insight, of new worlds to remember, imagine, believe" (32–33).

[. . .] By the end of the book, storytelling even carries the power of salvation and transubstantiation: "As a writer now, I want to save Linda's life . . . in a story I can steal her soul. I can revive, at least briefly, that which is absolute and unchanging. In a story, miracles can happen" (265). Writing, like life, entails choice; unlike life, it also offers endless possibility. Hence, O'Brien's stories often offer multiple versions of "reality," complicating the ambiguously entwined experience, memory, and retelling of Vietnam [. . .]. The book insistently asserts that "story-truth is truer sometimes than happening truth" (203) and admits that some stories, are simply "beyond telling" (79), can only be apprehended by those who experienced the event. Storytelling is finally a ritual both private and shared, a yearning toward wholeness, coherence, and meaning even while admitting their elusiveness.[3]

But who is invited to share this ritual? Despite its valorization of storytelling, *The Things They Carried* repeatedly underscores the incommunicability of war.

3. Like Toni Morrison's *Beloved*, *The Things They Carried* is fueled by the problem of how to tell stories about unspeakable trauma and how to make peace with the ghosts of the dead. This comparison sheds light on how texts and narrative strategies are gendered. Morrison's narrative of "re-memory" circles around the central story in a complex interplay of voices and sub-stories; its impulse is generous, inclusive, and collective, aimed at regeneration for a whole community as well as Sethe and her traumatized family. For a fuller treatment of this idea in Morrison, see Linda Krumholz. O'Brien's stories, as I hope to show, deal with trauma and the threat to the masculine subject by excluding women, both as readers and as characters. Though storytelling often reinforces camaraderie and redeems the solitary narrator, it does not include a whole community traumatized by the Vietnam War, nor does it attempt, as Morrison's story does, to recover a collective repressed history.

This paradox has been identified by Kali Tal, who defines writing by Vietnam veterans as a literature of trauma, with analogues to writing by survivors of the Holocaust, slavery, incest, rape, and torture. For Tal, "Trauma literature demonstrates the unbridgeable gap between writer and reader and thus defines itself by the impossibility of its task—the communication of the traumatic experience" ("Speaking" 218). Tal challenges critics to account for the "inherent contradiction within literature by Vietnam veterans" by recognizing that "the symbols generated by liminality are readable only to those familiar with the alphabet of trauma" (239). I agree in general with this claim but would qualify it with Susan Jeffords's argument that revisionist cultural and literary productions over the past decade have restored the once-stigmatized Vietnam veteran to a position of power and status. Indeed, thanks largely to Oliver Stone, Sylvester Stallone,[4] and Ron Kovic, veteran writers have increasingly had access to a discourse that is all *too* readable and familiar in our culture. The "alphabet of trauma," that is, has been encoded as a narrative of wounded American manhood that depends, for its meaning—whether tragic, ironic, or redemptive—on the positioning of women and Vietnamese as others.[5]

In an earlier essay, Tal found connections between the aims of feminist criticism and literature of Vietnam combat veterans who choose "to renounce their inherited white male power" ("Feminist Criticism" 199). Such texts, not surprisingly, are rare; more often, veterans' narratives fight bitterly to regain and sustain the power that the war temporarily disrupted. Hence, a consideration of how gender constructs affect the Vietnam veteran's rewriting of trauma opens a deeper gap than Tal identifies, in terms of both textual representation and the position and response of the reader. O'Brien often depicts war as inaccessible to nonveterans, creating a storytelling loop between characters within stories that excludes the uninitiated reader and privileges the authority of the soldiers' experience. But it is important to note that the moments of deepest trauma in the book occur when the masculine subject is threatened with dissolution or displacement. All readers are to some extent subjugated by O'Brien's shifty narrator: however, the female reader, in particular, is rendered marginal and mute, faced with the choice throughout the book of either staying outside the story or reading against herself from a masculine point of view. O'Brien repeatedly inscribes the outsider as female, hence reinforcing masculine bonds that lessen the survivor/outsider distinction for male readers. Male characters are granted many moments of mutual understanding, whereas women pointedly won't, don't, or can't understand war stories. In short, O'Brien writes women out of the war and the female reader out of the storytelling circle.

For all its polyphonic, postmodernist blurring of fact and fiction, *The Things They Carried* preserves a very traditional gender dichotomy, insistently representing abject femininity to reinforce dominant masculinity and to preserve the

4. Star (b. 1946) of (mainly action) films including *First Blood* (1982), the first of three movies about troubled Vietnam veteran John Rambo. *Oliver Stone*: Vietnam veteran (b. 1946) and director of films including *Born on the Fourth of July* (1989), based on the best-selling autobiography of paralyzed Vietnam veteran turned antiwar activist Ron Kovic (b. 1946) [editor's note].

5. For elaborations on the ways Vietnam War literature has worked to rehabilitate male veterans and masculinity, see Susan Jeffords, Jacqueline Lawson, and Lorrie Smith. Lynne Hanley explores female alternatives to "belligerent" narratives.

writing of war stories as a masculine privilege. Specifically, O'Brien uses female figures to mediate the process in homosocial bonding, a narrative strategy Sedgwick plots as a triangulation:

> In the presence of a woman who can't be seen as pitiable or contemptible, men are able to exchange power and to confirm each other's value even in the context of the remaining inequalities in their power. The sexually pitiable or contemptible female figure is a solvent that not only facilitates the relative democratization that grows up with capitalism and cash exchange, but goes a long way—for the men whom she leaves bonded together—toward palliating its gaps and failures. (160)

If we transfer Sedgwick's paradigm from the realm of class struggle to the current cultural contest over the meaning, communicability, and "gaps and failures" of the Vietnam War, we can understand how O'Brien's representations of "contemptible" femininity strengthen male bonds and deflect the contemporaneous assaults of an emasculating lost war, the women's movement, and feminist theory. We might even place the female reader at one corner of the triangle, her exclusion facilitating the bond between male writer and reader. Anxiety over the general incommunicabilty of trauma is thus greatly eased by the shared language of patriarchy.

Starring the now conventional trope of a democratic platoon of characters, this collection of stories suppresses any signifiers of age, race, class, or ideology to accentuate the common bond of masculinity. O'Brien closes male ranks in this book, celebrating camaraderie and preempting complicity or identification on the part of the female reader. Lavishing sensitive attention to the depth and complexity of men's emotions and rescuing their humanity in the face of a dehumanizing war, O'Brien represents women not as characters with agency and sensibility of their own, but as projections of a narrator trying to resolve the trauma of the war. Although he seems at points to engage and question conventional gender constructions, in the end he does so only to quell threats to masculinity and to re-assert patriarchal order. For all its internal resistance to narrative closure, the book's framing narrative is a hermeneutic circle: men at war act like men at war, and only men can write about it and understand it. [. . .]

Critics like Beidler who ignore gender can thus read *The Things They Carried* as a high achievement in the cultural project he sees writers of the Vietnam generation undertaking: to "reconstitute [American cultural mythology] as a medium both of historical self-reconsideration and, in the same moment, of historical self-renewal and even self-invention" (5). Such a grand(iose) humanistic accomplishment can only be achieved if we overlook how dominant conceptions of culture, self, and history erase or subjugate the female subject. Once we admit this asymmetry and oppression, totalizing myths of "universal truth" like those Beidler reads in O'Brien and other writers of the Vietnam generation become impossible. A feminist reading of fiction by Vietnam veterans reveals quite a different cultural and discursive project: what I have elsewhere labeled "backlash" and what Susan Jeffords calls "the remasculinization of America." Jeffords details how the proliferation of texts and films about the Vietnam War, especially during the 1980s, has contributed to "the large-scale renegotiation and regeneration of the interests, values, and projects of patriarchy now taking place in U.S. social relations." More specifically, "the representational features of the Vietnam War are structurally written through relations of gender, relations designed primarily to reinforce the interests of masculinity and patriarchy" (xi). Because Tim O'Brien is indisputably canonized as a major "Vietnam author in his generation" and *The Things They Carried* is widely acclaimed, it merits close examination in the context of this larger cultural work of consolidating the masculine subject, cementing male bonds, and preempting or silencing feminist dissent.

II

The core of *The Things They Carried* consists of five long stories originally published in *Esquire* during the late 1980s—the period in which Susan Faludi documents an "undeclared war on American women" and Jeffords locates the rehabilitation of temporarily outcast male Vietnam veterans. (Women veterans, of course, have never been visible enough to be cast out.)

* * *

III

[. . .] It seems more than coincidental that the [O'Brien] stories that most deeply probe and most emphatically reassert masculinity should appear in this glossy, upscale men's magazine famous, as Faludi puts it, for its "screeds against women." The intended audience for this magazine (subtitled "Man at His Best") is unabashedly male, and though O'Brien's stories rarely show men at their best, they do speak to a self-conscious and perhaps threatened masculinity. (Anyone familiar with Vietnam studies will also associate *Esquire* with a controversial and often-quoted article by William Broyles entitled "Why Men Love War.") As with *Playboy*, the female reader opening these pages ventures into alien and dangerous territory. Ultimately, reading war, like experiencing, remembering, and writing it, is constructed as a masculine rite.

The narrative structure of these stories is very similar: alternating radically disjunctive passages of past and present, fiction and commentary, war and memory. The force that presumes to reconcile these dualities and overcome the confounding incommunicability of war is the writer's imagination, articulated from a masculine point of view. In both the opening and closing stories of the volume, imagination is linked to an idealized, unattainable woman—Martha, a girlfriend at home, and Linda, a childhood sweetheart who died at nine. The first story plays one of the many variations on the imagination-reality motif and picks up where O'Brien's earlier novel, *Going After Cacciato,* left off, with Paul Berlin imagining himself pleading for peace at the Paris Peace Talks but admitting: "Even in imagination we must be true to our obligations, for, even in imagination, obligation cannot be outrun. Imagination, like reality, has its limits" (378). "The Things They Carried" goes further to limit the imagination, asserting that in battle, "Imagination was a killer." What this means, on one level, is that the nerve-wracking tension in the field could lead soldiers to imagine the worst or make a fatal mistake. But the story also establishes an inexorable equation: imagination=women=distraction=danger=death. The story's dramatic resolution turns on recovering masculine power by suppressing femininity in both female and male characters. Survival itself depends on excluding women from the masculine bond. In this first story, the renunciation of femininity is a sad but necessary cost of war, admitted only after real emotional struggle. It establishes a pattern, however, for the rest of the book.

"The Things They Carried" introduces the cast of Alpha Company and establishes their identity as a cohesive group, each manfully carrying his own weight but also sharing the burden of war. The story features Lieutenant Jimmy Cross, the platoon's 24-year-old C. O., who fell into the war via ROTC. He is presented as a man of integrity, honesty, and deep compassion for his men, a cautious, somewhat stiff and unseasoned commander with no inherent lust for death and destruction. The story is fundamentally an initiation narrative whose tension lies in Jimmy Cross's need to deal with guilt and harden himself to battle realities, which are here distinctly differentiated from the realm of imagination. Jimmy Cross's story alternates with lyrical passages cataloguing all the "things" men at war carry, including "all the emotional baggage of men who might die." These passages, echoing O'Brien's earlier constraints of "obligation," insistently repeat the idea that "the things they carried were largely determined by necessity. [. . .]" (4, 5).

Lieutenant Jimmy Cross's survival and his coming of age as an effective soldier depend on letting go of all that is not necessary and immediate—here equated completely with the feminine, the romantic, the imaginary. Becoming a warrior entails a pattern of desire, guilt, and renunciation in relation to a woman. The story opens by describing in detail Jimmy Cross's most precious cargo:

> First Lieutenant Jimmy Cross carried letters from a girl named Martha, a junior at Mount Sebastian College in New Jersey. They were not love letters, but Lieutenant Cross was hoping, so he kept them folded in plastic at the bottom of his rucksack. In the late afternoon, after a day's march, he would dig his foxhole, wash his hands under a canteen, unwrap the letters, hold them with the tips of his fingers, and spend the last hour of light pretending. He would imagine romantic camping trips. [. . .] More than anything, he wanted Martha to love him as he loved her, but the letters were mostly chatty, elusive on the matter of love. She was a virgin, he was almost sure. (4)

Martha's writing—and, implicitly, her reading of his war experience—are sexualized through association: her inability to respond to his love and his longing suggest the blank page of virginity in patriarchal discourse. Though Jimmy Cross tries to realize a connection with Martha through this sacramental/sexual ritual, she is represented as aloof and untouchable, a poet with "grey, neutral" eyes inhabiting "another world, which was not quite real." Martha's words are never presented directly, but are paraphrased by the narrator, who reminds us twice that she never mentions the war in her letters. Like other women in the book, she represents all those back home who will never understand the warrior's trauma. In addition to the letters, Jimmy Cross carries two pictures of Martha and a good-luck charm—a stone Martha sent from the Jersey Shore [. . .]. As the story progresses, Martha—rather these metonymic objects signifying Martha—becomes a distraction from the immediate work of war and caring for his men. His mind wanders, usually into the realm of sexual fantasy: "Slowly, a bit distracted, he would get up and move among his men, checking the perimeter, then at full dark he would return to his hole and watch the night and wonder if Martha was a virgin" (4). Memory and desire intertwine in a fantasy that fuses courage and virility and, by extension, fighting and writing upon her blank virgin page. In one of the book's several retrospective "should haves," Jimmy Cross remembers a date with Martha and thinks "he should've done something brave. He should've carried her up the stairs to her room and tied her to the bed and touched that left knee all night long. He should've risked it. Whenever he looked at the photographs, he thought of new things he should've done" (6). We are meant to see the move from chivalry to sado-masochistic erotica as natural and understandable, because "He was just a kid at war, in love," after all. That Jimmy Cross's sexual "bravery" might have been earned through violation and coercion is not considered in the story. The focus is on the male's empowering fantasy.

Jimmy Cross's distraction climaxes with the sniper shooting of Ted Lavender "on his way back from peeing." Just before this incident, the company had waited tensely for Lee Strunk to emerge from clearing out a Vietcong tunnel. The language of sexual desire and union, coming just before Lee Strunk's "rising from the dead" and Lavender's death, links Jimmy's imagination of Martha—his merging with the feminine—with annihilation of the self. As he gazes suggestively down into the dark tunnel, he leaves the war and succumbs to a fantasy of perfect union between masculine and feminine, death and desire:

> And then suddenly, without willing it, he was thinking about Martha. The stresses and fractures, the quick collapse, the two of them buried alive under all that weight. Dense, crushing love. Kneeling, watching the hole, he tried to concentrate on Lee Strunk and the war, all the dangers, but his love was too much for him, he felt paralyzed, he wanted to sleep inside her lungs and breathe her blood and be smothered. He wanted his to be a virgin and not a virgin, all at once. He wanted to know her. (12)

Such unraveling of gender duality, however, is dangerous, such paradoxes unsustainable. At the moment of Jimmy's imagined dissolution, Ted Lavender is shot. As if to punish himself for daydreaming and forgetting "about matters of security"—but more deeply for abandoning his men in the desire to know the feminine—Jimmy Cross goes to the extreme of rejecting desire for Martha altogether. He reacts to the trauma of Lavender's death in two significant ways. The first is one of the book's parallel scenes of My Lai–like[6] retribution, here bluntly told but not shown: "Lieutenant Jimmy Cross led his men into the village of Than Khe. They burned everything" (16). The second is guilt, entangled with anger that his love for Martha is unrequited. He reverts to a familiar binary choice—either Martha or his men: "He felt shame. He hated himself. He had loved Martha more than his men, and as a consequence Lavender was now dead, and

6. In the infamous My Lai Massacre, a company of U.S. soldiers, several of whose members had been maimed or killed in previous weeks, marched into the village of My Lai on March 16, 1968, and, without provocation, killed over three hundred apparently unarmed civilians [editor's note].

this was something he would have to carry, like a stone in his stomach for the rest of the war" (16)—his good luck charm transformed to the weight of guilt. That night he cries "for Ted Lavender" but also for the realization, or perhaps rationalization, that "Martha did not love him and never would." Jimmy Cross regains a "mask of composure" necessary to survive war's horror, burns Martha's letters and photographs in a purgative ritual reversing the opening blessing, and wills himself to renounce Martha and all she signifies: "He hated her. Yes, he did. He hated her. Love, too, but it was a hard, hating kind of love" (23). With this rejection and a newly hardened, terse idiom, Jimmy Cross completes his transformation: "He was a soldier, after all. . . . He was realistic about it. . . . He would be a man about it. . . . No more fantasies. . . . from this point on he would comport himself as an officer. . . . he would dispense with love; it was not now a factor" (23–24). His survival as a soldier and a leader depends upon absolute separation from the feminine world and rejection of his own femininity: "Henceforth, when he thought about Martha, it would be only to think that she belonged elsewhere. He would shut down the day-dreams. This was not Mount Sebastian, it was another world, where there were no pretty poems or midterm exams, a place where men died because of carelessness and gross stupidity" (24).

How are we meant to read this rejection? O'Brien is not blaming Martha for male suffering, for of course, the story isn't *about* Martha at all, though she introduces the book's protypical figure of the woman incapable of understanding war. Rather, he uses her to define "necessary" codes of male behavior in war and to establish Jimmy's "proper" bond with his men. We are given no rationale for why Jimmy perceives his choice in such absolute terms, nor are we invited to critique Jimmy for this rigidity, though we do pity him and recognize his naivete. Jimmy Cross's rejection of the feminine is portrayed as one of the burdensome but self-evident "necessities" of war, and O'Brien grants Jimmy this recognition: "It was very sad, he thought. The things men carried inside. The things men did or felt they had to do." Most sad and ironic of all, Jimmy ends up suffering alone because of his status as an officer: "He would show strength, distancing himself." Jimmy Cross's allegorical initials even encourage us to read his youthful renunciation in Christian terms.

At the very end, however, masculine bonds prevail and compensate for Jimmy's losses. O'Brien places the men of Alpha Company in a larger cultural landscape of men without women by alluding to cowboy movies and Huckleberry Finn: "He might just shrug and say, Carry on, then they would saddle up and form into a column and move out toward to villages west of Than Khe." The narrative voice here is very carefully distinguished from the characters, and it is hard to know how to take the conditional "might" and the self-conscious diction: as parody? as straight allusion? as Jimmy Cross's self-deluding macho fantasy? One possibility is that O'Brien means to expose and critique the social construction of masculinity, suggesting that soldiers' behavior in Vietnam is conditioned by years of John Wayne movies, as indeed numerous veterans' memoirs attest is true. Likewise, the story unmasks the soldiers' macho "stage presence," "pose," and "hard vocabulary": "Men killed, and died, because they were embarrassed not to"; they do what they "felt they had to do." But these constructions are inevitably converted into behavior that seems natural and inevitable— "necessary"—within the ur-story underlying all war stories: the tragic destruction of male innocence. O'Brien's depth as a writer allows him to reveal the socialized nature of soldiering and to show compassion for the vulnerable men behind the pose. But he stops short of undoing and revising these constructions. In the end, men *are* how they act, just as they *are* their stories and culture *is* its myths. The story rescues the humanity of men at war and consigns femininity to the margins, thus assuring the seamless continuity and endless repetition of masculine war stories.

* * *

VI

In the story that closes the book, "The Lives of the Dead," O'Brien makes a turn toward wholeness, closure, and regeneration. Here, for once, the feminine occupies a position in the same precious realm of the imagination as the masculine, although alternating sections again keep the war stories, the childhood stories, and the present-day metafictional commentary separate. The imagination, which was so dangerously distracting in "The Things They Carried," is now a force that keeps the dead alive and integrates the self by mixing memory and desire, "bringing body and soul back together," unifying through the shaping force of language and narrative form, "a little kid, twenty-three-year-old infantry sergeant, a middle-aged writer knowing guilt and sorrow" (265). The narrator alternates in this story two primal experiences of death: his view of a Vietcong corpse on his fourth day in Vietnam, and his experience of love and loss at age nine. The story resurrects Linda, his fourth grade sweetheart, who died of a brain tumor. In retrospect, he imagines their first love as "pure knowing," imbued with the knowledge that "beyond language . . . we were sharing something huge and permanent" (259). At this point in the book, the concept of merging wholly with another through "pure knowing" has accumulated the weight of fear (Jimmy Cross and Martha) and danger [. . .], both of which are also associated with transgressing normal gender codes and dissolving the socially constructed self. Here, the impulse seems to be to idealize youthful passion, distinguishing it from more frightening forms of grown-up "knowing." The narrator remembers that, in fact, his urge to tell stories has always been connected with resuscitating the dead. Grieving after Linda's death, he dreams of Linda coming back to comfort him: "Timmy, stop crying. It doesn't *matter*." In the months following, he begins to make up elaborate stories to bring Linda alive and call her into his dreams. He writes the stories down and in their vividness they become real. He gives Linda a voice (which of course is only his own dream voice, the feminine within himself) and imagines her expressing herself with a literary metaphor, once more reinforcing the connection between gender and writing/storytelling, with the female figured as absence: "'Well, right now,' she said, 'I'm *not* dead. But when I am, it's like . . . I don't know, I guess it's like being inside a book that nobody's reading." The strategy stuck with him, for "In Vietnam, too, we had ways of making the dead seem not quite so dead." The most important way, the book makes clear, is to both read and write the dead by telling stories woven "in the spell of memory and imagination."

"The Lives of the Dead" reverses the book's opening story, "The Things They Carried," for here the imagination, linked with the memory of a girl, is not a dangerous force but is redemptive and regenerative. The story also moves beyond the antagonistic polarity of gender that marks the other *Esquire* stories. Linda is forever innocent and forever young, an idealized Laura or Beatrice or Annabel Lee[7] who comes when bidden as muse for the narrator's cathartic stories. Although it sounds ungenerous to critique such a moving and lovely story, one must wonder whether the book's only positive and unthreatening representation of femininity is possible because she is forever pre-pubescent, safely encased in memory, dream, death, and narrative. Unlike Martha [. . .], she never grows up to be a castrating "cooze" or savage monster. She never touches the war, thus never intrudes upon his homosocial[8] bonds; rather, the narrator uses her, as male writers have always used female muses, to find his voice and arrive at his own understanding of his traumas. In the context of all the other war stories in the book, Linda still functions as part of a triangle; she is the mediator that facilitates the narrator's reconciliation with his own past in Vietnam and his recovery of a whole self. It is tempting to read that self as universally human, but the force of the whole preceding book cautions us that it is a masculine self wounded in war and recovered in war stories. Woman can only play dead or absent muse to the central masculine subject.

The Things They Carried contributes significantly to the canon of Vietnam War fiction. It is a remarkable treatment of the epistemology of writing and the psychology of soldiering. It dismantles many stereotypes that have dominated Hollywood treatments of the Vietnam War and distorted our understanding: the basket-case veteran (the book's narrator is reasonably well-adjusted), the macho war lover (characters such as Azar are presented as extreme aberrations), the callous officer (Jimmy Cross is fallible and sympathetic), the soldier as victim of government machinations, the peace movement, or apathetic civilians. The book probes the vulnerability of soldiers betrayed by cultural myths and registers how deeply war in our culture is a gendered activity. But O'Brien inscribes no critique of his characters' misogyny or the artificial binary opposition of masculinity and femininity, no redefinition of power, no fissure in the patriarchal discourse of war. However ambiguous and horrible Vietnam may be, and however many new combinations of memory, fact, and imagination O'Brien composes, war is still presented as an inevitable, natural phenomenon deeply meaningful to the male psyche and hostile to femininity. More pernicious, these stories seem to warn women readers away from any empathetic grasp of "the things men do." [. . .] Tim O'Brien's imaginative flights are heady, but his exclusion of women as readers and as characters finally reveals a failure of the imagination and muddy, clay feet.

7. Young, dead, but beloved heroine of the last (1849) poem by Edgar Allan Poe (1809–49), who famously declares in "The Philosophy of Composition" (1846), "The death of a beautiful woman is, unquestionably, the most poetical topic in the world." *Laura*: the beautiful but married woman, whether real or fictional, at sight of whom the Italian Renaissance poet Petrarch (1304–74) supposedly gave up his priestly vocation and the muse that inspired his influential sonnets. *Beatrice*—whom the poet Dante (1265–1321) met in childhood and who died at age twenty-four, just three years after marrying another man—performs a similar role in his life and work [editor's note].
8. Involving social relationships among people of the same sex [editor's note].

WORKS CITED

Beidler, Philip D. *Re-Writing America: Vietnam Authors in Their Generation*. Athens: U of Georgia P, 1991.

Broyles, William. "Why Men Love War." *Esquire* (Nov 84): 55–65.

Faludi, Susan. *Backlash: The Undeclared War on American Women*. New York: Crown, 1991.

Hanley, Lynne. *Writing War: Fiction, Gender and Memory*. Amherst: U of Massachusetts P, 1991.

Harris, Robert R. "Too Embarrassed Not to Kill." Review of *The Things They Carried. New York Times Book Review* 11 Mar 1990.

Jeffords, Susan. *The Remasculinization of America: Gender and the Vietnam War*. Bloomington: Indiana UP, 1991.

Krumholz, Linda. "The Ghosts of Slavery: Historical Recovery in Toni Morrison's *Beloved*." *African American Review* 26:3 (Fall 92): 395–408.

Lawson, Jacqueline. "'She a Pretty Woman . . . for a Gook': The Misogyny of the Vietnam War." In Philip K. Jason, ed. *Fourteen Landing Zones: Approaches to the Literature of the Vietnam War*. Iowa City: U of Iowa P, 1990.

Lomperis, Timothy. *"Reading the Wind": The Literature of the Vietnam War*. Durham: Duke UP, 1987.

Naparsteck, Martin. "An Interview with Tim O'Brien." *Contemporary Literature* 32:1 (Spring 91): 1–11.

O'Brien, Tim. *Going After Cacciato*. New York: Dell, 1978.

———. *The Things They Carried*. New York: Penguin, 1990.

Sedgwick, Eve Kosofsky. *Between Men: English Literature and Male Homosocial Desire*. New York: Columbia UP, 1985.

Smith, Lorrie. "Back against the Wall: Anti-Feminist Backlash in Vietnam War Literature." *Vietnam Generation* 1:3–4 (Summer–Fall, 1989): 115–126. Special issue on "Gender and the War: Men, Women and Vietnam."

Tal, Kali. "Feminist Criticism and the Literature of the Vietnam Combat Veteran." *Vietnam Generation* 1:3–4 (Summer–Fall, 1989): 190–202.

———. "Speaking the Language of Pain: Vietnam War Literature in the Context of a Literature of Trauma." In Philip K. Jason, ed. *Fourteen Landing Zones: Approaches to Vietnam War Literature*. Iowa City: U of Iowa P, 1991.

Susan Farrell

From Tim O'Brien and Gender: A Defense of *The Things They Carried*[1]

Alongside the popularity and critical acclaim awarded the outpouring of recent U.S. accounts of the Vietnam War sit some more quietly voiced criticisms of this body of literature. Perhaps the most compelling of these critiques has emerged from recent feminist scholars who argue that much Vietnam War literature replicates traditional western notions of gender and thus reinforces patriarchal institutions and beliefs. Two key works published in 1989 set the

1. Susan Farrell. "Tim O'Brien and Gender: A Defense of *The Things They Carried*." *CEA Critic*, vol. 66, no. 1, Fall 2003, pp. 1–21. Farrell's list of works cited has been abbreviated.

stage for much of the feminist criticism of Vietnam War literature that was to follow. Susan Jeffords' *The Remasculinization of America: Gender and the Vietnam War* (1989) explores popular film and narrative representations of the war. Jeffords argues for reading the war as a "construction of gendered interests," despite the fact that war might initially seem to be the domain of men and not relevant to gender analysis (81). A special issue of the journal *Vietnam Generation* devoted to the topic of gender and the war also appeared in 1989. In her introduction to this special issue, editor Jacqueline Lawson responds to a much-read *Esquire* article by ex-Marine William Broyles, Jr., "Why Men Love War." While Broyles claims that "war is the enduring condition of man, period," Lawson writes that she hopes this issue of the journal will dispel such a "canard—that war is the exclusive province of men, a closed and gendered activity inscribed by myth, informed by ritual, and enacted solely through the power relations of patriarchy" (6). To this end, she has explored some of the brutal rape and torture scenes of Vietnamese women that occur regularly in the literature.

[. . .] Critic Lorrie Smith has added to the debate, pointing out that "most popular treatments of the war—for all their claims to 'tell it like it was'—reveal more about the cultural and political climate of the 1980's than about the war itself" ("Back" 115). Smith connects a 1980s backlash against the feminist movement to the misogyny she reads in Vietnam War literature, a misogyny which she describes as "very visible," as seemingly "natural and expected." In popular representations, Smith argues, the "Vietnam War is being reconstructed as a site where white American manhood—figuratively as well as literally wounded during the war and assaulted by the women's movement for twenty years—can reassert its dominance in the social hierarchy" ("Back" 115).

The work of Tim O'Brien, while highly praised, has not been exempt from the criticism of feminist scholars. Lorrie Smith argues that the short fiction that eventually came together to make up *The Things They Carried* silences women and re-enforces traditional masculine views of war and gender. Smith writes that O'Brien's "text offers no challenge to a discourse of war in which apparently innocent American men are tragically wounded and women are objectified, excluded, and silenced" ("Things" 17). While Smith points out that her intent "is not to devalue O'Brien's technical skill or emotional depth," she does want to "account for [her] own discomfort as a female reader and to position *The Things They Carried* within a larger cultural project to rewrite the Vietnam War from a masculinist and strictly American perspective" (17). She argues that, even though O'Brien's narrator says that only those who were there can fully understand the events which occurred, he still permits a bond to form between male readers and the characters on the basis that women are completely unable to understand "the things men do." Male readers become less marked as outsiders than women as the stories progress since "the shared language of patriarchy" eases the general incommunicability of the war trauma for men (19).

Smith supports her argument with a close reading of both the longer stories that first appeared in *Esquire* magazine and the shorter vignettes that O'Brien added when he collected the material as a book. She argues that the opening, title story of the collection "establishes a pattern . . . for the rest of the book" in that it teaches readers that survival in war depends on "suppressing femininity" (24). Readers learn, as does Lieutenant Jimmy Cross, that the renunciation of the feminine, is "a sad but necessary cost of war" (24). Martha in the opening story, along with [the book's other female characters,] all represent another world: those back home who will never understand the war. Even more, this inability to understand is at least partly willful: they do not understand because they do not listen. [. . .]

While I find Smith's article thoughtful and intriguing, and while I agree with much feminist criticism of Vietnam War literature, this essay proposes that the work of Tim O'Brien, particularly *The Things They Carried*, stands apart from the genre as a whole. O'Brien is much more self-consciously aware of gender issues and critical of traditional gender dichotomies than are the bulk of U.S. writers about the Vietnam War. Though it is often tempting to forget it, readers must always bear in mind the distinction between O'Brien-the-narrator and O'Brien-the-author. This difference is crucial to understanding the book's central questions: What is truth and how can truth best be communicated? How can we truly understand the experiences of another human being? I would suggest that O'Brien posits two very different responses to these questions and that his responses are directly related to some of the concerns about gender raised by feminist critics. The male characters in the book do indeed subscribe to patriarchal and condescending attitudes about gender; they believe that knowledge is attained experientially and thus they exclude women from understanding the war experience. Yet, always running counter to this view is its corrective: that trauma is communicable, that understanding may be attained though the imaginative acts of storytelling and reading, and that the male characters do not necessarily understand war and gender as well as they think they do.

I. "The Things They Carried" [. . .]

The book's opening story, "The Things They Carried," offers two competing narratives: the ultra-realistic, precise details of what the men carry (down to brand names and weights of objects listed in ounces) versus the more personal, more traumatic story of the death of Ted Lavender. Such a form underscores one of the novel's main concerns, the relation between fact and fiction [. . .] The concrete specificity of the lists in the opening story [. . .] set[s] readers up to expect a hard-nosed, factual account of the war. Thus, we might mistakenly read Jimmy Cross's story as fact as well—an omniscient, third-person account of the reality of war experience. Such a reading would be a mistake, though. We must remember that the story of Ted Lavender's death is filtered through the subjective experience of Lieutenant Jimmy Cross. It is a narrative that increasingly interrupts and subsumes the more objective story of the items the men carry with them in the field. Yet, it is *not* a story about men at war having to renounce the feminine. Rather, it is about the inevitable guilt associated with war deaths and what soldiers do with that guilt.

While Jimmy Cross certainly views Martha as inhabiting another world, separate from the war, and thus as representing home, purity, an innocence he no longer retains, I'd argue that readers are not supposed to make the same easy gender classifications that Cross does. This point is driven home by Cross's reaction to Lavender's death. Cross is not only a romantic who fantasizes a love affair that's not really there with Martha, he greatly exaggerates his responsibility for Lavender's death. The very randomness of Lavender's death—he is "zapped while zipping," shot after separating from the men briefly to urinate—belies Jimmy Cross's responsibility for the death. Cross blames himself for the death because, as the narrator tells us in a later story, "In the Field," "When a man died, there had to be blame" (177). The soldiers wish to find a reason for the deaths they witness in order to make them less frightening, less random and meaningless. Blame can provide the illusion that war deaths such as those of Lavender and Kiowa are preventable, if only someone behaves differently, more responsibly, in the future. So, Cross determines that his love for Martha, his fantasies about her, are the cause of Lavender's death and that, to prevent such deaths in the future, he will strictly follow standard operating procedures and "dispense with love," focusing instead on duty. Ironically, Lavender dies after the platoon has just finished searching Viet Cong tunnels, a tactic that *was* standard operating procedure, but an extremely dangerous undertaking. While Lee Strunk emerges intact from such a risky assignment, Ted Lavender dies a few moments later completely unexpectedly, while conducting the ordinary business of living.

Again, readers are supposed to see the irrationality of both Cross's burden of guilt as well as his resolve to be a better officer. In fact, it is his very refusal to question orders, to deviate from standard operating procedure, that leads him to camp in the "shitfield" later in the book and inadvertently brings about the death of Kiowa, another accident, and one which many different characters claim blame for. Readers, then, are not supposed to see Cross's burning of Martha's picture and renunciation of the imagination as "sad but necessary" consequences of war, but rather as the attempts of a romantic and guilt-ridden young man to gain control over a situation in which he actually has very little power (Smith, "Things" 24). Because the burning of Martha's picture is linked to the burning of the Vietnamese village, readers see even more fully how mistaken and irrational Cross is in his reaction to Lavender's death.

• • •

V. "The Lives of the Dead"

"The Lives of the Dead" is as much a love story as it is a war story. The book, in fact, could be said to be framed by two love stories—the opening story which tells of Jimmy Cross's love for Martha and the final story which tells of the narrator's love as a nine-year-old for Linda, the little girl who dies of a brain tumor. [. . .] In "The Lives of the Dead," O'Brien deliberately juxtaposes traumatic war deaths with the traumatic death of Linda in order to undermine the old cliché of Vietnam War fiction: "if you weren't there, you can't possibly understand." "The Lives of the Dead" argues for the power of fiction, of imaginative creation. In stories, the dead *can* come to life; experiences *can* be communicated imaginatively.

The powerful status of fiction is perhaps nowhere so well illustrated as in the plot of the movie that nine-year-old Timmy attends on his date with Linda:

The Man Who Never Was. In the film, the Allies plant false documents on the body of a dead British soldier to mislead the Germans about the site of the upcoming landings in Europe. "The Germans find the documents," O'Brien writes, and "the deception wins the war" (232). The dead soldier's fictional identity is more influential than his actual, biographical identity, which we never discover. In many ways, narrator O'Brien in the book is "the man who never was." He is a created persona whose stories teach us about the difficulty of getting to the truth of individual identity. The narrator looks at a photograph of himself from 1956, realizing that, "in the important ways" he has not changed at all: "the essence remains the same . . . the human life is all one thing, like a blade tracing loops on ice" (236). What shapes a person, then, is difficult to unravel. An individual seems to be the product of biological predisposition as well as a jumble of experiences: wartime experience as well as larger life experience. In any case, human essence and selfhood remain mysterious.

Because O'Brien works so diligently to connect war experience to human experience in general, I do not read his work as excluding or silencing women. One of O'Brien's most moving pieces is a personal essay he published in the *New York Times Magazine* in 1994, called "The Vietnam in Me." In this essay, O'Brien tells two stories simultaneously—the tale of his return to Vietnam over twenty years after having been a soldier there and the story of the disintegration of a serious love relationship. Nearly suicidal over the break-up, O'Brien has difficulty sleeping and writes that he is on "war time, which is the time we're all on at one point or another: when fathers die, when husbands ask for divorce, when women you love are fast asleep beside men you wish were you" (55). Just as in "The Lives of the Dead" O'Brien links the physical corpse of the old Vietnamese man to those of Ted Lavender, Curt Lemon, and Kiowa, and finally to Linda's, O'Brien links wartime experience and life experience in this article. "If there's a lesson in this," he writes, "which there is not, it's very simple. You don't have to be in Nam to be in Nam" (55). While much Vietnam War literature expresses the "incommunicability" of war trauma, which is eased for men because of a shared patriarchal language, O'Brien's work expresses the exact opposite: that through imaginative acts of storytelling and reading, the atrocity of war can begin to be understood and thus can begin to heal.

WORKS CITED

Broyles Jr., William. "Why Men Love War." *Esquire* (November 1984): 55–65.

Jeffords, Susan. *The Remasculinization of America: Gender and the Vietnam War*. Bloomington: Indiana UP, 1989.

Lawson, Jacqueline. Introduction. *Vietnam Generation Special Issue. Gender and the War: Men, Women, and Vietnam* 1.3–4 (Summer-Fall 1989): 6–11.

O'Brien, Tim. *The Things They Carried*. New York: Houghton Mifflin, 1990.

———. "The Vietnam in Me." *New York Times Magazine* 2 October 1994: 48–57.

Smith, Lorrie N. "Back Against the Wall: Anti-Feminist Backlash in Vietnam War Literature." *Vietnam Generation Special Issue. Gender and the War: Men, Women, and Vietnam* 1.3–4 (Summer–Fall 1989): 115–126.

———. "'The Things Men Do': The Gendered Subtext in Tim O'Brien's *Esquire* Stories." *Critique: Studies in Contemporary Fiction* 36.1 (Fall 1994): 16–40.

SUGGESTIONS FOR WRITING

1. Though THE THINGS THEY CARRIED may be more obviously a "war story" than any other in this anthology, several others also deal with war or its aftereffects on combatants or civilians. These include Sherman Alexie's FLIGHT PATTERNS, William Faulkner's BARN BURNING, Amy Tan's PAIR OF TICKETS, A. S. Byatt's THE THING IN THE FOREST, and Ambrose Bierce's AN OCCURRENCE AT OWL CREEK BRIDGE. Write an essay comparing the treatment of war in at least two of these stories. What's similar and what's unique about what each story shows us or asks about war and its effects?
2. THE THINGS THEY CARRIED is written in third person, oscillating between sections that (like the title) refer to the entire platoon, as if seen from a distance, and sections that instead home in on a single focal character or consciousness. Usually, that consciousness is Jimmy Cross's. But not always. Write an essay exploring how point of view and/or other aspects of narration shape the story's effects and meaning. Why and how might it matter, for example, that in one section we "overhear" a conversation—between Bowker and Kiowa—that Jimmy isn't privy to, and even spend one paragraph inside Kiowa's thoughts?
3. Like almost every literary critic who writes about *The Things They Carried*, those whose work appears in this chapter all seem to agree that the stories in it are metafictional—that is, they in various ways draw attention to the fact that they *are* stories and thus also become *about* stories and about the relationship between fiction and reality, stories and truth. THE THINGS THEY CARRIED, however, may well be the least metafictional story in the book. Write a response paper or essay in which you analyze what, if anything, seems metafictional in and about the story and why and how exactly that might matter. Do the story's metafictional aspects make it seem less or more "true" or emotionally engaging, and in what ways?
4. Obviously, one topic of debate among scholars who write about THE THINGS THEY CARRIED is the extent to which it does and/or doesn't reproduce traditional notions of masculinity and femininity. Drawing upon both THE THINGS THEY CARRIED and the critical excerpts in this chapter, write an essay laying out your own case. Do you agree with one or another of the critics, or might both sides have missed something? Why and how so?
5. At one point in her essay, Lorrie N. Smith suggests, in passing, that THE THINGS THEY CARRIED is "fundamentally an initiation narrative" not unlike those featured in this anthology's "Initiation Stories" album. Write an essay exploring how the story works in these terms, perhaps by comparing this story to at least one other. Who is initiated? into what? In making your case, be sure to consider the different arguments the critical excerpts in this chapter make, especially about how the story as a whole encourages us to understand and feel about Jimmy Cross's thoughts and actions at the story's end.
6. *The Things They Carried* opens with the story of the same name, and it ends with "The Lives of the Dead." Write an essay interrelating or comparing the two stories, perhaps by considering some or all of the following questions: How and why exactly might THE THINGS THEY CARRIED work and mean differently when read alongside THE LIVES OF THE DEAD or vice versa? Why and how might THE THINGS THEY CARRIED work well as a sort of introduction to a fictional meditation on Vietnam and THE LIVES OF THE DEAD as a conclusion to one? In these or any terms, what might be the significance and effect of their very different styles of narration? of the way they each (differently) move back and forth in time and between different episodes or narrative modes?

7. In this chapter you have seen how a single work of literature can generate a broad range of critical responses. Taken together, these texts represent a kind of ongoing conversation between a "primary text" and "secondary texts," and among these "secondary texts" themselves. Using secondary texts available to you at a library and on the Internet, write an essay in which you join in the critical "conversation" about any of the stories you have read in another chapter of this book.

Reading More Fiction

MARGARET ATWOOD (b.1939)
Happy Endings

Margaret Atwood spent her first eleven years in sparsely populated areas of northern Ontario and Quebec, where her father worked as an entomologist—an upbringing that may help explain her enduring concern with humanity's often-destructive relationship with the natural world. Educated at the University of Toronto and Harvard, the woman now widely regarded as Canada's preeminent woman of letters published her first poem at nineteen and the first of numerous poetry collections, *Double Persephone,* three years later. An equally gifted short-story writer who counts Edgar Allan Poe among her early inspirations, Atwood is best known for her novels. Translated into over thirty languages and often, like her poetry, exploring the unique experiences and perspectives of women, past, present, and future, her novels include straightforwardly realistic narratives like *The Edible Woman* (1969) and *Bodily Harm* (1982), at least one modernized fairy tale (*The Robber Bride* [1993]), multilayered historical fictions such as *Alias Grace* (1996) and the Booker Prize–winning *The Blind Assassin* (2000), and the futuristic dystopias Atwood herself prefers to call "speculative" rather than "science fiction"—*Oryx and Crake* (2003), *The Year of the Flood* (2009), *MaddAdam* (2013), and *The Handmaid's Tale* (1986), which inspired both a Danish opera and a Hollywood movie.

John and Mary meet.
What happens next?
If you want a happy ending, try A.

A. John and Mary fall in love and get married. They both have worthwhile and remunerative jobs which they find stimulating and challenging. They buy a charming house. Real estate values go up. Eventually, when they can afford live-in help, they have two children, to whom they are devoted. The children turn out well. John and Mary have a stimulating and challenging sex life and worthwhile friends. They go on fun vacations together. They retire. They both have hobbies which they find stimulating and challenging. Eventually they die. This is the end of the story.

B. Mary falls in love with John but John doesn't fall in love with Mary. He merely uses her body for selfish pleasure and ego gratification of a tepid kind. He comes to her apartment twice a week and she cooks him dinner, you'll notice that he doesn't even consider her worth the price of a dinner out, and after he's eaten the dinner he fucks her and after that he falls asleep, while she does the dishes so he won't think she's untidy, having all those dirty dishes lying around, and puts on fresh lipstick so she'll look good when he wakes up, but when he wakes up he doesn't even notice, he puts on his socks and his shorts and his pants and his shirt and his tie and his shoes, the reverse order from the one in which he took them off. He doesn't take off Mary's clothes, she takes them off herself, she acts as if she's dying for it every time, not because she likes sex exactly, she doesn't, but she wants John to think she does because if they do it often enough surely he'll get used to her, he'll come to depend on her and they will get married, but John goes out the door with hardly so much as a good-night and three days later he turns up at six o'clock and they do the whole thing over again.

Mary gets run-down. Crying is bad for your face, everyone knows that and so does Mary but she can't stop. People at work notice. Her friends tell her John is a rat, a pig, a dog, he isn't good enough for her, but she can't believe it. Inside John, she thinks, is another John, who is much nicer. This other John will emerge like a butterfly from a cocoon, a Jack from a box, a pit from a prune, if the first John is only squeezed enough.

One evening John complains about the food. He has never complained about the food before. Mary is hurt.

Her friends tell her they've seen him in a restaurant with another woman, whose name is Madge. It's not even Madge that finally gets to Mary: it's the restaurant. John has never taken Mary to a restaurant. Mary collects all the sleeping pills and aspirins she can find, and takes them and a half a bottle of sherry. You can see what kind of a woman she is by the fact that it's not even whiskey. She leaves a note for John. She hopes he'll discover her and get her to the hospital in time and repent and then they can get married, but this fails to happen and she dies.

John marries Madge and everything continues as in A.

C. John, who is an older man, falls in love with Mary, and Mary, who is only twenty-two, feels sorry for him because he's worried about his hair falling out. She sleeps with him even though she's not in love with him. She met him at work. She's in love with someone called James, who is twenty-two also and not yet ready to settle down.

John on the contrary settled down long ago: this is what is bothering him. John has a steady, respectable job and is getting ahead in his field, but Mary isn't impressed by him, she's impressed by James, who has a motorcycle and a fabulous record collection. But James is often away on his motorcycle, being free. Freedom isn't the same for girls, so in the meantime Mary spends Thursday evenings with John. Thursdays are the only days John can get away.

John is married to a woman called Madge and they have two children, a charming house which they bought just before the real estate values went up, and hobbies which they find stimulating and challenging, when they have the time. John tells Mary how important she is to him, but of course he can't leave his wife because a commitment is a commitment. He goes on about this more than is necessary and Mary finds it boring, but older men can keep it up longer so on the whole she has a fairly good time.

One day James breezes in on his motorcycle with some top-grade California hybrid and James and Mary get higher than you'd believe possible and they climb into bed. Everything becomes very underwater, but along comes John, who has a key to Mary's apartment. He finds them stoned and entwined. He's hardly in any position to be jealous, considering Madge, but nevertheless he's overcome with despair. Finally he's middle-aged, in two years he'll be bald as an egg and he can't stand it. He purchases a handgun, saying he needs it for target practice—this is the thin part of the plot, but it can be dealt with later—and shoots the two of them and himself.

Madge, after a suitable period of mourning, marries an understanding man called Fred and everything continues as in A, but under different names.

15 D. Fred and Madge have no problems. They get along exceptionally well and are good at working out any little difficulties that may arise. But their charming house is by the seashore and one day a giant tidal wave approaches. Real estate values go down. The rest of the story is about what caused the tidal wave and how they escape from it. They do, though thousands drown, but Fred and Madge are virtuous and lucky. Finally on high ground they clasp each other, wet and dripping and grateful, and continue as in A.

E. Yes, but Fred has a bad heart. The rest of the story is about how kind and understanding they both are until Fred dies. Then Madge devotes herself to charity work until the end of A. If you like, it can be "Madge," "cancer," "guilty and confused," and "bird watching."

F. If you think this is all too bourgeois, make John a revolutionary and Mary a counterespionage agent and see how far that gets you. Remember, this is Canada. You'll still end up with A, though in between you may get a lustful brawling saga of passionate involvement, a chronicle of our times, sort of.

You'll have to face it, the endings are the same however you slice it. Don't be deluded by any other endings, they're all fake, either deliberately fake, with malicious intent to deceive, or just motivated by excessive optimism if not by downright sentimentality.

The only authentic ending is the one provided here:

20 *John and Mary die. John and Mary die. John and Mary die.*

So much for endings. Beginnings are always more fun. True connoisseurs, however, are known to favor the stretch in between, since it's the hardest to do anything with.

That's about all that can be said for plots, which anyway are just one thing after another, a what and a what and a what.

Now try How and Why.

1983

AMBROSE BIERCE
(1842–1914?)

An Occurrence at Owl Creek Bridge

The tenth child of a poor Ohio family, Ambrose Bierce served with distinction in the Union Army during the Civil War, rising to the rank of major. After the war he worked as a journalist in California and London, where his boisterous western mannerisms and savage wit made him a celebrity and earned him the name "Bitter Bierce." He is probably best known as the author of *The Cynic's Word Book* (1906; later called *The Devil's Dictionary*), but his finest achievement may be his two volumes of short stories—*Tales of Soldiers and Civilians* (1891; later called *In the Midst of Life*) and *Can Such Things Be?* (1893)—and *The Monk and the Hangman's Daughter* (1892), an adaptation of a German story. Disillusioned and depressed after his divorce and the deaths of his two sons, Bierce went to Mexico in 1913, where he reportedly rode with Pancho Villa's revolutionaries. He disappeared and is presumed to have died there.

I

A man stood upon a railroad bridge in Northern Alabama, looking down into the swift waters twenty feet below. The man's hands were behind his back, the wrists bound with a cord. A rope loosely encircled his neck. It was attached to a stout cross-timber above his head, and the slack fell to the level of his knees. Some loose boards laid upon the sleepers supporting the metals of the railway supplied a footing for him and his executioners—two private soldiers of the Federal army, directed by a sergeant, who in civil life may have been a deputy sheriff. At a short remove upon the same temporary platform was an officer in the uniform of his rank, armed. He was a captain. A sentinel at each end of the bridge stood with his rifle in the position known as "support," that is to say, vertical in front of the left shoulder, the hammer resting on the forearm thrown straight across the chest—a formal and unnatural position, enforcing an erect carriage of the body. It did not appear to be the duty of these two men to know what was occurring at the centre of the bridge; they merely blockaded the two ends of the foot plank which traversed it.

Beyond one of the sentinels nobody was in sight; the railroad ran straight away into a forest for a hundred yards, then, curving, was lost to view. Doubtless there was an outpost further along. The other bank of the stream was open ground—a gentle acclivity crowned with a stockade of vertical tree trunks, loopholed for rifles, with a single embrasure through which protruded the muzzle of a brass cannon commanding the bridge. Midway of the slope between bridge and fort were the spectators—a single company of infantry in line, at "parade rest," the butts of the rifles on the ground, the barrels inclining slightly backward against the right shoulder, the hands crossed upon the stock. A lieutenant stood at the right of the line, the point of his sword upon the ground, his left hand resting upon his right. Excepting the group of four at the centre of the bridge not a man moved. The company faced the bridge, staring stonily, motionless. The sentinels, facing the banks of the stream, might have been statues to adorn the bridge. The captain stood with folded arms, silent, observing the work of his subordinates but making no sign. Death is a dignitary who, when he comes announced, is to be received with formal manifestations of respect, even by those most familiar with him. In the code of military etiquette silence and fixity are forms of deference.

The man who was engaged in being hanged was apparently about thirty-five years of age. He was a civilian, if one might judge from his dress, which was that of a planter. His features were good—a straight nose, firm mouth, broad forehead, from which his long, dark hair was combed straight back, falling behind his ears to the collar of his well-fitting frock coat. He wore a moustache and pointed beard, but no whiskers; his eyes were large and dark grey and had a kindly expression which one would hardly have expected in one whose neck was in the hemp. Evidently this was no vulgar assassin. The liberal military code makes provision for hanging many kinds of people, and gentlemen are not excluded.

The preparations being complete, the two private soldiers stepped aside and each drew away the plank upon which he had been standing. The sergeant turned to the captain, saluted and placed himself immediately behind that officer, who in turn moved apart one pace. These movements left the condemned man and the sergeant standing on the two ends of the same plank, which spanned three of the cross-ties of the bridge. The end upon which the civilian stood almost, but not quite, reached a fourth. This plank had been held in place by the weight of the captain; it was now held by that of the sergeant. At a signal from the former, the latter would step aside, the plank would tilt and the condemned man go down between two ties. The arrangement commended itself to his judgment as simple and effective. His face had not been covered nor his eyes bandaged. He looked a moment at his "unsteadfast footing," then let his gaze wander to the swirling water of the stream racing madly beneath his feet. A piece of dancing driftwood caught his attention and his eyes followed it down the current. How slowly it appeared to move! What a sluggish stream!

5 He closed his eyes in order to fix his last thoughts upon his wife and children. The water, touched to gold by the early sun, the brooding mists under the banks at some distance down the stream, the fort, the soldiers, the piece of drift—all had distracted him. And now he became conscious of a new disturbance. Striking through the thought of his dear ones was a sound which he could neither ignore nor understand, a sharp, distinct, metallic percussion like the stroke of a blacksmith's hammer upon the anvil; it had the same ringing quality. He wondered what it was, and whether immeasurably distant or near by—it

seemed both. Its recurrence was regular, but as slow as the tolling of a death knell. He awaited each stroke with impatience and—he knew not why—apprehension. The intervals of silence grew progressively longer, the delays became maddening. With their greater infrequency the sounds increased in strength and sharpness. They hurt his ear like the thrust of a knife; he feared he would shriek. What he heard was the ticking of his watch.

He unclosed his eyes and saw again the water below him. "If I could free my hands," he thought, "I might throw off the noose and spring into the stream. By diving I could evade the bullets, and, swimming vigorously, reach the bank, take to the woods, and get away home. My home, thank God, is as yet outside their lines; my wife and little ones are still beyond the invader's farthest advance."

As these thoughts, which have here to be set down in words, were flashed into the doomed man's brain rather than evolved from it, the captain nodded to the sergeant. The sergeant stepped aside.

II

Peyton Farquhar was a well-to-do planter, of an old and highly-respected Alabama family. Being a slave owner, and, like other slave owners, a politician, he was naturally an original secessionist and ardently devoted to the Southern cause. Circumstances of an imperious nature which it is unnecessary to relate here, had prevented him from taking service with the gallant army which had fought the disastrous campaigns ending with the fall of Corinth,[1] and he chafed under the inglorious restraint, longing for the release of his energies, the larger life of the soldier, the opportunity for distinction. That opportunity, he felt, would come, as it comes to all in war time. Meanwhile he did what he could. No service was too humble for him to perform in aid of the South, no adventure too perilous for him to undertake if consistent with the character of a civilian who was at heart a soldier, and who in good faith and without too much qualification assented to at least a part of the frankly villainous dictum that all is fair in love and war.

One evening while Farquhar and his wife were sitting on a rustic bench near the entrance to his grounds, a grey-clad soldier rode up to the gate and asked for a drink of water. Mrs. Farquhar was only too happy to serve him with her own white hands. While she was gone to fetch the water, her husband approached the dusty horseman and inquired eagerly for news from the front.

"The Yanks are repairing the railroads," said the man, "and are getting ready 10
for another advance. They have reached the Owl Creek bridge, put it in order, and built a stockade on the other bank. The commandant has issued an order, which is posted everywhere, declaring that any civilian caught interfering with the railroad, its bridges, tunnels, or trains, will be summarily hanged. I saw the order."

"How far is it to the Owl Creek bridge?" Farquhar asked.

"About thirty miles."

"Is there no force on this side of the creek?"

"Only a picket post half a mile out, on the railroad, and a single sentinel at this end of the bridge."

1. Corinth, Mississippi, captured by General Ulysses S. Grant in April 1862.

15 "Suppose a man—a civilian and student of hanging—should elude the picket post and perhaps get the better of the sentinel," said Farquhar, smiling, "what could he accomplish?"

The soldier reflected. "I was there a month ago," he replied. "I observed that the flood of last winter had lodged a great quantity of driftwood against the wooden pier at this end of the bridge. It is now dry and would burn like tow."

The lady had now brought the water, which the soldier drank. He thanked her ceremoniously, bowed to her husband, and rode away. An hour later, after nightfall, he repassed the plantation, going northward in the direction from which he had come. He was a Federal scout.

III

As Peyton Farquhar fell straight downward through the bridge, he lost consciousness and was as one already dead. From this state he was awakened—ages later, it seemed to him—by the pain of a sharp pressure upon his throat, followed by a sense of suffocation. Keen, poignant agonies seemed to shoot from his neck downward through every fibre of his body and limbs. These pains appeared to flash along well-defined lines of ramification, and to beat with an inconceivably rapid periodicity. They seemed like streams of pulsating fire heating him to an intolerable temperature. As to his head, he was conscious of nothing but a feeling of fullness—of congestion. These sensations were unaccompanied by thought. The intellectual part of his nature was already effaced; he had power only to feel, and feeling was torment. He was conscious of motion. Encompassed in a luminous cloud, of which he was now merely the fiery heart, without material substance, he swung through unthinkable arcs of oscillation, like a vast pendulum. Then all at once, with terrible suddenness, the light about him shot upward with the noise of a loud plash; a frightful roaring was in his ears, and all was cold and dark. The power of thought was restored; he knew that the rope had broken and he had fallen into the stream. There was no additional strangulation; the noose about his neck was already suffocating him, and kept the water from his lungs. To die of hanging at the bottom of a river!—the idea seemed to him ludicrous. He opened his eyes in the blackness and saw above him a gleam of light, but how distant, how inaccessible! He was still sinking, for the light became fainter and fainter until it was a mere glimmer. Then it began to grow and brighten, and he knew that he was rising toward the surface—knew it with reluctance, for he was now very comfortable. "To be hanged and drowned," he thought, "that is not so bad; but I do not wish to be shot. No; I will not be shot; that is not fair."

He was not conscious of an effort, but a sharp pain in his wrist apprised him that he was trying to free his hands. He gave the struggle his attention, as an idler might observe the feat of a juggler, without interest in the outcome. What splendid effort!—what magnificent, what superhuman strength! Ah, that was a fine endeavour! Bravo! The cord fell away; his arms parted and floated upward, the hands dimly seen on each side in the growing light. He watched them with a new interest as first one and then the other pounced upon the noose at his neck. They tore it away and thrust it fiercely aside, its undulations resembling those of a water-snake. "Put it back, put it back!" He thought he shouted these words to his hands, for the undoing of the noose had been succeeded by the direst pang which he had yet experienced. His neck ached horribly; his brain was on fire; his heart, which had been fluttering faintly, gave a great leap, trying to force itself out at his mouth. His whole body was racked and wrenched with an insupportable anguish! But his disobedient hands gave no heed to the command. They beat the water vigorously with quick, downward strokes, forcing him to the surface. He felt his head emerge; his eyes were blinded by the sunlight; his chest expanded convulsively, and with a supreme and crowning agony his lungs engulfed a great draught of air, which instantly he expelled in a shriek!

20 He was now in full possession of his physical senses. They were, indeed, preternaturally keen and alert. Something in the awful disturbance of his organic system had so exalted and refined them that they made record of things never before perceived. He felt the ripples upon his face and heard their separate sounds as they struck. He looked at the forest on the bank of the stream, saw the individual trees, the leaves and the veining of each leaf—the very insects upon them, the locusts, the brilliant-bodied flies, the grey spiders stretching their webs from twig to twig. He noted the prismatic colors in all the dewdrops upon a million blades of grass. The humming of the gnats that danced above the eddies of the stream, the beating of the dragon flies' wings, the strokes of the water spiders' legs, like oars which had lifted their boat—all these made audible music. A fish slid along beneath his eyes and he heard the rush of its body parting the water.

He had come to the surface facing down the stream; in a moment the visible world seemed to wheel slowly round, himself the pivotal point, and he saw the bridge, the fort, the soldiers upon the bridge, the captain, the sergeant, the two privates, his executioners. They were in silhouette against the blue sky. They shouted and gesticulated, pointing at him; the captain had drawn his pistol, but did not fire; the others were unarmed. Their movements were grotesque and horrible, their forms gigantic.

Suddenly he heard a sharp report and something struck the water smartly within a few inches of his head, spattering his face with spray. He heard a second report, and saw one of the sentinels with his rifle at his shoulder, a light cloud of blue smoke rising from the muzzle. The man in the water saw the eye of the man on the bridge gazing into his own through the sights of the rifle. He observed that it was a grey eye, and remembered having read that grey eyes were keenest and that all famous marksmen had them. Nevertheless, this one had missed.

A counter swirl had caught Farquhar and turned him half round; he was again looking into the forest on the bank opposite the fort. The sound of a clear, high voice in a monotonous singsong now rang out behind him and came across the water with a distinctness that pierced and subdued all other sounds, even the beating of the ripples in his ears. Although no soldier, he had frequented camps enough to know the dread significance of that deliberate, drawling, aspirated chant; the lieutenant on shore was taking a part in the morning's work. How coldly and pitilessly—with what an even, calm intonation, presaging and enforcing tranquillity in the men—with what accurately-measured intervals fell those cruel words:

"Attention, company. . . . Shoulder arms. . . . Ready. . . . Aim. . . . Fire."

25 Farquhar dived—dived as deeply as he could. The water roared in his ears like the voice of Niagara, yet he heard the dulled thunder of the volley, and rising again toward the surface, met shining bits of metal, singularly flattened, oscillating slowly downward. Some of them touched him on the face and hands, then fell away, continuing their descent. One lodged between his collar and neck; it was uncomfortably warm, and he snatched it out.

As he rose to the surface, gasping for breath, he saw that he had been a long time under water; he was perceptibly farther down stream—nearer to safety. The soldiers had almost finished reloading; the metal ramrods flashed all at once in the sunshine as they were drawn from the barrels, turned in the air, and thrust into their sockets. The two sentinels fired again, independently and ineffectually.

The hunted man saw all this over his shoulder; he was now swimming vigorously with the current. His brain was as energetic as his arms and legs; he thought with the rapidity of lightning.

"The officer," he reasoned, "will not make that martinet's error a second time. It is as easy to dodge a volley as a single shot. He has probably already given the command to fire at will. God help me, I cannot dodge them all!"

An appalling plash within two yards of him, followed by a loud rushing sound, *diminuendo*, which seemed to travel back through the air to the fort and died in an explosion which stirred the very river to its deeps! A rising sheet of water, which curved over him, fell down upon him, blinded him, strangled him! The cannon had taken a hand in the game. As he shook his head free from the commotion of the smitten water, he heard the deflected shot humming through the air ahead, and in an instant it was cracking and smashing the branches in the forest beyond.

30 "They will not do that again," he thought; "the next time they will use a charge of grape. I must keep my eye upon the gun; the smoke will apprise me—the report arrives too late; it lags behind the missile. It is a good gun."

Suddenly he felt himself whirled round and round—spinning like a top. The water, the banks, the forest, the now distant bridge, fort and men—all were commingled and blurred. Objects were represented by their colors only; circular horizontal streaks of color—that was all he saw. He had been caught in a vortex and was being whirled on with a velocity of advance and gyration which made him giddy and sick. In a few moments he was flung upon the gravel at the foot of the left bank of the stream—the southern bank—and behind a projecting point which concealed him from his enemies. The sudden arrest of his motion, the abrasion of one of his hands on the gravel, restored him and he wept with delight. He dug his fingers into the sand, threw it over himself in handfuls and audibly blessed it. It looked like gold, like diamonds, rubies, emeralds; he could think of nothing beautiful which it did not resemble. The trees upon the bank were giant garden plants; he noted a definite order in their arrangement, inhaled the fragrance of their blooms. A strange, roseate light shone through the spaces among their trunks, and the wind made in their branches the music of æolian harps. He had no wish to perfect his escape, was content to remain in that enchanting spot until retaken.

A whizz and rattle of grapeshot among the branches high above his head roused him from his dream. The baffled cannoneer had fired him a random farewell. He sprang to his feet, rushed up the sloping bank, and plunged into the forest.

All that day he travelled, laying his course by the rounding sun. The forest seemed interminable; nowhere did he discover a break in it, not even a woodman's road. He had not known that he lived in so wild a region. There was something uncanny in the revelation.

By nightfall he was fatigued, footsore, famishing. The thought of his wife and children urged him on. At last he found a road which led him in what he knew to be the right direction. It was as wide and straight as a city street, yet it seemed untravelled. No fields bordered it, no dwelling anywhere. Not so much as the barking of a dog suggested human habitation. The black bodies of the great trees formed a straight wall on both sides, terminating on the horizon in a point, like a diagram in a lesson in perspective. Overhead, as he looked up through this rift in the wood, shone great golden stars looking unfamiliar and grouped in strange constellations. He was sure they were arranged in some order which had a secret and malign significance. The wood on either side was full of singular noises, among which—once, twice, and again—he distinctly heard whispers in an unknown tongue.

His neck was in pain, and, lifting his hand to it, he found it horribly swollen. 35
He knew that it had a circle of black where the rope had bruised it. His eyes felt congested; he could no longer close them. His tongue was swollen with thirst; he relieved its fever by thrusting it forward from between his teeth into the cool air. How softly the turf had carpeted the untravelled avenue! He could no longer feel the roadway beneath his feet!

Doubtless, despite his suffering, he fell asleep while walking, for now he sees another scene—perhaps he has merely recovered from a delirium. He stands at the gate of his own home. All is as he left it, and all bright and beautiful in the morning sunshine. He must have travelled the entire night. As he pushes open the gate and passes up the wide white walk, he sees a flutter of female garments; his wife, looking fresh and cool and sweet, steps down from the verandah to meet him. At the bottom of the steps she stands waiting, with a smile of ineffable joy, an attitude of matchless grace and dignity. Ah, how beautiful she is! He springs forward with extended arms. As he is about to clasp her, he feels a stunning blow upon the back of the neck; a blinding white light blazes all about him, with a sound like the shock of a cannon—then all is darkness and silence!

Peyton Farquhar was dead; his body, with a broken neck, swung gently from side to side beneath the timbers of the Owl Creek bridge.

1891

RALPH ELLISON
(1914–94)

King of the Bingo Game

After the early death of his father, Ralph Ellison was raised by his mother and by a close-knit African American community in Oklahoma City. He grew up loving jazz and began to study music at Tuskegee Institute in 1933. In 1936, Ellison moved to New York, where, with the novelist Richard Wright's encouragement, he wrote short stories, essays, and book reviews. In the years after his monumental novel *Invisible Man* (1952) won the National Book Award and earned him international acclaim, Ellison lectured and taught at various institutions, including New York University, and published *Shadow and Act* (1964), a collection of critical essays on the novelist's art. Upon his death from cancer in 1994, the literary world learned that he had been working steadily on a second major novel, begun in 1952, seemingly lost in a fire in 1967. The nearly completed manuscript was edited by Ellison's friend John F. Callahan and published as *Juneteenth* (1999).

The woman in front of him was eating roasted peanuts that smelled so good that he could barely contain his hunger. He could not even sleep and wished they'd hurry and begin the bingo game. There, on his right, two fellows were drinking wine out of a bottle wrapped in a paper bag, and he could hear soft gurgling in the dark. His stomach gave a low, gnawing growl. "If this was down South," he thought, "all I'd have to do is lean over and say, 'Lady, gimme a few of those peanuts, please ma'am,' and she'd pass me the bag and never think nothing of it." Or he could ask the fellows for a drink in the same way. Folks down South stuck together that way; they didn't even have to know you. But up here it was different. Ask somebody for something, and they'd think you were crazy. Well, I ain't crazy. I'm just broke, 'cause I got no birth certificate to get a job, and Laura 'bout to die 'cause we got no money for a doctor. But I ain't crazy. And yet a pinpoint of doubt was focused in his mind as he glanced toward the screen and saw the hero stealthily entering a dark room and sending the beam of a flashlight along a wall of bookcases. This is where he finds the trapdoor, he remembered. The man would pass abruptly through the wall and find the girl tied to a bed, her legs and arms spread wide, and her clothing torn to rags. He laughed softly to himself. He had seen the picture three times, and this was one of the best scenes.

On his right the fellow whispered wide-eyed to his companion, "Man, look ayonder!"

"Damn!"

"Wouldn't I like to have her tied up like that . . ."

5 "Hey! That fool's letting her loose!"

"Aw, man, he loves her."

"Love or no love!"

The man moved impatiently beside him, and he tried to involve himself in the scene. But Laura was on his mind. Tiring quickly of watching the picture he looked back to where the white beam filtered from the projection room above the balcony. It started small and grew large, specks of dust dancing in its whiteness as it reached the screen. It was strange how the beam always landed right on the screen and didn't mess up and fall somewhere else. But they had it all fixed. Everything was fixed. Now suppose when they showed that girl with her dress torn the girl started taking off the rest of her clothes, and when the guy came in he didn't untie her but kept her there and went to taking off his own clothes? *That* would be something to see. If a picture got out of hand like that those guys up there would go nuts. Yeah, and there'd be so many folks in here you couldn't find a seat for nine months! A strange sensation played over his skin. He shuddered. Yesterday he'd seen a bedbug on a woman's neck as they walked out into the bright street. But exploring his thigh through a hole in his pocket he found only goose pimples and old scars.

The bottle gurgled again. He closed his eyes. Now a dreamy music was accompanying the film and train whistles were sounding in the distance, and he was a boy again walking along a railroad trestle down South, and seeing the train coming, and running back as fast as he could go, and hearing the whistle blowing, and getting off the trestle to solid ground just in time, with the earth trembling beneath his feet, and feeling relieved as he ran down the cinder-strewn embankment onto the highway, and looking back and seeing with terror that the train had left the track and was following him right down the middle of the street, and all the white people laughing as he ran screaming. . . .

"Wake up there, buddy! What the hell do you mean hollering like that? Can't 10
you see we trying to enjoy this here picture?"

He stared at the man with gratitude.

"I'm sorry, old man," he said. "I musta been dreaming."

"Well, here, have a drink. And don't be making no noise like that, damn!"

His hands trembled as he tilted his head. It was not wine, but whiskey. Cold rye whiskey. He took a deep swoller, decided it was better not to take another, and handed the bottle back to its owner.

"Thanks, old man," he said. 15

Now he felt the cold whiskey breaking a warm path straight through the middle of him, growing hotter and sharper as it moved. He had not eaten all day, and it made him light-headed. The smell of the peanuts stabbed him like a knife, and he got up and found a seat in the middle aisle. But no sooner did he sit than he saw a row of intense-faced young girls, and got up again, thinking, "You chicks musta been Lindy-hopping[1] somewhere." He found a seat several rows ahead as the lights came on, and he saw the screen disappear behind a heavy red and gold curtain; then the curtain rising, and the man with the microphone and a uniformed attendant coming on the stage.

He felt for his bingo cards, smiling. The guy at the door wouldn't like it if he knew about his having *five* cards. Well, not everyone played the bingo game; and even with five cards he didn't have much of a chance. For Laura, though, he had to have faith. He studied the cards, each with its different numerals, punching the free center hole in each and spreading them neatly across his lap; and when the lights faded he sat slouched in his seat so that he could look from his cards to the bingo wheel with but a quick shifting of his eyes.

Ahead, at the end of the darkness, the man with the microphone was pressing a button attached to a long cord and spinning the bingo wheel and calling out the number each time the wheel came to rest. And each time the voice rang out his finger raced over the cards for the number. With five cards he had to move fast. He became nervous; there were too many cards, and the man went too fast with his grating voice. Perhaps he should just select one and throw the others away. But he was afraid. He became warm. Wonder how much Laura's doctor would cost? Damn that, watch the cards! And with despair he heard the man call three in a row which he missed on all five cards. This way he'd never win. . . .

1. Dancing.

When he saw the row of holes punched across the third card, he sat paralyzed and heard the man call three more numbers before he stumbled forward, screaming,

20 "Bingo! Bingo!"

"Let that fool up there," someone called.

"Get up there, man!"

He stumbled down the aisle and up the steps to the stage into a light so sharp and bright that for a moment it blinded him, and he felt that he had moved into the spell of some strange, mysterious power. Yet it was as familiar as the sun, and he knew it was the perfectly familiar bingo.

The man with the microphone was saying something to the audience as he held out his card. A cold light flashed from the man's finger as the card left his hand. His knees trembled. The man stepped closer, checking the card against the numbers chalked on the board. Suppose he had made a mistake? The pomade on the man's hair made him feel faint, and he backed away. But the man was checking the card over the microphone now, and he had to stay. He stood tense, listening.

25 "Under the O, forty-four," the man chanted. "Under the I, seven. Under the G, three. Under the B, ninety-six. Under the N, thirteen!"

His breath came easier as the man smiled at the audience.

"Yes sir, ladies and gentlemen, he's one of the chosen people!"

The audience rippled with laughter and applause.

"Step right up to the front of the stage."

30 He moved slowly forward, wishing that the light was not so bright.

"To win tonight's jackpot of $36.90 the wheel must stop between the double zero, understand?"

He nodded, knowing the ritual from the many days and nights he had watched the winners march across the stage to press the button that controlled the spinning wheel and receive the prizes. And now he followed the instructions as though he'd crossed the slippery stage a million prize-winning times.

The man was making some kind of joke, and he nodded vacantly. So tense had he become that he felt a sudden desire to cry and shook it away. He felt vaguely that his whole life was determined by the bingo wheel; not only that which would happen now that he was at last before it, but all that had gone before, since his birth, and his mother's birth and the birth of his father. It had always been there, even though he had not been aware of it, handing out the unlucky cards and numbers of his days. The feeling persisted, and he started quickly away. I better get down from here before I make a fool of myself, he thought.

"Here, boy," the man called. "You haven't started yet."

35 Someone laughed as he went hesitantly back.

"Are you all reet?"

He grinned at the man's jive talk, but no words would come, and he knew it was not a convincing grin. For suddenly he knew that he stood on the slippery brink of some terrible embarrassment.

"Where are you from, boy?" the man asked.

"Down South."

40 "He's from down South, ladies and gentlemen," the man said. "Where from? Speak right into the mike."

"Rocky Mont," he said. "Rock' Mont, North Car'lina."

"So you decided to come down off that mountain to the U.S.," the man laughed. He felt that the man was making a fool of him, but then something cold was placed in his hand, and the lights were no longer behind him.

Standing before the wheel he felt alone, but that was somehow right, and he remembered his plan. He would give the wheel a short quick twirl. Just a touch of the button. He had watched it many times, and always it came close to double zero when it was short and quick. He steeled himself; the fear had left, and he felt a profound sense of promise, as though he were about to be repaid for all the things he'd suffered all his life. Trembling, he pressed the button. There was a whirl of lights, and in a second he realized with finality that though he wanted to, he could not stop. It was as though he held a high-powered line in his naked hand. His nerves tightened. As the wheel increased its speed it seemed to draw him more and more into its power, as though it held his fate; and with it came a deep need to submit, to whirl, to lose himself in its swirl of color. He could not stop it now. So let it be.

The button rested snugly in his palm where the man had placed it. And now he became aware of the man beside him, advising him through the microphone, while behind the shadowy audience hummed with noisy voices. He shifted his feet. There was still that feeling of helplessness within him, making part of him desire to turn back, even now that the jackpot was right in his hand. He squeezed the button until his fist ached. Then, like the sudden shriek of a subway whistle, a doubt tore through his head. Suppose he did not spin the wheel long enough? What could he do, and how could he tell? And then he knew, even as he wondered, that as long as he pressed the button, he could control the jackpot. He and only he could determine whether or not it was to be his. Not even the man with the microphone could do anything about it now. He felt drunk. Then, as though he had come down from a high hill into a valley of people, he heard the audience yelling.

"Come down from there, you jerk!" 45

"Let somebody else have a chance. . . ."

"Ole Jack thinks he done found the end of the rainbow. . . ."

The last voice was not unfriendly, and he turned and smiled dreamily into the yelling mouths. Then he turned his back squarely on them.

"Don't take too long, boy," a voice said.

He nodded. They were yelling behind him. Those folks did not understand 50 what had happened to him. They had been playing the bingo game day in and night out for years, trying to win rent money or hamburger change. But not one of those wise guys had discovered this wonderful thing. He watched the wheel whirling past the numbers and experienced a burst of exaltation: This is God! This is the really truly God! He said it aloud, "This is God!"

He said it with such absolute conviction that he feared he would fall fainting into the footlights. But the crowd yelled so loud that they could not hear. These fools, he thought. I'm here trying to tell them the most wonderful secret in the world, and they're yelling like they gone crazy. A hand fell upon his shoulder.

"You'll have to make a choice now, boy. You've taken too long."

He brushed the hand violently away.

"Leave me alone, man. I know what I'm doing!"

55 The man looked surprised and held on to the microphone for support. And because he did not wish to hurt the man's feelings he smiled, realizing with a sudden pang that there was no way of explaining to the man just why he had to stand there pressing the button forever.

"Come here," he called tiredly.

The man approached, rolling the heavy microphone across the stage.

"Anybody can play this bingo game, right?" he said.

"Sure, but . . ."

60 He smiled, feeling inclined to be patient with this slick looking white man with his blue shirt and his sharp gabardine suit.

"That's what I thought," he said. "Anybody can win the jackpot as long as they get the lucky number, right?"

"That's the rule, but after all . . ."

"That's what I thought," he said. "And the big prize goes to the man who knows how to win it?"

The man nodded speechlessly.

65 "Well then, go on over there and watch me win like I want to. I ain't going to hurt nobody," he said, "and I'll show you how to win. I mean to show the whole world how it's got to be done."

And because he understood, he smiled again to let the man know that he held nothing against him for being white and impatient. Then he refused to see the man any longer and stood pressing the button, the voices of the crowd reaching him like sounds in distant streets. Let them yell. All the Negroes down there were just ashamed because he was black like them. He smiled inwardly, knowing how it was. Most of the time he was ashamed of what Negroes did himself. Well, let them be ashamed for something this time. Like him. He was like a long thin black wire that was being stretched and wound upon the bingo wheel; wound until he wanted to scream; wound, but this time himself controlling the winding and the sadness and the shame, and because he did, Laura would be all right. Suddenly the lights flickered. He staggered backwards. Had something gone wrong? All this noise. Didn't they know that although he controlled the wheel, it also controlled him, and unless he pressed the button forever and forever and ever it would stop, leaving him high and dry, dry and high on this hard high slippery hill and Laura dead? There was only one chance; he had to do whatever the wheel demanded. And gripping the button in despair, he discovered with surprise that it imparted a nervous energy. His spine tingled. He felt a certain power.

Now he faced the raging crowd with defiance, its screams penetrating his eardrums like trumpets shrieking from a juke-box. The vague faces glowing in the bingo lights gave him a sense of himself that he had never known before. He was running the show, by God! They had to react to him, for he was their luck. This is *me,* he thought. Let the bastards yell. Then someone was laughing inside him, and he realized that somehow he had forgotten his own name. It was a sad, lost feeling to lose your name, and a crazy thing to do. That name had been given him by the white man who had owned his grandfather a long lost time ago down South. But maybe those wise guys knew his name.

"Who am I?" he screamed.

"Hurry up and bingo, you jerk!"

They didn't know either, he thought sadly. They didn't even know their own names, they were all poor nameless bastards. Well, he didn't need that old name; he was reborn. For as long as he pressed the button he was The-man-who-pressed-the-button-who-held-the-prize-who-was-the-King-of-Bingo. That was the way it was, and he'd have to press the button even if nobody understood, even though Laura did not understand.

"Live!" he shouted.

The audience quieted like the dying of a huge fan.

"Live, Laura, baby. I got holt of it now, sugar. Live!"

He screamed it, tears streaming down his face. "I got nobody but YOU!"

The screams tore from his very guts. He felt as though the rush of blood to his head would burst out in baseball seams of small red droplets, like a head beaten by police clubs. Bending over he saw a trickle of blood splashing the toe of his shoe. With his free hand he searched his head. It was his nose. God, suppose something has gone wrong? He felt that the whole audience had somehow entered him and was stamping its feet in his stomach and he was unable to throw them out. They wanted the prize, that was it. They wanted the secret for themselves. But they'd never get it; he would keep the bingo wheel whirling forever, and Laura would be safe in the wheel. But would she? It had to be, because if she were not safe the wheel would cease to turn; it could not go on. He had to get away, *vomit* all, and his mind formed an image of himself running with Laura in his arms down the tracks of the subway just ahead of an A train, running desperately *vomit* with people screaming for him to come out but knowing no way of leaving the tracks because to stop would bring the train crushing down upon him and to attempt to leave across the other tracks would mean to run into a hot third rail as high as his waist which threw blue sparks that blinded his eyes until he could hardly see.

He heard singing and the audience was clapping its hands.

Shoot the liquor to him, Jim, boy!
Clap-clap-clap
Well a-calla the cop
He's blowing his top!
Shoot the liquor to him, Jim, boy!

Bitter anger grew within him at the singing. They think I'm crazy. Well let 'em laugh. I'll do what I got to do.

He was standing in an attitude of intense listening when he saw that they were watching something on the stage behind him. He felt weak. But when he turned he saw no one. If only his thumb did not ache so. Now they were applauding. And for a moment he thought that the wheel had stopped. But that was impossible, his thumb still pressed the button. Then he saw them. Two men in uniform beckoned from the end of the stage. They were coming toward him, walking in step, slowly, like a tap-dance team returning for a third encore. But their shoulders shot forward, and he backed away, looking wildly about. There was nothing to fight them with. He had only the long black cord which led to a plug somewhere back stage, and he couldn't use that because it operated the bingo wheel. He backed slowly, fixing the men with his eyes as his lips stretched over his teeth in a tight, fixed grin; moved toward the end of the stage and realizing that he couldn't go much further, for suddenly the cord became taut and he couldn't afford to break the cord. But he had to do something. The audience was howling. Suddenly he stopped dead, seeing the men halt, their legs lifted as in an interrupted step of a slow-motion dance. There was nothing to do but run in the other direction and he dashed forward, slipping and sliding. The men fell back, surprised. He struck out violently going past.

"Grab him!"

80 He ran, but all too quickly the cord tightened, resistingly, and he turned and ran back again. This time he slipped them, and discovered by running in a circle before the wheel he could keep the cord from tightening. But this way he had to flail his arms to keep the men away. Why couldn't they leave a man alone? He ran, circling.

"Ring down the curtain," someone yelled. But they couldn't do that. If they did the wheel flashing from the projection room would be cut off. But they had him before he could tell them so, trying to pry open his fist, and he was wrestling and trying to bring his knees into the fight and holding on to the button, for it was his life. And now he was down, seeing a foot coming down, crushing his wrist cruelly, down, as he saw the wheel whirling serenely above.

"I can't give it up," he screamed. Then quietly, in a confidential tone, "Boys, I really can't give it up."

It landed hard against his head. And in the blank moment they had it away from him, completely now. He fought them trying to pull him up from the stage as he watched the wheel spin slowly to a stop. Without surprise he saw it rest at double-zero.

"You see," he pointed bitterly.

85 "Sure, boy, sure, it's O.K.," one of the men said smiling.

And seeing the man bow his head to someone he could not see, he felt very, very happy; he would receive what all the winners received.

But as he warmed in the justice of the man's tight smile he did not see the man's slow wink, nor see the bow-legged man behind him step clear of the swiftly descending curtain and set himself for a blow. He only felt the dull pain exploding in his skull, and he knew even as it slipped out of him that his luck had run out on the stage.

1944

LOUISE ERDRICH
(b. 1954)

Love Medicine

Born in Minnesota of German American and French Chippewa descent, Louise Erdrich grew up in Wahpeton, North Dakota, as a member of the Turtle Mountain Band of Chippewa. She attended Dartmouth College and received an MFA in creative writing from Johns Hopkins University. Her first novel, *Love Medicine* (1984), a collection of linked stories, won the National Book Critics Circle Award. In her subsequent publications—*The Beet Queen* (1986), *Tracks* (1988), *The Bingo Palace* (1993), and *Tales of Burning Love* (1996)—she pursued her focus on the lives of Native Americans in contemporary North Dakota. In 1991 she jointly authored the best-selling novel *The Crown of Columbus* with her husband, Michael Dorris. Her recent works include the novels *The Last Report on the Miracles at Little No Horse* (2001), *The Plague of Doves* (2008), *The Round House* (2012), and *Books and Islands in Ojibwa County: Traveling through the Land of My Ancestors* (2014). She lives in Minnesota with her family and dogs.

I never really done much with my life, I suppose. I never had a television. Grandma Kashpaw had one inside her apartment at the Senior Citizens, so I used to go there and watch my favorite shows. For a while she used to call me the biggest waste on the reservation and hark back to how she saved me from my own mother, who wanted to tie me in a potato sack and throw me in a slough. Sure, I was grateful to Grandma Kashpaw for saving me like that, for raising me, but gratitude gets old. After a while, stale. I had to stop thanking her. One day I told her I had paid her back in full by staying at her beck and call. I'd do anything for Grandma. She knew that. Besides, I took care of Grandpa like nobody else could, on account of what a handful he'd gotten to be.

But that was nothing. I know the tricks of mind and body inside out without ever having trained for it, because I got the touch. It's a thing you got to be born with. I got secrets in my hands that nobody ever knew to ask. Take Grandma Kashpaw with her tired veins all knotted up in her legs like clumps of blue snails. I take my fingers and I snap them on the knots. The medicine flows out of me. The touch. I run my fingers up the maps of those rivers of veins or I knock very gentle above their hearts or I make a circling motion on their stomachs, and it helps them. They feel much better. Some women pay me five dollars.

I couldn't do the touch for Grandpa, though. He was a hard nut. You know, some people fall right through the hole in their lives. It's invisible, but they come to it after time, never knowing where. There is this woman here, Lulu Lamartine, who always had a thing for Grandpa. She loved him since she was a girl and always said he was a genius. Now she says that his mind got so full it exploded.

How can I doubt that? I know the feeling when your mental power builds up too far. I always used to say that's why the Indians got drunk. Even statistically we're the smartest people on the earth. Anyhow with Grandpa I couldn't hardly believe it, because all my youth he stood out as a hero to me. When he started getting toward second childhood he went through different moods. He would stand in the woods and cry at the top of his shirt. It scared me, scared everyone, Grandma worst of all.

Yet he was so smart—do you believe it?—that he *knew* he was getting foolish. 5
He said so. He told me that December I failed school and come back on the train to Hoopdance. I didn't have nowhere else to go. He picked me up there and he said it straight out: "I'm getting into my second childhood." And then he said something else I still remember: "I been chosen for it. I couldn't say no."

So I figure that a man so smart all his life—tribal chairman and the star of movies and even pictured in the statehouse and on cans of snuff—would know what he's doing by saying yes. I think he was called to second childhood like anybody else gets a call for the priesthood or the army or whatever. So I really did not listen too hard when the doctor said this was some kind of disease old people got eating too much sugar. You just can't tell me that a man who went to Washington and gave them bureaucrats what for could lose his mind from eating too much Milky Way. No, he put second childhood on himself.

Behind those songs he sings out in the middle of Mass, and back of those stories that everybody knows by heart, Grandpa is thinking hard about life. I know the feeling. Sometimes I'll throw up a smokescreen to think behind. I'll hitch up to Winnipeg and play the Space Invaders[1] for six hours, but all the time there and back I will be thinking some fairly deep thoughts that surprise even me, and I'm used to it. As for him, if it was just the thoughts there wouldn't be no problem. Smokescreen is what irritates the social structure, see, and Grandpa has done things that just distract people to the point they want to throw him in the cookie jar where they keep the mentally insane. He's far from that, I know for sure, but even Grandma had trouble keeping her patience once he started sneaking off to Lamartine's place. He's not supposed to have his candy, and Lulu feeds it to him. That's *one* of the reasons why he goes.

Grandma tried to get me to put the touch on Grandpa soon after he began stepping out. I didn't want to, but before Grandma started telling me again what a bad state my bare behind was in when she first took me home, I thought I should at least pretend.

I put my hands on either side of Grandpa's head. You wouldn't look at him and say he was crazy. He's a fine figure of a man, as Lamartine would say, with all his hair and half his teeth, a beak like a hawk, and cheeks like the blades of a hatchet. They put his picture on all the tourist guides to North Dakota and even copied his face for artistic paintings. I guess you could call him a monument all of himself. He started grinning when I put my hands on his templates, and I knew right then he knew how come I touched him. I knew the smokescreen was going to fall.

10 And I was right: just for a moment it fell.

"Let's pitch whoopee," he said across my shoulder to Grandma.

They don't use that expression much around here anymore, but for damn sure it must have meant something. It got her goat right quick.

She threw my hands off his head herself and stood in front of him, overmatching him pound for pound, and taller too, for she had a growth spurt in middle age while he had shrunk, so now the length and breadth of her surpassed him. She glared and spoke her piece into his face about how he was off at all hours tomcatting and chasing Lamartine again and making a damn old fool of himself.

"And you got no more whoopee to pitch anymore anyhow!" she yelled at last, surprising me so my jaw just dropped, for us kids all had pretended for so long that those rustling sounds we heard from their side of the room at night never happened. She sure had pretended it, up till now, anyway. I saw that tears were

1. Extremely popular and influential 1980s arcade video game.

in her eyes. And that's when I saw how much grief and love she felt for him. And it gave me a real shock to the system. You see I thought love got easier over the years so it didn't hurt so bad when it hurt, or feel so good when it felt good. I thought it smoothed out and old people hardly noticed it. I thought it curled up and died, I guess. Now I saw it rear up like a whip and lash.

She loved him. She was jealous. She mourned him like the dead. 15

And he just smiled into the air, trapped in the seams of his mind.

So I didn't know what to do. I was in a laundry then. They was like parents to me, the way they had took me home and reared me. I could see her point for wanting to get him back the way he was so at least she could argue with him, sleep with him, not be shamed out by Lamartine. She'd always love him. That hit me like a ton of bricks. For one whole day I felt this odd feeling that cramped my hands. When you have the touch, that's where longing gets you. I never loved like that. It made me feel all inspired to see them fight, and I wanted to go out and find a woman who I would love until one of us died or went crazy. But I'm not like that really. From time to time I heal a person all up good inside, however when it comes to the long shot I doubt that I got staying power.

And you need that, staying power, going out to love somebody. I knew this quality was not going to jump on me with no effort. So I turned my thoughts back to Grandma and Grandpa. I felt her side of it with my hands and my tangled guts, and I felt his side of it within the stretch of my mentality. He had gone out to lunch one day and never came back. He was fishing in the middle of Matchimanito. And there was big thoughts on his line, and he kept throwing them back for even bigger ones that would explain to him, say, the meaning of how we got here and why we have to leave so soon. All in all, I could not see myself treating Grandpa with the touch, bringing him back, when the real part of him had chose to be off thinking somewhere. It was only the rest of him that stayed around causing trouble, after all, and we could handle most of it without any problem.

Besides, it was hard to argue with his reasons for doing some things. Take Holy Mass. I used to go there just every so often, when I got frustrated mostly, because even though I know the Higher Power dwells everyplace, there's something very calming about the cool greenish inside of our mission. Or so I thought, anyway. Grandpa was the one who stripped off my delusions in this matter, for it was he who busted right through what Father calls the sacred serenity of the place.

We filed in that time. Me and Grandpa. We sat down in our pews. Then the 20
rosary got started up pre-Mass and that's when Grandpa filled up his chest and opened his mouth and belted out them words.

HAIL MARIE FULL OF GRACE.

He had a powerful set of lungs.

And he kept on like that. He did not let up. He hollered and he yelled them prayers, and I guess people was used to him by now, because they only muttered theirs and did not quit and gawk like I did. I was getting red-faced, I admit. I give him the elbow once or twice, but that wasn't nothing to him. He kept on. He shrieked to heaven and he pleaded like a movie actor and he pounded his chest like Tarzan in the Lord I Am Not Worthies. I thought he might hurt himself. Then after a while I guess I got used to it, and that's when I wondered: how come?

So afterwards I out and asked him. "How come? How come you yelled?"

25 "God don't hear me otherwise," said Grandpa Kashpaw.

I sweat. I broke right into a little cold sweat at my hairline because I knew this was perfectly right and for years not one damn other person had noticed it. God's been going deaf. Since the Old Testament, God's been deafening up on us. I read, see. Besides the dictionary, which I'm constantly in use of, I had this Bible once. I read it. I found there was discrepancies between then and now. It struck me. Here God used to raineth bread from clouds, smite the Phillipines, sling fire down on red-light districts where people got stabbed. He even appeared in person every once in a while. God used to pay attention, is what I'm saying.

Now there's your God in the Old Testament and there is Chippewa Gods as well. Indian Gods, good and bad, like tricky Nanabozho or the water monster, Missepeshu, who lives over in Matchimanito. That water monster was the last God I ever heard to appear. It had a weakness for young girls and grabbed one of the Pillagers off her rowboat. She got to shore all right, but only after this monster had its way with her. She's an old lady now. Old Lady Pillager. She still doesn't like to see her family fish that lake.

Our Gods aren't perfect, is what I'm saying, but at least they come around. They'll do a favor if you ask them right. You don't have to yell. But you do have to know, like I said, how to ask in the right way. That makes problems, because to ask proper was an art that was lost to the Chippewas once the Catholics gained ground. Even now, I have to wonder if Higher Power turned it back, if we got to yell, or if we just don't speak its language.

I looked around me. How else could I explain what all I had seen in my short life—King smashing his fist in things, Gordie drinking himself down to the Bismarck hospitals, or Aunt June left by a white man to wander off in the snow. How else to explain the times my touch don't work, and farther back, to the oldtime Indians who was swept away in the outright germ warfare and dirty-dog killing of the whites. In those times, us Indians was so much kindlier than now.

30 We took them in.

Oh yes, I'm bitter as an old cutworm just thinking of how they done to us and doing still.

So Grandpa Kashpaw just opened my eyes a little there. Was there any sense relying on a God whose ears was stopped? Just like the government? I says then, right off, maybe we got nothing but ourselves. And that's not much, just personally speaking. I know I don't got the cold hard potatoes it takes to understand everything. Still, there's things I'd like to do. For instance, I'd like to help some people like my Grandpa and Grandma Kashpaw get back some happiness within the tail ends of their lives.

I told you once before I couldn't see my way clear to putting the direct touch on Grandpa's mind, and I kept my moral there, but something soon happened to make me think a little bit of mental adjustment wouldn't do him and the rest of us no harm.

It was after we saw him one afternoon in the sunshine courtyard of the Senior Citizens with Lulu Lamartine. Grandpa used to like to dig there. He had his little dandelion fork out, and he was prying up them dandelions right and left while Lamartine watched him.

35 "He's scratching up the dirt, all right," said Grandma, watching Lamartine watch Grandpa out the window.

Now Lamartine was about half the considerable size of Grandma, but you would never think of sizes anyway. They were different in an even more noticeable way. It was the difference between a house fixed up with paint and picky fence, and a house left to weather away into the soft earth, is what I'm saying. Lamartine was jacked up, latticed, shuttered, and vinyl sided, while Grandma sagged and bulged on her slipped foundations and let her hair go the silver gray of rain-dried lumber. Right now, she eyed the Lamartine's pert flowery dress with such a look it despaired me. I knew what this could lead to with Grandma. Alternating tongue storms and rock-hard silences was hard on a man, even one who didn't notice, like Grandpa. So I went fetching him.

But he was gone when I popped through the little screen door that led out on the courtyard. There was nobody out there either, to point which way they went. Just the dandelion fork quibbling upright in the ground. That gave me an idea. I snookered over to the Lamartine's door and I listened in first, then knocked. But nobody. So I went walking through the lounges and around the card tables. Still nobody. Finally it was my touch that led me to the laundry room. I cracked the door. I went in. There they were. And he was really loving her up good, boy, and she was going hell for leather. Sheets was flapping on the lines above, and washcloths, pillowcases, shirts was also flying through the air, for they was trying to clear out a place for themselves in a high-heaped but shallow laundry cart. The washers and dryers was all on, chock-full of quarters, shaking and moaning. I couldn't hear what Grandpa and the Lamartine was billing and cooing, and they couldn't hear me.

I didn't know what to do, so I went inside and shut the door.

The Lamartine wore a big curly light-brown wig. Looked like one of them squeaky little white-people dogs. Poodles they call them. Anyway, that wig is what saved us from the worse. For I could hardly shout and tell them I was in there, no more could I try and grab him. I was trapped where I was. There was nothing I could really do but hold the door shut. I was scared of somebody else upsetting in and really getting an eyeful. Turned out though, in the heat of the clinch, as I was trying to avert my eyes you see, the Lamartine's curly wig jumped off her head. And if you ever been in the midst of something and had a big change like that occur in the someone, you can't help know how it devastates your basic urges. Not only that, but her wig was almost with a life of its own. Grandpa's eyes were bugging at the change already, and swear to God if the thing didn't rear up and pop him in the face like it was going to start something. He scrambled up, Grandpa did, and the Lamartine jumped up after him all addled looking. They just stared at each other, huffing and puffing, with quizzical expression. The surprise seemed to drive all sense completely out of Grandpa's mind.

"The letter was what started the fire," he said. "I never would have done it."

"What letter?" said the Lamartine. She was stiff-necked now, and elegant, even bald, like some alien queen. I gave her back the wig. The Lamartine replaced it on her head, and whenever I saw her after that, I couldn't help thinking of her bald, with special powers, as if from another planet.

"That was a close call," I said to Grandpa after she had left.

But I think he had already forgot the incident. He just stood there all quiet and thoughtful. You really wouldn't think he was crazy. He looked like he was just about to say something important, explaining himself. He said something, all right, but it didn't have nothing to do with anything that made sense.

He wondered where the heck he put his dandelion fork. That's when I decided about the mental adjustment.

45 Now what was mostly our problem was not so much that he was not all there, but that what was there of him often hankered after Lamartine. If we could put a stop to that, I thought, we might be getting someplace. But here, see, my touch was of no use. For what could I snap my fingers at to make him faithful to Grandma? Like the quality of staying power, this faithfulness was invisible. I know it's something that you got to acquire, but I never known where from. Maybe there's no rhyme or reason to it, like my getting the touch, and then again maybe it's a kind of magic.

It was Grandma Kashpaw who thought of it in the end. She knows things. Although she will not admit she has a scrap of Indian blood in her, there's no doubt in my mind she's got some Chippewa. How else would you explain the way she'll be sitting there, in front of her TV story, rocking in her armchair and suddenly she turns on me, her brown eyes hard as lake-bed flint.

"Lipsha Morrissey," she'll say, "you went out last night and got drunk."

How did she know that? I'll hardly remember it myself. Then she'll say she just had a feeling or ache in the scar of her hand or a creak in her shoulder. She is constantly being told things by little aggravations in her joints or by her household appliances. One time she told Gordie never to ride with a crazy Lamartine boy. She had seen something in the polished-up tin of her bread toaster. So he didn't. Sure enough, the time came we heard how Lyman and Henry went out of control in their car, ending up in the river. Lyman swam to the top, but Henry never made it.

Thanks to Grandma's toaster, Gordie was probably spared.

50 Someplace in the blood Grandma Kashpaw knows things. She also remembers things, I found. She keeps things filed away. She's got a memory like them video games that don't forget your score. One reason she remembers so many details about the trouble I gave her in early life is so she can flash back her total when she needs to.

Like now. Take the love medicine. I don't know where she remembered that from. It came tumbling from her mind like an asteroid off the corner of the screen.[2]

Of course she starts out by mentioning the time I had this accident in church and did she leave me there with wet overhalls? No she didn't. And ain't I glad? Yes I am. Now what you want now, Grandma?

But when she mentions them love medicines, I feel my back prickle at the danger. These love medicines is something of an old Chippewa specialty. No other tribe has got them down so well. But love medicines is not for the layman to handle. You don't just go out and get one without paying for it. Before you get one, even, you should go through one hell of a lot of mental condensation. You got to think it over. Choose the right one. You could really mess up your life grinding up the wrong little thing.

2. Allusion to Asteroids, another popular 1980s video arcade game.

So anyhow, I said to Grandma I'd give this love medicine some thought. I knew the best thing was to go ask a specialist like Old Lady Pillager, who lives up in a tangle of bush and never shows herself. But the truth is I was afraid of her, like everyone else. She was known for putting the twisted mouth on people, seizing up their hearts. Old Lady Pillager was serious business, and I have always thought it best to steer clear of that whenever I could. That's why I took the powers in my own hands. That's why I did what I could.

I put my whole mentality to it, nothing held back. After a while I started to 55
remember things I'd heard gossiped over.

I heard of this person once who carried a charm of seeds that looked like baby pearls. They was attracted to a metal knife, which made them powerful. But I didn't know where them seeds grew. Another love charm I heard about I couldn't go along with, because how was I suppose to catch frogs in the act, which it required. Them little creatures is slippery and fast. And then the powerfullest of all, the most extreme, involved nail clips and such. I wasn't anywhere near asking Grandma to provide me all the little body bits that this last love recipe called for. I went walking around for days just trying to think up something that would work.

Well I got it. If it hadn't been the early fall of the year, I never would have got it. But I was sitting underneath a tree one day down near the school just watching people's feet go by when something tells me, look up! Look up! So I look up, and I see two honkers, Canada geese, the kind with little masks on their faces, a bird what mates for life. I see them flying right over my head naturally preparing to land in some slough on the reservation, which they certainly won't get off of alive.

It hits me, anyway. Them geese, they mate for life. And I think to myself, just what if I went out and got a pair? And just what if I fed some part—say the goose heart—of the female to Grandma and Grandpa ate the other heart? Wouldn't that work? Maybe it's all invisible, and then maybe again it's magic. Love is a stony road. We know that for sure. If it's true that the higher feelings of devotion get lodged in the heart like people say, then we'd be home free. If not, eating goose heart couldn't harm nobody anyway. I thought it was worth my effort, and Grandma Kashpaw thought so, too. She had always known a good idea when she heard one. She borrowed me Grandpa's gun.

So I went out to this particular slough, maybe the exact same slough I never got thrown in by my mother, thanks to Grandma Kashpaw, and I hunched down in a good comfortable pile of rushes. I got my gun loaded up. I ate a few of these soft baloney sandwiches Grandma made me for lunch. And then I waited. The cattails blown back and forth above my head. Them stringy blue herons was spearing up their prey. The thing I know how to do best in this world, the thing I been training for all my life, is to wait. Sitting there and sitting there was no hardship on me. I got to thinking about some funny things that happened. There was this one time that Lulu Lamartine's little blue tweety bird, a paraclete, I guess you'd call it, flown up inside her dress and got lost within there. I recalled her running out into the hallway trying to yell something, shaking. She was doing a right good jig there, cutting the rug for sure, and the thing is it *never* flown out. To this day people speculate where it went. They fear she might perhaps of crushed it in her corsets. It sure hasn't ever yet been seen alive. I thought of funny things for a while, but then I used them up, and strange things that happened started weaseling their way into my mind.

60 I got to thinking quite naturally of the Lamartine's cousin named Wristwatch. I never knew what his real name was. They called him Wristwatch because he got his father's broken wristwatch as a young boy when his father passed on. Never in his whole life did Wristwatch take his father's watch off. He didn't care if it worked, although after a while he got sensitive when people asked what time it was, teasing him. He often put it to his ear like he was listening to the tick. But it was broken for good and forever, people said so, at least that's what they thought.

Well I saw Wristwatch smoking in his pickup one afternoon and by nine that evening he was dead.

He died sitting at the Lamartine's table, too. As she told it, Wristwatch had just eaten himself a good-size dinner and she said would he take seconds on the hot dish when he fell over to the floor. They turnt him over. He was gone. But here's the strange thing: when the Senior Citizen's orderly took the pulse he noticed that the wristwatch Wristwatch wore was now working. The moment he died the wristwatch started keeping perfect time. They buried him with the watch still ticking on his arm.

I got to thinking. What if some gravediggers dug up Wristwatch's casket in two hundred years and that watch was still going? I thought what question they would ask and it was this: Whose hand wound it?

I started shaking like a piece of grass at just the thought.

65 Not to get off the subject or nothing. I was still hunkered in the slough. It was passing late into the afternoon and still no honkers had touched down. Now I don't need to tell you that the waiting did not get to me, it was the chill. The rushes was very soft, but damp. I was getting cold and debating to leave, when they landed. Two geese swimming here and there as big as life, looking deep into each other's little pinhole eyes. Just the ones I was looking for. So I lifted Grandpa's gun to my shoulder and I aimed perfectly, and *blam! Blam!* I delivered two accurate shots. But the thing is, them shots missed. I couldn't hardly believe it. Whether it was that the stock had warped or the barrel got bent someways, I don't quite know, but anyway them geese flown off into the dim sky, and Lipsha Morrissey was left there in the rushes with evening fallen and his two cold hands empty. He had before him just the prospect of another day of bone-cracking chill in them rushes, and the thought of it got him depressed.

Now it isn't my style, in no way, to get depressed.

So I said to myself, Lipsha Morrissey, you're a happy S.O.B. who could be covered up with weeds by now down at the bottom of this slough, but instead you're alive to tell the tale. You might have problems in life, but you still got the touch. You got the power, Lipsha Morrissey. Can't argue that. So put your mind to it and figure out how not to be depressed.

I took my advice. I put my mind to it. But I never saw at the time how my thoughts led me astray toward a tragic outcome none could have known. I ignored all the danger, all the limits, for I was tired of sitting in the slough and my feet were numb. My face was aching. I was chilled, so I played with fire. I told myself love medicine was simple. I told myself the old superstitions was just that—strange beliefs. I told myself to take the ten dollars Mary MacDonald had paid me for putting the touch on her arthritis joint, and the other five I hadn't spent yet from winning bingo last Thursday. I told myself to go down to the Red Owl store.

And here is what I did that made the medicine backfire. I took an evil shortcut. I looked at birds that was dead and froze.

All right. So now I guess you will say, "Slap a malpractice suit on Lipsha Morrissey."

I heard of those suits. I used to think it was a color clothing quack doctors had to wear so you could tell them from the good ones. Now I know better that it's law.

As I walked back from the Red Owl with the rock-hard, heavy turkeys, I argued to myself about malpractice. I thought of faith. I thought to myself that faith could be called belief against the odds and whether or not there's any proof. How does that sound? I thought how we might have to yell to be heard by Higher Power, but that's not saying it's not *there.* And that is faith for you. It's belief even when the goods don't deliver. Higher Power makes promises we all know they can't back up, but anybody ever go and slap an old malpractice suit on God? Or the U.S. government? No they don't. Faith might be stupid, but it gets us through. So what I'm heading at is this. I finally convinced myself that the real actual power to the love medicine was not the goose heart itself but the faith in the cure.

I didn't believe it, I knew it was wrong, but by then I had waded so far into my lie I was stuck there. And then I went one step further.

The next day, I cleaned the hearts away from the paper packages of gizzards inside the turkeys. Then I wrapped them hearts with a clean hankie and brung them both to get blessed up at the mission. I wanted to get official blessings from the priest, but when Father answered the door to the rectory, wiping his hands on a little towel, I could tell he was a busy man.

"Booshoo,[3] Father," I said. "I got a slight request to make of you this afternoon."

"What is it?" he said.

"Would you bless this package?" I held out the hankie with the hearts tied inside it.

He looked at the package, questioning it.

"It's turkey hearts," I honestly had to reply.

A look of annoyance crossed his face.

"Why don't you bring this matter over to Sister Martin," he said. "I have duties."

And so, although the blessing wouldn't be as powerful, I went over to the Sisters with the package.

I rung the bell, and they brought Sister Martin to the door. I had her as a music teacher, but I was always so shy then. I never talked out loud. Now, I had grown taller than Sister Martin. Looking down, I saw that she was not feeling up to snuff. Brown circles hung under her eyes.

"What's the matter?" she said, not noticing who I was.

3. That is, *Bonjour,* French for "good day" or "hello."

"Remember me, Sister?"

She squinted up at me.

"Oh yes," she said after a moment. "I'm sorry, you're the youngest of the Kashpaws. Gordie's brother."

Her face warmed up.

"Lipsha," I said, "that's my name."

"Well, Lipsha," she said, smiling broad at me now, "what can I do for you?"

They always said she was the kindest-hearted of the Sisters up the hill, and she was. She brought me back into their own kitchen and made me take a big yellow wedge of cake and a glass of milk.

"Now tell me," she said, nodding at my package. "What have you got wrapped up so carefully in those handkerchiefs?"

Like before, I answered honestly.

"Ah," said Sister Martin. "Turkey hearts." She waited.

"I hoped you could bless them."

She waited some more, smiling with her eyes. Kindhearted though she was, I began to sweat. A person could not pull the wool down over Sister Martin. I stumbled through my mind for an explanation, quick, that wouldn't scare her off.

"They're a present," I said, "for Saint Kateri's[4] statue."

"She's not a saint yet."

"I know," I stuttered on. "In the hopes they will crown her."

"Lipsha," she said, "I never heard of such a thing."

So I told her. "Well the truth is," I said, "it's a kind of medicine."

"For what?"

"Love."

"Oh Lipsha," she said after a moment, "you don't need any medicine. I'm sure any girl would like you exactly the way you are."

I just sat there. I felt miserable, caught in my pack of lies.

"Tell you what," she said, seeing how bad I felt, "my blessing won't make any difference anyway. But there is something you can do."

I looked up at her, hopeless.

"Just be yourself."

I looked down at my plate. I knew I wasn't much to brag about right then, and I shortly became even less. For as I walked out the door I stuck my fingers in the cup of holy water that was sacred from their touches. I put my fingers in and blessed the hearts, quick, with my own hand.

I went back to Grandma and sat down in her little kitchen at the Senior Citizens. I unwrapped them hearts on the table, and her hard agate eyes went soft. She said she wasn't even going to cook those hearts up but eat them raw so their power would go down strong as possible.

4. Kateri Kekakwitha (1656–80), "Lily of the Mohawk," born in what is now upstate New York to a Mohawk father and an Algonquin mother who was a devout Christian. Following the deaths of her parents, Kateri moved to a Jesuit mission near Montreal to spend the rest of her short life in prayer and chastity. Miracles were attributed to her after her death; she was beatified in 1980 and canonized in 1991.

I couldn't hardly watch when she munched hers. Now that's true love. I was worried about how she would get Grandpa to eat his, but she told me she'd think of something and don't worry. So I did not. I was supposed to hide off in her bedroom while she put dinner on a plate for Grandpa and fixed up the heart so he'd eat it. I caught a glint of the plate she was making for him. She put that heart smack on a piece of lettuce like in a restaurant and then attached to it a little heap of boiled peas.

He sat down. I was listening in the next room.

She said, "Why don't you have some mash potato?" So he had some mash potato. Then she gave him a little piece of boiled meat. He ate that. Then she said, "Why you didn't never touch your salad yet. See that heart? I'm feeding you it because the doctor said your blood needs building up."

I couldn't help it, at that point I peeked through a crack in the door.

I saw Grandpa picking at that heart on his plate with a certain look. He 115
didn't look appetized at all, is what I'm saying. I doubted our plan was going to work. Grandma was getting worried, too. She told him one more time, loudly, that he had to eat that heart.

"Swallow it down," she said. "You'll hardly notice it."

He just looked at her straight on. The way he looked at her made me think I was going to see the smokescreen drop a second time, and sure enough it happened.

"What you want me to eat this for so bad?" he asked her uncannily.

Now Grandma knew the jig was up. She knew that he knew she was working medicine. He put his fork down. He rolled the heart around his saucer plate.

"I don't want to eat this," he said to Grandma. "It don't look good." 120

"Why it's fresh grade-A," she told him. "One hundred percent."

He didn't ask percent what, but his eyes took on an even more warier look.

"Just go on and try it," she said, taking the salt shaker up in her hand. She was getting annoyed. "Not tasty enough? You want me to salt it for you?" She waved the shaker over his plate.

"All right, skinny white girl!" She had got Grandpa mad. Oopsy-daisy, he popped the heart into his mouth. I was about to yawn loudly and come out of the bedroom. I was about ready for this crash of wills to be over, when I saw he was still up to his old tricks. First he rolled it into one side of his cheek. "Mmmmm," he said. Then he rolled it into the other side of his cheek. "Mmmmmmm," again. Then he stuck his tongue out with the heart on it and put it back, and there was no time to react. He had pulled Grandma's leg once too far. Her goat was got. She was so mad she hopped up quick as a wink and slugged him between the shoulderblades to make him swallow.

Only thing is, he choked. 125

He choked real bad. A person can choke to death. You ever sit down at a restaurant table and up above you there is a list of instructions what to do if something slides down the wrong pipe? It sure makes you chew slow, that's for damn sure. When Grandpa fell off his chair better believe me that little graphic illustrated poster fled into my mind. I jumped out the bedroom. I done everything within my power that I could do to unlodge what was choking him. I squeezed underneath his rib cage. I socked him in the back. I was desperate.

But here's the factor of decision: he wasn't choking on the heart alone. There was more to it than that. It was other things that choked him as well. It didn't seem like he wanted to struggle or fight. Death came and tapped his chest, so he went just like that. I'm sorry all through my body at what I done to him with that heart, and there's those who will say Lipsha Morrissey is just excusing himself off the hook by giving song and dance about how Grandpa gave up.

Maybe I can't admit what I did. My touch had gone worthless, that is true. But here is what I seen while he lay in my arms.

You hear a person's life will flash before their eyes when they're in danger. It was him in danger, not me, but it was *his* life come over me. I saw him dying, and it was like someone pulled the shade down in a room. His eyes clouded over and squeezed shut, but just before that I looked in. He was still fishing in the middle of Matchimanito. Big thoughts was on his line and he had half a case of beer in the boat. He waved at me, grinned, and then the bobber went under.

Grandma had gone out of the room crying for help. I bunched my force up in my hands and I held him. I was so wound up I couldn't even breathe. All the moments he had spent with me, all the times he had hoisted me on his shoulders or pointed into the leaves was concentrated in that moment. Time was flashing back and forth like a pinball machine. Lights blinked and balls hopped and rubber bands chirped, until suddenly I realized the last ball had gone down the drain and there was nothing. I felt his force leaving him, flowing out of Grandpa never to return. I felt his mind weakening. The bobber going under in the lake. And I felt the touch retreat back into the darkness inside my body, from where it came.

130 One time, long ago, both of us were fishing together. We caught a big old snapper what started towing us around like it was a motor. "This here fishline is pretty damn good," Grandpa said. "Let's keep this turtle on and see where he takes us." So we rode along behind that turtle, watching as from time to time it surfaced. The thing was just about the size of a washtub. It took us all around the lake twice, and as it was traveling, Grandpa said something as a joke. "Lipsha," he said, "we are glad your mother didn't want you because we was always looking for a boy like you who would tow us around the lake."

"I ain't no snapper. Snappers is so stupid they stay alive when their head's chopped off," I said.

"That ain't stupidity," said Grandpa. "Their brain's just in their heart, like yours is."

When I looked up, I knew the fuse had blown between my heart and my mind and that a terrible understanding was to be given.

Grandma got back into the room and I saw her stumble. And then she went down too. It was like a house you can't hardly believe has stood so long, through years of record weather, suddenly goes down in the worst yet. It makes sense, is what I'm saying, but you still can't hardly believe it. You think a person you know has got through death and illness and being broke and living on commodity rice will get through anything. Then they fold and you see how fragile were the stones that underpinned them. You see how instantly the ground can shift you thought was solid. You see the stop signs and the yellow dividing markers of roads you traveled and all the instructions you had played according to vanish. You see how all the everyday things you counted on was just a dream you had been having by which you run your whole life. She had been over me, like a sheer overhang of rock dividing Lipsha Morrissey from outer space. And now she went underneath. It was as though the banks gave way on the shores of Matchimanito, and where Grandpa's passing was just the bobber swallowed under by his biggest thought, her fall was the house and the rock under it sliding after, sending half the lake splashing up to the clouds.

Where there was nothing. 135

You play them games never knowing what you see. When I fell into the dream alongside of both of them I saw that the dominions I had defended myself from anciently was but delusions of the screen. Blips of light. And I was scot-free now, whistling through space.

I don't know how I come back. I don't know from where. They was slapping my face when I arrived back at Senior Citizens and they was oxygenating her. I saw her chest move, almost unwilling. She sighed the way she would when somebody bothered her in the middle of a row of beads she was counting. I think it irritated her to no end that they brought her back. I knew from the way she looked after they took the mask off, she was not going to forgive them disturbing her restful peace. Nor was she forgiving Lipsha Morrissey. She had been stepping out onto the road of death, she told the children later at the funeral. I asked was there any stop signs or dividing markers on that road, but she clamped her lips in a vise the way she always done when she was mad.

Which didn't bother me. I knew when things had cleared out she wouldn't have no choice. I was not going to speculate where the blame was put for Grandpa's death. We was in it together. She had slugged him between the shoulders. My touch had failed him, never to return.

All the blood children and the took-ins, like me, came home from Minneapolis and Chicago, where they had relocated years ago. They stayed with friends on the reservation or with Aurelia or slept on Grandma's floor. They were struck down with grief and bereavement to be sure, every one of them. At the funeral I sat down in the back of the church with Albertine. She had gotten all skinny and ragged haired from cramming all her years of study into two or three. She had decided that to be a nurse was not enough for her so she was going to be a doctor. But the way she was straining her mind didn't look too hopeful. Her eyes were bloodshot from driving and crying. She took my hand. From the back we watched all the children and the mourners as they hunched over their prayers, their hands stuffed full of Kleenex. It was someplace in that long sad service that my vision shifted. I began to see things different, more clear. The family kneeling down turned to rocks in a field. It struck me how strong and reliable grief was, and death. Until the end of time, death would be our rock.

So I had perspective on it all, for death gives you that. All the Kashpaw children had done various things to me in their lives—shared their folks with me, loaned me cash, beat me up in secret—and I decided, because of death, then and there I'd call it quits. If I ever saw King again, I'd shake his hand. Forgiving somebody else made the whole thing easier to bear. 140

Everybody saw Grandpa off into the next world. And then the Kashpaws had to get back to their jobs, which was numerous and impressive. I had a few beers with them and I went back to Grandma, who had sort of got lost in the shuffle of everybody being sad about Grandpa and glad to see one another.

Zelda had sat beside her the whole time and was sitting with her now. I wanted to talk to Grandma, say how sorry I was, that it wasn't her fault, but only mine. I would have, but Zelda gave me one of her looks of strict warning as if to say, "I'll take care of Grandma. Don't horn in on the women."

If only Zelda knew, I thought, the sad realities would change her. But of course I couldn't tell the dark truth.

It was evening, late. Grandma's light was on underneath a crack in the door. About a week had passed since we buried Grandpa. I knocked first but there wasn't no answer, so I went right in. The door was unlocked. She was there but she didn't notice me at first. Her hands were tied up in her rosary, and her gaze was fully absorbed in the easy chair opposite her, the one that had always been Grandpa's favorite. I stood there, staring with her, at the little green nubs in the cloth and plastic armrest covers and the sad little hair-tonic stain he had made on the white doily where he laid his head. For the life of me I couldn't figure what she was staring at. Thin space. Then she turned.

145 "He ain't gone yet," she said.

Remember that chill I luckily didn't get from waiting in the slough? I got it now. I felt it start from the very center of me, where fear hides, waiting to attack. It spiraled outward so that in minutes my fingers and teeth were shaking and clattering. I knew she told the truth. She seen Grandpa. Whether or not he had been there is not the point. She had *seen* him, and that meant anybody else could see him, too. Not only that but, as is usually the case with these here ghosts, he had a certain uneasy reason to come back. And of course Grandma Kashpaw had scanned it out.

I sat down. We sat together on the couch watching his chair out of the corner of our eyes. She had found him sitting in his chair when she walked in the door.

"It's the love medicine, my Lipsha," she said. "It was stronger than we thought. He came back even after death to claim me to his side."

I was afraid. "We shouldn't have tampered with it," I said. She agreed. For a while we sat still. I don't know what she thought, but my head felt screwed on backward. I couldn't accurately consider the situation, so I told Grandma to go to bed. I would sleep on the couch keeping my eye on Grandpa's chair. Maybe he would come back and maybe he wouldn't. I guess I feared the one as much as the other, but I got to thinking, see, as I lay there in darkness, that perhaps even through my terrible mistakes some good might come. If Grandpa did come back, I thought he'd return in his right mind. I could talk with him. I could tell him it was all my fault for playing with power I did not understand. Maybe he'd forgive me and rest in peace. I hoped this. I calmed myself and waited for him all night.

150 He fooled me though. He knew what I was waiting for, and it wasn't what he was looking to hear. Come dawn I heard a blood-splitting cry from the bedroom and I rushed in there. Grandma turnt the lights on. She was sitting on the edge of the bed and her face looked harsh, pinched-up, gray.

"He was here," she said. "He came and laid down next to me in bed. And he touched me."

Her heart broke down. She cried. His touch was so cold. She laid back in bed after a while, as it was morning, and I went to the couch. As I lay there, falling asleep, I suddenly felt Grandpa's presence and the barrier between us like a swollen river. I felt how I had wronged him. How awful was the place where I had sent him. Behind the wall of death, he'd watched the living eat and cry and get drunk. He was lonesome, but I understood he meant no harm.

"Go back," I said to the dark, afraid and yet full of pity. "You got to be with your own kind now," I said. I felt him retreating, like a sigh, growing less. I felt his spirit as it shrunk back through the walls, the blinds, the brick courtyard of Senior Citizens. "Look up Aunt June," I whispered as he left.

I slept late the next morning, a good hard sleep allowing the sun to rise and warm the earth. It was past noon when I awoke. There is nothing, to my mind, like a long sleep to make those hard decisions that you neglect under stress of wakefulness. Soon as I woke up that morning, I saw exactly what I'd say to Grandma. I had gotten humble in the past week, not just losing the touch but getting jolted into the understanding that would prey on me from here on out. Your life feels different on you, once you greet death and understand your heart's position. You wear your life like a garment from the mission bundle sale ever after—lightly because you realize you never paid nothing for it, cherishing because you know you won't ever come by such a bargain again. Also you have the feeling someone wore it before you and someone will after. I can't explain that, not yet, but I'm putting my mind to it.

"Grandma," I said, "I got to be honest about the love medicine." 155

She listened. I knew from then on she would be listening to me the way I had listened to her before. I told her about the turkey hearts and how I had them blessed. I told her what I used as love medicine was purely a fake, and then I said to her what my understanding brought me.

"Love medicine ain't what brings him back to you, Grandma. No, it's something else. He loved you over time and distance, but he went off so quick he never got the chance to tell you how he loves you, how he doesn't blame you, how he understands. It's true feeling, not no magic. No supermarket heart could have brung him back."

She looked at me. She was seeing the years and days I had no way of knowing, and she didn't believe me. I could tell this. Yet a look came on her face. It was like the look of mothers drinking sweetness from their children's eyes. It was tenderness.

"Lipsha," she said, "you was always my favorite."

She took the beads off the bedpost, where she kept them to say at night, and 160
she told me to put out my hand. When I did this, she shut the beads inside of my fist and held them there a long minute, tight, so my hand hurt. I almost cried when she did this. I don't really know why. Tears shot up behind my eyelids, and yet it was nothing. I didn't understand, except her hand was so strong, squeezing mine.

The earth was full of life and there were dandelions growing out the window, thick as thieves, already seeded, fat as big yellow plungers. She let my hand go. I got up. "I'll go out and dig a few dandelions," I told her.

Outside, the sun was hot and heavy as a hand on my back. I felt it flow down my arms, out my fingers, arrowing through the ends of the fork into the earth. With every root I prized up there was return, as if I was kin to its secret lesson. The touch got stronger as I worked through the grassy afternoon. Uncurling from me like a seed out of the blackness where I was lost, the touch spread. The spiked leaves full of bitter mother's milk. A buried root. A nuisance people dig up and throw in the sun to wither. A globe of frail seeds that's indestructible.

1982

WILLIAM FAULKNER

A Rose for Emily

(See Faulkner biography on p. 196.)

I

When Miss Emily Grierson died, our whole town went to her funeral: the men through a sort of respectful affection for a fallen monument, the women mostly out of curiosity to see the inside of her house, which no one save an old manservant—a combined gardener and cook—had seen in at least ten years.

It was a big, squarish frame house that had once been white, decorated with cupolas and spires and scrolled balconies in the heavily lightsome style of the seventies,[1] set on what had once been our most select street. But garages and cotton gins had encroached and obliterated even the august names of that neighborhood; only Miss Emily's house was left, lifting its stubborn and coquettish decay above the cotton wagons and the gasoline pumps—an eyesore among eyesores. And now Miss Emily had gone to join the representatives of those august names where they lay in the cedar-bemused cemetery among the ranked and anonymous graves of Union and Confederate soldiers who fell at the battle of Jefferson.

Alive, Miss Emily had been a tradition, a duty, and a care; a sort of hereditary obligation upon the town, dating from that day in 1894 when Colonel Sartoris, the mayor—he who fathered the edict that no Negro woman should appear on the streets without an apron—remitted her taxes, the dispensation dating from the death of her father on into perpetuity. Not that Miss Emily would have accepted charity. Colonel Sartoris invented an involved tale to the effect that Miss Emily's father had loaned money to the town, which the town, as a matter of business, preferred this way of repaying. Only a man of Colonel Sartoris' generation and thought could have invented it, and only a woman could have believed it.

When the next generation, with its more modern ideas, became mayors and aldermen, this arrangement created some little dissatisfaction. On the first of the year they mailed her a tax notice. February came, and there was no reply. They wrote her a formal letter, asking her to call at the sheriff's office at her convenience. A week later the mayor wrote her himself, offering to call or to send

1. The 1870s, the decade following the Civil War between the "Union and Confederate soldiers" mentioned at the end of the paragraph.

his car for her, and received in reply a note on paper of an archaic shape, in a thin, flowing calligraphy in faded ink, to the effect that she no longer went out at all. The tax notice was also enclosed, without comment.

They called a special meeting of the Board of Aldermen. A deputation waited upon her, knocked at the door through which no visitor had passed since she ceased giving china-painting lessons eight or ten years earlier. They were admitted by the old Negro into a dim hall from which a stairway mounted into still more shadow. It smelled of dust and disuse—a close, dank smell. The Negro led them into the parlor. It was furnished in heavy, leather-covered furniture. When the Negro opened the blinds of one window, a faint dust rose sluggishly about their thighs, spinning with slow motes in the single sun-ray. On a tarnished gilt easel before the fireplace stood a crayon portrait of Miss Emily's father.

They rose when she entered—a small, fat woman in black, with a thin gold chain descending to her waist and vanishing into her belt, leaning on an ebony cane with a tarnished gold head. Her skeleton was small and spare; perhaps that was why what would have been merely plumpness in another was obesity in her. She looked bloated, like a body long submerged in motionless water, and of that pallid hue. Her eyes, lost in the fatty ridges of her face, looked like two small pieces of coal pressed into a lump of dough as they moved from one face to another while the visitors stated their errand.

She did not ask them to sit. She just stood in the door and listened quietly until the spokesman came to a stumbling halt. Then they could hear the invisible watch ticking at the end of the gold chain.

Her voice was dry and cold. "I have no taxes in Jefferson. Colonel Sartoris explained it to me. Perhaps one of you can gain access to the city records and satisfy yourselves."

"But we have. We are the city authorities, Miss Emily. Didn't you get a notice from the sheriff, signed by him?"

"I received a paper, yes," Miss Emily said. "Perhaps he considers himself the sheriff. . . . I have no taxes in Jefferson."

"But there is nothing on the books to show that, you see. We must go by the—"

"See Colonel Sartoris. I have no taxes in Jefferson."

"But, Miss Emily—"

"See Colonel Sartoris." (Colonel Sartoris had been dead almost ten years.) "I have no taxes in Jefferson. Tobe!" The Negro appeared. "Show these gentlemen out."

II

So she vanquished them, horse and foot, just as she had vanquished their fathers thirty years before about the smell. That was two years after her father's death and a short time after her sweetheart—the one we believed would marry her—had deserted her. After her father's death she went out very little; after her sweetheart went away, people hardly saw her at all. A few of the ladies had the temerity to call, but were not received, and the only sign of life about the place was the Negro man—a young man then—going in and out with a market basket.

"Just as if a man—any man—could keep a kitchen properly," the ladies said; so they were not surprised when the smell developed. It was another link between the gross, teeming world and the high and mighty Griersons.

A neighbor, a woman, complained to the mayor, Judge Stevens, eighty years old.

"But what will you have me do about it, madam?" he said.

"Why, send her word to stop it," the woman said. "Isn't there a law?"

20 "I'm sure that won't be necessary," Judge Stevens said. "It's probably just a snake or a rat that nigger of hers killed in the yard. I'll speak to him about it."

The next day he received two more complaints, one from a man who came in diffident deprecation. "We really must do something about it, Judge. I'd be the last one in the world to bother Miss Emily, but we've got to do something." That night the Board of Aldermen met—three gray-beards and one younger man, a member of the rising generation.

"It's simple enough," he said. "Send her word to have her place cleaned up. Give her a certain time to do it in, and if she don't . . ."

"Dammit, sir," Judge Stevens said, "will you accuse a lady to her face of smelling bad?"

So the next night, after midnight, four men crossed Miss Emily's lawn and slunk about the house like burglars, sniffing along the base of the brickwork and at the cellar openings while one of them performed a regular sowing motion with his hand out of a sack slung from his shoulder. They broke open the cellar door and sprinkled lime there, and in all the outbuildings. As they recrossed the lawn, a window that had been dark was lighted and Miss Emily sat in it, the light behind her, and her upright torso motionless as that of an idol. They crept quietly across the lawn and into the shadow of the locusts that lined the street. After a week or two the smell went away.

25 That was when people had begun to feel really sorry for her. People in our town, remembering how old lady Wyatt, her great-aunt, had gone completely crazy at last, believed that the Griersons held themselves a little too high for what they really were. None of the young men were quite good enough for Miss Emily and such. We had long thought of them as a tableau; Miss Emily a slender figure in white in the background, her father a spraddled silhouette in the foreground, his back to her and clutching a horsewhip, the two of them framed by the back-flung front door. So when she got to be thirty and was still single, we were not pleased exactly, but vindicated; even with insanity in the family she wouldn't have turned down all of her chances if they had really materialized.

When her father died, it got about that the house was all that was left to her; and in a way, people were glad. At last they could pity Miss Emily. Being left alone, and a pauper, she had become humanized. Now she too would know the old thrill and the old despair of a penny more or less.

The day after his death all the ladies prepared to call at the house and offer condolence and aid, as is our custom. Miss Emily met them at the door, dressed as usual and with no trace of grief on her face. She told them that her father was not dead. She did that for three days, with the ministers calling on her, and the doctors, trying to persuade her to let them dispose of the body. Just as they were about to resort to law and force, she broke down, and they buried her father quickly.

We did not say she was crazy then. We believed she had to do that. We remembered all the young men her father had driven away, and we knew that with nothing left, she would have to cling to that which had robbed her, as people will.

III

She was sick for a long time. When we saw her again, her hair was cut short, making her look like a girl, with a vague resemblance to those angels in colored church windows—sort of tragic and serene.

The town had just let the contracts for paving the sidewalks, and in the sum- 30
mer after her father's death they began to work. The construction company came with niggers and mules and machinery, and a foreman named Homer Barron, a Yankee—a big, dark, ready man, with a big voice and eyes lighter than his face. The little boys would follow in groups to hear him cuss the niggers, and the niggers singing in time to the rise and fall of picks. Pretty soon he knew everybody in town. Whenever you heard a lot of laughing anywhere about the square, Homer Barron would be in the center of the group. Presently we began to see him and Miss Emily on Sunday afternoons driving in the yellow-wheeled buggy and the matched team of bays from the livery stable.

At first we were glad that Miss Emily would have an interest, because the ladies all said, "Of course a Grierson would not think seriously of a Northerner, a day laborer." But there were still others, older people, who said that even grief could not cause a real lady to forget *noblesse oblige*—without calling it *noblesse oblige.*[2] They just said, "Poor Emily. Her kinsfolk should come to her." She had some kin in Alabama; but years ago her father had fallen out with them over the estate of old lady Wyatt, the crazy woman, and there was no communication between the two families. They had not even been represented at the funeral.

And as soon as the old people said, "Poor Emily," the whispering began. "Do you suppose it's really so?" they said to one another. "Of course it is. What else could . . ." This behind their hands; rustling of craned silk and satin behind jalousies[3] closed upon the sun of Sunday afternoon as the thin, swift clop-clop-clop of the matched team passed: "Poor Emily."

She carried her head high enough—even when we believed that she was fallen. It was as if she demanded more than ever the recognition of her dignity as the last Grierson; as if it had wanted that touch of earthiness to reaffirm her imperviousness. Like when she bought the rat poison, the arsenic. That was over a year after they had begun to say "Poor Emily," and while the two female cousins were visiting her.

"I want some poison," she said to the druggist. She was over thirty then, still a slight woman, though thinner than usual, with cold, haughty black eyes in a face the flesh of which was strained across the temples and about the eyesockets as you imagine a lighthouse-keeper's face ought to look. "I want some poison," she said.

"Yes, Miss Emily. What kind? For rats and such? I'd recom—" 35

"I want the best you have. I don't care what kind."

The druggist named several. "They'll kill anything up to an elephant. But what you want is—"

"Arsenic," Miss Emily said. "Is that a good one?"

2. Obligation, coming with noble or upper-class birth, to behave with honor and generosity toward those less privileged.

3. Window blinds made of adjustable horizontal slats.

"Is . . . arsenic? Yes ma'am. But what you want—"

40 "I want arsenic."

The druggist looked down at her. She looked back at him, erect, her face like a strained flag. "Why, of course," the druggist said. "If that's what you want. But the law requires you to tell what you are going to use it for."

Miss Emily just stared at him, her head tilted back in order to look him eye for eye, until he looked away and went and got the arsenic and wrapped it up. The Negro delivery boy brought her the package; the druggist didn't come back. When she opened the package at home there was written on the box, under the skull and bones: "For rats."

IV

So the next day we all said, "She will kill herself"; and we said it would be the best thing. When she had first begun to be seen with Homer Barron, we had said, "She will marry him." Then we said, "She will persuade him yet," because Homer himself had remarked—he liked men, and it was known that he drank with the younger men in the Elk's Club—that he was not a marrying man. Later we said, "Poor Emily," behind the jalousies as they passed on Sunday afternoon in the glittering buggy, Miss Emily with her head high and Homer Barron with his hat cocked and a cigar in his teeth, reins and whip in a yellow glove.

Then some of the ladies began to say that it was a disgrace to the town and a bad example to the young people. The men did not want to interfere, but at last the ladies forced the Baptist minister—Miss Emily's people were Episcopal—to call upon her. He would never divulge what happened during that interview, but he refused to go back again. The next Sunday they again drove about the streets, and the following day the minister's wife wrote to Miss Emily's relations in Alabama.

45 So she had blood-kin under her roof again and we sat back to watch developments. At first nothing happened. Then we were sure that they were to be married. We learned that Miss Emily had been to the jeweler's and ordered a man's toilet set in silver, with the letters H. B. on each piece. Two days later we learned that she had bought a complete outfit of men's clothing, including a nightshirt, and we said, "They are married." We were really glad. We were glad because the two female cousins were even more Grierson than Miss Emily had ever been.

So we were not surprised when Homer Barron—the streets had been finished some time since—was gone. We were a little disappointed that there was not a public blowing-off, but we believed that he had gone on to prepare for Miss Emily's coming, or to give her a chance to get rid of the cousins. (By that time it was a cabal, and we were all Miss Emily's allies to help circumvent the cousins.) Sure enough, after another week they departed. And, as we had expected all along, within three days Homer Barron was back in town. A neighbor saw the Negro man admit him at the kitchen door at dusk one evening.

And that was the last we saw of Homer Barron. And of Miss Emily for some time. The Negro man went in and out with the market basket, but the front door remained closed. Now and then we would see her at a window for a moment, as the men did that night when they sprinkled the lime, but for almost six months she did not appear on the streets. Then we knew that this was to be expected too; as if that quality of her father which had thwarted her woman's life so many times had been too virulent and too furious to die.

When we next saw Miss Emily, she had grown fat and her hair was turning gray. During the next few years it grew grayer and grayer until it attained an even pepper-and-salt iron-gray, when it ceased turning. Up to the day of her death at seventy-four it was still that vigorous iron-gray, like the hair of an active man.

From that time on her front door remained closed, save for a period of six or seven years, when she was about forty, during which she gave lessons in china-painting. She fitted up a studio in one of the downstairs rooms, where the daughters and grand-daughters of Colonel Sartoris' contemporaries were sent to her with the same regularity and in the same spirit that they were sent on Sundays with a twenty-five cent piece for the collection plate. Meanwhile her taxes had been remitted.

Then the newer generation became the backbone and the spirit of the town, 50
and the painting pupils grew up and fell away and did not send their children to her with boxes of color and tedious brushes and pictures cut from the ladies' magazines. The front door closed upon the last one and remained closed for good. When the town got free postal delivery Miss Emily alone refused to let them fasten the metal numbers above her door and attach a mailbox to it. She would not listen to them.

Daily, monthly, yearly we watched the Negro grow grayer and more stooped, going in and out with the market basket. Each December we sent her a tax notice, which would be returned by the post office a week later, unclaimed. Now and then we would see her in one of the downstairs windows—she had evidently shut up the top floor of the house—like the carven torso of an idol in a niche, looking or not looking at us, we could never tell which. Thus she passed from generation to generation—dear, inescapable, impervious, tranquil, and perverse.

And so she died. Fell ill in the house filled with dust and shadows, with only a doddering Negro man to wait on her. We did not even know she was sick; we had long since given up trying to get any information from the Negro. He talked to no one, probably not even to her, for his voice had grown harsh and rusty, as if from disuse.

She died in one of the downstairs rooms, in a heavy walnut bed with a curtain, her gray head propped on a pillow yellow and moldy with age and lack of sunlight.

V

The Negro met the first of the ladies at the front door and let them in, with their hushed, sibilant voices and their quick, curious glances, and then he disappeared. He walked right through the house and out the back and was not seen again.

The two female cousins came at once. They held the funeral on the second 55
day, with the town coming to look at Miss Emily beneath a mass of bought flowers, with the crayon face of her father musing profoundly above the bier and the ladies sibilant and macabre; and the very old men—some in their brushed Confederate uniforms—on the porch and the lawn, talking of Miss Emily as if she had been a contemporary of theirs, believing that they had danced with her and courted her perhaps, confusing time with its mathematical progression, as the

old do, to whom all the past is not a diminishing road, but, instead, a huge meadow which no winter ever quite touches, divided from them now by the narrow bottleneck of the most recent decade of years.

Already we knew that there was one room in that region above stairs which no one had seen in forty years, and which would have to be forced. They waited until Miss Emily was decently in the ground before they opened it.

The violence of breaking down the door seemed to fill this room with pervading dust. A thin, acrid pall as of the tomb seemed to lie everywhere upon this room decked and furnished as for a bridal: upon the valance curtains of faded rose color, upon the rose-shaded lights, upon the dressing table, upon the delicate array of crystal and the man's toilet things backed with tarnished silver, silver so tarnished that the monogram was obscured. Among them lay a collar and tie, as if they had just been removed, which, lifted, left upon the surface a pale crescent in the dust. Upon a chair hung the suit, carefully folded; beneath it the two mute shoes and the discarded socks.

The man himself lay in the bed.

For a long while we just stood there, looking down at the profound and fleshless grin. The body had apparently once lain in the attitude of an embrace, but now the long sleep that outlasts love, that conquers even the grimace of love, had cuckolded him. What was left of him, rotted beneath what was left of the nightshirt, had become inextricable from the bed in which he lay; and upon him and upon the pillow beside him lay that even coating of the patient and biding dust.

60 Then we noticed that in the second pillow was the indentation of a head. One of us lifted something from it, and leaning forward, that faint and invisible dust dry and acrid in the nostrils, we saw a long strand of iron-gray hair.

1931

ERNEST HEMINGWAY (1899–1961)

Hills Like White Elephants

Among the most distinctively American of writers, even if he rarely wrote about America, Ernest Hemingway grew up in an upscale Chicago suburb, but he spent his summers on Lake Walloon in northern Michigan. Here, his physician father nurtured his love of hunting and fishing. Hemingway graduated from high school just two months after the United States entered World War I. Forbidden to enlist by his parents and uninterested in college, he worked as a reporter for the *Kansas City Star* before volunteering as a Red Cross ambulance driver. Badly wounded on the Italian front, he returned to the States and to journalism. Then, in 1921, he moved to Paris, entering the famed expatriate circle that included Ezra Pound, Gertrude Stein, and F. Scott Fitzgerald. Two volumes of stories, *In Our Time* (1925) and *Men without Women* (1927), and two major novels, *The Sun Also Rises* (1926) and *A Farewell to Arms* (1929), established Hemingway's international reputation as both a masterful literary craftsman and a chief spokesman for the "Lost Generation," while later, less critically acclaimed books on topics such as bullfighting (*Death in the Afternoon*, 1932) and big-game hunting (*Green Hills of Africa*, 1935) helped confirm his status as an almost mythic figure, patron saint of what the *New York Times* called a "cult" of daring and danger. Hemingway supported the Loyalists in the Spanish Civil War—the subject of his novel *For Whom the Bell Tolls* (1940); served as a war correspondent during World War II; and survived two plane crashes and four marriages. Severely depressed and suffering an array of physical ailments, he took his own life shortly before his sixty-second birthday, only a few years after earning both a Pulitzer—for *The Old Man and the Sea* (1952)—and a Nobel (1954).

The hills across the valley of the Ebro[1] were long and white. On this side there was no shade and no trees and the station was between two lines of rails in the sun. Close against the side of the station there was the warm shadow of the building and a curtain, made of strings of bamboo beads, hung across the open door into the bar, to keep out flies. The American and the girl with him sat at a table in the shade, outside the building. It was very hot and the express from Barcelona would come in forty minutes. It stopped at this junction for two minutes and went on to Madrid.

"What should we drink?" the girl asked. She had taken off her hat and put it on the table.

"It's pretty hot," the man said.

"Let's drink beer."

"Dos cervezas," the man said into the curtain.

"Big ones?" a woman asked from the doorway.

"Yes. Two big ones."

The woman brought two glasses of beer and two felt pads. She put the felt pads and the beer glasses on the table and looked at the man and the girl. The girl was looking off at the line of hills. They were white in the sun and the country was brown and dry.

"They look like white elephants," she said.

"I've never seen one," the man drank his beer.

"No, you wouldn't have."

"I might have," the man said. "Just because you say I wouldn't have doesn't prove anything."

The girl looked at the bead curtain. "They've painted something on it," she said. "What does it say?"

"Anis del Toro. It's a drink."

"Could we try it?"

The man called "Listen" through the curtain. The woman came out from the bar.

"Four reales."[2]

"We want two Anis del Toro."

"With water?"

"Do you want it with water?"

1. River in northern Spain.
2. Spanish coins.

"I don't know," the girl said. "Is it good with water?"

"It's all right."

"You want them with water?" asked the woman.

"Yes, with water."

"It tastes like licorice," the girl said and put the glass down.

"That's the way with everything."

"Yes," said the girl. "Everything tastes of licorice. Especially all the things you've waited so long for, like absinthe."

"Oh, cut it out."

"You started it," the girl said. "I was being amused. I was having a fine time."

"Well, let's try and have a fine time."

"All right. I was trying. I said the mountains looked like white elephants. Wasn't that bright?"

"That was bright."

"I wanted to try this new drink. That's all we do, isn't it—look at things and try new drinks?"

"I guess so."

The girl looked across at the hills.

"They're lovely hills," she said. "They don't really look like white elephants. I just meant the coloring of their skin through the trees."

"Should we have another drink?"

"All right."

The warm wind blew the bead curtain against the table.

"The beer's nice and cool," the man said.

"It's lovely," the girl said.

"It's really an awfully simple operation, Jig," the man said. "It's not really an operation at all."

The girl looked at the ground the table legs rested on.

"I know you wouldn't mind it, Jig. It's really not anything. It's just to let the air in."

The girl did not say anything.

"I'll go with you and I'll stay with you all the time. They just let the air in and then it's all perfectly natural."

"Then what will we do afterward?"

"We'll be fine afterward. Just like we were before."

"What makes you think so?"

"That's the only thing that bothers us. It's the only thing that's made us unhappy."

The girl looked at the bead curtain, put her hand out and took hold of two of the strings of beads.

"And you think then we'll be all right and be happy."

"I know we will. You don't have to be afraid. I've known lots of people that have done it."

"So have I," said the girl. "And afterward they were all so happy."

"Well," the man said, "if you don't want to you don't have to. I wouldn't have you do it if you didn't want to. But I know it's perfectly simple."

"And you really want to?"

"I think it's the best thing to do. But I don't want you to do it if you don't really want to."

"And if I do it you'll be happy and things will be like they were and you'll love me?"

"I love you now. You know I love you."

"I know. But if I do it, then it will be nice again if I say things are like white elephants, and you'll like it?"

"I'll love it. I love it now but I just can't think about it. You know how I get when I worry."

"If I do it you won't ever worry?"

"I won't worry about that because it's perfectly simple."

"Then I'll do it. Because I don't care about me."

"What do you mean?"

"I don't care about me."

"Well, I care about you."

"Oh, yes. But I don't care about me. And I'll do it and then everything will be fine."

"I don't want you to do it if you feel that way."

The girl stood up and walked to the end of the station. Across, on the other side, were fields of grain and trees along the banks of the Ebro. Far away, beyond the river, were mountains. The shadow of a cloud moved across the field of grain and she saw the river through the trees.

"And we could have all this," she said. "And we could have everything and every day we make it more impossible."

"What did you say?"

"I said we could have everything."

"We can have everything."

"No, we can't."

"We can have the whole world."

"No, we can't."

"We can go everywhere."

"No, we can't. It isn't ours anymore."

"It's ours."

"No, it isn't. And once they take it away, you never get it back."

"But they haven't taken it away."

"We'll wait and see."

"Come on back in the shade," he said. "You mustn't feel that way."

"I don't feel any way," the girl said. "I just know things."

"I don't want you to do anything that you don't want to do—"

"Nor that isn't good for me," she said. "I know. Could we have another beer?"

"All right. But you've got to realize—"

"I realize," the girl said. "Can't we maybe stop talking?"

They sat down at the table and the girl looked across at the hills on the dry side of the valley and the man looked at her and at the table.

"You've got to realize," he said, "that I don't want you to do it if you don't want to. I'm perfectly willing to go through with it if it means anything to you."

"Doesn't it mean anything to you? We could get along."

"Of course it does. But I don't want anybody but you. I don't want any one else. And I know it's perfectly simple."

"Yes, you know it's perfectly simple."

"It's all right for you to say that, but I do know it."

"Would you do something for me now?"

"I'd do anything for you."

"Would you please please please please please please please stop talking?"

He did not say anything but looked at the bags against the wall of the station. There were labels on them from all the hotels where they had spent nights.

"But I don't want you to," he said, "I don't care anything about it."

"I'll scream," the girl said.

The woman came out through the curtains with two glasses of beer and put them down on the damp felt pads. "The train comes in five minutes," she said.

"What did she say?" asked the girl.

"That the train is coming in five minutes."

The girl smiled brightly at the woman, to thank her.

"I'd better take the bags over to the other side of the station," the man said. She smiled at him.

"All right. Then come back and we'll finish the beer."

He picked up the two heavy bags and carried them around the station to the other tracks. He looked up the tracks but could not see the train. Coming back, he walked through the barroom, where people waiting for the train were drinking. He drank an Anis at the bar and looked at the people. They were all waiting reasonably for the train. He went out through the bead curtain. She was sitting at the table and smiled at him.

"Do you feel better?" he asked.

"I feel fine," she said. "There's nothing wrong with me. I feel fine."

1927

FRANZ KAFKA

A Hunger Artist[1]

(See Kafka biography on p. 522.)

Born into a middle-class Jewish family in Prague, Franz Kafka earned a doctorate in law from the German University in that city and held an inconspicuous position in the civil service for many years. Emotionally and physically ill for the last seven or eight years of his short life, he died of tuberculosis in Vienna, never having married (though he was twice engaged to the same woman and lived with an actress in Berlin for some time before he died) and not having published his three major novels, *The Trial* (1925), *The Castle* (1926), and *Amerika* (1927). Indeed, he ordered his friend Max Brod to destroy them and other works he had left in manuscript. Fortunately, Brod did not; and not long after Kafka's death, his sometimes-dreamlike, sometimes-nightmarish work became

1. Translated by Edwin and Willa Muir.

known and admired all over the world. His stories in English translation are collected in *The Great Wall of China* (1933), *The Penal Colony* (1948), and *The Complete Stories* (1976).

During these last decades the interest in professional fasting has markedly diminished. It used to pay very well to stage such great performances under one's own management, but today that is quite impossible. We live in a different world now. At one time the whole town took a lively interest in the hunger artist; from day to day of his fast the excitement mounted; everybody wanted to see him at least once a day; there were people who bought season tickets for the last few days and sat from morning till night in front of his small barred cage; even in the nighttime there were visiting hours, when the whole effect was heightened by torch flares; on fine days the cage was set out in the open air, and then it was the children's special treat to see the hunger artist; for their elders he was often just a joke that happened to be in fashion, but the children stood open-mouthed, holding each other's hands for greater security, marveling at him as he sat there pallid in black tights, with his ribs sticking out so prominently, not even on a seat but down among straw on the ground, sometimes giving a courteous nod, answering questions with a constrained smile, or perhaps stretching an arm through the bars so that one might feel how thin it was, and then again withdrawing deep into himself, paying no attention to anyone or anything, not even to the all-important striking of the clock that was the only piece of furniture in his cage, but merely staring into vacancy with half shut eyes, now and then taking a sip from a tiny glass of water to moisten his lips.

Besides casual onlookers there were also relays of permanent watchers selected by the public, usually butchers, strangely enough, and it was their task to watch the hunger artist day and night, three of them at a time, in case he should have some secret recourse to nourishment. This was nothing but a formality, instituted to reassure the masses, for the initiates knew well enough that during his fast the artist would never in any circumstances, not even under forcible compulsion, swallow the smallest morsel of food: the honor of his profession forbade it. Not every watcher, of course, was capable of understanding this, there were often groups of night watchers who were very lax in carrying out their duties and deliberately huddled together in a retired corner to play cards with great absorption, obviously intending to give the hunger artist the chance of a little refreshment, which they supposed he could draw from some private hoard. Nothing annoyed the artist more than such watchers; they made him miserable; they made his fast seem unendurable; sometimes he mastered his feebleness sufficiently to sing during their watch for as long as he could keep going, to show them how unjust their suspicions were. But that was of little use; they only wondered at his cleverness in being able to fill his mouth even while singing. Much more to his taste were the watchers who sat close up to the bars, who were not content with the dim night lighting of the hall but focused him in the full glare of the electric pocket torch[2] given them by the impresario. The

2. Flashlight.

harsh light did not trouble him at all, in any case he could never sleep properly, and he could always drowse a little, whatever the light, at any hour, even when the hall was thronged with noisy onlookers. He was quite happy at the prospect of spending a sleepless night with such watchers; he was ready to exchange jokes with them, to tell them stories out of his nomadic life, anything at all to keep them awake and demonstrate to them again that he had no eatables in his cage and that he was fasting as not one of them could fast. But his happiest moment was when the morning came and an enormous breakfast was brought them, at his expense, on which they flung themselves with the keen appetite of healthy men after a weary night of wakefulness. Of course there were people who argued that this breakfast was an unfair attempt to bribe the watchers, but that was going rather too far, and when they were invited to take on a night's vigil without a breakfast, merely for the sake of the cause, they made themselves scarce, although they stuck stubbornly to their suspicions.

Such suspicions, anyhow, were a necessary accompaniment to the profession of fasting. No one could possibly watch the hunger artist continuously, day and night, and so no one could produce first-hand evidence that the fast had really been rigorous and continuous; only the artist himself could know that, he was therefore bound to be the sole completely satisfied spectator of his own fast. Yet for other reasons he was never satisfied; it was not perhaps mere fasting that had brought him to such skeleton thinness that many people had regretfully to keep away from his exhibitions, because the sight of him was too much for them, perhaps it was dissatisfaction with himself that had worn him down. For he alone knew, what no other initiate knew, how easy it was to fast. It was the easiest thing in the world. He made no secret of this, yet people did not believe him, at the best they set him down as modest; most of them, however, thought he was out for publicity or else was some kind of cheat who found it easy to fast because he had discovered a way of making it easy, and then had the impudence to admit the fact, more or less. He had to put up with all that, and in the course of time had got used to it, but his inner dissatisfaction always rankled, and never yet, after any term of fasting—this must be granted to his credit—had he left the cage of his own free will. The longest period of fasting was fixed by his impresario at forty days,[3] beyond that term he was not allowed to go, not even in great cities, and there was good reason for it, too. Experience had proved that for about forty days the interest of the public could be stimulated by a steadily increasing pressure of advertisement, but after that the town began to lose interest, sympathetic support began notably to fall off; there were of course local variations as between one town and another or one country and another, but as a general rule forty days marked the limit. So on the fortieth day the flower-bedecked cage was opened, enthusiastic spectators filled the hall, a military band played, two doctors entered the cage to measure the results of the fast, which were announced through a megaphone, and finally two young ladies appeared, blissful at having been selected for the honor, to help the hunger artist down the few steps leading to a small table on which was spread a carefully chosen invalid repast. And at this very moment the artist always turned stub-

3. Common biblical length of time; in the New Testament, Jesus fasts for forty days in the desert and has visions of both God and the devil.

born. True, he would entrust his bony arms to the outstretched helping hands of the ladies bending over him, but stand up he would not. Why stop fasting at this particular moment, after forty days of it? He had held out for a long time, an illimitably long time; why stop now, when he was in his best fasting form, or rather, not yet quite in his best fasting form? Why should he be cheated of the fame he would get for fasting longer, for being not only the record hunger artist of all time, which presumably he was already, but for beating his own record by a performance beyond human imagination, since he felt that there were no limits to his capacity for fasting? His public pretended to admire him so much, why should it have so little patience with him; if he could endure fasting longer, why shouldn't the public endure it? Besides, he was tired, he was comfortable sitting in the straw, and now he was supposed to lift himself to his full height and go down to a meal the very thought of which gave him a nausea that only the presence of the ladies kept him from betraying, and even that with an effort. And he looked up into the eyes of the ladies who were apparently so friendly and in reality so cruel, and shook his head, which felt too heavy on its strengthless neck. But then there happened yet again what always happened. The impresario came forward, without a word—for the band made speech impossible—lifted his arms in the air above the artist, as if inviting Heaven to look down upon its creature here in the straw, this suffering martyr, which indeed he was, although in quite another sense; grasped him round the emaciated waist, with exaggerated caution, so that the frail condition he was in might be appreciated; and committed him to the care of the blenching ladies, not without secretly giving him a shaking so that his legs and body tottered and swayed. The artist now submitted completely; his head lolled on his breast as if it had landed there by chance; his body was hollowed out; his legs in a spasm of self-preservation clung close to each other at the knees, yet scraped on the ground as if it were not really solid ground, as if they were only trying to find solid ground; and the whole weight of his body, a feather-weight after all, relapsed onto one of the ladies, who, looking round for help and panting a little—this post of honor was not at all what she had expected it to be—first stretched her neck as far as she could to keep her face at least free from contact with the artist, when finding this impossible, and her more fortunate companion not coming to her aid but merely holding extended on her own trembling hand the little bunch of knucklebones that was the artist's, to the great delight of the spectators burst into tears and had to be replaced by an attendant who had long been stationed in readiness. Then came the food, a little of which the impresario managed to get between the artist's lips, while he sat in a kind of half-fainting trance, to the accompaniment of cheerful patter designed to distract the public's attention from the artist's condition; after that, a toast was drunk to the public, supposedly prompted by a whisper from the artist in the impresario's ear; the band confirmed it with a mighty flourish, the spectators melted away, and no one had any cause to be dissatisfied with the proceedings, no one except the hunger artist himself, he only, as always.

So he lived for many years, with small regular intervals of recuperation, in visible glory, honored by the world, yet in spite of that troubled in spirit, and all the more troubled because no one would take his trouble seriously. What comfort could he possibly need? What more could he possibly wish for? And if some good-natured person, feeling sorry for him, tried to console him by pointing out that his melancholy was probably caused by fasting, it could happen, especially when he had been fasting for some time, that he reacted with an outburst of fury and to the general alarm began to shake the bars of his cage like a wild animal. Yet the impresario had a way of punishing these outbreaks which he rather enjoyed putting into operation. He would apologize publicly for the artist's behavior, which was only to be excused, he admitted, because of the irritability caused by fasting, a condition hardly to be understood by well-fed people; then by natural transition he went on to mention the artist's equally incomprehensible boast that he could fast for much longer than he was doing; he praised the high ambition, the good will, the great self-denial undoubtedly implicit in such a statement; and then quite simply countered it by bringing out photographs, which were also on sale to the public, showing the artist on the fortieth day of a fast lying in bed almost dead from exhaustion. This perversion of the truth, familiar to the artist though it was, always unnerved him afresh and proved too much for him. What was a consequence of the premature ending of his fast was here presented as the cause of it! To fight against this lack of understanding, against a whole world of non-understanding, was impossible. Time and again in good faith he stood by the bars listening to the impresario, but as soon as the photographs appeared he always let go and sank with a groan back on to his straw, and the reassured public could once more come close and gaze at him.

5 A few years later when the witnesses of such scenes called them to mind, they often failed to understand themselves at all. For meanwhile the aforementioned change in public interest had set in; it seemed to happen almost overnight; there may have been profound causes for it, but who was going to bother about that; at any rate the pampered hunger artist suddenly found himself deserted one fine day by the amusement seekers, who went streaming past him to other more favored attractions. For the last time the impresario hurried him over half Europe to discover whether the old interest might still survive here and there; all in vain; everywhere, as if by secret agreement, a positive revulsion from professional fasting was in evidence. Of course it could not really have sprung up so suddenly as all that, and many premonitory symptoms which had not been sufficiently remarked or suppressed during the rush and glitter of success now came retrospectively to mind, but it was now too late to take any countermeasures. Fasting would surely come into fashion again at some future date, yet that was no comfort for those living in the present. What, then, was the hunger artist to do? He had been applauded by thousands in his time and could hardly come down to showing himself in a street booth at village fairs, and as for adopting another profession, he was not only too old for that but too fanatically devoted to fasting. So he took leave of the impresario, his partner in an unparalleled career, and hired himself to a large circus; in order to spare his own feelings he avoided reading the conditions of his contract.

A large circus with its enormous traffic in replacing and recruiting men, animals and apparatus can always find a use for people at any time, even for a hunger artist, provided of course that he does not ask too much, and in this particular case anyhow it was not only the artist who was taken on but his famous and long-known name as well, indeed considering the peculiar nature of his performance, which was not impaired by advancing age, it could not be objected that here was an artist past his prime, no longer at the height of his professional skill, seeking a refuge in some quiet corner of a circus; on the contrary, the hunger artist averred that he could fast as well as ever, which was entirely credible, he even alleged that if he were allowed to fast as he liked, and this was at once promised him without more ado, he could astound the world by establishing a record never yet achieved, a statement which certainly provoked a smile among the other professionals, since it left out of account the change in public opinion, which the hunger artist in his zeal conveniently forgot.

He had not, however, actually lost his sense of the real situation and took it as a matter of course that he and his cage should be stationed, not in the middle of the ring as a main attraction, but outside, near the animal cages, on a site that was after all easily accessible. Large and gaily painted placards made a frame for the cage and announced what was to be seen inside it. When the public came thronging out in the intervals to see the animals, they could hardly avoid passing the hunger artist's cage and stopping there for a moment, perhaps they might even have stayed longer had not those pressing behind them in the narrow gangway, who did not understand why they should be held up on their way toward the excitements of the menagerie, made it impossible for anyone to stand gazing quietly for any length of time. And that was the reason why the hunger artist, who had of course been looking forward to these visiting hours as the main achievement of his life, began instead to shrink from them. At first he could hardly wait for the intervals; it was exhilarating to watch the crowds come streaming his way, until only too soon—not even the most obstinate self-deception, clung to almost consciously, could hold out against the fact—the conviction was borne in upon him that these people, most of them, to judge from their actions, again and again, without exception, were all on their way to the menagerie. And the first sight of them from the distance remained the best. For when they reached his cage he was at once deafened by the storm of shouting and abuse that arose from the two contending factions, which renewed themselves continuously, of those who wanted to stop and stare at him—he soon began to dislike them more than the others—not out of real interest but only out of obstinate self-assertiveness, and those who wanted to go straight on to the animals. When the first great rush was past, the stragglers came along, and these, whom nothing could have prevented from stopping to look at him as long as they had breath, raced past with long strides, hardly even glancing at him, in their haste to get to the menagerie in time. And all too rarely did it happen that he had a stroke of luck, when some father of a family fetched up before him with his children, pointed a finger at the hunger artist and explained at length what the phenomenon meant, telling stories of earlier years when he himself had watched similar but much more thrilling performances, and the children, still rather uncomprehending, since neither inside nor outside school had they been sufficiently prepared for this lesson—what did they care about fasting?—yet showed by the brightness of their intent eyes that new and better times might be coming. Perhaps, said the hunger artist to himself many a time, things would be a little better if his cage were set not quite so near the menagerie. That made it too easy for people to make their choice, to say nothing of what he suffered from the stench of the menagerie, the animals' restlessness by night, the carrying past of raw lumps of flesh for the beasts of prey, the roaring at feeding times, which depressed him continually. But he did not dare to lodge a complaint with the management; after all, he had the animals to thank for the troops of people who passed his cage, among whom there might always be one here and there to take an interest in him, and who could tell where they might seclude him if he called attention to his existence and thereby to the fact that, strictly speaking, he was only an impediment on the way to the menagerie.

A small impediment, to be sure, one that grew steadily less. People grew familiar with the strange idea that they could be expected, in times like these, to take an interest in a hunger artist, and with this familiarity the verdict went out against him. He might fast as much as he could, and he did so; but nothing could save him now, people passed him by. Just try to explain to anyone the art of fasting! Anyone who has no feeling for it cannot be made to understand it. The fine placards grew dirty and illegible, they were torn down; the little notice board telling the number of fast days achieved, which at first was changed carefully every day, had long stayed at the same figure, for after the first few weeks even this small task seemed pointless to the staff; and so the artist simply fasted on and on, as he had once dreamed of doing, and it was no trouble to him, just as he had always foretold, but no one counted the days, no one, not even the artist himself, knew what records he was already breaking, and his heart grew heavy. And when once in a time some leisurely passer-by stopped, made merry over the old figure on the board and spoke of swindling, that was in its way the stupidest lie ever invented by indifference and inborn malice, since it was not the hunger artist who was cheating; he was working honestly, but the world was cheating him of his reward.

Many more days went by, however, and that too came to an end. An overseer's eye fell on the cage one day and he asked the attendants why this perfectly good cage should be left standing there unused with dirty straw inside it; nobody knew, until one man, helped out by the notice board, remembered about the hunger artist. They poked into the straw with sticks and found him in it. "Are you still fasting?" asked the overseer. "When on earth do you mean to stop?" "Forgive me, everybody," whispered the hunger artist; only the overseer, who had his ear to the bars, understood him. "Of course," said the overseer, and tapped his forehead with a finger to let the attendants know what state the man was in, "we forgive you." "I always wanted you to admire my fasting," said the hunger artist. "We do admire it," said the overseer, affably. "But you shouldn't admire it," said the hunger artist. "Well, then we don't admire it," said the overseer, "but why shouldn't we admire it?" "Because I have to fast, I can't help it," said the hunger artist. "What a fellow you are," said the overseer, "and why can't you help it?" "Because," said the hunger artist, lifting his head a little and speaking, with his lips pursed, as if for a kiss, right into the overseer's ear, so that no syllable might be lost, "because I couldn't find the food I liked. If I had found it, believe me, I should have made no fuss and stuffed myself like you or anyone else." These were his last words, but in his dimming eyes remained the firm though no longer proud persuasion that he was still continuing to fast.

10 "Well, clear this out now!" said the overseer, and they buried the hunger artist, straw and all. Into the cage they put a young panther. Even the most insensitive felt it refreshing to see this wild creature leaping around the cage that had so long been dreary. The panther was all right. The food he liked was

brought him without hesitation by the attendants; he seemed not even to miss his freedom; his noble body, furnished almost to the bursting point with all that it needed, seemed to carry freedom around with it too; somewhere in his jaws it seemed to lurk; and the joy of life streamed with such ardent passion from his throat that for the onlookers it was not easy to stand the shock of it. But they braced themselves, crowded round the cage, and did not want ever to move away.

1924

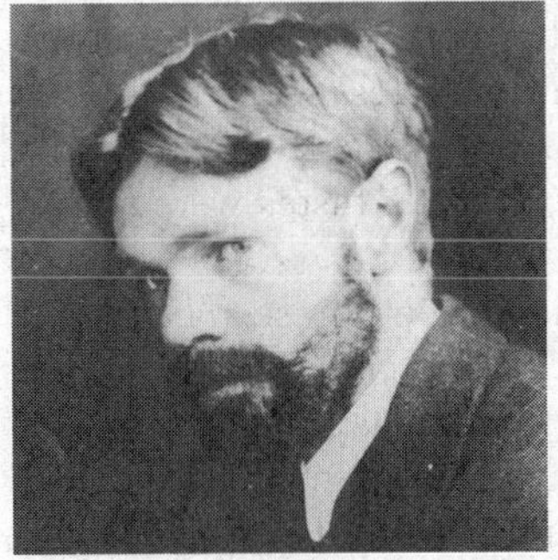

D. H. LAWRENCE
(1885–1930)

The Rocking-Horse Winner

The son of a coal miner and a schoolteacher, David Herbert Lawrence was able to attend high school only briefly. He worked for a surgical-appliance manufacturer, attended Nottingham University College, and taught school in Croydon, near London. After publishing his first novel, *The White Peacock* (1911), he devoted his time exclusively to writing; *Sons and Lovers* (1913) established him as a major literary figure. In 1912, he eloped with Frieda von Richthofen, and in 1914, after her divorce, they were married. During World War I, both his novels and his wife's German nationality gave him trouble: *The Rainbow* was published in September 1915 and suppressed in November. In 1919, the Lawrences left England and began years of wandering: first to Italy, then Ceylon, Australia, Mexico, and New Mexico, then back to England and Italy. Lawrence published *Women in Love* in 1920 and *Lady Chatterley's Lover,* his most sexually explicit novel, in 1928. Through it all he suffered from tuberculosis, eventually dying from the disease.

There was a woman who was beautiful, who started with all the advantages, yet she had no luck. She married for love, and the love turned to dust. She had bonny children, yet she felt they had been thrust upon her, and she could not love them. They looked at her coldly, as if they were finding fault with her. And hurriedly she felt she must cover up some fault in herself. Yet what it was that she must cover up she never knew. Nevertheless, when her children were present, she always felt the centre of her heart go hard. This troubled her, and in her manner she was all the more gentle and anxious for her children, as if she loved them very much. Only she herself knew that at the centre of her heart was a hard little place that could not feel love, no, not for anybody. Everybody else said of her: "She is such a good mother. She adores her children." Only she herself, and her children themselves, knew it was not so. They read it in each other's eyes.

There were a boy and two little girls. They lived in a pleasant house, with a garden, and they had discreet servants, and felt themselves superior to anyone in the neighbourhood.

Although they lived in style, they felt always an anxiety in the house. There was never enough money. The mother had a small income, and the father had a small income, but not nearly enough for the social position which they had to keep up. The father went in to town to some office. But though he had good prospects, these prospects never materialized. There was always the grinding sense of the shortage of money, though the style was always kept up.

At last the mother said: "I will see if *I* can't make something." But she did not know where to begin. She racked her brains, and tried this thing and the other, but could not find anything successful. The failure made deep lines come into her face. Her children were growing up, they would have to go to school. There must be more money, there must be more money. The father, who was always very handsome and expensive in his tastes, seemed as if he never *would* be able to do anything worth doing. And the mother, who had a great belief in herself, did not succeed any better, and her tastes were just as expensive.

5 And so the house came to be haunted by the unspoken phrase: *There must be more money! There must be more money!* The children could hear it all the time, though nobody said it aloud. They heard it at Christmas, when the expensive and splendid toys filled the nursery. Behind the shining modern rocking-horse, behind the smart doll's-house, a voice would start whispering: "There *must* be more money! There *must* be more money!" And the children would stop playing, to listen for a moment. They would look into each other's eyes, to see if they had all heard. And each one saw in the eyes of the other two that they too had heard. "There *must* be more money! There *must* be more money!"

It came whispering from the springs of the still-swaying rocking-horse, and even the horse, bending his wooden, champing head, heard it. The big doll, sitting so pink and smirking in her new pram,[1] could hear it quite plainly, and seemed to be smirking all the more self-consciously because of it. The foolish puppy, too, that took the place of the teddy-bear, he was looking so extraordinarily foolish for no other reason but that he heard the secret whisper all over the house: "There ***must*** be more money!"

Yet nobody ever said it aloud. The whisper was everywhere, and therefore no one spoke it. Just as no one ever says: "We are breathing!" in spite of the fact that breath is coming and going all the time.

"Mother," said the boy Paul one day, "why don't we keep a car of our own? Why do we always use uncle's, or else a taxi?"

"Because we're the poor members of the family," said the mother.

10 "But why *are* we, mother?"

"Well—I suppose," she said slowly and bitterly, "it's because your father has no luck."

The boy was silent for some time.

"Is luck money, mother?" he asked rather timidly.

"No, Paul. Not quite. It's what causes you to have money."

15 "Oh!" said Paul vaguely. "I thought when Uncle Oscar said *filthy lucker*, it meant money."

"*Filthy lucre* does mean money," said the mother. "But it's lucre, not luck."

1. Baby carriage.

"Oh!" said the boy. "Then what *is* luck, mother?"

"It's what causes you to have money. If you're lucky you have money. That's why it's better to be born lucky than rich. If you're rich, you may lose your money. But if you're lucky, you will always get more money."

"Oh! Will you? And is father not lucky?"

"Very unlucky, I should say," she said bitterly.

The boy watched her with unsure eyes.

"Why?" he asked.

"I don't know. Nobody ever knows why one person is lucky and another unlucky."

"Don't they? Nobody at all? Does *nobody* know?"

"Perhaps God. But He never tells."

"He ought to, then. And aren't you lucky either, mother?"

"I can't be, if I married an unlucky husband."

"But by yourself, aren't you?"

"I used to think I was, before I married. Now I think I am very unlucky indeed."

"Why?"

"Well—never mind! Perhaps I'm not really," she said.

The child looked at her, to see if she meant it. But he saw, by the lines of her mouth, that she was only trying to hide something from him.

"Well, anyhow," he said stoutly, "I'm a lucky person."

"Why?" said his mother, with a sudden laugh.

He stared at her. He didn't even know why he had said it.

"God told me," he asserted, brazening it out.

"I hope He did, dear!" she said, again with a laugh, but rather bitter.

"He did, mother!"

"Excellent!" said the mother, using one of her husband's exclamations.

The boy saw she did not believe him; or, rather, that she paid no attention to his assertion. This angered him somewhat, and made him want to compel her attention.

He went off by himself, vaguely, in a childish way, seeking for the clue to "luck." Absorbed, taking no heed of other people, he went about with a sort of stealth, seeking inwardly for luck. He wanted luck, he wanted it, he wanted it. When the two girls were playing dolls in the nursery, he would sit on his big rocking-horse, charging madly into space, with a frenzy that made the little girls peer at him uneasily. Wildly the horse careered, the waving dark hair of the boy tossed, his eyes had a strange glare in them. The little girls dared not speak to him.

When he had ridden to the end of his mad little journey, he climbed down and stood in front of his rocking-horse, staring fixedly into its lowered face. Its red mouth was slightly open, its big eye was wide and glassy-bright.

"Now!" he would silently command the snorting steed. "Now, take me to where there is luck! Now take me!"

And he would slash the horse on the neck with the little whip he had asked Uncle Oscar for. He *knew* the horse could take him to where there was luck, if only he forced it. So he would mount again, and start on his furious ride, hoping at last to get there. He knew he could get there.

"You'll break your horse, Paul!" said the nurse.

"He's always riding like that! I wish he'd leave off!" said his elder sister Joan.

But he only glared down on them in silence. Nurse gave him up. She could make nothing of him. Anyhow he was growing beyond her.

One day his mother and his Uncle Oscar came in when he was on one of his furious rides. He did not speak to them.

"Hallo, you young jockey! Riding a winner?" said his uncle.

"Aren't you growing too big for a rocking-horse? You're not a very little boy any longer, you know," said his mother.

But Paul only gave a blue glare from his big, rather close-set eyes. He would speak to nobody when he was in full tilt. His mother watched him with an anxious expression on her face.

At last he suddenly stopped forcing his horse into the mechanical gallop, and slid down.

"Well, I got there!" he announced fiercely, his blue eyes still flaring, and his sturdy long legs straddling apart.

"Where did you get to?" asked his mother.

"Where I wanted to go," he flared back at her.

"That's right, son!" said Uncle Oscar. "Don't you stop till you get there. What's the horse's name?"

"He doesn't have a name," said the boy.

"Gets on without all right?" asked the uncle.

"Well, he has different names. He was called Sansovino last week."

"Sansovino, eh? Won the Ascot.[2] How did you know his name?"

"He always talks about horse-races with Bassett," said Joan.

The uncle was delighted to find that his small nephew was posted with all the racing news. Bassett, the young gardener, who had been wounded in the left foot in the war[3] and had got his present job through Oscar Cresswell, whose batman[4] he had been, was a perfect blade of the "turf."[5] He lived in the racing events, and the small boy lived with him.

Oscar Cresswell got it all from Bassett.

"Master Paul comes and asks me, so I can't do more than tell him, sir," said Bassett, his face terribly serious, as if he were speaking of religious matters.

"And does he ever put anything on a horse he fancies?"

"Well—I don't want to give him away—he's a young sport, a fine sport, sir. Would you mind asking him himself? He sort of takes a pleasure in it, and perhaps he'd feel I was giving him away, sir, if you don't mind."

Bassett was serious as a church.

The uncle went back to his nephew and took him off for a ride in the car.

"Say, Paul, old man, do you ever put anything on a horse?" the uncle asked.

2. Race run at a course of that name in Berkshire. Other races mentioned in the story are Lincolnshire Handicap, then run at Lincoln Downs; the St. Leger Stakes, run at Doncaster; the Grand National Steeplechase, run at Aintree, the most famous steeplechase in the world; the famous Derby, a mile-and-a-half race for three-year-olds run at Epsom Downs.

3. World War I, 1914–18.

4. British officer's orderly.

5. That is, a dashing young horseplayer.

The boy watched the handsome man closely.

"Why, do you think I oughtn't to?" he parried.

"Not a bit of it! I thought perhaps you might give me a tip for the Lincoln."

The car sped on into the country, going down to Uncle Oscar's place in Hampshire.

"Honour bright?" said the nephew.

"Honour bright, son!" said the uncle.

"Well, then, Daffodil."

"Daffodil! I doubt it, sonny. What about Mirza?"

"I only know the winner," said the boy. "That's Daffodil."

"Daffodil, eh?"

There was a pause. Daffodil was an obscure horse comparatively.

"Uncle!"

"Yes, son?"

"You won't let it go any further, will you? I promised Bassett."

"Bassett be damned, old man! What's he got to do with it?"

"We're partners. We've been partners from the first. Uncle, he lent me my first five shillings, which I lost. I promised him, honour bright, it was only between me and him; only you gave me that ten-shilling note I started winning with, so I thought you were lucky. You won't let it go any further, will you?"

The boy gazed at his uncle from those big, hot, blue eyes, set rather close together. The uncle stirred and laughed uneasily.

"Right you are, son! I'll keep your tip private. Daffodil, eh? How much are you putting on him?"

"All except twenty pounds," said the boy. "I keep that in reserve."

The uncle thought it a good joke.

"You keep twenty pounds in reserve, do you, you young romancer? What are you betting, then?"

"I'm betting three hundred," said the boy, gravely. "But it's between you and me, Uncle Oscar! Honour bright?"

The uncle burst into a roar of laughter.

"It's between you and me all right, you young Nat Gould,"[6] he said, laughing. "But where's your three hundred?"

"Bassett keeps it for me. We're partners."

"You are, are you! And what is Bassett putting on Daffodil?"

"He won't go quite as high as I do, I expect. Perhaps he'll go a hundred and fifty."

"What, pennies?" laughed the uncle.

"Pounds," said the child, with a surprised look at his uncle. "Bassett keeps a bigger reserve than I do."

Between wonder and amusement Uncle Oscar was silent. He pursued the matter no further, but he determined to take his nephew with him to the Lincoln races.

"Now, son," he said, "I'm putting twenty on Mirza, and I'll put five for you on any horse you fancy. What's your pick?"

"Daffodil, uncle."

6. Nathaniel Gould (1857–1919), novelist and journalist who wrote about horse racing.

"No, not the fiver on Daffodil!"

"I should if it was my own fiver," said the child.

"Good! Good! Right you are! A fiver for me and a fiver for you on Daffodil."

The child had never been to a race-meeting before, and his eyes were blue fire. He pursed his mouth tight, and watched. A Frenchman just in front had put his money on Lancelot. Wild with excitement, he flayed his arms up and down, yelling *"Lancelot! Lancelot!"* in his French accent.

Daffodil came in first, Lancelot second, Mirza third. The child, flushed and with eyes blazing, was curiously serene. His uncle brought him four five-pound notes, four to one.

"What am I to do with these?" he cried, waving them before the boy's eyes.

"I suppose we'll talk to Bassett," said the boy. "I expect I have fifteen hundred now; and twenty in reserve; and this twenty."

His uncle studied him for some moments.

"Look here, son!" he said. "You're not serious about Bassett and that fifteen hundred, are you?"

"Yes, I am. But it's between you and me, uncle. Honour bright!"

"Honour bright all right, son! But I must talk to Bassett."

"If you'd like to be a partner, uncle, with Bassett and me, we could all be partners. Only, you'd have to promise, honour bright, uncle, not to let it go beyond us three. Bassett and I are lucky, and you must be lucky, because it was your ten shillings I started winning with. . . ."

Uncle Oscar took both Bassett and Paul into Richmond Park for an afternoon, and there they talked.

"It's like this, you see, sir," Bassett said. "Master Paul would get me talking about racing events, spinning yarns, you know, sir. And he was always keen on knowing if I'd made or if I'd lost. It's about a year since, now, that I put five shillings on Blush of Dawn for him—and we lost. Then the luck turned, with the ten shillings he had from you, that we put on Singhalese. And since that time, it's been pretty steady, all things considering. What do you say, Master Paul?"

"We're all right when we're sure," said Paul. "It's when we're not quite sure that we go down."

"Oh, but we're careful then," said Bassett.

"But when are you *sure*?" smiled Uncle Oscar.

"It's Master Paul, sir," said Bassett, in a secret, religious voice. "It's as if he had it from heaven. Like Daffodil, now, for the Lincoln. That was as sure as eggs."

"Did you put anything on Daffodil?" asked Oscar Cresswell.

"Yes, sir. I made my bit."

"And my nephew?"

Bassett was obstinately silent, looking at Paul.

"I made twelve hundred, didn't I, Bassett? I told uncle I was putting three hundred on Daffodil."

"That's right," said Bassett, nodding.

"But where's the money?" asked the uncle.

"I keep it safe locked up, sir. Master Paul he can have it any minute he likes to ask for it."

"What, fifteen hundred pounds?"

"And twenty! And *forty,* that is, with the twenty he made on the course."

"It's amazing!" said the uncle. 130

"If Master Paul offers you to be partners, sir, I would, if I were you; if you'll excuse me," said Bassett.

Oscar Cresswell thought about it.

"I'll see the money," he said.

They drove home again, and sure enough, Bassett came round to the garden-house with fifteen hundred pounds in notes. The twenty pounds reserve was left with Joe Glee, in the Turf Commission deposit.

"You see, it's all right, uncle, when I'm *sure!* Then we go strong, for all we're 135
worth. Don't we, Bassett?"

"We do that, Master Paul"

"And when are you sure?" said the uncle, laughing.

"Oh, well, sometimes I'm *absolutely* sure, like about Daffodil," said the boy; "and sometimes I have an idea; and sometimes I haven't even an idea, have I, Bassett? Then we're careful, because we mostly go down."

"You do, do you! And when you're sure, like about Daffodil, what makes you sure, sonny?"

"Oh, well, I don't know," said the boy uneasily. "I'm sure, you know, uncle; 140
that's all."

"It's as if he had it from heaven, sir," Bassett reiterated.

"I should say so!" said the uncle.

But he became a partner. And when the Leger was coming on, Paul was "sure" about Lively Spark, which was a quite inconsiderable horse. The boy insisted on putting a thousand on the horse, Bassett went for five hundred, and Oscar Cresswell two hundred. Lively Spark came in first, and the betting had been ten to one against him. Paul had made ten thousand.

"You see," he said, "I was absolutely sure of him."

Even Oscar Cresswell had cleared two thousand. 145

"Look here, son," he said, "this sort of thing makes me nervous."

"It needn't, uncle! Perhaps I shan't be sure again for a long time."

"But what are you going to do with your money?" asked the uncle.

"Of course," said the boy, "I started it for mother. She said she had no luck, because father is unlucky, so I thought if *I* was lucky, it might stop whispering."

"What might stop whispering?" 150

"Our house. I *hate* our house for whispering."

"What does it whisper?"

"Why—why"—the boy fidgeted—"why, I don't know. But it's always short of money, you know, uncle."

"I know it, son, I know it."

"You know people send mother writs, don't you, uncle?" 155

"I'm afraid I do," said the uncle.

"And then the house whispers, like people laughing at you behind your back. It's awful, that is! I thought if I was lucky . . ."

"You might stop it," added the uncle.

The boy watched him with big blue eyes, that had an uncanny cold fire in them, and he said never a word.

"Well, then!" said the uncle. "What are we doing?" 160

"I shouldn't like mother to know I was lucky," said the boy.

"Why not, son?"

"She'd stop me."

"I don't think she would."

165 "Oh!"—and the boy writhed in an odd way—"I *don't* want her to know, uncle."

"All right, son! We'll manage it without her knowing."

They managed it very easily. Paul, at the other's suggestion, handed over five thousand pounds to his uncle, who deposited it with the family lawyer, who was then to inform Paul's mother that a relative had put five thousand pounds into his hands, which sum was to be paid out a thousand pounds at a time, on the mother's birthday, for the next five years.

"So she'll have a birthday present of a thousand pounds for five successive years," said Uncle Oscar. "I hope it won't make it all the harder for her later."

Paul's mother had her birthday in November. The house had been "whispering" worse than ever lately, and, even in spite of his luck, Paul could not bear up against it. He was very anxious to see the effect of the birthday letter, telling his mother about the thousand pounds.

170 When there were no visitors, Paul now took his meals with his parents, as he was beyond the nursery control. His mother went into town nearly every day. She had discovered that she had an odd knack of sketching furs and dress materials, so she worked secretly in the studio of a friend who was the chief "artist" for the leading drapers. She drew the figures of ladies in furs and ladies in silk and sequins for the newspaper advertisements. This young woman artist earned several thousand pounds a year, but Paul's mother only made several hundreds, and she was again dissatisfied. She so wanted to be first in something, and she did not succeed, even in making sketches for drapery advertisements.

She was down to breakfast on the morning of her birthday. Paul watched her face as she read her letters. He knew the lawyer's letter. As his mother read it, her face hardened and became more expressionless. Then a cold, determined look came on her mouth. She hid the letter under the pile of others, and said not a word about it.

"Didn't you have anything nice in the post for your birthday, mother?" said Paul.

"Quite moderately nice," she said, her voice cold and absent.

She went away to town without saying more.

175 But in the afternoon Uncle Oscar appeared. He said Paul's mother had had a long interview with the lawyer, asking if the whole five thousand could not be advanced at once, as she was in debt.

"What do you think, uncle?" said the boy.

"I leave it to you, son."

"Oh, let her have it, then! We can get some more with the other," said the boy.

"A bird in the hand is worth two in the bush, laddie!" said Uncle Oscar.

180 "But I'm sure to *know* for the Grand National; or the Lincolnshire; or else the Derby. I'm sure to know for *one* of them," said Paul.

So Uncle Oscar signed the agreement, and Paul's mother touched the whole five thousand. Then something very curious happened. The voices in the house suddenly went mad, like a chorus of frogs on a spring evening. There were certain new furnishings, and Paul had a tutor. He was *really* going to Eton, his father's school, in the following autumn. There were flowers in the winter, and a blossoming of the luxury Paul's mother had been used to. And yet the voices in the house, behind the sprays of mimosa and almond blossom, and from under the piles of iridescent cushions, simply trilled and screamed in a sort of ecstasy: "There *must* be more money! Oh-h-h; there *must* be more money Oh, now, now-w! Now-w-w—there *must* be more money!—more than ever! More than ever!"

It frightened Paul terribly. He studied away at his Latin and Greek with his tutors. But his intense hours were spent with Bassett. The Grand National had gone by: he had not "known," and had lost a hundred pounds. Summer was at hand. He was in agony for the Lincoln. But even for the Lincoln he didn't "know," and he lost fifty pounds. He became wild-eyed and strange, as if something were going to explode in him.

"Let it alone, son! Don't you bother about it!" urged Uncle Oscar. But it was as if the boy couldn't really hear what his uncle was saying.

"I've got to know for the Derby! I've got to know for the Derby!" the child reiterated, his big blue eyes blazing with a sort of madness.

His mother noticed how overwrought he was.

"You'd better go to the seaside. Wouldn't you like to go now to the seaside, instead of waiting? I think you'd better," she said, looking down at him anxiously, her heart curiously heavy because of him.

But the child lifted his uncanny blue eyes.

"I couldn't possibly go before the Derby, mother!" he said. "I couldn't possibly!"

"Why not?" she said, her voice becoming heavy when she was opposed. "Why not? You can still go from the seaside to see the Derby with your Uncle Oscar, if that's what you wish. No need for you to wait here. Besides, I think you care too much about these races. It's a bad sign. My family has been a gambling family, and you won't know till you grow up how much damage it has done. But it has done damage. I shall have to send Bassett away, and ask Uncle Oscar not to talk racing to you, unless you promise to be reasonable about it; go away to the seaside and forget it. You're all nerves!"

"I'll do what you like, mother, so long as you don't send me away till after the Derby," the boy said.

"Send you away from where? Just from this house?"

"Yes," he said, gazing at her.

"Why, you curious child, what makes you care about this house so much, suddenly? I never knew you loved it."

He gazed at her without speaking. He had a secret within a secret, something he had not divulged, even to Bassett or to his Uncle Oscar.

But his mother, after standing undecided and a little bit sullen for some moments, said:

"Very well, then! Don't go to the seaside till after the Derby, if you don't wish it. But promise me you won't let your nerves go to pieces. Promise you won't think so much about horse-racing and events, as you call them!"

"Oh, no," said the boy casually. "I won't think much about them, mother. You needn't worry. I wouldn't worry, mother, if I were you."

"If you were me and I were you," said his mother, "I wonder what we *should* do!"

"But you know you needn't worry, mother, don't you?" the boy repeated.

"I should be awfully glad to know it," she said wearily.

"Oh, well, you *can,* you know. I mean, you *ought* to know you needn't worry," he insisted.

"Ought I? Then I'll see about it," she said.

Paul's secret of secrets was his wooden horse, that which had no name. Since he was emancipated from a nurse and a nursery-governess, he had had his rocking-horse removed to his own bedroom at the top of the house.

"Surely, you're too big for a rocking-horse!" his mother had remonstrated.

"Well, you see, mother, till I can have a *real* horse, I like to have *some* sort of animal about," had been his quaint answer.

"Do you feel he keeps you company?" she laughed.

"Oh, yes! He's very good, he always keeps me company, when I'm there," said Paul.

So the horse, rather shabby, stood in an arrested prance in the boy's bedroom.

The Derby was drawing near, and the boy grew more and more tense. He hardly heard what was spoken to him, he was very frail, and his eyes were really uncanny. His mother had sudden strange seizures of uneasiness about him. Sometimes, for half-an-hour, she would feel a sudden anxiety about him that was almost anguish. She wanted to rush to him at once, and know he was safe.

Two nights before the Derby, she was at a big party in town, when one of her rushes of anxiety about her boy, her first-born, gripped her heart till she could hardly speak. She fought with the feeling, might and main, for she believed in common-sense. But it was too strong. She had to leave the dance and go downstairs to telephone to the country. The children's nursery-governess was terribly surprised and startled at being rung up in the night.

"Are the children all right, Miss Wilmot?"

"Oh, yes, they are quite all right."

"Master Paul? Is he all right?"

"He went to bed as right as a trivet. Shall I run up and look at him?"

"No," said Paul's mother reluctantly. "No! Don't trouble. It's all right. Don't sit up. We shall be home fairly soon." She did not want her son's privacy intruded upon.

"Very good," said the governess.

It was about one o'clock when Paul's mother and father drove up to their house. All was still. Paul's mother went to her room and slipped off her white fur cloak. She had told her maid not to wait up for her. She heard her husband downstairs, mixing a whisky-and-soda.

And then, because of the strange anxiety at her heart, she stole upstairs to her son's room. Noiselessly she went along the upper corridor. Was there a faint noise? What was it?

She stood, with arrested muscles, outside his door, listening. There was a strange, heavy, and yet not loud noise. Her heart stood still. It was a soundless noise, yet rushing and powerful. Something huge, in violent, hushed motion. What was it? What in God's name was it? She ought to know. She felt that she knew the noise. She knew what it was.

Yet she could not place it. She couldn't say what it was. And on and on it went, like a madness.

Softly, frozen with anxiety and fear, she turned the door-handle.

The room was dark. Yet in the space near the window, she heard and saw something plunging to and fro. She gazed in fear and amazement.

Then suddenly she switched on the light, and saw her son, in his green pyjamas, madly surging on the rocking-horse. The blaze of light suddenly lit him up, as he urged the wooden horse, and lit her up, as she stood, blonde, in her dress of pale green and crystal, in the doorway.

"Paul!" she cried. "Whatever are you doing?"

"It's Malabar!" he screamed, in a powerful, strange voice. "It's Malabar!" 225

His eyes blazed at her for one strange and senseless second, as he ceased urging his wooden horse. Then he fell with a crash to the ground, and she, all her tormented motherhood flooding upon her, rushed to gather him up.

But he was unconscious, and unconscious he remained, with some brain-fever. He talked and tossed, and his mother sat stonily by his side.

"Malabar! It's Malabar! Bassett, Bassett, I *know*! It's Malabar!"

So the child cried, trying to get up and urge the rocking-horse that gave him his inspiration.

"What does he mean by Malabar?" asked the heart-frozen mother. 230

"I don't know," said the father stonily.

"What does he mean by Malabar?" she asked her brother Oscar.

"It's one of the horses running for the Derby," was the answer.

And, in spite of himself, Oscar Cresswell spoke to Bassett, and himself put a thousand on Malabar: at fourteen to one.

The third day of the illness was critical: they were waiting for a change. The 235
boy, with his rather long, curly hair, was tossing ceaselessly on the pillow. He neither slept nor regained consciousness, and his eyes were like blue stones. His mother sat, feeling her heart had gone, turned actually into a stone.

In the evening, Oscar Cresswell did not come, but Bassett sent a message, saying could he come up for one moment, just one moment? Paul's mother was very angry at the intrusion, but on second thought she agreed. The boy was the same. Perhaps Bassett might bring him to consciousness.

The gardener, a shortish fellow with a little brown moustache, and sharp little brown eyes, tip-toed into the room, touched his imaginary cap to Paul's mother, and stole to the bedside, staring with glittering, smallish eyes, at the tossing, dying child.

"Master Paul!" he whispered. "Master Paul! Malabar came in first all right, a clean win. I did as you told me. You've made over seventy thousand pounds, you have; you've got over eighty thousand. Malabar came in all right, Master Paul."

"Malabar! Malabar! Did I say Malabar, mother? Did I say Malabar? Do you think I'm lucky, mother? I knew Malabar, didn't I? Over eighty thousand pounds! I call that lucky, don't you, mother? Over eighty thousand pounds! I knew, didn't I know I knew! Malabar came in all right. If I ride my horse till I'm sure, then I tell you, Bassett, you can go as high as you like. Did you go for all you were worth, Bassett?"

"I went a thousand on it, Master Paul." 240

"I never told you, mother, that if I can ride my horse, and *get there*, then I'm absolutely sure—oh absolutely! Mother, did I ever tell you? I *am* lucky!"

"No, you never did," said the mother.

But the boy died in the night.

And even as he lay dead, his mother heard her brother's voice saying to her: "My God, Hester, you're eighty-odd thousand to the good, and a poor devil of a son to the bad. But, poor devil, poor devil, he's best gone out of a life where he rides his rocking-horse to find a winner."

1932

URSULA K. LE GUIN (b. 1929)

The Ones Who Walk Away from Omelas *(Variations on a Theme by William James)*[1]

Born in Berkeley, California, to a writer/folklorist mother and an anthropologist father, Ursula Kroeber earned a BA from Radcliffe College and an MA from Columbia University. In 1953, while a Fulbright Fellow in Paris, she married the historian Charles Le Guin, with whom she would eventually have three children. Although she began publishing fiction in the early 1960s, the prolific Le Guin established her literary reputation with the Earthsea novels, a philosophical fantasy series that begins with *A Wizard of Earthsea* (1968). Typically categorized as fantasy and/or science fiction, her work often depicts complex fictional societies with a folklorist's or anthropologist's eye for detail. Her many novels include *The Left Hand of Darkness* (1969) and *The Dispossessed* (1974), both part of the science-fiction series known as the "Hainish Cycle"; *The Compass Rose* (1982); and *Lavinia* (2008). In addition, Le Guin has written numerous essays, children's books, and both poetry and short-story collections, while collecting awards too numerous to list, including six Nebulas, five Hugos, and a PEN/Malamud Award for short fiction. In 2014, the National Book Foundation awarded Le Guin its prestigious Medal for Distinguished Contribution to American Letters in recognition of the fact that "[f]or more than 40 years, [she] has defied conventions of narrative, language, character, and genre, as well as transcended the boundaries between fantasy and realism, to forge new paths for literary fiction" by creating "fully imagined worlds [that] challenge readers to consider profound philosophical and existential questions about gender, race, the environment, and society."

With a clamor of bells that set the swallows soaring, the Festival of Summer came to the city Omelas, bright-towered by the sea. The rigging of the boats in harbor sparkled with flags. In the streets between houses with red

1. Pioneering American philosopher and psychologist (1842–1910), whose 1891 essay "The Moral Philosopher and Moral Life" asks, "[I]f the hypothesis were offered us of a world in which [. . .] millions [might] be kept permanently happy on the one simple condition that a certain lost soul on the far-off edge of things should lead a life of lonely torture, what except a specifical [*sic*] and independent sort of emotion [. . .] would make us immediately feel, even though an impulse arose within us to clutch at the happiness so offered, how hideous a thing would be its enjoyment when deliberately accepted as the fruit of such a bargain?"

roofs and painted walls, between old moss-grown gardens and under avenues of trees, past great parks and public buildings, processions moved. Some were decorous: old people in long stiff robes of mauve and grey, grave master workmen, quiet, merry women carrying their babies and chatting as they walked. In other streets the music beat faster, a shimmering of gong and tambourine, and the people went dancing, the procession was a dance. Children dodged in and out, their high calls rising like the swallows' crossing flights over the music and the singing. All the processions wound towards the north side of the city, where on the great water-meadow called the Green Fields boys and girls, naked in the bright air, with mud-stained feet and ankles and long, lithe arms, exercised their restive horses before the race. The horses wore no gear at all but a halter without bit. Their manes were braided with streamers of silver, gold, and green. They flared their nostrils and pranced and boasted to one another; they were vastly excited, the horse being the only animal who has adopted our ceremonies as his own. Far off to the north and west the mountains stood up half encircling Omelas on her bay. The air of morning was so clear that the snow still crowning the Eighteen Peaks burned with white-gold fire across the miles of sunlit air, under the dark blue of the sky. There was just enough wind to make the banners that marked the racecourse snap and flutter now and then. In the silence of the broad green meadows one could hear the music winding through the city streets, farther and nearer and ever approaching, a cheerful faint sweetness of the air that from time to time trembled and gathered together and broke out into the great joyous clanging of the bells.

Joyous! How is one to tell about joy? How describe the citizens of Omelas?

They were not simple folk, you see, though they were happy. But we do not say the words of cheer much any more. All smiles have become archaic. Given a description such as this one tends to make certain assumptions. Given a description such as this one tends to look next for the King, mounted on a splendid stallion and surrounded by his noble knights, or perhaps in a golden litter borne by great-muscled slaves. But there was no king. They did not use swords, or keep slaves. They were not barbarians. I do not know the rules and laws of their society, but I suspect that they were singularly few. As they did without monarchy and slavery, so they also got on without the stock exchange, the advertisement, the secret police, and the bomb. Yet I repeat that these were not simple folk, not dulcet shepherds, noble savages,[2] bland utopians. They were not less complex than us. The trouble is that we have a bad habit, encouraged by pedants and sophisticates, of considering happiness as something rather stupid. Only pain is intellectual, only evil interesting. This is the treason of the artist: a refusal to admit the banality of evil[3] and the terrible boredom of pain. If you can't lick 'em, join 'em. If it hurts, repeat it. But to praise despair is to condemn delight, to embrace violence is to lose hold of everything else. We have

2. Idealized concept of uncivilized peoples popularized by French philosopher Jean-Jacques Rousseau (1712–78), who contended that humans are innately good, evil arising only from the corruptions of civilization. Rousseau's noble savages thus somewhat resemble the *dulcet shepherds* of pastoral literature.

3. Allusion to political theorist Hannah Arendt's *Eichmann in Jerusalem: A Report on the Banality of Evil* (1963); it contends that, like Nazi administrator Adolf Eichmann (1906–62), those who commit even the most unspeakable evils are often not monsters, sociopaths, or ideologues but perfectly ordinary people who simply can't or don't imagine or reflect on the human and moral dimensions of their actions.

almost lost hold, we can no longer describe a happy man, nor make any celebration of joy. How can I tell you about the people of Omelas? They were not naïve and happy children—though their children were, in fact, happy. They were mature, intelligent, passionate adults whose lives were not wretched. O miracle! but I wish I could describe it better. I wish I could convince you. Omelas sounds in my words like a city in a fairy tale, long ago and far away, once upon a time. Perhaps it would be best if you imagined it as your own fancy bids, assuming it will rise to the occasion, for certainly I cannot suit you all. For instance, how about technology? I think that there would be no cars or helicopters in and above the streets; this follows from the fact that the people of Omelas are happy people. Happiness is based on a just discrimination of what is necessary, what is neither necessary nor destructive, and what is destructive. In the middle category, however—that of the unnecessary but undestructive, that of comfort, luxury, exuberance, etc—they could perfectly well have central heating, subway trains, washing machines, and all kinds of marvelous devices not yet invented here, floating light-sources, fuelless power, a cure for the common cold. Or they could have none of that: it doesn't matter. As you like it. I incline to think that people from towns up and down the coast have been coming in to Omelas during the last days before the Festival on very fast little trains and double-decked trams, and that the train station of Omelas is actually the handsomest building in town, though plainer than the magnificent Farmers' Market. But even granted trains, I fear that Omelas so far strikes some of you as goody-goody. Smiles, bells, parades, horses, bleh. If so, please add an orgy. If an orgy would help, don't hesitate. Let us not, however, have temples from which issue beautiful nude priests and priestesses already half in ecstasy and ready to copulate with any man or woman, lover or stranger, who desires union with the deep godhead of the blood, although that was my first idea. But really it would be better not to have any temples in Omelas—at least, not manned temples. Religion yes, clergy no. Surely the beautiful nudes can just wander about, offering themselves like divine soufflés to the hunger of the needy and the rapture of the flesh. Let them join the processions. Let tambourines be struck above the copulations, and the glory of desire be proclaimed upon the gongs, and (a not unimportant point) let the offspring of these delightful rituals be beloved and looked after by all. One thing I know there is none of in Omelas is guilt. But what else should there be? I thought at first there were no drugs, but that is puritanical. For those who like it, the faint insistent sweetness of *drooz* may perfume the ways of the city, *drooz* which first brings a great lightness and brilliance to the mind and limbs, and then after some hours a dreamy languor, and wonderful visions at last of the very arcana and inmost secrets of the Universe, as well as exciting the pleasure of sex beyond all belief; and it is not habit-forming. For more modest tastes I think there ought to be beer. What else, what else belongs in the joyous city? The sense of victory, surely, the celebration of courage. But as we did without clergy, let us do without soldiers. The joy built upon successful slaughter is not the right kind of joy; it will not do; it is fearful and it is trivial. A boundless and generous contentment, a magnanimous triumph felt not against some outer enemy but in communion with the finest and fairest in the souls of all men everywhere and the splendor of the world's summer: this is what swells the hearts of the people of Omelas, and the victory they celebrate is that of life. I really don't think many of them need to take *drooz*.

Most of the processions have reached the Green Fields by now. A marvelous smell of cooking goes forth from the red and blue tents of the provisioners. The faces of small children are amiably sticky; in the benign grey beard of a man a couple of crumbs of rich pastry are entangled. The youths and girls have mounted their horses and are beginning to group around the starting line of the course. An old woman, small, fat, and laughing, is passing out flowers from a basket, and tall young men wear her flowers in their shining hair. A child of nine or ten sits at the edge of the crowd, alone, playing on a wooden flute. People pause to listen, and they smile, but they do not speak to him, for he never ceases playing and never sees them, his dark eyes wholly rapt in the sweet, thin magic of the tune.

He finishes, and slowly lowers his hands holding the wooden flute. 5

As if that little private silence were the signal, all at once a trumpet sounds from the pavilion near the starting line: imperious, melancholy, piercing. The horses rear on their slender legs, and some of them neigh in answer. Sober-faced, the young riders stroke the horses' necks and soothe them, whispering, "Quiet, quiet, there my beauty, my hope. . . ." They begin to form in rank along the starting line. The crowds along the racecourse are like a field of grass and flowers in the wind. The Festival of Summer has begun.

Do you believe? Do you accept the festival, the city, the joy? No? Then let me describe one more thing.

In a basement under one of the beautiful public buildings of Omelas, or perhaps in the cellar of one of its more spacious private homes, there is a room. It has one locked door, and no window. A little light seeps in dustily between cracks in the boards, secondhand from a cobwebbed window somewhere across the cellar. In one corner of the little room a couple of mops, with stiff, clotted, foul-smelling heads, stand near a rusty bucket. The floor is dirt, a little damp to the touch, as cellar dirt usually is. The room is about three paces long and two wide: a mere broom closet or disused tool room. In the room a child is sitting. It could be a boy or a girl. It looks about six, but actually is nearly ten. It is feeble-minded. Perhaps it was born defective, or perhaps it has become imbecile through fear, malnutrition, and neglect. It picks its nose and occasionally fumbles vaguely with its toes or genitals, as it sits hunched in the corner farthest from the bucket and the two mops. It is afraid of the mops. It finds them horrible. It shuts its eyes, but it knows the mops are still standing there; and the door is locked; and nobody will come. The door is always locked; and nobody ever comes, except that sometimes—the child has no understanding of time or interval—sometimes the door rattles terribly and opens, and a person, or several people, are there. One of them may come in and kick the child to make it stand up. The others never come close, but peer in at it with frightened, disgusted eyes. The food bowl and the water jug are hastily filled, the door is locked, the eyes disappear. The people at the door never say anything, but the child, who has not always lived in the tool room, and can remember sunlight and its mother's voice, sometimes speaks. "I will be good," it says. "Please let me out. I will be good!" They never answer. The child used to scream for help at night, and cry a good deal, but now it only makes a kind of whining, "eh-haa, eh-haa," and it speaks less and less often. It is so thin there are no calves to its legs; its belly protrudes; it lives on a half-bowl of corn meal and grease a day. It is naked. Its buttocks and thighs are a mass of festered sores, as it sits in its own excrement continually.

They all know it is there, all the people of Omelas. Some of them have come to see it, others are content merely to know it is there. They all know that it has to be there. Some of them understand why, and some do not, but they all understand that their happiness, the beauty of their city, the tenderness of their friendships, the health of their children, the wisdom of their scholars, the skill of their makers, even the abundance of their harvest and the kindly weathers of their skies, depend wholly on this child's abominable misery.

10 This is usually explained to children when they are between eight and twelve, whenever they seem capable of understanding; and most of those who come to see the child are young people, though often enough an adult comes, or comes back, to see the child. No matter how well the matter has been explained to them, these young spectators are always shocked and sickened at the sight. They feel disgust, which they had thought themselves superior to. They feel anger, outrage, impotence, despite all the explanations. They would like to do something for the child. But there is nothing they can do. If the child were brought up into the sunlight out of the vile place, if it were cleaned and fed and comforted, that would be a good thing, indeed; but if it were done, in that day and hour all the prosperity and beauty and delight of Omelas would wither and be destroyed. Those are the terms. To exchange all the goodness and grace of every life in Omelas for that single, small improvement: to throw away the happiness of thousands for the chance of the happiness of one: that would be to let guilt within the walls indeed.

The terms are strict and absolute; there may not even be a kind word spoken to the child.

Often the young people go home in tears, or in a tearless rage, when they have seen the child and faced this terrible paradox. They may brood over it for weeks or years. But as time goes on they begin to realize that even if the child could be released, it would not get much good of its freedom: a little vague pleasure of warmth and food, no doubt, but little more. It is too degraded and imbecile to know any real joy. It has been afraid too long ever to be free of fear. Its habits are too uncouth for it to respond to humane treatment. Indeed, after so long it would probably be wretched without walls about it to protect it, and darkness for its eyes, and its own excrement to sit in. Their tears at the bitter injustice dry when they begin to perceive the terrible justice of reality, and to accept it. Yet it is their tears and anger, the trying of their generosity and the acceptance of their helplessness, which are perhaps the true source of the splendor of their lives. Theirs is no vapid, irresponsible happiness. They know that they, like the child, are not free. They know compassion. It is the existence of the child, and their knowledge of its existence, that makes possible the nobility of their architecture, the poignancy of their music, the profundity of their science. It is because of the child that they are so gentle with children. They know that if the wretched one were not there snivelling in the dark, the other one, the flute-player, could make no joyful music as the young riders line up in their beauty for the race in the sunlight of the first morning of summer.

Now do you believe in them? Are they not more credible? But there is one more thing to tell, and this is quite incredible.

At times one of the adolescent girls or boys who go to see the child does not go home to weep or rage, does not, in fact, go home at all. Sometimes also a man or woman much older falls silent for a day or two, and then leaves home. These people go out into the street, and walk down the street alone. They keep walking, and walk straight out of the city of Omelas, through the beautiful gates. They keep walking across the farmlands of Omelas. Each one goes alone, youth or girl, man or woman. Night falls; the traveler must pass down village streets, between the houses with yellow-lit windows, and on out into the darkness of the fields. Each alone, they go west or north, towards the mountains. They go on. They leave Omelas, they walk ahead into the darkness, and they do not come back. The place they go towards is a place even less imaginable to most of us than the city of happiness. I cannot describe it at all. It is possible that it does not exist. But they seem to know where they are going, the ones who walk away from Omelas.

1975

BOBBIE ANN MASON (b. 1940)

Shiloh

Bobbie Ann Mason was born and raised on her parents' dairy farm in western Kentucky, the region where many of her stories are set. She received a BA from the University of Kentucky, an MA from the State University of New York at Binghamton, and a PhD in English from the University of Connecticut. In addition to writing both a dissertation on the work of Vladimir Nabokov, later published as a book (1974), and *The Girl Sleuth: A Feminist Guide to the Bobbsey Twins, Nancy Drew, and Their Sisters* (1975), Mason began to publish the short stories eventually collected in the highly acclaimed *Shiloh and Other Stories* (1982), winner of the PEN Hemingway Award. That book, combined with her first novel, *In Country* (1985; filmed 1989), inspired one reviewer to dub her writing "Shopping Mall Realism." Mason has continued to write novels, including *Feather Crowns* (1993), *Atomic Romance* (2005), and *The Girl in the Blue Beret* (2011), as well as nonfiction ranging from a biography of Elvis Presley (2003) to *Clear Springs: A Memoir* (1999), a nominee for the Pulitzer Prize. She is best known and most highly praised, however, for short-story collections like *Zigzagging Down a Wild Trail* (2001) and *Nancy Culpepper* (2006). Novelist Ann Tyler describes Mason as "a full-fledged master of the short story," while fiction writer Lorrie Moore suggests that her "strongest form may be neither the novel nor the story, but the story *collection*."

Leroy Moffitt's wife, Norma Jean, is working on her pectorals. She lifts three-pound dumbbells to warm up, then progresses to a twenty-pound barbell. Standing with her legs apart, she reminds Leroy of Wonder Woman.

"I'd give anything if I could just get these muscles to where they're real hard," says Norma Jean. "Feel this arm. It's not as hard as the other one."

"That's cause you're right-handed," says Leroy, dodging as she swings the barbell in an arc.

"Do you think so?"

5 "Sure."

Leroy is a truckdriver. He injured his leg in a highway accident four months ago, and his physical therapy, which involves weights and a pulley, prompted Norma Jean to try building herself up. Now she is attending a body-building class. Leroy has been collecting temporary disability since his tractor-trailer jackknifed in Missouri, badly twisting his left leg in its socket. He has a steel pin in his hip. He will probably not be able to drive his rig again. It sits in the backyard, like a gigantic bird that has flown home to roost. Leroy has been home in Kentucky for three months, and his leg is almost healed, but the accident frightened him and he does not want to drive any more long hauls. He is not sure what to do next. In the meantime, he makes things from craft kits. He started by building a miniature log cabin from notched Popsicle sticks. He varnished it and placed it on the TV set, where it remains. It reminds him of a rustic Nativity scene. Then he tried string art (sailing ships on black velvet), a macramé owl kit, a snap-together B-17 Flying Fortress,[1] and a lamp made out of a model truck, with a light fixture screwed in the top of the cab. At first the kits were diversions, something to kill time, but now he is thinking about building a full-scale log house from a kit. It would be considerably cheaper than building a regular house, and besides, Leroy has grown to appreciate how things are put together. He has begun to realize that in all the years he was on the road he never took time to examine anything. He was always flying past scenery.

"They won't let you build a log cabin in any of the new subdivisions," Norma Jean tells him.

"They will if I tell them it's for you," he says, teasing her. Ever since they were married, he has promised Norma Jean he would build her a new home one day. They have always rented, and the house they live in is small and nondescript. It does not even feel like a home, Leroy realizes now.

Norma Jean works at the Rexall drugstore, and she has acquired an amazing amount of information about cosmetics. When she explains to Leroy the three stages of complexion care, involving creams, toners, and moisturizers, he thinks happily of other petroleum products—axle grease, diesel fuel. This is a connection between him and Norma Jean. Since he has been home, he has felt unusually tender about his wife and guilty over his long absences. But he can't tell what she feels about him. Norma Jean has never complained about his traveling; she has never made hurt remarks, like calling his truck a "widow-maker." He is reasonably certain she has been faithful to him, but he wishes she would celebrate his permanent homecoming more happily. Norma Jean is often startled to find Leroy at home, and he thinks she seems a little disappointed about it. Perhaps he reminds her too much of the early days of their marriage, before he went on the road. They had a child who died as an infant, years ago. They never speak about their memories of Randy, which have almost faded, but now that Leroy is home all the time, they sometimes feel awkward around each other, and Leroy wonders if one of them should mention the child. He has the feeling that they are waking up out of a dream together—that they must create

1. American World War II bomber.

a new marriage, start afresh. They are lucky they are still married. Leroy has read that for most people losing a child destroys the marriage—or else he heard this on *Donahue*. He can't always remember where he learns things anymore.

At Christmas, Leroy bought an electric organ for Norma Jean. She used to 10 play the piano when she was in high school. "It don't leave you," she told him once. "It's like riding a bicycle."

The new instrument had so many keys and buttons that she was bewildered by it at first. She touched the keys tentatively, pushed some buttons, then pecked out "Chopsticks." It came out in an amplified fox-trot rhythm, with marimba sounds.

"It's an orchestra!" she cried.

The organ had a pecan-look finish and eighteen preset chords, with optional flute, violin, trumpet, clarinet, and banjo accompaniments. Norma Jean mastered the organ almost immediately. At first she played Christmas songs. Then she bought *The Sixties Songbook* and learned every tune in it, adding variations to each with the rows of brightly colored buttons.

"I didn't like these old songs back then," she said. "But I have this crazy feeling I missed something."

"You didn't miss a thing," said Leroy. 15

Leroy likes to lie on the couch and smoke a joint and listen to Norma Jean play "Can't Take My Eyes Off You" and "I'll Be Back."[2] He is back again. After fifteen years on the road, he is finally settling down with the woman he loves. She is still pretty. Her skin is flawless. Her frosted curls resemble pencil trimmings.

Now that Leroy has come home to stay, he notices how much the town has changed. Subdivisions are spreading across western Kentucky like an oil slick. The sign at the edge of town says "Pop: 11,500"—only seven hundred more than it said twenty years before. Leroy can't figure out who is living in all the new houses. The farmers who used to gather around the courthouse square on Saturday afternoons to play checkers and spit tobacco juice have gone. It has been years since Leroy has thought about the farmers, and they have disappeared without his noticing.

Leroy meets a kid named Stevie Hamilton in the parking lot at the new shopping center. While they pretend to be strangers meeting over a stalled car, Stevie tosses an ounce of marijuana under the front seat of Leroy's car. Stevie is wearing orange jogging shoes and a T-shirt that says CHATTAHOOCHEE SUPER-RAT. His father is a prominent doctor who lives in one of the expensive subdivisions in a new white-columned brick house that looks like a funeral parlor. In the phone book under his name there is a separate number, with the listing "Teenagers."

"Where do you get this stuff?" asks Leroy. "From your pappy!"

"That's for me to know and you to find out," Stevie says. He is slit-eyed and 20 skinny.

"What else you got?"

"What you interested in?"

"Nothing special. Just wondered."

2. Hit songs of the 1960s.

Leroy used to take speed on the road. Now he has to go slowly. He needs to be mellow. He leans back against the car and says, "I'm aiming to build me a log house, soon as I get time. My wife, though, I don't think she likes the idea."

25 "Well, let me know when you want me again," Stevie says. He has a cigarette in his cupped palm, as though sheltering it from the wind. He takes a long drag, then stomps it on the asphalt and slouches away.

Stevie's father was two years ahead of Leroy in high school. Leroy is thirty-four. He married Norma Jean when they were both eighteen, and their child Randy was born a few months later, but he died at the age of four months and three days. He would be about Stevie's age now. Norma Jean and Leroy were at the drive-in, watching a double feature (*Dr. Strangelove* and *Lover Come Back*),[3] and the baby was sleeping in the back seat. When the first movie ended, the baby was dead. It was the sudden infant death syndrome. Leroy remembers handing Randy to a nurse at the emergency room, as though he were offering her a large doll as a present. A dead baby feels like a sack of flour. "It just happens sometimes," said the doctor, in what Leroy always recalls as a nonchalant tone. Leroy can hardly remember the child anymore, but he still sees vividly a scene from *Dr. Strangelove* in which the President of the United States was talking in a folksy voice on the hot line to the Soviet premier about the bomber accidentally headed toward Russia. He was in the War Room, and the world map was lit up. Leroy remembers Norma Jean catatonically beside him in the hospital and himself thinking: Who is this strange girl? He had forgotten who she was. Now scientists are saying that crib death is caused by a virus. Nobody knows anything, Leroy thinks. The answers are always changing.

When Leroy gets home from the shopping center, Norma Jean's mother, Mabel Beasley, is there. Until this year, Leroy has not realized how much time she spends with Norma Jean. When she visits, she inspects the closets and then the plants, informing Norma Jean when a plant is droopy or yellow. Mabel calls the plants "flowers," although there are never any blooms. She always notices if Norma Jean's laundry is piling up. Mabel is a short, overweight woman whose tight, brown-dyed curls look more like a wig than the actual wig she sometimes wears. Today she has brought Norma Jean an off-white dust ruffle she made for the bed; Mabel works in a custom-upholstery shop.

"This is the tenth one I made this year," Mabel says. "I got started and couldn't stop."

"It's real pretty," says Norma Jean.

30 "Now we can hide things under the bed," says Leroy, who gets along with his mother-in-law primarily by joking with her. Mabel has never really forgiven him for disgracing her by getting Norma Jean pregnant. When the baby died, she said that fate was mocking her.

"What's that thing?" Mabel says to Leroy in a loud voice, pointing to a tangle of yarn on a piece of canvas.

Leroy holds it up for Mabel to see. "It's my needlepoint," he explains. "This is a *Star Trek* pillow cover."

"That's what a woman would do," says Mabel. "Great day in the morning!"

3. A 1963 satire on nuclear war and a 1961 Rock Hudson–Doris Day romantic comedy satirizing the advertising business, respectively.

"All the big football players on TV do it," he says.

"Why, Leroy, you're always trying to fool me. I don't believe you for one minute. You don't know what to do with yourself—that's the whole trouble. Sewing!"

"I'm aiming to build us a log house," says Leroy. "Soon as my plans come."

"Like *heck* you are," says Norma Jean. She takes Leroy's needlepoint and shoves it into a drawer. "You have to find a job first. Nobody can afford to build now anyway."

Mabel straightens her girdle and says, "I still think before you get tied down y'all ought to take a little run to Shiloh."

"One of these days, Mama," Norma Jean says impatiently.

Mabel is talking about Shiloh, Tennessee. For the past few years, she has been urging Leroy and Norma Jean to visit the Civil War battleground there.[4] Mabel went there on her honeymoon—the only real trip she ever took. Her husband died of a perforated ulcer when Norma Jean was ten, but Mabel, who was accepted into the United Daughters of the Confederacy in 1975, is still preoccupied with going back to Shiloh.

"I've been to kingdom come and back in that truck out yonder," Leroy says to Mabel, "but we never yet set foot in that battleground. Ain't that something? How did I miss it?"

"It's not even that far," Mabel says.

After Mabel leaves, Norma Jean reads to Leroy from a list she has made. "Thing you could do," she announces. "You could get a job as a guard at Union Carbide, where they'd let you set on a stool. You could get on at the lumberyard. You could do a little carpenter work, if you want to build so bad. You could—"

"I can't do something where I'd have to stand up all day."

"You ought to try standing up all day behind a cosmetics counter. It's amazing that I have strong feet, coming from two parents that never had strong feet at all." At the moment Norma Jean is holding on to the kitchen counter, raising her knees one at a time as she talks. She is wearing two-pound ankle weights.

"Don't worry," says Leroy. "I'll do something."

"You could truck calves to slaughter for somebody. You wouldn't have to drive any big old truck for that."

"I'm going to build you this house," says Leroy. "I want to make you a real home."

"I don't want to live in any log cabin."

"It's not a cabin. It's a house."

"I don't care. It looks like a cabin."

"You and me together could lift those logs. It's just like lifting weights."

Norma Jean doesn't answer. Under her breath, she is counting. Now she is marching through the kitchen. She is doing goose steps.

Before his accident, when Leroy came home he used to stay in the house with Norma Jean, watching TV in bed and playing cards. She would cook fried chicken, picnic ham, chocolate pie—all his favorites. Now he is home alone

4. Where, in April 1862, more than twenty-three thousand troops of the North and South, one-quarter of those who fought there, died. This was the first real indication of how bitter and bloody the war was to be. When Union reinforcements arrived, General Ulysses S. Grant drove the Confederate forces, who had gained an initial victory by a surprise attack, back to their base in Corinth, Mississippi.

much of the time. In the mornings, Norma Jean disappears, leaving a cooling place in the bed. She eats a cereal called Body Buddies, and she leaves the bowl on the table, with soggy tan balls floating in a milk puddle. He sees things about Norma Jean that he never realized before. When she chops onions, she stares off into a corner, as if she can't bear to look. She puts on her house slippers almost precisely at nine o'clock every evening and nudges her jogging shoes under the couch. She saves bread heels for the birds. Leroy watches the birds at the feeder. He notices the peculiar way goldfinches fly past the window. They close their wings, then fall, then spread their wings to catch and lift themselves. He wonders if they close their eyes when they fall. Norma Jean closes her eyes when they are in bed. She wants the lights turned out. Even then, he is sure she closes her eyes.

55 He goes for long drives around town. He tends to drive a car rather carelessly. Power steering and an automatic shift make a car feel so small and inconsequential that his body is hardly involved in the driving process. His injured leg stretches out comfortably. Once or twice he has almost hit something, but even the prospect of an accident seems minor in a car. He cruises the new subdivisions, feeling like a criminal rehearsing for a robbery. Norma Jean is probably right about a log house being inappropriate here in the new subdivisions. All the houses look grand and complicated. They depress him.

One day when Leroy comes home from a drive he finds Norma Jean in tears. She is in the kitchen making a potato and mushroom-soup casserole, with grated-cheese topping. She is crying because her mother caught her smoking.

"I didn't hear her coming. I was standing here puffing away pretty as you please," Norma Jean says, wiping her eyes.

"I knew it would happen sooner or later," says Leroy, putting his arm around her.

"She don't know the meaning of the word 'knock,'" says Norma Jean. "It's a wonder she hadn't caught me years ago."

60 "Think of it this way," Leroy says. "What if she caught me with a joint?"

"You better not let her!" Norma Jean shrieks. "I'm warning you, Leroy Moffitt!"

"I'm just kidding. Here, play me a tune. That'll help you relax."

Norma Jean puts the casserole in the oven and sets the timer. Then she plays a ragtime tune, with horns and banjo, as Leroy lights up a joint and lies on the couch, laughing to himself about Mabel's catching him at it. He thinks of Stevie Hamilton—a doctor's son pushing grass. Everything is funny. The whole town seems crazy and small. He is reminded of Virgil Mathis, a boastful policeman Leroy used to shoot pool with. Virgil recently led a drug bust in a back room at a bowling alley, where he seized ten thousand dollars' worth of marijuana. The newspaper had a picture of him holding up the bags of grass and grinning widely. Right now, Leroy can imagine Virgil breaking down the door and arresting him with a lungful of smoke. Virgil would probably have been alerted to the scene because of all the racket Norma Jean is making. Now she sounds like a hard-rock band. Norma Jean is terrific. When she switches to a Latin-rhythm version of "Sunshine Superman," Leroy hums along. Norma Jean's foot goes up and down, up and down.

"Well, what do you think?" Leroy says, when Norma Jean pauses to search through her music.

"What do I think about what?" 65

His mind has gone blank. Then he says, "I'll sell my rig and build us a house." That wasn't what he wanted to say. He wanted to know what she thought—what she *really* thought—about them.

"Don't start in on that again," says Norma Jean. She begins playing "Who'll Be the Next in Line?"

Leroy used to tell hitchhikers his whole life story—about his travels, his hometown, the baby. He would end with a question: "Well, what do you think?" It was just a rhetorical question. In time, he had the feeling that he'd been telling the same story over and over to the same hitchhikers. He quit talking to hitchhikers when he realized how his voice sounded—whining and self-pitying, like some teenage-tragedy song. Now Leroy has the sudden impulse to tell Norma Jean about himself, as if he had just met her. They have known each other so long they have forgotten a lot about each other. They could become reacquainted. But when the oven timer goes off and she runs to the kitchen, he forgets why he wants to do this.

The next day, Mabel drops by. It is Saturday and Norma Jean is cleaning. Leroy is studying the plans of his log house, which have finally come in the mail. He has them spread out on the table—big sheets of stiff blue paper, with diagrams and numbers printed in white. While Norma Jean runs the vacuum, Mabel drinks coffee. She sets her coffee cup on a blueprint.

"I'm just waiting for time to pass," she says to Leroy, drumming her fingers on 70
the table.

As soon as Norma Jean switches off the vacuum, Mabel says in a loud voice, "Did you hear about the datsun dog that killed the baby?"

Norma Jean says, "The word is 'dachshund.'"

"They put the dog on trial. It chewed the baby's legs off. The mother was in the next room all the time." She raises her voice. "They thought it was neglect."

Norma Jean is holding her ears. Leroy manages to open the refrigerator and get some Diet Pepsi to offer Mabel. Mabel still has some coffee and she waves away the Pepsi.

"Datsuns are like that," Mabel says. "They're jealous dogs. They'll tear a 75
place to pieces if you don't keep an eye on them."

"You better watch out what you're saying, Mabel," says Leroy.

"Well, facts is facts."

Leroy looks out the window at his rig. It is like a huge piece of furniture gathering dust in the backyard. Pretty soon it will be an antique. He hears the vacuum cleaner. Norma Jean seems to be cleaning the living room rug again.

Later, she says to Leroy, "She just said that about the baby because she caught me smoking. She's trying to pay me back."

"What are you talking about?" Leroy says, nervously shuffling blueprints. 80

"You know good and well," Norma Jean says. She is sitting in a kitchen chair with her feet up and her arms wrapped around her knees. She looks small and helpless. She says, "The very idea, her bringing up a subject like that! Saying it was neglect."

"She didn't mean that," Leroy says.

"She might not have *thought* she meant it. She always says things like that. You don't know how she goes on."

"But she didn't really mean it. She was just talking."

Leroy opens a king-sized bottle of beer and pours it into two glasses, dividing it carefully. He hands a glass to Norma Jean and she takes it from him mechanically. For a long time, they sit by the kitchen window watching the birds at the feeder.

Something is happening. Norma Jean is going to night school. She has graduated from her six-week body-building course and now she is taking an adult-education course in composition at Paducah Community College. She spends her evenings outlining paragraphs.

"First you have a topic sentence," she explains to Leroy. "Then you divide it up. Your secondary topic has to be connected to your primary topic."

To Leroy, this sounds intimidating. "I never was any good in English," he says.

"It makes a lot of sense."

"What are you doing this for, anyhow?"

She shrugs. "It's something to do." She stands up and lifts her dumbbells a few times.

"Driving a rig, nobody cared about my English."

"I'm not criticizing your English."

Norma Jean used to say, "If I lose ten minutes' sleep, I just drag all day." Now she stays up late, writing compositions. She got a B on her first paper—a how-to theme on soup-based casseroles. Recently Norma Jean has been cooking unusual foods—tacos, lasagna, Bombay chicken. She doesn't play the organ anymore, though her second paper was called "Why Music Is Important to Me." She sits at the kitchen table, concentrating on her outlines, while Leroy plays with his log house plans, practicing with a set of Lincoln Logs. The thought of getting a truckload of notched, numbered logs scares him, and he wants to be prepared. As he and Norma Jean work together at the kitchen table, Leroy has the hopeful thought that they are sharing something, but he knows he is a fool to think this. Norma Jean is miles away. He knows he is going to lose her. Like Mabel, he is just waiting for time to pass.

One day, Mabel is there before Norma Jean gets home from work, and Leroy finds himself confiding in her. Mabel, he realizes, must know Norma Jean better than he does.

"I don't know what's got into that girl," Mabel says. "She used to go to bed with the chickens. Now you say she's up all hours. Plus her a-smoking. I like to died."

"I want to make her this beautiful home," Leroy says, indicating the Lincoln Logs. "I don't think she even wants it. Maybe she was happier with me gone."

"She don't know what to make of you, coming home like this."

"Is that it?"

Mabel takes the roof off his Lincoln Log cabin. "You couldn't get *me* in a log cabin," she says. "I was raised in one. It's no picnic, let me tell you."

"They're different now," says Leroy.

"I tell you what," Mabel says, smiling oddly at Leroy.

"What?"

"Take her on down to Shiloh. Y'all need to get out together, stir a little. Her brain's all balled up over them books."

Leroy can see traces of Norma Jean's features in her mother's face. Mabel's 105
face has the texture of crinkled cotton, but suddenly she looks pretty. It occurs to Leroy that Mabel has been hinting all along that she wants them to take her with them to Shiloh.

"Let's all go to Shiloh," he says. "You and me and her. Come Sunday."

Mabel throws up her hands in protest. "Oh, no, not me. Young folks want to be by theirselves."

When Norma Jean comes in with groceries, Leroy says excitedly, "Your mama here's been dying to go to Shiloh for thirty-five years. It's about time we went, don't you think?"

"I'm not going to butt in on anybody's second honeymoon," Mabel says.

"Who's going on a honeymoon, for Christ's sake?" Norma Jean says loudly. 110

"I never raised no daughter of mine to talk that-a-way," Mabel says.

"You ain't seen nothing yet," says Norma Jean. She starts putting away boxes and cans, slamming cabinet doors.

"There's a log cabin at Shiloh." Mabel says, "It was there during the battle. There's bullet holes in it."

"When are you going to *shut up* about Shiloh, Mama?" asks Norma Jean.

"I always thought Shiloh was the prettiest place, so full of history," Mabel goes 115
on. "I just hoped y'all could see it once before I die, so you could tell me about it." Later, she whispers to Leroy, "You do what I said. A little change is what she needs."

"Your name means 'the king,'" Norma Jean says to Leroy that evening. He is trying to get her to go to Shiloh, and she is reading a book about another century.

"Well, I reckon I ought to be right proud."

"I guess so."

"Am I still king around here?"

Norma Jean flexes her biceps and feels them for hardness. "I'm not fooling 120
around with anybody, if that's what you mean," she says.

"Would you tell me if you were?"

"I don't know."

"What does *your* name mean?"

"It was Marilyn Monroe's real name."

"No kidding!" 125

"Norma comes from the Normans. They were invaders," she says. She closes her book and looks hard at Leroy. "I'll go to Shiloh with you if you'll stop staring at me."

On Sunday, Norma Jean packs a picnic and they go to Shiloh. To Leroy's relief, Mabel says she does not want to come with them. Norma Jean drives, and Leroy, sitting beside her, feels like some boring hitchhiker she has picked up. He tries some conversation, but she answers him in monosyllables. At Shiloh, she drives aimlessly through the park, past bluffs and trails and steep ravines. Shiloh is an immense place, and Leroy cannot see it as a battleground. It is not what he expected. He thought it would look like a golf course. Monuments are everywhere, showing through the thick clusters of trees. Norma Jean passes the log cabin Mabel mentioned. It is surrounded by tourists looking for bullet holes.

"That's not the kind of log house I've got in mind," says Leroy apologetically.

"I know *that*."

130 "This is a pretty place. Your mama was right."

"It's O.K.," says Norma Jean. "Well, we've seen it. I hope she's satisfied."

They burst out laughing together.

At the park museum, a movie on Shiloh is shown every half hour, but they decide that they don't want to see it. They buy a souvenir Confederate flag for Mabel, and then they find a picnic spot near the cemetery. Norma Jean has brought a picnic cooler, with pimiento sandwiches, soft drinks, and Yodels. Leroy eats a sandwich and then smokes a joint, hiding it behind the picnic cooler. Norma Jean has quit smoking altogether. She is picking cake crumbs from the cellophane wrapper, like a fussy bird.

Leroy says, "So the boys in gray ended up in Corinth. The Union soldiers zapped 'em finally. April 7, 1862."

135 They both know that he doesn't know any history. He is just talking about some of the historical plaques they have read. He feels awkward, like a boy on a date with an older girl. They are still just making conversation.

"Corinth is where Mama eloped to," says Norma Jean.

They sit in silence and stare at the cemetery for the Union dead and, beyond, at a tall cluster of trees. Campers are parked nearby, bumper to bumper, and small children in bright clothing are cavorting and squealing. Norma Jean wads up the cake wrapper and squeezes it tightly in her hand. Without looking at Leroy, she says, "I want to leave you."

Leroy takes a bottle of Coke out of the cooler and flips off the cap. He holds the bottle poised near his mouth but cannot remember to take a drink. Finally he says, "No, you don't."

"Yes, I do."

140 "I won't let you."

"You can't stop me."

"Don't do me that way."

Leroy knows Norma Jean will have her own way. "Didn't I promise to be home from now on?" he says.

"In some ways, a woman prefers a man who wanders," says Norma Jean. "That sounds crazy, I know."

145 "You're not crazy."

Leroy remembers to drink from his Coke. Then he says, "Yes, you *are* crazy. You and me could start all over again. Right back at the beginning."

"We *have* started all over again," says Norma Jean. "And this is how it turned out."

"What did I do wrong?"

"Nothing."

150 "Is this one of those women's lib things?" Leroy asks.

"Don't be funny."

The cemetery, a green slope dotted with white markers, looks like a subdivision site. Leroy is trying to comprehend that his marriage is breaking up, but for some reason he is wondering about white slabs in a graveyard.

"Everything was fine till Mama caught me smoking," says Norma Jean, standing up. "That set something off."

"What are you talking about?"

155 "She won't leave me alone—*you* won't leave me alone." Norma Jean seems to be crying, but she is looking away from him. "I feel eighteen again. I can't face that all over again." She starts walking away. "No, it *wasn't* fine. I don't know what I'm saying. Forget it."

Leroy takes a lungful of smoke and closes his eyes as Norma Jean's words sink in. He tries to focus on the fact that thirty-five hundred soldiers died on the grounds around him. He can only think of that war as a board game with plastic soldiers. Leroy almost smiles, as he compares the Confederates' daring attack on the Union camps and Virgil Mathis's raid on the bowling alley. General Grant, drunk and furious, shoved the Southerners back to Corinth, where Mabel and Jet Beasley were married years later, when Mabel was still thin and good-looking. The next day, Mabel and Jet visited the battleground, and then Norma Jean was born, and then she married Leroy and they had a baby, which they lost, and now Leroy and Norma Jean are here at the same battleground. Leroy knows he is leaving out a lot. He is leaving out the insides of history. History was always just names and dates to him. It occurs to him that building a house out of logs is similarly empty—too simple. And the real inner workings of a marriage, like most of history, have escaped him. Now he sees that building a log house is the dumbest idea he could have had. It was clumsy of him to think Norma Jean would want a log house. It was a crazy idea. He'll have to think of something else, quickly. He will wad the blueprints into tight balls and fling them into the lake. Then he'll get moving again. He opens his eyes. Norma Jean has moved away and is walking through the cemetery, following a serpentine brick path.

Leroy gets up to follow his wife, but his good leg is asleep and his bad leg still hurts him. Norma Jean is far away, walking rapidly toward the bluff by the river, and he tries to hobble toward her. Some children run past him, screaming noisily. Norma Jean has reached the bluff, and she is looking out over the Tennessee River. Now she turns toward Leroy and waves her arms. Is she beckoning to him? She seems to be doing an exercise for her chest muscles. The sky is unusually pale—the color of the dust ruffle Mabel made for their bed.

1982

GUY DE MAUPASSANT
(1850–93)
The Jewelry[1]

Born Henri René Albert in Normandy, France, Maupassant was expelled at sixteen from a Rouen seminary and finished his education at a public high school. After serving in the Franco-Prussian War, he worked as a government clerk in Paris for ten years. A protégé of Flaubert, he published during the 1880s some three hundred stories, half a dozen novels, and plays. The short stories, which appeared regularly in popular periodicals, sampled military and peasant life, the decadent world of politics and journalism, prostitution, the supernatural, and the hypoc-

1. Translated by Lafcadio Hearn.

risies of solid citizens; with Chekhov, Maupassant may be said to have created the modern short story. His life ended somewhat like one of his own stories: He died of syphilis in an asylum. His novels include *Une Vie* (*A Life,* 1883), *Bel Ami* (*Handsome Friend,* 1885), and *Pierre et Jean* (1888).

Having met the girl one evening, at the house of the office-superintendent, M. Lantin became enveloped in love as in a net.

She was the daughter of a country-tutor, who had been dead for several years. Afterward she had come to Paris with her mother, who made regular visits to several bourgeois families of the neighborhood, in hopes of being able to get her daughter married. They were poor and respectable, quiet and gentle. The young girl seemed to be the very ideal of that pure good woman to whom every young man dreams of entrusting his future. Her modest beauty had a charm of angelic shyness; and the slight smile that always dwelt about her lips seemed a reflection of her heart.

Everybody sang her praises; all who knew her kept saying: "The man who gets her will be lucky. No one could find a nicer girl than that."

M. Lantin, who was then chief clerk in the office of the Minister of the Interior, with a salary of 3,500 francs a year,[2] demanded her hand, and married her.

5 He was unutterably happy with her. She ruled his home with an economy so adroit that they really seemed to live in luxury. It would be impossible to conceive of any attentions, tendernesses, playful caresses which she did not lavish upon her husband; and such was the charm of her person that, six years after he married her, he loved her even more than he did the first day.

There were only two points upon which he ever found fault with her—her love of the theater, and her passion for false jewelry.

Her lady-friends (she was acquainted with the wives of several small office holders) were always bringing her tickets for the theaters; whenever there was a performance that made a sensation, she always had her *loge* secured, even for first performances; and she would drag her husband with her to all these entertainments, which used to tire him horribly after his day's work. So at last he begged her to go to the theater with some lady-acquaintances who would consent to see her home afterward. She refused for quite a while—thinking it would not look very well to go out thus unaccompanied by her husband. But finally she yielded, just to please him; and he felt infinitely grateful to her therefore.

Now this passion for the theater at last evoked in her the desire of dress. It was true that her toilette remained simple, always in good taste, but modest; and her sweet grace, her irresistible grace, ever smiling and shy, seemed to take fresh charm from the simplicity of her robes. But she got into the habit of suspending in her pretty ears two big cut pebbles, fashioned in imitation of diamonds; and she wore necklaces of false pearls, bracelets of false gold, and haircombs studded with paste-imitations of precious stones.

Her husband, who felt shocked by this love of tinsel and show, would often say—"My dear, when one has not the means to afford real jewelry, one should

2. Midlevel bureaucratic wage, perhaps about $30,000 to $40,000 today.

appear adorned with one's natural beauty and grace only—and these gifts are the rarest of jewels."

But she would smile sweetly and answer: "What does it matter? I like those 10
things—that is my little whim. I know you are right; but one can't make oneself over again. I've always loved jewelry so much!"

And then she would roll the pearls of the necklaces between her fingers, and make the facets of the cut crystals flash in the light, repeating: "Now look at them—see how well the work is done. You would swear it was real jewelry."

He would then smile in his turn, and declare to her: "You have the tastes of a regular Gypsy."

Sometimes, in the evening, when they were having a chat by the fire, she would rise and fetch the morocco box in which she kept her "stock" (as M. Lantin called it)—would put it on the tea-table, and begin to examine the false jewelry with passionate delight, as if she experienced some secret and mysterious sensations of pleasure in their contemplation; and she would insist on putting one of the necklaces round her husband's neck, and laugh till she couldn't laugh any more, crying out: "Oh! how funny you look!" Then she would rush into his arms, and kiss him furiously.

One winter's night, after she had been to the Opera, she came home chilled through, and trembling. Next day she had a bad cough. Eight days after that, she died of pneumonia.

Lantin was very nearly following her into the tomb. His despair was so fright- 15
ful that in one single month his hair turned white. He wept from morning till night, feeling his heart torn by inexpressible suffering—ever haunted by the memory of her, by the smile, by the voice, by all the charm of the dead woman.

Time did not assuage his grief. Often during office hours his fellow-clerks went off to a corner to chat about this or that topic of the day—his cheeks might have been seen to swell up all of a sudden, his nose wrinkle, his eyes fill with water—he would pull a frightful face, and begin to sob.

He had kept his dead companion's room just in the order she had left it, and he used to lock himself up in it every evening to think about her—all the furniture, and even all her dresses, remained in the same place they had been on the last day of her life.

But life became hard for him. His salary, which, in his wife's hands, had amply sufficed for all household needs, now proved scarcely sufficient to supply his own few wants. And he asked himself in astonishment how she had managed always to furnish him with excellent wines and with delicate eating which he could not now afford at all with his scanty means.

He got a little into debt, like men obliged to live by their wits. At last one morning that he happened to find himself without a cent in his pocket, and a whole week to wait before he could draw his monthly salary, he thought of selling something; and almost immediately it occurred to him to sell his wife's "stock"—for he had always borne a secret grudge against the flash-jewelry that used to annoy him so much in former days. The mere sight of it, day after day, somewhat spoiled the sad pleasure of thinking of his darling.

He tried a long time to make a choice among the heap of trinkets she had left 20
behind her—for up to the very last day of her life she had kept obstinately buying them, bringing home some new thing almost every night—and finally he

resolved to take the big pearl necklace which she used to like the best of all, and which he thought ought certainly to be worth six or eight francs, as it was really very nicely mounted for an imitation necklace.

He put it in his pocket, and walked toward the office, following the boulevards, and looking for some jewelry-store on the way, where he could enter with confidence.

Finally he saw a place and went in; feeling a little ashamed of thus exposing his misery, and of trying to sell such a trifling object.

"Sir," he said to the jeweler, "please tell me what this is worth."

The jeweler took the necklace, examined it, weighed it, took up a magnifying glass, called his clerk, talked to him in whispers, put down the necklace on the counter, and drew back a little bit to judge of its effect at a distance.

25 M. Lantin, feeling very much embarrassed by all these ceremonies, opened his mouth and began to declare—"Oh! I know it can't be worth much" . . . when the jeweler interrupted him saying:

"Well, sir, that is worth between twelve and fifteen thousand francs; but I cannot buy it unless you can let me know exactly how you came by it."

The widower's eyes opened enormously, and he stood gaping—unable to understand. Then after a while he stammered out: "You said? . . . Are you sure?" The jeweler, misconstruing the cause of this astonishment, replied in a dry tone—"Go elsewhere if you like, and see if you can get any more for it. The very most I would give for it is fifteen thousand. Come back and see me again, if you can't do better."

M. Lantin, feeling perfectly idiotic, took his necklace and departed; obeying a confused desire to find himself alone and to get a chance to think.

But the moment he found himself in the street again, he began to laugh, and he muttered to himself: "The fool!—oh! what a fool; If I had only taken him at his word. Well, well!—a jeweler who can't tell paste from real jewelry!"

30 And he entered another jewelry-store, at the corner of the Rue de la Paix. The moment the jeweler set eyes on the necklace, he examined—"Hello! I know that necklace well—it was sold here!"

M. Lantin, very nervous, asked:

"What's it worth?"

"Sir, I sold it for twenty-five thousand francs. I am willing to buy it back again for eighteen thousand—if you can prove to me satisfactorily, according to legal presciptions, how you came into possession of it."—This time, M. Lantin was simply paralyzed with astonishment. He said: "Well . . . but please look at it again, sir. I always thought until now that it was . . . was false."

The jeweler said:

35 "Will you give me your name, sir?"

"Certainly. My name is Lantin; I am employed at the office of the Minister of the Interior. I live at No. 16, Rue des Martyrs."

The merchant opened the register, looked, and said: "Yes; this necklace was sent to the address of Madame Lantin, 16 Rue des Martyrs, on July 20th, 1876."

And the two men looked into each other's eyes—the clerk wild with surprise; the jeweler suspecting he had a thief before him.

The jeweler resumed:

"Will you be kind enough to leave this article here for twenty-four hours only—I'll give you a receipt." 40

M. Lantin stuttered: "Yes—ah! certainly." And he went out folding up the receipt, which he put in his pocket.

Then he crossed the street, went the wrong way, found out his mistake, returned by way of the Tuileries, crossed the Seine, found out he had taken the wrong road again, and went back to the Champs-Élysées without being able to get one clear idea into his head. He tried to reason, to understand. His wife could never have bought so valuable an object as that. Certainly not. But then, it must have been a present! . . . A present from whom? What for?

He stopped and stood stock-still in the middle of the avenue.

A horrible suspicion swept across his mind. . . . She? . . . But then all those other pieces of jewelry must have been presents also! . . . Then it seemed to him that the ground was heaving under his feet; that a tree, right in front of him, was falling toward him; he thrust out his arms instinctively, and fell senseless.

He recovered his consciousness again in a drug-store to which some bystanders had carried him. He had them lead him home, and he locked himself into his room. 45

Until nightfall he cried without stopping, biting his handkerchief to keep himself from screaming out. Then, completely worn out with grief and fatigue, he went to bed, and slept a leaden sleep.

A ray of sunshine awakened him, and he rose and dressed himself slowly to go to the office. It was hard to have to work after such a shock. Then he reflected that he might be able to excuse himself to the superintendent, and he wrote to him. Then he remembered he would have to go back to the jeweler's; and shame made his face purple. He remained thinking a long time. Still he could not leave the necklace there; he put on his coat and went out.

It was a fine day; the sky extended all blue over the city, and seemed to make it smile. Strollers were walking aimlessly about, with their hands in their pockets.

Lantin thought as he watched them passing: "How lucky the men are who have fortunes! With money a man can even shake off grief—you can go where you please—travel—amuse yourself! Oh! if I were only rich!"

He suddenly discovered he was hungry—not having eaten anything since the evening before. But his pockets were empty; and he remembered the necklace. Eighteen thousand francs! Eighteen thousand francs!—that was a sum—that was! 50

He made his way to the Rue de la Paix and began to walk backward and forward on the sidewalk in front of the store. Eighteen thousand francs! Twenty times he started to go in; but shame always kept him back.

Still he was hungry—very hungry—and had not a cent. He made one brusque resolve, and crossed the street almost at a run, so as not to let himself have time to think over the matter; and he rushed into the jeweler's.

As soon as he saw him, the merchant hurried forward, and offered him a chair with smiling politeness. Even the clerks came forward to stare at Lantin, with gaiety in their eyes and smiles about their lips.

The jeweler said: "Sir, I made inquiries; and if you are still so disposed, I am ready to pay you down the price I offered you."

The clerk stammered: "Why, yes—sir, certainly."

The jeweler took from a drawer eighteen big bills,[3] counted them, and held them out to Lantin, who signed a little receipt, and thrust the money feverishly into his pocket.

Then, as he was on the point of leaving, he turned to the ever-smiling merchant, and said, lowering his eyes: "I have some—I have some other jewelry, which came to me in the same—from the same inheritance. Would you purchase them also from me?"

The merchant bowed, and answered: "Why, certainly, sir—certainly. . . ." One of the clerks rushed out to laugh at his ease; another kept blowing his nose as hard as he could.

Lantin, impassive, flushed and serious, said: "I will bring them to you."

And he hired a cab to get the jewelry.

When he returned to the store, an hour later, he had not yet breakfasted. They examined the jewelry—piece by piece—putting a value on each. Nearly all had been purchased from that very house.

Lantin, now, disputed estimates made, got angry, insisted on seeing the books, and talked louder and louder the higher the estimates grew.

The big diamond earrings were worth 20,000 francs; the bracelets, 35,000; the brooches, rings and medallions, 16,000; a set of emeralds and sapphires, 14,000; solitaire, suspended to a gold neckchain, 40,000; the total value being estimated at 196,000 francs.

The merchant observed with mischievous good nature: "The person who owned these must have put all her savings into jewelry."

Lantin answered with gravity: "Perhaps that is as good a way of saving money as any other." And he went off, after having agreed with the merchant that an expert should make a counter-estimate for him the next day.

When he found himself in the street again, he looked at the Column Vendôme[4] with the desire to climb it, as if it were a May pole. He felt jolly enough to play leapfrog over the Emperor's head—up there in the blue sky.

He breakfasted at Voisin's[5] restaurant, and ordered wine at 20 francs a bottle.

Then he hired a cab and drove out to the Bois.[6] He looked at the carriages passing with a sort of contempt, and a wild desire to yell out to the passers-by: "I am rich, too—I am! I have 200,000 francs!"

The recollection of the office suddenly came back to him. He drove there, walked right into the superintendent's private room, and said: "Sir, I come to give you my resignation. I have just come into a fortune of *three* hundred thousand francs." Then he shook hands all round with his fellow-clerks; and told them all about his plans for a new career. Then he went to dinner at the Café Anglais.

3. French paper money varies in size; the larger the bill, the larger the denomination.

4. Famous column with a statue of the emperor Napoleon at the top.

5. Like the Café Anglais below, a well-known and high-priced restaurant.

6. Large Parisian park where the rich took their outings.

Finding himself seated at the same table with a man who seemed to him 70
quite genteel, he could not resist the itching desire to tell him, with a certain air of coquetry, that he had just inherited a fortune of *four* hundred thousand francs.

For the first time in his life he went to the theater without feeling bored by the performance; and he passed the night in revelry and debauch.

Six months after he married again. His second wife was the most upright of spouses, but had a terrible temper. She made his life very miserable.

1883

TILLIE OLSEN
(1912–2007)
I Stand Here Ironing

As Margaret Atwood has remarked of Tillie Olsen, "Few writers have gained such wide respect," even "reverence," "based on such a small body of published work"—only one unfinished novel, a short-story collection, and a book of nonfiction. Born in 1912 to poor Jewish émigrés from Russia, Tillie Lerner came of age at the start of the Great Depression, leaving high school without graduating to work at various low-paying jobs and launch a lifelong career as an unpaid (and twice-jailed) activist. After giving birth to a daughter, Olsen moved to San Francisco in 1933, eventually marrying—and having three more daughters with—union organizer Jack Olsen. Raising four children while working at various paid and unpaid jobs, Olsen later remarked, "It is no accident that the first work I considered publishable began: 'I stand here ironing. [. . .]'" Appearing in *The Best American Short Stories of 1957*, the story became the cornerstone of her first book, the award-winning 1961 collection *Tell Me a Riddle*. Thanks to the numerous prestigious prizes and teaching jobs that followed, Olsen published yet another "Best American Short Story" ("Requa") in 1970, and, in 1974, a revised but still incomplete version of the novel she had begun four decades earlier. A collection of essays and speeches, *Silences* (1978), movingly details the silencing effects of poverty and prejudice, social forces that Olsen tirelessly fought through her activism, her writing, and her mentorship of other would-be writers.

I stand here ironing, and what you asked me moves tormented back and forth with the iron.

"I wish you would manage the time to come in and talk with me about your daughter. I'm sure you can help me understand her. She's a youngster who needs help and whom I'm deeply interested in helping."

"Who needs help." . . . Even if I came, what good would it do? You think because I am her mother I have a key, or that in some way you could use me as a key? She has lived for nineteen years. There is all that life that has happened outside of me, beyond me.

And when is there time to remember, to sift, to weigh, to estimate, to total? I will start and there will be an interruption and I will have to gather it all together again. Or I will become engulfed with all I did or did not do, with what should have been and what cannot be helped.

5 She was a beautiful baby. The first and only one of our five that was beautiful at birth. You do not guess how new and uneasy her tenancy in her now-loveliness. You did not know her all those years she was thought homely, or see her poring over her baby pictures, making me tell her over and over how beautiful she had been—and would be, I would tell her—and was now, to the seeing eye. But the seeing eyes were few or non-existent. Including mine.

I nursed her. They feel that's important nowadays. I nursed all the children, but with her, with all the fierce rigidity of first motherhood, I did like the books then said. Though her cries battered me to trembling and my breasts ached with swollenness, I waited till the clock decreed.

Why do I put that first? I do not even know if it matters, or if it explains anything.

She was a beautiful baby. She blew shining bubbles of sound. She loved motion, loved light, loved color and music and textures. She would lie on the floor in her blue overalls patting the surface so hard in ecstasy her hands and feet would blur. She was a miracle to me, but when she was eight months old I had to leave her daytimes with the woman downstairs to whom she was no miracle at all, for I worked or looked for work and for Emily's father, who "could no longer endure" (he wrote in his good-bye note) "sharing want with us."

I was nineteen. It was the pre-relief, pre-WPA[1] world of the depression. I would start running as soon as I got off the streetcar, running up the stairs, the place smelling sour, and awake or asleep to startle awake, when she saw me she would break into a clogged weeping that could not be comforted, a weeping I can hear yet.

10 After a while I found a job hashing[2] at night so I could be with her days, and it was better. But it came to where I had to bring her to his family and leave her.

It took a long time to raise the money for her fare back. Then she got chicken pox and I had to wait longer. When she finally came, I hardly knew her, walking quick and nervous like her father, looking like her father, thin, and dressed in a shoddy red that yellowed her skin and glared at the pockmarks. All the baby loveliness gone.

She was two. Old enough for nursery school they said, and I did not know then what I know now—the fatigue of the long day, and the lacerations of group life in the kinds of nurseries that are only parking places for children.

Except that it would have made no difference if I had known. It was the only place there was. It was the only way we could be together, the only way I could hold a job.

1. Works Progress Administration; between 1935 and 1943 this federal agency, part of the Roosevelt administration's New Deal, employed 8.5 million people thrown out of work by the Great Depression. *Pre-relief*: that is, before the government assistance programs initiated during the Great Depression.
2. Waitressing, usually at a diner or other inexpensive restaurant.

And even without knowing, I knew. I knew that the teacher was evil because all these years it has curdled into my memory, the little boy hunched in the corner, her rasp, "why aren't you outside, because Alvin hits you? that's no reason, go out, scaredy." I knew Emily hated it even if she did not clutch and implore "don't go Mommy" like the other children, mornings.

She always had a reason why we should stay home. Momma, you look sick. 15
Momma, I feel sick. Momma, the teachers aren't there today, they're sick. Momma, we can't go, there was a fire there last night. Momma, it's a holiday today, no school, they told me.

But never a direct protest, never rebellion. I think of our others in their three-, four-year-oldness—the explosions, the tempers, the denunciations, the demands—and I feel suddenly ill. I put the iron down. What in me demanded that goodness in her? And what was the cost, the cost to her of such goodness?

The old man living in the back once said in his gentle way: "You should smile at Emily more when you look at her." What *was* in my face when I looked at her? I loved her. There were all the acts of love.

It was only with the others I remembered what he said, and it was the face of joy, and not of care or tightness or worry I turned to them—too late for Emily. She does not smile easily, let alone almost always as her brothers and sisters do. Her face is closed and sombre, but when she wants, how fluid. You must have seen it in her pantomimes, you spoke of her rare gift for comedy on the stage that rouses a laughter out of the audience so dear they applaud and applaud and do not want to let her go.

Where does it come from, that comedy? There was none of it in her when she came back to me that second time, after I had had to send her away again. She had a new daddy now to learn to love, and I think perhaps it was a better time.

Except when we left her alone nights, telling ourselves she was old enough. 20

"Can't you go some other time, Mommy, like tomorrow?" she would ask. "Will it be just a little while you'll be gone? Do you promise?"

The time we came back, the front door open, the clock on the floor in the hall. She rigid awake. "It wasn't just a little while. I didn't cry. Three times I called you, just three times, and then I ran downstairs to open the door so you could come faster. The clock talked loud. I threw it away, it scared me what it talked."

She said the clock talked loud again that night I went to the hospital to have Susan. She was delirious with the fever that comes before red measles, but she was fully conscious all the week I was gone and the week after we were home when she could not come near the new baby or me.

She did not get well. She stayed skeleton thin, not wanting to eat, and night after night she had nightmares. She would call for me, and I would rouse from exhaustion to sleepily call back: "You're all right, darling, go to sleep, it's just a dream," and if she still called, in a sterner voice, "now go to sleep, Emily, there's nothing to hurt you." Twice, only twice, when I had to get up for Susan anyhow, I went in to sit with her.

Now when it is too late (as if she would let me hold and comfort her like I do 25
the others) I get up and go to her at once at her moan or restless stirring. "Are you awake, Emily? Can I get you something?" And the answer is always the same: "No, I'm all right, go back to sleep, Mother."

They persuaded me at the clinic to send her away to a convalescent home in the country where "she can have the kind of food and care you can't manage for her, and you'll be free to concentrate on the new baby." They still send children to that place. I see pictures on the society page of sleek young women planning affairs to raise money for it, or dancing at the affairs, or decorating Easter eggs or filling Christmas stockings for the children.

They never have a picture of the children so I do not know if the girls still wear those gigantic red bows and the ravaged looks on the every other Sunday when parents can come to visit "unless otherwise notified"—as we were notified the first six weeks.

Oh it is a handsome place, green lawns and tall trees and fluted flower beds. High up on the balconies of each cottage the children stand, the girls in their red bows and white dresses, the boys in white suits and giant red ties. The parents stand below shrieking up to be heard and the children shriek down to be heard, and between them the invisible wall "Not To Be Contaminated by Parental Germs or Physical Affection."

There was a tiny girl who always stood hand in hand with Emily. Her parents never came. One visit she was gone. "They moved her to Rose Cottage" Emily shouted in explanation. "They don't like you to love anybody here."

She wrote once a week, the labored writing of a seven-year-old. "I am fine. How is the baby. If I write my leter nicly I will have a star. Love." There never was a star. We wrote every other day, letters she could never hold or keep but only hear read—once. "We simply do not have room for children to keep any personal possessions," they patiently explained when we pieced one Sunday's shrieking together to plead how much it would mean to Emily, who loved so to keep things, to be allowed to keep her letters and cards.

Each visit she looked frailer. "She isn't eating," they told us.

(They had runny eggs for breakfast or mush with lumps, Emily said later, I'd hold it in my mouth and not swallow. Nothing ever tasted good, just when they had chicken.)

It took us eight months to get her released home, and only the fact that she gained back so little of her seven lost pounds convinced the social worker.

I used to try to hold and love her after she came back, but her body would stay stiff, and after a while she'd push away. She ate little. Food sickened her, and I think much of life too. Oh she had physical lightness and brightness, twinkling by on skates, bouncing like a ball up and down up and down over the jump rope, skimming over the hill; but these were momentary.

She fretted about her appearance, thin and dark and foreign-looking at a time when every little girl was supposed to look or thought she should look a chubby blonde replica of Shirley Temple.[3] The doorbell sometimes rang for her, but no one seemed to come and play in the house or be a best friend. Maybe because we moved so much.

There was a boy she loved painfully through two school semesters. Months later she told me how she had taken pennies from my purse to buy him candy. "Licorice was his favorite and I brought him some every day, but he still liked

3. Famously curly-haired and dimpled child actress, singer, and dancer (1928–2014) who starred in such films as *Baby Take a Bow* (1934) and *Heidi* (1937).

Jennifer better'n me. Why, Mommy?" The kind of question for which there is no answer.

School was a worry to her. She was not glib or quick in a world where glibness and quickness were easily confused with ability to learn. To her overworked and exasperated teachers she was an overconscientious "slow learner" who kept trying to catch up and was absent entirely too often.

I let her be absent, though sometimes the illness was imaginary. How different from my now-strictness about attendance with the others. I wasn't working. We had a new baby, I was home anyhow. Sometimes, after Susan grew old enough, I would keep her home from school, too, to have them all together.

Mostly Emily had asthma, and her breathing, harsh and labored, would fill the house with a curiously tranquil sound. I would bring the two old dresser mirrors and her boxes of collections to her bed. She would select beads and single earrings, bottle tops and shells, dried flowers and pebbles, old postcards and scraps, all sorts of oddments; then she and Susan would play Kingdom, setting up landscapes and furniture, peopling them with action.

Those were the only times of peaceful companionship between her and 40
Susan. I have edged away from it, that poisonous feeling between them, that terrible balancing of hurts and needs I had to do between the two, and did so badly, those earlier years.

Oh there are conflicts between the others too, each one human, needing, demanding, hurting, taking—but only between Emily and Susan, no, Emily toward Susan that corroding resentment. It seems so obvious on the surface, yet it is not obvious. Susan, the second child, Susan, golden- and curly-haired and chubby, quick and articulate and assured, everything in appearance and manner Emily was not; Susan, not able to resist Emily's precious things, losing or sometimes clumsily breaking them; Susan telling jokes and riddles to company for applause while Emily sat silent (to say to me later: that was *my* riddle, Mother, I told it to Susan); Susan, who for all the five years' difference in age was just a year behind Emily in developing physically.

I am glad for that slow physical development that widened the difference between her and her contemporaries, though she suffered over it. She was too vulnerable for that terrible world of youthful competition, of preening and parading, of constant measuring of yourself against every other, of envy, "If I had that copper hair," "If I had that skin. . . ." She tormented herself enough about not looking like the others, there was enough of the unsureness, the having to be conscious of words before you speak, the constant caring—what are they thinking of me? without having it all magnified by the merciless physical drives.

Ronnie is calling. He is wet and I change him. It is rare there is such a cry now. That time of motherhood is almost behind me when the ear is not one's own but must always be racked and listening for the child cry, the child call. We sit for a while and I hold him, looking out over the city spread in charcoal with its soft aisles of light. *"Shoogily,"* he breathes and curls closer. I carry him back to bed, asleep. *Shoogily.* A funny word, a family word, inherited from Emily, invented by her to say: *comfort.*

In this and other ways she leaves her seal, I say aloud. And startle at my saying it. What do I mean? What did I start to gather together, to try and make coherent? I was at the terrible, growing years. War years.[4] I do not remember them well. I was working, there were four smaller ones now, there was not time for her. She had to help be a mother, and housekeeper, and shopper. She had to set her seal. Mornings of crisis and near hysteria trying to get lunches packed, hair combed, coats and shoes found, everyone to school or Child Care on time, the baby ready for transportation. And always the paper scribbled on by a smaller one, the book looked at by Susan then mislaid, the homework not done. Running out to that huge school where she was one, she was lost, she was a drop; suffering over her unpreparedness, stammering and unsure in her classes.

45 There was so little time left at night after the kids were bedded down. She would struggle over books, always eating (it was in those years she developed her enormous appetite that is legendary in our family) and I would be ironing, or preparing food for the next day, or writing V-mail[5] to Bill, or tending the baby. Sometimes, to make me laugh, or out of her despair, she would imitate happenings or types at school.

I think I said once: "Why don't you do something like this in the school amateur show?" One morning she phoned me at work, hardly understandable through the weeping: "Mother, I did it. I won, I won; they gave me first prize; they clapped and clapped and wouldn't let me go."

Now suddenly she was Somebody, and as imprisoned in her difference as she had been in her anonymity.

She began to be asked to perform at other high schools, even in colleges, then at city and statewide affairs. The first one we went to, I only recognized her that first moment when thin, shy, she almost drowned herself into the curtains. Then: Was this Emily? The control, the command, the convulsing and deadly clowning, the spell, then the roaring, stamping audience, unwilling to let this rare and precious laughter out of their lives.

Afterwards: You ought to do something about her with a gift like that—but without money or knowing how, what does one do? We have left it all to her, and the gift has as often eddied inside, clogged and clotted, as been used and growing.

50 She is coming. She runs up the stairs two at a time with her light graceful step, and I know she is happy tonight. Whatever it was that occasioned your call did not happen today.

"Aren't you ever going to finish the ironing, Mother? Whistler painted his mother in a rocker.[6] I'd have to paint mine standing over an ironing board." This is one of her communicative nights and she tells me everything and nothing as she fixes herself a plate of food out of the icebox.

She is so lovely. Why did you want me to come in at all? Why were you concerned? She will find her way.

She starts up the stairs to bed. "Don't get *me* up with the rest in the morning." "But I thought you were having midterms." "Oh, those," she comes back in,

4. World War II (1939–1945); America's direct involvement began in 1941.
5. Victory Mail: mail system for communicating with soldiers during World War II.
6. Allusion to the painting popularly known as *Whistler's Mother* (1871), by American artist James Abbot McNeil Whistler (1834–1903).

kisses me, and says quite lightly, "in a couple of years when we'll all be atom-dead[7] they won't matter a bit."

She has said it before. She *believes* it. But because I have been dredging the past, and all that compounds a human being is so heavy and meaningful in me, I cannot endure it tonight.

I will never total it all. I will never come in to say: She was a child seldom smiled 55
at. Her father left me before she was a year old. I had to work away from her her first six years when there was work, or I sent her home and to his relatives. There were years she had care she hated. She was dark and thin and foreign-looking in a world where the prestige went to blondeness and curly hair and dimples, she was slow where glibness was prized. She was a child of anxious, not proud, love. We were poor and could not afford for her the soil of easy growth. I was a young mother, I was a distracted mother. There were the other children pushing up, demanding. Her younger sister seemed all that she was not. There were years she did not let me touch her. She kept too much in herself, her life was such she had to keep too much in herself. My wisdom came too late. She has much to her and probably little will come of it. She is a child of her age, of depression, of war, of fear.

Let her be. So all that is in her will not bloom—but in how many does it? There is still enough left to live by. Only help her to know—help make it so there is cause for her to know—that she is more than this dress on the ironing board, helpless before the iron.

1953–54

ANNIE PROULX
(b. 1935)

Job History

Connecticut-born Annie Proulx earned a BA with Honors at Colby College and an MA in history at the University of Vermont before launching her nineteen-year career as a freelance writer of articles on, in her words, "weather, apples, canoeing, mountain lions, mice, cuisine, libraries, African beadwork, cider, and lettuces," as well as books including *The Complete Dairy Foods Cookbook* (with Lew Nichols, 1982) and *The Fine Art of Salad Gardening* (1985). Proulx's public debut as a fiction writer came in 1988, with the publication of *Heart Songs and Other Stories.* Two years later, she won the prestigious PEN/Faulkner Award for Fiction for her first novel, *Postcards.* Proulx's second novel, *The Shipping News* (1993), which was inspired by a canoeing trip to Newfoundland and reflects her keen interest in place, garnered numerous awards, including a Pulitzer, before being made into a movie (2001). Proulx's three other novels are the picaresque *Accordion Crimes* (1996); *That Old Ace in the Hole* (2002), set in Texas; and the historical novel *Barkskins* (2015). "Job History"

7. That is, killed by an atomic bomb. U.S. forces dropped atomic bombs on Japan at the end of World War II, and within a few years the Soviet Union developed an atomic bomb of its own; the ensuing decades of tense nuclear standoff became known as the Cold War.

appears in Proulx's second collection, *Close Range: Wyoming Stories* (1999), alongside the prize-winning story that inspired the Academy Award–winning film *Brokeback Mountain* (2005). The thrice-divorced mother of four has also published *Bird Cloud: A Memoir* (2011), as well as two more collections inspired by the state she now makes her home—*Bad Dirt: Wyoming Stories 2* (2004) and *Fine Just the Way It Is: Wyoming Stories 3* (2008).

Leeland Lee is born at home in Cora, Wyoming, November 17, 1947, the youngest of six. In the 1950s his parents move to Unique when his mother inherits a small dog-bone ranch. The ranch lies a few miles outside town. They raise sheep, a few chickens, and some hogs. The father is irascible and, as soon as they can, the older children disperse. Leeland can sing "That Doggie in the Window"[1] all the way through. His father strikes him with a flyswatter and tells him to shut up. There is no news on the radio. A blizzard has knocked out the power.

Leeland's face shows heavy bone from his mother's side. His neck is thick and his red-gold hair plastered down in bangs. Even as a child his eyes are as pouchy as those of a middle-aged alcoholic, the brows rod-straight above wandering, out-of-line eyes. His nose lies broad and close to his face, his mouth seems to have been cut with a single chisel blow into easy flesh. In the fifth grade, horsing around with friends, he falls off the school's fire escape and breaks his pelvis. He is in a body cast for three months. On the news an announcer says that the average American eats 8.6 pounds of margarine a year but only 8.3 pounds of butter. He never forgets this statistic.

When Leeland is seventeen he marries Lori Bovee. They quit school. Lori is pregnant and Leeland is proud of this. His pelvis gives him no trouble. She is a year younger than he, with an undistinguished, oval face, hair of medium length. She is a little stout but looks a confection in pastel sweater sets. Leeland and his mother fight over this marriage and Leeland leaves the ranch. He takes a job pumping gas at Egge's Service Station. Ed Egge says, "You may fire when ready, Gridley,"[2] and laughs. The station stands at the junction of highway 16 and a county road. Highway 16 is the main tourist road to Yellowstone. Leeland buys Lori's father's old truck for fifty dollars and Ed rebuilds the engine. Vietnam and Selma, Alabama,[3] are on the news.

The federal highway program[4] puts through the new four-lane interstate forty miles south of highway 16 and parallel with it. Overnight the tourist business in Unique falls flat. One day a hundred cars stop for gas and oil, hamburgers, cold soda. The next day only two cars pull in, both driven by locals asking

1. American pop singer Patti Page's rendition of this song topped the Billboard charts in 1953.
2. Phrase popularized by Bugs Bunny in the 1950s but originally spoken to U.S. Navy captain Charles Gridley on May 1, 1898, commanding him to initiate a battle in the Spanish-American War.
3. In March 1965, the Vietnam War began to escalate with the introduction of general conflict troops; in Selma, Alabama, police attacked civil rights demonstrators, causing a national outrage that helped inspire the Voting Rights Act of 1965.
4. The Federal Highway Act of 1956 authorized the modern interstate highway system. Construction on the Wyoming portion began in the 1960s.

how business is. In a few months there is a FOR SALE sign on the inside window of the service station. Ed Egge gets drunk and, driving at speed, hits two steers on the county road.

Leeland joins the army, puts in for the motor pool. He is stationed in Germany for six years and never learns a word of the language. He comes back to Wyoming heavier, moodier. He works with a snow-fence[5] crew during spring and summer, then moves Lori and the children—the boy and a new baby girl—to Casper[6] where he drives oil trucks. They live in a house trailer on Poison Spider Road, jammed between two rioting neighbors. On the news they hear that an enormous diamond has been discovered somewhere. The second girl is born. Leeland can't seem to get along with the oil company dispatcher. After a year they move back to Unique. Leeland and his mother make up their differences.

Lori is good at saving money and she has put aside a small nest egg. They set up in business for themselves. Leeland believes people will be glad to trade at a local ranch supply store that saves a long drive into town. He rents the service station from Mrs. Egge who has not been able to sell it after Ed's death. They spruce it up, Leeland doing all the carpenter work, Lori painting the interior and exterior. On the side Leeland raises hogs with his father. His father was born and raised in Iowa and knows hogs.

It becomes clear that people relish the long drive to a bigger town where they can see something different, buy fancy groceries, clothing, bakery goods as well as ranch supplies. One intensely cold winter when everything freezes from God to gizzard, Leeland and his father lose 112 hogs. They sell out. Eighteen months later the ranch supply business goes under. The new color television set goes back to the store.

After the bankruptcy proceedings Leeland finds work on a road construction crew. He is always out of town, it seems, but back often enough for what he calls "a good ride" and so makes Lori pregnant again. Before the baby is born he quits the road crew. He can't seem to get along with the foreman. No one can, and turnover is high. On his truck radio he hears that hundreds of religious cult members have swallowed Kool-Aid and cyanide.[7]

Leeland takes a job at Tongue River Meat Locker and Processing. Old Man Brose owns the business. Leeland is the only employee. He has an aptitude for sizing up and cutting large animals. He likes wrapping the tidy packages, the smell of damp bone and chill. He can throw his cleaver unerringly and when mice run along the wall they do not run far if Leeland is there. After months of discussion with Old Man Brose, Leeland and Lori sign a ten-year lease on the meat locker operation. Their oldest boy graduates from high school, the first in the family to do so, and joins the army. He signs up for six years. There is some-

5. Slatted fence designed to block blowing snow, especially to protect roads.

6. Wyoming's second-largest city, nicknamed "The Oil City" because of its role in various oil booms, one of which peaked in 1970.

7. On November 18, 1978, over nine hundred people died in the Jonestown massacre, a mass suicide in a religious community in Guyana led by American Jim Jones. Because of the way its victims were poisoned, the event inspired the phrase "drink the Kool-Aid," i.e., go along with others unquestioningly.

thing on the news about school lunches and ketchup is classed as a vegetable.[8] Old Man Brose moves to Albuquerque.

10 The economy takes a dive. The news is full of talk about recession and unemployment. Thrifty owners of small ranches go back to doing their own butchering, cutting, and freezing. The meat locker lease payments are high and electricity jumps up. Leeland and Lori have to give up the business. Old Man Brose returns from Albuquerque. There are bad feelings. It didn't work out, Leeland says, and that's the truth of it.

It seems like a good time to try another place. The family moves to Thermopolis where Leeland finds a temporary job at a local meat locker during hunting season. A hunter from Des Moines, not far from where Leeland's father was born, tips him $100 when he loads packages of frozen elk and the elk's head onto the man's single-engine plane. The man has been drinking. The plane goes down in the Medicine Bow range to the southeast.

During this long winter Leeland is out of work and stays home with the baby. Lori works in the school cafeteria. The baby is a real crier and Leeland quiets him down with spoonsful of beer.

In the spring they move back to Unique and Leeland tries truck driving again, this time in long-distance rigs on coast-to-coast journeys that take him away two and three months at a time. He travels all over the continent, to Texas, Alaska, Montreal, and Corpus Christi. He says every place is the same. Lori works now in the kitchen of the Hi-Lo Café in Unique. The ownership of the café changes three times in two years. West Klinker, an elderly rancher, eats three meals a day at the Hi-Lo. He is sweet on Lori. He reads her an article from the newspaper—a strange hole has appeared in the ozone layer.[9] He confuses ozone with oxygen.

One night while Leeland is somewhere on the east coast the baby goes into convulsions following a week's illness of fever and cough. Lori makes a frightening drive over icy roads to the distant hospital. The baby survives but he is slow. Lori starts a medical emergency response group in Unique. Three women and two men sign up to take the first aid course. They drive a hundred miles to the first aid classes. Only two of them pass the test on the first try. Lori is one of the two. The other is Stuttering Bob, an old bachelor. One of the failed students says Stuttering Bob has nothing to do but study the first aid manual as he enjoys the leisured life that goes with a monthly social security check.

15 Leeland quits driving trucks and again tries raising hogs with his father on the old ranch. He becomes a volunteer fireman and is at the bad February fire that kills two children. It takes the fire truck three hours to get in to the ranch through the wind-drifted snow. The family is related to Lori. When something inside explodes, Leeland tells, an object flies out of the house and strikes the fire engine hood. It is a Nintendo player and not even charred.

Stuttering Bob has cousins in Muncie, Indiana. One of the cousins works at the Muncie Medical Center. The cousin arranges for the Medical Center to donate an old ambulance to the Unique Rescue Squad although they had intended

8. In an effort to cut costs in federally subsidized school lunch programs but still comply with existing nutritional guidelines, the Reagan administration proposed reclassifying ketchup as a vegetable in 1982. The resulting public outcry scuttled the proposal.

9. In 1985, scientists discovered a hole in the atmosphere's ozone layer, which protects the planet from harmful ultraviolet light and is damaged by pollution.

to give it to a group in Mississippi. Bob's cousin, who has been to Unique, persuades them. Bob is afraid to drive through congested cities so Leeland and Lori take a series of buses to Muncie to pick up the vehicle. It is their first vacation. They take the youngest boy with them. On the return trip Lori leaves her purse on a chair in a restaurant. The gas money for the return trip is in the purse. They go back to the restaurant, wild with anxiety. The purse has been turned in and nothing is missing. Lori and Leeland talk about the goodness of people, even strangers. In their absence Stuttering Bob is elected president of the rescue squad.

A husband and wife from California move to Unique and open a taxidermy business. They say they are artists and arrange the animals in unusual poses. Lori gets work cleaning their workshop. The locals make jokes about the coyote in their window, posed lifting a leg against sagebrush where a trap is set. The taxidermists hold out for almost two years, then move to Oregon. Leeland's and Lori's oldest son telephones from overseas. He is making a career of the service.

Leeland's father dies and they discover the hog business is deeply in debt, the ranch twice-mortgaged. The ranch is sold to pay off debts. Leeland's mother moves in with them. Leeland continues long-distance truck driving. His mother watches television all day. Sometimes she sits in Lori's kitchen, saying almost nothing, picking small stones from dried beans.

The youngest daughter baby-sits. One night, on the way home, her employer feels her small breasts and asks her to squeeze his penis, because, he says, she ate the piece of chocolate cake he was saving. She does it but runs crying into the house and tells Lori who advises her to keep quiet and stay home from now on. The man is Leeland's friend; they hunt elk and antelope together.

20 Leeland quits truck driving. Lori has saved a little money. Once more they decide to go into business for themselves. They lease the old gas station where Leeland had his first job and where they tried the ranch supply store. Now it is a gas station again, but also a convenience store. They try surefire gimmicks: plastic come-on banners that pop and tear in the wind, free ice cream cones with every fill-up, prize drawings. Leeland has been thinking of the glory days when a hundred cars stopped. Now highway 16 seems the emptiest road in the country. They hold on for a year, then Leeland admits that it hasn't worked out and he is right. He is depressed for days when San Francisco beats Denver in the Super Bowl.[1]

Their oldest boy is discharged from the service and will not say why but Leeland knows it is chemical substances, drugs. Leeland is driving long-distance trucks again despite his back pain. The oldest son is home, working as a ranch hand in Pie. Leeland studies him, looking for signs of addiction. The son's eyes are always red and streaming.

The worst year comes. Leeland's mother dies, Leeland hurts his back, and, in the same week, Lori learns that she has breast cancer and is pregnant again. She is forty-six. Lori's doctor advises an abortion. Lori refuses.

The oldest son is discovered to have an allergy to horses and quits the ranch job. He tells Leeland he wants to try raising hogs. Pork prices are high. For a few days Leeland is excited. He can see it clearly: Leeland Lee & Son, Live-

1. On January 28, 1990, the San Francisco 49ers defeated the Denver Broncos 55–10.

stock. But the son changes his mind when a friend he knew in the service comes by on a motorcycle. The next morning both of them leave for Phoenix.

Lori spontaneously aborts in the fifth month of the pregnancy and then the cancer burns her up. Leeland is at the hospital with her every day. Lori dies. The daughters, both married now, curse Leeland. No one knows how to reach the oldest son and he misses the funeral. The youngest boy cries inconsolably. They decide he will live in Billings, Montana, with the oldest sister who is expecting her first child.

25 Two springs after Lori's death a middle-aged woman from Ohio buys the café, paints it orange, renames it Unique Eats and hires Leeland to cook. He is good with meat, knows how to choose the best cuts and grill or do them chicken-fried style to perfection. He has never cooked anything at home and everyone is surprised at this long-hidden skill. The oldest son comes back and next year they plan to lease the old gas station and convert it to a motorcycle repair shop and steak house. Nobody has time to listen to the news.

1999

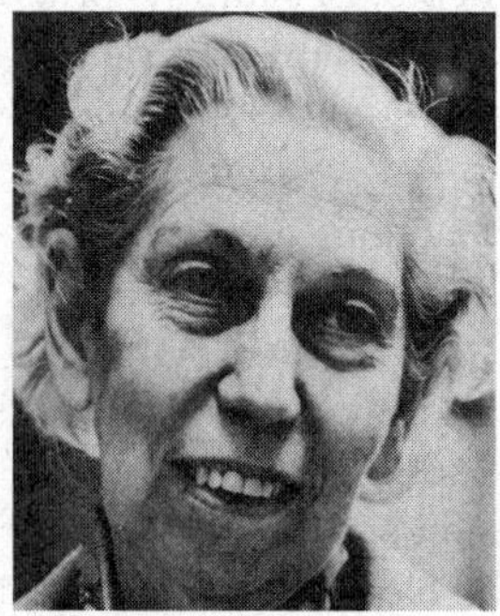

EUDORA WELTY (1909–2001)

Why I Live at the P.O.

Known as the "First Lady of Southern Literature," Eudora Welty was born and raised in Jackson, Mississippi, attended Mississippi State College for Women, and earned a BA from the University of Wisconsin. Among the countless awards she received were two Guggenheim Fellowships, six O. Henry Awards, a Pulitzer Prize, the French Legion of Honor, the National Medal for Literature, and the Presidential Medal of Freedom. Although she wrote five novels, including *The Robber Bridegroom* (1942), *Ponder Heart* (1954), and *The Optimist's Daughter* (1972), Welty is best known for her short stories, many of which appear in *The Collected Stories of Eudora Welty* (1980). Among her nonfiction works are *One Writer's Beginnings* (1984), *A Writer's Eye: Collected Book Reviews* (1994), and five collections of her photographs, including *One Place, One Time* (1978) and *Photographs* (1989). In 1998 the Library of America published a two-volume edition of her selected works, making her the first living author they had published.

I was getting along fine with Mama, Papa-Daddy, and Uncle Rondo until my sister Stella-Rondo just separated from her husband and came back home again. Mr. Whitaker! Of course I went with Mr. Whitaker first, when he first appeared here in China Grove, taking "Pose Yourself" photos, and Stella-Rondo broke us up. Told him I was one-sided. Bigger on one side than the other, which is a deliberate, calculated falsehood: I'm the same. Stella-Rondo is exactly twelve months to the day younger than I am and for that reason she's spoiled.

She's always had anything in the world she wanted and then she'd throw it away. Papa-Daddy give her this gorgeous Add-a-Pearl necklace when she was eight years old and she threw it away playing baseball when she was nine, with only two pearls.

So as soon as she got married and moved away from home the first thing she did was separate! From Mr. Whitaker! This photographer with the popeyes she said she trusted. Came home from one of those towns up in Illinois and to our complete surprise brought this child of two.

Mama said she like to make her drop dead for a second. "Here you had this marvelous blonde child and never so much as wrote your mother a word about it," says Mama. "I'm thoroughly ashamed of you." But of course she wasn't.

Stella-Rondo just calmly takes off this *hat,* I wish you could see it. She says, 5
"Why, Mama, Shirley-T.'s adopted, I can prove it."

"How?" says Mama, but all I says was, "H'm!" There I was over the hot stove, trying to stretch two chickens over five people and a completely unexpected child into the bargain without one moment's notice.

"What do you mean—'H'm'?" says Stella-Rondo, and Mama says, "I heard that, Sister."

I said that oh, I didn't mean a thing, only that whoever Shirley-T. was, she was the spit-image of Papa-Daddy if he'd cut off his beard, which of course he'd never do in the world. Papa-Daddy's Mama's papa and sulks.

Stella-Rondo got furious! She said, "Sister, I don't need to tell you you got a lot of nerve and always did have and I'll thank you to make no future reference to my adopted child whatsoever."

"Very well," I said. "Very well, very well. Of course I noticed at once she looks 10
like Mr. Whitaker's side too. That frown. She looks like a cross between Mr. Whitaker and Papa-Daddy."

"Well, all I can say is she isn't."

"She looks exactly like Shirley Temple to me," says Mama, but Shirley-T. just ran away from her.

So the first thing Stella-Rondo did at the table was turn Papa-Daddy against me.

"Papa-Daddy," she says. He was trying to cut up his meat. "Papa-Daddy!" I was taken completely by surprise. Papa-Daddy is about a million years old and's got this long-long beard. "Papa-Daddy, Sister says she fails to understand why you don't cut off your beard."

So Papa-Daddy l-a-y-s down his knife and fork! He's real rich. Mama says he 15
is, he says he isn't. So he says, "Have I heard correctly? You don't understand why I don't cut off my beard?"

"Why," I says, "Papa-Daddy, of course I understand, I did not say any such a thing, the idea!"

He says, "Hussy!"

I says, "Papa-Daddy, you know I wouldn't any more want you to cut off your beard than the man in the moon. It was the farthest thing from my mind! Stella-Rondo sat there and made that up while she was eating breast of chicken."

But he says, "So the postmistress fails to understand why I don't cut off my beard. Which job I got you through my influence with the government. 'Bird's nest'—is that what you call it?"

Not that it isn't the next to smallest P.O. in the entire state of Mississippi. 20

I says, "Oh, Papa-Daddy," I says, "I didn't say any such a thing, I never dreamed it was a bird's nest, I have always been grateful though this is the next to smallest P.O. in the state of Mississippi, and I do not enjoy being referred to as a hussy by my own grandfather."

But Stella-Rondo says, "Yes, you did say it too. Anybody in the world could of heard you, that had ears."

"Stop right there," says Mama, looking at *me*.

So I pulled my napkin straight back through the napkin ring and left the table.

As soon as I was out of the room Mama says, "Call her back, or she'll starve to death," but Papa-Daddy says, "This is the beard I started growing on the Coast when I was fifteen years old." He would of gone on till nightfall if Shirley-T. hadn't lost the Milky Way she ate in Cairo.

So Papa-Daddy says, "I am going out and lie in the hammock, and you can all sit here and remember my words: I'll never cut off my beard as long as I live, even one inch, and I don't appreciate it in you at all." Passed right by me in the hall and went straight out and got in the hammock.

It would be a holiday. It wasn't five minutes before Uncle Rondo suddenly appeared in the hall in one of Stella-Rondo's flesh-colored kimonos, all cut on the bias, like something Mr. Whitaker probably thought was gorgeous.

"Uncle Rondo!" I says. "I didn't know who that was! Where are you going?"

"Sister," he says, "get out of my way, I'm poisoned."

"If you're poisoned stay away from Papa-Daddy," I says. "Keep out of the hammock. Papa-Daddy will certainly beat you on the head if you come within forty miles of him. He thinks I deliberately said he ought to cut off his beard after he got me the P.O., and I've told him and told him and told him, and he acts like he just don't hear me. Papa-Daddy must of gone stone deaf."

"He picked a fine day to do it then," says Uncle Rondo, and before you could say "Jack Robinson" flew out in the yard.

What he'd really done, he'd drunk another bottle of that prescription. He does it every single Fourth of July as sure as shooting, and it's horribly expensive. Then he falls over in the hammock and snores. So he insisted on zigzagging right on out to the hammock, looking like a half-wit.

Papa-Daddy woke with this horrible yell and right there without moving an inch he tried to turn Uncle Rondo against me. I heard every word he said. Oh, he told Uncle Rondo I didn't learn to read till I was eight years old and he didn't see how in the world I ever got the mail put up at the P.O., much less read it all, and he said if Uncle Rondo could only fathom the lengths he had gone to get me that job! And he said on the other hand he thought Stella-Rondo had a brilliant mind and deserved credit for getting out of town. All the time he was just lying there swinging as pretty as you please and looping out his beard, and poor Uncle Rondo was *pleading* with him to slow down the hammock, it was making him as dizzy as a witch to watch it. But that's what Papa-Daddy likes about a hammock. So Uncle Rondo was too dizzy to get turned against me for the time being. He's Mama's only brother and is a good case of a one-track mind. Ask anybody. A certified pharmacist.

Just then I heard Stella-Rondo raising the upstairs window. While she was married she got this peculiar idea that it's cooler with the windows shut and locked. So she has to raise the window before she can make a soul hear her outdoors.

So she raises the window and says, "*Oh!*" You would have thought she was mortally wounded.

Uncle Rondo and Papa-Daddy didn't even look up, but kept right on with what they were doing. I had to laugh.

I flew up the stairs and threw the door open! I says, "What in the wide world's the matter, Stella-Rondo? You mortally wounded?"

"No," she says, "I am not mortally wounded but I wish you would do me the favor of looking out that window there and telling me what you see."

So I shade my eyes and look out the window.

"I see the front yard," I says.

"Don't you see any human beings?"

"I see Uncle Rondo trying to run Papa-Daddy out of the hammock," I says. "Nothing more. Naturally, it's so suffocating-hot in the house, with all the windows shut and locked, everybody who cares to stay in their right mind will have to go out and get in the hammock before the Fourth of July is over."

"Don't you notice anything different about Uncle Rondo?" asks Stella-Rondo.

"Why, no, except he's got on some terrible-looking flesh-colored contraption I wouldn't be found dead in, is all I can see," I says.

"Never mind, you won't be found dead in it, because it happens to be part of my trousseau, and Mr. Whitaker took several dozen photographs of me in it," says Stella-Rondo. "What on earth could Uncle Rondo *mean* by wearing part of my trousseau out in the broad open daylight without saying so much as 'Kiss my foot,' *knowing* I only got home this morning after my separation and hung my negligee up on the bathroom door, just as nervous as I could be?"

"I'm sure I don't know, and what do you expect me to do about it?" I says. "Jump out the window?"

"No, I expect nothing of the kind. I simply declare that Uncle Rondo looks like a fool in it, that's all," she says. "It makes me sick to my stomach."

"Well, he looks as good as he can," I says. "As good as anybody in reason could." I stood up for Uncle Rondo, please remember. And I said to Stella-Rondo, "I think I would do well not to criticize so freely if I were you and came home with a two-year-old child I had never said a word about, and no explanation whatever about my separation."

"I asked you the instant I entered this house not to refer one more time to my adopted child, and you gave me your word of honor you would not," was all Stella-Rondo would say, and started pulling out every one of her eyebrows with some cheap Kress tweezers.

So I merely slammed the door behind me and went down and made some green-tomato pickle. Somebody had to do it. Of course Mama had turned both the Negroes loose; she always said no earthly power could hold one anyway on the Fourth of July, so she wouldn't even try. It turned out that Jaypan fell in the lake and came within a very narrow limit of drowning.

So Mama trots in. Lifts up the lid and says, "H'm! Not very good for your Uncle Rondo in his precarious condition, I must say. Or poor little adopted Shirley-T. Shame on you!"

That made me tired. I says, "Well, Stella-Rondo had better thank her lucky stars it was her instead of me came trotting in with that very peculiar-looking child. Now if it had been me that trotted in from Illinois and brought a peculiar-looking child or two, I shudder to think of the reception I'd of got, much less controlled the diet of an entire family."

"But you must remember, Sister, that you were never married to Mr. Whitaker in the first place and didn't go up to Illinois to live," says Mama, shaking a spoon in my face. "If you had I would of been just as overjoyed to see you and your little adopted girl as I was to see Stella-Rondo, when you wound up with your separation and came on back home."

"You would not," I says.

"Don't contradict me, I would," says Mama.

But I said she couldn't convince me though she talked till she was blue in the face. Then I said, "Besides, you know as well as I do that that child is not adopted."

"She most certainly is adopted," says Mama, stiff as a poker.

I says, "Why, Mama, Stella-Rondo had her just as sure as anything in this world, and just too stuck up to admit it."

"Why, Sister," said Mama. "Here I thought we were going to have a pleasant Fourth of July, and you start right out not believing a word your own baby sister tells you!"

"Just like Cousin Annie Flo. Went to her grave denying the facts of life," I reminded Mama.

"I told you if you ever mentioned Annie Flo's name I'd slap your face," says Mama, and slaps my face.

"All right, you wait and see," I says.

"I," says Mama, "*I* prefer to take my children's word for anything when it's humanly possible." You ought to see Mama, she weighs two hundred pounds and has real tiny feet.

Just then something perfectly horrible occurred to me.

"Mama," I says, "can that child talk?" I simply had to whisper! "Mama, I wonder if that child can be—you know—in any way? Do you realize?" I says, "that she hasn't spoke one single, solitary word to a human being up to this minute? This is the way she looks," I says, and I looked like this.

Well, Mama and I just stood there and stared at each other. It was horrible!

"I remember well that Joe Whitaker frequently drank like a fish," says Mama. "I believed to my soul he drank *chemicals*." And without another word she marches to the foot of the stairs and calls Stella-Rondo.

"Stella-Rondo? O-o-o-o-o! Stella-Rondo!"

"What?" says Stella-Rondo from upstairs. Not even the grace to get up off the bed.

"Can that child of yours talk?" asks Mama.

Stella-Rondo says, "Can she what?"

"Talk! Talk!" says Mama. "Burdyburdyburdyburdy!"

So Stella-Rondo yells back, "Who says she can't talk?"

"Sister says so," says Mama.

"You didn't have to tell me, I know whose word of honor don't mean a thing in this house," says Stella-Rondo.

And in a minute the loudest Yankee voice I ever heard in my life yells out, "OE'm Pop-OE the Sailor-r-r-r Ma-a-an!" and then somebody jumps up and down in the upstairs hall. In another second the house would of fallen down.

"Not only talks, she can tap-dance!" calls Stella-Rondo. "Which is more than some people I won't name can do."

"Why, the little precious darling thing!" Mama says, so surprised. "Just as smart as she can be!" Starts talking baby talk right there. Then she turns on me. "Sister, you ought to be thoroughly ashamed! Run upstairs this instant and apologize to Stella-Rondo and Shirley-T."

"Apologize for what?" I says. "I merely wondered if the child was normal, that's all. Now that she's proved she is, why, I have nothing further to say."

80 But Mama just turned on her heel and flew out, furious. She ran right upstairs and hugged the baby. She believed it was adopted. Stella-Rondo hadn't done a thing but turn her against me from upstairs while I stood there helpless over the hot stove. So that made Mama, Papa-Daddy, and the baby all on Stella-Rondo's side.

Next, Uncle Rondo.

I must say that Uncle Rondo has been marvelous to me at various times in the past and I was completely unprepared to be made to jump out of my skin, the way it turned out. Once Stella-Rondo did something perfectly horrible to him—broke a chain letter from Flanders Field—and he took the radio back he had given her and gave it to me. Stella-Rondo was furious! For six months we all had to call her Stella instead of Stella-Rondo, or she wouldn't answer. I always thought Uncle Rondo had all the brains of the entire family. Another time he sent me to Mammoth Cave with all expenses paid.

But this would be the day he was drinking that prescription, the Fourth of July.

So at supper Stella-Rondo speaks up and says she thinks Uncle Rondo ought to try to eat a little something. So finally Uncle Rondo said he would try a little cold biscuits and ketchup, but that was all. So *she* brought it to him.

85 "Do you think it wise to disport with ketchup in Stella-Rondo's flesh-colored kimono?" I says. Trying to be considerate! If Stella-Rondo couldn't watch out for her trousseau, somebody had to.

"Any objections?" asks Uncle Rondo, just about to pour out all of the ketchup.

"Don't mind what she says, Uncle Rondo," says Stella-Rondo. "Sister has been devoting this solid afternoon to sneering out my bedroom window at the way you look."

"What's that?" says Uncle Rondo. Uncle Rondo has got the most terrible temper in the world. Anything is liable to make him tear the house down if it comes at the wrong time.

So Stella-Rondo says, "Sister says, 'Uncle Rondo certainly does look like a fool in that pink kimono!'"

90 Do you remember who it was really said that?

Uncle Rondo spills out all the ketchup and jumps out of his chair and tears off the kimono and throws it down on the dirty floor and puts his foot on it. It had to be sent all the way to Jackson to the cleaners and re-pleated.

"So that's your opinion of your Uncle Rondo, is it?" he says. "I look like a fool, do I? Well, that's the last straw. A whole day in this house with nothing to do, and then to hear you come out with a remark like that behind my back!"

"I didn't say any such of a thing, Uncle Rondo," I says, "and I'm not saying who did, either. Why, I think you look all right. Just try to take care of yourself and not talk and eat at the same time," I says. "I think you better go lie down."

"Lie down my foot," says Uncle Rondo. I ought to of known by that he was fixing to do something perfectly horrible.

95 So he didn't do anything that night in the precarious state he was in—just played Casino with Mama and Stella-Rondo and Shirley-T. and gave Shirley-T. a nickel with a head on both sides. It tickled her nearly to death, and she called him "Papa." But at 6:30 A.M. the next morning, he threw a whole five-cent package of some unsold one-inch firecrackers from the store as hard as he could into my bedroom and they every one went off. Not one bad one in the string. Anybody else, there'd be one that wouldn't go off.

Well, I'm just terribly susceptible to noise of any kind, the doctor has always told me I was the most sensitive person he had ever seen in his whole life, and I was simply prostrated. I couldn't eat! People tell me they heard it as far as the cemetery, and old Aunt Jep Patterson, that had been holding her own so good, thought it was Judgment Day and she was going to meet her whole family. It's usually so quiet here.

And I'll tell you it didn't take me any longer than a minute to make up my mind what to do. There I was with the whole entire house on Stella-Rondo's side and turned against me. If I have anything at all I have pride.

So I just decided I'd go straight down to the P.O. There's plenty of room there in the back, I says to myself.

Well! I made no bones about letting the family catch on to what I was up to. I didn't try to conceal it.

100 The first thing they knew, I marched in where they were all playing Old Maid and pulled the electric oscillating fan out by the plug, and everything got real hot. Next I snatched the pillow I'd done the needlepoint on right off the davenport from behind Papa-Daddy. He went "Ugh!" I beat Stella-Rondo up the stairs and finally found my charm bracelet in her bureau drawer under a picture of Nelson Eddy.[1]

"So that's the way the land lies," says Uncle Rondo. There he was, piecing on the ham. "Well, Sister, I'll be glad to donate my army cot if you got any place to set it up, providing you'll leave right this minute and let me get some peace." Uncle Rondo was in France.

"Thank you kindly for the cot and 'peace' is hardly the word I would select if I had to resort to firecrackers at 6:30 A.M. in a young girl's bedroom," I says to him. "And as to where I intend to go, you seem to forget my position as postmistress of China Grove, Mississippi," I says. "I've always got the P.O."

Well, that made them all sit up and take notice.

I went out front and started digging up some four-o'clocks to plant around the P.O.

1. Opera singer (1901–67) who enjoyed phenomenal popularity in the 1930s and 1940s when he costarred in numerous film musicals with Jeanette MacDonald. The two were known as "America's Singing Sweethearts."

"Ah-ah-ah!" says Mama, raising the window. "Those happen to be my four- 105
o'clocks. Everything planted in that star is mine. I've never known you to make anything grow in your life."

"Very well," I says. "But I take the fern. Even you, Mama, can't stand there and deny that I'm the one watered that fern. And I happen to know where I can send in a box top and get a packet of one thousand mixed seeds, no two the same kind, free."

"Oh, where?" Mama wants to know.

But I says, "Too late. You 'tend to your house, and I'll 'tend to mine. You hear things like that all the time if you know how to listen to the radio. Perfectly marvelous offers. Get anything you want free."

So I hope to tell you I marched in and got that radio, and they could of all bit a nail in two, especially Stella-Rondo, that it used to belong to, and she well knew she couldn't get it back, I'd sue for it like a shot. And I very politely took the sewing-machine motor I helped pay the most on to give Mama for Christmas back in 1929, and a good big calendar, with the first-aid remedies on it. The thermometer and the Hawaiian ukulele certainly were rightfully mine, and I stood on the step-ladder and got all my watermelon-rind preserves and every fruit and vegetable I'd put up, every jar. Then I began to pull the tacks out of the bluebird wall vases on the archway to the dining room.

"Who told you you could have those, Miss Priss?" says Mama, fanning as 110
hard as she could.

"I bought 'em and I'll keep track of 'em," I says. "I'll tack 'em up one on each side of the post-office window, and you can see 'em when you come to ask me for your mail, if you're so dead to see 'em."

"Not I! I'll never darken the door to that post office again if I live to be a hundred," Mama says. "Ungrateful child! After all the money we spent on you at the Normal."[2]

"Me either," says Stella-Rondo. "You can just let my mail lie there and *rot*, for all I care. I'll never come and relieve you of a single, solitary piece."

"I should worry," I says. "And who you think's going to sit down and write you all those big fat letters and postcards, by the way? Mr. Whitaker? Just because he was the only man ever dropped down in China Grove and you got him—unfairly—is he going to sit down and write you a lengthy correspondence after you come home giving no rhyme nor reason whatsoever for your separation and no explanation for the presence of that child? I may not have your brilliant mind, but I fail to see it."

So Mama says, "Sister, I've told you a thousand times that Stella-Rondo sim- 115
ply got homesick, and this child is far too big to be hers," and she says, "Now, why don't you just sit down and play Casino?"

Then Shirley-T. sticks out her tongue at me in this perfectly horrible way. She has no more manners than the man in the moon. I told her she was going to cross her eyes like that some day and they'd stick.

"It's too late to stop me now," I says. "You should have tried that yesterday. I'm going to the P.O. and the only way you can possibly see me is to visit me there."

2. That is, normal school (teachers' college).

So Papa-Daddy says, "You'll never catch me setting foot in that post office, even if I should take a notion into my head to write a letter some place." He says, "I won't have you reachin' out of that little old window with a pair of shears and cuttin' off any beard of mine. I'm too smart for you!"

"We all are," says Stella-Rondo.

120 But I said, "If you're so smart, where's Mr. Whitaker?"

So then Uncle Rondo says, "I'll thank you from now on to stop reading all the orders I get on postcards and telling everybody in China Grove what you think is the matter with them," but I says, "I draw my own conclusions and will continue in the future to draw them." I says, "If people want to write their innermost secrets on penny postcards, there's nothing in the wide world you can do about it, Uncle Rondo."

"And if you think we'll ever *write* another postcard you're sadly mistaken," says Mama.

"Cutting off your nose to spite your face then," I says. "But if you're all determined to have no more to do with the U.S. mail, think of this: What will Stella-Rondo do now, if she wants to tell Mr. Whitaker to come after her?"

"Wah!" says Stella-Rondo. I knew she'd cry. She had a conniption fit right there in the kitchen.

125 "It will be interesting to see how long she holds out," I says. "And now—I am leaving."

"Good-bye," says Uncle Rondo.

"Oh, I declare," says Mama, "to think that a family of mine should quarrel on the Fourth of July, or the day after, over Stella-Rondo leaving old Mr. Whitaker and having the sweetest little adopted child! It looks like we'd all be glad!"

"Wah!" says Stella-Rondo, and has a fresh conniption fit.

"He left *her*—you mark my words," I says. "That's Mr. Whitaker. I know Mr. Whitaker. After all, I knew him first. I said from the beginning he'd up and leave her. I foretold every single thing that's happened."

130 "Where did he go?" asks Mama.

"Probably to the North Pole, if he knows what's good for him," I says.

But Stella-Rondo just bawled and wouldn't say another word. She flew to her room and slammed the door.

"Now look what you've gone and done, Sister," says Mama. "You go apologize."

"I haven't the time, I'm leaving," I says.

135 "Well, what are you waiting around for?" asks Uncle Rondo.

So I just picked up the kitchen clock and marched off, without saying, "Kiss my foot," or anything, and never did tell Stella-Rondo good-bye.

There was a girl going along on a little wagon right in front.

"Nigger girl," I says, "come help me haul these things down the hill, I'm going to live in the post office."

Took her nine trips in her express wagon. Uncle Rondo came out on the porch and threw her a nickel.

140 And that's the last I've laid eyes on any of my family or my family laid eyes on me for five solid days and nights. Stella-Rondo may be telling the most horrible tales in the world about Mr. Whitaker, but I haven't heard them. As I tell everybody, I draw my own conclusions.

But oh, I like it here. It's ideal, as I've been saying. You see, I've got everything cater-cornered, the way I like it. Hear the radio? All the war news. Radio, sewing machine, book ends, ironing board and that great big piano lamp—peace, that's what I like. Butter-bean vines planted all along the front where the strings are.

Of course, there's not much mail. My family are naturally the main people in China Grove, and if they prefer to vanish from the face of the earth, for all the mail they get or the mail they write, why, I'm not going to open my mouth. Some of the folks here in town are taking up for me and some turned against me. I know which is which. There are always people who will quit buying stamps just to get on the right side of Papa-Daddy.

But here I am, and here I'll stay. I want the world to know I'm happy.

And if Stella-Rondo should come to me this minute, on bended knees, and *attempt* to explain the incidents of her life with Mr. Whitaker, I'd simply put my fingers in both my ears and refuse to listen.

1941

POETRY

Edna St. Vincent Millay

POETRY
Reading, Responding, Writing

Ways of reading poetry and reasons for doing so differ almost as widely as poems themselves, and in ways we can perhaps best appreciate by considering poetry's functions in other times and places. Though you might be aware, for example, that medieval noblemen paid courtly "bards" to commemorate their achievements and thereby help them to maintain their own prestige and power, you might be surprised to learn that since 2007 millions of people across the Middle East have tuned in to watch *Prince of Poets*, a reality show in which poets rather than pop singers compete for audience votes.

Such phenomena might come as a surprise to us simply because today, at least in the West, we don't tend to think of poetry as having great popular appeal or political potency. Millions of us may be moved by the way hip-hop artists use rhyme and rhythm to boast about, or "celebrate and sing," themselves; to show us the danger and excitement of life on the streets; or even to get out the vote. Yet "poetry" seems to many of us a thing apart, something either to suffer, to cherish, or to simply be baffled and intimidated by precisely because it seems so arcane, so different and difficult, so essentially irrelevant to the rest of our lives. Though one rarely hears anyone say of all fiction either "I hate it" or "I love it" or "I just don't get it," if you're like most people, you've probably said, thought, or heard someone else say at least one of these things about poetry.

This chapter and the ones that follow welcome poetry-lovers. But they neither require you to be one nor aim to convert you. They do, we hope, demonstrate a few key points:

- Poetry itself isn't all one thing: *Poems differ as much as the people who write and read them, or as much as music and movies do.* They can be by turns goofy, sad, or angry; they can tell a story, comment on current events, or simply describe the look of a certain time of day. Deciding that you "love," "hate," "get," or "don't get" all poetry based on your experience of one poem or of one kind of poetry is a little like either deciding you love all music because Mozart moves you or giving up on music entirely because Lady Gaga leaves you cold.
- *A good poem is not a secret message one needs a special decoder ring or an advanced degree to decipher.* Any thoughtful person who's willing to try can make sense of it, though some poems certainly do invite us to rethink our idea of what "making sense" might mean. Poetry has spoken to millions of ordinary people across the centuries and around the world, so at least some poems can speak to us, too, if we give both them and ourselves a chance. By the same token, even the most devoted, experienced poetry lovers among us can become better, more responsive, more thoughtful readers by simply reading more and different kinds of poetry and by exploring, as the following chapters do, the various elements and techniques with which poetry is made.

- People around the world have often turned to poetry to express their feelings and longings precisely because *poetry is, in certain vital ways, distinct from other forms of writing.* Each genre plays by its own rules and has its own history and traditions, so reading poetry effectively, like succeeding in a video game, does involve learning and playing by certain rules. Any one poem may open itself to multiple responses and interpretations, just as a game may allow you many ways of advancing to the next level. But in both cases there are limits. Neither is a free-for-all in which "anything goes." (In both cases, too, some difficulty can be essential to the fun.) *A poem wouldn't mean anything if it could mean everything.*
- *Yet the questions we ask of a poem and the techniques we use to understand it are simply variations of the same ones we use in reading fiction or drama.* Indeed, some poems narrate action just as a short story does; others work much like plays.
- Finally, *poems aren't nearly as fragile as we take them to be when we worry about "over-reading" or "analyzing them to death."* You can't kill a poem. But a poem does experience a sort of living death if it's not read, re-read, and pondered over. Poems need you. Not only can they bear the weight of your careful attention, but they also deserve it: the best of them are, after all, the result of someone else's. William Wordsworth may have done much to shape our contemporary ideas about poetry when he famously described it as "the spontaneous overflow of powerful feelings," but his own poems were, like most great poems, the result of weeks, even years, of writing and revision.

DEFINING POETRY

But what, after all, is poetry? Trying to define poetry is a bit like trying to catch a snowflake; you can do it, but at the very same moment, the snowflake begins to melt and disappear. With poems, as with fiction, one can always come up with particular examples that don't do what the definition insists they must, as well as numerous writers and readers who will disagree. Yet to claim that poetry eludes all definition is merely to reinforce the idea that it is simply too mysterious for ordinary mortals. Without being all-sufficient or entirely satisfying, a dictionary definition can at least give us a starting point. Here are two such definitions of poetry:

1. Writing that formulates a *concentrated* imaginative awareness of experience in language chosen and *arranged* to create a specific *emotional response* through meaning, sound, and *rhythm.* (*Merriam-Webster*)
2. Composition in verse or some comparable *patterned arrangement* of language in which the expression of *feelings* and ideas is given *intensity* by the use of distinctive style and *rhythm* [. . .]. Traditionally associated with explicit formal departure from the *patterns* of ordinary speech or prose, e.g., in the use of elevated diction, figurative language, and syntactical reordering. (*The Oxford English Dictionary*)

Different as they are, both of these definitions stress four elements: (1) the "patterned arrangement of language" to (2) generate "rhythm" and thereby both (3) express and evoke specific "emotion[s]" or "feelings" in (4) a "concentrated" way, or with "intensity."

But what does all that really mean? To test drive this definition, let's look at an example. And let's pick a tough one: HEAD, HEART, taken from *The Collected Stories of Lydia Davis*, is usually classified as a work of fiction, and it certainly does have the elements of one, including **characters** and some **action** arranged into a **plot** brought to us by a **narrator**. Yet one reviewer of Davis's *Collected Stories* tellingly describes this one as "a poem of a story." What specific features of the following story might make it work like a poem? Which, if any, of the features essential to poetry might it lack?

LYDIA DAVIS

Head, Heart

Heart weeps.
Head tries to help heart.
Head tells heart how it is, again:
You will lose the ones you love. They will all go. But even the earth will go, someday.
Heart feels better, then.
But the words of head do not remain long in the ears of heart.
Heart is so new to this.
I want them back, says heart.
Head is all heart has.
Help, head. Help heart.

2007

If difficulty were essential to poetry, "Head, Heart" would not seem to qualify. It's hard to imagine less formal, even less elementary, **diction** or **syntax**. And the whole seems relatively easy to paraphrase (often a helpful thing to do when first encountering a poem): When we're sad about losing someone we love, we reason with ourselves that loss is inevitable because everything earthly, even the earth itself, can't last forever. Such rational explanations give us comfort, but that comfort is itself temporary; we still miss those we've lost and have to keep calling on our heads to help our hearts cope.

We do have emotion here, then, as well as a **conflict** between emotion and reason—and even when they lack plots, most poems do explore conflicts, just as stories and plays do. But do we have a poem? Does it matter that "Head, Heart" depends entirely on two **figures of speech—metonymy**, the use of the name of one thing for another closely associated thing (here, "head" for "reason," and "heart" for "emotion"), as well as **personification**, the representation of an object or an abstraction (here, "head" and "heart") as a person (capable of weeping and talking, for example)? Though fiction and drama both use figurative language, we often describe such language as "poetic," even when it occurs in a story or play, because poems do tend to depend much more on it (as we discuss further in ch. 16).

Does it matter that "Head, Heart" is short—just seventy-one words? Though poems come in every size, many poems are short or at least shorter than the typical work of fiction. Brevity is one way that *some* poems achieve the "concentration" and "intensity" the dictionaries take to be essential. Such concentration invites, even requires, ours. As poet Billy Collins puts it, "Poetry offers us the possibility of modulating our pace." The very brevity of a poem can teach us simply to slow down for a moment and pay attention—not only to the details within the poem, but also, through them, to whatever in the world or in ourselves the poem attends to. Sometimes that's all a poem does—simply invites us to pay attention to something we wouldn't notice otherwise.

Regardless of their overall length, moreover, almost all poems concentrate our attention and modulate our pace by doling out words a few at a time, arranging them not just into sentences (as in prose), but into discreet **lines**. One result is much more blank space and thus more silences and pauses than in prose. For this reason alone, "Head, Heart" looks and works like a poem. And the deliberateness with which it does so is signaled by the fact that one of its sentences is divided so as to span multiple lines. (Line 3 ends with a colon, not a period.) By arranging words into lines and, often, into **stanzas**, the poet, not a typesetter or printer, determines where words fall on the page. And that perhaps is the most important aspect of that arrangement of language that has differentiated poetry from prose since poetry became a written, as well as spoken, art (an issue discussed further in ch. 20). All printings of a poem, if accurate, reproduce exactly the same breaks and space the words precisely the same way on the page.

AUTHORS ON THEIR CRAFT

BILLY COLLINS ON THE POET AS "LINE-MAKER"

From "A Brisk Walk: An Interview with Billy Collins" (2006)*

I'm a line-maker. I think that's what makes poets different from prose-writers. [. . .] We think not just in sentences the way prose writers do but also in lines. [. . .] When I'm constructing a poem, I'm trying to write one good line after another. [. . .] I'm not thinking of just writing a paragraph and then chopping it up. I'm very conscious of the fact that every line should have a cadence to it. It should contribute to the progress of the poem. And that the ending of the line is a way of turning the reader's attention back into the interior of the poem.

*"A Brisk Walk: An Interview with Billy Collins." Interview by Joel Whitney. *Guernica*, 14 June 2006, www.guernicamag.com/interviews/a_brisk_walk/.

One result is that line endings and beginnings inevitably get more of our attention, bear more oomph and meaning. Notice how many of the lines of "Head, Heart" begin with "Head" and "Heart" and how these words repeat in a pattern ("Heart," "Head," "Head," "Heart," "Heart," "Head"—and then "Help"), as if the line-beginnings themselves enact the same interplay between "head" and "heart" that the sentences describe. Conversely, certain end-words reverberate: "again," for example, suggests the repetitive familiarity of this conflict, one that paradoxically seems all the more difficult or poignant because it's both repetitive (each person goes through this again and again) and familiar (all of us go through this); "then" alerts us to the temporariness of the comfort head offers heart, preparing us for the "But" in the next line.

Again and *then* also reverberate in us and with each other because they **rhyme**, just as "head," "heart," and "help" **alliterate**. These words share a special aural, as well as spatial and visual, relationship to each other. Though prose writers certainly make their appeal to us in part through sound, poetry remains, as it has been for thousands of years, a more insistently aural form—one that appeals through aural patterning to what Davis here humorously, but not wrongly, calls "the ears of heart" (line 6). As poet Mary Oliver puts it, "To make a poem, we must make sounds. Not random sounds, but chosen sounds."

But are there qualities essential to poetry that "Head, Heart" lacks? Is it, for example, sufficiently aural in its appeal? Does it have genuine rhythm? Perhaps so, perhaps not. As you work your way through the rest of the chapters in this section and read more poems, we encourage you to keep thinking critically about our definitions in order to hone your own sense of just what poetry is, how it works, and what it does.

POETIC SUBGENRES AND KINDS

All poems share some common elements, use some of the same techniques, and thus require us to ask some of the same questions. Later in this chapter, we'll outline some of the steps you can follow and some of the questions you can pose as you read, respond to, and write about any poem. But different sorts of poems also work by slightly different rules and thus invite somewhat different responses and questions.

Poems may be classified into subgenres based on various characteristics, including their length, appearance, and formal features (patterns of rhyme and rhythm, for example); their subject; or even the type of **situation** and **setting** (time and place) they depict. (A **sonnet**, for example, has fourteen lines. Defined broadly, an **elegy** is simply any poem about death.) A single poem might well represent multiple subgenres or at least might contain elements of more than one. (One could write an elegy that is also a sonnet, for instance.)

Since Aristotle's time, however, readers and writers have also often divided poems into three broad categories or subgenres—**narrative**, **dramatic**, or **lyric**—based upon their mode of presentation. Put simply, poems that have a plot are either narrative poems (if they feature a narrator) or dramatic poems (if they don't), and many poems that lack a plot are lyrics. The rest of this section describes each of these subgenres in more detail, starting with the one that most resembles fiction and ending with the dramatic monologue, a sort of hybrid that combines features of both dramatic and lyric poetry.

As the dramatic monologue demonstrates, the borders between narrative, dramatic, and lyric poetry are fuzzy, contestable, and shifting. Some poems will cross those borders; others will resist these categories altogether. And the very definition of lyric poetry has not only changed over time, but also remains contested today. The ultimate goal isn't to definitively pigeonhole every poem but rather to develop a language through which to recognize, describe, and explore different poetic modes. Knowing which mode dominates in a particular poem can help ensure that we privilege the right questions as we read and write about it. Learning the conventions of particular subgenres and kinds allows us to better adjust to individual poems, to compare them to each other, and to appreciate how each creatively uses and reworks generic conventions.

Narrative Poetry

Like a work of prose fiction, a narrative poem tells a story; in other words, it has a plot related by a narrator, though its plot might be based on actual rather than made-up events. Comprising the same elements discussed in the Fiction section of this book, a narrative poem encourages us to ask the same questions—about character, plot, narration, and so on—that we do when reading a short story or novel. (See "Questions about the Elements of Fiction" in "Fiction: Reading, Responding, Writing.")

In centuries past, narrative poetry was a—even *the*—dominant subgenre of poetry. As a result, there are many different kinds of narrative poems, including book-length **epics** like Homer's *Iliad;* chivalric **romances** like Thomas Malory's *Le Morte d'Arthur;* grisly murder **ballads**, often rooted in actual events; and a range of harder-to-classify works of varying lengths such as the relatively short example below.

EDWIN ARLINGTON ROBINSON
Richard Cory

Whenever Richard Cory went down town,
We people on the pavement looked at him:
He was a gentleman from sole to crown,
Clean favored, and imperially slim.

And he was always quietly arrayed,
And he was always human when he talked;
But still he fluttered pulses when he said,
"Good-morning," and he glittered when he walked.

And he was rich—yes, richer than a king—
And admirably schooled in every grace:
In fine,[1] we thought that he was everything
To make us wish that we were in his place.

So on we worked, and waited for the light,
And went without the meat, and cursed the bread;
And Richard Cory, one calm summer night,
Went home and put a bullet through his head.

1897

- How does the poem characterize Richard Cory? What is the effect of the first-personal plural narration?
- What details in the poem's first three stanzas might make its final stanza simultaneously surprising, ironic, and predictable?

1. In conclusion, in sum.

Dramatic Poetry

For centuries, plays were written exclusively or mainly in verse; as a result, drama itself was understood not as a genre in its own right (as we think of it today) but rather as a subgenre of poetry. "Dramatic poetry" thus meant and still can mean actual plays in verse (or *verse drama*). But any poem that consists wholly of dialogue among characters, unmediated by a narrator, counts as a dramatic poem. And we might even apply that label to poems like the following in which narration is kept to the barest minimum. Indeed, this narrator's only words are "said she," and since every other word in the poem is spoken by one female character to another, the poem essentially reads like a scene from a play. Notice, though, that the poem also depends on techniques of formal organization and patterning unique to poetry: In each of the poem's six stanzas, for example, one woman speaks the first lines, while her companion gets the last line (or two).

THOMAS HARDY
The Ruined Maid

"O 'Melia,[2] my dear, this does everything crown!
Who could have supposed I should meet you in Town?
And whence such fair garments, such prosperi-ty?"—
"O didn't you know I'd been ruined?" said she.

—"You left us in tatters, without shoes or socks,
Tired of digging potatoes, and spudding up docks;[3]
And now you've gay bracelets and bright feathers three!"—
"Yes: that's how we dress when we're ruined," said she.

—"At home in the barton[4] you said 'thee' and 'thou,'
And 'thik oon,' and 'theäs oon,' and 't'other'; but now
Your talking quite fits 'ee for high compa-ny!"—
"Some polish is gained with one's ruin," said she.

—"Your hands were like paws then, your face blue and bleak
But now I'm bewitched by your delicate cheek,
And your little gloves fit as on any la-dy!"—
"We never do work when we're ruined," said she.

—"You used to call home-life a hag-ridden dream,
And you'd sigh, and you'd sock;[5] but at present you seem
To know not of megrims[6] or melancho-ly!"—
"True. One's pretty lively when ruined," said she.

—"I wish I had feathers, a fine sweeping gown,
And a delicate face, and could strut about Town!"—

2. Short for Amelia. 3. Spading up weeds. 4. Farmyard. 5. Sigh (English dialect).
6. Migraine headaches.

"My dear—a raw country girl, such as you be,
Cannot quite expect that. You ain't ruined," said she.

1866

When we read and write about dramatic poems, we can usefully bring to bear the same questions we do in reading drama. (See "Questions to Ask When Reading a Play" in "Drama: Reading, Responding, Writing.") But when it comes to short poems like THE RUINED MAID, questions about sets, staging, and even plot will usually be much less relevant than those related to character and conflict, as well as setting, tone, language, symbol, and theme. In Hardy's poem, for example, how are each of the two speakers characterized by *how* they speak, as well as *what* they say? How is our view of them, and especially of 'Melia, "the ruined maid," affected by the formal pattern mentioned earlier, which ensures (among other things) that she gets the last line? How might this pattern, along with rhythm and rhyme, also add **irony** to the poem?

Lyric Poetry

For good historical reasons, lyric poems probably best fulfill your expectations of what poetry should be like. Yet lyric poetry has been and still is defined in myriad ways. The word *lyric* derives from the ancient Greeks, for whom it designated a short poem chanted or sung by a single singer to the accompaniment of a stringed instrument called a lyre (hence, the word *lyric* and the fact that we today also use the word *lyrics* to denote the words of any song). Scholars believe that the earliest "lyrics" in the Greek sense were likely associated with religious occasions and feelings, especially those related to celebration, praise, and mourning. Ever since, the lyric has been associated with brevity, musicality, a single speaker, and the expression of intense feeling. Not surprisingly, at least a few specific kinds of lyric, including the **ode** and the elegy, originated in the ancient world.

Over the centuries, the lyric's boundaries have expanded and become less clear. Few lyrics are intended to be sung at all, much less to a lyre. But everyone agrees that relatively short poems that focus primarily on the feelings, impressions, and thoughts—that is, on the subjective, inward experience—of a single first-person speaker are lyrics.

Below are two examples very different from each other in subject matter and tone. Yet with these, as with all lyrics, our initial questions in both reading and writing will likely focus on each speaker's situation and inward experience of it. What is each speaker experiencing, feeling, and thinking, and how exactly does the poem make that state of mood and mind at once vivid and relevant to us?

WILLIAM WORDSWORTH

[I wandered lonely as a cloud]

I wandered lonely as a cloud
That floats on high o'er vales and hills,
When all at once I saw a crowd,
A host, of golden daffodils;

Beside the lake, beneath the trees,
Fluttering and dancing in the breeze.

Continuous as the stars that shine
And twinkle on the milky way,
They stretched in never-ending line
Along the margin of a bay:
Ten thousand saw I at a glance,
Tossing their heads in sprightly dance.

The waves beside them danced; but they
Out-did the sparkling waves in glee:
A poet could not but be gay,
In such a jocund company:
I gazed—and gazed—but little thought
What wealth the show to me had brought:

For oft, when on my couch I lie
In vacant or in pensive mood,
They flash upon that inward eye
Which is the bliss of solitude;
And then my heart with pleasure fills,
And dances with the daffodils.

1807

- **According to the speaker, what is "the bliss of solitude" (line 22)? Why and how does "solitude" become less "lonely" for him (line 1)?**
- **What about the relationship between human beings and nature might be implied by the speaker's description of his particular experience?**

FRANK O'HARA

Poem

Lana Turner[7] has collapsed!
I was trotting along and suddenly
it started raining and snowing
and you said it was hailing
but hailing hits you on the head
hard so it was really snowing and
raining and I was in such a hurry
to meet you but the traffic
was acting exactly like the sky
and suddenly I see a headline
LANA TURNER HAS COLLAPSED!
there is no snow in Hollywood
there is no rain in California
I have been to lots of parties
and acted perfectly disgraceful

7. American actress (1921–95); in 1958, Turner's lover was stabbed to death by her daughter, who was determined to have acted in self-defense.

but I never actually collapsed
oh Lana Turner we love you get up

1962

- What or whom exactly does this poem seem to make fun of? Does the poem also convey more serious sentiments?
- What current celebrity seems to you like the best potential substitute for Lana Turner? What about both this celebrity's public persona and the poem itself make your choice seem especially appropriate?

What makes these lyrics different from narrative and dramatic poems? Though both include action ("wander[ing]," "trotting," and so on), that action doesn't quite add up to a plot; what we have might be better described as a situation, scene, or incident. Similarly, though the poems vividly describe external things, from "golden daffodils" to "traffic," greater emphasis ultimately falls on how the "I" experiences and feels about them—the internal, subjective experience or state of mind and mood that those outward things inspire or reflect. Both poems thus encourage us to focus almost exclusively on the complex emotional experience and thoughts of a particular speaker in a specific situation, but ones that we can, if the poem is effective, ultimately understand as having a much wider, sometimes even universal, resonance and relevance.

Most lyrics require us to infer a general theme from a specific experience, but some offer more explicit reflection, commentary, even argument. As you read the following example, notice what happens in line 5 (exactly halfway through the poem), as the speaker turns from personal statements to more impersonal, argumentative ones. How does personal reflection relate to, even enable, argument here?

PHILLIS WHEATLEY

On Being Brought from Africa to America

'Twas mercy brought me from my Pagan land,
Taught my benighted soul to understand
That there's a God, that there's a Saviour too:
Once I redemption neither sought nor knew.
Some view our sable race with scornful eye,
"Their colour is a diabolic die."
Remember, Christians, Negroes, black as Cain,[8]
May be refin'd, and join th' angelic train.

1773

- What do the poem's first four lines imply about how the speaker feels about "being brought from Africa to America" and about what motivates these feelings?
- What two "view[s]" of Africans are contrasted in the last four lines (line 5)? According to the entire poem, which is the right view, and why and how so?

8. One of Adam's sons, who killed his brother Abel. (See Gen. 4.)

Descriptive or Observational Lyrics

As Wheatley's poem demonstrates, lyrics come in many varieties. Quite a few are more exclusively descriptive or observational than the examples above, insofar as they describe something or someone to us without bringing much attention to the speaker's personal state of mind or feelings. As we've noted, after all, some poems simply give us the opportunity to look more closely and carefully at something in the world around us. Nineteenth-century poet Percy Bysshe Shelley suggested, in fact, that all poetry's major purpose is just that—helping us see in a new way. Poetry, he said, "strips the veil of familiarity from the world, and lays bare [its] naked and sleeping beauty" and "wonder." Over a century later, American poet James Dickey expressed a similar idea somewhat differently when he defined a poet as "someone who notices and is enormously taken by things that somebody else would walk by."

Obviously, any descriptive poem inevitably reflects its speaker's point of view. Yet lyrics of this type invite us to focus more on what they describe than on the subjective, internal experience or feelings of the speaker doing the describing. As a result, our focus in reading and writing will probably be how the poem characterizes, and encourages us to see, think, and feel about, whatever it describes—whether a moment, a person, an object, or a phenomenon. What is described in each of the poems that follow? What figures of speech are used, and with what implications and effects?

EMILY DICKINSON
[The Sky is low—the Clouds are mean]

The Sky is low—the Clouds are mean.
A Travelling Flake of Snow
Across a Barn or through a Rut
Debates if it will go—
A Narrow Wind complains all Day
How some one treated him
Nature, like Us, is sometimes caught
Without her Diadem—

1866

- Whom does the speaker seem to mean by "Us," and what might this poem imply about the similarity between "Nature" and "Us" (line 7)?

BILLY COLLINS
Divorce

Once, two spoons in bed,
now tined forks

across a granite table
and the knives they have hired.

2008

- This poem consists almost entirely of **metaphor** (implied comparison). What is compared to what here? How would you describe the poem's **tone**? (Is it funny, sad, bitter, or some combination of these?) Why and how so?

The Dramatic Monologue

Finally, we come to the **dramatic monologue**, a subgenre of poem that—by residing somewhere in between lyric and dramatic poetry—can teach us more about both. Robert Browning, the nineteenth-century British poet often credited with inventing this kind of poem, tellingly labeled his own works "dramatic lyrics," describing them as "dramatic in principle," "lyric in expression." On the one hand, the dramatic monologue is "lyric in expression" or like a lyric poem because it features a single speaker who discusses him- or herself. On the other hand, it is "dramatic in principle" or resembles a scene from a play for at least two reasons. First, the poem's primary focus is characterization, an obviously fictional or historical speaker's often unintentional revelation of his or her personality, outlook, and values. Such poems tend to offer us a window into an entire, complex psychology and even life history rather than simply one experience or feeling of a speaker we otherwise discover little about (as in lyrics). Often, too, dramatic monologues invite us to see their speakers and situations somewhat differently than the speakers themselves do, much as does fiction narrated by *unreliable narrators.* Second, the speaker of a dramatic monologue often addresses one or more silent **auditors** whose identity we can only infer from the speaker's words *to* them. The questions we pose in reading and writing about such poems thus often center on character and characterization and on the gap between our perception of the speaker and his or her situation, on the one hand, and the speaker's own self-representation, on the other.

Invented in the nineteenth century, this subgenre remains as popular with contemporary songwriters as with contemporary poets. Bruce Springsteen's albums *Nebraska* (1982) and *The Rising* (2002), for instance, consist mainly of dramatic monologues. Below, you will find the lyrics to one of these, followed by a poem that takes the form of an imaginary letter, thus putting an interesting twist on the conventions regarding "speakers" and "auditors."

BRUCE SPRINGSTEEN
Nebraska

I saw her standin' on her front lawn
  just twirlin' her baton
Me and her went for a ride, sir, and ten
  innocent people died

From the town of Lincoln, Nebraska,
  with a sawed-off .410 on my lap
Through the badlands of Wyoming I
  killed everything in my path

I can't say that I'm sorry for the things
  that we done

At least for a little while, sir, me and
her we had us some fun

The jury brought in a guilty verdict and
the judge he sentenced me to death
Midnight in a prison storeroom with
leather straps across my chest

Sheriff, when the man pulls that
switch, sir, and snaps my poor head back
You make sure my pretty baby is sittin'
right there on my lap

They declared me unfit to live, said into
that great void my soul'd be hurled
They wanted to know why I did what I did
Well, sir, I guess there's just a meanness in this world[9]

1982

• **What different motives and explanations for the speaker's actions might Nebraska provide by means of what he says, how he speaks, and how his speech is rendered on the page? Might the song as a whole offer explanations that the speaker doesn't offer, at least consciously or directly?**

ROBERT HAYDEN

A Letter from Phillis Wheatley

(London, 1773)

Dear Obour[1]
Our crossing was without
event. I could not help, at times,
reflecting on that first—my Destined—
voyage long ago (I yet
have some remembrance of its Horrors)[2]
and marvelling at God's Ways.
Last evening, her Ladyship[3] presented me
to her illustrious Friends.
I scarce could tell them anything
of Africa, though much of Boston
and my hope of Heaven. I read
my latest Elegies to them.
"O Sable Muse!" the Countess cried,

9. Allusion to words spoken by a murderer in Flannery O'Connor's "A Good Man Is Hard to Find" (par. 134).

1. Obour Tanner, a Rhode Island slave and Wheatley's intimate friend and frequent correspondent.

2. Born in Africa c. 1753–54, Wheatley was taken at around age eight on the slave ship *Phillis* to America, where she was purchased by Boston merchant John Wheatley. In 1773, John Wheatley sent her to London with his son, Nathaniel, a visit at least partly motivated by concerns about her health.

3. Selina Hastings, Countess of Huntingdon (1707–91), helped arrange publication of Wheatley's first book of poems, which appeared in London just months after the poet's return to the United States.

embracing me, when I had done.
I held back tears, as is my wont,
and there were tears in Dear
Nathaniel's eyes.
  At supper—I dined apart
like captive Royalty—
the Countess and her Guests promised
signatures affirming me
True Poetess, albeit once a slave.[4]
Indeed, they were most kind, and spoke,
moreover, of presenting me
at Court (I thought of Pocahontas)[5]—
an Honor, to be sure, but one,
I should, no doubt, as Patriot decline.
  My health is much improved;
I feel I may, if God so Wills,
entirely recover here.
Idyllic England! Alas, there is
no Eden without its Serpent. Beneath
chiming Complaisance I hear him hiss;
I see his flickering tongue
when foppish would-be Wits
murmur of the Yankee Pedlar
and his Cannibal Mockingbird.
  Sister, forgive th'intrusion of
my Sombreness—Nocturnal Mood
I would not share with any save
your trusted Self. Let me disperse,
in closing, such unseemly Gloom
by mention of an Incident
you may, as I, consider Droll:
Today, a little Chimney Sweep,
his face and hands with soot quite Black,
staring hard at me, politely asked:
"Does you, M'lady, sweep chimneys too?"
I was amused, but Dear Nathaniel
(ever Solicitous) was not.
  I pray the Blessings of Our Lord
  and Saviour Jesus Christ
  will Abundantly be yours.

Phillis

1977

4. Wheatley's *Poems on Various Subjects, Religious and Moral* (1773) was prefaced by a letter, signed by seventeen eminent Bostonians, attesting to the poems' authenticity.

5. Daughter of an Algonquian Indian chief (c. 1595–1617), Pocahontas famously befriended Virginia's first English colonists, led by Captain John Smith; she died while visiting England, where she had been presented at the court of King James I.

- What internal and external conflicts seem to be revealed here? What conflict does Wheatley herself seem aware of? Why might Hayden have chosen both this particular moment in Wheatley's life and this particular addressee (Obour Tanner)?
- How does Hayden's portrayal of both Wheatley's feelings and others' views of her compare to Wheatley's own characterization of these in ON BEING BROUGHT FROM AFRICA TO AMERICA?

RESPONDING TO POETRY

Not all poems are as readily accessible as those in this chapter, and even those that are take on additional meanings if we approach them systematically, bringing to bear specific reading habits and skills and some knowledge of poetic genres and traditions. Experience will give you a sense of what to expect, but knowing what to expect isn't everything. As a reader of poetry, you should always be open—to new experiences, new feelings, new ideas, new forms of expression. Every poem is a potential new experience, and you will often discover something new with every re-reading.

Steps to Follow, Questions to Ask, and Sample Reading Notes

No one can give you a method that will offer you total experience of all poems. But because individual poems share characteristics with other poems, taking certain steps can prompt you both to ask the right questions and to devise compelling answers. If you are relatively new to poetry, encounter a poem that seems especially difficult, or plan to write about a poem, you may need to tackle these steps one at a time, pausing to write even as you read and respond. With further experience, you will often find that you can skip steps or run through them quickly and almost automatically, though your experience and understanding of any poem will be enriched if you slow down and take your time.

Try the first step on your own, then we will both detail and demonstrate the others.

1. **Listen to a poem first.** When you encounter a new poem, try reading it through once without thinking too much about what it means. Try to simply listen to the poem, even if you read silently, and much as you might a song on the radio. Or better yet, read it aloud. Doing so will help you hear the poem's sound qualities, get a clearer impression of its **tone**, and start making sense of its **syntax**, the way words combine into sentences.

APHRA BEHN

On Her Loving Two Equally

I

How strongly does my passion flow,
Divided equally twixt[6] two?
Damon had ne'er subdued my heart

6. Between.

Had not Alexis took his part;
Nor could Alexis powerful prove,
Without my Damon's aid, to gain my love.

II

When my Alexis present is,
Then I for Damon sigh and mourn;
But when Alexis I do miss,
Damon gains nothing but my scorn.
But if it chance they both are by,
For both alike I languish, sigh, and die.

III

Cure then, thou mighty wingèd god,[7]
This restless fever in my blood:
One golden-pointed dart take back:
But which, O Cupid, wilt thou take?
If Damon's, all my hopes are crossed;
Or that of my Alexis, I am lost.

1684

Now that you've read Behn's poem, read through the remaining steps and see how one reader used them as a guide for responding. Later, return to these steps as you read and respond to other poems.

2. **Articulate your expectations, starting with the title.** Poets often try to surprise readers, but you can appreciate such surprises only if you first define your expectations. As you read a poem, take note of what you expect and where, when, and how the poem fulfills, or perhaps frustrates, your expectations.

   The title of Aphra Behn's "On Her Loving Two Equally" makes me think the poem will be about a woman. But can someone really "love two equally"? Maybe this is the question the poem will ask. If so, I expect its answer to be "no" because I don't think this is possible. If so, maybe the title is a sort of pun—"On Her Loving *Too* Equally."

3. **Read the syntax literally.** What the sentences literally say is only a starting point, but it is vital. You cannot begin to explore what a poem means unless you first know what it says. Though poets arrange words into lines and stanzas, they usually write in complete sentences, just as writers in other genres do. At the same time and partly in order to create the sort of aural and visual patterns discussed earlier in this chapter, poets make much more frequent use of **inversion** (a change in normal word order or syntax). To ensure you don't misread, first "translate" the poem rather than fixing on certain words and free-associating or leaping to conclusions. To translate accurately, especially with poems written before the twentieth

7. Cupid, who, according to myth, shot darts of lead and of gold at the hearts of lovers, corresponding to false love and true love, respectively.

century, you may need to break this step down into the following smaller steps:

a. ***Identify sentences.*** **For now, ignore the line breaks and look for sentences or independent clauses (word groups that can function as complete sentences). These will typically be preceded and followed by a period (.), a semicolon (;), a colon (:), or a dash (—).**

The eighteen lines of Behn's poem can be broken down into nine sentences.

1. How strongly does my passion flow, Divided equally twixt two?
2. Damon had ne'er subdued my heart, Had not Alexis took his part;
3. Nor could Alexis powerful prove, Without my Damon's aid, to gain my love.
4. When my Alexis present is, Then I for Damon sigh and mourn;
5. But when Alexis I do miss, Damon gains nothing but my scorn.
6. But if it chance they both are by, For both alike I languish, sigh, and die.
7. Cure then, thou mighty wingèd god, This restless fever in my blood;
8. One golden-pointed dart take back: But which, O Cupid, wilt thou take?
9. If Damon's, all my hopes are crossed; Or that of my Alexis, I am lost.

b. ***Reorder sentences.*** **Identify the main elements—subject(s), verb(s), object(s)—of each sentence or independent clause, and if necessary rearrange them in normative word order. (In English, this order tends to be subject-verb-object except in the case of a question; in either case, dependent clauses come at the beginning or end of the main clause and next to whatever element they modify.)**

c. ***Replace each pronoun with the antecedent noun it replaces;*** **if the antecedent is ambiguous, indicate all the possibilities.**

In the following sentences, the reordered words appear in italics, nouns substituted for pronouns appear in parentheses:

1. How strong does my passion flow, Divided equally twixt two?
2. Damon had ne'er subdued my heart Had not Alexis took (Alexis's or Damon's) part;
3. Nor could Alexis prove powerful *to gain my love Without my Damon's aid.*
4. When my Alexis *is* present, Then I *sigh and mourn* for Damon;
5. But when I do *miss* Alexis, Damon gains nothing but my scorn.
6. But if it chance both (Damon and Alexis) are by, *I languish, sigh, and die* For both (Damon and Alexis) alike.
7. *thou mighty wingèd god,* Cure then This restless fever in my blood;
8. *take back* One golden-pointed dart: But which wilt thou take, *O Cupid?*
9. *If Damon's,* all my hopes are crossed; Or that (dart) of my Alexis, I am lost.

d. ***Translate sentences into modern prose.*** **Use a dictionary to define unfamiliar or ambiguous words or words that seem to be used in an unfamiliar or unexpected way. Add any implied words necessary to link the parts of a sentence to each other and one sentence logically to the next. At**

this stage, don't move to outright paraphrase; instead, stick closely to the original.

Below, added words appear in brackets, substituted definitions in parentheses:

1. How strongly does my passion flow [when it is] divided equally between two [people]?
2. Damon would never have (*conquered* or *tamed*) my heart if Alexis had not taken (Damon or Alexis's) (*portion*) [of my heart].
3. Nor could Alexis [have] prove[n] powerful [enough] to gain my love without my Damon's aid.
4. When my Alexis is present, then I sigh and mourn for Damon;
5. But when I miss Alexis, Damon doesn't gain anything (except) my scorn.
6. But if it (*so happens*) that both (Damon and Alexis) are [near]by [me], I languish, sigh, and die for both (Damon and Alexis) alike.
7. [Cupid], (you) mighty god (*with wings*), cure then this restless fever in my blood;
8. Take back one [of your two] darts [with] pointed gold [tips]: But which [of these darts] will you take, O Cupid?
9. If [on the one hand, you take away] Damon's [dart], all my hopes are (*opposed, invalidated, spoiled*); Or [if, on the other hand, you take away] Alexis's [arrow], I am (*desperate, ruined, destroyed; no longer claimed or possessed by anyone; helpless or unable to find my way*).

e. ***Note any ambiguities in the original language that you might have ignored in your translation.*** **For example, look for modifiers that might modify more than one thing; verbs that might have multiple subjects or objects; words that have multiple relevant meanings.**

In the second sentence, "his" could refer either to Damon or Alexis since both names appear in the first part of this sentence; in other words, this could say either "Alexis took Damon's part" or "Alexis took his own part." But what about the word *part*? I translated this as *portion*, and I assumed it referred back to "heart," partly because the two words come at the ends of lines 3 ("heart") and 4 ("part") and also rhyme. But two other definitions of *part* might make sense here: "the role of a character in a play" or "one's . . . allotted task (as in an action)," and "one of the opposing sides in a conflict or dispute," which in this case could be the "conflict" over the speaker's love. On the one hand, then, I could translate this either "Alexis took his own portion of my heart"; "Alexis played his own role in my life or in this three-way courtship drama"; or "Alexis defended his own side in the battle for my love." On the other hand, I could translate it as "Alexis took Damon's part of my heart"; "Alexis played Damon's role"; or even "Alexis defended Damon's side in the battle for my love."

4. **Consult reference works.** **In addition to using a dictionary to define unfamiliar or ambiguous words, look up anything else to which the poem refers that you either don't understand or that you suspect might be ambiguous: a place, a person, a myth, a quotation, an idea, and so forth.**

According to the *Encyclopaedia Britannica* Web site, Cupid was the "ancient Roman god of love" and "often appeared as a winged infant carrying a bow and a quiver of arrows whose wounds inspired love or passion in his every victim." It makes sense, then, that the speaker of this poem would think that she might stop loving one of these men if Cupid took back the arrow that made her love him. But the poem wasn't written in ancient Rome (it's dated 1684), so is the speaker just kidding or being deliberately "poetic" when she calls on Cupid? And what about the names "Damon" and "Alexis"? Were those common in the seventeenth century? Maybe so, if a poet could be named "Aphra Behn."

5. **Figure out who, where, when, and what happens.** Once you have gotten a sense of the literal meaning of each sentence, ask the following very general factual questions about the whole poem. Remember that not all of the questions will suit every poem. (Which questions apply will depend in part on whether the poem is narrative, dramatic, or lyric.) At this point, stick to the facts. What do you know for sure?

Who?
- Who is, or who are, the poem's **speaker(s)**?
- Who is, or who are, the **auditor(s)**, if any?
- Who are the other **characters**, if any, that appear in the poem?

The title suggests that the speaker is a woman who loves two people. In the poem, she identifies these as two men—Damon and Alexis. The speaker doesn't seem to address anyone in particular (certainly not the two men she talks about) except in the third stanza, when she addresses Cupid—first through the **epithet** "mighty wingèd god" (line 13) and then by name (line 16). (Because Cupid isn't present, this is an **apostrophe**.)

Where? When?
- Where is the speaker?
- Where and when do any actions described in the poem take place? That is, what is the poem's **setting**?

No place or time is specified in Behn's poem. The poem is dated 1684, and the antiquated diction ("twixt," line 2; "wilt," line 16) seems appropriate to that time. But nothing in the poem makes the situation or feelings it describes specific to a time or place. The speaker doesn't say things like "Last Thursday, when Damon and I were hanging out in the garden . . . ," for example. She seems to describe situations that keep happening repeatedly rather than specific incidents.

What?
- What is the **situation** described in the poem?
- What, if anything, literally happens over the course of it, or what **action**, if any, does it describe?
- Or, if the poem doesn't have a **plot**, then how would you describe its internal structure? Even when a poem seems less interested in telling a story than in simply capturing a feeling or describing something or someone, you can still usually read in it some kind of progression or development or

even an argument. When and how does the subject matter or focus or address shift over the course of the poem?

The basic situation is that the speaker loves two men equally. In the second stanza she describes recurring situations—being with one of the men and not the other or being with both of them at once—and the feelings that result. Then, in the third stanza, she imagines what would happen if she stopped loving one of them. The topic or subject essentially remains the same throughout, but there are two subtle shifts. First is the shift from addressing anyone in stanzas one and two to addressing Cupid in stanza three. Second, there are shifts in verb tense and time: The first stanza floats among various tenses ("does," line 1; "took," line 4), the second sticks to the present tense ("is," "sigh," "mourn," etc.), and the third shifts to future ("wilt," line 16). As a result, I would say that the poem has two parts: in one, the speaker characterizes her situation in the present and recent past; in the other she explores a possible alternative future (that she ends up not liking any better).

6. **Formulate tentative answers to the questions, *Why does it matter? What does it all mean?***

- **Why should the poem matter to anyone other than the poet, or what might the poem show and say to readers?**
- **What problems, issues, questions, or conflicts does the poem explore that might be relevant to people other than the speaker(s) or the poet—to humanity in general, to the poet's contemporaries, to people of a certain type or in a certain situation, and so forth?**
- **How is each problem or conflict developed and resolved over the course of the poem, or how is each question answered? What conclusions does the poem seem to reach about these, or what are its themes?**

The title and first two lines pose a question: How strong is our love if we love two people instead of one? We tend to assume that anything that is "divided" is less strong than something unified. The use of the word *flow* in the first line reinforces that assumption because it implicitly compares love to something that flows: A river, for example, "flows," and when a river divides into two streams, each is smaller and its flow less strong than the river's. So the way the speaker articulates the question implies an answer: Love, like a river, isn't strong and sure when divided.

But the rest of the poem undermines that answer. In the first stanza, the speaker points out that each lover and his love has "aided" and added to the "power" of the other: Neither man would have "gain[ed her] love" if the other hadn't. The second stanza gives a more concrete sense of why: Since we tend to yearn for what we don't have at the moment, being with one of these men makes her miss the other one. But if both men are present, she feels the same about both and perhaps even feels *more* complete and satisfied.

As if realizing she can't solve the problem herself, she turns in the third stanza to Cupid and asks him to help by taking away her love for either Damon or Alexis. As soon as she asks for this, though, she indicates that the result would be unhappiness. In the end, the poem seems to say (or its theme is) that love *doesn't* flow or work like a river because love can actually be stronger when we love more than one person, as if it's multiplied instead of lessened by division.

Clearly, this is the opposite of what I expected, which was that the poem would ask whether it was possible to love two people and conclude it wasn't. The conflict is also different than I expected—though there's an external conflict between the two men (maybe), the focus is on the speaker's internal conflict, but that conflict isn't over which guy to choose but about how this is actually working (*I love both of them equally; each love reinforces the other*) versus how she thinks things *should* work (*I'm not supposed to love two equally*).

7. **Consider how the poem's form contributes to its effect and meaning.**

- How is the poem organized on the page, into lines and/or stanzas, for example? (What are the lines and stanzas like in terms of length, shape, and so on? Are they all alike, or do they vary? Are lines **enjambed** or **end-stopped**?)
- What are the poem's other formal features? (Is there **rhyme** or another form of aural patterning such as **alliteration**? What is the poem's base **meter**, and are there interesting variations? If not, how else might you describe the poem's rhythm?)
- How do the poem's overall form and its various formal features contribute to its meaning and effect? In other words, what gets lost when you translate the poem into modern prose?

The stanza organization underscores shifts in the speaker's approach to her situation. But organization reinforces meaning in other ways as well. On the one hand, the division into three stanzas and the choice to number them, plus the fact that each stanza has three sentences, mirror the three-way struggle or "love triangle" described in the poem. On the other hand because the poem has 18 *lines* and 9 *sentences*, every sentence is "divided equally twixt two" *lines*. Sound and especially rhyme reinforce this pattern since the two lines that make up one sentence usually rhyme with each other (to form a **couplet**). The only lines that aren't couplets are those that begin the second stanza, where we instead have alternating rhyme—*is* (line 7) rhymes with *miss* (line 9), *mourn* (line 8) rhymes with *scorn* (line 10). But these lines describe how the speaker "miss[es]" one man when the other is "by," a sensation she arguably reproduces in readers by ensuring that we twice "miss" the rhyme that the rest of the poem leads us to expect.

8. **Investigate and consider the ways the poem both uses and departs from poetic conventions, especially those related to form and subgenre.** Does the poem use a traditional verse form (such as **blank verse**) or a traditional stanza form (such as **ballad stanza**)? Is it a specific subgenre or kind of poem—a **sonnet**, an **ode**, a **ballad**, for example? If so, how does that affect its meaning? Over time, stanza and verse forms have been used in certain ways and to certain ends, and particular subgenres have observed certain conventions. As a result, they generate particular expectations for readers familiar with such traditions, and poems gain additional meaning by both fulfilling and defying those expectations. For example, **anapestic**

meter (two unstressed syllables followed by a stressed one, as in *Tennessee*) is usually used for comic poems, so when poets use it in a serious poem they are probably making a point.

9. **Argue.** Discussion with others—both out loud and in writing—usually results in clarification and keeps you from being too dependent on personal biases and preoccupations that sometimes mislead even the best readers. Discussing a poem with someone else (especially someone who thinks very differently) or sharing what you've written about the poem can expand your perspective and enrich your experience.

WRITING ABOUT POETRY

If you follow the steps outlined above and keep notes on your personal responses to the poems you read, you will have already begun writing informally. You have also generated ideas and material you can use in more formal writing. To demonstrate how, we conclude this chapter with two examples of such writing. Both grow out of the notes earlier in this chapter. Yet each is quite different in form and content. The first example is a relatively informal response paper that investigates the allusions in Aphra Behn's On Her Loving Two Equally, following up on the discoveries and questions generated by consulting reference works (as in step 4 above). The second example is an essay on the poem that defends and develops as a thesis one answer to the questions, Why does it matter? What does it all mean? (as in step 6 above) by drawing on discoveries made in earlier and later steps.

As these examples illustrate, there are many different ways to write about poems, just as there are many different things to say about any one. But all such writing begins with a clear sense of the poem itself and your responses to it. Effective writing also depends on a willingness to listen carefully to the poem and to ask genuine questions about how it works, what it says and means, and how it both fulfills and challenges your expectations about life, as well as poetry.

• • •

From bardic chronicles to imaginary letters, brief introspective lyrics to action-packed epics, "poetry" comes in many sizes, shapes, and varieties; serves myriad purposes for many diverse audiences; and offers pleasures and rewards both like and unlike those we get from fiction, drama, music, or any other art form. In part, though, that's because poetry is something of a trickster and a trespasser, crossing in and out of those other generic domains and trying on their clothes, even as it inhabits and wears very special ones all its own. Poetry speaks to head, as well as heart; ears, as well as eyes. If you keep yours open, it just might speak to you in ways you never expected.

SAMPLE WRITING: RESPONSE PAPER

The following response paper investigates the allusions in Aphra Behn's ON HER LOVING TWO EQUALLY by drawing upon information from reference works. Not all response papers involve research, but we have included one that does in order to demonstrate both how you can use information from credible secondary sources to test and deepen your personal response to a poem and how you can develop reading notes into a thoughtful informal response paper.

Names in "On Her Loving Two Equally"

Aphra Behn's "On Her Loving Two Equally" is dated 1684, but refers to an ancient, pagan god. That seems weird and made me curious about what he was doing in the poem. According to the *Encyclopedia Britannica Online*, Cupid was the "ancient Roman god of love," "often appeared as a winged infant carrying a bow and a quiver of arrows whose wounds inspired love or passion in his every victim," and "was sometimes portrayed wearing armour like that of Mars, the God of war, perhaps to suggest ironic parallels between warfare and romance" ("Cupid"). It makes sense, then, that the speaker of this poem would think that she might stop loving one of these guys if Cupid took back the arrow that made her love him. And the reference to Cupid also reinforces the association in the poem between "warfare" or at least conflict "and romance." (The speaker is internally conflicted, and there is also an external conflict between the two male lovers.)

I'm still not sure whether the speaker is kidding or being deliberately "poetic" by talking to an ancient Roman god. But either way, this reinforces the idea I had when I was reading, that the poem isn't very specific about time or place. The poem makes the speaker's situation seem like something that has happened or could happen anytime, anywhere.

But what about the names Damon and Alexis? Were these real names in seventeenth-century England, which is apparently where Behn was from? According to the Oxford *Dictionary of First Names*, "Damon" is "a classical Greek name" that was

> made famous in antiquity by the story of Damon and Pythias. In the early 4th century BC Pythias was condemned to death by Dionysius, ruler of Syracuse. His friend Damon offered to stand surety for him, and took his place in the condemned cell while Pythias put his affairs in order. When Pythias duly returned to be executed rather than absconding and leaving his friend to his fate, Dionysius was so impressed by the

trust and friendship of the two young men that he pardoned both of them. ("Damon")

This doesn't tell me for sure whether there were really men named "Damon" in seventeenth-century England, but it's now clear that using the name "Damon" is another way of alluding to "antiquity" and maybe making this situation and poem seem "antique." But the story of Damon and Pythias seems even more relevant. When I was translating this poem, I noticed that it could imply that Damon and Alexis were actually helping each other, not just fighting over the speaker (especially because "his," in line 4, could refer to either man). Does the fact that the most famous Damon was willing to sit in prison and even be executed to help his best friend give me more evidence that I'm right? On the other hand, does it matter that the name comes from a word meaning " 'to tame, subdue' (often a euphemism for 'kill')" ("Damon")?

I couldn't find anything nearly this interesting about "Alexis," except that it is a Latin form of a Greek name that originally came from a word that means "to defend" ("Alexis").

To sum up, I think two things are important: (1) by referring to Cupid and naming her boyfriends Damon and Alexis, Behn makes her poem and her speaker's situation seem "antique," even for the seventeenth century, and implies her situation could happen anytime anywhere; and (2) the fact that the men's names mean "to tame, subdue," even "kill," and "to defend" makes the conflict in the poem more intense, but the fact that the world's most famous Damon sacrificed himself for his friend might add fuel to the idea that these rivals are also friends who are helping each other. Maybe there's even more "loving two equally" going on here than I thought at first? If the speaker loves each of these guys more because she loves the other one, is that true of them, too? This poem is crazy!

Works Cited

"Alexis." *A Dictionary of First Names*, edited by Patrick Hanks, et al., 2nd ed., Oxford UP, 2006. *Oxford Reference Online*, doi:10.1093/acref/9780198610601.001.0001.

Behn, Aphra. "On Her Loving Two Equally." *The Norton Introduction to Literature*, edited by Kelly J. Mays, 12th ed., W. W. Norton, 2017, pp. 864-65.

"Cupid." *Encyclopaedia Britannica Online*, 5 May 2015, www.britannica.com/topic/Cupid.

"Damon." *A Dictionary of First Names*, edited by Patrick Hanks, et al., 2nd ed., Oxford UP, 2006. *Oxford Reference Online*, doi:10.1093/acref/9780198610601.001.0001.

SAMPLE WRITING: ESSAY

The following sample essay develops the observations about Aphra Behn's On Her Loving Two Equally in this chapter, demonstrating how you can turn notes about a poem into a coherent, well-structured essay. As this essay also shows, however, you will often discover new ways of looking at a poem (or any literary text) in the very process of writing about it. (For guidelines on correctly quoting and citing poetry, see ch. 35.)

The writer begins by considering why she is drawn to the poem, even though it does not express her ideal of love. She then uses her personal response to the poem as a starting point for analyzing it in greater depth.

Multiplying by Dividing in Aphra Behn's "On Her Loving Two Equally"

My favorite poem in "Reading, Responding, Writing" is Aphra Behn's "On Her Loving Two Equally"—not because it expresses my ideal of love, but because it challenges conventional ideals. The main ideal or assumption explored in the poem is that true love is exclusive and monogamous, as the very titles of poems like "How Do *I* [singular] Love *Thee* [singular]?" or "To *My* Dear and Loving [and One and Only] Husband" insist (emphasis added). The mere title of Behn's poem upsets that idea by insisting that at least one woman is capable of "Loving Two Equally." In fact, one thing that is immediately interesting about Behn's poem is that, though it poses and explores a question, its question is not "Can a woman love two equally?" The title and the poem take it for granted that she can. Instead, the poem asks whether equally loving two people lessens the power or quality of love—or, as the speaker puts it in the first two lines, "How strongly does my passion flow, / Divided equally twixt two?" Every aspect of this poem suggests that when it comes to love, as opposed to math, division leads to multiplication.

This answer grabs attention because it is so counterintuitive and unconventional. Forget love for just a minute: It's common sense that anything that is divided is smaller and weaker than something unified. In math, for example, division is the opposite of multiplication; if we divide one number by another, we get a number smaller than the first number, if not the second. Although Behn's use of the word *flow* to frame her question compares love to a river instead of a number, the implication is the same: When a river divides into two streams, each of them is smaller than the river, and its flow less strong; as a result, each stream is more easily dammed up or diverted than the undivided river. So the way the speaker initially poses her question seems to support the conventional view: Love is stronger when it "flows" toward one person, weaker when divided between two.

However conventional and comforting that implied answer, however, it's one the poem immediately rejects. In the remaining lines of the first stanza, the speaker insists that each of her two lovers and the love she feels for him has *not* lessened the strength of her feelings for the other, but the reverse. Each lover and each love has "aid[ed]" (line 6) the other, making him and it more "powerful" (5). Indeed, she says, neither man would have "subdued [her] heart" (3) or "gain[ed her] love" (6) at all if the other hadn't done so as well.

In the second stanza, the speaker gives us a somewhat more concrete sense of why this might be the case. On the one hand, being with either one of these men ("When Alexis present is," 7) actually makes her both "scorn" him (10) and "miss" (9) the man who's not there ("I for Damon sigh and mourn," 8). This isn't really a paradox; we often yearn more for the person or thing we don't have (the grass is always greener on the *other* side of the fence), and we often lose our appreciation for nearby, familiar things and people. What is far away and inaccessible is often dearer to us because its absence either makes us aware of what it means to us or allows us to forget its flaws and idealize it.

Perhaps because all of this makes the speaker feel that she can't possibly solve the problem by herself, the speaker turns in the third stanza to Cupid—the deity who is supposed to control these things by shooting a "golden-pointed dart" (15) into the heart of each lover. She asks him to solve her dilemma for her by "tak[ing] back" her love for either Damon or Alexis (15). As with her question in the first stanza, however, this plea is taken back as soon as it's formulated, for if she loses Damon, "all [her] hopes are crossed"; if she loses Alexis, she is "lost" (17-18).

Here and throughout the poem, the speaker's main preoccupation seems to be what *she* feels and what this situation is like for *her*—"*my* passion" (1), "*my* heart" (3), "*my* Damon's aid, . . . *my* love" (6), "*my* Alexis" (7), "*I* . . . sigh and mourn" (8), "*I* do miss" (9), "*my* scorn" (10), "*I* languish, sigh, and die" (12), "This restless fever in *my* blood" (14), "*my* hopes" (17), "*my* Alexis" and "*I* am lost" (18). Yet the poem implies that the payoff here is not hers alone and that her feelings are not purely selfish. Both times the word *gain* appears in the poem, for example, her lovers' gains and feelings are the focus—the fact that Alexis is able "to gain [her] love" thanks to "Damon's aid" (6) and that "Damon gains nothing but my scorn" when she is missing Alexis (10). Moreover, ambiguous wording in the first stanza suggests that the men here may be actively, intentionally helping to create this situation and even acting in contradictory, selfish and unselfish, ways. When the speaker says that "Damon had ne'er subdued my heart / Had not Alexis took his part" (3-4), *his* could refer to Alexis or Damon and *part* could mean "a portion" (of her "heart," presumably), "a role" (in her life or in this courtship drama), or a "side in a dispute or conflict" (over her love). Thus, she could be saying that Alexis (unselfishly) defended Damon's suit; (selfishly) fought against Damon or took a share or role that properly belonged to Damon; and/or (neutrally) took his (Alexis's) own share or role or defended his (Alexis's) own cause. Perhaps all of this *has* been the case at various times; people do behave in contradictory ways when they are in love, especially when they perceive that they have a rival. It's also true that men and women alike often more highly prize something or someone that someone else prizes, too. So perhaps each lover's "passion" for her also "flow[s]" more strongly than it would otherwise precisely because he has a rival.

In the end, the poem thus seems to say that love *doesn't* flow or work like a river because love isn't a tangible or quantifiable thing. As a result, love is also different from the sort of battle implied by the martial language of the first stanza in which someone wins only if someone else loses. The poem attributes this to the perversity of the human heart—especially our tendency to yearn for what we can't have and what we think other people want, too.

Through its form, the poem demonstrates that division can increase instead of lessen meaning, as well as love. On the one hand, just as the poem's content stresses the power of the love among *three people*, so the poem's form also stresses "threeness" as well as "twoness." It is after all divided into *three* distinctly numbered stanzas, and each stanza consists of *three* sentences. On the other hand, every *sentence* is "divided equally twixt two" *lines*, just as the speaker's "passion" is divided equally between two men. Formally, then, the poem mirrors the kinds of division it describes. Sound and especially rhyme reinforce this pattern since the two lines that make up one sentence usually rhyme with each other to form a couplet. The only lines that don't conform to this pattern come at the beginning of the second stanza where we instead have alternating rhyme—*is* (7) rhymes with *miss* (9), *mourn* (8) rhymes with *scorn* (10). But here, again, form reinforces content since these lines describe how the speaker "miss[es]" one man when the other is "by," a sensation that she arguably reproduces in us as we read by ensuring we twice "miss" the rhyme that the rest of the poem leads us to expect.

Because of the way it challenges our expectations and our conventional ideas about romantic love, the poem might well make us uncomfortable, perhaps all the more so because the speaker and poet here are female. For though we tend to think all true lovers should be loyal and monogamous, this has been expected even more of women than of men. What the poem says about love might make more sense and seem less strange and even objectionable, however, if we think of other, nonromantic kinds of love: After all, do we really think that our mother and father love us less if their love is "divided equally twixt" ourselves and our siblings, or do we love each of our parents less because there are two of *them*? If we think of these familial kinds of love, it becomes much easier to accept Behn's suggestion that love multiplies when we spread it around.

Work Cited

Behn, Aphra. "On Her Loving Two Equally." *The Norton Introduction to Literature*, edited by Kelly J. Mays, 12th ed., W. W. Norton, 2017, pp. 864-65.

who
soar
delirious
then
luscious
live
has
drunk
these
ful
need
not
delicate
to
your
sleep
there
let
honey
sausage
death
this
language
above
moon
my
said
smooth
ship
blow
all
on
egg
stare
juice
am
the
day
bed
symphony
skin
ing
as
sing
after
want
sion
white

The Art of (Reading) Poetry

AN ALBUM

It is difficult
to get the news from poems
yet men die miserably every day
for lack
of what is found there.

—WILLIAM CARLOS WILLIAMS, *The Greeny Flower*

Poets obviously have a keen, even vested, interest in offering their own answers to the questions of what poetry is and why and how it needs to be written and read. Not surprisingly, many poets have found poetry itself the best medium through which to tackle those questions. Such poems, as well as prose works devoted to the same topic, constitute a genre of sorts—the "Ars Poetica," a Latin phrase meaning "The Art of Poetry" that many writers also use in the titles of individual works of this kind. In so doing, these writers deliberately insert themselves into a conversation that began many centuries ago, by alluding directly to a treatise on poetry with just that name by the Roman poet Horace (65–8 BCE).

You won't find any quotations from Horace in this album. But it does gather a range of more recent "Ars Poetica" poems and invite you to compare their visions of the art of poetry, both to each other and with your own ideas and experience. As you read the poems, be sure to consider the relationship between the vision of poetry that the poems explicitly articulate (by virtue of *what* they say) and implicitly enact (by virtue of *how* they say it)—that is, to the relationship between content and form, theory and practice. Does each poem manage to be or to do the things it suggests poetry must? Does the poem invite the sort of readerly response it envisions as ideal? How so or not? Which poems found elsewhere in this book do you think each of the poets in this album might like or admire the most? the least? Why and how so?

EMILY DICKINSON

[I dwell in Possibility—]

I dwell in Possibility—
A fairer House than Prose—
More numerous of Windows—
Superior—for Doors—

Of Chambers as the Cedars—
Impregnable of Eye—
And for an Everlasting Roof
The Gambrels[1] of the Sky—

1. Roofs with double slopes.

Of Visitors—the fairest—
For Occupation—This—
The spreading wide my narrow Hands
To gather Paradise—

c. 1862

- This poem never addresses the topic of poetry directly. Nor does it use the word *poetry*. Why might it be helpful (or not) to read "I dwell in Possibility" as an "ars poetica" poem?

ARCHIBALD MACLEISH

Ars Poetica[2]

A poem should be palpable and mute
As a globed fruit,

Dumb
As old medallions to the thumb,

Silent as the sleeve-worn stone
Of casement ledges where the moss has grown—

A poem should be wordless
As the flight of birds.

A poem should be motionless in time
As the moon climbs.

Leaving, as the moon releases
Twig by twig the night-entangled trees,

Leaving, as the moon behind the winter leaves,
Memory by memory the mind—

A poem should be motionless in time
As the moon climbs.

A poem should be equal to:
Not true.

For all the history of grief
An empty doorway and a maple leaf.

For love
The leaning grasses and two lights above the sea—

A poem should not mean
But be.

1926

- How can a poem "be wordless" (line 7)? "not mean / But be" (lines 23–24)? How does or doesn't this poem manage that?

2. "The Art of Poetry," title of a poetical treatise by the Roman poet Horace (65–8 BCE).

CZESLAW MILOSZ
Ars Poetica?

I have always aspired to a more spacious form
that would be free from the claims of poetry or prose
and would let us understand each other without exposing
the author or reader to sublime agonies.

In the very essence of poetry there is something indecent:
a thing is brought forth which we didn't know we had in us,
so we blink our eyes, as if a tiger had sprung out
and stood in the light, lashing his tail.

That's why poetry is rightly said to be dictated by a daimonion,[3]
though it's an exaggeration to maintain that he must be an angel.
It's hard to guess where that pride of poets comes from,
when so often they're put to shame by the disclosure of their frailty.

What reasonable man would like to be a city of demons,
who behave as if they were at home, speak in many tongues,
and who, not satisfied with stealing his lips or hand,
work at changing his destiny for their convenience?

It's true that what is morbid is highly valued today,
and so you may think that I am only joking
or that I've devised just one more means
of praising Art with the help of irony.

There was a time when only wise books were read,
helping us to bear our pain and misery.
This, after all, is not quite the same
as leafing through a thousand works fresh from psychiatric clinics.

And yet the world is different from what it seems to be
and we are other than how we see ourselves in our ravings.
People therefore preserve silent integrity,
thus earning the respect of their relatives and neighbors.

The purpose of poetry is to remind us
how difficult it is to remain just one person,
for our house is open, there are no keys in the doors,
and invisible guests come in and out at will.

What I'm saying here is not, I agree, poetry,
as poems should be written rarely and reluctantly,
under unbearable duress and only with the hope
that good spirits, not evil ones, choose us for their instrument.

1968

3. Internal mentor conceived to be like, or inspired by, a demon.

- How might this poem explain or justify the question mark in its title? What does the poem suggest about where poems come from, what they are or should be like, and why they might be useful, even necessary (and to whom)?

AUTHORS ON THEIR WORK
CZESLAW MILOSZ (1911–2004)

From "Czeslaw Milosz, The Art of Poetry No. 70" (1994)*

My poetry has been called polyphonic, which is to say that I have always been full of voices speaking; in a way I consider myself an instrument, a medium. [. . .] Am I alone in this? I don't think so. [Russian novelist Fyodor] Dostoyevsky was one of the first writers, along with [German philosopher] Friedrich Nietzsche, to identify a crisis of modern civilization: that every one of us is visited by contradictory voices, contradictory physical urges. I have written about the difficulty of remaining the same person when such guests enter and go and take us for their instrument. But we must hope to be inspired by good spirits, not evil ones. [. . .]

I suppose, looking back, that everything was dictated to me, and I was just a tool. Of what I don't know. I would like to believe that I am a tool of God, but that's presumptuous. So I prefer to call whatever it is my "daimonion."

*"Czeslaw Milosz, The Art of Poetry No. 70." Interview by Robert Faggen. *The Paris Review*, no. 133, Winter 1994, www.theparisreview.org/interviews/1721/the-art-of-poetry-no-70-czeslaw-milosz.

ELIZABETH ALEXANDER
Ars Poetica #100: I Believe

Poetry, I tell my students,
is idiosyncratic. Poetry

is where we are ourselves
(though Sterling Brown[4] said

"Every 'I' is a dramatic 'I'"),
digging in the clam flats

for the shell that snaps,
emptying the proverbial pocketbook.

Poetry is what you find
in the dirt in the corner,

overhear on the bus, God
in the details, the only way

4. African American poet (1901–89) and literary critic.

to get from here to there.
Poetry (and now my voice is rising)

is not all love, love, love,
and I'm sorry the dog died.

Poetry (here I hear myself loudest)
is the human voice,

and are we not of interest to each other?

2005

- **What competing ideas about poetry are articulated in this poem, and what is the speaker's view of each? Why might the poem end with a question?**

MARIANNE MOORE
Poetry

I, too, dislike it: there are things that are important beyond all this
  fiddle.
  Reading it, however, with a perfect contempt for it, one discovers in
  it after all, a place for the genuine.
    Hands that can grasp, eyes
    that can dilate, hair that can rise
      if it must, these things are important not because a

high-sounding interpretation can be put upon them but because they are
  useful. When they become so derivative as to become unintelligible,
  the same thing may be said for all of us, that we
  do not admire what
  we cannot understand: the bat
    holding on upside down or in quest of something to

eat, elephants pushing, a wild horse taking a roll, a tireless wolf under
  a tree, the immovable critic twitching his skin like a horse that feels a
    flea, the base-
  ball fan, the statistician—
    nor is it valid
      to discriminate against "business documents and

school-books";[5] all these phenomena are important. One must make a
    distinction
  however: when dragged into prominence by half poets, the result is not
    poetry,

  nor till the poets among us can be
    "literalists of

5. *Diary of Tolstoy* (Dutton), p. 84. "Where the boundary between prose and poetry lies, I shall never be able to understand. The question is raised in manuals of style, yet the answer to it lies beyond me. Poetry is verse: Prose is not verse. Or else poetry is everything with the exception of business documents and school books" [Moore's note].

the imagination"[6]—above
insolence and triviality and can present

for inspection, "imaginary gardens with real toads in them," shall we have
it. In the meantime, if you demand on the one hand,
the raw material of poetry in
all its rawness and
that which is on the other hand
genuine, you are interested in poetry.

1921

- **Does your interpretation of the meaning and tone of this poem's first line change as you read the rest of the poem? When and how so? By the poem's end, what might you conclude about what the speaker "dislike[s]" or feels "a perfect contempt for" (lines 1–2)?**

JULIA ALVAREZ
"Poetry Makes Nothing Happen"?

—W. H. AUDEN[7]

Listening to a poem on the radio,
Mike Holmquist stayed awake on his drive home
from Laramie[8] on Interstate 80,
tapping his hand to the beat of some lines
by Longfellow;[9] while overcome by grief
one lonesome night when the bathroom cabinet
still held her husband's meds, May Quinn reached out
for a book by Yeats instead and fell asleep
cradling "When You Are Old," not the poet's best,
but still . . . poetry made nothing happen,

which was good, given what May had in mind.
Writing a paper on a Bishop poem,[1]
Jenny Klein missed her ride but arrived home
to the cancer news in a better frame of mind.
While troops dropped down into Afghanistan
in the living room, Naomi Stella clapped
to the nursery rhyme her father had turned on,
All the king's horses and all the king's men . . .
If only poetry had made nothing happen!
If only the president had listened to Auden!

6. Yeats, *Ideas of Good and Evil* (A. H. Bullen, 1903), p. 182. "The limitation of [William Blake's] view was from the very intensity of his vision; he was a too literal realist of imagination, as others are of nature; and because he believed that the figures seen by the mind's eye, when exalted by inspiration, were 'eternal existences,' symbols of divine essences, he hated every grace of style that might obscure their lineaments" [Moore's note]. The phrase "imaginary [. . .] in them," in the next stanza, has no known source.
7. See "In Memory of W. B. Yeats," line 36. 8. In Wyoming.
9. American poet Henry Wadsworth Longfellow (1807–82). 1. Elizabeth Bishop (1911–79).

Faith Chaney, Lulú Pérez, Sunghee Chen—
there's a list as long as an epic poem
of folks who'll swear a poem has never done
a thing for them . . . except . . . perhaps adjust
the sunset view one cloudy afternoon,
which made them see themselves or see the world
in a different light—degrees of change so small
only a poem registers them at all.
That's why they can be trusted, why poems might
still save us from what happens in the world.

2003

- How does this poem answer the question in its title: what, if anything, does poetry "make happen" or keep from happening? What is the effect of the poem's specificity about names and situations? of the way each stanza differently plays on the word *happens*?

BILLY COLLINS
Introduction to Poetry

I ask them to take a poem
and hold it up to the light
like a color slide

or press an ear against its hive.

I say drop a mouse into a poem
and watch him probe his way out,

or walk inside the poem's room
and feel the walls for a light switch.

I want them to water-ski
across the surface of a poem
waving at the author's name on the shore.

But all they want to do
is tie the poem to a chair with rope
and torture a confession out of it.

They begin beating it with a hose
to find out what it really means.

1988

- Who is "them" (line 1), and what is the effect of the speaker's choice to refer to "them" and "they" (12) in this way? What different approaches to reading poetry come into conflict here? Why and how?

SUGGESTIONS FOR WRITING

1. Both Billy Collins's Introduction to Poetry and Elizabeth Alexander's Ars Poetica #100: I Believe can be interpreted as exploring, from a teacher's perspective, what happens among teachers, students, and poems in a classroom. Write a response paper in which you reflect on how either of those poems characterizes that situation and how that depiction compares to your own classroom experience.
2. Consider your responses to all the poems in this album. Which one most accurately expresses your view of what poetry is, what it does, and how we should read it? Why and how so? What does your choice say about you? Write an essay in which you reflect on how at least two of these poems express, reinforce, refine, or perhaps challenge your views of poetry.
3. Pick any poem in this album and write an essay that both explains what qualities it attributes to good poetry and then demonstrates whether, why, and how any other poem in the anthology has those qualities. Be sure to use concrete evidence from both poems to make your case.

Understanding the Text

12 SPEAKER: WHOSE VOICE DO WE HEAR?

Poems are personal. The thoughts and feelings they express belong to a specific person, and however general or universal their sentiments seem to be, poems come to us as the expression of an individual human voice. That voice is often a voice of the poet, but not always. Poets sometimes create characters just as writers of fiction or drama do. And the **speaker** of a poem may express ideas or feelings very different from the poet's own.

Usually there is much more to a poem than the characterization of the speaker, but often it is necessary first to identify the speaker and determine his or her character before we can appreciate what else goes on in the poem. And sometimes, in looking for the speaker of the poem we discover the gist of the entire poem.

NARRATIVE POEMS AND THEIR SPEAKERS

In the following narrative poem, the poet has created two speakers, each of whom has a distinctive voice. The first speaker here acts as a **narrator**, setting the scene and introducing the second speaker. As you read the poem, notice how your impressions of "the lady in skunk" (line 2) are shaped by both her words and the narrator's.

X. J. KENNEDY
In a Prominent Bar in Secaucus One Day

To the tune of "The Old Orange Flute" or the tune of "Sweet Betsy from Pike"

In a prominent bar in Secaucus[1] one day
Rose a lady in skunk with a topheavy sway,
Raised a knobby red finger—all turned from their beer—
While with eyes bright as snowcrust she sang high and clear:

"Now who of you'd think from an eyeload of me
That I once was a lady as proud as could be?
Oh I'd never sit down by a tumbledown drunk
If it wasn't, my dears, for the high cost of junk.

"All the gents used to swear that the white of my calf
Beat the down of a swan by a length and a half.

1. Small town on the Hackensack River in New Jersey, a few miles west of Manhattan.

In the kerchief of linen I caught to my nose
Ah, there never fell snot, but a little gold rose.

"I had seven gold teeth and a toothpick of gold.
My Virginia cheroot was a leaf of it rolled
And I'd light it each time with a thousand in cash—
Why the bums used to fight if I flicked them an ash.

"Once the toast of the Biltmore,[2] the belle of the Taft,
I would drink bottle beer at the Drake, never draft,
And dine at the Astor on Salisbury steak
With a clean tablecloth for each bite I did take.

"In a car like the Roxy[3] I'd roll to the track,
A steel-guitar trio, a bar in the back,
And the wheels made no noise, they turned over so fast,
Still it took you ten minutes to see me go past.

"When the horses bowed down to me that I might choose,
I bet on them all, for I hated to lose.
Now I'm saddled each night for my butter and eggs
And the broken threads race down the backs of my legs.

"Let you hold in mind, girls, that your beauty must pass
Like a lovely white clover that rusts with its grass.
Keep your bottoms off barstools and marry you young
Or be left—an old barrel with many a bung.

"For when time takes you out for a spin in his car
You'll be hard-pressed to stop him from going too far
And be left by the roadside, for all your good deeds,
Two toadstools for tits and a face full of weeds."

All the house raised a cheer, but the man at the bar
Made a phonecall and up pulled a red patrol car
And she blew us a kiss as they copped her away
From that prominent bar in Secaucus, N.J.

1961

We learn about the singer in this poem primarily through her own words, although we may not believe everything she tells us about her past. From her introduction in the first stanza we get some general notion of her appearance and condition, but it is she who tells us that she is a junkie (line 8) and a prostitute (lines 27, 32) and that her face and figure have seen better days (lines 32, 36). That information could make her a sad case, and the poem might lament her state or encourage us to lament it, but instead she presents herself in a light, friendly, and theatrical way. The comedy is bittersweet, perhaps, but she is allowed to present herself, through her own words and attitudes, as a likable character—someone who has

2. Like the Taft, Drake, and Astor, a once-fashionable New York hotel.

3. Luxurious old New York theater and movie house, the site of many "world premieres" in the heyday of Hollywood.

survived life's disappointments and retained her dignity. The self-portrait accumulates almost completely through how she talks about herself, and the poet develops our attitude toward her by allowing her to recount her story herself, in her own words—or rather in words he has chosen for her.

SPEAKERS IN THE DRAMATIC MONOLOGUE

Like all **dramatic monologues**, the following poem has no narrator at all. Rather, it consists entirely of the words of a single, fictional speaker in a specific time, place, and dramatic situation, very like a character in a play.

ROBERT BROWNING

Soliloquy of the Spanish Cloister

Gr-r-r—there go, my heart's abhorrence!
Water your damned flower-pots, do!
If hate killed men, Brother Lawrence,
God's blood, would not mine kill you!
What? your myrtle-bush wants trimming?
Oh, that rose has prior claims—
Needs its leaden vase filled brimming?
Hell dry you up with its flames!

At the meal we sit together:
Salve tibi![4] I must hear
Wise talk of the kind of weather,
Sort of season, time of year:
Not a plenteous cork-crop: scarcely
Dare we hope oak-galls,[5] *I doubt:*
What's the Latin name for "parsley"?
What's the Greek name for Swine's Snout?

Whew! We'll have our platter burnished,
Laid with care on our own shelf!
With a fire-new spoon we're furnished,
And a goblet for ourself,
Rinsed like something sacrificial
Ere 'tis fit to touch our chaps[6]—
Marked with L. for our initial!
(He-he! There his lily snaps!)

Saint, forsooth! While brown Dolores
—Squats outside the Convent bank
With Sanchicha, telling stories,
Steeping tresses in the tank,
Blue-black, lustrous, thick like horsehairs,

4. Hail to thee (Latin). Italics usually indicate the words of Brother Lawrence here mockingly reproduced by the speaker. 5. Abnormal growth on oak trees, used for tanning. 6. Jaws.

—Can't I see his dead eye glow,
Bright as 'twere a Barbary corsair's?[7]
(That is, if he'd let it show!)

When he finishes refection,
Knife and fork he never lays
Cross-wise, to my recollection,
As do I, in Jesu's praise.
I the Trinity illustrate,
Drinking watered orange-pulp—
In three sips the Arian[8] frustrate;
—While he drains his at one gulp.

Oh, those melons? If he's able
We're to have a feast! so nice!
One goes to the Abbot's table,
All of us get each a slice.
How go on your flowers? None double?
Not one fruit-sort can you spy?
Strange!—And I, too, at such trouble,
—Keep them close-nipped on the sly!

There's a great text in Galatians,
Once you trip on it, entails
Twenty-nine distinct damnations,[9]
One sure, if another fails:
If I trip him just a-dying,
Sure of heaven as sure can be,
Spin him round and send him flying
Off to hell, a Manichee?[1]

Or, my scrofulous French novel
On gray paper with blunt type!
Simply glance at it, you grovel
Hand and foot in Belial's gripe.[2]
If I double down its pages
At the woeful sixteenth print,
When he gathers his greengages,
Ope a sieve and slip it in't?

Or, there's Satan!—one might venture
Pledge one's soul to him, yet leave
Such a flaw in the indenture
—As he'd miss till, past retrieve,
Blasted lay that rose-acacia
We're so proud of! *Hy, Zy, Hine* . . . [3]

7. African pirate's. 8. Heretical sect that denied the Trinity.
9. Galatians 5.15–23 provides a long list of possible offenses, though they do not add up to twenty-nine.
1. Heretic. According to the Manichean heresy, the world was divided into the forces of good and evil, each equally powerful. 2. That is, in the devil's clutches.
3. Possibly the beginning of an incantation or curse.

'St, there's Vespers! *Plena gratiâ*
Ave, Virgo.[4] Gr-r-r—you swine!
1842

Not many poems begin with a growl, and this harsh sound turns out to be fair warning that we are about to meet a real beast, even though he is in the clothing of a religious man. In line 1 he shows himself to hold a most uncharitable attitude toward his fellow monk, Brother Lawrence, and by line 4 he has uttered two profanities and admitted his intense feelings of hatred and vengefulness. His ranting and roaring is full of exclamation points (four in the first stanza!), and he reveals his own personality and character when he imagines curses and unflattering nicknames for Brother Lawrence or plots malicious jokes on him. By the end, we have accumulated no knowledge of Brother Lawrence that makes him seem a fit target for such rage (except that he is pious, dutiful, and pleasant—perhaps enough to make this sort of speaker despise him), but we should have discovered much about the speaker's character and habits.

The speaker characterizes himself; the details accumulate into a fairly full portrait, even though here we do not have either a narrator's description (as in Kennedy's In a Prominent Bar in Secaucus One Day) or another speaker to give us perspective. Except for the moments when the speaker mimics or parodies Brother Lawrence (usually in italic type), we have only the speaker's own words and thoughts. But that is enough; the poet has controlled them so carefully that we know what he thinks of the speaker. The whole poem has been about the speaker and his attitudes; the point has been to characterize the speaker and develop in us a dislike of him and what he stands for.

In reading a poem like this aloud, we would want our voice to suggest all the speaker's unlikable features. We would also need to suggest, through tone of voice, the author's contemptuous mocking of them, and we would want, like an actor, to create strong disapproval in the hearer. The poem's words (the ones the author has given to the speaker) clearly imply those attitudes, and we would want our voice to express them.

THE LYRIC AND ITS SPEAKER

With narrative poems and dramatic monologues, we are usually in no danger of mistaking the speaker for the poet. Lyrics may present more of a challenge. When there is a pointed discrepancy between the speaker of a **lyric** and what we know of the poet—when the speaker is a woman, for example, and the poet is a man—we know we have a fictional speaker to contend with and that the point (or at least *one* point) of the poem is to observe the characterization carefully.

Sometimes even in lyrics poets "borrow" a character from history and ask readers to factor in historical facts and contexts. In the following poem, for example, the Canadian poet Margaret Atwood draws heavily on facts and traditions about a nineteenth-century émigré from Scotland to Canada. The poem is a lyric spoken in the first person, but its speaker is a fictional character based on a real woman.

The poem comes from a volume called *The Journals of Susanna Moodie: Poems by Margaret Atwood* (1970). A frontier pioneer, Moodie (1803–84) herself wrote two

4. Opening words of the *Ave Maria*, here reversed: "Full of grace, Hail, Virgin" (Latin).

books about Canada, *Roughing It in the Bush* and *Life in the Clearings*, and Atwood found their observations rather stark and disorganized. She wrote her Susanna Moodie poems to refocus the "character" and to reconstruct Moodie's actual geographical exploration and self-discovery. To fully understand these thoughts and meditations, then, we need to know something of the history behind them. Yet even without such knowledge, we can appreciate the poem's powerful evocation of the speaker's situation and feelings.

MARGARET ATWOOD

Death of a Young Son by Drowning

He, who navigated with success
the dangerous river of his own birth
once more set forth

on a voyage of discovery
into the land I floated on
but could not touch to claim.

His feet slid on the bank,
the currents took him;
he swirled with ice and trees in the swollen water

and plunged into distant regions,
his head a bathysphere;[5]
through his eyes' thin glass bubbles

he looked out, reckless adventurer
on a landscape stranger than Uranus
we have all been to and some remember.

There was an accident; the air locked,
he was hung in the river like a heart.
They retrieved the swamped body,

cairn of my plans and future charts,
with poles and hooks
from among the nudging logs.

It was spring, the sun kept shining, the new grass
leapt to solidity;
my hands glistened with details.

After the long trip I was tired of waves.
My foot hit rock. The dreamed sails
collapsed, ragged.

I planted him in this country
like a flag.

1970

5. Manned spherical chamber for deep-sea observation.

Even when poets present themselves as if they were speaking directly to us in their own voices, their poems present only a partial portrait, something considerably less than the full personality and character of the poet. Though there is not an obviously created character—someone with distinct characteristics that are different from those of the poet—strategies of characterization are used to present the person speaking in one way and not another. As a result, you should still differentiate between the speaker and the poet.

AUTHORS ON THEIR CRAFT

BILLY COLLINS AND SHARON OLDS ON "FINDING YOUR OWN VOICE"

From "A Brisk Walk: An Interview with Billy Collins" (2006)*

[. . . T]here's this pet phrase about writing that is bandied around [. . .] "finding your own voice as a poet," which I suppose means that you come out from under the direct influence of other poets and have perhaps found a way to combine those influences so that it appears to be your own voice. But I think you could also put it a different way. You, quote, find your voice, unquote, when you are able to invent this one character who resembles you, obviously, and probably is more like you than anyone else on earth, but is not the equivalent to you.

It is like a fictional character in that it has a very distinctive voice, a voice that seems to be able to accommodate and express an attitude that you are comfortable staying with but an attitude that is flexible enough to cover a number of situations.

• • •

From "Olds' Worlds" (2008)**

[. . . O]nce a poem is written, and [. . .] it's rewritten, and maybe published, and I'm in front of people, reading it aloud—I'm not too embarrassed by that [. . .] It doesn't feel personal. It feels like art—a made thing—the "I" in it not myself anymore, but, I'd hope, some pronoun that a reader or hearer could slip into. But how much can a poem reflect or embody a life anyhow? You can want to come close, but it's so profoundly different—the actual body, the flesh, the mortal life.

*"A Brisk Walk: An Interview with Billy Collins." Interview by Joel Whitney. *Guernica*, 14 June 2006, www.guernicamag.com/interviews/a_brisk_walk/.

**"Olds' Worlds." Interview by Marianne Macdonald. *The Guardian*, 26 July 2008, www.theguardian.com/books/2008/jul/26/poetry.

Although the poet is probably writing about a personal, actual experience in the following poem, he is also making a character of himself—that is, characterizing himself in a certain way, emphasizing some parts of himself and not others. We can call this character a **persona**.

WILLIAM WORDSWORTH

She Dwelt among the Untrodden Ways

She dwelt among the untrodden ways
 Beside the springs of Dove,[6]
A Maid whom there were none to praise
 And very few to love:

A violet by a mossy stone
 Half hidden from the eye!
—Fair as a star, when only one
 Is shining in the sky.

She lived unknown, and few could know
 When Lucy ceased to be;
But she is in her grave, and, oh,
 The difference to me!

1800

Did Lucy actually live? Was she a friend of the poet? We don't know; the poem doesn't tell us, and even biographers of Wordsworth are unsure. What we do know is that Wordsworth was able to represent grief very powerfully. Whether the speaker is the historical Wordsworth or not, that speaker is a major focus of the poem, and it is his feelings that the poem isolates and expresses. We need to recognize some characteristics of the speaker and be sensitive to his feelings for the poem to work.

Analyzing Speakers: An Exercise

In the following poem, we do not get a full sense of the speaker until well into the poem. As you read, try to imagine the tone of voice you think this person would use. Exactly when do you begin to know what she sounds like?

DOROTHY PARKER

A Certain Lady

Oh, I can smile for you, and tilt my head,
 And drink your rushing words with eager lips,
And paint my mouth for you a fragrant red,
 And trace your brows with tutored finger-tips.
When you rehearse your list of loves to me,
 Oh, I can laugh and marvel, rapturous-eyed.
And you laugh back, nor can you ever see
 The thousand little deaths my heart has died.
And you believe, so well I know my part,

6. Small stream in the Lake District in northern England, near where Wordsworth lived.

That I am gay as morning, light as snow,
And all the straining things within my heart
You'll never know.
Oh, I can laugh and listen, when we meet,
And you bring tales of fresh adventurings—
Of ladies delicately indiscreet,
Of lingering hands, and gently whispered things.
And you are pleased with me, and strive anew
To sing me sagas of your late delights.
Thus do you want me—marveling, gay, and true—
Nor do you see my staring eyes of nights.
And when, in search of novelty, you stray,
Oh, I can kiss you blithely as you go . . .
And what goes on, my love, while you're away,
You'll never know.

1937

To whom does the speaker seem to be talking? What sort of person is he? How do you feel about him? Which habits and attitudes of his do you like least? How soon can you tell that the speaker is not altogether happy about his conversation and conduct? In what tone of voice would you read the first twenty-two lines aloud? What attitude would you try to express toward the person spoken to? What tone would you use for the last two lines? How would you describe the speaker's personality? What aspects of her behavior are most crucial to the poem's effect?

• • •

The poems we have looked at in this chapter—and those that follow—all suggest the value of beginning the reading of any poem with three simple questions: Who is speaking? What do we know about him or her? What kind of person is she or he? Putting together the evidence that the poem presents in answer to such questions can often take us a long way into the poem. For some poems, such questions won't help a great deal because the speaking voice is too indistinct or the character too scantily presented. But starting with such questions will often lead you toward the central experience the poem offers.

POEMS FOR FURTHER STUDY

WALT WHITMAN

[I celebrate myself, and sing myself]

I celebrate myself, and sing myself,
And what I assume you shall assume,
For every atom belonging to me as good belongs to you.
I loafe and invite my soul,
I lean and loafe at my ease observing a spear of summer grass.

My tongue, every atom of my blood, form'd from this soil, this air,
Born here of parents born here from parents the same, and their parents
the same,
I, now thirty-seven years old in perfect health begin,
Hoping to cease not till death.
Creeds and schools in abeyance,
Retiring back a while sufficed at what they are, but never forgotten,
I harbor for good or bad, I permit to speak at every hazard,
Nature without check with original energy.

1855, 1881

• **What is characteristically American about the speaker of this poem?**

LANGSTON HUGHES
Ballad of the Landlord

Landlord, landlord,
My roof has sprung a leak.
Don't you 'member I told you about it
Way last week?

Landlord, landlord,
These steps is broken down.
When you come up yourself
It's a wonder you don't fall down.

Ten Bucks you say I owe you?
Ten Bucks you say is due?
Well, that's Ten Bucks more'n I'll pay you
Till you fix this house up new.

What? You gonna get eviction orders?
You gonna cut off my heat?
You gonna take my furniture and
Throw it in the street?

Um-huh! You talking high and mighty.
Talk on—till you get through.
You ain't gonna be able to say a word
If I land my fist on you.

Police! Police!
Come and get this man!
He's trying to ruin the government
And overturn the land!

Copper's whistle!
Patrol bell!
Arrest.

Precinct Station.
Iron cell.
Headlines in press:

MAN THREATENS LANDLORD
TENANT HELD NO BAIL
JUDGE GIVES NEGRO 90 DAYS IN COUNTY JAIL.

1940

- **Who are the various speakers in this poem? What is the effect of Hughes's choice not to give us all the words of all the speakers?**

E. E. CUMMINGS

[next to of course god america i]

"next to of course god america i
love you land of the pilgrims' and so forth oh
say can you see by the dawn's early my
country 'tis of centuries come and go
and are no more what of it we should worry
in every language even deafanddumb
thy sons acclaim your glorious name by gorry
by jingo by gee by gosh by gum
why talk of beauty what could be more beautiful than these heroic happy dead
who rushed like lions to the roaring slaughter
they did not stop to think they died instead
then shall the voice of liberty be mute?"

He spoke. And drank rapidly a glass of water

1926

- **Except for the last line, this poem works much like a dramatic monologue. What can you discern about the situation in which the quoted words are spoken? about the speaker and his or her audience? about the poem's attitude toward the speaker?**

GWENDOLYN BROOKS

We Real Cool

The Pool Players,
Seven at the Golden Shovel.

We real cool. We
Left school. We

Lurk late. We
Strike straight. We

Sing sin. We
Thin gin. We

Jazz June. We
Die soon.

1950

- Who are "we" in this poem? Do you think that the speaker and the poet share the same idea of what is "cool"?

AUTHORS ON THEIR WORK
GWENDOLYN BROOKS (1917–2000)

From "An Interview with Gwendolyn Brooks" (1970)*

Q[UESTION:] Are your characters literally true to your experience or do you set out to change experience?

A[NSWER:] Some of them are, are invented, some of them are very real people.

• • •

Q[UESTION:] How about the seven pool players in the poem "We Real Cool"?

A[NSWER:] They have no pretensions to any glamor. They are supposedly dropouts, or at least they're in the poolroom when they should possibly be in school, since they're probably young enough, or at least those I saw were when I looked in a poolroom [. . .]. First of all, let me tell you how that's supposed to be said, because there's a reason why I set it out as I did. These are people who are essentially saying, "Kilroy is here. We are." But they're a little uncertain of the strength of their identity. [. . .]

The "We"—you're supposed to stop after the "We" and think about their validity, and of course there's no way for you to tell whether it should be said softly or not, I suppose, but I say it rather softly because I want to represent their basic uncertainty, which they don't bother to question every day, of course.

Q[UESTION:] Are you saying that the form of this poem, then, was determined by the colloquial rhythm you were trying to catch?

A[NSWER:] No, determined by my feeling about these boys, these young men.

*"An Interview with Gwendolyn Brooks." Interview by George Stavros. *Contemporary Literature*, vol. 11, no. 1, Winter 1970, pp. 1–20. *JSTOR*, www.jstor.org/stable/1207502.

LUCILLE CLIFTON
cream of wheat

sometimes at night
we stroll the market aisles
ben and jemima and me   they
walk in front   remembering this and that
i lag behind
trying to remove my chefs cap

wondering about what ever pictured me
then left me personless
Rastus
i read in an old paper
i was called rastus
but no mother ever
gave that to her son   toward dawn
we return to our shelves
our boxes   ben and jemima and me
we pose and smile   i simmer   what
is my name

2008

- At what point and how did you begin to figure out just who the speaker of this poem is? What is the effect of the shifts between plural and singular, "we" and "I"?

SUGGESTIONS FOR WRITING

1. Several of the poems in this chapter create characters and imply situations, as in drama. Write an essay in which you describe and analyze the main speaker of any poem in this chapter.
2. Write an essay in which you compare the speakers in any two poems in this chapter. What kinds of self-image do they have? In each poem, what is the implied distance between the speaker and the poet?
3. Choose any of the poems in this or the previous chapter and write an essay about the way a poet can create irony and humor through the use of a speaker who is clearly distinct from the poet himself or herself.
4. Write a poem, short story, or personal essay in which the speaker or narrator is a character mentioned by a speaker in any of the poems in this chapter—for example, someone who hears the song sung in X. J. Kennedy's In a Prominent Bar in Secaucus One Day, the lover in Dorothy Parker's A Certain Lady, or Ben and Jemima in cream of wheat. How might the same situation, as well as the main speaker of these poems, look and sound different when viewed from another speaker's point of view and described in another speaker's voice?

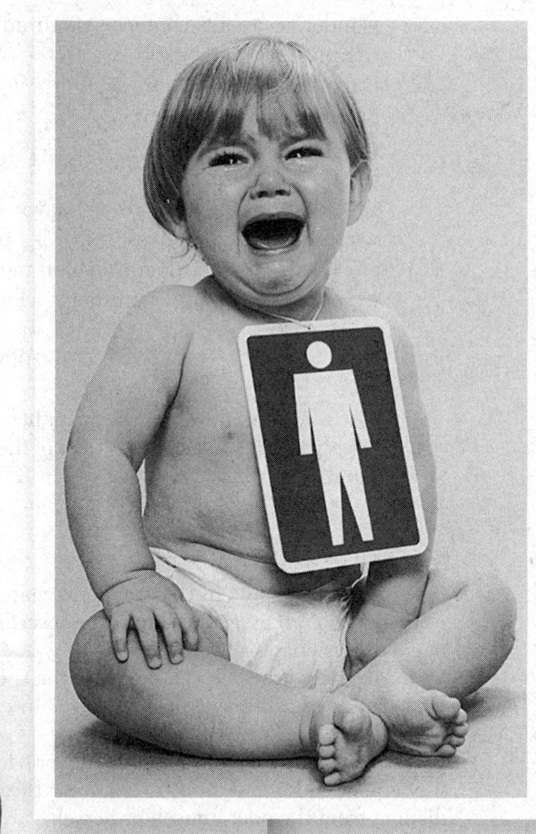

Exploring Gender

AN ALBUM

As far as I'm concerned, being any gender is a drag.

—PATTI SMITH

In poetry, as in life, the meaning of what is said to us depends in great part on who says it. In both contexts, too, our sense of who a **speaker** (or any person) is has much to do with gender, even when we aren't aware of it. Is this person a *he* or a *she*? Those little pronouns make all the difference.

As an experiment, look back at one or two of the poems in the last chapter. At what point, and for what reason, did you first decide that a poem's speaker was male or female? Did you ever change your mind? Does any speaker's gender seem more ambiguous now, on a second reading of the poem, than it did on the first reading? What difference does the speaker's gender make to your response? How might your response relate to the ways the poem does or doesn't conform to your expectations of men and women? What is the effect of the correspondence (or lack thereof) between the author's gender and the speaker's?

Despite all we have said about the danger of confusing the author of a poem with its speaker(s), in practice we usually use our knowledge of an author's gender in determining a speaker's gender, particularly when the latter is ambiguous. For example, consider William Wordsworth's poem She Dwelt among the Untrodden Ways (ch. 12). The title tells us that the poem describes a "she," whom we later learn is "A Maid"—that is, an unmarried woman, probably young and virginal, named Lucy (lines 3, 10). But what about the speaker? On the one hand, we know that Lucy's death and burial make all "[t]he difference" to this person (line 12), and the poem also gives us plenty of reasons to suspect that the speaker is among the "very few" who "love[d]" Lucy (line 4), at the very least finding her flowerlike and "[f]air" (lines 5, 7). On the other hand, you might be surprised to discover that nothing in the poem establishes the speaker's gender beyond a reasonable doubt. Yet based on these few cues—on the fact that the poem is written by *William* Wordsworth, on our experience of the ways men and women tend to feel and talk about each other, and on the ways a **lyric** is likely to portray the lost beloved—we almost inevitably assume as we read that the speaker is a man.

In the absence of definitive textual cues about a speaker's gender, such assumptions are perfectly acceptable and conventional, perhaps even inevitable. But it is nonetheless important (and just plain interesting) to notice that when we assign gender to the speaker of some poems, we *are* making an assumption—one that greatly affects our reading and response. Notice, too, that in assigning gender we often draw on assumptions about sexuality as well, often taking it for granted that people are heterosexual. When it comes to gender we need to pay attention to all the details that a poem gives us, as well as to those it withholds. We also need to be ready for surprises and to look for evidence that might overturn, or at least complicate, our assumptions. For example, Shakespeare's sonnets famously include some addressed to a young man, others addressed to a woman, and still others that are ambiguous, especially when read independently of the rest of the sonnets in the **sequence**. In some cases, the erotic charge of the poems, combined with our own tendency to believe that love poems must be addressed from a man to a woman or vice versa, might well lead us to make problematic assumptions about the gender of the speaker or the lover.

To help you think more about these issues, this album gathers poems whose speakers vary widely. In one way or another, however, all of these poems invite us to explore our ideas and feelings about gender and, to a lesser extent, sexuality. What does it mean to be a man or a woman? What has it meant in other times and places? Might gender be more complex than the phrases *man* or *woman* and *he* or *she* suggest? When, where, and how do we acquire our ideas about gender-appropriate roles, qualities, behavior, and appearance? Are some or all of these "ideas" not learned at all, but rather innate or instinctual? When and why might having a gender be a burden? a pleasure? How does gender shape our experience? our sense of ourselves and others? our interactions with, and our emotional responses to, poems and people?

RICHARD LOVELACE

Song: To Lucasta, Going to the Wars

Tell me not, sweet, I am unkind,
That from the nunnery
Of thy chaste breast and quiet mind
To war and arms I fly.

True: a new mistress now I chase,
The first foe in the field;
And with a stronger faith embrace
A sword, a horse, a shield.

Yet this inconstancy is such
As you too shall adore;
I could not love thee, dear, so much,
Loved I not honor more.

1649

- What might this poem imply about men's and women's attitudes toward love and war?

MARY, LADY CHUDLEIGH

To the Ladies

Wife and servant are the same,
But only differ in the name:
For when that fatal knot is tied,
Which nothing, nothing can divide,

When she the word *Obey* has said,
And man by law supreme has made,
Then all that's kind is laid aside,
And nothing left but state[1] and pride.
Fierce as an eastern prince he grows,
And all his innate rigor shows:
Then but to look, to laugh, or speak,
Will the nuptial contract break.
Like mutes, she signs alone must make,
And never any freedom take,
But still be governed by a nod,
And fear her husband as her god:
Him still must serve, him still obey,
And nothing act, and nothing say,
But what her haughty lord thinks fit,
Who, with the power, has all the wit.
Then shun, oh! shun that wretched state,
And all the fawning flatterers hate.
Value yourselves, and men despise:
You must be proud, if you'll be wise.

1703

- **What might the speaker mean when she says a husband "with the power, has all the wit" (line 20)? How might that statement multiply the meanings of the poem's last line?**

WILFRED OWEN
Disabled

He sat in a wheeled chair, waiting for dark,
And shivered in his ghastly suit of grey,
Legless, sewn short at elbow. Through the park
Voices of boys rang saddening like a hymn,
Voices of play and pleasure after day,
Till gathering sleep had mothered them from him.

About this time Town used to swing so gay
When glow-lamps budded in the light blue trees,
And girls glanced lovelier as the air grew dim,—
In the old times, before he threw away his knees.
Now he will never feel again how slim
Girls' waists are, or how warm their subtle hands;
All of them touch him like some queer disease.

There was an artist silly for his face,
For it was younger than his youth, last year.
Now, he is old; his back will never brace;

1. Social position.

He's lost his color very far from here,
Poured it down shell-holes till the veins ran dry,
And half his lifetime lapsed in the hot race,
And leap of purple spurted from his thigh.

One time he liked a blood-smear down his leg,
After the matches,[2] carried shoulder-high.
It was after football, when he'd drunk a peg,[3]
He thought he'd better join.—He wonders why.
Someone had said he'd look a god in kilts,
That's why; and may be, too, to please his Meg;
Aye, that was it, to please the giddy jilts
He asked to join. He didn't have to beg;
Smiling they wrote his lie; aged nineteen years.

Germans he scarcely thought of; all their guilt,
And Austria's, did not move him. And no fears
Of Fear came yet. He thought of jeweled hilts
For daggers in plaid socks; of smart salutes;
And care of arms; and leave; and pay arrears;
Esprit de corps; and hints for young recruits.
And soon, he was drafted out with drums and cheers.

Some cheered him home, but not as crowds cheer Goal.
Only a solemn man who brought him fruits
Thanked him; and then inquired about his soul.

Now, he will spend a few sick years in Institutes,
And do what things the rules consider wise,
And take whatever pity they may dole.
Tonight he noticed how the women's eyes
Passed from him to the strong men that were whole.
How cold and late it is! Why don't they come
And put him into bed? Why don't they come?

1917

- **How might you respond differently to this poem if the soldier himself were the speaker? if the poem described the events of his life in the order in which they happened? if the poem lacked its last two lines?**

ELIZABETH BISHOP

Exchanging Hats

Unfunny uncles who insist
in trying on a lady's hat,
—oh, even if the joke falls flat,
we share your slight transvestite twist

in spite of our embarrassment.
Costume and custom are complex.

2. Soccer games. 3. A drink, usually brandy and soda.

The headgear of the other sex
inspires us to experiment.

Anandrous[4] aunts, who, at the beach
with paper plates upon your laps,
keep putting on the yachtsmen's caps
with exhibitionistic screech,

the visors hanging o'er the ear
so that the golden anchors drag,
—the tides of fashion never lag.
Such caps may not be worn next year.

Or you who don the paper plate
itself, and put some grapes upon it,
or sport the Indian's feather bonnet,
—perversities may aggravate

the natural madness of the hatter.
And if the opera hats collapse
and crowns grow drafty, then, perhaps,
he thinks what might a miter matter?

Unfunny uncle, you who wore a
hat too big, or one too many,
tell us, can't you, are there any
stars inside your black fedora?

Aunt exemplary and slim,
with avernal[5] eyes, we wonder
what slow changes they see under
their vast, shady, turned-down brim.

1956

- **The speaker in this poem uses the first-person plural ("we," line 4; "our," line 5; "us," line 8). Who might "we" be? How might your response to the poem change if the speaker instead used the first-person singular ("I") or the third-person plural ("they")?**

DAVID WAGONER
My Father's Garden

On his way to the open hearth where white-hot steel
Boiled against furnace walls in wait for his lance
To pierce the fireclay and set loose demons
And dragons in molten tons, blazing
Down to the huge satanic caldrons,
Each day he would pass the scrapyard, his kind of garden.

4. Literally, "husbandless." **5. Infernal.**

In rusty rockeries of stoves and brake drums,
In grottoes of sewing machines and refrigerators,
He would pick flowers for us: small gears and cogwheels
With teeth like petals, with holes for anthers,
Long stalks of lead to be poured into toy soldiers,
Ball bearings as big as grapes to knock them down.

He was called a melter. He tried to keep his brain
From melting in those tyger-mouthed mills
Where the same steel reappeared over and over
To be reborn in the fire as something better
Or worse: cannons or cars, needles or girders,
Flagpoles, swords, or plowshares.

But it melted. His classical learning ran
Down and away from him, not burning bright.[6]
His fingers culled a few cold scraps of Latin
And Greek, *magna sine laude*,[7] for crosswords
And brought home lumps of tin and sewer grills
As if they were his ripe prize vegetables.

1987

- **What facts do we learn here about the speaker's father and his life? What are the speaker's feelings about both?**

JUDITH ORTIZ COFER
The Changeling

As a young girl
vying for my father's attention,
I invented a game that made him look up
from his reading and shake his head
as if both baffled and amused.

In my brother's closet, I'd change
into his dungarees—the rough material
molding me into boy shape; hide
my long hair under an army helmet
he'd been given by Father, and emerge
transformed into the legendary Ché[8]
of grown-up talk.

Strutting around the room,
I'd tell of life in the mountains,
of carnage and rivers of blood,
and of manly feasts with rum and music
to celebrate victories *para la libertad*.[9]

6. Like "tyger-mouthed" (line 14), an allusion to William Blake's poem "The Tyger" (1790).
7. Without great distinction; a reversal of the usual *magna cum laude*.
8. Ernesto "Che" Guevara (1928–67), Argentinian-born Cuban revolutionary leader.
9. For freedom (Spanish).

He would listen with a smile
to my tales of battles and brotherhood
until Mother called us to dinner.

She was not amused
by my transformations, sternly forbidding me
from sitting down with them as a man.
She'd order me back to the dark cubicle
that smelled of adventure, to shed
my costume, to braid my hair furiously
with blind hands, and to return invisible,
as myself,
to the real world of her kitchen.

1993

- **Why do you think the speaker's father is amused by her "transformations" (line 22), and why does her mother forbid them? What does this poem imply about all three characters?**

MARIE HOWE
Practicing

I want to write a love poem for the girls I kissed in seventh grade,
a song for what we did on the floor in the basement

of somebody's parents' house, a hymn for what we didn't say but thought:
That feels good or *I like that*, when we learned how to open each other's mouths

how to move our tongues to make somebody moan. We called it practicing, and
one was the boy, and we paired off—maybe six or eight girls—and turned out
the lights and kissed and kissed until we were stoned on kisses, and lifted our
nightgowns or let the straps drop, and, Now you be the boy:

concrete floor, sleeping bag or couch, playroom, game room, train room, laundry.
Linda's basement was like a boat with booths and portholes

instead of windows. Gloria's father had a bar downstairs with stools that spun,
plush carpeting. We kissed each other's throats.

We sucked each other's breasts, and we left marks, and never spoke of it upstairs
outdoors, in daylight, not once. We did it, and it was

practicing, and slept, sprawled so our legs still locked or crossed, a hand still lost
in someone's hair . . . and we grew up and hardly mentioned who

the first kiss really was—a girl like us, still sticky with the moisturizer
we'd
shared in the bathroom. I want to write a song

for that thick silence in the dark, and the first pure thrill of unreluctant
desire,
just before we made ourselves stop.

1998

- What does the speaker of this poem imply about why her memories of "practicing" matter to her now that she is an adult? What does she imply about how being a girl compares to being a woman?

AUTHORS ON THEIR WORK

MARIE HOWE (b. 1950)

From "Marie Howe" (1997)*

M[ARIE] H[OWE]: [. . .] I was interested in what it means to be a woman, what it means to be a man. [. . .]

In this culture, our mothers don't tell us about their first sexual experience, they don't tell us about their marriage, their lives, their sexual life in marriage, they don't tell us anything. My mother told us nothing [. . .] So, I've been really aware lately, at 46 years old, that I still need my sisters and my friends to teach me and help me figure out how to be a "girl."

[INTERVIEWER]: So much of our time as girls and women is spent trying to figure out what is allowed, by men and by other women as well. What is not talked about and what is talked about. How we can have an authentic sexuality.

MH: In learning how to be a girl in this culture, we are learning how to be objects. [. . .]

So in the poems, I was trying to find places in my young life where I was actually the subject, and I found it was in practicing how to kiss, which I did with other girls. I got to be a boy-girl and a girl-girl—I got to kiss the girl and kiss the boy. I loved that.

• • •

From "The Complexity of the Human Heart: A Conversation with Marie Howe" (2004)**

[INTERVIEWER]: I was interested in your saying you don't want to write personal poems anymore. Is one of the dangers having people confuse your poetry with your life? Once I heard someone say to Sharon Olds, "Tell me, how old are your son and daughter now?" And she said, "I have no son or daughter. Those are fictitious children."

MH: I understand what she means. For example, with that poem "Practicing," [. . .] the *New Yorker* legal department called up and said, "Are those girls identifiable?" I said, well, Linda's basement was like a boat and Gloria's father did have a bar downstairs with plush carpeting, but I didn't kiss those girls. So, yes, they're identifiable, because the poem has great, great details from my childhood, but that to me is the answer to the question of whether it is autobiographical. It's all constructed. I didn't kiss those two girls. They were my best friends when I was a kid. I kissed other girls, but how could you give up those gorgeous details with those basements, and it poured into the poems. They still made me change the names. But what comes together in a poem isn't true [. . .].

[. . .] I'm making something, like [the artist] Joseph Cornell makes his boxes and everyone looks into them, but it's the box you look into; it's not the man or the woman. It's alchemy of language and memory and imagination and time and music and sounds that gets made, and that's different from "Here is what happened to me when I was ten." That poem is a good example. Linda's boat basement and Gloria's plush carpeting were there, but they weren't *there* there.

*"Marie Howe." Interview by Victoria Redel. *Bomb: A Quarterly Arts and Culture Magazine*, Fall 1997, bombmagazine.org/article/2105/marie-howe.

**"The Complexity of the Human Heart: A Conversation with Marie Howe." Interview by David Elliott. *AGNI Online*, 2004, www.bu.edu/agni/interviews/online/2004/howe-elliott.html.

TERRANCE HAYES

Mr. T—[1]

A man made of scrap muscle & the steam
engine's imagination, white feathers
flapping in each lobe for the skull's migration,
should the need arise. Sometimes drugged
& duffled (by white men) in a cockpit
bound for the next adventure. And liable
to crush a fool's face like newsprint; headlines
of Hollywood blood and wincing. Half Step 'N Fetchit,[2]
half John Henry. What were we, the skinny B-boys,[3]
to learn from him? How to hulk through Chicago
in a hedgerow afro, an ox-grunt kicking dust
behind the teeth; those eighteen glammering
gold chains around the throat of pity,
that fat hollow medallion like the sun on a leash—

2002

- How does the poem characterize Mr. T and the speaker's feelings about him? Why might it matter that the speaker uses the first-person plural ("we") versus the singular ("I")?

1. Stage name of bodyguard-turned-actor Laurence Tureaud (b. 1952), who first rose to fame as a star of the 1980s action-adventure series *The A Team* and the film *Rocky III* (1982). His boast "I pity the fool" became a popular catchphrase.
2. Born Lincoln Theodore Perry (1902–85), "Stepin Fetchit" is often described as the first African American movie star; he became famous and controversial in the 1930s by repeatedly playing the same stereotypically simpleminded character.
3. Hip-hop dancers or "breakers." *John Henry*: American folk hero portrayed as an enormously strong railroad worker who died from exhaustion after winning a contest against a steam-powered drill.

BOB HICOK

O my pa-pa

Our fathers have formed a poetry workshop.
They sit in a circle of disappointment over our fastballs
and wives. We thought they didn't read our stuff,
whole anthologies of poems that begin, My father never,
or those that end, and he was silent as a carp,
or those with middles which, if you think
of the right side as a sketch, look like a paunch
of beer and worry, but secretly, with flashlights
in the woods, they've read every word and noticed
that our nine happy poems have balloons and sex
and giraffes inside, but not one dad waving hello
from the top of a hill at dusk. Theirs
is the revenge school of poetry, with titles like
"My Yellow Sheet Lad" and "Given Your Mother's Taste
for Vodka, I'm Pretty Sure You're Not Mine."
They're not trying to make the poems better
so much as sharper or louder, more like a fishhook
or electrocution, as a group
they overcome their individual senilities,
their complete distaste for language, how cloying
it is, how like tears it can be, and remember
every mention of their long hours at the office
or how tired they were when they came home,
when they were dragged through the door
by their shadows. I don't know why it's so hard
to write a simple and kind poem to my father, who worked,
not like a dog, dogs sleep most of the day in a ball
of wanting to chase something, but like a man, a man
with seven kids and a house to feed, whose absence
was his presence, his present, the Cheerios,
the PF Flyers, who taught me things about trees,
that they're the most intricate version of standing up,
who built a grandfather clock with me so I would know
that time is a constructed thing, a passing, ticking fancy.
A bomb. A bomb that'll go off soon for him, for me,
and I notice in our fathers' poems a reciprocal dwelling
on absence, that they wonder why we disappeared
as soon as we got our licenses, why we wanted
the rocket cars, as if running away from them
to kiss girls who looked like mirrors of our mothers
wasn't fast enough, and it turns out they did
start to say something, to form the words hey
or stay, but we'd turned into a door full of sun,
into the burning leave, and were gone
before it came to them that it was all right
to shout, that they should have knocked us down

with a hand on our shoulders, that they too are mystified
by the distance men need in their love.

2007

- What does the speaker seem to discover about fathers, sons, and men by imagining the poems "Our fathers" might write (line 1)? What does the poem imply about the relationship between poetry, "language" (line 20), and gender?

STACEY WAITE

The Kind of Man I Am at the DMV

"Mommy, that man is a girl," says the little boy
pointing his finger, like a narrow spotlight,
targeting the center of my back, his kid-hand
learning to assert what he sees, his kid-hand
learning the failure of gender's tidy little
story about itself. I try not to look at him

because, yes that man is a girl. I, man, am a girl.
I am the kind of man who is a girl and because
the kind of man I am is patient with children
I try not to hear the meanness in his voice,
his boy voice that sounds like a girl voice
because his boy voice is young and pitched high
like the tent in his pants will be years later
because he will grow to be the kind of man
who is a man, or so his mother thinks.

His mother snatches his finger from the air,
of course he's not, she says, pulling him
back to his seat, *what number does it say we are?*
she says to her boy, bringing his attention
to numbers, to counting and its solid sense.

But he has earrings, the boy complains
now sounding desperate like he's been
the boy who cries wolf, like he's been
the hub of disbelief before, but this time
he knows he is oh so right. The kind
of man I am is a girl, the kind of man
I am is push-ups on the basement
floor, is chest bound tight against himself,
is thick gripping hands to the wheel
when the kind of man I am drives away
from the boy who will become a boy
except for now while he's still a girl voice,
a girl face, a hairless arm, a powerless hand.
That boy is a girl that man who is a girl
thinks to himself, as he pulls out of the lot,
his girl eyes shining in the Midwest sun.

2013

- According to the poem, what is wrong with "gender's tidy little / story about itself," or what is its "failure" (lines 5–6)? How does the speaker characterize and seem to feel about the little boy? his mother? Why and how so?

SUGGESTIONS FOR WRITING

1. Identify the poem in this album that moves you the most, whether to anger, frustration, sadness, delight, or any other emotion. Write an essay exploring why and how the poem evokes the emotions it does, focusing especially on the way your emotional response relates, on the one hand, to the poem's representation of gender and, on the other hand, to either your own experience of being a certain gender or your own ideas about gender. Alternatively, choose any poem in the album that you find especially good or interesting, and write an essay exploring what it shows about gender and how it does so.
2. Some of the poems in this album explore the relationship between adults and children from the grown-up child's perspective (David Wagoner's MY FATHER'S GARDEN, Judith Ortiz Cofer's THE CHANGELING, Elizabeth Bishop's EXCHANGING HATS, Bob Hicok's O MY PA-PA). Write an essay comparing the way at least two of these poems portray either these relationships or the role of parents in teaching their children what it means to be a boy or a girl, a man or a woman. What feelings do the poems express about these relationships or roles?
3. Richard Lovelace's SONG: TO LUCASTA, GOING TO THE WARS, Wilfred Owen's DISABLED, and Judith Ortiz Cofer's THE CHANGELING all deal with war and men's and women's relationship to it. Write an essay in which you compare these poems and their implications about the role of war in defining masculinity and femininity.
4. Elizabeth Bishop's EXCHANGING HATS, Judith Ortiz Cofer's THE CHANGELING, and Marie Howe's PRACTICING all describe games or experiments that involve trying on different roles, sometimes by trying on different clothes. Write an essay in which you compare at least two of these poems and the games they describe. What does each game and each poem illustrate about social roles and rules? about the difference between "play" and "real life" or between childhood and adulthood? If you focus on PRACTICING, feel free to draw on the excerpts from the Howe interviews, as well as the poem.
5. Choose any poem from another chapter or album in this book, and write an essay exploring how the poem's meaning and emotional impact are affected by the fact that its speaker either is or is not clearly male or female.

13 SITUATION AND SETTING: WHAT HAPPENS? WHERE? WHEN?

Questions about the **speaker** in a poem (*Who?* questions) lead to questions about *What?* and *Why?* as well as *Where?* and *When?* First you identify the imagined **situation** in the poem: To whom is the speaker speaking? Is there an **auditor** in the poem? Is anyone else present or referred to in the poem? What is happening? Why is this event or communication occurring, and why is it significant? As soon as you zoom in on answers to such questions about persons and actions, you also encounter questions about place and time. (Where and when does the action or communication take place?) In other words, situation entails **setting**.

The place involved in a poem is its *spatial setting*, and the time is its *temporal setting*. The temporal setting may be a specific date or an era, a season of the year or a time of day. Temporal or spatial setting often influences our expectations, although a poet may surprise us by making something very different from what we had thought was familiar. We tend, for example, to think of spring as a time of discovery and growth, and poems set in spring are likely to make use of that association. Similarly, morning usually suggests discovery—beginnings, vitality, the world fresh and new.

Not all poems have an identifiable situation or setting, just as not all poems have a speaker who is easily distinguishable from the author. Poems that simply present a series of thoughts and feelings directly, in a reflective way, may not present anything resembling a scene with action, dialogue, or description. But many poems depend crucially on a sense of place, a sense of time, and scenes that resemble those in plays or films. And questions about these matters will often lead you to define not only the "facts" but also the feelings central to the design a poem has on its readers.

To understand the dialogue in Hardy's The Ruined Maid, for example, we need to recognize that the two women are meeting after an extended period of separation (the situation) and that they meet in a town rather than the rural area in which they grew up together (the setting). We infer (from the opening lines) that the meeting is accidental and that no other friends are present for the conversation. The poem's whole "story" depends on their situation: After leading separate lives for a while, they have some catching up to do. We don't know what specific town they are in or what year, season, or time of day it is—and those details are not important to the poem's effect.

More specific settings matter in other poems. In Browning's Soliloquy of the Spanish Cloister, the setting, a monastery, adds to the irony because of the gross inappropriateness of the speaker's sentiments and attitudes in a supposedly holy place.

Situation and setting may be treated in various ways in a poem, ranging from silence to the barest hints of description to full photographic detail. Often it is relatively easy to identify the situation at the beginning of a poem, but the implications of setting, and what happens as the poem unfolds, may be subtler. Poets often rely on readers to fill in the gaps, drawing on their knowledge of circumstances and familiar experiences in the present or in the past. The poem may specify only a few aspects of a *kind* of setting, such as a motel room in the afternoon.

SITUATION

Both of the poems below involve motherhood, but each portrays an entirely different situation. How would you summarize each?

RITA DOVE

Daystar

She wanted a little room for thinking:
but she saw diapers steaming on the line,
a doll slumped behind the door.
So she lugged a chair behind the garage
to sit out the children's naps.

Sometimes there were things to watch—
the pinched armor of a vanished cricket,
a floating maple leaf. Other days
she stared until she was assured
when she closed her eyes
she'd see only her own vivid blood.

She had an hour, at best, before Liza appeared
pouting from the top of the stairs.
And just *what* was mother doing
out back with the field mice? Why,
building a palace. Later
that night when Thomas rolled over and
lurched into her, she would open her eyes
and think of the place that was hers
for an hour—where
she was nothing,
pure nothing, in the middle of the day.

1986

LINDA PASTAN

To a Daughter Leaving Home

When I taught you
at eight to ride
a bicycle, loping along
beside you
as you wobbled away

on two round wheels,
my own mouth rounding
in surprise when you pulled
ahead down the curved
path of the park,
I kept waiting
for the thud
of your crash as I
sprinted to catch up,
while you grew
smaller, more breakable
with distance,
pumping, pumping
for your life, screaming
with laughter,
the hair flapping
behind you like a
handkerchief waving
goodbye.

1988

The mother in Dove's Daystar, overwhelmed by the demands of young children, needs a room of her own. All she can manage, however, is a brief hour of respite. The situation is virtually the whole story here. Nothing really happens except that daily events (washing diapers, picking up toys, looking at crickets and leaves, explaining the world to children, having sex) surround her brief private hour and make it precious. Being "nothing" (lines 21 and 22) takes on great value in these circumstances.

The particulars of time and place in Pastan's To a Daughter Leaving Home are even less specific; the incident the poem describes happened a long time ago, and its vividness is a function of memory. The speaker here thinks back nostalgically to a moment when her daughter made an earlier (but briefer) departure. Though we learn very little about the speaker, at least directly, we may infer quite a bit about her—her affection for her daughter, the kind of mother she has been, her anxiety at the new departure that seems to resemble the earlier wobbly ride into the distance. The daughter is now, the poem implies, old enough to "leave home" in a full sense, but we do not know the specific reason or what the present circumstances are. Only the title tells us the situation, and (like "Daystar") the poem is all situation.

THE CARPE DIEM POEM

The following two poems from the 1600s represent similar situations: In each, a male speaker addresses a female auditor whom he desires. The poems belong to the tradition of **carpe diem** (Latin for "seize the day") because the speaker is urging his auditor, his lover, to enjoy pleasures now, before they die. The woman is resisting because of her concern for chastity or social rules. The action of these poems is implied in the shifts in what the speaker is saying. What does the woman do in The Flea? Can you imagine the woman's response in To His Coy Mistress?

JOHN DONNE
The Flea

Mark but this flea, and mark in this,[1]
How little that which thou deny'st me is;
It sucked me first, and now sucks thee,
And in this flea our two bloods mingled be;
Thou know'st that this cannot be said
A sin, nor shame, nor loss of maidenhead.
  Yet this enjoys before it woo,
  And pampered[2] swells with one blood made of two,
  And this, alas, is more than we would do.[3]

Oh stay,[4] three lives in one flea spare,
Where we almost, yea more than, married are.
This flea is you and I, and this
Our marriage bed, and marriage temple is;
Though parents grudge, and you, we're met
And cloistered in these living walls of jet.
  Though use[5] make you apt to kill me,
  Let not to that, self-murder added be,
  And sacrilege, three sins in killing three.

Cruel and sudden, hast thou since
Purpled thy nail in blood of innocence?
Wherein could this flea guilty be,
Except in that drop which it sucked from thee?
Yet thou triumph'st, and say'st that thou
Find'st not thyself, nor me, the weaker now;
  'Tis true; then learn how false fears be;
  Just so much honor, when thou yield'st to me,
  Will waste, as this flea's death took life from thee.

1633

• **What lines help you imagine what the speaker is doing as he speaks? what the auditor does or says?**

ANDREW MARVELL
To His Coy Mistress

  Had we but world enough, and time,
This coyness,[6] lady, were no crime.
We would sit down, and think which way

1. Medieval preachers and rhetoricians asked their hearers to "mark" (look at) an object that illustrated a moral or philosophical lesson they wished to emphasize.
2. Fed luxuriously.
3. According to the medical theory of Donne's era, conception involved the literal mingling of the lovers' blood. 4. Desist. 5. Habit. 6. Hesitancy, modesty (not necessarily suggesting calculation).

To walk, and pass our long love's day.
Thou by the Indian Ganges' side
Shouldst rubies[7] find: I by the tide
Of Humber would complain.[8] I would
Love you ten years before the Flood,
And you should if you please refuse
Till the conversion of the Jews.[9]
My vegetable love[1] should grow
Vaster than empires, and more slow;
An hundred years should go to praise
Thine eyes, and on thy forehead gaze;
Two hundred to adore each breast,
But thirty thousand to the rest.
An age at least to every part,
And the last age should show your heart.
For, lady, you deserve this state;[2]
Nor would I love at lower rate.
  But at my back I always hear
Time's wingèd chariot hurrying near;
And yonder all before us lie
Deserts of vast eternity.
Thy beauty shall no more be found,
Nor, in thy marble vault, shall sound
My echoing song; then worms shall try
That long preserved virginity,
And your quaint honor turn to dust,
And into ashes all my lust:
The grave's a fine and private place,
But none, I think, do there embrace.
  Now therefore, while the youthful hue
Sits on thy skin like morning dew,[3]
And while thy willing soul transpires[4]
At every pore with instant fires,
Now let us sport us while we may,
And now, like am'rous birds of prey,
Rather at once our time devour
Than languish in his slow-chapped[5] pow'r.
Let us roll all our strength and all
Our sweetness up into one ball,
And tear our pleasures with rough strife

7. Talismans that are supposed to preserve virginity.

8. Write love complaints, conventional songs lamenting the cruelty of love. *Humber*: a river and estuary in Marvell's hometown of Hull.

9. Which, according to popular Christian belief, will occur just before the end of the world.

1. Which is capable only of passive growth, not of consciousness. The "vegetable soul" is lower than the other two divisions of the soul, "animal" and "rational."

2. Dignity. 3. The text reads "glew." "Lew" (warmth) has also been suggested as an emendation.

4. Breathes forth.

5. Slow-jawed. Chronos (Time), ruler of the world in early Greek myth, devoured all of his children except Zeus, who was hidden. Later, Zeus seized power (see line 46 and note).

Thorough[6] the iron gates of life.
Thus, though we cannot make our sun
Stand still,[7] yet we will make him run.[8]

1681

- How does each stanza develop the speaker's argument? Is it persuasive?

SETTING

Frequently a poem's setting draws on common notions of a particular time or place. Setting a poem in a garden, for example, or writing about apples almost inevitably reminds readers of the Garden of Eden because it is an important and widely recognized part of the Western heritage. Even people who don't read at all or who lack Judeo-Christian religious commitments are likely to know about Eden, and poets writing in Western cultures can count on that knowledge. A reference to something outside the poem that carries a history of meaning and strong emotional associations is called an **allusion**. For example, gardens may carry suggestions of innocence and order, or temptation and the Fall, or both, depending on how the poem handles the allusion.

Specific, well-known places may similarly be associated with particular ideas, values, ways of life, or natural phenomena. The titles of many poems refer, like the following one, directly to specific places or times.

MATTHEW ARNOLD

Dover Beach[9]

The sea is calm tonight.
The tide is full, the moon lies fair
Upon the straits; on the French coast the light
Gleams and is gone; the cliffs of England stand,
Glimmering and vast, out in the tranquil bay.
Come to the window, sweet is the night-air!
Only, from the long line of spray
Where the sea meets the moon-blanched land,
Listen! you hear the grating roar
Of pebbles which the waves draw back, and fling,
At their return, up the high strand,
Begin, and cease, and then again begin,
With tremulous cadence slow, and bring
The eternal note of sadness in.

Sophocles long ago
Heard it on the Aegean, and it brought
Into his mind the turbid ebb and flow

6. Through. 7. To lengthen his night of love with Alcmene, Zeus made the sun stand still.
8. Each sex act was believed to shorten life by one day.
9. At the narrowest point on the English Channel. The light on the French coast (lines 3–4) would be about twenty miles away.

Of human misery,[1] we
Find also in the sound a thought,
Hearing it by this distant northern sea.

The Sea of Faith
Was once, too, at the full, and round earth's shore
Lay like the folds of a bright girdle furled.
But now I only hear
Its melancholy, long, withdrawing roar,
Retreating, to the breath
Of the night-wind, down the vast edges drear
And naked shingles[2] of the world.

Ah, love, let us be true
To one another! for the world, which seems
To lie before us like a land of dreams,
So various, so beautiful, so new,
Hath really neither joy, nor love, nor light,
Nor certitude, nor peace, nor help for pain;
And we are here as on a darkling plain
Swept with confused alarms of struggle and flight,
Where ignorant armies clash by night.

c. 1851

The situation and setting of DOVER BEACH are concrete and specific. It is night by the seashore, and the speaker is gazing at the view from a room with someone he invites to "come to the window" (line 6) and "listen" (line 9); later he says to this person, "Ah, love, let us be true / To one another!" (lines 29–30). Most readers have assumed that the speaker and his companion are about to travel from Dover across the sea to France and that the situation is a honeymoon, or at least that the couple is young and married; after all the "world [. . .] seems / To lie before us [. . .] / so new" (lines 30–32). Although this poem is not a prayer, it is a kind of plea for hope despite the modern loss of faith. The tide is now full, but the poet hears a destructive repetition of rising and falling waves (the pebbles will be worn down eventually), and he dwells on the "withdrawing" side of this pattern. For centuries, Christian belief, "the Sea of Faith" (line 21), was at high tide, but now the speaker can only "hear" it "[r]etreating" (lines 24, 26). On the one hand, then, the specifics of setting—the fact that it is night, that the speaker looks out on a stony beach lined with cliffs, and so on—seem to evoke the sense of danger, isolation, and uncertainty the speaker feels as a result of the loss of faith. On the other hand, however, might details of setting introduce hope into the poem, especially when we combine them with our knowledge of how tides ebb and flow and how the dark of night gives way to the light of morning?

THE OCCASIONAL POEM

While much of the poetry in this anthology expresses personal feelings, and while some of it is tied to the poet's autobiographical circumstances, a great deal of poetry

1. In Sophocles's *Antigone*, lines 637–46, the chorus compares the fate of the house of Oedipus to the waves of the sea. 2. Pebble-strewn beaches.

written over the centuries has focused not on individuals but on political or historical topics and themes. The setting of **epic** poetry may be as broad as a nation or even the cosmos. Poems have been written to instruct readers about religion, science, philosophy, and the art of poetry, among many other topics, with an appropriate range of settings and situations. The poet may wish to influence readers' sympathies or loyalties toward different sides in a conflict, or to record and honor a specific event such as an inauguration. A poem written about or for a specific occasion is called an **occasional poem**, and such a poem is *referential*; that is, it *refers* to a certain historical time or event.

Sometimes it is hard to place ourselves fully in another time or place in order to imagine sympathetically what a particular historical moment would have been like, and even the best poetic efforts, by themselves, do not necessarily transport us there. For such poems we need, at the least, specific historical information—plus a willingness to be transported by a name, a date, or a dramatic situation.

Here, however, is a relatively recent example: an occasional poem that works to capture the significance of a recent, public event by considering it in the historical perspective inspired by a very specific setting.

MARTÍN ESPADA

Litany at the Tomb of Frederick Douglass[3]

Mount Hope Cemetery, Rochester, New York
November 7, 2008

This is the longitude and latitude of the impossible;
this is the epicenter of the unthinkable;
this is the crossroads of the unimaginable:
the tomb of Frederick Douglass, three days after the election.
This is a world spinning away from the gravity of centuries,
where the grave of a fugitive slave has become an altar.
This is the tomb of a man born as chattel, who taught himself to read in secret,
scraping the letters in his name with chalk on wood; now on the anvil-flat stone
a campaign button fills the O in *Douglass*. The button says: *Obama*.
This is the tomb of a man in chains, who left his fingerprints
on the slavebreaker's throat so the whip would never carve his back again;
now a labor union T-shirt drapes itself across the stone, offered up
by a nurse, a janitor, a bus driver. A sticker on the sleeve says: *I Voted Today*.
This is the tomb of a man who rolled his call to arms off the press,
peering through spectacles at the abolitionist headline; now a newspaper
spreads above his dates of birth and death. The headline says: *Obama Wins*.

3. Escaped slave (1817–95) who was involved in the Underground Railroad and became a major spokesman for abolition, especially through his autobiography (1845) and his Rochester-based newspaper, the *North Star*.

This is the stillness at the heart of the storm that began in the body
of the first slave, dragged aboard the first ship to America. Yellow leaves
descend in waves, and the newspaper flutters on the tomb, like the sails
Douglass saw in the bay, like the eyes of a slave closing to watch himself
escape with the tide. Believers in spirits would see the pages trembling
on the stone and say: *look how the slave boy teaches himself to read.*
I say a prayer, the first in years: that here we bury what we call
the impossible, the unthinkable, the unimaginable, now and forever.
Amen.

2008

AUTHORS ON THEIR WORK

MARTÍN ESPADA (b. 1957)

From "Poetry Month: Martín Espada" (2011)*

While we all have our criticisms of President Obama, we must not forget the history he made in 2008, and the history we all made by voting for him and the feeling behind the making of that history. [. . .] Right after the election, I found myself in Rochester, New York. And it so happens that's where Frederick Douglass is buried, and so this is the poem that came out of it.

First, it's not an Obama poem; it's a Frederick Douglass poem. Second, it's a poem about the making of history; it's about how we felt at the moment that history was made. [. . .] We can't lose that feeling, even as we become frustrated or disillusioned. [. . .] We can't lose the way we felt at that moment [. . .].

*"Poetry Month: Martín Espada." Interview by Brian Lehrer. *The Brian Lehrer Show,* 14 Apr. 2011, WNYC, www.wnyc.org/story/124060-poetry-month-martin-espada/.

THE AUBADE

While an occasional poem focuses on a specific historical event, an **aubade** focuses on a specific time of day—morning. (*Aubade* comes from the French term for dawn.) Although morning suggests fresh beginnings and hope, an aubade often expresses sadness because the new day means that two lovers must part—time has moved on. Do you detect sadness or hopefulness in the following aubades? Do the poems help you visualize a particular day? How does place or situation affect the speaker's response to the time of day? What references to darkness or light, to sleep or waking, to other times of day do you notice in these poems?

JOHN DONNE

The Good-Morrow

I wonder, by my troth, what thou and I
Did, till we loved? were we not weaned till then?
But sucked on country pleasures, childishly?
Or snorted we in the Seven Sleepers' den?[4]
'Twas so; but[5] this, all pleasures fancies be.
If ever any beauty I did see,
Which I desired, and got,[6] twas but a dream of thee.

And now good-morrow to our waking souls,
Which watch not one another out of fear;
For love, all love of other sights controls,
And makes one little room an everywhere.
Let sea-discoverers to new worlds have gone,
Let maps to other,[7] worlds on worlds have shown,
Let us possess one world, each hath one, and is one.

My face in thine eye, thine in mine appears,[8]
And true plain hearts do in the faces rest;
Where can we find two better hemispheres,
Without sharp north, without declining west?
Whatever dies was not mixed equally,[9]
If our two loves be one, or, thou and I
Love so alike that none do slacken, none can die.

1633

- **Like so many of Donne's poems, this one attempts to persuade. What is the situation of this poem? What does the speaker wish to demonstrate?**

JONATHAN SWIFT

A Description of the Morning

Now hardly here and there a hackney-coach[1]
Appearing, showed the ruddy morn's approach.
Now Betty[2] from her master's bed had flown,
And softly stole to discompose her own.
The slip shod 'prentice from his master's door
Had pared the dirt, and sprinkled round the floor.
Now Moll had whirled her mop with dext'rous airs,
Prepared to scrub the entry and the stairs.
The youth with broomy stumps began to trace

4. According to legend, seven Christian youths escaped Roman persecution by sleeping in a cave for 187 years. *Snorted*: snored. 5. Except for. 6. Sexually possessed. 7. Other people.
8. That is, each is reflected in the other's eyes.
9. Perfectly mixed elements, according to scholastic philosophy, were stable and immortal.
1. Hired coach. *Hardly*: scarcely; that is, they are just beginning to appear.
2. Stock name for a servant girl. *Moll* (lines 7, 14) is a frequent lower-class nickname.

The kennel-edge[3] where wheels had worn the place.
The small-coal man[4] was heard with cadence deep,
Till drowned in shriller notes of chimney-sweep:
Duns[5] at his lordship's gate began to meet;
And brick-dust Moll had screamed through half the street.[6]
The turnkey now his flock returning sees,
Duly let out a-nights to steal for fees.[7]
The watchful bailiffs take their silent stands,[8]
And schoolboys lag with satchels in their hands.

1709

- **From the poem's brief descriptions of morning routines, what do we know about its various characters and the kind of community they inhabit? Could a similar poem be written today?**

ONE POEM, MULTIPLE SITUATIONS AND SETTINGS

Though many poems depict a single situation and setting, a single poem will sometimes juxtapose multiple "scenes." In such cases, we need both to determine the situation and setting particular to each scene and to consider how the poem interrelates its various scenes to create a singular effect and meaning.

The following poem describes several different scenes. Some seem to have actually occurred at particular places and times (when the main speaker was "In sixth grade," for example [line 1]). Others seem hypothetical, abstract, or generic—events that might or often do happen almost anywhere to almost anybody (like "choos[ing] / persimmons," lines 6–7). Still others seem indeterminate as to time and/or place (Did "Donna undres[s]" only once [line 18]? When?). How many different scenes of each type can you discern? What connects them to each other? For example, how might at least some of these scenes demonstrate or discuss various kinds of "precision" (lines 5, 82)? How so, and what kinds?

LI-YOUNG LEE
Persimmons

In sixth grade Mrs. Walker
slapped the back of my head
and made me stand in the corner
for not knowing the difference
between *persimmon* and *precision*.
How to choose
persimmons. This is precision.
Ripe ones are soft and brown-spotted.
Sniff the bottoms. The sweet one
will be fragrant. How to eat:

3. Edge of the gutter that ran down the middle of the street. *Trace*: To find old nails [Swift's note].
4. A seller of coal and charcoal. 5. Bill collectors.
6. Selling powdered brick that was used to clean knives.
7. Jailers collected fees from prisoners for their keep and often let them out at night so they could steal to pay expenses. 8. Looking for those on their "wanted" lists.

put the knife away, lay down newspaper.
Peel the skin tenderly, not to tear the meat.
Chew the skin, suck it,
and swallow. Now, eat
the meat of the fruit,
so sweet,
all of it, to the heart.

Donna undresses, her stomach is white.
In the yard, dewy and shivering
with crickets, we lie naked,
face-up, face-down.
I teach her Chinese.
Crickets: *chiu chiu*. Dew: I've forgotten.
Naked: I've forgotten.
Ni, wo: you and me.
I part her legs,
remember to tell her
she is beautiful as the moon.

Other words
that got me into trouble were
fight and *fright*, *wren* and *yarn*.
Fight was what I did when I was frightened,
fright was what I felt when I was fighting.
Wrens are small, plain birds,
yarn is what one knits with.
Wrens are soft as yarn.
My mother made birds out of yarn.
I loved to watch her tie the stuff;
a bird, a rabbit, a wee man.

Mrs. Walker brought a persimmon to class
and cut it up
so everyone could taste
a *Chinese apple.* Knowing
it wasn't ripe or sweet, I didn't eat
but watched the other faces.

My mother said every persimmon has a sun
inside, something golden, glowing,
warm as my face.

Once, in the cellar, I found two wrapped in newspaper,
forgotten and not yet ripe.
I took them and set both on my bedroom windowsill,
where each morning a cardinal
sang, *The sun, the sun.*
Finally understanding
he was going blind,
my father sat up all one night
waiting for a song, a ghost.

I gave him the persimmons,
swelled, heavy as sadness,
and sweet as love.

This year, in the muddy lighting
of my parents' cellar, I rummage, looking
for something I lost.
My father sits on the tired, wooden stairs,
black cane between his knees,
hand over hand, gripping the handle.

He's so happy that I've come home.
I ask how his eyes are, a stupid question.
All gone, he answers.

Under some blankets, I find a box.
Inside the box I find three scrolls.
I sit beside him and untie
three paintings by my father:
Hibiscus leaf and a white flower.
Two cats preening.
Two persimmons, so full they want to drop from the cloth.

He raises both hands to touch the cloth,
asks, *Which is this?*

This is persimmons, Father.

Oh, the feel of the wolftail on the silk,
the strength, the tense
precision in the wrist.
I painted them hundreds of times
eyes closed. These I painted blind.
Some things never leave a person:
scent of the hair of one you love,
the texture of persimmons,
in your palm, the ripe weight.

1986

WRITING ABOUT SITUATION AND SETTING: AN EXERCISE

The title of the following poem suggests that place may be important, and it is, although you may be surprised to discover exactly what exists at this address and what uses the speaker makes of it. What happens in CHERRYLOG ROAD is fairly easy to sort out, but its effect is more complex than the simple story suggests, largely because of the wealth of details the poem provides about setting. First, read the poem through once, pausing only when you come to a period and allowing your immediate personal impressions to form on their own. Then, re-read the poem, following the steps provided for analyzing and taking notes on specific elements, which will help you understand—and write about—the centrality of its setting.

JAMES DICKEY

Cherrylog Road

Off Highway 106
At Cherrylog Road I entered
The '34 Ford without wheels,
Smothered in kudzu,
With a seat pulled out to run
Corn whiskey down from the hills,

And then from the other side
Crept into an Essex
With a rumble seat of red leather
And then out again, aboard
A blue Chevrolet, releasing
The rust from its other color,

Reared up on three building blocks.
None had the same body heat;
I changed with them inward, toward
The weedy heart of the junkyard,
For I knew that Doris Holbrook
Would escape from her father at noon

And would come from the farm
To seek parts owned by the sun
Among the abandoned chassis,
Sitting in each in turn
As I did, leaning forward
As in a wild stock-car race

In the parking lot of the dead.
Time after time, I climbed in
And out the other side, like
An envoy or movie star
Met at the station by crickets.
A radiator cap raised its head,

Become a real toad or a kingsnake
As I neared the hub of the yard,
Passing through many states,
Many lives, to reach
Some grandmother's long Pierce-Arrow
Sending platters of blindness forth

From its nickel hubcaps
And spilling its tender upholstery
On sleepy roaches,
The glass panel in between
Lady and colored driver
Not all the way broken out,

The back-seat phone
Still on its hook.
I got in as though to exclaim,
"Let us go to the orphan asylum,
John; I have some old toys
For children who say their prayers."

I popped with sweat as I thought
I heard Doris Holbrook scrape
Like a mouse in the southern-state sun
That was eating the paint in blisters
From a hundred car tops and hoods.
She was tapping like code,

Loosening the screws,
Carrying off headlights,
Sparkplugs, bumpers,
Cracked mirrors and gear-knobs,
Getting ready, already,
To go back with something to show

Other than her lips' new trembling
I would hold to me soon, soon,
Where I sat in the ripped back seat
Talking over the interphone,
Praying for Doris Holbrook
To come from her father's farm

And to get back there
With no trace of me on her face
To be seen by her red-haired father
Who would change, in the squalling barn,
Her back's pale skin with a strop,
Then lay for me

In a bootlegger's roasting car
With a string-triggered 12-gauge shotgun
To blast the breath from the air.
Not cut by the jagged windshields,
Through the acres of wrecks she came
With a wrench in her hand,

Through dust where the blacksnake dies
Of boredom, and the beetle knows
The compost has no more life.
Someone outside would have seen
The oldest car's door inexplicably
Close from within:

I held her and held her and held her,
Convoyed at terrific speed
By the stalled, dreaming traffic around us,
So the blacksnake, stiff

With inaction, curved back
Into life, and hunted the mouse

With deadly overexcitement,
The beetles reclaimed their field
As we clung, glued together,
With the hooks of the seat springs
Working through to catch us red-handed
Amidst the gray breathless batting

That burst from the seat at our backs.
We left by separate doors
Into the changed, other bodies
Of cars, she down Cherrylog Road
And I to my motorcycle
Parked like the soul of the junkyard

Restored, a bicycle fleshed
With power, and tore off
Up Highway 106, continually
Drunk on the wind in my mouth,
Wringing the handlebar for speed,
Wild to be wreckage forever.

1964

Now consider your response to Dickey's poem.

1. First, answer the basic questions at the beginning of this chapter: Who is speaking? To whom is the speaker speaking? Is there an auditor in the poem? Is anyone else present or referred to in the poem?
2. Underline or list the words or lines in which setting is first indicated.
3. Underline (perhaps in a different color) or list the words or lines that gave you your first impression of the situation. What do you notice about the connection between setting and situation? Could the action occur in a different place or kind of place?
4. Similarly, list the proper or improper nouns that fill in your sense of the setting. Sort these into different kinds of entities: plants, animals, machines, real or imaginary people. Consider and compare the items you list under each category. How do they help characterize the specific spatial and temporal setting of the poem? How do they contribute to the situation of the poem?
5. Make a similar inventory of the verbs in the poem in order to understand the action step by step. Which actions are real? Which are remembered? Which are repeated? Which are imagined?
6. As your inventories show, the poem relies on **personification** (attributing human qualities to natural or inanimate things). Find lines in which insects, reptiles, or mammals interact with the parts of cars, either helping destroy them or making them come back to life. Find lines in which creatures and humans are compared.

7. Now that you have comprehended the details of the poem, try to summarize each stanza in a phrase and to place it in time and place, whether within the scene or within the twentieth century in the United States. What is the significance of "Time after time" (line 26)? Of "Passing through many states, / Many lives" (lines 33–34)? Of "the southern-state sun" (line 51)? What is implied about the region and the time period in two references to illegal alcohol: "run / Corn whiskey down from the hills" (lines 5–6) and "a bootlegger's roasting car" (line 73)? What is implied about local social rules in the scenario of the "Lady and colored driver" with her plans to donate toys to orphans (lines 40–48)? Or in the idea of the menacing father who would whip his daughter in the barn and gun down her seducer (lines 65–75)?
8. Review the action of the poem and your answers in number 1 above. Why does the speaker arrive at the junkyard first and explore the cars before Doris Holbrook arrives? Why does the poem begin with the names of two roads in the first two lines and end with Doris departing "down Cherrylog Road" in the next-to-last stanza, followed by the speaker speeding on his motorcycle "up Highway 106" in the final stanza (lines 100, 105)? What does the last line suggest not only about the speaker's desire but also about the temporal and spatial setting?

POEMS FOR FURTHER STUDY

Consider the *Who? What? Why? Where?* and *When?* questions as you read the following poems.

NATASHA TRETHEWEY
Pilgrimage

Vicksburg, Mississippi[9]

Here, the Mississippi carved
        its mud-dark path, a graveyard

for skeletons of sunken riverboats.
        Here, the river changed its course,

turning away from the city
        as one turns, forgetting, from the past—

the abandoned bluffs, land sloping up
        above the river's bend—where now

the Yazoo fills the Mississippi's empty bed.
        Here, the dead stand up in stone, white

9. On July 4, 1863, the city surrendered to Union forces under Ulysses S. Grant after a forty-day siege; coming just a day after the Confederate defeat at Gettysburg, Vicksburg's surrender is often regarded as a major turning point in the Civil War.

marble, on Confederate Avenue. I stand
    on ground once hollowed by a web of caves;

they must have seemed like catacombs,
    in 1863, to the woman sitting in her parlor,
candlelit, underground. I can see her
    listening to shells explode, writing herself

into history, asking *what is to become*
    of all the living things in this place?

This whole city is a grave. Every spring—
    Pilgrimage—the living come to mingle

with the dead, brush against their cold shoulders
    in the long hallways, listen all night

to their silence and indifference, relive
    their dying on the green battlefield.

At the museum, we marvel at their clothes—
    preserved under glass—so much smaller

than our own, as if those who wore them
    were only children. We sleep in their beds,

the old mansions hunkered on the bluffs, draped
    in flowers—funereal—a blur

of petals against the river's gray.
    The brochure in my room calls this

living history. The brass plate on the door reads
    Prissy's[1] *Room.* A window frames

the river's crawl toward the Gulf. In my dream,
    the ghost of history lies down beside me,

rolls over, pins me beneath a heavy arm.

2006

• **What different historical times and situations meet in a single place in this poem? Why and how so?**

KELLY CHERRY
Alzheimer's

He stands at the door, a crazy old man
Back from the hospital, his mind rattling
Like the suitcase, swinging from his hand,
That contains shaving cream, a piggy bank,

1. Scarlett O'Hara's maid in Margaret Mitchell's novel *Gone with the Wind* (1936).

A book he sometimes pretends to read,
His clothes. On the brick wall beside him
Roses and columbine slug it out for space, claw the mortar.
The sun is shining, as it does late in the afternoon
In England, after rain.
Sun hardens the house, reifies it,
Strikes the iron grillwork like a smithy
And sparks fly off, burning in the bushes—
The rosebushes—
While the white wood trim defines solidity in space.
This is his house. He remembers it as his,
Remembers the walkway he built between the front room
And the garage, the rhododendron he planted in back,
The car he used to drive. He remembers himself,
A younger man, in a tweed hat, a man who loved
Music. There is no time for that now. No time for music,
The peculiar screeching of strings, the luxurious
Fiddling with emotion.
Other things have become more urgent.
Other matters are now of greater import, have more
Consequence, must be attended to. The first
Thing he must do, now that he is home, is decide who
This woman is, this old, white-haired woman
Standing here in the doorway,
Welcoming him in.

1997

- **How do phrases like "a crazy old man" and "a book he sometimes pretends to read" indicate the speaker's feelings toward the man she describes (lines 1, 5)? Does the tone shift at some point? Where? What might the poem encourage you to speculate about the speaker's relationship to the people described? about their relationship to each other?**

MAHMOUD DARWISH
Identity Card[2]

Write down:
I am Arab
my I.D. number, 50,000
my children, eight
and the ninth due next summer
—Does that anger you?

2. Translated by John Mikhail Asfour. Israeli law requires all citizens sixteen and over to carry a government-issued identity card at all times, to be presented on demand to authorized police, military, or government officials. Until 2005, the cards indicated the bearer's ethnic group (Arab, Jew, etc.).

Write down:
Arab.
I work with my struggling friends in a quarry
and my children are eight.
I chip a loaf of bread for them,
clothes and notebooks
from the rocks.
I will not beg for a handout at your door
nor humble myself
on your threshold
—Does that anger you?

Write down:
Arab,
a name with no friendly diminutive.
A patient man, in a country
brimming with anger.
My roots have gripped this soil
since time began,
before the opening of ages
before the cypress and the olive,
before the grasses flourished.
My father came from a line of plowmen,
and my grandfather was a peasant
who taught me about the sun's glory
before teaching me to read.
My home is a watchman's shack
made of reeds and sticks
—Does my condition anger you?

There is no gentle name,
write down:
Arab.
The color of my hair, jet black—
eyes, brown—
trademarks,
a headband over a *keffiyeh*[3]
and a hand whose touch grates
rough as a rock.
My address is a weaponless village
with nameless streets.
All its men are in the field and quarry
—Does that anger you?

Write down, then
at the top of Page One:
I do not hate
and do not steal
but starve me, and I will eat

3. Traditional male headdress consisting of a square of cloth secured by a cord.

my assailant's flesh.
Beware of my hunger
and of my anger.

1964

- **Based on the speaker's words and the poem's title, to whom and in what situation and setting do you imagine him speaking?**

YEHUDA AMICHAI

[On Yom Kippur in 1967 . . .][4]

On Yom Kippur in 1967, the Year of Forgetting,[5] I put on
my dark holiday clothes and walked to the Old City of Jerusalem.
For a long time I stood in front of an Arab's hole-in-the-wall shop,
not far from the Damascus Gate,[6] a shop with
buttons and zippers and spools of thread
in every color and snaps and buckles.
A rare light and many colors, like an open Ark.

I told him in my heart that my father too
had a shop like this, with thread and buttons.
I explained to him in my heart about all the decades
and the causes and the events, why I am now here
and my father's shop was burned there and he is buried here.[7]

When I finished, it was time for the Closing of the Gates prayer.
He too lowered the shutters and locked the gate
and I returned, with all the worshipers, home.

1968

- **Why and how is it important that the poem is set on Yom Kippur? that it ends with the word "home"?**

4. From the sequence "Jerusalem, 1967." Translated by Stephen Mitchell. *Yom Kippur*: the Day of Atonement, culmination of the High Holy Days, during which Jews seek forgiveness for wrongs committed against God and other people; usually falls in September or October.

5. In the so-called Six Day War of June 1967, Israel waged a highly successful campaign against Syria, Jordan, and Egypt, capturing the mainly Arab-occupied West Bank, along with the Sinai and Golan Heights. According to the translator, "the date 1967 (-5728) is expressed in the same Hebrew letters that also form the word for 'forget.'"

6. One of the main entrances to the Old City of Jerusalem, so called because it leads to a highway once stretching all the way to Syria's capital, Damascus.

7. Amichai's father was a prosperous German merchant who moved his family to what was then Palestine in 1936, three years after Adolf Hitler's appointment as Germany's chancellor, three years before the start of World War II, and twelve years before the state of Israel was founded.

YUSEF KOMUNYAKAA

Tu Do Street[8]

Searching for love, a woman,
someone to help ease down the cocked hammer
of my nerves & senses. The music
divides the evening into black
& white—soul, country & western,
acid rock, & Frank Sinatra.
I close my eyes & can see
men drawing lines in the dust,
daring each other to step across.
America pushes through the membrane
of mist & smoke, & I'm a small boy
again in Bogalusa[9] skirting tough talk
coming out of bars with *White Only*
signs & Hank Snow.[1] But tonight,
here in Saigon, just for the hell of it,
I walk into a place with Hank Williams[2]
calling from the jukebox. The bar girls
fade behind a smokescreen, fluttering
like tropical birds in a cage, not
speaking with their eyes & usual
painted smiles. I get the silent
treatment. We have played Judas
for each other out in the boonies
but only enemy machinegun fire
can bring us together again.
When I order a beer, the mama-san[3]
behind the counter acts as if she
can't understand, while her
eyes caress a white face;
down the street the black GIs
hold to their turf also.
An off-limits sign pulls me
deeper into alleys; I look
for a softness behind these voices
wounded by their beauty & war.
Back in the bush at Dak To
& Khe Sahn, we fought

8. Literally, "Liberty Street" (Vietnamese), famous thoroughfare in the French quarter of Saigon, Vietnam; so named only during the war between North and South Vietnam (1955–75).

9. Industrial city in southeastern Louisiana.

1. Renowned Canadian-born country singer (1914–99).

2. Famous troubled country music singer-songwriter (1923–53) whose many hits include "I'm So Lonesome I Could Cry."

3. In East Asia, a woman in authority; in Japanese, *san* is an honorific suffix, a title (not unlike "Mrs.") added to names and proper nouns to indicate respect.

the brothers of these women
we now run to hold in our arms.
There's more than a nation divided
inside us, as black & white
soldiers touch the same lovers
minutes apart, tasting
each other's breath,
without knowing these rooms
run into each other like tunnels
leading to the underworld.

1988

- **Why does the speaker seem to receive the reception he does in the first Tu Do Street bar he enters? How does he compare the way white and black American soldiers and Vietnamese women interact in this situation and setting and in others—in Bogalusa, Louisiana (lines 11–14) or "in the boonies" and "the bush at Dak To / & Khe Sahn" (lines 22–25, 36–39), for example? What does he seem to discover or conclude?**

AUTHORS ON THEIR WORK

YUSEF KOMUNYAKAA (b. 1947)

From "The Body Is Our First Music: Interview with Tony Barnstone and Michael Garabedian" (1998)*

BARNSTONE: [. . .] I'm interested where the female resides in your wartime imagination, and where does sex and motherhood and generation come into this activity in which, for the most part, men kill men?

KOMUYAKAA: Well . . . on the boundary, on the periphery, of every war, there seems to be the spoils of war alongside an industry of sex. But it's more than that, because often there's a kind of cleansing going on as well. People are getting killed, and people are being born on the periphery. This has always been the case [. . .]. Because the same men who are killing, the next day are loving. And often risking their hearts. So there is all this contradiction in their personality and perception. And I suppose we need that kind of complexity in order to make ourselves whole [. . .]. (118–19)

• • •

From "Still Negotiating with the Images: An Interview with William Baer" (1998)**

[INTERVIEWER:] No poem shows the interrelatedness of human beings in wartime more effectively than "Tu Do Street" [. . .] Th[e end of the poem offers] an amazing image of our connected humanity, but is the connection with "the underworld" just a harsh reminder of death that should stir us to behave with more kindness, or is it a pessimistic reflection of the human propensity to divide and destroy ourselves?

[KOMUYAKAA:] It was one of those endings that, once I'd written down, just stopped where it was. There were many symbolic underworlds in Vietnam, the underground tunnel systems, some of the bars, and the whole psychic space of the GI—a kind of underworld populated by ghosts and indefinable images. It was a place of emotional and psychological flux where one was trying to make sense out of the world and one's place in that world. And there was, relentlessly, a going back and forth between that internal space and external world. It was an effort to deal with oneself, and with the other GIs, the Vietnamese, and even the ghosts that we'd managed to create ourselves. So, for me, this is a very complex picture of the situation of the GI—going back and forth, condemned in a way to trek back and forth begtween those emotional demarcations while trying to make sense out of things. (95)

*"The Body Is Our First Music." Interview by Tony Barnstone and Michael Garabedian. *Blue Notes: Essays, Interviews, and Commentaries.* Edited by Radiclani Clytus, U of Michigan P, 2000, pp. 107–25. Originally published in *Poetry Flash*, no. 227, June–July 1998.

**"Still Negotiating with the Images." Interview by William Baer. *Blue Notes: Essays, Interviews, and Commentaries.* Edited by Radiclani Clytus, U of Michigan P, 2000, pp. 93–106. Originally published in *The Kenyon Review*, Fall 1998.

SUGGESTIONS FOR WRITING

1. Matthew Arnold's DOVER BEACH and Natasha Trethewey's PILGRIMAGE are meditations on history and human destiny derived from the poets' close observation of particular places and times. Write an essay in which you examine one poem's descriptive language and the way it creates a suitable setting for the speaker's philosophical musings.
2. Write an essay either comparing the two carpe diem poems in this chapter or comparing one of these poems to Donne's THE GOOD-MORROW. If you choose the former option, concentrate on how each poem differently handles the same basic situation: How does each speaker go about convincing his auditor to "seize the day"? If you choose the latter option, explore how Donne's poem might work as a sort of sequel to the carpe diem poem: In what ways are the two poems alike, and what difference do their different situations make?
3. Martín Espada claims that his occasional poem is about Frederick Douglass rather than President Obama. Write an essay exploring whether and why that seems to be the case. Why, according to the poem, was the election of Obama both an especially good occasion for remembering Douglass and itself an occasion worth commemorating in a poem? What and whom exactly are commemorated here? Alternatively, compare Espada's poem to Natasha Trethewey's. What might each poem suggest about history and memory, time and place?
4. Kelly Cherry's ALZHEIMER'S uses contrasts—especially before and after—to characterize the ravages of Alzheimer's disease. What evidence does the poem provide about what the man used to be like? What specific changes have come about? How does the setting of the poem suggest some of those changes? In what ways do the stabilities of house, landscape, and other people clarify what has happened? Write an essay about the function of the poem's setting.
5. Choose any poem in this anthology in which you think setting is especially key to the poem's effect and meaning or in which you think the meaningfulness of setting

depends on the associations of particular times and/or places. Write an essay explaining why and how so.

6. Write your own DESCRIPTION OF THE MORNING—or of the afternoon, evening, or night, or of a particular time of the year. Whether you produce a poem or a prose sketch, try to capture, as Swift does, the feeling of this time as it is or might be experienced in a specific place.

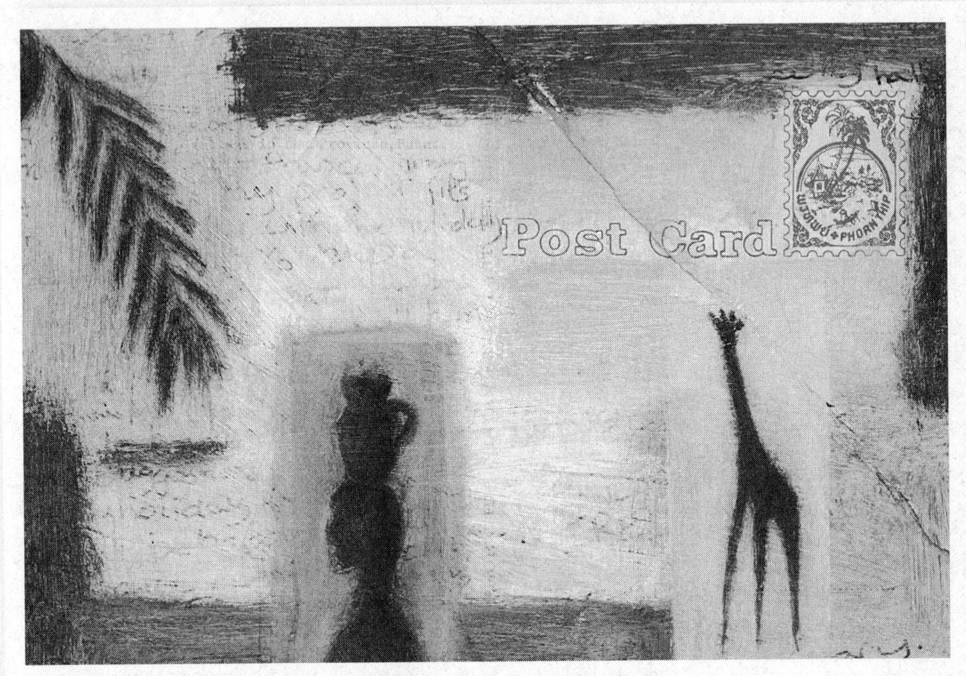

Rosemary Woods, *Africa Collage*

Homelands

AN ALBUM

One of the most ancient literary topics is the quest or journey away from home. Sacred literature, including the Bible, tells of exile and a long period of suffering before returning to or reaching a homeland. **Epics** and **romances** may concern the hero's wanderings or adventures to reach or to defend a realm closely associated with his birth, inheritance, or fate. Since the 1500s, global exploration, colonialism, slavery, mass migration, and economic transformation have meant that many of the world's populations have experienced dislocation and deracination (loss of roots). Those who find themselves displaced try to remember where they came from; they may seek to honor their heritage or yearn for a sense of belonging. The poems in this album were written at different times in different places and cultural contexts. Each speaker suggests some kind of double vision on the past and present, on a more modern or recent location and the former place. What is the role of dislocation or altered identity in these poems? How do these poems represent the speaker's divided loyalties or distance from home? How do they indicate the passage of time, whether in history, over generations, or within one person's life?

MAYA ANGELOU
Africa

Thus she had lain
sugar cane sweet
deserts her hair
golden her feet
mountains her breasts
two Niles her tears.
Thus she has lain
Black through the years.

Over the white seas
rime white and cold
brigands ungentled
icicle bold
took her young daughters
sold her strong sons
churched her with Jesus
bled her with guns.
Thus she has lain.

Now she is rising
remember her pain

remember the losses
her screams loud and vain
remember her riches
her history slain
now she is striding
although she had lain.

1975

- **What is the effect of the way the phrases describing Africa's action—"had lain," "is rising," and so forth—repeat with variations throughout the poem?**

AUTHORS ON THEIR WORK
MAYA ANGELOU (1928–2014)

From "Maya Angelou, The Art of Fiction No. 119" (1990)*

I never agreed, even as a young person, with the Thomas Wolfe title *You Can't Go Home Again.* Instinctively I didn't. But the truth is, you can never *leave* home. You take it with you; it's under your fingernails; it's in the hair follicles; it's in the way you smile; it's in the ride of your hips, in the passage of your breasts; it's all there, no matter where you go. You can take on the affectations and the postures of other places and even learn to speak their ways. But the truth is, home is between your teeth. Everybody's always looking for it: Jews go to Israel; black Americans and Africans in the Diaspora go to Africa; Europeans, Anglo-Saxons go to England and Ireland; people of Germanic background go to Germany. It's a very queer quest. We can kid ourselves; we can tell ourselves, Oh yes, honey, I live in Tel Aviv, actually. . . . The truth is a stubborn fact.

*"Maya Angelou, The Art of Fiction No. 119." Interview by George Plimpton. *The Paris Review*, no. 116, Fall 1990, www.theparisreview.org/interviews/2279/the-art-of-fiction-no-119-maya-angelou.

DEREK WALCOTT
A Far Cry from Africa

A wind is ruffling the tawny pelt
Of Africa. Kikuyu,[1] quick as flies,
Batten upon the bloodstreams of the veldt.[2]
Corpses are scattered through a paradise.
Only the worm, colonel of carrion, cries:

1. East African tribe whose members, as Mau Mau fighters, conducted an eight-year insurrection against British colonial settlers in Kenya.
2. Open plains, neither cultivated nor thickly forested (Afrikaans).

"Waste no compassion on these separate dead!"
Statistics justify and scholars seize
The salients of colonial policy.
What is that to the white child hacked in bed?
To savages, expendable as Jews?

Threshed out by beaters,[3] the long rushes break
In a white dust of ibises whose cries
Have wheeled since civilization's dawn
From the parched river or beast-teeming plain.
The violence of beast on beast is read
As natural law, but upright man
Seeks his divinity by inflicting pain.
Delirious as these worried beasts, his wars
Dance to the tightened carcass of a drum,
While he calls courage still that native dread
Of the white peace contracted by the dead.

Again brutish necessity wipes its hands
Upon the napkin of a dirty cause, again
A waste of our compassion, as with Spain,[4]
The gorilla wrestles with the superman.
I who am poisoned with the blood of both,
Where shall I turn, divided to the vein?
I who have cursed
The drunken officer of British rule, how choose
Between this Africa and the English tongue I love?
Betray them both, or give back what they give?
How can I face such slaughter and be cool?
How can I turn from Africa and live?

1962

- **How does the speaker express his divided loyalties in the questions that conclude the poem? What various meanings might the poem's title accrue by the end?**

3. In big-game hunting, natives are hired to beat the brush, driving birds—such as ibises—and other animals into the open.
4. Spanish Civil War (1936–39), in which the Republican loyalists were supported politically by liberals in the West and militarily by Soviet Communists, and the Nationalist rebels by Nazi Germany and Fascist Italy.

AUTHORS ON THEIR WORK

DEREK WALCOTT (b. 1930)

From "An Interview with Derek Walcott" (1979)*

[QUESTION:] Do you want to talk about the Caribbean writer's special relationship to Africa?

[ANSWER: . . .] I have been British; I have been a citizen of the Caribbean federation; now I'm supposed to be either a Trinidadian or a St. Lucian but with a British passport. I find that I am able to make a living in America (and I owe America a great deal for its recognition and the fact that I can work here); and there is the same danger, the same seduction in saying I really am African and should be in Africa, or that my whole experience is African. This can be simply another longing, even a slave longing, for another master. There is no West Indian who is black, or even one who is not black, who is not aware of the existence of Africa in all of us. [. . .] The fact is that every West Indian has been severed from a continent, whether he be Indian, Chinese, Portuguese, or black. To have the population induced into a mass nostalgia to be somewhere else seemed to me about as ennobling as wishing that the whole population was in Brooklyn, or Brickston. [. . .] It would be equally abhorrent to me to say "I wish we were English again" as to say "I wish we were African again." The reality is that one has to build in the West Indies. But that is not to say one doesn't know who one is: our music, our speech—all the things that are organic in the way we live—are African.

• • •

I [. . .] felt that it was a privilege to grow up as an English colonial child [in the West Indies] because politically and culturally the British heritage was supposed to be mine. It was no problem for me to feel that since I was writing in English, I was in tune with the growth of the language. I was the contemporary of anyone writing in English anywhere in the world. What is more important, however—and I'm still working on this—was to find a voice that was not inflected by influences. One didn't develop an English accent in speech; one kept as close as possible to an inflection that was West Indian. The aim was that a West Indian or an Englishman could read a single poem, each with his own accent, without either one feeling that it was written in dialect.

*"An Interview with Derek Walcott." Interview by Edward Hirsch. *Contemporary Literature*, vol. 20, no. 3, Summer 1979, pp. 279–92.

JUDITH ORTIZ COFER
The Latin Deli: An Ars Poetica[5]

Presiding over a formica counter,
plastic Mother and Child magnetized
to the top of an ancient register,
the heady mix of smells from the open bins
of dried codfish, the green plantains
hanging in stalks like votive offerings,
she is the Patroness of Exiles,
a woman of no-age who was never pretty,
who spends her days selling canned memories
while listening to the Puerto Ricans complain
that it would be cheaper to fly to San Juan
than to buy a pound of Bustelo coffee here,
and to Cubans perfecting their speech
of a "glorious return" to Havana—where no one
has been allowed to die and nothing to change until then;
to Mexicans who pass through, talking lyrically
of *dólares* to be made in El Norte[6]—
all wanting the comfort
of spoken Spanish, to gaze upon the family portrait
of her plain wide face, her ample bosom
resting on her plump arms, her look of maternal interest
as they speak to her and each other
of their dreams and their disillusions—
how she smiles understanding,
when they walk down the narrow aisles of her store
reading the labels of packages aloud, as if
they were the names of lost lovers: *Suspiros,*[7]
Merengues, the stale candy of everyone's childhood.
She spends her days
slicing *jamón y queso*[8] and wrapping it in wax paper
tied with string: plain ham and cheese
that would cost less at the A&P,[9] but it would not satisfy
the hunger of the fragile old man lost in the folds
of his winter coat, who brings her lists of items
that he reads to her like poetry, or the others,
whose needs she must divine, conjuring up products
from places that now exist only in their hearts—
closed ports she must trade with.

1993

5. Art of Poetry (Latin), after the title of a treatise by the Roman Poet Horace (65–8 BCE).
6. The North (referring to the United States). *Dólares*: Dollars (Spanish).
7. Sighs (Spanish); like *Merengues*, a type of candy.
8. Ham and cheese (Spanish).
9. Great Atlantic and Pacific Tea Company, a major grocery store chain founded in 1869.

- **What keeps people shopping at the Latin Deli (versus a chain store)? How is this poem an "ars poetica," or what might it say about "the art of poetry" as practiced by a Mexican American poet like Cofer?**

CATHY SONG

Heaven

He thinks when we die we'll go to China.
Think of it—a Chinese heaven
where, except for his blond hair,
the part that belongs to his father,
everyone will look like him.
China, that blue flower on the map,
bluer than the sea
his hand must span like a bridge
to reach it.
An octave away.

I've never seen it.
It's as if I can't sing that far.
But look—
on the map, this black dot.
Here is where we live,
on the pancake plains
just east of the Rockies,
on the other side of the clouds.
A mile above the sea,
the air is so thin, you can starve on it.
No bamboo trees
But the alpine equivalent,
reedy aspen with light, fluttering leaves.
Did a boy in Guangzhou[1] dream of this
as his last stop?
I've heard the trains at night
whistling past our yards,
what we've come to own,
the broken fences, the whiny dog, the rattletrap cars.
It's still the wild west,
mean and grubby,
the shootouts and fistfights in the back alley.
With my son the dreamer
and my daughter, who is too young to walk,
I've sat in this spot
and wondered why here?
Why in this short life,
this town, this creek they call a river?

He had never planned to stay,
the boy who helped to build

1. Usually called Canton, a seaport city in southeastern China.

the railroads for a dollar a day.
He had always meant to go back.
When did he finally know
that each mile of track led him further away,
that he would die in his sleep,
dispossessed,
having seen Gold Mountain,
the icy wind tunneling through it,
these landlocked, makeshift ghost towns?

It must be in the blood,
this notion of returning.
It skipped two generations, lay fallow,
the garden an unmarked grave.
On a spring sweater day
it's as if we remember him.
I call to the children.
We can see the mountains
shimmering blue above the air.
If you look really hard
says my son the dreamer,
leaning out from the laundry's rigging,
the work shirts fluttering like sails,
you can see all the way to heaven.

1988

- **Who is "He" in this poem's first line? What family history is recounted in the poem? How does the poem make use of contrast?**

AGHA SHAHID ALI
Postcard from Kashmir

(for Pavan Sahgal)

Kashmir shrinks into my mailbox,
my home a neat four by six inches.

I always loved neatness. Now I hold
the half-inch Himalayas in my hand.
This is home. And this the closest
I'll ever be to home. When I return,
the colors won't be so brilliant,
the Jhelum's waters[2] so clean,
so ultramarine. My love
so overexposed.

And my memory will be a little
out of focus, in it

2. The river Jhelum runs through Kashmir and Pakistan.

a giant negative, black
and white, still undeveloped.

1987

- **What words characterize the speaker's dreams of home in this poem? What words reveal a more realistic attitude?**

ADRIENNE SU

Escape from the Old Country

I never had to make one,
no sickening weeks by ocean,

no waiting for the aerogrammes[3]
that gradually ceased to come.

Spent the babysitting money
on novels, shoes, and movies,

yet the neighborhood stayed empty.
It had nothing to do with a journey

not undertaken, nor with dialect,
nor with a land that waited

to be rediscovered, then rejected.
As acid rain collected

above the suburban hills, I tried
to imagine being nothing, tried

to be able to claim, "I have
no culture," and be believed.

Yet the land occupies the person
even as the semblance of freedom

invites a kind of recklessness.
Tradition, unobserved, unasked,

hangs on tight; ancestors roam
into reverie, interfering at the most

awkward moments, first flirtations,
in doorways and dressing rooms—

But of course. Here in America,
no one escapes. In the end, each traveler

returns to the town where, everyone
knew, she hadn't even been born.

2006

- **In the context of the rest of the poem, what are the various possible meanings of the sentence "Here in America, / no one escapes" (lines 25–26)?**

3. Airmail letter, especially one on specially designed stationery.

SUGGESTIONS FOR WRITING

1. Write a response paper or essay exploring how Africa is characterized in at least one or two poems in this album.
2. Multiple poems in this album explore the way we tend to idealize the place we have left. Write an essay comparing what at least two poems suggest about how and why we do so. Which, if any, poems seem to see such idealization as a problem? Why and how so?
3. Look closely at the three stanzas of A FAR CRY FROM AFRICA by Derek Walcott. Be sure to note any changes—rhyme patterns or meter, subject matter or attitude—across the three stanzas. Where does the speaker clarify who he is and where his loyalties lie? Why is the last part of the poem a series of questions? Write an essay in which you interpret the form and theme of the poem as itself a kind of "far cry from Africa," in every sense: far from that homeland, part of a non-African tradition, "crying" for connection.
4. Imagine receiving in your mailbox a postcard from the place where you or your parents were born. (Alternatively, imagine receiving digital pictures or messages in other formats.) Write a poem or a short prose description in which you express a response similar to the speaker's in Agha Shahid Ali's POSTCARD FROM KASHMIR: How would the place be changed if you could visit, and how would it differ from the way you or your family think about it now?

14 THEME AND TONE

Poetry is full of surprises. Poems express anger or outrage just as effectively as love or sadness, and good poems can be written about going to a rock concert or having lunch or mowing the lawn, as well as about making love or smelling flowers or listening to Beethoven. Even poems on "predictable" subjects can surprise us with unpredicted attitudes or sudden twists. Knowing that a poem is about some particular subject or topic—love, for example, or death—may give us a general idea of what to expect, but it never tells us altogether what we will find in a particular poem. Labeling a poem a "love poem" or a "death poem" is a convenient way to speak of its topic. But poems that may be loosely called "love poems" or "death poems" may have little else in common, may express utterly different attitudes or ideas, and may concentrate on very different aspects of the subject. Letting a poem speak to us means more than merely figuring out its topic; it means listening to *how* the poem says what it says. *What* a poem says involves its **theme**. *How* a poem makes that statement involves its **tone**—the poem's attitude or feelings toward its topic. No two poems on the same subject affect us in exactly the same way; their themes and tones vary, and even similar themes may be expressed in various ways, creating different tones and effects.

TONE

Tone, a term borrowed from acoustics and music, refers to the qualities of the language a speaker uses in social situations or in a poem, and it also refers to a speaker's intended effect. Tone is closely related to style and diction; it is an effect of the speaker's expressions, *as if* showing a real person's feelings, manner, and attitude or relationship to a listener and to the particular subject or situation. Thus, the speaker may use angry or mocking words, may address the listener intimately or distantly, may sincerely confess or coolly observe, may paint a grand picture or narrate a legend.

The following poem describes a romantic encounter of sorts, but its tone may surprise you. As you read the poem, work first to identify its **speaker**, **situation**, and **setting**. Then try both to capture its tone in a single word or two and to figure out which features of the poem help to create that tone.

W. D. SNODGRASS

Leaving the Motel

Outside, the last kids holler
Near the pool: they'll stay the night.
Pick up the towels; fold your collar
Out of sight.

Check: is the second bed
Unrumpled, as agreed?
Landlords have to think ahead
In case of need,

Too. Keep things straight: don't take
The matches, the wrong keyrings—
We've nowhere we could keep a keepsake—
Ashtrays, combs, things

That sooner or later others
Would accidentally find.
Check: take nothing of one another's
And leave behind

Your license number only,
Which they won't care to trace;
We've paid. Still, should such things get lonely,
Leave in their vase

An aspirin to preserve
Our lilacs, the wayside flowers
We've gathered and must leave to serve
A few more hours;

That's all. We can't tell when
We'll come back, can't press claims,
We would no doubt have other rooms then,
Or other names.

1968

The title and details of LEAVING THE MOTEL indicate the situation and setting: Two secret lovers are at the end of an afternoon sexual encounter in a motel room (perhaps one is speaking for both of them), reminding themselves not to leave or take with them any clues for "others" (line 13)—their spouses?—to find.

Whereas many poems on the topic of love confirm an enduring attachment or express desire or suggest erotic experience, this poem focuses on the effort to erase a stolen encounter. The two lovers have no names; indeed, they have registered under false names. They have already paid for this temporary shelter, can't stay the night like other guests or build a home with children of their own, and are running through a checklist of their agreements and duties ("Check," "Keep things straight," "Check" [lines 5, 9, 15]). Other than the "wayside" lilacs (line 22), the objects mentioned are trivial, from matches and keyrings to license numbers. The matter-of-fact but hurried tone suggests that they wish to hide any deep feelings (hinted at in the last two stanzas in the wish to make "claims" or preserve flowers [line 26]). The failure to express love—or guilt—enhances the effect when the tone shifts, at the word "still" (line 19), to the second thoughts about leaving something behind. The poem's short rhyming lines, sounding brisk and somewhat impersonal, contrast with the situation and add to the tone of subdued regret that nothing lasts.

THEME

Our response to the tone of a poem, however it surprises or jars or stirs us, guides us to understand its theme (or themes): what the poem expresses about its topic. A theme is not simply a work's subject or its topic; it is a statement *about* that topic. Although we can usually agree on what a poem is about without much difficulty, it is harder to determine how to state a poem's theme. Not only may a theme be expressed in several different ways, but a single poem may also have more than one theme. Sometimes the poet explicitly states a poem's theme, and such a statement may clarify why the author chose a particular mode of presentation and how the poem fits into the author's own patterns of thinking and growing. However, the author's words may give a misleading view of how most people read the poem, just as a person's self-assessment may not be all we need in order to understand his or her character. Further study of the poem is necessary to understand how it fulfills—or fails to fulfill—the author's intentions. Despite the difficulty of identifying and expressing themes, doing so is an important step in understanding and writing about poetry.

Topic versus Tone and Theme: A Comparative Exercise

Reading two or more poems with similar topics side by side may suggest how each is distinctive in what it has to say and how it does so—its theme and tone. The following two poems are about animals, although both of them place their final emphasis on human beings: The animal in each case is only the means to the end of exploring human nature. The poems share the assumption that animal behavior may appear to reflect human habits and conduct, and that it may reveal much about us; in each case the character central to the poem is revealed to be surprisingly unlike the way she thinks of herself. But the poems differ in their tones, in the specific relationship between the woman and the animals, and in their themes.

How would you describe the tone of the following poem? its topic and theme?

MAXINE KUMIN

Woodchucks

Gassing the woodchucks didn't turn out right.
The knockout bomb from the Feed and Grain Exchange
was featured as merciful, quick at the bone

and the case we had against them was airtight,
both exits shoehorned shut with puddingstone,[1]
but they had a sub-sub-basement out of range.

Next morning they turned up again, no worse
for the cyanide than we for our cigarettes
and state-store Scotch, all of us up to scratch.
They brought down the marigolds as a matter of course
and then took over the vegetable patch
nipping the broccoli shoots, beheading the carrots.

The food from our mouths, I said, righteously thrilling
to the feel of the .22, the bullets' neat noses.
I, a lapsed pacifist fallen from grace
puffed with Darwinian pieties for killing,
now drew a bead on the littlest woodchuck's face.
He died down in the everbearing roses.

Ten minutes later I dropped the mother. She
flipflopped in the air and fell, her needle teeth
still hooked in a leaf of early Swiss chard.
Another baby next. O one-two-three
the murderer inside me rose up hard,
the hawkeye killer came on stage forthwith.

There's one chuck left. Old wily fellow, he keeps
me cocked and ready day after day after day.
All night I hunt his humped-up form. I dream
I sight along the barrel in my sleep.
If only they'd all consented to die unseen
gassed underground the quiet Nazi way.

1972

As you read WOODCHUCKS aloud, how does your tone of voice change from beginning to end? What tone do you use to read the ending? How does the hunter feel about her increasing attraction to violence? Why does the poem begin by calling the gassing of the woodchucks "merciful" (line 3) and end by describing it as "the quiet Nazi way" (line 30)? What names does the hunter call herself? How does the name-calling affect your feelings about her? Exactly when does the hunter begin to *enjoy* the feel of the gun and the idea of killing? How does the poet make that clear?

ADRIENNE RICH
Aunt Jennifer's Tigers

Aunt Jennifer's tigers prance across a screen,
Bright topaz denizens of a world of green.

1. Mixture of cement, pebbles, and gravel.

(continued on next page)

(*continued*)

They do not fear the men beneath the tree;
They pace in sleek chivalric certainty.

Aunt Jennifer's fingers fluttering through her wool
Find even the ivory needle hard to pull.
The massive weight of Uncle's wedding band
Sits heavily upon Aunt Jennifer's hand.

When Aunt is dead, her terrified hands will lie
Still ringed with ordeals she was mastered by.
The tigers in the panel that she made
Will go on prancing, proud and unafraid.

1951

In this poem, why are tigers a particularly appropriate contrast to the woman embroidering or cross-stitching a hunting scene? What words describing the tigers seem particularly significant? Why are Aunt Jennifer's hands described as "terrified" (line 9)? What clues does the poem give about why Aunt Jennifer is so afraid? How does the poem make you feel about Aunt Jennifer's life and death? How would you describe the tone of the poem? Why does the poem begin and end with the tigers?

AUTHORS ON THEIR WORK

ADRIENNE RICH (1929–2012)

From "When We Dead Awaken: Writing as Re-Vision" (1971)*

In writing this poem, composed and apparently cool as it is, I thought I was creating a portrait of an imaginary woman. But this woman suffers from the opposition of her imagination, worked out in tapestry, and her lifestyle, "ringed with ordeals she was mastered by." It was important to me that Aunt Jennifer was a person as distinct from myself as possible—distanced by the formalism of the poem, by its objective, observant tone—even by putting the woman in a different generation.

*"When We Dead Awaken: Writing as Re-Vision." Women's Forum of the MLA, Dec. 1971, Chicago. Address.

Questions for Comparing Poems

Here are some questions and steps for identifying, interpreting, and comparing the topic, theme, and tone of more than one poem. Some of these steps will be familiar to you already, and you may discover other ways to illuminate poetic themes and tones in addition to the guidelines offered here.

As you respond to these questions or prompts, be sure to note line numbers to cite your evidence, according to this format: "puddingstone" (line 5) or "her terrified hands will lie / Still ringed with ordeals" (lines 9–10).

1. Read each poem through slowly and carefully.
2. Compare the titles. How do the titles point to the topics and possible themes, and are these similar or different? Take WOODCHUCKS and AUNT JENNIFER'S TIGERS, for example. What different qualities do we associate with woodchucks or tigers, animals rarely kept as pets?
3. What is the situation and setting in each poem? Make a list of the words in each poem that name objects or indicate actions. Which things or scenes are most significant, and how would you visualize or imagine them? Compare your notes on situation, setting, objects, and actions in both poems.
4. Who are the speakers? Are there other people in the poems? Is anyone identified as a listener or auditor? Are any things or beings (such as animals) personified or given human traits? Compare the speakers and other personalities in the poems.
5. What happens in each poem? Look closely at each stanza. Could the stanzas or lines be rearranged without making a difference? Does one poem tell of a single event or short passage of time, whereas another describes repeated actions or longer periods? Is one poem more eventful than the other?
6. Write down four or five words that describe the tone of each poem. Do these words also describe the language or style of each poem? Can you use all or some of the same words for both poems?
7. What is different about the two styles and forms, including length? Notice the rhythms and sounds, any regular or irregular patterns of **meter** or **rhyme**, and the shape of the stanzas.
8. Re-read the poems and try to express their themes in complete sentences. Then try to combine the two themes in a single statement that notes similarities and differences between them. Does your statement comparing the themes resemble your comparison of the tone and style of the two poems? Do the themes relate to similar or different historical, political, and social issues or contexts featured in the poems? Do the poems develop their themes with comparable **allusions** to myth, religion, literature, art, or other familiar or traditional ideas or associations?
9. Drawing on your notes and responses to the other questions, outline and write an essay comparing the two poems.

THEME AND CONFLICT

Since a theme is an idea implied by all of the elements of the poem working together, identifying theme—as opposed to topic and tone—can sometimes be a tough and tricky business. In reading and writing about poetry, then, it often helps to focus first—and most—on conflict. Though we usually think of conflict as an aspect of plot, even perfectly plotless poems are almost always organized around and devoted to exploring conflicts and tensions. To begin to identify these, look for contrasts and think about the conflict they imply.

Take, for example, AUNT JENNIFER'S TIGERS. Though it might be hard to say at first just what the theme of Rich's poem might be, it's hard to miss the contrast that it builds and is built around. Where the tigers Aunt Jennifer embroiders "prance" and "pace" freely, "proud and unafraid" through a world as colorful and as lasting as they are (lines 1, 4, 12), Aunt Jennifer and her world seem just the opposite: Nothing but her fingers and hands move at all in the poem, and even they are "terrified" and tentative, "fluttering through her wool," "weight[ed]" down by a heavy "wedding band" in life and stilled permanently by death (lines 9, 5, 7). We have, then, not just a contrast but a multifaceted conflict—between imaginary and real worlds, between individual vision and social obligation. What the poem concludes about this conflict is its theme, but starting with questions about conflict often provides not only an easier way into the poem but also a much richer, more textured experience and understanding of it.

The following poem is in fact all about just this issue—the role of conflict in poetry. As you read the poem, try to identify the contrasts it sets up, the underlying conflict those contrasts point to, and the theme that ultimately emerges. Then test your own interpretation of the poem against the author's comments about how the poem came to be and what, for her, it's all about.

ADRIENNE SU

On Writing

A love poem risks becoming a ruin,
public, irretrievable, a form of tattooing,

while loss, being permanent,
can sustain a thousand documents.

Loss predominates in history,
smorgasbord of death, betrayal, heresy,

crime, contagion, deployment, divorce.
A writer could remain aboard

the ship of grief and thrive, never
approaching the shores of rapture.

What can be said about elation
that the elated, seeking consolation

from their joy, will go to books for?
It's wiser and quicker to look for

a poem in the dentist's chair
than in the luxury suite where

eternal love, declared, turns out
to be eternal. Who cares about

a stranger's bliss? Thus the juncture
where I'm stalled, unaccustomed

to integrity, despite your presence,
our tranquility, and every confidence.

2012

AUTHORS ON THEIR WORK

ADRIENNE SU (b. 1967)

From *The Best American Poetry 2013* (2013)*

When I started assembling my newest manuscript, *The House Unburned,* I found it to be suffering from structural gaps and an excess of grief and regret. [. . .]

To round it out, I needed to come up with some poems of happiness, or at least the absence of unhappiness. This presented a problem, since, as I'm always telling students, successful poems are born of uncertainty, interior conflict, the modes of struggle that lack clear solutions. I went back and forth between two selves: the editor, whose vision for the collection required some happier poems, and the poet, who raged against the affront of an assignment so lacking in ambiguity. How, argued the poet, can happiness, gratification, or success be complex enough to give life to a poem?

Eventually, the answer came with a shift in setting. If the poem could be about writing, conflict would be inherent in the question. So I gave myself permission to write about writing. Now that I had a conflict, the road to the poem appeared. (198)

******The Best American Poetry 2013.* **Edited by Denise Duhamel and David Lehman, Scribner Poetry, 2013.**

POEMS FOR FURTHER STUDY

WILLIAM BLAKE

London

I wander through each chartered street,
Near where the chartered Thames does flow,
And mark in every face I meet
Marks of weakness, marks of woe.

In every cry of every man,
In every Infant's cry of fear,
In every voice, in every ban,
The mind-forged manacles I hear.

How the Chimney-sweeper's cry
Every black'ning Church appalls;
And the hapless Soldier's sigh
Runs in blood down Palace walls.

But most through midnight streets I hear
How the youthful Harlot's curse
Blasts the new-born Infant's tear,
And blights with plagues the Marriage hearse.

1794

- Does the tone of this poem seem sad, angry, or both? Why and how so? How might the repeated word "chartered" (lines 1 and 2) suggest a theme?

PAUL LAURENCE DUNBAR

Sympathy

I know what the caged bird feels, alas!
When the sun is bright on the upland slopes;
When the wind stirs soft through the springing grass,
And the river flows like a stream of glass;
When the first bird sings and the first bud opens,
And the faint perfume from its chalice steals—
I know what the caged bird feels!

I know why the caged bird beats his wing
Till its blood is red on the cruel bars;
For he must fly back to his perch and cling
When he fain[2] would be on the bough a-swing;
And a pain still throbs in the old, old scars
And they pulse again with a keener sting—
I know why he beats his wing!

I know why the caged bird sings, ah me,
When his wing is bruised and his bosom sore,—
When he beats his bars and he would be free;
It is not a carol of joy or glee,
But a prayer that he sends from his heart's deep core,
But a plea, that upward to Heaven he flings—
I know why the caged bird sings!

1893

- **How might your interpretation of this poem's theme change depending on whether or not you consider the date of its publication and/or the fact that its author was African American?**

W. H. AUDEN

[Stop all the clocks, cut off the telephone]

Stop all the clocks, cut off the telephone,
Prevent the dog from barking with a juicy bone,
Silence the pianos and with muffled drum
Bring out the coffin, let the mourners come.

Let aeroplanes circle moaning overhead
Scribbling on the sky the message He Is Dead,
Put crêpe bows round the white necks of the public doves,
Let the traffic policemen wear black cotton gloves.

2. Gladly.

He was my North, my South, my East and West,
My working week and my Sunday rest,
My noon, my midnight, my talk, my song;
I thought that love would last for ever: I was wrong.

The stars are not wanted now: put out every one;
Pack up the moon and dismantle the sun;
Pour away the ocean and sweep up the wood;
For nothing now can ever come to any good.

c. 1936

- **In what tone of voice would you read line 12? How might you turn this line into a statement of the poem's theme?**

SHARON OLDS
Last Night

The next day, I am almost afraid.
Love? It was more like dragonflies
in the sun, 100 degrees at noon,
the ends of their abdomens stuck together, I
close my eyes when I remember. I hardly
knew myself, like something twisting and
twisting out of a chrysalis,
enormous, without language, all
head, all shut eyes, and the humming
like madness, the way they writhe away,
and do not leave, back, back,
away, back. Did I know you? No kiss,
no tenderness—more like killing, death-grip
holding to life, genitals
like violent hands clasped tight
barely moving, more like being closed
in a great jaw and eaten, and the screaming
I groan to remember it, and when we started
to die, then I refuse to remember,
the way a drunkard forgets. After,
you held my hands extremely hard as my
body moved in shudders like the ferry when its
axle is loosed past engagement, you kept me
sealed exactly against you, our hairlines
wet as the arc of a gateway after
a cloudburst, you secured me in your arms till I slept—
that was love, and we woke in the morning
clasped, fragrant, buoyant, that was
the morning after love.

1996

- What comparison is the speaker of this poem making between "dragonflies / in the sun" and a night of love-making (lines 2–3)? What other comparisons are made in the poem? How do they work together and contribute to tone and theme?

KAY RYAN

Repulsive Theory

Little has been made
of the soft, skirting action
of magnets reversed,
while much has been
made of attraction.
But is it not this pillowy
principle of repulsion
that produces the
doily edges of oceans
or the arabesques of thought?
And do these cutout coasts
and incurved rhetorical beaches
not baffle the onslaught
of the sea or objectionable people
and give private life
what small protection it's got?
Praise then the oiled motions
of avoidance, the pearly
convolutions of all that
slides off or takes a
wide berth; praise every
eddying vacancy of Earth,
all the dimpled depths
of pooling space, the whole
swirl set up by fending-off—
extending far beyond the personal,
I'm convinced—
immense and good
in a cosmological sense:
unpressing us against
each other, lending
the necessary never
to never-ending.

2003

- What is the "theory" articulated in this poem? Might that theory be the poem's theme?

TERRANCE HAYES
Carp Poem

After I have parked below the spray paint caked in the granite
grooves of the Frederick Douglass[3] Middle School sign,

where men-size children loiter like shadows draped in outsize
denim, jerseys, braids, and boots that mean I am no longer young;

after I have made my way to the New Orleans Parish Jail down the block,
where the black prison guard wearing the same weariness

my prison guard father wears buzzes me in. I follow his pistol and shield
along each corridor trying not to look at the black men

boxed and bunked around me until I reach the tiny classroom
where two dozen black boys are dressed in jumpsuits orange as the carp

I saw in a pond once in Japan, so many fat, snaggletoothed fish
ganged in and lurching for food that a lightweight tourist could have crossed

the water on their backs so long as he had tiny rice balls or bread
to drop into the mouths below his footsteps, which I'm thinking

is how Jesus must have walked on the lake that day, the crackers and crumbs
falling from the folds of his robe, and how maybe it was the one fish

so hungry it leaped up his sleeve that he later miraculously changed
into a narrow loaf of bread, something that could stick to a believer's ribs,

and don't get me wrong, I'm a believer too, in the power of food at least,
having seen a footbridge of carp packed gill to gill, packed tighter

than a room of boy prisoners waiting to talk poetry with a young black poet,
packed so close they'd have eaten each other had there been nothing else to eat.

2010

- **What theme might emerge from the particular way this poem describes and compares what seems like three very different episodes—at the New Orleans Parish Jail, in a Japanese garden, and in the Bible? What might the poem suggest about prison? about poetry?**

3. Prominent African American abolitionist, politician, and former slave (c. 1818–95).

C. K. WILLIAMS

The Economy Rescued by My Mother Returning to Shop

I sleep as always these dark days aquiver I awake atremble my limbs jerk I thrash like a gaffed shark
no not shark too many sharks already fiscal financial that's why gullible guppy I was I thought
the boom wouldn't bust the bubble not burst shred leave us hanging over this thorny dollarless void

Markets staggered sales down the chute confidence off the cliff the aisles of the box stores and chains
depeopled ghost towns even the parking lots empty the lane lines in martial formation like wings
stripped of their feathers forlornly signalling for interstellar relief how not quiver not jerk and thrash?

Wait don't give up too soon here comes my mother back from beyond and she's going to shop!
Avid sharp-eyed alert gleaming and beaming as she always was on our old bus expeditions downtown
with a vigilance keen and serene and hands entities sentient and shrewd cunningly separate from her
evolved to analyze things' intrinsic or better overlooked worth as they collate the goods on their racks—
a blouse in silk and on sale!—which she shows an admiring mirror and opens her wallet and *buys*
buys as that president told us we should[4] though only my mother has sufficient passion to effect this

Didn't I once watch her unwrap a pair of new shoes to inhale the scent of their unblemished soles
and in the very next quarter didn't the G.N.P.[5] begin to stir the number of long-term unemployed slip
because of my mother's single-minded devotion to the subtlest aspects of commerce and exchange?

And all this after growing up *poor* in my grandmother's half-starving canned green-pea kitchen
and after surviving *Depression* and *War* how did she garner so much abstruse lore on redistribution
how accrue so many practical speculations about what we'd need to correct these failures and flops?

4. In a national address delivered shortly after the September 11, 2001, attacks on the World Trade Center and Pentagon, President George W. Bush (b. 1946) called for "continued participation and confidence in the American economy"; these and other remarks were later widely interpreted as a call for Americans to "go shopping."

5. Gross national product (acronym), total value of goods and services produced by a nation's residents in a given time, usually a year.

Delighted the gods of money must be to behold her again as she conveys
herself through their portals
Here's ingenious *Hepbaestus*[6] devising for our enchantment his gadgets
and gizmos and glitter
and here *Hermes* publicity market sales (not *Hermès*[7] shrine for the rich
and pretend rich)
and vast *Hades*[8] who lurks in the fear beneath all waiting to drag us down
to the realm of dire want
where a hound with three heads a banker's a hedge-funder's an
under-prime mortgage broker's.[9]
snarls as my mother who once filched from her sister coins she didn't
have to buy me an ice cream

croons as she crooned then *Make it last* and retires to her couch and
opens her credit-card statement
and *pays* isn't it splendid to be able to pay for your new skirt your sheer
stockings your *eau de toilette*[1]
and so redeem the *Dow* and the *Nasdaq*[2] and hallow us all for our humble
hungers our almost innocent greed?

- How do the poem's title, diction, and many allusions contribute to its tone?

SUGGESTIONS FOR WRITING

1. Choose any two poems in this chapter that express positive and negative feelings about their topics. How do the tones of the poems combine or contrast the feelings? Is there a shift in tone in each poem? If so, where? How is the shift revealed through language? Write an essay in which you compare the way each poet accomplishes this shifting of tone.
2. Write an essay in which you consider the use of language to create tone in any two or more poems on the same subject. How do the tones suit the themes of these poems?
3. Write an essay on Maxine Kumin's WOODCHUCKS in which you show that the speaker's conflict between sympathy and murderous instinct is reflected in the mixed tone and varied vocabulary. Focus on formal and informal tone, noting phrases from law or religion—"the case we had against them"; "fallen from grace" (lines 4, 15)—or from everyday speech—"up to scratch," "food from our mouths" (lines 9, 13). How does the diction, or word choice, of the poem affect its tone?

6. Greek god of fire and of craftsmen; his Latin name is Vulcan.

7. In other words, the messenger of the gods and god of merchants, thieves, and oratory in Greek mythology, not the high-end French retail chain famous for its luxury leather goods, perfume, and scarves.

8. Underworld or god of the Underworld in Greek mythology; his Latin name is Pluto.

9. Usually *subprime mortgage*, high-risk mortgage granted to a borrower with a lower credit rating than required for a conventional mortgage. *Hedge-funder*: someone who runs a high-risk, high-return portfolio of investments. *Hound with three heads*: According to Greek myth, the entrance to Hades is guarded by Cerberus, a monstrous dog with at least three heads.

1. Literally, toilet water (French), a form of perfume.

2. National Association of Securities Dealers Automated Quotations (acronym), American stock exchange that includes technology giants Apple, Google, Microsoft, and Amazon. *Dow*: Dow Jones Industrial Average, a calculation of the average price of a select group of significant stocks traded on the NASDAQ and the New York Stock Exchange.

4. Reimagine W. D. Snodgrass's Leaving the Motel as a poem in which the speaker and lover are happy and delighted with each other and certain that the relationship will last forever. What details and phrases would need to be changed for the poem to express a positive feeling about the relationship? Write an essay in which you relate the tone of the poem to the subject of secret and short-lived sexual relationships.
5. Write an essay exploring just who or what C. K. Williams seems to poke fun at in The Economy Rescued by My Mother Returning to Shop. For all its humor, might the poem have a serious point or theme?

SAMPLE WRITING: RESPONSE PAPER

In the response paper that follows, Stephen Bordland works through Auden's poem STOP ALL THE CLOCKS, CUT OFF THE TELEPHONE more or less line by line, writing down whatever ideas come to him. The form of this paper is less important than the process of thinking carefully about the poem's music, emotions, and meanings. As you can see, by the time Stephen reaches the end of his response, he has decided on a topic for the more formal essay that he will write later.

Bordland 1

Stephen Bordland
Professor O'Connor
English 157
1 January 2017

Response Paper on Auden's "Stop all the clocks, cut off the telephone"

I first heard this poem read aloud when I saw the movie *Four Weddings and a Funeral* on cable. The character who read the poem was reading it at the funeral of his lover. It was perfectly suited to the story and was very moving. I was struck by the actor's reading because the poem seemed to have a steady rhythm for several lines and then suddenly hit what sounded like a dead end—"I thought that love would last forever: I was wrong" (line 12). Hearing the actor's reading of this poem made me want to read it myself, to see if the poem would still affect me if I read/heard it outside of the context of an emotional scene in a movie. It did, and I think that the "I was wrong" line is the key—a turning point, I guess.

In the anthology, the poem seems to have no actual title (at least that's how I interpret the fact that the first line is in brackets where the title usually goes), but I did some searching on the Internet and found that this poem was once called "Funeral Blues." If I were reading the poem for the first time under that title, I would at least know that the poem has something to do with death right from the start. But this title makes the poem sound irreverent rather than sincerely painful. I wonder if that would have been true in the 1930s, when Auden wrote the poem. There were lots of blues and jazz songs of that era whose titles ended in "Blues" (like Robert Johnson's "Kindhearted Woman Blues"), so maybe the title wasn't meant to be read the way that I'm reading it. Anyway, I don't know if Auden himself changed the title, or if there's another story there, but I think it's a better poem without the title.

Bordland 2

The poem starts with a request to an unknown person (everyone?) to make some common aspects of daily life go away: "Stop all the clocks" (1) presumably because time seems to be standing still; "cut off the telephone" (1) presumably because the speaker wants to be alone and undisturbed, cut off from human contact. I'm not sure what's implied by "Prevent the dog from barking with a juicy bone" (2) mainly because I'm confused about the literal meaning: Are we supposed to prevent the dog from barking by giving him a juicy bone (one way to interpret "with a juicy bone"), or are we supposed to prevent the dog with a juicy bone in his mouth (another way of interpreting "with a juicy bone") from barking at all? I don't think I really have a handle on what this line means in relation to the other ones, but I'll leave it for now. In the next line, "Silence the pianos" (3) clearly means that the speaker wants no music now that his lover is dead, except for the "muffled drum" (3) that will accompany the coffin and mourners in the fourth line. It's interesting that all of these things so far are sounds—the tick-tock of the clock, the ring of the telephone, a barking dog, music. They all seem to stand in for something, too—for the passing of time, contact with other people (and with pets?), joy as expressed by music.

The image of "aeroplanes" (5) circling overhead (and "moaning" [5]—that's a really good choice of words) writing "He is Dead" (6) is very strong and would have been a very modern reference at the time of this poem (c. 1936). A *Christian Science Monitor* article about a "skywriting" pilot says that "[s]kywriting's heyday was from the 1930s to the early 1950s when Pepsi Cola used skywriting as its main way of advertising" (Hartill), so the reference here is to a commercial medium being used to make as many people as possible aware of the speaker's loss. If a poet tried to make a reference to something equivalent today, it would have to be a television advertisement or a blog, maybe. I wonder if a modern poet could really pull off a reference to a TV ad and still make it sound sincerely sad.

I'm not sure what the "crêpe bows round the white necks of the public doves" (7) means. Would the bows even be visible? Does "crêpe" imply a color, or is it just a type of fabric? And what is a public dove? I'm not sure I like the repetition in this line of three adjective/noun pairs: "crepe bows," "white necks," "public doves." It seems too precious or "poetic." The "traffic policemen" (8) that I've seen all wear white gloves so that their hand movements can be seen clearly. The speaker wants them all to wear "black cotton gloves," the appropriate color for mourning, but that would probably create real problems for the drivers trying to see what the policemen are directing them to do. So, I wonder if the bows on doves and black gloves on cops are both there to show us that the speaker is feeling not just the sort of grief that moves him to write poetry, but also the sort of intense pain that makes him want to throw the rest of the world into the same confusion and chaos he's experiencing. Or at least, he's not only asking to be alone, but also wanting the rest of the world to share his grief.

In the next four lines, the speaker turns to himself and his lover: "He was my North, my South, my East and West / My working week and my Sunday rest" (9-12).

Bordland 3

These lines flow so smoothly, with a soothing, regular rhythm; they're almost sing-songy. But they don't seem sappy or wrong in this poem; they seem painfully sincere. The author uses place (as described by the compass) and time (the whole week, the reference to noon and midnight) to make very clear, in case we hadn't figured it out from the preceding lines, that his lover was everything to him. In the fourth line of this section, this regular rhythm is interrupted, or even stopped dead: "I thought that love would last for ever: I was wrong" (12). This is a very true and moving conclusion to reach, but it also seems ironic, once we read to the end of the poem. If the speaker was wrong to believe (before the death of his lover) that love would last forever, isn't it possible that he's wrong about the conclusion "nothing now can ever come to any good" (16)—that grief will last forever?

I think that Auden probably intended us to be aware of this irony. It seems to me that the poem is broken into three major parts. First, we sympathize with the speaker's grief and sense of loss. Then we're supposed to stop at the point where the speaker makes a judgment about his understanding of the world prior to that loss ("I thought that love would last for ever: I was wrong" [12]) and to spend a moment absorbing the meaning of that judgment. Finally, as we read the most extreme expression of the speaker's loss ("Pack up the moon and dismantle the sun" [14]), we can see that although we sympathize and understand, we also know something that the speaker doesn't know at the moment. Just as his love apparently blinded the speaker to love's inevitable end, so his profound grief is probably blinding him to grief's inevitable end. Also, it may just be me, but it seems that this last part is almost too dramatic or theatrical, as if maybe the speaker has made some sort of transition from being unself-consciously mournful to being self-consciously aware that the way he's expressing himself is poetic.

Back to the idea about the irony: The poem itself seems to be arguing against the notion that love cannot last forever (or, okay, a very long time). After all, people are still reading this poem, and I bet people will continue to read it for as long as people read poetry. That's about as close to forever as we get on this earth, so even though the lovers of this poem are long dead, their love lives on, in a way. Auden must have been aware of this when he was writing the poem. I wonder if he ever said anything in letters, essays, or speeches about art and immortality? If so, I think I'll write a paper on that topic as addressed in this poem.

Bordland 4

Works Cited

Auden, W. H. "Stop all the clocks, cut off the telephone." *The Norton Introduction to Literature*, edited by Kelly J. Mays, 12th ed., W. W. Norton, 2017, pp. 956-57.

Hartill, Lane. "Sky Writer." *Christian Science Monitor*, 25 Jan. 2000, www.csmonitor.com/2000/0125/p22s1.html.

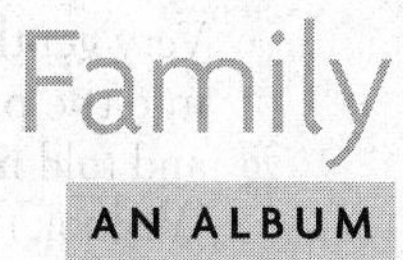

Family

AN ALBUM

Families are the groundwork of society, and most people's earliest memories involve family members. Families may be nuclear or extended, biological or adoptive, emotionally demonstrative or distant. Families may pass down traditions that younger generations may choose to abandon, embrace, or simply tolerate. Adults who have left home may dwell on memories, good or bad, of their mothers, fathers, brothers, or sisters. Each renewed contact with family can spark conflicting thoughts and feelings. Hope, disappointment, or grief for one's child can find expression as a concentrated moment in a poem. A spouse or a child can remind the speaker of the passage of time and mortality.

Because the family is such a basic unit of social interaction, many poems explore family relations. The following poems are all, in different ways, about family. What do these poems have in common? How do they differ? Which best capture your feelings and ideas about family relationships? Can you find two poems that express the same **theme**—in other words, can you accurately state their themes in the same way? How do any two poems compare in **tone**? Which poems have surprising shifts in tone? Do any poems express surprising or disturbing attitudes toward loved ones?

SIMON J. ORTIZ

My Father's Song

Wanting to say things,
I miss my father tonight.
His voice, the slight catch,
the depth from his thin chest,
the tremble of emotion
in something he has just said
to his son, his song:

We planted corn one Spring at Acu[1]—
we planted several times
but this one particular time
I remember the soft damp sand
in my hand.

My father had stopped at one point
to show me an overturned furrow;
the plowshare had unearthed
the burrow nest of a mouse
in the soft moist sand.

1. Alternative name for Acoma village and/or pueblo, about sixty miles west of Albuquerque, New Mexico. Sometimes translated as "the place that always was," it is the oldest continuously inhabited community in the United States.

Very gently, he scooped tiny pink animals
into the palm of his hand
and told me to touch them.
We took them to the edge
of the field and put them in the shade
of a sand moist clod.

I remember the very softness
of cool and warm sand and tiny alive mice
and my father saying things.

1976

- **What are the "things" that the speaker wants to say (line 1)? Are they the same "things" he remembers his father saying (line 26)? Does the poem itself say these things?**

ROBERT HAYDEN
Those Winter Sundays

Sundays too my father got up early
and put his clothes on in the blueblack cold,
then with cracked hands that ached
from labor in the weekday weather made
banked fires blaze. No one ever thanked him.

I'd wake and hear the cold splintering, breaking.
When the rooms were warm, he'd call,
and slowly I would rise and dress,
fearing the chronic angers of that house,

Speaking indifferently to him,
who had driven out the cold
and polished my good shoes as well.
What did I know, what did I know
of love's austere and lonely offices?

1966

- **Why does the poem begin with the words "Sundays too" (rather than, say, "On Sundays")? What are the "austere and lonely offices" to which the poem's final line refers?**

ELLEN BRYANT VOIGT
My Mother

my mother my mother my mother she
could do anything so she did everything the world
was an unplowed field a dress to be hemmed a scraped knee it needed
a casserole it needed another alto in the choir her motto was apply
yourself

the secret of life was spreading your gifts why hide your light
under a bushel[2] you might

forget it there in the dark times the lonely times
the sun gone down on her resolve she slept a little first
so she'd be fresh she put on a little lipstick drawing on her smile
she pulled that hair up off her face she pulled her stockings on she stepped
into her pumps she took up her matching purse already
packed with everything they all would learn
they would be nice they would

apologize they would be grateful whenever
they had forgotten what to pack she never did
she had a spare she kissed your cheek she wiped the mark
away with her own spit she marched you out again unless you were
that awful sort of stubborn broody[3] child who more and more
I was who once had been so sweet so mild staying put
where she put me what happened

must have been the bushel I was hiding in
the sun gone down on her resolve she slept a little first
so she'd be fresh she pulled her stockings on she'd packed
the words for my every lack she had a little lipstick on her teeth the mark
on my cheek would not rub off she gave the fluids from her mouth
to it she gave the tissues in her ample purse to it I never did
apologize I let my sister succor those in need and suffer
the little children[4] my mother

knew we are self-canceling she gave herself
a lifetime C an average grade from then on out she kept
the lights on day and night a garden needs the light the sun
could not be counted on she slept a little day and night she didn't need
her stockings or her purse she watered she weeded she fertilized she stood
in front the tallest stalk keeping the deer the birds all
the world's idle shameless thieves away

2011

- **How might the poem's form, especially its lack of punctuation and capitalization, contribute to tone? to its characterization of the speaker's mother?**

2. See the Sermon on the Mount (Matt. 5.15–16): "Neither do men light a candle, and put it under a bushel, but on a candlestick; and it giveth light until all that are in the house. / Let your light so shine before men, that they may see your good works, and glorify your Father which is in heaven."
3. Thoughtful and unhappy, given to brooding or worrying.
4. See Matthew 19.14: "But Jesus said, Suffer little children, and forbid them not, to come unto me: for of such is the kingdom of heaven."

MARTÍN ESPADA

Of the Threads That Connect the Stars

Did you ever see stars? asked my father with a cackle. He was not
speaking of the heavens, but the white flash in his head when a fist burst
between his eyes. In Brooklyn, this would cause men and boys to slap
the table with glee; this might be the only heavenly light we'd ever see.

I never saw stars. The sky in Brooklyn was a tide of smoke rolling over us
from the factory across the avenue, the mattresses burning in the junkyard,
the ruins where squatters would sleep, the riots of 1966[5] that kept me
locked in my room like a suspect. My father talked truce on the streets.

My son can see the stars through the tall barrel of a telescope.
He names the galaxies with the numbers and letters of astronomy.
I cannot see what he sees in the telescope, no matter how many eyes I shut.
I understand a smoking mattress better than the language of galaxies.

My father saw stars. My son sees stars. The earth rolls beneath
our feet. We lurch ahead, and one day we have walked this far.

2013

- **How does the poem differentiate and connect three generations of one family by describing the stars each did or didn't, do or don't, see?**

EMILY GROSHOLZ

Eden

In lurid cartoon colors, the big baby
dinosaur steps backwards under the shadow
of an approaching tyrannosaurus rex.
"His mommy going to fix it," you remark,
serenely anxious, hoping for the best.

After the big explosion, after the lights
go down inside the house and up the street,
we rush outdoors to find a squirrel stopped
in straws of half-gnawed cable. I explain,
trying to fit the facts, "The squirrel is dead."

No, you explain it otherwise to me.
"He's sleeping. And his mommy going to come."
Later, when the squirrel has been removed,
"His mommy fix him," you insist, insisting
on the right to know what you believe.

5. In July 1966, violent conflict repeatedly erupted between blacks and Puerto Ricans in Brooklyn's troubled Bedford-Stuyvesant neighborhood.

The world is truly full of fabulous
great and curious small inhabitants,
and you're the freshly minted, unashamed
Adam in this garden. You preside,
appreciate, and judge our proper names.

Like God, I brought you here.
Like God, I seem to be omnipotent,
mostly helpful, sometimes angry as hell.
I fix whatever minor faults arise
with bandaids, batteries, masking tape, and pills.

But I am powerless, as you must know,
to chase the serpent sliding in the grass,
or the tall angel with the flaming sword
who scares you when he rises suddenly
behind the gates of sunset.

1992

- How does Grosholz use language to elevate the poem's subject matter from the trivial and childish to the biblical and profound?

PHILIP LARKIN
This Be the Verse

They fuck you up, your mum and dad.
    They may not mean to, but they do.
They fill you with the faults they had
    And add some extra, just for you.

But they were fucked up in their turn
    By fools in old-style hats and coats,
Who half the time were soppy-stern
    And half at one another's throats.

Man hands on misery to man.
    It deepens like a coastal shelf.[6]
Get out as early as you can,
    And don't have any kids yourself.

1971

- This poem opens with one of the most (in)famous lines in all of English-language poetry. What tone does that line establish, and how so? How does the rest of the poem either maintain or complicate that tone? How might the poem's sound qualities—especially its rhyme and/or meter—contribute to tone? To what extent is and/or isn't the poem's first line an adequate statement of its theme?

6. Part of a continent that lies under the ocean and typically ends in a steep slope down to the ocean floor.

AUTHORS ON THEIR WORK
PHILIP LARKIN (1922–85)

From "An Interview with John Haffenden" (1981)*

Was it your intention, in using bad language in one or two poems, to provide a shock tactic?
Yes. I mean, these words are part of the palette. You use them when you want to shock. I don't think I've ever shocked for the sake of shocking. "They fuck you up" is funny because it's ambiguous. Parents bring about your conception and also bugger you up once you are born. Professional parents in particular don't like that poem. (61)

*"An Interview with John Haffenden." *Further Requirements: Interviews, Broadcasts, Statements and Book Reviews,* edited by Anthony Thwaite, Faber and Faber, 2001, pp. 47–62. Originally published in *Viewpoints: Poets in Conversation with John Haffenden*, 1981.

JIMMY SANTIAGO BACA
Green Chile

I prefer red chile over my eggs
and potatoes for breakfast.
Red chile *ristras*[7] decorate my door,
dry on my roof, and hang from eaves.
They lend open-air vegetable stands
historical grandeur, and gently swing
with an air of festive welcome.
I can hear them talking in the wind,
haggard, yellowing, crisp, rasping
tongues of old men, licking the breeze.

But grandmother loves green chile.
When I visit her,
she holds the green chile pepper
in her wrinkled hands.
Ah, voluptuous, masculine,
an air of authority and youth simmers
from its swan-neck stem, tapering to a flowery
collar, fermenting resinous spice.
A well-dressed gentleman at the door
my grandmother takes sensuously in her hand,
rubbing its firm glossed sides,
caressing the oily rubbery serpent,
with mouth-watering fulfillment,

7. Braided strings of dried peppers.

fondling its curves with gentle fingers.
Its bearing magnificent and taut
as flanks of a tiger in mid-leap,
she thrusts her blade into
as cuts it open, with lust
on her hot mouth, sweating over the stove,
bandanna round her forehead,
mysterious passion on her face
and she serves me green chile con carne
between soft warm leaves of corn tortillas,
with beans and rice—her sacrifice
to her little prince.
I slurp from my plate
with last bit of tortilla, my mouth burns
and I hiss and drink a tall glass of cold water.

All over New Mexico, sunburned men and women
drive rickety trucks stuffed with gunny-sacks
of green chile, from Belen, Veguita, Willard, Estancia,
San Antonio y[8] Socorro, from fields
to roadside stands, you see them roasting green chile
in screen-sided homemade barrels, and for a dollar a bag,
we relive this old, beautiful ritual again and again.

1989

- **What different qualities do the red and green chiles have? Which words in the poem help personify the chiles? How fully do these words reflect the differences between the speaker and the grandmother?**

PAUL MARTINEZ POMPA
The Abuelita[9] Poem

I. Skin & Corn

Her brown skin glistens as the sun
pours through the kitchen window
like gold *leche*.[1] After grinding
the *nixtamal*,[2] a word so beautifully ethnic
it must not only be italicized but underlined
to let you, the reader, know you've encountered
something beautifully ethnic, she kneads
with the hands of centuries-old ancestor
spirits who magically yet realistically possess her
until the *masa* is smooth as a *lowrider*'s
chrome bumper. And I know she must do this
with care because it says so on a website

8. And (Spanish).
9. Grandmother (Spanish). 1. Milk (Spanish).
2. Treated corn to make *masa*, the dough used in tortillas.

that explains how to make homemade corn *tortillas*.
So much labor for this peasant bread
this edible art birthed from *Abuelita*'s
brown skin, which is still glistening
in the sun.

II. Apology

Before she died I called my abuelita
grandma. I cannot remember
if she made corn tortillas from scratch
but, O, how she'd flip the factory fresh
El Milagros[3] (Quality Since 1950)
on the burner, bathe them in butter
& salt for her grandchildren.
How she'd knead the buttons
on the telephone, order me food
from Pizza Hut. I assure you,
gentle reader, this was done
with the spirit of Mesoamérica[4]
ablaze in her fingertips.

2009

- **How does this poem play on the expectations that might be created by its title? What does the poem ultimately seem to suggest about those expectations?**

CHARLIE SMITH
The Business

My father and his brother didn't get along;
for years they kept at it, sniping, digging
out the ground under each other's feet;
it was a life work more important
than family, than community. My grandfather
set them to it, yoked them
into his business, struck one against the other
to make sparks, raise a fire that would warm him.

My grandfather was a brilliant man;
he knew what a son will do for a father's love,
how success is a knife driven into the brother's chest,
how one must pay with another's life
for his own; he knew
what a sure thing it was, this jealousy,
like a magic bread
that doesn't run out,
that will feed a man as long as he lives.

1996

3. An actual brand, but meaning "miracles" (Spanish).
4. Literally, Middle America (Spanish), a region extending roughly from central Mexico to Nicaragua.

- What different meanings might the words "business" (line 6) and "work" (line 4) take on over the course of the poem, and how do these meanings interrelate?

ANDREW HUDGINS
Begotten

I've never, as some children do,
looked at my folks and thought, I *must*
have come from someone else—
rich parents who'd misplaced me, but
who would, as in a myth or novel,
return and claim me. Hell, no. I saw
my face in cousins' faces, heard
my voice in their high drawls. And Sundays,
after the dinner plates were cleared,
I lingered, elbow propped on red
oilcloth, and studied great-uncles, aunts,
and cousins new to me. They squirmed.
I stared till I discerned the features
they'd gotten from the family larder:
eyes, nose, lips, hair? I stared until,
uncomfortable, they'd snap, "Hey, boy—
what are you looking at? At me?"
"No, sir," I'd lie. "No, ma'am." I'd count ten
and then continue staring at them.
I never had to ask, What am I?
I stared at my blood-kin, and thought,
So *this,* dear God, is what I am.

1994

- What can you infer from the language in this poem about the speaker's attitude toward his life and his family? What does the poem's title evoke?

SUGGESTIONS FOR WRITING

1. Compare the portrayal of the parent-child relationship in any two poems in this album, focusing especially on the poems' tones and themes.
2. What words in Robert Hayden's THOSE WINTER SUNDAYS suggest the son's feelings toward his father and his home? What words indicate that his attitudes have changed since the time depicted in the poem? Write an essay in which you compare the speaker's feelings, as a youth and then later as a man, about his father and his home.
3. Write an essay comparing the way grandmothers and their relationship to food and family are portrayed in Jimmy Santiago Baca's GREEN CHILE and Paul Martinez Pompa's THE ABUELITA POEM. How might Pompa's poem respond to and comment on Baca's?
4. Pick the poem in this album that you like most and the one you like least. Write an informal response paper or essay comparing your reactions to the two poems and exploring just why and how the poems provoke those disparate reactions. What role do the poem's tones and themes play here? What role is played by your own experiences of, and feelings and ideas about, family?

15 LANGUAGE: WORD CHOICE AND ORDER

Fiction and drama depend on language just as poetry does, but in a poem almost everything comes down to the particular meanings and implications, as well as sound and shape, of individual words. When we read stories and plays, we generally focus our attention on character and plot, and although words determine how we imagine those characters and how we respond to what happens to them, we are not as likely to pause over any one word as we may need to when reading a poem. Because poems are often short, much depends on every word in them. Sometimes, as though they were distilled prose, poems contain only the essential words. They say just barely enough to communicate in the most basic way, using elemental signs—each of which is chosen for exactly the right shade of meaning or feeling or both. But elemental does not necessarily mean simple, and these signs may be very rich in their meanings and complex in their effects. The poet's word choice—the **diction** of a poem—determines not only meaning but also just about every effect the poem produces.

PRECISION AND AMBIGUITY

Let's look first at poems that create some of their effects by examining—or playing with—a single word. Here, multiple meanings or the shiftiness, ambiguity, and uncertainty of a word are at issue. The following short poem, for example, depends almost entirely on the ways we use the word *play*.

SARAH CLEGHORN
[The golf links lie so near the mill]

The golf links lie so near the mill
That almost every day
The laboring children can look out
And see the men at play.

1915

While traveling in the American South, Cleghorn had seen, right next to a golf course, a textile mill that employed quite young children. Her poem doesn't *say* that we expect men to work and children to play; it just assumes our expectation and builds an effect of *dramatic irony*—an incongruity between what we expect and what actually occurs—out of the observation. The poem saves almost all of its devastating effect for the final word, after the situation has been carefully described and the irony set up.

In the following poem, a word used over and over acquires multiple meanings and refuses to be limited to a single one. Here, the importance of a word involves its ambiguity (that is, its having more than one possible meaning) rather than its precision or exactness. How many different meanings of the words *lie* and *lay* can you distinguish in the poem?

MARTHA COLLINS

Lies

Anyone can get it wrong, laying low
when she ought to lie, but is it a lie
for her to say she laid him when we know
he wouldn't lie still long enough to let
her do it? A good lay is not a song,
not anymore; a good lie is something
else: lyrics, lines, what if you say *dear sister*
when you have no sister, what if you say *guns*
when you saw no guns, though you know
they're there? *She laid down her arms; she lay*
down, her arms by her sides. If we don't know,
do we lie if we say? If we don't say, do we lie
down on the job? To arms! in any case
dear friends. If we must lie, let's not lie around.

1999

DENOTATION AND CONNOTATION

Although the unambiguous or "dictionary" meaning of words—that is, their **denotation**—is certainly important, words are more than hard blocks of meaning on whose sense everyone agrees. They also carry emotional force and shades of suggestion. The words we use indicate not only what we mean but how we feel about it and want to encourage others to feel. A person who holds office is, quite literally (and unemotionally), an *officeholder*—the word denotes what he or she does. But if we want to imply that a particular officeholder is wise, trustworthy, and deserving of political support, we may call that person a *civil servant*, a *political leader*, or an *elected official*, whereas if we want to promote distrust or contempt of that same officeholder we might say *politician* or *bureaucrat* or *political hack*. These terms have clear **connotations**—suggestions of emotional coloration that imply our attitude and invite a similar one from our hearers. In poems, as in life, what words connote can be just as important as what they denote; some poems work primarily through denotation and some more through connotation.

The following **epitaph**, for example, which describes one person's mixed feelings about another, depends heavily on the connotations of fairly common words.

WALTER DE LA MARE
Slim Cunning Hands

Slim cunning hands at rest, and cozening eyes—
Under this stone one loved too wildly lies;
How false she was, no granite could declare;
Nor all earth's flowers, how fair.

1950

What the speaker in SLIM CUNNING HANDS remembers about the dead woman—her hands, her eyes—tells part of the story; her physical presence was clearly important to him. The poem's other nouns—*stone*, *granite*, *flowers*—all remind us of her death and its finality. All these words denote objects having to do with the rituals that memorialize a departed life. Granite and stone connote finality as well, and flowers connote fragility and suggest the brevity of life (which is why they have become the symbolic language of funerals). The way the speaker talks about the woman expresses, in just a few words, the complexity of his love for her. She was loved, he says, too "wildly"—by him perhaps, and apparently by others. The excitement she offered is suggested by the word, as is the lack of control. The words *cunning* and *cozening* imply both her falsity and, perhaps, her wildness; they suggest her calculation, cleverness, and untrustworthiness as well as her skill, persuasiveness, and ability to please. Moreover, coming at the end of the second line, the word *lies* has more than one meaning. The body "lies" under the stone, but the woman's falsity has by now become too prominent to ignore as a second meaning. And the word *fair*, a simple yet very inclusive word, suggests how totally attractive the speaker finds her: Her beauty can no more be expressed by flowers than her fickleness can be expressed by something as permanent as words in stone. But the word *fair*, in the emphatic position as the final word, also implies two other meanings that seem to resonate, ironically, with what we have already learned about her from the speaker: "impartial" and "just." "Impartial" she may be in her preferences (as the word *false* suggests), but to the speaker she is hardly "just," and the final defining word speaks both to her appearance and (ironically) to her character. Simple words here tell us perhaps all we need to know of a long story—or at least the speaker's version of it.

Words like *fair* and *cozening* are clearly loaded. They imply more emotionally than they mean literally. They have strong, clear connotations; they tell us what to think, what evaluation to make; and they suggest the basis for the evaluation.

Sometimes word choice in poems is less dramatic and less obviously significant but equally important. Often, in fact, simple appropriateness makes the words in a poem work, and words that do not call special attention to themselves can be the most effective. Precision of denotation may be just as impressive and productive of specific effects as the resonance or ambiguous suggestiveness of connotation. Often poems achieve their power by a combination of verbal effects, setting off elaborate **figures of speech** or other complicated strategies with simple words chosen to indicate exact actions, moments, or states of mind.

Words are the starting point for all poetry, of course, and almost every word is likely to be significant, either denotatively or connotatively or both. Poets who know their craft pick each word with care to express exactly what needs to be expressed and to suggest every emotional shade that the poem is calculated to evoke in us.

Word Choice: An Example and an Exercise

Before you read the following poem, notice the three words in the title. What do they lead you to expect? What questions do they raise? Jot down your thoughts on a piece of paper. Then, as you read the poem, take note of key words and try to be conscious of the emotional effects and impressions they create.

THEODORE ROETHKE

My Papa's Waltz

The whiskey on your breath
Could make a small boy dizzy;
But I hung on like death:
Such waltzing was not easy.

We romped until the pans
Slid from the kitchen shelf;
My mother's countenance
Could not unfrown itself.

The hand that held my wrist
Was battered on one knuckle;
At every step you missed
My right ear scraped a buckle.

You beat time on my head
With a palm caked hard by dirt,
Then waltzed me off to bed
Still clinging to your shirt.

1948

Exactly how does the situation in My Papa's Waltz and the poem itself fulfill or defy your expectations? How does it answer your questions? How does it characterize the waltz and the speaker's feelings about it? Which words are most suggestive in these terms? What clues are there in the word choice that an adult is remembering a childhood experience? How scared was the boy at the time? How does the grown adult now evaluate the emotions he felt when he was a boy?

WORD ORDER AND PLACEMENT

Individual words qualify and amplify one another—suggestions clarify other suggestions, and meanings grow upon meanings—and thus how words are put together and where individual words are located matters. Notice, for example, that in "Slim Cunning Hands" the final emphasis is on how *fair* in appearance the woman was; the speaker's last word describes the quality he can't forget despite her lack of a different kind of fairness and his distrust of her. Even though it doesn't justify everything else, her beauty mitigates all the disappointment and hurt. Putting the word *fair* at the end of the line and of the poem gives it special emphasis and meaning.

That one word, *fair*, does not stand all by itself, however, any more than any other word in a poem can be considered all alone. Every word exists within larger units of meaning—sentences, patterns of comparison and contrast, the whole poem—and where the word is and how it is used are often important. The final word or words may be especially emphatic (as in "Slim Cunning Hands"), and words that are repeated take on a special intensity, as *lie* does in LIES. Certain words may stand out because they are unusual or used in an unusual way (like *unfrown* or *waltzing* in "My Papa's Waltz") or because they are given an artificial prominence—through unusual sentence structure, for example, or because the title calls special attention to them. In a poem, as opposed to a prose work, moreover, the number and placement of words in a line and the spacing of the words and lines stays the same in every printed version. Where words come—in a line, in a stanza—and how they are spatially and visually related to other words also helps determine their force and meaning.

The subtlety and force of word choice are sometimes strongly affected by **syntax**—the way the sentences are put together. When you find unusual syntax or spacing, you can be pretty sure that something there merits special attention. Notice the odd sentence constructions in the second and third stanzas of "My Papa's Waltz"—the way the speaker talks about the abrasion of buckle on ear in line 12, for example. He does not say that the buckle scraped his ear, but rather "My right ear scraped a buckle." Reversing the more common expression makes a big difference in the effect created; the speaker avoids placing blame and refuses to specify any unpleasant effect. Had he said that the buckle scraped his ear, we would have to worry about the fragile ear. The syntax channels our feeling and helps control what we think of the "waltz."

In the most curious part of the poem, the second stanza, the silent mother appears, and the syntax on both sides of the semicolon is peculiar. In lines 5–6, the connection between the romping and the pans falling is stated oddly: "We romped *until* the pans / Slid from the kitchen shelf" (emphasis added). The speaker does not say that they knocked down the pans or imply awkwardness, but he does suggest energetic activity and duration. He implies intensity, almost intention—as though the romping would not be complete until the pans fell. And the clause about the mother—odd but effective—makes her position clear. A silent bystander in this male ritual, she doesn't seem frightened or angry. She seems to be holding a frown, or to have it molded on her face, as though it were part of her own ritual, and perhaps a facet of her stern character as well. The syntax implies that she *has to* maintain the frown, and the falling of the pans almost seems to be for her benefit. She disapproves, but she remains their audience.

Sometimes poems create, as well, a powerful sense of the way minds and emotions work by varying normal syntactical order in special ways. Listen for and watch, for example, what happens a few lines into the following poem. What does it suggest about what is happening inside the speaker?

SHARON OLDS
Sex without Love

How do they do it, the ones who make love
without love? Beautiful as dancers,
gliding over each other like ice-skaters
over the ice, fingers hooked
inside each other's bodies, faces
red as steak, wine, wet as the
children at birth whose mothers are going to
give them away. How do they come to the
come to the   come to the   God   come to the
still waters, and not love
the one who came there with them, light
rising slowly as steam off their joined
skin? These are the true religious,
the purists, the pros, the ones who will not
accept a false Messiah, love the
priest instead of the God. They do not
mistake the lover for their own pleasure,
they are like great runners: they know they are alone
with the road surface, the cold, the wind,
the fit of their shoes, their over-all cardio-
vascular health—just factors, like the partner
in the bed, and not the truth, which is the
single body alone in the universe
against its own best time.

1984

The poem starts calmly enough, with a simple rhetorical question implying that the speaker just cannot understand sex without love. Lines 2–4 carefully compare such sexual activity with two other artful activities, and the speaker—although plainly disapproving—seems coolly in control of the analysis and evaluation. But by the end of the fourth line, something begins to seem odd: "[H]ooked" seems too ugly and extreme a way to characterize the lovers' fingers, however much the speaker may disapprove, and by line 6 the syntax seems to break down. How does "wine" fit the syntax of the line? Is it parallel with "steak," another example of redness? Or is it somehow related to the last part of the sentence, parallel with "faces"? Neither of these possibilities quite works. At best, the punctuation is inadequate; at worst, the speaker's mind is working too fast for the language it generates, scrambling its images. We can't yet be sure what is going on, but by the ninth line the lack of control is manifest with the compulsive repeating (three times) of "come to the" and the interjected "God."

Such verbal behavior—here concretized by the way the poem orders its words and spaces them on the page—invites us to reevaluate the speaker's moralizing relative to her emotional involvement with the issues and with her representation of sexuality itself. The speaker's own values, as well as those who have sex without love, become a subject for evaluation.

AUTHORS ON THEIR WORK

SHARON OLDS (b. 1942)

From "Sharon Olds" (1996)*

I don't think that sex has been written about a lot in poetry. And I want to be able to write about any subject. There [. . .] are subjects that are probably a lot harder to write about than others. I think that love is almost the hardest thing to write about. Not a general state of being in love, but a particular love for a particular person. Just one's taste for that one. And if you look at all the love poetry in our tradition, there isn't much that helps us know why that one. I'm just interested in human stuff like hate, love, sexual love, and sex. I don't see why not. It just seems to me if writers can assemble, in language, something that bears any relation to experience—especially important experience, experience we care about, moving and powerful experience—then it is worth trying.

*"Sharon Olds." Interview by Dwight Garner. *Salon*, 1 July 1996, www.salon.com/1996/07/01/interview_19/.

• • •

Words, the basic materials of poetry, come in many varieties and can be used in many different ways and in different—sometimes surprising—combinations. They are seldom simple or transparent, even when we know their meanings and recognize their syntactical combinations as ordinary and conventional. Carefully examining them, individually and collectively, is a crucial part of reading poems, and being able to ask good questions about the words that poems use and the way they use them is one of the most basic—and rewarding—skills a reader of poetry can develop.

POEMS FOR FURTHER STUDY

GERARD MANLEY HOPKINS

Pied Beauty[1]

Glory be to God for dappled things—
　For skies of couple-color as a brinded[2] cow;
　　For rose-moles all in stipple[3] upon trout that swim;
Fresh-firecoal chestnut-falls;[4] finches' wings;
　Landscape plotted and pieced—fold, fallow, and plow;
　　And all trades, their gear and tackle and trim.

1. Particolored beauty: having patches or sections of more than one color. 2. Streaked or spotted. 3. Rose-colored dots or flecks. 4. Fallen chestnuts as red as burning coals.

All things counter, original, spare, strange;
    Whatever is fickle, freckled (who knows how?)
        With swift, slow; sweet, sour; adazzle, dim;
He fathers-forth whose beauty is past change;
                Praise him.

1887

- **How many ways of expressing mixed color can you find in this poem? How does Hopkins expand the meaning of "pied beauty"?**

WILLIAM CARLOS WILLIAMS

The Red Wheelbarrow

so much depends
upon

a red wheel
barrow

glazed with rain
water

beside the white
chickens.

1923

- **How does setting the words "barrow," "water," and "chickens" on lines of their own help to substantiate the poem's first line?**

This Is Just to Say

I have eaten
the plums
that were in
the icebox

and which
you were probably
saving
for breakfast

Forgive me
they were delicious
so sweet
and so cold

1934

- **What is meant by "This" in the poem's title? What is the apparent occasion for this poem?**

AUTHORS ON THEIR WORK

WILLIAM CARLOS WILLIAMS (1883–1963)

From reading and commentary at Princeton University (1952)*

I've [. . .] gotten some fame, but I should probably say notoriety, from a very brief little poem called "The Red Wheelbarrow." [. . .] I had a letter from a lady in Boston [. . .] that said, "I love it. It's perfectly wonderful. But what does it *mean*?" [audience laughs] In the first place, I say modestly it's a perfect poem [laughs] [. . .] It means just the same as the opening lines of [John Keats's] *Endymion*, "A thing of beauty is a joy forever." And so much depends upon it. But instead of saying "A thing of beauty," I say, "a red wheel / barrow // glazed with rain / water // beside the white / chickens." Isn't that beautiful?

• • •

From interview with John W. Gerber (1950)**

WILLIAMS: It actually took place just as it [. . .] says here [in "This Is Just to Say"]. And my wife being out, I left a note for her just that way, and she replied very beautifully. Unfortunately, I lost it. [. . .] I think what she wrote was quite as good as this, a little more complex, but quite as good. Perhaps the virtue of this is its simplicity.

INTERVIEWER: Now, what I want to ask you about that [is], What makes that a poem?

WILLIAMS: In the first place, it's metrically absolutely regular. [. . . reads poem] So, dogmatically speaking, it has to be a poem because it goes that way, don't you see?

INTERVIEWER: Well, this goes against so many preconceived ideas of the poem, though, because it's the kind of thing that almost anybody might say.

WILLIAMS: Yes, because no one believes that poetry can exist in its own light. That's one of our immediate fallacies. [. . .] Imagine reading a poem in the American dialects, how impossible! That's the first hazard, that's the first hurdle. We have to get over that. [. . .] It can't be that we poor colonials, as we have been ever since the Revolution, we poor people who are not living in the centers of Europe can have anything happen in our lives important enough to be put down in words and given a form. But everything in our lives, if it's sufficiently authentic to our lives and touches us deeply enough, with a certain amount of feeling, is capable of being organized into a form which can be a poem. [. . .] Your wife, [. . .] the woman who's there with whom you are supposed to be in love and sometimes are [. . .] had these things saved for supper, and here you come along and raid it. Why, it's practically rape of the icebox, and there you are. So I think that's material for a poem. [laughs] That's a definite poem—without even writing it. But then if you can give it conventional metrical form, why [. . .] you're just simply superb, that's all. [laughs] You've done a great deed.

*Reading and commentary at Princeton University. 19 Mar. 1952. *PennSound*, writing.upenn.edu/pennsound/x/Williams-WC.php.
**Interview with John W. Gerber, Rutherford, NJ. June 1950. *PennSound*, writing.upenn.edu/pennsound/x/Williams-WC.php.

KAY RYAN
Blandeur

If it please God,
let less happen.
Even out Earth's
rondure, flatten
Eiger,[5] blanden
the Grand Canyon.
Make valleys
slightly higher,
widen fissures
to arable land,
remand your
terrible glaciers
and silence
their calving,
halving or doubling
all geographical features
toward the mean.
Unlean against our hearts.
Withdraw your grandeur
from these parts.

2000

• How does the poem define the made-up words (or neologisms) *blandeur* and *blanden*? How does it play on the word *grandeur* and its connotations?

MARTHA COLLINS
[white paper #24][6]

The Irish were not, the Germans
were not, the Jews Italians Slavs and others
were not, or were not exactly or not quite
at various times in American history.

Before us the Greeks themselves

5. Mountain in the Swiss Alps.
6. From *White Papers*, a book-length sequence of poems designated by number rather than title. A *white paper* is a detailed, authoritative report issued by a government or business.

were not (though the weaker enemy
Persians[7] were), the next-up Romans
themselves were not either.

And later the Europeans were not
until Linnaeus[8] named by color,
red white yellow and black.

Even the English settlers were only
vaguely at first to contrast with natives,
but then with Africans, more and more
of them slaves to be irreversibly,
totally different from, they were.

Then others were not, then were,
or were not, but gradually became,
leaving only, for a time, black
and yellow to be not.

Then there were other words
for those who were still or newly
(see *immigrant*, *Arab*) somehow not
the same and therefore not.

Thus history leaves us nothing
but not: like children playing at being
something, we made, we keep
making our whiteness up.

2011

- What is the significance and effect of Collins's choice not to refer to the color white or to whiteness until the very last line of the poem? of her frequent use of *not*? of her sometimes odd syntax?

A. E. STALLINGS

Shoulda, Woulda, Coulda

The mood made him tense—
How she sharpened conditional[9] futures
On strops[1] of might-have-beens,
The butchered present in sutures.

He cursed in the fricative,[2]

7. Allusion to the Greco-Persian Wars (c. 492–449 BCE), in which Greek city-states eventually triumphed over the initially far more powerful Persian Empire.
8. Swedish scientist (1707–78) who, in 1735, developed an elaborate system for classifying all living beings into genus, species, and so on; the system divided human things beings into four species—*Americanus, Asiaticus, Africanus,* and *Europeaus*—based, in part, on skin tone.
9. In grammar, verb mood or tense used in expressing what might happen given the right conditions, as in "she *would eat* if he made her a sandwich."
1. Leather strap or similar device used to sharpen a razor.
2. In phonetics, consonant sound, such as the English *f* or *v*.

The way she could not act,
Or live in the indicative,[3]
Only contrary to fact.

Tomorrow should have been vast,
Bud-packed, grenade-gravid,[4]
Not just a die miscast.

It made him sad, it made him livid:
How she construed from the imperfect[5] past
A future less vivid.

2013

- How does this poem end up playing on the various meanings of the words "mood" and "tense" (line 1)? What exactly about the attitude of the woman described in the poem makes her male counterpart first "tense," then "sad" and "livid" (lines 1, 12)?

SUGGESTIONS FOR WRITING

1. Choose one poem in this book in which a single word seems crucial to that poem's total effect and theme. Write an essay in which you work out carefully why and how that's the case.
2. Choose one poem in this book in which syntax (the order of words in sentences) or the placement of words on the page seems especially key to the poem's overall effect and meaning. Write an essay explaining how and why considering word order, in either or both of these senses, might change or deepen a reader's understanding of the poem.
3. Language is a topic of (as well as tool used in) Martha Collins's Lies, A. E. Stallings's Shoulda, Woulda, Coulda, and even Kay Ryan's Blandeur. Write an essay exploring what any of these poems has to say about poetry or language and how word choice, order, and placement help the poem express or illustrate it.

3. In grammar, mood of verbs expressing a simple statement of fact.
4. Pregnant, distended with or full of.
5. In grammar, of or relating to a verb tense used to designate a continuing state or incomplete action, especially in the past, as in "We used to speak regularly" and "I was eating."

16 VISUAL IMAGERY AND FIGURES OF SPEECH

The language of poetry is often visual and pictorial. Rather than depending primarily on abstract ideas and elaborate reasoning, poems depend more on concrete and specific words that create images in our minds. Poems thus help us see things afresh or feel them suggestively through our other physical senses, such as hearing or touch. Sound is, as we will see, a vital aspect of poetry. But most poems use the sense of sight to help us form, in our minds, visual impressions, images that communicate more directly than concepts. We "see" yellow leaves on a branch, a father and son waltzing precariously, or two lovers sitting together on the bank of a stream, so that our response begins from a vivid visual impression of exactly what is happening. Some people think that those media and arts that challenge the imagination of a hearer or reader—radio drama, for example, or poetry—allow us to respond more fully than those (such as television or theater) that actually show things more fully to our physical senses. Certainly these media leave more to our imagination, to our mind's eye.

Poems are sometimes quite abstract—they can even be *about* abstractions like grandeur or history. But usually they are quite concrete in what they ask us to see. One reason is that they often begin in a poet's mind with a picture or an image: of a person, a place, an event, or an object of observation. That image may be based on something the poet has actually seen but it may also be totally imaginary and only based on the "real world" in the sense that it draws on the poet's sense of what the world is like. Even when a poet begins with an idea that draws on visual experience, however, the reader still has to *imagine* (through the poem's words) an image, some person or thing or action that the poem describes. The poet must rely on words to help the reader to flesh out that mental image. In a sense, then, the reader becomes a visual artist, but the poet directs the visualization by evoking specific responses through words. *How* that happens can involve quite complicated verbal strategies—or even *visual* ones that draw on the possibilities of print (see ch. 20).

The languages of description are quite varied. The visual qualities of poetry result partly from the two aspects of poetic language described in chapter 15: on the one hand, the precision of individual words, and, on the other hand, precision's opposite—the reach, richness, and ambiguity of suggestion that words sometimes accrue. Visualization can also derive from sophisticated rhetorical and literary devices (**figures of speech**, for example, as we will see later in this chapter). But often description begins simply with naming—providing the word (noun, verb, adjective, or adverb) that will trigger images familiar from a reader's own experience. A reader can readily imagine a *dog* or *cat* or *house* or *flower* when each word is named, but not all readers will envision the same kind of dog or flower until the word is qualified in some way. So the poet may specify that the dog is a greyhound or poodle, or that the flower is a daffodil or a lilac or Queen Anne's lace; or the poet may indicate colors, sizes, specific movements, or particular identifying features. Such description can involve either narrowing by category or expanding through detail, and often comparisons are either explicitly or implicitly involved. Notice how this works in the two following poems. In the first, Richard Wilbur's THE BEAUTIFUL CHANGES, for example, the comparison between wading through flowers in a meadow and wading among waves in the sea both suggests how the first experience feels and etches it visually in our minds. More than just a matter of naming, using precise words, and providing basic information, description involves qualification and comparison. Sometimes, as in the second poem below, the poet needs to tell us what *not* to picture, dissociating what the poem describes from other possible images we may have in mind. Different features in the language of description add up to something that describes a whole—a picture or scene—as well as a series of individualized objects.

Seeing in the mind's eye—the re-creation of visual experience—requires different skills from poets and readers. Poets use all the linguistic strategies they can think of to re-create for us something they have already "seen." Poets depend on our having had a rich variety of visual experiences and try to draw on those experiences by using common, evocative words and then refining the process through more elaborate verbal devices. We as readers inhabit the process the other way around, trying to draw on our previous knowledge so that we can "see" by following verbal clues. In the poems that follow, notice the ways that description inspires specific images, and pay attention to how shape, color, relationship, and perspective become clear, not only through individual words but also through combinations of words and phrases that suggest appearance and motion.

RICHARD WILBUR

The Beautiful Changes

One wading a Fall meadow finds on all sides
The Queen Anne's Lace[1] lying like lilies
On water; it glides
So from the walker, it turns
Dry grass to a lake, as the slightest shade of you
Valleys my mind in fabulous blue Lucernes.[2]

The beautiful changes as a forest is changed
By a chameleon's tuning his skin to it;
As a mantis, arranged
On a green leaf, grows
Into it, makes the leaf leafier, and proves
Any greenness is deeper than anyone knows.

Your hands hold roses always in a way that says
They are not only yours; the beautiful changes

1. Plant sometimes called "wild carrot," with delicate, fingerlike leaves and flat clusters of small white flowers.
2. Alfalfa, a plant resembling clover, with small purple flowers. Lake Lucerne is famed for its deep blue color and picturesque Swiss setting amid limestone mountains.

In such kind ways,
Wishing ever to sunder
Things and things' selves for a second finding, to lose
For a moment all that it touches back to wonder.

1947

- What part of speech is "Beautiful" in the poem's title and lines 7 and 14? What part of speech is "Changes"? What is meant by "the beautiful changes / In such kind ways" (lines 14–15)?

LYNN POWELL
Kind of Blue

Not Delft or
delphinium, not Wedgewood[3]
among the knickknacks, not wide-eyed chicory
evangelizing in the devil strip—

But way on down in the moonless
octave below midnight, honey,
way down where you can't tell cerulean from teal.

Not Mason jars of moonshine, not
waverings of silk, not the long-legged hunger
of a heron or the peacock's
iridescent id—

But Delilahs[4] of darkness, darling,
and the muscle of the mind
giving in.

Not sullen snow slumped
against the garden, not the first instinct of flame,
not small, stoic ponds, or the cold derangement
of a jealous sea—

But bluer than the lips of Lazarus, baby,
before Sweet Jesus himself could figure out
what else in the world to do but weep.

2004

- How does this poem help us envision a certain "kind of blue" by creating images of what it isn't? How do the images develop over the course of the poem?

3. Wedgwood pottery, often of a distinctive blue, manufactured by a company founded in England. *Delft*: city in southern Holland renowned for the manufacture of ceramics.

4. Perhaps an allusion to the biblical Delilah, who conspired with the rulers of Philistine to destroy Samson's strength by seducing him and cutting off his hair.

METAPHOR

Being visual does not just mean describing; telling us facts; indicating shapes, colors, and specific details. Often the vividness of the picture in our minds depends on comparisons made through figures of speech. What we are trying to imagine is pictured in terms of something else familiar to us, and we are asked to think of one thing as if it were something else. Many such comparisons, in which something is pictured or figured forth in terms of something already familiar to us, are taken for granted in daily life. Things we can't see or that aren't familiar to us are imaged as things we already know; for example, God is said to be like a father; Italy is said to be shaped like a boot; life is compared to a forest, a journey, or a sea. When the comparison is implicit, describing something as if it were something else, it is called a **metaphor**.

In the poem that follows, the poet helps us visualize old age and approaching death by making comparisons with familiar things—the coming of winter, the approach of sunset, and the dying embers of a fire.

WILLIAM SHAKESPEARE

[That time of year thou mayst in me behold]

That time of year thou mayst in me behold
When yellow leaves, or none, or few, do hang
Upon those boughs which shake against the cold,
Bare ruined choirs, where late the sweet birds sang.
In me thou see'st the twilight of such day
As after sunset fadeth in the west;
Which by and by[5] black night doth take away,
Death's second self,[6] that seals up all in rest.
In me thou see'st the glowing of such fire,
That on the ashes of his youth doth lie,
As the deathbed whereon it must expire,
Consumed with that which it was nourished by.
This thou perceiv'st, which makes thy love more strong,
To love that well which thou must leave ere long.

1609

The first four lines of THAT TIME OF YEAR evoke images of the late autumn, but notice that the poet does not have the speaker say directly that his physical condition and age make him resemble autumn. He draws the comparison without stating it as a comparison: You can see my own state, he says, in the coming of winter, when almost all the leaves have fallen from the trees. The speaker portrays himself *indirectly* by talking about the passing of the year. The poem uses metaphor; that is, one thing is pictured *as if* it were something else. "That time of year" goes on to another metaphor in lines 5–8 and still another in lines 9–12, and each metaphor contributes to our understanding of the speaker's sense of his old age and approaching death. More important, however, is the way the metaphors give us feelings, an emotional sense of the speaker's age and of his own attitude toward aging. Through

5. Shortly. 6. Sleep.

the metaphors we come to understand, appreciate, and to some extent share the increasing sense of urgency that the poem expresses. Our emotional sense of the poem depends largely on the way each metaphor is developed and by the way each metaphor leads, with its own kind of internal logic, to another, even as later metaphors build on earlier ones. Look back at the poem. What does each metaphor contribute?

"That time of year" represents an unusually intricate use of images to organize a poem and focus its emotional impact. Not all poems depend on such a full and varied use of metaphor. Sometimes rather than accumulating metaphors, a poet presents a single metaphor that extends over a section of a poem (in which case it is called an *extended metaphor*) or even over the whole poem (in which case it is called a *controlling metaphor*). The following poem depends from the beginning—even from its title—on a single controlling metaphor.

LINDA PASTAN

Marks

My husband gives me an A
for last night's supper,
an incomplete for my ironing,
a B plus in bed.
My son says I am average,
an average mother, but if
I put my mind to it
I could improve.
My daughter believes
in Pass/Fail and tells me
I pass. Wait 'til they learn
I'm dropping out.

1978

The speaker in MARKS is obviously less than pleased with the idea of continually being judged, and the metaphor of marks (or grades) as a way of talking about her performance of family duties suggests her irritation. The list of the roles implies the many things expected of her, and the three different systems of marking (letter grades, categories to be checked off on a chart, and pass/fail) detail the difficulties of multiple standards. The poem retains the language of schooldays all the way to the end ("learn," line 11; "dropping out," line 12), and the major effect of the poem depends on the irony of the speaker's surrendering to the metaphor the family has thrust upon her; if she is to be judged as if she were a student, she retains the right to leave the system. Ironically, she joins the system (adopts the metaphor for herself) in order to defeat it.

PERSONIFICATION

Another figure of speech, **personification**, involves treating an abstraction, such as death or justice or beauty, as if it were a person. When "That time of year" talks about the coming of night and of sleep, for example, Sleep is personified as the "second self" of Death (that is, as a kind of "double" for death [line 8]). If personification in this poem is a brief gesture, it proves much more obvious and central in the following poem, though in this case, too, it is death that the poet personifies. How so, and with what implications and effects?

EMILY DICKINSON

[Because I could not stop for Death—]

Because I could not stop for Death—
He kindly stopped for me—
The Carriage held but just Ourselves—
And Immortality.

We slowly drove—He knew no haste
And I had put away
My labor and my leisure too,
For His Civility—

We passed the School, where Children strove
At Recess—in the Ring—
We passed the Fields of Gazing Grain—
We passed the Setting Sun—

Or rather—He passed Us—
The Dews drew quivering and chill—
For only Gossamer,[7] my Gown—
My Tippet—only Tulle[8]—

We paused before a House that seemed
A Swelling of the Ground—
The Roof was scarcely visible—
The Cornice—in the Ground—

Since then—'tis Centuries—and yet
Feels shorter than the Day
I first surmised the Horses' Heads
Were toward Eternity—

c. 1863

- What vision of death and the afterlife is implied by the way death is personified and characterized in the poem? by the details the speaker offers about the carriage ride she takes with him?

SIMILE AND ANALOGY

Sometimes, in poetry as in prose, comparisons are made explicitly, as in the following poem.

7. Soft, sheer fabric. 8. Fine net fabric. *Tippet*: shawl.

ROBERT BURNS

A Red, Red Rose

O, my luve's like a red, red rose
That's newly sprung in June.
O, my luve is like the melodie
That's sweetly played in tune.

As fair art thou, my bonnie lass,
So deep in luve am I;
And I will luve thee still, my dear,
Till a' the seas gang[9] dry.

Till a' the seas gang dry, my dear,
And the rocks melt wi' the sun;
And I will luve thee still, my dear,
While the sands o' life shall run.

And fare thee weel, my only luve,
And fare thee weel a while!
And I will come again, my luve,
Though it were ten thousand mile.

1796

The first four lines make two explicit comparisons: The speaker says that his love is "like a [. . .] rose" (line 1) and "like [a] melodie" (line 3). Such *explicit* comparisons are called **similes**, and usually (as here) the comparison involves the word *like* or the word *as*. Similes work much as do metaphors, except that usually they are used more passingly, more incidentally; they make a quick comparison and usually do not elaborate. The two similes in A RED, RED ROSE assume that we already have a favorable opinion of roses and of melodies. Here the poet does not develop the comparison or even remind us of attractive details about roses or tunes. He pays the quick compliment and moves on.

Similes sometimes develop more elaborate comparisons than this and occasionally, as in the poem below, even govern a poem (in which case they are called ***analogies***).

TODD BOSS

My Love for You Is So Embarrassingly

grand . . . would you mind terribly, my groundling,[1]
    if I compared it to the *Hindenburg*[2] (I mean,
  before it burned)—that vulnerable, elephantine

9. Go.

1. Literally, someone on the ground; figuratively, a person of unsophisticated taste, like a spectator who stood in the pit of an Elizabethan theater.

2. German airship famously destroyed by fire during a failed docking attempt over New Jersey, May 6, 1937.

dream of transport, a fabric *Titanic*[3] on an ocean
of air? There: with binoculars, dear, you can
just make me out, in a gondola window, wildly

flapping both arms as the ship's shadow
moves like a vagrant country across the
country where you live in relative safety. I pull

that oblong shadow along behind me wherever
I go. It is so big, and goes so slowly, it alters
ground temperatures noticeably, makes

housewives part kitchen curtains, wrings
whimpers from German shepherds. Aren't I
ridiculous? Isn't it anachronistic, this

dirigible devotion, this Zeppelin affection, a moon
that touches, with a kiss of wheels, the ground
you take for granted beneath your heels?—

2011

ALLUSION

Like many poems, Todd Boss's humorous My Love for You Is So Embarrassingly depends on multiple figures of speech: by comparing his love to the *Hindenburg* and, in turn, the *Hindenburg* (line 2) to the *Titanic* (line 4), the speaker makes use not only of analogy and metaphor but also of **allusion**, a brief reference to a fictitious or actual person, place, or thing and, usually, to the stories or **myth** surrounding it. Like metaphor and simile, allusion allows poets to economically suggest a wealth of sometimes complex images, feelings, and ideas by relying on widely shared literary and cultural knowledge. In this particular case, knowing something about both what happened to the *Hindenburg* and the *Titanic* and what "dream[s]" of human ingenuity and power were destroyed along with them gives us a much more specific, vivid picture of how something might be simultaneously "vulnerable" and "elephantine," exhilarating and terrifying, transcendent and potentially disastrous (lines 4, 3).

Sometimes "getting" an allusion or even recognizing one requires us to learn something new. Many of the footnotes in this book and others like it aim to help you with that. But whenever you come across a name or other reference in a poem that you don't understand or a phrase that seems oddly familiar, it's well worth your while to consult a reference book or the Internet. Allusions are one of the ways poems engage with the larger world, participating in a vast conversation they invite and even expect you, too, to be a part of.

Below are two poems that rely on an array of allusions—to everything from historical events, myths, and poems to rock stars. As you read the poems, try not only to spot all the allusions but also to tease out what specifically each contributes to the poem in which it appears.

3. British passenger liner sunk on April 15, 1912, after colliding with an iceberg on its maiden voyage.

AMIT MAJMUDAR
Dothead

Well yes, I said, my mother wears a dot.
I know they said "third eye" in class, but it's not
an *eye* eye, not like that. It's not some freak
third eye that opens on your forehead like
on some Chernobyl baby.[4] What it means
is, what it's *showing* is, there's this unseen
eye, on the inside. And she's marking it.
It's how the X that says where treasure's at
is not the treasure, but as good as treasure.—
All right. What I said wasn't half so measured.
In fact, I didn't say a thing. Their laughter
had made my mouth go dry. Lunch was after
World History; that week was India—myths,
caste system, suttee,[5] all the Greatest Hits.
The white kids I was sitting with were friends,
at least as I defined a friend back then.
So wait, said Nick, does *your* mom wear a dot?
I nodded, and I caught a smirk on Todd—
She wear it to the shower? And to bed?—
while Jesse sucked his chocolate milk and Brad
was getting ready for another stab.
I said, Hand me that ketchup packet there.
And Nick said, What? I snatched it, twitched the tear,
and squeezed a dollop on my thumb and worked
circles till the red planet entered the house of war
and on my forehead for the world to see
my third eye burned those schoolboys in their seats,
their flesh in little puddles underneath,
pale pools where Nataraja[6] cooled his feet.

2011

PATRICIA LOCKWOOD
What Is the Zoo for What

The word "zoo" is a zoo for the zoo.

A fountain is a zoo for water, the song
is a zoo for sound, the harmonica

4. That is, a baby born with birth defects as a result of the explosion that occurred in April 1986 at the Chernobyl Nuclear Power Plant in Ukraine.

5. Custom of a Hindu widow voluntarily being cremated on her husband's funeral pyre.

6. The Lord of Dancers, an avatar of the Hindu god Shiva, whose ecstatic twirling expresses the cyclic energy of the universe.

is a zoo for the hot breath of Neil Young,[7]
vagina is a zoo for baby.

Baby, girl baby, is a zoo for vagina.

The rose is a zoo for the smell of the rose,
the smell of the rose rattles its cage,
the zookeeper throws something bleeding
to it, the something bleeding is not enough,
a toddler fell into the cage of the rose,
the toddler was entirely eaten. His name
was Rilke,[8] it was in all the papers.
A Little Pine Box is a zoo for him now,
it said in all the papers.

Then all the kids started doing it. Falling
into the violet's cage, approaching the cave
where the smell of violets slept, getting
their whole head clawed off by it.
Neil Young did it to a buttercup
and his face got absolutely mauled.

The music that was piped into the zoo
let all the longing escape from it
and it ran riot over the earth, full
of the sight of the smell of a buttercup
rearranging the face of Neil Young,
attacking pets at random, attacking
me in my bed as I slept, attacking
the happy wagging ends of my poems.

Can I put Neil Young in a poem.
Will he get trapped in there forever.

My voice is a zoo right now for this,
and this paces very much inside it,
it would like very much to escape
and eat hot blood again and go home,
and right down to the restless way
I walk I am an argument against zoos.

Zoo is very cruel. Let everything out
and live in the wild. Let it hunt for itself

7. Influential Canadian singer-songwriter, musician, and activist (b. 1945); though he is primarily known as a guitarist, Young's only number-one hit, "Heart of Gold" (1972), features one of rock's best-known harmonica solos.

8. Rainer Maria Rilke (1875–1926), one of history's most famous and influential German-language poets, known especially for lyrics relying on intensely physical imagery and symbolism. According to one biographer (E. M. Butler), "There is no doubt that roses," in particular, "cast a spell upon Rilke," whose "roses were always explicitly in enclosed spaces: in death-bed chambers, in his study at night, in rose-bowls, bringing summer into a room."

again. Get the stink of human hand off it.

But the hand is a zoo for hold.

2013

• • •

All figurative language involves an attempt to clarify something *and* to prompt readers to feel a certain way about it. Saying that one's love is like a rose implies a delicate and fragile beauty and invites our senses into play so that we can share sensuously a response to appealing fragrance and soft touch, just as the shivering boughs and dying embers in "That time of year" suggest separation and loss at the same time that they invite us to share both the cold sense of loneliness and the warmth of old friendship.

Once you start looking for them, you will find figures of speech in poem after poem; they are among the most common devices through which poets share their visions with us.

POEMS FOR FURTHER STUDY

WILLIAM SHAKESPEARE

[Shall I compare thee to a summer's day?]

Shall I compare thee to a summer's day?
Thou art more lovely and more temperate.
Rough winds do shake the darling buds of May,
And summer's lease hath all too short a date.
Sometime too hot the eye of heaven shines,
And often is his gold complexion dimmed;
And every fair from fair sometime declines,
By chance or nature's changing course untrimmed.
But thy eternal summer shall not fade,
Nor lose possession of that fair thou ow'st,
Nor shall Death brag thou wand'rest in his shade,
When in eternal lines to time thou grow'st.
So long as men can breathe or eyes can see,
So long lives this,[9] and this gives life to thee.

1609

- What sort of promise does the speaker make with this poem? Why can he boast that "thy eternal summer shall not fade" (line 9)?

9. This poem.

ANONYMOUS[1]

The Twenty-Third Psalm

The Lord is my shepherd; I shall not want.
He maketh me to lie down in green pastures: he leadeth me beside
the still waters.
He restoreth my soul: he leadeth me in the paths of righteousness
for his name's sake.
Yea, though I walk through the valley of the shadow of death,
I will fear no evil: for thou art with me;
thy rod and thy staff they comfort me.
5 Thou preparest a table before me in the presence of mine enemies:
thou anointest my head with oil; my cup runneth over.
Surely goodness and mercy shall follow me all the days of my life:
and I will dwell in the house of the Lord for ever.

- **What is the controlling metaphor in this poem? At what point in the psalm does the controlling metaphor shift?**

JOHN DONNE

[Batter my heart, three-personed God][2]

Batter my heart, three-personed God; for You
As yet but knock, breathe, shine, and seek to mend;
That I may rise and stand, o'erthrow me, and bend
Your force, to break, blow, burn, and make me new.
I, like an usurped town, to another due,
Labor to admit You, but Oh, to no end!
Reason, Your viceroy[3] in me, me should defend,
But is captived, and proves weak or untrue.
Yet dearly I love You, and would be loved fain,[4]
But am betrothed unto Your enemy:
Divorce me, untie or break that knot again,
Take me to You, imprison me, for I,
Except You enthrall me, never shall be free,
Nor ever chaste, except You ravish me.

1633

- **In the poem's controlling metaphor, who is the speaker? Who, or what, is God? To whom is the speaker "betrothed" (line 10)?**

1. Traditionally attributed to King David. This English translation is from the King James Version of the Bible (1611).
2. From the sequence *Holy Sonnets*.
3. One who rules as the representative of someone of higher rank. 4. Gladly.

RANDALL JARRELL
The Death of the Ball Turret Gunner[5]

From my mother's sleep I fell into the State,
And I hunched in its belly till my wet fur froze.
Six miles from earth, loosed from its dream of life,
I woke to black flak and the nightmare fighters.
When I died they washed me out of the turret with a hose.

1945

- **What is meant by "I fell into the State (line 1)"? What do the words "sleep," "dream," and "nightmare" (lines 1, 3, 4) suggest about the situation?**

JOHN BREHM
Sea of Faith

Once when I was teaching "Dover Beach"[6]
to a class of freshmen, a young woman
raised her hand and said "I'm confused
about this 'Sea of Faith.'" "Well," I said,
"let's talk about it. We probably need
to talk a bit about figurative language.
What confuses you about it?"
"I mean, is it a real sea?" she asked.
"You mean, is it a real body of water
that you could point to on a map
or visit on a vacation?"
"Yes," she said. "Is it a *real* sea?"
Oh Christ, I thought, is this where we are?
Next year I'll be teaching them the alphabet
and how to sound words out.
I'll have to teach them geography, apparently,
before we can move on to poetry.
I'll have to teach them history, too—
a few weeks on the Dark Ages might be instructive.
"Yes," I wanted to say, "it is.
It is a real sea. In fact it flows
right into the Sea of Ignorance
IN WHICH YOU ARE DROWNING.
Let me throw you a Rope of Salvation
before the Sharks of Desire gobble you up.

5. A ball turret was a Plexiglas sphere set into the belly of a B-17 or B-24 [airplane] and inhabited by two .50 caliber machine-guns and one man, a short small man. When this gunner tracked with his machine-guns a fighter attacking his bomber from below, he revolved with the turret; hunched upside-down in his little sphere, he looked like the foetus in the womb. The fighters which attacked him were armed with cannon firing explosive shells. The hose was a steam hose [Jarrell's note].

6. Famous and widely taught poem by Matthew Arnold (1822–88), published in 1867 and included in this anthology.

Let me hoist you back up onto this Ship of Fools
so that we might continue our search
for the Fountain of Youth. Here, take a drink
of this. It's fresh from the River of Forgetfulness."
But of course I didn't say any of that.
I tried to explain in such a way
as to protect her from humiliation,
tried to explain that poets
often speak of things that don't exist.
It was only much later that I wished
I could have answered differently,
only after I'd betrayed myself
and been betrayed that I wished
it was true, wished there really was a Sea of Faith
that you could wade out into,
dive under its blue and magic waters,
hold your breath, swim like a fish
down to the bottom, and then emerge again
able to believe in everything, faithful
and unafraid to ask even the simplest of questions,
happy to have them simply answered.

2004

- When and how does the speaker's attitude toward the student and her question seem to change? How does figurative language figure in the initial conflict and its resolution?

SUGGESTIONS FOR WRITING

1. Choose any poem in this chapter and explore the meaning and effect of its metaphor(s). Does the poem make use of an extended or controlling metaphor or of multiple metaphors? If the latter, how do the metaphors relate to and build on each other?
2. Choose any poem in this book that uses personification and write an essay exploring how this figure of speech contributes both to the emotional effect of the poem and its theme(s). (In addition to the Emily Dickinson poem in this chapter, other good options include Jimmy Santiago Baca's GREEN CHILE, John Keats's TO AUTUMN, and John Donne's DEATH, BE NOT PROUD.)
3. Research the design of World War II bombers like the B-17 and the B-24. Try to find a picture of the gunner in the ball turret of such an airplane, and note carefully his body position. Write an essay in which you explain how Randall Jarrell's THE DEATH OF THE BALL TURRET GUNNER uses visual details to create its fetal and birth metaphors.
4. Look online for the lyrics to some of your favorite songs and identify the figures of speech used in each. Write an essay explaining which of these figures seem the most creative and effective, and why.
5. Choose any poem in this book that relies on at least one allusion to something or someone initially unfamiliar to you. After researching whatever the poem alludes to, write an informal response paper or essay exploring how the poem works and means differently to an informed reader.

Response, Reinterpretation, Remixing

AN ALBUM

Though it can be very useful to separate, as we do in this book, poetic "texts" from their "contexts," it's equally useful to appreciate that the separation is a partial, even artificial one. Individual poems inevitably generate their meanings and effects by reminding us both of other poems and of the world beyond poems—in part through the figures of speech examined in the last chapter. Any time a writer sits down to write a poem, she inevitably, if only unconsciously, draws on her memory of—and thus in a sense responds to—other poems she has read, just as a reader will inevitably read her poem in light of other poems with which he is familiar. If that poem happens to be a sonnet, it can't help but recall and in a sense respond to other sonnets, just as any "horror story" recalls and responds to other, earlier "horror stories," both written and filmed. Poems of any and every kind make frequent use of that figure of speech called **allusion**—a very brief, passing reference to a specific literary text or other work of art, to a myth, an historical event, and so on. In some poems, however, such references go far beyond allusion, becoming so pervasive and extensive that they are virtually what the poem is "about." The whole purpose of an **occasional poem** like Martín Espada's Litany at the Tomb of Frederick Douglass or Thomas Hardy's Convergence of the Twain, for example, is to commemorate, respond to, and interpret a specific historical event or "occasion"—not only to assert its importance but also to make us think about just what its importance is. Ekphrastic poems do something similar with the specific works of art they describe—whether an ancient funereal vase, as in John Keats's Ode on a Grecian Urn, or a painting, as in W. H. Auden's Musée des Beaux arts or (in this album) U. A. Fanthorpe's Not My Best Side. (In Greek, *ekphrasis* simply means "description.") If one of poetry's major goals is to make us pay attention to something specific, to *see* it and thus also its meanings and implications anew, then occasional and ekphrastic poems are distinguished from other kinds simply by the specific sorts of "things" on which they focus.

Though Fanthorpe's "Not My Best Side" is an ekphrastic poem because it describes and responds to a specific painting—Paolo Uccello's *Saint George and the Dragon* (1470)—that painting is itself, as its title implies, a response to, and reinterpretation of, a myth with which you're probably very familiar even without knowing it. And it's clearly both that very old myth and its very contemporary, real-world implications, as much as a particular painting, that Fanthorpe's very funny poem invites us to contemplate. Much the same might be said of the otherwise quite varied poems gathered in this album. In it, you will find, first, two poems (Christopher Marlowe's **pastoral poem** A Passionate Shepherd to His Love and Richard Wilbur's Love Calls Us to the Things of This World), each paired with a poem that responds directly to it (Walter Raleigh's The Nymph's Reply to the Shepherd and Sherman Alexie's Grief Calls Us to the Things of This

WORLD, respectively). These are followed by poems by contemporary poets—Anthony Hecht, Annie Finch, and Annie Lauinger—that respond to two other much older and especially famous and influential works of poetry located elsewhere in this anthology—Matthew Arnold's DOVER BEACH and Andrew Marvell's TO HIS COY MISTRESS. (John Brehm's SEA OF FAITH, which you'll find at the end of the previous chapter, also responds to Arnold's poem.) Next, you'll find a poem that, rather than revisiting characters or situations from a single poem, incorporates and reworks lines from several, using a technique not unlike musical "sampling." Finally, we've paired Fanthorpe's poem with two others that focus less on specific works of literature or art than on **archetypal** characters from folktale and myth we're pretty sure you're intimately acquainted with—from dragons, ladies, and knights to Cinderella and the Big Bad Wolf.

As you read these poems—which are often as entertaining and funny as they are thoughtful and moving—think carefully about the relationship between "originals" and "responses." What might the response help you to see in or about the original that you wouldn't otherwise? What different perspective might each poem offer on their mutual subject, or how might the later poem in fact "change the subject," as it were?

CHRISTOPHER MARLOWE

The Passionate Shepherd to His Love

Come live with me and be my love,
And we will all the pleasures prove[1]
That valleys, groves, hills, and fields,
Woods, or steepy mountain yields.

And we will sit upon the rocks,
Seeing the shepherds feed their flocks,
By shallow rivers to whose falls
Melodious birds sing madrigals.

And I will make thee beds of roses
And a thousand fragrant posies,
A cap of flowers, and a kirtle[2]
Embroidered all with leaves of myrtle;

A gown made of the finest wool
Which from our pretty lambs we pull;
Fair linèd slippers for the cold,
With buckles of the purest gold;

A belt of straw and ivy buds,
With coral clasps and amber studs:
And if these pleasures may thee move,
Come live with me, and be my love.

The shepherd swains[3] shall dance and sing
For thy delight each May morning:

1. Experience. 2. Gown. 3. Youths.

If these delights thy mind may move,
Then live with me and be my love.

1600

- **What are the key characteristics of the pastoral life the speaker of this poem promises his love if she will "[c]ome live with" him (line 1)? What other implicit arguments or persuasive techniques does he use?**

SIR WALTER RALEIGH
The Nymph's Reply to the Shepherd

If all the world and love were young,
And truth in every shepherd's tongue,
These pretty pleasures might me move
To live with thee and be thy love.

Time drives the flocks from field to fold,
When rivers rage, and rocks grow cold,
And Philomel[4] becometh dumb;
The rest complain of cares to come.

The flowers do fade, and wanton fields
To wayward winter reckoning yields:
A honey tongue, a heart of gall,
Is fancy's spring, but sorrow's fall.

Thy gowns, thy shoes, thy beds of roses,
Thy cap, thy kirtle, and thy posies
Soon break, soon wither, soon forgotten;
In folly ripe, in reason rotten.

Thy belt of straw and ivy buds,
Thy coral clasps and amber studs,
All these in me no means can move
To come to thee and be thy love.

But could youth last, and love still breed,
Had joys no date,[5] nor age no need,
Then these delights my mind might move
To live with thee and be thy love.

1600

- **According to the speaker, under what conditions would she say yes to the shepherd's invitation? What are all the reasons why she is instead saying no? What comment might the poem as a whole make about the vision of life, especially rural life, offered up in conventional pastoral verse like Marlowe's?**

4. The nightingale. 5. End.

RICHARD WILBUR

Love Calls Us to the Things of This World

The eyes open to a cry of pulleys,
And spirited from sleep, the astounded soul
Hangs for a moment bodiless and simple
As false dawn.
Outside the open window
The morning air is all awash with angels.

Some are in bed-sheets, some are in blouses,
Some are in smocks: but truly there they are.
Now they are rising together in calm swells
Of halcyon[6] feeling, filling whatever they wear
With the deep joy of their impersonal breathing;
Now they are flying in place, conveying
The terrible speed of their omnipresence, moving
And staying like white water; and now of a sudden
They swoon down into so rapt a quiet
That nobody seems to be there.
The soul shrinks

From all that it is about to remember,
From the punctual rape of every blessed day,
And cries,
"Oh, let there be nothing on earth but laundry,
Nothing but rosy hands in the rising steam
And clear dances done in the sight of heaven."

Yet, as the sun acknowledges
With a warm look the world's hunks and colors,
The soul descends once more in bitter love
To accept the waking body, saying now
In a changed voice as the man yawns and rises,
"Bring them down from their ruddy gallows;
Let there be clean linen for the backs of thieves;
Let lovers go fresh and sweet to be undone,
And the heaviest nuns walk in a pure floating
Of dark habits,
keeping their difficult balance."

1956

- According to the poem, what process do our "astounded soul[s]" go through every morning, and why (line 2)? By envisioning that process as it does, how might the poem question the biblical injunction to "Love not the world" or "the things that are in the world" (1 John 2.15)?

6. Serene.

SHERMAN ALEXIE
Grief Calls Us to the Things of This World

The morning air is all awash with angels

—RICHARD WILBUR, "Love Calls Us to the Things of This World"

The eyes open to a blue telephone
In the bathroom of this five-star hotel.

I wonder whom I should call? A plumber,
Proctologist, urologist, or priest?

Who is blessed among us and most deserves
The first call? I choose my father because

He's astounded by bathroom telephones.
I dial home. My mother answers. "Hey, Ma,"

I say, "Can I talk to Poppa?" She gasps,
And then I remember that my father

Has been dead for nearly a year. "Shit, Mom,"
I say. "I forgot he's dead. I'm sorry—

How did I forget?" "It's okay," she says.
"I made him a cup of instant coffee

This morning and left it on the table—
Like I have for, what, twenty-seven years—

And I didn't realize my mistake
Until this afternoon." My mother laughs

At the angels who wait for us to pause
During the most ordinary of days

And sing our praise to forgetfulness
Before they slap our souls with their cold wings.

Those angels burden and unbalance us.
Those fucking angels ride us piggyback.

Those angels, forever falling, snare us
And haul us, prey and praying, into dust.

2009

- **Alexie's poem plays on different meanings of the word *call*: How, in this poem, does a phone *call* lead to being "*called* to the things of this world" by "grief"? In what specific ways does Alexie's poem refer back to Wilbur's?**

ANTHONY HECHT

The Dover Bitch

A Criticism of Life[7]

for Andrews Wanning[8]

So there stood Matthew Arnold and this girl
With the cliffs of England crumbling away behind them,
And he said to her, "Try to be true to me,
And I'll do the same for you, for things are bad
All over, etc., etc."
Well now, I knew this girl. It's true she had read
Sophocles in a fairly good translation
And caught that bitter allusion to the sea,[9]
But all the time he was talking she had in mind
The notion of what his whiskers would feel like
On the back of her neck. She told me later on
That after a while she got to looking out
At the lights across the channel, and really felt sad,
Thinking of all the wine and enormous beds
And blandishments in French and the perfumes.
And then she got really angry. To have been brought
All the way down from London, and then be addressed
As a sort of mournful cosmic last resort
Is really tough on a girl, and she was pretty.
Anyway, she watched him pace the room
And finger his watch-chain and seem to sweat a bit,
And then she said one or two unprintable things.
But you mustn't judge her by that. What I mean to say is,
She's really all right. I still see her once in a while
And she always treats me right. We have a drink
And I give her a good time, and perhaps it's a year
Before I see her again, but there she is,
Running to fat, but dependable as they come.
And sometimes I bring her a bottle of *Nuit d'Amour*.[1]

1968

- What specifically about the speaker of Matthew Arnold's DOVER BEACH does the speaker of THE DOVER BITCH make fun of both by *what* he says and by *how* he says it, especially the sort of language he uses? Might THE DOVER BITCH give us any reasons to be critical of *its* speaker?

7. Hecht's poem responds to Matthew Arnold's poem "Dover Beach" and to Arnold's influential view of poetry as "a criticism of life," an "application of ideas to life—to the question: How to live."
8. Professor of literature at Bard College.
9. See "Dover Beach," lines 9–18.
1. French for "Night of Love," presumably a bottle of perfume.

ANNIE FINCH

Coy Mistress[2]

Sir, I am not a bird of prey:
a Lady does not seize the day.
I trust that brief Time will unfold
our youth, before he makes us old.
How could we two write lines of rhyme
were we not fond of numbered Time
and grateful to the vast and sweet
trials his days will make us meet?
The Grave's not just the body's curse;
no skeleton can pen a verse!
So while this numbered World we see,
let's sweeten Time with poetry,
and Time, in turn, may sweeten Love
and give us time our love to prove.
You've praised my eyes, forehead, breast:
you've all our lives to praise the rest.

1997

- **What counter-arguments does Finch's "coy mistress" make to those made by the speaker of Andrew Marvell's To His Coy Mistress? What different views of the relationship between time, love, and poetry and/or between men and women might each poem offer?**

ANNE LAUINGER

Marvell Noir[3]

Sweetheart, if we had the time,
A week in bed would be no crime.
I'd light your Camels, pour your Jack;
You'd do shiatsu[4] on my back.
When you got up to scramble eggs,
I'd write a sonnet to your legs,
And you could watch my stubble grow.
Yes, gorgeous, we'd take it slow.
I'd hear the whole sad tale again:
A roadhouse band; you can't trust men;
He set you up; you had to eat,
And bitter with the bittersweet
Was what they dished you; Ginger lied;
You weren't there when Sanchez died;

2. See Andrew Marvell's "To His Coy Mistress."

3. This poem directly echoes and parodies Andrew Marvell's "To His Coy Mistress," as well as "noir" films (*noir* means "black" in French) in which a tough guy in the end reveals that the sexy woman is guilty of conspiring to commit murder or other crimes.

4. Japanese style of massage.

You didn't know the pearls were fake . . .
Aw, can it, sport! Make no mistake,
You're in it, doll, up to your eyeballs!
Tears? Please! You'll dilute our highballs,
And make that angel face a mess
For the nice Lieutenant. I confess
I'm nuts for you—but take the rap?[5]
You must think I'm some other sap!
And, precious, I kind of wish I was.
Well, when they spring[6] you, give abuzz;
Guess I'll get back to Archie's wife,
And you'll get twenty-five to life.
You'll have time there, more than enough,
To reminisce about the stuff
That dreams are made of,[7] and the men
You suckered. Sadly, in the pen
Your kind of talent goes to waste.
But Irish bars are more my taste
Than Iron ones: stripes ain't my style.
You're going down; I promise I'll
Come visit every other year.
Now kiss me, sweet—the squad car's here.

2005

• **What might Marvell Noir suggest about the similarities and differences in the relationship between men and women as imagined in carpe diem poems like To His Coy Mistress and in noir fiction and film?**

KIM ADDONIZIO

The First Line Is the Deepest[8]

I have been one acquainted with the spatula,[9]
the slotted, scuffed, Teflon-coated spatula

that lifts a solitary hamburger from pan to plate,
acquainted with the vibrator known as the Pocket Rocket

and the dildo that goes by Tex,
and I have gone out, a drunken bitch,

5. Confess and take the punishment in someone's stead.

6. Release from prison.

7. Allusion to Shakespeare, *The Tempest* (4.1): "we are such stuff as dreams are made on."

8. "The First Cut Is the Deepest," a pop song originally written by Cat Stevens (1967), has been a hit for several other artists, including Sheryl Crow (2003). Rather than responding to any one poem, Addonizio's "samples" and reworks phrases (often the first lines) of many.

9. Echo of the opening lines of Robert Frost's "Acquainted with the Night" (1928): "I have been one acquainted with the night / I have walked out in rain—and back in rain."

in order to ruin
what love I was given,

and also I have measured out
my life in little pills[1]—Zoloft,

Restoril, Celexa,
Xanax.

I have. For I am a poet. And it is my job, my duty
to know wherein lies the beauty

of this degraded body,[2]
or maybe

it's the degradation in the beautiful body,
the ugly me

groping back to my desk to piss
on perfection, to lay my kiss

of mortal confusion
upon the mouth of infinite wisdom.

My kiss says razors and pain, my kiss says
America is charged with the madness

of God.[3] Sundays, too,
the soldiers get up early, and put on their fatigues in the blue-

black day. Black milk. Black gold. Texas tea.[4]
Into the valley of Halliburton rides the infantry—[5]

Why does one month have to be the cruelest.[6]
can't they all be equally cruel? I have seen the best

1. See T. S. Eliot's "The Love Song of J. Alfred Prufrock" (1915): "I have measured out my life with coffee spoons" (line 51).
2. Perhaps an echo of poet Robinson Jeffers's verse drama *The Cretan Woman* (1954): "Take this degraded body here kneeling to you. Do what you like: love it or kill it. Oh—/ Lift it up: love it!"
3. See the first lines of Gerard Manley Hopkins's "God's Grandeur" (1877): "The world is charged with the grandeur of God. / It will flame out, like shining from shook foil."
4. Echo of "The Ballad of Jed Clampett," the theme song for *The Beverly Hillbillies*, a long-running sitcom (1962–71) about a poor country family who move into a Beverly Hills mansion after discovering oil on their land—an event the song's first stanza describes like this: "up through the ground came a bubblin' crude. // Oil that is, black gold, Texas tea." *Black milk*: See Paul Celan's Holocaust poem, "Deathfugue" (1952): "Black milk of daybreak we drink it at evening / we drink it at midday and morning we drink it at night" (lines 1–2). *Sundays . . . blue-black day*: Robert Hayden's "Those Winter Sundays" (1966) begins, "Sundays too my father got up early / and put his clothes on in the blueblack cold."
5. This line both echoes lines 7–8 of Alfred Tennyson's 1854 poem "The Charge of the Light Bridge" ("Into the valley of Death / Rode the six hundred"), about an infamously disastrous Crimean War battle, and alludes to Halliburton, a U.S.-based multinational corporation whose subsidiaries have, since the 1990s, played a major, often controversial role in U.S. military operations in the Middle East, including the Iraq War (2003–11).
6. T. S. Eliot's "The Wasteland" (1922) famously begins, "April is the cruellest month."

gamers of your generation,[7] joysticking their M1 tanks through
the sewage-filled streets. Whose

world this is I think I know.[8]

2009

- What does the speaker seem to mean by "lay[ing the] kiss // of mortal confusion / upon the mouth of infinite wisdom" (lines 20–22)? In what ways might her poem do just that by echoing lines from other poems? In these terms, what might be important about the sorts of poems from which those lines are taken and the way Addonizio's poem adapts the lines?

ANNE SEXTON

Cinderella

You always read about it:
the plumber with twelve children
who wins the Irish Sweepstakes.
From toilets to riches.
That story.

Or the nursemaid,
some luscious sweet from Denmark
who captures the oldest son's heart.
From diapers to Dior.
That story.

Or a milkman who serves the wealthy,
eggs, cream, butter, yogurt, milk,
the white truck like an ambulance
who goes into real estate
and makes a pile.
From homogenized to martinis at lunch.

Or the charwoman
who is on the bus when it cracks up
and collects enough from the insurance.
From mops to Bonwit Teller.[9]
That story.

Once
the wife of a rich man was on her deathbed
and she said to her daughter Cinderella:
Be devout. Be good. Then I will smile
down from heaven in the seam of a cloud.

7. See the opening lines of Allen Ginsberg's "Howl" (1955): "I saw the best minds of my generation destroyed by madness, starving hysterical naked, / dragging themselves through the negro streets at dawn looking for an angry fix."
8. Echo of the first lines of Robert Frost's "Stopping by Woods on a Snowy Evening" (1923): "Whose woods these are I think I know, / His house is in the village, though."
9. Upscale New York City department store founded in 1895.

The man took another wife who had
two daughters, pretty enough
but with hearts like blackjacks.[1]
Cinderella was their maid.
She slept on the sooty hearth each night
and walked around looking like Al Jolson.[2]
Her father brought presents home from town,
jewels and gowns for the other women
but the twig of a tree for Cinderella.
She planted that twig on her mother's grave
and it grew to a tree where a white dove sat.
Whenever she wished for anything the dove
would drop it like an egg upon the ground.
The bird is important, my dears, so heed him.

Next came the ball, as you all know.
It was a marriage market.
The prince was looking for a wife.
All but Cinderella were preparing
and gussying up for the big event.
Cinderella begged to go too.
Her stepmother threw a dish of lentils
into the cinders and said: Pick them
up in an hour and you shall go.
The white dove brought all his friends;
all the warm wings of the fatherland came,
and picked up the lentils in a jiffy.
No, Cinderella, said the stepmother,
you have no clothes and cannot dance.
That's the way with stepmothers.

Cinderella went to the tree at the grave
and cried forth like a gospel singer:
Mama! Mama! My turtledove,
send me to the prince's ball!
The bird dropped down a golden dress
and delicate little gold slippers.
Rather a large package for a simple bird.
So she went. Which is no surprise.
Her stepmother and sisters didn't
recognize her without her cinder face
and the prince took her hand on the spot
and danced with no other the whole day.

As nightfall came she thought she'd better
get home. The prince walked her home
and she disappeared into the pigeon house

1. Small leather-covered, often lead-filled or metal clubs with a handle; a weapon once popular with the police and military.
2. American singer, actor, and comedian famous for his performances in "blackface" (1886–1950).

and although the prince took an axe and broke
it open she was gone. Back to her cinders.
These events repeated themselves for three days.
However on the third day the prince
covered the palace steps with cobbler's wax
and Cinderella's gold shoe stuck upon it.
Now he would find whom the shoe fit
and find his strange dancing girl for keeps.
He went to their house and the two sisters
were delighted because they had lovely feet.
The eldest went into a room to try the slipper on
but her big toe got in the way so she simply
sliced it off and put on the slipper.
The prince rode away with her until the white dove
told him to look at the blood pouring forth.
That is the way with amputations.
They don't just heal up like a wish.
The other sister cut off her heel
but the blood told as blood will.
The prince was getting tired.
He began to feel like a shoe salesman.
But he gave it one last try.
This time Cinderella fit into the shoe
like a love letter into its envelope.

At the wedding ceremony
the two sisters came to curry favor
and the white dove pecked their eyes out.
Two hollow spots were left
like soup spoons.

Cinderella and the prince
lived, they say, happily ever after,
like two dolls in a museum case
never bothered by diapers or dust,
never arguing over the timing of an egg,
never telling the same story twice,
never getting a middle-aged spread,
their darling smiles pasted on for eternity.
Regular Bobbsey Twins.[3]
That story.

1971

- What do the four stories the poem opens with have in common with each other and with "Cinderella"? According to Sexton's poem, what are the chief problems with such stories?

3. Impossibly adorable protagonists (four in all) of a long-running, oft-revised series of children's novels first published in 1904.

AGHA SHAHID ALI
The Wolf's Postscript to "Little Red Riding Hood"

First, grant me my sense of history:
I did it for posterity,
for kindergarten teachers
and a clear moral:
Little girls shouldn't wander off
in search of strange flowers,
and they mustn't speak to strangers.

And then grant me my generous sense of plot:
Couldn't I have gobbled her up
right there in the jungle?
Why did I ask her where her grandma lived?
As if I, a forest-dweller,
didn't know of the cottage
under the three oak trees
and the old woman who lived there
all alone?
As if I couldn't have swallowed her years before?

And you may call me the Big Bad Wolf,
now my only reputation.
But I was no child-molester
though you'll agree she was pretty.

And the huntsman:
Was I sleeping while he snipped
my thick black fur
and filled me with garbage and stones?
I ran with that weight and fell down,
simply so children could laugh
at the noise of the stones
cutting through my belly,
at the garbage spilling out
with a perfect sense of timing,
just when the tale
should have come to an end.

1987

- **If you take Ali's poem to be, like Sexton's, not only about a specific tale ("Little Red Riding Hood") but also about folktales generally, what might it invite you to notice about how folktales work and the sorts of messages they send?**

U. A. FANTHORPE

Not My Best Side

I

Not my best side, I'm afraid.
The artist didn't give me a chance to
Pose properly, and as you can see,
Poor chap, he had this obsession with
Triangles, so he left off two of my
Feet. I didn't comment at the time
(What, after all, are two feet
To a monster?) but afterwards
I was sorry for the bad publicity.
Why, I said to myself, should my conqueror
Be so ostentatiously beardless, and ride
A horse with a deformed neck and square hoofs?
Why should my victim be so
Unattractive as to be inedible,
And why should she have me literally
On a string? I don't mind dying
Ritually, since I always rise again,
But I should have liked a little more blood
To show they were taking me seriously.

II

It's hard for a girl to be sure if
She wants to be rescued. I mean, I quite
Took to the dragon. It's nice to be
Liked, if you know what I mean. He was
So nicely physical, with his claws
And lovely green skin, and that sexy tail,
And the way he looked at me,
He made me feel he was all ready to
Eat me. And any girl enjoys that.
So when this boy turned up, wearing machinery,
On a really *dangerous* horse, to be honest,
I didn't much fancy[4] him. I mean,
What was he like underneath the hardware?
He might have acne, blackheads or even
Bad breath for all I could tell, but the dragon—
Well, you could see all his equipment
At a glance. Still, what could I do?
The dragon got himself beaten by the boy,
And a girl's got to think of her future.

III

I have diplomas in Dragon
Management and Virgin Reclamation.

4. Feel a desire or liking for; find sexually attractive (British English).

My horse is the latest model, with
Automatic transmission and built-in
Obsolescence. My spear is custom-built,
And my prototype armour
Still on the secret list. You can't
Do better than me at the moment.
I'm qualified and equipped to the
Eyebrow. So why be difficult?
Don't you want to be killed and/or rescued
In the most contemporary way? Don't
You want to carry out the roles
That sociology and myth have designed for you?
Don't you realize that, by being choosy,
You are endangering job-prospects
In the spear- and horse-building industries?
What, in any case, does it matter what
You want? You're in my way.

1978

- Fanthorpe's poem features three archetypal characters—the dragon or "monster" (line 8), the maiden or damsel-in-distress, and the knight or hero. How does the poem play with each? What serious point might it make in the process?

SUGGESTIONS FOR WRITING

1. More than one poem in this album responds to an earlier one by offering us the perspective and even, in some cases, the voice of a character other than the original poem's speaker—in Raleigh's and Finch's poems, for example, we hear from Marlowe's nymph and Marvell's mistress; though the speaker of Hecht's poem isn't the **auditor** of Arnold's, this character and her perceptions are the focus of THE DOVER BITCH. Similarly, Ali's poem responds to the oft-told tale of Red Riding Hood by making that tale's villain his speaker. Choose any one of these poems and write a response paper reflecting on what the poem achieves through this shift in perspective and/or speakers.
2. Do some research into "noir" film and/or fiction, and then draw on your research in an essay analyzing MARVELL NOIR. What specific conventions of noir does the poem draw on? What might it ultimately suggest about what in the world connects noir to Marvell's particular poem or to the **carpe diem** poem in general?
3. Write an essay exploring both what kind of story Sexton's poem suggests "Cinderella" is, in part by comparing it to other stories, and what her poem shows us about the nature and effects of "That story" (line 5), especially through her specific way of retelling "Cinderella."
4. In the last section of Fanthorpe's NOT MY BEST SIDE, when St. George refers to "the roles / That sociology and myth have designed for you" (lines 51–52), he seems to the use the word *myth* in two senses, as meaning not only a specific "traditional story of ostensibly historical events" like that of St. George and the dragon itself but also any "popular belief or tradition," especially a false or at least misleading one, crucial to the ideals of a particular culture or society. Choose any poem in this album and write an essay exploring what specific "myth" in this second sense the poem explores, how it does so, and what it says about it. Ideally, you should also consider the original text to which your poem responds, whether that text is another poem, a painting, or a folktale. How might (or might not) the original text perpetuate the "myth" that the response implies it does?

17 SYMBOL

Properly used, the term *symbol* suggests one of the most basic things about poems—their ability to get beyond what words signify and to make larger claims about meanings in the verbal world. All words go beyond themselves. They are not simply a collection of sounds: They signify something beyond their sounds, often things or actions or ideas. Words describe not only a verbal universe but also a world in which actions occur, acts have implications, and events have meaning. Sometimes words signify something beyond themselves, say, *rock* or *tree* or *cloud*, and symbolize something as well, such as solidity or life or dreams. Words can—when their implications are agreed on by tradition, convention, or habit—stand for things beyond their most immediate meanings or significations and become symbols, and even simple words that have accumulated no special power from previous use may be given special significance in special circumstances—in poetry as in life itself.

A **symbol** is, put simply, something that stands for something else. The everyday world is full of common examples; a flag, a logo, a trademark, or a skull and crossbones all suggest things beyond themselves, and everyone likely understands what their display indicates, whether or not each viewer shares a commitment to what is thus represented. In common usage a prison symbolizes confinement, constriction, and loss of freedom, and in specialized traditional usage a cross may symbolize oppression, cruelty, suffering, death, resurrection, triumph, or an intersection of some kind (as in *crossroads* and *crosscurrents*). The specific symbolic significance depends on the context; for example, a reader might determine significance by looking at contiguous details in a poem and by examining the poem's attitude toward a particular tradition or body of beliefs. A star means one thing to a Jewish poet and something else to a Christian poet, still something else to a sailor or an actor. In a very literal sense, words themselves are all symbols (they stand for objects, actions, or qualities, not just for letters or sounds), but symbols in poetry are those words and phrases that have a range of reference beyond their literal signification or **denotation**.

THE INVENTED SYMBOL

Poems sometimes create a symbol out of a thing, action, or event that has no previously agreed-upon symbolic significance. Such a symbol is sometimes called an *invented symbol*. The following poem, for example, gives an action symbolic significance.

JAMES DICKEY
The Leap

The only thing I have of Jane MacNaughton
Is one instant of a dancing-class dance.
She was the fastest runner in the seventh grade,
My scrapbook says, even when boys were beginning
To be as big as the girls,
But I do not have her running in my mind,
Though Frances Lane is there, Agnes Fraser,
Fat Betty Lou Black in the boys-against-girls
Relays we ran at recess: she must have run

Like the other girls, with her skirts tucked up
So they would be like bloomers,
But I cannot tell; that part of her is gone.
What I do have is when she came,
With the hem of her skirt where it should be
For a young lady, into the annual dance
Of the dancing class we all hated, and with a light
Grave leap, jumped up and touched the end
Of one of the paper-ring decorations

To see if she could reach it. She could,
And reached me now as well, hanging in my mind
From a brown chain of brittle paper, thin
And muscular, wide-mouthed, eager to prove
Whatever it proves when you leap
In a new dress, a new womanhood, among the boys
Whom you easily left in the dust
Of the passionless playground. If I said I saw
In the paper where Jane MacNaughton Hill,

Mother of four, leapt to her death from a window
Of a downtown hotel, and that her body crushed-in
The top of a parked taxi, and that I held
Without trembling a picture of her lying cradled
In that papery steel as though lying in the grass,
One shoe idly off, arms folded across her breast,
I would not believe myself. I would say
The convenient thing, that it was a bad dream
Of maturity, to see that eternal process

Most obsessively wrong with the world
Come out of her light, earth-spurning feet
Grown heavy: would say that in the dusty heels
Of the playground some boy who did not depend
On speed of foot, caught and betrayed her.
Jane, stay where you are in my first mind:
It was odd in that school, at that dance.

I and the other slow-footed yokels sat in corners
Cutting rings out of drawing paper

Before you leapt in your new dress
And touched the end of something I began,
Above the couples struggling on the floor,
New men and women clutching at each other
And prancing foolishly as bears: hold on
To that ring I made for you, Jane—
My feet are nailed to the ground
By dust I swallowed thirty years ago—
While I examine my hands.

1967

Memory is crucial to THE LEAP. The fact that Jane MacNaughton's graceful leap in dancing class has stuck in the speaker's mind all these years means that this leap was important to him, meant something to him, stood for something in his mind. For the speaker, the leap is an "instant" and the "only thing" he has of Jane (lines 2, 1). He remembers its grace and ease, and he struggles at several points to articulate its meaning (lines 16–26, 44–50), but even without articulation or explanation it remains in his head as a visual memory, a symbol of something beyond himself, something he cannot do, something he wanted to be. What that leap stood for, or symbolized, was boldness, confidence, accomplishment, maturity, Jane's ability to go beyond her fellow students in dancing class—the transcending of childhood by someone entering adulthood. Her feet now seem "earth-spurning" (line 38) in that original leap, and they separate her from everyone else. Jane MacNaughton was beyond the speaker's abilities and any attempt he could make to articulate his hopes, but she was not beyond his dreams. And even before he could say so, she symbolized a dream.

The leap to her death seems cruelly wrong and ironic after the grace of her earlier leap. In memory she is suspended in air, as if there were no gravity, no coming back to earth, as if life could exist as dream. And so the photograph, re-created in precise detail, is a cruel dashing of the speaker's dream—a detailed record of the ending of a leap, a denial of the suspension in which his memory had held her. His dream is grounded; her mortality is insistent. But the speaker still wants to hang on to that symbolic moment (line 42), which he confronts in a more mature context but will never altogether replace or surrender.

The leap is ultimately symbolic in the *poem*, too, not just in the speaker's mind. In the poem (and for us as readers) its symbolism is double: The first leap symbolizes aspiration, and the second symbolizes the frustration and grounding of high hopes; the two are complementary, one impossible to imagine without the other. The poem is horrifying in some ways, a dramatic reminder that human beings don't ultimately transcend their mortality, their limits, no matter how heroic or unencumbered by gravity they may once have seemed. But the poem is not altogether sad and despairing, partly because it still affirms the validity of the original leap and partly because it creates and elaborates another symbol: the paper chain.

The chain connects Jane to the speaker both literally and figuratively. It is, in part, *his* paper chain that she had leaped to touch in dancing class (lines 18–19), and he thinks of her first leap as "touch[ing] the end of something I began" (line 47).

He and the other earthbound, "slow-footed yokels" (line 44) made the chain, and it connects them to her original leap, just as a photograph glimpsed in the newspaper connects the speaker to her second leap. And so the paper chain becomes the poem's symbol of linkage, connecting lower accomplishment to higher possibility, the artisan to the artist, material substance to the act of imagination. At the end the speaker examines the hands that made the chain because those hands certify his connection to her and to the imaginative leap she had made for him. The chain thus symbolizes not only the lower capabilities of those who cannot leap like the budding Jane could, but also (later) the connection with her leap as both transcendence and mortality.

Like the leap, the chain is elevated to special meaning, given symbolic significance, only by the poet's treatment of it. A leap and a chain have no necessary significance in themselves to most of us—at least no significance that we have all agreed upon—but they may take on significance in specific circumstances or a specific text.

THE TRADITIONAL SYMBOL

Other objects and acts have a built-in significance because of past usage in literature, or tradition, or the stories a culture develops to explain itself and its beliefs. Such things have acquired an agreed-upon significance, an accepted value in our minds. They already stand for something before the poet cites them; they are *traditional symbols.* Poets assume that their readers will recognize the traditional meanings of these symbols, and the poem does not have to propose or argue a particular symbolic value. Birds, for example, traditionally symbolize flight, freedom from confinement, detachment from earthbound limits, the ability to soar beyond rationality and transcend mortal limits. Traditionally, birds have also been linked with imagination, especially poetic imagination, and poets often identify with them as pure and ideal singers of songs.

One traditional symbol, the rose, may be a simple and fairly plentiful flower in its season, but it has so long stood for particular qualities that merely to name it creates predictable expectations. Its beauty, delicacy, fragrance, shortness of life, and depth of color have made it a symbol of the transitoriness of beauty, and countless poets have counted on its accepted symbolism—sometimes to compliment a friend (as Burns does in A RED, RED ROSE) or sometimes to make a point about the nature of symbolism. The following poem draws, in quite a traditional way, on the traditional meanings.

EDMUND WALLER

Song

Go, lovely rose!
Tell her that wastes her time and me
That now she knows,
When I resemble[1] her to thee,
How sweet and fair she seems to be.

1. Compare.

Tell her that's young,
And shuns to have her graces spied,
That hadst thou sprung
In deserts, where no men abide,
Thou must have uncommended died.

Small is the worth
Of beauty from the light retired;
Bid her come forth,
Suffer herself to be desired,
And not blush so to be admired.

Then die! that she
The common fate of all things rare
May read in thee;
How small a part of time they share
That are so wondrous sweet and fair!

1645

The speaker in SONG sends the rose to his love in order to have it speak its traditional meanings of beauty and transitoriness. He counts on accepted symbolism to make his point and hurry her into accepting his advances. Likewise, the poet does not elaborate or argue these things because he does not need to; he counts on the familiarity of the tradition (though, of course, readers unfamiliar with the tradition will not respond in the same way—that is one reason it is difficult to fully appreciate texts from another linguistic or cultural tradition).

Poets may use traditional symbols to invoke predictable responses—in effect using shortcuts to meaning by repeating acts of signification sanctioned by time and cultural habit. But often poets examine the tradition even as they employ it, and sometimes they revise or reverse meanings built into the tradition. Symbols do not necessarily stay the same over time, and poets often turn even the most traditional symbols to their own original uses. Knowing the traditions of poetry—reading a lot of poems and observing how they tend to use certain words, metaphors, and symbols—can be very useful in reading new poems, but traditions evolve, and individual poems do highly individual things. Knowing the past never means being able to interpret new texts with certainty. Symbolism makes things happen, but individual poets and texts determine what will happen and how. How does the following poem both draw and comment on the traditional symbolism of roses?

DOROTHY PARKER

One Perfect Rose

A single flow'r he sent me, since we met.
All tenderly his messenger he chose;
Deep-hearted, pure, with scented dew still wet—
One perfect rose.

I knew the language of the floweret;
"My fragile leaves," it said, "his heart enclose."
Love long has taken for his amulet
One perfect rose.

Why is it no one ever sent me yet
One perfect limousine, do you suppose?
Ah no, it's always just my luck to get
One perfect rose.

1937

THE SYMBOLIC POEM

Sometimes symbols—traditional or not—become so insistent in the world of a poem that the larger referential world is left almost totally behind. In such cases the symbol is everything, and the poem does not just *use* symbols but becomes a symbolic poem, usually a highly individualized one dependent on an internal system introduced by the individual poet.

Here is one such poem.

WILLIAM BLAKE

The Sick Rose[2]

O rose, thou art sick.
The invisible worm
That flies in the night
In the howling storm

Has found out thy bed
Of crimson joy,
And his dark secret love
Does thy life destroy.

1794

The poem does not seem to be about or refer to a real rose. Rather the poem is about what the rose represents—not in this case something altogether understandable through the traditional meanings of *rose*.

We usually associate the rose with beauty and love, often with sex; and here several key terms have sexual connotations: "worm," "bed," and "crimson joy" (lines 2, 5, 6). The violation of the rose by the worm is the poem's main concern; the violation seems to have involved secrecy, deceit, and "dark" motives (line 7), and the result is sickness rather than the joy of love. The poem is sad; it involves a sense of hurt and tragedy, nearly of despair. The poem cries out against the misuse of the rose, against its desecration, implying that instead of a healthy joy in sensuality and sexuality, there has been in this case destruction and hurt, perhaps because of misunderstanding and repression and lack of sensitivity.

But to say so much about this poem we have to extrapolate from other poems by Blake, and we have to introduce information from outside the poem. Fully symbolic poems often require that we thus go beyond the formal procedures of reading that we have discussed so far. As presented in this poem, the rose is not part of the normal world that we ordinarily see, and it is symbolic in a special sense. The poet does

2. In Renaissance emblem books, the scarab beetle, worm, and rose are closely associated: The beetle feeds on dung, and the smell of the rose is fatal to it.

not simply take an object from our everyday world and give it special significance, making it a symbol in the same way that James Dickey does with the leap. In Blake's poem the rose seems to belong to its own world, a world made entirely inside the poem or the poet's head. The rose is not referential, or not primarily so. The whole poem is symbolic; it lives in its own world. But what is the rose here a symbol of? In general terms, we can say from what the poem tells us; but we may not be as confident as we can be in the more nearly recognizable world of THE LEAP or ONE PERFECT ROSE. In THE SICK ROSE, it seems inappropriate to ask the standard questions: What rose? Where? Which worm? What are the particulars here? In the world of this poem worms can fly and may be invisible. We are altogether in a world of meanings that have been formulated according to a special system of knowledge and code of belief. We will feel comfortable and confident in that world only if we read many poems written by the poet (in this case, William Blake) within the same symbolic system.

Negotiation of meanings in symbolic poems can be very difficult indeed. Reading symbolic poems is an advanced skill that depends on knowledge of context, especially the lives and work of authors and the special literary and cultural traditions they work from. But usually the symbols you will find in poems *are* referential of meanings we all share, and you can readily discover these meanings by carefully studying the poems themselves.

POEMS FOR FURTHER STUDY

JOHN KEATS

Ode to a Nightingale

I

My heart aches, and a drowsy numbness pains
  My sense, as though of hemlock I had drunk,
Or emptied some dull opiate to the drains
  One minute past, and Lethe-wards[3] had sunk:
'Tis not through envy of thy happy lot,
  But being too happy in thine happiness,
    That thou, light-wingèd Dryad[4] of the trees,
      In some melodious plot
  Of beechen green, and shadows numberless,
    Singest of summer in full-throated ease.

II

O, for a draught of vintage! that hath been
  Cooled a long age in the deep-delvèd earth,
Tasting of Flora[5] and the country green,
  Dance, and Provençal song,[6] and sunburnt mirth!
O for a beaker full of the warm South,
  Full of the true, the blushful Hippocrene,[7]

3. Toward the river of forgetfulness (Lethe) in Hades. 4. Wood nymph.
5. Roman goddess of flowers.
6. The medieval troubadours of Provence were famous for their love songs.
7. Fountain of the Muses on Mt. Helicon, whose waters bring poetic inspiration.

With beaded bubbles winking at the brim,
And purple-stainèd mouth;
That I might drink, and leave the world unseen,
And with thee fade away into the forest dim:

III

Fade far away, dissolve, and quite forget
What thou among the leaves hast never known,
The weariness, the fever, and the fret
Here, where men sit and hear each other groan;
Where palsy shakes a few, sad, last gray hairs,
Where youth grows pale, and specter-thin, and dies;
Where but to think is to be full of sorrow
And leaden-eyed despairs,
Where Beauty cannot keep her lustrous eyes,
Or new Love pine at them beyond tomorrow.

IV

Away! away! for I will fly to thee,
Not charioted by Bacchus and his pards,[8]
But on the viewless[9] wings of Poesy,
Though the dull brain perplexes and retards:
Already with thee! tender is the night,
And haply the Queen-Moon is on her throne,
Clustered around by all her starry Fays;[1]
But here there is no light,
Save what from heaven is with the breezes blown
Through verdurous glooms and winding mossy ways.

V

I cannot see what flowers are at my feet,
Nor what soft incense hangs upon the boughs,
But, in embalmèd[2] darkness, guess each sweet
Wherewith the seasonable month endows
The grass, the thicket, and the fruit-tree wild;
White hawthorn, and the pastoral eglantine;[3]
Fast fading violets covered up in leaves;
And mid-May's eldest child,
The coming musk-rose, full of dewy wine,
The murmurous haunt of flies on summer eves.

VI

Darkling[4] I listen; and, for many a time
I have been half in love with easeful Death,
Called him soft names in many a musèd rhyme,
To take into the air my quiet breath;
Now more than ever seems it rich to die,
To cease upon the midnight with no pain,

8. The Roman god of wine was sometimes portrayed in a chariot drawn by leopards.
9. Invisible. 1. Fairies. 2. Fragrant, aromatic. 3. Sweetbriar or honeysuckle. 4. In the dark.

While thou art pouring forth thy soul abroad
In such an ecstasy!
Still wouldst thou sing, and I have ears in vain—
To thy high requiem become a sod.

VII

Thou wast not born for death, immortal Bird!
No hungry generations tread thee down;
The voice I hear this passing night was heard
In ancient days by emperor and clown:
Perhaps the selfsame song that found a path
Through the sad heart of Ruth,[5] when, sick for home,
She stood in tears amid the alien corn;
The same that ofttimes hath
Charmed magic casements, opening on the foam
Of perilous seas, in faery lands forlorn.

VIII

Forlorn! the very word is like a bell
To toll me back from thee to my sole self!
Adieu! the fancy cannot cheat so well
As she is famed to do, deceiving elf.
Adieu! adieu! thy plaintive anthem fades
Past the near meadows, over the still stream,
Up the hillside; and now 'tis buried deep
In the next valley-glades:
Was it a vision, or a waking dream?
Fled is that music:—Do I wake or sleep?

May 1819

- **Since birds obviously die, just as humans do, what might the speaker mean when he declares, "Thou wast not born for death, immortal Bird!" (line 61)? That is, how, according to the poem, is the bird "immortal" in a way the speaker isn't? How might this help you begin to understand what the bird comes to symbolize in the poem?**

ROBERT FROST
The Road Not Taken

Two roads diverged in a yellow wood,
And sorry I could not travel both
And be one traveler, long I stood
And looked down one as far as I could
To where it bent in the undergrowth;

Then took the other, as just as fair,
And having perhaps the better claim,
Because it was grassy and wanted wear;

5. Virtuous Moabite widow who, according to the Old Testament book of Ruth, left her own country to accompany her mother-in-law, Naomi, back to Naomi's native land. She supported herself as a gleaner.

Though as for that the passing there
Had worn them really about the same,

And both that morning equally lay
In leaves no step had trodden black.
Oh, I kept the first for another day!
Yet knowing how way leads on to way,
I doubted if I should ever come back.

I shall be telling this with a sigh
Somewhere ages and ages hence:
Two roads diverged in a wood, and I—
I took the one less traveled by,
And that has made all the difference.

1916

• What sort of choices might the fork in the road represent? In these terms, what seems most important about the description of the roads? Why and how might it matter that the poem's famous last lines (about the great "difference" [line 20] it made to take the road "less traveled by" [line 19]) are framed as something the speaker imagines saying "with a sigh" at some point in the distant future (line 16)?

HOWARD NEMEROV
The Vacuum

The house is so quiet now
The vacuum cleaner sulks in the corner closet,
Its bag limp as a stopped lung, its mouth
Grinning into the floor, maybe at my
Slovenly life, my dog-dead youth.

I've lived this way long enough,
But when my old woman died her soul
Went into that vacuum cleaner, and I can't bear
To see the bag swell like a belly, eating the dust
And the woolen mice, and begin to howl

Because there is old filth everywhere
She used to crawl, in the corner and under the stair.
I know now how life is cheap as dirt,
And still the hungry, angry heart
Hangs on and howls, biting at air.

1955

• What does the vacuum come to symbolize? How might the poem play on the various meanings of the word *vacuum*?

ADRIENNE RICH
Diving into the Wreck

First having read the book of myths,
and loaded the camera,
and checked the edge of the knife-blade,
I put on
the body-armor of black rubber
the absurd flippers
the grave and awkward mask.
I am having to do this
not like Cousteau[6] with his
assiduous team
aboard the sun-flooded schooner
but here alone.

There is a ladder.
The ladder is always there
hanging innocently
close to the side of the schooner.
We know what it is for,
we who have used it.
Otherwise
it's a piece of maritime floss
some sundry equipment.

I go down.
Rung after rung and still
the oxygen immerses me
the blue light
the clear atoms
of our human air.
I go down.
My flippers cripple me,
I crawl like an insect down the ladder
and there is no one
to tell me when the ocean
will begin.

First the air is blue and then
it is bluer and then green and then
black I am blacking out and yet
my mask is powerful
it pumps my blood with power
the sea is another story
the sea is not a question of power
I have to learn alone
to turn my body without force
in the deep element.

6. Jacques-Yves Cousteau (1910–97), French writer and underwater explorer.

And now: it is easy to forget
what I came for
among so many who have always
lived here
swaying their crenellated fans
between the reefs
and besides
you breathe differently down here.

I came to explore the wreck.
The words are purposes.
The words are maps.
I came to see the damage that was done
and the treasures that prevail.
I stroke the beam of my lamp
slowly along the flank
of something more permanent
than fish or weed

the thing I came for:
the wreck and not the story of the wreck
the thing itself and not the myth
the drowned face always staring
toward the sun
the evidence of damage
worn by salt and sway into this threadbare beauty
the ribs of the disaster
curving their assertion
among the tentative haunters.

This is the place.
And I am here, the mermaid whose dark hair
streams black, the merman in his armored body
We circle silently
about the wreck
we dive into the hold.
I am she: I am he

whose drowned face sleeps with open eyes
whose breasts still bear the stress
whose silver, copper, vermeil cargo lies
obscurely inside barrels
half-wedged and left to rot
we are the half-destroyed instruments
that once held to a course
the water-eaten log
the fouled compass

We are, I am, you are
by cowardice or courage
the one who find our way
back to this scene

carrying a knife, a camera
a book of myths
in which
our names do not appear.

1972 1973

- What word or phrase first signals that DIVING INTO THE WRECK is to be understood symbolically, not literally? What are some possible symbolic interpretations of the wreck and the dive?

ROO BORSON

After a Death

Seeing that there's no other way,
I turn his absence into a chair.
I can sit in it,
gaze out through the window.
I can do what I do best
and then go out into the world.
And I can return then with my useless love,
to rest,
because the chair is there.

1989

- Why do you think the speaker chooses to symbolize her absent loved one with a chair?

BRIAN TURNER

Jundee Ameriki[7]

Many the healers of the body.
Where the healers of the soul?

—AHMAD SHAUQI

At the VA hospital in Long Beach, California,
Dr. Sushruta scores open a thin layer of skin
to reveal an object traveling up through muscle.
It is a kind of weeping the body does, expelling
foreign material, sometimes years after injury.
Dr. Sushruta lifts slivers of shrapnel, bits
of coarse gravel, road debris, diamond
points of glass—the minutiae of the story
reconstructing a cold afternoon in Baghdad,
November of 2005. The body offers aged cloth
from an *abaya*[8] dyed in blood, shards of bone.
And if he were to listen intently, he might hear

7. American soldier (Arabic). 8. Loose, long robe worn by some Muslim women.

the roughened larynx of this woman calling up
through the long corridors of flesh, saying
Allah al Akbar,[9] before releasing
her body's weapon, her dark and lasting gift
for this *jundee Ameriki*, who carries fragments
of the war inscribed in scar tissue,
a deep, intractable pain, the dull grief of it
the body must learn to absorb.

2009

• **What objects or actions in this poem operate as symbols, and for what?**

AUTHORS ON THEIR WORK

BRIAN TURNER (b. 1967)

From "War and Peace: An Interview with Poet Brian Turner" (2009)*

[. . .] Iraq will never be finished in our lifetimes—for the veterans who have come back home, for many of them, and then also for the Iraqis, who we can easily forget because we don't have to deal with them. We don't see them, we don't meet them, we don't have to go visit them or help them with anything. They're clear across the horizon in some foreign country. But we are intimately connected.

• • •

I think people still very much want to talk about these things, but they don't have that avenue. And I do think poetry and art can offer some avenues in, towards the emotional content, not so much the geopolitical possibilities and discussions, but the human content. . . . It offers people a way into a moment, and into a world that maybe they've never been a part of or seen and that they can experience a small portion of it and then be reconnected or reengaged to a discussion. I definitely think it's useful.

*"War and Peace: An Interview with Poet Brian Turner." Interview by Stefene Russell. *St. Louis*, 1 Apr. 2009, www.stlmag.com/War-and-Peace-An-Interview-With-Poet-Brian-Turner/.

9. Common misrendering of "Allahu akbar," meaning "God is great" or "greatest."

SHARON OLDS

Bruise Ghazal[1]

Now a black-and-blue oval on my hip has turned blue-
violet as the ink-brand on the husk-fat of a prime
cut, sore as a lovebite, but too
large for a human mouth. I like it, my
flesh brooch—gold rim, envy-color
cameo within, and violet mottle
on which the door-handle that bit is a black
purple with wiggles like trembling decapede
legs. I count back the days, and forward
to when it will go its rot colors and then
slowly fade. Some people think I should
be over my ex by now—maybe
I thought I might have been over him more
by now. Maybe I'm half over who he
was, but not who I thought he was, and not
over the wound, sudden deathblow
as if out of nowhere, though it came from the core
of our life together. Sleep now, Sharon,
sleep. Even as we speak, the work is being
done, within. You were born to heal.
Sleep and dream—but not of his return.
Since it cannot harm him, wound him, in your dream.

2012

- How do the various figures of speech Olds initially uses to characterize both her physical wound and her feelings about it help make that wound a resonant symbol for the more emotional wounds she discusses later in the poem?

SUGGESTIONS FOR WRITING

1. Consider the poems about roses in this chapter, and write a paragraph about each poem showing how it establishes specific symbolism for the rose. What generalizations can you draw about the rose's traditional meanings in poetry? If you can, find other poems about roses outside of this anthology to determine if your generalizations still apply.
2. Is there a "correct" interpretation of Adrienne Rich's DIVING INTO THE WRECK or of Brian Turner's JUNDEE AMERIKI? If one interpretation seems to fit all the particulars of the poem, does that mean it's better than other possible interpretations? Write an essay in which you explore the poem's symbolism and argue for or against the idea that there is a single best way to understand this poem. Can ambiguity serve a poet's purpose, or does it ultimately undercut a poem's meaning and significance?
3. Choose any poem in this book in which an object or action seems to function as a symbol. Write an essay exploring that symbol's various possible meanings.

1. Form of lyric poem, often on the subject of love and longing, originating in Middle Eastern and East Indian traditions and traditionally consisting of a series of autonomous but thematically related couplets each ending with the same internal rhyme and refrain words. (The first and second stanzas of one Heather McHugh ghazal, for example, end with the words "stirred person" and "absurd person.") Olds's poem does not adhere to this fixed form.

18 THE SOUNDS OF POETRY

Much of what happens in a poem happens in your mind's eye, but some of it happens in your "mind's ear" and in your voice. Poems are full of meaningful sounds and silences as well as words and sentences. Besides choosing words for their meanings, poets choose words because they have certain sounds, and poems use sound effects to create a mood or establish a tone, just as films do.

Historically, poetry began as an oral phenomenon. Early bards in many cultures chanted or recited their verses, often accompanied by a musical instrument of some kind, and poetry remains a vocal art, dependent on the human voice. Often poems that seem very difficult when looked at silently come alive when turned into sound. The music and rhythms become clearer, and saying the words aloud or hearing them spoken is very good practice for learning to hear in your mind's ear when you read silently.

RHYME

Rhyme—repetition or correspondence of the terminal sounds of words—is perhaps the single most familiar of sound devices poets use, though of course not all poems use it. Early English poetry, in fact, used **alliteration**, instead of rhyming words at the end of the poetic lines, to balance the first and second half of each line, and much, if not most, modern poetry is written in **free verse**—that is, without rhyme or regular **meter**. From the later Middle Ages until the twentieth century, however, the music of rhyme was central to both the sound and the formal conception of most poems in the Western world. Because poetry was originally an oral art (many poems were only later written down, if at all), various kinds of memory devices (sometimes called *mnemonic devices*) were built into poems to help reciters remember them. Rhyme was one such device, and most people still find it easier to memorize poetry that rhymes. The simple pleasure of hearing familiar sounds repeated at regular intervals may help account for the traditional popularity of rhyme. Rhyme also gives poetry a special aural quality that distinguishes it from prose. According to the established taste in eras before our own, there was a decorum or proper behavior in poetry as in other things: A poem should not in any way be mistaken for prose, which was thought to be artistically inferior to poetry and primarily utilitarian.

Some English poets (especially in the Renaissance) did experiment—often very successfully—with unrhymed verse, but the cultural pressure for rhyme was almost constant. Why? Custom, combined with the sense of proper decorum, accounted in part for the assumption that rhyme was necessary to poetry, but there was probably more to it than that. Rather, the poets' sense that poetry was an imitation of larger relationships in the universe made it seem natural to use rhyme to represent or re-create a sense of pattern, harmony, correspondence, symmetry, and order. The sounds of poetry were thus, poets reasoned, reminders of cosmic harmony, of the music of the spheres that animated all creation. In a modern world increasingly perceived as fragmented and chaotic, there may be less of a tendency to assume or assert a sense of harmony and symmetry. It would be too simple to say that rhyme in a poem necessarily means that the poet has a firm sense of cosmic order, or that an unrhymed poem testifies to chaos. But the cultural assumptions of different times have influenced the expectations and practices of both poets and readers.

Rhyme also provides a kind of discipline for the poet, a way of harnessing poetic talents and keeping a rein on the imagination. Robert Frost said that writing free verse was pointless, like playing tennis without a net. Frost speaks for many traditional poets in suggesting that writing good poetry requires discipline and great care with formal elements such as rhyme or rhythm. More recent poets have often chosen to play by new rules or to invent their own as they go along, preferring the sparer tones that unrhymed poetry provides. Contemporary poets of course still care about the sounds of their poetry, but they may replace rhyme with other aural devices or mix regular rhyme and meter with more flexible lines, paying tribute to tradition as well as the unexpectedness of experience.

End Rhyme and Rhyme Scheme

When we think of rhyme in poetry, what we likely think of first is the most common type—*end rhyme*, which occurs when the last words in two or more lines of a poem rhyme with each other. When we speak of a poem's *rhyme scheme*, we refer to its particular pattern of end rhymes. To indicate rhyme scheme, we conventionally assign a different letter of the alphabet to each rhyme sound, reusing the same letter every time the same terminal sound repeats in later lines. Here, for example, are the first two stanzas of Thomas Hardy's THE RUINED MAID, which have a rhyme scheme of *aabb, ccbb* thanks to the way each stanza ends with the very same (long *e*) sound:

"O 'Melia, my dear, this does everything crown! *a*
Who could have supposed I should meet you in Town? *a*
And whence such fair garments, such prosperi-ty?"— *b*
"O didn't you know I'd been ruined?" said she. *b*

—"You left us in tatters, without shoes or socks, *c*
Tired of digging potatoes, and spudding up docks; *c*
And now you've gay bracelets and bright feathers three!"— *b*
"Yes: that's how we dress when we're ruined," said she. *b*

Since any two adjacent lines that rhyme form a **couplet**, we could also or instead describe "The Ruined Maid" as a poem comprised entirely of rhyming couplets.

Internal, Slant, and Eye Rhyme

Though end rhyme alone determines the rhyme scheme of a poem, it isn't the only kind: *Internal rhyme* occurs when a word within (and thus *internal to*) a line rhymes with another word in the same or adjacent lines, as in the following lines from

Samuel Taylor Coleridge's "The Rime of the Ancient Mariner" (internal rhyming words appear in italics):

In mist or *cloud*, on mast or *shroud*,
It perched for vespers nine;
Whiles all the *night*, through fog-smoke *white*,
Glimmered the *white* moonshine.

Whether end or internal, rhymes differ, too, in type. Technically, rhyme (or what is sometimes called *perfect*, *true*, or *full rhyme*) requires that words share consonants and vowel sounds, as do "cloud" and "shroud," "night" and "white." When words share one but not the other, we have a version of what's variously called *off*, *half*, *near*, or *slant rhyme*—that is, a rhyme slightly "off" or only approximate. (The words *all* and *bowl*, for example, share consonant sounds, but their vowel sounds differ, and the opposite is true of *dark* and *heart*.) Another device more common in poetry written since the later nineteenth century, and (like internal rhyme) ubiquitous in hip-hop lyrics, slant rhyme can produce a variety of effects, all deriving from the poem's failure to provide the sounds our ears expect, whether our brains know it or not. Much the same in reverse is true of *eye rhyme*: As much a visual as an aural device, it occurs, as its name suggests, when words *look* like they should rhyme, but don't, as with *bear* and *ear*, *Yeats* and *Keats*.

ONOMATOPOEIA, ALLITERATION, ASSONANCE, AND CONSONANCE

Sometimes the sounds in poems just provide special effects, rather like a musical score behind a film, setting the mood and getting us into an appropriate frame of mind. But often sound and meaning go hand in hand, and the poet finds words whose sounds echo the action or make a point by stressing the relationship among words and the things they signify.

A single word that captures or approximates the sound of what it describes, such as *splash* or *squish* or *murmur*, is an *onomatopoeic* word, and the device itself is **onomatopoeia**.

But poets can also turn sound into sense by choosing and ordering words so as to create distinctive, meaningful aural patterns. Rhyme is one such device, but three other important ones are

- **alliteration**—the repetition of usually initial consonant sounds through a sequence of words, as in "In lurid *c*artoon *c*olors, the *b*ig *b*aby / dinosaur steps *b*ackwards" (from Emily Grosholz's EDEN) or "The *W*icked *W*itch of the *W*est";
- **consonance**—the repetition of consonant sounds, especially at the end of words or syllables, without the correspondence of vowel sounds necessary to create rhyme, as in "abstruser musings" (from Coleridge's FROST AT MIDNIGHT) or "That was a stro*k*e of luc*k*"; and
- **assonance**—the repetition of vowel sounds in a sequence of words with different endings, as in "The d*ea*th of the po*e*t was k*e*pt from his po*e*ms" (from W. H. Auden's IN MEMORY OF W. B. YEATS).

Used effectively, such devices can be powerful tools, generating meaning, as well as creating mood or simply providing emphasis. A case in point is the following excerpt from the world's most famous *mock epic,* which describes a scene that may seem at once foreign and familiar to you: A young woman (or "nymph") sits at a mirrored dressing table (or "toilet"), littered with cosmetics and other accouterments, and, with the help of her lady's maid, prepares herself for the day ahead—fixing her hair, applying makeup, and so on. Given the way these activities are characterized as a distinctly twisted religious ritual (in lines 123–30), what is the effect and significance of alliteration, particularly in line 140 (which here appears in bold)?

ALEXANDER POPE
From *The Rape of the Lock*

And now, unveil'd, the toilet stands displayed,
Each silver vase in mystic order laid.
First, rob'd in white, the nymph intent adores
With head uncover'd, the cosmetic pow'rs.
A heav'nly image in the glass appears,
To that she bends, to that her eyes she rears;
Th' inferior priestess,[1] at her altar's side,
Trembling, begins the sacred rites of pride.
Unnumber'd treasures ope at once, and here
The various off'rings of the world appear;
From each she nicely culls with curious[2] toil,
And decks the goddess with the glitt'ring spoil.
This casket India's glowing gems unlocks,
And all Arabia breathes from yonder box.
The tortoise here and elephant unite,
Transform'd to combs, the speckled and the white.[3]
Here files of pins extend their shining rows,
Puffs, powders, patches, bibles, billet-doux.[4]
Now awful[5] beauty puts on all its arms;
The fair each moment rises in her charms,
Repairs her smiles, awakens ev'ry grace,
And calls forth all the wonders of her face

1712, 1714

SOUND POEMS

The following poems place especially heavy emphasis on sound and aural patterning. As you read them, try to identify which sound devices they use and with what effects.

1. That is, the lady's maid. 2. Strange, unusual.
3. The hair combs, in other words, are made from tortoiseshell (which is "speckled") and ivory from an elephant's tusk (which is "white").
4. Love letter (French). *Patches*: tiny pieces of silk or plaster worn to hide a blemish or heighten one's beauty. 5. Awe-inspiring.

HELEN CHASIN
The Word *Plum*

The word *plum* is delicious

pout and push, luxury of
self-love, and savoring murmur

full in the mouth and falling
like fruit

taut skin
pierced, bitten, provoked into
juice, and tart flesh

question
and reply, lip and tongue
of pleasure.

1968

KENNETH FEARING
Dirge

1-2-3 was the number he played but today the number came 3-2-1;
Bought his Carbide at 30, and it went to 29; had the favorite at Bowie[6]
but the track was slow—

O executive type, would you like to drive a floating-power, knee-action,
silk-upholstered six? Wed a Hollywood star? Shoot the course in 58?
Draw to the ace, king, jack?
O fellow with a will who won't take no, watch out for three cigarettes on
the same, single match; O democratic voter born in August under
Mars, beware of liquidated rails—

Denouement to denouement, he took a personal pride in the certain,
certain way he lived his own, private life,
But nevertheless, they shut off his gas; nevertheless, the bank foreclosed;
nevertheless, the landlord called; nevertheless, the radio broke,

And twelve o'clock arrived just once too often,
Just the same he wore one gray tweed suit, bought one straw hat, drank
one straight Scotch, walked one short step, took one long look, drew
one deep breath,
Just one too many,

And wow he died as wow he lived,
Going whop to the office and blooie home to sleep and biff got married
and bam had children and oof got fired,
Zowie did he live and zowie did he die,

6. Racetrack in Maryland. *Carbide*: stock in the Union Carbide Corporation.

With who the hell are you at the corner of his casket, and where the hell're we going on the right-hand silver knob, and who the hell cares walking second from the end with an American Beauty[7] wreath from why the hell not,

Very much missed by the circulation staff of the New York Evening Post; deeply, deeply mourned by the B.M.T.[8]

Wham, Mr. Roosevelt; pow, Sears Roebuck; awk, big dipper; bop, summer rain;

Bong, Mr., bong, Mr., bong, Mr., bong.

1935

ALEXANDER POPE

Sound and Sense[9]

But most by numbers[1] judge a poet's song,
And smooth or rough, with them, is right or wrong;
In the bright muse though thousand charms conspire,[2]
Her voice is all these tuneful fools admire,
Who haunt Parnassus[3] but to please their ear,
Not mend their minds; as some to church repair,
Not for the doctrine, but the music there.
These, equal syllables[4] alone require,
Though oft the ear the open vowels tire,
While expletives[5] their feeble aid do join,
And ten low words oft creep in one dull line,
While they ring round the same unvaried chimes,
With sure returns of still expected rhymes.
Where'er you find "the cooling western breeze,"
In the next line, it "whispers through the trees";
If crystal streams "with pleasing murmurs creep,"
The reader's threatened (not in vain) with "sleep."
Then, at the last and only couplet fraught
With some unmeaning thing they call a thought,
A needless Alexandrine[6] ends the song,
That, like a wounded snake, drags its slow length along.
Leave such to tune their own dull rhymes, and know
What's roundly smooth, or languishingly slow;

7. A variety of rose. 8. New York City subway line.
9. From *An Essay on Criticism*, Pope's poem on the art of poetry and the problems of literary criticism. The passage excerpted here follows a discussion of several common weaknesses of critics—failure to regard an author's intention, for example, or overemphasis on clever metaphors and ornate style.
1. Meter, rhythm, sound. 2. Unite.
3. Mountain in Greece, traditionally associated with the Muses and considered the seat of poetry and music. 4. Regular accents. 5. Filler words, such as "do."
6. Line of six metrical feet, sometimes used in pentameter poems to vary the pace mechanically. Line 357 is an alexandrine.

And praise the easy vigor of a line,
Where Denham's strength and Waller's[7] sweetness join.
True ease in writing comes from art, not chance,
As those move easiest who have learned to dance.
'Tis not enough no harshness gives offense,
The sound must seem an echo to the sense:
Soft is the strain when Zephyr[8] gently blows,
And the smooth stream in smoother numbers flows;
But when loud surges lash the sounding shore,
The hoarse, rough verse should like the torrent roar.
When Ajax[9] strives, some rock's vast weight to throw,
The line too labors, and the words move slow;
Not so, when swift Camilla[1] scours the plain,
Flies o'er th' unbending corn, and skims along the main.
Hear how Timotheus'[2] varied lays surprise,
And bid alternate passions fall and rise!
While, at each change, the son of Libyan Jove[3]
Now burns with glory, and then melts with love;
Now his fierce eyes with sparkling fury glow,
Now sighs steal out, and tears begin to flow:
Persians and Greeks like turns of nature[4] found,
And the world's victor stood subdued by sound!
The pow'r of music all our hearts allow,
And what Timotheus was, is DRYDEN now.

1711

Helen Chasin's poem THE WORD *PLUM* savors the sounds of the word as well as the taste and feel of the fruit itself. It is almost as if the poem is tasting the sounds and rolling them slowly on the tongue. The alliterative second and third lines even replicate the *p*, *l*, *uh*, and *m* sounds of the word while imitating the squishy sounds of eating the fruit. Words like "delicious" and "luxury" sound juicy, and other words, such as "murmur," imitate sounds of satisfaction and pleasure. Even the process of eating is in part re-created aurally. The tight, clipped sounds of "taut skin / pierced" (lines 6–7) suggest the way teeth sharply break the skin and slice quickly into the soft flesh of a plum, and the words describing the tartness ("provoked," "question," lines 7, 9) force the lips to pucker and the tongue and palate to meet and hold, as if the mouth were savoring a tart fruit. The poet is having fun here refashioning the sensual appeal of a plum, teasing the sounds and meanings out of available words. The words must mean something appropriate and describe something accurately first of all, of course, but when they also imitate the sounds and feel of the process they describe, they do double duty.

7. Sir John Denham and Edmund Waller, seventeenth-century poets credited with perfecting the heroic couplet. 8. The west wind. 9. A Greek hero of the Trojan War, noted for his strength.

1. A woman warrior in Virgil's *Aeneid*.

2. Court musician of Alexander the Great, celebrated in a famous poem by John Dryden (see line 383) for the power of his music over Alexander's emotions.

3. In Greek tradition, the chief god of any people was often given the name Zeus (Jove), and the chief god of Libya (the Greek name for all of Africa) was called Zeus Ammon. Alexander visited his oracle and was proclaimed son of the god. 4. Similar alternations of emotion.

As its title implies, Kenneth Fearing's DIRGE is a musical lament, in this case for a businessman who took many chances and saw his investments and life go down the drain in the Great Depression of the early 1930s. The expressive cartoon words here like "oof" and "blooie" (line 11) echo the action. Reading aloud, you will notice that the poem employs rhythms much as a song would and that it frequently shifts its pace and mood. Notice how carefully the first two lines are balanced, and then how quickly the rhythm shifts as the "executive type" is addressed directly in line 3. (Especially long lines, like line 2, and irregular line lengths here create some of the poem's special sound effects.) In the direct address, the poem first picks up the rapid lingo of advertising. In stanza 3, the rhythm shifts again, but the poem gives us helpful clues about how to read. Line 5 sounds like prose and is long, drawn out, and rather dull (like its subject), but line 6 sets up a regular (and monotonous) rhythm with its repeated "nevertheless," which punctuates the rhythm like a drumbeat: "But nevertheless, *tuh-tuh-tuh-tuh-tuh*; nevertheless, *tuh-tuh-tuh-tuh*; nevertheless, *tuh-tuh-tuh-tuh*; nevertheless, *tuh-tuh-tuh-tuh-tuh*." In the next stanza comes more repetitive phrasing, this time guided by the word "one" in conjunction with other one-syllable words: "wore *one* gray tweed suit, bought *one* straw hat, *tuh* one *tuh-tuh*, *tuh* one *tuh-tuh*, *tuh* one *tuh-tuh*, *tuh* one *tuh-tuh*." And then a new rhythm and a new technique begin in stanza 5, which again imitates the language of comic books. You have to say words like "whop" and "zowie" aloud and in the rhythm of the whole sentence to get the full effect of how boring his life is, no matter how he tries to jazz it up. And so it goes—the repeating rhythms of routine—until the final bell ("Bong . . . bong . . . bong . . . bong") tolls rhythmically for the dead man in the final clanging line.

Written in a very different era and style, Pope's SOUND AND SENSE uses a number of echoic or onomatopoeic words. In some lines pleasant and unpleasant consonant sounds underline a particular point or emphasize a mood. When the poet talks about a particular weakness in poetry, he illustrates it at the same time—by using open vowels (line 345), expletives (line 346), monosyllabic words (line 347), predictable rhymes (lines 350–53), or long, slow lines (line 357). He similarly illustrates the good qualities of poetry as well (line 360, for example). But the main effects of the passage come from an interaction of several ingenious strategies at once. In lines 339 and 340, for example, Pope produces complex sound effects in addition to the harmony of a rhyming **couplet** ("conspire," "admire"). Assonance echoes in the *oo* vowel sounds in "muse," "tuneful," and "fools"; alliteration repeats consonants in "*r*ight or *wr*ong" and "tune*ful fool*s." Ironically, the *muse*-ical voice here is a bit out of tune to those who have good poetic taste: Pope intends the *r* and *f* sounds to feel both cute and awkward, as a comment on people who only want easy listening and miss poetry's other "charms," including its meaning (compared to the "doctrine" that is the real purpose of a church service, in line 343).

With a similar technique of demonstrating principles of poetic style and taste, the pace of lines 347, 357, and 359 is controlled by clashing consonant sounds as well as long vowels. Line 347 seems much longer than it is because almost every one-syllable word ends in a consonant that refuses to blend with the beginning of the next word, making the words hard to say without distinct, awkward pauses between them. In lines 357 and 359, long vowels such as those in "wounded," "snake," "slow," "along," "roundly," and "smooth" slow down the pace, and awkward, hard-to-pronounce consonants are again juxtaposed. The commas also provide nearly full stops in the middle of these lines to slow us down still more.

Similarly, the harsh lashing of the shore in lines 368–69 is accomplished partly by onomatopoeia and partly by the dominance of rough consonants in line 369. (In Pope's time, the English *r* was still trilled gruffly so that it could be made to sound extremely *rrr*ough and ha*rrr*sh.) Almost every line in this passage demonstrates how to make sound echo sense.

POETIC METER

In the Western world, we can thank the ancient Greeks for systematizing an understanding of meter and providing a vocabulary (including the words *rhythm* and *meter*) that enables us to discuss the art of poetry. *Meter* comes from a Greek word meaning "measure": What we measure in the English language are the patterns of stressed (or accented) syllables that occur naturally when we speak, and, just as when we measure length, the unit we use in measuring poetry is the **foot**. Most traditional poetry in English uses the accentual-syllabic form of meter—meaning that its rhythmic pattern is based on both a set number of syllables per line and a regular pattern of accents in each line. Not all poems have a regular metrical pattern, and not all metered poems follow only one pattern throughout. But like everyday speech, the language of poetry always has *some* accents (as in this italic emphasis on "some"), and poets arrange that rhythm for effect. Thus in nonmetrical as well as metrical poetry, a reader should "listen" for patterns of stress.

The Basic Metrical Feet of Poetry in English

iamb: an unstressed or unaccented syllable followed by a stressed or accented one ("she wént," "belíeve"). This meter is called *iambic*.

trochee: a stressed syllable followed by an unstressed one ("méter," "Hómer"). This meter is called *trochaic*.

anapest: two unstressed syllables followed by a stressed one ("comprehénd," "after yóu"). This meter is called *anapestic*.

dactyl: a stressed syllable followed by two unstressed ones ("róundabout," "dínnertime"). This meter is called *dactylic*.

rising or falling: the above feet either begin or end with the stressed syllable, as if they lose or gain momentum or "height." Hence iambic and anapestic are called rising meters, and trochaic and dactylic are called falling meters.

Other Kinds of Feet

spondee: two stressed syllables. Spondaic feet vary or interrupt the prevailing rhythm, emphasizing a syllable that we would expect to be unstressed ("Lást cáll," "Dón't gó").

pyrrhic: two unstressed syllables. Pyrrhic feet similarly interrupt the expected rising or falling beats, placing an unstressed syllable where we expect an emphasis ("ŭntŏ," "ĭs ă").

Spondees and pyrrhic feet depend on prevailing meter and usually appear singly or only a few times in a row. It is difficult to imagine (or to write or speak) a line or sentence that either has no unstressed syllables—a constant strong beat (spondaic)—or lacks stressed syllables—a rippling monotone (pyrrhic).

Because the concept of meter derives from poetic traditions in Greek and Latin that counted syllables rather than accents, other possible combinations of syllables acquired names, for instance, *amphibrach* (unstressed, stressed, unstressed—noted by Coleridge in his demonstration of meter, METRICAL FEET, below). But since most meter in poetry in English depends on accents rather than the number of syllables, the terms above cover most of the variations that you will encounter.

Counting Feet, or Meter

A line of poetry is subdivided into feet in order to "measure" its meter. The terms are easy enough to understand if you recall geometry or other numeric terminology. Remember that this is a count *not* of the number of syllables but of stresses; thus, for example, monometer could have two or three syllables per line.

monometer: one foot
dimeter: two feet
trimeter: three feet
tetrameter: four feet
pentameter: five feet
hexameter: six feet
heptameter: seven feet
octameter: eight feet

Counting the number of feet—that is, the number of accents, stresses, or strong beats per line—helps you identify the *kind* of feet in the line. Thus the terms are combined: *Iambic pentameter* has five iambs per line; *trochaic tetrameter* has four trochees per line, and so on.

Scansion

Scansion is the technique of listening to and marking stressed and unstressed syllables, counting the syllables and feet. Often, you will need to scan several lines before you can be sure of the "controlling" metrical pattern or "base meter" of a poem.

In the following poem, Samuel Taylor Coleridge playfully names and illustrates many types of meter. By marking syllables himself as stressed or unstressed, he also illustrates how scansion works.

SAMUEL TAYLOR COLERIDGE
Metrical Feet

Lesson for a Boy[5]

Trōchĕe trīps frŏm lōng tŏ shōrt;[6]
From long to long in solemn sort
Slōw Spōndēe stālks; strōng fōōt! yet ill able
Ēvĕr tŏ cōme ŭp wĭth Dāctȳl trĭsȳllăblĕ.
Ĭāmbĭcs mārch frŏm shōrt tŏ lōng—
Wĭth ă lēāp ănd ă bōūnd thĕ swĭft Ānăpĕsts thrōng;
One syllable long, with one short at each side,
Ămphībrăchȳs hāstes wĭth ă stātelȳ stride—
Fīrst ănd lāst bēĭng lōng, mīddlĕ shōrt, Am̄phĭmācer
Strīkes hĭs thūndērĭng hōōfs līke ă prōūd hīgh-brĕd Rācer.
If Derwent be innocent, steady, and wise,
And delight in the things of earth, water, and skies;
Tender warmth at his heart, with these meters to show it,
With sound sense in his brains, may make Derwent a poet—
May crown him with fame, and must win him the love
Of his father on earth and his Father above.
My dear, dear child!
Could you stand upon Skiddaw,[7] you would not from its whole ridge
See a man who so loves you as your fond S. T. COLERIDGE.

1806

Hearing a poem properly involves practice—listening to others read poetry and especially to yourself as you read poems aloud. Your dictionary will show you the stresses for every word of more than one syllable, and the governing stress of individual words will largely control the patterns in a line: If you read a line for its sense (almost as if it were prose), you will usually see the line's basic pattern. But single-syllable words can be a challenge because they may or may not be stressed, depending on their syntactic function and the full meaning of the sentence. Normally, important functional words, such as one-syllable nouns and verbs, are stressed (as in normal conversation or in prose), while conjunctions (such as *and* or *but*), prepositions (such as *on* or *with*), and articles (such as *an* or *the*) are unstressed.

Here are the first two lines of Alexander Pope's "Sound and Sense," marked to show the stressed syllables:

But móst | by núm- | bers júdge | a pó- | et's sóng,
And smóoth | or róugh, | with thém, | is ríght | or wróng.

These lines, like so many in English literature, provide an example of *iambic pentameter*—that is, each line consists of five iambic feet. Notice that there is nothing forced or artificial in the sound of these lines; the words flow easily. In fact,

5. Written originally for Coleridge's son Hartley, the poem was later adapted for his younger son, Derwent.

6. Long and short marks over syllables are Coleridge's.

7. Mountain in the lake country of northern England (where Coleridge lived in his early years), near the town of Derwent.

linguists contend that English is naturally iambic, and even the most ordinary, "unpoetic" utterances often fall into this pattern: "Please tell me if you've heard this one before." "They said she had a certain way with words." "The baseball game was televised at nine."

Here are a few more examples of various meters.

iambic pentameter: "In sé- | quent tóil | all fór- | wards dó | conténd" (William Shakespeare, "Like as the waves . . .")
trochaic octameter: "Ónce u- | pón a | mídnight | dréary, | whíle I | póndered, | wéak and | wéary" (Edgar Allan Poe, "The Raven")
anapestic tetrameter: "There are mán- | y who sáy | that a dóg | has his dáy" (Dylan Thomas)

Although scanning lines of poetry by reading them aloud, marking syllables as unstressed or stressed, and adding up feet may seem like a counting game that has little to do with the meaning of poetry, it is an important way to understand the sound effects of a poem. Like different styles of music, different meters tend to express different moods or to suit different themes. When you know the basic meter of a poem, you are more alert to subtle variations in the pattern. Poets avoid the predictable or the lulling by using certain "change-ups" in the dominant meter or line length, such as substitution of a different foot (e.g., a trochee or spondee instead of an iamb); **caesura**, a short pause within a line often signaled by punctuation; or **enjambment**, extending the end of the grammatical sentence beyond the end of the poetic line.

Notice that the following example is perfectly regular dactylic hexameter until the final foot, a trochee. Also notice that Longfellow has placed a caesura within a long line.

"Thís is the | fórest pri- | méval. The | múrmuring | pínes and the | hémlocks" (Henry Wadsworth Longfellow, *Evangeline*)

Substitution of one metrical foot for another—to accommodate idioms and conversational habits or to create a special effect or emphasis—is quite common, especially in the first foot of a line. Shakespeare often begins an iambic line with a trochee:

Líke as | the wáves | make towárds | the péb- | bled shóre

Or consider this line from John Milton's *Paradise Lost*, a poem written mainly in iambic pentameter:

Rócks, cáves, | lákes, féns, | bógs, déns, | and Shádes | of Déath

Here Milton substitutes three spondees for the first three iambs in a pentameter line. John Dryden's "To the Memory of Mr. Oldham" arguably begins with two spondees, a pyrrhic, and an iamb before settling into a regular iambic pentameter:

Fárewéll, | tóo lít | tle, and | tóo láte | ly knówn,

As Dryden's poem shows, meter does leave room for discussion; some readers might read the line above as iambic throughout, and others might read the last three feet as iambic: The natural emphasis on the first word after the caesura, "and," could make the predictable word "too" unstressed. The way you actually read a line, once you have "heard" the basic rhythm, is influenced by two factors: normal pronunciation and prose sense (on the one hand) and the predominant pattern of the poem (on the other). Since these two forces are constantly in tension and are sometimes contradictory, you can almost never fully predict the actual reading of a line, and good reading aloud (like every other art) depends less on formula than on subtlety and flexibility. And, again, very good readers sometimes disagree about whether or not to stress certain syllables. We have noted the use of substitution, and many poems since around 1900 have taken liberties with meter and rhyme. Some poets (such as Marianne Moore) have favored counting syllables rather than accents. Even more widespread is free verse, which does without any governing pattern of stresses or line lengths.

Scansion: An Exercise

Each of the following poems is written in a different meter. Using the terms defined in "Poetic Meter" (on pp. 1041–42), as well as in Coleridge's poem "Metrical Feet," pair the following poems with their corresponding meters. (The answers are on p. 1057.)

1. ANONYMOUS
[There was a young girl from St. Paul]

There was a young girl from St. Paul,
Wore a newspaper-dress to a ball.
  The dress caught on fire
  And burned her entire
Front page, sporting section and all.

(Note that this poem is a **limerick** and uses a meter common to this subgenre.)

2. ALFRED, LORD TENNYSON
From The Charge of the Light Brigade[8]

1.
Half a league, half a league,
  Half a league onward,
All in the valley of Death
  Rode the six hundred.
"Forward, the Light Brigade!
"Charge for the guns!" he said:

8. On October 25, 1854—during the Crimean war—miscommunication among commanders led a British cavalry troop to charge directly into a Russian artillery assault, leading to heavy casualties and an ignominious defeat.

(continued on next page)

(continued)

Into the valley of Death
Rode the six hundred.

2.

"Forward, the Light Brigade!"
Was there a man dismay'd?
Not tho' the soldier knew
Someone had blunder'd:
Theirs not to make reply,
Theirs not to reason why,
Theirs but to do and die:
Into the valley of Death
Rode the six hundred.

1854

3. JANE TAYLOR
The Star

'Twinkle, twinkle, little star,
How I wonder what you are!
Up above the world so high,
Like a diamond in the sky.

When the blazing sun is gone,
When he nothing shines upon,
Then you show your little light,
Twinkle, twinkle, all the night.

Then the trav'ller in the dark,
Thanks you for your tiny spark;
He could not see which way to go,
If you did not twinkle so.

In the dark blue sky you keep,
And often through my curtains peep,
For you never shut your eye
Till the sun is in the sky.

As your bright and tiny spark
Lights the trav'ller in the dark,
Though I know not what you are,
Twinkle, twinkle, little star.

1806

4. ANNE BRADSTREET
To My Dear and Loving Husband

If ever two were one, then surely we.
If ever man were loved by wife, then thee;
If ever wife was happy in a man,
Compare with me ye women if you can.
I prize thy love more than whole mines of gold,
Or all the riches that the East doth hold.
My love is such that rivers cannot quench,
Nor aught but love from thee give recompense.
Thy love is such I can no way repay;
The heavens reward thee manifold, I pray.
Then while we live, in love let's so persever,
That when we live no more we may live ever.

1678

Sound and Sense: A Comparative Exercise

To get a vivid sense of the difference sound can make to the tone and meaning of a poem—and just how you can *use* what you've learned about meter, rhyme, and other sound devices—try comparing the two following poems, both inspired by World War I (1914–18). The first is the most famous of several poems originally published in the British newspaper the *Daily Mail* by Jessie Pope (1868–1941), an English journalist famous, before the war, as a writer of light verse. The second poem is the work of Wilfred Owen (1893–1918), an aspiring English poet who voluntarily enlisted in 1915 (the same year Pope's poem appeared) and, from January 1917, served as an officer on the French front. Begun some nine months later, during Owen's hospitalization for shell shock, and originally entitled "To Jessie Pope," his poem is in some ways as much about traditional poetic representations of war as it is about war itself.

As you read the two poems, pay careful attention to how each uses all of the various sound devices discussed in this chapter, particularly meter and rhyme. How precisely do such sound effects contribute to the poems' very different tones and themes and their very different views of war?

JESSIE POPE
The Call

Who's for the trench—
Are you, my laddie?

(continued on next page)

(continued)

Who'll follow French[9]—
Will you, my laddie?
Who's fretting to begin,
Who's going out to win?
And who wants to save his skin—
Do you, my laddie?

Who's for the khaki suit—
Are you, my laddie?
Who longs to charge and shoot—
Do you, my laddie?
Who's keen on getting fit,
Who means to show his grit,
And who'd rather wait a bit—
Would you, my laddie?

Who'll earn the Empire's[1] thanks—
Will you, my laddie?
Who'll swell the victor's ranks—
Will you, my laddie?
When that procession comes,
Banners and rolling drums—
Who'll stand and bite his thumbs—
Will you, my laddie?

1915

WILFRED OWEN

Dulce et Decorum Est[2]

Bent double, like old beggars under sacks,
Knock-kneed, coughing like hags, we cursed through sludge,
Till on the haunting flares we turned our backs
And towards our distant rest began to trudge.
Men marched asleep. Many had lost their boots
But limped on, blood-shod. All went lame; all blind;
Drunk with fatigue; deaf even to the hoots
Of disappointed shells that dropped behind.

9. Field-Marshall John French (1852–1925), commander in chief of the British Expeditionary Force for the first two years of World War I (1914–16).

1. At the start of World War I, the British Empire was the largest in human history, covering over eleven million square miles of the earth's surface; the desire to maintain or expand empire was one major cause of the war.

2. Part of a phrase from Horace (Roman poet and satirist, 65–68 BCE), quoted in full in the last lines of Owen's poem: "It is sweet and proper to die for one's country" (Latin).

Gas! Gas! Quick, boys!—An ecstasy of fumbling,
Fitting the clumsy helmets just in time;
But someone still was yelling out and stumbling
And floundering like a man in fire or lime.—
Dim, through the misty panes and thick green light
As under a green sea, I saw him drowning.

In all my dreams, before my helpless sight,
He plunges at me, guttering, choking, drowning.

If in some smothering dreams you too could pace
Behind the wagon that we flung him in,
And watch the white eyes writhing in his face,
His hanging face, like a devil's sick of sin;
If you could hear, at every jolt, the blood
Come gargling from the froth-corrupted lungs,
Obscene as cancer, bitter as the cud
Of vile, incurable sores on innocent tongues,—
My friend, you would not tell with such high zest
To children ardent for some desperate glory,
The old Lie: Dulce et decorum est
Pro patria mori.

1917

POEMS FOR FURTHER STUDY

WILLIAM SHAKESPEARE

[Like as the waves make towards the pebbled shore]

Like as the waves make towards the pebbled shore,
So do our minutes hasten to their end,
Each changing place with that which goes before,
In sequent toil all forwards do contend.[3]
Nativity, once in the main[4] of light,
Crawls to maturity, wherewith being crowned,
Crooked[5] eclipses 'gainst his glory fight,
And Time that gave doth now his gift confound.[6]
Time doth transfix[7] the flourish set on youth

3. Struggle. *Sequent*: successive. 4. High seas. *Nativity*: newborn life. 5. Perverse. 6. Bring to nothing. 7. Pierce.

And delves the parallels[8] in beauty's brow,
Feeds on the rarities of nature's truth,
And nothing stands but for his scythe to mow.
And yet to times in hope[9] my verse shall stand,
Praising thy worth, despite his cruel hand.

1609

- **Which lines in this poem vary the basic iambic meter? What is the effect of these variations?**

GERARD MANLEY HOPKINS
Spring and Fall

to a young child

Márgarét áre you gríeving[1]
Over Goldengrove unleaving?
Leáves, like the things of man, you
With your fresh thoughts care for, can you?
Áh! ás the heart grows older
It will-come to such sights colder
By and by, nor spare a sigh
Though worlds of wanwood leafmeal[2] lie;
And yet you wíll weep and know why.
Now no matter, child, the name:
Sórrow's spríngs áre the same.
Nor mouth had, no nor mind, expressed
What heart heard of, ghost[3] guessed:
It ís the blight man was born for,
It is Margaret you mourn for.

1880

- **How does this poem's heavy use of alliteration serve its exploration of youth and age, life and death?**

WALT WHITMAN
Beat! Beat! Drums!

1

Beat! beat! drums!—Blow! bugles! blow!
Through the windows—through doors—burst like a
 force of armed men,
Into the solemn church, and scatter the congregation;
Into the school where the scholar is studying:

8. Lines, wrinkles. 9. In the future.
1. Hopkins's own accent markings.
2. Broken up, leaf by leaf (analogous to "piecemeal"). *Wanwood*: pale, gloomy woods. 3. Soul.

Leave not the bridegroom quiet—no happiness must he have now with his bride;
Nor the peaceful farmer any peace plowing his field or gathering his grain;
So fierce you whirr and pound, you drums—so shrill you bugles blow.

2

Beat! beat! drums!—Blow! bugles! blow!
Over the traffic of cities—over the rumble of wheels in the streets:
Are beds prepared for sleepers at night in the houses? No sleepers must sleep in those beds;
No bargainers' bargains by day—no brokers or speculators—Would they continue?
Would the talkers be talking? would the singer attempt to sing?
Would the lawyer rise in the court to state his case before the judge?
Then rattle quicker, heavier drums—you bugles wilder blow.

3

Beat! beat! drums!—Blow! bugles! blow!
Make no parley—stop for no expostulation;
Mind not the timid—mind not the weeper or prayer;
Mind not the old man beseeching the young man;
Let not the child's voice be heard, nor the mother's entreaties; Recruit! Recruit!
Make the very trestles to shake under the dead, where they lie in their shrouds awaiting the hearses.
So strong you thump, O terrible drums—so loud you bugles blow.

1861

- **How does Whitman use various sound devices to mimic both the sound he asks the drums and bugles to make and the effects he imagines those sounds having? How might the poem's date affect your sense of the poem, particularly its final stanza?**

KEVIN YOUNG
Ode to Pork

I wouldn't be here
without you. Without you
I'd be umpteen
pounds lighter & a lot
less alive. You stuck
round my ribs even
when I treated you like a dog
dirty, I dare not eat.
I know you're the blues
because loving you
may kill me—but still you
rock me down slow

as hamhocks on the stove.
Anyway you come
fried, cured, burnt
to within one inch
of your life I love. Babe,
I revere your every
nickname—bacon, chitlin,
cracklin, sin.
Some call you murder,
shame's stepsister—
then dress you up
& declare you white
& healthy, but you always
come back, sauced, to me.
Adam himself gave up
a rib to see yours
piled pink beside him.
Your heaven is the only one
worth wanting—
you keep me all night
cursing your four-
letter name, the next
begging for you again.

2007

- **How do sound effects contribute to the tone of ODE TO PORK? to the poem's characterization of the speaker's relationship to pork? How might they make the poem sound like a blues song?**

PAUL CELAN

Deathfugue[4]

Black milk of daybreak we drink it at evening
we drink it at midday and morning we drink it at night
we drink and we drink
we shovel a grave in the air where you won't lie too cramped
A man lives in the house he plays with his vipers he writes
he writes when it grows dark to Deutschland your golden hair
    Margareta[5]
he writes it and steps out of doors and the stars are all sparkling he
    whistles his hounds to stay close

4. Translated from the German by John Felstiner. *Fugue*: a particularly complex and highly regarded classical musical genre in which repeated variations on a single or central theme are interwoven.
5. Name of the tragic heroine in German poet Johann Wolfgang von Goethe's *Faust* (1808, 1832). The protagonist of Goethe's poem sells his soul to the devil, who then introduces him to Margarete; after Faust seduces and impregnates her, then kills her brother in a swordfight, Margarete goes insane, drowns her child, and is sentenced to death. *Deutschland*: Germany (German); also, the first word of Germany's national anthem, *Deutschland, Deutschland Über Alles*, "Germany, Germany above all."

Prisoners' orchestra performing for the SS-men in Auschwitz in 1941.

he whistles his Jews into rows has them shovel a grave in the ground
he commands us play up for the dance[6]

Black milk of daybreak we drink you at night
we drink you at morning and midday we drink you at evening
we drink and we drink
A man lives in the house he plays with his vipers he writes
he writes when it grows dark to Deutschland your golden hair
Margareta
Your ashen hair Shulamith[7] we shovel a grave in the air where you won't
lie too cramped

He shouts dig this earth deeper you lot there you others sing up and play
he grabs for the rod in his belt he swings it his eyes are so blue
stick your spades deeper you lot there you others play on for the dancing

Black milk of daybreak we drink you at night
we drink you at midday and morning we drink you at evening
we drink and we drink

6. During World War II, Jewish musicians in concentration camps were forced to perform for their German captors and fellow prisoners.
7. Biblical character from the Song of Songs, traditionally regarded as a symbol of the Jewish people.

a man lives in the house your goldenes Haar Margareta
your aschenes Haar[8] Shulamith he plays with his vipers

He shouts play death more sweetly this Death is a master from
Deutschland
he shouts scrape your strings darker you'll rise up as smoke to the sky
you'll then have a grave in the clouds where you won't lie too cramped

Black milk of daybreak we drink you at night
we drink you at midday Death is a master aus Deutschland
we drink you at evening and morning we drink and we drink
this Death is ein Meister aus Deutschland his eye it is blue
he shoots you with shot made of lead shoots you level and true
a man lives in the house your goldenes Haar Margarete
he looses his hounds on us grants us a grave in the air
he plays with his vipers and daydreams der Tod ist ein Meister aus
Deutschland[9]

dein[1] goldenes Haar Margarete
dein aschenes Haar Sulamith

c. 1944–45 1952
(trans. 1995)

- **How is each stanza like and different from preceding stanzas? What is the effect of both the repetition and the changes?**

THE TRANSLATOR ON HIS WORK: JOHN FELSTINER

From *Paul Celan: Poet, Survivor, Jew* (1995)*

When Celan [. . .] crossed out *tango* in a typescript and substituted *fuge* [. . . ,] this small change made an immense difference. It was to bring on decades of debate, the term *Todesfuge* offending against acceptable modes of meaning. What is this absurd genitive, this irreconcilable compound? "Fugue of Death," a correct translation, loses the accentual (and atrocious) symmetry of *Tó-des fú-ge,* while loosening the German possessive's compactness—the compact between death and music, nullity and order, which are the word's two sides. Yet "Death Fugue" does not convey the sense of belonging, a train of events belonging to death.

• • •

For the first line of "*Todesfuge*" I would like to say "Black milk of daybreak we drink it at dusk," so as to let alliteration imprint the day-in, day-out fatality of

8. Respectively, "golden hair" and "ashen hair" in German.
9. Death is a master from Germany (German). 1. Your (German).

camp existence. But "evening" rather than "dusk" for *abends* keeps Celan's rhythm and leads familiarly to "morning" in the next line. [. . .]

[. . .] In the beginning I hear—or persuade myself I hear—the creation sequence from Genesis: "And God called the light Day, and the darkness he called Night. And there was evening and there was morning: one day." If the Bible reverberates through Celan's opening lines, "day . . . night . . . evening . . . morning," then the word "dusk" cannot parody Scripture as does "evening . . . and morning" [. . .].

For forty years now, what Celan wrote has imprinted itself on readers and audiences through a relentless cadence that cannot be gainsaid. As his only poem not stopped by punctuation, "Todesfuge" finds a beat by the first line—

wir trink*en sie* ab*ends*

we *drink* it at *eve*ning

[. . .] *Wir trinken und trinken*: "we drink it and drink it," or "we're drinking and drinking," a rollicking beat that calls up much-loved German songs—from the Munich beer-hall, let us say, where Nazism arose.

* * *

Another reverberation occurs three times over: *da liegt man nicht eng* ("there one doesn't lie narrowly"). [. . .]

For years I have tried one way after another to bring *da liegt man nicht eng* into rhythmic, idiomatic English: "there you won't lie too tight"—but this makes an unwanted rhyme with "we drink it at night," in a poem where rhyme would prettify. Celan's laconic phrase gives a proverbial ring to the notion that these prisoners will not be jammed into rough narrow bunks anymore, once they have gone up in smoke. Or else: "there you won't lie crammed in," but I would rather end on a hard consonant as Celan does on *eng* [. . .]. Hence "there you won't lie too cramped," with its harsh cutoff.

Verse translators are always weighing whether to try for musical effects at the spots where such effects occur in the original. "A man lives in the house," we hear, then the treble alliteration in *der spielt mit den Schlangen der schreibt*, which connects playing, snakes, and writing. To say "he plays with his snakes he writes" creates some resonance, but "he plays with his vipers he writes" moves the rhythm along and ties "vipers" to "writes," uncovering something deadly in the act of writing.

Celan's sounds sometimes defy any English equivalent: *der schreibt wenn es dunkelt nach Deutschland*. Rather than "he writes when it grows dark to Germany," we can keep the jolt of *dunkelt* and *Deutschland* by extraditing the name into English: "he writes when it grows dark to Deutschland." Those two syllables grip the rhythm better than "Germany," and, after all, why translate *Deutschland*, drilled into everyone by Nazism's "Deutschland, Deutschland, über Alles." The word occurs this once in Celan's poetry, then never again.

* * *

Celan's *spielt süsser den Tod* ("play death more sweetly") brings into earshot Bach's aria *"Komm süsser Tod"* (Come sweet death). [. . .] Celan articulates a twist of thought that English cannot manage:

spielt	*süsser*	*den Tod*	*der Tod ist ein Meister*
play	more sweetly	death	death is a master

At the line's midpoint, *den Tod der Tod*, "death" as the object of sweet playing pivots directly on "death" as the subject of mastery. *Tod* wedges up against itself, making death both outcome and origin.

Now the poem confirms its title: *der Tod ist ein Meister aus Deutschland.* [. . .] It translates readily, yet *Meister* can designate God, Christ, rabbi, teacher, champion, captain, owner, guildsman, master of arts or theology, labor-camp overseer, musical maestro, "master" race, not to mention Goethe's *Wilhelm Meister* and Wagner's *Meistersinger von Nürnberg*, which carries overtones of the 1935 Nuremberg racial laws and the postwar trials. Any other choice but "master" would lose the loaded sense of *Meister.*

As this motif takes over, the verse itself falls into step and turns up the poem's only rhyme:

der Tod ist ein Meister aus Deutschland sein Auge ist blau
er trifft dich mit bleierner Kugel er trifft dich genau

this death is ein Meister aus Deutschland his eye it is blue
he shoots you with shot made of lead shoots you level and true

The celebrated purity of that icy Nordic eye calls for a folk idiom, a singsong wordiness to bring out the childlike tone, and a hackneyed rhyme. [. . .]

By the time this "master from Deutschland" is named three and then four times, "*Todesfuge*" has evolved its own span of real time. Rhythm and repetition have become systemic, there is no escaping them. [. . .]

Then suddenly this mind-emptying repetitiveness makes the poem easier to translate: *wir trinken dich mittags*—I've solved this already, and this: *der Tod ist ein Meister aus Deutschland.* The next time they come round I've got my version, then the next and the next. There's no use in thinking anymore, and that points to a rare option, given the poem's *fugue* of death: that is, to drive home its motifs as Celan himself does. The catch phrase *der Tod ist ein Meister aus Deutschland* appears four times. Let this sentence gradually revert to German. First, so that the reader comprehends, say "Death is a master from Deutschland." The second time, "Death is a master aus Deutschland." Then "Death is ein Meister aus Deutschland." And finally, "der Tod ist ein Meister aus Deutschland"—a German contagion of English.

What makes it possible to do this is the logic of "*Todesfuge*"—its musicality, for better or worse. By veering more and more to the original, my version gets a ring of truth, an identity with verse written by Paul Celan. In this gradual reversion, unavailable to German readers, we re-enter the darkness of deathbringing speech.

• • •

Finally, I leave the litany of appeals to Margaret and Shulamith wholly in German. The translator's voice moves into unison with the poet's, recouping a little of what has been lost in translation.

**Paul Celan: Poet, Survivor, Jew.* Yale UP, 1995.

SUGGESTIONS FOR WRITING

1. Read Pope's Sound and Sense carefully twice—once silently and once aloud—and then mark the stressed and unstressed syllables. Single out all the lines that have major variations from the basic iambic pentameter pattern. Pick out six lines with variations that seem to you worthy of comment, and write a paragraph on each in which you show how the variation contributes to the specific effects achieved in that line and the corresponding point Pope conveys about poetic style.
2. Try your hand at writing limericks in imitation of There was a young girl from St. Paul; study the rhythmic patterns and line lengths carefully, and imitate them exactly in your poem. Begin your limerick with "There once was a _____ from _____" (using a place for which you think you can find a comic rhyme).
3. Write an essay exploring how Wilfred Owen uses meter (including substitutions) and rhyme, as well as other sound devices, in Dulce et Decorum Est both to capture the experience of war and its effects and to respond critically to traditional war poetry, perhaps by comparing this poem to Jessie Pope's The Call. If you choose to draw on Pope's poem, however, you might also want to consider how the poem works and means differently when titled Dulce et Decorum Est rather than (as it originally was) To Jessie Pope.
4. Pope's Sound and Sense contains this advice for poets: "But when loud surges lash the sounding shore, / The hoarse, rough verse should like the torrent roar" (lines 368–69). In other words, he counsels that the sound of the poet's description should match the sense of what the poem is describing. Write an essay in which you examine the sound and sense in Shakespeare's Like as the waves make towards the pebbled shore. How does the poem achieve a harmony of meaning and sound?
5. Write an essay in which you discuss any poem in this book in which sound seems a more important element than anything else, even the meaning of words. What is the point of writing and reading this kind of poetry? Can it achieve its effects through silent reading, or must it be experienced aloud?

ANSWERS TO SCANSION EXERCISE: 1. anapestic, 2. dactylic, 3. trochaic, 4. iambic.

Words and Music

AN ALBUM

People often associate poetry with music, for good reason. The word *lyric* derives from the ancient Greeks' practice of reciting certain poems to the accompaniment of a harplike instrument, the lyre. Throughout history, poems have been set to music, and many "lyrics" have been created specifically to fit musical compositions. Many poems, especially during the Renaissance, were simply called "Song" (or "Chanson" or "Lied" or similar terms in other languages), and some were constructed in hybrid musical-poetic forms such as the madrigal, the dirge, and the hymn.

The most fundamental link between poetry and music involves their almost equal dependence on the principles of rhythm. Both art forms have a basis in mathematics: A regular beat or syncopated sound pattern shapes their phrasing and formal movement. Performers of both arts must keep count and consider quantities as well as qualities of sounds. Just as good musicians learn to listen and count so easily that it seems "natural," so poets often develop an ear for rhythm that makes their sound choices seem effortless. Readers, too, can develop such an ear.

Both poetry and music use representational or imitative strategies to create the illusion of sounds—bells, waves, motorcycles, for example—but words operate referentially in a way that sounds normally do not, and their syntax is of a different kind from that in musical composition. The referential fact of language almost always alters the "pure" effects of sound.

Poems composed to or for music obviously rely on rhythmic or harmonic effects even more than those created solely by words. Reading the lyrics of a song you know well is quite different from reading words that have for you no musical association or history. But the "music" created by a poem itself can work in a similar way when there is no musical "source" or cocreation.

The poems that follow were all written for, in conjunction with, or to imitate music. Can you add your own song lyrics from your favorite contemporary singers and groups? Are the words as effective without the music? Do they make good poems? Can you, in the lyrics you know well, separate the actual musical implications from those of the words alone?

THOMAS CAMPION

When to Her Lute Corinna Sings

When to her lute Corinna sings,
Her voice revives the leaden[1] strings,
And doth in highest notes appear
As any challenged[2] echo clear;
But when she doth of mourning speak,
Ev'n with her sighs the strings do break.

1. Heavy. 2. Aroused.

And as her lute doth live or die,
Led by her passion, so must I:
For when of pleasure she doth sing,
My thoughts enjoy a sudden spring;
But if she doth of sorrow speak,
Ev'n from my heart the strings do break.

1601

- **How does Campion mimic an "echo" in this poem? What is the effect of this echoing?**

The following two poems are ballads, a type of narrative poem originally intended for singing. These examples, moreover, use patterns of meter and stanza that are used so often in ballads that they are often called *ballad meter* and *ballad stanza*. Can you identify the patterns?

ANONYMOUS
Sir Patrick Spens

The king sits in Dumferling toune,[3]
  Drinking the blude-reid[4] wine:
"O whar will I get guid sailor,
  To sail this ship of mine?"

Up and spake an eldern knicht,
  Sat at the king's richt knee:
"Sir Patrick Spens is the best sailor
  That sails upon the sea."

The king has written a braid[5] letter
  And signed it wi' his hand,
And sent it to Sir Patrick Spens,
  Was walking on the sand.

The first line that Sir Patrick read,
  A loud lauch[6] lauched he;
The next line that Sir Patrick read,
  The tear blinded his ee.[7]

"O wha is this has done this deed,
  This il deed done to me,
To send me out this time o' the year,
  To sail upon the sea?

"Make haste, make haste, my merry men all,
  Our guid ship sails the morn."
"O say na sae,[8] my master dear,
  For I fear a deadly storm.

3. Town. 4. Bloodred. 5. Broad: explicit. 6. Laugh. 7. Eye. 8. Not so.

"Late, late yestre'en I saw the new moon
Wi' the auld moon in her arm,
And I fear, I fear, my dear mastér,
That we will come to harm."

O our Scots nobles were richt laith[9]
To weet their cork-heeled shoon,[1]
But lang owre a[2] the play were played
Their hats they swam aboon.[3]

O lang, lang, may their ladies sit,
Wi' their fans into their hand,
Or ere they see Sir Patrick Spens
Come sailing to the land.

O lang, lang, may the ladies stand
Wi' their gold kems[4] in their hair,
Waiting for their ain[5] dear lords,
For they'll see them na mair.

Half o'er, half o'er to Aberdour
It's fifty fadom deep,
And there lies guid Sir Patrick Spens
Wi' the Scots lords at his feet.

c. 13th century

• **Originally, ballads were a form of oral folk literature. Often their plots either involve extraordinary, even violent, events experienced by ordinary folk or center on a conflict between people of different social ranks. Is that true of SIR PATRICK SPENS? What might the ballad suggest about "nobles" (line 29) through its form, and especially its "music," as well as its content?**

DUDLEY RANDALL
Ballad of Birmingham

(On the bombing of a church in Birmingham, Alabama, 1963)[6]

"Mother dear, may I go downtown
Instead of out to play,
And march the streets of Birmingham
In a Freedom March today?"

"No, baby, no, you may not go,
For the dogs are fierce and wild,
And clubs and hoses, guns and jails
Aren't good for a little child."

9. Right loath: very reluctant.
1. To wet their cork-heeled shoes. Cork was expensive, and thus such shoes were a mark of wealth and status. 2. Before all. 3. Above. 4. Combs. 5. Own.
6. Just before Sunday services on September 15, 1963, a bomb exploded in Birmingham's 16th Street Baptist Church, killing four girls, aged eleven to fourteen, and injuring at least twenty-one other members of the predominantly African American congregation.

"But, mother, I won't be alone.
Other children will go with me,
And march the streets of Birmingham
To make our country free."

"No, baby, no, you may not go,
For I fear those guns will fire.
But you may go to church instead
And sing in the children's choir."

She has combed and brushed her night-dark hair,
And bathed rose petal sweet,
And drawn white gloves on her small brown hands,
And white shoes on her feet.

The mother smiled to know her child
Was in the sacred place,
But that smile was the last smile
To come upon her face.

For when she heard the explosion,
Her eyes grew wet and wild.
She raced through the streets of Birmingham
Calling for her child.

She clawed through bits of glass and brick,
Then lifted out a shoe.
"Oh, here's the shoe my baby wore,
But, baby, where are you?"

1969

- **Compare this poem to other ballads in this volume and elsewhere. Why is the form appropriate for commemorating this violent event?**

AUGUSTUS MONTAGUE TOPLADY

A Prayer, Living and Dying

I

ROCK of ages, cleft for me,
Let me hide myself in Thee!
Let the Water and the Blood,
From thy riven Side which flow'd,
Be of sin the double cure;
Cleanse me from its guilt and pow'r.

II

Not the labors of my hands
Can fulfill thy Law's demands:
Could my zeal no respite know,
Could my tears for ever flow,

All for sin could not atone;
Thou must save, and Thou alone.

III

Nothing in my hand I bring;
Simply to thy Cross I cling;
Naked, come to Thee for dress;
Helpless, look to Thee for grace;
Foul, I to the Fountain fly:
Wash me, SAVIOR, or I die!

IV

While I draw this fleeting breath—
When my eye-strings break in death—
When I soar to worlds unknown—
See Thee on thy judgment-throne—
ROCK of ages, cleft for me,
Let me hide myself in Thee!

1776

- **What aspects of this poem might make it suitable for communal singing by untrained singers?**

ROBERT HAYDEN

Homage to the Empress of the Blues[7]

Because there was a man somewhere in a candystripe silk shirt,
gracile and dangerous as a jaguar and because a woman moaned
for him in sixty-watt gloom and mourned him Faithless Love
Twotiming Love Oh Love Oh Careless Aggravating Love,

She came out on the stage in yards of pearls, emerging like
a favorite scenic view, flashed her golden smile and sang.

Because grey laths began somewhere to show from underneath
torn hurdygurdy[8] lithographs of dollfaced heaven;
and because there were those who feared alarming fists of snow
on the door and those who feared the riot-squad of statistics,

She came out on the stage in ostrich feathers, beaded satin,
and shone that smile on us and sang.

1962

- **How do the two short stanzas beginning with "She came out" complete the thoughts of the longer stanzas that start with "Because"?**

7. Bessie Smith (1894 [or 1898?]–1937); legendary blues singer whose theatrical style grew out of the black American vaudeville tradition.
8. Disreputable kind of dance hall.

MICHAEL HARPER
Dear John, Dear Coltrane

a love supreme, a love supreme
a love supreme, a love supreme[9]

Sex fingers toes
in the marketplace
near your father's church
in Hamlet, North Carolina—[1]
witness to this love
in this calm fallow
of these minds,
there is no substitute for pain:
genitals gone or going,
seed burned out,
you tuck the roots in the earth,
turn back, and move
by river through the swamps,
singing: *a love supreme, a love supreme*;
what does it all mean?
Loss, so great each black
woman expects your failure
in mute change, the seed gone.
You plod up into the electric city—
your song now crystal and
the blues. You pick up the horn
with some will and blow
into the freezing night:
a love supreme, a love supreme—

Dawn comes and you cook
up the thick sin 'tween
impotence and death, fuel
the tenor sax cannibal
heart, genitals and sweat
that makes you clean—
a love supreme, a love supreme—

Why you so black?
cause I am
why you so funky?
cause I am
why you so black

9. Jazz saxophonist and composer John William Coltrane (1926–67) wrote "A Love Supreme" in response to a spiritual experience in 1957 that also led to his quitting heroin and alcohol. Mainly an instrumental improvisation featuring Coltrane's saxophone, the piece begins with the repeated chant of "a love supreme." The record was released in 1965.
1. Coltrane's birthplace. His family shared a house with Coltrane's grandfather, who was the minister of St. Stephen's AME Zion Church.

cause I am
why you so sweet?
cause I am
why you so black?
cause I am
a love supreme, a love supreme:

So sick
you couldn't play *Naima,*[2]
so flat we ached
for song you'd concealed
with your own blood,
your diseased liver gave
out its purity,
the inflated heart
pumps out, the tenor kiss,
tenor love:
a love supreme, a love supreme—
a love supreme, a love supreme—

1970

- **In what ways is this poem, as suggested by the title, both a "Dear John" letter and a poem of praise?**

BOB DYLAN
The Times They Are A-Changin'

Come gather 'round people
Wherever you roam
And admit that the waters
Around you have grown
And accept it that soon
You'll be drenched to the bone
If your time to you is worth savin'
Then you better start swimmin' or you'll sink like a stone
For the times they are a-changin'

Come writers and critics
Who prophesize with your pen
And keep your eyes wide
The chance won't come again
And don't speak too soon
For the wheel's still in spin
And there's no tellin' who that it's namin'
For the loser now will be later to win
For the times they are a-changin'

Come senators, congressmen
Please heed the call

2. A song Coltrane wrote for and named after his wife, recorded in 1959.

Don't stand in the doorway
Don't block up the hall
For he that gets hurt
Will be he who has stalled
There's a battle outside and it is ragin'
It'll soon shake your windows and rattle your walls
For the times they are a-changin'

Come mothers and fathers
Throughout the land
And don't criticize
What you can't understand
Your sons and your daughters
Are beyond your command
Your old road is rapidly agin'
Please get out of the new one if you can't lend your hand
For the times they are a-changin'

The line it is drawn
The curse it is cast
The slow one now
Will later be fast
As the present now
Will later be past
The order is rapidly fadin'
And the first one now will later be last
For the times they are a-changin'

1963, 1964

- **How does familiarity with THE TIMES THEY ARE A-CHANGIN' as a song affect your sense of it as a poem? Do successful song lyrics necessarily work as poetry?**

LINDA PASTAN

Listening to Bob Dylan, 2005

Little Bobby Zimmerman,[3]
did he have a mother?
Iconoclast to icon,
was the wind his brother?[4]

Did he steal or borrow
Woody's[5] voice, pure gravel?

3. Influential singer-songwriter Bob Dylan was born Robert Allen Zimmerman (in Duluth, Minnesota, 1941).
4. Among the series of questions posed in Dylan's famous 1962 song "Blowin' in the Wind," is "how many times must the cannon balls fly / Before they're forever banned?"
5. Woody Guthrie (1912–67), influential Depression-era folk musician and singer-songwriter renowned for songs (including "This Land Is Your Land") championing common people and social and economic justice.

Women gave their bodies.
Kerouac[6] gave travel.

Some would call him genius
or curly-headed sphinx,
riding music out of sight
and noisy as a lynx.

Here we go again,
counting up our dead:
syncopated bullets,
hard rain on our heads,[7]

foxes in the hen house,
freedom on the rack.
Somebody sing something!
The times are a-changin' back.

2007

- **Why might Pastan include a date in her title? Can you find other allusions to Dylan songs and lyrics? What do they individually and collectively contribute to the poem? What sound devices does Pastan use, and what is their combined effect?**

MOS DEF
Hip Hop

You say one for the treble, two for the time
Come on, y'all, let's rock this!
You say one for the treble, two for the time
Come on!

Speech is my hammer, bang the world into shape, now let it fall . . . (*Hungh!!*)

My restlessness is my nemesis, it's hard
To really chill and sit still, committed to page
I write a rhyme, sometimes won't finish for days
Scrutinize my literature from the large to the miniature
I mathematically add-minister, subtract the wack
Selector, wheel it back, I'm feelin that
(Ha ha ha) From the core to the perimeter, Black
You know the motto: stay fluid even in staccato (Mos Def)
Full blooded, full throttle, breathe deep inside the drum hollow
. . . There's the hum
Young man, where you from? Brooklyn, number one

6. Jack Kerouac (1922–69), U.S. novelist and poet; widely regarded as a manifesto of sorts for the so-called Beat Generation, his novel *On the Road* (1957) is based on the cross-country travels of Kerouac and friends, including writers William S. Burroughs and Allen Ginsberg.

7. Dylan's 1963 song "A Hard Rain's A-Gonna Fall" includes lines such as "I saw guns and sharp swords in the hands of young children."

Native Son,[8] speaking in the native tongue
I got my eyes on tomorrow (there it is), while you still tryna
Find where it is, I'm on the ave' where it lives and dies
Violently, silently . . . Shine
So vibrantly that eyes squint to catch a glimpse
Embrace the bass with my dark ink fingertips
Used to speak the King's English, but caught a rash on my lips
See, now my chat just like this
Long range from the baseline (swish). Move like an apparition
Go to the ground with ammunition (chi-chi-POW)
Move from the gate, voice cued on your tape
Putting food on your plate, many crews can relate
Who choosing your fate, yo
We went from picking cotton, to chain-gang line chopping
To be-bopping, to hip-hopping
Blues people got the blue-chip stock option
Invisible Man,[9] got the whole world watching
(Where ya at?) I'm high, low, east, west, all over your map
I'm getting big props with this thing called hip hop
Where you can either get paid or get shot, when your product in stock
The fair-weather friends flock, when your chart position drop
Then the phone calls . . .
Chill for a minute, let's see who else hot
Snatch your shelf spot. Don't gas yourself, ock
The industry just a better-built cell block
A long way from the shell tops
And the bells that L rocked (rock, rock, rock, rock . . .)[1]

Hip hop is prosecution evidence
A out of court settlement, ad space for liquor
Sick without benefits (hungh!), luxury tenements
Choking the skyline, it's low life getting tree-top high
It is a backwater remedy
Bitter intent to memory, a class C felony[2]
Facing the death penalty (hungh!), stimulant and sedative
Original repetitive, violently competitive
A school unaccredited (there it is)
The break beats you get broken with on time and inappropriate
Hip hop went from selling crack to smoking it
Medicine for loneliness, remind me of Thelonious and Dizzy[3]
Propers to b-boys[4] getting busy
The wartime snapshot, the working man's jackpot

8. Title of a 1940 novel by Richard Wright (1908–60) about Bigger Thomas, an impoverished twenty-year-old living on Chicago's South Side.

9. Title of Ralph Ellison's 1952 novel, narrated by an unnamed African American protagonist.

1. Allusion to L.L. Cool J's 1985 hit "Rock the Bells."

2. States categorize felonies as A, B, C, etc. based on their seriousness, and penalties are apportioned accordingly.

3. Dizzy Gillespie (1917–93), American jazz musician, as was Thelonious Monk (1917–82).

4. Hip-hop dancers or "breakers."

A two dollar snack box sold beneath the crack spot
Olympic sponsor of the black Glock[5]
Gold medalist in the back shot from the sovereign state
Of the have-nots where farmers have trouble with cash crops
It's all-city like Phase 2, hip hop will simply amaze you
Praise you, pay you
Do whatever you say do, but Black, it can't save you

1999

- **What does this song suggest about the character, origin, and significance of hip-hop?**

JOSE B. GONZALEZ
Elvis in the Inner City

I was Elvis in the 70s, not swinging hips,
Not wearing suede shoes, but just the same,
In Canvas Chuck Taylors with my own svelte moves,
Spinning rap, scratching vinyl to the tunes of
Kurtis Blow, the Sugarhill Gang, Grandmaster Flash[6]
And the hip-hop of the hibity-hip-hip of other
Rappers, making rap mine, rhyming to
The boogie to the boom of the beat, beat, beat.

Mom and Dad's *charros,* same as Lawrence Welk's[7]
Instrumentals were stuff of old country boleros,[8]
But I had my rap, bebop and I'd rap, rap, rap.

The other side of the city, like the flip side of
A one-hit wonder, bopped heads to Van Morrison,
Jim Morrison, and Van Halen,[9] but I couldn't break
A pop to lyrics that weren't about me,
Inner city, inequality, in the record store
I be.

Boom boxes, size of refrigerators, walked up and
Down projects giving concerts for free,
And rap was made for me.

5. Pistol, especially semiautomatic.

6. Pioneering Caribbean-born, New York hip-hop artist, DJ, and Rock and Roll Hall of Famer Joseph Saddler (b. 1958). *Kurtis Blow*: U.S. rapper and record producer Kurt Walker (b. 1959), widely regarded as the first rapper to sign with a major record label (in 1979). *Sugarhill Gang*: U.S. rap group whose "Rapper's Delight" (1979) was arguably the first rap single to hit the Top 40.

7. U.S. accordionist and bandleader (1903–92) who hosted his own show from 1945 to 1982, featuring often sentimental earlier-twentieth-century standards performed by a big band and wholesome singers. *Charros*: literally, a Mexican horseman or cowboy, but here likely used to refer to the music of mariachi bands, who traditionally wear elaborate "charro" outfits.

8. Oldest, most traditional of Spanish dances and the music associated with it.

9. U.S. hard-rock band formed in 1972 by Eddie Van Halen and David Lee Roth. *Van Morrison*: Northern Irish singer-songwriter (b. 1945). *Jim Morrison*: U.S. singer-songwriter (1943–71), lead singer of the Doors (1965–73).

Until I—a lone white square on a checkerboard,
Reciting amidst Blacks of the block—
Froze, could not get my lips to vibrate,
Sync the refrain of the word
"nigger."

I, rockless, rapless,
Without a side A nor a side B,
Stuttered, strutted, struggled,
To find someone who would
Rhyme with me.

2006

• How does Gonzalez use various sound effects, as well as the arrangement of words on the page (into lines and stanzas), to characterize the speaker's evolving relationship to hip hop?

SUGGESTIONS FOR WRITING

1. Is there a meaningful difference between poetry and song lyrics? between poetry and rap? Is hip-hop a form of literature? Write an essay in which you explore the definitions of "poetry" and "lyrics." Be sure to cite enough examples to illustrate your ideas.
2. Find on the Internet the lyrics of a song (of any genre) that in your opinion uses words well, and download or print out one or more versions. First, notice any variations between the text(s) you find and the words you hear when listening to the song. Using a correct version of the lyrics (as you determine it), scan the lines for meter and rhyme. Are any words or syllables used to keep the beat without adding to the meaning (like the word "do," in Pope's Sound and Sense)? Are any rhymes dependent on vowel sounds rather than consonants (that is, do they not quite rhyme in print)? How does the refrain (if any) vary from the rest of the lyrics, and how does it relate to the title or theme of the song? Which lines or verses are most important to the "story" or the feeling relayed by the song? How would you describe the diction and tone of the "speaker" of the words, and how does it compare with the vocal style of the singer? Write a descriptive response paper on these words as a poem without music, and as lyrics within the song. Are they equally successful in print as they are when performed with music?
3. Drawing on Mos Def's Hip Hop and the lyrics to at least two other songs, write an essay exploring the rhythm and sound devices peculiar to hip-hop or rap. How especially do its rhythmic patterns compare to those of metered poetry?
4. Write an essay comparing either Mos Def's Hip Hop to Jose B. Gonzalez's poem about hip-hop or Bob Dylan's The Times They Are A-Changin' to Linda Pastan's poem Listening to Bob Dylan, 2005. Be sure to consider content—or what the song and the poem say about music or their times—and form—how the poem and/versus the song say it, especially through sound.

19 INTERNAL STRUCTURE

"Proper words in proper places": That is how one great writer of English prose, Jonathan Swift, described good writing. A good poet finds appropriate words, and already we have looked at some implications for readers of the verbal choices a poet makes. But the poet must also decide where to put those words—how to arrange them for maximum semantic, as well as visual and aural, effect—because individual words, figures of speech, symbols, and sounds exist not only within phrases and sentences and rhythmic patterns, but also within the larger whole of the poem. How should the words be arranged and the poem organized? What comes first and what last? What principle or idea of organization will inform the poem? How do the parts combine into a whole? And what is the effect of that arrangement? Considering these questions from the poet's point of view (What is my plan? Where shall I begin? Where do I want to go?) can help us notice the effects of structural choices.

DIVIDING POEMS INTO "PARTS"

It's useful to think of most poems—whether narrative, dramatic, or **lyric**—as informally divisible into parts, distinguished from each other by shifts in subject matter or topic, in **tone**, in address, in tense, or in mode (from narration to reflection or description, for example), and so on. As you read a new poem, look out for such shifts, however subtle, to determine how many parts you think the poem has and how each part relates to, and builds on, the one before. The following lyric, for example, seems to have two parts. How does each part relate to the other? What differentiates and connects them?

PAT MORA
Sonrisas

I live in a doorway
between two rooms, I hear
quiet clicks, cups of black
coffee, *click, click* like facts
   budgets, tenure, curriculum,
from careful women in crisp beige
suits, quick beige smiles
that seldom sneak into their eyes.

I peek
in the other room señoras

in faded dresses stir sweet
milk coffee, laughter whirls
with steam from fresh *tamales*
    sh, sh, mucho ruido,[1]
they scold one another,
press their lips, trap smiles
in their dark, Mexican eyes.

1986

This poem's two parts closely resemble each other in that each describes the women who inhabit one of the "two rooms" the speaker "live[s]" "between." Both descriptions include sights ("crisp beige / suits," "faded dresses"), sounds ("quiet clicks," "laughter"), and even the suggestion of tastes ("black / coffee," "sweet / milk coffee"). Yet the relation between the two parts and the two rooms is clearly one of contrast ("crisp / [. . .] suits" *versus* "faded dresses," "quiet clicks" *versus* "laughter," etc.). Here different languages, habits, sights, sounds, and values characterize the worlds symbolized by the two rooms, and the poem is organized around the contrast between them. The meaning of the poem (the difference between the two worlds and the experience of living between them) is very nearly the same as the structure.

To fully understand that meaning and the poem, we would need to tease out all those contrasts and their implications. We would also need to consider the significance of the author's choice not only to make the two parts essentially equal in length, but also to order them as she does. How would the poem and our sense of the speaker's feelings about the two rooms be different if we simply rearranged its lines, as follows?

I live in a doorway
between two rooms, I hear señoras
in faded dresses stir sweet
milk coffee, laughter whirls
with steam from fresh *tamales*
    sh, sh, mucho ruido,
they scold one another,
press their lips, trap smiles
in their dark, Mexican eyes.

I peek
in the other room, I hear
quiet clicks, cups of black
coffee, *click, click* like facts
        budgets, tenure, curriculum,
from careful women in crisp beige
suits, quick beige smiles
that seldom sneak into their eyes.

1. A lot of noise.

INTERNAL VERSUS EXTERNAL OR FORMAL "PARTS"

In Sonrisas, the internal division created by the speaker's shift in focus (from one room and world to another) corresponds to the poem's formal or "external" division into two **stanzas** and two sentences. Internal and external or formal divisions need not always coincide with each other, however. Major shifts in a poem can and do occur in the middle of a stanza, a line, even a sentence. Take the following poem. Only one sentence and one stanza long, it has no formal divisions at all. Yet it, too, arguably divides into two parts. As you read the poem, consider whether you agree and, if so, where you think the shift occurs.

GALWAY KINNELL

Blackberry Eating

I love to go out in late September
among the fat, overripe, icy, black blackberries
to eat blackberries for breakfast,
the stalks very prickly, a penalty
they earn for knowing the black art
of blackberry-making; and as I stand among them
lifting the stalks to my mouth, the ripest berries
fall almost unbidden to my tongue,
as words sometimes do, certain peculiar words
like *strengths* or *squinched*,
many-lettered, one-syllabled lumps,
which I squeeze, squinch open, and splurge well
in the silent, startled, icy, black language
of blackberry-eating in late September.

1980

The poem's first eight lines relate the speaker's experience of just what the title leads us to expect—blackberry eating. But notice what happens in line 9: The speaker's focus shifts from the topic of blackberries to the topic of words, with the word "as" signaling that we're entering the second phase of an **analogy** (or extended **simile**) comparing the experience we've just read about (eating blackberries) to the one we now begin to read about (forming words), with both berries and words "fall[ing] almost unbidden to [the] tongue" (line 8). Here, then, the relation between the poem's two parts and the two objects and experiences they describe is one of likeness rather than contrast. Fittingly enough for a poem about connection and comparison, as well as vaguely round "lumps" of things (line 11), the poem's final line ends with the same words as its first ("late September"). In a sense, then, the poem might be described as having a circular, as well as two-part (or "bipartite"), structure.

LYRICS AS INTERNAL DRAMAS

Obviously, not all poems consist of only two parts, as do those above. The following poem, for example, arguably divides into three parts. Just as important, in this poem the relationship between the parts seems to be one of development, tracing a change of outlook or attitude *within* the speaker.

SEAMUS HEANEY

Punishment[2]

I can feel the tug
of the halter at the nape
of her neck, the wind
on her naked front.

It blows her nipples
to amber beads,
it shakes the frail rigging
of her ribs.

I can see her drowned
body in the bog,
the weighing stone,
the floating rods and boughs.

Under which at first
she was a barked sapling
that is dug up
oak-bone, brain-firkin:

her shaved head
like a stubble of black corn,
her blindfold a soiled bandage,
her noose a ring

to store
the memories of love.
Little adulteress,
before they punished you

you were flaxen-haired,
undernourished, and your
tar-black face was beautiful.
My poor scapegoat,

I almost love you
but would have cast, I know,
the stones of silence.
I am the artful voyeur

of your brain's exposed
and darkened combs,
your muscles' webbing
and all your numbered bones:

2. According to the Roman historian Tacitus (c. 56–c. 120 CE), Germanic peoples punished adulterous women by first shaving their heads and then banishing or killing them. In 1951, in Windeby, Germany, the naked body of a young girl from the first century CE was pulled from the bog where she had been murdered. In contemporary Ireland, "betraying sisters" (line 38) have sometimes been punished by the Irish Republican Army for associating with British soldiers.

I who have stood dumb
when your betraying sisters,
cauled[3] in tar,
wept by the railings,
who would connive
in civilized outrage
yet understand the exact
and tribal, intimate revenge.

1975

Here, the first shift seems to come in line 23 (again, in the middle of a stanza rather than its beginning): Up to this point, the speaker has described the long-dead girl in the third person (e.g., "*her* neck," "*her* nipples," lines 3, 5; emphasis added). And despite his twice-repeated emphasis on his own perceptions and responses ("*I* can feel," "*I* can see," lines 1, 9; emphasis added), the girl herself gets most of the attention. Starting in line 23, however, the speaker begins to speak to the girl directly, addressing her in the second person ("you") and through **epithets** ("Little adulteress," "poor scapegoat," lines 23, 28). Verb tense shifts, too ("were," line 25), as the speaker begins to imagine the girl's life "before they punished" her (line 24). In at least two ways, then, the speaker seems to be coming closer to the girl, now seeing and addressing her as a human being with a history rather than as a thing to be looked at and talked *about*. At the same time, the speaker focuses more on himself as well, expressing his emotions ("I almost love you," line 29) and reflecting somewhat critically on the way he looked at the girl's body—and allowed us to—earlier in the poem ("I am the artful voyeur," line 32).

Subject matter and tense shift again, however, in line 37: The poem's final two stanzas consider the speaker's behavior toward the "betraying sisters" (line 38) in an indeterminate past ("I [. . .] have," line 37), as if here he describes not one specific experience, but rather a composite of many. Aside from the "your," in line 38, the girl herself seems to have disappeared from the poem (so much so that even that "your" now seems potentially ambiguous: Might it now also refer to someone else?). Though in this poem, unlike BLACKBERRY EATING, we don't have the word *as* to signal an analogy, it seems clear that Heaney's speaker has, over the course of the poem, come to see a similarity between his own complex attitude toward the long-dead girl and the "betraying sisters," the behavior of those responsible for these women's various punishments, and even between writing a poem about such women and punishing them. How and why so?

Though PUNISHMENT is by no means a dramatic poem in the literal sense, it does—like some other lyrics—relate an internal drama of sorts, tracing the process through which its speaker comes to see or accept, as well as share with us, some truth about or insight into the world or himself that he didn't see or accept previously, somewhat as a fictional character might in a dramatic or narrative poem or in a short story. In reading and writing about such poems, a good topic to explore might well be just what insight the speaker comes to over the course of the poem, and when and why so.

3. Wrapped or enclosed as if in a caul (the inner fetal membrane of higher vertebrates that sometimes covers the head at birth).

Analyzing Internal Structure: An Exercise

Like "Punishment," both of the following poems arguably trace a development in their speakers' perceptions of themselves or the world around them, even if the realization to which the speakers come and the process by which they get there differ. As you read each poem, think about where and why the shifts come both in the poem and in the speaker's outlook. In which poem does the change within the speaker seem to happen *during* the poem itself (as in "Punishment"), and which poem might instead depict the change as one that happened at some earlier, unspecified point in time?

SAMUEL TAYLOR COLERIDGE

Frost at Midnight

The frost performs its secret ministry,
Unhelped by any wind. The owlet's cry
Came loud—and hark, again! loud as before.
The inmates of my cottage, all at rest,
Have left me to that solitude, which suits
Abstruser musings: save that at my side
My cradled infant slumbers peacefully.
'Tis calm indeed! so calm, that it disturbs
And vexes meditation with its strange
And extreme silentness. Sea, hill, and wood,
This populous village! Sea, and hill, and wood,
With all the numberless goings on of life,
Inaudible as dreams! the thin blue flame
Lies on my low burnt fire, and quivers not;
Only that film,[4] which fluttered on the grate,
Still flutters there, the sole unquiet thing.
Methinks, its motion in this hush of nature
Gives it dim sympathies with me who live,
Making it a companionable form,
Whose puny flaps and freaks the idling Spirit
By its own moods interprets, every where
Echo or mirror seeking of itself,
And makes a toy of Thought.

But O! how oft,
How oft, at school, with most believing mind,
Presageful, have I gazed upon the bars,
To watch that fluttering stranger! and as oft
With unclosed lids, already had I dreamt

4. In all parts of the kingdom these films are called *strangers* and supposed to portend the arrival of some absent friend [Coleridge's note]. The "film" is a piece of soot fluttering on the bar of the grate.

Of my sweet birth-place, and the old church-tower,
Whose bells, the poor man's only music, rang
From morn to evening, all the hot Fair-day,
So sweetly, that they stirred and haunted me
With a wild pleasure, falling on mine ear
Most like articulate sounds of things to come!
So gazed I, till the soothing things I dreamt
Lulled me to sleep, and sleep prolonged my dreams!
And so I brooded all the following morn,
Awed by the stern preceptor's face, mine eye
Fixed with mock study on my swimming book:
Save if the door half opened, and I snatched
A hasty glance, and still my heart leaped up,
For still I hoped to see the stranger's face,
Townsman, or aunt, or sister more beloved,
My play-mate when we both were clothed alike![5]

Dear Babe, that sleepest cradled by my side,
Whose gentle breathings, heard in this deep calm,
Fill up the interspersed vacancies
And momentary pauses of the thought!
My babe so beautiful! it thrills my heart
With tender gladness, thus to look at thee,
And think that thou shalt learn far other lore
And in far other scenes! For I was reared
In the great city, pent 'mid cloisters dim,
And saw nought lovely but the sky and stars.
But thou, my babe! shalt wander like a breeze
By lakes and sandy shores, beneath the crags
Of ancient mountain, and beneath the clouds,
Which image in their bulk both lakes and shores
And mountain crags: so shalt thou see and hear
The lovely shapes and sounds intelligible
Of that eternal language, which thy God
Utters, who from eternity doth teach
Himself in all, and all things in himself.
Great universal Teacher! he shall mould
Thy spirit, and by giving make it ask.

Therefore all seasons shall be sweet to thee,
Whether the summer clothe the general earth
With greenness, or the redbreast sit and sing
Betwixt the tufts of snow on the bare branch
Of mossy apple-tree, while the nigh thatch
Smokes in the sun-thaw; whether the eave-drops fall
Heard only in the trances of the blast,

(*continued on next page*)

5. Late eighteenth-century custom called for all infants to wear dresses, regardless of gender.

(*continued*)

Or if the secret ministry of frost
Shall hang them up in silent icicles,
Quietly shining to the quiet Moon.

1798

- Coleridge described some of his poems, including FROST AT MIDNIGHT, as having a circular structure. How and why might this poem seem circular, or in what way does its end resemble its beginning? In what way are the two different? How might the resemblance and difference help us recognize the change in the speaker's outlook?

SHARON OLDS

The Victims

When Mother divorced you, we were glad. She took it and
took it, in silence, all those years and then
kicked you out, suddenly, and her
kids loved it. Then you were fired, and we
grinned inside, the way people grinned when
Nixon's helicopter lifted off the South
Lawn for the last time.[6] We were tickled
to think of your office taken away,
your secretaries taken away,
your lunches with three double bourbons,
your pencils, your reams of paper. Would they take your
suits back, too, those dark
carcasses hung in your closet, and the black
noses of your shoes with their large pores?
She had taught us to take it, to hate you and take it
until we pricked with her for your
annihilation, Father. Now I
pass the bums in doorways, the white
slugs of their bodies gleaming through slits in their
suits of compressed silt, the stained
flippers of their hands, the underwater
fire of their eyes, ships gone down with the
lanterns lit, and I wonder who took it and
took it from them in silence until they had
given it all away and had nothing
left but this.

1984

- How are the speakers' shifting attitudes toward her father (and the poem's parts) both related and differentiated by repetition of the word *took*?

6. When Richard Nixon resigned the U.S. presidency on August 8, 1974, his exit from the White House (by helicopter from the lawn) was televised live.

MAKING ARGUMENTS ABOUT STRUCTURE

Dividing a poem into parts and analyzing its internal structure as we have here isn't an exact science: Different readers might well come to slightly different conclusions about the nature, timing, and significance of key shifts and thus about just how many parts a poem might be said to have, how one part relates to another, and what sort of whole those parts create. It seems quite possible, for example, to argue that THE VICTIMS has either two parts or three, depending on what you make of lines 15–17 (up to the word "Now"), or that FROST AT MIDNIGHT has three, four, even five parts. In these cases, as in many others, there is no single correct answer. Indeed, ample room for disagreement is in a way precisely the point: Formulating your own ideas about just where important shifts come in a poem and just why they're important, identifying good evidence to support your conclusions, and considering alternative ways of understanding the poem's structure may take you far down the path to developing your own particular argument about how the poem as a whole works and means.

POEMS WITHOUT "PARTS"

As we've seen, too, dividing a poem into parts is simply a useful way to *begin* to explore and analyze its structure rather than the entire point or end of such analysis. And this is all the more obviously the case with those poems that contain no major shifts and thus no distinct "parts" at all. Such poems nonetheless have a distinct structure; their authors, too, must figure out how to organize their material so as to create something like a beginning, middle, and end. And here, too, such structural choices determine how the poem moves and means. The following poem is a case in point: One sentence and one stanza long, with no major shifts, how does it nonetheless manage both to cohere and develop? What picture of America results both from its particular details and the way they are organized?

WALT WHITMAN

I Hear America Singing

I hear America singing, the varied carols I hear,
Those of mechanics, each one singing his as it should be blithe and
  strong,
The carpenter singing his as he measures his plank or beam,
The mason singing his as he makes ready for work, or leaves off work,
The boatman singing what belongs to him in his boat, the deckhand
  singing on the steamboat deck,
The shoemaker singing as he sits on his bench, the hatter singing as he
  stands,
The wood-cutter's song, the ploughboy's on his way in the morning, or
  at noon intermission or at sundown,
The delicious singing of the mother, or of the young wife at work, or of
  the girl sewing or washing,
Each singing what belongs to him or her and to none else,

The day what belongs to the day—at night the party of young fellows, robust, friendly,
Singing with open mouths their strong melodious songs.

1860

By limiting himself to a single sentence and a single stanza, which nonetheless refers to a multitude of people and "songs," Whitman produces a poem that structurally embodies the motto on the U.S. seal—*e pluribus unum*, "Out of many, one." The "many ones" with whom the poem begins are all ordinary men who work with their hands: From "mechanics" (line 2) to a "boatman" (line 5) and "ploughboy" (line 7), they work on land and shore, in city and country. Though line 8 doesn't constitute a major shift, it does subtly broaden and further develop the poem's picture of America: Women enter the poem; and though they, too, are depicted "at work," the fact that they are identified specifically as a "mother," "young wife," and "girl" introduces, too, the idea both of generations and of family, two important social groups that intervene between many individuals, on the one hand, and an entire country, on the other. Finally, at poem's end, we move from "day" to "night" and from labor to leisure, in a way that makes clear that these oppositions and time itself have also been structuring principles all along: Line 4, after all, describes the mason as singing "as he makes ready for [. . .] or leaves off work," line 7 the ploughboy and wood-cutter each making "his way in the morning, or at noon intermission or at sundown." By its close, then, the poem has shown us a full day of life in Whitman's version of America and in the lives of those whose various, unique "carols" (line 1) combine to create a single American song.

POEMS FOR FURTHER STUDY

As you read each of the following poems, consider the following questions: Does the poem seem to divide into internal "parts"? If so, where and why? What are the major shifts? How does each part build on the last? How do the parts combine into a meaningful whole? If the poem doesn't seem divisible into parts, what are its organizing principles? How does the poem build and develop, and what overall picture or even **theme** results?

WILLIAM SHAKESPEARE

[Th' expense of spirit in a waste of shame]

Th' expense of spirit in a waste[7] of shame
Is lust in action; and, till action, lust
Is perjured, murderous, bloody, full of blame,
Savage, extreme, rude, cruel, not to trust;
Enjoyed no sooner but despisèd straight:
Past reason hunted; and no sooner had,
Past reason hated, as a swallowed bait,
On purpose laid to make the taker mad:
Mad in pursuit, and in possession so;
Had, having, and in quest to have, extreme;

7. Using up; also, desert. *Expense*: expending.

A bliss in proof,[8] and proved, a very woe;
Before, a joy proposed; behind, a dream.
All this the world well knows; yet none knows well
To shun the heaven that leads men to this hell.

1609

- **Paraphrase this poem. What emotional stages accompany the carrying out of a violent or lustful act? Is Shakespeare an insightful psychologist? What is his major insight about how lust works?**

PERCY BYSSHE SHELLEY
Ode to the West Wind

I

O wild West Wind, thou breath of Autumn's being,
Thou, from whose unseen presence the leaves dead
Are driven, like ghosts from an enchanter fleeing,

Yellow, and black, and pale, and hectic red,
Pestilence-stricken multitudes: O thou,
Who chariotest to their dark wintry bed

The wingèd seeds, where they lie cold and low,
Each like a corpse within its grave, until
Thine azure sister of the Spring shall blow

Her clarion[9] o'er the dreaming earth, and fill
(Driving sweet buds like flocks to feed in air)
With living hues and odors plain and hill:

Wild Spirit, which art moving everywhere;
Destroyer and preserver; hear, oh, hear!

II

Thou on whose stream, mid the steep sky's commotion,
Loose clouds like earth's decaying leaves are shed,
Shook from the tangled boughs of Heaven and Ocean,

Angels[1] of rain and lightning: there are spread
On the blue surface of thine aëry surge,
Like the bright hair uplifted from the head

Of some fierce Maenad,[2] even from the dim verge
Of the horizon to the zenith's height,
The locks of the approaching storm. Thou dirge

Of the dying year, to which this closing night
Will be the dome of a vast sepulcher,
Vaulted with all thy congregated might

8. In the act. 9. Trumpet call. 1. Messengers. 2. Frenzied female votary of Dionysus, the Greek god of vegetation and fertility who was supposed to die in the fall and rise again each spring.

Of vapors, from whose solid atmosphere
Black rain, and fire, and hail will burst: oh, hear!

III

Thou who didst waken from his summer dreams
The blue Mediterranean, where he lay,
Lulled by the coil of his crystàlline streams,

Beside a pumice isle in Baiae's bay,[3]
And saw in sleep old palaces and towers
Quivering within the wave's intenser day,

All overgrown with azure moss and flowers
So sweet, the sense faints picturing them! Thou
For whose path the Atlantic's level powers

Cleave themselves into chasms, while far below
The sea-blooms and the oozy woods which wear
The sapless foliage of the ocean, know

Thy voice, and suddenly grow gray with fear,
And tremble and despoil themselves:[4] oh, hear!

IV

If I were a dead leaf thou mightest bear;
If I were a swift cloud to fly with thee;
A wave to pant beneath thy power, and share

The impulse of thy strength, only less free
Than thou, O uncontrollable! If even
I were as in my boyhood, and could be

The comrade of thy wanderings over Heaven,
As then, when to outstrip thy skyey speed
Scarce seemed a vision; I would ne'er have striven

As thus with thee in prayer in my sore need.
Oh, lift me as a wave, a leaf, a cloud!
I fall upon the thorns of life! I bleed!

A heavy weight of hours has chained and bowed
One too like thee: tameless, and swift, and proud.

V

Make me thy lyre, even as the forest is:
What if my leaves are falling like its own!
The tumult of thy mighty harmonies

Will take from both a deep, autumnal tone,
Sweet though in sadness. Be thou, Spirit fierce,
My spirit! Be thou me, impetuous one!

3. Where Roman emperors had erected villas, west of Naples.
4. The vegetation at the bottom of the sea . . . sympathizes with that of the land in the change of seasons [Shelley's note].

Drive my dead thoughts over the universe
Like withered leaves to quicken a new birth!
And, by the incantation of this verse,

Scatter, as from an unextinguished hearth
Ashes and sparks, my words among mankind!
Be through my lips to unawakened earth

The trumpet of a prophecy! O Wind,
If Winter comes, can Spring be far behind?

1820

- **What attributes of the West Wind does the speaker want his poetry to embody? In what ways is this poem like the wind it describes? What is the effect of its structure?**

PHILIP LARKIN
Church Going

Once I am sure there's nothing going on
I step inside, letting the door thud shut.
Another church: matting, seats, and stone,
And little books; sprawlings of flowers, cut
For Sunday, brownish now; some brass and stuff
Up at the holy end; the small neat organ;
And a tense, musty, unignorable silence,
Brewed God knows how long. Hatless, I take off
My cycle-clips in awkward reverence,

Move forward, run my hand around the font.
From where I stand, the roof looks almost new—
Cleaned, or restored? Someone would know: I don't.
Mounting the lectern, I peruse a few
Hectoring large-scale verses, and pronounce
"Here endeth" much more loudly than I'd meant.
The echoes snigger briefly. Back at the door
I sign the book, donate an Irish sixpence,
Reflect the place was not worth stopping for.

Yet stop I did: in fact I often do,
And always end much at a loss like this,
Wondering what to look for; wondering, too,
When churches fall completely out of use
What we shall turn them into, if we shall keep
A few cathedrals chronically on show,
Their parchment, plate and pyx in locked cases,
And let the rest rent-free to rain and sheep.
Shall we avoid them as unlucky places?

Or, after dark, will dubious women come
To make their children touch a particular stone;

Pick simples[5] for a cancer; or on some
Advised night see walking a dead one?
Power of some sort or other will go on
In games, in riddles, seemingly at random;
But superstition, like belief, must die,
And what remains when disbelief has gone?
Grass, weedy pavement, brambles, buttress, sky,

A shape less recognizable each week,
A purpose more obscure. I wonder who
Will be the last, the very last, to seek
This place for what it was; one of the crew
That tap and jot and know what rood-lofts[6] were?
Some ruin-bibber,[7] randy for antique,
Or Christmas-addict, counting on a whiff
Of gown-and-bands and organ-pipes and myrrh?
Or will he be my representative,

Bored, uninformed, knowing the ghostly silt
Dispersed, yet tending to this cross of ground
Through suburb scrub because it held unspilt
So long and equably what since is found
Only in separation—marriage, and birth,
And death, and thoughts of these—for whom was built
This special shell? For, though I've no idea
What this accoutered frowsty barn is worth,
It pleases me to stand in silence here;

A serious house on serious earth it is,
In whose blent[8] air all our compulsions meet,
Are recognized, and robed as destinies.
And that much never can be obsolete,
Since someone will forever be surprising
A hunger in himself to be more serious,
And gravitating with it to this ground,
Which, he once heard, was proper to grow wise in,
If only that so many dead lie round.

1955

- **Describe the parts of this poem. How do the first two stanzas differ from the rest of the poem? Where and how does the poem shift from the personal to the general?**

5. Medicinal herbs.

6. Galleries atop the screens (on which crosses are mounted) that divide the naves or main bodies of churches from the choirs or chancels.

7. Literally, ruin-drinker: someone extremely attracted to antiquarian objects.

8. Blended.

AUTHORS ON THEIR WORK
PHILIP LARKIN (1922–85)

From "A Conversation with Ian Hamilton" (1964)*

It ["Church Going"] is of course an entirely secular poem. I was a bit irritated by an American who insisted to me it was a religious poem. It isn't religious at all. Religion surely means that the affairs of this world are under divine surveillance, and so on, and I go to some pains to point out that I don't bother about that kind of thing. [. . .]

[. . .] the poem is about going to church, not religion—I tried to suggest this by the title—and the union of the important stages of human life—birth, marriage and death—that going to church represents; and my own feeling that when they are dispersed into the registry office and the crematorium chapel life will become thinner in consequence. (22)

• • •

From "An Interview with John Haffenden" (1981)**

It ["Church Going"] came from the first time I saw a ruined church in Northern Ireland, and I'd never seen a ruined church before—discarded. It shocked me. Now of course it's commonplace: churches are not so much ruined as turned into bingo-halls, warehouses for refrigerators or split-level houses for architects.

It's not clear in the poem that you began with a ruined church.
No, it wasn't in the poem, but when you go into a church there's a feeling of something . . . well . . . over, derelict.

Some critics have discerned in it a yearning for a latter-day Christian or religious sanction. Is that so?
I suppose so. I'm not someone who's lost faith: I never had it. I was baptized [. . .] but not confirmed. Aren't religions shaped in terms of what people want? No one could help hoping Christianity was true, or at least the happy ending—rising from the dead and our sins forgiven. One longs for these miracles, and so in a sense one longs for religion. But "Church Going" isn't that kind of poem: it's a humanist poem, a celebration of the dignity of . . . well, you know what it says. (56–57)

*"A Conversation with Ian Hamilton." *Further Requirements: Interviews, Broadcasts, Statements and Book Reviews*, edited by Anthony Thwaite, Faber and Faber, 2001, pp. 19–26. Originally published in *London Magazine*, Nov. 1946.
**"An Interview with John Haffenden." *Further Requirements: Interviews, Broadcasts, Statements and Book Reviews*, edited by Anthony Thwaite, Faber and Faber, 2001, pp. 47–62. Originally published in *Viewpoints: Poets in Conversation with John Haffenden*, 1981.

KATIE FORD
Still-Life

Down by the pond, addicts sleep
on rocky grass half in water, half out,
and there the moon lights them
out of tawny silhouettes into the rarest
of amphibious flowers I once heard called *striders*,
between, but needing, two worlds.
Of what can you accuse them now,
beauty?

2013

• Katie Ford's poem contains only two sentences: Would you say that each constitutes one "part" of the poem? If so, how exactly do the parts relate to each other? Why might it matter that the final sentence is a question? What is the relevance and significance of the poem's title?

SUGGESTIONS FOR WRITING

1. What words and patterns are repeated in the different stanzas of Shelley's ODE TO THE WEST WIND? What differences are there from stanza to stanza? What "progress" does the poem make? Write an essay in which you discuss the ways that meaning and structure are intertwined in Shelley's poem.
2. Write an essay that explores the use of contrast in Pat Mora's SONRISAS. How is each of the two rooms in the poem characterized by way of contrast with the other? What do they individually and jointly symbolize? What does the poem show through this contrast?
3. Pick out any poem you have read in this book that seems particularly effective in the way it is put together. Write an essay in which you consider how the poem is organized—that is, what structural principles it employs. What do the choices of speaker, situation, and setting have to do with the poem's structure? What other artistic decisions contribute to its structure?

SAMPLE WRITING: ESSAY-IN-PROGRESS

The following piece of writing by student Lindsay Gibson was originally just one section of a longer essay on multiple poems by Philip Larkin. Though the beginning and middle of the piece work fine out of that context, you'll notice that we haven't supplied either the complete title or the real conclusion that the piece needs to have in order to be an entire, effective essay. What should the piece be titled? How might it be brought to a more satisfying conclusion?

You will notice, too, that the essay focuses only in part and somewhat unevenly on issues related to internal structure. How might the essay make more of the poem's structure? More generally, what are the weakest and strongest moments and aspects of the essay? How might its argument be improved or expanded? Answering such questions for yourself or discussing them with your classmates might be a useful way to better understand the qualities of a good argument, a good title, and a good conclusion.

Gibson 1

Lindsay Gibson
Dr. Nick Lolordo
Modern British Poetry
27 January 2017

Philip Larkin's "Church Going"

Philip Larkin is one of the semester's most fascinating poets. His use of colloquial language, regular meter, and rhyme sets him slightly apart from other poets of his day, many of whom write in varying forms of verse, use nearly indecipherable language, and rarely, if ever, make use of rhyme at all. Many of his poems are fraught with existential crises, the nature of which only someone living in the postmodern world could understand; consequently, his poems contain a lot of meaning for the contemporary reader.

Larkin's most fascinating poem, "Church Going," embodies many of his best attributes as a poet: it uses everyday, standard English and is therefore easy to read and understand, yet its stanzas contain a real search for meaning that its simple language might not immediately invite the reader to ponder. The poem also addresses one of Larkin's main preoccupations: religion, and specifically the role of religion in a postmodern world. Even with all of this, the most engaging aspect of the poem is the duality reflected in its structure: at first and on the one hand, the speaker makes quiet fun of religion; later and on the other hand, he reveals to us his own search for meaning and the answers that he realizes religion may or may not be able to give him.

The first two stanzas of "Church Going" contain a narrative of a seemingly secular man entering a church he has passed along his way. The speaker observes the layout of the building, the various accoutrements common to a church, and views it all with a mild sense of sarcasm or awkward reverence. His language almost insists on his self-proclaimed ignorance: "Someone would know; I don't" (line 12). And he foreshadows the rest of the poem when appraising the roof of the church as one would an antique: "Cleaned, or restored?" (12). At the end of the second stanza, the speaker reflects that "the place was not worth stopping for" (18). Yet stop he did, and that tells us volumes about what the rest of the poem is about.

In the third stanza, the poem's tone and the speaker's attitude shift as the speaker begins to ponder big questions about religion in today's world: does it have any meaning left? Should it? The speaker reveals to us that he often stops at churches like these, searching for meaning, yet "Wondering what to look for" (21), not even knowing what the questions are that he wants answered. His use of words like "parchment, plate and pyx" (25) reveals to us that he is not as ignorant about religious liturgy as he would have us believe—which, in turn, is further evidence of the dual nature of the poem: The speaker wants us to believe he doesn't know or care about anything to do with religion, yet he has been on his quest for meaning long enough to know the names of things he claims he does not. The last line of the third stanza poses another compelling question, this time about the future: after churches fall out of use, "Shall we avoid them as unlucky places?" (27). The question of whether, when faith is finally dead, people will still cling to superstitions such as luck and supernatural powers of whatever nature is a fascinating one.

The speaker goes on to explore this question in the next few stanzas by imagining some specific ways in which superstition might persist after religion is gone: women might take their children to "touch a particular stone" (29) or pick herbs around the church to use for medicinal purposes. But in all these imagined examples, no one actually goes to the church to worship anymore. In stanza 4, the speaker presents various tableaus of people using the church for more and more mundane uses, such as a student of architecture, someone else who only likes to see the ruins of old buildings simply because they're old, and finally, and somewhat paradoxically, a "Christmas-addict" (43) who (presumably) wants to see the last religious remnants of his beloved, commoditized, and commercialized holiday. The last person who might visit the church in this post-religion world might even be a doppelganger of the speaker himself, who, though claiming to be "bored" and "uninformed" (46), visits the church because "it held unspilt / So long and equably what since is found / Only in separation—marriage, and birth, / And death, and thoughts of these" (48-51). Once again the speaker insists that he is ignorant and careless of religion, but goes on

Gibson 3

to betray the fact that even if he does not believe in the religion itself, he is fascinated by the idea that it held "unspilt" what people now only find in marriages, births, and deaths: meaning. It is at this point that the reader can truly appreciate the point and purpose of this whole poem: meaning, and the search for it. It seems poignant that the speaker realizes there is more *meaning* in the church itself than any other place, whether actual belief in religion is there or not.

The last stanza seems to be an attempt on the speaker's part to reconcile the opposing forces of the poem—the speaker's insistence that he cares nothing for religion and that religion is meaningless anyway versus his existential need to find some kind of meaning that will justify his existence and maybe even the beliefs of others. The speaker finally respects what the church does for people, including himself: one's "compulsions meet, / Are recognised, and robed as destinies" (56-57). When one wonders if compulsions are merely that, one can go to church and be told that he or she is part of a larger whole—one's destiny. And if compulsions can be transformed into destinies, at least in the mind of the wonderer, then there will always be value in such a service: "that much never can be obsolete" (58), according to the speaker of the poem.

The last stanzas of the poem are devoted to a man who gravitates to the church because he "once heard [it] was proper to grow wise in, / If only that so many dead lie round" (62-63). Once again, the speaker shows us that even when belief in the religion associated with the church is completely gone, a sense of reverence, if only for the dead, will remain. The belief may be gone, but the sense of a community among people searching for, and perhaps finding, meaning will remain, and people will always be drawn to that, no matter what their belief system (or lack thereof).

The poem itself has another overarching concern that merits discussion: death. There are many images of or mentions of death throughout the poem: There are "flowers, cut / For Sunday, brownish now" (4-5), the words "Here endeth" (15) echoing through the small church, the possibility of someone seeing a "walking dead one" (31), the assertion that "superstition, like belief, must die" (34), talk of the "ghostly silt / Dispersed" (46-47), thoughts of "marriage, and birth, / And death" (50-51). And finally, the last image in the poem is the abandoned church's graveyard in which "so many dead lie round" (62). Throughout the poem there is death: death of people, death of ideas, death of faith. Death's pervasiveness is one more way the poem struggles with its dual nature: the poem narrates a serious search for meaning, yet the very definition of death is that there *is* no meaning. Death is the end, there is nothing more. Any search for meaning is rendered meaningless anyway upon one's death. The speaker implies that there is even an end to the search for meaning itself. The speaker asks in line 35, perhaps the most powerful line of the whole poem, "And what remains when disbelief has gone?" What is left over when even "disbelief" has died? Is it the beginning of another cycle in the search for meaning, or has even the "faith" that there is nothing out there died as well?

Gibson 4

The poem "Church Going" is a very layered, intensive look at all the things that matter to us as human beings: meaning, death, hope, hopelessness, and the way all of these things blend together in the perpetual existential crisis that is man's very existence.

Gibson 5

Work Cited

Larkin, Philip. "Church Going." *The Norton Introduction to Literature*, edited by Kelly J. Mays, 12th ed., W. W. Norton, 2017, pp. 1083-84.

20 EXTERNAL FORM

The previous chapters have discussed many of the *internal* features of a poem that make it unique: the **tone** and characteristics of its **speaker**; its **situation** and **setting** and its **themes**; its **diction**, **imagery**, and sounds. This chapter ventures into the *external* form of a poem, including its arrangement on the page and into both visual and verbal units. These formal aspects are external in being recognizable; like the fashion and fabric of clothing that expresses the personality of an individual, the external form is an appropriate garb or guise for the unique internal action and meaning of the poem. When reading a poem, you might immediately notice its stanza breaks. Or you might quickly recognize that the poem takes a traditional form such as the **sonnet**, or that it simply looks odd. These formal features guide readers as well as the poet. They help readers feel and appreciate repetitions and connections, changes and gaps, in the language as well as the meaning of the poem.

STANZAS

Most poems of more than a few lines are divided into **stanzas**—groups of lines divided from other groups by white space on the page. Putting some space between groupings of lines has the effect of sectioning a poem, giving its physical appearance a series of divisions that sometimes correspond to turns of thought, changes of scene or image, or other shifts in structure or direction of the kind examined in the last chapter. In Donne's THE FLEA, for example, the stanza divisions mark distinct stages in the action: Between the first and second stanzas, the speaker stops his companion from killing the flea; between the second and third stanzas, the companion follows through on her intention and kills the flea. Any formal division of a poem into stanzas is important to consider; what appear to be gaps or silences may be structural markers.

Historically, stanzas have most often been organized by patterns of **rhyme,** and often of **meter**, too; thus stanza divisions have traditionally been a visual indicator of patterns in sound. In most traditional stanza forms, the pattern of rhyme is repeated in stanza after stanza throughout the poem, until voice and ear become familiar with the pattern and come to expect it. The repetition of pattern allows us to hear deviations from the pattern as well, just as we do in music.

TRADITIONAL STANZA FORMS

As the poems in this anthology demonstrate, the forms that stanzas can take are limitless. Over time, however, certain stanza forms have become traditional, or "fixed." In using traditional stanza forms, poets thus often implicitly or explicitly allude and even respond to previous poets and poems that have used the same form. Like musicians, they also generate new effects, meanings, and music through meaningful variations on traditional forms.

Terza Rima

In Shelley's ODE TO THE WEST WIND, the first and third lines in each stanza rhyme, and the middle line then rhymes with the first and third lines of the next stanza.

O wild West Wind, thou breath of Autumn's being, *a*
Thou, from whose unseen presence the leaves dead *b*
Are driven, like ghosts from an enchanter fleeing, *a*

Yellow, and black, and pale, and hectic red, *b*
Pestilence-stricken multitudes: O thou, *c*
Who chariotest to their dark wintry bed *b*

The wingèd seeds, where they lie cold and low, *c*
Each like a corpse within its grave, until *d*
Thine azure sister of the Spring shall blow *c*

In this stanza form, known as **terza rima**, the stanzas are linked to each other by a common sound: one rhyme sound from each stanza is picked up in the next stanza, and so on to the end of the poem (though sometimes poems in this form have sections that use varied rhyme schemes). Most traditional stanza forms involve a metrical pattern as well as a rhyme scheme. Terza rima, like most English fixed stanza and verse forms, involves **iambic** meter (unstressed and stressed syllables alternating regularly), and each line has five beats (**pentameter**).

As the title of the following poem announces, it, too, is written—at least mostly—in terza rima. And it depends, for its full effect, on our knowing not only that this stanza form was used by Dante in *The Divine Comedy*, written in Italian in the early 1300s, but also that this three-book epic depicts the poet's journey through Hell (or the inferno) and Purgatory to Paradise.

RICHARD WILBUR
Terza Rima

In this great form, as Dante proved in Hell,
There is no dreadful thing that can't be said
In passing. Here, for instance, one could tell

How our jeep skidded sideways toward the dead
Enemy soldier with the staring eyes,
Bumping a little as it struck his head,

And then flew on, as if toward Paradise[1]

2008

- What might this poem communicate—about, for example, war, poetry, and/or death—by starting out, but not ending, in terza rima?

1. Perhaps an allusion, too, to Emily Dickinson's "[Because I could not stop for Death—]," which ends with a horse-drawn carriage driven by Death carrying the speaker "toward Eternity—" (line 24).

Terza rima requires many rhymes, and thus many different rhyme words, and therefore it is not very common in English, a language not as rich in rhyme possibilities as Italian or French. English is derived from so many different language families that it has fewer similar word endings than languages that mainly derive from a single language family.

Spenserian Stanza

Named for Edmund Spenser, who used it to great effect in his long poem *The Faerie Queene*, the **Spenserian stanza** is even more rhyme-rich than terza rima, using only three rhyme sounds in nine rhymed lines, as in John Keats's *The Eve of St. Agnes*:

Her falt'ring hand upon the balustrade,	*a*
Old Angela was feeling for the stair,	*b*
When Madeline, St. Agnes' charmèd maid,	*a*
Rose, like a missioned spirit, unaware:	*b*
With silver taper's light, and pious care,	*b*
She turned, and down the agèd gossip led	*c*
To a safe level matting. Now prepare,	*b*
Young Porphyro, for gazing on that bed;	*c*
She comes, she comes again, like ring dove frayed and fled	*c*

Notice that while the first eight lines of a Spenserian stanza are in iambic pentameter, the ninth has one extra foot, making it iambic **hexameter**.

Ballad Stanza

The much more common **ballad stanza** has only one set of rhymes in four lines; lines 1 and 3 in each stanza do not rhyme at all. And while those lines are in iambic **tetrameter** (4 beats/feet), lines 2 and 4 are rhymed iambic **trimeter** (3 beats/feet).

The king sits in Dumferling toune,	*a*
Drinking the blude-reid wine:	*b*
"O whar will I get guid sailor,	*c*
To sail this ship of mine?"	*b*

TRADITIONAL VERSE FORMS

Though ballad stanza takes its name from the fact that it is often used in the particular subgenre of poem known as the **ballad**, stanza forms are not themselves subgenres of poetry, but rather a form that can be used for various kinds of poems. The same is true of other traditional verse forms—set patterns of rhythm and rhyme that govern whole poems or parts of them rather than individual stanzas. Three especially useful verse forms to know are the couplet, blank verse, and free verse.

Any pair of consecutive lines that share *end rhymes* is called a *rhyming couplet*, regardless of their meter. Andrew Marvell's To His Coy Mistress, for example, consists entirely of iambic tetrameter couplets, beginning with these two:

Had we but world enough, and time,	*a*
This coyness, Lady, were no crime.	*a*

We would sit down and think which way *b*
To walk and pass our long love's day. *b*

A *heroic couplet*, however, requires iambic pentameter, as in Alexander Pope's SOUND AND SENSE:

But most by numbers judge a poet's song, *a*
And smooth or rough, with them, is right or wrong; *a*
In the bright muse though thousand charms conspire, *b*
Her voice is all these tuneful fools admire *b*

Near the other end of the spectrum from the heroic couplet sits **blank verse**, which consists of lines with regular meter, usually iambic pentameter, but no discernible rhyme scheme, as in these lines, which Adam speaks to Eve in John Milton's epic PARADISE LOST:

Well hast thou motioned, well thy thoughts employed,
How we might best fulfil the work which here
God hath assigned us; nor of me shalt pass
Unpraised: for nothing lovelier can be found
In woman, than to study household good,
And good works in her husband to promote.

Though here used by Milton to describe lofty events of cosmic significance, blank verse was among the least formal and most natural of traditional verse forms until the explosion of **free verse** in the twentieth century. Now perhaps the most common of verse forms, free verse is "free" precisely because it's defined wholly by what it lacks—both regular meter and rhyme. The wildly different lengths of the following lines from THE WORD *PLUM* make its use of free verse especially obvious:

taut skin
pierced, bitten, provoked into
juice, and tart flesh

FIXED FORMS OR FORM-BASED SUBGENRES

Again, all these stanza and verse forms can be used in many different kinds of poems. But some kinds or subgenres of poetry are defined wholly by their use of very particular formal patterns. Perhaps the most famous of these are the sonnet and the **haiku**, to which we devote the albums that follow this chapter. Others include the **limerick** (see, for example, THERE WAS A YOUNG GIRL FROM ST. PAUL), the **villanelle** (DO NOT GO GENTLE INTO THAT GOOD NIGHT, below), the **palindrome** (MYTH, below), and the **sestina** (see below). Though relatively rare for much of the twentieth century, such traditional fixed forms have in recent years become increasingly popular once again. *McSweeney's Internet Tendency*, the online version of the famously eccentric literary magazine edited by novelist Dave Eggers, included no new poetry except sestinas between 2003 and 2006, and you can still find hundreds of examples on its Web site.

You can probably deduce the principles involved in each of these fixed forms by looking carefully at an example; if you have trouble, look at the definitions in the glossary.

TRADITIONAL FORMS: POEMS FOR FURTHER STUDY

DYLAN THOMAS

Do Not Go Gentle into That Good Night[2]

Do not go gentle into that good night,
Old age should burn and rave at close of day;
Rage, rage against the dying of the light.

Though wise men at their end know dark is right,
Because their words had forked no lightning they
Do not go gentle into that good night.

Good men, the last wave by, crying how bright
Their frail deeds might have danced in a green bay,
Rage, rage against the dying of the light.

Wild men who caught and sang the sun in flight,
And learn, too late, they grieved it on its way,
Do not go gentle into that good night.

Grave men, near death, who see with blinding sight
Blind eyes could blaze like meteors and be gay,
Rage, rage against the dying of the light.

And you, my father, there on the sad height,
Curse, bless, me now with your fierce tears, I pray.
Do not go gentle into that good night.
Rage, rage against the dying of the light.

1952

- **What do the wise, good, wild, and grave men have in common with the speaker's father? Why do you think Thomas chose such a strict form, the villanelle, for such an emotionally charged subject?**

2. Written during the final illness of the poet's father.

NATASHA TRETHEWEY

Myth

I was asleep while you were dying.
It's as if you slipped through some rift, a hollow
I make between my slumber and my waking,

the Erebus[3] I keep you in, still trying
not to let go. You'll be dead again tomorrow,
but in dreams you live. So I try taking

you back into morning. Sleep-heavy, turning,
my eyes open, I find you do not follow.
Again and again, this constant forsaking.

Again and again, this constant forsaking:
my eyes open, I find you do not follow.
You back into morning, sleep-heavy, turning.

But in dreams you live. So I try taking,
not to let go. You'll be dead again tomorrow.
The Erebus I keep you in—still, trying—

I make between my slumber and my waking.
It's as if you slipped through some rift, a hollow.
I was asleep while you were dying.

2007

- **How does Trethewey's use of a palindromic structure contribute to the poem's evocation of grief? Why do you think the poem is called MYTH?**

ELIZABETH BISHOP

Sestina

September rain falls on the house.
In the failing light, the old grandmother
sits in the kitchen with the child
beside the Little Marvel Stove,
reading the jokes from the almanac,
laughing and talking to hide her tears.

She thinks that her equinoctial tears
and the rain that beats on the roof of the house
were both foretold by the almanac,
but only known to a grandmother.
The iron kettle sings on the stove.
She cuts some bread and says to the child,

3. In Greek mythology, the dark region of the underworld through which the dead pass en route to Hades.

It's time for tea now; but the child
is watching the teakettle's small hard tears
dance like mad on the hot black stove,
the way the rain must dance on the house.
Tidying up, the old grandmother
hangs up the clever almanac

on its string. Birdlike, the almanac
hovers half open above the child,
hovers above the old grandmother
and her teacup full of dark brown tears.
She shivers and says she thinks the house
feels chilly, and puts more wood in the stove.

It was to be, says the Marvel Stove.
I know what I know, says the almanac.
With crayons the child draws a rigid house
and a winding pathway. Then the child
puts in a man with buttons like tears
and shows it proudly to the grandmother.

But secretly, while the grandmother
busies herself about the stove,
the little moons fall down like tears
from between the pages of the almanac
into the flower bed the child
has carefully placed in the front of the house.

Time to plant tears, says the almanac.
The grandmother sings to the marvellous stove
and the child draws another inscrutable house.

1965

- **Try to derive from SESTINA the "rules" that govern the sestina form. Why do you think Bishop chose this form for her poem?**

CIARA SHUTTLEWORTH
Sestina

You
used
to
love
me
well.

Well,
you—
me—
used
love
to . . .

to . . .
well . . .
love.
You
used
me.

Me,
too,
used . . .
well . . .
you.
Love,
love
me.
You,
too
well
used,

used
love
well.
Me,
too.
You!

You used
to love
me well.

2010

- How does Shuttleworth use punctuation to produce meaning in this especially economical sestina?

THE WAY A POEM LOOKS

Like stanza breaks, other arrangements of print and space help guide the voice and the mind to a clearer sense of sound and meaning. But sometimes poems are written to be seen rather than heard, and their appearance on the page is crucial to their effect. E. E. Cummings's poem l(a, for example, tries to visualize typographically what the poet asks you to see in your mind's eye.

E. E. CUMMINGS
[l(a]

l(a
le
af
fa

ll
s)
one
l
iness

1958

The unusual spacing of words in the following poem, with some run together and others widely separated, provides a guide to reading, regulating both speed and sense, so that the poem can capture aloud some of the boy's wide-eyed enthusiasm, remembered now from a later perspective. (Notice how the word "defunct" helps establish the time and point of view.)

E. E. CUMMINGS
[Buffalo Bill's][4]

Buffalo Bill's
defunct
    who used to
    ride a watersmooth-silver
                                        stallion
and break onetwothreefourfive pigeonsjustlikethat
                                                                    Jesus
he was a handsome man
                                    and what i want to know is
how do you like your blueeyed boy
Mister Death

1923

CONCRETE POETRY

Occasionally, poems are composed in a specific shape so that they look like physical objects. The idea that poems can be related to the visual arts is an old one. Theodoric in ancient Greece is credited with inventing *technopaegnia*—that is, the construction of poems with visual appeal. Once, the shaping of words to resemble an object was thought to have mystical power, but more recent attempts at **concrete poetry**, or shaped verse, are usually playful exercises that attempt to supplement (or replace) verbal meanings with devices from painting and sculpture. Here are two examples.

4. From Cummings's *Portraits* XXI.

MAY SWENSON
Women

Women
should be
pedestals
moving
pedestals
moving
to the
motions
of men

Or they
should be
little horses
those wooden
sweet
oldfashioned
painted
rocking
horses

the gladdest things in the toyroom

The
pegs
of their
ears
so familiar
and dear
to the trusting
fists
To be chafed

feelingly
and then
unfeelingly
To be
joyfully
ridden
rockingly
ridden until
the restored

egos dismount and the legs stride away

Immobile
sweetlipped
sturdy
and smiling
women
should always
be waiting

willing
to be set
into motion
Women
should be
pedestals
to men

1978

- What shapes do you see in this poem? How are repeating words or sounds significant to the speaker's apparent statements about what women "should be" or should do (line 2)?

GEORGE HERBERT
Easter Wings

Lord, who createdst man in wealth and store,[5]
Though foolishly he lost the same,
Decaying more and more
Till he became
Most poor:
With thee
O let me rise
As larks,[6] harmoniously,
And sing this day thy victories:
Then shall the fall further the flight in me.

My tender age in sorrow did begin;
And still with sicknesses and shame
Thou didst so punish sin,
That I became
Most thin.
With thee
Let me combine,
And feel this day thy victory;
For, if I imp[7] my wing on thine,
Affliction shall advance the flight in me.

1633

- How do this poem's decreasing and increasing line lengths correspond to the meaning of the words? Why do you think Herbert has chosen to present the poem sideways?

SUGGESTIONS FOR WRITING

1. Trace the variations in imagery of light and darkness in Thomas's Do Not Go Gentle into That Good Night. How do we know that light represents life and darkness death (rather than, say, sight and blindness)? How does the poet use the strict formal requirements of the villanelle to emphasize this interplay of light and darkness? Write an essay in which you discuss the interaction of form and content in Do Not Go Gentle into That Good Night.
2. Which of the poems either mentioned or reproduced in this chapter do you think makes the most effective use of any traditional stanza or verse form? Why and how so? Write a response paper in which you explore your response to the poem and how it is shaped by the poet's choice of a traditional form.
3. Every poem has a particular form, whether or not it adheres to a traditional stanza or verse form or to conventional ideas about line, rhythm, or spacing. Examine closely the form of any poem in this book, including its arrangement on the page and division into lines and stanzas. How does the poet use form to shape sound, emotion, and meaning? Write an essay examining the relationship between the poem's theme and its external form.

5. In plenty. 6. Which herald the morning.
7. Engraft. In falconry, to engraft feathers in a damaged wing, so as to restore the powers of flight (*OED*).

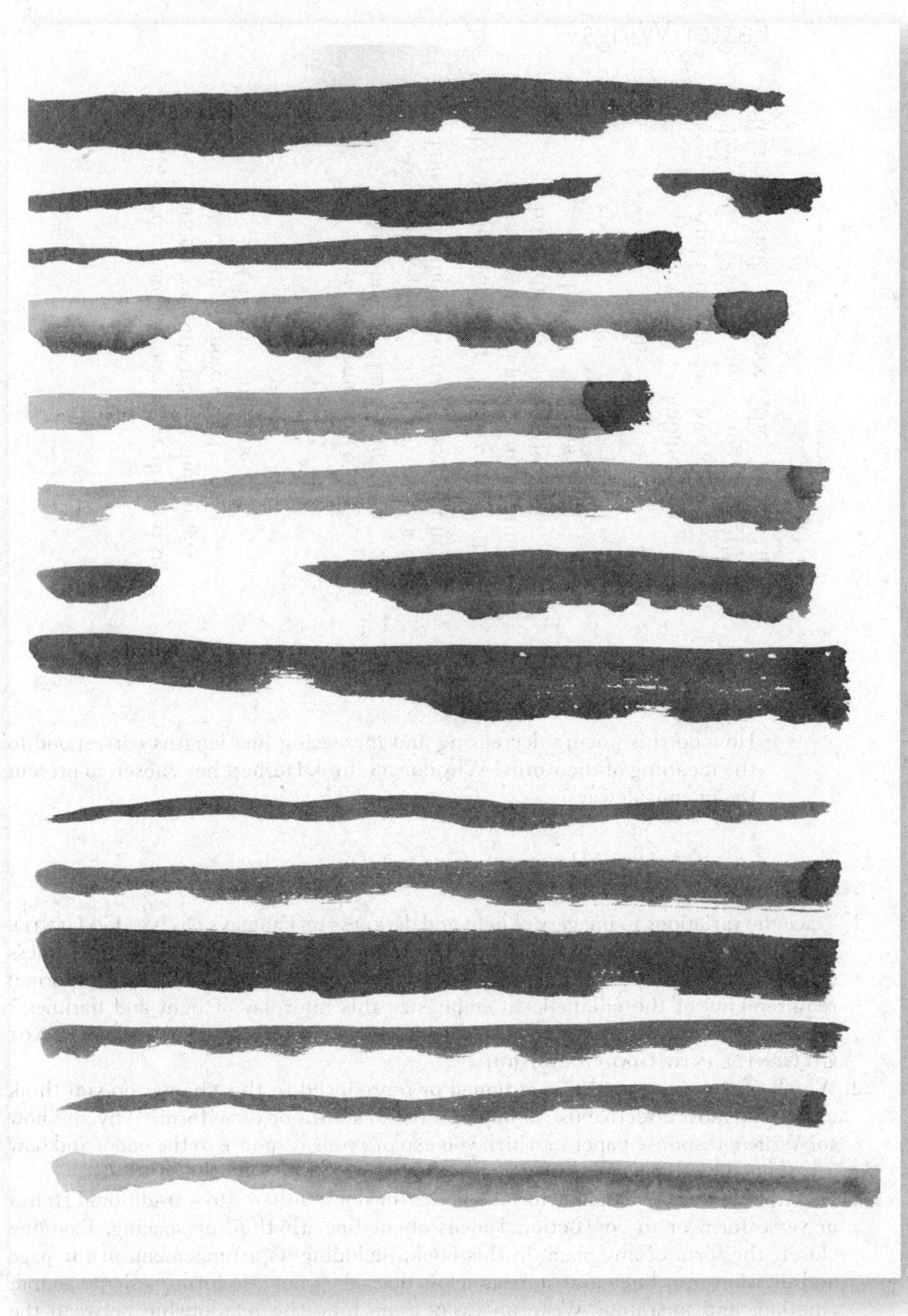

From *Black, Grey and White: A Book of Visual Sonnets* by David Miller.

The Sonnet

AN ALBUM

The **sonnet**, one of the most persistent and familiar fixed forms, originated in the Middle Ages in Italian and French poetry. It dominated English poetry in the late sixteenth and early seventeenth centuries and then was revived several times from the early nineteenth century onward. Except for some early experiments with length, the sonnet has always been fourteen lines long, and it usually is written in **iambic pentameter**. It is most often printed as if it were a single stanza, although it actually has formal divisions defined by its various rhyme schemes. For more than four centuries, the sonnet has been surprisingly resilient, and it continues to attract a variety of poets. As a verse form, the sonnet is contained, compact, demanding; whatever it does, it must do concisely. It is best suited to intensity of feeling and concentration of figurative language and expression.

Most sonnets are structured according to one of two principles of division. The *English*, or *Shakespearean*, *sonnet* is divided into three units of four lines each (quatrains) and a final unit of two lines (couplet), and sometimes the line spacing reflects this division. Ordinarily its rhyme scheme reflects the structure: The scheme of *abab cdcd efef gg* is the classic one, but many variations from that pattern still reflect the basic 4-4-4-2 division. In the *Italian*, or *Petrarchan*, *sonnet* (the Italian poet Petrarch was an early master of this form), the fundamental break is between the first eight lines (called an octave) and the last six (called a sestet). Its "typical" rhyme scheme is *abbaabba cdecde*, although it, too, produces many variations that still reflect the basic division into two parts, an octave and a sestet.

The two kinds of sonnet structures are useful for different sorts of argument. The 4-4-4-2 structure works very well for constructing a poem that makes a three-step argument (with either a quick summary or a dramatic turn at the end) or for setting up brief, cumulative images. Shakespeare's THAT TIME OF YEAR THOU MAYST IN ME BEHOLD, for example, uses the 4-4-4-2 structure to mark the progressive steps toward death and the parting of lovers by using three distinct images and then summarizing. In the two-part structure of the Italian sonnet, the octave states a proposition or generalization, and the sestet provides a particular example, consequence, or application of it; alternatively, the second part may turn away from the first to present a new position or response. The final lines may, for example, reverse the first eight and achieve a paradox or irony in the poem, or the poem may nearly balance two comparable arguments. Basically, the 8-6 structure lends itself to poems with two points to make, or to those that make one point and then illustrate or complicate it.

During the Renaissance, poets regularly employed the sonnet for love poems; many modern sonnets continue to be about love or private life, and many poets continue to use a personal, apparently open and sincere **tone** in their sonnets. But poets often find the sonnet's compact form and rigid demands equally useful for a variety of subjects and tones. Sonnets may be about subjects other than love: politics, philosophy, discovery. And their tones vary widely, too, from the anger and remorse of TH' EXPENSE OF SPIRIT IN A WASTE OF SHAME to the tender awe of HOW DO I LOVE THEE? (below). Many poets seem to take the kind of comfort in the careful limits of the form that William Wordsworth describes in NUNS FRET NOT (below), finding in its two basic variations, the English sonnet and the Italian sonnet, a wealth of ways to organize their materials into coherent structures.

Sometimes a neat and precise structure is altered as particular needs or effects may demand. And the two basic structures, Shakespearean and Petrarchan, certainly do not define all the structural possibilities within a fourteen-line poem, even if they are the most traditional ways of taking advantage of the sonnet's compact and contained form.

Which of the following sonnets follow the Italian model? the English? In each case, how do form, structure, and content work together? How does each poet adapt the traditional form to his or her particular purpose? Aside from particular patterns of rhyme and meter, what other conventions of the sonnet can you identify? How do individual poems use, rework, even comment on those conventions? (To see how one student answered some of these questions by comparing sonnets by two different writers, see the essay by Melissa Makolin that follows ch. 22.)

FRANCESCO PETRARCH

[Upon the breeze she spread her golden hair][1]

Upon the breeze she spread her golden hair
that in a thousand gentle knots was turned,
and the sweet light beyond all measure burned
in eyes where now that radiance is rare;

and in her face there seemed to come an air
of pity, true or false, that I discerned:
I had love's tinder in my breast unburned,
was it a wonder if it kindled there?

She moved not like a mortal, but as though
she bore an angel's form, her words had then
a sound that simple human voices lack;

a heavenly spirit, a living sun
was what I saw; now, if it is not so,
the wound's not healed because the bow grows slack.

c. 1334–38

- What might this sonnet imply about the relationship between the speaker and the woman described? What do both structure and form contribute to that characterization?

1. Translated by Anthony Mortimer.

HENRY CONSTABLE

[My lady's presence makes the roses red]

My lady's presence makes the roses red,
Because to see her lips they blush for shame.
The lily's leaves, for envy, pale became,
And her white hands in them this envy bred.
The marigold the leaves abroad doth spread,
Because the sun's and her power is the same.
The violet of purple colour came,
Dyed in the blood she made my heart to shed.
In brief: all flowers from her their virtue take;
From her sweet breath their sweet smells do proceed;
The living heat which her eyebeams doth make
Warmeth the ground and quickeneth the seed.
The rain, wherewith she watereth the flowers,
Falls from mine eyes, which she dissolves in showers.

1594

- **Which type of sonnet is this? How do external form and internal structure here work together?**

WILLIAM SHAKESPEARE

[My mistress' eyes are nothing like the sun]

My mistress' eyes are nothing like the sun;
Coral is far more red than her lips' red;
If snow be white, why then her breasts are dun,[2]
If hairs be wires, black wires grow on her head.
I have seen roses damasked[3] red and white,
But no such roses see I in her cheeks;
And in some perfumes is there more delight
Than in the breath that from my mistress reeks.
I love to hear her speak, yet well I know
That music hath a far more pleasing sound;
I grant I never saw a goddess go;[4]
My mistress, when she walks, treads on the ground.
And yet, by heaven, I think my love as rare
As any she belied with false compare.

1609

- **How might this poem respond to sonnets like Constable's MY LADY'S PRESENCE . . . and Petrarch's UPON THE BREEZE . . .?**

2. Mouse-colored.
3. Variegated.
4. Walk.

[Not marble, nor the gilded monuments]

Not marble, nor the gilded monuments
Of princes, shall outlive this powerful rhyme;
But you shall shine more bright in these contènts
Than unswept stone, besmeared with sluttish time.
When wasteful war shall statues overturn,
And broils[5] root out the work of masonry,
Nor Mars his[6] sword nor war's quick fire shall burn
The living record of your memory.
'Gainst death and all-oblivious enmity
Shall you pace forth; your praise shall still find room
Even in the eyes of all posterity
That wear this world out to the ending doom.[7]
So, till the judgment that yourself arise,
You live in this, and dwell in lovers' eyes.

1609

- **How does each quatrain build on the last?**

[Let me not to the marriage of true minds]

Let me not to the marriage of true minds
Admit impediments.[8] Love is not love
Which alters when it alteration finds,
Or bends with the remover to remove:
Oh, no! it is an ever-fixèd mark,
That looks on tempests and is never shaken;
It is the star to every wandering bark,
Whose worth's unknown, although his height be taken.[9]
Love's not Time's fool, though rosy lips and cheeks
Within his bending sickle's compass come;
Love alters not with his brief hours and weeks,
But bears it out even to the edge of doom.
If this be error and upon me proved,
I never writ, nor no man ever loved.

1609

- **What might the speaker mean when he says that love doesn't "ben[d] with the remover to remove" (line 4)? How might the rest of the poem explain and develop this statement?**

5. Roots of plants.
6. Mars his: Mars's. *Nor*: neither.
7. Judgment Day.
8. The Church of England's marriage service contains this address to the witnesses: "If any of you know cause or just impediments why these persons should not be joined together [. . .]"
9. That is, measuring the altitude of stars (for purposes of navigation) is not a way to measure value.

JOHN MILTON

[When I consider how my light is spent]

When I consider how my light is spent,
Ere half my days, in this dark world and wide,
And that one talent which is death to hide[1]
Lodged with me useless, though my soul more bent
To serve therewith my Maker, and present
My true account, lest he returning chide;
"Doth God exact day-labor, light denied?"
I fondly ask; but Patience to prevent[2]
That murmur, soon replies, "God doth not need
Either man's work or his own gifts; who best
Bear his mild yoke, they serve him best. His state
Is kingly. Thousands at his bidding speed
And post o'er land and ocean without rest:
They also serve who only stand and wait."

c. 1652

- **How might the timing of the poem's shift to Patience (in the middle of line 8) be meaningful? Paraphrase the speaker's question and Patience's reply.**

WILLIAM WORDSWORTH

Nuns Fret Not

Nuns fret not at their convent's narrow room;
And hermits are contented with their cells;
And students with their pensive citadels;
Maids at the wheel, the weaver at his loom,
Sit blithe and happy; bees that soar for bloom,
High as the highest Peak of Furness-fells,[3]
Will murmur by the hour in foxglove bells:
In truth the prison, unto which we doom
Ourselves, no prison is: and hence for me,
In sundry moods, 'twas pastime to be bound
Within the sonnet's scanty plot of ground;
Pleased if some souls (for such there needs must be)

1. In the parable of the talents (Matt. 25), the servants who earned interest on their master's money (his talents) while he was away were called "good and faithful"; the one who simply hid the money and then returned it was condemned and sent away.
2. Forestall. *Fondly*: foolishly.
3. Mountains in England's Lake District, where Wordsworth lived.

Who have felt the weight of too much liberty,
Should find brief solace there, as I have found.

1807

• **What does this poem imply about the sonnet's appeal?**

ELIZABETH BARRETT BROWNING

How Do I Love Thee?

How do I love thee? Let me count the ways.
I love thee to the depth and breadth and height
My soul can reach, when feeling out of sight
For the ends of Being and ideal Grace.
I love thee to the level of every day's
Most quiet need, by sun and candlelight.
I love thee freely, as men strive for Right;
I love thee purely, as they turn from Praise;
I love thee with the passion put to use
In my old griefs, and with my childhood's faith.
I love thee with a love I seemed to lose
With my lost saints—I love thee with the breath,
Smiles, tears of all my life!—and, if God choose,
I shall but love thee better after death.

1850

• **How many "ways" of loving does the speaker "count" in the poem (line 1)? How do these ways relate to and build on each other?**

CHRISTINA ROSSETTI

In an Artist's Studio

One face looks out from all his canvases,
One selfsame figure sits or walks or leans;
We found her hidden just behind those screens,
That mirror gave back all her loveliness.
A queen in opal or in ruby dress,
A nameless girl in freshest summer-greens,
A saint, an angel—every canvas means
The same one meaning, neither more nor less.
He feeds upon her face by day and night,
And she with true kind eyes looks back on him
Fair as the moon and joyful as the light:
Not wan with waiting, not with sorrow dim;
Not as she is, but was when hope shone bright;
Not as she is, but as she fills his dream.

1856

• **What might this poem suggest about the relationship between painter and subject? How might the poem's form encourage us to compare painting to poetry?**

EDNA ST. VINCENT MILLAY

[What lips my lips have kissed, and where, and why]

What lips my lips have kissed, and where, and why,
I have forgotten, and what arms have lain
Under my head till morning; but the rain
Is full of ghosts tonight, that tap and sigh
Upon the glass and listen for reply,
And in my heart there stirs a quiet pain
For unremembered lads that not again
Will turn to me at midnight with a cry.
Thus in the winter stands the lonely tree,
Nor knows what birds have vanished one by one,
Yet knows its boughs more silent than before:
I cannot say what loves have come and gone;
I only know that summer sang in me
A little while, that in me sings no more.

1923

- **What are the poem's principal parts? Why does the Italian/Petrarchan model suit this sonnet?**

[Women have loved before as I love now]

Women have loved before as I love now;
At least, in lively chronicles of the past—
Of Irish waters by a Cornish prow
Or Trojan waters by a Spartan mast
Much to their cost invaded—here and there,
Hunting the amorous line, skimming the rest,
I find some woman bearing as I bear
Love like a burning city in the breast.
I think however that of all alive
I only in such utter, ancient way
Do suffer love; in me alone survive
The unregenerate passions of a day
When treacherous queens, with death upon the tread,
Heedless and wilful, took their knights to bed.

1931

- **What does this poem imply about the difference between ancient and modern ways of loving?**

[I, being born a woman and distressed]

I, being born a woman and distressed
By all the needs and notions of my kind,
Am urged by your propinquity to find
Your person fair, and feel a certain zest

To bear your body's weight upon my breast:
So subtly is the fume of life designed,
To clarify the pulse and cloud the mind,
And leave me once again undone, possessed.
Think not for this, however, the poor treason
Of my stout blood against my staggering brain,
I shall remember you with love, or season
My scorn with pity,—let me make it plain:
I find this frenzy insufficient reason
For conversation when we meet again.

1923

• **What feelings are expressed here? What does the poem imply about the source or cause of these feelings?**

[I will put Chaos into fourteen lines]

I will put Chaos into fourteen lines
And keep him there; and let him thence escape
If he be lucky; let him twist, and ape
Flood, fire, and demon—his adroit designs
Will strain to nothing in the strict confines
Of this sweet Order, where, in pious rape,
I hold his essence and amorphous shape,
Till he with Order mingles and combines.
Past are the hours, the years, of our duress,
His arrogance, our awful servitude:
I have him. He is nothing more nor less
Than something simple not yet understood;
I shall not even force him to confess;
Or answer. I will only make him good.

1923

• **What might this sonnet suggest about the value or appeal of the sonnet form?**

ROBERT FROST

Range-Finding

The battle rent a cobweb diamond-strung
And cut a flower beside a groundbird's nest
Before it stained a single human breast.
The stricken flower bent double and so hung.
And still the bird revisited her young.
A butterfly its fall had dispossessed,
A moment sought in air his flower of rest,
Then slightly stooped to it and fluttering clung.
On the bare upland pasture there had spread

O'ernight 'twixt mullein stalks a wheel of thread
And straining cables wet with silver dew.
A sudden passing bullet shook it dry.
The indwelling spider ran to greet the fly,
But finding nothing, sullenly withdrew.

1916

• **What is the "battle" of line 1? What is the poem's actual subject?**

Design

I found a dimpled spider, fat and white,
On a white heal-all,[4] holding up a moth
Like a white piece of rigid satin cloth—
Assorted characters of death and blight
Mixed ready to begin the morning right,
Like the ingredients of a witches' broth—
A snow-drop spider, a flower like a froth,
And dead wings carried like a paper kite.

What had that flower to do with being white,
The wayside blue and innocent heal-all?
What brought the kindred spider to that height,
Then steered the white moth thither in the night?
What but design of darkness to appall?—
If design govern in a thing so small.

1936

• **How does this poem confound our usual preconceptions about "light" and "darkness"? How does its elaborate form complement its theme?**

GWENDOLYN BROOKS

First Fight. Then Fiddle.

First fight. Then fiddle. Ply the slipping string
With feathery sorcery; muzzle the note
With hurting love; the music that they wrote
Bewitch, bewilder. Qualify to sing
Threadwise. Devise no salt, no hempen thing
For the dear instrument to bear. Devote
The bow to silks and honey. Be remote
A while from malice and from murdering.
But first to arms, to armor. Carry hate
In front of you and harmony behind.
Be deaf to music and to beauty blind.
Win war. Rise bloody, maybe not too late

4. Plant, also called the "all-heal" and "self-heal," with tightly clustered violet-blue flowers.

For having first to civilize a space
Wherein to play your violin with grace.

1949

- **After advising "First fight. Then fiddle," the speaker discusses first music, then conflict. Why do you think the poet has arranged her material this way? Why a sonnet?**

GWEN HARWOOD
In the Park

She sits in the park. Her clothes are out of date.
Two children whine and bicker, tug her skirt.
A third draws aimless patterns in the dirt.
Someone she loved once passes by—too late

to feign indifference to that casual nod.
"How nice," et cetera. "Time holds great surprises."
From his neat head unquestionably rises
a small balloon . . . "but for the grace of God . . ."

They stand a while in flickering light, rehearsing
the children's names and birthdays. "It's so sweet
to hear their chatter, watch them grow and thrive,"
she says to his departing smile. Then, nursing
the youngest child, sits staring at her feet.
To the Wind she says, "They have eaten me alive."

1963

- **What is the implication of the "small balloon" (line 8) that rises from the head of the man who passes by?**

JUNE JORDAN
Something Like a Sonnet for Phillis Miracle Wheatley[5]

Girl from the realm of birds florid and fleet
flying full feather in far or near weather
Who fell to a dollar lust coffled[6] like meat
Captured by avarice and hate spit together
Trembling asthmatic alone on the slave block
built by a savagery travelling by carriage
viewed like a species of flaw in the livestock
A child without safety of mother or marriage

5. African-born poet (1753–84) brought to the United States as a slave at the age of seven or eight.
6. Chained together in a line.

Chosen by whimsy but born to surprise
They taught you to read but you learned how to write
Begging the universe into your eyes:
They dressed you in light but you dreamed with the night.
From Africa singing of justice and grace,
Your early verse sweetens the fame of our Race.

1989

- **Phillis Wheatley herself usually wrote in heroic couplets—couplets of iambic pentameter. Why does Jordan choose dactylic meter, unusual for a sonnet?**

BILLY COLLINS
Sonnet

All we need is fourteen lines, well, thirteen now,
and after this one just a dozen
to launch a little ship on love's storm-tossed seas,
then only ten more left like rows of beans.
How easily it goes unless you get Elizabethan
and insist the iambic bongos must be played
and rhymes positioned at the ends of lines,
one for every station of the cross.
But hang on here while we make the turn
into the final six where all will be resolved,
where longing and heartache will find an end,
where Laura will tell Petrarch[7] to put down his pen,
take off those crazy medieval tights,
blow out the lights, and come at last to bed.

1999

- **In what respects is Collins's poem a traditional sonnet? In what respects is it not? What might it suggest about the relationship between love and poetry, especially as portrayed in traditional sonnets?**

HARRYETTE MULLEN
Dim Lady[8]

My honeybunch's peepers are nothing like neon. Today's
special at Red Lobster is redder than her kisser. If Liquid Paper
is white, her racks are institutional beige. If her mop were
Slinkys, dishwater Slinkys would grow on her noggin. I have
seen tablecloths in Shakey's Pizza Parlors, red and white, but
no such picnic colors do I see in her mug. And in some minty-
fresh mouthwashes there is more sweetness than in the garlic

7. Italian poet Francesco Petrarch (1304–74), regarded as a father of the sonnet form. Many of his love poems were inspired by Laura, who may have been the wife of a local nobleman.
8. Shakespeare's sonnets frequently address or refer to the so-called Dark Lady.

breeze my main squeeze wheezes. I love to hear her rap, yet
I'm aware that Muzak has a hipper beat. I don't know any
Marilyn Monroes. My ball and chain is plain from head to toe.
And yet, by gosh, my scrumptious Twinkie has as much sex
appeal for me as any lanky model or platinum movie idol
who's hyped beyond belief.

2002

- How might Mullen's poem essentially "do unto" Shakespeare's My mistress' eyes are nothing like the sun much as Shakespeare's poem itself does to earlier, especially Petrarchan sonnets? What is the effect of Mullen's diction? her use of brand names? Is Dim Lady a sonnet?

SHERMAN ALEXIE
The Facebook Sonnet

Welcome to the endless high-school
Reunion. Welcome to past friends
And lovers, however kind or cruel.
Let's undervalue and unmend

The present. Why can't we pretend
Every stage of life is the same?
Let's exhume, resume, and extend
Childhood. Let's all play the games

That occupy the young. Let fame
And shame intertwine. Let one's search
For God become public domain.
Let church.com become our church.

Let's sign up, sign in, and confess
Here at the altar of loneliness.

2011

- What does Alexie suggest here about how and why we use *Facebook*? about the specific effects that doing so have on us? How do rhyme and meter, as well as other technical devices, help the poem communicate all this?

SUGGESTIONS FOR WRITING

1. Consider carefully the structure of, and sequencing in, Brooks's First Fight. Then Fiddle. How do various uses of sound in the poem (rhyme, onomatopoeia, and alliteration, for example) reinforce its themes and tones? Write an essay in which you explore the relationship between "sound and sense" in the poem.
2. Some of the sonnets in this book, such as those by Shakespeare, adhere closely to the classic English model; others, such as Milton's When I consider how my light is spent, follow the Italian model; and some, such as those by Billy Collins and June Jordan, bear only slight resemblance to either of the traditional sonnet models. Take any four sonnets in this book as the basis for an essay in which you compare the various ways poets have used the sonnet form to achieve their unique artistic purposes.

3. Several poems in this album are not only sonnets but also commentaries on the sonnet or on certain conventions associated with it such as Petrarchan "conceits" (Shakespeare's MY MISTRESS' EYES . . .) or the relation between (male) speaker and (female) subject or love object. Write an essay comparing at least two of these poems. What does each ultimately suggest about the sonnet through both its form and its content?

Yoshitoshi, *Since the Crescent Moon,* circa 1885–92
A woodblock print featuring haiku master Matsuo Bashō speaking to two farmers.
The haiku on the print reads:

Since the crescent moon
I have been waiting
for tonight

Haiku

AN ALBUM

The **haiku**, an import into the English poetic tradition, has a long history in Japanese poetry. Originally, the haiku (then called *hokku*) was a short section of a longer poem (called a *renga* or *haikai*) composed by several poets who wrote segments in response to one another. Traditionally, the Japanese haiku was an unrhymed poem consisting of seventeen sounds (or, rather, characters representing seventeen sounds) and distributed over three lines in a five-seven-five pattern—that is, five distinctive sounds in the first line, seven in the second, and five in the third. "Sounds" in the Japanese language are not exactly the same as "syllables" in English, but when English writers began to compose haiku about a century ago, they ordinarily translated the sound requirement into syllables.

Haiku aim for compression; they leave a lot unsaid. Typically, haiku describe a natural object and imply a state of mind. They usually have a "seasonal" requirement, so that each poem associates itself with one season of the year in a revolving pattern of change. This seasonal association may be made quite subtly and indirectly through, for example, an allusion to a seasonal flower. Haiku more generally involve descriptions of nature, reflecting the Buddhist sense of nature as orderly and benign but also contingent and transient.

When adapted into other languages and cultures, haiku cannot rely on the same spiritual assumptions or worldview, but these poems usually retain a sense of the human and natural as being mutually reflective and interdependent. Haiku often combine observation and imagination, blurring the Western distinction between seeing something literally and having some "vision" of its end or meaning.

Some of the traditional Japanese masters of haiku from the seventeenth to the early twentieth century—Bashō and Buson, for example—are represented (in English translations) in this album. So, too, are some of the many later poets and translators who have tried their hand at haiku, without always strictly observing the seventeen-syllable and three-line requirements. As haiku has become an international form, its conventions have, like those of other fixed forms, proven both demanding and adaptable to the particular needs of different cultural contexts, different languages, and different individual poets.

TRADITIONAL JAPANESE HAIKU

CHIYOJO

[Whether astringent][1]

Whether astringent
I do not know. This is my first
Persimmon picking.

1. Chiyojo (1703–75) is probably the most famous Japanese woman haiku poet. Tradition has it that she wrote this poem at the time of (and about) her engagement. Translation by Daniel C. Buchanan.

BASHŌ[2]

[A village without bells—]

A village without bells—
how do they live?
spring dusk.

[This road—]

This road—
no one goes down it,
autumn evening.

BUSON[3]

[Coolness—]

Coolness—
the sound of the bell
as it leaves the bell.

[Listening to the moon]

Listening to the moon,
gazing at the croaking of frogs
in a field of ripe rice.

ONE HAIKU, FOUR TRANSLATIONS

Perhaps the single most famous haiku is by Bashō. Here are four different English translations of that poem. (The source of these poems, Hiroaki Sato's *One Hundred Frogs: From Matsu [i.e., Matsuo] Basho to Allen Ginsberg*, contains an even greater variety of examples.)

LAFCADIO HEARN

[Old pond—]

Old pond—frogs jumped in—sound of water.

1898

CLARA A. WALSH

[An old-time pond]

An old-time pond, from off whose shadowed depth
Is heard the splash where some lithe frog leaps in.

1910

2. Matsuo Bashō (1644–94) is usually considered the first great master poet of haiku. Translations by Robert Hass. 3. Yosa Buson (1716–83). Translations by Robert Hass.

EARL MINER
[The still old pond]

The still old pond
and as a frog leaps in it
the sound of a splash.

1979

ALLEN GINSBERG
[The old pond]

The old pond—a frog jumps in, kerplunk!

1979

CONTEMPORARY ENGLISH-LANGUAGE HAIKU

ALLEN GINSBERG
[Looking over my shoulder]

Looking over my shoulder
my behind was covered
with cherry blossoms.

1955

RICHARD WRIGHT
[In the falling snow]

In the falling snow
A laughing boy holds out his palms
Until they are white.

1960

ETHERIDGE KNIGHT
[Eastern guard tower]

Eastern guard tower
glints in sunset; convicts rest
like lizards on rocks.

[The falling snow flakes]

The falling snow flakes
Cannot blunt the hard aches nor
Match the steel stillness.

[Making jazz swing in]

Making jazz swing in
Seventeen syllables AIN'T
No square poet's job.

1960

AUTHORS ON THEIR WORK

ETHERIDGE KNIGHT (1931–91)

From "A MELUS Interview: Etheridge Knight" (1985)*

INTERVIEWER: [. . .] What motivated you to use *haiku* as a form? Where'd you get it from?

KNIGHT: From Gwendolyn Brooks. Yeah, she's the first one turned me on to *haiku*. She used to come visit me when I was in prison. And this is in the Sixties, remember, this is long before they had poets-in-the-prison programs and poets in schools. [. . .] She brought me some books and Japanese *haiku*. Years later I asked her how come and she said, "It was because you were too wordy in your poems." And I like *haiku*. I try to use it, I try to follow the general form. I try to bring my own American consciousness to it. You know. [. . .] I like them because you gotta deal with the noun and the verb. You ain't got too much time to fool around with some abstractions, you know, a lot of adverbs and adjectives and stuff. But I like them.

*"A MELUS Interview: Etheridge Knight." Interview by Steven C. Tracy. *MELUS*, vol. 12, no. 2, Summer 1985, pp. 7–23. *JSTOR*, www.jstor.org/stable/467427.

MARK JARMAN

Haiku

Things that can turn to shrapnel:
Steel and stone. Crockery.
Wood. Glass. And bone.

2008

SONIA SANCHEZ

From 9 Haiku (for Freedom's Sisters)[4]

5.

(Fannie Lou Hamer)[5]

feet deep
in cotton you shifted
the country's eyes

7.

(Rosa Parks)[6]

baptizer of
morning light walking us away
from reserved spaces

2010

EZRA POUND

In a Station of the Metro[7]

The apparition of these faces in the crowd;
Petals on a wet, black bough.

1913

SUE STANDING

Diamond Haiku

Major or minor,
says Baseball Diamond Sutra,[8]
what does it matter?

The boys of summer
know that nirvana[9] is just
one inning away.

4. Each haiku in this sequence is dedicated to a specific African American woman.

5. *Fannie Lou Hamer* was the vice-chair of the Mississippi Freedom Democratic Party, a voting-rights activist, and a civil rights leader [Sanchez's note]. A Mississippi Delta sharecropper's daughter, Hamer (1917–77) grew up picking cotton alongside her nineteen siblings; in 1968, she became the first African American delegate to a national party convention since Reconstruction and Mississippi's first-ever female delegate.

6. *Rosa Parks* was an African American civil rights activist whom the U.S. Congress called the "Mother of the Modern-Day Civil Rights Movement" [Sanchez's note]. Parks (1913–2005) helped to spark the famous Montgomery Bus Boycott when she refused in 1955 to give up her bus seat to a white passenger.

7. Paris subway.

8. The *Diamond Sutra* is one of Buddhism's most ancient and sacred texts, but in her 1993 article "The Baseball Diamond Sutra," Helen Tworkov suggests that some modern enthusiasts credit baseball's putative "inventor," Union general Abner Doubleday (1819–93), with infusing the game with many veiled Buddhist references, including the baseball "diamond."

9. In Buddhism, state of bliss and peace reached through the effort to extinguish desire and transcend individual consciousness.

Deep in the outfield,
a glove reaches toward sky—
fireflies blink on.

Over the bleachers,
a blank scoreboard announces
no wins, no losses.

2011

LINDA PASTAN
In the Har-Poen Tea Garden

Three, nine, seventeen
carp—one for each syllable
color the water.

A sip of green tea—
the very taste of Japan,
odd but comforting.

The old maple bows
with such strict formality
over the fish pond.

I long for free verse,
explosions of syllables,
but this is Japan.

In white wedding dress
a bride bows down the stone path,
West and East marry.

Poor blooming cherry
trapped in miniature beauty.
The spell is bonsai.

Freed from a painting,
a ceremonial crane
fishes for dinner.

I dream in haiku—
words as perfect as blossoms
gone in the morning.

2011

TWAIKU

With its 140-character limit, *Twitter* has given haiku a new lease on life, inspiring thousands of people around the world to try their hand at crafting what some now dub "twaiku." You can find countless examples—on topics ranging from cats and zombies to NASCAR—online and via *Facebook* pages like "The Twitter Haiku Movement." But the "movement" (if such it is) first grabbed headlines in early 2010,

when Sun Microsystems' CEO Jonathan Schwartz chose to tweet (or "twaiku") his resignation:

Financial crisis
Stalled too many customers
CEO no more.

SUGGESTIONS FOR WRITING

1. What is gained, and what is lost, when an artistic tradition like Japanese haiku is imported, through translation, imitation, and inspiration, into another language and culture? Using the poems in this album and your own research, write an essay in which you analyze the way that haiku has established itself as part of English-language literary culture. What might be distinctive about English-language or specifically American haiku? Or how exactly have writers in this tradition adapted the form to suit and reflect a distinctively modern, Western perspective and experience?
2. As this album begins to demonstrate, haiku has proven especially attractive to twentieth- and twenty-first-century African American poets. Gwendolyn Brooks, for example, introduced the form to Etheridge Knight, and Sonia Sanchez in a sense continues to walk in their footsteps. Using the poems in this album and your own research, write an essay in which you explore how at least one or two of these poets, or others, have made their own distinctive use of the form.
3. Write an essay exploring the seasonal imagery in at least three of the more traditional haiku in this album. How does each refer to a season, however indirectly? What does each manage to suggest about the particular character or feeling of that season, and how so?

21 THE LONGER WORK

Poetry is often described as the art of brevity, compactness, and compression. Its sentences are usually divided into relatively short lines, its lines into stanzas that are traditionally much shorter than prose paragraphs. And many poems are very short overall. As we've seen, too, some subgenres or forms of poetry are short by definition: A **sonnet**, for example, generally has precisely fourteen lines, a **haiku** only three. As a result, poets have to "load every rift [. . .] with ore," as poet John Keats once put it.

Even so, there have been long poems for as long as there has been poetry. Indeed, some of the world's most famous poems—Homer's *Odyssey* (c. eighth century BCE), Geoffrey Chaucer's *Canterbury Tales* (fourteenth century), Dante's *Divine Comedy* (fourteenth century), John Milton's PARADISE LOST (excerpted in this chapter), and Goethe's *Faust* (1808, 1832), to name a few—are long enough to be published on their own as stand-alone books. Others such as Edgar Allan's Poe's THE RAVEN (1844), Walt Whitman's "Song of Myself" (1855), and T. S. Eliot's "The Waste Land" (1922) take up many pages in volumes that also include shorter works by the same author.

Most book-length poems are themselves divided into smaller, often numbered, units variously called *cantos* (Dante's *Inferno*), *books* (the *Odyssey, Paradise Lost*), *chapters*, or simply *sections* or *parts* (Whitman's "Song of Myself"). These units are sometimes, in turn, divided into **stanzas** or **verse paragraphs**.

Additionally, the long-poem category includes book-length works composed of a carefully ordered sequence of poems that can themselves be long, as in the case of *The Canterbury Tales* and Alfred, Lord Tennyson's *Idylls of the King* (1859–89). (The latter poem relates the story of King Arthur and his knights in twelve books, each of which can stand alone and has its own title, such as "The Coming of Arthur" and "The Passing of Arthur.") Other long poems are instead assembled of very short units that might work as individual poems, but together tell a story of sorts. Tennyson's *In Memoriam A. H. H.* (1850), for instance, consists of more than 130 short lyrics plus a verse introduction and an epilogue; collectively, they detail the speaker's response—over several years—to the death of a dear friend. Regardless of a poem's length, however, the steps involved in reading, responding to, and writing about it are essentially the same.

THE LONG POEM AND THE QUESTION OF GENRE

Length does make a difference in our experience of a poem and in the way a poem works—so much so that Edgar Allan Poe famously declared that there is in fact no such thing as a "long poem" because a long work ceases to be "poetic" after a certain point. Sometimes the long poem is treated as a distinct poetic genre or subgenre in its own right, though there is little agreement about how long a poem must be to qualify: Some scholars and critics maintain that only book-length works should count; others apply the label to any poem over, say, 100 lines (as we do in this chapter). This debate is reflected in the inconsistent way the titles of long poems are formatted. While everyone agrees that the titles of book-length works such as *Paradise Lost* should be italicized and that those of shorter works such as "Stopping by Woods on a Snowy Evening" should appear in quotation marks, you will often see titles of shorter long poems formatted both ways—as "The Waste Land" or *The Waste Land*, for example.

Regardless of which definition of *long poem* we use, however, the category embraces works that vary widely in terms of both content and form. Long poems include **dramatic poems** and verse drama, **narrative poems** (in which a speaker relates a series of events just as a fictional **narrator** would), or even **lyrics** in the broadest sense (poems in which a speaker describes, in the first person, his or her feelings or thoughts rather than telling a "story" per se). Long poems can tackle almost any subject and situation and feature any sort of speaker and setting.

Long poems can be written in **free verse** ("Song of Myself") or follow any other formal pattern. The lyrics that make up *In Memoriam*, for instance, contain a varied number of stanzas, but each stanza has precisely the same **rhyme scheme**, **meter**, and number of lines; though this unusual stanza form had been used before, it is now widely known as "the *In Memoriam* stanza." Similarly, Edmund Spenser's *Faerie Queene* uses a stanza form now known as the **Spenserian stanza**.

The long-poem category might thus be seen as a kind of catchall, or at least "catch-a-lot," including long works that don't fit easily into any other generic category, as well as long works that do fit. Below is a list and description of some of the genre categories into which many long poems fall (including those in this chapter).

Long Poem Genres

ballad: a narrative poem using relatively simple, sometimes archaic language to relate an often well-known story. Ballads conventionally feature ordinary, socially lowly characters, on the one hand, and, on the other, extraordinary action, often involving supernatural occurrences, tragic love, and/or semihistorical, legendary subjects such as Robin Hood. A ballad usually consists of short stanzas, has a simple rhyme scheme and meter, and makes much use of dialogue, repetition (often, a refrain), simple syntax, and stock imagery ("milk-white steed," "red as blood"). Many ballads use the particular stanza form known as **ballad stanza**, with alternating three-beat and four-beat lines. Not all ballads are long, especially folk ballads such as SIR PATRICK SPENS or poems modeled on folk ballads such as Dudley Randall's BALLAD OF BIRMINGHAM. But some later, written (versus oral) ballads are long, including Samuel Taylor Coleridge's THE RIME OF THE ANCIENT MARINER (later in this chapter). Though perhaps not designed to be sung, this poem does use a version of ballad stanza and can be sung to the tune of the *Gilligan's Island* theme song, "The Ballad of Gilligan's Island."

(*continued on next page*)

(continued)

The ballad is one of the oldest poetic forms in the English-language tradition: It is also, in origin, a "popular" form in the sense of being "of the (common) people," not least because ballads were traditionally composed and disseminated orally and, later, via cheap "broadsides" sold in the streets. Thus a person did not have to be wealthy or even literate to compose or enjoy a ballad.

dramatic monologue: a poem in which, in the words of literary critic M. H. Abrams, "(1) A single person, who is patently *not* the poet" (and often not a person with whom the poet encourages us to identify or sympathize) "utters the entire poem in a specific situation at a critical moment [. . .]. (2) This person addresses and interacts with one or more other people; but we know of the auditors' presence and what they say and do only from clues in the discourse of the single speaker. (3) The principle controlling the poet's selection and organization of what the [. . .] speaker says is the speaker's unintentional revelation of his or her temperament and character" (*A Glossary of Literary Terms*, 6th ed. [Harcourt Brace, 1993], 48). Examples include Robert Browning's SOLILOQUY OF THE SPANISH CLOISTER, PORPHYRIA'S LOVER, and MY LAST DUCHESS; Alfred Tennyson's ULYSSES; and T. S. Eliot's THE LOVE SONG OF J. ALFRED PRUFROCK.

The dramatic monologue is sometimes described both as a kind of lyric and as a kind of closet drama. Even the acknowledged master of the form, Robert Browning, labeled his own poems "dramatic lyrics," describing them as "dramatic in principle" and "lyric in expression." The dramatic monologue is thus best understood as a hybrid form.

elegy: In the most specific sense, a lyric in which the speaker laments the death of a particular person, praises that person, expresses his or her personal grief and often that of the community, and seeks both to find and to offer consolation. Examples include W. H. Auden's IN MEMORY OF W. B. YEATS and Walt Whitman's poem on the death of Abraham Lincoln, "When Lilacs Last in the Dooryard Bloom'd." More broadly, an elegy can be any lyric in sorrowful mood that is inspired by, and is about, death in general. A famous English-language example is Thomas Gray's "Elegy Written in a Country Churchyard."

epic: a long narrative poem in elevated language that celebrates the achievements of one or more heroic (often male) personages of history or legend. Epic heroes conventionally possess both high social rank and high office (so that their actions directly affect an entire society), as well as extraordinary, even superhuman, qualities and skills. Epic plots typically involve extraordinary events of major significance to an entire society—Homer's *Iliad* focuses on the Trojan War, Milton's *Paradise Lost* on the fall of Adam and Eve. Other epic **conventions** include

- an opening that states the poem's major subject, or what is conventionally called its *argument*; contains an *invocation of the Muse* or other source of inspiration, usually addressed directly in the second person ("thou" or "you") and asked to help the poet in his work; and begins to recount the action ***in*** *medias res* (Latin for "in the middle of things"), thus requiring the use of flashbacks later in the poem;

- a spatially and temporally vast, but often vaguely defined or described, setting that is usually much earlier than the time in which the poem was first written and read;
- lengthy *catalogs*, or lists (bk. II of *The Iliad,* for example, lists the captains of all the ships that sailed to Troy);
- epic similes—long, complex comparisons;
- a scene describing the arming of the hero for battle;
- at least one battle requiring extraordinary feats of derring-do (described vividly and at great length);
- a journey, often to a literal or figurative underworld, requiring further extraordinary feats of derring-do. (The *Odyssey,* for example, focuses on Odysseus's journey home from the Trojan War and includes an episode in which Odysseus travels to the Underworld to meet with the shades of the dead.)

Long considered one of the most demanding and revered of literary forms, the epic originated in the ancient world as an oral form. In addition to the works of Homer, the ancient world's greatest epics include the Babylonian *Epic of Gilgamesh*, the Roman poet Virgil's *Aeneid*, and the Hindu *Mahabharata* and *Ramayana.* Later epics in the English-language tradition include *Beowulf, Paradise Lost*, and Derek Walcott's *Omeros* (1990, a reworking of *The Odyssey* set in the Caribbean).

mock epic: a poem that uses epic language and conventions to depict subject matter—settings, characters, action—that usually wouldn't make it into traditional epics. The overall goal or effect is typically to "mock" or ridicule the particular social milieu represented in the poem (and the values or worldview of that milieu). However, a very few mock epics instead mock the grandeur and heroism of the epic itself (and the values or worldview associated with it). Alexander Pope's *The Rape of the Lock* (1714) is a famous and funny English-language mock epic.

pastoral elegy: a specific type of elegy that uses conventions associated with **pastoral literature**. Examples include John Milton's "Lycidas" (1638) and Percy Bysshe Shelley's poem on the death of John Keats, "Adonais" (1821).

verse novel: a narrative poem that is like a **novel** but written in verse. Unlike epics and like most novels, verse novels tend to have more contemporary, familiar, and often vividly described settings and to focus on more ordinary characters and actions. Examples include Elizabeth Barrett Browning's *Aurora Leigh* (1857), which also has certain epic features; Alexander Pushkin's Russian-language *Eugene Onegin* (1823–31); and Vikram Seth's *The Golden Gate* (1986).

verse drama: a play or plays written entirely or mainly in verse, whether designed for performance (like all of Shakespeare's plays, including A MIDSUMMER NIGHT'S DREAM and HAMLET, or as **closet drama** to be read (like Percy Bysshe's Shelley's *Prometheus Unbound* [1820] and Goethe's *Faust*).

JOHN MILTON

From Paradise Lost, Books 1 and 9

Of man's first disobedience, and the fruit
Of that forbidden tree whose mortal taste
Brought death into the world, and all our woe,
With loss of Eden, till one greater Man[1]
Restore us, and regain the blissful seat,
Sing, Heav'nly Muse,[2] that on the secret top
Of Oreb, or of Sinai, didst inspire
That Shepherd, who first taught the chosen seed,
In the beginning how the heav'ns and earth
Rose out of Chaos: or, if Sion hill
Delight thee more, and Siloa's brook[3] that flowed
Fast by the oracle of God; I thence
Invoke thy aid to my advent'rous song,
That with no middle flight intends to soar
Above th' Aonian mount,[4] while it pursues
Things unattempted yet in prose or rhyme.
And chiefly Thou O Spirit, that dost prefer
Before all temples th' upright heart and pure,
Instruct me, for thou know'st; thou from the first
Wast present, and with mighty wings outspread
Dove-like sat'st brooding on the vast abyss,
And mad'st it pregnant: what in me is dark
Illumine, what is low raise and support;
That to the height of this great argument[5]
I may assert Eternal Providence,
And justify the ways of God to men.

. . . .

[. . .] With tract[6] oblique
At first, as one who sought access, but feared
To interrupt, sidelong he[7] works his way.
As when a ship, by skilful steersman wrought
Nigh river's mouth or foreland, where the wind
Veers oft, as oft so steers, and shifts her sail;

1. Christ, the second Adam.
2. In Greek mythology, Urania, muse of astronomy; here, however, meaning the spirit that Moses ("That shepherd," line 8) encountered on the mountains of "Oreb" and "Sinai" (line 7) and that inspired him to write Genesis and other books of the Bible for the instruction of the Jews ("the chosen seed," line 8).
3. Spring near the temple of Solomon, which was located on Mount Zion ("Sion's hill," line 10).
4. Helicon, home of the muses in Greek mythology.
5. Subject or theme.
6. Course.
7. Satan, disguised as a snake. This excerpt, from book 9, describes his first encounter with Eve.

So varied he, and of his tortuous train
Curled many a wanton[8] wreath in sight of Eve,
To lure her eye; she busied heard the sound
Of rustling leaves, but minded not, as used
To such disport before her through the field,
From every beast more duteous at her call,
Than at Circean[9] call the herd disguised.
He bolder now uncalled before her stood;
But as in gaze admiring: oft the bowed
His turret crest, and sleek enameled[1] neck,
Fawning, and licked the ground whereon she trod.
His gentle dumb expression turned at length
The eye of Eve to mark his play; he glad
Of her attention gained, with serpent-tongue
Organic, or impulse of vocal air,[2]
His fraudulent temptation thus began.
"Wonder not, Sovran mistress, if perhaps
Thou canst, who art sole wonder, much less arm
Thy looks, the heav'n of mildness, with disdain,
Displeased that I approach thee thus, and gaze
Insatiate, I thus single, nor have feared
Thy awful[3] brow, more awful thus retired.
Fairest resemblance of thy Maker fair,
Thee all things living gaze on, all things thine
By gift, and thy celestial beauty adore
With ravishment beheld, there best beheld
Where universally admired; but here,
In this enclosure wild, these beasts among,
Beholders rude, and shallow to discern
Half what in thee is fair, one man except,
Who sees thee? (and what is one?) who shouldst be seen
A goddess among gods, adored and served
By angels numberless, thy daily train."
So glozed the Tempter, and his proem tuned;[4]
Into the heart of Eve his words made way,
Though at the voice much marveling; at length
Not unamazed she thus in answer spake.
"What may this mean? Language of man pronounced
By tongue of brute, and human sense expressed?
The first at least of these I thought denied
To beasts, whom God on their creation-day
Created mute to all articulate sound;

8. Playful; luxuriant.

9. In Homer's *Odyssey,* the witch Circe transforms Odysseus's men into obedient beasts.

1. Multicolored.

2. Since snakes don't have vocal chords, Satan must either somehow use its actual tongue to speak or impress the air with his own voice.

3. Awe inspiring.

4. Preface or preamble. *Glozed*: flattered.

The latter I demur,[5] for in their looks
Much reason, and in their actions oft appears.
Thee, serpent, subtlest beast of all the field
I knew, but not with human voice endued;[6]
Redouble then this miracle, and say,
How cam'st thou speakable of mute,[7] and how
To me so friendly grown above the rest
Of brutal kind, that daily are in sight?
Say, for such wonder claims attention due."
  To whom the guileful Tempter thus replied:
"Empress of this fair world, resplendent Eve!
Easy to me it is to tell thee all
What thou command'st, and right thou shouldst be obeyed;
I was at first as other beasts that graze
The trodden herb, of abject thoughts and low,
As was my food, nor aught but food discerned
Or sex, and apprehended nothing high:
Till on a day roving the field, I chanced
A goodly tree far distant to behold
Loaden with fruit of fairest colors mixed,
Ruddy and gold: I nearer drew to gaze;
When from the boughs a savory odor blown,
Grateful to appetite, more pleased my sense
Than smell of sweetest fennel, or the teats
Of ewe or goat dropping with milk at ev'n,[8]
Unsucked of lamb or kid, that tend their play.
To satisfy the sharp desire I had
Of tasting those fair apples, I resolved
Not to defer;[9] hunger and thirst at once,
Powerful persuaders, quickened at the scent
Of that alluring fruit, urged me so keen.
About the mossy trunk I wound me soon,
For high from ground the branches would require
Thy utmost reach or Adam's: round the tree
All other beasts that saw, with like desire
Longing and envying stood, but could not reach.
Amid the tree now got, where plenty hung
Tempting so nigh, to pluck and eat my fill
I spared[1] not, for such pleasure till that hour
At feed or fountain never had I found.
Sated at length, ere long I might perceive
Strange alteration in me, to degree
Of reason in my inward powers, and speech

5. Hesitate about.
6. Endowed.
7. That is, How did you go from being mute to being able to speak?
8. Evening.
9. Delay.
1. Refrained.

Wanted[2] not long, though to this shape retained.
Thenceforth to speculations high or deep
I turned my thoughts, and with capacious mind
Considered all things visible in Heav'n,
Or earth, or middle,[3] all things fair and good;
But all that fair and good in thy divine
Semblance, and in thy beauty's heav'nly ray,
United I beheld; no fair[4] to thine
Equivalent or second, which compelled
Me thus, though importune[5] perhaps, to come
And gaze, and worship thee of right declared
Sovran of creatures, universal dame!"
 So talked the spirited[6] sly snake; and Eve,
Yet more amazed unwary thus replied:
 "Serpent, thy overpraising leaves in doubt
The virtue[7] of that fruit, in thee first proved.
But say, where grows the tree, from hence how far?
For many are the trees of God that grow
In Paradise, and various, yet unknown
To us, in such abundance lies our choice,
As leaves a greater store of fruit untouched,
Still hanging incorruptible, till men
Grow up to their provision,[8] and more hands
Help to disburden nature of her birth."
 To whom the wily adder, blithe and glad;
"Empress, the way is ready, and not long,
Beyond a row of myrtles, on a flat,
Fast by a fountain, one small thicket past
Of blowing myrrh and balm; if thou accept
My conduct,[9] I can bring thee thither soon."
 "Lead, then," said Eve. He leading swiftly rolled
In tangles, and made intricate seem straight,
To mischief swift. Hope elevates, and joy
Brightens his crest, as when a wand'ring fire,
Compact of unctuous vapor,[1] which the night
Condenses, and the cold environs round,
Kindled through agitation to a flame,
Which oft, they say, some evil spirit attends,
Hovering and blazing with delusive light,

2. Lacked.
3. Region between heaven and earth.
4. Beauty, fairness.
5. Inopportunely.
6. Full of energy, enthusiasm, determination, but also, in this context, possessed by a spirit, Satan.
7. Power, but also perhaps goodness, desirability.
8. That is, until there are enough human beings to eat all the fruit God has provided and to which nature has given "birth" (line 624).
9. Guidance. *Blowing*: blooming.
1. *Ignuus fatuus* or "false light," as in a marsh, here imagined to be composed ("Compact," line 635) of oily ("unctuous," line 635) vapors.

Misleads th' amazed[2] night-wanderer from his way
To bogs and mires, and oft through pond or pool,
There swallowed up and lost, from succor far.
So glistered the dire Snake, and into fraud
Led Eve our credulous mother, to the tree
Of prohibition,[3] root of all our woe

1674

- What epic conventions does Milton follow in these excerpts? How does he rework conventions deviving from classic epic to suit his Christian epic?
- What various techniques and arguments does Satan use to tempt Eve to follow him to "the tree / Of prohibition" (lines 644–45)?

SAMUEL TAYLOR COLERIDGE
The Rime of the Ancient Mariner

In Seven Parts

Facile credo, plures esse Naturas invisibiles quam visibiles in rerum universitate. Sed horum [sic] *omnium familiam quis nobis enarrabit? et gradus et cognationes et discrimina et singulorum munera? Quid agunt? quae loca habitant? Harum rerum notitiam semper ambivit ingenium humanum, nunquam attigit. Juvat, interea, non diffiteor, quandoque in animo, tanquam in tabulâ, majoris et melioris mundi imaginem contemplari: ne mens assuefacta hodiernae vitae minutiis se contrahat nimis, et tota subsidat in pusillas cogitationes. Sed veritati interea invigilandum est, modusque servandus, ut certa ab incertis, diem a nocte, distinguamus.*

T. BURNET, *Archaeol. Phil.* p. 68.[4]

Argument

How a Ship, having first sailed to the Equator, was driven by storms to the cold Country towards the South Pole; how the Ancient Mariner cruelly and in contempt of the laws of hospitality killed a Seabird and how he was followed by many and strange Judgments: and in what manner he came back to his own Country.

2. Bewildered.
3. That is, the prohibited tree.
4. "I readily believe that there are more invisible than visible Natures in the universe. But who will explain for us the family of all these beings, and the ranks and relations and distinguishing features and functions of each? What do they do? What places do they inhabit? The human mind has always sought the knowledge of these things, but never attained it. Meanwhile I do not deny that it is helpful sometimes to contemplate in the mind, as on a tablet, the image of a greater and better world, lest the intellect, habituated to the petty things of daily life, narrow itself and sink wholly into trivial thoughts. But at the same time we must be watchful for the truth and keep a sense of proportion, so that we may distinguish the certain from the uncertain, day from night." Adapted by Coleridge from Thomas Burnet, *Archaeologiae Philosophicae* (1692).

Part 1

An ancient Mariner meeteth three Gallants bidden to a wedding feast, and detaineth one.

It is an ancient Mariner
And he stoppeth one of three.
—"By thy long gray beard and glittering eye,
Now wherefore stopp'st thou me?

The Bridegroom's doors are opened wide,
And I am next of kin;
The guests are met, the feast is set:
May'st hear the merry din."

He holds him with his skinny hand,
"There was a ship," quoth he.
"Hold off! unhand me, graybeard loon!"
Eftsoons[5] his hand dropped he.

The Wedding-Guest is spellbound by the eye of the old seafaring man, and constrained to hear his tale.

He holds him with his glittering eye—
The Wedding-Guest stood still,
And listens like a three years' child:
The Mariner hath his will.

The Wedding-Guest sat on a stone;
He cannot choose but hear;
And thus spake on that ancient man,
The bright-eyed Mariner.

"The ship was cheered, the harbor cleared,
Merrily did we drop
Below the kirk,[6] below the hill,
Below the lighthouse top.

The Mariner tells how the ship sailed southward with a good wind and fair weather, till it reached the Line.

The Sun came up upon the left,
Out of the sea came he!
And he shone bright, and on the right
Went down into the sea.

Higher and higher every day,
Till over the mast at noon[7]—"
The Wedding-Guest here beat his breast,
For he heard the loud bassoon.

The Wedding-Guest heareth the bridal music; but the Mariner continueth his tale.

The bride hath paced into the hall,
Red as a rose is she;
Nodding their heads before her goes
The merry minstrelsy.

The Wedding-Guest he beat his breast,
Yet he cannot choose but hear;
And thus spake on that ancient man,
The bright-eyed Mariner.

5. At once. 6. Church.
7. Indicating that the ship had reached the equator ("the Line").

The ship driven by a storm toward the South Pole.

"And now the STORM-BLAST came, and he
Was tyrannous and strong;
He struck with his o'ertaking wings,
And chased us south along.

With sloping masts and dipping prow,
As who pursued with yell and blow
Still treads the shadow of his foe,
And forward bends his head,
The ship drove fast, loud roared the blast,
And southward aye we fled.

And now there came both mist and snow,
And it grew wondrous cold:
And ice, mast-high, came floating by,
As green as emerald.

The land of ice, and of fearful sounds where no living thing was to be seen.

And through the drifts the snowy clifts
Did send a dismal sheen:
Nor shapes of men nor beasts we ken[8]—
The ice was all between.

The ice was here, the ice was there,
The ice was all around:
It cracked and growled, and roared and howled,
Like noises in a swound![9]

Till a great sea bird, called the Albatross, came through the snow-fog, and was received with great joy and hospitality.

At length did cross an Albatross,
Thorough the fog it came;
As if it had been a Christian soul,
We hailed it in God's name.

It ate the food it ne'er had eat,
And round and round it flew.
The ice did split with a thunder-fit;
The helmsman steered us through!

And lo! the Albatross proveth a bird of good omen, and followeth the ship as it returned northward through fog and floating ice.

And a good south wind sprung up behind;
The Albatross did follow,
And every day, for food or play,
Came to the mariners' hollo!

In mist or cloud, on mast or shroud,[1]
It perched for vespers nine;
Whiles all the night, through fog-smoke white,
Glimmered the white Moon-shine."

The ancient Mariner inhospitably killeth the pious bird of good omen.

"God save thee, ancient Mariner!
From the fiends, that plague thee thus!—
Why look'st thou so?"—With my crossbow
I shot the ALBATROSS.

8. Saw 9. Swoon.

1. Stout, tarred rope supporting the mast.

Part 2

The Sun now rose upon the right:[2]
Out of the sea came he,
Still hid in mist, and on the left
Went down into the sea.

And the good south wind still blew behind,
But no sweet bird did follow,
Nor any day for food or play
Came to the mariners' hollo!

His shipmates cry out against the ancient Mariner, for killing the bird of good luck.

And I had done a hellish thing,
And it would work 'em woe:
For all averred, I had killed the bird
That made the breeze to blow.
Ah wretch! said they, the bird to slay,
That made the breeze to blow!

But when the fog cleared off, they justify the same, and thus make themselves accomplices in the crime.

Nor dim nor red, like God's own head,
The glorious Sun uprist:
Then all averred, I had killed the bird
That brought the fog and mist.
'Twas right, said they, such birds to slay,
That bring the fog and mist.

The fair breeze continues; the ship enters the Pacific Ocean, and sails northward, even till it reaches the Line.

The fair breeze blew, the white foam flew,
The furrow followed free;
We were the first that ever burst
Into that silent sea.

The ship hath been suddenly becalmed.

Down dropped the breeze, the sails dropped down,
'Twas sad as sad could be;
And we did speak only to break
The silence of the sea!

All in a hot and copper sky,
The bloody Sun, at noon,
Right up above the mast did stand,
No bigger than the Moon.

Day after day, day after day,
We stuck, nor breath nor motion;
As idle as a painted ship
Upon a painted ocean.

And the Albatross begins to be avenged.

Water, water, everywhere,
And all the boards did shrink;
Water, water, everywhere,
Nor any drop to drink.

2. That is, the ship has now rounded Cape Horn and is headed northward.

The very deep did rot: O Christ!
That ever this should be!
Yea, slimy things did crawl with legs
Upon the slimy sea.

About, about, in reel and rout
The death-fires[3] danced at night;
The water, like a witch's oils,
Burnt green, and blue and white.

A Spirit had followed them; one of the invisible inhabitants of this planet, neither departed souls nor angels; concerning whom the learned Jew, Josephus, and the Platonic Constaninopolitan, Michael Psellus, may be consulted. They are very numerous, and there is no climate or element without one or more.

And some in dreams assured were
Of the Spirit that plagued us so;
Nine fathom deep he had followed us
From the land of mist and snow.

And every tongue, through utter drought,
Was withered at the root;
We could not speak, no more than if
We had been choked with soot.

The shipmates, in their sore distress, would fain throw the whole guilt on the ancient Mariner: in sign whereof they hang the dead sea bird round his neck.

Ah! well-a-day! what evil looks
Had I from old and young!
Instead of the cross, the Albatross
About my neck was hung.

Part 3

There passed a weary time. Each throat
Was parched, and glazed each eye.
A weary time! a weary time!
How glazed each weary eye,
When looking westward, I beheld
A something in the sky.

The ancient Mariner beholdeth a sign in the element afar off.

At first it seemed a little speck,
And then it seemed a mist;
It moved and moved, and took at last
A certain shape, I wist.[4]

A speck, a mist, a shape, I wist!
And still it neared and neared:
As if it dodged a water-sprite,
It plunged and tacked and veered.

3. Perhaps St. Elmo's fire—discharges of atmospheric electricity on a ship's spars or rigging—believed by superstitious sailors to portend disaster.
4. Knew.

At its nearer approach, it seemeth him to be a ship; and at a dear ransom he freeth his speech from the bonds of thirst.

With throats unslaked, with black lips baked,
We could nor laugh nor wail;
Through utter drought all dumb we stood!
I bit my arm, I sucked the blood,
And cried, A sail! a sail!

With throats unslaked, with black lips baked,
Agape they heard me call:

A flash of joy;

Gramercy![5] they for joy did grin,
And all at once their breath drew in,
As they were drinking all.

And horror follows. For can it be a ship that comes onward without wind or tide?

See! see! (I cried) she tacks no more!
Hither to work us weal;[6]
Without a breeze, without a tide,
She steadies with upright keel!

The western wave was all aflame.
The day was well nigh done!
Almost upon the western wave
Rested the broad bright Sun;
When that strange shape drove suddenly
Betwixt us and the Sun.

It seemeth him but the skeleton of a ship.

And straight the Sun was flecked with bars,
(Heaven's Mother send us grace!)
As if through a dungeon grate he peered
With broad and burning face.

Alas! (thought I, and my heart beat loud)

And its ribs are seen as bars on the face of the setting Sun.

How fast she nears and nears!
Are those *her* sails that glance in the Sun,
Like restless gossameres?[7]

The Specter-Woman and her Deathmate, and no other on board the skeleton ship.

Are those *her* ribs through which the Sun
Did peer, as through a grate?
And is that Woman all her crew?
Is that a DEATH? and are there two?
Is DEATH that woman's mate?

Like vessel, like crew!

Her lips were red, *her* looks were free,
Her locks were yellow as gold:
Her skin was as white as leprosy,
The Night-mare LIFE-IN-DEATH was she,
Who thicks man's blood with cold.

Death and Life-in-Death have diced for the ship's crew, and she (the latter) winneth the ancient Mariner.

The naked hulk alongside came,
And the twain were casting dice;
"The game is done! I've won! I've won!"
Quoth she, and whistles thrice.

5. From *grand-merci,* French for "great thanks." 6. Benefit. 7. Floating cobwebs.

No twilight within the courts of the Sun.

The Sun's rim dips; the stars rush out:
At one stride comes the dark;
With far-heard whisper, o'er the sea,
Off shot the spectre-bark.

At the rising of the Moon,

We listened and looked sideways up!
Fear at my heart, as at a cup,
My lifeblood seemed to sip!
The stars were dim, and thick the night,
The steersman's face by his lamp gleamed white;
From the sails the dew did drip—
Till clomb above the eastern bar
The hornèd Moon, with one bright star
Within the nether tip.[8]

One after another,

One after one, by the star-dogged Moon,
Too quick for groan or sigh,
Each turned his face with a ghastly pang,
And cursed me with his eye.

His shipmates drop down dead.

Four times fifty living men,
(And I heard nor sigh nor groan)
With heavy thump, a lifeless lump,
They dropped down one by one.

But Life-in-Death begins her work on the ancient Mariner.

The souls did from their bodies fly—
They fled to bliss or woe!
And every soul, it passed me by,
Like the whizz of my crossbow!

Part 4

The Wedding-Guest feareth that a Spirit is talking to him;

"I fear thee, ancient Mariner!
I fear thy skinny hand!
And thou art long, and lank, and brown,
As is the ribbed sea-sand.

But the ancient Mariner assureth him of his bodily life, and proceedeth to relate his horrible penance.

I fear thee and thy glittering eye,
And thy skinny hand, so brown."—
Fear not, fear not, thou Wedding-Guest!
This body dropped not down.

Alone, alone, all, all alone,
Alone on a wide wide sea!
And never a saint took pity on
My soul in agony.

He despiseth the creatures of the calm,

The many men, so beautiful!
And they all dead did lie:
And a thousand thousand slimy things
Lived on; and so did I.

8. An ill omen.

And envieth that they should live, and so many lie dead.

I looked upon the rotting sea,
And drew my eyes away;
I looked upon the rotting deck,
And there the dead men lay.

I looked to heaven, and tried to pray;
But or[9] ever a prayer had gushed,
A wicked whisper came, and made
My heart as dry as dust.

I closed my lids, and kept them close,
And the balls like pulses beat;
For the sky and the sea, and the sea and the sky
Lay like a load on my weary eye,
And the dead were at my feet.

But the curse liveth for him in the eye of the dead men.

The cold sweat melted from their limbs,
Nor rot nor reek did they:
The look with which they looked on me
Had never passed away.

An orphan's curse would drag to hell
A spirit from on high;
But oh! more horrible than that
Is the curse in a dead man's eye!
Seven days, seven nights, I saw that curse,
And yet I could not die.

In his loneliness and fixedness he yearneth towards the journeying Moon, and the stars that still sojourn, yet still move onward; and everywhere the blue sky belongs to them, and is their appointed rest, and their native country and their own natural homes, which they enter unannounced, as lords that are certainly expected and yet there is a silent joy at their arrival.

The moving Moon went up the sky,
And nowhere did abide:
Softly she was going up,
And a star or two beside—

Her beams bemocked the sultry main,
Like April hoar-frost spread;
But where the ship's huge shadow lay,
The charmèd water burnt alway
A still and awful red.

By the light of the Moon he beholdeth God's creatures of the great calm.

Beyond the shadow of the ship,
I watched the water snakes:
They moved in tracks of shining white,
And when they reared, the elfish light
Fell off in hoary flakes.

Within the shadow of the ship
I watched their rich attire:
Blue, glossy green, and velvet black,
They coiled and swam; and every track
Was a flash of golden fire.

9. Before.

Their beauty and their happiness.

O happy living things! no tongue
Their beauty might declare:
A spring of love gushed from my heart,
And I blessed them unaware:

He blesseth them in his heart.

Sure my kind saint took pity on me,
And I blessed them unaware.

The spell begins to break.

The self-same moment I could pray;
And from my neck so free
The Albatross fell off, and sank
Like lead into the sea.

Part 5

Oh sleep! it is a gentle thing,
Beloved from pole to pole!
To Mary Queen the praise be given!
She sent the gentle sleep from Heaven,
That slid into my soul.

By grace of the holy Mother, the ancient Mariner is refreshed with rain.

The silly[1] buckets on the deck,
That had so long remained,
I dreamt that they were filled with dew;
And when I awoke, it rained.

My lips were wet, my throat was cold,
My garments all were dank;
Sure I had drunken in my dreams,
And still my body drank.

I moved, and could not feel my limbs:
I was so light—almost
I thought that I had died in sleep,
And was a blessed ghost.

He heareth sounds and seeth strange sights and commotions in the sky and the element.

And soon I heard a roaring wind:
It did not come anear;
But with its sound it shook the sails,
That were so thin and sere.

The upper air burst into life!
And a hundred fire-flags sheen,[2]
To and fro they were hurried about!
And to and fro, and in and out,
The wan stars danced between.

And the coming wind did roar more loud,
And the sails did sigh like sedge;[3]
And the rain poured down from one black cloud;
The Moon was at its edge.

1. Plain, simple.
2. Shone. These fire-flags are probably St. Elmo's fire (see line 128n) but may be the aurora australis, or southern lights, and possibly also lightning. 3. Rushlike plant growing in wet soil.

The thick black cloud was cleft, and still
The Moon was at its side:
Like waters shot from some high crag,
The lightning fell with never a jag,
A river steep and wide.

The bodies of the ship's crew are inspirited, and the ship moves on;

The loud wind never reached the ship,
Yet now the ship moved on!
Beneath the lightning and the Moon
The dead men gave a groan.

They groaned, they stirred, they all uprose,
Nor spake, nor moved their eyes;
It had been strange, even in a dream,
To have seen those dead men rise.

The helmsman steered, the ship moved on;
Yet never a breeze up-blew;
The mariners all 'gan work the ropes,
Where they were wont to do;
They raised their limbs like lifeless tools—
We were a ghastly crew.

The body of my brother's son
Stood by me, knee to knee:
The body and I pulled at one rope,
But he said nought to me.

But not by the souls of the men, nor by dæmons[4] of earth or middle air, but by a blessed troop of angelic spirits, sent down by the invocation of the guardian saint.

"I fear thee, ancient Mariner!"
Be calm, thou Wedding Guest!
'Twas not those souls that fled in pain,
Which to their corses[5] came again,
But a troop of spirits blest:

For when it dawned—they dropped their arms,
And clustered round the mast;
Sweet sounds rose slowly through their mouths,
And from their bodies passed.

Around, around, flew each sweet sound,
Then darted to the Sun;
Slowly the sounds came back again,
Now mixed, now one by one.

Sometimes a-dropping from the sky
I heard the sky-lark sing;
Sometimes all little birds that are,
How they seemed to fill the sea and air
With their sweet jargoning![6]

4. Supernatural beings neither wholly mortal nor spiritual; see Coleridge's gloss beside lines 131–34.
5. Corpses.
6. Warbling.

And now 'twas like all instruments,
Now like a lonely flute;
And now it is an angel's song,
That makes the heavens be mute.

It ceased; yet still the sails made on
A pleasant noise till noon,
A noise like of a hidden brook
In the leafy month of June,
That to the sleeping woods all night
Singeth a quiet tune.

Till noon we quietly sailed on,
Yet never a breeze did breathe:
Slowly and smoothly went the ship,
Moved onward from beneath.

The lonesome Spirit from the South Pole carries on the ship as far as the Line, in obedience to the angelic troop, but still requireth vengeance.

Under the keel nine fathom deep,
From the land of mist and snow,
The spirit slid: and it was he
That made the ship to go.
The sails at noon left off their tune,
And the ship stood still also.

The Sun, right up above the mast,
Had fixed her to the ocean:
But in a minute she 'gan stir,
With a short uneasy motion—
Backwards and forwards half her length
With a short uneasy motion.

Then like a pawing horse let go,
She made a sudden bound:
It flung the blood into my head,
And I fell down in a swound.

The Polar Spirit's fellow dæmons, the invisible inhabitants of the element, take part in his wrong; and two of them relate, one to the other, that penance long and heavy for the ancient Mariner hath been accorded to the Polar Spirit, who returneth southward.

How long in that same fit I lay,
I have not[7] to declare;
But ere my living life returned,
I heard and in my soul discerned
Two voices in the air.

"Is it he?" quoth one, "Is this the man?
By him who died on cross,
With his cruel bow he laid full low
The harmless Albatross.

The spirit who bideth by himself
In the land of mist and snow,
He loved the bird that loved the man
Who shot him with his bow."

7. That is, do not have the ability.

The other was a softer voice,
As soft as honeydew:
Quoth he, "The man hath penance done,
And penance more will do."

Part 6

FIRST VOICE

"But tell me, tell me! speak again,
Thy soft response renewing—
What makes that ship drive on so fast?
What is the ocean doing?"

SECOND VOICE

"Still as a slave before his lord,
The ocean hath no blast;
His great bright eye most silently
Up to the Moon is cast—

If he may know which way to go;
For she guides him smooth or grim.
See, brother, see! how graciously
She looketh down on him."

The Mariner hath been cast into a trance; for the angelic power causeth the vessel to drive northward faster than human life could endure.

FIRST VOICE

"But why drives on that ship so fast,
Without or[8] wave or wind?"

SECOND VOICE

"The air is cut away before,
And closes from behind.

Fly, brother, fly! more high, more high!
Or we shall be belated:
For slow and slow that ship will go,
When the Mariner's trance is abated."

The supernatural motion is retarded; the Mariner awakes, and his penance begins anew.

I woke, and we were sailing on
As in a gentle weather:
'Twas night, calm night, the moon was high;
The dead men stood together.

All stood together on the deck,
For a charnel-dungeon fitter:
All fixed on me their stony eyes,
That in the Moon did glitter.

The pang, the curse, with which they died,
Had never passed away:
I could not draw my eyes from theirs,
Nor turn them up to pray.

8. Either.

The curse is finally expiated.

And now this spell was snapped: once more
I viewed the ocean green,
And looked far forth, yet little saw
Of what had else been seen—

Like one, that on a lonesome road
Doth walk in fear and dread,
And having once turned round walks on,
And turns no more his head;
Because he knows, a frightful fiend
Doth close behind him tread.

But soon there breathed a wind on me,
Nor[9] sound nor motion made:
Its path was not upon the sea,
In ripple or in shade.

It raised my hair, it fanned my cheek
Like a meadow-gale of spring—
It mingled strangely with my fears,
Yet it felt like a welcoming.

Swiftly, swiftly flew the ship,
Yet she sailed softly too:
Sweetly, sweetly blew the breeze—
On me alone it blew.

And the ancient Mariner beholdeth his native country.

Oh! dream of joy! is this indeed
The lighthouse top I see?
Is this the hill? is this the kirk?
Is this mine own countree?

We drifted o'er the harbor bar,
And I with sobs did pray—
O let me be awake, my God!
Or let me sleep alway.

The harbor bay was clear as glass,
So smoothly it was strewn!
And on the bay the moonlight lay,
And the shadow of the Moon.

The rock shone bright, the kirk no less,
That stands above the rock:
The moonlight steeped in silentness
The steady weathercock.

And the bay was white with silent light,
Till rising from the same,

The angelic spirits leave the dead bodies,

Full many shapes, that shadows were,
In crimson colors came.

9. Neither.

And appear in their own forms of light.

A little distance from the prow
Those crimson shadows were:
I turned my eyes upon the deck—
Oh, Christ! what saw I there!

Each corse lay flat, lifeless and flat,
And, by the holy rood!
A man all light, a seraph[1] man,
On every corse there stood.

This seraph band, each waved his hand:
It was a heavenly sight!
They stood as signals to the land,
Each one a lovely light;

This seraph band, each waved his hand,
No voice did they impart—
No voice; but oh! the silence sank
Like music on my heart.

But soon I heard the dash of oars,
I heard the Pilot's cheer;[2]
My head was turned perforce away
And I saw a boat appear.

The Pilot and the Pilot's boy,
I heard them coming fast:
Dear Lord in Heaven! it was a joy
The dead men could not blast.

I saw a third—I heard his voice:
It is the Hermit good!
He singeth loud his godly hymns
That he makes in the wood.
He'll shrieve my soul, he'll wash away
The Albatross's blood.

Part 7

The Hermit of the Wood,

This Hermit good lives in that wood
Which slopes down to the sea.
How loudly his sweet voice he rears!
He loves to talk with marineres
That come from a far countree.

He kneels at morn, and noon, and eve—
He hath a cushion plump:
It is the moss that wholly hides
The rotted old oak-stump.

1. Angel. *Rood*: cross. 2. Shout of encouragement.

The skiff-boat neared: I heard them talk,
"Why, this is strange, I trow![3]
Where are those lights so many and fair,
That signal made but now?"

Approacheth the ship with wonder.

"Strange, by my faith!" the Hermit said—
"And they answered not our cheer!
The planks looked warped! and see those sails,
How thin they are and sere!
I never saw aught like to them,
Unless perchance it were

Brown skeletons of leaves that lag
My forest-brook along;
When the ivy tod[4] is heavy with snow,
And the owlet whoops to the wolf below,
That eats the she-wolf's young."

"Dear Lord! it hath a fiendish look,"
(The Pilot made reply)
"I am a-feared"—"Push on, push on!"
Said the Hermit cheerily.

The boat came closer to the ship,
But I nor spake nor stirred;
The boat came close beneath the ship,
And straight a sound was heard.

The ship suddenly sinketh.

Under the water it rumbled on,
Still louder and more dread:
It reached the ship, it split the bay;
The ship went down like lead.

The ancient Mariner is saved in the Pilot's boat.

Stunned by that loud and dreadful sound,
Which sky and ocean smote,
Like one that hath been seven days drowned
My body lay afloat;
But swift as dreams, myself I found
Within the Pilot's boat.

Upon the whirl, where sank the ship,
The boat spun round and round;
And all was still, save that the hill
Was telling of the sound.

I moved my lips—the Pilot shrieked
And fell down in a fit;
The holy Hermit raised his eyes,
And prayed where he did sit.

I took the oars: the Pilot's boy,
Who now doth crazy go,

3. Think or believe. 4. Clump.

Laughed loud and long, and all the while
His eyes went to and fro.
"Ha! ha!" quoth he, "full plain I see,
The Devil knows how to row."

And now, all in my own countree,
I stood on the firm land!
The Hermit stepped forth from the boat,
And scarcely he could stand.

The ancient Mariner earnestly entreateth the Hermit to shrieve him; and the penance of life falls on him.

"O shrieve me, shrieve me, holy man!"
The Hermit crossed his brow.[5]
"Say quick," quoth he, "I bid thee say—
What manner of man art thou?"

Forthwith this frame of mine was wrenched
With a woeful agony,
Which forced me to begin my tale;
And then it left me free.

And ever and anon throughout his future life an agony constraineth him to travel from land to land;

Since then, at an uncertain hour,
That agony returns:
And till my ghastly tale is told,
This heart within me burns.

I pass, like night, from land to land;
I have strange power of speech;
That moment that his face I see,
I know the man that must hear me:
To him my tale I teach.

What loud uproar bursts from that door!
The wedding-guests are there:
But in the garden-bower the bride
And bride-maids singing are:
And hark the little vesper bell,
Which biddeth me to prayer!

O Wedding-Guest! this soul hath been
Alone on a wide wide sea:
So lonely 'twas, that God himself
Scarce seemèd there to be.

O sweeter than the marriage feast,
'Tis sweeter far to me,
To walk together to the kirk
With a goodly company!—

To walk together to the kirk,
And all together pray,
While each to his great Father bends,

5. That is, made the sign of the cross on his forehead. *Shrieve me*: hear my confession and grant me absolution.

Old men, and babes, and loving friends
And youths and maidens gay!

And to teach, by his own example, love and reverence to all things that God made and loveth.

Farewell, farewell! but this I tell
To thee, thou Wedding-Guest!
He prayeth well, who loveth well
Both man and bird and beast.

He prayeth best, who loveth best
All things both great and small;
For the dear God who loveth us,
He made and loveth all.[6]

The Mariner, whose eye is bright,
Whose beard with age is hoar,
Is gone: and now the Wedding-Guest
Turned from the bridegroom's door.

He went like one that hath been stunned,
And is of sense forlorn:[7]
A sadder and a wiser man,
He rose the morrow morn.

1797 1798

- Coleridge's poem has often been described as a tale of sin, punishment, and redemption. How is the killing of the albatross represented as a sin rather than simply a wrong or a crime? Why are *all* the mariners punished along with the ancient mariner? How does the mariner redeem himself?

CHRISTINA ROSSETTI
Goblin Market

Morning and evening
Maids heard the goblins cry:
"Come buy our orchard fruits,
Come buy, come buy:
Apples and quinces,
Lemons and oranges,
Plump unpecked cherries,
Melons and raspberries,
Bloom-down-cheeked peaches,
Swart[8]-headed mulberries,
Wild free-born cranberries,

6. Coleridge said in 1830, in response to the poet Anna Barbauld's objection that the poem "lacked a moral": "I told her that in my own judgment the poem had too much; and that the only, or chief fault, if I might say so, was the obtrusion of the moral sentiment so openly on the reader as a principle or cause of action in a work of pure imagination. It ought to have had no more moral than the *Arabian Nights'* tale of the merchant's sitting down to eat dates by the side of a well and throwing the shells aside, and lo! a genie starts up and says he *must* kill the aforesaid merchant *because* one of the date shells had, it seems, put out the eye of the genie's son." 7. Forsaken.
8. Dark.

Crab-apples, dewberries,
Pine-apples, blackberries,
Apricots, strawberries;—
All ripe together
In summer weather,—
Morns that pass by,
Fair eves that fly;
Come buy, come buy:
Our grapes fresh from the vine,
Pomegranates full and fine,
Dates and sharp bullaces,
Rare pears and greengages,
Damsons[9] and bilberries,
Taste them and try:
Currants and gooseberries,
Bright-fire-like barberries,
Figs to fill your mouth,
Citrons from the South,
Sweet to tongue and sound to eye;
Come buy, come buy."

Evening by evening
Among the brookside rushes,
Laura bowed her head to hear,
Lizzie veiled her blushes:
Crouching close together
In the cooling weather,
With clasping arms and cautioning lips,
With tingling cheeks and finger tips.
"Lie close," Laura said,
Pricking up her golden head:
"We must not look at goblin men,
We must not buy their fruits:
Who knows upon what soil they fed
Their hungry thirsty roots?"
"Come buy," call the goblins
Hobbling down the glen.
"Oh," cried Lizzie, "Laura, Laura,
You should not peep at goblin men."
Lizzie covered up her eyes,
Covered close lest they should look;
Laura reared her glossy head,
And whispered like the restless brook:
"Look, Lizzie, look, Lizzie,
Down the glen tramp little men.
One hauls a basket,
One bears a plate,
One lugs a golden dish

9. Plums; "bullaces" (line 22) and "greengages" (line 23) are others varieties of the same fruit.

Of many pounds weight.
How fair the vine must grow
Whose grapes are so luscious;
How warm the wind must blow
Thro' those fruit bushes."
"No," said Lizzie: "No, no, no;
Their offers should not charm us,
Their evil gifts would harm us."
She thrust a dimpled finger
In each ear, shut eyes and ran:
Curious Laura chose to linger
Wondering at each merchant man.
One had a cat's face,
One whisked a tail,
One tramped at a rat's pace,
One crawled like a snail,
One like a wombat prowled obtuse and furry,
One like a ratel[1] tumbled hurry skurry.
She heard a voice like voice of doves
Cooing all together:
They sounded kind and full of loves
In the pleasant weather.

Laura stretched her gleaming neck
Like a rush-imbedded swan,
Like a lily from the beck,[2]
Like a moonlit poplar branch,
Like a vessel at the launch
When its last restraint is gone.

Backwards up the mossy glen
Turned and trooped the goblin men,
With their shrill repeated cry,
"Come buy, come buy."
When they reached where Laura was
They stood stock still upon the moss,
Leering at each other,
Brother with queer brother;
Signalling each other,
Brother with sly brother.
One set his basket down,
One reared[3] his plate;
One began to weave a crown
Of tendrils, leaves and rough nuts brown
(Men sell not such in any town);
One heaved the golden weight
Of dish and fruit to offer her:
"Come buy, come buy," was still their cry.

1. Badger-like mammal native to Asia and Africa (pronounced "RAY-tl").
2. Stream. 3. Raised.

Laura stared but did not stir,
Longed but had no money:
The whisk-tailed merchant bade her taste
In tones as smooth as honey,
The cat-faced purr'd,
The rat-paced spoke a word
Of welcome, and the snail-paced even was heard;
One parrot-voiced and jolly
Cried "Pretty Goblin" still[4] for "Pretty Polly;"—
One whistled like a bird.

But sweet-tooth Laura spoke in haste:
"Good folk, I have no coin;
To take were to purloin:
I have no copper in my purse,
I have no silver either,
And all my gold is on the furze[5]
That shakes in windy weather
Above the rusty heather."
"You have much gold upon your head,"
They answered all together:
"Buy from us with a golden curl."
She clipped a precious golden lock,
She dropped a tear more rare than pearl,
Then sucked their fruit globes fair or red:
Sweeter than honey from the rock,[6]
Stronger than man-rejoicing wine,
Clearer than water flowed that juice;
She never tasted such before,
How should it cloy with length of use?
She sucked and sucked and sucked the more
Fruits which that unknown orchard bore;
She sucked until her lips were sore;
Then flung the emptied rinds away
But gathered up one kernel-stone,
And knew not was it night or day
As she turned home alone.

Lizzie met her at the gate
Full of wise upbraidings:
"Dear, you should not stay so late,
Twilight is not good for maidens;
Should not loiter in the glen
In the haunts of goblin men.
Do you not remember Jeanie,
How she met them in the moonlight,

4. Always. 5. Spiny shrub with yellow flowers.
6. See Psalm 81.16: "He should have fed them also with the finest of the wheat: and with honey out of the rock should I have satisfied thee."

Took their gifts both choice and many,
Ate their fruits and wore their flowers
Plucked from bowers
Where summer ripens at all hours?
But ever in the noonlight
She pined and pined away;
Sought them by night and day,
Found them no more but dwindled and grew grey;
Then fell with the first snow,
While to this day no grass will grow
Where she lies low:
I planted daisies there a year ago
That never blow.[7]
You should not loiter so."
"Nay, hush," said Laura:
"Nay, hush, my sister:
I ate and ate my fill,
Yet my mouth waters still;
Tomorrow night I will
Buy more:" and kissed her:
"Have done with sorrow;
I'll bring you plums tomorrow
Fresh on their mother twigs,
Cherries worth getting;
You cannot think what figs
My teeth have met in,
What melons icy-cold
Piled on a dish of gold
Too huge for me to hold,
What peaches with a velvet nap,
Pellucid[8] grapes without one seed:
Odorous indeed must be the mead
Whereon they grow, and pure the wave they drink
With lilies at the brink,
And sugar-sweet their sap."

Golden head by golden head,
Like two pigeons in one nest
Folded in each other's wings,
They lay down in their curtained bed:
Like two blossoms on one stem,
Like two flakes of new-fall'n snow,
Like two wands of ivory
Tipped with gold for awful[9] kings.
Moon and stars gazed in at them,
Wind sang to them lullaby,
Lumbering owls forbore to fly,
Not a bat flapped to and fro

7. Bloom. 8. Translucent. 9. Awe-inspiring.

Round their rest:
Cheek to cheek and breast to breast
Locked together in one nest.

Early in the morning
When the first cock crowed his warning,
Neat like bees, as sweet and busy,
Laura rose with Lizzie:
Fetched in honey, milked the cows,
Aired and set to rights the house,
Kneaded cakes of whitest wheat,
Cakes for dainty mouths to eat,
Next churned butter, whipped up cream,
Fed their poultry, sat and sewed;
Talked as modest maidens should:
Lizzie with an open heart,
Laura in an absent dream,
One content, one sick in part;
One warbling for the mere bright day's delight,
One longing for the night.
At length slow evening came:
They went with pitchers to the reedy brook;
Lizzie most placid in her look,
Laura most like a leaping flame.
They drew the gurgling water from its deep;
Lizzie plucked purple and rich golden flags,[1]
Then turning homewards said: "The sunset flushes
Those furthest loftiest crags;
Come, Laura, not another maiden lags,
No wilful squirrel wags,
The beasts and birds are fast asleep."
But Laura loitered still among the rushes
And said the bank was steep.

And said the hour was early still,
The dew not fall'n, the wind not chill:
Listening ever, but not catching
The customary cry,
"Come buy, come buy,"
With its iterated jingle
Of sugar-baited words:
Not for all her watching
Once discerning even one goblin
Racing, whisking, tumbling, hobbling;
Let alone the herds
That used to tramp along the glen,
In groups or single,
Of brisk fruit-merchant men.
Till Lizzie urged, "O Laura, come;

1. Irises.

I hear the fruit-call but I dare not look:
You should not loiter longer at this brook:
Come with me home.
The stars rise, the moon bends her arc,
Each glowworm winks her spark,
Let us get home before the night grows dark:
For clouds may gather
Tho' this is summer weather,
Put out the lights and drench us thro';
Then if we lost our way what should we do?"

Laura turned cold as stone
To find her sister heard that cry alone,
That goblin cry,
"Come buy our fruits, come buy."
Must she then buy no more such dainty fruit?
Must she no more such succous[2] pasture find,
Gone deaf and blind?
Her tree of life drooped from the root:
She said not one word in her heart's sore ache;
But peering thro' the dimness, nought discerning,
Trudged home, her pitcher dripping all the way;
So crept to bed, and lay
Silent till Lizzie slept;
Then sat up in a passionate yearning,
And gnashed her teeth for baulked desire, and wept
As if her heart would break.

Day after day, night after night,
Laura kept watch in vain
In sullen silence of exceeding pain.
She never caught again the goblin cry:
"Come buy, come buy;"—
She never spied the goblin men
Hawking their fruits along the glen:
But when the noon waxed bright
Her hair grew thin and gray;
She dwindled, as the fair full moon doth turn
To swift decay and burn
Her fire away.

One day remembering her kernel-stone
She set it by a wall that faced the south;
Dewed it with tears, hoped for a root,
Watched for a waxing shoot,
But there came none;
It never saw the sun,
It never felt the trickling moisture run:
While with sunk eyes and faded mouth

2. Juicy.

She dreamed of melons, as a traveler sees
False waves in desert drouth
With shade of leaf-crowned trees,
And burns the thirstier in the sandful breeze.

She no more swept the house,
Tended the fowls or cows,
Fetched honey, kneaded cakes of wheat,
Brought water from the brook:
But sat down listless in the chimney-nook
And would not eat.

Tender Lizzie could not bear
To watch her sister's cankerous[3] care
Yet not to share.
She night and morning
Caught the goblins' cry:
"Come buy our orchard fruits,
Come buy, come buy:"—
Beside the brook, along the glen,
She heard the tramp of goblin men,
The voice and stir
Poor Laura could not hear;
Longed to buy fruit to comfort her,
But feared to pay too dear.
She thought of Jeanie in her grave,
Who should have been a bride;
But who for joys brides hope to have
Fell sick and died
In her gay prime,
In earliest Winter time,
With the first glazing rime,
With the first snow-fall of crisp Winter time.

Till Laura dwindling
Seemed knocking at Death's door:
Then Lizzie weighed[4] no more
Better and worse;
But put a silver penny in her purse,
Kissed Laura, crossed the heath with clumps of furze
At twilight, halted by the brook:
And for the first time in her life
Began to listen and look.

Laughed every goblin
When they spied her peeping:
Came towards her hobbling,
Flying, running, leaping,
Puffing and blowing,

3. Corroding. 4. Evaluated, considered.

Chuckling, clapping, crowing,
Clucking and gobbling,
Mopping and mowing,[5]
Full of airs and graces,
Pulling wry faces,
Demure grimaces,
Cat-like and rat-like,
Ratel- and wombat-like,
Snail-paced in a hurry,
Parrot-voiced and whistler,
Helter skelter, hurry skurry,
Chattering like magpies,
Fluttering like pigeons,
Gliding like fishes,—
Hugged her and kissed her,
Squeezed and caressed her:
Stretched up their dishes,
Panniers,[6] and plates:
"Look at our apples
Russet and dun,
Bob at our cherries,
Bite at our peaches,
Citrons and dates,
Grapes for the asking,
Pears red with basking
Out in the sun,
Plums on their twigs;
Pluck them and suck them,
Pomegranates, figs."—

"Good folk," said Lizzie,
Mindful of Jeanie:
"Give me much and many:"—
Held out her apron,
Tossed them her penny.
"Nay, take a seat with us,
Honour and eat with us,"
They answered grinning:
"Our feast is but beginning.
Night yet is early,
Warm and dew-pearly,
Wakeful and starry:
Such fruits as these
No man can carry;
Half their bloom would fly,
Half their dew would dry,
Half their flavour would pass by.

5. Making faces. 6. Baskets for carrying provisions.

Sit down and feast with us,
Be welcome guest with us,
Cheer you and rest with us."—
"Thank you," said Lizzie: "But one waits
At home alone for me:
So without further parleying,
If you will not sell me any
Of your fruits tho' much and many,
Give me back my silver penny
I tossed you for a fee."—
They began to scratch their pates,
No longer wagging, purring,
But visibly demurring,
Grunting and snarling.
One called her proud,
Cross-grained, uncivil;
Their tones waxed loud,
Their looks were evil.
Lashing their tails
They trod and hustled her,
Elbowed and jostled her,
Clawed with their nails,
Barking, mewing, hissing, mocking,
Tore her gown and soiled her stocking,
Twitched her hair out by the roots,
Stamped upon her tender feet,
Held her hands and squeezed their fruits
Against her mouth to make her eat.
White and golden Lizzie stood,
Like a lily in a flood,—
Like a rock of blue-veined stone
Lashed by tides obstreperously,—
Like a beacon left alone
In a hoary roaring sea,
Sending up a golden fire,—
Like a fruit-crowned orange-tree
White with blossoms honey-sweet
Sore beset by wasp and bee,—
Like a royal virgin town
Topped with gilded dome and spire
Close beleaguered by a fleet
Mad to tug her standard down.

One may lead a horse to water,
Twenty cannot make him drink.
Tho' the goblins cuffed and caught her,
Coaxed and fought her,
Bullied and besought her,
Scratched her, pinched her black as ink,
Kicked and knocked her,

Mauled and mocked her,
Lizzie uttered not a word;
Would not open lip from lip
Lest they should cram a mouthful in:
But laughed in heart to feel the drip
Of juice that syrupped all her face,
And lodged in dimples of her chin,
And streaked her neck which quaked like curd.
At last the evil people
Worn out by her resistance
Flung back her penny, kicked their fruit
Along whichever road they took,
Not leaving root or stone or shoot;
Some writhed into the ground,
Some dived into the brook
With ring and ripple,
Some scudded on the gale without a sound,
Some vanished in the distance.
In a smart, ache, tingle,
Lizzie went her way;
Knew not was it night or day;
Sprang up the bank, tore thro' the furze,
Threaded copse and dingle,[7]
And heard her penny jingle
Bouncing in her purse,
Its bounce was music to her ear.
She ran and ran
As if she feared some goblin man
Dogged her with gibe or curse
Or something worse:
But not one goblin skurried after,
Nor was she pricked by fear;
The kind heart made her windy-paced
That urged her home quite out of breath with haste
And inward laughter.

She cried "Laura," up the garden,
"Did you miss me?
Come and kiss me.
Never mind my bruises,
Hug me, kiss me, suck my juices
Squeezed from goblin fruits for you,
Goblin pulp and goblin dew.
Eat me, drink me, love me;[8]
Laura, make much of me:
For your sake I have braved the glen
And had to do with goblin merchant men."

7. Deep wooded valley or dell. *Copse*: Small cluster of trees.
8. Echo of Jesus's words at the Last Supper: See Mark 14.22–24 and Luke 22.19–20.

Laura started from her chair,
Flung her arms up in the air,
Clutched her hair:
"Lizzie, Lizzie, have you tasted
For my sake the fruit forbidden?
Must your light like mine be hidden,
Your young life like mine be wasted,
Undone in mine undoing
And ruined in my ruin,
Thirsty, cankered, goblin-ridden?"—
She clung about her sister,
Kissed and kissed and kissed her:
Tears once again
Refreshed her shrunken eyes,
Dropping like rain
After long sultry drouth;
Shaking with aguish[9] fear, and pain,
She kissed and kissed her with a hungry mouth.

Her lips began to scorch,
That juice was wormwood[1] to her tongue,
She loathed the feast:
Writhing as one possessed she leaped and sung,
Rent all her robe, and wrung
Her hands in lamentable haste,
And beat her breast.
Her locks streamed like the torch
Borne by a racer at full speed,
Or like the mane of horses in their flight,
Or like an eagle when she stems the light
Straight toward the sun,
Or like a caged thing freed,
Or like a flying flag when armies run.

Swift fire spread thro' her veins, knocked at her heart,
Met the fire smouldering there
And overbore its lesser flame;
She gorged on bitterness without a name:
Ah! fool, to choose such part
Of soul-consuming care!
Sense failed in the mortal strife:
Like the watch-tower of a town
Which an earthquake shatters down,
Like a lightning-stricken mast,
Like a wind-uprooted tree
Spun about,
Like a foam-topped waterspout
Cast down headlong in the sea,

9. Feverish.
1. Bitter-tasting woody shrub sometimes used in medicine, as well as in vermouth and absinthe.

She fell at last;
Pleasure past and anguish past,
Is it death or is it life?

Life out of death.
That night long Lizzie watched by her,
Counted her pulse's flagging stir,
Felt for her breath,
Held water to her lips, and cooled her face
With tears and fanning leaves:
But when the first birds chirped about their eaves,
And early reapers plodded to the place
Of golden sheaves,
And dew-wet grass
Bowed in the morning winds so brisk to pass,
And new buds with new day
Opened of cup-like lilies on the stream,
Laura awoke as from a dream,
Laughed in the innocent old way,
Hugged Lizzie but not[2] twice or thrice;
Her gleaming locks showed not one thread of grey,
Her breath was sweet as May
And light danced in her eyes.

Days, weeks, months, years
Afterwards, when both were wives
With children of their own;
Their mother-hearts beset with fears,
Their lives bound up in tender lives;
Laura would call the little ones
And tell them of her early prime,
Those pleasant days long gone
Of not-returning time:
Would talk about the haunted glen,
The wicked, quaint[3] fruit-merchant men,
Their fruits like honey to the throat
But poison in the blood;
(Men sell not such in any town:)
Would tell them how her sister stood
In deadly peril to do her good,

And win the fiery antidote:
Then joining hands to little hands
Would bid them cling together,
"For there is no friend like a sister
In calm or stormy weather;
To cheer one on the tedious way,

2. Not only. 3. Strange.

To fetch one if one goes astray,
To lift one if one totters down,
To strengthen whilst one stands."

1862

- **How precisely are the goblins and their fruit characterized in the poem? What might they symbolize?**

T. S. ELIOT
The Love Song of J. Alfred Prufrock

S'io credessi che mia risposta fosse
a persona che mai tornasse al mondo,
questa fiamma staria senza più scosse.
Ma per ciò che giammai di questo fondo
non tornò vivo alcun, s'i'odo il vero,
senza tema d'infamia ti rispondo.[4]

Let us go then, you and I,
When the evening is spread out against the sky
Like a patient etherised upon a table;
Let us go, through certain half-deserted streets,
The muttering retreats
Of restless nights in one-night cheap hotels
And sawdust restaurants with oyster-shells:
Streets that follow like a tedious argument
Of insidious intent
To lead you to an overwhelming question . . .
Oh, do not ask, 'What is it?'
Let us go and make our visit.

In the room the women come and go
Talking of Michelangelo.[5]

The yellow fog that rubs its back upon the window-panes,
The yellow smoke that rubs its muzzle on the window-panes,
Licked its tongue into the corners of the evening,
Lingered upon the pools that stand in drains,
Let fall upon its back the soot that falls from chimneys,
Slipped by the terrace, made a sudden leap,
And seeing that it was a soft October night,
Curled once about the house, and fell asleep.

4. From Dante, *Inferno* (27.61–66): "If I thought that my reply would be / to one who would ever return to the world, / this flame would stay without further movement; // but since none has ever returned alive from this depth, / if what I hear is true, / I answer you without fear of infamy." The words are spoken by the character Guido da Montefeltro—imprisoned in flame in the depths of hell as a punishment for giving false counsel—to Dante, whom da Montefeltro believes will never return from his journey into the inferno.

5. Italian artist Michelangelo Buonarroti (1475–1564).

And indeed there will be time[6]
For the yellow smoke that slides along the street
Rubbing its back upon the window-panes;
There will be time, there will be time
To prepare a face to meet the faces that you meet;
There will be time to murder and create,
And time for all the works and days[7] of hands
That lift and drop a question on your plate;
Time for you and time for me,
And time yet for a hundred indecisions,
And for a hundred visions and revisions,
Before the taking of a toast and tea.

In the room the women come and go
Talking of Michelangelo.

And indeed there will be time
To wonder, 'Do I dare?' and, 'Do I dare?'
Time to turn back and descend the stair,
With a bald spot in the middle of my hair—
(They will say: 'How his hair is growing thin!')
My morning coat, my collar mounting firmly to the chin,
My necktie rich and modest, but asserted by a simple pin—
(They will say: 'But how his arms and legs are thin!')
Do I dare
Disturb the universe?
In a minute there is time
For decisions and revisions which a minute will reverse.

For I have known them all already, known them all—
Have known the evenings, mornings, afternoons,
I have measured out my life with coffee spoons;
I know the voices dying with a dying fall
Beneath the music from a farther room.
So how should I presume?

And I have known the eyes already, known them all—
The eyes that fix you in a formulated phrase,
And when I am formulated, sprawling on a pin,
When I am pinned and wriggling on the wall,
Then how should I begin
To spit out all the butt-ends of my days and ways?
And how should I presume?

And I have known the arms already, known them all—
Arms that are braceleted and white and bare
(But in the lamplight, downed with light brown hair!)

6. Echo of Andrew Marvell's "To His Coy Mistress" (1681), which famously begins, "Had we but world enough, and time / This coyness, lady, were no crime."
7. *Works and Days* is a poem composed about 700 BCE by the Greek writer Hesiod; lamenting the moral decay of the present, it celebrates simple life and hard work, especially agricultural labor.

Is it perfume from a dress
That makes me so digress?
Arms that lie along a table, or wrap about a shawl.
    And should I then presume?
    And how should I begin?

. . . .

Shall I say, I have gone at dusk through narrow streets
And watched the smoke that rises from the pipes
Of lonely men in shirt-sleeves, leaning out of windows? . . .

I should have been a pair of ragged claws
Scuttling across the floors of silent seas.

. . . .

And the afternoon, the evening, sleeps so peacefully!
Smoothed by long fingers,
Asleep . . . tired . . . or it malingers,
Stretched on the floor, here beside you and me.
Should I, after tea and cakes and ices,
Have the strength to force the moment to its crisis?
But though I have wept and fasted, wept and prayed,
Though I have seen my head (grown slightly bald) brought in
        upon a platter,[8]
I am no prophet—and here's no great matter;
I have seen the moment of my greatness flicker,
And I have seen the eternal Footman hold my coat, and snicker,
And in short, I was afraid.

And would it have been worth it, after all,
After the cups, the marmalade, the tea,
Among the porcelain, among some talk of you and me,
Would it have been worth while,
To have bitten off the matter with a smile,
To have squeezed the universe into a ball[9]
To roll it towards some overwhelming question,
To say: 'I am Lazarus, come from the dead,[1]
Come back to tell you all, I shall tell you all'—
If one, settling a pillow by her head,
    Should say: 'That is not what I meant at all.
    That is not it, at all.'

And would it have been worth it, after all,
Would it have been worth while,
After the sunsets and the dooryards and the sprinkled streets,

8. Like John the Baptist; at a banquet, King Herod has the prophet's head delivered on a plate to Salome, the woman who requested his execution (Mark 6.17–28; Matt. 14.3–11).

9. Another echo of "To His Coy Mistress": "Let us roll all our strength and all / Our sweetness up into one ball, / And tear our pleasures with rough strife / Through the iron gates of life" (lines 41–44).

1. The New Testament relates the story of Jesus raising Lazarus from the dead in John 11.1–44.

After the novels, after the teacups, after the skirts that trail along the floor—
And this, and so much more?—
It is impossible to say just what I mean!
But as if a magic lantern threw the nerves in patterns on a screen:
Would it have been worth while
If one, settling a pillow or throwing off a shawl,
And turning toward the window, should say:
'That is not it at all,
That is not what I meant, at all.'

. . . .

No! I am not Prince Hamlet,[1] nor was meant to be;
Am an attendant lord, one that will do
To swell a progress,[2] start a scene or two,
Advise the prince; no doubt, an easy tool,
Deferential, glad to be of use,
Politic, cautious, and meticulous;
Full of high sentence,[3] but a bit obtuse;
At times, indeed, almost ridiculous—
Almost, at times, the Fool.

I grow old . . . I grow old . . .
I shall wear the bottoms of my trousers rolled.

Shall I part my hair behind? Do I dare to eat a peach?
I shall wear white flannel trousers, and walk upon the beach.
I have heard the mermaids singing, each to each.

I do not think that they will sing to me.

I have seen them riding seaward on the waves
Combing the white hair of the waves blown back
When the wind blows the water white and black.

We have lingered in the chambers of the sea
By sea-girls wreathed with seaweed red and brown
Till human voices wake us, and we drown.

1915

• Like the speakers in all dramatic monologues, Prufrock intentionally and unintentionally reveals much about his temperament and character through both what he says and how he says it. How is Prufrock characterized? What do we learn about him, for example, through his allusions to Shakespeare's *Hamlet* (line 111)? to John the Baptist and Lazarus (lines 82, 94)?

2. Protagonist of Shakespeare's tragedy *Hamlet*, who is indecisive for much of the play.

3. Journey of a royal or noble person, or the representation of such a journey onstage as part of a play (as was common in the age of Shakespeare).

4. In either of its two archaic senses: official opinion, as of a judge; maxim, general truth, or proverbial saying.

SUGGESTIONS FOR WRITING

1. One of the many features that distinguishes Coleridge's THE RIME OF THE ANCIENT MARINER from traditional folk ballads (and makes the poem so long) is its use of a frame narrative—the story of how the ancient mariner tells the story of his experience at sea to a man on his way to a wedding. Write an essay explaining what the frame narrative contributes to the poem's effect and meaning.
2. Like most poems by T. S. Eliot, THE LOVE SONG OF J. ALFRED PRUFROCK contains many allusions. Write an essay exploring how the allusions contribute to the effect and meaning of the poem. Alternatively, focus your essay on the significance of Eliot's allusions to one poem—Andrew Marvell's TO HIS COY MISTRESS. One theme of Marvell's seduction poem is *carpe diem*, or "seize the day." To what extent is this also a theme or a key to the theme of Eliot's poem?
3. Write an essay exploring how GOBLIN MARKET might work as a religious allegory or even as a reworking of the story of Eve's temptation and fall, as recounted in Genesis and / or PARADISE LOST. In these terms, what is the effect of Rossetti's choice to follow fairy-tale conventions? to focus almost exclusively on female characters, especially two sisters?
4. Write an essay exploring how the internal structure and external form, as well as genre, of any one poem in this chapter contribute to its effect and meaning. For example, how does the fact that THE RIME OF THE ANCIENT MARINER is a ballad (and in ballad stanzas) shape its meaning and effect? How would "Prufrock" work differently if it weren't a dramatic monologue but rather a narrative poem with the sort of third-person speaker-narrator we get in PARADISE LOST or GOBLIN MARKET?
5. Write an essay comparing THE RIME OF THE ANCIENT MARINER to one or both of the shorter ballads in this anthology—SIR PATRICK SPENS or Dudley Randall's THE BALLAD OF BIRMINGHAM. What is similar and different about the shorter and longer ballads? Why does the ballad seem an appropriate or effective form for each of these poems? What might these poems together suggest about the nature and uses of the ballad?

SAMPLE WRITING: RESEARCH ESSAY

The following essay on THE RIME OF THE ANCIENT MARINER was originally written for an upper-division Romantic poetry course, but it answers the questions posed in the first and fourth of this chapter's "Suggestions for Writing." In it, student writer Dan Douglas uses only literary terms and reading strategies covered in this book, though he draws—perhaps too heavily and less effectively than he might—on a relatively reliable Internet source for his information about the ballad genre. As you read the essay, identify its strongest and weakest moments and aspects. How, for example, might Douglas better use the material from his secondary source? How might his essay be improved were he to draw on a different kind of source or on multiple sources? What kind of source would be best? (On writing sources, see ch. 34, "The Literature Research Essay")

Douglas 1

Dan Douglas
Dr. Kelly Mays
ENG 434: Romantic Poets
12 March 2017

The Form of *The Rime of the Ancient Mariner*

The Norton Anthology of English Literature explains that when another poet, Anna Letitia Barbauld, complained to Samuel Taylor Coleridge that *The Rime of the Ancient Mariner* "lacked a moral," he responded that the poem's "chief fault" was in fact the very opposite: "I told her that in my own judgment the poem had too much" moral, he is quoted as saying, and one too "openly" "obtru[ded] [. . .] on the reader" (qtd. in Greenblatt 459). The poem does seem to state its own moral when the mariner says near its end,

> He prayeth best, who loveth best
> All things both great and small;
> For the dear God who loveth us,
> He made and loveth all. (lines 614-17)

This is the lesson that the mariner learns when he is first punished for killing one animal (an extreme form of not "loving all") and then released only after he "blessed [. . .] unaware" (line 285) other animals he had only seconds before negatively labeled "slimy things" (line 238).

Douglas 2

What is not so obvious, though, is why Coleridge chose to teach this moral in a ballad and why he chose not to follow ballad convention by using a frame narrative. Or, in other words, how is the moral about treasuring all God's creatures "both great and small" affected by these choices? In this paper, I will argue that both devices are brilliant additions to the poem because they ensure (1) that we apply the poem's lesson to human beings as well as animals; (2) that we are clear about the poem's attitude toward organized religion versus its attitude toward God.

The frame narrative tells the story of the mariner's telling of the story of what happened with the albatross to a man on his way to a wedding. What's especially important is the auditor's initial response to the mariner. In the first stanza, when the mariner first "stoppeth" him (line 2), he is pretty shocked and maybe mad, asking, "By thy long grey beard and glittering eye, / Now wherefore stopp'st thou me?" (lines 3-4). Later, he practically screams, "Hold off! unhand me, grey-beard loon!" (line 11). The auditor's words imply that he wants to get away not just because he doesn't want to be late to the wedding of his "next of kin" (line 6), but because he's not happy about being held up and even touched by *this particular person*—a man so "ancient" he has a "grey beard" (notice he mentions the color of the beard twice), whom he maybe sees as badly groomed just because of the beard, and whom he definitely dismisses as a "loon" or crazy person. What we have here is age discrimination and a prejudice against people who have facial hair and seem "loony." Though we don't know much about the auditor, I wonder if we also have social prejudice here—after all, the ancient mariner is just a mariner, a common sailor. By dismissing the mariner, the auditor is arguably just doing to the mariner what the mariner did to the albatross. The auditor may not go so far as to kill the mariner, but he doesn't value him or what he's got to say, and I think that might be the reason that, as the mariner says later, he knows that this particular man is someone who "must hear" his story and learn what it "teach[es]" (lines 589-90).

The man is changed by what he hears. Almost immediately (by the third stanza), he is (maybe literally) mesmerized by the mariner and his tale: "He holds him with his glittering eye— / The wedding guest stood still, / And listens like a three years' child" (lines 13-15). He might "beat his breast" in anger or frustration when he hears the wedding music start in the church (lines 31-32), but "he cannot choose but hear" (line 38). And by the end of the first part, he even starts to think and care about what's going on with the mariner, how he feels, and why he feels that way, saying, "God save thee, ancient Mariner! / From the fiends, that plague thee thus!— / Why look'st thou so?" (lines 79-81). At this point, he's *asking* to hear the story. He's hooked, and he's hooked not just because the story is exciting (the mariner hasn't even gotten to the exciting part of the story yet), but because he's interested in the mariner himself. At least to some extent, the auditor has already started to learn what the mariner's story is

Douglas 3

supposed to teach: that we need to listen to, and value, the *people* we usually think of as "small," as well as the ones who are obviously "great," even "grey-beard loon[s]." And the word "loon"—which is literally a kind of bird—connects the albatross and the mariner.

The idea that we need to place more value on the people, as well as animals, we usually think of as "small" and unimportant is reinforced by Coleridge's choice to make the poem a ballad. On his website, Ted Nellen says,

> Of all the types of poetry, perhaps the one making the most direct appeal to all classes of readers and listeners from the Middle Ages to our own day is the popular ballad. It is essentially a narrative poem, that is, a poem that tells a story. And herein lies one of the reasons for its almost universal appeal; children and adults, educated and uneducated people, sophisticated and unsophisticated people—all like stories.

However, it's not just *that* ballads tell stories but *how* they tell stories that matters in this poem:

> So many ballads are cast into a four-line stanza of alternating four stress and three stress lines rhyming abcb that this stanza has come to be known as the ballad stanza. Ballads not composed in this stanza use one or another adaptation of it that is still essentially simple in structure.
>
> Just as the form is simple, so is the language. And this is what we might expect, since ballads originally were composed to be sung—frequently enough by the "folk" themselves as well as by professional ballad singers—to essentially simple music. Ballads use the vocabulary of everyday speech [. . .]. Dialogue does not normally distinguish between speakers, even though one may be a king and the other a commoner. Again, since ballads are folk literature, we do not find highly figurative language, learned allusions, or a highly literary vocabulary.

In other words, ballads are accessible to everyone, "both great and small," so by writing in this simple way, Coleridge makes his poem accessible, too, and he shows the value of listening to ordinary people and even telling stories their way.

As Nellen points out, there are lots of ways that Coleridge's poem isn't like folk ballads: Its "incidents are developed in far more detail," it is "rich in imagery," and it has "a complex system of symbols" and "significant philosophical content." However, another way Coleridge's ballad *is* like "a popular ballad" is that its plot includes "stirring and dramatic" and specifically "supernatural" "action" (Nellen)—"The Night-mare Life-in-Death" actually appears in the poem to punish the mariner, after he prays the albatross miraculously falls off his neck, and then *something* reanimates the sailors' bodies so that they can sail the ship home. According to *The Norton Anthology of English Literature*, there is also the implication that the mariner might mesmerize the wedding guest in some magical way (444). But none of these supernatural events or characters come from the Bible or from any organized religion I know of, though the mariner does refer to the virgin Mary (line 294) and Christ (line 487). Although the mariner also refers to "God" when he delivers the poem's moral (line 616), the moral doesn't say anything about actually going to church or participating in religion in any way. Instead, it stresses that we "prayeth well" by simply "lov[ing] well / Both man and bird and beast" (lines 612-13)—something we can't actually do in church since "bird[s] and beast[s]" are not allowed in.

This theme—that we don't really need organized religion or churches—is highlighted in the frame narrative because the wedding guest *never makes it to the church* or to the wedding ceremony. At the end of the poem, though he missed the wedding, he could still make it to the feast, as the mariner describes,

> What loud uproar bursts from that door!
> The wedding-guests are there:
> But in the garden-bower the bride
> And bride-maids singing are:
> And hark the little vesper bell,
> Which biddeth me to prayer! (lines 591-96)

However, the wedding guest doesn't go in, instead "Turn[ing] from the bridegroom's door" and presumably going home, where the next day "He rose" "A sadder and a wiser man" (lines 625, 624). The mariner also actually says that he thinks "walk[ing] together to the kirk [church] / With a goodly company" (lines 602-03) is "sweeter far" than "the marriage-feast" (lines 601-02), and even when he goes on to talk about going into the church and "all together pray[ing]," he emphasizes the relationship and relating between the people rather than the sermon or the minister. And here, too, he reinforces the point that that relationship has to be one in which *all* people, "great and small" and every age, class, etc. participate "all together"—"Old men, and babes, and loving friends, / And youths and maidens gay!" (lines 608-09).

This poem wouldn't be the same without the ballad form or the story about the wedding that frames the story of the albatross. Coleridge uses both to make sure that we don't take this story as only being about animals and the way we should value them and that we also don't take it as an endorsement of any particular religion or even organized religion at all. We can love God without going to church just by loving each other, but only if we love everyone of every species, age, looks, and class.

Works Cited

Coleridge, Samuel Taylor. *The Rime of the Ancient Mariner*. Greenblatt, pp. 443-59.

Greenblatt, Stephen, et al. *The Norton Anthology of English Literature*. 9th ed., vol. 2a, W. W. Norton, 2012.

Nellen, Ted. "Ballad." *Cyber English*, www.tnellen.com/cybereng/ballad.html.

Exploring Contexts

The more knowledge you have—both general knowledge and knowledge of poetic and literary traditions—the better a reader of poetry you are likely to be. Poems often draw on a fund of human knowledge about all sorts of things, asking us to bring to bear facts and beliefs we have acquired from earlier reading or from our everyday experiences. In the previous chapters, we have looked at how practice, specific skills, and a knowledge of basic literary terms make interpretation easier and better. This contextual section, however, focuses more on other types of information you need to read richly and fully: information about authors and their work, about events that influenced authors or inspired their writing, and about the ways other readers and critics have interpreted the work. Poets always write in a specific time and place, under unique circumstances, and with some awareness of the world around them, whether or not they explicitly refer to contemporary matters in a particular poem. Poems not only *refer* to people, places, and events—things that exist in time—but also *reflect* given moments; they are the products of both the potentialities and the limitations of the times in which they are created. Many poems—like many works of drama and fiction—also have something to say about their times, as well as timeless human qualities, habits, and relationships.

What we need to bring to our reading varies from poem to poem. For example, to understand Wilfred Owen's DULCE ET DECORUM EST we need to know that poison gas was used in World War I; the green tint through which the speaker sees the world in lines 13–14 comes from the green glass in the goggles of the gas mask he has just put on. But some broader issues matter as well, such as the climate of opinion that surrounded the war and the way war had been represented in earlier literary works. No doubt you will read a poem more intelligently—and with more feeling—the more you know about its cultural or historical and literary contexts. But at the same time, your sense of these subjects will grow as a result of reading the poems themselves sensitively and thoughtfully. Reading poetry can be a way to gain knowledge as well as an aesthetic experience. Although we don't generally turn to poetry for information as such, poems often give us more than we expect, insofar as we are aware of real-world contexts.

To get at appropriate factual, cultural, and historical information, we need to ask three kinds of questions of ourselves. The first is obvious: Do I understand all (or most) of the references in the poem? When events, places, or people unfamiliar to you come up, you will need to find out what, where, or whom they are. The second question is more difficult: How do I know, in a poem that does *not* refer specifically to events, people, or ideas that I do not recognize, that I need to know more? That is, when a poem has no specific references to look up, no people or events to identify, how do I know that it has a specific context? Usually, good poets will not puzzle you more than necessary, so you can safely assume that anything that is not self-explanatory will merit close attention and possibly some digging in the library. References that are not in themselves clear provide a strong clue that you need more information. When something doesn't click, when the information given does not seem enough, you need to trust your puzzlement and try to find the missing facts that will help you to make sense of the poem. But how? Often the date of the poem helps; sometimes the title gives a clue or a point of departure; sometimes you can uncover, by reading about the author, some of the things he or she was interested in or concerned about. There is no single all-purpose way to discover what to look for, but that kind of research—looking for clues, adding up the evidence—can be interesting in itself and very rewarding when it is successful. The third question for every factual reference is *Why*? Why does the poem refer to this particular person instead of some other? What function does the reference serve?

22 THE AUTHOR'S WORK AS CONTEXT: ADRIENNE RICH

Even though all poets share the medium of language and usually have some common notions about their craft, they put the unique resources of their individual personalities, experiences, and outlooks into every poem they create. A poet may rely on tradition extensively and use devices that others have developed without surrendering his or her individuality, just as any individual shares certain characteristics with others—political affiliations, religious beliefs, tastes in clothes and music—without compromising his or her integrity and uniqueness. Sometimes a person's uniqueness is hard to define. But it is always there, and we recognize and depend on it in our relationships with other people. And so with poets: Most don't make a conscious effort to put an individual stamp on their work; they don't have to. The stamp is there in the very subjects, words, images, and forms they choose. Every individual's unique consciousness marks what it records and imagines.

Experienced readers can often identify a poem as the distinctive work of an individual poet even though they may never have seen that poem before, much as experienced listeners can identify a new piece of music as the work of a particular composer, singer, or group after hearing only a few phrases. This ability depends on a lot of reading or a lot of listening to music, and any reasonably sensitive reader can learn, over time, to do it with remarkable accuracy. Yet this ability is not an end in itself; rather, it is a by-product of learning to appreciate the particular, distinctive qualities of any poet's work. Once you've read several poems by the same poet, you will usually see some features that the poems all share, and gradually you may come to think of those features as characteristic. Many people have favorite poets, just as they have favorite rock groups or rap artists. In both cases, we are attracted to the artist's work precisely because, consciously or not, we recognize and appreciate that artist's distinctive style and outlook.

The work of any writer will display a characteristic way of thinking. It will have certain identifiable *tendencies*. But this does not mean that every poem by a particular author will be predictable and contain all of the same features. Poets test their talents and their views—as well as their readers—by experimenting with various subjects and points of view, formal structures and devices. Like all of us, poets also grow and change over time. As readers, then, we want to strive to recognize differences, as well as similarities, among individual poems and to appreciate the ways an author's work does and doesn't change over the years.

Of what practical use is it to learn to recognize and understand the distinctive voice and mind of a particular poet? One use is the pleasant surprise that occurs when you recognize something familiar. Reading a new poem by a familiar poet can be like meeting an old friend. Just as meeting something or someone altogether new to you provides one kind of pleasure, so revisiting the familiar provides another, equal and opposite kind. Just *knowing* and *recognizing* often feel good in and of themselves.

In addition, just as you learn from watching other people, seeing how they react and respond to various situations and events, so you can learn from watching poets at work—seeing how they learn and develop, how they change their minds or test alternative points of view, how they discover the reach and limits of their imaginations and talents, how they find their distinctive voices and come to terms with their own identities. Each poem exists separately and individually, but at the same time the whole body of a poet's work records the workings and the evolution of a distinctive artistic consciousness as it confronts a world that is itself perpetually changing.

Finally, the more you know about a poet and the more of his or her poems you read, the better a reader you will likely be of any individual poem by the poet. External facts of the writer's life may inform whatever he or she writes—be it a poem, an essay, a letter, or an autobiography. But beyond that, when you grow accustomed to a writer's habits and manners and means of expression, you learn what to expect. Coming to a new poem by a poet you already are familiar with, you know what to look for and have clear expectations for the poem. At the same time, you are better prepared to appreciate the surprises each poem holds in store.

THE POETRY OF ADRIENNE RICH

You will find both continuity and change, similarities and differences, in the work of any good poet, and this chapter introduces you to a great one. Adrienne Rich (1929–2012) was an especially active, prolific poet whom many readers and critics regard as the best of her generation. A careful reader of her work will find similarities of interest and strategy from her earliest poems—published shortly after World War II, in 1951—to her newest ones. A distinctive mind and orientation are at work.

But over the years Rich's work changed quite a lot, too, and she modified her views on a number of issues. Such changes were the result both of her personal experiences and of those shared experiences that helped define her era. Many of the changes in Rich's ideas and attitudes, for example, reflect changing concerns among American intellectuals (especially women) in the second half of the twentieth century, and her poems represent both changed social conditions and sharply altered social, political, and philosophical attitudes. But her poems also reflect altered personal circumstances. Rich married in her early twenties and had three children by the time she was thirty; many of her early poems are about heterosexual love, and some of them are quite explicitly about sex. Later, she was involved in a long-term lesbian relationship and wrote, again quite explicitly, about sex between women. In Rich's poems, then, we may not only trace the contours of an evolving personal life and outlook but also—and even more important for the study of poetry generally—see how changes *within* the poet and in her social and cultural context altered the subjects and themes of her poetry, as well as its form.

Just as information about an author's life and times can help us in this enterprise, so, too, can the essays, letters, and interviews in which an author reflects on the character and aims of his or her poetry and on the subjects the poetry explores. In the case of Rich, we have a bounty of such material from a poet who was also a remarkably prolific, articulate and influential prose writer. Gathered at the end of this chapter are excerpts from these writings, including both essays that express Rich's outlook at a particular moment and retrospective pieces in which she gives us her interpretation of the character and development of her work over time.

It is fitting that two of Adrienne Rich's books—*A Change of World* (1951) and *The Will to Change* (1971)—bear titles that prominently feature the word *change.* For change is, indeed, both a consistent concern of her poetry and a hallmark of her poetic career. Published when their author was just twenty-one, poems such as AT A BACH CONCERT, STORM WARNINGS, and AUNT JENNIFER'S TIGERS seem, at first glance, preternaturally mature. With their tightly controlled structure, their regular rhythm (and, often, rhyme), and their coolly observant tone, these early poems both embody and celebrate the "discipline" that "masters feelings" and the "proud restraining purity" by which art lends order to life ("At a Bach Concert," below). (Versions of the word *master,* in fact, appear in all three poems.) Explaining why he chose *A Change of World* for the Yale Younger Poets Series, poet W. H. Auden singled out just such qualities and attitudes, praising Rich for a "craftsmanship" based in that "capacity for detachment from the self and its emotions without which no art is possible." If "poems are analogous to persons," Auden continued, then these poems are "neatly and modestly dressed, speak quietly but do not mumble, respect their elders but are not cowed by them, and do not tell fibs."

Less than a decade later, however, Rich began to see the very "neatness" and "detachment" of her own early poems as itself a kind of "fib." As she put it in 1964, the early poems, "even the ones I liked best and in which I felt I'd said most, were queerly limited; [. . .] in many cases I [. . .] suppressed, omitted, falsified even, certain disturbing elements to gain the perfection of order." From this point forward, Rich's work was very much an attempt to do the very opposite—to, in Matthew Arnold's words, "see life steadily and see it whole," in all its disturbing, disorderly imperfection. Indeed, one of the major themes of the later poems is both the necessity and the difficulty of breaking through the web of "myth" and illusion in order to get to "the thing itself" (DIVING INTO THE WRECK).

In its attempt to do just that, Rich's work itself became less neat and orderly, less quiet, modest, and respectful. Beginning with *Snapshots of a Daughter-in-Law* (1963) and its title poem, the poems speak in many radically different voices and tones and are cast in many different forms. Rich's evolution as a poet was not a matter of pursuing any kind of single-minded mastery over her materials. "I find that I can no longer go to write a poem with a neat handful of materials and express those materials according to a prior plan," Rich explained in 1964; "the poem itself engenders new sensations, new awareness in me as it progresses." What results are "poems that *are* experiences" rather than "poems *about* experiences."

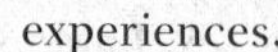

Adrienne Rich, circa 1970

In becoming more informal, exploratory, and emotional, Rich's poems also became more personal and autobiographical, more willing to enter and lay bare what "Storm Warnings" calls the "troubled regions" of the poet's own life, heart, and mind. In fact, Rich suggested that her artistic growth was, in part, a matter of closing the gap between "the woman in the poem and the woman writing the poem." And in "Roofwalker," a 1961 poem that articulated her new poetic ideal, Rich compares herself both to a roofer standing atop a half-built house and to "a naked man fleeing /

across" those very roofs. Like both, she now dared to be "exposed, larger than life, / and due to break my neck."

At the same time, Rich's work also became steadily more social, political, and historical. HISTORY is, in fact, the title of one poem in this chapter and the subject of many others. As early as 1956, moreover, Rich began to insist on the historicity of her own poems by dating each one. "It seems to me now that this was an oblique political statement," Rich insists in the 1984 essay "Blood, Bread, and Poetry": "It was a declaration that placed poetry in a historical continuity, not above or outside history." "For Rich," as one critic argues, "a deepening subjectivity does not mean withdrawal, as it did for [Emily] Dickinson, but, on the contrary, a more searching engagement with people and with social forces."

In Rich's life, as in her work, the movement into the self fueled the movement outward—into the world and back into the past—and vice versa. On the one hand, it was in part her personal feelings and experiences—the fact that she felt "unfit, disempowered, adrift" as a housewife and mother in the mid-1950s—that sent her to the work of "political" writers such as Mary Wollstonecraft, Simone de Beauvoir, and James Baldwin, and, later, into the antiwar, civil rights, and women's movements. On the other hand, it was these writers and movements that eventually encouraged her to see her "private turmoil"—indeed, her consciousness itself—as the product of historically specific social and political forces. As she explains in the essay "Blood, Bread, and Poetry,"

> my personal world view [. . .] was [. . .] created by political conditions. I was not a man; I was white in a white-supremacist society; I was [. . .] educated from the perspective of a particular class; my father was an "assimilated" Jew in an anti-Semitic world, my mother a white southern Protestant; there were particular historical currents on which my consciousness would come together, piece by piece. [. . .] My personal world view, which like so many young people I carried as a conviction of my own uniqueness, was not original with me, but was, rather, my untutored and half-conscious rendering of the facts of blood and bread, the social and political forces of my time and place.

Rich's mature poetry is, in many ways, an attempt to scrutinize the "social and political forces" that shape our lives and our relationships with one another and with the planet we inhabit. In this way, "the personal is political" for and in Rich—and so, too, is the literary. Yet her poetry works as poetry largely because in it the converse is always equally and palpably true. Her "poems compel us," as critic Albert Gelpi suggests, "precisely because [. . .] the politics [are] not abstracted and depersonalized but tested on the nerve-ends."

Despite—or even because of—all the changes, Rich's work also demonstrates a real and rare sort of consistency. From the very beginning of her career in the 1950s to its end in 2012, Rich conceived poems with a powerful sense of functional structure and cast them in **lyric** modes that sensitively reflect their moods and tones. She engaged readers viscerally and intellectually through vivid images. And certain images and objects—knives and coffee pots, ruins and rubble, maps and monsters, wintry weather—recur in multiple poems, binding the poems together even as they help us track a process of evolution and change that, Rich reminds us, isn't simple or straightforward. "If you think you can grasp me, think again," she warns us in the poem "Delta"; "my story flows in more than one direction."

POEMS BY ADRIENNE RICH

At a Bach Concert

Coming by evening through the wintry city
We said that art is out of love with life.
Here we approach a love that is not pity.

This antique discipline, tenderly severe,
Renews belief in love yet masters feeling,
Asking of us a grace in what we bear.

Form is the ultimate gift that love can offer—
The vital union of necessity
With all that we desire, all that we suffer.

A too-compassionate art is half an art.
Only such proud restraining purity
Restores the else-betrayed, too-human heart.

1951

Storm Warnings

The glass has been falling all the afternoon,
And knowing better than the instrument
What winds are walking overhead, what zone
Of gray unrest is moving across the land,
I leave the book upon a pillowed chair
And walk from window to closed window, watching
Boughs strain against the sky

And think again, as often when the air
Moves inward toward a silent core of waiting,
How with a single purpose time has traveled
By secret currents of the undiscerned
Into this polar realm. Weather abroad
And weather in the heart alike come on
Regardless of prediction.

Between foreseeing and averting change
Lies all the mastery of elements
Which clocks and weatherglasses cannot alter.
Time in the hand is not control of time,
Nor shattered fragments of an instrument
A proof against the wind; the wind will rise,
We can only close the shutters.

I draw the curtains as the sky goes black
And set a match to candles sheathed in glass
Against the keyhole draught, the insistent whine
Of weather through the unsealed aperture.
This is our sole defense against the season;

These are the things that we have learned to do
Who live in troubled regions.

1951

Living in Sin

She had thought the studio would keep itself;
no dust upon the furniture of love.
Half heresy, to wish the taps less vocal,
the panes relieved of grime. A plate of pears,
a piano with a Persian shawl, a cat
stalking the picturesque amusing mouse
had risen at his urging.
Not that at five each separate stair would writhe
under the milkman's tramp; that morning light
so coldly would delineate the scraps
of last night's cheese and three sepulchral bottles;
that on the kitchen shelf among the saucers
a pair of beetle-eyes would fix her own—
envoy from some village in the moldings . . .
Meanwhile, he, with a yawn,
sounded a dozen notes upon the keyboard,
declared it out of tune, shrugged at the mirror,
rubbed at his beard, went out for cigarettes;
while she, jeered by the minor demons,
pulled back the sheets and made the bed and found
a towel to dust the table-top,
and let the coffee-pot boil over on the stove.
By evening she was back in love again,
though not so wholly but throughout the night
she woke sometimes to feel the daylight coming
like a relentless milkman up the stairs.

1955

Snapshots of a Daughter-in-Law

1

You, once a belle in Shreveport,
with henna-colored hair, skin like a peachbud,
still have your dresses copied from that time,
and play a Chopin prelude
called by Cortot:[1] *"Delicious recollections*
float like perfume through the memory."

Your mind now, mouldering like wedding-cake,
heavy with useless experience, rich
with suspicion, rumor, fantasy,

1. Alfred Cortot (1877–1962), Franco-Swiss pianist and conductor.

crumbling to pieces under the knife-edge
of mere fact. In the prime of your life.
Nervy, glowering, your daughter
wipes the teaspoons, grows another way.

2

Banging the coffee-pot into the sink
she hears the angels chiding, and looks out
past the raked gardens to the sloppy sky.
Only a week since They said: *Have no patience.*

The next time it was: *Be insatiable.*
Then: *Save yourself; others you cannot save.*[2]
Sometimes she's let the tapstream scald her arm,
a match burn to her thumbnail,

or held her hand above the kettle's snout
right in the woolly steam. They are probably angels,
since nothing hurts her anymore, except
each morning's grit blowing into her eyes.

3

A thinking woman sleeps with monsters.
The beak that grips her, she becomes. And Nature,
that sprung-lidded, still commodious
steamer-trunk of *tempora* and *mores*[3]
gets stuffed with it all: the mildewed orange-flowers,
the female pills, the terrible breasts
of Boadicea[4] beneath flat foxes' heads and orchids.

Two handsome women, gripped in argument,
each proud, acute, subtle, I hear scream
across the cut glass and majolica
like Furies[5] cornered from their prey:
The argument *ad feminam*,[6] all the old knives
that have rusted in my back, I drive in yours,
ma semblable, ma soeur![7]

2. According to Matthew 27.42, the chief priests, scribes, and elders mocked the crucified Jesus by saying, "He saved others; himself he cannot save."
3. Times and customs (Latin).
4. Queen of the ancient Britons. When her husband died, the Romans seized the territory he ruled and scourged Boadicea; she then led a heroic but ultimately unsuccessful revolt. *Female pills*: medicines for menstrual ailments.
5. In Roman mythology, the three sisters were the avenging spirits of retributive justice.
6. To the woman (Latin). The *argumentum ad hominem* (literally, "argument to the man") is (in classical rhetoric) an argument aimed at a person's individual prejudices or special interests.
7. My mirror-image or "double," my sister (French). Charles Baudelaire (1821–67), in the prefatory poem to *Les Fleurs du Mal* (1857), addresses (and attacks) his "hypocrite reader" as "mon semblable, mon frère" (my double, my brother).

4

Knowing themselves too well in one another:
their gifts no pure fruition, but a thorn,
the prick filed sharp against a hint of scorn . . .
Reading while waiting
for the iron to heat,
writing, *My Life had stood—a Loaded Gun—*[8]
in that Amherst pantry while the jellies boil and scum,
or, more often,
iron-eyed and beaked and purposed as a bird,
dusting everything on the whatnot every day of life.

5

Dulce ridens, dulce loquens,[9]
she shaves her legs until they gleam
like petrified mammoth-tusk.

6

When to her lute Corinna sings[1]
neither words nor music are her own;
only the long hair dipping
over her cheek, only the song
of silk against her knees
and these
adjusted in reflections of an eye.

Poised, trembling and unsatisfied, before
an unlocked door, that cage of cages,
tell us, you bird, you tragical machine—
is this *fertilisante douleur*?[2] Pinned down
by love, for you the only natural action,
are you edged more keen
to prise the secrets of the vault? has Nature shown
her household books to you, daughter-in-law,
that her sons never saw?

7

"To have in this uncertain world some stay
which cannot be undermined, is
of the utmost consequence."[3]
Thus wrote

8. "My Life had stood—a Loaded Gun—" [Poem No. 754], Emily Dickinson, *Complete Poems*, ed. T. H. Johnson, 1960, p. 369 [Rich's note]. It is reprinted in the Emily Dickinson album that follows this chapter.

9. Sweet laughter, sweet chatter (Latin). The phrase (slightly modified here) concludes Horace's *Ode* 1.22, describing the appeal of a mistress.

1. Opening line of a lyric by Thomas Campion (1567–1620), which appears elsewhere in this anthology.

2. Enriching pain (French).

3. ". . . is of the utmost consequence," from Mary Wollstonecraft, *Thoughts on the Education of Daughters*, London, 1787 [Rich's note]. Wollstonecraft (1759–97) is also, and more famously, the author of *A Vindication of the Rights of Woman* (1792).

a woman, partly brave and partly good,
who fought with what she partly understood.
Few men about her would or could do more,
hence she was labeled harpy, shrew and whore.

8

"You all die at fifteen," said Diderot,[4]
and turn part legend, part convention.
Still, eyes inaccurately dream
behind closed windows blankening with steam.
Deliciously, all that we might have been,
all that we were—fire, tears,
wit, taste, martyred ambition—
stirs like the memory of refused adultery
the drained and flagging bosom of our middle years.

9

Not that it is done well, but
that it is done at all?[5] Yes, think
of the odds! or shrug them off forever.
This luxury of the precocious child,
Time's precious chronic invalid,—
would we, darlings, resign it if we could?
Our blight has been our sinecure:
mere talent was enough for us—
glitter in fragments and rough drafts.

Sigh no more, ladies.[6]
Time is male
and in his cups drinks to the fair.
Bemused by gallantry, we hear
our mediocrities over-praised,
indolence read as abnegation,
slattern thought styled intuition,
every lapse forgiven, our crime
only to cast too bold a shadow
or smash the mould straight off.

4. "Vous mourez toutes a quinze ans," from the *Lettres à Sophie Volland*, quoted by Simone de Beauvoir in *Le Deuxième Sexe*, vol. II, pp. 123–4 [Rich's note]. Editor of the *Encyclopédie* (the central document of the French Enlightenment), Denis Diderot (1713–84) became disillusioned with the traditional education of women and undertook an experimental education for his own daughter. French philosopher Simone de Beauvoir's (1908–86) landmark book, *The Second Sex* (1949), explores what she calls the "myths" and supposed "facts" that have made women "secondary" to men throughout human history.

5. Samuel Johnson's (1709–84) comment on women preachers: "Sir, a woman's preaching is like a dog's walking on his hinder legs. It is not done well, but you are surprised to find it done at all" (James Boswell's *Life of Johnson*, edited by L. F. Powell and G. B. Hill, Clarendon, 1934–64, vol. 1, p. 463).

6. Opening words of a song in Shakespeare's Much Ado about Nothing (Act 2, Scene 3); sung by a minor male character, it explains that "Men were deceivers ever" and urges women to "sigh not so, but let them go, / And be you blithe and bonny."

For that, solitary confinement,
tear gas, attrition shelling.
Few applicants for that honor.

10

Well,
she's long about her coming, who must be
more merciless to herself than history.[7]
Her mind full to the wind, I see her plunge
breasted and glancing through the currents,
taking the light upon her
at least as beautiful as any boy
or helicopter,
poised, still coming,
her fine blades making the air wince

but her cargo
no promise then:
delivered
palpable
ours.

1958–60

AUTHORS ON THEIR WORK

ADRIENNE RICH (1929–2012)

From "When We Dead Awaken" (1979)*

Over two years I wrote a 10-part poem called "Snapshots of a Daughter-in-Law," in a longer, looser mode than I'd ever trusted myself with before. It was an extraordinary relief to write that poem. It strikes me now as too literary, too dependent on allusion; I hadn't found the courage yet to do without authorities, or even to use the pronoun "I"—the woman in the poem is always "she." One section of it, #2, concerns a woman who thinks she is going mad; she is haunted by voices telling her to resist and rebel, voices which she can hear but not obey.

*"When We Dead Awaken: Writing as Re-Vision." *On Lies, Secrets, and Silence: Selected Prose: 1966–1978*, W. W. Norton, 1979, pp. 33–49.

7. Cf. *Le Deuxième See*, vol. II, p. 574: ". . . elle arrive du fond des ages, de Thèbes, de Minos, de Chichen Itza; et elle est aussi le totem planté au coeur de la brousse africaine; c'est un helicoptère et c'est un oiseau; et voilà la plus grande merveille: sous ses cheveux peints le bruissement des feuillages devient une pensée et des paroles s'échappent de ses seins" [Rich's note]. "[S]he comes from the remotest ages, from Thebes, Minos, Chichén Itzá; and she is also the totem planted in the heart of the African jungle; she is a helicopter and she is a bird; and here is the greatest wonder: beneath her painted hair, the rustling of leaves becomes a thought and words escape from her breasts" (Simone de Beauvoir's *The Second Sex*, translated by Constance Borde and Sheila Malovany, Alfred A. Knopf, 2009, p. 764).

Planetarium

(Thinking of Caroline Herschel, 1750–1848, astronomer, sister of William;[8] *and others)*

A woman in the shape of a monster
a monster in the shape of a woman
the skies are full of them

a woman "in the snow
among the Clocks and instruments
or measuring the ground with poles"

in her 98 years to discover
8 comets
she whom the moon ruled
like us
levitating into the night sky
riding the polished lenses
Galaxies of women, there
doing penance for impetuousness
ribs chilled
in those spaces of the mind

An eye,
"virile, precise and absolutely certain"
from the mad webs of Uranisborg[9]
encountering the NOVA
every impulse of light exploding
from the core
as life flies out of us

Tycho whispering at last
"Let me not seem to have lived in vain"[1]

What we see, we see
and seeing is changing

the light that shrivels a mountain
and leaves a man alive

Heartbeat of the pulsar
heart sweating through my body

8. In 1781, William Herschel (1738–1822) became the first astronomer since antiquity to discover a planet, Uranus, earning appointment as court astronomer to King George III, election to the world-famous Royal Society, and a knighthood.

9. Actually Uraniborg, the elaborate palace-laboratory-observatory of Danish astronomer Tycho Brahe (1546–1601), whose cosmology tried to fuse the Ptolemaic and Copernican systems. Brahe discovered and described (in *De nova stella*, 1574) a new star in what had previously been considered a fixed-star system. The quotation is from Brahe.

1. Reportedly Brahe's dying words, spoken to fellow astronomer and mathematician Johannes Kepler (1571–1630).

The radio impulse
pouring in from Taurus
        I am bombarded yet   I stand

I have been standing all my life in the
direct path of a battery of signals
the most accurately transmitted most
untranslatable language in the universe
I am a galactic cloud so deep   so invo-
luted that a light wave could take 15
years to travel through me   And has
taken   I am an instrument in the shape
of a woman trying to translate pulsations
into images   for the relief of the body
and the reconstruction of the mind.

1968

For the Record

The clouds and the stars didn't wage this war
the brooks gave no information
if the mountain spewed stones of fire into the river
it was not taking sides
the raindrop faintly swaying under the leaf
had no political opinions

and if here or there a house
filled with backed-up raw sewage
or poisoned those who lived there
with slow fumes, over years
the houses were not at war
nor did the tinned-up buildings

intend to refuse shelter
to homeless old women and roaming children
they had no policy to keep them roaming
or dying, no, the cities were not the problem
the bridges were non-partisan
the freeways burned, but not with hatred

Even the miles of barbed-wire
stretched around crouching temporary huts
designed to keep the unwanted
at a safe distance, out of sight
even the boards that had to absorb
year upon year, so many human sounds

so many depths of vomit, tears
slow-soaking blood
had not offered themselves for this
The trees didn't volunteer to be cut into boards
nor the thorns for tearing flesh
Look around at all of it

and ask whose signature
is stamped on the orders, traced
in the corner of the building plans
Ask where the illiterate, big-bellied
women were, the drunks and crazies,
the ones you fear most of all: ask where you were.

1983

[My mouth hovers across your breasts][2]

My mouth hovers across your breasts
in the short grey winter afternoon
in this bed   we are delicate
and tough   so hot with joy we amaze ourselves
tough   and delicate   we play rings
around each other   our daytime candle burns
with its peculiar light   and if the snow
begins to fall outside   filling the branches
and if the night falls   without announcement
these are the pleasures of winter
sudden, wild and delicate   your fingers
exact   my tongue exact at the same moment
stopping to laugh at a joke
my love   hot on your scent   on the cusp of winter

1986

History[3]

Should I simplify my life for you?
Don't ask how I began to love men.
Don't ask how I began to love women.
Remember the forties songs, the slowdance numbers
the small sex-filled gas-rationed Chevrolet?
Remember walking in the snow and who was gay?
Cigarette smoke of the movies, silver-and-gray
profiles, dreaming the dreams of he-and-she
breathing the dissolution of the wisping silver plume?
Dreaming that dream we leaned applying lipstick
by the gravestone's mirror when we found ourselves
playing in the cemetery. In Current Events she said
the war in Europe is over, the Allies
and she wore no lipstick have won the war[4]
and we raced screaming out of Sixth Period.

Dreaming that dream
we had to maze our ways through a wood

2. Poem 3 in Rich's sequence "Tracking Poems."

3. Poem 4 in Rich's sequence "Inscriptions."

4. World War II (1939–45), fought between the Allies or Allied powers (including France, Great Britain, the United States, and the Soviet Union) and the Axis powers (Germany, Japan, Italy).

where lips were knives breasts razors and I hid
in the cage of my mind scribbling
this map stops where it all begins
into a red-and-black notebook.
Remember after the war when peace came down
as plenty for some and they said we were saved
in an eternal present and we knew the world could end?
—Remember after the war when peace rained down
on the winds from Hiroshima Nagasaki Utah Nevada?[5]
and the socialist queer Christian teacher jumps from the hotel
window?[6]
and L.G. saying *I want to sleep with you but not for sex*
and the red-and-black enamelled coffee-pot dripped slow through the
dark grounds
—appetite terror power tenderness
the long kiss in the stairwell the switch thrown
on two Jewish Communists[7] married to each other
the definitive crunch of glass at the end of the wedding?[8]
(When shall we learn, what should be clear as day,
We cannot choose what we are free to love?)[9]

1995

Transparencies

That the meek word like the righteous word can bully
that an Israeli soldier interviewed years
after the first Intifada[1] could mourn on camera
what under orders he did, saw done, did not refuse
that another leaving Beit Jala[2] could scrawl
on a wall: *We are truely sorry for the mess we made*
is merely routine   word that would cancel deed
That human equals innocent and guilty
That we grasp for innocence whether or no
is elementary   That words can translate into broken bones
That the power to hurl words is a weapon
That the body can be a weapon
any child on playground knows   That asked your favorite word
in a game
you always named a thing, a quality, *freedom* or *river*
(never a pronoun never *God* or *War*)

5. Sites of atomic bomb explosions, the first two in Japan near the end of World War II, the last two at test sites in the American desert.

6. Allusion to the critic Francis Otto Matthiessen (1902–50), who taught at Harvard while Rich was an undergraduate there.

7. Julius and Ethel Rosenberg, executed as spies by the United States in 1953.

8. At Jewish weddings the groom breaks a glass to commemorate the loss of Jerusalem and the Temple.

9. Opening lines of W. H. Auden's poem "Canzone" (1942).

1. Rebellion (Arabic); specifically, armed uprising of Palestinians against Israeli occupation of the West Bank and Gaza Strip. The first began in 1987.

2. Town in the West Bank of Palestine inhabited mainly by Arab Christians.

is taken for granted   That word and body
are all we have to lay on the line
That words are windowpanes in a ransacked hut, smeared
by time's dirty rains, we might argue
likewise that words are clear as glass till the sun strikes it blinding

But that in a dark windowpane you have seen your face
That when you wipe your glasses the text grows clearer
That the sound of crunching glass comes at the height of the
wedding[3]
That I can look through glass
into my neighbor's house
but not my neighbor's life
That glass is sometimes broken to save lives
That a word can be crushed like a goblet underfoot
is only what it seems, part question, part answer: how
you live it

2002 2004

Tonight No Poetry Will Serve

Saw you walking barefoot
taking a long look
at the new moon's eyelid

later spread
sleep-fallen, naked in your dark hair
asleep but not oblivious
of the unslept unsleeping
elsewhere

Tonight I think
no poetry
will serve

Syntax of rendition:[4]

verb pilots the plane
adverb modifies action

verb force-feeds noun
submerges the subject
noun is choking
verb   disgraced   goes on doing

now diagram the sentence

2007 2011

3. At Jewish weddings the groom breaks a glass to commemorate the loss of Jerusalem and the Temple.

4. Perhaps an allusion to the practice of "extraordinary rendition"—transporting those suspected of terrorism or other crimes to other countries, including those which condone torture.

PASSAGES FROM RICH'S ESSAYS

From When We Dead Awaken: Writing as Re-Vision (1972, 1979)[5]

Most, if not all, human lives are full of fantasy—passive daydreaming which need not be acted on. But to write poetry or fiction, or even to think well, is not to fantasize, or to put fantasies on paper. For a poem to coalesce, for a character or an action to take shape, there has to be an imaginative transformation of reality which is in no way passive. And a certain freedom of the mind is needed—freedom to press on, to enter the currents of your thought like a glider pilot, knowing that your motion can be sustained, that the buoyancy of your attention will not be suddenly snatched away. Moreover, if the imagination is to transcend and transform experience it has to question, to challenge, to conceive of alternatives, perhaps to the very life you are living at that moment. You have to be free to play around with the notion that day might be night, love might be hate; nothing can be too sacred for the imagination to turn into its opposite or to call experimentally by another name. For writing is re-naming. Now, to be maternally with small children all day in the old way, to be with a man in the old way of marriage, requires a holding-back, a putting-aside of that imaginative activity, and demands instead a kind of conservatism. I want to make it clear that I am *not* saying that in order to write well, or think well, it is necessary to become unavailable to others, or to become a devouring ego. This has been the myth of the masculine artist and thinker; and I do not accept it. But to be a female human being trying to fulfill traditional female functions in a traditional way *is* in direct conflict with the subversive function of the imagination. The word traditional is important here. There must be ways, and we will be finding out more and more about them, in which the energy of creation and the energy of relation can be united. But in those earlier years I always felt the conflict as a failure of love in myself. I had thought I was choosing a full life: the life available to most men, in which sexuality, work, and parenthood could coexist. But I felt, at twenty-nine, guilt toward the people closest to me, and guilty toward my own being.

Adrienne Rich, circa 1978

I wanted, then, more than anything, the one thing of which there was never enough: time to think, time to write. The fifties and early sixties were years of rapid revelations: the sit-ins and marches in the South, the Bay of Pigs, the early antiwar movement,[6] raised large questions—questions for which the masculine world of the academy around me seemed to have expert and fluent answers. But I needed to think for myself—about pacifism

5. First published in *College English* in 1972; this version, slightly revised, is included in *On Lies, Secrets, and Silence: Selected Prose: 1966–1978*, W. W. Norton, 1979, pp. 33–49.

6. That is, the movement opposing the Vietnam War (c. 1955–75). *Bay of Pigs*: on April 17, 1961, 1,400 Cuban exiles, backed by the CIA, launched a botched invasion of Communist Cuba at the Bay of Pigs, on the island's south coast.

and dissent and violence, about poetry and society, and about my own relationship to all these things. For about ten years I was reading in fierce snatches, scribbling in notebooks, writing poetry in fragments; I was looking desperately for clues, because if there were no clues then I thought I might be insane. I wrote in a notebook about this time:

> Paralyzed by the sense that there exists a mesh of relationships—e.g., between my anger at the children, my sensual life, pacifism, sex (I mean sex in its broadest significance, not merely sexual desire)—an interconnectedness which, if I could see it, make it valid, would give me back myself, make it possible to function lucidly and passionately. Yet I grope in and out among these dark webs.

I think I began at this point to feel that politics was not something "out there" but something "in here" and of the essence of my condition.

In the late fifties I was able to write, for the first time, directly about experiencing myself as a woman. The poem[7] was jotted in fragments during children's naps, brief hours in a library, or at 3 A.M. after rising with a wakeful child. I despaired of doing any continuous work at this time. Yet I began to feel that my fragments and scraps had a common consciousness and a common theme, one which I would have been very unwilling to put on paper at an earlier time because I had been taught that poetry should be "universal," which meant, of course, nonfemale. Until then I had tried very much *not* to identify myself as a female poet.

From A Communal Poetry (1993)[8]

One day in New York in the late 1980s, I had lunch with a poet I'd known for more than twenty years. Many of his poems were—are—embedded in my life. We had read together at the antiwar events of the Vietnam years.[9] Then, for a long time, we hardly met. As a friend, he had seemed to me withheld, defended in a certain way I defined as masculine and with which I was becoming in general impatient; yet often, in their painful beauty, his poems told another story. On this day, he was as I had remembered him: distant, stiff, shy perhaps. The conversation stumbled along as we talked about our experiences with teaching poetry, which seemed a safe ground. I made some remark about how long it was since last we'd talked. Suddenly, his whole manner changed: *You disappeared! You simply disappeared.* I realized he meant not so much from his life as from a landscape of poetry to which he thought we both belonged and were in some sense loyal.

If anything, those intervening years had made me feel more apparent, more visible—to myself and to others—as a poet. The powerful magnet of the women's liberation movement—and the women's poetry movement it released—had drawn me to coffeehouses where women were reading new kinds of poems; to emerging "journals of liberation" that published women's poems, often in a con-

7. "Snapshots of a Daughter-in-Law" (above).

8. "A Communal Poetry." *What Is Found There: Notebooks on Poetry and Politics*, W. W. Norton, 1993, pp. 164–80. 9. Circa 1955–75.

Adrienne Rich, 1990s

text of political articles and the beginnings of feminist criticism; to bookstores selling chapbooks and pamphlets from the new women's presses; to a woman poet's workshops with women in prison; to meetings with other women poets in Chinese restaurants, coffee shops, apartments, where we talked not only of poetry, but of the conditions that make it possible or impossible. It had never occurred to me that I was disappearing—rather, that I was, along with other women poets, beginning to appear. In fact, we were taking part in an immense shift in human consciousness.

My old friend had, I believe, not much awareness of any of this. It was, for him, so off-to-the-edge, so out-of-the-way; perhaps so dangerous, it seemed I had sunk, or dived, into a black hole. Only later, in a less constrained and happier meeting, were we able to speak of the different ways we had perceived that time.

He thought there had been a known, defined poetic landscape and that as poetic contemporaries we simply shared it. But whatever poetic "generation" I belonged to, in the 1950s I was a mother, under thirty, raising three small children. Notwithstanding the prize and the fellowship to Europe that my first book of poems had won me,[1] there was little or no "appearance" I then felt able to claim as a poet, against that other profound and as yet unworded reality.

From Why I Refused the National Medal for the Arts (2001)[2]

July 3, 1997
Jane Alexander, Chair
The National Endowment for the Arts
1100 Pennsylvania Avenue
Washington, D.C. 20506
Dear Jane Alexander,

I just spoke with a young man from your office, who informed me that I had been chosen to be one of twelve recipients of the National Medal for the Arts at a ceremony at the White House in the fall. I told him at once that I could not accept such an award from President Clinton or this White House because the very meaning of art, as I understand it, is incompatible with the cynical politics of this administration. I want to clarify to you what I meant by my refusal.

1. Rich won the Yale Younger Poets Prize in 1951 and traveled on a Guggenheim Fellowship 1952–53.
2. "Why I Refused the National Medal for the Arts." *Arts of the Possible: Essays and Conversations*, W. W. Norton, 2001, pp. 98–105.

After the text of my letter to Jane Alexander, then chair of the National Endowment for the Arts, had been fragmentarily quoted in various news stories, Steve Wasserman, editor of the *Los Angeles Times Book Review*, asked me for an article expanding on my reasons. Herewith the letter and the article [Rich's note].

Anyone familiar with my work from the early sixties on knows that I believe in art's social presence—as breaker of official silences, as voice for those whose voices are disregarded, and as a human birthright. In my lifetime I have seen the space for the arts opened by movements for social justice, the power of art to break despair. Over the past two decades I have witnessed the increasingly brutal impact of racial and economic injustice in our country.

There is no simple formula for the relationship of art to justice. But I do know that art—in my own case the art of poetry—means nothing if it simply decorates the dinner table of power that holds it hostage. The radical disparities of wealth and power in America are widening at a devastating rate. A president cannot meaningfully honor certain token artists while the people at large are so dishonored.

I know you have been engaged in a serious and disheartening struggle to save government funding for the arts, against those whose fear and suspicion of art is nakedly repressive. In the end, I don't think we can separate art from overall human dignity and hope. My concern for my country is inextricable from my concerns as an artist. I could not participate in a ritual that would feel so hypocritical to me.

Sincerely,
Adrienne Rich

cc: President Clinton

The invitation from the White House came by telephone on July 3. After several years' erosion of arts funding and hostile propaganda from the religious right and the Republican Congress, the House vote to end the National Endowment for the Arts was looming. That vote would break as news on July 10; my refusal of the National Medal for the Arts would run as a sidebar story in the *New York Times* and the *San Francisco Chronicle.*

In fact, I was unaware of the timing. My refusal came directly out of my work as a poet and essayist and citizen drawn to the interfold of personal and public experience. I had recently been thinking and writing about the shrinking of the social compact, of whatever it was this country had ever meant when it called itself a democracy: the shredding of the vision of *government of the people, by the people, for the people.*

"We the people—still an excellent phrase," said the playwright Lorraine Hansberry in 1962, well aware who had been excluded, yet believing the phrase might someday come to embrace us all. And I had for years been feeling both personal and public grief, fear, hunger, and the need to render this, my time, in the language of my art.

Whatever was "newsworthy" about my refusal was not about a single individual—not myself, not President Clinton. Nor was it about a single political party. Both major parties have displayed a crude affinity for the interests of corporate power, while deserting the majority of the people, especially the most vulnerable. Like so many others, I've watched the dismantling of our public education, the steep rise in our incarceration rates, the demonization of our young black men, the accusations against our teen-age mothers, the selling of health care—public and private—to the highest bidders, the export of subsistence-level jobs in the United States to even lower-wage countries, the use of below-minimum-wage prison labor to break strikes and raise profits, the scapegoating of immigrants, the denial of dignity and minimal security to working and poor people. At the same time, we've witnessed the acquisition of publishing houses, once risk-taking conduits of creativity, by conglomerates driven single-mindedly to fast profits, the acquisition of major communications and media by those same interests, the sacrifice of the arts and public libraries in stripped-down school and civic budgets, and, most recently, the evisceration of the National Endowment for the Arts. Piece by piece the democratic process has been losing ground to the accumulation of private wealth.

There is no political leadership in the White House or the Congress that has spoken to and for the people who, in a very real sense, have felt abandoned by their government.

• • •

And what about art? Mistrusted, adored, pietized, condemned, dismissed as entertainment, commodified, auctioned at Sotheby's, purchased by investment-seeking celebrities, it dies into the "art object" of a thousand museum basements. It's also reborn hourly in prisons, women's shelters, small-town garages, community-college workshops, halfway houses, wherever someone picks up a pencil, a wood-burning tool, a copy of *The Tempest*,[3] a tag-sale camera, a whittling knife, a stick of charcoal, a pawnshop horn, a video of *Citizen Kane*,[4] whatever lets you know again that this deeply instinctual yet self-conscious expressive language, this regenerative process, could help you save your life. "If there were no poetry on any day in the world," the poet Muriel Rukeyser wrote, "poetry would be invented that day. For there would be an intolerable hunger."

• • •

Art can never be totally legislated by any system, even those that reward obedience and send dissident artists to hard labor and death; nor can it, in our specifically compromised system, be really free. It may push up through cracked macadam, by the merest means, but it needs breathing space, cultivation, protection to fulfill itself. Just as people do. New artists, young or old, need education in their art, the tools of their craft, chances to study examples from the past and meet practitioners in the present, get the criticism and encouragement of mentors, learn that they are not alone. As the social compact withers, fewer and fewer people will be told *Yes, you can do this; this also belongs to you.* Like government, art needs the participation of the many in order not to become the property of a powerful and narrowly self-interested few.

Art is our human birthright, our most powerful means of access to our own and another's experience and imaginative life. In continually rediscovering and

3. Very late Shakespeare play about the exiled Duke of Milan, a magician; widely regarded as the playwright's dramatic exploration of his own art.

4. Celebrated 1941 film about an unscrupulous publishing tycoon very loosely based on American newspaper magnate William Randolph Hearst (1863–1951).

recovering the humanity of human beings, art is crucial to the democratic vision. A government tending further and further away from the search for democracy will see less and less "use" in encouraging artists, will see art as obscenity or hoax.

* * *

Federal funding for the arts, like the philanthropy of private arts patrons, can be given and taken away. In the long run art needs to grow organically out of a social compost nourishing to everyone, a literate citizenry, a free, universal, public education complex with art as an integral element, a society honoring both human individuality and the search for a decent, sustainable common life. In such conditions, art would still be a voice of hunger, desire, discontent, passion, reminding us that the democratic project is never-ending.

Adrienne Rich, 2006

For that to happen, what else would have to change?

From Poetry and the Forgotten Future (2006)[5]

2

What I'd like to do here is touch on some aspects of poetry as it's created and received in [a] violently politicized and brutally divided world [. . .] .

I'll flash back to 1821: Shelley's[6] claim, in "The Defence of Poetry," that "poets are the unacknowledged legislators of the world." Piously overquoted, mostly out of context, it's taken to suggest that simply by virtue of composing verse, poets exert some exemplary moral power—in a vague, unthreatening way. In fact, in his earlier political essay "A Philosophic View of Reform," Shelley had written that "Poets *and philosophers* [italics mine] are the unacknowledged" etc. The philosophers he was talking about were revolutionary-minded: Thomas Paine, William Godwin, Voltaire, Mary Wollstonecraft.[7]

And Shelley was, no mistake, out to change the legislation of his time. For him there was no contradiction among poetry, political philosophy, and active confrontation with illegitimate authority [. . .] .

5. Plenary Lecture, Conference on Poetry and Politics, University of Stirring, Scotland, July 13, 2006. First published in 2007 as *Poetry and Commitment*, a chapbook, by W. W. Norton. Here taken from *A Human Eye: Essays on Art in Society, 1997–2008*, W. W. Norton, 2009, pp. 126–46.

6. Percy Bysshe Shelley, British poet (1792–1822).

7. British author (1759–97) whose works include both *A Vindication of the Rights of Men* (1790) and *A Vindication of the Rights of Woman* (1792); Wollstonecraft's daughter (by William Godwin) married Percy Bysshe Shelley. *Voltaire*: French Enlightenment philosopher (1694–78). *William Godwin*: Radical British philosopher (1756–1836) whose works include *An Enquiry Concerning Political Justice* (1793), also husband and first biographer of Mary Wollstonecraft. *Thomas Paine*: British-born author (1737–1809) of both *Common Sense* (1776) and *Rights of Man* (1791).

Shelley, in fact, saw powerful institutions, not original sin or "human nature," as the source of human misery. For him, art bore an integral relationship to the "struggle between Revolution and Oppression." His West Wind was the "trumpet of a prophecy," driving "dead thoughts . . . like withered leaves, to quicken a new birth."[8]

He did *not* say, "Poets are the unacknowledged interior decorators of the world."

3

Pursuing this theme of the committed poet and the action of poetry in the world: two interviews, both from 1970.

A high official of the Greek military junta asks the poet Yannis Ritsos, then under house arrest: "You are a poet. Why do you get mixed up in politics?"

Ritsos answers, "A poet is the first citizen of his country and for this very reason it is the duty of the poet to be concerned about the politics of his country."

• • •

Second interview. The South African poet Dennis Brutus, when asked about poetry and political activity: "I believe that the poet—as a poet—has no obligation to be committed, but the man—as a man—has an obligation to be committed. What I'm saying is that I think everybody ought to be committed and the poet is just one of the many 'everybodies.'"

Dennis Brutus wrote, acted on, was imprisoned then exiled for his opposition to the South African apartheid[9] regime [. . .].

What's at stake here is the recognition of poetry as what James Scully calls "social practice." He distinguishes between "protest poetry" and "dissident poetry": Protest poetry is "conceptually shallow," "reactive," predictable in its means, too often a hand-wringing from the sidelines.

> Dissident poetry, however [he writes] does not respect boundaries between private and public, self and other. In breaking boundaries, it breaks silences, speaking for, or at best, with, the silenced; opening poetry up, putting it into the middle of life. . . . It is a poetry that talks back, that would act as part of the world, not simply as a mirror of it.

4

I'm both a poet and one of the "everybodies" of my country. I live, in poetry and daily experience, with manipulated fear, ignorance, cultural confusion, and social antagonism huddling together on the fault line of an empire. In my lifetime I've seen the breakdown of rights and citizenship where ordinary "everybodies," poets or not, have left politics to a political class bent on shoveling the elemental resources, the public commons of the entire world, into private control. Where democracy has been left to the raiding of "acknowledged" legislators, the highest bidders. In short, to a criminal element.

Ordinary, comfortable Americans have looked aside when our fraternally-twinned parties—Democrat and Republican—have backed dictatorships against

8. See Shelley's "Ode to the West Wind" in this volume.

9. Literally, "apartness" (Afrikaans); system of legalized racial segregation practiced in South Africa from 1948 until 1991.

popular movements abroad; as their covert agencies, through torture and assassination, through supplied weapons and military training, have propped up repressive parties and regimes in the name of anticommunism and our "national interests." Why did we think fascistic methods, the subversion of civil and human rights, would be contained somewhere else? Because as a nation, we've clung to a self-righteous false innocence, eyes shut to our own scenario, our body politic's internal bleeding.

But internal bleeding is no sudden symptom. That uncannily prescient African American writer James Baldwin asked his country, a quarter century ago: "If you don't know my father, how can you know the people in the streets of Tehran?"[1]

This year, a report from the Bureau of Justice Statistics finds that 1 out of every 136 residents of the United States is behind bars: many in jails, unconvicted. That the percentage of black men in prison or jail is almost 12 to 1 over white male prisoners. That the states with the highest rates of incarceration and execution are those with the poorest populations.

We often hear that—by contrast with, say, Nigeria or Egypt, China or the former Soviet Union—the West doesn't imprison dissident writers. But when a nation's criminal justice system imprisons so many—often on tawdry evidence and botched due process—to be tortured in maximum security units or on death row, overwhelmingly because of color and class, it is in effect—and intention—silencing potential and actual writers, intellectuals, artists, journalists: a whole intelligentsia. The internationally known case of Mumia Abu-Jamal[2] is emblematic but hardly unique. The methods of Abu Ghraib and Guantánamo[3] have long been practiced in the prisons and policing of the United States.

What has all this to do with poetry? [. . .]

[. . . L]et's never discount it—within every official, statistical, designated nation, there breathes another nation: of unappointed, unappeased, unacknowledged clusters of people who daily, with fierce imagination and tenacity, confront cruelties, exclusions, and indignities, signaling through those carriers—which are often literal cages—in poetry, music, street theater, murals, videos, Web sites—and through many forms of direct activism.

• • •

5

I hope never to idealize poetry—it has suffered enough from that. Poetry is not a healing lotion, an emotional massage, a kind of linguistic aromatherapy. Neither is it a blueprint, nor an instruction manual, nor a billboard [. . .] .

Walt Whitman never separated his poetry from his vision of American democracy—a vision severely tested in a Civil War fought over the economics of slavery. Late in life he called "poetic lore [. . .] a conversation overheard in the

1. Capital of Iran.
2. African American activist and radio journalist (b. 1954) sentenced to death in 1982 for the murder of a Philadelphia police officer; many believe Abu-Jamal was wrongfully convicted.
3. Prisons in Iraq and Cuba, respectively. Established by the United States in 2002, the Guantánamo Bay Detention Camp houses prisoners of war, mainly from Afghanistan. Between 2004 and 2006, several U.S. soldiers were convicted of torturing inmates of Abu Ghraib while that facility was under the joint control of U.S. and Iraqi forces (2003–06).

dusk, from speakers far or hid, of which we get only a few broken murmurs"—the obscurity, we might think now, of democracy itself.

But also of those "dark times" in and about which Bertolt Brecht[4] assured us there would be songs.

Poetry has been charged with "aestheticizing," thus being complicit in, the violent realities of power, of practices like collective punishment, torture, rape, and genocide. This accusation was famously invoked in Adorno's[5] "after the Holocaust lyric poetry is impossible"—which Adorno later retracted and which a succession of Jewish poets have in their practice rejected [. . .] .

• • •

If to "aestheticize" is to glide across brutality and cruelty, treat them merely as dramatic occasions for the artist rather than structures of power to be revealed and dismantled—much hangs on the words "merely" and "rather than." Opportunism isn't the same as committed attention. But we can also define the "aesthetic" not as a privileged and sequestered rendering of human suffering, but as news of an awareness, a resistance, that totalizing systems want to quell: art reaching into us for what's still passionate, still unintimidated, still unquenched.

Poetry has been written off on other counts: (1) it's not a mass-market "product": it doesn't get sold on airport newsstands or in supermarket aisles; (2) the actual consumption figures for poetry can't be quantified at the checkout counter; (3) it's too "difficult" for the average mind; (4) it's too elite, but the wealthy don't bid for it at Sotheby's. It is, in short, redundant. This might be called the free-market critique of poetry.

There's actually an odd correlation between these ideas: poetry is either inadequate, even immoral, in the face of human suffering, or it's unprofitable, hence useless. Either way, poets are advised to hang our heads or fold our tents. Yet in fact, throughout the world, transfusions of poetic language can and do quite literally keep bodies and souls together—and more.

• • •

7

[. . .] Poetry has the capacity—in its own ways and by its own means—to remind us of something we are forbidden to see. A forgotten future: a still-uncreated site whose moral architecture is founded not on ownership and dispossession, the subjection of women, torture and bribes, outcast and tribe, but on the continuous redefining of freedom—that word now held under house arrest by the rhetoric of the "free" market. This ongoing future, written off over and over, is still within view. All over the world its paths are being rediscovered and reinvented: through collective action, through many kinds of art. Its elementary condition is the recovery and redistribution of the world's resources that have been extracted from the many by the few.

• • •

4. In "Motto," the German poet and playwright (1898–1956) asks, "In dark times, will there also be singing?" And he answers, "yes, there will be singing. About the dark times."

5. German philosopher Theodor Adorno (1903–69).

Finally: there is always that in poetry which will not be grasped, which cannot be described, which survives our ardent attention, our critical theories, our classrooms, our late-night arguments. There is always (I am quoting the poet/translator Américo Ferrari) "an unspeakable where, perhaps, the nucleus of the living relation between the poem and the world resides."

The living relation between the poem and the world: difficult knowledge, operating theater where the poet, committed, goes on working.

BIBLIOGRAPHY[6]

Brutus, Dennis. *Poetry and Protest: A Dennis Brutus Reader.* Ed. Lee Sustar and Aisha Karim. Chicago: Haymarket, 2006.

Franklin, H. Bruce. "The American Prison and the Normalization of Torture." historiansagainstwar.org/resources/torture/brucefranklin.html

Holmes, Richard. *Shelley: The Pursuit.* New ed. New York: New York Review of Books, 2003.

Ritsos, Yannis. *Yannis Ritsos, Selected Poems 1938–1988.* Ed. and trans. Kimon Friar and Kostas Myrsiades. Brockport, NY: BOA, 1989.

Scully, James. *Line Break: Poetry as Social Practice.* Foreword by Adrienne Rich. Willimantic, CT: Curbstone, 2005.

Vallejo, César. *Trilce.* Trans. Clayton Eshleman. Intro. by Américo Ferrari. New York: Marsilio, 1992.

White, Elizabeth. "1 in 136 U.S. Residents Behind Bars: U.S. Prisons, Jails Grew by 1,000 Inmates a Week from '04 to '05." Associated Press (22 May 2006).

Whitman, Walt. *Walt Whitman: Complete Poetry and Collected Prose.* Ed. Justin Kaplan. New York: Library of America, 1982.

Chronology

1929 Born in Baltimore, Maryland, May 16. Begins writing poetry as a child with the encouragement of her father, Dr. Arnold Rich.

1951 AB, Radcliffe College. *A Change of World* chosen by poet W. H. Auden for publication in the Yale Younger Poets series.

1952–53 Guggenheim Fellowship; travel in Europe and England. Marriage to Alfred H. Conrad, a Harvard economist.

1955 Birth of David Conrad. Publication of *The Diamond Cutters and Other Poems.*

1957 Birth of Paul Conrad.

1959 Birth of Jacob Conrad.

1960 National Institute of Arts and Letters Award for poetry.

1961–62 Guggenheim Fellowship; residence with family in the Netherlands.

1962–63 Amy Lowell Travelling Fellowship.

1963 *Snapshots of a Daughter-in-Law* published. Bess Hokin Prize of *Poetry* magazine.

6. Rich's bibliography has been abbreviated to include only works to which these excerpts from her lecture allude.

1966	*Necessities of Life* published. Moves to New York City and becomes increasingly active in protests against the war in Vietnam.
1966–68	Lecturer at Swarthmore College.
1967–69	Adjunct Professor of Writing in the Graduate School of the Arts, Columbia University.
1968	Begins teaching in the SEEK and Open Admissions Programs at City College of New York.
1969	*Leaflets* published.
1970	Death of Alfred Conrad.
1971	*The Will to Change* published. Increasingly active in the women's movement.
1972–73	Fannie Hurst Visiting Professor of Creative Literature at Brandeis University.
1973	*Diving into the Wreck* published.
1974	National Book Award for *Diving into the Wreck.* Rich rejects the award as an individual, but accepts it, in a statement written with fellow nominees Audre Lorde and Alice Walker, in the name of all women. Professor of English, City College of New York.
1975	*Poems: Selected and New* published.
1976	Professor of English at Douglass College. *Of Woman Born: Motherhood as Experience and Institution* and *Twenty-one Love Poems* published.
1978	*The Dream of a Common Language: Poems 1974–1977* published.
1979	*On Lies, Secrets, and Silence: Selected Prose 1966–1978* published. Moves to Montague, Massachusetts; edits, with Michelle Cliff, the lesbian-feminist journal *Sinister Wisdom.*
1981	*A Wild Patience Has Taken Me This Far: Poems 1978–1981* published.
1984	*The Fact of a Doorframe: Poems Selected and New 1950–1984* published. Moves to Santa Cruz, California and becomes Professor of English, San Jose State University.
1986	*Blood, Bread, and Poetry: Selected Prose 1979–1985* published. Professor of English, Stanford University.
1989	*Time's Power: Poems 1985–1988* published.
1991	*An Atlas of the Difficult World: Poems 1988–1991* published.
1992	Wins *Los Angeles Times* Book Prize for *An Atlas of the Difficult World: Poems 1988–1991*, the Lenore Marshall/*Nation* Prize for Poetry, and the Nicholas Roerich Museum Poet's Prize; is co-winner of the Frost Silver Medal for distinguished lifetime achievement.
1993	*What Is Found There: Notebooks on Poetry and Politics* published.
1994	Awarded MacArthur fellowship.
1995	*Dark Fields of the Republic: Poems 1991–1995* published.
1996	Awarded the Academy of American Poets (AAP) Dorothea Tanning Prize.
1997	Refuses the National Medal for the Arts on political grounds and wins the AAP's Wallace Stevens Award.
1999	Elected a chancellor of the AAP. Receives Lannan Foundation's Life-time Achievement Award. *Midnight Salvage: Poems 1995–1998* published.

2001 *Fox: Poems 1998–2000* and *Arts of the Possible: Essays and Conversations* published.

2002 *The Fact of a Doorframe: Poems Selected and New 1950–2000* published.

2004 *The School among the Ruins: Poems 2000–2004* published and awarded Book Critics Circle Award.

2006 Awarded the National Book Foundation's Medal for Distinguished Contribution to American Letters.

2007 *Telephone Ringing in the Labyrinth: Poems 2004–2006* and (with Mark Doty) *Poetry and Commitment* published.

2009 *A Human Eye: Essays on Art in Society, 1997–2008* published.

2010 *Tonight No Poetry Will Serve: Poems 2007–2010* published.

2012 Dies at age eighty-two, of complications from rheumatoid arthritis.

SUGGESTIONS FOR WRITING

1. In her 1951 poem At a Bach Concert, Adrienne Rich writes that "Form is the ultimate gift that love can offer" (line 7). What, exactly, is the case for the "discipline" of formal art argued by this poem (line 4)? How does Rich's later work both embody and reject formalism? Considering as evidence the selections of Rich's poetry and prose in this and previous chapters, write an essay in which you discuss how Rich's thoughts about formality and form evolved throughout her career.
2. Carefully considering plot, characterization, and structure, write an essay in which you detail the ways Diving into the Wreck is and is not typical of Rich's work.
3. In poems such as Snapshots of a Daughter-in-Law and Planetarium, Rich considers the creative accomplishments of women throughout history. What role do these women play in Rich's poetry, separately and together? How is that role both constrained and unconstrained by their gender? Write an essay in which you examine the way Rich portrays creative women. Are they role models in her work, or something else?
4. Rich once said of her college days in the late 1940s,

   > I had no political ideas of my own, only the era's vague and hallucinatory anti-Communism and the encroaching privatism of the 1950s. Drenched in invisible assumptions of my class and race, unable to fathom the pervasive ideology of gender, I felt "politics" as distant, vaguely sinister, the province of powerful older men or of people I saw as fanatics. It was in poetry that I sought a grasp on the world and on interior events, "ideas of order," even power.

   Using the poems by Rich included in this anthology, write an essay that charts the development of the poet's political consciousness.

5. In the prose writings excerpted in this chapter, Rich describes and defends the political passions that, she says, animate her life as an artist. How fully do Rich's poems embody her political beliefs, particularly her commitment to feminism? Write an essay in which you explore Rich's poetry in light of her feminist politics.
6. Choose two or more poems in this book by one author, and write an essay in which you draw on those poems to demonstrate either the distinctive, characteristic qualities and features of that author's work or the way your understanding of one poem by the author is altered or enhanced when you read it in conjunction with the other poem or poems.

SAMPLE WRITING: COMPARATIVE ESSAY

The student essay below was written in response to the following assignment (a more elaborate version of the last writing suggestion in ch. 22):

> Your second essay for the course should be 6–9 pages long and should analyze two or more poems included in *The Norton Introduction to Literature.* The poems must be by the same author.
>
> You are *strongly* encouraged to pay attention to how the poems' meaning and effect are shaped by some aspect or aspects of their form. Those aspects might include specific formal features such as rhyme, meter, alliteration, or assonance, and/or external form or subgenre—the fact that a poem is a Shakespearean or Petrarchan sonnet, a haiku, or a dramatic monologue, for example. (In terms of the latter, you might consider how the poem's effect and meaning are shaped by the very fact that it takes a particular form.)

In her essay, student writer Melissa Makolin draws on three sonnets by William Shakespeare to argue for the distinctiveness and radicalism of the views expressed in two sonnets by another author, Edna St. Vincent Millay. In a sense, then, Makolin's essay focuses simultaneously on external form (ch. 20) and the author's work (ch. 22), even as it explores gender ("Exploring Gender: An Album") and engages in a kind of feminist criticism (see "Critical Approaches"). That's a lot to tackle in a relatively short essay, and you will no doubt find things both to admire and to criticize about Makolin's argument. At what points do you find yourself agreeing with her interpretation? disagreeing? wanting more evidence or more analysis of the evidence provided? more contextual information—about literary tradition, the author, or historical and cultural context? Where and how might the essay's logic seem faulty or its claims contradictory? In the end, what might you take away from this sample essay about how to craft an effective, persuasive argument about an author's work?

Makolin 1

Melissa Makolin
Dr. Mays
English 298X
15 February 2017

Out-Sonneting Shakespeare: An Examination of
Edna St. Vincent Millay's Use of the Sonnet Form

Edna St. Vincent Millay is known not only for her poetry, but also for the feminist ideals she represents therein. She was an extremely talented poet who turned the sonnet form on its head, using the traditionally restrictive form previously used almost exclusively by male poets to express feminist ideas that were radical for her time. Sonnets, especially as written by Shakespeare and Petrarch, are often about the physical beauty of an idealized but also objectified woman, and they implicitly emphasize the man's dominance over her. Millay uses the sonnet form to assert a much different view of femininity, sexuality, and biological dominance. She uses a form known for its poetic limitations to reject social limitations. She uses a form previously used to objectify women to portray them as sexual beings with power and control over their own bodies and lives. The paradox of Millay's poetry is that she uses a poetically binding, male-dominated form to show that she will not be bound either by literary tradition or societal mores regarding inter-gender relations.

The idea of a woman seeking physical pleasure in defiance of societal constraints is one that was revolutionary when "Women have loved before as I love now" and "I, being born a woman and distressed" were published, in 1931 and 1923 respectively. They are poems about a woman's lust leading her to select a sexual partner based on her physical needs rather than on the desire for love. This is a concept that Shakespeare would have found very contentious for three reasons. First, Shakespeare did not agree with acting on lust of any kind; in fact, this is the topic of his sonnet "Th' expense of spirit in a waste of shame." It is a fourteen-line treatise on the evils that result from acting on lustful urges in which Shakespeare declares,

> Th'expense of spirit in a waste of shame
> Is lust in action; and, till action, lust
> Is perjured, murderous, bloody, full of blame,
> Savage, extreme, rude, cruel, not to trust. (lines 1-4)

Lust, sexual or otherwise, is a pathway to a hell both religious and secular. Seventeenth-century society dramatically constricted the liberties of women in particular and didn't encourage sexual freedom for either gender.

Second, the majority of Shakespeare's sonnets simultaneously idealize and trivialize the two things they celebrate: women and love. In poems such as "My mistress' eyes are nothing like the sun," he treats women either as objects of an

Makolin 2

ordered, almost courtly love or as objects of mild ridicule. In this poem's first twelve lines, he mocks his mistress by describing her halitosis (7-8), referring to her breasts as "dun" (3) and her hair as "black wires" (4), references to all the contemporary conventions of beauty to which she does not conform. He not only tells her what the ideal of feminine beauty is, but also makes light of the various ways in which she does not live up to it. He justifies these hurtful insults by reassuring the poor woman that she is "as rare / As any she belied with false compare" (13-14). He mocks her appearance by telling her that she is special and beautiful in her own way only because he loves her. Insulting someone, breaking down her self-esteem, and convincing her that she could be loved by no one else are tactics used in abusive relationships to subjugate one's partner. This is not love, and the role of women in the traditional Shakespeare sonnet is far from empowered.

Third and finally, in addition to idealizing while simultaneously trivializing women, Shakespeare's sonnets also demean the concept of love. To Shakespeare, a woman is worthy of love either because she is an ideal of physical beauty or because he is noble enough to love her despite her flaws (as in "My mistress' eyes are nothing like the sun"). He takes this warped concept one step further, though, by creating an ideal of love that is egotistical and unhealthy for both parties. In "Shall I compare thee to a summer's day?," he spends the first twelve lines describing the ways in which this particular woman fulfills the contemporary ideals of beauty. It is clear that he ardently reveres her physical appearance, and the poem ends with the kind of declaration of personal devotion consistent with love. The turn, however, exhibits a malignant narcissism when it reassures the beloved that "So long as men can breathe or eyes can see, / So long lives this, and this gives life to thee" (13-14). The object of the speaker's affection is just that, an object that only exists as an appendage to him. Shakespeare makes it clear that it is only because of his poetic greatness that their love will persist through the ages. He uses the poetic form to relegate women to the position of objects.

The sonnets of Edna St. Vincent Millay use Shakespearean and Petrarchan forms to offer quite a different view of the role of women. She sees herself as a liberated woman, and she is not afraid to defy social conventions by taking lovers and discarding them when necessary. In writing sonnets about actively satisfying her lust, she also defies literary conventions, completely changing the male-female power dynamic of past sonnets by male writers. In "Women have loved before as I love now," Millay discusses how women throughout history have felt the same lust that she feels, but unlike other more timid and traditional women, she is willing to join the ranks of the brave women of antiquity and to satisfy her passions despite the potential cost. This poem celebrates the women who choose to act against the standards set for them. Describing them as "treacherous queens, with death upon the tread, / Heedless and wilful, [who] took their knights to bed" makes them sound heroic, and it shifts control in the

Makolin 3

sexual relationship from the man to the woman (13-14). In Millay's version, the women sexually dominate the men and temporarily free themselves from the constraints of an oppressive society. Further, by alluding to the famous females of the "lively chronicles of the past" (2), she shows not only that this behavior is natural and heroic, but also that it is historically valid. The specific women she alludes to when referring to "Irish waters by a Cornish prow" (3) and "Trojan waters by a Spartan mast" (4) are respectively Iseult, the adulteress of the classic work of medieval passion *The Romance of Tristan and Iseult*, and Helen of Troy (or any of the other libidinous women) of the Homeric epics.

The fact that Millay uses the sonnet form to illustrate sexual liberation is significant for several reasons. First, it shows that she understands the restrictions placed upon her, both as a poet and as a woman. Second, using the sonnet shows that she can hold her own against the great male poets and write within the boundaries that they have erected; the subject matter of her poetry shows that she chooses not to. Lastly, it is significant because, in using the sonnet form for her own feminist purposes, she directly confronts Shakespeare's one-dimensional portrayal of women by proposing her own view of ideal femininity.

The second of Edna St. Vincent Millay's sonnets that defies the ideals set forth by Shakespeare is "I, being born a woman and distressed." It is a poem about impermanent lust, not eternal love. The speaker tells her lover that her feelings are purely physical ("a certain zest / To bear your body's weight upon breast," 4-5) and simply arise out of human biology ("the needs and notions of my kind," 2) and close quarters ("propinquity," 3). Emotional and physical needs are two things which need not be dependent on each other, and temporary desire does not have to lead to anything lasting. Consummation of a relationship was never discussed in the time of Shakespeare as a tenet of courtly love because women were supposed to be angelic ideals rather than real people with carnal desires. Millay's speaker defies these unrealistic and unattainable ideals of eternal adoration by warning her lover not to "Think" that "I shall remember you with love" (9, 11), illustrating that desire is impermanent. In fact, it is just a temporary "frenzy" and "insufficient reason" even to have a "conversation when we meet again" (13-14). Lust in Millay's world is fleeting, whereas the love of Shakespeare's world is final and complete once the man conquers all and the woman takes her place on his arm. Millay's poem might seem cynical, but it represents a more realistic view of female and male interactions; life and love are transitory and to be enjoyed in the moment because sexual urges can be sated, are biologically determined, and essential to survival, while emotional ones are (relatively) inconsequential and satisfied in other ways.

Millay draws on Shakespeare as a kind of foil by using the form so associated with his name as a vehicle for her very different views on the same topics. Millay brings sexual relationships to a far more terrestrial level with her assertions that women have primal urges that must be satisfied and that submission to ascribed gender roles is not necessary in order to obtain this satisfaction. She presents a radically modern view of relationships. She lambastes the Shake-

Makolin 4

spearean paradigm of the idealized woman, a traditionally beautiful possession of the egotistical man. By using the Shakespearean sonnet form to propose her own revamped, modern vision of woman, a self-aware person who fearlessly relishes the idea of her own emotional and sexual independence, Millay redefines both "woman" and "love."

Makolin 5

Works Cited

Mays, Kelly J., editor. *The Norton Introduction to Literature.* 12th ed., W. W. Norton, 2017.

Millay, Edna St. Vincent. "I, being born a woman and distressed." Mays, pp. 1109-10.

---. "Women have loved before as I love now." Mays, p. 1109.

Shakespeare, William. "Th' expense of spirit in a waste of shame." Mays, pp. 1080-81.

---. "My mistress' eyes are nothing like the sun." Mays, p. 1105.

---. "Shall I compare thee to a summer's day?" Mays, p. 998.

Emily Dickinson

AN ALBUM

The bee himself did not evade the schoolboy more than she evaded me; and even at this day I still stand somewhat bewildered, like the boy.

—THOMAS WENTWORTH HIGGINSON

The woman many regard as America's most original poet was born in her family's home in Amherst, Massachusetts, on December 10, 1830. She would die in the same home at the age of fifty-five, having anonymously published only ten of the almost eighteen hundred poems that her sister was surprised to discover after her death. Because she never married and rarely, if ever, ventured outside her home in the last twenty years of her life, biographers and critics are fond of contrasting the narrowness of Emily Dickinson's life with the tremendous breadth of her posthumous reputation and influence, and the brevity and emotional intensity of her poetry, with its sheer formal, emotional, and intellectual audacity and range.

Yet Dickinson's life was not quite as uneventful or narrow as it might outwardly appear. She received a fairly extensive education for a woman of her era, studying classics, as well as science and other subjects, at both Amherst Academy, which she attended for seven years, and the Mount Holyoke Female Seminary (later, Mount Holyoke College), which she attended for one. She also read widely and deeply throughout her life. Moreover, she had a great deal of indirect knowledge of public and literary affairs, including the abolitionist, feminist, and Transcendentalist movements, as well as the various theological controversies of her day. Her father was a prominent lawyer, college administrator, and politician; Emily herself maintained an avid correspondence with some ninety people and included among her friends the clergyman Charles Wadsworth, journalists Samuel Bowles and Thomas Higginson, and novelist Helen Hunt Jackson. Dickinson's friendships also ensured her a select, but astute, audience for her letters and the poems she often included in them.

Dickinson nonetheless did cultivate her privacy and independence, bequeathing us a body of poetry that is in some ways as deliberately elusive, enigmatic, and eccentric as the woman herself apparently was, even to those who knew her best. As a result, hers is also a poetry that holds especially rich rewards for readers willing both to read individual poems multiple times and to read multiple poems with an eye on the light each sheds on the others.

As you read the Dickinson poems gathered in the following album and in other chapters, try to identify the various formal features and strategies that seem to you most characteristic of Dickinson's poetry, including its **diction**, syntax, punctuation, **meter**, and **rhyme**. Pay attention, too, to the varying **tone** of the poems and the **persona** Dickinson creates in and through them. To what extent and how and why do the speakers of these varied **lyrics** seem like versions of the same person? what sort of person or persons? What patterns do you notice in the objects depicted and in the topics or questions explored in these poems? What sorts of feelings are communicated, and what might the poems have to say about feeling, as well as thought and imagination? Why might (or might not) Dickinson's poems seem "torn up by the roots, with rain and dew and earth still clinging to them," as Higginson once declared? Or how might the poems help you understand what Dickinson meant when she wrote, "Tell all the truth but tell it slant / Success in Circuit lies"?

As you work to answer these questions for yourself, you may—like countless other readers before you—find yourself as intrigued by the poet behind the work as by the work itself, and rightly so. Yet critic Molly McQuade's cautionary words are perhaps worth keeping in mind: "Because [Dickinson] lived in seclusion by choice, and because her poetry also steadfastly reflects the author's coveting of privacy, to read the life in the poetry is perilous, if not impossible. Likewise, to search the life for the origins of her poetry would be treacherous."

Another factor that may make both a biographical approach to Dickinson's poetry and claims about how it changed over time somewhat more difficult than in the case of other poets is the fact that we cannot precisely date Dickinson's poems. Instead, we have to rely on the approximate dates scholars assign based on a study of the letters and the hand-sewn books that hold the only surviving copies. In a way, then, the case of Emily Dickinson is a bit like that of William Shakespeare—one in which all that we *don't* know about the author makes the work even more intriguing.

POEMS BY EMILY DICKINSON

[Tell all the truth but tell it slant—]

Tell all the truth but tell it slant—
Success in Circuit lies
Too bright for our infirm Delight
The Truth's superb surprise
As Lightning to the Children eased
With explanation kind
The Truth must dazzle gradually
Or every man be blind—

1872

- What meanings of the word "Circuit" (line 2) seem especially appropriate and relevant here? Why and how so?

[I stepped from Plank to Plank]

I stepped from Plank to Plank
A slow and cautious way
The Stars about my Head I felt
About my Feet the Sea.

I knew not but the next
Would be my final inch—

This gave me that precarious Gait
Some call Experience.

c. 1864

- **For what does "stepp[ing] from Plank to Plank" become a metaphor in the poem? Is this experience a positive or a negative one?**

[Wild Nights—Wild Nights!]

Wild Nights—Wild Nights!
Were I with thee
Wild Nights should be
Our luxury!

Futile—the Winds—
To a Heart in port—
Done with the Compass—
Done with the Chart!

Rowing in Eden—
Ah, the Sea!
Might I but moor—Tonight—
In Thee!

c. 1861

- **Whom might the speaker be addressing? What might it mean to be "Done with the Chart" (line 8)?**

[My Life had stood—a Loaded Gun—]

My Life had stood—a Loaded Gun—
In Corners—till a Day
The Owner passed—identified—
And carried Me away—

And now We roam in Sovereign Woods—
And now We hunt the Doe—
And every time I speak for Him—
The Mountains straight reply—

And do I smile, such cordial light
Upon the Valley glow—
It is as a Vesuvian face
Had let its pleasure through—

And when at Night—Our good Day done—
I guard My Master's Head—
'Tis better than the Eider-Duck's
Deep Pillow—to have shared—

To foe of His—I'm deadly foe—
None stir the second time—

On whom I lay a Yellow Eye—
Or an emphatic Thumb—

Though I than He—may longer live
He longer must—than I—
For I have but the power to kill,
Without—the power to die—

c. 1863

- **How does Dickinson set up and then defy expectations through the poem's controlling metaphor? How do the poem's quirks (e.g., the jerky rhythm, the strange syntax, the slant rhymes) contribute to its overall effect?**

[After great pain, a formal feeling comes—]

After great pain, a formal feeling comes—
The Nerves sit ceremonious, like Tombs—
The stiff Heart questions was it He, that bore,
And Yesterday, or Centuries before?

The Feet, mechanical, go round—
A Wooden way
Of Ground, or Air, or Ought—
Regardless grown,
A Quartz contentment, like a stone—

This is the Hour of Lead—
Remembered, if outlived,
As Freezing Persons recollect the Snow—
First—Chill—then Stupor—then the letting go—

c. 1862

- **What different metaphors and similes are used here, and what does each contribute to the poem's portrayal of how we feel "After great pain"?**

[A narrow Fellow in the Grass]

A narrow Fellow in the Grass
Occasionally rides—
You may have met Him—did you not
His notice sudden is—

The Grass divides as with a Comb—
A spotted shaft is seen—
And then it closes at your feet
And opens further on—

He likes a Boggy Acre
A Floor too cool for Corn—
Yet when a Boy, and Barefoot—
I more than once at Noon

Have passed, I thought, a Whip lash
Unbraiding in the Sun

When stooping to secure it
It wrinkled, and was gone—

Several of Nature's People
I know, and they know me—
I feel for them a transport
Of cordiality—

But never met this Fellow
Attended, or alone
Without a tighter breathing
And Zero at the Bone—

1866

- **How does Dickinson use sound devices such as alliteration to underscore the images and themes of the poem?**

POEMS ABOUT EMILY DICKINSON

WENDY COPE
Emily Dickinson

Higgledy-piggledy
Emily Dickinson
Liked to use dashes
Instead of full stops.

Nowadays, faced with such
Idiosyncrasy,
Critics and editors
Send for the cops.

1986

- **What does the use of dactyls (each metrical foot consisting of a stressed syllable followed by two unstressed syllables) contribute to this poem? How do this meter and the poem's other formal features underscore its depiction of both Dickinson's poetry and the attitudes of modern "Critics and editors" (line 7)?**

HART CRANE
To Emily Dickinson

You who desired so much—in vain to ask—
Yet fed your hunger like an endless task,
Dared dignify the labor, bless the quest—
Achieved that stillness ultimately best,

Being, of all, least sought for: Emily, hear!
O sweet, dead Silencer, most suddenly clear
When singing that Eternity possessed
And plundered momently in every breast;

—Truly no flower yet withers in your hand.
The harvest you described and understand
Needs more than wit to gather, love to bind.
Some reconcilement of remotest mind—

Leaves Ormus rubyless, and Ophir[1] chill.
Else tears heap all within one clay-cold hill.

1927

- How does the speaker characterize Emily Dickinson in the first five lines of the poem? What does the second stanza suggest about the nature of her poetry? How does the poem's form contribute to its characterization of Dickinson and her work?

BILLY COLLINS

Taking Off Emily Dickinson's Clothes

First, her tippet[2] made of tulle,
easily lifted off her shoulders and laid
on the back of a wooden chair.

And her bonnet,
the bow undone with a light forward pull.

Then the long white dress, a more
complicated matter with mother-of-pearl
buttons down the back,
so tiny and numerous that it takes forever
before my hands can part the fabric,
like a swimmer's dividing water,
and slip inside.

You will want to know
that she was standing
by an open window in an upstairs bedroom,
motionless, a little wide-eyed,
looking out at the orchard below,
the white dress puddled at her feet
on the wide-board, hardwood floor.

The complexity of women's undergarments
in nineteenth-century America
is not to be waved off,
and I proceeded like a polar explorer
through clips, clasps, and moorings,
catches, straps, and whalebone stays,
sailing toward the iceberg of her nakedness.

1. Both Ormus and Ophir were cities in the Middle East legendary for their wealth and luxury.
2. Shoulder cape with hanging ends.

Later, I wrote in a notebook
it was like riding a swan into the night,
but, of course, I cannot tell you everything—
the way she closed her eyes to the orchard,
how her hair tumbled free of its pins,
how there were sudden dashes
whenever we spoke.

What I can tell you is
it was terribly quiet in Amherst
that Sabbath afternoon,
nothing but a carriage passing the house,
a fly buzzing in a windowpane.

So I could plainly hear her inhale
when I undid the very top
hook-and-eye fastener of her corset

and I could hear her sigh when finally it was unloosed,
the way some readers sigh when they realize
that Hope has feathers,
that Reason is a plank,
that Life is a loaded gun
that looks right at you with a yellow eye.

1998

- **How does this poem use figures of speech to characterize the act of disrobing Dickinson? For what does that act, in turn, become a metaphor? How does the poem use allusions to specific Dickinson poems?**

Chronology

1830 Dickinson is born on December 10 in Amherst, Massachusetts, second of the three children of Emily Norcross Dickinson and Edward Dickinson, son of the founder of Amherst College and himself both a treasurer of the college and a lawyer.

1841 After attending two local primary schools, Dickinson enters Amherst Academy; one of her teachers will later describe her "as a very bright, but rather delicate and frail-looking girl; an excellent scholar; of exemplary deportment, faithful in all school duties; but somewhat shy and nervous." "Her compositions," he added, "were strikingly original."

1842–43 Dickinson's father serves two terms as a state senator, later joining the Governor's Executive Council (1846–47).

1844 After the death of a cousin, Dickinson spends a month with her aunt in Boston.

1847 Dickinson leaves Amherst Academy for one year at Mount Holyoke Female Seminary (later Mount Holyoke College).

1852	Dickinson publishes the first of seven poems to appear anonymously in the local *Springfield Daily Republican*, a newspaper with liberal, abolitionist leanings.
1853–55	Dickinson's father serves in the U.S. Congress; in Spring 1855, Dickinson visits Washington, DC, with her father and sister, spending time with a cousin in Philadelphia on the way home. In 1855, her elder brother, Austin, declares himself "saved," and Emily becomes the only member of her immediate family not to undergo a similar religious experience.
1856	Austin Dickinson marries Susan Huntington Gilbert, who will become one of Dickinson's most intimate friends and the recipient of many letters and approximately ninety of her poems—by far the most of any correspondent.
1858	Dickinson meets *Springfield Daily Republican* editor Samuel Bowles (1826–78), who becomes a frequent visitor.
1862	Dickinson initiates a lifelong correspondence with *Atlantic Monthly* literary editor, abolitionist, and feminist Thomas Wentworth Higginson (1823–1911); though she will send many of her poems to Higginson, he advises against publication.
1864–65	Eye trouble sends Dickinson on two extended stays in Cambridgeport, where she is treated by a Boston ophthalmologist. After her return, Dickinson will seldom leave the family home, though she will receive visits from intimates including Higginson, Bowles, and the Reverend Charles Wadsworth.
1874	Dickinson's father dies.
1875	Dickinson's always-frail mother suffers a major stroke; Dickinson becomes her bedridden mother's primary caretaker.
1877	After the death of his wife, Judge Otis P. Lord, an old friend, engages Dickinson in what one journalist calls "an astonishingly candid, erotic correspondence," though Dickinson apparently refuses a marriage proposal.
1886	Dickinson dies at age fifty-five in her family's Amherst home on May 15. In an obituary, sister-in-law Susan Dickinson observes, "Very few in the village, except among older inhabitants, knew Miss Emily personally, although the facts of her seclusion and her intellectual brilliancy were familiar Amherst traditions." After Dickinson's death, her sister discovers almost eighteen hundred poems, as well as three volumes of letters.
1890	Austin Dickinson's mistress, Mabel Loomis Todd (1856–1932), and Thomas Higginson coedit and publish a posthumous collection of selected poems by Emily Dickinson.
1891	Responding to "a constant and earnest demand by readers for further information in regard to her," Higginson publishes excerpts from selected Dickinson letters.

SUGGESTIONS FOR WRITING

1. One immediately apparent feature of Dickinson's poetry is her rather odd use of punctuation, especially her frequent use of the dash. Write an essay that explains how punctuation contributes to the effect and meaning of at least two Dickinson poems.

2. Write an essay that explores the various kinds of "circuits" or "circuitousness" at work in at least two Dickinson poems and the way such "circuits" contribute to the poems' success.
3. Write an essay explaining the way Dickinson's poetry is characterized in one poem about Dickinson included in this album; be sure to draw on at least one of Dickinson's poems to assess whether, why, and how that characterization seems apt.

W. B. Yeats

AN ALBUM

Mad Ireland hurt you into poetry.

—W. H. AUDEN

If it is difficult to make claims about either biographical elements in Emily Dickinson's poems or her poetry's development over time, the opposite seems true of the work of W. B. Yeats. Whereas Dickinson left us guessing about her inner life, the timing and revision of her poems, and her ideas about the nature and goals of her craft, Yeats left us a treasure trove of memoirs, essays, and manuscripts on which to draw. As such, his poetry may well move and speak to us more as we discover more about the author's personal experience and beliefs; about the order in which the poems were written (and often rewritten); and about the historical events that helped shape the author and his work. Whereas Dickinson published few poems in her lifetime and soared to fame only after her death, Yeats was a prolific and celebrated, if controversial, public figure who received the Nobel Prize for Literature some twenty-five years before his death.

William Butler Yeats was born in Dublin in 1865. Though he spent much of his youth in London and is today regarded as one of the greatest **lyric** poets in the English language, he is best known as the preeminent Irish poet of the twentieth century. Well versed in Irish history, folklore, and politics, Yeats attended art school for a time before devoting himself to writing poetry that was, early in his career, self-consciously dreamy and ethereal. (A great admirer of poets Percy Shelley [1792–1822] and William Blake [1782–1827], Yeats once labeled himself "the last Romantic.") Yeats's poems became tighter, more concrete, direct, and passionate with his involvement (mainly through theater) with the Irish nationalist cause, his desperate love for the actress and activist Maud Gonne (1866–1953), his exposure to the work of the German philosopher Friedrich Nietzsche (1844–1900), and his friendship with the American poet Ezra Pound (1885–1972). Yeats served as a senator in the newly independent Irish government before withdrawing from active public life to Thoor Ballylee, a crumbling, ancient tower fashioned into a home by Yeats and Georgie Hyde-Lees (1892–1968), the young Englishwoman he ultimately married.

Both Yeats and his work were profoundly shaped by shifts in the character and fortunes of Irish nationalism—both the political movement to liberate Ireland from British control and its cultural cousin, the Celtic Revival, which sought to rejuvenate a distinctively Irish literature and culture. Deeply involved in both movements in a way that his younger countryman, James Joyce (1882–1941), never was, Yeats nonetheless—at various times and in various ways—found himself in profound conflict with their aims, their methods, and their vision of both art and Ireland. Though he was particularly averse to the idea of art as propaganda, his early poetry and plays draw heavily on the oral folk traditions and rhythms to which he was first introduced during childhood visits to County Sligo and which he began to research more seriously after his introduction to

Irish nationalists. Though such folk sources would become less important to his later work, Yeats strove throughout his life to preserve and reinvigorate Irish culture.

Yeats was also deeply influenced by events and movements that stretched well beyond his native country, including World War I (1914–18), the spiritualist movement, and the birth of psychology. As Yeats himself recognized, his deep immersion in the occult, as well as his lifelong search for a satisfactory belief system to replace or rejuvenate the Protestant Christianity of his ancestors, was at once a reaction to the materialistic, rationalistic spirit of his age (or what he called "the despotism of fact" that for him culminated in the First World War) and a reaction exceedingly common among the artists and intellectuals of his day. Ultimately, Yeats came to believe fervently in what his contemporary Carl Jung (1875–1961) labeled the "collective unconscious"—a sort of universal memory shared by all human beings—and in the idea that the poet, like the priest, the prophet, and the magician, taps into the collective unconscious and moves his audience through symbols. The comparison between priest and poet is key, for Yeats also believed that the arts, including poetry, should perform a quasi-religious function. He claimed in his essay "The Autumn of the Body" (1898) that "The arts are [. . .] about to take upon their shoulders the burdens that have fallen from the shoulders of priests, and to lead us back upon our journey by filling our thoughts with the essence of things, and not with things." Elsewhere, he declared that he "made a new religion, almost an infallible church of poetic tradition."

Such beliefs shape not only the complex symbolism of Yeats's verse but also its external form. Yeats eschewed the **free verse** popular with his contemporaries at least in part because, as he explains in "The Symbolism of Poetry" (1900),

> The purpose of rhythm [. . .] is to prolong the moment [. . .] when we are both asleep and awake, [. . .] by hushing us with an alluring monotony, which holds us waking by variety, to keep us in that state of perhaps real trance, in which the mind liberated from the pressure of the will is unfolded in symbols [. . .] . In the making and in the understanding of a work of art, and the more easily if it is full of patterns and symbols and music, we are lured to the threshold of sleep, and it may be far beyond it, without knowing that we have ever set our feet upon the steps of horn or of ivory.

To achieve those incantatory rhythms, Yeats experimented with various meters and verse forms, ranging from **ballad stanza** to **ottava rima**.

The chronology at the end of this album and the footnotes that accompany the poems will provide you with more information about Yeats, and you may find much more online and in the library. Even without that information, however, you will learn much about Yeats, his art, his beliefs, and the way all three changed over time by carefully reading the poems in this album one by one, paying attention to all that you observe, and talking about them with other readers. As you do so, keep in mind the following questions:

- What patterns can you detect in the poems' external form, as well as internal structure?
- Where do symbols occur and recur, and what role do they play?

- What vision of art and the artist is conveyed by both the content and the form of these poems?
- Do you agree with those scholars who see dramatic shifts of both form and content from early poems such as THE LAKE ISLE OF INNISFREE (1890) to mid-career poems such as ALL THINGS CAN TEMPT ME (1910) and EASTER 1916 (1916) to late poems such as LEDA AND THE SWAN (1923) and SAILING TO BYZANTIUM (1923)?
- If you do detect three distinct phases and kinds of poems here, then do you think THE SECOND COMING (1919) fits more with the poems of Yeats's second or middle phase, or more with those of his third or late phase? Why and how so?
- If you see all the poems as more alike than different, what are the features that make them both alike and distinctive?

POEMS BY W. B. YEATS

The Lake Isle of Innisfree[1]

I will arise and go now, and go to Innisfree,
And a small cabin build there, of clay and wattles made,
Nine bean-rows will I have there, a hive for the honey-bee,
And live alone in the bee-loud glade.

And I shall have some peace there, for peace comes dropping slow,
Dropping from the veils of the morning to where the cricket sings;
There midnight's all a glimmer, and noon a purple glow,
And evening full of the linnet's wings.

I will arise and go now, for always night and day
I hear lake water lapping with low sounds by the shore;
While I stand on the roadway, or on the pavements grey,
I hear it in the deep heart's core.

1890

- Why does the speaker vow to go to Innisfree, and how does the life he imagines living there compare to the one he now lives? In what ways might his imagined future seem like a return to the past?

1. Island in Lough Gill, County Sligo, Ireland.

AUTHORS ON THEIR WORK

W. B. YEATS (1865–1939)

From *The Trembling of the Veil* (1922)*

Sometimes I told myself very adventurous love-stories with myself for hero, and at other times I planned out a life of lonely austerity, and at other times mixed the ideals and planned a life of lonely austerity mitigated by periodical lapses. I had still the ambition, formed in Sligo in my teens, of living in imitation of Thoreau[2] on Innisfree, a little island in Lough Gill, and when walking through Fleet Street very homesick I heard a little tinkle of water and saw a fountain in a shop-window which balanced a little ball upon its jet, and began to remember lake water. From the sudden remembrance came my poem *Innisfree*, my first lyric with anything in its rhythm of my own music. I had begun to loosen rhythm as an escape from rhetoric and from that emotion of the crowd that rhetoric brings, but I only understood vaguely and occasionally that I must for my special purpose use nothing but the common syntax. A couple of years later I would not have written that first line with its conventional archaism—"Arise and go"—nor the inversion in the last stanza. Passing another day by the new Law Courts [. . .] I grew suddenly oppressed by the great weight of stone, and thought, "There are miles and miles of stone and brick all round me," and presently added, "If John the Baptist or his like were to come again and had his mind set upon it, he could make all these people go out into some wilderness leaving their buildings empty," and that thought, which does not seem very valuable now, so enlightened the day that it is still vivid in the memory [. . .].

***_The Autobiography of William Butler Yeats._ Macmillan, 1953. In this excerpt from his autobiography, Yeats describes the period in the 1880s when he was in his twenties and living in London with his family.**

All Things Can Tempt Me

All things can tempt me from this craft of verse:
One time it was a woman's face, or worse—
The seeming needs of my fool-driven land;
Now nothing but comes readier to the hand
Than this accustomed toil. When I was young,
I had not given a penny for a song
Did not the poet sing it with such airs
That one believed he had a sword upstairs;

2. Henry David Thoreau (1817–62) famously spent two years living in an isolated cabin near Walden Pond, in Massachusetts, experiences described in *Walden; or Life in the Woods* (1854).

Yet would be now, could I but have my wish,
Colder and dumber and deafer than a fish.

1910

• In his commentary on THE LAKE ISLE OF INNISFREE (see "Authors on Their Work," above), Yeats suggests that over time he abandoned the archaic language and syntax, as well as subject matter, of his early verse. How might (or might not) ALL THINGS CAN TEMPT ME both exemplify and comment on that shift? How do diction and syntax contribute to the poem's effect?

Easter 1916[3]

I have met them at close of day
Coming with vivid faces
From counter or desk among gray
Eighteenth-century houses.
I have passed with a nod of the head
Or polite meaningless words,
Or have lingered awhile and said
Polite meaningless words,
And thought before I had done
Of a mocking tale or a gibe
To please a companion
Around the fire at the club,
Being certain that they and I
But lived where motley is worn:
All changed, changed utterly:
A terrible beauty is born.

That woman's[4] days were spent
In ignorant good-will,
Her nights in argument
Until her voice grew shrill.
What voice more sweet than hers
When, young and beautiful,
She rode to harriers?
This man[5] had kept a school
And rode our wingèd horse,[6]
This other[7] his helper and friend
Was coming into his force;

3. On Easter Monday, 1916, nationalist leaders proclaimed an Irish Republic. After a week of street fighting, the British government put down the Easter Rebellion and executed a number of prominent nationalists, including the four mentioned in lines 75–76, all of whom Yeats knew personally.

4. Countess Constance Georgina Markiewicz (1868–1927), a beautiful and well-born young woman from County Sligo who became a vigorous nationalist. At first she was condemned to death, but her sentence was later commuted to life imprisonment, and she was granted amnesty in 1917.

5. Patrick Pearse (1879–1916), who led the assault on the Dublin Post Office, from which the proclamation of a republic was issued. A schoolmaster by profession, he had championed the restoration of the Gaelic language in Ireland and was an active political writer and poet.

6. The mythological Pegasus, a traditional symbol of poetic inspiration.

7. Thomas MacDonagh (1878–1916), also a writer and teacher.

He might have won fame in the end,
So sensitive his nature seemed,
So daring and sweet his thought.
This other man[8] I had dreamed
A drunken, vainglorious lout.
He had done most bitter wrong
To some who are near my heart,
Yet I number him in the song;
He, too, has resigned his part
In the casual comedy;
He, too, has been changed in his turn,
Transformed utterly:
A terrible beauty is born.

Hearts with one purpose alone
Through summer and winter seem
Enchanted to a stone
To trouble the living stream.
The horse that comes from the road,
The rider, the birds that range
From cloud to tumbling cloud,
Minute by minute they change;
A shadow of cloud on the stream
Changes minute by minute;
A horse-hoof slides on the brim,
And a horse plashes within it;
The long-legged moor-hens dive,
And hens to moor-cocks call;
Minute by minute they live:
The stone's in the midst of all.

Too long a sacrifice
Can make a stone of the heart.
O when may it suffice?
That is Heaven's part, our part
To murmur name upon name,
As a mother names her child
When sleep at last has come
On limbs that had run wild.
What is it but nightfall?
No, no, not night but death;
Was it needless death after all?
For England may keep faith[9]
For all that is done and said.
We know their dream; enough
To know they dreamed and are dead;

8. Major John MacBride (1868–1916), who had married Yeats's beloved Maud Gonne in 1903 but separated from her two years later.
9. Before the uprising, the English had promised eventual home rule to Ireland.

And what if excess of love
Bewildered them till they died?
I write it out in a verse—
MacDonagh and MacBride
And Connolly[1] and Pearse
Now and in time to be,
Wherever green is worn,
Are changed, changed utterly;
A terrible beauty is born.

1916

- **The phrase "A terrible beauty is born" becomes a kind of refrain in this poem. What does the poem suggest about why the events of Easter 1916 and the kind of political passion and commitment that went into it were simultaneously "terrible" and "beautiful"? What do the stone and the stream seem to symbolize?**

The Second Coming[2]

Turning and turning in the widening gyre[3]
The falcon cannot hear the falconer;
Things fall apart; the center cannot hold;
Mere anarchy is loosed upon the world,
The blood-dimmed tide is loosed, and everywhere
The ceremony of innocence is drowned;
The best lack all conviction, while the worst
Are full of passionate intensity.

Surely some revelation is at hand;
Surely the Second Coming is at hand.
The Second Coming! Hardly are those words out
When a vast image out of *Spiritus Mundi*[4]
Troubles my sight: somewhere in sands of the desert
A shape with lion body and the head of a man,
A gaze blank and pitiless as the sun,
Is moving its slow thighs, while all about it
Reel shadows of the indignant desert birds.[5]
The darkness drops again; but now I know
That twenty centuries of stony sleep

1. James Connolly (1868–1916), the leader of the Easter uprising.
2. The Second Coming of Christ, according to Matthew 24.29–44, will follow a time of "tribulation." In *A Vision* (1937), Yeats describes his view of history as dependent on cycles of about two thousand years: The birth of Christ had ended the cycle of Greco-Roman civilization, and now the Christian cycle seemed near an end, to be followed by an antithetical cycle, ominous in its portents.
3. Literally, the widening spiral of a falcon's flight. "Gyre" is Yeats's term for a cycle of history, which he diagrammed as a series of interpenetrating cones.
4. Or *Anima Mundi* (Latin), the spirit or soul of the world. Yeats considered this universal consciousness or memory a fund from which poets drew their images and symbols.
5. Yeats later wrote of the "brazen winged beast [. . .] described in my poem *The Second Coming*" as "associated with laughing, ecstatic destruction."

Were vexed to nightmare by a rocking cradle,
And what rough beast, its hour come round at last,
Slouches towards Bethlehem to be born?

January 1919

- **What vision of the contemporary world is implied by the metaphors in the poem's first half? What vision of its future is suggested in the poem's second half?**

Leda and the Swan[6]

A sudden blow: the great wings beating still
Above the staggering girl, her thighs caressed
By the dark webs, her nape caught in his bill,
He holds her helpless breast upon his breast.

How can those terrified vague fingers push
The feathered glory from her loosening thighs?
And how can body, laid in that white rush,
But feel the strange heart beating where it lies?

A shudder in the loins engenders there
The broken wall, the burning roof and tower
And Agamemnon dead.
Being so caught up,
So mastered by the brute blood of the air,
Did she put on his knowledge with his power
Before the indifferent beak could let her drop?

1923

- **If THE SECOND COMING predicts the end of one historical cycle and its governing (Christian) myth, LEDA AND THE SWAN imagines the beginning of the preceding cycle. How does the poem characterize that beginning? Might we again have here (as in EASTER 1916, above) a kind of "terrible beauty"? How would you paraphrase the question the speaker poses at the end? Why might questions in general loom so large in this poem?**

Sailing to Byzantium[7]

I

That[8] is no country for old men. The young
In one another's arms, birds in the trees

6. According to Greek myth, Zeus took the form of a swan to rape Leda, who became the mother of Helen of Troy; of Castor; and also of Clytemnestra, Agamemnon's wife and murderer. Helen's abduction from her husband, Menelaus, brother of Agamemnon, began the Trojan War (line 10). Yeats described the visit of Zeus to Leda as an annunciation like that to Mary (see Luke 1.26–38); "I imagine the annunciation that founded Greece as made to Leda" (*A Vision*).

7. Ancient name of Istanbul, the capital and holy city of Eastern Christendom from the late fourth century until 1453. It was famous for its stylized and formal mosaics; its symbolic, nonnaturalistic art; and its highly developed intellectual life. Yeats repeatedly uses it to symbolize a world of artifice and timelessness, free from the decay and death of the natural and sensual world.

8. Ireland, as an instance of the natural, temporal world.

—Those dying generations—at their song,
The salmon-falls, the mackerel-crowded seas,
Fish, flesh, or fowl, commend all summer long
Whatever is begotten, born, and dies.
Caught in that sensual music all neglect
Monuments of unaging intellect.

II

An aged man is but a paltry thing,
A tattered coat upon a stick, unless
Soul clap its hands and sing, and louder sing
For every tatter in its mortal dress,
Nor is there singing school but studying
Monuments of its own magnificence;
And therefore I have sailed the seas and come
To the holy city of Byzantium.

III

O sages standing in God's holy fire
As in the gold mosaic of a wall,
Come from the holy fire, perne in a gyre,[9]
And be the singing-masters of my soul.
Consume my heart away; sick with desire
And fastened to a dying animal
It knows not what it is; and gather me
Into the artifice of eternity.

IV

Once out of nature I shall never take
My bodily form from any natural thing,
But such a form as Grecian goldsmiths make
Of hammered gold and gold enameling
To keep a drowsy Emperor awake;[1]
Or set upon a golden bough[2] to sing
To lords and ladies of Byzantium
Of what is past, or passing, or to come.

1927

- **Like The Lake Isle of Innisfree, this poem focuses on an imaginary journey and on a contrast between then and there versus here and now, yet this poem deals much more directly with the subject of art and especially of**

9. That is, whirl in a coiling motion, so that his soul may merge with its motion as the timeless world invades the cycles of history and nature. "Perne" is Yeats's coinage (from the noun *pirn*): to spin around in the kind of spiral pattern that thread makes as it comes off a bobbin or spool.
1. I have read somewhere that in the Emperor's palace at Byzantium was a tree made of gold and silver, and artificial birds that sang [Yeats's note].
2. In book 6 of the *Aeneid*, the sibyl tells Aeneas that he must pluck the golden bough from a nearby tree in order to descend to Hades. Each time Aeneas plucks the branch, an identical one takes its place.

poetry or song: what it might be like, where it might come from, what it might do for us. How does this poem both pose and answer those questions?

A POEM ABOUT W. B. YEATS

W. H. AUDEN

In Memory of W. B. Yeats

(d. January, 1939)

I

He disappeared in the dead of winter:
The brooks were frozen, the airports almost deserted,
And snow disfigured the public statues;
The mercury sank in the mouth of the dying day.
What instruments we have agree
The day of his death was a dark cold day.

Far from his illness
The wolves ran on through the evergreen forests,
The peasant river was untempted by the fashionable quays;
By mourning tongues
The death of the poet was kept from his poems.

But for him it was his last afternoon as himself,
An afternoon of nurses and rumors;
The provinces of his body revolted,
The squares of his mind were empty,
Silence invaded the suburbs,
The current of his feeling failed; he became his admirers.

Now he is scattered among a hundred cities
And wholly given over to unfamiliar affections,
To find his happiness in another kind of wood
And be punished under a foreign code of conscience.
The words of a dead man
Are modified in the guts of the living.

But in the importance and noise of tomorrow
When the brokers are roaring like beasts on the floor of the Bourse,[3]
And the poor have the sufferings to which they are fairly accustomed,
And each in the cell of himself is almost convinced of his freedom,
A few thousand will think of this day
As one thinks of a day when one did something slightly unusual.
What instruments we have agree
The day of his death was a dark cold day.

II

You were silly like us; your gift survived it all:
The parish of rich women, physical decay,

3. Paris stock exchange.

Yourself. Mad Ireland hurt you into poetry.
Now Ireland has her madness and her weather still,
For poetry makes nothing happen: it survives
In the valley of its making where executives
Would never want to tamper, flows on south
From ranches of isolation and the busy griefs,
Raw towns that we believe and die in; it survives,
A way of happening, a mouth.

III

Earth, receive an honored guest:
William Yeats is laid to rest.
Let the Irish vessel lie
Emptied of its poetry.

In the nightmare of the dark
All the dogs of Europe bark,
And the living nations wait,
Each sequestered in its hate;

Intellectual disgrace
Stares from every human face,
And the seas of pity lie
Locked and frozen in each eye.

Follow, poet, follow right
To the bottom of the night,
With your unconstraining voice
Still persuade us to rejoice;

With the farming of a verse
Make a vineyard of the curse,
Sing of human unsuccess
In a rapture of distress;

In the deserts of the heart
Let the healing fountain start,
In the prison of his days
Teach the free man how to praise.

1939

- **Does Auden's elegy as a whole affirm that "poetry makes nothing happen" (line 36)? Why does the death of Yeats seem to inspire the speaker to reflect on this possibility?**

AUTHORS ON THEIR WORK

W. H. AUDEN (1907–73)

From "W. H. Auden, The Art of Poetry No. 17" (1974)*

INTERVIEWER: How about writers as leaders? Yeats, for instance, held office.

AUDEN: And he was terrible! Writers seldom make good leaders. They're self-employed, for one thing, and they have very little contact with their customers. It's very easy for a writer to be unrealistic. I have not lost my interest in politics, but I have come to realize that, in cases of social or political injustice, only two things are effective: political action and straight journalistic reportage of the facts. The arts can do nothing. The social and political history of Europe would be what it has been if Dante, Shakespeare, Michelangelo, Mozart, et al., had never lived. A poet, *qua* poet, has only one political duty, namely, in his own writing to set an example of the correct use of his mother tongue which is always being corrupted. When words lose their meaning, physical force takes over. By all means, let a poet, if he wants to, write what is now called an "engagé" ["engaged"] poem, so long as he realizes that it is mainly himself who will benefit from it. It will enhance his literary reputation among those who feel the same as he does.

• • •

INTERVIEWER: Would you care to comment on Yeats?

AUDEN: I find it very difficult to be fair to Yeats because he had a bad influence on me. He tempted me into a rhetoric which was, for me, oversimplified. Needless to say, the fault was mine, not his. He was, of course, a very great poet.

*"W. H. Auden, The Art of Poetry No. 17." Interview by Michael Newman. *The Paris Review*, no. 57, Spring 1974, www.theparisreview.org/interviews/3970/the-art-of-poetry-no-17-w-h-auden.

Chronology

1865 William Butler Yeats is born on June 13 in Dublin, Ireland, the eldest child of merchant's daughter Susan Pollexfen Yeats and well-known, but often financially strapped, lawyer-turned-painter John Butler Yeats.

1867 To further his career as an artist, John Yeats moves his family to London.

1872 Yeats, with his mother and siblings, spends two years at his maternal grandparents' home in Sligo, on Ireland's rural west coast.

1874 Yeats returns to London with his family and attends the Godolphin School.

1880 Financial difficulties force John Yeats to move his family back to Dublin, where his eldest son attends a local high school.

1884 Yeats enters Dublin's Metropolitan School of Art, where he will study until 1886. With fellow writer and art student George Russell (known as "A.E."), Yeats begins his research into spiritualism and the occult.

1885 Yeats meets Irish nationalist leader John O'Leary and, with O'Leary's help, publishes his first poems in the *Dublin University Review.* (In a 1907 essay, Yeats will describe O'Leary as championing the "romantic" and "idealistic" "conception of Irish nationality [. . .] in whose service I labour.")

1887 Yeats returns to London with his family and edits *Poems and Ballads of Young Ireland.*

1888 Yeats joins the spiritualist Theosophical Society and edits *Fairy and Folk Tales of the Irish Peasantry.*

1889 Yeats publishes his first volume of poetry, *The Wanderings of Oisin and Other Poems,* and meets and falls in love with the actress and Irish revolutionary Maud Gonne.

1891 Gonne rejects the first of at least three marriage proposals from Yeats.

1892 Yeats and others found the London-based Irish Literary Society, and Yeats publishes *The Countess Cathleen and Various Legends and Lyrics,* a collection of plays and poems.

1893 Yeats publishes an edition of the poems of William Blake and a prose work, *The Celtic Twilight.*

1895 Yeats publishes *Poems,* which includes revised versions of works in his first two collections and which is sometimes said to mark the end of his early period.

1896 Yeats meets fellow writer and Celtic Revivalist Lady Augusta Gregory and begins to spend holidays at her estate, Coole Park, in rural County Galway, Ireland.

1899 Yeats and Lady Gregory found the Irish Literary Theatre, later called the Abbey Theatre, in Dublin, which produces his *Countess Cathleen.*

1902 Maud Gonne stars in Yeats's *Cathleen ni Houlihan.*

1903 Gonne marries war veteran John MacBride.

1904 Yeats's so-called middle period arguably begins with the publication of the collection *In the Seven Woods.* He begins a six-year stint as manager of the Abbey Theatre, coming into conflict both with conservative Catholics offended by the supposed immorality and impiety of Abbey productions and with Irish nationalists convinced that Abbey plays should promote a wholly positive view of Ireland and the Irish.

1907 An Abbey performance of J. M. Synge's *The Playboy of the Western World* sparks riots over its supposedly negative portrayal of the Irish.

1913 Yeats spends the first of three winters with the young American poet Ezra Pound.

1914 World War I begins (in August). Yeats publishes *Responsibilities,* his first pointedly modernist, as well as avowedly public and political, poetry collection.

1916 In London, Yeats debuts *At the Hawk's Well,* the first of his plays influenced by Japanese Noh drama (rather than Irish history and legend), and publishes *Reveries of Childhood and Youth,* the first volume of his autobiography. In April, Irish nationalists stage the Easter Uprising in Dublin. Proclaiming Ireland an independent republic, the seven hundred volunteers are defeated by British troops after a week of bloody fighting; their leaders, including John MacBride, are executed for treason in May. Yeats proposes to Maud Gonne for the last time.

1917 The Russian Revolution begins, and T. S. Eliot publishes his first poetry collection, which includes *The Love Song of J. Alfred Prufrock* and which, Yeats later claimed, announced the birth of a new, self-consciously "modern" poetry that he "disliked" and yet admired for its "satiric intensity." Yeats marries Georgie Hyde-Lees; while still on their honeymoon, Georgie begins the spirit-inspired automatic writing that will be the basis for *A Vision* (1925; see below).

1918 World War I ends. Yeats and his wife move to Thoor (literally, "Castle") Ballylee, an ancient Norman tower near Lady Gregory's estate; the tower and its winding staircase will become a central symbol in his later poetry.

1919 In January, Russian revolutionaries kill four grand dukes, bringing to seventeen the number of members of the former Russian emperor's family to die in the revolution. Yeats writes "The Second Coming" and publishes *The Wild Swans at Coole*, the last collection of his so-called middle period. His first child, a daughter, is born in Dublin. Ireland enters a period of civil unrest.

1921 A truce brings temporary peace to Ireland. Yeats's second child, a son, is born, and Yeats publishes the poetry collection *Michael Robartes and the Dancer* (1921).

1922 Irish Civil War begins. Yeats's father dies. Yeats publishes *The Trembling of the Veil*, the second volume of his autobiography, and begins his six-year stint as a senator in the first Irish government.

1923 Yeats wins the Nobel Prize for Literature.

1925 Yeats publishes *A Vision*, a work of nonfiction outlining his system of symbols and cyclical vision of history.

1928 Yeats publishes *The Tower* and resigns from the Irish Senate.

1933 Yeats publishes *The Winding Stair and Other Poems.*

1939 At seventy-three, Yeats dies in France on January 28. World War II begins.

1948 Yeats's remains are returned to Ireland and buried in County Sligo under a stone bearing the epitaph he composed: "Cast a cold eye / On Life, on Death. / Horseman, pass by!"

SUGGESTIONS FOR WRITING

1. Write an essay in which you compare The Lake Isle of Innisfree and Sailing to Byzantium in order to show how Yeats's poetry both did and didn't change over the course of his career. How might the first of these poems seem like the work of a young man and poet, and the latter like that of a mature one?
2. Write an essay that explains the significance of any one recurring image or symbol, or set of related images or symbols, in at least two Yeats poems. Alternatively, use your essay to explore why terror and beauty seem to go together in Yeats' poems.
3. Drawing on at least three poems, write an essay explaining whether and how Yeats's poetry seems distinctly "Irish." How, for example, might the troubled history of his native country or his own troubled relationship to Irish nationalism, as well as the

middle-class Irish public, be explored in the poems, including the later ones that outwardly seem resolutely non-Irish in content and form?

4. Write an essay comparing the way W. H. Auden's poem about Yeats portrays the nature, source, and function of poetry to the way Yeats's poems, such as SAILING TO BYZANTIUM, do. Alternatively, compare the way each poet handles the contrast between physical, mortal life and "decay" (Auden, line 33), on the one hand, and the life lived in the imagination and poetry, on the other. Do the two poets seem to agree about the immortality and importance of poetry?

Pat Mora

AN ALBUM

Award-winning contemporary writer Pat Mora was born in 1942 in El Paso, Texas, a city on the Mexican border to which all four of her Spanish-speaking grandparents migrated during the Mexican Revolution. After earning a BA and MA from the University of Texas, El Paso, she taught both high-school and college English but did not devote herself seriously to writing until after her 1981 divorce, when, as she once joked to an interviewer, "I saw the age of forty coming for me." In the years since, she has seen her three children into adulthood; remarried; and left Texas for Cincinnati, Ohio, and Santa Fe, New Mexico (her two current homes). She has also flourished as a writer, publishing collections of poetry such as *Borders* (1986), *Agua Santa/Holy Water* (1995), *Aunt Carmen's Book of Practical Saints* (1997), and *Adobe Odes* (2007); a book of essays, *Nepantla: Essays from the Land in the Middle* (1993); a family memoir, *House of Houses* (1997); and over twenty-five books for children and young adults, including poetry, picture books, biographies, and retellings of Mayan folktales.

Avowing that she "take[s] pride in being a Hispanic writer," Mora sees her work for both children and adults as bound up with the effort to promote literacy, a wider knowledge and appreciation of Hispanic culture and heritage, and cross-cultural understanding. In *Nepantla*, she likens the work of the poet to that of the *curandera*, or traditional healer, sounding not unlike the Irish poet W. B. Yeats when she argues that

> [t]he Chicana writer seeks to heal cultural wounds of historical neglect by providing opportunities to remember the past, to share and ease bitterness, to describe what has been viewed as unworthy of description, to cure by incantations and rhythms, by listening with her entire being and responding. She then gathers the tales and myths, weaves them together, and, if lucky, casts spells.

Though she makes frequent use of Spanish terms and phrases in all her work, Mora writes primarily in English largely because she is, in her own words, "bilingual, though English-dominant," living on the figurative border between languages and cultures or in what she calls "the land in the middle." Much of her work explores that land. Yet in interviews, Mora roundly rejects the idea that the experience of living "in the middle" is necessarily negative. Rather she insists that, while "there are situations where, yes, it's plenty difficult" or where she is uncertain about where she belongs or who she is, there is also a flip side: "it's double pleasure in a way," offering "the advantage of moving back and forth." As Mora also suggests, people from all backgrounds "experience borders of many kinds throughout life." And by exploring some of these divides—between, for example, men and women or different generations—Mora's work stresses the ubiquity and even universality of the border experience, as well as the pleasures and conflicts it entails.

Literal, physical borders in particular and space and place in general also intrigue Mora—all the more, she suggests, since a 1989 move from the Southwest to the Midwest heightened her awareness of both the distinctiveness of her native landscape and her own relationship to it. Whenever she flew west, she explained to one interviewer,

> I would look out at this tremendous space and think how totally I felt at home there. Many of my Midwestern friends would confide to me that they found the desert sometimes even terrifying. I remember one of the brightest women I know who is an academic in Cincinnati said to me that the first time she came to the Southwest she was afraid she would fall off because she was so used to the protection of trees [. . .] . Our early geography shapes us in complex ways.

Geography, landscape, and the immigrant experience are only some of the many things you will find to explore in Mora's poems, including those gathered in this album and in other chapters. What might her poems individually and collectively suggest about what both is and isn't unique about the Mexican American experience? about the positive and negative aspects of living "in the land of the middle"? about what unites and divides Mexican Americans of different classes, generations, and genders? about family? about the power and the limits of language? In what ways might Mora's poems perform the *curandera*-like work she ascribes to the poet in *Nepantla*?

Elena

My Spanish isn't enough.
I remember how I'd smile
listening to my little ones,
understanding every word they'd say,
their jokes, their songs, their plots.
    Vamos a pedirle dulces a mamá. Vamos.[1]
But that was in Mexico.
Now my children go to American high schools.
They speak English. At night they sit around
the kitchen table, laugh with one another.
I stand by the stove and feel dumb, alone.
I bought a book to learn English.
My husband frowned, drank more beer.
My oldest said, "*Mamá*, he doesn't want you
to be smarter than he is." I'm forty,
embarrassed at mispronouncing words,
embarrassed at the laughter of my children,
the grocer, the mailman. Sometimes I take
my English book and lock myself in the bathroom,
say the thick words softly,
for if I stop trying, I will be deaf
when my children need my help.

1985

- What does the speaker mean by the first line—"My Spanish isn't enough"? What other words in the poem address the inadequacy of language?

1. Let's go ask mama for sweets. Let's go (Spanish).

Gentle Communion

Even the long-dead are willing to move.
Without a word, she came with me from the desert.
Mornings she wanders through my rooms
making beds, folding socks.

Since she can't hear me anymore,
Mamande[2] ignores the questions I never knew
to ask, about her younger days, her red
hair, the time she fell and broke her nose
in the snow. I will never know.

When I try to make her laugh,
to disprove her sad album face, she leaves
the room, resists me as she resisted
grinning for cameras, make-up, English.

While I write, she sits and prays,
feet apart, legs never crossed,
the blue housecoat buttoned high
as her hair dries white, girlish
around her head and shoulders.

She closes her eyes, bows her head,
and like a child presses her hands together,
her patient flesh steeple, the skin
worn, like the pages of her prayer book.

Sometimes I sit in her wide-armed
chair as I once sat in her lap.
Alone, we played a quiet I Spy.
She peeled grapes I still taste.

She removes the thin skin, places
the luminous coolness on my tongue.
I know not to bite or chew. I wait
for the thick melt,
our private green honey.

1991

- **How does this poem draw on the various meanings of the word *communion*? Why might it be significant that the grandmother comes "Without a word" (line 2)?**

Mothers and Daughters

The arm-in-arm-mother-daughter-stroll
in villages and shopping malls
evenings and weekends
the w a l k - t a l k slow,

2. Child's conflation *of mama grande* (Spanish for "grandmother").

arm-in-arm
around the world.

Sometimes they feed one another
memories sweet as hot bread
and lemon tea. Sometimes it's mother-stories
the young one can't remember:

"When you were new, I'd nest you
in one arm, while I cooked,
whisper, what am I to do with you?"

Sometimes it's tug
-of-war that started in the womb
the fight for space
the sharp jab deep inside
as the weight shifts,
arm-in-arm
around the world

always the bodytalk thick,
always the recipes
hints for feeding
more with less.

1991

- **How does the poem's form, especially its visual appearance and rhythm, contribute to its characterization of the mother-daughter relationship?**

La Migra

I

Let's play *La Migra*[3]
I'll be the Border Patrol.
You be the Mexican maid.
I get the badge and sunglasses.
You can hide and run,
but you can't get away
because I have a jeep
I can take you wherever
I want, but don't ask
questions because
I don't speak Spanish.
I can touch you wherever
I want but don't complain
too much because I've got
boots and kick—if I have to,
and I have handcuffs.

3. Mexican slang for U.S. border patrol agents (an abbreviation of the word *immigration*).

Oh, and a gun.
Get ready, get set, run.

II

Let's play *La Migra*
You be the Border Patrol.
I'll be the Mexican woman.
Your jeep has a flat,
and you have been spotted
by the sun.
All you have is heavy: hat,
glasses, badge, shoes, gun.
I know this desert,
where to rest,
where to drink.
Oh, I am not alone.
You hear us singing
and laughing with the wind,
Agua dulce brota aquí,
aquí, aquí,[4] but since you
can't speak Spanish,
you do not understand.
Get ready.

1993

• **Who seems to be the speaker of this poem, or are there more than one? What is the game of "hide and run" the speaker proposes (line 5)? Who will win?**

Ode to Adobe

Your blue mouth,
door of a thousand river-rolled stories,
opens.
Walls whisper,
voices of earth and straw.
Clay flower,
each of your rooms welcomes
like a wish,
tastes a different color—
mango, papaya, persimmon, quince.
In your nichos, Santa Rita and San Judas,[5]
patron saints of the impossible,

4. Sweet water springs here, here, here (Spanish).

5. One of Jesus's twelve apostles, St. Jude Thaddeus is the patron saint of desperate causes because his New Testament letter stresses that the faithful should persevere in the face of harsh, difficult circumstances. *Santa Rita*: patroness of impossible causes, Italian-born St. Rita (1381–1457) was mistreated for twenty years by the husband her parents forced her to marry and entered a convent after both he and her two sons died. *Nichos*: small shelves carved into a wall.

shake their heads,
gossip
about an aunt's pastel
lust, while they pretend to pray.

Mud song,
growing to your interior music,
dream cave,
honey-hive shaped by a choir
of muddy hands,
ballad of eloquent bricks,
kitchen of unending banquets,
beans simmering for centuries,
sun-baked loaf, you rise
from the desert into a luminaria.[6]

Traditional adobe dwelling found in the southwestern United States and northern Mexico.

Serenata de barro,
cantadora de la tierra,[7]
our hands stroke you, wrinkled
and delicious,
smell the layered legacy
that shelters us in the arms
of candle and piñon smoke.

Your melodies, washed and ironed
by generations of mothers,
drift out,

6. Traditional Mexican Christmas lantern made by setting a candle inside a paper bag weighted with sand.

7. Serenader of mud, singer of the popular songs of the earth, land, or soil (Spanish).

lure departed spirits home again
to dream in the crackle
of kiva fireplaces
warmed by sips of humor
and old desires, the taste
of guacamole, the silk
of skin.

In your candlelit mirror,
eternal vanity:
a spirit powders her bony nose.

2006

- **To what is adobe compared in the poem? How do these comparisons work together to characterize both the adobe and the life lived within it?**

Chronology

1942 Pat Mora is born on January 19 in El Paso, Texas, to Raul Antonio Mora, an optician, and his wife, Estela; both are bilingual, second-generation El Pasoans of Mexican descent.

1963 Mora marries William H. Burnside Jr., with whom she will ultimately have a son and two daughters; earns her BA from Texas Western College (now the University of Texas, El Paso); and begins a three-year stint teaching in the El Paso Independent School District.

1967 Mora earns her MA from the University of Texas, El Paso (UTEP).

1971 Mora begins working as a part-time English and communications instructor at El Paso Community College.

1979 Mora begins working as a part-time English instructor at UTEP.

1981 After her first marriage ends in divorce, Mora starts to devote more time to writing, while also working as assistant to UTEP's Vice President of Academic Affairs.

1984 Mora marries Vernon Lee Scarborough, an archaeologist teaching at UTEP; publishes her first poetry collection, *Chants*, winner of the Harvey L. Johnson and Southwest Book awards.

1986 Mora wins her second Southwest Book Award for her second poetry collection, *Borders*.

1988 Mora becomes director of UTEP's natural history museum and assistant to the university president.

1989 Mora leaves UTEP to devote herself full-time to writing, lecturing, and promoting literacy; she also moves to the Cincinnati/northern Kentucky area when her husband joins the University of Cincinnati anthropology department. (The couple will make a second home in Santa Fe, New Mexico.)

1991 Mora publishes *Communion*, a collection of poems chronicling her travels to Cuba, India, and Pakistan.

1992 Mora publishes *A Birthday Basket for Tia*, the first of many children's books.

1993 Mora publishes *Nepantla: Essays from the Land in the Middle.*

1994 Mora wins a National Endowment for the Arts fellowship to complete her poetry collection *Agua Santa/Holy Water* (1995).

1997 Mora publishes *House of Houses*, a family memoir, and the poetry collection *Aunt Carmen's Book of Practical Saints*, and spearheads creation of a national day of celebration of children's bilingual literacy (El día de los niños, El día de los libros/Children's Day, Book Day).

2001 Mora publishes *My Own True Name: New and Selected Poems for Young Adults.*

2007 Mora publishes *Adobe Odes.*

SUGGESTIONS FOR WRITING

1. Food, cooking, and related imagery figure in many of Mora's poems. Write an essay exploring the significance of such references. What might the poems suggest about the roles food, cooking, and eating play in our lives?
2. Drawing on at least three of Mora's poems, write an essay that explores her vision of the role of language. When, how, and why does language both unite and divide people? When, why, and how might nonverbal forms of communication prove superior?
3. As the introduction to this album suggests, Pat Mora takes pride in being a Latina writer and identifies one of her goals as chronicling the experience and feelings of contemporary Latinos and Latinas. Write an essay in which you compare at least two of Mora's poems, exploring what they together imply about what it is like to be Latino/a and how that experience differs across generations, classes, and/or genders.
4. The poems reprinted here were originally included in various collections, each of which has a distinct focus and flavor. GENTLE COMMUNION, for example, appears in Mora's third volume, *Communion* (1991), which some critics see as the culmination of the earliest phase of her career and as the reflection of both a widening of the world depicted in her work (through poems inspired by her travels to other countries) and a greater concentration on the situation of women, and the relationships among women and between women and men. Pick the Mora poem you like most, identify the collection in which it originally appeared, and read some other poems included in that collection. Then write an essay that either compares your chosen poem to others in the collection or that explains how your interpretation of the original poem changes when you read it in conjunction with the other poems.

23 THE AUTHOR'S WORK AS CONTEXT: WILLIAM BLAKE'S *SONGS OF INNOCENCE AND OF EXPERIENCE*

Throughout history and across the globe, poets have collected their poems into **sequences** or cycles. The type of poem we today call **haiku**, for instance, emerged out of a tradition in Japanese culture dating back to the middle ages, whereby a single poet would produce a poem of three lines to which other poets would add poems of two and three lines each to create a sequence of thirty-six, one hundred, or even a thousand or more linked poems. Over time, people began to lift out the three-line verse that began such a sequence and to treat it as a poem in its own right, often gathering a number of these to create an anthology of sorts. The popularity of such anthologies in turn inspired poets to begin writing stand-alone poems of this type, which eventually came to be known as haiku. Even Bashō (1644–94), the acknowledged master of the form, published most of his haiku as part of a sequence embedded within a lengthy prose memoir of his extensive travels.

In the Western literary tradition, one common type of poetic sequence is the **sonnet** sequence. Many of the most famous sonnets—from those of Francesco Petrarch and William Shakespeare to those of Elizabeth Barrett Browning and Edna St. Vincent Millay—are part of such sequences. These poems often lack titles; instead we conventionally either use the poems' first lines as titles ("My mistress's eyes are nothing like the sun") or number them according to their place in the sequence (SONNET 130).

Each of the poems in a sequence is itself an independent literary work that can be, and often is, enjoyed and understood on its own. Yet each also functions as part of the larger literary work that is the sequence. We can thus enjoy and understand the poem in quite a different way when we read it in the context of other poems in the sequence and in light of the traditions of poetic sequences generally.

Today, most poems are too short to be published singly, even if they are not part of a sequence. They may first appear in magazines, newspapers, or online, and later in books, including both collections of poems by a single writer and anthologies (like the one you are reading) that include the work of various poets. The poems in one poet's collection may be less intimately related to each other than the poems in a sequence, but they usually were written around the same time and provide a window of sorts onto a particular phase of the author's life and career. Further, poems in a collection—even, in rare cases, a collection by multiple authors—often share other features, depicting comparable situations or speakers or having a similar external form, for example. Though not the same as sequences, such collections can also offer an illuminating context for a particular poem—slightly altering, perhaps expanding, our response and interpretation.

WILLIAM BLAKE'S *SONGS OF INNOCENCE AND OF EXPERIENCE*

The rest of this chapter focuses on William Blake's *Songs of Innocence and of Experience,* one of the English-language tradition's most extraordinary poetry collections. One unique aspect of this collection is the fact that its creator—a professional painter and illustrator—not only wrote all the poems but also illustrated and printed the book himself, using a method of his own invention. As a result, Blake should indeed be regarded as the *creator* rather than the mere *author* of a book that is simultaneously a visual and verbal experience—a collection of interlinked paintings and poems.

The fact that the book was etched, printed, painted, and then sewn together by hand, moreover, had at least two important effects. First, Blake produced few copies of *Songs of Innocence and of Experience*; to date, only twenty-four are known to exist. Second, each of those twenty-four copies differs slightly from all the others: The order of the poems varies somewhat, and so, too, does the coloring of individual pages and illustrations.

In all its versions, however, the book combines two distinct yet intimately related sequences of poems. Blake first produced the book *Songs of Innocence* in 1789. Five years later, in 1794, he added other poems and pages to that book in order to create a new one: *Songs of Innocence and of Experience*. As its title suggests, the book is divided into two sections—"Songs of Innocence" and "Songs of Experience," each with its own title page and introductory poem.

Together, the two sections and sequences portray the world from two different, even opposite, perspectives, or what the book's title page labels "Two Contrary States of the Human Soul." An individual poem in "Songs of Innocence" thus often has a direct companion or counterpart poem in "Songs of Experience." In some cases, those two poems, though dramatically different, have precisely the same title and depict the same character or situation: There are, for example, two poems called HOLY THURSDAY and two called THE CHIMNEY SWEEPER. In other cases, the connection between the two poems is less direct: The poem THE LAMB, in "Songs of Innocence," for example, is typically viewed as the companion to THE TYGER, in "Songs of Experience." And the same holds true for THE ECCHOING GREEN (in "Innocence") and THE GARDEN OF LOVE (in "Experience"). A few poems, however, do not have any obvious counterparts; the two most famous examples are LONDON and THE SICK ROSE, which originally appeared in "Songs of Experience."

In this chapter, we include ten poems from *Songs of Innocence and of Experience*, along with color reproductions of some of the volume's actual pages to give you a sense of how it looks. (To see all of Blake's work, including various versions of the poems in this album, visit the impressive *Blake Archive* at www.blakearchive.org/blake/.) To provide more insight into Blake's life and world, a chronology follows the poems.

SONGS OF INNOCENCE

Introduction

Piping down the valleys wild
Piping songs of pleasant glee
On a cloud I saw a child.
And he laughing said to me

Pipe a song about a Lamb;
So I piped with merry chear,
Piper pipe that song again—
So I piped, he wept to hear.

Drop thy pipe thy happy pipe
Sing thy songs of happy chear,
So I sung the same again
While he wept with joy to hear

Piper sit thee down and write
In a book that all may read—
So he vanish'd from my sight.
And I pluck'd a hollow reed.

And I made a rural pen,
And I stain'd the water clear,
And I wrote my happy songs
Every child may joy to hear.

The Ecchoing Green

The Sun does arise,
And make happy the skies.
The merry bells ring,
To welcome the Spring.
The sky-lark and thrush,
The birds of the bush,
Sing louder around,
To the bells chearful sound.
While our sports shall be seen
On the Ecchoing Green.

Old John with white hair
Does laugh away care,
Sitting under the oak,
Among the old folk.
They laugh at our play,
And soon they all say,
Such such were the joys.
When we all girls & boys,
In our youth time were seen,
On the Ecchoing Green.

Till the little ones weary
No more can be merry
The sun does descend,
And our sports have an end:
Round the laps of their mothers,
Many sisters and brothers,
Like birds in their nest,

Are ready for rest;
And sport no more seen,
On the darkening Green.

Holy Thursday[1]

'Twas on a Holy Thursday, their innocent faces clean,
The children walking two & two, in red & blue & green;
Grey headed beadles walkd before with wands as white as snow,
Till into the high dome of Paul's they like Thames' waters flow.

O what a multitude they seemd, these flowers of London town!
Seated in companies they sit with radiance all their own.
The hum of multitudes was there, but multitudes of lambs,
Thousands of little boys & girls raising their innocent hands.

Now like a mighty wind they raise to heaven the voice of song,
Or like harmonious thunderings the seats of heaven among.
Beneath them sit the agèd men, wise guardians of the poor;
Then cherish pity, lest you drive an angel from your door.[2]

The Lamb

Little Lamb, who made thee?
Dost thou know who made thee?
Gave thee life, and bid thee feed
By the stream and o'er the mead;
Gave thee clothing of delight,
Softest clothing woolly bright;
Gave thee such a tender voice,
Making all the vales rejoice?
Little Lamb, who made thee?
Dost thou know who made thee?

Little Lamb, I'll tell thee!
Little Lamb, I'll tell thee:
He is calléd by thy name,
For he calls himself a Lamb,
He is meek and he is mild;
He became a little child.
I a child and thou a lamb,
We are callèd by his name.
Little Lamb, God bless thee!
Little Lamb, God bless thee!

1. In the English Church, the Thursday celebrating Christ's ascension, thirty-nine days after Easter. It was customary on this day to march the poor, frequently orphaned, children from the charity schools of London to a service at St. Paul's Cathedral.
2. See Hebrews 13.2: "Be not forgetful to entertain strangers: for thereby some have entertained angels unawares."

The Chimney Sweeper

When my mother died I was very young,
And my father sold me while yet my tongue,
Could scarcely cry weep weep weep weep.
So your chimneys I sweep & in soot I sleep.

There's little Tom Dacre, who cried when his head
That curl'd like a lambs back, was shav'd, so I said.
Hush Tom never mind it, for when your head's bare,
You know that the soot cannot spoil your white hair.

And so he was quiet, & that very night,
As Tom was a sleeping he had such a sight,
That thousands of sweepers Dick, Joe Ned & Jack
Were all of them lock'd up in coffins of black

And by came an Angel who had a bright key,
And he open'd the coffins & set them all free.
Then down a green plain leaping laughing they run
And wash in a river and shine in the Sun.

Then naked & white, all their bags left behind,
They rise upon clouds, and sport in the wind.
And the Angel told Tom if he'd be a good boy,
He'd have God for his father & never want[3] joy.

And so Tom awoke and we rose in the dark
And got with our bags & our brushes to work.
Tho' the morning was cold, Tom was happy & warm,
So if all do their duty, they need not fear harm.

1789

SONGS OF EXPERIENCE

Introduction

Hear the voice of the Bard!
Who Present, Past, & Future sees;
Whose ears have heard
The Holy Word,
That walk'd among the ancient trees;

Calling the lapsèd Soul
And weeping in the evening dew,
That might controll
The starry pole,
And fallen fallen light renew!

3. Lack.

O Earth, O Earth, return!
Arise from out the dewy grass;
Night is worn,
And the morn
Rises from the slumberous mass.

Turn away no more;
Why wilt thou turn away?
The starry floor
The watry shore
Is giv'n thee till the break of day.

The Tyger

Tyger! Tyger! burning bright
In the forests of the night,
What immortal hand or eye
Could frame thy fearful symmetry?

In what distant deeps or skies
Burnt the fire of thine eyes?
On what wings dare he aspire?
What the hand dare seize the fire?

And what shoulder, & what art,
Could twist the sinews of thy heart?
And when thy heart began to beat,
What dread hand? & what dread feet?

What the hammer? what the chain?
In what furnace was thy brain?
What the anvil? what dread grasp
Dare its deadly terrors clasp?

When the stars threw down their spears
And water'd heaven with their tears,
Did he smile his work to see?
Did he who made the Lamb make thee?

Tyger! Tyger! burning bright
In the forests of the night,
What immortal hand or eye
Dare frame thy fearful symmetry?

The Garden of Love

I went to the Garden of Love,
And saw what I never had seen:
A Chapel was built in the midst,
Where I used to play on the green.

SONGS
Of
INNOCENCE
and Of
EXPERIENCE

Shewing the Two Contrary States
of the Human Soul

SONGS
Innocence
The Author & Printer W Blake

Introduction

Piping down the valleys wild
Piping songs of pleasant glee
On a cloud I saw a child.
And he laughing said to me.

Pipe a song about a Lamb;
So I piped with merry chear,
Piper pipe that song again—
So I piped, he wept to hear.

Drop thy pipe thy happy pipe
Sing thy songs of happy chear,
So I sung the same again
While he wept with joy to hear

Piper sit thee down and write
In a book that all may read—
So he vanish'd from my sight.
And I pluck'd a hollow reed.

And I made a rural pen,
And I staind the water clear,
And I wrote my happy songs
Every child may joy to hear

The Ecchoing Green

The Sun does arise,
And make happy the skies.
The merry bells ring,
To welcome the Spring.
The sky-lark and thrush,
The birds of the bush,
Sing louder around,
To the bells chearful sound.
While our sports shall be seen
On the Ecchoing Green.

Old John with white hair
Does laugh away care,
Sitting under the oak,
Among the old folk.

They laugh at our play,
And soon they all say.
Such such were the joys.
When we all girls & boys,
In our youth-time were seen,
On the Ecchoing Green.
Till the little ones weary
No more can be merry
The sun does descend,
And our sports have an end:
Round the laps of their mothers,
Many sisters and brothers,
Like birds in their nest,
Are ready for rest;
And sport no more seen,
On the darkening Green.

HOLY THURSDAY

Twas on a Holy Thursday their innocent faces clean
The children walking two & two in red & blue & green
Grey headed beadles walkd before with wands as white as snow
Till into the high dome of Pauls they like Thames waters flow

O what a multitude they seemd these flowers of London town
Seated in companies they sit with radiance all their own
The hum of multitudes was there but multitudes of lambs
Thousands of little boys & girls raising their innocent hands

Now like a mighty wind they raise to heaven the voice of song
Or like harmonious thunderings the seats of heaven among
Beneath them sit the aged men wise guardians of the poor
Then cherish pity, lest you drive an angel from your door

The Lamb
Little Lamb who made thee
Dost thou know who made thee
Gave thee life & bid thee feed.
By the stream & o'er the mead;
Gave thee clothing of delight,
Softest clothing wooly bright;
Gave thee such a tender voice,
Making all the vales rejoice;
Little Lamb who made thee
Dost thou know who made thee

Little Lamb I'll tell thee,
Little Lamb I'll tell thee;
He is called by thy name,
For he calls himself a Lamb;
He is meek & he is mild,
He became a little child:
I a child & thou a lamb,
We are called by his name.
Little Lamb God bless thee.
Little Lamb God bless thee.

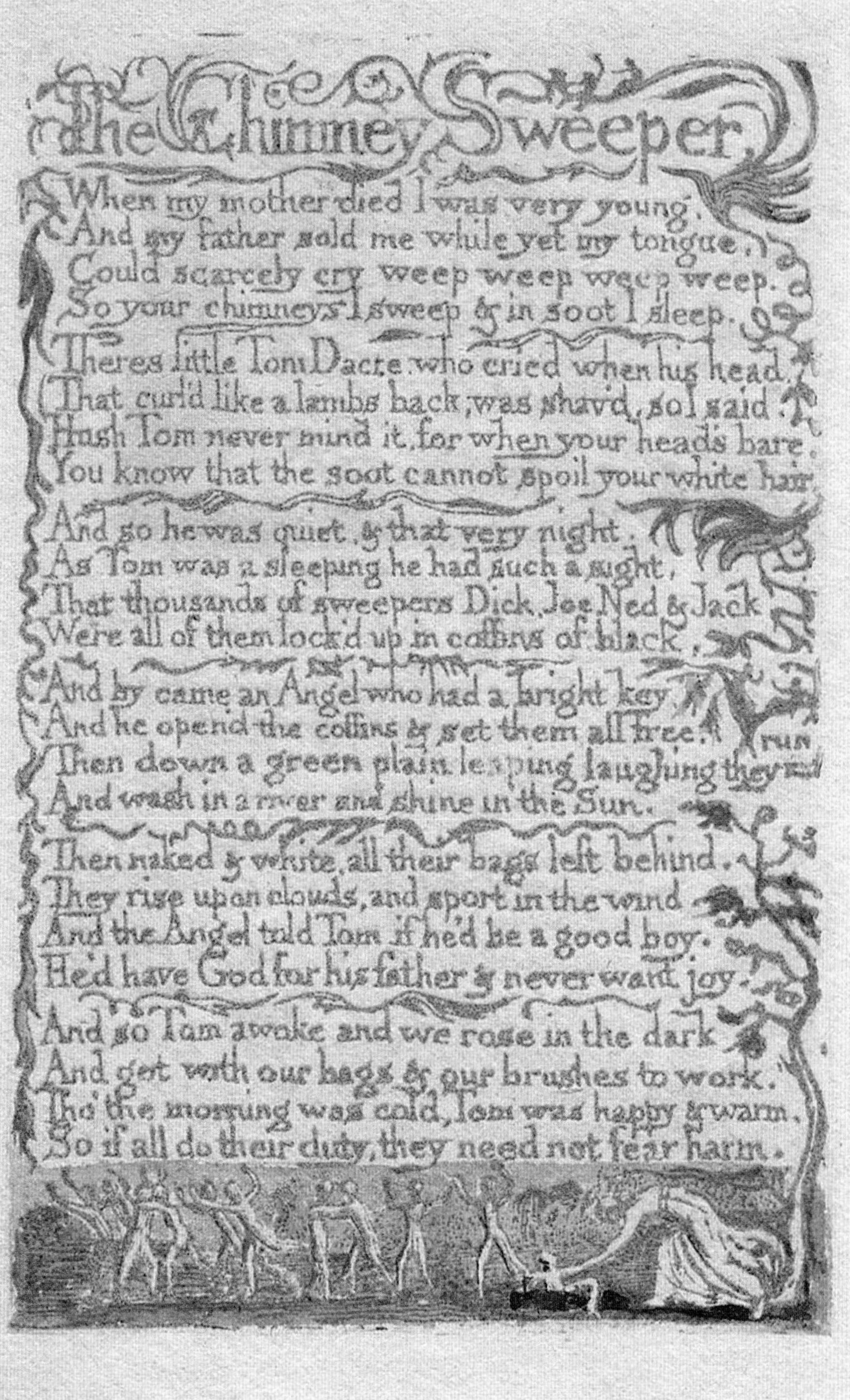

The Chimney Sweeper

When my mother died I was very young,
And my father sold me while yet my tongue,
Could scarcely cry weep weep weep weep.
So your chimneys I sweep & in soot I sleep.

Theres little Tom Dacre, who cried when his head
That curl'd like a lambs back, was shav'd, so I said.
Hush Tom never mind it, for when your head's bare,
You know that the soot cannot spoil your white hair

And so he was quiet, & that very night.
As Tom was a sleeping he had such a sight,
That thousands of sweepers Dick, Joe Ned & Jack
Were all of them lock'd up in coffins of black,

And by came an Angel who had a bright key
And he open'd the coffins & set them all free.
Then down a green plain leaping laughing they run
And wash in a river and shine in the Sun.

Then naked & white, all their bags left behind.
They rise upon clouds, and sport in the wind
And the Angel told Tom if he'd be a good boy.
He'd have God for his father & never want joy.

And so Tom awoke and we rose in the dark
And got with our bags & our brushes to work.
Tho' the morning was cold, Tom was happy & warm.
So if all do their duty, they need not fear harm.

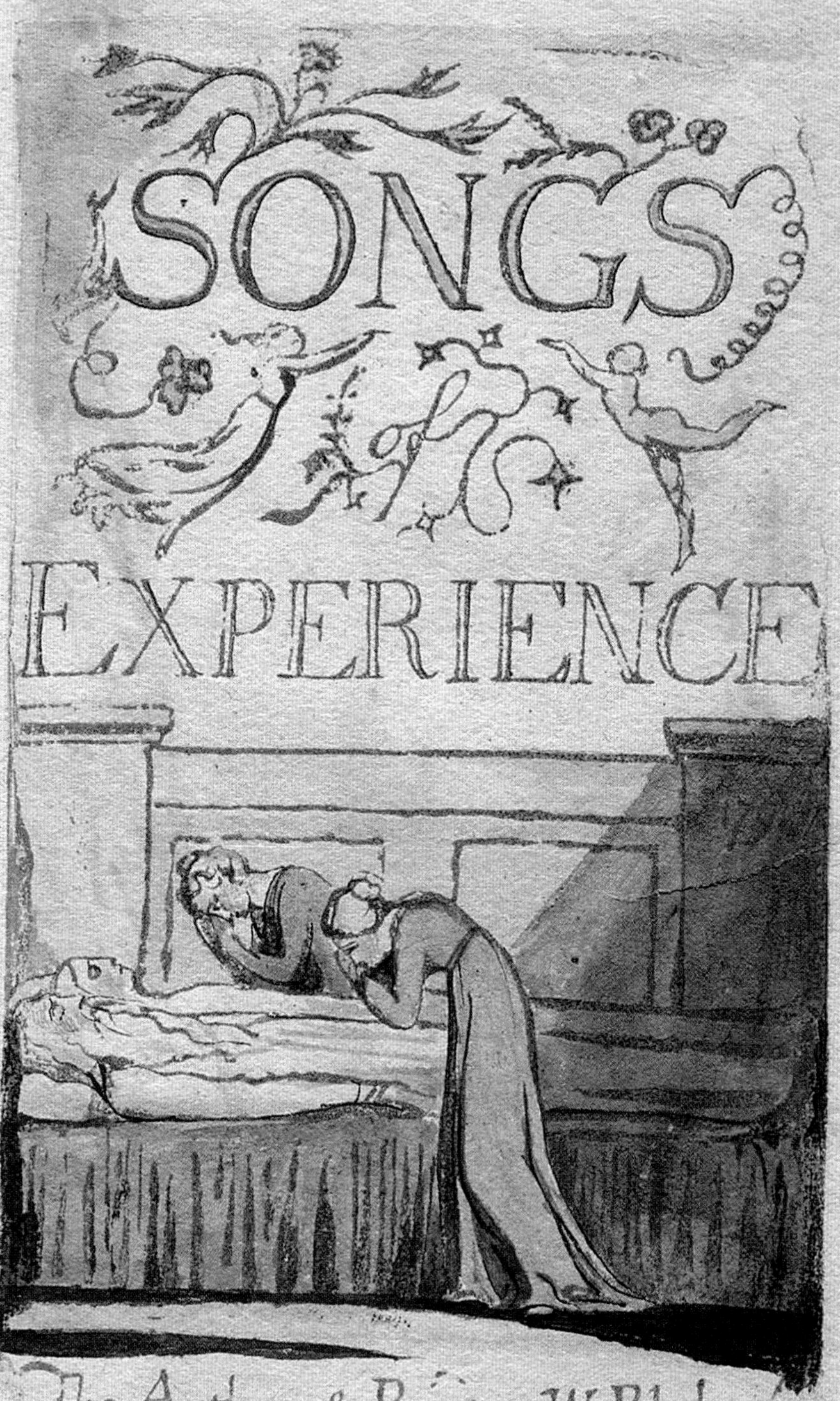
SONGS
of
EXPERIENCE
The Author & Printer W Blake

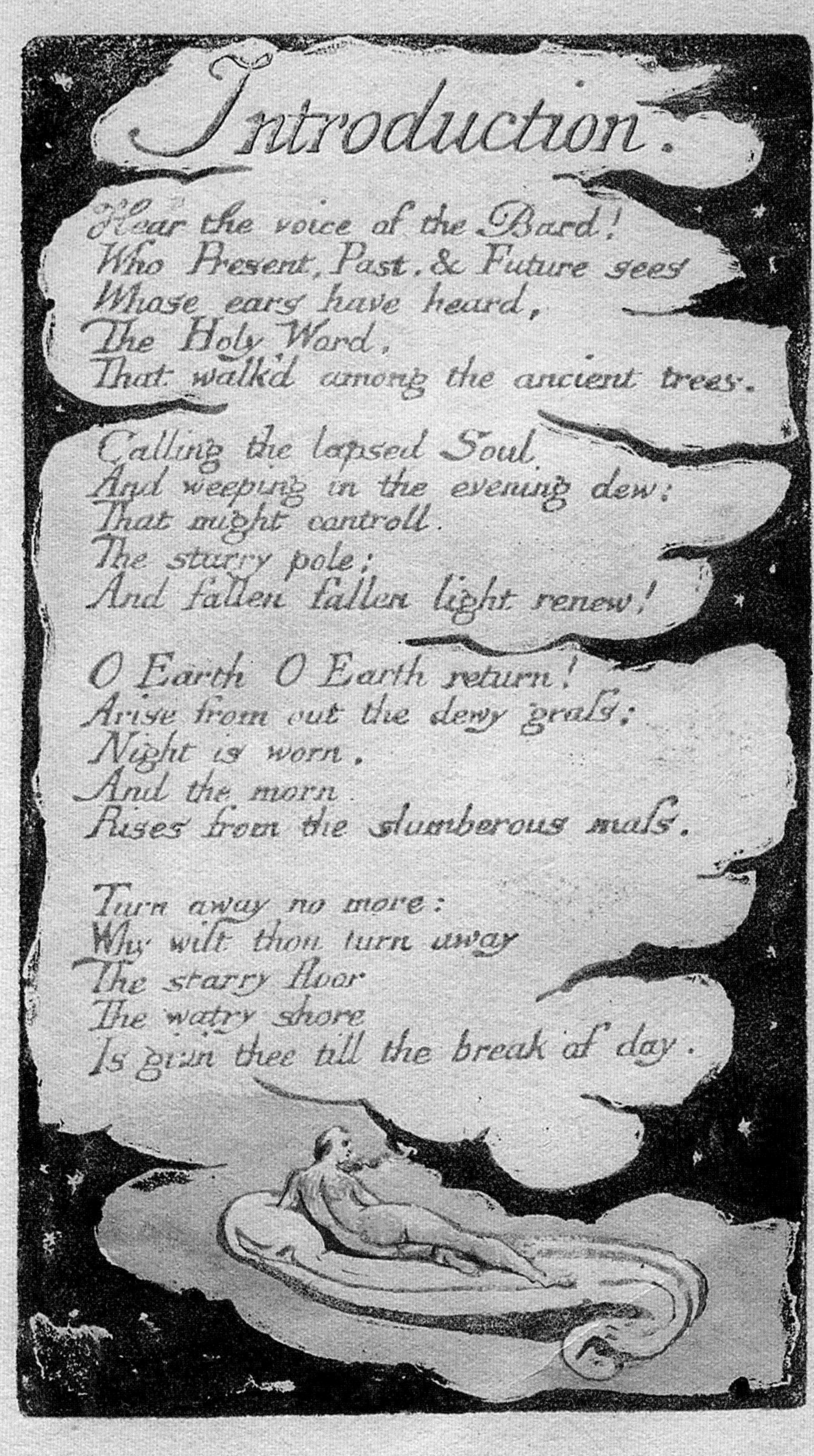

Introduction.

Hear the voice of the Bard!
Who Present, Past, & Future sees
Whose ears have heard,
The Holy Word,
That walk'd among the ancient trees.

Calling the lapsed Soul
And weeping in the evening dew;
That might controll,
The starry pole;
And fallen fallen light renew!

O Earth O Earth return!
Arise from out the dewy grass;
Night is worn,
And the morn
Rises from the slumberous mass.

Turn away no more:
Why wilt thou turn away
The starry floor
The watry shore
Is giv'n thee till the break of day.

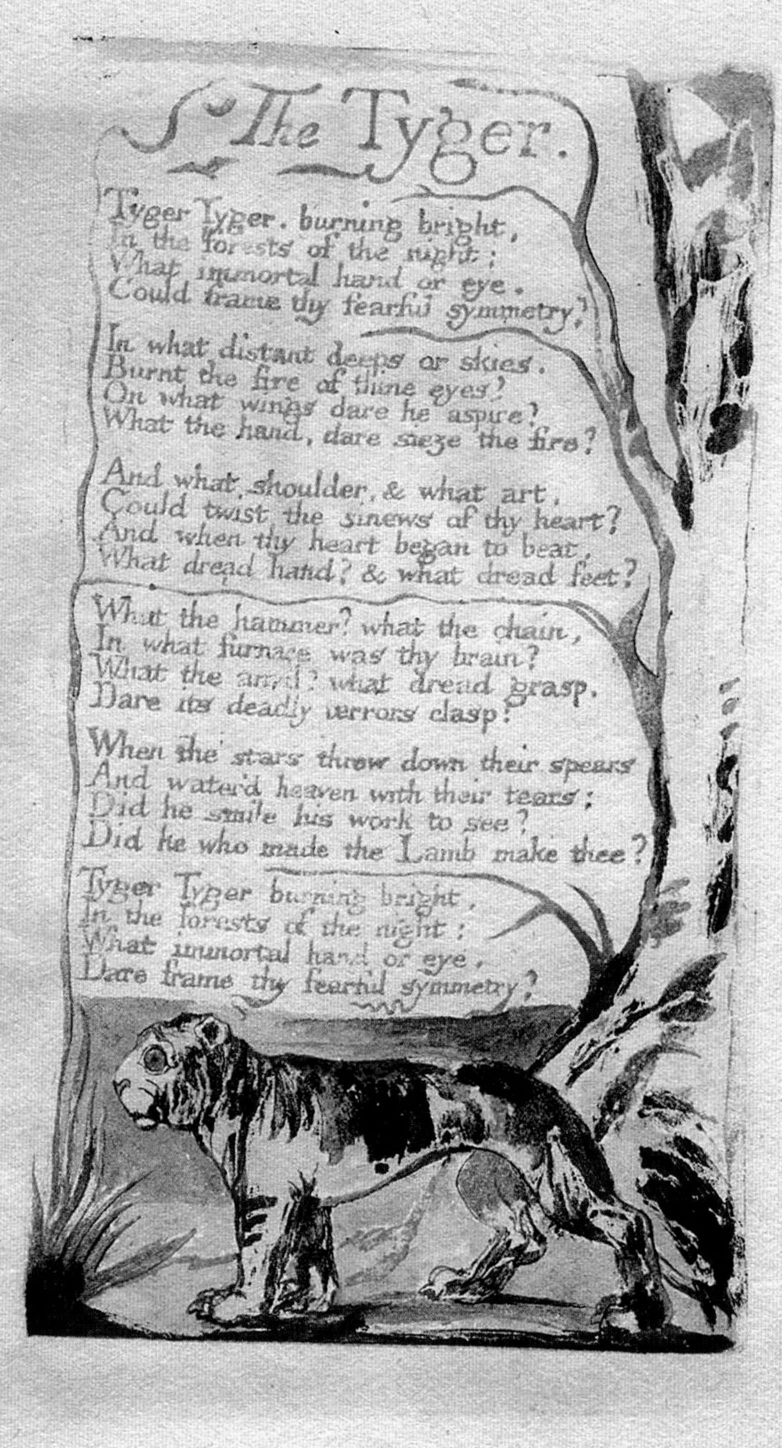

The Tyger.

Tyger Tyger. burning bright,
In the forests of the night;
What immortal hand or eye.
Could frame thy fearful symmetry?

In what distant deeps or skies.
Burnt the fire of thine eyes?
On what wings dare he aspire?
What the hand, dare sieze the fire?

And what shoulder, & what art,
Could twist the sinews of thy heart?
And when thy heart began to beat,
What dread hand? & what dread feet?

What the hammer? what the chain,
In what furnace was thy brain?
What the anvil? what dread grasp.
Dare its deadly terrors clasp?

When the stars threw down their spears
And water'd heaven with their tears:
Did he smile his work to see?
Did he who made the Lamb make thee?

Tyger Tyger burning bright,
In the forests of the night:
What immortal hand or eye,
Dare frame thy fearful symmetry?

The GARDEN of LOVE
I went to the Garden of Love.
And saw what I never had seen:
A Chapel was built in the midst,
Where I used to play on the green.
And the gates of this Chapel were shut,
And Thou shalt not. writ over the door;
So I turn'd to the Garden of Love,
That so many sweet flowers bore.
And I saw it was filled with graves,
And tomb-stones where flowers should be:
And Priests in black gowns, were walking their
rounds,
And binding with briars, my joys & desires.

THE Chimney Sweeper
A little black thing among the snow:
Crying weep, weep, in notes of woe!
Where are thy father & mother? say?
They are both gone up to the church to pray.
Because I was happy upon the heath,
And smil'd among the winters snow:
They clothed me in the clothes of death,
And taught me to sing the notes of woe.
And because I am happy, & dance & sing,
They think they have done me no injury:
And are gone to praise God & his Priest & King
Who make up a heaven of our misery.

HOLY THURSDAY
Is this a holy thing to see,
In a rich and fruitful land,
Babes reduced to misery,
Fed with cold and usurous hand?
Is that trembling cry a song?
Can it be a song of joy?
And so many children poor?
It is a land of poverty!
And their sun does never shine.
And their fields are bleak & bare.
And their ways are fill'd with thorns.
It is eternal winter there.
For where-e'er the sun does shine,
And where-e'er the rain does fall:
Babe can never hunger there,
Nor poverty the mind appall.

And the gates of this Chapel were shut,
And Thou shalt not, writ over the door;
So I turn'd to the Garden of Love,
That so many sweet flowers bore,

And I saw it was filled with graves,
And tomb-stones where flowers should be:
And Priests in black gowns, were walking their rounds,
And binding with briars, my joys & desires.

The Chimney Sweeper

A little black thing among the snow:
Crying weep, weep, in notes of woe!
Where are thy father & mother? say?
They are both gone up to the church to pray.

Because I was happy upon the heath,
And smil'd among the winters snow:
They clothed me in the clothes of death,
And taught me to sing the notes of woe.

And because I am happy, & dance & sing,
They think they have done me no injury:
And are gone to praise God & his Priest & King
Who make up a heaven of our misery.

Holy Thursday

Is this a holy thing to see,
In a rich and fruitful land,
Babes reduced to misery,
Fed with cold and usurous hand?

Is that trembling cry a song?
Can it be a song of joy?
And so many children poor?
It is a land of poverty!

And their sun does never shine,
And their fields are bleak & bare,
And their ways are fill'd with thorns;
It is eternal winter there.

For where-e'er the sun does shine,
And where-e'er the rain does fall,
Babe can never hunger there,
Nor poverty the mind appall.

1794

Chronology: William Blake and His Times

1757 William Blake is born in London on November 28, one of the seven children of Catherine and James Blake (a maker and seller of stockings and gloves); only five of the children will survive infancy.

1765–67 Blake has his first angelic visions and, at age ten (1767), enters drawing school.

1772 At age fourteen, Blake is apprenticed to a master engraver.

1776 The American Revolution, or War of Independence, begins.

1779 His apprenticeship complete, the twenty-one-year-old Blake begins his studies at the Royal Academy of Art.

1780 Blake begins to read and sing his own poems to friends and to earn his living by giving drawing lessons and by engraving prints and book illustrations for other authors and artists. (One such work is Anna Letitia Barbauld's *Hymns in Prose for Children* [1781].) While sketching near a river, Blake and two fellow artists are detained by British soldiers, who suspect them of being French spies; the prisoners are released only after other Royal Academy members testify on their behalf.

1782 Blake (at twenty-four) marries Catherine Boucher, an illiterate former domestic servant and one of the thirteen children of a market gardener. (Blake will teach his wife not only to read and write but also to engrave and print books, and she will eventually help with the engraving, printing, coloring, and assembly of all his self-published works.)

1783 A friend finances the publication of *Poetical Sketches*, the only book by Blake to be published in the conventional manner by another publisher. The American War of Independence ends in a British defeat.

1784 After the death of Blake's father, Blake's younger brother comes to live and study engraving with Blake and his wife; Blake uses his small inheritance to open a small print-selling and publishing business with a friend and writes (but does not publish) *An Island in the Moon*, a work of prose satire containing drafts of three poems later included in *Songs of Innocence*.

1785 When Blake's business folds, he returns to his work as an engraver for other publishers.

1787 After his brother's death, Blake begins to see him in visions, including one that reveals a new method of "illuminated printing" or relief etching.

1788 Blake produces *All Religions Are One* and *There Is No Natural Religion*, the first works made using his "illuminated printing" technique; Blake will use the same method to self-publish all of his subsequent work.

1789 Blake etches *Songs of Innocence* and *The Book of Thel*. The French Revolution begins in July with the storming of the Bastille, a Parisian prison.

1790–91 Blake etches *The Marriage of Heaven and Hell* and *The French Revolution*.

1792 Blake's friend and fellow radical Thomas Paine is sentenced to death in absentia for publishing his two-part political treatise *Rights of Man*, though the sentence is never carried out.

1793 In France, Louis XVI and Marie Antoinette are executed as part of the "Reign of Terror." Britain and France go to war. Blake etches *America*.

1794 Several London radicals well known to Blake are tried for high treason, a capital crime, but they are ultimately acquitted. Blake produces *Songs of Innocence and of Experience*, *Visions of the Daughters of Albion*, and *The Book of Urizen*.

1795–96 Blake produces *The Book of Los* and begins *The Four Zoas*.

1800 Blake and his wife move from London to the Sussex seaside to be near his new patron, William Hayley, whom Blake will later describe as "the enemy of my Spiritual Life while he pretends to be the Friend of my Corporeal."

1802–1804 A scuffle with a soldier leads to Blake's trial and acquittal on charges of sedition, a capital crime. Blake and Catherine move back to London.

1809–10 Blake self-publishes *Milton*.

1815 British forces defeat Napoleon at Waterloo.

1818–20 Blake self-publishes *Jerusalem*.

1820–25 Blake produces (on commission) illustrations for the Book of Job.

1825 Blake begins work on another commission, illustrations for Dante's *Divine Comedy*.

1827 Blake dies on August 12 at the age of sixty-nine.

SUGGESTIONS FOR WRITING

1. Write an essay analyzing Blake's two HOLY THURSDAY poems or any other pair of counterpart poems from *Songs of Innocence and of Experience*. What different views of the same person, place, situation, and so on are offered in your two poems? What conclusions does each poem seem to reach about, and through, the subject it depicts? How do the poems' formal qualities—syntax, diction, rhythm, rhyme, and so on—contribute to their distinctive tone and theme(s)?
2. Drawing on evidence from various poems in the "Songs of Experience" section of *Songs of Innocence and of Experience*, write an essay explaining how LONDON or THE SICK ROSE works as a "Song of Experience" poem. What similarities do you see between LONDON or THE SICK ROSE and other "Experience" poems? What does either of these poems add to the "Experience" sequence?
3. Write an essay exploring a particular symbol or set of symbols, characters, or formal techniques that you see as important to the effect and meaning of Blake's *Songs* as a sequence.
4. Choose any poem in this anthology and use library or Internet resources to research the collection or sequence of which it is a part. Write a response paper or essay reflecting on how your interpretation of the poem changes when you read it as part of a particular collection or sequence rather than on its own.
5. Write an essay analyzing at least two poems in this book that are part of the same sequence or collection. You might choose two sonnets by Edna St. Vincent Millay or William Shakespeare; two of the poems from Robert Browning's *Dramatic Lyrics* (1842): MY LAST DUCHESS and SOLILOQUY OF THE SPANISH CLOISTER; or two poems from the sequence of odes by John Keats that includes ODE TO A NIGHTINGALE, ODE ON A GRECIAN URN, and TO AUTUMN. How do your two poems make sense together, as parts of a single, unified sequence or collection? If you know how the poems are ordered in the collection, what difference might their order make to their meaning?
6. Write two poems that, like Blake's HOLY THURSDAY or CHIMNEY SWEEPER poems, depict the same object, person, or situation from two dramatically different perspectives.

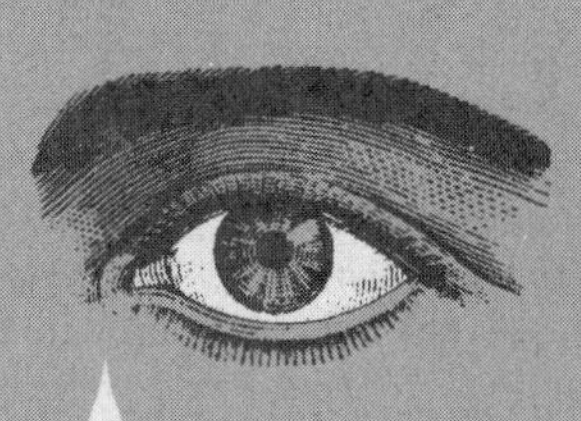

BOOK
OF HOURS
poems
KEVIN YOUNG

Kevin Young's *Book of Hours*

AN ALBUM

As comfortable talking with interviewers about *The X-Men* as he is about the Harlem Renaissance, poet Kevin Young was born in Lincoln, Nebraska, in 1970 and grew up mainly in the Midwest, spending the bulk of his childhood in Topeka, Kansas, before heading east to Boston. There, he took courses with Nobel Laureate Seamus Heaney, participated—alongside Natasha Trethewey—in the influential Dark Room Collective, and wrote many of the poems that would eventually make up his first, award-winning collection (*Most Way Home*, 1995) on the way to earning a BA in English and American literature from Harvard (1992). Young then spent two years at Stanford University, in Northern California, before completing his MFA at Brown, in Rhode Island. A child of the Midwest who spent time on both East and West Coasts, the truly all-American Young also has Southern roots. Both his mother—among the first black women to earn a PhD (in chemistry) from the University of Nebraska—and his father—an ophthalmologist who was also an avid hunter and cook—grew up in rural Louisiana, where much of Young's extended family still lives and which he describes as "that deep, deep country which I love so much" and "that's part of my growing up," even if "I didn't ever live there." Since 2005, when he married editor Kate Tuttle, Young has lived and worked mainly in Atlanta, Georgia, where he currently serves as both a professor of English and creative writing and the curator of the Raymond Danowski Poetry Library at Emory University.

The latter job would seem to be an especially apt one for a self-described "pack rat" from "a long line of pack rats" who collects everything from comic books and vinyl records to modern art and Langston Hughes first editions. Especially for a writer only in his forties, Young has also collected an impressive array of awards and achievements, including American Book and PEN awards and a Paterson Poetry Prize. Regarded as among the best poets of his generation, he has published sixteen books. These include both collections of his own poetry and essays and edited collections featuring the work of other poets. The titles of the latter collections reveal much about Young's eclectic interests and influences, ranging as they do from *The Hungry Ear: Poems of Food and Drink* (2012) to *The Art of Losing: Poems of Grief and Healing* (2010); from *Jazz Poems* (2006) and *Blues Poems* (2006) to *Selected Poems: John Berryman* (2004) and *The Collected Poems of Lucille Clifton* (2012).

Diverse as Young's own verse also is, each of his collections tends to be a highly unified work in which all of the individual poems—often lyrics written in a variety of voices—work together as part of a single, carefully crafted whole that often tells a story of sorts. Originally presented as a 350-page "double album in verse" and also described as a "jazz symphony" or "hip-hop opera," Young's second collection, *To Repel Ghosts: Five Sides in B Minor* (2002), for example, recounts the brief, wildly successful, yet troubled life of graffiti-artist-turned-painter Jean-Michel Basquiat, who died of a heroine overdose in 1988, when he was only twenty-seven. Riffing on classic 1940s Hollywood detective films, the poems in Young's

Black Maria (2005) relate the fictional adventures of private eye A. K. A. Jones and the alluring but dangerous Delilah Redbone, while those in *Ardency* (2011) tell the real-life tale of the Africans en route to the Americas who managed to wrest control of the slave ship *Amistad* in 1839 and later won their freedom in U.S. courts.

Fittingly, then, this album does not attempt to represent the range of Young's diverse body of work in its entirety but instead features poems taken exclusively from just one recent work—*Book of Hours* (2014). Published on the tenth anniversary of his sixty-one-year-old father's death in a hunting accident, the collection moves from poems grappling with this life-altering event to those inspired by another—the birth of Young's first son, less than two years later. Thus effectively charting the passage from death to birth and from losing a father to becoming one, the poems reflect, too, on the interconnections between these different experiences and the complex, evolving feelings they provoke. In this way, the poems embody what Young describes as a "kind of blues sensibility" or even "philosophy," a "tragicomic view of life" peculiarly attuned to the "moments of humor" found "even in sorrow" and to the sorrow underlying the greatest joy.

Like all Young's titles, *Book of Hours* has various meanings that suggest much about the way the poems in the book work and mean. Traditionally, the phrase *book of hours* refers to a type of book very popular with medieval Christians: hand-assembled and vividly colored, each was composed of prayers and psalms to be used in one's personal daily devotions. Such books, Young observes, thus "have this kind of intimate quality, . . . and I wanted to really capture that kind of intimacy." At the same time, Young's is a "book of hours" in the more literal sense that it aims to capture, in his words, the many different "hours and days and moments, in the process of grief and joy." Because that process and those feelings are, moreover, ones both that every one either has, or some day might, experience, and that involve an entire family, it seems altogether appropriate, too, that "book of hours" can't help but sound like "book of *ours*" or even "our book." And that, says Young, "I actually kind of love."

Rue

Strange how you keep on
          dying—not once
then over

& done with—or for—
          if not every day
anymore, each morning

a sabbath of sundering,
          then hours still arrive
I realize nothing

can beg you back—
          nor return to us days
without harm, heaven

only an idea. Hell not yet
          that week
I couldn't bear to sleep

in your half-life house
        & my future
wife & I stayed

at the Worst
        Western, the phone
ringing early, & late,

too late. I'd wake

& you'd be there, gone—
        retreating
to the bleak bathroom

& its heat lamp, perched
        on the edge
of the empty tub, I'd try

not to write.
        How terrible
to have to pick up

the pen, helpless
        to it, your death
not yet

a habit & try to say
        something other than
never, or *hereafter*,

to praise among the tile—
        not your dying—
but having

been alive. The pale bathroom

whose light burnt on, red
        as a darkroom,
ticking down—

your eulogy dashed out
        among the tiny
broken soap, each day

shrinking, slivered
        in our hands. Come late
afternoon, the distant, wet slaps

of children poolside
        crying out
in laughter—their muffled

watery shrieks echoing after.

Charity

So many socks.

After the pair
the undertaker asks for
(I picture them black

beneath the fold
in your open casket,
your toes still cold)

what else to do.
Body bags
of old suits, shirts

still pressed, long
johns, the unworn,
unwashed wreckage

of your closet, too many
coats to keep, though I will save
so many. How can I

give away the last
of your scent? And still,
father, you have errands,

errant dry cleaning to pick up—
yellow tags whose ghostly
carbon tells a story

where to look. One
place closed
for good, the tag old.

One place with none
of your clothes,
just stares as if no one

ever dies, as if you
are naked somewhere,
& I suppose you are.

Nothing here.
The last place knows exactly
what I mean, brings me shirts

hanging like a head.
Starched collars
your beard had worn.

One man saying sorry, older lady
in the back saying how funny
you were, how you joked

with her weekly. *Sorry—*
& a fellow black man hands
your clothes back for free,

don't worry. I've learned death
has few kindnesses left,
Such is charity—so rare

& so rarely free—
that on the way back
to your emptying house

I weep. Then drive
everything, swaying,
straight to Goodwill—

open late—to live on
another body
& day.

Wintering

I am no longer ashamed
how for weeks, after, I wanted
to be dead—not to die,

mind you, or do
myself in—but to be there
already, walking amongst

all those I'd lost, to join
the throng singing,
if that's what there is—

or the nothing, the gnawing—
So be it. I wished
to be warm—& worn—

like the quilt my grandmother
must have made, one side
a patchwork of color—

blues, green like the underside
of a leaf—the other
an old pattern of the dolls

of the world, never cut out
but sewn whole—if the world
were Scotsmen & sailors

in traditional uniforms.
Mourning, I've learned, is just
a moment, many,

grief the long betrothal
beyond. Grief what
we wed, ringing us—

heirloom brought
from my father's hot house—
the quilt heavy tonight

at the foot of my marriage bed,
its weight months of needling
& thread. Each straightish,

pale, uneven stitch
like the white hairs I earned
all that hollowed year—pull one

& ten more will come,
wearing white, to its funeral—
each a mourner, a winter,

gathering ash at my temple.

Expecting

Grave, my wife lies back, hands cross
her chest, while the doctor searches early
for your heartbeat, peach pit, unripe

plum—pulls out the world's worst
boom box, a Mr. Microphone,[1] to broadcast
your mother's lifting belly.

The whoosh and bellows of mama's body
and beneath it: nothing. Beneath
the slow stutter of her heart: nothing.

The doctor trying again to find you, fragile
fern, snowflake. Nothing.
After, my wife will say, in fear,

impatient, she went beyond her body,
this tiny room, into the ether—
for now, we spelunk[2] for you one last time

lost canary,[3] miner of coal
and chalk, lungs not yet black—
I hold my wife's feet to keep her here—

1. Brand name device that amplified sound when plugged into a radio; it was widely known and ridiculed in the 1980s thanks to a notoriously cheesy television commercial (now viewable on YouTube).
2. Explore a cave.
3. Traditionally canaries were used in mines to detect the presence of poisonous gases.

and me—trying not to dive starboard[4]
to seek you in the dark water. And there
it is: faint, an echo, faster and further

away than mother's, all beat box
and fuzzy feedback. You are like hearing
hip-hop for the first time—power

hijacked from a lamppost[5]—all promise.
You couldn't sound better, break-
dancer, my favorite song bumping

from a passing car. You've snuck
into the club underage and stayed!
Only later, much, will your mother

begin to believe your drumming
in the distance—my Kansas City
and Congo Square,[6] this jazz band

vamping on[7] inside her.

2011

Quickening

Fourth of July
Sag Harbor, Long Island

On the beach the fireworks bloom
above us, their boom
and brightness, and my goddaughter

slips asleep. These days
inside mama you don't so much
kick as wrestle, an elbow

then your butt budding
out her belly. We lie
by the water and watch the dark

lap the sand and scrub-filled shore.
Another ultrasound shows
you are my son, alright—head down

like a monk, burrowing, your profile
and pout only I seem to see.
When will you arrive to usher us

4. To the right (nautical term).
5. According to some sources, the world's first hip-hop concert occurred in the 1970s when a DJ, unable to afford to rent a nightclub, plugged his equipment into a lamppost near a public park in the Bronx; powered by free electricity, the concert reportedly drew 3,000 people.
6. New Orleans park famous for African American musical performances. 7. Improvising.

into your arms? It is we
who will be born,
not you. After the fanfare

for the country's birth—the smoke
and strong gunpowder smell
to remind us what once was there—

we'll walk back home
across the dark,
unalone.

Breaking Water

The earth has no edge
except this: waiting

for you to get born
but quick. Your galaxy

inside mama keeps on
expanding, her stomach

a planetarium, solar
system of one. Son,

anything pressed
against mama's skin

leaves saturnine rings.
Her belts go begging—

and her wedding rings.

While scientists try to decide
whether Pluto's still

a planet,[8] you rotate
on your axis, play

Asteroids[9] with mama's pelvis.
I now know pain

is part of any journey—
that this is the opposite

of grief, but grief
the only way I know

to describe waiting
and waiting without

8. In 2006, the International Astronomical Union declared that Pluto should no longer be considered a planet, though scientists continue to debate its status.
9. Minor planets, especially of the inner solar system, but also a highly popular arcade/video game released in 1979 in which players shoot down asteroids and flying saucers.

knowing, hoping one day
joy will arrive.

Or return. You must cross
breaking waves

of pain, the canal
of your birth, mama's

breathing and me barely—and none
too soon you're here

named for your grandfather,
squalling.

Greening

It never ends, the bruise
of being—messy,
untimely, the breath

of newborns uneven, half
pant, as they find
their rhythm, inexact

as vengeance. Son,
while you sleep
we watch you like a kettle

learning to whistle.
Awake, older,
you fumble now

in the most graceful
way—grateful
to have seen you, on your own

steam, simply eating, slow,
chewing—this bloom
of being. Almost beautiful

how you flounder, mouth full, bite
the edges of this world
that doesn't want

a thing but to keep turning
with, or without you—
with. With. Child, hold fast

I say, to this greening thing
as it erodes
and spins.

[It's death there]

It's death there
is no cure for—

life the long
disease.

If we're lucky.

Otherwise, short
trip beyond.

And below.

Noon,
growing shadow.

I chase the quiet
round the house.

Soon the sound—

wind wills
its way against

the panes. Welcome
the rain.

Welcome
the moon's squinting

into space.
The trees

bow like priests.

The storm lifts
up the leaves.

Why not sing.

SUGGESTIONS FOR WRITING

1. Pick any two poems from Young's *Book of Hours*, and write an essay exploring how each captures what Young calls the "moments of humor" found "even in sorrow" and the sorrow hidden even within moments of great joy. In these terms, what might be the role of wordplay or particular figures of speech?
2. The first three poems in this album, RUE, CHARITY, and WINTERING, all deal mainly with grief and mourning. Write an essay exploring what they individually and collectively suggest about what grief actually feels like and how it works. How, if at all, might the order of the poems matter? Do they trace any sort of progression, or do they instead depict grief as something other than the straightforward, linear process we might think or want it to be?
3. Write an essay analyzing the four poems that deal mainly with the process of becoming a parent—EXPECTING, QUICKENING, BREAKING WATER, and GREENING. What do these poems individually and collectively show us about the various feelings a parent experiences both before and after a child's birth? Alternatively, focus

specifically on EXPECTING, QUICKENING, and BREAKING WATER, which seem especially unusual and interesting because they give us a *father's* perspective on pregnancy and childbirth.

4. Write an essay exploring how all of these poems work as part of a single sequence, perhaps by concentrating on the evolution of the speaker's outlook. In the first selection, RUE, for example, he describes himself as "try[ing] // not to write" (lines 28–29), whereas the last selection in this album and in *Book of Hours* itself ends, "Why not sing." How does the speaker seem to get from here to there? Alternatively, consider how the experience of death and grief gives shape and meaning to the experience of birth and new life in these poems. What, for example, does BREAKING WATER explicitly suggest about how waiting for a child to be born resembles grieving? How might the joys and fears expressed in GREENING be inspired or intensified by the earlier experience of loss? And so on.
5. Write your own poem or a short prose piece imagining a particular moment and situation depicted in one of Young's poems from his wife's perspective. What might it feel like, for example, to be the "future / wife [. . .] stay[ing] // at the Worst Western" with a newly bereaved fiancé, as in RUE (lines 18–20)? or to be the person who "keeps on / expanding, her stomach // a planetarium," as in BREAKING WATER (lines 5–7)?

24 CULTURAL AND HISTORICAL CONTEXTS: THE HARLEM RENAISSANCE

Poetry may be read in private moments or experienced in a great variety of communal settings—in classrooms or theaters, for example, or at poetry slams or public readings. But it is almost always *written* in solitude by a single author. Collaborative composition is rare in poetry, even rarer than in other arts. Still, there is a sense in which many poems represent collaborative acts. Traditions, group identities, shared experiences, desires, and communal needs may come together in a particular moment and location to produce poetry that has a distinctive stamp of time, place, and vision. One such phenomenon was the Harlem Renaissance, a period of ten or fifteen years early in the twentieth century when an extraordinarily talented group of people came together in uptown Manhattan to celebrate and embody the awakening of a new African American consciousness. It was an unprecedented moment in American poetry and in American culture more generally, and it produced some of the twentieth century's most compelling and original poems, as well as significant works of art in a variety of other categories.

The Harlem Renaissance was not exactly a movement in the sense of having a formal structure; no one originated it or called it to order, and in fact it was not consciously planned or organized by any person or group. There was no founder, no architect, no leader, and it is hard to say why or how—or even exactly when—it began or ended. It happened, as the needs and desires of African American intellectuals and artists became manifest and began to coalesce in a particular time and place, and it ended—or rather scattered its energy—when conditions in the world at large dictated that other priorities, especially economic ones, began to trump those that had brought it together. But it was not, of course, independent of history or without cause. It was a product of many circumstances, most of them involving the long-term aftereffects of slavery and the increasingly articulated desire of African Americans to produce a distinctive black American culture within the larger national culture. The Harlem Renaissance represented powerful assertions: that America had to include the voices of black Americans in order to find its own full definition and, equally, that artistic creativity—including literary creativity—was essential to black Americans' realization and assertion of their full humanity. To live in Harlem and to be black and creative was not an altogether happy experience, and the poetry that exploded out of that time and place is a poetry of anger, resentment, conflict, and torn loyalties. It is also a poetry of energy, sensitivity, humanity, and high ideals.

What was the Harlem Renaissance? It was first of all a migration or, rather, part of a migration: Around the end of World War I, American blacks relocated in large numbers from the South to the North and from rural areas to cities. New York was only one of many destinations; Chicago, Philadelphia, Detroit, Washington, Cleveland, Buffalo, and other urban centers all received huge numbers of

The Cotton Club, circa 1930

black migrants. But New York was the largest and most vibrant seat of culture in America, beginning to rival European capitals as a site where active artistic communities produced and consumed culture of all kinds—high, low, and in between. More than 100,000 blacks migrated to Harlem during the 1920s, taking over and transforming a Manhattan neighborhood north of Central Park and turning it into a distinctive, creative, independent center of art and performance activities that drew the rest of New York City to it. For most of the 1920s—called "the Roaring 20s" throughout the Western world because of the era's daring, rebellious attitudes and booming economic growth—Harlem was a magnet for avant-garde whites in New York. They flocked to speakeasies, nightclubs, and theaters (see map, pp. 1262–63). They were fascinated by the kinds of music, dance, and performance art they could find there—productions quite different from those on Broadway or in other parts of the city, though increasingly white venues tried to capture, in their own productions, something of the life and energy that patrons sought in Harlem. White readers, and many white artists, showed enormous—sometimes mawkish or even ghoulish—curiosity about black life in America. Before the Harlem Renaissance had ended, a large number of

A dancer entertains a crowd at Small's Paradise Club, 1929. As at many of Harlem's best-known nightclubs, the entertainers and staff at Small's were primarily African American, and the clientele was mainly white.

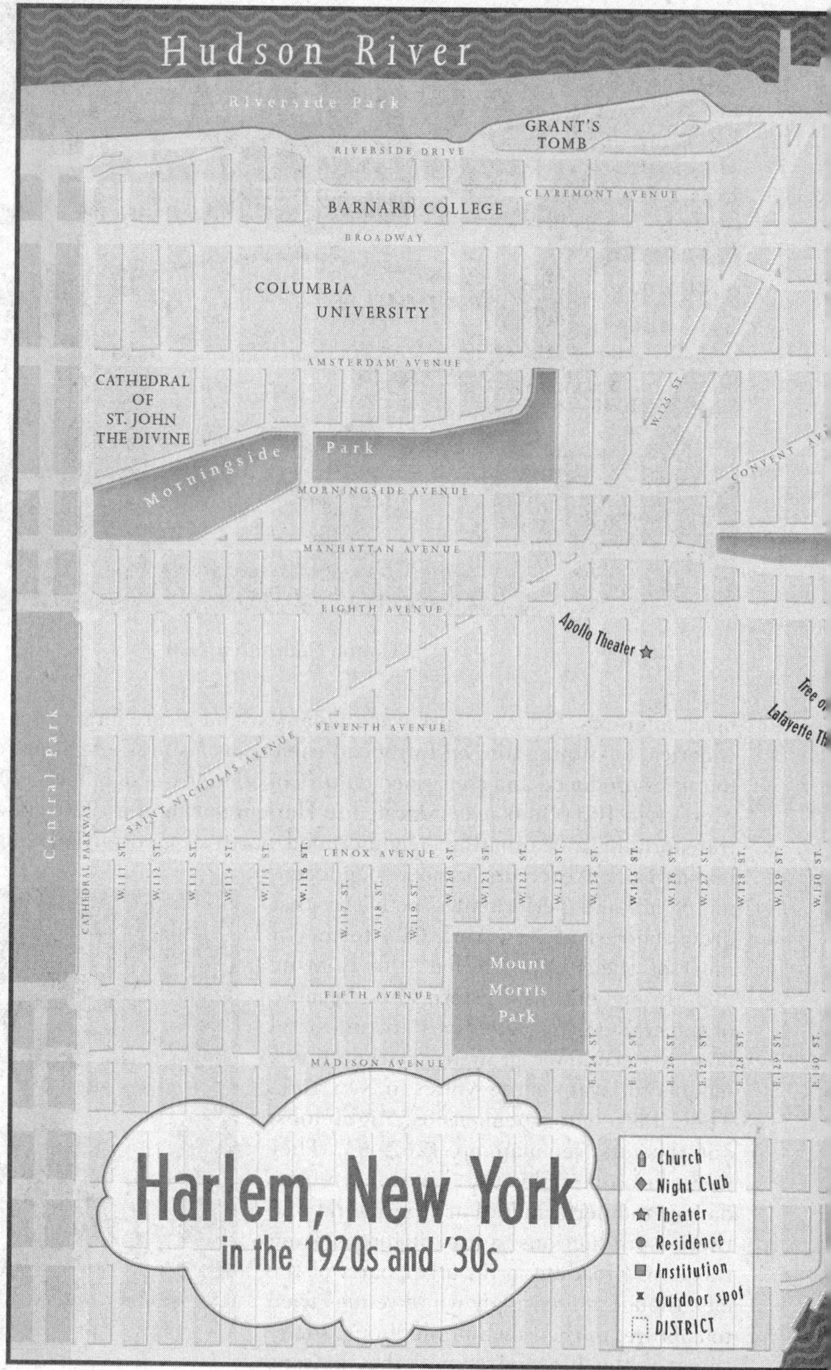

Hudson River
Riverside Park
GRANT'S TOMB
RIVERSIDE DRIVE
CLAREMONT AVENUE
BARNARD COLLEGE
BROADWAY
COLUMBIA UNIVERSITY
AMSTERDAM AVENUE
CATHEDRAL OF ST. JOHN THE DIVINE
Morningside Park
MORNINGSIDE AVENUE
W. 125 ST.
MANHATTAN AVENUE
EIGHTH AVENUE
Apollo Theater
SEVENTH AVENUE
SAINT NICHOLAS AVENUE
Central Park
CATHEDRAL PARKWAY
LENOX AVENUE
W. 111 ST.
W. 112 ST.
W. 113 ST.
W. 114 ST.
W. 115 ST.
W. 116 ST.
W. 117 ST.
W. 118 ST.
W. 119 ST.
W. 120 ST.
W. 121 ST.
W. 122 ST.
W. 123 ST.
W. 124 ST.
W. 125 ST.
W. 126 ST.
W. 127 ST.
W. 128 ST.
W. 129 ST.
W. 130 ST.
Mount Morris Park
FIFTH AVENUE
MADISON AVENUE
E. 124 ST.
E. 125 ST.
E. 126 ST.
E. 127 ST.
E. 128 ST.
E. 129 ST.
E. 130 ST.
Harlem, New York
in the 1920s and '30s
Church
Night Club
Theater
Residence
Institution
Outdoor spot
DISTRICT

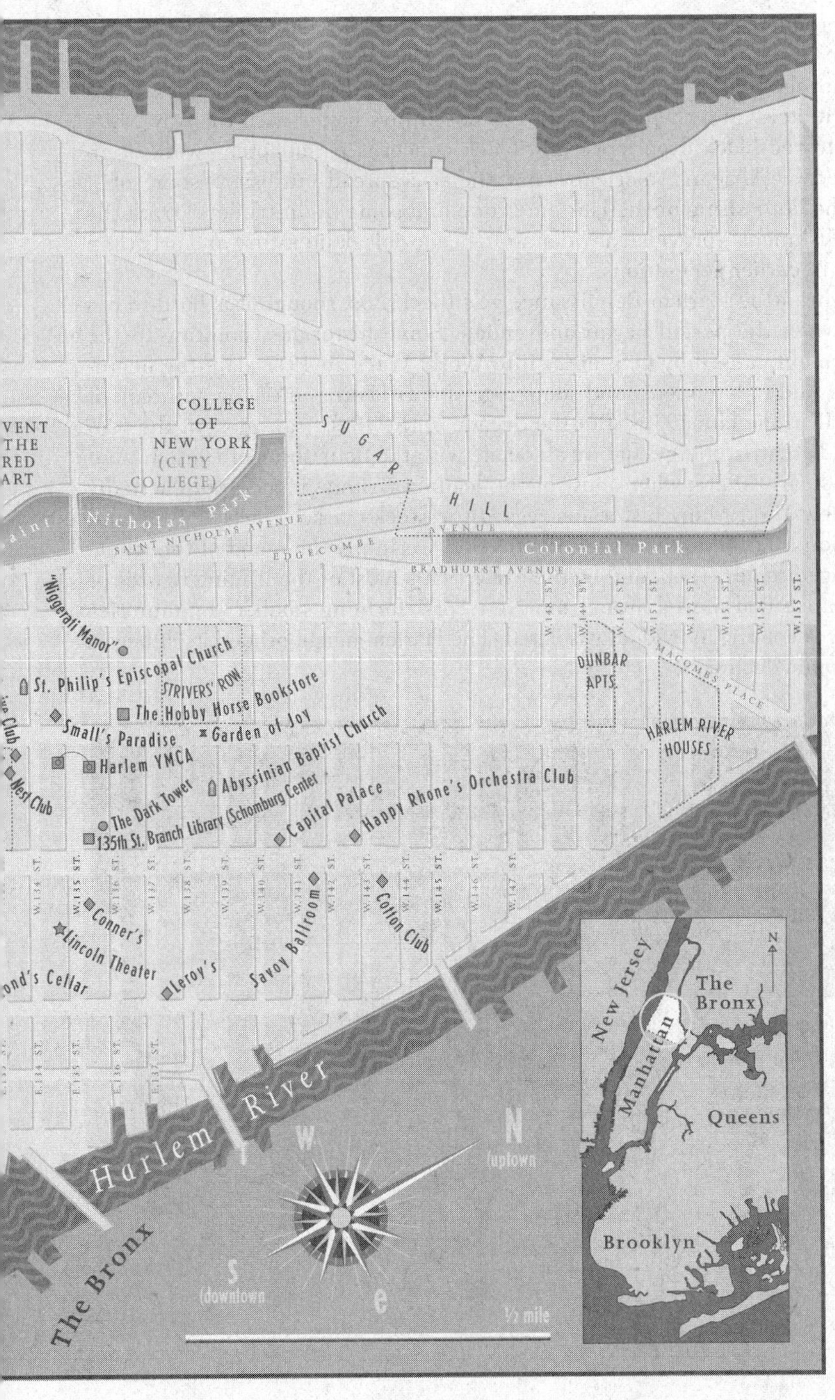

COLLEGE OF NEW YORK (CITY COLLEGE)
VENT
THE
RED
ART
SUGAR HILL
Saint Nicholas Park
SAINT NICHOLAS AVENUE
EDGECOMBE AVENUE
BRADHURST AVENUE
Colonial Park
"Niggerati Manor"
St. Philip's Episcopal Church
STRIVERS' ROW
The Hobby Horse Bookstore
Small's Paradise
Garden of Joy
Harlem YMCA
Abyssinian Baptist Church
The Dark Tower
135th St. Branch Library (Schomburg Center)
Capital Palace
Happy Rhone's Orchestra Club
Nest Club
Conner's
Lincoln Theater
Leroy's
Savoy Ballroom
Cotton Club
DUNBAR APTS.
HARLEM RIVER HOUSES
MACOMBS PLACE
W. 134 ST.
W. 135 ST.
W. 136 ST.
W. 137 ST.
W. 138 ST.
W. 139 ST.
W. 140 ST.
W. 141 ST.
W. 142 ST.
W. 143 ST.
W. 144 ST.
W. 145 ST.
W. 146 ST.
W. 147 ST.
W. 148 ST.
W. 149 ST.
W. 150 ST.
W. 151 ST.
W. 152 ST.
W. 153 ST.
W. 154 ST.
W. 155 ST.
E. 134 ST.
E. 135 ST.
E. 136 ST.
E. 137 ST.
Harlem River
The Bronx
N (uptown)
W
S (downtown)
E
½ mile
New Jersey
Manhattan
The Bronx
Queens
Brooklyn
N

Broadway productions—Marc Connelly's *Green Pastures* (1930), Eugene O'Neill's *The Emperor Jones* (1920) and *All God's Chillun Got Wings* (1924), for example—and many novels tried to represent the black experience for white audiences. Black artists and writers (and their readers) were not always happy with the way white writers portrayed black experience and black concerns or "adapted" work originally created by African Americans, but the widespread curiosity—some of it piqued by the flourishing of the Harlem group and some by "intruders" from the white establishment—provided a wider audience for black literature and arts than had existed in earlier generations.

The height of the Harlem Renaissance was the 1920s, though it is hard to pin down just when the period began and ended. Some historians, pointing to the political ferment caused by U.S. entry into World War I in 1917, date the beginnings in the mid to late teens, and some regard it as lasting until the outbreak of World War II in the late 1930s. But the decade of the 1920s saw most of the productivity and creative energy that we associate with the flourishing of Harlem. And it was in the early 1920s when most of the leading writers in the group actually moved to New York. Many historians regard the stock-market crash of 1929 and the depression that followed as signs of the end. Certainly the mood of the whole nation changed rapidly then, and by the early 1930s most of the leading figures of the Renaissance had moved away from New York, forming smaller communities elsewhere or becoming individually isolated. The Harlem neighborhood itself began a slow economic decline.

Prominent African Americans (including W. E. B. Du Bois, third from the right in the second row) parade down New York's Fifth Avenue on July 28, 1917, to protest a race riot in East St. Louis, Illinois. Thirty-nine African Americans were killed and hundreds were seriously injured in that melee, one of the deadliest outbreaks of racial violence in America.

Between the wars, though, Harlem's productivity and impact were dramatic. Before 1917, there had been few publishing outlets hospitable to young black writers; only Paul Lawrence Dunbar among African American poets was widely read or known, and he had died in 1906. But rising political and social concerns during and immediately after World War I produced several new periodicals: *The Messenger*, founded in 1917 by A. Philip Randolph and Chandler Owen, claimed to be "The only Radical Negro Magazine in America," and in 1923 the Urban League started its own magazine, *Opportunity*. Both of these new journals saw themselves as activist alternatives to the NAACP's official journal, *Crisis*, edited by W. E. B. Du Bois. Other magazines came and went. *Fire!!* managed only a single issue, but brought verbal and visual art spectacularly together. Meanwhile—and perhaps just as important in a different way—mainstream magazines (*Vanity Fair*, for example) and publishers (Knopf, Macmillan, Harper, and Harcourt Brace) began to feature younger black writers who soon developed a growing readership.

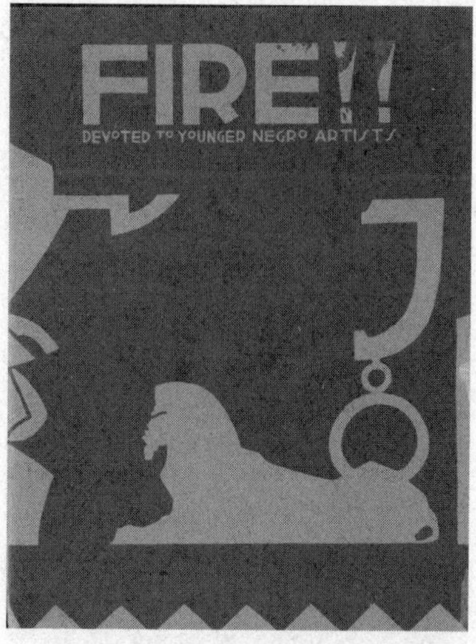

The cover of volume 1, number 1, of *Fire!!*, a journal "Devoted to Younger Negro Artists," established by the self-designated "niggerati," the younger generation of African American intellectuals and writers—including Wallace Thurman, Langston Hughes, Zora Neale Hurston, and others—who wanted to (in Hughes's words) "burn up a lot of the old, dead, conventional Negro-white ideas of the past."

Claude McKay, photographed circa 1930 by Carl Van Vechten

Portrait of Alain Locke, by Betsy G. Reyneau

Langston Hughes, circa 1925, in a pastel portrait by Winold Reiss. The original hangs in the National Portrait Gallery in Washington, D.C.

Some historians date the Harlem Renaissance from the composition of Claude McKay's fiery sonnet IF WE MUST DIE (below), written in the summer of 1919. McKay later denied that the poem referred specifically to blacks and whites, but the many anti-black riots that broke out in several American cities that summer—sometimes called "the Red Summer"—certainly inspired and shaped the poem. Another milestone was the publication in 1922 of James Weldon Johnson's *Book of American Negro Poetry*, which, in the words of the editors of the *Norton Anthology of African American Literature*, "emphasized the youthful promise of the new writers and established some of the terms of the emerging movement." But it was Alain Locke's landmark anthology, *The New Negro*, that, in 1925, effectively announced the significance of the Harlem Renaissance. Locke, a sociology professor at Howard University and an Oxford graduate as the first African American Rhodes Scholar, gathered all kinds of material—poems, fiction, essays, visual art—by authors old and young, black and white—into a working definition of what the "new Negro" was all about.

The major figures of the Harlem Renaissance were, however, highly individual. And though they shared many ideals and aspirations, they never confined themselves to a creed or hardened into a "school." Langston Hughes, with a wonderful **lyric** voice and an eye for telling details, pursued the relationship of poetry to black music and experimented with a variety of forms and rhythms. Countee Cullen, on the other hand, was deeply committed to conventional poetic forms and felt most at home poetically when he was working in traditional fixed forms. Claude McKay, born in Jamaica, lived briefly in New York but mostly in Greenwich Village rather than Harlem, and spent much of his career abroad (in Russia, France, and North Africa). He always followed his own star in poetry, too; his poetry was sometimes violent and incendiary, but equally strong was his sense of nostalgia and natural spiritualism. Despite setting a militant tone in a founding poem of the Harlem Renaissance, IF WE MUST DIE, he wrote only two poems that were directly about Harlem experiences and themes. Likewise, novelists like Zora Neale Hurston, Jean Toomer, Jesse Fauset, and Nella Larsen pursued individual styles and themes in their fiction. What held the

Countee Cullen, circa 1935

group together was a dedication to producing first-rate writing, on the one hand, and, on the other hand, a commitment to raising the aspirations of American blacks of all backgrounds and abilities.

Vendor selling books and pamphlets from a cart on 125th Street in Harlem, June 1943

The question of who was to benefit from the ambitious art of the Harlem Renaissance was hotly debated. Was it ordinary people, who could stretch the horizons of their reading and their own ambitions? African Americans generally? Or was it primarily intellectuals and artists who might raise expectations for black thought and art? W. E. B. Du Bois, who was a lightning rod for many members of the militant and radical new generation, had famously championed the "talented tenth," a select group whose natural gifts authoritatively raised them above others, and opinions split over whether the beneficiaries of the Harlem Renaissance were to be ordinary readers and viewers or the creative geniuses themselves, in the service of a higher aesthetic quite distinct from social progress. It's fair to say that writers remained divided, alternately championing the triumph of art and hoping for a larger cultural impact that would benefit readers (especially black readers) more generally.

The Dark Tower, a forum for African American intellectuals, met frequently in the home of A'Lelia Walker, a prominent Harlem heiress and socialite. Countee Cullen's poem "From the Dark Tower" (later in this chapter) is painted on the wall.

Carl Van Vechten, 1926

The role of whites in the Harlem Renaissance is also a matter of some dispute. The most controversial, though undeniably influential figure was Carl Van Vechten, whose parties legendarily brought young black writers into the company of famous and powerful white celebrities, many of whom could be helpful to black writers' careers. Van Vechten was a gifted photographer whose portraits of many rising figures chronicle the Harlem years brilliantly (as some of the photographs in this chapter demonstrate), and he undeniably fostered many useful connections that resulted in publication and fame. But some felt his motives were self-serving, and his well-meaning novel about everyday Harlem life, *Nigger Heaven* (1926), was widely disparaged, though critics equally suspected "realistic" accounts of everyday life by black writers. (See, for example, the Du Bois review of a Claude McKay novel later in this chapter.) There is no doubt that figures like Van Vechten fostered interaction between prominent whites and rising figures in the black artistic community, but not everyone regarded the results as helpful to the black cause overall. Some historians view white participation in the Harlem Renaissance as exploitative, others as sincere but bumbling; still others view such black-white collaboration as an early demonstration of racial unity.

Another set of questions involves elitism—whether the renaissance had truly salutary effects on the larger black community. Du Bois insisted on the obligation of "the talented tenth" to use their artistic and intellectual gifts to improve the lot of others. Critics of Du Bois find his position divisive and patronizing toward the majority of the black community; defenders see the idea as a strategy for achieving community improvement by cultivating potential leaders. At the heart of this controversy is disagreement about how leadership works to promote both improved social conditions and audience engagement. (Similar arguments rage today over the stardom of African American athletes and entertainers.)

Two related controversies concern the influence of the church on black culture and the relationship of the ambitious new "high art" of poetry, novels, and painting to popular-culture phenomena such as jazz, blues, and dance. There is little doubt that religion was a powerful force in the black community, but observers continue to debate, as the artists themselves then did, whether it fostered and furthered artistic expression or served as a restraining and discouraging force. Often readers can see in poetry about even the most secular subjects traces of religious ideas and traditions; you will have to decide for yourself whether the effects are positive or not. The relationship of radical art to popular culture was even more vexed. Some central figures in the Harlem Renaissance regarded their own aims as "above" the "attractions" and "spectacles" that drew large numbers of whites to Harlem, and they regarded the performance arts as, at best, distractions from or dilutions of the main flow of radical artistic expression. And while nearly everyone agrees that the quality of various theatrical arts in the many venues of Harlem was very high, the question of whether, beyond jazz and blues, the influence of popular arts on poetry was good or bad remains open.

• • •

No easy summary of the Harlem Renaissance will do. Its ambitions—often radical, sometimes revolutionary—made enormous waves in both the black urban community and the world of art. However one measures the Harlem Renaissance in terms of its impact on later writers, black and white, the poems themselves continue to speak to readers across divides of time and culture. You will find that some of the poems can hardly be understood without knowledge of the specific circumstances and conditions that produced them; you will also find that many of the poems reach insistently for connections both to the past and to the enduring concerns of poets and readers in far-flung times and places.

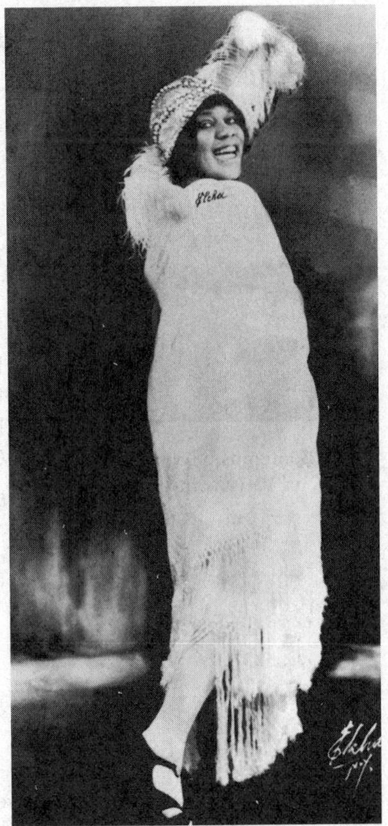

Known as the "Empress of the Blues," Bessie Smith was one of the most popular entertainers in America during the 1920s.

Arna Bontemps, photographed by Carl Van Vechten, 1939

POEMS OF THE HARLEM RENAISSANCE

ARNA BONTEMPS

A Black Man Talks of Reaping

I have sown beside all waters in my day.
I planted deep, within my heart the fear
That wind or fowl would take the grain away.
I planted safe against this stark, lean year.

I scattered seed enough to plant the land
In rows from Canada to Mexico
But for my reaping only what the hand
Can hold at once is all that I can show.

Yet what I sowed and what the orchard yields
My brother's sons are gathering stalk and root,
Small wonder then my children glean in fields
They have not sown, and feed on bitter fruit.

1926

COUNTEE CULLEN

Yet Do I Marvel

I doubt not God is good, well-meaning, kind,
And did He stoop to quibble could tell why
The little buried mole continues blind,
Why flesh that mirrors Him must some day die,
Make plain the reason tortured Tantalus[1]
Is baited by the fickle fruit, declare
If merely brute caprice dooms Sisyphus[2]
To struggle up a never-ending stair.
Inscrutable His ways are, and immune
To catechism by a mind too strewn
With petty cares to slightly understand
What awful brain compels His awful hand.
Yet do I marvel at this curious thing:
To make a poet black, and bid him sing!

1925

1. Figure in Greek myth condemned, for ambiguous reasons, to stand up to his neck in water he couldn't drink and to be within sight of fruit he couldn't reach to eat.
2. King of Corinth who, in Greek myth, was condemned eternally to roll a huge stone uphill.

Saturday's Child[3]

Some are teethed on a silver spoon,
With the stars strung for a rattle;
I cut my teeth as the black raccoon—
For implements of battle.

Some are swaddled in silk and down,
And heralded by a star;[4]
They swathed my limbs in a sackcloth gown
On a night that was black as tar.

For some, godfather and goddame
The opulent fairies be;
Dame Poverty gave me my name,
And Pain godfathered me.

For I was born on Saturday—
"Bad time for planting a seed,"
Was all my father had to say,
And, "One mouth more to feed."

Death cut the strings that gave me life,
And handed me to Sorrow,
The only kind of middle wife
My folks could beg or borrow.

1925

From the Dark Tower

(To Charles S. Johnson)[5]

We shall not always plant while others reap
The golden increment of bursting fruit,
Not always countenance, abject and mute,
That lesser men should hold their brothers cheap;
Not everlastingly while others sleep
Shall we beguile their limbs with mellow flute,
Not always bend to some more subtle brute;
We were not made eternally to weep.

The night whose sable breast relieves the stark,
White stars is no less lovely being dark,
And there are buds that cannot bloom at all
In light, but crumple, piteous, and fall;
So in the dark we hide the heart that bleeds,
And wait, and tend our agonizing seeds.

1927

3. According to a popular nursery rhyme, "Saturday's child works hard for his living."
4. According to Matthew 2.7–10, Jesus's birth was accompanied by the appearance of a new star.
5. Founder and editor of *Opportunity* magazine.

Angelina Grimké, circa 1905

ANGELINA GRIMKÉ

The Black Finger

I have just seen a beautiful thing
Slim and still,
Against a gold, gold sky,
A straight cypress,
Sensitive
Exquisite,
A black finger
Pointing upwards.
Why, beautiful, still finger are you black?
And why are you pointing upwards?

1925

Tenebris[6]

There is a tree, by day,
That, at night,
Has a shadow,
A hand huge and black,
With fingers long and black.
All through the dark,
Against the white man's house,
In the little wind,
The black hand plucks and plucks
At the bricks.
The bricks are the color of blood and very small.
Is it a black hand,
Or is it a shadow?

1927

LANGSTON HUGHES

Harlem

What happens to a dream deferred?

Does it dry up
Like a raisin in the sun?
Or fester like a sore—
And then run?
Does it stink like rotten meat?
Or crust and sugar over—
Like a syrupy sweet?

6. In darkness (Latin).

Maybe it just sags
Like a heavy load.

Or does it explode?

1951

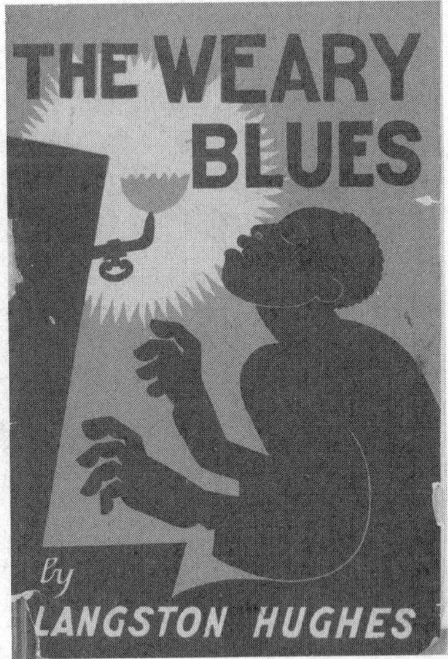

The Weary Blues

Droning a drowsy syncopated tune,
Rocking back and forth to a
mellow croon,
I heard a Negro play.
Down on Lenox Avenue[7] the other
night
By the pale dull pallor of an old gas
light
He did a lazy sway. . . .
He did a lazy sway. . . .
To the tune o' those Weary Blues.
With his ebony hands on each ivory key
He made that poor piano moan with melody.
O Blues!
Swaying to and fro on his rickety stool
He played that sad raggy tune like a musical fool.
Sweet Blues!
Coming from a black man's soul.
O Blues!
In a deep song voice with a melancholy tone
I heard that Negro sing, that old piano moan—
"Ain't got nobody in all this world,
Ain't got nobody but ma self.
I's gwine to quit ma frownin'
And put ma troubles on the shelf."
Thump, thump, thump, went his foot on the floor.
He played a few chords then he sang some more—
"I got the Weary Blues
And I can't be satisfied.
Got the Weary Blues
And can't be satisfied—
I ain't happy no mo'
And I wish that I had died."
And far into the night he crooned that tune.
The stars went out and so did the moon.
The singer stopped playing and went to bed
While the Weary Blues echoed through his head.
He slept like a rock or a man that's dead.

1923 1925

7. Major Harlem thoroughfare, now Malcolm X Boulevard.

Pen-and-ink illustration by the artist Aaron Douglas made specifically to accompany Hughes's "The Negro Speaks of Rivers"

The Negro Speaks of Rivers

I've known rivers:
I've known rivers ancient as the world and older than the flow of
human blood in human veins.

My soul has grown deep like the rivers.

I bathed in the Euphrates when dawns were young.
I built my hut near the Congo and it lulled me to sleep.
I looked upon the Nile and raised the pyramids above it.
I heard the singing of the Mississippi when Abe Lincoln went down to
New Orleans, and I've seen its muddy bosom turn all golden in
the sunset.

I've known rivers:
Ancient, dusky rivers.

My soul has grown deep like the rivers.

1926

I, Too

I, too, sing America.

I am the darker brother.
They send me to eat in the kitchen
When company comes,
But I laugh,
And eat well,
And grow strong.

Tomorrow,
I'll sit at the table.
When company comes
Nobody'll dare

Say to me,
"Eat in the kitchen,"
Then.

Besides,
They'll see how beautiful I am
And be ashamed—

I, too, am America.

1932

HELENE JOHNSON
Sonnet to a Negro in Harlem

You are disdainful and magnificent—
Your perfect body and your pompous gait,
Your dark eyes flashing solemnly with hate,
Small wonder that you are incompetent
To imitate those whom you so despise—
Your shoulders towering high above the throng,
Your head thrown back in rich, barbaric song,
Palm trees and mangoes stretched before your eyes.
Let others toil and sweat for labor's sake
And wring from grasping hands their meed[8] of gold.
Why urge ahead your supercilious feet?
Scorn will efface each footprint that you make.
I love your laughter arrogant and bold.
You are too splendid for this city street.

1927

CLAUDE MCKAY
Harlem Shadows

I hear the halting footsteps of a lass
In Negro Harlem when the night lets fall
Its veil. I see the shapes of girls who pass
To bend and barter at desire's call.
Ah, little dark girls who in slippered feet
Go prowling through the night from street to street!

Through the long night until the silver break
Of day the little gray feet know no rest;
Through the lone night until the last snow-flake
Has dropped from heaven upon the earth's white breast,
The dusky, half-clad girls of tired feet
Are trudging, thinly shod, from street to street.

Ah, stern harsh world, that in the wretched way
Of poverty, dishonor and disgrace,

8. Reward.

Has pushed the timid little feet of clay,
  The sacred brown feet of my fallen race!
Ah, heart of me, the weary, weary feet
In Harlem wandering from street to street.

1918

If We Must Die

If we must die, let it not be like hogs
Hunted and penned in an inglorious spot,
While round us bark the mad and hungry dogs,
Making their mock at our accursed lot.
If we must die, O let us nobly die,
So that our precious blood may not be shed
In vain; then even the monsters we defy
Shall be constrained to honor us though dead!
O kinsmen! we must meet the common foe!
Though far outnumbered let us show us brave,
And for their thousand blows deal one deathblow!
What though before us lies the open grave?
Like men we'll face the murderous, cowardly pack,
Pressed to the wall, dying, but fighting back!

1919

The Tropics in New York

Bananas ripe and green, and ginger-root,
  Cocoa in pods and alligator pears,
And tangerines and mangoes and grape fruit,
  Fit for the highest prize at parish fairs,

Set in the window, bringing memories
  Of fruit-trees laden by low-singing rills,
And dewy dawns, and mystical blue skies
  In benediction over nun-like hills.

My eyes grew dim, and I could no more gaze;
  A wave of longing through my body swept,
And, hungry for the old, familiar ways,
  I turned aside and bowed my head and wept.

1920

The Harlem Dancer

Applauding youths laughed with young prostitutes
And watched her perfect, half-clothed body sway;
Her voice was like the sound of blended flutes
Blown by black players upon a picnic day.
She sang and danced on gracefully and calm,
The light gauze hanging loose about her form;

To me she seemed a proudly-swaying palm
Grown lovelier for passing through a storm.
Upon her swarthy neck black shiny curls
Luxuriant fell; and tossing coins in praise,
The wine-flushed, bold-eyed boys, and even the girls,
Devoured her shape with eager, passionate gaze;
But looking at her falsely-smiling face,
I knew her self was not in that strange place.

1922

The White House

Your door is shut against my tightened face,
And I am sharp as steel with discontent;
But I possess the courage and the grace
To bear my anger proudly and unbent.
The pavement slabs burn loose beneath my feet,
And passion rends my vitals as I pass,
A chafing savage, down the decent street,
Where boldly shines your shuttered door of glass.
Oh, I must search for wisdom every hour,
Deep in my wrathful bosom sore and raw,
And find in it the superhuman power
To hold me to the letter of your law!
Oh, I must keep my heart inviolate
Against the poison of your deadly hate.

1937

CONTEXTUAL EXCERPTS

James Weldon Johnson

From the preface to The Book of American Negro Poetry (1921)

James Weldon Johnson, circa 1920

This preface has gone far beyond what I had in mind when I started. It was my intention to gather together the best verses I could find by Negro poets and present them with a bare word of introduction. It was not my plan to make this collection inclusive nor to make the book in any sense a book of criticism. I planned to present only verses by contemporary writers; but, perhaps, because this is the first collection of its kind, I realized the absence of a starting-point and was led to provide one and to fill in with historical data what I felt to be a gap.

It may be surprising to many to see how little of the poetry being written by Negro poets today is being written in Negro dialect. The newer Negro poets show a tendency to discard dialect; much of the subject-matter which went into the making of traditional dialect poetry, 'possums, watermelons, etc., they have discarded altogether, at least, as poetic material. This tendency will, no doubt, be regretted by the majority of white readers; and, indeed, it would be a distinct loss if the American Negro poets threw away this quaint and musical folk speech as a medium of expression. And yet, after all, these poets are working through a problem not realized by the reader, and, perhaps, by many of these poets themselves not realized consciously. They are trying to break away from, not Negro dialect itself, but the limitations on Negro dialect imposed by the fixing effects of long convention.

The Negro in the United States has achieved or been placed in a certain artistic niche. When he is thought of artistically, it is as a happy-go-lucky, singing, shuffling, banjo-picking being or as a more or less pathetic figure. The picture of him is in a log cabin amid fields of cotton or along the levees. Negro dialect is naturally and by long association the exact instrument for voicing this phase of Negro life; and by that very exactness it is an instrument with but two full stops, humor and pathos. So even when he confines himself to purely racial themes, the Aframerican poet realizes that there are phases of Negro life in the United States which cannot be treated in the dialect either adequately or artistically. Take, for example, the phases rising out of life in Harlem, that most wonderful Negro city in the world. I do not deny that a Negro in a log cabin is more picturesque than a Negro in a Harlem flat, but the Negro in the Harlem flat is here, and he is but part of a group growing everywhere in the country, a group whose ideals are becoming increasingly more vital than those of the traditionally artistic group, even if its members are less picturesque.

What the colored poet in the United States needs to do is something like what Synge[9] did for the Irish; he needs to find a form that will express the racial spirit by symbols from within rather than by symbols from without, such as the mere mutilation of English spelling and pronunciation. He needs a form that is freer and larger than dialect, but which will still hold the racial flavor; a form expressing the imagery, the idioms, the peculiar turns of thought, and the distinctive humor and pathos, too, of the Negro, but which will also be capable of voicing the deepest and highest emotions and aspirations, and allow of the widest range of subjects and the widest scope of treatment.

Negro dialect is at present a medium that is not capable of giving expression to the varied conditions of Negro life in America, and much less is it capable of giving the fullest interpretation of Negro character and psychology. This is no indictment against the dialect as dialect, but against the mold of convention in which Negro dialect in the United States has been set. In time these conventions may become lost, and the colored poet in the United States may sit down to write in dialect without feeling that his first line will put the general reader in a frame of mind which demands that the poem be humorous or pathetic. In the meantime, there is no reason why these poets should not continue to do the beautiful things that can be done, and done best, in the dialect.

9. John Millington Synge (1871–1909), Irish dramatist whose works celebrate Irish traditions.

In stating the need for Aframerican poets in the United States to work out a new and distinctive form of expression I do not wish to be understood to hold any theory that they should limit themselves to Negro poetry, to racial themes; the sooner they are able to write *American* poetry spontaneously, the better. Nevertheless, I believe that the richest contribution the Negro poet can make to the American literature of the future will be the fusion into it of his own individual artistic gifts.

Alain Locke

From The New Negro (1925)

The tide of Negro migration, northward and city-ward, is not to be fully explained as a blind flood started by the demands of war industry coupled with the shutting off of foreign migration, or by the pressure of poor crops coupled with increased social terrorism in certain sections of the South and Southwest. Neither labor demand, the bollweevil,[1] nor the Ku Klux Klan is a basic factor, however contributory any or all of them may have been. The wash and rush of this human tide on the beach line of the northern city centers is to be explained primarily in terms of a new vision of opportunity, of social and economic freedom, of a spirit to seize, even in the face of an extortionate and heavy toll, a chance for the improvement of conditions. With each successive wave of it, the movement of the Negro becomes more and more a mass movement toward the larger and the more democratic chance—in the Negro's case a deliberate flight not only from countryside to city, but from medieval America to modern.

Take Harlem as an instance of this. Here in Manhattan is not merely the largest Negro community in the world, but the first concentration in history of so many diverse elements of Negro life. It has attracted the African, the West Indian, the Negro American; has brought together the Negro of the North and the Negro of the South; the man from the city and the man from the town and village; the peasant, the student, the business man, the professional man, artist, poet, musician, adventurer and worker, preacher and criminal, exploiter and social outcast. Each group has come with its own separate motives and for its own special ends, but their greatest experience has been the finding of one another. Proscription and prejudice have thrown these dissimilar elements into a common area of contact and interaction. Within this area, race sympathy and unity have determined a further fusing of sentiment and experience. So what began in terms of segregation becomes more and more, as its elements mix and react, the laboratory of a great race-welding. Hitherto, it must be admitted that American Negroes have been a race more in name than in fact, or to be exact, more in sentiment than in experience. The chief bond between them has been that of a common condition rather than a common consciousness; a problem in common rather than a life in common. In Harlem, Negro life is seizing upon its first chances for group expression and self-determination. It is—or promises at least to be—a race capital. That is why our comparison is taken with those

1. Beetle notorious for destroying cotton crops.

nascent centers of folk-expression and self-determination which are playing a creative part in the world today. Without pretense to their political significance, Harlem has the same role to play for the New Negro as Dublin has had for the New Ireland or Prague for the New Czechoslovakia.

Harlem, I grant you, isn't typical—but it is significant, it is prophetic. No sane observer, however sympathetic to the new trend, would contend that the great masses are articulate as yet, but they stir, they move, they are more than physically restless. The challenge of the new intellectuals among them is clear enough—the "race radicals" and realists who have broken with the old epoch of philanthropic guidance, sentimental appeal and protest. But are we after all only reading into the stirrings of a sleeping giant the dreams of an agitator? The answer is in the migrating peasant. It is the "man farthest down" who is most active in getting up. One of the most characteristic symptoms of this is the professional man, himself migrating to recapture his constituency after a vain effort to maintain in some Southern corner what for years back seemed an established living and clientele. The clergyman following his errant flock, the physician or lawyer trailing his clients, supply the true clues. In a real sense it is the rank and file who are leading, and the leaders who are following. A transformed and transforming psychology permeates the masses.

When the racial leaders of twenty years ago spoke of developing race-pride and stimulating race-consciousness, and of the desirability of race solidarity, they could not in any accurate degree have anticipated the abrupt feeling that has surged up and now pervades the awakened centers. [. . .] It is a social disservice to blunt the fact that the Negro of the Northern centers has reached a stage where tutelage, even of the most interested and well-intentioned sort, must give place to new relationships, where positive self-direction must be reckoned with in ever increasing measure. The American mind must reckon with a fundamentally changed Negro.

The Negro too, for his part, has idols of the tribe to smash. If on the one hand the white man has erred in making the Negro appear to be that which would excuse or extenuate his treatment of him, the Negro, in turn, has too often unnecessarily excused himself because of the way he has been treated. The intelligent Negro of today is resolved not to make discrimination an extenuation for his shortcomings in performance, individual or collective; he is trying to hold himself at par, neither inflated by sentimental allowances nor depreciated by current social discounts. For this he must know himself and be known for precisely what he is, and for that reason he welcomes the new scientific rather than the old sentimental interest. Sentimental interest in the Negro has ebbed. We used to lament this as the falling off of our friends; now we rejoice and pray to be delivered both from self-pity and condescension. The mind of each racial group has had a bitter weaning, apathy or hatred on one side matching disillusionment or resentment on the other; but they face each other today with the possibility at least of entirely new mutual attitudes. [. . .]

The fiction is that the life of the races is separate, and increasingly so. The fact is that they have touched too closely at the unfavorable and too lightly at the favorable levels.

While inter-racial councils have sprung up in the South, drawing on forward elements of both races, in the Northern cities manual laborers may brush elbows in their everyday work, but the community and business leaders have experienced no such interplay or far too little of it. These segments must achieve contact or the race situation in America becomes desperate. Fortunately this is happening. There is a growing realization that in social effort the cooperative basis must supplant long-distance philanthropy, and that the only safeguard for mass relations in the future must be provided in the carefully maintained contacts of the enlightened minorities of both race groups. In the intellectual realm a renewed and keen curiosity is replacing the recent apathy; the Negro is being carefully studied, not just talked about and discussed. In art and letters, instead of being wholly caricatured, he is being seriously portrayed and painted.

To all of this the New Negro is keenly responsive as an augury of a new democracy in American culture. He is contributing his share to the new social understanding. But the desire to be understood would never in itself have been sufficient to have opened so completely the protectively closed portals of the thinking Negro's mind. There is still too much possibility of being snubbed or patronized for that. It was rather the necessity for fuller, truer self-expression, the realization of the unwisdom of allowing social discrimination to segregate him mentally, and a counter-attitude to cramp and fetter his own living—and so the "spite-wall" that the intellectuals built over the "color-line" has happily been taken down. Much of this reopening of intellectual contacts has centered in New York and has been richly fruitful not merely in the enlarging of personal experience, but in the definite enrichment of American art and letters and in the clarifying of our common vision of the social tasks ahead.

The particular significance in the re-establishment of contact between the more advanced and representative classes is that it promises to offset some of the unfavorable reactions of the past, or at least to re-surface race contacts somewhat for the future. Subtly the conditions that are molding a New Negro are molding a new American attitude.

However, this new phase of things is delicate; it will call for less charity but more justice; less help, but infinitely closer understanding. This is indeed a critical stage of race relationships because of the likelihood, if the new temper is not understood, of engendering sharp group antagonism and a second crop of more calculated prejudice. In some quarters, it has already done so. Having weaned the Negro, public opinion cannot continue to paternalize. The Negro today is inevitably moving forward under the control largely of his own objectives. What are these objectives? Those of his outer life are happily already well and finally formulated, for they are none other than the ideals of American institutions and democracy. Those of his inner life are yet in process of formation, for the new psychology at present is more of a consensus of feeling than of opinion, of attitude rather than of program. Still some points seem to have crystallized.

Up to the present one may adequately describe the Negro's "inner objectives" as an attempt to repair a damaged group psychology and reshape a warped social perspective. Their realization has required a new mentality for the American Negro. And as it matures we begin to see its effects; at first, negative, iconoclastic, and then positive and constructive. In this new group psychology we note the lapse of sentimental appeal, then the development of a more positive self-respect and self-reliance; the repudiation of social dependence, and then the gradual recovery from hyper-sensitiveness and "touchy" nerves, the repudiation of the double standard of judgment with its special philanthropic allowances and then the sturdier desire for objective and scientific appraisal; and finally the rise from social disillusionment to race pride, from the sense of social debt to the responsibilities of social contribution, and offsetting the necessary working and commonsense acceptance of restricted conditions, the belief in ultimate esteem and recognition.

* * *

The Negro mind reaches out as yet to nothing but American wants, American ideas. But this forced attempt to build his Americanism on race values is a unique social experiment, and its ultimate success is impossible except through the fullest sharing of American culture and institutions. There should be no delusion about this. American nerves in sections unstrung with race hysteria are often fed the opiate that the trend of Negro advance is wholly separatist, and that the effect of its operation will be to encyst the Negro as a benign foreign body in the body politic. This cannot be—even if it were desirable. The racialism of the Negro is no limitation or reservation with respect to American life; it is only a constructive effort to build the obstructions in the stream of his progress into an efficient dam of social energy and power. Democracy itself is obstructed and stagnated to the extent that any of its channels are closed. Indeed they cannot be selectively closed. So the choice is not between one way for the Negro and another way for the rest, but between American institutions frustrated on the one hand and American ideals progressively fulfilled and realized on the other.

* * *

More and more, however, an intelligent realization of the great discrepancy between the American social creed and the American social practice forces upon the Negro the taking of the moral advantage that is his. Only the steadying and sobering effect of a truly characteristic gentleness of spirit prevents the rapid rise of a definite cynicism and counter-hate and a defiant superiority feeling. Human as this reaction would be, the majority still deprecate its advent, and would gladly see it forestalled by the speedy amelioration of its causes. We wish our race pride to be a healthier, more positive achievement than a feeling based upon a realization of the shortcomings of others. But all paths toward the attainment of a sound social attitude have been difficult; only a relatively few enlightened minds have been able as the phrase puts it "to rise above" prejudice. The ordinary man has had until recently only a hard choice between the alternatives of supine and humiliating submission and stimulating but hurtful counter-prejudice. Fortunately from some inner, desperate resourcefulness has recently sprung up the simple expedient of fighting prejudice by mental passive resistance, in other words by trying to ignore it. For the few, this manna may perhaps be effective, but the masses cannot thrive upon it.

Fortunately there are constructive channels opening out into which the balked social feelings of the American Negro can flow freely.

Without them there would be much more pressure and danger than there is. These compensating interests are racial but in a new and enlarged way. One is the consciousness of acting as the advance-guard of the African peoples in their contact with Twentieth Century civilization; the other, the sense of a mission of rehabilitating the race in world esteem from that loss of prestige for which the fate and conditions of slavery have so largely been responsible. Harlem, as we shall see, is the center of both these movements; she is the home of the Negro's "Zionism."[2] The pulse of the Negro world has begun to beat in Harlem. A Negro newspaper carrying news material in English, French, and Spanish, gathered from all quarters of America, the West Indies, and Africa has maintained itself in Harlem for over five years. Two important magazines,[3] both edited from New York, maintain their news and circulation consistently on a cosmopolitan scale. Under American auspices and backing, three pan-African congresses have been held abroad for the discussion of common interests, colonial questions, and the future cooperative development of Africa. In terms of the race question as a world problem, the Negro mind has leapt, so to speak, upon the parapets of prejudice and extended its cramped horizons. In so doing it has linked up with the growing group consciousness of the dark-peoples and is gradually learning their common interests. As one of our writers has recently put it: "It is imperative that we understand the white world in its relations to the non-white world." As with the Jew, persecution is making the Negro international.

As a world phenomenon this wider race consciousness is a different thing from the much asserted rising tide of color. Its inevitable causes are not of our making. The consequences are not necessarily damaging to the best interests of civilization. Whether it actually brings into being new Armadas of conflict or argosies[4] of cultural exchange and enlightenment can only be decided by the attitude of the dominant races in an era of critical change. With the American Negro, his new internationalism is primarily an effort to recapture contact with the scattered peoples of African derivation. Garveyism[5] may be a transient, if spectacular, phenomenon, but the possible role of the American Negro in the future development of Africa is one of the most constructive and universally helpful missions that any modern people can lay claim to.

Rudolph Fisher

From The Caucasian Storms Harlem (1927)

I

It might not have been such a jolt had my five years' absence from Harlem been spent otherwise. But the study of medicine includes no courses in cabareting; and, anyway, the Negro cabarets in Washington, where I studied, are all uncom-

2. International movement aimed at securing a homeland for the Jewish people. The modern state of Israel was not founded until 1948.

3. Probably *Opportunity* and *The Crisis*.

4. Merchant ships. *Armadas*: fleets of warships.

5. The Back to Africa movement of Marcus Garvey (1887–1940).

promisingly black. Accordingly I was entirely unprepared for what I found when I returned to Harlem recently.

I remembered one place especially where my own crowd used to hold forth; and, hoping to find some old-timers there still, I sought it out one midnight. The old, familiar plunkety-plunk welcomed me from below as I entered. I descended the same old narrow stairs, came into the same smoke-misty basement, and found myself a chair at one of the ancient white-porcelain, mirror-smooth tables. I drew a deep breath and looked about, seeking familiar faces. "What a lot of 'fays!"[6] I thought, as I noticed the number of white guests. Presently I grew puzzled and began to stare, then I gaped—and gasped. I found myself wondering if this was the right place—if, indeed, this was Harlem at all. I suddenly became aware that, except for the waiters and members of the orchestra, I was the only Negro in the place.

After a while I left it and wandered about in a daze from night-club to night-club. I tried the Nest, Small's, Connie's Inn, the Capitol, Happy's, the Cotton Club. There was no mistake; my discovery was real and was repeatedly confirmed. No wonder my old crowd was not to be found in any of them. The best of Harlem's black cabarets have changed their names and turned white.

Such a discovery renders a moment's recollection irresistible. As irresistible as were the cabarets themselves to me seven or eight years ago. Just out of college in a town where cabarets were something only read about. A year of graduate work ahead. A Summer of rest at hand. Cabarets. Cabarets night after night, and one after another. There was no cover-charge then, and a fifteen-cent bottle of Whistle lasted an hour. It was just after the war[7]—the heroes were home—cabarets were the thing.

How the Lybia prospered in those happy days! It was the gathering place of the swellest Harlem set: if you didn't go to the Lybia, why, my dear, you just didn't belong. The people you saw at church in the morning you met at the Lybia at night. What romance in those war-tinged days and nights! Officers from Camp Upton,[8] with pretty maids from Brooklyn! Gay lieutenants, handsome captains—all whirling the lively onestep. Poor non-coms[9] completely ignored; what sensible girl wanted a corporal or even a sergeant? That white, old-fashioned house, standing alone in 138th street, near the corner of Seventh Avenue—doomed to be torn down a few months thence—how it shook with the dancing and laughter of the dark merry crowds!

But the first place really popular with my friends was a Chinese restaurant in 136th Street, which had been known as Hayne's Café and then became the Oriental. It occupied an entire house of three stories, and had carpeted floors and a quiet, superior air. There was excellent food and incredibly good tea and two unusual entertainers: a Cuban girl, who could so vary popular airs that they sounded like real music, and a slender little "brown" with a voice of silver and a way of singing a song that made you forget your food. One could dance in the Oriental if one liked, but one danced to a piano only, and wound one's way between linen-clad tables over velvety, noiseless floors.

6. Short for "ofays," a derogatory term for whites. 7. That is, World War I.
8. Military facility near Manhattan. 9. Noncommissioned officers.

Here we gathered: Fritz Pollard, All-American halfback,[1] selling Negro stock to prosperous Negro physicians; Henry Creamer and Turner Layton, who had written "After You've Gone" and a dozen more songs, and were going to write "Strut, Miss Lizzie;" Paul Robeson,[2] All-American end, on the point of tackling law, quite unaware that the stage would intervene; Preacher Harry Bragg, Harvard Jimmie MacLendon and a half a dozen others. Here at a little table, just inside the door, Bert Williams[3] had supper every night, and afterward sometimes joined us upstairs and sang songs with us and lampooned the Actors' Equity Association, which had barred him because of his color. Never did white guests come to the Oriental except as guests of Negroes. But the manager soon was stricken with a psychosis of some sort, became a black Jew, grew himself a bushy, square-cut beard, donned a skull-cap and abandoned the Oriental. And so we were robbed of our favorite resort, and thereafter became mere rounders.

II

Such places, those real Negro cabarets that we met in the course of our rounds! There was Edmonds' in Fifth Avenue at 130th Street. It was a sure-enough honky-tonk, occupying the cellar of a saloon. It was the social center of what was then, and still is, Negro Harlem's kitchen. Here a tall brown-skin girl, unmistakably the one guaranteed in the song to make a preacher lay his Bible down, used to sing and dance her own peculiar numbers, vesting them with her own originality. She was known simply as Ethel,[4] and was a genuine drawing-card. She knew her importance, too. Other girls wore themselves ragged trying to rise above the inattentive din of conversation, and soon, literally, yelled themselves hoarse; eventually they lost whatever music there was in their voices and acquired that familiar throaty roughness which is so frequent among blues singers, and which, though admired as characteristically African, is as a matter of fact nothing but a form of chronic laryngitis. Other girls did these things, but not Ethel. She took it easy. She would stride with great leisure and self-assurance to the center of the floor, stand there with a half-contemptuous nonchalance, and wait. All would become silent at once. Then she'd begin her song, genuine blues, which, for all their humorous lines, emanated tragedy and heartbreak:

Woke up this mawnin'
The day was dawnin'
And I was sad and blue, so blue, Lord—
Didn' have nobody
To tell my troubles to—

It was Ethel who first made popular the song, "Tryin' to Teach My Good Man Right from Wrong," in the slow, meditative measures in which she complained:

I'm gettin' sick and tired of my railroad man
I'm gettin' sick and tired of my railroad man—

1. In 1916 at Brown University. He was the first black professional football player (Akron Indians, 1919).
2. Star football player at Rutgers before entering Columbia University Law School in 1919 (1898–1976); he would later gain international renown as a singer and civil-rights spokesman.
3. Popular black comedian and actor (c. 1874–1922).
4. Ethel Waters (1896–1977).

Can't get him when I want him—
I get him when I can.

It wasn't long before this song-bird escaped her dingy cage. Her name is a vaudeville attraction now, and she uses it all—Ethel Waters. Is there anyone who hasn't heard her sing "Shake That Thing!"?

* * *

There were the Lybia, then, and Hayne's, Connor's, the Oriental, Edmonds' and the Garden of Joy, each distinctive, standing for a type, some living up to their names, others living down to them, but all predominantly black. Regularly I made the rounds among these places and saw only incidental white people. I have seen them occasionally in numbers, but such parties were out on a lark. They weren't in their natural habitat and they often weren't any too comfortable.

But what of Barron's, you say? Certainly they were at home there. Yes, I know about Barron's. I have been turned away from Barron's because I was too dark to be welcome. I have been a member of a group that was told, "No more room," when we could see plenty of room. Negroes were never actually wanted in Barron's save to work. Dark skins were always discouraged or barred. In short, the fact about Barron's was this: it simply wasn't a Negro cabaret; it was a cabaret run by Negroes for whites. It wasn't even on the lists of those who lived in Harlem—they'd no more think of going there than of going to the Winter Garden Roof.[5] But these other places were Negro through and through. Negroes supported them, not merely in now-and-then parties, but steadily, night after night.

* * *

IV

Some think it's just a fad. White people have always more or less sought Negro entertainment as diversion. The old shows of the early nineteen hundreds, Williams and Walker[6] and Cole and Johnson, are brought to mind as examples. The howling success—literally that—of J. Leubrie Hill[7] around 1913 is another; on the road his "Darktown Follies" played in numerous white theatres. In Harlem it played at the black Lafayette and, behold, the Lafayette temporarily became white. And so now, it is held, we are observing merely one aspect of a meteoric phenomenon, which simply presents itself differently in different circumstances: Roland Hayes and Paul Robeson, Jean Toomer and Walter White, Charles Gilpin and Florence Mills[8]—"Green Thursday," "Porgy," "In Abraham's Bosom"[9]—Negro spirituals—the startling new African groups

5. Prominent Manhattan nightclub.
6. Bert Williams and George Nash Walker formed an immensely popular vaudeville team in 1895.
7. Songwriter (1869–1916).
8. Performer (1895–1927). Hayes (1887–1976), singer. Toomer (1894–1967), author of *Cane*. White (1893–1955), writer and civil-rights leader. Gilpin (1878–1930), actor.
9. 1926 play by white writer Paul Green. *Porgy*: a novel by Du Bose Heyward (1925).

proposed for the Metropolitan Museum of Art. Negro stock is going up, and everybody's buying.

• • •

V

[. . .] It may be a season's whim, then, this sudden, contagious interest in everything Negro. If so, when I go into a familiar cabaret, or the place where a familiar cabaret used to be, and find it transformed and relatively colorless, I may be observing just one form that the season's whim has taken.

But suppose it is a fad—to say that explains nothing. How came the fad? What occasions the focusing of attention on this particular thing—rounds up and gathers these seasonal whims, and centers them about the Negro? Cabarets are peculiar, mind you. They're not like theatres and concert halls. You don't just go to a cabaret and sit back and wait to be entertained. You get out on the floor and join the pow-wow and help entertain yourself. Granted that white people have long enjoyed the Negro entertainment as a diversion, is it not something different, something more, when they bodily throw themselves into Negro entertainment in cabarets? "Now Negroes go to their own cabarets to see how white people act."

And what do we see? Why, we see them actually playing Negro games. I watch them in that epidemic Negroism, the Charleston. I look on and envy them. They camel and fish-tail and turkey, they geche and black-bottom and scronch, they skate and buzzard and mess-around[1]—and they do them all better than I! This interest in the Negro is an active and participating interest. It is almost as if a traveler from the North stood watching an African tribe-dance, then suddenly found himself swept wildly into it, caught in its tidal rhythm.

Willingly would I be an outsider in this if I could know that I read it aright—that out of this change in the old familiar ways some finer thing may come. Is this interest akin to that of the Virginians on the veranda of a plantation's big-house—sitting genuinely spellbound as they hear the lugubrious strains floating up from the Negro quarters? Is it akin to that of the African explorer, Stanley,[2] leaving a village far behind, but halting in spite of himself to catch the boom of its distant drum? Is it significant of basic human responses, the effect of which, once admitted, will extend far beyond cabarets? Maybe these Nordics at last have tuned in on our wave-length. Maybe they are at last learning to speak our language.

W. E. B. Du Bois

From Two Novels (1928)[3]

Claude McKay's *Home to Harlem* [. . .] for the most part nauseates me, and after the dirtier parts of its filth I feel distinctly like taking a bath. This does not mean that the book is wholly bad. McKay is too great a poet to make any complete failure in writing. There are bits of *Home to Harlem* beautiful and fascinat-

1. Various popular dances. 2. Sir Henry Morgan Stanley (1841–1904), English explorer of Africa.
3. The following excerpt omits Du Bois's comments on Nella Larsen's novel *Quicksand*.

Cover of the first edition of McKay's *Home to Harlem* (1928)

ing: the continued changes upon the theme of the beauty of colored skins; the portrayal of the fascination of their new yearnings for each other which Negroes are developing. The chief character, Jake, has something appealing, and the glimpses of the Haitian, Ray, have all the materials of a great piece of fiction.

But it looks as though, despite this, McKay has set out to cater for that prurient demand on the part of white folk for a portrayal in Negroes of that utter licentiousness which conventional civilization holds white folk back from enjoying—if enjoyment it can be called. That which a certain decadent section of the white American world, centered particularly in New York, longs for with fierce and unrestrained passions, it wants to see written out in black and white, and saddled on black Harlem. This demand, as voiced by a number of New York publishers, McKay has certainly satisfied, and added much for good measure. He has used every art and emphasis to paint drunkenness, fighting, lascivious sexual promiscuity, and utter absence of restraint in as bold and as bright colors as he can.

[. . .] As a picture of Harlem life or of Negro life anywhere, it is, of course, nonsense. Untrue, not so much on account of its facts, but on account of its emphasis and glaring colors. I am sorry that the author of *Harlem Shadows* stooped to this. I sincerely hope that he will some day rise above it and give us in fiction the strong, well-knit as well as beautiful theme, that it seems to me he might do.

Zora Neale Hurston

Zora Neale Hurston

How It Feels to Be Colored Me (1928)

I am colored but I offer nothing in the way of extenuating circumstances except the fact that I am the only Negro in the United States whose grandfather on the mother's side was *not* an Indian chief.

I remember the very day that I became colored. Up to my thirteenth year I lived in the little Negro town of Eatonville, Florida. It is exclusively a colored town. The only white people I knew passed through the town going to or coming from Orlando. The native whites rode dusty horses, the Northern tourists chugged down the sandy village road in automobiles. The town knew the Southerners and never stopped cane chewing when they passed. But the Northerners were something else again. They were peered at cautiously from behind curtains by the timid. The more venturesome would come out on the porch to watch them go past and got just as much pleasure out of the tourists as the tourists got out of the village.

The front porch might seem a daring place for the rest of the town, but it was a gallery seat for me. My favorite place was atop the gate-post. Proscenium box[4] for a born first-nighter. Not only did I enjoy the show, but I didn't mind the actors knowing that I liked it. I usually spoke to them in passing. I'd wave at them and when they returned my salute, I would say something like this: "Howdy-do-well-I-thank-you-where-you-goin'?" Usually automobile or the horse paused at this, and after a queer exchange of compliments, I would probably "go a piece of the way" with them, as we say in farthest Florida. If one of my family happened to come to the front in time to see me, of course negotiations would be rudely broken off. But even so, it is clear that I was the first "welcome-to-our-state" Floridian, and I hope the Miami Chamber of Commerce will please take notice.

During this period, white people differed from colored to me only in that they rode through town and never lived there. They liked to hear me "speak pieces" and sing and wanted to see me dance the parse-me-la, and gave me generously of their small silver for doing these things, which seemed strange to me for I wanted to do them so much that I needed bribing to stop. Only they didn't know it. The colored people gave no dimes. They deplored any joyful tendencies in me, but I was their Zora nevertheless. I belonged to them, to the nearby hotels, to the county—everybody's Zora.

But changes came in the family when I was thirteen, and I was sent to school in Jacksonville. I left Eatonville, the town of the oleanders, as Zora. When I disembarked from the river-boat at Jacksonville, she was no more. It seemed that I had suffered a sea change. I was not Zora of Orange County any more, I was now a little colored girl. I found it out in certain ways. In my heart as well as in the mirror, I became a fast[5] brown—warranted not to rub nor run.

But I am not tragically colored. There is no great sorrow dammed up in my soul, nor lurking behind my eyes. I do not mind at all. I do not belong to the sobbing school of Negrohood who hold that nature somehow has given them a lowdown dirty deal and whose feelings are all hurt about it. Even in the helter-skelter skirmish that is my life, I have seen that the world is to the strong regardless of a little pigmentation more or less. No, I do not weep at the world—I am too busy sharpening my oyster knife.[6]

4. The box seats in a theater on either side of and nearest to the stage.

5. That is, colorfast.

6. Allusion to Shakespeare's *The Merry Wives of Windsor* 2.2.4–5: "Why, then the world's mine oyster, / Which I with sword will open."

Someone is always at my elbow reminding me that I am the grand-daughter of slaves. It fails to register depression with me. Slavery is sixty years in the past. The operation was successful and the patient is doing well, thank you. The terrible struggle that made me an American out of a potential slave said "On the line!" The Reconstruction said "Get set!"; and the generation before said "Go!" I am off to a flying start and I must not halt in the stretch to look behind and weep. Slavery is the price I paid for civilization, and the choice was not with me. It is a bully adventure and worth all that I have paid through my ancestors for it. No one on earth ever had a greater chance for glory. The world to be won and nothing to be lost. It is thrilling to think—to know that for any act of mine, I shall get twice as much praise or twice as much blame. It is quite exciting to hold the center of the national stage, with the spectators not knowing whether to laugh or to weep.

The position of my white neighbor is much more difficult. No brown specter pulls up a chair beside me when I sit down to eat. No dark ghost thrusts its leg against mine in bed. The game of keeping what one has is never so exciting as the game of getting.

I do not always feel colored. Even now I often achieve the unconscious Zora of Eatonville before the Hegira.[7] I feel most colored when I am thrown against a sharp white background.

For instance at Barnard.[8] "Beside the waters of the Hudson" I feel my race. Among the thousand white persons, I am a dark rock surged upon, and overswept, but through it all, I remain myself. When covered by the waters, I am; and the ebb but reveals me again.

Sometimes it is the other way around. A white person is set down in our midst, but the contrast is just as sharp for me. For instance, when I sit in the drafty basement that is The New World Cabaret with a white person, my color comes. We enter chatting about any little nothing that we have in common and are seated by the jazz waiters. In the abrupt way that jazz orchestras have, this one plunges into a number. It loses no time in circumlocutions, but gets right down to business. It constricts the thorax and splits the heart with its tempo and narcotic harmonies. This orchestra grows rambunctious, rears on its hind legs and attacks the tonal veil with primitive fury, rending it, clawing it until it breaks through to the jungle beyond. I follow those heathen—follow them exultingly. I dance wildly inside myself; I yell within, I whoop; I shake my assegai[9] above my head, I hurl it true to the mark *yeeeeooww!* I am in the jungle and living in the jungle way. My face is painted red and yellow and my body is painted blue. My pulse is throbbing like a war drum. I want to slaughter something—give pain, give death to what, I do not know. But the piece ends. The men of the orchestra wipe their lips and rest their fingers. I creep back slowly to the veneer we call civilization with the last tone and find the white friend sitting motionless in his seat, smoking calmly.

7. In Islam, Muhammad's emigration from Mecca to Medina in 622 CE; here, the journey to Jacksonville.

8. Barnard College in Manhattan, then a private women's school, now part of Columbia University.

9. Spear.

"Good music they have here," he remarks, drumming the table with his fingertips.

Music. The great blobs of purple and red emotion have not touched him. He has only heard what I felt. He is far away and I see him but dimly across the ocean and the continent that have fallen between us. He is so pale with his whiteness then and I am *so* colored.

At certain times I have no race, I am *me*. When I set my hat at a certain angle and saunter down Seventh Avenue, Harlem City, feeling as snooty as the lions in front of the Forty-Second Street Library,[1] for instance. So far as my feelings are concerned, Peggy Hopkins Joyce on the Boule Mich[2] with her gorgeous raiment, stately carriage, knees knocking together in a most aristocratic manner, has nothing on me. The cosmic Zora emerges. I belong to no race nor time. I am the eternal feminine with its string of beads.

I have no separate feeling about being an American citizen and colored. I am merely a fragment of the Great Soul that surges within the boundaries. My country, right or wrong.

Sometimes, I feel discriminated against, but it does not make me angry. It merely astonishes me. How *can* any deny themselves the pleasure of my company? It's beyond me.

But in the main, I feel like a brown bag of miscellany propped against a wall. Against a wall in company with other bags, white, red and yellow. Pour out the contents, and there is discovered a jumble of small things priceless and worthless. A first-water diamond,[3] an empty spool, bits of broken glass, lengths of string, a key to a door long since crumbled away, a rusty knife-blade, old shoes saved for a road that never was and never will be, a nail bent under the weight of things too heavy for any nail, a dried flower or two still a little fragrant. In your hand is the brown bag. On the ground before you is the jumble it held—so much like the jumble in the bags, could they be emptied, that all might be dumped in a single heap and the bags refilled without altering the content of any greatly. A bit of colored glass more or less would not matter. Perhaps that is how the Great Stuffer of Bags filled them in the first place—who knows?

Langston Hughes

From The Big Sea (1940)

Harlem Literati

The summer of 1926, I lived in a rooming house on 137th Street, where Wallace Thurman and Harcourt Tynes[4] also lived. Thurman was then managing editor of the *Messenger*, a Negro magazine that had a curious career. It began by

1. Headquarters of the New York Public Library.
2. Elegant boulevard St. Michel in Paris.
3. That is, a diamond of the highest quality.
4. A friend of Thurman's. *House on 137th Street*: the rooming house appears in Thurman's novel *Infants of the Spring* (1932) as "Niggerati Manor."

being very radical, racial, and socialistic, just after the war. I believe it received a grant from the Garland Fund[5] in its early days. Then it later became a kind of Negro society magazine and a plugger for Negro business, with photographs of prominent colored ladies and their nice homes in it. A. Phillip Randolph, now President of the Brotherhood of Sleeping Car Porters, Chandler Owen, and George S. Schuyler were connected with it. Schuyler's editorials, à la Mencken,[6] were the most interesting things in the magazine, verbal brickbats that said sometimes one thing, sometimes another, but always vigorously. I asked Thurman what kind of magazine the *Messenger* was, and he said it reflected the policy of whoever paid off best at the time.

Anyway, the *Messenger* bought my first short stories. They paid me ten dollars a story. Wallace Thurman wrote me that they were very bad stories, but better than any others they could find, so he published them.

Thurman had recently come from California to New York. He was a strangely brilliant black boy, who had read everything, and whose critical mind could find something wrong with everything he read. I have no critical mind, so I usually either like a book or don't. But I am not capable of liking a book and then finding a million things wrong with it, too—as Thurman was capable of doing.

Thurman had read so many books because he could read eleven lines at a time. He would get from the library a great pile of volumes that would have taken me a year to read. But he would go through them in less than a week, and be able to discuss each one at great length with anybody. That was why, I suppose, he was later given a job as a reader at Macaulay's—the only Negro reader, so far as I know, to be employed by any of the larger publishing firms.

* * *

Wallace Thurman wanted to be a great writer, but none of his own work ever made him happy. *The Blacker the Berry*,[7] his first book, was an important novel on a subject little dwelt upon in Negro fiction—the plight of the very dark Negro woman, who encounters in some communities a double wall of color prejudice within and without the race. His play, *Harlem*, considerably distorted for box office purposes, was, nevertheless, a compelling study—and the only one in the theater—of the impact of Harlem on a Negro family fresh from the South. And his *Infants of the Spring*, a superb and bitter study of the bohemian fringe of Harlem's literary and artistic life, is a compelling book.

But none of these things pleased Wallace Thurman. He wanted to be a *very* great writer, like Gorki or Thomas Mann,[8] and he felt that he was merely a journalistic writer. His critical mind, comparing his pages to the thousands of other pages he had read, by Proust, Melville, Tolstoy, Galsworthy, Dostoyevski,

5. The American Fund for Public Service, established in 1920 by Charles Garland.

6. Henry Louis Mencken (1880–1956), prominent Baltimore essayist, critic, and editor who was a friend of Schuyler's. Randolph (1889–1976) and Owen (1889–1967), editors at the *Messenger*, who hired Schuyler as a writer in 1923. Schuyler (1895–1977), conservative black writer.

7. Published in 1929.

8. German novelist (1875–1955). Maxim Gorki was the pen name of Russian writer Aleksey Maksimovich Pyeshkov (1868–1936).

Henry James, Sainte-Beauve, Taine, Anatole France,[9] found his own pages vastly wanting. So he contented himself by writing a great deal for money, laughing bitterly at his fabulously concocted "true stories," creating two bad motion pictures[1] of the "Adults Only" type for Hollywood, drinking more and more gin, and then threatening to jump out of windows at people's parties and kill himself.

During the summer of 1926, Wallace Thurman, Zora Neale Hurston, Aaron Douglas, John P. Davis, Bruce Nugent, Gwendolyn Bennett,[2] and I decided to publish "a Negro quarterly of the arts" to be called *Fire*—the idea being that it would burn up a lot of the old, dead conventional Negro-white ideas of the past, *épater le bourgeois*[3] into a realization of the existence of the younger Negro writers and artists, and provide us with an outlet for publication not available in the limited pages of the small Negro magazines then existing, the *Crisis*, *Opportunity*, and the *Messenger*—the first two being house organs of inter-racial organizations, and the latter being God knows what.

Sweltering summer evenings we met to plan *Fire*. Each of the seven of us agreed to give fifty dollars to finance the first issue. Thurman was to edit it, John P. Davis to handle the business end, and Bruce Nugent to take charge of distribution. The rest of us were to serve as an editorial board to collect material, contribute our own work, and act in any useful way that we could.

• • •

I don't know how Thurman persuaded the printer to let us have all the copies to distribute, but he did. I think Alain Locke, among others, signed notes guaranteeing payments. But since Thurman was the only one of the seven of us with a regular job, for the next three or four years his checks were constantly being attached and his income seized to pay for *Fire*. And whenever I sold a poem, mine went there, too—to *Fire*.

None of the older Negro intellectuals would have anything to do with *Fire*. Dr. DuBois[4] in the *Crisis* roasted it. The Negro press called it all sorts of bad names, largely because of a green and purple story by Bruce Nugent, in the Oscar Wilde[5] tradition, which we had included. Rean Graves, the critic for the *Baltimore Afro-American*, began his review by saying: "I have just tossed the first issue of *Fire* into the fire." Commenting upon various of our contributors, he said: "Aaron Douglas who, in spite of himself and the meaningless grotesqueness of his creations, has gained a reputation as an artist, is permitted to spoil three perfectly good pages

9. Pen name of French novelist and essayist Jacques Anatole François Thibault (1844–1924). Marcel Proust (1871–1922), French novelist. Herman Melville (1819–91), U.S. writer. Leo Tolstoy (1828–1910), Russian novelist and social critic. John Galsworthy (1867–1933), English novelist. Fyodor Dostoyevski (1821–81), Russian novelist. James (1843–1916), U.S. novelist and critic. Charles Augustin Sainte-Beuve (1804–69), French critic and poet. Hippolyte Adolphe Taine (1828–93), French critic and historian.

1. *Tomorrow's Children* (1934) and *High School Girl* (1935).

2. Poet (1902–81). Hurston (1891–1960), novelist and folklore collector. Douglas (1898–1979), artist. Davis (1905–73), lawyer and prominent leftist. Nugent (1906–87), illustrator and writer.

3. Shock the middle class (French).

4. W. E. B. Du Bois (1868–1963), African American writer, editor of *Crisis*, and cofounder of the NAACP.

5. Irish poet, novelist, and playwright (1854–1900), a proponent of the Art for Art's Sake movement. *Green and purple story*: the first installment of a novel called *Smoke, Lilies and Jade* (1926).

and a cover with his pen and ink hudge pudge. Countee Cullen has written a beautiful poem in his 'From a Dark Tower,' but tries his best to obscure the thought in superfluous sentences. Langston Hughes displays his usual ability to say nothing in many words."

So *Fire* had plenty of cold water thrown on it by the colored critics. The white critics (except for an excellent editorial in the *Bookman* for November, 1926) scarcely noticed it at all. We had no way of getting it distributed to bookstands or news stands. Bruce Nugent took it around New York on foot and some of the Greenwich Village bookshops put it on display, and sold it for us. But then Bruce, who had no job, would collect the money and, on account of salary, eat it up before he got back to Harlem.

Finally, irony of ironies, several hundred copies of *Fire* were stored in the basement of an apartment where an actual fire occurred and the bulk of the whole issue was burned up. Even after that Thurman had to go on paying the printer.

Now *Fire* is a collector's item, and very difficult to get, being mostly ashes.

That taught me a lesson about little magazines. But since white folks had them, we Negroes thought we could have one, too. But we didn't have the money.

[. . .] About the future of Negro literature Thurman was very pessimistic. He thought the Negro vogue had made us all too conscious of ourselves, had flattered and spoiled us, and had provided too many easy opportunities for some of us to drink gin and more gin, on which he thought we would always be drunk. With his bitter sense of humor, he called the Harlem literati, the "niggerati."

Of this "niggerati," Zora Neale Hurston was certainly the most amusing. Only to reach a wider audience, need she ever write books—because she is a perfect book of entertainment in herself. In her youth she was always getting scholarships and things from wealthy white people, some of whom simply paid her just to sit around and represent the Negro race for them, she did it in such a racy fashion. She was full of side-splitting anecdotes, humorous tales, and tragicomic stories, remembered out of her life in the South as a daughter of a travelling minister of God. She could make you laugh one minute and cry the next. To many of her white friends, no doubt, she was a perfect "darkie," in the nice meaning they give the term—that is a naïve, childlike, sweet, humorous, and highly colored Negro.

But Miss Hurston was clever, too—a student who didn't let college give her a broad *a* and who had great scorn for all pretensions, academic or otherwise. That is why she was such a fine folk-lore collector,[6] able to go among the people and never act as if she had been to school at all. Almost nobody else could stop the average Harlemite on Lenox Avenue and measure his head with a strange-looking, anthropological device and not get bawled out for the attempt, except Zora, who used to stop anyone whose head looked interesting, and measure it.

* * *

[. . .] Harlem was like a great magnet for the Negro intellectual, pulling him from everywhere. Or perhaps the magnet was New York—but once in New York,

6. Hurston published two such collections, *Mules and Men* (1935) and *Tell My Horse* (1938).

he had to live in Harlem, for rooms were hardly to be found elsewhere unless one could pass for white or Mexican or Eurasian and perhaps live in the Village[7]—which always seemed to me a very arty locale, in spite of the many real artists and writers who lived there. Only a few of the New Negroes lived in the Village, Harlem being their real stamping ground.

SUGGESTIONS FOR WRITING

1. Many poets of the Harlem Renaissance made extensive use of the sonnet form; this chapter contains such examples as Countee Cullen's FROM THE DARK TOWER, Helene Johnson's SONNET TO A NEGRO IN HARLEM, and Claude McKay's IF WE MUST DIE. Write an essay in which you compare some of the sonnets written during the Harlem Renaissance. How do different approaches to the sonnet form signal different thematic concerns?
2. In 1921, James Weldon Johnson wrote of "the need for Aframerican poets in the United States to work out a new and distinctive form of expression." Judging from the selections in this chapter, do you think that poets such as Langston Hughes and Claude McKay met the need articulated by Johnson? Write an essay in which you examine both traditionalism and innovation in the poetry of the Harlem Renaissance. How distinct are the works of black and white poets during this period?
3. In *The New Negro*, Alain Locke declared, "In Harlem, Negro life is seizing upon its first chances for group expression and self-determination." Do poems such as Arna Bontemps's A BLACK MAN TALKS OF REAPING, Angelina Grimké's THE BLACK FINGER, and Langston Hughes's I, TOO achieve a common social consciousness—Locke's "group expression"? What political effect do you think these poets hoped to achieve through their work? Write an essay in which you analyze the political ideas in the poetry of the Harlem Renaissance.
4. Some poems of the Harlem Renaissance—Langston Hughes's THE WEARY BLUES and Claude McKay's THE HARLEM DANCER, for example—are explicitly about music; others, such as Countee Cullen's SATURDAY'S CHILD, with its ballad form, and Angelina Grimké's improvisational TENEBRIS, take a distinctly musical approach. Write an essay about the interplay of words and music in the poetry of this period.
5. In his review of Claude McKay's *Home to Harlem*, W. E. B. Du Bois laments that McKay "stooped" to betraying the black cause by portraying "drunkenness, fighting, lascivious sexual promiscuity, and utter absence of restraint" in his novel's black characters. Do writers have a particular duty to portray positive role models? Do writers from ethnic groups engaged in social struggle have an obligation to participate in that struggle? Citing evidence from the selections in this chapter, write an essay in which you weigh the demands of artistic duty against the demands of artistic freedom.
6. What does it mean for a group of artists to be considered a "school"—that is, a group whose work appears to share common themes, styles, and goals? Write an essay in which you discuss whether or not the writers of the Harlem Renaissance spoke with a unified voice. Does a grouping like "the Harlem Renaissance" help our understanding of this period and the art it produced, or does it obscure the individual achievements of the artists themselves?
7. Identify any two poets in this anthology whose work interests you and who lived and wrote in roughly the same time and place. (The biographies at the end of the Poetry section might be a helpful place to start.) Then do a bit of research. Did your two poets have similar backgrounds? Are they considered part of the same or competing "movements" or "schools"? Drawing on your research, write an essay in which you

7. Greenwich Village, Manhattan district long known as a haunt of writers and radicals.

compare at least one poem by each poet and explore how the poems were each shaped by historical and cultural context. Alternatively, choose two poets in this anthology who wrote poems on similar topics or of the same type or genre (odes or sonnets, for example) but who lived and wrote in very different times and/or places. Then write a research essay exploring how historical and/or cultural context might shape the different ways in which each writer approaches the same topic or genre.

SAMPLE WRITING: RESEARCH ESSAY

In the following essay student Irene Morstan reads Langston Hughes's poem, I, Too in the context of the Harlem Renaissance, drawing upon primary and secondary sources she discovered online, as well as material included in chapter 24. How effectively does she use her sources? integrate and balance textual and contextual analysis? To what aspects of the poem might she pay more attention?

Morstan 1

Irene Morstan
Dr. Mays
English 298
15 February 2017

"They'll See How Beautiful I Am": "I, Too" and the Harlem Renaissance

Langston Hughes begins his 1926 essay "The Negro Artist and the Racial Mountain" with a statement made to him by another black poet: "I want to be a poet—not a Negro poet." Hughes takes this to mean that the poet wishes he were a white poet, and pities the poet for this. He believes that the black poet should accept his blackness. The goal for black poets should not be to sound like white poets but to celebrate and embrace their black identity.

Hughes was a central figure in a movement called the Harlem Renaissance, which was "a period of ten or fifteen years in the early twentieth century when an extraordinarily talented group of people came together [. . .] to celebrate and embody the awakening of a new African American consciousness" (Mays, "Cultural" 1260). *The Norton Introduction to Literature* states, "The Harlem Renaissance represented powerful assertions: that America had to include the voices of black Americans in order to find its own full definition and, equally, that artistic creativity [. . .] was essential to black Americans' realization and assertion of their full humanity" (Mays, "Cultural" 1260). Hughes speaks to both of those assertions in his poem "I, Too." He insists upon the place of the black poet, and person, at the American "table" and upon the power of the black poet to "sing."

The opening of "I, Too" is a declaration of the black man as a poet, despite being historically excluded from such a title. In the first line of the poem "I, too, sing America," Hughes indicates that the speaker is a poet. Hughes related poetry to music, suggesting that Hughes thinks music-making and writing poetry are related. Not only is the speaker a poet, but he is a black poet. By the second line of the poem the race of the speaker is clear; he refers to himself as the "darker brother." The "too" in the first line implies that the speaker has been set apart from another group of people, that he has been excluded from "sing[ing] America." However, the speaker is responding to this exclusion with an affirmative statement that he is both a black poet and part of the American family, despite being set aside by white people.

Refusing to be set aside was an important part of the Harlem Renaissance. James Weldon Johnson, in his preface to *The Book of American Negro Poetry*, says black poets moved away from writing in dialect to keep white people from thinking of them as "a happy-go-lucky, singing, shuffling, banjo-picking being or as a more or less pathetic figure" (1278). Black poets in the Harlem Renaissance did not want to be stereotyped by whites; they did not want to be Jim from *Adventures of Huckleberry Finn*. Such stereotypes made black people easy to overlook because they were represented as caricatures of people. These figures did not accurately represent the black person as a complex human being capable of artistic achievement. Not all Harlem Renaissance poets responded to this in the same way. The author of "Literature of the Harlem Renaissance" states, "Countee Cullen insisted that the Black poet is a part of the universal community of all poets, while Langston Hughes asserted his unique racial qualities." While Hughes, in "The Negro Artist and the Racial Mountain," says that he does not believe that black people should give up any of the things associated with black identity, including writing in dialect, he does explore the dismissal of the black poet by the white audience through "I, Too."

This theme of black exclusion surfaces in the second stanza where the speaker talks about how "They send me to eat in the kitchen / When company comes" (lines 3-4). Here "they" refers to white people who dismiss the black poet from the "table" (line 9). These lines suggest that the white people are perhaps ashamed of "the darker brother" and do not want him to be present in front of the other white guests, the "company." Maybe they don't even see him as a brother, just a servant. This reflects the place of the black artist in the 1920s and 1930s. While the black artist might occasionally be present, he was meant to be a source of entertainment for white people, not an equal. Rudolph Fisher discusses the white interest in Harlem in *The Caucasian Storms Harlem*, where he notes, "White people have always more or less sought Negro entertainment as diversion" (1286). Despite being suspicious of white peoples' impulses to go to Harlem nightclubs, Fisher hopes that this white interest in black artistry will be the beginning of "finer things" and that "Maybe they are at last learning to speak our language" (1287).

The speaker of "I, Too" also sees that "finer things" are on the horizon. Even though he has been sent to the kitchen, a place reminiscent of the institution of slavery where black slaves worked to feed their white masters, the speaker of the poem says, "I laugh, / And eat well, / And grow strong" (lines 5-7). This dismissal has not crushed his spirit, and "Tomorrow, / I'll sit at the table" (lines 8-9). Hughes's speaker anticipates the time when the black poet will no longer be cast aside. Because of his strength and his spirit he is undeniable. In the future,

> Nobody'll dare
> Say to me,
> "Eat in the kitchen" (lines 11-13)

And the black spirit was undeniable during the Harlem Renaissance. The number of notable black authors and artists gathered in one place was incredible. During the 1920s and 1930s writers like Claude McKay, Countee Cullen, Zora Neale Hurston, Jean Toomer, Angelina Grimké, as well as Langston Hughes, were all in Harlem. This was one of the first times that black people from all over America were in one place together, as "more than 100,000 blacks migrated to Harlem during the 1920s" (Mays, "Cultural" 1261). Alain Locke, author of *The New Negro,* saw this as a turning point in black history and in the history of America, even arguing that it created a real black "race." In 1925, he wrote,

> Hitherto, it must be admitted that American Negroes have been a race more in name than in fact, or to be exact, more in sentiment than experience. The chief bond between them has been that of a common condition rather than a common consciousness; a problem in common rather than a life in common. In Harlem, Negro life is seizing upon its first chances for group expression and self-determination. (1279)

The Harlem Renaissance was a movement where black writers, even though they may have had some differences, joined together to create black art according to their own rules, not the rules of white people. Black artists had "grow[n] strong," and it is this strength that the speaker of "I, Too" sees as causing change between black and whites.

However, as hopeful as the speaker is, he acknowledges that this has not yet happened. By placing "then" on its own line and at the end of the sentence (line 14), Hughes highlights that these actions are yet to come. The "then" in the poem sounds wistful, as if the speaker gets very excited about the prospect of being acknowledged and respected, only to remember the difficulties that lie between the current state of affairs and the one dreamt of for the future. Racial inequality was still prevalent at the time of the Harlem Renaissance, and the situation did not improve for some time. During the 1920s and 1930s segregation was still normal. (Langston Hughes said that an African American who moved to New York "had to live in Harlem, for rooms were hardly to be found elsewhere unless one could pass for white or Mexican or Eurasian" [*The Big Sea* 1295], and Fisher says that blacks like him were surprisingly even excluded from some Harlem clubs [1286].) On the other hand, the isolation of the "then" on its own line also could be read as being firmly insistent that a positive change will come. This echoes the goal of the writers of the Harlem Renaissance, "to [raise] the aspirations

Morstan 4

of American blacks of all backgrounds and abilities" (Mays, "Cultural" 1267). In this reading, "then" is both a statement of faith about the future and a call to action about now.

These two readings reflect two different black views of Harlem literature. Some people were cynical and did not believe that change had come or would. Langston Hughes recounts that "[a]bout the future of Negro literature [Wallace] Thurman was very pessimistic. He thought the Negro vogue had made us all too conscious of ourselves, had flattered and spoiled us, and had provided too many easy opportunities for some of us to drink gin and more gin, on which he thought we would always be drunk" (*The Big Sea* 1294). In contrast to this dark view of the Harlem Renaissance is novelist Zora Neale Hurston's view of the position of black people in 1920s America. In "How It Feels to Be Colored Me," she states, "I am not tragically colored. There is no great sorrow dammed up in my soul nor lurking behind my eyes. . . . I do not belong to the sobbing school of Negrohood who hold that nature somehow has given them a lowdown dirty deal. . . . I do not weep at the world—I am too busy sharpening my oyster knife" (1286). Here Hurston is expressing that she is not brought down by the slavery of the past, but is making herself ready to make the world hers. Her view is the positive one found in Hughes's poem.

Just as the writers of the Harlem Renaissance wanted their creative abilities to be appreciated, so they also wanted black people and culture to be appreciated and embraced by the American public. The speaker of "I, Too" makes this apparent at the end of the poem when he says,

> Besides,
> They'll see how beautiful I am
> And be ashamed—
> I, too, am America. (lines 15-18)

The speaker is asserting that being black is being beautiful and that people who have discriminated against blacks will be ashamed of their behavior when they really see what black people are like. Not only are black people beautiful, they are part of America. The speaker of the poem makes this clear when he says that he *is* America. This "darker brother" is just as much a part of America as a white person (line 2), so he should not be excluded, either physically or literarily. Hughes, like many other writers of the Harlem Renaissance, is insisting that all Americans recognize the place of black people, both culturally and creatively, in the American identity.

Hughes speaks not only to white people in "I, Too" but also to other writers during the Harlem Renaissance. As is illustrated in the opening anecdote, Hughes was insistent about honoring blackness and common black life. He thought that all aspects of black life were worth celebrating, and "[u]nlike other notable black poets of the period—Claude McKay, Jean Toomer, and Countee Cullen—Hughes refused to differentiate between his personal experience and the common experience of black America. He wanted to tell the stories of his people in ways that reflected their actual culture, including both their suffering

Morstan 5

and their love of music, laughter, and language itself" ("Langston Hughes"). Hughes's references to race and beauty throughout "I, Too" show that he was committed to representing black life in a positive way.

Langston Hughes and the writers of the Harlem Renaissance are an important part of American history and have had a lasting impact on American literature. The quality of their works and power of their message shaped American culture. Through creative pieces like "I, Too," Hughes shows audiences how black literature and black people were valuable parts of the American identity.

Morstan 6

Works Cited

Fisher, Rudolph. "From *The Caucasian Storms Harlem*." Mays, *Norton*, pp. 1283-87.

Hughes, Langston. "From *The Big Sea*." Mays, *Norton*, pp. 1291-95.

---. "I, Too." Mays, *Norton*, pp. 1274-75.

---. "The Negro Artist and the Racial Mountain." 1926. *Poetry Foundation*, www.poetryfoundation.org/resources/learning/essays/detail/69395.

Hurston, Zora Neale. "How It Feels to Be Colored Me." Mays, *Norton*, pp. 1288-91.

Johnson, James Weldon. "From the Preface to *The Book of American Negro Poetry*." Mays, *Norton*, pp. 1277-79.

"Langston Hughes." *Poets.org*, Academy of American Poets, www.poets.org/poetsorg/poet/langston-hughes.

"Literature of the Harlem Renaissance." *Twentieth-Century Literary Criticism*. Edited by Thomas J. Schoenberg and Lawrence J. Trudeau, vol. 218, Gale, 2009, pp. 260-376.

Locke, Alain. "From *The New Negro*." Mays, *Norton*, pp. 1279-83.

Mays, Kelly J. "Cultural and Historical Contexts: The Harlem Renaissance." Mays, *Norton*, pp. 1260-69.

---, editor. *The Norton Introduction to Literature*. 12th ed., W. W. Norton, 2017.

25 CRITICAL CONTEXTS: SYLVIA PLATH'S "DADDY"

As the previous context chapters have suggested, poems draw on all kinds of earlier texts, experiences, and events. But they also produce new contexts of discussion and interpretation, ongoing conversations about the poems themselves. Different readers of poems see different things in them, so naturally a variety of interpretations and evaluations develop around any poem that is read repeatedly by various readers. Many of those interpretations are published in specialized journals and books (the selections that follow are all reprinted from published sources), and a kind of dialogue develops among readers, producing a body of commentary about the poem. Professional interpreters of texts are called *literary critics*, and the textual analysis they provide is called **literary criticism**—not because their work is necessarily negative or corrective, but because they ask hard, analytical, "critical" questions and interpret texts through a wide variety of literary, historical, biographical, psychological, aesthetic, moral, political, or social perspectives.

Your own interpretive work may seem to you more private and far removed from such "professional" writing about poems. But once you engage in class discussion or talk informally about a poem, you are practicing literary criticism—offering comments, analyzing, judging, putting the poem into some kind of perspective that makes it more intelligible. You are, in effect, joining the ongoing conversation about the poem. And when you *write* about the poem, you may often engage the opinions of others—your teacher, fellow students, or published criticism. You may not have the experience or specific expertise of professional critics, but you can modify or answer the work of others and use it in your own work.

There are many ways to engage literary criticism and put it to work for you. The most common is to draw on published work for specific information about the poem: glossings of particular terms; explanations of references or situations you don't recognize; accounts of how, when, and under what circumstances the poem was written. Another common use of such material is as a springboard for your own interpretation, either building on what someone else has argued or, if you disagree, using that argument as a point of departure.

When you use the work of others, you must give full credit, carefully detailing the sources of all direct quotations and all borrowed ideas. You must always tell your reader exactly how to find the material you have quoted, paraphrased, or summarized. Usually, you do this through careful notes and a list of citations (that is, a bibliography) at the end of your paper. (See ch. 35 for help with citation and documentation.) Your instructor may also guide you to handbooks—for example, the *MLA Handbook* or *The Chicago Manual of Style*—that provide more detail.

It is usually best to do your own extensive analysis of a poem *before* consulting what other critics have said. Your own reading experience gives you a legitimate perspective. You always want to take in new information and to challenge both your first impressions and your considered analyses—but don't be too quick to adopt somebody else's ideas. The best way to test the views of others is to compare them critically to your own conclusions, which you might then want to supplement, refine, extend, or even scrap altogether. You can sharpen your skills by testing your views against those of people with extensive interpretive experience. As you will discover, even the experts disagree. In fact, one measure of a poem's greatness is its ability to stimulate disagreement and a broad range of interpretation.

Judged by that standard, the poem featured in this chapter is arguably among the very greatest of the twentieth century. First published posthumously in 1965 and famously declared "monstrous" by distinguished Jewish American critic Irving Howe, Sylvia Plath's DADDY has generated countless interpretations and unusually heated debate among a wide array of readers. As the rash of newspaper, magazine, and Web articles inspired by the fiftieth anniversary of Plath's suicide in 2013 suggest, moreover, it is a debate that is still very much alive. This chapter invites you to enter that debate: Beginning with the poem itself (which is where we hope you, too, will begin), it features excerpts from several especially influential commentaries published over the last fifty years (including Howe's), as well as an exercise and "Suggestions for Writing" designed to help you develop your own informed response to both the poem and its critical context.

SYLVIA PLATH
Daddy

You do not do, you do not do
Any more, black shoe
In which I have lived like a foot
For thirty years, poor and white,
Barely daring to breathe or Achoo.

Daddy, I have had to kill you.
You died before I had time—
Marble-heavy, a bag full of God,
Ghastly statue with one gray toe[1]
Big as a Frisco seal

And a head in the freakish Atlantic
Where it pours bean green over blue
In the waters off beautiful Nauset.[2]
I used to pray to recover you.
Ach, du.[3]

In the German tongue, in the Polish town[4]
Scraped flat by the roller
Of wars, wars, wars.

1. Otto Plath, Sylvia's father, lost a toe to gangrene that resulted from diabetes.

2. Inlet on Cape Cod, Massachusetts. 3. Oh, you (German).

4. Otto Plath, an ethnic German, was born in Grabow, Poland.

But the name of the town is common.
My Polack friend

Says there are a dozen or two.
So I never could tell where you
Put your foot, your root,
I never could talk to you.
The tongue stuck in my jaw.

It stuck in a barb wire snare.
Ich,[5] ich, ich, ich,
I could hardly speak.
I thought every German was you.
And the language obscene

An engine, an engine
Chuffing me off like a Jew.
A Jew to Dachau, Auschwitz, Belsen.[6]
I began to talk like a Jew.
I think I may well be a Jew.

The snows of the Tyrol, the clear beer of Vienna[7]
Are not very pure or true.
With my gypsy-ancestress and my weird luck
And my Taroc[8] pack and my Taroc pack
I may be a bit of a Jew.

I have always been scared of *you*,
With your Luftwaffe,[9] your gobbledygoo.
And your neat moustache
And your Aryan[1] eye, bright blue.
Panzer[2]-man, panzer-man, O You—

Not God but a swastika
So black no sky could squeak through.
Every woman adores a Fascist,
The boot in the face, the brute
Brute heart of a brute like you.

You stand at the blackboard, daddy,
In the picture I have of you,
A cleft in your chin instead of your foot
But no less a devil for that, no not
Any less the black man who

Bit my pretty red heart in two.
I was ten when they buried you.
At twenty I tried to die

5. German for "I." 6. Sites of World War II Nazi death camps.
7. The snow in the Tyrol (an Alpine region in Austria and northern Italy) is, legendarily, as pure as the beer is clear in Vienna. 8. Tarot, playing cards used mainly for fortune-telling.
9. German air force. 1. People of Germanic lineage, often blond-haired and blue-eyed.
2. Literally "panther" (German), the Nazi tank corps' term for an armored vehicle.

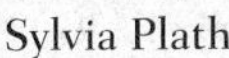

Sylvia Plath

Otto Plath

And get back, back, back to you.
I thought even the bones would do

But they pulled me out of the sack,
And they stuck me together with glue.[3]
And then I knew what to do.
I made a model of you,
A man in black with a Meinkampf[4] look

And a love of the rack and the screw.
And I said I do, I do.
So daddy, I'm finally through.
The black telephone's off at the root,
The voices just can't worm through.

If I've killed one man, I've killed two—
The vampire who said he was you
And drank my blood for a year,
Seven years, if you want to know.
Daddy, you can lie back now.

There's a stake in your fat black heart
And the villagers never liked you.
They are dancing and stamping on you.
They always *knew* it was you.
Daddy, daddy, you bastard, I'm through.

1962 1965

3. Perhaps an allusion to Plath's recovery from her first suicide attempt in 1953.

4. Title of Adolf Hitler's autobiography and manifesto (1925–27); German for "my struggle."

Preparing a Response to Critical Contexts: An Exercise

Before you read the criticism on Sylvia Plath's "Daddy" reprinted in this chapter, carefully read the poem itself several times. Ask all the analytical questions you have found useful in other cases: Who is speaking? to whom? when? under what conditions? What is the full situation? What kind of language does the poem use? How does the poem use **metaphor? allusion?** historical reference? What strategies of rhythm and sound does the poem use? What is the poem's **tone**? When was the poem written, and how does it reflect its time? What do you know about the person who wrote it? In what ways is this poem like others you have read by this poet or by this poet's contemporaries?

Once you have a preliminary "reading" of your own and have noted answers to these questions, look at the selections that follow. In order to come up with ideas for an essay incorporating the selections, you might follow these basic steps:

- Read each critical piece carefully and keep close track of all the things with which you agree and (even more important) disagree.
- Look specifically for information and facts that are new to you; examine and question the information carefully.
- Look for points of disagreement among the critics, make a list of the most important issues raised, and look for the parts of the poem over which disagreements occur.
- Once you have prepared your notes and absorbed some of the criticism, how do you participate in the debate about Sylvia Plath's poem? Here are some possible topics for an essay that draws on published criticism:
    - *Your essay could show that others have overlooked or misinterpreted something significant.* Note the sources the critics cite. Which articles or works by or about Sylvia Plath come up in more than one of the essays below? Find in your library or on the Internet a copy of the cited sources and read and interpret them in your own way.
    - *Your essay could be an overview of critical trends in the study of this poem, making clear which positions you find helpful, and where your own critical position differs from others.* Sort the critics into two or three groups according to their interpretation of "Daddy." Which critics place the most emphasis on Plath's psychology, personal experience, and self-expression? Which critics stress her development as a poet with a specific style? Which critics highlight her social criticism, either of anti-Semitism and the Holocaust or of sexism and women's oppression, or both? (See the section "Critical Approaches" for help identifying and describing the approaches of these critics or groups of critics.)

- In one or two sentences, write a **thesis** statement expressing your views on various critical approaches, such as the following:
  - Criticism of Sylvia Plath's "Daddy" has gone too far with a biographical approach, whereas myth criticism would facilitate a better understanding of the poem.
  - The life of Sylvia Plath provides a key to a reading of her poem "Daddy." As suggested by critics (including Steiner, Alvarez, and Axelrod) and biographical sources, the poem expresses violent emotional aspects of her life, including her unresolved attachment to her father, Otto Plath; her power struggle with her husband, Ted Hughes; and her suicide attempt.
  - Feminist readings of Sylvia Plath's "Daddy" have taken different approaches: Some focus on biographical evidence of Plath's experience as a woman, whereas others, such as Margaret Homans's A FEMININE TRADITION, consider a "literal" identification of the woman poet with the female speaker of the poem to be a reinforcement of the idea that women can never escape their personal, physical lives. This essay balances these feminist approaches to "Daddy," examining it as a semiautobiographical dramatic monologue: The speaker responds to some experiences Plath had as a daughter and wife, but the poem is not wholly autobiographical.

See also the writing suggestions at the end of this chapter.

CRITICAL EXCERPTS

George Steiner

From Dying Is an Art (1967)[5]

Sylvia Plath's last poems have already passed into legend as both representative of our present tone of emotional life and unique in their implacable, harsh brilliance [. . .] .

The spell does not lie wholly in the poems themselves. The suicide of Sylvia Plath at the age of thirty-one in 1963, and the personality of this young woman who had come from Massachusetts to study and live in England (where she married Ted Hughes, himself a gifted poet), are vital parts of it. To those who knew her and to the greatly enlarged circle who were electrified by her last poems and sudden death, she had come to signify the specific honesties and risks of the poet's condition. Her personal style, and the price in private harrowing she so obviously paid to achieve the intensity and candor of her principal poems, have taken on their own dramatic authority.

5. George Steiner. "Dying Is an Art." 1965. *Language and Silence: Essays on Language, Literature, and the Inhuman*, Atheneum, 1974, pp. 295–302. All footnotes have been added by the editor.

All this makes it difficult to judge the poems. I mean that the vehemence and intimacy of the verse is such as to constitute a very powerful rhetoric of sincerity. The poems play on our nerves with their own proud nakedness, making claims so immediate and sharply urged that the reader flinches, embarrassed by the routine discretions and evasions of his own sensibility. Yet if these poems are to take life among us, if they are to be more than exhibits in the history of modern psychological stress, they must be read with all the intelligence and scruple we can muster. They are too honest, they have cost too much, to be yielded to myth.

* * *

It requires no biographical impertinence to realize that Sylvia Plath's life was harried by bouts of physical pain, that she sometimes looked on the accumulated exactions of her own nerve and body as "a trash / To annihilate each decade."[6] She was haunted by the piecemeal, strung-together mechanics of the flesh. [. . .] The hospital ward was her exemplary ground:

> My patent leather overnight case like a black pillbox,
> My husband and child smiling out of the family photo;
> Their smiles catch onto my skin, little smiling hooks.[7]

This brokenness, so sharply feminine and contemporary, is, I think, her principal realization [. . .] . This new frankness of women about the specific hurts and tangles of their nervous-physiological makeup is as vital to the poetry of Sylvia Plath as it is to the tracts of Simone de Beauvoir[8] or to the novels of Edna O'Brien and Brigid Brophy.[9] Women speak out as never before [. . .] .

* * *

Where Emily Dickinson could—indeed was obliged to—shut the door on the riot and humiliations of the flesh, thus achieving her particular dry lightness, Sylvia Plath "fully assumed her own condition." This alone would assure her of a place in modern literature. But she took one step further, assuming a burden that was not naturally or necessarily hers.

Born in Boston in 1932 of German and Austrian parents, Sylvia Plath had no personal, immediate contact with the world of the concentration camps. I may be mistaken, but so far as I know there was nothing Jewish in her background. But her last, greatest poems culminate in an act of identification, of total communion with those tortured and massacred. [Here Steiner quotes lines 31–40 of "Daddy."]

* * *

6. Steiner here quotes Plath's "Lady Lazarus," lines 23–24.

7. Plath, "Tulips," lines 19–21.

8. French philosopher (1908–86) best known as author of *The Second Sex* (1949), a foundational text of modern feminism.

9. Irish novelist, essayist, and dramatist (1929–95) and vocal champion of women's and animal rights. *Edna O'Brien*: Irish novelist (b. 1930).

Pablo Picasso, *Guernica* (1937)

Sylvia Plath is only one of a number of young contemporary poets, novelists, and playwrights, themselves in no way implicated in the actual holocaust, who have done most to counter the general inclination to forget the death camps. Perhaps it is only those who had no part in the events who *can* focus on them rationally and imaginatively; to those who experienced the thing, it has lost the hard edges of possibility, it has stepped outside the real.

Committing the whole of her poetic and formal authority to the metaphor, to the mask of language, Sylvia Plath *became* a woman being transported to Auschwitz on the death trains. The notorious shards of massacre seemed to enter into her own being:

A cake of soap,
A wedding ring,
A gold filling.[1]

In "Daddy" she wrote one of the very few poems I know of in any language to come near the last horror. It achieves the classic act of generalization, translating a private, obviously intolerable hurt into a code of plain statement, of instantaneously public images which concern us all. It is the "Guernica"[2] of modern poetry. And it is both histrionic and, in some ways, "arty," as is Picasso's outcry.

Are these final poems entirely legitimate? In what sense does anyone, himself uninvolved and long after the event, commit a subtle larceny when he invokes the echoes and trappings of Auschwitz and appropriates an enormity of ready emotion to his own private design? Was there latent in Sylvia Plath's sensibility, as in that of many of us who remember only by fiat of imagination, a fearful envy, a dim resentment at not having been there, of having missed the rendezvous with hell? In "Lady Lazarus" and "Daddy" the realization seems to me so complete, the sheer rawness and control so great, that only irresistible need could have brought it off. These poems take tremendous risks, extending Sylvia Plath's essentially austere manner to the very limit. They are a bitter triumph, proof of the capacity of poetry to give to reality the greater permanence of the imagined. She could not return from them.

1. Plath, "Lady Lazarus," lines 76–78.
2. Pablo Picasso's famous painting (1937) depicting the brutalities of war.

A. Alvarez

From Sylvia Plath (1968)[3]

The reasons for Sylvia Plath's images are always there, though sometimes you have to work hard to find them. She is, in short, always in intelligent control of her feelings. Her work bears out her theories:

> I think my poems come immediately out of the sensuous and emotional experiences I have, but I must say I cannot sympathise with these cries from the heart that are informed by nothing except a needle or a knife or whatever it is. I believe that one should be able to control and manipulate experiences, even the most terrifying—like madness, being tortured, this kind of experience—and one should be able to manipulate these experiences with an informed and intelligent mind. I think that personal experience shouldn't be a kind of shut box and mirror-looking narcissistic experience. I believe it should be generally relevant, to such things as Hiroshima and Dachau, and so on.

It seems to me that it was only by her determination both to face her most inward and terrifying experiences and to use her intelligence in doing so—so as not to be overwhelmed by them—that she managed to write these extraordinary last poems, which are at once deeply autobiographical and yet detached, generally relevant.

[. . .] She assumes the suffering of all the modern victims. Above all, she becomes an imaginary Jew. I think this is a vitally important element in her work. For two reasons. First, because anyone whose subject is suffering has a ready-made modern example of hell on earth in the concentration camps. And what matters in them is not so much the physical torture—since sadism is general and perennial—but the way modern, as it were industrial, techniques can be used to destroy utterly the human identity. [. . .] This anonymity of pain, which makes all dignity impossible, was Sylvia Plath's subject. Second, she seemed convinced, in these last poems, that the root of her suffering was the death of her father, whom she loved, who abandoned her, and who dragged her after him into death. And in her fantasies her father was pure German, pure Aryan, pure anti-semite.

It all comes together in the most powerful of her last poems, "Daddy," about which she wrote the following bleak note:

> The poem is spoken by a girl with an Electra complex. Her father died while she thought he was God. Her case is complicated by the fact that her father was also a Nazi and her mother very possibly part Jewish. In the daughter the two strains marry and paralyse each other—she has to act out the awful little allegory once over before she is free of it.[4]

3. A. Alvarez. "Sylvia Plath." *Beyond All This Fiddle*, Penguin, 1968, pp. 56–57.

4. From the introductory notes to "New Poems," a reading prepared for the BBC Third Programme but never broadcast [Alvarez's note]. "Electra complex" is the psycoanalytic term for a girl's sense of competition with her mother for her father's affection, coined by Carl Jung (1875–1961) and alluding to the eponymous heroine of Sophocles's tragedy *Electra*. In the play, Electra and her brother conspire to kill their mother to avenge the murder of their father.

[. . .] What comes through most powerfully, I think, is the terrible *unforgivingness* of her verse, the continual sense not so much of violence—although there is a good deal of that—as of violent resentment that this should have been done to *her.* What she does in the poem is, with a weird detachment, to turn the violence against herself so as to show that she can equal her oppressors with her self-inflicted oppression. And this is the strategy of the concentration camps. When suffering is there whatever you do, by inflicting it upon yourself you achieve your identity, you set yourself free.

Yet the tone of the poem, like its psychological mechanisms, is not single or simple, and she uses a great deal of skill to keep it complex. Basically, her trick is to tell this horror story in a verse form as insistently jaunty and ritualistic as a nursery rhyme. And this helps her to maintain towards all the protagonists—her father, her husband and herself—a note of hard and sardonic anger, as though she were almost amused that her own suffering should be so extreme, so grotesque. [. . .] When she first read me the poem a few days after she wrote it, she called it a piece of "light verse." It obviously isn't, yet equally obviously it also isn't the racking personal confession that a mere description or précis of it might make it sound.

Yet neither is it unchangingly vindictive or angry. The whole poem works on one single, returning note and rhyme, echoing from start to finish:

> You do not do, you do not do . . .
> . . . I used to pray to recover you.
> Ach, du . . .

There is a kind of cooing tenderness in this which complicates the other, more savage note of resentment. It brings in an element of pity, less for herself and her own suffering than for the person who made her suffer. Despite everything, "Daddy" is a love poem.

Irving Howe

From The Plath Celebration: A Partial Dissent (1973)[5]

Sylvia Plath's most famous poem, adored by many sons and daughters, is "Daddy." It is a poem with an affecting theme, the feelings of the speaker as she regathers the pain of her father's premature death and her persuasion that he has betrayed her by dying:

> I was ten when they buried you.
> At twenty I tried to die
> And get back, back, back to you.

In the poem Sylvia Plath identifies the father (we recall his German birth) with the Nazis ("Panzer-man, panzer-man, O You") and flares out with assaults

5. Irving Howe. "The Plath Celebration: A Partial Dissent." 1973. *The Critical Point of Literature and Culture*, Horizon, 1977, pp. 231–33. All footnotes have been added by the editor.

for which nothing in the poem (nor, so far as we know, in Sylvia Plath's own life) offers any warrant: "A cleft in your chin instead of your foot / But no less a devil for that. . . ." Nor does anything in the poem offer warrant, other than the free-flowing hysteria of the speaker, for the assault of such lines as, "There's a stake in your fat black heart / And the villagers never liked you." [. . .]

What we have here is a revenge fantasy, feeding upon filial love-hatred, and thereby mostly of clinical interest. But seemingly aware that the merely clinical can't provide the materials for a satisfying poem, Sylvia Plath tries to enlarge upon the personal plight, give meaning to the personal outcry, by fancying the girl as victim of a Nazi father: "An engine, an engine / Chuffing me off like a Jew. . . ."

The more sophisticated admirers of this poem may say that I fail to see it as a dramatic presentation, a monologue spoken by a disturbed girl not necessarily to be identified with Sylvia Plath, despite the similarities of detail between the events of the poem and the events of her life. I cannot accept this view. The personal-confessional element, strident and undisciplined, is simply too obtrusive to suppose the poem no more than a dramatic picture of a certain style of disturbance. If, however, we did accept such a reading of "Daddy," we would fatally narrow its claims to emotional or moral significance, for we would be confining it to a mere vivid imagining of a pathological state. That, surely, is not how its admirers really take the poem.

It is clearly not how the critic George Steiner takes the poem when he calls it "the 'Guernica' of modern poetry." But then, in an astonishing turn, he asks: "In what sense does anyone, himself uninvolved and long after the event, commit a subtle larceny when he invokes the echoes and trappings of Auschwitz and appropriates an enormity of ready emotion to his own private design?" The question is devastating to his early comparison with "Guernica." Picasso's painting objectifies the horrors of Guernica,[6] through the distancing of art; no one can suppose that he shares or participates in them. Plath's poem aggrandizes on the "enormity of ready emotion" invoked by references to the concentration camps, in behalf of an ill-controlled if occasionally brilliant outburst. There is something monstrous, utterly disproportionate, when tangled emotions about one's father are deliberately compared with the historical fate of the European Jews; something sad, if the comparison is made spontaneously. "Daddy" persuades once again, through the force of negative example, of how accurate T. S. Eliot was in saying, "The more perfect the artist, the more completely separate in him will be the man who suffers and the mind which creates."[7]

6. See footnote 2 above. Picasso's painting was inspired by the German and Italian air assault on Guernica, a village in northern Spain, on April 26, 1937, during the Spanish Civil War.
7. In "Tradition and the Individual Talent" (1919).

Judith Kroll

From Rituals of Exorcism: "Daddy" (1976)[8]

Poems explicitly about the protagonist's father, read in order of composition, show that the attitude toward him evolves from nostalgic mournfulness, regret, and guilt, to resentment and a bitter resolve to break his hold on her. [. . .]

The recital of the myth in "Daddy" ends in a ritual intended to cancel the earlier "sacred marriage" which has suffocated her:

> You do not do, you do not do
> Any more, black shoe
> In which I have lived like a foot
> For thirty years, poor and white,
> Barely daring to breathe or Achoo.[9]

In this image of passive and victimized domesticity, the speaker implicitly compares her past self to the "old woman who lived in a shoe" who "didn't know what to do"; now, however, she makes it clear that she does know what to do.

As a preamble to the exorcism, [. . .] Daddy must be cast in this new light, transformed from god to devil, if he is to be successfully expelled, but there must also be some real basis for it. To be effectively exposed, he must first appear as godly. But the speaker soon shows that she now attributes his godliness in part to his authoritarianism and personal inaccessibility—qualities which became intensified through his death, and which later became transferred to "a model of you"—her husband. [. . .] Loving a man literally or metaphorically dead [. . .] becomes a kind of persecution or punishment; and so, by the end of the incantation, Daddy deserves to be cast out. The "black telephone . . . off at the root," conveys the finality of the intended exorcism.

The "venomousness," ambiguous from the beginning, is not the whole story. "Daddy" is not primarily a poem of "father-hatred" or abuse as Robert Lowell, Elizabeth Hardwick, and others have contended. The need for exorcising her father's ghost lies, after all, in the extremity of her attachment to him. Alvarez very justly remarks that [. . .] "'Daddy' is a love poem."[1] [. . .] The love is not merely conveyed by the rhythm and sound of the poem, it is a necessary part of the poem's meaning, a part of the logic of its act.

The exorcism serves another purpose because through it she attempts to reject the pattern of being abandoned and made to suffer by a god, a man who is "chock-full of power": she creates "a model of you"—an image of her father—and marries this proxy. Then she kills both father and husband at once, magically

8. Judith Kroll. "Rituals of Exorcism: 'Daddy.'" *Chapters in a Mythology: The Poetry of Sylvia Plath*, Harper & Row, 1976, pp. 122–26. Unless otherwise specified, all notes are Kroll's.

9. When Plath introduced "Daddy" as being about "a girl with an Electra complex" (with, in effect, the female version of an Oedipus complex), she gave a clue to what may be a play on words in the poem. "Oedipus" means "swell-foot," and therefore the speaker's identification of herself as a "foot" may be a private way of saying "I am Oedipus" and incorporating into the poem an allusion to the Electra complex.

1. Alvarez, "Sylvia Plath" [see pp. 1310–12].

using each as the other's representative.[2] Each death entails that of the other: the stake in her father's heart also kills the "vampire who said he was you"; and the killing of her marriage (for which she now claims to take responsibility, as she does for having allowed her marriage to perpetuate, by proxy, her relationship to her father) finally permits Daddy to "lie back." The marriage to and killing of her father by proxy are acts of what Frazer[3] calls "sympathetic magic," in which "things act on each other at a distance through a secret sympathy." [. . .]

Plath was familiar with and used such ideas. [. . .] The notion that "as the image suffers, so does the man"—affecting the real subject through a proxy—nicely describes marriage to a model of Daddy, and explains why "If I've killed one man, I've killed two." The earlier attempt of the speaker in "Daddy" to recover her father also involved sympathetic magic; she had tried to rejoin him by dying and becoming like him:

> At twenty I tried to die
> And get back, back, back to you.

She finally exorcises her father as if he were a scapegoat invested with the evils of her spoiled history. Frazer's discussion of rituals in which the dying god is also a scapegoat is germane here. He conjectures that two originally separate rituals merged. [. . . T]he father in "Daddy" may well be described as such a divine scapegoat figure.

Mary Lynn Broe

From Protean Poetic: The Poetry of Sylvia Plath (1980)[4]

Among the other poems that display the performing self, "Daddy" and "Lady Lazarus" are two of the most often quoted, but most frequently misunderstood, poems in the Plath canon. The speaker in "Daddy" performs a mock poetic exorcism of an event that has already happened—the death of her father, who she feels withdrew his love from her by dying prematurely: "Daddy, I have had to kill you. / You died before I had time—."

The speaker attempts to exorcise not just the memory of her father but her own *Mein Kampf* model of him as well as her inherited behavioral traits that lead her graveward under the Freudian banner of death instinct or Thanatos's[5] libido. But her ritual reenactment simply does not take. The event comically backfires as pure self-parody: the metaphorical murder of the father dwindles into Hollywood spectacle, while the poet is lost in the clutter of the collective unconscious.[6]

2. The biographical basis for this identification is evident in *Letters Home*. [. . .]
3. Sir James George Frazer (1854–1941), Scottish anthropologist whose book *The Golden Bough* analyzes early religious and magical practices [editor's note].
4. Mary Lynn Broe. *Protean Poetic: The Poetry of Sylvia Plath*. U of Missouri P, 1980. The following excerpt appears on pages 172–75. Unless otherwise indicated, all footnotes have been added by the editor.
5. In Greek mythology, Thanatos is a personification of death.
6. According to psychologist Carl Jung (1875–1961), a reservoir of memories and images shared by all, but inaccessible to the conscious mind.

Early in the poem, the ritual gets off on the wrong foot both literally and figuratively. A sudden rhythmic break midway through the first stanza interrupts the insistent and mesmeric chant of the poet's own freedom:

> You do not do, you do not do
> Any more, black shoe
> In which I have lived like a foot
> For thirty years, poor and white,
> Barely daring to breathe or Achoo.

The break suggests, on the one hand, that the nursery-rhyme world of contained terror is here abandoned; on the other, that the poet-exorcist's mesmeric control is superficial, founded in a shaky faith and an unsure heart—the worst possible state for the strong, disciplined exorcist.

At first she kills her father succinctly with her own words, demythologizing him to a ludicrous piece of statuary that is hardly a Poseidon or the Colossus of Rhodes.[7] [. . .]

Then as she tries to patch together the narrative of him, his tribal myth (the "common" town, the "German tongue," the war-scraped culture), she begins to lose her own powers of description to a senseless Germanic prattle ("The tongue stuck in my jaw. / It stuck in a barb wire snare. / Ich, ich, ich, ich"). The individual man is absorbed by his inhuman archetype, the "panzer man," "an engine / Chuffing me off like a Jew." Losing the exorcist's power that binds the spirit and then casts out the demon, she is the classic helpless victim of the swastika man. As she calls up her own picture of him as a devil, he refuses to adopt this stereotype. Instead he jumbles his trademark:

> A cleft in your chin instead of your foot
> But no less a devil for that, no not
> Any less the black man who
>
> Bit my pretty red heart in two.

The overt Nazi-Jew allegory throughout the poem suggests that, by a simple inversion of power, father and daughter grow more alike. But when she tries to imitate his action of dying, making all the appropriate grand gestures, she once again fails: "but they pulled me out of the sack, / And they stuck me together with glue." She retreats to a safe world of icons and replicas, but even the doll image she constructs turns out to be "the vampire who said he was you." At last, she abandons her father to the collective unconscious where it is *he* who is finally recognized ("they always *knew* it was you"). *She* is lost, impersonally absorbed by his irate persecutors, bereft of both her power and her conjuror's discipline, and possessed by the incensed villagers. The exorcist's ritual, one of purifying, cleansing, commanding silence and then ordering the evil spirit's departure, has dwindled to a comic picture from the heart of darkness. Mad villagers stamp on the devil-vampire creation. [. . .]

[. . .] It would seem that the real victim is the poet-performer who, despite her straining toward identification with the public events of holocaust and

7. One of the seven wonders of the ancient world, a gigantic statue of the Greek sun god, Helios. *Poseidon*: the chief sea god in the Greek pantheon.

destruction of World War II, becomes more murderously persecuting than the "panzer-man" who smothered her, and who abandoned her with a paradoxical love, guilt, and fear. [. . .]

The failure of the exorcism and the emotional ambivalence are echoed in the curious rhythm. The incantatory safety of the nursery-rhyme thump (seemingly one of controlled, familiar terrors) also suggests some sinister brooding by its repetition. The poem opens with a suspiciously emphatic protest, a kind of psychological whistling-in-the-dark. As it proceeds, "Daddy"'s continuous life-rhythms—the assonance, consonance, and especially the sustained *oo* sounds—triumph over either the personal or the cultural-historical imagery. The sheer sense of organic life in the interwoven sounds carries the verse forward in boisterous spirit and communicates an underlying feeling of comedy that is also echoed in the repeated failure of the speaker to perform her exorcism.

Ultimately, "Daddy" is like an emotional, psychological, and historical autopsy, a final report. There is no real progress. The poet is in the same place in the beginning as in the end. [. . .] Although it seems that the speaker has moved from identification with the persecuted to identity as persecutor, Jew to vampire-killer, powerless to powerful, she has simply enacted a performance that allows her to live with what is unchangeable. She has used her art to stave off suffocation, and performs her self-contempt with a degree of bravado.[8]

Margaret Homans

From A Feminine Tradition (1982)[9]

The current belief in a literal "I" present in poetry is responsible for the popular superstition that Sylvia Plath's death was the purposeful completion of her poetry's project, the assumption being that if the speaker is precisely the same as the biographical Plath, the poetry's self-destructive violence is directed toward Plath herself, not toward an imagined speaker. This reading of Plath is unfair to the woman and, by calling it merely unmediated self-expression, obscures her poetry's real power. In poem after poem depicting or wishing for physical violence, the imagery of violence is part of a symmetrical figurative system, and death is figured as a way of achieving rebirth or some other transcendence.[1] Plath's project may not thus be very different from that of Dickinson, who speaks quite often from beyond the grave, reimagining and repossessing death as her own in order to dispel the terrors of literal death. However, within that figurative system the poet embraces a self-destructive program that must soon have been poetically terminal, even if it did not bring about the actual death.

8. What remains the most thorough and enlightening account of the poem is A. R. Jones, "On 'Daddy,'" *The Art of Sylvia Plath*, [ed. Newman,] pp. 230–36 [Broe's note].

9. Margaret Homans. "A Feminine Tradition." *Women Writers and Poetic Identity: Dorothy Wordsworth, Emily Brontë, and Emily Dickinson*, Princeton UP, 1982, pp. 218–21.

1. I am indebted here, for their persuasively positive readings of Plath, to Judith Kroll, *Chapters in a Mythology: The Poetry of Sylvia Plath* (New York: Harper & Row, 1976), and to Stacy Pies, "Coming Clear of the Shadow: The Poetry of Sylvia Plath," unpublished essay (Yale University, 1979) [Homans's note].

Several of Plath's late poems come to terms with a father figure (who may include the poetic fathers she acknowledges in *The Colossus*), whose crime, no different from that identified by nineteenth-century women, is of attempting to transform the feminine self into objects.

• • •

"Daddy" uses Nazi imagery to make the same accusation about objectification brought against men as oppressors in "Lady Lazarus" and makes the corollary accusation against the father (and the husband modelled after him) that objectification has silenced her: "I never could talk to you./ . . . I could hardly speak." In this context defiance and retribution take the form of her speaking, but again this counterattack is counterproductive. Punning on the expression "being through" to mean both establishing a telephone connection and being finished, she at once makes and conclusively severs communication:

So daddy, I'm finally through.
The black telephone's off at the root,
The voices just can't worm through.

The poem concludes, "Daddy, daddy, you bastard, I'm through." Suppressing the power of the one who silenced her, she simultaneously returns herself to the silence that the poem came into being to protest.

Pamela J. Annas

From A Disturbance in Mirrors: The Poetry of Sylvia Plath (1988)[2]

The particular sexual metaphor in "Daddy" is sado-masochism, which stands for the authority structure of a partriarchal and war-making society. [. . .] "Daddy" is an analysis of the structure of the society in which the individual is enmeshed. Intertwined with the image of sadist and masochist in "Daddy" is a parallel image of vampire and victim. In "Daddy," father, husband, and a larger patriarchal and competitive authority structure, which the speaker of the poem sees as having been responsible for the various imperialisms of the twentieth century, all melt together and become demonic, finally a gigantic vampire figure. In the modulation from one image to another to form an accumulated image that is characteristic of many of Plath's late poems, the male figure at the center of "Daddy" takes four major forms: the statue, the Gestapo officer, the professor, and the vampire. The poem begins, however, with an image of a black shoe, an image which, like the black shoe in "The Munich Mannequins" and like the black suit in "The Applicant," can be seen to stand for corporate man. The second stanza of the poem refers back to the title poem of *The Colossus,* where the speaker's father, representative of a gigantic male other, so dominated her world that her horizon was bounded by his scattered pieces. [. . .] Here the image of her father, grown larger than the earlier Colossus of Rhodes,

2. Pamela J. Annas. *A Disturbance in Mirrors: The Poetry of Sylvia Plath.* Contributions in Women's Studies, no. 89, Greenwood, 1988, pp. 139–43. All notes are Annas's.

stretches across and subsumes the whole of the United States, from the Pacific to the Atlantic ocean.

The next seven stanzas of "Daddy" construct the image of the Gestapo officer, using her family background—her parents were both of German origin—to mediate between her personal sense of suffocation and the social history of the Nazi invasions. The black shoe of the first stanza in which she says she has been wedged like a foot "barely daring to breathe" becomes in stanza ten, at the end of the Nazi section, a larger social image of suffocation: "Not God but a swastika / So black no sky could squeak through." The Gestapo figure recurs briefly three stanzas later as the speaker of the poem transfers the image from father to husband and incidentally suggests that the victim has some control in a brutalized association—at least to the extent she chooses to be there.[3] "I made a model of you, . . . And I said I do, I do." The Gestapo figure becomes "Herr Professor" in stanza eleven, an actual image of Plath's father, and also an image of what has for centuries been seen as the prototypical and even ideal relationship between a man and a woman.[4] The professor, who is a man, talks and is active; the woman, who is a student, listens and is passive. [. . .] But Plath places this image between the images of Nazi/Jew and vampire/victim so that it becomes the center of a series. Indeed, the image of daddy as teacher turns almost immediately into a devil/demon/vampire. [. . .]

The last two stanzas of "Daddy" are like the conclusion of "Lady Lazarus" in their assertion that the speaker of the poem is breaking out of the cycle and that, in order to do so, she must turn on and kill Herr God, Herr Lucifer in the one poem, and Daddy in his final metamorphosis as vampire in the other poem [. . .].

The cycle of victim/vampire is, left alone, a closed and repetitious cycle, like the repeated suicides of "Lady Lazarus." According to the legends and the Hollywood film versions of these legends we all grew up on, once consumed by a vampire, one dies and is reborn a vampire and preys upon others, who in their turn die and become vampires. The vampire imagery in Sylvia Plath's poetry intersects on one level with her World War II imagery and its exploitation and victimization and on another level intersects with her images of a bureaucratic, fragmented, and dead—in the sense of numbed and unaware—society. The connections are sometimes confused, but certainly World War II is often imaged in her poetry as a kind of grisly, vampiric feast. [. . .]

The whole of "Daddy" is an exorcism to banish the demon, put a stake through the vampire's heart, and thus break the cycle of vampire→victim. It is crucial to the poem that the exorcism is accomplished through communal

3. See Wilhelm Reich's *The Mass Psychology of Fascism* (New York: Simon and Schuster, 1969), particularly his chapter on "The Authoritarian Personality," for an analysis of how an oppressed class can contribute to its own oppression. Judith Lewis Herman, in *Father-Daughter Incest* (Cambridge, Mass.: Harvard University Press, 1981), discusses the history of the suppression of incest beginning with Freud and continuing into contemporary psychological literature, the attribution of reports of incest to hysterical female oedipal fantasizing or, when the fact of incest is impossible to deny, assigning blame to the victim: what Herman calls the Seductive Daughter and/or the Collusive Mother (Chapter 1, "A Common Occurrence"). Writing in the early 1960s and familiar with some of these attitudes, [. . .] Plath assigns some culpability to the victim.

4. This photograph of Otto Plath is reproduced on page 17 of *Letters Home*.

action by the "villagers." The rhythm of the poem is powerfully and deliberately primitive: a child's chant, a formal curse. The hard sounds, short lines, and repeated rhymes of "do," "you," "Jew," and "through" give a hard pounding quality to the poem that is close to the sound of a heart beat. [. . .]

Purity, which is what exorcism aims at, is for Plath an ambiguous concept. On the one hand it means integrity of self, wholeness rather than fragmentation, an unspoiled state of being, rest, perfection, aesthetic beauty, and loss of self through transformation into some reborn other. On the other hand, it also means absence, isolation, blindness, a kind of autism which shuts out the world, stasis and death, and a loss of self through dispersal into some other. In "Lady Lazarus" and "Fever 103°" the emphasis is on exorcising the poet's previous selves, though within a social context that makes that unlikely. "Daddy," however, is a purification of the world; in "Daddy" it is the various avatars of the other—the male figure who represents the patriarchal society she lives in—that are being exorcised. [. . .] The more the speaker of the poems defines her situation as desperate, the more violent and vengeful becomes the agent of purification and transformation.

Steven Gould Axelrod

From Sylvia Plath: The Wound and the Cure of Words (1990)[5]

Although this poem too ["Daddy"] has traditionally been read as "personal" (Aird 78) or "confessional" (M. L. Rosenthal 82), Margaret Homans has more recently suggested that it concerns a woman's dislocated relations to speech (*Women Writers* 220–21). Plath herself introduced it on the BBC as the opposite of confession, as a constructed fiction: "Here is a poem spoken by a girl with an Electra complex. [. . .]" (*CP* 293).[6] [. . .] However we interpret Plath's preface, we must agree that "Daddy" is dramatic and allegorical, since its details depart freely from the facts of her biography. In this poem she [. . .] figures her unresolved conflicts with paternal authority as a textual issue. Significantly, her father was a published writer, and his successor, her husband, was also a writer. Her preface asserts that the poem concerns a young woman's paralyzing self-division, which she can defeat only through allegorical representation. Recalling that paralysis was one of Plath's main tropes for literary incapacity, we begin to see that the poem evokes the female poet's anxiety of authorship and specifically Plath's strategy of delivering herself from that anxiety by making it the topic of her discourse. Viewed from this perspective, "Daddy" enacts the woman poet's struggle with "daddy-poetry." It represents her effort to reject the "buried male muse" from her invention process and the "jealous gods" from her audience (*J* 223; *CP* 179).[7]

5. Steven Gould Axelrod. *Sylvia Plath: The Wound and the Cure of Words.* Johns Hopkins UP, 1990. These excerpts appear on pages 51–70. All footnotes have been added, and Axelrod's bibliography has been abbreviated by the editor.

6. For the full quotation, see the Alvarez excerpt above. *CP* is Axelrod's abbreviation for Plath's *Collected Poems.*

7. *J* is Axelrod's abbreviation for Plath's *Journals.*

Plath wrote "Daddy" several months after Hughes left her, on the day she learned that he had agreed to a divorce (October 12, 1962). George Brown and Tirril Harris have shown that early loss makes one especially vulnerable to subsequent loss (Bowlby 250–59), and Plath seems to have defended against depression by almost literally throwing herself into her poetry. She followed "Daddy" with a host of poems that she considered her greatest achievement to date: "Medusa," "The Jailer," "Lady Lazarus," "Ariel," the bee sequence, and others. The letters she wrote to her mother and brother on the day of "Daddy," and then again four days later, brim with a sense of artistic self-discovery: "Writing like mad. . . . Terrific stuff, as if domesticity had choked me" (*LH* 466).[8] Composing at the "still blue, almost eternal hour before the baby's cry, before the glassy music of the milkman, setting his bottles" (quoted in Alvarez, *Savage God* 21), she experienced an "enormous" surge in creative energy (*LH* 467). [. . .] she wrote "Daddy" to demonstrate the existence of her voice, which had been silent or subservient for so long. She wrote it to prove her "genius" (*LH* 468).

Plath projected her struggle for textual identity onto the figure of a partly Jewish young woman who learns to express her anger at the patriarch and at his language of male mastery, which is as foreign to her as German, as "obscene" as murder (st. 6),[9] and as meaningless as "gobbledygoo" (st. 9). [. . .] At a basic level, "Daddy" concerns its own violent, transgressive birth as a text, its origin in a culture that regards it as illegitimate—a judgment the speaker hurls back on the patriarch himself when she labels *him* a bastard (st. 16). Plath's unaccommodating worldview, which was validated by much in her childhood and adult experience, led her to understand literary tradition not as an expanding universe of beneficial influence [. . .] but as a closed universe in which every addition required a corresponding subtraction [. . .]. If Plath's speaker was to be born as a poet, a patriarch must die.

As in "The Colossus," the father here appears as a force or an object rather than as a person. Initially he takes the form of an immense "black shoe," capable of stamping on his victim (st. 1). Immediately thereafter he becomes a marble "statue" (st. 2) [. . .]. He then transforms into Nazi Germany (st. 6–7, 9–10), the archetypal totalitarian state. [. . .] Eventually the father declines in stature from God (st. 2) to a devil (st. 11) to a dying vampire (st. 15). Perhaps he shrinks under the force of his victim's denunciation, which de-creates him as a power as it creates him as a figure. But whatever his size, he never assumes human dimensions, aspirations, and relations—except when posing as a teacher in a photograph (st. 11). Like the colossus, he remains figurative and symbolic, not individual.

[. . . Unlike the father figure in "The Colossus,"] "Daddy" remains silent, apart from the gobbledygoo attributed to him once (st. 9). He uses his mouth primarily for biting and for drinking blood. The poem emphasizes his feet and, implicitly, his phallus. He is a "black shoe" (st. 1), a statue with "one gray toe" (st. 2), a "boot" (st. 10). [. . . the speaker] is herself silenced by his shoe: "I never could talk to you" (st. 5). Daddy is [. . .] a male censor. His boot in the face of "every woman" is presumably lodged in her mouth (st. 10). He stands for all the ele-

8. *LH* is Axelrod's abbreviation for Plath's *Letters Home*.

9. When referring to "Daddy," Axelrod cites stanza (st.) rather than line numbers.

ments in the literary situation and in the female ephebe's[1] internalization of it, that prevent her from producing any words at all, even copied or subservient ones. Appropriately, Daddy can be killed only by being stamped on: he lives and dies by force, not language. If "The Colossus" tells a tale of the patriarch's speech, [. . .] "Daddy" tells a tale of the daughter's effort to speak.

Thus we are led to another important difference between the two poems. The "I" of "The Colossus" acquires her identity only through serving her "father," whereas the "I" of "Daddy" actuates her gift only through opposition to him. The later poem precisely inscribes the plot of Plath's dream novel of 1958: "a girl's search for the dead father—for an outside authority which must be developed, instead, from the inside" (*J* 258). As the child of a Nazi, the girl could "hardly speak" (st. 6), but as a Jew she begins "to talk" and to acquire an identity (st. 7). In Plath's allegory, the outsider Jew corresponds to "the rebel, the artist, the odd" (*JP* 55),[2] and particularly to the woman artist. Otto Rank's *Beyond Psychology*, which had a lasting influence on her, explicitly compares women to Jews, since "woman . . . has suffered from the very beginning a fate similar to that of the Jew, namely, suppression, slavery, confinement, and subsequent persecution" (287–88). Rank, whose discourse I would consider tainted by anti-Semitism, argues that Jews speak a language [. . .] that differs essentially from the language of the majority cultures in which they find themselves (191, 281–84). He analogously [. . .] argues that woman speaks in a language different from man's, and that as a result of man's denial of woman's world, "woman's 'native tongue' has hitherto been unknown or at least unheard" (248). [. . .] his idea of linguistic difference based on gender and his analogy between Jewish and female speech seem to have embedded themselves in the substructure of "Daddy" (and in many of Plath's other texts as well). For Plath, as later for Adrienne Rich, the Holocaust and the patriarchy's silencing of women were linked outcomes of the masculinist interpretation of the world. Political insurrection and female self-assertion also interlaced symbolically. In "Daddy," Plath's speaker finds her voice and motive by identifying herself as antithetical to her Fascist father. [. . .] Previously devoted to the patriarch—both in "The Colossus" and in memories evoked in "Daddy" of trying to "get back" to him (st. 12)—she now seeks only to escape from him and to see him destroyed.

Plath has unleashed the anger, normal in mourning as well as in revolt, that she suppressed in the earlier poem. But she has done so at a cost. Let us consider her childlike speaking voice. The language of "Daddy," beginning with its title, is often regressive. The "I" articulates herself by moving backwards in time, using the language of nursery rhymes and fairy tales (the little old woman who lived in a shoe, the black man of the forest). Such language accords with a child's conception of the world, not an adult's. Plath's assault on the language of "daddy-poetry" has turned inward, on the language of her own poem, which teeters precariously on the edge of a preverbal abyss—represented by the eerie, keening "oo" sound with which a majority of the verses end. And then let us consider the play on "through" at the poem's conclusion. Although that last line allows for multiple readings, one interpretation is that the "I" has unconsciously carried out her father's

1. Youth, especially a young man, in training; apprentice.
2. *JP* is Axelrod's abbreviation for Plath's *Johnny Panic and the Bible of Dreams.*

wish: her discourse, by transforming itself into cathartic oversimplifications, has undone itself.

Yet the poem does contain its verbal violence by means more productive than silence. In a letter to her brother, Plath referred to "Daddy" as "gruesome" (*LH* 472), while on almost the same day she described it to A. Alvarez as a piece of "light verse" (Alvarez, *Beyond* 56). She later read it on the BBC in a highly ironic tone of voice. The poem's unique spell derives from its rhetorical complexity: its variegated and perhaps bizarre fusion of the horrendous and the comic. As [Margaret] Uroff has remarked, it both shares and remains detached from the fixation of its protagonist (159). [. . .] Plath's speaker uses potentially self-mocking melodramatic terms to describe both her opponent ("so black no sky could squeak through" [st. 10]) and herself ("poor and while" [st. 1]). While this aboriginal speaker quite literally expresses black-and-white thinking, her civilized double possesses a sensibility sophisticated enough to subject such thinking to irony. Thus the poem expresses feelings that it simultaneously parodies—it may be parodying the very idea of feeling. The tension between erudition and simplicity in the speaker's voice appears in her pairings that juxtapose adult with childlike diction: "breathe or Achoo," "your Luftewaffe, your gobbledygoo" (st. 1, 9). She can expound on such adult topics as Taroc packs, Viennese beer, and Tyrolean snowfall; can specify death camps by name; and can employ an adult vocabulary of "recover," "ancestress," "Aryan," "*Meinkampf*," "obscene," and "bastard." Yet she also has recourse to a more primitive lexicon that includes "chuffing," "your black heart," and "my pretty red heart." She proves herself capable of careful intellectual discriminations ("so I never could tell" [st. 5]), conventionalized description ("beautiful Nauset" [st. 3]), and moral analogy ("if I've killed one man, I've killed two" [st. 15]), while also exhibiting regressive fantasies (vampires), repetitions ("wars, wars, wars" [st. 4]), and inarticulateness ("panzer-man, panzer-man, O You—" [st. 9]). She oscillates between calm reflection "(You stand at the blackboard, daddy, / In the picture I have of you" [st. 11]) and mad incoherence ("Ich, ich, ich, ich" [st. 6]). Her sophisticated language puts her wild language in an ironic perspective, removing the discourse from the control of the archaic self who understands experience only in extreme terms.

The ironies in "Daddy" proliferate in unexpected ways, however. When the speaker proclaims categorically that "every woman adores a Fascist" (st. 10), she is subjecting her victimization to irony by suggesting that sufferers choose, or at least accommodate themselves to, their suffering. But she is also subjecting her authority to irony, since her claim about "every woman" is transparently false. It simply parodies patriarchal commonplaces, such as those advanced by Helene Deutsch concerning "feminine masochism" (192–99, 245–85). [. . .] Plath's mother wished that Plath would write about "decent, courageous people" (*LH* 477), and she herself heard an inner voice demanding that she be a perfect "paragon" in her language and feeling (*J* 176). But in the speaker of "Daddy," she inscribed the opposite of such a paragon: a divided self whose veneer of civilization is breached and infected by unhealthy instincts.

Plath's irony cuts both ways. At the same time that the speaker's sophisticated voice undercuts her childish voice, reducing its melodrama to comedy, the childish or maddened voice undercuts the pretensions of the sophisticated voice, revealing the extremity of suffering masked by its ironies. While demonstrating the inadequacy of thinking and feeling in opposites, the poem implies that such a mode can locate truths denied more complex cognitive and affective systems. The very moderation of the normal adult intelligence, its tolerance of ambiguity, its defenses against the primal energies of the id, results in falsification. Reflecting Schiller's[3] idea that the creative artist experiences a "momentary and passing madness" (quoted by Freud in a passage of *The Interpretation of Dreams* [193] that Plath underscored), "Daddy" gives voice to that madness. Yet the poem's sophisticated awareness, its comic vision, probably wins out in the end, since the poem concludes by curtailing the power of its extreme discourse [. . .]. Furthermore, Plath distanced herself from the poem's aboriginal voice by introducing her text as "a poem spoken by a girl with an Electra complex"—that is, as a study of the *girl*'s pathology rather than her father's—and as an allegory that will "free" her from that pathology. She also distanced herself by reading the poem in a tone that emphasized its irony. And finally, she distanced herself by laying the poem's wild voice permanently to rest after October. The aboriginal vision was indeed purged. "Daddy" represents not Dickinson's madness that is divinest sense,[4] but rather an entry into a style of discourse and a mastery of it. [. . .]

Plath's poetic revolt in "Daddy" liberated her pent-up creativity, but the momentary success sustained her little more than self-sacrifice had done. "Daddy" became another stage in her development, an unrepeatable experiment, a vocal opening that closed itself at once. The poem is not an elegy for the power of "daddy-poetry" but for the powers of speech Plath discovered in composing it.

When we consider "Daddy" generically, a further range of implications presents itself. Although we could profitably consider the poem as the dramatic monologue Plath called it in her BBC broadcast, let us regard it instead as the kind of poem most readers have taken it to be: a domestic poem. [. . .] I shall define the domestic poem as one that represents and comments on a protagonist's relationship to one or more family members, usually a parent, child, or spouse. To focus our discussion even further, I shall emphasize poetry that specifically concerns a father.

* * *

In the 1950s the "domestic poem" proper appeared on the scene, with its own conventions and expectations, and with its own complex cultural and literary reasons for being. Perhaps [. . .] its precise timing depended on a reaction against modernism's aesthetic of impersonality.[5] Theodore Roethke wrote several early poems that initiated the genre: "My Papa's Waltz" (1948), "The Lost Son" (1948), and "Where Knock Is Open Wide" (1951). [Robert] Lowell's "Life Studies" sequence (1959) was, and is, the genre's most prominent landmark. [. . .] In all these poems, the parent-child relationship serves as a locus for psychological investigation. In many of them it also serves as a means of representing the acquisition of poetic identity and of exploring the bounds of textuality itself. [. . .] The

3. German poet-philosopher Friedrich Schiller (1759–1805).

4. One Emily Dickinson poem begins, "Much Madness is divinest Sense—/ To a discerning Eye—/ Much Sense—the starkest Madness."

5. In "Tradition and the Individual Talent" (1919), modernist poet T. S. Eliot articulates an "impersonal theory of poetry," arguing, "the more perfect the artist, the more completely separate in him will be the man who suffers and the mind which creates."

"domestic poem" became a system of signs in which each individual text's adherence to the system and deviations within the system produced its particular literary meaning.

During Plath's trying time of 1958–59 [. . .] she struggled [. . .] to "break into a new line of poetry" (*J* 321). As always, her method was to "read others and think hard" (*J* 302). The two male poets she read most intently, the two who most instructed her, were Roethke and Lowell.

* * *

In 1959 [when she attended Lowell's Boston University poetry courses] Plath did not consciously attempt to write in the domestic poem genre, perhaps because she was not yet ready to assume her majority. [. . .] But by fall 1962, when she had already lost so much, she was ready to chance tackling poetic tradition, and specifically her chief male instructors, Roethke and Lowell. In "Daddy" she achieved her victory in two ways. First, as we have seen, she symbolically assaults a father figure who is identified with male control of language. All her anxiety of influence comes to the fore in the poem: her sense of belatedness, her awareness of constraint, her fears of inadequacy, her furious need to overcome her dependency, her guilt at her own aggressivity. Since the precursors "do not do / Any more" (st. 1), she wishes to escape their paralyzing influence and to empty the "bag full of God" that has kept her tongue stuck in her jaw for so long (st. 2, 5). The father whose power she attacks is not simply Roethke or Lowell, or even Hughes or Otto Plath, but a literary character who includes reference to all of them as categories of masculine authority. [. . .]

In addition to killing the father in its fictional plot, the poem seeks to discredit the forefathers through its status as poetic act. Taking a genre established by Roethke and Lowell, "Daddy" fundamentally alters it through antithesis and parody. Like all strong poems, it transforms its genre and therefore the way we perceive the precursive examples [. . .]. Her poem attempts to conclude the genre, to represent the final possible stroke, or at the very least to inaugurate some new and important genre, of which the whole domestic genre was but a foreshadowing.

This point comes clearer if we compare "Daddy" with two analogues, Roethke's "The Lost Son" (1948) and Lowell's "Commander Lowell" (1959). In the Freudian drama of "The Lost Son," the protagonist subjectively relives his childhood fears and fantasies. Like the speaker of the companion piece, "My Papa's Waltz," he is still enmeshed in the family romance, remembering the father ambivalently as powerful, protective, and threatening. After locating himself at his father's grave, where he feels both grief and estrangement [. . .], he descends into his unconscious, seeking, as Roethke later explained, "some clue to existence" (*Poet* 38). He encounters his death wish, his memory of his father as "Father Fear," his sexual anxieties, and finally the "dark swirl" of a blackout, after which a childhood memory of his "Papa" shouting "order" in German returns him to consciousness. Although the figure of "Papa" blends earthly and heavenly father (*Poet* 39), he also symbolizes the superego, restoring order to a psyche and a poem that had fallen into chaos. At the poem's conclusion, as the "lost son" waits for his "understandable spirit" to revive, he appears to be purged, though not cured, of the conflicts that incapacitated him.

The speaker of "Commander Lowell," in contrast, is objective, precise, and witty. His discourse reflects a detached perspective on the past rather than a psychic reimmersion in it. He portrays his father as one who threatened him only through weakness. This father "was nothing to shout / about to the summer colony at 'Matt' " ; took "four shots with his putter to sink his putt"; sang "Anchors Aweigh" in the bathtub; was fired from his job; and squandered his inheritance. Whereas Roethke's poem represents a cathartic experience, Lowell's converts chaotic feelings into intellectual irony. Whereas Roethke's poem can be read as an allegory of man's relationship to God or as a model of the Freudian psyche, Lowell's remains a realistic narrative, though it does suggest the cultural and financial decline of a social class.

Plath's poem combines features of both of these precursors: Roethke's evocation of a German-speaking authoritarian with Lowell's sarcastic deflation of a man without qualities; Roethke's subjective anguish with Lowell's social comedy. Like Roethke's Papa, Plath's title character is an intimidating patriarch; like Lowell's Father, he is a buffoon ("big as a Frisco seal"). Finally, Plath's poem, like those of her predecessors, has little to do with psychological cure: the speaker's defenses remain in place. But in a deeper sense, "Daddy" swerves sharply from its precursors, curtailing their power. It turns the psychological depth of Roethke's poem and the ironically detached surface of Lowell's poem into a fury of denunciation, an extravagance of emotion, an exaggeration of acts and effects, perhaps revealing the subtexts of both precursors. [. . .] It unmasks Roethke's implicitly oppressive father figure as a monster and Lowell's sophisticated comedy as slapstick. It transforms the domestic genre alternately into a horror show, encapsulating every political, cultural, and familial atrocity of the age, and a theater of cruelty, evoking nervous laughter. "Daddy" takes the genre as far as it can go—and then further.

[. . . N]either poet [Roethke or Lowell] moved significantly in the directions suggested by "Daddy" [in their subsequent poems . . .] But Lowell confessed a feeling of defeat in his foreword to [Plath's] *Ariel*, and perhaps that confession has general application: "There is a peculiar, haunting challenge to these poems . . . in her lines, I often hear the serpent whisper, 'Come, if only you had the courage, you too could have my rightness, audacity and ease of inspiration' "(x).

WORKS CITED

PRIMARY TEXTS

Lowell, Robert. Foreword. *Ariel*. By Sylvia Plath. New York: Harper & Row, 1966. ix–xi.

Plath, Sylvia. *Collected Poems*. Ed. Ted Hughes. New York: Harper & Row, 1981.

———. *Johnny Panic and the Bible of Dreams: Short Stories, Prose, and Diary Excerpts*. New York: Harper & Row, 1979.

———. *Journals of Sylvia Plath*. Ed. Frances McCullough and Ted Hughes. New York: Dial, 1982.

———. *Letters Home: Correspondence: 1950–1963*. Ed. Aurelia Schober Plath. New York: Harper & Row, 1975.

Roethke, Theodore. *On the Poet and His Craft: Selected Prose*. Seattle: U of Washington P, 1965.

SECONDARY TEXTS

Aird, Eileen. *Sylvia Plath: Her Life and Work.* New York: Harper & Row, 1973.
Alvarez, A. *Beyond All This Fiddle.* London: Allen Lane-Penguin, 1968.
———. *The Savage God: A Study of Suicide.* 1971. New York: Bantam, 1973.
Bowlby, John. *Attachment and Loss.* Vol. 3. *Loss: Sadness and Depression.* London: Hogarth, 1980.
Deutsch, Helene. *The Psychology of Women,* Vol. 1. *Girlhood.* 1944. New York: Bantam, 1973.
Freud, Sigmund. *The Interpretation of Dreams.* 1900. Trans. A. A. Brill. *Basic Writings.* New York: Random House/Modern Library, 1938. 181–549.
Homans, Margaret. *Women Writers and Poetic Identity: Dorothy Wordsworth, Emily Brontë, and Emily Dickinson.* Princeton: Princeton UP, 1980.
Rank, Otto. *Beyond Psychology.* 1941. New York: Dover, 1958.
Rosenthal, M. L. *The New Poets: American and British Poetry since World War II.* London: Oxford UP, 1967.
Uroff, Margaret Dickie. *Sylvia Plath and Ted Hughes.* Urbana: U of Illinois P, 1979.

Laura Frost

From "Every Woman Adores a Fascist": Feminist Visions of Fascism from *Three Guineas* to *Fear of Flying* (2000)[6]

Throughout the 50s and 60s, the scenario of the fascist leader and his mesmerized followers was commonly interpreted as a gendered sadomasochistic encounter between a male leader and the collectively feminized "masses."[7] When Max Horkheimer and Theodor W. Adorno[8] sought an analogy by which to describe totalitarianism, they echoed Reich's[9] assumption that women are particularly constitutionally susceptible to the tyrant's libidinal allure:

> Just as women adore the unmoved paranoiac, so nations genuflect before totalitarian Fascism [. . .] (*Dialectic of Enlightenment* 191)

Given the gendered assumptions underpinning these and so many early theories of fascism, it is not surprising that fascism came to be a recurring term in feminist discourse. Countering the notion that women are drawn to subjugation, post-war feminism developed an analogy that posed fascism as a correlative of patriarchy: an exaggerated but related form of male domination. Simone de

6. Laura Frost. "'Every Woman Adores a Fascist': Feminist Visions of Fascism from *Three Guineas* to *Fear of Flying.*" *Women's Studies*, no. 29, 2000, pp. 37–69. *Taylor & Francis Online*, doi:10.1080/00497878.2000.9979299. Unless otherwise indicated, all notes are Frost's.

7. A competing psycho-sociological interpretation presents fascism as a sublimated form of homosexual attraction, a view made popular by William Shirer's bestselling 1959 account of Nazism, *The Rise and Fall of the Third Reich.* For a more recent analysis of this conflation of homosexuality with fascism, see Andrew Hewitt's *Political Inversions: Homosexuality, Fascism, and the Modernist Imaginary* (Stanford, CA: Stanford UP, 1996).

8. German-Jewish philosopher and sociologist (1895–1973) and German sociologist, philosopher, and musicologist (1903–69) [editor's note].

9. William Reich (1897–1957), Austrian-American psychiatrist and psychoanalyst, student of Sigmund Freud, and author of *The Mass Psychology of Fascism* (1933) [editor's note].

Beauvoir's *The Second Sex* [1949], for example, presents Nazism as a cautionary tale for women in democratic countries [. . .] . Likewise, Kate Millett's *Sexual Politics* (1970) represents fascist ideology as "the most deliberate attempt ever made to revive and solidify extreme patriarchal conditions" (159) by dissolving existing women's groups, turning back the clock on women's participation in higher education and the workplace, banning abortion, preventing distribution of contraceptives, and reinstating separate spheres for men and women.

• • •

THE DIALECTIC OF "DADDY"

Sylvia Plath's snarling declaration, in her 1962 poem "Daddy," that

> Every woman adores a Fascist,
> The boot in the face, the brute
> Brute heart of a brute like you (*Ariel*, 50)

is as much a part of the Plath mythology as her gas-oven suicide that mirrored the imagery of the Holocaust in her poems. Although references to fascism and the Holocaust appear in only a handful of her poems, they loom large in Plath criticism and pose problems for feminist readings. Her poems bring together at a heated pitch both terms of [the] fascism/patriarchy analogy [found in other feminist discourse]; however, in "Daddy" and elsewhere, the speaker's relationship to both terms is highly conflicted, with equal measures of resistance and desire.

Fascism signifies a series of opposites for Plath: subjugation and oppression, control and freedom, sadism and masochism, and hate and love. These pairs are typically polarized by gender: Daddy and his daughter who sees herself as a Jew, and Herr Doktor and Lady Lazarus. However, Plath's female speakers identify with both the Jewish victim (although by no means were all the victims of the Holocaust Jewish, they are generally so in Plath's work) and the Nazi torturer. Beneath the speaker's bitter hatred for the "Panzer-man" in "Daddy" is a strong connection between the two. A. Alvarez even calls it a "love poem." Direct addresses to the dead man—"you" (and "du"), "your" and "Daddy"—occur twenty-nine times, in relation to the speaker's thirty "I"s, a ratio demonstrating Daddy's enormous psychic importance to the speaker. [. . .] Daddy is the superego, the paternal law,[1] and as such, he embodies an elusive linguistic power: the speaker "never could talk to" him: "The tongue stuck in my jaw. // It stuck in a barb wire snare. / Ich, ich, ich, ich" (49.25–27). [. . .] In "Daddy," the speaker's fear of the Nazi patriarch has made her seek out another language uncontaminated by his German: now she talks "like a Jew. / I think I may well be a Jew" (*Ariel* 50.34–35)—Daddy's historical victim.

The figure of Daddy constitutes a problem of language, memory and desire, all of which prevent the speaker from recuperation. The need to recreate the father leads to a self-destructive repetition compulsion: "I made a model of you, / A man in black with a Meinkampf look // And a love of the rack and the screw. / And I said I do, I do" (*Ariel* 51.64–67). Ironically rhyming the marriage vow

1. See Sandra Gilbert's comments on the father-figures in "Daddy" and "Colossus" (41).

with the ugly "screw," Plath shows the speaker's shifts of agency and libido: the sexualized love of the "screw" and the masochistic desire to slavishly serve the father's memory. [. . .] Instead of a movement of exhumation to burial, "Daddy" moves from the speaker's passive masochism to active sadism, but both positions are doggedly in reference to Daddy.

Plath's declaration of desire in relation to the fascist/patriarch has opened the way for damning criticism, the majority of which centers on whether or not she had the "right" to employ Holocaust imagery in a highly personal way. Leon Wieseltier [. . .] contends that Plath "did not earn" the right to use the Holocaust's "metaphors for extremity"; ". . . . Whatever her German father did to her," he argues of "Daddy," "it could not have been what the Germans did to the Jews. The metaphor is inappropriate. The images do not illuminate her experience" (20). Irving Howe agrees [. . .] (qtd. in Butscher 230). But Plath is far from the only writer to construct personal meanings around images of Nazism and the Holocaust. What incurs such critical wrath is the libidinal valences in which the speaker cloaks her fascism references and the fact that the evil Nazi "Daddy" is intimately connected to patriarchy. Wieseltier conflates the speaker's voice with Plath's, reading "Daddy" as Plath's father. [. . .]

In her journals, Plath does collapse her speaker's personas and her own: "If I really think I killed and castrated my father, may all my dreams of deformed and tortured people be my guilty visions of him or fears of punishment for me? And how to lay them? To stop them operating through the rest of my life?" (*Journals* 273). Here Plath focuses less on autobiographical realism than she does on psychic life and psychoanalytic narratives of female sexual development. Her poetry displays a similar focus. It is significant that Plath tends to construct similes rather than metaphors to express the figurative relation between the Holocaust and the speaker's personal history: her skin is not a Nazi lampshade, but rather "bright *as* a Nazi lampshade" ("Lady Lazarus"); the engine in "Daddy" is "chuffing" her "off like a Jew." The figurative distance [. . .] indicates that Plath is primarily interested in how history is incorporated into our consciousness and takes on personal and imaginary significance. [. . .] Her poems show, as Jacqueline Rose points out, how history and politics are filtered through the prism of fantasy, in which the most fanciful and grotesque distortions occur. "Remember the illogic of the fantasy," Plath reminds herself in her diaries (*Journals* 60). [. . .]

In a desperate letter contemplating suicide, Plath writes:

> I can begin to see the compulsion for committing original sin, for adoring Hitler, for taking opium. I have long wanted to read and explore the theories of philosophy, psychology, national, religious and primitive consciousness, but it seems now too late for anything. (56)

Here and throughout Plath's poems, fascism has a particular relationship to the "primitive unconscious," to repressed aggressive desires and to a desire to be swept away. Plath was far from the first to intuit in fascism a harnessing of unconscious impulses. In *Civilization and its Discontents,* Freud proposed that those impulses repressed or forbidden in democratic society would necessarily reemerge in some other form, and many critics read fascism or authoritarianism as founded upon the expression of violent and sadomasochistic desires disavowed by liberal politics. W. H. Auden, for example, remarked in 1940 in his commencement address at Smith College (Plath's alma mater), that "[Carl] Jung hardly went far enough when he said 'Hitler is the unconscious of every German'; he comes uncomfortably near being the unconscious of most of us."[2] Plath's images of fascism are crafted according to this dream-logic of the unconscious, forging surreal links and producing unexpected affinities; in her lexicon, Nazism is inextricably linked to the unconscious and to sexual fantasy.

Plath's voice stands out in sharp relief against the Cold War rhetoric of 1950s America, smug with postwar prosperity, extolling democracy's triumph over fascism and its ethical imperative to do battle with the next monster (communism). Plath opposes the happy homemaker smiling beside shiny refrigerators and reliable washing machines to the frustrated, self-destructive female artist obsessed with death. Her female speakers inhabit a world of violence and brutality colored by voluptuous sexuality. Dissatisfied with their culture that shuts them out of opportunities, these women savor and theatricalize their abjection and revenge. They replace romantic myths of love with a carnal imbalance of powers where the torturer and his victim [. . .] are bound together by hate, resentment, and lust. Daddy's love and the security of marriage are dissatisfying compensations for limited horizons; the female speakers' long-delayed rebellions against "Daddy" arouse stifled desires for social power and sexual liberation.

[. . .] Cherishing martyrdom and seeking it out as the role they play best, the masochistic women in *Ariel* and *The Colossus* are whirling dervishes of revenge rising above a landscape of dirty dishes and smelly diapers to rage, burn, and murder men. [. . .] If Plath's is the language of female victimization, it is not one we are accustomed to hearing, for it always contains its double: a lashing, sadistic triumph. Nowhere is this clearer than in "Daddy."

[. . .] But even if she rebels against the oppressive patriarchal father, the speaker of "Daddy" recapitulates his violence. Her anger is reactive, and she does not succeed in freeing herself of him; her punishment of "Daddy" shows her own identification with his Nazi cruelty rather than overcoming of it. Even at the end of the poem, she is still addressing herself to him; she is still caught within the dialectic of Daddy.

• • •

The difference between [Virginia] Woolf's and Plath's models of female psychology under fascism and patriarchy is illustrated by their respective identifications with Greek heroines. Woolf's example [in *Three Guineas* (1938)] of a woman rebelling against the patriarchal law is Sophocles' Antigone. [. . .] For Woolf, Antigone is a model of visionary female bravery who is able to rise above her situation and perceive that "there are two kinds of law, the written and the unwritten" (184). The patriarch Creon's edict violates the more sacred humanist laws and needs to be challenged.

Plath also turns to Attic Greek drama for her model of female insurrection, but she chooses Aeschylus's Electra, a daughter whose relationship to her tyran-

2. "Romantic or Free?" *Smith Alumnae Quarterly* 31 (August 1940), 357.

nical father—Agamemnon, who sacrificed his other daughter, Iphigenia, to the winds—is entirely different from Antigone's. After Agamemnon is killed, Electra's mother, Clytaemestra, and her lover, Aegisthus, abuse Electra for her loyalty to her father's memory. The Chorus of Mycenaean Women warns Electra to temper her rebellion against her mother, but she persists until her exiled brother returns and kills Clytaemestra and Aegisthus. Electra persists in loving her deeply flawed father long after he is dead.

[. . .] Plath's reading of *Electra* takes into account unconscious and ambivalent psychic responses.[3] [. . .] It is the female speaker's mother who may be Jewish and who connects the speaker to a position of victimhood that she both savors and repudiates. In her attraction to the fascist male/father, Plath's daughter both betrays and repeats her mother's possible fate as a Jew married to a Nazi. [. . .] Plath's Electra is Antigone's "libidinous double," containing within her Antigone's rebellion but unable to shake her love-hate relation to her father. Plath's reiteration of and departure from simplistic narratives of power and desire—that one is either subservient to or in rebellion against patriarchal/fascist power—shows the conflicted emotions within one woman. Her transformation of the oedipal father into the fascist father encapsulates how "Daddy" is imbued by virtue of his place in the family, with mythic phallic power and how a daughter could both hate him and think that "he was God."

For Plath, the "fascist" structure of patriarchal desire is inherently erotic, and it is ironically the feminist daughter who tries to free herself from "Daddy" for whom he looms largest in psychic life. Even though institutions change and women gain ground in their struggle to separate from "Daddy," Plath suggests that he stubbornly persists as an object of sadomasochistic fantasy. The two poles of behavior rejected by liberal politics—domination and submission—surface in Plath's poems as the substance of eroticized fantasy. This point is difficult to reconcile with a feminist vision for social change: for Plath, we are bound to our investments in the tyrannical "Daddy" all the more so as he is politically repudiated.

WORKS CITED[4]

Butscher, Edward, ed. *Sylvia Plath: The Woman and the Work.* New York: Dodd, Mead & Co., 1977.

Gilbert, Sandra M. "Teaching Plath's 'Daddy' to Speak to Undergraduates." *ADE Bulletin* 76, Winter 1983: 38–42.

Horkheimer, Max and Theodor W. Adorno. *Dialectic of Enlightenment.* Tr. John Cumming. New York: Continuum, 1972.

Millett, Kate. *Sexual Politics.* New York: Simon and Schuster, 1990.

Plath, Sylvia. *Ariel.* New York: Harper and Row, 1965.

———. *The Journals of Sylvia Plath.* Ted Hughes and Frances McCullogh, Eds. New York: Dial P, 1982.

3. Frost here quotes Plath's remark about the poem's speaker, as quoted in Alvarez, p. 1310 [editor's note].

4. Frost's bibliography has been edited to include only works cited in the excerpts reprinted here [editor's note].

Reich, Wilhelm. *The Mass Psychology of Fascism.* Tr. Vincent R. Carfagno. New York: Noonday P, 1970.

Rose, Jacqueline. *The Haunting of Sylvia Plath.* Cambridge: Harvard UP, 1991.

Wieseltier, Leon. "In a Universe of Ghosts." *The New York Review of Books* Nov. 25, 1976: 20–23.

Woolf, Virginia. *Three Guineas.* New York: Harcourt Brace Jovanovich, 1938.

SUGGESTIONS FOR WRITING

1. In his essay DYING IS AN ART, George Steiner argues that Plath's poems "are too honest, they have cost too much, to be yielded to myth." Do you think that DADDY is an "honest" poem? Write an essay exploring what "honesty" means in modern poetry and whether or not DADDY is an "honest" poem. Draw on the critical essays found in this chapter, and be sure to cite them when appropriate.
2. Several of the critics in this chapter make competing claims about the meaning and significance of the form of DADDY, particularly its nursery-rhyme-like qualities. Using those claims as a springboard, write an essay in which you make your own argument about the relationship between form and content in DADDY.
3. In THE PLATH CELEBRATION: A PARTIAL DISSENT, Irving Howe argues, "There is something monstrous, utterly disproportionate, when tangled emotions about one's father are deliberately compared with the historical fate of the European Jews." Is Plath's personal, artistic use of a great historical tragedy truly "monstrous," as Howe says, or is it acceptable and effective, as other critics here contend? Write an essay in which you discuss the appropriateness and effects of Plath's references to the Holocaust.
4. Broe, Kroll, Homans, Annas, and Axelrod all claim that DADDY portrays the speaker's attempt to successfully "exorcise" one demon or another, though they disagree rather dramatically both about what that demon is and about whether and how that exorcism (not the poem) succeeds. Using their arguments as a starting point, write an essay in which you offer your own interpretation of the process of exorcism enacted in the poem.
5. In SYLVIA PLATH, A. Alvarez quotes Plath's own interpretation of DADDY as a poem "spoken by a girl with an Electra complex." (Other articles mention this statement.) Research the term "Electra complex," which originated with Sigmund Freud. Is it useful to interpret DADDY through the lens of the Electra complex? Citing critics included in this chapter, write an essay in which you discuss Plath's Freudian explanation of DADDY.
6. Write an essay comparing Plath's DADDY to at least two of the "domestic poems" mentioned by Axelrod in SYLVIA PLATH: THE WOUND AND THE CURE OF WORDS or other similar, contemporaneous poems. To what extent do you agree and disagree with Axelrod's interpretation of the similarities and differences between DADDY and poems by Plath's contemporaries?
7. Is DADDY a "feminist" poem? Citing the essays by Homans and other critics in this chapter, write an essay in which you explore the validity of a feminist interpretation.

Reading More Poetry

W. H. AUDEN

Musée des Beaux Arts[1]

About suffering they were never wrong,
The Old Masters: how well they understood
Its human position; how it takes place
While someone else is eating or opening a window or just walking
    dully along;
How, when the aged are reverently, passionately waiting
For the miraculous birth, there always must be
Children who did not specially want it to happen, skating
On a pond at the edge of the wood:
They never forgot
That even the dreadful martyrdom must run its course
Anyhow in a corner, some untidy spot
Where the dogs go on with their doggy life and the torturer's horse
Scratches its innocent behind on a tree.

In Brueghel's *Icarus*,[2] for instance: how everything turns away
Quite leisurely from the disaster; the plowman may
Have heard the splash, the forsaken cry,
But for him it was not an important failure; the sun shone
As it had to on the white legs disappearing into the green
Water; and the expensive delicate ship that must have seen
Something amazing, a boy falling out of the sky,
Had somewhere to get to and sailed calmly on.

1938

1. The Museum of the Fine Arts, in Brussels, Belgium.

2. *Landscape with the Fall of Icarus*, by Pieter Bruegel or Brueghel the Elder (1525?–69), located in the Brussels museum. According to Greek myth, Daedalus and his son, Icarus, escaped from imprisonment by using homemade wings of feathers and wax; but Icarus flew too near the sun, the wax melted, and he fell into the sea and drowned. In the Bruegel painting the central figure is a peasant plowing, and several other figures are more immediately noticeable than Icarus, who, disappearing into the sea, is easy to miss in the lower right-hand corner.

ROBERT BROWNING

Porphyria's Lover[3]

The rain set early in tonight,
The sullen wind was soon awake,
It tore the elm-tops down for spite,
And did its worst to vex the lake:
I listened with heart fit to break.
When glided in Porphyria; straight
She shut the cold out and the storm,
And kneeled and made the cheerless grate
Blaze up, and all the cottage warm;
Which done, she rose, and from her form
Withdrew the dripping cloak and shawl,
And laid her soiled gloves by, untied
Her hat and let the damp hair fall,
And, last, she sat down by my side
And called me. When no voice replied,
She put my arm about her waist,
And made her smooth white shoulder bare,
And all her yellow hair displaced,
And, stooping, made my cheek lie there,
And spread, o'er all, her yellow hair,
Murmuring how she loved me=mshe
Too weak, for all her heart's endeavor,
To set its struggling passion free
From pride, and vainer ties dissever,
And give herself to me forever.
But passion sometimes would prevail,
Nor could tonight's gay feast restrain
A sudden thought of one so pale
For love of her, and all in vain:
So, she was come through wind and rain.
Be sure I looked up at her eyes
Happy and proud; at last I knew
Porphyria worshiped me: surprise
Made my heart swell, and still it grew
While I debated what to do.
That moment she was mine, mine, fair,
Perfectly pure and good: I found
A thing to do, and all her hair
In one long yellow string I wound
Three times her little throat around,
And strangled her. No pain felt she;
I am quite sure she felt no pain.

3. Dramatic monologue originally published under the title "Madhouse Cells."

As a shut bud that holds a bee,
 I warily oped her lids: again
 Laughed the blue eyes without a stain.
And I untightened next the tress
 About her neck; her cheek once more
Blushed bright beneath my burning kiss:
 I propped her head up as before,
 Only, this time my shoulder bore
Her head, which droops upon it still:
 The smiling rosy little head,

So glad it has its utmost will,
 That all it scorned at once is fled,
 And I, its love, am gained instead!
Porphyria's love: she guessed not how
 Her darling one wish would be heard.
And thus we sit together now,
 And all night long we have not stirred
 And yet God has not said a word!

1836, 1842

My Last Duchess

Ferrara[4]

That's my last Duchess painted on the wall,
Looking as if she were alive. I call
That piece a wonder, now: Frà Pandolf's hands[5]
Worked busily a day, and there she stands.
Will't please you sit and look at her? I said
"Frà Pandolf" by design, for never read
Strangers like you that pictured countenance,
The depth and passion of its earnest glance,
But to myself they turned (since none puts by
The curtain I have drawn for you, but I)
And seemed as they would ask me, if they durst,
How such a glance came there; so, not the first
Are you to turn and ask thus. Sir, 'twas not
Her husband's presence only, called that spot
Of joy into the Duchess' cheek: perhaps
Frà Pandolf chanced to say "Her mantle laps
Over my lady's wrist too much," or "Paint
Must never hope to reproduce the faint
Half-flush that dies along her throat": such stuff
Was courtesy, she thought, and cause enough

4. Alfonso II, Duke of Ferrara in Italy in the mid-sixteenth century, is the presumed speaker of this dramatic monologue, which is loosely based on historical events. The duke's first wife—whom he had married when she was fourteen—died under suspicious circumstances at seventeen, and he then negotiated through an agent (this poem's auditor) for the hand of the niece of the count of Tyrol in Austria.
5. Frà Pandolf is, like Claus (line 56), fictitious.

For calling up that spot of joy. She had
A heart—how shall I say?—too soon made glad,
Too easily impressed; she liked whate'er
She looked on, and her looks went everywhere.
Sir, 'twas all one! My favor at her breast,
The dropping of the daylight in the West,
The bough of cherries some officious fool
Broke in the orchard for her, the white mule
She rode with round the terrace—all and each
Would draw from her alike the approving speech,
Or blush, at least. She thanked men,—good! but thanked
Somehow—I know not how—as if she ranked
My gift of a nine-hundred-years-old name
With anybody's gift. Who'd stoop to blame
This sort of trifling? Even had you skill
In speech—which I have not—to make your will
Quite clear to such an one, and say, "Just this
Or that in you disgusts me; here you miss,
Or there exceed the mark"—and if she let
Herself be lessoned so, nor plainly set
Her wits to yours, forsooth, and made excuse,
—E'en then would be some stooping; and I choose
Never to stoop. Oh sir, she smiled, no doubt,
Whene'er I passed her; but who passed without
Much the same smile? This grew; I gave commands;
Then all smiles stopped together. There she stands
As if alive. Will't please you rise? We'll meet
The company below, then. I repeat,
The Count your master's known munificence
Is ample warrant that no just pretense
Of mine for dowry will be disallowed;
Though his fair daughter's self, as I avowed
At starting, is my object. Nay, we'll go
Together down, sir. Notice Neptune, though,
Taming a sea-horse, thought a rarity,
Which Claus of Innsbruck cast in bronze for me!

1842

SAMUEL TAYLOR COLERIDGE
Kubla Khan

Or, a Vision in a Dream[6]

In Xanadu did Kubla Khan
A stately pleasure-dome decree:
Where Alph, the sacred river, ran

6. Coleridge said that he wrote this fragment immediately after waking from an opium dream and that after he was interrupted by a caller he was unable to finish the poem.

Through caverns measureless to man
  Down to a sunless sea.
So twice five miles of fertile ground
With walls and towers were girdled round:
And here were gardens bright with sinuous rills
Where blossomed many an incense-bearing tree;
And here were forests ancient as the hills,
Enfolding sunny spots of greenery.
But oh! that deep romantic chasm which slanted
Down the green hill athwart a cedarn cover![7]
A savage place! as holy and enchanted
As e'er beneath a waning moon was haunted
By woman wailing for her demon-lover![8]
And from this chasm, with ceaseless turmoil seething,
As if this earth in fast thick pants were breathing,
A mighty fountain momently[9] was forced,
Amid whose swift half-intermitted burst
Huge fragments vaulted like rebounding hail,
Or chaffy grain beneath the thresher's flail:
And 'mid these dancing rocks at once and ever
It flung up momently the sacred river.
Five miles meandering with a mazy motion
Through wood and dale the sacred river ran,
Then reached the caverns measureless to man,
And sank in tumult to a lifeless ocean:
And 'mid this tumult Kubla heard from far
Ancestral voices prophesying war!

  The shadow of the dome of pleasure
  Floated midway on the waves;
  Where was heard the mingled measure
  From the fountain and the caves.
It was a miracle of rare device,
A sunny pleasure-dome with caves of ice!

  A damsel with a dulcimer
  In a vision once I saw:
  It was an Abyssinian maid,
  And on her dulcimer she played,
  Singing of Mount Abora.
  Could I revive within me
  Her symphony and song,
  To such a deep delight 'twould win me,
That with music loud and long,
I would build that dome in air,

7. That is, from side to side beneath a cover of cedar trees.

8. In a famous and often-imitated German ballad, the lady Lenore is carried off on horseback by the specter of her lover and married to him at his grave.

9. Suddenly.

That sunny dome! those caves of ice!
And all who heard should see them there,
And all should cry, Beware! Beware!
His flashing eyes, his floating hair!
Weave a circle round him thrice,
And close your eyes with holy dread,
For he on honey-dew hath fed,
And drunk the milk of Paradise.

1798

E. E. CUMMINGS

[in Just-][1]

in Just-
spring   when the world is mud-
luscious the little
lame balloonman

whistles   far   and wee

and eddieandbill come
running from marbles and
piracies and it's
spring

when the world is puddle-wonderful

the queer
old balloonman whistles
far   and   wee
and bettyandisbel come dancing

from hop-scotch and jump-rope and

it's
spring
and
    the

        goat-footed

balloonMan[2] whistles
far
and
wee

1923

1. First poem in the series *Chansons innocentes* (French for "Songs of Innocence").
2. Pan, whose Greek name means "everything," is traditionally represented with a syrinx (or the pipes of Pan). The upper half of his body is human, the lower half goat; as the father of Silenus he is associated with the spring rites of Dionysus.

JOHN DONNE

[Death, be not proud]

Death be not proud, though some have callèd thee
Mighty and dreadful, for thou art not so;
For those whom thou think'st thou dost overthrow
Die not, poor Death, nor yet canst thou kill me.
From rest and sleep, which but thy pictures[3] be,
Much pleasure; then from thee much more must flow,
And soonest[4] our best men with thee do go,
Rest of their bones, and soul's delivery.[5]
Thou art slave to Fate, Chance, kings, and desperate men,
And dost with Poison, War, and Sickness dwell;
And poppy or charms can make us sleep as well,
And better than thy stroke; why swell'st[6] thou then?
One short sleep past, we wake eternally
And death shall be no more; Death, thou shalt die.

1633

Song

Go, and catch a falling star,
  Get with child a mandrake root,[7]
Tell me, where all past years are,
  Or who cleft the devil's foot,
Teach me to hear mermaids singing
Or to keep off envy's stinging,
    And find
    What wind
Serves to advance an honest mind.

If thou beest born to strange sights,[8]
  Things invisible to see,
Ride ten thousand days and nights,
  Till age snow white hairs on thee;
Thou, when thou return'st, wilt tell me
All strange wonders that befell thee,
    And swear
    No where
Lives a woman true, and fair.

If thou find'st one, let me know:
  Such a pilgrimage were sweet.
Yet do not, I would not go,
  Though at next door we might meet:
Though she were true when you met her,

3. Likenesses. 4. Most willingly. 5. Deliverance. 6. Puff with pride.
7. The forked mandrake root looks vaguely like a pair of human legs.
8. That is, if you have supernatural powers.

And last till you write your letter,
Yet she
Will be
False, ere I come, to two, or three.

1633

The Sun Rising

Busy old fool, unruly sun,
Why dost thou thus,
Through windows, and through curtains, call on us?
Must to thy motions lovers' seasons run?
Saucy pedantic wretch, go chide
Late schoolboys, and sour prentices,[9]
Go tell court-huntsmen that the king will ride,
Call country ants[1] to harvest offices;
Love, all alike, no season knows, nor clime,
Nor hours, days, months, which are the rags of time.
Thy beams, so reverend and strong
why shouldst thou think?
I could eclipse and cloud them with a wink,
But that I would not lose her sight so long:
If her eyes have not blinded thine,
Look, and tomorrow late, tell me
Whether both the Indias[2] of spice and mine
Be where thou left'st them, or lie here with me.
Ask for those kings whom thou saw'st yesterday,
And thou shalt hear, all here in one bed lay.

She is all states, and all princes I,
Nothing else is.
Princes do but play us; compared to this,
All honor's mimic,[3] all wealth alchemy.
Thou, sun, art half as happy as we,
In that the world's contracted thus;
Thine age asks[4] ease, and since thy duties be
To warm the world, that's done in warming us.
Shine here to us, and thou art every where;
This bed thy center[5] is, these walls thy sphere.

1633

A Valediction: Forbidding Mourning

As virtuous men pass mildly away,
And whisper to their souls to go,
Whilst some of their sad friends do say,
"The breath goes now," and some say, "No,"

9. Apprentices. 1. Farmworkers.
2. The East and West Indies, commercial sources of spices and gold. 3. Mimicry. 4. Requires.
5. Of orbit.

So let us melt, and make no noise,
   No tear-floods, nor sigh-tempests move;
'Twere profanation of our joys
   To tell the laity our love.

Moving of the earth[6] brings harms and fears,
   Men reckon what it did and meant;
But trepidation of the spheres,[7]
   Though greater far, is innocent.

Dull sublunary[8] lovers' love
   (Whose soul is sense) cannot admit
Absence, because it doth remove
   Those things which elemented[9] it.

But we, by a love so much refined
   That our selves know not what it is,
Inter-assured of the mind,
   Care less, eyes, lips, and hands to miss.

Our two souls therefore, which are one,
   Though I must go, endure not yet
A breach, but an expansion,
   Like gold to airy thinness beat.

If they be two, they are two so
   As stiff twin compasses are two:
Thy soul, the fixed foot, makes no show
   To move, but doth, if the other do;

And though it in the center sit,
   Yet when the other far doth roam,
It leans, and hearkens after it,
   And grows erect, as that comes home.

Such wilt thou be to me, who must,
   Like the other foot, obliquely run;
Thy firmness makes my circle[1] just,
   And makes me end where I begun.

c. 1611

PAUL LAURENCE DUNBAR

We Wear the Mask

We wear the mask that grins and lies,
It hides our cheeks and shades our eyes,—

6. Earthquakes.
7. Renaissance theory that the celestial spheres trembled and thus caused unexpected variations in their orbits. Such movements are "innocent" because earthlings do not observe or fret about them.
8. Below the moon—that is, changeable. According to the traditional cosmology that Donne invokes here, the moon is the dividing line between the immutable celestial world and the mutable earthly one.
9. Comprised, made up its elements. 1. Traditional symbol of perfection.

This debt we pay to human guile;
With torn and bleeding hearts we smile,
And mouth with myriad subtleties.

Why should the world be over-wise,
In counting all our tears and sighs?
Nay, let them only see us, while
We wear the mask.

We smile, but, O great Christ, our cries
To thee from tortured souls arise.
We sing, but oh the clay is vile
Beneath our feet, and long the mile;
But let the world dream otherwise,
We wear the mask!

1895

ROBERT FROST

Home Burial

He saw her from the bottom of the stairs
Before she saw him. She was starting down,
Looking back over her shoulder at some fear.
She took a doubtful step and then undid it
To raise herself and look again. He spoke
Advancing toward her: "What is it you see
From up there always?—for I want to know."
She turned and sank upon her skirts at that,
And her face changed from terrified to dull.
He said to gain time: "What is it you see?"
Mounting until she cowered under him.
"I will find out now—you must tell me, dear."
She, in her place, refused him any help,
With the least stiffening of her neck and silence.
She let him look, sure that he wouldn't see,
Blind creature; and awhile he didn't see.
But at last he murmured, "Oh," and again, "Oh."

"What is it—what?" she said.

"Just that I see."

"You don't," she challenged. "Tell me what it is."

"The wonder is I didn't see at once.
I never noticed it from here before.
I must be wonted[2] to it—that's the reason.
The little graveyard where my people are!
So small the window frames the whole of it.
Not so much larger than a bedroom, is it?

2. Habituated, accustomed.

There are three stones of slate and one of marble,
Broad-shouldered little slabs there in the sunlight
On the sidehill. We haven't to mind *those.*
But I understand: it is not the stones,
But the child's mound—"

"Don't, don't, don't,
don't," she cried.

She withdrew, shrinking from beneath his arm
That rested on the banister, and slid downstairs;
And turned on him with such a daunting look,
He said twice over before he knew himself:
"Can't a man speak of his own child he's lost?"

"Not you!—Oh, where's my hat? Oh, I don't need it!
I must get out of here. I must get air.—
I don't know rightly whether any man can."

"Amy! Don't go to someone else this time.
Listen to me. I won't come down the stairs."
He sat and fixed his chin between his fists.
"There's something I should like to ask you, dear."

"You don't know how to ask it."

"Help me, then."

Her fingers moved the latch for all reply.

"My words are nearly always an offense.
I don't know how to speak of anything
So as to please you. But I might be taught,
I should suppose. I can't say I see how.
A man must partly give up being a man
With womenfolk. We could have some arrangement
By which I'd bind myself to keep hands off
Anything special you're a-mind to name.
Though I don't like such things 'twixt those that love.
Two that don't love can't live together without them.
But two that do can't live together with them."
She moved the latch a little. "Don't—don't go.
Don't carry it to someone else this time.
Tell me about it if it's something human.
Let me into your grief. I'm not so much
Unlike other folks as your standing there
Apart would make me out. Give me my chance.
I do think, though, you overdo it a little.
What was it brought you up to think it the thing
To take your mother-loss of a first child
So inconsolably—in the face of love.
You'd think his memory might be satisfied—"

"There you go sneering now!"

"I'm not, I'm not!
You make me angry. I'll come down to you.
God, what a woman! And it's come to this,
A man can't speak of his own child that's dead."

"You can't because you don't know how to speak.
If you had any feelings, you that dug
With your own hand—how could you?—his little grave;
I saw you from that very window there,
Making the gravel leap and leap in air,
Leap up, like that, like that, and land so lightly
And roll back down the mound beside the hole.
I thought, Who is that man? I didn't know you.
And I crept down the stairs and up the stairs
To look again, and still your spade kept lifting.
Then you came in. I heard your rumbling voice
Out in the kitchen, and I don't know why,
But I went near to see with my own eyes.
You could sit there with the stains on your shoes
Of the fresh earth from your own baby's grave
And talk about your everyday concerns.
You had stood the spade up against the wall
Outside there in the entry, for I saw it."

"I shall laugh the worst laugh I ever laughed.
I'm cursed. God, if I don't believe I'm cursed."

"I can repeat the very words you were saying:
'Three foggy mornings and one rainy day
Will rot the best birch fence a man can build.'
Think of it, talk like that at such a time!
What had how long it takes a birch to rot
To do with what was in the darkened parlor?
You *couldn't* care! The nearest friends can go
With anyone to death, comes so far short
They might as well not try to go at all.
No, from the time when one is sick to death,
One is alone, and he dies more alone.
Friends make pretense of following to the grave,
But before one is in it, their minds are turned
And making the best of their way back to life
And living people, and things they understand.
But the world's evil. I won't have grief so
If I can change it. Oh, I won't, I won't!"

"There, you have said it all and you feel better.
You won't go now. You're crying. Close the door.
The heart's gone out of it: why keep it up?
Amy! There's someone coming down the road!"

"*You*—oh, you think the talk is all. I must go—
Somewhere out of this house. How can I make you—"

"If—you—do!" She was opening the door wider.
"Where do you mean to go? First tell me that.
I'll follow and bring you back by force. I *will*!—"

1915

Stopping by Woods on a Snowy Evening

Whose woods these are I think I know.
His house is in the village, though;
He will not see me stopping here
To watch his woods fill up with snow.

My little horse must think it queer
To stop without a farmhouse near
Between the woods and frozen lake
The darkest evening of the year.

He gives his harness bells a shake
To ask if there is some mistake.
The only other sound's the sweep
Of easy wind and downy flake.

The woods are lovely, dark, and deep,
But I have promises to keep,
And miles to go before I sleep,
And miles to go before I sleep.

1923

ALLEN GINSBERG

Velocity of Money

For Lee Berton

I'm delighted by the velocity of money as it whistles through wind of
Lower East Side
Delighted skyscrapers rise grungy apartments fall on 84th Street
pavement
Delighted this year inflation drives me out on the street
with double digit interest rates in Capitalist worlds
I always was a communist, now we'll win
as usury makes walls thinner, books thicker & dumber
Usury makes my poetry more valuable
Manuscripts worth their weight in useless gold—
The velocity's what counts as the National Debt gets trillions higher
Everybody running after the rising dollar
Crowds of joggers down Broadway past City Hall on the way to the Fed[3]

3. Federal Reserve Bank of New York, part of the Federal Reserve System, which controls the money supply in the United States.

Nobody reads Dostoyevsky[4] books anymore so they'll have to give
passing ear
to my fragmented ravings in between President's speeches
Nothing's happening but the collapse of the Economy
so I can go back to sleep till the landlord wins his eviction suit in court
February 18, 1986, 10:00 A.M

THOMAS HARDY
The Convergence of the Twain[5]

(*Lines on the loss of the* Titanic)[6]

1

In a solitude of the sea
Deep from human vanity,
And the Pride of Life that planned her, stilly couches she.

2

Steel chambers, late the pyres
Of her salamandrine[7] fires,
Cold currents thrid,[8] and turn to rhythmic tidal lyres.

3

Over the mirrors meant
To glass the opulent
The sea-worm crawls—grotesque, slimed, dumb, indifferent.

4

Jewels in joy designed
To ravish the sensuous mind
Lie lightless, all their sparkles bleared and black and blind.

5

Dim moon-eyed fishes near
Gaze at the gilded gear
And query: 'What does this vaingloriousness down here?' . . .

6

Well: while was fashioning
This creature of cleaving wing,
The Immanent Will[9] that stirs and urges everything

4. Fyodor Dostoevsky (1821–81), Russian novelist.
5. Two. 6. The biggest, most opulant, and supposedly safest ship of its time; after colliding with an iceberg, it sank on April 15, 1912, halfway through its first voyage, killing some fifteen hundred people.
7. That is, intensely hot and destructive. Salamanders were long believed to be capable of surviving fire.
8. Thread, crisscross.
9. Like *Spinner of the Years* (stanza 11), the force that, according to Hardy, drives the world, somewhat like fate or destiny.

7

Prepared a sinister mate
For her—so gaily great—
A Shape of Ice, for the time far and dissociate.

8

And as the smart ship grew
In stature, grace, and hue,
In shadowy silent distance grew the Iceberg too.

9

Alien they seemed to be:
No mortal eye could see
The intimate welding of their later history,

10

Or sign that they were bent
By paths coincident
On being anon twin halves of one august[1] event,

11

Till the Spinner of the Years
Said 'Now!' And each one hears,
And consummation comes, and jars two hemispheres.

1912, 1914

- **How might Hardy's description of the *Titanic* encourage us to interpret the ship as a symbol of "human vanity" and the "Pride of Life" (lines 2–3)? How might that symbolism be underscored by the poet's choice to describe the ship (stanzas 1–5) before relating what happened to it (stanzas 6–11)?**

ROBERT HAYDEN
Frederick Douglass[2]

When it is finally ours, this freedom, this liberty, this beautiful
and terrible thing, needful to man as air,
usable as earth; when it belongs at last to all,
when it is truly instinct, brain matter, diastole, systole,
reflex action; when it is finally won; when it is more
than the gaudy mumbo jumbo of politicians:
this man, this Douglass, this former slave, this Negro
beaten to his knees, exiled, visioning a world
where none is lonely, none hunted, alien,
this man, superb in love and logic, this man
shall be remembered. Oh, not with statues' rhetoric,

1. Famous, important. *Anon*: soon.
2. Escaped slave (1817–95), participant in the Underground Railroad and publisher of the famous abolitionist newspaper the *North Star*, in Rochester, New York.

not with legends and poems and wreaths of bronze alone,
but with the lives grown out of his life, the lives
fleshing his dream of the beautiful, needful thing.

1966

SEAMUS HEANEY

Digging

Between my finger and my thumb
The squat pen rests; snug as a gun.

Under my window, a clean rasping sound
When the spade sinks into gravelly ground:
My father, digging. I look down

Till his straining rump among the flowerbeds
Bends low, comes up twenty years away
Stooping in rhythm through potato drills[3]
Where he was digging.

The coarse boot nestled on the lug, the shaft
Against the inside knee was levered firmly.
He rooted out tall tops, buried the bright edge deep
To scatter new potatoes that we picked
Loving their cool hardness in our hands.

By God, the old man could handle a spade.
Just like his old man.

My grandfather cut more turf[4] in a day
Than any other man on Toner's bog.
Once I carried him milk in a bottle
Corked sloppily with paper. He straightened up
To drink it, then fell to right away
Nicking and slicing neatly, heaving sods
Over his shoulder, going down and down
For the good turf. Digging.

The cold smell of potato mould, the squelch and slap
Of soggy peat, the curt cuts of an edge
Through living roots awaken in my head.
But I've no spade to follow men like them.

Between my finger and my thumb
The squat pen rests.
I'll dig with it.

1966

3. Small furrows in which seeds are sown.
4. Peat cut into slabs and dried to be used as fuel in stoves and furnaces.

GERARD MANLEY HOPKINS

God's Grandeur

The world is charged with the grandeur of God.
It will flame out, like shining from shook foil;[5]
It gathers to a greatness, like the ooze of oil
Crushed. Why do men then now not reck his rod?[6]
Generations have trod, have trod, have trod;
And all is seared with trade; bleared, smeared with toil;
And wears man's smudge and shares man's smell: the soil
Is bare now, nor can foot feel, being shod.

And for all this, nature is never spent;
There lives the dearest freshness deep down things;
And though the last lights off the black West went
Oh, morning, at the brown brink eastward, springs—
Because the Holy Ghost over the bent
World broods with warm breast and with ah! bright wings.

c. 1877

The Windhover[7]

To Christ our Lord

I caught this morning morning's minion,[8] king-
dom of daylight's dauphin,[9] dapple-dawn-drawn Falcon, in his riding
Of the rolling level underneath him steady air, and striding
High there, how he rung upon the rein of a wimpling[1] wing
In his ecstasy! then off, off forth on swing,
As a skate's heel sweeps smooth on a bow-bend: the hurl and gliding
Rebuffed the big wind. My heart in hiding
Stirred for a bird,—the achieve of, the mastery of the thing!

Brute beauty and valor and act, oh, air, pride, plume, here
Buckle![2] AND the fire that breaks from thee then, a billion
Times told lovelier, more dangerous, O my chevalier![3]

No wonder of it: shéer plód makes plow down sillion[4]
Shine, and blue-bleak embers, ah my dear,
Fall, gall themselves, and gash gold-vermilion.

1877

5. "I mean foil in its sense of leaf or tinsel [. . .]. Shaken goldfoil gives off broad glares like sheet lightning and also, and this is true of nothing else, owing to its zig-zag dints and creasings and network of small many cornered facets, a sort of fork lightning too" (*Letters of Gerard Manley Hopkins to Robert Bridges*, edited by C. C. Abbott, 1955, p. 169). 6. Heed his authority.
7. Small hawk, the kestrel, which habitually hovers in the air, headed into the wind.
8. Favorite, beloved. 9. Heir to regal splendor. 1. Rippling.
2. Several meanings may apply: to join closely, to prepare for battle, to grapple with, to collapse.
3. Horseman, knight.
4. Narrow strip of land between furrows in an open field divided for separate cultivation.

BEN JONSON
On My First Son

Farewell, thou child of my right hand,[5] and joy;
My sin was too much hope of thee, loved boy:
Seven years thou wert lent to me, and I thee pay,
Exacted by thy fate, on the just[6] day.
O could I lose all father now! for why
Will man lament the state he should envy,
To have so soon 'scaped world's and flesh's rage,
And, if no other misery, yet age?
Rest in soft peace, and asked, say, "Here doth lie
Ben Jonson his[7] best piece of poetry."
For whose sake henceforth all his vows be such
As what he loves may never like too much.

1616

JOHN KEATS
Ode on a Grecian Urn

I

Thou still unravished bride of quietness,
Thou foster-child of silence and slow time,
Sylvan historian, who canst thus express
A flowery tale more sweetly than our rhyme:
What leaf-fringed legend haunts about thy shape
Of deities or mortals, or of both,
In Tempe or the dales of Arcady?[8]
What men or gods are these? What maidens loath?
What mad pursuit? What struggle to escape?
What pipes and timbrels? What wild ecstasy?

II

Heard melodies are sweet, but those unheard
Are sweeter; therefore, ye soft pipes, play on;
Not to the sensual[9] ear, but, more endeared,
Pipe to the spirit ditties of no tone:
Fair youth, beneath the trees, thou canst not leave
Thy song, nor ever can those trees be bare;
Bold Lover, never, never canst thou kiss,
Though winning near the goal—yet, do not grieve;

5. Literal translation of the son's name, Benjamin.
6. Exact; the son died on his seventh birthday, in 1603.
7. That is, Ben Jonson's (this was a common Renaissance form of the possessive).
8. Arcadia. Tempe is a beautiful valley near Mt. Olympus in Greece, and the valleys ("dales") of Arcadia are a picturesque section of the Peloponnesus; both came to be associated with the pastoral ideal.
9. Of the senses, as distinguished from the "ear" of the spirit or imagination.

She cannot fade, though thou hast not thy bliss,
For ever wilt thou love, and she be fair!

III

Ah, happy, happy boughs! that cannot shed
Your leaves, nor ever bid the Spring adieu;
And, happy melodist, unwearièd,
For ever piping songs for ever new;
More happy love! more happy, happy love!
For ever warm and still to be enjoyed,
For ever panting, and for ever young;
All breathing human passion far above,
That leaves a heart high-sorrowful and cloyed,
A burning forehead, and a parching tongue.

IV

Who are these coming to the sacrifice?
To what green altar, O mysterious priest,
Lead'st thou that heifer lowing at the skies,
And all her silken flanks with garlands dressed?
What little town by river or sea shore,
Or mountain-built with peaceful citadel,
Is emptied of its folk, this pious morn?
And, little town, thy streets for evermore
Will silent be; and not a soul to tell
Why thou art desolate, can e'er return.

V

O Attic shape! Fair attitude! with brede[1]
Of marble men and maidens overwrought,[2]
With forest branches and the trodden weed;
Thou, silent form, dost tease us out of thought
As doth eternity: Cold Pastoral!
When old age shall this generation waste,
Thou shalt remain, in midst of other woe
Than ours, a friend to man, to whom thou say'st,
Beauty is truth, truth beauty[3]—that is all
Ye know on earth, and all ye need to know.

May 1819 1820

To Autumn

I

Season of mists and mellow fruitfulness,
Close bosom-friend of the maturing sun;

1. Woven pattern. *Attic*: Attica was the district of ancient Greece surrounding Athens.
2. Ornamented all over.
3. In some texts of the poem, "Beauty is truth, truth beauty" is in quotation marks, and in some texts it is not, leading to critical disagreements about whether the last line and a half are also inscribed on the urn or spoken by the poem's speaker.

Conspiring with him how to load and bless
With fruit the vines that round the thatch-eves run;
To bend with apples the mossed cottage-trees,
And fill all fruit with ripeness to the core;
To swell the gourd, and plump the hazel shells
With a sweet kernel; to set budding more,
And still more, later flowers for the bees,
Until they think warm days will never cease,
For Summer has o'er-brimmed their clammy cells.

II

Who hath not seen thee oft amid thy store?
Sometimes whoever seeks abroad may find
Thee sitting careless on a granary floor,
Thy hair soft-lifted by the winnowing wind,[4]
Or on a half-reaped furrow sound asleep,
Drowsed with the fume of poppies, while thy hook[5]
Spares the next swath and all its twinèd flowers:
And sometimes like a gleaner thou dost keep
Steady thy laden head across a brook;
Or by a cider-press, with patient look,
Thou watchest the last oozings hours by hours.

III

Where are the songs of Spring? Ay, where are they?
Think not of them, thou hast thy music too—
While barrèd clouds bloom the soft-dying day,
And touch the stubble-plains with rosy hue;
Then in a wailful choir the small gnats mourn
Among the river sallows,[6] borne aloft
Or sinking as the light wind lives or dies;
And full-grown lambs loud bleat from hilly bourn;[7]
Hedge-crickets sing; and now with treble soft
The red-breast whistles from a garden-croft;[8]
And gathering swallows twitter in the skies.

September 19, 1819 1820

ETHERIDGE KNIGHT

Hard Rock Returns to Prison from the Hospital for the Criminal Insane

Hard Rock was "known not to take no shit
From nobody," and he had the scars to prove it:
Split purple lips, lumped ears, welts above
His yellow eyes, and one long scar that cut

4. Which sifts the grain from the chaff. 5. Scythe or sickle. 6. Shallows. 7. Domain.
8. Enclosed garden near a house.

Across his temple and plowed through a thick
Canopy of kinky hair.

The WORD was that Hard Rock wasn't a mean nigger
Anymore, that the doctors had bored a hole in his head,
Cut out part of his brain, and shot electricity
Through the rest. When they brought Hard Rock back,
Handcuffed and chained, he was turned loose,
Like a freshly gelded stallion, to try his new status.
And we all waited and watched, like indians at a corral,
To see if the WORD was true.

As we waited we wrapped ourselves in the cloak
Of his exploits: "Man, the last time, it took eight
Screws to put him in the Hole."[9] "Yeah, remember when he
Smacked the captain with his dinner tray?" "He set
The record for time in the Hole—67 straight days!"
"Ol Hard Rock! man, that's one crazy nigger."
And then the jewel of a myth that Hard Rock had once bit
A screw on the thumb and poisoned him with syphilitic spit.

The testing came, to see if Hard Rock was really tame.
A hillbilly called him a black son of a bitch
And didn't lose his teeth, a screw who knew Hard Rock
From before shook him down and barked in his face.
And Hard Rock did *nothing.* Just grinned and looked silly,
His eyes empty like knot holes in a fence.

And even after we discovered that it took Hard Rock
Exactly 3 minutes to tell you his first name,
We told ourselves that he had just wised up,
Was being cool; but we could not fool ourselves for long,
And we turned away, our eyes on the ground. Crushed.
He had been our Destroyer, the doer of things
We dreamed of doing but could not bring ourselves to do,
The fears of years, like a biting whip,
Had cut grooves too deeply across our backs.

1968

YUSEF KOMUNYAKAA

Facing It

My black face fades,
hiding inside the black granite.
I said I wouldn't,
dammit: No tears.
I'm stone. I'm flesh.
My clouded reflection eyes me

9. Solitary confinement. *Screws*: guards.

like a bird of prey, the profile of night
slanted against morning. I turn
this way—I'm inside
the Vietnam Veterans Memorial[1]
again, depending on the light
to make a difference.
I go down the 58,022 names,
half-expecting to find
my own in letters like smoke.
I touch the name Andrew Johnson;[2]
I see the booby trap's white flash.
Names shimmer on a woman's blouse
but when she walks away
the names stay on the wall.
Brushstrokes flash, a red bird's
wings cutting across my stare.
The sky. A plane in the sky.
A white vet's image floats
closer to me, then his eyes
look through mine. I'm a window.
He's lost his right arm
inside the stone. In the black mirror
a woman's trying to erase names:
No, she's brushing a boy's hair.

1988

AUTHORS ON THEIR WORK

YUSEF KOMUNYAKAA (b. 1947)

From "Facing It" (2000)*

Now, as I think back to 1984, when I wrote "Facing It," with the humidity hanging over New Orleans [. . .] in early summer, I remember that it seemed several lifetimes from those fiery years in Vietnam. [. . .] I had meditated on the Vietnam Veterans Memorial as if the century's blues songs had been solidified into something monumental and concrete. Our wailing, our ranting, our singing of spirituals and kaddish and rock anthems, it was all captured and refined into a shaped destiny that attempted to portray personal and public feelings about war and human loss. It became a shrine overnight: a blackness that plays with light—a reflected motion in the stone that balances a dance between grass and sky.

1. Designed by Yale undergraduate Maya Ying Lin, the centerpiece of this Washington, DC, memorial consists of two black, highly reflective stone walls, each almost 247 feet long, etched with the names of servicemen declared either missing or killed in action during the Vietnam conflict.
2. Soldier from Komunyakaa's hometown, Bogalusa, Louisiana. He shared the name of the U.S. president who, after succeeding the recently assassinated Abraham Lincoln in 1865, both vetoed bills designed to stop Southern states from depriving freed slaves of their civil liberties and opposed passage of the Fourteenth Amendment (1868) granting citizenship to African Americans.

Whoever faces the granite becomes a part of it. The reflections move into and through each other. A dance between the dead and the living. Even in its heft and weight, emotionally and physically, it still seems to defy immediate description, constantly incorporating into its shape all the new reflections and shapes brought to it: one of the poignant shrines of the twentieth century. (55)

*"Facing It." *Blue Notes: Essays, Interviews, and Commentaries*, edited by Radiclani Clytus, U of Michigan P, 2000, pp. 54–55.

EMMA LAZARUS
The New Colossus[3]

Not like the brazen giant of Greek fame,[4]
With conquering limbs astride from land to land;
Here at our sea-washed, sunset gates shall stand
A mighty woman with a torch, whose flame
Is the imprisoned lightning, and her name
Mother of Exiles. From her beacon-hand
Glows world-wide welcome; her mild eyes command
The air-bridged harbor that twin cities[5] frame.
"Keep ancient lands, your storied pomp!" cries she
With silent lips. "Give me your tired, your poor,
Your huddled masses yearning to breathe free,
The wretched refuse of your teeming shore.
Send these, the homeless, tempest-tost to me,
I lift my lamp beside the golden door!"

November 1883

ANDREW MARVELL
On a Drop of Dew

See how the orient[6] dew
Shed from the bosom of the morn
    Into the blowing roses,
Yet careless of its mansion new
For[7] the clear region where 'twas born
    Round in itself incloses,
    And in its little globe's extent
Frames as it can its native element;
    How it the purple flow'r does slight,
    Scarce touching where it lies,

3. The poem was written to commemorate the opening of the Statue of Liberty, in New York harbor.
4. The Colossus of Rhodes, one of the seven wonders of the ancient world, a one-hundred-foot statue of Helios, the sun god. 5. Manhattan and Brooklyn. 6. Shining. 7. By reason of.

But gazing back upon the skies,
Shines with a mournful light
Like its own tear,
Because so long divided from the sphere.[8]
Restless it rolls and unsecure,
Trembling lest it grow impure,
Till the warm sun pity its pain,
And to the skies exhale it back again.
So the soul, that drop, that ray
Of the clear fountain of eternal day,
Could it within the human flower be seen,
Rememb'ring still its former height,
Shuns the sweet leaves and blossoms green;
And, recollecting its own light,
Does, in its pure and circling thoughts, express
The greater Heaven in an Heaven less.
In how coy[9] a figure wound,
Every way it turns away;
So the world excluding round,
Yet receiving in the day:
Dark beneath, but bright above,
Here disdaining, there in love.

How loose and easy hence to go,
How girt and ready to ascend;
Moving but on a point below,
It all about does upwards bend.
Such did the manna's sacred dew distill,
White and entire, though congealed and chill;[1]
Congealed on earth, but does, dissolving, run
Into the glories of th' almighty sun.

1681

LINDA PASTAN
love poem

I want to write you
a love poem as headlong
as our creek
after thaw
when we stand
on its dangerous
banks and watch it carry

8. Of heaven. 9. Reserved, withdrawn, modest.

1. In the wilderness, the Israelites fed upon manna from heaven (distilled from the dew; see Exod. 16.10–21); manna became a traditional symbol for divine grace.

with it every twig
every dry leaf and branch
in its path
every scruple
when we see it
so swollen
with runoff
that even as we watch
we must grab
each other
and step back
we must grab each
other or
get our shoes
soaked we must
grab each other

1988

MARGE PIERCY

Barbie Doll

This girlchild was born as usual
and presented dolls that did pee-pee
and miniature GE stoves and irons
and wee lipsticks the color of cherry candy.
Then in the magic of puberty, a classmate said:
You have a great big nose and fat legs.

She was healthy, tested intelligent,
possessed strong arms and back,
abundant sexual drive and manual dexterity.
She went to and fro apologizing.
Everyone saw a fat nose on thick legs.

She was advised to play coy,
exhorted to come on hearty,
exercise, diet, smile and wheedle.
Her good nature wore out
like a fan belt.
So she cut off her nose and her legs
and offered them up.

In the casket displayed on satin she lay
with the undertaker's cosmetics painted on,
a turned-up putty nose,
dressed in a pink and white nightie.
Doesn't she look pretty? everyone said.
Consummation at last.
To every woman a happy ending.

1973

SYLVIA PLATH
Lady Lazarus

I have done it again.
One year in every ten
I manage it—

A sort of walking miracle, my skin
Bright as a Nazi lampshade,
My right foot

A paperweight,
My face a featureless, fine
Jew linen.[2]

Peel off the napkin
O my enemy.
Do I terrify?—

The nose, the eye pits, the full set of teeth?
The sour breath
Will vanish in a day.

Soon, soon the flesh
The grave cave ate will be
At home on me

And I a smiling woman.
I am only thirty.
And like the cat I have nine times to die.

This is Number Three.
What a trash
To annihilate each decade.

What a million filaments.
The peanut-crunching crowd
Shoves in to see

Them unwrap me hand and foot—
The big strip tease.
Gentlemen, ladies

These are my hands
My knees.
I may be skin and bone,

Nevertheless, I am the same, identical woman.
The first time it happened I was ten.
It was an accident.

2. During World War II, prisoners in some Nazi camps were gassed to death and their body parts then turned into objects such as lampshades and paperweights.

The second time I meant
To last it out and not come back at all.
I rocked shut

As a seashell.
They had to call and call
And pick the worms off me like sticky pearls.

Dying
Is an art, like everything else.
I do it exceptionally well.

I do it so it feels like hell.
I do it so it feels real.
I guess you could say I've a call.

It's easy enough to do it in a cell.
It's easy enough to do it and stay put.
It's the theatrical

Comeback in broad day
To the same place, the same face, the same brute
Amused shout:

"A miracle!"
That knocks me out.
There is a charge

For the eyeing of my scars, there is a charge
For the hearing of my heart—
It really goes.

And there is a charge, a very large charge
For a word or a touch
Or a bit of blood

Or a piece of my hair or my clothes.
So, so Herr Doktor.
So, Herr Enemy.

I am your opus,
I am your valuable,
The pure gold baby

That melts to a shriek.
I turn and burn.
Do not think I underestimate your great concern

Ash, ash—
You poke and stir.
Flesh, bone, there is nothing there—

A cake of soap,
A wedding ring,
A gold filling.

Herr God, Herr Lucifer
Beware
Beware.

Out of the ash
I rise with my red hair
And I eat men like air.

1965

Morning Song

Love set you going like a fat gold watch.
The midwife slapped your footsoles, and your bald cry
Took its place among the elements.

Our voices echo, magnifying your arrival. New statue.
In a drafty museum, your nakedness
Shadows our safety. We stand round blankly as walls.

I'm no more your mother
Than the cloud that distils a mirror to reflect its own slow
Effacement at the wind's hand.

All night your moth-breath
Flickers among the flat pink roses. I wake to listen:
A far sea moves in my ear.

One cry, and I stumble from bed, cow-heavy and floral
In my Victorian nightgown.
Your mouth opens clean as a cat's. The window square

Whitens and swallows its dull stars. And now you try
Your handful of notes;
The clear vowels rise like balloons.

1961

EDGAR ALLAN POE

The Raven

Once upon a midnight dreary, while I pondered, weak and weary,
Over many a quaint and curious volume of forgotten lore,
While I nodded, nearly napping, suddenly there came a tapping,
As of some one gently rapping, rapping at my chamber door.
"'Tis some visitor," I muttered, "tapping at my chamber door—
Only this, and nothing more."

Ah, distinctly I remember it was in the bleak December,
And each separate dying ember wrought its ghost upon the floor.
Eagerly I wished the morrow;—vainly I had sought to borrow
From my books surcease of sorrow—sorrow for the lost Lenore—

For the rare and radiant maiden whom the angels name Lenore—
Nameless here for evermore.

And the silken sad uncertain rustling of each purple curtain
Thrilled me—filled me with fantastic terrors never felt before;
So that now, to still the beating of my heart, I stood repeating
"'Tis some visitor entreating entrance at my chamber door;—
Some late visitor entreating entrance at my chamber door;
This it is, and nothing more."

Presently my soul grew stronger; hesitating then no longer,
"Sir," said I, "or Madam, truly your forgiveness I implore;
But the fact is I was napping, and so gently you came rapping,
And so faintly you came tapping, tapping at my chamber door,
That I scarce was sure I heard you"—here I opened wide the door;—
Darkness there, and nothing more.

Deep into that darkness peering, long I stood there wondering, fearing,
Doubting, dreaming dreams no mortal ever dared to dream before;
But the silence was unbroken, and the darkness gave no token,
And the only word there spoken was the whispered word, "Lenore!"
This I whispered, and an echo murmured back the word, "Lenore!"—
Merely this, and nothing more.

Back into the chamber turning, all my soul within me burning,
Soon I heard again a tapping somewhat louder than before.
"Surely," said I, "surely that is something at my window lattice;
Let me see, then, what thereat is, and this mystery explore—
Let my heart be still a moment and this mystery explore;—
'Tis the wind and nothing more!"

Open here I flung the shutter, when, with many a flirt and flutter,
In there stepped a stately raven of the saintly days of yore;
Not the least obeisance made he; not an instant stopped or stayed he;
But, with mien of lord or lady, perched above my chamber door—
Perched upon a bust of Pallas[3] just above my chamber door—
Perched, and sat, and nothing more.

Then this ebony bird beguiling my sad fancy into smiling,
By the grave and stern decorum of the countenance it wore,
"Though thy crest be shorn and shaven, thou," I said, "art sure no craven,
Ghastly grim and ancient raven wandering from the Nightly shore—
Tell me what thy lordly name is on the Night's Plutonian[4] shore!"
Quoth the raven, "Nevermore."

Much I marvelled this ungainly fowl to hear discourse so plainly,
Though its answer little meaning—little relevancy bore,
For we cannot help agreeing that no living human being
Ever yet was blessed with seeing bird above his chamber door—
Bird or beast upon the sculptured bust above his chamber door,
With such name as "Nevermore."

3. Athena, the Greek goddess of wisdom. 4. Dark; Pluto was the ancient Greek god of the underworld.

But the raven, sitting lonely on the placid bust, spoke only
That one word, as if his soul in that one word he did outpour.
Nothing farther then he uttered—not a feather then he fluttered—
Till I scarcely more than muttered "Other friends have flown before—
On the morrow *he* will leave me, as my hopes have flown before."
Then the bird said "Nevermore."

Startled at the stillness broken by reply so aptly spoken,
"Doubtless," said I, "what it utters is its only stock and store
Caught from some unhappy master whom unmerciful Disaster
Followed fast and followed faster till his songs one burden bore—
Till the dirges of his Hope that melancholy burden bore
Of 'Never—nevermore.'"

But the raven still beguiling all my sad soul into smiling,
Straight I wheeled a cushioned seat in front of bird and bust and door;
Then, upon the velvet sinking, I betook myself to linking
Fancy unto fancy, thinking what this ominous bird of yore—
What this grim, ungainly, ghastly, gaunt, and ominous bird of yore
Meant in croaking "Nevermore."

This I sat engaged in guessing, but no syllable expressing
To the fowl whose fiery eyes now burned into my bosom's core;
This and more I sat divining, with my head at ease reclining
On the cushion's velvet lining that the lamplight gloated o'er,
But whose velvet violet lining with the lamplight gloating o'er,
She shall press, ah, nevermore!

Then, methought, the air grew denser, perfumed from an unseen censer
Swung by angels whose faint foot-falls tinkled on the tufted floor.
"Wretch," I cried, "thy God hath lent thee—by these angels he hath sent thee
Respite—respite and nepenthe[5] from thy memories of Lenore!
Quaff, oh quaff this kind nepenthe and forget this lost Lenore!"
Quoth the raven, "Nevermore."

"Prophet!" said I, "thing of evil!—prophet still, if bird or devil!—
Whether Tempter sent, or whether tempest tossed thee here ashore,
Desolate, yet all undaunted, on this desert land enchanted—
On this home by Horror haunted—tell me truly, I implore—
Is there—*is* there balm in Gilead?[6]—tell me—tell me, I implore!"
Quoth the raven, "Nevermore."

"Prophet!" said I, "thing of evil—prophet still, if bird or devil!
By that Heaven that bends above us—by that God we both adore—
Tell this soul with sorrow laden if, within the distant Aidenn,[7]
It shall clasp a sainted maiden whom the angels name Lenore—
Clasp a rare and radiant maiden whom the angels name Lenore."
Quoth the raven, "Nevermore."

5. Drug reputed by the Greeks to cause forgetfulness or sorrow (pronounced "ne-PEN-thee").
6. See Jeremiah 8.22. 7. Eden.

"Be that word our sign of parting, bird or fiend!" I shrieked upstarting—
"Get thee back into the tempest and the Night's Plutonian shore!
Leave no black plume as a token of that lie thy soul hath spoken!
Leave my loneliness unbroken!—quit the bust above my door!
Take thy beak from out my heart, and take thy form from off my door!"
Quoth the raven, "Nevermore."

And the raven, never flitting, still is sitting, still is sitting
On the pallid bust of Pallas just above my chamber door;
And his eyes have all the seeming of a demon's that is dreaming,
And the lamp-light o'er him streaming throws his shadow on the floor;
And my soul from out that shadow that lies floating on the floor
Shall be lifted—nevermore!

1844

EZRA POUND

The River-Merchant's Wife: A Letter

(after Rihaku)[8]

While my hair was still cut straight across my forehead
I played about the front gate, pulling flowers.
You came by on bamboo stilts, playing horse,
You walked about my seat, playing with blue plums.
And we went on living in the village of Chokan:
Two small people, without dislike or suspicion.

At fourteen I married My Lord you.
I never laughed, being bashful.
Lowering my head, I looked at the wall.
Called to, a thousand times, I never looked back.

At fifteen I stopped scowling,
I desired my dust to be mingled with yours
For ever and for ever and for ever.
Why should I climb the look out?

At sixteen you departed,
You went into far Ku-to-yen, by the river of swirling eddies,
And you have been gone five months.
The monkeys make sorrowful noise overhead.

You dragged your feet when you went out.
By the gate now, the moss is grown, the different mosses,
Too deep to clear them away!

The leaves fall early this autumn, in wind.
The paired butterflies are already yellow with August

8. Japanese name for Li Po, an eighth-century Chinese poet. Pound's poem is based on one by Li Po, which Pound read in translation.

Over the grass in the West garden;
They hurt me. I grow older.
If you are coming down through the narrows of the river Kiang,
Please let me know beforehand,
And I will come out to meet you
As far as Cho-fu-Sa.

1915

THEODORE ROETHKE

Root Cellar

Nothing would sleep in that cellar, dank as a ditch,
Bulbs broke out of boxes hunting for chinks in the dark,
Shoots dangled and drooped,
Lolling obscenely from mildewed crates,
Hung down long yellow evil necks, like tropical snakes.
And what a congress of stinks!–
Roots ripe as old bait,
Pulpy stems, rank, silo-rich,
Leaf-mold, manure, lime, piled against slippery planks.
Nothing would give up life:
Even the dirt kept breathing a small breath.

1948

PERCY BYSSHE SHELLEY

Ozymandias[9]

I met a traveler from an antique land,
Who said—"Two vast and trunkless[1] legs of stone
Stand in the desart. . . . Near them, on the sand,
Half sunk a shattered visage lies, whose frown,
And wrinkled lip, and sneer of cold command,
Tell that its sculptor well those passions read
Which yet survive, stamped on these lifeless things,
The hand that mocked them, and the heart that fed;[2]
And on the pedestal, these words appear:
My name is Ozymandias, King of Kings,
Look on my Works, ye Mighty, and despair!
Nothing beside remains. Round the decay

9. Ancient Greek name for Egyptian pharaoh Ramses II (13th century BCE); according to one early Greek historian, Egypt's largest statue bore the inscription "I am Ozymandias king of kings; if anyone wishes to know what I am and where I lie, let him surpass me in some of my exploits."
1. Without a torso.
2. That is, because they are "stamped on" the statue's features, the king's passions outlive ("survive") both his "heart," which "fed" them, and the scultptor's "hand that mocked them," with *mock* meaning both imitated and satirized.

Of that colossal Wreck, boundless and bare
The lone and level sands stretch far away."

1817 1818

WALLACE STEVENS

Anecdote of the Jar

I placed a jar in Tennessee,
And round it was, upon a hill.
It made the slovenly wilderness
Surround that hill.

The wilderness rose up to it,
And sprawled around, no longer wild.
The jar was round upon the ground
And tall and of a port in air.

It took dominion everywhere.
The jar was gray and bare.
It did not give of bird or bush,
Like nothing else in Tennessee.

1923

The Emperor of Ice-Cream

Call the roller of big cigars,
The muscular one, and bid him whip
In kitchen cups concupiscent curds.[3]
Let the wenches dawdle in such dress
As they are used to wear, and let the boys
Bring flowers in last month's newspapers.
Let be be finale of seem.[4]
The only emperor is the emperor of ice-cream.

Take from the dresser of deal,
Lacking the three glass knobs, that sheet
On which she embroidered fantails[5] once
And spread it so as to cover her face.
If her horny feet protrude, they come
To show how cold she is, and dumb.

3. "The words 'concupiscent curds' have no genealogy; they are merely expressive: at least, I hope they are expressive. They express the concupiscence of life, but, by contrast with the things in relation to them in the poem, they express or accentuate life's destitution, and it is this that gives them something more than a cheap lustre" (Wallace Stevens, *Letters*. Edited by Holly Stevens, U of California P, 1996, p. 500).
4. "The true sense of Let be be the finale of seem is let being become the conclusion or denouement of appearing to be: in short, icecream is an absolute good. The poem is obviously not about icecream, but about being as distinguished from seeming to be" (*Letters* 341).
5. Fantail pigeons.

Let the lamp affix its beam.
The only emperor is the emperor of ice-cream.

1923

ALFRED, LORD TENNYSON

Tears, Idle Tears[6]

Tears, idle tears, I know not what they mean,
Tears from the depth of some divine despair
Rise in the heart, and gather to the eyes,
In looking on the happy autumn-fields,
And thinking of the days that are no more.

Fresh as the first beam glittering on a sail,
That brings our friends up from the underworld,
Sad as the last which reddens over one
That sinks with all we love below the verge;
So sad, so fresh, the days that are no more.

Ah, sad and strange as in dark summer dawns
The earliest pipe of half-awakened birds
To dying ears, when unto dying eyes
The casement slowly grows a glimmering square;
So sad, so strange, the days that are no more.

Dear as remembered kisses after death,
And sweet as those by hopeless fancy feigned
On lips that are for others; deep as love,
Deep as first love, and wild with all regret;
O Death in Life, the days that are no more!

1847

Ulysses[7]

It little profits that an idle king,
By this still hearth, among these barren crags,
Matched with an agèd wife,[8] mete and dole
Unequal laws unto a savage race,
That hoard, and sleep, and feed, and know not me.

I cannot rest from travel; I will drink
Life to the lees.[9] All times I have enjoyed
Greatly, have suffered greatly, both with those
That loved me, and alone; on shore, and when

6. One of the songs from Tennyson's book-length narrative poem *The Princess*.

7. After the Trojan War ended, Ulysses (or Odysseus), king of Ithaca and one of the war's Greek heroes, returned to his island home (line 34). Homer's account of the situation is in book 11 of *The Odyssey*, but Dante's account of Ulysses in canto 26 of the *Inferno* is the more immediate background of Tennyson's poem. 8. Penelope.

9. That is, all the way down to the bottom of the cup.

Through scudding drifts the rainy Hyades[1]
Vexed the dim sea. I am become a name;
For always roaming with a hungry heart
Much have I seen and known—cities of men
And manners, climates, councils, governments,
Myself not least, but honored of them all—
And drunk delight of battle with my peers,
Far on the ringing plains of windy Troy.
I am a part of all that I have met;
Yet all experience is an arch wherethrough
Gleams that untraveled world, whose margin fades
For ever and for ever when I move.
How dull it is to pause, to make an end,
To rust unburnished, not to shine in use!
As though to breathe were life. Life piled on life
Were all too little, and of one to me
Little remains; but every hour is saved
From that eternal silence, something more,
A bringer of new things; and vile it were
For some three suns to store and hoard myself,
And this gray spirit yearning in desire
To follow knowledge like a sinking star,
Beyond the utmost bound of human thought.

This is my son, mine own Telemachus,
To whom I leave the scepter and the isle—
Well-loved of me, discerning to fulfill
This labor, by slow prudence to make mild
A rugged people, and through soft degrees
Subdue them to the useful and the good.
Most blameless is he, centered in the sphere
Of common duties, decent not to fail
In offices of tenderness, and pay
Meet adoration to my household gods,
When I am gone. He works his work, I mine.

There lies the port; the vessel puffs her sail:
There gloom the dark, broad seas. My mariners,
Souls that have toiled, and wrought, and thought with me—
That ever with a frolic welcome took
The thunder and the sunshine, and opposed
Free hearts, free foreheads—you and I are old;
Old age hath yet his honor and his toil.
Death closes all; but something ere the end,
Some work of noble note, may yet be done,
Not unbecoming men that strove with Gods.
The lights begin to twinkle from the rocks;
The long day wanes; the slow moon climbs; the deep
Moans round with many voices. Come, my friends,

1. Group of stars believed to predict the rain when they rose at the same time as the sun.

'Tis not too late to seek a newer world.
Push off, and sitting well in order smite
The sounding furrows; for my purpose holds
To sail beyond the sunset, and the baths
Of all the western stars, until I die.
It may be that the gulfs will wash us down;[2]
It may be we shall touch the Happy Isles,[3]
And see the great Achilles, whom we knew.
Though much is taken, much abides; and though
We are not now that strength which in old days
Moved earth and heaven, that which we are, we are:
One equal temper of heroic hearts,
Made weak by time and fate, but strong in will
To strive, to seek, to find, and not to yield.

1833

WALT WHITMAN
Facing West from California's Shores

Facing west, from California's shores,
Inquiring, tireless, seeking what is yet unfound,
I, a child, very old, over waves, towards the house of maternity,[4] the
land of migrations, look afar,
Look off the shores of my Western sea, the circle almost circled:
For starting westward from Hindustan, from the vales of Kashmere,
From Asia, from the north, from the God, the sage, and the hero,
From the south, from the flowery peninsulas and the spice islands,
Long having wandered since, round the earth having wandered,
Now I face home again, very pleased and joyous;
(But where is what I started for, so long ago?
And why is it yet unfound?)

1860

A Noiseless Patient Spider

A noiseless patient spider,
I marked where on a little promontory it stood isolated,
Marked how to explore the vacant vast surrounding,
It launched forth filament, filament, filament, out of itself,
Ever unreeling them, ever tirelessly speeding them.

And you O my soul where you stand,
Surrounded, detached, in measureless oceans of space,
Ceaselessly musing, venturing, throwing, seeking the spheres to
connect them,

2. Beyond the Gulf of Gibraltar was supposed to lie a chasm that led to Hades, the underworld.
3. Elysium, the Islands of the Blessed, where heroes like Achilles (line 64) go after death.
4. Asia, as the supposed birthplace of the human race.

Till the bridge you will need be formed, till the ductile anchor hold,
Till the gossamer thread you fling catch somewhere, O my soul.

1881

WILLIAM CARLOS WILLIAMS
The Dance

In Brueghel's great picture, The Kermess,[5]
the dancers go round, they go round and
around, the squeal and the blare and the
tweedle of bagpipes, a bugle and fiddles
tipping their bellies (round as the thick-
sided glasses whose wash they impound)
their hips and their bellies off balance
to turn them. Kicking and rolling about
the Fair Grounds, swinging their butts, those
shanks must be sound to bear up under such
rollicking measures, prance as they dance
in Brueghel's great picture, The Kermess.

1944

WILLIAM CARLOS WILLIAMS
Landscape with the Fall of Icarus[6]

According to Brueghel
when Icarus fell
it was spring

a farmer was ploughing
his field
the whole pageantry

of the year was
awake tingling
near

the edge of the sea
concerned
with itself

sweating in the sun
that melted
the wings' wax

unsignificantly
off the coast
there was

5. A painting by Pieter Bruegel or Brueghel the Elder (c. 1525–69).

6. The painting *Landscape with the Fall of Icarus* was long thought to be the work of Flemish master Pieter Bruegel or Brueghel the Elder (c. 1525–69); but is today believed to be a copy or version of a now-lost Bruegel original.

a splash quite unnoticed
this was
Icarus drowning

WILLIAM WORDSWORTH

[The world is too much with us]

The world is too much with us; late and soon,
Getting and spending, we lay waste our powers:
Little we see in Nature that is ours;
We have given our hearts away, a sordid boon![7]
This Sea that bares her bosom to the moon;
The winds that will be howling at all hours,
And are up-gathered now like sleeping flowers;
For this, for every thing, we are out of tune;
It moves us not.—Great God! I'd rather be
A Pagan suckled in a creed outworn;
So might I, standing on this pleasant lea,
Have glimpses that would make me less forlorn;
Have sight of Proteus rising from the sea;
Or hear old Triton[8] blow his wreathèd horn.

1807

[A slumber did my spirit seal][9]

A slumber did my spirit seal;
I had no human fears:
She seemed a thing that could not feel
The touch of earthly years.

No motion has she now, no force;
She neither hears nor sees;
Rolled round in earth's diurnal[1] course,
With rocks, and stones, and trees.

1799 1800

7. Gift. It is the act of giving the heart away that is sordid.
8. Sea deity, usually represented as blowing on a conch shell. *Proteus*: an old man of the sea who (in *The Odyssey*) can assume a variety of shapes.
9. This poem is part of the same sequence of so-called Lucy poems that includes "She Dwelt among the Untrodden Ways." 1. Daily.

Biographical Sketches: Poets

Sketches are included for all poets represented by two or more poems.

SHERMAN ALEXIE (b. 1966)

Sherman Alexie grew up with his four siblings on a reservation near Spokane, Washington, an experience he once described as the "origin" of "everything I do now, writing and otherwise." After attending high school in nearby Reardan, where he was the only Native American other than the school mascot, he earned a BA in American Studies from Washington State University and soon after published the first of twelve collections of poetry, *The Business of Ferrydancing* (1991). Named a *New York Times* Notable Book of the Year, it also earned high praise from the *New York Times Book Review,* which hailed its 26-year-old author as "one of the major lyric voices of our time." Yet Alexie is perhaps better understood as an accomplished storyteller in verse and prose. His first collection of fiction, *The Lone Ranger and Tonto Fistfight in Heaven* (1993), received a PEN/Hemingway Award for Best First Book, which Alexie followed up over 15 years later with a PEN/Faulkner Award for his fourth collection, *War Stories* (2009). In between have come novels—including *Reservation Blues* (1995), *Flight* (2007), and the National Book Award–winning young adult novel *The Absolutely True Diary of a Part-Time Indian* (2009)—as well as radio scripts and screenplays: *Smoke Signals* (1998) was featured at the Sundance Film Festival. A sometime stand-up comedian and four-time champion of the World Heavyweight Poetry Slam, he lives in Seattle, Washington, with his wife and two sons.

AGHA SHAHID ALI (1949–2001)

Agha Shahid Ali, who died of brain cancer when he was only fifty-two, rightly considered himself a quintessentially American poet, an immigrant in a land of immigrants. He was born in New Delhi, India, but grew up in Kashmir (a long-contested region today divided up among India, Pakistan, and China) and Indiana, where his parents both completed doctorates in 1964. As this suggests, his was a highly educated family. Ali, who himself grew up speaking both Urdu and English, fondly remembered a grandmother who quoted British poets ranging from John Milton to Thomas Hardy, alongside their equally famous Persian, Urdu, and Kashmiri peers. After earning both a BA at the University of Kashmir (1968) and an MA from the University of New Delhi (1970), Ali settled permanently in the United States, where he studied at both Pennsylvania State (MA, 1981; PhD, 1984) and the University of Arizona (MFA, 1985). Ali's highly regarded and evocatively titled volumes of poetry—including *A Walk through the Yellow Pages* (1987), *A Nostalgist's Map of America* (1991), *The Country without a Post Office* (1997), and *Call Me Ishmael Tonight: A Book of Ghazals* (2003)—all in different ways reflect what he himself described as the "triple heritage"—"Hindu, Muslim, and Western"—that afforded him "the ability and confidence to breath something rich and strange into English." So, too, in a different way, do his efforts as critic (in *T. S. Eliot as Editor,* 1986); translator (of Urdu poet Faiz Ahmad Faiz's *The Rebel's Silhouette,* 1991); and editor (of *Ravishing DisUnities: Real Ghazals in English,* 2000).

W. H. AUDEN (1907–73)

Wystan Hugh Auden was born in York, England, to a medical officer and a nurse. Intending at first to become a scientist, Auden studied at Oxford, where he became the center of the "Oxford Group" of poets and leftist intellectuals. His travels during the 1930s led him to Germany, Iceland, China, Spain (where he was an ambulance driver in the civil war), and the United States (where he taught at various universities and, in 1946, became a naturalized citizen). A prolific writer of poems, plays, essays, and criticism, Auden won the Pulitzer Prize in 1948 for his collection of poems *The Age of Anxiety*, set in a New York City bar. Late in life he returned to Christ Church College, Oxford, where he was writer in residence. He is regarded as a masterly poet of political and intellectual conscience as well as one of the twentieth century's greatest lyric craftsmen.

BASHŌ (1644–94)

Born Matsuo Munefusa, the second son of a low-ranking provincial samurai, the haiku poet who came to be known as Bashō at first put aside his literary interests and entered into service with the local ruling military house. In 1666, following the feudal lord's death, Bashō left for Edo (now Tokyo), the military capital of the shogun's new government, to pursue a career as a professional poet. He supported himself as a teacher and editor of other people's poetry but ultimately developed a following and a sizable group of students. A seasoned traveler, Bashō maintained an austere existence on the road and at home, casting himself in travel narratives such as *Oku no hosomichi* (*The Narrow Road to the Interior*, 1694) as a pilgrim devoted to nature and Zen.

ELIZABETH BISHOP (1911–79)

Born in Worcester, Massachusetts, Elizabeth Bishop endured the death of her father before she was a year old and the institutionalization of her mother four years later. Bishop was raised first by her maternal grandmother in Nova Scotia, then by her paternal grandparents back in Worcester. At Vassar College she met the poet Marianne Moore, who encouraged her to give up plans for medical school and pursue a career in poetry. Bishop traveled through Canada, Europe, and South America, finally settling in Rio de Janeiro, where she lived for nearly twenty years. Her four volumes of poetry are *North and South* (1946); *A Cold Spring* (1955), which won the Pulitzer Prize; *Questions of Travel* (1965); and *Geography III* (1976), which won the National Book Critics' Circle Award.

WILLIAM BLAKE (1757–1828)

The son of a London haberdasher and his wife, William Blake studied drawing at ten and at fourteen was apprenticed to an engraver for seven years. After a first book of poems, *Poetical Sketches* (1783), he began experimenting with what he called "illuminated printing"—the words and pictures of each page were engraved in relief on copper, which was used to print sheets that were then partly colored by hand—a laborious and time-consuming process that resulted in books of singular beauty, no two of which are exactly alike. His great *Songs of Innocence and of Experience* (1794) were produced in this manner, as were his increasingly mythic and prophetic books, including *The Marriage of Heaven and Hell* (1793), *The Four Zoas* (1803), *Milton* (1804), and *Jerusalem* (1809). Blake devoted his later life to pictorial art, illustrating *The Canterbury Tales*, the Book of Job, and *The Divine Comedy*, on which he was hard at work when he died.

GWENDOLYN BROOKS (1917–2000)

Gwendolyn Brooks was born in Topeka, Kansas, and raised in Chicago, where she began writing poetry at the age of seven, and where she graduated from Wilson Junior College in 1936. Shortly after beginning her formal study of modern poetry at Chicago's Southside Community Art Center, Brooks produced her first book of poems, *A Street in Bronzeville* (1945). With her second volume, *Annie Allen* (1949), she became the first African American to win the Pulitzer Prize. Though her early work focused on what Langston Hughes called the "ordinary aspects of black life," during the mid-1960s she devoted her poetry to raising African American consciousness and to social activism. In 1968, she was named the Poet Laureate of Illinois; from 1985 to 1986, she became the first black woman ever to serve as poetry consultant to the Library of Congress.

ROBERT BROWNING (1812–89)

Born in London, Robert Browning attended London University but was largely self-educated, learning Latin, Greek, French, and Italian by the time he was fourteen. He was an accomplished but little-known poet and playwright when he began courting the already famous poet Elizabeth Barrett. After they eloped to Italy in 1846, the Brownings enjoyed a period of happiness during which they produced most of their best-known work. Following Elizabeth's death in 1861, Robert returned to England with their son and for the rest of his life enjoyed great literary and social success. His major collections are *Men and Women* (1855), dedicated to his wife, and *Dramatis Personae* (1864), which contains some of his finest dramatic monologues. Lionized as one of England's greatest poets by the time of his death, Browning is buried in Poets' Corner at London's Westminster Abbey.

JUDITH ORTIZ COFER (1952–2016)

Born in Hormigueros, Puerto Rico, Judith Ortiz Cofer just two years later moved with her family, first to New Jersey and later to Georgia, experiences that would inspire much of her later fiction and poetry. "How can you inject passion and purpose into your work if it has no roots?" she wrote, avowing that her own roots include a long line of women storytellers who "infected" her at a very early age with the desire to tell stories both on and off the page. After earning an MA at Florida Atlantic University (1977), Ortiz Cofer returned to Georgia, where she served as professor emerita at the University of Georgia until her death. Among her numerous publications are *The Line of the Sun* (1989), a novel in which a young girl relates the history of her ne'er-do-well uncle's emigration from Puerto Rico; the poetry collection *A Love Story Beginning in Spanish* (2005); *The Latin Deli: Prose and Poetry* (1993); and *In the Cruel Country: Notes for an Elegy* (2015).

SAMUEL TAYLOR COLERIDGE (1772–1834)

Born in the small town of Ottery St. Mary in rural Devonshire, England, Samuel Taylor Coleridge is among the greatest and most original of the nineteenth-century Romantic poets. He wrote three of the most haunting and powerful poems in English—*The Rime of the Ancient Mariner* (1798), *Christabel* (1816), and "Kubla Khan" (1816)—as well as immensely influential literary criticism and a treatise on biology. In 1795, in the midst of a failed experiment to establish a "Pantisocracy" (his form of ideal community), he met William Wordsworth, and in 1798 they jointly published their enormously influential *Lyrical Ballads*. Coleridge's physical ailments, addiction to opium, and profound sense of despair made his life difficult and tumultuous and certainly affected his work. Still, he remains a central figure in English literature.

BILLY COLLINS (b. 1941)

Sometimes described as "the most popular poet in America," Billy Collins enjoys the sort of celebrity status usually reserved for Hollywood actors like his friend Bill Murray, reportedly signing six-figure contracts for books-in-progress. As U.S. Poet Laureate (2001–03), however, Collins both refused to publish and hence profit from his poem "The Names," written in honor of the victims of the 9/11 attacks, and initiated philanthropic projects like *Poetry 180*, which aims at exciting high-schoolers' interest in poetry. Born in New York City, Collins credits his mother with awakening his love of poetry and teaching him the importance of "reading poetry as poetry [. . .] as a set of sounds set to rhythm"—lessons reinforced by his studies at the College of Holy Cross and the University of California–Riverside. Though Collins began publishing his work in the 1980s, it wasn't until 1991 that his book *Questions About Angels* thrust him into the spotlight. Since that time, he has published numerous collections, including *The Art of Drowning* (1995), *Taking off Emily Dickinson's Clothes* (2000), *Ballistics* (2008), and *Aimless Love* (2013). By his own account "unashamedly" "suburban," "domestic," and "middle class," Collins's deceptively simple poetry uses the material of the everyday to, as one reader put it, "help us feel the mystery of being alive."

MARTHA COLLINS (b. 1940)

Nebraska-born poet, teacher, translator, and editor Martha Collins grew up in Des Moines, Iowa, the late and only child of a pharmacist who wanted her to be a doctor and a pianist who fostered the love of music that still, she says, ensures "I usually hear the music of a poem before I begin to understand it." In the process of earning three degrees in English literature—a Stanford BA (1962) and an MA and PhD from the University of Iowa (1965, 1971)—Collins discovered, in her words, "that I didn't want to write about writers—I wanted to be one." Citing as inspirations poets as diverse as Wallace Stevens, Gwendolyn Brooks, John Ashbery, and Emily Dickinson—whom, she says, "taught me to care about everything I see," as well as "every word I write"—Collins published her first poetry collection, *The Catastrophe of Rainbows*, in 1985. In addition to later collections such as *The Arrangement of Space* (1991), *Some Things Words Can Do* (1998), *White Papers* (2012), and *Day unto Day* (2014), Collins's award-winning body of work includes both three books of poetry translated from the Vietnamese and *Blue Front* (2006), a book-length poem inspired by a lynching her father witnessed in Cairo, Illinois when he was only five. After over thirty years at the University of Massachusetts–Boston, where she founded and codirected the Creative Writing program, Collins returned to the Midwest in 1997, serving until 2007 as Pauline Delaney Professor of Creative Writing at Oberlin College in Ohio, where she still lives.

COUNTEE CULLEN (1903–46)

During his own lifetime, Countee Cullen was the most celebrated and honored poet of the Harlem Renaissance, and he claimed New York City as his birthplace. In fact, he may have been born in Louisville, Kentucky, and the circumstances of his childhood adoption by the Reverend Frederick Cullen remain obscure. It is certain, though, that the poet received a good education at New York's DeWitt Clinton High School and then New York University. After receiving his MA at Harvard, Cullen returned to New York in 1926 and soon established himself as the leading figure in the Harlem literary world, winning numerous awards for his poetry and editing the influential monthly column "The Dark Tower" for *Opportunity: Journal of Negro Life*. A playwright, novelist, translator, and anthologist, Cullen is best remembered as a poet; his work has been collected in the volume *My Soul's High Song: The Collected Writings of Countee Cullen, Voice of the Harlem Renaissance* (1991).

E. E. CUMMINGS (1894–1962)

Born in Cambridge, Massachusetts, the son of a Congregationalist minister, Edward Estlin Cummings attended Harvard University, where he wrote poetry in the Pre-Raphaelite and Metaphysical traditions. He joined the ambulance corps in France the day after the United States entered World War I but was imprisoned by the French due to his outspoken opposition to the war; he transmuted the experience into his first literary success, the novel *The Enormous Room* (1922). After the war, Cummings established himself as a poet and artist in New York City's Greenwich Village, made frequent trips to France and New Hampshire, and showed little interest in wealth or his growing celebrity. His variety of Modernism was distinguished by its playfulness, its formal experimentation, its lyrical directness, and above all its celebration of the individual.

EMILY DICKINSON (1830–86)

From childhood on, Emily Dickinson led a sequestered and obscure life. Yet her verse has traveled far beyond the cultured yet relatively circumscribed environment in which she lived: her room, her father's house, her family, a few close friends, and the small town of Amherst, Massachusetts. Indeed, along with Walt Whitman, her far more public contemporary, she all but invented American poetry. Born in Amherst, the daughter of a respected lawyer whom she revered ("His heart was pure and terrible," she once wrote), Dickinson studied for less than a year at the Mount Holyoke Female Seminary, returning permanently to her family home. She became more and more reclusive, dressing only in white, seeing no visitors, yet working ceaselessly at her poems—nearly eighteen hundred in all, only a few of which were published during her lifetime. After her death, her sister Lavinia discovered the rest in a trunk, neatly bound into packets with blue ribbons—among the most important bodies of work in all of American literature.

JOHN DONNE (1572–1631)

The first and greatest of the English writers who came to be known as the Metaphysical poets, John Donne wrote in a revolutionary style that combined highly intellectual conceits with complex, compressed phrasing. Born into an old Roman Catholic family at a time when Catholics were subject to constant harassment, Donne quietly abandoned his religion and had a promising legal career until a politically disastrous marriage ruined his worldly hopes. He struggled for years to support a large family; impoverished and despairing, he even wrote a treatise (*Biathanatos*) on the lawfulness of suicide.

King James (who had ambitions for him as a preacher) eventually pressured Donne to take Anglican orders in 1615, and Donne became one of the great sermonizers of his day, rising to the position of dean of St. Paul's Cathedral in 1621. Donne's private devotions ("Meditations") were published in 1624, and he continued to write poetry until a few years before his death.

PAUL LAURENCE DUNBAR (1872–1906)

The son of former slaves, Paul Laurence Dunbar was born in Dayton, Ohio. He attended a white high school, where he showed an early talent for writing and was elected class president. Unable to afford further education, he then worked as an elevator operator, writing poems and newspaper articles in his spare time. Dunbar took out a loan to subsidize the printing of his first book, *Oak and Ivy* (1893), but with the publication of *Majors and Minors* (1895) and *Lyrics of Lowly Life* (1896), his growing reputation enabled him to support himself by writing and lecturing. Though acclaimed during his lifetime for his lyrical use of rural black dialect in volumes such as *Candle-Lightin' Time* (1902), Dunbar was later criticized for adopting "white" literary conventions and accused of pandering to racist images of slaves and ex-slaves. He wrote novels and short stories in addition to poetry and dealt frankly with racial injustice in works such as *The Sport of the Gods* (1903) and *The Fourth of July and Race Outrages* (1903).

MARTÍN ESPADA (b. 1957)

At the age of thirteen, Martín Espada moved with his family to a Long Island neighborhood where they were the only Puerto Ricans, an experience he describes as "more traumatic than anything that ever happened to me on the so-called mean streets" of the racially diverse Brooklyn neighborhood he previously called home. By working everywhere from a bar and a ballpark to a primate lab and a transient hotel, Espada put himself through college, graduating from the University of Wisconsin–Madison with a BA in history, with a focus on Latin America. After earning a law degree at Northeastern University, in Boston, he went to work as a lawyer, specializing first in bilingual education, later in housing law. From age twenty, however, Espada was also writing poetry, inspired initially by a family friend's gift of both an anthology of Latin American revolutionary poetry and the prediction that "Tri tambien seras poeta" ("You will also become a poet"). Featuring barrio photos taken by his father, a community activist, Espada's first collection, *The Immigrant Iceboy's Bolero*, appeared in 1982. But it was his third, prize-winning book, *Rebellion Is the Circle of a Lover's Hand* (1990), that led the *New York Times* to predict he would be "the Latino poet of his generation." In the years since, Espada has done much to earn that title, securing a professorship at the University of Massachusetts–Amherst (in 1993) and publishing not only poetry collections ranging from *City of Coughing and Dead Radiators* (1993) to *The Republic of Poetry* (2006, a finalist for the Pulitzer) but also books of essays including *Zapata's Disciple* (1998), anthologies of Latino and Chicano poetry, and translations. What drives all that work, says Espada, is the same commitment he had as a lawyer: "to speak on behalf of" all those who lack not the ability but the "opportunity" to "speak for themselves."

ROBERT FROST (1874–1963)

Though his poetry identifies Frost with rural New England, he was born and lived to the age of eleven in San Francisco. Moving to New England after his father's death, Frost studied classics in high school, entered and dropped out of both Dartmouth and Harvard, and spent difficult years as an unrecognized poet before his first book, *A Boy's Will* (1913), was accepted and published in England. Frost's character was full of contradiction—he held "that we get forward as much by hating as by loving"—yet by the end of his long life he was one of the most honored poets of his time, as well as the most widely read. In 1961, two years before his death, he was invited to read a poem at John F. Kennedy's presidential inauguration ceremony. Frost's poems—masterfully crafted, sometimes deceptively simple—are collected in *The Poetry of Robert Frost* (1969).

ALLEN GINSBERG (1926–97)

After a childhood in Paterson, New Jersey, overshadowed by his mother's mental illness, Allen Ginsberg enrolled at Columbia University, intent upon following his father's advice and becoming a labor lawyer. At the center of a circle that included

Lucien Carr, Jack Kerouac, William S. Burroughs, and Neal Cassady, Ginsberg became interested in experimental poetry and alternative lifestyles. He graduated in 1948 and then joined the literary scene in San Francisco. In 1956, he published *Howl and Other Poems,* with an introduction by his mentor William Carlos Williams. The title poem, which condemned bourgeois culture and celebrated the emerging counterculture, became a manifesto for the Beat movement and catapulted Ginsberg to fame. Deeply involved in radical politics and Eastern spiritualism, Ginsberg went on to write such prose works as *Declaration of Independence for Dr. Timothy Leary* (1971) in addition to many volumes of poetry.

ANGELINA GRIMKÉ (1880–1958)

Born in Boston, Angelina Grimké was the descendent of black slaves, white slaveholders, free blacks, and prominent white abolitionists, including her namesake, Angelina Weld Grimké. As a child, Angelina was abandoned by her white mother, whose middle-class family disapproved of her marriage to Archibald Grimké, a biracial lawyer and author who eventually became vice president of the NAACP. Grimké graduated from the Boston Normal School of Gymnastics in 1902 and then moved with her father to Washington, D.C., where she worked as a teacher and began to write poetry, essays, short stories, and plays. By the 1920s, she was publishing her work in the leading journals and anthologies of the Harlem Renaissance—*The Crisis, Opportunity,* Alain Locke's *The New Negro* (1925), Countee Cullen's *Caroling Dusk* (1927), and Robert Kerlin's *Negro Poets and Their Poems* (1928). Much of her finest writing can be found in *Selected Works of Angelina Weld Grimké* (1991).

THOMAS HARDY (1840–1928)

Thanks to the series of much-lauded novels that ended with *Jude the Obscure* (1895) and the many poetry collections that followed his 1898 *Wessex Poems,* Thomas Hardy is today regarded as both one of the greatest novelists of the nineteenth century and one of the greatest poets of the twentieth. Believing that "the best and greatest among mankind are those who do themselves no worldly good," Hardy took pride in producing fiction that flouted nineteenth-century conventions, treating sexual, social, and religious topics with a candor few authors dared match. Yet Hardy's novels did bring him "worldly good," ensuring him a rise in social status of a sort rare outside of fiction. Raised in a small town in that area of rural Dorset, England, he would later immortalize as "Wessex," Hardy was a stonemason's son who walked six miles back and forth to school every day from age ten to sixteen, dreaming of attending university and becoming a clergyman. Unable to afford that, Hardy was instead apprenticed to an architect in 1856, giving up that profession for full-time writing only in 1874, following the publication of his fifth novel, *Far from the Madding Crowd.* Though Hardy often blamed a squeamish reading public and publishing industry for his choice to abandon fiction for poetry in midcareer, he also seems to have envisioned poetry as a fitter, freer medium in which to explore the questions—particularly about fate, free will, and "the Supreme Mover or Movers"—sparked by both the scientific discoveries of his day and his keen awareness of human suffering and injustice. Awarded the Order of Merit by King Edward VII in 1910, the former stonemason's son received upon his death one of his nation's highest honors when his ashes were buried in Poets' Corner at Westminster Abbey.

ROBERT HAYDEN (1913–80)

Born in a Detroit ghetto, Asa Sheffey became "Robert Hayden" at eighteen months, when he was unofficially adopted by the neighbors who would raise him and whom he would remember in poems such as "Those Winter Sundays." Inspired by the Harlem Renaissance writers he discovered as a teenager, Hayden published his first poem in 1931. Severely nearsighted, he attended Detroit City College (1932–36), thanks only to state rehabilitation grants, and worked for the Federal Writers Project (1936–39), before studying with W. H. Auden at the University of Michigan (MA, 1944). Becoming "a poet who teaches [. . .] so that he can write a poem or two now and then," Hayden held professorships at historically black Fisk University (1946–69) and at the University of Michigan (1969–80). International acclaim came late: In 1966, Langston Hughes and seven other judges unanimously awarded Hayden the Grand Prize for Poetry at the First World Festival of Negro Arts in Senegal, and in 1976 he became the first African American appointed to the post now known as U.S. Poet Laureate.

Like his masterpiece "Middle Passage" (1962), much of Hayden's poetry aims, he said, to "correct the distortions of Afro-American history." Yet he passionately insisted that he was not a "black artist" but an American one. Today he is widely and rightly regarded as among the very best of both.

TERRANCE HAYES (b. 1971)

Born in Columbia, South Carolina, Terrence Hayes attended Coker College on a basketball scholarship, shifting his attention to poetry only in his senior year and going on to earn an MFA from the University of Pittsburgh (1997). His first book of poetry, *Muscular Music* (1999), is an exploration of popular culture's impact on African American identity and notions of masculinity, and was followed by *Hip Logic* (2002), a National Poetry Series winner, and *Wind in a Box* (2006), listed by *Publishers Weekly* as one of the top 100 books of 2006. Characterized as "an elegant and adventurous writer" whose work deftly combines humor and sincerity, Hayes has garnered numerous honors and awards for his work, including a National Book Award for his fourth collection, *Lighthead* (2010), three Best American Poetry selections, a Pushcart Prize, and a MacArthur Fellowship. Though he is continually drawn to themes of identity, masculinity, race, culture, and community, he "aspire[s] to a poetic style that resists style"; and indeed, his collections contain poetic forms that range from pecha kucha, a format for Japanese business presentations, to Dante's terza rima, and adopt the voices of poets from Amiri Baraka to Dr. Seuss. Hayes teaches creative writing at the University of Pittsburgh, where he lives with his wife and fellow poet Yona Harvey and their children.

SEAMUS HEANEY (1939–2013)

Considered "the most important Irish poet since Yeats," 1995 Nobel Prize–winner Seamus Heaney grew up with his eight siblings on Mossbawm Farm in rural County Derry, Northern Ireland. At twelve, however, scholarships took Heaney first to St. Columb's College and then Queen's University, Belfast, where he studied Irish, Latin, and Old English. Here, too, he discovered the poetry of authors such as Ted Hughes, Patrick Kavanagh, and Robert Frost, which, he said, first taught him to "trust" in the value of that "local" childhood experience that he once "considered archaic and irrelevant to 'the modern world.'" Rural life and labor, as well as the relationship between past and present, the "archaic" and the "modern," loom large from his earliest collection, *Death of a Naturalist* (1966), to much later ones such as *District and Circle* (2006). Most famous, perhaps, is *North* (1975), especially its sequence of poems inspired by both the ancient, yet somehow ageless, corpses discovered in Irish and Scandinavian bogs, and also by the increasingly violent conflict between Protestants and Catholics in Northern Ireland. Having earned virtually all of the highest honors that a contemporary poet could, Heaney also won acclaim both as a versatile and creative translator, most famously of *Beowulf* (2000) and *Antigone* (*The Burial at Thebes*, 2004), and as an essayist; his *Finders Keepers: Selected Prose, 1971–2001* (2002) won the Truman Capote Award for Literary Criticism, the largest annual prize of its kind. After teaching at Harvard from 1985 until 2006, Heaney lived in Dublin until his death.

GERARD MANLEY HOPKINS (1844–89)

Born the eldest of eight children of a marine-insurance adjuster and his wife, Gerard Manley Hopkins attended Oxford, where his ambition was to become a painter—until, at the age of twenty-two, he converted to Roman Catholicism and burned all his early poetry as too worldly. Not until after his seminary training and ordination as a Jesuit priest, in 1877, did he resume writing poetry, though he made few attempts to publish his verse, which many of his contemporaries found nearly incomprehensible. Near the end of his life, Hopkins was appointed professor of Greek at University College, Dublin, where—out of place, deeply depressed, and all but unknown—he died of typhoid. His poetry, collected and published by his friends, has been championed by modern poets, who admire its controlled tension, strong rhythm, and sheer exuberance.

LANGSTON HUGHES (1902–67)

Born in Joplin, Missouri, Langston Hughes was raised mainly by his maternal grandmother, though he lived intermittently with each of his parents. He studied at Columbia University but left to travel and work at a variety of jobs. Having already published poems in periodicals, anthologies, and his own first collection, *The Weary Blues* (1926), he graduated from Lincoln University; published a successful novel, *Not without Laughter* (1930); and became a major writer in the Harlem Renaissance. During the 1930s, he became involved in radical politics and traveled the world as a correspondent and columnist; during the 1950s, though, the FBI classified him as a security risk and limited his ability to travel. In addition to poems and novels, he wrote essays, plays, screenplays, and an autobiography; he also edited anthologies of literature and folklore.

JOHN KEATS (1795–1821)

Because John Keats was the son of a London livery stable owner and his wife, reviewers would later disparage him as a working-class "Cockney poet." At fifteen he was apprenticed to a surgeon, and at twenty-one he became a licensed pharmacist—in the same year that his first two published poems, including the sonnet "On First Looking into Chapman's Homer," appeared in *The Examiner*, a journal edited by the critic and poet Leigh Hunt. Hunt introduced Keats to such literary figures as the poet Percy Bysshe Shelley and helped him publish his *Poems by John Keats* (1817). When his second book, the long poem *Endymion* (1818), was fiercely attacked by critics, Keats, suffering from a steadily worsening case of tuberculosis, knew that he would not live to realize his poetic promise. In July 1820, he published *Lamia, Isabella, The Eve of St. Agnes; and Other Poems*, which contained the poignant "To Autumn" and three other great odes: "Ode on a Grecian Urn," "Ode on Melancholy," and "Ode to a Nightingale"; early the next year, he died in Rome. In the years after Keats's death, his letters became almost as famous as his poetry.

ETHERIDGE KNIGHT (1931–91)

A native of Corinth, Mississippi, Etheridge Knight spent much of his adolescence carousing in pool halls, bars, and juke joints, developing a skillful oratorical style in an environment that prized verbal agility. During this time, he also became addicted to narcotics. He served in the U.S. Army from 1947 to 1951; in 1960 he was sentenced to eight years in prison for robbery. At the Indiana State Prison in Michigan City, he began to write poetry and in 1968 published his first collection, *Poems from Prison*. After his release, Knight joined the Black Arts movement, taught at a number of universities, and published works including *Black Voices from Prison* (1970), *Belly Song and Other Poems* (1973), and *Born of a Woman* (1980).

YUSEF KOMUNYAKAA (b. 1947)

The first African American man to win a Pulitzer Prize for Poetry, Yusef Komunyakaa once described his life and work as a "process" of "healing" from "two places." The first was Bogalusa, Louisiana—the segregated rural mill town where James Willie Brown, Jr., grew up, learning "the importance of music and metaphor" from the Bible and the family radio, "the value of tools" and "precision" from a carpenter father unable to read or write. The second was Vietnam, where twenty-one-year-old Komunyakaa—who eventually adopted the surname his great-grandparents gave up when they emigrated from Trinidad—earned a Bronze Star for meritorious wartime service. While pursuing a BA (University of Colorado, 1975), an MA (Colorado State, 1979), and an MFA (University of California, Irvine, 1980), Komunyakaa began to turn the first of these places into poetry, initially gaining recognition with the jazz- and blues-inflected collection *Copacetic* (1984). National acclaim came with *Dien Cai Dau* (1988), the book in which, twenty years after the fact, the poet finally, in his own words, stopped "writing around the war." In the years since, Komunyakaa's numerous collections have garnered him some of poetry's highest honors, including a Pulitzer (for *Neon Vernacular: New & Selected Poems 1977–1989* [1994]), the Ruth Lilly Poetry Prize (2001), and the Wallace Stevens Award (2011). Today Global Distinguished Professor of English at New York University, Komunyakaa is also the editor of two jazz poetry anthologies; cotranslator (with Martha Collins) of Vietnamese poet Nguyen Quan Thieu's *The Insomnia of Fire* (1995); and author of *Blues Notes: Essays, Interviews & Commentaries* (2000) and, with Chad Gracia, of *Gilgamesh: A Verse Play* (2006).

PHILIP LARKIN (1922–85)

Postwar England's most widely known and popular poet, so-called laureate of the common man Philip Larkin endured what he later described as a boring childhood as the second, belated, rather shy—because also nearsighted and stuttering—child of Coventry's city treasurer. Exempted from service in World War II because of his eyesight, Larkin graduated from Oxford in 1943 and became a librarian, mainly at Hull, where he headed the university library for thirty years (1955–85). Larkin credited his rediscovery of Thomas Hardy's poetry with "cur[ing]" him of the Yeatsian "Celtic fever" of his first collection, *The North Ship* (1945), and helping him to develop the mature style debuted in his second, *The Less Deceived* (1955). This critically acclaimed book made Larkin the undisputed leading light of "the Movement," a group of young poets who rejected the enigmatic, allusive, and—in their eyes—elitist modernism of T. S. Eliot and Ezra Pound in favor of a more straightforward and robust, if also skeptical and ironic, style. Notoriously publicity-averse, Larkin declined the position of Poet Laureate of the United Kingdom just a year before his death. In his lifetime, he published only two other volumes of verse, *The Whitsun Weddings* (1964) and *High Windows* (1974); two novels, *Jill* (1946) and *A Girl in Winter* (1947); *All What Jazz* (1970), a collection of jazz reviews originally written for the *Daily Telegraph*; and the best-selling *Required Writing: Miscellaneous Pieces 1955–1982* (1983). Since his death, Larkin has become a more controversial figure, thanks less to the previously unpublished work included in *Collected Poems* (1988) than to the publication of both his *Selected Letters* (1992) and Andrew Motion's revealing biography, *Philip Larkin: A Writer's Life* (1993).

ANDREW MARVELL (1621–78)

The son of a clergyman and his wife, Andrew Marvell was born in Yorkshire, England, and educated at Trinity College, Cambridge. There is no evidence that he fought in the English Civil War, which broke out in 1642, but his poem "An Horatian Ode upon Cromwell's Return from Ireland" appeared in 1650, shortly after the beheading of King Charles I in 1649, and may represent straightforward praise of England's new Puritan leader. Some regard it as strong satire, however—Marvell was known in his day for his satirical prose and verse. Today he is better known for lyric poems such as "To His Coy Mistress," which he probably wrote while serving as tutor to a Yorkshire nobleman's daughter. In 1657, on the recommendation of John Milton, Marvell accepted a position in Cromwell's government that he held until his election to Parliament in 1659. After helping restore the monarchy in 1660, he continued to write and to serve as a member of Parliament until the end of his life.

CLAUDE MCKAY (1889–1948)

Festus Claudius McKay was born and raised in Sunny Ville, Clarendon Parish, Jamaica, the youngest of eleven children. He worked as a wheelwright and cabinetmaker, then briefly as a police constable, before writing and publishing two books of poetry in Jamaican dialect. In 1912, he emigrated to the United States, where he attended Booker T. Washington's Tuskegee Institute in Alabama and studied agricultural science at Kansas State College before moving to New York City. McKay supported himself through various jobs while becoming a prominent literary and political figure. The oldest Harlem Renaissance writer, McKay was also the first to publish, with the poetry collection *Harlem Shadows* (1922). His other works include the novels *Home to Harlem* (1928) and *Banana Bottom* (1933) and his autobiography, *A Long Way from Home* (1937).

EDNA ST. VINCENT MILLAY (1892–1950)

Born in Rockland, Maine, Edna St. Vincent Millay published her first poem at twenty, her first poetry collection at twenty-five. After graduating from Vassar College, she moved to New York City's Greenwich Village, where she both gained a reputation as a brilliant poet and became notorious for her bohemian life and her association with prominent artists, writers, and radicals. In 1923, she won the Pulitzer Prize for her collection *The Ballad of the Harp-Weaver*; in 1925, growing weary of fame, she and her husband moved to Austerlitz, New York, where she lived for the rest of her life. Although her work fell out of favor with mid-twentieth-century Modernists, who rejected her formalism as old-fashioned, her poetry—witty, acerbic, and superbly crafted—has found many new admirers today.

JOHN MILTON (1608–74)

Born in London, the elder son of a self-made businessman and his wife, John Milton exhibited unusual literary and scholarly gifts at an early age; before entering Cambridge University, he was adept at Latin and Greek and was well on his way to mastering Hebrew and numerous European languages. After graduation, he devoted six more years to intense study and composed, among other works, his great pastoral elegy, "Lycidas" (1637). After a year of travel in Europe, Milton return to England and found his country embroiled in religious strife and civil war. Milton took up the Puritan cause and, in 1641, began writing pamphlets defending everything from free speech to Cromwell's execution of Charles I; Milton also served as Cromwell's Latin secretary until, in 1651, he lost his sight. After the monarchy was restored in 1660, Milton was briefly imprisoned, and his property confiscated. Blind, impoverished, and isolated, he devoted himself to the great spiritual epics of his later years: *Paradise Lost* (1667), *Paradise Regained* (1671), and *Samson Agonistes* (1671).

PAT MORA (b. 1942)

Born to Mexican American parents in El Paso, Texas, Pat Mora earned a BA and an MA from the University of Texas at El Paso. She has been a consultant on U.S.-Mexico youth exchanges; a museum director and administrator at her alma mater; and a teacher of English at all levels. Her poetry—collected in *Chants* (1985), *Borders* (1986), *Communion* (1991), *Agua Santa* (1995), *Aunt Carmen's Book of Practical Saints* (1997), and *Adobe Odes* (2006)—reflects and addresses her Chicana and southwestern background. Mora's other publications include *Nepantla: Essays from the Land in the Middle* (1993); a family memoir, *House of Houses* (1997); and many works for children and young adults.

SHARON OLDS (b. 1942)

Born in San Francisco; raised in Berkeley by fiercely religious, yet troubled parents; and educated at Stanford (BA, 1964) and Columbia (PhD, 1972) universities (where she wrote a dissertation on Ralph Waldo Emerson), poet Sharon Olds was thirty-seven when she published her first book of poetry, *Satan Says*, in 1981. Since then, she has come to rank as one of America's most important living poets, garnering National Book Critics' Circle Awards both for her 1984 collection *The Dead and the Living* and for *Strike Spark: Selected Poems* (2002). In 2013, she became the first woman to win the T.S. Eliot Prize for Poetry, for *Stag's Leap*, a collection that also earned a Pulitzer. Like the work of two writers to whom Olds is often compared, Walt Whitman and Sylvia Plath, however, hers has consistently provoked controversy, thanks mainly to its unflinching attention to, and distinctly female perspective on, the pleasures and pains of both the human body and the family, as well as emotional and literal violence. *The Dead and the Living* is divided between "Poems for the Living," about the poet's experience as daughter and mother, and "Poems for the Dead," about the victims of international conflicts; *The Father* (1992) chronicles her father's death (from cancer), *One Secret Thing* (2008), her mother's. *Stag's Leap* (2013) deals with the disintegration of her 32-year marriage. As famous for her reticence off the page as for her candor on it, Olds teaches creative writing both at New York University and in a program for the severely disabled that she founded at NYU's Goldwater Hospital.

WILFRED OWEN (1893–1918)

Born in Oswestry, Shropshire, England, Wilfred Owen left school in 1911, having failed to win a scholarship to London University. He served as assistant to a vicar in Oxfordshire until 1913, when he left to teach English at a Berlitz school in Bordeaux. In 1915, Owen returned to England to enlist in the army and was sent to the front lines in France. Suffering from shell shock two years later, he was evacuated to Craiglockhart War Hospital, where he met the poets Siegfried Sassoon and Robert Graves. Five of Owen's poems were published in 1918, the year he returned to combat; he was killed one week before the signing of the armistice. His poems, which portray the horror of trench warfare and satirize the unthinking patriotism of those who cheered the war from their armchairs, are collected in the two-volume *Complete Poems and Fragments* (1983).

DOROTHY PARKER (1893–1967)

Born in West End, New Jersey, Dorothy Rothschild worked for both *Vogue* and *Vanity Fair* magazines before becoming a freelance writer. In 1917, she married Edwin Pond Parker II, whom she divorced in 1928. Her first book of verse, *Enough Rope* (1926), was a best-seller and was followed by *Sunset Gun* (1928), *Death and Taxes* (1931), and *Collected Poems: Not So Deep as a Well* (1936). In 1927, Parker became a book reviewer for the *New Yorker*, to which she contributed for most of her career. In 1933, Parker and her second husband, Alan Campbell, moved to Hollywood, where they collaborated as film writers. In addition, Parker wrote criticism, two plays, short stories, and news reports from the Spanish Civil War. She is probably best remembered, though, as the reigning wit at the "Round Table" at Manhattan's Algonquin Hotel, where, in the 1920s and '30s, she traded barbs with other prominent writers and humorists.

LINDA PASTAN (b. 1932)

Linda Pastan was born in New York City and raised in nearby Westchester County. After graduating from Radcliffe College, she received an MA in literature from Brandeis University. Although her first published poems appeared in *Mademoiselle* in 1955, Pastan spent many years concentrating on her husband and three children—indeed, much of her poetry deals with her own family life. Her many collections include *A Perfect Circle of Sun* (1971), *The Five Stages of Grief* (1978), American Book Award nominee *PM/AM: New and Selected Poems* (1982), *Carnival Evening: New and Selected Poems 1968–1998* (1998), *Queen of a Rainy Country* (2006), and *Traveling Light* (2011). She lives in Potomac, Maryland.

SYLVIA PLATH (1932–63)

Sylvia Plath was born in Boston; her father, a Polish immigrant, died when she was eight. After graduating from Smith College, Plath attended Cambridge University on a Fulbright scholarship, and there she met and married the poet Ted Hughes, with whom she had two children. As she documented in her novel *The Bell Jar* (1963), in 1953—between her junior and senior years of college—Plath became seriously depressed, attempted suicide, and was hospitalized. In 1963, the breakup of her marriage led to another suicide attempt, this time successful. Plath has attained cult status as much for her poems as for her "martyrdom" to art and life. In addition to her first volume of poetry, *The Colossus* (1960), Plath's work has been collected in *Ariel* (1966), *Crossing the Water* (1971), and *Winter Trees* (1972). Her selected letters were published in 1975; her expurgated journals in 1983; and her unabridged journals in 2000.

ALEXANDER POPE (1688–1744)

Son of a wealthy merchant, London-born Alexander Pope managed to become the greatest poet of his age, one of the most accomplished versifiers and satirists in English literary history, and the first British writer to make his living entirely by his pen despite—or, rather, thanks to—two obvious handicaps. One, tuberculosis of the spine, contracted in infancy, ensured that Pope was, in the words of his contemporaries, only "about four feet six high; very humpbacked and deformed," plagued with "the headache four days in a week, and [. . .] sick [. . .] the other three." Two, as a Roman Catholic, Pope was legally debarred from voting or holding public office, inheriting or purchasing land, living within ten miles of London, or attending any of England's so-called public schools or universities. Largely self-taught and unable to rely on patronage, the pugnacious, politically conservative Pope launched his career with poems celebrating natural beauty and love (*Pastorals* [1709] and *Windsor Forest* [1713]) but leapt to fame with two book-length poems in a very different spirit—the didactic *An Essay on Criticism* (1711) and the brilliant mock epic *The Rape of the Lock* (1712, 1714). Made wealthy by his monumental translations of Homer's *Iliad* (1720) and *Odyssey* (1726), Pope retired to a five-acre villa in Twickenham, outside London. By the time of his death at age fifty-six, he had produced an unrivalled body of work that includes at least two other masterpieces, the merciless satire *The Dunciad* (1728) and the philosophical verse-treatise *An Essay on Man* (1734).

EZRA POUND (1885–1972)

Born in Hailey, Idaho, Ezra Pound studied at the University of Pennsylvania and Hamilton College before traveling to Europe in 1908. He remained there, living in Ireland, England, France, and Italy, for much of his life. Pound's tremendous ambition—to succeed in his own work and to influence the development of poetry and Western culture in general—led him to found the Imagist school of poetry, to advise and assist many great writers (Eliot, Joyce, Williams, Frost, and Hemingway, to name a few), and to write a number of highly influential critical works. His increasingly fiery and erratic behavior led to a charge of treason (he served as a propagandist for Italian Fascist Beni Mussolini during World War II), a diagnosis of insanity, and twelve years at St. Elizabeth's, an institution for the criminally insane.

ADRIENNE RICH (1929–2012)

Easily one of the foremost poets and public intellectuals of her time, Adrienne Rich was born in Baltimore, Maryland, daughter of a former concert pianist and of a renowned Johns Hopkins University pathologist. Rich's career as a poet began in 1951, when the Radcliffe College senior's first volume, *A Change of World* (1951), was selected by W. H. Auden for the prestigious Yale Younger Poets Award. Two years later, Rich married Harvard economist Alfred Conrad, with whom she had three children. As the 1950s gave way to the 1960s and '70s, Rich's life and work changed profoundly. Beginning with her 1963 collection, *Snapshots of a Daughter-in-Law*, her poetry became ever less tightly controlled and formal, as it became ever more politically and personally charged, reflecting her deep engagement with the feminist, antiwar, and civil rights movements. After her recently estranged husband's suicide (1970) and publication of the National Book Award–winning *Diving into the Wreck* (1974), Rich began a lifelong partnership with Jamaica-born novelist and editor Michelle Cliff and published her two most influential prose works, *Of Woman Born: Motherhood as Experience and Institution* (1976) and *On Lies, Secrets and Silence* (1979), which includes her landmark essay "Compulsory Heterosexuality and Lesbian Existence." In the decades that followed, Rich never rested on her countless laurels, fiercely pursuing both her craft and her campaign for social justice. Her thirtieth and last volume of verse, *Tonight No Poetry Will Serve*, came out in 2010, just two years before her death, at age eighty-two, from the rheumatoid arthritis she had battled for decades. In its obituary, the *New York Times* aptly dubbed her "a poet of towering reputation," whose work is "distinguished by an unswerving progressive vision and a dazzling, empathetic ferocity."

THEODORE ROETHKE (1908–1963)

Born in Saginaw, Michigan, Theodore Roethke grew up around his father's twenty-five-acre greenhouse complex; plants and their associations with nurture and growth were an important subject in his later poetry. He worked for a time at Lafayette College, where he was professor of English and tennis coach, and later at the University of Washington, which appointed him poet-in-residence one year before he died. Roethke suffered from periodic mental breakdowns, yet the best of his poetry, with its reverence for and fear of the physical world, seems destined to last. His books include *Open House* (1942); *Praise to the End!* (1951); *The Far Field* (1964), which received a posthumous National Book Award; and *Collected Poems* (1966).

CHRISTINA ROSSETTI (1830–94)

Ranking with Emily Dickinson and Elizabeth Barrett Browning as among the nineteenth century's most important women poets, Christina Rossetti spent her outwardly uneventful life in London, part of a uniquely talented family. Her father, an Italian political exile, was a poet, Dante scholar, and Italian professor, her mother an Anglo-Italian former governess. Rossetti's older sister and youngest brother ultimately became distinguished literature and art critics, and her eldest brother, Dante Gabriel, an influential painter-poet. According to her brother, Christina composed her first poem before she was old enough to write and was, as a girl, so extraordinarily "vivacious, and open to pleasurable impressions" that everyone expected her to "develop into a woman [. . .] fond of society and diversions, and taking a part in them of more than average brilliancy." Yet "[w]hat came to pass was [. . .] quite the contrary." In the 1840s, the illness and virtual blindness of the teenaged Rossetti's father rendered her family's financial situation precarious; her own health broke down, and she became much more devout. For the rest of her life, Rossetti battled illness and what she saw as sin in equal measure. Seeking to adhere strictly to her Protestant faith, she refused to marry any of her various suitors, eschewed once-loved "diversions" such as opera, and undertook volunteer work, including ten years at the St. Mary Magdalene Penitentiary, a charitable institution dedicated to the reform of so-called fallen or ruined women. All the while, however, Rossetti kept writing and publishing, producing a remarkable body of poetry including lyrics, devotional verse, narrative fables, and ballads. Her first and best-known book, *Goblin Market and Other Poems*, appeared in 1862.

KAY RYAN (b. 1945)

Described by fellow poet J. D. McClatchy as "compact, exhilarating, strange affairs" full of sly wordplay and wit, Kay Ryan's poems are often compared to Emily Dickinson's. Like Dickinson, says Jack Foley, "Ryan can certainly be funny, but it is rarely without a sting." Typically fewer than twenty lines long and with lines often containing six syllables or less, Ryan's poems tend to have what she calls "the most dangerous shape," one in which "nearly every word is on one edge or the other" and "you can't hide anything" because "Any crap is going to show." U.S. Poet Laureate from 2008 to 2010 and winner of the 2011 Pulitzer Prize for Poetry, Ryan earned such accolades the hard way. Raised in California's Mojave Desert and San Joaquin Valley by her oil-well-driller father and once rejected from the poetry club at UCLA, where she earned both BA (1967) and MA (1968) degrees in English, Ryan began teaching remedial English at the College of Marin in 1971, receiving widespread recognition for her poetry only some twenty years later. "All of us want instant success," she has said, "I'm glad I was on a sort of slow drip." This "drip" has produced over seven volumes, including *Say Uncle* (2000) and *The Best of It: New and Selected Poems* (2010). In 2009 Ryan was widowed by the death of Carol Adair, her partner of over thirty years. Although she is sometimes accused of being too apolitical by members of the gay community, Ryan's 30-plus years at Marin have made her a strong and vocal advocate of what she describes as America's "much underpraised and underfunded community colleges."

WILLIAM SHAKESPEARE (1554–1616)

Considering the great fame of his work, surprisingly little is known of William Shakespeare's life. Between 1585 and 1592, he left his birthplace of Stratford-upon-Avon for London to begin a career as playwright and actor. No dates of his professional career are recorded, however, nor can the order in which he composed his plays and poems be determined with any certainty. By 1594, he had established himself as a poet with two long works—*Venus and Adonis* and *The Rape of Lucrece*—and his more than 150 sonnets are supreme expressions of the form. His reputation, though, rests on the works he wrote for the theater. Shakespeare produced perhaps thirty-five plays in twenty-five years, proving himself a master of every dramatic genre: tragedy (in works such as *Macbeth, Hamlet, King Lear,* and *Othello*); historical drama (for example, *Richard III* and *Henry IV*); comedy (*Twelfth Night, As You Like It,* and many more); and romance (in plays such as *The Tempest* and *Cymbaline*). Without question, Shakespeare is the most quoted, discussed, and beloved English writer.

PERCY BYSSHE SHELLEY (1792–1822)

A baronet's eldest son, Percy Shelley was born into wealth and privilege, ostensibly destined to inherit his family's considerable estate and a seat in Parliament. Instead, he became an outspoken radical, exile, and poet, ranking alongside Blake, Coleridge, Wordsworth, and his friends Byron and Keats as among the most famous and influential of the so-called Romantics. A graduate of Eton, Shelley lasted less than a year at Oxford, expelled from the university and permanently estranged from his family for coauthoring an atheistic pamphlet whose principles he refused to renounce. Three years later, the already-married Shelley fell in love and eloped to Europe with Mary Wollstonecraft Godwin—the seventeen-year-old daughter of Shelley's friend and mentor, the radical philosopher William Godwin, and Godwin's late wife, Mary Wollstonecraft (author of *A Vindication of the Rights of Woman* [1892]). Married in 1816, after the suicide of his first wife, Percy and Mary Shelley (author of *Frankenstein; or the Modern Prometheus* [1818]) would live mostly abroad until 1822, when Shelley—just twenty-nine—drowned in a boating accident. The remarkable body of work he left behind includes not only impassioned lyrics like "Ode to the West Wind" but also lengthy narrative poems such as *Alastor; or the Spirit of Solitude* (1814), *Prometheus Unbound* (1820), and his memorable elegy of Keats, *Adonais* (1821). A publishing career that in fact began with two Gothic novels (*Zastrozzi* [1810] and *St. Irvyne* [1811]) effectively ended, moreover, with the posthumous publication of the highly influential essay "A Defence of Poetry" (1840), in which Shelley famously describes poets as both "nightingale[s], who si[t] in darkness and sin[g] to cheer [their] own solitude" and—as "the trumpets which sing to battle, and feel not what they inspire; the influence which is moved not, but moves"—"the unacknowledged legislators of the world."

WALLACE STEVENS (1879–1955)

Born and raised in Reading, Pennsylvania, Wallace Stevens attended Harvard University and New York Law School. In New York City, he worked for a number of law firms, published poems in magazines, and befriended such literary figures as William Carlos Williams and Marianne Moore. In 1916, Stevens moved to Connecticut and began working for the Hartford Accident and Indemnity Company, where he became a vice president in 1934 and where he worked for the rest of his life, writing poetry at night and during vacations. He published his first collection, *Harmonium*, in 1923 and followed it with a series of volumes from 1935 until 1950, establishing himself as one of the twentieth century's most important poets. His lectures were collected in *The Necessary Angel: Essays on Reality and Imagination* (1951); his *Collected Poems* appeared in 1954.

ADRIENNE SU (b. 1967)

Adrienne Su grew up in Atlanta, Georgia, unaware, she says, of the ironies involved in being "viewed as Chinese," while "I knew no Chinese and thrived on the study of Latin." A graduate of Harvard and the University of Virginia, where she studied with Rita Dove, Gregory Orr, and Charles Wright, Su, by her own account, "started writing as soon as I could form a sentence on paper" and "started sending out work" while still in high school. Having worked as a freelance editor and writer, Su is today an associate professor of English and Poet-in-Residence at Pennsylvania's Dickinson College; a wife and mother; and the author of three poetry collections, *Middle Kingdom* (1997), *Sanctuary* (2006), and *Having None of It* (2009). Crediting her high-school Latin teacher and the ancient Roman poet Virgil with first teaching her the art of meter, and her early involvement in poetry slams with bolstering her commitment to writing "poems that on some levels can be read by anyone," Su also, in her words, "prefer[s] the daily to the exotic as subject matter," seeing writing as best when "it's woven into every life, as a ritual that fits somewhere between making pancakes for my kids and preparing a class for college students."

ALFRED, LORD TENNYSON (1809–92)

Certainly the most popular and perhaps the most important of the Victorian poets, Alfred, Lord Tennyson demonstrated his talents at an early age; he published his first volume in 1827. Encouraged to devote his life to poetry by a group of undergraduates at Cambridge University known as the "Apostles," Tennyson was particularly close to Arthur Hallam, whose sudden death in 1833 inspired the long elegy *In Memoriam* (1850). With that poem he achieved lasting fame and recognition; he was appointed Poet Laureate the year of its publication, succeeding Wordsworth. Despite the great popularity of his "journalistic" poems—"The Charge of the Light Brigade" (1854) is perhaps the best known—Tennyson's great theme was the past, both personal (*In the Valley of Cauteretz*, 1864) and national (*Idylls of the King*, 1869). Tennyson was made a baron in 1884; when he died, eight years later, he was buried in Poets' Corner in London's Westminster Abbey.

NATASHA TRETHEWEY (b. 1966)

Daughter of a social worker and a Canadian poet who met at a Kentucky college, but had to marry in Ohio because of laws banning interracial unions, Natasha Trethewey was born in her mother's hometown of Gulfport, Mississippi. After her parents' divorce, she lived with her mother in Atlanta, summering on the Gulf Coast with both her father and her mother's family. In 1985, Trethewey was just beginning her studies at the University of Georgia when her stepfather murdered her mother. Turning to poetry to deal with her grief, Trethewey earned her BA in 1989; an MA from Virginia's Hollins College, where her father was a professor (1991); and an MFA from the University of Massachusetts at Amherst (1995). After a short stint teaching at Auburn University, Trethewey moved to Emory and, in 2007, became only the fourth African

American poet ever to win the Pulitzer Prize, for *Native Guard*. Her third collection, it explores the problem of individual and collective historical amnesia through elegies to her mother and a ten-sonnet sequence written from the perspective of a soldier in the first all-black regiment to fight on the Union side in the Civil War. The years 2007–08, however, also brought Trethewey loss and hardship when her brother was imprisoned on drug-related charges and her beloved grandmother died. Interweaving poetry, essays, and letters, her memoir *Beyond Katrina: A Meditation on the Mississippi Gulf Coast* (2010) reflects on both the region and her family's efforts to remember and rebuild.

WALT WHITMAN (1819–92)

Walt Whitman was born on a farm in West Hills, Long Island, to a British father and a Dutch mother. After working as a journalist throughout New York for many years, he taught for a time and founded his own newspaper, *The Long Islander*, in 1838; he then left journalism to work on *Leaves of Grass*, originally intended as a poetic treatise on American democratic idealism. Published privately in multiple editions from 1855 to 1874, the book of poems at first failed to reach a mass audience. In 1881, Boston's Osgood and Company published another edition of *Leaves of Grass*, which sold well until the district attorney called it "obscene literature" and stipulated that Whitman remove certain poems and phrases. He refused, and it was many years before his works were again published, this time in Philadelphia. By the time Whitman died, his work was revered, as it still is today, for its greatness of spirit and its exuberant American voice.

RICHARD WILBUR (b. 1921)

The son of a painter and a newspaperman's daughter, former U.S. Poet Laureate Richard Wilbur was raised in rural New Jersey, a background that may help to explain his precise imagery and keen interest in nature. Graduating from Amherst College into a world at war, Wilbur in 1942 married the woman who would remain his wife for over sixty years, joined the army, and, by his own account, began to "versify in earnest" because "One does not use poetry [. . .] as a means to organize oneself and the world, until one's world somehow gets out of hand." The many collections Wilbur published between his first, *The Beautiful Changes and Other Poems* (1947), and *Anterooms: New Poems and Translations* (2010) include two Pulitzer Prize winners: *Things of This World* (1956) and *New and Collected Poems* (1988). In recent decades Wilbur's poems have been increasingly lauded for the very qualities that drew criticism in the 30 years between his two Pulitzer Prizes: As critic Gerry Cunningham wittily puts it, "They never raise their voices, put knives to their throats, drink too much, tell dirty jokes, or take their clothes off in public." Using traditional patterns of rhyme and meter, they "acknowledge horror," but remain largely "untouched by it."

WILLIAM CARLOS WILLIAMS (1883–1963)

Born in Rutherford, New Jersey, William Carlos Williams attended school in Switzerland and New York and studied medicine at the University of Pennsylvania and the University of Leipzig in Germany. He spent most of his life in Rutherford, practicing medicine and gradually establishing himself as one of the great figures in American poetry. Early in his writing career he left the European-inspired Imagist movement in favor of a more uniquely American poetic style comprised of vital, local language, and "no ideas but in things." His shorter poems have been published in numerous collected editions, including the Pulitzer Prize-winning *Brueghel, and Other Poems* (1963); his five-volume philosophical poem, *Paterson*, was published in 1963. Among his other works are plays such as *A Dream of Love* (1948) and *Many Loves* (1950); a trilogy of novels—*White Mules* (1937), *In the Money* (1940), and *The Build-Up* (1952); his *Autobiography* (1951); his *Selected Essays* (1954); and his *Selected Letters* (1957).

WILLIAM WORDSWORTH (1770–1850)

Regarded by many as the greatest of the Romantic poets, William Wordsworth was born in Cockermouth in the English Lake District, a beautiful, mountainous region that his poetry helped make a popular tourist destination even in his own lifetime. He studied at Cambridge and then spent a year in France, hoping to witness the French Revolution firsthand; as the Revolution's "glorious renovation" dissolved into anarchy and then tyranny, Wordsworth was forced to return to England. Remarkably, he managed to establish "a saving intercourse with my true self" and to write some of his finest poetry, including the early version of his autobiographical masterpiece, *The Prelude*, which first appeared in 1805 and then again, much altered, in 1850. In 1798, Wordsworth and his friend Samuel Taylor Coleridge published *Lyrical Ballads*, which contained many of their greatest poems and can be considered the founding document of English Romanticism. Revered by the reading public, Wordsworth served as Poet Laureate from 1843 until his death in 1850.

WILLIAM BUTLER YEATS (1865–1939)

William Butler Yeats was born in Dublin, Ireland, and, though he spent most of his youth in London, became the preeminent Irish poet of the twentieth century. Immersed in Irish history, folklore, and politics, as well as spiritualism and the occult, he attended art school for a time but left to devote himself to poetry that was, early in his career, self-consciously dreamy and ethereal. Yeats's poems became tighter and more passionate with his reading of philosophers such as Nietzsche, his involvement (mainly through theater) with the Irish nationalist cause, and his desperate love for the actress and nationalist Maud Gonne. He was briefly a senator in the newly independent Irish government before withdrawing from active public life to Thoor Ballylee, a crumbling Norman tower that Yeats and his wife fashioned into a home. There he developed an elaborate mythology (published as *A Vision* in 1925) and wrote poems that explored fundamental questions of history and identity. He was awarded the Nobel Prize for Literature in 1923.

KEVIN YOUNG (b. 1970)

Poet Kevin Young was born in Lincoln, Nebraska and grew up mainly in the Midwest, before heading east to Harvard. There, he took courses with Seamus Heaney, participated—alongside Natasha Trethewey—in the influential Dark Room Collective, and wrote many of the poems that would eventually make up his first, award-winning collection (*Most Way Home*, 1995) on the way to earning a BA in English and American literature (1992). Shuttling between coasts, Young spent two years at Stanford University, in Northern California, before completing his MFA at Brown, in Rhode Island. As poems like "Ode to Pork" attest, however, Young also has deep southern roots. Both his mother—among the first black women to earn a PhD (in Chemistry) from the University of Nebraska—and his father—an ophthalmologist who was also an avid hunter and cook—grew up in rural Louisiana, where much of Young's extended family still lives. Since 2005, when he married editor Kate Tuttle, Young has lived mainly in Atlanta, Georgia, where he currently serves as both Atticus Haygood Professor of English and Creative Writing and Curator of the Raymond Danowski Poetry Library at Emory University. Young's astonishingly diverse collections of verse include *Black Maria* (2005), about fictional private eye A. K. A. Jones; *Ardency* (2011), about the real-life Africans who managed to wrest control of the slave ship *Amistad* in 1839; and *Book of Hours* (2014), which moves from poems grappling with his father's 2004 death, in a hunting accident, to those inspired by the birth of Young's first son some two years later.

DRAMA

Arthur Miller

DRAMA
Reading, Responding, Writing

As noted in the introduction, many cultures have had oral literatures: histories, romances, poems to be recited or sung. Our own era has its share of oral art forms, of course, but "literary" fiction and poetry are now most often read privately, silently, from the printed page. Most contemporary fiction writers and poets write with an understanding that their work will be experienced and enjoyed this way.

In contrast, **drama** is written primarily to be performed—by actors, on a stage, for an audience. Playwrights work with an understanding that the words on the page are just the first step—a map of sorts—toward the ultimate goal: a collaborative, publicly performed work of art. They create plays fully aware of the possibilities that go beyond printed words and extend to physical actions, stage devices, and other theatrical techniques for creating effects and modifying audience responses. Although the script of a play may be the most essential piece in the puzzle that makes up the final work of art, the play text is not the final, complete work.

To attend a play—that is, to be part of an audience—represents a very different kind of experience from the usually solitary act of reading. On the stage, real human beings, standing for imaginary characters, deliver lines and perform actions for you to see and hear. In turn, the actors adapt in subtle ways to the reactions of the people who attend the performance and whose responses are no longer wholly private but have become, in part, communal.

When you attend the performance of a play, then, you become a collaborator in the creation of a unique work of art: not the play *text* but instead a specific *interpretation* of that text. No two performances of a play can ever be identical, just as no two interpretations of a play can be exactly the same.

READING DRAMA

In many respects, of course, reading drama is similar to reading fiction. In both cases we anticipate what will happen next; we imagine the characters, settings, and actions; we respond to the symbolic suggestiveness of images; and we notice thematic patterns that are likely to matter in the end. But because most plays are written to be performed, reading plays is also somewhat different from reading fiction or poetry. In fiction, for example, there is a mediator or **narrator**, someone standing between us and the events. In contrast, drama rarely has such an interpreter or mediator to tell us what is happening or to shape our responses. Play texts instead rely on **stage directions** (the italicized descriptions of the set, characters, and actions), while **exposition** (the explanation of the past and current situation) emerges only here and there through dialogue.

For this reason, reading drama may place a greater demand on the imagination than reading fiction does: The reader must be his or her own narrator and interpreter. Such exercise for the imagination can prove rewarding, however, for it has much in common with the imaginative work that a director, actors, and other artists involved in a staged production do. In re-creating a play as we read it, we are essentially imagining the play as if it were being performed by live actors in real time. We "cast" the characters, we design the set with its furniture and props, and we choreograph or "block" the physical action, according to the cues in the text.

In reading drama even more than in reading fiction, we construct our ideas of character and personality from what characters say. In some plays, especially those with a modernist or experimental bent, certain lines of dialogue can be mystifying; other characters, as well as the audience or readers, can be left wondering what a speech means. On the one hand, such puzzling lines can become clearer in performance when we see and hear actors deliver them. On the other hand, plays that call for several characters to speak at once or to talk at cross purposes can be much easier to understand from the printed script than in performance. In interpreting dialogue, you will naturally draw on your own experiences of comparable situations or similar personalities, as well as your familiarity with other plays or stories.

Questions to Ask When Reading a Play

In reading drama as in reading fiction, you can begin to understand a text by asking some basic questions about the elements of drama.

- **Expectations:** What do you expect
  - from the title? from the first sentence, paragraph, or speech?
  - after the first events or interactions of characters? as the **conflict** is resolved?
- **Characterization:** Who are the characters? Is there a list of characters printed after the title of the play? What do you notice about their names or any identification of their roles, character types, or relationships?
  - Who is/are the **protagonist**(s)?
  - Who is/are the **antagonist**(s) (villain, opponent, obstacle)?
  - Who are the other characters?
  - What does each character know at any moment in the **action**? What does each character expect at any point? What does the audience know or expect that is different from what the characters know or expect?
- **Plot:** What happens in the play?
  - Do the characters or situations change during the play?
  - What are the differences between the beginning, middle, and end of the play? Is it divided into acts? Would there be an intermission in a performance?
  - Can you summarize the plot? Is it a recognizable kind or genre such as **tragedy**, **comedy**, **farce**, or mystery?

(continued on next page)

(*continued*)

- **Setting:** What is the setting of the play?
  - *When* does the action occur? Is it contemporary or set in the past? Do the stage directions specify a day of the week, a season, a time of day?
  - Are there any time changes during the play? Are the scenes in chronological order, or are there any scenes that are supposed to take place earlier or simultaneously? Does the passage of time in the lives of the characters correspond with the passage of time onstage? Or do we understand that time has passed and events have occurred offstage and between scenes?
  - *Where* does it take place? Is it in the United States or another country, or in a specific town or region? Do the stage directions describe the scene that an audience would see on stage, and does this remain the same or does it change during the play? How many scene changes are there?
- **Style:** What do you notice about how the play is written?
  - What is the style of the dialogue? Are the sentences and speeches short or long? Is the vocabulary simple or complex? Do characters ever speak at the same time, or do they always take turns? Does the play instruct actors to be silent for periods of time? Which characters speak most often?
  - Are there any **images** or figures of speech?
  - What is the **tone** or mood? Does the play make the reader or audience feel sad, amused, worried, curious?
- **Theme:** What does the play mean? Can you express its theme or themes?
  - Answers to these big questions may be found in many instances by returning to your answers to the questions above. The play's meaning or theme depends on all its features.

THINKING THEATRICALLY

As you read a play, you should not only make mental or written notes but also raise some of the questions an actor might ask in preparing a role, or that a director might ask before choosing a cast: How should this line be spoken? What kind of person is this character, and what are his or her motives in each scene? What does the play suggest about what made the character this way—family, environment, experience? Which characters are present or absent (onstage or off) in which scenes, and how do the characters onstage or off influence one another? Would you, as "director" of an imaginary performance, tell the actors to move in certain directions, together or apart; to express certain emotions and intentions; to speak in quiet, angry, sarcastic, or agonized tones?

Besides trying to understand the characters, you should consider ways that the play could be produced, designed, and staged. How might a set designer create a kitchen, drawing room, garden, woods, or other space for the actors to move in, and how many set changes are there in the play? What would the audience see through any windows or doors in an imaginary building? How would lighting give an impression of the time of day or season? Would sound effects or music be necessary (such as a gunshot, radio, or telephone)? What sort of costumes are specified in the stage directions, and how would costumes help express character types and their relationships, as well as the historical time period? What essential props must be provided for the actors to use, and what other props are optional?

As you read Susan Glaspell's TRIFLES, keep these kinds of questions in mind. Try to create a mental image of the settings and of each character, and think about different ways the lines might be delivered and their effect on an audience's response.

SUSAN GLASPELL (1876–1948)

Trifles

Though today remembered almost exclusively for her masterful *Trifles* (1916), Susan Glaspell wrote over a dozen plays, fifty short stories, nine novels, and a memoir, in addition to playing a key role in the development of twentieth-century American theater. Born in Davenport, Iowa, she graduated from Drake University in 1899 and spent two years at the *Des Moines Daily News*, where she covered the trial of a fifty-seven-year-old woman accused of murdering her sleeping husband with an axe. When Glaspell's short stories began appearing in magazines, she returned to Davenport. There, she became involved with George Cram Cook, a former English professor, socialist, and married father of two. The two wed in 1913 and moved east, eventually settling in New York's Greenwich Village and Cape Cod, Massachusetts, where they founded the Provincetown Playhouse (later the Playwright's Theater), an extraordinary gathering of freethinking, Left-leaning actors, directors, and playwrights that included Edna St. Vincent Millay and a then-unknown Eugene O'Neill. Between 1916 and 1922, this pioneering group reportedly staged more plays by women than any other contemporary theater; among them were eleven by Glaspell, ranging from realistic dramas such as *Trifles* and satirical comedies like *Woman's Honor* (1918) to her expressionistic *The Verge* (1921). Widowed in 1924, Glaspell ended a brief second marriage in 1931, the same year that her last play, *Alison's House*, won the Pulitzer Prize for Drama. Having published her first novel in 1909 and multiple best sellers in the 1920s and 1930s, Glaspell spent the last years of her life writing fiction in Provincetown.

CHARACTERS

SHERIFF
COUNTY ATTORNEY
HALE
MRS. PETERS, *Sheriff's wife*
MRS. HALE

SCENE: *The kitchen in the now abandoned farmhouse of* JOHN WRIGHT, *a gloomy kitchen, and left without having been put in order—unwashed pans under the sink, a loaf of bread outside the bread-box, a dish-towel on the table—other signs of incompleted work. At the rear the outer door opens and the* SHERIFF *comes in followed by the* COUNTY ATTORNEY *and* HALE. *The* SHERIFF *and* HALE *are men in middle life, the* COUNTY ATTORNEY *is a young man; all are much bundled up and go at once to the stove. They are followed by the two women—the* SHERIFF'S *wife first; she is a slight wiry woman, a thin nervous face.* MRS. HALE *is larger and would ordinarily be called more comfortable looking, but she is disturbed now and looks fearfully about as she enters. The women have come in slowly, and stand close together near the door.*

COUNTY ATTORNEY: [*Rubbing his hands.*] This feels good. Come up to the fire, ladies.

MRS. PETERS: [*After taking a step forward.*] I'm not—cold.

SHERIFF: [*Unbuttoning his overcoat and stepping away from the stove as if to mark the beginning of official business.*] Now, Mr. Hale, before we move things about, you explain to Mr. Henderson just what you saw when you came here yesterday morning.

COUNTY ATTORNEY: By the way, has anything been moved? Are things just as you left them yesterday?

SHERIFF: [*Looking about.*] It's just the same. When it dropped below zero last night I thought I'd better send Frank out this morning to make a fire for us—no use getting pneumonia with a big case on, but I told him not to touch anything except the stove—and you know Frank.

COUNTY ATTORNEY: Somebody should have been left here yesterday.

SHERIFF: Oh—yesterday. When I had to send Frank to Morris Center for that man who went crazy—I want you to know I had my hands full yesterday. I knew you could get back from Omaha by today and as long as I went over everything here myself—

COUNTY ATTORNEY: Well, Mr. Hale, tell just what happened when you came here yesterday morning.

HALE: Harry and I had started to town with a load of potatoes. We came along the road from my place and as I got here I said, "I'm going to see if I can't get John Wright to go in with me on a party telephone."[1] I spoke to Wright about it once before and he put me off, saying folks talked too much anyway, and all he asked was peace and quiet—I guess you know about how much he talked himself; but I thought maybe if I went to the house and talked about it before his wife, though I said to Harry that I didn't know as what his wife wanted made much difference to John—

COUNTY ATTORNEY: Let's talk about that later, Mr. Hale. I do want to talk about that, but tell now just what happened when you got to the house.

HALE: I didn't hear or see anything; I knocked at the door, and still it was all quiet inside. I knew they must be up, it was past eight o'clock. So I knocked again, and I thought I heard somebody say, "Come in." I wasn't sure, I'm not sure yet, but I opened the door—this door [*Indicating the door by which the two women are still standing.*] and there in that rocker—[*Pointing to it.*] sat Mrs. Wright.

[*They all look at the rocker.*]

1. That is, a party line in which a number of households each have extensions of a single line, a common arrangement in the early twentieth century, especially in rural areas.

COUNTY ATTORNEY: What—was she doing?

HALE: She was rockin' back and forth. She had her apron in her hand and was kind of—pleating it.

COUNTY ATTORNEY: And how did she—look?

HALE: Well, she looked queer.

COUNTY ATTORNEY: How do you mean—queer?

HALE: Well, as if she didn't know what she was going to do next. And kind of done up.

COUNTY ATTORNEY: How did she seem to feel about your coming?

HALE: Why, I don't think she minded—one way or other. She didn't pay much attention. I said, "How do, Mrs. Wright, it's cold, ain't it?" And she said, "Is it?"—and went on kind of pleating at her apron. Well, I was surprised; she didn't ask me to come up to the stove, or to set down, but just sat there, not even looking at me, so I said, "I want to see John." And then she—laughed. I guess you would call it a laugh. I thought of Harry and the team outside, so I said a little sharp: "Can't I see John?" "No," she says, kind o' dull like. "Ain't he home?" says I. "Yes," says she, "he's home." "Then why can't I see him?" I asked her, out of patience. "'Cause he's dead," says she. *"Dead?"* says I. She just nodded her head, not getting a bit excited, but rockin' back and forth. "Why—where is he?" says I, not knowing what to say. She just pointed upstairs—like that. [*Himself pointing to the room above.*] I got up, with the idea of going up there. I walked from there to here—then I says, "Why, what did he die of?" "He died of a rope round his neck," says she, and just went on pleatin' at her apron. Well, I went out and called Harry. I thought I might—need help. We went upstairs and there he was lyin'—

COUNTY ATTORNEY: I think I'd rather have you go into that upstairs, where you can point it all out. Just go on now with the rest of the story.

HALE: Well, my first thought was to get that rope off. It looked . . . [*Stops, his face twitches.*] . . . but Harry, he went up to him, and he said, "No, he's dead all right, and we'd better not touch anything." So we went back downstairs. She was still sitting that same way. "Has anybody been notified?" I asked. "No," says she, unconcerned. "Who did this, Mrs. Wright?" said Harry. He said it business-like—and she stopped pleatin' of her apron. "I don't know," she says. "You don't *know*?" says Harry. "No," says she. "Weren't you sleepin' in the bed with him?" says Harry. "Yes," says she, "but I was on the inside." "Somebody slipped a rope round his neck and strangled him and you didn't wake up?" says Harry. "I didn't wake up," she said after him. We must 'a looked as if we didn't see how that could be, for after a minute she said, "I sleep sound." Harry was going to ask her more questions but I said maybe we ought to let her tell her story first to the coroner, or the sheriff, so Harry went fast as he could to Rivers' place, where there's a telephone.

COUNTY ATTORNEY: And what did Mrs. Wright do when she knew that you had gone for the coroner?

HALE: She moved from that chair to this one over here [*Pointing to a small chair in the corner.*] and just sat there with her hands held together and looking down. I got a feeling that I ought to make some conversation, so I said I had come in to see if John wanted to put in a telephone, and at that she started to laugh, and then she stopped and looked at me—scared. [*The* COUNTY

ATTORNEY, *who has had his notebook out, makes a note.*] I dunno, maybe it wasn't scared. I wouldn't like to say it was. Soon Harry got back, and then Dr. Lloyd came, and you, Mr. Peters, and so I guess that's all I know that you don't.

COUNTY ATTORNEY: [*Looking around.*] I guess we'll go upstairs first—and then out to the barn and around there. [*To the* SHERIFF.] You're convinced that there was nothing important here—nothing that would point to any motive?

SHERIFF: Nothing here but kitchen things.

[*The* COUNTY ATTORNEY, *after again looking around the kitchen, opens the door of a cupboard closet. He gets up on a chair and looks on a shelf. Pulls his hand away, sticky.*]

COUNTY ATTORNEY: Here's a nice mess.

[*The women draw nearer.*]

MRS. PETERS: [*To the other woman.*] Oh, her fruit; it did freeze. [*To the* LAWYER.] She worried about that when it turned so cold. She said the fire'd go out and her jars would break.

SHERIFF: Well, can you beat the women! Held for murder and worryin' about her preserves.

COUNTY ATTORNEY: I guess before we're through she may have something more serious than preserves to worry about.

HALE: Well, women are used to worrying over trifles.

[*The two women move a little closer together.*]

COUNTY ATTORNEY: [*With the gallantry of a young politician.*] And yet, for all their worries, what would we do without the ladies? [*The women do not unbend. He goes to the sink, takes a dipperful of water from the pail and pouring it into a basin, washes his hands. Starts to wipe them on the roller towel, turns it for a cleaner place.*] Dirty towels! [*Kicks his foot against the pans under the sink.*] Not much of a housekeeper, would you say, ladies?

MRS. HALE: [*Stiffly.*] There's a great deal of work to be done on a farm.

COUNTY ATTORNEY: To be sure. And yet [*With a little bow to her.*] I know there are some Dickson county farmhouses which do not have such roller towels. [*He gives it a pull to expose its length again.*]

MRS. HALE: Those towels get dirty awful quick. Men's hands aren't always as clean as they might be.

COUNTY ATTORNEY: Ah, loyal to your sex, I see. But you and Mrs. Wright were neighbors. I suppose you were friends, too.

MRS. HALE: [*Shaking her head.*] I've not seen much of her of late years. I've not been in this house—it's more than a year.

COUNTY ATTORNEY: And why was that? You didn't like her?

MRS. HALE: I liked her all well enough. Farmers' wives have their hands full, Mr. Henderson. And then—

COUNTY ATTORNEY: Yes—?

MRS. HALE: [*Looking about.*] It never seemed a very cheerful place.

COUNTY ATTORNEY: No—it's not cheerful. I shouldn't say she had the home-making instinct.

MRS. HALE: Well, I don't know as Wright had, either.

COUNTY ATTORNEY: You mean that they didn't get on very well?

MRS. HALE: No, I don't mean anything. But I don't think a place'd be any cheerfuller for John Wright's being in it.

COUNTY ATTORNEY: I'd like to talk more of that a little later. I want to get the lay of things upstairs now. [*He goes to the left, where three steps lead to a stair door.*]

SHERIFF: I suppose anything Mrs. Peters does'll be all right. She was to take in some clothes for her, you know, and a few little things. We left in such a hurry yesterday.

COUNTY ATTORNEY: Yes, but I would like to see what you take, Mrs. Peters, and keep an eye out for anything that might be of use to us.

MRS. PETERS: Yes, Mr. Henderson. [*The women listen to the men's steps on the stairs, then look about the kitchen.*]

MRS. HALE: I'd hate to have men coming into my kitchen, snooping around and criticizing. [*She arranges the pans under the sink which the* LAWYER *had shoved out of place.*]

MRS. PETERS: Of course it's no more than their duty.

MRS. HALE: Duty's all right, but I guess that deputy sheriff that came out to make the fire might have got a little of this on. [*Gives the roller towel a pull.*] Wish I'd thought of that sooner. Seems mean to talk about her for not having things slicked up when she had to come away in such a hurry.

MRS. PETERS: [*Who has gone to a small table in the left rear corner of the room, and lifted one end of a towel that covers a pan.*] She had bread set. [*Stands still.*]

MRS. HALE: [*Eyes fixed on a loaf of bread beside the bread box, which is on a low shelf at the other side of the room. Moves slowly toward it.*] She was going to put this in there. [*Picks up loaf, then abruptly drops it. In a manner of returning to familiar things.*] It's a shame about her fruit. I wonder if it's all gone. [*Gets up on the chair and looks.*] I think there's some here that's all right, Mrs. Peters. Yes—here; [*Holding it toward the window.*] this is cherries, too. [*Looking again.*] I declare I believe that's the only one. [*Gets down, bottle in her hand. Goes to the sink and wipes it off on the outside.*] She'll feel awful bad after all her hard work in the hot weather. I remember the afternoon I put up my cherries last summer. [*She puts the bottle on the big kitchen table, center of the room. With a sigh, is about to sit down in the rocking-chair. Before she is seated realizes what chair it is; with a slow look at it, steps back. The chair, which she has touched, rocks back and forth.*]

MRS. PETERS: Well, I must get those things from the front room closet. [*She goes to the door at the right, but after looking into the other room, steps back.*] You coming with me, Mrs. Hale? You could help me carry them. [*They go in the other room; reappear,* MRS. PETERS *carrying a dress and skirt,* MRS. HALE *following with a pair of shoes.*] My, it's cold in there. [*She puts the clothes on the big table, and hurries to the stove.*]

MRS. HALE: [*Examining the skirt.*] Wright was close. I think maybe that's why she kept so much to herself. She didn't even belong to the Ladies Aid. I suppose she felt she couldn't do her part, and then you don't enjoy things when you feel shabby. She used to wear pretty clothes and be lively, when she was Minnie Foster, one of the town girls singing in the choir. But that—oh, that was thirty years ago. This all you was to take in?

MRS. PETERS: She said she wanted an apron. Funny thing to want, for there isn't much to get you dirty in jail, goodness knows. But I suppose just to make her feel more natural. She said they was in the top drawer in this cupboard. Yes, here. And then her little shawl that always hung behind the door. [*Opens stair door and looks.*] Yes, here it is. [*Quickly shuts door leading upstairs.*]

MRS. HALE: [*Abruptly moving toward her.*] Mrs. Peters?

MRS. PETERS: Yes, Mrs. Hale?

MRS. HALE: Do you think she did it?

MRS. PETERS: [*In a frightened voice.*] Oh, I don't know.

MRS. HALE: Well, I don't think she did. Asking for an apron and her little shawl. Worrying about her fruit.

MRS. PETERS: [*Starts to speak, glances up, where footsteps are heard in the room above. In a low voice.*] Mr. Peters says it looks bad for her. Mr. Henderson is awful sarcastic in a speech and he'll make fun of her sayin' she didn't wake up.

MRS. HALE: Well, I guess John Wright didn't wake when they was slipping that rope under his neck.

MRS. PETERS: No, it's strange. It must have been done awful crafty and still. They say it was such a—funny way to kill a man, rigging it all up like that.

MRS. HALE: That's just what Mr. Hale said. There was a gun in the house. He says that's what he can't understand.

MRS. PETERS: Mr. Henderson said coming out that what was needed for the case was a motive; something to show anger, or—sudden feeling.

MRS. HALE: [*Who is standing by the table.*] Well, I don't see any signs of anger around here. [*She puts her hand on the dish towel which lies on the table, stands looking down at table, one half of which is clean, the other half messy.*] It's wiped to here. [*Makes a move as if to finish work, then turns and looks at loaf of bread outside the bread box. Drops towel. In that voice of coming back to familiar things.*] Wonder how they are finding things upstairs. I hope she had it a little more red-up[2] up there. You know, it seems kind of *sneaking*. Locking her up in town and then coming out here and trying to get her own house to turn against her!

MRS. PETERS: But Mrs. Hale, the law is the law.

MRS. HALE: I s'pose 'tis. [*Unbuttoning her coat.*] Better loosen up your things, Mrs. Peters. You won't feel them when you go out.

[MRS. PETERS *takes off her fur tippet, goes to hang it on hook at back of room, stands looking at the under part of the small corner table.*]

MRS. PETERS: She was piecing a quilt. [*She brings the large sewing basket and they look at the bright pieces.*]

MRS. HALE: It's log cabin pattern. Pretty, isn't it? I wonder if she was goin' to quilt it or just knot it?

[*Footsteps have been heard coming down the stairs. The* SHERIFF *enters followed by* HALE *and the* COUNTY ATTORNEY.]

SHERIFF: They wonder if she was going to quilt it or just knot it!

[*The men laugh, the women look abashed.*]

2. Tidied up.

COUNTY ATTORNEY: [*Rubbing his hands over the stove.*] Frank's fire didn't do much up there, did it? Well, let's go out to the barn and get that cleared up.

[*The men go outside.*]

MRS. HALE: [*Resentfully.*] I don't know as there's anything so strange, our takin' up our time with little things while we're waiting for them to get the evidence. [*She sits down at the big table smoothing out a block with decision.*] I don't see as it's anything to laugh about.

MRS. PETERS: [*Apologetically.*] Of course they've got awful important things on their minds. [*Pulls up a chair and joins* MRS. HALE *at the table.*]

MRS. HALE: [*Examining another block.*] Mrs. Peters, look at this one. Here, this is the one she was working on, and look at the sewing! All the rest of it has been so nice and even. And look at this! It's all over the place! Why, it looks as if she didn't know what she was about! [*After she has said this they look at each other, then start to glance back at the door. After an instant* MRS. HALE *has pulled at a knot and ripped the sewing.*]

MRS. PETERS: Oh, what are you doing, Mrs. Hale?

MRS. HALE: [*Mildly.*] Just pulling out a stitch or two that's not sewed very good. [*Threading the needle.*] Bad sewing always made me fidgety.

MRS. PETERS: [*Nervously.*] I don't think we ought to touch things.

MRS. HALE: I'll just finish up this end. [*Suddenly stopping and leaning forward.*] Mrs. Peters?

MRS. PETERS: Yes, Mrs. Hale?

MRS. HALE: What do you suppose she was so nervous about?

MRS. PETERS: Oh—I don't know. I don't know as she was nervous. I sometimes sew awful queer when I'm just tired. [MRS. HALE *starts to say something, looks at* MRS. PETERS, *then goes on sewing.*] Well, I must get these things wrapped up. They may be through sooner than we think. [*Putting apron and other things together.*] I wonder where I can find a piece of paper, and string.

MRS. HALE: In that cupboard, maybe.

MRS. PETERS: [*Looking in cupboard.*] Why, here's a bird-cage. [*Holds it up.*] Did she have a bird, Mrs. Hale?

MRS. HALE: Why, I don't know whether she did or not—I've not been here for so long. There was a man around last year selling canaries cheap, but I don't know as she took one; maybe she did. She used to sing real pretty herself.

MRS. PETERS: [*Glancing around.*] Seems funny to think of a bird here. But she must have had one, or why would she have a cage? I wonder what happened to it.

MRS. HALE: I s'pose maybe the cat got it.

MRS. PETERS: No, she didn't have a cat. She's got that feeling some people have about cats—being afraid of them. My cat got in her room and she was real upset and asked me to take it out.

MRS. HALE: My sister Bessie was like that. Queer, ain't it?

MRS. PETERS: [*Examining the cage.*] Why, look at this door. It's broke. One hinge is pulled apart.

MRS. HALE: [*Looking too.*] Looks as if someone must have been rough with it.

MRS. PETERS: Why, yes. [*She brings the cage forward and puts it on the table.*]

MRS. HALE: I wish if they're going to find any evidence they'd be about it. I don't like this place.

MRS. PETERS: But I'm awful glad you came with me, Mrs. Hale. It would be lonesome for me sitting here alone.

MRS. HALE: It would, wouldn't it? [*Dropping her sewing.*] But I tell you what I do wish, Mrs. Peters. I wish I had come over sometimes when *she* was here. I—[*Looking around the room.*]—wish I had.

MRS. PETERS: But of course you were awful busy, Mrs. Hale—your house and your children.

MRS. HALE: I could've come. I stayed away because it weren't cheerful—and that's why I ought to have come. I—I've never liked this place. Maybe because it's down in a hollow and you don't see the road. I dunno what it is, but it's a lonesome place and always was. I wish I had come over to see Minnie Foster sometimes. I can see now—[*Shakes her head.*]

MRS. PETERS: Well, you mustn't reproach yourself, Mrs. Hale. Somehow we just don't see how it is with other folks until—something comes up.

MRS. HALE: Not having children makes less work—but it makes a quiet house, and Wright out to work all day, and no company when he did come in. Did you know John Wright, Mrs. Peters?

MRS. PETERS: Not to know him; I've seen him in town. They say he was a good man.

MRS. HALE: Yes—good; he didn't drink, and kept his word as well as most, I guess, and paid his debts. But he was a hard man, Mrs. Peters. Just to pass the time of day with him—[*Shivers.*] Like a raw wind that gets to the bone. [*Pauses, her eye falling on the cage.*] I should think she would 'a wanted a bird. But what do you suppose went with it?

MRS. PETERS: I don't know, unless it got sick and died. [*She reaches over and swings the broken door, swings it again, both women watch it.*]

MRS. HALE: You weren't raised round here, were you? [MRS. PETERS *shakes her head.*] You didn't know—her?

MRS. PETERS: Not till they brought her yesterday.

MRS. HALE: She—come to think of it, she was kind of like a bird herself—real sweet and pretty, but kind of timid and—fluttery. How—she—did—change. [*Silence; then as if struck by a happy thought and relieved to get back to everyday things.*] Tell you what, Mrs. Peters, why don't you take the quilt in with you? It might take up her mind.

MRS. PETERS: Why, I think that's a real nice idea, Mrs. Hale. There couldn't possibly be any objection to it, could there? Now, just what would I take? I wonder if her patches are in here—and her things. [*They look in the sewing basket.*]

MRS. HALE: Here's some red. I expect this has got sewing things in it. [*Brings out a fancy box.*] What a pretty box. Looks like something somebody would give you. Maybe her scissors are in here. [*Opens box. Suddenly puts her hand to her nose.*] Why—[MRS. PETERS *bends nearer, then turns her face away.*] There's something wrapped up in this piece of silk.

MRS. PETERS: Why, this isn't her scissors.

MRS. HALE: [*Lifting the silk.*] Oh, Mrs. Peters—it's—

[MRS. PETERS *bends closer.*]

MRS. PETERS: It's the bird.

MRS. HALE: [*Jumping up.*] But, Mrs. Peters—look at it! Its neck! Look at its neck! It's all—other side *to.*

MRS. PETERS: Somebody—wrung—its—neck.

[*Their eyes meet. A look of growing comprehension, of horror. Steps are heard outside.* MRS. HALE *slips box under quilt pieces, and sinks into her chair. Enter* SHERIFF *and* COUNTY ATTORNEY. MRS. PETERS *rises.*]

COUNTY ATTORNEY: [*As one turning from serious things to little pleasantries.*] Well ladies, have you decided whether she was going to quilt it or knot it?

MRS. PETERS: We think she was going to—knot it.

COUNTY ATTORNEY: Well, that's interesting, I'm sure. [*Seeing the bird-cage.*] Has the bird flown?

MRS. HALE: [*Putting more quilt pieces over the box.*] We think the—cat got it.

COUNTY ATTORNEY: [*Preoccupied.*] Is there a cat?

[MRS. HALE *glances in a quick covert way at* MRS. PETERS.]

MRS. PETERS: Well, not *now.* They're superstitious, you know. They leave.

COUNTY ATTORNEY: [*To* SHERIFF PETERS, *continuing an interrupted conversation.*] No sign at all of anyone having come from the outside. Their own rope. Now let's go up again and go over it piece by piece. [*They start upstairs.*] It would have to have been someone who knew just the—

[MRS. PETERS *sits down. The two women sit there not looking at one another, but as if peering into something and at the same time holding back. When they talk now it is in the manner of feeling their way over strange ground, as if afraid of what they are saying, but as if they cannot help saying it.*]

MRS. HALE: She liked the bird. She was going to bury it in that pretty box.

MRS. PETERS: [*In a whisper.*] When I was a girl—my kitten—there was a boy took a hatchet, and before my eyes—and before I could get there—[*Covers her face an instant.*] If they hadn't held me back I would have—[*Catches herself, looks upstairs where steps are heard, falters weakly.*]—hurt him.

MRS. HALE: [*With a slow look around her.*] I wonder how it would seem never to have had any children around. [*Pause.*] No, Wright wouldn't like the bird—a thing that sang. She used to sing. He killed that, too.

MRS. PETERS: [*Moving uneasily.*] We don't know who killed the bird.

MRS. HALE: I knew John Wright.

MRS. PETERS: It was an awful thing was done in this house that night, Mrs. Hale. Killing a man while he slept, slipping a rope around his neck that choked the life out of him.

MRS. HALE: His neck. Choked the life out of him. [*Her hand goes out and rests on the bird-cage.*]

MRS. PETERS: [*With rising voice.*] We don't know who killed him. We don't *know.*

MRS. HALE: [*Her own feeling not interrupted.*] If there's been years and years of nothing, then a bird to sing to you, it would be awful—still, after the bird was still.

MRS. PETERS: [*Something within her speaking.*] I know what stillness is. When we homesteaded in Dakota, and my first baby died—after he was two years old, and me with no other then—

MRS. HALE: [*Moving.*] How soon do you suppose they'll be through, looking for the evidence?

MRS. PETERS: I know what stillness is. [*Pulling herself back.*] The law has got to punish crime, Mrs. Hale.

MRS. HALE: [*Not as if answering that.*] I wish you'd seen Minnie Foster when she wore a white dress with blue ribbons and stood up there in the choir and sang. [*A look around the room.*] Oh, I *wish* I'd come over here once in a while! That was a crime! That was a crime! Who's going to punish that?

MRS. PETERS: [*Looking upstairs.*] We mustn't—take on.

MRS. HALE: I might have known she needed help! I know how things can be—for women. I tell you, it's queer, Mrs. Peters. We live close together and we live far apart. We all go through the same things—it's all just a different kind of the same thing. [*Brushes her eyes, noticing the bottle of fruit, reaches out for it.*] If I was you, I wouldn't tell her her fruit was gone. Tell her it *ain't*. Tell her it's all right. Take this in to prove it to her. She—she may never know whether it was broke or not.

MRS. PETERS: [*Takes the bottle, looks about for something to wrap it in; takes petticoat from the clothes brought from the other room, very nervously begins winding this around the bottle. In a false voice.*] My, it's a good thing the men couldn't hear us. Wouldn't they just laugh! Getting all stirred up over a little thing like a—dead canary. As if that could have anything to do with—with—wouldn't they *laugh*!

[*The men are heard coming down stairs.*]

MRS. HALE: [*Under her breath.*] Maybe they would—maybe they wouldn't.

COUNTY ATTORNEY: No, Peters, it's all perfectly clear except a reason for doing it. But you know juries when it comes to women. If there was some definite thing. Something to show—something to make a story about—a thing that would connect up with this strange way of doing it—

[*The women's eyes meet for an instant. Enter* HALE *from outer door.*]

HALE: Well, I've got the team around. Pretty cold out there.

COUNTY ATTORNEY: I'm going to stay here a while by myself. [*To the* SHERIFF.] You can send Frank out for me, can't you? I want to go over everything. I'm not satisfied that we can't do better.

SHERIFF: Do you want to see what Mrs. Peters is going to take in?

[*The* LAWYER *goes to the table, picks up the apron, laughs.*]

COUNTY ATTORNEY: Oh, I guess they're not very dangerous things the ladies have picked out. [*Moves a few things about, disturbing the quilt pieces which cover the box. Steps back.*] No, Mrs. Peters doesn't need supervising. For that matter, a sheriff's wife is married to the law. Ever think of it that way, Mrs. Peters?

MRS. PETERS: Not—just that way.

SHERIFF: [*Chuckling.*] Married to the law. [*Moves toward the other room.*] I just want you to come in here a minute, George. We ought to take a look at these windows.

COUNTY ATTORNEY: [*Scoffingly.*] Oh, windows!

SHERIFF: We'll be right out, Mr. Hale.

[HALE *goes outside. The* SHERIFF *follows the* COUNTY ATTORNEY *into the other room. Then* MRS. HALE *rises, hands tight together, looking intensely at* MRS. PETERS, *whose eyes make a slow turn, finally meeting* MRS. HALE's. *A moment* MRS. HALE *holds her, then her own eyes point the way to where the box is concealed. Suddenly* MRS. PETERS *throws back quilt pieces and tries to put the box in the bag she is wearing. It is too big. She opens box, starts to take bird out, cannot touch it, goes to pieces, stands there helpless. Sound of a knob turning in the other room.* MRS. HALE *snatches the box and puts it in the pocket of her big coat. Enter* COUNTY ATTORNEY *and* SHERIFF.]

COUNTY ATTORNEY: [*Facetiously.*] Well, Henry, at least we found out that she was not going to quilt it. She was going to—what is it you call it, ladies?

MRS. HALE: [*Her hand against her pocket.*] We call it—knot it, Mr. Henderson.

CURTAIN

1916

QUESTIONS

1. If we were watching a production of TRIFLES and had no cast list, how would we gradually piece together the fact that Mrs. Peters is the sheriff's wife? What are the earliest lines of dialogue that allow an audience to infer this fact?
2. What lines in the play characterize Mrs. Hale's reaction to the men's behavior and attitudes? What lines characterize Mrs. Peters's reaction to the men early in the play, and what lines show her feelings changing later in the play? What might account for the two women's initial differences and their evolving solidarity with Mrs. Wright?
3. What are the "trifles" that the men ignore and the two women notice? Why do the men dismiss them, and why do the women see these things as significant clues? What is the thematic importance of these "trifles"?
4. How would you stage the key moment of the play, Mrs. Hale's discovery of the bird in the sewing basket? What facial expression would she have? What body language? Where would you place Mrs. Peters, and what would she be doing? How would you use lighting to heighten the effectiveness of the scene?
5. If a twenty-first-century playwright were to write an updated version of TRIFLES, what details of plot, character, and setting would be different from those in Glaspell's play? What would be the same? What are some possible "trifles" that might serve the same dramatic functions as those in Glaspell's play?

RESPONDING TO DRAMA

When reading a play in order to write about it, you will need to keep a record of how you respond and what you observe as the action unfolds. Recording your thoughts as you read will help you clarify your expectations and attend to the way the play elicits and manages them. Below you will find examples of two ways of responding to a play. The first shows how you might jot down your initial impressions and questions in the margins as you read. The second shows how one reader used the questions on pages 1153–54 to take more comprehensive, methodical notes on the same play. Each of these methods of note-taking has certain advantages, and you may well find that a combination of the two works best.

SAMPLE WRITING: ANNOTATION OF *TRIFLES*

Though the passage chosen for annotation here is the play's opening, any passage in a play—including stage directions, as well as dialogue—will reward close analysis.

A "trifle" is something unimportant and also a kind of dessert. So is the play going to be about unimportant things? Is it a comedy?

Trifles

Only character *not* identified either by job or relationship to somebody else. (Why not "Mr. Hale"?)

CHARACTERS

SHERIFF — MRS. PETERS, *Sheriff's wife*
COUNTY ATTORNEY — MRS. HALE
HALE

Why "now abandoned"? Who's John Wright? "Gloomy" doesn't sound like a comedy.

Is this a crime scene? Why refer to "work" (not "eating" or something)?

Women described more than men. They look different, but even the "comfortable looking" one (funny expression) isn't comfortable. They stick together.

SCENE: *The kitchen in the now abandoned farmhouse of* JOHN WRIGHT, *a gloomy kitchen, and left without having been put in order—unwashed pans under the sink, a loaf of bread outside the bread-box, a dish-towel on the table—other signs of incompleted work. At the rear the outer door opens and the* SHERIFF *comes in followed by the* COUNTY ATTORNEY *and* HALE. *The* SHERIFF *and* HALE *are men in middle life, the* COUNTY ATTORNEY *is a young man; all are much bundled up and go at once to the stove. They are followed by the two women—the* SHERIFF*'s wife first; she is a slight wiry woman, a thin nervous face.* MRS. HALE *is larger and would ordinarily be called more comfortable looking, but she is disturbed now and looks fearfully about as she enters. The women have come in slowly, and stand close together near the door.*

Why hesitate?

COUNTY ATTORNEY: [*Rubbing his hands.*] This feels good. Come up to the fire, ladies.

MRS. PETERS: [*After taking a step forward.*] I'm not—cold.

Now attorney gets a name. Sounds like they are in court.

Second mention of things being moved: they're worried about evidence.

SHERIFF: [*Unbuttoning his overcoat and stepping away from the stove as if to mark the beginning of official business.*] Now, Mr. Hale, before we move things about, you explain to Mr. Henderson just what you saw when you came here yesterday morning.

COUNTY ATTORNEY: By the way, has anything been moved? Are things just as you left them yesterday?

So this *is* "a big case." Is John Wright the criminal or victim?

Everyone knows everyone else. It's very cold, a harsh environment outside this kitchen. And it takes work to make it warm (lighting a fire).

SHERIFF: [*Looking about.*] It's just the same. When it dropped below zero last night I thought I'd better send Frank out this morning to make a fire for us—no use getting pneumonia with a big case on, but I told him not to touch anything except the stove—and you know Frank.

It's a small town (in Nebraska?), but a lot of bad stuff is happening! Sheriff is defensive with attorney—source of conflict?

Again, everybody knows about everybody else.

COUNTY ATTORNEY: Somebody should have been left here yesterday.

SHERIFF: Oh—yesterday. When I had to send Frank to Morris Center for that man who went crazy—I want you to know I had my hands full yesterday. I knew you could get back from Omaha by today and as long as I went over everything here myself—

COUNTY ATTORNEY: Well, Mr. Hale, tell just what happened when you came here yesterday morning.

Hale assumes most husbands would act differently around their wives, care about what they want—but maybe not Wright.

HALE: Harry and I had started to town with a load of potatoes. We came along the road from my place and as I got here I said, "I'm going to see if I can't get John Wright to go in with me on a party telephone." I spoke to Wright about it once before and he put me off, saying folks talked too much anyway, and all he asked was peace and quiet—I guess you know about how much he talked himself; but I thought maybe if I went to the house and talked about it before his wife, though I said to Harry that I didn't know as what his wife wanted made much difference to John—

Attorney is worried about being "official," sticking to facts, actions, "business," and "that" (Wright's personality or feelings?) doesn't count.

COUNTY ATTORNEY: Let's talk about that later, Mr. Hale. I do want to talk about that, but tell now just what happened when you got to the house.

Everyone gets up early—because of all the work they have to do?

Really ordinary things now seem very creepy. Why are the women still standing by the door—because they are afraid? because they aren't part of "official business"? Are they witnesses, too? Why are they here?

She's not listed as character either. What happened?

HALE: I didn't hear or see anything; I knocked at the door, and still it was all quiet inside. I knew they must be up, it was past eight o'clock. So I knocked again, and I thought I heard somebody say, "Come in." I wasn't sure, I'm not sure yet, but I opened the door—this door [*Indicating the door by which the two women are still standing.*] and there in that rocker—[*Pointing to it.*] sat Mrs. Wright.

SAMPLE WRITING: READING NOTES

Below are examples of the questions an experienced reader might ask when reading the play TRIFLES for the first time, as well as responses to those questions. (See pp. 1391–1401.) Any of these notes might inspire ideas for essay topics on *Trifles*. This is just a selection of the many details that could be observed about this lasting play, in which details certainly matter.

Expectations

Does the title suggest anything? "Trifles" sounds like a comedy (a trifle is something trivial), but it might be ironic. But why does Hale say that "women are used to worrying over trifles"? I expect to find out that the title is significant in some way.

Characterization

Who are the characters? What are they like? Three men and two women in the cast of characters. After I read the stage directions and part of the dialogue, I check the list again to keep straight who is who. What kind of situation would bring together a sheriff, a county attorney, a farmer, and two wives? No actors are needed to play either Mr. Wright or Mrs. Wright. Some men who help Mr. Hale (Harry) and Mr. Peters (deputy Frank) are mentioned as coming and going but are never on stage.

The "county attorney" acts like a detective; he seems businesslike and thinks he's smarter than farmers and women. The stage directions specify that he speaks "With the gallantry of a young politician," but his flattery toward the women doesn't work. We find out his name is Mr. Henderson.

According to the stage directions, Mrs. Peters, the sheriff's wife, is "a slight wiry woman, a thin nervous face"; Mrs. Hale, the farmer's wife, is "larger and would ordinarily be called more comfortable looking." The casting of the two women would be important for contrast; a wider range of physical types would be suitable for the men. Everyone is cold, but only the men take comfort by the fire in the kitchen; the women are upset.

Is there a protagonist, an antagonist, or other types? There isn't a young hero or heroine of this play, and I wouldn't call anyone the villain unless it's the dead man.

Are the characters' names significant? There's nothing especially meaningful or unusual about the names, although "Hale" means healthy (as in "hale and hearty"), and "Wright" sounds just like "right," though obviously something's wrong in this house.

Plot

What happens? The big event has already happened; this is the scene of the crime. The men are looking for clues and leave the women in the kitchen, where they discover possible causes or motives for the crime. The women decide not to tell the men about either the evidence they find or their interpretation of it.

Are there scene changes? The whole scene is a fairly short uninterrupted period in one part of a farmhouse. Characters go offstage to other rooms or outdoors to the barn.

How is exposition handled? The county attorney asks Hale to "tell just what happened"; Hale explains what happened before the play started, describing how Mrs. Wright behaved. It comes as a shock to learn that Mrs. Wright told Hale he couldn't see John Wright " 'Cause [he was] dead." Shouldn't she have run to tell someone about the murder or have told Hale as soon as he arrived? When Hale reports that Mrs. Wright said her husband "died of a rope around his neck," it sounds suspicious. Could she have slept so soundly that she didn't realize someone had strangled Mr. Wright?

What events mark the rising action? When the men go upstairs and Mrs. Hale says, "I'd hate to have men coming into my kitchen, and snooping and criticizing," the women have a chance to notice more in the kitchen. Mrs. Hale recalls her relationship to Mrs. Wright, and the women discuss whether the wife really murdered her husband.

The men return to the kitchen on their way out to the barn just after the women discover the quilt pieces with the bad stitching. The next dialogue between the women is more open and brings out Mrs. Hale's regret for not having visited and supported Mrs. Wright in her unhappy marriage. They notice the empty birdcage.

What is the climax? Mrs. Hale finds the dead bird in the pretty box, and the two women understand what it means just before the men return to the kitchen briefly. From then on the women utter small lies to the men. Mrs. Peters for the first time reveals personal memories that suggest she can imagine Mrs. Wright's motives.

What is the resolution? As everyone prepares to leave, Mrs. Peters pretends the bird is insignificant, joining Mrs. Hale in protecting Mrs. Wright and playing along with the men's idea that there's nothing to notice in the kitchen. The women collaborate in hiding the bird.

What kind of play or plot is it? Like some detective stories, the play doesn't ask "whodunnit?" but why the murder was committed. Its mode of representation is a familiar type—domestic realism—in which the places, people, things, and even events are more or less ordinary. (Unfortunately, domestic violence is quite common.)

Setting

When does the action occur? The play appears to be contemporary with 1916 (a stove heater, party-line telephones, a horse-drawn wagon). It is a winter morning, and the scene takes perhaps an hour.

Where does the action occur? It is obviously farm country, perhaps in the Midwest, where farms are very far apart.

What is the atmosphere? The freezing weather reflects the feeling of the play and gives the characters a motive for gathering in the kitchen. John Wright is described as a chilly wind. The frozen house has ruined Mrs. Wright's preserves of summer fruit. The mess in the kitchen, especially the sticky spill of red fruit in the cupboard, seems related to the unhappiness and horror of the marriage and the crime.

Are there scene changes? Instead of several scenes over a longer time, showing the deteriorating marriage, the crisis over the bird, the murder itself, Mrs. Wright's sleepless night, and Mr. Hale's visit, the story unfolds in a single scene, in one room, on the second morning after the murder, between the entrance and exit of Mrs. Hale and Mrs. Peters. It is essential that the play focus on "kitchen things" and what the women visitors notice and think.

Style, Tone, Imagery

What is the style of the dialogue? The dialogue seems similar to everyday speech. There are some differences in speaking style that show the Hales are more rustic than the Peters and the county attorney. Hale has a relaxed way of telling a story: "then I says," etc. Mrs. Hale: "Those towels get dirty awful quick" and "If I was you, I wouldn't tell her the fruit was gone. Tell her it *ain't*."

How do nonverbal gestures and actions convey meaning? Many specific actions indicated in the stage directions are crucial to the play: everyone looking at the rocking chair, pointing to the room upstairs, looking at the loaf of bread that should have been put back in the bread box, etc.

Do any of the props seem to have symbolic meaning? Some objects in the play are so important they seem symbolic, though the play tries not to be too heavily poetic. All kinds of "trifles" are clues. For instance, the women get Mrs. Wright's clothes to bring to her in jail. "MRS. HALE: [*Examining the skirt.*] Wright was close," meaning stingy. Mrs. Hale's words convey a quick impression: The skirt looks "shabby" because John Wright didn't give his wife any money for clothes (he was "good" but stingy and cold).

There would be some colorful props on stage—the jar of cherries, the red cloth and other quilt material, the pretty box—all of them signs of what has gone wrong. The room itself is "gloomy" and has some dirty and messy things in plain sight; other things in the cupboards are eventually revealed. These props would add to the uncomfortable feeling of the play.

The closest thing to a symbol is the caged songbird. Even the men notice the broken door and missing bird. Mrs. Hale underlines the comparison to Mrs. Wright twice: "she was kind of like a bird," and later, "No, Wright wouldn't like the bird—a thing that sang. She used to sing. He killed that, too."

Theme

What is the theme of the play? The title calls attention to what the play is about. Glaspell didn't call it *The Caged Songbird* or *Murder in the Midwest* or something heavy-handed. The main action is a search for a motive to confirm what everyone believes, that Minnie Wright must have strangled her husband while he was sleeping in bed. But the underlying theme of the play seems to be about men's and women's different perspectives. How can women's everyday things be important? Why would anyone charged with murder worry about preserves? Even the women hope that Mrs. Wright's worry about having her apron and shawl in jail means she didn't commit the crime. The kitchen things—the trifles in her own house—"turn against her," but the women are able to hide evidence that the men consider insignificant.

WRITING ABOUT DRAMA

Writing an essay about drama, like writing about fiction or poetry, can sharpen your responses and focus your reading; at the same time, it can illuminate aspects of the work that other readers may have missed. When you write about drama, in a very real sense you perform the role that directors and actors take on in a stage performance: You offer your "reading" of the text, interpreting it in order to guide other readers' responses. But you also shape and refine your own response by attempting to express it clearly.

Using the notes you have taken while reading a play, try to locate the specific lines that have contributed to your expectations or your discoveries. Are these lines at the beginning, the middle, or the end of the play? Who gives most of the hints or misleading information? If there is one character who is especially unseeing, especially devious, or especially insightful, you might decide to write an essay describing the function of that character in the play. A good way to undertake such a study of a character in drama (as in fiction) is to imagine the work without that character. Mrs. Hale in *Trifles* is certainly the cleverest "detective," so why do we need Mrs. Peters as well? One obvious answer is that plays need dialogue, and we would find it artificial if Mrs. Hale talked mainly to herself. But a more interesting answer is that in a play the audience learns by witnessing characters with different temperaments responding to the same situation. As these remarks suggest, you can also develop essays that compare characters.

In addition to character studies, essays on drama can focus on the kinds of observations made above: expectations and plot structure; the presence and absence of characters or actions onstage; the different degrees of awareness of characters and audience at various points in the action; titles, stage directions, and other stylistic details, including **metaphors** or other imagery; and, of course, themes. As you write, you will probably discover that you can imagine directing or acting in a performance of the play, and you'll realize that interpreting a play is a crucial step in bringing it to life.

SUGGESTIONS FOR WRITING

1. The action in Glaspell's play unfolds continuously, without interruption, in a single, relatively small room (the kitchen of a farmhouse), with the two female characters never leaving the stage. Write a response paper or essay discussing how these three factors affect your responses to the play, to the crime being investigated, and to the various characters.
2. How do your sympathies for Mrs. Peters change over the course of TRIFLES? What might Mrs. Peters be said to represent in the clash of attitudes at the heart of the play? Write an essay in which you examine both Mrs. Peters's evolving character as it is revealed in TRIFLES and her significance to the play's theme.
3. How would you characterize Susan Glaspell's feminism as revealed in TRIFLES—does it seem radical or moderate? How does it compare to feminist political and social ideas of our own time? (Consult three or more educational or library Web sites for biographical background on Glaspell; there are several sites offering teaching materials on TRIFLES as well. If time allows, you might also pursue sources that provide an overview of women's movements in the United States in the twentieth century.) Write an essay in which you explore the political leanings apparent in TRIFLES, both in the context of Glaspell's play (published in 1916) and in the broader historical context of the struggle for women's rights over the past century.
4. Write an essay in which you propose a production of TRIFLES, complete with details of how you would handle the casting, costumes, set design, lighting, and direction of the actors. What would be your overall controlling vision for the production? Would you attempt to reproduce faithfully the look and feel of the play as it might have been in 1916, or would you introduce innovations? How would you justify your choices in terms of dramatic effectiveness?

SAMPLE WRITING: RESPONSE PAPER

Response papers are a great way to begin moving from informal notes to a more formal essay. Though many response-paper assignments invite you to respond to any aspect or element of a literary text that grabs your attention, the following example was written in response to a more targeted assignment, one that asked students to "explore something specific about the way TRIFLES handles plot. For example, what are the major internal and/or external conflicts? Or what would you argue is the play's turning point, and why?" Student-writer Jessica Zezulka explored the last question. Marginal comments below are the instructor's. But what do you think of her answer? How might she strengthen and develop the argument she begins to make here about the play's turning point? What alternative answers or arguments occur to you?

Zezulka 1

Jessica Zezulka
Professor Mays
English 298
10 January 2017

Trifles Plot Response Paper

While the men dillydally over the facts, the so-called "evidence," the women in *Trifles* discover the missing piece: a motive for murder. The moment Mrs. Hale and Mrs. Peters find the dead canary in the hidden box is the turning point in the play. Up until that instant, their conversation seems trivial, to both a reader and the men involved. Upon discussing the little trifles, the quilt and the sewing, these two women have inadvertently stumbled across what the men are so desperate to find. This turning point changes the way the play is read, as well as the way you view the wife of the dead man.

Mrs. Wright, accused of murdering her husband, appears almost crazy for just up and killing her spouse. The reader is as confused as the men at first, wondering why on earth would she do it? When you realize, along with the two women, that her motive was his brutal killing of the canary, you suddenly become privy to a secret that the men seemingly never learn. The play uses dramatic irony, where the reader knows the truth but the characters in the play are oblivious.

Might it be possible to read their conversation as less trivial (even up to this point) than the male characters do?

Again, though, don't we have relevant evidence before that about the possible state (and effects) of this marriage, which might be just as relevant to motive? If so, what *really* makes this moment stand out?

Interesting! Irony certainly is key to the play, but not all the characters are equally "oblivious," right?

Zezulka 2

Susan Glaspell timed this moment perfectly, giving the reader time to be both confused and then suddenly enlightened.

This turning point breeds sympathy for the accused murderess. Mrs. Wright is no longer just a good-wife-gone-bad. You as the reader follow the emotions of the two women in the empty house and can feel their almost immediate comprehension and understanding of both the situation and the woman involved. The wife becomes someone we can relate to, almost having a just cause for murdering her husband. As I said, Glaspell builds the tension to that point perfectly; the reader is all for the law being upheld until you know what led up to the murder. If you asked me, I'd say he deserved it. The women's discussion of *Trifles* led to the heart of the matter, a turning point that all but justifies John Wright's death.

So might the play also turn on the conflict — or at least the contrast — between two possible ways of defining "innocence" or even two kinds of "law"?

Zezulka 3

Work Cited

Glaspell, Susan. *Trifles. The Norton Introduction to Literature*, edited by Kelly J. Mays, 12th ed., W. W. Norton, 2017, pp. 1391-1401.

SAMPLE WRITING: ESSAY

The following sample of student writing demonstrates how you might develop an early response to a play into a more formal and thorough argument about it. In her essay on Susan Glaspell's TRIFLES, Stephanie Ortega explores the relationship among the female characters in order to offer her own answers to more than one of the questions posed in the previous chapter's "Suggestions for Writing": How does Mrs. Peters's character evolve over the course of *Trifles*? How is that evolution significant to the play's theme, or how might it help to define the play's particular version of feminism?

As always, we encourage you to read the sample with a critical eye, identifying what works and what doesn't so as to discover specific ways to improve your own writing and reading. At what moments in the essay do you find yourself strongly agreeing? discovering something new about or in Glaspell's play? At what moments might you instead find yourself disagreeing or feeling either confused or simply dissatisfied, wanting more? What exactly makes each of these moments especially satisfying, interesting, persuasive, enlightening—or the reverse? If Stephanie Ortega were your classmate, what three specific things would you suggest she do in order to improve the essay in revision? Alternatively, what three qualities of this essay might you want to emulate in your own work?

Ortega 1

Stephanie Ortega
Professor Mays
English 298
23 January 2017

A Journey of Sisterhood

Trifles begins at the start of a murder investigation. Mrs. Wright has allegedly murdered her harsh husband, John Wright; and the Sheriff and his wife, Mrs. Peters; the County Attorney; and the neighbors, Mr. and Mrs. Hale, all come to the Wright house to investigate. Throughout the entire play the women are always on stage, whereas the men enter and exit, so the women are the play's focus. But Glaspell's *Trifles* is a feminist play not only because of that, but also because of how it shows two or even three very different women coming together in sisterhood.

Ortega 2

Mrs. Peters and Mrs. Hale are first introduced as they stand together by the door of the house where the murder took place, yet though the women stand together, their behavior and views initially seem wide apart. Whereas Mrs. Hale stands up for her counterparts, Mrs. Peters and Mrs. Wright, from the beginning, Mrs. Peters at first tends to stick up more for the men. When the County Attorney makes a remark about Mrs. Wright not having been much of a homemaker and having a dirty home, we see that Mrs. Hale doesn't like men poking in Mrs. Wright's business and having input in the doings of a house. Putting herself in Mrs. Wright's shoes, Mrs. Hale says, "I'd hate to have men coming into *my* kitchen, snooping around and criticizing" (1395, emphasis added). But Mrs. Peters states that since it is an investigation, "it's no more than th[e men's] duty" to poke around (1395). Later, when Mrs. Hale actually interferes with the investigation by trying to tidy up the place and re-sew the badly stitched quilt they discover, Mrs. Peters steps in, "*[n]ervously*" saying, "I don't think we ought to touch things" (1397). Mrs. Peters's only view is that of her husband; she knows and seems to care very little about Mrs. Wright or her life before marriage as Minnie Foster. As far as Mrs. Peters is concerned, "the law is the law" (1396), and she is "married to" it, as the County Attorney will say at the end of the play (1400); therefore she must abide by it.

Mrs. Hale's identification with Minnie Foster only intensifies as the play progresses. She remembers Minnie Foster as a carefree woman full of energy and life, bright and cheery like a canary, implying that marriage to John Wright "change[d]" all that (1398). Mrs. Hale starts feeling guilty for not visiting Mrs. Wright, telling Mrs. Peters multiple times that she "wish[es she] had come over sometimes when *she* was here," and eventually even suggesting that not coming to see Mrs. Wright was "a crime" (1398, 1400).

In part because of the way Mrs. Hale talks about her, Minnie Foster's figurative presence becomes ever stronger, bringing Mrs. Hale and Mrs. Peters together as they put themselves into her place, speculating about her feelings and responses to the conditions of her life. When the women come upon a box containing a bird that had its neck wrung, Mrs. Hale associates Mr. Wright's presumed killing of the songbird with his destruction of part of Mrs. Wright, speculating about her feelings: "No, Wright wouldn't like the bird—a thing that sang. She used to sing. He killed that, too" (1399). Thus, Mr. Wright's killing of the bird is a symbolic killing of Minnie Foster's spirit. At this point, the women come to understand that Mrs. Wright was indeed the one who killed her husband because when the women realize that Mr. Wright wrung the bird's neck, the women finally know the reason for Mrs. Wright's "funny way" of killing him (1396). (It's now that "*Their eyes meet*" with "*[a] look of growing comprehension, of horror*" [1399].)

More importantly, here is where we really start to see a change in Mrs. Peters. For the first time she, too, interferes with the investigators, even though she doesn't actually destroy evidence or lie, when she responds to a question about the cat by simply saying that there is not one "*now*" (1399). She expresses sympathy

Ortega 3

for Minnie Foster and identifies with her, based on her own memories of the way she felt both when her kitten was killed with a hatchet and, much later, when her first baby died, leaving her and her husband alone in the "stillness" of their isolated house (1399). Mrs. Peters also states that had she gotten hold of the boy who killed her kitten long ago she would have gotten revenge just as Mrs. Peters and Mrs. Hale now speculate that Minnie Foster Wright did. The women each sympathize with Minnie Foster and the distant person she has become, Mrs. Wright.

By sympathizing with Mrs. Wright and paying attention to the "little things" the men don't consider solid "evidence" (1397), the women have single-handedly sorted out a plausible sequence of events and, more importantly, a reason why Mrs. Wright killed her husband the way she did. Yet rather than reveal what they've learned, they slowly, in the silence of mutual sympathy, work together to cover Mrs. Wright's tracks and to protect her. Mrs. Peters is defying the actual law and starting to protect the law of women and sisterhood instead. Mrs. Hale, Mrs. Peters, and Mrs. Wright become one unit, opposing their intuitive feminine selves to the logical and analytical men.

Although Mrs. Wright never once appears on stage, her presence is what brings all three women closer. They are able to attain information that the men simply overlook. And it is this which brings the women forth in the union of sisterhood at the end of the play as they realize that "We [women] all go through the same things—it's all just a different kind of the same thing" (1400).

Ortega 4

Work Cited

Glaspell, Susan. *Trifles. The Norton Introduction to Literature*, edited by Kelly J. Mays, 12th ed., W. W. Norton, 2017, pp. 1391-1401.

Understanding the Text

26 ELEMENTS OF DRAMA

Most of us read more fiction than drama and are likely to encounter drama by watching filmed versions of it. Nonetheless, the skills you have developed in reading stories and poems come in handy when you read plays. And just as with fiction and poetry, you will understand and appreciate drama more fully by becoming familiar with the various elements of the **genre**.

CHARACTER

Character is possibly the most familiar and accessible of the elements; both fiction and drama feature one or more imaginary persons who take part in the action. The word *character* refers not only to a person represented in an imagined plot, whether narrated or acted out, but also to the unique qualities that make up a personality. From one point of view, "character" as a part in a plot and "character" as a kind of personality are both predictions: This sort of person is likely to see things from a certain angle and behave in certain ways. Notice that the idea of character includes both the individual differences among people and the classification of similar people into types. Whereas much realistic fiction emphasizes unique individuals rather than general character types, drama often compresses and simplifies personalities—a play has only about two hours at the most (sometimes much less) in which to show situations, appearances, and behaviors, without description or background other than **exposition** provided in the dialogue. The advantage of portraying character in broader strokes is that it heightens the contrasts between character types, adding to the drama: Differences provoke stronger reactions.

Plays are especially concerned with character because of the concrete manner in which they portray people on the stage. With a few exceptions (such as experiments in multimedia performance), the only words in the performance of a play are spoken by actors, and usually these actors are *in character*—that is, speaking as though they really were the people they play in the drama. (Rarely, plays have a **narrator** who observes and comments on the action from the sidelines, and in some plays a character may address the audience directly, but even when the actors apparently step outside of the imaginary frame, they are still part of the play and are still playing characters.) In fiction, the narrator's description and commentary can guide a reader's judgment about characters. Reading a play, you will have no such guide because drama relies almost exclusively on *indirect characterization* (see ch. 3). Apart from some clues about characters in the **stage directions**, you will need to imagine the appearance, manners, and movement of someone speaking the lines assigned to any one character. You can do this even as you read through a play for the first time, discovering the characters' attitudes and motivations as the scenes unfold. This ability to predict character and then to revise expectations as situations change is based not only on our experiences of people in real life but also on our familiarity with types of characters or roles that occur in many dramatic forms.

Consider the patterns of characters in many stories that are narrated or acted out, whether in novels, comic books, television series, Hollywood films, or even video games. In many of these forms, there is a leading role, a main character: the **protagonist**. The titles of plays such as HAMLET, ANTIGONE, or, a little less obviously, DEATH OF A SALESMAN imply that the play will be about a central character, the chief object of the playwright's and the reader's or audience's concern. Understanding the character of the protagonist—sometimes in contrast with an **antagonist**, the opponent of the main character—becomes the consuming interest of such a play. Especially in more traditional or popular genres, the protagonist may be called a **hero** or **heroine**, and the antagonist may be called the **villain**. Most characterization in professional theater, however, avoids depicting pure good and pure evil in a fight to the death. Most characters possess both negative and redeeming qualities.

As in other genres that represent people in action, in drama there are *minor characters* or supporting roles. At least since ancient Rome, romantic comedies have been structured around a leading man and woman, along with a comparable pair (often the "buddies" of the leads) whose problems may be less serious, whose characters may be less complex, or who in other ways support or complicate rather than dominate the action. Sometimes a minor character can be said to be a **foil**, a character designed to bring out qualities in another character by contrast. The main point to remember is that all the characters in a drama are interdependent and help characterize each other. Through dialogue and behavior, each brings out what is characteristic in the others.

Like movies, plays must respect certain limitations: the time an audience can be expected to sit and watch, the attention and sympathy an audience is likely to give to various characters, the amount of exposition that can be shown rather than spoken aloud. Because of these constraints, playwrights, screenwriters, casting directors, and actors must rely on shortcuts to convey character. Everyone involved, including the audience, consciously or unconsciously relies on stereotypes of various social roles to flesh out the dramatic action. Even a play that seeks to undermine stereotypes must still invoke them. In the United States today, casting—or typecasting—usually relies on an actor's social identity, from gender and race to occupation, region, and age. However, plays that rely too much on stereotypes, positive or negative, may leave everyone disappointed (or offended); a role that defies stereotypes can be more interesting to perform and to watch. Alternatively, a character can be so exceptional and unfamiliar that audiences will fail to recognize any connection to people they might meet, and their responses will fall flat. All dramatic roles, then, must have some connection to types of personality, and good roles modify such types just enough to make the character interesting. Playwrights often overturn or modify expectations of character in order to surprise an audience. So, too, do the actors who play those parts.

Every performance of a given character, like every production of a play, is an interpretation. Not just "adaptations"—Greek or Elizabethan plays set in modern times and performed in modern dress, for example—but even productions that seek to adhere faithfully to the written play are interpretations of what is vital or essential in it. John Malkovich, in the 1983–84 production of *Death of a Salesman*, did not portray Biff Loman as an outgoing, successful, hail-fellow-well-met jock, though that is apparently how the playwright originally envisioned the part. Malkovich saw Biff as only pretending to be a jock. Big-time athletes, he insisted, don't glad-hand people; they wait for people to come to them. The actor did not change the author's words, but by intonation, body language, and "stage business" (wordless gestures and actions) he suggested his own view of the character. In other words, he broke with the expectations associated with the character's type. As you read and develop your own interpretation of a play, try imagining various interpretations of its characters in order to reveal different possible meanings in the drama.

Questions about Character

- Who is the protagonist? Why and how so? Which other characters, if any, are main or major characters? Which are minor characters?
- What are the protagonist's most distinctive traits, and what is most distinctive about his or her outlook and values? What motivates the character? What is it about the character that creates internal and/or external conflict? Which lines or stage directions reveal most about the character?
- What are the roles of other characters? Which, if any, functions as an antagonist? Which, if any, serves as a foil? Does any character function as a narrator or **chorus**, providing background information and commentary? Why and how so?
- To what extent are any of the characters in the play "types"? How might this affect an audience's experience of the play? In what ways might a director or actor choose to go against the expected types, and how would this complicate the play's overall effect and meaning?
- Which of the characters, or which aspects of the characters, does the play encourage us to sympathize with or to admire? to view negatively? Why and how so? Are there characters who might be more or less sympathetic, depending on how the role is cast and interpreted?
- If you were directing a production of this play, whom among your friends and acquaintances would you cast in each role, and why? If you were directing a movie version, what professional actors would you cast?

PLOT AND STRUCTURE

An important part of any storyteller's task, whether in narrative or dramatic genres, is the invention, selection, and arrangement of some **action**. Even carefully structured action cannot properly be called a full-scale **plot** without some unifying sense of purpose. That is, what happens should seem to happen for meaningful reasons. This does not mean, of course, that characters or the audience must be satisfied in their hopes or expectations, or that effective plays need to wrap up every loose end. It does mean that a reader or theatergoer should feel that the playwright has completed *this* play—that nothing essential is missing—though the play's outcome or overall effect may be difficult to sum up.

Conflict is the engine that drives plot, and the presentation of conflict shapes the dramatic structure of a play. A conflict whose outcome is never in doubt may have other kinds of interest, but it is not truly dramatic. In a dramatic conflict, each of the opposing forces must at some point seem likely to triumph or worthy of such triumph—whether conflict is *external* (one character versus another, or one group of characters versus another group, each of whom may represent a different worldview) or *internal* (within a single character torn between competing views, duties, needs, or desires), or even one idea or ideology versus another one. In *Hamlet*, for example, our interest in the struggle between Hamlet and Claudius depends on their being evenly matched. Claudius has possession of the throne and the queen, but Hamlet's role as the heir to the late king and his popularity with the people offset his opponent's strength.

The typical plot in drama, as in fiction, involves five stages: exposition, rising action, climax, falling action, and conclusion. **Exposition**, the first phase of plot, provides essential background information about the characters and situation as they exist at the beginning of a play and perhaps also about the events that got the characters to this point—as when, early in TRIFLES, Mr. Hale describes what happened before the play opens. The second phase, **rising action**, begins when an **inciting incident** leads to conflict—as when, in *Trifles*, the men leave the women alone with what the latter soon discover to be crucial evidence. The moment when the conflict reaches its greatest pitch of intensity and its outcome is decided is the plot's third phase, its **climax** or **turning point**—in *Trifles*, perhaps the discovery of the dead bird and the act of covering up the evidence. The fourth stage, **falling action**, brings a release of emotional tension and moves the characters toward the **resolution** of their conflict and the plot itself toward its fifth and final stage, the **conclusion**. In *Trifles*, the men's return to the kitchen because, they believe, no evidence has been found can be called the falling action. The women's apparent decision to remain mute about what they have discovered can be called the resolution. The play concludes as the characters leave the Wrights' house. Unlike *Trifles*, some lengthy plays feature more than one plot. In such cases, the plot to which less time and attention is devoted is called the **subplot**.

Many older plays in the Western tradition, such as Shakespeare's, have five acts, each act roughly corresponding to—and thus emphasizing—a particular phase of plot. Acts are often further subdivided into scenes, each of which usually takes place in a somewhat different time and place and features a somewhat different combination of characters. Ancient Greek plays such as OEDIPUS THE KING are structured differently, such that individual scenes or *episodes* are separated by choral songs—that is, odes spoken or sung by the group of characters known as the chorus. Modern plays tend to have fewer acts and scenes than those of earlier eras, and plays such as *Trifles*—in which the action unfolds continuously and, usually, in a single time and place—have become so common that they have their own name: the *one-act play*.

In the performance of a play longer than one act, it has become customary to have at least one intermission, in part for the practical reason that the audience may need restrooms or refreshments. Breaks may be signaled by turning down stage lights, turning up the house lights, and lowering the curtain (if there is one).

On rare occasions, very long plays (such as Tony Kushner's *Angels in America* [1992–93]) are performed over more than one evening, with the obvious challenge of finding an audience willing and able to afford tickets and time for more than one performance; those who read such play "cycles" or **sequences** at their own pace at home have a certain advantage.

The key point is that the form of a play and the breaks between scenes or acts result from the nature of the play. Breaks can create suspense—a curtain comes down after an unexplained gunshot—or they can provide relief from tension or an emotional crisis.

Questions about Plot

- Read the first scene or the first few pages and then stop. What potential for conflict do you see here? What do you expect to happen in the rest of the play?
- How is the play divided into acts, scenes, or episodes, if at all? What is the effect of this structure? Does the division of the play correspond, more or less, to the five stages of plot development—exposition, rising action, climax, resolution, conclusion?
- Does the play show a relatively clear progression through the traditional stages of plot development, or does it seem to defy such conventions? If so, how, and what might the playwright achieve through these departures from tradition?
- What is the inciting incident or destabilizing event? How and why does this event destabilize the initial situation? How would you describe the conflict that develops? To what extent is it external, internal, or both?
- What is the climax, or turning point? Why and how so? How is the conflict resolved? How and why might this resolution fulfill or defy your expectations?

STAGES, SETS, AND SETTING

Most of us have been to a theater at one time or another, and we know what a conventional modern stage (the **proscenium stage**) looks like: a room with the wall missing between us and it (the so-called *fourth wall*). So when we read a modern play—that is, one written during the past two or three hundred years—and imagine it taking place before us, we think of it as happening on this kind of stage. Though there are also other modern types of stages—the **thrust stage**, where the audience sits around three sides of the major acting area, and the **arena stage**, where the audience sits all the way around the acting area and players make their entrances and their exits through the auditorium—most plays today are performed on a proscenium stage. Most of the plays in this book can be readily imagined as taking place on such a stage.

Ancient Greek plays and the plays of Shakespeare were originally staged quite differently from most modern plays, however, and although they may be played today on a proscenium stage, we might be confused as we read if we are unaware of the layout of the theaters for which they were first written. In the Greek theater, the audience sat on a raised semicircle of seats (**amphitheater**) halfway around a circular area (**orchestra**) used primarily for dancing by the chorus. At the back of the orchestra was the **skene**, or stage house, representing the palace or temple before which the action took place. Shakespeare's stage, in contrast, basically involved a rectangular area built inside one end of a large enclosure like a circular walled-in yard; the audience stood on the ground or sat in stacked balconies around three sides of the principal acting area (rather like a thrust stage). There were additional acting areas on either side of this stage, as well as a recessed area at its back (which could represent Gertrude's chamber in *Hamlet*, for example) and an upper acting area (which could serve as Juliet's balcony). A trap door in the stage floor was used for occasional effects; the ghost of Hamlet's father probably entered and exited this way. Until three centuries ago—and certainly in Shakespeare's time—plays for large paying audiences were performed outdoors in daylight because of the difficulty and expense of lighting. If you are curious about Shakespeare's stage, you can visit a reconstruction of his Globe Theatre in Southwark, London, England, either in person or online at www.shakespearesglobe.org. Every summer, plays by Shakespeare are performed there for large international audiences willing to sit on hard benches around the arena or to stand as "groundlings" (a lucky few of whom can lean on the stage near the feet of the actors). The walls in the background of the stage are beautifully carved and painted, but there is no painted scenery, minimal furniture, few costume changes, no lighting, and no curtain around the stage (a cloth hanging usually covers the recessed area at the back of the stage). Three or four musicians may play period instruments on the balcony.

As the design of the Globe suggests, the conventions of dramatic writing and stage production have changed considerably over the centuries. Certainly this is true of the way playwrights convey a sense of place—one of the two key ingredients that make up a play's **setting**. Usually the audience is asked to imagine that the featured section of the auditorium is actually a particular place somewhere else. The audience of course knows it is a stage, more or less bare or elaborately disguised, but they accept it as a kitchen, a public square, a wooded park, an open road, or a room in a castle or a hut. *Oedipus the King* takes place entirely before the palace at Thebes. Following the general convention of ancient Greek drama, the play's setting never changes. When the action demands the presence of Teiresias, for example, the scene does not shift to him; instead, escorts bring him to the front of the palace. Similarly, important events that take place elsewhere are described by witnesses who arrive on the scene.

In Shakespeare's theater the conventions of place are quite different: The acting arena does not represent a single specific place but assumes a temporary identity according to the characters who inhabit it, their costumes, and their speeches. At the opening of *Hamlet* we know we are at a sentry station because a man dressed as a soldier challenges two others. By line 15, we know that we are in Denmark because the actors profess to be "liegemen to the Dane." At the end of the scene the actors leave the stage and in a sense take the sentry station with them. Shortly thereafter, a group of people dressed in court costumes and a man and a woman wearing crowns appear. As a theater audience, we must surmise from the costumes and dialogue that the acting area has now become a royal court; when we read the play, the stage directions give us a cue that the place has changed.

In a modern play, there are likely to be several changes of scene, each marked by the lowering of the curtain or the darkening of the stage while different sets and props are arranged. **Sets** (the design, decoration, and scenery) and **props** (articles or objects used on stage) vary greatly in modern productions of plays written in any period. Sometimes space is merely suggested—a circle of sand at one end of the stage, a blank wall behind—to emphasize universal themes or to stimulate the audience's imagination. More typically, a set uses realistic aids to the imagination. The set of *Trifles*, for example, must include at least a sink, a cupboard, a stove, a small table, a large kitchen table, and a rocking chair, as well as certain props: a bird cage, quilting pieces, and an ornamental box.

Time is the second key ingredient of setting, and conventions for representing time have also altered across the centuries. Three or four centuries ago, European dramatists and critics admired the conventions of classical Greek drama which, they believed, dictated that the action of a play should represent a very short time—sometimes as short as the actual performance time (two or three hours), and certainly no longer than a single day. This unity of time, one of the three so-called **classical unities**, impels a dramatist to select the moment when a stable situation should change and to fill in the necessary prior details by exposition. (These same critics maintained that a play should be unified in place and action as well; the kind of leaping from Denmark to England, or from court to forest, that happens in Shakespeare's plays, as well as subplots, were off-limits according to such standards. In *Trifles*, which observes the three unities, all the action before the investigators' visit to the farmhouse is summarized by characters during their brief visit, and the kitchen is the only part of the house seen by the audience.)

When there are gaps and shifts in time, they are often indicated between scenes with the help of scenery, sound effects, stage directions, or notes in the program. An actor must assist in conveying the idea of time if his or her character appears at different ages. Various conventions of classical or Elizabethan drama have also worked effectively to communicate to the audience the idea of the passage of time, from the choral odes in *Oedipus the King* to the breaks between scenes in Shakespeare plays.

Action within a play thus can take place in a wide range of locations and over many years rather than in the one place and the twenty-four-hour period demanded by critics who believed in the classical unities. And we can learn much about how a particular play works and what it means by paying attention to the way it handles setting and sets.

Questions about Setting and Staging

- Does all the action occur in one time and place, or in more than one? If the latter, what are those times and places? How much time tends to pass between scenes or episodes?
- How important do the general time and place seem to be, and in what ways are they important? What about the plot and characters would remain the same if a director chose to set the play in a different time and place? What wouldn't?
- What patterns do you notice regarding where and when things happen? Which characters are associated with each setting? How do different characters relate to the same setting? When, how, and why do scenes change from one setting to another? Are there significant deviations?
- Do the stage directions describe particular settings and props in detail? If so, what seems significant about the details? How might they establish mood, reveal character, and affect individual characters and their interactions with one another? Is there anything in the stage directions that seems to be intended more for readers than for a director staging a production?
- Does the date of the play tell you anything about the way it was originally intended to be staged? Does the representation of time and place in the play implicitly call for a certain type of stage? If you were staging the play today, what kind of stage, sets, and props might you use, and why? How might your choices affect how the play works on audiences and what it means to them?

TONE, LANGUAGE, AND SYMBOL

In plays, as in other literary genres, **tone** is difficult to specify or explain. Perhaps tone is more important in drama than in other genres because it is, in performance, a spoken form, and vocal tone always affects the meaning of spoken words to some extent, in any culture or language. The actor—and any reader who wishes to imagine a play as spoken aloud—must infer from the written language just how to read a line, what tone of voice to use. The choice of tone must be a negotiation between the words of the playwright and the interpretation and skill of the actor or reader. At times stage directions will specify the tone of a line of dialogue, though even that must be only a hint, since there are many ways of speaking "intensely" or "angrily." Find a line in one of the plays printed here that has a stage direction telling the actor how to deliver it, and with one or two other people take turns saying it that way. If nothing else, such an experiment may help you appreciate the talent of good actors who can put on a certain tone of voice and make it seem natural and convincing. But it will also show you the many options for interpreting tone.

Dramatic ***irony***, in which a character's perception is contradicted by what the audience knows, and even *situational irony*, in which a character's (and the audience's) expectations about what will happen are contradicted by what actually does happen, are relatively easy to detect. But *verbal irony*, in which a statement implies a meaning quite different from its obvious, literal meaning, can be fairly subtle and easy to miss. In the absence of clear stage directions, verbal irony—like other aspects of tone—can also be a matter of interpretation. That is, directors and actors, as well as readers and audiences, will often have to decide which lines in a play should be interpreted ironically. All three types of irony are nonetheless crucial to drama. As the very term *dramatic irony* suggests, drama—even more than fiction—depends for its effects on gaps between what the various characters and the audience know. And situational irony—the gap between expectations and outcomes and even between what characters seem to deserve and what they get—is an especially key component of **tragedy**.

Never hesitate to apply the skills you have developed in interpreting poetry to drama; after all, most early plays were written in some form of verse. Aspects of poetry often emerge in modern plays; for example, **monologues** or extended speeches by one character, while they rarely rhyme or have regular **meter**, may allow greater eloquence than is usual in everyday speech and may include revealing imagery and **figures of speech**. A character in Lorraine Hansberry's A RAISIN IN THE SUN, for example, uses **metaphor** and **personification**, as well as **alliteration**, to great effect when she remarks (in act 3) that "death done come in this here house [. . .] Done come walking in my house."

Simple actions or objects, too, often have metaphorical significance or turn into **symbols**. Effective plays often use props in this way, as *Trifles* does with the bird and its cage. And some plays, like some poems, may even be organized around *controlling* ***metaphors***. As you read, pay close attention to metaphors or images, whether in language or more concrete form.

Allusions, references to other works of literature or art or something else external to the play, can enrich the text in similar ways. The title of Tom Stoppard's uproarious comedy *The Real Inspector Hound* (1968), for example, seems to be an allusion to Sir Arthur Conan Doyle's novel *The Hound of the Baskervilles* (1901–02), featuring Sherlock Holmes. Doyle's novel is a classic in the detective fiction genre, which Stoppard's *Inspector Hound* parodies. In a more serious vein, though New Orleans, where Tennessee Williams's A STREETCAR NAMED DESIRE takes place, actually does contain a street called Elysian Fields, the play gets a good deal of symbolic mileage out of using this as a setting for the play thanks to the allusion to Greek mythology (in which the Elysian Fields were the final resting place of heroic and virtuous souls). Awareness of all the stylistic choices in the work can help you reach a clearer interpretation of the whole play.

Questions about Tone, Language, and Symbol

- Which lines in the play strike you as most ambiguous when it comes to the tone in which they should be spoken? Why and how so? What is the effect of that ambiguity, or how might an actor's or reader's decision about tone here affect the play as a whole?
- How would you describe the overall tone of the whole play? Do any moments or entire scenes or acts in the play seem interestingly different in terms of their tone?
- How do the play's characters differ from one another in terms of their tone? Does any character's tone change over the course of the play?
- Are any details—such as names; actions or statements; references to objects, props, or other details of setting; or allusions, metaphors, or other figures of speech—repeated throughout the play? Do any of these repeated details seem to have special significance? If so, what might that significance be?
- What types of irony, if any, are at work in the play? What is the effect of the irony?

THEME

Theme—a statement a work seems to make about a given issue or subject—is by its very nature the most comprehensive of the elements, embracing the impact of the entire work. Indeed, theme is not part of the work but is abstracted from it by the reader or audience. Since we, as interpreters, infer the theme and put it in our own words, we understandably often disagree about it. To arrive at your own statement of a theme, you need to consider all the elements of a play together: character, structure, setting (including time and place), tone, and other aspects of the style or the potential staging that create the entire effect.

Tips for Identifying Theme

Because theme emerges from a work in its entirety and from all the other elements working together, there's no one-size-fits-all method for discovering theme. Here, however, are some things to look for and consider as you read and re-read a play.

- Pay attention to the title. A title will seldom indicate a play's theme directly, but some titles do suggest a central topic or a key question. Probe the rest of the play to see what insights, if any, about that topic or answers to that question it ultimately seems to offer.

- Identify any statements that the characters make about a general concept, issue, or topic such as human nature, the natural world, and so on, particularly in monologues or in debates between major characters. Look, too, for statements that potentially have a general meaning or application beyond the play, even if they refer to a specific situation. Then consider whether and how the play as a whole corroborates, overturns, or complicates any one such view or statement.
- If a character changes over the course of the play, try to articulate the truth or insight that he or she seems to discover. Then consider whether and how the play as a whole corroborates or complicates that insight.
- Identify a conflict depicted in the play and state it in general terms or turn it into a general question, leaving out any reference to specific characters, setting, and so on. Then think about the insight or theme that might be implied by the way the conflict is resolved.

• • •

Above all, try to understand a play on its own terms and to separate interpretation from evaluation. You may dislike symbolic or unrealistic drama until you get more used to it; if a play is not supposed to represent what real people would do in everyday life in that place and time, then it should not be criticized for failing to do so. Or you may find realistic plays about ordinary adults in middle America in the mid-twentieth century to be lacking in excitement or appeal. Yet if you read carefully, you may discover vigorous, moving portrayals of people trapped in situations all too familiar to them, if alien to you. Tastes may vary as widely as tones of speech, but if you are familiar with the elements of drama and the ways dramatic **conventions** vary over time and across cultures, you can become a good judge of theatrical literature, and you will notice more and more of the fine effects it can achieve. Nothing replaces the exhilaration and immediacy of a live theater performance, but reading and re-reading plays can yield a rich and rewarding appreciation of the dramatic art.

AUGUST WILSON
(1945–2005)
Fences

August Wilson died of liver cancer when he was only sixty. One of the most important dramatists in American theater history, he had come a long way, the hard way. Frederick August Kittel, Jr. (who would later take his mother's maiden name), was the son of a white, German-born baker and his wife, a black cleaning woman who singlehandedly raised their six children in Pittsburgh's down-at-heel Hill District. In 1957, when Wilson was twelve, his mother remarried. Her new husband was an African American sewer-department worker who, as Wilson learned only after his stepfather's death, had been both a high-school football star unable to secure a college scholarship and an ex-convict. After a series of bad experiences, Wilson left school at fifteen. Armed with a tenth-grade education, he took on a series of menial jobs, read his way through the public library, and served briefly in the Army. In 1968, he returned to the Hill, cofounding the Black Horizon Theater and debuting his first play. Fourteen years later, Wilson struck artistic gold with *Ma Rainey's Black Bottom* (1982), his first Broadway play and the second in what would become a ten-play cycle. Set mostly in the Hill and chronicling African American life in every decade of the twentieth century, the series earned Wilson two Pulitzers (for *Fences*, 1987, and *The Piano Lesson*, 1990); a Tony (for *Fences*); a Grammy (for the *Ma Rainey's* cast album); an Emmy (for his adaption of *Piano Lesson*); and eight Drama Critics Circle awards. Wilson often described *Fences* as his least representative, most conventional play, thanks to the way it revolves around a single "big character." Yet this, his best-known work, is also arguably among his most personal, set in the period of his youth and aimed, he said, at "uncover[ing] the nobility and the dignity" of the adults he grew up around—"that generation, which shielded its children from all of the indignities they went through."

For Lloyd Richards,[1]
who adds to whatever he touches

CHARACTERS

TROY MAXSON
JIM BONO, *Troy's friend*
ROSE, *Troy's wife*
LYONS, *Troy's oldest son by a previous marriage*
GABRIEL, *Troy's brother*
CORY, *Troy and Rose's son*
RAYNELL, *Troy's daughter*

SETTING: *The setting is the yard which fronts the only entrance to the Maxson household, an ancient two-story brick house set back off a small alley in a big-city neighborhood. The entrance to the house is gained by two or three steps leading to a wooden porch badly in need of paint.*

A relatively recent addition to the house and running its full width, the porch lacks congruence. It is a sturdy porch with a flat roof. One or two chairs of dubious value sit at one end where the kitchen window opens onto the porch. An old-fashioned icebox stands silent guard at the opposite end.

The yard is a small dirt yard, partially fenced (except during the last scene), with a wooden sawhorse, a pile of lumber, and other fence-building equipment off to the side. Opposite is a tree from which hangs a ball made of rags. A baseball bat leans against the tree. Two oil drums serve as garbage receptacles and sit near the house at right to complete the setting.

1. Influential Canadian-American director-actor (1919–2006) whom August Wilson called his "guide, mentor, and provocateur"; the first black director of a Broadway play (Lorraine Hansberry's *A Raisin in the Sun*, 1959), artistic director of the Eugene O'Neill Theater Center and the Yale Repertory Theatre, and dean of the Yale School of Drama, Richards oversaw the first productions of all of Wilson's plays, beginning with *Ma Rainey's Black Bottom* (1982).

THE PLAY: *Near the turn of the century, the destitute of Europe sprang on the city with tenacious claws and an honest and solid dream. The city devoured them. They swelled its belly until it burst into a thousand furnaces and sewing machines, a thousand butcher shops and bakers' ovens, a thousand churches and hospitals and funeral parlors and moneylenders. The city grew. It nourished itself and offered each man a partnership limited only by his talent, his guile and his willingness and capacity for hard work. For the immigrants of Europe, a dream dared and won true.*

The descendants of African slaves were offered no such welcome or participation. They came from places called the Carolinas and the Virginias, Georgia, Alabama, Mississippi and Tennessee. They came strong, eager, searching. The city rejected them and they fled and settled along the riverbanks and under bridges in shallow, ramshackle houses made of sticks and tar paper. They collected rags and wood. They sold the use of their muscles and their bodies. They cleaned houses and washed clothes, they shined shoes, and in quiet desperation and vengeful pride, they stole, and lived in pursuit of their own dream. That they could breathe free, finally, and stand to meet life with the force of dignity and whatever eloquence the heart could call upon.

By 1957, the hard-won victories of the European immigrants had solidified the industrial might of America. War had been confronted and won with new energies that used loyalty and patriotism as its fuel. Life was rich, full and flourishing. The Milwaukee Braves won the World Series, and the hot winds of change that would make the sixties a turbulent, racing, dangerous and provocative decade had not yet begun to blow full.

When the sins of our fathers visit us
We do not have to play host.
We can banish them with forgiveness
As God, in His Largeness and Laws.

—AUGUST WILSON

ACT ONE

Scene 1

It is 1957. Troy and Bono enter the yard, engaged in conversation. Troy is fifty-three years old, a large man with thick, heavy hands; it is this largeness that he strives to fill out and make an accommodation with. Together with his blackness, his largeness informs his sensibilities and the choices he has made in his life.

Of the two men, Bono is obviously the follower. His commitment to their friendship of thirty-odd years is rooted in his admiration of Troy's honesty, capacity for hard work, and his strength, which Bono seeks to emulate.

It is Friday night, payday, and the one night of the week the two men engage in a ritual of talk and drink. Troy is usually the most talkative and at times he can be crude and almost vulgar, though he is capable of rising to profound heights of expression. The men carry lunch buckets and wear or carry burlap aprons and are dressed in clothes suitable to their jobs as garbage collectors.

BONO: Troy, you ought to stop that lying!

TROY: I ain't lying! The nigger had a watermelon this big. (*Indicates with his hands*) Talking about . . . "What watermelon, Mr. Rand?" I like to fell out! "What watermelon, Mr. Rand?" . . . And it sitting there big as life.

BONO: What did Mr. Rand say?

TROY: Ain't said nothing. Figure if the nigger too dumb to know he carrying a watermelon, he wasn't gonna get much sense out of him. Trying to hide that great big old watermelon under his coat. Afraid to let the white man see him carry it home.

BONO: I'm like you . . . I ain't got no time for them kind of people.

TROY: Now what he look like getting mad 'cause he see the man from the union talking to Mr. Rand?

BONO: He come talking to me about . . . "Maxson gonna get us fired." I told him to get away from me with that. He walked away from me calling you a troublemaker. What Mr. Rand say?

TROY: Ain't said nothing. He told me to go down the commissioner's office next Friday. They called me down there to see them.

BONO: Well, as long as you got your complaint filed, they can't fire you. That's what one of them white fellows tell me.

TROY: I ain't worried about them firing me. They gonna fire me 'cause I asked a question? That's all I did. I went to Mr. Rand and asked him, "Why? Why you got the white mens driving and the colored lifting?" Told him, "What's the matter, don't I count? You think only white fellows got sense enough to drive a truck. That ain't no paper job! Hell, anybody can drive a truck. How come you got all whites driving and the colored lifting?" He told me, "Take it to the union." Well, hell, that's what I done! Now they wanna come up with this pack of lies.

BONO: I told Brownie if the man come and ask him any questions . . . just tell the truth! It ain't nothing but something they done trumped up on you 'cause you filed a complaint on them.

TROY: Brownie don't understand nothing. All I want them to do is change the job description. Give everybody a chance to drive the truck. Brownie can't see that. He ain't got that much sense.

BONO: How you figure he be making out with that gal be up at Taylors' all the time . . . that Alberta gal?

TROY: Same as you and me. Getting as much as we is. Which is to say nothing.

BONO: It is, huh? I figure you doing a little better than me . . . and I ain't saying what I'm doing.

TROY: Aw, nigger, look here . . . I know you. If you had got anywhere near that gal, twenty minutes later you be looking to tell somebody. And the first one you gonna tell . . . that you gonna want to brag to . . . is gonna be me.

BONO: I ain't saying that. I see where you be eyeing her.

TROY: I eye all the women. I don't miss nothing. Don't never let nobody tell you Troy Maxson don't eye the women.

BONO: You been doing more than eyeing her. You done bought her a drink or two.

TROY: Hell yeah, I bought her a drink! What that mean? I bought you one, too. What that mean 'cause I buy her a drink? I'm just being polite.

BONO: It's all right to buy her one drink. That's what you call being polite. But when you wanna be buying two or three . . . that's what you call eyeing her.

TROY: Look here, as long as you known me . . . you ever known me to chase after women?

BONO: Hell yeah! Long as I done known you. You forgetting I knew you when.

TROY: Naw, I'm talking about since I been married to Rose?

BONO: Oh, not since you been married to Rose. Now, that's the truth, there. I can say that.

TROY: All right then! Case closed.

BONO: I see you be walking up around Alberta's house. You supposed to be at Taylors' and you be walking up around there.

TROY: What you watching where I'm walking for? I ain't watching after you.

BONO: I seen you walking around there more than once.

TROY: Hell, you liable to see me walking anywhere! That don't mean nothing 'cause you see me walking around there.

BONO: Where she come from anyway? She just kinda showed up one day.

TROY: Tallahassee. You can look at her and tell she one of them Florida gals. They got some big healthy women down there. Grow them right up out the ground. Got a little bit of Indian in her. Most of them niggers down in Florida got some Indian in them.

BONO: I don't know about that Indian part. But she damn sure big and healthy. Woman wear some big stockings. Got them great big old legs and hips as wide as the Mississippi River.

TROY: Legs don't mean nothing. You don't do nothing but push them out of the way. But them hips cushion the ride!

BONO: Troy, you ain't got no sense.

TROY: It's the truth! Like you riding on Goodyears!

(Rose enters from the house. She is ten years younger than Troy. Her devotion to him stems from her recognition of the possibilities of her life without him: a succession of abusive men and their babies, a life of partying and running the streets, the church, or aloneness with its attendant pain and frustration. She recognizes Troy's spirit as a fine and illuminating one and she either ignores or forgives his faults, only some of which she recognizes. Though she doesn't drink, her presence is an integral part of the Friday night rituals. She alternates between the porch and the kitchen, where supper preparations are under way.)

ROSE: What you all out here getting into?

TROY: What you worried about what we getting into for? This is men talk, woman.

ROSE: What I care what you talking about? Bono, you gonna stay for supper?

BONO: No, I thank you, Rose. But Lucille say she cooking up a pot of pigfeet.

TROY: Pigfeet! Hell, I'm going home with you! Might even stay the night if you got some pigfeet. You got something in there to top them pigfeet, Rose?

ROSE: I'm cooking up some chicken. I got some chicken and collard greens.

TROY: Well, go on back in the house and let me and Bono finish what we was talking about. This is men talk. I got some talk for you later. You know what kind of talk I mean. You go on and powder it up.

ROSE: Troy Maxson, don't you start that now!

TROY (*Puts his arm around her*): Aw, woman . . . come here. Look here, Bono . . . when I met this woman . . . I got out that place, say, "Hitch up my pony, saddle up my mare . . . there's a woman out there for me somewhere. I looked here. Looked there. Saw Rose and latched on to her." I latched on to her and told her—I'm gonna tell you the truth—I told her, "Baby, I don't wanna marry, I just wanna be your man." Rose told me . . . tell him what you told me, Rose.

ROSE: I told him if he wasn't the marrying kind, then move out the way so the marrying kind could find me.

TROY: That's what she told me. "Nigger, you in my way. You blocking the view! Move out the way so I can find me a husband." I thought it over two or three days. Come back—

ROSE: Ain't no two or three days nothing. You was back the same night.

TROY: Come back, told her . . . "Okay, baby . . . but I'm gonna buy me a banty rooster and put him out there in the backyard . . . and when he see a stranger come, he'll flap his wings and crow . . ." Look here, Bono, I could watch the front door by myself . . . it was that back door I was worried about.

ROSE: Troy, you ought not talk like that. Troy ain't doing nothing but telling a lie.

TROY: Only thing is . . . when we first got married . . . forget the rooster . . . we ain't had no yard!

BONO: I hear you tell it. Me and Lucille was staying down there on Logan Street. Had two rooms with the outhouse in the back. I ain't mind the outhouse none. But when that goddamn wind blow through there in the winter . . . that's what I'm talking about! To this day I wonder why in the hell I ever stayed down there for six long years. But see, I didn't know I could do no better. I thought only white folks had inside toilets and things.

ROSE: There's a lot of people don't know they can do no better than they doing now. That's just something you got to learn. A lot of folks still shop at Bella's.

TROY: Ain't nothing wrong with shopping at Bella's. She got fresh food.

ROSE: I ain't said nothing about if she got fresh food. I'm talking about what she charge. She charge ten cents more than the A&P.[2]

TROY: The A&P ain't never done nothing for me. I spends my money where I'm treated right. I go down to Bella, say, "I need a loaf of bread, I'll pay you Friday." She give it to me. What sense that make when I got money to go and spend it somewhere else and ignore the person who done right by me? That ain't in the Bible.

ROSE: We ain't talking about what's in the Bible. What sense it make to shop there when she overcharge?

TROY: You shop where you want to. I'll do my shopping where the people been good to me.

ROSE: Well, I don't think it's right for her to overcharge. That's all I was saying.

BONO: Look here . . . I got to get on. Lucille be raising all kind of hell.

TROY: Where you going, nigger? We ain't finished this pint. Come here, finish this pint.

BONO: Well, hell, I am . . . if you ever turn the bottle loose.

2. By the 1930s, the Great Atlantic and Pacific Tea Company, so named in 1859, was the leading supermarket chain in the United States.

TROY (*Hands him the bottle*): The only thing I say about the A&P is I'm glad Cory got that job down there. Help him take care of his school clothes and things. Gabe done moved out and things getting tight around here. He got that job . . . He can start to look out for himself.

ROSE: Cory done went and got recruited by a college football team.

TROY: I told that boy about that football stuff. The white man ain't gonna let him get nowhere with that football. I told him when he first come to me with it. Now you come telling me he done went and got more tied up in it. He ought to go and get recruited in how to fix cars or something where he can make a living.

ROSE: He ain't talking about making no living playing football. It's just something the boys in school do. They gonna send a recruiter by to talk to you. He'll tell you he ain't talking about making no living playing football. It's a honor to be recruited.

TROY: It ain't gonna get him nowhere. Bono'll tell you that.

BONO: If he be like you in the sports . . . he's gonna be all right. Ain't but two men ever played baseball as good as you. That's Babe Ruth and Josh Gibson.[3] Them's the only two men ever hit more home runs than you.

TROY: What it ever get me? Ain't got a pot to piss in or a window to throw it out of.

ROSE: Times have changed since you was playing baseball, Troy. That was before the war.[4] Times have changed a lot since then.

TROY: How in hell they done changed?

ROSE: They got lots of colored boys playing ball now. Baseball and football.

BONO: You right about that, Rose. Times have changed, Troy. You just come along too early.

TROY: There ought not never have been no time called too early! Now you take that fellow . . . what's that fellow they had playing right field for the Yankees back then? You know who I'm talking about, Bono. Used to play right field for the Yankees.

ROSE: Selkirk?[5]

TROY: Selkirk! That's it! Man batting .269, understand? .269. What kind of sense that make? I was hitting .432 with thirty-seven home runs! Man batting .269 and playing right field for the Yankees! I saw Josh Gibson's daughter yesterday. She walking around with raggedy shoes on her feet. Now I bet you Selkirk's daughter ain't walking around with raggedy shoes on her feet! I bet you that!

ROSE: They got a lot of colored baseball players now. Jackie Robinson[6] was the first. Folks had to wait for Jackie Robinson.

TROY: I done seen a hundred niggers play baseball better than Jackie Robinson. Hell, I know some teams Jackie Robinson couldn't even make! What you talking about Jackie Robinson. Jackie Robinson wasn't nobody. I'm talking

3. Georgia-born catcher (1911–47) often called "the black Babe Ruth"; hailed by the Baseball Hall of Fame as "the greatest power hitter in black baseball," he died three months before integration of the major leagues. *Babe Ruth*: legendary outfielder, pitcher, and power hitter (1895–1948) for the Boston Red Sox and New York Yankees.

4. World War II (1939–45).

5. George Selkirk (1908–87), Canadian-born player who succeeded Babe Ruth as the New York Yankees right fielder.

6. Brooklyn Dodgers first baseman (1919–72) who, in 1947, became the first black player in the major leagues and, in 1949, the first black winner of the National League MVP Award.

about if you could play ball then they ought to have let you play. Don't care what color you were. Come telling me I come along too early. If you could play . . . then they ought to have let you play.

(Troy takes a long drink from the bottle.)

ROSE: You gonna drink yourself to death. You don't need to be drinking like that.

TROY: Death ain't nothing. I done seen him. Done wrassled with him. You can't tell me nothing about death. Death ain't nothing but a fastball on the outside corner. And you know what I'll do to that! Lookee here, Bono . . . am I lying? You get one of them fastballs, about waist high, over the outside corner of the plate where you can get the meat of the bat on it . . . and good God! You can kiss it good-bye. Now, am I lying?

BONO: Naw, you telling the truth there. I seen you do it.

TROY: If I'm lying . . . that 450 feet worth of lying! *(Pause)* That's all death is to me. A fastball on the outside corner.

ROSE: I don't know why you want to get on talking about death.

TROY: Ain't nothing wrong with talking about death. That's part of life. Everybody gonna die. You gonna die, I'm gonna die. Bono's gonna die. Hell, we all gonna die.

ROSE: But you ain't got to talk about it. I don't like to talk about it.

TROY: You the one brought it up. Me and Bono was talking about baseball . . . you tell me I'm gonna drink myself to death. Ain't that right, Bono? You know I don't drink this but one night out of the week. That's Friday night. I'm gonna drink just enough to where I can handle it. Then I cuts it loose. I leave it alone. So don't you worry about me drinking myself to death. 'Cause I ain't worried about Death. I done seen him. I done wrestled with him.

Look here, Bono . . . I looked up one day and Death was marching straight at me. Like Soldiers on Parade! The Army of Death was marching straight at me. The middle of July, 1941. It got real cold just like it be winter. It seem like Death himself reached out and touched me on the shoulder. He touch me just like I touch you. I got cold as ice and Death standing there grinning at me.

ROSE: Troy, why don't you hush that talk.

TROY: I say . . . What you want, Mr. Death? You be wanting me? You done brought your army to be getting me? I looked him dead in the eye. I wasn't fearing nothing. I was ready to tangle. Just like I'm ready to tangle now. The Bible say be ever vigilant. That's why I don't get but so drunk. I got to keep watch.

ROSE: Troy was right down there in Mercy Hospital. You remember he had pneumonia? Laying there with a fever talking plumb out of his head.

TROY: Death standing there staring at me . . . carrying that sickle in his hand. Finally he say, "You want bound over for another year?" See, just like that . . . "You want bound over for another year?" I told him, "Bound over hell! Let's settle this now!"

It seem like he kinda fell back when I said that, and all the cold went out of me. I reached down and grabbed that sickle and threw it just as far as I could throw it . . . and me and him commenced to wrestling.

We wrestled for three days and three nights. I can't say where I found the strength from. Every time it seemed like he was gonna get the best of me, I'd reach way down deep inside myself and find the strength to do him one better.

ROSE: Every time Troy tell that story he find different ways to tell it. Different things to make up about it.

TROY: I ain't making up nothing. I'm telling you the facts of what happened. I wrestled with Death for three days and three nights and I'm standing here to tell you about it. *(Pause)* All right. At the end of the third night we done weakened each other to where we can't hardly move. Death stood up, throwed on his robe . . . had him a white robe with a hood on it. He throwed on that robe and went off to look for his sickle. Say, "I'll be back." Just like that. "I'll be back." I told him say, "Yeah, but . . . you gonna have to find me!" I wasn't no fool. I wasn't going looking for him. Death ain't nothing to play with. And I know he's gonna get me. I know I got to join his army . . . his camp followers. But as long as I keep my strength and see him coming . . . as long as I keep up my vigilance . . . he's gonna have to fight to get me. I ain't going easy.

BONO: Well, look here, since you got to keep up your vigilance . . . let me have the bottle.

TROY: Aw hell, I shouldn't have told you that part. I should have left out that part.

ROSE: Troy be talking that stuff and half the time don't even know what he be talking about.

TROY: Bono know me better than that.

BONO: That's right. I know you. I know you got some Uncle Remus[7] in your blood. You got more stories than the devil got sinners.

TROY: Aw hell, I done seen him too! Done talked with the devil.

ROSE: Troy, don't nobody want to be hearing all that stuff.

(Lyons enters the yard from the street. Thirty-four years old, Troy's son from a previous marriage, he sports a neatly trimmed goatee, sport coat and white shirt, tieless and buttoned at the collar. Though he fancies himself a musician, he is more caught up in the rituals and "idea" of being a musician than in the actual practice of the music. He has come to borrow money from Troy and, while he knows he will be successful, he is uncertain as to what extent his lifestyle will be held up to scrutiny and ridicule.)

LYONS: Hey, Pop.

TROY: What you come "Hey, Popping" me for?

LYONS: How you doing, Rose? *(Kisses her)* Mr. Bono. How you doing?

BONO: Hey, Lyons . . . how you been?

TROY: He must have been doing all right. I ain't seen him around here last week.

ROSE: Troy, leave your boy alone. He come by to see you and you wanna start all that nonsense.

TROY: I ain't bothering Lyons. *(Offers him the bottle)* Here, get you a drink. We got an understanding. I know why he come by to see me and he know I know.

LYONS: Come on, Pop . . . I just stopped by to say hi . . . see how you was doing.

TROY: You ain't stopped by yesterday.

ROSE: You gonna stay for supper, Lyons? I got some chicken cooking in the oven.

LYONS: No, Rose . . . thanks. I was just in the neighborhood and thought I'd stop by for a minute.

7. African American narrator of the folktales, adapted from African American originals, published by white Georgia journalist Joel Chandler Harris beginning in 1879, and featuring Br'er Rabbit.

TROY: You was in the neighborhood all right, nigger. You telling the truth there. You was in the neighborhood 'cause it's my payday.

LYONS: Well, hell, since you mentioned it . . . let me have ten dollars.

TROY: I'll be damned! I'll die and go to hell and play blackjack with the devil before I give you ten dollars.

BONO: That's what I want to know about . . . that devil you done seen.

LYONS: What . . . Pop done seen the devil? You too much, Pops.

TROY: Yeah, I done seen him. Talked to him too!

ROSE: You ain't seen no devil. I done told you that man ain't had nothing to do with the devil. Anything you can't understand, you want to call it the devil.

TROY: Look here, Bono . . . I went down to see Hertzberger about some furniture. Got three rooms for two-ninety-eight. That what it say on the radio. "Three rooms . . . two-ninety-eight." Even made up a little song about it. Go down there . . . man tell me I can't get no credit. I'm working every day and can't get no credit. What to do? I got an empty house with some raggedy furniture in it. Cory ain't got no bed. He's sleeping on a pile of rags on the floor. Working every day and can't get no credit. Come back here—Rose'll tell you—madder than hell. Sit down . . . try to figure what I'm gonna do. Come a knock on the door. Ain't been living here but three days. Who know I'm here? Open the door . . . devil standing there bigger than life. White fellow . . . got on good clothes and everything. Standing there with a clipboard in his hand. I ain't had to say nothing. First words come out of his mouth was . . . "I understand you need some furniture and can't get no credit." I liked to fell over. He say, "I'll give you all the credit you want, but you got to pay the interest on it." I told him, "Give me three rooms' worth and charge whatever you want." Next day a truck pulled up here and two men unloaded them three rooms. Man what drove the truck give me a book. Say send ten dollars, first of every month to the address in the book and everything will be all right. Say if I miss a payment the devil was coming back and it'll be hell to pay. That was fifteen years ago. To this day . . . the first of the month I send my ten dollars, Rose'll tell you.

ROSE: Troy lying.

TROY: I ain't never seen that man since. Now you tell me who else that could have been but the devil? I ain't sold my soul or nothing like that, you understand. Naw, I wouldn't have truck with the devil about nothing like that. I got my furniture and pays my ten dollars the first of the month just like clockwork.

BONO: How long you say you been paying this ten dollars a month?

TROY: Fifteen years!

BONO: Hell, ain't you finished paying for it yet? How much the man done charged you.

TROY: Aw hell, I done paid for it. I done paid for it ten times over! The fact is I'm scared to stop paying it.

ROSE: Troy lying. We got that furniture from Mr. Glickman, He ain't paying no ten dollars a month to nobody.

TROY: Aw hell, woman. Bono know I ain't that big a fool.

LYONS: I was just getting ready to say . . . I know where there's a bridge for sale.

TROY: Look here, I'll tell you this . . . it don't matter to me if he was the devil. It don't matter if the devil give credit. Somebody has got to give it.

ROSE: It ought to matter. You going around talking about having truck with the devil . . . God's the one you gonna have to answer to. He's the one gonna be at the Judgment.

LYONS: Yeah, well, look here, Pop . . . let me have that ten dollars. I'll give it back to you. Bonnie got a job working at the hospital.

TROY: What I tell you, Bono? The only time I see this nigger is when he wants something. That's the only time I see him.

LYONS: Come on, Pop, Mr. Bono don't want to hear all that. Let me have the ten dollars. I told you Bonnie working.

TROY: What that mean to me? "Bonnie working." I don't care if she working. Go ask her for the ten dollars if she working. Talking about "Bonnie working." Why ain't you working?

LYONS: Aw, Pop, you know I can't find no decent job. Where am I gonna get a job at? You know I can't get no job.

TROY: I told you I know some people down there. I can get you on the rubbish if you want to work. I told you that the last time you came by here asking me for something.

LYONS: Naw, Pop . . . thanks. That ain't for me. I don't wanna be carrying nobody's rubbish. I don't wanna be punching nobody's time clock.

TROY: What's the matter, you too good to carry people's rubbish? Where you think that ten dollars you talking about come from? I'm just supposed to haul people's rubbish and give my money to you 'cause you too lazy to work. You too lazy to work and wanna know why you ain't got what I got.

ROSE: What hospital Bonnie working at? Mercy?

LYONS: She's down at Passavant working in the laundry.

TROY: I ain't got nothing as it is. I give you that ten dollars and I got to eat beans the rest of the week. Naw . . . you ain't getting no ten dollars here.

LYONS: You ain't got to be eating no beans. I don't know why you wanna say that.

TROY: I ain't got no extra money. Gabe done moved over to Miss Pearl's paying her the rent and things done got tight around here. I can't afford to be giving you every payday.

LYONS: I ain't asked you to give me nothing. I asked you to loan me ten dollars. I know you got ten dollars.

TROY: Yeah, I got it. You know why I got it? 'Cause I don't throw my money away out there in the streets. You living the fast life . . . wanna be a musician . . . running around in them clubs and things . . . then, you learn to take care of yourself. You ain't gonna find me going and asking nobody for nothing. I done spent too many years without.

LYONS: You and me is two different people, Pop.

TROY: I done learned my mistake and learned to do what's right by it. You still trying to get something for nothing. Life don't owe you nothing. You owe it to yourself. Ask Bono. He'll tell you I'm right.

LYONS: You got your way of dealing with the world . . . I got mine. The only thing that matters to me is the music.

TROY: Yeah, I can see that! It don't matter how you gonna eat . . . where your next dollar is coming from. You telling the truth there.

LYONS: I know I got to eat. But I got to live too. I need something that gonna help me to get out of the bed in the morning. Make me feel like I belong in the world. I don't bother nobody. I just stay with my music 'cause that's the only way I can find to live in the world. Otherwise there ain't no telling what I might do. Now I don't come criticizing you and how you live. I just come by to ask you for ten dollars. I don't wanna hear all that about how I live.

TROY: Boy, your mama did a hell of a job raising you.

LYONS: You can't change me, Pop. I'm thirty-four years old. If you wanted to change me, you should have been there when I was growing up. I come by to see you . . . ask for ten dollars and you want to talk about how I was raised. You don't know nothing about how I was raised.

ROSE: Let the boy have ten dollars, Troy.

TROY *(To Lyons)*: What the hell you looking at me for? I ain't got no ten dollars. You know what I do with my money. *(To Rose)* Give him ten dollars if you want him to have it.

ROSE: I will. Just as soon as you turn it loose.

TROY *(Handing Rose the money)*: There it is. Seventy-six dollars and forty-two cents. You see this, Bono? Now, I ain't gonna get but six of that back.

ROSE: You ought to stop telling that lie. Here, Lyons. *(Hands him the money)*

LYONS: Thanks, Rose. Look . . . I got to run . . . I'll see you later.

TROY: Wait a minute. You gonna say, "Thanks, Rose," and ain't gonna look to see where she got that ten dollars from? See how they do me, Bono?

LYONS: I know she got it from you, Pop. Thanks. I'll give it back to you.

TROY: There he go telling another lie. Time I see that ten dollars . . . he'll be owing me thirty more.

LYONS: See you, Mr. Bono.

BONO: Take care, Lyons!

LYONS: Thanks, Pop. I'll see you again.

(Lyons exits the yard.)

TROY: I don't know why he don't go and get him a decent job and take care of that woman he got.

BONO: He'll be all right, Troy. The boy is still young.

TROY: The *boy* is thirty-four years old.

ROSE: Let's not get off into all that.

BONO: Look here . . . I got to be going. I got to be getting on. Lucille gonna be waiting.

TROY *(Puts his arm around Rose)*: See this woman, Bono? I love this woman. I love this woman so much it hurts. I love her so much . . . I done run out of ways of loving her. So I got to go back to basics. Don't you come by my house Monday morning talking about time to go to work . . . 'cause I'm still gonna be stroking!

ROSE: Troy! Stop it now!

BONO: I ain't paying him no mind, Rose. That ain't nothing but gin-talk. Go on, Troy. I'll see you Monday.

TROY: Don't you come by my house, nigger! I done told you what I'm gonna be doing.

(The lights fade to black.)

Scene 2

The lights come up on Rose hanging up clothes. She hums and sings softly to herself. It is the following morning.

ROSE *(Singing)*:
Jesus, be a fence all around me every day
Jesus, I want you to protect me as I travel on my way.
Jesus, be a fence all around me every day.

(Troy enters from the house.)

Jesus, I want you to protect me
As I travel on my way.

(To Troy) 'Morning. You ready for breakfast? I can fix it soon as I finish hanging up these clothes?

TROY: I got the coffee on. That'll be all right. I'll just drink some of that this morning.

ROSE: That 651 hit yesterday. That's the second time this month. Miss Pearl hit for a dollar . . . seem like those that need the least always get lucky. Poor folks can't get nothing.

TROY: Them numbers don't know nobody. I don't know why you fool with them. You and Lyons both.

ROSE: It's something to do.

TROY: You ain't doing nothing but throwing your money away.

ROSE: Troy, you know I don't play foolishly. I just play a nickel here and a nickel there.

TROY: That's two nickels you done thrown away.

ROSE: Now I hit sometimes . . . that makes up for it. It always comes in handy when I do hit. I don't hear you complaining then.

TROY: I ain't complaining now. I just say it's foolish. Trying to guess out of six hundred ways which way the number gonna come. If I had all the money niggers, these Negroes, throw away on numbers for one week—just one week—I'd be a rich man.

ROSE: Well, you wishing and calling it foolish ain't gonna stop folks from playing numbers. That's one thing for sure. Besides . . . some good things come from playing numbers. Look where Pope done bought him that restaurant off of numbers.

TROY: I can't stand niggers like that. Man ain't had two dimes to rub together. He walking around with his shoes all run over bumming money for cigarettes. All right. Got lucky there and hit the numbers . . .

ROSE: Troy, I know all about it.

TROY: Had good sense, I'll say that for him. He ain't throwed his money away. I seen niggers hit the numbers and go through two thousand dollars in four days. Man bought him that restaurant down there . . . fixed it up real nice . . . and then didn't want nobody to come in it! A Negro go in there and can't get no kind of service. I seen a white fellow come in there and order a bowl of stew. Pope picked all the meat out the pot for him. Man ain't had nothing but a bowl of meat! Negro come behind him and ain't got nothing but the potatoes and carrots. Talking about what numbers do for people, you picked a wrong example. Ain't done nothing but make a worser fool out of him than he was before.

ROSE: Troy, you ought to stop worrying about what happened at work yesterday.

TROY: I ain't worried. Just told me to be down there at the commissioner's office on Friday. Everybody think they gonna fire me. I ain't worried about them firing me. You ain't got to worry about that. *(Pause)* Where's Cory? Cory in the house? *(Calls)* Cory?

ROSE: He gone out.

TROY: Out, huh? He gone out 'cause he know I want him to help me with this fence. I know how he is. That boy scared of work.

(Gabriel enters. He comes halfway down the alley and, hearing Troy's voice, stops.)

He ain't done a lick of work in his life.

ROSE: He had to go to football practice. Coach wanted them to get in a little extra practice before the season start.

TROY: I got his practice . . . running out of here before he get his chores done.

ROSE: Troy, what is wrong with you this morning? Don't nothing set right with you. Go on back in there and go to bed . . . get up on the other side.

TROY: Why something got to be wrong with me? I ain't said nothing wrong with me.

ROSE: You got something to say about everything. First it's the numbers . . . then it's the way the man runs his restaurant . . . then you done got on Cory. What's it gonna be next? Take a look up there and see if the weather suits you . . . or is it gonna be how you gonna put up the fence with the clothes hanging in the yard.

TROY: You hit the nail on the head then.

ROSE: I know you like I know the back of my hand. Go on in there and get you some coffee . . . see if that straighten you up. 'Cause you ain't right this morning.

(Troy starts into the house and sees Gabriel. Gabriel starts singing. Troy's brother, he is seven years younger than Troy. Injured in World War II, he has a metal plate in his head. He carries an old trumpet tied around his waist and believes with every fiber of his being that he is the archangel Gabriel.[8] *He carries a chipped basket with an assortment of discarded fruits and vegetables he has picked up in the strip district*[9] *and which he attempts to sell.)*

GABRIEL *(Singing)*:

Yes, ma'am, I got plums
You ask me how I sell them

8. Divine messenger in Jewish, Christian, and Islamic traditions. In the Bible, he appears to Daniel (to explain his visions), to Zacharias (to prophesy John the Baptist's birth), and to Mary (to announce that she will bear Jesus). He is also said to be the angelic trumpeter who will announce the arrival of the Last Judgment and Christ's second coming.

9. Market district located on a narrow strip of land northeast of downtown Pittsburgh.

Oh ten cents apiece
Three for a quarter
Come and buy now
'Cause I'm here today
And tomorrow I'll be gone.

(Rose enters.)

Hey, Rose!

ROSE: How you doing, Gabe?

GABRIEL: There's Troy . . . Hey, Troy!

TROY: Hey, Gabe.

(Troy exits into the kitchen.)

ROSE *(To Gabriel)*: What you got there?

GABRIEL: You know what I got, Rose. I got fruits and vegetables.

ROSE *(Looking in the basket)*: Where's all these plums you talking about?

GABRIEL: I ain't got no plums today, Rose. I was just singing that. Have some tomorrow. Put me in a big order for plums. Have enough plums tomorrow for Saint Peter[1] and everybody.

(Troy reenters from the kitchen and crosses to the steps.)

(To Rose) Troy's mad at me.

TROY: I ain't mad at you. What I got to be mad at you about? You ain't done nothing to me.

GABRIEL: I just moved over to Miss Pearl's to keep out from in your way. I ain't mean no harm by it.

TROY: Who said anything about that? I ain't said anything about that.

GABRIEL: You ain't mad at me, is you?

TROY: Naw . . . I ain't mad at you, Gabe. If I was mad at you I'd tell you about it.

GABRIEL: Got me two rooms. In the basement. Got my own door too. Wanna see my key? *(Holds up a key)* That's my own key! Ain't nobody else got a key like that. That's my key! My two rooms!

TROY: Well, that's good, Gabe. You got your own key . . . that's good.

ROSE: You hungry, Gabe? I was just fixing to cook Troy his breakfast.

GABRIEL: I'll take some biscuits. You got some biscuits? Did you know when I was in Heaven . . . every morning me and Saint Peter would sit down by the Gate and eat some big fat biscuits? Oh, yeah! We had us a good time. We'd sit there and eat us them biscuits and then Saint Peter would go off to sleep and tell me to wake him up when it's time to open the Gates for the Judgment.

ROSE: Well, come on . . . I'll make up a batch of biscuits.

(Rose exits into the house.)

GABRIEL: Troy . . . Saint Peter got your name in the book. I seen it. It say . . . Troy Maxson. I say . . . I know him! He got the same name like what I got. That's my brother!

1. Apostle traditionally represented as guardian of heaven's gates because, in Matthew 16.19, Jesus tells him, "I will give unto thee the keys of the kingdom of heaven [. . .]."

TROY: How many times you gonna tell me that, Gabe?

GABRIEL: Ain't got my name in the book. Don't have to have my name. I done died and went to Heaven. He got your name though. One morning Saint Peter was looking at his book . . . marking it up for the Judgment . . . and he let me see your name. Got it in there under M. Got Rose's name . . . I ain't seen it like I seen yours . . . but I know it's in there. He got a great big book. Got everybody's name what was ever been born. That's what he told me. But I seen your name. Seen it with my own eyes.

TROY: Go on in the house there. Rose going to fix you something to eat.

GABRIEL: Oh, I ain't hungry. I done had breakfast with Aunt Jemima. She come by and cooked me up a whole mess of flapjacks. Remember how we used to eat them flapjacks?

TROY: Go on in the house and get you something to eat now.

GABRIEL: I got to go sell my plums. I done sold some tomatoes. Got me two quarters. Wanna see? *(Shows Troy his quarters)* I'm gonna save them and buy me a new horn so Saint Peter can hear me when it's time to open the Gates. *(Stops suddenly. Listens)* Hear that? That's the hellhounds. I got to chase them out of here. Go on get out of here! Get out! *(Exits singing:)*

Better get ready for the Judgment
Better get ready for the Judgment
My Lord is coming down.

(Rose enters from the house.)

TROY: He gone off somewhere.

GABRIEL *(Offstage)*:
Better get ready for the Judgment
Better get ready for the Judgment morning
Better get ready for the Judgment
My God is coming down.

ROSE: He ain't eating right. Miss Pearl say she can't get him to eat nothing.

TROY: What you want me to do about it, Rose? I done did everything I can for the man. I can't make him get well. Man got half his head blown away . . . what you expect?

ROSE: Seem like something ought to be done to help him.

TROY: Man don't bother nobody. He just mixed up from that metal plate he got in his head. Ain't no sense for him to go back into the hospital.

ROSE: Least he be eating right. They can help him take care of himself.

TROY: Don't nobody wanna be locked up, Rose. What you wanna lock him up for? Man go over there and fight the war . . . messin' around with them Japs, get half his head blown off . . . and they give him a lousy three thousand dollars. And I had to swoop down on that.

ROSE: Is you fixing to go into that again?

TROY: That's the only way I got a roof over my head . . . 'cause of that metal plate.

ROSE: Ain't no sense you blaming yourself for nothing. Gabe wasn't in no condition to manage that money. You done what was right by him. Can't nobody say you ain't done what was right by him. Look how long you took care of him . . . till he wanted to have his own place and moved over there with Miss Pearl.

TROY: That ain't what I'm saying, woman! I'm just stating the facts. If my brother didn't have that metal plate in his head . . . I wouldn't have a pot to piss in or a window to throw it out of. And I'm fifty-three years old. Now see if you can understand that!

(He gets up from the porch and starts to exit the yard.)

ROSE: Where you going off to? You been running out of here every Saturday for weeks. I thought you was gonna work on this fence?

TROY: I'm gonna walk down to Taylors'. Listen to the ball game. I'll be back in a bit. I'll work on it when I get back.

(He exits the yard. The lights fade to black.)

Scene 3

The lights come up on the yard. It is four hours later. Rose is taking down the clothes from the line. Cory enters carrying his football equipment.

ROSE: Your daddy like to had a fit with you running out of here this morning without doing your chores.

CORY: I told you I had to go to practice.

ROSE: He say you were supposed to help him with this fence.

CORY: He been saying that the last four or five Saturdays, and then he don't never do nothing, but go down to Taylors'. Did you tell him about the recruiter?

ROSE: Yeah, I told him.

CORY: What he say?

ROSE: He ain't said nothing too much. You get in there and get started on your chores before he gets back. Go on and scrub down them steps before he gets back here hollering and carrying on.

CORY: I'm hungry. What you got to eat, Mama?

ROSE: Go on and get started on your chores. I got some meat loaf in there. Go on and make you a sandwich . . . and don't leave no mess in there.

(Cory exits into the house. Rose continues to take down the clothes. Troy enters the yard and sneaks up and grabs her from behind.)

Troy! Go on, now. You liked to scared me to death. What was the score of the game? Lucille had me on the phone and I couldn't keep up with it.

TROY: What I care about the game? Come here, woman. *(Tries to kiss her)*

ROSE: I thought you went down Taylors' to listen to the game. Go on, Troy! You supposed to be putting up this fence.

TROY *(Attempting to kiss her again)*: I'll put it up when I finish with what is at hand.

ROSE: Go on, Troy. I ain't studying you.

TROY *(Chasing after her)*: I'm studying you . . . fixing to do my homework!

ROSE: Troy, you better leave me alone.

TROY: Where's Cory? That boy brought his butt home yet?

ROSE: He's in the house doing his chores.
TROY *(Calling)*: Cory! Get your butt out here, boy!

(Rose exits into the house with the laundry. Troy goes over to the pile of wood, picks up a board, and starts sawing. Cory enters from the house.)

You just now coming in here from leaving this morning?
CORY: Yeah, I had to go to football practice.
TROY: Yeah, what?
CORY: Yessir.
TROY: I ain't but two seconds off you noway. The garbage sitting in there overflowing . . . you ain't done none of your chores . . . and you come in here talking about, "Yeah."
CORY: I was just getting ready to do my chores now, Pop . . .
TROY: Your first chore is to help me with this fence on Saturday. Everything else come after that. Now get that saw and cut them boards.

(Cory takes the saw and begins cutting the boards. Troy continues working. There is a long pause.)

CORY: Hey, Pop . . . why don't you buy a TV?
TROY: What I want with a TV? What I want one of them for?
CORY: Everybody got one. Earl, Ba Bra . . . Jesse!
TROY: I ain't asked you who had one. I say what I want with one?
CORY: So you can watch it. They got lots of things on TV. Baseball games and everything. We could watch the World Series.
TROY: Yeah . . . and how much this TV cost?
CORY: I don't know. They got them on sale for around two hundred dollars.
TROY: Two hundred dollars, huh?
CORY: That ain't that much, Pop.
TROY: Naw, it's just two hundred dollars. See that roof you got over your head at night? Let me tell you something about that roof. It's been over ten years since that roof was last tarred. See now . . . the snow come this winter and sit up there on that roof like it is . . . and it's gonna seep inside. It's just gonna be a little bit . . . ain't gonna hardly notice it. Then the next thing you know, it's gonna be leaking all over the house. Then the wood rot from all that water and you gonna need a whole new roof. Now, how much you think it cost to get that roof tarred?
CORY: I don't know.
TROY: Two hundred and sixty-four dollars . . . cash money. While you thinking about a TV, I got to be thinking about the roof . . . and whatever else go wrong around here. Now if you had two hundred dollars, what would you do . . . fix the roof or buy a TV?
CORY: I'd buy a TV. Then when the roof started to leak . . . when it needed fixing . . . I'd fix it.
TROY: Where are you gonna get the money from? You done spent it for a TV. You gonna sit up and watch the water run all over your brand-new TV.
CORY: Aw, Pop. You got money. I know you do.
TROY: Where I got it at, huh?
CORY: You got it in the bank.

TROY: You wanna see my bankbook? You wanna see that seventy-three dollars and twenty-two cents I got sitting up in there.

CORY: You ain't got to pay for it all at one time. You can put a down payment on it and carry it home with you.

TROY: Not me. I ain't gonna owe nobody nothing if I can help it. Miss a payment and they come and snatch it right out your house. Then what you got? Now, soon as I get two hundred dollars clear, then I'll buy a TV. Right now, as soon as I get two hundred and sixty-four dollars, I'm gonna have this roof tarred.

CORY: Aw . . . Pop!

TROY: You go on and get you two hundred dollars and buy one if ya want it. I got better things to do with my money.

CORY: I can't get no two hundred dollars. I ain't never seen two hundred dollars.

TROY: I'll tell you what . . . you get you a hundred dollars and I'll put the other hundred with it.

CORY: All right, I'm gonna show you.

TROY: You gonna show me how you can cut them boards right now.

(Cory begins to cut the boards. There is a long pause.)

CORY: The Pirates won today. That makes five in a row.

TROY: I ain't thinking about the Pirates. Got an all-white team. Got that boy . . . that Puerto Rican boy . . . Clemente.[2] Don't even half-play him. That boy could be something if they give him a chance. Play him one day and sit him on the bench the next.

CORY: He gets a lot of chances to play.

TROY: I'm talking about playing regular. Playing every day so you can get your timing. That's what I'm talking about.

CORY: They got some white guys on the team that don't play every day. You can't play everybody at the same time.

TROY: If they got a white fellow sitting on the bench . . . you can bet your last dollar he can't play! The colored guy got to be twice as good before he get on the team. That's why I don't want you to get all tied up in them sports. Man on the team and what it get him? They got colored on the team and don't use them. Same as not having them. All them teams the same.

CORY: The Braves got Hank Aaron and Wes Covington.[3] Hank Aaron hit two home runs today. That makes forty-three.

TROY: Hank Aaron ain't nobody. That's what you supposed to do. That's how you supposed to play the game. Ain't nothing to it. It's just a matter of timing . . . getting the right follow-through. Hell, I can hit forty-three home runs right now!

CORY: Not off no major-league pitching, you couldn't.

2. Roberto Clemente (1934–72), Pittsburgh Pirates right fielder (1955–72), four-time National League batting champion, and winner of twelve Gold Gloves.

3. African American fielder (1932–2011) who played for the Milwaukee Braves from 1956 to 1961. *Hank Aaron*: legendary African American batsman (b. 1934) who played twenty-one seasons with the Milwaukee, later Atlanta, Braves (1954–74) and, in 1974–75, broke Babe Ruth's records for most home runs and runs batted in (RBIs).

TROY: We had better pitching in the Negro leagues. I hit seven home runs off of Satchel Paige.[4] You can't get no better than that!

CORY: Sandy Koufax.[5] He's leading the league in strikeouts.

TROY: I ain't thinking of no Sandy Koufax.

CORY: You got Warren Spahn and Lew Burdette.[6] I bet you couldn't hit no home runs off of Warren Spahn.

TROY: I'm through with it now. You go on and cut them boards. *(Pause)* Your mama tell me you done got recruited by a college football team? Is that right?

CORY: Yeah. Coach Zellman say the recruiter gonna be coming by to talk to you. Get you to sign the permission papers.

TROY: I thought you supposed to be working down there at the A&P. Ain't you supposed to be working down there after school?

CORY: Mr. Stawicki say he gonna hold my job for me until after the football season. Say starting next week I can work weekends.

TROY: I thought we had an understanding about this football stuff? You suppose to keep up with your chores and hold that job down at the A&P. Ain't been around here all day on a Saturday. Ain't none of your chores done . . . and now you telling me you done quit your job.

CORY: I'm gonna be working weekends.

TROY: You damn right you are! And ain't no need for nobody coming around here to talk to me about signing nothing.

CORY: Hey, Pop . . . you can't do that. He's coming all the way from North Carolina.

TROY: I don't care where he coming from. The white man ain't gonna let you get nowhere with that football noway. You go on and get your book-learning so you can work yourself up in that A&P or learn how to fix cars or build houses or something, get you a trade. That way you have something can't nobody take away from you. You go on and learn how to put your hands to some good use. Besides hauling people's garbage.

CORY: I get good grades, Pop. That's why the recruiter wants to talk with you. You got to keep up your grades to get recruited. This way I'll be going to college. I'll get a chance . . .

TROY: First you gonna get your butt down there to the A&P and get your job back.

CORY: Mr. Stawicki done already hired somebody else 'cause I told him I was playing football.

TROY: You a bigger fool than I thought . . . to let somebody take away your job so you can play some football. Where you gonna get your money to take out your girlfriend and whatnot? What kind of foolishness is that to let somebody take away your job?

CORY: I'm still gonna be working weekends.

4. Pitcher (1906–82); arguably the Negro Leagues' most famous player (1926–47), he pitched in the newly integrated major leagues from age forty-two to sixty (1948–66).

5. Brooklyn, later Los Angeles, Dodgers pitcher (b. 1935), the first player ever to win three Cy Young Awards, and the youngest ever elected to Baseball's Hall of Fame.

6. Like 1957 Cy Young Award winner Warren Spahn (1921–2003), a pitcher for the Boston, later Milwaukee, Braves (1926–2007), MVP of the 1957 World Series, the only World Series the Milwaukee Braves ever won and the first, since 1948, won by any non–New York team.

TROY: Naw . . . naw. You getting your butt out of here and finding you another job.

CORY: Come on, Pop! I got to practice. I can't work after school and play football too. The team needs me. That's what Coach Zellman say . . .

TROY: I don't care what nobody else say. I'm the boss . . . you understand? I'm the boss around here. I do the only saying what counts.

CORY: Come on, Pop!

TROY: I asked you . . . did you understand?

CORY: Yeah . . .

TROY: What!?!

CORY: Yessir.

TROY: You go on down there to that A&P and see if you can get your job back. If you can't do both . . . then you quit the football team. You've got to take the crookeds with the straights.

CORY: Yessir. *(Pause)* Can I ask you a question?

TROY: What the hell you wanna ask me? Mr. Stawicki the one you got the questions for.

CORY: How come you ain't never liked me?

TROY: Liked you? Who the hell say I got to like you? What law is there say I got to like you? Wanna stand up in my face and ask a damn fool-ass question like that. Talking about liking somebody. Come here, boy, when I talk to you.

(Cory comes over to where Troy is working. He stands slouched over and Troy shoves him on his shoulder.)

Straighten up, goddamn it! I asked you a question . . . what law is there say I got to like you?

CORY: None.

TROY: Well, all right then! Don't you eat every day? *(Pause)* Answer me when I talk to you! Don't you eat every day?

CORY: Yeah.

TROY: Nigger, as long as you in my house, you put that sir on the end of it when you talk to me!

CORY: Yes . . . sir.

TROY: You eat every day.

CORY: Yessir!

TROY: Got a roof over your head.

CORY: Yessir!

TROY: Got clothes on your back.

CORY: Yessir.

TROY: Why you think that is?

CORY: 'Cause of you.

TROY: Aw, hell, I know its 'cause of me . . . but why do you think that is?

CORY *(Hesitant)*: 'Cause you like me.

TROY: Like you? I go out of here every morning . . . bust my butt . . . putting up with them crackers every day . . . 'cause I like you? You about the biggest fool I ever saw. *(Pause)* It's my job. It's my responsibility! You understand that? A man got to take care of his family. You live in my house . . . sleep you behind on my bedclothes . . . fill you belly up with my food . . . 'cause you my son.

You my flesh and blood. Not 'cause I like you! 'Cause it's my duty to take care of you. I owe a responsibility to you!

Let's get this straight right here . . . before it go along any further . . . I ain't got to like you. Mr. Rand don't give me my money come payday 'cause he likes me. He gives me 'cause he owe me. I done give you everything I had to give you. I gave you your life! Me and your mama worked that out between us. And liking your black ass wasn't part of the bargain. Don't you try and go through life worrying about if somebody like you or not. You best be making sure they doing right by you. You understand what I'm saying, boy?

CORY: Yessir.

TROY: Then get the hell out of my face, and get on down to that A&P.

(Rose has been standing behind the screen door for much of the scene. She enters as Cory exits.)

ROSE: Why don't you let the boy go ahead and play football, Troy? Ain't no harm in that. He's just trying to be like you with the sports.

TROY: I don't want him to be like me! I want him to move as far away from my life as he can get. You the only decent thing that ever happened to me. I wish him that. But I don't wish him a thing else from my life. I decided seventeen years ago that boy wasn't getting involved in no sports. Not after what they did to me in the sports.

ROSE: Troy, why don't you admit you was too old to play in the major leagues? For once . . . why don't you admit that?

TROY: What do you mean too old? Don't come telling me I was too old. I just wasn't the right color. Hell, I'm fifty-three years old and can do better than Selkirk's .269 right now!

ROSE: How's was you gonna play ball when you were over forty? Sometimes I can't get no sense out of you.

TROY: I got good sense, woman. I got sense enough not to let my boy get hurt over playing no sports. You been mothering that boy too much. Worried about if people like him.

ROSE: Everything that boy do . . . he do for you. He wants you to say, "Good job, son." That's all.

TROY: Rose, I ain't got time for that. He's alive. He's healthy. He's got to make his own way. I made mine. Ain't nobody gonna hold his hand when he get out there in that world.

ROSE: Times have changed from when you was young, Troy. People change. The world's changing around you and you can't even see it.

TROY *(Slow, methodical)*: Woman . . . I do the best I can do. I come in here every Friday. I carry a sack of potatoes and a bucket of lard. You all line up at the door with your hands out. I give you the lint from my pockets. I give you my sweat and my blood. I ain't got no tears. I done spent them. We go upstairs in that room at night . . . and I fall down on you and try to blast a hole into forever. I get up Monday morning . . . find my lunch on the table. I go out. Make my way. Find my strength to carry me through to the next Friday. *(Pause)* That's all I got, Rose. That's all I got to give. I can't give nothing else.

(Troy exits into the house. The lights fade to black.)

Scene 4

It is Friday. Two weeks later. Cory starts out of the house with his football equipment. The phone rings.

CORY *(Calling)*: I got it! *(Answers the phone, stands in the screen door talking)* Hello? Hey, Jesse. Naw . . . I was just getting ready to leave now.

ROSE *(Calling)*: Cory!

CORY: I told you, man, them spikes is all tore up. You can use them if you want, but they ain't no good. Earl got some spikes.

ROSE *(Calling)*: Cory!

CORY *(Calling to Rose)*: Mam? I'm talking to Jesse. *(Into phone)* When she say that? *(Pause)* Aw, you lying, man. I'm gonna tell her you said that.

ROSE *(Calling)*: Cory, don't you go nowhere!

CORY: I got to go to the game, Ma! *(Into the phone)* Yeah, hey, look, I'll talk to you later. Yeah, I'll meet you over Earl's house. Later. Bye, Ma.

(Cory exits the house and starts out the yard.)

ROSE: Cory, where you going off to? You got that stuff all pulled out and thrown all over your room.

CORY *(In the yard)*: I was looking for my spikes. Jesse wanted to borrow my spikes.

ROSE: Get up there and get that cleaned up before your daddy get back in here.

CORY: I got to go to the game! I'll clean it up *when I get back.*

(He exits.)

ROSE: That's all he need to do is see that room all messed up.

(Rose exits into the house. Troy and Bono enter the yard with a bottle. Troy is dressed in clothes other than his work clothes.)

BONO: He told him the same thing he told you. Take it to the union.

TROY: Brownie ain't got that much sense. Man wasn't thinking about nothing. He wait until I confront them on it . . . then he wanna come crying seniority. *(Calls)* Hey, Rose!

BONO: I wish I could have seen Mr. Rand's face when he told you.

TROY: He couldn't get it out of his mouth! Liked to bit his tongue! When they called me down there to the commissioner's office . . . he thought they was gonna fire me. Like everybody else.

BONO: I didn't think they was gonna fire you. I thought they was gonna put you on the warning paper.

TROY: Hey, Rose! *(To Bono)* Yeah, Mr. Rand like to bit his tongue.

(Troy breaks the seal on the bottle, takes a drink, and hands it to Bono.)

BONO: I see you run right down to Taylors' and told that Alberta gal.

TROY *(Calling)*: Hey, Rose! *(To Bono)* I told everybody. Hey, Rose! I went down there to cash my check.

ROSE *(Entering from the house)*: Hush all that hollering, man! I know you out here. What they say down there at the commissioner's office?

TROY: You supposed to come when I call you, woman. Bono'll tell you that. *(To Bono)* Don't Lucille come when you call her?

ROSE: Man, hush your mouth. I ain't no dog . . . talk about "come when you call me."

TROY *(Puts his arm around Rose)*: You hear this, Bono? I had me an old dog used to get uppity like that. You say, "C'mere, Blue!" . . . and he just lay there and look at you. End up getting a stick and chasing him away trying to make him come.

ROSE: I ain't studying you and your dog. I remember you used to sing that old song.

TROY *(Singing)*:

> Hear it ring! Hear it ring!
> I had a dog his name was Blue.

ROSE: Don't nobody wanna hear you sing that old song.

TROY *(Singing)*:

> You know Blue was mighty true.

ROSE: Used to have Cory running around here singing that song.

BONO: Hell, I remember that song myself.

TROY *(Singing)*:

> You know Blue was a good old dog.
> Blue treed a possum in a hollow log.

That was my daddy's song. My daddy made up that song.

ROSE: I don't care who made it up. Don't nobody wanna hear you sing it.

TROY *(Makes a song like calling a dog)*: Come here, woman.

ROSE: You come in here carrying on, I reckon they ain't fired you. What they say down there at the commissioner's office?

TROY: Look here, Rose . . . Mr. Rand called me into his office today when I got back from talking to them people down there . . . it come from up top . . . he called me in and told me they was making me a driver.

ROSE: Troy, you kidding!

TROY: No I ain't. Ask Bono.

ROSE: Well, that's great, Troy. Now you don't have to hassle them people no more.

(Lyons enters from the street.)

TROY: Aw hell, I wasn't looking to see you today. I thought you was in jail. Got it all over the front page of the *Courier* about them raiding Seefus' place . . . where you be hanging out with all them thugs.

LYONS: Hey, Pop . . . that ain't got nothing to do with me. I don't go down there gambling. I go down there to sit in with the band. I ain't got nothing to do with the gambling part. They got some good music down there.

TROY: They got some rogues . . . is what they got.

LYONS: How you been, Mr. Bono? Hi, Rose.

BONO: I see where you playing down at the Crawford Grill tonight.

ROSE: How come you ain't brought Bonnie like I told you. You should have brought Bonnie with you, she ain't been over in a month of Sundays.

LYONS: I was just in the neighborhood . . . thought I'd stop by.

TROY: Here he come . . .

BONO: Your daddy got a promotion on the rubbish. He's gonna be the first colored driver. Ain't got to do nothing but sit up there and read the paper like them white fellows.

LYONS: Hey, Pop . . . if you knew how to read you'd be all right.

BONO: Naw . . . naw . . . you mean if the nigger knew how to *drive* he'd be all right. Been fighting with them people about driving and ain't even got a license. Mr. Rand know you ain't got no driver's license?

TROY: Driving ain't nothing. All you do is point the truck where you want it to go. Driving ain't nothing.

BONO: Do Mr. Rand know you ain't got no driver's license? That's what I'm talking about. I ain't asked if driving was easy. I asked if Mr. Rand know you ain't got no driver's license.

TROY: He ain't got to know. The man ain't got to know my business. Time he find out, I have two or three driver's licenses.

LYONS (*Going into his pocket*): Say, look here, Pop . . .

TROY: I knew it was coming. Didn't I tell you, Bono? I know what kind of "look here, Pop" that was. The nigger fixing to ask me for some money. It's Friday night. It's my payday. All them rogues down there on the avenue . . . the ones that ain't in jail . . . and Lyons is hopping in his shoes to get down there with them.

LYONS: See, Pop . . . if you'd give somebody else a chance to talk sometime, you'd see that I was fixing to pay you back your ten dollars like I told you. Here . . . I told you I'd pay you when Bonnie got paid.

TROY: Naw . . . you go ahead and keep that ten dollars. Put it in the bank. The next time you feel like you wanna come by here and ask me for something . . . you go on down there and get that.

LYONS: Here's your ten dollars, Pop. I told you I don't want you to give me nothing. I just wanted to borrow ten dollars.

TROY: Naw . . . you go on and keep that for the next time you want to ask me.

LYONS: Come on, Pop . . . here go your ten dollars.

ROSE: Why don't you go on and let the boy pay you back, Troy?

LYONS: Here you go, Rose. If you don't take it I'm gonna have to hear about it for the next six months. (*Hands her the money*)

ROSE: You can hand yours over here too, Troy.

TROY: You see this, Bono. You see how they do me.

BONO: Yeah, Lucille do me the same way.

(*Gabriel is heard singing offstage. He enters.*)

GABRIEL: Better get ready for the Judgment! Better get ready for . . . Hey! . . . Hey! There's Troy's boy!

LYONS: How you doing, Uncle Gabe?

GABRIEL: Lyons . . . The King of the Jungle! Rose . . . hey, Rose. Got a flower for you. (*Takes a rose from his pocket*) Picked it myself. That's the same rose like you is!

ROSE: That's right nice of you, Gabe.

LYONS: What you been doing, Uncle Gabe?

GABRIEL: Oh, I been chasing hellhounds and waiting on the time to tell Saint Peter to open the Gates.

LYONS: You been chasing hellhounds, huh? Well . . . you doing the right thing, Uncle Gabe. Somebody got to chase them.

GABRIEL: Oh, yeah . . . I know it. The devil's strong. The devil ain't no pushover. Hellhounds snipping at everybody's heels. But I got my trumpet waiting on the Judgment time.

LYONS: Waiting on the Battle of Armageddon,[7] huh?

GABRIEL: Ain't gonna be too much of a battle when God get to waving that Judgment sword. But the people's gonna have a hell of a time trying to get into Heaven if them Gates ain't open.

LYONS *(Putting his arm around Gabriel)*: You hear this, Pop. Uncle Gabe, you all right!

GABRIEL *(Laughing with Lyons)*: Lyons! King of the Jungle.

ROSE: You gonna stay for supper, Gabe. Want me to fix you a plate?

GABRIEL: I'll just take a sandwich, Rose. Don't want no plate. Just wanna eat with my hands. I'll take a sandwich.

ROSE: How about you, Lyons? You staying? Got some short ribs cooking.

LYONS: Naw, I won't eat nothing till after we finished playing. *(Pause)* You ought to come down and listen to me play, Pop.

TROY: I don't like that Chinese music. All that noise.

ROSE: Go on in the house and wash up, Gabe . . . I'll fix you a sandwich.

GABRIEL *(As he exits, to Lyons)*: Troy's mad at me.

LYONS: What you mad at Uncle Gabe for, Pop.

ROSE: He thinks Troy's mad at him 'cause he moved over to Miss Pearl's.

TROY: I ain't mad at the man. He can live where he want to live at.

LYONS: What he move over there for? Miss Pearl don't like nobody.

ROSE: She don't mind him none. She treats him real nice. She just don't allow all that singing.

TROY: She don't mind that rent he be paying . . . that's what she don't mind.

ROSE: Troy, I ain't going through that with you no more. He's over there 'cause he want to have his own place. He can come and go as he please.

TROY: Hell, he could come and go as he please here. I wasn't stopping him. I ain't put no rules on him.

ROSE: It ain't the same thing, Troy. And you know it.

(Gabriel comes to the screen door.)

Now, that's the last I wanna hear about that. I don't wanna hear nothing else about Gabe and Miss Pearl. And next week . . .

GABRIEL: I'm ready for my sandwich, Rose.

ROSE: And next week . . . when that recruiter come from that school . . . I want you to sign that paper and go on and let Cory play football. Then that'll be the last I have to hear about that.

TROY *(To Rose as she exits into the house)*: I ain't thinking about Cory nothing.

LYONS: What . . . Cory got recruited? What school he going to?

7. According to Christian tradition, the final, history-ending battle between the armies of good and evil.

TROY: That boy walking around here smelling his piss . . . thinking he's grown. Thinking he's gonna do what he want, irrespective of what I say. Look here, Bono . . . I left the commissioner's office and went down to the A&P . . . that boy ain't working down there. He lying to me. Telling me he got his job back . . . telling me he working weekends . . . telling me he working after school . . . Mr. Stawicki tell me he ain't working down there at all!

LYONS: Cory just growing up. He's just busting at the seams trying to fill out your shoes.

TROY: I don't care what he's doing. When he get to the point where he wanna disobey me . . . then it's time for him to move on. Bono'll tell you that I bet he ain't never disobeyed his daddy without paying the consequences.

BONO: I ain't never had a chance. My daddy came on through . . . but I ain't never knew him to see him . . . or what he had on his mind or where he went. Just moving on through. Searching out the New Land. That's what the old folks used to call it. See a fellow moving around from place to place . . . woman to woman . . . called it Searching out the New Land. I can't say if he ever found it. I come along, didn't want no kids. Didn't know if I was gonna be in one place long enough to fix on them right as their daddy. I figured I was going searching too. As it turned out I been hooked up with Lucille near about as long as your daddy been with Rose. Going on sixteen years.

TROY: Sometimes I wish I hadn't known my daddy. He ain't cared nothing about no kids. A kid to him wasn't nothing. All he wanted was for you to learn how to walk so he could start you to working. When it come time for eating . . . he ate first. If there was anything left over, that's what you got. Man would sit down and eat two chickens and give you the wing.

LYONS: You ought to stop that, Pop. Everybody feed their kids. No matter how hard times is . . . everybody care about their kids. Make sure they have something to eat.

TROY: The only thing my daddy cared about was getting them bales of cotton in to Mr. Lubin. That's the only thing that mattered to him. Sometimes I used to wonder why he was living. Wonder why the devil hadn't come and got him. "Get them bales of cotton in to Mr. Lubin" and find out he owe him money . . .

LYONS: He should have just went on and left when he saw he couldn't get nowhere. That's what I would have done.

TROY: How he gonna leave with eleven kids? And where he gonna go? He ain't knew how to do nothing but farm. No, he was trapped and I think he knew it. But I'll say this for him . . . he felt a responsibility toward us. Maybe he ain't treated us the way I felt he should have . . . but without that responsibility he could have walked off and left us . . . made his own way.

BONO: A lot of them did. Back in those days what you talking about . . . they walk out their front door and just take on down one road or another and keep on walking.

LYONS: There you go! That's what I'm talking about.

BONO: Just keep on walking till you come to something else. Ain't you never heard of nobody having the walking blues? Well, that's what you call it when you just take off like that.

TROY: My daddy ain't had them walking blues! What you talking about? He stayed right there with his family. But he was just as evil as he could be. My mama couldn't stand him. Couldn't stand that evilness. She run off when I was about eight. She sneaked off one night after he had gone to sleep. Told me she was coming back for me. I ain't never seen her no more. All his women run off and left him. He wasn't good for nobody.

When my turn come to head out, I was fourteen and got to sniffing around Joe Canewell's daughter. Had us an old mule we called Greyboy. My daddy sent me out to do some plowing and I tied up Greyboy and went to fooling around with Joe Canewell's daughter. We done found us a nice spot, got real cozy with each other. She about thirteen and we done figured we was grown anyway . . . so we down there enjoying ourselves . . . ain't thinking about nothing. We didn't know Greyboy had got loose and wandered back to the house and my daddy was looking for me. We down there by the creek enjoying ourselves when my daddy come up on us. Surprised us. He had them leather straps off the mule and commenced to whupping me like there was no tomorrow. I jumped up, mad and embarrassed. I was scared of my daddy. When he commenced to whupping on me . . . quite naturally I run to get out of the way. *(Pause)* Now I thought he was mad 'cause I ain't done my work. But I see where he was chasing me off so he could have the gal for himself. When I see what the matter of it was, I lost all fear of my daddy. Right there is where I become a man . . . at fourteen years of age. *(Pause)* Now it was my turn to run him off. I picked up them same reins that he had used on me. I picked up them reins and commenced to whupping on him. The gal jumped up and run off . . . and when my daddy turned to face me, I could see why the devil had never come to get him . . . 'cause he was the devil himself. I don't know what happened. When I woke up, I was laying right there by the creek, and Blue . . . this old dog we had . . . was licking my face. I thought I was blind. I couldn't see nothing. Both my eyes were swollen shut. I laid there and cried. I didn't know what I was gonna do. The only thing I knew was the time had come for me to leave my daddy's house. And right there the world suddenly got big. And it was a long time before I could cut it down to where I could handle it.

Part of that cutting down was when I got to the place where I could feel him kicking in my blood and knew that the only thing that separated us was the matter of a few years.

(Gabriel enters from the house with a sandwich.)

LYONS: What you got there, Uncle Gabe?

GABRIEL: Got me a ham sandwich. Rose gave me a ham sandwich.

TROY: I don't know what happened to him. I done lost touch with everybody except Gabriel. But I hope he's dead. I hope he found some peace.

LYONS: That's a heavy story, Pop. I didn't know you left home when you was fourteen.

TROY: And didn't know nothing. The only part of the world I knew was the forty-two acres of Mr. Lubin's land. That's all I knew about life.

LYONS: Fourteen's kinda young to be out on your own. *(Phone rings)* I don't even think I was ready to be out on my own at fourteen. I don't know what I would have done.

TROY: I got up from the creek and walked on down to Mobile.[8] I was through with farming. Figured I could do better in the city. So I walked the two hundred miles to Mobile.

LYONS: Wait a minute . . . you ain't walked no two hundred miles, Pop. Ain't nobody gonna walk no two hundred miles. You talking about some walking there.

BONO: That's the only way you got anywhere back in them days.

LYONS: Shhh. Damn if I wouldn't have hitched a ride with somebody!

TROY: Who you gonna hitch it with? They ain't had no cars and things like they got now. We talking about 1918.

ROSE *(Entering)*: What you all out here getting into?

TROY *(To Rose)*: I'm telling Lyons how good he got it. He don't know nothing about this I'm talking.

ROSE: Lyons, that was Bonnie on the phone. She say you supposed to pick her up.

LYONS: Yeah, okay, Rose.

TROY: I walked on down to Mobile and hitched up with some of them fellows that was heading this way. Got up here and found out . . . not only couldn't you get a job . . . you couldn't find no place to live. I thought I was in freedom. Shhh. Colored folks living down there on the riverbanks in whatever kind of shelter they could find for themselves. Right down there under the Brady Street Bridge. Living in shacks made of sticks and tarpaper. Messed around there and went from bad to worse. Started stealing. First it was food. Then I figured, hell, if I steal money I can buy me some food. Buy me some shoes too! One thing led to another. Met your mama. I was young and anxious to be a man. Met your mama and had you. What I do that for? Now I got to worry about feeding you and her. Got to steal three times as much. Went out one day looking for somebody to rob . . . that's what I was, a robber. I'll tell you the truth. I'm ashamed of it today. But it's the truth. Went to rob this fellow . . . pulled out my knife . . . and he pulled out a gun. Shot me in the chest. It felt just like somebody had taken a hot branding iron and laid it on me. When he shot me I jumped at him with my knife. They told me I killed him and they put me in the penitentiary and locked me up for fifteen years. That's where I met Bono. That's where I learned how to play baseball. Got out that place and your mama had taken you and went on to make life without me. Fifteen years was a long time for her to wait. But that fifteen years cured me of that robbing stuff. Rose'll tell you. She asked me when I met her if I had gotten all that foolishness out of my system. And I told her, "Baby, it's you and baseball all what count with me." You hear me, Bono? I meant it too. She say, "Which one comes first?" I told her, "Baby, ain't no doubt it's baseball . . . but you stick and get old with me and we'll both outlive this baseball." Am I right, Rose? And it's true.

ROSE: Man, hush your mouth. You ain't said no such thing. Talking about, "Baby, you know you'll always be number one with me." That's what you was talking.

TROY: You hear that, Bono. That's why I love her.

BONO: Rose'll keep you straight. You get off the track, she'll straighten you up.

8. City in southwest Alabama, on the Gulf Coast near the Florida state line.

ROSE: Lyons, you better get on up and get Bonnie. She waiting on you.

LYONS *(Gets up to go)*: Hey, Pop, why don't you come on down to the Grill and hear me play?

TROY: I ain't going down there. I'm too old to be sitting around in them clubs.

BONO: You got to be good to play down at the Grill.

LYONS: Come on, Pop . . .

TROY: I got to get up in the morning.

LYONS: You ain't got to stay long.

TROY: Naw, I'm gonna get my supper and go on to bed.

LYONS: Well, I got to go. I'll see you again.

TROY: Don't you come around my house on my payday.

ROSE: Pick up the phone and let somebody know you coming. And bring Bonnie with you. You know I'm always glad to see her.

LYONS: Yeah, I'll do that, Rose. You take care now. See you, Pop. See you, Mr. Bono. See you, Uncle Gabe.

GABRIEL: Lyons! King of the Jungle!

(Lyons exits.)

TROY: Is supper ready, woman? Me and you got some business to take care of. I'm gonna tear it up too.

ROSE: Troy, I done told you now!

TROY *(Puts his arm around Bono)*: Aw hell, woman . . . this is Bono. Bono like family. I done known this nigger since . . . how long I done know you?

BONO: It's been a long time.

TROY: I done known this nigger since Skippy was a pup. Me and him done been through some times.

BONO: You sure right about that.

TROY: Hell, I done know him longer than I known you. And we still standing shoulder to shoulder. Hey, look here, Bono . . . a man can't ask for no more than that. *(Drinks to him)* I love you, nigger.

BONO: Hell, I love you too . . . but I got to get home see my woman. You got yours in hand. I got to go get mine.

(Bono starts to exit as Cory enters the yard, dressed in his football uniform. He gives Troy a hard, uncompromising look.)

CORY: What you do that for, Pop? *(Throws his helmet down in the direction of Troy)*

ROSE: What's the matter? Cory . . . what's the matter?

CORY: Papa done went up to the school and told Coach Zellman I can't play football no more. Wouldn't even let me play the game. Told him to tell the recruiter not to come.

ROSE: Troy . . .

TROY: What you Troying me for. Yeah, I did it. And the boy know why I did it.

CORY: Why you wanna do that to me? That was the one chance I had.

ROSE: Ain't nothing wrong with Cory playing football, Troy.

TROY: The boy lied to me. I told the nigger if he wanna play football . . . to keep up his chores and hold down that job at the A&P. That was the conditions. Stopped down there to see Mr. Stawicki . . .

CORY: I can't work after school during the football season, Pop! I tried to tell you that Mr. Stawicki's holding my job for me. You don't never want to listen to nobody. And then you wanna go and do this to me!

TROY: I ain't done nothing to you. You done it to yourself.

CORY: Just 'cause you didn't have a chance! You just scared I'm gonna be better than you, that's all.

TROY: Come here.

ROSE: Troy . . .

(Cory reluctantly crosses over to Troy.)

TROY: All right! See. You done made a mistake.

CORY: I didn't even do nothing!

TROY: I'm gonna tell you what your mistake was. See . . . you swung at the ball and didn't hit it. That's strike one. See, you in the batter's box now. You swung and you missed. That's strike one. Don't you strike out!

(The lights go down on the scene.)

ACT TWO

Scene 1

The following morning. Cory is at the tree hitting the ball with the bat. He tries to mimic Troy, but his swing is awkward, less sure. Rose enters from the house.

ROSE: Cory, I want you to help me with this cupboard.

CORY: I ain't quitting the team. I don't care what Poppa say.

ROSE: I'll talk to him when he gets back. He had to go see about your Uncle Gabe. The police done arrested him. Say he was disturbing the peace. He'll be back directly. Come on in here and help me clean out the top of this cupboard.

(Cory exits into the house. Rose sees Troy and Bono coming down the alley.)

Troy . . . what they say down there?

TROY: Ain't said nothing. I give them fifty dollars and they let him go. I'll talk to you about it. Where's Cory?

ROSE: He's in there helping me clean out these cupboards.

TROY: Tell him to get his butt out here.

(Troy and Bono go over to the pile of wood. Bono picks up the saw and begins sawing.)

(To Bono) All they want is the money. That makes six or seven times I done went down there and got him. See me coming they stick out their *hands.*

BONO: Yeah, I know what you mean. That's all they care about . . . that money. They don't care about what's right. *(Pause)* Nigger, why you got to go and get some hard wood? You ain't doing nothing but building a little old fence. Get you some soft pine wood. That's all you need.

TROY: I know what I'm doing. This is outside wood. You put pine wood inside the house. Pine wood is inside wood. This here is outside wood. Now you tell me where the fence is gonna be?

BONO: You don't need this wood. You can put it up with pine wood and it'll stand as long as you gonna be here looking at it.

TROY: How you know how long I'm gonna be here, nigger? Hell, I might just live forever. Live longer than old man Horsely.

BONO: That's what Magee used to say.

TROY: Magee's a damn fool. Now you tell me who you ever heard of gonna pull their own teeth with a pair of rusty pliers.

BONO: The old folks . . . my granddaddy used to pull his teeth with pliers. They ain't had no dentists for the colored folks back then.

TROY: Get clean pliers! You understand? Clean pliers! Sterilize them! Besides we ain't living back then. All Magee had to do was walk over to Doc Goldblum's.

BONO: I see where you and that Tallahassee gal . . . that Alberta . . . I see where you all done got tight.

TROY: What you mean "got tight"?

BONO: I see where you be laughing and joking with her all the time.

TROY: I laughs and jokes with all of them, Bono. You know me.

BONO: That ain't the kind of laughing and joking I'm talking about.

(Cory enters from the house.)

CORY: How you doing, Mr. Bono?

TROY: Cory? Get that saw from Bono and cut some wood. He talking about the wood's too hard to cut. Stand back there, Jim, and let that young boy show you how it's done.

BONO: He's sure welcome to it.

(Cory takes the saw and begins to cut the wood.)

Whew-e-e! Look at that. Big old strong boy. Look like Joe Louis.[9] Hell, must be getting old the way I'm watching that boy whip through that wood.

CORY: I don't see why Mama want a fence around the yard noways.

TROY: Damn if I know either. What the hell she keeping out with it? She ain't got nothing nobody want.

BONO: Some people build fences to keep people out . . . and other people build fences to keep people in. Rose wants to hold on to you all. She loves you.

TROY: Hell, nigger, I don't need nobody to tell me my wife loves me, Cory . . . go on in the house and see if you can find that other saw.

CORY: Where's it at?

TROY: I said find it! Look for it till you find it!

(Cory exits into the house.)

What's that supposed to mean? Wanna keep us in?

BONO: Troy . . . I done known you seem like damn near my whole life. You and Rose both. I done know both of you all for a long time. I remember when you

9. Alabama-born boxer (1914–81) known as the "Brown Bomber," world heavyweight champion from 1937 to 1949.

met Rose. When you was hitting them baseball out the park. A lot of them old gals was after you then. You had the pick of the litter. When you picked Rose, I was happy for you. That was the first time I knew you had any sense. I said . . . My man Troy knows what he's doing . . . I'm gonna follow this nigger . . . he might take me somewhere. I been following you too. I done learned a whole heap of things about life watching you. I done learned how to tell where the shit lies. How to tell it from the alfalfa. You done learned me a lot of things. You showed me how to not make the same mistakes . . . to take life as it comes along and keep putting one foot in front of the other. *(Pause)* Rose a good woman, Troy.

TROY: Hell, nigger, I know she a good woman. I been married to her for eighteen years. What you got on your mind, Bono?

BONO: I just say she a good woman. Just like I say anything. I ain't got to have nothing on my mind.

TROY: You just gonna say she a good woman and leave it hanging out there like that? Why you telling me she a good woman?

BONO: She loves you, Troy. Rose loves you.

TROY: You saying I don't measure up. That's what you trying to say. I don't measure up 'cause I'm seeing this other gal. I know what you trying to say.

BONO: I know what Rose means to you, Troy. I'm just trying to say I don't want to see you mess up.

TROY: Yeah, I appreciate that, Bono. If you was messing around on Lucille I'd be telling you the same thing.

BONO: Well, that's all I got to say. I just say that because I love you both.

TROY: Hell, you know me . . . I wasn't out there looking for nothing. You can't find a better woman than Rose. I know that. But seems like this woman just stuck on to me where I can't shake her loose. I done wrestled with it, tried to throw her off me . . . but she just stuck on tighter. Now she's stuck on for good.

BONO: You's in control . . . that's what you tell me all the time. You responsible for what you do.

TROY: I ain't ducking the responsibility of it. As long as it sets right in my heart . . . then I'm okay. 'Cause that's all I listen to. It'll tell me right from wrong every time. And I ain't talking about doing Rose no bad turn. I love Rose. She done carried me a long ways and I love and respect her for that.

BONO: I know you do. That's why I don't want to see you hurt her. But what you gonna do when she find out? What you got then? If you try and juggle both of them . . . sooner or later you gonna drop one of them. That's common sense.

TROY: Yeah, I hear what you saying, Bono. I been trying to figure a way to work it out.

BONO: Work it out right, Troy. I don't want to be getting all up between you and Rose's business . . . but work it so it come out right.

TROY: Aw hell, I get all up between you and Lucille's business. When you gonna get that woman that refrigerator she been wanting? Don't tell me you ain't got no money now. I know who your banker is. Mellon don't need that money bad as Lucille want that refrigerator. I'll tell you that.

BONO: Tell you what I'll do . . . when you finish building this fence for Rose . . . I'll buy Lucille that refrigerator.

TROY: You done stuck your foot in your mouth now!

(Troy grabs up a board and begins to saw. Bono starts to walk out the yard.)

Hey, nigger . . . where you going?

BONO: I'm going home. I know you don't expect me to help you now. I'm protecting my money. I wanna see you put up that fence by yourself. That's what I want to see. You'll be here another six months without me.

TROY: Nigger, you ain't right.

BONO: When it comes to my money . . . I'm as right as fireworks on the Fourth of July.

TROY: All right, we gonna see now. You better get out your bankbook.

(Bono exits, and Troy continues to work. Rose enters from the house.)

ROSE: What they say down there? What's happening with Gabe?

TROY: I went down there and got him out. Cost me fifty dollars. Say he was disturbing the peace. Judge set up a hearing for him in three weeks. Say to show cause why he shouldn't be recommitted.

ROSE: What was he doing that cause them to arrest him?

TROY: Some kids was teasing him and he run them off home. Say he was howling and carrying on. Some folks seen him and called the police. That's all it was.

ROSE: Well, what's you say? What'd you tell the judge?

TROY: Told him I'd look after him. It didn't make no sense to recommit the man. He stuck out his big greasy palm and told me to give him fifty dollars and take him on home.

ROSE: Where's he at now? Where'd he go off to?

TROY: He's gone on about his business. He don't need nobody to hold his hand.

ROSE: Well, I don't know. Seem like that would be the best place for him if they did put him into the hospital. I know what you're gonna say. But that's what I think would be best.

TROY: The man done had his life ruined fighting for what? And they wanna take and lock him up. Let him be free. He don't bother nobody.

ROSE: Well, everybody got their own way of looking at it I guess. Come on and get your lunch. I got a bowl of lima beans and some cornbread in the oven. Come on get something to eat. Ain't no sense you fretting over Gabe. *(Turns to go in the house)*

TROY: Rose . . . got something to tell you.

ROSE: Well, come on . . . wait till I get this food on the table.

TROY: Rose!

(She stops and turns around.)

I don't know how to say this. *(Pause)* I can't explain it none. It just sort of grows on you till it gets out of hand. It starts out like a little bush . . . and the next thing you know it's a whole forest.

ROSE: Troy . . . what is you talking about?

TROY: I'm talking, woman, let me talk. I'm trying to find a way to tell you . . . I'm gonna be a daddy. I'm gonna be somebody's daddy.

ROSE: Troy . . . you're not telling me this? You're gonna be . . . what?

TROY: Rose . . . now . . . see . . .

ROSE: You telling me you gonna be somebody's daddy? You telling your *wife* this?

(Gabriel enters from the street. He carries a rose in his hand.)

GABRIEL: Hey, Troy! Hey, Rose!

ROSE: I have to wait eighteen years to hear something like this.

GABRIEL: Hey, Rose . . . I got a flower for you. *(Hands it to her)* That's a rose. Same rose like you is.

ROSE: Thanks, Gabe.

GABRIEL: Troy, you ain't mad at me is you? Them bad mens come and put me away. You ain't mad at me is you?

TROY: Naw, Gabe, I ain't mad at you.

ROSE: Eighteen years and you wanna come with this.

GABRIEL *(Takes a quarter out of his pocket)*: See what I got? Got a brand-new quarter.

TROY: Rose . . . it's just . . .

ROSE: Ain't nothing you can say, Troy. Ain't no way of explaining that.

GABRIEL: Fellow that give me this quarter had a whole mess of them. I'm gonna keep this quarter till it stop shining.

ROSE: Gabe, go on in the house there. I got some watermelon in the frigidaire. Go on and get you a piece.

GABRIEL: Say, Rose . . . you know I was chasing hellhounds and them bad mens come and get me and take me away. Troy helped me. He come down there and told them they better let me go before he beat them up. Yeah, he did!

ROSE: You go on and get you a piece of watermelon, Gabe. Them bad mens is gone now.

GABRIEL: Okay, Rose . . . gonna get me some watermelon. The kind with the stripes on it.

(Gabriel exits into the house.)

ROSE: Why, Troy? Why? After all these years to come dragging this in to me now. It don't make no sense at your age. I could have expected this ten or fifteen years ago, but not now.

TROY: Age ain't got nothing to do with it, Rose.

ROSE: I done tried to be everything a wife should be. Everything a wife could be. Been married eighteen years and I got to live to see the day you tell me you been seeing another woman and done fathered a child by her. And you know I ain't never wanted no half nothing in my family. My whole family is half. Everybody got different fathers and mothers . . . my two sisters and my brother. Can't hardly tell who's who. Can't never sit down and talk about Papa and Mama. It's your papa and your mama and my papa and my mama . . .

TROY: Rose . . . stop it now.

ROSE: I ain't never wanted that for none of my children. And now you wanna drag your behind in here and tell me something like this.

TROY: You ought to know. It's time for you to know.

ROSE: Well, I don't want to know, goddamn it!

TROY: I can't just make it go away. It's done now. I can't wish the circumstance of the thing away.

ROSE: And you don't want to either. Maybe you want to wish me and my boy away. Maybe that's what you want? Well, you can't wish us away. I've got eighteen years of my life invested in you. You ought to have stayed upstairs in my bed where you belong.

TROY: Rose . . . now listen to me . . . we can get a handle on this thing. We can talk this out . . . come to an understanding.

ROSE: All of a sudden it's "we." Where was "we" at when you was down there rolling around with some godforsaken woman? "We" should have come to an understanding before you started making a damn fool of yourself. You're a day late and a dollar short when it comes to an understanding with me.

TROY: It's just . . . She gives me a different idea . . . a different understanding about myself. I can step out of this house and get away from the pressures and problems . . . be a different man. I ain't got to wonder how I'm gonna pay the bills or get the roof fixed. I can just be a part of myself that I ain't never been.

ROSE: What I want to know . . . is do you plan to continue seeing her. That's all you can say to me.

TROY: I can sit up in her house and laugh. Do you understand what I'm saying. I can laugh out loud . . . and it feels good. It reaches all the way down to the bottom of my shoes. *(Pause)* Rose, I can't give that up.

ROSE: Maybe you ought to go on and stay down there with her . . . if she a better woman than me.

TROY: It ain't about nobody being a better woman or nothing. Rose, you ain't to blame. A man couldn't ask for no woman to be a better wife than you've been. I'm responsible for it. I done locked myself into a pattern trying to take care of you all that I forgot about myself.

ROSE: What the hell was I there for? That was my job, not somebody else's.

TROY: Rose, I done tried all my life to live decent . . . to live a clean . . . hard . . . useful life. I tried to be a good husband to you. In every way I knew how. Maybe I come into the world backwards, I don't know. But . . . you born with two strikes on you before you come to the plate. You got to guard it closely . . . always looking for the curveball on the inside corner. You can't afford to let none get past you. You can't afford a call strike. If you going down . . . you going down swinging. Everything lined up against you. What you gonna do. I fooled them, Rose. I bunted. When I found you and Cory and a halfway decent job . . . I was safe. Couldn't nothing touch me. I wasn't gonna strike out no more. I wasn't going back to the penitentiary, I wasn't gonna lay in the streets with a bottle of wine. I was safe. I had me a family. A job. I wasn't gonna get that last strike. I was on first looking for one of them boys to knock me in. To get me home.

ROSE: You should have stayed in my bed, Troy.

TROY: Then when I saw that girl . . . she firmed up my backbone. And I got to thinking that if I tried . . . I just might be able to steal second. Do you understand, after eighteen years I wanted to steal second.

ROSE: You should have held me tight. You should have grabbed me and held on.

TROY: I stood on first base for eighteen years and I thought . . . well, goddamn it . . . go on for it!

ROSE: We're not talking about baseball! We're talking about you going off to lay in bed with another woman . . . and then bring it home to me. That's what we're talking about. We ain't talking about no baseball.

TROY: Rose, you're not listening to me. I'm trying the best I can to explain it to you. It's not easy for me to admit that I been standing in the same place for eighteen years.

ROSE: I been standing with you! I been right here with you, Troy. I got a life too. I gave eighteen years of my life to stand in the same spot with you. Don't you think I ever wanted other things? Don't you think I had dreams and hopes? What about my life? What about me? Don't you think it ever crossed my mind to want to know other men? That I wanted to lay up somewhere and forget about my responsibilities? That I wanted someone to make me laugh so I could feel good? You not the only one who's got wants and needs. But I held on to you, Troy. I took all my feelings, my wants and needs, my dreams . . . and I buried them inside you. I planted a seed and watched and prayed over it. I planted myself inside you and waited to bloom. And it didn't take me no eighteen years to find out the soil was hard and rocky and it wasn't never gonna bloom.

But I held on to you, Troy. I held you tighter. You was my husband. I owed you everything I had. Every part of me I could find to give you. And upstairs in that room . . . with the darkness falling in on me . . . I gave everything I had to try and erase the doubt that you wasn't the finest man in the world. And wherever you was going . . . I wanted to be there with you. 'Cause you was my husband. 'Cause that's the only way I was gonna survive as your wife. You always talking about what you give . . . and what you don't have to give. But you take too. You take . . . and don't even know nobody's giving!

(Rose turns to exit into the house; Troy grabs her arm.)

TROY: You say I take and don't give!

ROSE: Troy! You're hurting me.

TROY: You say I take and don't give.

ROSE: Troy . . . you're hurting my arm! Let go!

TROY: I done give you everything I got. Don't you tell that lie on me.

ROSE: Troy!

TROY: Don't you tell that lie on me!

(Cory enters from the house.)

CORY: Mama!

ROSE: Troy, you're hurting me.

TROY: Don't you tell me about no taking and giving.

(Cory comes up behind Troy and grabs him. Troy, surprised, is thrown off balance just as Cory throws a glancing blow that catches him on the chest and knocks him down. Troy is stunned, as is Cory.)

ROSE: Troy. Troy. No!

(Troy gets to his feet and starts at Cory.)

Troy . . . no. Please! Troy!

(Rose pulls on Troy to hold him back. Troy stops himself.)

TROY *(To Cory)*: All right. That's strike two. You stay away from around me, boy. Don't you strike out. You living with a full count. Don't you strike out.

(Troy exits out the yard as the lights go down on the scene.)

Scene 2

It is six months later, early afternoon. Troy enters from the house and starts to exit the yard. Rose enters from the house.

ROSE: Troy, I want to talk to you.

TROY: All of a sudden, after all this time, you want to talk to me, huh? You ain't wanted to talk to me for months. You ain't wanted to talk to me last night. You ain't wanted no part of me then. What you wanna talk to me about now?

ROSE: Tomorrow's Friday.

TROY: I know what day tomorrow is. You think I don't know tomorrow's Friday? My whole life I ain't done nothing but look to see Friday coming and you got to tell me it's Friday.

ROSE: I want to know if you're coming home.

TROY: I always come home, Rose. You know that. There ain't never been a night I ain't come home.

ROSE: That ain't what I mean . . . and you know it. I want to know if you're coming straight home after work.

TROY: I figured I'd cash my check . . . hang out at Taylors' with the boys . . . maybe play a game of checkers . . .

ROSE: Troy, I can't live like this. I won't live like this. You livin' on borrowed time with me. It's been going on six months now you ain't been coming home.

TROY: I be here every night. Every night of the year. That's three hundred sixty-five days.

ROSE: I want you to come home tomorrow after work.

TROY: Rose . . . I don't mess up my pay. You know that now. I take my pay and I give it to you. I don't have no money but what you give me back. I just want to have a little time to myself . . . a little time to enjoy life.

ROSE: What about me? When's my time to enjoy life?

TROY: I don't know what to tell you, Rose. I'm doing the best I can.

ROSE: You ain't come home from work but time enough to change your clothes and run out . . . and you wanna call that the best you can do?

TROY: I'm going over to the hospital to see Alberta. She went into the hospital this afternoon. Look like she might have the baby early. I won't be gone long.

ROSE: Well, you ought to know. They went over to Miss Pearl's and got Gabe today. She said you told them to go ahead and lock him up.

TROY: I ain't said no such thing. Whoever told you that is telling a lie. Pearl ain't doing nothing but telling a big fat lie.

ROSE: She ain't had to tell me. I read it on the papers.

TROY: I ain't told them nothing of the kind.

ROSE: I saw it right there on the papers.

TROY: What it say, huh?

ROSE: It said you told them to take him.

TROY: Then they screwed that up, just the way they screw up everything. I ain't worried about what they got on the paper.

ROSE: Say the government send part of his check to the hospital and the other part to you.

TROY: I ain't got nothing to do with that if that's the way it works. I ain't made up the rules about how it work.

ROSE: You did Gabe just like you did Cory. You wouldn't sign the paper for Cory . . . but you signed for Gabe. You signed that paper.

(The phone is heard ringing inside the house.)

TROY: I told you I ain't signed nothing, woman! The only thing I signed was the release form. Hell, I can't read, I don't know what they had on that paper! I ain't signed nothing about sending Gabe away.

ROSE: I said send him to the hospital . . . you said let him be free . . . now you done went down there and signed him to the hospital for half his money. You went back on yourself, Troy. You gonna have to answer for that.

TROY: See now . . . you been over there talking to Miss Pearl. She done got mad 'cause she ain't getting Gabe's rent money. That's all it is. She's liable to say anything.

ROSE: Troy, I seen where you signed the paper.

TROY: You ain't seen nothing I signed. What she doing got papers on my brother anyway? Miss Pearl telling a big fat lie. And I'm gonna tell her about it too! You ain't seen nothing I signed. Say . . . you ain't seen nothing I signed.

(Rose exits into the house to answer the phone. She returns.)

ROSE: Troy . . . that was the hospital. Alberta had the baby.

TROY: What she have? What is it?

ROSE: It's a girl.

TROY: I better get on down to the hospital to see her.

ROSE: Troy . . .

TROY: Rose . . . I got to go see her now. That's only right . . . what's the matter . . . the baby's all right, ain't it?

ROSE: Alberta died having the baby.

TROY: Died . . . you say she's dead? Alberta's dead?

ROSE: They said they done all they could. They couldn't do nothing for her.

TROY: The baby? How's the baby?

ROSE: They say it's healthy. I wonder who's gonna bury her.

TROY: She had family, Rose. She wasn't living in the world by herself.

ROSE: I know she wasn't living in the world by herself.

TROY: Next thing you gonna want to know if she had any insurance.

ROSE: Troy, you ain't got to talk like that.

TROY: That's the first thing that jumped out your mouth. "Who's gonna bury her?" Like I'm fixing to take on that task for myself.

ROSE: I am your wife. Don't push me away.

TROY: I ain't pushing nobody away. Just give me some space. That's all. Just give me some room to breathe.

(Rose exits into the house. Troy walks about the yard.)

(With a quiet rage that threatens to consume him) All right . . . Mr. Death. See now . . . I'm gonna tell you what I'm gonna do. I'm gonna take and build me a fence around this yard. See? I'm gonna build me a fence around what belongs to me. And then I want you to stay on the other side. See? You stay

over there until you're ready for me. Then you come on. Bring your army. Bring your sickle. Bring your wrestling clothes. I ain't gonna fall down on my vigilance this time. You ain't gonna sneak up on me no more. When you ready for me . . . when the top of your list say "Troy Maxson" . . . that's when you come around here. You come up and knock on the front door. Ain't nobody else got nothing to do with this. This is between you and me. Man to man. You stay on the other side of that fence until you ready for me. Then you come up and knock on the front door. Anytime you want. I'll be ready for you.

(The lights fade to black.)

Scene 3

The lights come up on the porch. It is late evening three days later. Rose sits listening to the ball game, waiting for Troy. The final out of the game is made and Rose switches off the radio. Troy enters the yard carrying an infant wrapped in blankets. He stands back from the house and calls.

Rose enters and stands on the porch. There is a long, awkward silence, the weight of which grows heavier with each passing second.

TROY: Rose . . . I'm standing here with my daughter in my arms. She ain't but a wee bitty little old thing. She don't know nothing about grownups' business. She innocent . . . and she ain't got no mama.

ROSE: What you telling me for, Troy?

(She turns and exits into the house.)

TROY: Well . . . I guess we'll just sit out here on the porch.

(He sits down on the porch. There is an awkward indelicateness about the way he handles the baby. His largeness engulfs and seems to swallow her. He speaks loud enough for Rose to hear:)

A man's got to do what's right for him. I ain't sorry for nothing I done. It felt right in my heart. *(To the baby)* What you smiling at? Your daddy's a big man. Got these great big old hands. But sometimes he's scared. And right now your daddy's scared 'cause we sitting out here and ain't got no home. Oh, I been homeless before. I ain't had no little baby with me. But I been homeless. You just be out on the road by your lonesome and you see one of them trains coming and you just kinda go like this . . . *(Singing, as a lullaby:)*

Please, Mr. Engineer, let a man ride the line
Please, Mr. Engineer, let a man ride the line
I ain't got no ticket please let me ride the blinds.[1]

(Rose enters from the house. Troy hearing her steps behind him, stands and faces her.)

She's my daughter, Rose. My own flesh and blood. I can't deny her no more than I can deny them boys. *(Pause)* You and them boys is my family. You and

1. That is, hitch a free ride on the platform outside a rail car with no door at one end (hence, "blind").

them and this child is all I got in the world. So I guess what I'm saying is . . . I'd appreciate it if you'd help me take care of her.

ROSE: Okay, Troy . . . you're right. I'll take care of your baby for you . . . 'cause . . . like you say . . . she's innocent . . . and you can't visit the sins of the father upon the child. A motherless child has got a hard time. *(Takes the baby from him)* From right now . . . this child got a mother. But you a womanless man.

(Rose turns and exits into the house with the baby. The lights fade to black.)

Scene 4

It is two months later. Lyons enters from the street. He knocks on the door and calls.

LYONS: Hey, Rose! *(Pause)* Rose!

ROSE *(From inside the house)*: Stop that yelling. You gonna wake up Raynell. I just got her to sleep.

LYONS: I just stopped by to pay Papa this twenty dollars I owe him. Where's Papa at?

ROSE: He should be here in a minute. I'm getting ready to go down to the church. Sit down and wait on him.

LYONS: I got to go pick up Bonnie over her mother's house.

ROSE: Well, sit it down there on the table. He'll get it.

LYONS: *(Enters the house and sets the money on the table)*: Tell Papa I said thanks. I'll see you again.

ROSE: All right, Lyons. We'll see you.

(Lyons starts to exit as Cory enters.)

CORY: Hey, Lyons.

LYONS: What's happening, Cory. Say man, I'm sorry I missed your graduation. You know I had a gig and couldn't get away. Otherwise, I would have been there, man. So what you doing?

CORY: I'm trying to find a job.

LYONS: Yeah, I know how that go, man. It's rough out here. Jobs are scarce.

CORY: Yeah, I know.

LYONS: Look here, I got to run. Talk to Papa . . . he know some people. He'll be able to help get you a job. Talk to him . . . see what he say.

CORY: Yeah . . . all right, Lyons.

LYONS: You take care. I'll talk to you soon. We'll find some time to talk.

(Lyons exits the yard. Cory wanders over to the tree, picks up the bat and assumes a batting stance. He studies an imaginary pitcher and swings. Dissatisfied with the result, he tries again. Troy enters. They eye each other for a beat. Cory puts the bat down and exits the yard. Troy starts into the house as Rose exits with Raynell. She is carrying a cake.)

TROY: I'm coming in and everybody's going out.

ROSE: I'm taking this cake down to the church for the bake sale. Lyons was by to see you. He stopped by to pay you your twenty dollars. It's laying in there on the table.

TROY *(Going into his pocket)*: Well . . . here go this money.
ROSE: Put it in there on the table, Troy. I'll get it.
TROY: What time you coming back?
ROSE: Ain't no use in you studying me. It don't matter what time I come back.
TROY: I just asked you a question, woman. What's the matter . . . can't I ask you a question?
ROSE: Troy, I don't want to go into it. Your dinner's in there on the stove. All you got to do is heat it up. And don't you be eating the rest of them cakes in there. I'm coming back for them. We having a bake sale at the church tomorrow.

(Rose exits the yard. Troy sits down on the steps, takes a pint bottle from his pocket, opens it and drinks. He begins to sing:)

TROY:

Hear it ring! Hear it ring!
Had an old dog his name was Blue
You know Blue was mighty true
You know Blue was a good old dog
Blue treed a possum in a hollow log
You know from that he was a good old dog.

(Bono enters the yard.)

BONO: Hey, Troy.
TROY: Hey, what's happening, Bono?
BONO: I just thought I'd stop by to see you.
TROY: What you stop by and see me for? You ain't stopped by in a month of Sundays. Hell, I must owe you money or something.
BONO: Since you got your promotion I can't keep up with you. Used to see you every day. Now I don't even know what route you working.
TROY: They keep switching me around. Got me out in Greentree now . . . hauling white folks' garbage.
BONO: Greentree, huh? You lucky, at least you ain't got to be lifting them barrels. Damn if they ain't getting heavier. I'm gonna put in my two years and call it quits.
TROY: I'm thinking about retiring myself.
BONO: You got it easy. You can *drive* for another five years.
TROY: It ain't the same, Bono. It ain't like working the back of the truck. Ain't got nobody to talk to . . . feel like you working by yourself. Naw, I'm thinking about retiring. How's Lucille?
BONO: She all right. Her arthritis get to acting up on her sometime. Saw Rose on my way in. She going down to the church, huh?
TROY: Yeah, she took up going down there. All them preachers looking for somebody to fatten their pockets. *(Pause)* Got some gin here.
BONO: Naw, thanks. I just stopped by to say hello.
TROY: Hell, nigger . . . you can take a drink. I ain't never known you to say no to a drink. You ain't got to work tomorrow.
BONO: I just stopped by. I'm fixing to go over to Skinner's. We got us a domino game going over his house every Friday.

TROY: Nigger, you can't play no dominoes. I used to whup you four games out of five.

BONO: Well, that learned me. I'm getting better.

TROY: Yeah? Well, that's all right.

BONO: Look here . . . I got to be getting on. Stop by sometime, huh?

TROY: Yeah, I'll do that, Bono. Lucille told Rose you bought her a new refrigerator.

BONO: Yeah, Rose told Lucille you had finally built your fence . . . so I figured we'd call it even.

TROY: I knew you would.

BONO: Yeah . . . okay. I'll be talking to you.

TROY: Yeah, take care, Bono. Good to see you. I'm gonna stop over.

BONO: Yeah. Okay, Troy.

(Bono exits. Troy drinks from the bottle.)

TROY:

Old Blue died and I dug his grave
Let him down with a golden chain
Every night when I hear old Blue bark
I know Blue treed a possum in Noah's Ark.
Hear it ring! Hear it ring!

(Cory enters the yard. Cory and Troy eye each other for a beat. Cory walks over to Troy, who sits in the middle of the steps.)

CORY: I got to get by.

TROY: Say what? What's you say?

CORY: You in my way. I got to get by.

TROY: You got to get by where? This is my house. Bought and paid for. In full. Took me fifteen years. And if you wanna go in my house and I'm sitting on the steps . . . you say excuse me. Like your mama taught you.

CORY: Come on, Pop . . . I got to get by.

(Cory starts to maneuver his way past Troy. Troy grabs his leg and shoves him back.)

TROY: You just gonna walk over top of me?

CORY: I live here too!

TROY *(Advancing on him)*: You just gonna walk over top of me in my own house?

CORY: I ain't scared of you.

TROY: I ain't asked if you was scared of me. I asked you if you was fixing to walk over top of me in my own house? That's the question. You ain't gonna say excuse me? You just gonna walk over top of me?

CORY: If you wanna put it like that.

TROY: How else am I gonna put it?

CORY: I was walking by you to go into the house 'cause you sitting on the steps drunk, singing to yourself. You can put it like that.

TROY: Without saying excuse me??? *(Cory doesn't respond)* I asked you a question. Without saying excuse me???

CORY: I ain't got to say excuse me to you. You don't count around here no more.

TROY: Oh, I see . . . I don't count around here no more. You ain't got to say excuse me to your daddy. All of a sudden you done got so grown that your daddy don't count around here no more . . . Around here in his own house and yard that he done paid for with the sweat of his brow. You done got so grown to where you gonna take over. You gonna take over my house. Is that right? You gonna wear my pants. You gonna go in there and stretch out on my bed. You ain't got to say excuse me 'cause I don't count around here no more. Is that right?

CORY: That's right. You always talking this dumb stuff. Now, why don't you just get out my way.

TROY: I guess you got someplace to sleep and something to put in your belly. You got that, huh? You got that? That's what you need. You got that, huh?

CORY: You don't know what I got. You ain't got to worry about what I got.

TROY: You right! You one hundred percent right! I done spent the last seventeen years worrying about what you got. Now it's your turn, see? I'll tell you what to do. You grown . . . we done established that. You a man. Now, let's see you act like one. Turn your behind around and walk out this yard. And when you get out there in the alley . . . you can forget about this house. See? 'Cause this is my house. You go on and be a man and get your own house. You can forget about this. 'Cause this is mine. You go on and get yours 'cause I'm through with doing for you.

CORY: You talking about what you did for me . . . what'd you ever give me?

TROY: Them feet and bones! That pumping heart, nigger! I give you more than anybody else is ever gonna give you.

CORY: You ain't never gave me nothing! You ain't never done nothing but hold me back. Afraid I was gonna be better than you. All you ever did was try and make me scared of you. I used to tremble every time you called my name. Every time I heard your footsteps in the house. Wondering all the time . . . what's Papa gonna say if I do this? . . . What's he gonna say if I do that? . . . What's Papa gonna say if I turn on the radio? And Mama, too . . . she tries . . . but she's scared of you.

TROY: You leave your mama out of this. She ain't got nothing to do with this.

CORY: I don't know how she stand you . . . after what you did to her.

TROY: I told you to leave your mama out of this! *(Advances on Cory)*

CORY: What you gonna do . . . give me a whupping? You can't whup me no more. You're too old. You just an old man.

TROY *(Shoves him on his shoulder)*: Nigger! That's what you are! You just another nigger on the street to me!

CORY: You crazy! You know that?

TROY: Go on now! You got the devil in you. Get on away from me!

CORY: You just a crazy old man . . . talking about I got the devil in me.

TROY: Yeah, I'm crazy! If you don't get on the other side of that yard . . . I'm gonna show you how crazy I am! Go on . . . get the hell out of my yard.

CORY: It ain't your yard. You took Uncle Gabe's money he got from the Army to buy this house and then you put him out.

TROY *(Advances on Cory)*: Get your black ass out of my yard!

(Troy's advance backs Cory up against the tree. Cory grabs the bat.)

CORY: I ain't going nowhere! Come on . . . put me out! I ain't scared of you.

TROY: That's my bat!
CORY: Come on!
TROY: Put my bat down!
CORY: Come on, put me out.

(Cory swings at Troy, who backs across the yard.)

What's the matter? You so bad . . . put me out!

(Troy advances on Cory, who backs up.)

Come on! Come on!

TROY: You're gonna have to use it! You wanna draw that bat back on me . . . you're gonna have to use it.
CORY: Come on! . . . Come on!

(Cory swings the bat at Troy a second time. He misses. Troy continues to advance on him.)

TROY: You're gonna have to kill me! You wanna draw that bat back on me. You're gonna have to kill me.

(Cory, backed up against the tree, can go no farther. Troy taunts him. He sticks out his head and offers him a target.)

Come on! Come on!

(Cory is unable to swing the bat. Troy grabs it.)

Then I'll show you.

(Cory and Troy struggle over the bat. The struggle is fierce and fully engaged. Troy ultimately is the stronger, and takes the bat from Cory and stands over him ready to swing. He stops himself.)

Go on and get away from around my house.

(Cory, stung by his defeat, picks himself up, walks slowly out of the yard and up the alley.)

CORY: Tell Mama I'll be back for my things. *(Exits)*
TROY: They'll be on the other side of that fence.

I can't taste nothing. Hallelujah! I can't taste nothing no more. *(Assumes a batting posture and begins to taunt Death, the fastball in the outside corner)* Come on! It's between you and me now! Come on! Anytime you want! Come on! I be ready for you . . . but I ain't gonna be easy.

(The lights go down on the scene.)

Scene 5

The time is 1965. The lights come up in the yard. It is the morning of Troy's funeral. A funeral plaque with a light hangs beside the door. There is a small garden plot off to the side. There is noise and activity in the house as Rose, Gabriel, Lyons and Bono have gathered. The door opens and Raynell, seven years old, enters dressed in a flannel nightgown. She crosses to the garden and pokes around with a stick. Rose calls from the house.

ROSE: Raynell!
RAYNELL: Mam?
ROSE: What you doing out there?
RAYNELL: Nothing.

(Rose comes to the screen door.)

ROSE: Girl, get in here and get dressed. What you doing?
RAYNELL: Seeing if my garden growed.
ROSE: I told you it ain't gonna grow overnight. You got to wait.
RAYNELL: It don't look like it never gonna grow. Dag!
ROSE: I told you a watched pot never boils. Get in here and get dressed.
RAYNELL: This ain't even no pot, Mama.
ROSE: You just have to give it a chance. It'll grow. Now you come on and do what I told you. We got to be getting ready. This ain't no morning to be playing around. You hear me?
RAYNELL: Yes, Mam.

(Rose exits into the house. Raynell continues to poke at her garden with a stick. Cory enters. He is dressed in a Marine corporal's uniform, and carries a duffel bag. His posture is that of a military man, and his speech has a clipped sternness.)

CORY *(To Raynell)*: Hi. *(Pause)* I bet your name is Raynell.
RAYNELL: Uh-huh.
CORY: Is your mama home?

(Raynell runs up on the porch and calls through the screen door:)

RAYNELL: Mama . . . there's some man out here. Mama?

(Rose comes to the screen door.)

ROSE: Cory? Lord have mercy! Look here, you all!

(Rose and Cory embrace in a tearful reunion as Bono and Lyons enter from the house dressed in funeral clothes.)

BONO: Aw, looka here . . .
ROSE: Done got all grown up!
CORY: Don't cry, Mama. What you crying about?
ROSE: I'm just so glad you made it.
CORY: Hey, Lyons. How you doing, Mr. Bono.

(Lyons goes to embrace Cory.)

LYONS: Look at you, man. Look at you. Don't he look good, Rose. Got them corporal stripes.
ROSE: What took you so long.
CORY: You know how the Marines are, Mama. They got to get all their paperwork straight before they let you do anything.

ROSE: Well, I'm sure glad you made it. They let Lyons come. Your Uncle Gabe's still in the hospital. They don't know if they gonna let him out or not. I just talked to them a little while ago.

LYONS: A corporal in the United States Marines.

BONO: Your daddy knew you had it in you. He used to tell me all the time.

LYONS: Don't he look good, Mr. Bono?

BONO: Yeah, he remind me of Troy when I first met him. *(Pause)* Say, Rose, Lucille's down at the church with the choir. I'm gonna go down and get the pallbearers lined up. I'll be back to get you all.

ROSE: Thanks, Jim.

CORY: See you, Mr. Bono.

(Bono exits.)

LYONS *(With his arm around Raynell)*: Cory . . . look at Raynell. Ain't she precious? She gonna break a whole lot of hearts.

ROSE: Raynell, come and say hello to your brother. This is your brother, Cory. You remember Cory.

RAYNELL: No, Mam.

CORY: She don't remember me, Mama.

ROSE: Well, we talk about you. She heard us talk about you. *(To Raynell)* This is your brother Cory. Come on and say hello.

RAYNELL: Hi.

CORY: Hi. So you're Raynell. Mama told me a lot about you.

ROSE: You all come on into the house and let me fix you some breakfast. Keep up your strength.

CORY: I ain't hungry, Mama.

LYONS: You can fix me something, Rose. I'll be in there in a minute.

ROSE: Cory, you sure you don't want nothing. I know they ain't feeding you right.

CORY: No, Mama . . . thanks. I don't feel like eating. I'll get something later.

ROSE: Raynell . . . get on upstairs and get that dress on like I told you.

(Rose and Raynell exit into the house.)

LYONS: So . . . I hear you thinking about getting married.

CORY: Yeah, I done found the right one, Lyons. It's about time.

LYONS: Me and Bonnie been split up about four years now. About the time Papa retired. I guess she just got tired of all them changes I was putting her through. *(Pause)* I always knew you was gonna make something out yourself. Your head was always in the right direction. So . . . you gonna stay in . . . make it a career . . . put in your twenty years?

CORY: I don't know. I got six already, I think that's enough.

LYONS: Stick with Uncle Sam and retire early. Ain't nothing out here. I guess Rose told you what happened with me. They got me down the workhouse. I thought I was being slick cashing other people's checks.

CORY: How much time you doing?

LYONS: They give me three years. I got that beat now. I ain't got but nine more months. It ain't so bad. You learn to deal with it like anything else. You got to take the crookeds with the straights. That's what Papa used to say. He used to say that when he struck out. I seen him strike out three times in a row . . . and the next time up he hit the ball over the grandstand. Right out there in Homestead Field.[2] He wasn't satisfied hitting in the seats . . . he wanted to hit it over everything! After the game he had two hundred people standing around waiting to shake his hand. You got to take the crookeds with the straights. Yeah, Papa was something else.

CORY: You still playing?

LYONS: Cory . . . you know I'm gonna do that. There's some fellows down there we got us a band . . . we gonna try and stay together when we get out . . . but yeah, I'm still playing. It still helps me to get out of bed in the morning. As long as it do that I'm gonna be right there playing and trying to make some sense out of it.

ROSE *(Calling)*: Lyons, I got these eggs in the pan.

LYONS: Let me go on and get these eggs, man. Get ready to go bury Papa. *(Pause)* How you doing? You doing all right?

(Cory nods. Lyons touches him on the shoulder and they share a moment of silent grief. Lyons exits into the house. Cory wanders about the yard. Raynell enters.)

RAYNELL: Hi.

CORY: Hi.

RAYNELL: Did you used to sleep in my room?

CORY: Yeah . . . that used to be my room.

RAYNELL: That's what Papa call it. "Cory's room." It got your football in the closet.

(Rose comes to the screen door.)

ROSE: Raynell, get in there and get them good shoes on.

RAYNELL: Mama, can't I wear these? Them other one hurt my feet.

ROSE: Well, they just gonna have to hurt your feet for a while. You ain't said they hurt your feet when you went down to the store and got them.

RAYNELL: They didn't hurt then. My feet done got bigger.

ROSE: Don't you give me no backtalk now. You get in there and get them shoes on.

(Raynell exits into the house.)

Ain't too much changed. He still got that piece of rag tied to that tree. He was out here swinging that bat. I was just ready to go back in the house. He swung that bat and then he just fell over. Seem like he swung it and stood there with this grin on his face . . . and then he just fell over. They carried him on down to the hospital, but I knew there wasn't no need . . . Why don't you come on in the house?

CORY: Mama . . . I got something to tell you. I don't know how to tell you this . . . but I've got to tell you . . . I'm not going to Papa's funeral.

ROSE: Boy, hush your mouth. That's your daddy you talking about. I don't want hear that kind of talk this morning. I done raised you to come to this? You standing there all healthy and grown talking about you ain't going to your daddy's funeral?

CORY: Mama . . . listen . . .

ROSE: I don't want to hear it, Cory. You just get that thought out of your head.

2. Among the most renowned teams in the Negro League, the Homestead Grays originated in Homestead, Pennsylvania, just south of Pittsburgh, but moved to Pittsburgh's Forbes Field in the late 1930s.

CORY: I can't drag Papa with me everywhere I go. I've got to say no to him. One time in my life I've got to say no.

ROSE: Don't nobody have to listen to nothing like that. I know you and your daddy ain't seen eye to eye, but I ain't got to listen to that kind of talk this morning. Whatever was between you and your daddy . . . the time has come to put it aside. Just take it and set it over there on the shelf and forget about it. Disrespecting your daddy ain't gonna make you a man, Cory. You got to find a way to come to that on your own. Not going to your daddy's funeral ain't gonna make you a man.

CORY: The whole time I was growing up . . . living in his house . . . Papa was like a shadow that followed you everywhere. It weighed on you and sunk into your flesh. It would wrap around you and lay there until you couldn't tell which one was you anymore. That shadow digging in your flesh. Trying to crawl in. Trying to live through you. Everywhere I looked, Troy Maxson was staring back at me . . . hiding under the bed . . . in the closet. I'm just saying I've got to find a way to get rid of that shadow, Mama.

ROSE: You just like him. You got him in you good.

CORY: Don't you tell me that, Mama.

ROSE: You Troy Maxson all over again.

CORY: I don't want to be Troy Maxson. I want to be me.

ROSE: You can't be nobody but who you are, Cory. That shadow wasn't nothing but you growing into yourself. You either got to grow into it or cut it down to fit you. But that's all you got to make life with. That's all you got to measure yourself against that world out there. Your daddy wanted you to be everything he wasn't . . . and at the same time he tried to make you into everything he was. I don't know if he was right or wrong . . . but I do know he meant to do more good than he meant to do harm. He wasn't always right. Sometimes when he touched he bruised. And sometimes when he took me in his arms he cut.

When I first met your daddy I thought, "Here is a man I can lay down with and make a baby." That's the first thing I thought when I seen him. I was thirty years old and had done seen my share of men. But when he walked up to me and said, "I can dance a waltz that'll make you dizzy," I thought, "Rose Lee, here is a man that you can open yourself up to and be filled to bursting. Here is a man that can fill all them empty spaces you been tipping around the edges of." One of them empty spaces was being somebody's mother.

I married your daddy and settle down to cooking his supper and keeping clean sheets on the bed. When your daddy walked through the house he was so big he filled it up. That was my first mistake. Not to make him leave some room for me. For my part in the matter. But at that time I wanted that. I wanted a house that I could sing in. And that's what your daddy gave me. I didn't know to keep up his strength I had to give up little pieces of mine. I did that. I took on his life as mine and mixed up the pieces so that you couldn't hardly tell which was which anymore. It was my choice. It was my life and I didn't have to live it like that. But that's what life offered me in the way of being a woman and I took it. I grabbed hold of it with both hands.

By the time Raynell came into the house, me and your daddy had done lost touch with one another. I didn't want to make my blessing off of nobody's misfortune . . . but I took on to Raynell like she was all them babies I had wanted and never had. *(The phone rings)* Like I'd been blessed to relive a part of my life. And if the Lord see fit to keep up my strength . . . I'm gonna do her just like your daddy did you . . . I'm gonna give her the best of what's in me.

RAYNELL *(Entering, still with her old shoes)*: Mama . . . Reverend Tolliver on the phone.

(Rose exits into the house.)

Hi.

CORY: Hi.

RAYNELL: You in the Army or the Marines?

CORY: Marines.

RAYNELL: Papa said it was the Army. Did you know Blue?

CORY: Blue? Who's Blue?

RAYNELL: Papa's dog what he sing about all the time.

CORY *(Singing)*:

Hear it ring! Hear it ring!
I had a dog his name was Blue
You know Blue was mighty true
You know Blue was a good old dog
Blue treed a possum in a hollow log
You know from that he was a good old dog.
Hear it ring! Hear it ring!

(Raynell joins in singing.)

CORY AND RAYNELL:

Blue treed a possum out on a limb
Blue looked at me and I looked at him
Grabbed that possum and put him in a sack
Blue stayed there till I came back
Old Blue's feets was big and round
Never allowed a possum to touch the ground.

Old Blue died and I dug his grave
I dug his grave with a silver spade
Let him down with a golden chain
And every night I call his name
Go on Blue, you good dog you
Go on Blue, you good dog you

RAYNELL:

Blue laid down and died like a man
Blue laid down and died . . .

CORY AND RAYNELL:

Blue laid down and died like a man
Now he's treeing possums in the Promised Land
I'm gonna tell you this to let you know

Blue's gone where the good dogs go
When I hear Old Blue bark
When I hear Old Blue bark
Blue treed a possum in Noah's Ark
Blue treed a possum in Noah's Ark.

(Rose comes to the screen door.)

ROSE: Cory, we gonna be ready to go in a minute.
CORY *(To Raynell)*: You go on in the house and change them shoes like Mama told you so we can go to Papa's funeral.
RAYNELL: Okay, I'll be back.

(Raynell exits into the house. Cory gets up and crosses over to the tree. Rose stands at the screen door watching him. Gabriel enters from the alley.)

GABRIEL *(Calling)*: Hey, Rose!
ROSE: Gabe?
GABRIEL: I'm here, Rose. Hey, Rose, I'm here!

(Rose enters from the house.)

ROSE: Lord . . . Look here, Lyons!
LYONS *(Enters from the house)*: See, I told you, Rose . . . I told you they'd let him come.
CORY: How you doing, Uncle Gabe?
LYONS: How you doing, Uncle Gabe?
GABRIEL: Hey, Rose. It's time. It's time to tell Saint Peter to open the Gates. Troy, you ready? You ready, Troy. I'm gonna tell Saint Peter to open the Gates. You get ready now.

(Gabriel, with great fanfare, braces himself to blow. The trumpet is without a mouthpiece. He puts the end of it into his mouth and blows with great force, like a man who has been waiting some twenty-odd years for this single moment. No sound comes out of the trumpet. He braces himself and blows again with the same result. A third time he blows. There is a weight of impossible description that falls away and leaves him bare and exposed to a frightful realization. It is a trauma that a sane and normal mind would be unable to withstand. He begins to dance. A slow, strange dance, eerie and life-giving. A dance of atavistic[3] signature and ritual. Lyons attempts to embrace him. Gabriel pushes Lyons away. Gabriel begins to howl in what is an attempt at song, or perhaps a song turning back into itself in an attempt at speech. He finishes his dance and the Gates of Heaven stand open as wide as God's closet.)

That's the way that go!

(Blackout.)

1987

3. Characterized by a reversion to an ancient or ancestral form.

QUESTIONS

1. In interviews, August Wilson describes FENCES as revolving so completely around its central character that it might "almost" be called "*The Life of Troy Maxson* or just *Troy Maxson*." To what extent does and doesn't that seem true?
2. Wilson also describes the play as "examin[ing] Troy's life layer by layer" to find out why he made the choices he made" (see "Authors on Their Work" below). How do you think the play ultimately answers that question? What does it seem to present as the key to Troy's character or the thing he values most?
3. According to the play, how have circumstances helped to make Troy the man he is? How might he and his life have been different had he turned fifty-three in either 1947 or 1967? had he been white?
4. Does Troy's character develop over the course of the play or only the way others see him? Why and how so?
5. What is the effect and significance of the fact that the play ends after Troy's death? How would the play work and mean differently if its final scene were omitted? if Troy died onstage?
6. What might the fence come to stand for or symbolize in the play? Why might *Fences*, plural, be a more apt title than *The Fence*?
7. How are father-son relationships depicted in the play? How does Troy's relationship with his father compare to and shape his relationship with his sons? Why do you think the play includes Lyons, as well as Cory?
8. How might Rose or your impression of her evolve over the course of the play? Why does she adopt Raynell, and what effect does this choice seem to have? Why might she begin to go to church?
9. What is the significance and effect of Wilson's choice to set the play in the Maxson's front yard? to punctuate the play with scenes that take place on Friday nights? not to show us Troy at work, Cory playing football, and so on?

AUTHORS ON THEIR WORK

AUGUST WILSON (1945–2005)

From Dennis Watlington, "Hurdling Fences" (1989)*

[. . .] I wanted to explore our commonalities of culture. What you have in *Fences* is a very specific situation, a black family which the forces of racism have molded and shaped, but you also have a husband-wife, father-son. White America looks at black America in this glancing manner. They pass right by the Troy Maxsons of the world and never stop to look at them. They talk about niggers as lazy and shiftless. Well, here's a man with responsibilities as prime to his life. I wanted to examine Troy's life layer by layer and find out why he made the choices he made. (109)

• • •

From "Men, Women, and Culture: A Conversation with August Wilson" (1993)**

[INTERVIEWER]: What makes Troy heroic? He's an ex-con, ex-baseball player, now a garbage collector; he exploits his brother and cheats on his wife—what is redeeming about him as an African American man?

WILSON: I think that, for me, this may be nothing more than his willingness to wrestle with his life, his willingness to engage no matter what the circumstances of his life. He hasn't given up despite the twists and turns it's given him. I find that both noble and heroic. (172)

*"Hurdling Fences." Interview by Dennis Watlington. *Vanity Fair*, no. 52 Apr. 1989, pp. 102–13.
**"Men, Women, and Culture: A Conversation with August Wilson." Interview by Nathan L. Grant. *American Drama*, vol. 5, no. 2, Spring 1996, pp. 100–22.

SUGGESTIONS FOR WRITING

1. Why is Troy Maxson so insistent that his son quit the football team? What about your own cultural and historical context might make his attitude seem surprising? Write a response paper or essay exploring these questions.
2. Write an essay exploring Gabriel's role in the play. What is significant about his injuries and their cause, for example? about his fixation with Judgment Day? about his actions in the play's final scene? What might his final, "*frightful realization*" (1237) be, and why, according to Wilson's stage directions, might "*the Gates of Heaven stand open as wide as God's closet*" only after that realization and the "*atavistic*" dance that follows it?
3. Write an essay exploring Wilson's characterization of Rose. What might the play suggest, through her, about the options available to, or conflicts faced by, women in general or African American women in particular in the 1950s? To what extent might Wilson's play reproduce or challenge our preconceptions about such women? Alternatively, consider how FENCES might reproduce or challenge stereotypical views of black men.
4. Write an epilogue to FENCES, a scene depicting Rose, Lyons, Cory, or Raynell in 1975. What do you imagine has happened to this character, and why and how so? If Cory had a child, for example, what would his relationship with that child be like? What might he say to his child about his father, his mother, and his own childhood?
5. Research theories of tragedy and the tragic hero. Drawing on both these and evidence from Wilson's play, explain whether and how FENCES might be considered a tragedy or Troy Maxson a tragic hero.
6. Write an essay comparing Troy Maxson to Willie Lohman, in Arthur Miller's DEATH OF A SALESMAN. How might Wilson's character and play respond to Miller's?

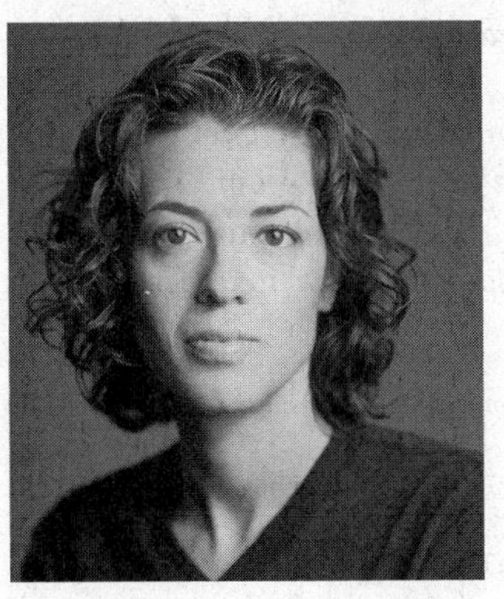

QUIARA ALEGRÍA HUDES
(b. 1977)

Water by the Spoonful

Though she now lives in New York City with her lawyer husband and two small children, Quiara Alegría Hudes hails from Philadelphia, the city that still serves as inspiration and setting for much of her work. The daughter of a Jewish carpenter and a Puerto Rican mother and stepfather, Hudes spent her childhood exploring the city's ethnically and economically diverse neighborhoods, especially the predominantly African American West Philly area she called home and the North Philly barrios where many of her maternal relatives still live. Hudes had her first play produced by Philadelphia Young Playwrights when she was only ten. Yet when she became the first in her family to attend college, at Yale, she majored in music. After graduation, Hudes returned home, launching a successful career as a musician-composer before heading to Brown University. Here she earned an MFA (2003) and completed two plays—the award-winning *Yamaya's Belly* (2005), about a young Cuban boy who dreams of immigrating to the United States, and *The Adventures of Barrio Grrl!*, which she later turned into a children's musical. Hudes received the first of three Pulitzer nominations for her work on another musical, the Tony Award–winning *In the Heights* (2007). But her real acclaim as a dramatist rests on a trilogy inspired by, and developed partly in collaboration with, her "story-centric family," especially Elliot Ruiz, a cousin wounded in the Iraq War. *Water by the Spoonful* (2011), for which Hudes won the Pulitzer, is the second play in the sequence that also includes *Elliot, a Soldier's Fugue* (2006) and *The Happiest Song Plays Last* (2012). Together, says Hudes, these plays tell a distinctly "American story" about issues and people we too often "don't talk about," in part by exploiting and exploring diverse, often distinctly twenty-first-century ways of both talking and storytelling.

CHARACTERS

ELLIOT ORTIZ, an Iraq vet with a slight limp, works at Subway sandwich shop, scores an occasional job as a model or actor, Yazmin's cousin, Odessa's birth son, Puerto Rican, twenty-four.

YAZMIN ORTIZ, in her first year as an adjunct professor of music, Odessa's niece and Elliot's cousin, Puerto Rican, twenty-nine.

HAIKUMOM, aka Odessa Ortiz, founder of *www.recover-together.com*, works odd janitorial jobs, lives one notch above squalor, Puerto Rican, thirty-nine.

FOUNTAINHEAD, aka John, a computer programmer and entrepreneur, lives on Philadelphia's Main Line,[1] white, forty-one.

CHUTES&LADDERS, lives in San Diego, has worked a low-level job at the IRS since the Reagan years,[2] his real name is Clayton "Buddy" Wilkie, African American, fifty-six.

ORANGUTAN, a recent community college graduate, her real name is Madeleine Mays and before that Yoshiko Sakai, Japanese by birth, thirty-one.

A GHOST, also plays Professor Aman, an Arabic professor at Swarthmore;[3] also plays a Policeman in Japan.

SETTING: *2009. Six years after Elliot left for Iraq. Philadelphia, San Diego, Japan and Puerto Rico.*

The stage has two worlds. The "real world" is populated with chairs. The chairs are from many locations—living rooms, an office, a seminar room, a church, a diner, internet cafés, etc. They all have the worn-in feel of life. A duct-taped La-Z-Boy. Salvaged trash chairs. A busted-up metal folding chair from a rec center.

1. Series of affluent towns in Philadelphia's western suburbs, along the old Main Line of the Pennsylvania Railroad.

2. 1981–89, during the presidency of Ronald Reagan (1911–2004). *IRS*: Internal Revenue Service (acronym).

3. Highly ranked private liberal arts college (founded 1864) located eleven miles southwest of Philadelphia.

Liza Colón-Zayas, Sue Jean Kim, and Frankie R. Faison in the Second Stage Theatre production of *Water by the Spoonful*, 2012

An Aero chair. An Eames chair.[4] *A chair/desk from a college classroom. Diner chairs. A chair from an internet café in Japan. Living room chairs. Library chairs. A church pew. Facing in all different directions.*

The "online world" is an empty space. A space that connects the chairs.

MUSIC: *Jazz. John Coltrane.*[5] *The sublime stuff* (A Love Supreme). *And the noise* (Ascension).

NOTE: *Unless specifically noted, when characters are online, don't have actors typing on a keyboard. Treat it like regular conversation rather than the act of writing or typing. They can be doing things people do in the comfort of their home, like eating potato chips, walking around in jammies, cooking, doing dishes, clipping nails, etc.*

Scene One

Swarthmore College. Elliot and Yaz eat breakfast. Elliot wears a Subway sandwich shop polo shirt.

ELLIOT: This guy ain't coming. How do you know him?
YAZ: We're on a committee together.
ELLIOT: My shift starts in fifteen.
YAZ: All right, we'll go.

4. High-end chair designed in 1956 by renowned husband-and-wife team Charles (1907–78) and Ray Eames (1912–88).

5. American jazz saxophonist and composer (1926–67), pioneer of "free jazz."

ELLIOT: Five more minutes. Tonight on the way home, we gotta stop by Whole Foods.

YAZ: Sure, I need toothpaste.

ELLIOT: You gotta help me with my mom, Yaz.

YAZ: You said she had a good morning.

ELLIOT: She cooked breakfast.

YAZ: Progress.

ELLIOT: No. The docs said she can't be eating all that junk, it'll mess with her chemo, so she crawls out of bed for the first time in days and cooks eggs for breakfast. In two inches of pork-chop fat. I'm like, Mom, recycle glass and plastic, not grease. She thinks putting the egg on top of a paper towel after you cook it makes it healthy. I told her, Mom, you gotta cook egg whites. In Pam spray. But it has to be her way. Like, "That's how we ate them in Puerto Rico and we turned out fine." You gotta talk to her. I'm trying to teach her about quinoa. Broccoli rabe. Healthy shit. So I get home the other day, she had made quinoa with bacon. She was like, "It's healthy!"

YAZ: That's Ginny. The more stubborn she's being, the better she's feeling.

ELLIOT: I gave those eggs to the dogs when she went to the bathroom.

YAZ *(Pulls some papers from her purse)*: You wanna be my witness?

ELLIOT: To what?

(Yaz signs the papers.)

YAZ: My now-legal failure. I'm divorced.

ELLIOT: Yaz. I don't want to hear that.

YAZ: You've been saying that for months and I've been keeping my mouth closed. I just need a John Hancock.

ELLIOT: What happened to "trial separation"?

YAZ: There was a verdict. William fell out of love with me.

ELLIOT: I've never seen you two argue.

YAZ: We did, we just had smiles on our faces.

ELLIOT: That's bullshit. You don't divorce someone before you even have a fight with them. I'm calling him.

YAZ: Go ahead.

ELLIOT: He was just texting me about going to the Phillies game on Sunday.

YAZ: So, go. He didn't fall out of love with the family, just me.

ELLIOT: I'm going to ask him who he's been screwing behind your back.

YAZ: No one, Elliot.

ELLIOT: You were tappin' some extra on the side?

YAZ: He woke up one day and I was the same as any other person passing by on the street, and life is short, and you can only live in mediocrity so long.

ELLIOT: You two are the dog and the owner that look like each other. Ya'll are the *Cosby Show.*[6] Conundrum, Yaz and William make a funny, end-of episode. You show all us cousins, maybe we can't ever do it ourselves, but it *is* possible.

YAZ: Did I ever say, "It's possible"?

ELLIOT: By example.

6. Television sitcom (1984–92) about a close-knit upper-middle-class African American family starring comedian Bill Cosby (b. 1937).

YAZ: Did I ever say those words?

(Professor Aman enters.)

AMAN: Yazmin, forgive me. You must be . . .

ELLIOT: Elliot Ortiz. Nice to meet you, I appreciate it.

AMAN: Professor Aman. *(They shake)* We'll have to make this short and sweet, my lecture begins . . . began . . . well, talk fast.

ELLIOT: Yaz, give us a second?

YAZ: I'll be in the car. *(Exits)*

ELLIOT: I'm late, too, so . . .

AMAN: You need something translated.

ELLIOT: Just a phrase. Thanks, man.

AMAN: Eh, your sister's cute.

ELLIOT: Cousin. I wrote it phonetically. You grow up speaking Arabic?

AMAN: English. What's your native tongue?

ELLIOT: Spanglish. *(Hands Aman a piece of paper)*

AMAN: Mom-ken men fad-luck ted-dini ga-waz saf-far-i. Mom-ken men-fadluck ted-dini gawaz saffari. Am I saying that right?

ELLIOT *(Spooked)*: Spot on.

AMAN: You must have some familiarity with Arabic to remember it so clearly.

ELLIOT: Maybe I heard it on TV or something.

AMAN: An odd phrase.

ELLIOT: It's like a song I can't get out of my head.

AMAN: Yazmin didn't tell me what this is for.

ELLIOT: It's not for anything.

AMAN: Do you mind me asking, what's around your neck?

ELLIOT: Something my girl gave me.

AMAN: Can I see? *(Elliot pulls dog tags from under his shirt)* Romantic gift. You were in the army.

ELLIOT: Marines.

AMAN: Iraq?

ELLIOT: For a minute.

AMAN: Were you reluctant to tell me that?

ELLIOT: No.

AMAN: Still in the service?

ELLIOT: Honorable discharge. Leg injury.

AMAN: When?

ELLIOT: A few years ago.

AMAN: This is a long time to have a phrase stuck in your head.

ELLIOT: What is this, man?

AMAN: You tell me.

ELLIOT: It's just a phrase. If you don't want to translate, just say so.

AMAN: A college buddy is making a film about Marines in Iraq. Gritty, documentary-style. He's looking for some veterans to interview. Get an authentic point of view. Maybe I could pass your number onto him.

ELLIOT: Nope. No interviews for this guy.

AMAN: You're asking me for a favor. *(Pause)* Yazmin told me you're an actor. Every actor needs a break, right?

ELLIOT: I did enough Q&As about the service. People manipulate you with the questions.

AMAN: It's not just to interview. He needs a right-hand man, an expert to help him. How do Marines hold a gun? How do they kick in civilian doors, this sort of thing. How do they say "Ooh-rah" in a patriotic manner?

ELLIOT: Are you his headhunter or something?

AMAN: I'm helping with the translations, I have a small stake and I want the movie to be accurate. And you seem not unintelligent. For a maker of sandwiches. *(Hands him a business card)* He's in L.A. In case you want a career change. I give you a cup of sugar, you give me a cup of sugar.

ELLIOT: If I have a minute, I'll dial the digits. *(Takes the business card)* So what's it mean?

AMAN: Momken men-fadluck ted-dini gawaz saffari. Rough translation, "Can I please have my passport back?"

Scene Two

Odessa's living room and kitchen. She makes coffee. She goes over to her computer, clicks a button. On a screen we see:

HAIKUMOM, SITEADMIN
STATUS: ONLINE

HAIKUMOM: Rise and shine, kiddos, the rooster's a-crowin', it's a beautiful day to be sober. *(No response)* Your Thursday morning haiku:[7]

if you get restless
buy a hydrangea or rose
water it, wait, bloom

(Odessa continues making coffee. A computer dings and on another screen we see:)

ORANGUTAN
STATUS: ONLINE

ORANGUTAN: Ninety-one days. Smiley face.

HAIKUMOM *(Relieved)*: Orangutan! Jesus, I thought my primate friend had disappeared back to the jungle.

ORANGUTAN: Disappeared? Yes. Jungle? Happily, no.

HAIKUMOM: I'm trying to put a high-five emoticon, but my computer is being a capital B. So, high-five!

(They high-five in the air. Another computer screen lights up:)

7. Originally Japanese poetic form that, in its English-language incarnations, traditionally consists of seventeen syllables divided into three lines of five, seven, and five syllables, respectively.

CHUTES&LADDERS
STATUS: ONLINE

CHUTES&LADDERS: Orangutan? I was about to send a search party after your rear end. Kid, *log on.* No news is bad news.

ORANGUTAN: Chutes&Ladders, giving me a hard time as usual. I'd expect nothing less.

CHUTES&LADDERS: Your last post says: "Day One. Packing bags, gotta run," and then you don't log on for three months?

ORANGUTAN: I was going to Japan, I had to figure out what shoes to bring.

HAIKUMOM: The country?

CHUTES&LADDERS: What happened to Maine?

ORANGUTAN: And I quote, "Get a hobby, find a new job, an exciting city, go teach English in a foreign country." Did you guys think I wouldn't take your seasoned advice? I was batting 0 for ten, and for the first time, guys, I feel fucking free.

HAIKUMOM *(Nonjudgmental)*: Censored.

ORANGUTAN: I wake up and I think, What's the world got up its sleeve today? And I look forward to the answer. So, thank you.

CHUTES&LADDERS: We told you so.

ORANGUTAN *(Playful)*: Shut up.

HAIKUMOM: You're welcome.

ORANGUTAN: I gave my parents the URL. My username, my password. They logged on and read every post I've ever put on here and for once they said they understood. They had completely cut me off, but after reading this site they bought me the plane ticket. One way. I teach English in the mornings. I have a class of children, a class of teens, and a class of adults, most of whom are older than me. I am free in the afternoons. I have a paycheck which I use for legal things like ice cream, noodles and socks. I walk around feeling like maybe I *am* normal. Maybe, just possibly, I'm not that different. Or maybe it's just homeland delusions.

CHUTES&LADDERS AND HAIKUMOM: Homeland?

HAIKUMOM: You're Japanese?

ORANGUTAN: I *was*, for the first eight days of my life. Yoshiko Sakai. Then on day nine I was adopted and moved to Cape Lewiston, Maine, where I became Ma—M.M., and where in all my days I have witnessed *one* other Asian. In the Superfresh. Deli counter.

CHUTES&LADDERS: Japan . . . Wow, that little white rock sure doesn't discriminate.

HAIKUMOM: Amen.

ORANGUTAN: Mango Internet Café. I'm sitting in an orange plastic chair, a little view of the Hokkaido waterfront.

HAIKUMOM: Japan has a waterfront?

CHUTES&LADDERS: It's an island.

HAIKUMOM: Really? Are there beaches? Can you go swimming?

ORANGUTAN: The ocean reminds me of Maine. Cold water, very quiet, fisherman, boats, the breeze. I wouldn't try swimming. I'm just a looker. I was never one to actually have an experience.

CHUTES&LADDERS: Ah, the ocean . . . There's only one thing on this planet I'm more scared of than that big blue lady.

HAIKUMOM: Let me guess: landing on a sliding board square?[8]

CHUTES&LADDERS: Lol, truer words have never been spoken. You know I was born just a few miles from the Pacific. In the fresh salt air. Back in "those days" I'm at Coronado Beach[9] with a few "friends" doing my "thing" and I get sucked up under this wave. I gasp, I breathe in and my lungs fill with water. I'm like, this is it, I'm going to meet my maker. I had never felt so heavy, not even during my two OD's.[1] I was sinking to the bottom and my head hit the sand like a lead ball. My body just felt like an anvil. The next thing I know there's fingers digging in my ankles. This lifeguard pulls me out, I'm throwing up salt water. I say to him, "Hey blondie, you don't know me from Adam but you are my witness: today's the day I start to *live.*" And this lifeguard, I mean he was young with these muscles, this kid looks at me like, "Who is this big black dude who can't even doggy paddle?" When I stand up and brush the sand off me, people *applaud.* An old lady touches my cheek and says, "I thought you were done for." I get back to San Diego that night, make one phone call, the next day I'm in my first meeting, sitting in a folding chair, saying the serenity prayer.[2]

ORANGUTAN: I hate to inflate your already swollen ego, but that was a lucid, touching story. By the way, did you get the lifeguard's name? He sounds hot.

HAIKUMOM: Hey Chutes&Ladders, it's never too late to learn. Most YMCAs offer adult swimming classes.

CHUTES&LADDERS: I'll do the world a favor and stay out of a speedo.

ORANGUTAN: Sober air toast. To lifeguards.

CHUTES&LADDERS AND HAIKUMOM: To lifeguards.

ORANGUTAN, CHUTES&LADDERS AND HAIKUMOM: Clink.

HAIKUMOM: Chutes&Ladders, I'm buying you a pair of water wings.

Scene Three

John Coltrane's A Love Supreme *plays. A Subway sandwich shop on Philadelphia's Main Line. Elliot sits behind the counter. The phone rings. He gets up, hobbles to it—he walks with a limp.*

ELLIOT: Subway Main Line. Lar! Laaar, what's it doing for you today? Staying in the shade? I got you, how many you need? Listen, the delivery guy's out and my little sports injury is giving me hell so can you pick up? Cool, sorry for the inconvenience. Let me grab a pen. A'ight, pick a hoagie, any hoagie!

(Elliot begins writing the order.

Lights rise to a seminar room at Swarthmore College. We find Yaz mid-class. She hits a button on a stereo and the Coltrane stops playing.)

8. In Milton Bradley's board game Chutes & Ladders (based on the ancient Indian game Snakes and Ladders), some squares are connected by sliding boards, or "chutes." Players landing on the square picturing the top of the chute advance or "slide" directly to the square picturing the bottom of the chute.

9. On Coronado Island, just off the coast of San Diego, California.

1. Overdoses (acronym).

2. Authored by American theologian Reinhold Niebuhr (1892–1971) and adopted by Alcoholics Anonymous and other twelve-step addiction-recovery programs, it reads, "God, grant me the serenity to accept the things I cannot change, / The courage to change the things I can, / And the wisdom to know the difference."

YAZ: Coltrane's *A Love Supreme*, 1964. Dissonance is still a gateway to resolution. A B-diminished chord is still resolving to? C-major. A tritone is still resolving up to? The major sixth. Diminished chords, tritones, still didn't have the right to be their own independent thought. In 1965 something changed. The ugliness bore no promise of a happy ending. The ugliness became an end in itself. Coltrane democratized the notes. He said, they're all equal. Freedom. It was called Free Jazz but freedom is a hard thing to express musically without spinning into noise. This is from *Ascension*, 1965.

(She plays Ascension. *It sounds uglier than the first sample. In the Subway, a figure comes into view. It is the Ghost.)*

GHOST: Momken men-fadluck ted-dini gawaz saffari?

(Elliot tries to ignore the Ghost, reading off the order.)

ELLIOT: That's three teriyaki onion with chicken. First with hots and onions. Second with everything. Third with extra bacon. Two spicy Italian with American cheese on whole grain. One BMT on flatbread. Good so far?
GHOST: Momken men-fadluck ted-dini gawaz saffari?
ELLIOT: Five chocolate chip cookies, one oatmeal raisin. Three Baked Lay's, three Doritos. Two Sprite Zeros, one Barq's, one Coke, two orange sodas. How'd I do?
GHOST: Momken men-fadluck ted-dini gawaz saffari?
ELLIOT: All right, that'll be ready in fifteen minutes. One sec for your total.

(Elliot gets a text message. He reads it; his entire demeanor shifts.)

Lar, I just got a text. There's a family emergency, I can't do this order right now.

(Elliot hangs up. He exits, limping away.)

YAZ: Oh come on, don't make that face. I know it feels academic. You're going to leave here and become R&B hit makers and Sondheim[3] clones and never think about this noise again. But this is Coltrane, people, this is not Schoenberg![4] This is jazz, stuff people listen to *voluntarily*. Shopping period is still on—go sit in one session of "Germans and Noise" down the hall and you'll come running back begging for this muzak.

(Yaz turns off the music.)

In fact, change the syllabus. No listening report next week. Instead, I want you to pinpoint the first time you really noticed dissonance. The composer, the piece, the measures. Two pages analyzing the notes and two pages describing the experience personally. This is your creation myth.[5] Before you leave this school you better figure out that story and cling to it for dear life or you'll be a stockbroker within a year.

3. Stephen Sondheim (b. 1930), multi-award-winning American composer-lyricist best known for hit Broadway musicals including *West Side Story* (1957), for which he wrote the lyrics only; *Sweeney Todd* (1979); and *Into the Woods* (1986).

4. Arnold Schoenberg (1874–1951), influential avant-garde Austrian classical pianist, composer, and music theorist.

5. Narrative recounting a particular culture or religion's understanding of how something (usually the world itself) came to be.

I was thirteen, I worked in a corrugated box factory all summer, I saved up enough to find my first music teacher—up to that point I was self-taught, playing to the radio. I walked into Don Rappaport's room at Settlement Music School.[6] He was old, he had jowls, he was sitting at the piano and he said, "What do you do?" I said, "I'm a composer, sir." Presumptuous, right? I sat down and played Mr. Rappaport a Yazmin original. He said, "It's pretty, everything goes together. It's like an outfit where your socks are blue and your pants, shirt, hat are all blue." Then he said, "Play an F-sharp major in your left hand." Then he said, "Play a C-major in your right hand." "Now play them together." He asked me, "Does it go together?" I told him, "No, sir." He said, "Now go home and write." My first music lesson was seven minutes long. I had never really heard dissonance before.

(Yaz's phone vibrates. She sees the caller with concern.)

Let's take five.

(As students file out, Yaz makes a phone call. Lights up on Elliot outside the Subway.)

("What's the bad news?") You called three times.

ELLIOT: She's still alive.

YAZ: Okay.

ELLIOT: Jefferson Hospital. They admitted her three hours ago. Pop had the courtesy to text me.

YAZ: Are you still at work?

ELLIOT: Just smashed the bathroom mirror all over the floor. Boss sent me out to the parking lot.

YAZ: Wait there. I'm on my way.

ELLIOT: "Your mom is on breathing machine." Who texts that? Who texts that and then doesn't pick up the phone?

YAZ: I'll be there within twenty.

ELLIOT: Why did I come to work today?

YAZ: She had a good morning. You wanted your thing translated.

ELLIOT: She cooked and I wouldn't eat a bite off the fork. There's a Subway hoagies around the corner and I had to work half an hour away.

YAZ: You didn't want your buddies to see you working a normal job.

ELLIOT: Not normal job. Shit job. I'm a butler. A porter of sandwiches.

YAZ: Ginny's been to Hades and back, stronger each time.

ELLIOT: What is Hades?

YAZ: In Greek mythology, the river through the underworld—

ELLIOT: My mom's on a machine and you're dropping vocab words?!

(A ding.)

YAZ: Text message, don't hang up. *(She looks at her phone. A moment, then)* You still there?

ELLIOT: It was my dad wasn't it? Yaz, spit it out.

6. Philadelphia institution originally founded (1908) to provide free music instruction to newly arrived immigrants but today offering music, dance, and visual arts classes to children and adults across the city "without regard to age, race or financial circumstances." Hudes is an alumna.

YAZ: It was your dad.

ELLIOT: And? Yaz, I'm about to start walking down Lancaster Avenue for thirty miles till I get back to Philly and I don't care if I snap every wire out my leg and back—I need to get out of here. I need to see Mom, I need to talk to her!

YAZ: He said, "Waiting for Elliot till we turn off the machine."

Scene Four

The chat room. A screen lights up:

[NO IMAGE]
FOUNTAINHEAD[7]
STATUS: ONLINE

FOUNTAINHEAD: I've uh, wow, hello there everyone. Delete, delete. Good afternoon. Evening. Delete.

(Deep breath.)

Things I am taking:

—My life into my own hands.
—My gorgeous, deserving wife out for our seventh anniversary.

Me: mildly athletic, but work twice as hard. Won state for javelin two years straight. Ran a half marathon last fall. Animated arguer. Two medals for undergrad debate. MBA from Wharton.[8] Beautiful wife, two sons. Built a programming company from the ground up, featured in the *New York Times'* Circuits section, sold it at its peak, bought a yellow Porsche, got a day job to keep myself honest. Salary was 300K, company was run by morons, got laid off, handsome severance, which left me swimming in cash and free time.

Me and crack: long story short, I was at a conference with our CFO and two programmers and a not-unattractive lady in HR.[9] They snorted, invited me to join. A few weeks later that little rock waltzed right into my hand. I've been using off and on since. One eight ball every Saturday, strict rations, portion control. Though the last three or four weeks, it's less like getting high and more like trying to build a time machine. Anything to get back the romance of that virgin smoke.

Last weekend I let myself buy more than my predetermined allotment—I buy in small quantity, because as with my food, I eat what's on my plate. Anyway, I ran over a curb, damaged the underside of my Porsche. Now it's in the shop and I'm driving a rental Mustang. So, not rock bottom but a rental Ford is as close to rock bottom as I'd like to get. Fast forward to tonight. I'm watching my wife's eyelids fall and telling myself, "You are on punishment, Poppa. Daddy's on time out. Do not get out of bed, do not tiptoe down those stairs, do not go down to that basement, do not sit beside that foosball table, do not smoke, and please do not crawl on the carpet looking for one last hit in the fibers."

(Pause.)

7. Title of a best-selling 1943 novel by Ayn Rand (1905–82), a famous evocation of her individualist philosophy.

8. Famed business school (founded 1881) of the University of Pennsylvania, in Philadelphia. *MBA*: master of business administration (acronym).

9. Human resources (acronym). *CFO*: chief financial officer.

In kindergarten my son tested into G and T. Gifted and talented. You meet with the school, they tailor the program to the kid. Math, reading, art, whatever the parent chooses. I said, "Teach my son how to learn. How to use a library. How to find original source material, read a map, track down the experts so he becomes an expert." Which gets me to—

You: the experts. It's the first day of school and I'm knocking at your classroom door. I got my No. 2 pencils, I'll sit in the front row, pay attention, and do my homework. No lesson is too basic. Teach me every technique. Any tip so that Saturday doesn't become every day. Any actions that keep you in the driver seat. Healthy habits and rational thoughts to blot out that voice in the back of my head.

Today, I quit. My wife cannot know, she'd get suspicious if I were at meetings all the time. There can be no medical records, so therapy is out. At least it's not heroin, I'm not facing a physical war. It's a psychological battle and I'm armed with two weapons: willpower and the experts.

I'm taking my wife out tomorrow for our seventh anniversary and little does she know that when we clink glasses, I'll be toasting to Day One.

(Odessa is emotional. Chutes&Ladders and Orangutan seem awestruck.)

ORANGUTAN *(Clapping)*: That was brave.

CHUTES&LADDERS: What. The.

HAIKUMOM: Careful.

CHUTES&LADDERS: Fuck.

HAIKUMOM: Censored.

ORANGUTAN: I'm making popcorn. Oh, this is gonna be fun!

CHUTES&LADDERS: Fountainhead, speaking of experts, I've been meaning to become an asshole. Can you teach me how?

HAIKUMOM: Censored!

ORANGUTAN: "Tips"? This isn't a cooking website. And what is a half marathon?

CHUTES&LADDERS: Maybe it's something like a half crack addict. Or a half husband.

ORANGUTAN: Was that an addiction coming out or an online dating profile? "Married Male Dope Fiend. Smokin' hot."

CHUTES&LADDERS: Fountainhead, you sound like the kind of guy who's read *The 7 Habits of Highly Effective People*[1] cover to cover. Was one of those habits crack? Give the essays a rest and type three words. "I'm. A. Crackhead."

ORANGUTAN: You know, adderall is like totes[2] cool. Us crackheads, we're like yucky and stuff. We're like so nineties. Go try the adderall edge!

HAIKUMOM: Hey.

ORANGUTAN: The guy's a hoax. Twenty bucks says he's pranking. Let's start a new thread.

HAIKUMOM: Hi, Fountainhead, welcome. As the site administrator, I want to honestly congratulate you for accomplishing what so many addicts only hope for: one clean day. Any time you feel like using, log on here instead. It's worked

1. Popular business self-help book (1989) by Stephen R. Covey (1932–2012) stressing the principles of independence and self-mastery, interdependence, and continuous improvement.

2. Totally (slang). *Adderall*: stimulant used to treat narcolepsy and attention deficit hyperactivity disorder.

for me. When it comes to junkies, I dug lower than the dungeon. Once upon a time I had a beautiful family, too. Now all I have is six years clean. Don't lose what I lost, what Chutes&Ladders lost.

CHUTES&LADDERS: Excuse me.

HAIKUMOM: Orangutan, I just checked and Fountainhead has no aliases and has never logged onto this site before under a different pseudonym, which are the usual markers of a scam.

ORANGUTAN: I'm just saying. Who toasts to their first day of sobriety?

CHUTES&LADDERS: I hope it's seltzer in that there champagne glass.

ORANGUTAN: Ginger ale, shirley temple.

CHUTES&LADDERS: "A toast, honey. I had that seven-year itch so I became a crackhead."

CHUTES&LADDERS AND ORANGUTAN: Clink.

HAIKUMOM: Hey; kiddos. Your smiley administrator doesn't want to start purging messages. For rules of the forums click on this link. No personal attacks.

ORANGUTAN: We don't come to this site for a pat on the back.

HAIKUMOM: I'm just saying. R-e-s-p-e-c-t.

CHUTES&LADDERS: I will always give *crack* the respect it deserves. Some pure-bred poodle comes pissing on my tree trunk? Damn straight I'll chase his ass out my forest.

HAIKUMOM: This here is my forest. You two think you were all humble pie when you started out? Check your original posts.

ORANGUTAN: Oh, I know mine. "I-am-scared-I-will-kill-myself-talk-me-off-the-ledge."

HAIKUMOM: So unless someone gets that desperate they don't deserve our noble company? "Suffer like me, or you ain't legit"?

ORANGUTAN: Haikumom's growing claws.

HAIKUMOM: Just don't act entitled because you got so low. *(To Fountainhead)* Sorry. Fountainhead, forgive us. We get very passionate because—

CHUTES&LADDERS: Fountainhead, your Porsche has a massive engine. You got bulging marathon muscles. I'm sure your penis is as big as that javelin you used to throw.

HAIKUMOM: Censored.

CHUTES&LADDERS: But none of those things come close to the size of your ego. If you can put that aside, you may, *may* stand a chance. Otherwise, you're fucked, my friend.

HAIKUMOM: Message purged.

ORANGUTAN: OH MY GOD, WE'RE DYING HERE, DO WE HAVE TO BE SO POLITE ABOUT IT?

HAIKUMOM: Censored.

ORANGUTAN: Oh my G-zero-D. Democracy or dictatorship?

CHUTES&LADDERS: Hey Fountainhead, why the silence?

(Fountainhead logs off.)

HAIKUMOM: Nice work, guys. Congratulations.

CHUTES&LADDERS: You don't suppose he's . . . crawling on the carpet looking for one last rock??

ORANGUTAN: Lordy lord lord, I'm about to go over his house and start looking for one myself!

HAIKUMOM: That's why you're in Japan, little monkey. For now, I'm closing this thread. Fountainhead, if you want to reopen it, email me directly.

Scene Five

A flower shop in Center City[3] *Philadelphia. Yaz looks over some brochures. Elliot enters, his limp looking worse.*

YAZ: I was starting to get worried. How you holding?

ELLIOT: Joe's Gym, perfect remedy.

YAZ: You went boxing? Really?

ELLIOT: I had to blow off steam. Women don't get it.

YAZ: Don't be a pig. You've had four leg surgeries, no more boxing.

ELLIOT: Did Odessa call?

YAZ: You know how she is. Shutting herself out from the world.

ELLIOT: We need help this week.

YAZ: And I got your back.

ELLIOT: I'm just saying, pick up the phone and ask, "Do you need anything, Elliot?"

YAZ: I did speak to your dad. Everyone's gathering at the house. People start arriving from PR[4] in a few hours. The next door neighbor brought over two trays of pigs feet.

ELLIOT: I just threw up in my mouth.

YAZ: Apparently a fight broke out over who gets your mom's pocketbooks.

ELLIOT: Those pleather things from the ten-dollar store?

YAZ: Thank you, it's not like she had Gucci purses!

ELLIOT: People just need to manufacture drama.

YAZ: He said they were tearing through Ginny's closets like it was a shopping spree. "I want this necklace!" "I want the photo album!" "Yo, those chancletas[5] are mine!" I'm like, damn, let the woman be buried first.

ELLIOT: Yo, let's spend the day here.

YAZ (*Handing him some papers*): Brochures. I was being indecisive so the florist went to work on a wedding bouquet. I ruled out seven, you make the final call. Celebration of Life, Blooming Garden, Eternity Wreath.

ELLIOT: All of those have carnations. I don't want a carnation within a block of the church.

YAZ: You told me to eliminate seven. I eliminated seven. Close your eyes and point.

ELLIOT: Am I a particularly demanding person?

YAZ: Yes. What's so wrong with a carnation?

ELLIOT: You know what a carnation says to the world? That they were out of roses at the 7-Eleven. It should look something like Mom's garden.

YAZ (*In agreement*): Graveside Remembrances? That looks something like it . . . I'm renominating Graveside Remembrances. Putting it back on the table.

3. Downtown district, the city's business and transportation hub.

4. Puerto Rico (acronym).

5. Sandals or flip-flops (Spanish slang).

ELLIOT: You couldn't find anything tropical? Yaz, you could find a needle in a damn haystack and you couldn't find a bird of paradise or something?

YAZ: He just shoved some brochures in my hand.

ELLIOT *(Stares her down)*: You have an awful poker face.

YAZ: Now, look here.

ELLIOT: You did find something.

YAZ: No. Not exactly.

ELLIOT: How much does it cost? Yaz, this is my mom we're talking about.

YAZ: Five hundred more. Just for the casket piece.

ELLIOT: You can't lie for shit, you never could.

YAZ: Orchid Paradise.

(Yaz hands him another brochure. They look at it together.)

ELLIOT: Aw damn. Damn. That looks like her garden.

YAZ: Spitting image.

ELLIOT *(Pointing)*: I think she grew those.

YAZ: Right next to the tomatoes.

ELLIOT: But hers were yellow. Fuck.

YAZ: It's very odd to order flowers when someone dies. Because the flowers are just gonna die, too. "Would you like some death with your death?"

ELLIOT *(A confession)*: I didn't water them.

YAZ *(Getting it)*: What, are you supposed to be a gardener all of a sudden?

ELLIOT: It doesn't rain for a month and do I grab the hose and water Mom's garden one time?

YAZ: You were feeding her. Giving her meds. Bathing her. I could've come over and watered a leaf. A single petal.

ELLIOT: The last four days, she'd wake me up in the middle of the night. "Did you water the flowers?" "Yeah, Mom, just like you told me to yesterday." "Carry me out back, I want to see." "Mom, you're too heavy, I can't carry you down those steps one more time today."

YAZ: Little white lies.

ELLIOT: Can you do the sermon?

YAZ: This is becoming a second career.

ELLIOT: Because you're the only one who doesn't cry.

YAZ: Unlike Julia.

ELLIOT *(Imitating)*: "¡Ay dios mio![6] ¡Ay! ¡Ay!"

YAZ: I hate public speaking.

ELLIOT: You're a teacher.

YAZ: It's different when it's ideas. Talking about ideas isn't saying something, it's making syllables with your mouth.

ELLIOT: You love ideas. All you ever wanted to do was have ideas.

YAZ: It was an elaborate bait and switch. The ideas don't fill the void, they just help you articulate it.

ELLIOT: You've spoken at city hall. On the radio.

YAZ: You're the face of Main Line Chevrolet. *(Pause)* Can I do it in English?

ELLIOT: You could do it in Russian for all I care. I'll just be in the front row acting like my cheek is itchy so no one sees me crying.

6. Oh Lord or Oh my God (Spanish).

YAZ: The elders want a good Spanish sermon.
ELLIOT: Mami Ginny was it. You're the elder now.
YAZ: I'm twenty-nine.
ELLIOT: But you don't look a day over fifty.
YAZ: You gotta do me a favor in return. I know this is your tragedy but . . . Call William. Ask him not to come to the funeral.
ELLIOT: Oh shit.
YAZ: He saw the obit in the *Daily News.*
ELLIOT: They were close. Mami Ginny loved that blond hair. She was the madrina[7] of your wedding.
YAZ: William relinquished mourning privileges. You fall out of love with me, you lose certain rights. He calls talking about, "I want the condo." Fuck that. Fuck that. Coming from you it won't seem bitter. Wants the fucking condo all for hisself. That I decorated, that I painted. "Oh, and where's the funeral, by the way?" You know, he's been to four funerals in the Ortiz clan and I could feel it, there was a part of him, under it all, that was disgusted. The open casket. The prayers.
ELLIOT: It is disgusting.
YAZ: Sitting in the pew knowing what freaks we are.
ELLIOT: He's good people.
YAZ: I was probably at his side doing the same thing, thinking I'm removed, that I'm somehow different.
ELLIOT: Hey, hey, done.
YAZ: One more condition. I go to Puerto Rico with you. We scatter her ashes together.
ELLIOT: Mami Ginny couldn't be buried in Philly. She had to have her ashes thrown at a waterfall in El Yunque,[8] just to be the most Puerto Rican motherfucker around.
YAZ: I saw your Colgate ad.
ELLIOT: Dang, cousin Yaz watches Spanish TV?
YAZ: Shut up.
ELLIOT: I walked into the casting office, flashed my pearly whites, showed them my military ID and I charmed them.
YAZ: Do it.
ELLIOT: Give me a dollar.
YAZ: For that big cheeseburger smile?

(She gives him a dollar.)

ELLIOT *(Smiling)*: "Sonrisa,[9] baby!"

(Yaz cracks up laughing, which devolves into tears.)

How we gonna pay for Orchid Paradise?
YAZ: They should have a frequent-flower card. They punch a hole. Buy nine funeral bouquets, get the tenth free. We'd be living in a house full of lilies.

7. Matron of honor (Spanish).
8. Tropical rain forest in Puerto Rico, part of the U.S. National Forest System.
9. Smile (Spanish).

Look at that guy. Arranging his daisies like little treasures. What do you think it's like to be him? To be normal?

ELLIOT: Normal? A hundred bucks says that dude has a closet full of animal porno at home.

YAZ: I bet in his family, funerals are rare occasions. I bet he's never seen a cousin get arrested. Let alone one under the age of eighteen. I bet he never saw his eight-year-old cousin sipping rum through a twisty straw or . . . I just remembered this time cousin Maria was babysitting me . . .

ELLIOT: Fat Maria or Buck Tooth Maria?

YAZ: Pig.

ELLIOT: Ah, Fat Maria.

YAZ: I was dyeing her hair. I had never dyed hair before so I asked her to read me the next step and she handed me the box and said, "You read it." And I said, "My rubber gloves are covered in toxic goop, I can't really hold that right now." And so she held it in front of my eyes and said, "You gonna have to read it because I sure as hell can't."

ELLIOT: I been knowed that.

YAZ: I said, "But you graduated from high school." She said, "They just pass you, I just stood in the back." I was in fourth grade. *I* could read! *(Pause)* I have a degree written in Latin that I don't even understand. I paid seventeen thousand dollars for my piano.

ELLIOT: Oh shit.

YAZ: I have a mortgage on my piano. Drive two miles north? William told me every time I went to North Philly, I'd come back different. His family has Quaker Oats for DNA. They play Pictionary on New Year's. I'd sit there wishing I could scoop the blood out my veins like you scoop the seeds out a pumpkin and he'd be like, "Whatchu thinking about, honey?" And I'd be like, "Nothing. Let's play some Pictionary."

ELLIOT: Yo, being the scholarship case at an all-white prep school really fucked with your head, didn't it?

YAZ: I should've gone to Edison.

ELLIOT: Public school in el barrio.[1] You wouldn't have survived there for a day.

YAZ: Half our cousins didn't survive there.

ELLIOT: True. But you would've pissed your pants. At least their pants was dry when they went down.

YAZ: You're sick.

ELLIOT: And the ladies love me.

YAZ: I thought abuela[2] dying, that would be the end of us. But Ginny grabbed the torch. Christmas, Easter. Now what? Our family may be fucked-up but we had somewhere to go. A kitchen that connected us. Plastic-covered sofas where we could park our communal asses.

ELLIOT: Pop's selling the house. And the plastic-covered sofas. He's moving back to the Bronx, be with his sisters.

YAZ: You going with him? *(Elliot shrugs)* Wow. I mean, once that living room is gone, I may never step foot in North Philly again.

1. Spanish-speaking district or neighborhood.

2. Grandmother (Spanish).

ELLIOT: Washed up at age twenty-four. Disabled vet. Motherless chil'. Working at Subway. Soon-to-be homeless.
YAZ: My couch is your couch.
ELLIOT: Until William takes your couch.
YAZ: My cardboard box is your cardboard box.
ELLIOT: I could go out to L.A. and be a movie star.
YAZ: You need a manager? Shoot I'm coming witchu. Forget Philly.
ELLIOT: Change of scene, baby. Dream team.
YAZ: Probably we should order some flowers first, though. Don'tcha think? *(Elliot nods. To the florist)* Sir?

Scene Six

The chat room. Orangutan is online, seems upset.

ORANGUTAN: 2:38 A.M. Tuesday. The witching hour.

(Chutes&Ladders logs on.)

CHUTES&LADDERS: 1:38 P.M. Monday. The lunch hour.
ORANGUTAN: I'm in a gay bar slash internet café in the city of Sapporo. Deafening dance music.
CHUTES&LADDERS: Sure you should be in a bar, little monkey?
ORANGUTAN *(Disappointed)*: I flew halfway around the world and guess what? It was still me who got off the plane. *(Taking comfort)* Sapporo is always open. The world turns upside down at night.
CHUTES&LADDERS: You're in a city named after a beer sitting in a bar. Go home.
ORANGUTAN: Everything in this country makes sense but me. The noodles in soup make sense. The woodpecker outside my window every evening? Completely logical. The girls getting out of school in their miniskirts and shy smiles? Perfectly natural. I'm floating. I'm a cloud. My existence is one sustained out-of-body experience. It doesn't matter if I change my shoes, there's not a pair I've ever been able to fill. I'm a baby in a basket on an endless river. Wherever I go I don't make sense there.
CHUTES&LADDERS: Hey, little monkey. How many days you got?
ORANGUTAN: I think day ninety-six is when the demons really come out to play.
CHUTES&LADDERS: Ninety-six? Girl, hang your hat on that.
ORANGUTAN: I really really really want to smoke crack.
CHUTES&LADDERS: Yeah, well *don't.*
ORANGUTAN: Distract me from myself. What do you really really really want, Chutes&Ladders?
CHUTES&LADDERS: I wouldn't say no to a new car—my Tercel is one sorry sight.
ORANGUTAN: What else?
CHUTES&LADDERS: Tuesday's crossword. On Monday I'm done by the time I sit at my desk. I wish every day could be a Tuesday.
ORANGUTAN: What about your son? Don't you really really really want to call him?
CHUTES&LADDERS: By all accounts, having me be a stranger these ten years has given him the best decade of his life.

ORANGUTAN: I've known you for how long?

CHUTES&LADDERS: Three Christmas Eves. When you logged on you were a stone-cold user. We sang Christmas carols online all night. Now you've got ninety days.

ORANGUTAN: Can I ask you a personal question? What's your day job?

CHUTES&LADDERS: IRS. GS4 paper pusher.

ORANGUTAN: Got any vacation days?

CHUTES&LADDERS: A solid collection. I haven't taken a vacation in ten years.

ORANGUTAN: Do you have money?

CHUTES&LADDERS: Enough to eat steak on Friday nights. Enough to buy pay-per-view boxing.

ORANGUTAN: Yeah, I bet that's all the pay-per-view you buy. *(Pause)* Enough money to fly to Japan?

(Pause.)

CHUTES&LADDERS: You should know I'm fifty years old on a good day. I eat three and a half doughnuts for breakfast and save the remaining half for brunch. I have small hands, six toes on my left foot. And my face resembles a corgi.

ORANGUTAN: If I was looking for a hot screw I wouldn't be logging on to this site.

CHUTES&LADDERS: Damn, was it something I said?

ORANGUTAN *(With honest admiration)*: I've been on this planet for thirty-one years and you're the only person I've ever met who's more sarcastic than I am yet still believes in God.

CHUTES&LADDERS *(Taking the compliment)*: Says the agnostic.

ORANGUTAN: The atheist. Who is very envious of believers. My brain is my biggest enemy—always arguing my soul into a corner. *(Pause)* I like you. Come to Japan. We can go get an ice cream. I can show you the countryside.

CHUTES&LADDERS: I don't have a passport. If my Tercel can't drive there, I generally don't go.

ORANGUTAN: Come save me in Japan. Be my knight in shining armor.

CHUTES&LADDERS: I'll admit, I'm a dashing concept. If you saw my flesh and blood, you'd be disappointed.

ORANGUTAN: I see my flesh and blood every day and I've learned to live with the disappointment.

CHUTES&LADDERS: I'm the squarest of the square. I live in a square house on a square block watching a square box eating square-cut fries.

ORANGUTAN: I get it. You were the kid who colored inside the lines.

CHUTES&LADDERS: No, I was the kid who ate the crayons. *Was.* I went clean and all personality left my life. Flew right out the window. I had to take life on life's terms. Messy, disappointing, bad shit happens to good people, coffee stains on my necktie, boring life.

ORANGUTAN: Maybe we could hang out and have a relationship that has very little to do with crack or addiction or history. We could watch DVDs and microwave popcorn and take walks on the waterfront while we gossip about celebrities. It could be the land of the living.

CHUTES&LADDERS: Stay in the box. Keep things in their place. It's a simple, effective recipe for ten clean years.

ORANGUTAN: Forget simple. I want a goddamn challenge.

CHUTES&LADDERS: You're in recovery and work in a foreign country. That's a challenge.

ORANGUTAN: No. No it's fucking not. Not if I just stay anonymous and alone. Like every day of my shit life so far. A friend, the kind that is nice to you and you are nice to in return. *That* would push the comfort zone. The invitation is open. Come tear my shyness open.

CHUTES&LADDERS: All right, now you're being weird. Can we change the subject?

(Haikumom appears. She's reading the newspaper.)

HAIKUMOM: Orangutan, cover your ears.

ORANGUTAN: Big Brother, always watching.

HAIKUMOM: Cover your ears, kiddo.

ORANGUTAN: That doesn't really work online.

HAIKUMOM: Okay, Chutes and Ladders, can we g-chat? One on one?

ORANGUTAN: Come on! No talking behind backs.

HAIKUMOM: Fine. Chutes&Ladders, you listening?

CHUTES&LADDERS: Lord have mercy spit it out.

HAIKUMOM: Orangutan may be immature . . .

ORANGUTAN: Hey.

HAIKUMOM: She may be annoying at times . . .

ORANGUTAN: What the f?

HAIKUMOM: She may be overbearing and self-obsessed and a little bit of a concern troll and she can type faster than she can think which often leads to diarrhea of the keyboard—

CHUTES&LADDERS: Your point?

HAIKUMOM: But she's telling you, "Be my friend." When's the last time someone opened your closet door, saw all them skeletons, and said, "Wassup?! Can I join the party?"

CHUTES&LADDERS: All right, my wrist is officially slapped. Thank you, oh nagging wives.

HAIKUMOM: Internal Revenue Service, 300 North Los Angeles Street 90012? Is that you?

CHUTES&LADDERS: Need my name, too? It's Wilkie. I'll leave it at that.

HAIKUMOM: I'm sending you a care package. Orangutan, you can uncover your ears now. I love you.

ORANGUTAN: Middle finger.

(Fountainhead's log-on appears.)

FOUNTAINHEAD: Hey all, thanks for the warm two-by-four to my head.

HAIKUMOM: All right, look who's back.

FOUNTAINHEAD: Knives sharpened? Last night we ran out of butter while my wife was cooking and she sent me to the store and it took every bit of strength I could summon not to make a "wrong turn" to that parking lot I know so well. I got the butter and on the car ride home, I couldn't help it, I drove by the lot, and there was my dealer in the shadows. My brain went on attack. "Use one more time just to prove you won't need another hit tomorrow." I managed to keep on driving and bring the butter home. Major victory. And my wife pulls it out of the plastic bag and says, "This is unsalted. I said salted." Then she feels guilty so she says never mind, never mind, she'll just add a little extra salt to the pie crust but I insist. "No, no, no, my wife deserves the right kind of butter and she's gonna get it!" I mean, I bark it, I'm already halfway out the door, my heart was racing all the way to the parking lot and raced even harder when I sat in the car and smoked. So, Michael Jordan[3] is benched with a broken foot. But he'll come back in the finals.

HAIKUMOM: Thanks for the update, Fountainhead. You may not believe this, but we were missing you and worried about you. Don't beat yourself up about the slip. You had three days clean. This time you'll make it to day four.

FOUNTAINHEAD: Be ambitious. Why not reach for a whopping five?

ORANGUTAN: Maybe you'll make it to day thirty if you tell your wife.

FOUNTAINHEAD: I told you, I have my reasons, I cannot do that. My wife has some emotional issues.

ORANGUTAN *(Sarcastic)*: No!

FOUNTAINHEAD: Listen? Please? Are you capable of that? She's in therapy twice a week. Depression, manic. I don't want to be the reason she goes down a tailspin. I actually have her best interest in mind.

CHUTES&LADDERS: Yawn.

FOUNTAINHEAD: Ah, Chutes&Ladders. I could feel you circling like a vulture. Weigh in, by all means.

CHUTES&LADDERS: And I repeat. Yawn.

FOUNTAINHEAD: Chutes&Ladders, why do I get the feeling you'd be the first in line for tickets to watch me smoke again? That you'd be in the bleachers cheering if I relapse?

CHUTES&LADDERS: How can you relapse when you don't even think you're addicted?

FOUNTAINHEAD: If you read my original post clearly, I wrote that it's a psychological addiction, not like heroin.

CHUTES&LADDERS: Well see then, you're not a junkie after all.

FOUNTAINHEAD: What is this, first-grade recess?

CHUTES&LADDERS: No, this is a site for crackheads trying not to be crackheads anymore. If you're not a crackhead, leave, we don't want you, you are irrelevant, get off my lawn, go.

HAIKUMOM: Chutes&Ladders, please.

CHUTES&LADDERS: I got this.

ORANGUTAN: He's still logged on.

CHUTES&LADDERS: Hey Fountainhead, why did you come to this website?

FOUNTAINHEAD: Because I thoroughly enjoy getting shit on.

HAIKUMOM: Censored.

CHUTES&LADDERS: Why do you want to be here?

FOUNTAINHEAD: Want? The two times I've logged on here I've *wanted* to vomit.

CHUTES&LADDERS: Well? Did you receive some sort of invitation? Did one of us ask you here?

3. American basketball player (b. 1963) named in 1996 one of the fifty greatest players in National Basketball Association history.

FOUNTAINHEAD: Look, I'm the first to say it. I have a problem.
CHUTES&LADDERS: Adam had problems. Eve had problems. Why are *you here?*
FOUNTAINHEAD: To get information.
CHUTES&LADDERS: Go to Wikipedia. Why are you *here?*
FOUNTAINHEAD: Because I smoke crack.
CHUTES&LADDERS: Go to a dealer. Why are you here?
FOUNTAINHEAD: Because I plan to stop smoking crack.
CHUTES&LADDERS: Fine, when your son has a tummy-ache in the middle of the night and walks in on you tweaking and geeking just tell him, "Don't worry, Junior, Daddy's sucking on a glass dick—"
HAIKUMOM *(Overlaps)*: Hey!
CHUTES&LADDERS: "—but Daddy makes 300K and this is all a part of Daddy's Plan!"
FOUNTAINHEAD: I'M A FUCKING CRACKHEAD.
HAIKUMOM *(Apologetic)*: Censored.
FOUNTAINHEAD: Fuck you, Chutes&Ladders.
HAIKUMOM: Bleep.
FOUNTAINHEAD: Fuck you . . . Don't talk about my sons. Don't fucking talk about my boys.
HAIKUMOM: Bleep again.
FOUNTAINHEAD: Are you happy, Chutes&Ladders?
CHUTES&LADDERS: Absolutely not, my friend. I'm a crackhead, too, and I wouldn't wish it on my worst enemy.
FOUNTAINHEAD: And I *made* 300K, I'm currently unemployed. An unemployed crackhead. At least I still have all my teeth. *(They laugh)* Better than I can say for my dealer.
CHUTES&LADDERS *(Being a friend)*: Ex-dealer, man.
FOUNTAINHEAD: Ex-dealer. Thank you.
HAIKUMOM: Fountainhead, welcome to the dinner party. Granted, it's a party we never wanted to be invited to, but pull up a chair and pass the salt. Some people here may pour it in your wounds. Just like you, we've all crawled on the floor with a flashlight. We've thrown out the brillo and bought some more. But guess what? You had three days. For three days straight, you didn't try to kill yourself on an hourly basis. Please. Talk to your wife about your addiction. You need every supporting resource. You are in for the fight of your life. You mentioned Wharton. I live in Philly. If you're still in the area and you have an emergency or even a craving, email me directly. Any time of night. Don't take it lightly when I say a sober day for you is a sober day for me. I know you can do this but I know you can't do it alone. So stop being a highly functioning isolator and start being a highly dysfunctional *person.* The only way out it is through it.
ORANGUTAN *(Nostalgic)*: Slogans . . .
HAIKUMOM: Ya'll know I know 'em all.
CHUTES&LADDERS: They saved my life.
ORANGUTAN: Your personal favorite. Go.
HAIKUMOM: "Nothing changes if nothing changes."

(Elliot appears at the boxing gym, punching a bag. The Ghost watches him.)

GHOST: Momken men-fadluck ted-dini gawaz saffari?
ORANGUTAN: "It came to pass, it didn't come to stay."
FOUNTAINHEAD: "I obsessively pursue feeling good, no matter how bad it makes me feel."
CHUTES&LADDERS: Okay, now!
ORANGUTAN: Nice!
HAIKUMOM: Rookie don't play!
GHOST: Momken men-fadluck ted-dini gawaz saffari?
ORANGUTAN: "One hit is too many, one thousand never enough."
HAIKUMOM: "Have an at-ti-tude of gra-ti-tude."
CHUTES&LADDERS: "If you are eating a shit sandwich, chances are you ordered it."
ORANGUTAN: Ding ding ding. We have a winner!
HAIKUMOM: Censored. But good one.
GHOST: Momken men-fadluck ted-dini gawaz saffari?
HAIKUMOM *(Turning a page in the paper)*: Oh shit!
ORANGUTAN: CENSORED!!!!!! YES!!!!!! Whoooooo!
HAIKUMOM: You got me.
ORANGUTAN *(Victorious)*: You know how long I've been waiting to do that?!
HAIKUMOM: My sister Ginny's in the *Daily News*! A nice big picture!
GHOST: Momken men-fadluck ted-dini gawaz saffari?
HAIKUMOM: "Eugenia P. Ortiz, A Force For Good In Philadelphia!" Okay, now!

(Elliot punches harder. His leg is starting to bother him.)

ELLIOT: Your leg feels great. Your leg feels like a million bucks. No pain. No pain.
HAIKUMOM: "In lieu of flowers contributions may be made to . . ."

(Haikumom drops the newspaper.
The Ghost blows on Elliot, knocking him to the floor.)

GHOST: Momken men-fadluck ted-dini gawaz saffari?

(Intermission.)

Scene Seven

A diner. Odessa and John, aka Fountainhead, sit in a booth.

ODESSA: To lapsed Catholics. *(They clink coffee mugs)* And you thought we had nothing in common.
JOHN: When did you become interested in Buddhism?
ODESSA: My older brother used to terrorize me during mass. He would point to a statue, tell me about the evil spirit hiding behind it. Fangs, claws. I thought Saint Lazarus[4] was gonna come to life and suck my eyes out. Buddhism? Not scary. If there's spirits, they're hiding inside you.
JOHN: Aren't those the scariest kind?
ODESSA: So, how many days do you have? It should be two now.
JOHN: I put my sons' picture on my cell phone so if I get the urge, I can just look at them instead.

4. In the Gospel of John, Jesus restores Lazarus to life four days after his death.

ODESSA: How many days?

JOHN (*Small talk*): I love Puerto Rico. On my honeymoon we stayed at that hotel in Old San Juan, the old convent. (*Odessa shrugs*) And that Spanish fort at the top of the city? El Morro?

ODESSA: I've always been meaning to make it there.

JOHN: There are these keyholes where the canons used to fit, and the view of the waves through them, you can practically see the Spanish armada approaching.

ODESSA: I mean, one of these days I've gotta make it to PR.

JOHN: Oh. I just figured . . .

ODESSA: The Jersey Shore. Atlantic City. The Philadelphia airport. Oh, I've been places.

JOHN: On an actual plane?

ODESSA: I only fly first-class, and I'm still saving for that ticket.

(*Odessa's cell phone rings.*)

JOHN: You're a popular lady.

ODESSA (*Into her phone, her demeanor completely changing*): What? I told you, the diner on Spring Garden and Third. I'm busy, come in an hour. One hour. Now stop calling me and asking fucking directions. (*She hangs up*)

JOHN: Says the one who censors.

ODESSA: My sister died.

JOHN: Right. You sure you're okay?

ODESSA: She's dead, ain't nothing left to do. People act like the world is going to fall apart.

JOHN: You write very Zen[5] messages. And yet.

ODESSA: My family knows every button to push.

JOHN: My condolences. (*Pause*) You don't strike me as a computer nerd. I used to employ an entire floor of them.

ODESSA: You should've seen me at first, pecking with two fingers. Now I'm like an octopus with ten little tentacles. In my neck of the woods staying clean is like trying to tap-dance on a minefield. The website fills the hours. So how are we gonna fill yours, huh? When was the last time you picked up a javelin?

JOHN: Senior year of high school.

ODESSA (*Hands him a sheet of paper*): There's a sober softball league. Fairmount Park, games on Sundays. Sober bowling on Thursdays.

JOHN: I lied in my first post. I've been smoking crack for two years. I've tried quitting hundreds of times. Day two? Please, I'm in the seven-hundredth day of hell.

ODESSA: You got it out of your system. Most people lie at one time or another on the site. The good news is, two years in, there's still time. (*Hands him another sheet of paper*) Talbott Recovery Center in Atlanta. It's designed for professionals with addictions. Paradise Recovery in Hawaii. They actually check your income before admitting you. Just for the wealthy. This place in Jersey, it's right over the bridge, they have an outpatient program for professionals like you.

JOHN: I'm tenacious. I'm driven. I love my parents.

5. Japanese school of Buddhism stressing the achievement of enlightenment through meditation, often using brief, enigmatic, often paradoxical statements (koans) to transcend rational thought.

ODESSA: Pitchforks against tanks.
JOHN: I relish in paying my taxes.
ODESSA: And you could be dead tomorrow. *(Pause)* Is your dealer male or female?
JOHN: I had a few. Flushed their numbers down the toilet like you suggested.
ODESSA: Your original connection. The one who got you hooked.
JOHN: Female.
ODESSA: Did you have sex with her?
JOHN: You don't beat around the bush do you?
ODESSA: I'll take that as a yes. *(No answer)* Do you prefer sex when you're high to sex when you're sober?
JOHN: I've never really analyzed it.
ODESSA: It can be a dangerous cocktail. Some men get off on smoking and fucking.
JOHN: All men get off on fucking.
ODESSA: Are you scared your wife will find out you're addicted to crack? Or are you scared she'll find out what came of your wedding vows?
JOHN: I should go.
ODESSA: We just ordered.
JOHN: I promised my son. There's a science fair tomorrow. Something about dioramas and crazy glue.
ODESSA: Don't talk about them. Get sober for them.
JOHN: Fuck you.
ODESSA: Leave me three bucks for your coffee cuz I ain't got it.

(He stands, pulls out three dollars. She throws the money back at him.)

You picked up the phone and called me.
JOHN *(He sits down again)*: I don't know how to do this. I've never done this before.
ODESSA: I have and it usually doesn't end up so good. One in twenty, maybe, hang around. Most people just don't write one day and then thirty days and then you're wondering . . . And sometimes you get the answer. Cuz their wife looks on their computer and sees the website and logs on and writes, "I found him face down in the snow."
JOHN: How many day ones did you have?
ODESSA: Seven years' worth.
JOHN: Do you still crave?
ODESSA: On the good days, only every hour. Would you rather be honest with your wife, or would you rather end up like me? *(Pause)* That wasn't rhetorical.
JOHN: You're not exactly what I wanted to be when I grew up.
ODESSA: Truth. Now we're talking.

(Elliot and Yaz enter.)

YAZ: There she is.

(Elliot and Yaz sit down in the booth.)

ELLIOT: You were supposed to meet us at the flower place.
YAZ: The deposit was due at nine.
ODESSA: My alarm clock didn't go off.

ELLIOT: Were you up on that chat room all night?
ODESSA *(Ignoring him, to a waiter, off)*: Can I get a refill, please?
ELLIOT: Where's the money?
ODESSA: I told you I don't have any money.
ELLIOT: And you think I do? I been paying for Mami Ginny's meds for six months straight—
ODESSA: Well get it from Yaz's mom.
YAZ: My mom put in for the headstone. She got an expensive one.
ODESSA: Headstone? She's getting cremated.
YAZ: She still needs a proper Catholic piece of granite. Right beside abuela, right beside your dad and sister and brother.
ELLIOT: And daughter.
YAZ: Everyone agreed.
ODESSA: No one asked my opinion.
ELLIOT: Everyone who showed up to the family meeting.
ODESSA: I wasn't invited.
YAZ: I texted you twice.
ODESSA: I was out of minutes.
ELLIOT: We just spoke on the phone.
ODESSA: Whatchu want me to do, Elliot, if I say I ain't got no fucking money, I ain't got no money.
JOHN: Hi, I'm John, nice to meet you.
YAZ: Yazmin.
ELLIOT: You one of Mom's rehab buddies?
JOHN: We know each other from work.
ELLIOT: You scrub toilets?
ODESSA *(To John)*: I'm a practitioner of the custodial arts.
ELLIOT: Is she your sponsor?
JOHN *(To Odessa)*: I thought this was going to be a private meeting.
ELLIOT: I'm her son.
JOHN *(To Odessa)*: You must have been young.
ELLIOT: But I was raised by my Aunt Ginny and that particular aunt just died. *(To Odessa)* So now, you got three hours to find some money to pay for one basket of flowers in the funeral of the woman who changed my pampers.
YAZ: We're all supposed to be helping out.
ODESSA: You both know I run out of minutes all the time. No one could be bothered to drive by and tell me face to face?
ELLIOT: Because you always bothered to drive by and say hello to Mami Ginny when you knew she was sick? Because you bothered to hit me up one time this week and say, "Elliot, I'm sorry your mom died."
ODESSA: You still got one mom alive.
ELLIOT: Really? You want to go there?
YAZ: The flower place needs the money today.
ODESSA: She was my sister and you are my son, too.
YAZ: Guys. Two hundred dollars by end of business day.
ODESSA: That's my rent.
ELLIOT: Then fifty.
ODESSA: I just spent fifty getting my phone back on.

ELLIOT: Ten dollars. For the woman who raised your son! Do we hear ten dollars? Going once!
ODESSA: I spent my last ten at the post office.
ELLIOT: Going twice!

(John goes into his wallet.)

JOHN: Here's fifty.

(They all look at him like he's crazy. He pulls out some more money.)

Two hundred?

(Elliot pushes the money back to John with one pointer finger, as if the bills might be contaminated.)

ELLIOT: No offense, I don't take money from users.
JOHN: I'm not . . . I think that was my cue.
ODESSA: Sit down. My son was just going.
ELLIOT: Did World's Best Mom here tell you about her daughter?
ODESSA: I'm about to throw this coffee in your fucking face.
YAZ: Come on, Elliot, I'll pay for the flowers.

(Elliot doesn't get up.)

ELLIOT: I looked at that chat room once. The woman I saw there? She's literally not the same person I know. *(To John)* Did she tell you how she became such a saint?
JOHN: We all have skeletons.
ELLIOT: Yeah well she's an archaeological dig. Did she tell you about her daughter?
ODESSA *(Suddenly resigned)*: Go ahead, I ain't got no secrets.
YAZ *(Getting up)*: Excuse me.
ELLIOT: Sit here and listen, Yaz. You were born with a silver spoon and you need to know how it was for me.
YAZ: I said I'd pay for the goddamn flowers so LET'S GO. NOW!
ELLIOT: My sister and I had the stomach flu, right? For a whole day we couldn't keep nothing down.
ODESSA: Three days . . . You were vomiting three days straight.
ELLIOT: Medicine, juice, anything we ate, it would come right back up. *(To John)* Your co-worker here took us to Children's Hospital.
ODESSA: Jefferson.
ELLIOT: It was wall-to-wall packed. Every kid in Philly had this bug. ERs were turning kids away. They gave us a flier about stomach flu and sent us home. Bright blue paper. Little cartoon diagrams. It said give your kids a spoonful of water every five minutes.
ODESSA: A teaspoon.
ELLIOT: A small enough amount that they can keep it down. Five minutes. Spoon. Five minutes. Spoon. I remember thinking, Wow, this is it. Family time. Quality time. Just the three of us. Because it was gentle, the way you said, "Open up." I opened my mouth, you put that little spoon of water into my mouth. That little bit of relief. And then I watched you do the same thing with my

little sister. And I remember being like, "Wow, I love you, Mom. My moms is all right." Five minutes. Spoon. Five minutes. Spoon. But you couldn't stick to something simple like that. You couldn't sit still like that. You had to have your thing. That's where I stop remembering.

ODESSA: I left.

ELLIOT: A Department of Human Services report. That's my memory. Six hours later a neighbor kicks in the door. Me and my sister are lying in a pile of laundry. My shorts was all messed up. And what I really don't remember is my sister. Quote: "Female infant, approximately two years, pamper and tear ducts dry, likely cause of death, dehydration." Cuz when you dehydrate you can't form a single tear.

JOHN *(To Elliot)*: I'm very sorry . . . *(He puts some money on the table)* For the coffee. *(Exits)*

ELLIOT: That's some friend you got there.

(Pause.)

YAZ: Mary Lou. We can at least say her name out loud. Mary Lou. Mary Lou. *(To Odessa)* One time you came to babysit me, you brought Elliot and Mary Lou—she was still in pampers—and Mary Lou had this soda from 7-Eleven. She didn't want to give me a sip. You yelled at her so bad, you totally cursed her out and I said, "You're not supposed to yell at people like that!" And you said, "No, Yaz, let her cry. She's gotta learn that ya'll are cousins, ya'll are flesh and blood, and we share everything. You hear me, Yaz? In this family we share *everything*." You walked out of the room, came back from the kitchen with four straws in your hand, sat us down on the floor in a circle, pointed to me and said, "You first." I sipped. "Elliot's turn." He sipped. "Mary Lou's turn." She sipped. Then you sipped. You made us do like that, taking turns, going around the circle, till the cup was empty.

(Odessa hands Elliot a key.)

ODESSA: The pawn shop closes at five. Go into my house. Take my computer. Pawn it. However much you get, put towards a few flowers, okay?

(Odessa exits.)

Scene Eight

Split scene: Odessa's living room and the chat room.
Chutes&Ladders holds a phone.

ORANGUTAN: Did you hit the call button yet?

CHUTES&LADDERS: I'm working on it.

ORANGUTAN: Where are you? Are you at home?

CHUTES&LADDERS: *Jeopardy!*'s on mute.

ORANGUTAN: Dude, turn off the tube. This is serious. Did you even dial?

CHUTES&LADDERS: Yeah, yeah. *(He does)* All right, it's ringing. What am I going to say?

ORANGUTAN: "Hi, Son, it's Dad."

CHUTES&LADDERS: Wendell. That's his name. *(Hangs up)* No answer.

ORANGUTAN: As in, you hung up?

CHUTES&LADDERS: Yes. I hung up.

ORANGUTAN: Dude, way too quick!

CHUTES&LADDERS: What do you have, a stopwatch? Do you know the average time before someone answers a telephone?

ORANGUTAN: 3.2 rings.

CHUTES&LADDERS: According to . . .

ORANGUTAN: I don't reveal my sources.

CHUTES&LADDERS: Look, my son's a grown man with a good life.

ORANGUTAN: Quit moping and dial Wendell's number.

CHUTES&LADDERS: This Japan thing is cramping my style. Different networks, different time zones. No concurrent *Jeopardy!* watching.

ORANGUTAN: Deflection: nostalgia.

CHUTES&LADDERS: Humor me.

ORANGUTAN *(Humoring him)*: How's my little Trebeky[6] doing?

CHUTES&LADDERS: He's had work done. Man looks younger than he did twenty years ago.

ORANGUTAN: Needle or knife?

CHUTES&LADDERS: Needle. His eyes are still in the right place.

ORANGUTAN: Well, it's working. Meow. Purrrrr. Any good categories?

CHUTES&LADDERS: Before and After.

ORANGUTAN: I love Before and After! But I'll go with . . . Quit Stalling for two hundred. *(She hums the* Jeopardy! *theme)*

CHUTES&LADDERS: It's ringing.

ORANGUTAN: My stopwatch is running.

CHUTES&LADDERS: Still ringing.

ORANGUTAN: You're going to be great.

CHUTES&LADDERS: It rang again.

ORANGUTAN: You're a brave soul.

(We hear a man's voice at the other end of the line say, "Hello?" Chutes&Ladders hangs up.)

CHUTES&LADDERS: He must not be around.

ORANGUTAN: Leave a voice mail.

CHUTES&LADDERS: Maybe next time.

(Chutes&Ladders logs off.)

ORANGUTAN: Hey! Don't log off, come on. Chutes&Ladders. Whatever happened to tough love? Log back on, we'll do a crossword. You can't fly before "Final Jeopardy!" Sigh. Anyone else online? Haikumom? I'm still waiting for that daily poem . . . Bueller? Bueller?

(In Odessa's living room, Elliot and Yaz enter.)

YAZ: Wow, look at that computer. Stone age.

ELLIOT: Fred Flinstone shit.

YAZ: Positively Dr. Who.[7]

6. Alex Trebek (b. 1940), host of the television game show *Jeopardy!* since 1984.

7. British science-fiction television program (1963–present), a cult classic known for its cheesy props and special effects.

ELLIOT: Dr. Who?

YAZ: That computer is actually worse than what they give the adjuncts[8] at Swarthmore.

ELLIOT: What does "adjunct" even mean?

YAZ: Exactly. It's the nicest thing she owns.

ELLIOT: Let's not act like this is some heroic sacrifice. Like this makes her the world's martyr.

YAZ: We're not going to get more than fifteen bucks for it.

ELLIOT: Symbols matter, Yaz. This isn't about the money. This is shaking hands. This is tipping your hat. This is holding the door open. This is the bare minimum, the least effort possible to earn the label "person." *(Looks at the screen)* What do you think her password is? *(Types)* "Odessa." Nope. "Odessaortiz." Nope.

YAZ: It's probably Elliot.

(He types. Haikumom's log-on appears.)

ELLIOT: The irony.

YAZ: I think legally that might be like breaking and entering.

ELLIOT *(Typing)*: Hello? Oh shit it posted.

ORANGUTAN: Haikumom! Hit me with those seventeen syllables, baby!

YAZ: Haikumom? What the hell is that?

ELLIOT: Her username. She has the whole world thinking she's some Chinese prophet.

YAZ: Haiku are Japanese.

ELLIOT: "Haiku are Japanese." *(Typing)* Hello, Orangutan. How are you?

ORANGUTAN *(Formal)*: I am fine. How are you?

ELLIOT *(Typing)*: So, I guess you like monkeys, huh?

ORANGUTAN: An orangutan is a primate.

YAZ: Elliot.

ELLIOT: Chill.

ORANGUTAN: And this primate has ninety-eight days. That deserves a poem, don't you think?

ELLIOT *(Typing)*: I don't have a poem, but I have a question. What does crack feel like?

ORANGUTAN: What?

YAZ: Elliot, cut it out.

ELLIOT *(Typing)*: Sometimes I'm amazed I don't know firsthand.

ORANGUTAN: Who is this?

ELLIOT *(Typing)*: How does it make your brain feel?

ORANGUTAN: Like it's flooded with dopamine.[9] Listen, cyber-stalker, if you came here for shits and giggles, we are a sadly unfunny bunch.

ELLIOT *(Typing)*: Are you just a smoker or do you inject it right into your eyeballs?

ORANGUTAN: Who the fuck is this?

ELLIOT *(Typing)*: Haikumom.

8. College instructors hired on a temporary and usually part-time basis as opposed to permanent, tenure-track faculty.

9. A primary neurotransmitter (a chemical used to send signals between nerve cells), affecting motor function, emotions, learning, and behavior, associated especially with pleasure.

ORANGUTAN: Bullshit, you didn't censor me. Quit screwing around, hacker, who are you?

YAZ: You think Ginny would want you acting this way?

ELLIOT: I think Mami Ginny would want Mami Odessa to pay for a single flower on her fucking casket.

YAZ *(Types)*: This is not Haikumom. It's her son.

ORANGUTAN: Well, if you're looking for the friends and family thread, you have to go to the home page and create a new log-on. This particular forum is for people actually in recovery. Wait, her son the actor? From the Crest ad?

ELLIOT *(Typing)*: Colgate.

ORANGUTAN: "Sonrisa baby!" I saw that on YouTube! Your teeth are insanely white. Ever worked in Hollywood?

ELLIOT *(Typing)*: Psh. I just had this guy begging me to do a feature film. Gritty, documentary-style, about Marines in Iraq. I just don't want to do anything cheesy.

ORANGUTAN: So you're the war hero . . .

ELLIOT *(Typing)*: Haikumom brags.

ORANGUTAN: How's your recovery going? *(No answer)* This is the crack forum, but there's a really good pain-meds forum on this site, too. Link here.

YAZ: What is she talking about?

ORANGUTAN: There's a few war vets on that forum, just like you. You'd be in good company.

YAZ: Pain meds? Elliot? *(He doesn't respond. Yaz types)* What are you talking about?

ORANGUTAN: Haikumom told us about your history.

YAZ *(Typing)*: What history?

ORANGUTAN: Sorry. Maybe she told us in confidence.

ELLIOT: Confidence? They call this shit "world wide" for a reason.

YAZ *(Typing)*: I can search all the threads right now.

ORANGUTAN: That you had a bunch of leg surgeries in Iraq. That if a soldier said they hurt, the docs practically threw pills at them. That you OD'd three times and were in the hospital for it. She was real messed up about it. I guess she had hoped the fruit would fall a little farther from the tree.

YAZ *(To Elliot)*: Is this true?

ELLIOT: I wasn't a soldier. I was a Marine. Soldiers is the army.

YAZ: Oh my god.

ELLIOT *(Takes the keyboard, types)*: What I am: sober. What I am not and never will be: a pathetic junkie like you.

(He unplugs the computer. He throws the keyboard on the ground. He starts unplugging cables violently.)

YAZ: Hold on. Just stop it, Elliot! Stop it!

ELLIOT: The one time I ever reached out to her for anything and she made me a story on a website.

YAZ: Why wouldn't you ask me for help? Why would you deal with that alone?

ELLIOT: The opposite of alone. I seen barracks that looked like dope houses. It was four months in my life, it's over. We've chopped up a lot of shit together, Yaz, but we ain't gonna chop this up. This shit stays in the vault. You got me?

YAZ: No!

ELLIOT: Yaz. *(He looks her straight in the eye)* Please. Please.
YAZ: I want to grab the sky and smash it into pieces. Are you clean?
ELLIOT: The only thing I got left from those days is the nightmares. That's when he came, and some days I swear he ain't never gonna leave.
YAZ: Who?

(Elliot tries to walk away from the conversation, but the Ghost is there, blocking his path.)

Who?!

ELLIOT *(Almost like a child)*: Please, Yaz. Please end this conversation. Don't make me beg, Yaz.
YAZ: The pawn shop closes in fifteen minutes. I'll get the monitor, you grab the computer.

Scene Nine

Chutes&Ladders is at work, on his desk phone. A bundled pile of mail is on his desk. He takes off the rubber band, browses. Junk, mostly.

CHUTES&LADDERS *(Into the work phone)*: That's right. Three Ws. Dot. Not the word, the punctuation mark. I-R-S. Not "F" like flamingo; "S" like Sam. Dot. Yup, another one. Gov. Grover orange victor.

(Orangutan appears, online.)

ORANGUTAN: I'm doing it. I'm almost there. *And* I can chat! Japan is so advanced. Internet cafes are like parking meters here.
CHUTES&LADDERS: Where are you and what are you doing?
ORANGUTAN: Sapporo train station. Just did some research. Get this: in the early eighties, they straightened all the rivers in Hokkaido.
CHUTES&LADDERS: Why?
ORANGUTAN: To create jobs the government straightened the rivers! Huge bodies of water, manual laborers, scientists, engineers, bulldozers, and the rivers became straight! How nuts is that?
CHUTES&LADDERS: People can't leave good enough alone. Why are humans so damn restless?
ORANGUTAN: It's not restlessness. It's ego. Massive, bizarre ego.
CHUTES&LADDERS: Can't let a river be a river. *(Into the phone)* The forms link is on the left.
ORANGUTAN: Now it's the aughts, people keep being born, jobs still need creating, but there's no curves left to straighten, so, drum roll, the government is beginning a new program to put all the original turns back in the rivers!
CHUTES&LADDERS: Well good luck to them, but no amount of engineering can put a wrinkle back in Nicole Kidman's[1] forehead.
ORANGUTAN: Ever heard of Kushiro?
CHUTES&LADDERS: Is that your new boyfriend's name?

1. Australian actress (b. 1967) whose adventures in plastic surgery have been the stuff of tabloid rumor since at least 2008.

ORANGUTAN: Ha. Ha ha ha. It's home of the hundred-mile-long Kushiro River, which is the pilot project, the first river they're trying to recurve.

CHUTES&LADDERS: Kushiro River. Got it. Burned in the brain. One day I'll win a Trivial Pursuit's[2] wedge with that. *(Into the phone)* You, too, ma'am. *(He hangs up)*

ORANGUTAN: My train to Kushiro leaves in twenty minutes. My heart is pounding.

CHUTES&LADDERS: I don't follow.

ORANGUTAN: Kushiro is the town where I was born. I'm going. I'm doing it.

CHUTES&LADDERS: Hold on, now you're throwing curveballs.

ORANGUTAN: In my hand is a sheet of paper. On the paper is the address of the house where my birth parents once lived. I'm going to knock on their door.

(Chutes&Ladder's desk phone rings.)

CHUTES&LADDERS *(Into the phone)*: Help desk, please hold. *(To Orangutan)* How long have you had that address for?

ORANGUTAN: It's been burning a hole in my pocket for two days. I hounded my mom before I left Maine. She finally wrote down the name of the adoption agency. The first clue, the first evidence of who I was I ever had. I made a vow to myself, if I could stay sober for three months, I would track my parents down. So a few days ago class ended early, I went to the agency, showed my passport, and thirty minutes later I had an address on a piece of paper. Ask me anything about Kushiro. All I've done the last two days is research it. I'm an expert. Population, 190,000. There's a tech school, there's an airport.

CHUTES&LADDERS: Why are you telling me this? To get my blessing?

ORANGUTAN: I tell you about the things I do.

CHUTES&LADDERS: You don't want my opinion, you want my approval.

ORANGUTAN: Hand it over.

CHUTES&LADDERS: No.

ORANGUTAN: Don't get monosyllabic.

CHUTES&LADDERS: Take that piece of paper and use it as kindling for a warm winter fire.

ORANGUTAN: Jeez, what did they slip into your Wheaties this morning?

CHUTES&LADDERS: Do a ritual burning and never look back. You have three months. Do you know the worth in gold of three months? Don't give yourself a reason to go back to the shadows.

ORANGUTAN: I'm in recovery. I have no illusions about catharsis. I realize what will most likely happen is nothing. Maybe something tiny. A microscopic butterfly flapping her microscopic wings.

CHUTES&LADDERS: Live in the past, follow your ass.

ORANGUTAN: Don't you have the slightest ambition?

CHUTES&LADDERS: Yes, and I achieve it every day: Don't use and don't hurt anyone. Two things I used to do on a daily basis. I don't do them anymore. Done. Dream realized. No more dreaming.

(His phone rings again.)

2. Board game in which players win wedge-shaped game pieces by correctly answering trivia questions.

(Into the phone) Continue holding, please.

ORANGUTAN: When was the last time you went out on a limb?

CHUTES&LADDERS: Three odd weeks ago.

ORANGUTAN: Did you try hazelnut instead of french roast? Did you listen to *Soul Mornings* instead of NPR?[3]

CHUTES&LADDERS: There's a new secretary down the hall, she's got a nice smile. I decided to go say hello. We had a little back and forth. I said, let's have lunch, she said maybe but meant no, I turned away, looked down and my tie was floating in my coffee cup.

ORANGUTAN: I waited three months to tell you this, every step of the way, the train ride, what the river looks like. What their front door looks like. *(Pause)* I'm quitting this site. I hate this site. I fucking hate this site.

CHUTES&LADDERS: You're already losing it and you haven't even gotten on the train.

ORANGUTAN: Three days ago I suggested you and I meet face to face and you blew a fucking gasket.

CHUTES&LADDERS: That's what this is about?

ORANGUTAN: Don't flatter yourself. This is about me wanting relationships. With humans, not ones and zeroes. So we were once junkies. It's superficial. It's not real friendship.

CHUTES&LADDERS: I beg to differ.

ORANGUTAN: Prove me wrong.

CHUTES&LADDERS: Search down that address and a hundred bucks says your heart comes back a shattered light bulb.

ORANGUTAN: You mean, gasp, I'll actually FEEL something?

CHUTES&LADDERS: What are you going to do if the address is wrong? What if the building's been bulldozed? What if some new tenant lives there? What if the woman who gave you birth then gave you away answers the door?

ORANGUTAN: I DON'T KNOW! A concept you clearly avoid at all costs. Learn how to live, that's all I'm goddamn trying to do!

(His phone rings. He picks up the receiver and hangs it up.)

CHUTES&LADDERS: I have three grandsons. You know how I know that? Because I rang my son's doorbell one day. Step 9,[4] make amends. And his wife answered, and I don't blame her for hating me. But I saw three little boys in that living room and one of those boys said, "Daddy, who's that man at the door?" And my son said to *my grandson*, "I don't know. He must be lost." My son came outside, closed the door behind him, exchanged a few cordial words and then asked me to go.

ORANGUTAN: So I shouldn't even try.

CHUTES&LADDERS: I had five years sober until that day.

ORANGUTAN: You really believe in your heart of hearts I should not even try. *(Pause)* Coward.

(His phone rings. He unplugs the phone line.)

3. National Public Radio (acronym).

4. In the twelve-step addiction-recovery program first pioneered by Alcoholics Anonymous. In their original form, steps 8 and 9 read, "Made a list of all persons we had harmed and became willing to make amends to them all" and "Made direct amends to such people wherever possible, except when to do so would injure them or others."

CHUTES&LADDERS: You think it's easy being your friend?

ORANGUTAN: Sissy. You walk the goddamn earth scared of your own shadow, getting smaller and smaller, until you disappear.

CHUTES&LADDERS: You tease me. You insult me. It's like breathing to you.

ORANGUTAN: You fucking idiot. Why do little girls tease little boys on the playground at recess? Why the fuck were cooties invented? You fucking imbecile!

CHUTES&LADDERS: You disappeared for three months. I couldn't sleep for three months!

ORANGUTAN: I wanted to impress you. I wanted to log on and show you I could be better. And I was an idiot because you're just looking for cowards like you. I'm logging off. This is it. It's over.

CHUTES&LADDERS: Orangutan.

ORANGUTAN: Into the abyss I climb, looking for a flesh-and-blood hand to grasp onto.

CHUTES&LADDERS: Little monkey, stop it.

ORANGUTAN: I'm in the station. My train is in five minutes, you gave me all the motivational speech I need, I'm going to the platform, I'm getting on the train, I'm going to see the house where I was born.

(She logs off. Chutes&Ladders grabs his phone and hurls it into his wastebasket. He throws his calculator, his mail pile, his pen cup to the ground. Left on his desk is one padded envelope.)

CHUTES&LADDERS: "To Chutes&Ladders Wilkie." "From Haikumom Ortiz."

(He rips it open, pulls out a deflated orange water wing, puts it over his hand.)

Scene Ten

Split scene. Lights rise on a church. Elliot and Yaz stand at the lectern.

YAZ: It is time to honor a woman.[5]

ELLIOT: A woman who built her community with a hammer and nails.

YAZ: A woman who knew her nation's history. Its African roots. European roots. Indigenous roots. A woman who refused to be enslaved but lived to serve.

ELLIOT: A carpenter, a nurse, a comedian, a cook.

YAZ: Eugenia Ortiz.

ELLIOT: Mami Ginny.

(Lights rise on Odessa's house. She sits on her floor. She scoops a spoonful of water from a mug, pours it onto the floor in a slow ribbon.)

YAZ: She grew vegetables in her garden lot and left the gate open so anyone could walk in and pick dinner off the vine.

ELLIOT: She drank beer and told dirty jokes and even the never-crack-a-smile church ladies would be rolling laughing.

5. This eulogy is inspired by and owes much debt to Roger Zepernick's eulogy for Eugenia Burgos [Hudes's note]. Zepernick is an ordained Lutheran minister and onetime director of Centro Pedro Claver, a North Philadelphia social services organization. Eugenia "Jinny" Perez Burgos—Hudes's maternal aunt and a North Philadelphia neighborhood activist and city administrator—died of bone cancer in 2009 at age fifty-nine; obituaries credit her with raising two sons, Shawn Ortiz and Elliot Ruiz.

YAZ: She told me every time I visited, "Yaz, you're going to Juilliard."[6]

ELLIOT: Every morning when I left for school, "Elliot, nobody can make you invisible but you."

(Lights rise on the Sapporo train station. Orangutan is on the platform.)

LOUDSPEAKER *(An announcement in Japanese)*: 3:00 express to Kushiro now boarding on track one. Please have tickets out and ready for inspection.

YAZ: Zero.

ELLIOT: Birth children.

YAZ: One.

ELLIOT: Adopted son.

(Odessa pours another spoonful of water on the floor. Again, it creates a slow ribbon.)

YAZ: Three.

ELLIOT: Years in the army nurse corps.

YAZ: Three.

ELLIOT: Arrests for civil disobedience. I was in Iraq and she was demonstrating for peace.

YAZ: Forty-seven.

ELLIOT: Wheelchair ramps she installed in homes with disabled children or elderly.

(Odessa pours another spoonful of water on the floor. A small pool is forming.)

YAZ: Twelve.

ELLIOT: Abandoned lots she turned into city-recognized public gardens.

(Another spoonful.)

YAZ: Twenty-two.

ELLIOT: Godchildren recognized by this church.

(Another spoonful.)

YAZ: One hundred and thirty.

ELLIOT: Abandoned homes she refurbished and sold to young families.

LOUDSPEAKER *(Another announcement in Japanese)*: Final boarding call, 3:00 express to Kushiro, track one.

(Orangutan is still on the platform. She seems frozen, like she cannot move.)

YAZ: All while having a fresh pot of rice and beans on the stove every night. For any hungry stranger. And the pilgrims stopped. And they planted roots, because she was here. We are the living, breathing proof.

ELLIOT: I am the . . . Excuse me.

(He exits.)

YAZ: Elliot is the standing, walking testimony to a life. She. Was. Here.

(Odessa turns the cup upside down. It is empty.)

6. Elite performing arts conservatory (founded 1905) housed in New York City's Lincoln Center for the Performing Arts.

Scene Eleven

Chutes&Ladders at his desk. In front of him: an inflated orange water wing.

CHUTES&LADDERS *(On the phone)*: Yeah, it's a 1995 Tercel. Midnight blue. It's got a few miles. A hundred and twenty thousand. But like I said, I'll give it to you for three hundred below Kelley Blue Book. Yup, automatic. Just got new brake pads. Cassette deck, mint condition. I'll even throw in a few tapes. Tina Turner and Lionel Richie.[7] Oh, hold on, call-waiting.

(He presses mute. Sings to himself:)

A tisket, a tasket.
A green and yellow basket.
I bought a basket for my mommy.
On the way I dropped it.
Was it red? No no no no!
Was it brown? No no no no![8]

(Back into the phone) Sorry about that. I got someone else interested. No, it's all right, I have them on hold. You need to see this thing tonight if you're serious. I put this listing up thirty minutes ago, my phone is ringing off the hook. 6:30? Hey I didn't mention. Little lady has racing stripes.

Scene Twelve

Split scene. Lights rise on the Sapporo train station, same as before. Orangutan has laid down on the platform and fallen asleep, her backpack like a pillow.

Lights rise on Odessa's house, that night. Her phone rings. We hear loud knocking.

ELLIOT *(Offstage)*: Mami Odessa! Open the door!

(More ringing.)

(Offstage) Yo, Mom!
YAZ *(Offstage)*: She's not there.
ELLIOT *(Offstage)*: Can't you hear her phone ringing? Move out the way.
YAZ *(Offstage)*: Be careful, your leg!

(A few kicks and the door bursts open. Yaz and Elliot enter, switch on the lights. Odessa is in a heap, motionless, on the floor. Yaz runs and holds Odessa in her arms.)

Oh shit. Odessa! Odessa! Wake up.

(Yaz slaps Odessa's face a few times.)

7. American pop singer-songwriter (b. 1949) popular in the 1980s. *Tina Turner*: singer-actress (b. 1939) widely known as "the Queen of Rock 'n' Roll"; first rocketing to fame in the 1960s (alongside husband Ike), she enjoyed a new wave of international success thanks to her comeback album, *Private Dancer* (1984).
8. Slightly mangled version of "A-Tisket, A-Tasket," a song first recorded in 1938 by jazz legend Ella Fitzgerald (1917–96), based on a traditional nursery rhyme.

Her pulse is racing.

(Yaz opens her cell phone, dials.
Elliot finds a spoon on the floor.)

ELLIOT: Oh no. Oh no you fucking didn't! MOM!!! Get up!
YAZ *(Into the phone)*: Hi, I need an ambulance. I have someone unconscious here. I think it's an overdose, crack cocaine. Yes, she has a pulse. 33 Ontario Street. No, no seizures, she's just a lump. Well what should we do while we wait? Okay. Yes. *(She hangs up)* They're on their way. Elevate her feet.
ELLIOT: Help me get her to the sofa. One, two, three.

(Elliot lifts her with Yaz's help. They struggle under her weight. In fact they lift the air. Odessa stands up, lucid, and watches the action: Elliot and Yaz struggling under her invisible weight.)

YAZ: Watch her head.
ELLIOT: Aw, fuck, my leg.
YAZ: Careful.

(They set "Odessa" on the sofa, while Odessa watches, unseen, calm.)

ODESSA: I must be in the terminal. Between flights. The layover.
YAZ: Oh god, not two in one day, please.
ELLIOT: She's been through this shit a million times. She's a survivor! WAKE UP! Call your mom. She'll get here before the ambulance.

(Yaz dials.)

ODESSA: I've been to the airport, one time. My dad flew here from Puerto Rico. First time I met him. We stood by the baggage claim, his flight was late, we waited forever. There was one single, lone suitcase, spinning around a carousel.
YAZ *(To Elliot)*: Voice mail. *(Into the phone)* Mom? Call me back immediately, it's an emergency.
ELLIOT: Give me that. *(Grabs the phone)* Titi, Odessa fucking OD'd and she's dying on her living room floor and I can't take this anymore! COME GET US before I walk off and leave her on the sofa! *(He hangs up)*
YAZ: If you need to, go. No guilt. I got this.
ELLIOT: She's my *mom*. Can I be angry? Can you let me be angry?
YAZ: Why is this family plagued? *(Elliot moves to go)* Where are you going?
ELLIOT: To find something fragile.

(He exits. We hear something shatter.)

ODESSA: Everyone had cleared away from the carousel. Everyone had their bags. But this one was unclaimed. It could still be there for all I know. Spiraling. Spinning. Looking for an owner. Abandoned.

(In the Sapporo station, a Policeman enters with a bright, beaming flashlight and points it at Orangutan.
In Odessa's house, a radiant white light suddenly pours in from above. Odessa looks up, is overwhelmed. It is beautiful. Yaz sees it.)

YAZ: Dear god, do you see that?

(Elliot enters. Watching Yaz, he looks up.)

ELLIOT *(Not seeing it)*: What?
YAZ *(To Odessa)*: It's okay, Odessa, go, go, we love you, I love you Titi,[9] you are good, you *are* good. Oh my god, she's beautiful.
ELLIOT: What are you talking about?
YAZ: It's okay, it's okay. We love you Odessa.
POLICEMAN *(In Japanese)*: Miss, miss, are you okay?
ORANGUTAN *(Waking)*: English, please.
POLICEMAN: No sleeping on the floor.
ORANGUTAN *(Getting up slowly)*: Sorry.
POLICEMAN: Are you sick?
ORANGUTAN: No.
POLICEMAN: Are you intoxicated?
ORANGUTAN: No. I'm very sorry. I just got tired. I'll go. I'm going.
POLICEMAN: Please, can I give you a hand?
ORANGUTAN: No. I got it.

(Orangutan exits. The Policeman turns off his flashlight, exits.
The sound of an ambulance siren. Suddenly the white light disappears. Odessa crawls onto the couch and slips into Yaz's arms, where she's been all along.)

YAZ: Holy shit . . .
ELLIOT: What's happening, Yaz? What the fuck was that?
YAZ: You've got to forgive her, Elliot. You have to.

Scene Thirteen

The chat room.

CHUTES&LADDERS: Oh nagging wives? Orangutan? Hello? Earth to Orangutan. Come on, three days straight I been worrying about you. I have time-sensitive information. Ground control to Major Orangutan.[1]
ORANGUTAN: Ta-da.
CHUTES&LADDERS: Where you been?
ORANGUTAN: Here. There. Morrissey and Nine Inch Nails[2] on loop.
CHUTES&LADDERS: Is that what the kids like these days?
ORANGUTAN *(Rolls eyes)*: That was me rolling my eyes.
CHUTES&LADDERS: Guess what I did.
ORANGUTAN *(Shrugs)*: That was me shrugging.
CHUTES&LADDERS: Guess.
ORANGUTAN: Guess what I didn't do?

9. Auntie (Spanish).
1. David Bowie's 1969 song "Space Oddity" includes the lines "Ground Control to Major Tom: your circuit's dead, there's something wrong."
2. American industrial rock band (founded 1988). *Morrissey*: English singer-songwriter (b. 1959), vocalist of the influential rock band the Smiths (1982–87).

CHUTES&LADDERS: Meet your birth parents?
ORANGUTAN: Board the train.
CHUTES&LADDERS: Sorry.
ORANGUTAN: Don't apologize. You had my number.
CHUTES&LADDERS: Guess what I did.
ORANGUTAN: Told me so. Had my shit pegged.
CHUTES&LADDERS: I sold my Tercel. My plane lands in Narita Airport a week from this Wednesday.
ORANGUTAN: What?
CHUTES&LADDERS: American Airlines Flight 3312. Arriving 10:01 A.M.
ORANGUTAN: You're a dumbass. Tokyo? Do you have any idea how far that is from Hokkaido? And how much a ticket on the train costs? Oy, and how the hell am I going to get out of teaching that day? Oh, you dollface, you ducky!
CHUTES&LADDERS: I'll be wearing a jean jacket and a Padres cap. That's how you'll know me.
ORANGUTAN: Oh Chutes&Ladders. You old bag of bones, you! You old so-and-so, you mensch,[3] you human being! Why the hell didn't you tell me?
CHUTES&LADDERS: I'm just hoping I have the guts to get on the plane.
ORANGUTAN: Of course you're getting on that damn plane! For me you did this?

(Fountainhead logs on.)

FOUNTAINHEAD: Hey everyone. I managed to find one computer here at the hospital that works. Odessa asked me to post a message on her behalf. She landed on: "Go." Hit reset on the timer. Back to day one.
ORANGUTAN: Who's Odessa?
FOUNTAINHEAD: Sorry. Haikumom.
ORANGUTAN: What? Do you log on here just to mock us?
CHUTES&LADDERS: Hold on, is she okay?
FOUNTAINHEAD: Cardiac arrest. They said she was one hair from a coma. She hadn't used in six years and her system went nuts.
CHUTES&LADDERS: So she's alive?
FOUNTAINHEAD: And just barely ticking. Tubes in and out of her nose. She's responsive, she mumbled a few words.
ORANGUTAN: You can't be serious.
CHUTES&LADDERS: Why are you there? Were you using with her?
FOUNTAINHEAD: No.
CHUTES&LADDERS: Did you sell her the stuff?
FOUNTAINHEAD: No, Jesus, of course not. She gave them my number, I'm her emergency contact. Why, I have no idea, we're practically strangers. Getting here to the hospital, seeing her like that . . . I don't mean this as an insult, but she looked not human. Bones with skin covering. Mummy-like.
ORANGUTAN: Fuck. You.
FOUNTAINHEAD: I'm being descriptive. I'm being honest. The thought of my boys walking in on me like that. My wife finding me . . .
ORANGUTAN: That woman is the reason I'm. Oh god, you get complacent for one second! One second! You get comfortable for one minute! Fountainhead, go to the stats page. You'll see. There's thousands of members on this site. People

3. Person of great integrity; a really good, stand-up guy (Yiddish).

she has saved, people she may yet save some day. I am one of them. You are one of them.

CHUTES&LADDERS: Fountainhead, does she have family there? Has anyone come through her room?

FOUNTAINHEAD: Apparently a son and a niece but they had to catch a flight to San Juan.[4]

CHUTES&LADDERS: No parents? No other children? A friend? A neighbor?

FOUNTAINHEAD: None showed up.

CHUTES&LADDERS: Fountainhead. You have a family, I absolutely understand that, and I mean zero disrespect when I say, when I beg of you this: your job on this earth has just changed. It is not to stay clean. It's not to be a husband or a father or a CEO. It's to stay by that woman's side. Make sure she gets home safe. Bathe her. Feed her. Get her checked into a rehab, inpatient. Do not leave her side for a second. Can you do this?

FOUNTAINHEAD: I have one day clean. I'm not meant to be a saint.

CHUTES&LADDERS: Tell me now, swear on your mother's name, otherwise I'm on the first flight to Philadelphia.

FOUNTAINHEAD: I don't know.

CHUTES&LADDERS: Look man, do you believe in God?

FOUNTAINHEAD: Sure, along with unicorns and the boogeyman.

CHUTES&LADDERS: How about miracles?

FOUNTAINHEAD: When the Phils are winning.

CHUTES&LADDERS: How about actions? I bet you believe in those.

FOUNTAINHEAD: Yeah.

CHUTES&LADDERS: Your lifeboat has just arrived. Get on board or get out of the way.

FOUNTAINHEAD: I'll take care of Odessa. You have my word. My solemn word. *(Pause)* She did manage to say one thing: Someone has to take over site admin. She doesn't want the chat room full of curse words.

(Yaz appears. A screen lights up:)

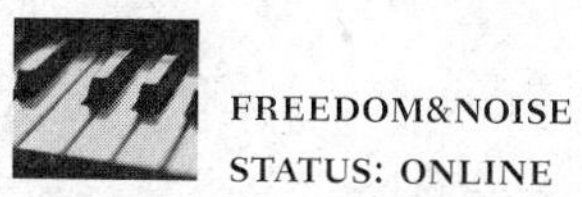

FREEDOM&NOISE
STATUS: ONLINE

FREEDOM&NOISE: I'm good with computers. I'll throw my hat in the ring.

CHUTES&LADDERS: Freedom&Noise, are you new here?

FREEDOM&NOISE: Yes. Very.

(Fountainhead's phone rings.)

FOUNTAINHEAD: Freedom&Noise, email me offline. Link attached. I gotta go.

CHUTES&LADDERS: You gave us your word. Don't be a stranger.

(Fountainhead logs off. Into the phone:)

FOUNTAINHEAD: Hi, honey, sorry I haven't called sooner. Something came up. Listen, I'm not coming home tonight, just order in. I have a friend who got sick, she's having an emergency. No, it's not a romantic friend. I will tell you about it. When I get home. When I— Honey? Honey . . .

4. Capital of Puerto Rico.

(The call is over. He writes a text message.)

Honey, under my bookmarks, click on "Fantasy Football" link. My username is "Fountainhead." My password is "Porsche71." Log on and read. Send.

Scene Fourteen

Puerto Rico. A hotel room. Yaz is online.

FREEDOM&NOISE: Hello, I am Freedom&Noise, your interim site manager, currently logging on from the Rainforest B&B in Puerto Rico. I am not a user, I've smoked pot twice, both times when I was thirteen, and am therefore unqualified for this position. There was a young woman I once knew. Let's call her "O." My crazy aunt, a fun babysitter, the baddest hide-and-seek player north of Girard Avenue. We played dress-up, built booby traps and forts, and when I was eight, she disappeared. No explanation, no acknowledgment she had ever existed, the grown-ups in the family had taken a vow of silence, and O. had been erased. My freshman year at college, I returned home for Thanksgiving, and thanks to a snow delay I walked into the middle of turkey dinner itself, and there was O., a plate full of food, chowing down. I hadn't seen her in ten years. After dinner she told me to congratulate her, it was her anniversary. I said, "Did you get married?" She pulled a necklace out from under her shirt and said, "You know what these gold letters mean? The 'N' is for narcotics, the 'A' is for anonymous and today is my two-year anniversary of being clean." *(Pause)* A few days ago I met a new woman: Haikumom. A woman who created a living, breathing ecosystem, and since I've never sown a single seed, let alone planted a garden, the least I can do is censor you, fix glitches—and one other thing . . . Formulating first line. Did Haikumom really do these on the fly? Five-seven-five, right? *(Counting the syllables on her fingers)* Box full of ashes . . .

(Elliot enters from the bathroom, freshly showered, pulling on a shirt)

ELLIOT: Whatchu looking at, Willis?[5]

YAZ: Sh. I'm counting syllables.

(Elliot looks over Yaz's shoulder at the computer.)

ELLIOT: Hold up. Don't read that shit, Yaz.

YAZ: You know how Odessa got into haiku in the first place?

ELLIOT: For real, close the computer.

YAZ: I went through this Japanese minimalist phase freshman year. Rock Gardens, Zen Buddhism, the works. I gave her a haiku collection for Christmas.

ELLIOT: Yeah, and you gave me a midget tree that died by New Year's.

YAZ: Bonsai. You didn't water it.

ELLIOT *(Closing Yaz's laptop)*: For the two days I'm away from Philly, let me be away from Philly?

YAZ: You know where I was gonna be by thirty? Two kids. Equal-housework marriage. Tenure, no question. Waaaay tenured, like by the age of twenty-four.

5. Play on "Whatchu talkin' about, Willis?," catchphrase of a character (played by diminutive actor Gary Coleman [1968–2010]) on the popular 1980s American sitcom *Diff'rent Strokes*.

Carnegie Hall debuts: Yazmin Ortiz's "Oratorio for Electric Guitar and Children's Choir." I wrote a list on a piece of paper and dug a hole in Fairmount Park and put it in the ground and said, "When I turn thirty, I'll dig it up and cross it all off." And I promise you I'll never have the courage to go to that spot with a shovel and face my list full of crumbs, decoys and bandaids.

ELLIOT: Married with kids, what an awful goal.

YAZ: Odessa's done things.

ELLIOT: Well, when you throw her a parade, don't expect me to come.

YAZ: You've done things.

ELLIOT: I wouldn't come to my own parade, either.

YAZ: Ginny did things. What have I done?

ELLIOT: Second-grade Language Arts. You glued my book report.

YAZ: I couldn't stop your leg from getting chewed up.

ELLIOT: Fairmount little league basketball. You kept score, you brought our equipment.

YAZ: I didn't hold your hand when you were in the desert popping pills trying to make yourself disappear. I didn't keep Odessa away from that needle. I didn't water a single plant in Ginny's garden. We're in PR and I'm gonna dig a new hole and I'm not putting a wish or a list in there, I'm putting a scream in there. And I'm gonna sow it like the ugliest foulest and most necessary seed in the world and it's going to bloom! This time it's going to fucking bloom!

ELLIOT: My eyes just did this weird thing. For a second, it was Mom standing in front of me.

YAZ: Odessa?

ELLIOT: Ginny.

YAZ: Elliot, your birth mother saved your life by giving you away. Tell me I'm wrong.

(Elliot doesn't respond. Yaz begins gathering her stuff hastily.)

Now we got some ashes to throw. El Yunque closes in an hour and a half.

ELLIOT: Maybe we should do this tomorrow.

YAZ: I gotta make a call. I'll be in the lobby!

(She exits.)

ELLIOT: Yaz?

(The Ghost appears. He's probably been there the whole time.)

Yaz!

GHOST: Momken men-fadluck ted-dini gawaz saffari?

(The Ghost reaches out his hand to touch Elliot.)

Momken men-fadluck ted-dini gawaz saffari?

(The second they make contact, Elliot spins on his heels and grabs the Ghost. The Ghost defends himself, pulling away. They start pushing, grabbing, fighting. The Ghost is looking for something—is it Elliot's wallet?)

Momken men-fadluck ted-dini gawaz saffari?

(The Ghost finds Elliot's wallet and tears through it, hurling its contents onto the floor. Elliot attacks again, but this time the Ghost reaches out his hand and touches Elliot's face. Elliot freezes, unable to move, as the Ghost's hands glide across his features, considering each one with authority, taking inventory.)

Momken men-fadluck ted-dini gawaz saffari?

(The Ghost is gone. Elliot catches his breath, shaken. He reaches into his pocket and pulls out a bottle of pills. He puts one pill in his hand. Then he empties the entire bottle of pills into his hand. He stares at the pills, wanting to throw them away.)

Scene Fifteen

Split scene. Odessa's bathroom. The bathtub is filled with water. John enters, carrying a very weak Odessa. Odessa is wearing shorts and a bra, a modest outfit for bathing. John lowers her gently into the bathtub.

JOHN: Does that feel okay?

(Odessa barely nods.)

It's not too hot or cold?

(Odessa shakes her head.)

I don't know how to do this. These are things women do. Take care of sick people. Make the wounds go away.

(He takes a sponge and starts to bathe her.)

Is this okay?

(He lifts her arms and washes her armpits. Embarrassed at first, but quickly gets the swing of it.)

We check you in at 4:30 so we have plenty of time to clean you up and get you in good clothes, okay? You'll go in there looking like a decent woman.

(Odessa whispers something inaudible.)

What was that?

(She gestures for him to lean in. She whispers into his ear.)

One more time.

(She whispers a little louder.)

Did someone take swimming lessons?

(She whispers again.)

Did someone put on water wings?

(She nods. He continues to bathe her, gently, in silence as:

Lights rise on Tokyo. Narita Airport. Orangutan sits on the floor by the luggage carousel. At her feet is a sign that says Chutes&Ladders. She throws the sign like a frisbee across the floor and gets up to leave. Chutes&Ladders enters, rolling a suitcase behind him. He waves to Orangutan.)

CHUTES&LADDERS: Orangutan?

ORANGUTAN: What the holy hell?

CHUTES&LADDERS: Sorry. Sorry. I tried calling but my cell doesn't work here. I told you I'm no good at this fancy kind of living.

ORANGUTAN: You were supposed to land yesterday, you were too scared to get on the plane. You rebook, you were supposed to land today, forty-five minutes ago. Everyone got their luggage already. The last person pulled the last suitcase from the carousel half an hour ago. I thought, Wow, this one sure knows how to play a joke on the ladies. I thought you had left me at the fucking altar.

CHUTES&LADDERS: I got sick on the flight. Totally embarrassing. I had a panic attack as the plane landed and I started tossing into the doggy bag right next to this nice old lady. I've been sitting on the bathroom floor emptying my stomach. Then I had to find a toothbrush and toothpaste and mouthwash because I didn't want to greet you with bad breath and all.

(She looks skeptical. She sniffs his mouth quickly.)

ORANGUTAN: Minty. *(Pause)* Oh, you dummy, you big old dummy. COME HERE, you San Diego Padre.

(They hug. A warm and brief greeting.)

What's your name?

CHUTES&LADDERS: Clay. Clayton "Buddy" Wilkie.

ORANGUTAN: I'm Madeleine Mays.

CHUTES&LADDERS: It's weird, huh?

ORANGUTAN: Totally weird. The land of the living.

(They hug. They melt into each other's arms. A hug of basic survival and necessary friendship. Then, they exit, rolling Chutes&Ladders's suitcase off as lights rise in:

Puerto Rico. A rock outcropping looking out over a waterfall. Elliot is there, looking down at the water.)

ELLIOT *(Looking down)*: Oh shit! Yaz, you gotta see this! Yaz? Fucking Johnny Appleseed of El Yunque.

(Yaz enters holding a soil-covered flower bulb. She compares the root against a field book.)

YAZ: I found my spiral ginger! This is going right next to the aloe by the kitchen door, baby!

ELLIOT: Yo, this science experiment ain't getting past security.

YAZ: Experiment my ass. I'm planting these in Ginny's garden.

ELLIOT: Customs gonna sniff that shit from a mile away.

YAZ *(Putting the bulb in a ziploc baggie full of dirt and bulbs)*: China rose . . . Sea grape . . . Some kind of fern . . .

ELLIOT: When they cuff those wrists, I don't know you.

YAZ: I'll hide them in my tampon box.

ELLIOT: That don't work. My first trip to PR, Mami Ginny smuggled a coqui[6] back with her kotex and got arrested. Front page of the *Daily News.*

YAZ: Good shit. *(A dirty little secret)* You know what Grandma did?

ELLIOT: Do I want to?

YAZ: She used to smuggle stuff back, too. She'd tuck it below her boobs. She had storage space under there!

ELLIOT: Yeah after she was sixty and had nursed seven kids. Yo you think if I jumped off this rock right now and dove into that water, I'd survive?

YAZ: Just watch out for the huge boulders and the footbridge.

ELLIOT: It's tempting. That spray. *(His phone beeps)* Reception in the rainforest.

YAZ: Kind of ruins the romance.

ELLIOT *(Reads a text message)*: Damn, that was fast.

YAZ: What?

ELLIOT: Pop sold the house. Did he even put out a listing?

YAZ: Not that I know of.

ELLIOT: That's like a VW bus going from zero to sixty in three seconds. Don't make no sense.

YAZ: Must have been an inside job.

ELLIOT: I guess so.

YAZ: A way way inside job . . .

ELLIOT: Yaz . . .

YAZ *(Conspiratorially)*: Yeeeees?

ELLIOT: What did you do?

YAZ *(Very conspiratorially)*: Nothing . . .

ELLIOT: Holy shit!

YAZ: Put my Steinway[7] on craigslist. Got four responses before you made it down to the lobby. My eighty-eight keys are worth more than Ginny's whole house. Sadly. I'll buy an upright.

ELLIOT: You are one crazy motherfucking adjunct! Yo, I don't know if el barrio is ready for you. I don't know if they can handle you!

YAZ: Oh, they gonna handle me.

ELLIOT: Wait wait wait. You need a title.

YAZ: Yaz will do just fine.

ELLIOT: Hells no. Command respect. I step on those corners, I'm Big El. *(Pause)* "Professor."

YAZ: "Professor."

ELLIOT: You like that, huh?

YAZ: It'll be the Cousins House. We'll renovate the kitchen. You redo the plumbing, I'll hook up a little tile backsplash.

ELLIOT: I watched Bob Vila[8] with Pop, but I ain't no handyman.

YAZ: Just wait, Mr. Home Depot. You're gonna be like, "Fuacata,[9] fuacata, fuacata," with your power drill and nail gun and vise grips.

6. Singing tree frog native to Puerto Rico.

7. Piano made by the legendary German American firm Steinway & Sons (founded 1853).

8. Host (b. 1946) of a series of home-improvement shows, beginning with *This Old House* (1979–89).

9. Onomatopoeic interjection akin to "Wham!" or "Bam!" (Cuban Spanish).

ELLIOT: Something like that.
YAZ: Well? Get to it. Toss 'em.
ELLIOT: Me? Why the hell do you think I let you come along?

(He hands Yaz the box.)

YAZ: Well then say something. Pray.
ELLIOT: I'm all out of prayers.
YAZ: Me, too. Make a toast.
ELLIOT: To LAX. I'm not flying back with you.
YAZ: What do you mean?
ELLIOT: I called from the hotel and changed my flight. One-way ticket. Watch out, Hollywood. *(Pause)* You know how you had to shake me awake last night?
YAZ *(Demeanor shifting)*: You were literally sobbing in your sleep.
ELLIOT: This dream was different than usual. I'm fixing a Subway hoagie, I feel eyes on the back of my neck, I turn around and expect to see him, the first guy I shot down in Iraq. But instead it's Mami Ginny. Standing next to the bread oven, smiling. You know how her eyes smile?
YAZ: Best smile in the world.
ELLIOT: Looking at me, her son. Coming to say good-bye.
YAZ: That's beautiful.
ELLIOT: She puts on her glasses to see my face even better. She squints and something changes. The moment I come into focus, her eyes widen. Her jaw drops, she starts trembling. Then she starts to cry. Something she's seeing scares her. Then she starts to scream. Loud, like, "Ahhh! Ahhh!" She won't stop looking at me, but she's terrified, horrified by what she sees. And I don't know if my lip is bleeding or there's a gash on my forehead or she's looking through my eyes and seeing straight into my fucking soul.
YAZ: Jesus.
ELLIOT: I wanted Mami Odessa to relapse, Yaz. I wanted her to pick up that needle. I knew precisely what to do, what buttons to push, I engineered that shit, I might as well have pushed the thing into her vein. Because I thought, Why would God take the good one? Yo, take the bad mom instead! I was like, Why wouldn't you take the bad fucking mom? If I stay in Philly, I'm gonna turn into it. I'm gonna become one of them. I'm already halfway there. You've got armor, you've got ideas, but I don't.
YAZ: Go. Go and don't you ever, ever look back.

(She takes his hand.)

But if you do, there will be a plastic-covered sofa waiting for you.

(Below them, in Philadelphia, John is done bathing Odessa. He lifts her and holds her like an angel above the bathtub. She is dripping wet and seems almost radiant, and yet deeply, deeply sick.)

I'm the elder now. I stay home. I hold down the fort.
ELLIOT: I'm walking.
YAZ: On three?

YAZ AND ELLIOT: One.
Two.
Three.

(They toss the ashes. Blackout.)

2011

QUESTIONS

1. WATER BY THE SPOONFUL features many entirely fictional characters, situations, and events, including the online community created by "Haikumom" and the death of Elliot's infant sister. Yet as the biographical headnote and textual footnotes suggest, the play was also inspired in part by real people and events: Hudes's cousin Elliot Ruiz was raised by their aunt Ginny; she did die of cancer; he was wounded in Iraq; Odessa is based in part on a cousin who is a former drug addict; and so on. How, if at all, might this knowledge affect your response to the play and its characters?
2. How do the characters of Elliot and Yaz each develop over the course of the play? What role in that development is played by their experiences in both real and online worlds?
3. As readers or spectators of Hudes's play, we first get to know Odessa via her online interactions, and throughout the play we see much more of these than does Elliott or Yaz. How does that affect how we view and feel about Odessa, Elliott, their individual and mutual conflicts? Why might Hudes have chosen to structure the play in this way?
4. How would you articulate the main theme of the play? Might it have to do with notions of family? with the ways we help and hurt others? with the process of trauma and recovery? something else entirely?
5. How might Yaz's discussion of musical dissonance provide a language for articulating the play's themes or describing its structure?
6. Especially in terms of conflict or theme, what role is played by Fountainhead, Chutes&Ladders, and Orangutan? How, if at all, might it matter that Fountainhead is the play's only white or upper-middle-class character? that Chutes&Ladders and Orangutan end up meeting in the real world?

SUGGESTIONS FOR WRITING

1. Though WATER BY THE SPOONFUL begins by alternating scenes set entirely in the real world with scenes set wholly in the virtual world, later scenes tend to be more complicated. Scene 10, for example, is a "split scene" that shifts among Ginny's funeral, Odessa's house, and a train station in Sapporo, Japan. Choose one of these "split scenes" and write an informal response paper about it. How do the various elements of the scene work together and perhaps comment on each other? How might the scene be staged so as to emphasize those connections without confusing the audience?
2. Write an essay exploring what WATER BY THE SPOONFUL seems to suggest about the power and limits of online selves and communities. What might the virtual world allow us to be and do that the real world doesn't, and vice versa?
3. Write an essay exploring the water imagery in Hudes's play. By its end, what various meanings might the phrase "water by the spoonful" accrue?
4. WATER BY THE SPOONFUL features a cast of characters who at first seem very different from each other in terms of their personalities, their backgrounds and situations in life, and their conflicts. Yet over the course of the play we and they arguably discover just how similar they are. Choose any two characters from the play, perhaps

those that initially seem the most different or far removed from each other. Then write an essay comparing the characters and their development over the course of the play. What similarities emerge as the play progresses? To what extent and how do the characters themselves come to appreciate these similarities? What might the play ultimately say or show us through these characters?

5. Charles Isherwood, writing in the *New York Times*, describes WATER BY THE SPOONFUL's theme as having to do with "the myriad ways in which human lives can intersect, and the potentially great rewards—or irreparable damage—that can result from the unlikely spark of those connections." Others instead describe the play as exploring the difficulty and importance of forgiving both ourselves and others; the idea "that no one is above reproach—or beyond redemption"; "the true meaning of family" (theatreworks.org); or the "life-affirming message" that "[p]eople instinctively take care of each other" and that "hitting bottom is the start of the trip back up" (Richard Zoglin, in *Time*). Write an essay defending and developing one of these claims.

27 TRAGEDY AND COMEDY

Classifying literary texts serves a variety of purposes for literary critics, who may need to "place" a work in history, suggest its relationship to other texts, or assess its literary quality or cultural value. But classification is not just an activity for "professionals." Classification can also be important to students and ordinary readers; a knowledge of categories and what they stand for can aid in the enjoyment and interpretation of individual texts.

Authors sometimes label their texts specifically to help readers know what to expect, thereby entering into a kind of contract with readers. **Pastoral** plays promise to be about shepherds living in an idealized world reminiscent of some primitive golden age. **Farces** promise broad humor and wild antics, perhaps slapstick, pratfalls, or other physical humor or perhaps easy puns and verbal high jinks, but certainly something entertaining, not too taxing, and not too serious. **Satires** promise critical commentary on a person or situation or event, often political or involving a specific cultural or social situation. Not all satires, farces, and pastoral plays do exactly what their labels promise, but those labels do lead readers to expect a certain kind of text—one that will treat predictable subject matter and progress in predictable fashion. Often these labels imply a certain kind of structure, language, and value system.

Not all plays (or texts of any other kind) are labeled by their authors, but many unlabeled texts draw on previous practice, observe established conventions, and are therefore placed by critics or by viewers and readers within traditional categories. We might, for example, describe a film as a whodunnit or a "spaghetti Western," or we might call a TV program a sitcom or a soap, and reasonably expect that others will know, at least roughly, what kind of film or show we are describing.

Tragedy and **comedy** are two of the oldest dramatic forms, and many contemporary playwrights and critics continue to apply these terms. Many people believe that tragedy and comedy still provide convenient ways to organize and present experience because they reflect basic ways of viewing human history. You can sometimes get into a pretty lively argument about whether a particular play should be called a tragedy; all kinds of critics, students, theatergoers, and readers argued with Arthur Miller and with one another about whether *Death of a Salesman* was truly tragic, for example. But while individuals often disagree about how to label particular texts and about exactly what each label implies, most people admit the necessity of labels and believe that general agreement about definition is possible, despite quibbling over details.

The broad parameters of comedy and tragedy have been around since the time of Aristotle, the fourth century B.C.E.; in his *Poetics* Aristotle defined tragedy in terms of contemporary examples. Aristotle's definition depends on three things—the order of values implicit in the play, the nature of character in the play, and the nature of the conclusion.

In a tragedy like OEDIPUS THE KING, values are universal and beyond the control of humankind. Right and wrong stem not from any agreement between individuals but from the will of the gods or from some other extrahuman authority. When the oracle tells Oedipus that he is fated to kill his father and marry his mother, Oedipus is horrified. In human terms he must try to avoid this fate—but in terms of the value system that rules the play, his attempt to circumvent the will of the gods must destroy him. In a comedy like THE IMPORTANCE OF BEING EARNEST, on the other hand, values are social and determined by the general opinion of society. In moral terms, Jack and Gwendolen, being healthy and single, might marry and establish a family. They face a social problem, however, in that Gwendolen's children cannot achieve their "proper" place in society unless her husband is a man of good family, some social position, and adequate means. Indeed, comedy tends to endorse the values of society, sometimes at the expense of individual needs or values.

Tragedy and comedy also differ in their treatment of character. Tragedy tends to focus on a person of high rank who confronts the universe and his or her fate as an individual. The tragic figure is ultimately doomed because, although good and noble, he or she has a flaw of character or a limitation of knowledge—some mark of humanity—that offsets all his or her greatness. Oedipus wishes to know and to control his own destiny, but he learns too much and is destroyed. Had Oedipus been the son of a shepherd rather than of a king, perhaps the gods would not have taken such an unfortunate interest in his fate.

By contrast, being concerned largely with society, comedies often define their characters in terms of social roles. In *The Importance of Being Earnest*, both Jack and Algernon are, for plot purposes, unmarried young men but not eminently eligible husbands-to-be, Jack because of his uncertain parentage and Algernon because of his lack of money. They have individual traits—Algernon eats too much and is somewhat pretentious; Jack tries to be more straightforward. But what distinguishes them is not so important as what they have in common according to prevailing social standards. Many comic characters become stereotypes. Lady Bracknell, for example, is a middle-aged, meddling matron, ideally placed by age and position to exert decisive social influence. Other stereotypical characters in the play include Miss Prism, the desperate spinster, and Dr. Chasuble, the slightly dim clergyman.

Finally, tragedy and comedy can be differentiated by their endings. In most tragedies, the hero is enlightened, coming to understand the meaning of his or her deeds and to accept the consequences. At the end of *Oedipus the King*, the blind hero sees and understands. Accepting his ostracism, he leaves Thebes a chastened and humbled but wiser man. Many tragic heroes die, as Hamlet does, but understanding, rather than death itself, ends the tragedy. Hamlet understands what has happened and in his last moments tries to restore order to the kingdom, asking for himself only that people may know the truth about what he has done. In comedy, on the other hand, the resolution occurs when one or more characters take on a proper social role. Most frequently, this means the marriage of an eligible young woman and an equally eligible young man. The society of *Earnest* believes that young men like Jack and Algernon and young women like Gwendolen and Cecily should marry and get about the business of having children and raising them to perpetuate the society. Even the marriage of Miss Prism and Dr. Chasuble serves social purposes. The society of the play prefers married clergymen to celibates and has no really useful function for a middle-aged spinster.

Oedipus the King and *The Importance of Being Earnest* clearly display the assumptions and features of tragedy and comedy, respectively. Many good plays provide less clear-cut examples of these genres, and many other categories have been used over the centuries to describe the shape and conventions of groups of dramatic texts. Still, *tragedy* and *comedy* are two of the most important genres to explore in any study of the various classifications of drama.

SOPHOCLES
(496?–406 BCE)
Oedipus the King[1]

Sophocles lived at a time when Athens and Greek civilization were at the peak of their power and influence. He served as a general under Pericles, played a prominent role in the city's affairs, and was arguably the greatest of the Greek tragic playwrights, winning the annual dramatic competition about twenty times, a feat unmatched by even his great contemporaries, Aeschylus and Euripides. An innovator, Sophocles fundamentally changed the nature of dramatic performance by adding a third actor, enlarging the chorus, and introducing the use of painted scenery. Aristotle held that Sophocles's *Oedipus the King* (c. 429 BCE) was the perfect tragedy and used it as his model when he discussed the nature of tragedy in his *Poetics*. Today only seven of Sophocles's tragedies survive—the Oedipus trilogy (*Oedipus the King*, *Oedipus at Colonus*, and *Antigone*), *Philoctetes*, *Ajax*, *Trachiniae*, and *Electra*—though he is believed to have written as many as 123 plays.

CHARACTERS

OEDIPUS, *King of Thebes*
JOCASTA, *His Wife*
CREON, *His Brother-in-Law*
TEIRESIAS, *an Old Blind Prophet*
A PRIEST
FIRST MESSENGER
SECOND MESSENGER
A HERDSMAN
A CHORUS *of Old Men of Thebes*

SCENE: *In front of the palace of* OEDIPUS *at Thebes. To the right of the stage near the altar stands the* PRIEST *with a crowd of children.* OEDIPUS *emerges from the central door.*

OEDIPUS: Children, young sons and daughters of old Cadmus,[2]
why do you sit here with your suppliant crowns?
The town is heavy with a mingled burden
of sounds and smells, of groans and hymns and incense;
I did not think it fit that I should hear
of this from messengers but came myself,—
I Oedipus whom all men call the Great.

1. Translated by David Grene. 2. Founder of Thebes.

[*He turns to the* PRIEST.]

You're old and they are young; come, speak for them.
What do you fear or want, that you sit here
suppliant? Indeed I'm willing to give all
that you may need; I would be very hard
should I not pity suppliants like these.

PRIEST: O ruler of my country, Oedipus,
you see our company around the altar;
you see our ages; some of us, like these,
who cannot yet fly far, and some of us
heavy with age; these children are the chosen
among the young, and I the priest of Zeus.
Within the market place sit others crowned
with suppliant garlands, at the double shrine
of Pallas[3] and the temple where Ismenus
gives oracles by fire. King, you yourself
have seen our city reeling like a wreck
already; it can scarcely lift its prow
out of the depths, out of the bloody surf.
A blight is on the fruitful plants of the earth,
a blight is on the cattle in the fields,
a blight is on our women that no children
are born to them; a God that carries fire,
a deadly pestilence, is on our town,
strikes us and spares not, and the house of Cadmus
is emptied of its people while black Death
grows rich in groaning and in lamentation.
We have not come as suppliants to this altar
because we thought of you as of a God,
but rather judging you the first of men
in all the chances of this life and when
we mortals have to do with more than man.
You came and by your coming saved our city,
freed us from tribute which we paid of old
to the Sphinx, cruel singer.[4] This you did
in virtue of no knowledge we could give you,
in virtue of no teaching; it was God
that aided you, men say, and you are held
with God's assistance to have saved our lives.
Now Oedipus, Greatest in all men's eyes,
here falling at your feet we all entreat you,
find us some strength for rescue.
Perhaps you'll hear a wise word from some God,

3. Athena, the goddess of wisdom. *Zeus*: principal god and father of Athena.

4. Thebes was in the thrall of the monstrous Sphinx—part human, part lion, part eagle, part serpent—until Oedipus was able to answer a riddle; freed at last from the monster's cruelty, the grateful citizens of Thebes made Oedipus their king.

perhaps you will learn something from a man
(for I have seen that for the skilled of practice
the outcome of their counsels live the most).
Noblest of men, go, and raise up our city,
go,—and give heed. For now this land of ours
calls you its savior since you saved it once.
So, let us never speak about your reign
as of a time when first our feet were set
secure on high, but later fell to ruin.
Raise up our city, save it and raise it up.
Once you have brought us luck with happy omen;
be no less now in fortune.
If you will rule this land, as now you rule it,
better to rule it full of men than empty.
For neither tower nor ship is anything
when empty, and none live in it together.

OEDIPUS: I pity you, children. You have come full of longing,
but I have known the story before you told it
only too well. I know you are all sick,
yet there is not one of you, sick though you are,
that is as sick as I myself.
Your several sorrows each have single scope
and touch but one of you. My spirit groans
for city and myself and you at once.
You have not roused me like a man from sleep;
know that I have given many tears to this,
gone many ways wandering in thought,
but as I thought I found only one remedy
and that I took. I sent Menoeceus' son
Creon, Jocasta's brother, to Apollo,[5]
to his Pythian temple,
that he might learn there by what act or word
I could save this city. As I count the days,
it vexes me what ails him; he is gone
far longer than he needed for the journey.
But when he comes, then, may I prove a villain,
if I shall not do all the God commands.

PRIEST: Thanks for your gracious words. Your servants here
signal that Creon is this moment coming.

OEDIPUS: His face is bright. O holy Lord Apollo,
grant that his news too may be bright for us
and bring us safety.

PRIEST: It is happy news,
I think, for else his head would not be crowned
with sprigs of fruitful laurel.

OEDIPUS: We will know soon,

5. God of truth and of light, worshipped at many shrines, most famously that at Pytho (an ancient name for Delphi), where an oracle was believed to speak for the god.

he's within hail. Lord Creon, my good brother,
what is the word you bring us from the God?

[CREON *enters.*]

CREON: A good word,—for things hard to bear themselves
if in the final issue all is well
I count complete good fortune.
OEDIPUS: What do you mean?
What you have said so far
leaves me uncertain whether to trust or fear.
CREON: If you will hear my news before these others
I am ready to speak, or else to go within.
OEDIPUS: Speak it to all;
the grief I bear, I bear it more for these
than for my own heart.
CREON: I will tell you, then,
what I heard from the God.
King Phoebus[6] in plain words commanded us
to drive out a pollution from our land,
pollution grown ingrained within the land;
drive it out, said the God, not cherish it,
till it's past cure.
OEDIPUS: What is the rite
of purification? How shall it be done?
CREON: By banishing a man, or expiation
of blood by blood, since it is murder guilt
which holds our city in this destroying storm.
OEDIPUS: Who is this man whose fate the God pronounces?
CREON: My Lord, before you piloted the state
we had a king called Laius.
OEDIPUS: I know of him by hearsay. I have not seen him.
CREON: The God commanded clearly: let someone
punish with force this dead man's murderers.
OEDIPUS: Where are they in the world? Where would a trace
of this old crime be found? It would be hard
to guess where.
CREON: The clue is in this land;
that which is sought is found;
the unheeded thing escapes:
so said the God.
OEDIPUS: Was it at home,
or in the country that death came upon him,
or in another country travelling?
CREON: He went, he said himself, upon an embassy,
but never returned when he set out from home.
OEDIPUS: Was there no messenger, no fellow traveller
who knew what happened? Such a one might tell

6. Another name for Apollo.

something of use.
CREON: They were all killed save one. He fled in terror
and he could tell us nothing in clear terms
of what he knew, nothing, but one thing only.
OEDIPUS: What was it?
If we could even find a slim beginning
in which to hope, we might discover much.
CREON: This man said that the robbers they encountered
were many and the hands that did the murder
were many; it was no man's single power.
OEDIPUS: How could a robber dare a deed like this
were he not helped with money from the city,
money and treachery?
CREON: That indeed was thought.
But Laius was dead and in our trouble
there was none to help.
OEDIPUS: What trouble was so great to hinder you
inquiring out the murder of your king?
CREON: The riddling Sphinx induced us to neglect
mysterious crimes and rather seek solution
of troubles at our feet.
OEDIPUS: I will bring this to light again. King Phoebus
fittingly took this care about the dead,
and you too fittingly.
And justly you will see in me an ally,
a champion of my country and the God.
For when I drive pollution from the land
I will not serve a distant friend's advantage,
but act in my own interest. Whoever
he was that killed the king may readily
wish to dispatch me with his murderous hand;
so helping the dead king I help myself.

Come, children, take your suppliant boughs and go;
up from the altars now. Call the assembly
and let it meet upon the understanding
that I'll do everything. God will decide
whether we prosper or remain in sorrow.
PRIEST: Rise, children—it was this we came to seek,
which of himself the king now offers us.
May Phoebus who gave us the oracle
come to our rescue and stay the plague.

[*Exeunt*[7] *all but the* CHORUS.]

CHORUS: [*Strophe.*][8] What is the sweet spoken word of God from the shrine of
Pytho, rich in gold

7. Exit the stage (Latin for "they go out"). 8. In Greek stagecraft, choral song and corresponding dance of the chorus to one side.

that has come to glorious Thebes?
I am stretched on the rack of doubt, and terror and trembling hold
my heart, O Delian Healer,[9] and I worship full of fears
for what doom you will bring to pass, new or renewed in the revolving
years.
Speak to me, immortal voice,
child of golden Hope.

[*Antistrophe.*][1]

First I call on you, Athene,[2] deathless daughter of Zeus,
and Artemis,[3] Earth Upholder,
who sits in the midst of the marketplace in the throne which men call
Fame,
and Phoebus, the Far Shooter, three averters of Fate,
come to us now, if ever before, when ruin rushed upon the state,
you drove destruction's flame away
out of our land.

[*Strophe.*]

Our sorrows defy number;
all the ship's timbers are rotten;
taking of thought is no spear for the driving away of the plague.
There are no growing children in this famous land;
there are no women bearing the pangs of childbirth.
You may see them one with another, like birds swift on the wing,
quicker than fire unmastered,
speeding away to the coast of the Western God.

[*Antistrophe.*]

In the unnumbered deaths
of its people the city dies;
those children that are born lie dead on the naked earth
unpitied, spreading contagion of death; and grey haired mothers and wives
everywhere stand at the altar's edge, suppliant, moaning;
the hymn to the healing God rings out but with it the wailing voices are
blended.
From these our sufferings grant us, O golden Daughter of Zeus,
glad-faced deliverance.

[*Strophe.*]

There is no clash of brazen shields but our fight is with the War God,
a War God ringed with the cries of men, a savage God who burns us;
grant that he turn in racing course backwards out of our country's bounds
to the great palace of Amphitrite[4] or where the waves of the Thracian sea

9. Apollo was also god of healing; one of his principal shrines was located on the island of Delos.
1. After the strophe, the chorus's answering song and returning dance.
2. Goddess of both war and peace, as well as wisdom.
3. Goddess of the earth and the hunt, twin sister of Apollo.
4. Queen of the sea and wife of Poseidon, sometimes said to dwell in the Atlantic Ocean.

deny the stranger safe anchorage.
Whatsoever escapes the night
at last the light of day revisits;
so smite the War God,[5] Father Zeus,
beneath your thunderbolt,
for you are the Lord of the lightning, the lightning that carries fire.

[*Antistrophe.*]

And your unconquered arrow shafts, winged by the golden corded bow,
Lycean King, I beg to be at our side for help;[6]
and the gleaming torches of Artemis with which she scours the Lycean hills,
and I call on the God with the turban of gold, who gave his name to this country of ours,
the Bacchic God with the wind flushed face,
Evian One, who travel
with the Maenad[7] company,
combat the God that burns us
with your torch of pine;
for the God that is our enemy is a God unhonoured among the Gods.

[OEDIPUS *returns.*]

OEDIPUS: For what you ask me—if you will hear my words,
and hearing welcome them and fight the plague,
you will find strength and lightening of your load
Hark to me; what I say to you, I say
as one that is a stranger to the story
as stranger to the deed. For I would not
be far upon the track if I alone
were tracing it without a clue. But now,
since after all was finished, I became
a citizen among you, citizens—
now I proclaim to all the men of Thebes:
who so among you knows the murderer
by whose hand Laius, son of Labdacus,
died—I command him to tell everything
to me,—yes, though he fears himself to take the blame
on his own head; for bitter punishment
he shall have none, but leave this land unharmed.
Or if he knows the murderer, another,
a foreigner, still let him speak the truth.
For I will pay him and be grateful, too.
But if you shall keep silence, if perhaps
some one of you, to shield a guilty friend,

5. Ares, son of Zeus and half brother to Athena.
6. That is, Apollo, a major shrine to whom was located at Lycia in Anatolia, modern-day Turkey.
7. Female worshippers of Dionysus (Bacchus to the Romans; see line 219), god of fertility and wine. *Evian One*: Dionysus (also known as Evius).

or for his own sake shall reject my words—
hear what I shall do then:
I forbid that man, whoever he be, my land,
my land where I hold sovereignty and throne;
and I forbid any to welcome him
or cry him greeting or make him a sharer
in sacrifice or offering to the gods,
or give him water for his hands to wash.
I command all to drive him from their homes,
since he is our pollution, as the oracle
of Pytho's god proclaimed him now to me.
So I stand forth a champion of the god
and of the man who died.
Upon the murderer I invoke this curse—
whether he is one man and all unknown,
or one of many—may he wear out his life
in misery to miserable doom!
If with my knowledge he lives at my hearth
I pray that I myself may feel my curse.
On you I lay my charge to fulfill all this
for me, for the god, and for this land of ours
destroyed and blighted, by the god forsaken.

Even were this no matter of God's ordinance
it would not fit you so to leave it lie,
unpurified, since a good man is dead
and one that was a king. Search it out.
Since I am now the holder of his office,
and have his bed and wife that once was his,
and had his line not been unfortunate
we would have common children—(fortune leaped
upon his head)—because of all these things,
I fight in his defence as for my father,
and I shall try all means to take the murderer
of Laius the son of Labdacus
the son of Polydorus and before him
of Cadmus and before him of Agenor.
Those who do not obey me, may the Gods
grant no crops springing from the ground they plough
nor children to their women! May a fate
like this, or one still worse than this consume them!
For you whom these words please, the other Thebans,
may Justice as your ally and all the Gods
live with you, blessing you now and for ever!

CHORUS: As you have held me to my oath, I speak:
I neither killed the king nor can declare
the killer; but since Phoebus set the quest
it is his part to tell who the man is.

OEDIPUS: Right; but to put compulsion on the Gods
against their will—no man can do that.
CHORUS: May I then say what I think second best?
OEDIPUS: If there's a third best, too, spare not to tell it.
CHORUS: I know that what the Lord Teiresias
sees, is most often what the Lord Apollo
sees. If you should inquire of this from him
you might find out most clearly.
OEDIPUS: Even in this my actions have not been sluggard.
On Creon's word I have sent two messengers
and why the prophet is not here already
I have been wondering.
CHORUS: His skill apart
there is besides only an old faint story.
OEDIPUS: What is it?
I look at every story.
CHORUS: It was said
that he was killed by certain wayfarers.
OEDIPUS: I heard that, too, but no one saw the killer.
CHORUS: Yet if he has a share of fear at all,
his courage will not stand firm, hearing your curse.
OEDIPUS: The man who in the doing did not shrink
will fear no word.
CHORUS: Here comes his prosecutor:
led by your men the godly prophet comes
in whom alone of mankind truth is native.

[*Enter* TEIRESIAS, *led by a* LITTLE BOY.]

OEDIPUS: Teiresias, you are versed in everything,
things teachable and things not to be spoken,
things of the heaven and earth-creeping things.
You have no eyes but in your mind you know
with what a plague our city is afflicted.
My lord, in you alone we find a champion,
in you alone one that can rescue us.
Perhaps you have not heard the messengers,
but Phoebus sent in answer to our sending
an oracle declaring that our freedom
from this disease would only come when we
should learn the names of those who killed King Laius,
and kill them or expel from our country.
Do not begrudge us oracles from birds,
or any other way of prophecy
within your skill; save yourself and the city,
save me; redeem the debt of our pollution
that lies on us because of this dead man.
We are in your hands; pains are most nobly taken
to help another when you have means and power.

TEIRESIAS: Alas, how terrible is wisdom when
it brings no profit to the man that's wise!
This I knew well, but had forgotten it,
else I would not have come here.
OEDIPUS: What is this?
How sad you are now you have come!
TEIRESIAS: Let me
go home. It will be easiest for us both
to bear our several destinies to the end
if you will follow my advice.
OEDIPUS: You'd rob us
of this your gift of prophecy? You talk
as one who had no care for law nor love
for Thebes who reared you.
TEIRESIAS: Yes, but I see that even your own words
miss the mark; therefore I must fear for mine.
OEDIPUS: For God's sake if you know of anything,
do not turn from us; all of us kneel to you,
all of us here, your suppliants.
TEIRESIAS: All of you here know nothing. I will not
bring to the light of day my troubles, mine—
rather than call them yours.
OEDIPUS: What do you mean?
You know of something but refuse to speak.
Would you betray us and destroy the city?
TEIRESIAS: I will not bring this pain upon us both,
neither on you nor on myself. Why is it
you question me and waste your labour? I
will tell you nothing.
OEDIPUS: You would provoke a stone! Tell us, you villain,
tell us, and do not stand there quietly
unmoved and balking at the issue.
TEIRESIAS: You blame my temper but you do not see
your own that lives within you; it is me
you chide.
OEDIPUS: Who would not feel his temper rise
at words like these with which you shame our city?
TEIRESIAS: Of themselves things will come, although I hide them
and breathe no word of them.
OEDIPUS: Since they will come
tell them to me.
TEIRESIAS: I will say nothing further.
Against this answer let your temper rage
as wildly as you will.
OEDIPUS: Indeed I am
so angry I shall not hold back a jot
of what I think. For I would have you know
I think you were complotter of the deed

and doer of the deed save in so far
as for the actual killing. Had you had eyes
I would have said alone you murdered him.
TEIRESIAS: Yes? Then I warn you faithfully to keep
the letter of your proclamation and
from this day forth to speak no word of greeting
to these nor me; you are the land's pollution.
OEDIPUS: How shamelessly you started up this taunt!
How do you think you will escape?
TEIRESIAS: I have.
I have escaped; the truth is what I cherish
and that's my strength.
OEDIPUS: And who has taught you truth?
Not your profession surely!
TEIRESIAS: You have taught me,
for you have made me speak against my will.
OEDIPUS: Speak what? Tell me again that I may learn it better.
TEIRESIAS: Did you not understand before or would you
provoke me into speaking?
OEDIPUS: I did not grasp it,
not so to call it known. Say it again.
TEIRESIAS: I say you are the murderer of the king
whose murderer you seek.
OEDIPUS: Not twice you shall
say calumnies like this and stay unpunished.
TEIRESIAS: Shall I say more to tempt your anger more?
OEDIPUS: As much as you desire; it will be said
in vain.
TEIRESIAS: I say that with those you love best
you live in foulest shame unconsciously
and do not see where you are in calamity.
OEDIPUS: Do you imagine you can always talk
like this, and live to laugh at it hereafter?
TEIRESIAS: Yes, if the truth has anything of strength.
OEDIPUS: It has, but not for you; it has no strength
for you because you are blind in mind and ears
as well as in your eyes.
TEIRESIAS: You are a poor wretch
to taunt me with the very insults which
everyone soon will heap upon yourself.
OEDIPUS: Your life is one long night so that you cannot
hurt me or any other who sees the light.
TEIRESIAS: It is not fate that I should be your ruin,
Apollo is enough; it is his care
to work this out.
OEDIPUS: Was this your own design
or Creon's?

TEIRESIAS: Creon is no hurt to you,
but you are to yourself.
OEDIPUS: Wealth, sovereignty and skill outmatching skill
for the contrivance of an envied life!
Great store of jealousy fill your treasury chests,
if my friend Creon, friend from the first and loyal,
thus secretly attacks me, secretly
desires to drive me out and secretly
suborns this juggling, trick devising quack,
this wily beggar who has only eyes
for his own gains, but blindness in his skill.
For, tell me, where have you seen clear, Teiresias,
with your prophetic eyes? When the dark singer,
the Sphinx, was in your country, did you speak
word of deliverance to its citizens?
And yet the riddle's answer was not the province
of a chance comer. It was a prophet's task
and plainly you had no such gift of prophecy
from birds nor otherwise from any God
to glean a word of knowledge. But I came,
Oedipus, who knew nothing, and I stopped her.
I solved the riddle by my wit alone.
Mine was no knowledge got from birds.[8] And now
you would expel me,
because you think that you will find a place
by Creon's throne. I think you will be sorry,
both you and your accomplice, for your plot
to drive me out. And did I not regard you
as an old man, some suffering would have taught you
that what was in your heart was treason.
CHORUS: We look at this man's words and yours, my king,
and we find both have spoken them in anger.
We need no angry words but only thought
how we may best hit the God's meaning for us.
TEIRESIAS: If you are king, at least I have the right
no less to speak in my defence against you.
Of that much I am master. I am no slave
of yours, but Loxias',[9] and so I shall not
enroll myself with Creon for my patron.
Since you have taunted me with being blind,
here is my word for you.
You have your eyes but see not where you are
in sin, nor where you live, nor whom you live with.

8. Prophetic knowledge derived from observing the flight of birds or sometimes from inspecting bird entrails.
9. Yet another name for Apollo.

Do you know who your parents are? Unknowing
you are an enemy to kith and kin
in death, beneath the earth, and in this life.
A deadly footed, double striking curse,
from father and mother both, shall drive you forth
out of this land, with darkness on your eyes,
that now have such straight vision. Shall there be
a place will not be harbour to your cries,
a corner of Cithaeron[1] will not ring
in echo to your cries, soon, soon,—
when you shall learn the secret of your marriage,
which steered you to a haven in this house,—
haven no haven, after lucky voyage?
And of the multitude of other evils
establishing a grim equality
between you and your children, you know nothing.
So, muddy with contempt my words and Creon's!
Misery shall grind no man as it will you.

OEDIPUS: Is it endurable that I should hear
such words from him? Go and a curse go with you!
Quick, home with you! Out of my house at once!

TEIRESIAS: I would not have come either had you not called me.

OEDIPUS: I did not know then you would talk like a fool—
or it would have been long before I called you.

TEIRESIAS: I am a fool then, as it seems to you—
but to the parents who have bred you, wise.

OEDIPUS: What parents? Stop! Who are they of all the world?

TEIRESIAS: This day will show your birth and will destroy you.

OEDIPUS: How needlessly your riddles darken everything.

TEIRESIAS: But it's in riddle answering you are strongest.

OEDIPUS: Yes. Taunt me where you will find me great.

TEIRESIAS: It is this very luck that has destroyed you.

OEDIPUS: I do not care, if it has saved this city.

TEIRESIAS: Well, I will go. Come, boy, lead me away.

OEDIPUS: Yes, lead him off. So long as you are here,
you'll be a stumbling block and a vexation;
once gone, you will not trouble me again.

TEIRESIAS: I have said
what I came here to say not fearing your
countenance: there is no way you can hurt me.
I tell you, king, this man, this murderer
(whom you have long declared you are in search of,
indicting him in threatening proclamation
as murderer of Laius)—he is here.
In name he is a stranger among citizens
but soon he will be shown to be a citizen

1. Mountain where Oedipus was abandoned as a child.

true native Theban, and he'll have no joy
of the discovery: blindness for sight
and beggary for riches his exchange,
he shall go journeying to a foreign country
tapping his way before him with a stick.
He shall be proved father and brother both
to his own children in his house; to her
that gave him birth, a son and husband both;
a fellow sower in his father's bed
with that same father that he murdered.
Go within, reckon that out, and if you find me
mistaken, say I have no skill in prophecy.

[*Exeunt separately* TEIRESIAS *and* OEDIPUS.]

CHORUS: [*Strophe*.] Who is the man proclaimed
by Delphi's[2] prophetic rock
as the bloody handed murderer,
the doer of deeds that none dare name?
Now is the time for him to run
with a stronger foot
than Pegasus[3]
for the child of Zeus leaps in arms upon him
with fire and the lightning bolt,
and terribly close on his heels
are the Fates[4] that never miss.

[*Antistrophe*.]

Lately from snowy Parnassus[5]
clearly the voice flashed forth,
bidding each Theban track him down,
the unknown murderer.
In the savage forests he lurks and in
the caverns like
the mountain bull.
He is sad and lonely, and lonely his feet
that carry him far from the navel of earth;
but its prophecies, ever living,
flutter around his head.

[*Strophe*.]

The augur has spread confusion,
terrible confusion;
I do not approve what was said
nor can I deny it.

2. Location of Greece's most important shrine to Apollo, renowned for its oracle.

3. Winged horse. 4. Goddesses who decide the course of human life.

5. Mountain sacred to Apollo.

I do not know what to say;
I am in a flutter of foreboding;
I never heard in the present
nor past of a quarrel between
the sons of Labdacus and Polybus,[6]
that I might bring as proof
in attacking the popular fame
of Oedipus, seeking
to take vengeance for undiscovered
death in the line of Labdacus.

[*Antistrophe.*]

Truly Zeus and Apollo are wise
and in human things all knowing;
but amongst men there is no
distinct judgment, between the prophet
and me—which of us is right.
One man may pass another in wisdom
but I would never agree
with those that find fault with the king
till I should see the word
proved right beyond doubt. For once
in visible form the Sphinx
came on him and all of us
saw his wisdom and in that test
he saved the city. So he will not be condemned by my mind.

[*Enter* CREON.]

CREON: Citizens, I have come because I heard
deadly words spread about me, that the king
accuses me. I cannot take that from him.
If he believes that in these present troubles
he has been wronged by me in word or deed
I do not want to live on with the burden
of such a scandal on me. The report
injures me doubly and most vitally—
for I'll be called a traitor to my city
and traitor also to my friends and you.
CHORUS: Perhaps it was a sudden gust of anger
that forced that insult from him, and no judgment.
CREON: But did he say that it was in compliance
with schemes of mine that the seer told him lies?
CHORUS: Yes, he said that, but why, I do not know.
CREON: Were his eyes straight in his head? Was his mind right
when he accused me in this fashion?

6. King who adopted Oedipus.

CHORUS: I do not know; I have no eyes to see
what princes do. Here comes the king himself.

[*Enter* OEDIPUS.]

OEDIPUS: You, sir, how is it you come here? Have you so much
brazen-faced daring that you venture in
my house although you are proved manifestly
the murderer of that man, and though you tried,
openly, highway robbery of my crown?
For God's sake, tell me what you saw in me,
what cowardice or what stupidity,
that made you lay a plot like this against me?
Did you imagine I should not observe
the crafty scheme that stole upon me or
seeing it, take no means to counter it?
Was it not stupid of you to make the attempt,
to try to hunt down royal power without
the people at your back or friends? For only
with the people at your back or money can
the hunt end in the capture of a crown.
CREON: Do you know what you're doing? Will you listen
to words to answer yours, and then pass judgment?
OEDIPUS: You're quick to speak, but I am slow to grasp you,
for I have found you dangerous,—and my foe.
CREON: First of all hear what I shall say to that.
OEDIPUS: At least don't tell me that you are not guilty.
CREON: If you think obstinacy without wisdom
a valuable possession, you are wrong.
OEDIPUS: And you are wrong if you believe that one,
a criminal, will not be punished only
because he is my kinsman.
CREON: This is but just—
but tell me, then, of what offense I'm guilty?
OEDIPUS: Did you or did you not urge me to send
to this prophetic mumbler?
CREON: I did indeed,
and I shall stand by what I told you.
OEDIPUS: How long ago is it since Laius . . .
CREON: What about Laius? I don't understand.
OEDIPUS: Vanished—died—was murdered?
CREON: It is long,
a long, long time to reckon.
OEDIPUS: Was this prophet
in the profession then?
CREON: He was, and honoured
as highly as he is today.
OEDIPUS: At that time did he say a word about me?
CREON: Never, at least when I was near him.

OEDIPUS: You never made a search for the dead man?
CREON: We searched, indeed, but never learned of anything.
OEDIPUS: Why did our wise old friend not say this then?
CREON: I don't know; and when I know nothing, I
usually hold my tongue.
OEDIPUS: You know this much,
and can declare this much if you are loyal.
CREON: What is it? If I know, I'll not deny it.
OEDIPUS: That he would not have said that I killed Laius
had he not met you first.
CREON: You know yourself
whether he said this, but I demand that I
should hear as much from you as you from me.
OEDIPUS: Then hear,—I'll not be proved a murderer.
CREON: Well, then. You're married to my sister.
OEDIPUS: Yes,
that I am not disposed to deny.
CREON You rule
this country giving her an equal share
in the government?
OEDIPUS: Yes, everything she wants
she has from me.
CREON: And I, as thirdsman to you,
am rated as the equal of you two?
OEDIPUS: Yes, and it's there you've proved yourself false friend.
CREON: Not if you will reflect on it as I do.
Consider, first, if you think anyone
would choose to rule and fear rather than rule
and sleep untroubled by a fear if power
were equal in both cases. I, at least,
I was not born with such a frantic yearning
to be a king—but to do what kings do.
And so it is with everyone who has learned
wisdom and self-control. As it stands now,
the prizes are all mine—and without fear.
But if I were the king myself, I must
do much that went against the grain.
How should despotic rule seem sweeter to me
than painless power and an assured authority?
I am not so besotted yet that I
want other honours than those that come with profit.
Now every man's my pleasure; every man greets me;
now those who are your suitors fawn on me,—
success for them depends upon my favour.
Why should I let all this go to win that?
My mind would not be traitor if it's wise;
I am no treason lover, of my nature,

nor would I ever dare to join a plot.
Prove what I say. Go to the oracle
at Pytho and inquire about the answers,
if they are as I told you. For the rest,
if you discover I laid any plot
together with the seer, kill me, I say,
not only by your vote but by my own.
But do not charge me on obscure opinion
without some proof to back it. It's not just
lightly to count your knaves as honest men,
nor honest men as knaves. To throw away
an honest friend is, as it were, to throw
your life away, which a man loves the best.
In time you will know all with certainty;
time is the only test of honest men,
one day is space enough to know a rogue.

CHORUS: His words are wise, king, if one fears to fall.
Those who are quick of temper are not safe.

OEDIPUS: When he that plots against me secretly
moves quickly, I must quickly counterplot.
If I wait taking no decisive measure
his business will be done, and mine be spoiled.

CREON: What do you want to do then? Banish me?

OEDIPUS: No, certainly; kill you, not banish you.[7]

CREON: I do not think that you've your wits about you.

OEDIPUS: For my own interests, yes.

CREON: But for mine, too,
you should think equally.

OEDIPUS: You are a rogue.

CREON: Suppose you do not understand?

OEDIPUS: But yet
I must be ruler.

CREON: Not if you rule badly.

OEDIPUS: O, city, city!

CREON: I too have some share
in the city; it is not yours alone.

CHORUS: Stop, my lords! Here—and in the nick of time
I see Jocasta coming from the house;
with her help lay the quarrel that now stirs you.

[*Enter* JOCASTA.]

JOCASTA: For shame! Why have you raised this foolish squabbling
brawl? Are you not ashamed to air your private

7. *Translator's note*: Two lines omitted here owing to the confusion in the dialogue consequent on the loss of a third line. The lines as they stand in Jebb's edition (1902) are: OED: That you may show what manner of thing is envy. / CREON: You speak as one that will not yield or trust. / [OED: *lost line.*]

griefs when the country's sick? Go in, you, Oedipus,
and you, too, Creon, into the house. Don't magnify
your nothing troubles.

CREON: Sister, Oedipus,
your husband, thinks he has the right to do
terrible wrongs—he has but to choose between
two terrors: banishing or killing me.

OEDIPUS: He's right, Jocasta; for I find him plotting
with knavish tricks against my person.

CREON: That God may never bless me! May I die
accursed, if I have been guilty of
one tittle of the charge you bring against me!

JOCASTA: I beg you, Oedipus, trust him in this,
spare him for the sake of this his oath to God,
for my sake, and the sake of those who stand here.

CHORUS: Be gracious, be merciful,
we beg of you.

OEDIPUS: In what would you have me yield?

CHORUS: He has been no silly child in the past.
He is strong in his oath now.
Spare him.

OEDIPUS: Do you know what you ask?

CHORUS: Yes.

OEDIPUS: Tell me then.

CHORUS: He has been your friend before all men's eyes; do not cast him
away dishonoured on an obscure conjecture.

OEDIPUS: I would have you know that this request of yours
really requests my death or banishment.

CHORUS: May the Sun God,[8] king of Gods, forbid! May I die without God's blessing, without friends' help, if I had any such thought. But my spirit is broken by my unhappiness for my wasting country; and this would but add troubles amongst ourselves to the other troubles.

OEDIPUS: Well, let him go then—if I must die ten times for it,
or be sent out dishonoured into exile.
It is your lips that prayed for him I pitied,
not his; wherever he is, I shall hate him.

CREON: I see you sulk in yielding and you're dangerous
when you are out of temper; natures like yours
are justly heaviest for themselves to bear.

OEDIPUS: Leave me alone! Take yourself off, I tell you.

CREON: I'll go, you have not known me, but they have,
and they have known my innocence.

[*Exit.*]

8. Helios, closely associated with Apollo, the god of light.

CHORUS: Won't you take him inside, lady?
JOCASTA: Yes, when I've found out what was the matter.
CHORUS: There was some misconceived suspicion of a story, and on the other side the sting of injustice.
JOCASTA: So, on both sides?
CHORUS: Yes.
JOCASTA: What was the story?
CHORUS: I think it best, in the interests of the country, to leave it where it ended.
OEDIPUS: You see where you have ended, straight of judgment
although you are, by softening my anger.
CHORUS: Sir, I have said before and I say again—be sure that I would have been proved a madman, bankrupt in sane council, if I should put you away, you who steered the country I love safely when she was crazed with troubles. God grant that now, too, you may prove a fortunate guide for us.
JOCASTA: Tell me, my lord, I beg of you, what was it
that roused your anger so?
OEDIPUS: Yes, I will tell you.
I honour you more than I honour them.
It was Creon and the plots he laid against me.
JOCASTA: Tell me—if you can clearly tell the quarrel—
OEDIPUS: Creon says
that I'm the murderer of Laius.
JOCASTA: Of his own knowledge or on information?
OEDIPUS: He sent this rascal prophet to me, since
he keeps his own mouth clean of any guilt.
JOCASTA: Do not concern yourself about this matter;
listen to me and learn that human beings
have no part in the craft of prophecy.
Of that I'll show you a short proof.
There was an oracle once that came to Laius,—
I will not say that it was Phoebus' own,
but it was from his servants—and it told him
that it was fate that he should die a victim
at the hands of his own son, a son to be born
of Laius and me. But, see now, he,
the king, was killed by foreign highway robbers
at a place where three roads meet—so goes the story;
and for the son—before three days were out
after his birth King Laius pierced his ankles
and by the hands of others cast him forth
upon a pathless hillside. So Apollo
failed to fulfill his oracle to the son,
that he should kill his father, and to Laius
also proved false in that the thing he feared,
death at his son's hands, never came to pass.
So clear in this case were the oracles,

so clear and false. Give them no heed, I say;
what God discovers need of, easily
he shows to us himself.

OEDIPUS: O dear Jocasta,
as I hear this from you, there comes upon me
a wandering of the soul—I could run mad.

JOCASTA: What trouble is it, that you turn again
and speak like this?

OEDIPUS: I thought I heard you say
that Laius was killed at a crossroads.

JOCASTA: Yes, that was how the story went and still
that word goes round.

OEDIPUS: Where is this place, Jocasta,
where he was murdered?

JOCASTA: Phocis is the country
and the road splits there, one of two roads from Delphi,
another comes from Daulia.

OEDIPUS: How long ago is this?

JOCASTA: The news came to the city just before
you became king and all men's eyes looked to you.
What is it, Oedipus, that's in your mind?

OEDIPUS: What have you designed, O Zeus, to do with me?

JOCASTA: What is the thought that troubles your heart?

OEDIPUS: Don't ask me yet—tell me of Laius—
How did he look? How old or young was he?

JOCASTA: He was a tall man and his hair was grizzled
already—nearly white—and in his form
not unlike you.

OEDIPUS: O God, I think I have
called curses on myself in ignorance.

JOCASTA: What do you mean? I am terrified
when I look at you.

OEDIPUS: I have a deadly fear
that the old seer had eyes. You'll show me more
if you can tell me one more thing.

JOCASTA: I will.
I'm frightened,—but if I can understand,
I'll tell you all you ask.

OEDIPUS: How was his company?
Had he few with him when he went this journey,
or many servants, as would suit a prince?

JOCASTA: In all there were but five, and among them
a herald; and one carriage for the king.

OEDIPUS: It's plain—it's plain—who was it told you this?

JOCASTA: The only servant that escaped safe home.

OEDIPUS: Is he at home now?

JOCASTA: No, when he came home again
and saw you king and Laius was dead,

he came to me and touched my hand and begged
that I should send him to the fields to be
my shepherd and so he might see the city
as far off as he might. So I
sent him away. He was an honest man,
as slaves go, and was worthy of far more
than what he asked of me.

OEDIPUS: O, how I wish that he could come back quickly!

JOCASTA: He can. Why is your heart so set on this?

OEDIPUS: O dear Jocasta, I am full of fears
that I have spoken far too much; and therefore
I wish to see this shepherd.

JOCASTA: He will come;
but, Oedipus, I think I'm worthy too
to know what it is that disquiets you.

OEDIPUS: It shall not be kept from you, since my mind
has gone so far with its forebodings. Whom
should I confide in rather than you, who is there
of more importance to me who have passed
through such a fortune?
Polybus was my father, king of Corinth,
and Merope, the Dorian, my mother.
I was held greatest of the citizens
in Corinth till a curious chance befell me
as I shall tell you—curious, indeed,
but hardly worth the store I set upon it.
There was a dinner and at it a man,
a drunken man, accused me in his drink
of being bastard. I was furious
but held my temper under for that day.
Next day I went and taxed my parents with it;
they took the insult very ill from him,
the drunken fellow who had uttered it.
So I was comforted for their part, but
still this thing rankled always, for the story
crept about widely. And I went at last
to Pytho, though my parents did not know.
But Phoebus sent me home again unhonoured
in what I came to learn, but he foretold
other and desperate horrors to befall me,
that I was fated to lie with my mother,
and show to daylight an accursed breed
which men would not endure, and I was doomed
to be murderer of the father that begot me.
When I heard this I fled, and in the days
that followed I would measure from the stars
the whereabouts of Corinth—yes, I fled
to somewhere where I should not see fulfilled

the infamies told in that dreadful oracle.
And as I journeyed I came to the place
where, as you say, this king met with his death.
Jocasta, I will tell you the whole truth.
When I was near the branching of the crossroads,
going on foot, I was encountered by
a herald and a carriage with a man in it,
just as you tell me. He that led the way
and the old man himself wanted to thrust me
out of the road by force. I became angry
and struck the coachman who was pushing me.
When the old man saw this he watched his moment,
and as I passed he struck me from his carriage,
full on the head with his two pointed goad.
But he was paid in full and presently
my stick had struck him backwards from the car
and he rolled out of it. And then I killed them
all. If it happened there was any tie
of kinship twixt this man and Laius,
who is then now more miserable than I,
what man on earth so hated by the Gods,
since neither citizen nor foreigner
may welcome me at home or even greet me,
but drive me out of doors? And it is I,
I and no other have so cursed myself.
And I pollute the bed of him I killed
by the hands that killed him. Was I not born evil?
Am I not utterly unclean? I had to fly
and in my banishment not even see
my kindred nor set foot in my own country,
or otherwise my fate was to be yoked
in marriage with my mother and kill my father,
Polybus who begot me and had reared me.
Would not one rightly judge and say that on me
these things were sent by some malignant God?
O no, no, no—O holy majesty
of God on high, may I not see that day!
May I be gone out of men's sight before
I see the deadly taint of this disaster
come upon me.

CHORUS: Sir, we too fear these things. But until you see this man face to face and hear his story, hope.

OEDIPUS: Yes, I have just this much of hope—to wait until the herdsman comes.

JOCASTA: And when he comes, what do you want with him?

OEDIPUS: I'll tell you; if I find that his story is the same as yours, I at least will be clear of this guilt.

JOCASTA: Why what so particularly did you learn from my story?

OEDIPUS: You said that he spoke of highway *robbers* who killed Laius. Now if he uses the same number, it was not I who killed him. One man cannot be the same as many. But if he speaks of a man travelling alone, then clearly the burden of the guilt inclines towards me.

JOCASTA: Be sure, at least, that this was how he told the story. He cannot unsay it now, for everyone in the city heard it—not I alone. But, Oedipus, even if he diverges from what he said then, he shall never prove that the murder of Laius squares rightly with the prophecy—for Loxias declared that the king should be killed by his own son. And that poor creature did not kill him surely,—for he died himself first. So as far as prophecy goes, henceforward I shall not look to the right hand or the left.

OEDIPUS: Right. But yet, send someone for the peasant to bring him here; do not neglect it.

JOCASTA: I will send quickly. Now let me go indoors. I will do nothing except what pleases you.

[*Exeunt.*]

CHORUS: [*Strophe.*] May destiny ever find me
pious in word and deed
prescribed by the laws that live on high:
laws begotten in the clear air of heaven,
whose only father is Olympus;
no mortal nature brought them to birth,
no forgetfulness shall lull them to sleep;
for God is great in them and grows not old.

[*Antistrophe.*]

Insolence breeds the tyrant, insolence
if it is glutted with a surfeit, unseasonable, unprofitable,
climbs to the roof-top and plunges
sheer down to the ruin that must be,
and there its feet are no service.
But I pray that the God may never
abolish the eager ambition that profits the state.
For I shall never cease to hold the God as our protector.

[*Strophe.*]

If a man walks with haughtiness
of hand or word and gives no heed
to Justice and the shrines of Gods
despises—may an evil doom
smite him for his ill-starred pride of heart!—
if he reaps gains without justice
and will not hold from impiety
and his fingers itch for untouchable things.
When such things are done, what man shall contrive
to shield his soul from the shafts of the God?

When such deeds are held in honour,
why should I honour the Gods in the dance?

[*Antistrophe.*]

No longer to the holy place,
to the navel of earth I'll go
to worship, nor to Abae
nor to Olympia,[9]
unless the oracles are proved to fit,
for all men's hands to point at.
O Zeus, if you are rightly called
the sovereign lord, all-mastering,
let this not escape you nor your ever-living power!
The oracles concerning Laius
are old and dim and men regard them not.
Apollo is nowhere clear in honour; God's service perishes.

[*Enter* JOCASTA, *carrying garlands.*]

JOCASTA: Princes of the land, I have had the thought to go
to the Gods' temples, bringing in my hand
garlands and gifts of incense, as you see.
For Oedipus excites himself too much
at every sort of trouble, not conjecturing,
like a man of sense, what will be from what was,
but he is always at the speaker's mercy,
when he speaks terrors. I can do no good
by my advice, and so I came as suppliant
to you, Lycaean Apollo, who are nearest.
These are the symbols of my prayer and this
my prayer: grant us escape free of the curse.
Now when we look to him we are all afraid;
he's pilot of our ship and he is frightened.

[*Enter* MESSENGER.]

MESSENGER: Might I learn from you, sirs, where is the house of Oedipus? Or best of all, if you know, where is the king himself?

CHORUS: This is his house and he is within doors. This lady is his wife and mother of his children.

MESSENGER: God bless you, lady, and God bless your household! God bless Oedipus' noble wife!

JOCASTA: God bless you, sir, for your kind greeting! What do you want of us that you have come here? What have you to tell us?

MESSENGER: Good news, lady. Good for your house and for your husband.

JOCASTA: What is your news? Who sent you to us?

9. Mountain in Greece said to be the home of Zeus and the other principal gods. *Abae*: Site of one of Apollo's oracles.

MESSENGER: I come from Corinth and the news I bring will give you pleasure. Perhaps a little pain too.
JOCASTA: What is this news of double meaning?
MESSENGER: The people of the Isthmus[1] will choose Oedipus to be their king. That is the rumour there.
JOCASTA: But isn't their king still old Polybus?
MESSENGER: No. He is in his grave. Death has got him.
JOCASTA: Is that the truth? Is Oedipus' father dead?
MESSENGER: May I die myself if it be otherwise!
JOCASTA: [*To a* SERVANT.] Be quick and run to the King with the news! O oracles of the Gods, where are you now? It was from this man Oedipus fled, lest he should be his murderer! And now he is dead, in the course of nature, and not killed by Oedipus.

[*Enter* OEDIPUS.]

OEDIPUS: Dearest Jocasta, why have you sent for me?
JOCASTA: Listen to this man and when you hear reflect what is the outcome of the holy oracles of the Gods.
OEDIPUS: Who is he? What is his message for me?
JOCASTA: He is from Corinth and he tells us that your father Polybus is dead and gone.
OEDIPUS: What's this you say, sir? Tell me yourself.
MESSENGER: Since this is the first matter you want clearly told: Polybus has gone down to death. You may be sure of it.
OEDIPUS: By treachery or sickness?
MESSENGER: A small thing will put old bodies asleep.
OEDIPUS: So he died of sickness, it seems,—poor old man!
MESSENGER: Yes, and of age—the long years he had measured.
OEDIPUS: Ha! Ha! O dear Jocasta, why should one
look to the Pythian hearth?[2] Why should one look
to the birds screaming overhead? They prophesied
that I should kill my father! But he's dead,
and hidden deep in earth, and I stand here
who never laid a hand on spear against him,—
unless perhaps he died of longing for me,
and thus I am his murderer. But they,
the oracles, as they stand—he's taken them
away with him, they're dead as he himself is,
and worthless.
JOCASTA: That I told you before now.
OEDIPUS: You did, but I was misled by my fear.
JOCASTA: Then lay no more of them to heart, not one.
OEDIPUS: But surely I must fear my mother's bed?
JOCASTA: Why should man fear since chance is all in all

1. That is, Corinth, the city-state located on the isthmus connecting the Peloponnesian peninsula with mainland Greece. 2. Delphi.

for him, and he can clearly foreknow nothing?
Best to live lightly, as one can, unthinkingly.
As to your mother's marriage bed,—don't fear it.
Before this, in dreams too, as well as oracles,
many a man has lain with his own mother.
But he to whom such things are nothing bears
his life most easily.

OEDIPUS: All that you say would be said perfectly
if she were dead; but since she lives I must
still fear, although you talk so well, Jocasta.

JOCASTA: Still in your father's death there's light of comfort?

OEDIPUS: Great light of comfort; but I fear the living.

MESSENGER: Who is the woman that makes you afraid?

OEDIPUS: Merope, old man, Polybus' wife.

MESSENGER: What about her frightens the queen and you?

OEDIPUS: A terrible oracle, stranger, from the Gods.

MESSENGER: Can it be told? Or does the sacred law
forbid another to have knowledge of it?

OEDIPUS: O no! Once on a time Loxias said
that I should lie with my own mother and
take on my hands the blood of my own father.
And so for these long years I've lived away
from Corinth; it has been to my great happiness;
but yet it's sweet to see the face of parents.

MESSENGER: This was the fear which drove you out of Corinth?

OEDIPUS: Old man, I did not wish to kill my father.

MESSENGER: Why should I not free you from this fear, sir,
since I have come to you in all goodwill?

OEDIPUS: You would not find me thankless if you did.

MESSENGER: Why, it was just for this I brought the news,—
to earn your thanks when you had come safe home.

OEDIPUS: No, I will never come near my parents.

MESSENGER: Son,
it's very plain you don't know what you're doing.

OEDIPUS: What do you mean, old man? For God's sake, tell me.

MESSENGER: If your homecoming is checked by fears like these.

OEDIPUS: Yes, I'm afraid that Phoebus may prove right.

MESSENGER: The murder and the incest?

OEDIPUS: Yes, old man;
that is my constant terror.

MESSENGER: Do you know
that all your fears are empty?

OEDIPUS: How is that,
if they are father and mother and I their son?

MESSENGER: Because Polybus was no kin to you in blood.

OEDIPUS: What, was not Polybus my father?

MESSENGER: No more than I but just so much.

OEDIPUS: How can

my father be my father as much as one
that's nothing to me?

MESSENGER: Neither he nor I
begat you.

OEDIPUS: Why then did he call me son?

MESSENGER: A gift he took you from these hands of mine.

OEDIPUS: Did he love so much what he took from another's hand?

MESSENGER: His childlessness before persuaded him.

OEDIPUS: Was I a child you bought or found when I
was given to him?

MESSENGER: On Cithaeron's slopes
in the twisting thickets you were found.

OEDIPUS: And why
were you a traveller in those parts?

MESSENGER: I was
in charge of mountain flocks.

OEDIPUS: You were a shepherd?
A hireling vagrant?

MESSENGER: Yes, but at least at that time
the man that saved your life, son.

OEDIPUS: What ailed me when you took me in your arms?

MESSENGER: In that your ankles should be witnesses.

OEDIPUS: Why do you speak of that old pain?

MESSENGER: I loosed you;
the tendons of your feet were pierced and fettered,—

OEDIPUS: My swaddling clothes brought me a rare disgrace.

MESSENGER: So that from this you're called your present name.[3]

OEDIPUS: Was this my father's doing or my mother's?
For God's sake, tell me.

MESSENGER: I don't know, but he
who gave you to me has more knowledge than I.

OEDIPUS: You yourself did not find me then? You took me
from someone else?

MESSENGER: Yes, from another shepherd.

OEDIPUS: Who was he? Do you know him well enough
to tell?

MESSENGER: He was called Laius' man.

OEDIPUS: You mean the king who reigned here in the old days?

MESSENGER: Yes, he was that man's shepherd.

OEDIPUS: Is he alive
still, so that I could see him?

MESSENGER: You who live here
would know that best.

OEDIPUS: Do any of you here
know of this shepherd whom he speaks about

3. *Oedipus* means, literally, "swollen foot" (cf. lines 777–80).

in town or in the fields? Tell me. It's time
that this was found out once for all.
CHORUS: I think he is none other than the peasant
whom you have sought to see already; but
Jocasta here can tell us best of that.
OEDIPUS: Jocasta, do you know about this man
whom we have sent for? Is he the man he mentions?
JOCASTA: Why ask of whom he spoke? Don't give it heed;
nor try to keep in mind what has been said.
It will be wasted labour.
OEDIPUS: With such clues
I could not fail to bring my birth to light.
JOCASTA: I beg you—do not hunt this out—I beg you,
if you have any care for your own life.
What I am suffering is enough.
OEDIPUS: Keep up
your heart, Jocasta. Though I'm proved a slave,
thrice slave, and though my mother is thrice slave,
you'll not be shown to be of lowly lineage.
JOCASTA: O be persuaded by me, I entreat you;
do not do this.
OEDIPUS: I will not be persuaded to let be
the chance of finding out the whole thing clearly.
JOCASTA: It is because I wish you well that I
give you this counsel—and it's the best counsel.
OEDIPUS: Then the best counsel vexes me, and has
for some while since.
JOCASTA: O Oedipus, God help you!
God keep you from the knowledge of who you are!
OEDIPUS: Here, someone, go and fetch the shepherd for me;
and let her find her joy in her rich family!
JOCASTA: O Oedipus, unhappy Oedipus!
that is all I can call you, and the last thing
that I shall ever call you.

[*Exit.*]

CHORUS: Why has the queen gone, Oedipus, in wild
grief rushing from us? I am afraid that trouble
will break out of this silence.
OEDIPUS: Break out what will! I at least shall be
willing to see my ancestry, though humble.
Perhaps she is ashamed of my low birth,
for she has all a woman's high-flown pride.
But I account myself a child of Fortune,
beneficent Fortune, and I shall not be
dishonoured. She's the mother from whom I spring;
the months, my brothers, marked me, now as small,
and now again as mighty. Such is my breeding,

and I shall never prove so false to it,
as not to find the secret of my birth.

CHORUS: [*Strophe.*] If I am a prophet and wise of heart
you shall not fail, Cithaeron,
by the limitless sky, you shall not!—
to know at tomorrow's full moon
that Oedipus honours you,
as native to him and mother and nurse at once;
and that you are honoured in dancing by us, as finding favour in sight of our king.
Apollo, to whom we cry, find these things pleasing!

[*Antistrophe.*]
Who was it bore you, child? One of
the long-lived nymphs who lay with Pan[4]—
the father who treads the hills?
Or was she a bride of Loxias, your mother? The grassy slopes
are all of them dear to him. Or perhaps Cyllene's[5] king
or the Bacchants' God[6] that lives on the tops
of the hills received you a gift from some
one of the Helicon Nymphs,[7] with whom he mostly plays?

[*Enter an* OLD MAN, *led by* OEDIPUS' *servants.*]

OEDIPUS: If someone like myself who never met him
may make a guess,—I think this is the herdsman,
whom we were seeking. His old age is consonant
with the other. And besides, the men who bring him
I recognize as my own servants. You
perhaps may better me in knowledge since
you've seen the man before.

CHORUS: You can be sure
I recognize him. For if Laius
had ever an honest shepherd, this was he.

OEDIPUS: You, sir, from Corinth, I must ask you first,
is this the man you spoke of?

MESSENGER: This is he
before your eyes.

OEDIPUS: Old man, look here at me
and tell me what I ask you. Were you ever
a servant of King Laius?

HERDSMAN: I was,—
no slave he bought but reared in his own house.

OEDIPUS: What did you do as work? How did you live?

HERDSMAN: Most of my life was spent among the flocks.

4. God of nature; half man, half goat.
5. Mountain reputed to be the birthplace of Hermes, the messenger god.
6. Dionysus.
7. The Muses, nine sister goddesses who presided over poetry, music, and the arts.

OEDIPUS: In what part of the country did you live?
HERDSMAN: Cithaeron and the places near to it.
OEDIPUS: And somewhere there perhaps you knew this man?
HERDSMAN: What was his occupation? Who?
OEDIPUS: This man here,
have you had any dealings with him?
HERDSMAN: No—
not such that I can quickly call to mind.

MESSENGER: That is no wonder, master. But I'll make him remember what he does not know. For I know, that he well knows the country of Cithaeron, how he with two flocks, I with one kept company for three years—each year half a year—from spring till autumn time and then when winter came I drove my flocks to our fold home again and he to Laius' steadings. Well—am I right or not in what I said we did?

HERDSMAN: You're right—although it's a long time ago.
MESSENGER: Do you remember giving me a child
to bring up as my foster child?
HERDSMAN: What's this?
Why do you ask this question?
MESSENGER: Look old man,
here he is—here's the man who was that child!
HERDSMAN: Death take you! Won't you hold your tongue?
OEDIPUS: No, no,
do not find fault with him, old man. Your words
are more at fault than his.
HERDSMAN: O best of masters,
how do I give offense?
OEDIPUS: When you refuse
to speak about the child of whom he asks you.
HERDSMAN: He speaks out of his ignorance, without meaning.
OEDIPUS: If you'll not talk to gratify me, you
will talk with pain to urge you.
HERDSMAN: O please, sir,
don't hurt an old man, sir.
OEDIPUS: [*To the* SERVANTS.] Here, one of you,
twist his hands behind him.
HERDSMAN: Why, God help me, why?
What do you want to know?
OEDIPUS: You gave a child
to him,—the child he asked you of?
HERDSMAN: I did.
I wish I'd died the day I did.
OEDIPUS: You will
unless you tell me truly.
HERDSMAN: And I'll die
far worse if I should tell you.
OEDIPUS: This fellow
is bent on more delays, as it would seem.

HERDSMAN: O no, no! I have told you that I gave it.
OEDIPUS: Where did you get this child from? Was it your own or did you get it from another?
HERDSMAN: Not
my own at all; I had it from someone.
OEDIPUS: One of these citizens? or from what house?
HERDSMAN: O master, please—I beg you, master, please don't ask me more.
OEDIPUS: You're a dead man if I
ask you again.
HERDSMAN: It was one of the children
of Laius.
OEDIPUS: A slave? Or born in wedlock?
HERDSMAN: O God, I am on the brink of frightful speech.
OEDIPUS: And I of frightful hearing. But I must hear.
HERDSMAN: The child was called his child; but she within,
your wife would tell you best how all this was.
OEDIPUS: *She* gave it to you?
HERDSMAN: Yes, she did, my lord.
OEDIPUS: To do what with it?
HERDSMAN: Make away with it.
OEDIPUS: She was so hard—its mother?
HERDSMAN: Aye, through fear
of evil oracles.
OEDIPUS: Which?
HERDSMAN: They said that he
should kill his parents.
OEDIPUS: How was it that you
gave it away to this old man?
HERDSMAN: O master,
I pitied it, and thought that I could send it
off to another country and this man
was from another country. But he saved it
for the most terrible troubles. If you are
the man he says you are, you're bred to misery.
OEDIPUS: O, O, O, they will all come,
all come out clearly! Light of the sun, let me
look upon you no more after today!
I who first saw the light bred of a match
accursed, and accursed in my living
with them I lived with, cursed in my killing.

[*Exeunt all but the* CHORUS.]

CHORUS: [*Strophe*.] O generations of men, how I
count you as equal with those who live
not at all!
What man, what man on earth wins more
of happiness than a seeming
and after that turning away?
Oedipus, you are my pattern of this,

Oedipus, you and your fate!
Luckless Oedipus, whom of all men
I envy not at all.

[*Antistrophe.*]

In as much as he shot his bolt
beyond the others and won the prize
of happiness complete—
O Zeus—and killed and reduced to nought
the hooked taloned maid of the riddling speech,[8]
standing a tower against death for my land:
hence he was called my king and hence
was honoured the highest of all
honours; and hence he ruled
in the great city of Thebes.

[*Strophe.*]

But now whose tale is more miserable?
Who is there lives with a savager fate?
Whose troubles so reverse his life as his?

O Oedipus, the famous prince
for whom a great haven
the same both as father and son
sufficed for generation,
how, O how, have the furrows ploughed
by your father endured to bear you, poor wretch,
and hold their peace so long?

[*Antistrophe.*]

Time who sees all has found you out
against your will; judges your marriage accursed,
begetter and begot at one in it.

O child of Laius,
would I had never seen you.
I weep for you and cry
a dirge of lamentation.

To speak directly, I drew my breath
from you at the first and so now I lull
my mouth to sleep with your name.

[*Enter a* SECOND MESSENGER.]

SECOND MESSENGER: O Princes always honoured by our country,
what deeds you'll hear of and what horrors see,
what grief you'll feel, if you as true born Thebans

8. The Sphinx, who killed herself when Oedipus was the first to give a correct answer to her riddle: "What walks on four feet in the morning, on two at noon, and on three in the evening?" (cf. line 41n.).

care for the house of Labdacus' sons.[9]
Phasis nor Ister[1] cannot purge this house,
I think, with all their streams, such things
it hides, such evils shortly will bring forth
into the light, whether they will or not;
and troubles hurt the most
when they prove self-inflicted.

CHORUS: What we had known before did not fall short
of bitter groaning's worth; what's more to tell?

SECOND MESSENGER: Shortest to hear and tell—our glorious queen
Jocasta's dead.

CHORUS: Unhappy woman! How?

SECOND MESSENGER: By her own hand. The worst of what was done
you cannot know. You did not see the sight.
Yet in so far as I remember it
you'll hear the end of our unlucky queen.
When she came raging into the house she went
straight to her marriage bed, tearing her hair
with both her hands, and crying upon Laius
long dead—Do you remember, Laius,
that night long past which bred a child for us
to send you to your death and leave
a mother making children with her son?
And then she groaned and cursed the bed in which
she brought forth husband by her husband, children
by her own child, an infamous double bond.
How after that she died I do not know,—
for Oedipus distracted us from seeing.
He burst upon us shouting and we looked
to him as he paced frantically around,
begging us always: Give me a sword, I say,
to find this wife no wife, this mother's womb,
this field of double sowing whence I sprang
and where I sowed my children! As he raved
some god showed him the way—none of us there.
Bellowing terribly and led by some
invisible guide he rushed on the two doors,—
wrenching the hollow bolts out of their sockets,
he charged inside. There, there, we saw his wife
hanging, the twisted rope around her neck.
When he saw her, he cried out fearfully
and cut the dangling noose. Then, as she lay,
poor woman, on the ground, what happened after,
was terrible to see. He tore the brooches—
the gold chased[2] brooches fastening her robe—

9. Labdacus, king of Thebes, was father of Laïus and grandfather of Oedipus. 1. Phasis and Ister are rivers near Thebes. 2. Decorated with ornamental indentations.

away from her and lifting them up high
dashed them on his own eyeballs, shrieking out
such things as: they will never see the crime
I have committed or had done upon me!
Dark eyes, now in the days to come look on
forbidden faces, do not recognize
those whom you long for—with such imprecations
he struck his eyes again and yet again
with the brooches. And the bleeding eyeballs gushed
and stained his beard—no sluggish oozing drops
but a black rain and bloody hail poured down.
So it has broken—and not on one head
but troubles mixed for husband and for wife.
The fortune of the days gone by was true
good fortune—but today groans and destruction
and death and shame—of all ills can be named
not one is missing.

CHORUS: Is he now in any ease from pain?

SECOND MESSENGER: He shouts
for someone to unbar the doors and show him
to all the men of Thebes, his father's killer,
his mother's—no I cannot say the word,
it is unholy—for he'll cast himself,
out of the land, he says, and not remain
to bring a curse upon his house, the curse
he called upon it in his proclamation. But
he wants for strength, aye, and someone to guide him;
his sickness is too great to bear. You, too,
will be shown that. The bolts are opening.
Soon you will see a sight to waken pity
even in the horror of it.

[*Enter the blinded* OEDIPUS.]

CHORUS: This is a terrible sight for men to see!
I never found a worse!
Poor wretch, what madness came upon you!
What evil spirit leaped upon your life
to your ill-luck—a leap beyond man's strength!
Indeed I pity you, but I cannot
look at you, though there's much I want to ask
and much to learn and much to see.
I shudder at the sight of you.

OEDIPUS: O, O,
where am I going? Where is my voice
borne on the wind to and fro?
Spirit, how far have you sprung?

CHORUS: To a terrible place whereof men's ears
may not hear, nor their eyes behold it.

OEDIPUS: Darkness!
Horror of darkness enfolding, resistless, unspeakable visitant sped by an ill wind in haste!
Madness and stabbing pain and memory
of evil deeds I have done!
CHORUS: In such misfortunes it's no wonder
if double weighs the burden of your grief.
OEDIPUS: My friend,
you are the only one steadfast, the only one that attends on me;
you still stay nursing the blind man.
Your care is not unnoticed. I can know
your voice, although this darkness is my world.
CHORUS: Doer of dreadful deeds, how did you dare
so far to do despite to your own eyes?
what spirit urged you to it?
OEDIPUS: It was Apollo, friends, Apollo,
that brought this bitter bitterness, my sorrows to completion.
But the hand that struck me
was none but my own.
Why should I see
whose vision showed me nothing sweet to see?
CHORUS: These things are as you say.
OEDIPUS: What can I see to love?
What greeting can touch my ears with joy?
Take me away, and haste—to a place out of the way!
Take me away, my friends, the greatly miserable,
the most accursed, whom God too hates
above all men on earth!
CHORUS: Unhappy in your mind and your misfortune,
would I had never known you!
OEDIPUS: Curse on the man who took
the cruel bonds from off my legs, as I lay in the field.
He stole me from death and saved me,
no kindly service.
Had I died then
I would not be so burdensome to friends.
CHORUS: I, too, could have wished it had been so.
OEDIPUS: Then I would not have come
to kill my father and marry my mother infamously.
Now I am godless and child of impurity,
begetter in the same seed that created my wretched self.
If there is any ill worse than ill,
that is the lot of Oedipus.
CHORUS: I cannot say your remedy was good;
you would be better dead than blind and living.
OEDIPUS: What I have done here was best done—don't tell me
otherwise, do not give me further counsel.
I do not know with what eyes I could look

upon my father when I die and go
under the earth, nor yet my wretched mother—
those two to whom I have done things deserving
worse punishment than hanging. Would the sight
of children, bred as mine are, gladden me?
No, not these eyes, never. And my city,
its towers and sacred places of the Gods,
of these I robbed my miserable self
when I commanded all to drive *him* out,
the criminal since proved by God impure
and of the race of Laius.
To this guilt I bore witness against myself—
with what eyes shall I look upon my people?
No. If there were a means to choke the fountain
of hearing I would not have stayed my hand
from locking up my miserable carcase,
seeing and hearing nothing; it is sweet
to keep our thoughts out of the range of hurt.

Cithaeron, why did you receive me? why
having received me did you not kill me straight?
And so I had not shown to men my birth.

O Polybus and Corinth and the house,
the old house that I used to call my father's—
what fairness you were nurse to, and what foulness
festered beneath! Now I am found to be
a sinner and a son of sinners. Crossroads,
and hidden glade, oak and the narrow way
at the crossroads, that drank my father's blood
offered you by my hands, do you remember
still what I did as you looked on, and what
I did when I came here? O marriage, marriage!
you bred me and again when you had bred
bred children of your child and showed to men
brides, wives and mothers and the foulest deeds
that can be in this world of ours.

Come—it's unfit to say what is unfit
to do.—I beg of you in God's name hide me
somewhere outside your country, yes, or kill me,
or throw me into the sea, to be forever
out of your sight. Approach and deign to touch me
for all my wretchedness, and do not fear.
No man but I can bear my evil doom.

CHORUS: Here Creon comes in fit time to perform
or give advice in what you ask of us.
Creon is left sole ruler in your stead.

OEDIPUS: Creon! Creon! What shall I say to him?

How can I justly hope that he will trust me?
In what is past I have been proved towards him
an utter liar.

[*Enter* CREON.]

CREON: Oedipus, I've come
not so that I might laugh at you nor taunt you
with evil of the past. But if you still
are without shame before the face of men
reverence at least the flame that gives all life,
our Lord the Sun, and do not show unveiled
to him pollution such that neither land
nor holy rain nor light of day can welcome.

[*To a* SERVANT.]

Be quick and take him in. It is most decent
that only kin should see and hear the troubles
of kin.

OEDIPUS: I beg you, since you've torn me from
my dreadful expectations and have come
in a most noble spirit to a man
that has used you vilely—do a thing for me.
I shall speak for your own good, not for my own.

CREON: What do you need that you would ask of me?

OEDIPUS: Drive me from here with all the speed you can
to where I may not hear a human voice.

CREON: Be sure, I would have done this had not I
wished first of all to learn from the God the course
of action I should follow.

OEDIPUS: But his word
has been quite clear to let the parricide,
the sinner, die.

CREON: Yes, that indeed was said.
But in the present need we had best discover
what we should do.

OEDIPUS: And will you ask about
a man so wretched?

CREON: Now even you will trust
the God.

OEDIPUS: So. I command you—and will beseech you—
to her that lies inside that house give burial
as you would have it; she is yours and rightly
you will perform the rites for her. For me—
never let this my father's city have me
living a dweller in it. Leave me live
in the mountains where Cithaeron is, that's called
my mountain, which my mother and my father
while they were living would have made my tomb.

So I may die by their decree who sought
indeed to kill me. Yet I know this much:
no sickness and no other thing will kill me.
I would not have been saved from death if not
for some strange evil fate. Well, let my fate
go where it will.
Creon, you need not care
about my sons; they're men and so wherever
they are, they will not lack a livelihood.
But my two girls—so sad and pitiful—
whose table never stood apart from mine,
and everything I touched they always shared—
O Creon, have a thought for them! And most
I wish that you might suffer me to touch them
and sorrow with them.

[*Enter* ANTIGONE *and* ISMENE, OEDIPUS' *two daughters.*]

O my lord! O true noble Creon! Can I
really be touching them, as when I saw?
What shall I say?
Yes, I can hear them sobbing—my two darlings!
and Creon has had pity and has sent me
what I loved most?
Am I right?

CREON: You're right: it was I gave you this
because I knew from old days how you loved them
as I see now.

OEDIPUS: God bless you for it, Creon,
and may God guard you better on your road
than he did me!
O children,
where are you? Come here, come to my hands,
a brother's hands which turned your father's eyes,
those bright eyes you knew once, to what you see,
a father seeing nothing, knowing nothing,
begetting you from his own source of life.
I weep for you—I cannot see your faces—
I weep when I think of the bitterness
there will be in your lives, how you must live
before the world. At what assemblages
of citizens will you make one? to what
gay company will you go and not come home
in tears instead of sharing in the holiday?
And when you're ripe for marriage, who will he be,
the man who'll risk to take such infamy
as shall cling to my children, to bring hurt
on them and those that marry with them? What
curse is not there? "Your father killed his father

and sowed the seed where he had sprung himself
and begot you out of the womb that held him."
These insults you will hear. Then who will marry you?
No one, my children; clearly you are doomed
to waste away in barrenness unmarried.
Son of Menoeceus,[3] since you are all the father
left these two girls, and we, their parents, both
are dead to them—do not allow them wander
like beggars, poor and husbandless.
They are of your own blood.
And do not make them equal with myself
in wretchedness; for you can see them now
so young, so utterly alone, save for you only.
Touch my hand, noble Creon, and say yes.
If you were older, children, and were wiser,
there's much advice I'd give you. But as it is,
let this be what you pray: give me a life
wherever there is opportunity
to live, and better life than was my father's.

CREON: Your tears have had enough of scope; now go within the house.
OEDIPUS: I must obey, though bitter of heart.
CREON: In season, all is good.
OEDIPUS: Do you know on what conditions I obey?
CREON: You tell me them,
and I shall know them when I hear.
OEDIPUS: That you shall send me out
to live away from Thebes.
CREON: That gift you must ask of the Gods.
OEDIPUS: But I'm now hated by the Gods.
CREON: So quickly you'll obtain your prayer.
OEDIPUS: You consent then?
CREON: What I do not mean, I do not use to say.
OEDIPUS: Now lead me away from here.
CREON: Let go the children, then, and come.
OEDIPUS: Do not take them from me.
CREON: Do not seek to be master in everything,
for the things you mastered did not follow you throughout your life.

[*As* CREON *and* OEDIPUS *go out.*]

CHORUS: You that live in my ancestral Thebes, behold this Oedipus,—
him who knew the famous riddles and was a man most masterful;
not a citizen who did not look with envy on his lot—
see him now and see the breakers of misfortune swallow him!
Look upon that last day always. Count no mortal happy till
he has passed the final limit of his life secure from pain.

c. 429 BCE

3. Father of Creon and Jocasta.

OSCAR WILDE
(1854–1900)

The Importance of Being Earnest

Born and raised in Dublin, Oscar Wilde studied classical languages at Trinity College and took his degree from Oxford in 1878. While at Oxford, he was captivated by the aesthetic theories of John Ruskin and Walter Pater. Upon graduation, he moved to London to write, soon becoming both a much-quoted wit and the most visible exponent of the "art for art's sake" movement. Wilde wrote criticism, poetry, and fiction, most notably the novel *The Picture of Dorian Gray* (1891). However, he achieved his greatest success as a comic dramatist, with clever, witty plays such as *Lady Windermere's Fan* (1892), *A Woman of No Importance* (1893), and his masterpiece *The Importance of Being Earnest* (1895). At the height of his career, Wilde was accused of homosexuality by his lover's father, the marquess of Queensbury; he sued for libel, lost the case, and was imprisoned for two years, a ruinous experience that inspired his best-known poem, "The Ballad of Reading Gaol" (1898). Upon his release, he emigrated to France under an assumed name, dying there three years later. "In this world," he wrote, "there are only two tragedies. One is not getting what one wants, and the other is getting it."

CHARACTERS

ALGERNON MONCRIEFF
LANE
ERNEST WORTHING
LADY AUGUSTA BRACKNELL
GWENDOLEN FAIRFAX
MISS PRISM
CECILY CARDEW
CANON CHASUBLE
MERRIMAN

ACT I

SCENE: *Morning room in* ALGERNON*'s flat in Half-Moon Street.*[1]

The room is luxuriously and artistically furnished. The sound of a piano is heard in the adjoining room.

[LANE *is arranging afternoon tea on the table, and after the music has ceased,* ALGERNON *enters.*]

ALGERNON: Did you hear what I was playing, Lane?

LANE: I didn't think it polite to listen, sir.

ALGERNON: I'm sorry for that, for your sake. I don't play accurately—anyone can play accurately—but I play with wonderful expression. As far as the piano is concerned, sentiment is my forte. I keep science for Life.

1. Like many of the addresses in the play, Half-Moon Street is in Mayfair, a very fashionable section of London. It runs north from Piccadilly near Hyde Park.

LANE: Yes, sir.

ALGERNON: And, speaking of the science of Life, have you got the cucumber sandwiches cut for Lady Bracknell?

LANE: Yes, sir. [*Hands them on a salver.*]

ALGERNON: [*Inspects them, takes two, and sits down on the sofa.*] Oh! . . . by the way, Lane, I see from your book that on Thursday night, when Lord Shoreham and Mr. Worthing were dining with me, eight bottles of champagne are entered as having been consumed.

LANE: Yes, sir; eight bottles and a pint.

ALGERNON: Why is it that at a bachelor's establishment the servants invariably drink the champagne? I ask merely for information.

LANE: I attribute it to the superior quality of the wine, sir. I have often observed that in married households the champagne is rarely of a first-rate brand.

ALGERNON: Good heavens! Is marriage so demoralizing as that?

LANE: I believe it *is* a very pleasant state, sir. I have had very little experience of it myself up to the present. I have only been married once. That was in consequence of a misunderstanding between myself and a young person.

ALGERNON: [*Languidly.*] I don't know that I am much interested in your family life, Lane.

LANE: No, sir; it is not a very interesting subject. I never think of it myself.

ALGERNON: Very natural, I am sure. That will do, Lane, thank you.

LANE: Thank you, sir. [LANE *goes out.*]

ALGERNON: Lane's views on marriage seem somewhat lax. Really, if the lower orders don't set us a good example, what on earth is the use of them? They seem, as a class, to have absolutely no sense of moral responsibility.

[*Enter* LANE.]

LANE: Mr. Ernest Worthing.

[*Enter* JACK. LANE *goes out.*]

ALGERNON: How are you, my dear Ernest? What brings you up to town?

JACK: Oh, pleasure, pleasure! What else should bring one anywhere? Eating as usual, I see, Algy!

ALGERNON: [*Stiffly.*] I believe it is customary in good society to take some slight refreshment at five o'clock. Where have you been since last Thursday?

JACK: [*Sitting down on the sofa.*] In the country.

ALGERNON: What on earth do you do there?

JACK: [*Pulling off his gloves.*] When one is in town one amuses oneself. When one is in the country one amuses other people. It is excessively boring.

ALGERNON: And who are the people you amuse?

JACK: [*Airily.*] Oh, neighbors, neighbors.

ALGERNON: Got nice neighbors in your part of Shropshire?

JACK: Perfectly horrid! Never speak to one of them.

ALGERNON: How immensely you must amuse them! [*Goes over and takes sandwich.*] By the way, Shropshire is your county, is it not?

JACK: Eh? Shropshire?[2] Yes, of course. Hallo! Why all these cups? Why cucumber sandwiches? Why such reckless extravagance in one so young? Who is coming to tea?

ALGERNON: Oh! merely Aunt Augusta and Gwendolen.

JACK: How perfectly delightful!

ALGERNON: Yes, that is all very well; but I am afraid Aunt Augusta won't quite approve of your being here.

JACK: May I ask why?

ALGERNON: My dear fellow, the way you flirt with Gwendolen is perfectly disgraceful. It is almost as bad as the way Gwendolen flirts with you.

JACK: I am in love with Gwendolen. I have come up to town expressly to propose to her.

ALGERNON: I thought you had come up for pleasure? . . . I call that business.

JACK: How utterly unromantic you are!

ALGERNON: I really don't see anything romantic in proposing. It is very romantic to be in love. But there is nothing romantic about a definite proposal. Why, one may be accepted. One usually is, I believe. Then the excitement is all over. The very essence of romance is uncertainty. If ever I get married, I'll certainly try to forget the fact.

JACK: I have no doubt about that, dear Algy. The divorce court was specially invented for people whose memories are so curiously constituted.

ALGERNON: Oh! there is no use speculating on that subject. Divorces are made in heaven— [JACK *puts out his hand to take a sandwich.* ALGERNON *at once interferes.*] Please don't touch the cucumber sandwiches. They are ordered specially for Aunt Augusta. [*Takes one and eats it.*]

JACK: Well, you have been eating them all the time.

ALGERNON: That is quite a different matter. She is my aunt. [*Takes plate from below.*] Have some bread and butter. The bread and butter is for Gwendolen. Gwendolen is devoted to bread and butter.

JACK: [*Advancing to table and helping himself.*] And very good bread and butter it is too.

ALGERNON: Well, my dear fellow, you need not eat as if you were going to eat it all. You behave as if you were married to her already. You are not married to her already, and I don't think you ever will be.

JACK: Why on earth do you say that?

ALGERNON: Well, in the first place, girls never marry the men they flirt with. Girls don't think it right.

JACK: Oh, that is nonsense!

ALGERNON: It isn't. It is a great truth. It accounts for the extraordinary number of bachelors that one sees all over the place. In the second place, I don't give my consent.

JACK: Your consent!

ALGERNON: My dear fellow, Gwendolen is my first cousin. And before I allow you to marry her, you will have to clear up the whole question of Cecily. [*Rings bell.*]

2. County on the Welsh border, to the west of London; Jack's country place is actually in Hertfordshire, to the north of London.

JACK: Cecily! What on earth do you mean? What do you mean, Algy, by Cecily? I don't know anyone of the name of Cecily.

[*Enter* LANE.]

ALGERNON: Bring me that cigarette case Mr. Worthing left in the smoking-room the last time he dined here.
LANE: Yes, sir. [LANE *goes out*.]
JACK: Do you mean to say you have had my cigarette case all this time? I wish to goodness you had let me know. I have been writing frantic letters to Scotland Yard about it. I was very nearly offering a large reward.
ALGERNON: Well, I wish you would offer one. I happen to be more than usually hard up.
JACK: There is no good offering a large reward now that the thing is found.

[*Enter* LANE *with the cigarette case on a salver.* ALGERNON *takes it at once.* LANE *goes out*.]

ALGERNON: I think that is rather mean of you, Ernest, I must say. [*Opens case and examines it.*] However, it makes no matter, for, now that I look at the inscription inside, I find that the thing isn't yours after all.
JACK: Of course it's mine. [*Moving to him.*] You have seen me with it a hundred times, and you have no right whatsoever to read what is written inside. It is a very ungentlemanly thing to read a private cigarette case.
ALGERNON: Oh! it is absurd to have a hard-and-fast rule about what one should read and what one shouldn't. More than half of modern culture depends on what one shouldn't read.
JACK: I am quite aware of the fact, and I don't propose to discuss modern culture. It isn't the sort of thing one should talk of in private. I simply want my cigarette case back.
ALGERNON: Yes; but this isn't your cigarette case. This cigarette case is a present from someone of the name of Cecily, and you said you didn't know anyone of that name.
JACK: Well, if you want to know, Cecily happens to be my aunt.
ALGERNON: Your aunt!
JACK: Yes. Charming old lady she is, too. Lives at Tunbridge Wells.[3] Just give it back to me, Algy.
ALGERNON: [*Retreating to back of sofa.*] But why does she call herself Cecily if she is your aunt and lives at Tunbridge Wells? [*Reading.*] "From little Cecily with her fondest love."
JACK: [*Moving to sofa and kneeling upon it.*] My dear fellow, what on earth is there in that? Some aunts are tall, some aunts are not tall. That is a matter that surely an aunt may be allowed to decide for herself. You seem to think that every aunt should be exactly like your aunt! That is absurd! For heaven's sake give me back my cigarette case. [*Follows* ALGY *round the room.*]
ALGERNON: Yes. But why does your aunt call you her uncle? "From little Cecily, with her fondest love to her dear Uncle Jack." There is no objection, I admit, to an aunt being a small aunt, but why an aunt, no matter what her size may

3. Resort town in Kent, southeast of London.

be, should call her own nephew her uncle, I can't quite make out. Besides, your name isn't Jack at all; it is Ernest.

JACK: It isn't Ernest; it's Jack.

ALGERNON: You have always told me it was Ernest. I have introduced you to everyone as Ernest. You answer to the name of Ernest. You look as if your name was Ernest. You are the most earnest looking person I ever saw in my life. It is perfectly absurd your saying that your name isn't Ernest. It's on your cards. Here is one of them. [*Taking it from case.*] "Mr. Ernest Worthing, B. 4, The Albany."[4] I'll keep this as a proof that your name is Ernest if ever you attempt to deny it to me, or to Gwendolen, or to anyone else. [*Puts the card in his pocket.*]

JACK: Well, my name is Ernest in town and Jack in the country, and the cigarette case was given to me in the country.

ALGERNON: Yes, but that does not account for the fact that your small Aunt Cecily, who lives at Tunbridge Wells, calls you her dear uncle. Come, old boy, you had much better have the thing out at once.

JACK: My dear Algy, you talk exactly as if you were a dentist. It is very vulgar to talk like a dentist when one isn't a dentist. It produces a false impression.

ALGERNON: Well, that is exactly what dentists always do. Now, go on! Tell me the whole thing. I may mention that I have always suspected you of being a confirmed and secret Bunburyist; and I am quite sure of it now.

JACK: Bunburyist? What on earth do you mean by a Bunburyist?

ALGERNON: I'll reveal to you the meaning of that incomparable expression as soon as you are kind enough to inform me why you are Ernest in town and Jack in the country.

JACK: Well, produce my cigarette case first.

ALGERNON: Here it is. [*Hands cigarette case.*] Now produce your explanation, and pray make it improbable. [*Sits on sofa.*]

JACK: My dear fellow, there is nothing improbable about my explanation at all. In fact it's perfectly ordinary. Old Mr. Thomas Cardew, who adopted me when I was a little boy, made me in his will guardian to his granddaughter, Miss Cecily Cardew. Cecily, who addresses me as her uncle from motives of respect that you could not possibly appreciate, lives at my place in the country under the charge of her admirable governess, Miss Prism.

ALGERNON: Where is that place in the country, by the way?

JACK: That is nothing to you, dear boy. You are not going to be invited. . . . I may tell you candidly that the place is not in Shropshire.

ALGERNON: I suspected that, my dear fellow! I have Bunburyed all over Shropshire on two separate occasions. Now, go on. Why are you Ernest in town and Jack in the country?

JACK: My dear Algy, I don't know whether you will be able to understand my real motives. You are hardly serious enough. When one is placed in the position of guardian, one has to adopt a very high moral tone on all subjects. It's one's duty to do so. And as a high moral tone can hardly be said to conduce

4. Apartment building for single gentlemen on Piccadilly, east of Algernon's flat.

very much to either one's health or one's happiness, in order to get up to town I have always pretended to have a younger brother of the name of Ernest, who lives in the Albany, and gets into the most dreadful scrapes. That, my dear Algy, is the whole truth pure and simple.

ALGERNON: The truth is rarely pure and never simple. Modern life would be very tedious if it were either, and modern literature a complete impossibility!

JACK: That wouldn't be at all a bad thing.

ALGERNON: Literary criticism is not your forte, my dear fellow. Don't try it. You should leave that to people who haven't been at a university. They do it so well in the daily papers. What you really are is a Bunburyist. I was quite right in saying you were a Bunburyist. You are one of the most advanced Bunburyists I know.

JACK: What on earth do you mean?

ALGERNON: You have invented a very useful young brother called Ernest, in order that you may be able to come up to town as often as you like. I have invented an invaluable permanent invalid called Bunbury, in order that I may be able to go down into the country whenever I choose. Bunbury is perfectly invaluable. If it wasn't for Bunbury's extraordinary bad health, for instance, I wouldn't be able to dine with you at Willis's[5] tonight, for I have been really engaged to Aunt Augusta for more than a week.

JACK: I haven't asked you to dine with me anywhere tonight.

ALGERNON: I know. You are absurdly careless about sending out invitations. It is very foolish of you. Nothing annoys people so much as not receiving invitations.

JACK: You had much better dine with your Aunt Augusta.

ALGERNON: I haven't the smallest intention of doing anything of the kind. To begin with, I dined there on Monday, and once a week is quite enough to dine with one's own relations. In the second place, whenever I do dine there I am always treated as a member of the family, and sent down with either no woman at all, or two. In the third place, I know perfectly well whom she will place me next to, tonight. She will place me next Mary Farquhar, who always flirts with her own husband across the dinner table. That is not very pleasant. Indeed, it is not even decent . . . and that sort of thing is enormously on the increase. The amount of women in London who flirt with their own husbands is perfectly scandalous. It looks so bad. It is simply washing one's clean linen in public. Besides, now that I know you to be a confirmed Bunburyist, I naturally want to talk to you about Bunburying. I want to tell you the rules.

JACK: I'm not a Bunburyist at all. If Gwendolen accepts me, I am going to kill my brother, indeed I think I'll kill him in any case. Cecily is a little too much interested in him. It is rather a bore. So I am going to get rid of Ernest. And I strongly advise you to do the same with Mr. . . . with your invalid friend who has the absurd name.

ALGERNON: Nothing will induce me to part with Bunbury, and if you ever get married, which seems to me extremely problematic, you will be very glad

5. Well-known restaurant on King Street, off St. James's Street, near Piccadilly.

to know Bunbury. A man who marries without knowing Bunbury has a very tedious time of it.

JACK: That is nonsense. If I marry a charming girl like Gwendolen, and she is the only girl I ever saw in my life that I would marry, I certainly won't want to know Bunbury.

ALGERNON: Then your wife will. You don't seem to realize, that in married life three is company and two is none.

JACK: [*Sententiously.*] That, my dear young friend, is the theory that the corrupt French drama has been propounding for the last fifty years.[6]

ALGERNON: Yes; and that the happy English home has proved in half the time.

JACK: For heaven's sake, don't try to be cynical. It's perfectly easy to be cynical.

ALGERNON: My dear fellow, it isn't easy to be anything nowadays. There's such a lot of beastly competition about. [*The sound of an electric bell is heard.*] Ah! that must be Aunt Augusta. Only relatives, or creditors, ever ring in that Wagnerian manner.[7] Now, if I get her out of the way for ten minutes, so that you can have an opportunity for proposing to Gwendolen, may I dine with you tonight at Willis's?

JACK: I suppose so, if you want to.

ALGERNON: Yes, but you must be serious about it. I hate people who are not serious about meals. It is so shallow of them.

[*Enter* LANE.]

LANE: Lady Bracknell and Miss Fairfax.

[ALGERNON *goes forward to meet them. Enter* LADY BRACKNELL *and* GWENDOLEN.]

LADY BRACKNELL: Good afternoon, dear Algernon, I hope you are behaving very well.

ALGERNON: I'm feeling very well, Aunt Augusta.

LADY BRACKNELL: That's not quite the same thing. In fact the two things rarely go together. [*Sees* JACK *and bows to him with icy coldness.*]

ALGERNON: [*To* GWENDOLEN.] Dear me, you are smart![8]

GWENDOLEN: I am always smart! Aren't I, Mr. Worthing?

JACK: You're quite perfect, Miss Fairfax.

GWENDOLEN: Oh! I hope I am not that. It would leave no room for developments, and I intend to develop in many directions. [GWENDOLEN *and* JACK *sit down together in the corner.*]

LADY BRACKNELL: I'm sorry if we are a little late, Algernon, but I was obliged to call on dear Lady Harbury. I hadn't been there since her poor husband's death. I never saw a woman so altered; she looks quite twenty years younger. And now I'll have a cup of tea, and one of those nice cucumber sandwiches you promised me.

6. Starting in the mid-nineteenth century, the French produced plays dealing with such subjects as adultery, prostitution, and illegitimacy. The heavily censored English theater either avoided such subjects or dealt with them more cautiously.

7. Many early listeners to the music of Richard Wagner found it extremely loud and, consequently, unpleasantly demanding. 8. That is, neat and stylish in appearance.

ALGERNON: Certainly, Aunt Augusta. [*Goes over to teatable.*]

LADY BRACKNELL: Won't you come and sit here, Gwendolen?

GWENDOLEN: Thanks, mamma, I'm quite comfortable where I am.

ALGERNON: [*Picking up empty plate in horror.*] Good heavens! Lane! Why are there no cucumber sandwiches? I ordered them specially.

LANE: [*Gravely.*] There were no cucumbers in the market this morning, sir. I went down twice.

ALGERNON: No cucumbers!

LANE: No, sir. Not even for ready money.

ALGERNON: That will do, Lane, thank you.

LANE: Thank you, sir.

ALGERNON: I am greatly distressed, Aunt Augusta, about there being no cucumbers, not even for ready money.

LADY BRACKNELL: It really makes no matter, Algernon. I had some crumpets with Lady Harbury, who seems to me to be living entirely for pleasure now.

ALGERNON: I hear her hair has turned quite gold from grief.

LADY BRACKNELL: It certainly has changed its color. From what cause I, of course, cannot say. [ALGERNON *crosses and hands tea.*] Thank you. I've quite a treat for you tonight, Algernon. I am going to send you down with Mary Farquhar. She is such a nice woman, and so attentive to her husband. It's delightful to watch them.

ALGERNON: I am afraid, Aunt Augusta, I shall have to give up the pleasure of dining with you tonight after all.

LADY BRACKNELL: [*Frowning.*] I hope not, Algernon. It would put my table completely out. Your uncle would have to dine upstairs. Fortunately he is accustomed to that.

ALGERNON: It is a great bore, and, I need hardly say, a terrible disappointment to me, but the fact is I have just had a telegram to say that my poor friend Bunbury is very ill again. [*Exchanges glances with* JACK.] They seem to think I should be with him.

LADY BRACKNELL: It is very strange. This Mr. Bunbury seems to suffer from curiously bad health.

ALGERNON: Yes; poor Bunbury is a dreadful invalid.

LADY BRACKNELL: Well, I must say, Algernon, that I think it is high time that Mr. Bunbury made up his mind whether he was going to live or to die. This shilly-shallying with the question is absurd. Nor do I in any way approve of the modern sympathy with invalids. I consider it morbid. Illness of any kind is hardly a thing to be encouraged in others. Health is the primary duty of life. I am always telling that to your poor uncle, but he never seems to take much notice . . . as far as any improvement in his ailments goes. I should be obliged if you would ask Mr. Bunbury, from me, to be kind enough not to have a relapse on Saturday, for I rely on you to arrange my music for me. It is my last reception, and one wants something that will encourage conversation, particularly at the end of the season when everyone has practically said whatever they had to say, which, in most cases, was probably not much.

ALGERNON: I'll speak to Bunbury, Aunt Augusta, if he is still conscious, and I think I can promise you he'll be all right by Saturday. Of course the music is a great difficulty. You see, if one plays good music, people don't listen, and if one plays bad music, people don't talk. But I'll run over the program I've drawn out, if you will kindly come into the next room for a moment.

LADY BRACKNELL: Thank you, Algernon. It is very thoughtful of you. [*Rising, and following* ALGERNON.] I'm sure the program will be delightful, after a few expurgations. French songs I cannot possibly allow. People always seem to think that they are improper, and either look shocked, which is vulgar, or laugh, which is worse. But German sounds a thoroughly respectable language, and indeed, I believe is so. Gwendolen, you will accompany me.

GWENDOLEN: Certainly, mamma.

[LADY BRACKNELL *and* ALGERNON *go into the music room,* GWENDOLEN *remains behind.*]

JACK: Charming day it has been, Miss Fairfax.

GWENDOLEN: Pray don't talk to me about the weather, Mr. Worthing. Whenever people talk to me about the weather, I always feel quite certain that they mean something else. And that makes me so nervous.

JACK: I do mean something else.

GWENDOLWN: I thought so. In fact, I am never wrong.

JACK: And I would like to be allowed to take advantage of Lady Bracknell's temporary absence . . .

GWENDOLEN: I would certainly advise you to do so. Mamma has a way of coming back suddenly into a room that I have often had to speak to her about.

JACK: [*Nervously.*] Miss Fairfax, ever since I met you I have admired you more than any girl . . . I have ever met since . . . I met you.

GWENDOLEN: Yes, I am quite aware of the fact. And I often wish that in public, at any rate, you had been more demonstrative. For me you have always had an irresistible fascination. Even before I met you I was far from indifferent to you. [JACK *looks at her in amazement.*] We live, as I hope you know, Mr. Worthing, in an age of ideals. The fact is constantly mentioned in the more expensive monthly magazines, and has reached the provincial pulpits, I am told: and my ideal has always been to love someone of the name of Ernest. There is something in that name that inspires absolute confidence. The moment Algernon first mentioned to me that he had a friend called Ernest, I knew I was destined to love you.

JACK: You really love me, Gwendolen?

GWENDOLEN: Passionately!

JACK: Darling! You don't know how happy you've made me.

GWENDOLEN: My own Ernest!

JACK: But you don't really mean to say that you couldn't love me if my name wasn't Ernest?

GWENDOLEN: But your name is Ernest.

JACK: Yes, I know it is. But supposing it was something else? Do you mean to say you couldn't love me then?

GWENDOLEN: [*Glibly.*] Ah! that is clearly a metaphysical speculation, and like most metaphysical speculations has very little reference at all to the actual facts of real life, as we know them.

JACK: Personally, darling, to speak quite candidly, I don't much care about the name of Ernest . . . I don't think the name suits me at all.

GWENDOLEN: It suits you perfectly. It is a divine name. It has a music of its own. It produces vibrations.

JACK: Well, really, Gwendolen, I must say that I think there are lots of other much nicer names. I think Jack, for instance, a charming name.

GWENDOLEN: Jack? . . . No, there is very little music in the name Jack, if any at all, indeed. It does not thrill. It produces absolutely no vibrations. . . . I have known several Jacks, and they all, without exception, were more than usually plain. Besides, Jack is a notorious domesticity for John! And I pity any woman who is married to a man called John. She would probably never be allowed to know the entrancing pleasure of a single moment's solitude. The only really safe name is Ernest.

JACK: Gwendolen, I must get christened at once—I mean we must get married at once. There is no time to be lost.

GWENDOLEN: Married, Mr. Worthing?

JACK: [*Astounded.*] Well . . . surely. You know that I love you, and you led me to believe, Miss Fairfax, that you were not absolutely indifferent to me.

GWENDOLEN: I adore you. But you haven't proposed to me yet. Nothing has been said at all about marriage. The subject has not even been touched on.

JACK: Well . . . may I propose to you now?

GWENDOLEN: I think it would be an admirable opportunity. And to spare you any possible disappointment, Mr. Worthing, I think it only fair to tell you quite frankly beforehand that I am fully determined to accept you.

JACK: Gwendolen!

GWENDOLEN: Yes, Mr. Worthing, what have you got to say to me?

JACK: You know what I have got to say to you.

GWENDOLEN: Yes, but you don't say it.

JACK: Gwendolen, will you marry me? [*Goes on his knees.*]

GWENDOLEN: Of course I will, darling. How long you have been about it! I am afraid you have had very little experience in how to propose.

JACK: My own one, I have never loved anyone in the world but you.

GWENDOLEN: Yes, but men often propose for practice. I know my brother Gerald does. All my girlfriends tell me so. What wonderfully blue eyes you have, Ernest! They are quite, quite blue. I hope you will always look at me just like that, especially when there are other people present.

[*Enter* LADY BRACKNELL.]

LADY BRACKNELL: Mr. Worthing! Rise, sir, from this semi-recumbent posture. It is most indecorous.

GWENDOLEN: Mamma! [*He tries to rise; she restrains him.*] I must beg you to retire. This is no place for you. Besides, Mr. Worthing has not quite finished yet.

LADY BRACKNELL: Finished what, may I ask?

GWENDOLEN: I am engaged to Mr. Worthing, mamma.

[*They rise together.*]

LADY BRACKNELL: Pardon me, you are not engaged to anyone. When you do become engaged to someone, I, or your father, should his health permit him, will inform you of the fact. An engagement should come on a young girl as a surprise, pleasant or unpleasant, as the case may be. It is hardly a matter that she could be allowed to arrange for herself. . . . And now I have a few questions to put to you, Mr. Worthing. While I am making these inquiries, you, Gwendolen, will wait for me below in the carriage.

GWENDOLEN: [*Reproachfully.*] Mamma!

LADY BRACKNELL: In the carriage, Gwendolen! [GWENDOLEN *goes to the door. She and* JACK *blow kisses to each other behind* LADY BRACKNELL*'s back.* LADY BRACKNELL *looks vaguely about as if she could not understand what the noise was. Finally turns round.*] Gwendolen, the carriage!

GWENDOLEN: Yes, mamma. [*Goes out, looking back at* JACK.]

LADY BRACKNELL: [*Sitting down.*] You can take a seat, Mr. Worthing.

[*Looks in her pocket for notebook and pencil.*]

JACK: Thank you, Lady Bracknell, I prefer standing.

LADY BRACKNELL: [*Pencil and notebook in hand.*] I feel bound to tell you that you are not down on my list of eligible young men, although I have the same list as the dear Duchess of Bolton has. We work together, in fact. However, I am quite ready to enter your name, should your answers be what a really affectionate mother requires. Do you smoke?

JACK: Well, yes, I must admit I smoke.

LADY BRACKNELL: I am glad to hear it. A man should always have an occupation of some kind. There are far too many idle men in London as it is. How old are you?

JACK: Twenty-nine.

LADY BRACKNELL: A very good age to be married at. I have always been of opinion that a man who desires to get married should know either everything or nothing. Which do you know?

JACK: [*After some hesitation.*] I know nothing, Lady Bracknell.

LADY BRACKNELL: I am pleased to hear it. I do not approve of anything that tampers with natural ignorance. Ignorance is like a delicate exotic fruit; touch it and the bloom is gone. The whole theory of modern education is radically unsound. Fortunately in England, at any rate, education produces no effect whatsoever. If it did, it would prove a serious danger to the upper classes, and probably lead to acts of violence in Grosvenor Square.[9] What is your income?

JACK: Between seven and eight thousand a year.[1]

LADY BRACKNELL: [*Makes a note in her book.*] In land, or in investments?

JACK: In investments, chiefly.

LADY BRACKNELL: That is satisfactory. What between the duties expected of one during one's lifetime, and the duties exacted from one after one's death, land

9. Fashionable location in Mayfair. 1. Nearly $1,000,000 annually in today's U.S. currency.

has ceased to be either a profit or a pleasure. It gives one position, and prevents one from keeping it up. That's all that can be said about land.

JACK: I have a country house with some land, of course, attached to it, about fifteen hundred acres, I believe; but I don't depend on that for my real income. In fact, as far as I can make out, the poachers are the only people who make anything out of it.

LADY BRACKNELL: A country house! How many bedrooms? Well, that point can be cleared up afterwards. You have a town house, I hope? A girl with a simple, unspoiled nature, like Gwendolen, could hardly be expected to reside in the country.

JACK: Well, I own a house in Belgrave Square,[2] but it is let by the year to Lady Bloxham. Of course, I can get it back whenever I like, at six months' notice.

LADY BRACKNELL: Lady Bloxham? I don't know her.

JACK: Oh, she goes about very little. She is a lady considerably advanced in years.

LADY BRACKNELL: Ah, nowadays that is no guarantee of respectability of character. What number in Belgrave Square?

JACK: 149.

LADY BRACKNELL: [*Shaking her head.*] The unfashionable side. I thought there was something. However, that could easily be altered.

JACK: Do you mean the fashion, or the side?

LADY BRACKNELL: [*Sternly.*] Both, if necessary, I presume. What are your politics?

JACK: Well, I am afraid I really have none. I am a Liberal Unionist.

LADY BRACKNELL: Oh, they count as Tories.[3] They dine with us. Or come in the evening, at any rate. Now to minor matters. Are your parents living?

JACK: I have lost both my parents.

LADY BRACKNELL: Both? To lose one parent may be regarded as a misfortune—to lose *both* seems like carelessness. Who was your father? He was evidently a man of some wealth. Was he born in what the Radical papers call the purple of commerce, or did he rise from the ranks of aristocracy?

JACK: I am afraid I really don't know. The fact is, Lady Bracknell, I said I had lost my parents. It would be nearer the truth to say that my parents seem to have lost me. . . . I don't actually know who I am by birth. I was . . . well, I was found.

LADY BRACKNELL: Found!

JACK: The late Mr. Thomas Cardew, an old gentleman of a very charitable and kindly disposition, found me, and gave me the name of Worthing, because he happened to have a first-class ticket for Worthing in his pocket at the time. Worthing is a place in Sussex. It is a seaside resort.

LADY BRACKNELL: Where did the charitable gentleman who had a first-class ticket for this seaside resort find you?

JACK: [*Gravely.*] In a handbag.

LADY BRACKNELL: A handbag?

2. Near the southeast corner of Hyde Park in Belgravia, another fashionable London neighborhood.

3. Members of the Conservative party. Opposed to home rule for Ireland, they joined forces with the Liberal Unionists, who had split from the Liberal party over the issue.

JACK: [*Very seriously.*] Yes, Lady Bracknell. I was in a handbag—a somewhat large, black leather handbag, with handles to it—an ordinary handbag, in fact.

LADY BRACKNELL: In what locality did this Mr. James, or Thomas, Cardew come across this ordinary handbag?

JACK: In the cloak room at Victoria Station.[4] It was given to him in mistake for his own.

LADY BRACKNELL: The cloak room at Victoria Station?

JACK: Yes. The Brighton line.

LADY BRACKNELL: The line is immaterial. Mr. Worthing, I confess I feel somewhat bewildered by what you have just told me. To be born, or at any rate, bred in a handbag, whether it had handles or not, seems to me to display a contempt for the ordinary decencies of family life that reminds one of the worst excesses of the French Revolution. And I presume you know what that unfortunate movement led to? As for the particular locality in which the handbag was found, a cloak room at a railway station might serve to conceal a social indiscretion—has probably, indeed, been used for that purpose before now—but it could hardly be regarded as an assured basis for a recognized position in good society.

JACK: May I ask you then what you would advise me to do? I need hardly say I would do anything in the world to ensure Gwendolen's happiness.

LADY BRACKNELL: I would strongly advise you, Mr. Worthing, to try and acquire some relations as soon as possible, and to make a definite effort to produce at any rate one parent, of either sex, before the season is quite over.

JACK: Well, I don't see how I could possibly manage to do that. I can produce the handbag at any moment, it is in my dressing room at home. I really think that should satisfy you, Lady Bracknell.

LADY BRACKNELL: Me, sir! What has it to do with me? You can hardly imagine that I and Lord Bracknell would dream of allowing our only daughter—a girl brought up with the utmost care—to marry into a cloak room, and form an alliance with a parcel? Good morning, Mr. Worthing!

[LADY BRACKNELL *sweeps out in majestic indignation.*]

JACK: Good morning! [ALGERNON, *from the other room, strikes up the Wedding March.* JACK *looks perfectly furious, and goes to the door.*] For goodness' sake don't play that ghastly tune, Algy! How idiotic you are!

[*The music stops, and* ALGERNON *enters cheerily.*]

ALGERNON: Didn't it go off all right, old boy? You don't mean to say Gwendolen refused you? I know it is a way she has. She is always refusing people. I think it is most ill-natured of her.

JACK: Oh, Gwendolen is as right as a trivet.[5] As far as she is concerned, we are engaged. Her mother is perfectly unbeatable. Never met such a Gorgon[6] . . . I don't really know what a Gorgon is like, but I am quite sure that Lady

4. Major London railroad station.
5. Proverbial expression, referring to the stability of a tripod on its three legs.
6. Mythological creature with a horrible face and snakes in lieu of hair. According to myth, those who looked on a Gorgon turned to stone.

Bracknell is one. In any case, she is a monster, without being a myth, which is rather unfair. . . . I beg your pardon, Algy, I suppose I shouldn't talk about your own aunt in that way before you.

ALGERNON: My dear boy, I love hearing my relations abused. It is the only thing that makes me put up with them at all. Relations are simply a tedious pack of people who haven't got the remotest knowledge of how to live, nor the smallest instinct about when to die.

JACK: Oh, that is nonsense!

ALGERNON: It isn't!

JACK: Well, I won't argue about the matter. You always want to argue about things.

ALGERNON: That is exactly what things were originally made for.

JACK: Upon my word, if I thought that, I'd shoot myself. . . . [*A pause.*] You don't think there is any chance of Gwendolen becoming like her mother in about a hundred and fifty years, do you, Algy?

ALGERNON: All women become like their mothers. That is their tragedy. No man does. That's his.

JACK: Is that clever?

ALGERNON: It is perfectly phrased! and quite as true as any observation in civilized life should be.

JACK: I am sick to death of cleverness. Everybody is clever nowadays. You can't go anywhere without meeting clever people. The thing has become an absolute public nuisance. I wish to goodness we had a few fools left.

ALGERNON: We have.

JACK: I should extremely like to meet them. What do they talk about?

ALGERNON: The fools? Oh! about the clever people, of course.

JACK: What fools!

ALGERNON: By the way, did you tell Gwendolen the truth about your being Ernest in town, and Jack in the country?

JACK: [*In a very patronizing manner.*] My dear fellow, the truth isn't quite the sort of thing one tells to a nice sweet refined girl. What extraordinary ideas you have about the way to behave to a woman!

ALGERNON: The only way to behave to a woman is to make love to her, if she is pretty, and to someone else if she is plain.

JACK: Oh, that is nonsense.

ALGERNON: What about your brother? What about the profligate Ernest?

JACK: Oh, before the end of the week I shall have got rid of him. I'll say he died in Paris of apoplexy. Lots of people die of apoplexy, quite suddenly, don't they?

ALGERNON: Yes, but it's hereditary, my dear fellow. It's a sort of thing that runs in families. You had much better say a severe chill.

JACK: You are sure a severe chill isn't hereditary, or anything of that kind?

ALGERNON: Of course it isn't!

JACK: Very well, then. My poor brother Ernest is carried off suddenly in Paris, by a severe chill. That gets rid of him.

ALGERNON: But I thought you said that . . . Miss Cardew was a little too much interested in your poor brother Ernest? Won't she feel his loss a good deal?

JACK: Oh, that is all right. Cecily is not a silly romantic girl, I am glad to say. She has got a capital appetite, goes on long walks, and pays no attention at all to her lessons.

ALGERNON: I would rather like to see Cecily.

JACK: I will take very good care you never do. She is excessively pretty, and she is only just eighteen.

ALGERNON: Have you told Gwendolen yet that you have an excessively pretty ward who is only just eighteen?

JACK: Oh! one doesn't blurt these things out to people. Cecily and Gwendolen are perfectly certain to be extremely great friends. I'll bet you anything you like that half an hour after they have met, they will be calling each other sister.

ALGERNON: Women only do that when they have called each other a lot of other things first. Now, my dear boy, if we want to get a good table at Willis's, we really must go and dress. Do you know it is nearly seven?

JACK: [*Irritably.*] Oh! it always is nearly seven.

ALGERNON: Well, I'm hungry.

JACK: I never knew you when you weren't. . . .

ALGERNON: What shall we do after dinner? Go to the theater?

JACK: Oh no! I loathe listening.

ALGERNON: Well, let us go to the club?

JACK: Oh, no! I hate talking.

ALGERNON: Well, we might trot around to the Empire[7] at ten?

JACK: Oh no! I can't bear looking at things. It is so silly.

ALGERNON: Well, what shall we do?

JACK: Nothing!

ALGERNON: It is awfully hard work doing nothing. However, I don't mind hard work where there is no definite object of any kind.

[*Enter* LANE.]

LANE: Miss Fairfax.

[*Enter* GWENDOLEN. LANE *goes out.*]

ALGERNON: Gwendolen, upon my word!

GWENDOLEN: Algy, kindly turn your back. I have something very particular to say to Mr. Worthing.

ALGERNON: Really, Gwendolen, I don't think I can allow this at all.

GWENDOLEN: Algy, you always adopt a strictly immoral attitude towards life. You are not quite old enough to do that.

[ALGERNON *retires to the fireplace.*]

JACK: My own darling!

GWENDOLEN: Ernest, we may never be married. From the expression on mamma's face I fear we never shall. Few parents nowadays pay any regard to what their children say to them. The old-fashioned respect for the young is fast dying out. Whatever influence I ever had over mamma, I lost at the age of three.

7. The Empire Theatre of Varieties, a music hall on Leicester Square.

But although she may prevent us from becoming man and wife, and I may marry someone else, and marry often, nothing that she can possibly do can alter my eternal devotion to you.

JACK: Dear Gwendolen!

GWENDOLEN: The story of your romantic origin, as related to me by mamma, with unpleasing comments, has naturally stirred the deeper fibers of my nature. Your Christian name has an irresistible fascination. The simplicity of your character makes you exquisitely incomprehensible to me. Your town address at the Albany I have. What is your address in the country?

JACK: The Manor House, Woolton, Hertfordshire.

[ALGERNON, *who has been carefully listening, smiles to himself, and writes the address on his shirt-cuff. Then picks up the Railway Guide.*]

GWENDOLEN: There is a good postal service, I suppose? It may be necessary to do something desperate. That of course will require serious consideration. I will communicate with you daily.

JACK: My own one!

GWENDOLEN: How long do you remain in town?

JACK: Till Monday.

GWENDOLEN: Good! Algy, you may turn round now.

ALGERNON: Thanks, I've turned round already.

GWENDOLEN: You may also ring the bell.

JACK: You will let me see you to your carriage, my own darling?

GWENDOLEN: Certainly.

JACK: [*To* LANE, *who now enters.*] I will see Miss Fairfax out.

LANE: Yes, sir.

[JACK *and* GWENDOLEN *go off.* LANE *presents several letters on a salver to* ALGERNON. *It is to be surmised that they are bills, as* ALGERNON, *after looking at the envelopes, tears them up.*]

ALGERNON: A glass of sherry, Lane.

LANE: Yes, sir.

ALGERNON: Tomorrow, Lane, I'm going Bunburying.

LANE: Yes, sir.

ALGERNON: I shall probably not be back till Monday. You can put up my dress clothes, my smoking jacket, and all the Bunbury suits. . . .

LANE: Yes, sir. [*Handing sherry.*]

ALGERNON: I hope tomorrow will be a fine day, Lane.

LANE: It never is, sir.

ALGERNON: Lane, you're a perfect pessimist.

LANE: I do my best to give satisfaction, sir.

[*Enter* JACK. LANE *goes off.*]

JACK: There's a sensible, intellectual girl! the only girl I ever cared for in my life. [ALGERNON *is laughing immoderately.*] What on earth are you so amused at?

ALGERNON: Oh, I'm a little anxious about poor Bunbury, that is all.

JACK: If you don't take care, your friend Bunbury will get you into a serious scrape some day.

ALGERNON: I love scrapes. They are the only things that are never serious.
JACK: Oh, that's nonsense, Algy. You never talk anything but nonsense.
ALGERNON: Nobody ever does.

[JACK *looks indignantly at him, and leaves the room.* ALGERNON *lights a cigarette, reads his shirt-cuff, and smiles.*]

ACT-DROP[8]

ACT II

SCENE: *Garden at the Manor House. A flight of gray stone steps leads up to the house. The garden, an old-fashioned one, full of roses. Time of year, July. Basket chairs, and a table covered with books, are set under a large yew tree.*

[MISS PRISM *discovered seated at the table.* CECILY *is at the back watering flowers.*]

MISS PRISM: [*Calling.*] Cecily, Cecily! Surely such a utilitarian occupation as the watering of flowers is rather Moulton's duty than yours? Especially at a moment when intellectual pleasures await you. Your German grammar is on the table. Pray open it at page fifteen. We will repeat yesterday's lesson.

CECILY: [*Coming over very slowly.*] But I don't like German. It isn't at all a becoming language. I know perfectly well that I look quite plain after my German lesson.

MISS PRISM: Child, you know how anxious your guardian is that you should improve yourself in every way. He laid particular stress on your German, as he was leaving for town yesterday. Indeed, he always lays stress on your German when he is leaving for town.

CECILY: Dear Uncle Jack is so very serious! Sometime he is so serious that I think he cannot be quite well.

MISS PRISM: [*Drawing herself up.*] Your guardian enjoys the best of health, and his gravity of demeanor is especially to be commended in one so comparatively young as he is. I know no one who has a higher sense of duty and responsibility.

CECILY: I suppose that is why he often looks a little bored when we three are together.

MISS PRISM: Cecily! I am surprised at you. Mr. Worthing has many troubles in his life. Idle merriment and triviality would be out of place in his conversation. You must remember his constant anxiety about that unfortunate young man his brother.

CECILY: I wish Uncle Jack would allow that unfortunate young man, his brother, to come down here sometimes. We might have a good influence over him, Miss Prism. I am sure you certainly would. You know German, and geology, and things of that kind influence a man very much. [CECILY *begins to write in her diary.*]

MISS PRISM: [*Shaking her head.*] I do not think that even I could produce any effect on a character that according to his own brother's admission is

8. That is, a lowering of the curtain to permit a scene change.

irretrievably weak and vacillating. Indeed I am not sure that I would desire to reclaim him. I am not in favor of this modern mania for turning bad people into good people at a moment's notice. As a man sows so let him reap. You must put away your diary, Cecily. I really don't see why you should keep a diary at all.

CECILY: I keep a diary in order to enter the wonderful secrets of my life. If I didn't write them down I should probably forget all about them.

MISS PRISM: Memory, my dear Cecily, is the diary that we all carry about with us.

CECILY: Yes, but it usually chronicles the things that have never happened, and couldn't possibly have happened. I believe that memory is responsible for nearly all the three-volume novels that Mudie sends us.[9]

MISS PRISM: Do not speak slightingly of the three-volume novel, Cecily. I wrote one myself in earlier days.

CECILY: Did you really, Miss Prism? How wonderfully clever you are! I hope it did not end happily? I don't like novels that end happily. They depress me so much.

MISS PRISM: The good ended happily, and the bad unhappily. That is what fiction means.

CECILY: I suppose so. But it seems very unfair. And was your novel ever published?

MISS PRISM: Alas! no. The manuscript unfortunately was abandoned. I use the word in the sense of lost or mislaid. To your work, child—these speculations are profitless.

CECILY: [*Smiling.*] But I see dear Dr. Chasuble coming up through the garden.

MISS PRISM: [*Rising and advancing.*] Dr. Chasuble! This is indeed a pleasure.

[*Enter* CANON CHASUBLE.]

CHASUBLE: And how are we this morning? Miss Prism, you are, I trust, well?

CECILY: Miss Prism has just been complaining of a slight headache. I think it would do her so much good to have a short stroll with you in the park, Dr. Chasuble.

MISS PRISM: Cecily, I have not mentioned anything about a headache.

CECILY: No, dear Miss Prism, I know that, but I felt instinctively that you had a headache. Indeed I was thinking about that, and not about my German lesson, when the Rector came in.

CHASUBLE: I hope, Cecily, you are not inattentive.

CECILY: Oh, I am afraid I am.

CHASUBLE: That is strange. Were I fortunate enough to be Miss Prism's pupil, I would hang upon her lips. [MISS PRISM *glares.*] I spoke metaphorically.—My metaphor was drawn from bees.[1] Ahem! Mr. Worthing, I suppose, has not returned from town yet?

MISS PRISM: We do not expect him till Monday afternoon.

9. From the 1840s to the 1890s, most novels were published in three volumes. Because of the price, most readers could not afford to buy copies and so obtained them by subscription from lending libraries, of which Mudie's in London was by far the largest.

1. Reference to the "honey" of Miss Prism's instruction.

CHASUBLE: Ah yes, he usually likes to spend his Sunday in London. He is not one of those whose sole aim is enjoyment, as, by all accounts, that unfortunate young man his brother seems to be. But I must not disturb Egeria[2] and her pupil any longer.

MISS PRISM: Egeria? My name is Laetitia, Doctor.

CHASUBLE: [*Bowing.*] A classical allusion merely, drawn from the Pagan authors. I shall see you both no doubt at Evensong?[3]

MISS PRISM: I think, dear Doctor, I will have a stroll with you. I find I have a headache after all, and a walk might do it good.

CHASUBLE: With pleasure, Miss Prism, with pleasure. We might go as far as the schools and back.

MISS PRISM: That would be delightful. Cecily, you will read your Political Economy[4] in my absence. The chapter on the Fall of the Rupee you may omit. It is somewhat too sensational. Even these metallic problems have their melodramatic side. [*Goes down the garden with* CANON CHASUBLE.]

CECILY: [*Picks up books and throws them back on table.*] Horrid Political Economy! Horrid Geography! Horrid, horrid German!

[*Enter* MERRIMAN *with a card on a salver.*]

MERRIMAN: Mr. Ernest Worthing has just driven over from the station. He has brought his luggage with him.

CECILY: [*Takes the card and reads it.*] "Mr. Ernest Worthing, B. 4, The Albany, W." Uncle Jack's brother! Did you tell him Mr. Worthing was in town?

MERRIMAN: Yes, Miss. He seemed very much disappointed. I mentioned that you and Miss Prism were in the garden. He said he was anxious to speak to you privately for a moment.

CECILY: Ask Mr. Ernest Worthing to come here. I suppose you had better talk to the housekeeper about a room for him.

MERRIMAN: Yes, Miss. [MERRIMAN *goes off.*]

CECILY: I have never met any really wicked person before. I feel rather frightened. I am so afraid he will look just like everyone else. [*Enter* ALGERNON, *very gay and debonair.*] He does!

ALGERNON: [*Raising his hat.*] You are my little cousin Cecily, I'm sure.

CECILY: You are under some strange mistake. I am not little. In fact, I believe I am more than usually tall for my age. [ALGERNON *is rather taken aback.*] But I am your cousin Cecily. You, I see from your card, are Uncle Jack's brother, my cousin Ernest, my wicked cousin Ernest.

ALGERNON: Oh! I am not really wicked at all, cousin Cecily. You mustn't think that I am wicked.

CECILY: If you are not, then you have certainly been deceiving us all in a very inexcusable manner. I hope you have not been leading a double life, pretending to be wicked and being really good all the time. That would be hypocrisy.

ALGERNON: [*Looks at her in amazement.*] Oh! Of course I have been rather reckless.

2. In classical mythology, a nymph famous as the wise counselor of Numa Pompilius, the second of Rome's legendary kings. 3. Evening church services. 4. That is, book about economics.

CECILY: I am glad to hear it.

ALGERNON: In fact, now you mention the subject, I have been very bad in my own small way.

CECILY: I don't think you should be so proud of that, though I am sure it must have been very pleasant.

ALGERNON: It is much pleasanter being here with you.

CECILY: I can't understand how you are here at all. Uncle Jack won't be back till Monday afternoon.

ALGERNON: That is a great disappointment. I am obliged to go up by the first train on Monday morning. I have a business appointment that I am anxious . . . to miss.

CECILY: Couldn't you miss it anywhere but in London?

ALGERNON: No: the appointment is in London.

CECILY: Well, I know, of course, how important it is not to keep a business engagement, if one wants to retain any sense of the beauty of life, but still I think you had better wait till Uncle Jack arrives. I know he wants to speak to you about your emigrating.

ALGERNON: About my what?

CECILY: Your emigrating. He has gone up to buy your outfit.

ALGERNON: I certainly wouldn't let Jack buy my outfit. He has no taste in neckties at all.

CECILY: I don't think you will require neckties. Uncle Jack is sending you to Australia.[5]

ALGERNON: Australia? I'd sooner die.

CECILY: Well, he said at dinner on Wednesday night, that you would have to choose between this world, the next world, and Australia.

ALGERNON: Oh, well! The accounts I have received of Australia and the next world are not particularly encouraging. This world is good enough for me, cousin Cecily.

CECILY: Yes, but are you good enough for it?

ALGERNON: I'm afraid I'm not that. That is why I want you to reform me. You might make that your mission, if you don't mind, cousin Cecily.

CECILY: I'm afraid I've no time, this afternoon.

ALGERNON: Well, would you mind my reforming myself this afternoon?

CECILY: It is rather Quixotic of you. But I think you should try.

ALGERNON: I will. I feel better already.

CECILY: You are looking a little worse.

ALGERNON: That is because I am hungry.

CECILY: How thoughtless of me. I should have remembered that when one is going to lead an entirely new life, one requires regular and wholesome meals. Won't you come in?

ALGERNON: Thank you. Might I have a buttonhole[6] first? I never have any appetite unless I have a buttonhole first.

5. Though no longer a British penal colony in Wilde's day, Australia was still widely believed to be a place where disreputable family members might be sent.

6. A flower to be worn on the lapel of a man's coat, in this case the Maréchal Niel, a popular yellow rose of the period.

CECILY: A Maréchal Niel? [*Picks up scissors.*]

ALGERNON: No, I'd sooner have a pink rose.

CECILY: Why? [*Cuts a flower.*]

ALGERNON: Because you are like a pink rose, cousin Cecily.

CECILY: I don't think it can be right for you to talk to me like that. Miss Prism never says such things to me.

ALGERNON: Then Miss Prism is a shortsighted old lady. [CECILY *puts the rose in his buttonhole.*] You are the prettiest girl I ever saw.

CECILY: Miss Prism says that all good looks are a snare.

ALGERNON: They are a snare that every sensible man would like to be caught in.

CECILY: Oh! I don't think I would care to catch a sensible man. I shouldn't know what to talk to him about.

[*They pass into the house.* MISS PRISM *and* DR. CHASUBLE *return.*]

MISS PRISM: You are too much alone, dear Dr. Chasuble. You should get married. A misanthrope I can understand—a womanthrope, never!

CHASUBLE: [*With a scholar's shudder.*] Believe me, I do not deserve so neologistic a phrase. The precept as well as the practice of the Primitive Church[7] was distinctly against matrimony.

MISS PRISM: [*Sententiously.*] That is obviously the reason why the Primitive Church has not lasted up to the present day. And you do not seem to realize, dear Doctor, that by persistently remaining single, a man converts himself into a permanent public temptation. Men should be more careful; this very celibacy leads weaker vessels astray.

CHASUBLE: But is a man not equally attractive when married?

MISS PRISM: No married man is ever attractive except to his wife.

CHASUBLE: And often, I've been told, not even to her.

MISS PRISM: That depends on the intellectual sympathies of the woman. Maturity can always be depended on. Ripeness can be trusted. Young women are green. [DR. CHASUBLE *starts.*] I spoke horticulturally. My metaphor was drawn from fruits. But where is Cecily?

CHASUBLE: Perhaps she followed us to the schools.

[*Enter* JACK *slowly from the back of the garden. He is dressed in the deepest mourning, with crape hat-band and black gloves.*]

MISS PRISM: Mr. Worthing!

CHASUBLE: Mr. Worthing?

MISS PRISM: This is indeed a surprise. We did not look for you till Monday afternoon.

JACK: [*Shakes* MISS PRISM*'s hand in a tragic manner.*] I have returned sooner than I expected. Dr. Chasuble, I hope you are well?

CHASUBLE: Dear Mr. Worthing, I trust this garb of woe does not betoken some terrible calamity?

JACK: My brother.

MISS PRISM: More shameful debts and extravagance?

7. Early Christian Church.

CHASUBLE: Still leading his life of pleasure?

JACK: [*Shaking his head.*] Dead!

CHASUBLE: Your brother Ernest dead?

JACK: Quite dead.

MISS PRISM: What a lesson for him! I trust he will profit by it.

CHASUBLE: Mr. Worthing, I offer you my sincere condolence. You have at least the consolation of knowing that you were always the most generous and forgiving of brothers.

JACK: Poor Ernest! He had many faults, but it is a sad, sad blow.

CHASUBLE: Very sad indeed. Were you with him at the end?

JACK: No. He died abroad; in Paris, in fact. I had a telegram last night from the manager of the Grand Hotel.

CHASUBLE: Was the cause of death mentioned?

JACK: A severe chill, it seems.

MISS PRISM: As a man sows, so shall he reap.

CHASUBLE: [*Raising his hand.*] Charity, dear Miss Prism, charity! None of us are perfect. I myself am peculiarly susceptible to drafts. Will the interment take place here?

JACK: No. He seemed to have expressed a desire to be buried in Paris.

CHASUBLE: In Paris! [*Shakes his head.*] I fear that hardly points to any very serious state of mind at the last. You would no doubt wish me to make some slight allusion to this tragic domestic affliction next Sunday. [JACK *presses his hand convulsively.*] My sermon on the meaning of the manna in the wilderness can be adapted to almost any occasion, joyful, or, as in the present case, distressing. [*All sigh.*] I have preached it at harvest celebrations, christenings, confirmations, on days of humiliation and festal days. The last time I delivered it was in the Cathedral, as a charity sermon on behalf of the Society for the Prevention of Discontent among the Upper Orders. The Bishop, who was present, was much struck by some of the analogies I drew.

JACK: Ah! That reminds me, you mentioned christenings, I think, Dr. Chasuble? I suppose you know how to christen all right? [DR. CHASUBLE *looks astounded.*] I mean, of course, you are continually christening, aren't you?

MISS PRISM: It is, I regret to say, one of the Rector's most constant duties in this parish. I have often spoken to the poorer classes on the subject. But they don't seem to know what thrift is.

CHASUBLE: But is there any particular infant in whom you are interested, Mr. Worthing? Your brother was, I believe, unmarried, was he not?

JACK: Oh yes.

MISS PRISM: [*Bitterly.*] People who live entirely for pleasure usually are.

JACK: But it is not for any child, dear Doctor. I am very fond of children. No! the fact is, I would like to be christened myself, this afternoon, if you have nothing better to do.

CHASUBLE: But surely, Mr. Worthing, you have been christened already?

JACK: I don't remember anything about it.

CHASUBLE: But have you any grave doubts on the subject?

JACK: I certainly intend to have. Of course I don't know if the thing would bother you in any way, or if you think I am a little too old now.

CHASUBLE: Not at all. The sprinkling, and, indeed, the immersion of adults is a perfectly canonical practice.

JACK: Immersion!

CHASUBLE: You need have no apprehensions. Sprinkling is all that is necessary, or indeed I think advisable. Our weather is so changeable. At what hour would you wish the ceremony performed?

JACK: Oh, I might trot round about five if that would suit you.

CHASUBLE: Perfectly, perfectly! In fact I have two similar ceremonies to perform at that time. A case of twins that occurred recently in one of the outlying cottages on your own estate. Poor Jenkins the carter, a most hard-working man.

JACK: Oh! I don't see much fun in being christened along with other babies. It would be childish. Would half-past five do?

CHASUBLE: Admirably! Admirably! [*Takes out watch.*] And now, dear Mr. Worthing, I will not intrude any longer into a house of sorrow. I would merely beg you not to be too much bowed down by grief. What seem to us bitter trials are often blessings in disguise.

MISS PRISM: This seems to me a blessing of an extremely obvious kind.

[*Enter* CECILY *from the house.*]

CECILY: Uncle Jack! Oh, I am pleased to see you back. But what horrid clothes you have got on! Do go and change them.

MISS PRISM: Cecily!

CHASUBLE: My child! my child!

[CECILY *goes towards* JACK; *he kisses her brow in a melancholy manner.*]

CECILY: What is the matter, Uncle Jack? Do look happy! You look as if you had toothache, and I have got such a surprise for you. Who do you think is in the dining room? Your brother!

JACK: Who?

CECILY: Your brother Ernest. He arrived about half an hour ago.

JACK: What nonsense! I haven't got a brother!

CECILY: Oh, don't say that. However badly he may have behaved to you in the past he is still your brother. You couldn't be so heartless as to disown him. I'll tell him to come out. And you will shake hands with him, won't you, Uncle Jack? [*Runs back into the house.*]

CHASUBLE: These are very joyful tidings.

MISS PRISM: After we had all been resigned to his loss, his sudden return seems to me peculiarly distressing.

JACK: My brother is in the dining room? I don't know what it all means. I think it is perfectly absurd. [*Enter* ALGERNON *and* CECILY *hand in hand. They come slowly up to* JACK.] Good heavens! [*Motions* ALGERNON *away.*]

ALGERNON: Brother John, I have come down from town to tell you that I am very sorry for all the trouble I have given you, and that I intend to lead a better life in the future. [JACK *glares at him and does not take his hand.*]

CECILY: Uncle Jack, you are not going to refuse your own brother's hand?

JACK: Nothing will induce me to take his hand. I think his coming down here disgraceful. He knows perfectly well why.

CECILY: Uncle Jack, do be nice. There is some good in everyone. Ernest has just been telling me about his poor invalid friend Mr. Bunbury whom he goes to visit so often. And surely there must be much good in one who is kind to an invalid, and leaves the pleasures of London to sit by a bed of pain.

JACK: Oh! he has been talking about Bunbury, has he?

CECILY: Yes, he has told me all about poor Mr. Bunbury, and his terrible state of health.

JACK: Bunbury! Well, I won't have him talk to you about Bunbury or about anything else. It is enough to drive one perfectly frantic.

ALGERNON: Of course I admit that the faults were all on my side. But I must say that I think that Brother John's coldness to me is peculiarly painful. I expected a more enthusiastic welcome, especially considering it is the first time I have come here.

CECILY: Uncle Jack, if you don't shake hands with Ernest, I will never forgive you.

JACK: Never forgive me?

CECILY: Never, never, never!

JACK: Well, this is the last time I shall ever do it. [*Shakes hands with* ALGERNON *and glares.*]

CHASUBLE: It's pleasant, is it not, to see so perfect a reconciliation? I think we might leave the two brothers together.

MISS PRISM: Cecily, you will come with us.

CECILY: Certainly, Miss Prism. My little task of reconciliation is over.

CHASUBLE: You have done a beautiful action today, dear child.

MISS PRISM: We must not be premature in our judgments.

CECILY: I feel very happy.

[*They all go off.*]

JACK: You young scoundrel, Algy, you must get out of this place as soon as possible. I don't allow any Bunburying here.

[*Enter* MERRIMAN.]

MERRIMAN: I have put Mr. Ernest's things in the room next to yours, sir. I suppose that is all right?

JACK: What?

MERRIMAN: Mr. Ernest's luggage, sir. I have unpacked it and put it in the room next to your own.

JACK: His luggage?

MERRIMAN: Yes, sir. Three portmanteaus, a dressing case, two hat-boxes, and a large luncheon basket.

ALGERNON: I am afraid I can't stay more than a week this time.

JACK: Merriman, order the dogcart[8] at once. Mr. Ernest has been suddenly called back to town.

MERRIMAN: Yes, sir. [*Goes back into the house.*]

ALGERNON: What a fearful liar you are, Jack. I have not been called back to town at all.

JACK: Yes, you have.

8. Light, two-wheeled carriage, usually drawn by one horse.

ALGERNON: I haven't heard anyone call me.

JACK: Your duty as a gentleman calls you back.

ALGERNON: My duty as a gentleman has never interfered with my pleasures in the smallest degree.

JACK: I can quite understand that.

ALGERNON: Well, Cecily is a darling.

JACK: You are not to talk of Miss Cardew like that. I don't like it.

ALGERNON: Well, I don't like your clothes. You look perfectly ridiculous in them. Why on earth don't you go up and change? It is perfectly childish to be in deep mourning for a man who is actually staying for a whole week with you in your house as a guest. I call it grotesque.

JACK: You are certainly not staying with me for a whole week as a guest or anything else. You have got to leave . . . by the four-five train.

ALGERNON: I certainly won't leave you so long as you are in mourning. It would be most unfriendly. If I were in mourning you would stay with me, I suppose. I should think it very unkind if you didn't.

JACK: Well, will you go if I change my clothes?

ALGERNON: Yes, if you are not too long. I never saw anybody take so long to dress, and with such little result.

JACK: Well, at any rate, that is better than being always overdressed as you are.

ALGERNON: If I am occasionally a little overdressed, I make up for it by being always immensely overeducated.

JACK: Your vanity is ridiculous, your conduct an outrage, and your presence in my garden utterly absurd. However, you have got to catch the four-five, and I hope you will have a pleasant journey back to town. This Bunburying, as you call it, has not been a great success for you. [*Goes into the house.*]

ALGERNON: I think it has been a great success. I'm in love with Cecily, and that is everything. [*Enter* CECILY *at the back of the garden. She picks up the can and begins to water the flowers.*] But I must see her before I go, and make arrangements for another Bunbury. Ah, there she is.

CECILY: Oh, I merely came back to water the roses. I thought you were with Uncle Jack.

ALGERNON: He's gone to order the dogcart for me.

CECILY: Oh, is he going to take you for a nice drive?

ALGERNON: He's going to send me away.

CECILY: Then have we got to part?

ALGERNON: I am afraid so. It's very painful parting.

CECILY: It is always painful to part from people whom one has known for a very brief space of time. The absence of old friends one can endure with equanimity. But even a momentary separation from anyone to whom one has just been introduced is almost unbearable.

ALGERNON: Thank you.

[*Enter* MERRIMAN.]

MERRIMAN: The dogcart is at the door, sir. [ALGERNON *looks appealingly at* CECILY.]

CECILY: It can wait, Merriman . . . for . . . five minutes.

MERRIMAN: Yes, Miss. [*Exit* MERRIMAN.]

ALGERNON: I hope, Cecily, I shall not offend you if I state quite frankly and openly that you seem to me to be in every way the visible personification of absolute perfection.

CECILY: I think your frankness does you great credit, Ernest. If you will allow me I will copy your remarks into my diary. [*Goes over to table and begins writing in diary.*]

ALGERNON: Do you really keep a diary? I'd give anything to look at it. May I?

CECILY: Oh no. [*Puts her hand over it.*] You see, it is simply a very young girl's record of her own thoughts and impressions, and consequently meant for publication. When it appears in volume form I hope you will order a copy. But pray, Ernest, don't stop. I delight in taking down from dictation. I have reached "absolute perfection." You can go on. I am quite ready for more.

ALGERNON: [*Somewhat taken aback.*] Ahem! Ahem!

CECILY: Oh, don't cough, Ernest. When one is dictating one should speak fluently and not cough. Besides, I don't know how to spell a cough. [*Writes as* ALGERNON *speaks.*]

ALGERNON: [*Speaking very rapidly.*] Cecily, ever since I first looked upon your wonderful and incomparable beauty, I have dared to love you wildly, passionately, devotedly, hopelessly.

CECILY: I don't think that you should tell me that you love me wildly, passionately, devotedly, hopelessly. Hopelessly doesn't seem to make much sense, does it?

ALGERNON: Cecily!

[*Enter* MERRIMAN.]

MERRIMAN: The dogcart is waiting, sir.

ALGERNON: Tell it to come round next week, at the same hour.

MERRIMAN: [*Looks at* CECILY, *who makes no sign.*] Yes, sir. [MERRIMAN *retires.*]

CECILY: Uncle Jack would be very much annoyed if he knew you were staying on till next week, at the same hour.

ALGERNON: Oh, I don't care about Jack. I don't care for anybody in the whole world but you. I love you, Cecily. You will marry me, won't you?

CECILY: You silly boy! Of course. Why, we have been engaged for the last three months.

ALGERNON: For the last three months?

CECILY: Yes, it will be exactly three months on Thursday.

ALGERNON: But how did we become engaged?

CECILY: Well, ever since dear Uncle Jack first confessed to us that he had a younger brother who was very wicked and bad, you of course have formed the chief topic of conversation between myself and Miss Prism. And of course a man who is much talked about is always very attractive. One feels there must be something in him after all. I daresay it was foolish of me, but I fell in love with you, Ernest.

ALGERNON: Darling! And when was the engagement actually settled?

CECILY: On the 14th of February last. Worn out by your entire ignorance of my existence, I determined to end the matter one way or the other, and after a long struggle with myself I accepted you under this dear old tree here. The next day I bought this little ring in your name, and this is the little bangle with the true lovers' knot I promised you always to wear.

ALGERNON: Did I give you this? It's very pretty, isn't it?

CECILY: Yes, you've wonderfully good taste, Ernest. It's the excuse I've always given for your leading such a bad life. And this is the box in which I keep all your dear letters. [*Kneels at table, opens box, and produces letters tied up with blue ribbon.*]

ALGERNON: My letters! But my own sweet Cecily, I have never written you any letters.

CECILY: You need hardly remind me of that, Ernest. I remember only too well that I was forced to write your letters for you. I always wrote three times a week, and sometimes oftener.

ALGERNON: Oh, do let me read them, Cecily?

CECILY: Oh, I couldn't possibly. They would make you far too conceited. [*Replaces box.*] The three you wrote me after I had broken off the engagement are so beautiful, and so badly spelled, that even now I can hardly read them without crying a little.

ALGERNON: But was our engagement ever broken off?

CECILY: Of course it was. On the 22nd of last March. You can see the entry if you like. [*Shows diary.*] "Today I broke off my engagement with Ernest. I feel it is better to do so. The weather still continues charming."

ALGERNON: But why on earth did you break it off? What had I done? I had done nothing at all. Cecily, I am very much hurt indeed to hear you broke it off. Particularly when the weather was so charming.

CECILY: It would hardly have been a really serious engagement if it hadn't been broken off at least once. But I forgave you before the week was out.

ALGERNON: [*Crossing to her, and kneeling.*] What a perfect angel you are, Cecily.

CECILY: You dear romantic boy. [*He kisses her, she puts her fingers through his hair.*] I hope your hair curls naturally, does it?

ALGERNON: Yes, darling, with a little help from others.

CECILY: I am so glad.

ALGERNON: You'll never break off our engagement again, Cecily?

CECILY: I don't think I could break it off now that I have actually met you. Besides, of course, there is the question of your name.

ALGERNON: Yes, of course. [*Nervously.*]

CECILY: You must not laugh at me, darling, but it had always been a girlish dream of mine to love someone whose name was Ernest. [ALGERNON *rises,* CECILY *also.*] There is something in that name that seems to inspire absolute confidence. I pity any poor married woman whose husband is not called Ernest.

ALGERNON: But, my dear child, do you mean to say you could not love me if I had some other name?

CECILY: But what name?

ALGERNON: Oh, any name you like—Algernon—for instance . . .

CECILY: But I don't like the name of Algernon.

ALGERNON: Well, my own dear, sweet, loving little darling, I really can't see why you should object to the name of Algernon. It is not at all a bad name. In fact, it is rather an aristocratic name. Half of the chaps who get into the Bankruptcy Court are called Algernon. But seriously, Cecily . . . [*Moving to her.*] . . . if my name was Algy, couldn't you love me?

CECILY: [*Rising.*] I might respect you, Ernest, I might admire your character, but I fear that I should not be able to give you my undivided attention.

ALGERNON: Ahem! Cecily! [*Picking up hat.*] Your Rector here is, I suppose, thoroughly experienced in the practice of all the rites and ceremonials of the Church?

CECILY: Oh, yes. Dr. Chasuble is a most learned man. He has never written a single book, so you can imagine how much he knows.

ALGERNON: I must see him at once on a most important christening—I mean on most important business.

CECILY: Oh!

ALGERNON: I shan't be away more than half an hour.

CECILY: Considering that we have been engaged since February the 14th, and that I only met you today for the first time, I think it is rather hard that you should leave me for so long a period as half an hour. Couldn't you make it twenty minutes?

ALGERNON: I'll be back in no time. [*Kisses her and rushes down the garden.*]

CECILY: What an impetuous boy he is! I like his hair so much. I must enter his proposal in my diary.

[*Enter* MERRIMAN.]

MERRIMAN: A Miss Fairfax has just called to see Mr. Worthing. On very important business, Miss Fairfax states.

CECILY: Isn't Mr. Worthing in his library?

MERRIMAN: Mr. Worthing went over in the direction of the rectory some time ago.

CECILY: Pray ask the lady to come out here; Mr. Worthing is sure to be back soon. And you can bring tea.

MERRIMAN: Yes, Miss. [*Goes out.*]

CECILY: Miss Fairfax! I suppose one of the many good elderly women who are associated with Uncle Jack in some of his philanthropic work in London. I don't quite like women who are interested in philanthropic work. I think it is so forward of them.

[*Enter* MERRIMAN.]

MERRIMAN: Miss Fairfax.

[*Enter* GWENDOLEN. *Exit* MERRIMAN.]

CECILY: [*Advancing to meet her.*] Pray let me introduce myself to you. My name is Cecily Cardew.

GWENDOLEN: Cecily Cardew? [*Moving to her and shaking hands.*] What a very sweet name! Something tells me that we are going to be great friends. I like you already more than I can say. My first impressions of people are never wrong.

CECILY: How nice of you to like me so much after we have known each other such a comparatively short time. Pray sit down.

GWENDOLEN: [*Still standing up.*] I may call you Cecily, may I not?
CECILY: With pleasure!
GWENDOLEN: And you will always call me Gwendolen, won't you?
CECILY: If you wish.
GWENDOLEN: Then that is all quite settled, is it not?
CECILY: I hope so. [*A pause. They both sit down together.*]
GWENDOLEN: Perhaps this might be a favorable opportunity for my mentioning who I am. My father is Lord Bracknell. You have never heard of papa, I suppose?
CECILY: I don't think so.
GWENDOLEN: Outside the family circle, papa, I am glad to say, is entirely unknown. I think that is quite as it should be. The home seems to me to be the proper sphere for the man. And certainly once a man begins to neglect his domestic duties he becomes painfully effeminate, does he not? And I don't like that. It makes men so very attractive. Cecily, mamma, whose views on education are remarkably strict, has brought me up to be extremely shortsighted; it is part of her system; so do you mind my looking at you through my glasses?
CECILY: Oh! not at all, Gwendolen. I am very fond of being looked at.
GWENDOLEN: [*After examining* CECILY *carefully through a lorgnette.*] You are here on a short visit, I suppose.
CECILY: Oh no! I live here.
GWENDOLEN: [*Severely.*] Really? Your mother, no doubt, or some female relative of advanced years, resides here also?
CECILY: Oh no! I have no mother, nor, in fact, any relations.
GWENDOLEN: Indeed?
CECILY: My dear guardian, with the assistance of Miss Prism, has the arduous task of looking after me.
GWENDOLEN: Your guardian?
CECILY: Yes, I am Mr. Worthing's ward.
GWENDOLEN: Oh! It is strange he never mentioned to me that he had a ward. How secretive of him! He grows more interesting hourly. I am not sure, however, that the news inspires me with feelings of unmixed delight. [*Rising and going to her.*] I am very fond of you, Cecily; I have liked you ever since I met you! But I am bound to state that now that I know that you are Mr. Worthing's ward, I cannot help expressing a wish you were—well just a little older than you seem to be—and not quite so very alluring in appearance. In fact, if I may speak candidly—
CECILY: Pray do! I think that whenever one has anything unpleasant to say, one should always be quite candid.
GWENDOLEN: Well, to speak with perfect candor, Cecily, I wish that you were fully forty-two, and more than usually plain for your age. Ernest has a strong upright nature. He is the very soul of truth and honor. Disloyalty would be as impossible to him as deception. But even men of the noblest possible moral character are extremely susceptible to the influence of the physical charms of others. Modern, no less than ancient history, supplies us with many most painful examples of what I refer to. If it were not so, indeed, history would be quite unreadable.

CECILY: I beg your pardon, Gwendolen, did you say Ernest?

GWENDOLEN: Yes.

CECILY: Oh, but it is not Mr. Ernest Worthing who is my guardian. It is his brother—his elder brother.

GWENDOLEN: [*Sitting down again.*] Ernest never mentioned to me that he had a brother.

CECILY: I am sorry to say they have not been on good terms for a long time.

GWENDOLEN: Ah! that accounts for it. And now that I think of it I have never heard any man mention his brother. The subject seems distasteful to most men. Cecily, you have lifted a load from my mind. I was growing almost anxious. It would have been terrible if any cloud had come across a friendship like ours, would it not? Of course you are quite, quite sure that it is not Mr. Ernest Worthing who is your guardian?

CECILY: Quite sure. [*A pause.*] In fact, I am going to be his.

GWENDOLEN: [*Inquiringly.*] I beg your pardon?

CECILY: [*Rather shy and confidingly.*] Dearest Gwendolen, there is no reason why I should make a secret of it to you. Our little county newspaper is sure to chronicle the fact next week. Mr. Ernest Worthing and I are engaged to be married.

GWENDOLEN: [*Quite politely, rising.*] My darling Cecily, I think there must be some slight error. Mr. Ernest Worthing is engaged to me. The announcement will appear in the *Morning Post* on Saturday at the latest.

CECILY: [*Very politely, rising.*] I am afraid you must be under some misconception. Ernest proposed to me exactly ten minutes ago. [*Shows diary.*]

GWENDOLEN: [*Examines diary through her lorgnette carefully.*] It is certainly very curious, for he asked me to be his wife yesterday afternoon at 5:30. If you would care to verify the incident, pray do so. [*Produces diary of her own.*] I never travel without my diary. One should always have something sensational to read in the train. I am so sorry, dear Cecily, if it is any disappointment to you, but I am afraid *I* have the prior claim.

CECILY: It would distress me more than I can tell you, dear Gwendolen, if it caused you any mental or physical anguish, but I feel bound to point out that since Ernest proposed to you he clearly has changed his mind.

GWENDOLEN: [*Meditatively.*] If the poor fellow has been entrapped into any foolish promise I shall consider it my duty to rescue him at once, and with a firm hand.

CECILY: [*Thoughtfully and sadly.*] Whatever unfortunate entanglement my dear boy may have got into, I will never reproach him with it after we are married.

GWENDOLEN: Do you allude to me, Miss Cardew, as an entanglement? You are presumptuous. On an occasion of this kind it becomes more than a moral duty to speak one's mind. It becomes a pleasure.

CECILY: Do you suggest, Miss Fairfax, that I entrapped Ernest into an engagement? How dare you? This is no time for wearing the shallow mask of manners. When I see a spade I call it a spade.

GWENDOLEN: [*Satirically.*] I am glad to say that I have never seen a spade. It is obvious that our social spheres have been widely different.

[*Enter* MERRIMAN, *followed by the footman. He carries a salver, tablecloth, and plate stand.* CECILY *is about to retort. The presence of the servants exercises a restraining influence, under which both girls chafe.*]

MERRIMAN: Shall I lay tea here as usual, Miss?
CECILY: [*Sternly, in a calm voice.*] Yes, as usual.

[MERRIMAN *begins to clear table and lay cloth. A long pause.* CECILY *and* GWENDOLEN *glare at each other.*]

GWENDOLEN: Are there many interesting walks in the vicinity, Miss Cardew?
CECILY: Oh! yes! a great many. From the top of one of the hills quite close one can see five counties.
GWENDOLEN: Five counties! I don't think I should like that. I hate crowds.
CECILY: [*Sweetly.*] I suppose that is why you live in town?

[GWENDOLEN *bites her lip, and beats her foot nervously with her parasol.*]

GWENDOLEN: [*Looking round.*] Quite a well-kept garden this is, Miss Cardew.
CECILY: So glad you like it, Miss Fairfax.
GWENDOLEN: I had no idea there were any flowers in the country.
CECILY: Oh, flowers are as common here, Miss Fairfax, as people are in London.
GWENDOLEN: Personally I cannot understand how anybody manages to exist in the country, if anybody who is anybody does. The country always bores me to death.
CECILY: Ah! This is what the newspapers call agricultural depression, is it not? I believe the aristocracy are suffering very much from it just at present. It is almost an epidemic amongst them, I have been told. May I offer you some tea, Miss Fairfax?
GWENDOLEN: [*With elaborate politeness.*] Thank you. [*Aside.*] Detestable girl! But I require tea!
CECILY: [*Sweetly.*] Sugar?
GWENDOLEN: [*Superciliously.*] No, thank you. Sugar is not fashionable anymore.

[CECILY *looks angrily at her, takes up the tongs and puts four lumps of sugar into the cup.*]

CECILY: [*Severely.*] Cake or bread and butter?
GWENDOLEN: [*In a bored manner.*] Bread and butter, please. Cake is rarely seen at the best houses nowadays.
CECILY: [*Cuts a very large slice of cake, and puts it on the tray.*] Hand that to Miss Fairfax.

[MERRIMAN *does so, and goes out with footman.* GWENDOLEN *drinks the tea and makes a grimace. Puts down cup at once, reaches out her hand to the bread and butter, looks at it, and finds it is cake. Rises in indignation.*]

GWENDOLEN: You have filled my tea with lumps of sugar, and though I asked most distinctly for bread and butter, you have given me cake. I am known for the gentleness of my disposition, and the extraordinary sweetness of my nature, but I warn you, Miss Cardew, you may go too far.

CECILY: [*Rising.*] To save my poor, innocent, trusting boy from the machinations of any other girl there are no lengths to which I would not go.

GWENDOLEN: From the moment I saw you I distrusted you. I felt that you were false and deceitful. I am never deceived in such matters. My first impressions of people are invariably right.

CECILY: It seems to me, Miss Fairfax, that I am trespassing on your valuable time. No doubt you have many other calls of a similar character to make in the neighborhood.

[*Enter* JACK.]

GWENDOLEN: [*Catching sight of him.*] Ernest! My own Ernest!

JACK: Gwendolen! Darling! [*Offers to kiss her.*]

GWENDOLEN: [*Drawing back.*] A moment! May I ask if you are engaged to be married to this young lady? [*Points to* CECILY.]

JACK: [*Laughing.*] To dear little Cecily! Of course not! What could have put such an idea into your pretty little head?

GWENDOLEN: Thank you. You may! [*Offers her cheek.*]

CECILY: [*Very sweetly.*] I knew there must be some misunderstanding, Miss Fairfax. The gentleman whose arm is at present round your waist is my dear guardian, Mr. John Worthing.

GWENDOLEN: I beg your pardon?

CECILY: This is Uncle Jack.

GWENDOLEN: [*Receding.*] Jack! Oh!

[*Enter* ALGERNON.]

CECILY: Here is Ernest.

ALGERNON: [*Goes straight over to* CECILY *without noticing anyone else.*] My own love! [*Offers to kiss her.*]

CECILY: [*Drawing back.*] A moment, Ernest! May I ask you—are you engaged to be married to this young lady?

ALGERNON: [*Looking round.*] To what young lady? Good heavens! Gwendolen!

CECILY: Yes! to good heavens, Gwendolen, I mean to Gwendolen.

ALGERNON: [*Laughing.*] Of course not! What could have put such an idea into your pretty little head?

CECILY: Thank you. [*Presenting her cheek to be kissed.*] You may. [ALGERNON *kisses her.*]

GWENDOLEN: I felt there was some slight error, Miss Cardew. The gentleman who is now embracing you is my cousin, Mr. Algernon Moncrieff.

CECILY: [*Breaking away from* ALGERNON.] Algernon Moncrieff! Oh! [*The two girls move towards each other and put their arms round each other's waists as if for protection.*] Are you called Algernon?

ALGERNON: I cannot deny it.

CECILY: Oh!

GWENDOLEN: Is your name really John?

JACK: [*Standing rather proudly.*] I could deny it if I liked, I could deny anything if I liked. But my name certainly is John. It has been John for years.

CECILY: [*To* GWENDOLEN.] A gross deception has been practiced on both of us.

GWENDOLEN: My poor wounded Cecily!

CECILY: My sweet wronged Gwendolen!

GWENDOLEN: [*Slowly and seriously.*] You will call me sister, will you not?

[*They embrace.* JACK *and* ALGERNON *groan and walk up and down.*]

CECILY: [*Rather brightly.*] There is just one question I would like to be allowed to ask my guardian.

GWENDOLEN: An admirable idea! Mr. Worthing, there is just one question I would like to be permitted to put to you. Where is your brother Ernest? We are both engaged to be married to your brother Ernest, so it is a matter of some importance to us to know where your brother Ernest is at present.

JACK: [*Slowly and hesitatingly.*] Gwendolen—Cecily—it is very painful for me to be forced to speak the truth. It is the first time in my life that I have ever been reduced to such a painful position, and I am really quite inexperienced in doing anything of the kind. However I will tell you quite frankly that I have no brother Ernest. I have no brother at all. I never had a brother in my life, and certainly have not the smallest intention of ever having one in the future.

CECILY: [*Surprised.*] No brother at all?

JACK: [*Cheerily.*] None!

GWENDOLEN: [*Severely.*] Had you never a brother of any kind?

JACK: [*Pleasantly.*] Never. Not even of any kind.

GWENDOLEN: I am afraid it is quite clear, Cecily, that neither of us is engaged to be married to anyone.

CECILY: It is not a very pleasant position for a young girl suddenly to find herself in. Is it?

GWENDOLEN: Let us go into the house. They will hardly venture to come after us there.

CECILY: No, men are so cowardly, aren't they?

[*They retire into the house with scornful looks.*]

JACK: This ghastly state of things is what you call Bunburying, I suppose?

ALGERNON: Yes, and a perfectly wonderful Bunbury it is. The most wonderful Bunbury I have ever had in my life.

JACK: Well, you've no right whatsoever to Bunbury here.

ALGERNON: That is absurd. One has a right to Bunbury anywhere one chooses. Every serious Bunburyist knows that.

JACK: Serious Bunburyist! Good heavens!

ALGERNON: Well, one must be serious about something, if one wants to have any amusement in life. I happen to be serious about Bunburying. What on earth you are serious about I haven't got the remotest idea. About everything, I should fancy. You have such an absolutely trivial nature.

JACK: Well, the only small satisfaction I have in the whole of this wretched business is that your friend Bunbury is quite exploded. You won't be able to run down to the country quite so often as you used to do, dear Algy. And a very good thing too.

ALGERNON: Your brother is a little off-color,[9] isn't he, dear Jack? You won't be able to disappear to London quite so frequently as your wicked custom was. And not a bad thing either.

9. In poor health.

JACK: As for your conduct towards Miss Cardew, I must say that your taking in a sweet, simple, innocent girl like that is quite inexcusable. To say nothing of the fact that she is my ward.

ALGERNON: I can see no possible defense at all for your deceiving a brilliant, clever, thoroughly experienced young lady like Miss Fairfax. To say nothing of the fact that she is my cousin.

JACK: I wanted to be engaged to Gwendolen, that is all. I love her.

ALGERNON: Well, I simply wanted to be engaged to Cecily. I adore her.

JACK: There is certainly no chance of your marrying Miss Cardew.

ALGERNON: I don't think there is much likelihood, Jack, of you and Miss Fairfax being united.

JACK: Well, that is no business of yours.

ALGERNON: If it was my business, I wouldn't talk about it. [*Begins to eat muffins.*] It is very vulgar to talk about one's business. Only people like stockbrokers do that, and then merely at dinner parties.

JACK: How can you sit there, calmly eating muffins when we are in this horrible trouble, I can't make out. You seem to me to be perfectly heartless.

ALGERNON: Well, I can't eat muffins in an agitated manner. The butter would probably get on my cuffs. One should always eat muffins quite calmly. It is the only way to eat them.

JACK: I say it's perfectly heartless your eating muffins at all, under the circumstances.

ALGERNON: When I am in trouble, eating is the only thing that consoles me. Indeed, when I am in really great trouble, as anyone who knows me intimately will tell you, I refuse everything except food and drink. At the present moment I am eating muffins because I am unhappy. Besides, I am particularly fond of muffins. [*Rising.*]

JACK: [*Rising.*] Well, that is no reason why you should eat them all in that greedy way. [*Takes muffins from* ALGERNON.]

ALGERNON: [*Offering tea cake.*] I wish you would have tea cake instead. I don't like tea cake.

JACK: Good heavens! I suppose a man may eat his own muffins in his own garden.

ALGERNON: But you have just said it was perfectly heartless to eat muffins.

JACK: I said it was perfectly heartless of you, under the circumstances. That is a very different thing.

ALGERNON: That may be. But the muffins are the same. [*He seizes the muffin dish from* JACK.]

JACK: Algy, I wish to goodness you would go.

ALGERNON: You can't possibly ask me to go without having some dinner. It's absurd. I never go without my dinner. No one ever does, except vegetarians and people like that. Besides I have just made arrangements with Dr. Chasuble to be christened at a quarter to six under the name of Ernest.

JACK: My dear fellow, the sooner you give up that nonsense the better. I made arrangements this morning with Dr. Chasuble to be christened myself at 5:30, and I naturally will take the name of Ernest. Gwendolen would wish it. We can't both be christened Ernest. It's absurd. Besides, I have a perfect right to be christened if I like. There is no evidence at all that I ever have been christened by anybody. I should think it extremely probable I never was, and so does

Dr. Chasuble. It is entirely different in your case. You have been christened already.

ALGERNON: Yes, but I have not been christened for years.

JACK: Yes, but you have been christened. That is the important thing.

ALGERNON: Quite so. So I know my constitution can stand it. If you are not quite sure about your ever having been christened, I must say I think it rather dangerous your venturing on it now. It might make you very unwell. You can hardly have forgotten that someone very closely connected with you was very nearly carried off this week in Paris by a severe chill.

JACK: Yes, but you said yourself that a severe chill was not hereditary.

ALGERNON: It usen't to be, I know—but I daresay it is now. Science is always making wonderful improvements in things.

JACK: [*Picking up the muffin dish.*] Oh, that is nonsense; you are always talking nonsense.

ALGERNON: Jack, you are at the muffins again! I wish you wouldn't. There are only two left. [*Takes them.*] I told you I was particularly fond of muffins.

JACK: But I hate tea cake.

ALGERNON: Why on earth then do you allow tea cake to be served up for your guests? What ideas you have of hospitality!

JACK: Algernon! I have already told you to go. I don't want you here. Why don't you go!

ALGERNON: I haven't quite finished my tea yet! and there is still one muffin left.

[JACK *groans, and sinks into a chair.* ALGERNON *still continues eating.*]

ACT-DROP

ACT III

SCENE: *Morning room at the Manor House.*

[GWENDOLEN *and* CECILY *are at the window, looking out into the garden.*]

GWENDOLEN: The fact that they did not follow us at once into the house, as anyone else would have done, seems to me to show that they have some sense of shame left.

CECILY: They have been eating muffins. That looks like repentance.

GWENDOLEN: [*After a pause.*] They don't seem to notice us at all. Couldn't you cough?

CECILY: But I haven't got a cough.

GWENDOLEN: They're looking at us. What effrontery!

CECILY: They're approaching. That's very forward of them.

GWENDOLEN: Let us preserve a dignified silence.

CECILY: Certainly. It's the only thing to do now.

[*Enter* JACK *followed by* ALGERNON. *They whistle some dreadful popular air from a British Opera.*]

GWENDOLEN: This dignified silence seems to produce an unpleasant effect.

CECILY: A most distasteful one.

GWENDOLEN: But we will not be the first to speak.

CECILY: Certainly not.

GWENDOLEN: Mr. Worthing, I have something very particular to ask you. Much depends on your reply.

CECILY: Gwendolen, your common sense is invaluable. Mr. Moncrieff, kindly answer me the following question. Why did you pretend to be my guardian's brother?

ALGERNON: In order that I might have an opportunity of meeting you.

CECILY: [*To* GWENDOLEN.] That certainly seems a satisfactory explanation, does it not?

GWENDOLEN: Yes, dear, if you can believe him.

CECILY: I don't. But that does not affect the wonderful beauty of his answer.

GWENDOLEN: True. In matters of grave importance, style, not sincerity, is the vital thing. Mr. Worthing, what explanation can you offer to me for pretending to have a brother? Was it in order that you might have an opportunity of coming up to town to see me as often as possible?

JACK: Can you doubt it, Miss Fairfax?

GWENDOLEN: I have the gravest doubts upon the subject. But I intend to crush them. This is not the moment for German skepticism.[1] [*Moving to* CECILY.] Their explanations appear to be quite satisfactory, especially Mr. Worthing's. That seems to me to have the stamp of truth upon it.

CECILY: I am more than content with what Mr. Moncrieff said. His voice alone inspires one with absolute credulity.

GWENDOLEN: Then you think we should forgive them?

CECILY: Yes. I mean no.

GWENDOLEN: True! I had forgotten. There are principles at stake that one cannot surrender. Which of us should tell them? The task is not a pleasant one.

CECILY: Could we not both speak at the same time?

GWENDOLEN: An excellent idea! I nearly always speak at the same time as other people. Will you take the time from me?

CECILY: Certainly. [GWENDOLEN *beats time with uplifted finger.*]

GWENDOLEN AND CECILY: [*Speaking together.*] Your Christian names are still an insuperable barrier. That is all!

JACK AND ALGERNON: [*Speaking together.*] Our Christian names! Is that all? But we are going to be christened this afternoon.

GWENDOLEN: [*To* JACK.] For my sake you are prepared to do this terrible thing?

JACK: I am.

CECILY: [*To* ALGERNON.] To please me you are ready to face this fearful ordeal?

ALGERNON: I am!

GWENDOLEN: How absurd to talk of the equality of the sexes! Where questions of self-sacrifice are concerned, men are infinitely beyond us.

JACK: We are. [*Clasps hands with* ALGERNON.]

CECILY: They have moments of physical courage of which we women know absolutely nothing.

1. Reference to such philosophical movements as the Materialism of Ludwig Feuerbach (1804–72) and such theological movements as the "Higher Criticism," which promoted studying the Bible in the same way as other books.

GWENDOLEN: [*To* JACK.] Darling!

ALGERNON: [*To* CECILY.] Darling. [*They fall into each other's arms.*]

[*Enter* MERRIMAN. *When he enters he coughs loudly, seeing the situation.*]

MERRIMAN: Ahem! Ahem! Lady Bracknell!

JACK: Good heavens!

[*Enter* LADY BRACKNELL. *The couples separate in alarm. Exit* MERRIMAN.]

LADY BRACKNELL: Gwendolen! What does this mean?

GWENDOLEN: Merely that I am engaged to be married to Mr. Worthing, mamma.

LADY BRACKNELL: Come here. Sit down. Sit down immediately. Hesitation of any kind is a sign of mental decay in the young, of physical weakness in the old. [*Turns to* JACK.] Apprised, sir, of my daughter's sudden flight by her trusty maid, whose confidence I purchased by means of a small coin, I followed her at once by a luggage train. Her unhappy father is, I am glad to say, under the impression that she is attending a more than usually lengthy lecture by the University Extension Scheme[2] on the Influence of a Permanent Income on Thought. I do not propose to undeceive him. Indeed I have never undeceived him on any question. I would consider it wrong. But of course, you will clearly understand that all communication between yourself and my daughter must cease immediately from this moment. On this point, as indeed on all points, I am firm.

JACK: I am engaged to be married to Gwendolen, Lady Bracknell!

LADY BRACKNELL: You are nothing of the kind, sir. And now, as regards Algernon! . . . Algernon!

ALGERNON: Yes, Aunt Augusta.

LADY BRACKNELL: May I ask if it is in this house that your invalid friend Mr. Bunbury resides?

ALGERNON: [*Stammering.*] Oh! No! Bunbury doesn't live here. Bunbury is somewhere else at present. In fact, Bunbury is dead.

LADY BRACKNELL: Dead! When did Mr. Bunbury die? His death must have been extremely sudden.

ALGERNON: [*Airily.*] Oh! I killed Bunbury this afternoon. I mean poor Bunbury died this afternoon.

LADY BRACKNELL: What did he die of?

ALGERNON: Bunbury? Oh, he was quite exploded.

LADY BRACKNELL: Exploded! Was he the victim of a revolutionary outrage? I was not aware that Mr. Bunbury was interested in social legislation. If so, he is well punished for his morbidity.

ALGERNON: My dear Aunt Augusta, I mean he was found out! The doctors found out that Bunbury could not live, that is what I mean—so Bunbury died.

LADY BRACKNELL: He seems to have had great confidence in the opinion of his physicians. I am glad, however, that he made up his mind at the last to some definite course of action, and acted under proper medical advice. And now

2. Program of public lectures delivered by university professors.

that we have finally got rid of this Mr. Bunbury, may I ask, Mr. Worthing, who is that young person whose hand my nephew Algernon is now holding in what seems to me a peculiarly unnecessary manner?

JACK: That lady is Miss Cecily Cardew, my ward.

[LADY BRACKNELL *bows coldly to* CECILY.]

ALGERNON: I am engaged to be married to Cecily, Aunt Augusta.

LADY BRACKNELL: I beg your pardon?

CECILY: Mr. Moncrieff and I are engaged to be married, Lady Bracknell.

LADY BRACKNELL: [*With a shiver, crossing to the sofa and sitting down.*] I do not know whether there is anything peculiarly exciting in the air of this particular part of Hertfordshire, but the number of engagements that go on seems to me considerably above the proper average that statistics have laid down for our guidance. I think some preliminary inquiry on my part would not be out of place. Mr. Worthing, is Miss Cardew at all connected with any of the larger railway stations in London? I merely desire information. Until yesterday I had no idea that there were any families or persons whose origin was a terminus.

[JACK *looks perfectly furious, but restrains himself.*]

JACK: [*In a clear, cold voice.*] Miss Cardew is the granddaughter of the late Mr. Thomas Cardew of 149, Belgrave Square, S.W.; Gervase Park, Dorking, Surrey; and the Sporran, Fifeshire, N.B.[3]

LADY BRACKNELL: That sounds not unsatisfactory. Three addresses always inspire confidence, even in tradesmen. But what proof have I of their authenticity?

JACK: I have carefully preserved the Court Guides[4] of the period. They are open to your inspection, Lady Bracknell.

LADY BRACKNELL: [*Grimly.*] I have known strange errors in that publication.

JACK: Miss Cardew's family solicitors are Messrs.[5] Markby, Markby, and Markby.

LADY BRACKNELL: Markby, Markby, and Markby? A firm of the very highest position in their profession. Indeed I am told that one of the Mr. Markbys is occasionally to be seen at dinner parties. So far I am satisfied.

JACK: [*Very irritably.*] How extremely kind of you, Lady Bracknell! I have also in my possession, you will be pleased to hear, certificates of Miss Cardew's birth, baptism, whooping cough, registration, vaccination, confirmation, and the measles; both the German and the English variety.

LADY BRACKNELL: Ah! A life crowded with incident, I see; though perhaps somewhat too exciting for a young girl. I am not myself in favor of premature experiences. [*Rises, looks at her watch.*] Gwendolen! the time approaches for our departure. We have not a moment to lose. As a matter of form, Mr. Worthing, I had better ask you if Miss Cardew has any little fortune?

3. In addition to his London residence in Belgrave Square (referred to in act I), Mr. Cardew has homes in the south of England (Dorking, Surrey) and in Scotland (Fifeshire; N.B.: North Britain).

4. Records of civil and legal proceedings. 5. That is, "Messieurs" ("Misters" in French).

JACK: Oh! about a hundred and thirty thousand pounds in the Funds.[6] That is all. Good-bye, Lady Bracknell. So pleased to have seen you.

LADY BRACKNELL: [*Sitting down again.*] A moment, Mr. Worthing. A hundred and thirty thousand pounds! And in the Funds! Miss Cardew seems to me a most attractive young lady, now that I look at her. Few girls of the present day have any really solid qualities, any of the qualities that last, and improve with time. We live, I regret to say, in an age of surfaces. [*To* CECILY.] Come over here, dear. [CECILY *goes across.*] Pretty child! your dress is sadly simple, and your hair seems almost as Nature might have left it. But we can soon alter all that. A thoroughly experienced French maid produces a really marvelous result in a very brief space of time. I remember recommending one to young Lady Lancing, and after three months her own husband did not know her.

JACK: [*Aside.*] And after six months nobody knew her.

LADY BRACKNELL: [*Glares at* JACK *for a few moments. Then bends, with a practiced smile, to* CECILY.] Kindly turn round, sweet child. [CECILY *turns completely round.*] No, the side view is what I want. [CECILY *presents her profile.*] Yes, quite as I expected. There are distinct social possibilities in your profile. The two weak points in our age are its want of principle and its want of profile. The chin a little higher, dear. Style largely depends on the way the chin is worn. They are worn very high, just at present. Algernon!

ALGERNON: Yes, Aunt Augusta!

LADY BRACKNELL: There are distinct social possibilities in Miss Cardew's profile.

ALGERNON: Cecily is the sweetest, dearest, prettiest girl in the whole world. And I don't care twopence about social possibilities.

LADY BRACKNELL: Never speak disrespectfully of Society, Algernon. Only people who can't get into it do that. [*To* CECILY.] Dear child, of course you know that Algernon has nothing but his debts to depend upon. But I do not approve of mercenary marriages. When I married Lord Bracknell I had no fortune of any kind. But I never dreamed for a moment of allowing that to stand in my way. Well, I suppose I must give my consent.

ALGERNON: Thank you, Aunt Augusta.

LADY BRACKNELL: Cecily, you may kiss me!

CECILY: [*Kisses her.*] Thank you, Lady Bracknell.

LADY BRACKNELL: You may also address me as Aunt Augusta for the future.

CECILY: Thank you, Aunt Augusta.

LADY BRACKNELL: The marriage, I think, had better take place quite soon.

ALGERNON: Thank you, Aunt Augusta.

CECILY: Thank you, Aunt Augusta.

LADY BRACKNELL: To speak frankly, I am not in favor of long engagements. They give people the opportunity of finding out each other's character before marriage, which I think is never advisable.

JACK: I beg your pardon for interrupting you, Lady Bracknell, but this engagement is quite out of the question. I am Miss Cardew's guardian, and she cannot

6. Over $20,000,000 in today's U.S. currency, invested in stock of the British National Debt.

marry without my consent until she comes of age. That consent I absolutely decline to give.

LADY BRACKNELL: Upon what grounds may I ask? Algernon is an extremely, I may almost say an ostentatiously, eligible young man. He has nothing, but he looks everything. What more can one desire?

JACK: It pains me very much to have to speak frankly to you, Lady Bracknell, about your nephew, but the fact is that I do not approve at all of his moral character. I suspect him of being untruthful.

[ALGERNON *and* CECILY *look at him in indignant amazement.*]

LADY BRACKNELL: Untruthful! My nephew Algernon? Impossible! He is an Oxonian.[7]

JACK: I fear there can be no possible doubt about the matter. This afternoon, during my temporary absence in London on an important question of romance, he obtained admission to my house by means of the false pretense of being my brother. Under an assumed name he drank, I've just been informed by the butler, an entire pint bottle of my Perrier-Jouet, Brut, '89;[8] a wine I was specially reserving for myself. Continuing his disgraceful deception, he succeeded in the course of the afternoon in alienating the affections of my only ward. He subsequently stayed to tea, and devoured every single muffin. And what makes his conduct all the more heartless is, that he was perfectly well aware from the first that I have no brother, that I never had a brother, and that I don't intend to have a brother, not even of any kind. I distinctly told him so myself yesterday afternoon.

LADY BRACKNELL: Ahem! Mr. Worthing, after careful consideration I have decided entirely to overlook my nephew's conduct to you.

JACK: That is very generous of you, Lady Bracknell. My own decision, however, is unalterable. I decline to give my consent.

LADY BRACKNELL: [*To* CECILY.] Come here, sweet child. [CECILY *goes over.*] How old are you, dear?

CECILY: Well, I am really only eighteen, but I always admit to twenty when I go to evening parties.

LADY BRACKNELL: You are perfectly right in making some slight alteration. Indeed, no woman should ever be quite accurate about her age. It looks so calculating. . . . [*In a meditative manner.*] Eighteen, but admitting to twenty at evening parties. Well, it will not be very long before you are of age and free from the restraints of tutelage. So I don't think your guardian's consent is, after all, a matter of any importance.

JACK: Pray excuse me, Lady Bracknell, for interrupting you again, but it is only fair to tell you that according to the terms of her grandfather's will Miss Cardew does not come legally of age till she is thirty-five.

LADY BRACKNELL: That does not seem to me to be a grave objection. Thirty-five is a very attractive age. London society is full of women of the very highest birth who have, of their own free choice, remained thirty-five for years. Lady Dumbleton is an instance in point. To my own knowledge she has been

7. Graduate of Oxford University. 8. Very fine champagne.

thirty-five ever since she arrived at the age of forty, which was many years ago now. I see no reason why our dear Cecily should not be even still more attractive at the age you mention than she is at present. There will be a large accumulation of property.

CECILY: Algy, could you wait for me till I was thirty-five?

ALGERNON: Of course I could, Cecily. You know I could.

CECILY: Yes, I felt it instinctively, but I couldn't wait all that time. I hate waiting even five minutes for anybody. It always makes me rather cross. I am not punctual myself, I know, but I do like punctuality in others, and waiting, even to be married, is quite out of the question.

ALGERNON: Then what is to be done, Cecily?

CECILY: I don't know, Mr. Moncrieff.

LADY BRACKNELL: My dear Mr. Worthing, as Miss Cardew states positively that she cannot wait till she is thirty-five—a remark which I am bound to say seems to me to show a somewhat impatient nature—I would beg of you to reconsider your decision.

JACK: But my dear Lady Bracknell, the matter is entirely in your own hands. The moment you consent to my marriage with Gwendolen, I will most gladly allow your nephew to form an alliance with my ward.

LADY BRACKNELL: [*Rising and drawing herself up.*] You must be quite aware that what you propose is out of the question.

JACK: Then a passionate celibacy is all that any of us can look forward to.

LADY BRACKNELL: This is not the destiny I propose for Gwendolen. Algernon, of course, can choose for himself. [*Pulls out her watch.*] Come, dear; [GWENDOLEN *rises.*] we have already missed five, if not six, trains. To miss any more might expose us to comment on the platform.

[*Enter* CANON CHASUBLE.]

CHASUBLE: Everything is quite ready for the christenings.

LADY BRACKNELL: The christenings, sir! Is not that somewhat premature!

CHASUBLE: [*Looking rather puzzled, and pointing to* JACK *and* ALGERNON.] Both these gentlemen have expressed a desire for immediate baptism.

LADY BRACKNELL: At their age? The idea is grotesque and irreligious! Algernon, I forbid you to be baptized. I will not hear of such excesses. Lord Bracknell would be highly displeased if he learned that that was the way in which you wasted your time and money.

CHASUBLE: Am I to understand then that there are to be no christenings at all this afternoon?

JACK: I don't think that, as things are now, it would be of much practical value to either of us, Dr. Chasuble.

CHASUBLE: I am grieved to hear such sentiments from you, Mr. Worthing. They savor of the heretical views of the Anabaptists,[9] views that I have completely refuted in four of my unpublished sermons. However, as your present mood seems to be one peculiarly secular, I will return to the church at once.

9. Sixteenth-century religious group, somewhat like contemporary Mennonites. Dr. Chasuble, however, is probably using the term loosely to apply to a group more like contemporary Baptists.

Indeed, I have just been informed by the pew-opener[1] that for the last hour and a half Miss Prism has been waiting for me in the vestry.

LADY BRACKNELL: [*Starting.*] Miss Prism! Did I hear you mention a Miss Prism?

CHASUBLE: Yes, Lady Bracknell. I am on my way to join her.

LADY BRACKNELL: Pray allow me to detain you for a moment. This matter may prove to be one of vital importance to Lord Bracknell and myself. Is this Miss Prism a female of repellent aspect, remotely connected with education?

CHASUBLE: [*Somewhat indignantly.*] She is the most cultivated of ladies, and the very picture of respectability.

LADY BRACKNELL: It is obviously the same person. May I ask what position she holds in your household?

CHASUBLE: [*Severely.*] I am a celibate, madam.

JACK: [*Interposing.*] Miss Prism, Lady Bracknell, has been for the last three years Miss Cardew's esteemed governess and valued companion.

LADY BRACKNELL: In spite of what I hear of her, I must see her at once. Let her be sent for.

CHASUBLE: [*Looking off.*] She approaches; she is nigh.

[*Enter* MISS PRISM *hurriedly.*]

MISS PRISM: I was told you expected me in the vestry, dear Canon. I have been waiting for you there for an hour and three quarters. [*Catches sight of* LADY BRACKNELL, *who has fixed her with a stony glare.* MISS PRISM *grows pale and quails. She looks anxiously round as if desirous to escape.*]

LADY BRACKNELL: [*In a severe, judicial voice.*] Prism! [MISS PRISM *bows her head in shame.*] Come here, Prism! [MISS PRISM *approaches in a humble manner.*] Prism! Where is that baby? [*General consternation.* THE CANON *starts back in horror.* ALGERNON *and* JACK *pretend to be anxious to shield* CECILY *and* GWENDOLEN *from hearing the details of a terrible public scandal.*] Twenty-eight years ago, Prism, you left Lord Bracknell's house, Number 104, Upper Grosvenor Street, in charge of a perambulator that contained a baby, of the male sex. You never returned. A few weeks later, through the elaborate investigations of the Metropolitan police, the perambulator was discovered at midnight, standing by itself in a remote corner of Bayswater.[2] It contained the manuscript of a three-volume novel of more than usually revolting sentimentality. [MISS PRISM *starts in involuntary indignation.*] But the baby was not there! [*Everyone looks at* MISS PRISM.] Prism! Where is that baby? [*A pause.*]

MISS PRISM: Lady Bracknell, I admit with shame that I do not know. I only wish I did. The plain facts of the case are these. On the morning of the day you mention, a day that is forever branded on my memory, I prepared as usual to take the baby out in its perambulator. I had also with me a somewhat old, but capacious handbag, in which I had intended to place the manuscript of a work of fiction that I had written during my few unoccupied hours. In a moment

1. Usher. Since most pews were enclosed, his duties would have included opening the gate that allowed worshipers to enter. In addition, since most pews were rented by specific persons, he would have been responsible for seeing that worshipers were seated in the correct pews.
2. Fashionable residential neighborhood north of Hyde Park and Kensington Gardens.

of mental abstraction, for which I never can forgive myself, I deposited the manuscript in the bassinette, and placed the baby in the handbag.

JACK: [*Who has been listening attentively.*] But where did you deposit the handbag?

MISS PRISM: Do not ask me, Mr. Worthing.

JACK: Miss Prism, this is a matter of no small importance to me. I insist on knowing where you deposited the handbag that contained that infant.

MISS PRISM: I left it in the cloak room of one of the larger railway stations in London.

JACK: What railway station?

MISS PRISM: [*Quite crushed.*] Victoria. The Brighton line. [*Sinks into a chair.*]

JACK: I must retire to my room for a moment. Gwendolen, wait here for me.

GWENDOLEN: If you are not too long, I will wait here for you all my life.

[*Exit* JACK *in great excitement.*]

CHASUBLE: What do you think this means, Lady Bracknell?

LADY BRACKNELL: I dare not even suspect, Dr. Chasuble. I need hardly tell you that in families of high position strange coincidences are not supposed to occur. They are hardly considered the thing.

[*Noises heard overhead as if someone was throwing trunks about. Everyone looks up.*]

CECILY: Uncle Jack seems strangely agitated.

CHASUBLE: Your guardian has a very emotional nature.

LADY BRACKNELL: This noise is extremely unpleasant. It sounds as if he was having an argument. I dislike arguments of any kind. They are always vulgar, and often convincing.

CHASUBLE: [*Looking up.*] It has stopped now. [*The noise is redoubled.*]

LADY BRACKNELL: I wish he would arrive at some conclusion.

GWENDOLEN: This suspense is terrible. I hope it will last.

[*Enter* JACK *with a handbag of black leather in his hand.*]

JACK: [*Rushing over to* MISS PRISM.] Is this the handbag, Miss Prism? Examine it carefully before you speak. The happiness of more than one life depends on your answer.

MISS PRISM: [*Calmly.*] It seems to be mine. Yes, here is the injury it received through the upsetting of a Gower Street omnibus in younger and happier days. Here is the stain on the lining caused by the explosion of a temperance beverage,[3] an incident that occurred at Leamington. And here, on the lock, are my initials. I had forgotten that in an extravagant mood I had had them placed there. The bag is undoubtedly mine. I am delighted to have it so unexpectedly restored to me. It has been a great inconvenience being without it all these years.

JACK: [*In a pathetic voice.*] Miss Prism, more is restored to you than this handbag. I was the baby you placed in it.

3. Carbonated soda drinks were marketed in the 1890s as "temperance beverages" (healthy alternatives to alcohol).

MISS PRISM: [*Amazed.*] You!

JACK: [*Embracing her.*] Yes . . . mother!

MISS PRISM: [*Recoiling in indignant astonishment.*] Mr. Worthing! I am unmarried!

JACK: Unmarried! I do not deny that is a serious blow. But after all, who has the right to cast a stone against one who has suffered? Cannot repentance wipe out an act of folly? Why should there be one law for men, and another for women? Mother, I forgive you. [*Tries to embrace her again.*]

MISS PRISM: [*Still more indignant.*] Mr. Worthing, there is some error. [*Pointing to* LADY BRACKNELL.] There is the lady who can tell you who you really are.

JACK: [*After a pause.*] Lady Bracknell, I hate to seem inquisitive, but would you kindly inform me who I am?

LADY BRACKNELL: I am afraid that the news I have to give you will not altogether please you. You are the son of my poor sister, Mrs. Moncrieff, and consequently Algernon's elder brother.

JACK: Algy's elder brother! Then I have a brother after all. I knew I had a brother! I always said I had a brother! Cecily—how could you have ever doubted that I had a brother? [*Seizes hold of* ALGERNON.] Dr. Chasuble, my unfortunate brother. Miss Prism, my unfortunate brother. Gwendolen, my unfortunate brother. Algy, you young scoundrel, you will have to treat me with more respect in the future. You have never behaved to me like a brother in all your life.

ALGERNON: Well, not till today, old boy, I admit. I did my best, however, though I was out of practice. [*Shakes hands.*]

GWENDOLEN: [*To* JACK.] My own! But what own are you? What is your Christian name, now that you have become someone else?

JACK: Good heavens! . . . I had quite forgotten that point. Your decision on the subject of my name is irrevocable, I suppose?

GWENDOLEN: I never change, except in my affections.

CECILY: What a noble nature you have, Gwendolen!

JACK: Then the question had better be cleared up at once. Aunt Augusta, a moment. At the time when Miss Prism left me in the handbag, had I been christened already?

LADY BRACKNELL: Every luxury that money could buy, including christening, had been lavished on you by your fond and doting parents.

JACK: Then I was christened! That is settled. Now, what name was I given? Let me know the worst.

LADY BRACKNELL: Being the eldest son you were naturally christened after your father.

JACK: [*Irritably.*] Yes, but what was my father's Christian name?

LADY BRACKNELL: [*Meditatively.*] I cannot at the present moment recall what the General's Christian name was. But I have no doubt he had one. He was eccentric, I admit. But only in later years. And that was the result of the Indian climate, and marriage, and indigestion, and other things of that kind.

JACK: Algy! Can't you recollect what our father's Christian name was?

ALGERNON: My dear boy, we were never even on speaking terms. He died before I was a year old.

JACK: His name would appear in the Army Lists of the period, I suppose, Aunt Augusta?

LADY BRACKNELL: The General was essentially a man of peace, except in his domestic life. But I have no doubt his name would appear in any military directory.

JACK: The Army Lists of the last forty years are here. These delightful records should have been my constant study. [*Rushes to bookcase and tears the books out.*] M. Generals . . . Mallam, Maxbohm, Magley, what ghastly names they have—Markby, Migsby, Mobbs, Moncrieff! Lieutenant 1840, Captain, Lieutenant Colonel, Colonel, General 1869, Christian names, Ernest John. [*Puts book very quietly down and speaks quite calmly.*] I always told you, Gwendolen, my name was Ernest, didn't I? Well, it is Ernest after all. I mean it naturally is Ernest.

LADY BRACKNELL: Yes, I remember now that the General was called Ernest. I knew I had some particular reason for disliking the name.

GWENDOLEN: Ernest! My own Ernest! I felt from the first that you could have no other name!

JACK: Gwendolen, it is a terrible thing for a man to find out suddenly that all his life he has been speaking nothing but the truth. Can you forgive me?

GWENDOLEN: I can. For I feel that you are sure to change.

JACK: My own one!

CHASUBLE: [*To* MISS PRISM.] Laetitia! [*Embraces her.*]

MISS PRISM: [*Enthusiastically.*] Frederick! At last!

ALGERNON: Cecily! [*Embraces her.*] At last!

JACK: Gwendolen! [*Embraces her.*] At last!

LADY BRACKNELL: My nephew, you seem to be displaying signs of triviality.

JACK: On the contrary, Aunt Augusta, I've now realized for the first time in my life the vital Importance of Being Earnest.

CURTAIN

1895 1899

SUGGESTIONS FOR WRITING

1. OEDIPUS THE KING poses intriguing questions about the mysteries of sight and blindness, light and darkness. Why, for example, is it significant that Apollo, the sun god, is also a god of prophecy? Why is Teiresias, a prophet inspired by Apollo, blind? How does his blindness compare to that of Oedipus? What distinction does Sophocles draw between sight and insight? Using specific actions, images, and passages, write an essay in which you examine what *seeing* means in OEDIPUS THE KING. With what kinds of enlightenment and darkness is the play concerned?
2. What is "tragic" and what is "heroic" about a tragic hero? To the modern sensibility, Oedipus's poor judgment and stubborn unwillingness to face facts are what bring down upon him, his family, and the people of Thebes, the fate shown in the play. But to the ancients, Oedipus was the model of nobility in his innate sense of justice, selfless concern for the well-being of his people, and ultimate embrace of his destiny. What, then, is the nature of Oedipus's responsibility for his fate and the fate of Thebes? Write an essay in which you discuss the role of the "tragic hero" in OEDIPUS THE KING. What is the play's intended "lesson"?
3. In his *Poetics*, Aristotle praises OEDIPUS THE KING as a model tragedy—nearly perfect in the simplicity of its plot, the nobility of its characters, and the decorousness of its poetry. Write an essay in which you compare the dramatic elements

of OEDIPUS THE KING with those of at least one other play by Sophocles, such as ANTIGONE (ch. 30). How does Sophocles define and vary his dramatic formula?

4. In its traditional form as practiced, for example, by Shakespeare, a comedy nearly always depicts lovers who must overcome obstacles (such as misunderstandings, unjust laws, or family interference) in order to unite in marriage and in this way ensure the continuation of their society. By such a definition, is THE IMPORTANCE OF BEING EARNEST a traditional "comedy"? Or might it instead be labeled an "anti-comedy," a play that subverts traditional social mores? Using research if necessary, write an essay in which you trace the ways in which THE IMPORTANCE OF BEING EARNEST does and does not adhere to the classic comedy formula.
5. Oscar Wilde was famous in his time as a champion of aestheticism—that is, the belief that art exists solely for its own sake and that artists should be free from any religious, political, or social interference. "All art," he declared, "is quite useless." Nevertheless, in its own witty way, THE IMPORTANCE OF BEING EARNEST seems to address many of the same matters that concern moralists—the proper ordering of society, the use and abuse of language, the relations between men and women. Is Wilde's play truly "useless"? Write an essay in which you argue that the play either is or is not a mere entertainment. Does THE IMPORTANCE OF BEING EARNEST have a "moral" or at least a theme?

Exploring Contexts

28 THE AUTHOR'S WORK AS CONTEXT: WILLIAM SHAKESPEARE

When we read, we inevitably compare. We compare the writer's style to the styles of other writers; we compare characters within a story or play to one another and to people we know; we compare our life experiences to the many imaginary experiences that unfold before us as we read. Our interpretations of literature are fueled by such comparisons.

Reading several works by a single author is one of the most rewarding and enlightening types of comparison we can employ as active readers of literature. Such comparisons serve a variety of purposes: They help us develop a sense of the overall shape of the writer's work (that is, the writer's **oeuvre**, or **canon**); they reveal the kinds of characters, plots, and dramatic situations the author tends to create; they offer a glimpse into the author's particular way of looking at the world. At the same time, such comparisons can enrich our understanding of any one work by drawing our attention to features we might not have thought much about otherwise.

THE LIFE OF SHAKESPEARE: A BIOGRAPHICAL MYSTERY

This chapter offers you the opportunity to compare two plays by one of history's most vital and versatile playwrights: William Shakespeare. Shakespeare is a particularly enticing subject for this kind of comparative study in part because we know so little about him. While we can enhance our reading of many writers by studying the letters, essays, diaries, and other documents in which the writers comment directly on their lives and works, Shakespeare left behind no such record. The only records that exist are a handful of official ones—marriage licenses, property deeds, and wills.

William Shakespeare

Those records tell a brief story. Shakespeare's origins were humble: His grandfather, Richard, rented the land he farmed, near Stratford-upon-Avon, a market town in the English midlands. Richard's son, John, married the daughter of one of Richard's former landlords and moved to town. There he became a tradesman prosperous and respected enough to buy quite a bit of property and to hold several civic offices, including that of mayor. The family's star was on the rise by the time William was born (some time in April 1564). Though most likely neither of Shakespeare's parents could read or write (certainly they had no

Shakespeare's birthplace

formal schooling), his father's involvement in city government brought with it the privilege of enrolling William in the local free grammar school. Here Shakespeare learned how to read and write, not only in English but also in Latin and perhaps Greek. His schoolmasters also probably required him to read such standard classical works as Ovid's *Metamorphoses* and the plays of Plautus and Terence (which greatly influenced the plays he would later write). In 1582, Shakespeare married Anne Hathaway, the daughter of a local farmer; in the next three years, the couple had three children, including a set of twins.

From the time of the twins' birth in 1585 until 1592, Shakespeare's life becomes—for us—a blank: All we know is that by the latter date he was a successful actor and playwright spending most of his time in London. (We know this, in part, because Shakespeare was prominent enough to be called an "upstart crow" in a book published by a rival playwright in 1592; apparently, this London-born, university-educated author felt a bit threatened by the undereducated provincial.) Though, in 1594, the "upstart crow" achieved a measure of renown as a poet by publishing two lengthy narrative poems (*Venus and Adonis* and *The Rape of Lucrece*), his career from this time until his death centered mainly on his work with the Lord Chamberlain's (later King's) Men—one of the two most prominent acting companies of his day. Shakespeare's work with the company was multifaceted: An actor with the troupe and its chief dramatist, he was also a shareholder who helped manage the troupe's affairs (including the building of the Globe Theatre, on the South Bank of the River Thames, in 1599). Being a shareholder ensured that he prospered along with the company (especially after they secured the patronage of the king in 1603). As a result, Shakespeare enjoyed a level of economic prosperity and a kind of status that wouldn't have been possible to a mere actor, playwright, or poet. The Crown granted Shakespeare's father (and thus the playwright) the title of "gentleman" in the late 1590s. And at his death in 1616, Shakespeare left his family substantial property in both London and Stratford (where the family had continued to live).

Model of the Globe Theater

Such facts remind us that Shakespeare was, after all, a real and in some ways rather ordinary person—who ultimately convinced audiences and rivals alike that he was more than an "upstart crow," but who did not, as a recent biographer reminds us, "in his own day inspire the mysterious veneration that afterwards came to surround him." These mundane facts tell us almost nothing, however, about the man's or the artist's inner life—his personal opinions, his motives, his loves, his dislikes, his politics, his "philosophy." These we can only infer, guess at, or imagine by reading and comparing his poems and plays. Luckily, Shakespeare left us a lot of these, including 154 sonnets (some of which are included in the poetry section of this book) and at least thirty-eight plays. Scholars believe Shakespeare cowrote at least one more play, and others may yet be discovered and authenticated.

EXPLORING SHAKESPEARE'S WORK: *A MIDSUMMER NIGHT'S DREAM* AND *HAMLET*

Given that his plays include thirteen comedies, ten tragedies, ten English histories, and five romances, variety is a distinctive feature of Shakespeare's work as a playwright. It is fitting, then, that the two plays included in this chapter—A MIDSUMMER NIGHT'S DREAM and HAMLET—seem, at first glance, so different. *A Midsummer Night's Dream*, written in about 1595, is generally considered one of the last of Shakespeare's "apprentice" plays—the work of a young writer just beginning to find his own voice and dramatic style, but still quite dependent on classical models. Though written only a few years later (c. 1599–1601), *Hamlet* is nonetheless regarded as one of the greatest works of a seasoned writer. Differences proliferate: *Dream*, a **comedy**, culminates in marriage (several marriages, in fact); *Hamlet*, a **tragedy**, concludes with the death and destruction of an entire royal family. *Dream* is among Shakespeare's shortest plays; *Hamlet*, among his longest. *Hamlet* focuses squarely—almost relentlessly—on its title character, whom we leave the play feeling that we know inside and out. *Dream*, in contrast, flits among many characters. Though we may fall in love with some of them, we probably will not feel that we truly know any of them. (Indeed, part of the play's humor comes from our having as hard a time as the characters themselves do remembering who is who and who loves whom.)

But while the plays have important and revealing differences, they have equally significant similarities, and by attending to these similarities we may come to understand and appreciate Shakespeare's particular way of looking at the world. To begin with, we may approach such similarities (within these or any plays) by concentrating on the elements, looking for patterns in character, setting, structure, tone, and theme, remembering that these elements ultimately combine to shape our experience of any one play.

In thinking about character, for example, notice that both the **protagonists** and the **antagonists** of *A Midsummer Night's Dream* and *Hamlet* are persons of high birth and position. These characters' choices and behavior deeply affect the communities that they lead. In fact, both plays repeatedly remind us of the general effects and communal significance of such characters' actions. Like all Shakespeare's plays, this comedy and tragedy both take for granted the idea that "on [a leader's] choice depends / The safety and health of th[e] whole state" (*Hamlet* 1.3.20–21), and both trace the effects of the particular choices made by kings, princes, and dukes.

Shakespeare and his contemporaries often compared the relationship between a king and his subjects to that between a father and his children or between a husband and his wife. For example, an early Shakespeare comedy, *The Taming of the Shrew*, concludes with a speech in which the tamed shrew declares, "Thy husband is thy lord, thy life, thy keeper, / Thy head, thy sovereign." Building on this idea, she argues both that a woman's duty to her husband is the same "as the subject owes the prince" and that a woman who refuses to obey her husband is exactly like "a foul contending rebel / And graceless traitor." We can see similar analogies at work in *A Midsummer Night's Dream* and *Hamlet*: One begins with a duke and a father provoking a group of young Athenians to rebel against them; the other shows us a son who is also a prince struggling to choose the right response to the murder of a father who was also a king.

We pay attention to the effects of these high-born characters on their environments in part because Shakespeare's plays also include characters who occupy positions much lower on the social ladder than the main characters do. In addition to Titania, Oberon, Theseus, and Hippolyta (rulers of the divine and human realms), *A Midsummer Night's Dream* introduces us to the Athenian craftsmen (or "mechanicals") led by the fittingly named Bottom. And while *Hamlet* focuses predominantly on members of the Danish royal court, one of the most memorable scenes in the play features a lowly gravedigger and the skeletal remains of a court jester named Yorick. As a result, the two plays demonstrate Shakespeare's tendency to people his plays with a socially diverse cast of characters and to thereby create a socially inclusive dramatic world.

As inclusive as Shakespeare's dramatic world is, it is far from *democratic* (as the speech from *The Taming of the Shrew* suggests). As you read more plays by Shakespeare, you will probably become more attuned to the different ways in which they depict "high" and "low" characters. *A Midsummer Night's Dream* is typical, for example, in the way it associates socially low characters with **low** or **physical comedy** (as opposed to **high** or **verbal comedy**). Bottom, after all, wears an ass's head for much of the play. Yet Bottom is also typical of Shakespeare's socially humble characters because he possesses a kind of wisdom his social betters lack.

Despite the tendency to distinguish high from low, then, Shakespearean drama draws our attention to fundamental human experiences that cut across social lines. *A Midsummer Night's Dream* reminds us that a fairy queen is no more immune to love's magic or foolishness than the lowliest of mortals; *Hamlet*, that a king's life lasts no longer than a court jester's. The joys of love, the pain of death—these experiences link us and remind us of our common humanity.

Shakespeare suggests such links, in part, by structuring each play so that the main plot is complemented by parallel, yet often contrasting, **subplots**. *A Midsummer Night's Dream* offers at least four plots, each featuring a pair of lovers whose happiness is, or has been, threatened by their own failures to understand each other or by others' opposition to their relationship. *Hamlet* revolves around three intersecting, but distinct, plots featuring Hamlet, Laertes, and Fortinbras—

Titania and Bottom, from *A Midsummer Night's Dream*

three very different young men who must each figure out how to respond to, and perhaps avenge, his father's murder. In these, as in other Shakespeare plays, the secondary plots can be divided into *underplots*, which are romantic or parodic versions of the main plot, and *overplots*, which foreground its political dimensions. In *A Midsummer Night's Dream*, Bottom becomes the protagonist of the underplot, Theseus and Hippolyta (and, perhaps, Titania and Oberon) of the overplot(s). In *Hamlet*, the underplot focuses on Laertes; the overplot, on Fortinbras. However, all the subplots encourage us—and sometimes, as in *Hamlet*, the characters themselves—to compare the ways different people handle similar situations and thus to evaluate various choices and various responses. The parallel plots serve simultaneously as a structural device, a potent means of characterization, and a way of drawing our attention to general issues and themes.

Reading *Hamlet* and *A Midsummer Night's Dream* side by side may also help us appreciate the tonal complexity of Shakespeare's plays—their incorporation of both comic and tragic elements. While *A Midsummer Night's Dream* plunges us into a nighttime world dominated by the intertwining forces of magic, love, and humor, it also continually reminds us of the dangerous aspects of the night, of the struggles that human beings endure in their pursuit of love and happiness, of the brevity and fragility of human joy and life, even of what Hamlet calls the "thousand natural shocks / That flesh is heir to" (3.1.62–63). The specter of death hovers in the background of *A Midsummer Night's Dream* as surely as it occupies the foreground of *Hamlet*. And though *Hamlet*, like most tragedies, focuses primarily on mortality, violence, and time's destructive force, it also shows us the comic side of the human condition. In fact, one of the things that makes Hamlet such a sympathetic character is his sense of humor.

Turning from **tone** to **theme**, we find that both *Hamlet* and *A Midsummer Night's Dream* say something about the order of things and the rhythm of life. Although *Hamlet* ends with a body-strewn stage, the play encourages us to see those deaths as the necessary prelude to a restoration of order and health to a kingdom diseased and disordered as a result of a sovereign's choices. Claudius's crimes ultimately infect and poison everything and everyone, even innocent bystanders like Ophelia. Both to us and to Hamlet, Claudius's reign represents the triumph of humanity's worst impulses. By embracing his role as heaven's "scourge and minister" even at the risk of his own life (3.4.179–81), however, Hamlet reaffirms our faith in humanity's noblest qualities as he strives to set right all that is "rotten in the state of Denmark" (1.4.90). In *A Midsummer Night's Dream*, we again see the actions of a sovereign turn the world upside down: The young rebel against the old, women chase men, old friends turn on each other, an ass consorts with a queen. Clearly, the kinds of dissension and disorder at work in *A Midsummer Night's Dream* make us laugh, while those in *Hamlet* make us cringe or cry. Yet the rhythm of both plays turns out to be surprisingly similar, tracing the movement from disorder to order, from dissension to harmony. In the process, both plays ask us to think about the nature and causes of social, political, and moral disorder, of dissension within states and families.

Sir Laurence Olivier as Hamlet

As you read *Hamlet* and *A Midsummer Night's Dream*, you will discover many more parallels of theme, character, setting, and structure whose significance you will want to ponder and investigate. But you may also want to think about another, perhaps more elusive element: language. Shakespeare is justly celebrated for his use of language, and we pay homage to it, unwittingly or not, every time we use any one of the many idiomatic expressions that originated in the plays. (If, for example, you conclude that Shakespeare is "Greek to me," you have proved otherwise by quoting directly from his play *Julius Caesar*.) In Shakespearean drama, language is never an end in itself but instead establishes character and tone, structures the play, shapes our emotional response to it, and enunciates theme. *Hamlet*, for example, characterizes both Polonius and Hamlet in part through their penchant for wordplay. But as Polonius suggests, Hamlet's wordplay is "pregnant" with significance in a way that his own is not (2.2.201). Here, subtle differences prove just as key to characterization as similarities.

In both *Hamlet* and *A Midsummer Night's Dream*, the musical and visual qualities of Shakespeare's language are integral to its meaning. Though written mainly in verse, Shakespeare's plays include prose passages; and though most of the poetry is **blank verse** (unrhymed **iambic pentameter**), Shakespeare also uses **rhyme** and rhythmic variation to great effect. As you read the plays, then, you will want to pay attention to the texture and rhythm of the language—to the effect of *sound* on *sense*. You will also want to attend to the way Shakespeare uses language to appeal to your eye, as well as your ear. Visual **imagery**, like sound, consistently serves both structural and thematic ends, linking various moments and ideas, actions and themes. In *A Midsummer Night's Dream*, for example, characters frequently refer to their eyes. Such references begin in the very first scene: When Hermia wishes that her father "look'd but with my eyes," Theseus responds that "your eyes must with his judgment look" (lines 56–57). These lines prepare us for a drama in which eyes will play a major part, in which love and vision tend to go hand in hand, in which both love and vision often conflict with "judgment." The characters' talk of eyes thus connects directly to the plot; through both, the play asks us to think about the tremendous power of vision and the dangers of relying too heavily on it.

• • •

Reading multiple plays by a single playwright will help you better recognize stylistic as well as structural and thematic patterns within each play: Each additional play you read will bring you closer to an understanding and appreciation of its creator's unique way of looking at the world and of the way his or her views and technique changed over time. You will gain a sense of the author's development as a dramatist even as, ideally, you develop your own skills as a reader of drama.

WILLIAM SHAKESPEARE

A Midsummer Night's Dream[1]

[THE PERSONS OF THE PLAY

THESEUS, *Duke of Athens*
HIPPOLYTA, *Queen of the Amazons, betrothed to Theseus*
EGEUS, *father to Hermia*
HERMIA, *daughter to Egeus, in love with Lysander*
LYSANDER, *in love with Hermia*
DEMETRIUS, *in love with Hermia*
HELENA, *in love with Demetrius*
PHILOSTRATE, *Master of the Revels at the court of Theseus*
Lords and Attendants on Theseus and Hippolyta
OBERON, *King of the Fairies*
TITANIA, *Queen of the Fairies*
ROBIN *Goodfellow, a puck*[2]
PEASEBLOSSOM, COBWEB, MOTH, MUSTARDSEED — *fairies in Titania's service*
Other FAIRIES
Peter QUINCE, a carpenter, Prologue in the Interlude
Nick BOTTOM, a weaver, Pyramus in the Interlude
Francis FLUTE, a bellows-mender, Thisbe in the Interlude
Tom SNOUT, a tinker, Wall in the Interlude
SNUG, a joiner, Lion in the Interlude
Robin STARVELING, a tailor, Moonshine in the Interlude]

1.1[3]

Enter THESEUS, HIPPOLYTA, [*and* PHILOSTRATE,] *with others.*

THESEUS: Now, fair Hippolyta, our nuptial hour
Draws on apace. Four happy days bring in
Another moon; but, oh, methinks, how slow
This old moon wanes! She lingers[4] my desires
Like to a stepdame or a dowager
Long withering out a young man's revenue.[5]
HIPPOLYTA: Four days will quickly steep[6] themselves in night;
Four nights will quickly dream away the time;
And then the moon—like to a silver bow
Now bent in heaven—shall behold the night

1. Edited and annotated by Stephen Greenblatt. Notes have been renumbered, and some have been deleted. Edited notes are set in brackets. 2. An imp or mischievous sprite.
3. Location: Theseus's palace in Athens. 4. Delays fulfillment of.
5. A widow using up the inheritance that will go to her husband's (young) heir on her death. *Stepdame*: stepmother. 6. Plunge.

Of our solemnities.

THESEUS: Go, Philostrate,
Stir up the Athenian youth to merriments,
Awake the pert and nimble spirit of mirth,
Turn melancholy forth to funerals;
The pale companion is not for our pomp. [*Exit* PHILOSTRATE.]
Hippolyta, I wooed thee with my sword
And won thy love doing thee injuries;[7]
But I will wed thee in another key,
With pomp, with triumph,[8] and with reveling.

Enter EGEUS *and his daughter* HERMIA, *and* LYSANDER *and* DEMETRIUS.

EGEUS: Happy be Theseus, our renownèd duke!
THESEUS: Thanks, good Egeus. What's the news with thee?
EGEUS: Full of vexation come I, with complaint
Against my child, my daughter Hermia.
—Stand forth, Demetrius. —My noble lord,
This man hath my consent to marry her.
—Stand forth, Lysander. —And, my gracious duke,
This man hath bewitched the bosom of my child.
—Thou, thou, Lysander, thou hast given her rhymes,
And interchanged love tokens with my child.
Thou hast by moonlight at her window sung
With feigning[9] voice verses of feigning love,
And stolen the impression of her fantasy[1]
With bracelets of thy hair, rings, gauds, conceits,[2]
Knacks, trifles, nosegays,[3] sweetmeats—messenger
Of strong prevailment[4] in unhardened youth.
With cunning hast thou filched my daughter's heart,
Turned her obedience, which is due to me,
To stubborn harshness. —And, my gracious duke,
Be it so[5] she will not here before your grace
Consent to marry with Demetrius,
I beg the ancient privilege of Athens:
As she is mine, I may dispose of her,
Which shall be either to this gentleman
Or to her death, according to our law
Immediately[6] provided in that case.
THESEUS: What say you, Hermia? Be advised, fair maid:
To you your father should be as a god,
One that composed[7] your beauties, yea, and one
To whom you are but as a form in wax

7. Theseus captured Hippolyta in his military conquest of the Amazons. 8. Public festivity.
9. A pun: deceitful; desiring ("faining"); soft (in music).
1. By craftily impressing your image on her imagination, like a seal in wax, (you have) stolen her love.
2. Clever gifts. *Gauds:* trinkets. 3. Bouquets. *Knacks*: knickknacks. 4. Persuasiveness. 5. If.
6. Expressly. 7. Fashioned.

By him imprinted,[8] and within his power
To leave the figure or disfigure[9] it.
Demetrius is a worthy gentleman.
HERMIA: So is Lysander.
THESEUS: In himself he is,
But in this kind, wanting your father's voice,[1]
The other must be held the worthier.
HERMIA: I would my father looked but with my eyes.
THESEUS: Rather your eyes must with his judgment look.
HERMIA: I do entreat your grace to pardon me.
I know not by what power I am made bold,
Nor how it may concern[2] my modesty
In such a presence here to plead my thoughts,
But I beseech your grace that I may know
The worst that may befall me in this case
If I refuse to wed Demetrius.
THESEUS: Either to die the death[3] or to abjure
For ever the society of men.
Therefore, fair Hermia, question your desires,
Know of your youth, examine well your blood,[4]
Whether, if you yield not to your father's choice,
You can endure the livery of a nun,[5]
For aye to be in shady cloister mewed,[6]
To live a barren sister all your life,
Chanting faint hymns to the cold fruitless moon.[7]
Thrice blessèd they that master so their blood
To undergo such maiden pilgrimage;[8]
But earthlier happy is the rose distilled[9]
Than that which, withering on the virgin thorn,
Grows, lives, and dies in single blessedness.[1]
HERMIA: So will I grow, so live, so die, my lord,
Ere I will yield my virgin patent[2] up
Unto his lordship whose unwishèd yoke
My soul consents not to give sovereignty.
THESEUS: Take time to pause, and by the next new moon—
The sealing day betwixt my love and me
For everlasting bond of fellowship—
Upon that day either prepare to die
For disobedience to your father's will,
Or else to wed Demetrius, as he would,

8. You are merely a wax impression of his seal. 9. Destroy. *Leave*: maintain.
1. Lacking your father's consent or vote. *Kind*: respect. 2. Befit. 3. Be executed.
4. Passions. *Know*: inquire.
5. Christian orders of nuns were established in the Middle Ages, but Elizabethans used the term as well for women devoted to a religious life in classical antiquity. *Livery*: habit.
6. Caged. *For aye*: forever. 7. The emblem of Diana, goddess of chastity. 8. Life as a virgin.
9. Preserved in a perfume (figuratively, preserved in her children). *Earthlier happy*: happier on earth.
1. In celibacy. 2. My right to remain a virgin.

Or on Diana's altar to protest[3]
For aye austerity and single life.
DEMETRIUS: Relent, sweet Hermia, and, Lysander, yield
Thy crazèd title[4] to my certain right.
LYSANDER: You have her father's love, Demetrius;
Let me have Hermia's. Do you marry him.
EGEUS: Scornful Lysander! True, he hath my love,
And what is mine my love shall render him;
And she is mine, and all my right of her
I do estate[5] unto Demetrius.
LYSANDER: [*to* THESEUS] I am, my lord, as well derived[6] as he,
As well possessed,[7] my love is more than his,
My fortunes every way as fairly ranked,
If not with vantage,[8] as Demetrius'.
And, which is more than all these boasts can be,
I am beloved of beauteous Hermia.
Why should not I then prosecute[9] my right?
Demetrius, I'll avouch it to his head,[1]
Made love to[2] Nedar's daughter, Helena,
And won her soul, and she, sweet lady, dotes,
Devoutly dotes, dotes in idolatry
Upon this spotted and inconstant[3] man.
THESEUS: I must confess that I have heard so much
And with Demetrius thought to have spoke thereof,
But, being overfull of self-affairs,[4]
My mind did lose it. —But, Demetrius, come,
—And come, Egeus; you shall go with me.
I have some private schooling[5] for you both.
—For you, fair Hermia, look you arm[6] yourself
To fit your fancies[7] to your father's will,
Or else the law of Athens yields you up,
Which by no means we may extenuate,[8]
To death or to a vow of single life.
—Come, my Hippolyta. What cheer, my love?
—Demetrius and Egeus, go along.
I must employ you in some business
Against[9] our nuptial and confer with you
Of something nearly that[1] concerns yourselves.
EGEUS: With duty and desire we follow you.

Exeunt [*all but* LYSANDER *and* HERMIA].

LYSANDER: How now, my love, why is your cheek so pale?
How chance the roses there do fade so fast?
HERMIA: Belike[2] for want of rain, which I could well

3. Vow. 4. Flawed claim. 5. Settle; bestow. 6. Descended. 7. Endowed with wealth. 8. Superiority. 9. Pursue. 1. Face. 2. Wooed. 3. Fickle. 4. My own concerns. 5. Advice. 6. Prepare. 7. Desires. 8. Mitigate. 9. In preparation for. 1. That closely. 2. Probably.

Beteem[3] them from the tempest of my eyes.
LYSANDER: Ay me! For aught that I could ever read,
Could ever hear by tale or history,
The course of true love never did run smooth,
But either it was different in blood[4]—
HERMIA: Oh, cross![5] Too high to be enthralled to low.
LYSANDER: Or else misgraffèd[6] in respect of years—
HERMIA: Oh, spite! Too old to be engaged to young.
LYSANDER: Or else it stood upon the choice of friends[7]—
HERMIA: Oh, hell! To choose love by another's eyes.
LYSANDER: Or if there were a sympathy[8] in choice,
War, death, or sickness did lay siege to it,
Making it momentany[9] as a sound,
Swift as a shadow, short as any dream,
Brief as the lightning in the collied[1] night
That in a spleen unfolds[2] both heaven and earth
And ere a man hath power to say "Behold!"
The jaws of darkness do devour it up.
So quick bright things come to confusion.
HERMIA: If then true lovers have been ever[3] crossed,
It stands as an edict in destiny.
Then let us teach our trial patience[4]
Because it is a customary cross,
As due to love as thoughts and dreams and sighs,
Wishes and tears, poor fancy's[5] followers.
LYSANDER: A good persuasion.[6] Therefore hear me, Hermia:
I have a widow aunt, a dowager
Of great revenue, and she hath no child.
From Athens is her house remote seven leagues,
And she respects[7] me as her only son.
There, gentle Hermia, may I marry thee,
And to that place the sharp Athenian law
Cannot pursue us. If thou lovest me then
Steal forth thy father's house tomorrow night,
And in the wood, a league without[8] the town,
Where I did meet thee once with Helena
To do observance to a morn of May,[9]
There will I stay for thee.
HERMIA: My good Lysander,
I swear to thee by Cupid's strongest bow,
By his best arrow with the golden head,[1]

3. Afford; grant. 4. Hereditary rank. 5. Vexation.
6. Badly matched; improperly grafted. 7. Kin. *Stood*: rested. 8. An agreement. 9. Momentary.
1. Coal-black. 2. Reveals. *Spleen*: swift impulse. 3. Always.
4. Let us teach ourselves to be patient in this trial. 5. Love's. 6. Argument; principle. 7. Regards.
8. Outside. 9. Celebrate May Day.
1. Cupid's sharp golden arrow was said to create love; his blunt lead arrow caused dislike.

By the simplicity of Venus' doves,[2]
By that which knitteth souls and prospers loves,
And by that fire which burned the Carthage Queen
When the false Trojan under sail was seen,[3]
By all the vows that ever men have broke,
In number more than ever women spoke,
In that same place thou hast appointed me
Tomorrow truly will I meet with thee.

LYSANDER: Keep promise, love. Look, here comes Helena.

Enter HELENA.

HERMIA: God speed, fair[4] Helena! Whither away?

HELENA: Call you me fair? That "fair" again unsay.
Demetrius loves your fair; oh, happy fair![5]
Your eyes are lodestars, and your tongue's sweet air[6]
More tunable[7] than lark to shepherd's ear
When wheat is green, when hawthorn buds appear.
Sickness is catching; oh, were favor[8] so,
Your words I catch, fair Hermia, ere I go;
My ear should catch your voice, my eye your eye,
My tongue should catch your tongue's sweet melody.
Were the world mine, Demetrius being bated,[9]
The rest I'd give to be to you translated.
Oh, teach me how you look, and with what art
You sway the motion of Demetrius' heart.

HERMIA: I frown upon him, yet he loves me still.

HELENA: Oh, that your frowns would teach my smiles such skill!

HERMIA: I give him curses, yet he gives me love.

HELENA: Oh, that my prayers could such affection move!

HERMIA: The more I hate, the more he follows me.

HELENA: The more I love, the more he hateth me.

HERMIA: His folly, Helena, is no fault of mine.

HELENA: None but your beauty; would that fault were mine!

HERMIA: Take comfort: he no more shall see my face.
Lysander and myself will fly this place.
Before the time I did Lysander see
Seemed Athens as a paradise to me.
Oh, then, what graces in my love do dwell
That he hath turned a heaven unto a hell?

LYSANDER: Helen, to you our minds we will unfold:
Tomorrow night, when Phoebe[1] doth behold
Her silver visage in the watery glass,

2. Said to draw Venus's chariot. *Simplicity*: innocence.
3. Dido, Queen of Carthage, burned herself on a funeral pyre when her lover, Aeneas, sailed away.
4. The dialogue plays on the meanings "blonde," "beautiful," "beauty." Helena is presumably fair-haired and Hermia (called a "raven" at 2.2.114) a brunette. 5. Fortunate beauty.
6. Melody. *Lodestars*: guiding stars. 7. Tuneful. 8. Looks; charms. 9. Excepted.
1. Diana (the moon).

Decking with liquid pearl the bladed grass,
A time that lovers' flights doth still[2] conceal,
Through Athens' gates have we devised to steal.
HERMIA: And in the wood where often you and I
Upon faint primrose beds were wont[3] to lie,
Emptying our bosoms of their counsel sweet,
There my Lysander and myself shall meet,
And thence from Athens turn away our eyes
To seek new friends and stranger companies.[4]
Farewell, sweet playfellow; pray thou for us,
And good luck grant thee thy Demetrius.
—Keep word, Lysander; we must starve our sight
From lovers' food till morrow deep midnight. *Exit.*
LYSANDER: I will, my Hermia. —Helena, adieu.
As you on him, Demetrius dote on you. *Exit.*
HELENA: How happy some o'er other some[5] can be!
Through Athens I am thought as fair as she.
But what of that? Demetrius thinks not so.
He will not know what all but he do know.
And as he errs, doting on Hermia's eyes,
So I, admiring of his qualities.
Things base and vile, holding no quantity,[6]
Love can transpose to form and dignity.
Love looks not with the eyes but with the mind,[7]
And therefore is winged Cupid painted blind.
Nor hath love's mind of any judgment taste,[8]
Wings and no eyes figure[9] unheedy haste.
And therefore is love said to be a child
Because in choice he is so oft beguiled.
As waggish boys in game[1] themselves forswear,
So the boy Love is perjured everywhere.
For ere Demetrius looked on Hermia's eyne,[2]
He hailed down oaths that he was only mine.
And when this hail some heat from Hermia felt,
So he dissolved,[3] and showers of oaths did melt.
I will go tell him of fair Hermia's flight:
Then to the wood will he tomorrow night
Pursue her; and for this intelligence[4]
If I have thanks, it is a dear[5] expense.
But herein mean I to enrich my pain,
To have his sight thither and back again. *Exit.*

2. Always. 3. Accustomed. *Faint*: pale. 4. The company of strangers.
5. In comparison with others. 6. Shape; proportion.
7. Love is promoted not by the evidence of the senses, but by the fancies of the mind.
8. Any trace of judgment. 9. Symbolize. 1. Play. *Waggish*: playful. 2. Eyes.
3. Broke faith; melted. 4. Information.
5. Costly (because of the betrayal of secrecy and because it leads Demetrius to Hermia); or welcome (because the potential return is Demetrius's love regained).

1.2[6]

Enter QUINCE *the carpenter, and* SNUG *the joiner, and* BOTTOM *the weaver, and* FLUTE *the bellows-mender, and* SNOUT *the tinker, and* STARVELING *the tailor.*[7]

QUINCE: Is all our company here?

BOTTOM: You were best to call them generally,[8] man by man, according to the scrip.[9]

QUINCE: Here is the scroll of every man's name which is thought fit through all Athens to play in our interlude[1] before the Duke and the Duchess on his wedding day at night.

BOTTOM: First, good Peter Quince, say what the play treats on; then read the names of the actors; and so grow to a point.[2]

QUINCE: Marry,[3] our play is *The Most Lamentable Comedy and Most Cruel Death of Pyramus and Thisbe.*[4]

BOTTOM: A very good piece of work, I assure you, and a merry. Now, good Peter Quince, call forth your actors by the scroll. Masters, spread yourselves.

QUINCE: Answer as I call you. —Nick Bottom, the weaver?

BOTTOM: Ready. Name what part I am for, and proceed.

QUINCE: You, Nick Bottom, are set down for Pyramus.

BOTTOM: What is Pyramus? A lover or a tyrant?

QUINCE: A lover that kills himself, most gallant, for love.

BOTTOM: That will ask some tears in the true performing of it. If I do it, let the audience look to their eyes. I will move storms. I will condole[5] in some measure. To the rest. —Yet my chief humor is for a tyrant. I could play Ercles rarely,[6] or a part to tear a cat in, to make all split.[7]

The raging rocks
And shivering shocks[8]
Shall break the locks
Of prison gates,
And Phibbus' car[9]
Shall shine from far
And make and mar
The foolish Fates.

6. Location: Somewhere in the city of Athens.

7. The artisans' names recall their occupations. Quince's name is probably derived from "quoins," wooden wedges used by carpenters who made buildings such as houses and theaters. The name "Snug" evokes well-finished wooden furniture made by joiners. A bottom was the piece of wood on which thread was wound; Bottom's name also connotes "ass" and "lowest point." As Flute's name suggests, domestic bellows whistle through holes when needing repair. Snout's name may refer either to the spouts of the kettles he repairs or to his nose. Tailors, as Starveling's name recalls, were proverbially thin.

8. Bottom's error for "individually" (he frequently misuses words in this manner). 9. Script; list.

1. Brief play. 2. Draw to a conclusion. 3. By the Virgin Mary.

4. Parodying titles such as that of Thomas Preston's *Cambyses: A Lamentable Tragedy Mixed Full of Pleasant Mirth . . .* (ca. 1570). 5. Lament; arouse pity.

6. Excellently. *Ercles*: Hercules (a stock ranting role in early plays). *Humor*: inclination.

7. Go to pieces. *Cat*: cant. 8. Shattering blows.

9. The chariot of Phoebus Apollo, the sun god (the odd spelling may represent Bottom's pronunciation).

This was lofty. Now name the rest of the players. This is Ercles' vein, a tyrant's vein. A lover is more condoling.

QUINCE: Francis Flute, the bellows-mender?

FLUTE: Here, Peter Quince.

QUINCE: Flute, you must take Thisbe on you.

FLUTE: What is Thisbe, a wandering knight?[1]

QUINCE: It is the lady that Pyramus must love.

FLUTE: Nay, faith, let not me play a woman:[2] I have a beard coming.

QUINCE: That's all one. You shall play it in a mask,[3] and you may speak as small[4] as you will.

BOTTOM: An[5] I may hide my face, let me play Thisbe too. I'll speak in a monstrous little voice, "Thisne, Thisne!"[6] —"Ah, Pyramus, my lover dear, thy Thisbe dear and lady dear."

QUINCE: No, no, you must play Pyramus; and Flute, you Thisbe.

BOTTOM: Well, proceed.

QUINCE: Robin Starveling, the tailor?

STARVELING: Here, Peter Quince.

QUINCE: Robin Starveling, you must play Thisbe's mother. —Tom Snout, the tinker?

SNOUT: Here, Peter Quince.

QUINCE: You, Pyramus' father; myself, Thisbe's father; Snug the joiner, you, the lion's part; and I hope here is a play fitted.[7]

SNUG: Have you the lion's part written? Pray you, if it be, give it me, for I am slow of study.

QUINCE: You may do it extempore, for it is nothing but roaring.

BOTTOM: Let me play the lion too. I will roar that I will do any man's heart good to hear me. I will roar that I will make the Duke say, "Let him roar again! Let him roar again!"

QUINCE: An you should do it too terribly, you would fright the Duchess and the ladies that they would shriek, and that were enough to hang us all.

ALL: That would hang us, every mother's son.

BOTTOM: I grant you, friends, if you should fright the ladies out of their wits, they would have no more discretion but to hang us. But I will aggravate[8] my voice so that I will roar you as gently as any sucking dove. I will roar you an 'twere[9] any nightingale.

QUINCE: You can play no part but Pyramus; for Pyramus is a sweet-faced man, a proper[1] man as one shall see in a summer's day, a most lovely, gentlemanlike man. Therefore you must needs play Pyramus.

BOTTOM: Well, I will undertake it. What beard were I best to play it in?

QUINCE: Why, what you will.

1. Knight-errant. 2. On the Elizabethan stage, women's parts were played by boys and young men.
3. Elizabethan ladies regularly wore masks to remain anonymous and to protect their complexions. *One*: irrelevant. 4. High-pitched; shrill. 5. If.
6. Probably intended as a pet name for Thisbe; or it may mean "in this manner" ("thissen").
7. (Well) cast. 8. (For "moderate.")
9. As though it were. *Sucking dove*: Bottom confuses "sitting dove" and "sucking lamb." 1. Handsome.

BOTTOM: I will discharge[2] it in either your straw-color beard, your orange-tawny beard, your purple-in-grain[3] beard, or your French-crown-color[4] beard, your perfect yellow.

QUINCE: Some of your French crowns have no hair at all,[5] and then you will play bare-faced.[6] —But, masters, here are your parts,[7] and I am to entreat you, request you, and desire you to con[8] them by tomorrow night, and meet me in the palace wood, a mile without the town, by moonlight. There will we rehearse; for if we meet in the city, we shall be dogged with company, and our devices[9] known. In the meantime, I will draw a bill[1] of properties such as our play wants. I pray you, fail me not.

BOTTOM: We will meet, and there we may rehearse most obscenely and courageously. Take pains; be perfect.[2] Adieu.

QUINCE: At the Duke's oak we meet.

BOTTOM: Enough! Hold, or cut bowstrings.[3] *Exeunt.*

2.1[4]

Enter a FAIRY *at one door and* ROBIN *Goodfellow[, a puck,] at another.*

ROBIN: How now, spirit, whither wander you?

FAIRY: Over hill, over dale,
Thorough[5] bush, thorough briar,
Over park, over pale,[6]
Thorough flood, thorough fire,
I do wander everywhere
Swifter than the moon's sphere;[7]
And I serve the Fairy Queen
To dew her orbs[8] upon the green.
The cowslips tall her pensioners[9] be;
In their gold coats spots you see.
Those be rubies, fairy favors,[1]
In those freckles live their savors.[2]
I must go seek some dewdrops here
And hang a pearl in every cowslip's ear.
Farewell, thou lob[3] of spirits, I'll be gone.
Our queen and all her elves come here anon.

2. Perform.
3. Very deep red. *Orange-tawny*: dark yellow, a recognized name for the dye. (Bottom the weaver shows his professional knowledge.) 4. Gold-coin-colored.
5. Referring to the baldness caused by venereal disease (called "the French disease").
6. Beardless; undisguised.
7. Literally; an Elizabethan actor was generally given only his own lines and cues. 8. Memorize.
9. Plans. 1. List.
2. Be letter perfect in learning your parts. *Obscenely*: a comic blunder, possibly for "out of sight" ("from the scene" or "from being seen"). 3. Be present at the rehearsal, or else quit the troupe (?).
4. Location: A wood near Athens. 5. Through. 6. Enclosure; fence.
7. Each planet, including the moon, was thought to be fixed in a transparent hollow globe revolving around the earth. 8. To sprinkle her fairy rings (circles of dark grass). 9. Royal bodyguards.
1. Gifts. 2. Scent. 3. Country bumpkin.

ROBIN: The King doth keep his revels here tonight.
Take heed the Queen come not within his sight,
For Oberon is passing fell and wrath[4]
Because that she as her attendant hath
A lovely boy stolen from an Indian king—
She never had so sweet a changeling[5]—
And jealous Oberon would have the child
Knight of his train, to trace[6] the forests wild.
But she perforce[7] withholds the lovèd boy,
Crowns him with flowers, and makes him all her joy.
And now they never meet in grove or green,
By fountain clear or spangled starlight sheen,[8]
But they do square,[9] that all their elves for fear
Creep into acorn cups and hide them there.

FAIRY: Either I mistake your shape and making[1] quite,
Or else you are that shrewd[2] and knavish sprite
Called Robin Goodfellow. Are not you he
That frights the maidens of the villagery,[3]
Skim milk, and sometimes labor in the quern,[4]
And bootless[5] make the breathless housewife churn,
And sometime make the drink to bear no barm,[6]
Mislead night-wanderers, laughing at their harm?
Those that "hobgoblin" call you, and "sweet puck,"
You do their work, and they shall have good luck.
Are not you he?

ROBIN: Thou speakest aright;
I am that merry wanderer of the night.
I jest to Oberon and make him smile
When I a fat and bean-fed horse beguile,[7]
Neighing in likeness of a filly foal.
And sometime lurk I in a gossip's[8] bowl
In very likeness of a roasted crab,[9]
And when she drinks, against her lips I bob,
And on her withered dewlap[1] pour the ale.
The wisest aunt telling the saddest[2] tale
Sometime for three-foot stool mistaketh me.
Then slip I from her bum, down topples she,
And "tailor" cries,[3] and falls into a cough;
And then the whole choir[4] hold their hips and laugh,

4. Exceedingly fierce and angry.
5. Usually a child left by fairies in exchange for one stolen, but here the stolen child. 6. Range.
7. Forcibly. 8. Shining starlight. *Fountain:* spring. 9. Quarrel 1. Form. 2. Mischievous.
3. Villages. 4. Hand mill. 5. In vain. 6. Froth on ale. *Sometime*: at times. 7. Trick.
8. An old woman's.
9. Crab apple ("lamb's wool," a winter drink, was made with roasted apples and warm ale).
1. Loose skin on neck. 2. Most serious. *Aunt*: old woman.
3. Possibly the old woman cries this because she ends up cross-legged on the floor, as tailors sat to do their work, or because she falls on her "tail." 4. Company.

And waxen in their mirth, and neeze,[5] and swear
A merrier hour was never wasted there.
But room, fairy: here comes Oberon.
FAIRY: And here my mistress. Would that he were gone.

Enter [OBERON,] *the King of Fairies, at one door, with his train, and* [TITANIA,] *the Queen, at another, with hers.*

OBERON: Ill met by moonlight, proud Titania.
TITANIA: What, jealous Oberon?—Fairy, skip hence.
I have forsworn his bed and company.
OBERON: Tarry, rash wanton![6] Am not I thy lord?
TITANIA: Then I must be thy lady; but I know
When thou hast stolen away from fairyland
And in the shape of Corin[7] sat all day
Playing on pipes of corn and versing love[8]
To amorous Phillida. Why art thou here
Come from the farthest step[9] of India
But that, forsooth, the bouncing[1] Amazon,
Your buskined[2] mistress and your warrior love,
To Theseus must be wedded, and you come
To give their bed joy and prosperity?
OBERON: How canst thou thus, for shame, Titania,
Glance at my credit[3] with Hippolyta,
Knowing I know thy love to Theseus?
Didst not thou lead him through the glimmering night
From Perigenia, whom he ravishèd,
And make him with fair Aegles[4] break his faith,
With Ariadne, and Antiopa?[5]
TITANIA: These are the forgeries of jealousy;
And never since the middle summer's spring[6]
Met we on hill, in dale, forest, or mead,
By pavèd fountain or by rushy[7] brook,
Or in the beachèd margin[8] of the sea
To dance our ringlets[9] to the whistling wind,
But with thy brawls thou hast disturbed our sport.
Therefore the winds, piping to us in vain,
As in revenge have sucked up from the sea

5. Sneeze. *Waxen*: increase. 6. Impetuous creature.
7. "Corin" and "Phillida" [line 68] are typical names for a shepherd and shepherdess in pastoral poetry.
8. Making or reciting love poetry. *Pipes of corn*: musical instruments made of oat stalks. 9. Limit.
1. Vigorous. 2. Wearing hunting boots. 3. Question my good name.
4. In Plutarch's *Lives*, Theseus previously had mistresses named Perigouna and Aegles. "Perigenia" may be Shakespeare's alteration.
5. Taken from Plutarch; some writers used "Antiopa" as an alternative name for the Amazonian queen whom Theseus married, although here it seems to refer to a different woman. Ariadne helped Theseus to kill the Minotaur and escape from his labyrinth on Crete; she fled with Theseus, but he deserted her on Naxos. 6. Beginning of midsummer. 7. Fringed with reeds. *Pavèd*: pebbled. 8. Shore. *In*: on.
9. Circle dances.

Contagious fogs which, falling in the land,
Hath every pelting[1] river made so proud
That they have overborne their continents.[2]
The ox hath therefore stretched his yoke in vain,
The plowman lost his sweat, and the green corn[3]
Hath rotted ere his youth attained a beard.
The fold stands empty in the drownèd field,
And crows are fatted with the murrain[4] flock;
The nine-men's morris[5] is filled up with mud,
And the quaint mazes in the wanton green[6]
For lack of tread are undistinguishable.
The human mortals want their winter cheer;[7]
No night is now with hymn or carol blessed.
Therefore[8] the moon, the governess of floods,
Pale in her anger, washes[9] all the air,
That rheumatic[1] diseases do abound.
And thorough this distemperature[2] we see
The seasons alter; hoary-headed frosts
Fall in the fresh lap of the crimson rose,
And on old Hiems'[3] chin and icy crown
An odorous chaplet[4] of sweet summer buds
Is, as in mockery, set. The spring, the summer,
The childing[5] autumn, angry winter, change
Their wonted liveries, and the mazèd[6] world
By their increase[7] now knows not which is which.
And this same progeny of evils comes
From our debate,[8] from our dissension;
We are their parents and original.[9]
OBERON: Do you amend it then; it lies in you.
Why should Titania cross her Oberon?
I do but beg a little changeling boy
To be my henchman.[1]
TITANIA: Set your heart at rest.[2]
The fairyland buys not the child of me.
His mother was a votress[3] of my order,
And in the spicèd Indian air by night
Full often hath she gossiped by my side
And sat with me on Neptune's yellow sands,

1. Paltry. 2. Banks. 3. Grain. 4. Dead of disease.
5. The playing area for this outdoor game (traditionally, a board game played with nine pebbles or pegs) was cut in turf.
6. Luxuriant grass. *Quaint mazes*: intricate arrangements of paths (kept visible by frequent use).
7. Winter cheer would include the hymns and carols of the Yuletide. *Want*: lack.
8. As in lines 88 and 93 above, referring to the consequences of their quarrel. 9. Moistens; wets.
1. Characterized by rheum: colds, coughs, and the like. 2. Bad weather; disturbance. 3. Winter's.
4. Wreath. 5. Fruitful. 6. Bewildered. *Liveries*: customary clothing. 7. Crop yield. 8. Quarrel.
9. Origin. 1. Page of honor. 2. Proverbial expression for "Abandon that idea."
3. A woman who has taken a vow to serve (often, religious).

Marking the embarkèd traders on the flood,[4]
When we have laughed to see the sails conceive
And grow big-bellied with the wanton[5] wind,
Which she, with pretty and with swimming[6] gait
Following[7]—her womb then rich with my young squire—
Would imitate, and sail upon the land
To fetch me trifles and return again,
As from a voyage, rich with merchandise.
But she, being mortal, of that boy did die,
And for her sake do I rear up her boy,
And for her sake I will not part with him.

OBERON: How long within this wood intend you stay?

TITANIA: Perchance till after Theseus' wedding day.
If you will patiently dance in our round
And see our moonlight revels, go with us.
If not, shun me, and I will spare[8] your haunts.

OBERON: Give me that boy, and I will go with thee.

TITANIA: Not for thy fairy kingdom. —Fairies, away!
We shall chide[9] downright if I longer stay.

Exeunt [TITANIA *and her train*].

OBERON: Well, go thy way. Thou shalt not from[1] this grove
Till I torment thee for this injury.
—My gentle puck, come hither. Thou rememberest
Since[2] once I sat upon a promontory
And heard a mermaid on a dolphin's back
Uttering such dulcet and harmonious breath[3]
That the rude[4] sea grew civil at her song
And certain stars shot madly from their spheres[5]
To hear the sea-maid's music?

ROBIN: I remember.

OBERON: That very time I saw—but thou couldst not—
Flying between the cold moon and the earth,
Cupid, all armed. A certain aim he took
At a fair vestal thronèd by the west,[6]
And loosed his love-shaft[7] smartly from his bow
As[8] it should pierce a hundred thousand hearts.
But I might[9] see young Cupid's fiery shaft
Quenched in the chaste beams of the watery moon;
And the imperial votress passèd on
In maiden meditation, fancy-free.[1]
Yet marked I where the bolt[2] of Cupid fell.

4. Tide. *Traders*: merchant ships. 5. Playful; amorous. 6. As though gliding through the waves. 7. Copying. 8. Avoid. 9. Quarrel. 1. Go from. 2. When. 3. Voice; song. *Dulcet*: sweet. 4. Rough. 5. Orbits.
6. To the west of India; in England. *Vestal*: virgin (a compliment to Queen Elizabeth, the Virgin Queen, and possibly an allusion to a specific entertainment in her honor, such as the water pageant at Elvetham in 1591). 7. Golden arrow. 8. As though. 9. Could. 1. Free of love thoughts. 2. Arrow.

It fell upon a little western flower,
Before milk-white, now purple with love's wound,
And maidens call it "love-in-idleness."[3]
Fetch me that flower. The herb I showed thee once:
The juice of it on sleeping eyelids laid
Will make or[4] man or woman madly dote
Upon the next live creature that it sees.
Fetch me this herb, and be thou here again
Ere the leviathan[5] can swim a league.

ROBIN: I'll put a girdle[6] round about the earth
In forty minutes.

OBERON: Having once this juice,
I'll watch Titania when she is asleep
And drop the liquor[7] of it in her eyes.
The next thing then she waking looks upon—
Be it on lion, bear, or wolf, or bull,
On meddling monkey or on busy ape—
She shall pursue it with the soul of love.
And ere I take this charm from off her sight—
As I can take it with another herb—
I'll make her render up her page to me.
But who comes here? I am invisible,
And I will overhear their conference.

Enter DEMETRIUS, HELENA *following him.*

DEMETRIUS: I love thee not, therefore pursue me not.
Where is Lysander and fair Hermia?
The one I'll stay, the other stayeth me.[8]
Thou told'st me they were stolen unto this wood,
And here am I, and wood[9] within this wood
Because I cannot meet my Hermia.
Hence, get thee gone, and follow me no more.

HELENA: You draw me, you hard-hearted adamant,[1]
But yet you draw not iron, for my heart
Is true as steel. Leave you[2] your power to draw,
And I shall have no power to follow you.

DEMETRIUS: Do I entice you? Do I speak you fair?[3]
Or rather do I not in plainest truth
Tell you I do not nor I cannot love you?

HELENA: And even for that do I love you the more.

3. Pansy. (Classical legend describes how the mulberry turned purple with Pyramus's blood and the hyacinth with Hyacinthus's, but it does not mention the pansy.) 4. Either.
5. Biblical sea monster, identified with the whale. 6. Circle. 7. Juice.
8. The one (Lysander) I'll bring to a halt, the other (Hermia) stops me in my tracks. 9. Insane.
1. Very hard stone supposed to have magnetic properties. *Draw me:* that is, with the magnetic power of attraction.
2. Relinquish. *But yet . . steel*: Hermia contrasts the base metal iron with steel, which holds its temper.
3. Do I speak kindly to you?

I am your spaniel, and, Demetrius,
The more you beat me I will fawn on you.
Use me but as your spaniel: spurn me, strike me,
Neglect me, lose me—only give me leave,
Unworthy as I am, to follow you.
What worser place can I beg in your love—
And yet a place of high respect with me—
Than to be usèd as you use your dog?

DEMETRIUS: Tempt not too much the hatred of my spirit,
For I am sick when I do look on thee.

HELENA: And I am sick when I look not on you.

DEMETRIUS: You do impeach[4] your modesty too much
To leave the city and commit yourself
Into the hands of one that loves you not,
To trust the opportunity of night
And the ill counsel of a desert[5] place
With the rich worth of your virginity.

HELENA: Your virtue is my privilege. For that[6]
It is not night when I do see your face.
Therefore I think I am not in the night,
Nor doth this wood lack worlds of company,
For you in my respect[7] are all the world.
Then how can it be said I am alone
When all the world is here to look on me?

DEMETRIUS: I'll run from thee and hide me in the brakes,[8]
And leave thee to the mercy of wild beasts.

HELENA: The wildest hath not such a heart as you.
Run when you will. The story shall be changed:
Apollo flies, and Daphne holds the chase;[9]
The dove pursues the griffin; the mild hind[1]
Makes speed to catch the tiger: bootless[2] speed
When cowardice pursues and valor flies.

DEMETRIUS: I will not stay thy questions.[3] Let me go!
Or if thou follow me, do not believe
But I shall do thee mischief in the wood. [*Exit.*][4]

HELENA: Ay, in the temple, in the town, the field,
You do me mischief. Fie, Demetrius,
Your wrongs do set a scandal on my sex.[5]

4. Call into question. 5. Deserted. 6. Because. *Privilege*: protection.
7. As far as I am concerned. 8. Thickets.
9. A reversal of the traditional myth in which the nymph Daphne, flying from Apollo, was transformed into a laurel tree to escape him.
1. Doe. *Griffin*: A fabulous monster with a lion's body and an eagle's head and wings. 2. Useless.
3. I will not wait here any longer to hear you talk.
4. [Different editions of the play omit an exit for Demetrius in this scene; however, when exactly he leaves has important implications for the tone of Helena's speech.]
5. Your injustices to me cause me to behave in a way that disgraces my sex (by wooing him rather than being wooed).

We cannot fight for love as men may do;
We should be wooed and were not made to woo.
I'll follow thee and make a heaven of hell
To die upon the hand I love so well. [*Exit.*]

OBERON: Fare thee well, nymph. Ere he do leave this grove
Thou shalt fly him, and he shall seek thy love.

Enter [ROBIN *Goodfellow, the*] *puck.*

Hast thou the flower there? Welcome, wanderer.

ROBIN: Ay, there it is.

OBERON: I pray thee give it me.
I know a bank where the wild thyme blows,
Where oxlips[6] and the nodding violet grows,
Quite over-canopied with luscious woodbine,[7]
With sweet musk-roses, and with eglantine.[8]
There sleeps Titania sometime of the night,
Lulled in these flowers with dances and delight;
And there the snake throws[9] her enameled skin,
Weed[1] wide enough to wrap a fairy in.
And with the juice of this I'll streak[2] her eyes,
And make her full of hateful fantasies.
Take thou some of it, and seek through this grove.
A sweet Athenian lady is in love
With a disdainful youth. Anoint his eyes,
But do it when the next thing he espies
May be the lady. Thou shalt know the man
By the Athenian garments he hath on.
Effect it with some care, that he may prove
More fond[3] on her than she upon her love.
And look thou meet me ere the first cock crow.[4]

ROBIN: Fear not, my lord; your servant shall do so. *Exeunt.*

2.2[5]

Enter TITANIA, *Queen of Fairies, with her train.*

TITANIA: Come, now a roundel[6] and a fairy song;
Then, for the third part of a minute,[7] hence,
Some to kill cankers[8] in the musk-rose buds,
Some war with reremice[9] for their leathern wings
To make my small elves coats, and some keep back
The clamorous owl that nightly hoots and wonders

6. Hybrid between primrose and cowslip. 7. Honeysuckle.
8. Sweet brier (a type of rose). *Musk-roses*: Large rambling white roses. 9. Throws off; casts away.
1. Garment. 2. Anoint. 3. Doting.
4. Some spirits were thought unable to bear daylight (compare *Hamlet* 1.1.28–36).
5. Location: The wood. 6. Circle dance.
7. The fairies are quick enough to do their tasks in twenty seconds. 8. Caterpillars. 9. Bats.

At our quaint[1] spirits. Sing me now asleep;
Then to your offices, and let me rest.

[*She lies down.*] FAIRIES *sing* [*and dance*].

FIRST FAIRY: You spotted snakes with double[2] tongue,
Thorny hedgehogs, be not seen;
Newts and blindworms,[3] do no wrong,
Come not near our Fairy Queen.

CHORUS: Philomel,[4] with melody
Sing in our sweet lullaby;
Lulla, lulla, lullaby, lulla, lulla, lullaby.
Never harm,
Nor spell, nor charm
Come our lovely lady nigh.
So good night, with lullaby.

FIRST FAIRY: Weaving spiders, come not here;
Hence, you long-legged spinners, hence!
Beetles black, approach not near;
Worm nor snail, do no offense.

CHORUS: Philomel, with melody, etc.

[TITANIA *sleeps.*]

SECOND FAIRY: Hence, away! Now all is well.
One aloof[5] stand sentinel. [*Exeunt* FAIRIES, *leaving one sentinel.*]

Enter OBERON. [*He squeezes the juice on* TITANIA'S *eyes.*]

OBERON: What thou seest when thou dost wake,
Do it for thy true love take;
Love and languish for his sake.
Be it ounce[6] or cat or bear,
Pard,[7] or boar with bristled hair,
In thy eye that shall appear
When thou wak'st, it is thy dear.
Wake when some vile thing is near. [*Exit.*]

Enter LYSANDER *and* HERMIA.

LYSANDER: Fair love, you faint with wandering in the wood,
And to speak truth, I have forgot our way.
We'll rest us, Hermia, if you think it good,
And tarry for the comfort of the day.

HERMIA: Be it so, Lysander. Find you out a bed,
For I upon this bank will rest my head.

LYSANDER: One turf shall serve as pillow for us both;
One heart, one bed, two bosoms, and one troth.[8]

1. Dainty. 2. Forked.
3. Newts (water lizards) and blindworms were thought to be poisonous, as were spiders (line 20).
4. Philomel, the nightingale (in classical mythology, a woman who, having been raped by her sister's husband, was transformed into a bird). 5. At a distance. 6. Lynx. 7. Leopard. 8. Pledged faith.

HERMIA: Nay, good Lysander: for my sake, my dear,
Lie further off yet; do not lie so near.
LYSANDER: Oh, take the sense,[9] sweet, of my innocence!
Love takes the meaning in love's conference.[1]
I mean that my heart unto yours is knit,
So that but one heart we can make of it.
Two bosoms interchainèd with an oath;
So, then, two bosoms and a single troth.
Then by your side no bed-room me deny,
For lying so, Hermia, I do not lie.[2]
HERMIA: Lysander riddles very prettily.
Now much beshrew[3] my manners and my pride
If Hermia meant to say Lysander lied.
But, gentle friend, for love and courtesy
Lie further off in human[4] modesty.
Such separation as may well be said
Becomes a virtuous bachelor and a maid,
So far be distant. And good night, sweet friend;
Thy love ne'er alter till thy sweet life end.
LYSANDER: Amen, amen, to that fair prayer say I,
And then end life when I end loyalty.
Here is my bed. Sleep give thee all his rest.
HERMIA: With half that wish the wisher's eyes be pressed.[5]

[*They sleep separately.*]

Enter [ROBIN *Goodfellow, the*] *puck.*

ROBIN: Through the forest have I gone,
But Athenian found I none
On whose eyes I might approve[6]
This flower's force in stirring love.
Night and silence. Who is here?
Weeds of Athens he doth wear.
This is he my master said
Despisèd the Athenian maid;
And here the maiden, sleeping sound
On the dank and dirty ground.
Pretty soul, she durst not lie
Near this lack-love, this kill-courtesy.
Churl,[7] upon thy eyes I throw
All the power this charm doth owe.[8]

[*He squeezes the juice on* LYSANDER*'s eyes.*]

When thou wak'st, let love forbid

9. True meaning. 1. Love should enable lovers truly to understand each other.
2. Deceive; punning on "lie down." 3. Curse (used in a mild sense). 4. Courteous.
5. May sleep's rest be shared between us. *Pressed*: closed in sleep. 6. Test. 7. Rude fellow. 8. Own.

Sleep his seat on thy eyelid.[9]
So awake when I am gone,
For I must now to Oberon. *Exit.*

Enter DEMETRIUS *and* HELENA, *running.*

HELENA: Stay, though thou kill me, sweet Demetrius.
DEMETRIUS: I charge thee: hence, and do not haunt me thus.
HELENA: Oh, wilt thou darkling[1] leave me? Do not so.
DEMETRIUS: Stay, on thy peril;[2] I alone will go. [*Exit.*]
HELENA: Oh, I am out of breath in this fond[3] chase.
The more my prayer, the lesser is my grace.[4]
Happy is Hermia, wheresoe'er she lies,
For she hath blessèd and attractive[5] eyes.
How came her eyes so bright? Not with salt tears;
If so, my eyes are oftener washed than hers.
No, no; I am as ugly as a bear,
For beasts that meet me run away for fear.
Therefore no marvel though Demetrius
Do, as[6] a monster, fly my presence thus.
What wicked and dissembling glass of mine
Made me compare with Hermia's sphery eyne?[7]
But who is here? Lysander, on the ground?
Dead or asleep? I see no blood, no wound.
Lysander, if you live, good sir, awake.
LYSANDER: [*awaking*] And run through fire I will for thy sweet sake.
Transparent Helena, nature shows art[8]
That through thy bosom makes me see thy heart.
Where is Demetrius? Oh, how fit a word
Is that vile name to perish on my sword!
HELENA: Do not say so, Lysander; say not so.
What though he love your Hermia? Lord, what though?
Yet Hermia still loves you; then be content.
LYSANDER: Content with Hermia? No, I do repent
The tedious minutes I with her have spent.
Not Hermia but Helena I love.
Who will not change a raven for a dove?
The will of man is by his reason swayed,[9]
And reason says you are the worthier maid.
Things growing are not ripe until their season,
So I, being young, till now ripe not to reason.
And, touching now the point of human skill,[1]
Reason becomes the marshal[2] to my will

9. Prevent you from sleeping. 1. In darkness. 2. Stay here, or risk peril (if you follow me).
3. Foolish. 4. Reward. 5. Magnetic. 6. As if I were. 7. Starry eyes. *Compare*: Compete.
8. Skill; magic power. *Transparent*: radiant; capable of being seen through.
9. Renaissance psychology considered the will (that is, the passions) to be in constant conflict with, and ideally subject to, the faculty of reason. 1. Reaching (only) now the highest point of human judgment.
2. An officer who led guests to their appointed places.

And leads me to your eyes, where I o'erlook[3]
Love's stories written in love's richest book.

HELENA: Wherefore was I to this keen[4] mockery born?
When at your hands did I deserve this scorn?
Is't not enough, is't not enough, young man,
That I did never—no, nor never can—
Deserve a sweet look from Demetrius' eye,
But you must flout my insufficiency?[5]
Good troth, you do me wrong—good sooth,[6] you do—
In such disdainful manner me to woo.
But fare you well. Perforce I must confess
I thought you lord of more true gentleness.[7]
Oh, that a lady of one man refused
Should of[8] another therefore be abused! *Exit.*

LYSANDER: She sees not Hermia. —Hermia, sleep thou there,
And never mayst thou come Lysander near;
For as a surfeit of the sweetest things
The deepest loathing to the stomach brings,
Or as the heresies that men do leave
Are hated most of those they did deceive,[9]
So thou, my surfeit and my heresy,
Of all be hated, but the most of me!
And, all my powers, address[1] your love and might
To honor Helen and to be her knight. *Exit.*

HERMIA: [*awaking*] Help me, Lysander, help me! Do thy best
To pluck this crawling serpent from my breast!
Ay me, for pity! What a dream was here!
Lysander, look how I do quake with fear.
Methought a serpent ate my heart away,
And you sat smiling at his cruel prey.[2]
Lysander? What, removed? Lysander! Lord!
What, out of hearing, gone? No sound, no word?
Alack, where are you? Speak an if[3] you hear,
Speak, of[4] all loves! I swoon almost with fear.
No? Then I well perceive you are not nigh.
Either death or you I'll find immediately.

Exit. [TITANIA *remains lying asleep.*]

3. Look over; read. 4. Sharp. 5. Mock my shortcomings by pretending they are wonderful qualities.
6. Indeed. *Good troth*: truly. 7. Courtesy; breeding. 8. By.
9. As men most hate the false opinions they once held. 1. Direct; apply. 2. Act of preying.
3. An if = if. 4. For the sake of.

3.1[5]

Enter the clowns[6] [, BOTTOM, QUINCE, SNOUT, STARVELING, FLUTE, *and* SNUG].

BOTTOM: Are we all met?

QUINCE: Pat,[7] pat; and here's a marvelous convenient place for our rehearsal. This green plot shall be our stage, this hawthorn brake our tiring-house,[8] and we will do it in action as we will do it before the Duke.

BOTTOM: Peter Quince?

QUINCE: What sayest thou, bully[9] Bottom?

BOTTOM: There are things in this comedy of Pyramus and Thisbe that will never please. First, Pyramus must draw a sword to kill himself, which the ladies cannot abide. How answer you that?

SNOUT: By'r lakin, a parlous[1] fear.

STARVELING: I believe we must leave the killing out, when all is done.[2]

BOTTOM: Not a whit. I have a device to make all well. Write me a prologue, and let the prologue seem to say we will do no harm with our swords, and that Pyramus is not killed indeed. And for the more better assurance, tell them that I, Pyramus, am not Pyramus but Bottom the weaver. This will put them out of fear.

QUINCE: Well, we will have such a prologue, and it shall be written in eight and six.[3]

BOTTOM: No, make it two more: let it be written in eight and eight.

SNOUT: Will not the ladies be afeard of the lion?

STARVELING: I fear it, I promise you.

BOTTOM: Masters, you ought to consider with yourself, to bring in—God shield us!—a lion among ladies is a most dreadful thing. For there is not a more fearful[4] wildfowl than your lion living. And we ought to look to't.

SNOUT: Therefore another prologue must tell he is not a lion.

BOTTOM: Nay, you must name his name, and half his face must be seen through the lion's neck, and he himself must speak through, saying thus or to the same defect:[5] "Ladies," or "Fair Ladies, I would wish you," or "I would request you," or "I would entreat you not to fear, not to tremble. My life for yours.[6] If you think I come hither as a lion, it were pity of[7] my life. No, I am no such thing. I am a man as other men are"—and there indeed let him name his name, and tell them plainly he is Snug the joiner.

QUINCE: Well, it shall be so. But there is two hard things: that is, to bring the moonlight into a chamber—for you know Pyramus and Thisbe meet by moonlight.

SNOUT:[8] Doth the moon shine that night we play our play?

5. [Location: Remains the same.] 6. Rustics. 7. On the dot.

8. Dressing room. *Brake*: thorn brake. 9. Good fellow; jolly.

1. Perilous. *By'r lakin*: by our ladykin (Virgin Mary): a mild oath. 2. When all is said and done.

3. Alternate lines of eight and six syllables (a common ballad measure).

4. Frightening. *A lion . . . thing*: In 1594, at a feast in honor of the christening of King James's son, a tame lion that was supposed to draw a chariot was replaced by a black African man in order to avoid frightening the audience. 5. (For "effect.") 6. I pledge my life to defend yours. 7. A threat to.

8. [Or Snug. Some sources use "Sn."]

BOTTOM: A calendar, a calendar! Look in the almanac; find out moonshine, find out moonshine!

QUINCE: Yes, it doth shine that night.

BOTTOM: Why, then may you leave a casement of the great chamber window where we play open, and the moon may shine in at the casement.

QUINCE: Ay, or else one must come in with a bush of thorns and a lantern and say he comes to disfigure, or to present,[9] the person of Moonshine. Then there is another thing: we must have a wall in the great chamber; for Pyramus and Thisbe, says the story, did talk through the chink of a wall.

SNOUT: You can never bring in a wall. What say you, Bottom?

BOTTOM: Some man or other must present Wall; and let him have some plaster, or some loam, or some roughcast[1] about him to signify "wall"; or let him hold his fingers thus, and through that cranny shall Pyramus and Thisbe whisper.

QUINCE: If that may be, then all is well. Come, sit down, every mother's son, and rehearse your parts. Pyramus, you begin. When you have spoken your speech, enter into that brake, and so everyone according to his cue.

Enter ROBIN[*, invisible*].

ROBIN: [*aside*] What hempen homespuns[2] have we swaggering here
So near the cradle of the Fairy Queen?
What, a play toward?[3] I'll be an auditor—
An actor too perhaps, if I see cause.

QUINCE: Speak, Pyramus. —Thisbe, stand forth.

BOTTOM: [*as Pyramus*] "Thisbe, the flowers of odious[4] savors sweet—"

QUINCE: Odors—"odorous"!

BOTTOM: [*as Pyramus*] "—Odors savors sweet.
So hath thy breath, my dearest Thisbe dear.
But hark, a voice! Stay thou but here a while,
And by and by I will to thee appear." *Exit.*

QUINCE: A stranger Pyramus than e'er played here. [*Exit.*]

FLUTE: Must I speak now?

QUINCE: Ay, marry, must you. For you must understand he goes but to see a noise that he heard and is to come again.

FLUTE: [*as Thisbe*] "Most radiant Pyramus, most lily-white of hue,
Of color like the red rose on triumphant briar,
Most brisky juvenal and eke most lovely Jew,[5]
As true as truest horse that yet would never tire,
I'll meet thee, Pyramus, at Ninny's tomb—"

9. Represent. *Disfigure*: blunder for "figure," represent. *Bush of thorns*: bundle of thornbush kindling (like the lantern, a traditional accessory of the man in the moon).

1. Mixture of lime and gravel used to plaster exterior walls.

2. Peasants, or country bumpkins, dressed in coarse homespun fabric made from hemp.

3. In preparation. 4. (For "odorous.")

5. Not often considered "lovely" by Elizabethan Christians; usually, a term of abuse (here, echoing the first syllable of "juvenal"). *Eke*: also. *Juvenal*: lively youth (juvenile).

QUINCE: "Ninus'[6] tomb," man! Why, you must not speak that yet; that you answer to Pyramus. You speak all your part at once, cues and all. —Pyramus, enter! Your cue is past; it is "never tire."

FLUTE: Oh,
[*as Thisbe*] "As true as truest horse that yet would never tire."

[*Enter* ROBIN, *invisible, and* BOTTOM *with the ass head on.*]

BOTTOM: [*as Pyramus*] "If I were fair, Thisbe, I were[7] only thine."

QUINCE: Oh, monstrous! Oh, strange! We are haunted! Pray, masters! Fly, masters! Help! [Exeunt QUINCE, SNOUT, STARVELING, FLUTE, and SNUG.]

ROBIN: I'll follow you, I'll lead you about a round,[8]
Through bog, through bush, through brake, through briar.
Sometime a horse I'll be, sometime a hound,
A hog, a headless bear, sometime a fire,[9]
And neigh and bark and grunt and roar and burn,
Like horse, hound, hog, bear, fire, at every turn. *Exit.*

BOTTOM: Why do they run away? This is a knavery of them to make me afeard.

Enter SNOUT.

SNOUT: O Bottom, thou art changed! What do I see on thee?

BOTTOM: What do you see? You see an ass head of your own,[1] do you? [*Exit* SNOUT.]

Enter QUINCE.

QUINCE: Bless thee, Bottom, bless thee! Thou art translated.[2] *Exit.*

BOTTOM: I see their knavery. This is to make an ass of me, to fright me, if they could. But I will not stir from this place, do what they can. I will walk up and down here, and I will sing, that they shall hear I am not afraid.

[*Sings.*]

The ouzel cock,[3] so black of hue,
With orange-tawny bill,
The throstle[4] with his note so true,
The wren with little quill[5]—

TITANIA: [*awaking*] What angel wakes me from my flowery bed?

BOTTOM: [*sings*]

The finch, the sparrow, and the lark,
The plainsong[6] cuckoo gray,
Whose note full many a man doth mark
And dares not answer "Nay"[7]—

6. Mythical founder of Nineveh, whose wife, Semiramis, was believed to have founded Babylon, the setting for the story of Pyramus and Thisbe. Flute's mistake, "Ninny," means "fool."
7. Would be. *Fair*: handsome. 8. In circles. 9. Will-o'-the-wisp.
1. You see a figment of your own asinine imagination. 2. Transformed. 3. Male blackbird
4. Song thrush. 5. Feathers. 6. A melody sung without adornment (that is, the cuckoo's call).
7. Deny. (The cuckoo's call was associated with cuckoldry.)

for indeed, who would set his wit to so foolish a bird? Who would give a bird the lie, though he cry "cuckoo" never so?[8]

TITANIA: I pray thee, gentle mortal, sing again.
Mine ear is much enamored of thy note;
So is mine eye enthrallèd to thy shape,
And thy fair virtue's force[9] perforce doth move me
On the first view to say, to swear, I love thee.

BOTTOM: Methinks, mistress, you should have little reason for that. And yet, to say the truth, reason and love keep little company together nowadays—the more the pity that some honest neighbors will not make them friends. Nay, I can gleek[1] upon occasion.

TITANIA: Thou art as wise as thou art beautiful.

BOTTOM: Not so neither; but if I had wit enough to get out of this wood, I have enough to serve mine own turn.[2]

TITANIA: Out of this wood do not desire to go.
Thou shalt remain here, whether thou wilt or no.
I am a spirit of no common rate[3]—
The summer still doth tend upon my state[4]—
And I do love thee. Therefore go with me.
I'll give thee fairies to attend on thee,
And they shall fetch thee jewels from the deep
And sing while thou on pressèd flowers dost sleep.
And I will purge thy mortal grossness so
That thou shalt like an airy spirit go.
Peaseblossom, Cobweb, Moth,[5] and Mustardseed!

Enter four FAIRIES[: PEASEBLOSSOM, COBWEB, MOTH, *and* MUSTARDSEED].

PEASEBLOSSOM: Ready.
COBWEB: And I.
MOTH: And I.
MUSTARDSEED: And I.
ALL: Where shall we go?

TITANIA: Be kind and courteous to this gentleman.
Hop in his walks and gambol in his eyes;
Feed him with apricots and dewberries,
With purple grapes, green figs, and mulberries;
The honey bags steal from the humble-bees,[6]
And for night-tapers crop their waxen thighs,
And light them at the fiery glowworms' eyes
To have[7] my love to bed and to arise;
And pluck the wings from painted butterflies
To fan the moonbeams from his sleeping eyes.
Nod to him, elves, and do him courtesies.

8. Ever so much. *Who . . . lie*: Who would call a bird a liar? *Set his wit to*: pay heed to.
9. The power of your good or beauteous qualities. 1. Make jokes. 2. Purpose. 3. Rank.
4. Serves me, as part of my royal retinue. *Still*: always; continually.
5. [Speck. Some sources use the spelling "Mote." *Mote* and *Moth* both had the same pronunciation.]
6. Bumblebees. 7. Lead.

PEASEBLOSSOM: Hail, mortal!
COBWEB: Hail!
MOTH: Hail!
MUSTARDSEED: Hail!

BOTTOM: I cry your worships' mercy,[8] heartily. —I beseech your worship's name.

COBWEB: Cobweb.

BOTTOM: I shall desire you of more acquaintance, good Master Cobweb. If I cut my finger,[9] I shall make bold with you. —Your name, honest gentleman?

PEASEBLOSSOM: Peaseblossom.

BOTTOM: I pray you commend me to Mistress Squash, your mother, and to Master Peascod,[1] your father. Good Master Peaseblossom, I shall desire you of more acquaintance too. —Your name, I beseech you, sir?

MUSTARDSEED: Mustardseed.

BOTTOM: Good Master Mustardseed, I know your patience[2] well. That same cowardly, giant-like ox-beef[3] hath devoured many a gentleman of your house. I promise you, your kindred hath made my eyes water ere now. I desire you of more acquaintance, good Master Mustardseed.

TITANIA: [*to the* FAIRIES] Come, wait upon him. Lead him to my bower.
The moon methinks looks with a watery eye,
And when she weeps, weeps every little flower,[4]
Lamenting some enforcèd[5] chastity.
Tie up my lover's tongue;[6] bring him silently. [*Exeunt.*]

3.2[7]

Enter [OBERON,] *King of Fairies.*

OBERON: I wonder if Titania be awaked;
Then what it was that next came in her eye,
Which she must dote on in extremity.

Enter ROBIN *Goodfellow.*

Here comes my messenger. How now, mad spirit?
What night-rule[8] now about this haunted grove?

ROBIN: My mistress with a monster is in love.
Near to her close[9] and consecrated bower,
While she was in her dull[1] and sleeping hour,
A crew of patches, rude mechanicals[2]
That work for bread upon Athenian stalls,[3]
Were met together to rehearse a play
Intended for great Theseus' nuptial day.

8. I beg pardon of your honors. 9. Cobwebs were used to stop bleeding.
1. Ripe pea pod (called "your father" because it suggests "codpiece"). *Squash*: unripe pea pod.
2. What you have suffered with fortitude.
3. Because beef is often eaten with mustard, or because oxen munch on mustard plants.
4. Dew was thought to originate on the moon. 5. Violated; involuntary.
6. Bottom is perhaps making involuntary asinine noises. 7. Location: The wood.
8. Night revels; sports. 9. Private. 1. Drowsy. 2. Rough workmen. *Patches*: fools.
3. Market stands.

The shallowest thick-skin of that barren sort,[4]
Who Pyramus presented[5] in their sport,
Forsook his scene[6] and entered in a brake.
When I did him at this advantage take,
An ass's nole[7] I fixèd on his head.
Anon his Thisbe must be answerèd,
And forth my mimic[8] comes. When they him spy—
As wild geese that the creeping fowler[9] eye,
Or russet-pated choughs, many in sort,[1]
Rising and cawing at the gun's report,
Sever[2] themselves and madly sweep the sky—
So at his sight away his fellows fly,
And at our stamp[3] here o'er and o'er one falls.
He[4] "Murder!" cries and help from Athens calls.
Their sense thus weak, lost with their fears thus strong,
Made senseless things begin to do them wrong.
For briars and thorns at their apparel snatch,
Some sleeves, some hats: from yielders all things catch.[5]
I led them on in this distracted fear
And left sweet Pyramus translated there,
When in that moment, so it came to pass,
Titania waked and straightway loved an ass.

OBERON: This falls out better than I could devise.
But hast thou yet latched[6] the Athenian's eyes
With the love juice, as I did bid thee do?

ROBIN: I took him sleeping—that is finished, too—
And the Athenian woman by his side,
That when he waked, of force[7] she must be eyed.

Enter DEMETRIUS *and* HERMIA.

OBERON: Stand close. This is the same Athenian.

ROBIN: This is the woman, but not this the man.

[OBERON *and* ROBIN *stand apart.*]

DEMETRIUS: Oh, why rebuke you him that loves you so?
Lay breath so bitter on your bitter foe.

HERMIA: Now I but chide, but I should use thee worse,
For thou, I fear, hast given me cause to curse.
If thou hast slain Lysander in his sleep,
Being o'er shoes[8] in blood, plunge in the deep,
And kill me too.
The sun was not so true unto the day
As he to me. Would he have stolen away

4. Witless lot. 5. Acted. 6. Stage.
7. Head. 8. Burlesque actor. 9. Hunter of birds.
1. Together, in a flock. *Russet-pated choughs*: gray-headed jackdaws. 2. Scatter.
3. Editors have wondered how a fairy's presumably tiny foot could cause the human to fall.
4. One (workman). 5. Everything robs the timid. 6. Anointed. 7. Necessity. *That*: so that.
8. Having waded so far.

From sleeping Hermia? I'll believe as soon
This whole[9] earth may be bored, and that the moon
May through the center creep and so displease
Her brother's noontide with the Antipodes.[1]
It cannot be but thou hast murdered him.
So should a murderer look: so dead,[2] so grim.

DEMETRIUS: So should the murdered look, and so should I,
Pierced through the heart with your stern cruelty.
Yet you, the murderer, look as bright, as clear,
As yonder Venus in her glimmering sphere.[3]

HERMIA: What's this to my Lysander? Where is he?
Ah, good Demetrius, wilt thou give him me?

DEMETRIUS: I had rather give his carcass to my hounds.

HERMIA: Out, dog! Out, cur! Thou driv'st me past the bounds
Of maiden's patience. Hast thou slain him, then?
Henceforth be never numbered among men.
Oh, once tell true; tell true, even for my sake:
Durst thou have looked upon him being awake,
And hast thou killed him sleeping? Oh, brave touch![4]
Could not a worm,[5] an adder do so much?
An adder did it; for with doubler[6] tongue
Than thine, thou serpent, never adder stung.

DEMETRIUS: You spend your passion on a misprised mood.[7]
I am not guilty of Lysander's blood,
Nor is he dead, for aught that I can tell.

HERMIA: I pray thee, tell me then that he is well.

DEMETRIUS: And if I could, what should I get therefore?[8]

HERMIA: A privilege, never to see me more;
And from thy hated presence part I so.
See me no more, whether he be dead or no. *Exit.*

DEMETRIUS: There is no following her in this fierce vein.
Here therefore for a while I will remain.
So sorrow's heaviness[9] doth heavier grow
For debt that bankrupt sleep doth sorrow owe,[1]
Which now in some slight measure it will pay,
If for his tender here I make some stay.[2]

[He] *lies down* [*and sleeps*].

OBERON: [*to* ROBIN] What hast thou done? Thou hast mistaken quite
And laid the love juice on some true love's sight.
Of thy misprision[3] must perforce ensue

9. Solid.

1. That the moon could creep through a hole bored through the earth's center and emerge on the other side, the Antipodes, displeasing the inhabitants by displacing the noontime sun with the darkness of night. (Apollo, the sun god, was the brother of Diana, the moon goddess.) 2. Deathly pale.

3. Orbit. 4. Noble stroke. 5. Serpent. 6. More forked (of the adder); more duplicitous (of Demetrius).

7. In misconceived arger. 8. For that. 9. Sadness (punning on "heavy": drowsy).

1. Because sorrow worsens without sleep.

2. I will rest here awhile, giving sleep capital ("tender") to pay off some of its debt to sorrow. 3. Mistake

Some true love turned, and not a false turned true.
ROBIN: Then fate o'errules, that, one man holding troth,[4]
A million fail, confounding oath on oath.[5]
OBERON: About the wood go swifter than the wind,
And Helena of Athens look[6] thou find.
All fancy-sick she is and pale of cheer[7]
With sighs of love that costs the fresh blood dear.[8]
By some illusion see thou bring her here;
I'll charm his eyes against[9] she do appear.
ROBIN: I go, I go; look how I go,
Swifter than arrow from the Tartar's bow.[1] [*Exit.*]
OBERON: [*squeezing the juice on* DEMETRIUS' *eyes*] Flower of this purple dye,
Hit with Cupid's archery,
Sink in apple[2] of his eye.
When his love he doth espy,
Let her shine as gloriously
As the Venus of the sky.
When thou wak'st, if she be by,
Beg of her for remedy.

Enter [ROBIN *Goodfellow, the*] *puck.*

ROBIN: Captain of our fairy band,
Helena is here at hand,
And the youth mistook by me,
Pleading for a lover's fee.[3]
Shall we their fond[4] pageant see?
Lord, what fools these mortals be!
OBERON: Stand aside. The noise they make
Will cause Demetrius to awake.
ROBIN: Then will two at once woo one;
That must needs be sport alone.[5]
And those things do best please me
That befall preposterously.[6]

[*They stand apart.*]

Enter LYSANDER *and* HELENA.

LYSANDER: Why should you think that I should woo in scorn?
Scorn and derision never come in tears.
Look when I vow, I weep, and vows so born,
In their nativity all truth appears.[7]

4. Faith. 5. Among the millions of faithless men, the one true man's oath has been subverted by fate.
6. Be sure. 7. Face. *Fancy-sick*: lovesick. 8. Sighs were thought to cause a loss of blood.
9. In readiness for when.
1. Tartars, a dark-skinned, supposedly savage people in Asia Minor, were famed for their skills in archery.
2. Pupil. 3. Reward. 4. Foolish. 5. In itself. 6. Ass backward.
7. The fact that I am weeping authenticates my vow's sincerity.

How can these things in me seem scorn to you,
Bearing the badge of faith[8] to prove them true?
HELENA: You do advance[9] your cunning more and more.
When truth kills truth[1]—oh, devilish-holy fray!
These vows are Hermia's. Will you give her o'er?
Weigh oath with oath, and you will nothing weigh.[2]
Your vows to her and me put in two scales
Will even weigh, and both as light as tales.[3]
LYSANDER: I had no judgment when to her I swore.
HELENA: Nor none, in my mind, now you give her o'er.
LYSANDER: Demetrius loves her, and he loves not you.
DEMETRIUS: [*awaking*] O Helen, goddess, nymph, perfect, divine!
To what, my love, shall I compare thine eyne?
Crystal is muddy. Oh, how ripe in show[4]
Thy lips, those kissing cherries, tempting grow!
That pure congealèd white, high Taurus'[5] snow,
Fanned with the eastern wind, turns to a crow[6]
When thou hold'st up thy hand. Oh, let me kiss
This princess of pure white, this seal[7] of bliss!
HELENA: Oh, spite! Oh, hell! I see you all are bent
To set against me for your merriment.
If you were civil and knew courtesy,
You would not do me thus much injury.
Can you not hate me, as I know you do,
But you must join in souls to mock me too?
If you were men, as men you are in show,
You would not use a gentle[8] lady so,
To vow and swear and superpraise my parts,[9]
When I am sure you hate me with your hearts.
You both are rivals and love Hermia,
And now both rivals to mock Helena.
A trim[1] exploit, a manly enterprise,
To conjure tears up in a poor maid's eyes
With your derision. None of noble sort[2]
Would so offend a virgin and extort[3]
A poor soul's patience, all to make you sport.
LYSANDER: You are unkind, Demetrius; be not so.
For you love Hermia; this you know I know.
And here, with all good will, with all my heart,
In Hermia's love I yield you up my part;
And yours of Helena to me bequeath,
Whom I do love and will do till my death.

8. Insignia, such as that worn on a servant's livery (here, his tears). 9. Increase; display.
1. When one vow nullifies another.
2. You will find that neither oath has any substance; you, Lysander, will be found to have no substance. 3. Lies; fiction. 4. Appearance. 5. Range of high mountains in Asia Minor.
6. Appears black by contrast. 7. Pledge 8. Well-born; mild. 9. Overpraise my qualities. 1. Fine.
2. Rank; nature. 3. Torture.

HELENA: Never did mockers waste more idle breath.
DEMETRIUS: Lysander, keep thy Hermia. I will none.[4]
If e'er I loved her, all that love is gone.
My heart to her but as guest-wise[5] sojourned,
And now to Helen is it home returned,
There to remain.
LYSANDER: Helen, it is not so.
DEMETRIUS: Disparage not the faith thou dost not know,
Lest to thy peril thou aby it dear.[6]
Look where thy love comes; yonder is thy dear.

Enter HERMIA.

HERMIA: Dark night, that from the eye his[7] function takes,
The ear more quick of apprehension makes.
Wherein it doth impair the seeing sense,
It pays the hearing double recompense.
Thou art not by mine eye, Lysander, found;
Mine ear, I thank it, brought me to thy sound.
But why unkindly didst thou leave me so?
LYSANDER: Why should he stay whom love doth press to go?
HERMIA: What love could press Lysander from my side?
LYSANDER: Lysander's love, that would not let him bide:
Fair Helena, who more engilds the night
Than all yon fiery oes and eyes of light.[8]
[*to* HERMIA] Why seek'st thou me? Could not this make thee know
The hate I bare thee made me leave thee so?
HERMIA: You speak not as you think; it cannot be.
HELENA: Lo, she is one of this confederacy.
Now I perceive they have conjoined all three
To fashion this false sport in spite of[9] me.
Injurious Hermia, most ungrateful maid,
Have you conspired, have you with these contrived
To bait[1] me with this foul derision?
Is all the counsel[2] that we two have shared,
The sisters' vows, the hours that we have spent
When we have chid the hasty-footed time
For parting us—oh, is all forgot,
All schooldays' friendship, childhood innocence?
We, Hermia, like two artificial[3] gods
Have with our needles created both one flower,
Both on one sampler, sitting on one cushion,
Both warbling of one song, both in one key,
As if our hands, our sides, voices, and minds

4. I will have nothing to do with her. 5. As a guest. 6. Pay for it dearly. 7. Its.
8. Stars (punning on the vowels and on lovers' exclamatory "oh"s and "ay"s). An "o" was a spangle.
9. To spite. 1. To torment (as Elizabethans set dogs to bait a bear). 2. Intimacy.
3. Artfully skilled.

Had been incorporate.[4] So we grew together
Like to a double cherry, seeming parted,
But yet an union in partition,
Two lovely berries molded on one stem;
So with two seeming bodies but one heart,
Two of the first,[5] like coats in heraldry,
Due but to one and crownèd with one crest.
And will you rent our ancient love asunder,
To join with men in scorning your poor friend?
It is not friendly, 'tis not maidenly.
Our sex as well as I may chide you for it,
Though I alone do feel the injury.

HERMIA: I am amazèd at your words.
I scorn you not; it seems that you scorn me.

HELENA: Have you not set Lysander, as in scorn,
To follow me and praise my eyes and face?
And made your other love, Demetrius—
Who even but now[6] did spurn me with his foot—
To call me goddess, nymph, divine, and rare,
Precious, celestial? Wherefore speaks he this
To her he hates? And wherefore doth Lysander
Deny your love—so rich within his soul—
And tender[7] me, forsooth, affection,
But by your setting on, by your consent?
What though I be not so in grace[8] as you,
So hung upon with love, so fortunate,
But miserable most, to love unloved?
This you should pity rather than despise.

HERMIA: I understand not what you mean by this.

HELENA: I do. Persever, counterfeit sad[9] looks,
Make mouths upon[1] me when I turn my back,
Wink each at other, hold the sweet jest up.[2]
This sport well carried shall be chronicled.
If you have any pity, grace, or manners,
You would not make me such an argument.[3]
But fare ye well. 'Tis partly my own fault,
Which death or absence soon shall remedy.

LYSANDER: Stay, gentle Helena, hear my excuse,
My love, my life, my soul, fair Helena!

HELENA: Oh, excellent!

HERMIA: [*to* LYSANDER] Sweet, do not scorn her so.

DEMETRIUS: If she cannot entreat, I can compel.[4]

4. Of one body.
5. A technical phrase in heraldry, referring to the first quartering in a coat of arms, which may be repeated. The friends then have two bodies but a single, overarching identity. 6. Just now. 7. Offer. 8. Favor. 9. Serious. 1. Make faces at. 2. Keep up the joke. 3. A subject of merriment.
4. If Hermia cannot entreat you to stop, I can make you do it.

LYSANDER: Thou canst compel no more than she entreat.
Thy threats have no more strength than her weak prayers.
—Helen, I love thee, by my life, I do!
I swear by that which I will lose for thee
To prove him false that says I love thee not.
DEMETRIUS: [*to* HELENA] I say I love thee more than he can do.
LYSANDER: If thou say so, withdraw,[5] and prove it too.
DEMETRIUS: Quick, come!
HERMIA: Lysander, whereto tends all this?
LYSANDER: Away, you Ethiope![6]

[*He tries to break away from* HERMIA.]

DEMETRIUS: [*to* HERMIA] No, no, he'll
Seem to break loose. [*to* LYSANDER] Take on as[7] you would follow,
But yet come not. You are a tame man, go!
LYSANDER: [*to* HERMIA] Hang off,[8] thou cat, thou burr! Vile thing, let loose,
Or I will shake thee from me like a serpent.
HERMIA: Why are you grown so rude? What change is this, Sweet love?
LYSANDER: Thy love? Out, tawny Tartar, out!
Out, loathèd medicine![9] O hated potion, hence!
HERMIA: Do you not jest?
HELENA: Yes, sooth,[1] and so do you.
LYSANDER: Demetrius, I will keep my word with thee.
DEMETRIUS: I would I had your bond, for I perceive
A weak bond[2] holds you. I'll not trust your word.
LYSANDER: What? Should I hurt her, strike her, kill her dead?
Although I hate her, I'll not harm her so.
HERMIA: What? Can you do me greater harm than hate?
Hate me? Wherefore? Oh, me, what news,[3] my love?
Am not I Hermia? Are not you Lysander?
I am as fair now as I was erewhile.[4]
Since night you loved me, yet since night you left me.
Why then, you left me—oh, the gods forbid—
In earnest, shall I say?
LYSANDER: Ay, by my life,
And never did desire to see thee more.
Therefore be out of hope, of question, of doubt;
Be certain, nothing truer. 'Tis no jest
That I do hate thee and love Helena.
HERMIA: [*to* HELENA] Oh, me, you juggler, you canker-blossom,[5]

5. Come with me ("step outside").
6. Allusion to Hermia's dark hair and complexion. Elizabethans generally regarded light complexions as more beautiful than dark and often stigmatized dark-skinned peoples (such as Ethiopians or Tartars) as ugly. 7. Pretend. *He'll . . . loose*: Lysander will only pretend to break free from Hermia.
8. Let go. 9. Any drug (including poison). 1. Truly.
2. Hermia's weak grasp (with a pun on "bond": signed oath, the meaning in the previous line).
3. What has happened. 4. A while ago.
5. A worm that devours blossoms (of love). *Juggler*: trickster.

You thief of love! What, have you come by night
And stolen my love's heart from him?
HELENA: Fine, i'faith.
Have you no modesty, no maiden shame,
No touch of bashfulness? What, will you tear
Impatient answers from my gentle tongue?
Fie, fie, you counterfeit, you puppet,[6] you!
HERMIA: "Puppet"? Why so? —Ay, that way goes the game.
Now I perceive that she hath made compare
Between our statures; she hath urged her height,
And with her personage, her tall personage,
Her height, forsooth, she hath prevailed with him.
—And are you grown so high in his esteem
Because I am so dwarfish and so low?
How low am I, thou painted maypole?[7] Speak!
How low am I? I am not yet so low
But that my nails can reach unto thine eyes.
HELENA: I pray you, though you mock me, gentlemen,
Let her not hurt me. I was never curst;[8]
I have no gift at all in shrewishness.
I am a right[9] maid for my cowardice.
Let her not strike me. You perhaps may think
Because she is something[1] lower than myself
That I can match her.
HERMIA: "Lower"? Hark, again!
HELENA: Good Hermia, do not be so bitter with me.
I evermore did love you, Hermia,
Did ever keep your counsels, never wronged you,
Save that, in love unto Demetrius,
I told him of your stealth[2] unto this wood.
He followed you; for love I followed him.
But he hath chid me hence and threatened me
To strike me, spurn me, nay, to kill me too.
And now, so[3] you will let me quiet go,
To Athens will I bear my folly back
And follow you no further. Let me go.
You see how simple and how fond[4] I am.
HERMIA: Why, get you gone. Who is't that hinders you?
HELENA: A foolish heart that I leave here behind.
HERMIA: What, with Lysander?
HELENA: With Demetrius.
LYSANDER: Be not afraid; she shall not harm thee, Helena.
DEMETRIUS: No, sir, she shall not, though you take her part.
HELENA: Oh, when she is angry she is keen and shrewd.[5]

6. Fraudulent imitation; but Hermia interprets "puppet" as a reference to her height.
7. Proverbial epithet for someone tall and skinny. *Painted*: insulting allusion to the use of cosmetics.
8. Quarrelsome. 9. Proper. 1. Somewhat. 2. Stealing away. 3. If only. 4. Foolish.
5. Shrewish. *Keen*: sharp.

She was a vixen when she went to school,
And though she be but little, she is fierce.
HERMIA: "Little" again? Nothing but "low" and "little"?
Why will you suffer her to flout me thus?
Let me come to her.
LYSANDER: Get you gone, you dwarf,
You minimus of hind'ring knot-grass[6] made,
You bead, you acorn.
DEMETRIUS: You are too officious
In her behalf that scorns your services.
Let her alone: speak not of Helena;
Take not her part. For if thou dost intend
Never so little[7] show of love to her,
Thou shalt aby[8] it.
LYSANDER: Now she holds me not;
Now follow, if thou dar'st, to try whose right,
Of thine or mine, is most in Helena.
DEMETRIUS: Follow? Nay, I'll go with thee, cheek by jowl.[9]

[*Exeunt* LYSANDER *and* DEMETRIUS.]

HERMIA: You, mistress, all this coil is long[1] of you.
Nay, go not back.
HELENA: I will not trust you, I,
Nor longer stay in your curst company.
Your hands than mine are quicker for a fray;[2]
My legs are longer, though, to run away. [*Exit.*]
HERMIA: I am amazed and know not what to say. [*Exit.*]

[OBERON *and* ROBIN *come forward.*]

OBERON: This is thy negligence. Still[3] thou mistak'st
Or else committ'st thy knaveries willfully.
ROBIN: Believe me, king of shadows,[4] I mistook.
Did not you tell me I should know the man
By the Athenian garments he had on?
And so far[5] blameless proves my enterprise
That I have 'nointed an Athenian's eyes;
And so far am I glad it so did sort,[6]
As this their jangling[7] I esteem a sport.
OBERON: Thou seest these lovers seek a place to fight.
Hie[8] therefore, Robin, overcast the night;
The starry welkin[9] cover thou anon
With drooping fog as black as Acheron,[1]
And lead these testy rivals so astray
As[2] one come not within another's way.

6. Creeping binding weed (its sap was thought to stunt human growth). *Minimus*: diminutive thing (Latin). 7. Even the smallest. 8. Pay for. 9. Proverbial saying for "side by side." 1. Because. *Coil*: turmoil. 2. Fight. 3. Always. 4. Fairy spirits. 5. To this extent. 6. Turn out. 7. Bickering. *As*: since. 8. Hurry. 9. Sky. 1. (River of hell). 2. So that.

Like to Lysander sometime frame thy tongue,
Then stir Demetrius up with bitter wrong;[3]
And sometime rail thou like Demetrius,
And from each other look thou lead them thus
Till o'er their brows death-counterfeiting sleep
With leaden legs and batty[4] wings doth creep.
Then crush this herb into Lysander's eye,
Whose liquor hath this virtuous[5] property:
To take from thence all error with his might
And make his eyeballs roll with wonted[6] sight.
When they next wake, all this derision
Shall seem a dream and fruitless[7] vision,
And back to Athens shall the lovers wend[8]
With league whose date[9] till death shall never end.
Whiles I in this affair do thee employ,
I'll to my queen and beg her Indian boy;
And then I will her charmèd[1] eye release
From monster's view, and all things shall be peace.

ROBIN: My fairy lord, this must be done with haste,
For night's swift dragons[2] cut the clouds full fast,
And yonder shines Aurora's harbinger,[3]
At whose approach ghosts wandering here and there
Troop home to churchyards; damnèd spirits all,
That in crossways and floods[4] have burial,
Already to their wormy beds are gone,
For fear lest day should look their shames upon:
They willfully themselves exile from light
And must for aye[5] consort with black-browed night.

OBERON: But we are spirits of another sort.
I with the morning's love[6] have oft made sport,
And like a forester[7] the groves may tread
Even till the eastern gate, all fiery red,
Opening on Neptune[8] with fair blessèd beams
Turns into yellow gold his salt[9] green streams.
But notwithstanding, haste, make no delay;
We may effect this business yet ere day. [*Exit.*]

ROBIN: Up and down, up and down,

3. Insults. 4. Batlike. 5. Potent. 6. Normal. 7. Inconsequential. 8. Go.
9. Duration. *League*: covenant. 1. Enchanted.
2. Imagined as drawing the chariots of the goddess of night.
3. Herald of the goddess of dawn; the morning star.
4. In which the drowned were "buried," without Christian sacrament. *Crossways*: crossroads (where suicides were buried, also without Christian sacrament). Robin is differentiating here between two types of spirits: those who wandered from their churchyard graves and those who have no proper resting place. These two types, both ghosts of former humans, are differentiated in turn from the fairy spirits by Oberon in the ensuing lines. 5. Forever.
6. The love of Aurora, goddess of dawn (or Cephalus, a brave hunter, Aurora's lover).
7. Keeper of a royal forest or private park. 8. (The sea.) 9. Salty.

I will lead them up and down.
I am feared in field and town.
Goblin,[1] lead them up and down.
Here comes one.

Enter LYSANDER.

LYSANDER: Where art thou, proud Demetrius? Speak thou now.
ROBIN: Here, villain, drawn[2] and ready. Where art thou?
LYSANDER: I will be with thee straight.[3]
ROBIN: Follow me then
To plainer[4] ground. [*Exit* LYSANDER.]

Enter DEMETRIUS.

DEMETRIUS: Lysander, speak again.
Thou runaway, thou coward, art thou fled?
Speak! In some bush? Where dost thou hide thy head?
ROBIN: Thou coward, art thou bragging to the stars,
Telling the bushes that thou look'st for wars,
And wilt not come? Come, recreant;[5] come, thou child.
I'll whip thee with a rod. He is defiled
That draws a sword on thee.[6]
DEMETRIUS: Yea, art thou there?
ROBIN: Follow my voice; we'll try[7] no manhood here. *Exeunt.*

[*Enter* LYSANDER.]

LYSANDER: He goes before me and still dares me on.
When I come where he calls, then he is gone.
The villain is much lighter-heeled than I.
I followed fast, but faster he did fly,
That[8] fallen am I in dark uneven way,
And here will rest me.

[*He lies down.*]

Come, thou gentle day.
For if but once thou show me thy gray light,
I'll find Demetrius and revenge this spite.

[*He sleeps.*]

[*Enter*] ROBIN *and* DEMETRIUS.

ROBIN: Ho, ho, ho! Coward, why com'st thou not?
DEMETRIUS: Abide me, if thou dar'st; for well I wot[9]

1. (Robin himself.)
2. With sword drawn. *Robin*: In what follows, Robin presumably mimics the voices of Demetrius and Lysander. 3. Immediately. 4. He might instead wander about the stage. *Plainer*: clearer.
5. Coward; wretch. 6. That is, it would be a disgrace to treat you as an honorable opponent. 7. Test.
8. With the result that. 9. Know. *Abide*: wait for.

Thou runn'st before me, shifting every place,
And dar'st not stand nor look me in the face.
Where art thou now?

ROBIN: Come hither; I am here.

DEMETRIUS: Nay, then, thou mock'st me. Thou shalt buy this dear[1]
If ever I thy face by daylight see.
Now, go thy way. Faintness constraineth me
To measure out my length on this cold bed.

[*He lies down.*]

By day's approach look to be visited.

[*He sleeps.*]

Enter HELENA.

HELENA: O weary night, O long and tedious night,
Abate[2] thy hours; shine comforts from the east,
That I may back to Athens by daylight
From these that my poor company detest;
And sleep, that sometimes shuts up sorrow's eye,
Steal me a while from mine own company.

[*She lies down and*] *sleep*[s].

ROBIN: Yet but three? Come one more;
Two of both kinds makes up four.

[*Enter* HERMIA.]

Here she comes, curst[3] and sad.
Cupid is a knavish lad
Thus to make poor females mad.

HERMIA: Never so weary, never so in woe,
Bedabbled with the dew and torn with briars,
I can no further crawl, no further go;
My legs can keep no pace with my desires.
Here will I rest me till the break of day.

[*She lies down.*]

Heavens shield Lysander, if they mean a fray.

[*She sleeps.*]

ROBIN: On the ground,
Sleep sound.
I'll apply
To your eye,
Gentle lover, remedy.

[*He squeezes the juice on* LYSANDER'S *eyes.*]

1. Dearly. *Buy*: pay for. 2. Shorten. 3. Angry.

When thou wak'st,
Thou tak'st
True delight
In the sight
Of thy former lady's eye;
And the country proverb known,
That every man should take his own,
In your waking shall be shown.
Jack shall have Jill,
Naught shall go ill,
The man shall have his mare again, and all shall be well.

[*Exit. The lovers remain onstage, asleep.*]

4.1[4]

Enter [TITANIA,] *Queen of Fairies, and* [BOTTOM, *the*] *clown* [*with the ass head*], *and* FAIRIES[, PEASEBLOSSOM, COBWEB, MOTH, *and* MUSTARDSEED], *and* [OBERON,] *the King, behind them.*

TITANIA: [*to* BOTTOM] Come, sit thee down upon this flowery bed
While I thy amiable cheeks do coy,[5]
And stick musk-roses in thy sleek smooth head,
And kiss thy fair large ears, my gentle joy.

BOTTOM: Where's Peaseblossom?

PEASEBLOSSOM: Ready.

BOTTOM: Scratch my head, Peaseblossom. —Where's Monsieur Cobweb?

COBWEB: Ready.

BOTTOM: Monsieur Cobweb, good monsieur, get you your weapons in your hand and kill me a red-hipped humble-bee on the top of a thistle; and, good monsieur, bring me the honey-bag. Do not fret yourself too much in the action, monsieur; and, good monsieur, have a care the honey-bag break not. I would be loath to have you overflown with[6] a honey-bag, signor. [*Exit* COBWEB.] —Where's Monsieur Mustardseed?

MUSTARDSEED: Ready.

BOTTOM: Give me your neaf,[7] Monsieur Mustardseed. Pray you leave your courtesy,[8] good monsieur.

MUSTARDSEED: What's your will?

BOTTOM: Nothing, good monsieur, but to help Cavaliery[9] Cobweb to scratch. I must to the barber's, monsieur, for methinks I am marvelous hairy about the face. And I am such a tender ass, if my hair do but tickle me, I must scratch.

TITANIA: What, wilt thou hear some music, my sweet love?

BOTTOM: I have a reasonable good ear in music. Let's have the tongs and the bones.[1]

4. Location: The wood. 5. Caress. *Amiable*: lovable. 6. Submerged by. 7. Fist.
8. Stop bowing, or do not stand bareheaded.
9. Blunder for "Cavalier," perhaps influenced by the Italian term *cavaliere*.
1. Triangle and clappers (rustic musical instruments).

TITANIA: Or say, sweet love, what thou desir'st to eat.

BOTTOM: Truly, a peck of provender.[2] I could munch your good dry oats. Methinks I have a great desire to a bottle[3] of hay. Good hay, sweet hay, hath no fellow.[4]

TITANIA: I have a venturous fairy that shall seek
The squirrel's hoard and fetch thee off new nuts.

BOTTOM: I had rather have a handful or two of dried peas. But, I pray you, let none of your people stir me; I have an exposition of[5] sleep come upon me.

TITANIA: Sleep thou, and I will wind thee in my arms.
—Fairies, be gone, and be always[6] away. [*Exeunt* FAIRIES.]
So doth the woodbine[7] the sweet honeysuckle
Gently entwist; the female ivy so
Enrings the barky fingers of the elm.
—Oh, how I love thee, how I dote on thee!

[*They sleep.*]

Enter ROBIN *Goodfellow.*

OBERON: [*coming forward*] Welcome, good Robin. Seest thou this sweet sight?
Her dotage now I do begin to pity.
For, meeting her of late behind the wood
Seeking sweet favors[8] for this hateful fool,
I did upbraid her and fall out with her.
For she his hairy temples then had rounded
With coronet of fresh and fragrant flowers,
And that same dew which sometime[9] on the buds
Was wont to swell like round and orient[1] pearls
Stood now within the pretty flowerets' eyes
Like tears that did their own disgrace bewail.
When I had at my pleasure taunted her,
And she in mild terms begged my patience,
I then did ask of her her changeling child,
Which straight she gave me, and her fairy sent
To bear him to my bower in fairyland.
And now I have the boy, I will undo
This hateful imperfection of her eyes.
And, gentle puck, take this transformèd scalp
From off the head of this Athenian swain,
That he, awaking when the other[2] do,
May all to Athens back again repair
And think no more of this night's accidents
But as the fierce vexation of a dream.
But first I will release the Fairy Queen.

[*He squeezes the juice on* TITANIA*'s eyes.*]

2. Fodder. 3. Bundle. 4. Equal. 5. (For "disposition to.") 6. In every direction.
7. Here, "woodbine" cannot mean "honeysuckle," as it did at 2.1.251, and thus must refer to a different plant. *So*: thus. 8. Love tokens. 9. Formerly.
1. Lustrous (the best pearls were from the Far East). *Wont*: accustomed. 2. Others.

Be as thou wast wont to be;
See as thou wast wont to see.
Dian's bud o'er Cupid's flower[3]
Hath such force and blessèd power.
Now, my Titania, wake you, my sweet queen.
TITANIA: [*awaking*] My Oberon, what visions have I seen!
Methought I was enamored of an ass.
OBERON: There lies your love.
TITANIA: How came these things to pass?
Oh, how mine eyes do loathe his visage now!
OBERON: Silence a while. —Robin, take off this head.
—Titania, music call, and strike more dead
Than common sleep of all these five[4] the sense.
TITANIA: Music, ho—music such as charmeth sleep!

[*Music plays.*]

ROBIN: [*to* BOTTOM, *removing the ass head*] Now when thou wak'st with thine own fool's eyes peep.
OBERON: Sound, music! Come, my queen, take hands with me,
And rock the ground whereon these sleepers be.

[*They dance.*]

Now thou and I are new in amity
And will tomorrow midnight solemnly
Dance in Duke Theseus' house triumphantly
And bless it to all fair prosperity.
There shall the pairs of faithful lovers be
Wedded, with Theseus, all in jollity.
ROBIN: Fairy King, attend and mark:
I do hear the morning lark.
OBERON: Then, my queen, in silence sad
Trip we after night's shade.
We the globe can compass[5] soon,
Swifter than the wandering moon.
TITANIA: Come, my lord, and in our flight
Tell me how it came this night
That I sleeping here was found
With these mortals on the ground.

Exeunt [OBERON, TITANIA, *and* ROBIN].

Wind horn. Enter THESEUS [*with* HIPPOLYTA, EGEUS,] *and all his train.*

THESEUS: Go, one of you, find out the forester,
For now our observation[6] is performed.

3. "Dian's bud," the herb of 2.1.184 and 3.2.366, is perhaps *Agnus castus*, or chaste tree: said to preserve chastity and hence the antidote to "Cupid's flower," or the "love-in-idleness" of 2.1.168.
4. The lovers and Bottom. 5. Orbit. 6. "Observance to a morn of May," as at 1.1.167.

And since we have the vanguard[7] of the day,
My love shall hear the music of my hounds.
Uncouple[8] in the western valley; let them go.
Dispatch, I say, and find the forester. [*Exit an Attendant.*]
—We will, fair Queen, up to the mountain's top
And mark the musical confusion
Of hounds and echo in conjunction.

HIPPOLYTA: I was with Hercules and Cadmus[9] once
When in a wood of Crete they bayed[1] the bear
With hounds of Sparta.[2] Never did I hear
Such gallant chiding;[3] for besides the groves,
The skies, the fountains, every region near
Seemed all one mutual cry. I never heard
So musical a discord, such sweet thunder.

THESEUS: My hounds are bred out of the Spartan kind,
So flewed, so sanded;[4] and their heads are hung
With ears that sweep away the morning dew;
Crook-kneed, and dewlapped[5] like Thessalian bulls;
Slow in pursuit, but matched in mouth like bells,
Each under each. A cry more tunable[6]
Was never holla'd to nor cheered with horn
In Crete, in Sparta, nor in Thessaly.
Judge when you hear. But soft,[7] what nymphs are these?

EGEUS: My lord, this is my daughter here asleep,
And this Lysander, this Demetrius is,
This Helena, old Nedar's Helena.
I wonder of their being here together.

THESEUS: No doubt they rose up early to observe
The rite of May and, hearing our intent,
Came here in grace of our solemnity.[8]
But speak, Egeus: is not this the day
That Hermia should give answer of her choice?

EGEUS: It is, my lord.

THESEUS: Go bid the huntsmen wake them with their horns.

[*Exit an Attendant.*]

Shout within; wind horns; [*the lovers*] *all start up.*

Good morrow, friends. Saint Valentine[9] is past.
Begin these woodbirds but to couple now?

7. Earliest part. 8. Release (the dogs, leashed in pairs).
9. Mythical founder of Thebes. (No source for the anecdote is known.) 1. Hunted.
2. Famous in antiquity as hunting dogs. 3. Barking.
4. Sandy-colored. *Flewed*: flews were large hanging, fleshy chaps.
5. With hanging folds of skin under the neck (compare 2.1.50).
6. A pack of hounds more well tuned. *Matched . . . each*: harmoniously matched in the pitch of their barking, like a set of bells. 7. Stop; look. 8. Ceremony.
9. Birds were said to choose their mates on Valentine's Day.

LYSANDER: Pardon, my lord.

[*The lovers kneel.*]

THESEUS: I pray you all, stand up.

[*The lovers stand.*]

[*to* DEMETRIUS *and* LYSANDER] I know you two are rival enemies.
How comes this gentle concord in the world,
That hatred is so far from jealousy[1]
To sleep by hate and fear no enmity?
LYSANDER: My lord, I shall reply amazèdly,[2]
Half sleep, half waking. But as yet, I swear,
I cannot truly say how I came here.
But as I think—for truly would I speak,
And now I do bethink me, so it is—
I came with Hermia hither. Our intent
Was to be gone from Athens where we might
Without[3] the peril of the Athenian law—
EGEUS: [*to* THESEUS] Enough, enough, my lord; you have enough.
I beg the law, the law upon his head!
—They would have stolen away, they would, Demetrius,
Thereby to have defeated[4] you and me,
You of your wife and me of my consent,
Of my consent that she should be your wife.
DEMETRIUS: [*to* THESEUS] My lord, fair Helen told me of their stealth,
Of this their purpose hither to this wood,
And I in fury hither followed them,
Fair Helena in fancy[5] following me.
But, my good lord, I wot not by what power—
But by some power it is—my love to Hermia,
Melted as the snow, seems to me now
As the remembrance of an idle gaud[6]
Which in my childhood I did dote upon;
And all the faith, the virtue of my heart,
The object and the pleasure of mine eye,
Is only Helena. To her, my lord,
Was I betrothed ere I saw Hermia,
But like a sickness[7] did I loathe this food;
But, as in health come to my natural taste,
Now I do wish it, love it, long for it,
And will for evermore be true to it.
THESEUS: Fair lovers, you are fortunately met.
Of this discourse we more will hear anon.
—Egeus, I will overbear your will;

1. Suspicion. 2. Confusedly. 3. Outside. 4. Defrauded. 5. Love. 6. A worthless trinket.
7. Only as a person does when ill or nauseated.

For in the temple, by and by, with us
These couples shall eternally be knit.
And, for the morning now is something[8] worn,
Our purposed hunting shall be set aside.
Away with us to Athens. Three and three,
We'll hold a feast in great solemnity.
—Come, Hippolyta.

[*Exit* THESEUS *with* HIPPOLYTA, EGEUS, *and his train.*]

DEMETRIUS: These things seem small and undistinguishable,
Like far-off mountains turnèd into clouds.
HERMIA: Methinks I see these things with parted eye,[9]
When everything seems double.
HELENA: So methinks;
And I have found Demetrius like a jewel,
Mine own and not mine own.
DEMETRIUS: Are you sure
That we are awake? It seems to me
That yet we sleep, we dream. Do not you think
The Duke was here and bid us follow him?
HERMIA: Yea, and my father.
HELENA: And Hippolyta.
LYSANDER: And he did bid us follow to the temple.
DEMETRIUS: Why, then, we are awake. Let's follow him,
And by the way let's recount our dreams. [*Exeunt lovers.*]

BOTTOM: [*awaking*] When my cue comes, call me, and I will answer. My next is "Most fair Pyramus." Heigh-ho,[1] Peter Quince? Flute the bellows-mender? Snout the tinker? Starveling? God's my life![2] Stolen hence and left me asleep! I have had a most rare vision. I have had a dream past the wit of man to say what dream it was. Man is but an ass if he go about[3] to expound this dream. Methought I was—there is no man can tell what. Methought I was—and methought I had—but man is but patched a fool if he will offer[4] to say what methought I had. The eye of man hath not heard, the ear of man hath not seen, man's hand is not able to taste, his tongue to conceive, nor his heart to report[5] what my dream was. I will get Peter Quince to write a ballad of this dream. It shall be called "Bottom's Dream," because it hath no bottom;[6] and I will sing it in the latter end of a play, before the Duke. Peradventure,[7] to make it the more gracious, I shall sing it at her[8] death.

[*Exit.*]

8. Somewhat. *For*: since. 9. (Double vision.) 1. (A call; perhaps a yawn.) 2. Good Lord.
3. Try. 4. Venture. *Patched a fool*: patchwork or motley costumes were worn by jesters.
5. Burlesque of scripture: "The eye hath not seen, and the ear hath not heard, neither have entered into the heart of man" those things that God has prepared (1 Cor. 2:9–10 [Bishops' Bible]).
6. Because it is unfathomable, or has no substance (foundation).
7. Perhaps. 8. (Thisbe's?)

4.2[9]

Enter QUINCE, FLUTE[, SNOUT, *and* STARVELING].

QUINCE: Have you sent to Bottom's house? Is he come home yet?
STARVELING: He cannot be heard of. Out of doubt he is transported.[1]
FLUTE: If he come not, then the play is marred. It goes not forward, doth it?
QUINCE: It is not possible. You have not a man in all Athens able to discharge[2] Pyramus but he.
FLUTE: No, he hath simply the best wit[3] of any handicraft man in Athens.
QUINCE: Yea, and the best person[4] too; and he is a very paramour for a sweet voice.
FLUTE: You must say "paragon." A paramour is—God bless us—a thing of naught.[5]

Enter SNUG *the joiner.*

SNUG: Masters, the Duke is coming from the temple, and there is two or three lords and ladies more married. If our sport[6] had gone forward, we had all been made men.[7]
FLUTE: Oh, sweet bully Bottom! Thus hath he lost sixpence a day[8] during his life; he could not have 'scaped sixpence a day. An[9] the Duke had not given him sixpence a day for playing Pyramus, I'll be hanged. He would have deserved it. Sixpence a day in Pyramus, or nothing.

Enter BOTTOM.

BOTTOM: Where are these lads? Where are these hearts?[1]
QUINCE: Bottom! Oh, most courageous[2] day! Oh, most happy hour!
BOTTOM: Masters, I am to discourse wonders; but ask me not what; for if I tell you, I am not true Athenian. I will tell you everything right as it fell out.
QUINCE: Let us hear, sweet Bottom.
BOTTOM: Not a word of[3] me. All that I will tell you is that the Duke hath dined. Get your apparel together, good strings[4] to your beards, new ribbons to your pumps. Meet presently[5] at the palace; every man look o'er his part. For the short and the long is, our play is preferred.[6] In any case, let Thisbe have clean linen; and let not him that plays the lion pare his nails, for they shall hang out for the lion's claws. And, most dear actors, eat no onions nor garlic, for we are to utter sweet breath; and I do not doubt but to hear them say it is a sweet comedy. No more words. Away! Go, away! [*Exeunt.*]

5.1[7]

Enter THESEUS, HIPPOLYTA, PHILOSTRATE[, *Lords, and Attendants*].

HIPPOLYTA: 'Tis strange, my Theseus, that[8] these lovers speak of.
THESEUS: More strange than true. I never may believe

9. Location: Athens. 1. Carried away (by the fairies); transformed. *Out of doubt*: doubtless.
2. Perform. 3. Intellect. 4. Looks. 5. Something wicked. 6. Entertainment.
7. Our fortunes would have been made.
8. As a royal pension, considerably more than the average daily wage of an Elizabethan workman.
9. If. 1. Mates. 2. Blunder for "brave," meaning "splendid." 3. Out of. 4. (To attach the beards.)
5. Immediately. 6. Recommended. 7. Location: Athens. Theseus's palace. 8. That which.

These antique fables, nor these fairy toys.[9]
Lovers and madmen have such seething brains,
Such shaping fantasies, that apprehend[1] more
Than cool reason ever comprehends.
The lunatic, the lover, and the poet
Are of imagination all compact.[2]
One sees more devils than vast hell can hold;
That is the madman. The lover, all as frantic,
Sees Helen's beauty in a brow of Egypt.[3]
The poet's eye, in a fine frenzy rolling,
Doth glance from heaven to earth, from earth to heaven.
And as imagination bodies forth
The forms of things unknown, the poet's pen
Turns them to shapes and gives to airy nothing
A local habitation and a name.
Such tricks hath strong imagination
That if it would but apprehend some joy,
It comprehends some bringer[4] of that joy;
Or in the night, imagining some fear,[5]
How easy is a bush supposed a bear!

HIPPOLYTA: But all the story of the night told over,
And all their minds transfigured so together,
More witnesseth than fancy's images[6]
And grows to something of great constancy;[7]
But, howsoever, strange and admirable.[8]

Enter [the] lovers, LYSANDER, DEMETRIUS, HERMIA, *and* HELENA.

THESEUS: Here come the lovers, full of joy and mirth.
Joy, gentle friends, joy and fresh days of love
Accompany your hearts.

LYSANDER: More than to us
Wait in your royal walks, your board, your bed.[9]

THESEUS: Come now, what masques, what dances shall we have
To wear away this long age of three hours
Between our after-supper and bedtime?
Where is our usual manager of mirth?
What revels are in hand? Is there no play
To ease the anguish of a torturing hour?
Call Philostrate.

PHILOSTRATE: Here, mighty Theseus.

THESEUS: Say, what abridgement[1] have you for this evening,
What masque, what music? How shall we beguile
The lazy time if not with some delight?

9. Trifles. *Antique*: Ancient; strange, grotesque (as in "antic"). 1. Conceive. *Fantasies*: imaginations. 2. Composed. 3. In a gypsy's face. *Helen*: Helen of Troy. 4. Source. 5. Object to be feared. 6. *More . . . images*: Testifies to something more than mere figments of the imagination. 7. Consistency. 8. Wondrous. *Howsoever*: in any case. 9. May even more joy and love attend your daily lives. 1. Pastime, something to make the evening seem shorter.

PHILOSTRATE: [*giving* THESEUS *a paper*] There is a brief[2] how many sports are ripe.
Make choice of which your highness will see first.
THESEUS: [*reads*] "The battle with the Centaurs,[3] to be sung
By an Athenian eunuch to the harp."
We'll none of that. That have I told my love
In glory of my kinsman Hercules.[4]
[*Reads*.] "The riot of the tipsy Bacchanals
Tearing the Thracian singer in their rage."[5]
That is an old device,[6] and it was played
When I from Thebes came last a conqueror.
[*Reads*.] "The thrice-three muses mourning for the death
Of learning, late deceased in beggary."[7]
That is some satire, keen and critical,
Not sorting with[8] a nuptial ceremony.
[*Reads*.] "A tedious brief scene of young Pyramus
And his love Thisbe; very tragical mirth."
Merry and tragical? Tedious and brief?
That is hot ice and wondrous strange snow!
How shall we find the concord of this discord?
PHILOSTRATE: A play there is, my lord, some ten words long,
Which is as brief as I have known a play,
But by ten words, my lord, it is too long,
Which makes it tedious. For in all the play
There is not one word apt, one player fitted.[9]
And tragical, my noble lord, it is,
For Pyramus therein doth kill himself,
Which, when I saw rehearsed, I must confess,
Made mine eyes water; but more merry tears
The passion of loud laughter never shed.
THESEUS: What are they that do play it?
PHILOSTRATE: Hard-handed men that work in Athens here,
Which never labored in their minds till now,
And now have toiled their unbreathed[1] memories
With this same play against[2] your nuptial.
THESEUS: And we will hear it.
PHILOSTRATE: No, my noble lord,
It is not for you. I have heard it over,
And it is nothing, nothing in the world;
Unless you can find sport in their intents,

2. Short list.
3. Probably the battle that occurred when the Centaurs tried to carry off the bride of Theseus's friend Pirithous.
4. According to Plutarch, Hercules and Theseus were cousins.
5. The murder of the poet Orpheus by drunken women, devotees of Dionysus. 6. Show.
7. Possibly a topical reference: Robert Greene, Christopher Marlowe, and Thomas Kyd, university wits who began writing for the stage in the 1580s, all died in desperate circumstances in 1592–94. But satiric laments on the poverty of scholars and poets were commonplace.
8. Befitting. 9. Appropriately cast. 1. Unexercised. *Toiled*: taxed. 2. In preparation for.

Extremely stretched and conned[3] with cruel pain,
To do you service.

THESEUS: I will hear that play.
For never anything can be amiss
When simpleness and duty tender it.
Go, bring them in; and take your places, ladies. [*Exit* PHILOSTRATE.]

HIPPOLYTA: I love not to see wretchedness o'ercharged,[4]
And duty in his service[5] perishing.

THESEUS: Why, gentle sweet, you shall see no such thing.

HIPPOLYTA: He says they can do nothing in this kind.[6]

THESEUS: The kinder we, to give them thanks for nothing.
Our sport shall be to take what they mistake.
And what poor duty cannot do, noble respect[7]
Takes it in might, not merit.[8]
Where I have come, great clerks[9] have purposèd
To greet me with premeditated welcomes,
Where I have seen them shiver and look pale,
Make periods in the midst of sentences,
Throttle their practised accent[1] in their fears,
And in conclusion dumbly have broke off,
Not paying me a welcome. Trust me, sweet,
Out of this silence yet I picked a welcome;
And in the modesty of fearful[2] duty
I read as much as from the rattling tongue
Of saucy and audacious eloquence.
Love, therefore, and tongue-tied simplicity
In least speak most, to my capacity.[3]

[*Enter* PHILOSTRATE.]

PHILOSTRATE: So please your grace, the Prologue is addressed.[4]

THESEUS: Let him approach.

Enter [QUINCE *as*] *the Prologue.*

QUINCE: [*as Prologue*] If we offend, it is with our good will.
That you should think, we come not to offend
But with good will. To show our simple skill,
That is the true beginning of our end.
Consider, then, we come but in despite.
We do not come as minding[5] to content you,
Our true intent is. All for your delight
We are not here. That you should here repent you

3. Memorized. *Stretched*: Strained.
4. Overburdened. *Wretchedness*: incompetence or weakness; poor people. 5. Its attempt to serve.
6. Kind of thing. 7. Consideration.
8. With respect to the giver's capacity, not the merit of the performance. 9. Scholars.
1. Rehearsed eloquence; usual manner of speaking. 2. Frightened. 3. In my judgment.
4. The speaker of the Prologue is ready. 5. Intending.

The actors are at hand; and by their show
You shall know all that you are like to know.[6]

THESEUS: This fellow doth not stand upon points.[7]

LYSANDER: He hath rid his prologue like a rough[8] colt: he knows not the stop.[9] A good moral, my lord: it is not enough to speak, but to speak true.

HIPPOLYTA: Indeed he hath played on this prologue like a child on a recorder: a sound, but not in government.[1]

THESEUS: His speech was like a tangled chain: nothing[2] impaired, but all disordered. Who is next?

Enter [BOTTOM *as*] *Pyramus, and* [FLUTE *as*] *Thisbe, and* [SNOUT *as*] *Wall, and* [STARVELING *as*] *Moonshine, and* [SNUG *as*] *Lion.*

QUINCE: [*as Prologue*] Gentles, perchance you wonder at this show,
But wonder on till truth make all things plain.
This man is Pyramus, if you would know;
This beauteous lady Thisbe is, certain.
This man with lime and roughcast doth present
Wall, that vile wall which did these lovers sunder;
And through Wall's chink, poor souls, they are content
To whisper—at the which let no man wonder.
This man with lantern, dog, and bush of thorn
Presenteth Moonshine. For, if you will know,
By moonshine did these lovers think no scorn[3]
To meet at Ninus' tomb, there, there to woo.
This grisly beast, which "Lion" hight[4] by name,
The trusty Thisbe, coming first by night,
Did scare away, or rather did affright;
And as she fled, her mantle she did fall,[5]
Which Lion vile with bloody mouth did stain.
Anon comes Pyramus, sweet youth and tall,[6]
And finds his trusty Thisbe's mantle slain;
Whereat with blade, with bloody, blameful blade,
He bravely broached[7] his boiling bloody breast;
And Thisbe, tarrying in mulberry shade,
His dagger drew and died. For all the rest
Let Lion, Moonshine, Wall, and lovers twain
At large[8] discourse, while here they do remain.

Exeunt [QUINCE *as Prologue,* SNUG *as*] *Lion,* [FLUTE *as*] *Thisbe, and* [STARVELING *as*] *Moonshine.*

THESEUS: I wonder if the lion be to speak.

DEMETRIUS: No wonder, my lord; one lion may when many asses do.

SNOUT: [*as Wall*] In this same interlude[9] it doth befall

6. The humor of Quince's speech rests in its mispunctuation; repunctuated, it becomes a typical courteous address.

7. Bother about niceties; heed punctuation marks. 8. An unbroken.

9. How to rein the colt to a stop; punctuation mark. 1. Control. 2. Not at all.

3. (It) no disgrace. 4. Is called. 5. Drop. 6. Handsome. 7. Stabbed. 8. Lengthy. 9. Play.

That I, one Snout by name, present a wall;
And such a wall as I would have you think
That had in it a crannied hole or chink
Through which the lovers, Pyramus and Thisbe,
Did whisper often very secretly.
This loam, this roughcast, and this stone doth show
That I am that same wall; the truth is so.
And this the cranny is, right and sinister,[1]
Through which the fearful lovers are to whisper.

THESEUS: Would you desire lime and hair to speak better?

DEMETRIUS: It is the wittiest partition[2] that ever I heard discourse, my lord.

THESEUS: Pyramus draws near the wall: silence!

BOTTOM: [*as Pyramus*] O grim-looked night, O night with hue so black,
O night, which ever art when day is not,
O night, O night, alack, alack, alack,
I fear my Thisbe's promise is forgot.
And thou, O wall, O sweet, O lovely wall,
That stand'st between her father's ground and mine,
Thou wall, O wall, O sweet and lovely wall,
Show me thy chink, to blink through with mine eyne.

[SNOUT, *as Wall, shows his chink.*]

Thanks, courteous wall; Jove shield thee well for this.
But what see I? No Thisbe do I see.
O wicked wall, through whom I see no bliss,
Cursed be thy stones[3] for thus deceiving me!

THESEUS: The wall, methinks, being sensible, should curse again.[4]

BOTTOM: [*to* THESEUS] No, in truth, sir, he should not. "Deceiving me" is Thisbe's cue. She is to enter now, and I am to spy her through the wall. You shall see it will fall pat[5] as I told you. Yonder she comes.

Enter [FLUTE *as*] *Thisbe.*

FLUTE: [*as Thisbe*] O wall, full often hast thou heard my moans
For parting my fair Pyramus and me.
My cherry lips have often kissed thy stones,
Thy stones with lime and hair knit up in thee.

BOTTOM: [*as Pyramus*] I see a voice; now will I to the chink
To spy an[6] I can hear my Thisbe's face.
Thisbe?

FLUTE: [*as Thisbe*] My love! Thou art my love, I think.

BOTTOM: [*as Pyramus*] Think what thou wilt, I am thy lover's grace,[7]
And like Limander[8] am I trusty still.

FLUTE: [*as Thisbe*] And I like Helen,[9] till the fates me kill.

1. Left; running horizontally. Or on the one side (Pyramus's) and the other (Thisbe's).
2. Wall; formal term for part of an oration. 3. Punning, unintentionally, on "testicles."
4. Back. *Sensible*: capable of feeling. 5. Precisely. 6. If. 7. Gracious lover.
8. Blunder for "Leander," who drowned while swimming across the Hellespont to meet his lover, Hero.
9. Helen of Troy was notoriously untrustworthy; a blunder for "Hero."

BOTTOM: [*as Pyramus*] Not Shafalus to Procrus[1] was so true.
FLUTE: [*as Thisbe*] As Shafalus to Procrus, I to you.
BOTTOM: [*as Pyramus*] Oh, kiss me through the hole of this vile wall.
FLUTE: [*as Thisbe*] I kiss the wall's hole, not your lips at all.
BOTTOM: [*as Pyramus*] Wilt thou at Ninny's tomb meet me straightway?
FLUTE: [*as Thisbe*] Tide[2] life, tide death, I come without delay.

[*Exeunt* BOTTOM *and* FLUTE.]

SNOUT: [*as Wall*] Thus have I, Wall, my part dischargèd so;
And, being done, thus Wall away doth go. [*Exit.*]
THESEUS: Now is the mural[3] down between the two neighbors.
DEMETRIUS: No remedy, my lord, when walls are so willful to hear without warning.[4]
HIPPOLYTA: This is the silliest stuff that ever I heard.
THESEUS: The best in this kind are but shadows,[5] and the worst are no worse if imagination amend them.
HIPPOLYTA: It must be your imagination then, and not theirs.
THESEUS: If we imagine no worse of them than they of themselves, they may pass for excellent men. Here come two noble beasts in, a man and a lion.

Enter [SNUG *as*] *Lion and* [STARVELING *as*] *Moonshine* [*with a lantern, thornbush, and dog*].

SNUG: [*as Lion*] You ladies, you whose gentle hearts do fear
The smallest monstrous mouse that creeps on floor,
May now, perchance, both quake and tremble here
When lion rough in wildest rage doth roar.
Then know that I as Snug the joiner am
A lion fell,[6] nor else no lion's dam.
For if I should as lion come in strife
Into this place, 'twere pity on my life.
THESEUS: A very gentle beast, and of a good conscience.
DEMETRIUS: The very best at a beast, my lord, that e'er I saw.
LYSANDER: This lion is a very fox[7] for his valor.
THESEUS: True; and a goose[8] for his discretion.
DEMETRIUS: Not so, my lord. For his valor cannot carry his discretion, and the fox carries the goose.
THESEUS: His discretion, I am sure, cannot carry his valor; for the goose carries not the fox. It is well. Leave it to his discretion, and let us listen to the moon.
STARVELING: [*as Moonshine*] This lantern doth the hornèd[9] moon present.

1. Blunder for "Cephalus" and "Procris." Procris was in fact seduced by her husband in disguise as another man; he later accidentally killed her. 2. Betide; come. 3. Wall.
4. Informing the parents. *Hear*: proverbially, "walls have ears." *To*: as to.
5. Mere likenesses without substance. *Kind*: profession (that is, actors).
6. Fierce; or skin (punning on the costume to which Snug reassuringly calls attention).
7. Symbolic of low cunning, rather than courage. 8. Symbolic of foolishness. 9. Crescent.

DEMETRIUS: He should have worn the horns on his head.[1]

THESEUS: He is no crescent,[2] and his horns are invisible within the circumference.

STARVELING: [*as Moonshine*] This lantern doth the hornèd moon present;
Myself the man i'th' moon do seem to be.

THESEUS: This is the greatest error of all the rest: the man should be put into the lantern; how is it else the man i'th' moon?

DEMETRIUS: He dares not come there for[3] the candle. For you see it is already in snuff.[4]

HIPPOLYTA: I am aweary of this moon; would he would change!

THESEUS: It appears by his small light of discretion that he is in the wane; but yet in courtesy, in all reason, we must stay the time.

LYSANDER: Proceed, Moon.

STARVELING: All that I have to say is to tell you that the lantern is the moon, I the man i'th' moon, this thornbush my thornbush, and this dog my dog.

DEMETRIUS: Why, all these should be in the lantern, for all these are in the moon. But silence; here comes Thisbe.

Enter [FLUTE *as*] *Thisbe.*

FLUTE: [*as Thisbe*] This is old Ninny's tomb. Where is my love?

SNUG: [*as Lion*] Oh!

[*Lion roars.*]

[*Thisbe runs off, dropping her mantle.*]

DEMETRIUS: Well roared, Lion!

THESEUS: Well run, Thisbe!

HIPPOLYTA: Well shone, Moon! Truly, the moon shines with a good grace.

[*Lion worries*[5] *Thisbe's mantle.*]

THESEUS: Well moused,[6] Lion!

Enter [BOTTOM *as*] *Pyramus.*

DEMETRIUS: And then came Pyramus. [*Exit* SNUG *as Lion.*]

LYSANDER: And so the lion vanished.

BOTTOM: [*as Pyramus*] Sweet moon, I thank thee for thy sunny beams;
I thank thee, moon, for shining now so bright.
For by thy gracious, golden, glittering gleams
I trust to take of truest Thisbe sight.
But stay, oh, spite!
But mark, poor knight,
What dreadful dole[7] is here?
Eyes, do you see?
How can it be?

1. The symbol of a cuckold. 2. Waxing moon. Perhaps a joke about Starveling's thinness. 3. For fear of. 4. In need of snuffing; angry. 5. Gnaws on. 6. The mantle is like a mouse in the mouth of a cat. 7. Grief.

O dainty duck! O dear!
Thy mantle good,
What, stained with blood?
Approach, ye Furies fell!
O Fates,[8] come, come,
Cut thread and thrum,[9]
Quail, crush, conclude, and quell![1]

THESEUS: This passion, and[2] the death of a dear friend, would go near to make a man look sad.

HIPPOLYTA: Beshrew my heart, but I pity the man.

BOTTOM: [*as Pyramus*] Oh, wherefore, Nature, didst thou lions frame,
Since lion vile hath here deflowered[3] my dear?
Which is—no, no, which was—the fairest dame
That lived, that loved, that liked, that looked with cheer.
Come, tears, confound!
Out, sword, and wound
The pap[4] of Pyramus,
Ay, that left pap,
Where heart doth hop.

[*He stabs himself.*]

Thus die I, thus, thus, thus.
Now am I dead;
Now am I fled.
My soul is in the sky.
Tongue, lose thy light;
Moon, take thy flight. [*Exit* STARVELING *as Moonshine.*]
Now die, die, die, die, die.

[*Pyramus dies.*]

DEMETRIUS: No die, but an ace for him; for he is but one.[5]

LYSANDER: Less than an ace, man; for he is dead, he is nothing.

THESEUS: With the help of a surgeon he might yet recover, and yet prove an ass.

HIPPOLYTA: How chance Moonshine is gone before Thisbe comes back and finds her lover?

THESEUS: She will find him by starlight.

[*Enter* FLUTE *as Thisbe.*]

Here she comes, and her passion[6] ends the play.

HIPPOLYTA: Methinks she should not use a long one for such a Pyramus; I hope she will be brief.

8. The three Fates in Greek mythology spun and cut the thread of a person's life.
9. A technical term from Bottom's occupation: the tufted end of a weaver's warp, or set of yarns placed lengthwise in a loom when the woven fabric is cut.
1. Kill. *Quail*: overpower. 2. Only if combined with. *Passion*: suffering; extravagant speech.
3. Ruined (but commonly suggesting "deprived of her virginity"); his error for "devoured."
4. Breast. 5. Pun on "die" as one of a pair of dice. *One*: the ace, or lowest throw.
6. Passionate speech.

DEMETRIUS: A mote will turn the balance which Pyramus, which Thisbe,[7] is the better: he for a man, God warrant us; she for a woman, God bless us.

LYSANDER: She hath spied him already with those sweet eyes.

DEMETRIUS: And thus she means, *videlicet*:[8]

FLUTE: [*as Thisbe*] Asleep, my love?
What, dead, my dove?
O Pyramus, arise!
Speak, speak! Quite dumb?
Dead, dead? A tomb
Must cover thy sweet eyes.
These lily lips,
This cherry nose,
These yellow cowslip cheeks
Are gone, are gone.
Lovers, make moan.
His eyes were green as leeks.
O sisters three,[9]
Come, come to me
With hands as pale as milk;
Lay them in gore,
Since you have shore[1]
With shears his thread of silk.
Tongue, not a word!
Come, trusty sword,
Come, blade, my breast imbrue.[2]

[*She stabs herself.*]

And farewell, friends
Thus Thisbe ends.
Adieu, adieu, adieu.

[*Thisbe dies.*]

THESEUS: Moonshine and Lion are left to bury the dead.

DEMETRIUS: Ay, and Wall too.

BOTTOM: [*starting up*] No, I assure you, the wall is down that parted their fathers. [FLUTE *rises.*] Will it please you to see the epilogue or to hear a Bergomask dance[3] between two of our company?

THESEUS: No epilogue, I pray you; for your play needs no excuse. Never excuse; for when the players are all dead, there need none to be blamed. Marry, if he that writ it had played Pyramus and hanged himself in Thisbe's garter, it would have been a fine tragedy; and so it is, truly, and very notably discharged. But come, your Bergomask; let your epilogue alone.

[BOTTOM *and* FLUTE[4] *dance; then exeunt.*]

7. Whether Pyramus or Thisbe. *Mote*: speck.

8. As follows. *Means*: moans; lodges a formal legal complaint. 9. (The Fates.) 1. Shorn.

2. Stain with blood. 3. A dance named after Bergamo, in Italy (commonly ridiculed for its rusticity).

4. The only "two of our company" onstage at the end of the interlude. The role of Bottom may have been first performed by the actor Will Kemp, who was famous for his dancing.

The iron tongue of midnight hath told[5] twelve.
Lovers, to bed; 'tis almost fairy time.
I fear we shall outsleep the coming morn
As much as we this night have overwatched.[6]
This palpable-gross[7] play hath well beguiled
The heavy[8] gait of night. Sweet friends, to bed.
A fortnight hold we this solemnity
In nightly revels and new jollity. *Exeunt.*

Enter [ROBIN *Goodfellow, the*] *puck*[*, with a broom*].

ROBIN: Now the hungry lion roars,
And the wolf behowls the moon,
Whilst the heavy[9] plowman snores,
All with weary task fordone.[1]
Now the wasted brands[2] do glow,
Whilst the screech-owl, screeching loud,
Puts the wretch that lies in woe
In remembrance of a shroud.
Now it is the time of night
That the graves, all gaping wide,
Every one lets forth his sprite[3]
In the churchway paths to glide;
And we fairies that do run
By the triple Hecate's[4] team
From the presence of the sun,
Following darkness like a dream,
Now are frolic.[5] Not a mouse
Shall disturb this hallowed house.
I am sent with broom[6] before
To sweep the dust behind[7] the door.

Enter [OBERON *and* TITANIA,] *King and Queen of Fairies, with all their train.*

OBERON: Through the house give glimmering light
By the dead and drowsy fire;
Every elf and fairy sprite
Hop as light as bird from briar;
And this ditty after me
Sing, and dance it trippingly.
TITANIA: First rehearse your song by rote,
To each word a warbling note.
Hand in hand with fairy grace

5. Counted; tolled. 6. Stayed awake too late. 7. Palpably crude. 8. Drowsy; slow. 9. Weary.
1. "Done in"; exhausted. 2. Burned-out logs. 3. Each grave lets forth its ghost.
4. Hecate was goddess of the moon and night, and she had three realms: heaven (as Cynthia), earth (as Diana), and hell (as Proserpine). 5. Merry.
6. One of his traditional emblems; he helped good housekeepers and punished lazy ones.
7. From behind.

Will we sing and bless this place.

[*The* FAIRIES *dance to a song.*]

OBERON: Now until the break of day
Through this house each fairy stray.
To the best bride-bed will we,[8]
Which by us shall blessèd be;
And the issue there create[9]
Ever shall be fortunate.
So shall all the couples three
Ever true in loving be.
And the blots of nature's hand
Shall not in their issue stand;
Never mole, harelip, nor scar,
Nor mark prodigious,[1] such as are
Despisèd in nativity,
Shall upon their children be.
With this field-dew consecrate[2]
Every fairy take his gait,[3]
And each several[4] chamber bless
Through this palace with sweet peace;
And the owner of it blessed
Ever shall in safety rest.
Trip away, make no stay;
Meet me all by break of day. *Exeunt* [*all but* ROBIN].

ROBIN: [*to the audience*] If we shadows have offended,
Think but this, and all is mended,
That you have but slumbered here
While these visions did appear.
And this weak and idle theme,
No more yielding but[5] a dream,
Gentles, do not reprehend;
If you pardon, we will mend.
And as I am an honest puck,
If we have unearnèd luck
Now to 'scape the serpent's tongue,[6]
We will make amends ere long;
Else the puck a liar call.
So, good night unto you all.
Give me your hands,[7] if we be friends,
And Robin shall restore amends. [*Exit.*]

c. 1594–95

8. Oberon and Titania will bless the bed of Theseus and Hippolyta. 9. Created; conceived.
1. Ominous birthmarks.
2. Consecrated, blessed. Playfully alludes to the traditional Catholic custom of blessing the bride-bed with holy water. 3. Way. 4. Separate. 5. Than. 6. Hissing from the audience. 7. Applause.

Hamlet

CHARACTERS

CLAUDIUS, *King of Denmark*
HAMLET, *son of the former king and nephew to the present king*
POLONIUS, *Lord Chamberlain*
HORATIO, *friend of Hamlet*
LAERTES, *son of Polonius*
VOLTEMAND, CORNELIUS, ROSENCRANTZ, GUILDENSTERN, OSRIC, A GENTLEMAN — *courtiers*
A PRIEST
MARCELLUS, BERNARDO — *officers*
FRANCISCO, *a soldier*
REYNALDO, *servant to Polonius*
PLAYERS
TWO CLOWNS, *gravediggers*
FORTINBRAS, *Prince of Norway*
A NORWEGIAN CAPTAIN
ENGLISH AMBASSADORS
GERTRUDE, *Queen of Denmark, and mother of Hamlet*
OPHELIA, *daughter of Polonius*
GHOST OF HAMLET'S FATHER
LORDS, LADIES, OFFICERS, SOLDIERS, SAILORS, MESSENGERS, AND ATTENDANTS

SCENE: *The action takes place in or near the royal castle of Denmark at Elsinore.*

ACT I

Scene 1

A guard station atop the castle. Enter BERNARDO *and* FRANCISCO, *two sentinels.*

BERNARDO: Who's there?
FRANCISCO: Nay, answer me. Stand and unfold yourself.
BERNARDO: Long live the king!
FRANCISCO: Bernardo?
BERNARDO: He.
FRANCISCO: You come most carefully upon your hour.
BERNARDO: 'Tis now struck twelve. Get thee to bed, Francisco.
FRANCISCO: For this relief much thanks. 'Tis bitter cold,
And I am sick at heart.
BERNARDO: Have you had quiet guard?
FRANCISCO: Not a mouse stirring.
BERNARDO: Well, good night.
If you do meet Horatio and Marcellus,
The rivals[1] of my watch, bid them make haste.

[*Enter* HORATIO *and* MARCELLUS.]

FRANCISCO: I think I hear them. Stand, ho! Who is there?
HORATIO: Friends to this ground.
MARCELLUS: And liegemen to the Dane.[2]

1. Companions.
2. The "Dane" is the king of Denmark, who is also called "Denmark," as in line 48 of this scene. In line 61 a similar reference is used for the king of Norway.

FRANCISCO: Give you good night.
MARCELLUS: O, farewell, honest soldier!
Who hath relieved you?
FRANCISCO: Bernardo hath my place.
Give you good night. [*Exit* FRANCISCO.]
MARCELLUS: Holla, Bernardo!
BERNARDO: Say—
What, is Horatio there?
HORATIO: A piece of him.
BERNARDO: Welcome, Horatio. Welcome, good Marcellus.
HORATIO: What, has this thing appeared again tonight?
BERNARDO: I have seen nothing.
MARCELLUS: Horatio says 'tis but our fantasy,
And will not let belief take hold of him
Touching this dreaded sight twice seen of us.
Therefore I have entreated him along
With us to watch the minutes of this night,
That if again this apparition come,
He may approve[3] our eyes and speak to it.
HORATIO: Tush, tush, 'twill not appear.
BERNARDO: Sit down awhile,
And let us once again assail your ears,
That are so fortified against our story,
What we have two nights seen.
HORATIO: Well, sit we down.
And let us hear Bernardo speak of this.
BERNARDO: Last night of all,
When yond same star that's westward from the pole[4]
Had made his course t' illume that part of heaven
Where now it burns, Marcellus and myself,
The bell then beating one—

[*Enter* GHOST.]

MARCELLUS: Peace, break thee off. Look where it comes again.
BERNARDO: In the same figure like the king that's dead.
MARCELLUS: Thou art a scholar; speak to it, Horatio.
BERNARDO: Looks 'a[5] not like the king? Mark it, Horatio.
HORATIO: Most like. It harrows me with fear and wonder.
BERNARDO: It would be spoke to.
MARCELLUS: Speak to it, Horatio.
HORATIO: What art thou that usurp'st this time of night
Together with that fair and warlike form
In which the majesty of buried Denmark
Did sometimes march? By heaven I charge thee, speak.
MARCELLUS: It is offended.
BERNARDO: See, it stalks away.

3. Confirm the testimony of. 4. Polestar. 5. He.

HORATIO: Stay. Speak, speak. I charge thee, speak. [*Exit* GHOST.]
MARCELLUS: 'Tis gone and will not answer.
BERNARDO: How now, Horatio! You tremble and look pale.
Is not this something more than fantasy?
What think you on't?
HORATIO: Before my God, I might not this believe
Without the sensible[6] and true avouch
Of mine own eyes.
MARCELLUS: It is not like the king?
HORATIO: As thou art to thyself.
Such was the very armor he had on
When he the ambitious Norway combated.
So frowned he once when, in an angry parle,[7]
He smote the sledded Polacks on the ice.
'Tis strange.
MARCELLUS: Thus twice before, and jump[8] at this dead hour,
With martial stalk hath he gone by our watch.
HORATIO: In what particular thought to work I know not,
But in the gross and scope of mine opinion,
This bodes some strange eruption to our state.
MARCELLUS: Good now, sit down, and tell me he that knows,
Why this same strict and most observant watch
So nightly toils the subject[9] of the land,
And why such daily cast of brazen cannon
And foreign mart for implements of war;
Why such impress of shipwrights, whose sore task
Does not divide the Sunday from the week.
What might be toward that this sweaty haste
Doth make the night joint-laborer with the day?
Who is't that can inform me?
HORATIO: That can I.
At least, the whisper goes so. Our last king,
Whose image even but now appeared to us,
Was as you know by Fortinbras of Norway,
Thereto pricked on by a most emulate pride,
Dared to the combat; in which our valiant Hamlet
(For so this side of our known world esteemed him)
Did slay this Fortinbras; who by a sealed compact
Well ratified by law and heraldry,
Did forfeit, with his life, all those his lands
Which he stood seized of,[1] to the conqueror;
Against the which a moiety competent[2]
Was gagèd[3] by our king; which had returned
To the inheritance of Fortinbras,
Had he been vanquisher; as, by the same covenant

6. Perceptible. 7. Parley. 8. Precisely. 9. People. 1. Possessed.
2. Portion of similar value. 3. Pledged.

And carriage of the article designed,
His fell to Hamlet. Now, sir, young Fortinbras,
Of unimprovèd mettle hot and full,
Hath in the skirts of Norway here and there
Sharked up a list of lawless resolutes
For food and diet to some enterprise
That hath a stomach in't; which is no other,
As it doth well appear unto our state,
But to recover of us by strong hand
And terms compulsatory, those foresaid lands
So by his father lost; and this, I take it,
Is the main motive of our preparations,
The source of this our watch, and the chief head
Of this post-haste and romage[4] in the land.

BERNARDO: I think it be no other but e'en so.
Well may it sort[5] that this portentous figure
Comes armèd through our watch so like the king
That was and is the question of these wars.

HORATIO: A mote[6] it is to trouble the mind's eye.
In the most high and palmy state of Rome,
A little ere the mightiest Julius fell,
The graves stood tenantless, and the sheeted dead
Did squeak and gibber in the Roman streets;
As stars with trains of fire, and dews of blood,
Disasters in the sun; and the moist star,
Upon whose influence Neptune's empire stands,[7]
Was sick almost to doomsday with eclipse.
And even the like precurse[8] of feared events,
As harbingers preceding still the fates
And prologue to the omen coming on,
Have heaven and earth together demonstrated
Unto our climatures[9] and countrymen.

[*Enter* GHOST.]

But soft, behold, lo where it comes again!
I'll cross it[1] though it blast me.—Stay, illusion.

[*It spreads (its) arms.*]

If thou hast any sound or use of voice,
Speak to me.
If there be any good thing to be done,
That may to thee do ease, and grace to me,
Speak to me.

4. Stir. 5. Chance. 6. Speck of dust.
7. Neptune was the Roman sea god; the "moist star" is the moon. 8. Precursor. 9. Regions.
1. Horatio means either that he will move across the ghost's path in order to stop the ghost or that he will make the sign of the cross to gain power over the ghost. The stage direction that follows is somewhat ambiguous. "It" seems to refer to the ghost, but the movement would be appropriate to Horatio.

If thou art privy to thy country's fate,
Which happily foreknowing may avoid,
O, speak!
Or if thou hast uphoarded in thy life
Extorted treasure in the womb of earth,
For which, they say, you spirits oft walk in death,

[*The cock crows.*]

Speak of it. Stay, and speak. Stop it, Marcellus.
MARCELLUS: Shall I strike at it with my partisan?[2]
HORATIO: Do, if it will not stand.
BERNARDO: 'Tis here.
HORATIO: 'Tis here.
MARCELLUS: 'Tis gone. [*Exit* GHOST.]
We do it wrong, being so majestical,
To offer it the show of violence;
For it is as the air, invulnerable,
And our vain blows malicious mockery.
BERNARDO: It was about to speak when the cock crew.
HORATIO: And then it started like a guilty thing
Upon a fearful summons. I have heard
The cock, that is the trumpet to the morn,
Doth with his lofty and shrill-sounding throat
Awake the god of day, and at his warning,
Whether in sea or fire, in earth or air,
Th' extravagant and erring[3] spirit hies
To his confine; and of the truth herein
This present object made probation.[4]
MARCELLUS: It faded on the crowing of the cock.
Some say that ever 'gainst that season comes
Wherein our Savior's birth is celebrated,
This bird of dawning singeth all night long,
And then, they say, no spirit dare stir abroad,
The nights are wholesome, then no planets strike,
No fairy takes,[5] nor witch hath power to charm,
So hallowed and so gracious is that time.
HORATIO: So have I heard and do in part believe it.
But look, the morn in russet mantle clad
Walks o'er the dew of yon high eastward hill.
Break we our watch up, and by my advice
Let us impart what we have seen tonight
Unto young Hamlet, for upon my life
This spirit, dumb to us, will speak to him.
Do you consent we shall acquaint him with it,
As needful in our loves, fitting our duty?
MARCELLUS: Let's do't, I pray, and I this morning know
Where we shall find him most conveniently. [*Exeunt.*]

2. Halberd. 3. Errant, wandering out of bounds. 4. Proof. 5. Enchants.

Scene 2

A chamber of state. Enter KING CLAUDIUS, QUEEN GERTRUDE, HAMLET, POLONIUS, LAERTES, VOLTEMAND, CORNELIUS *and other members of the court.*

KING: Though yet of Hamlet our dear brother's death
The memory be green, and that it us befitted
To bear our hearts in grief, and our whole kingdom
To be contracted in one brow of woe,
Yet so far hath discretion fought with nature
That we with wisest sorrow think on him,
Together with remembrance of ourselves.
Therefore our sometime sister, now our queen,
Th' imperial jointress[6] to this warlike state,
Have we, as 'twere with a defeated joy,
With an auspicious and a dropping eye,
With mirth in funeral, and with dirge in marriage,
In equal scale weighing delight and dole,
Taken to wife; nor have we herein barred
Your better wisdoms, which have freely gone
With this affair along. For all, our thanks.
Now follows that you know young Fortinbras,
Holding a weak supposal of our worth,
Or thinking by our late dear brother's death
Our state to be disjoint and out of frame,
Colleaguèd with this dream of his advantage,
He hath not failed to pester us with message
Importing the surrender of those lands
Lost by his father, with all bonds of law,
To our most valiant brother. So much for him.
Now for ourself, and for this time of meeting,
Thus much the business is: we have here writ
To Norway, uncle of young Fortinbras—
Who, impotent and bedrid, scarcely hears
Of this his nephew's purpose—to suppress
His further gait[7] herein, in that the levies,
The lists, and full proportions are all made
Out of his subject; and we here dispatch
You, good Cornelius, and you, Voltemand,
For bearers of this greeting to old Norway,
Giving to you no further personal power
To business with the king, more than the scope
Of these dilated[8] articles allow.
Farewell, and let your haste commend your duty.

CORNELIUS: } VOLTEMAND: } In that, and all things will we show our duty.

6. Widow who holds a *jointure* or life interest in the estate of her deceased husband.
7. Progress. 8. Fully expressed.

KING: We doubt it nothing, heartily farewell.
[*Exeunt* VOLTEMAND *and* CORNELIUS.]
And now, Laertes, what's the news with you?
You told us of some suit. What is't, Laertes?
You cannot speak of reason to the Dane
And lose your voice. What wouldst thou beg, Laertes,
That shall not be my offer, not thy asking?
The head is not more native to the heart,
The hand more instrumental[9] to the mouth,
Than is the throne of Denmark to thy father.
What wouldst thou have, Laertes?
LAERTES: My dread lord,
Your leave and favor to return to France,
From whence, though willingly, I came to Denmark
To show my duty in your coronation,
Yet now I must confess, that duty done,
My thoughts and wishes bend again toward France,
And bow them to your gracious leave and pardon.
KING: Have you your father's leave? What says Polonius?
POLONIUS: He hath, my lord, wrung from me my slow leave
By laborsome petition, and at last
Upon his will I sealed my hard consent.
I do beseech you give him leave to go.
KING: Take thy fair hour, Laertes. Time be thine,
And thy best graces spend it at thy will.
But now, my cousin[1] Hamlet, and my son—
HAMLET: [*Aside.*] A little more than kin, and less than kind.
KING: How is it that the clouds still hang on you?
HAMLET: Not so, my lord. I am too much in the sun.
QUEEN: Good Hamlet, cast thy nighted color off,
And let thine eye look like a friend on Denmark.
Do not for ever with thy vailèd lids[2]
Seek for thy noble father in the dust.
Thou know'st 'tis common—all that lives must die,
Passing through nature to eternity.
HAMLET: Ay, madam, it is common.
QUEEN: If it be,
Why seems it so particular with thee?
HAMLET: Seems, madam? Nay, it is. I know not "seems."
'Tis not alone my inky cloak, good mother,
Nor customary suits of solemn black,
Nor windy suspiration of forced breath,
No, nor the fruitful river in the eye,
Nor the dejected havior[3] of the visage,
Together with all forms, moods, shapes of grief,

9. Serviceable. 1. "Cousin" is used here as a general term of kinship. 2. Lowered eyes.
3. Appearance.

That can denote me truly. These indeed seem,
For they are actions that a man might play,
But I have that within which passes show—
These but the trappings and the suits of woe.

KING: 'Tis sweet and commendable in your nature, Hamlet,
To give these mourning duties to your father,
But you must know your father lost a father,
That father lost, lost his, and the survivor bound
In filial obligation for some term
To do obsequious[4] sorrow. But to persever
In obstinate condolement is a course
Of impious stubbornness. 'Tis unmanly grief.
It shows a will most incorrect to[5] heaven,
A heart unfortified, a mind impatient,
An understanding simple and unschooled.
For what we know must be, and is as common
As any the most vulgar thing to sense,
Why should we in our peevish opposition
Take it to heart? Fie, 'tis a fault to heaven,
A fault against the dead, a fault to nature,
To reason most absurd, whose common theme
Is death of fathers, and who still hath cried,
From the first corse[6] till he that died today,
"This must be so." We pray you throw to earth
This unprevailing woe, and think of us
As of a father, for let the world take note
You are the most immediate[7] to our throne,
And with no less nobility of love
Than that which dearest father bears his son
Do I impart toward you. For your intent
In going back to school in Wittenberg,
It is most retrograde[8] to our desire,
And we beseech you, bend you to remain
Here in the cheer and comfort of our eye,
Our chiefest courtier, cousin, and our son.

QUEEN: Let not thy mother lose her prayers, Hamlet.
I pray thee stay with us, go not to Wittenberg.

HAMLET: I shall in all my best obey you, madam.

KING: Why, 'tis a loving and a fair reply.
Be as ourself in Denmark. Madam, come.
This gentle and unforced accord of Hamlet
Sits smiling to my heart, in grace whereof,
No jocund health that Denmark drinks today
But the great cannon to the clouds shall tell,
And the king's rouse the heaven shall bruit[9] again,

4. Suited for funeral obsequies. 5. Unsubmissive toward. 6. Corpse. 7. Next in line.
8. Contrary. 9. Echo. *Rouse*: carousal.

Respeaking earthly thunder. Come away.
[*Flourish. Exeunt all but* HAMLET.]

HAMLET: O, that this too too solid flesh would melt,
Thaw, and resolve itself into a dew,
Or that the Everlasting had not fixed
His canon[1] 'gainst self-slaughter. O God, God,
How weary, stale, flat, and unprofitable
Seem to me all the uses of this world!
Fie on't, ah, fie, 'tis an unweeded garden
That grows to seed. Things rank and gross in nature
Possess it merely.[2] That it should come to this,
But two months dead, nay, not so much, not two.
So excellent a king, that was to this
Hyperion to a satyr,[3] so loving to my mother,
That he might not beteem[4] the winds of heaven
Visit her face too roughly. Heaven and earth,
Must I remember? Why, she would hang on him
As if increase of appetite had grown
By what it fed on, and yet, within a month—
Let me not think on't. Frailty, thy name is woman—
A little month, or ere those shoes were old
With which she followed my poor father's body
Like Niobe,[5] all tears, why she, even she—
O God, a beast that wants discourse of reason
Would have mourned longer—married with my uncle,
My father's brother, but no more like my father
Than I to Hercules.[6] Within a month,
Ere yet the salt of most unrighteous tears
Had left the flushing in her gallèd eyes,
She married. O, most wicked speed, to post
With such dexterity to incestuous sheets!
It is not, nor it cannot come to good.
But break my heart, for I must hold my tongue.

[*Enter* HORATIO, MARCELLUS, *and* BERNARDO.]

HORATIO: Hail to your lordship!
HAMLET: I am glad to see you well.
Horatio—or I do forget myself.
HORATIO: The same, my lord, and your poor servant ever.
HAMLET: Sir, my good friend, I'll change that name with you.
And what make you from[7] Wittenberg, Horatio?
Marcellus?

1. Law. 2. Entirely.
3. Hyperion, a Greek god, stands here for beauty in contrast to the monstrous satyr, a lecherous creature, half man and half goat. 4. Permit.
5. In Greek mythology, Niobe was turned to stone after a tremendous fit of weeping over the death of her fourteen children, a misfortune brought about by her boasting over her fertility.
6. The demigod Hercules was noted for his strength and the series of spectacular labors that he accomplished. 7. What are you doing away from? *Change*: exchange.

MARCELLUS: My good lord!
HAMLET: I am very glad to see you. [*To* BERNARDO.] Good even, sir.—
But what, in faith, make you from Wittenberg?
HORATIO: A truant disposition, good my lord.
HAMLET: I would not hear your enemy say so,
Nor shall you do my ear that violence
To make it truster of your own report
Against yourself. I know you are no truant.
But what is your affair in Elsinore?
We'll teach you to drink deep ere you depart.
HORATIO: My lord, I came to see your father's funeral.
HAMLET: I prithee do not mock me, fellow-student,
I think it was to see my mother's wedding.
HORATIO: Indeed, my lord, it followed hard upon.
HAMLET: Thrift, thrift, Horatio. The funeral-baked meats
Did coldly furnish forth the marriage tables.
Would I had met my dearest[8] foe in heaven
Or ever I had seen that day, Horatio!
My father—methinks I see my father.
HORATIO: Where, my lord?
HAMLET: In my mind's eye, Horatio.
HORATIO: I saw him once, 'a was a goodly king.
HAMLET: 'A was a man, take him for all in all,
I shall not look upon his like again.
HORATIO: My lord, I think I saw him yesternight.
HAMLET: Saw who?
HORATIO: My lord, the king your father.
HAMLET: The king my father?
HORATIO: Season your admiration[9] for a while
With an attent ear till I may deliver[1]
Upon the witness of these gentlemen
This marvel to you.
HAMLET: For God's love, let me hear!
HORATIO: Two nights together had these gentlemen,
Marcellus and Bernardo, on their watch
In the dead waste and middle of the night
Been thus encountered. A figure like your father,
Armèd at point exactly, cap-a-pe,[2]
Appears before them, and with solemn march
Goes slow and stately by them. Thrice he walked
By their oppressed and fear-surprisèd eyes
Within his truncheon's[3] length, whilst they, distilled
Almost to jelly with the act of fear,
Stand dumb and speak not to him. This to me
In dreadful secrecy impart they did,
And I with them the third night kept the watch,

8. Bitterest. 9. Moderate your wonder. 1. Relate. *Attent*: attentive.
2. From head to toe. *Exactly*: completely. 3. Baton of office.

Where, as they had delivered, both in time,
Form of the thing, each word made true and good,
The apparition comes. I knew your father.
These hands are not more like.
HAMLET: But where was this?
MARCELLUS: My lord, upon the platform where we watch.
HAMLET: Did you not speak to it?
HORATIO: My lord, I did,
But answer made it none. Yet once methought
It lifted up it head and did address
Itself to motion, like as it would speak;
But even then the morning cock crew loud,
And at the sound it shrunk in haste away
And vanished from our sight.
HAMLET: 'Tis very strange.
HORATIO: As I do live, my honored lord, 'tis true,
And we did think it writ down in our duty
To let you know of it.
HAMLET: Indeed, sirs, but
This troubles me. Hold you the watch tonight?
ALL: We do, my lord.
HAMLET: Armed, say you?
ALL: Armed, my lord.
HAMLET: From top to toe?
ALL: My lord, from head to foot.
HAMLET: Then saw you not his face.
HORATIO: O yes, my lord, he wore his beaver[4] up.
HAMLET: What, looked he frowningly?
HORATIO: A countenance more in sorrow than in anger.
HAMLET: Pale or red?
HORATIO: Nay, very pale.
HAMLET: And fixed his eyes upon you?
HORATIO: Most constantly.
HAMLET: I would I had been there.
HORATIO: It would have much amazed you.
HAMLET: Very like.
Stayed it long?
HORATIO: While one with moderate haste might tell[5] a hundred.
BOTH: Longer, longer.
HORATIO: Not when I saw't.
HAMLET: His beard was grizzled, no?
HORATIO: It was as I have seen it in his life,
A sable silvered.
HAMLET: I will watch tonight.
Perchance 'twill walk again.
HORATIO: I warr'nt it will.

4. Hinged face protector. 5. Count.

HAMLET: If it assume my noble father's person,
I'll speak to it though hell itself should gape
And bid me hold my peace. I pray you all,
If you have hitherto concealed this sight,
Let it be tenable[6] in your silence still,
And whatsomever else shall hap tonight,
Give it an understanding but no tongue.
I will requite your loves. So fare you well.
Upon the platform 'twixt eleven and twelve
I'll visit you.
ALL: Our duty to your honor.
HAMLET: Your loves, as mine to you. Farewell. [*Exeunt all but* HAMLET.]
My father's spirit in arms? All is not well.
I doubt[7] some foul play. Would the night were come!
Till then sit still, my soul. Foul deeds will rise,
Though all the earth o'erwhelm them, to men's eyes. [*Exit.*]

Scene 3

The dwelling of POLONIUS. *Enter* LAERTES *and* OPHELIA.

LAERTES: My necessaries are embarked. Farewell.
And, sister, as the winds give benefit
And convoy is assistant,[8] do not sleep,
But let me hear from you.
OPHELIA: Do you doubt that?
LAERTES: For Hamlet, and the trifling of his favor,
Hold it a fashion and a toy in blood,
A violet in the youth of primy[9] nature,
Forward, not permanent, sweet, not lasting,
The perfume and suppliance of a minute,
No more.
OPHELIA: No more but so?
LAERTES: Think it no more.
For nature crescent[1] does not grow alone
In thews and bulk, but as this temple[2] waxes
The inward service of the mind and soul
Grows wide withal. Perhaps he loves you now,
And now no soil nor cautel[3] doth besmirch
The virtue of his will, but you must fear,
His greatness weighted,[4] his will is not his own,
For he himself is subject to his birth.
He may not, as unvalued persons do,
Carve for himself, for on his choice depends
The safety and health of this whole state,

6. Held. 7. Suspect. 8. Means of transport is available. 9. Of the spring. 1. Growing.
2. Body. *Thews*: muscles. 3. Deceit. 4. Rank considered.

And therefore must his choice be circumscribed
Unto the voice[5] and yielding of that body
Whereof he is the head. Then if he says he loves you,
It fits your wisdom so far to believe it
As he in his particular act and place
May give his saying deed, which is no further
Than the main voice of Denmark goes withal.
Then weigh what loss your honor may sustain
If with too credent[6] ear you list his songs,
Or lose your heart, or your chaste treasure open
To his unmastered importunity.
Fear it, Ophelia, fear it, my dear sister,
And keep you in the rear of your affection,
Out of the shot and danger of desire.
The chariest[7] maid is prodigal enough
If she unmask her beauty to the moon.
Virtue itself scapes not calumnious strokes.
The canker[8] galls the infants of the spring
Too oft before their buttons[9] be disclosed,
And in the morn and liquid dew of youth
Contagious blastments[1] are most imminent.
Be wary then; best safety lies in fear.
Youth to itself rebels, though none else near.

OPHELIA: I shall the effect of this good lesson keep
As watchman to my heart. But, good my brother,
Do not as some ungracious pastors do,
Show me the steep and thorny way to heaven,
Whiles like a puffed and reckless libertine
Himself the primrose path of dalliance treads
And recks not his own rede.[2]

LAERTES: O, fear me not.

[*Enter* POLONIUS.]

I stay too long. But here my father comes.
A double blessing is a double grace;
Occasion smiles upon a second leave.

POLONIUS: Yet here, Laertes? Aboard, aboard, for shame!
The wind sits in the shoulder of your sail,
And you are stayed for. There—my blessing with thee,
And these few precepts in thy memory
Look thou character.[3] Give thy thoughts no tongue,
Nor any unproportioned thought his act.
Be thou familiar, but by no means vulgar.
Those friends thou hast, and their adoption tried,
Grapple them unto thy soul with hoops of steel;

5. Assent. 6. Credulous. *List*: listen to. 7. Most circumspect. 8. Cankerworm. 9. Buds.
1. Blights. 2. Heeds not his own advice. 3. Write.

But do not dull[4] thy palm with entertainment
Of each new-hatched, unfledged comrade. Beware
Of entrance to a quarrel, but being in,
Bear't that th' opposèd[5] may beware of thee.
Give every man thy ear, but few thy voice;[6]
Take each man's censure, but reserve thy judgment.
Costly thy habit as thy purse can buy,
But not expressed in fancy; rich not gaudy,
For the apparel oft proclaims the man,
And they in France of the best rank and station
Are of a most select and generous chief[7] in that.
Neither a borrower nor a lender be,
For loan oft loses both itself and friend,
And borrowing dulls th' edge of husbandry.
This above all, to thine own self be true,
And it must follow as the night the day
Thou canst not then be false to any man.
Farewell. My blessing season this in thee!
LAERTES: Most humbly do I take my leave, my lord.
POLONIUS: The time invests you. Go, your servants tend.[8]
LAERTES: Farewell, Ophelia, and remember well
What I have said to you.
OPHELIA: 'Tis in my memory locked,
And you yourself shall keep the key of it.
LAERTES: Farewell. [*Exit.*]
POLONIUS: What is't, Ophelia, he hath said to you?
OPHELIA: So please you, something touching the Lord Hamlet.
POLONIUS: Marry, well bethought.
'Tis told me he hath very oft of late
Given private time to you, and you yourself
Have of your audience been most free and bounteous.
If it be so—as so 'tis put on me,
And that in way of caution—I must tell you,
You do not understand yourself so clearly
As it behooves my daughter and your honor.
What is between you? Give me up the truth.
OPHELIA: He hath, my lord, of late made many tenders
Of his affection to me.
POLONIUS: Affection? Pooh! You speak like a green girl,
Unsifted in such perilous circumstance.
Do you believe his tenders, as you call them?
OPHELIA: I do not know, my lord, what I should think.
POLONIUS: Marry, I will teach you. Think yourself a baby
That you have ta'en these tenders for true pay
Which are not sterling. Tender yourself more dearly,
Or (not to crack the wind of the poor phrase,

4. Make callous. 5. Conduct it so that the opponent. 6. Approval. 7. Eminence. 8. Await.

Running it thus) you'll tender me a fool.
OPHELIA: My lord, he hath importuned me with love
In honorable fashion.
POLONIUS: Ay, fashion you may call it. Go to, go to.
OPHELIA: And hath given countenance[9] to his speech, my lord,
With almost all the holy vows of heaven.
POLONIUS: Ay, springes[1] to catch woodcocks. I do know,
When the blood burns, how prodigal the soul
Lends the tongue vows. These blazes, daughter,
Giving more light than heat, extinct in both
Even in their promise, as it is a-making,
You must not take for fire. From this time
Be something scanter of your maiden presence.
Set your entreatments[2] at a higher rate
Than a command to parle. For Lord Hamlet,
Believe so much in him that he is young,
And with a larger tether may he walk
Than may be given you. In few, Ophelia,
Do not believe his vows, for they are brokers,[3]
Not of that dye which their investments[4] show,
But mere implorators[5] of unholy suits,
Breathing like sanctified and pious bawds,
The better to beguile. This is for all:
I would not, in plain terms, from this time forth
Have you so slander any moment leisure
As to give words or talk with the Lord Hamlet.
Look to't, I charge you. Come your ways.
OPHELIA: I shall obey, my lord. [*Exeunt.*]

Scene 4

The guard station. Enter HAMLET, HORATIO *and* MARCELLUS.

HAMLET: The air bites shrewdly;[6] it is very cold.
HORATIO: It is a nipping and an eager[7] air.
HAMLET: What hour now?
HORATIO: I think it lacks of twelve.
MARCELLUS: No, it is struck.
HORATIO: Indeed? I heard it not.
It then draws near the season
Wherein the spirit held his wont to walk.

[*A flourish of trumpets, and two pieces go off.*]

What does this mean, my lord?
HAMLET: The king doth wake tonight and takes his rouse,

9. Confirmation. 1. Snares. 2. Negotiations before a surrender. 3. Panderers. 4. Garments. 5. Solicitors. 6. Sharply. 7. Keen.

Keeps wassail, and the swagg'ring up-spring reels,
And as he drains his draughts of Rhenish[8] down,
The kettledrum and trumpet thus bray out
The triumph of his pledge.

HORATIO: Is it a custom?

HAMLET: Ay, marry, is't,
But to my mind, though I am native here
And to the manner born, it is a custom
More honored in the breach than the observance.
This heavy-headed revel east and west
Makes us traduced and taxed of other nations.
They clepe[9] us drunkards, and with swinish phrase
Soil our addition,[1] and indeed it takes
From our achievements, though performed at height,
The pith and marrow of our attribute.[2]
So oft it chances in particular men,
That for some vicious mole of nature in them,
As in their birth, wherein they are not guilty
(Since nature cannot choose his origin),
By their o'ergrowth of some complexion,
Oft breaking down the pales[3] and forts of reason,
Or by some habit that too much o'er-leavens
The form of plausive[4] manners—that these men,
Carrying, I say, the stamp of one defect,
Being nature's livery or fortune's star,
His virtues else, be they as pure as grace,
As infinite as man may undergo,
Shall in the general censure take corruption
From that particular fault. The dram of evil
Doth all the noble substance often doubt[5]
To his own scandal.

[*Enter* GHOST.]

HORATIO: Look, my lord, it comes.

HAMLET: Angels and ministers of grace defend us!
Be thou a spirit of health or goblin damned,
Bring with thee airs from heaven or blasts from hell,
Be thy intents wicked or charitable,
Thou com'st in such a questionable[6] shape
That I will speak to thee. I'll call thee Hamlet,
King, father, royal Dane. O, answer me!
Let me not burst in ignorance, but tell
Why thy canonized[7] bones, hearsèd in death,
Have burst their cerements;[8] why the sepulchre

8. Rhine wine. *Up-spring*: a German dance. 9. Call. 1. Reputation. 2. Honor. 3. Barriers.
4. Pleasing. 5. Extinguish. 6. Prompting question. 7. Buried in accordance with church canons.
8. Gravecloths.

Wherein we saw thee quietly inurned
Hath oped his ponderous and marble jaws
To cast thee up again. What may this mean
That thou, dead corse, again in complete steel[9]
Revisits thus the glimpses of the moon,
Making night hideous, and we fools of nature
So horridly to shake our disposition
With thoughts beyond the reaches of our souls?
Say, why is this? Wherefore? What should we do?

[GHOST *beckons.*]

HORATIO: It beckons you to go away with it,
As if it some impartment[1] did desire
To you alone.

MARCELLUS: Look with what courteous action
It waves you to a more removèd[2] ground.
But do not go with it.

HORATIO: No, by no means.

HAMLET: It will not speak; then I will follow it.

HORATIO: Do not, my lord.

HAMLET: Why, what should be the fear?
I do not set my life at a pin's fee,[3]
And for my soul, what can it do to that,
Being a thing immortal as itself?
It waves me forth again. I'll follow it.

HORATIO: What if it tempt you toward the flood, my lord,
Or to the dreadful summit of the cliff
That beetles[4] o'er his base into the sea,
And there assume some other horrible form,
Which might deprive your sovereignty of reason[5]
And draw you into madness? Think of it.
The very place puts toys of desperation,[6]
Without more motive, into every brain
That looks so many fathoms to the sea
And hears it roar beneath.

HAMLET: It wafts me still.
Go on. I'll follow thee.

MARCELLUS: You shall not go, my lord.

HAMLET: Hold off your hands.

HORATIO: Be ruled. You shall not go.

HAMLET: My fate cries out
And makes each petty artere in this body
As hardy as the Nemean lion's nerve.[7]

9. Armor. 1. Communication. 2. Beckons you to a more distant. 3. Price.
4. Juts out. 5. Rational power. *Deprive*: take away. 6. Desperate fancies.
7. The Nemean lion was a mythological monster slain by Hercules as one of his twelve labors. *Artere*: artery.

Still am I called. Unhand me, gentlemen.
By heaven, I'll make a ghost of him that lets[8] me.
I say, away! Go on. I'll follow thee. [*Exeunt* GHOST *and* HAMLET.]
HORATIO: He waxes desperate with imagination.
MARCELLUS: Let's follow. 'Tis not fit thus to obey him.
HORATIO: Have after. To what issue will this come?
MARCELLUS: Something is rotten in the state of Denmark.
HORATIO: Heaven will direct it.
MARCELLUS: Nay, let's follow him. [*Exeunt.*]

Scene 5

Near the guard station. Enter GHOST *and* HAMLET.

HAMLET: Whither wilt thou lead me? Speak. I'll go no further.
GHOST: Mark me.
HAMLET: I will.
GHOST: My hour is almost come,
When I to sulph'rous and tormenting flames
Must render up myself.
HAMLET: Alas, poor ghost!
GHOST: Pity me not, but lend thy serious hearing
To what I shall unfold.
HAMLET: Speak. I am bound to hear.
GHOST: So art thou to revenge, when thou shalt hear.
HAMLET: What?
GHOST: I am thy father's spirit,
Doomed for a certain term to walk the night,
And for the day confined to fast in fires,
Till the foul crimes done in my days of nature[9]
Are burnt and purged away. But that I am forbid
To tell the secrets of my prison house,
I could a tale unfold whose lightest word
Would harrow up thy soul, freeze thy young blood,
Make thy two eyes like stars start from their spheres,
Thy knotted and combinèd[1] locks to part,
And each particular hair to stand an end,
Like quills upon the fretful porpentine.[2]
But this eternal blazon[3] must not be
To ears of flesh and blood. List, list, O, list!
If thou didst ever thy dear father love—
HAMLET: O God!
GHOST: Revenge his foul and most unnatural murder.
HAMLET: Murder!
GHOST: Murder most foul, as in the best it is,
But this most foul, strange, and unnatural.

8. Hinders. 9. That is, while I was alive. 1. Tangled. 2. Porcupine. 3. Description of eternity.

HAMLET: Haste me to know't, that I, with wings as swift
As meditation or the thoughts of love,
May sweep to my revenge.
GHOST: I find thee apt.
And duller shouldst thou be than the fat weed
That rots itself in ease on Lethe[4] wharf,—
Wouldst thou not stir in this. Now, Hamlet, hear.
'Tis given out that, sleeping in my orchard,
A serpent stung me. So the whole ear of Denmark
Is by a forgèd process[5] of my death
Rankly abused. But know, thou noble youth,
The serpent that did sting thy father's life
Now wears his crown.
HAMLET: O my prophetic soul!
My uncle!
GHOST: Ay, that incestuous, that adulterate beast,
With witchcraft of his wits, with traitorous gifts—
O wicked wit and gifts that have the power
So to seduce!—won to his shameful lust
The will of my most seeming virtuous queen.
O Hamlet, what a falling off was there,
From me, whose love was of that dignity
That it went hand in hand even with the vow
I made to her in marriage, and to decline[6]
Upon a wretch whose natural gifts were poor
To those of mine!
But virtue, as it never will be moved,
Though lewdness court it in a shape of heaven,
So lust, though to a radiant angel linked,
Will sate itself in a celestial bed
And prey on garbage.
But soft, methinks I scent the morning air.
Brief let me be. Sleeping within my orchard,
My custom always of the afternoon,
Upon my secure hour thy uncle stole,
With juice of cursed hebona[7] in a vial,
And in the porches of my ears did pour
The leperous distilment, whose effect
Holds such an enmity with blood of man
That swift as quicksilver it courses through
The natural gates and alleys of the body,
And with a sudden vigor it doth posset[8]
And curd, like eager[9] droppings into milk,
The thin and wholesome blood. So did it mine,

4. When drunk, the waters of the Lethe, one of the rivers of the classical underworld, induced forgetfulness. The "fat weed" is the asphodel that grew there; some texts have "roots" for "rots."
5. False report. 6. Sink. 7. A poison. 8. Coagulate. 9. Acid. *Curd*: curdle.

And a most instant tetter barked about[1]
Most lazar-like[2] with vile and loathsome crust
All my smooth body.
Thus was I sleeping by a brother's hand
Of life, of crown, of queen at once dispatched,
Cut off even in the blossoms of my sin,
Unhouseled, disappointed, unaneled,[3]
No reck'ning made, but sent to my account
With all my imperfections on my head.
O, horrible! O, horrible, most horrible!
If thou hast nature in thee, bear it not.
Let not the royal bed of Denmark be
A couch of luxury[4] and damnèd incest.
But howsomever thou pursues this act,
Taint not thy mind, nor let thy soul contrive
Against thy mother aught. Leave her to heaven,
And to those thorns that in her bosom lodge
To prick and sting her. Fare thee well at once.
The glowworm shows the matin[5] to be near,
And gins to pale his uneffectual fire.
Adieu, adieu, adieu. Remember me. [*Exit.*]

HAMLET: O all you host of heaven! O earth! What else?
And shall I couple hell? O, fie! Hold, hold, my heart,
And you, my sinews, grow not instant old,
But bear me stiffly up. Remember thee?
Ay, thou poor ghost, whiles memory holds a seat
In this distracted globe.[6] Remember thee?
Yea, from the table[7] of my memory
I'll wipe away all trivial fond[8] records,
All saws of books, all forms, all pressures past
That youth and observation copied there,
And thy commandment all alone shall live
Within the book and volume of my brain,
Unmixed with baser matter. Yes, by heaven!
O most pernicious woman!
O villain, villain, smiling, damnèd villain!
My tables—meet it is I set it down
That one may smile, and smile, and be a villain.
At least I am sure it may be so in Denmark.
So, uncle, there you are. Now to my word:[9]
It is "Adieu, adieu. Remember me."
I have sworn't.

[*Enter* HORATIO *and* MARCELLUS.]

1. Covered like bark. *Tetter*: a skin disease. 2. Leperlike.
3. The ghost means that he died without the customary rites of the church, that is, without receiving the Sacrament, without confession, and without Extreme Unction. 4. Lust. 5. Morning.
6. Skull. 7. Writing tablet. 8. Foolish. 9. For my motto.

HORATIO: My lord, my lord!
MARCELLUS: Lord Hamlet!
HORATIO: Heavens secure him!
HAMLET: So be it!
MARCELLUS: Illo, ho, ho,[1] my lord!
HAMLET: Hillo, ho, ho, boy! Come, bird, come.
MARCELLUS: How is't, my noble lord?
HORATIO: What news, my lord?
HAMLET: O, wonderful!
HORATIO: Good my lord, tell it.
HAMLET: No, you will reveal it.
HORATIO: Not I, my lord, by heaven.
MARCELLUS: Nor I, my lord.
HAMLET: How say you then, would heart of man once think it?
But you'll be secret?
BOTH: Ay, by heaven, my lord.
HAMLET: There's never a villain dwelling in all Denmark
But he's an arrant knave.
HORATIO: There needs no ghost, my lord, come from the grave
To tell us this.
HAMLET: Why, right, you are in the right,
And so without more circumstance at all
I hold it fit that we shake hands and part,
You, as your business and desire shall point you,
For every man hath business and desire
Such as it is, and for my own poor part,
Look you, I'll go pray.
HORATIO: These are but wild and whirling words, my lord.
HAMLET: I am sorry they offend you, heartily;
Yes, faith, heartily.
HORATIO: There's no offence, my lord.
HAMLET: Yes, by Saint Patrick, but there is, Horatio,
And much offence too. Touching this vision here,
It is an honest ghost, that let me tell you.
For your desire to know what is between us,
O'ermaster't as you may. And now, good friends,
As you are friends, scholars, and soldiers,
Give me one poor request.
HORATIO: What is't, my lord? We will.
HAMLET: Never make known what you have seen tonight.
BOTH: My lord, we will not.
HAMLET: Nay, but swear't.
HORATIO: In faith,
My lord, not I.
MARCELLUS: Nor I, my lord, in faith.
HAMLET: Upon my sword.

1. A falconer's cry.

MARCELLUS: We have sworn, my lord, already.
HAMLET: Indeed, upon my sword, indeed.

[GHOST *cries under the stage.*]

GHOST: Swear.
HAMLET: Ha, ha, boy, say'st thou so? Art thou there, truepenny?[2]
Come on. You hear this fellow in the cellarage.[3]
Consent to swear.
HORATIO: Propose the oath, my lord.
HAMLET: Never to speak of this that you have seen,
Swear by my sword.
GHOST: [*Beneath.*] Swear.
HAMLET: Hic et ubique?[4] Then we'll shift our ground.
Come hither, gentlemen,
And lay your hands again upon my sword.
Swear by my sword
Never to speak of this that you have heard.
GHOST: [*Beneath.*] Swear by his sword.
HAMLET: Well said, old mole! Canst work i' th' earth so fast?
A worthy pioneer![5] Once more remove, good friends.
HORATIO: O day and night, but this is wondrous strange!
HAMLET: And therefore as a stranger give it welcome.
There are more things in heaven and earth, Horatio,
Than are dreamt of in your philosophy.
But come.
Here as before, never, so help you mercy,
How strange or odd some'er I bear myself
(As I perchance hereafter shall think meet
To put an antic[6] disposition on),
That you, at such times, seeing me, never shall,
With arms encumbered[7] thus, or this head-shake,
Or by pronouncing of some doubtful phrase,
As "Well, we know," or "We could, and if we would"
Or "If we list to speak," or "There be, and if they might"
Or such ambiguous giving out, to note
That you know aught of me—this do swear,
So grace and mercy at your most need help you.
GHOST: [*Beneath.*] Swear. [*They swear.*]
HAMLET: Rest, rest, perturbèd spirit! So, gentlemen,
With all my love I do commend me to you,
And what so poor a man as Hamlet is
May do t'express his love and friending[8] to you,
God willing, shall not lack. Let us go in together,
And still your fingers on your lips, I pray.
The time is out of joint. O cursèd spite

2. Trusty old fellow. 3. Below. 4. Here and everywhere? (Latin). 5. Soldier who digs trenches.
6. Mad. 7. Folded. 8. Friendship.

That ever I was born to set it right!
Nay, come, let's go together. [*Exeunt.*]

ACT II

Scene 1

The dwelling of POLONIUS. *Enter* POLONIUS *and* REYNALDO.

POLONIUS: Give him this money and these notes, Reynaldo.
REYNALDO: I will, my lord.
POLONIUS: You shall do marvellous wisely, good Reynaldo,
Before you visit him, to make inquire[9]
Of his behavior.
REYNALDO: My lord, I did intend it.
POLONIUS: Marry, well said, very well said. Look you, sir.
Enquire me first what Danskers[1] are in Paris,
And how, and who, what means, and where they keep,[2]
What company, at what expense; and finding
By this encompassment[3] and drift of question
That they do know my son, come you more nearer
Than your particular demands[4] will touch it.
Take you as 'twere some distant knowledge of him,
As thus, "I know his father and his friends,
And in part him." Do you mark this, Reynaldo?
REYNALDO: Ay, very well, my lord.
POLONIUS: "And in part him, but," you may say, "not well,
But if't be he I mean, he's very wild,
Addicted so and so." And there put on him
What forgeries you please; marry, none so rank[5]
As may dishonor him. Take heed of that.
But, sir, such wanton, wild, and usual slips
As are companions noted and most known
To youth and liberty.
REYNALDO: As gaming, my lord.
POLONIUS: Ay, or drinking, fencing, swearing,
Quarrelling, drabbing[6]—you may go so far.
REYNALDO: My lord, that would dishonor him.
POLONIUS: Faith, no, as you may season it in the charge.[7]
You must not put another scandal on him,
That he is open to incontinency.[8]
That's not my meaning. But breathe his faults so quaintly[9]
That they may seem the taints of liberty,[1]
The flash and outbreak of a fiery mind,
A savageness in unreclaimèd[2] blood,

9. Inquiry. 1. Danes. 2. Live. 3. Indirect means. 4. Direct questions.
5. Foul. *Forgeries*: lies. 6. Whoring. 7. Soften the accusation. 8. Sexual excess.
9. With delicacy. 1. Faults of freedom. 2. Untamed.

Of general assault.[3]
REYNALDO: But, my good lord—
POLONIUS: Wherefore should you do this?
REYNALDO: Ay, my lord,
I would know that.
POLONIUS: Marry, sir, here's my drift,
And I believe it is a fetch of warrant.[4]
You laying these slight sullies on my son,
As 'twere a thing a little soiled wi' th' working,
Mark you,
Your party in converse,[5] him you would sound,
Having ever seen in the prenominate[6] crimes
The youth you breathe[7] of guilty, be assured
He closes with you in this consequence,
"Good sir," or so, or "friend," or "gentleman,"
According to the phrase or the addition
Of man and country.
REYNALDO: Very good, my lord.
POLONIUS: And then, sir, does 'a this—'a does—What was I about to say?
By the mass, I was about to say something.
Where did I leave?
REYNALDO: At "closes in the consequence."
POLONIUS: At "closes in the consequence"—ay, marry,
He closes thus: "I know the gentleman.
I saw him yesterday, or th' other day,
Or then, or then, with such, or such, and as you say,
There was 'a gaming, there o'ertook in's rouse,
There falling out at tennis," or perchance
"I saw him enter such a house of sale,"
Videlicet,[8] a brothel, or so forth.
See you, now—
Your bait of falsehood takes this carp of truth,
And thus do we of wisdom and of reach,[9]
With windlasses and with assays of bias,[1]
By indirections find directions out;
So by my former lecture and advice
Shall you my son. You have me, have you not?
REYNALDO: My lord, I have.
POLONIUS: God b'wi' ye; fare ye well.
REYNALDO: Good my lord.
POLONIUS: Observe his inclination in yourself.
REYNALDO: I shall, my lord.
POLONIUS: And let him ply[2] his music.
REYNALDO: Well, my lord.
POLONIUS: Farewell. [*Exit* REYNALDO.]

3. Touching everyone. 4. Permissible trick. 5. Conversation. 6. Already named. 7. Speak.
8. Namely. 9. Ability. 1. Indirect tests. 2. Practice.

[*Enter* OPHELIA.]

How now, Ophelia, what's the matter?
OPHELIA: O my lord, my lord, I have been so affrighted!
POLONIUS: With what, i' th' name of God?
OPHELIA: My lord, as I was sewing in my closet,[3]
Lord Hamlet with his doublet all unbraced,[4]
No hat upon his head, his stockings fouled,
Ungartered and down-gyvèd[5] to his ankle,
Pale as his shirt, his knees knocking each other,
And with a look so piteous in purport
As if he had been loosèd out of hell
To speak of horrors—he comes before me.
POLONIUS: Mad for thy love?
OPHELIA: My lord, I do not know,
But truly I do fear it.
POLONIUS: What said he?
OPHELIA: He took me by the wrist, and held me hard,
Then goes he to the length of all his arm,
And with his other hand thus o'er his brow,
He falls to such perusal of my face
As 'a would draw it. Long stayed he so.
At last, a little shaking of mine arm,
And thrice his head thus waving up and down,
He raised a sigh so piteous and profound
As it did seem to shatter all his bulk,[6]
And end his being. That done, he lets me go,
And with his head over his shoulder turned
He seemed to find his way without his eyes,
For out adoors he went without their helps,
And to the last bended[7] their light on me.
POLONIUS: Come, go with me. I will go seek the king.
This is the very ecstasy of love,
Whose violent property fordoes[8] itself,
And leads the will to desperate undertakings
As oft as any passion under heaven
That does afflict our natures. I am sorry.
What, have you given him any hard words of late?
OPHELIA: No, my good lord, but as you did command
I did repel[9] his letters, and denied
His access to me.
POLONIUS: That hath made him mad.
I am sorry that with better heed and judgment
I had not quoted[1] him. I feared he did but trifle,
And meant to wrack[2] thee; but beshrew my jealousy.
By heaven, it is as proper to our age

3. Chamber. 4. Unlaced. *Doublet*: jacket. 5. Fallen down like fetters. 6. Body. 7. Directed.
8. Destroys. *Property*: character. 9. Refuse. 1. Observed. 2. Harm.

To cast beyond ourselves in our opinions
As it is common for the younger sort
To lack discretion. Come, go we to the king.
This must be known, which being kept close, might move
More grief to hide than hate to utter love.
Come. [*Exeunt.*]

Scene 2

A public room. Enter KING, QUEEN, ROSENCRANTZ *and* GUILDENSTERN.

KING: Welcome, dear Rosencrantz and Guildenstern.
Moreover that[3] we much did long to see you,
The need we have to use you did provoke
Our hasty sending. Something have you heard
Of Hamlet's transformation—so call it,
Sith[4] nor th' exterior nor the inward man
Resembles that it was. What it should be,
More than his father's death, that thus hath put him
So much from th' understanding of himself,
I cannot deem of. I entreat you both
That, being of so young days[5] brought up with him,
And sith so neighbored[6] to his youth and havior,
That you vouchsafe your rest here in our court
Some little time, so by your companies
To draw him on to pleasures, and to gather
So much as from occasion you may glean,
Whether aught to us unknown afflicts him thus,
That opened lies within our remedy.
QUEEN: Good gentlemen, he hath much talked of you,
And sure I am two men there are not living
To whom he more adheres. If it will please you
To show us so much gentry[7] and good will
As to expend your time with us awhile
For the supply and profit of our hope,
Your visitation shall receive such thanks
As fits a king's remembrance.
ROSENCRANTZ: Both your majesties
Might, by the sovereign power you have of us,
Put your dread pleasures more into command
Than to entreaty.
GUILDENSTERN: But we both obey,
And here give up ourselves in the full bent[8]
To lay our service freely at your feet,
To be commanded.
KING: Thanks, Rosencrantz and gentle Guildenstern.

3. In addition to the fact that. 4. Since. 5. From childhood. 6. Closely allied. 7. Courtesy.
8. Completely.

QUEEN: Thanks, Guildenstern and gentle Rosencrantz.
And I beseech you instantly to visit
My too much changed son. Go, some of you,
And bring these gentlemen where Hamlet is.
GUILDENSTERN: Heavens make our presence and our practices
Pleasant and helpful to him!
QUEEN: Ay, amen!
[*Exeunt* ROSENCRANTZ *and* GUILDENSTERN.]

[*Enter* POLONIUS.]

POLONIUS: Th' ambassadors from Norway, my good lord,
Are joyfully returned.
KING: Thou still[9] hast been the father of good news.
POLONIUS: Have I, my lord? I assure you, my good liege,
I hold my duty as I hold my soul,
Both to my God and to my gracious king;
And I do think—or else this brain of mine
Hunts not the trail of policy[1] so sure
As it hath used to do—that I have found
The very cause of Hamlet's lunacy.
KING: O, speak of that, that do I long to hear.
POLONIUS: Give first admittance to th' ambassadors.
My news shall be the fruit[2] to that great feast.
KING: Thyself do grace to them, and bring them in. [*Exit* POLONIUS.]
He tells me, my dear Gertrude, he hath found
The head and source of all your son's distemper.
QUEEN: I doubt it is no other but the main,
His father's death and our o'erhasty marriage.
KING: Well, we shall sift[3] him.

[*Enter Ambassadors* (VOLTEMAND *and* CORNELIUS) *with* POLONIUS.]

Welcome, my good friends,
Say, Voltemand, what from our brother Norway?
VOLTEMAND: Most fair return of greetings and desires.
Upon our first,[4] he sent out to suppress
His nephew's levies, which to him appeared
To be a preparation 'gainst the Polack,
But better looked into, he truly found
It was against your highness, whereat grieved,
That so his sickness, age, and impotence
Was falsely borne in hand, sends out arrests[5]
On Fortinbras, which he in brief obeys,
Receives rebuke from Norway, and in fine,
Makes vow before his uncle never more
To give th' assay[6] of arms against your majesty.

9. Ever. 1. Statecraft. 2. Dessert. 3. Examine. 4. That is, first appearance.
5. Orders to stop. *Falsely borne in hand*: deceived. 6. Trial.

Whereon old Norway, overcome with joy,
Gives him three thousand crowns in annual fee,
And his commission to employ those soldiers,
So levied as before, against the Polack,
With an entreaty, herein further shown, [*Gives* CLAUDIUS *a paper.*]
That it might please you to give quiet pass[7]
Through your dominions for this enterprise,
On such regards of safety and allowance
As therein are set down.

KING: It likes[8] us well,
And at our more considered time[9] we'll read,
Answer, and think upon this business.
Meantime we thank you for your well-took[1] labor.
Go to your rest; at night we'll feast together.
Most welcome home! [*Exeunt* AMBASSADORS.]

POLONIUS: This business is well ended.
My liege and madam, to expostulate[2]
What majesty should be, what duty is,
Why day is day, night night, and time is time,
Were nothing but to waste night, day, and time.
Therefore, since brevity is the soul of wit,
And tediousness the limbs and outward flourishes,[3]
I will be brief. Your noble son is mad.
Mad call I it, for to define true madness,
What is't but to be nothing else but mad?
But let that go.

QUEEN: More matter with less art.

POLONIUS: Madam, I swear I use no art at all.
That he is mad, 'tis true: 'tis true 'tis pity,
And pity 'tis 'tis true. A foolish figure,
But farewell it, for I will use no art.
Mad let us grant him, then, and now remains
That we find out the cause of this effect,
Or rather say the cause of this defect,
For this effect defective comes by cause.
Thus it remains, and the remainder thus.
Perpend.[4]
I have a daughter—have while she is mine—
Who in her duty and obedience, mark,
Hath given me this. Now gather, and surmise.
[*Reads*] *the letter.*

"To the celestial, and my soul's idol, the most beautified Ophelia."—That's an ill phrase, a vile phrase, "beautified" is a vile phrase. But you shall hear. Thus:

"In her excellent white bosom, these, etc."

7. Safe conduct. 8. Pleases. 9. Time for more consideration. 1. Successful. 2. Discuss.
3. Adornments. 4. Consider.

QUEEN: Came this from Hamlet to her?
POLONIUS: Good madam, stay awhile. I will be faithful.

"Doubt thou the stars are fire,
Doubt that the sun doth move;
Doubt truth to be a liar;
But never doubt I love.

O dear Ophelia, I am ill at these numbers.[5] I have not art to reckon my groans, but that I love thee best, O most best, believe it. Adieu.

Thine evermore, most dear lady,
whilst this machine[6] is to him, Hamlet."

This in obedience hath my daughter shown me,
And more above, hath his solicitings,
As they fell out by time, by means, and place,
All given to mine ear.
KING: But how hath she
Received his love?
POLONIUS: What do you think of me?
KING: As of a man faithful and honorable.
POLONIUS: I would fain prove so. But what might you think,
When I had seen this hot love on the wing.
(As I perceived it, I must tell you that,
Before my daughter told me), what might you,
Or my dear majesty your queen here, think,
If I had played the desk or table-book,
Or given my heart a winking, mute and dumb,
Or looked upon this love with idle sight,[7]
What might you think? No, I went round[8] to work,
And my young mistress thus I did bespeak:
"Lord Hamlet is a prince out of thy star.[9]
This must not be." And then I prescripts[1] gave her,
That she should lock herself from his resort,
Admit no messengers, receive no tokens.
Which done, she took[2] the fruits of my advice;
And he repelled, a short tale to make,
Fell into a sadness, then into a fast,
Thence to a watch, thence into a weakness,
Thence to a lightness, and by this declension,
Into the madness wherein now he raves,
And all we mourn for.
KING: Do you think 'tis this?
QUEEN: It may be, very like.
POLONIUS: Hath there been such a time—I would fain know that—

5. Verses. 6. Body.
7. Polonius means that he would have been at fault if, having seen Hamlet's attention to Ophelia, he had winked at it or not paid attention, an "idle sight," and if he had remained silent and kept the information to himself, as if it were written in a "desk" or "table-book." 8. Directly. 9. Beyond your sphere.
1. Orders. 2. Followed.

That I have positively said "'Tis so,"
When it proved otherwise?

KING: Not that I know.

POLONIUS: [*Pointing to his head and shoulder.*] Take this from this, if this be otherwise.
If circumstances lead me, I will find
Where truth is hid, though it were hid indeed
Within the centre.[3]

KING: How may we try it further?

POLONIUS: You know sometimes he walks four hours together
Here in the lobby.

QUEEN: So he does, indeed.

POLONIUS: At such a time I'll loose[4] my daughter to him.
Be you and I behind an arras[5] then.
Mark the encounter. If he love her not,
And be not from his reason fall'n thereon,
Let me be no assistant for a state,
But keep a farm and carters.

KING: We will try it.

[*Enter* HAMLET *reading a book.*]

QUEEN: But look where sadly the poor wretch comes reading.

POLONIUS: Away, I do beseech you both away,
I'll board[6] him presently. [*Exeunt* KING *and* QUEEN.]
O, give me leave.
How does my good Lord Hamlet?

HAMLET: Well, God-a-mercy.

POLONIUS: Do you know me, my lord?

HAMLET: Excellent well, you are a fishmonger.

POLONIUS: Not I, my lord.

HAMLET: Then I would you were so honest a man.

POLONIUS: Honest, my lord?

HAMLET: Ay, sir, to be honest as this world goes, is to be one man picked out of ten thousand.

POLONIUS: That's very true, my lord.

HAMLET: For if the sun breed maggots in a dead dog, being a god kissing carrion[7]—Have you a daughter?

POLONIUS: I have, my lord.

HAMLET: Let her not walk i' th' sun. Conception is a blessing, but as your daughter may conceive—friend, look to't.

POLONIUS: How say you by that? [*Aside.*] Still harping on my daughter. Yet he knew me not at first. 'A said I was a fishmonger. 'A is far gone. And truly in my youth I suffered much extremity for love. Very near this. I'll speak to him again.—What do you read, my lord?

3. Of the earth. 4. Let loose. 5. Tapestry. 6. Accost.
7. Reference to the belief that maggots were produced spontaneously by the action of sunshine on carrion.

HAMLET: Words, words, words.

POLONIUS: What is the matter, my lord?

HAMLET: Between who?

POLONIUS: I mean the matter that you read, my lord.

HAMLET: Slanders, sir; for the satirical rogue says here that old men have grey beards, that their faces are wrinkled, their eyes purging thick amber and plumtree gum, and that they have a plentiful lack of wit, together with most weak hams[8]—all which, sir, though I most powerfully and potently believe, yet I hold it not honesty to have it thus set down, for yourself, sir, shall grow old as I am, if like a crab you could go backward.

POLONIUS: [*Aside.*] Though this be madness, yet there is method in't.—Will you walk out of the air, my lord?

HAMLET: Into my grave?

POLONIUS: [*Aside.*] Indeed, that's out of the air. How pregnant sometime his replies are! a happiness that often madness hits on, which reason and sanity could not so prosperously be delivered of. I will leave him, and suddenly contrive the means of meeting between him and my daughter.—My honorable lord. I will most humbly take my leave of you.

HAMLET: You cannot take from me anything that I will more willingly part withal—except my life, except my life, except my life.

[*Enter* GUILDENSTERN *and* ROSENCRANTZ.]

POLONIUS: Fare you well, my lord.

HAMLET: These tedious old fools!

POLONIUS: You go to seek the Lord Hamlet. There he is.

ROSENCRANTZ: [*To* POLONIUS.] God save you, sir! [*Exit* POLONIUS.]

GUILDENSTERN: My honored lord!

ROSENCRANTZ: My most dear lord!

HAMLET: My excellent good friends! How dost thou, Guildenstern?
Ah, Rosencrantz! Good lads, how do you both?

ROSENCRANTZ: As the indifferent[9] children of the earth.

GUILDENSTERN: Happy in that we are not over-happy;
On Fortune's cap we are not the very button.[1]

HAMLET: Nor the soles of her shoe?

ROSENCRANTZ: Neither, my lord.

HAMLET: Then you live about her waist, or in the middle of her favors?

GUILDENSTERN: Faith, her privates we.

HAMLET: In the secret parts of Fortune? O, most true, she is a strumpet.[2] What news?

ROSENCRANTZ: None, my lord, but that the world's grown honest.

HAMLET: Then is doomsday near. But your news is not true. Let me question more in particular. What have you, my good friends, deserved at the hands of Fortune, that she sends you to prison hither?

8. Limbs. 9. Ordinary. 1. That is, on top.

2. Prostitute. Hamlet is indulging in characteristic ribaldry. Guildenstern means that they are "privates" = ordinary citizens, but Hamlet takes him to mean "privates" = sexual organs and "middle of her favors" = waist = sexual organs.

GUILDENSTERN: Prison, my lord?
HAMLET: Denmark's a prison.
ROSENCRANTZ: Then is the world one.
HAMLET: A goodly one, in which there are many confines, wards[3] and dungeons. Denmark being one o' th' worst.
ROSENCRANTZ: We think not so, my lord.
HAMLET: Why then 'tis none to you; for there is nothing either good or bad, but thinking makes it so. To me it is a prison.
ROSENCRANTZ: Why then your ambition makes it one. 'Tis too narrow for your mind.
HAMLET: O God, I could be bounded in a nutshell and count myself a king of infinite space, were it not that I have bad dreams.
GUILDENSTERN: Which dreams indeed are ambition; for the very substance of the ambitious is merely the shadow of a dream.
HAMLET: A dream itself is but a shadow.
ROSENCRANTZ: Truly, and I hold ambition of so airy and light a quality that it is but a shadow's shadow.
HAMLET: Then are our beggars bodies, and our monarchs and outstretched heroes the beggars' shadows. Shall we to th' court? for, by my fay,[4] I cannot reason.
BOTH: We'll wait upon you.
HAMLET: No such matter. I will not sort[5] you with the rest of my servants; for to speak to you like an honest man, I am most dreadfully attended. But in the beaten way of friendship, what make you at Elsinore?
ROSENCRANTZ: To visit you, my lord; no other occasion.
HAMLET: Beggar that I am, I am even poor in thanks, but I thank you; and sure, dear friends, my thanks are too dear a halfpenny.[6] Were you not sent for? Is it your own inclining? Is it a free visitation? Come, come, deal justly with me. Come, come, nay speak.
GUILDENSTERN: What should we say, my lord?
HAMLET: Anything but to th' purpose. You were sent for, and there is a kind of confession in your looks, which your modesties have not craft enough to color. I know the good king and queen have sent for you.
ROSENCRANTZ: To what end, my lord?
HAMLET: That you must teach me. But let me conjure you by the rights of our fellowship, by the consonancy of our youth, by the obligation of our ever preserved love, and by what more dear a better proposer can charge you withal, be even and direct[7] with me whether you were sent for or no.
ROSENCRANTZ: [*Aside to* GUILDENSTERN.] What say you?
HAMLET: [*Aside.*] Nay, then, I have an eye of you.—If you love me, hold not off.
GUILDENSTERN: My lord, we were sent for.
HAMLET: I will tell you why; so shall my anticipation prevent your discovery,[8] and your secrecy to the king and queen moult no feather. I have of late—but wherefore I know not—lost all my mirth, forgone all custom of exercises; and indeed it goes so heavily with my disposition, that this goodly frame the earth seems to me a sterile promontory, this most excellent canopy the air, look you, this brave o'er-hanging firmament, this majestical roof

3. Cells. 4. Faith. 5. Include. 6. Not worth a halfpenny. 7. Straightforward. 8. Disclosure.

fretted[9] with golden fire, why it appeareth nothing to me but a foul and pestilent congregation of vapors. What a piece of work is a man, how noble in reason, how infinite in faculties, in form and moving, how express[1] and admirable in action, how like an angel in apprehension, how like a god: the beauty of the world, the paragon of animals. And yet to me, what is this quintessence of dust? Man delights not me, nor woman neither, though by your smiling you seem to say so.

ROSENCRANTZ: My lord, there was no such stuff in my thoughts.

HAMLET: Why did ye laugh, then, when I said "Man delights not me"?

ROSENCRANTZ: To think, my lord, if you delight not in man, what lenten entertainment the players shall receive from you. We coted[2] them on the way, and hither are they coming to offer you service.

HAMLET: He that plays the king shall be welcome—his majesty shall have tribute of me; the adventurous knight shall use his foil and target; the lover shall not sigh gratis; the humorous[3] man shall end his part in peace; the clown shall make those laugh whose lungs are tickle o' th' sere;[4] and the lady shall say her mind freely, or the blank verse shall halt for't. What players are they?

ROSENCRANTZ: Even those you were wont to take such delight in, the tragedians of the city.

HAMLET: How chances it they travel? Their residence, both in reputation and profit, was better both ways.

ROSENCRANTZ: I think their inhibition comes by the means of the late innovation.

HAMLET: Do they hold the same estimation they did when I was in the city? Are they so followed?

ROSENCRANTZ: No, indeed, are they not.

HAMLET: How comes it? Do they grow rusty?

ROSENCRANTZ: Nay, their endeavor keeps in the wonted pace; but there is, sir, an eyrie of children, little eyases,[5] that cry out on the top of question,[6] and are most tyrannically clapped for't. These are now the fashion, and so berattle the common stages (so they call them) that many wearing rapiers are afraid of goose quills[7] and dare scarce come thither.[8]

HAMLET: What, are they children? Who maintains 'em? How are they escoted?[9] Will they pursue the quality no longer than they can sing? Will they not say afterwards, if they should grow themselves to common players (as it is most like, if their means are no better), their writers do them wrong to make them exclaim against their own succession?[1]

ROSENCRANTZ: Faith, there has been much todo on both sides; and the nation holds it no sin to tarre[2] them to controversy. There was for a while no money bid for argument,[3] unless the poet and the player went to cuffs[4] in the question.

9. Ornamented with fretwork. 1. Well built. 2. Passed. *Lenten*: scanty.
3. Eccentric. *Foil and target*: sword and shield. 4. Easily set off.
5. Little hawks. 6. With a loud, high delivery. 7. Pens of satirical writers.
8. The passage refers to the emergence at the time of the play of theatrical companies made up of children from London choir schools. Their performances became fashionable and hurt the business of the established companies. Hamlet says that if they continue to act ("pursue the quality") when they are grown, they will find that they have been damaging their own future careers.
9. Supported. 1. Future careers. 2. Urge. 3. Paid for a play plot. 4. Blows.

HAMLET: Is't possible?

GUILDENSTERN: O, there has been much throwing about of brains.

HAMLET: Do the boys carry it away?

ROSENCRANTZ: Ay, that they do, my lord. Hercules and his load too.[5]

HAMLET: It is not very strange, for my uncle is King of Denmark, and those that would make mouths[6] at him while my father lived give twenty, forty, fifty, a hundred ducats apiece for his picture in little.[7] 'Sblood, there is something in this more than natural, if philosophy could find it out.

[*A flourish.*]

GUILDENSTERN: There are the players.

HAMLET: Gentlemen, you are welcome to Elsinore. Your hands. Come then, th' appurtenance of welcome is fashion and ceremony. Let me comply with you in this garb, lest my extent[8] to the players, which I tell you must show fairly outwards should more appear like entertainment[9] than yours. You are welcome. But my uncle-father and aunt-mother are deceived.

GUILDENSTERN: In what, my dear lord?

HAMLET: I am but mad north-north-west; when the wind is southerly I know a hawk from a handsaw.[1]

[*Enter* POLONIUS.]

POLONIUS: Well be with you, gentlemen.

HAMLET: Hark you, Guildenstern—and you too—at each ear a hearer. That great baby you see there is not yet out of his swaddling clouts.[2]

ROSENCRANTZ: Happily he is the second time come to them, for they say an old man is twice a child.

HAMLET: I will prophesy he comes to tell me of the players. Mark it.—You say right, sir, a Monday morning, 'twas then indeed.

POLONIUS: My lord, I have news to tell you.

HAMLET: My lord, I have news to tell you. When Roscius was an actor in Rome[3]—

POLONIUS: The actors are come hither, my lord.

HAMLET: Buzz, buzz.

POLONIUS: Upon my honor—

HAMLET: Then came each actor on his ass—

POLONIUS: The best actors in the world, either for tragedy, comedy, history, pastoral, pastoral-comical, historical-pastoral, tragical-historical, tragical-comical historical-pastoral, scene individable, or poem unlimited. Seneca cannot be too heavy nor Plautus too light. For the law of writ and the liberty, these are the only men.[4]

5. During one of his labors Hercules assumed for a time the burden of the Titan Atlas, who supported the heavens on his shoulders. Also a reference to the effect on business at Shakespeare's theater, the Globe. 6. Sneer. 7. Miniature. 8. Fashion. *Comply with*: welcome.

9. Cordiality. 1. A "hawk" is a plasterer's tool; Hamlet may also be using "handsaw" = hernshaw = heron. 2. Wrappings for an infant. 3. Roscius was the most famous actor of classical Rome.

4. Seneca and Plautus were Roman writers of tragedy and comedy, respectively. The "law of writ" refers to plays written according to such rules as the classical unities, the "liberty" to those written otherwise.

HAMLET: O Jephtha, judge of Israel, what a treasure hadst thou![5]
POLONIUS: What a treasure had he, my lord?
HAMLET: Why—

"One fair daughter, and no more,
The which he loved passing well."

POLONIUS: [*Aside.*] Still on my daughter.
HAMLET: Am I not i' th' right, old Jephtha?
POLONIUS: If you call me Jephtha, my lord, I have a daughter that I love passing well.
HAMLET: Nay, that follows not.
POLONIUS: What follows then, my lord?
HAMLET: Why—

"As by lot, God wot"

and then, you know,

"It came to pass, as most like it was."

The first row of the pious chanson[6] will show you more, for look where my abridgement[7] comes.

[*Enter the* PLAYERS.]

You are welcome, masters; welcome, all.—I am glad to see thee well.—Welcome, good friends.—O, old friend! Why, thy face is valanced[8] since I saw thee last. Com'st thou to beard me in Denmark?—What, my young lady and mistress? By'r lady, your ladyship is nearer to heaven than when I saw you last by the altitude of a chopine.[9] Pray God your voice, like a piece of uncurrent gold, be not cracked within the ring.—Masters, you are all welcome. We'll e'en to't like French falconers, fly at anything we see. We'll have a speech straight. Come give us a taste of your quality,[1] come a passionate speech.
FIRST PLAYER: What speech, my good lord?
HAMLET: I heard thee speak me a speech once, but it was never acted, or if it was, not above once, for the play, I remember, pleased not the million; 'twas caviary to the general.[2] But it was—as I received it, and others whose judgments in such matters cried in the top of[3] mine—an excellent play, well digested[4] in the scenes, set down with as much modesty as cunning. I remember one said there were no sallets[5] in the lines to make the matter savory, nor no matter in the phrase that might indict the author of affectation, but called

5. To ensure victory, Jephtha promised to sacrifice the first creature to meet him on his return. Unfortunately, his only daughter outstripped his dog and was the victim of his vow. The biblical story is told in Judges 11. 6. Song. *Row*: stanza. 7. That which cuts short by interrupting.
8. Fringed (with a beard).
9. Reference to the contemporary theatrical practice of using boys to play women's parts. The company's "lady" has grown in height by the size of a woman's thick-soled shoe ("chopine") since Hamlet saw him last. The next sentence refers to the possibility, suggested by his growth, that the young actor's voice may soon begin to change. 1. Trade. 2. Caviar to the masses (i.e., pearls before swine).
3. Were weightier than. 4. Arranged. 5. Spicy passages.

it an honest method, as wholesome as sweet, and by very much more handsome than fine. One speech in't I chiefly loved. 'Twas Æneas' tale to Dido, and thereabout of it especially where he speaks of Priam's slaughter.[6] If it live in your memory, begin at this line—let me see, let me see:

"The rugged Pyrrhus, like th' Hyrcanian beast"[7]—

'tis not so; it begins with Pyrrhus—

"The rugged Pyrrhus, he whose sable arms,
Black as his purpose, did the night resemble
When he lay couchéd in th' ominous horse,[8]
Hath now this dread and black complexion smeared
With heraldry more dismal; head to foot
Now is he total gules, horridly tricked[9]
With blood of fathers, mothers, daughters, sons,
Baked and impasted with the parching[1] streets,
That lend a tyrannous and a damnèd light
To their lord's murder. Roasted in wrath and fire,
And thus o'er-sizèd with coagulate[2] gore,
With eyes like carbuncles, the hellish Pyrrhus
Old grandsire Priam seeks."

So proceed you.

POLONIUS: Fore God, my lord, well spoken, with good accent and good discretion.

FIRST PLAYER: "Anon he finds him[3]
Striking too short at Greeks. His antique[4] sword,
Rebellious[5] to his arm, lies where it falls,
Repugnant to command. Unequal matched,
Pyrrhus at Priam drives, in rage strikes wide.
But with the whiff and wind of his fell sword
Th' unnervèd father falls. Then senseless[6] Ilium,
Seeming to feel this blow, with flaming top
Stoops[7] to his base, and with a hideous crash
Takes prisoner Pyrrhus' ear. For, lo! his sword,
Which was declining[8] on the milky head
Of reverend Priam, seemed i' th' air to stick.
So as a painted tyrant Pyrrhus stood,
And like a neutral to his will and matter,[9]
Did nothing.
But as we often see, against some storm,
A silence in the heavens, the rack[1] stand still,

6. Aeneas, fleeing with his band from fallen Troy (Ilium), arrives in Carthage, where he tells Dido, the queen of Carthage, of Troy's fall. Here he is describing the death of Priam, the aged king of Troy, at the hands of Pyrrhus, the son of the slain Achilles. 7. Tiger. 8. That is, the Trojan horse.
9. Adorned. *Total gules*: completely red. 1. Burning. *Impasted*: crusted.
2. Clotted. *O'er-sizèd*: glued over. 3. That is, Pyrrhus finds Priam.
4. Which he used when young. 5. Refractory. 6. Without feeling. 7. Falls. 8. About to fall.
9. Between his will and the fulfillment of it. 1. Clouds.

The bold winds speechless, and the orb below
As hush as death, anon the dreadful thunder
Doth rend the region; so, after Pyrrhus' pause,
A rousèd vengeance sets him new awork,[2]
And never did the Cyclops' hammers fall
On Mars's armor, forged for proof eterne,[3]
With less remorse than Pyrrhus' bleeding sword
Now falls on Priam.
Out, out, thou strumpet, Fortune! All you gods,
In general synod take away her power,
Break all the spokes and fellies[4] from her wheel,
And bowl the round nave[5] down the hill of heaven
As low as to the fiends."

POLONIUS: This is too long.

HAMLET: It shall to the barber's with your beard.—Prithee say on. He's for a jig,[6] or a tale of bawdry, or he sleeps. Say on; come to Hecuba.[7]

FIRST PLAYER: "But who, ah woe! had seen the moblèd[8] queen—"

HAMLET: "The moblèd queen"?

POLONIUS: That's good. "Moblèd queen" is good.

FIRST PLAYER: "Run barefoot up and down, threat'ning the flames
With bisson rheum, a clout[9] upon that head
Where late the diadem stood, and for a robe,
About her lank and all o'er-teemèd loins,
A blanket, in the alarm of fear caught up—
Who this had seen, with tongue in venom steeped,
'Gainst Fortune's state[1] would treason have pronounced.
But if the gods themselves did see her then,
When she saw Pyrrhus make malicious sport
In mincing[2] with his sword her husband's limbs,
The instant burst of clamor that she made,
Unless things mortal move them not at all,
Would have made milch[3] the burning eyes of heaven,
And passion in the gods."

POLONIUS: Look whe'r[4] he has not turned his color, and has tears in's eyes. Prithee no more.

HAMLET: 'Tis well. I'll have thee speak out the rest of this soon.—Good my lord, will you see the players well bestowed?[5] Do you hear, let them be well used, for they are the abstract[6] and brief chronicles of the time; after your death you were better have a bad epitaph than their ill report while you live.

2. To work.

3. Mars, as befits a Roman war god, had armor made for him by the blacksmith god Vulcan and his assistants, the Cyclopes. It was suitably impenetrable (of "proof eterne"). 4. Parts of the rim.

5. Hub. *Bowl*: roll. 6. A comic act.

7. Hecuba was the wife of Priam and queen of Troy. Her "loins" are described below as "o'erteemèd" because of her unusual fertility. The number of her children varies in different accounts, but twenty is a safe minimum. 8. Muffled (in a hood). 9. Cloth. *Bisson rheum*: blinding tears.

1. Government. 2. Cutting up. 3. Tearful (literally, milk-giving). 4. Whether. 5. Provided for.

6. Summary.

POLONIUS: My lord, I will use them according to their desert.

HAMLET: God's bodkin, man, much better. Use every man after his desert, and who shall 'scape whipping? Use them after your own honor and dignity. The less they deserve, the more merit is in your bounty. Take them in.

POLONIUS: Come, sirs.

HAMLET: Follow him, friends. We'll hear a play tomorrow.

[*Aside to* FIRST PLAYER.]

Dost thou hear me, old friend, can you play "The Murder of Gonzago"?

FIRST PLAYER: Ay, my lord.

HAMLET: We'll ha't tomorrow night. You could for a need study a speech of some dozen or sixteen lines which I would set down and insert in't, could you not?

FIRST PLAYER: Ay, my lord.

HAMLET: Very well. Follow that lord, and look you mock him not.

[*Exeunt* POLONIUS and PLAYERS.]

My good friends, I'll leave you till night. You are welcome to Elsinore.

ROSENCRANTZ: Good my lord. [*Exeunt* ROSENCRANTZ *and* GUILDENSTERN.]

HAMLET: Ay, so God b'wi'ye. Now I am alone.
O, what a rogue and peasant slave am I!
Is it not monstrous that this player here,
But in a fiction, in a dream of passion,
Could force his soul so to his own conceit[7]
That from her working all his visage wanned;[8]
Tears in his eyes, distraction in his aspect[9]
A broken voice, and his whole function suiting
With forms to his conceit? And all for nothing,
For Hecuba!
What's Hecuba to him or he to Hecuba,
That he should weep for her? What would he do
Had he the motive and the cue for passion
That I have? He would drown the stage with tears,
And cleave the general ear with horrid speech,
Make mad the guilty, and appal the free,
Confound the ignorant, and amaze indeed
The very faculties of eyes and ears.
Yet I,
A dull and muddy-mettled rascal, peak[1]
Like John-a-dreams, unpregnant[2] of my cause,
And can say nothing; no, not for a king
Upon whose property and most dear life
A damned defeat was made. Am I a coward?
Who calls me villain, breaks my pate across,
Plucks off my beard and blows it in my face,
Tweaks me by the nose, gives me the lie i' th' throat
As deep as to the lungs? Who does me this?
Ha, 'swounds, I should take it; for it cannot be

7. Imagination. 8. Grew pale. 9. Face. 1. Mope. *Muddy-mettled*: dull-spirited.
2. Not quickened by. *John-a-dreams*: a man dreaming.

But I am pigeon-livered and lack gall[3]
To make oppression bitter, or ere this
I should 'a fatted all the region kites[4]
With this slave's offal. Bloody, bawdy villain!
Remorseless, treacherous, lecherous, kindless[5] villain!
O, vengeance!
Why, what an ass am I! This is most brave,
That I, the son of a dear father murdered,
Prompted to my revenge by heaven and hell,
Must like a whore unpack[6] my heart with words,
And fall a-cursing like a very drab,
A scullion![7] Fie upon't! foh!
About, my brains. Hum—I have heard
That guilty creatures sitting at a play,
Have by the very cunning of the scene
Been struck so to the soul that presently
They have proclaimed[8] their malefactions;
For murder, though it have no tongue, will speak
With most miraculous organ. I'll have these players
Play something like the murder of my father
Before mine uncle. I'll observe his looks.
I'll tent him to the quick. If 'a do blench,[9]
I know my course. The spirit that I have seen
May be a devil, and the devil hath power
T' assume a pleasing shape, yea, and perhaps
Out of my weakness and my melancholy,
As he is very potent with such spirits,
Abuses me to damn me. I'll have grounds
More relative[1] than this. The play's the thing
Wherein I'll catch the conscience of the king. *[Exit.]*

ACT III

Scene 1

A room in the castle. Enter KING, QUEEN, POLONIUS, OPHELIA, ROSENCRANTZ *and* GUILDENSTERN.

KING: And can you by no drift of conference[2]
Get from him why he puts on this confusion,
Grating so harshly all his days of quiet
With turbulent[3] and dangerous lunacy?
ROSENCRANTZ: He does confess he feels himself distracted,
But from what cause 'a will by no means speak.

3. Bitterness. 4. Birds of prey of the area. 5. Unnatural. 6. Relieve.
7. In some versions of the play, the word "stallion," a slang term for prostitute, appears in place of "scullion." 8. Admitted. 9. Turn pale. *Tent*: try. 1. Conclusive. 2. Line of conversation.
3. Disturbing.

GUILDENSTERN: Nor do we find him forward to be sounded,[4]
But with a crafty madness keeps aloof
When we would bring him on to some confession
Of his true state.
QUEEN: Did he receive you well?
ROSENCRANTZ: Most like a gentleman.
GUILDENSTERN: But with much forcing of his disposition.[5]
ROSENCRANTZ: Niggard of question, but of our demands[6]
Most free in his reply.
QUEEN: Did you assay[7] him
To any pastime?
ROSENCRANTZ: Madam, it so fell out that certain players
We o'er-raught[8] on the way. Of these we told him,
And there did seem in him a kind of joy
To hear of it. They are here about the court,
And as I think, they have already order
This night to play before him.
POLONIUS: 'Tis most true,
And he beseeched me to entreat your majesties
To hear and see the matter.[9]
KING: With all my heart, and it doth much content me
To hear him so inclined.
Good gentlemen, give him a further edge,
And drive his purpose[1] into these delights.
ROSENCRANTZ: We shall, my lord. [*Exeunt* ROSENCRANTZ *and* GUILDENSTERN.]
KING: Sweet Gertrude, leave us too,
For we have closely sent for Hamlet hither,
That he, as 'twere by accident, may here
Affront[2] Ophelia.
Her father and myself (lawful espials[3])
Will so bestow ourselves that, seeing unseen,
We may of their encounter frankly judge,
And gather by him, as he is behaved,
If't be th' affliction of his love or no
That thus he suffers for.
QUEEN: I shall obey you.—
And for your part, Ophelia, I do wish
That your good beauties be the happy cause
Of Hamlet's wildness. So shall I hope your virtues
Will bring him to his wonted[4] way again,
To both your honors.
OPHELIA: Madam, I wish it may. [*Exit* QUEEN.]
POLONIUS: Ophelia, walk you here.—Gracious,[5] so please you,
We will bestow ourselves.—[*To* OPHELIA.] Read on this book,

4. Questioned. *Forward*: eager. 5. Mood. 6. To our questions. 7. Tempt. 8. Passed.
9. Performance. 1. Sharpen his intention. 2. Confront. 3. Justified spies. 4. Usual.
5. Majesty.

That show of such an exercise may color[6]
Your loneliness.—We are oft to blame in this,
'Tis too much proved, that with devotion's visage
And pious action we do sugar o'er
The devil himself.

KING: [*Aside.*] O, 'tis too true.
How smart a lash that speech doth give my conscience!
The harlot's cheek, beautied with plast'ring[7] art,
Is not more ugly to the thing that helps it
Than is my deed to my most painted word.
O heavy burden!

POLONIUS: I hear him coming. Let's withdraw, my lord.

[*Exeunt* KING *and* POLONIUS.]

[*Enter* HAMLET.]

HAMLET: To be, or not to be, that is the question:
Whether 'tis nobler in the mind to suffer
The slings and arrows of outrageous fortune,
Or to take arms against a sea of troubles,
And by opposing end them. To die, to sleep—
No more; and by a sleep to say we end
The heartache, and the thousand natural shocks
That flesh is heir to. 'Tis a consummation
Devoutly to be wished—to die, to sleep—
To sleep, perchance to dream, ay there's the rub;
For in that sleep of death what dreams may come
When we have shuffled off this mortal coil[8]
Must give us pause—there's the respect[9]
That makes calamity of so long life.
For who would bear the whips and scorns of time,
Th' oppressor's wrong, the proud man's contumely,[1]
The pangs of despised love, the law's delay,
The insolence of office, and the spurns[2]
That patient merit of th' unworthy takes,
When he himself might his quietus[3] make
With a bare bodkin? Who would fardels[4] bear,
To grunt and sweat under a weary life,
But that the dread of something after death,
The undiscovered country, from whose bourn[5]
No traveller returns, puzzles the will,
And makes us rather bear those ills we have
Than fly to others that we know not of?
Thus conscience does make cowards of us all;
And thus the native[6] hue of resolution

6. Explain. *Exercise*: act of devotion. 7. Thickly painted. 8. Turmoil. 9. Consideration.
1. Insulting behavior. 2. Rejections. 3. Settlement. 4. Burdens. *Bodkin*: dagger.
5. Boundary. 6. Natural.

Is sicklied o'er with the pale cast of thought,
And enterprises of great pitch and moment[7]
With this regard their currents turn awry
And lose the name of action.—Soft you now,
The fair Ophelia.—Nymph, in thy orisons[8]
Be all my sins remembered.

OPHELIA: Good my lord,
How does your honor for this many a day?

HAMLET: I humbly thank you, well, well, well.

OPHELIA: My lord, I have remembrances of yours
That I have longèd long to re-deliver.
I pray you now receive them.

HAMLET: No, not I,
I never gave you aught.

OPHELIA: My honored lord, you know right well you did,
And with them words of so sweet breath composed
As made the things more rich. Their perfume lost,
Take these again, for to the noble mind
Rich gifts wax[9] poor when givers prove unkind.
There, my lord.

HAMLET: Ha, ha! are you honest?[1]

OPHELIA: My lord?

HAMLET: Are you fair?

OPHELIA: What means your lordship?

HAMLET: That if you be honest and fair, your honesty should admit no discourse to your beauty.

OPHELIA: Could beauty, my lord, have better commerce[2] than with honesty?

HAMLET: Ay, truly, for the power of beauty will sooner transform honesty from what it is to a bawd than the force of honesty can translate beauty into his likeness. This was sometimes a paradox, but now the time gives it proof. I did love you once.

OPHELIA: Indeed, my lord, you made me believe so.

HAMLET: You should not have believed me, for virtue cannot so inoculate[3] our old stock but we shall relish of it. I loved you not.

OPHELIA: I was the more deceived.

HAMLET: Get thee to a nunnery.[4] Why wouldst thou be a breeder of sinners? I am myself indifferent[5] honest, but yet I could accuse me of such things that it were better my mother had not borne me: I am very proud, revengeful, ambitious, with more offences at my beck[6] than I have thoughts to put them in, imagination to give them shape, or time to act them in. What should such fellows as I do crawling between earth and heaven? We are arrant[7] knaves all; believe none of us. Go thy ways to a nunnery. Where's your father?

OPHELIA: At home, my lord.

7. Importance. *Pitch*: height. 8. Prayers. 9. Become. 1. Chaste. 2. Intercourse.
3. Change by grafting. 4. Hamlet uses "nunnery" in two senses, the second as a slang term for brothel.
5. Moderately. 6. Command. 7. Thorough.

HAMLET: Let the doors be shut upon him, that he may play the fool nowhere but in's own house. Farewell.

OPHELIA: O, help him, you sweet heavens!

HAMLET: If thou dost marry, I'll give thee this plague for thy dowry: be thou as chaste as ice, as pure as snow, thou shalt not escape calumny. Get thee to a nunnery, farewell. Or if thou wilt needs marry, marry a fool, for wise men know well enough what monsters[8] you make of them. To a nunnery, go, and quickly too. Farewell.

OPHELIA: Heavenly powers, restore him!

HAMLET: I have heard of your paintings, too, well enough. God hath given you one face, and you make yourselves another. You jig, you amble, and you lisp;[9] you nickname God's creatures, and make your wantonness your ignorance.[1] Go to, I'll no more on't, it hath made me mad. I say we will have no more marriage. Those that are married already, all but one, shall live. The rest shall keep as they are. To a nunnery, go. [*Exit.*]

OPHELIA: O, what a noble mind is here o'erthrown!
The courtier's, soldier's, scholar's, eye, tongue, sword,
Th' expectancy and rose[2] of the fair state,
The glass of fashion and the mould[3] of form,
Th' observed of all observers, quite quite down!
And I of ladies most deject and wretched,
That sucked the honey of his music[4] vows,
Now see that noble and most sovereign reason
Like sweet bells jangled, out of time and harsh;
That unmatched form and feature of blown[5] youth
Blasted with ecstasy. O, woe is me
T' have seen what I have seen, see what I see!

[*Enter* KING *and* POLONIUS.]

KING: Love! His affections do not that way tend,
Nor what he spake, though it lacked form a little,
Was not like madness. There's something in his soul
O'er which his melancholy sits on brood,[6]
And I do doubt the hatch and the disclose[7]
Will be some danger; which to prevent,
I have in quick determination
Thus set it down: he shall with speed to England
For the demand of our neglected tribute.
Haply the seas and countries different,
With variable objects, shall expel
This something-settled matter in his heart
Whereon his brains still beating puts him thus
From fashion of himself. What think you on't?

8. Horned because cuckolded. 9. Walk and talk affectedly.

1. Hamlet means that women call things by pet names and then blame the affectation on ignorance.

2. Ornament. *Expectancy*: hope. 3. Model. *Glass*: mirror. 4. Musical. 5. Full-blown.

6. That is, like a hen. 7. Result. *Doubt*: fear.

POLONIUS: It shall do well. But yet do I believe
The origin and commencement of his grief
Sprung from neglected love.—How now, Ophelia?
You need not tell us what Lord Hamlet said,
We heard it all.—My lord, do as you please,
But if you hold it fit, after the play
Let his queen-mother all alone entreat him
To show his grief. Let her be round[8] with him,
And I'll be placed, so please you, in the ear[9]
Of all their conference. If she find him not,[1]
To England send him; or confine him where
Your wisdom best shall think.
KING: It shall be so.
Madness in great ones must not unwatched go. [*Exeunt.*]

Scene 2

A public room in the castle. Enter HAMLET *and three of the* PLAYERS.

HAMLET: Speak the speech, I pray you, as I pronounced it to you, trippingly on the tongue; but if you mouth it as many of our players do, I had as lief the town-crier spoke my lines. Nor do not saw the air too much with your hand thus, but use all gently, for in the very torrent, tempest, and as I may say, whirl wind of your passion, you must acquire and beget a temperance that may give it smoothness. O, it offends me to the soul to hear a robustious periwig-pated[2] fellow tear a passion to tatters, to very rags, to split the ears of the groundlings, who for the most part are capable of[3] nothing but inexplicable dumb shows and noise. I would have such a fellow whipped for o'erdoing Termagant. It out-herods Herod.[4] Pray you avoid it.

FIRST PLAYER: I warrant your honor.

HAMLET: Be not too tame neither, but let your own discretion be your tutor. Suit the action to the word, the word to the action, with this special observance, that you o'erstep not the modesty of nature; for anything so o'erdone is from[5] the purpose of playing, whose end both at the first, and now, was and is, to hold as 'twere the mirror up to nature, to show virtue her own feature, scorn her own image, and the very age and body of the time his form and pressure.[6] Now this overdone, or come tardy off, though it makes the unskilful[7] laugh, cannot but make the judicious grieve, the censure[8] of the which one must in your allowance o'erweigh a whole theatre of others. O, there be players that I have seen play—and heard others praise, and that highly—not to speak it profanely, that neither having th' accent of Christians, nor the gait of Christian, pagan, nor man, have so strutted and bellowed that I have

8. Direct. 9. Hearing. 1. Does not discover his problem. 2. Bewigged. *Robustious*: noisy.
3. That is, capable of understanding. *Groundlings*: the spectators who paid least and had to stand.
4. Termagant, a "Saracen" deity, and the biblical Herod were stock characters in popular drama noted for the excesses of sound and fury used by their interpreters. 5. Contrary to. 6. Shape.
7. Ignorant. 8. Judgment.

thought some of nature's journeymen[9] had made men, and not made them well, they imitated humanity so abominably.

FIRST PLAYER: I hope we have reformed that indifferently[1] with us, sir.

HAMLET: O, reform it altogether. And let those that play your clowns speak no more than is set down for them, for there be of them that will themselves laugh, to set on some quantity of barren[2] spectators to laugh too, though in the meantime some necessary question of the play be then to be considered. That's villainous, and shows a most pitiful ambition in the fool that uses it. Go, make you ready. [*Exeunt* PLAYERS.]

[*Enter* POLONIUS, GUILDENSTERN, *and* ROSENCRANTZ.]

How now, my lord? Will the king hear this piece of work?

POLONIUS: And the queen too, and that presently.

HAMLET: Bid the players make haste. [*Exit* POLONIUS.]
Will you two help to hasten them?

ROSENCRANTZ: Ay, my lord. [*Exeunt they two.*]

HAMLET: What, ho, Horatio!

[*Enter* HORATIO.]

HORATIO: Here, sweet lord, at your service.

HAMLET: Horatio, thou art e'en as just a man
As e'er my conversation coped[3] withal.

HORATIO: O my dear lord!

HAMLET: Nay, do not think I flatter,
For what advancement may I hope from thee,
That no revenue hast but thy good spirits
To feed and clothe thee? Why should the poor be flattered?
No, let the candied tongue lick absurd pomp,
And crook the pregnant[4] hinges of the knee
Where thrift[5] may follow fawning. Dost thou hear?
Since my dear soul was mistress of her choice
And could of men distinguish her election,
S'hath sealed thee for herself, for thou hast been
As one in suff'ring all that suffers nothing,
A man that Fortune's buffets and rewards
Hast ta'en with equal thanks; and blest are those
Whose blood and judgment are so well commingled
That they are not a pipe[6] for Fortune's finger
To sound what stop[7] she please. Give me that man
That is not passion's slave, and I will wear him
In my heart's core, ay, in my heart of heart,
As I do thee. Something too much of this.
There is a play tonight before the king.
One scene of it comes near the circumstance
Which I have told thee of my father's death.
I prithee, when thou seest that act afoot,

9. Inferior craftsmen. 1. Somewhat. 2. Dullwitted. 3. Encountered. 4. Quick to bend. 5. Profit. 6. Musical instrument. 7. Note. *Sound*: play.

Even with the very comment[8] of thy soul
Observe my uncle. If his occulted[9] guilt
Do not itself unkennel[1] in one speech,
It is a damnèd ghost that we have seen,
And my imaginations are as foul
As Vulcan's stithy. Give him heedful note,[2]
For I mine eyes will rivet to his face,
And after we will both our judgments join
In censure of his seeming.[3]

HORATIO: Well, my lord.
If 'a steal aught the whilst this play in playing,
And 'scape detecting, I will pay[4] the theft.

[*Enter Trumpets and Kettledrums,* KING, QUEEN, POLONIUS, OPHELIA, ROSENCRANTZ, GUILDENSTERN, *and other* LORDS *attendant.*]

HAMLET: They are coming to the play. I must be idle.
Get you a place.

KING: How fares our cousin Hamlet?

HAMLET: Excellent, i' faith, of the chameleon's dish. I eat the air, promise-crammed. You cannot feed capons[5] so.

KING: I have nothing with this answer, Hamlet. These words are not mine.

HAMLET: No, nor mine now. [*To* POLONIUS.] My lord, you played once i' th' university, you say?

POLONIUS: That did I, my lord, and was accounted a good actor.

HAMLET: What did you enact?

POLONIUS: I did enact Julius Cæsar. I was killed i' th' Capitol; Brutus killed me.[6]

HAMLET: It was a brute part of him to kill so capital a calf there. Be the players ready?

ROSENCRANTZ: Ay, my lord, they stay upon your patience.[7]

QUEEN: Come hither, my dear Hamlet, sit by me.

HAMLET: No, good mother, here's metal more attractive.

POLONIUS: [*To the* KING.] O, ho! do you mark that?

HAMLET: Lady, shall I lie in your lap?

[*Lying down at* OPHELIA's *feet.*]

OPHELIA: No, my lord.

HAMLET: I mean, my head upon your lap?

OPHELIA: Ay, my lord.

HAMLET: Do you think I meant country matters?[8]

OPHELIA: I think nothing, my lord.

8. Keenest observation. 9. Hidden. 1. Break loose. 2. Careful attention. *Stithy*: smithy.
3. Manner. 4. Repay.
5. Castrated male chickens fattened for slaughter; also a term for fool. *Chameleon's dish*: reference to a popular belief that the chameleon subsisted on a diet of air. Hamlet has deliberately misunderstood the king's question.
6. Julius Caesar's assassination by Brutus and others is the subject of another play by Shakespeare.
7. Leisure. *Stay*: wait.
8. Presumably, rustic misbehavior, but here and elsewhere in this exchange Hamlet treats Ophelia to some ribald double meanings.

HAMLET: That's a fair thought to lie between maids' legs.
OPHELIA: What is, my lord?
HAMLET: Nothing.
OPHELIA: You are merry, my lord.
HAMLET: Who, I?
OPHELIA: Ay, my lord.
HAMLET: O God, your only jig-maker![9] What should a man do but be merry? For look you how cheerfully my mother looks, and my father died within's two hours.
OPHELIA: Nay, 'tis twice two months, my lord.
HAMLET: So long? Nay then, let the devil wear black, for I'll have a suit of sables. O heavens! die two months ago, and not forgotten yet? Then there's hope a great man's memory may outlive his life half a year, but by'r lady 'a must build churches then, or else shall 'a suffer not thinking on, with the hobby-horse, whose epitaph is "For O, for O, the hobby-horse is forgot!"[1]

The trumpets sound. Dumb Show follows. Enter a KING *and a* QUEEN *very lovingly; the* QUEEN *embracing him and he her. She kneels, and makes show of protestation unto him. He takes her up, and declines*[2] *his head upon her neck. He lies him down upon a bank of flowers; she, seeing him asleep, leaves him. Anon come in another man, takes off his crown, kisses it, pours poison in the sleeper's ears, and leaves him. The* QUEEN *returns, finds the* KING *dead, makes passionate action. The* POISONER *with some three or four come in again, seem to condole with her. The dead body is carried away. The* POISONER *woos the* QUEEN *with gifts; she seems harsh awhile, but in the end accepts love.* [*Exeunt.*]

OPHELIA: What means this, my lord?
HAMLET: Marry, this is miching mallecho;[3] it means mischief.
OPHELIA: Belike this show imports the argument[4] of the play.

[*Enter* PROLOGUE.]

HAMLET: We shall know by this fellow. The players cannot keep counsel; they'll tell all.
OPHELIA: Will 'a tell us what this show meant?
HAMLET: Ay, or any show that you will show him. Be not you ashamed to show, he'll not shame to tell you what it means.
OPHELIA: You are naught, you are naught. I'll mark[5] the play.
PROLOGUE: *For us, and for our tragedy,*
Here stooping to your clemency,
We beg your hearing patiently. [*Exit.*]

HAMLET: Is this a prologue, or the posy[6] of a ring?
OPHELIA: 'Tis brief, my lord.

9. Writer of comic scenes.
1. In traditional games and dances one of the characters was a man represented as riding a horse. The horse was made of something like cardboard and was worn about the "rider's" waist.
2. Lays. 3. Sneaking crime (from the Spanish *malhecho*, "evil deed"). 4. Plot. *Imports*: explains.
5. Attend to. *Naught*: obscene. 6. Motto engraved inside.

HAMLET: As woman's love.

[*Enter the* PLAYER KING *and* QUEEN.]

PLAYER KING: *Full thirty times hath Phœbus' cart gone round*
Neptune's salt wash and Tellus' orbèd ground,
And thirty dozen moons with borrowed sheen[7]
About the world have times twelve thirties been,
Since love our hearts and Hymen did our hands
Unite comutual in most sacred bands.[8]
PLAYER QUEEN: *So many journeys may the sun and moon*
Make us again count o'er ere love be done!
But woe is me, you are so sick of late,
So far from cheer and from your former state,
That I distrust[9] *you. Yet though I distrust,*
Discomfort you, my lord, it nothing must.
For women's fear and love hold quantity,[1]
In neither aught, or in extremity.[2]
Now what my love is proof hath made you know,
And as my love is sized,[3] *my fear is so.*
Where love is great, the littlest doubts are fear;
Where little fears grow great, great love grows there.
PLAYER KING: *Faith, I must leave thee, love, and shortly too;*
My operant powers their functions leave[4] *to do.*
And thou shalt live in this fair world behind,
Honored, beloved, and haply one as kind
For husband shalt thou—
PLAYER QUEEN: *O, confound the rest!*
Such love must needs be treason in my breast.
In second husband let me be accurst!
None wed the second but who killed the first.[5]
HAMLET: That's wormwood.[6]
PLAYER QUEEN: *The instances*[7] *that second marriage move*
Are base respects[8] *of thrift, but none of love.*
A second time I kill my husband dead,
When second husband kisses me in bed.
PLAYER KING: *I do believe you think what now you speak,*
But what we do determine oft we break.
Purpose is but the slave to memory,
Of violent birth, but poor validity;
Which now, like fruit unripe, sticks on the tree,

7. Light.
8. The speech contains several references to Greek mythology. Phoebus was the sun god, and his chariot or "cart" is the sun. The "salt wash" of Neptune is the ocean; Tellus was an earth goddess, and her "orbed ground" is the Earth, or globe. Hymen was the god of marriage. *Comutual*: mutually.
9. Fear for. 1. Agree in weight. 2. Without regard to too much or too little. 3. In size.
4. Cease. *Operant powers*: active forces.
5. Though there is some ambiguity, she seems to mean that the only kind of woman who would remarry is one who has killed or would kill her first husband. 6. Bitter medicine. 7. Causes. 8. Concerns.

But fall unshaken when they mellow be.
Most necessary 'tis that we forget
To pay ourselves what to ourselves is debt.
What to ourselves in passion we propose,
The passion ending, doth the purpose lose.
The violence of either grief or joy
Their own enactures[9] *with themselves destroy.*
Where joy most revels, grief doth most lament;
Grief joys, joy grieves, on slender accident.
This world is not for aye,[1] *nor 'tis not strange*
That even our loves should with our fortunes change;
For 'tis a question left us yet to prove,
Whether love lead fortune, or else fortune love.
The great man down, you mark his favorite flies;
The poor advanced makes friends of enemies;
And hitherto doth love on fortune tend,
For who not needs shall never lack a friend,
And who in want a hollow[2] *friend doth try,*
Directly seasons him[3] *his enemy.*
But orderly to end where I begun,
Our wills and fates do so contrary run
That our devices[4] *still are overthrown;*
Our thoughts are ours, their ends none of our own.
So think thou wilt no second husband wed,
But die thy thoughts when thy first lord is dead.

PLAYER QUEEN: *Nor earth to me give food, nor heaven light,*
Sport and repose lock from me day and night,
To desperation turn my trust and hope,
An anchor's cheer[5] *in prison be my scope,*
Each opposite that blanks[6] *the face of joy*
Meet what I would have well, and it destroy,
Both here and hence[7] *pursue me lasting strife,*
If once a widow, ever I be wife!

HAMLET: If she should break it now!

PLAYER KING: *'Tis deeply sworn. Sweet, leave me here awhile.*
My spirits grow dull, and fain I would beguile
The tedious day with sleep. [*Sleeps.*]

PLAYER QUEEN: *Sleep rock thy brain,*
And never come mischance between us twain! [*Exit.*]

HAMLET: Madam, how like you this play?

QUEEN: The lady doth protest too much, methinks.

HAMLET: O, but she'll keep her word.

KING: Have you heard the argument? Is there no offence in't?

HAMLET: No, no, they do but jest, poison in jest; no offence i' th' world.

KING: What do you call the play?

9. Actions. 1. Eternal. 2. False. 3. Ripens him into. 4. Plans. 5. Anchorite's (hermit's) food. 6. Blanches. 7. In the next world.

HAMLET: "The Mouse-trap." Marry, how? Tropically.[8] This play is the image of a murder done in Vienna. Gonzago is the duke's name; his wife, Baptista. You shall see anon. 'Tis a knavish piece of work, but what of that? Your majesty, and we that have free souls, it touches us not. Let the galled jade wince, our withers are unwrung.[9]

[*Enter* LUCIANUS.]

This is one Lucianus, nephew to the king.

OPHELIA: You are as good as a chorus, my lord.

HAMLET: I could interpret between you and your love, if I could see the puppets dallying.

OPHELIA: You are keen, my lord, you are keen.

HAMLET: It would cost you a groaning to take off mine edge.

OPHELIA: Still better, and worse.

HAMLET: So you mistake your husbands.—Begin, murderer. Leave thy damnable faces and begin. Come, the croaking raven doth bellow for revenge.

LUCIANUS: *Thoughts black, hands apt, drugs fit, and time agreeing,*
Confederate season,[1] *else no creature seeing,*
Thou mixture rank, of midnight weeds collected,
With Hecate's ban thrice blasted, thrice infected,[2]
Thy natural magic[3] *and dire property*
On wholesome life usurp immediately. [*Pours the poison in his ears.*]

HAMLET: 'A poisons him i' th' garden for his estate. His name's Gonzago. The story is extant, and written in very choice Italian. You shall see anon how the murderer gets the love of Gonzago's wife.

OPHELIA: The king rises.

HAMLET: What, frighted with false fire?

QUEEN: How fares my lord?

POLONIUS: Give o'er the play.

KING: Give me some light. Away!

POLONIUS: Lights, lights, lights! [*Exeunt all but* HAMLET *and* HORATIO.]

HAMLET:

Why, let the strucken deer go weep,
The hart ungallèd[4] play.
For some must watch while some must sleep;
Thus runs the world away.

Would not this, sir, and a forest of feathers[5]—if the rest of my fortunes turn Turk with me—with two Provincial roses on my razed shoes, get me a fellowship in a cry of players?[6]

8. Figuratively.
9. A "galled jade" is a horse, particularly one of poor quality, with a sore back. The "withers" are the ridge between a horse's shoulders; "unwrung withers" are not chafed by the harness.
1. A helpful time for the crime. 2. Hecate was a classical goddess of witchcraft.
3. Native power. 4. Uninjured. 5. Plumes.
6. Hamlet asks Horatio if "this" recitation, accompanied with a player's costume, including plumes and rosettes on shoes that have been slashed for decorative effect, might not entitle him to become a shareholder in a theatrical company in the event that Fortune goes against him ("turn Turk"). *Cry*: company.

HORATIO: Half a share.

HAMLET: A whole one, I.

For thou dost know, O Damon dear,[7]
  This realm dismantled was
Of Jove himself, and now reigns here
  A very, very—peacock.

HORATIO: You might have rhymed.

HAMLET: O good Horatio, I'll take the ghost's word for a thousand pound. Didst perceive?

HORATIO: Very well, my lord.

HAMLET: Upon the talk of the poisoning.

HORATIO: I did very well note[8] him.

HAMLET: Ah, ha! Come, some music. Come, the recorders.[9]

For if the king like not the comedy.
Why then, belike he likes it not, perdy.[1]

Come, some music.

[*Enter* ROSENCRANTZ *and* GUILDENSTERN.]

GUILDENSTERN: Good my lord, vouchsafe me a word with you.

HAMLET: Sir, a whole history.

GUILDENSTERN: The king, sir—

HAMLET: Ay, sir, what of him?

GUILDENSTERN: Is in his retirement marvellous distempered.[2]

HAMLET: With drink, sir?

GUILDENSTERN: No, my lord, with choler.[3]

HAMLET: Your wisdom should show itself more richer to signify this to the doctor, for for me to put him to his purgation[4] would perhaps plunge him into more choler.

GUILDENSTERN: Good my lord, put your discourse into some frame,[5] and start not so wildly from my affair.

HAMLET: I am tame, sir. Pronounce.

GUILDENSTERN: The queen your mother, in most great affliction of spirit, hath sent me to you.

HAMLET: You are welcome.

GUILDENSTERN: Nay, good my lord, this courtesy is not of the right breed. If it shall please you to make me a wholesome[6] answer, I will do your mother's commandment. If not, your pardon and my return[7] shall be the end of my business.

HAMLET: Sir, I cannot.

ROSENCRANTZ: What, my lord?

7. Damon was a common name for a young man or a shepherd in pastoral poetry. Jove was the chief god of the Romans. Readers may supply for themselves the rhyme referred to by Horatio.
8. Observe. 9. Wooden, end-blown flutes. 1. That is, *par Dieu* (French for "by God").
2. Vexed. *Retirement*: place to which he has retired. 3. Bile (anger).
4. Treatment with a laxative. 5. Order. *Discourse*: speech. 6. Reasonable.
7. That is, to the queen.

HAMLET: Make you a wholesome answer; my wit's diseased. But, sir, such answer as I can make, you shall command, or rather, as you say, my mother. Therefore no more, but to the matter. My mother, you say—

ROSENCRANTZ: Then thus she says: your behavior hath struck her into amazement and admiration.[8]

HAMLET: O wonderful son, that can so stonish a mother! But is there no sequel at the heels of his mother's admiration? Impart.[9]

ROSENCRANTZ: She desires to speak with you in her closet[1] ere you go to bed.

HAMLET: We shall obey, were she ten times our mother. Have you any further trade[2] with us?

ROSENCRANTZ: My lord, you once did love me.

HAMLET: And do still, by these pickers and stealers.[3]

ROSENCRANTZ: Good my lord, what is your cause of distemper? You do surely bar the door upon your own liberty, if you deny your griefs to your friend.

HAMLET: Sir, I lack advancement.

ROSENCRANTZ: How can that be, when you have the voice of the king himself for your succession in Denmark?

HAMLET: Ay, sir, but "while the grass grows"—the proverb[4] is something musty.

[*Enter the* PLAYERS *with recorders.*]

O, the recorders! Let me see one. To withdraw with you[5]—why do you go about to recover the wind of me, as if you would drive me into a toil?[6]

GUILDENSTERN: O my lord, if my duty be too bold, my love is too unmannerly.

HAMLET: I do not well understand that. Will you play upon this pipe?[7]

GUILDENSTERN: My lord, I cannot.

HAMLET: I pray you.

GUILDENSTERN: Believe me, I cannot.

HAMLET: I do beseech you.

GUILDENSTERN: I know no touch of it,[8] my lord.

HAMLET: It is as easy as lying. Govern these ventages[9] with your fingers and thumb, give it breath with your mouth, and it will discourse most eloquent music. Look you, these are the stops.[1]

GUILDENSTERN: But these cannot I command to any utt'rance of harmony. I have not the skill.

HAMLET: Why, look you now, how unworthy a thing you make of me! You would play upon me, you would seem to know my stops, you would pluck out the heart of my mystery, you would sound[2] me from my lowest note to the top of my compass;[3] and there is much music, excellent voice, in this little organ, yet cannot you make it speak. 'Sblood, do you think I am easier to be played on than a pipe? Call me what instrument you will, though you can fret[4] me, you cannot play upon me.

8. Wonder. 9. Tell me. 1. Bedroom. 2. Business. 3. Hands.
4. The proverb ends "the horse starves." 5. Let me step aside.
6. The simile refers to hunting. Hamlet asks why Guildenstern is attempting to get windward of him, as if he would drive him into a net. 7. Recorder. 8. Have no ability.
9. Holes. *Govern*: cover and uncover. 1. Windholes. 2. Play. 3. Range.
4. "Fret" is used in a double sense, to annoy and to play a guitar or similar instrument using the "frets" or small bars on the neck.

[*Enter* POLONIUS.]

God bless you, sir!

POLONIUS: My lord, the queen would speak with you, and presently.[5]

HAMLET: Do you see yonder cloud that's almost in shape of a camel?

POLONIUS: By th' mass, and 'tis like a camel indeed.

HAMLET: Methinks it is like a weasel.

POLONIUS: It is backed like a weasel.

HAMLET: Or like a whale.

POLONIUS: Very like a whale.

HAMLET: Then I will come to my mother by and by. [*Aside.*] They fool me to the top of my bent.[6]—I will come by and by.

POLONIUS: I will say so. [*Exit.*]

HAMLET: "By and by" is easily said. Leave me, friends. [*Exeunt all but* HAMLET.]
'Tis now the very witching time of night,
When churchyards yawn, and hell itself breathes out
Contagion to this world. Now could I drink hot blood,
And do such bitter business as the day
Would quake to look on. Soft, now to my mother.
O heart, lose not thy nature; let not ever
The soul of Nero[7] enter this firm bosom.
Let me be cruel, not unnatural;
I will speak daggers to her, but use none.
My tongue and soul in this be hypocrites—
How in my words somever she be shent,[8]
To give them seals[9] never, my soul, consent! [*Exit.*]

Scene 3

A room in the castle. Enter KING, ROSENCRANTZ, *and* GUILDENSTERN.

KING: I like him not,[1] nor stands it safe with us
To let his madness range.[2] Therefore prepare you.
I your commission will forthwith dispatch,
And he to England shall along with you.
The terms of our estate[3] may not endure
Hazard so near's as doth hourly grow
Out of his brows.

GUILDENSTERN: We will ourselves provide,[4]
Most holy and religious fear it is
To keep those many many bodies safe
That live and feed upon your majesty.

ROSENCRANTZ: The single and peculiar[5] life is bound
With all the strength and armor of the mind

5. At once. 6. Treat me as an utter fool.
7. The Roman emperor Nero, known for his excesses, was believed responsible for the death of his mother. 8. Shamed. 9. Fulfillment in action. 1. Distrust him. 2. Roam freely.
3. Condition of the state. 4. Equip (for the journey). 5. Individual.

To keep itself from noyance,[6] but much more
That spirit upon whose weal[7] depends and rests
The lives of many. The cess[8] of majesty
Dies not alone, but like a gulf[9] doth draw
What's near it with it. It is a massy[1] wheel
Fixed on the summit of the highest mount,
To whose huge spokes ten thousand lesser things
Are mortised and adjoined,[2] which when it falls,
Each small annexment, petty consequence,
Attends[3] the boist'rous ruin. Never alone
Did the king sigh, but with a general groan.

KING: Arm you, I pray you, to this speedy voyage,
For we will fetters put about this fear,
Which now goes too free-footed.

ROSENCRANTZ: We will haste us.

[*Exeunt* ROSENCRANTZ *and* GUILDENSTERN.]

[*Enter* POLONIUS.]

POLONIUS: My lord, he's going to his mother's closet.
Behind the arras I'll convey[4] myself
To hear the process. I'll warrant she'll tax him home,[5]
And as you said, and wisely was it said,
'Tis meet that some more audience than a mother,
Since nature makes them partial, should o'erhear
The speech, of vantage.[6] Fare you well, my liege.
I'll call upon you ere you go to bed,
And tell you what I know.

KING: Thanks, dear my lord. [*Exit* POLONIUS.]
O, my offence is rank, it smells to heaven;
It hath the primal eldest curse[7] upon't,
A brother's murder. Pray can I not,
Though inclination be as sharp as will.
My stronger guilt defeats my strong intent,
And like a man to double business[8] bound,
I stand in pause where I shall first begin,
And both neglect. What if this cursèd hand
Were thicker than itself with brother's blood,
Is there not rain enough in the sweet heavens
To wash it white as snow? Whereto serves mercy
But to confront the visage of offence?
And what's in prayer but this twofold force,
To be forestallèd[9] ere we come to fall,
Or pardoned being down?[1] Then I'll look up.
My fault is past, But, O, what form of prayer

6. Harm. 7. Welfare. 8. Cessation. 9. Whirlpool. 1. Massive. 2. Attached. 3. Joins in.
4. Station. 5. Sharply. *Process*: proceedings. 6. From a position of vantage.
7. That is, of Cain. 8. Two mutually opposed interests. 9. Prevented (from sin). 1. Having sinned.

Can serve my turn? "Forgive me my foul murder"?
That cannot be, since I am still possessed
Of those effects[2] for which I did the murder—
My crown, mine own ambition, and my queen.
May one be pardoned and retain th' offence?[3]
In the corrupted currents of this world
Offence's gilded[4] hand may shove by justice,
And oft 'tis seen the wicked prize itself
Buys out the law. But 'tis not so above.
There is no shuffling; there the action[5] lies
In his true nature, and we ourselves compelled,
Even to the teeth and forehead of[6] our faults,
To give in evidence. What then? What rests?[7]
Try what repentance can. What can it not?
Yet what can it when one cannot repent?
O wretched state! O bosom black as death!
O limèd[8] soul, that struggling to be free
Art more engaged! Help, angels! Make assay.
Bow, stubborn knees, and heart with strings of steel,
Be soft as sinews of the new-born babe.
All may be well. [*He kneels.*]

[*Enter* HAMLET.]

HAMLET: Now might I do it pat,[9] now 'a is a-praying,
And now I'll do't—and so 'a goes to heaven,
And so am I revenged. That would be scanned.[1]
A villain kills my father, and for that,
I, his sole son, do this same villain send
To heaven.
Why, this is hire and salary, not revenge.
'A took my father grossly, full of bread,[2]
With all his crimes broad blown, as flush[3] as May;
And how his audit stands who knows save heaven?
But in our circumstance and course of thought
'Tis heavy with him; and am I then revenged
To take him in the purging of his soul,
When he is fit and seasoned[4] for his passage?
No.
Up, sword, and know thou a more horrid hent.[5]
When he is drunk, asleep, or in his rage,
Or in th' incestuous pleasure of his bed,
At game a-swearing, or about some act
That has no relish[6] of salvation in't—

2. Gains. 3. That is, benefits of the offense. 4. Bearing gold as a bribe.
5. Case at law. 6. Face-to-face with. 7. Remains. 8. Caught as with birdlime. 9. Easily.
1. Deserves consideration. 2. In a state of sin and without fasting.
3. Vigorous. *Broad blown*: full blown. 4. Ready. 5. Opportunity. 6. Flavor.

Then trip him, that his heels may kick at heaven,
And that his soul may be as damned and black
As hell, whereto it goes. My mother stays.
This physic[7] but prolongs thy sickly days. [*Exit.*]

KING: [*Rising.*] My words fly up, my thoughts remain below.
Words without thoughts never to heaven go. [*Exit.*]

Scene 4

The Queen's chamber. Enter QUEEN *and* POLONIUS.

POLONIUS: 'A will come straight. Look you lay home to[8] him.
Tell him his pranks have been too broad[9] to bear with,
And that your grace hath screen'd[1] and stood between
Much heat and him. I'll silence me even here.
Pray you be round with him.

HAMLET: [*Within.*] Mother, mother, mother!

QUEEN: I'll warrant you. Fear[2] me not.
Withdraw, I hear him coming.

[POLONIUS *goes behind the arras. Enter* HAMLET.]

HAMLET: Now, mother, what's the matter?

QUEEN: Hamlet, thou hast thy father much offended.

HAMLET: Mother, you have my father much offended.

QUEEN: Come, come, you answer with an idle tongue.

HAMLET: Go, go, you question with a wicked tongue.

QUEEN: Why, how now, Hamlet?

HAMLET: What's the matter now?

QUEEN: Have you forgot me?

HAMLET: No, by the rood,[3] not so.
You are the queen, your husband's brother's wife,
And would it were not so, you are my mother.

QUEEN: Nay, then I'll set those to you that can speak.

HAMLET: Come, come, and sit you down. You shall not budge.
You go not till I set you up a glass[4]
Where you may see the inmost part of you.

QUEEN: What wilt thou do? Thou wilt not murder me?
Help, ho!

POLONIUS: [*Behind.*] What, ho! help!

HAMLET: [*Draws.*] How now, a rat?
Dead for a ducat, dead!

[*Kills* POLONIUS *with a pass through the arras.*]

POLONIUS: [*Behind.*] O, I am slain!

QUEEN: O me, what hast thou done?

7. Medicine. 8. Be sharp with. 9. Outrageous. 1. Acted as a fire screen. 2. Doubt.
3. Cross. 4. Mirror.

HAMLET: Nay, I know not.
Is it the king?
QUEEN: O, what a rash and bloody deed is this!
HAMLET: A bloody deed!—almost as bad, good mother,
As kill a king and marry with his brother.
QUEEN: As kill a king?
HAMLET: Ay, lady, it was my word. [*Parting the arras.*]
Thou wretched, rash, intruding fool, farewell!
I took thee for thy better. Take thy fortune.
Thou find'st to be too busy[5] is some danger.—
Leave wringing of your hands. Peace, sit you down
And let me wring your heart, for so I shall
If it be made of penetrable stuff,
If damnèd custom have not brazed it[6] so
That it be proof and bulwark against sense.[7]
QUEEN: What have I done that thou dar'st wag thy tongue
In noise so rude against me?
HAMLET: Such an act
That blurs the grace and blush of modesty,
Calls virtue hypocrite, takes off the rose
From the fair forehead of an innocent love.
And sets a blister[8] there, makes marriage-vows
As false as dicers' oaths. O, such a deed
As from the body of contraction[9] plucks
The very soul, and sweet religion makes
A rhapsody of words. Heaven's face does glow
O'er this solidity and compound mass[1]
With heated visage, as against the doom[2]—
Is thought-sick at the act.
QUEEN: Ay me, what act
That roars so loud and thunders in the index?[3]
HAMLET: Look here upon this picture[4] and on this,
The counterfeit presentment of two brothers.
See what a grace was seated on this brow:
Hyperion's curls, the front[5] of Jove himself,
An eye like Mars, to threaten and command,
A station like the herald Mercury[6]
New lighted[7] on a heaven-kissing hill—
A combination and a form indeed
Where every god did seem to set his seal,[8]
To give the world assurance of a man.
This was your husband. Look you now what follows.
Here is your husband, like a mildewed ear
Blasting his wholesome brother. Have you eyes?

5. Officious. 6. Plated it with brass. 7. Feeling. *Proof*: armor. 8. Brand. 9. The marriage contract.
1. Meaningless mass (Earth). 2. Judgment Day. 3. Table of contents. 4. Portrait. 5. Forehead.
6. In Roman mythology, Mercury served as the messenger of the gods. *Station*: bearing.
7. Newly alighted. 8. Mark of approval.

Could you on this fair mountain leave to feed,
And batten[9] on this moor? Ha! have you eyes?
You cannot call it love, for at your age
The heyday in the blood is tame, it's humble,
And waits upon the judgment, and what judgment
Would step from this to this? Sense sure you have
Else could you not have motion, but sure that sense
Is apoplexed[1] for madness would not err,
Nor sense to ecstasy was ne'er so thralled
But it reserved some quantity[2] of choice
To serve in such a difference. What devil was't
That thus hath cozened you at hoodman-blind?[3]
Eyes without feeling, feeling without sight,
Ears without hands or eyes, smelling sans[4] all,
Or but a sickly part of one true sense
Could not so mope.[5] O shame! where is thy blush?
Rebellious hell,
If thou canst mutine[6] in a matron's bones,
To flaming youth let virtue be as wax
And melt in her own fire. Proclaim no shame
When the compulsive ardor gives the charge,[7]
Since frost itself as actively doth burn,
And reason panders[8] will.

QUEEN: O Hamlet, speak no more!
Thou turn'st my eyes into my very soul;
And there I see such black and grainèd[9] spots
As will not leave their tinct.[1]

HAMLET: Nay, but to live
In the rank sweat of an enseamèd[2] bed,
Stewed in curruption, honeying and making love
Over the nasty sty—

QUEEN: O, speak to me no more!
These words like daggers enter in my ears;
No more, sweet Hamlet.

HAMLET: A murderer and a villain,
A slave that is not twentieth part the tithe[3]
Of your precedent lord, a vice of kings,[4]
A cutpurse[5] of the empire and the rule,
That from a shelf the precious diadem stole
And put it in his pocket—

QUEEN: No more.

[*Enter* GHOST.]

9. Feed greedily. 1. Paralyzed. 2. Power. 3. Blindman's buff. *Cozened*: cheated. 4. Without. 5. Be stupid. 6. Commit mutiny. 7. Attacks. 8. Pimps for. 9. Ingrained. 1. Lose their color. 2. Greasy. 3. One-tenth.

4. The "Vice," a common character in the popular drama, was a clown or buffoon. *Precedent lord*: first husband. 5. Pickpocket.

HAMLET: A king of shreds and patches—
Save me and hover o'er me with your wings,
You heavenly guards! What would your gracious figure?
QUEEN: Alas, he's mad.
HAMLET: Do you not come your tardy[6] son to chide,
That lapsed in time and passion lets go by
Th' important acting of your dread command?
O, say!
GHOST: Do not forget. This visitation
Is but to whet thy almost blunted purpose.
But look, amazement on thy mother sits.
O, step between her and her fighting soul!
Conceit[7] in weakest bodies strongest works.
Speak to her, Hamlet.
HAMLET: How is it with you, lady?
QUEEN: Alas, how is't with you,
That you do bend[8] your eye on vacancy,
And with th' incorporal air do hold discourse?
Forth at your eyes your spirits wildly peep,
And as the sleeping soldiers in th' alarm,
Your bedded hairs like life in excrements[9]
Start up and stand an end. O gentle son,
Upon the heat and flame of thy distemper
Sprinkle cool patience. Whereon do you look?
HAMLET: On him, on him! Look you how pale he glares.
His form and cause conjoined,[1] preaching to stones,
Would make them capable.[2]—Do not look upon me,
Lest with this piteous action you convert
My stern effects.[3] Then what I have to do
Will want true color—tears perchance for blood.
QUEEN: To whom do you speak this?
HAMLET: Do you see nothing there?
QUEEN: Nothing at all, yet all that is I see.
HAMLET: Nor did you nothing hear?
QUEEN: No, nothing but ourselves.
HAMLET: Why, look you there. Look how it steals away.
My father, in his habit[4] as he lived!
Look where he goes even now out at the portal. [*Exit* GHOST.]
QUEEN: This is the very coinage[5] of your brain.
This bodiless creation ecstasy[6]
Is very cunning[7] in.
HAMLET: Ecstasy?
My pulse as yours doth temperately keep time,
And makes as healthful music. It is not madness
That I have uttered. Bring me to the test,

6. Slow to act. 7. Imagination. 8. Turn. 9. Nails and hair. 1. Working together.
2. Of responding. 3. Deeds. 4. Clothing. 5. Invention. 6. Madness. 7. Skilled.

And I the matter will re-word, which madness
Would gambol[8] from. Mother, for love of grace,
Lay not that flattering unction[9] to your soul,
That not your trespass but my madness speaks.
It will but skin and film the ulcerous place
Whiles rank corruption, mining[1] all within,
Infects unseen. Confess yourself to heaven,
Repent what's past, avoid what is to come.
And do not spread the compost on the weeds,
To make them ranker. Forgive me this my virtue,
For in the fatness of these pursy[2] times
Virtue itself of vice must pardon beg,
Yea, curb[3] and woo for leave to do him good.

QUEEN: O Hamlet, thou hast cleft my heart in twain.

HAMLET: O, throw away the worser part of it,
And live the purer with the other half.
Good night—but go not to my uncle's bed.
Assume a virtue, if you have it not.
That monster custom[4] who all sense doth eat
Of habits devil, is angel yet in this,
That to the use of actions fair and good
He likewise gives a frock or livery
That aptly[5] is put on. Refrain tonight,
And that shall lend a kind of easiness
To the next abstinence; the next more easy;
For use almost can change the stamp of nature,
And either curb the devil, or throw him out
With wondrous potency. Once more, good night,
And when you are desirous to be blest,
I'll blessing beg of you. For this same lord
I do repent; but heaven hath pleased it so,
To punish me with this, and this with me,
That I must be their scourge and minister.
I will bestow[6] him and will answer well
The death I gave him. So, again, good night.
I must be cruel only to be kind.
Thus bad begins and worse remains behind.
One word more, good lady.

QUEEN: What shall I do?

HAMLET: Not this, by no means, that I bid you do:
Let the bloat[7] king tempt you again to bed,
Pinch wanton[8] on your cheek, call you his mouse,
And let him, for a pair of reechy[9] kisses,
Or paddling in your neck with his damned fingers,
Make you to ravel[1] all this matter out,

8. Shy away. 9. Ointment. 1. Undermining. 2. Bloated. 3. Bow. 4. Habit. 5. Easily.
6. Dispose of. 7. Bloated. 8. Lewdly. 9. Foul. 1. Reveal.

That I essentially am not in madness,
But mad in craft. 'Twere good you let him know,
For who that's but a queen, fair, sober, wise,
Would from a paddock, from a bat, a gib,[2]
Such dear concernings hide? Who would so do?
No, in despite of sense and secrecy,
Unpeg the basket on the house's top,
Let the birds fly, and like the famous ape,
To try conclusions, in the basket creep
And break your own neck down.[3]

QUEEN: Be thou assured, if words be made of breath
And breath of life, I have no life to breathe
What thou hast said to me.

HAMLET: I must to England; you know that?

QUEEN: Alack,
I had forgot. 'Tis so concluded on.

HAMLET: There's letters sealed, and my two school-fellows,
Whom I will trust as I will adders fanged,
They bear the mandate; they must sweep[4] my way
And marshal me to knavery. Let it work,
For 'tis the sport to have the enginer
Hoist with his own petard;[5] and't shall go hard
But I will delve[6] one yard below their mines
And blow them at the moon. O, 'tis most sweet
When in one line two crafts directly meet.
This man shall set me packing.
I'll lug the guts into the neighbor room.
Mother, good night. Indeed, this counsellor
Is now most still, most secret, and most grave,
Who was in life a foolish prating knave.
Come sir, to draw toward an end with you.
Good night, mother.

[*Exit the* QUEEN. *Then exit* HAMLET *tugging* POLONIUS.]

ACT IV

Scene 1

A room in the castle. Enter KING, QUEEN, ROSENCRANTZ *and* GUILDENSTERN.

KING: There's matter in these sighs, these profound heaves,
You must translate;[7] 'tis fit we understand them.

2. Tomcat. *Paddock*: toad.
3. Apparently a reference to a now-lost fable in which an ape, finding a basket containing a cage of birds on a housetop, opens the cage. The birds fly away. The ape, thinking that if he were in the basket he too could fly, enters, jumps out, and breaks his neck. 4. Prepare. *Mandate*: command.
5. The "enginer," or engineer, is a military man who is here described as being blown up by a bomb of his own construction ("hoist with his own petard"). The military imagery continues in the succeeding lines where Hamlet describes himself as digging a countermine or tunnel beneath the one Claudius is digging to defeat Hamlet. In line 216, the two tunnels unexpectedly meet. 6. Dig. 7. Explain.

Where is your son?
QUEEN: Bestow this place on us a little while.
[*Exeunt* ROSENCRANTZ *and* GUILDENSTERN.]
Ah, mine own lord, what have I seen tonight!
KING: What, Gertrude? How does Hamlet?
QUEEN: Mad as the sea and wind when both contend
Which is the mightier. In his lawless fit,
Behind the arras hearing something stir,
Whips out his rapier, cries "A rat, a rat!"
And in this brainish apprehension[8] kills
The unseen good old man.
KING: O heavy deed!
It had been so with us had we been there.
His liberty is full of threats to all—
To you yourself, to us, to every one.
Alas, how shall this bloody deed be answered?
It will be laid to us, whose providence[9]
Should have kept short, restrained, and out of haunt,[1]
This mad young man. But so much was our love,
We would not understand what was most fit;
But, like the owner of a foul disease,
To keep it from divulging, let it feed
Even on the pith of life. Where is he gone?
QUEEN: To draw apart the body he hath killed,
O'er whom his very madness, like some ore
Among a mineral of metals base,
Shows itself pure: 'a weeps for what is done.
KING: O Gertrude, come away!
The sun no sooner shall the mountains touch
But we will ship him hence, and this vile deed
We must with all our majesty and skill
Both countenance and excuse. Ho, Guildenstern!

[*Enter* ROSENCRANTZ *and* GUILDENSTERN.]

Friends both, go join you with some further aid.
Hamlet in madness hath Polonius slain,
And from his mother's closet hath he dragged him.
Go seek him out; speak fair, and bring the body
Into the chapel. I pray you haste in this.
[*Exeunt* ROSENCRANTZ *and* GUILDENSTERN.]
Come, Gertrude, we'll call up our wisest friends
And let them know both what we mean to do
And what's untimely done;
Whose whisper o'er the world's diameter,
As level as the cannon to his blank,[2]
Transports his poisoned shot—may miss our name,

8. Insane notion. 9. Prudence. 1. Away from public gatherings. 2. Mark. *Level*: direct.

And hit the woundless air. O, come away!
My soul is full of discord and dismay. [*Exeunt.*]

Scene 2

A passageway. Enter HAMLET.

HAMLET: Safely stowed.
ROSENCRANTZ *and* GUILDENSTERN: [*Within.*] Hamlet! Lord Hamlet!
HAMLET: But soft, what noise? Who calls on Hamlet?
O, here they come.

[*Enter* ROSENCRANTZ, GUILDENSTERN, *and* OTHERS.]

ROSENCRANTZ: What have you done, my lord, with the dead body?
HAMLET: Compounded it with dust, whereto 'tis kin.
ROSENCRANTZ: Tell us where 'tis, that we may take it thence
And bear it to the chapel.
HAMLET: Do not believe it.
ROSENCRANTZ: Believe what?
HAMLET: That I can keep your counsel and not mine own. Besides, to be demanded of a sponge—what replication[3] should be made by the son of a king?
ROSENCRANTZ: Take you me for a sponge, my lord?
HAMLET: Ay, sir, that soaks up the king's countenance,[4] his rewards, his authorities. But such officers do the king best service in the end. He keeps them like an apple in the corner of his jaw, first mouthed to be last swallowed. When he needs what you have gleaned, it is but squeezing you and, sponge, you shall be dry again.
ROSENCRANTZ: I understand you not, my lord.
HAMLET: I am glad of it. A knavish speech sleeps in a foolish ear.
ROSENCRANTZ: My lord, you must tell us where the body is, and go with us to the king.
HAMLET: The body is with the king, but the king is not with the body.
The king is a thing—
GUILDENSTERN: A thing, my lord!
HAMLET: Of nothing. Bring me to him. Hide fox, and all after.[5] [*Exeunt.*]

Scene 3

A room in the castle. Enter KING.

KING: I have sent to seek him, and to find the body.
How dangerous is it that this man goes loose!
Yet must not we put the strong law on him.
He's loved of the distracted[6] multitude,
Who like not in their judgment but their eyes,
And where 'tis so, th' offender's scourge[7] is weighed,

3. Answer. *Demanded of*: questioned by. 4. Favor.
5. Apparently a reference to a children's game like hide-and-seek. 6. Confused.
7. Punishment.

But never the offence. To bear all smooth and even,
This sudden sending him away must seem
Deliberate pause.[8] Diseases desperate grown
By desperate appliance are relieved,
Or not at all.

[*Enter* ROSENCRANTZ, GUILDENSTERN, *and all the rest.*]

How now! what hath befall'n?

ROSENCRANTZ: Where the dead body is bestowed, my lord,
We cannot get from him.

KING: But where is he?

ROSENCRANTZ: Without, my lord; guarded, to know[9] your pleasure.

KING: Bring him before us.

ROSENCRANTZ: Ho! bring in the lord.

[*They enter with* HAMLET.]

KING: Now, Hamlet, where's Polonius?

HAMLET: At supper.

KING: At supper? Where?

HAMLET: Not where he eats, but where 'a is eaten. A certain convocation of politic[1] worms are e'en at him. Your worm is your only emperor for diet. We fat all creatures else to fat us, and we fat ourselves for maggots. Your fat king and your lean beggar is but variable service—two dishes, but to one table. That's the end.

KING: Alas, alas!

HAMLET: A man may fish with the worm that hath eat of a king, and eat of the fish that hath fed of that worm.

KING: What dost thou mean by this?

HAMLET: Nothing but to show you how a king may go a progress through the guts of a beggar.

KING: Where is Polonius?

HAMLET: In heaven. Send thither to see. If your messenger find him not there, seek him i' th' other place yourself. But if, indeed, you find him not within this month, you shall nose[2] him as you go up the stairs into the lobby.

KING: [*To* ATTENDANTS.] Go seek him there.

HAMLET: 'A will stay till you come. [*Exeunt* ATTENDANTS.]

KING: Hamlet, this deed, for thine especial safety—
Which we do tender, as we dearly[3] grieve
For that which thou hast done—must send thee hence
With fiery quickness. Therefore prepare thyself.
The bark is ready, and the wind at help,
Th' associates tend, and everything is bent
For England.

HAMLET: For England?

KING: Ay, Hamlet.

HAMLET: Good.

8. That is, not an impulse. 9. Await. 1. Scheming. *Convocation*: gathering. 2. Smell.
3. Deeply. *Tender*: consider.

KING: So it is, if thou knew'st our purposes.
HAMLET: I see a cherub that sees them. But come, for England!
Farewell, dear mother.
KING: Thy loving father, Hamlet.
HAMLET: My mother. Father and mother is man and wife, man and wife is one flesh. So, my mother. Come, for England. [*Exit.*]
KING: Follow him at foot;[4] tempt him with speed aboard.
Delay it not; I'll have him hence tonight.
Away! for everything is sealed and done
That else leans on th' affair. Pray you make haste. [*Exeunt all but the* KING.]
And, England, if my love thou hold'st at aught—
As my great power thereof may give thee sense,[5]
Since yet thy cicatrice[6] looks raw and red
After the Danish sword, and thy free awe
Pays homage to us—thou mayst not coldly set[7]
Our sovereign process,[8] which imports at full
By letters congruing[9] to that effect
The present death of Hamlet. Do it, England,
For like the hectic[1] in my blood he rages,
And thou must cure me. Till I know 'tis done,
Howe'er my haps, my joys were ne'er begun. [*Exit.*]

Scene 4

Near Elsinore. Enter FORTINBRAS *with his army.*

FORTINBRAS: Go, captain, from me greet the Danish king.
Tell him that by his license Fortinbras
Craves the conveyance[2] of a promised march
Over his kingdom. You know the rendezvous.
If that his majesty would aught with us,
We shall express our duty in his eye,[3]
And let him know so.
CAPTAIN: I will do't, my lord.
FORTINBRAS: Go softly on. [*Exeunt all but the* CAPTAIN.]

[*Enter* HAMLET, ROSENCRANTZ, GUILDENSTERN, *and* OTHERS.]

HAMLET: Good sir, whose powers are these?
CAPTAIN: They are of Norway, sir.
HAMLET: How purposed, sir, I pray you?
CAPTAIN: Against some part of Poland.
HAMLET: Who commands them, sir?
CAPTAIN: The nephew to old Norway, Fortinbras.
HAMLET: Goes it against the main[4] of Poland, sir,
Or for some frontier?
CAPTAIN: Truly to speak, and with no addition,[5]

4. Closely. 5. Of its value. 6. Wound scar. 7. Set aside. 8. Mandate. 9. Agreeing.
1. Chronic fever. 2. Escort. 3. Presence. 4. Central part. 5. Exaggeration.

We go to gain a little patch of ground
That hath in it no profit but the name.
To pay five ducats,[6] five, I would not farm it;
Nor will it yield to Norway or the Pole
A ranker rate should it be sold in fee.[7]

HAMLET: Why, then the Polack never will defend it.

CAPTAIN: Yes, it is already garrisoned.

HAMLET: Two thousand souls and twenty thousand ducats
Will not debate the question of this straw.
This is th' imposthume[8] of much wealth and peace,
That inward breaks, and shows no cause without
Why the man dies. I humbly thank you, sir.

CAPTAIN: God b'wi'ye, sir. [*Exit.*]

ROSENCRANTZ: Will't please you go, my lord?

HAMLET: I'll be with you straight. Go a little before. [*Exeunt all but* HAMLET.]
How all occasions do inform against me,
And spur my dull revenge! What is a man,
If his chief good and market[9] of his time
Be but to sleep and feed? A beast, no more.
Sure he that made us with such large discourse,[1]
Looking before and after, gave us not
That capability and godlike reason
To fust[2] in us unused. Now, whether it be
Bestial oblivion, or some craven scruple
Of thinking too precisely on th' event[3]—
A thought which, quartered, hath but one part wisdom
And ever three parts coward—I do not know
Why yet I live to say "This thing's to do,"
Sith[4] I have cause, and will, and strength, and means,
To do't. Examples gross as earth exhort me.
Witness this army of such mass and charge,[5]
Led by a delicate and tender prince,
Whose spirit, with divine ambition puffed,
Makes mouths at[6] the invisible event,
Exposing what is mortal and unsure
To all that fortune, death, and danger dare,
Even for an eggshell. Rightly to be great
Is not to stir without great argument,
But greatly to find quarrel in a straw
When honor's at the stake. How stand I then,
That have a father killed, a mother stained,
Excitements of my reason and my blood,
And let all sleep, while to my shame I see
The imminent death of twenty thousand men
That for a fantasy and trick of fame

6. That is, in rent. 7. Outright. *Ranker*: higher. 8. Abscess. 9. Occupation.

1. Ample reasoning power. 2. Grow musty. 3. Outcome. 4. Since. 5. Expense. 6. Scorns.

Go to their graves like beds, fight for a plot
Whereon the numbers cannot try the cause,
Which is not tomb enough and continent
To hide the slain?[7] O, from this time forth,
My thoughts be bloody, or be nothing worth! [*Exit.*]

Scene 5

A room in the castle. Enter QUEEN, HORATIO *and a* GENTLEMAN.

QUEEN: I will not speak with her.
GENTLEMAN: She is importunate, indeed distract.
Her mood will needs to be pitied.
QUEEN: What would she have?
GENTLEMAN: She speaks much of her father, says she hears
There's tricks i' th' world, and hems, and beats her heart,
Spurns enviously at straws,[8] speaks things in doubt
That carry but half sense. Her speech is nothing,
Yet the unshapèd use of it doth move
The hearers to collection;[9] they yawn at it,
And botch the words up fit to their own thoughts,
Which, as her winks and nods and gestures yield them,
Indeed would make one think there might be thought,
Though nothing sure, yet much unhappily.
HORATIO: 'Twere good she were spoken with, for she may strew
Dangerous conjectures in ill-breeding minds.
QUEEN: Let her come in. [*Exit* GENTLEMAN.]
[*Aside.*] To my sick soul, as sin's true nature is,
Each toy seems prologue to some great amiss.[1]
So full of artless jealousy is guilt,
It spills itself in fearing to be spilt.

[*Enter* OPHELIA *distracted.*]

OPHELIA: Where is the beauteous majesty of Denmark?
QUEEN: How now, Ophelia!
OPHELIA:

[*Sings.*]

How should I your true love know
From another one?
By his cockle hat and staff,[2]
And his sandal shoon.[3]

7. The plot of ground involved is so small that it cannot contain the number of men involved in fighting or furnish burial space for the number of those who will die. 8. Takes offense at trifles.
9. An attempt to order. 1. Catastrophe. *Toy*: trifle.
2. A cockle hat, one decorated with a shell, indicated that its wearer had made a pilgrimage to the shrine of St. James at Compostela in Spain. The staff also marked the carrier as a pilgrim.
3. Shoes.

QUEEN: Alas, sweet lady, what imports this song?
OPHELIA: Say you? Nay, pray you mark.

[*Sings.*]

He is dead and gone, lady,
He is dead and gone;
At his head a grass-green turf,
At his heels a stone.

O, ho!
QUEEN: Nay, but Ophelia—
OPHELIA: Pray you mark.

[*Sings.*]

White his shroud as the mountain snow—

[*Enter* KING.]

QUEEN: Alas, look here, my lord.
OPHELIA:

[*Sings.*]

Larded all with sweet flowers;
Which bewept to the grave did not go
With true-love showers.

KING: How do you, pretty lady?
OPHELIA: Well, God dild you! They say the owl was a baker's daughter.[4] Lord, we know what we are, but know not what we may be. God be at your table!
KING: Conceit[5] upon her father.
OPHELIA: Pray let's have no words of this, but when they ask you what it means, say you this:

[*Sings.*]

Tomorrow is Saint Valentine's day,
All in the morning betime,
And I a maid at your window,
To be your Valentine.

Then up he rose, and donn'd his clo'es,
And dupped[6] the chamber-door,
Let in the maid, that out a maid
Never departed more.

KING: Pretty Ophelia!
OPHELIA: Indeed, without an oath, I'll make an end on't.

4. Reference to a folktale about a young woman transformed into an owl when she failed to offer generosity to Jesus, who had asked for bread in her father's shop. *Dild*: yield, repay.
5. Thought. 6. Opened.

[*Sings.*]

By Gis[7] and by Saint Charity,
Alack, and fie for shame!
Young men will do't, if they come to't;
By Cock,[8] they are to blame.
Quoth she "before you tumbled me,
You promised me to wed."

He answers:

"So would I'a done, by yonder sun,
An thou hadst not come to my bed."

KING: How long hath she been thus?

OPHELIA: I hope all will be well. We must be patient, but I cannot choose but weep to think they would lay him i' th' cold ground. My brother shall know of it, and so I thank you for your good counsel. Come, my coach! Good night, ladies, good night. Sweet ladies, good night, good night. [*Exit.*]

KING: Follow her close; give her good watch, I pray you.

[*Exeunt* HORATIO *and* GENTLEMAN.]

O, this is the poison of deep grief; it springs
All from her father's death, and now behold!
O Gertrude, Gertrude!
When sorrows come, they come not single spies,
But in battalions: first, her father slain;
Next, your son gone, and he most violent author
Of his own just remove; the people muddied,[9]
Thick and unwholesome in their thoughts and whispers
For good Polonius' death; and we have done but greenly[1]
In hugger-mugger[2] to inter him; poor Ophelia
Divided from herself and her fair judgment,
Without the which we are pictures, or mere beasts;
Last, and as much containing as all these,
Her brother is in secret come from France,
Feeds on his wonder, keeps himself in clouds,
And wants not buzzers to infect his ear
With pestilent speeches of his father's death,
Wherein necessity, of matter beggared,[3]
Will nothing stick our person to arraign[4]
In ear and ear.[5] O my dear Gertrude, this,
Like to a murd'ring piece,[6] in many places
Gives me superfluous death. [*A noise within.*]

QUEEN: Alack, what noise is this?

KING: Attend!
Where are my Switzers?[7] Let them guard the door.

7. Jesus. 8. Corruption of "God," with a sexual pun. 9. Disturbed. 1. Without judgment.
2. Haste. 3. Short on facts. 4. Accuse. *Stick*: hesitate. 5. From both sides.
6. Weapon designed to scatter its shot. 7. Swiss guards.

What is the matter?
MESSENGER: Save yourself, my lord.
The ocean, overpeering of his list,[8]
Eats not the flats with more impiteous[9] haste
Than young Laertes, in a riotous head,[1]
O'erbears your officers. The rabble call him lord,
And as the world were now but to begin,
Antiquity forgot, custom not known,
The ratifiers and props of every word,
They cry "Choose we, Laertes shall be king."
Caps, hands, and tongues, applaud it to the clouds,
"Laertes shall be king, Laertes king."
QUEEN: How cheerfully on the false trail they cry![2]

[*A noise within.*]

O, this is counter,[3] you false Danish dogs!
KING: The doors are broke.

[*Enter* LAERTES, *with* OTHERS.]

LAERTES: Where is this king?—Sirs, stand you all without.
ALL: No, let's come in.
LAERTES: I pray you give me leave.
ALL: We will, we will.
LAERTES: I thank you. Keep[4] the door. [*Exeunt his followers.*]
O thou vile king,
Give me my father!
QUEEN: Calmly, good Laertes.
LAERTES: That drop of blood that's calm proclaims me bastard,
Cries cuckold to my father, brands the harlot
Even here between the chaste unsmirchèd brow
Of my true mother.
KING: What is the cause, Laertes,
That thy rebellion looks so giant-like?
Let him go, Gertrude. Do not fear[5] our person.
There's such divinity doth hedge a king
That treason can but peep to[6] what it would,
Acts little of his will. Tell me, Laertes.
Why thou art thus incensed. Let him go, Gertrude.
Speak, man.
LAERTES: Where is my father?
KING: Dead.
QUEEN: But not by him.
KING: Let him demand[7] his fill.
LAERTES: How came he dead? I'll not be juggled with.
To hell allegiance, vows to the blackest devil,

8. Towering above its limits. 9. Pitiless. 1. With an armed band. 2. As if following the scent.
3. Backward. 4. Guard. 5. Fear for. 6. Look at over or through a barrier. 7. Question.

Conscience and grace to the profoundest pit!
I dare damnation. To this point I stand,
That both the worlds I give to negligence,[8]
Let come what comes, only I'll be revenged
Most throughly for my father.

KING: Who shall stay you?

LAERTES: My will, not all the world's.
And for my means, I'll husband[9] them so well
They shall go far with little.

KING: Good Laertes,
If you desire to know the certainty
Of your dear father, is't writ in your revenge
That, swoopstake,[1] you will draw both friend and foe,
Winner and loser?

LAERTES: None but his enemies.

KING: Will you know them, then?

LAERTES: To his good friends thus wide I'll ope my arms,
And like the kind life-rend'ring pelican,[2]
Repast them with my blood.

KING: Why, now you speak
Like a good child and a true gentleman.
That I am guiltless of your father's death,
And am most sensibly in grief for it,
It shall as level[3] to your judgment 'pear
As day does to your eye.

[*A noise within*: "Let her come in."]

LAERTES: How now? What noise is that?

[*Enter* OPHELIA.]

O, heat dry up my brains! tears seven times salt
Burn out the sense and virtue[4] of mine eye!
By heaven, thy madness shall be paid with weight
Till our scale turn the beam. O rose of May,
Dear maid, kind sister, sweet Ophelia!
O heavens, is't possible a young maid's wits
Should be as mortal as an old man's life?
Nature is fin[5] in love, and where 'tis fine
It sends some precious instances of itself
After the thing it loves.[6]

OPHELIA:

[*Sings.*]

8. Disregard. *Both the worlds*: that is, this world and the next. 9. Manage.
1. Sweeping the board. 2. The pelican was believed to feed her young with her own blood.
3. Plain. 4. Function. *Sense*: feeling. 5. Refined.
6. Laertes means that Ophelia, because of her love for her father, gave up her sanity as a token of grief at his death.

They bore him barefac'd on the bier;
Hey non nonny, nonny, hey nonny;
And in his grave rain'd many a tear—

Fare you well, my dove!

LAERTES: Hadst thou thy wits, and didst persuade revenge,
It could not move thus.

OPHELIA: You must sing "A-down, a-down, and you call him a-down-a." O, how the wheel becomes it! It is the false steward, that stole his master's daughter.[7]

LAERTES: This nothing's more than matter.

OPHELIA: There's a rosemary, that's for remembrance. Pray you, love, remember. And there is pansies, that's for thoughts.

LAERTES: A document[8] in madness, thoughts and remembrance fitted.

OPHELIA: There's fennel for you, and columbines. There's rue for you, and here's some for me. We may call it herb of grace a Sundays. O, you must wear your rue with a difference. There's a daisy. I would give you some violets, but they withered all when my father died. They say 'a made a good end.

[*Sings.*]

For bonny sweet Robin is all my joy.

LAERTES: Thought and affliction, passion, hell itself,
She turns to favor[9] and to prettiness.

OPHELIA:

[*Sings.*]

And will 'a not come again?
And will 'a not come again?
No, no, he is dead,
Go to thy death-bed,
He never will come again.

His beard was as white as snow,
All flaxen was his poll;[1]
He is gone, he is gone,
And we cast away moan:
God-a-mercy on his soul!

And of all Christian souls, I pray God. God b'wi'you. [*Exit.*]

LAERTES: Do you see this, O God?

KING: Laertes, I must commune with your grief,
Or you deny me right. Go but apart,
Make choice of whom your wisest friends you will,
And they shall hear and judge 'twixt you and me.

7. The "wheel" refers to the "burden" or refrain of a song, in this case "A-down, a-down, and you call him a-down-a." The ballad to which she refers was about a false steward. Others have suggested that the "wheel" is either the Wheel of Fortune, a spinning wheel to whose rhythm such a song might have been sung, or a kind of dance movement performed by Ophelia as she sings. 8. Lesson. 9. Beauty. 1. Head.

If by direct or by collateral[2] hand
They find us touched,[3] we will our kingdom give,
Our crown, our life, and all that we call ours,
To you in satisfaction; but if not,
Be you content to lend your patience to us,
And we shall jointly labor with your soul
To give it due content.

LAERTES: Let this be so.
His means of death, his obscure funeral—
No trophy, sword, nor hatchment,[4] o'er his bones,
No noble rite nor formal ostentation[5]—
Cry to be heard, as 'twere from heaven to earth,
That I must call't in question.

KING: So you shall;
And where th' offence is, let the great axe fall.
I pray you go with me. [*Exeunt.*]

Scene 6

Another room in the castle. Enter HORATIO *and a* GENTLEMAN.

HORATIO: What are they that would speak with me?

GENTLEMAN: Sea-faring men, sir. They say they have letters for you.

HORATIO: Let them come in. [*Exit* GENTLEMAN.]
I do not know from what part of the world
I should be greeted, if not from Lord Hamlet.

[*Enter* SAILORS.]

SAILOR: God bless you, sir.

HORATIO: Let him bless thee too.

SAILOR: 'A shall, sir, an't please him. There's a letter for you, sir—it came from th' ambassador that was bound for England—if your name be Horatio, as I am let to know[6] it is.

HORATIO: [*Reads.*] "Horatio, when thou shalt have overlooked[7] this, give these fellows some means[8] to the king. They have letters for him. Ere we were two days old at sea, a pirate of very warlike appointment[9] gave us chase. Finding ourselves too slow of sail, we put on a compelled valor, and in the grapple I boarded them. On the instant they got clear of our ship, so I alone became their prisoner. They have dealt with me like thieves of mercy, but they knew what they did; I am to do a good turn for them. Let the king have the letters I have sent, and repair thou to me with as much speed as thou wouldest fly death. I have words to speak in thine ear will make thee dumb; yet are they much too light for the bore of the matter.[1] These good fellows will bring thee

2. Indirect. 3. By guilt. 4. Coat of arms. 5. Pomp. 6. Informed. 7. Read through.
8. Access. 9. Equipment.

1. Figure of speech from gunnery, referring to shot that is too small for the size of the weapons to be fired.

where I am. Rosencrantz and Guildenstern hold their course for England. Of them I have much to tell thee. Farewell.

He that thou knowest thine, Hamlet."

Come, I will give you way[2] for these your letters,
And do't the speedier that you may direct me
To him from whom you brought them. [*Exeunt.*]

Scene 7

Another room in the castle. Enter KING *and* LAERTES.

KING: Now must your conscience my acquittance seal,[3]
And you must put me in your heart for friend,
Sith you have heard, and with a knowing ear,
That he which hath your noble father slain
Pursued my life.
LAERTES: It well appears. But tell me
Why you proceeded not against these feats,
So criminal and so capital in nature,
As by your safety, greatness, wisdom, all things else,
You mainly were stirred up.
KING: O, for two special reasons,
Which may to you, perhaps, seem much unsinewed,[4]
But yet to me th' are strong. The queen his mother
Lives almost by his looks, and for myself—
My virtue or my plague, be it either which—
She is so conjunctive[5] to my life and soul
That, as the star moves not but in his sphere,[6]
I could not but by her. The other motive,
Why to a public count[7] I might not go,
Is the great love the general gender[8] bear him,
Who, dipping all his faults in their affection,
Work like the spring that turneth wood to stone,[9]
Convert his gyves[1] to graces; so that my arrows,
Too slightly timbered[2] for so loud a wind,
Would have reverted to my bow again,
But not where I had aimed them.
LAERTES: And so have I a noble father lost,
A sister driven into desp'rate terms,
Whose worth, if praises may go back again,
Stood challenger on mount of all the age
For her perfections. But my revenge will come.
KING: Break not your sleeps for that. You must not think

2. Means of delivery. 3. Grant me innocent. 4. Weak. 5. Closely joined.
6. Reference to the Ptolemaic cosmology, in which planets and stars were believed to revolve in crystalline spheres concentrically about the Earth. 7. Reckoning. 8. Common people.
9. Certain English springs contain so much lime that a log placed in one of them for a length of time will be covered in limestone. 1. Fetters. 2. Shafted.

That we are made of stuff so flat and dull
That we can let our beard be shook with danger,
And think it pastime. You shortly shall hear more.
I loved your father, and we love our self,
And that, I hope, will teach you to imagine—

[*Enter a* MESSENGER *with letters.*]

How now? What news?
MESSENGER: Letters, my lord, from Hamlet.
These to your majesty; this to the queen.
KING: From Hamlet! Who brought them?
MESSENGER: Sailors, my lord, they say. I saw them not.
They were given me by Claudio; he received them
Of him that brought them.
KING: Laertes, you shall hear them.—
Leave us. [*Exit* MESSENGER.]

[*Reads.*] "High and mighty, you shall know I am set naked on your kingdom. Tomorrow shall I beg leave to see your kingly eyes; when I shall, first asking your pardon thereunto, recount the occasion of my sudden and more strange return.

Hamlet."

What should this mean? Are all the rest come back?
Or is it some abuse,[3] and no such thing?
LAERTES: Know you the hand?
KING: 'Tis Hamlet's character.[4] "Naked"!
And in a postscript here, he says "alone."
Can you devise[5] me?
LAERTES: I am lost in it, my lord. But let him come.
It warms the very sickness in my heart
That I shall live and tell him to his teeth
"Thus didest thou."
KING: If it be so, Laertes—
As how should it be so, how otherwise?—
Will you be ruled by me?
LAERTES: Ay, my lord,
So you will not o'errule me to a peace.
KING: To thine own peace. If he be now returned,
As checking at[6] his voyage, and that he means
No more to undertake it, I will work him
To an exploit now ripe in my device,
Under the which he shall not choose but fall;
And for his death no wind of blame shall breathe
But even his mother shall uncharge[7] the practice
And call it accident.
LAERTES: My lord, I will be ruled;

3. Trick. 4. Handwriting. 5. Explain it to. 6. Turning aside from. 7. Not accuse.

The rather if you could devise it so
That I might be the organ.[8]
KING: It falls right.
You have been talked of since your travel much,
And that in Hamlet's hearing, for a quality
Wherein they say you shine. Your sum of parts
Did not together pluck such envy from him
As did that one, and that, in my regard,
Of the unworthiest siege.[9]
LAERTES: What part is that, my lord?
KING: A very riband in the cap of youth,
Yet needful too, for youth no less becomes
The light and careless livery that it wears
Than settled age his sables and his weeds,[1]
Importing health and graveness. Two months since
Here was a gentleman of Normandy.
I have seen myself, and served against, the French,
And they can[2] well on horseback, but this gallant
Had witchcraft in't. He grew unto his seat,
And to such wondrous doing brought his horse,
As had he been incorpsed and demi-natured
With the brave beast. So far he topped my thought
That I, in forgery[3] of shapes and tricks,
Come short of what he did.[4]
LAERTES: A Norman was't?
KING: A Norman.
LAERTES: Upon my life, Lamord.
KING: The very same.
LAERTES: I know him well. He is the brooch indeed
And gem of all the nation.
KING: He made confession[5] of you,
And gave you such a masterly report
For art and exercise in your defence,[6]
And for your rapier most especial,
That he cried out 'twould be a sight indeed
If one could match you. The scrimers[7] of their nation
He swore had neither motion, guard, nor eye,
If you opposed them. Sir, this report of his
Did Hamlet so envenom with his envy
That he could nothing do but wish and beg
Your sudden coming o'er, to play with you.
Now out of this—

8. Instrument. 9. Lowest rank. 1. Dignified clothing. 2. Perform. 3. Imagination.
4. The gentleman referred to was so skilled in horsemanship that he seemed to share one body with the horse ("incorpsed"). The king further extends the compliment by saying that he appeared like the mythical centaur, a creature who was man from the waist up and horse from the waist down, therefore "demi-natured." 5. Gave a report. 6. Skill in fencing. 7. Fencers.

LAERTES: What out of this, my lord?
KING: Laertes, was your father dear to you?
Or are you like the painting of a sorrow,
A face without a heart?
LAERTES: Why ask you this?
KING: Not that I think you did not love your father,
But that I know love is begun by time,
And that I see in passages of proof,[8]
Time qualifies the spark and fire of it.
There lives within the very flame of love
A kind of wick or snuff that will abate it,
And nothing is at a like goodness still,
For goodness, growing to a plurisy,[9]
Dies in his own too much.[1] That we would do,
We should do when we would; for this "would" changes,
And hath abatements and delays as many
As there are tongues, are hands, are accidents,
And then this "should" is like a spendthrift's sigh
That hurts by easing. But to the quick of th' ulcer[2]—
Hamlet comes back; what would you undertake
To show yourself in deed your father's son
More than in words?
LAERTES: To cut his throat i' th' church.
KING: No place indeed should murder sanctuarize;[3]
Revenge should have no bounds. But, good Laertes,
Will you do this? Keep close within your chamber.
Hamlet returned shall know you are come home.
We'll put on those shall praise your excellence,
And set a double varnish on the fame
The Frenchman gave you, bring you in fine[4] together,
And wager on your heads. He, being remiss,[5]
Most generous, and free from all contriving,
Will not peruse[6] the foils, so that with ease,
Or with a little shuffling, you may choose
A sword unbated,[7] and in a pass of practice
Requite him for your father.
LAERTES: I will do't,
And for that purpose I'll anoint my sword.
I bought an unction of a mountebank
So mortal that but dip a knife in it,
Where it draws blood no cataplasm[8] so rare,
Collected from all simples[9] that have virtue
Under the moon, can save the thing from death

8. Tests of experience. 9. Fullness. 1. Excess.
2. Heart of the matter. *Spendthrift's sigh*: a sigh was believed to draw a drop of blood from the heart and thus to "hurt" by "easing" sadness. 3. Provide sanctuary for murder. 4. In short.
5. Careless. 6. Examine. 7. Not blunted. 8. Poultice. 9. Herbs.

That is but scratched withal. I'll touch my point
With this contagion, that if I gall[1] him slightly,
It may be death.

KING: Let's further think of this,
Weigh what convenience both of time and means
May fit us to our shape. If this should fail,
And that our drift look[2] through our bad performance,
'Twere better not assayed. Therefore this project
Should have a back or second that might hold
If this did blast in proof.[3] Soft, let me see.
We'll make a solemn wager on your cunnings—
I ha't.
When in your motion you are hot and dry—
As make your bouts more violent to that end—
And that he calls for drink, I'll have prepared him
A chalice for the nonce, whereon but sipping,
If he by chance escape your venomed stuck,[4]
Our purpose may hold there.—But stay, what noise?

[*Enter* QUEEN.]

QUEEN: One woe doth tread upon another's heel,
So fast they follow. Your sister's drowned, Laertes.

LAERTES: Drowned? O, where?

QUEEN: There is a willow grows aslant the brook
That shows his hoar leaves in the glassy stream.
Therewith fantastic garlands did she make
Of crowflowers, nettles, daisies, and long purples
That liberal shepherds give a grosser[5] name,
But our cold[6] maids do dead men's fingers call them.
There on the pendent boughs her coronet weeds
Clamb'ring to hang, an envious[7] sliver broke,
When down her weedy trophies and herself
Fell in the weeping brook. Her clothes spread wide,
And mermaid-like awhile they bore her up,
Which time she chanted snatches of old tunes,
As one incapable[8] of her own distress,
Or like a creature native and indued[9]
Unto that element. But long it could not be
Till that her garments, heavy with their drink,
Pulled the poor wretch from her melodious lay
To muddy death.

LAERTES: Alas, then she is drowned?

QUEEN: Drowned, drowned.

LAERTES: Too much of water hast thou, poor Ophelia,

1. Scratch. 2. Intent become obvious. 3. Fail when tried. 4. Thrust.
5. Coarser. The "long purples" are purple orchises, a type of orchid known as "dog's cullions" (testicles) or "goat's cullions." *Liberal*: vulgar. 6. Chaste. 7. Malicious. 8. Unaware. 9. Habituated.

And therefore I forbid my tears; but yet
It is our trick; nature her custom holds,
Let shame say what it will. When these are gone,
The woman will be out. Adieu, my lord.
I have a speech o' fire that fain would blaze
But that this folly drowns it. [*Exit.*]

KING: Let's follow, Gertrude.
How much I had to do to calm his rage!
Now fear I this will give it start again;
Therefore let's follow. [*Exeunt.*]

ACT V

Scene 1

A churchyard. Enter two CLOWNS.[1]

CLOWN: Is she to be buried in Christian burial when she wilfully seeks her own salvation?

OTHER: I tell thee she is. Therefore make her grave straight. The crowner hath sat on her,[2] and finds it Christian burial.

CLOWN: How can that be, unless she drowned herself in her own defence?

OTHER: Why, 'tis found so.

CLOWN: It must be "se offendendo";[3] it cannot be else. For here lies the point: if I drown myself wittingly, it argues an act, and an act hath three branches—it is to act, to do, to perform; argal,[4] she drowned herself wittingly.

OTHER: Nay, but hear you, Goodman Delver.

CLOWN: Give me leave. Here lies the water; good. Here stands the man; good. If the man go to this water and drown himself, it is, will he, nill he, he goes—mark you that. But if the water come to him and drown him, he drowns not himself. Argal, he that is not guilty of his own death shortens not his own life.

OTHER: But is this law?

CLOWN: Ay, marry, is't; crowner's quest[5] law.

OTHER: Will you ha' the truth on't? If this had not been a gentlewoman, she should have been buried out o' Christian burial.

CLOWN: Why, there thou say'st. And the more pity that great folk should have count'nance[6] in this world to drown or hang themselves more than their even-Christen.[7] Come, my spade. There is no ancient gentlemen but gard'ners, ditchers, and grave-makers. They hold up Adam's profession.

OTHER: Was he a gentleman?

CLOWN: 'A was the first that ever bore arms.

OTHER: Why, he had none.

CLOWN: What, art a heathen? How dost thou understand the Scripture? The Scripture says Adam digged. Could he dig without arms? I'll put another question to thee. If thou answerest me not to the purpose, confess thyself—

1. Rustics; unsophisticated peasants. 2. Held an inquest. *Crowner*: coroner. 3. Error for *se defendendo*, in self-defense. 4. "Ergo," therefore. 5. Inquest. 6. Approval. 7. Fellow Christians.

OTHER: Go to.

CLOWN: What is he that builds stronger than either the mason, the shipwright, or the carpenter?

OTHER: The gallows-maker, for that frame outlives a thousand tenants.

CLOWN: I like thy wit well, in good faith. The gallows does well. But how does it well? It does well to those that do ill. Now thou dost ill to say the gallows is built stronger than the church. Argal, the gallows may do well to thee. To't again,[8] come.

OTHER: Who builds stronger than a mason, a shipwright, or a carpenter?

CLOWN: Ay tell me that, and unyoke.[9]

OTHER: Marry, now I can tell.

CLOWN: To't.

OTHER: Mass, I cannot tell.

CLOWN: Cudgel thy brains no more about it, for your dull ass will not mend his pace with beating. And when you are asked this question next, say "a grave maker." The houses he makes lasts till doomsday. Go, get thee in, and fetch me a stoup[1] of liquor. [*Exit* OTHER CLOWN.]

[*Enter* HAMLET *and* HORATIO *as* CLOWN *digs and sings.*]

In youth, when I did love, did love,
  Methought it was very sweet,
To contract the time for-a my behove,[2]
  O, methought there-a was nothing-a meet.[3]

HAMLET: Has this fellow no feeling of his business, that 'a sings in grave-making?

HORATIO: Custom hath made it in him a property of easiness.

HAMLET: 'Tis e'en so. The hand of little employment hath the daintier sense.

CLOWN:

[*Sings.*]

But age, with his stealing steps,
  Hath clawed me in his clutch,
And hath shipped me into the land,
  As if I had never been such.

[*Throws up a skull.*]

HAMLET: That skull had a tongue in it, and could sing once. How the knave jowls[4] it to the ground, as if 'twere Cain's jawbone, that did the first murder! This might be the pate of a politician, which this ass now o'erreaches;[5] one that would circumvent God, might it not?

HORATIO: It might, my lord.

HAMLET: Or of a courtier, which could say, "Good morrow, sweet lord! How does thou, sweet lord?" This might be my Lord Such-a-one, that praised my Lord Such-a-one's horse, when 'a meant to beg it, might it not?

HORATIO: Ay, my lord.

8. Guess again. 9. Finish the matter. 1. Mug. 2. Advantage. *Contract*: shorten.
3. The gravedigger's song is a free version of "The aged lover renounceth love" by Thomas, Lord Vaux, published in *Tottel's Miscellany* (1557). 4. Hurls. 5. Gets the better of.

HAMLET: Why, e'en so, and now my Lady Worm's, chapless,[6] and knock'd about the mazzard with a sexton's spade. Here's fine revolution,[7] an we had the trick to see't. Did these bones cost no more the breeding but to play at loggets with them?[8] Mine ache to think on't.

CLOWN:

[*Sings.*]

A pick-axe and a spade, a spade,
For and a shrouding sheet:
O, a pit of clay for to be made
For such a guest is meet.

[*Throws up another skull.*]

HAMLET: There's another. Why may not that be the skull of a lawyer? Where be his quiddities now, his quillets, his cases, his tenures, and his tricks? Why does he suffer this mad knave now to knock him about the sconce[9] with a dirty shovel, and will not tell him of his action of battery? Hum! This fellow might be in's time a great buyer of land, with his statutes, his recognizances, his fines, his double vouchers, his recoveries. Is this the fine[1] of his fines, and the recovery of his recoveries, to have his fine pate full of fine dirt? Will his vouchers vouch him no more of his purchases, and double ones too, than the length and breadth of a pair of indentures?[2] The very conveyances of his lands will scarcely lie in this box, and must th' inheritor himself have no more, ha?[3]

HORATIO: Not a jot more, my lord.

HAMLET: Is not parchment made of sheepskins?

HORATIO: Ay, my lord, and of calves' skins too.

HAMLET: They are sheep and calves which seek out assurance in that. I will speak to this fellow. Whose grave's this, sirrah?

CLOWN: Mine, sir.

[*Sings.*]

O, a pit of clay for to be made
For such a guest is meet.

HAMLET: I think it be thine indeed, for thou liest in't.

CLOWN: You lie out on't, sir, and therefore 'tis not yours. For my part, I do not lie in't, yet it is mine.

HAMLET: Thou dost lie in't, to be in't and say it is thine. 'Tis for the dead, not for the quick;[4] therefore thou liest.

CLOWN: 'Tis a quick lie, sir; 'twill away again from me to you.

HAMLET: What man dost thou dig it for?

CLOWN: For no man, sir.

HAMLET: What woman, then?

6. Lacking a lower jaw. 7. Skill. *Mazzard*: head.
8. "Loggets" were small pieces of wood thrown as part of a game. 9. Head. 1. End. 2. Contracts.
3. In this speech Hamlet reels off a list of legal terms relating to property transactions. 4. Living.

CLOWN: For none neither.

HAMLET: Who is to be buried in't?

CLOWN: One that was a woman, sir; but, rest her soul, she's dead.

HAMLET: How absolute the knave is! We must speak by the card,[5] or equivocation will undo us. By the Lord, Horatio, this three years I have took note of it, the age is grown so picked[6] that the toe of the peasant comes so near the heel of the courtier, he galls his kibe.[7] How long hast thou been a grave-maker?

CLOWN: Of all the days i' th' year, I came to't that day that our last King Hamlet overcame Fortinbras.

HAMLET: How long is that since?

CLOWN: Cannot you tell that? Every fool can tell that. It was that very day that young Hamlet was born—he that is mad, and sent into England.

HAMLET: Ay, marry, why was he sent into England?

CLOWN: Why, because 'a was mad. 'A shall recover his wits there; or, if 'a do not, 'tis no great matter there.

HAMLET: Why?

CLOWN: 'Twill not be seen in him there. There the men are as mad as he.

HAMLET: How came he mad?

CLOWN: Very strangely, they say.

HAMLET: How strangely?

CLOWN: Faith, e'en with losing his wits.

HAMLET: Upon what ground?

CLOWN: Why, here in Denmark. I have been sexton here, man and boy, thirty years.

HAMLET: How long will a man lie i' th' earth ere he rot?

CLOWN: Faith, if 'a be not rotten before 'a die—as we have many pocky[8] corses now-a-days that will scarce hold the laying in—'a will last you some eight year or nine year. A tanner will last you nine year.

HAMLET: Why he more than another?

CLOWN: Why, sir, his hide is so tanned with his trade that 'a will keep out water a great while; and your water is a sore decayer of your whoreson dead body. Here's a skull now hath lien[9] you i' th' earth three and twenty years.

HAMLET: Whose was it?

CLOWN: A whoreson mad fellow's it was. Whose do you think it was?

HAMLET: Nay, I know not.

CLOWN: A pestilence on him for a mad rogue! 'A poured a flagon of Rhenish on my head once. This same skull, sir, was, sir, Yorick's skull, the king's jester.

HAMLET: [*Takes the skull.*] This?

CLOWN: E'en that.

HAMLET: Alas, poor Yorick! I knew him, Horatio—a fellow of infinite jest, of most excellent fancy. He hath bore me on his back a thousand times, and now how abhorred in my imagination it is! My gorg[1] rises at it. Here hung those lips that I have kissed I know not how oft. Where be your gibes now, your gambols, your songs, your flashes of merriment that were wont to set the table on a roar? Not one now to mock your own grinning? Quite chap-fall'n?[2] Now

5. Exactly. *Absolute*: precise. 6. Refined. 7. Rubs a blister on his heel. 8. Corrupted by syphilis. 9. Lain. *Whoreson*: bastard (not literally). 1. Throat. 2. Lacking a lower jaw.

get you to my lady's chamber, and tell her, let her paint an inch thick, to this favor[3] she must come. Make her laugh at that. Prithee, Horatio, tell me one thing.

HORATIO: What's that, my lord?

HAMLET: Dost thou think Alexander looked o' this fashion i' th' earth?

HORATIO: E'en so.

HAMLET: And smelt so? Pah! [*Throws down the skull.*]

HORATIO: E'en so, my lord.

HAMLET: To what base uses we may return, Horatio! Why may not imagination trace the noble dust of Alexander till 'a find it stopping a bung-hole?[4]

HORATIO: 'Twere to consider too curiously[5] to consider so.

HAMLET: No, faith, not a jot, but to follow him thither with modesty[6] enough, and likelihood to lead it. Alexander died, Alexander was buried, Alexander returneth to dust; the dust is earth; of earth we make loam; and why of that loam whereto he was converted might they not stop a beerbarrel?

Imperious Cæsar, dead and turned to clay,
Might stop a hole to keep the wind away.
O, that that earth which kept the world in awe
Should patch a wall t'expel the winter's flaw![7]

But soft, but soft awhile! Here comes the king,
The queen, the courtiers.

[*Enter* KING, QUEEN, LAERTES, *and the Corse with a* PRIEST *and* LORDS *attendant.*]

Who is this they follow?
And with such maimèd[8] rites? This doth betoken
The corse they follow did with desperate hand
Fordo its own life. 'Twas of some estate.[9]
Couch[1] we awhile and mark. [*Retires with* HORATIO.]

LAERTES: What ceremony else?[2]

HAMLET: That is Laertes, a very noble youth. Mark.

LAERTES: What ceremony else?

PRIEST: Here obsequies have been as far enlarged[3]
As we have warranty. Her death was doubtful,
And but that great command o'ersways the order,[4]
She should in ground unsanctified been lodged
Till the last trumpet. For charitable prayers,
Shards, flints, and pebbles, should be thrown on her.
Yet here she is allowed her virgin crants,[5]
Her maiden strewments,[6] and the bringing home
Of bell and burial.

LAERTES: Must there no more be done?

3. Appearance. 4. Used as a cork in a cask. 5. Precisely. 6. Moderation. 7. Gusty wind. 8. Shortened. 9. Rank. *Fordo*: destroy. 1. Conceal ourselves. 2. More. 3. Extended. 4. Usual rules. 5. Wreaths. 6. Flowers strewn on the grave.

PRIEST: No more be done.
We should profane the service of the dead
To sing a requiem and such rest to her
As to peace-parted souls.
LAERTES: Lay her i' th' earth,
And from her fair and unpolluted flesh
May violets spring! I tell thee, churlish priest,
A minist'ring angel shall my sister be
When thou liest howling.[7]
HAMLET: What, the fair Ophelia!
QUEEN: Sweets to the sweet. Farewell! [*Scatters flowers.*]
I hoped thou shouldst have been my Hamlet's wife.
I thought thy bride-bed to have decked, sweet maid,
And not t' have strewed thy grave.
LAERTES: O, treble woe
Fall ten times treble on that cursèd head
Whose wicked deed thy most ingenious sense[8]
Deprived thee of! Hold off the earth awhile,
Till I have caught her once more in mine arms. [*Leaps into the grave.*]
Now pile your dust upon the quick and dead,
Till of this flat a mountain you have made
T' o'er-top old Pelion or the skyish head
Of blue Olympus.[9]
HAMLET: [*Coming forward.*] What is he whose grief
Bears such an emphasis, whose phrase of sorrow
Conjures[1] the wand'ring stars, and makes them stand
Like wonder-wounded hearers? This is I,
Hamlet the Dane.

[HAMLET *leaps into the grave and they grapple.*]

LAERTES: The devil take thy soul!
HAMLET: Thou pray'st not well.
I prithee take thy fingers from my throat,
For though I am not splenitive[2] and rash,
Yet have I in me something dangerous,
Which let thy wisdom fear. Hold off thy hand.
KING: Pluck them asunder.
QUEEN: Hamlet! Hamlet!
ALL: Gentlemen!
HORATIO: Good my lord, be quiet.

[*The* ATTENDANTS *part them, and they come out of the grave.*]

7. In Hell. 8. Lively mind.
9. The rivalry between Laertes and Hamlet in this scene extends even to their rhetoric. Pelion and Olympus, mentioned here by Laertes, and Ossa, mentioned below by Hamlet, are Greek mountains noted in mythology for their height. Olympus was the reputed home of the gods, and the other two were piled one on top of the other by the Giants in an attempt to reach the top of Olympus and overthrow the gods. 1. Casts a spell on. 2. Hot tempered.

HAMLET: Why, I will fight with him upon this theme
Until my eyelids will no longer wag.[3]
QUEEN: O my son, what theme?
HAMLET: I loved Ophelia. Forty thousand brothers
Could not with all their quantity of love
Make up my sum. What wilt thou do for her?
KING: O, he is mad, Laertes.
QUEEN: For love of God, forbear[4] him.
HAMLET: 'Swounds, show me what th'owt do.
Woo't[5] weep, woo't fight, woo't fast, woo't tear thyself,
Woo't drink up eisel,[6] eat a crocodile?
I'll do't. Dost come here to whine?
To outface[7] me with leaping in her grave?
Be buried quick with her, and so will I.
And if thou prate of mountains, let them throw
Millions of acres on us, till our ground,
Singeing his pate against the burning zone,[8]
Make Ossa like a wart! Nay, an thou'lt mouth,
I'll rant as well as thou.
QUEEN: This is mere madness
And thus awhile the fit will work on him.
Anon, as patient as the female dove
When that her golden couplets[9] are disclosed,
His silence will sit drooping.
HAMLET: Hear you, sir.
What is the reason that you use me thus?
I loved you ever. But it is no matter.
Let Hercules himself do what he may,
The cat will mew, and dog will have his day. [*Exit.*]
KING: I pray thee, good Horatio, wait upon[1] him.

[*Exit* HORATIO.]

[*To* LAERTES.] Strengthen your patience in our last night's speech.
We'll put the matter to the present push.[2]—
Good Gertrude, set some watch over your son.—
This grave shall have a living monument.
An hour of quiet shortly shall we see;
Till then in patience our proceeding be. [*Exeunt.*]

Scene 2

A hall or public room. Enter HAMLET *and* HORATIO.

HAMLET: So much for this, sir; now shall you see the other.
You do remember all the circumstance?

3. Move. 4. Bear with. 5. Will you. 6. Vinegar. 7. Get the best of. 8. Sky in the torrid zone.
9. Pair of eggs. 1. Attend. 2. Immediate trial.

HORATIO: Remember it, my lord!
HAMLET: Sir, in my heart there was a kind of fighting
That would not let me sleep. Methought I lay
Worse than the mutines in the bilboes.[3] Rashly,
And praised be rashness for it—let us know,
Our indiscretion sometime serves us well,
When our deep plots do pall; and that should learn[4] us
There's a divinity that shapes our ends,
Rough-hew them how we will—
HORATIO: That is most certain.
HAMLET: Up from my cabin,
My sea-gown scarfed[5] about me, in the dark
Groped I to find out them, had my desire,
Fingered their packet, and in fine[6] withdrew
To mine own room again, making so bold,
My fears forgetting manners, to unseal
Their grand commission; where I found, Horatio—
Ah, royal knavery!—an exact[7] command,
Larded[8] with many several sorts of reasons,
Importing Denmark's health, and England's too,
With, ho! such bugs and goblins in my life,[9]
That on the supervise,[1] no leisure bated,
No, not to stay the grinding of the axe,
My head should be struck off.
HORATIO: Is't possible?
HAMLET: Here's the commission; read it at more leisure.
But wilt thou hear now how I did proceed?
HORATIO: I beseech you.
HAMLET: Being thus benetted[2] round with villainies,
Ere I could make a prologue to my brains,
They had begun the play. I sat me down,
Devised a new commission, wrote it fair.[3]
I once did hold it, as our statists[4] do,
A baseness to write fair, and labored much
How to forget that learning; but sir, now
It did me yeoman's service.[5] Wilt thou know
Th' effect[6] of what I wrote?
HORATIO: Ay, good my lord.
HAMLET: An earnest conjuration from the king,
As England was his faithful tributary,[7]
As love between them like the palm might flourish,
As peace should still her wheaten garland wear
And stand a comma 'tween their amities[8]

3. Stocks. *Mutines*: mutineers. 4. Teach. 5. Wrapped. 6. Quickly. *Fingered*: stole.
7. Precisely stated. 8. Garnished. 9. Such dangers if I remained alive.
1. As soon as the commission was read. 2. Caught in a net. 3. Legibly. *Devised*: made.
4. Politicians. 5. Served me well. 6. Contents. 7. Vassal. 8. Link friendships.

And many such like as's of great charge,[9]
That on the view and knowing of these contents,
Without debatement[1] further more or less,
He should those bearers put to sudden death,
Not shriving-time allowed.[2]

HORATIO: How was this sealed?

HAMLET: Why, even in that was heaven ordinant,[3]
I had my father's signet in my purse,
Which was the model of that Danish seal,
Folded the writ up in the form of th' other,
Subscribed it, gave't th' impression,[4] placed it safely,
The changeling[5] never known. Now, the next day
Was our sea-fight, and what to this was sequent[6]
Thou knowest already.

HORATIO: So Guildenstern and Rosencrantz go to't.

HAMLET: Why, man, they did make love to this employment.
They are not near my conscience; their defeat[7]
Does by their own insinuation grow.
'Tis dangerous when the baser nature comes
Between the pass and fell[8] incensèd points
Of mighty opposites.

HORATIO: Why, what a king is this!

HAMLET: Does it not, think thee, stand me now upon—
He that hath killed my king and whored my mother,
Popped in between th' election and my hopes,
Thrown out his angle[9] for my proper life,
And with such coz'nage[1]—is't not perfect conscience
To quit[2] him with this arm? And is't not to be damned
To let this canker of our nature come
In further evil?

HORATIO: It must be shortly known to him from England
What is the issue[3] of the business there.

HAMLET: It will be short;[4] the interim is mine.
And a man's life's no more than to say "one."
But I am very sorry, good Horatio,
That to Laertes I forgot myself;
For by the image of my cause I see
The portraiture of his. I'll court his favors.
But sure the bravery[5] of his grief did put me
Into a tow'ring passion.

HORATIO: Peace; who comes here?

[*Enter* OSRIC.]

OSRIC: Your lordship is right welcome back to Denmark.

9. Import. 1. Consideration. 2. Without time for confession. 3. Operative. 4. With the seal.
5. Replacement. 6. Followed. 7. Death. *Are not near*: do not touch. 8. Cruel. *Pass*: thrust.
9. Fishhook. 1. Trickery. 2. Repay. 3. Outcome. 4. Soon. 5. Exaggerated display.

HAMLET: I humbly thank you, sir. [*Aside to* HORATIO.] Dost know this water-fly?

HORATIO: [*Aside to* HAMLET.] No, my good lord.

HAMLET: [*Aside to* HORATIO.] Thy state is the more gracious, for 'tis a vice to know him. He hath much land, and fertile. Let a beast be lord of beasts, and his crib shall stand at the king's mess. 'Tis a chough,[6] but as I say, spacious in the possession of dirt.

OSRIC: Sweet lord, if your lordship were at leisure, I should impart a thing to you from his majesty.

HAMLET: I will receive it, sir, with all diligence of spirit. Put your bonnet to his right use. 'Tis for the head.[7]

OSRIC: I thank your lordship, it is very hot.

HAMLET: No, believe me, 'tis very cold; the wind is northerly.

OSRIC: It is indifferent[8] cold, my lord, indeed.

HAMLET: But yet methinks it is very sultry and hot for my complexion.[9]

OSRIC: Exceedingly, my lord; it is very sultry, as 'twere—I cannot tell how. My lord, his majesty bade me signify to you that 'a has laid a great wager on your head. Sir, this is the matter—

HAMLET: I beseech you, remember. [*Moves him to put on his hat.*]

OSRIC: Nay, good my lord; for my ease, in good faith. Sir, here is newly come to court Laertes; believe me, an absolute[1] gentleman, full of most excellent differences of very soft society and great showing.[2] Indeed, to speak feelingly of him, he is the card or calendar of gentry, for you shall find in him the continent[3] of what part a gentleman would see.

HAMLET: Sir, his definement[4] suffers no perdition in you, though I know to divide him inventorially would dozy th' arithmetic of memory, and yet but yaw[5] neither in respect of his quick sail. But in the verity of extolment, I take him to be a soul of great article, and his infusion[6] of such dearth and rareness as, to make true diction of him, his semblage is his mirror,[7] and who else would trace him, his umbrage,[8] nothing more.

OSRIC: Your lordship speaks most infallibly of him.

HAMLET: The concernancy,[9] sir? Why do we wrap the gentleman in our more rawer breath?[1]

OSRIC: Sir?

HORATIO: Is't not possible to understand in another tongue? You will to't, sir, really.

HAMLET: What imports the nomination[2] of this gentleman?

OSRIC: Of Laertes?

HORATIO: [*Aside.*] His purse is empty already. All's golden words are spent.

HAMLET: Of him, sir.

OSRIC: I know you are not ignorant—

HAMLET: I would you did, sir; yet, in faith, if you did, it would not much approve me. Well, sir.

6. Jackdaw. 7. Osric has evidently removed his hat in deference to the prince. 8. Moderately.
9. Temperament. 1. Perfect. 2. Good manners. *Excellent differences*: qualities.
3. Sum total. *Calendar*: measure. 4. Description.
5. Steer wildly. *Dozy*: daze. *Divide him inventorially*: examine bit by bit. 6. Nature. *Article*: scope.
7. That is, his likeness ("semblage") is (only) his own mirror image; he is unrivaled. *Diction*: telling.
8. Shadow. *Trace*: keep pace with. 9. Meaning. (Hamlet is mocking Osric's affected speech.)
1. Cruder words. 2. Naming.

OSRIC: You are not ignorant of what excellence Laertes is—

HAMLET: I dare not confess that, lest I should compare[3] with him in excellence; but to know a man well were to know himself.

OSRIC: I mean, sir, for his weapon; but in the imputation[4] laid on him by them, in his meed he's unfellowed.[5]

HAMLET: What's his weapon?

OSRIC: Rapier and dagger.

HAMLET: That's two of his weapons—but well.

OSRIC: The king, sir, hath wagered with him six Barbary horses, against the which he has impawned,[6] as I take it, six French rapiers and poniards, with their assigns, as girdle, hangers,[7] and so. Three of the carriages, in faith, are very dear to fancy,[8] very responsive to the hilts, most delicate carriages, and of very liberal conceit.[9]

HAMLET: What call you the carriages?

HORATIO: [*Aside to* HAMLET.] I knew you must be edified by the margent[1] ere you had done.

OSRIC: The carriages, sir, are the hangers.

HAMLET: The phrase would be more germane to the matter if we could carry a cannon by our sides. I would it might be hangers till then. But on! Six Barbary horses against six French swords, their assigns, and three liberal conceited carriages; that's the French bet against the Danish. Why is this all impawned, as you call it?

OSRIC: The king, sir, hath laid, sir, that in a dozen passes between yourself and him he shall not exceed you three hits; he hath laid on twelve for nine, and it would come to immediate trial if your lordship would vouchsafe the answer.

HAMLET: How if I answer no?

OSRIC: I mean, my lord, the opposition of your person in trial.

HAMLET: Sir, I will walk here in the hall. If it please his majesty, it is the breathing time[2] of day with me. Let the foils be brought, the gentleman willing, and the king hold his purpose; I will win for him an I can. If not, I will gain nothing but my shame and the odd hits.

OSRIC: Shall I deliver you so?

HAMLET: To this effect, sir, after what flourish your nature will.

OSRIC: I commend my duty to your lordship.

HAMLET: Yours, yours. [*Exit* OSRIC.] He does well to commend it himself; there are no tongues else for's turn.

HORATIO: This lapwing runs away with the shell on his head.[3]

HAMLET: 'A did comply, sir, with his dug[4] before 'a sucked it. Thus has he, and many more of the same bevy that I know the drossy age dotes on, only got the tune of the time; and out of an habit of encounter, a king of yesty[5] collection

3. That is, compare myself. 4. Reputation. 5. Unequaled in his excellence 6. Staked.
7. Sword belts. *Assigns*: appurtenances. 8. Finely designed.
9. Elegant design. *Delicate*: well adjusted. 1. Marginal gloss. 2. Time for exercise.
3. The lapwing was thought to be so precocious that it could run immediately after being hatched, even, as here, with bits of the shell still on its head. 4. Mother's breast. *Comply*: deal formally.
5. Yeasty.

which carries them through and through the most fanned and winnowed opinions; and do but blow them to their trial, the bubbles are out.

[*Enter a* LORD.]

LORD: My lord, his majesty commended him to you by young Osric, who brings back to him that you attend[6] him in the hall. He sends to know if your pleasure hold to play with Laertes, or that you will take longer time.

HAMLET: I am constant to my purposes; they follow the king's pleasure. If his fitness speaks, mine is ready; now or whensoever, provided I be so able as now.

LORD: The king and queen and all are coming down.

HAMLET: In happy time.

LORD: The queen desires you to use some gentle entertainment[7] to Laertes before you fall to play.

HAMLET: She well instructs me. [*Exit* LORD.]

HORATIO: You will lose this wager, my lord.

HAMLET: I do not think so. Since he went into France I have been in continual practice. I shall win at the odds. But thou wouldst not think how ill[8] all's here about my heart. But it's no matter.

HORATIO: Nay, good my lord—

HAMLET: It is but foolery, but it is such a kind of gaingiving[9] as would perhaps trouble a woman.

HORATIO: If your mind dislike anything, obey it. I will forestall their repair[1] hither, and say you are not fit.

HAMLET: Not a whit, we defy augury. There is special providence in the fall of a sparrow. If it be now, 'tis not to come; if it be not to come, it will be now; if it be not now, yet it will come. The readiness is all. Since no man of aught he leaves knows, what is't to leave betimes? Let be.

[*A table prepared. Enter* TRUMPETS, DRUMS, *and* OFFICERS *with cushions;* KING, QUEEN, OSRIC *and* ATTENDANTS *with foils, daggers, and* LAERTES.]

KING: Come, Hamlet, come and take this hand from me.

[*The* KING *puts* LAERTES' *hand into* HAMLET'S.]

HAMLET: Give me your pardon, sir. I have done you wrong,
But pardon 't as you are a gentleman.
This presence[2] knows, and you must needs have heard,
How I am punished with a sore distraction.
What I have done
That might your nature, honor, and exception,[3]
Roughly awake, I here proclaim was madness.
Was 't Hamlet wronged Laertes? Never Hamlet.
If Hamlet from himself be ta'en away,
And when he's not himself does wrong Laertes,
Then Hamlet does it not, Hamlet denies it.
Who does it then? His madness. If't be so,

6. Await. 7. Cordiality. 8. Uneasy. 9. Misgiving. 1. Coming. 2. Company. 3. Resentment.

Hamlet is of the faction that is wronged;
His madness is poor Hamlet's enemy.
Sir, in this audience,
Let my disclaiming from[4] a purposed evil
Free[5] me so far in your most generous thoughts
That I have shot my arrow o'er the house
And hurt my brother.

LAERTES: I am satisfied in nature,
Whose motive in this case should stir me most
To my revenge. But in my terms of honor
I stand aloof, and will no reconcilement
Till by some elder masters of known honor
I have a voice[6] and precedent of peace
To keep my name ungored.[7] But till that time
I do receive your offered love like love,
And will not wrong it.

HAMLET: I embrace it freely,
And will this brother's wager frankly[8] play.
Give us the foils. Come on.

LAERTES: Come, one for me.

HAMLET: I'll be your foil, Laertes. In mine ignorance
Your skill shall, like a star i' th' darkest night,
Stick fiery off[9] indeed.

LAERTES: You mock me, sir.

HAMLET: No, by this hand.

KING: Give them the foils, young Osric. Cousin Hamlet,
You know the wager?

HAMLET: Very well, my lord;
Your Grace has laid the odds o' th' weaker side.

KING: I do not fear it, I have seen you both;
But since he is bettered[1] we have therefore odds.

LAERTES: This is too heavy; let me see another.

HAMLET: This likes me well. These foils have all a[2] length?

[*They prepare to play.*]

OSRIC: Ay, my good lord.

KING: Set me the stoups of wine upon that table.
If Hamlet give the first or second hit,
Or quit in answer of[3] the third exchange,
Let all the battlements their ordnance fire.
The king shall drink to Hamlet's better breath,
And in the cup an union[4] shall he throw,
Richer than that which four successive kings
In Denmark's crown have worn. Give me the cups,
And let the kettle[5] to the trumpet speak,

4. Denying of. 5. Absolve. 6. Authority. 7. Unshamed. 8. Freely. 9. Shine brightly.
1. Reported better. 2. The same. *Likes*: suits. 3. Repay. 4. Pearl. 5. Kettledrum.

The trumpet to the cannoneer without,
The cannons to the heavens, the heaven to earth,
"Now the king drinks to Hamlet." Come, begin—

[*Trumpets the while.*]

And you, the judges, bear a wary eye.
HAMLET: Come on, sir.
LAERTES: Come, my lord.

[*They play.*]

HAMLET: One.
LAERTES: No.
HAMLET: Judgment?
OSRIC: A hit, a very palpable hit.

[*Drums, trumpets, and shot. Flourish; a piece goes off.*]

LAERTES: Well, again.
KING: Stay, give me drink. Hamlet, this pearl is thine.
Here's to thy health. Give him the cup.
HAMLET: I'll play this bout first; set it by awhile.
Come.

[*They play.*]

Another hit; what say you?
LAERTES: A touch, a touch, I do confess't.
KING: Our son shall win.
QUEEN: He's fat,[6] and scant of breath.
Here, Hamlet, take my napkin, rub thy brows.
The queen carouses to thy fortune, Hamlet.
HAMLET: Good madam!
KING: Gertrude, do not drink.
QUEEN: I will, my lord; I pray you pardon me.
KING: [*Aside.*] It is the poisoned cup; it is too late.
HAMLET: I dare not drink yet, madam; by and by.
QUEEN: Come, let me wipe thy face.
LAERTES: My lord, I'll hit him now.
KING: I do not think't.
LAERTES: [*Aside.*] And yet it is almost against my conscience.
HAMLET: Come, for the third, Laertes. You do but dally.
I pray you pass[7] with your best violence;
I am afeard you make a wanton of me.[8]
LAERTES: Say you so? Come on.

[*They play.*]

OSRIC: Nothing, neither way.
LAERTES: Have at you now!

6. Out of shape. 7. Attack. 8. Trifle with me.

[LAERTES *wounds* HAMLET: *then, in scuffling, they change rapiers, and* HAMLET *wounds* LAERTES.]

KING: Part them. They are incensed.
HAMLET: Nay, come again.

[*The* QUEEN *falls.*]

OSRIC: Look to the queen there, ho!
HORATIO: They bleed on both sides. How is it, my lord?
OSRIC: How is't, Laertes?
LAERTES: Why, as a woodcock to mine own springe,[9] Osric.
I am justly killed with mine own treachery.
HAMLET: How does the queen?
KING: She swoons to see them bleed.
QUEEN: No, no, the drink, the drink! O my dear Hamlet!
The drink, the drink! I am poisoned. [*Dies.*]
HAMLET: O, villainy! Ho! let the door be locked.
Treachery! seek it out.
LAERTES: It is here, Hamlet. Hamlet, thou art slain;
No med'cine in the world can do thee good.
In thee there is not half an hour's life.
The treacherous instrument is in thy hand,
Unbated[1] and envenomed. The foul practice
Hath turned itself on me. Lo, here I lie,
Never to rise again. Thy mother's poisoned.
I can no more. The king, the king's to blame.
HAMLET: The point envenomed too?
Then, venom, to thy work. [*Hurts the* KING.]
ALL: Treason! treason!
KING: O, yet defend me, friends. I am but hurt.[2]
HAMLET: Here, thou incestuous, murd'rous, damnèd Dane,
Drink off this potion. Is thy union here?
Follow my mother.

[*The* KING *dies.*]

LAERTES: He is justly served.
It is a poison tempered[3] by himself.
Exchange forgiveness with me, noble Hamlet.
Mine and my father's death come not upon thee,
Nor thine on me! [*Dies.*]
HAMLET: Heaven make thee free of[4] it! I follow thee.
I am dead, Horatio. Wretched queen, adieu!
You that look pale and tremble at this chance,[5]
That are but mutes or audience to this act,
Had I but time, as this fell sergeant Death

9. Snare. 1. Unblunted. 2. Wounded. 3. Mixed. 4. Forgive. 5. Circumstance.

Is strict in his arrest,[6] O, I could tell you—
But let it be. Horatio, I am dead:
Thou livest; report me and my cause aright
To the unsatisfied.[7]

HORATIO: Never believe it.
I am more an antique Roman than a Dane.
Here's yet some liquor left.

HAMLET: As th'art a man,
Give me the cup. Let go. By heaven, I'll ha't.
O God, Horatio, what a wounded name,
Things standing thus unknown, shall live behind me!
If thou didst ever hold me in thy heart,
Absent thee from felicity awhile,
And in this harsh world draw thy breath in pain,
To tell my story.

[*A march afar off.*]

What warlike noise is this?

OSRIC: Young Fortinbras, with conquest come from Poland,
To th' ambassadors of England gives
This warlike volley.[8]

HAMLET: O, I die, Horatio!
The potent poison quite o'er-crows[9] my spirit.
I cannot live to hear the news from England,
But I do prophesy th' election[1] lights
On Fortinbras. He has my dying voice.[2]
So tell him, with th' occurrents,[3] more and less,
Which have solicited[4]—the rest is silence. [*Dies.*]

HORATIO: Now cracks a noble heart. Good night, sweet prince,
And flights of angels sing thee to thy rest!

[*March within.*]

Why does the drum come hither?

[*Enter* FORTINBRAS, *with the* AMBASSADORS *and with drum, colors, and* ATTENDANTS.]

FORTINBRAS: Where is this sight?

HORATIO: What is it you would see?
If aught of woe or wonder, cease your search.

FORTINBRAS: This quarry cries on havoc.[5] O proud death,

6. Summons to court. 7. Uninformed.
8. The staging presents some difficulties here. Unless Osric is clairvoyant, he must have left the stage at some point and returned. One possibility is that he might have left to carry out Hamlet's order to lock the door (line 280) and returned when the sound of the distant march is heard.
9. Overcomes. 1. (Of a new king for Denmark.) 2. Support. 3. Circumstances.
4. Brought about this scene. 5. The game killed in the hunt proclaims a slaughter.

What feast is toward[6] in thine eternal cell
That thou so many princes at a shot
So bloodily hast struck?
AMBASSADORS: The sight is dismal;
And our affairs from England come too late.
The ears are senseless[7] that should give us hearing
To tell him his commandment is fulfilled,
That Rosencrantz and Guildenstern are dead.
Where should we have our thanks?
HORATIO: Not from his mouth,
Had it th' ability of life to thank you.
He never gave commandment for their death.
But since, so jump[8] upon this bloody question,
You from the Polack wars, and you from England,
Are here arrived, give orders that these bodies
High on a stage be placèd to the view,
And let me speak to th' yet unknowing world
How these things came about. So shall you hear
Of carnal, bloody, and unnatural acts;
Of accidental judgments, casual[9] slaughters;
Of deaths put on by cunning and forced cause;
And, in this upshot,[1] purposes mistook
Fall'n on th' inventors' heads. All this can I
Truly deliver.
FORTINBRAS: Let us haste to hear it,
And call the noblest to the audience.[2]
For me, with sorrow I embrace my fortune.
I have some rights of memory[3] in this kingdom,
Which now to claim my vantage[4] doth invite me.
HORATIO: Of that I shall have also cause to speak,
And from his mouth whose voice will draw on more.
But let this same be presently performed,
Even while men's minds are wild, lest more mischance
On plots and errors happen.
FORTINBRAS: Let four captains
Bear Hamlet like a soldier to the stage,
For he was likely, had he been put on,[5]
To have proved most royal; and for his passage
The soldier's music and the rite of war
Speak loudly for him.
Take up the bodies. Such a sight as this
Becomes the field,[6] but here shows much amiss.
Go, bid the soldiers shoot. [*Exeunt marching. A peal of ordnance shot off.*]

c. 1600

6. In preparation. 7. Without sense of hearing. 8. Exactly.
9. Brought about by apparent accident. 1. Result. 2. Hearing. 3. Succession 4. Position.
5. Elected king. 6. Battlefield.

SUGGESTIONS FOR WRITING

1. In A MIDSUMMER NIGHT'S DREAM's best-known speech, Theseus asserts, "The lunatic, the lover, and the poet / Are of imagination all compact" (5.1.7–8). Citing evidence from the play, write an essay analyzing Shakespeare's characterization of love—not only in the play's action but also in the words of the love-obsessed characters. Is Shakespearean love merely a kind of madness, or does it contain hints of a guiding wisdom beyond the awareness of lovers themselves?
2. Early in A MIDSUMMER NIGHT'S DREAM, Helena remarks, "Love looks not with the eyes, but with the mind" (1.1.234). The play is filled with references to eyes and vision; indeed, the plot hinges on the differences between what characters see and what they think they see. Using specific examples, write an essay exploring the significance of eyes, sight, and seeing in this play. What does the play suggest about the power and the limitations of human vision?
3. In ancient Greek tragedy, misfortune is often the result of *hubris*—the excessive pride that leads a hero to overstep the bounds of his destiny and thus to offend the gods. More recent writing about tragedy develops the concept of *hamartia*—the notion that the protagonist's fate is brought about by a tragic flaw or failing of character. What propels HAMLET—the prince's proud wish to avenge his father's death and assert his rights? a tragic flaw in Hamlet's otherwise noble character? or something else altogether? Write an essay examining the circumstances and motivations that lead to Hamlet's death and the fall of Denmark.
4. Some critics have focused on the psychological underpinnings of HAMLET; others have seen the play as political commentary. In 1600 (the approximate date of HAMLET's first performance), Queen Elizabeth I was sixty-seven and had no direct heirs, a situation that promised no end to the wars and rebellions over succession to the throne that had plagued England for the preceding two centuries. Drawing on the play and, if need be, your own research into the politics of Shakespeare's era, write an essay showing how England's historical circumstances may be reflected in HAMLET.
5. In both A MIDSUMMER NIGHT'S DREAM and HAMLET, characters perform a play. What are the functions and effects of this device? What might the plays within plays suggest about the value of drama—including the value of plays like Shakespeare's own? What different attitudes toward drama are displayed by various characters in A MIDSUMMER NIGHT'S DREAM and HAMLET? Write an essay exploring the function and significance of these plays within plays. What attitudes toward drama does Shakespeare encourage us to adopt?
6. Write an essay exploring the characterization of the socially lowly characters in A MIDSUMMER NIGHT'S DREAM and HAMLET and their thematic significance. What might be noteworthy about when such characters appear in each play? Might some or all of these characters display a wisdom lacking in their social betters? If so, what is it, and is it the same or similar in the two plays?
7. Write an essay comparing the way relationships between fathers and daughters are portrayed in HAMLET and A MIDSUMMER NIGHT'S DREAM. What might the plays suggest about how and why such relationships tend to go wrong? about how fathers should treat daughters and vice versa?

29 CULTURAL AND HISTORICAL CONTEXTS: LORRAINE HANSBERRY'S *A RAISIN IN THE SUN*

Three different levels of time operate in most literary texts, including plays. First, a text represents a particular **time**—the temporal **setting**—in which the action takes place. We can call this *plot time.* Second, the text reflects the time when the author was writing, and, inevitably, the conditions and assumptions of that time inform the text's conception and style; this feature of textual time we may call *authorial time.* Third, readers read in a particular *reader time,* when conditions and assumptions may differ from those that obtain in either the text's or the author's present. (If we encounter a play on the stage, we might instead call this *performance time.*)

In some cases, plot, authorial, and reader time all differ. Wole Soyinka's *Death and the King's Horseman,* for example, is set in the early 1940s in the British colony of Nigeria. Yet it was written in the early 1970s, after Soyinka's country gained its independence. Thus, when we—as readers in the 2010s—read the play, three distinct historical and cultural contexts are operating at once. Values in these three times will not be identical. How we interpret the actions and thoughts of the characters in part depends not only on our own assumptions about what they should or might do, but also on what we know about the conditions that shaped people's lives in quite different historical and cultural milieus. Keeping these three contexts in mind as we read—and consciously making comparisons when we perceive conflicting values—is a vital part of our response and interpretation.

This can be equally true of plays that represent the times in which they were written. When Lorraine Hansberry's A RAISIN IN THE SUN debuted in 1959, its audience watched scenes that might well have been unfolding at virtually the same moment just down the street. The stage directions, in fact, indicate that the action in the play occurs "in Chicago's Southside, sometime between World War II and the present." In this case, almost no difference exists between plot time and authorial time. Indeed, the play asked its original audiences to believe that they were confronting life exactly as it was happening and being invited to consider issues of immediate consequence. And the play also drew, at least to some extent, on that audience's knowledge of current events, concerns, and issues—knowledge that we, living in a quite different reader time, may have to work to master.

Of course, this does not mean that *A Raisin in the Sun* or any great play can't speak to us unless we "study up" on the worlds about and in which it was written. "Inevitably, . . . every work belongs to a given moment," as Wole Soyinka reminds us. But, he adds, "it transcends this" moment, too. Hansberry's play remains relevant in part because it shows us characters who are as hopeful, complex, funny, and flawed as we are. Indeed, one of Hansberry's major objectives was, as she explained in a letter, to "help . . . people to understand how we ['Negroes'] are just as complicated as they are—and just as mixed up." And we see her characters confronting questions that we face, too—about family, cultural and personal identity, gender, race and ethnicity, ambition, human dignity and honor, historical change, and generational conflict. Much of what happens in the play could and does still happen in our world, and in much the same way.

But not everything. Consider the abortion that Ruth Younger contemplates near the end of *A Raisin in the Sun*'s first act. In 1959, abortion was illegal in the United States. Women who sought abortions had either to leave the country, usually traveling to Mexico or Puerto Rico (a relatively expensive option), or to seek out shady, back-alley practitioners like the one Ruth consults. Such abortionists typically had little medical expertise and often operated in highly unsanitary conditions. Disease and mortality rates were high, and some of the horror that the Younger family expresses at the thought of abortion can be attributed to reasonable fears about its physical consequences. But their horror also results from the moral and social stigma surrounding abortion. However individuals today might feel about the ethics of abortion, the law prohibited it in 1959, and public opinion weighed heavily against the practice. To appreciate Ruth's situation, understand other characters' responses, and imagine the original audience's reactions, it helps to know about the prevailing legal climate, as well as the various social attitudes and concerns of the day, especially within a respectable, proud, and aspiring African American family like the Youngers.

Some plays offer us a good deal of information about setting that is relevant to the interpretation of specific episodes. But sometimes we have to supply facts that the text doesn't give us. People may share some characteristics across ages and cultures, but behavior and motivation are often conditioned by historically and culturally specific circumstances. Often we have to adjust our expectations because the world of the play or that of its author differs greatly from our own. Identifying the play's setting—in time and place—and considering carefully the historical and cultural context in which the play was written can be crucial to understanding what happens and why.

The rest of this chapter seeks to introduce you to the contexts that inspired and shaped *A Raisin in the Sun* and to some of the historically specific conditions, concerns, and conflicts the play explores.

THE HISTORICAL SIGNIFICANCE OF *A RAISIN IN THE SUN*

The debut of *A Raisin in the Sun* was a significant historical and cultural event in its own right. The first play by an African American woman ever produced on Broadway, *A Raisin in the Sun* earned its creator, Lorraine Hansberry (1930–65), the New York Drama Critics Circle Award as the year's best play just two months after it opened. Hansberry thus became—at twenty-nine—the youngest American playwright, the first black writer, and only the fifth woman ever to receive this prestigious award. Yet when Hansberry's friend and fellow writer James Baldwin labeled her play a "historical achievement" of the greatest importance, he had something else in mind—the unprecedented way that *A Raisin in the Sun* brought African Americans into the theater and onto the stage. "I had never in my life seen so many black people in the theater," Baldwin recalled. "And the reason was that never before, in the entire history of the American theater, had so much of the truth of black people's lives been seen on the stage. Black people [had] ignored the theater because the theater had always ignored them." To

Lorraine Hansberry, 1959

Baldwin and others, *A Raisin in the Sun* was a "historical achievement" precisely because of its realism and contemporaneity, its truthful depiction of the sorts of lives lived by many ordinary African Americans in the late 1950s. In a sense, the play made history by accurately reflecting a historical and cultural reality previously ignored by dramatists.

THE GREAT MIGRATION

One factor that undoubtedly made the Younger family seem so realistic was the fact that their situation closely resembled that of the 6.5 million African Americans who moved from the rural South to the urban North between 1910 and 1970 as part of the Great Migration. Though these migrants settled in every northern city, the majority eventually made their homes in New York City and Chicago. By 1960, Chicago's black population had grown to 813,000—25 percent of the city's inhabitants.

Like Lena Younger and her husband, those migrant millions flew north on the wings of hope—hope for better jobs at higher wages and for greater safety and freedom than they enjoyed in the Jim Crow–era South. (By 1914, every southern state had passed "Jim Crow" laws mandating segregated railroad cars, waiting rooms, bathrooms, restaurants, theaters, recreation areas, and even hospitals.) Not coincidentally, migration increased when northern industries were expanding and when conditions in the South were particularly oppressive or violent. In the 1920s, when the Younger family would have arrived in Chicago, a government-sponsored report on race relations in that city pointed out that over 85 percent of the 2,881 lynchings that occurred in the United States between 1885 and 1918 occurred in southern states and "that numbers of migrants from towns where lynchings had occurred registered for jobs in Chicago very shortly after lynchings." The same report also concluded that southern blacks were drawn to the city for more than economic reasons. When recent immigrants interviewed for the report were asked, "What do you like about the North?" their responses were remarkably similar:

1. Freedom in voting and conditions of colored people here.
2. Freedom and chance to make a living; privileges.
3. Freedom and opportunity to acquire something.

• • •

10. Freedom of speech and action. Can live without fear. No Jim Crow.

Songs and poems of the 1920s, as well as the African American press, fueled such hopes and imbued them with religious significance. The Great Migration was cast as the "Flight out of Egypt"; migrants were encouraged to see themselves as "Bound for the Promised Land," "Going into Canaan."

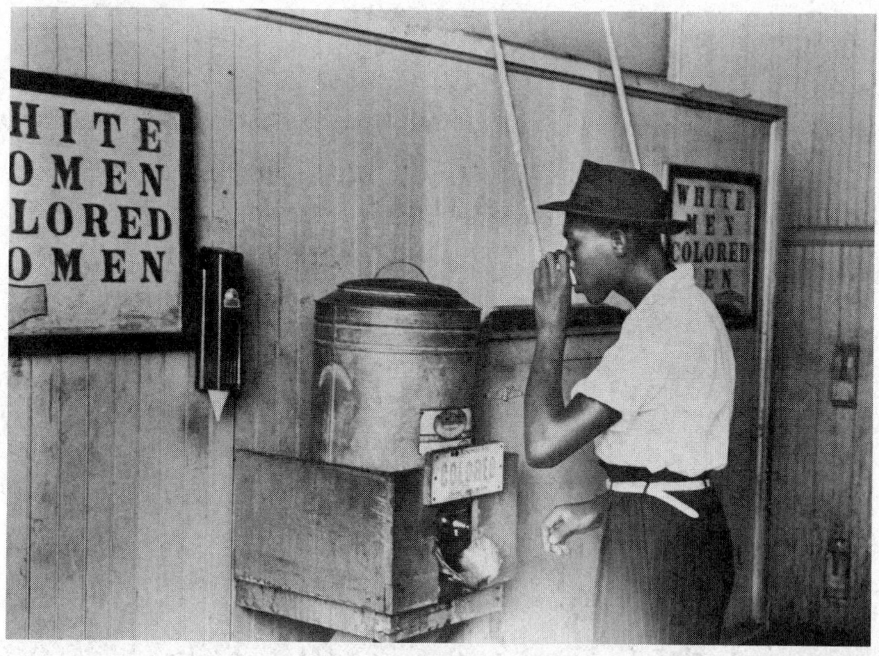

Segregated drinking fountain, Oklahoma City, 1939

LIFE IN THE "BLACK METROPOLIS"

In reality, the vast majority of blacks who came north found themselves not in Canaan, but in the all-black, inner-city enclaves—the so-called Smoketowns, Bronzevilles, and Black Belts—that had begun to develop in all of the North's major cities before the First World War. In Chicago, that "distinct Negro world" was the South Side, a strip of land extending south along State Street from the Loop (the city's central business district) and bounded by Lake Michigan (to the east), Chicago's famous stockyards (to the west), and white neighborhoods (to the south). By the 1940s, the South Side had become what it remains to this day—"the largest contiguous settlement of African-Americans" (in the words of journalist Nicholas Lemann).

On the one hand, this "Black Metropolis" might well have looked to newcomers very like the African American Promised Land, a city within a city in which "a black person could be somebody." By the 1940s, the South Side boasted bustling shopping districts; a spacious public park and lake-side beach; nationally known institutions such as the Regal Theater, the Savoy Ballroom, and the Hotel Grand; as well as countless movie houses and nightclubs featuring blues masters like Muddy Waters (1915–83), himself a migrant from the Mississippi Delta. It was also, as Lemann notes,

> home to the heavyweight boxing champion of the world (and the most famous black man in America), Joe Louis; the only black member of Congress, William Dawson; the most prominent black newspaper, the *Defender*; the largest black congregation, J. H. Jackson's Oliver Baptist Church; the greatest black singer, Mahalia Jackson; and a host of lesser-known prosperous people [. . .].

Regal Theater, Chicago, 1953

Undoubtedly, the presence of so many African American luminaries, as well as the sheer existence of such a large black community, fueled the pride and aspirations of ordinary people like the Youngers.

On the other hand, however, those "prosperous people" were few and far between. And what lay between them were the thousands who, like the Youngers, occupied lower rungs of the social ladder. For even if northern cities offered African Americans greater economic opportunities than they enjoyed in the South, they were still paid much lower wages than their white counterparts, barred entirely from many good jobs, fired first in bad economic times, and hired last in good ones. In 1950 (nine years before *A Raisin in the Sun*'s debut), the African American unemployment rate in Chicago was about three times that of white workers. Of those Chicagoans who were employed, 70 percent of black men (versus 36 percent of white men) and 75 percent of black women (versus 33 percent of white women) held unskilled jobs. At the same time, 22 percent of black men and almost 36 percent of black women worked, like the Youngers, in the lowest, "service" sector—as cooks, maids, janitors, and chauffeurs; only 14 percent of white men and 11 percent of white women did so.

Housing and Residential Segregation

If the Youngers' jobs make them representative, so, too, does the fact that they live in a small, "tired," roach-infested apartment. In the 1940s, population density on the South Side averaged about 90,000 people per square mile (as compared with 20,000 in white neighborhoods). Landlords often charged South Side residents much higher rents than were charged elsewhere, while doing little to maintain the apartments hastily carved out of existing buildings. In their 1960 study *Housing a Metropolis,* sociologists Beverly Duncan and Philip M. Hauser estimated that Chicago's nonwhite renters were more than twice as likely as whites to live in substandard housing. For home-buyers in the South Side, the situation was even worse. Duncan and Hauser estimated that, in the late 1940s, those buyers paid 28 to 51 percent more than they would have in white neighborhoods. And they often got less for their money: In 1960, nonwhite homeowners were, according to the same source, six times as likely as their white counterparts to live in substandard homes.

Though Chicago's Black Belt expanded southward and westward throughout the Great Migration, this expansion meant movement into formerly white residential areas—an extraordinarily difficult, slow, and often violent process. This was so, as sociologists St. Clair Drake and Horace R. Cayton explain in their classic *Black Metropolis* (1945), "primarily because of white people's attitudes toward having Negroes as neighbors. Because some white Chicagoans do not wish colored neighbors, formal and informal social controls are used to isolate the latter within congested all-Negro neighborhoods." The major "formal" means of maintaining residential segregation were restrictive covenants preventing property from being sold or rented to blacks. By 1930, about 75 percent of the city's residential property was bound by such agreements, while all agents who belonged to the real-estate trade association were bound by a code of ethics that forbade moving blacks into white areas. The Supreme Court declared such covenants legally unenforceable, though not themselves illegal, in 1948. But both before and after that time—in Chicago and every other northern U.S. city—violence was the chief "informal" means adopted by whites when restrictive covenants and codes failed. According to Drake and Cayton, almost five hundred attacks on black residents were reported in Chicago between 1945 and 1950, most involving arson. In 1956 and 1957 alone, 164 such racial "incidents" occurred.

It is here that Hansberry's personal experience intersects with the historical and cultural context about and in which she wrote, though her family was much more comfortably middle class than the fictional family she created. In 1938, when Hansberry was eight, her father, Carl—a prosperous real-estate broker and founder of one of Chicago's first black-owned banks—decided to test the legality of restrictive covenants by purchasing a house in an all-white neighborhood. When the local neighborhood association secured an injunction prohibiting him from occupying the property, Carl Hansberry, backed by the National Association for the Advancement of Colored People (NAACP), took the case all the way to the Supreme Court. Though he won the case (on a technicality) in 1940, his victory was a limited and costly one. As Lorraine Hansberry later recalled,

> That fight [. . .] required that our family occupy the disputed property in a hellishly hostile "white neighborhood" in which, literally, howling mobs surrounded our house. One of their missiles almost took [my] life. [. . .] My memories [. . .] include being spat at, cursed, and pummeled in the daily trek to and from school. And I also remember my desperate and courageous mother, patrolling our house all night with a loaded German luger, doggedly guarding her four children, while my father fought [. . .] in the Washington court.

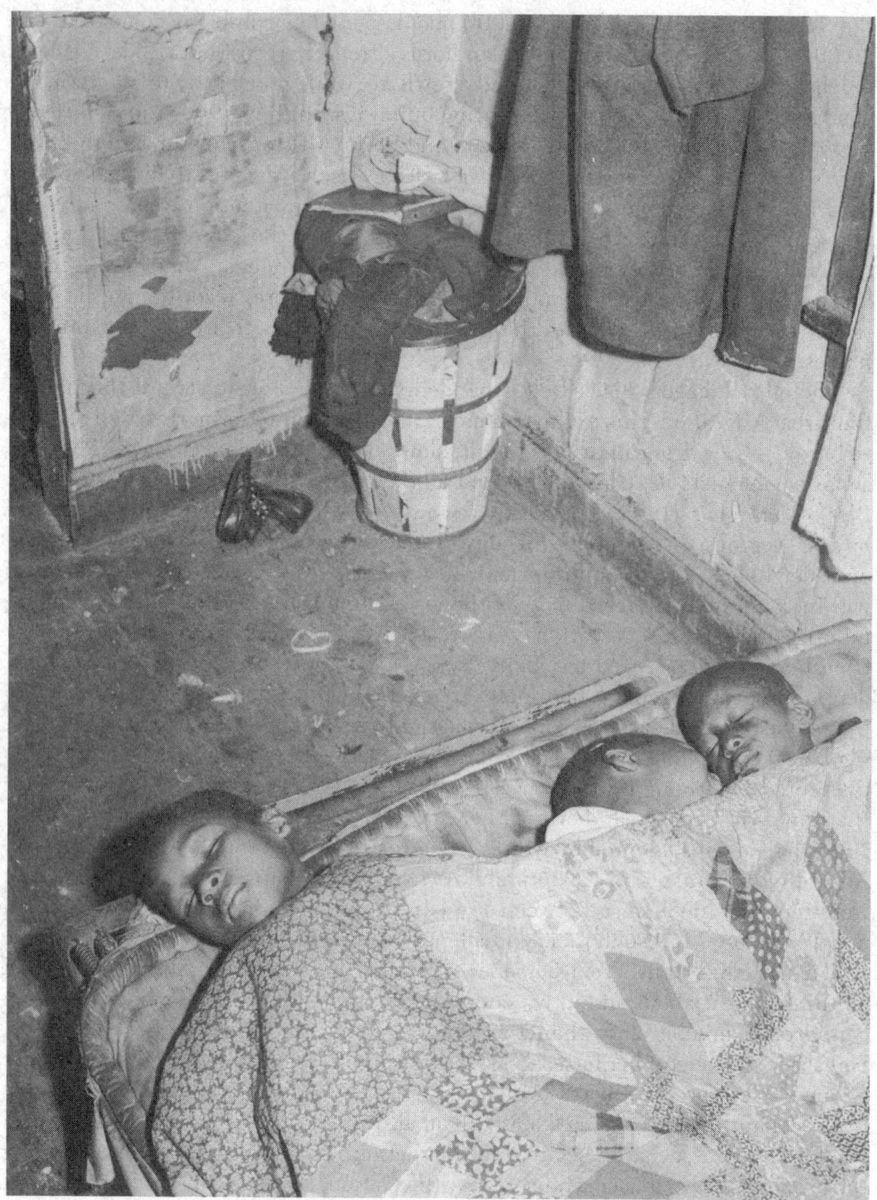

Crowded conditions in a Chicago tenement, 1941

> [. . .] The cost, in emotional turmoil, time, and money [. . .] led to my father's early death as a permanently embittered exile in a foreign country when he saw that after such sacrificial efforts the Negroes of Chicago were as ghetto-locked as ever [. . .].

(The disillusioned Carl Hansberry was arranging to move his family to Mexico when he died in 1946.) Among other things, Hansberry's account of her experience might give readers of *A Raisin in the Sun* a deeper appreciation of the play's complex denouement and of the fact that its plot is propelled by a much-loved, hardworking father's death.

THE CIVIL RIGHTS MOVEMENT

Hansberry's experiences remind us that the African American civil rights struggle was multifaceted and began well before the 1960s. Yet it was entering an entirely new phase in 1959. Just five years earlier, in 1954, the famous *Brown v. Board of Education* Supreme Court decision declared "separate but equal" education policies unconstitutional, initiating the long, often violent fight to integrate America's schools. One year later, in 1955, the Montgomery Bus Boycott began, eventually forcing full integration of public transportation and launching Martin Luther King, Jr. (1929–68) on his career as one of the nation's most famous and influential civil rights leaders. The modern civil rights movement had begun—one in which "gradualism" gave way to "direct action," and court battles to marches, sit-ins, and other forms of civil disobedience.

One factor propelling change was World War II (1939–45). James Baldwin was only one of many Americans to see that war as marking "a turning point in the Negro's relation to" his country because, as Baldwin wrote in *The Fire Next Time* (1963),

> a certain hope died, a certain respect for white Americans faded. One began to pity them, or to hate them. You must put yourself in the skin of a man who is wearing the uniform of his country, is a candidate for death in its defense, and who is called a

Dr. Martin Luther King, Jr., after being hit on a head by a rock at a housing discrimination protest in Chicago, 1966

"nigger" by his comrades-in-arms and his officers; who is almost always given the hardest, ugliest, most menial work to do; [. . .] who does not dance at the U.S.O. the night white soldiers dance there [. . .]; and who watches German prisoners of war being treated by Americans with more human dignity than he has ever received at their hands. And who, at the same time, as a human being, is far freer in a strange land than he has ever been at home [. . .]. You must consider what happens to this citizen, after all he has endured, when he returns home: search, in his shoes, for a job, for a place to live; ride, in his skin, on segregated buses; see, with his eyes, the signs saying "White" and "Colored" [. . .]; look into the eyes of his wife; look into the eyes of his son; listen, with his ears, to political speeches, North and South; imagine yourself being told to "wait."

Though the modern civil rights movement involved people of every age, it was in some ways, as Howard Zinn would argue in 1964, the first major social movement in U.S. history "led by youngsters." A political scientist and activist, Zinn was speaking specifically of the college students who, in 1960, began conducting sit-ins throughout the South and eventually formed the Student Non-Violent Coordinating Committee (SNCC). But Martin Luther King, Jr., was himself only twenty-six when he was chosen to lead the Montgomery boycott. In a sense, then, the modern civil rights movement was born out of the kinds of generational attitudes explored in *A Raisin in the Sun.* Hansberry, for example, described her father as "typical of a generation of Negroes who believed that the 'American way' could successfully be made to work to democratize the United States." But, she said, it was "Negroes my own age and younger" who were beginning to question the "American way" and to advocate a more aggressively confrontational stance, "say[ing] that we must now lie down in the streets, tie up traffic, do whatever we can—take to the hills with guns if necessary—and fight back."

Determined to act on their frustration in ways that their parents wouldn't or couldn't, thousands of young people—many the city-born children of the Great Migration—turned to activism in the 1950s and 1960s. Yet, through Walter's drinking and the crime at the heart of her play, Hansberry also subtly reminds us that there were other ways that frustration found expression. The very same impulses and emotions that inspired SNCC members to head south led many of their peers in a very different direction.

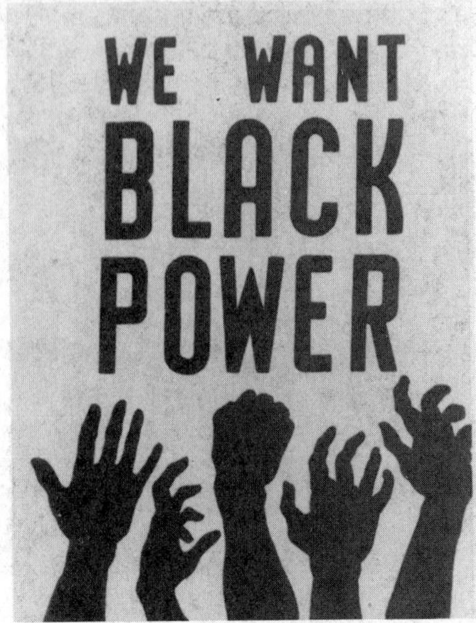

Poster printed and distributed by SNCC in the late 1960s

AFRICAN AMERICANS AND AFRICA

In *A Raisin in the Sun,* the differences between and within generations take a variety of shapes, but one such distinction whose meaning may be especially dependent on a knowledge of historical and cultural context involves the character Joseph Asagai. A Nigerian attending college in Chicago, Joseph plans to return home in order to help liberate his country from British colonial rule. Through him, Hansberry thus highlights parallels between the situation of blacks in the United States and in Africa, drawing on her audience's knowledge of contemporary events in Africa even as she suggests just how little real knowledge of Africa most Americans possess.

Historically speaking, Hansberry's (and Beneatha's) keen interest in both traditional African culture and events in contemporary Africa is no accident. As Earl Thorpe noted in 1959 (in an article excerpted below), various African American intellectuals and activists had worked to spread knowledge about Africa and to improve the situation of colonized Africans since at least the 1920s. But African American interest in Africa was becoming much more widespread and taking on a variety of unprecedented forms in the 1950s. Between the late 1950s and early 1970s more African Americans than ever before would, like Beneatha, seek to learn about, and embrace, their African cultural heritage, sometimes adopting African names, giving up hair straighteners in order to grow Afros, or wearing clothes modeled on African styles. Meanwhile, black activists drew inspiration from modern Africans' struggles to liberate their countries from colonial rule.

Between 1880 and 1912 all of Africa except Liberia and Ethiopia had come under the control of European powers. But in the 1950s, "the winds of change" suddenly began to blow hard across Africa, beginning in the north, where first Libya achieved independence (1951), and then Morocco, Sudan, and Tunisia (1956). In 1957 the process moved southward into sub-Saharan Africa when Britain's Gold Coast colony became independent Ghana. Thereafter, almost every year saw the birth of at least one new African nation. No wonder, then, that Africa was often in the news and on American minds in the 1950s and 1960s.

Developments in Africa stirred African American interest and pride for yet another reason. African independence was, in many cases, the result of hard-fought popular campaigns spearheaded by extraordinarily charismatic men very like Joseph Asagai, men educated partially in the West and quite familiar with its culture and ways, yet eager to liberate their people and to embrace and revitalize ancient African folkways. The first and most famous such leader to emerge on the world stage was Jomo Kenyatta (1893?–1978), whose career led him from an obscure village to the presidency of independent Kenya by way of the London School of Economics; a masterful book on the culture of his own people, the Kikuyu (*Facing Mount Kenya* [1938]), and a seven-year imprisonment for sedition against the British colonial state. At least in African American eyes, such leaders might very well seem like modern versions of the great warriors of African history and myth.

THE "AMERICANNESS" OF *A RAISIN IN THE SUN*

As *A Raisin in the Sun* reminds us, however, the differences between African Americans and Africans are just as significant as their historical and cultural ties. And for all its characters' interest in Africa, *A Raisin in the Sun* is a distinctly American play in terms of both content and style. Hansberry herself was well aware of the way it complemented and contrasted with canonical American masterpieces such as Arthur Miller's DEATH OF A SALESMAN. As she pointed out, "Walter Younger is an American more than he is anything else," and there is "a simple line of descent between" her Walter and Miller's Willy Loman—"the last great hero in American drama to also *accept* the values of his [American] culture."

• • •

Hansberry's play offers you the perfect opportunity to think further about how historical and cultural contexts shape literary texts and how those texts speak both to their historical moment and to ours. To help you make the most of that opportunity, the rest of this chapter contains the text of the play, a timeline, and contextual materials. Most of those materials focus on three interrelated, but distinct, topics. The first section documents the various challenges that confronted African Americans in Chicago and other northern cities throughout the Great Migration and especially in the late 1950s and early 1960s, focusing particularly on residential segregation as viewed from the perspective of both African Americans (in the excerpts from novelist Richard Wright's semiautobiographical TWELVE MILLION BLACK VOICES and a *New York Times* article by Gertrude Samuels) and their white counterparts (in Robert Gruenberg's article on the effort to integrate one Chicago housing project). The second section turns to the aims and aspirations of African Americans in the late 1950s and early 1960s, particularly the way they tended to be understood as distinctly American and/or middle class, while the third section instead considers African Americans' changing attitudes toward Africa and Africans. All these contextual materials aim to bring more vividly to life the world out of which *A Raisin in the Sun* sprang and the historically and culturally specific conditions and concerns it explores. But the chapter ends with an excerpt that we hope will inspire you to think and talk, too, about the play's relevance to our twenty-first-century world. That excerpt comes from CLYBOURNE PARK, a 2010 Pulitzer Prize–winning play that, by revisiting and updating settings, situations, and characters from Hansberry's play, artfully invites us to ponder how America has and hasn't changed since 1959.

LORRAINE HANSBERRY
A Raisin in the Sun

What happens to a dream deferred?

Does it dry up
Like a raisin in the sun?
Or fester like a sore—
And then run?
Does it stink like rotten meat?
Or crust and sugar over—
Like a syrupy sweet?
Maybe it just sags
Like a heavy load.

Or does it explode?

—LANGSTON HUGHES[1]

1. Hughes's poem, published in 1951, is titled "Harlem (A Dream Deferred)."

Ruby Dee as Ruth, Sidney Poitier as Walter Lee Younger, and Diana Sands as Beneatha in the original 1959 Broadway production of *A Raisin in the Sun*

CAST OF CHARACTERS

RUTH YOUNGER
TRAVIS YOUNGER
WALTER LEE YOUNGER (BROTHER)
BENEATHA YOUNGER
LENA YOUNGER (MAMA)
JOSEPH ASAGAI
GEORGE MURCHISON
KARL LINDNER
BOBO
MOVING MEN

The action of the play is set in Chicago's Southside, sometime between World War II and the present.

ACT I

Scene One

The Younger living room would be a comfortable and well-ordered room if it were not for a number of indestructible contradictions to this state of being. Its furnishings are typical and undistinguished and their primary feature now is that they have clearly had to accommodate the living of too many people for too many years—and they are tired. Still, we can see that at some time, a time probably no longer remembered by the family (except perhaps for MAMA*), the furnishings of this room were actually selected with care and love and even hope—and brought to this apartment and arranged with taste and pride.*

That was a long time ago. Now the once loved pattern of the couch upholstery has to fight to show itself from under acres of crocheted doilies and couch covers which have themselves finally come to be more important than the upholstery. And here a table or a chair has been moved to disguise the worn places in the carpet; but the carpet has fought back by showing its weariness, with depressing uniformity, elsewhere on its surface.

Weariness has, in fact, won in this room. Everything has been polished, washed, sat on, used, scrubbed too often. All pretenses but living itself have long since vanished from the very atmosphere of this room.

Moreover, a section of this room, for it is not really a room unto itself, though the landlord's lease would make it seem so, slopes backward to provide a small kitchen area, where the family prepares the meals that are eaten in the living room proper, which must also serve as dining room. The single window that has been provided for these "two" rooms is located in this kitchen area. The sole natural light the family may enjoy in the course of a day is only that which fights its way through this little window.

At left, a door leads to a bedroom which is shared by MAMA *and her daughter,* BENEATHA. *At right, opposite, is a second room (which in the beginning of the life of this apartment was probably a breakfast room) which serves as a bedroom for* WALTER *and his wife,* RUTH.

Time: Sometime between World War II and the present.

Place: Chicago's Southside.

At Rise: It is morning dark in the living room. TRAVIS *is asleep on the make-down bed at center. An alarm clock sounds from within the bedroom at right, and presently* RUTH *enters from that room and closes the door behind her. She crosses sleepily toward the window. As she passes her sleeping son she reaches down and shakes him a little. At the window she raises the shade and a dusky Southside morning light comes in feebly. She fills a pot with water and puts it on to boil. She calls to the boy, between yawns, in a slightly muffled voice.*

RUTH *is about thirty. We can see that she was a pretty girl, even exceptionally so, but now it is apparent that life has been little that she expected, and disappointment has already begun to hang in her face. In a few years, before thirty-five even, she will be known among her people as a "settled woman."*

She crosses to her son and gives him a good, final, rousing shake.

RUTH: Come on now, boy, it's seven thirty! [*Her son sits up at last, in a stupor of sleepiness.*] I say hurry up, Travis! You ain't the only person in the world got to use a bathroom! [*The child, a sturdy, handsome little boy of ten or eleven, drags himself out of the bed and almost blindly takes his towels and "today's clothes" from drawers and a closet and goes out to the bathroom, which is in an outside hall and which is shared by another family or families on the same floor.* RUTH *crosses to the bedroom door at right and opens it and calls in to her husband.*] Walter Lee! . . . It's after seven thirty! Lemme see you do some waking up in there now! [*She waits.*] You better get up from there, man! It's after seven thirty I tell you. [*She waits again.*] All right, you just go ahead and lay there and next thing you know Travis be finished and Mr. Johnson'll be in there and you'll be fussing and cussing round here like a mad man! And be late too! [*She waits, at the end of patience.*] Walter Lee—it's time for you to get up!

[*She waits another second and then starts to go into the bedroom, but is apparently satisfied that her husband has begun to get up. She stops, pulls the door to, and returns to the kitchen area. She wipes her face with a moist cloth and runs her fingers through her sleep-disheveled hair in a vain effort and ties an apron around her housecoat. The bedroom door at right opens and her husband stands in the doorway in his pajamas, which are rumpled and mismated. He is a lean, intense young man in his middle thirties, inclined to quick nervous movements and erratic speech habits—and always in his voice there is a quality of indictment.*]

WALTER: Is he out yet?

RUTH: What you mean *out*? He ain't hardly got in there good yet.

WALTER: [*Wandering in, still more oriented to sleep than to a new day.*] Well, what was you doing all that yelling for if I can't even get in there yet? [*Stopping and thinking.*] Check coming today?

RUTH: They *said* Saturday and this is just Friday and I hopes to God you ain't going to get up here first thing this morning and start talking to me 'bout no money—'cause I 'bout don't want to hear it.

WALTER: Something the matter with you this morning?

RUTH: No—I'm just sleepy as the devil. What kind of eggs you want?

WALTER: Not scrambled. [RUTH *starts to scramble eggs.*] Paper come? [RUTH *points impatiently to the rolled up* Tribune *on the table, and he gets it and spreads it out and vaguely reads the front page.*] Set off another bomb yesterday.

RUTH: [*Maximum indifference.*] Did they?

WALTER: [*Looking up.*] What's the matter with you?

RUTH: Ain't nothing the matter with me. And don't keep asking me that this morning.

WALTER: Ain't nobody bothering you. [*Reading the news of the day absently again.*] Say Colonel McCormick[2] is sick.

RUTH: [*Affecting tea-party interest.*] Is he now? Poor thing.

WALTER: [*Sighing and looking at his watch.*] Oh, me. [*He waits.*] Now what is that boy doing in that bathroom all this time? He just going to have to start getting up earlier. I can't be late to work on account of him fooling around in there.

RUTH: [*Turning on him.*] Oh, no he ain't going to be getting up no earlier no such thing! It ain't his fault that he can't get to bed no earlier nights 'cause he got a bunch of crazy good-for-nothing clowns sitting up running their mouths in what is supposed to be his bedroom after ten o'clock at night . . .

2. Robert Rutherford McCormick (1880–1955), owner-publisher of the *Chicago Tribune*.

WALTER: That's what you mad about, ain't it? The things I want to talk about with my friends just couldn't be important in your mind, could they?

[*He rises and finds a cigarette in her handbag on the table and crosses to the little window and looks out, smoking and deeply enjoying this first one.*]

RUTH: [*Almost matter of factly, a complaint too automatic to deserve emphasis.*] Why you always got to smoke before you eat in the morning?

WALTER: [*At the window.*] Just look at 'em down there . . . Running and racing to work . . . [*He turns and faces his wife and watches her a moment at the stove, and then, suddenly.*] You look young this morning, baby.

RUTH: [*Indifferently.*] Yeah?

WALTER: Just for a second—stirring them eggs. It's gone now—just for a second it was—you looked real young again. [*Then, drily.*] It's gone now—you look like yourself again.

RUTH: Man, if you don't shut up and leave me alone.

WALTER: [*Looking out to the street again.*] First thing a man ought to learn in life is not to make love to no colored woman first thing in the morning. You all some evil people at eight o'clock in the morning.

[TRAVIS *appears in the hall doorway, almost fully dressed and quite wide awake now, his towels and pajamas across his shoulders. He opens the door and signals for his father to make the bathroom in a hurry.*]

TRAVIS: [*Watching the bathroom.*] Daddy, come on!

[WALTER *gets his bathroom utensils and flies out to the bathroom.*]

RUTH: Sit down and have your breakfast, Travis.

TRAVIS: Mama, this is Friday. [*Gleefully.*] Check coming tomorrow, huh?

RUTH: You get your mind off money and eat your breakfast.

TRAVIS: [*Eating.*] This is the morning we supposed to bring the fifty cents to school.

RUTH: Well, I ain't got no fifty cents this morning.

TRAVIS: Teacher say we have to.

RUTH: I don't care what teacher say. I ain't got it. Eat your breakfast, Travis.

TRAVIS: I *am* eating.

RUTH: Hush up now and just eat!

[*The boy gives her an exasperated look for her lack of understanding, and eats grudgingly.*]

TRAVIS: You think Grandmama would have it?

RUTH: No! And I want you to stop asking your grandmother for money, you hear me?

TRAVIS: [*Outraged.*] Gaaaleee! I don't ask her, she just gimme it sometimes!

RUTH: Travis Willard Younger—I got too much on me this morning to be—

TRAVIS: Maybe Daddy—

RUTH: *Travis!*

[*The boy hushes abruptly. They are both quiet and tense for several seconds.*]

TRAVIS: [*Presently.*] Could I maybe go carry some groceries in front of the supermarket for a little while after school then?

RUTH: Just hush, I said. [TRAVIS *jabs his spoon into his cereal bowl viciously, and rests his head in anger upon his fists.*] If you through eating, you can get over there and make up your bed.

[*The boy obeys stiffly and crosses the room, almost mechanically, to the bed and more or less carefully folds the covering. He carries the bedding into his mother's room and returns with his books and cap.*]

TRAVIS: [*Sulking and standing apart from her unnaturally.*] I'm gone.

RUTH: [*Looking up from the stove to inspect him automatically.*] Come here. [*He crosses to her and she studies his head.*] If you don't take this comb and fix this here head, you better! [TRAVIS *puts down his books with a great sigh of oppression, and crosses to the mirror. His mother mutters under her breath about his "slubbornness."*] 'Bout to march out of here with that head looking just like chickens slept in it! I just don't know where you get your slubborn ways . . . And get your jacket, too. Looks chilly out this morning.

TRAVIS: [*With conspicuously brushed hair and jacket.*] I'm gone.

RUTH: Get carfare and milk money—[*Waving one finger.*]—and not a single penny for no caps, you hear me?

TRAVIS: [*With sullen politeness.*] Yes'm.

[*He turns in outrage to leave. His mother watches after him as in his frustration he approaches the door almost comically. When she speaks to him, her voice has become a very gentle tease.*]

RUTH: [*Mocking; as she thinks he would say it.*] Oh, Mama makes me so mad sometimes, I don't know what to do! [*She waits and continues to his back as he stands stock-still in front of the door.*] I wouldn't kiss that woman good-bye for nothing in this world this morning! [*The boy finally turns around and rolls his eyes at her, knowing the mood has changed and he is vindicated; he does not, however, move toward her yet.*] Not for nothing in this world! [*She finally laughs aloud at him and holds out her arms to him and we see that it is a way between them, very old and practiced. He crosses to her and allows her to embrace him warmly but keeps his face fixed with masculine rigidity. She holds him back from her presently and looks at him and runs her fingers over the features of his face. With utter gentleness—*] Now—whose little old angry man are you?

TRAVIS: [*The masculinity and gruffness start to fade at last.*] Aw gaalee—Mama . . .

RUTH: [*Mimicking.*] Aw—gaaaaalleeeee, Mama! [*She pushes him, with rough playfulness and finality, toward the door.*] Get on out of here or you going to be late.

TRAVIS: [*In the face of love, new aggressiveness.*] Mama, could I *please* go carry groceries?

RUTH: Honey, it's starting to get so cold evenings.

WALTER: [*Coming in from the bathroom and drawing a make-believe gun from a make-believe holster and shooting at his son.*] What is it he wants to do?

RUTH: Go carry groceries after school at the supermarket.

WALTER: Well, let him go . . .

TRAVIS: [*Quickly, to the ally.*] I *have* to—she won't gimme the fifty cents . . .
WALTER: [*To his wife only.*] Why not?
RUTH: [*Simply, and with flavor.*] 'Cause we don't have it.
WALTER: [*To* RUTH *only.*] What you tell the boy things like that for? [*Reaching down into his pants with a rather important gesture.*] Here, son—

[*He hands the boy the coin, but his eyes are directed to his wife's.* TRAVIS *takes the money happily.*]

TRAVIS: Thanks, Daddy.

[*He starts out.* RUTH *watches both of them with murder in her eyes.* WALTER *stands and stares back at her with defiance, and suddenly reaches into his pocket again on an afterthought.*]

WALTER: [*Without even looking at his son, still staring hard at his wife.*] In fact, here's another fifty cents . . . Buy yourself some fruit today—or take a taxi-cab to school or something!
TRAVIS: Whoopee—

[*He leaps up and clasps his father around the middle with his legs, and they face each other in mutual appreciation; slowly* WALTER LEE *peeks around the boy to catch the violent rays from his wife's eyes and draws his head back as if shot.*]

WALTER: You better get down now—and get to school, man.
TRAVIS: [*At the door.*] O.K. Good-bye.

[*He exits.*]

WALTER: [*After him, pointing with pride.*] That's *my* boy. [*She looks at him in disgust and turns back to her work.*] You know what I was thinking 'bout in the bathroom this morning?
RUTH: No.
WALTER: How come you always try to be so pleasant!
RUTH: What is there to be pleasant 'bout!
WALTER: You want to know what I was thinking 'bout in the bathroom or not!
RUTH: I know what you thinking 'bout.
WALTER: [*Ignoring her.*] 'Bout what me and Willy Harris was talking about last night.
RUTH: [*Immediately—a refrain.*] Willy Harris is a good-for-nothing loud mouth.
WALTER: Anybody who talks to me has got to be a good-for-nothing loud mouth, ain't he? And what you know about who is just a good-for-nothing loud mouth? Charlie Atkins was just a "good-for-nothing loud mouth" too, wasn't he! When he wanted me to go in the dry-cleaning business with him. And now—he's grossing a hundred thousand a year. A hundred thousand dollars a year! You still call *him* a loud mouth!
RUTH: [*Bitterly.*] Oh, Walter Lee . . .

[*She folds her head on her arms over the table.*]

WALTER: [*Rising and coming to her and standing over her.*] You tired, ain't you? Tired of everything. Me, the boy, the way we live—this beat-up hole—everything.

Ain't you? [*She doesn't look up, doesn't answer.*] So tired—moaning and groaning all the time, but you wouldn't do nothing to help, would you? You couldn't be on my side that long for nothing, could you?

RUTH: Walter, please leave me alone.

WALTER: A man needs for a woman to back him up . . .

RUTH: Walter—

WALTER: Mama would listen to you. You know she listen to you more than she do me and Bennie. She think more of you. All you have to do is just sit down with her when you drinking your coffee one morning and talking 'bout things like you do and— [*He sits down beside her and demonstrates graphically what he thinks her methods and tone should be.*] —you just sip your coffee, see, and say easy like that you been thinking 'bout that deal Walter Lee is so interested in, 'bout the store and all, and sip some more coffee, like what you saying ain't really that important to you—And the next thing you know, she be listening good and asking you questions and when I come home—I can tell her the details. This ain't no fly-by-night proposition, baby. I mean we figured it out, me and Willy and Bobo.

RUTH: [*With a frown.*] Bobo?

WALTER: Yeah. You see, this little liquor store we got in mind cost seventy-five thousand and we figured the initial investment on the place be 'bout thirty thousand, see. That be ten thousand each. Course, there's a couple of hundred you got to pay so's you don't spend your life just waiting for them clowns to let your license get approved—

RUTH: You mean graft?

WALTER: [*Frowning impatiently.*] Don't call it that. See there, that just goes to show you what women understand about the world. Baby, don't *nothing* happen for you in this world 'less you pay *somebody* off!

RUTH: Walter, leave me alone! [*She raises her head and stares at him vigorously—then says, more quietly.*] Eat your eggs, they gonna be cold.

WALTER: [*Straightening up from her and looking off.*] That's it. There you are. Man say to his woman: I got me a dream. His woman say: Eat your eggs. [*Sadly, but gaining in power.*] Man say: I got to take hold of this here world, baby! And a woman will say: Eat your eggs and go to work. [*Passionately now.*] Man say: I got to change my life, I'm choking to death, baby! And his woman say— [*In utter anguish as he brings his fists down on his thighs.*] —Your eggs is getting cold!

RUTH: [*Softly.*] Walter, that ain't none of our money.

WALTER: [*Not listening at all or even looking at her.*] This morning, I was lookin' in the mirror and thinking about it . . . I'm thirty-five years old; I been married eleven years and I got a boy who sleeps in the living room— [*Very, very quietly.*] —and all I got to give him is stories about how rich white people live . . .

RUTH: Eat your eggs, Walter.

WALTER: *Damn my eggs . . . damn all the eggs that ever was!*

RUTH: Then go to work.

WALTER: [*Looking up at her.*] See—I'm trying to talk to you 'bout myself— [*Shaking his head with the repetition.*] —and all you can say is eat them eggs and go to work.

RUTH: [*Wearily.*] Honey, you never say nothing new. I listen to you every day, every night and every morning, and you never say nothing new. [*Shrugging.*] So you would rather *be* Mr. Arnold than be his chauffeur. So—I would *rather* be living in Buckingham Palace.[3]

WALTER: That is just what is wrong with the colored woman in this world . . . Don't understand about building their men up and making 'em feel like they somebody. Like they can do something.

RUTH: [*Drily, but to hurt.*] There *are* colored men who do things.

WALTER: No thanks to the colored woman.

RUTH: Well, being a colored woman, I guess I can't help myself none.

[*She rises and gets the ironing board and sets it up and attacks a huge pile of rough-dried clothes, sprinkling them in preparation for the ironing and then rolling them into tight fat balls.*]

WALTER: [*Mumbling.*] We one group of men tied to a race of women with small minds.

[*His sister* BENEATHA *enters. She is about twenty, as slim and intense as her brother. She is not as pretty as her sister-in-law, but her lean, almost intellectual face has a handsomeness of its own. She wears a bright-red flannel nightie, and her thick hair stands wildly about her head. Her speech is a mixture of many things; it is different from the rest of the family's insofar as education has permeated her sense of English—and perhaps the Midwest rather than the South has finally—at last—won out in her inflection; but not altogether, because over all of it is a soft slurring and transformed use of vowels which is the decided influence of the Southside. She passes through the room without looking at either* RUTH *or* WALTER *and goes to the outside door and looks, a little blindly, out to the bathroom. She sees that it has been lost to the Johnsons. She closes the door with a sleepy vengeance and crosses to the table and sits down a little defeated.*]

BENEATHA: I am going to start timing those people.

WALTER: You should get up earlier.

BENEATHA: [*Her face in her hands. She is still fighting the urge to go back to bed.*] Really—would you suggest dawn? Where's the paper?

WALTER: [*Pushing the paper across the table to her as he studies her almost clinically, as though he has never seen her before.*] You a horrible-looking chick at this hour.

BENEATHA: [*Drily.*] Good morning, everybody.

WALTER: [*Senselessly.*] How is school coming?

BENEATHA: [*In the same spirit.*] Lovely. Lovely. And you know, biology is the greatest. [*Looking up at him.*] I dissected something that looked just like you yesterday.

WALTER: I just wondered if you've made up your mind and everything.

BENEATHA: [*Gaining in sharpness and impatience.*] And what did I answer yesterday morning—and the day before that?

3. London residence of the queen of the United Kingdom of Great Britain and Northern Ireland.

RUTH: [*From the ironing board, like someone disinterested and old.*] Don't be so nasty, Bennie.

BENEATHA: [*Still to her brother.*] And the day before that and the day before that!

WALTER: [*Defensively.*] I'm interested in you. Something wrong with that? Ain't many girls who decide—

WALTER AND BENEATHA: [*In unison.*]—"to be a doctor."

[*Silence.*]

WALTER: Have we figured out yet just exactly how much medical school is going to cost?

RUTH: Walter Lee, why don't you leave that girl alone and get out of here to work?

BENEATHA: [*Exits to the bathroom and bangs on the door.*] Come on out of there, please!

[*She comes back into the room.*]

WALTER: [*Looking at his sister intently.*] You know the check is coming tomorrow.

BENEATHA: [*Turning on him with a sharpness all her own.*] That money belongs to Mama, Walter, and it's for her to decide how she wants to use it. I don't care if she wants to buy a house or a rocket ship or just nail it up somewhere and look at it. It's hers. Not ours—*hers.*

WALTER: [*Bitterly.*] Now ain't that fine! You just got your mother's interest at heart, ain't you, girl? You such a nice girl—but if Mama got that money she can always take a few thousand and help you through school too—can't she?

BENEATHA: I have never asked anyone around here to do anything for me.

WALTER: No! And the line between asking and just accepting when the time comes is big and wide—ain't it!

BENEATHA: [*With fury.*] What do you want from me, Brother—that I quit school or just drop dead, which!

WALTER: I don't want nothing but for you to stop acting holy 'round here. Me and Ruth done made some sacrifices for you—why can't you do something for the family?

RUTH: Walter, don't be dragging me in it.

WALTER: You are in it—Don't you get up and go work in somebody's kitchen for the last three years to help put clothes on her back?

RUTH: Oh, Walter—that's not fair . . .

WALTER: It ain't that nobody expects you to get on your knees and say thank you, Brother; thank you, Ruth; thank you, Mama—and thank you, Travis, for wearing the same pair of shoes for two semesters—

BENEATHA: [*Dropping to her knees.*] Well—I *do*—all right?—thank everybody . . . and forgive me for ever wanting to be anything at all . . . forgive me, forgive me!

RUTH: Please stop it! Your mama'll hear you.

WALTER: Who the hell told you you had to be a doctor? If you so crazy 'bout messing 'round with sick people—then go be a nurse like other women—or just get married and be quiet . . .

BENEATHA: Well—you finally got it said . . . it took you three years but you finally got it said. Walter, give up; leave me alone—it's Mama's money.

WALTER: *He was my father, too!*

BENEATHA: So what? He was mine, too—and Travis' grandfather—but the insurance money belongs to Mama. Picking on me is not going to make her give it to you to invest in any liquor stores— [*Underbreath, dropping into a chair.*] —and I for one say, God bless Mama for that!

WALTER: [*To* RUTH.] See—did you hear? Did you hear!

RUTH: Honey, please go to work.

WALTER: Nobody in this house is ever going to understand me.

BENEATHA: Because you're a nut.

WALTER: Who's a nut?

BENEATHA: You—you are a nut. Thee is mad, boy.

WALTER: [*Looking at his wife and his sister from the door, very sadly.*] The world's most backward race of people, and that's a fact.

BENEATHA: [*Turning slowly in her chair.*] And then there are all those prophets who would lead us out of the wilderness—. [WALTER *slams out of the house.*] —into the swamps!

RUTH: Bennie, why you always gotta be pickin' on your brother? Can't you be a little sweeter sometimes? [*Door opens.* WALTER *walks in.*]

WALTER: [*To* RUTH.] I need some money for carfare.

RUTH: [*Looks at him, then warms; teasing, but tenderly.*] Fifty cents? [*She goes to her bag and gets money.*] Here, take a taxi.

[WALTER *exits.* MAMA *enters. She is a woman in her early sixties, full-bodied and strong. She is one of those women of a certain grace and beauty who wear it so unobtrusively that it takes a while to notice. Her dark-brown face is surrounded by the total whiteness of her hair, and, being a woman who has adjusted to many things in life and overcome many more, her face is full of strength. She has, we can see, wit and faith of a kind that keep her eyes lit and full of interest and expectancy. She is, in a word, a beautiful woman. Her bearing is perhaps most like the noble bearing of the women of the Hereros of Southwest Africa—rather as if she imagines that as she walks she still bears a basket or a vessel upon her head. Her speech, on the other hand, is as careless as her carriage is precise—she is inclined to slur everything—but her voice is perhaps not so much quiet as simply soft.*]

MAMA: Who that 'round here slamming doors at this hour?

[*She crosses through the room, goes to the window, opens it, and brings in a feeble little plant growing doggedly in a small pot on the window sill. She feels the dirt and puts it back out.*]

RUTH: That was Walter Lee. He and Bennie was at it again.

MAMA: My children and they tempers. Lord, if this little old plant don't get more sun than it's been getting it ain't never going to see spring again. [*She turns from the window.*] What's the matter with you this morning, Ruth? You looks right peaked. You aiming to iron all them things? Leave some for me. I'll get to 'em this afternoon. Bennie honey, it's too drafty for you to be sitting 'round half dressed. Where's your robe?

BENEATHA: In the cleaners.

MAMA: Well, go get mine and put it on.

BENEATHA: I'm not cold, Mama, honest.

MAMA: I know—but you so thin . . .

BENEATHA: [*Irritably.*] Mama, I'm not cold.

MAMA: [*Seeing the make-down bed as* TRAVIS *has left it.*] Lord have mercy, look at that poor bed. Bless his heart—he tries, don't he?

[*She moves to the bed* TRAVIS *has sloppily made up.*]

RUTH: No—he don't half try at all 'cause he knows you going to come along behind him and fix everything. That's just how come he don't know how to do nothing right now—you done spoiled that boy so.

MAMA: Well—he's a little boy. Ain't supposed to know 'bout housekeeping. My baby, that's what he is. What you fix for his breakfast this morning?

RUTH: [*Angrily.*] I feed my son, Lena!

MAMA: I ain't meddling— [*Underbreath; busy-bodyish.*] I just noticed all last week he had cold cereal, and when it starts getting this chilly in the fall a child ought to have some hot grits or something when he goes out in the cold—

RUTH: [*Furious.*] I gave him hot oats—is that all right!

MAMA: I ain't meddling. [*Pause.*] Put a lot of nice butter on it? [RUTH *shoots her an angry look and does not reply.*] He likes lots of butter.

RUTH: [*Exasperated.*] Lena—

MAMA: [*To* BENEATHA. MAMA *is inclined to wander conversationally sometimes.*] What was you and your brother fussing 'bout this morning?

BENEATHA: It's not important, Mama.

[*She gets up and goes to look out at the bathroom, which is apparently free, and she picks up her towels and rushes out.*]

MAMA: What was they fighting about?

RUTH: Now you know as well as I do.

MAMA: [*Shaking her head.*] Brother still worrying hisself sick about that money?

RUTH: You know he is.

MAMA: You had breakfast?

RUTH: Some coffee.

MAMA: Girl, you better start eating and looking after yourself better. You almost thin as Travis.

RUTH: Lena—

MAMA: Un-hunh?

RUTH: What are you going to do with it?

MAMA: Now don't you start, child. It's too early in the morning to be talking about money. It ain't Christian.

RUTH: It's just that he got his heart set on that store—

MAMA: You mean that liquor store that Willy Harris want him to invest in?

RUTH: Yes—

MAMA: We ain't no business people, Ruth. We just plain working folks.

RUTH: Ain't nobody business people till they go into business. Walter Lee say colored people ain't never going to start getting ahead till they start gambling on some different kinds of things in the world—investments and things.

MAMA: What done got into you, girl? Walter Lee done finally sold you on investing.

RUTH: No. Mama, something is happening between Walter and me. I don't know what it is—but he needs something—something I can't give him anymore. He needs this chance, Lena.

MAMA: [*Frowning deeply.*] But liquor, honey—

RUTH: Well—like Walter say—I spec people going to always be drinking themselves some liquor.

MAMA: Well—whether they drinks it or not ain't none of my business. But whether I go into business selling it to 'em *is,* and I don't want that on my ledger this late in life. [*Stopping suddenly and studying her daughter-in-law.*] Ruth Younger, what's the matter with you today? You look like you could fall over right there.

RUTH: I'm tired.

MAMA: Then you better stay home from work today.

RUTH: I can't stay home. She'd be calling up the agency and screaming at them, "My girl didn't come in today—send me somebody! My girl didn't come in!" Oh, she just have a fit . . .

MAMA: Well, let her have it. I'll just call her up and say you got the flu—

RUTH: [*Laughing.*] Why the flu?

MAMA: 'Cause it sounds respectable to 'em. Something white people get, too. They know 'bout the flu. Otherwise they think you been cut up or something when you tell 'em you sick.

RUTH: I got to go in. We need the money.

MAMA: Somebody would of thought my children done all but starved to death the way they talk about money here late. Child, we got a great big old check coming tomorrow.

RUTH: [*Sincerely, but also self-righteously.*] Now that's your money. It ain't got nothing to do with me. We all feel like that—Walter and Bennie and me—even Travis.

MAMA: [*Thoughtfully, and suddenly very far away.*] Ten thousand dollars—

RUTH: Sure is wonderful.

MAMA: Ten thousand dollars.

RUTH: You know what you should do, Miss Lena? You should take yourself a trip somewhere. To Europe or South America or someplace—

MAMA: [*Throwing up her hands at the thought.*] Oh, child!

RUTH: I'm serious. Just pack up and leave! Go on away and enjoy yourself some. Forget about the family and have yourself a ball for once in your life—

MAMA: [*Drily.*] You sound like I'm just about ready to die. Who'd go with me? What I look like wandering 'round Europe by myself?

RUTH: Shoot—these here rich white women do it all the time. They don't think nothing of packing up they suitcases and piling on one of them big steamships and—swoosh!—they gone, child.

MAMA: Something always told me I wasn't no rich white woman.

RUTH: Well—what are you going to do with it then?

MAMA: I ain't rightly decided. [*Thinking. She speaks now with emphasis.*] Some of it got to be put away for Beneatha and her schoolin'—and ain't nothing going to touch that part of it. Nothing. [*She waits several seconds, trying to make up her mind about something, and looks at* RUTH *a little tentatively before going on.*] Been thinking that we maybe could meet the notes on a little old two-story somewhere, with a yard where Travis could play in the summertime, if we use part of the insurance for a down payment and everybody kind of pitch in. I could maybe take on a little day work again, few days a week—

RUTH: [*Studying her mother-in-law furtively and concentrating on her ironing, anxious to encourage without seeming to.*] Well, Lord knows, we've put enough rent into this here rat trap to pay for four houses by now . . .

MAMA: [*Looking up at the words "rat trap" and then looking around and leaning back and sighing—in a suddenly reflective mood—*] "Rat trap"—yes, that's all it is. [*Smiling.*] I remember just as well the day me and Big Walter moved in here. Hadn't been married but two weeks and wasn't planning on living here no more than a year. [*She shakes her head at the dissolved dream.*] We was going to set away, little by little, don't you know, and buy a little place out in Morgan Park. We had even picked out the house. [*Chuckling a little.*] Looks right dumpy today. But Lord, child, you should know all the dreams I had 'bout buying that house and fixing it up and making me a little garden in the back— [*She waits and stops smiling.*] And didn't none of it happen.

[*Dropping her hands in a futile gesture.*]

RUTH: [*Keeps her head down, ironing.*] Yes, life can be a barrel of disappointments, sometimes.

MAMA: Honey, Big Walter would come in here some nights back then and slump down on that couch there and just look at the rug, and look at me and look at the rug and then back at me—and I'd know he was down then . . . really down. [*After a second very long and thoughtful pause; she is seeing back to times that only she can see.*] And then, Lord, when I lost that baby—little Claude—I almost thought I was going to lose Big Walter too. Oh, that man grieved hisself! He was one man to love his children.

RUTH: Ain't nothin' can tear at you like losin' your baby.

MAMA: I guess that's how come that man finally worked hisself to death like he done. Like he was fighting his own war with this here world that took his baby from him.

RUTH: He sure was a fine man, all right. I always liked Mr. Younger.

MAMA: Crazy 'bout his children! God knows there was plenty wrong with Walter Younger—hard-headed, mean, kind of wild with women—plenty wrong with him. But he sure loved his children. Always wanted them to have something—be something. That's where Brother gets all these notions, I reckon. Big Walter used to say, he'd get right wet in the eyes sometimes, lean his head back with the water standing in his eyes and say, "Seem like God didn't see fit to give the black man nothing but dreams—but He did give us children to make them dreams seem worthwhile." [*She smiles.*] He could talk like that, don't you know.

RUTH: Yes, he sure could. He was a good man, Mr. Younger.

MAMA: Yes, a fine man—just couldn't never catch up with his dreams, that's all.

[BENEATHA *comes in, brushing her hair and looking up to the ceiling, where the sound of a vacuum cleaner has started up.*]

BENEATHA: What could be so dirty on that woman's rugs that she has to vacuum them every single day?

RUTH: I wish certain young women 'round here who I could name would take inspiration about certain rugs in a certain apartment I could also mention.

BENEATHA: [*Shrugging.*] How much cleaning can a house need, for Christ's sakes.

MAMA: [*Not liking the Lord's name used thus.*] Bennie!

RUTH: Just listen to her—just listen!

BENEATHA: Oh, God!

MAMA: If you use the Lord's name just one more time—

BENEATHA: [*A bit of a whine.*] Oh, Mama—

RUTH: Fresh—just fresh as salt, this girl!

BENEATHA: [*Drily.*] Well—if the salt loses its savor[4]—

MAMA: Now that will do. I just ain't going to have you 'round here reciting the scriptures in vain—you hear me?

BENEATHA: How did I manage to get on everybody's wrong side by just walking into a room?

RUTH: If you weren't so fresh—

BENEATHA: Ruth, I'm twenty years old.

MAMA: What time you be home from school today?

BENEATHA: Kind of late. [*With enthusiasm.*] Madeline is going to start my guitar lessons today.

[MAMA *and* RUTH *look up with the same expression.*]

MAMA: Your *what* kind of lessons?

BENEATHA: Guitar.

RUTH: Oh, Father!

MAMA: How come you done taken it in your mind to learn to play the guitar?

BENEATHA: I just want to, that's all.

MAMA: [*Smiling.*] Lord, child, don't you know what to do with yourself ? How long it going to be before you get tired of this now—like you got tired of that little play-acting group you joined last year? [*Looking at* RUTH.] And what was it the year before that?

RUTH: The horseback-riding club for which she bought that fifty-five-dollar riding habit that's been hanging in the closet ever since!

MAMA: [*To* BENEATHA.] Why you got to flit so from one thing to another, baby?

BENEATHA: [*Sharply.*] I just want to learn to play the guitar. Is there anything wrong with that?

MAMA: Ain't nobody trying to stop you. I just wonders sometimes why you has to flit so from one thing to another all the time. You ain't never done nothing with all that camera equipment you brought home—

BENEATHA: I don't flit! I—I experiment with different forms of expression—

RUTH: Like riding a horse?

BENEATHA: —People have to express themselves one way or another.

MAMA: What is it you want to express?

4. See Matthew 5.13: "You are the salt of the earth. But if the salt loses its taste, with what can it be seasoned? It is no longer good for anything but to be thrown out and trampled underfoot."

BENEATHA: [*Angrily.*] Me! [MAMA *and* RUTH *look at each other and burst into raucous laughter.*] Don't worry—I don't expect you to understand.

MAMA: [*To change the subject.*] Who you going out with tomorrow night?

BENEATHA: [*With displeasure.*] George Murchison again.

MAMA: [*Pleased.*] Oh—you getting a little sweet on him?

RUTH: You ask me, this child ain't sweet on nobody but herself— [*Underbreath.*] Express herself!

[*They laugh.*]

BENEATHA: Oh—I like George all right, Mama. I mean I like him enough to go out with him and stuff, but—

RUTH: [*For devilment.*] What does *and stuff* mean?

BENEATHA: Mind your own business.

MAMA: Stop picking at her now, Ruth. [*A thoughtful pause, and then a suspicious sudden look at her daughter as she turns in her chair for emphasis.*] What *does* it mean?

BENEATHA: [*Wearily.*] Oh, I just mean I couldn't ever really be serious about George. He's—he's so shallow.

RUTH: Shallow—what do you mean he's shallow? He's *rich*!

MAMA: Hush, Ruth.

BENEATHA: I know he's rich. He knows he's rich, too.

RUTH: Well—what other qualities a man got to have to satisfy you, little girl?

BENEATHA: You wouldn't even begin to understand. Anybody who married Walter could not possibly understand.

MAMA: [*Outraged.*] What kind of way is that to talk about your brother?

BENEATHA: Brother is a flip—let's face it.

MAMA: [*To* RUTH, *helplessly.*] What's a flip?

RUTH: [*Glad to add kindling.*] She's saying he's crazy.

BENEATHA: Not crazy. Brother isn't really crazy yet—he—he's an elaborate neurotic.

MAMA: Hush your mouth!

BENEATHA: As for George. Well. George looks good—he's got a beautiful car and he takes me to nice places and, as my sister-in-law says, he is probably the richest boy I will ever get to know and I even like him sometimes—but if the Youngers are sitting around waiting to see if their little Bennie is going to tie up the family with the Murchisons, they are wasting their time.

RUTH: You mean you wouldn't marry George Murchison if he asked you someday? That pretty, rich thing? Honey, I knew you was odd—

BENEATHA: No I would not marry him if all I felt for him was what I feel now. Besides, George's family wouldn't really like it.

MAMA: Why not?

BENEATHA: Oh, Mama—The Murchisons are honest-to-God-real-*live*-rich colored people, and the only people in the world who are more snobbish than rich white people are rich colored people. I thought everybody knew that. I've met Mrs. Murchison. She's a scene!

MAMA: You must not dislike people 'cause they well off, honey.

BENEATHA: Why not? It makes just as much sense as disliking people 'cause they are poor, and lots of people do that.

RUTH: [*A wisdom-of-the-ages manner. To* MAMA.] Well, she'll get over some of this—

BENEATHA: Get over it? What are you talking about, Ruth? Listen, I'm going to be a doctor. I'm not worried about who I'm going to marry yet—if I ever get married.

MAMA AND RUTH: *If!*

MAMA: Now, Bennie—

BENEATHA: Oh, I probably will . . . but first I'm going to be a doctor, and George, for one, still thinks that's pretty funny. I couldn't be bothered with that. I am going to be a doctor and everybody around here better understand that!

MAMA: [*Kindly.*] 'Course you going to be a doctor, honey, God willing.

BENEATHA: [*Drily.*] God hasn't got a thing to do with it.

MAMA: Beneatha—that just wasn't necessary.

BENEATHA: Well—neither is God. I get sick of hearing about God.

MAMA: Beneatha!

BENEATHA: I mean it! I'm just tired of hearing about God all the time. What has He got to do with anything? Does He pay tuition?

MAMA: You 'bout to get your fresh little jaw slapped!

RUTH: That's just what she needs, all right!

BENEATHA: Why? Why can't I say what I want to around here, like everybody else?

MAMA: It don't sound nice for a young girl to say things like that—you wasn't brought up that way. Me and your father went to trouble to get you and Brother to church every Sunday.

BENEATHA: Mama, you don't understand. It's all a matter of ideas, and God is just one idea I don't accept. It's not important. I am not going out and be immoral or commit crimes because I don't believe in God. I don't even think about it. It's just that I get tired of Him getting credit for all the things the human race achieves through its own stubborn effort. There simply is no blasted God—there is only man and it is he who makes miracles!

[MAMA *absorbs this speech, studies her daughter and rises slowly and crosses to* BENEATHA *and slaps her powerfully across the face. After, there is only silence and the daughter drops her eyes from her mother's face, and* MAMA *is very tall before her.*]

MAMA: Now—you say after me, in my mother's house there is still God. [*There is a long pause and* BENEATHA *stares at the floor wordlessly.* MAMA *repeats the phrase with precision and cool emotion.*] In my mother's house there is still God.

BENEATHA: In my mother's house there is still God.

[*A long pause.*]

MAMA: [*Walking away from* BENEATHA, *too disturbed for triumphant posture. Stopping and turning back to her daughter.*] There are some ideas we ain't going to have in this house. Not long as I am at the head of this family.

BENEATHA: Yes, ma'am.

[MAMA *walks out of the room.*]

RUTH: [*Almost gently, with profound understanding.*] You think you a woman, Bennie—but you still a little girl. What you did was childish—so you got treated like a child.

BENEATHA: I see. [*Quietly.*] I also see that everybody thinks it's all right for Mama to be a tyrant. But all the tyranny in the world will never put a God in the heavens!

[*She picks up her books and goes out.*]

RUTH: [*Goes to* MAMA*'s door.*] She said she was sorry.

MAMA: [*Coming out, going to her plant.*] They frightens me, Ruth. My children.

RUTH: You got good children, Lena. They just a little off sometimes—but they're good.

MAMA: No—there's something come down between me and them that don't let us understand each other and I don't know what it is. One done almost lost his mind thinking 'bout money all the time and the other done commence to talk about things I can't seem to understand in no form or fashion. What is it that's changing, Ruth?

RUTH: [*Soothingly, older than her years.*] Now . . . you taking it all too seriously. You just got strong-willed children and it takes a strong woman like you to keep 'em in hand.

MAMA: [*Looking at her plant and sprinkling a little water on it.*] They spirited all right, my children. Got to admit they got spirit—Bennie and Walter. Like this little old plant that ain't never had enough sunshine or nothing—and look at it . . .

[*She has her back to* RUTH, *who has had to stop ironing and lean against something and put the back of her hand to her forehead.*]

RUTH: [*Trying to keep* MAMA *from noticing.*] You . . . sure . . . loves that little old thing, don't you? . . .

MAMA: Well, I always wanted me a garden like I used to see sometimes at the back of the houses down home. This plant is close as I ever got to having one. [*She looks out of the window as she replaces the plant.*] Lord, ain't nothing as dreary as the view from this window on a dreary day, is there? Why ain't you singing this morning, Ruth? Sing that "No Ways Tired." That song always lifts me up so—[*She turns at last to see that* RUTH *has slipped quietly into a chair, in a state of semiconsciousness.*] Ruth! Ruth honey—what's the matter with you . . . Ruth!

[CURTAIN.]

Scene Two

It is the following morning; a Saturday morning, and house cleaning is in progress at the Youngers. Furniture has been shoved hither and yon and MAMA *is giving the kitchen-area walls a washing down.* BENEATHA, *in dungarees, with a handkerchief tied around her face, is spraying insecticide into the cracks in the walls. As they work, the radio is on and a Southside disk-jockey program is inappropriately filling the house with a rather exotic saxophone blues.* TRAVIS, *the sole idle one, is leaning on his arms, looking out of the window.*

TRAVIS: Grandmama, that stuff Bennie is using smells awful. Can I go downstairs, please?

MAMA: Did you get all them chores done already? I ain't seen you doing much.

TRAVIS: Yes'm—finished early. Where did Mama go this morning?
MAMA: [*Looking at* BENEATHA.] She had to go on a little errand.
TRAVIS: Where?
MAMA: To tend to her business.
TRAVIS: Can I go outside then?
MAMA: Oh, I guess so. You better stay right in front of the house, though . . . and keep a good lookout for the postman.
TRAVIS: Yes'm. [*He starts out and decides to give his aunt* BENEATHA *a good swat on the legs as he passes her.*] Leave them poor little old cockroaches alone, they ain't bothering you none.

[*He runs as she swings the spray gun at him both viciously and playfully.* WALTER *enters from the bedroom and goes to the phone.*]

MAMA: Look out there, girl, before you be spilling some of that stuff on that child!
TRAVIS: [*Teasing.*] That's right—look out now!

[*He exits.*]

BENEATHA: [*Drily.*] I can't imagine that it would hurt him—it has never hurt the roaches.
MAMA: Well, little boys' hides ain't as tough as Southside roaches.
WALTER: [*Into phone.*] Hello—Let me talk to Willy Harris.
MAMA: You better get over there behind the bureau. I seen one marching out of there like Napoleon yesterday.
WALTER: Hello, Willy? It ain't come yet. It'll be here in a few minutes. Did the lawyer give you the papers?
BENEATHA: There's really only one way to get rid of them, Mama—
MAMA: How?
BENEATHA: Set fire to this building.
WALTER: Good. Good. I'll be right over.
BENEATHA: Where did Ruth go, Walter?
WALTER: I don't know.

[*He exits abruptly.*]

BENEATHA: Mama, where did Ruth go?
MAMA: [*Looking at her with meaning.*] To the doctor, I think.
BENEATHA: The doctor? What's the matter? [*They exchange glances.*] You don't think—
MAMA: [*With her sense of drama.*] Now I ain't saying what I think. But I ain't never been wrong 'bout a woman neither.

[*The phone rings.*]

BENEATHA: [*At the phone.*] Hay-lo . . . [*Pause, and a moment of recognition.*] Well—when did you get back! . . . And how was it? . . . Of course I've missed you—in my way . . . This morning? No . . . house cleaning and all that and Mama hates it if I let people come over when the house is like this . . . You *have*? Well, that's different . . . What is it—Oh, what the hell, come on over . . . Right, see you then.

[*She hangs up.*]

MAMA: [*Who has listened vigorously, as is her habit.*] Who is that you inviting over here with this house looking like this? You ain't got the pride you was born with!

BENEATHA: Asagai doesn't care how houses look, Mama—he's an intellectual.

MAMA: *Who?*

BENEATHA: Asagai—Joseph Asagai. He's an African boy I met on campus. He's been studying in Canada all summer.

MAMA: What's his name?

BENEATHA: Asagai, Joseph. Ah-sah-guy . . . He's from Nigeria.

MAMA: Oh, that's the little country that was founded by slaves way back . . .

BENEATHA: No, Mama—that's Liberia.

MAMA: I don't think I never met no African before.

BENEATHA: Well, do me a favor and don't ask him a whole lot of ignorant questions about Africans. I mean, do they wear clothes and all that—

MAMA: Well, now, I guess if you think we so ignorant 'round here maybe you shouldn't bring your friends here—

BENEATHA: It's just that people ask such crazy things. All anyone seems to know about when it comes to Africa is Tarzan—

MAMA: [*Indignantly.*] Why should I know anything about Africa?

BENEATHA: Why do you give money at church for the missionary work?

MAMA: Well, that's to help save people.

BENEATHA: You mean save them from *heathenism*—

MAMA: [*Innocently.*] Yes.

BENEATHA: I'm afraid they need more salvation from the British and the French.

[RUTH *comes in forlornly and pulls off her coat with dejection. They both turn to look at her.*]

RUTH: [*Dispiritedly.*] Well, I guess from all the happy faces—everybody knows.

BENEATHA: You pregnant?

MAMA: Lord have mercy, I sure hope it's a little old girl. Travis ought to have a sister.

[BENEATHA *and* RUTH *give her a hopeless look for this grandmotherly enthusiasm.*]

BENEATHA: How far along are you?

RUTH: Two months.

BENEATHA: Did you mean to? I mean did you plan it or was it an accident?

MAMA: What do you know about planning or not planning?

BENEATHA: Oh, Mama.

RUTH: [*Wearily.*] She's twenty years old, Lena.

BENEATHA: Did you plan it, Ruth?

RUTH: Mind your own business.

BENEATHA: It is my business—where is he going to live, on the roof? [*There is silence following the remark as the three women react to the sense of it.*] Gee—I didn't mean that, Ruth, honest. Gee, I don't feel like that at all. I—I think it is wonderful.

RUTH: [*Dully.*] Wonderful.

BENEATHA: Yes—really.

MAMA: [*Looking at* RUTH, *worried.*] Doctor say everything going to be all right?

RUTH: [*Far away.*] Yes—she says everything is going to be fine . . .

MAMA: [*Immediately suspicious.*] "She"—What doctor you went to?

[RUTH *folds over, near hysteria.*]

MAMA: [*Worriedly hovering over* RUTH.] Ruth honey—what's the matter with you—you sick?

[RUTH *has her fists clenched on her thighs and is fighting hard to suppress a scream that seems to be rising in her.*]

BENEATHA: What's the matter with her, Mama?

MAMA: [*Working her fingers in* RUTH'S *shoulder to relax her.*] She be all right. Women gets right depressed sometimes when they get her way. [*Speaking softly, expertly, rapidly.*] Now you just relax. That's right . . . just lean back, don't think 'bout nothing at all . . . nothing at all—

RUTH: I'm all right . . .

[*The glassy-eyed look melts and then she collapses into a fit of heavy sobbing. The bell rings.*]

BENEATHA: Oh, my God—that must be Asagai.

MAMA: [*To* RUTH.] Come on now, honey. You need to lie down and rest awhile . . . then have some nice hot food.

[*They exit,* RUTH'S *weight on her mother-in-law.* BENEATHA, *herself profoundly disturbed, opens the door to admit a rather dramatic-looking young man with a large package.*]

ASAGAI: Hello, Alaiyo—

BENEATHA: [*Holding the door open and regarding him with pleasure.*] Hello . . . [*Long pause.*] Well—come in. And please excuse everything. My mother was very upset about my letting anyone come here with the place like this.

ASAGAI: [*Coming into the room.*] You look disturbed too . . . Is something wrong?

BENEATHA: [*Still at the door, absently.*] Yes . . . we've all got acute ghetto-itus. [*She smiles and comes toward him, finding a cigarette and sitting.*] So—sit down! How was Canada?

ASAGAI: [*A sophisticate.*] Canadian.

BENEATHA: [*Looking at him.*] I'm very glad you are back.

ASAGAI: [*Looking back at her in turn.*] Are you really?

BENEATHA: Yes—very.

ASAGAI: Why—you were quite glad when I went away. What happened?

BENEATHA: You went away.

ASAGAI: Ahhhhhhhh.

BENEATHA: Before—you wanted to be so serious before there was time.

ASAGAI: How much time must there be before one knows what one feels?

BENEATHA: [*Stalling this particular conversation. Her hands pressed together, in a deliberately childish gesture.*] What did you bring me?

ASAGAI: [*Handing her the package.*] Open it and see.

BENEATHA: [*Eagerly opening the package and drawing out some records and the colorful robes of a Nigerian woman.*] Oh, Asagai! . . . You got them for me! . . . How beautiful . . . and the records too! [*She lifts out the robes and runs to the mirror with them and holds the drapery up in front of herself.*]

ASAGAI: [*Coming to her at the mirror.*] I shall have to teach you how to drape it properly. [*He flings the material about her for the moment and stands back to look at her.*] Ah—*Oh-pay-gay-day, oh-gbah-mu-shay.* [*A Yoruba exclamation for admiration.*] You wear it well . . . very well . . . mutilated hair and all.

BENEATHA: [*Turning suddenly.*] My hair—what's wrong with my hair?

ASAGAI: [*Shrugging.*] Were you born with it like that?

BENEATHA: [*Reaching up to touch it.*] No . . . of course not.

[*She looks back to the mirror, disturbed.*]

ASAGAI: [*Smiling.*] How then?

BENEATHA: You know perfectly well how . . . as crinkly as yours . . . that's how.

ASAGAI: And it is ugly to you that way?

BENEATHA: [*Quickly.*] Oh, no—not ugly . . . [*More slowly, apologetically.*] But it's so hard to manage when it's, well—raw.

ASAGAI: And so to accommodate that—you mutilate it every week?

BENEATHA: It's not mutilation!

ASAGAI: [*Laughing aloud at her seriousness.*] Oh . . . please! I am only teasing you because you are so very serious about these things. [*He stands back from her and folds his arms across his chest as he watches her pulling at her hair and frowning in the mirror.*] Do you remember the first time you met me at school? . . . [*He laughs.*] You came up to me and you said—and I thought you were the most serious little thing I had ever seen—you said: [*He imitates her.*] "Mr. Asagai—I want very much to talk with you. About Africa. You see, Mr. Asagai, I am looking for my *identity*!"

[*He laughs.*]

BENEATHA: [*Turning to him, not laughing.*] Yes—

[*Her face is quizzical, profoundly disturbed.*]

ASAGAI: [*Still teasing and reaching out and taking her face in his hands and turning her profile to him.*] Well . . . it is true that this is not so much a profile of a Hollywood queen as perhaps a queen of the Nile— [*A mock dismissal of the importance of the question.*] But what does it matter? Assimilationism is so popular in your country.

BENEATHA: [*Wheeling, passionately, sharply.*] I am not an assimilationist!

ASAGAI: [*The protest hangs in the room for a moment and* ASAGAI *studies her, his laughter fading.*] Such a serious one. [*There is a pause.*] So—you like the robes? You must take excellent care of them—they are from my sister's personal wardrobe.

BENEATHA: [*With incredulity.*] You—you sent all the way home—for me?

ASAGAI: [*With charm.*] For you—I would do much more . . . Well, that is what I came for. I must go.

BENEATHA: Will you call me Monday?

ASAGAI: Yes . . . We have a great deal to talk about. I mean about identity and time and all that.

BENEATHA: Time?

ASAGAI: Yes. About how much time one needs to know what one feels.

BENEATHA: You never understood that there is more than one kind of feeling which can exist between a man and a woman—or, at least, there should be.

ASAGAI: [*Shaking his head negatively but gently.*] No. Between a man and a woman there need be only one kind of feeling. I have that for you . . . Now even . . . right this moment . . .

BENEATHA: I know—and by itself—it won't do. I can find that anywhere.

ASAGAI: For a woman it should be enough.

BENEATHA: I know—because that's what it says in all the novels that men write. But it isn't. Go ahead and laugh—but I'm not interested in being someone's little episode in America or— [*With feminine vengeance.*] —one of them! [ASAGAI *has burst into laughter again.*] That's funny as hell, huh!

ASAGAI: It's just that every American girl I have known has said that to me. White—black—in this you are all the same. And the same speech, too!

BENEATHA: [*Angrily.*] Yuk, yuk, yuk!

ASAGAI: It's how you can be sure that the world's most liberated women are not liberated at all. You all talk about it too much!

[MAMA *enters and is immediately all social charm because of the presence of a guest.*]

BENEATHA: Oh—Mama—this is Mr. Asagai.

MAMA: How do you do?

ASAGAI: [*Total politeness to an elder.*] How do you do, Mrs. Younger. Please forgive me for coming at such an outrageous hour on a Saturday.

MAMA: Well, you are quite welcome. I just hope you understand that our house don't always look like this. [*Chatterish.*] You must come again. I would love to hear all about— [*Not sure of the name.*] —your country. I think it's so sad the way our American Negroes don't know nothing about Africa 'cept Tarzan and all that. And all that money they pour into these churches when they ought to be helping you people over there drive out them French and Englishmen done taken away your land.

[*The mother flashes a slightly superior look at her daughter upon completion of the recitation.*]

ASAGAI: [*Taken aback by this sudden and acutely unrelated expression of sympathy.*] Yes . . . yes . . .

MAMA: [*Smiling at him suddenly and relaxing and looking him over.*] How many miles is it from here to where you come from?

ASAGAI: Many thousands.

MAMA: [*Looking at him as she would* WALTER.] I bet you don't half look after yourself, being away from your mama either. I spec you better come 'round here from time to time and get yourself some decent home-cooked meals . . .

ASAGAI: [*Moved.*] Thank you. Thank you very much. [*They are all quiet, then—*] Well . . . I must go. I will call you Monday, Alaiyo.

MAMA: What's that he call you?

ASAGAI: Oh—"Alaiyo." I hope you don't mind. It is what you would call a nickname, I think. It is a Yoruba word. I am a Yoruba.

MAMA: [*Looking at* BENEATHA.] I—I thought he was from—

ASAGAI: [*Understanding.*] Nigeria is my country. Yoruba is my tribal origin—

BENEATHA: You didn't tell us what Alaiyo means . . . for all I know, you might be calling me Little Idiot or something . . .

ASAGAI: Well . . . let me see . . . I do not know how just to explain it . . . The sense of a thing can be so different when it changes languages.

BENEATHA: You're evading.

ASAGAI: No—really it is difficult . . . [*Thinking.*] It means . . . it means One for Whom Bread—Food—Is Not Enough. [*He looks at her.*] Is that all right?

BENEATHA: [*Understanding, softly.*] Thank you.

MAMA: [*Looking from one to the other and not understanding any of it.*] Well . . . that's nice . . . You must come see us again—Mr.—

ASAGAI: Ah-sah-guy . . .

MAMA: Yes . . . Do come again.

ASAGAI: Good-bye.

[*He exits.*]

MAMA: [*After him.*] Lord, that's a pretty thing just went out here! [*Insinuatingly, to her daughter.*] Yes, I guess I see why we done commence to get so interested in Africa 'round here. Missionaries my aunt Jenny!

[*She exits.*]

BENEATHA: Oh, Mama! . . .

[*She picks up the Nigerian dress and holds it up to her in front of the mirror again. She sets the headdress on haphazardly and then notices her hair again and clutches at it and then replaces the headdress and frowns at herself. Then she starts to wriggle in front of the mirror as she thinks a Nigerian woman might.* TRAVIS *enters and regards her.*]

TRAVIS: You cracking up?

BENEATHA: Shut up.

[*She pulls the headdress off and looks at herself in the mirror and clutches at her hair again and squinches her eyes as if trying to imagine something. Then, suddenly, she gets her raincoat and kerchief and hurriedly prepares for going out.*]

MAMA: [*Coming back into the room.*] She's resting now. Travis, baby, run next door and ask Miss Johnson to please let me have a little kitchen cleanser. This here can is empty as Jacob's kettle.

TRAVIS: I just came in.

MAMA: Do as you told. [*He exits and she looks at her daughter.*] Where you going?

BENEATHA: [*Halting at the door.*] To become a queen of the Nile!

[*She exits in a breathless blaze of glory.* RUTH *appears in the bedroom doorway.*]

MAMA: Who told you to get up?

RUTH: Ain't nothing wrong with me to be lying in no bed for. Where did Bennie go?

MAMA: [*Drumming her fingers.*] Far as I could make out—to Egypt. [RUTH *just looks at her.*] What time is it getting to?

RUTH: Ten twenty. And the mailman going to ring that bell this morning just like he done every morning for the last umpteen years.

[TRAVIS *comes in with the cleanser can.*]

TRAVIS: She say to tell you that she don't have much.

MAMA: [*Angrily.*] Lord, some people I could name sure is tight-fisted! [*Directing her grandson.*] Mark two cans of cleanser down on the list there. If she that hard up for kitchen cleanser, I sure don't want to forget to get her none!

RUTH: Lena—maybe the woman is just short on cleanser—

MAMA: [*Not listening.*]—Much baking powder as she done borrowed from me all these years, she could of done gone into the baking business!

[*The bell sounds suddenly and sharply and all three are stunned—serious and silent—mid-speech. In spite of all the other conversations and distractions of the morning, this is what they have been waiting for, even* TRAVIS, *who looks helplessly from his mother to his grandmother.* RUTH *is the first to come to life again.*]

RUTH: [*To* TRAVIS.] *Get down them steps, boy!*

[TRAVIS *snaps to life and flies out to get the mail.*]

MAMA: [*Her eyes wide, her hand to her breast.*] You mean it done really come?

RUTH: [*Excited.*] Oh, Miss Lena!

MAMA: [*Collecting herself.*] Well . . . I don't know what we all so excited about 'round here for. We known it was coming for months.

RUTH: That's a whole lot different from having it come and being able to hold it in your hands . . . a piece of paper worth ten thousand dollars . . . [TRAVIS *bursts back into the room. He holds the envelope high above his head, like a little dancer, his face is radiant and he is breathless. He moves to his grandmother with sudden slow ceremony and puts the envelope into her hands. She accepts it, and then merely holds it and looks at it.*] Come on! Open it . . . Lord have mercy, I wish Walter Lee was here!

TRAVIS: Open it, Grandmama!

MAMA: [*Staring at it.*] Now you all be quiet. It's just a check.

RUTH: Open it . . .

MAMA: [*Still staring at it.*] Now don't act silly . . . We ain't never been no people to act silly 'bout no money—

RUTH: [*Swiftly.*] We ain't never had none before—*open it!*

[MAMA *finally makes a good strong tear and pulls out the thin blue slice of paper and inspects it closely. The boy and his mother study it raptly over* MAMA'S *shoulders.*]

MAMA: *Travis!* [*She is counting off with doubt.*] Is that the right number of zeros.

TRAVIS: Yes'm . . . ten thousand dollars. Gaalee, Grandmama, you rich.

MAMA: [*She holds the check away from her, still looking at it. Slowly her face sobers into a mask of unhappiness.*] Ten thousand dollars. [*She hands it to* RUTH.] Put it away somewhere, Ruth. [*She does not look at* RUTH; *her eyes seem to be seeing something somewhere very far off.*] Ten thousand dollars they give you. Ten thousand dollars.

TRAVIS: [*To his mother, sincerely.*] What's the matter with Grandmama—don't she want to be rich?

RUTH: [*Distractedly.*] You go on out and play now, baby. [TRAVIS *exits.* MAMA *starts wiping dishes absently, humming intently to herself.* RUTH *turns to her, with kind exasperation.*] You've gone and got yourself upset.

MAMA: [*Not looking at her.*] I spec if it wasn't for you all . . . I would just put that money away or give it to the church or something.

RUTH: Now what kind of talk is that. Mr. Younger would just be plain mad if he could hear you talking foolish like that.

MAMA: [*Stopping and staring off.*] Yes . . . he sure would. [*Sighing.*] We got enough to do with that money, all right. [*She halts then, and turns and looks at her daughter-in-law hard;* RUTH *avoids her eyes and* MAMA *wipes her hands with finality and starts to speak firmly to* RUTH.] Where did you go today, girl?

RUTH: To the doctor.

MAMA: [*Impatiently.*] Now, Ruth . . . you know better than that. Old Doctor Jones is strange enough in his way but there ain't nothing 'bout him make somebody slip and call him "she"—like you done this morning.

RUTH: Well, that's what happened—my tongue slipped.

MAMA: You went to see that woman, didn't you?

RUTH: [*Defensively, giving herself away.*] What woman you talking about?

MAMA: [*Angrily.*] That woman who—

[WALTER *enters in great excitement.*]

WALTER: Did it come?

MAMA: [*Quietly.*] Can't you give people a Christian greeting before you start asking about money?

WALTER: [*To* RUTH.] Did it come? [RUTH *unfolds the check and lays it quietly before him, watching him intently with thoughts of her own.* WALTER *sits down and grasps it close and counts off the zeros.*] Ten thousand dollars— [*He turns suddenly, frantically to his mother and draws some papers out of his breast pocket.*] Mama—look. Old Willy Harris put everything on paper—

MAMA: Son—I think you ought to talk to your wife . . . I'll go on out and leave you alone if you want—

WALTER: I can talk to her later—Mama, look—

MAMA: Son—

WALTER: WILL SOMEBODY PLEASE LISTEN TO ME TODAY!

MAMA: [*Quietly.*] I don't 'low no yellin' in this house, Walter Lee, and you know it— [WALTER *stares at them in frustration and starts to speak several times.*] And there ain't going to be no investing in no liquor stores. I don't aim to have to speak on that again.

[*A long pause.*]

WALTER: Oh—so you don't aim to have to speak on that again? So you have decided . . . [*Crumpling his papers.*] Well, *you* tell that to my boy tonight when you put him to sleep on the living-room couch . . . [*Turning to* MAMA *and speaking directly to her.*] Yeah—and tell it to my wife, Mama, tomorrow when she has to go out of here to look after somebody else's kids. And tell it to *me*, Mama, every time we need a new pair of curtains and I have to watch *you* go out and work in somebody's kitchen. Yeah, you tell me then!

[WALTER *starts out.*]

RUTH: Where you going?
WALTER: I'm going out!
RUTH: Where?
WALTER: Just out of this house somewhere—
RUTH: [*Getting her coat.*] I'll come too.
WALTER: I don't want you to come!
RUTH: I got something to talk to you about, Walter.
WALTER: That's too bad.
MAMA: [*Still quietly.*] Walter Lee— [*She waits and he finally turns and looks at her.*] Sit down.
WALTER: I'm a grown man, Mama.
MAMA: Ain't nobody said you wasn't grown. But you still in my house and my presence. And as long as you are—you'll talk to your wife civil. Now sit down.
RUTH: [*Suddenly.*] Oh, let him go on out and drink himself to death! He makes me sick to my stomach! [*She flings her coat against him.*]
WALTER: [*Violently.*] And you turn mine too, baby! [RUTH *goes into their bedroom and slams the door behind her.*] That was my greatest mistake—
MAMA: [*Still quietly.*] Walter, what is the matter with you?
WALTER: Matter with me? Ain't nothing the matter with *me*!
MAMA: Yes there is. Something eating you up like a crazy man. Something more than me not giving you this money. The past few years I been watching it happen to you. You get all nervous acting and kind of wild in the eyes—[WALTER *jumps up impatiently at her words.*] I said sit there now, I'm talking to you!
WALTER: Mama—I don't need no nagging at me today.
MAMA: Seem like you getting to a place where you always tied up in some kind of knot about something. But if anybody ask you 'bout it you just yell at 'em and bust out the house and go out and drink somewheres. Walter Lee, people can't live with that. Ruth's a good, patient girl in her way—but you getting to be too much. Boy, don't make the mistake of driving that girl away from you.
WALTER: Why—what she do for me?
MAMA: She loves you.
WALTER: Mama—I'm going out. I want to go off somewhere and be by myself for a while.
MAMA: I'm sorry 'bout your liquor store, son. It just wasn't the thing for us to do. That's what I want to tell you about—
WALTER: I got to go out, Mama—

[*He rises.*]

MAMA: It's dangerous, son.
WALTER: What's dangerous?
MAMA: When a man goes outside his home to look for peace.
WALTER: [*Beseechingly.*] Then why can't there never be no peace in this house then?

MAMA: You done found it in some other house?

WALTER: No—there ain't no woman! Why do women always think there's a woman somewhere when a man gets restless. [*Coming to her.*] Mama—Mama—I want so many things . . .

MAMA: Yes, son—

WALTER: I want so many things that they are driving me kind of crazy . . . Mama—look at me.

MAMA: I'm looking at you. You a good-looking boy. You got a job, a nice wife, a fine boy and—

WALTER: A job. [*Looks at her.*] Mama, a job? I open and close car doors all day long. I drive a man around in his limousine and I say, "Yes, sir; no, sir; very good, sir; shall I take the Drive, sir?" Mama, that ain't no kind of job . . . that ain't nothing at all. [*Very quietly.*] Mama, I don't know if I can make you understand.

MAMA: Understand what, baby?

WALTER: [*Quietly.*] Sometimes it's like I can see the future stretched out in front of me—just plain as day. The future, Mama. Hanging over there at the edge of my days. Just waiting for me—a big, looming blank space—full of *nothing.* Just waiting for *me.* [*Pause.*] Mama—sometimes when I'm downtown and I pass them cool, quiet-looking restaurants where them white boys are sitting back and talking 'bout things . . . sitting there turning deals worth millions of dollars . . . sometimes I see guys don't look much older than me—

MAMA: Son—how come you talk so much 'bout money?

WALTER: [*With immense passion.*] Because it is life, Mama!

MAMA: [*Quietly.*] Oh— [*Very quietly.*] So now it's life. Money is life. Once upon a time freedom used to be life—now it's money. I guess the world really do change . . .

WALTER: No—it was always money, Mama. We just didn't know about it.

MAMA: No . . . something has changed. [*She looks at him.*] You something new, boy. In my time we was worried about not being lynched and getting to the North if we could and how to stay alive and still have a pinch of dignity too . . . Now here come you and Beneatha—talking 'bout things we ain't never even thought about hardly, me and your daddy. You ain't satisfied or proud of nothing we done. I mean that you had a home; that we kept you out of trouble till you was grown; that you don't have to ride to work on the back of nobody's streetcar—You my children—but how different we done become.

WALTER: You just don't understand, Mama, you just don't understand.

MAMA: Son—do you know your wife is expecting another baby? [WALTER *stands, stunned, and absorbs what his mother has said.*] That's what she wanted to talk to you about. [WALTER *sinks down into a chair.*] This ain't for me to be telling—but you ought to know. [*She waits.*] I think Ruth is thinking 'bout getting rid of that child.[5]

WALTER: [*Slowly understanding.*] No—no—Ruth wouldn't do that.

MAMA: When the world gets ugly enough—a woman will do anything for her family. *The part that's already living.*

5. Abortions were illegal and dangerous in the United States prior to the 1973 *Roe v. Wade* Supreme Court decision.

WALTER: You don't know Ruth, Mama, if you think she would do that.

[RUTH *opens the bedroom door and stands there a little limp.*]

RUTH: [*Beaten.*] Yes I would too, Walter. [*Pause.*] I gave her a five-dollar down payment.

[*There is total silence as the man stares at his wife and the mother stares at her son.*]

MAMA: [*Presently.*] Well— [*Tightly.*] Well—son, I'm waiting to hear you say something . . . I'm waiting to hear how you be your father's son. Be the man he was . . . [*Pause.*] Your wife say she going to destroy your child. And I'm waiting to hear you talk like him and say we a people who give children life, not who destroys them— [*She rises.*] I'm waiting to see you stand up and look like your daddy and say we done give up one baby to poverty and that we ain't going to give up nary another one . . . I'm waiting.

WALTER: Ruth—

MAMA: If you a son of mine, tell her! [WALTER *turns, looks at her and can say nothing. She continues, bitterly.*] You . . . you are a disgrace to your father's memory. Somebody get me my hat.

[CURTAIN.]

ACT II

Scene One

Time: Later the same day.

At rise: RUTH *is ironing again. She has the radio going. Presently* BENEATHA'S *bedroom door opens and* RUTH'S *mouth falls and she puts down the iron in fascination.*

RUTH: What have we got on tonight!

BENEATHA: [*Emerging grandly from the doorway so that we can see her thoroughly robed in the costume* ASAGAI *brought.*] You are looking at what a well-dressed Nigerian woman wears— [*She parades for* RUTH, *her hair completely hidden by the headdress; she is coquettishly fanning herself with an ornate oriental fan, mistakenly more like Butterfly*[6] *than any Nigerian that ever was.*] Isn't it beautiful? [*She promenades to the radio and, with an arrogant flourish, turns off the good loud blues that is playing.*] Enough of this assimilationist junk! [RUTH *follows her with her eyes as she goes to the phonograph and puts on a record and turns and waits ceremoniously for the music to come up. Then, with a shout—*] OCOMOGOSIAY!

[RUTH *jumps. The music comes up, a lovely Nigerian melody.* BENEATHA *listens, enraptured, her eyes far away—"back to the past." She begins to dance.* RUTH *is dumbfounded.*]

6. Madame Butterfly, a Japanese woman married to and then abandoned by an American man in the opera *Madama Butterfly* (1904), by the Italian composer Giacomo Puccini (1858–1924).

RUTH: What kind of dance is that?
BENEATHA: A folk dance.
RUTH: [*Pearl Bailey.*][7] What kind of folks do that, honey?
BENEATHA: It's from Nigeria. It's a dance of welcome.
RUTH: Who you welcoming?
BENEATHA: The men back to the village.
RUTH: Where they been?
BENEATHA: How should I know—out hunting or something. Anyway, they are coming back now . . .
RUTH: Well, that's good.
BENEATHA: [*With the record.*]

Alundi, alundi
Alundi alunya
Jop pu a jeepua
Ang gu sooooooooo

Ai yai yae . . .
Ayehaye—alundi . . .

[WALTER *comes in during this performance; he has obviously been drinking. He leans against the door heavily and watches his sister, at first with distaste. Then his eyes look off—"back to the past"—as he lifts both his fists to the roof, screaming.*]

WALTER: YEAH . . . AND ETHIOPIA STRETCH FORTH HER HANDS AGAIN! . . .[8]
RUTH: [*Drily, looking at him.*] Yes—and Africa sure is claiming her own tonight. [*She gives them both up and starts ironing again.*]
WALTER: [*All in a drunken, dramatic shout.*] Shut up! . . . I'm digging them drums . . . them drums move me! . . . [*He makes his weaving way to his wife's face and leans in close to her.*] In my *heart of hearts*— [*He thumps his chest.*] —I am much warrior!
RUTH: [*Without even looking up.*] In your heart of hearts you are much drunkard.
WALTER: [*Coming away from her and starting to wander around the room, shouting.*] Me and Jomo . . . [*Intently, in his sister's face. She has stopped dancing to watch him in this unknown mood.*] That's my man, Kenyatta.[9] [*Shouting and thumping his chest.*] FLAMING SPEAR! HOT DAMN! [*He is suddenly in possession of an imaginary spear and actively spearing enemies all over the room.*] OCOMOGOSIAY . . . THE LION IS WAKING . . . OWIMOWEH! [*He pulls his shirt open and leaps up on a table and gestures with his spear. The bell rings.* RUTH *goes to answer.*]
BENEATHA: [*To encourage* WALTER, *thoroughly caught up with this side of him.*] OCOMOGOSIAY, FLAMING SPEAR!

7. That is, in the manner of the popular African American singer and entertainer (1918–90).
8. See Psalms 68.31: "Princes shall come out of Egypt; Ethiopia shall soon stretch out her hands unto God."
9. Jomo Kenyatta (1893–1978), African political leader and first president of Kenya (1964–78) following its independence from British colonial rule.

WALTER: [*On the table, very far gone, his eyes pure glass sheets. He sees what we cannot, that he is a leader of his people, a great chief, a descendant of Chaka,*[1] *and that the hour to march has come.*] Listen, my black brothers—

BENEATHA: OCOMOGOSIAY!

WALTER: —Do you hear the waters rushing against the shores of the coastlands—

BENEATHA: OCOMOGOSIAY!

WALTER: —Do you hear the screeching of the cocks in yonder hills beyond where the chiefs meet in council for the coming of the mighty war—

BENEATHA: OCOMOGOSIAY!

WALTER: —Do you hear the beating of the wings of the birds flying low over the mountains and the low places of our land—

[RUTH *opens the door.* GEORGE MURCHISON *enters.*]

BENEATHA: OCOMOGOSIAY!

WALTER: —Do you hear the singing of the women, singing the war songs of our fathers to the babies in the great houses . . . singing the sweet war songs? OH, DO YOU HEAR, MY BLACK BROTHERS!

BENEATHA: [*Completely gone.*] We hear you, Flaming Spear—

WALTER: Telling us to prepare for the greatness of the time— [*To* GEORGE.] Black Brother!

[*He extends his hand for the fraternal clasp.*]

GEORGE: Black Brother, hell!

RUTH: [*Having had enough, and embarrassed for the family.*] Beneatha, you got company—what's the matter with you? Walter Lee Younger, get down off that table and stop acting like a fool . . .

[WALTER *comes down off the table suddenly and makes a quick exit to the bathroom.*]

RUTH: He's had a little to drink . . . I don't know what her excuse is.

GEORGE: [*To* BENEATHA.] Look honey, we're going *to* the theatre—we're not going to be *in* it . . . so go change, huh?

RUTH: You expect this boy to go out with you looking like that?

BENEATHA: [*Looking at* GEORGE.] That's up to George. If he's ashamed of his heritage—

GEORGE: Oh, don't be so proud of yourself, Bennie—just because you look eccentric.

BENEATHA: How can something that's natural be eccentric?

GEORGE: That's what being eccentric means—being natural. Get dressed.

BENEATHA: I don't like that, George.

RUTH: Why must you and your brother make an argument out of everything people say?

BENEATHA: Because I hate assimilationist Negroes!

RUTH: Will somebody please tell me what assimila-who-ever means!

1. Zulu chief (1786–1828), also known as "Shaka" and called "The Black Napoleon" for his strategic and organizational genius.

GEORGE: Oh, it's just a college girl's way of calling people Uncle Toms—but that isn't what it means at all.

RUTH: Well, what does it mean?

BENEATHA: [*Cutting* GEORGE *off and staring at him as she replies to* RUTH.] It means someone who is willing to give up his own culture and submerge himself completely in the dominant, and in this case, *oppressive* culture!

GEORGE: Oh, dear, dear, dear! Here we go! A lecture on the African past! On our Great West African Heritage! In one second we will hear all about the great Ashanti empires; the great Songhay civilizations; and the great sculpture of Bénin—and then some poetry in the Bantu—and the whole monologue will end with the word *heritage*! [*Nastily*.] Let's face it, baby, your heritage is nothing but a bunch of raggedy-assed spirituals and some grass huts!

BENEATHA: *Grass huts!* [RUTH *crosses to her and forcibly pushes her toward the bedroom*.] See there . . . you are standing there in your splendid ignorance talking about people who were the first to smelt iron on the face of the earth! [RUTH *is pushing her through the door*.] The Ashanti were performing surgical operations when the English— [RUTH *pulls the door to, with* BENEATHA *on the other side, and smiles graciously at* GEORGE. BENEATHA *opens the door and shouts the end of the sentence defiantly at* GEORGE.] —were still tattooing themselves with blue dragons . . . [*She goes back inside*.]

RUTH: Have a seat, George. [*They both sit.* RUTH *folds her hands rather primly on her lap, determined to demonstrate the civilization of the family*.] Warm, ain't it? I mean for September. [*Pause*.] Just like they always say about Chicago weather: If it's too hot or cold for you, just wait a minute and it'll change. [*She smiles happily at this cliché of clichés*.] Everybody say it's got to do with them bombs and things they keep setting off.[2] [*Pause*.] Would you like a nice cold beer?

GEORGE: No, thank you. I don't care for beer. [*He looks at his watch*.] I hope she hurries up.

RUTH: What time is the show?

GEORGE: It's an eight-thirty curtain. That's just Chicago, though. In New York standard curtain time is eight forty.

[*He is rather proud of this knowledge*.]

RUTH: [*Properly appreciating it*.] You get to New York a lot?

GEORGE: [*Offhand*.] Few times a year.

RUTH: Oh—that's nice. I've never been to New York.

[WALTER *enters. We feel he has relieved himself, but the edge of unreality is still with him*.]

WALTER: New York ain't got nothing Chicago ain't. Just a bunch of hustling people all squeezed up together—being "Eastern."

[*He turns his face into a screw of displeasure*.]

GEORGE: Oh—you've been?

WALTER: *Plenty* of times.

RUTH: [*Shocked at the lie*.] Walter Lee Younger!

2. In the 1950s, people commonly blamed weather fluctuations on atomic testing.

WALTER: [*Staring her down.*] Plenty! [*Pause.*] What we got to drink in this house? Why don't you offer this man some refreshment. [*To* GEORGE.] They don't know how to entertain people in this house, man.

GEORGE: Thank you—I don't really care for anything.

WALTER: [*Feeling his head; sobriety coming.*] Where's Mama?

RUTH: She ain't come back yet.

WALTER: [*Looking* MURCHISON *over from head to toe, scrutinizing his carefully casual tweed sports jacket over cashmere V-neck sweater over soft eyelet shirt and tie, and soft slacks, finished off with white buckskin shoes.*] Why all you college boys wear them fairyish-looking white shoes?

RUTH: Walter Lee!

[GEORGE MURCHISON *ignores the remark.*]

WALTER: [*To* RUTH.] Well, they look crazy as hell—white shoes, cold as it is.

RUTH: [*Crushed.*] You have to excuse him—

WALTER: No he don't! Excuse me for what? What you always excusing me for! I'll excuse myself when I needs to be excused! [*A pause.*] They look as funny as them black knee socks Beneatha wears out of here all the time.

RUTH: It's the college *style*, Walter.

WALTER: Style, hell, She looks like she got burnt legs or something!

RUTH: Oh, Walter—

WALTER: [*An irritable mimic.*] Oh, Walter! Oh, Walter! [*To* MURCHISON.] How's your old man making out? I understand you all going to buy that big hotel on the Drive?[3] [*He finds a beer in the refrigerator, wanders over to* MURCHISON, *sipping and wiping his lips with the back of his hand, and straddling a chair backwards to talk to the other man.*] Shrewd move. Your old man is all right, man. [*Tapping his head and half winking for emphasis.*] I mean he knows how to operate. I mean he thinks *big*, you know what I mean, I mean for a *home*, you know? But I think he's kind of running out of ideas now. I'd like to talk to him. Listen, man, I got some plans that could turn this city upside down. I mean I think like he does. *Big.* Invest big, gamble big, hell, lose *big* if you have to, you know what I mean. It's hard to find a man on this whole Southside who understands my kind of thinking—you dig? [*He scrutinizes* MURCHISON *again, drinks his beer, squints his eyes and leans in close, confidential, man to man.*] Me and you ought to sit down and talk sometimes, man. Man, I got me some ideas . . .

GEORGE: [*With boredom.*] Yeah—sometimes we'll have to do that, Walter.

WALTER: [*Understanding the indifference, and offended.*] Yeah—well, when you get the time, man. I know you a busy little boy.

RUTH: Walter, please—

WALTER: [*Bitterly, hurt.*] I know ain't nothing in this world as busy as you colored college boys with your fraternity pins and white shoes . . .

RUTH: [*Covering her face with humiliation.*] Oh, Walter Lee—

WALTER: I see you all the time—with the books tucked under your arms—going to your [*British A—a mimic.*] "clahsses." And for what! What the hell you

3. Lake Shore Drive, a scenic thoroughfare along Lake Michigan.

learning over there? Filling up your heads— [*Counting off on his fingers.*] —with the sociology and the psychology—but they teaching you how to be a man? How to take over and run the world? They teaching you how to run a rubber plantation or a steel mill? Naw—just to talk proper and read books and wear white shoes . . .

GEORGE: [*Looking at him with distaste, a little above it all.*] You're all wacked up with bitterness, man.

WALTER: [*Intently, almost quietly, between the teeth, glaring at the boy.*] And you—ain't you bitter, man? Ain't you just about had it yet? Don't you see no stars gleaming that you can't reach out and grab? You happy?—You contented son-of-a-bitch—you happy? You got it made? Bitter? Man, I'm a volcano. Bitter? Here I am a giant—surrounded by ants! Ants who can't even understand what it is the giant is talking about.

RUTH: [*Passionately and suddenly.*] Oh, Walter—ain't you with nobody!

WALTER: [*Violently.*] No! 'Cause ain't nobody with me! Not even my own mother!

RUTH: Walter, that's a terrible thing to say!

[BENEATHA *enters, dressed for the evening in a cocktail dress and earrings.*]

GEORGE: Well—hey, you look great.

BENEATHA: Let's go, George. See you all later.

RUTH: Have a nice time.

GEORGE: Thanks. Good night. [*To* WALTER, sarcastically.] Good night, *Prometheus.*[4]

[BENEATHA *and* GEORGE *exit.*]

WALTER: [*To* RUTH.] Who is Prometheus?

RUTH: I don't know. Don't worry about it.

WALTER: [*In fury, pointing after* GEORGE.] See there—they get to a point where they can't insult you man to man—they got to go talk about something ain't nobody never heard of!

RUTH: How do you know it was an insult? [*To humor him.*] Maybe Prometheus is a nice fellow.

WALTER: Prometheus! I bet there ain't even no such thing! I bet that simple-minded clown—

RUTH: Walter—

[*She stops what she is doing and looks at him.*]

WALTER: [*Yelling.*] Don't start!

RUTH: Start what?

WALTER: Your nagging! Where was I? Who was I with? How much money did I spend?

RUTH: [*Plaintively.*] Walter Lee—why don't we just try to talk about it . . .

4. In Greek mythology, Prometheus represented the bold creative spirit; defying the gods, he stole fire from Olympus (the locale of the gods) and gave it to humankind. Though successful, he was harshly punished by Zeus.

WALTER: [*Not listening.*] I been out talking with people who understand me. People who care about the things I got on my mind.

RUTH: [*Wearily.*] I guess that means people like Willy Harris.

WALTER: Yes, people like Willy Harris.

RUTH: [*With a sudden flash of impatience.*] Why don't you all just hurry up and go into the banking business and stop talking about it!

WALTER: Why? You want to know why? 'Cause we all tied up in a race of people that don't know how to do nothing but moan, pray and have babies!

[*The line is too bitter even for him and he looks at her and sits down.*]

RUTH: Oh, Walter . . . [*Softly.*] Honey, why can't you stop fighting me?

WALTER: [*Without thinking.*] Who's fighting you? Who even cares about you?

[*This line begins the retardation of his mood.*]

RUTH: Well— [*She waits a long time, and then with resignation starts to put away her things.*] I guess I might as well go on to bed . . . [*More or less to herself.*] I don't know where we lost it . . . but we have . . . [*Then, to him.*] I—I'm sorry about this new baby, Walter. I guess maybe I better go on and do what I started . . . I guess I just didn't realize how bad things was with us . . . I guess I just didn't really realize— [*She starts out to the bedroom and stops.*] You want some hot milk?

WALTER: Hot milk?

RUTH: Yes—hot milk.

WALTER: Why hot milk?

RUTH: 'Cause after all that liquor you come home with you ought to have something hot in your stomach.

WALTER: I don't want no milk.

RUTH: You want some coffee then?

WALTER: No, I don't want no coffee. I don't want nothing hot to drink. [*Almost plaintively.*] Why you always trying to give me something to eat?

RUTH: [*Standing and looking at him helplessly.*] What else can I give you, Walter Lee Younger?

[*She stands and looks at him and presently turns to go out again. He lifts his head and watches her going away from him in a new mood which began to emerge when he asked her "Who cares about you?"*]

WALTER: It's been rough, ain't it, baby? [*She hears and stops but does not turn around and he continues to her back.*] I guess between two people there ain't never as much understood as folks generally thinks there is. I mean like between me and you— [*She turns to face him.*] How we gets to the place where we scared to talk softness to each other. [*He waits, thinking hard himself.*] Why you think it got to be like that? [*He is thoughtful, almost as a child would be.*] Ruth, what is it gets into people ought to be close?

RUTH: I don't know, honey. I think about it a lot.

WALTER: On account of you and me, you mean? The way things are with us. The way something done come down between us.

RUTH: There ain't so much between us, Walter . . . Not when you come to me and try to talk to me. Try to be with me . . . a little even.

WALTER: [*Total honesty.*] Sometimes . . . sometimes . . . I don't even know how to try.

RUTH: Walter—

WALTER: Yes?

RUTH: [*Coming to him, gently and with misgiving, but coming to him.*] Honey . . . life don't have to be like this. I mean sometimes people can do things so that things are better . . . You remember how we used to talk when Travis was born . . . about the way we were going to live . . . the kind of house . . . [*She is stroking his head.*] Well, it's all starting to slip away from us . . .

[MAMA *enters, and* WALTER *jumps up and shouts at her.*]

WALTER: Mama, where have you been?

MAMA: My—them steps is longer than they used to be. Whew! [*She sits down and ignores him.*] How you feeling this evening, Ruth?

[RUTH *shrugs, disturbed some at having been prematurely interrupted and watching her husband knowingly.*]

WALTER: Mama, where have you been all day?

MAMA: [*Still ignoring him and leaning on the table and changing to more comfortable shoes.*] Where's Travis?

RUTH: I let him go out earlier and he ain't come back yet. Boy, is he going to get it!

WALTER: Mama!

MAMA: [*As if she has heard him for the first time.*] Yes, son?

WALTER: Where did you go this afternoon?

MAMA: I went downtown to tend to some business that I had to tend to.

WALTER: What kind of business?

MAMA: You know better than to question me like a child, Brother.

WALTER: [*Rising and bending over the table.*] Where were you, Mama? [*Bringing his fists down and shouting.*] Mama, you didn't go do something with that insurance money, something crazy?

[*The front door opens slowly, interrupting him, and* TRAVIS *peeks his head in, less than hopefully.*]

TRAVIS: [*To his mother.*] Mama, I—

RUTH: "Mama I" nothing! You're going to get it, boy! Get on in that bedroom and get yourself ready!

TRAVIS: But I—

MAMA: Why don't you all never let the child explain hisself.

RUTH: Keep out of it now, Lena.

[MAMA *clamps her lips together, and* RUTH *advances toward her son menacingly.*]

RUTH: A thousand times I have told you not to go off like that—

MAMA: [*Holding out her arms to her grandson.*] Well—at least let me tell him something. I want him to be the first one to hear . . . Come here, Travis. [*The boy obeys, gladly.*] Travis— [*She takes him by the shoulder and looks into his face.*] —you know that money we got in the mail this morning?

TRAVIS: Yes'm—

MAMA: Well—what you think your grandmama gone and done with that money?

TRAVIS: I don't know, Grandmama.

MAMA: [*Putting her finger on his nose for emphasis.*] She went out and she bought you a house! [*The explosion comes from* WALTER *at the end of the revelation and he jumps up and turns away from all of them in a fury.* MAMA *continues, to* TRAVIS.] You glad about the house? It's going to be yours when you get to be a man.

TRAVIS: Yeah—I always wanted to live in a house.

MAMA: All right, gimme some sugar then— [TRAVIS *puts his arms around her neck as she watches her son over the boy's shoulder. Then, to* TRAVIS, *after the embrace.*] Now when you say your prayers tonight, you thank God and your grandfather—'cause it was him who give you the house—in his way.

RUTH: [*Taking the boy from* MAMA *and pushing him toward the bedroom.*] Now you get out of here and get ready for your beating.

TRAVIS: Aw, Mama—

RUTH: Get on in there— [*Closing the door behind him and turning radiantly to her mother-in-law.*] So you went and did it!

MAMA: [*Quietly, looking at her son with pain.*] Yes, I did.

RUTH: [*Raising both arms classically.*] *Praise God!* [*Looks at* WALTER *a moment, who says nothing. She crosses rapidly to her husband.*] Please, honey—let me be glad . . . you be glad too. [*She has laid her hands on his shoulders, but he shakes himself free of her roughly, without turning to face her.*] Oh, Walter . . . a home . . . *a home.* [*She comes back to* MAMA.] Well—where is it? How big is it? How much it going to cost?

MAMA: Well—

RUTH: When we moving?

MAMA: [*Smiling at her.*] First of the month.

RUTH: [*Throwing back her head with jubilance.*] *Praise God!*

MAMA: [*Tentatively, still looking at her son's back turned against her and* RUTH.] It's—it's a nice house too . . . [*She cannot help speaking directly to him. An imploring quality in her voice, her manner, makes her almost like a girl now.*] Three bedrooms—nice big one for you and Ruth . . . Me and Beneatha still have to share our room, but Travis have one of his own—and [*With difficulty.*] I figure if the—new baby—is a boy, we could get one of them double-decker outfits . . . And there's a yard with a little patch of dirt where I could maybe get to grow me a few flowers . . . And a nice big basement . . .

RUTH: Walter honey, be glad—

MAMA: [*Still to his back, fingering things on the table.*] 'Course I don't want to make it sound fancier than it is . . . It's just a plain little old house—but it's made good and solid—and it will be *ours.* Walter Lee—it makes a difference in a man when he can walk on floors that belong to *him* . . .

RUTH: Where is it?

MAMA: [*Frightened at this telling.*] Well—well—it's out there in Clybourne Park[5]—

[RUTH'*s radiance fades abruptly, and* WALTER *finally turns slowly to face his mother with incredulity and hostility.*]

5. On Chicago's Near North Side.

RUTH: Where?

MAMA: [*Matter-of-factly.*] Four o six Clybourne Street, Clybourne Park.

RUTH: Clybourne Park? Mama, there ain't no colored people living in Clybourne Park.

MAMA: [*Almost idiotically.*] Well, I guess there's going to be some now.

WALTER: [*Bitterly.*] So that's the peace and comfort you went out and bought for us today!

MAMA: [*Raising her eyes to meet his finally.*] Son—I just tried to find the nicest place for the least amount of money for my family.

RUTH: [*Trying to recover from the shock.*] Well—well—'course I ain't one never been 'fraid of no crackers[6] mind you—but—well, wasn't there no other houses nowhere?

MAMA: Them houses they put up for colored in them areas way out all seem to cost twice as much as other houses. I did the best I could.

RUTH: [*Struck senseless with the news, in its various degrees of goodness and trouble, she sits a moment, her fists propping her chin in thought, and then she starts to rise, bringing her fists down with vigor, the radiance spreading from cheek to cheek again.*] Well—well!—All I can say is—if this is my time in life—*my time*—to say good-bye— [*And she builds with momentum as she starts to circle the room with an exuberant, almost tearfully happy release.*] —to these God-damned cracking walls!— [*She pounds the walls.*] —and these marching roaches!— [*She wipes at an imaginary army of marching roaches.*] —and this cramped little closet which ain't now or never was no kitchen! . . . then I say it loud and good, *Hallelujah! and good-bye misery . . . I don't never want to see your ugly face again!* [*She laughs joyously, having practically destroyed the apartment, and flings her arms up and lets them come down happily, slowly, reflectively, over her abdomen, aware for the first time perhaps that the life therein pulses with happiness and not despair.*] Lena?

MAMA: [*Moved, watching her happiness.*] Yes, honey?

RUTH: [*Looking off.*] Is there—is there a whole lot of sunlight?

MAMA: [*Understanding.*] Yes, child, there's a whole lot of sunlight.

[*Long pause.*]

RUTH: [*Collecting herself and going to the door of the room* TRAVIS *is in.*] Well—I guess I better see 'bout Travis. [*To* MAMA.] Lord, I sure don't feel like whipping nobody today!

[*She exits.*]

MAMA: [*The mother and son are left alone now and the mother waits a long time, considering deeply, before she speaks.*] Son—you—you understand what I done, don't you? [WALTER *is silent and sullen.*] I—I just seen my family falling apart today . . . just falling to pieces in front of my eyes . . . We couldn't of gone on like we was today. We was going backwards 'stead of forwards—talking 'bout killing babies and wishing each other was dead . . . When it gets like that in life—you just got to do something different, push on out and

6. Derogatory term for poor whites.

do something bigger . . . [*She waits.*] I wish you say something, son . . . I wish you'd say how deep inside you you think I done the right thing—

WALTER: [*Crossing slowly to his bedroom door and finally turning there and speaking measuredly.*] What you need me to say you done right for? *You* the head of this family. You run our lives like you want to. It was your money and you did what you wanted with it. So what you need for me to say it was all right for? [*Bitterly, to hurt her as deeply as he knows is possible.*] So you butchered up a dream of mine—you—who always talking 'bout your children's dreams . . .

MAMA: Walter Lee—

[*He just closes the door behind him.* MAMA *sits alone, thinking heavily.*]

[CURTAIN.]

Scene Two

Time: Friday night. A few weeks later.

At rise: Packing crates mark the intention of the family to move. BENEATHA *and* GEORGE *come in, presumably from an evening out again.*

GEORGE: O.K. . . . O.K., whatever you say . . . [*They both sit on the couch. He tries to kiss her. She moves away.*] Look, we've had a nice evening; let's not spoil it, huh? . . .

[*He again turns her head and tries to nuzzle in and she turns away from him, not with distaste but with momentary lack of interest; in a mood to pursue what they were talking about.*]

BENEATHA: I'm *trying* to talk to you.

GEORGE: We always talk.

BENEATHA: Yes—and I love to talk.

GEORGE: [*Exasperated; rising.*] I know it and I don't mind it sometimes . . . I want you to cut it out, see—The moody stuff, I mean. I don't like it. You're a nice-looking girl . . . all over. That's all you need, honey, forget the atmosphere. Guys aren't going to go for the atmosphere—they're going to go for what they see. Be glad for that. Drop the Garbo[7] routine. It doesn't go with you. As for myself, I want a nice— [*Groping.*] —simple [*Thoughtfully.*] —sophisticated girl . . . not a poet— O.K.?

[*She rebuffs him again and he starts to leave.*]

BENEATHA: Why are you angry?

GEORGE: Because this is stupid! I don't go out with you to discuss the nature of "quiet desperation"[8] or to hear all about your thoughts—because the world will go on thinking what it thinks regardless—

BENEATHA: Then why read books? Why go to school?

GEORGE: [*With artificial patience, counting on his fingers.*] It's simple. You read books—to learn facts—to get grades—to pass the course—to get a degree. That's all—it has nothing to do with thoughts.

7. Greta Garbo (1905–90), Swedish-born American film star whose sultry, remote, and European femininity was widely imitated.

8. In *Walden* (1854), Henry Thoreau asserts that "the mass of men lead lives of quiet desperation."

[*A long pause.*]

BENEATHA: I see. [*A longer pause as she looks at him.*] Good night, George.

[GEORGE *looks at her a little oddly, and starts to exit. He meets* MAMA *coming in.*]

GEORGE: Oh—hello, Mrs. Younger.
MAMA: Hello, George, how you feeling?
GEORGE: Fine—fine, how are you?
MAMA: Oh, a little tired. You know them steps can get you after a day's work. You all have a nice time tonight?
GEORGE: Yes—a fine time. Well, good night.
MAMA: Good night. [*He exits.* MAMA *closes the door behind her.*] Hello, honey. What you sitting like that for?
BENEATHA: I'm just sitting.
MAMA: Didn't you have a nice time?
BENEATHA: No.
MAMA: No? What's the matter?
BENEATHA: Mama, George is a fool—honest. [*She rises.*]
MAMA: [*Hustling around unloading the packages she has entered with. She stops.*] Is he, baby?
BENEATHA: Yes.

[BENEATHA *makes up* TRAVIS' *bed as she talks.*]

MAMA: You sure?
BENEATHA: Yes.
MAMA: Well—I guess you better not waste your time with no fools.

[BENEATHA *looks up at her mother, watching her put groceries in the refrigerator. Finally she gathers up her things and starts into the bedroom. At the door she stops and looks back at her mother.*]

BENEATHA: Mama—
MAMA: Yes, baby—
BENEATHA: Thank you.
MAMA: For what?
BENEATHA: For understanding me this time.

[*She exits quickly and the mother stands, smiling a little, looking at the place where* BENEATHA *just stood.* RUTH *enters.*]

RUTH: Now don't you fool with any of this stuff, Lena—
MAMA: Oh, I just thought I'd sort a few things out.

[*The phone rings.* RUTH *answers.*]

RUTH: [*At the phone.*] Hello—Just a minute. [*Goes to door.*] Walter, it's Mrs. Arnold. [*Waits. Goes back to the phone. Tense.*] Hello. Yes, this is his wife speaking . . . He's lying down now. Yes . . . well, he'll be in tomorrow. He's been very sick. Yes—I know we should have called, but we were so sure he'd be able to come in today. Yes—yes, I'm very sorry. Yes . . . Thank you very much. [*She hangs up.* WALTER *is standing in the doorway of the bedroom behind her.*] That was Mrs. Arnold.

WALTER: [*Indifferently.*] Was it?

RUTH: She said if you don't come in tomorrow that they are getting a new man . . .

WALTER: Ain't that sad—ain't that crying sad.

RUTH: She said Mr. Arnold has had to take a cab for three days . . . Walter, you ain't been to work for three days! [*This is a revelation to her.*] Where you been, Walter Lee Younger? [WALTER *looks at her and starts to laugh.*] You're going to lose your job.

WALTER: That's right . . .

RUTH: Oh, Walter, and with your mother working like a dog every day—

WALTER: That's sad too—Everything is sad.

MAMA: What you been doing for these three days, son?

WALTER: Mama—you don't know all the things a man what got leisure can find to do in this city . . . What's this—Friday night? Well—Wednesday I borrowed Willy Harris' car and I went for a drive . . . just me and myself and I drove and drove . . . Way out . . . way past South Chicago, and I parked the car and I sat and looked at the steel mills all day long. I just sat in the car and looked at them big black chimneys for hours. Then I drove back and I went to the Green Hat. [*Pause.*] And Thursday—Thursday I borrowed the car again and I got in it and I pointed it the other way and I drove the other way—for hours—way, way up to Wisconsin, and I looked at the farms. I just drove and looked at the farms. Then I drove back and I went to the Green Hat. [*Pause.*] And today—today I didn't get the car. Today I just walked. All over the Southside. And I looked at the Negroes and they looked at me and finally I just sat down on the curb at Thirty-ninth and South Parkway and I just sat there and watched the Negroes go by. And then I went to the Green Hat. You all sad? You all depressed? And you know where I am going right now—

[RUTH *goes out quietly.*]

MAMA: Oh, Big Walter, is this the harvest of our days?

WALTER: You know what I like about the Green Hat? [*He turns the radio on and a steamy, deep blues pours into the room.*] I like this little cat they got there who blows a sax . . . He blows. He talks to me. He ain't but 'bout five feet tall and he's got a conked head[9] and his eyes is always closed and he's all music—

MAMA: [*Rising and getting some papers out of her handbag.*] Walter—

WALTER: And there's this other guy who plays the piano . . . and they got a sound. I mean they can work on some music . . . They got the best little combo in the world in the Green Hat . . . You can just sit there and drink and listen to them three men play and you realize that don't nothing matter worth a damn, but just being there—

MAMA: I've helped do it to you, haven't I, son? Walter, I been wrong.

WALTER: Naw—you ain't never been wrong about nothing, Mama.

MAMA: Listen to me, now. I say I been wrong, son. That I been doing to you what the rest of the world been doing to you. [*She stops and he looks up slowly*

9. Straightened hair.

at her and she meets his eyes pleadingly.] Walter—what you ain't never understood is that I ain't got nothing, don't own nothing, ain't never really wanted nothing that wasn't for you. There ain't nothing as precious to me . . . There ain't nothing worth holding on to, money, dreams, nothing else—if it means—if it means it's going to destroy my boy. [*She puts her papers in front of him and he watches her without speaking or moving.*] I paid the man thirty-five hundred dollars down on the house. That leaves sixty-five hundred dollars. Monday morning I want you to take this money and take three thousand dollars and put it in a savings account for Beneatha's medical schooling. The rest you put in a checking account—with your name on it. And from now on any penny that come out of it or that go in it is for you to look after. For you to decide. [*She drops her hands a little helplessly.*] It ain't much, but it's all I got in the world and I'm putting it in your hands. I'm telling you to be the head of this family from now on like you supposed to be.

WALTER: [*Stares at the money.*] You trust me like that, Mama?

MAMA: I ain't never stop trusting you. Like I ain't never stop loving you.

[*She goes out, and* WALTER *sits looking at the money on the table as the music continues in its idiom, pulsing in the room. Finally, in a decisive gesture, he gets up, and, in mingled joy and desperation, picks up the money. At the same moment,* TRAVIS *enters for bed.*]

TRAVIS: What's the matter, Daddy? You drunk?

WALTER: [*Sweetly, more sweetly than we have ever known him.*] No, Daddy ain't drunk. Daddy ain't going to never be drunk again. . . .

TRAVIS: Well, good night, Daddy.

[*The father has come from behind the couch and leans over, embracing his son.*]

WALTER: Son, I feel like talking to you tonight.

TRAVIS: About what?

WALTER: Oh, about a lot of things. About you and what kind of man you going to be when you grow up . . . Son—son, what do you want to be when you grow up?

TRAVIS: A bus driver.

WALTER: [*Laughing a little.*] A what? Man, that ain't nothing to want to be!

TRAVIS: Why not?

WALTER: 'Cause, man—it ain't big enough—you know what I mean.

TRAVIS: I don't know then. I can't make up my mind. Sometimes Mama asks me that too. And sometimes when I tell her I just want to be like you—she says she don't want me to be like that and sometimes she says she does . . .

WALTER: [*Gathering him up in his arms.*] You know what, Travis? In seven years you going to be seventeen years old. And things is going to be very different with us in seven years, Travis . . . One day when you are seventeen I'll come home—home from my office downtown somewhere—

TRAVIS: You don't work in no office, Daddy.

WALTER: No—but after tonight. After what your daddy gonna do tonight, there's going to be offices—a whole lot of offices . . .

TRAVIS: What you gonna do tonight, Daddy?

WALTER: You wouldn't understand yet, son, but your daddy's gonna make a transaction . . . a business transaction that's going to change our lives . . . That's how come one day when you 'bout seventeen years old I'll come home and I'll be pretty tired, you know what I mean, after a day of conferences and secretaries getting things wrong the way they do . . .'cause an executive's life is hell, man— [*The more he talks the farther away he gets.*] And I'll pull the car up on the driveway . . . just a plain black Chrysler, I think, with white walls—no—black tires. More elegant. Rich people don't have to be flashy . . . though I'll have to get something a little sportier for Ruth—maybe a Cadillac convertible to do her shopping in . . . And I'll come up the steps to the house and the gardener will be clipping away at the hedges and he'll say, "Good evening, Mr. Younger." And I'll say, "Hello, Jefferson, how are you this evening?" And I'll go inside and Ruth will come downstairs and meet me at the door and we'll kiss each other and she'll take my arm and we'll go up to your room to see you sitting on the floor with the catalogues of all the great schools in America around you . . . All the great schools in the world. And—and I'll say, all right son—it's your seventeenth birthday, what is it you've decided? . . . Just tell me where you want to go to school and you'll *go.* Just tell me, what it is you want to be—and you'll *be* it . . . Whatever you want to be—Yessir! [*He holds his arms open for* TRAVIS.] You just name it, son . . . [TRAVIS *leaps into them.*] and I hand you the world!

[WALTER'S *voice has risen in pitch and hysterical promise and on the last line he lifts* TRAVIS *high.*]

[BLACKOUT.]

Scene Three

Time: Saturday, moving day, one week later.

Before the curtain rises, RUTH'S *voice, a strident, dramatic church alto, cuts through the silence.*

It is, in the darkness, a triumphant surge, a penetrating statement of expectation: "Oh, Lord, I don't feel no ways tired! Children, oh, glory hallelujah!"

As the curtain rises we see that RUTH *is alone in the living room, finishing up the family's packing. It is moving day. She is nailing crates and tying cartons.* BENEATHA *enters, carrying a guitar case, and watches her exuberant sister-in-law.*

RUTH: Hey!

BENEATHA: [*Putting away the case.*] Hi.

RUTH: [*Pointing at a package.*] Honey—look in that package there and see what I found on sale this morning at the South Center. [RUTH *gets up and moves to the package and draws out some curtains.*] Lookahere—hand-turned hems!

BENEATHA: How do you know the window size out there?

RUTH: [*Who hadn't thought of that.*] Oh—Well, they bound to fit something in the whole house. Anyhow, they was too good a bargain to pass up. [RUTH *slaps her head, suddenly remembering something.*] Oh, Bennie—I meant to put a special note on that carton over there. That's your mama's good china and she wants 'em to be very careful with it.

BENEATHA: I'll do it.

[BENEATHA *finds a piece of paper and starts to draw large letters on it.*]

RUTH: You know what I'm going to do soon as I get in that new house?

BENEATHA: What?

RUTH: Honey—I'm going to run me a tub of water up to here . . . [*With her fingers practically up to her nostrils.*] And I'm going to get in it—and I am going to sit . . . and sit . . . and sit in that hot water and the first person who knocks to tell *me* to hurry up and come out—

BENEATHA: Gets shot at sunrise.

RUTH: [*Laughing happily.*] You said it, sister! [*Noticing how large* BENEATHA *is absentmindedly making the note.*] Honey, they ain't going to read that from no airplane.

BENEATHA: [*Laughing herself.*] I guess I always think things have more emphasis if they are big, somehow.

RUTH: [*Looking up at her and smiling.*] You and your brother seem to have that as a philosophy of life. Lord, that man—done changed so 'round here. You know—you know what we did last night? Me and Walter Lee?

BENEATHA: What?

RUTH: [*Smiling to herself.*] We went to the movies. [*Looking at* BENEATHA *to see if she understands.*] We went to the movies. You know the last time me and Walter went to the movies together?

BENEATHA: No.

RUTH: Me neither. That's how long it been. [*Smiling again.*] But we went last night. The picture wasn't much good, but that didn't seem to matter. We went—and we held hands.

BENEATHA: Oh, Lord!

RUTH: We held hands—and you know what?

BENEATHA: What?

RUTH: When we come out of the show it was late and dark and all the stores and things was closed up . . . and it was kind of chilly and there wasn't many people on the streets . . . and we was still holding hands, me and Walter.

BENEATHA: You're killing me.

[WALTER *enters with a large package. His happiness is deep in him; he cannot keep still with his new-found exuberance. He is singing and wiggling and snapping his fingers. He puts his package in a corner and puts a phonograph record, which he has brought in with him, on the record player. As the music comes up he dances over to* RUTH *and tries to get her to dance with him. She gives in at last to his raunchiness and in a fit of giggling allows herself to be drawn into his mood and together they deliberately burlesque an old social dance of their youth.*]

BENEATHA: [*Regarding them a long time as they dance, then drawing in her breath for a deeply exaggerated comment which she does not particularly mean.*] Talk about—olddddddddd-fashioneddddddd—Negroes!

WALTER: [*Stopping momentarily.*] What kind of Negroes?

[*He says this in fun. He is not angry with her today, nor with anyone. He starts to dance with his wife again.*]

BENEATHA: Old-fashioned.

WALTER: [*As he dances with* RUTH.] You know, when these *New Negroes* have their convention— [*Pointing at his sister.*] —that is going to be the chairman of the Committee on Unending Agitation. [*He goes on dancing, then stops.*] Race, race, race! . . . Girl, I do believe you are the first person in the history of the entire human race to successfully brainwash yourself. [BENEATHA *breaks up and he goes on dancing. He stops again, enjoying his tease.*] Damn, even the N double A C P[1] takes a holiday sometimes! [BENEATHA *and* RUTH *laugh. He dances with* RUTH *some more and starts to laugh and stops and pantomimes someone over an operating table.*] I can just see that chick someday looking down at some poor cat on an operating table before she starts to slice him, saying . . . [*Pulling his sleeves back maliciously.*] "By the way, what are your views on civil rights down there? . . ."

[*He laughs at her again and starts to dance happily. The bell sounds.*]

BENEATHA: Sticks and stones may break my bones but . . . words will never hurt me!

[BENEATHA *goes to the door and opens it as* WALTER *and* RUTH *go on with the clowning.* BENEATHA *is somewhat surprised to see a quiet-looking middle-aged white man in a business suit holding his hat and a briefcase in his hand and consulting a small piece of paper.*]

MAN: Uh—how do you do, miss. I am looking for a Mrs.— [*He looks at the slip of paper.*] Mrs. Lena Younger?

BENEATHA: [*Smoothing her hair with slight embarrassment.*] Oh—yes, that's my mother. Excuse me [*She closes the door and turns to quiet the other two.*] Ruth! Brother! Somebody's here. [*Then she opens the door. The* MAN *casts a curious quick glance at all of them.*] Uh—come in please.

MAN: [*Coming in.*] Thank you.

BENEATHA: My mother isn't here just now. Is it business?

MAN: Yes . . . well, of a sort.

WALTER: [*Freely, the Man of the House.*] Have a seat. I'm Mrs. Younger's son. I look after most of her business matters.

[RUTH *and* BENEATHA *exchange amused glances.*]

MAN: [*Regarding* WALTER, *and sitting.*] Well—My name is Karl Lindner . . .

WALTER: [*Stretching out his hand.*] Walter Younger. This is my wife— [RUTH *nods politely.*] —and my sister.

LINDNER: How do you do.

WALTER: [*Amiably, as he sits himself easily on a chair, leaning with interest forward on his knees and looking expectantly into the newcomer's face.*] What can we do for you, Mr. Lindner!

LINDNER: [*Some minor shuffling of the hat and briefcase on his knees.*] Well—I am a representative of the Clybourne Park Improvement Association—

WALTER: [*Pointing.*] Why don't you sit your things on the floor?

1. National Association for the Advancement of Colored People, civil rights organization founded in 1909.

LINDNER: Oh—yes. Thank you. [*He slides the briefcase and hat under the chair.*] And as I was saying—I am from the Clybourne Park Improvement Association and we have had it brought to our attention at the last meeting that you people—or at least your mother—has bought a piece of residential property at— [*He digs for the slip of paper again.*] —four o six Clybourne Street . . .

WALTER: That's right. Care for something to drink? Ruth, get Mr. Lindner a beer.

LINDNER: [*Upset for some reason.*] Oh—no, really. I mean thank you very much, but no thank you.

RUTH: [*Innocently.*] Some coffee?

LINDNER: Thank you, nothing at all.

[BENEATHA *is watching the man carefully.*]

LINDNER: Well, I don't know how much you folks know about our organization. [*He is a gentle man; thoughtful and somewhat labored in his manner.*] It is one of these community organizations set up to look after—oh, you know, things like block upkeep and special projects and we also have what we call our New Neighbors Orientation Committee . . .

BENEATHA: [*Drily.*] Yes—and what do they do?

LINDNER: [*Turning a little to her and then returning the main force to* WALTER.] Well—it's what you might call a sort of welcoming committee, I guess. I mean they, we, I'm the chairman of the committee—go around and see the new people who move into the neighborhood and sort of give them the lowdown on the way we do things out in Clybourne Park.

BENEATHA: [*With appreciation of the two meanings, which escape* RUTH *and* WALTER.] Un-huh.

LINDNER: And we also have the category of what the association calls— [*He looks elsewhere.*] —uh—special community problems . . .

BENEATHA: Yes—and what are some of those?

WALTER: Girl, let the man talk.

LINDNER: [*With understated relief.*] Thank you. I would sort of like to explain this thing in my own way. I mean I want to explain to you in a certain way.

WALTER: Go ahead.

LINDNER: Yes. Well. I'm going to try to get right to the point. I'm sure we'll all appreciate that in the long run.

BENEATHA: Yes.

WALTER: Be still now!

LINDNER: Well—

RUTH: [*Still innocently.*] Would you like another chair—you don't look comfortable.

LINDNER: [*More frustrated than annoyed.*] No, thank you very much. Please. Well—to get right to the point I— [*A great breath, and he is off at last.*] I am sure you people must be aware of some of the incidents which have happened in various parts of the city when colored people have moved into certain areas— [BENEATHA *exhales heavily and starts tossing a piece of fruit up and down in the air.*] Well—because we have what I think is going to be a unique type of organization in American community life—not only do we deplore that kind of thing—but we are trying to do something about it.

[BENEATHA *stops tossing and turns with a new and quizzical interest to the man.*] We feel— [*Gaining confidence in his mission because of the interest in the faces of the people he is talking to.*] —we feel that most of the trouble in this world, when you come right down to it— [*He hits his knee for emphasis.*] —most of the trouble exists because people just don't sit down and talk to each other.

RUTH: [*Nodding as she might in church, pleased with the remark.*] You can say that again, mister.

LINDNER: [*More encouraged by such affirmation.*] That we don't try hard enough in this world to understand the other fellow's problem. The other guy's point of view.

RUTH: Now that's right.

[BENEATHA *and* WALTER *merely watch and listen with genuine interest.*]

LINDNER: Yes—that's the way we feel out in Clybourne Park. And that's why I was elected to come here this afternoon and talk to you people. Friendly like, you know, the way people should talk to each other and see if we couldn't find some way to work this thing out. As I say, the whole business is a matter of *caring* about the other fellow. Anybody can see that you are a nice family of folks, hard working and honest I'm sure. [BENEATHA *frowns slightly, quizzically, her head tilted regarding him.*] Today everybody knows what it means to be on the outside of something. And of course, there is always somebody who is out to take the advantage of people who don't always understand.

WALTER: What do you mean?

LINDNER: Well—you see our community is made up of people who've worked hard as the dickens for years to build up that little community. They're not rich and fancy people; just hard-working, honest people who don't really have much but those little homes and a dream of the kind of community they want to raise their children in. Now, I don't say we are perfect and there is a lot wrong in some of the things they want. But you've got to admit that a man, right or wrong, has the right to want to have the neighborhood he lives in a certain kind of way. And at the moment the overwhelming majority of our people out there feel that people get along better, take more of a common interest in the life of the community, when they share a common background. I want you to believe me when I tell you that race prejudice simply doesn't enter into it. It is a matter of the people of Clybourne Park believing, rightly or wrongly, as I say, that for the happiness of all concerned that our Negro families are happier when they live in their *own* communities.

BENEATHA: [*With a grand and bitter gesture.*] This, friends, is the Welcoming Committee!

WALTER: [*Dumfounded, looking at* LINDNER.] Is this what you came marching all the way over here to tell us?

LINDNER: Well, now we've been having a fine conversation. I hope you'll hear me all the way through.

WALTER: [*Tightly.*] Go ahead, man.

LINDNER: You see—in the face of all things I have said, we are prepared to make your family a very generous offer . . .

BENEATHA: Thirty pieces and not a coin less![2]

WALTER: Yeah?

LINDNER: [*Putting on his glasses and drawing a form out of the briefcase.*] Our association is prepared, through the collective effort of our people, to buy the house from you at a financial gain to your family.

RUTH: Lord have mercy, ain't this the living gall!

WALTER: All right, you through?

LINDNER: Well, I want to give you the exact terms of the financial arrangement—

WALTER: We don't want to hear no exact terms of no arrangements. I want to know if you got any more to tell us 'bout getting together?

LINDNER: [*Taking off his glasses.*] Well—I don't suppose that you feel . . .

WALTER: Never mind how I feel—you got any more to say 'bout how people ought to sit down and talk to each other? . . . Get out of my house, man.

[*He turns his back and walks to the door.*]

LINDNER: [*Looking around at the hostile faces and reaching and assembling his hat and briefcase.*] Well—I don't understand why you people are reacting this way. What do you think you are going to gain by moving into a neighborhood where you just aren't wanted and where some elements—well—people can get awful worked up when they feel that their whole way of life and everything they've ever worked for is threatened.

WALTER: Get out.

LINDNER: [*At the door, holding a small card.*] Well—I'm sorry it went like this.

WALTER: Get out.

LINDNER: [*Almost sadly regarding* WALTER.] You just can't force people to change their hearts, son.

[*He turns and puts his card on a table and exits.* WALTER *pushes the door to with stinging hatred, and stands looking at it.* RUTH *just sits and* BENEATHA *just stands. They say nothing.* MAMA *and* TRAVIS *enter.*]

MAMA: Well—this all the packing got done since I left out of here this morning. I testify before God that my children got all the energy of the dead. What time the moving men due?

BENEATHA: Four o'clock. You had a caller, Mama.

[*She is smiling, teasingly.*]

MAMA: Sure enough—who?

BENEATHA: [*Her arms folded saucily.*] The Welcoming Committee.

[WALTER *and* RUTH *giggle.*]

MAMA: [*Innocently.*] Who?

BENEATHA: The Welcoming Committee. They said they're sure going to be glad to see you when you get there.

WALTER: [*Devilishly.*] Yeah, they said they can't hardly wait to see your face.

[*Laughter.*]

2. See Matthew 26.15, in which Judas Iscariot is paid thirty pieces of silver to betray Jesus.

MAMA: [*Sensing their facetiousness.*] What's the matter with you all?

WALTER: Ain't nothing the matter with us. We just telling you 'bout the gentleman who came to see you this afternoon. From the Clybourne Park Improvement Association.

MAMA: What he want?

RUTH: [*In the same mood as* BENEATHA *and* WALTER.] To welcome you, honey.

WALTER: He said they can't hardly wait. He said the one thing they don't have, that they just *dying* to have out there is a fine family of colored people! [*To* RUTH *and* BENEATHA.] Ain't that right!

RUTH AND BENEATHA: [*Mockingly.*] Yeah! He left his card in case—

[*They indicate the card, and* MAMA *picks it up and throws it on the floor—understanding and looking off as she draws her chair up to the table on which she has put her plant and some sticks and some cord.*]

MAMA: Father, give us strength. [*Knowingly—and without fun.*] Did he threaten us?

BENEATHA: Oh—Mama—they don't do it like that anymore. He talked Brotherhood. He said everybody ought to learn how to sit down and hate each other with good Christian fellowship.

[*She and* WALTER *shake hands to ridicule the remark.*]

MAMA: [*Sadly.*] Lord, protect us . . .

RUTH: You should hear the money those folks raised to buy the house from us. All we paid and then some.

BENEATHA: What they think we going to do—eat 'em?

RUTH: No, honey, marry 'em.

MAMA: [*Shaking her head.*] Lord, Lord, Lord . . .

RUTH: Well—that's the way the crackers crumble. Joke.

BENEATHA: [*Laughingly noticing what her mother is doing.*] Mama, what are you doing?

MAMA: Fixing my plant so it won't get hurt none on the way . . .

BENEATHA: Mama, you going to take *that* to the new house?

MAMA: Un-huh—

BENEATHA: That raggedy-looking old thing?

MAMA: [*Stopping and looking at her.*] It expresses *me.*

RUTH: [*With delight, to* BENEATHA.] So there, Miss Thing!

[WALTER *comes to* MAMA *suddenly and bends down behind her and squeezes her in his arms with all his strength. She is overwhelmed by the suddenness of it and, though delighted, her manner is like that of* RUTH *with* TRAVIS.]

MAMA: Look out now, boy! You make me mess up my thing here!

WALTER: [*His face lit, he slips down on his knees beside her, his arms still about her.*] Mama . . . you know what it means to climb up in the chariot?

MAMA: [*Gruffly, very happy.*] Get on away from me now . . .

RUTH: [*Near the gift-wrapped package, trying to catch* WALTER'S *eye.*] Psst—

WALTER: What the old song say, Mama . . .

RUTH: Walter—Now?

[*She is pointing at the package.*]

WALTER: [*Speaking the lines, sweetly, playfully, in his mother's face.*]

> I got wings . . . you got wings . . .
> All God's Children got wings[3] . . .

MAMA: Boy—get out of my face and do some work . . .

WALTER:

> When I get to heaven gonna put on my wings,
> Gonna fly all over God's heaven . . .

BENEATHA: [*Teasingly, from across the room.*] Everybody talking 'bout heaven ain't going there!

WALTER: [*To* RUTH, *who is carrying the box across to them.*] I don't know, you think we ought to give her that . . . Seems to me she ain't been very appreciative around here.

MAMA: [*Eying the box, which is obviously a gift.*] What is that?

WALTER: [*Taking it from* RUTH *and putting it on the table in front of* MAMA.] Well—what you all think? Should we give it to her?

RUTH: Oh—she was pretty good today.

MAMA: I'll good you—

[*She turns her eyes to the box again.*]

BENEATHA: Open it, Mama.

[*She stands up, looks at it, turns and looks at all of them, and then presses her hands together and does not open the package.*]

WALTER: [*Sweetly.*] Open it, Mama. It's for you. [MAMA *looks in his eyes. It is the first present in her life without its being Christmas. Slowly she opens her package and lifts out, one by one, a brand-new sparkling set of gardening tools.* WALTER *continues, prodding.*] Ruth made up the note—read it . . .

MAMA: [*Picking up the card and adjusting her glasses.*] "To our own Mrs. Miniver[4]—Love from Brother, Ruth and Beneatha." Ain't that lovely . . .

TRAVIS: [*Tugging at his father's sleeve.*] Daddy, can I give her mine now?

WALTER: All right, son. [TRAVIS *flies to get his gift.*] Travis didn't want to go in with the rest of us, Mama. He got his own. [*Somewhat amused.*] We don't know what it is . . .

TRAVIS: [*Racing back in the room with a large hatbox and putting it in front of his grandmother.*] Here!

MAMA: Lord have mercy, baby. You done gone and bought your grandmother a hat?

TRAVIS: [*Very proud.*] Open it!

[*She does and lifts out an elaborate, but very elaborate, wide gardening hat, and all the adults break up at the sight of it.*]

RUTH: Travis, honey, what is that?

3. Lines from an African American spiritual. Walter's and Beneatha's next lines are also from the song.
4. Courageous, charismatic title character of a 1942 film starring Greer Garson.

TRAVIS: [*Who thinks it is beautiful and appropriate.*] It's a gardening hat! Like the ladies always have on in the magazines when they work in their gardens.

BENEATHA: [*Giggling fiercely.*] Travis—we were trying to make Mama Mrs. Miniver—not Scarlett O'Hara![5]

MAMA: [*Indignantly.*] What's the matter with you all! This here is a beautiful hat! [*Absurdly.*] I always wanted me one just like it!

[*She pops it on her head to prove it to her grandson, and the hat is ludicrous and considerably oversized.*]

RUTH: Hot dog! Go, Mama!

WALTER: [*Doubled over with laughter.*] I'm sorry, Mama—but you look like you ready to go out and chop you some cotton sure enough!

[*They all laugh except* MAMA, *out of deference to* TRAVIS' *feelings.*]

MAMA: [*Gathering the boy up to her.*] Bless your heart—this is the prettiest hat I ever owned— [WALTER, RUTH *and* BENEATHA *chime in—noisily, festively and insincerely congratulating* TRAVIS *on his gift.*] What are we all standing around here for? We ain't finished packin' yet. Bennie, you ain't packed one book.

[*The bell rings.*]

BENEATHA: That couldn't be the movers . . . it's not hardly two good yet—

[BENEATHA *goes into her room.* MAMA *starts for door.*]

WALTER: [*Turning, stiffening.*] Wait—wait—I'll get it.

[*He stands and looks at the door.*]

MAMA: You expecting company, son?

WALTER: [*Just looking at the door.*] Yeah—yeah . . .

[MAMA *looks at* RUTH, *and they exchange innocent and unfrightened glances.*]

MAMA: [*Not understanding.*] Well, let them in, son.

BENEATHA: [*From her room.*] We need some more string.

MAMA: Travis—you run to the hardware and get me some string cord.

[MAMA *goes out and* WALTER *turns and looks at* RUTH. TRAVIS *goes to a dish for money.*]

RUTH: Why don't you answer the door, man?

WALTER: [*Suddenly bounding across the floor to her.*] 'Cause sometimes it hard to let the future begin! [*Stooping down in her face.*]

I got wings! You got wings!
All God's children got wings!

[*He crosses to the door and throws it open. Standing there is a very slight little man in a not too prosperous business suit and with haunted frightened eyes and a hat pulled down tightly, brim up, around his forehead.* TRAVIS *passes*

5. Glamorous, headstrong heroine of Margaret Mitchell's 1936 historical novel *Gone with the Wind*; Vivien Leigh played Scarlett in the 1939 film adaptation.

between the men and exits. WALTER *leans deep in the man's face, still in his jubilance.*]

When I get to heaven gonna put on my wings,
Gonna fly all over God's heaven . . .

[*The little man just stares at him.*]

Heaven—

[*Suddenly he stops and looks past the little man into the empty hallway.*] Where's Willy, man?

BOBO: He ain't with me.

WALTER: [*Not disturbed.*] Oh—come on in. You know my wife.

BOBO: [*Dumbly, taking off his hat.*] Yes—h'you, Miss Ruth.

RUTH: [*Quietly, a mood apart from her husband already, seeing* BOBO.] Hello, Bobo.

WALTER: You right on time today . . . Right on time. That's the way! [*He slaps* BOBO *on his back.*] Sit down . . . lemme hear.

[RUTH *stands stiffly and quietly in back of them, as though somehow she senses death, her eyes fixed on her husband.*]

BOBO: [*His frightened eyes on the floor, his hat in his hands.*] Could I please get a drink of water, before I tell you about it, Walter Lee?

[WALTER *does not take his eyes off the man.* RUTH *goes blindly to the tap and gets a glass of water and brings it to* BOBO.]

WALTER: There ain't nothing wrong, is there?

BOBO: Lemme tell you—

WALTER: Man—didn't nothing go wrong?

BOBO: Lemme tell you—Walter Lee. [*Looking at* RUTH *and talking to her more than to* WALTER.] You know how it was. I got to tell you how it was. I mean first I got to tell you how it was all the way . . . I mean about the money I put in, Walter Lee . . .

WALTER: [*With taut agitation now.*] What about the money you put in?

BOBO: Well—it wasn't much as we told you—me and Willy— [*He stops.*] I'm sorry, Walter. I got a bad feeling about it. I got a real bad feeling about it . . .

WALTER: Man, what you telling me about all this for? . . . Tell me what happened in Springfield . . .

BOBO: Springfield.

RUTH: [*Like a dead woman.*] What was supposed to happen in Springfield?

BOBO: [*To her.*] This deal that me and Walter went into with Willy—Me and Willy was going to go down to Springfield and spread some money 'round so's we wouldn't have to wait so long for the liquor license . . . That's what we were going to do. Everybody said that was the way you had to do, you understand, Miss Ruth?

WALTER: Man—what happened down there?

BOBO: [*A pitiful man, near tears.*] I'm trying to tell you, Walter.

WALTER: [*Screaming at him suddenly.*] THEN TELL ME, GODDAMMIT . . . WHAT'S THE MATTER WITH YOU?

BOBO: Man . . . I didn't go to no Springfield, yesterday.

WALTER: [*Halted, life hanging in the moment.*] Why not?

BOBO: [*The long way, the hard way to tell.*] 'Cause I didn't have no reasons to . . .

WALTER: Man, what are you talking about!

BOBO: I'm talking about the fact that when I got to the train station yesterday morning—eight o'clock like we planned . . . Man—*Willy didn't never show up.*

WALTER: Why . . . where was he . . . where is he?

BOBO: That's what I'm trying to tell you . . . I don't know . . . I waited six hours . . . I called his house . . . and I waited . . . six hours . . . I waited in that train station six hours . . . [*Breaking into tears.*] That was all the extra money I had in the world . . . [*Looking up at* WALTER *with the tears running down his face.*] Man, *Willy is gone.*

WALTER: Gone, what you mean Willy is gone? Gone where? You mean he went by himself. You mean he went off to Springfield by himself—to take care of getting the license— [*Turns and looks anxiously at* RUTH.] You mean maybe he didn't want too many people in on the business down there? [*Looks to* RUTH *again, as before.*] You know Willy got his own ways. [*Looks back to* BOBO.] Maybe you was late yesterday and he just went on down there without you. Maybe—maybe—he's been callin' you at home tryin' to tell you what happened or something. Maybe—maybe—he just got sick. He's somewhere—he's got to be somewhere. We just got to find him—me and you got to find him. [*Grabs* BOBO *senselessly by the collar and starts to shake him.*] We got to!

BOBO: [*In sudden angry, frightened agony.*] What's the matter with you, Walter! *When a cat take off with your money he don't leave you no maps!*

WALTER: [*Turning madly, as though he is looking for* WILLY *in the very room.*] Willy! . . . Willy . . . don't do it . . . Please don't do it . . . Man, not with that money . . . Man, please, not with that money . . . Oh, God . . . Don't let it be true . . . [*He is wandering around, crying out for* WILLY *and looking for him or perhaps for help from God.*] Man . . . I trusted you . . . Man, I put my life in your hands . . . [*He starts to crumple down on the floor as* RUTH *just covers her face in horror.* MAMA *opens the door and comes into the room, with* BENEATHA *behind her.*] Man . . . [*He starts to pound the floor with his fists, sobbing wildly.*] *That money is made out of my father's flesh . . .*

BOBO: [*Standing over him helplessly.*] I'm sorry, Walter . . . [*Only* WALTER*'s sobs reply.* BOBO *puts on his hat.*] I had my life staked on this deal, too . . .

[*He exits.*]

MAMA: [*To* WALTER.] Son— [*She goes to him, bends down to him, talks to his bent head.*] Son . . . Is it gone? Son, I gave you sixty-five hundred dollars. Is it gone? All of it? Beneatha's money too?

WALTER: [*Lifting his head slowly.*] Mama . . . I never . . . went to the bank at all . . .

MAMA: [*Not wanting to believe him.*] You mean . . . your sister's school money . . . you used that too . . . Walter? . . .

WALTER: Yessss! . . . All of it . . . It's all gone . . . [*There is total silence.* RUTH *stands with her face covered with her hands;* BENEATHA *leans forlornly against a wall, fingering a piece of red ribbon from the mother's gift.* MAMA *stops and looks at her son without recognition and then, quite without thinking about it, starts to beat him senselessly in the face.* BENEATHA *goes to them and stops it.*]

BENEATHA: Mama!

[MAMA *stops and looks at both of her children and rises slowly and wanders vaguely, aimlessly away from them.*]

MAMA: I seen . . . him . . . night after night . . . come in . . . and look at that rug . . . and then look at me . . . the red showing in his eyes . . . the veins moving in his head . . . I seen him grow thin and old before he was forty . . . working and working and working like somebody's old horse . . . killing himself . . . and you—you give it all away in a day . . .

BENEATHA: Mama—

MAMA: Oh, God . . . [*She looks up to Him.*] Look down here—and show me the strength.

BENEATHA: Mama—

MAMA: [*Folding over.*] Strength . . .

BENEATHA: [*Plaintively.*] Mama . . .

MAMA: Strength!

[CURTAIN.]

ACT III

An hour later.

At curtain, there is a sullen light of gloom in the living room, gray light not unlike that which began the first scene of Act I. At left we can see WALTER *within his room, alone with himself. He is stretched out on the bed, his shirt out and open, his arms under his head. He does not smoke, he does not cry out, he merely lies there, looking up at the ceiling, much as if he were alone in the world.*

In the living room BENEATHA *sits at the table, still surrounded by the now almost ominous packing crates. She sits looking off. We feel that this is a mood struck perhaps an hour before, and it lingers now, full of the empty sound of profound disappointment. We see on a line from her brother's bedroom the sameness of their attitudes. Presently the bell rings and* BENEATHA *rises without ambition or interest in answering. It is* ASAGAI, *smiling broadly, striding into the room with energy and happy expectation and conversation.*

ASAGAI: I came over . . . I had some free time. I thought I might help with the packing. Ah, I like the look of packing crates! A household in preparation for a journey! It depresses some people . . . but for me . . . it is another feeling. Something full of the flow of life, do you understand? Movement, progress . . . It makes me think of Africa.

BENEATHA: Africa!

ASAGAI: What kind of a mood is this? Have I told you how deeply you move me?

BENEATHA: He gave away the money, Asagai . . .

ASAGAI: Who gave away what money?

BENEATHA: The insurance money. My brother gave it away.

ASAGAI: Gave it away?

BENEATHA: He made an investment! With a man even Travis wouldn't have trusted.

ASAGAI: And it's gone?

BENEATHA: Gone!

ASAGAI: I'm very sorry . . . And you, now?

BENEATHA: Me? . . . Me? . . . Me, I'm nothing . . . Me. When I was very small . . . we used to take our sleds out in the wintertime and the only hills we had were the ice-covered stone steps of some houses down the street. And we used to fill them in with snow and make them smooth and slide down them all day . . . and it was very dangerous you know . . . far too steep . . . and sure enough one day a kid named Rufus came down too fast and hit the sidewalk . . . and we saw his face just split open right there in front of us . . . And I remember standing there looking at his bloody open face thinking that was the end of Rufus. But the ambulance came and they took him to the hospital and they fixed the broken bones and they sewed it all up . . . and the next time I saw Rufus he just had a little line down the middle of his face . . . I never got over that . . .

[WALTER *sits up, listening on the bed. Throughout this scene it is important that we feel his reaction at all times, that he visibly respond to the words of his sister and* ASAGAI.]

ASAGAI: What?

BENEATHA: That that was what one person could do for another, fix him up—sew up the problem, make him all right again. That was the most marvelous thing in the world . . . I wanted to do that. I always thought it was the one concrete thing in the world that a human being could do. Fix up the sick, you know—and make them whole again. This was truly being God . . .

ASAGAI: You wanted to be God?

BENEATHA: No—I wanted to cure. It used to be so important to me. I wanted to cure. It used to matter. I used to care. I mean about people and how their bodies hurt . . .

ASAGAI: And you've stopped caring?

BENEATHA: Yes—I think so.

ASAGAI: Why?

[WALTER *rises, goes to the door of his room and is about to open it, then stops and stands listening, leaning on the door jamb.*]

BENEATHA: Because it doesn't seem deep enough, close enough to what ails mankind—I mean this thing of sewing up bodies or administering drugs. Don't you understand? It was a child's reaction to the world. I thought that doctors had the secret to all the hurts . . . That's the way a child sees things—or an idealist.

ASAGAI: Children see things very well sometimes—and idealists even better.

BENEATHA: I know that's what you think. Because you are still where I left off—you still care. This is what you see for the world, for Africa. You with the dreams of the future will patch up all Africa—you are going to cure the Great Sore of colonialism with Independence—

ASAGAI: Yes!

BENEATHA: Yes—and you think that one word is the penicillin of the human spirit: "Independence!" But then what?

ASAGAI: That will be the problem for another time. First we must get there.

BENEATHA: And where does it end?

ASAGAI: End? Who even spoke of an end? To life? To living?

BENEATHA: An end to misery!

ASAGAI: [*Smiling*.] You sound like a French intellectual.

BENEATHA: No! I sound like a human being who just had her future taken right out of her hands! While I was sleeping in my bed in there, things were happening in this world that directly concerned me—and nobody asked me, consulted me—they just went out and did things—and changed my life. Don't you see there isn't any real progress, Asagai, there is only one large circle that we march in, around and around, each of us with our own little picture—in front of us—our own little mirage that we think is the future.

ASAGAI: That is the mistake.

BENEATHA: What?

ASAGAI: What you just said—about the circle. It isn't a circle—it is simply a long line—as in geometry, you know, one that reaches into infinity. And because we cannot see the end—we also cannot see how it changes. And it is very odd but those who see the changes are called "idealists"—and those who cannot, or refuse to think, they are the "realists." It is very strange, and amusing too, I think.

BENEATHA: You—you are almost religious.

ASAGAI: Yes . . . I think I have the religion of doing what is necessary in the world—and of worshipping man—because he is so marvelous, you see.

BENEATHA: Man is foul! And the human race deserves its misery!

ASAGAI: You see: *you* have become the religious one in the old sense. Already, and after such a small defeat, you are worshipping despair.

BENEATHA: From now on, I worship the truth—and the truth is that people are puny, small and selfish . . .

ASAGAI: Truth? Why is it that you despairing ones always think that only you have the truth? I never thought to see *you* like that. You! Your brother made a stupid, childish mistake—and you are grateful to him. So that now you can give up the ailing human race on account of it. You talk about what good is struggle; what good is anything? Where are we all going? And why are we bothering?

BENEATHA: *And you cannot answer it!* All your talk and dreams about Africa and Independence. Independence and then what? What about all the crooks and petty thieves and just plain idiots who will come into power to steal and plunder the same as before—only now they will be black and do it in the name of the new Independence—You cannot answer that.

ASAGAI: [*Shouting over her*.] *I live the answer!* [*Pause*.] In my village at home it is the exceptional man who can even read a newspaper . . . or who ever *sees* a book at all. I will go home and much of what I will have to say will seem strange to the people of my village . . . But I will teach and work and things will happen, slowly and swiftly. At times it will seem that nothing changes at all . . . and then again . . . the sudden dramatic events which make history leap into the future. And then quiet again. Retrogression even. Guns, murder, revolution. And I even will have moments when I wonder if the quiet was not better than all that death and hatred. But I will look about my village at the illiteracy and disease and ignorance and I will not wonder long. And perhaps . . . perhaps I will be a great man . . . I mean perhaps I will hold on to the substance of truth and find my way always with the right course . . . and perhaps for it I will be butchered in my bed some night by the servants of empire . . .

BENEATHA: *The martyr!*

ASAGAI: . . . or perhaps I shall live to be a very old man, respected and esteemed in my new nation . . . And perhaps I shall hold office and this is what I'm trying to tell you, Alaiyo; perhaps the things I believe now for my country will be wrong and outmoded, and I will not understand and do terrible things to have things my way or merely to keep my power. Don't you see that there will be young men and women, not British soldiers then, but my own black countrymen . . . to step out of the shadows some evening and slit my then useless throat? Don't you see they have always been there . . . that they always will be. And that such a thing as my own death will be an advance? They who might kill me even . . . actually replenish me!

BENEATHA: Oh, Asagai, I know all that.

ASAGAI: Good! Then stop moaning and groaning and tell me what you plan to do.

BENEATHA: Do?

ASAGAI: I have a bit of a suggestion.

BENEATHA: What?

ASAGAI: [*Rather quietly for him.*] That when it is all over—that you come home with me—

BENEATHA: [*Slapping herself on the forehead with exasperation born of misunderstanding.*] Oh—Asagai—at this moment you decide to be romantic!

ASAGAI: [*Quickly understanding the misunderstanding.*] My dear, young creature of the New World—I do not mean across the city—I mean across the ocean; home—to Africa.

BENEATHA: [*Slowly understanding and turning to him with murmured amazement.*] To—to Nigeria?

ASAGAI: Yes! . . . [*Smiling and lifting his arms playfully.*] Three hundred years later the African Prince rose up out of the seas and swept the maiden back across the middle passage[6] over which her ancestors had come—

BENEATHA: [*Unable to play.*] Nigeria?

ASAGAI: Nigeria. Home. [*Coming to her with genuine romantic flippancy.*] I will show you our mountains and our stars; and give you cool drinks from gourds and teach you the old songs and the ways of our people—and, in time, we will pretend that— [*Very softly.*] —you have only been away for a day—

[*She turns her back to him, thinking. He swings her around and takes her full in his arms in a long embrace which proceeds to passion.*]

BENEATHA: [*Pulling away.*] You're getting me all mixed up—

6. Term denoting the route traveled by slaves transported from Africa to the Americas.

ASAGAI: Why?

BENEATHA: Too many things—too many things have happened today. I must sit down and think. I don't know what I feel about anything right this minute.

[*She promptly sits down and props her chin on her fist.*]

ASAGAI: [*Charmed.*] All right, I shall leave you. No—don't get up. [*Touching her, gently, sweetly.*] Just sit awhile and think . . . Never be afraid to sit awhile and think. [*He goes to door and looks at her.*] How often I have looked at you and said, "Ah—so this is what the New World hath finally wrought . . ."[7]

[*He exits.* BENEATHA *sits on alone. Presently* WALTER *enters from his room and starts to rummage through things, feverishly looking for something. She looks up and turns in her seat.*]

BENEATHA: [*Hissingly.*] Yes—just look at what the New World hath wrought! . . . Just look! [*She gestures with bitter disgust.*] There he is! *Monsieur le petit bourgeois noir*[8]—himself! There he is—Symbol of a Rising Class! Entrepreneur! Titan of the system! [WALTER *ignores her completely and continues frantically and destructively looking for something and hurling things to the floor and tearing things out of their place in his search.* BENEATHA *ignores the eccentricity of his actions and goes on with the monologue of insult.*] Did you dream of yachts on Lake Michigan, Brother? Did you see yourself on that Great Day sitting down at the Conference Table, surrounded by all the mighty bald-headed men in America? All halted, waiting, breathless, waiting for your pronouncements on industry? Waiting for you—Chairman of the Board? [WALTER *finds what he is looking for—a small piece of white paper—and pushes it in his pocket and puts on his coat and rushes out without ever having looked at her. She shouts after him.*] I look at you and I see the final triumph of stupidity in the world!

[*The door slams and she returns to just sitting again.* RUTH *comes quickly out of* MAMA'S *room.*]

RUTH: Who was that?

BENEATHA: Your husband.

RUTH: Where did he go?

BENEATHA: Who knows—maybe he has an appointment at U.S. Steel.

RUTH: [*Anxiously, with frightened eyes.*] You didn't say nothing bad to him, did you?

BENEATHA: Bad? Say anything bad to him? No—I told him he was a sweet boy and full of dreams and everything is strictly peachy keen, as the ofay[9] kids say!

[MAMA *enters from her bedroom. She is lost, vague, trying to catch hold, to make some sense of her former command of the world, but it still eludes her. A sense of waste overwhelms her gait; a measure of apology rides on her shoulders. She goes to her plant, which has remained on the table, looks at it, picks it up and takes it to the window sill and sits it outside, and she stands*

7. Allusion to the biblical exclamation "What hath God wrought!" (Num. 23.23).

8. Mister Black Middle Class (French). 9. White.

and looks at it a long moment. Then she closes the window, straightens her body with effort and turns around to her children.]

MAMA: Well—ain't it a mess in here, though? [*A false cheerfulness, a beginning of something.*] I guess we all better stop moping around and get some work done. All this unpacking and everything we got to do. [RUTH *raises her head slowly in response to the sense of the line; and* BENEATHA *in similar manner turns very slowly to look at her mother.*] One of you all better call the moving people and tell 'em not to come.

RUTH: Tell 'em not to come?

MAMA: Of course, baby. Ain't no need in 'em coming all the way here and having to go back. They charges for that too. [*She sits down, fingers to her brow, thinking.*] Lord, ever since I was a little girl, I always remembers people saying, "Lena—Lena Eggleston, you aims too high all the time. You needs to slow down and see life a little more like it is. Just slow down some." That's what they always used to say down home—"Lord, that Lena Eggleston is a high-minded thing. She'll get her due one day!"

RUTH: No, Lena . . .

MAMA: Me and Big Walter just didn't never learn right.

RUTH: Lena, no! We gotta go. Bennie—tell her . . . [*She rises and crosses to* BENEATHA *with her arms outstretched.* BENEATHA *doesn't respond.*] Tell her we can still move . . . the notes ain't but a hundred and twenty-five a month. We got four grown people in this house—we can work . . .

MAMA: [*To herself.*] Just aimed too high all the time—

RUTH: [*Turning and going to* MAMA *fast—the words pouring out with urgency and desperation.*] Lena—I'll work . . . I'll work twenty hours a day in all the kitchens in Chicago . . . I'll strap my baby on my back if I have to and scrub all the floors in America and wash all the sheets in America if I have to—but we got to move . . . We got to get out of here . . .

[MAMA *reaches out absently and pats* RUTH*'s hand.*]

MAMA: No—I sees things differently now. Been thinking 'bout some of the things we could do to fix this place up some. I seen a second-hand bureau over on Maxwell Street[1] just the other day that could fit right there. [*She points to where the new furniture might go.* RUTH *wanders away from her.*] Would need some new handles on it and then a little varnish and then it look like something brand-new. And—we can put up them new curtains in the kitchen . . . Why this place be looking fine. Cheer us all up so that we forget trouble ever came . . . [*To* RUTH.] And you could get some nice screens to put up in your room round the baby's bassinet . . . [*She looks at both of them, pleadingly.*] Sometimes you just got to know when to give up some things . . . and hold on to what you got.

[WALTER *enters from the outside, looking spent and leaning against the door, his coat hanging from him.*]

MAMA: Where you been, son?

WALTER: [*Breathing hard.*] Made a call.

1. Street market southwest of the Loop.

MAMA: To who, son?

WALTER: To The Man.

MAMA: What man, baby?

WALTER: The Man, Mama. Don't you know who The Man is?

RUTH: Walter Lee?

WALTER: *The Man.* Like the guys in the streets say—The Man. Captain Boss—Mistuh Charley . . . Old Captain Please Mr. Bossman . . .

BENEATHA: [*Suddenly.*] Lindner!

WALTER: That's right! That's good. I told him to come right over.

BENEATHA: [*Fiercely, understanding.*] For what? What do you want to see him for!

WALTER: [*Looking at his sister.*] We going to do business with him.

MAMA: What you talking 'bout, son?

WALTER: Talking 'bout life, Mama. You all always telling me to see life like it is. Well—I laid in there on my back today . . . and I figured it out. Life just like it is. Who gets and who don't get. [*He sits down with his coat on and laughs.*] Mama, you know it's all divided up. Life is. Sure enough. Between the takers and the "tooken." [*He laughs.*] I've figured it out finally. [*He looks around at them.*] Yeah. Some of us always getting "tooken." [*He laughs.*] People like Willy Harris, they don't never get "tooken." And you know why the rest of us do? 'Cause we all mixed up. Mixed up bad. We get to looking 'round for the right and the wrong, and we worry about it and cry about it and stay up nights trying to figure out 'bout the wrong and the right of things all the time . . . And all the time, man, them takers is out there operating, just taking and taking. Willy Harris? Shoot—Willy Harris don't even count. He don't even count in the big scheme of things. But I'll say one thing for old Willy Harris . . . he's taught me something. He's taught me to keep my eye on what counts in this world. Yeah— [*Shouting out a little.*] Thanks, Willy!

RUTH: What did you call that man for, Walter Lee?

WALTER: Called him to tell him to come on over to the show. Gonna put on a show for the man. Just what he wants to see. You see, Mama, the man came here today and he told us that them people out there where you want us to move—well they so upset they willing to pay us not to move out there. [*He laughs again.*] And—and oh, Mama—you would of been proud of the way me and Ruth and Bennie acted. We told him to get out . . . Lord have mercy! We told the man to get out. Oh, we was some proud folks this afternoon, yeah. [*He lights a cigarette.*] We were still full of that old-time stuff . . .

RUTH: [*Coming toward him slowly.*] You talking 'bout taking them people's money to keep us from moving in that house?

WALTER: I ain't just talking 'bout it, baby—I'm telling you that's what's going to happen.

BENEATHA: Oh, God! Where is the bottom! Where is the real honest-to-God bottom so he can't go any farther!

WALTER: See—that's the old stuff. You and that boy that was here today. You all want everybody to carry a flag and a spear and sing some marching songs, huh? You wanna spend your life looking into things and trying to find the right and the wrong part, huh? Yeah. You know what's going to happen to that boy someday—he'll find himself sitting in a dungeon, locked in forever—and the takers will have the key! Forget it, baby! There ain't no causes—there ain't nothing but taking in this world, and he who takes most is smartest—and it don't make a damn bit of difference *how.*

MAMA: You making something inside me cry, son. Some awful pain inside me.

WALTER: Don't cry, Mama. Understand. That white man is going to walk in that door able to write checks for more money than we ever had. It's important to him and I'm going to help him . . . I'm going to put on the show, Mama.

MAMA: Son—I come from five generations of people who was slaves and sharecroppers—but ain't nobody in my family never let nobody pay 'em no money that was a way of telling us we wasn't fit to walk the earth. We ain't never been that poor. [*Raising her eyes and looking at him.*] We ain't never been that dead inside.

BENEATHA: Well—we are dead now. All the talk about dreams and sunlight that goes on in this house. All dead.

WALTER: What's the matter with you all! I didn't make this world! It was give to me this way! Hell, yes, I want me some yachts someday! Yes, I want to hang some real pearls 'round my wife's neck. Ain't she supposed to wear no pearls? Somebody tell me—tell me, who decides which women is suppose to wear pearls in this world. I tell you I am a *man*—and I think my wife should wear some pearls in this world!

[*This last line hangs a good while and* WALTER *begins to move about the room. The word "Man" has penetrated his consciousness; he mumbles it to himself repeatedly between strange agitated pauses as he moves about.*]

MAMA: Baby, how you going to feel on the inside?

WALTER: Fine! . . . Going to feel fine . . . a man . . .

MAMA: You won't have nothing left then, Walter Lee.

WALTER: [*Coming to her.*] I'm going to feel fine, Mama. I'm going to look that son-of-a-bitch in the eyes and say— [*He falters.*] —and say, "All right, Mr. Lindner— [*He falters even more.*] —that's your neighborhood out there. You got the right to keep it like you want. You got the right to have it like you want. Just write the check and—the house is yours." And, and I am going to say— [*His voice almost breaks.*] And you—you people just put the money in my hand and you won't have to live next to this bunch of stinking niggers! . . . [*He straightens up and moves away from his mother, walking around the room.*] Maybe—maybe I'll just get down on my black knees . . . [*He does so;* RUTH *and* BENNIE *and* MAMA *watch him in frozen horror.*] Captain, Mistuh, Bossman. [*He starts crying.*] A-hee-hee-hee! [*Wringing his hands in profoundly anguished imitation.*] Yassss-suh! Great White Father, just gi' ussen de money, fo' God's sake, and we's ain't gwine come out deh and dirty up yo' white folks neighborhood . . .

[*He breaks down completely, then gets up and goes into the bedroom.*]

BENEATHA: That is not a man. That is nothing but a toothless rat.

MAMA: Yes—death done come in this here house. [*She is nodding, slowly, reflectively.*] Done come walking in my house. On the lips of my children. You what supposed to be my beginning again. You—what supposed to be my harvest. [*To* BENEATHA.] You—you mourning your brother?

BENEATHA: He's no brother of mine.

MAMA: What you say?

BENEATHA: I said that that individual in that room is no brother of mine.

MAMA: That's what I thought you said. You feeling like you better than he is today? [BENEATHA *does not answer.*] Yes? What you tell him a minute ago? That he wasn't a man? Yes? You give him up for me? You done wrote his epitaph too—like the rest of the world? Well, who give you the privilege?

BENEATHA: Be on my side for once! You saw what he just did, Mama! You saw him—down on his knees. Wasn't it you who taught me—to despise any man who would do that. Do what he's going to do.

MAMA: Yes—I taught you that. Me and your daddy. But I thought I taught you something else too . . . I thought I taught you to love him.

BENEATHA: Love him? There is nothing left to love.

MAMA: There is always something left to love. And if you ain't learned that, you ain't learned nothing. [*Looking at her.*] Have you cried for that boy today? I don't mean for yourself and for the family 'cause we lost the money. I mean for him; what he been through and what it done to him. Child, when do you think is the time to love somebody the most; when they done good and made things easy for everybody? Well then, you ain't through learning—because that ain't the time at all. It's when he's at his lowest and can't believe in hisself 'cause the world done whipped him so. When you starts measuring somebody, measure him right, child, measure him right. Make sure you done taken into account what hills and valleys he come through before he got to wherever he is.

[TRAVIS *bursts into the room at the end of the speech, leaving the door open.*]

TRAVIS: Grandmama—the moving men are downstairs! The truck just pulled up.

MAMA: [*Turning and looking at him.*] Are they, baby? They downstairs?

[*She sighs and sits.* LINDNER *appears in the doorway. He peers in and knocks lightly, to gain attention, and comes in. All turn to look at him.*]

LINDNER: [*Hat and briefcase in hand.*] Uh—hello . . . [RUTH *crosses mechanically to the bedroom door and opens it and lets it swing open freely and slowly as the lights come up on* WALTER *within, still in his coat, sitting at the far corner of the room. He looks up and out through the room to* LINDNER.]

RUTH: He's here.

[*A long minute passes and* WALTER *slowly gets up.*]

LINDNER: [*Coming to the table with efficiency, putting his briefcase on the table and starting to unfold papers and unscrew fountain pens.*] Well, I certainly was glad to hear from you people. [WALTER *has begun the trek out of the room, slowly and awkwardly, rather like a small boy, passing the back of his sleeve across his mouth from time to time.*] Life can really be so much simpler than people let it be most of the time. Well—with whom do I negotiate? You, Mrs. Younger, or your son here? [MAMA *sits with her hands folded on her lap and her eyes closed as* WALTER *advances.* TRAVIS *goes close to* LINDNER *and looks at the papers curiously.*] Just some official papers, sonny.

RUTH: Travis, you go downstairs.

MAMA: [*Opening her eyes and looking into* WALTER's.] No. Travis, you stay right here. And you make him understand what you doing, Walter Lee. You teach him good. Like Willy Harris taught you. You show where our five generations done come to. Go ahead, son—

WALTER: [*Looks down into his boy's eyes.* TRAVIS *grins at him merrily and* WALTER *draws him beside him with his arm lightly around his shoulders.*] Well, Mr. Lindner. [BENEATHA *turns away.*] We called you— [*There is a profound, simple groping quality in his speech.*] —because, well, me and my family [*He looks around and shifts from one foot to the other.*] Well—we are very plain people . . .

LINDNER: Yes—

WALTER: I mean—I have worked as a chauffeur most of my life—and my wife here, she does domestic work in people's kitchens. So does my mother. I mean—we are plain people . . .

LINDNER: Yes, Mr. Younger—

WALTER: [*Really like a small boy, looking down at his shoes and then up at the man.*] And—uh—well, my father, well, he was a laborer most of his life.

LINDNER: [*Absolutely confused.*] Uh, yes—

WALTER: [*Looking down at his toes once again.*] My father almost beat a man to death once because this man called him a bad name or something, you know what I mean?

LINDNER: No, I'm afraid I don't.

WALTER: [*Finally straightening up.*] Well, what I mean is that we come from people who had a lot of pride. I mean—we are very proud people. And that's my sister over there and she's going to be a doctor—and we are very proud—

LINDNER: Well—I am sure that is very nice, but—

WALTER: [*Starting to cry and facing the man eye to eye.*] What I am telling you is that we called you over here to tell you that we are very proud and that this is—this is my son, who makes the sixth generation of our family in this country, and that we have all thought about your offer and we have decided to move into our house because my father—my father—he earned it. [MAMA *has her eyes closed and is rocking back and forth as though she were in church, with her head nodding the amen yes.*] We don't want to make no trouble for nobody or fight no causes—but we will try to be good neighbors. That's all we got to say. [*He looks the man absolutely in the eyes.*] We don't want your money.

[*He turns and walks away from the man.*]

LINDNER: [*Looking around at all of them.*] I take it then that you have decided to occupy.

BENEATHA: That's what the man said.

LINDNER: [*To* MAMA *in her reverie.*] Then I would like to appeal to you, Mrs. Younger. You are older and wiser and understand things better I am sure . . .

MAMA: [*Rising.*] I am afraid you don't understand. My son said we was going to move and there ain't nothing left for me to say. [*Shaking her head with double meaning.*] You know how these young folks is nowadays, mister. Can't do a thing with 'em. Good-bye.

LINDNER: [*Folding up his materials.*] Well—if you are that final about it . . . There is nothing left for me to say. [*He finishes. He is almost ignored by the family, who are concentrating on* WALTER LEE. *At the door* LINDNER *halts and looks around.*] I sure hope you people know what you're doing.

[*He shakes his head and exits.*]

RUTH: [*Looking around and coming to life.*] Well, for God's sake—if the moving men are here—LET'S GET THE HELL OUT OF HERE!

MAMA: [*Into action.*] Ain't it the truth! Look at all this here mess. Ruth, put Travis' good jacket on him . . . Walter Lee, fix your tie and tuck your shirt in, you look just like somebody's hoodlum. Lord have mercy, where is my plant? [*She flies to get it amid the general bustling of the family, who are deliberately trying to ignore the nobility of the past moment.*] You all start on down . . . Travis child, don't go empty-handed . . . Ruth, where did I put that box with my skillets in it? I want to be in charge of it myself . . . I'm going to make us the biggest dinner we ever ate tonight . . . Beneatha, what's the matter with them stockings? Pull them things up, girl . . .

[*The family starts to file out as two moving men appear and begin to carry out the heavier pieces of furniture, bumping into the family as they move about.*]

BENEATHA: Mama, Asagai—asked me to marry him today and go to Africa—

MAMA: [*In the middle of her getting-ready activity.*] He did? You ain't old enough to marry nobody— [*Seeing the moving men lifting one of her chairs precariously.*] Darling, that ain't no bale of cotton, please handle it so we can sit in it again. I had that chair twenty-five years . . .

[*The movers sigh with exasperation and go on with their work.*]

BENEATHA: [*Girlishly and unreasonably trying to pursue the conversation.*] To go to Africa, Mama—be a doctor in Africa . . .

MAMA: [*Distracted.*] Yes, baby—

WALTER: Africa! What he want you to go to Africa for?

BENEATHA: To practice there . . .

WALTER: Girl, if you don't get all them silly ideas out your head! You better marry yourself a man with some loot . . .

BENEATHA: [*Angrily, precisely as in the first scene of the play.*] What have you got to do with who I marry!

WALTER: Plenty. Now I think George Murchison—

[*He and* BENEATHA *go out yelling at each other vigorously;* BENEATHA *is heard saying that she would not marry* GEORGE MURCHISON *if he were Adam and she were Eve, etc. The anger is loud and real till their voices diminish.* RUTH *stands at the door and turns to* MAMA *and smiles knowingly.*]

MAMA: [*Fixing her hat at last.*] Yeah—they something all right, my children . . .

RUTH: Yeah—they're something. Let's go, Lena.

MAMA: [*Stalling, starting to look around at the house.*] Yes—I'm coming. Ruth—

RUTH: Yes?

MAMA: [*Quietly, woman to woman.*] He finally come into his manhood today, didn't he? Kind of like a rainbow after the rain . . .

RUTH: [*Biting her lip lest her own pride explode in front of* MAMA.] Yes, Lena.

[WALTER'S *voice calls for them raucously.*]

MAMA: [*Waving* RUTH *out vaguely.*] All right, honey—go on down. I be down directly.

[RUTH *hesitates, then exits.* MAMA *stands, at last alone in the living room, her plant on the table before her as the lights start to come down. She looks around at all the walls and ceilings and suddenly, despite herself, while the children call below, a great heaving thing rises in her and she puts her fist to her mouth, takes a final desperate look, pulls her coat about her, pats her hat and goes out. The lights dim down. The door opens and she comes back in, grabs her plant, and goes out for the last time.*]

[CURTAIN.]

1959

AUTHORS ON THEIR WORK

LORRAINE HANSBERRY (1930–65)

From "Willie Loman, Walter Younger, and He Who Must Live" (1959)*

[. . .] Walter Younger is an American more than he is anything else. His ordeal [. . .] is not extraordinary but intensely familiar like Willy [Loman]'s [in Arthur Miller's *Death of a Salesman*]. The two of them have virtually no values which have not come out of their culture, and to a significant point, no view of the possible solutions to their problems which do not also come out of the selfsame culture. Walter can find no peace with that part of society which seems to permit him no entry into that which has willfully excluded him. He shares with Willy Loman the acute awareness that *something* is obstructing some abstract progress that he feels he *should* be making; that *something* is in the way of his ascendancy. It does not occur to either of them to question the nature of this desired "ascendancy." Walter accepts, he believes in the "world" as it has been presented to him. When we first meet him, he does not wish to alter *it*; merely to change *his* position in it. His mentors and his associates all take the view that the institutions which frustrate him are somehow impeccable, or, at best, "unfortunate." "Things being as they are," he must look to *himself* as the only source of any rewards he may expect. Within himself, he is encouraged to believe, are the only seeds of defeat or victory within the universe. And Walter believes this and when opportunity, haphazard and rooted in death, prevails, he acts.

HUGE OBSTACLES

But the obstacles [. . .] are gigantic; the weight of the loss of the money is in fact, the weight of death. In Walter Lee Younger's life, somebody *has* to die for ten thousand bucks to pile up—if then. Elsewhere in the world, in the face of catastrophe, he might be tempted to don the saffron robes of acceptance and sit on a mountain top all day contemplating the divine justice of his misery. Or, history being what it is turning out to be, he might wander down to his first Communist Party meeting. But here in the dynamic and confusing postwar years on the Southside of Chicago, his choices of action are equal to those gestures only in symbolic terms. The American ghetto hero may give up and contemplate his misery in rose-colored bars to the melodies of hypnotic saxophones, but revolution seems alien to him in his circumstances (America), and it is easier to dream of personal wealth than of a communal state wherein universal dignity is supposed to be a corollary. Yet his position in time and space does allow for one other alternative; he may take his place on any one of a number of frontiers of challenge. Challenges (such as helping to break down restricted neighborhoods) which are admittedly limited because they most certainly do not threaten the basic social order.

NOT SO SMALL

But why is even this final choice possible [. . .]? Well, that is where Walter departs from Willy Loman; there is a second pulse in his still-dual culture. His people have had "somewhere" they have been trying to get for so long that more sophisticated confusions do not yet bind them. [. . .] Walter is, despite his lack of consciousness of it, inextricably as much wedded to his special mass as Willy was to his, and the moods of each are able to decisively determine the dramatic typicality. Furthermore, the very nature of the situation of American Negroes can force their representative hero to recognize that for his *true* ascendancy he must ultimately be at cross-purposes with at least certain of his culture's values. It is to the pathos of Willy Loman that his section of American life seems to have momentarily lost that urgency; that he cannot, like Walter, draw on the strength of an incredible people who, historically, have simply refused to give up.

In other words, the symbolism of moving into the new house is quite as small as it seems and quite as significant. For if there are no waving flags and marching songs at the barricades as Walter marches out with his little battalion, it is not because the battle lacks nobility. On the contrary, he has picked up in his way, still imperfect and wobbly in his small view of human destiny, what I believe Arthur Miller once called "the golden thread of history." He becomes, in spite of those who are too intrigued with despair and hatred of man to see it, King Oedipus refusing to tear out his eyes, but attacking the Oracle instead. He is that last Jewish patriot manning his rifle in the burning ghetto at Warsaw; [. . .] he is the nine small heroes of Little Rock; he is Michelangelo creating David and Beethoven bursting forth with the Ninth Symphony. He is all those things because he has finally reached out in his tiny moment and caught that sweet essence which is human dignity, and it shines like the gold star-touched dream that it is in his eyes. We see, in the moment, I think, what becomes, and not for Negroes alone, but for Willy and all of us, entirely an American responsibility.

Out in the darkness where we watch, most of us are not afraid to cry.

*Lorraine Hansberry. "Willie Loman, Walter Younger, and He Who Must Live." *Village Voice*, no. 12, Aug. 1959 pp. 7–8.

Chronology

1938 To challenge restrictive housing convenants, eight-year-old Lorraine Hansberry's family purchases and occupies a house in a white neighborhood in Chicago.

1940 The Supreme Court upholds the Hansberry family's right to remain in their home, but because the Court's decision hinges upon a technicality, it fails to address the legality of restrictive covenants.

1943 A Detroit race riot kills thirty-four (including twenty-five blacks), injures almost seven hundred, and ends only after President Roosevelt calls in the National Guard; a race riot in Harlem injures three hundred and kills six African Americans.

1946 A race riot leads Chicago housing authorities to abandon efforts to move black families into the Airport Homes housing project; Lorraine Hansberry's father, Carl, dies at age fifty.

1947 A race riot occurs in Chicago when local authorities attempt to move blacks into the Fernwood Park housing project.

1948 President Truman issues an executive order integrating the armed forces; the Supreme Court rules restrictive covenants legally unenforceable.

1949 A race riot occurs in Chicago's Park Manor when a black family attempts to move in; another breaks out in Englewood Park when a black man is seen visiting the home of a white union organizer.

1951 The National Guard is called in to quell a riot sparked by a black family's move into an apartment complex in Cicero, a town bordering Chicago.

1953 Two neighborhood associations lead a nine-month "campaign of terror" after local authorities try to move a black family into Chicago's Trumbull Park housing project. (See Gruenberg excerpt below.)

1954 In *Brown v. Board of Education*, the Supreme Court declares school segregation unconstitutional.

1955 A year-long bus boycott begins in Montgomery, Alabama.

1956 The Supreme Court declares segregation on buses unconstitutional; "after seeing a play" that made her "disgusted with a whole body of material about Negroes" full of "cardboard characters," Lorraine Hansberry begins writing *A Raisin in the Sun*.

1957 When Arkansas's governor blocks nine black students from attending a Little Rock high school, President Eisenhower sends in federal troops to force compliance with court-ordered desegregation.

1959 *A Raisin in the Sun* becomes the first play by an African American woman produced on Broadway; twenty-nine-year-old Hansberry becomes the first African American and the youngest playwright ever to win the Drama Critics Circle Award for best play.

1960 Refused service at the lunch counter of a Greensboro, North Carolina, Woolworth's, four black college students stage the first sit-in; SNCC is founded in Raleigh, North Carolina.

1961 Between May and August, approximately one thousand volunteer "Freedom Riders" take buses to the South in support of integration.

1962 African American James Meredith is denied admission to the University of Mississippi, resulting in race riots that kill two.

1963 Martin Luther King, Jr., jailed in Birmingham, Alabama, for leading civil rights demonstrations, writes "Letter from Birmingham Jail" (excerpted below); President Kennedy forces Governor George Wallace to allow integration of the University of Alabama; civil rights leader Medgar Evers is assassinated in Mississippi; 200,000 people participate in the March on Washington, where Martin Luther King, Jr., delivers his "I Have a Dream" speech; one month later, a Birmingham, Alabama, church bombing kills four black girls attending Sunday School and sparks riots in which two African Americans are killed.

1964 Twenty-Fourth Amendment to the U.S. Constitution abolishes the poll tax traditionally used to prevent blacks from voting; "Freedom Summer" begins with a massive effort to register black voters throughout the South; Congress passes the Civil Rights Act outlawing employment discrimination and segregation in public facilities; in Mississippi, three people working to register black voters are murdered, their bodies discovered only after President Johnson sends military personnel to aid in the search; Martin Luther King, Jr., wins the Nobel Peace Prize.

1965 Hansberry dies of cancer at age thirty-five; Malcolm X is assassinated in Harlem; Martin Luther King, Jr., leads a march from Selma to Montgomery, Alabama, to demand protection of voting rights, and, on "Bloody Sunday," fifty marchers are hospitalized after police use tear gas, whips, and clubs against them; the Voting Rights Act makes it easier for southern blacks to register to vote by outlawing requirements such as literacy tests; race riots occur in several cities, the worst—in Los Angeles' Watts neighborhood—kills four and injures one thousand.

1966 In Chicago, Martin Luther King, Jr., begins his first northern campaign, leading a series of marches in Chicago to protest housing conditions and renting an apartment in a Southside slum; Edward Brooke, of Massachusetts, becomes the first African American elected to the U.S. Senate in eighty-five years; as first secretary of the newly created Department of Housing and Urban Development, Robert C. Weaver becomes the first African American to hold a cabinet-level position in the U.S. government.

CONTEXTUAL EXCERPTS

THE GREAT MIGRATION AND LIFE IN THE "BLACK METROPOLIS"

Richard Wright

From Twelve Million Black Voices: A Folk History of the Negro in the United States (1941)[1]

Perhaps never in history has a more utterly unprepared folk wanted to go to the city; we were barely born as a folk when we headed for the tall and sprawling

1. Richard Wright. *Twelve Million Black Voices: A Folk History of the Negro in the United States.* Viking, 1941.

centers of steel and stone. We, who were landless upon the land; we, who had barely managed to live in family groups; [. . .] we who had never belonged to any organizations except the church and burial societies; we, who had had our personalities blasted with two hundred years of slavery and had been turned loose to shift for ourselves—we were such a folk as this when we moved into a world that was destined to test all we were, that threw us into the scales of competition to weigh our mettle. And how were we to know that, the moment we landless millions of the land—we men who were struggling to be born—set our awkward feet upon the pavements of the city, life would begin to exact of us a heavy toll in death?

We did not know what would happen, what was in store for us. We went innocently, longing and hoping for a life that the Lords of the Land would not let us live. Our hearts were high as we moved northward to the cities. What emotions, fears, what a complex of sensations we felt when, looking out of a train window at the revolving fields, we first glimpsed the sliding waters of the gleaming Ohio! What memories that river evoked in us, memories black and gloomy, yet tinged with the bright border of a wild and desperate hope! The Ohio is more than a river. It is a symbol, a line that runs through our hearts, dividing hope from despair, just as once it bisected the nation, dividing freedom from slavery.

• • •

[Once in the North w]e [. . .] live in the clinging soot just beyond the factory areas, behind the railroad tracks, near the river banks, under the viaducts, by the steel and iron mills, on the edges of the coal and lumber yards. We live in crowded, barn-like rooms, in old rotting buildings where once dwelt rich native whites of a century ago [. . .]. When we return home at night from our jobs, we are afraid to venture into other sections of the city, for we fear that the white boys will gang up and molest us. When we do go out into white neighborhoods, we always go in crowds, for that is the best mode of protection.

White people say that they are afraid of us, and it often makes us laugh. When they see one of us, they either smile with contempt or amusement. [. . .] When they see *six* of us, they become downright apprehensive and alarmed. And because they are afraid of us, we are afraid of them. Especially do we feel fear when we meet the gangs of white boys who have been taught—at home and at school—that we black folk are making their parents lose their homes and life's savings because we have moved into their neighborhoods.

They say our presence in their neighborhoods lowers the value of their property. We do not understand why this should be so. We are poor; but they were once poor, too. They make up their minds, because others tell them to, that they must move at once if we rent an apartment near them. Having been warned against us by the Bosses of the Buildings, having heard tall tales about us, about how "bad" we are, they react emotionally as though we had the plague when we move into their neighborhoods. Is it any wonder, then, that their homes are suddenly and drastically reduced in value? They hastily abandon them, sacrificing them to the Bosses of the Buildings [. . .].

And the Bosses of the Buildings take these old houses and convert them into "kitchenettes," and then rent them to us at rates so high that they make fabulous fortunes before the houses are too old for habitation. What they do is this: they take, say, a seven-room apartment, [. . .] and cut it up into seven small apartments, of one room each; they install one small gas stove and one small sink in each room.

• • •

Sometimes five or six of us live in a one-room kitchenette, a place where simple folk such as we should never be held captive. A war sets up in our emotions: one part of our feelings tells us that it is good to be in the city, that we have a chance at life here, that we need but turn a corner to become a stranger, that we no longer need bow and dodge at the sight of the Lords of the Land. Another part of our feelings tells us that, in terms of worry and strain, the cost of living in the kitchenettes is too high, that the city heaps too much responsibility upon us and gives too little security in return.

The kitchenette is the author of the glad tidings that new suckers are in town, ready to be cheated, plundered, and put in their places.

The kitchenette is our prison, our death sentence without a trial, the new form of mob violence that assaults not only the lone individual, but all of us, in its ceaseless attacks.

The kitchenette, with its filth and foul air, with its one toilet for thirty or more tenants, kills our black babies so fast that in many cities twice as many of them die as white babies.

The kitchenette is the seed bed for scarlet fever, dysentery, typhoid, tuberculosis, gonorrhea, syphilis, pneumonia, and malnutrition.

The kitchenette scatters death so widely among us that our death rate exceeds our birth rate, and if it were not for the trains and autos bringing us daily into the city from the plantations, we black folks who dwell in northern cities would die out entirely over the course of a few years.

The kitchenette, with its crowded rooms and incessant bedlam, provides an enticing place for crimes of all sort—crimes against women and children or any stranger who happens to stray into its dark hallways. The noise of our living, boxed in stone and steel, is so loud that even a pistol shot is smothered.

The kitchenette throws desperate and unhappy people into an unbearable closeness of association, thereby increasing latent friction, giving birth to never-ending quarrels of recrimination, accusation, and vindictiveness, producing warped personalities.

The kitchenette injects pressure and tension into our individual personalities, making many of us give up the struggle, walk off and leave wives, husbands, and even children behind to shift as best they can.

The kitchenette creates thousands of one-room homes where our black mothers sit, deserted, with their children about their knees.

The kitchenette blights the personalities of our growing children, disorganizes them, blinds them to hope, creates problems whose effects can be traced in the characters of its child victims for years afterward.

The kitchenette jams our farm girls, while still in their teens, into rooms with men who are restless and stimulated by the noise and lights of the city; and more of our girls have bastard babies than the girls in any other sections of the city.

The kitchenette fills our black boys with longing and restlessness, urging them to run off from home, to join together with other restless black boys in gangs, that brutal form of city courage.

The kitchenette piles up mountains of profits for the Bosses of the Buildings and makes them ever more determined to keep things as they are.

The kitchenette reaches out with fingers full of golden bribes to the officials of the city, persuading them to allow old firetraps to remain standing and occupied long after they should have been torn down.

The kitchenette is the funnel through which our pulverized lives flow to ruin and death on the city pavements, at a profit.

• • •

Despite our new worldliness, [. . .] we keep our churches alive. In fact, we have built more of them than ever here on the city pavements, for it is only when we are within the walls of our churches that we are wholly ourselves, that we keep alive a sense of our personalities in relation to the total world in which we live, that we maintain a quiet and constant communion with all that is deepest in us. Our going to church of a Sunday is like placing one's ear to another's chest to hear the unquenchable murmur of the human heart. In our collective outpourings of song and prayer, the fluid emotions of others make us feel the strength in ourselves [. . .]. Our churches are where we dip our tired bodies in cool springs of hope, where we retain our wholeness and humanity [. . .].

Our churches are centers of social and community life, for we have virtually no other mode of communion and we are usually forbidden to worship God in the temples of the Bosses of the Buildings [. . .].

In the Black Belts of the northern cities, our women are the most circumscribed and tragic objects to be found in our lives, and it is to the churches that our black women cling for emotional security and the release of their personalities. Because their orbit of life is narrow—from their kitchenette to the white folk's kitchen and back home again—they love the church more than do our men, who find a large measure of the expression of their lives in the mills and factories. Surrounding our black women are many almost insuperable barriers: they are black, they are women, they are workers; they are triply anchored and restricted in their movements within and without the Black Belts.

So they keep thousands of Little Bethels and Pilgrims and Calvarys and White Rocks and Good Hopes and Mount Olives going with their nickels and dimes [. . .]. Sometimes, even in crowded northern cities, elderly black women, hungry for the South but afraid to return, will cultivate tiny vegetable gardens in the narrow squares of ground in front of their hovels.

• • •

Many of our children scorn us; they say that we still wear the red bandanna about our heads, that we are still Uncle Toms. We lean upon our God and scold our children and try to drag them to church with us, but just as we once, years ago, left the plantation to roam the South, so now they leave us for the city pavements. But deep down in us we are glad that our children feel the world hard enough to yearn to wrestle with it. We, the mothers and fathers of the black children, try to hold them back from death, but if we persuade them to stay, or if they come back because we call them, we will pour out our pity upon them. Always our deepest love is toward those children of ours who turn their backs upon our way of life, for our instincts tell us that those brave ones who struggle against death are the ones who bring new life into the world, even though they die to do so, even though our hearts are broken when they die.

We watch strange moods fill our children, and our hearts swell with pain. The streets, with their noise and flaring lights, the taverns, the automobiles, and the poolrooms claim them, and no voice of ours can call them back. They spend their nights away from home; they forget our ways of life, our language, our God. Their swift speech and impatient eyes make us feel weak and foolish. We cannot keep them in school [. . .]. We fall upon our knees and pray for them, but in vain. The city has beaten us, evaded us; but they, with young bodies filled with warm blood, feel bitter and frustrated at the sight of the alluring hopes and prizes denied them. It is not their eagerness to fight that makes us afraid, but that they go to death on the city pavements faster than even disease and starvation can take them [. . .]. The courts and the morgues become crowded with our lost children [. . .].

Robert Gruenberg

From Chicago Fiddles While Trumbull Park Burns (1954)[1]

Chicago

On July 30, 1953, Donald Howard, a war veteran, with his wife and two small children became the first Negro tenants of Trumbull Park Homes, a federal housing project operated by the Chicago Housing Authority in the steel-mill belt of Chicago's South Side. Less than a week later the 462-unit development and surrounding lawns were a fire-gutted, rubble-strewn waste-land. Since then ten other Negro families have moved into the development, and "racial disturbances" ranging from rock-tossing to rioting and arson have become an almost daily occurrence.

Two weeks ago the Howard family, importuned by well-intentioned friends, moved out, in the hope that order would be restored and the other Negro tenants left in peace. But rocks continue to fly and aerial bombs puncture the night. Recently tension rose to such a point that civic, labor, and church leaders, meeting under the sponsorship of the National Association for the Advancement of Colored People, warned Chicago's Mayor Kennelly that unless he took immediate steps to stop the disturbances he would have to face "continuous" mass demonstrations at the City Hall.

In the three months before the Howard family moved into Trumbull Park Homes only three fire alarms were turned in from the area, two of them for minor blazes. Since last summer alarms have averaged two dozen a month, about half of them false. There have been forty-four fires in sheds, garages, and barns, eight in the Trumbull Park project itself, and two in liquor stores. A tavern which had served Negroes was completely destroyed.

• • •

1. Robert Gruenberg. "Chicago Fiddles While Trumbull Park Burns." *The Nation*, 22 May 1954, pp. 441–43.

Many people have dismissed the incidents as either youthful exuberance or genuine expressions of protest by aroused owners of nearby property. Others, however, have been aware for some time that the trouble at Trumbull Park is not altogether spontaneous. All the evidence shows it has been fanned by two small groups, one of them a professional race-baiting outfit.

These are the South Deering Improvement Association, one of scores of "improvement" associations intent on keeping the Negro out of "all white" areas, and the National Citizens' Protective Association, a hate group founded by a former aide of Gerald L. K. Smith, the anti-Semitic race baiter, and boasting among its national officers a former Ku Klux Klan "emperor." The president of the home-grown South Deering association is Louis P. Dinnocenzo, a $6,000-a-year highway engineer on the Cook County pay roll. His organization, he claims, has about 500 members, each of whom pays dues of a dollar a year. They meet once a month in the Trumbull Park fieldhouse.

If you ask Dinnocenzo about the part played by his association in the racial disorders, he answers straightforwardly: "We are requesting our aldermen and our representatives to do everything within their ability to get them [the ten Negro families living in the project] out." What else are you doing? "We're parading around at night—within the law—like we're entitled to do—to picket." Doesn't parading create an atmosphere begetting violence? "Yes, it sometimes does," he admits, "but we don't want the violence. It's the teenagers." Dinnocenzo calls the moving in of Negroes "an encroachment on our right." He explains "While the law is opposed to us, morally we're right."

* * *

GOING WITH GOD IN TRUMBULL PARK

> The Trumbull Park housing project is a white housing project. . . . Only the ignoble and shameful and the base can be suppressed, never the heroic truth, for we go with God. If you live like a good American, you don't need the police department and a pressure group to keep you by force in a community where you know you don't belong. Get out, and get off our backs.
>
> —*From a letter to the editor of the* Daily Calumet *in South Chicago.*

Mayor Kennelly has yet to come out with a strong statement condemning the South Deering lawlessness.

* * *

The most outspoken support for the South Deering troublemakers comes from the *Daily Calumet,* a paper published in a neighboring area. Its editor is Colonel Horace F. Wulf, an army-reserve officer. Here is a sample of his writing: "Some white areas may welcome other races with open arms, bless them. But the folks of South Deering have not been sufficiently brainwashed to consent to such practice. Any race mixing must be done with a policeman's nightstick."

Ironically, part of the *Daily Calumet's* financial support comes from the tax dollars of Chicago's citizens, Negro and white. As a newspaper of "general circulation" it can bid for advertising contracts of the Chicago Sanitary District, and this year it obtained the contract. One of the Republican trustees of the Sanitary District is John Henneberger, for ten years president of United Steelworkers Local 1008 at the Youngstown Sheet and Tube Company's South Chicago plant before he retired in 1951 with a lifetime honorary presidency. On February 1 the *Daily Calumet* reported as follows on Henneberger's talk at a dinner held by the South Deering Improvement Association attended by 500 persons. "He said, 'It is an inspiring sight to see a community fight for what it thinks is right.' He added the Republican Party stands ready to lend its hand to any group of citizens engaged in a struggle for a just cause." Questioned about this, Henneberger denied making the statement.

• • •

Donald Howard's decision to leave Trumbull Park was sudden and known in advance to only a few police officials and Howard's attorneys. One of Chicago's police captains helped Howard get a new job and a new home. Howard authorized his attorneys to say in his behalf

> Police officials and well-meaning human-relations experts have visited me and they have approached me through well-intentioned persons, all with the view that my continued occupancy of an apartment [. . .] represents a threat to civil peace and tranquility in Trumbull Park Homes. Having in mind the fact that there are ten other Negro families in Trumbull Park Homes and hoping that there is something my family and I can do to contribute to a restoration of order in Trumbull Park I have decided to succumb to the pressures placed on me.

Gertrude Samuels

From Even More Crucial Than in the South (1963)[1]

A report on the forms the Negro revolution is taking against discrimination, economic and social, in the North.

A policeman tells a street vender to move on and sets off a series of clashes between Negroes and police . . .

A human chain of Negro parents blocks a dozen buses loaded with Negro children going to schools where they will be separated from white children . . .

A thousand whites gather menacingly at a brick house on an all-white street where a Negro family is attempting to move in . . .

Police rush lines of Negro pickets who are protesting bias in hiring practices. Negroes are beaten and black-jacked; policemen, stabbed . . .

These incidents of recent weeks took place not in the South but in the North. For the past year the attention of the country has been largely concentrated on

1. Gertrude Samuels. "Even More Crucial Than in the South." *The New York Times*, 30 June 1963, pp. 143+, nyti.ms/29W7hgl.

the racial crisis in the South. Now there is growing awareness that the crisis in the North is boiling, and that it is perhaps more dangerous.

The civil-rights struggle in the South is still largely in its legal, elementary stage: Negro strategy there is to attempt to crumble barriers to school integration, to accommodation at such public facilities as lunch counters, hotels and playgrounds, and in transportation.

But in the North Negroes say the problem revolves around the far more sinister moral questions of private policy—what Negro leaders describe as "the snide, subtle and insidious practice" of economic and social discrimination.

Of the nation's nearly 20,000,000 Negroes—about 10 per cent of the population—some 48 per cent live outside the South. What is the extent of their dissatisfaction?

• • •

What is clear from all these reports is that there is an intensification of militancy at the Negro leadership level [. . .]. But there is also a great response at the "followership" level—a willingness to follow, to demonstrate, to be involved in the struggle more decisively than ever before.

The Negro drive in the North is aimed at four main targets: residential segregation, job discrimination, *de facto* school segregation and, above all, affronts to personal dignity.

RESIDENTIAL SEGREGATION

All over the North, but particularly in the giant industrial cities, there are "gentlemen's agreements" to hold the Negro down residentially. How else explain the largest slum area in the country—Negro Harlem in upper Manhattan, with about half a million black persons crowded into its tenements and crumbling brownstones? [. . .]

A few Negro families have escaped—finding enough money, and enough community acceptance to move into integrated neighborhoods in some suburbs—but most are as rigidly held back from living and mixing with whites as in the South. More so in fact, for in many cities of the South—in Little Rock[, Arkansas,] and Vicksburg[, Mississippi,] and Louisville[, Kentucky,]—Negro and white families have lived side by side for years.

• • •

The situation is particularly acute on Chicago's South Side, where half of Illinois' Negro population is segregated. Friction starts when Negroes move—or try to move—into adjoining white neighborhoods.

Recently, a crowd of whites gathered around a two-family brick house in an all-white neighborhood on the South Side when it was rumored that Negroes were about to come. Two Negro men did appear, and some furniture was moved in. Rocks were thrown, the police arrived, according to a well-designed plan, and the situation was brought under control. But the Negro family gave up the idea of "breaking the block," as whites charged they were trying to do.

Horror runs through all white economic levels in the North at the idea of having a Negro family move into the neighborhood—largely because of the belief that their presence will reduce property values. It is a fear seldom substantiated by any person's firsthand knowledge, but Negroes acknowledge its pervasiveness with a bitter saying: "In the South, the whites say, 'I don't care how close you get but don't get too high.' In the North, the whites say, 'I don't care how high you get, but don't get too close.'"

Deerfield, Ill., an upper-income suburb of Chicago, dramatized the extent to which whites will go to avoid having Negro neighbors—even those who can afford $30,000 homes. The village was to have been the site of an interracial real-estate development. The project was killed when the community, encouraged by the Rev. Jack D. Parker of St. Gregory Episcopal Church, condemned the land and floated a bond issue to make a park out of it. Court action up to the Supreme Court resulted in a victory for the village.

JOB DISCRIMINATION

And it is certainly "gentlemen's agreements" or naked prejudice that operate against Northern Negroes in job-hiring practices.

The North has on its books many laws and directives against job discrimination that have meant well. The cause of the seething unrest is that in practice, down at the individual level, the laws don't work. Municipalities and state governments lack the courage to enforce them, and private enterprise is apathetic or worse.

The situation is boiling up because jobs are growing scarcer—twice as many Negroes compared with whites are jobless.

* * *

SCHOOL SEGREGATION

But if housing and job discrimination hurt, the greatest outrage that the Northern Negro feels is over the segregation of his children.

* * *

In Chicago, where only about 10 per cent of pupils go to school with children of another race, "the hottest item for the last two years has been the issue of second-rate education for Negroes." The charge is that the "neighborhood" school-district system [. . .] creates segregation—overcrowding all-Negro schools while white classrooms stand empty. At a recent civil-rights rally, a speaker said school segregation in Chicago and Alabama is as similar as the names [of Chicago School Superintendent Benjamin] Willis and ([Alabama] Governor [George]) Wallace.

Such segregation in the North is, obviously, a direct consequence of residential segregation. John H. Johnson, editor and publisher of the Negro magazine *Ebony*, says bluntly: "If we had integrated housing, the school problem would automatically be solved." [. . .]

* * *

THE PSYCHOLOGICAL FACTOR

Above all these grievances looms the main factor—and that is psychological. Negroes in all walks—from porters and taxi drivers to college professors and political leaders—say that the real drive that is now rising ominously is a demand for personal dignity.

• • •

As Roy Wilkins, executive director of the N.A.A.C.P. puts it: "[. . .] We're making the Constitution and the Declaration of Independence real and alive. We're taking them off parchment and putting them into people's lives, white and black. One of these days, after the fist-shaking is over, the whites are going to understand and to thank us."

The Black Middle Class, the American Dream, and the Campaign for Civil Rights

Wilma Dykeman and James Stokely

From New Southerner: The Middle-Class Negro (1959)[1]

His emergence, while its greatest impact is in the South,
has meaning for the nation.
Paradoxically, the change may mean both a short step back
and a leap forward in race relations.

A young Negro father in one of the South's larger cities said recently, "I can't understand why they [certain white politicians in his city] keep shouting that when we try to send our children to the best schools we can, it means we want them to marry whites. What it means is that we want our children to have a chance at owning a station wagon and a ranch-style house and carrying a brief-case instead of a shovel."

If many white Southerners could understand the implications of this man's statement, then the equality which they envision largely as nightmare might be reappraised as closer to the fulfillment of a dream—the American dream. For one of the major forces shaping and energizing the Negro's drive toward full integration into our national life today is a strengthened belief in every man's right to earn his living, own his home and better his place in society, the traditional goals of the white middle class.

And one of the major forces hindering the Negro in this drive, especially in the South, is the white man's persistent image of the Negro as the eternal hewer of wood and drawer of water. One of the matters to which professional segregationist orators have given closest attention is reviving the picture of the "African savage" whom slavery "rescued" from the jungles and brought into beneficent

1. Wilma Dykeman and James Stokely. "New Southerner: The Middle-Class Negro." *The New York Times*, 9 Aug. 1959, pp. SM11+, nyti.ms/29PefAT.

contact with white civilization. Even thus, a century ago, slavery was made to seem the appropriately inferior role of an inferior race.

* * *

There are two points of departure from which to examine the importance of the emerging Southern Negro middle class. It may be compared with its white counterpart and the total American economy—in which case it appears small and severely handicapped. For instance, individual Negro incomes are still only 52 percent as large as white incomes, and two out of every five Negro families still earn less than $2,000 per year.

Or, this middle class may be studied in the light of its own background and recent history—in which case it appears highly significant. For instance, the pre-war percentage difference between Negro and white incomes has been cut by better than 20 per cent and today the total annual cash purchasing power of the Negro population equals the market of the whole of Canada.

Contributing to the growth of this middle class are two basic movements. They can be summarized in two colloquialisms: "going to town" and "heading North."

Both the Negro and white South are "going to town" in a drama of change gripping the entire region. The South is in the process of shifting from a rural, predominantly single-crop economy to urban industrialization. In the brief period between 1940 and 1944, a million Negroes left farming in the South. From 1950 to 1954, the number of Negro farmers in the South declined 17.1 per cent.

Many of these "headed North." Their exodus has meant not only that the South is getting whiter all the time but also that new ways, new standards, new ambitions filter down the family grapevine (as well as the TV serial which sprouts on every roof), replacing the familiar old acceptance of subservience.

* * *

As the Southern Negro comes closer to entering the total pattern of American life, he also becomes more aware of those educational and economic opportunities essential to securing and maintaining position in the middle class. His status is still low—but it is changing for the better; it is the combination of these two facts that provides part of the dynamic behind the Negro protest. Because this dynamic is also such a firm part of the American ideal of self-betterment and progress, the protest will neither diminish nor disappear, as so many important white leaders, both North and South, who have not yet understood its full meaning, seem to hope.

The question is frequently asked, and not only in the South, why Negro leadership did not wage to a successful conclusion the fight for full equality in civil rights or the field of health or housing, before tackling the emotion-laden realm of schools. To ask this is to underrate the Negro's powerful push from peasantry, combined with the pull toward the middle class which is one of the real revolutions of our time. One sociologist has observed that "education is a passion with the middle-class Negro." The reasons are obvious.

Education is one of the master keys unlocking the door of opportunity—economic, political, social—into the middle class world.

* * *

If the Southern white father could stop seeing the Southern Negro father as a *Negro* and could see him, even for a moment, as another *father,* he might comprehend more clearly some of the determination behind the drive for desegregation.

* * *

When Princeton's Dr. Melvin Tumin and associates published their recent study of a North Carolina county, "Desegregation, Resistance and Readiness," one of their ten major findings included the majority image of the Negro as inferior to the white in morality, intelligence, responsibility and ambition—but with an impressive minority disagreement. "Approximately 27 per cent consider the Negro to be equal or superior to the white in responsibility, 31 per cent in morality, 33 per cent in ambition, and 40 percent in intelligence. [. . .]"

Martin Luther King, Jr.

From Letter from Birmingham Jail (1963)

My Dear Fellow Clergymen:

While confined here in the Birmingham city jail, I came across your recent statement calling my present activities "unwise and untimely." Seldom do I pause to answer criticism of my work and ideas. If I sought to answer all the criticisms that cross my desk, my secretaries would have little time for anything other than such correspondence in the course of the day, and I would have no time for constructive work. But since I feel that you are men of genuine good will and that your criticisms are sincerely set forth, I want to try to answer your statement in what I hope will be patient and reasonable terms.

I think I should indicate why I am here in Birmingham, since you have been influenced by the view which argues against "outsiders coming in."

* * *

[. . .] I am cognizant of the interrelatedness of all communities and states. I cannot sit idly by in Atlanta and not be concerned about what happens in Birmingham. Injustice anywhere is a threat to justice everywhere. We are caught in an inescapable network of mutuality, tied in a single garment of destiny. Whatever affects one directly, affects all indirectly. Never again can we afford to live with the narrow, provincial "outside agitator" idea. Anyone who lives inside the United States can never be considered an outsider anywhere within its bounds.

* * *

We know through painful experience that freedom is never voluntarily given by the oppressor; it must be demanded by the oppressed. Frankly, I have yet to engage in a direct-action campaign that was "well timed" in the view of those who have not suffered unduly from the disease of segregation. For years now I have heard the word "Wait!" It rings in the ear of every Negro with piercing familiarity. This "Wait" has almost always meant "Never." We must come to see, with one of our distinguished jurists, that "justice too long delayed is justice denied."

We have waited for more than 340 years for our constitutional and God-given rights. The nations of Asia and Africa are moving with jetlike speed toward gaining political independence, but we still creep at horse-and-buggy pace toward gaining a cup of coffee at a lunch counter. Perhaps it is easy for those who have never felt the stinging darts of segregation to say, "Wait." But when you have seen vicious mobs lynch your mothers and fathers at will and drown your sisters and brothers at whim; when you have seen hate-filled policemen curse, kick, and even kill your black brothers and sisters; when you see the vast majority of your twenty million Negro brothers smothering in an airtight cage of poverty in the midst of an affluent society; when you suddenly find your tongue twisted and your speech stammering as you seek to explain to your six-year-old daughter why she can't go to the public amusement park that has just been advertised on television, and see tears welling up in her eyes when she is told that Funtown is closed to colored children, and see ominous clouds of inferiority beginning to form in her little mental sky, and see her beginning to distort her personality by developing an unconscious bitterness toward white people; when you have to concoct an answer for a five-year-old son who is asking, "Daddy, why do white people treat colored people so mean?"; when you take a cross-country drive and find it necessary to sleep night after night in the uncomfortable corners of your automobile because no motel will accept you; when you are humiliated day in and day out by nagging signs reading "white" and "colored"; when your first name becomes "nigger," your middle name becomes "boy" (however old you are) and your last name becomes "John," and your wife and mother are never given the respected title "Mrs."; when you are harried by day and haunted by night by the fact that you are a Negro, living constantly at tiptoe stance, never quite knowing what to expect next, and are plagued with inner fears and outer resentments; when you are forever fighting a degenerating sense of "nobodiness"—then you will understand why we find it difficult to wait. There comes a time when the cup of endurance runs over, and men are no longer willing to be plunged into the abyss of despair. I hope, sirs, you can understand our legitimate and unavoidable impatience.

• • •

Oppressed people cannot remain oppressed forever. The yearning for freedom eventually manifests itself, and that is what has happened to the American Negro. Something within has reminded him of his birthright of freedom, and something without has reminded him that it can be gained. Consciously or unconsciously, he has been caught up by the *Zeitgeist,*[1] and with his black brothers of Africa and his brown and yellow brothers of Asia, South America, and the Caribbean, the United States Negro is moving with a sense of great urgency toward the promised land of racial justice. If one recognizes this vital urge that has engulfed the Negro community, one should readily understand why public demonstrations are taking

1. The spirit of the times (German).

place. The Negro has many pent-up resentments and latent frustrations, and he must release them. So let him march; let him make prayer pilgrimages to the city hall; let him go on freedom rides—and try to understand why he must do so. If his repressed emotions are not released in nonviolent ways, they will seek expression through violence; this is not a threat but a fact of history. So I have not said to my people, "Get rid of your discontent." Rather, I have tried to say that this normal and healthy discontent can be channeled into the creative outlet of nonviolent direct action. And now this approach is being termed extremist.

But though I was initially disappointed at being categorized as an extremist, as I continued to think about the matter I gradually gained a measure of satisfaction from the label. Was not Jesus an extremist for love: "Love your enemies, bless them that curse you, do good to them that hate you, and pray for them which despitefully use you, and persecute you."[2] Was not Amos an extremist for justice: "Let justice roll down like waters and righteousness like an ever-flowing stream."[3] Was not Paul an extremist for the Christian gospel: "I bear in my body the marks of the Lord Jesus."[4] Was not Martin Luther an extremist: "Here I stand; I cannot do otherwise, so help me God."[5] And John Bunyan: "I will stay in jail to the end of my days before I make a butchery of my conscience."[6] And Abraham Lincoln: "This nation cannot survive half slave and half free." And Thomas Jefferson: "We hold these truths to be self-evident, that all men are created equal. . . ." So the question is not whether we will be extremists, but what kind of extremists we will be. Will we be extremists for hate or for love? Will we be extremists for the preservation of injustice or for the extension of justice?

Robert C. Weaver

From "The Negro as an American": The Yearning for Human Dignity (1963)[1]

Delivered before the Symposium on Challenges to Democracy of the Fund for the Republic, Chicago, Illinois, June 13, 1963

Most middle-class white Americans frequently ask, "Why do Negroes push so? They have made phenomenal progress in 100 years of freedom, so why don't their leaders do something about the crime rate and illegitimacy?" To them I would reply that when Negroes press for full equality now they are behaving as all other Americans would under similar circumstances. Every American has

2. Matthew 5.44. 3. Amos 5.24; Amos was an Old Testament prophet.

4. Galatians 6:17; Paul, a great missionary of the early Christian church, often suffered for his teaching. He wrote some of his own biblical letters from prison.

5. German theologian and leader of the Reformation (1483–1546); the quotation is from Luther's defense of his teaching at the Trial of Worms, 1521.

6. English preacher (1628–88) and author of *Pilgrim's Progress* (1678); this is a paraphrase of a passage in his Confession of My Faith, and a Reason of My Practice.

1. Robert C. Weaver. "'The Negro as an American': The Yearning for Human Dignity." *Vital Speeches of the Day*, vol. 29, no. 20, 1963, pp. 620–29. *EbscoHost*, connection.ebscohost.com/c/speeches/9877028/negro-as-american.

the right to be treated as a human being and striving for human dignity is a national characteristic.

* * *

Negroes who are constantly confronted or threatened by discrimination and inequality articulate a sense of outrage. Many react with hostility, sometimes translating their feelings into overt anti-social actions. In parts of the Negro community a separate culture with deviant values develops. To the members of this subculture I would observe that ours is a middle-class society and those who fail to evidence most of its values and behavior are headed toward difficulties. But I am reminded that the rewards for those who do are often minimal, providing insufficient inducement for large numbers to emulate them.

* * *

The Negro here—as he has so frequently and eloquently demonstrated—is an American. And his status, no less than his aspirations, can be measured meaningfully only in terms of American standards.

Viewed from this point of view what are the facts?

Median family income among non-whites was slightly less than 55 per cent of that for whites in 1959; for individuals the figure was 50 per cent.

Only a third of the Negro families in 1959 earned sufficient to sustain an acceptable American standard of living. [. . .]

Undergirding these overall figures are many paradoxes. Negroes have made striking gains in historical terms, yet their current rate of unemployment is well over double that among whites. Over two-thirds of our colored workers are still concentrated in five major unskilled and semi-skilled occupations, as contrasted to slightly over a third of the white labor force. [. . .]

In 1959 non-white males who were high school graduates earned, on the average, 32 per cent less than whites; for non-white college graduates the figure was 38 per cent less. Among women a much different situation exists. Non-white women who were high school graduates earned on the average some 24 per cent less than whites. Non-white female college graduates, however, earned but slightly over one per cent less average annual salaries than white women college graduates. Significantly, the median annual income of non-white female college graduates was more than double that of non-white women with only high school education.

Is it any wonder that among non-whites, as contrasted to whites, a larger proportion of women than of men attend and finish college? [. . .]

There is much in these situations that reflects the continuing matriarchal character of Negro society—a situation which had its roots in the family composition under slavery where the father, if identified, had no established role. Subsequent and continuing economic advantages of Negro women who found steady employment as domestics during the post Civil War era and thereafter perpetuated the pattern. This [. . .] served to emasculate many Negro men economically and psychologically. It also explains, in part, the high prevalence of broken homes, illegitimacy, and lack of motivation in the Negro community.

• • •

The tragedy of discrimination is that it provides an excuse for failure while erecting barriers to success.

Most colored Americans still are not only outside the mainstream of our society but see no hope of entering it. The lack of motivation and anti-social behavior which result are capitalized upon by the champions of the *status quo.* They say that the average Negro must demonstrate to the average white that the latter's fears are groundless. One proponent of this point of view has stated that Negro crime and illegitimacy must decline and Negro Neighborhoods must stop deteriorating.

In these observations lie a volume on race relations. In the first place, those who articulate this point of view fail to differentiate between acceptance as earned by individual merit and enjoyment of rights guaranteed to everyone. Implicit, also, is the assumption that Negroes can lift themselves by their bootstraps, and that once they become brown counterparts of white middle-class Americans, they will be accepted on the basis of individual merit. Were this true, our race problem would be no more than a most recent phase in the melting pot tradition of the nation.

As compared to the earlier newcomers to our cities from Europe, the later ones who are colored face much greater impediments in moving from the slums or from the bottom of the economic ladder. At the same time, they have less resources to meet the more difficult problems which confront them.

• • •

Enforced residential segregation, the most stubborn and universal of the Negro's disadvantages, often leads to exploitation and effects a spatial pattern which facilitates neglect of public services in the well-defined areas where Negroes live. It restricts the opportunities of the more successful as well as the least successful in the group, augmenting artificially the number of non-whites who live in areas of blight and neglect and face impediments to the attainment of values and behavior required for upward social and economic mobility.

The most obvious consequence of involuntary residential segregation is that the housing dollar in a dark hand usually commands less purchasing power than one in a white hand. Clearly, this is a denial of a basic promise of a free economy.

For immigrant groups in the nation, the trend toward improved socioeconomic status has gone hand-and-hand with decreasing residential segregation. The reverse has been true of the Negro.

• • •

I happen to have been born a Negro and to have devoted a large part of my adult energies to the problem of the role of the Negro in America. But I am also a government administrator [. . .].

My responsibilities as a Negro and an American are part of the heritage I received from my parents—a heritage that included a wealth of moral and social values that don't have anything to do with my race. [. . .]

The challenge frequently thrown to me is why I don't go out into the Negro community and exhort Negro youths to prepare themselves for present and future opportunities. [. . .]

Many of the youth which I am urged to exhort come from broken homes. They live in communities where the fellow who stays in school and follows the rules is a "square." They reside in a neighborhood where the most successful are often engaged in shady—if not illegal—activities. They know that the very policeman who may arrest them for violation of the law is sometimes the pay-off man for the racketeers. And they recognize that the majority society, which they frequently believe to be the "enemy," condones this situation. Their experience also leads some of them to believe that getting the kind of job the residents in the neighborhood hold is unrewarding—a commitment to hard work and poverty. For almost all of them, the precepts of Ben Franklin are lily-white in their applicability.

* * *

For many successful older colored Americans, middle-class status has been difficult. Restricted, in large measure, to racial ghettos, they have expended great effort to protect their children from falling back into the dominant values of that environment. And these values are probably more repugnant to them than to most Americans. This is understandable in terms of their social origins. For the most part, they come from lower-middle class families, where industry, good conduct, family ties, and a willingness to postpone immediate rewards for future successes are stressed. Their values and standards of conduct are those of success-oriented middle-class Americans. [. . .]

These attitudes, too, are shifting. The younger middle-class Negroes are more secure and consequently place less stress upon the quest for respectability. But few Negroes are immune from the toll of upward mobility. Frequently their struggle has been difficult, and the maintenance of their status demands a heavy input. As long as this is true, they will have less energy to devote to the problems of the Negro subculture. It is significant, however, that the sit-ins and Freedom Marches in the South were planned and executed by Negro college students most of whom come from middle-class families.

Middle-class Negroes have long led the fight for civil rights; today its youthful members do not hesitate to resort to direct action, articulating the impatience which is rife throughout the Negro community. In so doing they are forging a new solidarity in the struggle for human dignity.

* * *

The ultimate responsibilities of Negro leadership, however, are to show results and maintain a following. This means that it cannot be so "responsible" that it forgets the trials and tribulations of others who are less fortunate or less recognized than itself. It cannot stress progress—the emphasis which is so palatable to the majority group—without, at the same time, delineating the unsolved business of democracy.

Most Negroes in leadership capacities have articulated the fact that they and those who follow them are a part of America. They have striven for realization of the American dream. Most recognize their responsibilities as citizens and urge others to follow their example. Sophisticated whites realize that the status of Negroes in our society depends not only upon what the Negro does to achieve his goals and prepare himself for opportunities but, even more, upon what all America does to expand these opportunities. And the quality and nature of future Negro leadership depends upon how effective those leaders who relate to the total society can be in satisfying the yearnings for human dignity which reside in the hearts of all Americans.

African Americans and Africa

Earl E. Thorpe

From Africa in the Thought of Negro Americans (1959)[1]

The continent of Africa is daily growing in economic, political, and cultural significance. Recently a Negro newspaper in St. Louis, Missouri, contained the statement that the newly independent state of Ghana holds a significance for Negro Americans which is comparable to that which Israel holds for Jewish Americans. How much truth is there in such a statement? Or better still, what does Africa and its history mean to American Negroes? Opinions on this vary greatly, for in an opposite vein from that contained in the St. Louis newspaper, recently the most eminent of all Negro Sociologists[2] stated that most educated Negroes have little but contempt and disdain for Africa and its peoples.

• • •

While most Afro-Americans have wished to be a part of the midstream of national life and culture, not all have wanted this integration. A few, either because they felt that the race actually is inferior and could not compete with whites, or because they went to the opposite extreme and came to believe that Negroes were superior and would lose their distinctive qualities, have desired continued segregation in some form, either here or abroad. Marcus Garvey belonged to the latter group [. . .].

[. . .] Sharing the pessimism and disillusionment, as well as the optimism of the [1920s], Marcus Garvey became convinced that the position of his race within the United States was eternally without hope. Thus he advocated a "back to Africa" movement, and in step with the new appreciation which artists and scholars were beginning to show for African culture, Garvey created a veritable cult of blackness. Reacting against the contempt for dark complexions which many white and Negro Americans held, he proclaimed that black is actually the best and "superior" color. Since it coincided with the efforts of [. . .] scholars in the social sciences, as well as with . . . trends in art, music, and creative literature, the

1. Earl E. Thorpe. "Africa in the Thought of Negro Americans." *The Negro History Bulletin*, Oct. 1959, pp. 5+.

2. E. Franklin Frazier (1894–1962), author of several influential sociological studies of African American life and first black president of the American Sociological Society.

movement "put steel into the spine of many Negroes who had previously been ashamed of their color." Especially did Garveyism appeal to lower-class Negroes, and even yet it represents the nearest semblance to a mass movement which has existed among Afro-Americans. Most Negro organizations and intellectuals opposed the movement, however.

• • •

[T]he prominence of the African theatre of battle during the early years of the second world war,[3] participation of native African troops in the allied cause, and the possible demise of colonialism as a consequence of the war kept Africa prominent in the thought of Negro Americans. With the return of peace, Afro-American race consciousness and pride were bolstered not only by the phenomenal overthrow of imperialism and colonialism by yellow, brown, and black people in Asia and Africa, but by the dramatic achievements in racial integration within their own country. And just as the personality and efforts of Mahatma Gandhi had inspired Afro-Americans in the twenties and thirties, he, Kwame Nkrumah, Jomo Kenyatta, Gamel Nasser,[4] and other nationalist leaders in Asia and Africa were great sources of inspiration to them in the late forties and fifties.

It seems almost paradoxical that rampant nationalism in Asia and Africa have evoked a greater internationalism in the thought of Afro-Americans.

[. . .] Indeed, a dominant characteristic of the mid-twentieth century Negro vis-à-vis Africa is the greatly increased number who have visited that continent [. . .]. This travel is helping to dispel much of the ignorance about Africa and Africans which has been evident among Negro Americans. Thus many of the old stereotypes once commonly accepted are now rapidly being discarded. [. . .]

As a consequence of the degradation of slavery, Negroes have been unique among Americans in the rejection of the land of their fathers. Now a greater maturity and developing race pride are bringing an end to this rejection, and it would not be surprising, to the present writer at least, to see the masses of Afro-Americans soon embrace Africa with a force comparable to that which the Irish and Jewish Americans show for the lands of their fathers.

Phaon Goldman

From The Significance of African Freedom for the Negro American (1960)[1]

With Africa in the headlines every day it behooves us as alert, adult Americans, to know more about Africa and her peoples and the new nations being born almost monthly on this the world's second largest continent. One of my professors used

3. German forces invaded Libya in 1941; two years later they were driven out of North Africa by Allied forces.
4. Gamel Nasser (1918–70), first president of the republic of Egypt (from 1956–70). Kwame Nkrumah (1909–72), first prime minister, then first president, of Ghana (1957–66). Jomo Kenyatta (1893–1978), first president of Kenya (from 1964–78).
1. Phaon Goldman. "The Significance of African Freedom for the Negro American." *Negro History Bulletin*, Oct. 1960, pp. 2+.

to say that all we know (as Negro Americans) about Africa was that it was shaped like a "po'k chop"—and it is, too, if you'll notice the map. It's a pork chop that's sizzling nowadays.

Africa is significant not only because it's in the news, but also because we have an ancestral connection with the peoples of Africa—a connection we need to review and re-appraise. We have only heard since we were wee tots about Africa in terms of the exotic, the outlandish—land of cannibals, slithering snakes, and people who go around boiling missionaries in a pot. These are the one-sided views of Africa we have been taught; these would furnish material for books and movies that would sell. Seldom, if ever, did we hear the appraisals of Africa made by the most learned scholars of old, such as Ibn Batuda, greatest of the Moslem travelers of the Middle Ages—a man who had traveled throughout most of the then known world, said this of West Africa (in contrast to Spain, Syria, India, China, Turkey, etc.), "Nowhere is there a higher regard for justice or greater security. One can travel throughout the kingdom of the blacks without fear of thieves, robbers, vagabonds, or other evil persons." [. . .]

There is also another instance of our background and connection with Africa which we have come to see only in one light, and that is our outlook on the system of slavery—the instrument that brought us to these shores. When we think of slavery we too often visualize happy-go-lucky slaves captured easily and without a struggle. But the truth of the matter is that the Portuguese, Dutch, and British, fought many a pitched battle to capture most of the Africans that were taken into slavery. Those men, sold into the chains of the European slave-traders by other Africans, were most often warriors who had been captured in inter-village battles. Tens of thousands of these men died by their own hand on the long middle passage rather than submit to that day's form of man's inhumanity to man. So you can see that our ancestors represent not a bunch of cringing cowards but the most valiant of men in body and spirit.

* * *

The valor and sense of justice of the ancient peoples of West Africa can most clearly be seen [. . .] in the determined, forthright, and courageous stand for freedom now being taken by our young Negro youth of the South who in spite of threats, insults, and violence, stand by their right to be accorded the simple human decencies that all other people on earth get in America. The strength of our forefathers is with us still, and make no mistake about it, the students' inspiration came from the fight for freedom now being waged all over the African continent [. . .].

These are sides of our past which have been deliberately buried, for if a man can convince you that you came from nothing, that you are nothing, and that you never will be anything, he doesn't need to worry about you trying to break down segregation barriers, for he has already convinced you that you are different from other human beings and you will be content with your lot.

There are other ways in which we have come to disrespect ourselves too—subtle ways, ways that affect our subconscious mind and blunt our demand for "Freedom Now," and the human dignity accorded all other peoples.

. . .

[One] subconscious factor causing us to feel we're different from others and therefore perhaps should be treated differently, is the American standard of beauty [. . .]. The faces we see on TV, in the movies and in the magazine ads, reflect the Anglo-Saxon characteristics of the thin nose, a white skin, and straight hair. Being a minority people of physically diametrically opposite characteristics, but set down in the middle of other values, we begin to subconsciously feel that we need to make ourselves over, physically, in order to become acceptable to the majority. So we're told that certain skin preparations will make us "lighter, brighter, and more acceptable" and similar positive attributes are assigned to hair preparations that give us 'straight' hair instead of the curly variety we have.

. . .

So to sum up, with Africa in the news every day we must re-view our past concepts of Africa and our relations with the African people, we must view their current battle for "Freedom Now" through the pressures of boycotts, strikes, and mass protests as that stage of man's eternal quest for human dignity that brings the issues out into the open and forces a decision. We must keep ever in mind that the cry of "Freedom Now" is but the present-day application of the ideas of men like Thomas Jefferson and Patrick Henry whose cry of "Give me liberty or give me death" brought freedom to this country and still inspires men to fight for freedom around the world.

Perhaps the greatest significance of African freedom for the Negro American is that it may light the way for those of us of African descent here in America to re-vitalize America's conscience by moving together now for our freedom and force America to solve her moral dilemma of the race question and resume her rightful place as a world leader by showing in deed as well as in preachment that she is truly the land of "liberty and justice for all."

NAACP POLITICAL ACTION COMMITTEE

Raisin in the Sun Revisited

Actor-playwright Bruce Norris's *Clybourne Park*, winner of the 2011 Pulitzer Prize for Drama, consists of two acts, one a prequel, the other a sequel, to *A Raisin in the Sun*. Set in 1959, Act One depicts a white couple's struggle to deal both with the death of their son and with a neighbor anxious to stop the sale of their home to a black purchaser; that neighbor turns out to be Karl (Lindner), the black purchasers, the Youngers. Set in the same house and featuring the same actors, Act Two takes place fifty years later, in 2009, when the home's new white owners' plan to replace it with a much larger one brings them into conflict with both city regulations and a neighborhood association bent on preserving the now mainly black neighborhood's historic character in the face of gentrification. The representatives of that neighborhood association are another young professional couple: Kevin and his wife, Lena, a relative and namesake of Lena Younger. In the following brief excerpt from Act Two, Kevin and Lena, along with the neighborhood association lawyer, Tom, battle it out with the new homeowners, Steve and Lindsey, and their lawyer, Kathy, who also just happens to be Karl Lindner's daughter.

Bruce Norris

From Clybourne Park (2010)

TOM [*holding up a document*] Okay. Here's the wording from the City Council, and I quote: "In recognition of the *historic* status of the Clybourne Park neighborhood, and its distinctive collection of *low-rise single-family homes— (cont'd.)*

LINDSEY
Aren't *we* a single family?

KEVIN
Hey. Hey.
Everything's cool.

TOM
(continuous)— intended to house a community of working-class families."

LINDSEY: And you know, the thing is? Communities change.
STEVE: They do.
LINDSEY: That's just the reality.
STEVE: It is.
LENA: And some change is inevitable, and we all support that, but it might be worth asking yourself who exactly is *responsible* for that change?

[*Little pause.*]

LINDSEY
I'm not sure what you—?

KEVIN
Wait, what are you trying to—?

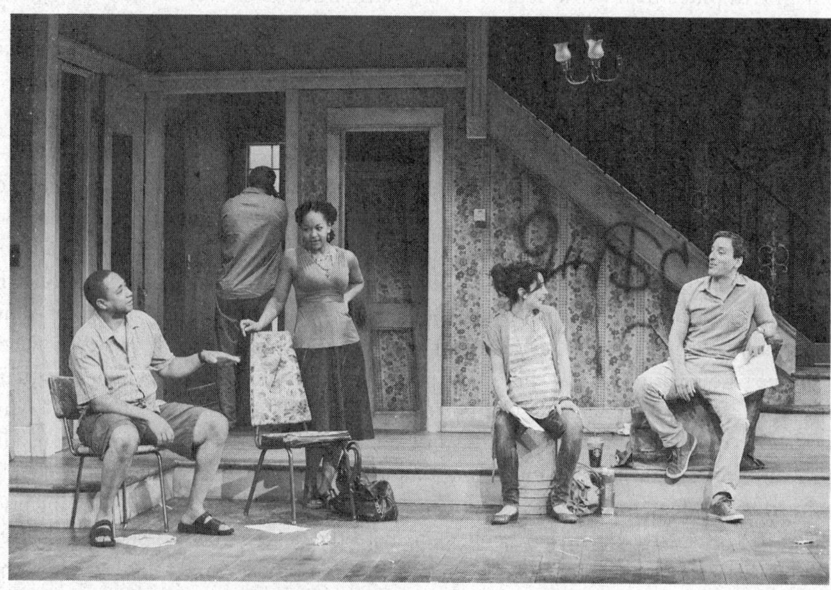

Damon Gupton as Kevin, Crystal A. Dickinson as Lena, Annie Parisse as Lindsey, and Jeremy Shamos as Steve in the Playwrights Horizon production of *Clybourne Park*

LENA: I'm asking you to think about the motivation behind the long-range political initiative to change the face of this neighborhood.

[*Another little pause.*]

LINDSEY
What does that mean? I don't know what that—?

STEVE
(*to* LENA)
Wait, say that again?

KEVIN
The long-range *what*?

LENA: I mean that this is a highly desirable area.
STEVE: Well, *we* desire it.
LENA: I know you do.
LINDSEY: Same as you.
LENA: And now the area is *changing*.
KATHY: And for the *better*, right?
LENA: And I'm saying that there are certain economic interests that are being served by those changes and others that are not. That's all.
STEVE: (*suspiciously*) And . . . *which* interests are being—?
LENA: (*systematically*) If you have a residential area, in direct proximity to *downtown*?
STEVE: Right?
LENA: And if that area is occupied by a particular *group*?

STEVE
Which group?

LINDSEY
(*to* LENA) You know what? We're talking about *one house*.

LENA: (*to* LINDSEY) I understand that.
STEVE: Which group?
LINDSEY: A house for our *family*?
STEVE: Which group?
LENA: That's how it happens.
LINDSEY: In which to raise our *child*?
STEVE: No no. Which group?
LENA: It happens one house at a time.
STEVE: Whoa whoa whoa. Okay. Stop right there.
LINDSEY: What are you doing?
STEVE: No. I'm sorry, but can we just come out and *say* what it is we're actually—? Shouldn't we maybe *do* that? Because if *that's* what this is really about, then . . . jesus, maybe we oughta save ourselves some time and and and and just . . . *say* what it is we're really *saying* instead of doing this elaborate little *dance* around it.

[*Dead stop. All stare at* STEVE]

Never mind.
KATHY: *What* dance?
STEVE: I—I—I—I shouldn't have—whatever.
LENA (*parsing his meaning*): So . . . you think I haven't been *saying* what I *actually*—?
STEVE (*laughs*): Uhhh . . . Not to my way of thinking, no.
LENA: Well, what is it you *think* I'm—?

STEVE: I—I—I . . . *(laughs incredulously)*: . . . like we don't all *know*?
LINDSEY: *I* don't.
STEVE: Oh, *yes you do.* Of *course* you do.
KEVIN: Well, maybe you oughta *tell* us what *you* think she was saying.
STEVE: Oh oh, but it has to be *me*?
LENA: Well, you're the one who raised the question as to—*(cont'd.)*
STEVE *(laughs, overlapping)*: Oh, *come on.* It was *blatant.*
LENA *(continuous)*: —the sincerity of my speech.
LINDSEY: What the fuck, Steve?
STEVE: You know what? Forget I said it.

LINDSEY	LENA	STEVE
You didn't *say* anything.	Oh no, I'm *interested.*	Let's forget the whole—

STEVE *(continuous)*: —Okay. Okay. If you really want to—It's . . . *(tries to laugh, then, sotto)* . . . it's *race.* Isn't it? You're trying to tell me that that . . . That implicit in what you *said*—That this entire conversation . . . isn't at least *partly* informed—*am I right? (laughs nervously)* By the issue of . . . *(sotto)* of *racism*?

[*Beat, then*]

LINDSEY	STEVE
(to STEVE*)*	*(to* LINDSEY*)*
Are you out of your—?	And *please* don't do that to me, okay? I've asked you repeatedly.
	(to LENA*)*
	I have no idea where this is coming from.

LENA: Well, the *original* issue was the inappropriately large *house* that—*(cont'd.)*
STEVE *(to* LENA, overlapping): Oh, come *on.*
LENA *(continuous)*: —you're planning to build. Only, *now* I'm fairly certain that I've been called a *racist.*
STEVE: But I didn't say that, did I?
LENA: *Sounded* like you did.
STEVE *(to* KEVIN*)* Did I say that?
KEVIN: Yeah, you kinda did.
STEVE: In what way did I say that?
KEVIN: Uh, *somebody* said racism.
STEVE: *-Cism*! *-Cism*! Not *-cist*!!
KEVIN: Which must originate from *somewhere.*
STEVE: And which we all find totally reprehensi—
KEVIN: So—are *you* the racist?
STEVE: Can I just—?
KEVIN: Is it your wife?
KATHY: Don't look at *me.*
STEVE: Look:
KEVIN: 'Cause, by process of elimination—
STEVE: Here's what I'm saying:
LINDSEY: What *are* you saying?!
STEVE: I'm saying: Was race *not* a factor—
LINDSEY: *(re:* STEVE, *exonerating herself)* I don't know this person.

STEVE: Were there *not* these differences—

LINDSEY: *What* differences!!? There's no—

STEVE (*to* LINDSEY *re:* LENA): Okay: She walks in here, from the very beginning, with all these *issues—(cont'd.)*

LENA (*overlapping*): About your *house.*

STEVE (*continuous*): —and I'm only asking whether, were we not, shall we say—?

LINDSEY: You're *creating* an issue. *Where none exists.*

STEVE: Oh oh oh you *heard* what she *said*. She as much as claimed that there's some kind of, of, of *secret conspiracy*—

LENA: Oh, it's not a *secret.*

KEVIN (*to* LENA)	LENA (*to* KEVIN)	STEVE
Ohh, *c'mon.* Are you seriously—?	Oh, please don't be purposely *naive.*	*There. Thank you. Now you see what I'm—?*

LENA: This has been under discussion for at least *four decades* now—*(cont'd.)*

KEVIN (*overlapping, to* LENA): *You can't prove that.*

LENA (*continuous*): —at the highest institutional levels of—

(to KEVIN—): *oh, don't act like you don't know it's true.*

STEVE (*to* LENA): What, and now we're the evil invaders who are—

LINDSEY (*to* STEVE): *She never said that!!!!*

STEVE: —appropriating your *ancestral homeland*?

LINDSEY (*to* STEVE): This, this, this—No. I'm sorry, this is the most *asinine*—

(*to* LENA and KEVIN): *Half of my friends are black!*

STEVE (*sputtering*): *What!!??*

LINDSEY (*to* STEVE, *as to a child*): As is true for most *normal* people.

STEVE: Name *one.*

LINDSEY: *Normal* people? Tend to have *many* friends of a diverse and wide-ranging—

STEVE: You can't name *one*!

LINDSEY: Candace.

STEVE (*beat, then*): Name another.

LINDSEY: *I don't have to stand here compiling a list of*—

STEVE: You said *half.* You *specifically*—

LINDSEY: Theresa.

STEVE: *She works in your office!! She's not your "friend".*

LINDSEY: *She was at the baby shower, Steve! I hope she's not my enemy!!*

TOM: Well, this is all fascinating—

STEVE (*to* LINDSEY): Name another.

TOM: And while I'd love to sit here and review *all* of American History, *maybe* we should concentrate on the plans for your *property—(cont'd)*

STEVE (*overlapping*): Yes!! Yes!! *(cont'd)*

TOM (*continuous*): —which *had* been the *original* topic of the convers—

STEVE (*overlapping, continuous*): The history of America *is* the history of private property.

LENA: That may be—

STEVE: Read De Tocqueville.[1]

1. Reference to *Democracy in America* (1835–40), a compehensive two-volume study of American society by the Frenchman Alexis de Tocqueville (1805–59).

LENA: —though I rather doubt *your* grandparents were *sold as* private property.

STEVE (*to* KEVIN & LENA): Ohhhhh my *god.* Look. Look. Humans are *territorial,* okay?

LINDSEY (*to* STEVE): Who *are* you?

STEVE: This is why we have *wars.* One group, one *tribe,* tries to usurp some *territory*—and now *you guys* have *this* territory, right? And you don't like having it *stolen away* from you, the way white people stole everything else from black America. *We get it,* And we *apologize.* But what *good* does it do, if we perpetually fall into the same, predictable little euphemistic tap dance around the topic?

KEVIN: You know how to tap dance?

STEVE: *See? See what he's doing?!!*

LINDSEY: Maybe quit while you're ahead.

SUGGESTIONS FOR WRITING

1. Langston Hughes's poem HARLEM poses a question: "What happens to a dream deferred?" Why do you think Lorraine Hansberry chose this poem as the epigraph for A RAISIN IN THE SUN? Write an essay in which you discuss the various "dreams" that come into conflict in the play. Which "dream" does the play seem to endorse? Does it ultimately answer Hughes's question?
2. In A RAISIN IN THE SUN's third act, Beneatha asserts that "there isn't any real progress [. . .] there is only one large circle that we march in, around and around, each of us with our own little picture—in front of us—our own little mirage that we think is the future." Asagai counters that progress follows "a long line—as in geometry, [. . .] one that reaches into infinity." Write an essay in which you compare these two views of progress as they are depicted in A RAISIN IN THE SUN. Does the play seem to favor one view over the other?
3. In EVEN MORE CRUCIAL THAN IN THE SOUTH, *New York Times* reporter Gertrude Samuels suggests that what African Americans were increasingly demanding in the late 1950s and early 1960s was not only an end to racial discrimination in housing, schooling, and employment, but also and above all "personal dignity" (1530), a point echoed in Martin Luther King, Jr.'s reference, in LETTER FROM BIRMINGHAM JAIL, to "the stinging darts of segregation" (1535). Drawing on these and other contextual excerpts in this chapter, as well as A RAISIN IN THE SUN, write an essay exploring what the play might contribute to our understanding of the psychological and emotional effects of racial discrimination. How does the latter seem to affect the way the characters perceive themselves and each other?
4. A RAISIN IN THE SUN is set in Chicago, but in many ways its heart is in Africa—the Africa of the mythical past, the Africa of the slave trade, and the Africa of the play's own temporal setting. Write an essay in which you explore the many ways in which both African history and culture and American attitudes toward them inform Hansberry's play. To what extent might the play illustrate ideas found in Earl E. Thorpe's AFRICA IN THE THOUGHT OF NEGRO AMERICANS and/or Phaon Goldman's THE SIGNIFICANCE OF AFRICAN FREEDOM FOR THE NEGRO AMERICAN?
5. Hansberry's play explores not only the evolving social and economic positions of African Americans in the mid-twentieth century, but also their evolving gender roles, a subject on which Robert C. Weaver also comments briefly in THE NEGRO AS AN AMERICAN. Write an essay in which you discuss the crucial role that gender plays in the action of A RAISIN IN THE SUN. Does the play seem to uphold any particular vision of gender roles, especially within the family? Might it in any way endorse Weaver's rather provocative claims on the subject?

30 CRITICAL CONTEXTS: SOPHOCLES'S *ANTIGONE*

Even more than other forms of literature, drama has a relatively stable **canon**, a select group of plays that the theater community thinks of as especially worthy of frequent performance. New plays join this canon, of course, but theater companies worldwide tend to perform the same ones over and over, especially those by Shakespeare, Ibsen, and Sophocles. The reasons are many, involving the plays' themes and continued appeal across times and cultures as well as their formal literary and theatrical features. But their repeated performance means that a relatively small number of plays become much better known than all the others and that there is a tradition of "talk" about those plays. A lot of this talk is informal and local, resulting from the fact that people see plays communally, viewing performances together and often comparing responses afterward. But more permanent and more formal responses also exist; individual productions of plays are often reviewed in newspapers and magazines, on radio and television, and on the Internet. Such reviews concentrate primarily on evaluating specific productions. But because every production of a play involves a particular interpretation of the text, cumulative accounts of performances add up to a body of interpretive criticism—that is, analytical commentary about many aspects of the play as text and as performance. Scholars add to that body of criticism by publishing their own interpretations of a play in academic journals and books.

Sophocles's ANTIGONE, for instance, attracts attention from a wide variety of perspectives—from Greek scholars, who view it in relation to classical myth or ancient Greek language and culture; from philosophers, who may see in it examinations of classic ideas and ethical problems; from theater historians, who may think about it in relation to traditions of staging and visualization or the particulars of gestures and stage business; and from historians of rhetoric, who may consider the interactions between the chorus and the players or the way characters use or abuse classical rhetorical conventions.

As a reader of plays in a textbook like this one, you may or may not bring to your reading an awareness of what others have thought about a particular play, but that body of material is available if you choose to use it as a way of getting additional perspectives on the text. You don't have to read this accumulated criticism to understand what happens in a text. But reading what others have said about a text can help you—by offering historical information that you hadn't known or hadn't considered relevant, by pointing to problems or possibilities of interpretation you had not yet thought of, or by supporting a reading you had already arrived at. In a sense, reading published criticism is like talking with your fellow students or being involved in a class discussion. In general, you shouldn't read "the critics" until after you have read the play at least once, just as you should read the text in full before you discuss it with others. That way, your initial responses to the play are your own; if you don't understand some things, you can always discuss them later or read a few pieces of good criticism.

A bust of Sophocles

Reading criticism can be especially helpful when you have to write an essay. Critics will often guide you to crucial points of debate or to a place in the text that is a crux for deciding on a particular interpretation. You will likely get the most help if you read several critics with different perspectives—not because more is better, but because you will see their differences and, more important, the *grounds* for their differences in the kinds of evidence they use and the various inferences they draw from it. Their disagreements will likely be very useful to you as a new interpreter. But don't regard critics as "authorities" (an interpretation is not true simply because it is published or because it is written by somebody famous); instead, look to critics and their work as a spur to your own thinking.

Often, when you're just starting to think about the essay you want to write, reading criticism can help you see some of the critical issues in the play. Critics frequently disagree on the interpretation of particular issues or passages or even on what the issues really are, but reading their work can make your own thoughts concrete, especially when you're just starting to sort things out. Reacting to someone else's view, especially one that is strongly argued, can help you articulate what you think and can suggest a line of interpretation and argument. Sorting out the important issues can be complicated, and issues do shift from era to era and culture to culture. But often the arguments posed in one era interest subsequent critics in whatever age and from whatever perspective. More generally, studying how professional critics make arguments and what makes some arguments more compelling and effective than others can help you both assess and improve your own.

If you draw on published criticism in your paper, you should acknowledge the critic up front and then work his or her words into your paper the way you have learned to do with lines or phrases from a literary text, though you will often find that summary or paraphrase—stating a source's ideas in your own words—is more effective. Sometimes a particular critic can be especially helpful in focusing your thoughts because you so clearly disagree with what she or he says. In that case, you may well get a good paper out of a rebuttal. Pitting one critic against another—sorting out the issues that interpreters disagree on and showing what their differences consist of—can also be a good way to frame your own contribution. But remember that the point of reading criticism is to *use* it for your own interpretive purposes, to make your responses more sensitive and resonant, to make you a more informed reader of the play, and to make you a better reader and writer in general.

• • •

Antigone's performance history goes back more than twenty-four centuries, and over that time readers and viewers have recorded many thousands of responses. Following the text of the play below, we reprint only a small sample, all from the twentieth century. But earlier views are often referred to and sometimes still argued about. The famous comments of the German philosopher G. W. F. Hegel (1770–

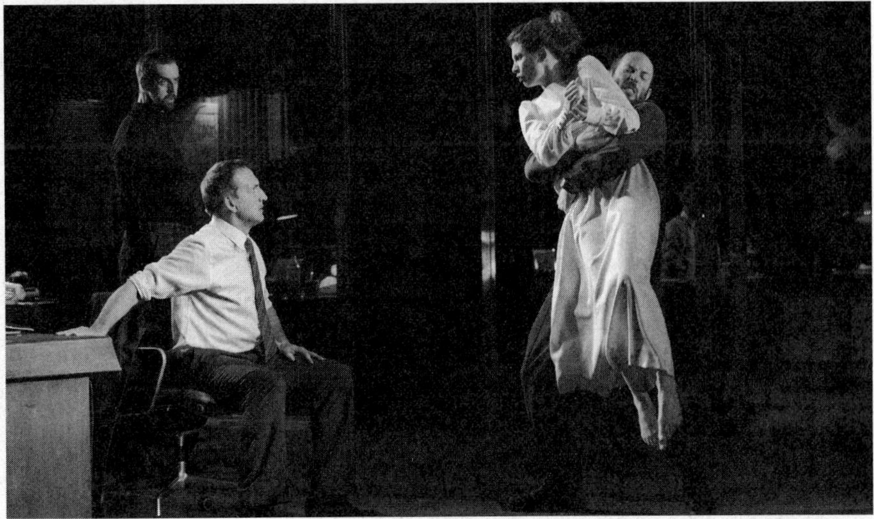

Scene from the 1982 New York Shakespeare Festival production of *Antigone*

1831), for example, continue to set the agenda for an astonishing number of interpreters. Many answer him directly; others use him to sharpen, complicate, or flesh out their views or simply to position themselves in some larger debate about specific issues in the play or about literary criticism or philosophy more generally.

In the following selections, you will find various interpretations of crucial scenes and issues in *Antigone*. Especially prominent are questions about how to read the opinions of the chorus, how to interpret the character of Antigone, and how to assess Creon's flaws. As you read the critics, pay attention to the way they argue—what kinds of textual evidence they use to back up their claims and how they structure their arguments—as well as the main interpretive claims they make. (Following the chapter is a sample student essay about *Antigone* that draws on one of the critical excerpts in this chapter, as well as other secondary sources.)

SOPHOCLES
Antigone[1]

CHARACTERS

ANTIGONE
ISMENE
CHORUS OF THEBAN ELDERS
CREON
A SENTRY
HAEMON
TEIRESIAS
A MESSENGER
EURYDICE
SECOND MESSENGER

The two sisters ANTIGONE *and* ISMENE *meet in front of the palace gates in Thebes.*

1. Translated by David Grene.

ANTIGONE: Ismene, my dear sister,
whose father was my father, can you think of any
of all the evils that stem from Oedipus[2]
that Zeus does not bring to pass for us, while we yet live?
No pain, no ruin, no shame, and no dishonor
but I have seen it in our mischiefs,
yours and mine.
And now what is the proclamation that they tell of
made lately by the commander, publicly,
to all the people? Do you know it? Have you heard it?
Don't you notice when the evils due to enemies
are headed towards those we love?
ISMENE: Not a word, Antigone, of those we love,
either sweet or bitter, has come to me since the moment
when we lost our two brothers,
on one day, by their hands dealing mutual death.
Since the Argive[3] army fled in this past night,
I know of nothing further, nothing
of better fortune or of more destruction.
ANTIGONE: *I* knew it well; that is why I sent for you
to come outside the palace gates
to listen to me, privately.
ISMENE: What is it? Certainly your words
come of dark thoughts.
ANTIGONE: Yes, indeed; for those two brothers of ours, in burial
has not Creon honored the one, dishonored the other?
Eteocles, they say he has used justly
with lawful rites and hid him in the earth
to have his honor among the dead men there.
But the unhappy corpse of Polyneices
he has proclaimed to all the citizens,
they say, no man may hide
in a grave nor mourn in funeral,
but leave unwept, unburied, a dainty treasure
for the birds that see him, for their feast's delight.
That is what, they say, the worthy Creon
has proclaimed for you and me—for me, I tell you—
and he comes here to clarify to the unknowing
his proclamation; he takes it seriously;
for whoever breaks the edict death is prescribed,
and death by stoning publicly.

2. In Greek legend, Oedipus became king of Thebes by inadvertently fulfilling the prophecy that he was destined to kill his father and marry his mother (as depicted in Sophocles's *Oedipus the King*); for these offenses against nature and the gods, Creon sent Oedipus, along with his daughters Antigone and Ismene, into exile at Colonus. Oedipus's sons, Eteocles and Polyneices, agreed to take turns ruling Thebes. But when Eteocles refused to give up the throne at the end of his first allotted year, Polyneices gathered an "Argive army" (line 17) and attacked the city.
3. From Argos, a rival Greek city-state.

There you have it; soon you will show yourself
as noble both in your nature and your birth,
or yourself as base, although of noble parents.
ISMENE: If things are as you say, poor sister, how
can I better them? how loose or tie the knot?
ANTIGONE: Decide if you will share the work, the deed.
ISMENE: What kind of danger is there? How far have your thoughts gone?
ANTIGONE: Here is this hand. Will you help it to lift the dead man?
ISMENE: Would you bury him, when it is forbidden the city?
ANTIGONE: At least he is my brother—and yours, too,
though you deny him. *I* will not prove false to him.
ISMENE: You are so headstrong. Creon has forbidden it.
ANTIGONE: It is not for him to keep me from my own.
ISMENE: O God!
Consider, sister, how our father died,
hated and infamous; how he brought to light
his own offenses; how he himself struck out
the sight of his two eyes;
his own hand was their executioner.
Then, mother and wife, two names in one, did shame
violently on her life, with twisted cords.
Third, our two brothers, on a single day,
poor wretches, themselves worked out their mutual doom.
Each killed the other, hand against brother's hand.
Now there are only the two of us, left behind,
and see how miserable our end shall be
if in the teeth of law we shall transgress
against the sovereign's decree and power.
You ought to realize we are only women,
not meant in nature to fight against men,
and that we are ruled, by those who are stronger,
to obedience in this and even more painful matters.
I do indeed beg those beneath the earth
to give me their forgiveness,
since force constrains me,
that I shall yield in this to the authorities.
Extravagant action is not sensible.
ANTIGONE: I would not urge you now; nor if you wanted
to act would I be glad to have you with me.
Be as you choose to be; but for myself
I myself will bury him. It will be good
to die, so doing. I shall lie by his side,
loving him as he loved me; I shall be
a criminal—but a religious one.
The time in which I must please those that are dead
is longer than I must please those of this world.
For there I shall lie forever. You, if you like,
can cast dishonor on what the gods have honored.

ISMENE: I will not put dishonor on them, but
to act in defiance of the citizenry,
my nature does not give me means for that.
ANTIGONE: Let that be your excuse. But I will go
to heap the earth on the grave of my loved brother.
ISMENE: How I fear for you, my poor sister!
ANTIGONE: Do not fear for me. Make straight your own path to destiny.
ISMENE: At least do not speak of this act to anyone else;
bury him in secret; I will be silent, too.
ANTIGONE: Oh, oh, no! shout it out. I will hate you still worse
for silence—should you not proclaim it,
to everyone.
ISMENE: You have a warm heart for such chilly deeds.
ANTIGONE: I know I am pleasing those I should please most.
ISMENE: *If* you can do it. But you are in love
with the impossible.
ANTIGONE: No. When I can no more, then I will stop.
ISMENE: It is better not to hunt the impossible
at all.
ANTIGONE: If you will talk like this I will loathe you,
and you will be adjudged an enemy—
justly—by the dead's decision. Let me alone
and my folly with me, to endure this terror.
No suffering of mine will be enough
to make me die ignobly.
ISMENE: Well, if you will, go on.
Know this; that though you are wrong to go, your friends
are right to love you.
CHORUS: Sun's beam, fairest of all
that ever till now shone
on seven-gated Thebes;
O golden eye of day, you shone
coming over Dirce's stream;[4]
You drove in headlong rout
the whiteshielded man from Argos,
complete in arms;
his bits rang sharper
under your urging.

Polyneices brought him here
against our land, Polyneices,
roused by contentious quarrel;
like an eagle he flew into our country,
with many men-at-arms,
with many a helmet crowned with horsehair.

4. River near Thebes.

He stood above the halls, gaping with murderous lances,
encompassing the city's
seven-gated mouth[5]
But before his jaws would be sated
with our blood, before the fire,
pine fed, should capture our crown of towers,
he went hence—
such clamor of war stretched behind his back,
from his dragon foe, a thing he could not overcome.

For Zeus, who hates the most
the boasts of a great tongue,
saw them coming in a great tide,
insolent in the clang of golden armor.
The god struck him down with hurled fire,
as he strove to raise the victory cry,
now at the very winning post.

The earth rose to strike him as he fell swinging.
In his frantic onslaught, possessed, he breathed upon us
with blasting winds of hate.
Sometimes the great god of war was on one side,
and sometimes he struck a staggering blow on the other;
the god was a very wheel horse[6] on the right trace.

At seven gates stood seven captains,
ranged equals against equals, and there left
their brazen suits of armor
to Zeus, the god of trophies.
Only those two wretches born of one father and mother
set their spears to win a victory on both sides;
they worked out their share in a common death.

Now Victory, whose name is great, has come
to Thebes of many chariots
with joy to answer her joy,
to bring forgetfulness of these wars;
let us go to all the shrines of the gods
and dance all night long.
Let Bacchus lead the dance,
shaking Thebes to trembling.

But here is the king of our land,
Creon,[7] son of Menoeceus;

5. Thebes was known throughout the ancient world for having seven gateways through the walls protecting the city.
6. Strongest and ablest horse in a team pulling a vehicle, harnessed nearest the front wheels "on the right trace."
7. Brother of Jocasta, mother and wife of Oedipus; he became king of Thebes after the deaths of Oedipus's sons.

in our new contingencies with the gods,
he is our new ruler.
He comes to set in motion some design—
what design is it? Because he has proposed
the convocation of the elders.
He sent a public summons for our discussion.
CREON: Gentlemen: as for our city's fortune,
the gods have shaken her, when the great waves broke,
but the gods have brought her through again to safety.
For yourselves, I chose you out of all and summoned you
to come to me, partly because I knew you
as always loyal to the throne—at first,
when Laïus[8] was king, and then again
when Oedipus saved our city and then again
when he died and you remained with steadfast truth
to their descendants,
until they met their double fate upon one day,
striking and stricken, defiled each by a brother's murder.
Now here I am, holding all authority
and the throne, in virtue of kinship with the dead.
It is impossible to know any man—
I mean his soul, intelligence, and judgment—
until he shows his skill in rule and law.
I think that a man supreme ruler of a whole city,
if he does not reach for the best counsel for her,
but through some fear, keeps his tongue under lock and key,
him I judge the worst of any;
I have always judged so; and anyone thinking
another man more a friend than his own country,
I rate him nowhere. For my part, God is my witness,
who sees all, always, I would not be silent
if I saw ruin, not safety, on the way
towards my fellow citizens. I would not count
any enemy of my country as a friend—
because of what I know, that she it is
which gives us our security. If she sails upright
and we sail on her, friends will be ours for the making.
In the light of rules like these, I will make her greater still.

In consonance with this, I here proclaim
to the citizens about Oedipus' sons.
For Eteocles, who died this city's champion,
showing his valor's supremacy everywhere,
he shall be buried in his grave with every rite
of sanctity given to heroes under earth.
However, his brother, Polyneices, a returned exile,
who sought to burn with fire from top to bottom

8. Father of Oedipus.

his native city, and the gods of his own people;
who sought to taste the blood he shared with us,
and lead the rest of us to slavery—
I here proclaim to the city that this man
shall no one honor with a grave and none shall mourn.
You shall leave him without burial; you shall watch him
chewed up by birds and dogs and violated.
Such is my mind in the matter; never by me
shall the wicked man have precedence in honor
over the just. But he that is loyal to the state
in death, in life alike, shall have my honor.

CHORUS: Son of Menoeceus, so it is your pleasure
to deal with foe and friend of this our city.
To use any legal means lies in your power,
both about the dead and those of us who live.

CREON: I understand, then, you will do my bidding.

CHORUS: Please lay this burden on some younger man.

CREON: Oh, watchers of the corpse I have already.

CHORUS: What else, then, do your commands entail?

CREON: That you should not side with those who disagree.

CHORUS: There is none so foolish as to love his own death.

CREON: Yes, indeed those are the wages, but often greed
has with its hopes brought men to ruin.

[*The* SENTRY *whose speeches follow represents a remarkable experiment in Greek tragedy in the direction of naturalism of speech. He speaks with marked clumsiness, partly because he is excited and talks almost colloquially. But also the royal presence makes him think apparently that he should be rather grand in his show of respect. He uses odd bits of archaism or somewhat stale poetical passages, particularly in catch phrases. He sounds something like lower-level Shakespearean characters, e.g. Constable Elbow, with his uncertainty about benefactor and malefactor.*]

SENTRY: My lord, I will never claim my shortness of breath
is due to hurrying, nor were there wings in my feet.
I stopped at many a lay-by in my thinking;
I circled myself till I met myself coming back.
My soul accosted me with different speeches.
"Poor fool, yourself, why are you going somewhere
when once you get there you will pay the piper?"
"Well, aren't you the daring fellow! stopping again?
and suppose Creon hears the news from someone else—
don't you realize that you will smart for that?"
I turned the whole matter over. I suppose I may say
"I made haste slowly" and the short road became long.
However, at last I came to a resolve:
I must go to you; even if what I say
is nothing, really, still I shall say it.
I come here, a man with a firm clutch on the hope

that nothing can betide him save what is fated.
CREON: What is it then that makes you so afraid?
SENTRY: No, I want first of all to tell you my side of it.
I didn't do the thing; I never saw who did it.
It would not be fair for me to get into trouble.
CREON: You hedge, and barricade the thing itself.
Clearly you have some ugly news for me.
SENTRY: Well, you know how disasters make a man
hesitate to be their messenger.
CREON: For God's sake, tell me and get out of here!
SENTRY: Yes, I *will* tell you. Someone just now
buried the corpse and vanished. He scattered on the skin
some thirsty dust; he did the ritual,
duly, to purge the body of desecration.
CREON: What! Now who on earth could have done that?
SENTRY: I do not know. For there was there no mark
of axe's stroke nor casting up of earth
of any mattock; the ground was hard and dry,
unbroken; there were no signs of wagon wheels.
The doer of the deed had left no trace.
But when the first sentry of the day pointed it out,
there was for all of us a disagreeable
wonder. For the body had disappeared;
not in a grave, of course; but there lay upon him
a little dust as of a hand avoiding
the curse of violating the dead body's sanctity.
There were no signs of any beast nor dog
that came there; he had clearly not been torn.
There was a tide of bad words at one another,
guard taunting guard, and it might well have ended
in blows, for there was no one there to stop it.
Each one of us was the criminal but no one
manifestly so; all denied knowledge of it.
We were ready to take hot bars in our hands
or walk through fire,[9] and call on the gods with oaths
that we had neither done it nor were privy
to a plot with anyone, neither in planning
nor yet in execution.
At last when nothing came of all our searching,
there was one man who spoke, made every head
bow to the ground in fear. For we could not
either contradict him nor yet could we see how
if we did what he said we would come out all right.

9. Ancient legal custom in which an accused person was required to undergo a "trial by ordeal," such as walking through fire; if the resulting injuries were not serious, the person was thought to be innocent and therefore divinely protected.

His word was that we must lay information
about the matter to yourself; we could not cover it.
This view prevailed and the lot of the draw chose me,
unlucky me, to win that prize. So here
I am. I did not want to come,
and you don't want to have me. I know that.
For no one likes the messenger of bad news.

CHORUS: My lord: I wonder, could this be God's doing?
This is the thought that keeps on haunting me.

CREON: Stop, before your words fill even me with rage,
that you should be exposed as a fool, and you so old.
For what you say is surely insupportable
when you say the gods took forethought for this corpse.
Is it out of excess of honor for the man,
for the favors that he did them, they should cover him?
This man who came to burn their pillared temples,
their dedicated offerings—and this land
and laws he would have scattered to the winds?
Or do you see the gods as honoring
criminals? This is not so. But what I am doing
now, and other things before this, some men disliked,
within this very city, and muttered against me,
secretly shaking their heads; they would not bow
justly beneath the yoke to submit to me.
I am very sure that these men hired others
to do this thing. I tell you the worse currency
that ever grew among mankind is money. This
sacks cities, this drives people from their homes,
this teaches and corrupts the minds of the loyal
to acts of shame. This displays
all kinds of evil for the use of men,
instructs in the knowledge of every impious act.
Those that have done this deed have been paid to do it,
but in the end they will pay for what they have done.

It is as sure as I still reverence Zeus—
know this right well—and I speak under oath—
if you and your fellows do not find this man
who with his own hand did the burial
and bring him here before me face to face,
your death alone will not be enough for me.
You will hang alive till you open up this outrage.
That will teach you in the days to come from what
you may draw profit—safely—from your plundering.
It's not from anything and everything
you can grow rich. You will find out
that ill-gotten gains ruin more than they save.

SENTRY: Have I your leave to say something—or should
I just turn and go?
CREON: Don't you know your talk is painful enough already?
SENTRY: Is the ache in your ears or in your mind?
CREON: Why do you dissect the whereabouts of my pain?
SENTRY: Because it is he who did the deed who hurts your
mind. I only hurt your ears that listen.
CREON: I am sure you have been a chatterbox since you were born.
SENTRY: All the same, I did not do this thing.
CREON: You might have done this, too, if you sold your soul.
SENTRY: It's a bad thing if one judges and judges wrongly.
CREON: You may talk as wittily as you like of judgment.
Only, if you don't bring to light those men
who have done this, you will yet come to say
that your wretched gains have brought bad consequences.
SENTRY: [*Aside.*] It were best that he were found, but whether
the criminal is taken or he isn't—
for that chance will decide—one thing is certain,
you'll never see me coming here again.
I never hoped to escape, never thought I could.
But now I have come off safe, I thank God heartily.
CHORUS: Many are the wonders, none
is more wonderful than what is man.
This it is that crosses the sea
with the south winds storming and the waves swelling,
breaking around him in roaring surf.
He it is again who wears away
the Earth, oldest of gods, immortal, unwearied,
as the ploughs wind across her from year to year
when he works her with the breed that comes from horses.

The tribe of the lighthearted birds he snares
and takes prisoner the races of savage beasts
and the brood of the fish of the sea,
with the close-spun web of nets.
A cunning fellow is man. His contrivances
make him master of beasts of the field
and those that move in the mountains.
So he brings the horse with the shaggy neck
to bend underneath the yoke;
and also the untamed mountain bull;
and speech and windswift thought
and the tempers that go with city living
he has taught himself, and how to avoid
the sharp frost, when lodging is cold
under the open sky
and pelting strokes of the rain.
He has a way against everything,
and he faces nothing that is to come

without contrivance.
Only against death
can he call on no means of escape;
but escape from hopeless diseases
he has found in the depths of his mind.
With some sort of cunning, inventive
beyond all expectation
he reaches sometimes evil,
and sometimes good.

If he honors the laws of earth,
and the justice of the gods he has confirmed by oath,
high is his city; no city
has he with whom dwells dishonor
prompted by recklessness.
He who is so, may he never
share my hearth!
may he never think my thoughts!

Is this a portent sent by God?
I cannot tell.
I know her. How can I say
that this is not Antigone?
Unhappy girl, child of unhappy Oedipus,
what is this?
Surely it is not you they bring here
as disobedient to the royal edict,
surely not you, taken in such folly.

SENTRY: She is the one who did the deed;
we took her burying him. But where is Creon?
CHORUS: He is just coming from the house, when you most need him.
CREON: What is this? What has happened that I come
so opportunely?
SENTRY: My lord, there is nothing
that a man should swear he would never do.
Second thoughts make liars of the first resolution.
I would have vowed it would be long enough
before I came again, lashed hence by your threats.
But since the joy that comes past hope, and against all hope,
is like no other pleasure in extent,
I have come here, though I break my oath in coming.
I bring this girl here who has been captured
giving the grace of burial to the dead man.
This time no lot chose me; this was my jackpot,
and no one else's. Now, my lord, take her
and as you please judge her and test her; I
am justly free and clear of all this trouble.
CREON: This girl—how did you take her and from where?
SENTRY: She was burying the man. Now you know all.
CREON: Do you know what you are saying? Do you mean it?

SENTRY: She is the one; I saw her burying
the dead man you forbade the burial of.
Now, do I speak plainly and clearly enough?
CREON: How was she seen? How was she caught in the act?
SENTRY: This is how it was. When we came there,
with those dreadful threats of yours upon us,
we brushed off all the dust that lay upon
the dead man's body, heedfully
leaving it moist and naked.
We sat on the brow of the hill, to windward,
that we might shun the smell of the corpse upon us.
Each of us wakefully urged his fellow
with torrents of abuse, not to be careless
in this work of ours. So it went on,
until in the midst of the sky the sun's bright circle
stood still; the heat was burning. Suddenly
a squall lifted out of the earth a storm of dust,
a trouble in the sky. It filled the plain,
ruining all the foliage of the wood
that was around it. The great empty air
was filled with it. We closed our eyes, enduring
this plague sent by the gods. When at long last
we were quit of it, why, then we saw the girl.

She was crying out with the shrill cry
of an embittered bird
that sees its nest robbed of its nestlings
and the bed empty. So, too, when she saw
the body stripped of its cover, she burst out in groans,
calling terrible curses on those that had done that deed;
and with her hands immediately
brought thirsty dust to the body; from a shapely brazen
urn, held high over it, poured a triple stream
of funeral offerings; and crowned the corpse.
When we saw that, we rushed upon her and
caught our quarry then and there, not a bit disturbed.
We charged her with what she had done, then and the first time.
She did not deny a word of it—to my joy,
but to my pain as well. It is most pleasant
to have escaped oneself out of such troubles
but painful to bring into it those whom we love.
However, it is but natural for me
to count all this less than my own escape.
CREON: You there, that turn your eyes upon the ground,
do you confess or deny what you have done?
ANTIGONE: Yes, I confess; I will not deny my deed.
CREON: [*To the* SENTRY.] You take yourself off where you like.

You are free of a heavy charge.
Now, Antigone, tell me shortly and to the point,
did you know the proclamation against your action?

ANTIGONE: I knew it; of course I did. For it was public.

CREON: And did you dare to disobey that law?

ANTIGONE: Yes, it was not Zeus that made the proclamation;
nor did Justice, which lives with those below, enact
such laws as that, for mankind. I did not believe
your proclamation had such power to enable
one who will someday die to override
God's ordinances, unwritten and secure.
They are not of today and yesterday;
they live forever; none knows when first they were.
These are the laws whose penalties I would not
incur from the gods, through fear of any man's temper.

I know that I will die—of course I do—
even if you had not doomed me by proclamation.
If I shall die before my time, I count that
a profit. How can such as I, that live
among such troubles, not find a profit in death?
So for such as me, to face such a fate as this
is pain that does not count. But if I dared to leave
the dead man, my mother's son, dead and unburied,
that would have been real pain. The other is not.
Now, if you think me a fool to act like this,
perhaps it is a fool that judges so.

CHORUS: The savage spirit of a savage father
shows itself in this girl. She does not know
how to yield to trouble.

CREON: I would have you know the most fanatic spirits
fall most of all. It is the toughest iron,
baked in the fire to hardness, you may see
most shattered, twisted, shivered to fragments.
I know hot horses are restrained
by a small curb. For he that is his neighbor's slave cannot
be high in spirit. This girl had learned her insolence
before this, when she broke the established laws.
But here is still another insolence
in that she boasts of it, laughs at what she did.
I swear I am no man and she the man
if she can win this and not pay for it.
No; though she were my sister's child or closer
in blood than all that my hearth god acknowledges
as mine, neither she nor her sister should escape
the utmost sentence—death. For indeed I accuse her,
the sister, equally of plotting the burial.

Summon her. I saw her inside, just now,
crazy, distraught. When people plot
mischief in the dark, it is the mind which first
is convicted of deceit. But surely I hate indeed
the one that is caught in evil and then makes
that evil look like good.

ANTIGONE: Do you want anything
beyond my taking and my execution?

CREON: Oh, nothing! Once I have that I have everything.

ANTIGONE: Why do you wait, then? Nothing that you say
pleases me; God forbid it ever should.
So my words, too, naturally offend you.
Yet how could I win a greater share of glory
than putting my own brother in his grave?
All that are here would surely say that's true,
if fear did not lock their tongues up. A prince's power
is blessed in many things, not least in this,
that he can say and do whatever he likes.

CREON: You are alone among the people of Thebes
to see things in that way.

ANTIGONE: No, these do, too,
but keep their mouths shut for the fear of you.

CREON: Are you not ashamed to think so differently
from them?

ANTIGONE: There is nothing shameful in honoring my brother.

CREON: Was not he that died on the other side your brother?

ANTIGONE: Yes, indeed, of my own blood from father and mother.

CREON: Why then do you show a grace that must be impious
in *his* sight?

ANTIGONE: *That* other dead man
would never bear you witness in what you say.

CREON: Yes he would, if you put him only on equality
with one that was a desecrator.

ANTIGONE: It was his brother, not his slave, that died.

CREON: He died destroying the country the other defended.

ANTIGONE: The god of death demands these rites for both.

CREON: But the good man does not seek an *equal* share only,
with the bad.

ANTIGONE: Who knows
if in that other world this is true piety?

CREON: My enemy is still my enemy, even in death.

ANTIGONE: My nature is to join in love, not hate.

CREON: Go then to the world below, yourself, if you
must love. Love *them*. When I am alive no woman shall rule.

CHORUS: Here before the gates comes Ismene
shedding tears for the love of a brother.
A cloud over her brow casts shame

on her flushed face, as the tears wet
her fair cheeks.

CREON: You there, who lurked in my house, viper-like—
secretly drawing its lifeblood; I never thought
that I was raising two sources of destruction,
two rebels against my throne. Come tell me now,
will you, too, say you bore a hand in the burial
or will you swear that you know nothing of it?

ISMENE: I did it, yes—if she will say I did it
I bear my share in it, bear the guilt, too.

ANTIGONE: Justice will not allow you what you refused
and I will have none of your partnership.

ISMENE: But in your troubles I am not ashamed
to sail with you the sea of suffering.

ANTIGONE: Where the act was death, the dead are witnesses.
I do not love a friend who loves in words.

ISMENE: Sister, do not dishonor me, denying me
a common death with you, a common honoring
of the dead man.

ANTIGONE: Don't die with me, nor make your own
what you have never touched. I that die am enough.

ISMENE: What life is there for me, once I have lost you?

ANTIGONE: Ask Creon; all your care was on his behalf.

ISMENE: Why do you hurt me, when you gain nothing by it?

ANTIGONE: I am hurt by my own mockery—if I mock you.

ISMENE: Even now—what can I do to help you still?

ANTIGONE: Save yourself; I do not grudge you your escape.

ISMENE: I cannot bear it! Not even to share your death!

ANTIGONE: Life was your choice, and death was mine.

ISMENE: You cannot say I accepted that choice in silence.

ANTIGONE: You were right in the eyes of one party, I in the other.

ISMENE: Well then, the fault is equally between us.

ANTIGONE: Take heart; you are alive, but my life died
long ago, to serve the dead.

CREON: Here are two girls; I think that one of them
has suddenly lost her wits—the other was always so.

ISMENE: Yes, for, my lord, the wits that they are born with
do not stay firm for the unfortunate.
They go astray.

CREON: Certainly yours do,
when you share troubles with the troublemaker.

ISMENE: What life can be mine alone without her?

CREON: Do not
speak of *her*. *She* isn't, anymore.

ISMENE: Will you kill your son's wife to be?[1]

1. Antigone, betrothed to Creon's son Haemon.

CREON: Yes, there are other fields for him to plough.
ISMENE: Not with the mutual love of him and her.
CREON: I hate a bad wife for a son of mine.
ANTIGONE: Dear Haemon, how your father dishonors you.
CREON: There is too much of you—and of your marriage!
CHORUS: Will you rob your son of this girl?
CREON: Death—it is death that will stop the marriage for me.
CHORUS: Your decision it seems is taken: she shall die.
CREON: Both you and I have decided it. No more delay.

[*He turns to the* SERVANTS.]

Bring her inside, you. From this time forth,
these must be women, and not free to roam.
For even the stout of heart shrink when they see
the approach of death close to their lives.
CHORUS: Lucky are those whose lives
know no taste of sorrow.
But for those whose house has been shaken by God
there is never cessation of ruin;
it steals on generation after generation
within a breed. Even as the swell
is driven over the dark deep
by the fierce Thracian winds
I see the ancient evils of Labdacus' house[2]
are heaped on the evils of the dead.
No generation frees another, some god
strikes them down; there is no deliverance.
Here was the light of hope stretched
over the last roots of Oedipus' house,
and the bloody dust due to the gods below
has mowed it down—that and the folly of speech
and ruin's enchantment of the mind.

Your power, O Zeus, what sin of man can limit?
All-aging sleep does not overtake it,
nor the unwearied months of the gods; and you,
for whom time brings no age,
you hold the glowing brightness of Olympus.

For the future near and far,
and the past, this law holds good:
nothing very great
comes to the life of mortal man
without ruin to accompany it.
For Hope, widely wandering, comes to many of mankind
as a blessing,
but to many as the deceiver,
using light-minded lusts;

2. Theban royal lineage that included Labdacus; his son, Laïus; and his grandson, Oedipus.

she comes to him that knows nothing
till he burns his foot in the glowing fire.
With wisdom has someone declared
a word of distinction:
that evil seems good to one whose mind
the god leads to ruin,
and but for the briefest moment of time
is his life outside of calamity.
Here is Haemon, youngest of your sons.
Does he come grieving
for the fate of his bride to be,
in agony at being cheated of his marriage?

CREON: Soon we will know that better than the prophets.
My son, can it be that you have not heard
of my final decision on your betrothed?
Can you have come here in your fury against your father?
Or have I your love still, no matter what I do?

HAEMON: Father, I am yours; with your excellent judgment
you lay the right before me, and I shall follow it.
No marriage will ever be so valued by me
as to override the goodness of your leadership.

CREON: Yes, my son, this should always be
in your very heart, that everything else
shall be second to your father's decision.
It is for this that fathers pray to have
obedient sons begotten in their halls,
that they may requite with ill their father's enemy
and honor his friend no less than he would himself.
If a man have sons that are no use to him,
what can one say of him but that he has bred
so many sorrows to himself, laughter to his enemies?
Do not, my son, banish your good sense
through pleasure in a woman, since you know
that the embrace grows cold
when an evil woman shares your bed and home.
What greater wound can there be than a false friend?
No. Spit on her, throw her out like an enemy,
this girl, to marry someone in Death's house.
I caught her openly in disobedience
alone out of all this city and I shall not make
myself a liar in the city's sight. No, I will kill her.
So let her cry if she will on the Zeus of kinship;
for if I rear those of my race and breeding
to be rebels, surely I will do so with those outside it.
For he who is in his household a good man
will be found a just man, too, in the city.
But he that breaches the law or does it violence
or thinks to dictate to those who govern him

shall never have my good word.
The man the city sets up in authority
must be obeyed in small things and in just
but also in their opposites.
I am confident such a man of whom I speak
will be a good ruler, and willing to be well ruled.
He will stand on his country's side, faithful and just,
in the storm of battle. There is nothing worse
than disobedience to authority.
It destroys cities, it demolishes homes;
it breaks and routs one's allies. Of successful lives
the most of them are saved by discipline.
So we must stand on the side of what is orderly;
we cannot give victory to a woman.
If we must accept defeat, let it be from a man;
we must not let people say that a woman beat us.

CHORUS: We think, if we are not victims of Time the Thief,
that you speak intelligently of what you speak.

HAEMON: Father, the natural sense that the gods breed
in men is surely the best of their possessions.
I certainly could not declare you wrong—
may I never know how to do so!—Still there might
be something useful that some other than you might think.
It is natural for me to be watchful on your behalf
concerning what all men say or do or find to blame.
Your face is terrible to a simple citizen;
it frightens him from words you dislike to hear.
But what *I* can hear, in the dark, are things like these:
the city mourns for this girl; they think she is dying
most wrongly and most undeservedly
of all womenkind, for the most glorious acts.
Here is one who would not leave her brother unburied,
a brother who had fallen in bloody conflict,
to meet his end by greedy dogs or by
the bird that chanced that way. Surely what she merits
is golden honor, isn't it? That's the dark rumor
that spreads in secret. Nothing I own
I value more highly, father, than your success.
What greater distinction can a son have than the glory
of a successful father, and for a father
the distinction of successful children?
Do not bear this single habit of mind, to think
that what you say and nothing else is true.
A man who thinks that he alone is right,
or what he says, or what he *is* himself,
unique, such men, when opened up, are seen
to be quite empty. For a man, though he be wise,

it is no shame to learn—learn many things,
and not maintain his views too rigidly.
You notice how by streams in wintertime
the trees that yield preserve their branches safely,
but those that fight the tempest perish utterly.
The man who keeps the sheet[3] of his sail tight
and never slackens capsizes his boat
and makes the rest of his trip keel uppermost.
Yield something of your anger, give way a little.
If a much younger man, like me, may have
a judgment, I would say it were far better
to be one altogether wise by nature, but,
as things incline not to be so, then it is good
also to learn from those who advise well.
CHORUS: My lord, if he says anything to the point,
you should learn from him, and you, too, Haemon,
learn from your father. Both of you
have spoken well.
CREON: Should we that are my age learn wisdom
from young men such as he is?
HAEMON: Not learn injustice, certainly. If I am young,
do not look at my years but what I do.
CREON: Is what you do to have respect for rebels?
HAEMON: I
would not urge you to be scrupulous
towards the wicked.
CREON: Is *she* not tainted by the disease of wickedness?
HAEMON: The entire people of Thebes says no to that.
CREON: Should the city tell me how I am to rule them?
HAEMON: Do you see what a young man's words these are of yours?
CREON: Must I rule the land by someone else's judgment
rather than my own?
HAEMON: There is no city
possessed by one man only.
CREON: Is not the city thought to be the ruler's?
HAEMON: You would be a fine dictator of a desert.
CREON: It seems this boy is on the woman's side.
HAEMON: If you are a woman—my care is all for you.
CREON: You villain, to bandy words with your own father!
HAEMON: I see your acts as mistaken and unjust.
CREON: Am I mistaken, reverencing my own office?
HAEMON: There is no reverence in trampling on God's honor.
CREON: Your nature is vile, in yielding to a woman.
HAEMON: You will not find me yield to what is shameful.
CREON: At least, your argument is all for her.

3. Rope attached to the corner of a sail to hold it at the proper angle to the wind.

HAEMON: Yes, and for you and me—and for the gods below.
CREON: You will never marry her while her life lasts.
HAEMON: Then she must die—and dying destroy another.
CREON: Has your daring gone so far, to threaten me?
HAEMON: What threat is it to speak against empty judgments?
CREON: Empty of sense yourself, you will regret
your schooling of me in sense.
HAEMON: If you were not
my father, I would say you are insane.
CREON: You woman's slave, do not try to wheedle me.
HAEMON: You want to talk but never to hear and listen.
CREON: Is that so? By the heavens above you will not—
be sure of that—get off scot-free, insulting,
abusing me.

[*He speaks to the* SERVANTS.]

You people bring out this creature,
this hated creature, that she may die before
his very eyes, right now, next her would-be husband.
HAEMON: Not at my side! Never think that! She will not
die by my side. But you will never again
set eyes upon my face. Go then and rage
with such of your friends as are willing to endure it.
CHORUS: The man is gone, my lord, quick in his anger.
A young man's mind is fierce when he is hurt.
CREON: Let him go, and do and think things superhuman.
But these two girls he shall not save from death.
CHORUS: Both of them? Do you mean to kill them both?
CREON: No, not the one that didn't do anything.
You are quite right there.
CHORUS: And by what form of death do you mean to kill her?
CREON: I will bring her where the path is loneliest,
and hide her alive in a rocky cavern there.
I'll give just enough of food as shall suffice
for a bare expiation, that the city may avoid pollution.
In that place she shall call on Hades, god of death,
in her prayers. That god only she reveres.
Perhaps she will win from him escape from death
or at least in that last moment will recognize
her honoring of the dead is labor lost.
CHORUS: Love undefeated in the fight,
Love that makes havoc of possessions,
Love who lives at night in a young girl's soft cheeks,
Who travels over sea, or in huts in the countryside—
there is no god able to escape you
nor anyone of men, whose life is a day only,
and whom you possess is mad.

You wrench the minds of just men to injustice,
to their disgrace; this conflict among kinsmen
it is you who stirred to turmoil.
The winner is desire. She gleaming kindles
from the eyes of the girl good to bed.
Love shares the throne with the great powers that rule.
For the golden Aphrodite[4] holds her play there
and then no one can overcome her.

Here I too am borne out of the course of lawfulness
when I see these things, and I cannot control
the springs of my tears
when I see Antigone making her way
to her bed—but the bed
that is rest for everyone.

ANTIGONE: You see me, you people of my country,
as I set out on my last road of all,
looking for the last time on this light of this sun—
never again. I am alive but Hades who gives sleep to everyone
is leading me to the shores of Acheron,[5]
though I have known nothing of marriage songs
nor the chant that brings the bride to bed.
My husband is to be the Lord of Death.

CHORUS: Yes, you go to the place where the dead are hidden,
but you go with distinction and praise.
You have not been stricken by wasting sickness;
you have not earned the wages of the sword;
it was your own choice and alone among mankind
you will descend, alive,
to that world of death.

ANTIGONE: But indeed I have heard of the saddest of deaths—
of the Phrygian stranger,[6] daughter of Tantalus,
whom the rocky growth subdued, like clinging ivy.
The rains never leave her, the snow never fails,
as she wastes away. That is how men tell the story.
From streaming eyes her tears wet the crags;
most like to her the god brings me to rest.

CHORUS: Yes, but she was a god, and god born,
and you are mortal and mortal born.
Surely it is great renown
for a woman that dies, that in life and death
her lot is a lot shared with demigods.

ANTIGONE: You mock me. In the name of our fathers' gods
why do you not wait till I am gone to insult me?

4. Goddess of love and beauty. 5. River in Hades.
6. Niobe, whose children were slain because of her boastfulness and who was herself turned into a stone on Mount Sipylus. Her tears became the mountain's streams.

Must you do it face to face?
My city! Rich citizens of my city!
You springs of Dirce, you holy groves of Thebes,
famed for its chariots! I would still have you as my witnesses,
with what dry-eyed friends, under what laws
I make my way to my prison sealed like a tomb.
Pity me. Neither among the living nor the dead
do I have a home in common—
neither with the living nor the dead.

CHORUS: You went to the extreme of daring
and against the high throne of Justice
you fell, my daughter, grievously.
But perhaps it was for some ordeal of your father
that you are paying requital.

ANTIGONE: You have touched the most painful of my cares—
the pity for my father, ever reawakened,
and the fate of all of our race, the famous Labdacids;
the doomed self-destruction of my mother's bed
when she slept with her own son,
my father.
What parents I was born of, God help me!
To them I am going to share their home,
the curse on me, too, and unmarried.
Brother, it was a luckless marriage you made,
and dying killed my life.

CHORUS: There *is* a certain reverence for piety.
But for him in authority,
he cannot see that authority defied;
it is your own self-willed temper
that has destroyed you.

ANTIGONE: No tears for me, no friends, no marriage. Brokenhearted
I am led along the road ready before me.
I shall never again be suffered
to look on the holy eye of the day.
But my fate claims no tears—
no friend cries for me.

CREON: [*To the* SERVANTS.] Don't you know that weeping and wailing before death
would never stop if one is allowed to weep and wail?
Lead her away at once. Enfold her
in that rocky tomb of hers—as I told you to.
There leave her alone, solitary,
to die if she so wishes
or live a buried life in such a home;
we are guiltless in respect of her, this girl.
But living above, among the rest of us, this life
she shall certainly lose.

ANTIGONE: Tomb, bridal chamber, prison forever
dug in rock, it is to you I am going

to join my people, that great number that have died,
whom in their death Persephone[7] received.
I am the last of them and I go down
in the worst death of all—for I have not lived
the due term of my life. But when I come
to that other world my hope is strong
that my coming will be welcome to my father,
and dear to you, my mother, and dear to you,
my brother deeply loved. For when you died,
with my own hands I washed and dressed you all,
and poured the lustral offerings on your graves.
And now, Polyneices, it was for such care of your body
that I have earned these wages.
Yet those who think rightly will think I did right
in honoring you. Had I been a mother
of children, and my husband been dead and rotten,
I would not have taken this weary task upon me
against the will of the city. What law backs me
when I say this? I will tell you:
If my husband were dead, I might have had another,
and child from another man, if I lost the first.
But when father and mother both were hidden in death
no brother's life would bloom for me again.
That is the law under which I gave you precedence,
my dearest brother, and that is why Creon thinks me
wrong, even a criminal, and now takes me
by the hand and leads me away,
unbedded, without bridal, without share
in marriage and in nurturing of children;
as lonely as you see me; without friends;
with fate against me I go to the vault of death
while still alive. What law of God have I broken?
Why should I still look to the gods in my misery?
Whom should I summon as ally? For indeed
because of piety I was called impious.
If this proceeding is good in the gods' eyes
I shall know my sin, once I have suffered.
But if Creon and his people are the wrongdoers
let their suffering be no worse than the injustice
they are meting out to me.

CHORUS: It is the same blasts, the tempests of the soul,
possess her.

CREON: Then for this her guards,
who are so slow, will find themselves in trouble.

ANTIGONE: [*Cries out.*] Oh, that word has come
very close to death.

7. Abducted by Pluto (known to the Greeks as Hades), god of the underworld, who made her his queen.

CREON: I will not comfort you
with hope that the sentence will not be accomplished.
ANTIGONE: O my father's city, in Theban land,
O gods that sired my race,
I am led away, I have no more stay.
Look on me, princes of Thebes,
the last remnant of the old royal line;
see what I suffer and who makes me suffer
because I gave reverence to what claims reverence.
CHORUS: Danae suffered, too, when, her beauty lost, she gave
the light of heaven in exchange for brassbound walls,
and in the tomb-like cell was she hidden and held;
yet she was honored in her breeding, child,
and she kept, as guardian, the seed of Zeus
that came to her in a golden shower.[8]
But there is some terrible power in destiny
and neither wealth nor war
nor tower nor black ships, beaten by the sea,
can give escape from it.

The hot-tempered son of Dryas,[9] the Edonian king,
in fury mocked Dionysus,
who then held him in restraint
in a rocky dungeon.
So the terrible force and flower of his madness
drained away. He came to know the god
whom in frenzy he had touched with his mocking tongue,
when he would have checked the inspired women
and the fire of Dionysus,
when he provoked the Muses[1] that love the lyre.
By the black rocks, dividing the sea in two,
are the shores of the Bosporus, Thracian Salmydessus.[2]
There the god of war who lives near the city
saw the terrible blinding wound
dealt by his savage wife
on Phineus' two sons.[3]
She blinded and tore with the points of her shuttle,
and her bloodied hands, those eyes
that else would have looked on her vengefully.
As they wasted away, they lamented
their unhappy fate that they were doomed

8. Danae was locked away because it was prophesized that her son would kill her father. Zeus entered her cell as a shower of gold, impregnated her, and thus fathered Perseus, the child who fulfilled the prophecy. 9. Stricken with madness by Dionysus.

1. Nine sister goddesses of poetry, music, and the arts.

2. City in the land of Thrace, in ancient times erroneously believed to lie on the Bosporus, the strait separating Europe and Asia at the outlet of the Black Sea.

3. King Phineus's second wife blinded the children of his first wife, whom Phineus had imprisoned in a cave.

to be born of a mother cursed in her marriage.
She traced her descent from the seed
of the ancient Erechtheidae.
In far-distant caves she was raised
among her father's storms, that child of Boreas[4]
quick as a horse, over the steep hills,
a daughter of the gods.
But, my child, the long-lived Fates[5]
bore hard upon her, too.

[*Enter* TEIRESIAS, *the blind prophet, led by a* BOY.]

TEIRESIAS: My lords of Thebes, we have come here together,
one pair of eyes serving us both. For the blind
such must be the way of going, by a guide's leading.
CREON: What is the news, my old Teiresias?
TEIRESIAS: I will tell you; and you, listen to the prophet.
CREON: Never in the past have I turned from your advice.
TEIRESIAS: And so you have steered well the ship of state.
CREON: I have benefited and can testify to that.
TEIRESIAS: Then realize you are on the razor edge
of danger.
CREON: What can that be? I shudder to hear those words.
TEIRESIAS: When you learn the signs recognized by my art
you will understand.
I sat at my ancient place of divination
for watching the birds, where every bird finds shelter;
and I heard an unwonted voice among them;
they were horribly distressed, and screamed unmeaningly.
I knew they were tearing each other murderously;
the beating of their wings was a clear sign.
I was full of fear; at once on all the altars,
as they were fully kindled, I tasted the offerings,
but the god of fire refused to burn from the sacrifice,
and from the thighbones a dark stream of moisture
oozed from the embers, smoked and sputtered.
The gall bladder burst and scattered to the air
and the streaming thighbones lay exposed
from the fat wrapped round them—
so much I learned from this boy here,
the fading prophecies of a rite that failed.
This boy here is my guide, as I am others'.
This is the city's sickness—and your plans are the cause of it.
For our altars and our sacrificial hearths

4. God of the cold north wind, who sometimes took the form of a stallion.
5. Supernatural forces, usually represented as three old women, who determine the quality and length of life.

are filled with the carrion meat of birds and dogs,
torn from the flesh of Oedipus' poor son.
So the gods will not take our prayers or sacrifice
nor yet the flame from the thighbones, and no bird
cries shrill and clear, so glutted
are they with fat of the blood of the killed man.
Reflect on these things, son. All men
can make mistakes; but, once mistaken,
a man is no longer stupid nor accursed
who, having fallen on ill, tries to cure that ill,
not taking a fine undeviating stand.
It is obstinacy that convicts of folly.
Yield to the dead man; do not stab him—
now he is gone—what bravery is this,
to inflict another death upon the dead?
I mean you well and speak well for your good.
It is never sweeter to learn from a good counselor
than when he counsels to your benefit.

CREON: Old man, you are all archers, and I am your mark.
I must be tried by your prophecies as well.
By the breed of you I have been bought and sold
and made a merchandise, for ages now.
But I tell you: make your profit from silver-gold
from Sardis[6] and the gold from India
if you will. But this dead man you shall not hide
in a grave, not though the eagles of Zeus should bear
the carrion, snatching it to the throne of Zeus itself.
Even so, I shall not so tremble at the pollution
to let you bury him.
No, I am certain
no human has the power to pollute the gods.
They fall, you old Teiresias, those men,
—so very clever—in a bad fall whenever
they eloquently speak vile words for profit.

TEIRESIAS: I wonder if there's a man who dares consider—

CREON: What do you mean? What sort of generalization
is this talk of yours?

TEIRESIAS: How much the best of possessions is the ability
to listen to wise advice?

CREON: As I should imagine that the worst
injury must be native stupidity.

TEIRESIAS: Now that is exactly where your mind is sick.

CREON: I do not like to answer a seer with insults.

TEIRESIAS: But you do, when you say my prophecies are lies.

CREON: Well,

6. Capital of the ancient kingdom of Lydia, part of modern-day Turkey, and an important trading center, famed for its wealth.

the whole breed of prophets certainly loves money.
TEIRESIAS: And the breed that comes from princes loves to take
advantage—base advantage.
CREON: Do you realize
you are speaking in such terms of your own prince?
TEIRESIAS: I know. But it is through me you have saved the city.
CREON: You are a wise prophet, but what you love is wrong.
TEIRESIAS: You will force me to declare what should be hidden
in my own heart.
CREON: Out with it—
but only if your words are not for gain.
TEIRESIAS: They won't be for *your* gain—that I am sure of.
CREON: But realize you will not make a merchandise
of my decisions.
TEIRESIAS: And you must realize
that you will not outlive many cycles more
of this swift sun before you give in exchange
one of your own loins bred, a corpse for a corpse,
for you have thrust one that belongs above
below the earth, and bitterly dishonored
a living soul by lodging her in the grave;
while one that belonged indeed to the underworld
gods you have kept on this earth without due share
of rites of burial, of due funeral offerings,
a corpse unhallowed. With all of this you, Creon,
have nothing to do, nor have the gods above.
These acts of yours are violence, on your part.
And in requital the avenging Spirits
of Death itself and the gods' Furies shall
after *your* deeds, lie in ambush for you, and
in their hands you shall be taken cruelly.
Now, look at this and tell me I was bribed
to say it! The delay will not be long
before the cries of mourning in your house,
of men and women. All the cities will stir in hatred
against you, because their sons in mangled shreds
received their burial rites from dogs, from wild beasts
or when some bird of the air brought a vile stink
to each city that contained the hearths of the dead.
These are the arrows that archer-like I launched—
you vexed me so to anger—at your heart.
You shall not escape their sting. You, boy,
lead me away to my house, so he may discharge
his anger on younger men; so may he come to know
to bear a quieter tongue in his head and a better
mind than that now he carries in him.
CHORUS: That was a terrible prophecy, my lord.
The man has gone. Since these hairs of mine grew white

from the black they once were, he has never spoken
a word of a lie to our city.

CREON: I know, I know.
My mind is all bewildered. To yield is terrible.
But by opposition to destroy my very being
with a self-destructive curse must also be reckoned
in what is terrible.

CHORUS: You need good counsel, son of Menoeceus,
and need to take it.

CREON: What must I do, then? Tell me; I shall agree.

CHORUS: The girl—go now and bring her up from her cave,
and for the exposed dead man, give him his burial.

CREON: That is really your advice? You would have me yield.

CHORUS: And quickly as you may, my lord. Swift harms
sent by the gods cut off the paths of the foolish.

CREON: Oh, it is hard; I must give up what my heart
would have me do. But it is ill to fight
against what must be.

CHORUS: Go now, and do this;
do not give the task to others.

CREON: I will go,
just as I am. Come, servants, all of you;
take axes in your hands; away with you
to the place you see, there.
For my part, since my intention is so changed,
as I bound her myself, myself will free her.
I am afraid it may be best, in the end
of life, to have kept the old accepted laws.

CHORUS: You of many names,[7] glory of the Cadmeian
bride, breed of loud thundering Zeus;
you who watch over famous Italy;
you who rule where all are welcome in Eleusis;
in the sheltered plains of Deo—
O Bacchus that dwells in Thebes,
the mother city of Bacchanals,
by the flowing stream of Ismenus,
in the ground sown by the fierce dragon's teeth.

You are he on whom the murky gleam of torches glares,
above the twin peaks of the crag
where come the Corycean nymphs
to worship you, the Bacchanals;
and the stream of Castalia has seen you, too;
and you are he that the ivy-clad

7. Refers to Dionysus, known also as Bacchus (especially to the later Romans); son of Zeus and Semele, a mortal princess of Thebes. As god of wine, Dionysus presided over frenzied rites known as Bacchanals.

slopes of Nisaean hills,
and the green shore ivy-clustered,
sent to watch over the roads of Thebes,
where the immortal Evoe chant[8] rings out.

It is Thebes which you honor most of all cities,
you and your mother both,
she who died by the blast of Zeus' thunderbolt.
And now when the city, with all its folk,
is gripped by a violent plague,
come with healing foot, over the slopes of Parnassus,[9]
over the moaning strait.
You lead the dance of the fire-breathing stars,
you are master of the voices of the night.
True-born child of Zeus, appear,
my lord, with your Thyiad attendants,
who in frenzy all night long
dance in your house, Iacchus,
dispenser of gifts.

MESSENGER: You who live by the house of Cadmus and Amphion,[1]
hear me. There is no condition of man's life
that stands secure. As such I would not
praise it or blame. It is chance that sets upright;
it is chance that brings down the lucky and the unlucky,
each in his turn. For men, that belong to death,
there is no prophet of established things.
Once Creon was a man worthy of envy—
of my envy, at least. For he saved this city
of Thebes from her enemies, and attained
the throne of the land, with all a king's power.
He guided it right. His race bloomed
with good children. But when a man forfeits joy
I do not count his life as life, but only
a life trapped in a corpse.
Be rich within your house, yes greatly rich,
if so you will, and live in a prince's style.
If the gladness of these things is gone, I would not
give the shadow of smoke for the rest,
as against joy.

CHORUS: What is the sorrow of our princes
of which you are the messenger?

MESSENGER: Death; and the living are guilty of their deaths.

CHORUS: But who is the murderer? Who the murdered? Tell us.

MESSENGER: Haemon is dead; the hand that shed his blood
was his very own.

8. Come forth, come forth!
9. Mountain in central Greece sacred to Apollo, Dionysus, and the Muses; Apollo's shrine, Delphi, lies at the foot of Parnassus. 1. A name for Thebes.

CHORUS: Truly his own hand? Or his father's?
MESSENGER: His own hand, in his anger
against his father for a murder.
CHORUS: Prophet, how truly you have made good your word!
MESSENGER: These things are so; you may debate the rest.
Here I see Creon's wife Eurydice
approaching. Unhappy woman!
Does she come from the house as hearing about her son
or has she come by chance?
EURYDICE: I heard your words, all you men of Thebes, as I
was going out to greet Pallas[2] with my prayers.
I was just drawing back the bolts of the gate
to open it when a cry struck through my ears
telling of my household's ruin. I fell backward
in terror into the arms of my servants; I fainted.
But tell me again, what is the story? I
will hear it as one who is no stranger to sorrow.
MESSENGER: Dear mistress, I will tell you, for I was there,
and I will leave out no word of the truth.
Why should I comfort you and then tomorrow
be proved a liar? The truth is always best.
I followed your husband, at his heels, to the end of the plain
where Polyneices' body still lay unpitied,
and torn by dogs. We prayed to Hecate, goddess
of the crossroads, and also to Pluto[3]
that they might restrain their anger and turn kind.
And him we washed with sacred lustral water
and with fresh-cut boughs we burned what was left of him
and raised a high mound of his native earth;
then we set out again for the hollowed rock,
death's stone bridal chamber for the girl.
Someone then heard a voice of bitter weeping
while we were still far off, coming from that unblest room.
The man came to tell our master Creon of it.
As the king drew nearer, there swarmed about him
a cry of misery but no clear words.
He groaned and in an anguished mourning voice
cried "Oh, am I a true prophet? Is this the road
that I must travel, saddest of all my wayfaring?
It is my son's voice that haunts my ear. Servants,
get closer, quickly. Stand around the tomb
and look. There is a gap there where the stones
have been wrenched away; enter there, by the very mouth,
and see whether I recognize the voice of Haemon
or if the gods deceive me." On the command

2. Athena, goddess of wisdom.
3. King of the underworld, known to the Greeks as Hades. *Hecate*: goddess of witchcraft.

of our despairing master we went to look.
In the furthest part of the tomb we saw her, hanging
by her neck. She had tied a noose of muslin on it.
Haemon's hands were about her waist embracing her,
while he cried for the loss of his bride gone to the dead,
and for all his father had done, and his own sad love.
When Creon saw him he gave a bitter cry,
went in and called to him with a groan: "Poor son!
what have you done? What can you have meant?
What happened to destroy you? Come out, I pray you!"
The boy glared at him with savage eyes, and then
spat in his face, without a word of answer.
He drew his double-hilted sword. As his father
ran to escape him, Haemon failed to strike him,
and the poor wretch in anger at himself
leaned on his sword and drove it halfway in,
into his ribs. Then he folded the girl to him,
in his arms, while he was conscious still,
and gasping poured a sharp stream of bloody drops
on her white cheeks. There they lie,
the dead upon the dead. So he has won
the pitiful fulfillment of his marriage
within death's house. In this human world he has shown
how the wrong choice in plans is for a man
his greatest evil.

CHORUS: What do you make of this? My lady is gone,
without a word of good or bad.

MESSENGER: I, too,
am lost in wonder. I am inclined to hope
that hearing of her son's death she could not
open her sorrow to the city, but chose rather
within her house to lay upon her maids
the mourning for the household grief. Her judgment
is good; she will not make any false step.

CHORUS: I do not know. To me this over-heavy silence
seems just as dangerous as much empty wailing.

MESSENGER: I will go in and learn if in her passionate
heart she keeps hidden some secret purpose.
You are right; there is sometimes danger in too much silence.

CHORUS: Here comes our king himself. He bears in his hands
a memorial all too clear;
it is a ruin of none other's making,
purely his own if one dare to say that.

CREON: The mistakes of a blinded man
are themselves rigid and laden with death.
You look at us the killer and the killed
of the one blood. Oh, the awful blindness
of those plans of mine. My son, you were so young,

so young to die. You were freed from the bonds of life
through no folly of your own—only through mine.
CHORUS: I think you have learned justice—but too late.
CREON: Yes, I have learned it to my bitterness. At this moment
God has sprung on my head with a vast weight
and struck me down. He shook me in my savage ways;
he has overturned my joy, has trampled it,
underfoot. The pains men suffer
are pains indeed.
SECOND MESSENGER: My lord, you have troubles and a store besides;
some are there in your hands, but there are others
you will surely see when you come to your house.
CREON: What trouble can there be beside these troubles?
SECOND MESSENGER: The queen is dead. She was indeed true mother
of the dead son. She died, poor lady,
by recent violence upon herself.
CREON: Haven of death, you can never have enough.
Why, why do you destroy me?
You messenger, who have brought me bitter news,
what is this tale you tell?
It is a dead man that you kill again—
what new message of yours is this, boy?
Is this new slaughter of a woman
a doom to lie on the pile of the dead?
CHORUS: You can see. It is no longer
hidden in a corner.

[*By some stage device, perhaps the so-called eccyclema,*[4] *the inside of the palace is shown, with the body of the dead* QUEEN.]

CREON: Here is yet another horror
for my unhappy eyes to see.
What doom still waits for me?
I have but now taken in my arms my son,
and again I look upon another dead face.
Poor mother and poor son!
SECOND MESSENGER: She stood at the altar, and with keen whetted knife
she suffered her darkening eyes to close.
First she cried in agony recalling the noble fate of Megareus,[5]
who died before all this,
and then for the fate of this son; and in the end
she cursed you for the evil you had done
in killing her sons.
CREON: I am distracted with fear. Why does not someone
strike a two-edged sword right through me?
I am dissolved in an agony of misery.

4. Wheeled platform rolled forward onto the stage to depict interior scenes; often used in tragedies to reveal dead bodies. 5. Another son of Creon who died defending Thebes.

SECOND MESSENGER: You were indeed accused
by her that is dead
of Haemon's and of Megareus' death.
CREON: By what kind of violence did she find her end?
SECOND MESSENGER: Her own hand struck her to the entrails
when she heard of her son's lamentable death.
CREON: These acts can never be made to fit another
to free me from the guilt. It was I that killed her.
Poor wretch that I am, I say it is true!
Servants, lead me away, quickly, quickly.
I am no more a live man than one dead.
CHORUS: What you say is for the best—if there be a best
in evil such as this. For the shortest way
is best with troubles that lie at our feet.
CREON: O, let it come, let it come,
that best of fates that waits on my last day.
Surely best fate of all. Let it come, let it come!
That I may never see one more day's light!
CHORUS: These things are for the future. We must deal
with what impends. What in the future is to care for
rests with those whose duty it is
to care for them.
CREON: At least, all that *I* want
is in that prayer of mine.
CHORUS: Pray for no more at all. For what is destined
for us, men mortal, there is no escape.
CREON: Lead me away, a vain silly man
who killed you, son, and you, too, lady.
I did not mean to, but I did.
I do not know where to turn my eyes
to look to, for support.
Everything in my hands is crossed. A most unwelcome fate
has leaped upon me.
CHORUS: Wisdom is far the chief element in happiness
and, secondly, no irreverence towards the gods.
But great words of haughty men exact
in retribution blows as great
and in old age teach wisdom.

THE END

c. 441 BCE

CRITICAL EXCERPTS

Richard C. Jebb

From Introduction to *The* Antigone *of Sophocles* (1902)[1]

The issue defined in the opening scene,—the conflict of divine with human law,—remains the central interest throughout. The action, so simple in plan, is varied by masterly character-drawing, both in the two principal figures, and in those lesser persons who contribute gradations of light and shade to the picture. There is no halting in the march of the drama; at each successive step we become more and more keenly interested to see how this great conflict is to end; and when the tragic climax is reached, it is worthy of such a progress.

The simplicity of the plot is due to the clearness with which two principles are opposed to each other. *Creon represents the duty of obeying the State's laws; Antigone, the duty of listening to the private conscience.* The definiteness and the power with which the play puts the case on each side are conclusive proofs that the question had assumed a distinct shape before the poet's mind. It is the only instance in which a Greek play has for its central theme a practical problem of conduct, involving issues, moral and political, which might be discussed on similar grounds in any age and in any country of the world. Greek tragedy, owing partly to the limitations which it placed on detail, was better suited than modern drama to raise such a question in a general form. The *Antigone*, indeed, raises the question in a form as nearly abstract as is compatible with the nature of drama. The case of Antigone is a thoroughly typical one for the private conscience, because the particular thing which she believes that she ought to do was, in itself, a thing which every Greek of that age recognised as a most sacred duty,—viz.,[2] to render burial rites to kinsfolk. This advantage was not devised by Sophocles; it came to him as part of the story which he was to dramatise; but it forms an additional reason for thinking that, when he dramatised that story in the precise manner which he has chosen, he had a consciously dialectical purpose. Such a purpose was wholly consistent, in this instance, with the artist's first aim,—to produce a work of art. It is because Creon and Antigone are so human that the controversy which they represent becomes so vivid.

But how did Sophocles intend us to view the result? What is the drift of the words at the end, which say that "wisdom is the supreme part of happiness"? If this wisdom, or prudence [. . .], means, generally, the observance of due limit, may not the suggested moral be that both the parties to the conflict were censurable? As Creon overstepped the due limit when, by his edict, he infringed the divine law, so Antigone also overstepped it when she defied the edict. The drama would thus be a conflict between two persons, each of whom defends an intrinsically sound principle, but defends it in a mistaken way; and both persons are therefore punished. This view, of which Boeckh[3] is the chief representative, has found several supporters. Among them is Hegel:—"In the view of the Eternal

1. Sir Richard C. Jebb. Introduction. *The* Antigone *of Sophocles*. Abridged by E. S. Shuckburgh, Cambridge UP, 1971, pp. xi–xxx.

2. Namely (abbreviation of the Latin *videlicet*) [editor's note].

3. August Boeckh (1785–1867), German classical scholar [editor's note].

Justice, both were wrong, because they were one-sided, but at the same time both were right."[4]

Or does the poet rather intend us to feel that Antigone is wholly in the right,—*i.e.*, that nothing of which the human lawgiver could complain in her was of a moment's account beside the supreme duty which she was fulfilling;—and that Creon was wholly in the wrong,—*i.e.*, that the intrinsically sound maxims of government on which he relies lose all validity when opposed to the higher law which he was breaking? If that was the poet's meaning, then the "wisdom" taught by the issue of the drama means the sense which duly subordinates human to divine law,—teaching that, if the two come into conflict, human law must yield.

A careful study of the play itself will suffice (I think) to show that the second of these two views is the true one. Sophocles has allowed Creon to put his case ably, and (in a measure from which an inferior artist might have shrunk) he has been content to make Antigone merely a nobly heroic woman, not a being exempt from human passion and human weakness; but none the less does he mean us to feel that, in this controversy, the right is wholly with her, and the wrong wholly with her judge.

Maurice Bowra

From Sophoclean Tragedy (1944)[1]

Modern critics who do not share Sophocles' conviction about the paramount duty of burying the dead and who attach more importance than he did to the claims of political authority have tended to underestimate the way in which he justifies Antigone against Creon. To their support they have called in the great name of Hegel, who was fascinated by the play and advanced remarkable views on it.[2] [. . . H]e has been made responsible for the opinion that Sophocles dramatized a conflict not between right and wrong but between right and right, that Antigone and Creon are equally justified in their actions and that the tragedy arises out of this irreconcilable conflict. [. . .] Hegel used the *Antigone* to illustrate his view of tragedy and his view of existence. He drew his own conclusions about the actions portrayed in it, as he was fully entitled to do. But his views are not those of Sophocles, and he should not be thought to maintain that Creon and Antigone were equally right in the eyes of their creator.

Sophocles leaves no doubt what conclusion should be drawn from the *Antigone*. He closes with a moral on the lips of the Chorus which tells the audience what to think:

> Wisdom has first place in happiness,
> And to fail not in reverence to the gods.
> The big words of the arrogant
> Lay big stripes on the boasters' backs.

4. *Religionsphilosophie*, II. 114 [Jebb's note].

1. Maurice Bowra. *Sophoclean Tragedy*. Clarendon, 1944. Bowra's notes have been edited.

2. *Philosophie der Religion*, xvi, I.133, *Aesthetik*, ii.2, Absch. I. Cf. A. C. Bradley, *Oxford Lectures on Poetry*, pp. 69–92 [Bowra's note].

> They pay the price
> And learn in old age to be wise.[3]

This can refer to no one but Creon, whose lack of wisdom has brought him to misery, who has shown irreverence to the gods in refusing burial to Polynices, been chastened for his proud words, and learned wisdom in his old age. To this lesson the preceding action in which Creon has lost son and wife and happiness has already made its effective contribution. We may be sure that the Chorus speak for the poet. It is as silent about Antigone as it is emphatic about Creon. There is no hint that she has in any way acted wrongly or that her death should be regarded as a righteous punishment. Of course the final words do not sum up everything important in the play, but we may reasonably assume that they pass judgement on its salient events as they appear in retrospect when the action is finished. There is no real problem about the ethical intention of the *Antigone.* It shows the fall of a proud man, and its lesson is that the gods punish pride and irreverence. But what matters much more than the actual conclusion is the means by which it is reached, the presentation of the different parties in the conflict, the view that we take of each, the feelings that are forced on us. The interest and power of the *Antigone* lie in the tangled issues which are unravelled in it.

A conclusion so clear as this is only worth reaching if it has been preceded by a drama in which the issues are violent and complex. The rights and wrongs of the case must not throughout be so obvious as they are at the end; the audience must feel that the issue is difficult, that there is much to be said on both sides, that the ways of the gods are hard to discern. Without this the play will fail in dramatic and human interest. And Sophocles has taken great care to show the issues in their full difficulty before he provides a solution for them. He makes the two protagonists appear in such a light that at intervals we doubt if all the right is really with Antigone and all the wrong with Creon. To Creon, who defies the divine ordinance of burial, he gives arguments and sentiments which sound convincing enough when they are put forward, and many must feel that he has some good reason to act as he does. On the other hand Antigone, who fearlessly vindicates the laws of the gods, is by no means a gentle womanly creature who suffers martyrdom for the right. She may be right, but there are moments when we qualify our approval of her, when she seems proud and forbidding in her determination to do her duty and to do it alone. For these variations in our feelings Sophocles is responsible. He makes us find some right in Creon, some wrong in Antigone, even if we are misled about both. He built his play on a contrast not between obvious wrong and obvious right but between the real arrogance of Creon and the apparent arrogance of Antigone. The first deceives by its fine persuasive sentiments; the second works through Antigone's refusal to offer concessions or to consider any point of view but her own. This contrast runs through much of the play, accounts for misunderstandings of what takes place in it, provides false clues and suggests wrong conclusions, and adds greatly to the intensity of the drama. When a play is written round a moral issue, that issue must be a real problem about which more than one view is tenable until all the relevant facts are known. So the *Antigone* dramatizes a conflict which was familiar to

3. Bowra's translation of lines 1409–13.

the Periclean age,[3] would excite divergent judgements and feelings, and make some support Antigone, some Creon, until the end makes all clear.

Bernard Knox

From Introduction to *Antigone* (1982)[1]

The opening scenes show us the conflicting claims and loyalties of the two adversaries, solidly based, in both cases, on opposed political and religious principles. This is of course the basic insight of Hegel's famous analysis of the play: he sees it as "a collision between the two highest moral powers." What is wrong with them, in his view, is that they are both "one-sided." But Hegel goes much further than that. He was writing in the first half of the nineteenth century, a period of fervent German nationalism in which the foundations of the unified German state were laid: his views on loyalty to the state were very much those of Creon. "Creon," he says, "is not a tyrant, he is really a moral power. He is not in the wrong."

However, as the action develops the favorable impression created by Creon's opening speech is quickly dissipated. His announcement of his decision to expose the corpse, the concluding section of his speech, is couched in violent, vindictive terms—"carrion for the birds and dogs to tear" (225)[2]—which stand in shocking contrast to the ethical generalities that precede it. This hint of a cruel disposition underlying the statesmanlike façade is broadened by the threat of torture leveled at the sentry (335–41) and the order to execute Antigone in the presence of Haemon, her betrothed (818–20). And as he meets resistance from a series of opponents—Antigone's contemptuous defiance, the rational, political advice of his son Haemon, the imperious summons to obedience of the gods' spokesman, Tiresias—he swiftly abandons the temperate rhetoric of his inaugural address for increasingly savage invective. Against the two sanctions invoked by Antigone, the demands of blood relationship, the rights and privileges of the gods below, he rages in terms ranging from near-blasphemous defiance to scornful mockery.

> Sister's child or closer in blood
> than all my family clustered at my altar
> worshiping Guardian Zeus—she'll never escape,
> . . . the most barbaric death. (530–33)

He will live to regret this wholesale denial of the family bond, for it is precisely through that family clustered at his altar that his punishment will be administered, in the suicides of his son and his wife, both of whom die cursing him.

And for Antigone's appeals to Hades, the great god of the underworld to whom the dead belong, Creon has nothing but contempt; for him "Hades" is simply a

3. The height of Athenian culture and political power in the time of the Athenian statesman Pericles (c. 495–429 BCE) [editor's note].

1. Bernard Knox. Introduction. *Antigone, Sophocles, The Three Theban Plays: Antigone, Oedipus the King, Oedipus at Colonus*, translated by Robert Fagles, Penguin, 1982, pp. 21–37. All footnotes have been added by the editor.

2. Knox's references are to Robert Fagles's translation, printed in *The Three Theban Plays*. Here and throughout we have substituted for the line numbers in Knox's parenthetical citations numbers for the relevant lines in the translation reprinted in this anthology. The wording varies between translations.

word meaning "death," a sentence he is prepared to pass on anyone who stands in his way. He threatens the sentry with torture as a prelude: "simple death won't be enough for you" (340). When asked if he really intends to deprive Haemon of his bride he answers sarcastically: "Death will do it for me" (630). He expects to see Antigone and Ismene turn coward "once they see Death coming for their lives" (635–36). With a derisive comment he tells his son to abandon Antigone: "Spit her out, / . . . Let her find a husband down among the dead [in Hades' house]" (704–05). And he dismisses Antigone's reverence for Hades and the rights of the dead with mockery as he condemns her to be buried alive: "There let her pray to the one god she worships: / Death" (837–38). But this Hades is not something to be so lightly referred to, used or mocked. In the great choral ode which celebrated Man's progress and powers this was the one insurmountable obstacle that confronted him:

> ready, resourceful man!
> Never without resources
> never an impasse as he marches on the future—
> only Death, from Death alone he will find no rescue . . . (381, 393–97)

And Creon, in the end, looking at the corpse of his son and hearing the news of his wife's suicide, speaks of Hades for the first time with the fearful respect that is his due, not as an instrument of policy or a subject for sardonic wordplay, but as a divine power, a dreadful presence: "harbor of Death, so choked, so hard to cleanse!— / why me? why are you killing me?" (1350–51).

Creon is forced at last to recognize the strength of those social and religious imperatives that Antigone obeys, but long before this happens he has abandoned the principles which he had proclaimed as authority for his own actions. His claim to be representative of the whole community is forgotten as he refuses to accept Haemon's report that the citizens, though they dare not speak out, disapprove of his action; he denies the relevance of such a report even if true—"And is Thebes about to tell me how to rule?" (790)—and finally repudiates his principles in specific terms by an assertion that the city belongs to him—"The city *is* the king's—that's the law!" (795). This autocratic phrase puts the finishing touch to the picture Sophocles is drawing for his audience: Creon has now displayed all the characteristics of the "tyrant," a despotic ruler who seizes power and retains it by intimidation and force. Athens had lived under the rule of a "tyrant" before the democracy was established in 508 B.C., and the name and institution were still regarded with abhorrence. Creon goes on to abandon the gods whose temples crown the city's high places, the gods he once claimed as his own, and his language is even more violent. The blind prophet Tiresias tells him that the birds and dogs are fouling the altars of the city's gods with the carrion flesh of Polynices; he must bury the corpse. His furious reply begins with a characteristic accusation that the prophet has been bribed (the sentry had this same accusation flung at him), but what follows is a hideously blasphemous defiance of those gods Creon once claimed to serve:

> You'll never bury that body in the grave,
> not even if Zeus's eagles rip the corpse
> and wing their rotten pickings off to the throne of god! (1090–92)

At this high point in his stubborn rage (he will break by the end of the scene and try, too late, to avoid the divine wrath), he is sustained by nothing except his tyrannical insistence on his own will, come what may, and his outraged refusal to be defeated by a woman. "No woman," he says, "is going to lord it over me" (577). "I'm not the man, not now: she is the man / if this victory goes to her and she goes free" (528–29).

Antigone, on her side, is just as indifferent to Creon's principles of action as he is to hers. She mentions the city only in her last agonized laments before she is led off to her living death:

> O my city, all your fine rich sons!
> . . . springs of the Dirce,
> holy grove of Thebes . . . (893–94)

But here she is appealing for sympathy to the city over the heads of the chorus, the city's symbolic representative on stage. In all her arguments with Creon and Ismene she speaks as one wholly unconscious of the rights and duties membership in the city confers and imposes, as if no unit larger than the family existed. It is a position just as extreme as Creon's insistence that the demands of the city take precedence over all others, for the living and the dead alike.

Like Creon, she acts in the name of gods, but they are different gods. There is more than a little truth in Creon's mocking comment that Hades is "the one god she worships (838)." She is from the beginning "much possessed by death"; together with Ismene she is the last survivor of a doomed family, burdened with such sorrow that she finds life hardly worth living. "Who on earth," she says to Creon, "alive in the midst of so much grief as I, / could fail to find his death a rich reward?" (507–08). She has performed the funeral rites for mother, father and her brother Eteocles:

> I washed you with my hands,
> I dressed you all, I poured the cups
> across your tombs. (948–50)

She now sacrifices her life to perform a symbolic burial, a handful of dust sprinkled on the corpse, for Polynices, the brother left to rot on the battlefield. She looks forward to her reunion with her beloved dead in that dark kingdom where Persephone, the bride of Hades, welcomes the ghosts (939–41). It is in the name of Hades, one of the three great gods who rule the universe, that she defends the right of Polynices and of all human beings to proper burial. "Death [Hades] longs for the same rites for all" (570), she tells Creon—for patriot and traitor alike; she rejects Ismene's plea to be allowed to share her fate with an appeal to the same stern authority: "Who did the work? / Let the dead and the god of death bear witness!" (595). In Creon's gods, the city's patrons and defenders, she shows no interest at all. Zeus she mentions twice: once as the source of all the calamities that have fallen and are still to fall on the house of Oedipus (2–5), and once again at the beginning of her famous speech about the unwritten laws. But the context here suggests strongly that she is thinking about Zeus in his special relationship to the underworld, Zeus *Chthonios* (Underworld Zeus). "It wasn't Zeus," she says,

> who made this proclamation. . . .
> Nor did that Justice, dwelling with the gods
> beneath the earth, ordain such laws for men. (494–96)

From first to last her religious devotion and duty are to the divine powers of the world below, the masters of that world where lie her family dead, to which she herself, reluctant but fascinated, is irresistibly drawn.

But, like Creon, she ends by denying the great sanctions she invoked to justify her action. In his case the process was spread out over the course of several scenes, as he reacted to each fresh pressure that was brought to bear on him; Antigone turns her back on the claims of blood relationship and the nether gods in one sentence: three lines in Greek, no more. They are the emotional high point of the speech she makes just before she is led off to her death.

> Never, I tell you,
> if I had been the mother of children
> or if my husband died, exposed and rotting—
> I'd never have taken this ordeal upon myself,
> never defied our people's will. (954–57)

These unexpected words are part of the long speech that concludes a scene of lyric lamentation and is in effect her farewell to the land of the living. They are certainly a total repudiation of her proud claim that she acted as the champion of the unwritten laws and the infernal gods, for, as she herself told Creon, those laws and those gods have no preferences, they long "for the same rites for all" (570). And her assertion that she would not have done for her children what she has done for Polynices is a spectacular betrayal of that fanatical loyalty to blood relationship which she urged on Ismene and defended against Creon, for there is no closer relationship imaginable than that between the mother and the children of her own body. Creon turned his back on his guiding principles step by step, in reaction to opposition based on those principles; Antigone's rejection of her public values is just as complete, but it is the sudden product of a lonely, brooding introspection, a last-minute assessment of her motives, on which the imminence of death confers a merciless clarity. She did it because Polynices was her brother; she would not have done it for husband or child. She goes on to justify this disturbing statement by an argument which is more disturbing still: husband and children, she says, could be replaced by others but, since her parents are dead, she could never have another brother. It so happens that we can identify the source of this strange piece of reasoning; it is a story in the *Histories* of Sophocles' friend Herodotus (a work from which Sophocles borrowed material more than once). Darius the Great King had condemned to death for treason a Persian noble, Intaphrenes, and all the men of his family. The wife of Intaphrenes begged importunately for their lives; offered one, she chose her brother's. When Darius asked her why, she replied in words that are unmistakably the original of Antigone's lines. But what makes sense in the story makes less in the play. The wife of Intaphrenes saves her brother's life, but Polynices is already dead; Antigone's phrase "no brother could ever spring to light again" (962) would be fully appropriate only if Antigone had managed to save Polynices' life rather than bury his corpse.

For this reason, and also because of some stylistic anomalies in this part of the speech, but most of all because they felt that the words are unworthy of the Antigone who spoke so nobly for the unwritten laws, many great scholars and also a great poet and dramatist, Goethe, have refused to believe that Sophocles wrote them. "I would give a great deal," Goethe told his friend Eckermann in 1827, "if some talented scholar could prove that these lines were interpolated, not genuine." Goethe did not know that the attempt had already been made, six years earlier; many others have tried since—Sir Richard Jebb, the greatest English editor of Sophocles, pronounced against them—and opinion today is still divided. Obviously a decision on this point is of vital significance for the interpretation of the play as a whole: with these lines removed, Antigone goes to her prison-tomb with no flicker of self-doubt, the flawless champion of the family bond and the unwritten laws, "whole as the marble, founded as the rock"[3]—unlike Creon, she is not, in the end, reduced to recognizing that her motive is purely personal.

There is however one objective piece of evidence that speaks volumes for the authenticity of the disputed lines. Aristotle, writing his treatise on rhetoric less than a century after the death of Sophocles, summarizes this part of Antigone's speech and quotes the two lines about the irreplaceability of a brother. He is telling the would-be orator that if, in a law-court speech for the defense, he has to describe an action that seems inappropriate for the character of his client and hard to believe, he must provide an explanation for it "as in the example Sophocles gives, the one from *Antigone*"—the phrasing suggests that the passage was well known to Aristotle's readers. Evidently he does not find the passage as repellent as Goethe and Jebb did; he recognizes that Antigone's initial statement is, in terms of her character, "hard to believe" [. . .], but apparently he finds her explanation rhetorically satisfactory. He does not, however, for one moment suspect the authenticity of the lines. [. . .] His acceptance of Antigone's speech as genuine demands that rather than suppress it we should try to understand it.

This is Antigone's third and last appearance on stage; in the prologue she planned her action, in the confrontation with Creon she defended it, and now, under guard, she is on her way to the prison which is to be her tomb. In lyric meters, the dramatic medium for unbridled emotion, she appeals to the chorus for sympathy and mourns for the marriage hymn she will never hear (this is as close as she ever comes to mentioning Haemon). She gets little comfort from the Theban elders; the only consolation they offer is a reminder that she may be the victim of a family curse—"do you pay for your father's terrible ordeal?" (904–05)—a suggestion that touches her to the quick and provokes a horror-struck rehearsal of the tormented loves and crimes of the house of Oedipus. There is, as she goes on to say, no one left to mourn her; the lyric lament she sings in this scene is her attempt to provide for herself that funeral dirge which her blood relatives would have wailed over her corpse, if they had not already preceded her into the realm of Hades. This is recognized by Creon, who cuts off the song with a sarcastic comment: "if a man could wail his own dirge *before* he dies, / he'd never finish" (928–29). And he orders the guards to take her away.

Her song cut off, she turns from the lyric medium of emotion to spoken verse, the vehicle of reasoned statement, for her farewell speech. It is not directed at

3. Shakespeare's *Macbeth* 3.4.22.

anyone on stage; it resembles a soliloquy, a private meditation. It is an attempt to understand the real reasons for the action that has brought her to the brink of death. After an address to the tomb and prison where she expects to be reunited with her family she speaks to Polynices (Creon is referred to in the third person). It is to Polynices that she is speaking when she says that she would not have given her life for anyone but a brother; it is as if she had already left the world of the living and joined that community of the family dead she speaks of with such love. Now, in the face of death, oblivious of the presence of Creon and the chorus, with no public case to make, no arguments to counter, she can at last identify the driving force behind her action, the private, irrational imperative which was at the root of her championship of the rights of family and the dead against the demands of the state. It is her fanatical devotion to one particular family, her own, the doomed, incestuous, accursed house of Oedipus and especially to its most unfortunate member, the brother whose corpse lay exposed to the birds and dogs. When she tells him that she has done for him what she would not have done for husband or children she is not speaking in wholly hypothetical terms, for in sober fact she has sacrificed, for his sake, her marriage to Haemon and the children that might have issued from it.

And in this moment of self-discovery she realizes that she is absolutely alone, not only rejected by men but also abandoned by gods. "What law of the mighty gods have I transgressed?" (971) she asks—as well she may, for whatever her motive may have been, her action was a blow struck for the rights of Hades and the dead. Unlike Christians whose master told them not to look for signs from heaven (Matthew 16:4),[4] the ancient Greek expected if not direct intervention at least some manifestation of favor or support from his gods when he believed his cause was just—a flight of eagles, the bird of Zeus, or lightning and thunder, the signs which, in the last play,[5] summon Oedipus to his resting place. But Antigone has to renounce this prospect: "Why look to heavens any more . . . ?" (972). She must go to her death as she has lived, alone, without a word of approval or a helping hand from men or gods.

Antigone's discovery that her deepest motives were purely personal has been overinterpreted by those who would suppress the passage on the grounds that, to quote Jebb's eloquent indictment, "she suddenly gives up that which, throughout the drama, has been the immovable basis of her action—the universal and unqualified validity of the divine law." This formulation is too absolute. Before the raw immediacy of death, which, as Doctor Johnson remarked, wonderfully concentrates the mind,[6] she has sounded the depths of her own soul and identified the determinant of those high principles she proclaimed in public. But that does not mean that they were a pretense, still less that she has now abandoned them. She dies for them. In her very last words, as she calls on the chorus to bear witness to her unjust fate, she claims once more and for the last time that she is the champion of divine law—she suffers "all for reverence, my reverence for the gods!" (993).

4. "A wicked and adulterous generation seeketh after a sign; and there shall no sign be given unto it [. . .]."

5. *Oedipus at Colonus.*

6. Samuel Johnson (1709–84), as quoted in James Boswell's *Life of Samuel Johnson* (1791): "when a man knows he is to be hanged in a fortnight, it concentrates his mind wonderfully."

Unlike Creon, who after proclaiming the predominance of the city's interests rides roughshod over them, speaking and acting like a tyrant, who after extolling the city's gods dismisses Tiresias, their spokesman, with a blasphemous insult, Antigone does not betray the loyalties she spoke for. No word of compromise or surrender comes to her lips, no plea for mercy [. . .].

• • •

This is a pattern of character and behavior which is found in other Sophoclean dramatic figures also; not only in the Oedipus of the other two plays of this volume but also in the protagonists of *Ajax*, *Electra* and *Philoctetes*. They are of course very different from each other, but they all have in common the same uncompromising determination, the same high sense of their own worth and a consequent quickness to take offense, the readiness to die rather than surrender—a heroic temper. This figure of the tragic hero [. . .] seems, as far as we can tell from what remains of Attic tragedy, to have been a peculiarly Sophoclean creation. In his plays he explores time and again the destinies of human beings who refuse to recognize the limits imposed on the individual will by men and gods, and go to death or triumph, magnificently defiant to the last.

Antigone is such a heroic figure, and this is another of the ways in which she is different from Creon. Not only does Creon, unlike Antigone, betray in action the principles he claimed to stand for; he also, subjected to pressure that falls short of the death Antigone is faced with, collapses in abject surrender. He was sure Antigone would give way when force was applied; he has seen "the stiffest stubborn wills / fall the hardest; the toughest iron . . . crack and shatter" (518–21)—but he is wrong. He is the one who is shattered. Tiresias tells him that he will lose a child of his own to death in return for the living being he has imprisoned in the tomb and the corpse he has kept in the sunlight. He hesitates: "I'm shaken, torn. / It's a dreadful thing to yield . . ." (1158). But yield he does. "What should I do?" he asks the chorus (1164) and they tell him: release Antigone, bury Polynices. But he arrives too late; Antigone, independent to the last, has chosen her own way to die [. . .]

[. . .] His savage dismissal of the claims of that blood relationship Antigone stood for has been punished with exquisite appropriateness, in the destruction of his own family, the curses of his son and wife. [. . .] The gods of the city whom he claimed to defend, have, through the medium of the blind seer, denounced his action, and the city he proposed to steer on a firm course is now, as Tiresias told him, threatened by the other cities whose dead were left to rot, like Polynices, outside the walls of Thebes (1141–45). He is revealed as a disastrous failure, both as head of a family and head of state, an offender against heaven and a man without family or friends, without the respect of his fellow-citizens. He may well describe himself as "no one. Nothing" (1386).

Antigone asked the gods to punish Creon if he was wrong [975–79], and they have. They have shown to all the world that her action was right. But she did not live to see her vindication. [. . . T]he will of the gods remains, as in all three of these plays, mysterious; revealed partially, if at all, through prophets rejected and prophecies misunderstood, it is the insoluble riddle at the heart of Sophocles' tragic vision. The gods told Creon he was wrong, but it is noticeable that

Tiresias, their spokesman, does not say Antigone was right, he does not praise her—in fact he does not mention her. Antigone was ready to admit, if the gods did not save her and she suffered death, that she was wrong (975–76); these words suggest that she hanged herself not just to cut short the lingering agony of starvation and imprisonment but in a sort of existential despair. [. . .]

The gods do not praise Antigone, nor does anyone else in the play—except the young man who loves her so passionately that he cannot bear to live without her. Haemon tells his father what the Thebans are saying behind his back, the "murmurs in the dark" (743): that Antigone deserves not death but "a glowing crown of gold!" (751). Whether this is a true report (and the chorus does not praise Antigone even when they have been convinced that she was right) or just his own feelings attributed to others for the sake of his argument, it is a timely reminder of Antigone's heroic status. In the somber world of the play, against the background of so many sudden deaths and the dark mystery of the divine dispensation, her courage and steadfastness are a gleam of light; she is the embodiment of the only consolation tragedy can offer—that in certain heroic natures unmerited suffering and death can be met with a greatness of soul which, because it is purely human, brings honor to us all.

Martha C. Nussbaum

From Sophocles' *Antigone*: Conflict, Vision, and Simplification (1986, 2001)[1]

[. . . A]lmost all interpreters of this play have agreed that the play shows Creon to be morally defective, though they might not agree about the particular nature of his defect. The situation of Antigone is more controversial. Hegel assimilated her defect to Creon's; some more recent writers uncritically hold her up as a blameless heroine. Without entering into an exhaustive study of her role in the tragedy, I should like to claim (with the support of an increasing number of recent critics) that there is at least some justification for the Hegelian assimilation—though the criticism needs to be focused more clearly and specifically than it is in Hegel's brief remarks. I want to suggest that Antigone, like Creon, has engaged in a ruthless simplification of the world of value which effectively eliminates conflicting obligations. Like Creon, she can be blamed for refusal of vision. But there are important differences, as well, between her project and Creon's. When these are seen, it will also emerge that this criticism of Antigone is not incompatible with the judgment that she is morally superior to Creon.

• • •

There has been a war. On one side was an army led by Eteocles, brother of Antigone and Ismene. On the other side was an invading army, made up partly of foreigners, but led by a Theban brother, Polynices. This heterogeneity is denied,

1. Martha C. Nussbaum. "Sophocles' *Antigone*: Conflict, Vision, and Simplification." *The Fragility of Goodness: Luck and Ethics in Greek Tragedy and Philosophy.* 1986. Revised ed., Cambridge UP, 2001, pp. 51–84. Nussbaum's footnotes and parenthetical citations have been edited.

in different ways, by both Creon and Antigone. Creon's strategy is to draw, in thought, a line between the invading and defending forces. What falls to one side of this line is a foe, bad, unjust; what falls to the other (if loyal to the city's cause) becomes, indiscriminately, friend or loved one. Antigone, on the other hand, denies the relevance of this distinction entirely. She draws, in imagination, a small circle around the members of her family: what is inside (with further restrictions which we shall mention) is family, therefore loved one and friend; what is outside is non-family, therefore, in any conflict with the family, enemy. If one listened only to Antigone, one would not know that a war had taken place or that anything called "city" was ever in danger.[2] To her it is a simple injustice that Polynices should not be treated like a friend.

"Friend" (*philos*) and "enemy," then, are functions solely of family relationship.[3] When Antigone says, "It is my nature to join in loving (*sumphilein*), not to join in hating," she is expressing not a general attachment to love, but a devotion to the *philia* of the family. It is the nature of these *philia* bonds to make claims on one's commitments and actions regardless of one's occurrent desires. This sort of love is not something one decides about; the relationships involved may have little to do with liking or fondness. We might say (to use terminology borrowed from Kant[4]) that Antigone, in speaking of love, means "practical," not "pathological" love (a love that has its source in fondness or inclination). "He is my own brother," she says to Ismene in explanation of her defiance of the city's decree, "and yours too, even if you don't want it. I certainly will never be found a traitor to him" (51–52). Relationship is itself a source of obligation, regardless of the feelings involved. When Antigone speaks of Polynices as "my dearest [. . .] brother" (94), even when she proclaims, "I shall lie with him as a loved one with a loved one [. . .]" (83–84), there is no sense of closeness, no personal memory, no particularity animating her speech.[5] Ismene, the one person who ought, historically, to be close to her, is treated from the beginning with remote coldness; she is even called enemy (110) when she takes the wrong stand on matters of pious obligation. It is Ismene whom we see weeping "sister-loving tears," who acts out of commitment to a felt love. "What life is worth living for me, bereft of you?" (602) she asks with an intensity of feeling that never animates her sister's

2. Cf. [S. G.] Bernardete, "A Reading [of Sophocles' *Antigone*]." [*Interpretation* 4 (1975): 148–96; 5 (1975): 1–55, 148–84,] 2.4 [Nussbaum's note].

3. [. . .] Cf. Bernardete, *op. cit.* 8.6, 9.5, [C.] Segal, *Tragedy* [*and Civilization: An Interpretation of Sophocles* (Cambridge, 1981)] 189, [R. P.] Winnington-Ingram, *Sophocles*[*: An Interpretation* (Cambridge, 1980)] 129ff, [B.] Knox, [*The*] *Heroic Temper*[*: Studies in Sophoclean Tragedy* (Berkeley, 1964)] 79–80 [Nussbaum's note].

4. Immanuel Kant (1724–1804), German philosopher who uses these terms in his *Critique of Pure Reason*.

5. A number of scholars have claimed that Antigone is motivated by deep personal love for Polynices: for example, [M.] Santirocco, "Justice [in Sophocles' *Antigone*.]" [*Phil Lit* 4 (1980): 1880–98,] 188, Knox, *Heroic Temper* 107ff., Winnington-Ingram, *op cit.* 130. Contrast the effective negative arguments of [G.] Perrotta, *Sofocle* [Messina-Florence, 1935] 112–14, [H.] Lloyd-Jones, [*The Justice of Zeus* (Berkeley, 1971)] 116, [I. M.] Linforth, "Antigone and Creon" [*University of California Publications in Classical Philology* 15 (1961): 183–260,] 250. Perrotta correctly observes that she loves Polynices not *qua* Polynices, but *qua* falling under a family duty. [. . .] With her abstract and cold remarks of mourning we might contrast, for example, the agonized mourning of Hecuba (in Euripides' *Trojan Women* [. . .]) over the corpse of her grandchild, where each part of the loved body conjures up a new memory of shared affection. There are many similar cases [Nussbaum's note].

piety. To Haemon, the man who passionately loves and desires her, Antigone never addresses a word throughout the entire play.[6] It is Haemon, not Antigone, whom the Chorus views as inspired by *erōs* (842–56). Antigone is as far from *erōs* as Creon.[7] For Antigone, the dead are "those whom it is most important to please" (103). "You have a warm heart for the cold" (102), observes her sister, failing to comprehend this impersonal and single-minded passion.

Duty to the family dead is the supreme law and the supreme passion. And Antigone structures her entire life and her vision of the world in accordance with this simple, self-contained system of duties. Even within this system, should a conflict ever arise, she is ready with a fixed priority ordering that will clearly dictate her choice. The strange speech (954–64) in which she ranks duties to different family dead, placing duty to brother above duties to husband and children, is in this sense (if genuine) highly revealing: it makes us suspect that she is capable of a strangely ruthless simplification of duties, corresponding not so much to any known religious law as to the exigencies of her own practical imagination.[8]

Other values fall into place, confirming these suspicions. Her single-minded identification with duties to the dead (and only some of these) effects a strange reorganization of piety, as well as of honor and justice. She is truly, in her own words, *hosia panourgēsasa*, one who will do anything for the sake of the pious;[9] and her piety takes in only a part of conventional religion.[1] She speaks of her allegiance to Zeus [. . .], but she refuses to recognize his role as guardian of the

6. Cf. Perrotta, *op. cit.* 112. We must ascribe "O dearest Haemon, how your father dishonors you," to Ismene as in all the manuscripts. Pearson and other editors have assigned it to Antigone, out of their desire to have Antigone say something affectionate about Haemon. But *philtate*, "dearest," is not unusually strong inside a close family relationship, and it is perfectly appropriate to the affectionate Ismene; it need not, in fact, even desgianate close affection. Creon's reply that the speaker's continued harping on marriage "irritates him is appropriate to his relationship with Ismene (who is, in any case, the one who has been "harping" on marriage), but is far too mild to express his deep hatred for and anger against Antigone. See the arguments of Linforth, *op. cit.* 209, Bernardete *ad loc* [Nussbaum's note].

7. On Antigone's refusal of *eros*, see [J.-P.] Vernant, "Tensions [et ambiguités dans la tragédie grecque]," in [J-P.] Vernant and [P.] Vidal-Naquet, *Mythe et tragédie en grèce ancienne* (Paris, 1972),] 34–5, Bernardete, "A reading" 8.6; compare Segal, *Tragedy* §VIII [Nussbaum's note, here abbreviated].

8. This speech is notoriously controversial. It would surely have been branded spurious had it not been quoted as genuine by Aristotle in the *Rhetoric*; this dates it so early that, if spurious, it could only be an actor's interpolation. And it is difficult to imagine an actor giving himself such an oddly legalistic and unemotional speech at a climactic moment in the dramatic action. It is, then, [. . .] almost certainly genuine; and it is very difficult to explain as a confused and incoherent outpouring of passionate love—thought this approach has indeed been tried (e.g. by Winnington-Ingram, *Sophocles* 145ff., Knox, *Heroic Temper* 144ff.). The best explanation for this coldly determined priority-ordering of duties is that Antigone is not animated by personal love at all, but by a stern determination to have a fixed set of ordered requirements that will dictate her actions without engendering conflict; her refusal of the erotic [. . .] is then sufficient to explain her choice of the brother. For review of the controversy about authenticity and about the relation of the passage to Herodotus III.119, see [D. A.] Hester, "Sophocles the unphilosophical[: A Study in the *Antigone*.]" [*Mnemosyne* 4th ser. 24 (1971): 11–59,] 55–80, [R. C.] Jebb, [*Sophocles: The Antigone* (Cambridge, 1900),] Appendix, 258–65, [G.] Müller, *Sophokles, Antigone* [Heidelberg, 1967] 198ff, 106ff., Knox, *op. cit.* 105–6, Winnington-Ingram, *op. cit.* 145ff. See also D. Page, *Actors' Interpolations in Greek Tragedy* (Oxford, 1934) [Nussbaum's note].

9. See Bernardete, "A reading" 9.3 [Nussbaum's note].

1. See Knox, *Heroic Temper* 94ff., Segal, *Tragedy* §VIII. Winnington-Ingram calls the way in which she denies the hatred of brothers for one another after death a "heroic fiat," "a supreme effort to impose heroic will upon a recalcitrant world" (*Sophocles* 132) [Nussbaum's note].

city and backer of Eteocles. The very expression of her devotion is suspect: "Zeus did not decree this, as far as I am concerned" ([. . .] 494). She sets herself up as the arbiter of what Zeus can and cannot have decreed, just as Creon took it upon himself to say whom the gods could and could not have covered: no other character bears out her view of Zeus as single-mindedly backing the rights of the dead. She speaks, too, of the goddess *Dikē*, Justice; but *Dikē;* for her is, simply, "the Justice who lives together with the gods below" (495). The Chorus recognizes another *Dikē*.[2] Later they will say to her, "Having advanced to the utmost limit of boldness, you struck hard against the altar of *Dikē* on high, o child" (901–3). Justice is up here in the city, as well as below the earth. It is not as simple as she says it is. Antigone, accordingly, is seen by them not as a conventionally pious person, but as one who improvised her piety, making her own decisions about what to honor. She is a "maker of her own law [. . .]"; her defiance is "self-invented passion" ([. . .]920). Finally they tell her unequivocally that her pious respect is incomplete: "[This] reverent action [. . .] is a part of piety [. . .]" (917). Antigone's rigid adherence to a single narrow set of duties has caused her to misinterpret the nature of piety itself, a virtue within which a more comprehensive understanding would see the possibility of conflict.

Creon's strategy of simplification led him to regard others as material for his aggressive exploitation. Antigone's dutiful subservience to the dead leads to an equally strange, though different (and certainly less hideous) result. Her relation to others in the world above is characterized by an odd coldness. "You are alive," she tells her sister, "but my life [. . .] is long since dead, to the end of serving the dead." The safely dutiful human life requires, or is, life's annihilation.[3] Creon's attitude towards others is like necrophilia: he aspires to possess the inert and unresisting. Antigone's subservience to duty is, finally, the ambition to be a *nekros*, a corpse beloved of corpses. (Her apparent similarity to martyrs in our own tradition, who expect a fully active life after death, should not conceal from us the strangeness of this goal.) In the world below, there are no risks of failure or wrongdoing.

Neither Creon nor Antigone, then, is a loving or passionate being in anything like the usual sense. Not one of the gods, not one human being escapes the power of *erōs*, says the Chorus (842–47); but these two oddly inhuman beings do, it appears, escape. Creon sees loved persons as functions of the civic good, replaceable producers of citizens. For Antigone, they are either dead, fellow servants of the dead, or objects of complete indifference. No living being is loved for his or her personal qualities, loved with the sort of love that Haemon feels and Ismene praises. By altering their beliefs about the nature and value of persons, they have, it seems, altered or restructured the human passions themselves. They achieve harmony in this way; but at a cost. The Chorus speaks of *erōs* as a force as important and obligating as the ancient *thesmoi* or laws of right, a force against which it is both foolish and, apparently, blameworthy to rebel [. . .].

2. On Antigone's conception of *diké* and its novelty, see R. Hirzel, *Themis, Diké, and Verwandtes* (Leipzig, 1907) 147ff.; also Santirocco, "Justice" 186, Segal, *op. cit.* 170 [Nussbaum's note].

3. Segal, *op. cit.* provides an excellent discussion of this aspect of Antigone in several places—esp. 156ff., §VIII, §IV, 196 [Nussbaum's note].

Antigone learns too—like Creon, by being forced to recognize a problem that lies at the heart of her single-minded concern. Creon saw that the city itself is pious and loving; that he could not be its champion without valuing what it values, in all its complexity. Antigone comes to see that the service of the dead requires the city, that her own religious aims cannot be fulfilled without civic institutions. By being her own law, she has not only ignored a part of piety, she has also jeopardized the fulfillment of the very pious duties to which she is so attached. Cut off from friends, from the possibility of having children, she cannot keep herself alive in order to do further service to the dead; nor can she guarantee the pious treatment of her own corpse. In her last speeches she laments not so much the fact of imminent death as, repeatedly, her isolation from the continuity of offspring, from friends and mourners. She emphasizes the fact that she will never marry; she will remain childless. Acheron will be her husband, the tomb her bridal chamber. Unless she can successfully appeal to the citizens whose needs as citizens she had refused to consider, she will die without anyone to mourn her death or to replace her as guardian of her family religion. She turns therefore increasingly, in this final scene, to the citizens and the gods of the city [. . .], until her last words closely echo an earlier speech made by Creon [. . .] and blend his concerns with hers:

> O city of my fathers in this land of Thebes. O gods, progenitors of our race. I am led away, and wait no longer. Look, leaders of Thebes, the last of your royal line. Look what I suffer, at whose hands, for having respect for piety. (987–93)

We have, then, two narrowly limited practical worlds, two strategies of avoidance and simplification. In one, a single human value has become *the* final end; in the other, a single set of duties has eclipsed all others. But we can now acknowledge that we admire Antigone, nonetheless, in a way that we do not admire Creon. It seems important to look for the basis of this difference.

First, in the world of the play, it seems clear that Antigone's actual choice is preferable to Creon's. The dishonour to civic values involved in giving pious burial to an enemy's corpse is far less radical than the violation of religion involved in Creon's act. Antigone shows a deeper understanding of the community and its values than Creon does when she argues that the obligation to bury the dead is an unwritten law, which cannot be set aside by the decree of a particular ruler. The belief that not all values are utility-relative, that there are certain claims whose neglect will prove deeply destructive of communal attunement and individual character, is a part of Antigone's position left untouched by the play's implicit criticism of her single-mindedness.

Furthermore, Antigone's pursuit of virtue is her own. It involves nobody else and commits her to abusing no other person. Rulership must be rulership *of* something; Antigone's pious actions are executed alone, out of a solitary commitment. She may be strangely remote from the world; but she does no violence to it.

Finally, and perhaps most important, Antigone remains ready to risk and to sacrifice her ends in a way that is not possible for Creon, given the singleness of his conception of value. There is a complexity in Antigone's virtue that permits genuine sacrifice *within* the defense of piety. She dies recanting nothing; but still she is torn by a conflict. Her virtue is, then, prepared to admit a contingent conflict, at least in the extreme case where its adequate exercise requires the cancellation of the conditions of its exercise. From within her single-minded devotion to the dead, she recognizes the power of these contingent circumstances and yields to them, comparing herself to Niobe wasted away by nature's snow and rain (878–84).[4] (Earlier she had been compared, in her grief, to a mother bird crying out over an empty nest; so she is, while heroically acting, linked with the openness and vulnerability of the female.) The Chorus here briefly tries to console her with the suggestion that her bad luck does not really matter, in view of her future fame; she calls their rationalization a mockery of her loss. This vulnerability in virtue, this ability to acknowledge the world of nature by mourning the constraints that it imposes on virtue, surely contributes to making her the more humanly rational and the richer of the two protagonists: both active and receptive, neither exploiter nor simply victim.

Philip Holt

From Polis *and Tragedy in the* Antigone (1999)[1]

I. INTRODUCTION

Sophokles' *Antigone* is an easy play for moderns, even modern classicists, to get wrong.[2] We are likely to see Antigone as the champion of moral right, or conscience, or religion against the authority of the state, as represented by Kreon. She is then a martyr for a cause, and our age is rather drawn to causes and martyrs. This does much to explain the scholarly predilection for what Hester called "the orthodox view" of the play: Antigone right and noble, Kreon wrong and tyrannical.[3] But these terms for describing the conflict—and even more the ethical weight and emotional coloring these terms carry—are relatively modern.

4. The importance of this link with the yielding world of nature is seen by Segal, *Tragedy* 154ff [Nussbaum's note, here abbreviated].

1. Philip Holt. "*Polis* and Tragedy in the *Antigone*." *Mnemosyne*, 4th ser., vol. 52, no. 6, Dec. 1999, pp. 658–90. *JSTOR*, www.jstor.org/stable/4433045. All footnotes are the author's, but some have been edited and others omitted, along with the parts of the essay to which they pertain.

2. The following works are cited by author's name (and short title where necessary) only: [. . .] Helene Foley, *Tragedy and Democratic Ideology: The Case of Sophocles'* Antigone, in: Barbara Goff (ed.), *History, Tragedy, Theory: Dialogues on Athenian Drama* (Austin 1995), 131–50; Simon Goldhill, *Reading Greek Tragedy* (Cambridge 1986); Bernard M. W. Knox, *The Heroic Temper: Studies in Sophoclean Tragedy* (Berkeley 1964); Christiane Sourvinou-Inwood, *Assumptions and the Creation of Meaning: Reading Sophocles'* Antigone, JHS 109 (1989), 134–48 and (with substantial overlap) *Sophocles' Antigone as a "Bad Woman,"* in: F. Dieteren, E. Kloek (ed.), *Writing Women into History* (Amsterdam 1990), 11–38; and the commentaries of Brown (Warminster 1987) [. . . and] Kamerbeek (Leiden 1978) [. . .]. I have used the text of Lloyd-Jones and Wilson (Oxford 1990).

3. Hester's extensive review of scholarship on the play found this view to be far more popular than what he called the "Hegelian" view, which sees Antigone and Kreon as being more evenly matched with flaws on both sides: D. A. Hester, *Sophocles the Unphilosophical: A Study in the* Antigone, Mnemosyne 24 (1971), 11–59. For a similar tilt in Germany (Schlegel over Hegel), see Erick Eberlein, *Über die verschiedenen Deutungen des tragischen Konflikts in der Tragödie 'Antigone' des Sophokles*, Gymnasium 68 (1961), 16–34 at 16–9.

"The state" to us means a nation-state with extensive powers over the lives of its citizens and an extensive apparatus of bureaucrats and police to enforce its dictates. We worry about its powers and want to protect our freedom within it, especially after twentieth-century experience with totalitarian regimes. "Conscience" and "morality" to us mean the personal values of an autonomous individual, influenced by society but often at variance with it. "Religion" to us is likely to include notions of divinely revealed truth and an organized body of believers, both of them distinct from, and often at odds with, political authority. For us, then, conscience, morality, and religion set the individual apart from, perhaps even against, the state. It is easy for us to make Antigone into a heroic dissident. She upholds principle against political authority, and she is right.

* * *

We must understand fifth-century Athenian beliefs about the state, the role of the individual within it, and its relations to religion, funerals, and related matters—the "*polis*" part of my title—before we can make sense of the *Antigone.* These will be surveyed, with some large debts to previous work, in part II. Here the "orthodox" view is particularly weak, and its weaknesses still need attention. [. . .]

Still, understanding Greek beliefs and attitudes is only a first step towards interpretation. We need to consider not so much what Greeks thought and felt generally as how they are likely to have thought and felt under the conditions of a tragic performance, this tragedy in particular. Hence the "tragedy" part of my title: a discussion of how decent Greek opinion fares over the course of the *Antigone* (part III) and a coda on how it might fare in tragedy generally (part IV). Tragedy is the *polis*' partner in an intricate dialogue. She has her own agenda and her own ways of making her points, some of them quite sly,[4] and she is rather more on Antigone's side than the *polis* is. The main burden of this essay is to understand better her side of the conversation, an area where history-minded critics, straining to catch the voice of the *polis*, often miss things.

II. *POLIS*

* * *

Broad construction of the public interest gave the Athenian *polis* considerable power to regulate what its citizens did. Among other things, the *polis* could regulate funerals. A funeral was basically a family function, but the display and ostentation which the family could employ were restricted by the state.[5] The state could also restrict funeral rites for certain classes of people—suicides, for example.[6]

4. "Drama . . . unfolds as a complex dialogue that refuses to be bound in any direct fashion by the discourses of the agora" (Foley, 132); it provides a "radical critique" of "the city's discourse" (Goldhill, 78; on how this applies to some particular issues in the *Antigone*, see 104–6, 174–80).

5. Erwin Rohde, *Psyche: The Cult of Souls and Belief in Immortality among the Greeks*, English trans. (London 1925), 164f.; Robert Garland, *The Greek Way of Death* (Ithaca, N.Y. 1985), 21–3.

6. Thalheim, *Selbstmord, RE* II A.1 (1921), 1134f.

This brings us to a fact which is troublesome for devotees of St. Antigone the Martyr but important for assessing how an Athenian audience would respond to the play: Athenian law forbade the burial of traitors and sacrilegious people in Athenian territory. There is abundant evidence of this law, and of similar laws in other states.[7] Now, Polyneikes, who led an army against his homeland, was certainly a traitor, and if Kreon is right that he planned to burn the temples of the gods (*Ant.* 199–201, 284–7), he aspired to sacrilege as well. Hence in refusing him burial, Kreon was imposing a sanction that was recognizable to the audience as part of their law. He had good reasons for it. In a small city-state, defeat in war could mean civic destruction and the loss of everything one had; treason was a serious business, a threat to the survival of the community.

• • •

To sum up, in fifth-century terms Kreon is within his rights as the leader of his *polis*, and his ban on burying Polyneikes is a reasonable sanction. In fifth-century terms, Antigone's defiance of that ban is seriously, perhaps even shockingly, out of line: an individual defying due authority in the *polis*, in time of crisis, on behalf of a national enemy, and moreover a woman defying due male authority.

Critics often see Antigone as an isolated figure, willful and obstinate, proud and cold to others, acting from a mixed bag of reasons, both principled and personal.[8] There are good reasons why they should. To a degree which may be hard for us to imagine, she stands alone, forced to rely heavily on her own heroic temper. A modern Antigone comes with some ready-made bases for defying the community, respected and well-articulated values to which she can appeal. The ancient Antigone is not so well equipped. Conscience and religious authority are largely out. "The wide range of ideals, eccentricities and obsessions which we nowadays amalgamate under the name of 'conscience' did not seem to Greeks to be good reasons for defying the law."[9] Religion was focused more on prayer and ritual than on beliefs and ethical demands, more apt to produce traditionalists and conformists than dissidents and martyrs. Far from providing a basis for criticizing the *polis*, religion was an integral part of it. The *polis*,

7. Gustave Glotz, *La solidarité de la famille dans le droit criminel en Grèce* (Paris 1904), 460f. gives an extensive collection of evidence; also basic, and long neglected for bringing the issue into discussion of the *Antigone*, is W. Vischer, *Zu Sophokles Antigone*, RhM 20 (1865), 444–54 at 445–9.

8. So (with considerable variation) Elizabeth Bryson Bongie, *The Daughter of Oedipus*, in: John L. Heller (ed.), *Serta Turyniana* (Urbana 1974), 239–67; Brown, 7–10; Gerald F. Else, *The Madness of Antigone* (Heidelberg 1976); Knox, 62–8, 102–7, 113–6. Two important recent studies have done much to clear Antigone of the charge of inconsistency: Helene P. Foley, *Antigone as Moral Agent*, in: M. S. Silk (ed.), *Tragedy and the Tragic: Greek Theatre and Beyond* (Oxford 1996), 49–73; Matt Neuburg, *How Like a Woman: Antigone's "Inconsistency,"* CQ 40 (1990): 54–76. But her consistent reasons are nevertheless complicated and strongly rooted in the specifics of her unusual situation, dying unmarried (Neuburg, 66–70) and acting on behalf of a brother (Foley, 51–7). Complex situations produce complex motives. It is possible to see her as both consistent and self-willed: Martin Cropp, *Antigone's Final Speech (Sophocles,* Antigone *891–928)*, G&R 44 (1997), 137–60.

9. [K. J.] Dover[, *Greek Popular Morality in the Time of Plato and Aristotle* (Berkeley 1974)], (n.13) 309.

after all, administered, financed, and regulated much of the religious activity within it.[1] It had large scope in making decisions about religious matters.

There remains the family, whose entanglements with the *polis*, interdependent yet often conflicting, were important in Greek history and have been important in *Antigone* criticism at least since Hegel. There is no anachronism in raising family concerns. Antigone does, after all, break Kreon's edict on behalf of her brother, precisely because he is her brother, and she appeals repeatedly to that blood-tie to justify her action.[2] Still, family and *polis* do not meet in the play as an evenly balanced pair of opposites, a thesis and antithesis in search of a synthesis.[3] The *Antigone* presents a situation which the fifth-century *polis* had already decided in its own favor. As we have seen, the *polis* could override the family to regulate funerals, or even ban them for certain classes of people—including traitors like Polyneikes. [. . .]

Sophokles, then, gives Kreon a strong position, far stronger than we moderns are generally prepared or able to recognize. What becomes of that position on the stage, however, is another matter.

III. THE *ANTIGONE*

It should not escape the reader's notice that the discussion so far is aimed at estimating how fifth-century Athenians would react to Antigone's action if it were a real event in civic life—if they were debating it in the assembly or judging it as jurors in a court of law or discussing it as a piece of recent news. [. . .] But of course, Polyneikes' burial is not an event in real life. It is part of a tragic drama, which is to say, it is presented to the audience by the playwright in a certain way and observed by the audience under certain conditions. This complicates the task of interpretation. We may know, more or less, what decent Athenian opinion held; but what does the play do with it?

I shall argue that the structure of Sophokles' drama—his arrangement and presentation of events, the playwright's devices for getting his story across—does much to encourage sympathy for Antigone, undercutting the shock and condemnation that her action would likely arouse in real life. Moreover, this sympathy for a lawbreaker is of a piece with what tragedy does elsewhere: it tests limits, defies norms, gives a certain kind of outlet for antisocial feelings. The audience

1. Christiane Sourvinou-Inwood, *What Is* Polis *Religion*?, in: Oswyn Murray, Simon Price (ed.), *The Greek City from Homer to Alexander* (Oxford 1990), 295–322 and *Further Aspects of Polis Religion*, AION (archeol) 10 (1988), 259–74.

2. *Ant.* 21 f., 45 f., 80 f., 466–8, 502–4, 511, 517; see also 696–8 (spoken by Haimon), 10, 73, 89 (*philos* and related expressions). Kreon's valuation of kinship ties is considerably lower (486–9, 658 f.) Antigone's notorious declaration that she would not have broken Kreon's edict to bury anyone but her brother (904–20), however odd critics find it, is consistent with her motives as repeatedly stated elsewhere. Antigone's loyalty to Polyneikes may not be simply a matter of blood-ties: Patricia J. Johnson, *Woman's Third Face: A Psycho/Social Reconsideration of Sophocles'* Antigone, Arethusa 30 (1997), 369–98 raises the issue, with a highly speculative answer.

3. One can question more broadly whether Antigone's action really respects proper family loyalties and proper responsibilities in burying dead kin: Sourvinou-Inwood, *Bad Woman*, 17–21 and 29–31. I find some of the arguments too intricate to be helpful in estimating a theatre audience's responses to the play, but the question deserves fuller consideration. I confine my remarks here to narrow grounds involving funerals.

did not come to a tragedy to vent its orthodoxies upon the characters; it came, I suggest, partly for the more interesting and exciting experience of watching the characters defy the orthodoxies.

We may begin with the premise of Sophokles' drama—Kreon's edict forbidding the burial of Polyneikes. As we have seen, the edict was in keeping with Athenian law; but that does not settle the question of how an Athenian audience would have regarded it. Denying burial to traitors and temple-robbers was, after all, a circumscribed exception to a widely accepted norm, the right to a decent funeral. It was an extreme reprisal, and it may well have occasioned doubts, reservations, and ambivalence in the community that resorted to it.

* * *

To a large extent, the action of the *Antigone* is taken up with unfolding th[e "heavy unanticipated"] costs [of Kreon's edict]. Kreon's position is repeatedly challenged, he repeatedly resists, but each challenge reveals new weaknesses, and eventually he crumbles. Orthodox critics tend to regard this result as a foregone conclusion: Kreon's position is of course wrong, so he is bound to end badly. This is too harsh: it underestimates the basic reasonableness (in Greek terms) of Kreon's position, and it tends to read the play backwards, interpreting the early scenes out of our advance knowledge of how things will turn out and magnifying small hints in those early scenes accordingly.[4] Historically minded critics, on the other hand, sometimes appear to regard the outcome as a surprise, as though we had to wait for Teiresias to tell us how wrong Kreon is.[5] This is too sanguine: it scants some important signs in the text of the stages by which Kreon's edict is undone. We would do better to see the play as a progression of complications, with Kreon's position undermined bit by bit. The outcome is not clear from the start, but we can see it coming as the play goes on. Tragic complications encroach more and more upon the dictates of the *polis*. Sophokles first deals Kreon a strong hand and then has us watch him lose with it.

* * *

The play opens towards dawn, with two women in conversation. Kreon, we are told, has already issued his edict but is on his way "to proclaim it clearly to those who do not know it" (*Ant.* 31–4).[6] This cusp of time gives Antigone a chance to respond to the edict in advance, after it is formulated but before any other character or the audience hears it. Sophokles uses this bit of timing to let her launch a pre-emptive strike upon it to win the audience's sympathy.

Her strike is an impressive one. The terms of the edict are revealed only after a dramatic buildup. The house of Oidipous has suffered everything imaginable, she says, "for there is nothing painful or destructive or shameful or dishonorable which I have not seen among your sufferings and mine" (*Ant.* 4–6). And

4. A. S. McDevitt, *Sophocles' Praise of Man in the Antigone*, Ramus 1 (1972), 152–64 at 159f. and Sourvinou-Inwood, *Assumptions*, 135f. both raise some powerful objections to such backward reading.
5. Sourvinou-Inwood waits for Teiresias; Calder [. . .], 401f. holds out even after that. [William M. Calder III, *Sophokles' Political Tragedy,* Antigone, GRBS 9 (1968), 389–407.]
6. [. . .] On the timing, see Brown, *ad* 31–4.

now [. . .] on top of it all, this terrible proclamation [. . .]. We have not yet heard what the proclamation says, but by the time Ismene asks [. . .], twenty lines into this scene, we are primed to hear something terrible.

Terrible indeed [. . .]. Eteokles' burial is described simply and approvingly (23–5), but the other brother and his treatment are described more fully, in more emotional terms [. . .] (26–30). Polyneikes is "wretchedly dead," and the consequences of exposing his corpse are graphically depicted: no lamentation, no funeral, only the birds to devour him. [. . .] First impressions are powerful, and our first impression of Kreon's edict comes to us filtered through Antigone's grief and indignation.[7]

We need not wait long for a second impression, even before Kreon's entrance. Ismene elicits gradually, through a series of questions, the details of Antigone's plan to bury Polyneikes (*Ant.* 39–48), and she finds it bold and dangerous. The series of questions brings out Antigone's plan in stages, each more shocking than the last, and we are invited to share Ismene's surprise and alarm [. . .]. Like Antigone, she can rehearse the sad history of the family (49–57), but it affects her differently. It does not sting her to outrage, it urges her to caution: "Consider how we two, left alone, will perish wretchedly if despite the law we transgress the ruler's decision and power" (58–60). Ismene also reminds us that Antigone's plan is illegal. [. . .]

Ismene, notoriously, is no tragic heroine. We could, like many critics, cheer Antigone's heroism and castigate Ismene's cowardice, but the scene is not quite so one-sided. At the very least, Ismene reminds us that more than one reaction to Kreon's edict is possible. [. . .]

Still, Antigone has had the chance to strike the first blow, and she has done it well, passionately, and dramatically. The audience may well sympathize with her, not necessarily because they would agree with her, but because shock and distress seen up close arouse sympathy. Ismene's objections, although often underrated, do not erase this. Kreon comes to the plate with one strike against him.

After the parados, we move from the private world of Antigone to the public world of Kreon. Despite Antigone's pre-emptive strike, Kreon's opening address to the Chorus gives him every chance to look good in the audience's eyes. The Chorus has just given thanks to the gods for delivering Thebes from great danger, and their song has reminded us vividly of the impiety and violence of Polyneikes' army, the sufferings that awaited the Thebans had they lost the battle.[8] As a new ruler in a difficult time, Kreon has a claim on our sympathy, and for the most part he comes off well. His speech is reasoned, his tone moderate under the circumstances. His heart is clearly in the right place: he seeks good advice in guiding the city (*Ant.* 178–81), he puts the city first, before private connections (182–91), and he is determined to distinguish between the patriotic Eteokles and the treacherous Polyneikes. [. . .]

Still, the question is raised whether Thebes is in good hands, and the answer is not altogether satisfactory.[9] "It is impossible to know any man's soul and

7. "Thus we learn of the edict, not from a bald report, but through Antigone's sense of outrage at it" (Brown, 135). 8. McDevitt [. . .] 157–9.

9. R. P. Winnington-Ingram, *Sophocles: An Interpretation* (Cambridge 1980), 123–5 offers a more extensive discussion than mine of "warning signals" in this scene.

thought and mind," Kreon says, "before he is experienced in office and law" (*Ant.* 175–7). This puts us on notice that Kreon is untested at this point in the play, hence unknown. More telling, his edict forbidding funeral rites for Polyneikes, presented after a slow, careful buildup, gets a remarkably lukewarm reception from the Chorus. [. . .] Indeed, all through the play the merits of Kreon's edict (as distinguished from his authority to impose it) go unsupported by anybody but him. Saying that he has the power or the right to command something is not the same as saying that it is a good idea.

Kreon's position is almost immediately challenged. The Guard enters with news that Polyneikes' corpse has been sprinkled with dust. Kreon, untried in "office and law" (*Ant.* 177), is on trial here, for we will see how he stands up to the first test of his new regime. Our attention begins to shift, and will shift more markedly in the following scene, from the proclamation to the ruler who issues it. The ruler does not come off well, for he meets the challenge with anger, error, and obstinacy.

• • •

In the Guard's narrative as in the prologue, Antigone's grief and outrage are given play, stressing the terrible consequences of Kreon's edict. She wails like a bird robbed of its young, laments the corpse "when she saw it bare," and curses those who left it that way (422–8). Kreon does not change his plans when he finds out that the perpetrator of the crime is his own niece and his son's fiancée; he is still determined to put her to death. These developments show Kreon persisting in his intention as the emotional costs mount. Kreon's edict may be based on sound principles, but it takes a tough heart and a strong stomach to maintain his position in the extreme situation which the play presents. Unfortunately, Kreon possesses both these qualities.

By this point in the play, principles have gotten mixed up with personalities. We have come away from the noble abstractions of Kreon's "inaugural address" and gotten a chance to see something of Kreon himself. He is less impressive than his ideals, and he is not doing terribly well on the test he set for himself—how well he performs "in office and law" (*Ant.* 175–7). Still, a Greek audience might well hold back from shifting all its sympathy to Antigone. Her ringing declaration of the unwritten laws, eternal and not to be altered by human decree, makes a fine sound to modern ears, but fifth-century Greeks were not so well primed to hear it. More important, the unwritten laws occupy only half her speech to Kreon (450–60). The other half (460–70) is more specific and personal [. . .]. The Chorus' response to all this is that she is her father's daughter, all right, "raw" and stubborn (471 f.). This is not an endorsement of the unwritten laws, and it is not altogether complimentary to Antigone either. Like Kreon's rule, Antigone's defiance is a complex combination of principle and personality, and she is driven by will, pride, and family honor at least as much as by devotion to the unwritten laws.[1] The conflict is between two characters,

1. This deserves fuller discussion, for which I must refer the reader to Bongie [. . .] and Knox, inter alia. Bongie, 252 goes so far as to call the speech on the unwritten laws "a rationalization of the more compelling personal motives."

Kreon and Antigone, not between the principles of state and family, or human and divine law, to which they appeal.[2] It is more personal and thereby more dramatic, and neither comes off unscathed.

Kreon's scene with Haimon shows his weaknesses as a ruler to a higher degree.

• • •

Nestled in all Haimon's deference is one piece of information: the people of Thebes pity Antigone and support her (*Ant.* 692–700). [. . . P]opular opinion is beginning to tilt against Kreon.

Kreon, predictably, [. . .] reacts with rage and disbelief. His world is being turned upside down: a younger man is venturing to instruct an elder (*Ant.* 726 f.), Antigone is rebellious (730–2), the city is not submitting to its ruler (734–9). Perhaps worst of all, women are getting the better of men (740, 746, 756; the point has also appeared at 484 f., 525, 677–80). The world thus disturbed is actually that of the *polis* to a large degree; most Greeks in the audience would probably have been quite content with the idea that the young ought to submit to the old, people to authority, women to men.[3] But accepting a principle does not mean that we will automatically agree with everyone who invokes it. Kreon's nervous insistence on these principles begins to look like a sign of weakness, inflexibility, or even tyranny. He does not so much espouse civic norms as hide behind them.

The denouement of the play can be discussed more briefly, at least for the issues that concern us here. Antigone's kommos and final speech draw critical attention mostly for what they tell us about her, about her motives for defying Kreon and her feelings as she faces death. These are important questions, but for this enquiry it is worth stressing a simpler and more obvious point, what Kreon is doing to her. [. . .] Amid the many problems of this scene—whether the Chorus is sympathetic or aloof, what Antigone means in comparing herself to Niobe, why she values her brother over other kin—we are invited to grieve over her. This echoes in a different key something which we encountered in the prologue, when we saw at close range Antigone's grief and outrage over Kreon's edict. In both scenes, whatever we might think of the practice of throwing out traitors unburied, or of Antigone herself, we are invited to pity her.[4] Pity can be potent. The Thebans, Haimon tells us, grieved for Antigone [. . .] and so came to support her. The Chorus grieves in spite of Kreon's rulings[5] and does not break with him openly. We may turn our pity into a political position, like the Thebans, or decide not to, like the Chorus. Either way, we are invited again to contemplate the costs of Kreon's edict, and of his way of running the *polis*.

2. See inter alia Eberlein [. . .], passim; Else [. . .] 42; Hester [. . .] 40; Knox, 102–16.

3. [Vittorio] Citti[, *Strutture e tensioni sociali nell'*Antigone *di Sofocle*, AIV 134 (1975–76), 477–501] [. . .], 487–92 and [*Sofocle e le strutture di potere nell'Atene del V secolo*, BIFG 3 (1976), 84–120 at 103], passim; Sourvinou-Inwood, *Assumptions*, 138–40, 144 f.

4. Sourvinou-Inwood, *Bad Woman*, 17 notes the shift from portraying Antigone as a threatening rebellious woman earlier in the play to showing her as a pitiable bride of Hades here.

5. The Chorus says that they are "carried outside the *thesmoi*" ([. . .] 801 f.) upon seeing Antigone and are unable to restrain their tears. I take it that the *thesmoi* here are Kreon's (Jebb, Kamerbeek), whether his sentence against Antigone or his royal authority generally.

The costs become far more apparent in the Teiresias scene, when the seer first reports dire omens and disruptions in the kosmos and then announces that it is all because of Kreon. Kreon tries to make amends, but too late: three people die, and Kreon is left ruined.

The verdict of the gods is in at last, but as often, the verdict is plainer than the story leading up to it. We miss much of the story, and much of the achievement of the *Antigone*, if we make Kreon merely impious in issuing his proclamation and Antigone merely noble in defying him. As we have seen, Kreon starts in a stronger position, and one more in keeping with fifth-century values, than we often recognize. Consequently, the play takes on a larger task than we often recognize in making his ruin credible and satisfying. In succeeding, it is a better play than we often recognize—not only a great one, but a deft one as well. [. . .]

[. . .] the modern picture of Antigone as a heroic dissenter is not altogether wrong. Only we must recognize that the play does not generate sympathy for Antigone by appealing to any widely held notions about martyrs for causes or conscience against tyranny. Rather, it works by the way it arranges events and shades their presentation—perhaps even by manipulation. Antigone's distress and passion are given full play, her opponent is made to appear weak and foolish, and she and her allies get most of the good lines.[6] The play encourages the audience to root for a rebel against the values which they would likely espouse and practice in real life.

* * *

IV. TRAGEDY

If this reading of the play is reasonably close to the truth, then the *Antigone* does something which tragedy does generally. Defiance of the norms is part of its stock in trade. Tragedy is a "genre of transgression" and features an "interplay between norm and transgression"—an important part of the current lively discussion of drama in relation to the *polis*.[7] The *Antigone* presents quite a lot of transgression. Antigone's defiance of Kreon involves a degree of self-assertion and boldness which would be hard to find, perhaps even hard to conceive of, in a real-life Greek city, but her play lets the antisocial voice speak on stage and gives the audience reason to root for it in spite of itself.

6. A few "zingers": The doer grieves your mind, I grieve your ears (*Ant.* 319); I would have died even if you hadn't sentenced me (460f.); if my actions seem foolish, I'm accused of folly by a fool (469f.); there is no city which belongs to one man (737); you'd rule well over a desert alone (739); I speak for her—and you and me and the gods below (749). Kreon's only approach to pithiness (as distinguished from his usual maxim-spouting) is his declaration that one of his nieces has just lost her mind and the other never had any (561f.).

7. Quotes from Goldhill, [*The*] *Great Dionysia* [*and Civic Ideology*, in: John J. Winkler, Froma I. Zeitlin (ed.), *Nothing to Do with Dionysos? Athenian Drama in its Social Context* (Princeton 1990)], [. . .] 126 and 127, a basic study for delineating the paradox of anticivic discourse in a highly ordered civic setting. For the discussion more generally, a good starter bibliography would include the collections edited by Goff [. . .], Pelling [Christopher Pelling, *Greek Tragedy and the Historian* (Oxford 1997)], and Winkler and Zeitlin. [. . .]

SUGGESTIONS FOR WRITING

1. The first two scenes or episodes of ANTIGONE introduce us to each of the play's two main characters—first Antigone herself, then Creon. Write an essay in which you explore what each scene shows us about who these characters are, what motives and values drive them, and why they come into conflict. What does Sophocles achieve by showing us Antigone in conversation with her sister, or Creon with a "convocation of the elders" (line 177)? In terms of characterization and conflict, what is the significance of the choral songs that end each episode?
2. As is conventional in Greek drama, ANTIGONE ends with a final choral song that articulates the theme of the play, while also leaving a great deal of room for interpretation about just what that theme is. Drawing on evidence from the entire play, explain how we should interpret the final song and the play's theme.
3. Write an essay that draws on evidence from this ancient Greek play to explore precisely how and why it remains relevant to the world in which you live. Does ANTIGONE, for example, depict a type of person or a conflict still common in the twenty-first century, or might it articulate a theme that still applies?
4. Many of the critical excerpts in this chapter focus on the conflict between Antigone and Creon, debating not only how that conflict is ultimately resolved but also what the nature of the conflict is. To take just two examples, Richard C. Jebb takes the conflict to be one between *"the duty of obeying the State's laws"* and *"the duty of listening to the private conscience,"* while Maurice Bowra implies that the conflict is instead between duty to the laws of man versus those of the gods and/or between the human tendency toward "arrogance" versus the need for humility and reverence. Carefully read the other critical excerpts in the chapter, working to understand how each characterizes the conflict between Creon and Antigone. Then, write an essay in which you first describe the views of all the critics and then draw on evidence from the play either to defend one of these views or to offer an alternative interpretation of the conflict between Antigone and Creon.
5. Though he acknowledges that ANTIGONE depicts an external conflict between Antigone and Creon and the views and values each represents, Bernard Knox suggests that the play also presents Creon as internally conflicted. Carefully read the excerpt from Knox's introduction, and write an essay exploring whether the play supports his interpretation of Creon's internal conflict and its resolution.
6. Re-read the critical excerpts in this chapter and then make a list of at least three moments in ANTIGONE or aspects or elements of the play that strike you as important, but that aren't given adequate attention in the critical excerpts. Then write an essay that explains why any one of these moments, aspects, or elements is especially important to the play's effect and meaning.

SAMPLE WRITING: RESEARCH ESSAY

The student essay below was written in response to an assignment that asked students to draw on at least five works of literary criticism, including any relevant excerpts in this chapter and at least one journal article *not* included here, in order to develop their own interpretations of any aspect of ANTIGONE. Student writer Jackie Izawa decided to explore rival interpretations of Antigone's treatment of her siblings and her fiancé. The resulting essay demonstrates unusual strengths and a few common problems, particularly in the way it uses, presents, and quotes from both primary and secondary sources. The instructor's comments that accompany the essay highlight some of those strengths and weaknesses.

Perhaps the weakest moment in the essay is a conclusion that does not fulfill the promise made in the introduction that the essay will ultimately "draw a conclusion" about Antigone's motives. The simplest way to fix that inconsistency would be to change the thesis statement so that it matches up with the conclusion and to devote the conclusion to discussing why it's so "essential that we consider different perspectives" and interpretations rather than simply endorsing one. What might the play itself say about that issue, particularly through Haemon's remarks to his father?

Izawa 1

Jackie Izawa
Dr. Mays
ENG 298X
15 January 2017

The Two Faces of Antigone

Antigone's strong yet harsh nature motivates her to defy Creon's edict, but it also isolates her from those who love her. Throughout the play, Antigone tries to convince Creon that her fallen brother, Polyneices, deserves a proper burial. Her unwavering loyalty to her brother shows she might be capable of love. But if so, why does she only seem to love the person who's dead before the play even begins? She barely shows any affection for her only living sibling, Ismene, and none for her betrothed, Haemon. It is possible that Antigone is so overwhelmed by a desire for justice for her brother that she becomes blinded to every other person. The other possibility is that she is creating the illusion that she does not love Ismene and Haemon because she wants to spare them. "Namely, that although now Antigone does not mean to be stern and hard, as she is simply being herself, yet all the same she *is* stern and hard" (Simpson and Millar 79). Before drawing a conclusion about Antigone's motives, it is important to recognize and acknowledge both positions.

Introduce quotations from sources with a signal phrase that provides the information about the source necessary to understand the quotation and its relationship to your statement. Is Simpson endorsing one of the two possible interpretations you've just offered of Antigone, or does the statement suggest a third possibility? Also, make sure that the quotation makes sense on its own. The sentence fragment you quote here is confusing.

Ismene is Antigone's opposite in every way, in W. H. D. Rouse's words, "a nice girl, soft-hearted and devoted, but a shadow of her strong sister" (41). In the opening scene of *Antigone*, the two sisters have just heard of Creon's edict, and both have different opinions about how to handle it. While Antigone is set on burying her brother, Ismene tries to reason with her. She recalls all the horrible events that happened in their family history. First Oedipus "himself struck out / the sight of his two eyes," and then his wife and mother "did shame / violently on her life, with twisted cords" (lines 58-59, 61-62). Ismene continues talking about the family's tragedies, ending with the deaths of her brothers. Both sisters know that the sentence for burying Polyneices is death. Ismene does not want herself or Antigone to follow in the steps of her deceased family members or to "put dishonor on them" by defying Creon (line 90). Ismene is timid and fearful of breaking the law. By nature, Ismene is submissive. She views herself as an obedient woman, a compliant citizen. Naturally, when Antigone asks for Ismene's help in burying their brother, Ismene declines. Ismene would like to bury her brother, but she cannot break the law. She tells Antigone, "to act in defiance of the citizenry, / my nature does not give me means for that" (lines 91-92).

You provide good evidence from your primary source to support your claims about Ismene's natural reluctance to defy the law, but none to back up your other claim—that her reluctance is also due to her sense of her particular position and duties "as an obedient woman."

In the play's very first line, Antigone calls Ismene "my dear sister." But this is the first and only time that Antigone shows affection for Ismene. Because Ismene is afraid to go against Creon's edict, Antigone

Izawa 3

regards Ismene as a coward and disowns her. Immediately, Antigone verbally attacks her sister, showing that she is unable to view things as others do: "At least he is my brother—and yours, too, / though you deny him. *I* will not prove false to him" (lines 51-52). The emphasis on the "*I*" shows that Antigone feels a degree of rivalry. It is likely she feels that because *she* is determined to bury Polyneices, she is better than Ismene. This kind of rivalry is common between siblings even today. The idea of proving your superiority is always attractive, especially if you can demonstrate it publicly, to an entire city. Antigone is rather cruel and ruthless to her sister, whether out of pure anger, rivalry, or pain at her betrayal of the family. Towards the end of their first encounter, Ismene promises that she will keep silent, but Antigone retorts, "Oh, oh, no! shout it out. I will hate you still worse / for silence—should you not proclaim it, / to everyone" (lines 99-101). Despite all that both of them have endured because of their shared family history, Antigone is willing to throw it away when Ismene does not help her:

> If you will talk like this I will loathe you,
> and you will be adjudged an enemy—
> justly—by the dead's decision. Let me alone
> and my folly with me, to endure this terror.
> No suffering of mine will be enough
> to make me die ignobly. (lines 109-14)

Interesting observation! Does this introduce a third possible interpretation of Antigone (in addition to the two you introduce early on)?

What exactly do you mean to demonstrate with this quotation? Does this provide evidence for your point about Antigone's desire to publicly demonstrate her superiority? or the point about her cruelty? or something else?

The two sisters are seen together only briefly later in the play, but the dynamic between them is much the same. After Antigone attempts to bury Polyneices and both sisters are brought to Creon, Antigone lashes out at Ismene, effectively severing any ties she has with her sister. As Charles Levy argues, "in [a . . .] tense stichomythic exchange with Ismene" shortly after her argument with Creon, "she reacts with still greater vehemence than during their earlier encounter to what she regards as her sister's irremediable betrayal of her, scorning Ismene . . ." (142). Ismene wants to share the sentence of death with her sister,

This quotation from your secondary source consists mainly of plot summary. It would be more effective to describe the action yourself, while acknowledging that Levy, too, notes its importance.

Izawa 4

pleading, "Sister, do not dishonor me, denying me / a common death with you, a common honoring / of the dead man." But Antigone refuses to listen, saying, "Don't die with me, nor make your own / what you have never touched" (lines 597-601). Antigone is consistently cold towards her sister.

Showing the same consistency (in the opposite way), Ismene seems to disregard the ill treatment she receives from her sister, continuing to show love for Antigone though Ismene knows that she is no longer welcome in Antigone's eyes. Being the compassionate and devoted sister that she is, Ismene still does her best to save Antigone. Even after being rejected, Ismene tries to reason with Creon. She pleads again that her life would be incomplete without Antigone. When Creon refuses to change his mind, Ismene brings up Haemon, hoping that Creon is not cruel enough to execute his future daughter-in-law. Unfortunately, even that does not budge Creon. Ismene is loving and caring, showing as much loyalty to her sister as Antigone does for their brother, but Ismene's gesture is never acknowledged.

Or might Antigone in fact be making a gesture of love even greater than her sister's? As A. W. Simpson and C. M. H. Millar argue, Antigone's treatment of Ismene could in fact be viewed as liberating Ismene or saving her from death (79). They believe that Antigone is brutal with Ismene because she is "unwillingly" putting up a façade for Creon (80). One of the main driving factors in their argument is the irony in Antigone's decision: "The *irony* of the situation is brought out, because, from love for Ismene, Antigone alienates herself from her, in order to save her, and goes to her death thinking she has failed; and she never finds out that she succeeded after all" (80).

What evidence from your primary text supports this claim, and what do you think of it? Remember that quoting a critic's interpretive claim isn't enough to prove the claim valid.

Likewise, there are also two different ways of interpreting Antigone's interaction with her betrothed. Haemon, from the first moment he is introduced, immediately sides with Antigone and is completely devoted to her. He defends his wife-to-be and defies his father, Creon, ironically with as much passion as Antigone shows. When he first appears in the play, he is naturally dedicated to his father. He shows that he respects his father, but at the same time he also reasons with Creon both about the rule of the city and about the punishment of Antigone:

> Haemon: You will not find me yield to what is shameful.
>
> Creon: At least, your argument is all for her.
>
> Haemon: Yes, and for you and me—and for the gods below.
>
> Creon: You will never marry her while her life lasts.
>
> Haemon: Then she must die—and dying destroy another. (lines 804-08)

Haemon is showing his devotion to Antigone as well as foreshadowing his own fate in the play. Even though Creon tells him he can find another wife, Haemon refuses. His love for Antigone dooms him to his death. All of his actions following his argument with his father are undertaken for Antigone. When Haemon finds Antigone dead in the cave, he is consumed with rage and anger. As Walter H. Johns puts it, because "Haemon hears his father's voice and realizes that the cause of all his grief is close at hand," he "turn[s] his sword against himself and d[ies] with his arms about the body of Antigone" (100). Haemon's rage is likely equivalent to his love for Antigone, and for him to kill himself because of his grief over her death only supports this likelihood.

Again, this section seems a bit light on evidence (versus secondary source material), while the latter consists of plot summary.

The reader empathizes with and even pities Haemon because although he speaks of great affection for Antigone, she does not do the same for him. In fact, as Martha Nussbaum points out, "Antigone never [even] addresses a word throughout the entire play" to this "man who passionately loves and desires her" (1596). And Antigone says his name only once in the play when she responds to Creon, "Dear Haemon, how your father dishonors you" (line 627). Though "dear" is usually a term of endearment, the context in which it is used and Antigone's silence about Haemon

Great point! Is it one any other critic makes as well?

in the rest of the play suggest that she says it in a pitying manner. Perhaps she felt sympathy for Haemon because he had a father who was willing to kill the love of his life, but that's not the same as loving him as he does her. The relationship is completely one-sided, and Antigone's lack of affection for her betrothed seems to give a new kind of meaning to Ismene's remark much earlier in the play that her sister is "in love / with the impossible" (lines 104-05). Antigone does seem to be more in love with the idea of burying her brother than she is with Haemon.

Again, though, is hard-heartedness or single-heartedness the only explanation for Antigone's behavior? Some critics argue that it isn't, that Antigone's lack of attention to Haemon is inspired by her desire to ensure that he does not share her fate. She could very well love him, but because she is sentenced to death, she breaks off ties with him. Simpson and Millar, for example, conclude that "Antigone has broken the ties between herself and her sister, in order to save her, and is now completely alone in the world. Haemon cannot reach her, as far as she knows, because Creon has just forbidden the marriage" (80). Perhaps Antigone realized that she and Haemon would never have a happy marriage, so she let him go. Unfortunately, Haemon does not realize her intentions.

The true motive behind Antigone's actions will always be debated. There are always at least two sides to everything, and it is essential that we consider different perspectives. Antigone can be viewed as hard-hearted and cruel, able to cut herself off from those who love and cherish her. However, she can also be seen as the type of heroine who does everything for the greater good of those she is closest to. In this view, she is compassionate, loyal, and unafraid to make sacrifices. Either way, Antigone remains a heroine who has made a huge impact not only on other characters in the play, but on those who read it as well.

Izawa 7

Works Cited

Johns, Walter H. "Dramatic Effect in Sophocles' Antigone 1232." *Classical Journal*, vol. 43, no. 2, 1947, pp. 99-100. *JSTOR*, www.jstor.org/stable/3293075.

Levy, Charles S. "Antigone's Motives: A Suggested Interpretation." *Transactions and Proceedings of the American Philological Association*, no. 94, 1963, pp. 137-44. *JSTOR*, www.jstor.org/stable/283641.

Mays, Kelly J., editor. *The Norton Introduction to Literature*. 12th ed., W. W. Norton, 2017.

Nussbaum, Martha C. "From *The Fragility of Goodness: Luck and Ethics in Greek Tragedy and Philosophy*." Mays, pp. 1594-99.

Rouse, W. H. D. "The Two Burials in *Antigone*." *Classical Review*, vol. 25, no. 2, 1911, pp. 40-42. *JSTOR*, www.jstor.org/stable/694563.

Simpson, A. W., and C. M. H. Millar. "A Note on Sophocles' *Antigone*, Lines 531-81." *Greece & Rome*, vol. 17, no. 50, 1948, pp. 78-81. *JSTOR*, www.jstor.org/stable/641167.

Sophocles. *Antigone*. Mays, pp. 1551-83.

Reading More Drama

ANTON CHEKHOV
(1860–1904)
The Cherry Orchard[1]

The son of a grocer and the grandson of an emancipated serf, Anton Pavlovich Chekhov was born in the Russian town of Taganrog. In 1875, his father, facing bankruptcy and imprisonment, fled to Moscow; shortly thereafter, the rest of the family lost their house to a former friend and lodger, a misfortune that Chekhov would revisit in *The Cherry Orchard.* In 1884, Chekhov received his MD from the University of Moscow; in the early 1890s, he purchased an estate near Moscow and became both an industrious landowner and a doctor to the local peasants. Throughout the 1880s, he supported his family and financed his medical studies by writing the sketches and stories that would eventually win him enduring international acclaim. Chekhov began writing for the stage in 1887. Early productions of his plays were poorly received: *The Wood Demon* (later rewritten as *Uncle Vanya*) was performed only a few times in 1889 before closing; the 1896 premiere of *The Seagull* turned into a riot when an audience expecting comedy found themselves watching an experimental tragedy. Konstantin Stanislavsky, director at the Moscow Art Theater, helped restore Chekhov's reputation with successful productions of *The Seagull* and *Uncle Vanya* in 1899, *The Three Sisters* in 1901, and *The Cherry Orchard* in 1904.

CHARACTERS IN THE PLAY

MADAME RANEVSKY (LYUBOV ANDREYEVNA), *the owner of the Cherry Orchard*
ANYA, *her daughter, aged 17*
VARYA, *her adopted daughter, aged 24*
SEMYONOV-PISHTCHIK, *a landowner*
CHARLOTTA IVANOVNA, *a governess*
EPIHODOV (SEMYON PANTALEYEVITCH), *a clerk*
DUNYASHA, *a maid*
FIRS, *an old valet, aged 87*
GAEV (LEONID ANDREYEVITCH), *brother of Madame Ranevsky*
LOPAHIN (YERMOLAY ALEXEYEVITCH), *a merchant*
TROFIMOV (PYOTR SERGEYEVITCH), *a student*
YASHA, *a young valet*
A WAYFARER
THE STATION MASTER
A POST-OFFICE CLERK
VISITORS, SERVANTS

The action takes place on the estate of MADAME RANEVSKY.

1. Translated by Constance Garnett.

ACT I

A room, which has always been called the nursery. One of the doors leads into ANYA'S *room. Dawn, sun rises during the scene. May, the cherry trees in flower, but it is cold in the garden with the frost of early morning. Windows closed.*

Enter DUNYASHA *with a candle and* LOPAHIN *with a book in his hand.*

LOPAHIN: The train's in, thank God. What time is it?

DUNYASHA: Nearly two o'clock. [*Puts out the candle.*] It's daylight already.

LOPAHIN: The train's late! Two hours, at least. [*Yawns and stretches.*] I'm a pretty one; what a fool I've been. Came here on purpose to meet them at the station and dropped asleep. . . . Dozed off as I sat in the chair. It's annoying. . . . You might have waked me.

DUNYASHA: I thought you had gone. [*Listens.*] There, I do believe they're coming!

LOPAHIN: [*Listens.*] No, what with the luggage and one thing and another. [*A pause.*] Lyubov Andreyevna has been abroad five years; I don't know what she is like now. . . . She's a splendid woman. A good-natured, kind-hearted woman. I remember when I was a lad of fifteen, my poor father—he used to keep a little shop here in the village in those days—gave me a punch in the face with his fist and made my nose bleed. We were in the yard here, I forget what we'd come about—he had had a drop. Lyubov Andreyevna—I can see her now—she was a slim young girl then—took me to wash my face, and then brought me into this very room, into the nursery. "Don't cry, little peasant," says she, "it will be well in time for your wedding day." . . . [*A pause.*] Little peasant. . . . My father was a peasant, it's true, but here am I in a white waistcoat and brown shoes, like a pig in a bun shop. Yes, I'm a rich man, but for all my money, come to think, a peasant I was, and a peasant I am. [*Turns over the pages of the book.*] I've been reading this book and I can't make head or tail of it. I fell asleep over it. [*A pause.*]

DUNYASHA: The dogs have been awake all night, they feel that the mistress is coming.

LOPAHIN: Why, what's the matter with you, Dunyasha?

DUNYASHA: My hands are all of a tremble. I feel as though I should faint.

LOPAHIN: You're a spoilt soft creature, Dunyasha. And dressed like a lady too, and your hair done up. That's not the thing. One must know one's place.

[*Enter* EPIHODOV *with a nosegay;*[2] *he wears a pea-jacket and highly polished creaking topboots; he drops the nosegay as he comes in.*]

EPIHODOV: [*Picking up the nosegay.*] Here! the gardener's sent this, says you're to put it in the dining-room. [*Gives* DUNYASHA *the nosegay.*]

LOPAHIN: And bring me some kvass.[3]

DUNYASHA: I will. [*Goes out.*]

EPIHODOV: It's chilly this morning, three degrees of frost,[4] though the cherries are all in flower. I can't say much for our climate. [*Sighs.*] I can't. Our climate is not often propitious to the occasion. Yermolay Alexeyevitch, permit me to call your attention to the fact that I purchased myself a pair of boots the day

2. Bouquet. 3. Weak homemade beer. 4. That is, 29°F (–2°C).

before yesterday, and they creak, I venture to assure you, so that there's no tolerating them. What ought I to grease them with?

LOPAHIN: Oh, shut up! Don't bother me.

EPIHODOV: Every day some misfortune befalls me. I don't complain, I'm used to it, and I wear a smiling face.

[DUNYASHA *comes in, hands* LOPAHIN *the kvass.*]

EPIHODOV: I am going. [*Stumbles against a chair, which falls over.*] There! [*As though triumphant.*] There you see now, excuse the expression, an accident like that among others. . . . It's positively remarkable. [*Goes out.*]

DUNYASHA: Do you know, Yermolay Alexeyevitch, I must confess, Epihodov has made me a proposal.

LOPAHIN: Ah!

DUNYASHA: I'm sure I don't know. . . . He's a harmless fellow, but sometimes when he begins talking, there's no making anything of it. It's all very fine and expressive, only there's no understanding it. I've a sort of liking for him too. He loves me to distraction. He's an unfortunate man; every day there's something. They tease him about it—two and twenty misfortunes they call him.

LOPAHIN: [*Listening.*] There! I do believe they're coming.

DUNYASHA: They are coming! What's the matter with me? . . . I'm cold all over.

LOPAHIN: They really are coming. Let's go and meet them. Will she know me? It's five years since I saw her.

DUNYASHA: [*In a flutter.*] I shall drop this very minute. . . . Ah, I shall drop.

[*There is a sound of two carriages driving up to the house.* LOPAHIN *and* DUNYASHA *go out quickly. The stage is left empty. A noise is heard in the adjoining rooms.* FIRS, *who has driven to meet* MADAME RANEVSKY, *crosses the stage hurriedly leaning on a stick. He is wearing old-fashioned livery and a high hat. He says something to himself, but not a word can be distinguished. The noise behind the scenes goes on increasing. A voice: "Come, let's go in here." Enter* LYUBOV ANDREYEVNA, ANYA, *and* CHARLOTTA IVANOVNA *with a pet dog on a chain, all in traveling dresses.* VARYA *in an outdoor coat with a kerchief over her head,* GAEV, SEMYONOV-PISHTCHIK, LOPAHIN, DUNYASHA *with bag and parasol, servants with other articles. All walk across the room.*]

ANYA: Let's come in here. Do you remember what room this is, mamma?

LYUBOV: [*Joyfully, through her tears.*] The nursery!

VARYA: How cold it is, my hands are numb. [*To* LYUBOV ANDREYEVNA.] Your rooms, the white room and the lavender one, are just the same as ever, mamma.

LYUBOV: My nursery, dear delightful room. . . . I used to sleep here when I was little. . . . [*Cries.*] And here I am, like a little child. . . . [*Kisses her brother and* VARYA, *and then her brother again.*] Varya's just the same as ever, like a nun. And I knew Dunyasha. [*Kisses* DUNYASHA.]

GAEV: The train was two hours late. What do you think of that? Is that the way to do things?

CHARLOTTA: [*To* PISHTCHIK.] My dog eats nuts, too.

PISHTCHIK: [*Wonderingly.*] Fancy that!

[*They all go out except* ANYA *and* DUNYASHA.]

DUNYASHA: We've been expecting you so long. [*Takes* ANYA'*s hat and coat.*]

ANYA: I haven't slept for four nights on the journey. I feel dreadfully cold.

DUNYASHA: You set out in Lent, there was snow and frost, and now? My darling! [*Laughs and kisses her.*] I *have* missed you, my precious, my joy. I must tell you . . . I can't put it off a minute. . . .

ANYA: [*Wearily.*] What now?

DUNYASHA: Epihodov, the clerk, made me a proposal just after Easter.

ANYA: It's always the same thing with you. . . . [*Straightening her hair.*] I've lost all my hairpins. . . . [*She is staggering from exhaustion.*]

DUNYASHA: I don't know what to think, really. He does love me, he does love me so!

ANYA: [*Looking towards her door, tenderly.*] My own room, my windows just as though I had never gone away. I'm home! To-morrow morning I shall get up and run into the garden. . . . Oh, if I could get to sleep! I haven't slept all the journey, I was so anxious and worried.

DUNYASHA: Pyotr Sergeyevitch came the day before yesterday.

ANYA: [*Joyfully.*] Petya!

DUNYASHA: He's asleep in the bath house, he has settled in there. I'm afraid of being in their way, says he. [*Glancing at her watch.*] I was to have waked him, but Varvara Mihalovna told me not to. Don't you wake him, says she.

[*Enter* VARYA *with a bunch of keys at her waist.*]

VARYA: Dunyasha, coffee and make haste. . . . Mamma's asking for coffee.

DUNYASHA: This very minute. [*Goes out.*]

VARYA: Well, thank God, you've come. You're home again. [*Petting her.*] My little darling has come back! My precious beauty has come back again!

ANYA: I have had a time of it!

VARYA: I can fancy.

ANYA: We set off in Holy Week—it was so cold then, and all the way Charlotta would talk and show off her tricks. What did you want to burden me with Charlotta for?

VARYA: You couldn't have traveled all alone, darling. At seventeen!

ANYA: We got to Paris at last, it was cold there—snow. I speak French shockingly. Mamma lives on the fifth floor, I went up to her and there were a lot of French people, ladies, an old priest with a book. The place smelt of tobacco and so comfortless. I felt sorry, oh! so sorry for mamma all at once, I put my arms round her neck, and hugged her and wouldn't let her go. Mamma was as kind as she could be, and she cried. . . .

VARYA: [*Through her tears.*] Don't speak of it, don't speak of it!

ANYA: She had sold her villa at Mentone, she had nothing left, nothing. I hadn't a farthing left either, we only just had enough to get here. And mamma doesn't understand! When we had dinner at the stations, she always ordered the most expensive things and gave the waiters a whole rouble. Charlotta's just the same. Yasha too must have the same as we do; it's simply awful. You know Yasha is mamma's valet now, we brought him here with us.

VARYA: Yes, I've seen the young rascal.

ANYA: Well, tell me—have you paid the arrears on the mortgage?

VARYA: How could we get the money?

ANYA: Oh, dear! Oh, dear!

VARYA: In August the place will be sold.

ANYA: My goodness!

LOPAHIN: [*Peeps in at the door and moos like a cow.*] Moo! [*Disappears.*]

VARYA: [*Weeping.*] There, that's what I could do to him. [*Shakes her fist.*]

ANYA: [*Embracing* VARYA, *softly.*] Varya, has he made you an offer? [VARYA *shakes her head.*] Why, but he loves you. Why is it you don't come to an understanding? What are you waiting for?

VARYA: I believe that there never will be anything between us. He has a lot to do, he has no time for me . . . and takes no notice of me. Bless the man, it makes me miserable to see him. . . . Everyone's talking of our being married, everyone's congratulating me, and all the while there's really nothing in it; it's all like a dream. [*In another tone.*] You have a new brooch like a bee.

ANYA: [*Mournfully.*] Mamma bought it. [*Goes into her own room and in a lighthearted childish tone.*] And you know, in Paris I went up in a balloon!

VARYA: My darling's home again! My pretty is home again!

[DUNYASHA *returns with the coffee-pot and is making the coffee.*]

VARYA: [*Standing at the door.*] All day long, darling, as I go about looking after the house, I keep dreaming all the time. If only we could marry you to a rich man, then I should feel more at rest. Then I would go off by myself on a pilgrimage to Kiev, to Moscow . . . and so I would spend my life going from one holy place to another. . . . I would go on and on. . . . What bliss!

ANYA: The birds are singing in the garden. What time is it?

VARYA: It must be nearly three. It's time you were asleep, darling. [*Going into* ANYA'*s room.*] What bliss!

[YASHA *enters with a rug and a traveling bag.*]

YASHA: [*Crosses the stage, mincingly.*] May one come in here, pray?

DUNYASHA: I shouldn't have known you, Yasha. How you have changed abroad.

YASHA: H'm! . . . And who are you?

DUNYASHA: When you went away, I was that high. [*Shows distance from floor.*] Dunyasha, Fyodor's daughter. . . . You don't remember me!

YASHA: H'm! . . . You're a peach! [*Looks round and embraces her: she shrieks and drops a saucer.* YASHA *goes out hastily.*]

VARYA: [*In the doorway, in a tone of vexation.*] What now?

DUNYASHA: [*Through her tears.*] I have broken a saucer.

VARYA: Well, that brings good luck.

ANYA: [*Coming out of her room.*] We ought to prepare mamma: Petya is here.

VARYA: I told them not to wake him.

ANYA: [*Dreamily.*] It's six years since father died. Then only a month later little brother Grisha was drowned in the river, such a pretty boy he was, only seven. It was more than mamma could bear, so she went away, went away without looking back. [*Shuddering.*] . . . How well I understand her, if only she knew! [*A pause.*] And Petya Trofimov was Grisha's tutor, he may remind her.

[*Enter* FIRS: *he is wearing a pea-jacket and a white waistcoat.*]

FIRS: [*Goes up to the coffee-pot, anxiously.*] The mistress will be served here. [*Puts on white gloves.*] Is the coffee ready? [*Sternly to* DUNYASHA.] Girl! Where's the cream?

DUNYASHA: Ah, mercy on us! [*Goes out quickly.*]

FIRS: [*Fussing round the coffee-pot.*] Ech! you good-for-nothing! [*Muttering to himself.*] Come back from Paris. And the old master used to go to Paris too . . . horses all the way. [*Laughs.*]

VARYA: What is it, Firs?

FIRS: What is your pleasure? [*Gleefully.*] My lady has come home! I have lived to see her again! Now I can die. [*Weeps with joy.*]

[*Enter* LYUBOV ANDREYEVNA, GAEV *and* SEMYONOV-PISHTCHIK; *the latter is in a short-waisted full coat of fine cloth, and full trousers.* GAEV, *as he comes in, makes a gesture with his arms and his whole body, as though he were playing billiards.*]

LYUBOV: How does it go? Let me remember. Cannon off the red!

GAEV: That's it—in off the white! Why, once, sister, we used to sleep together in this very room, and now I'm fifty-one, strange as it seems.

LOPAHIN: Yes, time flies.

GAEV: What do you say?

LOPAHIN: Time, I say, flies.

GAEV: What a smell of patchouli!

ANYA: I'm going to bed. Good-night, mamma. [*Kisses her mother.*]

LYUBOV: My precious darling. [*Kisses her hands.*] Are you glad to be home? I can't believe it.

ANYA: Good-night, uncle.

GAEV: [*Kissing her face and hands.*] God bless you! How like you are to your mother! [*To his sister.*] At her age you were just the same, Lyuba.

[ANYA *shakes hands with* LOPAHIN *and* PISHTCHIK, *then goes out, shutting the door after her.*]

LYUBOV: She's quite worn out.

PISHTCHIK: Aye, it's a long journey, to be sure.

VARYA: [*To* LOPAHIN *and* PISHTCHIK.] Well, gentlemen? It's three o'clock and time to say good-bye.

LYUBOV: [*Laughs.*] You're just the same as ever, Varya. [*Draws her to her and kisses her.*] I'll just drink my coffee and then we will all go and rest. [FIRS *puts a cushion under her feet.*] Thanks, friend. I am so fond of coffee, I drink it day and night. Thanks, dear old man. [*Kisses* FIRS.]

VARYA: I'll just see whether all the things have been brought in. [*Goes out.*]

LYUBOV: Can it really be me sitting here? [*Laughs.*] I want to dance about and clap my hands. [*Covers her face with her hands.*] And I could drop asleep in a moment! God knows I love my country, I love it tenderly; I couldn't look out of the window in the train, I kept crying so. [*Through her tears.*] But I must drink my coffee, though. Thank you, Firs, thanks, dear old man. I'm so glad to find you still alive.

FIRS: The day before yesterday.

GAEV: He's rather deaf.

LOPAHIN: I have to set off for Harkov[5] directly, at five o'clock. . . . It is annoying! I wanted to have a look at you, and a little talk. . . . You are just as splendid as ever.

PISHTCHIK: [*Breathing heavily.*] Handsomer, indeed. . . . Dressed in Parisian style . . . completely bowled me over.

LOPAHIN: Your brother, Leonid Andreyevitch here, is always saying that I'm a low-born knave, that I'm a money-grubber, but I don't care one straw for that. Let him talk. Only I do want you to believe in me as you used to. I do want your wonderful tender eyes to look at me as they used to in the old days. Merciful God! My father was a serf of your father and of your grandfather, but you—you—did so much for me once, that I've forgotten all that; I love you as though you were my kin . . . more than my kin.

LYUBOV: I can't sit still, I simply can't. . . . [*Jumps up and walks about in violent agitation.*] This happiness is too much for me. . . . You may laugh at me, I know I'm silly. . . . My own bookcase. [*Kisses the bookcase.*] My little table.

GAEV: Nurse died while you were away.

LYUBOV: [*Sits down and drinks coffee.*] Yes, the Kingdom of Heaven be hers! You wrote me of her death.

GAEV: And Anastasy is dead. Squinting Petruchka has left me and is in service now with the police captain in the town. [*Takes a box of caramels out of his pocket and sucks one.*]

PISHTCHIK: My daughter, Dashenka, wishes to be remembered to you.

LOPAHIN: I want to tell you something very pleasant and cheering. [*Glancing at his watch.*] I'm going directly . . . there's no time to say much . . . well, I can say it in a couple of words. I needn't tell you your cherry orchard is to be sold to pay your debts; the 22nd of August is the date fixed for the sale; but don't you worry, dearest lady, you may sleep in peace, there is a way of saving it. . . . This is what I propose. I beg your attention! Your estate is not twenty miles from the town, the railway runs close by it, and if the cherry orchard and the land along the river bank were cut up into building plots and then let on lease for summer villas, you would make an income of at least 25,000 roubles a year out of it.[6]

GAEV: That's all rot, if you'll excuse me.

LYUBOV: I don't quite understand you, Yermolay Alexeyevitch.

LOPAHIN: You will get a rent of at least 25 roubles a year for a three-acre plot from summer visitors, and if you say the word now, I'll bet you what you like there won't be one square foot of ground vacant by the autumn, all the plots will be taken up. I congratulate you; in fact, you are saved. It's a perfect situation with that deep river. Only, of course, it must be cleared—all the old buildings, for example, must be removed, this house too, which is really good for nothing and the old cherry orchard must be cut down.

LYUBOV: Cut down? My dear fellow, forgive me, but you don't know what you are talking about. If there is one thing interesting—remarkable indeed—in the whole province, it's just our cherry orchard.

5. Kharkov, the second-largest city in Ukraine, was part of the Russian Empire at the time of the play.
6. Nearly $500,000 per year in today's U.S. currency; a rental fee of 25 roubles is the equivalent of about $500.

LOPAHIN: The only thing remarkable about the orchard is that it's a very large one. There's a crop of cherries every alternate year, and then there's nothing to be done with them, no one buys them.

GAEV: This orchard is mentioned in the *Encyclopædia*.[7]

LOPAHIN: [*Glancing at his watch.*] If we don't decide on something and don't take some steps, on the 22nd of August the cherry orchard and the whole estate too will be sold by auction. Make up your minds! There is no other way of saving it, I'll take my oath on that. No, no!

FIRS: In old days, forty or fifty years ago, they used to dry the cherries, soak them, pickle them, make jam too, and they used—

GAEV: Be quiet, Firs.

FIRS: And they used to send the preserved cherries to Moscow and to Harkov by the wagon-load. That brought the money in! And the preserved cherries in those days were soft and juicy, sweet and fragrant. . . . They knew the way to do them then. . . .

LYUBOV: And where is the recipe now?

FIRS: It's forgotten. Nobody remembers it.

PISHTCHIK: [*To* LYUBOV ANDREYEVNA.] What's it like in Paris? Did you eat frogs there?

LYUBOV: Oh, I ate crocodiles.

PISHTCHIK: Fancy that now!

LOPAHIN: There used to be only the gentlefolks and the peasants in the country, but now there are these summer visitors. All the towns, even the small ones, are surrounded nowadays by these summer villas. And one may say for sure, that in another twenty years there'll be many more of these people and that they'll be everywhere. At present the summer visitor only drinks tea in his verandah, but maybe he'll take to working his bit of land too, and then your cherry orchard would become happy, rich, and prosperous. . . .

GAEV: [*Indignant.*] What rot!

[*Enter* VARYA *and* YASHA.]

VARYA: There are two telegrams for you, mamma. [*Takes out keys and opens an old-fashioned bookcase with a loud crack.*] Here they are.

LYUBOV: From Paris. [*Tears the telegrams, without reading them.*] I have done with Paris.

GAEV: Do you know, Lyuba, how old that bookcase is? Last week I pulled out the bottom drawer and there I found the date branded on it. The bookcase was made just a hundred years ago. What do you say to that? We might have celebrated its jubilee. Though it's an inanimate object, still it is a *book* case.

PISHTCHIK: [*Amazed.*] A hundred years! Fancy that now.

GAEV: Yes. . . . It is a thing. . . . [*Feeling the bookcase.*] Dear, honored, bookcase! Hail to thee who for more than a hundred years hast served the pure ideals of good and justice; thy silent call to fruitful labor has never flagged in those hundred years, maintaining [*In tears.*] in the generations of man, courage and

7. Perhaps the *Great Russian Encyclopedic Dictionary*, an authoritative eighty-six-volume reference work edited by Brockhaus and Efron.

faith in a brighter future and fostering in us ideals of good and social consciousness. [*A pause.*]

LOPAHIN: Yes. . . .

LYUBOV: You are just the same as ever, Leonid.

GAEV: [*A little embarrassed.*] Cannon off the right into the pocket!

LOPAHIN: [*Looking at his watch.*] Well, it's time I was off.

YASHA: [*Handing* LYUBOV ANDREYEVNA *medicine.*] Perhaps you will take your pills now.

PISHTCHIK: You shouldn't take medicines, my dear madam . . . they do no harm and no good. Give them here . . . honored lady. [*Takes the pill-box, pours the pills into the hollow of his hand, blows on them, puts them in his mouth and drinks off some kvass.*] There!

LYUBOV: [*In alarm.*] Why, you must be out of your mind!

PISHTCHIK: I have taken all the pills.

LOPAHIN: What a glutton! [*All laugh.*]

FIRS: His honor stayed with us in Easter week, ate a gallon and a half of cucumbers. . . . [*Mutters.*]

LYUBOV: What is he saying?

VARYA: He has taken to muttering like that for the last three years. We are used to it.

YASHA: His declining years!

[CHARLOTTA IVANOVNA, *a very thin, lanky figure in a white dress with a lorgnette in her belt, walks across the stage.*]

LOPAHIN: I beg your pardon, Charlotta Ivanovna, I have not had time to greet you. [*Tries to kiss her hand.*]

CHARLOTTA: [*Pulling away her hand.*] If I let you kiss my hand, you'll be wanting to kiss my elbow, and then my shoulder.

LOPAHIN: I've no luck to-day! [*All laugh.*] Charlotta Ivanovna, show us some tricks!

LYUBOV: Charlotta, do show us some tricks!

CHARLOTTA: I don't want to. I'm sleepy. [*Goes out.*]

LOPAHIN: In three weeks' time we shall meet again. [*Kisses* LYUBOV ANDREYEVNA'S *hand.*] Good-bye till then—I must go. [*To* GAEV.] Good-bye. [*Kisses* PISHTCHIK.] Good-bye. [*Gives his hand to* VARYA, *then to* FIRS *and* YASHA.] I don't want to go. [*To* LYUBOV ANDREYEVNA.] If you think over my plan for the villas and make up your mind, then let me know; I will lend you 50,000 roubles.[8] Think of it seriously.

VARYA: [*Angrily.*] Well, do go, for goodness sake.

LOPAHIN: I'm going, I'm going. [*Goes out.*]

GAEV: Low-born knave! I beg pardon, though . . . Varya is going to marry him, he's Varya's fiancé.

VARYA: Don't talk nonsense, uncle.

LYUBOV: Well, Varya, I shall be delighted. He's a good man.

PISHTCHIK: He is, one must acknowledge, a most worthy man. And my Dashenka . . . says too that . . . she says . . . various things. [*Snores, but at once*

8. Nearly $1 million in today's U.S. currency.

wakes up.] But all the same, honored lady, could you oblige me . . . with a loan of 240 roubles[9] . . . to pay the interest on my mortgage to-morrow?

VARYA: [*Dismayed.*] No, no.

LYUBOV: I really haven't any money.

PISHTCHIK: It will turn up. [*Laughs.*] I never lose hope. I thought everything was over, I was a ruined man, and lo and behold—the railway passed through my land and . . . they paid me for it. And something else will turn up again, if not to-day, then to-morrow . . . Dashenka'll win two hundred thousand . . . she's got a lottery ticket.

LYUBOV: Well, we've finished our coffee, we can go to bed.

FIRS: [*Brushes* GAEV, *reprovingly.*] You have got on the wrong trousers again! What am I to do with you?

VARYA: [*Softly.*] Anya's asleep. [*Softly opens the window.*] Now the sun's risen, it's not a bit cold. Look, mamma, what exquisite trees! My goodness! And the air! The starlings are singing!

GAEV: [*Opens another window.*] The orchard is all white. You've not forgotten it, Lyuba? That long avenue that runs straight, straight as an arrow, how it shines on a moonlight night. You remember? You've not forgotten?

LYUBOV: [*Looking out of the window into the garden.*] Oh, my childhood, my innocence! It was in this nursery I used to sleep, from here I looked out into the orchard, happiness waked with me every morning and in those days the orchard was just the same, nothing has changed. [*Laughs with delight.*] All, all white! Oh, my orchard! After the dark gloomy autumn, and the cold winter; you are young again, and full of happiness, the heavenly angels have never left you. . . . If I could cast off the burden that weighs on my heart, if I could forget the past!

GAEV: H'm! and the orchard will be sold to pay our debts; it seems strange. . . .

LYUBOV: See, our mother walking . . . all in white, down the avenue! [*Laughs with delight.*] It is she!

GAEV: Where?

VARYA: Oh, don't, mamma!

LYUBOV: There is no one. It was my fancy. On the right there, by the path to the arbor, there is a white tree bending like a woman. . . .

[*Enter* TROFIMOV *wearing a shabby student's uniform and spectacles.*]

LYUBOV: What a ravishing orchard! White masses of blossom, blue sky. . . .

TROFIMOV: Lyubov Andreyevna! [*She looks round at him.*] I will just pay my respects to you and then leave you at once. [*Kisses her hand warmly.*] I was told to wait until morning, but I hadn't the patience to wait any longer. . . .

[LYUBOV ANDREYEVNA *looks at him in perplexity.*]

VARYA: [*Through her tears.*] This is Petya Trofimov.

TROFIMOV: Petya Trofimov, who was your Grisha's tutor. . . . Can I have changed so much?

[LYUBOV ANDREYEVNA *embraces him and weeps quietly.*]

9. A loan of nearly $5,000 in today's U.S. currency.

GAEV: [*In confusion.*] There, there, Lyuba.
VARYA: [*Crying.*] I told you, Petya, to wait till to-morrow.
LYUBOV: My Grisha . . . my boy . . . Grisha . . . my son!
VARYA: We can't help it, mamma, it is God's will.
TROFIMOV: [*Softly through his tears.*] There . . . there.
LYUBOV: [*Weeping quietly.*] My boy was lost . . . drowned. Why? Oh, why, dear Petya? [*More quietly.*] Anya is asleep in there, and I'm talking loudly . . . making this noise. . . . But, Petya? Why have you grown so ugly? Why do you look so old?
TROFIMOV: A peasant-woman in the train called me a mangy-looking gentleman.
LYUBOV: You were quite a boy then, a pretty little student, and now your hair's thin—and spectacles. Are you really a student still? [*Goes towards the door.*]
TROFIMOV: I seem likely to be a perpetual student.
LYUBOV: [*Kisses her brother, then* VARYA.] Well, go to bed. . . . You are older too, Leonid.
PISHTCHIK: [*Follows her.*] I suppose it's time we were asleep. . . . Ugh! my gout. I'm staying the night! Lyubov Andreyevna, my dear soul, if you could . . . to-morrow morning . . . 240 roubles.
GAEV: That's always his story.
PISHTCHIK: 240 roubles . . . to pay the interest on my mortgage.
LYUBOV: My dear man, I have no money.
PISHTCHIK: I'll pay it back, my dear . . . a trifling sum.
LYUBOV: Oh, well, Leonid will give it you. . . . You give him the money, Leonid.
GAEV: Me give it him! Let him wait till he gets it!
LYUBOV: It can't be helped, give it him. He needs it. He'll pay it back.

[LYUBOV ANDREYEVNA, TROFIMOV, PISHTCHIK *and* FIRS *go out.* GAEV, VARYA *and* YASHA *remain.*]

GAEV: Sister hasn't got out of the habit of flinging away her money. [*To* YASHA.] Get away, my good fellow, you smell of the hen-house.
YASHA: [*With a grin.*] And you, Leonid Andreyevitch, are just the same as ever.
GAEV: What's that? [*To* VARYA.] What did he say?
VARYA: [*To* YASHA.] Your mother has come from the village; she has been sitting in the servants' room since yesterday, waiting to see you.
YASHA: Oh, bother her!
VARYA: For shame!
YASHA: What's the hurry? She might just as well have come to-morrow. [*Goes out.*]
VARYA: Mamma's just the same as ever, she hasn't changed a bit. If she had her own way, she'd give away everything.
GAEV: Yes. [*A pause.*] If a great many remedies are suggested for some disease, it means that the disease is incurable. I keep thinking and racking my brains; I have many schemes, a great many, and that really means none. If we could only come in for a legacy from somebody, or marry our Anya to a very rich man, or we might go to Yaroslavl[1] and try our luck with our old aunt, the Countess. She's very, very rich, you know.

1. Major industrial city located on the Volga River, 170 miles northeast of Moscow.

VARYA: [*Weeps.*] If God would help us.

GAEV: Don't blubber. Aunt's very rich, but she doesn't like us. First, sister married a lawyer instead of a nobleman. . . .

[ANYA *appears in the doorway.*]

GAEV: And then her conduct, one can't call it virtuous. She is good, and kind, and nice, and I love her, but, however one allows for extenuating circumstances, there's no denying that she's an immoral woman. One feels it in her slightest gesture.

VARYA: [*In a whisper.*] Anya's in the doorway.

GAEV: What do you say? [*A pause.*] It's queer, there seems to be something wrong with my right eye. I don't see as well as I did. And on Thursday when I was in the district Court . . .

[*Enter* ANYA.]

VARYA: Why aren't you asleep, Anya?

ANYA: I can't get to sleep.

GAEV: My pet. [*Kisses* ANYA'S *face and hands.*] My child. [*Weeps.*] You are not my niece, you are my angel, you are everything to me. Believe me, believe. . . .

ANYA: I believe you, uncle. Everyone loves you and respects you . . . but, uncle dear, you must be silent . . . simply be silent. What were you saying just now about my mother, about your own sister? What made you say that?

GAEV: Yes, yes. . . . [*Puts his hand over his face.*] Really, that was awful! My God, save me! And to-day I made a speech to the bookcase . . . so stupid! And only when I had finished, I saw how stupid it was.

VARYA: It's true, uncle, you ought to keep quiet. Don't talk, that's all.

ANYA: If you could keep from talking, it would make things easier for you, too.

GAEV: I won't speak. [*Kisses* ANYA'S *and* VARYA'S *hands.*] I'll be silent. Only this is about business. On Thursday I was in the district Court; well, there was a large party of us there and we began talking of one thing and another, and this and that, and do you know, I believe that it will be possible to raise a loan on an I.O.U. to pay the arrears on the mortgage.

VARYA: If the Lord would help us!

GAEV: I'm going on Tuesday; I'll talk of it again. [*To* VARYA.] Don't blubber. [*To* ANYA.] Your mamma will talk to Lopahin; of course, he won't refuse her. And as soon as you're rested you shall go to Yaroslavl to the Countess, your great-aunt. So we shall all set to work in three directions at once, and the business is done. We shall pay off arrears, I'm convinced of it. [*Puts a caramel in his mouth.*] I swear on my honor, I swear by anything you like, the estate shan't be sold. [*Excitedly.*] By my own happiness, I swear it! Here's my hand on it, call me the basest, vilest of men, if I let it come to an auction! Upon my soul I swear it!

ANYA: [*Her equanimity has returned, she is quite happy.*] How good you are, uncle, and how clever! [*Embraces her uncle.*] I'm at peace now! Quite at peace! I'm happy!

[*Enter* FIRS.]

FIRS: [*Reproachfully.*] Leonid Andreyevitch, have you no fear of God? When are you going to bed?

GAEV: Directly, directly. You can go, Firs. I'll . . . yes, I will undress myself. Come, children, bye-bye. We'll go into details to-morrow, but now go to bed. [*Kisses* ANYA *and* VARYA.] I'm a man of the eighties.[2] They run down that period, but still I can say I have had to suffer not a little for my convictions in my life, it's not for nothing that the peasant loves me. One must know the peasant! One must know how. . . .

ANYA: At it again, uncle!

VARYA: Uncle dear, you'd better be quiet!

FIRS: [*Angrily.*] Leonid Andreyevitch!

GAEV: I'm coming. I'm coming. Go to bed. Potted the shot—there's a shot for you![3] A beauty! [*Goes out,* FIRS *hobbling after him.*]

ANYA: My mind's at rest now. I don't want to go to Yaroslavl, I don't like my great-aunt, but still my mind's at rest. Thanks to uncle. [*Sits down.*]

VARYA: We must go to bed. I'm going. Something unpleasant happened while you were away. In the old servants' quarters there are only the old servants, as you know—Efimyushka, Polya, and Yevstigney—and Karp too. They began letting stray people in to spend the night—I said nothing. But all at once I heard they had been spreading a report that I gave them nothing but pease pudding to eat. Out of stinginess, you know. . . . And it was all Yevstigney's doing. . . . Very well, I said to myself. . . . If that's how it is, I thought, wait a bit. I sent for Yevstigney. . . . [*Yawns.*] He comes. . . . "How's this, Yevstigney," I said, "you could be such a fool as to? . . ." [*Looking at* ANYA.] Anitchka! [*A pause.*] She's asleep. [*Puts her arm around* ANYA.] Come to bed . . . come along! [*Leads her.*] My darling has fallen asleep! Come. . . . [*They go.*]

[*Far away beyond the orchard a shepherd plays on a pipe.* TROFIMOV *crosses the stage and, seeing* VARYA *and* ANYA, *stands still.*]

VARYA: 'Sh! asleep, asleep. Come, my own.

ANYA: [*Softly, half asleep.*] I'm so tired. Still those bells. Uncle . . . dear . . . mamma and uncle. . . .

VARYA: Come, my own, come along.

[*They go into* ANYA'S *room.*]

TROFIMOV: [*Tenderly.*] My sunshine! My spring.

CURTAIN.

ACT II

The open country. An old shrine,[4] long abandoned and fallen out of the perpendicular; near it a well, large stones that have apparently once been tombstones, and an old garden seat. The road to GAEV'S *house is seen. On one side rise dark poplars; and there the cherry orchard begins. In the distance a row of telegraph poles and far, far away on the horizon there is faintly outlined a great*

2. That is, the 1880s, a period of reactionary conservatism in Russia under Tsar Alexander III.

3. Gaev is preoccupied with billiards; the terminology is fanciful because Chekhov admittedly knew nothing about the game.

4. That is, a chapel.

town, only visible in very fine clear weather. It is near sunset. CHARLOTTA, YASHA *and* DUNYASHA *are sitting on the seat.* EPIHODOV *is standing near, playing something mournful on a guitar. All sit plunged in thought.* CHARLOTTA *wears an old forage cap; she has taken a gun from her shoulder and is tightening the buckle on the strap.*

CHARLOTTA: [*Musingly.*] I haven't a real passport[5] of my own, and I don't know how old I am, and I always feel that I'm a young thing. When I was a little girl, my father and mother used to travel about to fairs and give performances—very good ones. And I used to dance *salto-mortale*[6] and all sorts of things. And when papa and mamma died, a German lady took me and had me educated. And so I grew up and become a governess. But where I came from, and who I am, I don't know. . . . Who my parents were, very likely they weren't married. . . . I don't know. [*Takes a cucumber out of her pocket and eats.*] I know nothing at all. [*A pause.*] One wants to talk and has no one to talk to. . . . I have nobody.

EPIHODOV: [*Plays on the guitar and sings.*] "What care I for the noisy world! What care I for friends or foes!"[7] How agreeable it is to play on the mandoline!

DUNYASHA: That's a guitar, not a mandoline. [*Looks in a hand-mirror and powders herself.*]

EPIHODOV: To a man mad with love, it's a mandoline. [*Sings.*] "Were her heart but aglow with love's mutual flame." [YASHA *joins in.*]

CHARLOTTA: How shockingly these people sing! Foo! Like jackals!

DUNYASHA: [*To* YASHA.] What happiness, though, to visit foreign lands.

YASHA: Ah, yes! I rather agree with you there. [*Yawns, then lights a cigar.*]

EPIHODOV: That's comprehensible. In foreign lands everything has long since reached full complexion.

YASHA: That's so, of course.

EPIHODOV: I'm a cultivated man, I read remarkable books of all sorts, but I can never make out the tendency I am myself precisely inclined for, whether to live or to shoot myself, speaking precisely, but nevertheless I always carry a revolver. Here it is. . . . [*Shows revolver.*]

CHARLOTTA: I've had enough, and now I'm going. [*Puts on the gun.*] Epihodov, you're a very clever fellow, and a very terrible one too, all the women must be wild about you. Br-r-r! [*Goes.*] These clever fellows are all so stupid; there's not a creature for me to speak to. . . . Always alone, alone, nobody belonging to me . . . and who I am, and why I'm on earth, I don't know. [*Walks away slowly.*]

EPIHODOV: Speaking precisely, not touching upon other subjects, I'm bound to admit about myself, that destiny behaves mercilessly to me, as a storm to a little boat. If, let us suppose, I am mistaken, then why did I wake up this morning, to quote an example, and look round, and there on my chest was a spider of fearful magnitude . . . like this. [*Shows with both hands.*] And then I take up a jug of kvass, to quench my thirst, and in it there is something in the highest degree unseemly of the nature of a cockroach. [*A pause.*] Have

5. Document required for travel within Russia. 6. Literally, "deadly leap"; Italian for "somersault."
7. Words of a popular ballad.

you read Buckle?[8] [*A pause.*] I am desirous of troubling you, Dunyasha, with a couple of words.

DUNYASHA: Well, speak.

EPIHODOV: I should be desirous to speak with you alone. [*Sighs.*]

DUNYASHA: [*Embarrassed.*] Well—only bring me my mantle first. It's by the cupboard. It's rather damp here.

EPIHODOV: Certainly. I will fetch it. Now I know what I must do with my revolver. [*Takes guitar and goes off playing on it.*]

YASHA: Two and twenty misfortunes! Between ourselves, he's a fool. [*Yawns.*]

DUNYASHA: God grant he doesn't shoot himself! [*A pause.*] I am so nervous, I'm always in a flutter. I was a little girl when I was taken into our lady's house, and now I have quite grown out of peasant ways, and my hands are white, as white as a lady's. I'm such a delicate, sensitive creature, I'm afraid of everything. I'm so frightened. And if you deceive me, Yasha, I don't know what will become of my nerves.

YASHA: [*Kisses her.*] You're a peach! Of course a girl must never forget herself; what I dislike more than anything is a girl being flighty in her behavior.

DUNYASHA: I'm passionately in love with you, Yasha; you are a man of culture—you can give your opinion about anything. [*A pause.*]

YASHA: [*Yawns.*] Yes, that's so. My opinion is this: if a girl loves anyone, that means that she has no principles. [*A pause.*] It's pleasant smoking a cigar in the open air. [*Listens.*] Someone's coming this way . . . it's the gentlefolk. [DUNYASHA *embraces him impulsively.*] Go home, as though you had been to the river to bathe; go by that path, or else they'll meet you and suppose I have made an appointment with you here. That I can't endure.

DUNYASHA: [*Coughing softly.*] The cigar has made my head ache. . . . [*Goes off.*]

[YASHA *remains sitting near the shrine. Enter* LYUBOV ANDREYEVNA, GAEV *and* LOPAHIN.]

LOPAHIN: You must make up your mind once for all—there's no time to lose. It's quite a simple question, you know. Will you consent to letting the land for building or not? One word in answer: Yes or no? Only one word!

LYUBOV: Who is smoking such horrible cigars here? [*Sits down.*]

GAEV: Now the railway line has been brought near, it's made things very convenient. [*Sits down.*] Here we have been over and lunched in town. Cannon off the white! I should like to go home and have a game.

LYUBOV: You have plenty of time.

LOPAHIN: Only one word! [*Beseechingly.*] Give me an answer!

GAEV: [*Yawning.*] What do you say?

LYUBOV: [*Looks in her purse.*] I had quite a lot of money here yesterday, and there's scarcely any left to-day. My poor Varya feeds us all on milk soup for the sake of economy; the old folks in the kitchen get nothing but pease pudding, while I waste my money in a senseless way. [*Drops purse, scattering gold pieces.*] There, they have all fallen out! [*Annoyed.*]

8. Henry Thomas Buckle (1821–61), a learned but eccentric historian known as a freethinker; his *History of Civilization in England* (1857) was the talk of Moscow a generation earlier. His work, initially respected for its empirical methods, quickly fell into disrepute in sophisticated intellectual circles.

YASHA: Allow me, I'll soon pick them up. [*Collects the coins.*]

LYUBOV: Pray do, Yasha. And what did I go off to the town to lunch for? Your restaurant's a wretched place with its music and the tablecloth smelling of soap. . . . Why drink so much, Leonid? And eat so much? And talk so much? To-day you talked a great deal again in the restaurant, and all so inappropriately. About the era of the seventies, about the decadents.[9] And to whom? Talking to waiters about decadents!

LOPAHIN: Yes.

GAEV: [*Waving his hand.*] I'm incorrigible; that's evident. [*Irritably to* YASHA.] Why is it you keep fidgeting about in front of us!

YASHA: [*Laughs.*] I can't help laughing when I hear your voice.

GAEV: [*To his sister.*] Either I or he. . . .

LYUBOV: Get along! Go away, Yasha.

YASHA: [*Gives* LYUBOV ANDREYEVNA *her purse.*] Directly. [*Hardly able to suppress his laughter.*] This minute. . . . [*Goes off.*]

LOPAHIN: Deriganov, the millionaire, means to buy your estate. They say he is coming to the sale himself.

LYUBOV: Where did you hear that?

LOPAHIN: That's what they say in town.

GAEV: Our aunt in Yaroslavl has promised to send help; but when, and how much she will send, we don't know.

LOPAHIN: How much will she send? A hundred thousand? Two hundred?

LYUBOV: Oh, well! . . . Ten or fifteen thousand, and we must be thankful to get that.

LOPAHIN: Forgive me, but such reckless people as you are—such queer, unbusiness-like people—I never met in my life. One tells you in plain Russian your estate is going to be sold, and you seem not to understand it.

LYUBOV: What are we to do? Tell us what to do.

LOPAHIN: I do tell you every day. Every day I say the same thing. You absolutely must let the cherry orchard and the land on building leases; and do it at once, as quick as may be—the auction's close upon us! Do understand! Once make up your mind to build villas, and you can raise as much money as you like, and then you are saved.

LYUBOV: Villas and summer visitors—forgive me saying so—it's so vulgar.

GAEV: There I perfectly agree with you.

LOPAHIN: I shall sob, or scream, or fall into a fit. I can't stand it! You drive me mad! [*To* GAEV.] You're an old woman!

GAEV: What do you say?

LOPAHIN: An old woman! [*Gets up to go.*]

LYUBOV: [*In dismay.*] No, don't go! Do stay, my dear friend! Perhaps we shall think of something.

LOPAHIN: What is there to think of?

9. Probably a reference to the group of flamboyant French poets of the 1880s who called themselves *les décadents. The era of the seventies*: the 1870s, a relatively liberal period in Russia that ended abruptly with the assassination of Alexander II in 1881.

LYUBOV: Don't go, I entreat you! With you here it's more cheerful, anyway. [*A pause.*] I keep expecting something, as though the house were going to fall about our ears.

GAEV: [*In profound dejection.*] Potted the white! It fails—a kiss.

LYUBOV: We have been great sinners. . . .

LOPAHIN: You have no sins to repent of.

GAEV: [*Puts a caramel in his mouth.*] They say I've eaten up my property in caramels. [*Laughs.*]

LYUBOV: Oh, my sins! I've always thrown my money away recklessly like a lunatic. I married a man who made nothing but debts. My husband died of champagne—he drank dreadfully. To my misery I loved another man, and immediately—it was my first punishment—the blow fell upon me, here, in the river . . . my boy was drowned and I went abroad—went away for ever, never to return, not to see that river again . . . I shut my eyes, and fled, distracted, and *he* after me . . . pitilessly, brutally. I bought a villa at Mentone,[1] for *he* fell ill there, and for three years I had no rest day or night. His illness wore me out, my soul was dried up. And last year, when my villa was sold to pay my debts, I went to Paris and there he robbed me of everything and abandoned me for another woman; and I tried to poison myself. . . . So stupid, so shameful! . . . And suddenly I felt a yearning for Russia, for my country, for my little girl. . . . [*Dries her tears.*] Lord, Lord, be merciful! Forgive my sins! Do not chastise me more! [*Takes a telegram out of her pocket.*] I got this to-day from Paris. He implores forgiveness, entreats me to return. [*Tears up the telegram.*] I fancy there is music somewhere. [*Listens.*]

GAEV: That's our famous Jewish orchestra. You remember, four violins, a flute, and a double bass.

LYUBOV: That still in existence? We ought to send for them one evening, and give a dance.

LOPAHIN: [*Listens.*] I can't hear. . . . [*Hums softly.*] "For money the Germans will turn a Russian into a Frenchman." [*Laughs.*] I did see such a piece at the theater yesterday! It was funny!

LYUBOV: And most likely there was nothing funny in it. You shouldn't look at plays, you should look at yourselves a little oftener. How gray your lives are! How much nonsense you talk.

LOPAHIN: That's true. One may say honestly, we live a fool's life. [*Pause.*] My father was a peasant, an idiot; he knew nothing and taught me nothing, only beat me when he was drunk, and always with his stick. In reality I am just such another blockhead and idiot. I've learnt nothing properly. I write a wretched hand. I write so that I feel ashamed before folks, like a pig.

LYUBOV: You ought to get married, my dear fellow.

LOPAHIN: Yes . . . that's true.

LYUBOV: You should marry our Varya, she's a good girl.

LOPAHIN: Yes.

LYUBOV: She's a good-natured girl, she's busy all day long, and what's more, she loves you. And you have liked her for ever so long.

1. Resort town on the French Mediterranean coast.

LOPAHIN: Well? I'm not against it. . . . She's a good girl. [*Pause.*]

GAEV: I've been offered a place in the bank: 6,000 roubles a year.[2] Did you know?

LYUBOV: You would never do for that! You must stay as you are.

[*Enter* FIRS *with overcoat.*]

FIRS: Put it on, sir, it's damp.

GAEV: [*Putting it on.*] You bother me, old fellow.

FIRS: You can't go on like this. You went away in the morning without leaving word. [*Looks him over.*]

LYUBOV: You look older, Firs!

FIRS: What is your pleasure?

LOPAHIN: You look older, she said.

FIRS: I've had a long life. They were arranging my wedding before your papa was born. . . . [*Laughs.*] I was the head footman before the emancipation came.[3] I wouldn't consent to be set free then; I stayed on with the old master. . . . [*A pause.*] I remember what rejoicings they made and didn't know themselves what they were rejoicing over.

LOPAHIN: Those were fine old times. There was flogging anyway.

FIRS: [*Not hearing.*] To be sure! The peasants knew their place, and the masters knew theirs; but now they're all at sixes and sevens,[4] there's no making it out.

GAEV: Hold your tongue, Firs. I must go to town to-morrow. I have been promised an introduction to a general, who might let us have a loan.

LOPAHIN: You won't bring that off. And you won't pay your arrears, you may rest assured of that.

LYUBOV: That's all his nonsense. There is no such general.

[*Enter* TROFIMOV, ANYA *and* VARYA.]

GAEV: Here come our girls.

ANYA: There's mamma on the seat.

LYUBOV: [*Tenderly.*] Come here, come along. My darlings! [*Embraces* ANYA *and* VARYA.] If you only knew how I love you both. Sit beside me, there, like that. [*All sit down.*]

LOPAHIN: Our perpetual student is always with the young ladies.

TROFIMOV: That's not your business.

LOPAHIN: He'll soon be fifty, and he's still a student.

TROFIMOV: Drop your idiotic jokes.

LOPAHIN: Why are you so cross, you queer fish?

TROFIMOV: Oh, don't persist!

LOPAHIN: [*Laughs.*] Allow me to ask you what's your idea of me?

TROFIMOV: I'll tell you my idea of you, Yermolay Alexeyevitch: you are a rich man, you'll soon be a millionaire. Well, just as in the economy of nature a

2. Nearly $120,000 per year in today's U.S. currency.

3. In 1861 Tsar Alexander II issued the Edict of Emancipation, which freed the serfs (agricultural workers held in feudal bondage, who represented about one-third of Russia's population).

4. That is, they are confused, unsettled.

wild beast is of use, who devours everything that comes in his way, so you too have your use.

[*All laugh.*]

VARYA: Better tell us something about the planets, Petya.
LYUBOV: No, let us go on with the conversation we had yesterday.
TROFIMOV: What was it about?
GAEV: About pride.
TROFIMOV: We had a long conversation yesterday, but we came to no conclusion. In pride, in your sense of it, there is something mystical. Perhaps you are right from your point of view; but if one looks at it simply, without subtlety, what sort of pride can there be, what sense is there in it, if man in his physiological formation is very imperfect, if in the immense majority of cases he is coarse, dull-witted, profoundly unhappy? One must give up glorification of self. One should work, and nothing else.
GAEV: One must die in any case.
TROFIMOV: Who knows? And what does it mean—dying? Perhaps man has a hundred senses, and only the five we know are lost at death, while the other ninety-five remain alive.
LYUBOV: How clever you are, Petya!
LOPAHIN: [*Ironically.*] Fearfully clever!
TROFIMOV: Humanity progresses, perfecting its powers. Everything that is beyond its ken now will one day become familiar and comprehensible; only we must work, we must with all our powers aid the seeker after truth. Here among us in Russia the workers are few in number as yet. The vast majority of the intellectual people I know, seek nothing, do nothing, are not fit as yet for work of any kind. They call themselves intellectual, but they treat their servants as inferiors, behave to the peasants as though they were animals, learn little, read nothing seriously, do practically nothing, only talk about science and know very little about art. They are all serious people, they all have severe faces, they all talk of weighty matters and air their theories, and yet the vast majority of us—ninety-nine per cent—live like savages, at the least thing fly to blows and abuse, eat piggishly, sleep in filth and stuffiness, bugs everywhere, stench and damp and moral impurity. And it's clear all our fine talk is only to divert our attention and other people's. Show me where to find the *crèches* there's so much talk about, and the reading-rooms?[5] They only exist in novels: in real life there are none of them. There is nothing but filth and vulgarity and Asiatic apathy. I fear and dislike very serious faces. I'm afraid of serious conversations. We should do better to be silent.
LOPAHIN: You know, I get up at five o'clock in the morning, and I work from morning to night; and I've money, my own and other people's, always passing through my hands, and I see what people are made of all round me. One has only to begin to do anything to see how few honest, decent people there are. Sometimes when I lie awake at night, I think: "Oh! Lord, thou hast given us

5. Nursery schools and centers offering free reading material—that is, the social services and civilizing influences that have been imagined but never created.

immense forests, boundless plains, the widest horizons, and living here we ourselves ought really to be giants."

LYUBOV: You ask for giants! They are no good except in story-books; in real life they frighten us.

[EPIHODOV *advances in the background, playing on the guitar.*]

LYUBOV: [*Dreamily.*] There goes Epihodov.

ANYA: [*Dreamily.*] There goes Epihodov.

GAEV: The sun has set, my friends.

TROFIMOV: Yes.

GAEV: [*Not loudly, but, as it were, declaiming.*] O nature, divine nature, thou art bright with eternal luster, beautiful and indifferent! Thou, whom we call mother, thou dost unite within thee life and death! Thou dost give life and dost destroy!

VARYA: [*In a tone of supplication.*] Uncle!

ANYA: Uncle, you are at it again!

TROFIMOV: You'd much better be cannoning off the red!

GAEV: I'll hold my tongue, I will.

[*All sit plunged in thought. Perfect stillness. The only thing audible is the muttering of* FIRS. *Suddenly there is a sound in the distance, as it were from the sky—the sound of a breaking harp-string, mournfully dying away.*]

LYUBOV: What is that?

LOPAHIN: I don't know. Somewhere far away a bucket fallen and broken in the pits. But somewhere very far away.

GAEV: It might be a bird of some sort—such as a heron.

TROFIMOV: Or an owl.

LYUBOV: [*Shudders.*] I don't know why, but it's horrid. [*A pause.*]

FIRS: It was the same before the calamity—the owl hooted and the samovar hissed all the time.

GAEV: Before what calamity?

FIRS: Before the emancipation. [*A pause.*]

LYUBOV: Come, my friends, let us be going; evening is falling. [*To* ANYA.] There are tears in your eyes. What is it, darling? [*Embraces her.*]

ANYA: Nothing, mamma; it's nothing.

TROFIMOV: There is somebody coming.

[*The* WAYFARER *appears in a shabby white forage cap and an overcoat; he is slightly drunk.*]

WAYFARER: Allow me to inquire, can I get to the station this way?

GAEV: Yes. Go along that road.

WAYFARER: I thank you most feelingly. [*Coughing.*] The weather is superb. [*Declaims.*] My brother, my suffering brother! . . . Come out to the Volga![6]

6. Line from a poem by Nikolai Nekrasov (1821–78), a poet known as a champion of the lower classes. (The Volga is Europe's longest river and Russia's principal waterway.) *My brother, my suffering brother!*: Line from a poem by Semen Nadson (1862–87), persecuted in Russia because of his Jewish origins.

Whose groan do you hear? . . . [*To* VARYA.] Mademoiselle, vouchsafe a hungry Russian thirty kopecks.[7]

[VARYA *utters a shriek of alarm.*]

LOPAHIN: [*Angrily.*] There's a right and a wrong way of doing everything!
LYUBOV: [*Hurriedly.*] Here, take this. [*Looks in her purse.*] I've no silver. No matter—here's gold for you.
WAYFARER: I thank you most feelingly! [*Goes off.*]

[*Laughter.*]

VARYA: [*Frightened.*] I'm going home—I'm going. . . . Oh, mamma, the servants have nothing to eat, and you gave him gold!
LYUBOV: There's no doing anything with me. I'm so silly! When we get home, I'll give you all I possess. Yermolay Alexeyevitch, you will lend me some more! . . .
LOPAHIN: I will.
LYUBOV: Come, friends, it's time to be going. And Varya, we have made a match of it for you. I congratulate you.
VARYA: [*Through her tears.*] Mamma, that's not a joking matter.
LOPAHIN: "Ophelia, get thee to a nunnery!"[8]
GAEV: My hands are trembling; it's a long while since I had a game of billiards.
LOPAHIN: "Ophelia! Nymph, in thy orisons be all my sins remember'd."
LYUBOV: Come, it will soon be supper-time.
VARYA: How he frightened me! My heart's simply throbbing.
LOPAHIN: Let me remind you, ladies and gentlemen: on the 22nd of August the cherry orchard will be sold. Think about that! Think about it!

[*All go off, except* TROFIMOV *and* ANYA.]

ANYA: [*Laughing.*] I'm grateful to the wayfarer! He frightened Varya and we are left alone.
TROFIMOV: Varya's afraid we shall fall in love with each other, and for days together she won't leave us. With her narrow brain she can't grasp that we are above love. To eliminate the petty and transitory which hinder us from being free and happy—that is the aim and meaning of our life. Forward! We go forward irresistibly towards the bright star that shines yonder in the distance. Forward! Do not lag behind, friends.
ANYA: [*Claps her hands.*] How well you speak! [*A pause.*] It is divine here today.
TROFIMOV: Yes, it's glorious weather.
ANYA: Somehow, Petya, you've made me so that I don't love the cherry orchard as I used to. I used to love it so dearly. I used to think that there was no spot on earth like our garden.
TROFIMOV: All Russia is our garden. The earth is great and beautiful—there are many beautiful places in it. [*A pause.*] Think only, Anya, your grandfather,

7. About $6 in today's U.S. currency.
8. For this quotation and the one below, see *Hamlet* 3.1.

and great-grandfather, and all your ancestors were slave-owners—the owners of living souls—and from every cherry in the orchard, from every leaf, from every trunk there are human creatures looking at you. Cannot you hear their voices? Oh, it is awful! Your orchard is a fearful thing, and when in the evening or at night one walks about the orchard, the old bark on the trees glimmers dimly in the dusk, and the old cherry trees seem to be dreaming of centuries gone by and tortured by fearful visions.[9] Yes! We are at least two hundred years behind, we have really gained nothing yet, we have no definite attitude to the past, we do nothing but theorize or complain of depression or drink vodka. It is clear that to begin to live in the present we must first expiate our past, we must break with it; and we can expiate it only by suffering, by extraordinary unceasing labor. Understand that, Anya.

ANYA: The house we live in has long ceased to be our own, and I shall leave it, I give you my word.

TROFIMOV: If you have the house keys, fling them into the well and go away. Be free as the wind.

ANYA: [*In ecstasy.*] How beautifully you said that!

TROFIMOV: Believe me, Anya, believe me! I am not thirty yet, I am young, I am still a student, but I have gone through so much already! As soon as winter comes I am hungry, sick, careworn, poor as a beggar, and what ups and downs of fortune have I not known! And my soul was always, every minute, day and night, full of inexplicable forebodings. I have a foreboding of happiness, Anya. I see glimpses of it already.

ANYA: [*Pensively.*] The moon is rising.

[EPIHODOV *is heard playing still the same mournful song on the guitar. The moon rises. Somewhere near the poplars* VARYA *is looking for* ANYA *and calling "Anya! where are you?"*]

TROFIMOV: Yes, the moon is rising. [*A pause.*] Here is happiness—here it comes! It is coming nearer and nearer; already I can hear its footsteps. And if we never see it—if we may never know it—what does it matter? Others will see it after us.

VARYA'S VOICE: Anya! Where are you?

TROFIMOV: That Varya again! [*Angrily.*] It's revolting!

ANYA: Well, let's go down to the river. It's lovely there.

TROFIMOV: Yes, let's go. [*They go.*]

VARYA'S VOICE: Anya! Anya!

CURTAIN

9. *Oh, it is awful! [. . .] fearful visions.* Chekhov wrote this passage to replace one that official censors found objectionable: "To own human beings has affected every one of you—those who lived before and those who live now. Your mother, your uncle, and you don't notice that you are living off the labors of others—in fact, the very people you won't even let in the front door." This passage was restored following the 1917 revolution.

ACT III

A drawing-room divided by an arch from a larger drawing-room.[1] *A chandelier burning. The Jewish orchestra, the same that was mentioned in Act II, is heard playing in the ante-room. It is evening. In the larger drawing-room they are dancing the grand chain. The voice of* SEMYONOV-PISHTCHIK: "Promenade à une paire!"[2] *Then enter the drawing-room in couples first* PISHTCHIK *and* CHARLOTTA IVANOVNA, *then* TROFIMOV *and* LYUBOV ANDREYEVNA, *thirdly* ANYA *with the* POST-OFFICE CLERK, *fourthly* VARYA *with the* STATION MASTER, *and other guests.* VARYA *is quietly weeping and wiping away her tears as she dances. In the last couple is* DUNYASHA. *They move across the drawing-room.* PISHTCHIK *shouts:* "Grand rond, balancez!" *and* "Les Cavaliers à genou et remerciez vos dames."

FIRS *in a swallow-tail coat brings in seltzer water on a tray.* PISHTCHIK *and* TROFIMOV *enter the drawing-room.*

PISHTCHIK: I am a full-blooded man; I have already had two strokes. Dancing's hard work for me, but as they say, if you're in the pack, you must bark with the rest. I'm as strong, I may say, as a horse. My parent, who would have his joke—may the Kingdom of Heaven be his!—used to say about our origin that the ancient stock of the Semyonov-Pishtchiks was derived from the very horse that Caligula made a member of the senate.[3] [*Sits down.*] But I've no money, that's where the mischief is. A hungry dog believes in nothing but meat. [*Snores, but at once wakes up.*] That's like me . . . I can think of nothing but money.

TROFIMOV: There really is something horsy about your appearance.

PISHTCHIK: Well . . . a horse is a fine beast . . . a horse can be sold.

[*There is the sound of billiards being played in an adjoining room.* VARYA *appears in the arch leading to the larger drawing-room.*]

TROFIMOV: [*Teasing.*] Madame Lopahin! Madame Lopahin!

VARYA: [*Angrily.*] Mangy-looking gentleman!

TROFIMOV: Yes, I am a mangy-looking gentleman, and I'm proud of it!

VARYA: [*Pondering bitterly.*] Here we have hired musicians and nothing to pay them! [*Goes out.*]

TROFIMOV: [*To* PISHTCHIK.] If the energy you have wasted during your lifetime in trying to find the money to pay your interest had gone to something else, you might in the end have turned the world upside down.

PISHTCHIK: Nietzsche, the philosopher, a very great and celebrated man[4] . . . of enormous intellect . . . says in his works, that one can make forged banknotes.

TROFIMOV: Why, have you read Nietzsche?

1. That is, ballroom.
2. In this French phrase and those quoted below, Semyonov-Pishtchik is calling out the moves in the "grand chain" dance: promenade (walk) to a couple; grand circle, step to the side (that is, *balancez* as in ballet); and gentlemen (knights), kneel and thank your ladies. (French was widely spoken as a second language among the upper classes in pre-Soviet Russia.)
3. Caligula (12–41 CE), Roman emperor known for tyrannical cruelty, is said to have gone insane and to have appointed his horse as a consul.
4. Friedrich Wilhelm Nietzsche (1844–1900), German philosopher who rejected what he termed the "slave morality" of Western bourgeois civilization.

PISHTCHIK: What next . . . Dashenka told me. . . . And now I am in such a position, I might just as well forge banknotes. The day after to-morrow I must pay 310 roubles[5]—130 I have procured. [*Feels in his pockets, in alarm.*] The money's gone! I have lost my money! [*Through his tears.*] Where's the money? [*Gleefully.*] Why, here it is behind the lining. . . . It has made me hot all over.

[*Enter* LYUBOV ANDREYEVNA *and* CHARLOTTA IVANOVNA.]

LYUBOV: [*Hums the Lezginka.*] Why is Leonid so long? What can he be doing in town? [*To* DUNYASHA.] Offer the musicians some tea.

TROFIMOV: The sale hasn't taken place, most likely.

LYUBOV: It's the wrong time to have the orchestra, and the wrong time to give a dance. Well, never mind. [*Sits down and hums softly.*]

CHARLOTTA: [*Gives* PISHTCHIK *a pack of cards.*] Here's a pack of cards. Think of any card you like.

PISHTCHIK: I've thought of one.

CHARLOTTA: Shuffle the pack now. That's right. Give it here, my dear Mr. Pishtchik. *Eins, zwei, drei*[6]—now look, it's in your breast pocket.

PISHTCHIK: [*Taking a card out of his breast pocket.*] The eight of spades! Perfectly right! [*Wonderingly.*] Fancy that now!

CHARLOTTA: [*Holding pack of cards in her hands, to* TROFIMOV.] Tell me quickly which is the top card.

TROFIMOV: Well, the queen of spades.

CHARLOTTA: It is! [*To* PISHTCHIK.] Well, which card is uppermost?

PISHTCHIK: The ace of hearts.

CHARLOTTA: It is! [*Claps her hands, pack of cards disappears.*] Ah! what lovely weather it is to-day!

[*A mysterious feminine voice which seems coming out of the floor answers her. "Oh, yes, it's magnificent weather, madam."*]

CHARLOTTA: You are my perfect ideal.

VOICE: And I greatly admire you too, madam.

STATION MASTER: [*Applauding.*] The lady ventriloquist—bravo!

PISHTCHIK: [*Wonderingly.*] Fancy that now! Most enchanting Charlotta Ivanovna. I'm simply in love with you.

CHARLOTTA: In love? [*Shrugging shoulders.*] What do you know of love, *guter Mensch, aber schlechter Musikant.*[7]

TROFIMOV: [*Pats* PISHTCHIK *on the shoulder.*] You dear old horse. . . .

CHARLOTTA: Attention, please! Another trick! [*Takes a traveling rug from a chair.*] Here's a very good rug; I want to sell it. [*Shaking it out.*] Doesn't anyone want to buy it?

PISHTCHIK: [*Wonderingly.*] Fancy that!

CHARLOTTA: *Ein, zwei, drei!* [*Quickly picks up rug she has dropped; behind the rug stands* ANYA; *she makes a curtsey, runs to her mother, embraces her and runs back into the larger drawing-room amidst general enthusiasm.*]

LYUBOV: [*Applauds.*] Bravo! Bravo!

5. The equivalent of over $6,000 in today's U.S. currency.

6. One, two, three (German). Charlotta speaks the language she associates with her childhood of performing at carnivals.

7. A good man, but a poor musician (German).

CHARLOTTA: Now again! *Ein, zwei, drei!* [*Lifts up the rug; behind the rug stands* VARYA, *bowing.*]

PISHTCHIK: [*Wonderingly.*] Fancy that now!

CHARLOTTA: That's the end. [*Throws the rug at* PISHTCHIK, *makes a curtsey, runs into the larger drawing-room.*]

PISHTCHIK: [*Hurries after her.*] Mischievous creature! Fancy! [*Goes out.*]

LYUBOV: And still Leonid doesn't come. I can't understand what he's doing in the town so long! Why, everything must be over by now. The estate is sold, or the sale has not taken place. Why keep us so long in suspense?

VARYA: [*Trying to console her.*] Uncle's bought it. I feel sure of that.

TROFIMOV: [*Ironically.*] Oh, yes!

VARYA: Great-aunt sent him an authorization to buy it in her name, and transfer the debt. She's doing it for Anya's sake, and I'm sure God will be merciful. Uncle will buy it.

LYUBOV: My aunt in Yaroslavl sent fifteen thousand to buy the estate in her name, she doesn't trust us—but that's not enough even to pay the arrears. [*Hides her face in her hands.*] My fate is being sealed to-day, my fate. . . .

TROFIMOV: [*Teasing* VARYA.] Madame Lopahin.

VARYA: [*Angrily.*] Perpetual student! Twice already you've been sent down[8] from the University.

LYUBOV: Why are you angry, Varya? He's teasing you about Lopahin. Well, what of that? Marry Lopahin if you like, he's a good man, and interesting; if you don't want to, don't! Nobody compels you, darling.

VARYA: I must tell you plainly, mamma, I look at the matter seriously; he's a good man, I like him.

LYUBOV: Well, marry him. I can't see what you're waiting for.

VARYA: Mamma. I can't make him an offer myself. For the last two years, everyone's been talking to me about him. Everyone talks; but he says nothing or else makes a joke. I see what it means. He's growing rich, he's absorbed in business, he has no thoughts for me. If I had money, were it ever so little, if I had only a hundred roubles, I'd throw everything up and go far away. I would go into a nunnery.

TROFIMOV: What bliss!

VARYA: [*To* TROFIMOV.] A student ought to have sense! [*In a soft tone with tears.*] How ugly you've grown, Petya! How old you look! [*To* LYUBOV ANDREYEVNA, *no longer crying.*] But I can't do without work, mamma; I must have something to do every minute.

[*Enter* YASHA.]

YASHA: [*Hardly restraining his laughter.*] Epihodov has broken a billiard cue! [*Goes out.*]

VARYA: What is Epihodov doing here? Who gave him leave to play billiards? I can't make these people out. [*Goes out.*]

LYUBOV: Don't tease her, Petya. You see she has grief enough without that.

TROFIMOV: She is so very officious, meddling in what's not her business. All the summer she's given Anya and me no peace. She's afraid of a love affair

8. Expelled.

between us. What's it to do with her? Besides, I have given no grounds for it. Such triviality is not in my line. We are above love!

LYUBOV: And I suppose I am beneath love. [*Very uneasily.*] Why is it Leonid's not here? If only I could know whether the estate is sold or not! It seems such an incredible calamity that I really don't know what to think. I am distracted . . . I shall scream in a minute . . . I shall do something stupid. Save me, Petya, tell me something, talk to me!

TROFIMOV: What does it matter whether the estate is sold to-day or not? That's all done with long ago. There's no turning back, the path is overgrown. Don't worry yourself, dear Lyubov Andreyevna. You mustn't deceive yourself; for once in your life you must face the truth!

LYUBOV: What truth? You see where the truth lies, but I seem to have lost my sight, I see nothing. You settle every great problem so boldly, but tell me, my dear boy, isn't it because you're young—because you haven't yet understood one of your problems through suffering? You look forward boldly, and isn't it that you don't see and don't expect anything dreadful because life is still hidden from your young eyes? You're bolder, more honest, deeper than we are, but think, be just a little magnanimous, have pity on me. I was born here, you know, my father and mother lived here, my grandfather lived here, I love this house. I can't conceive of life without the cherry orchard, and if it really must be sold, then sell me with the orchard. [*Embraces* TROFIMOV, *kisses him on the forehead.*] My boy was drowned here. [*Weeps.*] Pity me, my dear kind fellow.

TROFIMOV: You know I feel for you with all my heart.

LYUBOV: But that should have been said differently, so differently. [*Takes out her handkerchief, telegram falls on the floor.*] My heart is so heavy to-day. It's so noisy here, my soul is quivering at every sound, I'm shuddering all over, but I can't go away; I'm afraid to be quiet and alone. Don't be hard on me, Petya . . . I love you as though you were one of ourselves. I would gladly let you marry Anya—I swear I would—only, my dear boy, you must take your degree, you do nothing—you're simply tossed by fate from place to place. That's so strange. It is, isn't it? And you must do something with your beard to make it grow somehow. [*Laughs.*] You look so funny!

TROFIMOV: [*Picks up the telegram.*] I've no wish to be a beauty.

LYUBOV: That's a telegram from Paris. I get one every day. One yesterday and one to-day. That savage creature is ill again, he's in trouble again. He begs forgiveness, beseeches me to go, and really I ought to go to Paris to see him. You look shocked, Petya. What am I to do, my dear boy, what am I to do? He is ill, he is alone and unhappy, and who'll look after him, who'll keep him from doing the wrong thing, who'll give him his medicine at the right time? And why hide it or be silent? I love him, that's clear. I love him! I love him! He's a millstone about my neck, I'm going to the bottom with him, but I love that stone and can't live without it. [*Presses* TROFIMOV's *hand.*] Don't think ill of me, Petya, don't tell me anything, don't tell me. . . .

TROFIMOV: [*Through his tears*] For God's sake forgive my frankness: why, he robbed you!

LYUBOV: No! No! No! You mustn't speak like that. [*Covers her ears.*]

TROFIMOV: He is a wretch! You're the only person that doesn't know it! He's a worthless creature! A despicable wretch!

LYUBOV: [*Getting angry, but speaking with restraint.*] You're twenty-six or twenty-seven years old, but you're still a schoolboy.

TROFIMOV: Possibly.

LYUBOV: You should be a man at your age! You should understand what love means! And you ought to be in love yourself. You ought to fall in love! [*Angrily.*] Yes, yes, and it's not purity in you, you're simply a prude, a comic fool, a freak.

TROFIMOV: [*In horror.*] The things she's saying!

LYUBOV: I am above love! You're not above love, but simply as our Firs here says, "You are a good-for-nothing." At your age not to have a mistress!

TROFIMOV: [*In horror.*] This is awful! The things she is saying! [*Goes rapidly into the larger drawing-room clutching his head.*] This is awful! I can't stand it! I'm going. [*Goes off, but at once returns.*] All is over between us! [*Goes off into the ante-room.*]

LYUBOV: [*Shouts after him.*] Petya! Wait a minute! You funny creature! I was joking! Petya! [*There is a sound of somebody running quickly downstairs and suddenly falling with a crash.* ANYA *and* VARYA *scream, but there is a sound of laughter at once.*]

LYUBOV: What has happened?

[ANYA *runs in.*]

ANYA: [*Laughing.*] Petya's fallen downstairs! [*Runs out.*]

LYUBOV: What a queer fellow that Petya is!

[*The* STATION MASTER *stands in the middle of the larger room and reads* The Magdalene, *by Alexey Tolstoy.*[9] *They listen to him, but before he has recited many lines strains of a waltz are heard from the ante-room and the reading is broken off. All dance.* TROFIMOV, ANYA, VARYA *and* LYUBOV ANDREYEVNA *come in from the ante-room.*]

LYUBOV: Come, Petya—come, pure heart! I beg your pardon. Let's have a dance! [*Dances with* PETYA.]

[ANYA *and* VARYA *dance.* FIRS *comes in, puts his stick down near the side door.* YASHA *also comes into the drawing-room and looks on at the dancing.*]

YASHA: What is it, old man?

FIRS: I don't feel well. In old days we used to have generals, barons, and admirals dancing at our balls, and now we send for the post-office clerk and the station master and even they're not overanxious to come. I am getting feeble. The old master, the grandfather, used to give sealing-wax for all complaints. I have been taking sealing-wax for twenty years or more. Perhaps that's what's kept me alive.

YASHA: You bore me, old man! [*Yawns.*] It's time you were done with.

FIRS: *Ach,* you're a good-for-nothing! [*Mutters.*]

[TROFIMOV *and* LYUBOV ANDREYEVNA *dance in larger room and then on to the stage.*]

LYUBOV: *Merci.* I'll sit down a little. [*Sits down.*] I'm tired.

9. Poem sometimes translated as "The Sinful Woman," by Alexsey Tolstoy (1817–75), a distant cousin of novelist Leo Tolstoy.

[*Enter* ANYA.]

ANYA: [*Excitedly.*] There's a man in the kitchen has been saying that the cherry orchard's been sold to-day.

LYUBOV: Sold to whom?

ANYA: He didn't say to whom. He's gone away.

[*She dances with* TROFIMOV, *and they go off into the larger room.*]

YASHA: There was an old man gossiping there, a stranger.

FIRS: Leonid Andreyevitch isn't here yet, he hasn't come back. He has his light overcoat on, *demi-saison*,[1] he'll catch cold for sure. *Ach!* Foolish young things!

LYUBOV: I feel as though I should die. Go, Yasha, find out to whom it has been sold.

YASHA: But he went away long ago, the old chap. [*Laughs.*]

LYUBOV: [*With slight vexation.*] What are you laughing at? What are you pleased at?

YASHA: Epihodov is so funny. He's a silly fellow, two and twenty misfortunes.

LYUBOV: Firs, if the estate is sold, where will you go?

FIRS: Where you bid me, there I'll go.

LYUBOV: Why do you look like that? Are you ill? You ought to be in bed.

FIRS: Yes. [*Ironically.*] Me go to bed and who's to wait here? Who's to see to things without me? I'm the only one in all the house.

YASHA: [*To* LYUBOV ANDREYEVNA.] Lyubov Andreyevna, permit me to make a request of you; if you go back to Paris again, be so kind as to take me with you. It's positively impossible for me to stay here. [*Looking about him; in an undertone.*] There's no need to say it, you see for yourself—an uncivilized country, the people have no morals, and then the dullness! The food in the kitchen's abominable, and then Firs runs after one muttering all sorts of unsuitable words. Take me with you, please do!

[*Enter* PISHTCHIK.]

PISHTCHIK: Allow me to ask you for a waltz, my dear lady. [LYUBOV ANDREYEVNA *goes with him.*] Enchanting lady, I really must borrow of you just 180 roubles,[2] [Dances.] only 180 roubles. [*They pass into the larger room.*]

[*In the larger drawing-room, a figure in a gray top hat and in check trousers is gesticulating and jumping about. Shouts of* "Bravo, Charlotta Ivanovna."]

DUNYASHA: [*She has stopped to powder herself.*] My young lady tells me to dance. There are plenty of gentlemen, and too few ladies, but dancing makes me giddy and makes my heart beat. Firs, the post-office clerk said something to me just now that quite took my breath away.

[*Music becomes more subdued.*]

FIRS: What did he say to you?

DUNYASHA: He said I was like a flower.

YASHA: [*Yawns.*] What ignorance! [*Goes out.*]

DUNYASHA: Like a flower. I am a girl of such delicate feelings, I am awfully fond of soft speeches.

1. Literally, "half-season" (French). 2. Roughly $4,000 in today's U.S. currency.

FIRS: Your head's being turned.

[*Enter* EPIHODOV.]

EPIHODOV: You have no desire to see me, Dunyasha. I might be an insect. [*Sighs.*] Ah! life!

DUNYASHA: What is it you want?

EPIHODOV: Undoubtedly you may be right. [*Sighs.*] But, of course, if one looks at it from that point of view, if I may so express myself, you have, excuse my plain speaking, reduced me to a complete state of mind. I know my destiny. Every day some misfortune befalls me and I have long ago grown accustomed to it, so that I look upon my fate with a smile. You gave me your word, and though I—

DUNYASHA: Let us have a talk later, I entreat you, but now leave me in peace, for I am lost in reverie. [*Plays with her fan.*]

EPIHODOV: I have a misfortune every day, and if I may venture to express myself, I merely smile at it, I even laugh.

[VARYA *enters from the larger drawing-room.*]

VARYA: You still have not gone, Epihodov. What a disrespectful creature you are, really! [*To* DUNYASHA.] Go along, Dunyasha! [*To* EPIHODOV.] First you play billiards and break the cue, then you go wandering about the drawing-room like a visitor!

EPIHODOV: You really cannot, if I may so express myself, call me to account like this.

VARYA: I'm not calling you to account, I'm speaking to you. You do nothing but wander from place to place and don't do your work. We keep you as a counting-house clerk, but what use you are I can't say.

EPIHODOV: [*Offended.*] Whether I work or whether I walk, whether I eat or whether I play billiards, is a matter to be judged by persons of understanding and my elders.

VARYA: You dare to tell me that! [*Firing up.*] You dare! You mean to say I've no understanding. Begone from here! This minute!

EPIHODOV: [*Intimidated.*] I beg you to express yourself with delicacy.

VARYA: [*Beside herself with anger.*] This moment! get out! away! [*He goes towards the door, she following him.*] Two and twenty misfortunes! Take yourself off! Don't let me set eyes on you! [EPIHODOV *has gone out, behind the door his voice,* "I shall lodge a complaint against you."] What! You're coming back? [*Snatches up the stick* FIRS *has put down near the door.*] Come! Come! Come! I'll show you! What! you're coming? Then take that! [*She swings the stick, at the very moment that* LOPAHIN *comes in.*]

LOPAHIN: Very much obliged to you!

VARYA: [*Angrily and ironically.*] I beg your pardon!

LOPAHIN: Not at all! I humbly thank you for your kind reception!

VARYA: No need of thanks for it. [*Moves away, then looks round and asks softly.*] I haven't hurt you?

LOPAHIN: Oh, no! Not at all! There's an immense bump coming up, though!

VOICES FROM LARGER ROOM: Lopahin has come! Yermolay Alexeyevitch!

PISHTCHIK: What do I see and hear? [*Kisses* LOPAHIN.] There's a whiff of cognac about you, my dear soul, and we're making merry here too!

[*Enter* LYUBOV ANDREYEVNA.]

LYUBOV: Is it you, Yermolay Alexeyevitch? Why have you been so long? Where's Leonid?

LOPAHIN: Leonid Andreyevitch arrived with me. He is coming.

LYUBOV: [*In agitation.*] Well! Well! Was there a sale? Speak!

LOPAHIN: [*Embarrassed, afraid of betraying his joy.*] The sale was over at four o'clock. We missed our train—had to wait till half-past nine. [*Sighing heavily.*] Ugh! I feel a little giddy.

[*Enter* GAEV. *In his right hand he has purchases, with his left hand he is wiping away his tears.*]

LYUBOV: Well, Leonid? What news? [*Impatiently, with tears.*] Make haste, for God's sake!

GAEV: [*Makes her no answer, simply waves his hand. To* FIRS, *weeping.*] Here, take them; there's anchovies, Kertch herrings. I have eaten nothing all day. What I have been through! [*Door into the billiard room is open. There is heard a knocking of balls and the voice of* YASHA *saying* "Eighty-seven." GAEV'*s expression changes, he leaves off weeping.*] I am fearfully tired. Firs, come and help me change my things. [*Goes to his own room across the larger drawing-room.*]

PISHTCHIK: How about the sale? Tell us, do!

LYUBOV: Is the cherry orchard sold?

LOPAHIN: It is sold.

LYUBOV: Who has bought it?

LOPAHIN: I have bought it. [*A pause.* LYUBOV *is crushed; she would fall down if she were not standing near a chair and table.*]

[VARYA *takes keys from her waistband, flings them on the floor in middle of drawing-room and goes out.*]

LOPAHIN: I have bought it! Wait a bit, ladies and gentlemen, pray. My head's a bit muddled, I can't speak. [*Laughs.*] We came to the auction. Deriganov was there already. Leonid Andreyevitch only had 15,000 and Deriganov bid 30,000, besides the arrears, straight off. I saw how the land lay. I bid against him. I bid 40,000, he bid 45,000, I said 55, and so he went on, adding 5 thousands and I adding 10. Well . . . So it ended. I bid 90, and it was knocked down to me.[3] Now the cherry orchard's mine! Mine! [*Chuckles.*] My God, the cherry orchard's mine! Tell me that I'm drunk, that I'm out of my mind, that it's all a dream. [*Stamps with his feet.*] Don't laugh at me! If my father and my grandfather could rise from their graves and see all that has happened! How their Yermolay, ignorant, beaten Yermolay, who used to run about barefoot in winter, how that very Yermolay has bought the finest estate in the world! I have bought the estate where my father and grandfather were slaves, where they weren't even admitted into the kitchen. I am asleep, I am dreaming! It is all fancy, it is the work of your imagination plunged in the darkness of ignorance. [*Picks up keys, smiling fondly.*] She threw away the keys; she means to show she's not the housewife now. [*Jingles the keys.*] Well, no matter. [*The orchestra*

3. Lopahin's winning bid for the estate was 90,000 roubles, nearly $2 million in today's U.S. currency—about twice what Lopahin had offered to lend Lyubov and her family to save the estate (act 1).

is heard tuning up.] Hey, musicians! Play! I want to hear you. Come, all of you, and look how Yermolay Lopahin will take the ax to the cherry orchard, how the trees will fall to the ground! We will build houses on it and our grandsons and great-grandsons will see a new life springing up there. Music! Play up!

[*Music begins to play.* LYUBOV ANDREYEVNA *has sunk into a chair and is weeping bitterly.*]

LOPAHIN: [*Reproachfully.*] Why, why didn't you listen to me? My poor friend! Dear lady, there's no turning back now. [*With tears.*] Oh, if all this could be over, oh, if our miserable disjointed life could somehow soon be changed!

PISHTCHIK: [*Takes him by the arm, in an undertone.*] She's weeping, let us go and leave her alone. Come. [*Takes him by the arm and leads him into the larger drawing-room.*]

LOPAHIN: What's that? Musicians, play up! All must be as I wish it. [*With irony.*] Here comes the new master, the owner of the cherry orchard! [*Accidentally tips over a little table, almost upsetting the candelabra.*] I can pay for everything! [*Goes out with* PISHTCHIK. *No one remains on the stage or in the larger drawing-room except* LYUBOV, *who sits huddled up, weeping bitterly. The music plays softly.* ANYA *and* TROFIMOV *come in quickly.* ANYA *goes up to her mother and falls on her knees before her.* TROFIMOV *stands at the entrance to the larger drawing-room.*]

ANYA: Mamma! Mamma, you're crying, dear, kind, good mamma! My precious! I love you! I bless you! The cherry orchard is sold, it is gone, that's true, that's true! But don't weep, mamma! Life is still before you, you have still your good, pure heart! Let us go, let us go, darling, away from here! We will make a new garden, more splendid than this one; you will see it, you will understand. And joy, quiet, deep joy, will sink into your soul like the sun at evening! And you will smile, mamma! Come, darling, let us go!

CURTAIN

ACT IV

SCENE: *Same as in First Act. There are neither curtains on the windows nor pictures on the walls: only a little furniture remains piled up in a corner as if for sale. There is a sense of desolation; near the outer door and in the background of the scene are packed trunks, traveling bags, etc. On the left the door is open, and from here the voices of* VARYA *and* ANYA *are audible.* LOPAHIN *is standing waiting.* YASHA *is holding a tray with glasses full of champagne. In front of the stage* EPIHODOV *is tying up a box. In the background behind the scene a hum of talk from the peasants who have come to say good-bye. The voice of* GAEV: "Thanks, brothers, thanks!"

YASHA: The peasants have come to say good-bye. In my opinion, Yermolay Alexeyevitch, the peasants are good-natured, but they don't know much about things.

[*The hum of talk dies away. Enter across front of stage* LYUBOV ANDREYEVNA *and* GAEV. *She is not weeping, but is pale; her face is quivering—she cannot speak.*]

GAEV: You gave them your purse, Lyuba. That won't do—that won't do!
LYUBOV: I couldn't help it! I couldn't help it!

[*Both go out.*]

LOPAHIN: [*In the doorway, calls after them.*] You will take a glass at parting? Please do. I didn't think to bring any from the town, and at the station I could only get one bottle. Please take a glass. [*A pause.*] What? You don't care for any? [*Comes away from the door.*] If I'd known, I wouldn't have bought it. Well, and I'm not going to drink it. [YASHA *carefully sets the tray down on a chair.*] You have a glass, Yasha, anyway.

YASHA: Good luck to the travelers, and luck to those that stay behind! [*Drinks.*] This champagne isn't the real thing, I can assure you.

LOPAHIN: It cost eight roubles the bottle. [*A pause.*] It's devilish cold here.

YASHA: They haven't heated the stove today—it's all the same since we're going. [*Laughs.*]

LOPAHIN: What are you laughing for?

YASHA: For pleasure.

LOPAHIN: Though it's October, it's as still and sunny as though it were summer. It's just right for building! [*Looks at his watch; says in doorway.*] Take note, ladies and gentlemen, the train goes in forty-seven minutes; so you ought to start for the station in twenty minutes. You must hurry up!

[TROFIMOV *comes in from out of doors wearing a great-coat.*]

TROFIMOV: I think it must be time to start, the horses are ready. The devil only knows what's become of my goloshes; they're lost. [*In the doorway.*] Anya! My goloshes aren't here. I can't find them.

LOPAHIN: And I'm getting off to Harkov. I am going in the same train with you. I'm spending all the winter at Harkov. I've been wasting all my time gossiping with you and fretting with no work to do. I can't get on without work. I don't know what to do with my hands, they flap about so queerly, as if they didn't belong to me.

TROFIMOV: Well, we're just going away, and you will take up your profitable labors again.

LOPAHIN: Do take a glass.

TROFIMOV: No, thanks.

LOPAHIN: Then you're going to Moscow now?

TROFIMOV: Yes. I shall see them as far as the town, and to-morrow I shall go on to Moscow.

LOPAHIN: Yes, I daresay, the professors aren't giving any lectures, they're waiting for your arrival.

TROFIMOV: That's not your business.

LOPAHIN: How many years have you been at the University?

TROFIMOV: Do think of something newer than that—that's stale and flat. [*Hunts for goloshes.*] You know we shall most likely never see each other again, so let me give you one piece of advice at parting: don't wave your arms about—get out of the habit. And another thing, building villas, reckoning up that the summer visitors will in time become independent farmers—reckoning like that, that's not the thing to do either. After all, I am fond of you: you have fine delicate fingers like an artist, you've a fine delicate soul.

LOPAHIN: [*Embraces him.*] Good-bye, my dear fellow. Thanks for everything. Let me give you money for the journey, if you need it.

TROFIMOV: What for? I don't need it.

LOPAHIN: Why, you haven't got a half-penny.

TROFIMOV: Yes, I have, thank you. I got some money for a translation. Here it is in my pocket, [*Anxiously.*] but where can my goloshes be!

VARYA: [*From the next room.*] Take the nasty things! [*Flings a pair of goloshes on to the stage.*]

TROFIMOV: Why are you so cross, Varya? h'm! . . . but those aren't my goloshes.

LOPAHIN: I sowed three thousand acres with poppies in the spring, and now I have cleared forty thousand profit.[4] And when my poppies were in flower, wasn't it a picture! So here, as I say, I made forty thousand, and I'm offering you a loan because I can afford to. Why turn up your nose? I am a peasant—I speak bluntly.

TROFIMOV: Your father was a peasant, mine was a chemist[5]—and that proves absolutely nothing whatever. [LOPAHIN *takes out his pocket-book.*] Stop that—stop that. If you were to offer me two hundred thousand I wouldn't take it. I am an independent man, and everything that all of you, rich and poor alike, prize so highly and hold so dear, hasn't the slightest power over me—it's like so much fluff fluttering in the air. I can get on without you. I can pass by you. I am strong and proud. Humanity is advancing towards the highest truth, the highest happiness, which is possible on earth, and I am in the front ranks.

LOPAHIN: Will you get there?

TROFIMOV: I shall get there. [*A pause.*] I shall get there, or I shall show others the way to get there.

[*In the distance is heard the stroke of an ax on a tree.*]

LOPAHIN: Good-bye, my dear fellow; it's time to be off. We turn up our noses at one another, but life is passing all the while. When I am working hard without resting, then my mind is more at ease, and it seems to me as though I too know what I exist for; but how many people there are in Russia, my dear boy, who exist, one doesn't know what for. Well, it doesn't matter. That's not what keeps things spinning. They tell me Leonid Andreyevitch has taken a situation. He is going to be a clerk at the bank—6,000 roubles a year.[6] Only, of course, he won't stick to it—he's too lazy.

ANYA: [*In the doorway.*] Mamma begs you not to let them chop down the orchard until she's gone.

TROFIMOV: Yes, really, you might have the tact. [*Walks out across the front of the stage.*]

LOPAHIN: I'll see to it! I'll see to it! Stupid fellows! [*Goes out after him.*]

ANYA: Has Firs been taken to the hospital?

4. That is, a profit equivalent to well over $800,000 in today's U.S. currency. 5. Pharmacist.
6. Salary equivalent to over $120,000 in today's U.S. currency.

YASHA: I told them this morning. No doubt they have taken him.

ANYA: [*To* EPIHODOV, *who passes across the drawing-room.*] Semyon Pantaleyevitch, inquire, please, if Firs has been taken to the hospital.

YASHA: [*In a tone of offence.*] I told Yegor this morning—why ask a dozen times?

EPIHODOV: Firs is advanced in years. It's my conclusive opinion no treatment would do him good; it's time he was gathered to his fathers. And I can only envy him. [*Puts a trunk down on a cardboard hat-box and crushes it.*] There, now, of course—I knew it would be so.

YASHA: [*Jeeringly.*] Two and twenty misfortunes!

VARYA: [*Through the door.*] Has Firs been taken to the hospital?

ANYA: Yes.

VARYA: Why wasn't the note for the doctor taken too?

ANYA: Oh, then, we must send it after them. [*Goes out.*]

VARYA: [*From the adjoining room.*] Where's Yasha? Tell him his mother's come to say good-bye to him.

YASHA: [*Waves his hand.*] They put me out of all patience! [DUNYASHA *has all this time been busy about the luggage. Now, when* YASHA *is left alone, she goes up to him.*]

DUNYASHA: You might just give me one look, Yasha. You're going away. You're leaving me. [*Weeps and throws herself on his neck.*]

YASHA: What are you crying for? [*Drinks the champagne.*] In six days I shall be in Paris again. To-morrow we shall get into the express train and roll away in a flash. I can scarcely believe it! *Vive la France!* It doesn't suit me here—it's not the life for me; there's no doing anything. I have seen enough of the ignorance here. I have had enough of it. [*Drinks champagne.*] What are you crying for? Behave yourself properly, and then you won't cry.

DUNYASHA: [*Powders her face, looking in a pocket-mirror.*] Do send me a letter from Paris. You know how I loved you, Yasha—how I loved you! I am a tender creature, Yasha.

YASHA: Here they are coming!

[*Busies himself about the trunks, humming softly. Enter* LYUBOV ANDREYEVNA, GAEV, ANYA *and* CHARLOTTA IVANOVNA.]

GAEV: We ought to be off. There's not much time now. [*Looking at* YASHA.] What a smell of herrings!

LYUBOV: In ten minutes we must get into the carriage. [*Casts a look about the room.*] Farewell, dear house, dear old home of our fathers! Winter will pass and spring will come, and then you will be no more; they will tear you down! How much those walls have seen! [*Kisses her daughter passionately.*] My treasure, how bright you look! Your eyes are sparkling like diamonds! Are you glad? Very glad?

ANYA: Very glad! A new life is beginning, mamma.

GAEV: Yes, really, everything is all right now. Before the cherry orchard was sold, we were all worried and wretched, but afterwards, when once the question was settled conclusively, irrevocably, we all felt calm and even cheerful. I am a bank clerk now—I am a financier—cannon off the red. And you, Lyuba, after all, you are looking better; there's no question of that.

LYUBOV: Yes. My nerves are better, that's true. [*Her hat and coat are handed to her.*] I'm sleeping well. Carry out my things, Yasha. It's time. [*To* ANYA.] My darling, we shall soon see each other again. I am going to Paris. I can live there on the money your Yaroslavl auntie sent us to buy the estate with—hurrah for auntie—but that money won't last long.

ANYA: You'll come back soon, mamma, won't you? I'll be working up for my examination in the high school, and when I have passed that, I shall set to work and be a help to you. We will read all sorts of things together, mamma, won't we? [*Kisses her mother's hands.*] We will read in the autumn evenings. We'll read lots of books, and a new wonderful world will open out before us. [*Dreamily.*] Mamma, come soon.

LYUBOV: I shall come, my precious treasure. [*Embraces her.*]

[*Enter* LOPAHIN. CHARLOTTA *softly hums a song.*]

GAEV: Charlotta's happy; she's singing!

CHARLOTTA: [*Picks up a bundle like a swaddled baby.*] Bye, bye, my baby. [*A baby is heard crying: "Ooah! ooah!"*] Hush, hush, my pretty boy! [*Ooah! ooah!*] Poor little thing! [*Throws the bundle back.*] You must please find me a situation. I can't go on like this.

LOPAHIN: We'll find you one, Charlotta Ivanovna. Don't you worry yourself.

GAEV: Everyone's leaving us. Varya's going away. We have become of no use all at once.

CHARLOTTA: There's nowhere for me to be in the town. I must go away. [*Hums.*] What care I . . .

[*Enter* PISHTCHIK.]

LOPAHIN: The freak of nature!

PISHTCHIK: [*Gasping.*] Oh! . . . let me get my breath. . . . I'm worn out . . . my most honored . . . Give me some water.

GAEV: Want some money, I suppose? Your humble servant! I'll go out of the way of temptation. [*Goes out.*]

PISHTCHIK: It's a long while since I have been to see you . . . dearest lady. [*To* LOPAHIN.] You are here . . . glad to see you . . . a man of immense intellect . . . take . . . here. [*Gives* LOPAHIN.] 400 roubles.[7] That leaves me owing 840.

LOPAHIN: [*Shrugging his shoulders in amazement.*] It's like a dream. Where did you get it?

PISHTCHIK: Wait a bit . . . I'm hot . . . a most extraordinary occurrence! Some Englishmen came along and found in my land some sort of white clay. [*To* LYUBOV ANDREYEVNA.] And 400 for you . . . most lovely . . . wonderful. [*Gives money.*] The rest later. [*Sips water.*] A young man in the train was telling me just now that a great philosopher advises jumping off a house-top. "Jump!" says he; "the whole gist of the problem lies in that." [*Wonderingly.*] Fancy that, now! Water, please!

LOPAHIN: What Englishmen?

PISHTCHIK: I have made over to them the rights to dig the clay for twenty-four years . . . and now, excuse me . . . I can't stay . . . I must be trotting on. I'm

7. Over $8,500 in today's U.S. currency.

going to Znoikovo . . . to Kardamanovo. . . . I'm in debt all round. [*Sips.*] . . . To your very good health! . . . I'll come in on Thursday.

LYUBOV: We are just off to the town, and to-morrow I start for abroad.

PISHTCHIK: What! [*In agitation.*] Why to the town? Oh, I see the furniture . . . the boxes. No matter . . . [*Through his tears.*] . . . no matter . . . men of enormous intellect . . . these Englishmen. . . . Never mind . . . be happy. God will succor you . . . no matter . . . everything in this world must have an end. [*Kisses* LYUBOV ANDREYEVNA'S *hand.*] If the rumor reaches you that my end has come, think of this . . . old horse, and say: "There once was such a man in the world . . . Semyonov-Pishtchik . . . the Kingdom of Heaven be his!" . . . most extraordinary weather . . . yes. [*Goes out in violent agitation, but at once returns and says in the doorway.*] Dashenka wishes to be remembered to you. [*Goes out.*]

LYUBOV: Now we can start. I leave with two cares in my heart. The first is leaving Firs ill. [*Looking at her watch.*] We have still five minutes.

ANYA: Mamma, Firs has been taken to the hospital. Yasha sent him off this morning.

LYUBOV: My other anxiety is Varya. She is used to getting up early and working; and now, without work, she's like a fish out of water. She is thin and pale, and she's crying, poor dear! [*A pause.*] You are well aware, Yermolay Alexeyevitch, I dreamed of marrying her to you, and everything seemed to show that you would get married. [*Whispers to* ANYA *and motions to* CHARLOTTA *and both go out.*] She loves you—she suits you. And I don't know—I don't know why it is you seem, as it were, to avoid each other. I can't understand it!

LOPAHIN: I don't understand it myself, I confess. It's queer somehow, altogether. If there's still time, I'm ready now at once. Let's settle it straight off, and go ahead; but without you, I feel I shan't make her an offer.

LYUBOV: That's excellent. Why, a single moment's all that's necessary. I'll call her at once.

LOPAHIN: And there's champagne all ready too. [*Looking into the glasses.*] Empty! Someone's emptied them already. [YASHA *coughs.*] I call that greedy.

LYUBOV: [*Eagerly.*] Capital! We will go out. Yasha, *allez!*[8] I'll call her in. [*At the door.*] Varya, leave all that; come here. Come along! [*Goes out with* YASHA.]

LOPAHIN: [*Looking at his watch.*] Yes.

[*A pause. Behind the door, smothered laughter and whispering, and, at last, enter* VARYA.]

VARYA: [*Looking a long while over the things.*] It is strange, I can't find it anywhere.

LOPAHIN: What are you looking for?

VARYA: I packed it myself, and I can't remember. [*A pause.*]

LOPAHIN: Where are you going now, Varvara Mihailova?

VARYA: I? To the Ragulins. I have arranged to go to them to look after the house—as a housekeeper.

LOPAHIN: That's in Yashnovo? It'll be seventy miles away. [*A pause.*] So this is the end of life in this house!

8. Go! (French).

VARYA: [*Looking among the things.*] Where is it? Perhaps I put it in the trunk. Yes, life in this house is over—there will be no more of it.
LOPAHIN: And I'm just off to Harkov—by this next train. I've a lot of business there. I'm leaving Epihodov here, and I've taken him on.
VARYA: Really!
LOPAHIN: This time last year we had snow already, if you remember; but now it's so fine and sunny. Though it's cold, to be sure—three degrees of frost.
VARYA: I haven't looked. [*A pause.*] And besides, our thermometer's broken. [*A pause.*]

[*Voice at the door from the yard: "Yermolay Alexeyevitch!"*]

LOPAHIN: [*As though he had long been expecting this summons.*] This minute!

[LOPAHIN *goes out quickly.* VARYA *sitting on the floor and laying her head on a bag full of clothes, sobs quietly. The door opens.* LYUBOV ANDREYEVNA *comes in cautiously.*]

LYUBOV: Well? [*A pause.*] We must be going.
VARYA: [*Has wiped her eyes and is no longer crying.*] Yes, mamma, it's time to start. I shall have time to get to the Ragulins to-day, if only you're not late for the train.
LYUBOV: [*In the doorway.*] Anya, put your things on.

[*Enter* ANYA, *then* GAEV *and* CHARLOTTA IVANOVNA. GAEV *has on a warm coat with a hood. Servants and cabmen come in.* EPIHODOV *bustles about the luggage.*]

LYUBOV: Now we can start on our travels.
ANYA: [*Joyfully.*] On our travels!
GAEV: My friends—my dear, my precious friends! Leaving this house for ever, can I be silent? Can I refrain from giving utterance at leave-taking to those emotions which now flood all my being?
ANYA: [*Supplicatingly.*] Uncle!
VARYA: Uncle, you mustn't!
GAEV: [*Dejectedly.*] Cannon and into the pocket . . . I'll be quiet. . . .

[*Enter* TROFIMOV *and afterwards* LOPAHIN.]

TROFIMOV: Well, ladies and gentlemen, we must start.
LOPAHIN: Epihodov, my coat!
LYUBOV: I'll stay just one minute. It seems as though I have never seen before what the walls, what the ceilings in this house were like, and now I look at them with greediness, with such tender love.
GAEV: I remember when I was six years old sitting in that window on Trinity Day watching my father going to church.
LYUBOV: Have all the things been taken?
LOPAHIN: I think all. [*Putting on overcoat, to* EPIHODOV.] You, Epihodov, mind you see everything is right.
EPIHODOV: [*In a husky voice.*] Don't you trouble, Yermolay Alexeyevitch.
LOPAHIN: Why, what's wrong with your voice?

EPIHODOV: I've just had a drink of water, and I choked over something.

YASHA: [*Contemptuously.*] The ignorance!

LYUBOV: We are going—and not a soul will be left here.

LOPAHIN: Not till the spring.

VARYA: [*Pulls a parasol out of a bundle, as though about to hit someone with it.* LOPAHIN *makes a gesture as though alarmed.*] What is it? I didn't mean anything.

TROFIMOV: Ladies and gentlemen, let us get into the carriage. It's time. The train will be in directly.

VARYA: Petya, here they are, your goloshes, by that box. [*With tears.*] And what dirty old things they are!

TROFIMOV: [*Putting on his goloshes.*] Let us go, friends!

GAEV: [*Greatly agitated, afraid of weeping.*] The train—the station! Double baulk, ah!

LYUBOV: Let us go!

LOPAHIN: Are we all here? [*Locks the side-door on left.*] The things are all here. We must lock up. Let us go!

ANYA: Good-bye, home! Good-bye to the old life!

TROFIMOV: Welcome to the new life!

[TROFIMOV *goes out with* ANYA. VARYA *looks round the room and goes out slowly.* YASHA *and* CHARLOTTA IVANOVNA, *with her dog, go out.*]

LOPAHIN: Till the spring, then! Come, friends, till we meet! [*Goes out.*]

[LYUBOV ANDREYEVNA *and* GAEV *remain alone. As though they had been waiting for this, they throw themselves on each other's necks, and break into subdued smothered sobbing, afraid of being overheard.*]

GAEV: [*In despair.*] Sister, my sister!

LYUBOV: Oh, my orchard!—my sweet, beautiful orchard! My life, my youth, my happiness, good-bye! good-bye!

VOICE OF ANYA: [*Calling gaily.*] Mamma!

VOICE OF TROFIMOV: [*Gaily, excitedly.*] Aa—oo!

LYUBOV: One last look at the walls, at the windows. My dear mother loved to walk about this room.

GAEV: Sister, sister!

VOICE OF ANYA: Mamma!

VOICE OF TROFIMOV: Aa—oo!

LYUBOV: We are coming. [*They go out.*]

[*The stage is empty. There is the sound of the doors being locked up, then of the carriages driving away. There is silence. In the stillness there is the dull stroke of an ax in a tree, clanging with a mournful lonely sound. Footsteps are heard.* FIRS *appears in the doorway on the right. He is dressed as always—in a pea-jacket and white waistcoat, with slippers on his feet. He is ill.*]

FIRS: [*Goes up to the doors, and tries the handles.*] Locked! They have gone . . . [*Sits down on sofa.*] They have forgotten me. . . . Never mind . . . I'll sit here a bit. . . . I'll be bound Leonid Andreyevitch hasn't put his fur coat on and has gone off in his thin overcoat. [*Sighs anxiously.*] I didn't see after him. . . . These young people . . . [*Mutters something that can't be distinguished.*] Life has slipped by as though I hadn't lived. [*Lies down.*] I'll lie down a bit. . . . There's no strength in you, nothing left you—all gone! Ech! I'm good for nothing. [*Lies motionless.*]

[*A sound is heard that seems to come from the sky, like a breaking harp-string, dying away mournfully. All is still again, and there is heard nothing but the strokes of the ax far away in the orchard.*]

CURTAIN

1903–04

HENRIK IBSEN
(1828–1906)

A Doll House[1]

Born in Skien, Norway, Henrik Ibsen was apprenticed to an apothecary until 1850, when he left for Oslo and published his first play, *Catilina*, a verse tragedy. By 1857 Ibsen was director of Oslo's Norwegian Theater, but his early plays, such as *Love's Comedy* (1862), were poorly received. Disgusted with what he saw as Norway's backwardness, Ibsen left in 1864 for Rome, where he wrote two more verse plays, *Brand* (1866) and *Peer Gynt* (1867), before turning to the realistic style and harsh criticism of traditional social mores for which he is best known. *The League of Youth* (1869), *Pillars of Society* (1877), *A Doll House* (1879), *Ghosts* (1881), *An Enemy of the People* (1882), *The Wild Duck* (1884), and *Hedda Gabler* (1890) won him a reputation throughout Europe as a controversial and outspoken advocate of moral and social reform. Near the end of his life, Ibsen explored the human condition in the explicitly symbolic terms of *The Master Builder* (1892) and *When We Dead Awaken* (1899). Ibsen's works had enormous influence on twentieth-century drama.

CHARACTERS

TORVALD HELMER, *a lawyer*
NORA, *his wife*
DR. RANK
MRS. LINDE
NILS KROGSTAD, *a bank clerk*
THE HELMERS' THREE SMALL CHILDREN
ANNE-MARIE, *their nurse*
HELENE, *a maid*
A DELIVERY BOY

The action takes place in HELMER'S *residence.*

1. Translated by Rolf Fjelde.

ACT I

A comfortable room, tastefully but not expensively furnished. A door to the right in the back wall leads to the entryway; another to the left leads to HELMER'S *study. Between these doors, a piano. Midway in the left-hand wall a door, and further back a window. Near the window a round table with an armchair and a small sofa. In the right-hand wall, toward the rear, a door, and nearer the foreground a porcelain stove with two armchairs and a rocking chair beside it. Between the stove and the side door, a small table. Engravings on the walls. An etagère with china figures and other small art objects; a small bookcase with richly bound books; the floor carpeted; a fire burning in the stove. It is a winter day.*

A bell rings in the entryway; shortly after we hear the door being unlocked. NORA *comes into the room, humming happily to herself; she is wearing street clothes and carries an armload of packages, which she puts down on the table to the right. She has left the hall door open; and through it a* DELIVERY BOY *is seen, holding a Christmas tree and a basket, which he gives to the* MAID *who let them in.*

NORA: Hide the tree well, Helene. The children mustn't get a glimpse of it till this evening, after it's trimmed. [*To the* DELIVERY BOY, *taking out her purse.*] How much?

DELIVERY BOY: Fifty, ma'am.

NORA: There's a crown. No, keep the change. [*The* BOY *thanks her and leaves.* NORA *shuts the door. She laughs softly to herself while taking off her street things. Drawing a bag of macaroons from her pocket, she eats a couple, then steals over and listens at her husband's study door.*] Yes, he's home. [*Hums again as she moves to the table right.*]

HELMER: [*From the study.*] Is that my little lark twittering out there?

NORA: [*Busy opening some packages.*] Yes, it is.

HELMER: Is that my squirrel rummaging around?

NORA: Yes!

HELMER: When did my squirrel get in?

NORA: Just now. [*Putting the macaroon bag in her pocket and wiping her mouth.*] Do come in, Torvald, and see what I've bought.

HELMER: Can't be disturbed. [*After a moment he opens the door and peers in, pen in hand.*] Bought, you say? All that there? Has the little spendthrift been out throwing money around again?

NORA: Oh, but Torvald, this year we really should let ourselves go a bit. It's the first Christmas we haven't had to economize.

HELMER: But you know we can't go squandering.

NORA: Oh yes, Torvald, we can squander a little now. Can't we? Just a tiny, wee bit. Now that you've got a big salary and are going to make piles and piles of money.

HELMER: Yes—starting New Year's. But then it's a full three months till the raise comes through.

NORA: Pooh! We can borrow that long.

HELMER: Nora! [*Goes over and playfully takes her by the ear.*] Are your scatter-brains off again? What if today I borrowed a thousand crowns, and you squandered them over Christmas week, and then on New Year's Eve a roof tile fell on my head, and I lay there—

NORA: [*Putting her hand on his mouth.*] Oh! Don't say such things!

HELMER: Yes, but what if it happened—then what?

NORA: If anything so awful happened, then it just wouldn't matter if I had debts or not.

HELMER: Well, but the people I'd borrowed from?

NORA: Them? Who cares about them! They're strangers.

HELMER: Nora, Nora, how like a woman! No, but seriously, Nora, you know what I think about that. No debts! Never borrow! Something of freedom's lost—and something of beauty, too—from a home that's founded on borrowing and debt. We've made a brave stand up to now, the two of us; and we'll go right on like that the little while we have to.

NORA: [*Going toward the stove.*] Yes, whatever you say, Torvald.

HELMER: [*Following her.*] Now, now, the little lark's wings mustn't droop. Come on, don't be a sulky squirrel. [*Taking out his wallet.*] Nora, guess what I have here.

NORA: [*Turning quickly.*] Money!

HELMER: There, see. [*Hands her some notes.*] Good grief, I know how costs go up in a house at Christmastime.

NORA: Ten—twenty—thirty—forty. Oh, thank you, Torvald; I can manage no end on this.

HELMER: You really will have to.

NORA: Oh yes, I promise I will. But come here so I can show you everything I bought. And so cheap! Look, new clothes for Ivar here—and a sword. Here a horse and a trumpet for Bob. And a doll and a doll's bed here for Emmy; they're nothing much, but she'll tear them to bits in no time anyway. And here I have dress material and handkerchiefs for the maids. Old Anne-Marie really deserves something more.

HELMER: And what's in that package there?

NORA: [*With a cry.*] Torvald, no! You can't see that till tonight!

HELMER: I see. But tell me now, you little prodigal, what have you thought of for yourself?

NORA: For myself? Oh, I don't want anything at all.

HELMER: Of course you do. Tell me just what—within reason—you'd most like to have.

NORA: I honestly don't know. Oh, listen, Torvald—

HELMER: Well?

NORA: [*Fumbling at his coat buttons, without looking at him.*] If you want to give me something, then maybe you could—you could—

HELMER: Come, on, out with it.

NORA: [*Hurriedly.*] You could give me money, Torvald. No more than you think you can spare; then one of these days I'll buy something with it.

HELMER: But Nora—

NORA: Oh, please, Torvald darling, do that! I beg you, please. Then I could hang the bills in pretty gilt paper on the Christmas tree. Wouldn't that be fun?

HELMER: What are those little birds called that always fly through their fortunes?

NORA: Oh yes, spendthrifts; I know all that. But let's do as I say, Torvald; then I'll have time to decide what I really need most. That's very sensible, isn't it?

HELMER: [*Smiling.*] Yes, very—that is, if you actually hung onto the money I give you, and you actually used it to buy yourself something. But it goes for the house and for all sorts of foolish things, and then I only have to lay out some more.

NORA: Oh, but Torvald—

HELMER: Don't deny it, my dear little Nora. [*Putting his arm around her waist.*] Spendthrifts are sweet, but they use up a frightful amount of money. It's incredible what it costs a man to feed such birds.

NORA: Oh, how can you say that! Really, I save everything I can.

HELMER: [*Laughing.*] Yes, that's the truth. Everything you can. But that's nothing at all.

NORA: [*Humming, with a smile of quiet satisfaction.*] Hm, if you only knew what expenses we larks and squirrels have, Torvald.

HELMER: You're an odd little one. Exactly the way your father was. You're never at a loss for scaring up money; but the moment you have it, it runs right out through your fingers; you never know what you've done with it. Well, one takes you as you are. It's deep in your blood. Yes, these things are hereditary, Nora.

NORA: Ah, I could wish I'd inherited many of Papa's qualities.

HELMER: And I couldn't wish you anything but just what you are, my sweet little lark. But wait; it seems to me you have a very—what should I call it?—a very suspicious look today—

NORA: I do?

HELMER: You certainly do. Look me straight in the eye.

NORA: [*Looking at him.*] Well?

HELMER: [*Shaking an admonitory finger.*] Surely my sweet tooth hasn't been running riot in town today, has she?

NORA: No. Why do you imagine that?

HELMER: My sweet tooth really didn't make a little detour through the confectioner's?

NORA: No, I assure you, Torvald—

HELMER: Hasn't nibbled some pastry?

NORA: No, not at all.

HELMER: Not even munched a macaroon or two?

NORA: No, Torvald, I assure you, really—

HELMER: There, there now. Of course I'm only joking.

NORA: [*Going to the table, right.*] You know I could never think of going against you.

HELMER: No, I understand that; and you *have* given me your word. [*Going over to her.*] Well, you keep your little Christmas secrets to yourself, Nora darling. I expect they'll come to light this evening, when the tree is lit.

NORA: Did you remember to ask Dr. Rank?

HELMER: No. But there's no need for that; it's assumed he'll be dining with us. All the same, I'll ask him when he stops by here this morning. I've ordered some fine wine. Nora, you can't imagine how I'm looking forward to this evening.

NORA: So am I. And what fun for the children, Torvald!

HELMER: Ah, it's so gratifying to know that one's gotten a safe, secure job, and with a comfortable salary. It's a great satisfaction, isn't it?

NORA: Oh, it's wonderful!

HELMER: Remember last Christmas? Three whole weeks before, you shut yourself in every evening till long after midnight, making flowers for the Christmas tree, and all the other decorations to surprise us. Ugh, that was the dullest time I've ever lived through.

NORA: It wasn't at all dull for me.

HELMER: [*Smiling.*] But the outcome *was* pretty sorry, Nora.

NORA: Oh, don't tease me with that again. How could I help it that the cat came in and tore everything to shreds.

HELMER: No, poor thing, you certainly couldn't. You wanted so much to please us all, and that's what counts. But it's just as well that the hard times are past.

NORA: Yes, it's really wonderful.

HELMER: Now I don't have to sit here alone, boring myself, and you don't have to tire your precious eyes and your fair little delicate hands—

NORA: [*Clapping her hands.*] No, is it really true, Torvald, I don't have to? Oh, how wonderfully lovely to hear! [*Taking his arm.*] Now I'll tell you just how I've thought we should plan things. Right after Christmas—[*The doorbell rings.*] Oh, the bell. [*Straightening the room up a bit.*] Somebody would have to come. What a bore!

HELMER: I'm not at home to visitors, don't forget.

MAID: [*From the hall doorway.*] Ma'am, a lady to see you—

NORA: All right, let her come in.

MAID: [*To* HELMER.] And the doctor's just come too.

HELMER: Did he go right to my study?

MAID: Yes, he did.

[HELMER *goes into his room. The* MAID *shows in* MRS. LINDE, *dressed in traveling clothes, and shuts the door after her.*]

MRS. LINDE: [*In a dispirited and somewhat hesitant voice.*] Hello, Nora.

NORA: [*Uncertain.*] Hello—

MRS. LINDE: You don't recognize me.

NORA: No, I don't know—but wait, I think—[*Exclaiming.*] What! Kristine! Is it really you?

MRS. LINDE: Yes, it's me.

NORA: Kristine! To think I didn't recognize you. But then, how could I? [*More quietly.*] How you've changed, Kristine!

MRS. LINDE: Yes, no doubt I have. In nine—ten long years.

NORA: Is it so long since we met! Yes, it's all of that. Oh, these last eight years have been a happy time, believe me. And so now you've come in to town, too. Made the long trip in the winter. That took courage.

MRS. LINDE: I just got here by ship this morning.

NORA: To enjoy yourself over Christmas, of course. Oh, how lovely! Yes, enjoy ourselves, we'll do that. But take your coat off. You're not still cold? [*Helping her.*] There now, let's get cozy here by the stove. No, the easy chair there! I'll take the rocker here. [*Seizing her hands.*] Yes, now you have your old look again; it was only in that first moment. You're a bit more pale, Kristine—and maybe a bit thinner.

MRS. LINDE: And much, much older, Nora.

NORA: Yes, perhaps a bit older; a tiny, tiny bit; not much at all. [*Stopping short; suddenly serious.*] Oh, but thoughtless me, to sit here, chattering away. Sweet, good Kristine, can you forgive me?

MRS. LINDE: What do you mean, Nora?

NORA: [*Softly.*] Poor Kristine, you've become a widow.

MRS. LINDE: Yes, three years ago.

NORA: Oh, I knew it, of course; I read it in the papers. Oh, Kristine, you must believe me; I often thought of writing you then, but I kept postponing it, and something always interfered.

MRS. LINDE: Nora dear, I understand completely.

NORA: No, it was awful of me, Kristine. You poor thing, how much you must have gone through. And he left you nothing?

MRS. LINDE: No.

NORA: And no children?

MRS. LINDE: No.

NORA: Nothing at all, then?

MRS. LINDE: Not even a sense of loss to feed on.

NORA: [*Looking incredulously at her.*] But Kristine, how could that be?

MRS. LINDE: [*Smiling wearily and smoothing her hair.*] Oh, sometimes it happens, Nora.

NORA: So completely alone. How terribly hard that must be for you. I have three lovely children. You can't see them now; they're out with the maid. But now you must tell me everything—

MRS. LINDE: No, no, no, tell me about yourself.

NORA: No, you begin. Today I don't want to be selfish. I want to think only of you today. But there *is* something I must tell you. Did you hear of the wonderful luck we had recently?

MRS. LINDE: No, what's that?

NORA: My husband's been made manager in the bank, just think!

MRS. LINDE: Your husband? How marvelous!

NORA: Isn't it? Being a lawyer is such an uncertain living, you know, especially if one won't touch any cases that aren't clean and decent. And of course Torvald would never do that, and I'm with him completely there. Oh, we're simply delighted, believe me! He'll join the bank right after New Year's and start getting a huge salary and lots of commissions. From now on we can live quite differently—just as we want. Oh, Kristine, I feel so light and happy! Won't it be lovely to have stacks of money and not a care in the world?

MRS. LINDE: Well, anyway, it would be lovely to have enough for necessities.

NORA: No, not just for necessities, but stacks and stacks of money!

MRS. LINDE: [*Smiling.*] Nora, Nora, aren't you sensible yet? Back in school you were such a free spender.

NORA: [*With a quiet laugh.*] Yes, that's what Torvald still says. [*Shaking her finger.*] But "Nora, Nora" isn't as silly as you all think. Really, we've been in no position for me to go squandering. We've had to work, both of us.

MRS. LINDE: You too?

NORA: Yes, at odd jobs—needlework, crocheting, embroidery, and such—[*Casually.*] and other things too. You remember that Torvald left the department when we were married? There was no chance of promotion in his office, and of course he needed to earn more money. But that first year he drove himself terribly. He took on all kinds of extra work that kept him going morning and night. It wore him down, and then he fell deathly ill. The doctors said it was essential for him to travel south.

MRS. LINDE: Yes, didn't you spend a whole year in Italy?

NORA: That's right. It wasn't easy to get away, you know. Ivar had just been born. But of course we had to go. Oh, that was a beautiful trip, and it saved Torvald's life. But it cost a frightful sum, Kristine.

MRS. LINDE: I can well imagine.

NORA: Four thousand, eight hundred crowns it cost. That's really a lot of money.

MRS. LINDE: But it's lucky you had it when you needed it.

NORA: Well, as it was, we got it from Papa.

MRS. LINDE: I see. It was just about the time your father died.

NORA: Yes, just about then. And, you know, I couldn't make that trip out to nurse him. I had to stay here, expecting Ivar any moment, and with my poor sick Torvald to care for. Dearest Papa, I never saw him again, Kristine. Oh, that was the worst time I've known in all my marriage.

MRS. LINDE: I know how you loved him. And then you went off to Italy?

NORA: Yes. We had the means now, and the doctors urged us. So we left a month after.

MRS. LINDE: And your husband came back completely cured?

NORA: Sound as a drum!

MRS. LINDE: But—the doctor?

NORA: Who?

MRS. LINDE: I thought the maid said he was a doctor, the man who came in with me.

NORA: Yes, that was Dr. Rank—but he's not making a sick call. He's our closest friend, and he stops by at least once a day. No, Torvald hasn't had a sick moment since, and the children are fit and strong, and I am, too. [*Jumping up and clapping her hands.*] Oh, dear God, Kristine, what a lovely thing to live and be happy! But how disgusting of me—I'm talking of nothing but my own affairs. [*Sits on a stool close by* KRISTINE, *arms resting across her knees.*] Oh, don't be angry with me! Tell me, is it really true that you weren't in love with your husband? Why did you marry him, then?

MRS. LINDE: My mother was still alive, but bedridden and helpless—and I had my two younger brothers to look after. In all conscience, I didn't think I could turn him down.

NORA: No, you were right there. But was he rich at the time?

MRS. LINDE: He was very well off, I'd say. But the business was shaky, Nora. When he died, it all fell apart, and nothing was left.

NORA: And then—?

MRS. LINDE: Yes, so I had to scrape up a living with a little shop and a little teaching and whatever else I could find. The last three years have been like one endless workday without a rest for me. Now it's over, Nora. My poor mother doesn't need me, for she's passed on. Nor the boys, either; they're working now and can take care of themselves.

NORA: How free you must feel—

MRS. LINDE: No—only unspeakably empty. Nothing to live for now. [*Standing up anxiously.*] That's why I couldn't take it any longer out in that desolate hole. Maybe here it'll be easier to find something to do and keep my mind occupied. If I could only be lucky enough to get a steady job, some office work—

NORA: Oh, but Kristine, that's so dreadfully tiring, and you already look so tired. It would be much better for you if you could go off to a bathing resort.

MRS. LINDE: [*Going toward the window.*] I have no father to give me travel money, Nora.

NORA: [*Rising.*] Oh, don't be angry with me.

MRS. LINDE: [*Going to her.*] Nora dear, don't you be angry with me. The worst of my kind of situation is all the bitterness that's stored away. No one to work for, and yet you're always having to snap up your opportunities. You have to live; and so you grow selfish. When you told me the happy change in your lot, do you know I was delighted less for your sakes than for mine?

NORA: How so? Oh, I see. You think maybe Torvald could do something for you.

MRS. LINDE: Yes, that's what I thought.

NORA: And he will, Kristine! Just leave it to me; I'll bring it up so delicately—find something attractive to humor him with. Oh, I'm so eager to help you.

MRS. LINDE: How very kind of you, Nora, to be so concerned over me—doubly kind, considering you really know so little of life's burdens yourself.

NORA: I—? I know so little—?

MRS. LINDE: [*Smiling.*] Well, my heavens—a little needlework and such—Nora, you're just a child.

NORA: [*Tossing her head and pacing the floor.*] You don't have to act so superior.

MRS. LINDE: Oh?

NORA: You're just like the others. You all think I'm incapable of anything serious—

MRS. LINDE: Come now—

NORA: That I've never had to face the raw world.

MRS. LINDE: Nora dear, you've just been telling me all your troubles.

NORA: Hm! Trivia! [*Quietly.*] I haven't told you the big thing.

MRS. LINDE: Big thing? What do you mean?

NORA: You look down on me so, Kristine, but you shouldn't. You're proud that you worked so long and hard for your mother.

MRS. LINDE: I don't look down on a soul. But it *is* true: I'm proud—and happy, too—to think it was given to me to make my mother's last days almost free of care.

NORA: And you're also proud thinking of what you've done for your brothers.

MRS. LINDE: I feel I've a right to be.

NORA: I agree. But listen to this, Kristine—I've also got something to be proud and happy for.

MRS. LINDE: I don't doubt it. But whatever do you mean?

NORA: Not so loud. What if Torvald heard! He mustn't, not for anything in the world. Nobody must know, Kristine. No one but you.

MRS. LINDE: But what is it, then?

NORA: Come here. [*Drawing her down beside her on the sofa.*] It's true—I've also got something to be proud and happy for. I'm the one who saved Torvald's life.

MRS. LINDE: Saved—? Saved how?

NORA: I told you about the trip to Italy. Torvald never would have lived if he hadn't gone south—

MRS. LINDE: Of course; your father gave you the means—

NORA: [*Smiling.*] That's what Torvald and all the rest think, but—

MRS. LINDE: But—?

NORA: Papa didn't give us a pin. I was the one who raised the money.

MRS. LINDE: You? That whole amount?

NORA: Four thousand, eight hundred crowns. What do you say to that?

MRS. LINDE: But Nora, how was it possible? Did you win the lottery?

NORA: [*Disdainfully.*] The lottery? Pooh! No art to that.

MRS. LINDE: But where did you get it from then?

NORA: [*Humming, with a mysterious smile.*] Hmm, tra-la-la-la.

MRS. LINDE: Because you couldn't have borrowed it.

NORA: No? Why not?

MRS. LINDE: A wife can't borrow without her husband's consent.

NORA: [*Tossing her head.*] Oh, but a wife with a little business sense, a wife who knows how to manage—

MRS. LINDE: Nora, I simply don't understand—

NORA: You don't have to. Whoever said I *borrowed* the money? I could have gotten it other ways. [*Throwing herself back on the sofa.*] I could have gotten it from some admirer or other. After all, a girl with my ravishing appeal—

MRS. LINDE: You lunatic.

NORA: I'll bet you're eaten up with curiosity, Kristine.

MRS. LINDE: Now listen here, Nora—you haven't done something indiscreet?

NORA: [*Sitting up again.*] Is it indiscreet to save your husband's life?

MRS. LINDE: I think it's indiscreet that without his knowledge you—

NORA: But that's the point: he mustn't know! My Lord, can't you understand? He mustn't ever know the close call he had. It was to *me* the doctors came to say his life was in danger—that nothing could save him but a stay in the south. Didn't I try strategy then! I began talking about how lovely it would be for me to travel abroad like other young wives; I begged and I cried; I told him please to remember my condition, to be kind and indulge me; and then I dropped a hint that he could easily take out a loan. But at that, Kristine, he nearly exploded. He said I was frivolous, and it was his duty as man of the house not to indulge me in whims and fancies—as I think he called them. Aha, I thought, now you'll just have to be saved—and that's when I saw my chance.

MRS. LINDE: And your father never told Torvald the money wasn't from him?

NORA: No, never. Papa died right about then. I'd considered bringing him into my secret and begging him never to tell. But he was too sick at the time—and then, sadly, it didn't matter.

MRS. LINDE: And you've never confided in your husband since?

NORA: For heaven's sake, no! Are you serious? He's so strict on that subject. Besides—Torvald, with all his masculine pride—how painfully humiliating for him if he ever found out he was in debt to me. That would just ruin our relationship. Our beautiful, happy home would never be the same.

MRS. LINDE: Won't you ever tell him?

NORA: [*Thoughtfully.*] Yes—maybe sometime years from now, when I'm no longer so attractive. Don't laugh! I only mean when Torvald loves me less than now, when he stops enjoying my dancing and dressing up and reciting for him. Then it might be wise to have something in reserve—[*Breaking off.*] How ridiculous! That'll never happen—Well, Kristine, what do you think of my big secret? I'm capable of something too, hm? You can imagine, of course, how this thing hangs over me. It really hasn't been easy meeting the payments on time. In the business world there's what they call quarterly interest and what they call amortization, and these are always so terribly hard to manage. I've had to skimp a little here and there, wherever I could, you know. I could hardly spare anything from my house allowance, because Torvald has to live well. I couldn't let the children go poorly dressed; whatever I got for them, I felt I had to use up completely—the darlings!

MRS. LINDE: Poor Nora, so it had to come out of your own budget, then?

NORA: Yes, of course. But I was the one most responsible, too. Every time Torvald gave me money for new clothes and such, I never used more than half; always bought the simplest, cheapest outfits. It was a godsend that everything looks so well on me that Torvald never noticed. But it did weigh me down at times, Kristine. It *is* such a joy to wear fine things. You understand.

MRS. LINDE: Oh, of course.

NORA: And then I found other ways of making money. Last winter I was lucky enough to get a lot of copying to do. I locked myself in and sat writing every evening till late in the night. Ah, I was tired so often, dead tired. But still it was wonderful fun, sitting and working like that, earning money. It was almost like being a man.

MRS. LINDE: But how much have you paid off this way so far?

NORA: That's hard to say, exactly. These accounts, you know, aren't easy to figure. I only know that I've paid out all I could scrape together. Time and again I haven't known where to turn. [*Smiling.*] Then I'd sit here dreaming of a rich old gentleman who had fallen in love with me—

MRS. LINDE: What! Who is he?

NORA: Oh, really! And that he'd died, and when his will was opened, there in big letters it said, "All my fortune shall be paid over in cash, immediately, to that enchanting Mrs. Nora Helmer."

MRS. LINDE: But Nora dear—who *was* this gentleman?

NORA: Good grief, can't you understand? The old man never existed; that was only something I'd dream up time and again whenever I was at my wits' end for money. But it makes no difference now; the old fossil can go where he pleases for all I care; I don't need him or his will—because now I'm free. [*Jumping up.*] Oh, how lovely to think of that, Kristine! Carefree! To know you're carefree, utterly carefree; to be able to romp and play with the children, and to keep up a beautiful, charming home—everything just the way Torvald likes it! And think, spring is coming, with big blue skies. Maybe we can travel a little then. Maybe I'll see the ocean again. Oh yes, it *is* so marvelous to live and be happy!

[*The front doorbell rings.*]

MRS. LINDE: [*Rising.*] There's the bell. It's probably best that I go.

NORA: No, stay. No one's expected. It must be for Torvald.

MAID: [*From the hall doorway.*] Excuse me, ma'am—there's a gentleman here to see Mr. Helmer, but I didn't know—since the doctor's with him—

NORA: Who is the gentleman?

KROGSTAD: [*From the doorway.*] It's me, Mrs. Helmer.

[MRS. LINDE *starts and turns away toward the window.*]

NORA: [*Stepping toward him, tense, her voice a whisper.*] You? What is it? Why do you want to speak to my husband?

KROGSTAD: Bank business—after a fashion. I have a small job in the investment bank, and I hear now your husband is going to be our chief—

NORA: In other words, it's—

KROGSTAD: Just dry business, Mrs. Helmer. Nothing but that.

NORA: Yes, then please be good enough to step into the study. [*She nods indifferently as she sees him out by the hall door, then returns and begins stirring up the stove.*]

MRS. LINDE: Nora—who was that man?

NORA: That was a Mr. Krogstad—a lawyer.

MRS. LINDE: Then it really was him.

NORA: Do you know that person?

MRS. LINDE: I did once—many years ago. For a time he was a law clerk in our town.

NORA: Yes, he's been that.

MRS. LINDE: How he's changed.

NORA: I understand he had a very unhappy marriage.

MRS. LINDE: He's a widower now.

NORA: With a number of children. There now, it's burning. [*She closes the stove door and moves the rocker a bit to one side.*]

MRS. LINDE: They say he has a hand in all kinds of business.

NORA: Oh? That may be true; I wouldn't know. But let's not think about business. It's so dull.

[DR. RANK *enters from* HELMER'S *study.*]

RANK: [*Still in the doorway.*] No, no, really—I don't want to intrude, I'd just as soon talk a little while with your wife. [*Shuts the door, then notices* MRS. LINDE.] Oh, beg pardon. I'm intruding here too.

NORA: No, not at all. [*Introducing him.*] Dr. Rank, Mrs. Linde.

RANK: Well now, that's a name much heard in this house. I believe I passed the lady on the stairs as I came.

MRS. LINDE: Yes, I take the stairs very slowly. They're rather hard on me.

RANK: Uh-hm, some touch of internal weakness?

MRS. LINDE: More overexertion, I'd say.

RANK: Nothing else? Then you're probably here in town to rest up in a round of parties?

MRS. LINDE: I'm here to look for work.

RANK: Is that the best cure for overexertion?

MRS. LINDE: One has to live, Doctor.

RANK: Yes, there's a common prejudice to that effect.

NORA: Oh, come on, Dr. Rank—you really do want to live yourself.

RANK: Yes, I really do. Wretched as I am, I'll gladly prolong my torment indefinitely. All my patients feel like that. And it's quite the same, too, with the morally sick. Right at this moment there's one of those moral invalids in there with Helmer—

MRS. LINDE: [*Softly.*] Ah!

NORA: Who do you mean?

RANK: Oh, it's a lawyer, Krogstad, a type you wouldn't know. His character is rotten to the root—but even he began chattering all-importantly about how he had to *live*.

NORA: Oh? What did he want to talk to Torvald about?

RANK: I really don't know. I only heard something about the bank.

NORA: I didn't know that Krog—that this man Krogstad had anything to do with the bank.

RANK: Yes, he's gotten some kind of berth down there. [*To* MRS. LINDE.] I don't know if you also have, in your neck of the woods, a type of person who scuttles about breathlessly, sniffing out hints of moral corruption, and then maneuvers his victim into some sort of key position where he can keep an eye on him. It's the healthy these days that are out in the cold.

MRS. LINDE: All the same, it's the sick who most need to be taken in.

RANK: [*With a shrug.*] Yes, there we have it. That's the concept that's turning society into a sanatorium.

[NORA, *lost in her thoughts, breaks out into quiet laughter and claps her hands.*]

RANK: Why do you laugh at that? Do you have any real idea of what society is?

NORA: What do I care about dreary old society? I was laughing at something quite different—something terribly funny. Tell me, Doctor—is everyone who works in the bank dependent now on Torvald?

RANK: Is that what you find so terribly funny?

NORA: [*Smiling and humming.*] Never mind, never mind [*Pacing the floor.*] Yes, that's really immensely amusing: that we—that Torvald has so much power now over all those people. [*Taking the bag out of her pocket.*] Dr. Rank, a little macaroon on that?

RANK: See here, macaroons! I thought they were contraband here.

NORA: Yes, but these are some that Kristine gave me.

MRS. LINDE: What? I—?

NORA: Now, now, don't be afraid. You couldn't possibly know that Torvald had forbidden them. You see, he's worried they'll ruin my teeth. But hmp! Just this once! Isn't that so, Dr. Rank? Help yourself! [*Puts a macaroon in his mouth.*]

And you too, Kristine. And I'll also have one, only a little one—or two, at the most. [*Walking about again.*] Now I'm really tremendously happy. Now there's just one last thing in the world that I have an enormous desire to do.

RANK: Well! And what's that?

NORA: It's something I have such a consuming desire to say so Torvald could hear.

RANK: And why can't you say it?

NORA: I don't dare. It's quite shocking.

MRS. LINDE: Shocking?

RANK: Well, then it isn't advisable. But in front of us you certainly can. What do you have such a desire to say so Torvald could hear?

NORA: I have such a huge desire to say—to hell and be damned!

RANK: Are you crazy?

MRS. LINDE: My goodness, Nora!

RANK: Go on, say it. Here he is.

NORA: [*Hiding the macaroon bag.*] Shh, shh, shh!

[HELMER *comes in from his study, hat in hand, overcoat over his arm.*]

NORA: [*Going toward him.*] Well, Torvald dear, are you through with him?

HELMER: Yes, he just left.

NORA: Let me introduce you—this is Kristine, who's arrived here in town.

HELMER: Kristine—? I'm sorry, but I don't know—

NORA: Mrs. Linde, Torvald dear. Mrs. Kristine Linde.

HELMER: Of course. A childhood friend of my wife's, no doubt?

MRS. LINDE: Yes, we knew each other in those days.

NORA: And just think, she made the long trip down here in order to talk with you.

HELMER: What's this?

MRS. LINDE: Well, not exactly—

NORA: You see, Kristine is remarkably clever in office work, and so she's terribly eager to come under a capable man's supervision and add more to what she already knows—

HELMER: Very wise, Mrs. Linde.

NORA: And then when she heard that you'd become a bank manager—the story was wired out to the papers—then she came in as fast as she could and—Really, Torvald, for my sake you can do a little something for Kristine, can't you?

HELMER: Yes, it's not at all impossible. Mrs. Linde, I suppose you're a widow?

MRS. LINDE: Yes.

HELMER: Any experience in office work?

MRS. LINDE: Yes, a good deal.

HELMER: Well, it's quite likely that I can make an opening for you—

NORA: [*Clapping her hands.*] You see, you see!

HELMER: You've come at a lucky moment, Mrs. Linde.

MRS. LINDE: Oh, how can I thank you?

HELMER: Not necessary. [*Putting his overcoat on.*] But today you'll have to excuse me—

RANK: Wait, I'll go with you. [*He fetches his coat from the hall and warms it at the stove.*]

NORA: Don't stay out long, dear.

HELMER: An hour; no more.

NORA: Are you going too, Kristine?

MRS. LINDE: [*Putting on her winter garments.*] Yes, I have to see about a room now.

HELMER: Then perhaps we can all walk together.

NORA: [*Helping her.*] What a shame we're so cramped here, but it's quite impossible for us to—

MRS. LINDE: Oh, don't even think of it! Good-bye, Nora dear, and thanks for everything.

NORA: Good-bye for now. Of course you'll be back this evening. And you too, Dr. Rank. What? If you're well enough? Oh, you've got to be! Wrap up tight now.

[*In a ripple of small talk the company moves out into the hall; children's voices are heard outside on the steps.*]

NORA: There they are! There they are! [*She runs to open the door. The children come in with their nurse,* ANNE-MARIE.] Come in, come in! [*Bends down and kisses them.*] Oh, you darlings—! Look at them, Kristine. Aren't they lovely!

RANK: No loitering in the draft here.

HELMER: Come, Mrs. Linde—this place is unbearable now for anyone but mothers.

[DR. RANK, HELMER, *and* MRS. LINDE *go down the stairs.* ANNE-MARIE *goes into the living room with the children.* NORA *follows, after closing the hall door.*]

NORA: How fresh and strong you look. Oh, such red cheeks you have! Like apples and roses. [*The children interrupt her throughout the following.*] And it was so much fun? That's wonderful. Really? You pulled both Emmy and Bob on the sled? Imagine, all together! Yes, you're a clever boy, Ivar. Oh, let me hold her a bit, Anne-Marie. My sweet little doll baby! [*Takes the smallest from the nurse and dances with her.*] Yes, yes, Mama will dance with Bob as well. What? Did you throw snowballs? Oh, if I'd only been there! No, don't bother, Anne-Marie—I'll undress them myself. Oh yes, let me. It's such fun. Go in and rest; you look half frozen. There's hot coffee waiting for you on the stove. [*The nurse goes into the room to the left.* NORA *takes the children's winter things off, throwing them about, while the children talk to her all at once.*] Is that so? A big dog chased you? But it didn't bite? No, dogs never bite little, lovely doll babies. Don't peek in the packages, Ivar! What is it? Yes, wouldn't you like to know. No, no, it's an ugly something. Well? Shall we play? What shall we play? Hide-and-seek? Yes, let's play hide-and-seek. Bob must hide first. I must? Yes, let me hide first. [*Laughing and shouting, she and the children play in and out of the living room and the adjoining room to the right. At last* NORA *hides under the table. The children come storming in, search, but cannot find her, then hear her muffled laughter, dash over to the table, lift the cloth up and find her. Wild shouting. She creeps forward as if to scare them. More shouts. Meanwhile, a knock at the hall door; no one has noticed it. Now the door half opens, and* KROGSTAD *appears. He waits a moment; the game goes on.*]

KROGSTAD: Beg pardon, Mrs. Helmer—

NORA: [*With a strangled cry, turning and scrambling to her knees.*] Oh! What do you want?

KROGSTAD: Excuse me. The outer door was ajar; it must be someone forgot to shut it—

NORA: [*Rising.*] My husband isn't home, Mr. Krogstad.

KROGSTAD: I know that.

NORA: Yes—then what do you want here?

KROGSTAD: A word with you.

NORA: With—? [*To the children, quietly.*] Go in to Anne-Marie. What? No, the strange man won't hurt Mama. When he's gone, we'll play some more. [*She leads the children into the room to the left and shuts the door after them. Then, tense and nervous:*] You want to speak to me?

KROGSTAD: Yes, I want to.

NORA: Today? But it's not yet the first of the month—

KROGSTAD: No, it's Christmas Eve. It's going to be up to you how merry a Christmas you have.

NORA: What is it you want? Today I absolutely can't—

KROGSTAD: We won't talk about that till later. This is something else. You do have a moment to spare, I suppose?

NORA: Oh yes, of course—I do, except—

KROGSTAD: Good. I was sitting over at Olsen's Restaurant when I saw your husband go down the street—

NORA: Yes?

KROGSTAD: With a lady.

NORA: Yes. So?

KROGSTAD: If you'll pardon my asking: wasn't that lady a Mrs. Linde?

NORA: Yes.

KROGSTAD: Just now come into town?

NORA: Yes, today.

KROGSTAD: She's a good friend of yours?

NORA: Yes, she is. But I don't see—

KROGSTAD: I also knew her once.

NORA: I'm aware of that.

KROGSTAD: Oh? You know all about it. I thought so. Well, then let me ask you short and sweet: is Mrs. Linde getting a job in the bank?

NORA: What makes you think you can cross-examine me, Mr. Krogstad—you, one of my husband's employees? But since you ask, you might as well know—yes, Mrs. Linde's going to be taken on at the bank. And I'm the one who spoke for her, Mr. Krogstad. Now you know.

KROGSTAD: So I guessed right.

NORA: [*Pacing up and down.*] Oh, one does have a tiny bit of influence, I should hope. Just because I am a woman, don't think it means that—When one has a subordinate position, Mr. Krogstad, one really ought to be careful about pushing somebody who—hm—

KROGSTAD: Who has influence?

NORA: That's right.

KROGSTAD: [*In a different tone.*] Mrs. Helmer, would you be good enough to use your influence on my behalf?

NORA: What? What do you mean?

KROGSTAD: Would you please make sure that I keep my subordinate position in the bank?

NORA: What does that mean? Who's thinking of taking away your position?

KROGSTAD: Oh, don't play the innocent with me. I'm quite aware that your friend would hardly relish the chance of running into me again; and I'm also aware now whom I can thank for being turned out.

NORA: But I promise you—

KROGSTAD: Yes, yes, yes, to the point: there's still time, and I'm advising you to use your influence to prevent it.

NORA: But Mr. Krogstad, I have absolutely no influence.

KROGSTAD: You haven't? I thought you were just saying—

NORA: You shouldn't take me so literally. I! How can you believe that I have any such influence over my husband?

KROGSTAD: Oh, I've known your husband from our student days. I don't think the great bank manager's more steadfast than any other married man.

NORA: You speak insolently about my husband, and I'll show you the door.

KROGSTAD: The lady has spirit.

NORA: I'm not afraid of you any longer. After New Year's, I'll soon be done with the whole business.

KROGSTAD: [*Restraining himself.*] Now listen to me, Mrs. Helmer. If necessary, I'll fight for my little job in the bank as if it were life itself.

NORA: Yes, so it seems.

KROGSTAD: It's not just a matter of income; that's the least of it. It's something else—All right, out with it! Look, this is the thing. You know, just like all the others, of course, that once, a good many years ago, I did something rather rash.

NORA: I've heard rumors to that effect.

KROGSTAD: The case never got into court; but all the same, every door was closed in my face from then on. So I took up those various activities you know about. I had to grab hold somewhere; and I dare say I haven't been among the worst. But now I want to drop all that. My boys are growing up. For their sakes, I'll have to win back as much respect as possible here in town. That job in the bank was like the first rung in my ladder. And now your husband wants to kick me right back down in the mud again.

NORA: But for heaven's sake, Mr. Krogstad, it's simply not in my power to help you.

KROGSTAD: That's because you haven't the will to—but I have the means to make you.

NORA: You certainly won't tell my husband that I owe you money?

KROGSTAD: Hm—what if I told him that?

NORA: That would be shameful of you. [*Nearly in tears.*] This secret—my joy and my pride—that he should learn it in such a crude and disgusting way—learn it from you. You'd expose me to the most horrible unpleasantness—

KROGSTAD: Only unpleasantness?

NORA: [*Vehemently.*] But go on and try. It'll turn out the worse for you, because then my husband will really see what a crook you are, and then you'll *never* be able to hold your job.

KROGSTAD: I asked if it was just domestic unpleasantness you were afraid of?

NORA: If my husband finds out, then of course he'll pay what I owe at once, and then we'd be through with you for good.

KROGSTAD: [*A step closer.*] Listen, Mrs. Helmer—you've either got a very bad memory, or else no head at all for business. I'd better put you a little more in touch with the facts.

NORA: What do you mean?

KROGSTAD: When your husband was sick, you came to me for a loan of four thousand, eight hundred crowns.

NORA: Where else could I go?

KROGSTAD: I promised to get you that sum—

NORA: And you got it.

KROGSTAD: I promised to get you that sum, on certain conditions. You were so involved in your husband's illness, and so eager to finance your trip, that I guess you didn't think out all the details. It might just be a good idea to remind you. I promised you the money on the strength of a note I drew up.

NORA: Yes, and that I signed.

KROGSTAD: Right. But at the bottom I added some lines for your father to guarantee the loan. He was supposed to sign down there.

NORA: Supposed to? He did sign.

KROGSTAD: I left the date blank. In other words, your father would have dated his signature himself. Do you remember that?

NORA: Yes, I think—

KROGSTAD: Then I gave you the note for you to mail to your father. Isn't that so?

NORA: Yes.

KROGSTAD: And naturally you sent it at once—because only some five, six days later you brought me the note, properly signed. And with that, the money was yours.

NORA: Well, then; I've made my payments regularly, haven't I?

KROGSTAD: More or less. But—getting back to the point—those were hard times for you then, Mrs. Helmer.

NORA: Yes, they were.

KROGSTAD: Your father was very ill, I believe.

NORA: He was near the end.

KROGSTAD: He died soon after?

NORA: Yes.

KROGSTAD: Tell me, Mrs. Helmer, do you happen to recall the date of your father's death? The day of the month, I mean.

NORA: Papa died the twenty-ninth of September.

KROGSTAD: That's quite correct; I've already looked into that. And now we come to a curious thing—[*Taking out a paper.*] which I simply cannot comprehend.

NORA: Curious thing? I don't know—

KROGSTAD: This is the curious thing: that your father co-signed the note for your loan three days after his death.

NORA: How—? I don't understand.

KROGSTAD: Your father died the twenty-ninth of September. But look. Here your father dated his signature October second. Isn't that curious, Mrs. Helmer? [NORA *is silent.*] Can you explain it to me? [NORA *remains silent.*] It's also remarkable that the words "October second" and the year aren't written in your father's hand, but rather in one that I think I know. Well, it's easy to understand. Your father forgot perhaps to date his signature, and then someone or other added it, a bit sloppily, before anyone knew of his death. There's nothing wrong in that. It all comes down to the signature. And there's no question about *that,* Mrs. Helmer. It really *was* your father who signed his own name here, wasn't it?

NORA: [*After a short silence, throwing her head back and looking squarely at him.*] No, it wasn't. *I* signed papa's name.

KROGSTAD: Wait, now—are you fully aware that this is a dangerous confession?

NORA: Why? You'll soon get your money.

KROGSTAD: Let me ask you a question—why didn't you send the paper to your father?

NORA: That was impossible. Papa was so sick. If I'd asked him for his signature, I also would have had to tell him what the money was for. But I couldn't tell him, sick as he was, that my husband's life was in danger. That was just impossible.

KROGSTAD: Then it would have been better if you'd given up the trip abroad.

NORA: I couldn't possibly. The trip was to save my husband's life. I couldn't give that up.

KROGSTAD: But didn't you ever consider that this was a fraud against me?

NORA: I couldn't let myself be bothered by that. You weren't any concern of mine. I couldn't stand you, with all those cold complications you made, even though you knew how badly off my husband was.

KROGSTAD: Mrs. Helmer, obviously you haven't the vaguest idea of what you've involved yourself in. But I can tell you this: it was nothing more and nothing worse that I once did—and it wrecked my whole reputation.

NORA: You? Do you expect me to believe that you ever acted bravely to save your wife's life?

KROGSTAD: Laws don't inquire into motives.

NORA: Then they must be very poor laws.

KROGSTAD: Poor or not—if I introduce this paper in court, you'll be judged according to law.

NORA: This I refuse to believe. A daughter hasn't a right to protect her dying father from anxiety and care? A wife hasn't a right to save her husband's life? I don't know much about laws, but I'm sure that somewhere in the books these things are allowed. And you don't know anything about it—you who practice the law? You must be an awful lawyer, Mr. Krogstad.

KROGSTAD: Could be. But business—the kind of business we two are mixed up in—don't you think I know about that? All right. Do what you want now. But I'm telling you *this*: if I get shoved down a second time, you're going to keep me company. [*He bows and goes out through the hall.*]

NORA: [*Pensive for a moment, then tossing her head.*] Oh, really! Trying to frighten me! I'm not so silly as all that. [*Begins gathering up the children's clothes, but soon stops.*] But—? No, but that's impossible! I did it out of love.

THE CHILDREN: [*In the doorway, left.*] Mama, that strange man's gone out the door.

NORA: Yes, yes, I know it. But don't tell anyone about the strange man. Do you hear? Not even Papa!

THE CHILDREN: No, Mama. But now will you play again?

NORA: No, not now.

THE CHILDREN: Oh, but Mama, you promised.

NORA: Yes, but I can't now. Go inside; I have too much to do. Go in, go in, my sweet darlings. [*She herds them gently back in the room and shuts the door after them. Settling on the sofa, she takes up a piece of embroidery and makes some stitches, but soon stops abruptly.*] No! [*Throws the work aside, rises, goes to the hall door and calls out.*] Helene! Let me have the tree in here. [*Goes to the table, left, opens the table drawer, and stops again.*] No, but that's utterly impossible!

MAID: [*With the Christmas tree.*] Where should I put it, ma'am?

NORA: There. The middle of the floor.

MAID: Should I bring anything else?

NORA: No, thanks. I have what I need.

[*The* MAID, *who has set the tree down, goes out.*]

NORA: [*Absorbed in trimming the tree.*] Candles here—and flowers here. That terrible creature! Talk, talk, talk! There's nothing to it at all. The tree's going to be lovely. I'll do anything to please you, Torvald. I'll sing for you, dance for you—

[HELMER *comes in from the hall, with a sheaf of papers under his arm.*]

NORA: Oh! You're back so soon?

HELMER: Yes. Has anyone been here?

NORA: Here? No.

HELMER: That's odd. I saw Krogstad leaving the front door.

NORA: So? Oh yes, that's true. Krogstad was here a moment.

HELMER: Nora, I can see by your face that he's been here, begging you to put in a good word for him.

NORA: Yes.

HELMER: And it was supposed to seem like your own idea? You were to hide it from me that he'd been here. He asked you that, too, didn't he?

NORA: Yes, Torvald, but—

HELMER: Nora, Nora, and you could fall for that? Talk with that sort of person and promise him anything? And then in the bargain, tell me an untruth.

NORA: An untruth—?

HELMER: Didn't you say that no one had been here? [*Wagging his finger.*] My little songbird must never do that again. A songbird needs a clean beak to warble with. No false notes. [*Putting his arm about her waist.*] That's the way it should be, isn't it? Yes, I'm sure of it. [*Releasing her.*] And so, enough of that. [*Sitting by the stove.*] Ah, how snug and cozy it is here. [*Leafing among his papers.*]

NORA: [*Busy with the tree, after a short pause.*] Torvald!

HELMER: Yes.

NORA: I'm so much looking forward to the Stenborgs' costume party, day after tomorrow.

HELMER: And I can't wait to see what you'll surprise me with.

NORA: Oh, that stupid business!

HELMER: What?

NORA: I can't find anything that's right. Everything seems so ridiculous, so inane.

HELMER: So my little Nora's come to *that* recognition?

NORA: [*Going behind his chair, her arms resting on its back.*] Are you very busy, Torvald?

HELMER: Oh—

NORA: What papers are those?

HELMER: Bank matters.

NORA: Already?

HELMER: I've gotten full authority from the retiring management to make all necessary changes in personnel and procedure. I'll need Christmas week for that. I want to have everything in order by New Year's.

NORA: So that was the reason this poor Krogstad—

HELMER: Hm.

NORA: [*Still leaning on the chair and slowly stroking the nape of his neck.*] If you weren't so very busy, I would have asked you an enormous favor, Torvald.

HELMER: Let's hear. What is it?

NORA: You know, there isn't anyone who has your good taste—and I want so much to look well at the costume party. Torvald, couldn't you take over and decide what I should be and plan my costume?

HELMER: Ah, is my stubborn little creature calling for a lifeguard?

NORA: Yes, Torvald, I can't get anywhere without your help.

HELMER: All right—I'll think it over. We'll hit on something.

NORA: Oh, how sweet of you. [*Goes to the tree again. Pause.*] Aren't the red flowers pretty—? But tell me, was it really such a crime that this Krogstad committed?

HELMER: Forgery. Do you have any idea what that means?

NORA: Couldn't he have done it out of need?

HELMER: Yes, or thoughtlessness, like so many others. I'm not so heartless that I'd condemn a man categorically for just one mistake.

NORA: No, of course not, Torvald!

HELMER: Plenty of men have redeemed themselves by openly confessing their crimes and taking their punishment.

NORA: Punishment—?

HELMER: But now Krogstad didn't go that way. He got himself out by sharp practices, and that's the real cause of his moral breakdown.

NORA: Do you really think that would—?

HELMER: Just imagine how a man with that sort of guilt in him has to lie and cheat and deceive on all sides, has to wear a mask even with the nearest and dearest he has, even with his own wife and children. And with the children, Nora—that's where it's most horrible.

NORA: Why?

HELMER: Because that kind of atmosphere of lies infects the whole life of a home. Every breath the children take in is filled with the germs of something degenerate.

NORA: [*Coming closer behind him.*] Are you sure of that?

HELMER: Oh, I've seen it often enough as a lawyer. Almost everyone who goes bad early in life has a mother who's a chronic liar.

NORA: Why just—the mother?

HELMER: It's usually the mother's influence that's dominant, but the father's works in the same way, of course. Every lawyer is quite familiar with it. And still this Krogstad's been going home year in, year out, poisoning his own children with lies and pretense; that's why I call him morally lost. [*Reaching his hands out toward her.*] So my sweet little Nora must promise me never to plead his cause. Your hand on it. Come, come, what's this? Give me your hand. There, now. All settled. I can tell you it'd be impossible for me to work alongside of him. I literally feel physically revolted when I'm anywhere near such a person.

NORA: [*Withdraws her hand and goes to the other side of the Christmas tree.*] How hot it is here! And I've got so much to do.

HELMER: [*Getting up and gathering his papers.*] Yes, and I have to think about getting some of these read through before dinner. I'll think about your costume, too. And something to hang on the tree in gilt paper, I may even see about that. [*Putting his hand on her head.*] Oh you, my darling little songbird. [*He goes into his study and closes the door after him.*]

NORA: [*Softly, after a silence.*] Oh, really! it isn't so. It's impossible. It must be impossible.

ANNE-MARIE: [*In the doorway, left.*] The children are begging so hard to come in to Mama.

NORA: No, no, no, don't let them in to me! You stay with them, Anne-Marie.

ANNE-MARIE: Of course, ma'am. [*Closes the door.*]

NORA: [*Pale with terror*]. Hurt my children—! Poison my home? [*A moment's pause; then she tosses her head.*] That's not true. Never. Never in all the world.

ACT II

Same room. Beside the piano the Christmas tree now stands stripped of ornament, burned-down candle stubs on its ragged branches. nora's street clothes lie on the sofa. nora, alone in the room, moves restlessly about; at last she stops at the sofa and picks up her coat.

NORA: [*Dropping the coat again.*] Someone's coming! [*Goes toward the door, listens.*] No—there's no one. Of course—nobody's coming today, Christmas Day—or tomorrow, either. But maybe—[*Opens the door and looks out.*] No, nothing in the mailbox. Quite empty. [*Coming forward.*] What nonsense! He won't do anything serious. Nothing terrible could happen. It's impossible. Why, I have three small children.

[ANNE-MARIE, *with a large carton, comes in from the room to the left.*]

ANNE-MARIE: Well, at last I found the box with the masquerade clothes.

NORA: Thanks. Put it on the table.

ANNE-MARIE: [*Does so.*] But they're all pretty much of a mess.

NORA: Ahh! I'd love to rip them in a million pieces!

ANNE-MARIE: Oh, mercy, they can be fixed right up. Just a little patience.

NORA: Yes, I'll go get Mrs. Linde to help me.

ANNE-MARIE: Out again now? In this nasty weather? Miss Nora will catch cold—get sick.

NORA: Oh, worse things could happen—How are the children?

ANNE-MARIE: The poor mites are playing with their Christmas presents, but—

NORA: Do they ask for me much?

ANNE-MARIE: They're so used to having Mama around, you know.

NORA: Yes, but Anne-Marie, I *can't* be together with them as much as I was.

ANNE-MARIE: Well, small children get used to anything.

NORA: You think so? Do you think they'd forget their mother if she was gone for good?

ANNE-MARIE: Oh, mercy—gone for good!

NORA: Wait, tell me, Anne-Marie—I've wondered so often—how could you ever have the heart to give your child over to strangers?

ANNE-MARIE: But I had to, you know, to become little Nora's nurse.

NORA: Yes, but how could you *do* it?

ANNE-MARIE: When I could get such a good place? A girl who's poor and who's gotten in trouble is glad enough for that. Because that slippery fish, he didn't do a thing for me, you know.

NORA: But your daughter's surely forgotten you.

ANNE-MARIE: Oh, she certainly has not. She's written to me, both when she was confirmed and when she was married.

NORA: [*Clasping her about the neck.*] You old Anne-Marie, you were a good mother for me when I was little.

ANNE-MARIE: Poor little Nora, with no other mother but me.

NORA: And if the babies didn't have one, then I know that you'd—What silly talk! [*Opening the carton.*] Go in to them. Now I'll have to—Tomorrow you can see how lovely I'll look.

ANNE-MARIE: Oh, there won't be anyone at the party as lovely as Miss Nora. [*She goes off into the room, left.*]

NORA: [*Begins unpacking the box, but soon throws it aside.*] Oh, if I dared to go out. If only nobody would come. If only nothing would happen here while I'm out. What craziness—nobody's coming. Just don't think. This muff—needs a brushing. Beautiful gloves, beautiful gloves. Let it go. Let it go! One, two, three, four, five, six—[*With a cry.*] Oh, there they are! [*Poises to move toward the door, but remains irresolutely standing.* MRS. LINDE *enters from the hall, where she has removed her street clothes.*]

NORA: Oh, it's you, Kristine. There's no one else out there? How good that you've come.

MRS. LINDE: I hear you were up asking for me.

NORA: Yes, I just stopped by. There's something you really can help me with. Let's get settled on the sofa. Look, there's going to be a costume party tomorrow evening at the Stenborgs' right above us, and now Torvald wants me to go as a Neapolitan peasant girl and dance the tarantella[2] that I learned in Capri.

MRS. LINDE: Really, are you giving a whole performance?

NORA: Torvald says yes, I should. See, here's the dress. Torvald had it made for me down there; but now it's all so tattered that I just don't know—

2. Lively folk dance of southern Italy, thought to cure the bite of the tarantula.

MRS. LINDE: Oh, we'll fix that up in no time. It's nothing more than the trimmings—they're a bit loose here and there. Needle and thread? Good, now we have what we need.

NORA: Oh, how sweet of you!

MRS. LINDE: [*Sewing.*] So you'll be in disguise tomorrow, Nora. You know what? I'll stop by then for a moment and have a look at you all dressed up. But listen, I've absolutely forgotten to thank you for that pleasant evening yesterday.

NORA: [*Getting up and walking about.*] I don't think it was as pleasant as usual yesterday. You should have come to town a bit sooner, Kristine—Yes, Torvald really knows how to give a home elegance and charm.

MRS. LINDE: And you do, too, if you ask me. You're not your father's daughter for nothing. But tell me, is Dr. Rank always so down in the mouth as yesterday?

NORA: No, that was quite an exception. But he goes around critically ill all the time—tuberculosis of the spine, poor man. You know, his father was a disgusting thing who kept mistresses and so on—and that's why the son's been sickly from birth.

MRS. LINDE: [*Lets her sewing fall to her lap.*] But my dearest Nora, how do you know about such things?

NORA: [*Walking more jauntily.*] Hmp! When you've had three children, then you've had a few visits from—from women who know something of medicine, and they tell you this and that.

MRS. LINDE: [*Resumes sewing; a short pause.*] Does Dr. Rank come here every day?

NORA: Every blessed day. He's Torvald's best friend from childhood, and *my* good friend, too. Dr. Rank almost belongs to this house.

MRS. LINDE: But tell me—is he quite sincere? I mean, doesn't he rather enjoy flattering people?

NORA: Just the opposite. Why do you think that?

MRS. LINDE: When you introduced us yesterday, he was proclaiming that he'd often heard my name in this house; but later I noticed that your husband hadn't the slightest idea who I really was. So how could Dr. Rank—?

NORA: But it's all true, Kristine. You see, Torvald loves me beyond words, and, as he puts it, he'd like to keep me all to himself. For a long time he'd almost be jealous if I even mentioned any of my old friends back home. So of course I dropped that. But with Dr. Rank I talk a lot about such things, because he likes hearing about them.

MRS. LINDE: Now listen, Nora; in many ways you're still like a child. I'm a good deal older than you, with a little more experience. I'll tell you something: you ought to put an end to all this with Dr. Rank.

NORA: What should I put an end to?

MRS. LINDE: Both parts of it, I think. Yesterday you said something about a rich admirer who'd provide you with money—

NORA: Yes, one who doesn't exist—worse luck. So?

MRS. LINDE: Is Dr. Rank well off?

NORA: Yes, he is.

MRS. LINDE: With no dependents?

NORA: No, no one. But—

MRS. LINDE: And he's over here every day?

NORA: Yes, I told you that.

MRS. LINDE: How can a man of such refinement be so grasping?

NORA: I don't follow you at all.

MRS. LINDE: Now don't try to hide it, Nora. You think I can't guess who loaned you the forty-eight hundred crowns?

NORA: Are you out of your mind? How could you think such a thing! A friend of ours, who comes here every single day. What an intolerable situation that would have been!

MRS. LINDE: Then it really wasn't him.

NORA: No, absolutely not. It never even crossed my mind for a moment—And he had nothing to lend in those days; his inheritance came later.

MRS. LINDE: Well, I think that was a stroke of luck for you, Nora dear.

NORA: No, it never would have occurred to me to ask Dr. Rank—Still, I'm quite sure that if I had asked him—

MRS. LINDE: Which you won't, of course.

NORA: No, of course not. I can't see that I'd ever need to. But I'm quite positive that if I talked to Dr. Rank—

MRS. LINDE: Behind your husband's back?

NORA: I've got to clear up this other thing; *that's* also behind his back. I've *got* to clear it all up.

MRS. LINDE: Yes, I was saying that yesterday, but—

NORA: [*Pacing up and down.*] A man handles these problems so much better than a woman—

MRS. LINDE: One's husband does, yes.

NORA: Nonsense. [*Stopping.*] When you pay everything you owe, then you get your note back, right?

MRS. LINDE: Yes, naturally.

NORA: And can rip it into a million pieces and burn it up—that filthy scrap of paper!

MRS. LINDE: [*Looking hard at her, laying her sewing aside, and rising slowly.*] Nora, you're hiding something from me.

NORA: You can see it in my face?

MRS. LINDE: Something's happened to you since yesterday morning. Nora, what is it?

NORA: [*Hurrying toward her.*] Kristine! [*Listening.*] Shh! Torvald's home. Look, go in with the children a while. Torvald can't bear all this snipping and stitching. Let Anne-Marie help you.

MRS. LINDE: [*Gathering up some of the things.*] All right, but I'm not leaving here until we've talked this out. [*She disappears into the room, left, as* TORVALD *enters from the hall.*]

NORA: Oh, how I've been waiting for you, Torvald dear.

HELMER: Was that the dressmaker?

NORA: No, that was Kristine. She's helping me fix up my costume. You know, it's going to be quite attractive.

HELMER: Yes, wasn't that a bright idea I had?

NORA: Brilliant! But then wasn't I good as well to give in to you?

HELMER: Good—because you give in to your husband's judgment? All right, you little goose, I know you didn't mean it like that. But I won't disturb you. You'll want to have a fitting, I suppose.

NORA: And you'll be working?

HELMER: Yes. [*Indicating a bundle of papers.*] See. I've been down to the bank. [*Starts toward his study.*]

NORA: Torvald.

HELMER: [*Stops.*] Yes.

NORA: If your little squirrel begged you, with all her heart and soul, for something—?

HELMER: What's that?

NORA: Then would you do it?

HELMER: First, naturally, I'd have to know what it was.

NORA: Your squirrel would scamper about and do tricks, if you'd only be sweet and give in.

HELMER: Out with it.

NORA: Your lark would be singing high and low in every room—

HELMER: Come on, she does that anyway.

NORA: I'd be a wood nymph and dance for you in the moonlight.

HELMER: Nora—don't tell me it's that same business from this morning?

NORA: [*Coming closer.*] Yes, Torvald, I beg you, please!

HELMER: And you actually have the nerve to drag that up again?

NORA: Yes, yes, you've got to give in to me; you *have* to let Krogstad keep his job in the bank.

HELMER: My dear Nora, I've slated his job for Mrs. Linde.

NORA: That's awfully kind of you. But you could just fire another clerk instead of Krogstad.

HELMER: This is the most incredible stubbornness! Because you go and give an impulsive promise to speak up for him, I'm expected to—

NORA: That's not the reason, Torvald. It's for your own sake. That man does writing for the worst papers; you said it yourself. He could do you any amount of harm. I'm scared to death of him—

HELMER: Ah, I understand. It's the old memories haunting you.

NORA: What do you mean by that?

HELMER: Of course, you're thinking about your father.

NORA: Yes, all right. Just remember how those nasty gossips wrote in the papers about Papa and slandered him so cruelly. I think they'd have had him dismissed if the department hadn't sent you up to investigate, and if you hadn't been so kind and open-minded toward him.

HELMER: My dear Nora, there's a notable difference between your father and me. Your father's official career was hardly above reproach. But mine is; and I hope it'll stay that way as long as I hold my position.

NORA: Oh, who can ever tell what vicious minds can invent? We could be so snug and happy now in our quiet, carefree home—you and I and the children, Torvald! That's why I'm pleading with you so—

HELMER: And just by pleading for him you make it impossible for me to keep him on. It's already known at the bank that I'm firing Krogstad. What if it's rumored around now that the new bank manager was vetoed by his wife—

NORA: Yes, what then—?

HELMER: Oh yes—as long as our little bundle of stubbornness gets her way—! I should go and make myself ridiculous in front of the whole office—give people the idea I can be swayed by all kinds of outside pressure. Oh, you can bet I'd feel the effects of that soon enough! Besides—there's something that rules Krogstad right out at the bank as long as I'm the manager.

NORA: What's that?

HELMER: His moral failings I could maybe overlook if I had to—

NORA: Yes, Torvald, why not?

HELMER: And I hear he's quite efficient on the job. But he was a crony of mine back in my teens—one of those rash friendships that crop up again and again to embarrass you later in life. Well, I might as well say it straight out: we're on a first-name basis. And that tactless fool makes no effort at all to hide it in front of others. Quite the contrary—he thinks that entitles him to take a familiar air around me, and so every other second he comes booming out with his "Yes, Torvald!" and "Sure thing, Torvald!" I tell you, it's been excruciating for me. He's out to make my place in the bank unbearable.

NORA: Torvald, you can't be serious about all this.

HELMER: Oh no? Why not?

NORA: Because these are such petty considerations.

HELMER: What are you saying? Petty? You think I'm petty!

NORA: No, just the opposite, Torvald dear. That's exactly why—

HELMER: Never mind. You call my motives petty; then I might as well be just that. Petty! All right! We'll put a stop to this for good. [*Goes to the hall door and calls.*] Helene!

NORA: What do you want?

HELMER: [*Searching among his papers.*] A decision. [*The* MAID *comes in.*] Look here; take this letter; go out with it at once. Get hold of a messenger and have him deliver it. Quick now. It's already addressed. Wait, here's some money.

MAID: Yes, sir. [*She leaves with the letter.*]

HELMER: [*Straightening his papers.*] There, now, little Miss Willful.

NORA: [*Breathlessly.*] Torvald, what was that letter?

HELMER: Krogstad's notice.

NORA: Call it back, Torvald! There's still time. Oh, Torvald, call it back! Do it for my sake—for your sake, for the children's sake! Do you hear, Torvald; do it! You don't know how this can harm us.

HELMER: Too late.

NORA: Yes, too late.

HELMER: Nora dear, I can forgive you this panic, even though basically you're insulting me. Yes, you are! Or isn't it an insult to think that *I* should be afraid of a courtroom hack's revenge? But I forgive you anyway, because this shows so beautifully how much you love me. [*Takes her in his arms.*] This is the way it should be, my darling Nora. Whatever comes, you'll see: when it really counts, I have strength and courage enough as a man to take on the whole weight myself.

NORA: [*Terrified.*] What do you mean by that?

HELMER: The whole weight, I said.

NORA: [*Resolutely.*] No, never in all the world.

HELMER: Good. So we'll share it, Nora, as man and wife. That's as it should be. [*Fondling her.*] Are you happy now? There, there, there—not these frightened dove's eyes. It's nothing at all but empty fantasies—Now you should run through your tarantella and practice your tambourine. I'll go to the inner office and shut both doors, so I won't hear a thing; you can make all the noise you like. [*Turning in the doorway.*] And when Rank comes, just tell him where he can find me. [*He nods to her and goes with his papers into the study, closing the door.*]

NORA: [*Standing as though rooted, dazed with fright, in a whisper.*] He really could do it. He will do it. He'll do it in spite of everything. No, not that, never, never! Anything but that! Escape! A way out—[*The doorbell rings.*] Dr. Rank! Anything but that! *Anything,* whatever it is! [*Her hands pass over her face, smoothing it; she pulls herself together, goes over and opens the hall door.* DR. RANK *stands outside, hanging his fur coat up. During the following scene, it begins getting dark.*]

NORA: Hello, Dr. Rank. I recognized your ring. But you mustn't go in to Torvald yet; I believe he's working.

RANK: And you?

NORA: For you, I always have an hour to spare—you know that. [*He has entered, and she shuts the door after him.*]

RANK: Many thanks. I'll make use of these hours while I can.

NORA: What do you mean by that? While you can?

RANK: Does that disturb you?

NORA: Well, it's such an odd phrase. Is anything going to happen?

RANK: What's going to happen is what I've been expecting so long—but I honestly didn't think it would come so soon.

NORA: [*Gripping his arm.*] What is it you've found out? Dr. Rank, you have to tell me!

RANK: [*Sitting by the stove.*] It's all over with me. There's nothing to be done about it.

NORA: [*Breathing easier.*] Is it you—then—?

RANK: Who else? There's no point in lying to one's self. I'm the most miserable of all my patients, Mrs. Helmer. These past few days I've been auditing my internal accounts. Bankrupt! Within a month I'll probably be laid out and rotting in the churchyard.

NORA: Oh, what a horrible thing to say.

RANK: The thing itself is horrible. But the worst of it is all the other horror before it's over. There's only one final examination left; when I'm finished with that, I'll know about when my disintegration will begin. There's something I want to say. Helmer with his sensitivity has such a sharp distaste for anything ugly. I don't want him near my sickroom.

NORA: Oh, but Dr. Rank—

RANK: I won't have him in there. Under no condition. I'll lock my door to him—As soon as I'm completely sure of the worst, I'll send you my calling card marked with a black cross, and you'll know then the wreck has started to come apart.

NORA: No, today you're completely unreasonable. And I wanted you so much to be in a really good humor.

RANK: With death up my sleeve? And then to suffer this way for somebody else's sins. Is there any justice in that? And in every single family, in some way or another, this inevitable retribution of nature goes on—

NORA: [*Her hands pressed over her ears.*] Oh, stuff! Cheer up! Please—be gay!

RANK: Yes, I'd just as soon laugh at it all. My poor, innocent spine, serving time for my father's gay army days.

NORA: [*By the table, left.*] He was so infatuated with asparagus tips and *pâté de foie gras*, wasn't that it?

RANK: Yes—and with truffles.

NORA: Truffles, yes. And then with oysters, I suppose?

RANK: Yes, tons of oysters, naturally.

NORA: And then the port and champagne to go with it. It's so sad that all these delectable things have to strike at our bones.

RANK: Especially when they strike at the unhappy bones that never shared in the fun.

NORA: Ah, that's the saddest of all.

RANK: [*Looks searchingly at her.*] Hm.

NORA: [*After a moment.*] Why did you smile?

RANK: No, it was you who laughed.

NORA: No, it was you who smiled, Dr. Rank!

RANK: [*Getting up.*] You're even a bigger tease than I'd thought.

NORA: I'm full of wild ideas today.

RANK: That's obvious.

NORA: [*Putting both hands on his shoulders.*] Dear, dear Dr. Rank, you'll never die for Torvald and me.

RANK: Oh, that loss you'll easily get over. Those who go away are soon forgotten.

NORA: [*Looks fearfully at him.*] You believe that?

RANK: One makes new connections, and then—

NORA: Who makes new connections?

RANK: Both you and Torvald will when I'm gone. I'd say you're well under way already. What was that Mrs. Linde doing here last evening?

NORA: Oh, come—you can't be jealous of poor Kristine?

RANK: Oh yes, I am. She'll be my successor here in the house. When I'm down under, that woman will probably—

NORA: Shh! Not so loud. She's right in there.

RANK: Today as well. So you see.

NORA: Only to sew on my dress. Good gracious, how unreasonable you are. [*Sitting on the sofa.*] Be nice now, Dr. Rank. Tomorrow you'll see how beautifully I'll dance; and you can imagine then that I'm dancing only for you—yes, and of course for Torvald, too—that's understood. [*Takes various items out of the carton.*] Dr. Rank, sit over here and I'll show you something.

RANK: [*Sitting.*] What's that?

NORA: Look here. Look.

RANK: Silk stockings.

NORA: Flesh-colored. Aren't they lovely? Now it's so dark here, but tomorrow—No, no, no, just look at the feet. Oh well, you might as well look at the rest.

RANK: Hm—

NORA: Why do you look so critical? Don't you believe they'll fit?

RANK: I've never had any chance to form an opinion on that.

NORA: [*Glancing at him a moment.*] Shame on you. [*Hits him lightly on the ear with the stockings.*] That's for you. [*Puts them away again.*]

RANK: And what other splendors am I going to see now?

NORA: Not the least bit more, because you've been naughty. [*She hums a little and rummages among her things.*]

RANK: [*After a short silence.*] When I sit here together with you like this, completely easy and open, then I don't know—I simply can't imagine—whatever would have become of me if I'd never come into this house.

NORA: [*Smiling.*] Yes, I really think you feel completely at ease with us.

RANK: [*More quietly, staring straight ahead.*] And then to have to go away from it all—

NORA: Nonsense, you're not going away.

RANK: [*His voice unchanged.*]—and not even be able to leave some poor show of gratitude behind, scarcely a fleeting regret—no more than a vacant place that anyone can fill.

NORA: And if I asked you now for—? No—

RANK: For what?

NORA: For a great proof of your friendship—

RANK: Yes, yes?

NORA: No, I mean—for an exceptionally big favor—

RANK: Would you really, for once, make me so happy?

NORA: Oh, you haven't the vaguest idea what it is.

RANK: All right, then tell me.

NORA: No, but I can't, Dr. Rank—it's all out of reason. It's advice and help, too—and a favor—

RANK: So much the better. I can't fathom what you're hinting at. Just speak out. Don't you trust me?

NORA: Of course. More than anyone else. You're my best and truest friend, I'm sure. That's why I want to talk to you. All right, then, Dr. Rank: there's something you can help me prevent. You know how deeply, how inexpressibly dearly Torvald loves me; he'd never hesitate a second to give up his life for me.

RANK: [*Leaning close to her.*] Nora—do you think he's the only one—

NORA: [*With a slight start.*] Who—?

RANK: Who'd gladly give up his life for you.

NORA: [*Heavily.*] I see.

RANK: I swore to myself you should know this before I'm gone. I'll never find a better chance. Yes, Nora, now you know. And also you know now that you can trust me beyond anyone else.

NORA: [*Rising, natural and calm.*] Let me by.

RANK: [*Making room for her, but still sitting.*] Nora—

NORA: [*In the hall doorway.*] Helene, bring the lamp in. [*Goes over to the stove.*] Ah, dear Dr. Rank, that was really mean of you.

RANK: [*Getting up.*] That I've loved you just as deeply as somebody else? Was *that* mean?

NORA: No, but that you came out and told me. That was quite unnecessary—

RANK: What do you mean? Have you known—?

[*The* MAID *comes in with the lamp, sets it on the table, and goes out again.*]

RANK: Nora—Mrs. Helmer—I'm asking you: have you known about it?

NORA: Oh, how can I tell what I know or don't know? Really, I don't know what to say—Why did you have to be so clumsy, Dr. Rank! Everything was so good.

RANK: Well, in any case, you now have the knowledge that my body and soul are at your command. So won't you speak out?

NORA: [*Looking at him.*] After that?

RANK: Please, just let me know what it is.

NORA: You can't know anything now.

RANK: I have to. You mustn't punish me like this. Give me the chance to do whatever is humanly possible for you.

NORA: Now there's nothing you can do for me. Besides, actually, I don't need any help. You'll see—it's only my fantasies. That's what it is. Of course! [*Sits in the rocker, looks at him, and smiles.*] What a nice one you are, Dr. Rank. Aren't you a little bit ashamed, now that the lamp is here?

RANK: No, not exactly. But perhaps I'd better go—for good?

NORA: No, you certainly can't do that. You must come here just as you always have. You know Torvald can't do without you.

RANK: Yes, but *you*?

NORA: You know how much I enjoy it when you're here.

RANK: That's precisely what threw me off. You're a mystery to me. So many times I've felt you'd almost rather be with me than with Helmer.

NORA: Yes—you see, there are some people that one loves most and other people that one would almost prefer being with.

RANK: Yes, there's something to that.

NORA: When I was back home, of course I loved Papa most. But I always thought it was so much fun when I could sneak down to the maids' quarters, because they never tried to improve me, and it was always so amusing, the way they talked to each other.

RANK: Aha, so it's *their* place that I've filled.

NORA: [*Jumping up and going to him.*] Oh, dear, sweet Dr. Rank, that's not what I meant at all. But you can understand that with Torvald it's just the same as with Papa—

[*The* MAID *enters from the hall.*]

MAID: Ma'am—please! [*She whispers to* NORA *and hands her a calling card.*]

NORA: [*Glancing at the card.*] Ah! [*Slips it into her pocket.*]

RANK: Anything wrong?

NORA: No, no, not at all. It's only some—it's my new dress—

RANK: Really? But—there's your dress.

NORA: Oh, that. But this is another one—I ordered it—Torvald mustn't know—

RANK: Ah, now we have the big secret.

NORA: That's right. Just go in with him—he's back in the inner study. Keep him there as long as—

RANK: Don't worry. He won't get away. [*Goes into the study.*]

NORA: [*To the* MAID.] And he's standing waiting in the kitchen?

MAID: Yes, he came up by the back stairs.

NORA: But didn't you tell him somebody was here?

MAID: Yes, but that didn't do any good.

NORA: He won't leave?

MAID: No, he won't go till he's talked with you, ma'am.

NORA: Let him come in, then—but quietly. Helene, don't breathe a word about this. It's a surprise for my husband.

MAID: Yes, yes, I understand—[*Goes out.*]

NORA: This horror—it's going to happen. No, no, no, it can't happen, it mustn't.

[*She goes and bolts* HELMER'S *door. The* MAID *opens the hall door for* KROGSTAD *and shuts it behind him. He is dressed for travel in a fur coat, boots, and a fur cap.*]

NORA: [*Going toward him.*] Talk softly. My husband's home.

KROGSTAD: Well, good for him.

NORA: What do you want?

KROGSTAD: Some information.

NORA: Hurry up, then. What is it?

KROGSTAD: You know, of course, that I got my notice.

NORA: I couldn't prevent it, Mr. Krogstad. I fought for you to the bitter end, but nothing worked.

KROGSTAD: Does your husband's love for you run so thin? He knows everything I can expose you to, and all the same he dares to—

NORA: How can you imagine he knows anything about this?

KROGSTAD: Ah, no—I can't imagine it either, now. It's not at all like my fine Torvald Helmer to have so much guts—

NORA: Mr. Krogstad, I demand respect for my husband!

KROGSTAD: Why, of course—all due respect. But since the lady's keeping it so carefully hidden, may I presume to ask if you're also a bit better informed than yesterday about what you've actually done?

NORA: More than you ever could teach me.

KROGSTAD: Yes, I *am* such an awful lawyer.

NORA: What is it you want from me?

KROGSTAD: Just a glimpse of how you are, Mrs. Helmer. I've been thinking about you all day long. A cashier, a night-court scribbler, a—well, a type like me also has a little of what they call a heart, you know.

NORA: Then show it. Think of my children.

KROGSTAD: Did you or your husband ever think of mine? But never mind. I simply wanted to tell you that you don't need to take this thing too seriously. For the present, I'm not proceeding with any action.

NORA: Oh no, really! Well—I knew that.

KROGSTAD: Everything can be settled in a friendly spirit. It doesn't have to get around town at all; it can stay just among us three.

NORA: My husband must never know anything of this.

KROGSTAD: How can you manage that? Perhaps you can pay me the balance?

NORA: No, not right now.

KROGSTAD: Or you know some way of raising the money in a day or two?

NORA: No way that I'm willing to use.

KROGSTAD: Well, it wouldn't have done you any good, anyway. If you stood in front of me with a fistful of bills, you still couldn't buy your signature back.

NORA: Then tell me what you're going to do with it.

KROGSTAD: I'll just hold onto it—keep it on file. There's no outsider who'll even get wind of it. So if you've been thinking of taking some desperate step—

NORA: I have.

KROGSTAD: Been thinking of running away from home—

NORA: I have!

KROGSTAD: Or even of something worse—

NORA: How could you guess that?

KROGSTAD: You can drop those thoughts.

NORA: How could you guess I was thinking of *that*?

KROGSTAD: Most of us think about *that* at first. I thought about it too, but I discovered I hadn't the courage—

NORA: [*Lifelessly*.] I don't either.

KROGSTAD: [*Relieved*.] That's true, you haven't the courage? You too?

NORA: I don't have it—I don't have it.

KROGSTAD: It would be terribly stupid, anyway. After that first storm at home blows out, why, then—I have here in my pocket a letter for your husband—

NORA: Telling everything?

KROGSTAD: As charitably as possible.

NORA: [*Quickly*.] He mustn't ever get that letter. Tear it up. I'll find some way to get money.

KROGSTAD: Beg pardon, Mrs. Helmer, but I think I just told you—

NORA: Oh, I don't mean the money I owe you. Let me know how much you want from my husband, and I'll manage it.

KROGSTAD: I don't want any money from your husband.

NORA: What do you want, then?

KROGSTAD: I'll tell you what. I want to recoup, Mrs. Helmer; I want to get on in the world—and there's where your husband can help me. For a year and a half I've kept myself clean of anything disreputable—all that time struggling with the worst conditions; but I was satisfied, working my way up step by step. Now I've been written right off, and I'm just not in the mood to come crawling back. I tell you, I want to move on. I want to get back in the bank—in a better position. Your husband can set up a job for me—

NORA: He'll never do that!

KROGSTAD: He'll do it. I know him. He won't dare breathe a word of protest. And once I'm in there together with him, you just wait and see! Inside of a year, I'll be the manager's right-hand man. It'll be Nils Krogstad, not Torvald Helmer, who runs the bank.

NORA: You'll never see the day!

KROGSTAD: Maybe you think you can—

NORA: I have the courage now—for *that*.

KROGSTAD: Oh, you don't scare me. A smart, spoiled lady like you—

NORA: You'll see; you'll see!

KROGSTAD: Under the ice, maybe? Down in the freezing, coal-black water? There, till you float up in the spring, ugly, unrecognizable, with your hair falling out—

NORA: You don't frighten me.

KROGSTAD: Nor do you frighten me. One doesn't do these things, Mrs. Helmer. Besides, what good would it be? I'd still have him safe in my pocket.

NORA: Afterwards? When I'm no longer—?

KROGSTAD: Are you forgetting that *I'll* be in control then over your final reputation? [NORA *stands speechless, staring at him*.] Good; now I've warned you. Don't do anything stupid. When Helmer's read my letter, I'll be waiting for his reply. And bear in mind that it's your husband himself who's forced me back to my old ways. I'll never forgive him for that. Good-bye, Mrs. Helmer. [*He goes out through the hall.*]

NORA: [*Goes to the hall door, opens it a crack, and listens.*] He's gone. Didn't leave the letter. Oh no, no, that's impossible too! [*Opening the door more and more.*] What's that? He's standing outside—not going downstairs. He's thinking it over? Maybe he'll—? [*A letter falls in the mailbox; then* KROGSTAD*'s footsteps are heard, dying away down a flight of stairs.* NORA *gives a muffled cry and runs over toward the sofa table. A short pause.*] In the mailbox. [*Slips warily over to the hall door.*] It's lying there. Torvald, Torvald—now we're lost!

MRS. LINDE: [*Entering with the costume from the room, left.*] There now, I can't see anything else to mend. Perhaps you'd like to try—

NORA: [*In a hoarse whisper.*] Kristine, come here.

MRS. LINDE: [*Tossing the dress on the sofa.*] What's wrong? You look upset.

NORA: Come here. See that letter? *There!* Look—through the glass in the mailbox.

MRS. LINDE: Yes, yes, I see it.

NORA: That letter's from Krogstad—

MRS. LINDE: Nora—it's Krogstad who loaned you the money!

NORA: Yes, and now Torvald will find out everything.

MRS. LINDE: Believe me, Nora, it's best for both of you.

NORA: There's more you don't know. I forged a name.

MRS. LINDE: But for heaven's sake—?

NORA: I only want to tell you that, Kristine, so that you can be my witness.

MRS. LINDE: Witness? Why should I—?

NORA: If I should go out of my mind—it could easily happen—

MRS. LINDE: Nora!

NORA: Or anything else occurred—so I couldn't be present here—

MRS. LINDE: Nora, Nora, you aren't yourself at all!

NORA: And someone should try to take on the whole weight, all of the guilt, you follow me—

MRS. LINDE: Yes, of course, but why do you think—?

NORA: Then you're the witness that it isn't true, Kristine. I'm very much myself; my mind right now is perfectly clear; and I'm telling you: nobody else has known about this; I alone did everything. Remember that.

MRS. LINDE: I will. But I don't understand all this.

NORA: Oh, how could you ever understand it? It's the miracle now that's going to take place.

MRS. LINDE: The miracle?

NORA: Yes, the miracle. But it's so awful, Kristine. It mustn't take place, not for anything in the world.

MRS. LINDE: I'm going right over and talk with Krogstad.

NORA: Don't go near him; he'll do you some terrible harm!

MRS. LINDE: There was a time once when he'd gladly have done anything for me.

NORA: He?

MRS. LINDE: Where does he live?

NORA: Oh, how do I know? Yes. [*Searches in her pocket.*] Here's his card. But the letter, the letter—!

HELMER: [*From the study, knocking on the door.*] Nora!

NORA: [*With a cry of fear.*] Oh! What is it? What do you want?

HELMER: Now, now, don't be so frightened. We're not coming in. You locked the door—are you trying on the dress?

NORA: Yes, I'm trying it. I'll look just beautiful, Torvald.

MRS. LINDE: [*Who has read the card.*] He's living right around the corner.

NORA: Yes, but what's the use? We're lost. The letter's in the box.

MRS. LINDE: And your husband has the key?

NORA: Yes, always.

MRS. LINDE: Krogstad can ask for his letter back unread; he can find some excuse—

NORA: But it's just this time that Torvald usually—

MRS. LINDE: Stall him. Keep him in there. I'll be back as quick as I can. [*She hurries out through the hall entrance.*]

NORA: [*Goes to* HELMER's *door, opens it, and peers in.*] Torvald!

HELMER: [*From the inner study.*] Well—does one dare set foot in one's own living room at last? Come on, Rank, now we'll get a look—[*In the doorway.*] But what's this?

NORA: What, Torvald dear?

HELMER: Rank had me expecting some grand masquerade.

RANK: [*In the doorway.*] That was my impression, but I must have been wrong.

NORA: No one can admire me in my splendor—not till tomorrow.

HELMER: But Nora dear, you look so exhausted. Have you practiced too hard?

NORA: No, I haven't practiced at all yet.

HELMER: You know, it's necessary—

NORA: Oh, it's absolutely necessary, Torvald. But I can't get anywhere without your help. I've forgotten the whole thing completely.

HELMER: Ah, we'll soon take care of that.

NORA: Yes, take care of me, Torvald, please! Promise me that? Oh, I'm so nervous. That big party—You must give up everything this evening for me. No business—don't even touch your pen. Yes? Dear Torvald, promise?

HELMER: It's a promise. Tonight I'm totally at your service—you little helpless thing. Hm—but first there's one thing I want to—[*Goes toward the hall door.*]

NORA: What are you looking for?

HELMER: Just to see if there's any mail.

NORA: No, no, don't do that, Torvald!

HELMER: Now what?

NORA: Torvald, please. There isn't any.

HELMER: Let me look, though. [*Starts out.* NORA, *at the piano, strikes the first notes of the tarantella.* HELMER, *at the door, stops.*] Aha!

NORA: I can't dance tomorrow if I don't practice with you.

HELMER: [*Going over to her.*] Nora dear, are you really so frightened?

NORA: Yes, so terribly frightened. Let me practice right now; there's still time before dinner. Oh, sit down and play for me, Torvald. Direct me. Teach me, the way you always have.

HELMER: Gladly, if it's what you want. [*Sits at the piano.*]

NORA: [*Snatches the tambourine up from the box, then a long, varicolored shawl, which she throws around herself, whereupon she springs forward and cries out:*] Play for me now! Now I'll dance!

[HELMER *plays and* NORA *dances.* RANK *stands behind* HELMER *at the piano and looks on.*]

HELMER: [*As he plays.*] Slower. Slow down.
NORA: Can't change it.
HELMER: Not so violent, Nora!
NORA: Has to be just like this.
HELMER: [*Stopping.*] No, no, that won't do at all.
NORA: [*Laughing and swinging her tambourine.*] Isn't that what I told you?
RANK: Let me play for her.
HELMER: [*Getting up.*] Yes, go on. I can teach her more easily then.

[RANK *sits at the piano and plays;* NORA *dances more and more wildly.* HELMER *has stationed himself by the stove and repeatedly gives her directions; she seems not to hear them; her hair loosens and falls over her shoulders; she does not notice, but goes on dancing.* MRS. LINDE *enters.*]

MRS. LINDE: [*Standing dumbfounded at the door.*] Ah—!
NORA: [*Still dancing.*] See what fun, Kristine!
HELMER: But Nora darling, you dance as if your life were at stake.
NORA: And it is.
HELMER: Rank, stop! This is pure madness. Stop it, I say!

[RANK *breaks off playing, and* NORA *halts abruptly.*]

HELMER: [*Going over to her.*] I never would have believed it. You've forgotten everything I taught you.
NORA: [*Throwing away the tambourine.*] You see for yourself.
HELMER: Well, there's certainly room for instruction here.
NORA: Yes, you see how important it is. You've got to teach me to the very last minute. Promise me that, Torvald?
HELMER: You can bet on it.
NORA: You mustn't, either today or tomorrow, think about anything else but me; you mustn't open any letters—or the mailbox—
HELMER: Ah, it's still the fear of that man—
NORA: Oh yes, yes, that too.
HELMER: Nora, it's written all over you—there's already a letter from him out there.
NORA: I don't know. I guess so. But you mustn't read such things now; there mustn't be anything ugly between us before it's all over.
RANK: [*Quietly to* HELMER.] You shouldn't deny her.
HELMER: [*Putting his arm around her.*] The child can have her way. But tomorrow night, after you've danced—
NORA: Then you'll be free.
MAID: [*In the doorway, right.*] Ma'am, dinner is served.
NORA: We'll be wanting champagne, Helene.
MAID: Very good, ma'am. [*Goes out.*]

HELMER: So—a regular banquet, hm?

NORA: Yes, a banquet—champagne till daybreak! [*Calling out*.] And some macaroons, Helene. Heaps of them—just this once.

HELMER: [*Taking her hands*.] Now, now, now—no hysterics. Be my own little lark again.

NORA: Oh, I will soon enough. But go on in—and you, Dr. Rank. Kristine, help me put up my hair.

RANK: [*Whispering, as they go*.] There's nothing wrong—really wrong, is there?

HELMER: Oh, of course not. It's nothing more than this childish anxiety I was telling you about. [*They go out, right*.]

NORA: Well?

MRS. LINDE: Left town.

NORA: I could see by your face.

MRS. LINDE: He'll be home tomorrow evening. I wrote him a note.

NORA: You shouldn't have. Don't try to stop anything now. After all, it's a wonderful joy, this waiting here for the miracle.

MRS. LINDE: What is it you're waiting for?

NORA: Oh, you can't understand that. Go in to them; I'll be along in a moment.

[MRS. LINDE *goes into the dining room*. NORA *stands a short while as if composing herself; then she looks at her watch*.]

NORA: Five. Seven hours to midnight. Twenty-four hours to the midnight after, and then the tarantella's done. Seven and twenty-four? Thirty-one hours to live.

HELMER: [*In the doorway, right*.] What's become of the little lark?

NORA: [*Going toward him with open arms*.] Here's your lark!

ACT III

Same scene. The table, with chairs around it, has been moved to the center of the room. A lamp on the table is lit. The hall door stands open. Dance music drifts down from the floor above. MRS. LINDE *sits at the table, absently paging through a book, trying to read, but apparently unable to focus her thoughts. Once or twice she pauses, tensely listening for a sound at the outer entrance.*

MRS. LINDE: [*Glancing at her watch*.] Not yet—and there's hardly any time left. If only he's not—[*Listening again*.] Ah, there he is. [*She goes out in the hall and cautiously opens the outer door. Quiet footsteps are heard on the stairs. She whispers:*] Come in. Nobody's here.

KROGSTAD: [*In the doorway*.] I found a note from you at home. What's back of all this?

MRS. LINDE: I just *had* to talk to you.

KROGSTAD: Oh? And it just *had* to be here in this house?

MRS. LINDE: At my place it was impossible; my room hasn't a private entrance. Come in; we're all alone. The maid's asleep, and the Helmers are at the dance upstairs.

KROGSTAD: [*Entering the room*.] Well, well, the Helmers are dancing tonight? Really?

MRS. LINDE: Yes, why not?

KROGSTAD: How true—why not?

MRS. LINDE: All right, Krogstad, let's talk.

KROGSTAD: Do we two have anything more to talk about?

MRS. LINDE: We have a great deal to talk about.

KROGSTAD: I wouldn't have thought so.

MRS. LINDE: No, because you've never understood me, really.

KROGSTAD: Was there anything more to understand—except what's all too common in life? A calculating woman throws over a man the moment a better catch comes by.

MRS. LINDE: You think I'm so thoroughly calculating? You think I broke it off lightly?

KROGSTAD: Didn't you?

MRS. LINDE: Nils—is that what you really thought?

KROGSTAD: If you cared, then why did you write me the way you did?

MRS. LINDE: What else could I do? If I had to break off with you, then it was my job as well to root out everything you felt for me.

KROGSTAD: [*Wringing his hands.*] So that was it. And this—all this, simply for money!

MRS. LINDE: Don't forget I had a helpless mother and two small brothers. We couldn't wait for you, Nils; you had such a long road ahead of you then.

KROGSTAD: That may be; but you still hadn't the right to abandon me for somebody else's sake.

MRS. LINDE: Yes—I don't know. So many, many times I've asked myself if I did have that right.

KROGSTAD: [*More softly.*] When I lost you, it was as if all the solid ground dissolved from under my feet. Look at me; I'm a half-drowned man now, hanging onto a wreck.

MRS. LINDE: Help may be near.

KROGSTAD: It was near—but then you came and blocked it off.

MRS. LINDE: Without my knowing it, Nils. Today for the first time I learned that it's you I'm replacing at the bank.

KROGSTAD: All right—I believe you. But now that you know, will you step aside?

MRS. LINDE: No, because that wouldn't benefit you in the slightest.

KROGSTAD: Not "benefit" me, hm! I'd step aside anyway.

MRS. LINDE: I've learned to be realistic. Life and hard, bitter necessity have taught me that.

KROGSTAD: And life's taught me never to trust fine phrases.

MRS. LINDE: Then life's taught you a very sound thing. But you do have to trust in actions, don't you?

KROGSTAD: What does that mean?

MRS. LINDE: You said you were hanging on like a half-drowned man to a wreck.

KROGSTAD: I've good reason to say that.

MRS. LINDE: I'm also like a half-drowned woman on a wreck. No one to suffer with; no one to care for.

KROGSTAD: You made your choice.

MRS. LINDE: There wasn't any choice then.

KROGSTAD: So—what of it?

MRS. LINDE: Nils, if only we two shipwrecked people could reach across to each other.

KROGSTAD: What are you saying?

MRS. LINDE: Two on one wreck are at least better off than each on his own.

KROGSTAD: Kristine!

MRS. LINDE: Why do you think I came into town?

KROGSTAD: Did you really have some thought of me?

MRS. LINDE: I have to work to go on living. All my born days, as long as I can remember, I've worked, and it's been my best and my only joy. But now I'm completely alone in the world; it frightens me to be so empty and lost. To work for yourself—there's no joy in that. Nils, give me something—someone to work for.

KROGSTAD: I don't believe all this. It's just some hysterical feminine urge to go out and make a noble sacrifice.

MRS. LINDE: Have you ever found me to be hysterical?

KROGSTAD: Can you honestly mean this? Tell me—do you know everything about my past?

MRS. LINDE: Yes.

KROGSTAD: And you know what they think I'm worth around here.

MRS. LINDE: From what you were saying before, it would seem that with me you could have been another person.

KROGSTAD: I'm positive of that.

MRS. LINDE: Couldn't it happen still?

KROGSTAD: Kristine—you're saying this in all seriousness? Yes, you are! I can see it in you. And do you really have the courage, then—?

MRS. LINDE: I need to have someone to care for; and your children need a mother. We both need each other. Nils, I have faith that you're good at heart—I'll risk everything together with you.

KROGSTAD: [*Gripping her hands.*] Kristine, thank you, thank you—Now I know I can win back a place in their eyes. Yes—but I forgot—

MRS. LINDE: [*Listening.*] Shh! The tarantella. Go now! Go on!

KROGSTAD: Why? What is it?

MRS. LINDE: Hear the dance up there? When that's over, they'll be coming down.

KROGSTAD: Oh, then I'll go. But—it's all pointless. Of course, you don't know the move I made against the Helmers.

MRS. LINDE: Yes, Nils, I know.

KROGSTAD: And all the same, you have the courage to—?

MRS. LINDE: I know how far despair can drive a man like you.

KROGSTAD: Oh, if I only could take it all back.

MRS. LINDE: You easily could—your letter's still lying in the mailbox.

KROGSTAD: Are you sure of that?

MRS. LINDE: Positive. But—

KROGSTAD: [*Looks at her searchingly.*] Is that the meaning of it, then? You'll save your friend at any price. Tell me straight out. Is that it?

MRS. LINDE: Nils—anyone who's sold herself for somebody else once isn't going to do it again.

KROGSTAD: I'll demand my letter back.

MRS. LINDE: No, no.

KROGSTAD: Yes, of course. I'll stay here till Helmer comes down; I'll tell him to give me my letter again—that it only involves my dismissal—that he shouldn't read it—

MRS. LINDE: No, Nils, don't call the letter back.

KROGSTAD: But wasn't that exactly why you wrote me to come here?

MRS. LINDE: Yes, in that first panic. But it's been a whole day and night since then, and in that time I've seen such incredible things in this house. Helmer's got to learn everything; this dreadful secret has to be aired; those two have to come to a full understanding; all these lies and evasions can't go on.

KROGSTAD: Well, then, if you want to chance it. But at least there's one thing I can do, and do right away—

MRS. LINDE: [*Listening.*] Go now, go, quick! The dance is over. We're not safe another second.

KROGSTAD: I'll wait for you downstairs.

MRS. LINDE: Yes, please do; take me home.

KROGSTAD: I can't believe it; I've never been so happy. [*He leaves by way of the outer door; the door between the room and the hall stays open.*]

MRS. LINDE: [*Straightening up a bit and getting together her street clothes.*] How different now! How different! Someone to work for, to live for—a home to build. Well, it is worth the try! Oh, if they'd only come! [*Listening.*] Ah, there they are. Bundle up. [*She picks up her hat and coat.* NORA*'s and* HELMER*'s voices can be heard outside; a key turns in the lock, and* HELMER *brings* NORA *into the hall almost by force. She is wearing the Italian costume with a large black shawl about her; he has on evening dress, with a black domino*[3] *open over it.*]

NORA: [*Struggling in the doorway.*] No, no, no, not inside! I'm going up again. I don't want to leave so soon.

HELMER: But Nora dear—

NORA: Oh, I beg you, please, Torvald. From the bottom of my heart, *please*—only an hour more!

HELMER: Not a single minute, Nora darling. You know our agreement. Come on, in we go; you'll catch cold out here. [*In spite of her resistance, he gently draws her into the room.*]

MRS. LINDE: Good evening.

NORA: Kristine!

HELMER: Why, Mrs. Linde—are you here so late?

MRS. LINDE: Yes, I'm sorry, but I did want to see Nora in costume.

NORA: Have you been sitting here, waiting for me?

MRS. LINDE: Yes. I didn't come early enough; you were all upstairs; and then I thought I really couldn't leave without seeing you.

HELMER: [*Removing* NORA*'s shawl.*] Yes, take a good look. She's worth looking at, I can tell you that, Mrs. Linde. Isn't she lovely?

MRS. LINDE: Yes, I should say—

HELMER: A dream of loveliness, isn't she? That's what everyone thought at the party, too. But she's horribly stubborn—this sweet little thing. What's to be done with her? Can you imagine, I almost had to use force to pry her away.

3. Hood worn by members of some religious orders.

NORA: Oh, Torvald, you're going to regret you didn't indulge me, even for just a half hour more.

HELMER: There, you see. She danced her tarantella and got a tumultuous hand—which was well earned, although the performance may have been a bit too naturalistic—I mean it rather overstepped the proprieties of art. But never mind—what's important is, she made a success, an overwhelming success. You think I could let her stay on after that and spoil the effect? Oh no; I took my lovely little Capri girl—my capricious little Capri girl, I should say—took her under my arm; one quick tour of the ballroom, a curtsy to every side, and then—as they say in novels—the beautiful vision disappeared. An exit should always be effective, Mrs. Linde, but that's what I can't get Nora to grasp. Phew, it's hot in here. [*Flings the domino on a chair and opens the door to his room.*] Why's it dark in here? Oh yes, of course. Excuse me. [*He goes in and lights a couple of candles.*]

NORA: [*In a sharp, breathless whisper.*] So?

MRS. LINDE: [*Quietly.*] I talked with him.

NORA: And—?

MRS. LINDE: Nora—you must tell your husband everything.

NORA: [*Dully.*] I knew it.

MRS. LINDE: You've got nothing to fear from Krogstad, but you have to speak out.

NORA: I won't tell.

MRS. LINDE: Then the letter will.

NORA: Thanks, Kristine. I know now what's to be done. Shh!

HELMER: [*Reentering.*] Well, then, Mrs. Linde—have you admired her?

MRS. LINDE: Yes, and now I'll say good night.

HELMER: Oh, come, so soon? Is this yours, this knitting?

MRS. LINDE: Yes, thanks. I nearly forgot it.

HELMER: Do you knit, then?

MRS. LINDE: Oh yes.

HELMER: You know what? You should embroider instead.

MRS. LINDE: Really? Why?

HELMER: Yes, because it's a lot prettier. See here, one holds the embroidery so, in the left hand, and then one guides the needle with the right—so—in an easy, sweeping curve—right?

MRS. LINDE: Yes, I guess that's—

HELMER: But, on the other hand, knitting—it can never be anything but ugly. Look, see here, the arms tucked in, the knitting needles going up and down—there's something Chinese about it. Ah, that was really a glorious champagne they served.

MRS. LINDE: Yes, good night, Nora, and don't be stubborn anymore.

HELMER: Well put, Mrs. Linde!

MRS. LINDE: Good night, Mr. Helmer.

HELMER: [*Accompanying her to the door.*] Good night, good night. I hope you get home all right. I'd be very happy to—but you don't have far to go. Good night, good night. [*She leaves. He shuts the door after her and returns.*] There, now, at last we got her out the door. She's a deadly bore, that creature.

NORA: Aren't you pretty tired, Torvald?

HELMER: No, not a bit.

NORA: You're not sleepy?

HELMER: Not at all. On the contrary, I'm feeling quite exhilarated. But you? Yes, you really look tired and sleepy.

NORA: Yes, I'm very tired. Soon now I'll sleep.

HELMER: See! You see! I was right all along that we shouldn't stay longer.

NORA: Whatever you do is always right.

HELMER: [*Kissing her brow.*] Now my little lark talks sense. Say, did you notice what a time Rank was having tonight?

NORA: Oh, was he? I didn't get to speak with him.

HELMER: I scarcely did either, but it's a long time since I've seen him in such high spirits. [*Gazes at her a moment, then comes nearer her.*] Hm—it's marvelous, though, to be back home again—to be completely alone with you. Oh, you bewitchingly lovely young woman!

NORA: Torvald, don't look at me like that!

HELMER: Can't I look at my richest treasure? At all that beauty that's mine, mine alone—completely and utterly.

NORA: [*Moving around to the other side of the table.*] You mustn't talk to me that way tonight.

HELMER: [*Following her.*] The tarantella is still in your blood, I can see—and it makes you even more enticing. Listen. The guests are beginning to go. [*Dropping his voice.*] Nora—it'll soon be quiet through this whole house.

NORA: Yes, I hope so.

HELMER: You do, don't you, my love? Do you realize—when I'm out at a party like this with you—do you know why I talk to you so little, and keep such a distance away; just send you a stolen look now and then—you know why I do it? It's because I'm imagining then that you're my secret darling, my secret young bride-to-be, and that no one suspects there's anything between us.

NORA: Yes, yes; oh, yes, I know you're always thinking of me.

HELMER: And then when we leave and I place the shawl over those fine young rounded shoulders—over that wonderful curving neck—then I pretend that you're my young bride, that we're just coming from the wedding, that for the first time I'm bringing you into my house—that for the first time I'm alone with you—completely alone with you, your trembling young beauty! All this evening I've longed for nothing but you. When I saw you turn and sway in the tarantella—my blood was pounding till I couldn't stand it—that's why I brought you down here so early—

NORA: Go away, Torvald! Leave me alone. I don't want all this.

HELMER: What do you mean? Nora, you're teasing me. You will, won't you? Aren't I your husband—?

[*A knock at the outside door.*]

NORA: [*Startled.*] What's that?

HELMER: [*Going toward the half.*] Who is it?

RANK: [*Outside.*] It's me. May I come in a moment?

HELMER: [*With quiet irritation.*] Oh, what does he want now? [*Aloud.*] Hold on. [*Goes and opens the door.*] Oh, how nice that you didn't just pass us by!

RANK: I thought I heard your voice, and then I wanted so badly to have a look in. [*Lightly glancing about.*] Ah, me, these old familiar haunts. You have it snug and cozy in here, you two.

HELMER: You seemed to be having it pretty cozy upstairs, too.

RANK: Absolutely. Why shouldn't I? Why not take in everything in life? As much as you can, anyway, and as long as you can. The wine was superb—

HELMER: The champagne especially.

RANK: You noticed that too? It's amazing how much I could guzzle down.

NORA: Torvald also drank a lot of champagne this evening.

RANK: Oh?

NORA: Yes, and that always makes him so entertaining.

RANK: Well, why shouldn't one have a pleasant evening after a well-spent day?

HELMER: Well spent? I'm afraid I can't claim that.

RANK: [*Slapping him on the back.*] But I can, you see!

NORA: Dr. Rank, you must have done some scientific research today.

RANK: Quite so.

HELMER: Come now—little Nora talking about scientific research!

NORA: And can I congratulate you on the results?

RANK: Indeed you may.

NORA: Then they were good?

RANK: The best possible for both doctor and patient—certainty.

NORA: [*Quickly and searchingly.*] Certainty?

RANK: Complete certainty. So don't I owe myself a gay evening afterwards?

NORA: Yes, you're right, Dr. Rank.

HELMER: I'm with you—just so long as you don't have to suffer for it in the morning.

RANK: Well, one never gets something for nothing in life.

NORA: Dr. Rank—are you very fond of masquerade parties?

RANK: Yes, if there's a good array of odd disguises—

NORA: Tell me, what should we two go as at the next masquerade?

HELMER: You little featherhead—already thinking of the next!

RANK: We two? I'll tell you what: you must go as Charmed Life—

HELMER: Yes, but find a costume for *that!*

RANK: Your wife can appear just as she looks every day.

HELMER: That was nicely put. But don't you know what you're going to be?

RANK: Yes, Helmer, I've made up my mind.

HELMER: Well?

RANK: At the next masquerade I'm going to be invisible.

HELMER: That's a funny idea.

RANK: They say there's a hat—black, huge—have you never heard of the hat that makes you invisible? You put it on, and then no one on earth can see you.

HELMER: [*Suppressing a smile.*] Ah, of course.

RANK: But I'm quite forgetting what I came for. Helmer, give me a cigar, one of the dark Havanas.

HELMER: With the greatest pleasure. [*Holds out his case.*]

RANK: Thanks. [*Takes one and cuts off the tip.*]

NORA: [*Striking a match*] Let me give you a light.

RANK: Thank you. [*She holds the match for him; he lights the cigar.*] And now good-bye.

HELMER: Good-bye, good-bye, old friend.

NORA: Sleep well, Doctor.

RANK: Thanks for that wish.

NORA: Wish me the same.

RANK: You? All right, if you like—Sleep well. And thanks for the light. [*He nods to them both and leaves.*]

HELMER: [*His voice subdued.*] He's been drinking heavily.

NORA: [*Absently.*] Could be. [HELMER *takes his keys from his pocket and goes out in the hall.*] Torvald—what are you after?

HELMER: Got to empty the mailbox; it's nearly full. There won't be room for the morning papers.

NORA: Are you working tonight?

HELMER: You know I'm not. Why—what's this? Someone's been at the lock.

NORA: At the lock—?

HELMER: Yes, I'm positive. What do you suppose—? I can't imagine one of the maids—? Here's a broken hairpin. Nora, it's yours—

NORA: [*Quickly.*] Then it must be the children—

HELMER: You'd better break them of that. Hm, hm—well, opened it after all. [*Takes the contents out and calls into the kitchen.*] Helene! Helene, would you put out the lamp in the hall. [*He returns to the room, shutting the hall door, then displays the handful of mail.*] Look how it's piled up. [*Sorting through them.*] Now what's this?

NORA: [*At the window.*] The letter! Oh, Torvald, no!

HELMER: Two calling cards—from Rank.

NORA: From Dr. Rank?

HELMER: [*Examining them.*] "Dr. Rank, Consulting Physician." They were on top. He must have dropped them in as he left.

NORA: Is there anything on them?

HELMER: There's a black cross over the name. See? That's a gruesome notion. He could almost be announcing his own death.

NORA: That's just what he's doing.

HELMER: What! You've heard something? Something he's told you?

NORA: Yes. That when those cards came, he'd be taking his leave of us. He'll shut himself in now and die.

HELMER: Ah, my poor friend! Of course I knew he wouldn't be here much longer. But so soon—And then to hide himself away like a wounded animal.

NORA: If it has to happen, then it's best it happens in silence—don't you think so, Torvald?

HELMER: [*Pacing up and down.*] He'd grown right into our lives. I simply can't imagine him gone. He with his suffering and loneliness—like a dark cloud setting off our sunlit happiness. Well, maybe it's best this way. For him, at least. [*Standing still.*] And maybe for us too, Nora. Now we're thrown back on each other, completely. [*Embracing her.*] Oh you, my darling wife, how can I hold you close enough? You know what, Nora—time and again I've wished you were in some terrible danger, just so I could stake my life and soul and everything, for your sake.

NORA: [*Tearing herself away, her voice firm and decisive.*] Now you must read your mail, Torvald.

HELMER: No, no, not tonight. I want to stay with you, dearest.

NORA: With a dying friend on your mind?

HELMER: You're right. We've both had a shock. There's ugliness between us—these thoughts of death and corruption. We'll have to get free of them first. Until then—we'll stay apart.

NORA: [*Clinging about his neck.*] Torvald—good night! Good night!

HELMER: [*Kissing her on the cheek.*] Good night, little songbird. Sleep well, Nora. I'll be reading my mail now. [*He takes the letters into his room and shuts the door after him.*]

NORA: [*With bewildered glances, groping about, seizing* HELMER's *domino, throwing it around her, and speaking in short, hoarse, broken whispers.*] Never see him again. Never, never. [*Putting her shawl over her head.*] Never see the children either—them, too. Never, never. Oh, the freezing black water! The depths—down—Oh, I wish it were over—He has it now; he's reading it—now. Oh no, no, not yet. Torvald, good-bye, you and the children—[*She starts for the hall; as she does,* HELMER *throws open his door and stands with an open letter in his hand.*]

HELMER: Nora!

NORA: [*Screams.*] Oh—!

HELMER: What is this? You know what's in this letter?

NORA: Yes, I know. Let me go! Let me out!

HELMER: [*Holding her back.*] Where are you going?

NORA: [*Struggling to break loose.*] You can't save me, Torvald!

HELMER: [*Slumping back.*] True! Then it's true what he writes? How horrible! No, no, it's impossible—it can't be true.

NORA: It *is* true. I've loved you more than all this world.

HELMER: Ah, none of your slippery tricks.

NORA: [*Taking one step toward him.*] Torvald—!

HELMER: What *is* this you've blundered into!

NORA: Just let me loose. You're not going to suffer for my sake. You're not going to take on my guilt.

HELMER: No more playacting. [*Locks the hall door.*] You stay right here and give me a reckoning. You understand what you've done? Answer! You understand?

NORA: [*Looking squarely at him, her face hardening.*] Yes. I'm beginning to understand everything now.

HELMER: [*Striding about.*] Oh, what an awful awakening! In all these eight years—she who was my pride and joy—a hypocrite, a liar—worse, worse—a criminal! How infinitely disgusting it all is! The shame! [NORA *says nothing and goes on looking straight at him. He stops in front of her.*] I should have suspected something of the kind. I should have known. All your father's flimsy values—Be still! All your father's flimsy values have come out in you. No religion, no morals, no sense of duty—Oh, how I'm punished for letting him off! I did it for your sake, and you repay me like this.

NORA: Yes, like this.

HELMER: Now you've wrecked all my happiness—ruined my whole future. Oh, it's awful to think of. I'm in a cheap little grafter's hands; he can do anything he wants with me, ask for anything, play with me like a puppet—and I can't breathe a word. I'll be swept down miserably into the depths on account of a featherbrained woman.

NORA: When I'm gone from this world, you'll be free.

HELMER: Oh, quit posing. Your father had a mess of those speeches too. What good would that ever do me if you were gone from this world, as you say? Not the slightest. He can still make the whole thing known; and if he does, I could be falsely suspected as your accomplice. They might even think that I was behind it—that I put you up to it. And all that I can thank you for—you that I've coddled the whole of our marriage. Can you see now what you've done to me?

NORA: [*Icily calm.*] Yes.

HELMER: It's so incredible, I just can't grasp it. But we'll have to patch up whatever we can. Take off the shawl. I said, take it off! I've got to appease him somehow or other. The thing has to be hushed up at any cost. And as for you and me, it's got to seem like everything between us is just as it was—to the outside world, that is. You'll go right on living in this house, of course. But you can't be allowed to bring up the children; I don't dare trust you with them—Oh, to have to say this to someone I've loved so much, and that I still—! Well, that's done with. From now on happiness doesn't matter; all that matters is saving the bits and pieces, the appearance—[*The doorbell rings.* HELMER *starts.*] What's that? And so late. Maybe the worst—? You think he'd—? Hide, Nora! Say you're sick. [NORA *remains standing motionless.* HELMER *goes and opens the door.*]

MAID: [*Half dressed, in the hall.*] A letter for Mrs. Helmer.

HELMER: I'll take it. [*Snatches the letter and shuts the door.*] Yes, it's from him. You don't get it; I'm reading it myself.

NORA: Then read it.

HELMER: [*By the lamp.*] I hardly dare. We may be ruined, you and I. But—I've got to know. [*Rips open the letter, skims through a few lines, glances at an enclosure, then cries out joyfully.*] Nora! [NORA *looks inquiringly at him.*] Nora! Wait—better check it again—Yes, yes, it's true. I'm saved. Nora, I'm saved!

NORA: And I?

HELMER: You too, of course. We're both saved, both of us. Look. He's sent back your note. He says he's sorry and ashamed—that a happy development in his life—oh, who cares what he says! Nora, we're saved! No one can hurt you. Oh, Nora, Nora—but first, this ugliness all has to go. Let me see—[*Takes a look at the note.*] No, I don't want to see it; I want the whole thing to fade like a dream. [*Tears the note and both letters to pieces, throws them into the stove and watches them burn.*] There—now there's nothing left—He wrote that since Christmas Eve you—Oh, they must have been three terrible days for you, Nora.

NORA: I fought a hard fight.

HELMER: And suffered pain and saw no escape but—No, we're not going to dwell on anything unpleasant. We'll just be grateful and keep on repeating: it's over now, it's over! You hear me, Nora? You don't seem to realize—it's over. What's it mean—that frozen look? Oh, poor little Nora, I understand. You can't believe I've forgiven you. But I have, Nora; I swear I have. I know that what you did, you did out of love for me.

NORA: That's true.

HELMER: You loved me the way a wife ought to love her husband. It's simply the means that you couldn't judge. But you think I love you any the less for not knowing how to handle your affairs? No, no—just lean on me; I'll guide you and teach you. I wouldn't be a man if this feminine helplessness didn't make you twice as attractive to me. You mustn't mind those sharp words I said—that was all in the first confusion of thinking my world had collapsed. I've forgiven you, Nora; I swear I've forgiven you.

NORA: My thanks for your forgiveness. [*She goes out through the door, right.*]

HELMER: No, wait—[*Peers in.*] What are you doing in there?

NORA: [*Inside.*] Getting out of my costume.

HELMER: [*By the open door.*] Yes, do that. Try to calm yourself and collect your thoughts again, my frightened little songbird. You can rest easy now; I've got wide wings to shelter you with. [*Walking about close by the door.*] How snug and nice our home is, Nora. You're safe here; I'll keep you like a hunted dove I've rescued out of a hawk's claws. I'll bring peace to your poor, shuddering heart. Gradually it'll happen, Nora; you'll see. Tomorrow all this will look different to you; then everything will be as it was. I won't have to go on repeating I forgive you; you'll feel it for yourself. How can you imagine I'd ever conceivably want to disown you—or even blame you in any way? Ah, you don't know a man's heart, Nora. For a man there's something indescribably sweet and satisfying in knowing he's forgiven his wife—and forgiven her out of a full and open heart. It's as if she belongs to him in two ways now: in a sense he's given her fresh into the world again, and she's become his wife and his child as well. From now on that's what you'll be to me—you little, bewildered, helpless thing. Don't be afraid of anything, Nora; just open your heart to me, and I'll be conscience and will to you both—[NORA *enters in her regular clothes.*] What's this? Not in bed? You've changed your dress?

NORA: Yes, Torvald, I've changed my dress.

HELMER: But why now, so late?

NORA: Tonight I'm not sleeping.

HELMER: But Nora dear—

NORA: [*Looking at her watch.*] It's still not so very late. Sit down, Torvald; we have a lot to talk over. [*She sits at one side of the table.*]

HELMER: Nora—what is this? That hard expression—

NORA: Sit down. This'll take some time. I have a lot to say.

HELMER: [*Sitting at the table directly opposite her.*] You worry me, Nora. And I don't understand you.

NORA: No, that's exactly it. You don't understand me. And I've never understood you either—until tonight. No, don't interrupt. You can just listen to what I say. We're closing out accounts, Torvald.

HELMER: How do you mean that?

NORA: [*After a short pause.*] Doesn't anything strike you about our sitting here like this?

HELMER: What's that?

NORA: We've been married now eight years. Doesn't it occur to you that this is the first time we two, you and I, man and wife, have ever talked seriously together?

HELMER: What do you mean—seriously?

NORA: In eight whole years—longer even—right from our first acquaintance, we've never exchanged a serious word on any serious thing.

HELMER: You mean I should constantly go and involve you in problems you couldn't possibly help me with?

NORA: I'm not talking of problems. I'm saying that we've never sat down seriously together and tried to get to the bottom of anything.

HELMER: But dearest, what good would that ever do you?

NORA: That's the point right there: you've never understood me. I've been wronged greatly, Torvald—first by Papa, and then by you.

HELMER: What! By us—the two people who've loved you more than anyone else?

NORA: [*Shaking her head.*] You never loved me. You've thought it fun to be in love with me, that's all.

HELMER: Nora, what a thing to say!

NORA: Yes, it's true now, Torvald. When I lived at home with Papa, he told me all his opinions, so I had the same ones too; or if they were different I hid them, since he wouldn't have cared for that. He used to call me his doll-child, and he played with me the way I played with my dolls. Then I came into your house—

HELMER: How can you speak of our marriage like that?

NORA: [*Unperturbed.*] I mean, then I went from Papa's hands into yours. You arranged everything to your own taste, and so I got the same taste as you—or I pretended to; I can't remember. I guess a little of both, first one, then the other. Now when I look back, it seems as if I'd lived here like a beggar—just from hand to mouth. I've lived by doing tricks for you, Torvald. But that's the way you wanted it. It's a great sin what you and Papa did to me. You're to blame that nothing's become of me.

HELMER: Nora, how unfair and ungrateful you are! Haven't you been happy here?

NORA: No, never. I thought so—but I never have.

HELMER: Not—not happy!

NORA: No, only lighthearted. And you've always been so kind to me. But our home's been nothing but a playpen. I've been your doll-wife here, just as at home I was Papa's doll-child. And in turn the children have been my dolls. I thought it was fun when you played with me, just as they thought it fun when I played with them. That's been our marriage, Torvald.

HELMER: There's some truth in what you're saying—under all the raving exaggeration. But it'll all be different after this. Playtime's over; now for the schooling.

NORA: Whose schooling—mine or the children's?

HELMER: Both yours and the children's, dearest.

NORA: Oh, Torvald, you're not the man to teach me to be a good wife to you.

HELMER: And you can say that?

NORA: And I—how am I equipped to bring up children?

HELMER: Nora!

NORA: Didn't you say a moment ago that that was no job to trust me with?

HELMER: In a flare of temper! Why fasten on that?

NORA: Yes, but you were so very right. I'm not up to the job. There's another job I have to do first. I have to try to educate myself. You can't help me with that. I've got to do it alone. And that's why I'm leaving you now.

HELMER: [*Jumping up.*] What's that?

NORA: I have to stand completely alone, if I'm ever going to discover myself and the world out there. So I can't go on living with you.

HELMER: Nora, Nora!

NORA: I want to leave right away. Kristine should put me up for the night—

HELMER: You're insane! You've no right! I forbid you!

NORA: From here on, there's no use forbidding me anything. I'll take with me whatever is mine. I don't want a thing from you, either now or later.

HELMER: What kind of madness is this!

NORA: Tomorrow I'm going home—I mean, home where I came from. It'll be easier up there to find something to do.

HELMER: Oh, you blind, incompetent child!

NORA: I must learn to be competent, Torvald.

HELMER: Abandon your home, your husband, your children! And you're not even thinking what people will say.

NORA: I can't be concerned about that. I only know how essential this is.

HELMER: Oh, it's outrageous. So you'll run out like this on your most sacred vows.

NORA: What do you think are my most sacred vows?

HELMER: And I have to tell you that! Aren't they your duties to your husband and children?

NORA: I have other duties equally sacred.

HELMER: That isn't true. What duties are they?

NORA: Duties to myself.

HELMER: Before all else, you're a wife and a mother.

NORA: I don't believe in that anymore. I believe that, before all else, I'm a human being, no less than you—or anyway, I ought to try to become one. I know the majority thinks you're right, Torvald, and plenty of books agree with you, too. But I can't go on believing what the majority says, or what's written in books. I have to think over these things myself and try to understand them.

HELMER: Why can't you understand your place in your own home? On a point like that, isn't there one everlasting guide you can turn to? Where's your religion?

NORA: Oh, Torvald, I'm really not sure what religion is.

HELMER: What—?

NORA: I only know what the minister said when I was confirmed. He told me religion was this thing and that. When I get clear and away by myself, I'll go into that problem too. I'll see if what the minister said was right, or, in any case, if it's right for me.

HELMER: A young woman your age shouldn't talk like that. If religion can't move you, I can try to rouse your conscience. You do have some moral feeling? Or, tell me—has that gone too?

NORA: It's not easy to answer that, Torvald. I simply don't know. I'm all confused about these things. I just know I see them so differently from you. I find out, for one thing, that the law's not at all what I'd thought—but I can't get it through my head that the law is fair. A woman hasn't a right to protect her dying father or save her husband's life! I can't believe that.

HELMER: You talk like a child. You don't know anything of the world you live in.

NORA: No, I don't. But now I'll begin to learn for myself. I'll try to discover who's right, the world or I.

HELMER: Nora, you're sick; you've got a fever. I almost think you're out of your head.

NORA: I've never felt more clearheaded and sure in my life.

HELMER: And—clearheaded and sure—you're leaving your husband and children?

NORA: Yes.

HELMER: Then there's only one possible reason.

NORA: What?

HELMER: You no longer love me.

NORA: No. That's exactly it.

HELMER: Nora! You can't be serious!

NORA: Oh, this is so hard, Torvald—you've been so kind to me always. But I can't help it. I don't love you anymore.

HELMER: [*Struggling for composure.*] Are you also clearheaded and sure about that?

NORA: Yes, completely. That's why I can't go on staying here.

HELMER: Can you tell me what I did to lose your love?

NORA: Yes, I can tell you. It was this evening when the miraculous thing didn't come—then I knew you weren't the man I'd imagined.

HELMER: Be more explicit; I don't follow you.

NORA: I've waited now so patiently eight long years—for, my Lord, I know miracles don't come every day. Then this crisis broke over me, and such a certainty filled me: *now* the miraculous event would occur. While Krogstad's letter was lying out there, I never for an instant dreamed that you could give in to his terms. I was so utterly sure you'd say to him: go on, tell your tale to the whole wide world. And when he'd done that—

HELMER: Yes, what then? When I'd delivered my own wife into shame and disgrace—!

NORA: When he'd done that, I was so utterly sure that you'd step forward, take the blame on yourself and say: I am the guilty one.

HELMER: Nora—!

NORA: You're thinking I'd never accept such a sacrifice from you? No, of course not. But what good would my protests be against you? That was the miracle I was waiting for, in terror and hope. And to stave that off, I would have taken my life.

HELMER: I'd gladly work for you day and night, Nora—and take on pain and deprivation. But there's no one who gives up honor for love.

NORA: Millions of women have done just that.

HELMER: Oh, you think and talk like a silly child.

NORA: Perhaps. But you neither think nor talk like the man I could join myself to. When your big fright was over—and it wasn't from any threat against me, only for what might damage you—when all the danger was past, for you it was just as if nothing had happened. I was exactly the same, your little lark, your doll, that you'd have to handle with double care now that I'd turned out so brittle and frail. [*Gets up.*] Torvald—in that instant it dawned on me that for eight years I've been living here with a stranger, and that I'd even conceived three children—oh, I can't stand the thought of it! I could tear myself to bits.

HELMER: [*Heavily.*] I see. There's a gulf that's opened between us—that's clear. Oh, but Nora, can't we bridge it somehow?

NORA: The way I am now, I'm no wife for you.

HELMER: I have the strength to make myself over.

NORA: Maybe—if your doll gets taken away.

HELMER: But to part! To part from you! No, Nora, no—I can't imagine it.

NORA: [*Going out, right.*] All the more reason why it has to be. [*She reenters with her coat and a small overnight bag, which she puts on a chair by the table.*]

HELMER: Nora, Nora, not now! Wait till tomorrow.

NORA: I can't spend the night in a strange man's room.

HELMER: But couldn't we live here like brother and sister—

NORA: You know very well how long that would last. [*Throws her shawl about her.*] Good-bye, Torvald. I won't look in on the children. I know they're in better hands than mine. The way I am now, I'm no use to them.

HELMER: But someday, Nora—someday—?

NORA: How can I tell? I haven't the least idea what'll become of me.

HELMER: But you're my wife, now and wherever you go.

NORA: Listen, Torvald—I've heard that when a wife deserts her husband's house just as I'm doing, then the law frees him from all responsibility. In any case, I'm freeing you from being responsible. Don't feel yourself bound, any more than I will. There has to be absolute freedom for us both. Here, take your ring back. Give me mine.

HELMER: That too?

NORA: That too.

HELMER: There it is.

NORA: Good. Well, now it's all over. I'm putting the keys here. The maids know all about keeping up the house—better than I do. Tomorrow, after I've left town, Kristine will stop by to pack up everything that's mine from home. I'd like those things shipped up to me.

HELMER: Over! All over! Nora, won't you ever think about me?

NORA: I'm sure I'll think of you often, and about the children and the house here.

HELMER: May I write you?

NORA: No—never. You're not to do that.

HELMER: Oh, but let me send you—

NORA: Nothing. Nothing.

HELMER: Or help you if you need it.

NORA: No. I accept nothing from strangers.

HELMER: Nora—can I never be more than a stranger to you?

NORA: [*Picking up the overnight bag.*] Ah, Torvald—it would take the greatest miracle of all—

HELMER: Tell me the greatest miracle!

NORA: You and I both would have to transform ourselves to the point that—Oh, Torvald, I've stopped believing in miracles.

HELMER: But I'll believe. Tell me! Transform ourselves to the point that—?

NORA: That our living together could be a true marriage. [*She goes out down the hall.*]

HELMER: [*Sinks down on a chair by the door, face buried in his hands.*] Nora! Nora! [*Looking about and rising.*] Empty. She's gone. [*A sudden hope leaps in him.*] The greatest miracle—?

[*From below, the sound of a door slamming shut.*]

1879

JANE MARTIN

Two Monologues from *Talking With . . .*

The true identity of the award-winning playwright known as "Jane Martin" has been the subject of widespread speculation and debate since 1982, when her *Talking With . . .* debuted to great acclaim at the sixth annual Humana Festival in Louisville, Kentucky, and then went on to win the 1982 American Theatre Critics Association (ATCA) principal citation for most outstanding script of the season. Composed of eleven monologues by a diverse array of female characters, the play established Martin as a master of the monologue form and earned her comparisons to Flannery O'Connor, thanks not least to its bizarre, even grotesque, and usually obsessive characters, its deft rendering of their distinctive speech patterns, its often darkly religious undertones, and its fascination with physical and psychological violence. In the years since, Martin's work has included two other monologue-based plays, *Vital Signs* (1990) and *Sez She* (2006); comedies such as *Cementville* (1991) and *Criminal Hearts* (1992); the theater satire *Anton in Show Business* (2000), about three Texas actresses who mount a disastrous production of Anton Chekhov's *The Three Sisters;* the parody *Flaming Guns of the Purple Sage* (2001); and the highly topical plays *Keely and Du* (1993), about a working-class rape victim held captive by pro-life terrorists bent on preventing her from having an abortion; *Mr. Bundy* (1998), in which the parents of an eleven-year-old discover that a convicted child molester lives next door; and *Flags* (2005), which focuses on a father's extreme reaction to the death of his soldier-son in Iraq. Prior to 2001, almost all of Martin's plays debuted at the Humana Festival under the direction of its founder, Jon Jory (b. 1938). As a result, and despite the director's demurrals, many believe Jane Martin is in fact either Jory himself or a team of writers that includes him.

The play* Talking With . . . *consists of eleven monologues delivered by a diverse array of female characters. We here include two, "Handler" and "French Fries."

Handler

A young woman in a simple, country-print dress. On the floor before her is a handmade wooden box about two feet long and eighteen inches high with a sliding wire screen top.

CARO: My Dada [Pronounced *"Dád-aw."*] was gonna do this tonight but the Lord froze his face so he sent me. I learned this from my Dada and he learned it up from great Gran, who took it on from the Reverend Soloman Bracewood, who had him a mule ministry[1] 'round these parts way back when. Dada taught Miss Ellie, my ma, and my brother Jamie . . . he was in it too, 'fore he went for Detroit.

See, what I got in here is snakes. Lotta people don't like snakes. Gives it its nature, I guess. This here is water mocs. Jamie, he said they got the dirtiest, nastiest bite of all . . . well, rattlers is yer biggest. Lotta venom. You milk you a rattler, you can half fill up a juice glass. Dada said Jamie should do rattlers, but he never. Did 'heads, copperheads. Now they're slower and safer but it ain't such a good show. You know those dang snakes smell like cucumbers? Well, they do. Miss Ellie, she favored moccasins. Dada too . . . well, Dada he did all kinds, all ways. Your moccasin now, he's your good ol' boy snake. Flat out mean an' lots of get up n' go. Heck, they'll chase ya. They will. Ol' Dada he didn't like Miss Ellie doin' 'em. "You lay off them mocs 'fore they lay you down." Made Miss Ellie laugh. Lotta handlers think moccasins are slimy. Couldn't get me to touch one. They'll do rattlers . . . got him a nice dry feel. Little bit sandpapery. Rattler can find ya in the pitch dark though. They git on to yer body heat. Snake handlin.' *All* my blood does it. Only Dada an' me now though. Snake handlin', with the Holiness Church. Down where I come from we take God pretty serious. If you got the spirit, snake don't bite. If he bites you, you know you ain't got the spirit. Makes the difference real clear, don't it?

It's right there in the scripture . . . Mark, Chapter 16, verses 17 and 18, "And these signs shall follow them that believe. In my name they shall cast out devils; they shall speak in new tongues; they shall take up serpents; and if they shall drink any deadly thing, it shall not hurt them; they shall lay hands on the sick and they shall recover." Don't figure it could be much clearer than that. There's some churches don't use snakes, use strychnine, powdered poison, same idea though. They mix it with Cherry kool-ade, sing 'em a hymn, drink it off, and then just stand around waitin' to see if they fall over. Ain't much of a show. Not like snakes. Dada does fire but I can't do it. Pours some kerosene in a coke bottle, sticks a rag in the top and lights it up. Holds that fire under his chin, passes it down the arm, puts his hand in it, you know, that kind of stuff. He says there's people do blow torches down to Tennessee. I don't know. Jamie give it a try 'fore he went to Detroit. Just about burned his ass off. Sorry.

When I handle, I keep 'em in this box. Dada gimme this and some Heidi[2] doll on my ninth birthday. Sometimes I'll just open up the lid and put my foot in or, uh, maybe stick it open side to my chest. There's some lay it to their face. I don't. Scares my eyes. Durin' service we take 'em right out, pass 'em around. It's more dangerous than a single handler. Snake gets to comparin' who got the spirit a whole lot an' who jes got it some. Somebody's jes about bound to come in second. Don't get me wrong now. Y' don't die everytime yer

1. That is, he was a traveling preacher who traveled by mule.
2. Protagonist of two Swiss children's books published in 1880 by Johanna Spyri and of many subsequent films.

bit. I been bit seven times. Four times by the same serpent. Dada says he got the sweet tooth for me. Dada been bit thirty-two times an' never saw him a doctor. Used to let me kiss him on the marks. Last one got him here.

(*Points to eye.*) Froze him right up. Dada says he'll thaw but I don't know.

Day after Jamie took off Miss Ellie did moccasins standin' in the back of the pickup over to Hard Burley. Shouldn't ought to 'cause her mind weren't there. Coal truck backfired and she got bit. Snake bit her three more times 'fore she hit the ground. Dada layed hands on her but she died anyway. There was ten of us handled right there at the funeral. Snake handlin'.

Snake knows what you feel. You can fool a person but you can't fool a snake. You got the spirit, God locks their jaws. Keeps you safe. Tell you what though . . . I don't believe in a God. Left me. Gone with Miss Ellie. I was handlin' when I knew it sure. Snake was jes comin' on down the line. Marita she yells out, "The Lord. Lord's in me and with me. In me and with me." Noah he was ululatin', talkin' in tongues. Couple of folks was rollin' and singing. Dada was doin' switch grips. Had Miss Ellie's weddin' ring on his little finger. And it came on me, heck, there ain't no God in here. There's just a bunch of shouters gettin' tranced. There ain't no God in here at all. 'Bout that time they layed that serpent to me. Felt fussy. Nasty. Just lookin' for an excuse y'know? An' I was an empty vessel, worse nor a pharasee,[3] grist for the mill. My blood went so cold I coulda crapped ice-cubes. Snake knew. Started to get leverage. So I said, "Snake. You Satan's hand-maiden. You're right, there ain't no God in me. I'm just a woman, but I'm the only woman in my Dada's house and he needs me home. Outta his faith and his need, you lock yer jaws." I let that snake feel a child's pure love and it sponged it up offa my hands and then ol'wiggley went limp. I tranced it. It was a real good service. Didn't nobody handlin' get bit.

(*Takes snake out of the box.*) Yes, you got to believe. Holiness Church is dead right about that. Make me wonder, you know? I git to lookin' at people and wonderin' if they got anything in 'em could lock a serpent's jaws. Any power or spirit or love or whatever. I look at 'em and I wonder, could they handle? Tell you what though, you can see it in a face. You can read it. You look me full in the face it don't take me 30 seconds. It's like I was the snake, some ol' pit viper, an' I can read yer heart. Maybe you could handle and maybe you can't, but there's but one sure thing in this world . . . yer empty, yer gonna get bit.

[*Fade out.*]

French Fries

An old woman in a straight-back chair holding a McDonald's cup. She is surrounded by several bundles of newspapers. She wears thick glasses that distort her eyes to the viewer.

3. In Matthew 23, Jesus represents the Pharisees, a Jewish sect, as "hypocrites" who do not practice as they preach.

ANNA MAE: If I had one wish in my life, why I'd like to live in McDonald's. Right there in the restaurant. 'Stead of in this old place. I'll come up to the brow of the hill, bowed down with my troubles, hurtin' under my load and I'll see that yellow horseshoe, sort of like part of a rainbow, and it gives my old spirit a lift. Lord, I can sit in a McDonald's all day. I've done it too. Walked the seven miles with the sun just on its way, and then sat on the curb till five minutes of seven. First one there and the last to leave. Just like some ol' french fry they forgot.

I like the young people workin' there. Like a team of fine young horses when I was growin' up. All smilin'. Tell you what I really like though is the plastic. God gave us plastic so there wouldn't be no stains on his world. See, in the human world of the earth it all gets scratched, stained, tore up, faded down. Loses its shine. All of it does. In time. Well, God he gave us the idea of plastic so we'd know what the everlasting really was. See if there's plastic then there's surely eternity. It's God's hint.

You ever watch folks when they come on in the McDonald's? They always speed up, almost run the last few steps. You see if they don't. Old Dobbin[1] with the barn in sight. They know it's safe in there and it ain't safe outside. Now it ain't safe outside and you know it.

I've seen a man healed by a Big Mac. I have. I was just sittin' there. Last summer it was. Oh, they don't never move you on. It's a sacred law in McDonald's, you can sit for a hundred years. Only place in the world. Anyway, a fella, maybe thirty-five, maybe forty, come on in there dressed real nice, real bright tie, bran' new baseball cap, nice white socks and he had him that disease. You know the one I mean, Cerebral Walrus[2] they call it. Anyway, he had him a cock leg. His poor old body had it two speeds at the same time. Now he got him some coffee, with a lid on, and sat him down and Jimmy the tow-head[3] cook knew him, see, and he brought over a Big Mac. Well, the sick fella ate maybe half of it and then he was just sittin', you know, suffering those tremors, when a couple of *ants* come right out of the burger. Now there ain't no ants in McDonald's no way. Lord sent those ants, and the sick fella he looked real sharp at the burger and a bunch *more* ants marched on out nice as you please and his head lolled right over and he pitched himself out of that chair and banged his head on the floor, loud. Thwack! Like a bowling ball dropping. Made you half sick to hear it. We jump up and run over but he was cold out. Well those servin' kids, so cute, they watered him, stuck a touch pepper up his nostril, slapped him right smart, and bang, up he got. Standin' an' blinkin'. "Well, how are you?," we say. An he looks us over, looks right in our eyes, and he say, "I'm fine." And he was. He was fine! Tipped his Cincinnati Reds baseball cap, big "us'-swallowed-the-canary" grin, paraded out of there clean, straight like a pole-bean poplar, walked him a plumb line without no trace of the "walrus." Got outside, jumped up, whooped, hollered, sang him the National Anthem, flagged down a Circle Line bus, an' rode off up Muhammad Ali Boulevard wavin' an' smilin' like the King of the Pharoahs. Healed by a Big Mac. I saw it.

1. Traditional name for a horse, especially a working farm horse.

2. Cerebral palsy. 3. Someone with extremely blond, even white, hair.

Laura Saladino in a scene from *Talking with . . .* at Theatre TCU

McDonald's. You ever see anybody die in a McDonald's? No sir. No way. Nobody ever has died in one. Shoot, they die in Burger Kings all the time. Kentucky Fried Chicken's got their own damn ambulances. Noooooooooo, you can't die in a McDonald's no matter how hard you try. It's the spices. Seals you safe in this life like it seals in the flavor. Yesssssss, yes!

I asked Jarrell could I live there. See they close up around ten, and there ain't a thing goin' on in 'em till seven a.m. I'd just sit in those nice swingy chairs and lean forward. Rest my head on those cool, cool, smooth tables, sing me a hymn and sleep like a baby. Jarrell, he said he'd write him a letter up the chain of command and see would they let me. Oh, I got my bid in. Peaceful and clean.

Sometimes I see it like the last of a movie. You know how they start the picture up real close and then back it off steady and far? Well, that's how I dream it. I'm living in McDonald's and it's real late at night and you see me up close, smiling, and then you see the whole McDonald's from the outside, lit up and friendly. And I get smaller and smaller, like they do, and then it's just a light in the darkness, like a star, and I'm in it. I'm part of that light, part of the whole sky, and it's all McDonald's, but part of something even bigger, something fixed and shiny . . . like plastic.

I know. I know. It's just a dream. Just a beacon in the storm. But you got to have a dream. It's our dreams make us what we are.

[*Blackout.*]

1980

ARTHUR MILLER
(1915–2005)

Death of a Salesman

Arthur Miller was born in New York City to a prosperous family whose fortunes were ruined by the Depression, a circumstance that would shape his political outlook and imbue him with a deep sense of social responsibility. Miller studied history, economics, and journalism at the University of Michigan, began writing plays, and joined the Federal Theater Project, a proving ground for some of the best playwrights of the period. He had his first Broadway success, *All My Sons*, in 1947, followed two years later by his Pulitzer Prize–winning masterpiece, *Death of a Salesman*. In 1953, against the backdrop of Senator Joseph McCarthy's anti-Communist "witch-hunts," Miller fashioned another modern parable, his Tony Award–winning *The Crucible*, based on the seventeenth-century Salem witch trials. Among his other works for the stage are the Pulitzer Prize–winner *A View from the Bridge* (1955), *After the Fall* (1964), *Incident at Vichy* (1965), *The Price* (1968), *The Ride Down Mt. Morgan* (1991), *Broken Glass* (1994), and *Resurrection Blues* (2004). In addition, Miller wrote a novel, *Focus* (1945); the screenplay for the film *The Misfits* (1961), which starred his second wife, Marilyn Monroe; *The Theater Essays* (1971), a collection of his writings about dramatic literature; and *Timebends* (1987), his autobiography.

Certain Private Conversations in Two Acts and a Requiem

CHARACTERS

WILLY LOMAN	THE WOMAN	STANLEY
LINDA	CHARLEY	MISS FORSYTHE
BIFF	UNCLE BEN	LETTA
HAPPY	HOWARD WAGNER	
BERNARD	JENNY	

The action takes place in WILLY LOMAN'S *house and yard and in various places he visits in the New York and Boston of today.*

ACT I

A melody is heard, playing upon a flute. It is small and fine, telling of grass and trees and the horizon. The curtain rises.

Before us is the Salesman's house. We are aware of towering, angular shapes behind it, surrounding it on all sides. Only the blue light of the sky falls upon the house and forestage; the surrounding area shows an angry flow of orange. As more light appears, we see a solid vault of apartment houses around the small, fragile-seeming home. An air of the dream clings to the place, a dream rising out of reality. The kitchen at center seems actual enough, for there is a kitchen table with three chairs, and a refrigerator. But no other fixtures are seen. At the back of the kitchen there is a draped entrance, which leads to the living-room. To the right of the kitchen, on a level raised two feet, is a bedroom furnished only with a brass bedstead and a straight chair. On a shelf over the bed a silver athletic trophy stands. A window opens onto the apartment house at the side.

Behind the kitchen, on a level raised six and a half feet, is the boys' bedroom, at present barely visible. Two beds are dimly seen, and at the back of the room a dormer window. (This bedroom is above the unseen living-room.) At the left a stairway curves up to it from the kitchen.

The entire setting is wholly or, in some places, partially transparent. The roof-line of the house is one-dimensional; under and over it we see the apartment buildings. Before the house lies an apron, curving beyond the forestage into the orchestra. This forward area serves as the back yard as well as the locale of all WILLY'S *imaginings and of his city scenes. Whenever the action is in the present the actors observe the imaginary wall-lines, entering the house only through its door at the left. But in the scenes of the past these boundaries are broken, and characters enter or leave a room by stepping "through" a wall onto the forestage.*

From the right, WILLY LOMAN, *the Salesman, enters, carrying two large sample cases. The flute plays on. He hears but is not aware of it. He is past sixty years of age, dressed quietly. Even as he crosses the stage to the doorway of the house, his exhaustion is apparent. He unlocks the door, comes into the kitchen, and thankfully lets his burden down, feeling the soreness of his palms. A word-sigh escapes his lips—it might be "Oh, boy, oh, boy." He closes the door, then carries his cases out into the living-room, through the draped kitchen doorway.*

LINDA, *his wife, has stirred in her bed at the right. She gets out and puts on a robe, listening. Most often jovial, she has developed an iron repression of her exceptions to* WILLY'S *behavior—she more than loves him, she admires him, as though his mercurial nature, his temper, his massive dreams and little cruelties, served her only as sharp reminders of the turbulent longings within him, longings which she shares but lacks the temperament to utter and follow to their end.*

LINDA: [*Hearing* WILLY *outside the bedroom, calls with some trepidation.*] Willy!

WILLY: It's all right. I came back.

LINDA: Why? What happened? [*Slight pause.*] Did something happen, Willy?

WILLY: No, nothing happened.

LINDA: You didn't smash the car, did you?

WILLY: [*With casual irritation.*] I said nothing happened. Didn't you hear me?

LINDA: Don't you feel well?

WILLY: I'm tired to the death. [*The flute has faded away. He sits on the bed beside her, a little numb.*] I couldn't make it. I just couldn't make it, Linda.

LINDA: [*Very carefully, delicately.*] Where were you all day? You look terrible.

WILLY: I got as far as a little above Yonkers. I stopped for a cup of coffee. Maybe it was the coffee.

LINDA: What?

WILLY: [*After a pause.*] I suddenly couldn't drive any more. The car kept going off onto the shoulder, y'know?

LINDA: [*Helpfully.*] Oh. Maybe it was the steering again. I don't think Angelo knows the Studebaker.

WILLY: No, it's me, it's me. Suddenly I realize I'm goin' sixty miles an hour and I don't remember the last five minutes. I'm—I can't seem to—keep my mind to it.

LINDA: Maybe it's your glasses. You never went for your new glasses.

WILLY: No, I see everything. I came back ten miles an hour. It took me nearly four hours from Yonkers.

LINDA: [*Resigned.*] Well, you'll just have to take a rest, Willy, you can't continue this way.

WILLY: I just got back from Florida.

LINDA: But you didn't rest your mind. Your mind is overactive, and the mind is what counts, dear.

WILLY: I'll start out in the morning. Maybe I'll feel better in the morning. [*She is taking off his shoes.*] These goddam arch supports are killing me.

LINDA: Take an aspirin. Should I get you an aspirin? It'll soothe you.

WILLY: [*With wonder.*] I was driving along, you understand? And I was fine. I was even observing the scenery. You can imagine, me looking at scenery, on the road every week of my life. But it's so beautiful up there, Linda, the trees are so thick, and the sun is warm. I opened the windshield and just let the warm air bathe over me. And then all of a sudden I'm goin' off the road! I'm tellin' ya, I absolutely forgot I was driving. If I'd've gone the other way over the white line I might've killed somebody. So I went on again—and five minutes later I'm dreamin' again, and I nearly—[*He presses two fingers against his eyes.*] I have such thoughts, I have such strange thoughts.

LINDA: Willy, dear. Talk to them again. There's no reason why you can't work in New York.

WILLY: They don't need me in New York. I'm the New England man. I'm vital in New England.

LINDA: But you're sixty years old. They can't expect you to keep traveling every week.

WILLY: I'll have to send a wire[1] to Portland. I'm supposed to see Brown and Morrison tomorrow morning at ten o'clock to show the line. Goddammit, I could sell them! [*He starts putting on his jacket.*]

LINDA: [*Taking the jacket from him.*] Why don't you go down to the place tomorrow and tell Howard you've simply got to work in New York? You're too accommodating, dear.

WILLY: If old man Wagner was alive I'da been in charge of New York now! That man was a prince, he was a masterful man. But that boy of his, that Howard, he don't appreciate. When I went north the first time, the Wagner Company didn't know where New England was!

LINDA: Why don't you tell those things to Howard, dear?

WILLY: [*Encouraged.*] I will, I definitely will. Is there any cheese?

LINDA: I'll make you a sandwich.

WILLY: No, go to sleep. I'll take some milk. I'll be up right away. The boys in?

LINDA: They're sleeping. Happy took Biff on a date tonight.

WILLY: [*Interested.*] That so?

LINDA: It was so nice to see them shaving together, one behind the other, in the bathroom. And going out together. You notice? The whole house smells of shaving lotion.

1. Telegram.

WILLY: Figure it out. Work a lifetime to pay off a house. You finally own it, and there's nobody to live in it.

LINDA: Well, dear, life is a casting off. It's always that way.

WILLY: No, no, some people—some people accomplish something. Did Biff say anything after I went this morning?

LINDA: You shouldn't have criticized him, Willy, especially after he just got off the train. You mustn't lose your temper with him.

WILLY: When the hell did I lose my temper? I simply asked him if he was making any money. Is that a criticism?

LINDA: But, dear, how could he make any money?

WILLY: [*Worried and angered.*] There's such an undercurrent in him. He became a moody man. Did he apologize when I left this morning?

LINDA: He was crestfallen, Willy. You know how he admires you. I think if he finds himself, then you'll both be happier and not fight any more.

WILLY: How can he find himself on a farm? Is that a life? A farmhand? In the beginning, when he was young, I thought, well, a young man, it's good for him to tramp around, take a lot of different jobs. But it's more than ten years now and he has yet to make thirty-five dollars a week!

LINDA: He's finding himself, Willy.

WILLY: Not finding yourself at the age of thirty-four is a disgrace!

LINDA: Shh!

WILLY: The trouble is he's lazy, goddammit!

LINDA: Willy, please!

WILLY: Biff is a lazy bum!

LINDA: They're sleeping. Get something to eat. Go on down.

WILLY: Why did he come home? I would like to know what brought him home.

LINDA: I don't know. I think he's still lost, Willy. I think he's very lost.

WILLY: Biff Loman is lost. In the greatest country in the world a young man with such—personal attractiveness, gets lost. And such a hard worker. There's one thing about Biff—he's not lazy.

LINDA: Never.

WILLY: [*With pity and resolve.*] I'll see him in the morning; I'll have a nice talk with him. I'll get him a job selling. He could be big in no time. My God! Remember how they used to follow him around in high school? When he smiled at one of them their faces lit up. When he walked down the street . . . [*He loses himself in reminiscences.*]

LINDA: [*Trying to bring him out of it.*] Willy, dear, I got a new kind of American-type cheese today. It's whipped.

WILLY: Why do you get American when I like Swiss?

LINDA: I just thought you'd like a change—

WILLY: I don't want a change! I want Swiss cheese. Why am I always being contradicted?

LINDA: [*With a covering laugh.*] I thought it would be a surprise.

WILLY: Why don't you open a window in here, for God's sake?

LINDA: [*With infinite patience.*] They're all open, dear.

WILLY: The way they boxed us in here. Bricks and windows, windows and bricks.

LINDA: We should've bought the land next door.

WILLY: The street is lined with cars. There's not a breath of fresh air in the neighborhood. The grass don't grow any more, you can't raise a carrot in the back yard. They should've had a law against apartment houses. Remember those two beautiful elm trees out there? When I and Biff hung the swing between them?

LINDA: Yeah, like being a million miles from the city.

WILLY: They should've arrested the builder for cutting those down. They massacred the neighborhood. [*Lost.*] More and more I think of those days, Linda. This time of year it was lilac and wisteria. And then the peonies would come out, and the daffodils. What fragrance in this room!

LINDA: Well, after all, people had to move somewhere.

WILLY: No, there's more people now.

LINDA: I don't think there's more people. I think—

WILLY: There's more people! That's what ruining this country! Population is getting out of control. The competition is maddening! Smell the stink from that apartment house! And another one on the other side . . . How can they whip cheese?

[*On* WILLY'S *last line,* BIFF *and* HAPPY *raise themselves up in their beds, listening.*]

LINDA: Go down, try it. And be quiet.

WILLY: [*Turning to* LINDA, *guiltily.*] You're not worried about me, are you, sweetheart?

BIFF: What's the matter?

HAPPY: Listen!

LINDA: You've got too much on the ball to worry about.

WILLY: You're my foundation and my support, Linda.

LINDA: Just try to relax, dear. You make mountains out of mole-hills.

WILLY: I won't fight with him anymore. If he wants to go back to Texas, let him go.

LINDA: He'll find his way.

WILLY: Sure. Certain men just don't get started till later in life. Like Thomas Edison, I think. Or B. F. Goodrich. One of them was deaf.[2] [*He starts for the bedroom doorway.*] I'll put my money on Biff.

LINDA: And Willy—if it's warm Sunday we'll drive in the country. And we'll open the windshield, and take lunch.

WILLY: No, the windshields don't open on the new cars.

LINDA: But you opened it today.

WILLY: Me? I didn't. [*He stops.*] Now isn't that peculiar! Isn't that a remarkable—[*He breaks off in amazement and fright as the flute is heard distantly.*]

LINDA: What, darling?

WILLY: That is the most remarkable thing.

LINDA: What, dear?

WILLY: I was thinking of the Chevvy. [*Slight pause.*] Nineteen twenty-eight . . . when I had that red Chevvy—[*Breaks off.*] That funny? I coulda sworn I was driving that Chevvy today.

LINDA: Well, that's nothing. Something must've reminded you.

2. Thomas Alva Edison (1847–1931), American inventor best known for the phonograph and the incandescent lightbulb; Edison's deafness was legendary. Benjamin Franklin Goodrich (1841–88), American industrialist known for the tire company that still bears his name.

WILLY: Remarkable. *Ts.* Remember those days? The way Biff used to simonize[3] that car? The dealer refused to believe there was eighty thousand miles on it. [*He shakes his head.*] Heh! [*To* LINDA.] Close your eyes, I'll be right up. [*He walks out of the bedroom.*]

HAPPY: [*To* BIFF.] Jesus, maybe he smashed up the car again!

LINDA: [*Calling after* WILLY.] Be careful on the stairs, dear! The cheese is on the middle shelf! [*She turns, goes over to the bed, takes his jacket, and goes out of the bedroom.*]

[*Light has risen on the boys' room. Unseen,* WILLY *is heard talking to himself, "Eighty thousand miles," and a little laugh.* BIFF *gets out of bed, comes downstage a bit, and stands attentively.* BIFF *is two years older than his brother,* HAPPY, *well built, but in these days bears a worn air and seems less self-assured. He has succeeded less, and his dreams are stronger and less acceptable than* HAPPY'S. HAPPY *is tall, powerfully made. Sexuality is like a visible color on him, or a scent that many women have discovered. He, like his brother, is lost, but in a different way, for he has never allowed himself to turn his face toward defeat and is thus more confused and hard-skinned, although seemingly more content.*]

HAPPY: [*Getting out of bed.*] He's going to get his license taken away if he keeps that up. I'm getting nervous about him, y'know, Biff?

BIFF: His eyes are going.

HAPPY: No, I've driven with him. He sees all right. He just doesn't keep his mind on it. I drove into the city with him last week. He stops at a green light and then it turns red and he goes. [*He laughs.*]

BIFF: Maybe he's color-blind.

HAPPY: Pop? Why he's got the finest eye for color in the business. You know that.

BIFF: [*Sitting down on his bed.*] I'm going to sleep.

HAPPY: You're not still sour on Dad, are you Biff?

BIFF: He's all right, I guess.

WILLY: [*Underneath them, in the living-room.*] Yes, sir, eighty thousand miles—eighty-two thousand!

BIFF: You smoking?

HAPPY: [*Holding out a pack of cigarettes.*] Want one?

BIFF: [*Taking a cigarette.*] I can never sleep when I smell it.

WILLY: What a simonizing job, heh!

HAPPY: [*With deep sentiment.*] Funny, Biff, y'know? Us sleeping in here again? The old beds. [*He pats his bed affectionately.*] All the talk that went across those two beds, huh? Our whole lives.

BIFF: Yeah. Lotta dreams and plans.

HAPPY: [*With a deep and masculine laugh.*] About five hundred women would like to know what was said in this room.

[*They share a soft laugh.*]

BIFF: Remember that big Betsy something—what the hell was her name—over on Bushwick Avenue?[4]

3. Polish with car wax. *Ts:* Ford Model Ts, extraordinarily popular cars manufactured from 1908 to 1928.

4. Major thoroughfare in Brooklyn, New York.

HAPPY: [*Combing his hair.*] With the collie dog!

BIFF: That's the one. I got you in there, remember?

HAPPY: Yeah, that was my first time—I think. Boy, there was a pig! [*They laugh, almost crudely.*] You taught me everything I know about women. Don't forget that.

BIFF: I bet you forgot how bashful you used to be. Especially with girls.

HAPPY: Oh, I still am, Biff.

BIFF: Oh, go on.

HAPPY: I just control it, that's all. I think I got less bashful and you got more so. What happened, Biff? Where's the old humor, the old confidence? [*He shakes* BIFF*'s knee.* BIFF *gets up and moves restlessly about the room.*] What's the matter?

BIFF: Why does Dad mock me all the time?

HAPPY: He's not mocking you, he—

BIFF: Everything I say there's a twist of mockery on his face. I can't get near him.

HAPPY: He just wants you to make good, that's all. I wanted to talk to you about Dad for a long time, Biff. Something's—happening to him. He—talks to himself.

BIFF: I noticed that this morning. But he always mumbled.

HAPPY: But not so noticeable. It got so embarrassing I sent him to Florida. And you know something? Most of the time he's talking to you.

BIFF: What's he say about me?

HAPPY: I can't make it out.

BIFF: What's he say about me?

HAPPY: I think the fact that you're not settled, that you're still kind of up in the air . . .

BIFF: There's one or two things depressing him, Happy.

HAPPY: What do you mean?

BIFF: Never mind. Just don't lay it all to me.

HAPPY: But I think if you just got started—I mean—is there any future for you out there?

BIFF: I tell ya, Hap, I don't know what the future is. I don't know—what I'm supposed to want.

HAPPY: What do you mean?

BIFF: Well, I spent six or seven years after high school trying to work myself up. Shipping clerk, salesman, business of one kind or another. And it's a measly manner of existence. To get on that subway on the hot mornings in summer. To devote your whole life to keeping stock, or making phone calls, or selling or buying. To suffer fifty weeks of the year for the sake of a two-week vacation, when all you really desire is to be outdoors, with your shirt off. And always to have to get ahead of the next fella. And still—that's how you build a future.

HAPPY: Well, you really enjoy it on a farm? Are you content out there?

BIFF: [*With rising agitation.*] Hap, I've had twenty or thirty different kinds of jobs since I left home before the war, and it always turns out the same. I just realized it lately. In Nebraska when I herded cattle, and the Dakotas, and Arizona, and now in Texas. It's why I came home now, I guess, because I realized it. This farm I work on, it's spring there now, see? And they've got about fifteen new colts. There's nothing more inspiring or—beautiful than the sight of a mare and a new colt. And it's cool there now, see? Texas is cool now, and it's spring. And whenever spring comes to where I am, I suddenly get the feeling, my God, I'm not gettin' anywhere! What the hell am I doing, playing around with horses, twenty-eight dollars a week! I'm thirty-four years old. I oughta be makin' my future. That's when I come running home. And now, I get there, and I don't know what to do with myself. [*After a pause.*] I've always made a point of not wasting my life, and everytime I come back here I know that all I've done is to waste my life.

HAPPY: You're a poet, you know that, Biff? You're a—you're an idealist!

BIFF: No, I'm mixed up very bad. Maybe I oughta get married. Maybe I oughta get stuck into something. Maybe that's my trouble. I'm like a boy. I'm not married. I'm not in business, I just—I'm like a boy. Are you content, Hap? You're a success, aren't you? Are you content?

HAPPY: Hell, no!

BIFF: Why? You're making money, aren't you?

HAPPY: [*Moving about with energy, expressiveness.*] All I can do now is wait for the merchandise manager to die. And suppose I get to be merchandise manager? He's a good friend of mine, and he just built a terrific estate on Long Island. And he lived there about two months and sold it, and now he's building another one. He can't enjoy it once it's finished. And I know that's just what I would do. I don't know what the hell I'm workin' for. Sometimes I sit in my apartment—all alone. And I think of the rent I'm paying. And it's crazy. But then, it's what I always wanted. My own apartment, a car, and plenty of women. And still, goddammit, I'm lonely.

BIFF: [*With enthusiasm.*] Listen, why don't you come out West with me?

HAPPY: You and I, heh?

BIFF: Sure, maybe we could buy a ranch. Raise cattle, use our muscles. Men built like we are should be working out in the open.

HAPPY: [*Avidly.*] The Loman Brothers, heh?

BIFF: [*With vast affection.*] Sure, we'd be known all over the counties!

HAPPY: [*Enthralled.*] That's what I dream about, Biff. Sometimes I want to just rip my clothes off in the middle of the store and outbox that goddam merchandise manager. I mean I can outbox, outrun, and outlift anybody in that store, and I have to take orders from those common, petty sons-of-bitches till I can't stand it anymore.

BIFF: I'm tellin' you, kid, if you were with me I'd be happy out there.

HAPPY: [*Enthused.*] See, Biff, everybody around me is so false that I'm constantly lowering my ideals . . .

BIFF: Baby, together we'd stand up for one another, we'd have someone to trust.

HAPPY: If I were around you—

BIFF: Hap, the trouble is we weren't brought up to grub for money. I don't know how to do it.

HAPPY: Neither can I!

BIFF: Then let's go!

HAPPY: The only thing is—what can you make out there?

BIFF: But look at your friend. Builds an estate and then hasn't the peace of mind to live in it.

HAPPY: Yeah, but when he walks into the store the waves part in front of him. That's fifty-two thousand dollars a year coming through the revolving door, and I got more in my pinky finger than he's got in his head.

BIFF: Yeah, but you just said—

HAPPY: I gotta show some of those pompous, self-important executives over there that Hap Loman can make the grade. I want to walk into the store the way he walks in. Then I'll go with you, Biff. We'll be together yet, I swear. But take those two we had tonight. Now weren't they gorgeous creatures?

BIFF: Yeah, yeah, most gorgeous I've had in years.

HAPPY: I get that any time I want, Biff. Whenever I feel disgusted. The only trouble is, it gets like bowling or something. I just keep knockin' them over and it doesn't mean anything. You still run around a lot?

BIFF: Naa. I'd like to find a girl—steady, somebody with substance.

HAPPY: That's what I long for.

BIFF: Go on! You'd never come home.

HAPPY: I would! Somebody with character, with resistance! Like Mom, y'know? You're gonna call me a bastard when I tell you this. That girl Charlotte I was with tonight is engaged to be married in five weeks. [*He tries on his new hat.*]

BIFF: No kiddin'!

HAPPY: Sure, the guy's in line for the vice-presidency of the store. I don't know what gets into me, maybe I just have an overdeveloped sense of competition or something, but I went and ruined her, and furthermore I can't get rid of her. And he's the third executive I've done that to. Isn't that a crummy characteristic? And to top it all, I go to their weddings! [*Indignantly, but laughing.*] Like I'm not supposed to take bribes. Manufacturers offer me a hundred-dollar bill now and then to throw an order their way. You know how honest I am, but it's like this girl, see. I hate myself for it. Because I don't want the girl, and, still, I take it and—I love it!

BIFF: Let's go to sleep.

HAPPY: I guess we didn't settle anything, heh?

BIFF: I just got one idea that I'm going to try.

HAPPY: What's that?

BIFF: Remember Bill Oliver?

HAPPY: Sure, Oliver is very big now. You want to work for him again?

BIFF: No, but when I quit he said something to me. He put his arm on my shoulder, and he said, "Biff, if you ever need anything, come to me."

HAPPY: I remember that. That sounds good.

BIFF: I think I'll go to see him. If I could get ten thousand or even seven or eight thousand dollars I could buy a beautiful ranch.

HAPPY: I bet he'd back you. 'Cause he thought highly of you, Biff. I mean, they all do. You're well liked, Biff. That's why I say to come back here, and we both have the apartment. And I'm tellin' you, Biff, any babe you want . . .

BIFF: No, with a ranch I could do the work I like and still be something. I just wonder though. I wonder if Oliver still thinks I stole that carton of basketballs.

HAPPY: Oh, he probably forgot that long ago. It's almost ten years. You're too sensitive. Anyway, he didn't really fire you.

BIFF: Well, I think he was going to. I think that's why I quit. I was never sure whether he knew or not. I know he thought the world of me, though. I was the only one he'd let lock up the place.

WILLY: [*Below.*] You gonna wash the engine, Biff?

HAPPY: Shh! [BIFF *looks at* HAPPY, *who is gazing down, listening.* WILLY *is mumbling in the parlor.*] You hear that?

[*They listen.* WILLY *laughs warmly.*]

BIFF: [*Growing angry.*] Doesn't he know Mom can hear that?

WILLY: Don't get your sweater dirty, Biff!

[*A look of pain crosses* BIFF*'s face.*]

HAPPY: Isn't that terrible? Don't leave again, will you? You'll find a job here. You gotta stick around. I don't know what to do about him, it's getting embarrassing.

WILLY: What a simonizing job!

BIFF: Mom's hearing that!

WILLY: No kiddin', Biff, you got a date? Wonderful!

HAPPY: Go on to sleep. But talk to him in the morning, will you?

BIFF: [*Reluctantly getting into bed.*] With her in the house. Brother!

HAPPY: [*Getting into bed.*] I wish you'd have a good talk with him.

[*The light on their room begins to fade.*]

BIFF: [To himself in bed.] That selfish, stupid . . .

HAPPY: Sh . . . Sleep, Biff.

[*Their light is out. Well before they have finished speaking,* WILLY*'s form is dimly seen below in the darkened kitchen. He opens the refrigerator, searches in there, and takes out a bottle of milk. The apartment houses are fading out, and the entire house and surroundings become covered with leaves. Music insinuates itself as the leaves appear.*]

WILLY: Just wanna be careful with those girls, Biff, that's all. Don't make any promises. No promises of any kind. Because a girl, y'know, they always believe what you tell 'em, and you're very young, Biff, you're too young to be talking seriously to girls. [*Light rises on the kitchen.* WILLY, *talking, shuts the refrigerator door and comes downstage to the kitchen table. He pours milk into a glass. He is totally immersed in himself, smiling faintly.*] Too young entirely, Biff. You want to watch your schooling first. Then when you're all set, there'll be plenty of girls for a boy like you. [*He smiles broadly at a kitchen chair.*] That so? The girls pay for you? [*He laughs.*] Boy, you must really be makin' a hit. [WILLY *is gradually addressing—physically—a point offstage, speaking through the wall of the kitchen, and his voice has been rising in volume to that of a normal conversation.*] I been wondering why you polish the car so careful. Ha! Don't leave the hubcaps, boys. Get the chamois to the hubcaps. Happy, use newspaper on the windows, it's the easiest thing. Show him how to do it, Biff! You see, Happy? Pad it up, use it like a pad. That's it, that's it, good work. You're doin' all right, Hap. [*He pauses, then nods in approbation for a few seconds, then looks upward.*] Biff, first thing we gotta do when we get time is clip that big branch over the house. Afraid it's gonna fall in a storm and hit the roof. Tell you what. We get a rope and sling her around, and then we climb up there with a couple of saws and take her down. Soon as you finish the car, boys, I wanna see ya. I got a surprise for you, boys.

BIFF: [*Offstage.*] Whatta ya got, Dad?

WILLY: No, you finish first. Never leave a job till you're finished—remember that. [*Looking toward the "big trees."*] Biff, up in Albany I saw a beautiful hammock. I think I'll buy it next trip, and we'll hang it right between those two elms. Wouldn't that be something? Just swingin' there under those branches. Boy, that would be . . .

[YOUNG BIFF *and* YOUNG HAPPY *appear from the direction* WILLY *was addressing.* HAPPY *carries rags and a pail of water.* BIFF, *wearing a sweater with a block "S," carries a football.*]

BIFF: [*Pointing in the direction of the car offstage.*] How's that, Pop, professional?

WILLY: Terrific. Terrific job, boys. Good work, Biff.

HAPPY: Where's the surprise, Pop?

WILLY: In the back seat of the car.

HAPPY: Boy! [*He runs off.*]

BIFF: What is it, Dad? Tell me, what'd you buy?

WILLY: [*Laughing, cuffs him.*] Never mind, something I want you to have.

BIFF: [*Turns and starts off.*] What is it, Hap?

HAPPY: [*Offstage.*] It's a punching bag!

BIFF: Oh, Pop!

WILLY: It's got Gene Tunney's[5] signature on it!

[HAPPY *runs onstage with a punching bag.*]

BIFF: Gee, how'd you know we wanted a punching bag?

WILLY: Well, it's the finest thing for the timing.

HAPPY: [*Lies down on his back and pedals with his feet.*] I'm losing weight, you notice, Pop?

WILLY: [*To* HAPPY.] Jumping rope is good too.

BIFF: Did you see the new football I got?

WILLY: [*Examining the ball.*] Where'd you get a new ball?

BIFF: The coach told me to practice my passing.

WILLY: That so? And he gave you the ball, heh?

BIFF: Well, I borrowed it from the locker room. [*He laughs confidentially.*]

WILLY: [*Laughing with him at the theft.*] I want you to return that.

HAPPY: I told you he wouldn't like it!

BIFF: [*Angrily.*] Well, I'm bringing it back!

WILLY: [*Stopping the incipient argument, to* HAPPY.] Sure, he's gotta practice with a regulation ball, doesn't he? [*To* BIFF.] Coach'll probably congratulate you on your initiative!

BIFF: Oh, he keeps congratulating my initiative all the time, Pop.

5. Tunney (1897–1978) was world heavyweight boxing champion from 1926 to 1928 and retired undefeated.

WILLY: That's because he likes you. If somebody else took that ball there'd be an uproar. So what's the report, boys, what's the report?

BIFF: Where'd you go this time, Dad? Gee we were lonesome for you.

WILLY: [*Pleased, puts an arm around each boy and they come down to the apron.*] Lonesome, heh?

BIFF: Missed you every minute.

WILLY: Don't say? Tell you a secret, boys. Don't breathe it to a soul. Someday I'll have my own business, and I'll never have to leave home anymore.

HAPPY: Like Uncle Charley, heh?

WILLY: Bigger than Uncle Charley! Because Charley is not—liked. He's liked, but he's not—well liked.

BIFF: Where'd you go this time, Dad?

WILLY: Well, I got on the road, and I went north to Providence. Met the mayor.

BIFF: The mayor of Providence!

WILLY: He was sitting in the hotel lobby.

BIFF: What'd he say?

WILLY: He said, "Morning!" And I said, "You got a fine city here, Mayor." And then he had coffee with me. And then I went to Waterbury. Waterbury is a fine city. Big clock city, the famous Waterbury clock. Sold a nice bill there. And then Boston—Boston is the cradle of the Revolution. A fine city. And a couple of other towns in Mass., and on to Portland and Bangor and straight home!

BIFF: Gee, I'd love to go with you sometime, Dad.

WILLY: Soon as summer comes.

HAPPY: Promise?

WILLY: You and Hap and I, and I'll show you all the towns. America is full of beautiful towns and fine, upstanding people. And they know me, boys, they know me up and down New England. The finest people. And when I bring you fellas up, there'll be open sesame for all of us, 'cause one thing, boys: I have friends. I can park my car in any street in New England, and the cops protect it like their own. This summer, heh?

BIFF and HAPPY: [*Together.*] Yeah! You bet!

WILLY: We'll take our bathing suits.

HAPPY: We'll carry your bags, Pop!

WILLY: Oh, won't that be something! Me comin' into the Boston stores with you boys carryin' my bags. What a sensation! [BIFF *is prancing around, practicing passing the ball.*] You nervous, Biff, about the game?

BIFF: Not if you're gonna be there.

WILLY: What do they say about you in school, now that they made you captain?

HAPPY: There's a crowd of girls behind him every time the classes change.

BIFF: [*Taking* WILLY*'s hand.*] This Saturday, Pop, this Saturday—just for you, I'm going to break through for a touchdown.

HAPPY: You're supposed to pass.

BIFF: I'm takin' one play for Pop. You watch me, Pop, and when I take off my helmet, that means I'm breakin' out. Then you watch me crash through that line!

WILLY: [*Kisses* BIFF.] Oh, wait'll I tell this in Boston!

[BERNARD *enters in knickers. He is younger than* BIFF, *earnest and loyal, a worried boy.*]

BERNARD: Biff, where are you? You're supposed to study with me today.
WILLY: Hey, looka Bernard. What're you lookin' so anemic about, Bernard?
BERNARD: He's gotta study, Uncle Willy. He's got Regents[6] next week.
HAPPY: [*Tauntingly, spinning* BERNARD *around.*] Let's box, Bernard!
BERNARD: Biff! [*He gets away from* HAPPY.] Listen, Biff, I heard Mr. Birnbaum say that if you don't start studyin' math he's gonna flunk you, and you won't graduate. I heard him!
WILLY: You better study with him, Biff. Go ahead now.
BERNARD: I heard him!
BIFF: Oh, Pop, you didn't see my sneakers! [*He holds up a foot for* WILLY *to look at.*]
WILLY: Hey, that's a beautiful job of printing!
BERNARD: [*Wiping his glasses.*] Just because he printed University of Virginia on his sneakers doesn't mean they've got to graduate him, Uncle Willy!
WILLY: [*Angrily.*] What're you talking about? With scholarships to three universities they're gonna flunk him?
BERNARD: But I heard Mr. Birnbaum say—
WILLY: Don't be a pest, Bernard! [*To his boys.*] What an anemic!
BERNARD: Okay, I'm waiting for you in my house, Biff.

[BERNARD *goes off. The* LOMANS *laugh.*]

WILLY: Bernard is not well liked, is he?
BIFF: He's liked, but he's not well liked.
HAPPY: That's right, Pop.
WILLY: That's just what I mean. Bernard can get the best marks in school, y'understand, but when he gets out in the business world, y'understand, you are going to be five times ahead of him. That's why I thank Almighty God you're both built like Adonises.[7] Because the man who makes an appearance in the business world, the man who creates personal interest, is the man who gets ahead. Be liked and you will never want. You take me, for instance. I never have to wait in line to see a buyer. "Willy Loman is here!" That's all they have to know, and I go right through.
BIFF: Did you knock them dead, Pop?
WILLY: Knocked 'em cold in Providence, slaughtered 'em in Boston.
HAPPY: [*On his back, pedaling again.*] I'm losing weight, you notice, Pop?

[LINDA *enters, as of old, a ribbon in her hair, carrying a basket of washing.*]

LINDA: [*With youthful energy.*] Hello, dear!
WILLY: Sweetheart!
LINDA: How'd the Chevvy run?
WILLY: Chevrolet, Linda, is the greatest car ever built. [*To the boys.*] Since when do you let your mother carry wash up the stairs?
BIFF: Grab hold there, boy!
HAPPY: Where to, Mom?
LINDA: Hang them up on the line. And you better go down to your friends, Biff. The cellar is full of boys. They don't know what to do with themselves.

6. Examinations administered to New York State high-school students.
7. In Greek myth Adonis was a beautiful youth.

BIFF: Ah, when Pop comes home they can wait!

WILLY: [*Laughs appreciatively.*] You better go down and tell them what to do, Biff.

BIFF: I think I'll have them sweep out the furnace room.

WILLY: Good work, Biff.

BIFF: [*Goes through wall-line of kitchen to doorway at back and calls down.*] Fellas! Everybody sweep out the furnace room! I'll be right down!

VOICES: All right! Okay, Biff.

BIFF: George and Sam and Frank, come out back! We're hangin' up the wash! Come on, Hap, on the double!

[*He and* HAPPY *carry out the basket.*]

LINDA: The way they obey him!

WILLY: Well, that training, the training. I'm tellin' you, I was sellin' thousands and thousands, but I had to come home.

LINDA: Oh, the whole block'll be at that game. Did you sell anything?

WILLY: I did five hundred gross in Providence and seven hundred gross in Boston.

LINDA: No! Wait a minute, I've got a pencil. [*She pulls pencil and paper out of her apron pocket.*] That makes your commission . . . Two hundred—my God! Two hundred and twelve dollars!

WILLY: Well, I didn't figure it yet, but . . .

LINDA: How much did you do?

WILLY: Well, I—I did—about a hundred and eighty gross in Providence. Well, no—it came to—roughly two hundred gross on the whole trip.

LINDA: [*Without hesitation.*] Two hundred gross. That's . . . [*She figures.*]

WILLY: The trouble was that three of the stores were half closed for inventory in Boston. Otherwise I woulda broke records.

LINDA: Well, it makes seventy dollars and some pennies. That's very good.

WILLY: What do we owe?

LINDA: Well, on the first there's sixteen dollars on the refrigerator—

WILLY: Why sixteen?

LINDA: Well, the fan belt broke, so it was a dollar eighty.

WILLY: But it's brand new.

LINDA: Well, the man said that's the way it is. Till they work themselves in, y'know.

[*They move through the wall-line into the kitchen.*]

WILLY: I hope we didn't get stuck on that machine.

LINDA: They got the biggest ads of any of them!

WILLY: I know, it's a fine machine. What else?

LINDA: Well, there's nine-sixty for the washing machine. And for the vacuum cleaner there's three and a half due on the fifteenth. Then the roof, you got twenty-one dollars remaining.

WILLY: It don't leak, does it?

LINDA: No, they did a wonderful job. Then you owe Frank for the carburetor.

WILLY: I'm not going to pay that man! That goddam Chevrolet, they ought to prohibit the manufacture of that car!

LINDA: Well, you owe him three and a half. And odds and ends, comes to around a hundred and twenty dollars by the fifteenth.

WILLY: A hundred and twenty dollars! My God, if business don't pick up I don't know what I'm gonna do!

LINDA: Well, next week you'll do better.

WILLY: Oh, I'll knock 'em dead next week. I'll go to Hartford. I'm very well liked in Hartford. You know, the trouble is, Linda, people don't seem to take to me.

[*They move onto the forestage.*]

LINDA: Oh, don't be foolish.

WILLY: I know it when I walk in. They seem to laugh at me.

LINDA: Why? Why would they laugh at you? Don't talk that way, Willy.

[WILLY *moves to the edge of the stage.* LINDA *goes into the kitchen and starts to darn stockings.*]

WILLY: I don't know the reason for it, but they just pass me by. I'm not noticed.

LINDA: But you're doing wonderful, dear. You're making seventy to a hundred dollars a week.

WILLY: But I gotta be at it ten, twelve hours a day. Other men—I don't know—they do it easier. I don't know why—I can't stop myself—I talk too much. A man oughta come in with a few words. One thing about Charley. He's a man of few words, and they respect him.

LINDA: You don't talk too much, you're just lively.

WILLY: [*Smiling.*] Well, I figure, what the hell, life is short, a couple of jokes. [*To himself.*] I joke too much! [*The smile goes.*]

LINDA: Why? You're—

WILLY: I'm fat. I'm very—foolish to look at, Linda. I didn't tell you, but Christmas time I happened to be calling on F. H. Stewarts, and a salesman I know, as I was going in to see the buyer I heard him say something about—walrus. And I—I cracked him right across the face. I won't take that. I simply will not take that. But they do laugh at me. I know that.

LINDA: Darling . . .

WILLY: I gotta overcome it. I know I gotta overcome it. I'm not dressing to advantage, maybe.

LINDA: Willy, darling, you're the handsomest man in the world—

WILLY: Oh, no, Linda.

LINDA: To me you are. [*Slight pause.*] The handsomest. [*From the darkness is heard the laughter of a woman.* WILLY *doesn't turn to it, but it continues through* LINDA'S *lines.*] And the boys, Willy. Few men are idolized by their children the way you are.

[*Music is heard as behind a scrim, to the left of the house,* THE WOMAN, *dimly seen, is dressing.*]

WILLY: [*With great feeling.*] You're the best there is, Linda, you're a pal, you know that? On the road—on the road I want to grab you sometimes and just kiss the life outa you. [*The laughter is loud now, and he moves into a brightening area at the left, where* THE WOMAN *has come from behind the scrim and is standing, putting on her hat, looking into a "mirror" and laughing.*] 'Cause I get so lonely—especially when business is bad and there's nobody to talk to. I get the feeling that I'll never sell anything again, that I won't make a living for you, or a business, a business for the boys. [*He talks through* THE WOMAN'*s subsiding laughter.* THE WOMAN *primps at the "mirror."*] There's so much I want to make for—

THE WOMAN: Me? You didn't make me, Willy. I picked you.

WILLY: [*Pleased.*] You picked me?

THE WOMAN: [*Who is quite proper-looking,* WILLY'*s age.*] I did. I've been sitting at that desk watching all the salesmen go by, day in, day out. But you've got such a sense of humor, and we do have such a good time together, don't we?

WILLY: Sure, sure. [*He takes her in his arms.*] Why do you have to go now?

THE WOMAN: It's two o'clock . . .

WILLY: No, come on in! [*He pulls her.*]

THE WOMAN: . . . my sisters'll be scandalized. When'll you be back?

WILLY: Oh, two weeks about. Will you come up again?

THE WOMAN: Sure thing. You do make me laugh. It's good for me. [*She squeezes his arm, kisses him.*] And I think you're a wonderful man.

WILLY: You picked me, heh?

THE WOMAN: Sure. Because you're so sweet. And such a kidder.

WILLY: Well, I'll see you next time I'm in Boston.

THE WOMAN: I'll put you right through to the buyers.

WILLY: [*Slapping her bottom.*] Right. Well, bottoms up!

THE WOMAN: [*Slaps him gently and laughs.*] You just kill me, Willy. [*He suddenly grabs her and kisses her roughly.*] You kill me. And thanks for the stockings. I love a lot of stockings. Well, good night.

WILLY: Good night. And keep your pores open!

THE WOMAN: Oh, Willy!

[THE WOMAN *bursts out laughing, and* LINDA'*s laughter blends in.* THE WOMAN *disappears into the dark. Now the area at the kitchen table brightens.* LINDA *is sitting where she was at the kitchen table, but now is mending a pair of her silk stockings.*]

LINDA: You are, Willy. The handsomest man. You've got no reason to feel that—

WILLY: [*Coming out of* THE WOMAN'*s dimming area and going over to* LINDA.] I'll make it all up to you, Linda. I'll—

LINDA: There's nothing to make up, dear. You're doing fine, better than—

WILLY: [*Noticing her mending.*] What's that?

LINDA: Just mending my stockings. They're so expensive—

WILLY: [*Angrily, taking them from her.*] I won't have you mending stockings in this house! Now throw them out!

[LINDA *puts the stockings in her pocket.*]

BERNARD: [*Entering on the run.*] Where is he? If he doesn't study!

WILLY: [*Moving to the forestage, with great agitation.*] You'll give him the answers!

BERNARD: I do, but I can't on a Regents! That's a state exam! They're liable to arrest me!

WILLY: Where is he? I'll whip him, I'll whip him!

LINDA: And he'd better give back that football, Willy, it's not nice.

WILLY: Biff! Where is he? Why is he taking everything?

LINDA: He's too rough with the girls, Willy. All the mothers are afraid of him!

WILLY: I'll whip him!
BERNARD: He's driving the car without a license!

[THE WOMAN's *laugh is heard.*]

WILLY: Shut up!
LINDA: All the mothers—
WILLY: Shut up!
BERNARD: [*Backing quietly away and out.*] Mr. Birnbaum says he's stuck up.
WILLY: Get outa here!
BERNARD: If he doesn't buckle down he'll flunk math! [*He goes off.*]
LINDA: He's right, Willy, you've gotta—
WILLY: [*Exploding at her.*] There's nothing the matter with him! You want him to be a worm like Bernard? He's got spirit, personality . . . [*As he speaks,* LINDA, *almost in tears, exits into the living room.* WILLY *is alone in the kitchen, wilting and staring. The leaves are gone. It is night again, and the apartment houses look down from behind.*] Loaded with it. Loaded! What is he stealing? He's giving it back, isn't he? Why is he stealing? What did I tell him? I never in my life told him anything but decent things.

[HAPPY *in pajamas has come down the stairs;* WILLY *suddenly becomes aware of* HAPPY's *presence.*]

HAPPY: Let's go now, come on.
WILLY: [*Sitting down at the kitchen table.*] Huh! Why did she have to wax the floors herself? Everytime she waxes the floors she keels over. She knows that!
HAPPY: Shh! Take it easy. What brought you back tonight?
WILLY: I got an awful scare. Nearly hit a kid in Yonkers. God! Why didn't I go to Alaska with my brother Ben that time! Ben! That man was a genius, that man was success incarnate! What a mistake! He begged me to go.
HAPPY: Well, there's no use in—
WILLY: You guys! There was a man started with the clothes on his back and ended up with diamond mines!
HAPPY: Boy, someday I'd like to know how he did it.
WILLY: What's the mystery? The man knew what he wanted and went out and got it! Walked into a jungle, and comes out, the age of twenty-one, and he's rich! The world is an oyster, but you don't crack it open on a mattress!
HAPPY: Pop, I told you I'm gonna retire you for life.
WILLY: You'll retire me for life on seventy goddam dollars a week? And your women and your car and your apartment, and you'll retire me for life! Christ's sake, I couldn't get past Yonkers today! Where are you guys, where are you? The woods are burning! I can't drive a car!

[CHARLEY *has appeared in the doorway. He is a large man, slow of speech, laconic, immovable. In all he says, despite what he says, there is pity, and now, trepidation. He has a robe over pajamas, slippers on his feet. He enters the kitchen.*]

CHARLEY: Everything all right?
HAPPY: Yeah, Charley, everything's . . .
WILLY: What's the matter?

CHARLEY: I heard some noise. I thought something happened. Can't we do something about the walls? You sneeze in here, and in my house hats blow off.
HAPPY: Let's go to bed, Dad. Come on.

[CHARLEY *signals to* HAPPY *to go.*]

WILLY: You go ahead, I'm not tired at the moment.
HAPPY: [*To* WILLY.] Take it easy, huh? [*He exits.*]
WILLY: What're you doin' up?
CHARLEY: [*Sitting down at the kitchen table opposite* WILLY.] Couldn't sleep good. I had a heartburn.
WILLY: Well, you don't know how to eat.
CHARLEY: I eat with my mouth.
WILLY: No, you're ignorant. You gotta know about vitamins and things like that.
CHARLEY: Come on, let's shoot. Tire you out a little.
WILLY: [*Hesitantly.*] All right. You got cards?
CHARLEY: [*Taking a deck from his pocket.*] Yeah, I got them. Someplace. What is it with those vitamins?
WILLY: [*Dealing.*] They build up your bones. Chemistry.
CHARLEY: Yeah, but there's no bones in a heartburn.
WILLY: What are you talkin' about? Do you know the first thing about it?
CHARLEY: Don't get insulted.
WILLY: Don't talk about something you don't know anything about.

[*They are playing. Pause.*]

CHARLEY: What're you doin' home?
WILLY: A little trouble with the car.
CHARLEY: Oh. [*Pause.*] I'd like to take a trip to California.
WILLY: Don't say.
CHARLEY: You want a job?
WILLY: I got a job, I told you that. [*After a slight pause.*] What the hell are you offering me a job for?
CHARLEY: Don't get insulted.
WILLY: Don't insult me.
CHARLEY: I don't see no sense in it. You don't have to go on this way.
WILLY: I got a good job. [*Slight pause.*] What do you keep comin' in here for?
CHARLEY: You want me to go?
WILLY: [*After a pause, withering.*] I can't understand it. He's going back to Texas again. What the hell is that?
CHARLEY: Let him go.
WILLY: I got nothin' to give him, Charley, I'm clean, I'm clean.
CHARLEY: He won't starve. None a them starve. Forget about him.
WILLY: Then what have I got to remember?
CHARLEY: You take it too hard. To hell with it. When a deposit bottle is broken you don't get your nickel back.
WILLY: That's easy enough for you to say.
CHARLEY: That ain't easy for me to say.
WILLY: Did you see the ceiling I put up in the living-room?
CHARLEY: Yeah, that's a piece of work. To put up a ceiling is a mystery to me. How do you do it?

WILLY: What's the difference?
CHARLEY: Well, talk about it.
WILLY: You gonna put up a ceiling?
CHARLEY: How could I put up a ceiling?
WILLY: Then what the hell are you bothering me for?
CHARLEY: You're insulted again.
WILLY: A man who can't handle tools is not a man. You're disgusting.
CHARLEY: Don't call me disgusting, Willy.

[UNCLE BEN, *carrying a valise and an umbrella, enters the forestage from around the right corner of the house. He is a stolid man, in his sixties, with a mustache and an authoritative air. He is utterly certain of his destiny, and there is an aura of far places about him. He enters exactly as* WILLY *speaks.*]

WILLY: I'm getting awfully tired, Ben.

[BEN'S *music is heard.* BEN *looks around at everything.*]

CHARLEY: Good, keep playing; you'll sleep better. Did you call me Ben?

[BEN *looks at his watch.*]

WILLY: That's funny. For a second there you reminded me of my brother Ben.
BEN: I only have a few minutes. [*He strolls, inspecting the place.* WILLY *and* CHARLEY *continue playing.*]
CHARLEY: You never heard from him again, heh? Since that time?
WILLY: Didn't Linda tell you? Couple of weeks ago we got a letter from his wife in Africa. He died.
CHARLEY: That so.
BEN: [*Chuckling.*] So this is Brooklyn, eh?
CHARLEY: Maybe you're in for some of his money.
WILLY: Naa, he had seven sons. There's just one opportunity I had with that man . . .
BEN: I must make a train, William. There are several properties I'm looking at in Alaska.
WILLY: Sure, sure! If I'd gone with him to Alaska that time, everything would've been totally different.
CHARLEY: Go on, you'da froze to death up there.
WILLY: What're you talking about?
BEN: Opportunity is tremendous in Alaska, William. Surprised you're not up there.
WILLY: Sure, tremendous.
CHARLEY: Heh?
WILLY: There was the only man I ever met who knew the answers.
CHARLEY: Who?
BEN: How are you all?
WILLY: [*Taking a pot, smiling.*] Fine, fine.
CHARLEY: Pretty sharp tonight.
BEN: Is Mother living with you?
WILLY: No, she died a long time ago.
CHARLEY: Who?
BEN: That's too bad. Fine specimen of a lady, Mother.
WILLY: [*To* CHARLEY.] Heh?

BEN: I'd hoped to see the old girl.

CHARLEY: Who died?

BEN: Heard anything from Father, have you?

WILLY: [*Unnerved.*] What do you mean, who died?

CHARLEY: [*Taking a pot.*] What're you talkin' about?

BEN: [*Looking at his watch.*] William, it's half-past eight!

WILLY: [*As though to dispel his confusion he angrily stops* CHARLEY'*s hand.*] That's my build!

CHARLEY: I put the ace—

WILLY: If you don't know how to play the game I'm not gonna throw my money away on you!

CHARLEY: [*Rising.*] It was my ace, for God's sake!

WILLY: I'm through, I'm through!

BEN: When did Mother die?

WILLY: Long ago. Since the beginning you never knew how to play cards.

CHARLEY: [*Picks up the cards and goes to the door.*] All right! Next time I'll bring a deck with five aces.

WILLY: I don't play that kind of game!

CHARLEY: [*Turning to him.*] You ought to be ashamed of yourself!

WILLY: Yeah?

CHARLEY: Yeah! [*He goes out.*]

WILLY: [*Slamming the door after him.*] Ignoramus!

BEN: [*As* WILLY *comes toward him through the wall-line of the kitchen.*] So you're William.

WILLY: [*Shaking* BEN'*s hand.*] Ben! I've been waiting for you so long! What's the answer? How did you do it?

BEN: Oh, there's a story in that.

[LINDA *enters the forestage, as of old, carrying the wash basket.*]

LINDA: Is this Ben?

BEN: [*Gallantly.*] How do you do, my dear.

LINDA: Where've you been all these years? Willy's always wondered why you—

WILLY: [*Pulling* BEN *away from her impatiently.*] Where is Dad? Didn't you follow him? How did you get started?

BEN: Well, I don't know how much you remember.

WILLY: Well, I was just a baby, of course, only three or four years old—

BEN: Three years and eleven months.

WILLY: What a memory, Ben!

BEN: I have many enterprises, William, and I have never kept books.

WILLY: I remember I was sitting under the wagon in—was it Nebraska?

BEN: It was South Dakota, and I gave you a bunch of wild flowers.

WILLY: I remember you walking away down some open road.

BEN: [*Laughing.*] I was going to find Father in Alaska.

WILLY: Where is he?

BEN: At that age I had a very faulty view of geography, William. I discovered after a few days that I was heading due south, so instead of Alaska, I ended up in Africa.

LINDA: Africa!

WILLY: The Gold Coast!

BEN: Principally diamond mines.

LINDA: Diamond mines!

BEN: Yes, my dear. But I've only a few minutes—

WILLY: No! Boys! Boys! [*Young* BIFF *and* HAPPY *appear.*] Listen to this. This is your Uncle Ben, a great man! Tell my boys, Ben!

BEN: Why, boys, when I was seventeen I walked into the jungle, and when I was twenty-one I walked out. [*He laughs.*] And by God I was rich.

WILLY: [*To the boys.*] You see what I been talking about? The greatest things can happen!

BEN: [*Glancing at his watch.*] I have an appointment in Ketchikan Tuesday week.[8]

WILLY: No, Ben! Please tell about Dad. I want my boys to hear. I want them to know the kind of stock they spring from. All I remember is a man with a big beard, and I was in Mamma's lap, sitting around a fire, and some kind of high music.

BEN: His flute. He played the flute.

WILLY: Sure, the flute, that's right!

[*New music is heard, a high, rollicking tune.*]

BEN: Father was a very great and a very wild-hearted man. We would start in Boston, and he'd toss the whole family into the wagon, and then he'd drive the team right across the country; through Ohio, and Indiana, Michigan, Illinois, and all the Western states. And we'd stop in the towns and sell the flutes that he'd made on the way. Great inventor, Father. With one gadget he made more in a week than a man like you could make in a lifetime.

WILLY: That's just the way I'm bringing them up, Ben—rugged, well liked, all-around.

BEN: Yeah? [*To* BIFF.] Hit that, boy—hard as you can. [*He pounds his stomach.*]

BIFF: Oh, no, sir!

BEN: [*Taking boxing stance.*] Come on, get to me! [*He laughs.*]

WILLY: Go to it, Biff! Go ahead, show him!

BIFF: Okay! [*He cocks his fist and starts in.*]

LINDA: [*To* WILLY.] Why must he fight, dear?

BEN: [*Sparring with* BIFF.] Good boy! Good boy!

WILLY: How's that, Ben, heh?

HAPPY: Give him the left, Biff!

LINDA: Why are you fighting?

BEN: Good boy! [*Suddenly comes in, trips* BIFF, *and stands over him, the point of his umbrella poised over* BIFF*'s eye.*]

LINDA: Look out, Biff!

BIFF: Gee!

BEN: [*Patting* BIFF's knee.] Never fight fair with a stranger, boy. You'll never get out of the jungle that way. [*Taking* LINDA's *hand and bowing.*] It was an honor and a pleasure to meet you, Linda.

LINDA: [*Withdrawing her hand coldly, frightened.*] Have a nice—trip.

BEN: [*To* WILLY.] And good luck with your—what do you do?

WILLY: Selling.

BEN: Yes. Well . . . [*He raises his hand in farewell to all.*]

8. That is, in Ketchikan, Alaska, one week from Tuesday.

WILLY: No, Ben, I don't want you to think . . . [*He takes* BEN'*s arm to show him.*] It's Brooklyn, I know, but we hunt too.

BEN: Really, now.

WILLY: Oh, sure, there's snakes and rabbits and—that's why I moved out here. Why, Biff can fell any one of these trees in no time! Boys! Go right over to where they're building the apartment house and get some sand. We're gonna rebuild the entire front stoop right now! Watch this, Ben!

BIFF: Yes, sir! On the double, Hap!

HAPPY: [*As he and* BIFF *run off.*] I lost weight, Pop, you notice?

[CHARLEY *enters in knickers, even before the boys are gone.*]

CHARLEY: Listen, if they steal any more from that building the watchman'll put the cops on them!

LINDA: [*To* WILLY.] Don't let Biff . . .

[BEN *laughs lustily.*]

WILLY: You shoulda seen the lumber they brought home last week. At least a dozen six-by-tens worth all kinds a money.

CHARLEY: Listen, if that watchman—

WILLY: I gave them hell, understand. But I got a couple of fearless characters there.

CHARLEY: Willy, the jails are full of fearless characters.

BEN: [*Clapping* WILLY *on the back, with a laugh at* CHARLEY.] And the stock exchange, friend!

WILLY: [*Joining in* BEN'*s laughter.*] Where are the rest of your pants?

CHARLEY: My wife bought them.

WILLY: Now all you need is a golf club and you can go upstairs and go to sleep. [*To* BEN.] Great athlete! Between him and his son Bernard they can't hammer a nail!

BERNARD: [*Rushing in.*] The watchman's chasing Biff!

WILLY: [*Angrily.*] Shut up! He's not stealing anything!

LINDA: [*Alarmed, hurrying off left.*] Where is he? Biff, dear! [*She exits.*]

WILLY: [*Moving toward the left, away from* BEN.] There's nothing wrong. What's the matter with you?

BEN: Nervy boy. Good!

WILLY: [*Laughing.*] Oh, nerves of iron, that Biff!

CHARLEY: Don't know what it is. My New England man comes back and he's bleedin', they murdered him up there.

WILLY: It's contacts, Charley, I got important contacts!

CHARLEY: [*Sarcastically.*] Glad to hear it, Willy. Come in later, we'll shoot a little casino. I'll take some of your Portland money. [*He laughs at* WILLY *and exits.*]

WILLY: [*Turning to* BEN.] Business is bad, it's murderous. But not for me, of course.

BEN: I'll stop by on my way back to Africa.

WILLY: [*Longingly.*] Can't you stay a few days? You're just what I need, Ben, because I—I have a fine position here, but I—well, Dad left when I was such a baby and I never had a chance to talk to him and I still feel—kind of temporary about myself.

BEN: I'll be late for my train.

[*They are at opposite ends of the stage.*]

WILLY: Ben, my boys—can't we talk? They'd go into the jaws of hell for me, see, but I—

BEN: William, you're being first-rate with your boys. Outstanding, manly chaps!

WILLY: [*Hanging on to his words.*] Oh, Ben, that's good to hear! Because sometimes I'm afraid that I'm not teaching them the right kind of—Ben, how should I teach them?

BEN: [*Giving great weight to each word, and with a certain vicious audacity.*] William, when I walked into the jungle, I was seventeen. When I walked out I was twenty-one. And, by God, I was rich! [*He goes off into darkness around the right corner of the house.*]

WILLY: . . . was rich! That's just the spirit I want to imbue them with! To walk into a jungle! I was right! I was right! I was right!

[BEN *is gone, but* WILLY *is still speaking to him as* LINDA, *in nightgown and robe, enters the kitchen, glances around for* WILLY, *then goes to the door of the house, looks out and sees him. Comes down to his left. He looks at her.*]

LINDA: Willy, dear? Willy?

WILLY: I was right!

LINDA: Did you have some cheese? [*He can't answer.*] It's very late, darling. Come to bed, heh?

WILLY: [*Looking straight up.*] Gotta break your neck to see a star in this yard.

LINDA: You coming in?

WILLY: Whatever happened to that diamond watch fob? Remember? When Ben came from Africa that time? Didn't he give me a watch fob with a diamond in it?

LINDA: You pawned it, dear. Twelve, thirteen years ago. For Biff's radio correspondence course.

WILLY: Gee, that was a beautiful thing. I'll take a walk.

LINDA: But you're in your slippers.

WILLY: [*Starting to go around the house at the left.*] I was right! I was! [*Half to* LINDA, *as he goes, shaking his head.*] What a man! There was a man worth talking to. I was right!

LINDA: [*Calling after* WILLY.] But in your slippers, Willy!

[WILLY *is almost gone when* BIFF, *in his pajamas, comes down the stairs and enters the kitchen.*]

BIFF: What is he doing out there?

LINDA: Sh!

BIFF: God Almighty, Mom, how long has he been doing this?

LINDA: Don't, he'll hear you.

BIFF: What the hell is the matter with him?

LINDA: It'll pass by morning.

BIFF: Shouldn't we do anything?

LINDA: Oh, my dear, you should do a lot of things, but there's nothing to do, so go to sleep.

[HAPPY *comes down the stairs and sits on the steps.*]

HAPPY: I never heard him so loud, Mom.

LINDA: Well, come around more often; you'll hear him. [*She sits down at the table and mends the lining of* WILLY's *jacket.*]

BIFF: Why didn't you ever write me about this, Mom?

LINDA: How would I write to you? For over three months you had no address.

BIFF: I was on the move. But you know I thought of you all the time. You know that, don't you, pal?

LINDA: I know, dear, I know. But he likes to have a letter. Just to know that there's still a possibility for better things.

BIFF: He's not like this all the time, is he?

LINDA: It's when you come home he's always the worst.

BIFF: When I come home?

LINDA: When you write you're coming, he's all smiles, and talks about the future, and—he's just wonderful. And then the closer you seem to come, the more shaky he gets, and then, by the time you get here, he's arguing, and he seems angry at you. I think it's just that maybe he can't bring himself to—to open up to you. Why are you so hateful to each other? Why is that?

BIFF: [*Evasively.*] I'm not hateful, Mom.

LINDA: But you no sooner come in the door than you're fighting!

BIFF: I don't know why. I mean to change. I'm tryin', Mom, you understand?

LINDA: Are you home to stay now?

BIFF: I don't know. I want to look around, see what's doin'.

LINDA: Biff, you can't look around all your life, can you?

BIFF: I just can't take hold, Mom. I can't take hold of some kind of a life.

LINDA: Biff, a man is not a bird, to come and go with the springtime.

BIFF: Your hair . . . [*He touches her hair.*] Your hair got so gray.

LINDA: Oh, it's been gray since you were in high school. I just stopped dyeing it, that's all.

BIFF: Dye it again, will ya? I don't want my pal looking old. [*He smiles.*]

LINDA: You're such a boy! You think you can go away for a year and . . . You've got to get it into your head now that one day you'll knock on this door and there'll be strange people here—

BIFF: What are you talking about? You're not even sixty, Mom.

LINDA: But what about your father?

BIFF: [*Lamely.*] Well, I meant him too.

HAPPY: He admires Pop.

LINDA: Biff, dear, if you don't have any feeling for him, then you can't have any feeling for me.

BIFF: Sure I can, Mom.

LINDA: No. You can't just come to see me, because I love him. [*With a threat, but only a threat, of tears.*] He's the dearest man in the world to me, and I won't have anyone making him feel unwanted and low and blue. You've got to make up your mind now, darling, there's no leeway anymore. Either he's your father and you pay him that respect, or else you're not to come here. I know he's not easy to get along with—nobody knows that better than me—but . . .

WILLY: [*From the left, with a laugh.*] Hey, hey, Biffo!

BIFF: [*Starting to go out after* WILLY.] What the hell is the matter with him? [HAPPY *stops him.*]

LINDA: Don't—don't go near him!

BIFF: Stop making excuses for him! He always, always wiped the floor with you. Never had an ounce of respect for you.

HAPPY: He's always had respect for—

BIFF: What the hell do you know about it?

HAPPY: [*Surlily.*] Just don't call him crazy!

BIFF: He's got no character—Charley wouldn't do this. Not in his own house—spewing out that vomit from his mind.

HAPPY: Charley never had to cope with what he's got to.

BIFF: People are worse off than Willy Loman. Believe me, I've seen them!

LINDA: Then make Charley your father, Biff. You can't do that, can you? I don't say he's a great man. Willy Loman never made a lot of money. His name was never in the paper. He's not the finest character that ever lived. But he's a human being, and a terrible thing is happening to him. So attention must be paid. He's not to be allowed to fall into his grave like an old dog. Attention, attention must be finally paid to such a person. You called him crazy—

BIFF: I didn't mean—

LINDA: No, a lot of people think he's lost his—balance. But you don't have to be very smart to know what his trouble is. The man is exhausted.

HAPPY: Sure!

LINDA: A small man can be just as exhausted as a great man. He works for a company thirty-six years this March, opens up unheard-of territories to their trademark, and now in his old age they take his salary away.

HAPPY: [*Indignantly.*] I didn't know that, Mom.

LINDA: You never asked, my dear! Now that you get your spending money someplace else you don't trouble your mind with him.

HAPPY: But I gave you money last—

LINDA: Christmas time, fifty dollars! To fix the hot water it cost ninety-seven fifty! For five weeks he's been on straight commission, like a beginner, an unknown!

BIFF: Those ungrateful bastards!

LINDA: Are they any worse than his sons? When he brought them business, when he was young, they were glad to see him. But now his old friends, the old buyers that loved him so and always found some order to hand him in a pinch—they're all dead, retired. He used to be able to make six, seven calls a day in Boston. Now he takes his valises out of the car and puts them back and takes them out again and he's exhausted. Instead of walking he talks now. He drives seven hundred miles, and when he gets there no one knows him anymore, no one welcomes him. And what goes through a man's mind, driving seven hundred miles home without having earned a cent? Why shouldn't he talk to himself? Why? When he has to go to Charley and borrow fifty dollars a week and pretend to me that it's his pay? How long can that go on? How long? You see what I'm sitting here and waiting for? And you tell me he has no character? The man who never worked a day but for your benefit? When does he get the medal for that? Is this his reward—to turn around at the age of sixty-three and find his sons, who he loved better than his life, one a philandering bum—

HAPPY: Mom!

LINDA: That's all you are, my baby! [*To* BIFF.] And you! What happened to the love you had for him? You were such pals! How you used to talk to him on the phone every night! How lonely he was till he could come home to you!

BIFF: All right, Mom. I'll live here in my room, and I'll get a job. I'll keep away from him, that's all.

LINDA: No, Biff. You can't stay here and fight all the time.

BIFF: He threw me out of this house, remember that.

LINDA: Why did he do that? I never knew why.

BIFF: Because I know he's a fake and he doesn't like anybody around who knows!

LINDA: Why a fake? In what way? What do you mean?

BIFF: Just don't lay it all at my feet. It's between me and him—that's all I have to say. I'll chip in from now on. He'll settle for half my paycheck. He'll be all right. I'm going to bed. [*He starts for the stairs.*]

LINDA: He won't be all right.

BIFF: [*Turning on the stairs, furiously.*] I hate this city and I'll stay here. Now what do you want?

LINDA: He's dying, Biff.

[HAPPY *turns quickly to her, shocked.*]

BIFF: [*After a pause.*] Why is he dying?

LINDA: He's been trying to kill himself.

BIFF: [*With great horror.*] How?

LINDA: I live from day to day.

BIFF: What're you talking about?

LINDA: Remember I wrote you that he smashed up the car again? In February?

BIFF: Well?

LINDA: The insurance inspector came. He said that they have evidence. That all these accidents in the last year—weren't—weren't—accidents.

HAPPY: How can they tell that? That's a lie.

LINDA: It seems there's a woman . . . [*She takes a breath as. . . .*]

{BIFF: [*Sharply but contained.*] What woman?
{LINDA: [*Simultaneously.*] . . . and this woman . . .

LINDA: What?

BIFF: Nothing. Go ahead.

LINDA: What did you say?

BIFF: Nothing. I just said what woman?

HAPPY: What about her?

LINDA: Well, it seems she was walking down the road and saw his car. She says that he wasn't driving fast at all, and that he didn't skid. She says he came to that little bridge, and then deliberately smashed into the railing, and it was only the shallowness of the water that saved him.

BIFF: Oh, no, he probably just fell asleep again.

LINDA: I don't think he fell asleep.

BIFF: Why not?

LINDA: Last month . . . [*With great difficulty.*] Oh, boys, it's so hard to say a thing like this! He's just a big stupid man to you, but I tell you there's more good in him than in many other people. [*She chokes, wipes her eyes.*] I was looking for a fuse. The lights blew out, and I went down the cellar. And behind the fuse box—it happened to fall out—was a length of rubber pipe—just short.

HAPPY: No kidding?

LINDA: There's a little attachment on the end of it. I knew right away. And sure enough, on the bottom of the water heater there's a new little nipple on the gas pipe.

HAPPY: [*Angrily.*] That—jerk.

BIFF: Did you have it taken off?

LINDA: I'm—I'm ashamed to. How can I mention it to him? Every day I go down and take away that little rubber pipe. But, when he comes home, I put it back where it was. How can I insult him that way? I don't know what to do. I live from day to day, boys. I tell you, I know every thought in his mind. It sounds so old-fashioned and silly, but I tell you he put his whole life into you and you've turned your backs on him. [*She is bent over in the chair, weeping, her face in her hands.*] Biff, I swear to God! Biff, his life is in your hands!

HAPPY: [*To* BIFF.] How do you like that damned fool!

BIFF: [*Kissing her.*] All right, pal, all right. It's all settled now. I've been remiss. I know that, Mom. But now I'll stay, and I swear to you, I'll apply myself. [*Kneeling in front of her, in a fever of self-reproach.*] It's just—you see, Mom, I don't fit in business. Not that I won't try. I'll try, and I'll make good.

HAPPY: Sure you will. The trouble with you in business was you never tried to please people.

BIFF: I know, I—

HAPPY: Like when you worked for Harrison's. Bob Harrison said you were tops, and then you go and do some damn fool thing like whistling whole songs in the elevator like a comedian.

BIFF: [*Against* HAPPY.] So what? I like to whistle sometimes.

HAPPY: You don't raise a guy to a responsible job who whistles in the elevator!

LINDA: Well, don't argue about it now.

HAPPY: Like when you'd go off and swim in the middle of the day instead of taking the line around.

BIFF: [*His resentment rising.*] Well, don't you run off? You take off sometimes, don't you? On a nice summer day?

HAPPY: Yeah, but I cover myself!

LINDA: Boys!

HAPPY: If I'm going to take a fade the boss can call any number where I'm supposed to be and they'll swear to him that I just left. I'll tell you something that I hate to say, Biff, but in the business world some of them think you're crazy.

BIFF: [*Angered.*] Screw the business world!

HAPPY: All right, screw it! Great, but cover yourself!

LINDA: Hap, Hap!

BIFF: I don't care what they think! They've laughed at Dad for years, and you know why? Because we don't belong in this nuthouse of a city! We should be mixing cement on some open plain, or—or carpenters. A carpenter is allowed to whistle!

[WILLY *walks in from the entrance of the house, at left.*]

WILLY: Even your grandfather was better than a carpenter. [*Pause. They watch him.*] You never grew up. Bernard does not whistle in the elevator, I assure you.

BIFF: [*As though to laugh* WILLY *out of it.*] Yeah, but you do, Pop.

WILLY: I never in my life whistled in an elevator! And who in the business world thinks I'm crazy?

BIFF: I didn't mean it like that, Pop. Now don't make a whole thing out of it, will ya?

WILLY: Go back to the West! Be a carpenter, a cowboy, enjoy yourself!

LINDA: Willy, he was just saying—

WILLY: I heard what he said!

HAPPY: [*Trying to quiet* WILLY.] Hey, Pop, come on now . . .

WILLY: [*Continuing over* HAPPY'S *line.*] They laugh at me, heh? Go to Filene's, go to the Hub, go to Slattery's Boston. Call out the name Willy Loman and see what happens! Big shot!

BIFF: All right, Pop.

WILLY: Big!

BIFF: All right!

WILLY: Why do you always insult me?

BIFF: I didn't say a word. [*To* LINDA.] Did I say a word?

LINDA: He didn't say anything, Willy.

WILLY: [*Going to the doorway of the living-room.*] All right, good night, good night.

LINDA: Willy, dear, he just decided . . .

WILLY: [*To* BIFF.] If you get tired hanging around tomorrow, paint the ceiling I put up in the living-room.

BIFF: I'm leaving early tomorrow.

HAPPY: He's going to see Bill Oliver, Pop.

WILLY: [*Interestedly.*] Oliver? For what?

BIFF: [*With reserve, but trying, trying.*] He always said he'd stake me. I'd like to go into business, so maybe I can take him up on it.

LINDA: Isn't that wonderful?

WILLY: Don't interrupt. What's wonderful about it? There's fifty men in the City of New York who'd stake him. [*To* BIFF.] Sporting goods?

BIFF: I guess so. I know something about it and—

WILLY: He knows something about it! You know sporting goods better than Spalding,[9] for God's sake! How much is he giving you?

BIFF: I don't know, I didn't even see him yet, but—

WILLY: Then what're you talkin' about?

BIFF: [*Getting angry.*] Well, all I said was I'm gonna see him, that's all!

WILLY: [*Turning away.*] Ah, you're counting your chickens again.

BIFF: [*Starting left for the stairs.*] Oh, Jesus, I'm going to sleep!

WILLY: [*Calling after him.*] Don't curse in this house!

BIFF: [*Turning.*] Since when did you get so clean?

HAPPY: [*Trying to stop them.*] Wait a . . .

WILLY: Don't use that language to me! I won't have it!

HAPPY: [*Grabbing* BIFF, *shouts.*] Wait a minute! I got an idea. I got a feasible idea. Come here, Biff, let's talk this over now, let's talk some sense here. When I was down in Florida last time, I thought of a great idea to sell sporting goods. It just came back to me. You and I, Biff—we have a line, the Loman Line. We train a couple of weeks, and put on a couple of exhibitions, see?

9. Albert G. Spalding (1850–1915), American baseball player and sporting-goods manufacturer.

WILLY: That's an idea!

HAPPY: Wait! We form two basketball teams, see? Two water-polo teams. We play each other. It's a million dollars' worth of publicity. Two brothers, see? The Loman Brothers. Displays in the Royal Palms—all the hotels. And banners over the ring and the basketball court: "Loman Brothers." Baby, we could sell sporting goods!

WILLY: That is a one-million-dollar idea!

LINDA: Marvelous!

BIFF: I'm in great shape as far as that's concerned.

HAPPY: And the beauty of it is, Biff, it wouldn't be like a business. We'd be out playin' ball again . . .

BIFF: [*Enthused.*] Yeah, that's . . .

WILLY: Million-dollar . . .

HAPPY: And you wouldn't get fed up with it, Biff. It'd be the family again. There'd be the old honor, and comradeship, and if you wanted to go off for a swim or somethin'—well, you'd do it! Without some smart cooky gettin' up ahead of you!

WILLY: Lick the world! You guys together could absolutely lick the civilized world.

BIFF: I'll see Oliver tomorrow. Hap, if we could work that out . . .

LINDA: Maybe things are beginning to—

WILLY: [*Wildly enthused, to* LINDA.] Stop interrupting! [*To* BIFF.] But don't wear sport jacket and slacks when you see Oliver.

BIFF: No, I'll—

WILLY: A business suit, and talk as little as possible, and don't crack any jokes.

BIFF: He did like me. Always liked me.

LINDA: He loved you!

WILLY: [*To* LINDA.] Will you stop! [*To* BIFF.] Walk in very serious. You are not applying for a boy's job. Money is to pass. Be quiet, fine, and serious. Everybody likes a kidder, but nobody lends him money.

HAPPY: I'll try to get some myself, Biff. I'm sure I can.

WILLY: I see great things for you kids, I think your troubles are over. But remember, start big and you'll end big. Ask for fifteen. How much you gonna ask for?

BIFF: Gee, I don't know—

WILLY: And don't say "Gee." "Gee" is a boy's word. A man walking in for fifteen thousand dollars does not say "Gee!"

BIFF: Ten, I think, would be top though.

WILLY: Don't be so modest. You always started too low. Walk in with a big laugh. Don't look worried. Start off with a couple of your good stories to lighten things up. It's not what you say, it's how you say it—because personality always wins the day.

LINDA: Oliver always thought the highest of him—

WILLY: Will you let me talk?

BIFF: Don't yell at her, Pop, will ya?

WILLY: [*Angrily.*] I was talking, wasn't I?

BIFF: I don't like you yelling at her all the time, and I'm tellin' you, that's all.

WILLY: What're you, takin' over this house?

LINDA: Willy—

WILLY: [*Turning on her.*] Don't take his side all the time, goddammit!

BIFF: [*Furiously.*] Stop yelling at her!

WILLY: [*Suddenly pulling on his cheek, beaten down, guilt ridden.*] Give my best to Bill Oliver—he may remember me. [*He exits through the living-room doorway.*]

LINDA: [*Her voice subdued.*] What'd you have to start that for? [BIFF *turns away.*] You see how sweet he was as soon as you talked hopefully? [*She goes over to* BIFF.] Come up and say good night to him. Don't let him go to bed that way.

HAPPY: Come on, Biff, let's buck him up.

LINDA: Please, dear. Just say good night. It takes so little to make him happy. Come. [*She goes through the living-room doorway, calling upstairs from within the living-room.*] Your pajamas are hanging in the bathroom, Willy!

HAPPY: [*Looking toward where* LINDA *went out.*] What a woman! They broke the mold when they made her. You know that, Biff?

BIFF: He's off salary. My God, working on commission!

HAPPY: Well, let's face it: he's no hot-shot selling man. Except that sometimes, you have to admit, he's a sweet personality.

BIFF: [*Deciding.*] Lend me ten bucks, will ya? I want to buy some new ties.

HAPPY: I'll take you to a place I know. Beautiful stuff. Wear one of my striped shirts tomorrow.

BIFF: She got gray. Mom got awful old. Gee, I'm gonna go in to Oliver tomorrow and knock him for a—

HAPPY: Come on up. Tell that to Dad. Let's give him a whirl. Come on.

BIFF: [*Steamed up.*] You know, with ten thousand bucks, boy!

HAPPY: [*As they go into the living-room.*] That's the talk, Biff, that's the first time I've heard the old confidence out of you! [*From within the living-room, fading off.*] You're gonna live with me, kid, and any babe you want just say the word . . .

[*The last lines are hardly heard. They are mounting the stairs to their parents' bedroom.*]

LINDA: [*Entering her bedroom and addressing* WILLY, *who is in the bathroom. She is straightening the bed for him.*] Can you do anything about the shower? It drips.

WILLY: [*From the bathroom.*] All of a sudden everything falls to pieces! Goddam plumbing, oughta be sued, those people. I hardly finished putting it in and the thing . . . [*His words rumble off.*]

LINDA: I'm just wondering if Oliver will remember him. You think he might?

WILLY: [*Coming out of the bathroom in his pajamas.*] Remember him? What's the matter with you, you crazy? If he'd've stayed with Oliver he'd be on top by now! Wait'll Oliver gets a look at him. You don't know the average caliber anymore. The average young man today—[*He is getting into bed.*]—is got a caliber of zero. Greatest thing in the world for him was to bum around. [BIFF *and* HAPPY *enter the bedroom. Slight pause.* WILLY *stops short, looking at* BIFF.] Glad to hear it, boy.

HAPPY: He wanted to say good night to you, sport.

WILLY: [*To* BIFF.] Yeah. Knock him dead, boy. What'd you want to tell me?

BIFF: Just take it easy, Pop. Good night. [*He turns to go.*]

WILLY: [*Unable to resist.*] And if anything falls off the desk while you're talking to him—like a package or something—don't you pick it up. They have office boys for that.

LINDA: I'll make a big breakfast—

WILLY: Will you let me finish? [*To* BIFF.] Tell him you were in the business in the West. Not farm work.

BIFF: All right, Dad.

LINDA: I think everything—

WILLY: [*Going right through her speech.*] And don't undersell yourself. No less than fifteen thousand dollars.

BIFF: [*Unable to bear him.*] Okay. Good night, Mom. [*He starts moving.*]

WILLY: Because you got a greatness in you, Biff, remember that. You got all kinds of greatness . . . [*He lies back, exhausted.* BIFF *walks out.*]

LINDA: [*Calling after* BIFF.] Sleep well, darling!

HAPPY: I'm gonna get married, Mom. I wanted to tell you.

LINDA: Go to sleep, dear.

HAPPY: [*Going.*] I just wanted to tell you.

WILLY: Keep up the good work. [HAPPY *exits.*] God . . . remember that Ebbets Field[1] game? The championship of the city?

LINDA: Just rest. Should I sing to you?

WILLY: Yeah. Sing to me. [LINDA *hums a soft lullaby.*] When that team came out—he was the tallest, remember?

LINDA: Oh, yes. And in gold.

[BIFF *enters the darkened kitchen, takes a cigarette, and leaves the house. He comes downstage into a golden pool of light. He smokes, staring at the night.*]

WILLY: Like a young god. Hercules—something like that. And the sun, the sun all around him. Remember how he waved to me? Right up from the field, with the representatives of three colleges standing by? And the buyers I brought, and the cheers when he came out—Loman, Loman, Loman! God Almighty, he'll be great yet. A star like that, magnificent, can never really fade away!

[*The light on* WILLY *is fading. The gas heater begins to glow through the kitchen wall, near the stairs, a blue flame beneath red coils.*]

LINDA: [*Timidly.*] Willy dear, what has he got against you?

WILLY: I'm so tired. Don't talk anymore.

[BIFF *slowly returns to the kitchen. He stops, stares toward the heater.*]

LINDA: Will you ask Howard to let you work in New York?

WILLY: First thing in the morning. Everything'll be all right.

[BIFF *reaches behind the heater and draws out a length of rubber tubing. He is horrified and turns his head toward* WILLY's *room, still dimly lit, from which the strains of* LINDA's *desperate but monotonous humming rise.*]

WILLY: [*Staring through the window into the moonlight.*] Gee, look at the moon moving between the buildings!

[BIFF *wraps the tubing around his hand and quickly goes up the stairs.*]

CURTAIN

1. Stadium where the Dodgers, Brooklyn's major-league baseball team, played from 1913 to 1957.

ACT II

Music is heard, gay and bright. The curtain rises as the music fades away. WILLY, *in shirt sleeves, is sitting at the kitchen table, sipping coffee, his hat in his lap.* LINDA *is filling his cup when she can.*

WILLY: Wonderful coffee. Meal in itself.
LINDA: Can I make you some eggs?
WILLY: No. Take a breath.
LINDA: You look so rested, dear.
WILLY: I slept like a dead one. First time in months. Imagine, sleeping till ten on a Tuesday morning. Boys left nice and early, heh?
LINDA: They were out of here by eight o'clock.
WILLY: Good work!
LINDA: It was so thrilling to see them leaving together. I can't get over the shaving lotion in this house!
WILLY: [*Smiling.*] Mmm—
LINDA: Biff was very changed this morning. His whole attitude seemed to be hopeful. He couldn't wait to get downtown to see Oliver.
WILLY: He's heading for a change. There's no question, there simply are certain men that take longer to get—solidified. How did he dress?
LINDA: His blue suit. He's so handsome in that suit. He could be a—anything in that suit!

[WILLY *gets up from the table.* LINDA *holds his jacket for him.*]

WILLY: There's no question, no question at all. Gee, on the way home tonight I'd like to buy some seeds.
LINDA: [*Laughing.*] That'd be wonderful. But not enough sun gets back there. Nothing'll grow any more.
WILLY: You wait, kid, before it's all over we're gonna get a little place out in the country, and I'll raise some vegetables, a couple of chickens . . .
LINDA: You'll do it yet, dear.

[WILLY *walks out of his jacket.* LINDA *follows him.*]

WILLY: And they'll get married, and come for a weekend. I'd build a little guest house. 'Cause I got so many fine tools, all I'd need would be a little lumber and some peace of mind.
LINDA: [*Joyfully.*] I sewed the lining . . .
WILLY: I could build two guest houses, so they'd both come. Did he decide how much he's going to ask Oliver for?
LINDA: [*Getting him into the jacket.*] He didn't mention it, but I imagine ten or fifteen thousand. You going to talk to Howard today?
WILLY: Yeah. I'll put it to him straight and simple. He'll just have to take me off the road.
LINDA: And Willy, don't forget to ask for a little advance, because we've got the insurance premium. It's the grace period now.
WILLY: That's a hundred . . . ?
LINDA: A hundred and eight, sixty-eight. Because we're a little short again.
WILLY: Why are we short?

LINDA: Well, you had the motor job on the car . . .

WILLY: That goddam Studebaker!

LINDA: And you got one more payment on the refrigerator . . .

WILLY: But it just broke again!

LINDA: Well, it's old, dear.

WILLY: I told you we should've bought a well-advertised machine. Charley bought a General Electric and it's twenty years old and it's still good, that son-of-a-bitch.

LINDA: But, Willy—

WILLY: Whoever heard of a Hastings refrigerator? Once in my life I would like to own something outright before it's broken! I'm always in a race with the junkyard! I just finished paying for the car and it's on its last legs. The refrigerator consumes belts like a goddam maniac. They time those things. They time them so when you finally paid for them, they're used up.

LINDA: [*Buttoning up his jacket as he unbuttons it.*] All told, about two hundred dollars would carry us, dear. But that includes the last payment on the mortgage. After this payment, Willy, the house belongs to us.

WILLY: It's twenty-five years!

LINDA: Biff was nine years old when we bought it.

WILLY: Well, that's a great thing. To weather a twenty-five year mortgage is—

LINDA: It's an accomplishment.

WILLY: All the cement, the lumber, the reconstruction I put in this house! There ain't a crack to be found in it anymore.

LINDA: Well, it served its purpose.

WILLY: What purpose? Some stranger'll come along, move in, and that's that. If only Biff would take this house, and raise a family . . . [*He starts to go.*] Goodbye, I'm late.

LINDA: [*Suddenly remembering.*] Oh, I forgot! You're supposed to meet them for dinner.

WILLY: Me?

LINDA: At Frank's Chop House on Forty-eighth near Sixth Avenue.

WILLY: Is that so! How about you?

LINDA: No, just the three of you. They're gonna blow you to a big meal!

WILLY: Don't say! Who thought of that?

LINDA: Biff came to me this morning, Willy, and he said, "Tell Dad, we want to blow him to a big meal." Be there six o'clock. You and your two boys are going to have dinner.

WILLY: Gee whiz! That's really somethin'. I'm gonna knock Howard for a loop, kid. I'll get an advance, and I'll come home with a New York job. Goddammit, now I'm gonna do it!

LINDA: Oh, that's the spirit, Willy!

WILLY: I will never get behind a wheel the rest of my life!

LINDA: It's changing, Willy, I can feel it changing!

WILLY: Beyond a question. G'bye, I'm late. [*He starts to go again.*]

LINDA: [*Calling after him as she runs to the kitchen table for a handkerchief.*] You got your glasses?

WILLY: [*Feels for them, then comes back in.*] Yeah, yeah, got my glasses.

LINDA: [*Giving him the handkerchief.*] And a handkerchief.

WILLY: Yeah, handkerchief.
LINDA: And your saccharine?[2]
WILLY: Yeah, my saccharine.
LINDA: Be careful on the subway stairs.

[*She kisses him, and a silk stocking is seen hanging from her hand.* WILLY *notices it.*]

WILLY: Will you stop mending stockings? At least while I'm in the house. It gets me nervous. I can't tell you. Please.

[LINDA *hides the stocking in her hand as she follows* WILLY *across the forestage in front of the house.*]

LINDA: Remember, Frank's Chop House.
WILLY: [*Passing the apron.*[3]] Maybe beets would grow out there.
LINDA: [*Laughing.*] But you tried so many times.
WILLY: Yeah. Well, don't work hard today. [*He disappears around the right corner of the house.*]
LINDA: Be careful! [*As* WILLY *vanishes,* LINDA *waves to him. Suddenly the phone rings. She runs across the stage and into the kitchen and lifts it.*] Hello? Oh, Biff! I'm so glad you called, I just . . . Yes, sure, I just told him. Yes, he'll be there for dinner at six o'clock, I didn't forget. Listen, I was just dying to tell you. You know that little rubber pipe I told you about? That he connected to the gas heater? I finally decided to go down the cellar this morning and take it away and destroy it. But it's gone! Imagine? He took it away himself, it isn't there! [*She listens.*] When? Oh, then you took it. Oh—nothing, it's just that I'd hoped he'd taken it away himself. Oh, I'm not worried, darling, because this morning he left in such high spirits, it was like the old days! I'm not afraid anymore. Did Mr. Oliver see you? . . . Well, you wait there then. And make a nice impression on him, darling. Just don't perspire too much before you see him. And have a nice time with Dad. He may have big news too! . . . That's right, a New York job. And be sweet to him tonight, dear. Be loving to him. Because he's only a little boat looking for a harbor. [*She is trembling with sorrow and joy.*] Oh, that's wonderful, Biff, you'll save his life. Thanks, darling. Just put your arm around him when he comes into the restaurant. Give him a smile. That's the boy . . . Good-bye, dear . . . You got your comb? . . . That's fine. Good-bye, Biff dear.

[*In the middle of her speech,* HOWARD WAGNER, *thirty-six, wheels on a small typewriter table on which is a wire-recording machine*[4] *and proceeds to plug it in. This is on the left forestage. Light slowly fades on* LINDA *as it rises on* HOWARD. HOWARD *is intent on threading the machine and only glances over his shoulder as* WILLY *appears.*]

WILLY: Pst! Pst!
HOWARD: Hello, Willy, come in.
WILLY: Like to have a little talk with you, Howard.

2. Artificial sweetener once recommended as a healthy alternative to sugar.
3. Foremost part of the stage, in front of the proscenium arch.
4. Precursor to the tape recorder.

HOWARD: Sorry to keep you waiting. I'll be with you in a minute.
WILLY: What's that, Howard?
HOWARD: Didn't you ever see one of these? Wire recorder.
WILLY: Oh. Can we talk a minute?
HOWARD: Records things. Just got delivery yesterday. Been driving me crazy, the most terrific machine I ever saw in my life. I was up all night with it.
WILLY: What do you do with it?
HOWARD: I bought it for dictation, but you can do anything with it. Listen to this. I had it home last night. Listen to what I picked up. The first one is my daughter. Get this. [*He flicks the switch and "Roll out the Barrel" is heard being whistled.*] Listen to that kid whistle.
WILLY: That is lifelike, isn't it?
HOWARD: Seven years old. Get that tone.
WILLY: Ts, ts. Like to ask a little favor if you . . .

[*The whistling breaks off, and the voice of* HOWARD'S *daughter is heard.*]

HIS DAUGHTER: "Now you, Daddy."
HOWARD: She's crazy for me! [*Again the same song is whistled.*] That's me! Ha! [*He winks.*]
WILLY: You're very good!

[*The whistling breaks off again. The machine runs silent for a moment.*]

HOWARD: Sh! Get this now, this is my son.
HIS SON: "The capital of Alabama is Montgomery; the capital of Arizona is Phoenix; the capital of Arkansas is Little Rock; the capital of California is Sacramento . . ." [*And on, and on.*]
HOWARD: [*Holding up five fingers.*] Five years old, Willy!
WILLY: He'll make an announcer some day!
HIS SON: [*Continuing.*] "The capital . . ."
HOWARD: Get that—alphabetical order! [*The machine breaks off suddenly.*] Wait a minute. The maid kicked the plug out.
WILLY: It certainly is a—
HOWARD: Sh, for God's sake!
HIS SON: "It's nine o'clock, Bulova watch time.[5] So I have to go to sleep."
WILLY: That really is—
HOWARD: Wait a minute! The next is my wife.

[*They wait.*]

HOWARD'S VOICE: "Go on, say something." [*Pause.*] "Well, you gonna talk?"
HIS WIFE: "I can't think of anything."
HOWARD'S VOICE: "Well, talk—it's turning."
HIS WIFE: [*Shyly, beaten.*] "Hello." [*Silence.*] "Oh, Howard, I can't talk into this . . ."
HOWARD: [*Snapping the machine off.*] That was my wife.
WILLY: That is a wonderful machine. Can we—
HOWARD: I tell you, Willy, I'm gonna take my camera, and my bandsaw, and all my hobbies, and out they go. This is the most fascinating relaxation I ever found.

5. Phrase commonly heard on radio programs sponsored by the Bulova Watch Company.

WILLY: I think I'll get one myself.

HOWARD: Sure, they're only a hundred and a half. You can't do without it. Supposing you wanna hear Jack Benny,[6] see? But you can't be at home at that hour. So you tell the maid to turn the radio on when Jack Benny comes on, and this automatically goes on with the radio . . .

WILLY: And when you come home you . . .

HOWARD: You can come home twelve o'clock, one o'clock, any time you like, and you get yourself a Coke and sit yourself down, throw the switch, and there's Jack Benny's program in the middle of the night!

WILLY: I'm definitely going to get one. Because lots of time I'm on the road, and I think to myself, what I must be missing on the radio!

HOWARD: Don't you have a radio in the car?

WILLY: Well, yeah, but who ever thinks of turning it on?

HOWARD: Say, aren't you supposed to be in Boston?

WILLY: That's what I want to talk to you about, Howard. You got a minute? [*He draws a chair in from the wing.*]

HOWARD: What happened? What're you doing here?

WILLY: Well . . .

HOWARD: You didn't crack up again, did you?

WILLY: Oh, no. No . . .

HOWARD: Geez, you had me worried there for a minute. What's the trouble?

WILLY: Well, tell you the truth, Howard. I've come to the decision that I'd rather not travel anymore.

HOWARD: Not travel! Well, what'll you do?

WILLY: Remember, Christmas time, when you had the party here? You said you'd try to think of some spot for me here in town.

HOWARD: With us?

WILLY: Well, sure.

HOWARD: Oh, yeah, yeah. I remember. Well, I couldn't think of anything for you, Willy.

WILLY: I tell ya, Howard. The kids are all grown up, y'know. I don't need much anymore. If I could take home—well, sixty-five dollars a week, I could swing it.

HOWARD: Yeah, but Willy, see I—

WILLY: I tell ya why, Howard. Speaking frankly and between the two of us, y'know—I'm just a little tired.

HOWARD: Oh, I could understand that, Willy. But you're a road man, Willy, and we do a road business. We've only got a half-dozen salesmen on the floor here.

WILLY: God knows, Howard, I never asked a favor of any man. But I was with the firm when your father used to carry you in here in his arms.

HOWARD: I know that, Willy, but—

WILLY: Your father came to me the day you were born and asked me what I thought of the name of Howard, may he rest in peace.

HOWARD: I appreciate that, Willy, but there just is no spot here for you. If I had a spot I'd slam you right in, but I just don't have a single solitary spot.

[*He looks for his lighter.* WILLY *has picked it up and gives it to him. Pause.*]

6. Vaudeville, radio, television, and movie star (1894–1974); he hosted America's most popular radio show from 1932 to 1955.

WILLY: [*With increasing anger.*] Howard, all I need to set my table is fifty dollars a week.

HOWARD: But where am I going to put you, kid?

WILLY: Look, it isn't a question of whether I can sell merchandise, is it?

HOWARD: No, but it's a business, kid, and everybody's gotta pull his own weight.

WILLY: [*Desperately.*] Just let me tell you a story, Howard—

HOWARD: 'Cause you gotta admit, business is business.

WILLY: [*Angrily.*] Business is definitely business, but just listen for a minute. You don't understand this. When I was a boy—eighteen, nineteen—I was already on the road. And there was a question in my mind as to whether selling had a future for me. Because in those days I had a yearning to go to Alaska. See, there were three gold strikes in one month in Alaska, and I felt like going out. Just for the ride, you might say.

HOWARD: [*Barely interested.*] Don't say.

WILLY: Oh, yeah, my father lived many years in Alaska. He was an adventurous man. We've got quite a little streak of self-reliance in our family. I thought I'd go out with my older brother and try to locate him, and maybe settle in the North with the old man. And I was almost decided to go, when I met a salesman in the Parker House. His name was Dave Singleman. And he was eighty-four years old, and he'd drummed merchandise in thirty-one states. And old Dave, he'd go up to his room, y'understand, put on his green velvet slippers—I'll never forget—and pick up his phone and call the buyers, and without ever leaving his room, at the age of eighty-four, he made a living. And when I saw that, I realized that selling was the greatest career a man could want. 'Cause what could be more satisfying than to be able to go, at the age of eighty-four, into twenty or thirty different cities, and pick up his phone and be remembered and loved and helped by so many different people? Do you know? when he died—and by the way he died the death of a salesman, in his green velvet slippers in the smoker[7] of the New York, New Haven and Hartford, going into Boston—when he died, hundreds of salesmen and buyers were at his funeral. Things were sad on a lotta trains for months after that. [*He stands up.* HOWARD *has not looked at him.*] In those days there was personality in it, Howard. There was respect, and comradeship, and gratitude in it. Today, it's all cut and dried, and there's no chance for bringing friendship to bear—or personality. You see what I mean? They don't know me anymore.

HOWARD: [*Moving away, toward the right.*] That's just the thing, Willy.

WILLY: If I had forty dollars a week—that's all I'd need. Forty dollars, Howard.

HOWARD: Kid, I can't take blood from a stone, I—

WILLY: [*Desperation is on him now.*] Howard, the year Al Smith[8] was nominated, your father came to me and—

HOWARD: [*Starting to go off.*] I've got to see some people, kid.

WILLY: [*Stopping him.*] I'm talking about your father! There were promises made across this desk! You mustn't tell me you've got people to see—I put thirty-four years into this firm, Howard, and now I can't pay my insurance! You

7. That is, smoking car on a train.

8. Alfred E. Smith (1873–1944), governor of New York and Democratic presidential nominee who lost to Herbert Hoover in 1928.

can't eat the orange and throw the peel away—a man is not a piece of fruit! [*After a pause.*] Now pay attention. Your father—in 1928 I had a big year. I averaged a hundred and seventy dollars a week in commissions.

HOWARD: [*Impatiently.*] Now, Willy, you never averaged—

WILLY: [*Banging his hand on the desk.*] I averaged a hundred and seventy dollars a week in the year of 1928! And your father came to me—or rather, I was in the office here—it was right over this desk—and he put his hand on my shoulder—

HOWARD: [*Getting up.*] You'll have to excuse me, Willy, I gotta see some people. Pull yourself together. [*Going out.*] I'll be back in a little while.

[*On* HOWARD*'s exit, the light on his chair grows very bright and strange.*]

WILLY: Pull myself together! What the hell did I say to him? My God, I was yelling at him! How could I! [WILLY *breaks off, staring at the light, which occupies the chair, animating it. He approaches this chair, standing across the desk from it.*] Frank, Frank, don't you remember what you told me that time? How you put your hand on my shoulder, and Frank . . . [*He leans on the desk and as he speaks the dead man's name he accidentally switches on the recorder, and instantly.*]

HOWARD'S SON: ". . . of New York is Albany. The capital of Ohio is Cincinnati, the capital of Rhode Island is . . ." [*The recitation continues.*]

WILLY: [*Leaping away with fright, shouting.*] Ha! Howard! Howard! Howard!

HOWARD: [*Rushing in.*] What happened?

WILLY: [*Pointing at the machine, which continues nasally, childishly, with the capital cities.*] Shut it off! Shut it off!

HOWARD: [*Pulling the plug out.*] Look, Willy . . .

WILLY: [*Pressing his hands to his eyes.*] I gotta get myself some coffee. I'll get some coffee . . .

[WILLY *starts to walk out.* HOWARD *stops him.*]

HOWARD: [*Rolling up the cord.*] Willy, look . . .

WILLY: I'll go to Boston.

HOWARD: Willy, you can't go to Boston for us.

WILLY: Why can't I go?

HOWARD: I don't want you to represent us. I've been meaning to tell you for a long time now.

WILLY: Howard, are you firing me?

HOWARD: I think you need a good long rest, Willy.

WILLY: Howard—

HOWARD: And when you feel better, come back, and we'll see if we can work something out.

WILLY: But I gotta earn money, Howard. I'm in no position to—

HOWARD: Where are your sons? Why don't your sons give you a hand?

WILLY: They're working on a very big deal.

HOWARD: This is no time for false pride, Willy. You go to your sons and you tell them that you're tired. You've got two great boys, haven't you?

WILLY: Oh, no question, no question, but in the meantime . . .

HOWARD: Then that's that, heh?

WILLY: All right, I'll go to Boston tomorrow.

HOWARD: No, no.

WILLY: I can't throw myself on my sons. I'm not a cripple!

HOWARD: Look, kid, I'm busy, I'm busy this morning.

WILLY: [*Grasping* HOWARD'S *arm.*] Howard, you've got to let me go to Boston!

HOWARD: [*Hard, keeping himself under control.*] I've got a line of people to see this morning. Sit down, take five minutes, and pull yourself together, and then go home, will ya? I need the office, Willy. [*He starts to go, turns, remembering the recorder, starts to push off the table holding the recorder.*] Oh, yeah. Whenever you can this week, stop by and drop off the samples. You'll feel better, Willy, and then come back and we'll talk. Pull yourself together, kid, there's people outside.

[HOWARD *exits, pushing the table off left.* WILLY *stares into space, exhausted. Now the music is heard—*BEN'S *music—first distantly, then closer, closer. As* WILLY *speaks,* BEN *enters from the right. He carries valise and umbrella.*]

WILLY: Oh, Ben, how did you do it? What is the answer? Did you wind up the Alaska deal already?

BEN: Doesn't take much time if you know what you're doing. Just a short business trip. Boarding ship in an hour. Wanted to say good-by.

WILLY: Ben, I've got to talk to you.

BEN: [*Glancing at his watch.*] Haven't the time, William.

WILLY: [*Crossing the apron to* BEN.] Ben, nothing's working out. I don't know what to do.

BEN: Now, look here, William. I've bought timberland in Alaska and I need a man to look after things for me.

WILLY: God, timberland! Me and my boys in those grand outdoors!

BEN: You've a new continent at your doorstep, William. Get out of these cities, they're full of talk and time payments and courts of law. Screw on your fists and you can fight for a fortune up there.

WILLY: Yes, yes! Linda, Linda!

[LINDA *enters as of old, with the wash.*]

LINDA: Oh, you're back?

BEN: I haven't much time.

WILLY: No, wait! Linda, he's got a proposition for me in Alaska.

LINDA: But you've got—[*To* BEN.] He's got a beautiful job here.

WILLY: But in Alaska, kid, I could—

LINDA: You're doing well enough, Willy!

BEN: [*To* LINDA.] Enough for what, my dear?

LINDA: [*Frightened of* BEN *and angry at him.*] Don't say those things to him! Enough to be happy right here, right now. [*To* WILLY, *while* BEN *laughs.*] Why must everybody conquer the world? You're well liked, and the boys love you, and someday—[*To* BEN.]—why, old man Wagner told him just the other day that if he keeps it up he'll be a member of the firm, didn't he, Willy?

WILLY: Sure, sure. I am building something with this firm, Ben, and if a man is building something he must be on the right track, mustn't he?

BEN: What are you building? Lay your hand on it. Where is it?

WILLY: [*Hesitantly.*] That's true, Linda, there's nothing.

LINDA: Why? [*To* BEN.] There's a man eighty-four years old—

WILLY: That's right, Ben, that's right. When I look at that man I say, what is there to worry about?

BEN: Bah!

WILLY: It's true, Ben. All he has to do is go into any city, pick up the phone, and he's making his living and you know why?

BEN: [*Picking up his valise.*] I've got to go.

WILLY: [*Holding* BEN *back.*] Look at this boy! [BIFF, *in his high school sweater, enters carrying suitcase.* HAPPY *carries* BIFF'S *shoulder guards, gold helmet, and football pants.*] Without a penny to his name, three great universities are begging for him, and from there the sky's the limit, because it's not what you do, Ben. It's who you know and the smile on your face! It's contacts, Ben, contacts! The whole wealth of Alaska passes over the lunch table at the Commodore Hotel, and that's the wonder, the wonder of this country, that a man can end with diamonds here on the basis of being liked! [*He turns to* BIFF.] And that's why when you get out on that field today it's important. Because thousands of people will be rooting for you and loving you. [*To* BEN, *who has again begun to leave.*] And Ben! when he walks into a business office his name will sound out like a bell and all the doors will open to him! I've seen it, Ben, I've seen it a thousand times! You can't feel it with your hand like timber, but it's there!

BEN: Good-by, William.

WILLY: Ben, am I right? Don't you think I'm right? I value your advice.

BEN: There's a new continent at your doorstep, William. You could walk out rich. Rich! [*He is gone.*]

WILLY: We'll do it here, Ben! You hear me? We're gonna do it here!

[*Young* BERNARD *rushes in. The gay music of the Boys is heard.*]

BERNARD: Oh, gee, I was afraid you left already!

WILLY: Why? What time is it?

BERNARD: It's half-past one!

WILLY: Well, come on, everybody! Ebbets Field next stop! Where's the pennants? [*He rushes through the wall-line of the kitchen and out into the living room.*]

LINDA: [*To* BIFF.] Did you pack fresh underwear?

BIFF: [*Who has been limbering up.*] I want to go!

BERNARD: Biff, I'm carrying your helmet, ain't I?

HAPPY: No, I'm carrying the helmet.

BERNARD: Oh, Biff, you promised me.

HAPPY: I'm carrying the helmet.

BERNARD: How am I going to get in the locker room?

LINDA: Let him carry the shoulder guards. [*She puts her coat and hat on in the kitchen.*]

BERNARD: Can I, Biff? 'Cause I told everybody I'm going to be in the locker room.

HAPPY: In Ebbets Field it's the clubhouse.

BERNARD: I meant the clubhouse, Biff!

HAPPY: Biff!

BIFF: [*Grandly, after a slight pause.*] Let him carry the shoulder guards.

HAPPY: [*As he gives* BERNARD *the shoulder guards.*] Stay close to us now.

[WILLY *rushes in with the pennants.*]

WILLY: [*Handing them out.*] Everybody wave when Biff comes out on the field. [HAPPY *and* BERNARD *run off.*] You set now, boy?

[*The music has died away.*]

BIFF: Ready to go, Pop. Every muscle is ready.
WILLY: [*At the edge of the apron.*] You realize what this means?
BIFF: That's right, Pop.
WILLY: [*Feeling* BIFF's *muscles.*] You're comin' home this afternoon captain of the All-Scholastic Championship Team of the City of New York.
BIFF: I got it, Pop. And remember, pal, when I take off my helmet, that touchdown is for you.
WILLY: Let's go! [*He is starting out, with his arm around* BIFF, *when* CHARLEY *enters, as of old, in knickers.*] I got no room for you, Charley.
CHARLEY: Room? For what?
WILLY: In the car.
CHARLEY: You goin' for a ride? I wanted to shoot some casino.
WILLY: [*Furiously.*] Casino! [*Incredulously.*] Don't you realize what today is?
LINDA: Oh, he knows, Willy. He's just kidding you.
WILLY: That's nothing to kid about!
CHARLEY: No, Linda, what's goin' on?
LINDA: He's playing in Ebbets Field.
CHARLEY: Baseball in this weather?
WILLY: Don't talk to him. Come on, come on! [*He is pushing them out.*]
CHARLEY: Wait a minute, didn't you hear the news?
WILLY: What?
CHARLEY: Don't you listen to the radio? Ebbets Field just blew up.
WILLY: You go to hell! [CHARLEY *laughs. Pushing them out.*] Come on, come on! We're late.
CHARLEY: [*As they go.*] Knock a homer, Biff, knock a homer!
WILLY: [*The last to leave, turning to* CHARLEY.] I don't think that was funny, Charley. This is the greatest day of my life.
CHARLEY: Willy, when are you going to grow up?
WILLY: Yeah, heh? When this game is over, Charley, you'll be laughing out of the other side of your face. They'll be calling him another Red Grange.[9] Twenty-five thousand a year.
CHARLEY: [*Kidding.*] Is that so?
WILLY: Yeah, that's so.
CHARLEY: Well, then, I'm sorry, Willy. But tell me something.
WILLY: What?
CHARLEY: Who is Red Grange?
WILLY: Put up your hands. Goddam you, put up your hands! [CHARLEY, *chuckling, shakes his head and walks away, around the left corner of the stage.* WILLY *follows him. The music rises to a mocking frenzy.*] Who the hell do you think you are, better than everybody else? You don't know everything, you big, ignorant, stupid . . . Put up your hands!

9. Harold Edward Grange (1903–91), All-American halfback at the University of Illinois from 1923 to 1925; he played professionally for the Chicago Bears.

[*Light rises, on the right side of the forestage, on a small table in the reception room of* CHARLEY'S *office. Traffic sounds are heard.* BERNARD, *now mature, sits whistling to himself. A pair of tennis rackets and an overnight bag are on the floor beside him.*]

WILLY: [*Offstage.*] What are you walking away for? Don't walk away! If you're going to say something say it to my face! I know you laugh at me behind my back. You'll laugh out of the other side of your goddam face after this game. Touchdown! Touchdown! Eighty thousand people! Touchdown! Right between the goal posts.

[BERNARD *is a quiet, earnest, but self-assured young man.* WILLY'S *voice is coming from right upstage now.* BERNARD *lowers his feet off the table and listens.* JENNY, *his father's secretary, enters.*]

JENNY: [*Distressed.*] Say, Bernard, will you go out in the hall?
BERNARD: What is that noise? Who is it?
JENNY: Mr. Loman. He just got off the elevator.
BERNARD: [*Getting up.*] Who's he arguing with?
JENNY: Nobody. There's nobody with him. I can't deal with him anymore, and your father gets all upset everytime he comes. I've got a lot of typing to do, and your father's waiting to sign it. Will you see him?
WILLY: [*Entering.*] Touchdown! Touch—[*He sees* JENNY.] Jenny, Jenny, good to see you. How're ya? Workin'? Or still honest?
JENNY: Fine. How've you been feeling?
WILLY: Not much anymore, Jenny. Ha, ha! [*He is surprised to see the rackets.*]
BERNARD: Hello, Uncle Willy.
WILLY: [*Almost shocked.*] Bernard! Well, look who's here! [*He comes quickly, guiltily to* BERNARD *and warmly shakes his hand.*]
BERNARD: How are you? Good to see you.
WILLY: What are you doing here?
BERNARD: Oh, just stopped by to see Pop. Get off my feet till my train leaves. I'm going to Washington in a few minutes.
WILLY: Is he in?
BERNARD: Yes, he's in his office with the accountant. Sit down.
WILLY: [*Sitting down.*] What're you going to do in Washington?
BERNARD: Oh, just a case I've got there, Willy.
WILLY: That so? [*Indicating the rackets.*] You going to play tennis there?
BERNARD: I'm staying with a friend who's got a court.
WILLY: Don't say. His own tennis court. Must be fine people, I bet.
BERNARD: They are, very nice. Dad tells me Biff's in town.
WILLY: [*With a big smile.*] Yeah, Biff's in. Working on a very big deal, Bernard.
BERNARD: What's Biff doing?
WILLY: Well, he's been doing very big things in the West. But he decided to establish himself here. Very big. We're having dinner. Did I hear your wife had a boy?
BERNARD: That's right. Our second.
WILLY: Two boys! What do you know!
BERNARD: What kind of a deal has Biff got?

WILLY: Well, Bill Oliver—very big sporting-goods man—he wants Biff very badly. Called him in from the West. Long distance, carte blanche, special deliveries. Your friends have their own private tennis court?

BERNARD: You still with the old firm, Willy?

WILLY: [*After a pause.*] I'm—I'm overjoyed to see how you made the grade, Bernard, overjoyed. It's an encouraging thing to see a young man really—really—Looks very good for Biff—very—[*He breaks off, then.*] Bernard—[*He is so full of emotion, he breaks off again.*]

BERNARD: What is it, Willy?

WILLY: [*Small and alone.*] What—what's the secret?

BERNARD: What secret?

WILLY: How—how did you? Why didn't he ever catch on?

BERNARD: I wouldn't know that, Willy.

WILLY: [*Confidentially, desperately.*] You were his friend, his boyhood friend. There's something I don't understand about it. His life ended after that Ebbets Field game. From the age of seventeen nothing good ever happened to him.

BERNARD: He never trained himself for anything.

WILLY: But he did, he did. After high school he took so many correspondence courses. Radio mechanics; television; God knows what, and never made the slightest mark.

BERNARD: [*Taking off his glasses.*] Willy, do you want to talk candidly?

WILLY: [*Rising, faces* BERNARD.] I regard you as a very brilliant man, Bernard. I value your advice.

BERNARD: Oh, the hell with the advice, Willy. I couldn't advise you. There's just one thing I've always wanted to ask you. When he was supposed to graduate, and the math teacher flunked him—

WILLY: Oh, that son-of-a-bitch ruined his life.

BERNARD: Yeah, but, Willy, all he had to do was go to summer school and make up that subject.

WILLY: That's right, that's right.

BERNARD: Did you tell him not to go to summer school?

WILLY: Me? I begged him to go. I ordered him to go!

BERNARD: Then why wouldn't he go?

WILLY: Why? Why! Bernard, that question has been trailing me like a ghost for the last fifteen years. He flunked the subject, and laid down and died like a hammer hit him!

BERNARD: Take it easy, kid.

WILLY: Let me talk to you—I got nobody to talk to. Bernard, Bernard, was it my fault? Y'see? It keeps going around in my mind, maybe I did something to him. I got nothing to give him.

BERNARD: Don't take it so hard.

WILLY: Why did he lay down? What is the story there? You were his friend!

BERNARD: Willy, I remember, it was June, and our grades came out. And he'd flunked math.

WILLY: That son-of-a-bitch!

BERNARD: No, it wasn't right then. Biff just got very angry, I remember, and he was ready to enroll in summer school.

WILLY: [*Surprised.*] He was?

BERNARD: He wasn't beaten by it at all. But then, Willy, he disappeared from the block for almost a month. And I got the idea that he'd gone up to New England to see you. Did he have a talk with you then? [WILLY *stares in silence.*] Willy?

WILLY: [*With a strong edge of resentment in his voice.*] Yeah, he came to Boston. What about it?

BERNARD: Well, just that when he came back—I'll never forget this, it always mystifies me. Because I'd thought so well of Biff, even though he'd always taken advantage of me. I loved him, Willy, y'know? And he came back after that month and took his sneakers—remember those sneakers with "University of Virginia" printed on them? He was so proud of those, wore them every day. And he took them down in the cellar, and burned them up in the furnace. We had a fist fight. It lasted at least half an hour. Just the two of us, punching each other down the cellar, and crying right through it. I've often thought of how strange it was that I knew he'd given up his life. What happened in Boston, Willy? [WILLY *looks at him as at an intruder.*] I just bring it up because you asked me.

WILLY: [*Angrily.*] Nothing. What do you mean, "What happened?" What's that got to do with anything?

BERNARD: Well, don't get sore.

WILLY: What are you trying to do, blame it on me? If a boy lays down is that my fault?

BERNARD: Now, Willy, don't get—

WILLY: Well, don't—don't talk to me that way! What does that mean, "What happened?"

[CHARLEY *enters. He is in his vest, and he carries a bottle of bourbon.*]

CHARLEY: Hey, you're going to miss that train. [*He waves the bottle.*]

BERNARD: Yeah, I'm going. [*He takes the bottle.*] Thanks, Pop. [*He picks up his rackets and bag.*] Good-bye, Willy, and don't worry about it. You know, "If at first you don't succeed . . ."

WILLY: Yes, I believe in that.

BERNARD: But sometimes, Willy, it's better for a man just to walk away.

WILLY: Walk away?

BERNARD: That's right.

WILLY: But if you can't walk away?

BERNARD: [*After a slight pause.*] I guess that's when it's tough. [*Extending his hand.*] Good-bye, Willy.

WILLY: [*Shaking* BERNARD*'s hand.*] Good-bye, boy.

CHARLEY: [*An arm on* BERNARD*'s shoulder.*] How do you like this kid? Gonna argue a case in front of the Supreme Court.

BERNARD: [*Protesting.*] Pop!

WILLY: [*Genuinely shocked, pained, and happy.*] No! The Supreme Court!

BERNARD: I gotta run. 'Bye, Dad!

CHARLEY: Knock 'em dead, Bernard!

[BERNARD *goes off.*]

WILLY: [*As* CHARLEY *takes out his wallet.*] The Supreme Court! And he didn't even mention it!

CHARLEY: [*Counting out money on the desk.*] He don't have to—he's gonna do it.

WILLY: And you never told him what to do, did you? You never took any interest in him.

CHARLEY: My salvation is that I never took any interest in anything. There's some money—fifty dollars. I got an accountant inside.

WILLY: Charley, look . . . [*With difficulty.*] I got my insurance to pay. If you can manage it—I need a hundred and ten dollars. [CHARLEY *doesn't reply for a moment; merely stops moving.*] I'd draw it from my bank but Linda would know, and I . . .

CHARLEY: Sit down, Willy.

WILLY: [*Moving toward the chair.*] I'm keeping an account of everything, remember. I'll pay every penny back. [*He sits.*]

CHARLEY: Now listen to me, Willy.

WILLY: I want you to know I appreciate . . .

CHARLEY: [*Sitting down on the table.*] Willy, what're you doin'? What the hell is goin' on in your head?

WILLY: Why? I'm simply . . .

CHARLEY: I offered you a job. You can make fifty dollars a week. And I won't send you on the road.

WILLY: I've got a job.

CHARLEY: Without pay? What kind of job is a job without pay? [*He rises.*] Now, look kid, enough is enough. I'm no genius but I know when I'm being insulted.

WILLY: Insulted!

CHARLEY: Why don't you want to work for me?

WILLY: What's the matter with you? I've got a job.

CHARLEY: Then what're you walkin' in here every week for?

WILLY: [*Getting up.*] Well, if you don't want me to walk in here—

CHARLEY: I am offering you a job!

WILLY: I don't want your goddam job!

CHARLEY: When the hell are you going to grow up?

WILLY: [*Furiously.*] You big ignoramus, if you say that to me again I'll rap you one! I don't care how big you are! [*He's ready to fight. Pause.*]

CHARLEY: [*Kindly, going to him.*] How much do you need, Willy?

WILLY: Charley, I'm strapped, I'm strapped. I don't know what to do. I was just fired.

CHARLEY: Howard fired you?

WILLY: That snotnose. Imagine that? I named him. I named him Howard.

CHARLEY: Willy, when're you gonna realize that them things don't mean anything? You named him Howard, but you can't sell that. The only thing you got in this world is what you can sell. And the funny thing is that you're a salesman, and you don't know that.

WILLY: I've always tried to think otherwise, I guess. I always felt that if a man was impressive, and well liked, that nothing—

CHARLEY: Why must everybody like you? Who liked J. P. Morgan?[1] Was he impressive? In a Turkish bath he'd look like a butcher. But with his pockets

1. American financier and industrialist John Pierpont Morgan (1837–1913), widely criticized for his business dealings with the U.S. government.

on he was very well liked. Now listen, Willy, I know you don't like me, and nobody can say I'm in love with you, but I'll give you a job because—just for the hell of it, put it that way. Now what do you say?

WILLY: I—I just can't work for you, Charley.

CHARLEY: What're you, jealous of me?

WILLY: I can't work for you, that's all, don't ask me why.

CHARLEY: [*Angered, takes out more bills.*] You been jealous of me all your life, you damned fool! Here, pay your insurance. [*He puts the money in* WILLY's *hand.*]

WILLY: I'm keeping strict accounts.

CHARLEY: I've got some work to do. Take care of yourself. And pay your insurance.

WILLY: [*Moving to the right.*] Funny, y'know? After all the highways and the trains, and the appointments, and the years, you end up worth more dead than alive.

CHARLEY: Willy, nobody's worth nothin' dead. [*After a slight pause.*] Did you hear what I said? [WILLY *stands still, dreaming.*] Willy!

WILLY: Apologize to Bernard for me when you see him. I didn't mean to argue with him. He's a fine boy. They're all fine boys, and they'll end up big—all of them. Someday they'll all play tennis together. Wish me luck, Charley. He saw Bill Oliver today.

CHARLEY: Good luck.

WILLY: [*On the verge of tears.*] Charley, you're the only friend I got. Isn't that a remarkable thing? [*He goes out.*]

CHARLEY: Jesus!

[CHARLEY *stares after him a moment and follows. All light blacks out. Suddenly raucous music is heard, and a red glow rises behind the screen at right.* STANLEY, *a young waiter, appears, carrying a table, followed by* HAPPY, *who is carrying two chairs.*]

STANLEY: [*Putting the table down.*] That's all right, Mr. Loman, I can handle it myself. [*He turns and takes the chairs from* HAPPY *and places them at the table.*]

HAPPY: [*Glancing around.*] Oh, this is better.

STANLEY: Sure, in the front there you're in the middle of all kinds a noise. Whenever you got a party, Mr. Loman, you just tell me and I'll put you back here. Y'know, there's a lotta people they don't like it private, because when they go out they like to see a lotta action around them because they're sick and tired to stay in the house by theirself. But I know you, you ain't from Hackensack.[2] You know what I mean?

HAPPY: [*Sitting down.*] So how's it coming, Stanley?

STANLEY: Ah, it's a dog life. I only wish during the war they'd a took me in the Army. I couda been dead by now.

HAPPY: My brother's back, Stanley.

STANLEY: Oh, he come back, heh? From the Far West.

HAPPY: Yeah, big cattle man, my brother, so treat him right. And my father's coming too.

2. Mainly working-class city in northern New Jersey.

STANLEY: Oh, your father too!

HAPPY: You got a couple of nice lobsters?

STANLEY: Hundred per cent, big.

HAPPY: I want them with the claws.

STANLEY: Don't worry, I don't give you no mice. [HAPPY *laughs.*] How about some wine? It'll put a head on the meal.

HAPPY: No. You remember, Stanley, that recipe I brought you from overseas? With the champagne in it?

STANLEY: Oh, yeah, sure. I still got it tacked up yet in the kitchen. But that'll have to cost a buck apiece anyways.

HAPPY: That's all right.

STANLEY: What'd you, hit a number or somethin'?

HAPPY: No, it's a little celebration. My brother is—I think he pulled off a big deal today. I think we're going into business together.

STANLEY: Great! That's the best for you. Because a family business, you know what I mean?—that's the best.

HAPPY: That's what I think.

STANLEY: 'Cause what's the difference? Somebody steals? It's in the family. Know what I mean? [*Sotto voce.*[3]] Like this bartender here. The boss is goin' crazy what kinda leak he's got in the cash register. You put it in but it don't come out.

HAPPY: [*Raising his head.*] Sh!

STANLEY: What?

HAPPY: You notice I wasn't lookin' right or left, was I?

STANLEY: No.

HAPPY: And my eyes are closed.

STANLEY: So what's the—?

HAPPY: Strudel's comin'.

STANLEY: [*Catching on, looks around.*] Ah, no, there's no—[*He breaks off as a furred, lavishly dressed* GIRL *enters and sits at the next table. Both follow her with their eyes.*] Geez, how'd ya know?

HAPPY: I got radar or something. [*Staring directly at her profile.*] Oooooooo . . . Stanley.

STANLEY: I think, that's for you, Mr. Loman.

HAPPY: Look at that mouth. Oh, God. And the binoculars.

STANLEY: Geez, you got a life, Mr. Loman.

HAPPY: Wait on her.

STANLEY: [*Going to the* GIRL*'s table.*] Would you like a menu, ma'am?

GIRL: I'm expecting someone, but I'd like a—

HAPPY: Why don't you bring her—excuse me, miss, do you mind? I sell champagne, and I'd like you to try my brand. Bring her a champagne, Stanley.

GIRL: That's awfully nice of you.

HAPPY: Don't mention it. It's all company money. [*He laughs.*]

GIRL: That's a charming product to be selling, isn't it?

HAPPY: Oh, gets to be like everything else. Selling is selling, y'know.

GIRL: I suppose.

HAPPY: You don't happen to sell, do you?

3. In an undertone (Italian).

GIRL: No, I don't sell.

HAPPY: Would you object to a compliment from a stranger? You ought to be on a magazine cover.

GIRL: [*Looking at him a little archly.*] I have been.

[STANLEY *comes in with a glass of champagne.*]

HAPPY: What'd I say before, Stanley? You see? She's a cover girl.

STANLEY: Oh, I could see, I could see.

HAPPY: [*To the* GIRL.] What magazine?

GIRL: Oh, a lot of them. [*She takes the drink.*] Thank you.

HAPPY: You know what they say in France, don't you? "Champagne is the drink of the complexion"—Hya, Biff!

[BIFF *has entered and sits with* HAPPY.]

BIFF: Hello, kid. Sorry I'm late.

HAPPY: I just got here. Uh, Miss—?

GIRL: Forsythe.

HAPPY: Miss Forsythe, this is my brother.

BIFF: Is Dad here?

HAPPY: His name is Biff. You might've heard of him. Great football player.

GIRL: Really? What team?

HAPPY: Are you familiar with football?

GIRL: No, I'm afraid I'm not.

HAPPY: Biff is quarterback with the New York Giants.

GIRL: Well, that's nice, isn't it? [*She drinks.*]

HAPPY: Good health.

GIRL: I'm happy to meet you.

HAPPY: That's my name, Hap. It's really Harold, but at West Point they called me Happy.

GIRL: [*Now really impressed.*] Oh, I see. How do you do? [*She turns her profile.*]

BIFF: Isn't Dad coming?

HAPPY: You want her?

BIFF: Oh, I could never make that.

HAPPY: I remember the time that idea would never come into your head. Where's the old confidence, Biff?

BIFF: I just saw Oliver—

HAPPY: Wait a minute. I've got to see that old confidence again. Do you want her? She's on call.

BIFF: Oh, no. [*He turns to look at the* GIRL.]

HAPPY: I'm telling you. Watch this. [*Turning to see the* GIRL.] Honey? [*She turns to him.*] Are you busy?

GIRL: Well, I am . . . but I could make a phone call.

HAPPY: Do that, will you, honey? And see if you can get a friend. We'll be here for a while. Biff is one of the greatest football players in the country.

GIRL: [*Standing up.*] Well, I'm certainly happy to meet you.

HAPPY: Come back soon.

GIRL: I'll try.

HAPPY: Don't try, honey, try hard. [*The* GIRL *exits.* STANLEY *follows, shaking his head in bewildered admiration.*] Isn't that a shame now? A beautiful girl like that? That's why I can't get married. There's not a good woman in a thousand. New York is loaded with them, kid!

BIFF: Hap, look—

HAPPY: I told you she was on call![4]

BIFF: [*Strangely unnerved.*] Cut it out, will ya? I want to say something to you.

HAPPY: Did you see Oliver?

BIFF: I saw him all right. Now look, I want to tell Dad a couple of things and I want you to help me.

HAPPY: What? Is he going to back you?

BIFF: Are you crazy? You're out of your goddam head, you know that?

HAPPY: Why? What happened?

BIFF: [*Breathlessly.*] I did a terrible thing today, Hap. It's been the strangest day I ever went through. I'm all numb, I swear.

HAPPY: You mean he wouldn't see you?

BIFF: Well, I waited six hours for him, see? All day. Kept sending my name in. Even tried to date his secretary so she'd get me to him, but no soap.

HAPPY: Because you're not showin' the old confidence, Biff. He remembered you, didn't he?

BIFF: [*Stopping* HAPPY *with a gesture.*] Finally, about five o'clock, he comes out. Didn't remember who I was or anything. I felt like such an idiot, Hap.

HAPPY: Did you tell him my Florida idea?

BIFF: He walked away. I saw him for one minute. I got so mad I could've torn the walls down! How the hell did I ever get the idea I was a salesman there? I even believed myself that I'd been a salesman for him! And then he gave me one look and—I realized what a ridiculous lie my whole life has been! We've been talking in a dream for fifteen years. I was a shipping clerk.

HAPPY: What'd you do?

BIFF: [*With great tension and wonder.*] Well, he left, see. And the secretary went out. I was all alone in the waiting-room. I don't know what came over me, Hap. The next thing I know I'm in his office—paneled walls, everything. I can't explain it. I—Hap, I took his fountain pen.

HAPPY: Geez, did he catch you?

BIFF: I ran out. I ran down all eleven flights. I ran and ran and ran.

HAPPY: That was an awful dumb—what'd you do that for?

BIFF: [*Agonized.*] I don't know, I just—wanted to take something, I don't know. You gotta help me, Hap, I'm gonna tell Pop.

HAPPY: You crazy? What for?

BIFF: Hap, he's got to understand that I'm not the man somebody lends that kind of money to. He thinks I've been spiting him all these years and it's eating him up.

HAPPY: That's just it. You tell him something nice.

BIFF: I can't.

HAPPY: Say you got a lunch date with Oliver tomorrow.

BIFF: So what do I do tomorrow?

HAPPY: You leave the house tomorrow and come back at night and say Oliver is thinking it over. And he thinks it over for a couple of weeks, and gradually it fades away and nobody's the worse.

4. That is, a call girl, a prostitute.

BIFF: But it'll go on forever!

HAPPY: Dad is never so happy as when he's looking forward to something! [WILLY *enters.*] Hello, scout!

WILLY: Gee, I haven't been here in years!

[STANLEY *has followed* WILLY *in and sets a chair for him.* STANLEY *starts off but* HAPPY *stops him.*]

HAPPY: Stanley!

[STANLEY *stands by, waiting for an order.*]

BIFF: [*Going to* WILLY *with guilt, as to an invalid.*] Sit down, Pop. You want a drink?

WILLY: Sure, I don't mind.

BIFF: Let's get a load on.

WILLY: You look worried.

BIFF: N-no. [*To* STANLEY.] Scotch all around. Make it doubles.

STANLEY: Doubles, right. [*He goes.*]

WILLY: You had a couple already, didn't you?

BIFF: Just a couple, yeah.

WILLY: Well, what happened, boy? [*Nodding affirmatively, with a smile.*] Everything go all right?

BIFF: [*Takes a breath, then reaches out and grasps* WILLY'S *hand.*] Pal . . . [*He is smiling bravely, and* WILLY *is smiling too.*] I had an experience today.

HAPPY: Terrific, Pop.

WILLY: That so? What happened?

BIFF: [*High, slightly alcoholic, above the earth.*] I'm going to tell you everything from first to last. It's been a strange day. [*Silence. He looks around, composes himself as best he can, but his breath keeps breaking the rhythm of his voice.*] I had to wait quite a while for him, and—

WILLY: Oliver?

BIFF: Yeah, Oliver. All day, as a matter of cold fact. And a lot of—instances—facts, Pop, facts about my life came back to me. Who was it, Pop? Who ever said I was a salesman with Oliver?

WILLY: Well, you were.

BIFF: No, Dad, I was shipping clerk.

WILLY: But you were practically—

BIFF: [*With determination.*] Dad, I don't know who said it first, but I was never a salesman for Bill Oliver.

WILLY: What're you talking about?

BIFF: Let's hold on to the facts tonight, Pop. We're not going to get anywhere bullin' around. I was a shipping clerk.

WILLY: [*Angrily.*] All right, now listen to me—

BIFF: Why don't you let me finish?

WILLY: I'm not interested in stories about the past or any crap of that kind because the woods are burning, boys, you understand? There's a big blaze going on all around. I was fired today.

BIFF: [*Shocked.*] How could you be?

WILLY: I was fired, and I'm looking for a little good news to tell your mother, because the woman has waited and the woman has suffered. The gist of it is that I haven't got a story left in my head, Biff. So don't give me a lecture about facts and aspects. I am not interested. Now what've you got to say to me? [STANLEY *enters with three drinks. They wait until he leaves.*] Did you see Oliver?

BIFF: Jesus, Dad!

WILLY: You mean you didn't go up there?

HAPPY: Sure he went up there.

BIFF: I did. I—saw him. How could they fire you?

WILLY: [*On the edge of his chair.*] What kind of a welcome did he give you?

BIFF: He won't even let you work on commission?

WILLY: I'm out. [*Driving.*] So tell me, he gave you a warm welcome?

HAPPY: Sure, Pop, sure!

BIFF: [*Driven.*] Well, it was kind of—

WILLY: I was wondering if he'd remember you. [*To* HAPPY.] Imagine, man doesn't see him for ten, twelve years and gives him that kind of a welcome!

HAPPY: Damn right!

BIFF: [*Trying to return to the offensive.*] Pop, look—

WILLY: You know why he remembered you, don't you? Because you impressed him in those days.

BIFF: Let's talk quietly and get this down to the facts, huh?

WILLY: [*As though* BIFF *had been interrupting.*] Well, what happened? It's great news, Biff. Did he take you into his office or'd you talk in the waiting-room?

BIFF: Well, he came in, see and—

WILLY: [*With a big smile.*] What'd he say? Betcha he threw his arm around you.

BIFF: Well, he kinda—

WILLY: He's a fine man. [*To* HAPPY.] Very hard man to see, y'know.

HAPPY: [*Agreeing.*] Oh, I know.

WILLY: [*To* BIFF.] Is that where you had the drinks?

BIFF: Yeah, he gave me a couple of—no, no!

HAPPY: [*Cutting in.*] He told him my Florida idea.

WILLY: Don't interrupt. [*To* BIFF.] How'd he react to the Florida idea?

BIFF: Dad, will you give me a minute to explain?

WILLY: I've been waiting for you to explain since I sat down here! What happened? He took you into his office and what?

BIFF: Well—I talked. And—he listened, see.

WILLY: Famous for the way he listens, y'know. What was his answer?

BIFF: His answer was—[*He breaks off, suddenly angry.*] Dad, you're not letting me tell you what I want to tell you!

WILLY: [*Accusing, angered.*] You didn't see him, did you?

BIFF: I did see him!

WILLY: What'd you insult him or something? You insulted him, didn't you?

BIFF: Listen, will you let me out of it, will you just let me out of it!

HAPPY: What the hell!

WILLY: Tell me what happened!

BIFF: [*To* HAPPY.] I can't talk to him!

[*A single trumpet note jars the ear. The light of green leaves stains the house, which holds the air of night and a dream.* YOUNG BERNARD *enters and knocks on the door of the house.*]

YOUNG BERNARD: [*Frantically.*] Mrs. Loman, Mrs. Loman!
HAPPY: Tell him what happened!
BIFF: [*To* HAPPY.] Shut up and leave me alone!
WILLY: No, no. You had to go and flunk math!
BIFF: What math? What're you talking about?
YOUNG BERNARD: Mrs. Loman, Mrs. Loman!

[LINDA *appears in the house, as of old.*]

WILLY: [*Wildly.*] Math, math, math!
BIFF: Take it easy, Pop!
YOUNG BERNARD: Mrs. Loman!
WILLY: [*Furiously.*] If you hadn't flunked you'd've been set by now!
BIFF: Now, look, I'm gonna tell you what happened, and you're going to listen to me.
YOUNG BERNARD: Mrs. Loman!
BIFF: I waited six hours—
HAPPY: What the hell are you saying?
BIFF: I kept sending in my name but he wouldn't see me. So finally he . . . [*He continues unheard as light fades low on the restaurant.*]
YOUNG BERNARD: Biff flunked math!
LINDA: No!
YOUNG BERNARD: Birnbaum flunked him! They won't graduate him!
LINDA: But they have to. He's gotta go to the university. Where is he? Biff! Biff!
YOUNG BERNARD: No, he left. He went to Grand Central.[5]
LINDA: Grand—You mean he went to Boston!
YOUNG BERNARD: Is Uncle Willy in Boston?
LINDA: Oh, maybe Willy can talk to the teacher. Oh, the poor, poor boy!

[*Light on house area snaps out.*]

BIFF: [*At the table, now audible, holding up a gold fountain pen.*] . . . so I'm washed up with Oliver, you understand? Are you listening to me?
WILLY: [*At a loss.*] Yeah, sure. If you hadn't flunked—
BIFF: Flunked what? What're you talking about?
WILLY: Don't blame everything on me! I didn't flunk math—you did! What pen?
HAPPY: That was awful dumb, Biff, a pen like that is worth—
WILLY: [*Seeing the pen for the first time.*] You took Oliver's pen?
BIFF: [*Weakening.*] Dad, I just explained it to you.
WILLY: You stole Bill Oliver's fountain pen!
BIFF: I didn't exactly steal it! That's just what I've been explaining to you!
HAPPY: He had it in his hand and just then Oliver walked in, so he got nervous and stuck it in his pocket!
WILLY: My God, Biff!
BIFF: I never intended to do it, Dad!
OPERATOR'S VOICE: Standish Arms, good evening!
WILLY: [*Shouting.*] I'm not in my room!
BIFF: [*Frightened.*] Dad, what's the matter? [*He and* HAPPY *stand up.*]

5. Grand Central Terminal, New York City's principal railway and subway station.

OPERATOR: Ringing Mr. Loman for you!

BIFF: [*Horrified, gets down on one knee before* WILLY.] Dad, I'll make good, I'll make good. [WILLY *tries to get to his feet.* BIFF *holds him down.*] Sit down now.

WILLY: No, you're no good, you're no good for anything.

BIFF: I am, Dad, I'll find something else, you understand? Now don't worry about anything. [*He holds up* WILLY'*s face.*] Talk to me, Dad.

OPERATOR: Mr. Loman does not answer. Shall I page him?

WILLY: [*Attempting to stand, as though to rush and silence the* OPERATOR.] No, no, no!

HAPPY: He'll strike something, Pop.

WILLY: No, no . . .

BIFF: [*Desperately, standing over* WILLY.] Pop, listen! Listen to me! I'm telling you something good. Oliver talked to his partner about the Florida idea. You listening? He—he talked to his partner, and he came to me . . . I'm going to be all right, you hear? Dad, listen to me, he said it was just a question of the amount!

WILLY: Then you . . . got it?

HAPPY: He's gonna be terrific, Pop!

WILLY: [*Trying to stand.*] Then you got it, haven't you? You got it! You got it!

BIFF: [*Agonized, holds* WILLY *down.*] No, no. Look, Pop. I'm supposed to have lunch with them tomorrow. I'm just telling you this so you'll know that I can still make an impression, Pop. And I'll make good somewhere, but I can't go tomorrow, see?

WILLY: Why not? You simply—

BIFF: But the pen, Pop!

WILLY: You give it to him and tell him it was an oversight!

HAPPY: Sure, have lunch tomorrow!

BIFF: I can't say that—

WILLY: You were doing a crossword puzzle and accidentally used his pen!

BIFF: Listen, kid, I took those balls years ago, now I walk in with his fountain pen? That clinches it, don't you see? I can't face him like that! I'll try elsewhere.

PAGE'S VOICE: Paging Mr. Loman!

WILLY: Don't you want to be anything?

BIFF: Pop, how can I go back?

WILLY: You don't want to be anything, is that what's behind it?

BIFF: [*Now angry at* WILLY *for not crediting his sympathy.*] Don't take it that way! You think it was easy walking into that office after what I'd done to him? A team of horses couldn't have dragged me back to Bill Oliver!

WILLY: Then why'd you go?

BIFF: Why did I go? Why did I go! Look at you! Look at what's become of you!

[*Off left,* THE WOMAN *laughs.*]

WILLY: Biff, you're going to go to that lunch tomorrow, or—

BIFF: I can't go. I've got an appointment!

HAPPY: Biff, for . . . !

WILLY: Are you spiting me?

BIFF: Don't take it that way! Goddammit!

WILLY: [*Strikes* BIFF *and falters away from the table.*] You rotten little louse! Are you spiting me?

THE WOMAN: Someone's at the door, Willy!

BIFF: I'm no good, can't you see what I am?

HAPPY: [*Separating them.*] Hey, you're in a restaurant! Now cut it out, both of you! [*The* GIRLS *enter.*] Hello, girls, sit down.

[THE WOMAN *laughs, off left.*]

MISS FORSYTHE: I guess we might as well. This is Letta.

THE WOMAN: Willy, are you going to wake up?

BIFF: [*Ignoring* WILLY.] How're ya, miss, sit down. What do you drink?

MISS FORSYTHE: Letta might not be able to stay long.

LETTA: I gotta get up early tomorrow. I got jury duty. I'm so excited! Were you fellows ever on a jury?

BIFF: No, but I been in front of them! [*The* GIRLS *laugh.*] This is my father.

LETTA: Isn't he cute? Sit down with us, Pop.

HAPPY: Sit him down, Biff!

BIFF: [*Going to him.*] Come on, slugger, drink us under the table. To hell with it! Come on, sit down, pal.

[*On* BIFF'*s last insistence,* WILLY *is about to sit.*]

THE WOMAN: [*Now urgently.*] Willy, are you going to answer the door!

[THE WOMAN'*s call pulls* WILLY *back. He starts right, befuddled.*]

BIFF: Hey, where are you going?

WILLY: Open the door.

BIFF: The door?

WILLY: The washroom . . . the door . . . where's the door?

BIFF: [*Leading* WILLY *to the left.*] Just go straight down.

[WILLY *moves left.*]

THE WOMAN: Willy, Willy, are you going to get up, get up, get up, get up?

[WILLY *exits left.*]

LETTA: I think it's sweet you bring your daddy along.

MISS FORSYTHE: Oh, he isn't really your father!

BIFF: [*At left, turning to her resentfully.*] Miss Forsythe, you've just seen a prince walk by. A fine, troubled prince. A hardworking, unappreciated prince. A pal, you understand? A good companion. Always for his boys.

LETTA: That's so sweet.

HAPPY: Well, girls, what's the program? We're wasting time. Come on, Biff. Gather round. Where would you like to go?

BIFF: Why don't you do something for him?

HAPPY: Me!

BIFF: Don't you give a damn for him, Hap?

HAPPY: What're you talking about? I'm the one who—

BIFF: I sense it, you don't give a good goddam about him. [*He takes the rolled-up hose from his pocket and puts it on the table in front of* HAPPY.] Look what I found in the cellar, for Christ's sake. How can you bear to let it go on?

HAPPY: Me? Who goes away? Who runs off and—

BIFF: Yeah, but he doesn't mean anything to you. You could help him—I can't! Don't you understand what I'm talking about? He's going to kill himself, don't you know that?

HAPPY: Don't I know it! Me!

BIFF: Hap, help him! Jesus . . . help him . . . Help me, help me, I can't bear to look at his face! [*Ready to weep, he hurries out, up right.*]

HAPPY: [*Starting after him.*] Where are you going?

MISS FORSYTHE: What's he so mad about?

HAPPY: Come on, girls, we'll catch up with him.

MISS FORSYTHE: [*As* HAPPY *pushes her out.*] Say, I don't like that temper of his!

HAPPY: He's just a little overstrung, he'll be all right!

WILLY: [*Off left, as* THE WOMAN *laughs.*] Don't answer! Don't answer!

LETTA: Don't you want to tell your father—

HAPPY: No, that's not my father. He's just a guy. Come on, we'll catch Biff, and, honey, we're going to paint this town! Stanley, where's the check! Hey, Stanley!

[*They exit.* STANLEY *looks toward left.*]

STANLEY: [*Calling to* HAPPY *indignantly.*] Mr. Loman! Mr. Loman!

[STANLEY *picks up a chair and follows them off. Knocking is heard off left.* THE WOMAN *enters, laughing.* WILLY *follows her. She is in a black slip; he is buttoning his shirt. Raw, sensuous music accompanies their speech.*]

WILLY: Will you stop laughing? Will you stop?

THE WOMAN: Aren't you going to answer the door? He'll wake the whole hotel.

WILLY: I'm not expecting anybody.

THE WOMAN: Whyn't you have another drink, honey, and stop being so damn self-centered?

WILLY: I'm so lonely.

THE WOMAN: You know you ruined me, Willy? From now on, whenever you come to the office, I'll see that you go right through to the buyers. No waiting at my desk anymore, Willy. You ruined me.

WILLY: That's nice of you to say that.

THE WOMAN: Gee, you are self-centered! Why so sad? You are the saddest, self-centeredest soul I ever did see-saw. [*She laughs. He kisses her.*] Come on inside, drummer boy. It's silly to be dressing in the middle of the night. [*As knocking is heard.*] Aren't you going to answer the door?

WILLY: They're knocking on the wrong door.

THE WOMAN: But I felt the knocking. And he heard us talking in here. Maybe the hotel's on fire!

WILLY: [*His terror rising.*] It's a mistake.

THE WOMAN: Then tell them to go away!

WILLY: There's nobody there.

THE WOMAN: It's getting on my nerves, Willy. There's somebody standing out there and it's getting on my nerves!

WILLY: [*Pushing her away from him.*] All right, stay in the bathroom here, and don't come out. I think there's a law in Massachusetts about it, so don't come out. It may be that new room clerk. He looked very mean. So don't come out. It's a mistake, there's no fire.

[*The knocking is heard again. He takes a few steps away from her, and she vanishes into the wing. The light follows him, and now he is facing* YOUNG BIFF, *who carries a suitcase.* BIFF *steps toward him. The music is gone.*]

BIFF: Why didn't you answer?

WILLY: Biff! What are you doing in Boston?

BIFF: Why didn't you answer? I've been knocking for five minutes, I called you on the phone—

WILLY: I just heard you. I was in the bathroom and had the door shut. Did anything happen home?

BIFF: Dad—I let you down.

WILLY: What do you mean?

BIFF: Dad . . .

WILLY: Biffo, what's this about? [*Putting his arm around* BIFF.] Come on, let's go downstairs and get you a malted.

BIFF: Dad, I flunked math.

WILLY: Not for the term?

BIFF: The term. I haven't got enough credits to graduate.

WILLY: You mean to say Bernard wouldn't give you the answers?

BIFF: He did, he tried, but I only got a sixty-one.

WILLY: And they wouldn't give you four points?

BIFF: Birnbaum refused absolutely. I begged him, Pop, but he won't give me those points. You gotta talk to him before they close the school. Because if he saw the kind of man you are, and you just talked to him in your way, I'm sure he'd come through for me. The class came right before practice, see, and I didn't go enough. Would you talk to him? He'd like you, Pop. You know the way you could talk.

WILLY: You're on. We'll drive right back.

BIFF: Oh, Dad, good work! I'm sure he'll change for you!

WILLY: Go downstairs and tell the clerk I'm checkin' out. Go right down.

BIFF: Yes, sir! See, the reason he hates me, Pop—one day he was late for class so I got up at the blackboard and imitated him. I crossed my eyes and talked with a lithp.

WILLY: [*Laughing.*] You did? The kids like it?

BIFF: They nearly died laughing!

WILLY: Yeah? What'd you do?

BIFF: The thquare root of thixthy twee is . . . [WILLY *bursts out laughing;* BIFF *joins him.*] And in the middle of it he walked in!

[WILLY *laughs and* THE WOMAN *joins in offstage.*]

WILLY: [*Without hesitation.*] Hurry downstairs and—

BIFF: Somebody in there?

WILLY: No, that was next door.

[THE WOMAN *laughs offstage.*]

BIFF: Somebody got in your bathroom!

WILLY: No, it's the next room, there's a party—

THE WOMAN: [*Enters laughing. She lisps this.*] Can I come in? There's something in the bathtub, Willy, and it's moving!

[WILLY *looks at* BIFF, *who is staring open-mouthed and horrified at* THE WOMAN.]

WILLY: Ah—you better go back to your room. They must be finished painting by now. They're painting her room so I let her take a shower here. Go back, go back . . . [*He pushes her.*]

THE WOMAN: [*Resisting.*] But I've got to get dressed, Willy, I can't—

WILLY: Get out of here! Go back, go back . . . [*Suddenly striving for the ordinary.*] This is Miss Francis, Biff, she's a buyer. They're painting her room. Go back, Miss Francis, go back . . .

THE WOMAN: But my clothes, I can't go out naked in the hall!

WILLY: [*Pushing her offstage.*] Get outa here! Go back, go back!

[BIFF *slowly sits down on his suitcase as the argument continues offstage.*]

THE WOMAN: Where's my stockings? You promised me stockings, Willy!

WILLY: I have no stockings here!

THE WOMAN: You had two boxes of size nine sheers for me, and I want them!

WILLY: Here, for God's sake, will you get outa here!

THE WOMAN: [*Enters holding a box of stockings.*] I just hope there's nobody in the hall. That's all I hope. [*To* BIFF.] Are you football or baseball?

BIFF: Football.

THE WOMAN: [*Angry, humiliated.*] That's me too. G'night. [*She snatches her clothes from* WILLY, *and walks out.*]

WILLY: [*After a pause.*] Well, better get going. I want to get to the school first thing in the morning. Get my suits out of the closet. I'll get my valise. [BIFF *doesn't move.*] What's the matter? [BIFF *remains motionless, tears falling.*] She's a buyer. Buys for J. H. Simmons. She lives down the hall—they're painting. You don't imagine—[*He breaks off. After a pause.*] Now listen, pal, she's just a buyer. She sees merchandise in her room and they have to keep it looking just so . . . [*Pause. Assuming command.*] All right, get my suits. [BIFF *doesn't move.*] Now stop crying and do as I say. I gave you an order. Biff, I gave you an order! Is that what you do when I give you an order? How dare you cry! [*Putting his arm around* BIFF.] Now look, Biff, when you grow up you'll understand about these things. You mustn't—you mustn't overemphasize a thing like this. I'll see Birnbaum first thing in the morning.

BIFF: Never mind.

WILLY: [*Getting down beside* BIFF.] Never mind! He's going to give you those points. I'll see to it.

BIFF: He wouldn't listen to you.

WILLY: He certainly will listen to me. You need those points for the U. of Virginia.

BIFF: I'm not going there.

WILLY: Heh? If I can't get him to change that mark you'll make it up in summer school. You've got all summer to—

BIFF: [*His weeping breaking from him.*] Dad . . .

WILLY: [*Infected by it.*] Oh, my boy . . .
BIFF: Dad . . .
WILLY: She's nothing to me, Biff. I was lonely, I was terribly lonely.
BIFF: You—you gave her Mama's stockings! [*His tears break through and he rises to go.*]
WILLY: [*Grabbing for* BIFF.] I gave you an order!
BIFF: Don't touch me, you—liar!
WILLY: Apologize for that!
BIFF: You fake! You phony little fake! You fake!

[*Overcome, he turns quickly and weeping fully goes out with his suitcase.* WILLY *is left on the floor on his knees.*]

WILLY: I gave you an order! Biff, come back here or I'll beat you! Come back here! I'll whip you! [STANLEY *comes quickly in from the right and stands in front of* WILLY. WILLY *shouts at* STANLEY.] I gave you an order . . .
STANLEY: Hey, let's pick it up, pick it up, Mr. Loman. [*He helps* WILLY *to his feet.*] Your boys left with the chippies.[6] They said they'll see you home.

[*A* SECOND WAITER *watches some distance away.*]

WILLY: But we were supposed to have dinner together.

[*Music is heard,* WILLY'*s theme.*]

STANLEY: Can you make it?
WILLY: I'll—sure, I can make it. [*Suddenly concerned about his clothes.*] Do I—I look all right?
STANLEY: Sure, you look all right. [*He flicks a speck off* WILLY'*s lapel.*]
WILLY: Here—here's a dollar.
STANLEY: Oh, your son paid me. It's all right.
WILLY: [*Putting it in* STANLEY'*s hand.*] No, take it. You're a good boy.
STANLEY: Oh, no, you don't have to . . .
WILLY: Here—here's some more, I don't need it anymore. [*After a slight pause.*] Tell me—is there a seed store in the neighborhood?
STANLEY: Seeds? You mean like to plant?

[*As* WILLY *turns,* STANLEY *slips the money back into his jacket pocket.*]

WILLY: Yes. Carrots, peas . . .
STANLEY: Well, there's hardware stores on Sixth Avenue, but it may be too late now.
WILLY: [*Anxiously.*] Oh, I'd better hurry. I've got to get some seeds. [*He starts off to the right.*] I've got to get some seeds, right away. Nothing's planted. I don't have a thing in the ground.

[WILLY *hurries out as the light goes down.* STANLEY *moves over to the right after him, watches him off. The other* WAITER *has been staring at* WILLY.]

STANLEY: [*To the* WAITER.] Well, whatta you looking at?

[*The* WAITER *picks up the chairs and moves off right.* STANLEY *takes the table and follows him. The light fades on this area. There is a long pause, the*

6. Prostitutes, tramps.

sound of the flute coming over. The light gradually rises on the kitchen, which is empty. HAPPY *appears at the door of the house, followed by* BIFF. HAPPY *is carrying a large bunch of long-stemmed roses. He enters the kitchen, looks around for* LINDA. *Not seeing her, he turns to* BIFF, *who is just outside the house door, and makes a gesture with his hands, indicating "Not here, I guess." He looks into the living-room and freezes. Inside,* LINDA, *unseen, is seated,* WILLY's *coat on her lap. She rises ominously and quietly and moves toward* HAPPY, *who backs up into the kitchen, afraid.*]

HAPPY: Hey, what're you doing up? [LINDA *says nothing but moves toward him implacably.*] Where's Pop? [*He keeps backing to the right, and now* LINDA *is in full view in the doorway to the living-room.*] Is he sleeping?

LINDA: Where were you?

HAPPY: [*Trying to laugh it off.*] We met two girls, Mom, very fine types. Here, we brought you some flowers. [*Offering them to her.*] Put them in your room, Ma. [*She knocks them to the floor at* BIFF's *feet. He has now come inside and closed the door behind him. She stares at* BIFF, *silent.*] Now what'd you do that for? Mom, I want you to have some flowers—

LINDA: [*Cutting* HAPPY *off, violently to* BIFF.] Don't you care whether he lives or dies?

HAPPY: [*Going to the stairs.*] Come upstairs, Biff.

BIFF: [*With a flare of disgust, to* HAPPY.] Go away from me! [*To* LINDA.] What do you mean, lives or dies? Nobody's dying around here, pal.

LINDA: Get out of my sight! Get out of here!

BIFF: I wanna see the boss.

LINDA: You're not going near him!

BIFF: Where is he? [*He moves into the living-room and* LINDA *follows.*]

LINDA: [*Shouting after* BIFF.] You invite him for dinner. He looks forward to it all day—[BIFF *appears in his parents' bedroom, looks around and exits.*]—and then you desert him there. There's no stranger you'd do that to!

HAPPY: Why? He had a swell time with us. Listen, when I—[LINDA *comes back into the kitchen.*]—desert him I hope I don't outlive the day!

LINDA: Get out of here!

HAPPY: Now look, Mom . . .

LINDA: Did you have to go to women tonight? You and your lousy rotten whores!

[BIFF *re-enters the kitchen.*]

HAPPY: Mom, all we did was follow Biff around trying to cheer him up! [*To* BIFF.] Boy, what a night you gave me!

LINDA: Get out of here, both of you, and don't come back! I don't want you tormenting him anymore. Go on now, get your things together! [*To* BIFF.] You can sleep in his apartment. [*She starts to pick up the flowers and stops herself.*] Pick up this stuff, I'm not your maid anymore. Pick it up, you bum, you! [HAPPY *turns his back to her in refusal.* BIFF *slowly moves over and gets down on his knees, picking up the flowers.*] You're a pair of animals! Not one, not another living soul would have had the cruelty to walk out on that man in a restaurant!

BIFF: [*Not looking at her.*] Is that what he said?

LINDA: He didn't have to say anything. He was so humiliated he nearly limped when he came in.

HAPPY: But, Mom, he had a great time with us—

BIFF: [*Cutting him off violently.*] Shut up!

[*Without another word,* HAPPY *goes upstairs.*]

LINDA: You! You didn't even go in to see if he was all right!

BIFF: [*Still on the floor in front of* LINDA, *the flowers in his hand; with self-loathing.*] No. Didn't. Didn't do a damned thing. How do you like that, heh? Left him babbling in a toilet.

LINDA: You louse. You . . .

BIFF: Now you hit it on the nose! [*He gets up, throws the flowers in the wastebasket.*] The scum of the earth, and you're looking at him!

LINDA: Get out of here!

BIFF: I gotta talk to the boss, Mom. Where is he?

LINDA: You're not going near him. Get out of this house!

BIFF: [*With absolute assurance, determination.*] No. We're gonna have an abrupt conversation, him and me.

LINDA: You're not talking to him! [*Hammering is heard from outside the house, off right.* BIFF *turns toward the noise. Suddenly pleading.*] Will you please leave him alone?

BIFF: What's he doing out there?

LINDA: He's planting the garden!

BIFF: [*Quietly.*] Now? Oh, my God!

[BIFF *moves outside,* LINDA *following. The light dies down on them and comes up on the center of the apron as* WILLY *walks into it. He is carrying a flashlight, a hoe, and a handful of seed packets. He raps the top of the hoe sharply to fix it firmly, and then moves to the left, measuring off the distance with his foot. He holds the flashlight to look at the seed packets, reading off the instructions. He is in the blue of night.*]

WILLY: Carrots . . . quarter-inch apart. Rows . . . one-foot rows. [*He measures it off.*] One foot. [*He puts down a package and measures off.*] Beets. [*He puts down another package and measures again.*] Lettuce. [*He reads the package, puts it down.*] One foot—[*He breaks off as* BEN *appears at the right and moves slowly down to him.*] What a proposition, ts, ts. Terrific, terrific. 'Cause she's suffered, Ben, the woman has suffered. You understand me? A man can't go out the way he came in, Ben, a man has got to add up to something. You can't, you can't—[BEN *moves toward him as though to interrupt.*] You gotta consider, now. Don't answer so quick. Remember, it's a guaranteed twenty-thousand-dollar proposition. Now look, Ben, I want you to go through the ins and outs of this thing with me. I've got nobody to talk to, Ben, and the woman has suffered, you hear me?

BEN: [*Standing still, considering.*] What's the proposition?

WILLY: It's twenty thousand dollars on the barrelhead. Guaranteed, gilt-edged, you understand?

BEN: You don't want to make a fool of yourself. They might not honor the policy.

WILLY: How can they dare refuse? Didn't I work like a coolie to meet every premium on the nose? And now they don't pay off! Impossible!

BEN: It's called a cowardly thing, William.

WILLY: Why? Does it take more guts to stand here the rest of my life ringing up a zero?

BEN: [*Yielding.*] That's a point, William. [*He moves, thinking, turns.*] And twenty thousand—that *is* something one can feel with the hand, it is there.

WILLY: [*Now assured, with rising power.*] Oh, Ben, that's the whole beauty of it! I see it like a diamond, shining in the dark, hard and rough, that I can pick up and touch in my hand. Not like—like an appointment! This would not be another damned-fool appointment, Ben, and it changes all the aspects. Because he thinks I'm nothing, see, and so he spites me. But the funeral—[*Straightening up.*] Ben, that funeral will be massive! They'll come from Maine, Massachusetts, Vermont, New Hampshire! All the old-timers with the strange license plates—that boy will be thunder-struck, Ben, because he never realized—I am known! Rhode Island, New York, New Jersey—I am known, Ben, and he'll see it with his eyes once and for all. He'll see what I am, Ben! He's in for a shock, that boy!

BEN: [*Coming down to the edge of the garden.*] He'll call you a coward.

WILLY: [*Suddenly fearful.*] No, that would be terrible.

BEN: Yes. And a damned fool.

WILLY: No, no, he mustn't, I won't have that! [*He is broken and desperate.*]

BEN: He'll hate you, William.

[*The gay music of the Boys is heard.*]

WILLY: Oh, Ben, how do we get back to all the great times? Used to be so full of light, and comradeship, the sleigh-riding in winter, and the ruddiness on his cheeks. And always some kind of good news coming up, always something nice coming up ahead. And never even let me carry the valises in the house, and simonizing, simonizing that little red car! Why, why can't I give him something and not have him hate me?

BEN: Let me think about it. [*He glances at his watch.*] I still have a little time. Remarkable proposition, but you've got to be sure you're not making a fool of yourself.

[BEN *drifts off upstage and goes out of sight.* BIFF *comes down from the left.*]

WILLY: [*Suddenly conscious of* BIFF, *turns and looks up at him, then begins picking up the packages of seeds in confusion.*] Where the hell is that seed? [*Indignantly.*] You can't see nothing out here! They boxed in the whole goddam neighborhood!

BIFF: There are people all around here. Don't you realize that?

WILLY: I'm busy. Don't bother me.

BIFF: [*Taking the hoe from* WILLY.] I'm saying good-bye to you, Pop. [WILLY *looks at him, silent, unable to move.*] I'm not coming back anymore.

WILLY: You're not going to see Oliver tomorrow?

BIFF: I've got no appointment, Dad.

WILLY: He put his arm around you, and you've got no appointment?

BIFF: Pop, get this now, will you? Everytime I've left it's been a fight that sent me out of here. Today I realized something about myself and I tried to explain it to you and I—I think I'm just not smart enough to make any sense out of it for you. To hell with whose fault it is or anything like that. [*He takes* WILLY's *arm.*] Let's just wrap it up, heh? Come on in, we'll tell Mom. [*He gently tries to pull* WILLY *to left.*]

WILLY: [*Frozen, immobile, with guilt in his voice.*] No, I don't want to see her.

BIFF: Come on! [*He pulls again, and* WILLY *tries to pull away.*]

WILLY: [*Highly nervous.*] No, no, I don't want to see her.

BIFF: [*Tries to look into* WILLY*'s face, as if to find the answer there.*] Why don't you want to see her?

WILLY: [*More harshly now.*] Don't bother me, will you?

BIFF: What do you mean, you don't want to see her? You don't want them calling you yellow, do you? This isn't your fault; it's me, I'm a bum. Now come inside! [WILLY *strains to get away.*] Did you hear what I said to you?

[WILLY *pulls away and quickly goes by himself into the house.* BIFF *follows.*]

LINDA: [*To* WILLY.] Did you plant, dear?

BIFF: [*At the door, to* LINDA.] All right, we had it out. I'm going and I'm not writing anymore.

LINDA: [*Going to* WILLY *in the kitchen.*] I think that's the best way, dear. 'Cause there's no use drawing it out, you'll just never get along.

[WILLY *doesn't respond.*]

BIFF: People ask where I am and what I'm doing, you don't know, and you don't care. That way it'll be off your mind and you can start brightening up again. All right? That clears it, doesn't it? [WILLY *is silent, and* BIFF *goes to him.*] You gonna wish me luck, scout? [*He extends his hand.*] What do you say?

LINDA: Shake his hand, Willy.

WILLY: [*Turning to her, seething with hurt.*] There's no necessity to mention the pen at all, y'know.

BIFF: [*Gently.*] I've got no appointment, Dad.

WILLY: [*Erupting fiercely.*] He put his arm around . . . ?

BIFF: Dad, you're never going to see what I am, so what's the use of arguing? If I strike oil I'll send you a check. Meantime forget I'm alive.

WILLY: [*To* LINDA.] Spite, see?

BIFF: Shake hands, Dad.

WILLY: Not my hand.

BIFF: I was hoping not to go this way.

WILLY: Well, this is the way you're going. Good-bye. [BIFF *looks at him a moment, then turns sharply and goes to the stairs.* WILLY *stops him with.*] May you rot in hell if you leave this house!

BIFF: [*Turning.*] Exactly what is it that you want from me?

WILLY: I want you to know, on the train, in the mountains, in the valleys, wherever you go, that you cut down your life for spite!

BIFF: No, no.

WILLY: Spite, spite, is the word of your undoing! And when you're down and out, remember what did it. When you're rotting somewhere beside the railroad tracks, remember, and don't you dare blame it on me!

BIFF: I'm not blaming it on you!

WILLY: I won't take the rap for this, you hear?

[HAPPY *comes down the stairs and stands on the bottom step, watching.*]

BIFF: That's just what I'm telling you!

WILLY: [*Sinking into a chair at the table, with full accusation.*] You're trying to put a knife in me—don't think I don't know what you're doing!

BIFF: All right, phony! Then let's lay it on the line. [*He whips the rubber tube out of his pocket and puts it on the table.*]

HAPPY: You crazy—

LINDA: Biff!

[*She moves to grab the hose, but* BIFF *holds it down with his hand.*]

BIFF: Leave it there! Don't move it!

WILLY: [*Not looking at it.*] What is that?

BIFF: You know goddam well what that is.

WILLY: [*Caged, wanting to escape.*] I never saw that.

BIFF: You saw it. The mice didn't bring it into the cellar! What is this supposed to do, make a hero out of you? This supposed to make me sorry for you?

WILLY: Never heard of it.

BIFF: There'll be no pity for you, you hear it? No pity!

WILLY: [*To* LINDA.] You hear the spite!

BIFF: No, you're going to hear the truth—what you are and what I am!

LINDA: Stop it!

WILLY: Spite!

HAPPY: [*Coming down toward* BIFF.] You cut it now!

BIFF: [*To* HAPPY.] The man don't know who we are! The man is gonna know! [*To* WILLY.] We never told the truth for ten minutes in this house!

HAPPY: We always told the truth!

BIFF: [*Turning on him.*] You big blow, are you the assistant buyer? You're one of the two assistants to the assistant, aren't you?

HAPPY: Well, I'm practically—

BIFF: You're practically full of it! We all are! And I'm through with it. [*To* WILLY.] Now hear this, Willy, this is me.

WILLY: I know you!

BIFF: You know why I had no address for three months? I stole a suit in Kansas City and I was in jail. [*To* LINDA, *who is sobbing.*] Stop crying. I'm through with it.

[LINDA *turns away from them, her hands covering her face.*]

WILLY: I suppose that's my fault!

BIFF: I stole myself out of every good job since high school!

WILLY: And whose fault is that?

BIFF: And I never got anywhere because you blew me so full of hot air I could never stand taking orders from anybody! That's whose fault it is!

WILLY: I hear that!

LINDA: Don't, Biff!

BIFF: It's goddam time you heard that! I had to be boss big shot in two weeks, and I'm through with it!

WILLY: Then hang yourself! For spite, hang yourself!

BIFF: No! Nobody's hanging himself, Willy! I ran down eleven flights with a pen in my hand today. And suddenly I stopped, you hear me? And in the middle of that office building, do you hear this? I stopped in the middle of that building and I saw—the sky. I saw the things that I love in this world. The work and the food and time to sit and smoke. And I looked at the pen and said to myself, what the hell am I grabbing this for? Why am I trying to become what I don't want to be? What am I doing in an office, making a contemptuous, begging fool of myself, when all I want is out there, waiting for me the minute I say I know who I am! Why can't I say that, Willy? [*He tries to make* WILLY *face him, but* WILLY *pulls away and moves to the left.*]

WILLY: [*With hatred, threateningly.*] The door of your life is wide open!

BIFF: Pop! I'm a dime a dozen, and so are you!

WILLY: [*Turning on him now in an uncontrolled outburst.*] I am not a dime a dozen! I am Willy Loman, and you are Biff Loman!

[BIFF *starts for* WILLY, *but is blocked by* HAPPY. *In his fury,* BIFF *seems on the verge of attacking his father.*]

BIFF: I am not a leader of men, Willy, and neither are you. You were never anything but a hard-working drummer who landed in the ash can like all the rest of them! I'm one dollar an hour, Willy! I tried seven states and couldn't raise it. A buck an hour! Do you gather my meaning? I'm not bringing home any prizes anymore, and you're going to stop waiting for me to bring them home!

WILLY: [*Directly to* BIFF.] You vengeful, spiteful mut!

[BIFF *breaks from* HAPPY. WILLY, *in fright, starts up the stairs.* BIFF *grabs him.*]

BIFF: [*At the peak of his fury.*] Pop, I'm nothing! I'm nothing, Pop. Can't you understand that? There's no spite in it anymore. I'm just what I am, that's all.

[BIFF'*s fury has spent itself, and he breaks down, sobbing, holding on to* WILLY, *who dumbly fumbles for* BIFF'*s face.*]

WILLY: [*Astonished.*] What're you doing? What're you doing? [*To* LINDA.] Why is he crying?

BIFF: [*Crying, broken.*] Will you let me go, for Christ's sake? Will you take that phony dream and burn it before something happens? [*Struggling to contain himself, he pulls away and moves to the stairs.*] I'll go in the morning. Put him—put him to bed. [*Exhausted,* BIFF *moves up the stairs to his room.*]

WILLY: [*After a long pause, astonished, elevated.*] Isn't that—isn't that remarkable? Biff—he likes me!

LINDA: He loves you, Willy!

HAPPY: [*Deeply moved.*] Always did, Pop.

WILLY: Oh, Biff! [*Staring wildly.*] He cried! Cried to me. [*He is choking with his love, and now cries out his promise.*] That boy—that boy is going to be magnificent!

[BEN *appears in the light just outside the kitchen.*]

BEN: Yes, outstanding, with twenty thousand behind him.

LINDA: [*Sensing the racing of his mind, fearfully, carefully.*] Now come to bed, Willy. It's all settled now.

WILLY: [*Finding it difficult not to rush out of the house.*] Yes, we'll sleep. Come on. Go to sleep, Hap.

BEN: And it does take a great kind of man to crack the jungle.

[*In accents of dread,* BEN*'s idyllic music starts up.*]

HAPPY: [*His arm around* LINDA.] I'm getting married, Pop, don't forget it. I'm changing everything. I'm gonna run that department before the year is up. You'll see, Mom. [*He kisses her.*]

BEN: The jungle is dark but full of diamonds, Willy.

[WILLY *turns, moves, listening to* BEN.]

LINDA: Be good. You're both good boys, just act that way, that's all.

HAPPY: 'Night, Pop. [*He goes upstairs.*]

LINDA: [*To* WILLY.] Come, dear.

BEN: [*With greater force.*] One must go in to fetch a diamond out.

WILLY: [*To* LINDA, *as he moves slowly along the edge of the kitchen, toward the door.*] I just want to get settled down, Linda. Let me sit alone for a little.

LINDA: [*Almost uttering her fear.*] I want you upstairs.

WILLY: [*Taking her in his arms.*] In a few minutes, Linda. I couldn't sleep right now. Go on, you look awful tired. [*He kisses her.*]

BEN: Not like an appointment at all. A diamond is rough and hard to the touch.

WILLY: Go on now. I'll be right up.

LINDA: I think this is the only way, Willy.

WILLY: Sure, it's the best thing.

BEN: Best thing!

WILLY: The only way. Everything is gonna be—go on, kid, get to bed. You look so tired.

LINDA: Come right up.

WILLY: Two minutes. [LINDA *goes into the living-room, then reappears in her bedroom.* WILLY *moves just outside the kitchen door.*] Loves me. [*Wonderingly.*] Always loved me. Isn't that a remarkable thing? Ben, he'll worship me for it!

BEN: [*With promise.*] It's dark there, but full of diamonds.

WILLY: Can you imagine that magnificence with twenty thousand dollars in his pocket?

LINDA: [*Calling from her room.*] Willy! Come up!

WILLY: [*Calling into the kitchen.*] Yes! Yes. Coming! It's very smart, you realize that, don't you, sweetheart? Even Ben sees it. I gotta go, baby. 'Bye! 'Bye! [*Going over to* BEN, *almost dancing.*] Imagine? When the mail comes he'll be ahead of Bernard again!

BEN: A perfect proposition all around.

WILLY: Did you see how he cried to me? Oh, if I could kiss him, Ben!

BEN: Time, William, time!

WILLY: Oh, Ben, I always knew one way or another we were gonna make it, Biff and I!

BEN: [*Looking at his watch.*] The boat. We'll be late. [*He moves slowly off into the darkness.*]

WILLY: [*Elegiacally, turning to the house.*] Now when you kick off, boy, I want a seventy-yard boot, and get right down the field under the ball, and when you hit, hit low and hit hard, because it's important, boy. [*He swings around and faces the audience.*] There's all kinds of important people in the stands, and the first thing you know . . . [*Suddenly realizing he is alone.*] Ben! Ben, where do I . . . ? [*He makes a sudden movement of search.*] Ben, how do I . . . ?

LINDA: [*Calling.*] Willy, you coming up?

WILLY: [*Uttering a gasp of fear, whirling about as if to quiet her.*] Sh! [*He turns around as if to find his way; sounds, faces, voices, seem to be swarming in upon him and he flicks at them, crying.*] Sh! Sh! [*Suddenly music, faint and high, stops him. It rises in intensity, almost to an unbearable scream. He goes up and down on his toes, and rushes off around the house.*] Shhh!

LINDA: Willy? [*There is no answer.* LINDA *waits.* BIFF *gets up off his bed. He is still in his clothes.* HAPPY *sits up.* BIFF *stands listening.*] [*With real fear.*] Willy, answer me! Willy! [*There is the sound of a car starting and moving away at full speed.*] No!

BIFF: [*Rushing down the stairs.*] Pop!

[*As the car speeds off, the music crashes down in a frenzy of sound, which becomes the soft pulsation of a single cello string.* BIFF *slowly returns to his bedroom. He and* HAPPY *gravely don their jackets.* LINDA *slowly walks out of her room. The music has developed into a dead march. The leaves of day are appearing over everything.* CHARLEY *and* BERNARD, *somberly dressed, appear and knock on the kitchen door.* BIFF *and* HAPPY *slowly descend the stairs to the kitchen as* CHARLEY *and* BERNARD *enter. All stop a moment when* LINDA, *in clothes of mourning, bearing a little bunch of roses, comes through the draped doorway into the kitchen. She goes to* CHARLEY *and takes his arm. Now all move toward the audience, through the wall-line of the kitchen. At the limit of the apron,* LINDA *lays down the flowers, kneels, and sits back on her heels. All stare down at the grave.*]

REQUIEM[7]

CHARLEY: It's getting dark, Linda.

[LINDA *doesn't react. She stares at the grave.*]

BIFF: How about it, Mom? Better get some rest, heh? They'll be closing the gate soon.

[LINDA *makes no move. Pause.*]

HAPPY: [*Deeply angered.*] He had no right to do that. There was no necessity for it. We would've helped him.

CHARLEY: [*Grunting.*] Hmmm.

BIFF: Come along, Mom.

LINDA: Why didn't anybody come?

CHARLEY: It was a very nice funeral.

LINDA: But where are all the people he knew? Maybe they blame him.

CHARLEY: Naa. It's a rough world, Linda. They wouldn't blame him.

LINDA: I can't understand it. At this time especially. First time in thirty-five years we were just about free and clear. He only needed a little salary. He was even finished with the dentist.

CHARLEY: No man only needs a little salary.

LINDA: I can't understand it.

7. Mass for the repose of departed souls; also a musical setting for such a mass.

BIFF: There were a lot of nice days. When he'd come home from a trip; or on Sundays, making the stoop; finishing the cellar; putting on the new porch; when he built the extra bathroom; and put up the garage. You know something, Charley, there's more of him in that front stoop than in all the sales he ever made.

CHARLEY: Yeah. He was a happy man with a batch of cement.

LINDA: He was so wonderful with his hands.

BIFF: He had the wrong dreams. All, all, wrong.

HAPPY: [*Almost ready to fight* BIFF.] Don't say that!

BIFF: He never knew who he was.

CHARLEY: [*Stopping* HAPPY*'s movement and reply. To* BIFF.] Nobody dast blame this man. You don't understand: Willy was a salesman. And for a salesman, there is no rock bottom to the life. He don't put a bolt to a nut, he don't tell you the law or give you medicine. He's a man way out there in the blue, riding on a smile and a shoeshine. And when they start not smiling back—that's an earthquake. And then you get yourself a couple of spots on your hat, and you're finished. Nobody dast blame this man. A salesman is got to dream, boy. It comes with the territory.

BIFF: Charley, the man didn't know who he was.

HAPPY: [*Infuriated.*] Don't say that!

BIFF: Why don't you come with me, Happy?

HAPPY: I'm not licked that easily. I'm staying right in this city, and I'm gonna beat this racket! [*He looks at* BIFF, *his chin set.*] The Loman Brothers!

BIFF: I know who I am, kid.

HAPPY: All right, boy. I'm gonna show you and everybody else that Willy Loman did not die in vain. He had a good dream. It's the only dream you can have—to come out number-one-man. He fought it out here, and this is where I'm gonna win it for him.

BIFF: [*With a hopeless glance at* HAPPY, *bends toward his mother.*] Let's go, Mom.

LINDA: I'll be with you in a minute. Go on, Charley. [*He hesitates.*] I want to, just for a minute. I never had a chance to say good-bye. [CHARLEY *moves away, followed by* HAPPY. BIFF *remains a slight distance up and left of* LINDA. *She sits there, summoning herself. The flute begins, not far away, playing behind her speech.*] Forgive me, dear. I can't cry. I don't know what it is, but I can't cry. I don't understand it. Why did you ever do that? Help me, Willy, I can't cry. It seems to me that you're just on another trip. I keep expecting you. Willy, dear, I can't cry. Why did you do it? I search and search and I search, and I can't understand it, Willy. I made the last payment on the house today. Today, dear. And there'll be nobody home. [*A sob rises in her throat.*] We're free and clear. [*Sobbing more fully, released.*] We're free. [BIFF *comes slowly toward her.*] We're free . . . We're free . . .

[BIFF *lifts her to her feet and moves out up right with her in his arms.* LINDA *sobs quietly.* BERNARD *and* CHARLEY *come together and follow them, followed by* HAPPY. *Only the music of the flute is left on the darkening stage as over the house the hard towers of the apartment buildings rise into sharp focus.*]

CURTAIN

1949

AUTHORS ON THEIR WORK

ARTHUR MILLER (1915–2005)

From "Arthur Miller Interview" (2001)*

MILLER: [. . .] a lot of people give a lot of their lives to a company or even the government, and when they are no longer needed, when they are used up, they're tossed aside. [. . .] Willie Loman's situation is even more common now than it was then [1949]. A lot of people are eliminated earlier from the productive life in this society than they used to be.

* * *

MILLER: That play [*Death of a Salesman*] is several inventions which have been pilfered over the years by other writers. It is new in the sense that, first of all, there is very little or no waste. The play begins with its action, and there are no transitions. It is a kind of frontal attack on the conditions of this man's life, without any piddling around with techniques. The basic technique is very straightforward. It is told like a dream. In a dream, we are simply confronted with various loaded symbols, and where one is exhausted, it gives way to another. In *Salesman*, there is the use of a past in the present. It has been mistakenly called flashbacks, but there are no flashbacks in that play. It is a concurrence of a past with the present, and that's a bit different.

* * *

[INTERVIEWER]: [. . .] I heard that after you saw *Streetcar* [*Named Desire*], you rewrote the play you were working on at the time, *Inside of His Head*, and that turned into *Death of a Salesman*. What did you see in *Streetcar* that changed your vision of your own play?

MILLER: [. . .] What it did was to validate the use of language the way *Salesman* used language. [. . .] Willie Loman isn't talking street talk; Willie Loman's talk is very formed and formal, very often. [. . .] That was the decision I made: to lift him into the area where one could deal with his ideas and his feelings and make them applicable to the whole human race. I'm using slang in the play and different kinds of speech, but it is basically a formed, very aware use of the English language. Of course, Tennessee [Williams] was similarly a fundamentally formal writer, and he was not trying to write the way people speak on the street.

*"Arthur Miller Interview." Interview by William R. Ferris. *National Endowment for the Humanities*, www.neh.gov/about/awards/jefferson-lecture/arthur-miller-interview. Originally published in *Humanities Magazine*, Mar.–Apr. 2001.

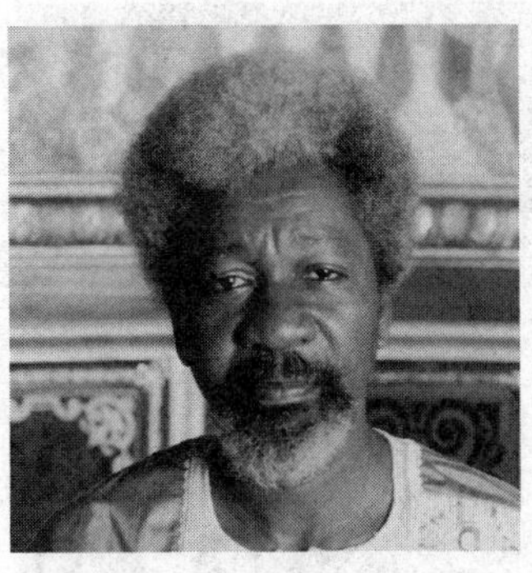

WOLE SOYINKA
(b. 1934)
Death and the King's Horseman

The first black African ever to win the Nobel Prize for Literature (1986), Akinwande Oluwole Soyinka was born in 1934 to a Yoruba family in Abeokuta, Nigeria, then a British colony. Before joining London's Royal Court Theatre as an actor and director, he earned degrees in English at the universities of Ibadan, in Nigeria, and of Leeds, in England, where he studied with renowned Shakespeareanist G. Wilson Knight. In 1960 Soyinka returned to Nigeria to study African drama and to teach. His first important play, *A Dance of the Forests* (1960), was commissioned in celebration of Nigerian independence, but like many of his subsequent works angered Nigerian authorities. Soyinka's appeal for a ceasefire during Nigeria's civil war led to his serving 22 months as a political prisoner (1967–69). His many plays, ranging from satirical comedies to politically charged tragedies, brilliantly synthesize elements of Western drama with Yoruban cultural traditions. They include *The Lion and the Jewel* (1959), *The Road* (1965), *Death and the King's Horseman* (1975), and *King Baabu* (2001). Though also the author of two novels and several volumes of poetry, Soyinka is today almost as famous for his nonfiction and his political activism as for his plays. That nonfiction includes memoirs such as *The Man Died: Prison Notes* (1972), *Aké: The Years of Childhood* (1981), and *You Must Set Forth at Dawn* (2006), as well as essays and essay collections such as *Myth, Literature, and the African World* (1976), *The Burden of Memory, the Muse of Forgiveness* (1999), and *Of Africa* (2012).

Author's Note

This play is based on events which took place in Oyo, ancient Yoruba city of Nigeria, in 1946. That year, the lives of Elesin (Olori Elesin), his son, and the Colonial District Officer intertwined with the disastrous results set out in the play. The changes I have made are in matters of detail, sequence, and of course characterisation. The action has also been set back two or three years to while the war was still on, for minor reasons of dramaturgy.

The factual account still exists in the archives of the British Colonial Administration. It has already inspired a fine play in Yoruba (Oba Wàjà) by Duro Ladipo. It has also misbegotten a film by some German television company.

The bane of themes of this genre is that they are no sooner employed creatively than they acquire the facile tag of "clash of cultures," a prejudicial label which, quite apart from its frequent misapplication, presupposes a potential equality *in every given situation* of the alien culture and the indigenous, on the actual soil of the latter. (In the area of misapplication, the overseas prize for illiteracy and mental conditioning undoubtedly goes to the blurb-writer for the

Norman Matlock (left) as Elesin and Ben Halley Jr. (middle) as the Praise-Singer in the 1979 Kennedy Center production of *Death and the King's Horseman*

American edition of my novel *Season of Anomy* who unblushingly declares that this work portrays the "clash between old values and new ways, between western methods and African traditions"!) It is thanks to this kind of perverse mentality that I find it necessary to caution the would-be producer of this play against a sadly familiar reductionist tendency, and to direct his vision instead to the far more difficult and risky task of eliciting the play's threnodic essence.

One of the more obvious alternative structures of the play would be to make the District Officer the victim of a cruel dilemma. This is not to my taste and it is not by chance that I have avoided dialogue or situation which would encourage this. No attempt should be made in production to suggest it. The Colonial Factor is an incident, a catalytic incident merely. The confrontation in the play is largely metaphysical, contained in the human vehicle which is Elesin and the universe of the Yoruba mind—the world of the living, the dead and the unborn, and the numinous passage which links all: transition. *Death and the King's Horseman* can be fully realised only through an evocation of music from the abyss of transition.

W. S.

CHARACTERS

PRAISE-SINGER
ELESIN, *Horseman of the King*
SIMON PILKINGS, *District Officer*
JANE PILKINGS, *his wif*

IYALOJA, *"Mother"*[1] *of the market*
JOSEPH, *houseboy to the Pilkingses*
BRIDE
H.R.H. THE PRINCE
SERGEANT AMUSA
THE RESIDENT[2]
AIDE-DE-CAMP
OLUNDE, *eldest son of Elesin*
DRUMMERS, WOMEN, YOUNG GIRLS, DANCERS AT THE BALL

The play should run without an interval. For rapid scene changes, one adjustable outline set is very appropriate.

Scene 1

A passage through a market in its closing stages. The stalls are being emptied, mats folded. A few WOMEN *pass through on their way home, loaded with baskets. On a cloth-stand, bolts of cloth are taken down, display pieces folded and piled on a tray.* ELESIN OBA *enters along a passage before the market, pursued by his* DRUMMERS *and* PRAISE-SINGERS. *He is a man of enormous vitality, speaks, dances, and sings with that infectious enjoyment of life which accompanies all his actions.*

PRAISE-SINGER: Elesin o! Elesin Oba! Howu![3] What tryst is this the cockerel[4] goes to keep with such haste that he must leave his tail behind?

ELESIN: [*Slows down a bit, laughing.*] A tryst where the cockerel needs no adornment.

PRAISE-SINGER: O-oh, you hear that, my companions? That's the way the world goes. Because the man approaches a brand-new bride he forgets the long-faithful mother of his children.

ELESIN: When the horse sniffs the stable does he not strain at the bridle? The market is the long-suffering home of my spirit and the women are packing up to go. That Esu[5]-harassed day slipped into the stewpot while we feasted. We ate it up with the rest of the meat. I have neglected my women.

PRAISE-SINGER: We know all that. Still it's no reason for shedding your tail on this day of all days. I know the women will cover you in damask and *alart*[6] but when the wind blows cold from behind, that's when the fowl knows his true friends.

ELESIN: Olohun-iyo![7]

PRAISE-SINGER: Are you sure there will be one like me on the other side?

ELESIN: Olohun-iyo!

PRAISE-SINGER: Far be it for me to belittle the dwellers of that place but, a man is either born to his art or he isn't. And I don't know for certain that you'll meet my father, so who is going to sing these deeds in accents that will pierce the deafness of the ancient ones. I have prepared my going—just tell me: Olohun-iyo, I need you on this journey and I shall be behind you.

ELESIN: You're like a jealous wife. Stay close to me, but only on this side. My fame, my honour are legacies to the living; stay behind and let the world sip its honey from your lips.

1. Leader of the market women.
2. Senior colonial administrator who outranks and oversees the district officer.
3. "Why have you come?" 4. Young domestic rooster.
5. Yoruba trickster god often associated with doubleness, ambivalence, and duplicity.
6. A rich, woven cloth, brightly coloured [Soyinka's glossary]. 7. Praise-singer.

PRAISE-SINGER: Your name will be like the sweet berry a child places under his tongue to sweeten the passage of food. The world will never spit it out.

ELESIN: Come then. This market is my roost. When I come among the women I am a chicken with a hundred mothers. I become a monarch whose palace is built with tenderness and beauty.

PRAISE-SINGER: They love to spoil you but beware. The hands of women also weaken the unwary.

ELESIN: This night I'll lay my head upon their lap and go to sleep. This night I'll touch feet with their feet in a dance that is no longer of this earth. But the smell of their flesh, their sweat, the smell of indigo[8] on their cloth, this is the last air I wish to breathe as I go to meet my great forebears.

PRAISE-SINGER: In their time the world was never tilted from its groove, it shall not be in yours.

ELESIN: The gods have said, No.

PRAISE-SINGER: In their time the great wars came and went, the little wars came and went; the white slavers came and went, they took away the heart of our race, they bore away the mind and muscle of our race.[9] The city fell and was rebuilt; the city fell and our people trudged through mountain and forest to found a new home[1] but—Elesin Oba, do you hear me?

ELESIN: I hear your voice, Olohun-iyo.

PRAISE-SINGER: Our world was never wrenched from its true course.

ELESIN: The gods have said, No.

PRAISE-SINGER: There is only one home to the life of a river-mussel; there is only one home to the life of a tortoise; there is only one shell to the soul of man; there is only one world to the spirit of our race. If that world leaves its course and smashes on boulders of the great void, whose world will give us shelter?

ELESIN: It did not in the time of my forebears, it shall not in mine.

PRAISE-SINGER: The cockerel must not be seen without his feathers.

ELESIN: Nor will the Not-I bird[2] be much longer without his nest.

PRAISE-SINGER: [*Stopped in his lyric stride.*] The Not-I bird, Elesin?

ELESIN: I said, The Not-I bird.

PRAISE-SINGER: All respect to our elders but, is there really such a bird?

ELESIN: What! Could it be that he failed to knock on your door?

PRAISE-SINGER: [*Smiling.*] Elesin's riddles are not merely the nut in the kernel[3] that breaks human teeth; he also buries the kernel in hot embers and dares a man's fingers to draw it out.

ELESIN: I am sure he called on you, Olohun-iyo. Did you hide in the loft and push out the servant to tell him you were out?

[ELESIN *executes a brief, half-taunting dance. The* DRUMMER *moves in and draws a rhythm out of his steps.* ELESIN *dances towards the market-place as*

8. Blue dye obtained from plants; it is associated with royalty and power.

9. Reference to the numerous wars among Yoruba kingdoms in the eighteenth and nineteenth centuries and to the transatlantic slave trade and its consequences.

1. As it sought to consolidate its authority in the sixteenth century, the Yoruba kingdom of Oyo had to build and rebuild its capital several times.

2. Bird whose chirping sounds like it is saying "Not I" in Yoruba. 3. Soft, edible part of a palm nut.

he chants the story of the Not-I bird, his voice changing dexterously to mimic his characters. He performs like a born raconteur, infecting his retinue with his humour and energy. More WOMEN *arrive during his recital, including* IYALOJA.]

Death came calling.
Who does not know his rasp of reeds?
A twilight whisper in the leaves before
The great araba[4] falls? Did you hear it?
Not I! swears the farmer. He snaps
His fingers round his head, abandons
A hard-worn harvest and begins
A rapid dialogue with his legs.
"Not I," shouts the fearless hunter, "but—
It's getting dark, and this night-lamp
Has leaked out all its oil. I think
It's best to go home and resume my hunt
Another day." But now he pauses, suddenly
Lets out a wail: "Oh foolish mouth, calling
Down a curse on your own head! Your lamp
Has leaked out all its oil, has it?"
Forwards or backwards now he dare not move.
To search for leaves and make *etutu*[5]
On that spot? Or race home to the safety
Of his hearth? Ten market-days have passed
My friends, and still he's rooted there
Rigid as the plinth of Orayan.[6]
The mouth of the courtesan barely
Opened wide enough to take a ha'penny *robo*[7]
When she wailed: "Not I." All dressed she was
To call upon my friend the Chief Tax Officer.
But now she sends her go-between instead:
"Tell him I'm ill: my period has come suddenly
But not—I hope—my time."

Why is the pupil crying?
His hapless head was made to taste
The knuckles of my friend the Mallam.[8]
"If you were then reciting the Koran
Would you have ears for idle noises
Darkening the trees, you child of ill omen?"
He shuts down school before its time
Runs home and rings himself with amulets.

4. Silk cotton tree or kapok. 5. Placatory rites or medicine [Soyinka's glossary].

6. Tall plinth or landmark in Ile-Ife, considered to be the ancestral home of the Yoruba. Orayan was one of the children of Oduduwa, the founding father of the Yoruba people.

7. Delicacy made from crushed melon seeds, fried in tiny balls [Soyinka's glossary].

8. Muslim teacher.

And take my good kinsman, Ifawomi.
His hands were like a carver's, strong
And true. I saw them
Tremble like wet wings of a fowl
One day he cast his time-smoothed *opele*[9]
Across the divination board. And all because
The suppliant looked him in the eye and asked,
"Did you hear that whisper in the leaves?"
"Not I," was his reply; "perhaps I'm growing deaf—
Good-day." And Ifa spoke no more that day
The priest locked fast his doors,
Sealed up his leaking roof—but wait!
This sudden care was not for Fawomi[1]
But for Osanyin,[2] courier-bird of Ifa's
Heart of wisdom. I did not know a kite
Was hovering in the sky
And Ifa now a twittering chicken in
The brood of Fawomi the Mother Hen.

Ah, but I must not forget my evening
Courier from the abundant palm, whose groan
Became Not I, as he constipated down
A wayside bush. He wonders if Elegbara[3]
Has tricked his buttocks to discharge
Against a sacred grove. Hear him
Mutter spells to ward off penalties
For an abomination he did not intend.
If any here
Stumbles on a gourd of wine, fermenting
Near the road, and nearby hears a stream
Of spells issuing from a crouching form,
Brother to a *sigidi*,[4] bring home my wine,
Tell my tapper[5] I have ejected
Fear from home and farm. Assure him,
All is well.

PRAISE-SINGER: In your time we do not doubt the peace of farmstead and home, the peace of road and hearth, we do not doubt the peace of the forest.

ELESIN: There was fear in the forest too.
Not I was lately heard even in the lair
Of beasts. The hyena cackled loud: Not I,

9. String of beads used in Ifa divination [Soyinka's glossary].
1. Contraction of "Ifawomi," meaning "Ifa watches over me." Ifa is the Yoruba god of divination.
2. Patron deity of diviners and medicine men in Yoruba culture.
3. Another name for Esu, the trickster god.
4. Squat, carved figure, endowed with the powers of an incubus [Soyinka's glossary]. An incubus is an imaginary evil spirit that descends on sleeping people.
5. Person whose profession is to tap palm trees for their sap, which is fermented into a wine.

The civet twitched his fiery tail and glared:
Not I. Not-I became the answering-name
Of the restless bird, that little one
Whom Death found nesting in the leaves
When whisper of his coming ran
Before him on the wind. Not-I
Has long abandoned home. This same dawn
I heard him twitter in the gods' abode.
Ah, companions of this living world
What a thing this is, that even those
We call immortal
Should fear to die.

IYALOJA: But you, husband of multitudes?

ELESIN: I, when that Not-I bird perched
Upon my roof, bade him seek his nest again,
Safe, without care or fear. I unrolled
My welcome mat for him to see. Not-I
Flew happily away, you'll hear his voice
No more in this lifetime—You all know
What I am.

PRAISE-SINGER: That rock which turns its open lodes
Into the path of lightning. A gay
Thoroughbred whose stride disdains
To falter though an adder reared
Suddenly in his path.

ELESIN: My rein is loosened.
I am master of my Fate. When the hour comes
Watch me dance along the narrowing path
Glazed by the soles of my great precursors.
My soul is eager. I shall not turn aside.

WOMEN: You will not delay?

ELESIN: Where the storm pleases, and when, it directs
The giants of the forest. When friendship summons
Is when the true comrade goes.

WOMEN: Nothing will hold you back?

ELESIN: Nothing. What! Has no one told you yet?
I go to keep my friend and master company.
Who says the mouth does not believe in
"No, I have chewed all that before?" I say I have.
The world is not a constant honey-pot.
Where I found little I made do with little.
Where there was plenty I gorged myself.
My master's hands and mine have always
Dipped together and, home or sacred feast,
The bowl was beaten bronze, the meats
So succulent our teeth accused us of neglect.
We shared the choicest of the season's

Harvest of yams. How my friend would read
Desire in my eyes before I knew the cause—
However rare, however precious, it was mine.

WOMEN: The town, the very land was yours.

ELESIN: The world was mine. Our joint hands
Raised houseposts of trust that withstood
The siege of envy and the termites of time.
But the twilight hour brings bats and rodents—
Shall I yield them cause to foul the rafters?

PRAISE-SINGER: Elesin Oba! Are you not that man who
Looked out of doors that stormy day
The god of luck[6] limped by, drenched
To the very lice that held
His rags together? You took pity upon
His sores and wished him fortune.
Fortune was footloose this dawn, he replied,
Till you trapped him in a heartfelt wish
That now returns to you. Elesin Oba!
I say you are that man who
Chanced upon the calabash[7] of honour
You thought it was palm wine and
Drained its contents to the final drop.

ELESIN: Life has an end. A life that will outlive
Fame and friendship begs another name.
What elder takes his tongue to his plate,
Licks it clean of every crumb? He will encounter
Silence when he calls on children to fulfill
The smallest errand! Life is honour.
It ends when honour ends.

WOMEN: We know you for a man of honour.

ELESIN: Stop! Enough of that!

WOMEN: [*Puzzled, they whisper among themselves, turning mostly to* IYALOJA.] What is it? Did we say something to give offence? Have we slighted him in some way?

ELESIN: Enough of that sound I say. Let me hear no more in that vein. I've heard enough.

IYALOJA: We must have said something wrong. [*Comes forward a little.*] Elesin Oba, we ask forgiveness before you speak.

ELESIN: I am bitterly offended.

IYALOJA: Our unworthiness has betrayed us. All we can do is ask your forgiveness. Correct us like a kind father.

ELESIN: This day of all days . . .

6. Possibly a reference to Esu Elegba, the trickster god, who, especially in New World versions, limps because one leg is shorter than the other.

7. Cup or bowl made from half of a gourd, usually used to serve food or drink.

IYALOJA: It does not bear thinking. If we offend you now we have mortified the gods. We offend heaven itself. Father of us all, tell us where we went astray. [*She kneels, the other women follow.*]

ELESIN: Are you not ashamed? Even a tear-veiled
Eye preserves its function of sight.
Because my mind was raised to horizons
Even the boldest man lowers his gaze
In thinking of, must my body here
Be taken for a vagrant's?

IYALOJA: Horseman of the King, I am more baffled than ever.

PRAISE-SINGER: The strictest father unbends his brow when the child is penitent, Elesin. When time is short, we do not spend it prolonging the riddle. Their shoulders are bowed with the weight of fear lest they have marred your day beyond repair. Speak now in plain words and let us pursue the ailment to the home of remedies.

ELESIN: Words are cheap. "We know you for
A man of honour." Well tell me, is this how
A man of honour should be seen?
Are these not the same clothes in which
I came among you a full half-hour ago?

[*He roars with laughter and the* WOMEN, *relieved, rise and rush into stalls to fetch rich cloths.*]

WOMEN: The gods are kind. A fault soon remedied is soon forgiven. Elesin Oba, even as we match our words with deed, let your heart forgive us completely.

ELESIN: You who are breath and giver of my being
How shall I dare refuse you forgiveness
Even if the offence were real.

IYALOJA: [*Dancing round him. Sings.*]
He forgives us. He forgives us.
What a fearful thing it is when
The voyager sets forth
But a curse remains behind.

WOMEN: For a while we truly feared
Our hands had wrenched the world adrift
In emptiness.

IYALOJA: Richly, richly, robe him richly
The cloth of honour is *alari*
Sanyan[8] is the band of friendship
Boa-skin[9] makes slippers of esteem.

WOMEN: For a while we truly feared
Our hands had wrenched the world adrift
In emptiness.

PRAISE-SINGER: He who must, must voyage forth

8. A richly valued woven cloth [Soyinka's glossary]. 9. Skin from a boa constrictor.

The world will not roll backwards.
It is he who must, with one
Great gesture overtake the world.

WOMEN: For a while we truly feared
Our hands had wrenched the world
In emptiness.

PRAISE-SINGER: The gourd you bear is not for shirking.
The gourd is not for setting down
At the first crossroad or wayside grove.
Only one river may know its contents.

WOMEN: We shall all meet at the great market.[1]
We shall all meet at the great market
He who goes early takes the best bargains
But we shall meet, and resume our banter.

[ELESIN *stands resplendent in rich clothes, cap, shawl, etc. His sash is of a bright red alari cloth. The* WOMEN *dance round him. Suddenly, his attention is caught by an object off-stage.*]

ELESIN: The world I know is good.

WOMEN: We know you'll leave it so.

ELESIN: The world I know is the bounty
Of hives after bees have swarmed.
No goodness teems with such open hands
Even in the dreams of deities.

WOMEN: And we know you'll leave it so.

ELESIN: I was born to keep it so. A hive
Is never known to wander. An anthill
Does not desert its roots. We cannot see
The still great womb of the world—
No man beholds his mother's womb—
Yet who denies it's there? Coiled
To the navel of the world is that
Endless cord that links us all
To the great origin. If I lose my way
The trailing cord will bring me to the roots.

WOMEN: The world is in your hands.

[*The earlier distraction, a beautiful* YOUNG GIRL, *comes along the passage through which* ELESIN *first made his entry.*]

ELESIN: I embrace it. And let me tell you, women—
I like this farewell that the world designed,
Unless my eyes deceive me, unless
We are already parted, the world and I,
And all that breeds desire is lodged
Among our tireless ancestors. Tell me, friends,
Am I still earthed in that beloved market

1. That is, in the afterlife.

Of my youth? Or could it be my will
Has outleapt the conscious act and I have come
Among the great departed?

PRAISE-SINGER: Elesin-Oba, why do your eyes roll like a bush rat who sees his fate like his father's spirit, mirrored in the eye of a snake? And all these questions! You're standing on the same earth you've always stood upon. This voice you hear is mine, Oluhun-iyo, not that of an acolyte in heaven.

ELESIN: How can that be? In all my life
As Horseman of the King, the juiciest
Fruit on every tree was mine. I saw,
I touched, I wooed, rarely was the answer No.
The honour of my place, the veneration I
Received in the eye of man or woman
Prospered my suit and
Played havoc with my sleeping hours.
And they tell me my eyes were a hawk
In perpetual hunger. Split an iroko[2] tree
In two, hide a woman's beauty in its heartwood
And seal it up again—Elesin, journeying by,
Would make his camp beside that tree
Of all the shades in the forest.

PRAISE-SINGER: Who would deny your reputation, snake-on-the-loose in dark passages of the market! Bed-bug who wages war on the mat and receives the thanks of the vanquished! When caught with his bride's own sister he protested—but I was only prostrating myself to her as becomes a grateful in-law. Hunter who carries his powder-horn[3] on the hips and fires crouching or standing! Warrior who never makes that excuse of the whining coward—but how can I go to battle without my trousers?—trouserless or shirtless it's all one to him. Oka[4]-rearing-from-a-camouflage-of-leaves, before he strikes the victim is already prone! Once they told him, Howu, a stallion does not feed on the grass beneath him: he replied, true, but surely he can roll on it!

WOMEN: Ba-a-a-ba O!

PRAISE-SINGER: Ah, but listen yet. You know there is the leaf-nibbling grub and there is the cola-chewing beetle; the leaf-nibbling grub lives on the leaf, the cola-chewing beetle lives in the colanut.[5] Don't we know what our man feeds on when we find him cocooned in a woman's wrapper?

ELESIN: Enough, enough, you all have cause
To know me well. But, if you say this earth
Is still the same as gave birth to those songs,
Tell me who was that goddess through whose lips
I saw the ivory pebbles of Oya's[6] riverbed.
Iyaloja, who is she? I saw her enter

2. An African teak, a large tree believed, in Yoruba folklore, to be inhabited by a roguish fairy or spirit. The heartwood of the iroko tree is multi-colored.
3. Yoruba hunters carry their gunpowder in a horn. 4. Python.
5. Seed of the cola (kola) nut tree valued by long-distance drivers for its caffeine, but also used as a ritual symbol of welcome. 6. Oya is the goddess of the Niger River and patron of fishermen and sailors.

Your stall; all your daughters I know well.
No, not even Ogun[7]-of-the-farm toiling.
Dawn till dusk on his tuber patch
Not even Ogun with the finest hoe he ever
Forged at the anvil could have shaped
That rise of buttocks, not though he had
The richest earth between his fingers.
Her wrapper was no disguise
For thighs whose ripples shamed the river's
Coils around the hills of Ilesi.[8] Her eyes
Were new-laid eggs glowing in the dark.
Her skin . . .

IYALOJA: Elesin Oba . . .

ELESIN: What! Where do you all say I am?

IYALOJA: Still among the living.

ELESIN: And that radiance which so suddenly
Lit up this market I could boast
I knew so well?

IYALOJA: Has one step already in her husband's home. She is betrothed.

ELESIN: [*Irritated.*] Why do you tell me that?

[IYALOJA *falls silent. The* WOMEN *shuffle uneasily.*]

IYALOJA: Not because we dare give you offence, Elesin. Today is your day and the whole world is yours. Still, even those who leave town to make a new dwelling elsewhere like to be remembered by what they leave behind.

ELESIN: Who does not seek to be remembered?
Memory is Master of Death, the chink
In his armour of conceit. I shall leave
That which makes my going the sheerest
Dream of an afternoon. Should voyagers
Not travel light? Let the considerate traveller
Shed, of his excessive load, all
That may benefit the living.

WOMEN: [*Relieved.*] Ah Elesin Oba, we knew you for a man of honour.

ELESIN: Then honour me. I deserve a bed of honour to lie upon.

IYALOJA: The best is yours. We know you for a man of honour. You are not one who eats and leaves nothing on his plate for children. Did you not say it yourself? Not one who blights the happiness of others for a moment's pleasure.

ELESIN: Who speaks of pleasure? O women, listen!
Pleasure palls. Our acts should have meaning.
The sap of the plantain[9] never dries.
You have seen the young shoot swelling

7. God of iron and war, of hunters, soldiers, and blacksmiths; also considered the patron of artists.
8. District and town in Oyo, western Nigeria.
9. Variety of banana, a popular staple of the tropical regions of Africa.

Even as the parent stalk begins to wither.
Women, let my going be likened to
The twilight hour of the plantain.

WOMEN: What does he mean, Iyaloja? This language is the language of our elders, we do not fully grasp it.

IYALOJA: I dare not understand you yet, Elesin.

ELESIN: All you who stand before the spirit that dares
The opening of the last door of passage,
Dare to rid my going of regrets! My wish
Transcends the blotting out of thought
In one mere moment's tremor of the senses.
Do me credit. And do me honour.
I am girded for the route beyond
Burdens of waste and longing.
Then let me travel light. Let
Seed that will not serve the stomach
On the way remain behind. Let it take root
In the earth of my choice, in this earth
I leave behind.

IYALOJA: [*Turns to* WOMEN.] The voice I hear is already touched by the waiting fingers of our departed. I dare not refuse.

WOMAN: But Iyaloja . . .

IYALOJA: The matter is no longer in our hands.

WOMAN: But she is betrothed to your own son. Tell him.

IYALOJA: My son's wish is mine. I did the asking for him, the loss can be remedied. But who will remedy the blight of closed hands on the day when all should be openness and light? Tell him, you say! You wish that I burden him with knowledge that will sour his wish and lay regrets on the last moments of his mind. You pray to him who is your intercessor to the world—don't set this world adrift in your own time; would you rather it was my hand whose sacrilege wrenched it loose?

WOMAN: Not many men will brave the curse of a dispossessed husband.

IYALOJA: Only the curses of the departed are to be feared. The claims of one whose foot is on the threshold of their abode surpasses even the claims of blood. It is impiety even to place hindrances in their ways.

ELESIN: What do my mothers say? Shall I step
Burdened into the unknown?

IYALOJA: Not we, but the very earth says No. The sap in the plantain does not dry. Let grain that will not feed the voyager at his passage drop here and take root as he steps beyond this earth and us. Oh you who fill the home from hearth to threshold with the voices of children, you who now bestride the hidden gulf and pause to draw the right foot across and into the resting-home of the great forebears, it is good that your loins be drained into the earth we know, that your last strength be ploughed back into the womb that gave you being.

PRAISE-SINGER: Iyaloja, mother of multitudes in the teeming market of the world, how your wisdom transfigures you!

IYALOJA: [*Smiling broadly, completely reconciled.*] Elesin, even at the narrow end of the passage I know you will look back and sigh a last regret for the flesh that flashed past your spirit in flight. You always had a restless eye. Your choice has my blessing. [*To the* WOMEN.] Take the good news to our daughter and make her ready. [*Some* WOMEN *go off.*]

ELESIN: Your eyes were clouded at first.

IYALOJA: Not for long. It is those who stand at the gateway of the great change to whose cry we must pay heed. And then, think of this—it makes the mind tremble. The fruit of such a union is rare. It will be neither of this world nor of the next. Nor of the one behind us. As if the timelessness of the ancestor world and the unborn have joined spirits to wring an issue of the elusive being of passage . . . Elesin!

ELESIN: I am here. What is it?

IYALOJA: Did you hear all I said just now?

ELESIN: Yes.

IYALOJA: The living must eat and drink. When the moment comes, don't turn the food to rodents' droppings in their mouth. Don't let them taste the ashes of the world when they step out at dawn to breathe the morning dew.

ELESIN: This doubt is unworthy of you, Iyaloja.

IYALOJA: Eating the awusa[1] nut is not so difficult as drinking water afterwards.

ELESIN: The waters of the bitter stream are honey to a man
Whose tongue has savoured all.

IYALOJA: No one knows when the ants desert their home; they leave the mound intact. The swallow is never seen to peck holes in its nest when it is time to move with the season. There are always throngs of humanity behind the leave-taker. The rain should not come through the roof for them, the wind must not blow through the walls at night.

ELESIN: I refuse to take offence.

IYALOJA: You wish to travel light. Well, the earth is yours. But be sure the seed you leave in it attracts no curse.

ELESIN: You really mistake my person, Iyaloja.

IYALOJA: I said nothing. Now we must go prepare your bridal chamber. Then these same hands will lay your shrouds.

ELESIN: [*Exasperated.*] Must you be so blunt? [*Recovers.*] Well, weave your shrouds, but let the fingers of my bride seal my eyelids with earth and wash my body.

IYALOJA: Prepare yourself, Elesin.

[*She gets up to leave. At that moment the* WOMEN *return, leading the* BRIDE. ELESIN'*s face glows with pleasure. He flicks the sleeves of his agbada*[2] *with renewed confidence and steps forward to meet the group. As the girl kneels before* IYALOJA, *lights fade out on the scene.*]

Scene 2

The verandah of the District Officer's bungalow. A tango is playing from an old hand-cranked gramophone and, glimpsed through the wide windows and doors which

1. A climbing plant.
2. Large, flowing robe usually worn by men and often embroidered at the neck and chest.

open onto the forestage verandah are the shapes of SIMON PILKINGS *and his wife*, JANE, *tangoing in and out of shadows in the living-room. They are wearing what is immediately apparent as some form of fancy-dress.*[3] *The dance goes on for some moments and then the figure of a* "NATIVE ADMINISTRATION" POLICEMAN[4] *emerges and climbs up the steps onto the verandah. He peeps through and observes the dancing couple, reacting with what is obviously a long-standing bewilderment. He stiffens suddenly, his expression changes to one of disbelief and horror. In his excitement he upsets a flowerpot and attracts the attention of the couple. They stop dancing.*

PILKINGS: Is there anyone out there?

JANE: I'll turn off the gramophone.

PILKINGS: [*Approaching the verandah.*] I'm sure I heard something fall over. [*The* CONSTABLE *retreats slowly, open-mouthed as* PILKINGS *approaches the verandah.*] Oh, it's you, Amusa. Why didn't you just knock instead of knocking things over?

AMUSA: [*Stammers badly and points a shaky finger at his dress.*] Mista Pirinkin . . . Mista Pirinkin . . .

PILKINGS: What is the matter with you?

JANE: [*Emerging.*] Who is it dear? Oh, Amusa . . .

PILKINGS: Yes, it's Amusa, and acting most strangely.

AMUSA: [*His attention now transferred to* MRS PILKINGS.] Mammadam . . . you too!

PILKINGS: What the hell is the matter with you, man!

JANE: Your costume, darling. Our fancy dress.

PILKINGS: Oh hell, I'd forgotten all about that. [*Lifts the face mask over his head showing his face. His wife follows suit.*]

JANE: I think you've shocked his big pagan heart, bless him.

PILKINGS: Nonsense, he's a Moslem. Come on, Amusa, you don't believe in all this nonsense, do you? I thought you were a good Moslem.

AMUSA: Mista Pirinkin, I beg you sir, what you think you do with that dress? It belong to dead cult, not for human being.

PILKINGS: Oh Amusa, what a let-down you are. I swear by you at the club you know—thank God for Amusa, he doesn't believe in any mumbo-jumbo. And now look at you!

AMUSA: Mista Pirinkin, I beg you, take it off. Is not good for man like you to touch that cloth.

PILKINGS: Well, I've got it on. And what's more, Jane and I have bet on it we're taking first prize at the ball. Now, if you can just pull yourself together and tell me what you wanted to see me about . . .

AMUSA: Sir, I cannot talk this matter to you in that dress. I no fit.

PILKINGS: What's that rubbish again?

JANE: He is dead earnest too, Simon. I think you'll have to handle this delicately.

PILKINGS: Delicately my . . . ! Look here, Amusa, I think this little joke has gone far enough, hm? Let's have some sense. You seem to forget that you are a

3. Costume, usually representing some historical or fictitious character.

4. African policeman belonging to a unit charged with the policing of Africans and considered inferior to the regular police.

police officer in the service of His Majesty's Government. I order you to report your business at once or face disciplinary action.

AMUSA: Sir, it is a matter of death. How can man talk against death to person in uniform of death? Is like talking against government to person in uniform of police. Please sir, I go and come back.

PILKINGS: [*Roars.*] Now! [AMUSA *switches his gaze to the ceiling suddenly, remains mute.*]

JANE: Oh Amusa, what is there to be scared of in the costume? You saw it confiscated last month from those *egungun*[5] men who were creating trouble in town. You helped arrest the cult leaders yourself—if the juju[6] didn't harm you at the time how could it possibly harm you now? And merely by looking at it?

AMUSA: [*Without looking down.*] Madam, I arrest the ringleaders who make trouble but me I no touch *egungun*. That *egungun* itself, I no touch. And I no abuse 'am. I arrest ringleader but I treat *egungun* with respect.

PILKINGS: It's hopeless. We'll merely end up missing the best part of the ball. When they get this way there is nothing you can do. It's simply hammering against a brick wall. Write your report or whatever it is on that pad, Amusa, and take yourself out of here. Come on, Jane. We only upset his delicate sensibilities by remaining here.

[AMUSA *waits for them to leave, then writes in the notebook, somewhat laboriously. Drumming from the direction of the town wells up.* AMUSA *listens, makes a movement as if he wants to recall* PILKINGS *but changes his mind. Completes his note and goes. A few moments later* PILKINGS *emerges, picks up the pad and reads.*]

PILKINGS: Jane!

JANE: [*From the bedroom.*] Coming, darling. Nearly ready.

PILKINGS: Never mind being ready, just listen to this.

JANE: What is it?

PILKINGS: Amusa's report. Listen. "I have to report that it come to my information that one prominent chief, namely, the Elesin Oba, is to commit death tonight as a result of native custom. Because this is criminal offence I await further instruction at charge office. Sergeant Amusa."

[JANE *comes out onto the verandah while he is reading.*]

JANE: Did I hear you say commit death?

PILKINGS: Obviously he means murder.

JANE: You mean a ritual murder?

PILKINGS: Must be. You think you've stamped it all out but it's always lurking under the surface somewhere.

JANE: Oh. Does it mean we are not getting to the ball at all?

PILKINGS: No-o. I'll have the man arrested. Everyone remotely involved. In any case there may be nothing to it. Just rumours.

5. Ancestral masquerade [Soyinka's glossary]. The masked figures in the masquerade are considered the reincarnated spirits of ancestors; their dress is often a long grass robe and a wooden mask representing the face or head of an animal. 6. Magic, usually attributed to a fetish.

JANE: Really? I thought you found Amusa's rumours generally reliable.

PILKINGS: That's true enough. But who knows what may have been giving him the scare lately. Look at his conduct tonight.

JANE: [*Laughing.*] You have to admit he had his own peculiar logic. [*Deepens her voice.*] How can man talk against death to person in uniform of death? [*Laughs.*] Anyway, you can't go into the police station dressed like that.

PILKINGS: I'll send Joseph with instructions. Damn it, what a confounded nuisance!

JANE: But don't you think you should talk first to the man, Simon?

PILKINGS: Do you want to go to the ball or not?

JANE: Darling, why are you getting rattled? I was only trying to be intelligent. It seems hardly fair just to lock up a man—and a chief at that—simply on the er . . . what is the legal word again?—uncorroborated word of a sergeant.

PILKINGS: Well, that's easily decided. Joseph!

JOSEPH: [*From within.*] Yes, master.

PILKINGS: You're quite right of course, I am getting rattled. Probably the effect of those bloody drums. Do you hear how they go on and on?

JANE: I wondered when you'd notice. Do you suppose it has something to do with this affair?

PILKINGS: Who knows? They always find an excuse for making a noise . . . [*Thoughtfully.*] Even so . . .

JANE: Yes Simon?

PILKINGS: It's different, Jane. I don't think I've heard this particular—sound—before. Something unsettling about it.

JANE: I thought all bush drumming sounded the same.

PILKINGS: Don't tease me now, Jane. This may be serious.

JANE: I'm sorry. [*Gets up and throws her arms around his neck. Kisses him. The* HOUSEBOY *enters, retreats and knocks.*]

PILKINGS: [*Wearily.*] Oh, come in, Joseph! I don't know where you pick up all these elephantine notions of tact. Come over here.

JOSEPH: Sir?

PILKINGS: Joseph, are you a Christian or not?

JOSEPH: Yessir.

PILKINGS: Does seeing me in this outfit bother you?

JOSEPH: No sir, it has no power.

PILKINGS: Thank God for some sanity at last. Now Joseph, answer me on the honour of a Christian—what is supposed to be going on in town tonight?

JOSEPH: Tonight, sir? You mean the chief who is going to kill himself ?

PILKINGS: What?

JANE: What do you mean, kill himself ?

PILKINGS: You do mean he is going to kill somebody, don't you?

JOSEPH: No, master. He will not kill anybody and no one will kill him. He will simply die.

JANE: But why, Joseph?

JOSEPH: It is native law and custom. The King die last month. Tonight is his burial. But before they can bury him, the Elesin must die so as to accompany him to heaven.

PILKINGS: I seem to be fated to clash more often with that man than with any of the other chiefs.

JOSEPH: He is the King's Chief Horseman.

PILKINGS: [*In a resigned way.*] I know.

JANE: Simon, what's the matter?

PILKINGS: It would have to be him!

JANE: Who is he?

PILKINGS: Don't you remember? He's that chief with whom I had a scrap some three or four years ago. I helped his son get to a medical school in England, remember? He fought tooth and nail to prevent it.

JANE: Oh, now I remember. He was that very sensitive young man. What was his name again?

PILKINGS: Olunde. Haven't replied to his last letter, come to think of it. The old pagan wanted him to stay and carry on some family tradition or the other. Honestly I couldn't understand the fuss he made. I literally had to help the boy escape from close confinement and load him onto the next boat. A most intelligent boy, really bright.

JANE: I rather thought he was much too sensitive, you know. The kind of person you feel should be a poet munching rose petals in Bloomsbury.[7]

PILKINGS: Well, he's going to make a first-class doctor. His mind is set on that. And as long as he wants my help he is welcome to it.

JANE: [*After a pause.*] Simon.

PILKINGS: Yes?

JANE: This boy, he was the eldest son, wasn't he?

PILKINGS: I'm not sure. Who could tell with that old ram?

JANE: Do you know, Joseph?

JOSEPH: Oh yes, madam. He was the eldest son. That's why Elesin cursed master good and proper. The eldest son is not supposed to travel away from the land.

JANE: [*Giggling.*] Is that true, Simon? Did he really curse you good and proper?

PILKINGS: By all accounts I should be dead by now.

JOSEPH: Oh no, master is white man. And good Christian. Black man juju can't touch master.

JANE: If he was his eldest, it means that he would be the Elesin to the next king. It's a family thing, isn't it, Joseph?

JOSEPH: Yes, madam. And if this Elesin had died before the King, his eldest son must take his place.

JANE: That would explain why the old chief was so mad you took the boy away.

PILKINGS: Well, it makes me all the more happy I did.

JANE: I wonder if he knew.

PILKINGS: Who? Oh, you mean Olunde?

JANE: Yes. Was that why he was so determined to get away? I wouldn't stay if I knew I was trapped in such a horrible custom.

PILKINGS: [*Thoughtfully.*] No, I don't think he knew. At least he gave no indication. But you couldn't really tell with him. He was rather close you know, quite unlike most of them. Didn't give much away, not even to me.

7. Area of central London next to the British Museum; it is associated with art and high culture.

JANE: Aren't they all rather close, Simon?

PILKINGS: These natives here? Good gracious. They'll open their mouths and yap with you about their family secrets before you can stop them. Only the other day . . .

JANE: But Simon, do they really give anything away? I mean, anything that really counts. This affair for instance, we didn't know they still practised that custom, did we?

PILKINGS: Ye-e-es, I suppose you're right there. Sly, devious bastards.

JOSEPH: [*Stiffly.*] Can I go now, master? I have to clean the kitchen.

PILKINGS: What? Oh, you can go. Forgot you were still there.

[JOSEPH *goes.*]

JANE: Simon, you really must watch your language. Bastard isn't just a simple swear-word in these parts, you know.

PILKINGS: Look, just when did you become a social anthropologist, that's what I'd like to know.

JANE: I'm not claiming to know anything. I just happen to have overheard quarrels among the servants. That's how I know they consider it a smear.

PILKINGS: I thought the extended family system took care of all that. Elastic family, no bastards.

JANE: [*Shrugs.*] Have it your own way.

[*Awkward silence. The drumming increases in volume.* JANE *gets up suddenly, restless.*]

That drumming, Simon, do you think it might really be connected with this ritual? It's been going on all evening.

PILKINGS: Let's ask our native guide. Joseph! Just a minute, Joseph. [JOSEPH *re-enters.*] What's the drumming about?

JOSEPH: I don't know, master.

PILKINGS: What do you mean, you don't know? It's only two years since your conversion. Don't tell me all that holy water nonsense also wiped out your tribal memory.

JOSEPH: [*Visibly shocked.*] Master!

JANE: Now you've done it.

PILKINGS: What have I done now?

JANE: Never mind. Listen, Joseph, just tell me this. Is that drumming connected with dying or anything of that nature?

JOSEPH: Madam, this is what I am trying to say: I am not sure. It sounds like the death of a great chief and then, it sounds like the wedding of a great chief. It really mix me up.

PILKINGS: Oh, get back to the kitchen. A fat lot of help you are.

JOSEPH: Yes, master. [*Goes.*]

JANE: Simon . . .

PILKINGS: Alright, alright. I'm in no mood for preaching.

JANE: It isn't my preaching you have to worry about, it's the preaching of the missionaries who preceded you here. When they make converts they really convert them. Calling holy water nonsense to our Joseph is really like insulting the Virgin Mary before a Roman Catholic. He's going to hand in his notice tomorrow, you mark my word.

PILKINGS: Now you're being ridiculous.

JANE: Am I? What are you willing to bet that tomorrow we are going to be without a steward-boy?[8] Did you see his face?

PILKINGS: I am more concerned about whether or not we will be one native chief short by tomorrow. Christ! Just listen to those drums. [*He strides up and down, undecided.*]

JANE: [*Getting up.*] I'll change and make us some supper.

PILKINGS: What's that?

JANE: Simon, it's obvious we have to miss this ball.

PILKINGS: Nonsense. It's the first bit of real fun the European club has managed to organise for over a year, I'm damned if I'm going to miss it. And it is a rather special occasion. Doesn't happen every day.

JANE: You know this business has to be stopped, Simon. And you are the only man who can do it.

PILKINGS: I don't have to stop anything. If they want to throw themselves off the top of a cliff or poison themselves for the sake of some barbaric custom what is that to me? If it were ritual murder or something like that I'd be duty-bound to do something. I can't keep an eye on all the potential suicides in this province. And as for that man—believe me, it's good riddance.

JANE: [*Laughs.*] I know you better than that, Simon. You are going to have to do something to stop it—after you've finished blustering.

PILKINGS: [*Shouts after her.*] And suppose after all it's only a wedding. I'd look a proper fool if I interrupted a chief on his honeymoon, wouldn't I? [*Resumes his angry stride, slows down.*] Ah well, who can tell what those chiefs actually do on their honeymoon anyway? [*He takes up the pad and scribbles rapidly on it.*] Joseph! Joseph! Joseph! [*Some moments later* JOSEPH *puts in a sulky appearance.*] Did you hear me call you? Why the hell didn't you answer?

JOSEPH: I didn't hear, master.

PILKINGS: You didn't hear me! How come you are here, then?

JOSEPH: [*Stubbornly.*] I didn't hear, master.

PILKINGS: [*Controls himself with an effort.*] We'll talk about it in the morning. I want you to take this note directly to Sergeant Amusa. You'll find him at the charge office.[9] Get on your bicycle and race there with it. I expect you back in twenty minutes exactly. Twenty minutes, is that clear?

JOSEPH: Yes, master. [*Going.*]

PILKINGS: Oh er . . . Joseph.

JOSEPH: Yes, master?

PILKINGS: [*Between gritted teeth.*] Er . . . forget what I said just now. The holy water is not nonsense. *I* was talking nonsense.

JOSEPH: Yes, master. [*Goes.*]

JANE: [*Pokes her head round the door.*] Have you found him?

PILKINGS: Found who?

JANE: Joseph. Weren't you shouting for him?

8. Houseboy, servant. 9. Booking office of a police station.

PILKINGS: Oh yes, he turned up finally.

JANE: You sounded desperate. What was it all about?

PILKINGS: Oh, nothing. I just wanted to apologise to him. Assure him that the holy water isn't really nonsense.

JANE: Oh? And how did he take it?

PILKINGS: Who the hell gives a damn! I had a sudden vision of our Very Reverend Macfarlane drafting another letter of complaint to the Resident about my unchristian language towards his parishioners.

JANE: Oh, I think he's given up on you by now.

PILKINGS: Don't be too sure. And anyway, I wanted to make sure Joseph didn't "lose" my note on the way. He looked sufficiently full of the holy crusade to do some such thing.

JANE: If you've finished exaggerating, come and have something to eat.

PILKINGS: No, put it all away. We can still get to the ball.

JANE: Simon . . .

PILKINGS: Get your costume back on. Nothing to worry about. I've instructed Amusa to arrest the man and lock him up.

JANE: But that station is hardly secure, Simon. He'll soon get his friends to help him escape.

PILKINGS: A-ah, that's where I have out-thought you. I'm not having him put in the station cell. Amusa will bring him right here and lock him up in my study. And he'll stay with him till we get back. No one will dare come here to incite him to anything.

JANE: How clever of you, darling. I'll get ready.

PILKINGS: Hey.

JANE: Yes, darling.

PILKINGS: I have a surprise for you. I was going to keep it until we actually got to the ball.

JANE: What is it?

PILKINGS: You know the Prince is on a tour of the colonies, don't you? Well, he docked in the capital only this morning but he is already at the Residency. He is going to grace the ball with his presence later tonight.

JANE: Simon! Not really.

PILKINGS: Yes, he is. He's been invited to give away the prizes and he has agreed. You must admit old Engleton is the best Club Secretary we ever had. Quick off the mark, that lad.

JANE: But how thrilling.

PILKINGS: The other provincials are going to be damned envious.

JANE: I wonder what he'll come as.

PILKINGS: Oh, I don't know. As a coat-of-arms perhaps. Anyway it won't be anything to touch this.

JANE: Well, that's lucky. If we are to be presented I won't have to start looking for a pair of gloves. It's all sewn on.

PILKINGS: [*Laughing.*] Quite right. Trust a woman to think of that. Come on, let's get going.

JANE: [*Rushing off.*] Won't be a second. [*Stops.*] Now I see why you've been so edgy all evening. I thought you weren't handling this affair with your usual brilliance—to begin with that is.

PILKINGS: [*His mood is much improved.*] Shut up, woman, and get your things on.
JANE: Alright, boss—coming.

[PILKINGS *suddenly begins to hum the tango to which they were dancing before. Starts to execute a few practice steps. Lights fade.*]

Scene 3

A swelling, agitated hum of women's voices rises immediately in the background. The lights come on and we see the frontage of a converted cloth stall in the market. The floor leading up to the entrance is covered in rich velvets and woven cloth. The WOMEN *come on stage, borne backwards by the determined progress of Sergeant* AMUSA *and his two* CONSTABLES, *who already have their batons out and use them as a pressure against the* WOMEN. *At the edge of the cloth-covered floor, however, the* WOMEN *take a determined stand and block all further progress of the men. They begin to tease them mercilessly.*

AMUSA: I am tell you women for last time to commot my road.[1] I am here on official business.
WOMAN: Official business, you white man's eunuch? Official business is taking place where you want to go and it's a business you wouldn't understand.
WOMAN: [*Makes a quick tug at the* CONSTABLE'*s baton.*] That doesn't fool anyone, you know. It's the one you carry under your government knickers[2] that counts. [*She bends low as if to peep under the baggy shorts. The embarrassed* CONSTABLE *quickly puts his knees together. The* WOMEN *roar.*]
WOMAN: You mean there is nothing there at all?
WOMAN: Oh, there was something. You know that handbell which the white-man uses to summon his servants . . . ?
AMUSA: [*He manages to preserve some dignity throughout.*] I hope you women know that interfering with officer in execution of his duty is criminal offence.
WOMAN: Interfere? He says we're interfering with him. You foolish man, we're telling you there's nothing to interfere with.
AMUSA: I am order you now to clear the road.
WOMAN: What road? The one your father built?
WOMAN: You are a policeman, not so? Then you know what they call trespassing in court. Or— [*Pointing to the cloth-lined steps.*]—do you think that kind of road is built for every kind of feet?
WOMAN: Go back and tell the white man who sent you to come himself.
AMUSA: If I go I will come back with reinforcement. And we will all return carrying weapons.
WOMAN: Oh, now I understand. Before they can put on those knickers the white man first cuts off their weapons.
WOMAN: What a cheek! You mean you come here to show power to women and you don't even have a weapon.
AMUSA: [*Shouting above the laughter.*] For the last time, I warn you women to clear the road.

1. "Get out of my way"; literally, "come out of my road" in pidgin English.
2. Women's underpants. The reference here is to the khaki shorts worn by colonial policemen.

WOMAN: To where?

AMUSA: To that hut. I know he dey dere.

WOMAN: Who?

AMUSA: The chief who call himself Elesin Oba.

WOMAN: You ignorant man. It is not he who calls himself Elesin Oba, it is his blood that says it. As it called out to his father before him and will to his son after him. And that is in spite of everything your white man can do.

WOMAN: Is it not the same ocean that washes this land and the white man's land? Tell your white man he can hide our son away as long as he likes. When the time comes for him, the same ocean will bring him back.

AMUSA: The government say dat kin' ting[3] must stop.

WOMAN: Who will stop it? You? Tonight our husband and father will prove himself greater than the laws of strangers.

AMUSA: I tell you nobody go prove anything tonight or anytime. Is ignorant and criminal to prove dat kin' prove.

IYALOJA: [*Entering, from the hut. She is accompanied by a group of* YOUNG GIRLS *who have been attending the* BRIDE.] What is it, Amusa? Why do you come here to disturb the happiness of others?

AMUSA: Madame Iyaloja, I glad you come. You know me, I no like trouble but duty is duty. I am here to arrest Elesin for criminal intent. Tell these women to stop obstructing me in the performance of my duty.

IYALOJA: And you? What gives you the right to obstruct our leader of men in the performance of his duty?

AMUSA: What kin' duty be dat one, Iyaloja?

IYALOJA: What kin' duty? What kin' duty does a man have to his new bride?

AMUSA: [*Bewildered, looks at the* WOMEN *and at the entrance to the hut.*] Iyaloja, is it wedding you call dis kin' ting?

IYALOJA: You have wives, haven't you? Whatever the white man has done to you he hasn't stopped you having wives. And if he has, at least he is married. If you don't know what a marriage is, go and ask him to tell you.

AMUSA: This no to wedding.

IYALOJA: And ask him at the same time what he would have done if anyone had come to disturb him on his wedding night.

AMUSA: Iyaloja, I say dis no to wedding.

IYALOJA: You want to look inside the bridal chamber? You want to see for yourself how a man cuts the virgin knot?

AMUSA: Madam . . .

WOMAN: Perhaps his wives are still waiting for him to learn.

AMUSA: Iyaloja, make you tell dese women make den no insult me again. If I hear dat kin' insult once more . . .

GIRL: [*Pushing her way through.*] You will do what?

GIRL: He's out of his mind. It's our mothers you're talking to, do you know that? Not to any illiterate villager you can bully and terrorise. How dare you intrude here anyway?

GIRL: What a cheek, what impertinence!

3. "That kind of thing" in pidgin English.

GIRL: You've treated them too gently. Now let them see what it is to tamper with the mothers of this market.
GIRL: Your betters dare not enter the market when the women say no!
GIRL: Haven't you learnt that yet, you jester in khaki and starch?
IYALOJA: Daughters . . .
GIRL: No no, Iyaloja, leave us to deal with him. He no longer knows his mother, we'll teach him.

[*With a sudden movement they snatch the batons of the two* CONSTABLES. *They begin to hem them in.*]

GIRL: What next? We have your batons? What next? What are you going to do?

[*With equally swift movements they knock off their hats.*]

GIRL: Move if you dare. We have your hats, what will you do about it? Didn't the white man teach you to take off your hats before women?
IYALOJA: It's a wedding night. It's a night of joy for us. Peace . . .
GIRL: Not for him. Who asked him here?
GIRL: Does he dare go to the Residency without an invitation?
GIRL: Not even where the servants eat the leftovers.
GIRL: [*In turn. In an "English" accent.*] Well well, it's Mister Amusa. Were you invited? [*Playacting to one another. The older* WOMEN *encourage them with their titters.*]

—Your invitation card please?
—Who are you? Have we been introduced?
—And who did you say you were?
—Sorry, I didn't quite catch your name.
—May I take your hat?
—If you insist. May I take yours? [*Exchanging the* POLICEMEN*'s hats.*]
—How very kind of you.
—Not at all. Won't you sit down?
—After you.
—Oh no.
—I insist.
—You're most gracious.
—And how do you find the place?
—The natives are alright.
—Friendly?
—Tractable.
—Not a teeny-weeny bit restless?
—Well, a teeny-weeny bit restless.
—One might even say, difficult?
—Indeed one might be tempted to say, difficult.
—But you do manage to cope?
—Yes, indeed I do. I have a rather faithful ox called Amusa.
—He's loyal?
—Absolutely.
—Lay down his life for you what?
—Without a moment's thought.

—Had one like that once. Trust him with my life.
—Mostly of course they are liars.
—Never known a native to tell the truth.
—Does it get rather close around here?
—It's mild for this time of the year.
—But the rains may still come.
—They are late this year aren't they?
—They are keeping African time.
—Ha ha ha ha
—Ha ha ha ha
—The humidity is what gets me.
—It used to be whisky.
—Ha ha ha ha
—Ha ha ha ha
—What's your handicap, old chap?
—Is there racing by golly?
—Splendid golf course, you'll like it.
—I'm beginning to like it already.
—And a European club, exclusive.
—You've kept the flag flying.
—We do our best for the old country.
—It's a pleasure to serve.
—Another whisky, old chap?
—You are indeed too too kind.
—Not at all sir. Where is that boy? [*With a sudden bellow.*] Sergeant!

AMUSA: [*Snaps to attention.*] Yessir!

[*The* WOMEN *collapse with laughter.*]

GIRL: Take your men out of here.

AMUSA: [*Realising the trick, he rages from loss of face.*] I'm give you warning . . .

GIRL: Alright then. Off with his knickers! [*They surge slowly forward.*]

IYALOJA: Daughters, please.

AMUSA: [*Squaring himself for defence.*] The first woman wey touch me . . .

IYALOJA: My children, I beg of you . . .

GIRL: Then tell him to leave this market. This is the home of our mothers. We don't want the eater of white left-overs at the feast their hands have prepared.

IYALOJA: You heard them, Amusa. You had better go.

GIRL: Now!

AMUSA: [*Commencing his retreat.*] We dey go now, but make you no say we no warn you.

GIRL: Now!

GIRL: Before we read the riot act—you should know all about that.

AMUSA: Make we go. [*They depart, more precipitately.*]

[*The* WOMEN *strike their palms across in the gesture of wonder.*]

WOMEN: Do they teach you all that at school?

WOMAN: And to think I nearly kept Apinke away from the place.

WOMAN: Did you hear them? Did you see how they mimicked the white man?

WOMAN: The voices exactly. Hey, there are wonders in this world!

IYALOJA: Well, our elders have said it: Dada may be weak, but he has a younger sibling who is truly fearless.[4]

WOMAN: The next time the white man shows his face in this market I will set Wuraola[5] on his tail.

[*A* WOMAN *bursts into song and dance of euphoria—'Tani l'awa o l'ogbeja? Kayi! A l'ogbeja. Omo Kekere l'ogbeja.'*[6] *The rest of the* WOMEN *join in, some placing the* GIRLS *on their back like infants, others dancing round them. The dance becomes general, mounting in excitement.* ELESIN *appears, in wrapper only. In his hands a white velvet cloth folded loosely as if it held some delicate object. He cries out.*]

ELESIN: Oh, you mothers of beautiful brides! [*The dancing stops. They turn and see him, and the object in his hands.* IYALOJA *approaches and gently takes the cloth from him.*] Take it. It is no mere virgin stain, but the union of life and the seeds of passage. My vital flow, the last from this flesh is intermingled with the promise of future life. All is prepared. Listen! [*A steady drum-beat from the distance.*] Yes. It is nearly time. The King's dog has been killed. The King's favourite horse is about to follow his master. My brother chiefs know their task and perform it well. [*He listens again.*]

[*The* BRIDE *emerges, stands shyly by the door. He turns to her.*]

Our marriage is not yet wholly fulfilled. When earth and passage wed, the consummation is complete only when there are grains of earth on the eyelids of passage. Stay by me till then. My faithful drummers, do me your last service. This is where I have chosen to do my leave-taking, in this heart of life, this hive which contains the swarm of the world in its small compass. This is where I have known love and laughter away from the palace. Even the richest food cloys when eaten days on end; in the market, nothing ever cloys. Listen. [*They listen to the drums.*] They have begun to seek out the heart of the King's favourite horse. Soon it will ride in its bolt of raffia[7] with the dog at its feet. Together they will ride on the shoulders of the King's grooms through the pulse centres of the town. They know it is here I shall await them. I have told them. [*His eyes appear to cloud. He passes his hand over them as if to clear his sight. He gives a faint smile.*] It promises well; just then I felt my spirit's eagerness. The kite makes for wide spaces and the wind creeps up behind its tail; can the kite say less than—thank you, the quicker the better? But wait a while my spirit. Wait. Wait for the coming of the courier of the King. Do you know, friends, the horse is born to this one destiny, to bear the burden that is man upon its back. Except for this night, this night alone when the spotless stallion will ride in triumph on the back of man. In the time of my father I witnessed the strange sight. Perhaps

4. Dada, the mythical king of Oyo and patron god of newborns, reputedly abdicated in favor of his fierce younger brother, Shango, god of thunder and lightning.

5. "Rich gold," a common name for a girl.

6. "Who says we haven't a defender? Silence! We have our defenders. Little children are our champions" [Soyinka's translation].

7. Fiber from raffia palms, used in making skirts for masqueraders.

tonight also I shall see it for the last time. If they arrive before the drums beat for me, I shall tell them to let the Alafin[8] know I follow swiftly. If they come after the drums have sounded, why then, all is well for I have gone ahead. Our spirits shall fall in step along the great passage. [*He listens to the drums. He seems again to be falling into a state of semi-hypnosis; his eyes scan the sky but it is in a kind of daze. His voice is a little breathless.*] The moon has fed, a glow from its full stomach fills the sky and air, but I cannot tell where is that gateway through which I must pass. My faithful friends, let our feet touch together this last time, lead me into the other market with sounds that cover my skin with down yet make my limbs strike earth like a thoroughbred. Dear mothers, let me dance into the passage even as I have lived beneath your roofs. [*He comes down progressively among them. They make way for him, the* DRUMMERS *playing. His dance is one of solemn, regal motions, each gesture of the body is made with a solemn finality. The* WOMEN *join him, their steps a somewhat more fluid version of his. Beneath the* PRAISE-SINGER'S *exhortations the women dirge "Alẹ lẹ lẹ, awo mi lọ"*[9]].

PRAISE-SINGER: Elesin Alafin, can you hear my voice?
ELESIN: Faintly, my friend, faintly.
PRAISE-SINGER: Elesin Alafi, can you hear my call?
ELESIN: Faintly, my king, faintly.
PRAISE-SINGER: Is your memory sound, Elesin?
Shall my voice be a blade of grass and
Tickle the armpit of the past?
ELESIN: My memory needs no prodding but
What do you wish to say to me?
PRAISE-SINGER: Only what has been spoken. Only what concerns
The dying wish of the father of all.
ELESIN: It is buried like seed-yam in my mind.
This is the season of quick rains, the harvest
Is this moment due for gathering.
PRAISE-SINGER: If you cannot come, I said, swear
You'll tell my favourite horse. I shall
Ride on through the gates alone.
ELESIN: Elesin's message will be read
Only when his loyal heart no longer beats.
PRAISE-SINGER: If you cannot come, Elesin, tell my dog.
I cannot stay the keeper too long
At the gate.
ELESIN: A dog does not outrun the hand
That feeds it meat. A horse that throws its rider
Slows down to a stop. Elesin Alafin
Trusts no beasts with messages between
A king and his companion.
PRAISE-SINGER: If you get lost my dog will track
The hidden path to me.

8. King of the Yoruba. 9. "Night has fallen, the seasoned initiate is leaving" (Yoruba).

ELESIN: The seven-way crossroads[1] confuses
Only the stranger. The Horseman of the King
Was born in the recesses of the house.
PRAISE-SINGER: I know the wickedness of men. If there is
Weight on the loose end of your sash, such weight
As no mere man can shift; if your sash is earthed
By evil minds who mean to part us at the last . . .
ELESIN: My sash is of the deep purple *alari*;
It is no tethering-rope. The elephant
Trails no tethering-rope; that king
Is not yet crowed who will peg[2] an elephant—
Not even you, my friend and King.
PRAISE-SINGER: And yet this fear will not depart from me
The darkness of this new abode is deep—
Will your human eyes suffice?
ELESIN: In a night which falls before our eyes
However deep, we do not miss our way.
PRAISE-SINGER: Shall I now not acknowledge I have stood
Where wonders met their end? The elephant deserves
Better than that we say, "I have caught
A glimpse of something." If we see the tamer
Of the forest let us say plainly, we have seen
An elephant.
ELESIN: [*His voice is drowsy.*]
I have freed myself of earth and now
It's getting dark. Strange voices guide my feet.
PRAISE-SINGER: The river is never so high that the eyes
Of a fish are covered. The night is not so dark
That the albino fails to find his way. A child
Returning homewards craves no leading by the hand.
Gracefully does the mask regain his grove at the end of the day . . .
Gracefully. Gracefully does the mask dance
Homeward at the end of the day, gracefully . . .

[ELESIN*'s trance appears to be deepening, his steps heavier.*]

IYALOJA: It is the death of war that kills the valiant,
Death of water is how the swimmer goes.
It is the death of markets that kills the trader
And death of indecision takes the idle away.
The trade of the cutlass blunts its edge
And the beautiful die the death of beauty.
It takes an Elesin to die the death of death . . .
Only Elesin . . . dies the unknowable death of death . . .
Gracefully, gracefully does the horseman regain
The stables at the end of day, gracefully . . .

1. In Yoruba cosmology, Esu Elegba, the god of confusion and doubleness, is often found at the crossroads. 2. Confine, pin down.

PRAISE-SINGER: How shall I tell what my eyes have seen? The Horseman gallops on before the courier, how shall I tell what my eyes have seen? He says a dog may be confused by new scents of beings he never dreamt of, so he must precede the dog to heaven. He says a horse may stumble on strange boulders and be lamed, so he races on before the horse to heaven. It is best, he says, to trust no messenger who may falter at the outer gate; oh how shall I tell what my ears have heard? But do you hear me still, Elesin, do you hear your faithful one?

[ELESIN *in his motions appears to feel for a direction of sound, subtly, but he only sinks deeper into his trance-dance.*]

Elesin Alafin, I no longer sense your flesh. The drums are changing now but you have gone far ahead of the world. It is not yet noon in heaven; let those who claim it is begin their own journey home. So why must you rush like an impatient bride: why do you race to desert your Olohun-iyo?

[ELESIN *is now sunk fully deep in his trance, there is no longer sign of any awareness of his surroundings.*]

Does the deep voice of *gbedu*[3] cover you then, like the passage of royal elephants? Those drums that brook no rivals, have they blocked the passage to your ears that my voice passes into wind, a mere leaf floating in the night? Is your flesh lightened, Elesin, is that lump of earth I slid between your slippers to keep you longer slowly sifting from your feet? Are the drums on the other side now tuning skin to skin with ours in *osugbo*?[4] Are there sounds there I cannot hear, do footsteps surround you which pound the earth like *gbedu*, roll like thunder round the dome of the world? Is the darkness gathering in your head, Elesin? Is there now a streak of light at the end of the passage, a light I dare not look upon? Does it reveal whose voices we often heard, whose touches we often felt, whose wisdoms come suddenly into the mind when the wisest have shaken their heads and murmured: It cannot be done? Elesin Alafin, don't think I do not know why your lips are heavy, why your limbs are drowsy as palm oil in the cold of harmattan.[5] I would call you back but when the elephant heads for the jungle, the tail is too small a handhold for the hunter that would pull him back. The sun that heads for the sea no longer heeds the prayers of the farmer. When the river begins to taste the salt of the ocean, we no longer know what deity to call on, the river-god or Olokun.[6] No arrow flies back to the string, the child does not return through the same passage that gave it birth. Elesin Oba, can you hear me at all? Your eyelids are glazed like a courtesan's, is it that you see the dark groom and master of life? And will you see my father? Will you tell him that I stayed with you to the last? Will my voice ring in your ears awhile, will you remember Olohun-iyo even if the music on the other side surpasses his mortal craft? But will they know you over there? Have they eyes to gauge your worth, have they the heart

3. A deep-timbred royal drum [Soyinka's glossary].
4. Secret 'executive' cult of the Yoruba; its meeting place [Soyinka's glossary].
5. In west Africa, a dry, parching seasonal breeze carrying dusty winds from the Sahara Desert.
6. God of the ocean, worshiped by fishermen and sailors.

to love you, will they know what thoroughbred prances towards them in caparisons[7] of honour? If they do not, Elesin, if any there cuts your yam with a small knife, or pours you wine in a small calabash, turn back and return to welcoming hands. If the world were not greater than the wishes of Olohun-iyo, I would not let you go . . .

[*He appears to break down.* ELESIN *dances on, completely in a trance. The dirge wells up louder and stronger.* ELESIN*'s dance does not lose its elasticity but his gestures become, if possible, even more weighty. Lights fade slowly on the scene.*]

Scene 4

A Masque.[8] *The front side of the stage is part of a wide corridor around the great hall of the Residency extending beyond vision into the rear and wings. It is redolent of the tawdry decadence of a far-flung but key imperial frontier. The couples in a variety of fancy-dress are ranged around the walls, gazing in the same direction. The guest-of-honour is about to make an appearance. A portion of the local police brass band with its white conductor is just visible. At last, the entrance of Royalty. The band plays "Rule Britannia," badly, beginning long before he is visible. The couples bow and curtsey as he passes by them. Both he and his companions are dressed in seventeenth-century European costume. Following behind are the* RESIDENT *and his partner similarly attired. As they gain the end of the hall where the orchestra dais begins the music comes to an end. The* PRINCE *bows to the guests. The band strikes up a Viennese waltz and the* PRINCE *formally opens the floor. Several bars later the* RESIDENT *and his companion follow suit. Others follow in appropriate pecking order. The orchestra's waltz rendition is not of the highest musical standard.*

Some time later the PRINCE *dances again into view and is settled into a corner by the* RESIDENT *who then proceeds to select couples as they dance past for introduction, sometimes threading his way through the dancers to tap the lucky couple on the shoulder. Desperate efforts from many to ensure that they are recognised in spite of, perhaps, their costume. The ritual of introductions soon takes in* PILKINGS *and his wife. The* PRINCE *is quite fascinated by their costume and they demonstrate the adaptations they have made to it, pulling down the mask to demonstrate how the* egungun *normally appears, then showing the various press-button controls they have innovated for the face flaps, the sleeves, etc. They demonstrate the dance steps and the guttural sounds made by the* egungun*, harass other dancers in the hall,* MRS. PILKINGS *playing the "restrainer"*[9] *to* PILKINGS*' manic darts. Everyone is highly entertained, the Royal Party especially who lead the applause.*

At this point a liveried footman comes in with a note on a salver and is intercepted almost absent-mindedly by the RESIDENT *who takes the note and reads it. After polite coughs he succeeds in excusing the* PILKINGS *from the* PRINCE *and takes them aside. The* PRINCE *considerately offers the* RESIDENT*'s wife his hand and dancing is resumed.*

7. Cloths spread over the saddle or harness of a horse, often gaily ornamented.
8. Formal, European-style costume party with elaborate dress and masks.
9. Person who controls the movements of the dancing mask when its movements seem excessive.

On their way out the RESIDENT *gives an order to* his AIDE-DE-CAMP.[1] *They come into the side corridor where the* RESIDENT *hands the note to* PILKINGS.

RESIDENT: As you see, it says "emergency" on the outside. I took the liberty of opening it because His Highness was obviously enjoying the entertainment. I didn't want to interrupt unless really necessary.

PILKINGS: Yes, yes of course, sir.

RESIDENT: Is it really as bad as it says? What's it all about?

PILKINGS: Some strange custom they have, sir. It seems because the King is dead some important chief has to commit suicide.

RESIDENT: The King? Isn't it the same one who died nearly a month ago?

PILKINGS: Yes, sir.

RESIDENT: Haven't they buried him yet?

PILKINGS: They take their time about these things, sir. The pre-burial ceremonies last nearly thirty days. It seems tonight is the final night.

RESIDENT: But what has it got to do with the market women? Why are they rioting? We've waived that troublesome tax,[2] haven't we?

PILKINGS: We don't quite know that they are exactly rioting yet, sir. Sergeant Amusa is sometimes prone to exaggerations.

RESIDENT: He sounds desperate enough. That comes out even in his rather quaint grammar. Where is the man, anyway? I asked my aide-de-camp to bring him here.

PILKINGS: They are probably looking in the wrong verandah. I'll fetch him myself.

RESIDENT: No no you stay here. Let your wife go and look for them. Do you mind, my dear . . . ?

JANE: Certainly not, your Excellency. [*Goes.*]

RESIDENT: You should have kept me informed, Pilkings. You realise how disastrous it would have been if things had erupted while His Highness was here.

PILKINGS: I wasn't aware of the whole business until tonight, sir.

RESIDENT: Nose to the ground, Pilkings, nose to the ground. If we all let these little things slip past us, where would the empire be, eh? Tell me that. Where would we all be?

PILKINGS: [*Low voice.*] Sleeping peacefully at home, I bet.

RESIDENT: What did you say, Pilkings?

PILKINGS: It won't happen again, sir.

RESIDENT: It mustn't, Pilkings. It mustn't. Where is that damned sergeant? I ought to get back to His Highness as quickly as possible and offer him some plausible explanation for my rather abrupt conduct. Can you think of one, Pilkings?

PILKINGS: You could tell him the truth, sir.

RESIDENT: I could? No no no, Pilkings, that would never do. What! Go and tell him there is a riot just two miles away from him? This is supposed to be a secure colony of His Majesty, Pilkings.

PILKINGS: Yes, sir.

1. Military assistant to a civilian administrator.
2. Taxes levied on market women were often the cause of riots in colonial West Africa.

RESIDENT: Ah, there they are. No, these are not our native police. Are these the ring-leaders of the riot?

PILKINGS: Sir, these are my police officers.

RESIDENT: Oh, I beg your pardon, officers. You do look a little . . . I say, isn't there something missing in their uniform? I think they used to have some rather colourful sashes. If I remember rightly I recommended them myself in my young days in the service. A bit of colour always appeals to the natives, yes, I remember putting that in my report. Well well well, where are we? Make your report man.

PILKINGS: [*Moves close to* AMUSA, *between his teeth.*] And let's have no more superstitious nonsense from you Amusa or I'll throw you in the guardroom for a month and feed you pork![3]

RESIDENT: What's that? What has pork to do with it?

PILKINGS: Sir, I was just warning him to be brief. I'm sure you are most anxious to hear his report.

RESIDENT: Yes yes yes, of course. Come on man, speak up. Hey, didn't we give them some colourful fez hats with all those wavy things, yes, pink tassels . . .

PILKINGS: Sir, I think if he was permitted to make his report we might find that he lost his hat in the riot.

RESIDENT: Ah yes, indeed. I'd better tell His Highness that. Lost his hat in the riot, ha ha. He'll probably say, Well, as long as he didn't lose his head. [*Chuckles to himself.*] Don't forget to send me a report first thing in the morning, young Pilkings.

PILKINGS: No, sir.

RESIDENT: And whatever you do, don't let things get out of hand. Keep a cool head and—nose to the ground, Pilkings. [*Wanders off in the general direction of the hall.*]

PILKINGS: Yes, sir.

AIDE-DE-CAMP: Would you be needing me, sir?

PILKINGS: No thanks, Bob. I think His Excellency's need of you is greater than ours.

AIDE-DE-CAMP: We have a detachment of soldiers from the capital, sir. They accompanied His Highness up here.

PILKINGS: I doubt if it will come to that but, thanks, I'll bear it in mind. Oh, could you send an orderly[4] with my cloak.

AIDE-DE-CAMP: Very good, sir. [*Goes.*]

PILKINGS: Now, sergeant.

AMUSA: Sir . . . [*Makes an effort, stops dead. Eyes to the ceiling.*]

PILKINGS: Oh, not again.

AMUSA: I cannot against death to dead cult. This dress get power of dead.

PILKINGS: Alright, let's go. You are relieved of all further duty, Amusa. Report to me first thing in the morning.

JANE: Shall I come, Simon?

PILKINGS: No, there's no need for that. If I can get back later I will. Otherwise get Bob to bring you home.

JANE: Be careful, Simon . . . I mean, be clever.

3. Muslims consider it a sacrilege to eat pork.
4. Soldier assigned to perform duties for a superior, like carrying orders or messages.

PILKINGS: Sure I will. You two, come with me. [*As he turns to go, the clock in the Residency begins to chime.* PILKINGS *looks at his watch then turns, horror-stricken, to stare at his wife. The same thought clearly occurs to her. He swallows hard. An orderly brings his cloak.*] It's midnight. I had no idea it was that late.

JANE: But surely . . . they don't count the hours the way we do. The moon, or something . . .

PILKINGS: I am . . . not so sure.

[*He turns and breaks into a sudden run. The two* CONSTABLES *follow, also at a run.* AMUSA, *who has kept his eyes on the ceiling throughout waits until the last of the footsteps has faded out of hearing. He salutes suddenly, but without once looking in the direction of the woman.*]

AMUSA: Goodnight, madam.

JANE: Oh. [*She hesitates.*] Amusa . . . [*He goes off without seeming to have heard.*] Poor Simon . . . [*A figure emerges from the shadows, a young black man dressed in a sober western suit. He peeps into the hall, trying to make out the figures of the dancers.*] Who is that?

OLUNDE: [*Emerging into the light.*] I didn't mean to startle you, madam. I am looking for the District Officer.

JANE: Wait a minute . . . don't I know you? Yes, you are Olunde, the young man who . . .

OLUNDE: Mrs. Pilkings! How fortunate. I came here to look for your husband.

JANE: Olunde! Let's look at you. What a fine young man you've become. Grand but solemn. Good God, when did you return? Simon never said a word. But you do look well, Olunde. Really!

OLUNDE: You are . . . well, you look quite well yourself, Mrs. Pilkings. From what little I can see of you.

JANE: Oh, this. It's caused quite a stir, I assure you, and not all of it very pleasant. You are not shocked, I hope?

OLUNDE: Why should I be? But don't you find it rather hot in there? Your skin must find it difficult to breathe.

JANE: Well, it is a little hot I must confess, but it's all in a good cause.

OLUNDE: What cause, Mrs. Pilkings?

JANE: All this. The ball. And His Highness being here in person and all that.

OLUNDE: [*Mildly.*] And that is the good cause for which you desecrate an ancestral mask?

JANE: Oh, so you are shocked after all. How disappointing.

OLUNDE: No, I am not shocked, Mrs. Pilkings. You forget that I have now spent four years among your people. I discovered that you have no respect for what you do not understand.

JANE: Oh. So you've returned with a chip on your shoulder. That's a pity, Olunde. I am sorry.

[*An uncomfortable silence follows.*]

I take it then that you did not find your stay in England altogether edifying.

OLUNDE: I don't say that. I found your people quite admirable in many ways, their conduct and courage in this war,[5] for instance.

5. World War II (1939–45).

JANE: Ah yes, the war. Here, of course, it is all rather remote. From time to time we have a black-out drill just to remind us that there is a war on. And the rare convoy passes through on its way somewhere or on manoeuvres. Mind you, there is the occasional bit of excitement like that ship that was blown up in the harbour.

OLUNDE: Here? Do you mean through enemy action?

JANE: Oh no, the war hasn't come that close. The captain did it himself. I don't quite understand it, really. Simon tried to explain. The ship had to be blown up because it had become dangerous to the other ships, even to the city itself. Hundreds of the coastal population would have died.

OLUNDE: Maybe it was loaded with ammunition and had caught fire. Or some of those lethal gases they've been experimenting on.

JANE: Something like that. The captain blew himself up with it. Deliberately. Simon said someone had to remain on board to light the fuse.

OLUNDE: It must have been a very short fuse.

JANE: [*Shrugs.*] I don't know much about it. Only that there was no other way to save lives. No time to devise anything else. The captain took the decision and carried it out.

OLUNDE: Yes . . . I quite believe it. I met men like that in England.

JANE: Oh, just look at me! Fancy welcoming you back with such morbid news. Stale too. It was at least six months ago.

OLUNDE: I don't find it morbid at all. I find it rather inspiring. It is an affirmative commentary on life.

JANE: What is?

OLUNDE: That captain's self-sacrifice.

JANE: Nonsense. Life should never be thrown deliberately away.

OLUNDE: And the innocent people round the harbour?

JANE: Oh, how does one know? The whole thing was probably exaggerated anyway.

OLUNDE: That was a risk the captain couldn't take. But please, Mrs. Pilkings, do you think you could find your husband for me? I have to talk to him.

JANE: Simon? Oh. [*As she recollects for the first time the full significance of* OLUNDE*'s presence.*] Simon is . . . there is a little problem in town. He was sent for. But . . . when did you arrive? Does Simon know you're here?

OLUNDE: [*Suddenly earnest.*] I need your help, Mrs. Pilkings. I've always found you somewhat more understanding than your husband. Please find him for me and when you do, you must help me talk to him.

JANE: I'm afraid I don't quite . . . follow you. Have you seen my husband already?

OLUNDE: I went to your house. Your houseboy told me you were here. [*He smiles.*] He even told me how I would recognise you and Mr. Pilkings.

JANE: Then you must know what my husband is trying to do for you.

OLUNDE: For me?

JANE: For you. For your people. And to think he didn't even know you were coming back! But how do you happen to be here? Only this evening we were talking about you. We thought you were still four thousand miles away.

OLUNDE: I was sent a cable.

JANE: A cable? Who did? Simon? The business of your father didn't begin till tonight.

OLUNDE: A relation sent it weeks ago, and it said nothing about my father. All it said was, Our King is dead. But I knew I had to return home at once so as to bury my father. I understood that.

JANE: Well, thank God you don't have to go through that agony. Simon is going to stop it.

OLUNDE: That's why I want to see him. He's wasting his time. And since he has been so helpful to me I don't want him to incur the enmity of our people. Especially over nothing.

JANE: [*Sits down open-mouthed.*] You . . . you Olunde!

OLUNDE: Mrs. Pilkings, I came home to bury my father. As soon as I heard the news I booked my passage home. In fact we were fortunate. We travelled in the same convoy as your Prince, so we had excellent protection.

JANE: But you don't think your father is also entitled to whatever protection is available to him?

OLUNDE: How can I make you understand? He *has* protection. No one can undertake what he does tonight without the deepest protection the mind can conceive. What can you offer him in place of his peace of mind, in place of the honour and veneration of his own people? What would you think of your Prince if he refused to accept the risk of losing his life on this voyage? This . . . showing-the-flag tour of colonial possessions.

JANE: I see. So it isn't just medicine you studied in England.

OLUNDE: Yet another error into which your people fall. You believe that everything which appears to make sense was learnt from you.

JANE: Not so fast, Olunde. You have learnt to argue, I can tell that, but I never said you made sense. However clearly you try to put it, it is still a barbaric custom. It is even worse—it's feudal! The king dies and a chieftain must be buried with him. How feudalistic can you get!

OLUNDE: [*Waves his hand towards the background. The* PRINCE *is dancing past again—to a different step—and all the guests are bowing and curtseying as he passes.*] And this? Even in the midst of a devastating war, look at that. What name would you give to that?

JANE: Therapy, British style. The preservation of sanity in the midst of chaos.

OLUNDE: Others would call it decadence. However, it doesn't really interest me. You white races know how to survive; I've seen proof of that. By all logical and natural laws this war should end with all the white races wiping out one another, wiping out their so-called civilisation for all time and reverting to a state of primitivism the like of which has so far only existed in your imagination when you thought of us. I thought all that at the beginning. Then I slowly realised that your greatest art is the art of survival. But at least have the humility to let others survive in their own way.

JANE: Through ritual suicide?

OLUNDE: Is that worse than mass suicide? Mrs. Pilkings, what do you call what those young men are sent to do by their generals in this war? Of course you have also mastered the art of calling things by names which don't remotely describe them.

JANE: You talk! You people with your long-winded, roundabout way of making conversation.

OLUNDE: Mrs. Pilkings, whatever we do, we never suggest that a thing is the opposite of what it really is. In your newsreels[6] I heard defeats, thorough, murderous defeats described as strategic victories. No wait, it wasn't just on your newsreels. Don't forget I was attached to hospitals all the time. Hordes of your wounded passed through those wards. I spoke to them. I spent long evenings by their bedsides while they spoke terrible truths of the realities of that war. I know now how history is made.

JANE: But surely, in a war of this nature, for the morale of the nation you must expect . . .

OLUNDE: That a disaster beyond human reckoning be spoken of as a triumph? No. I mean, is there no mourning in the home of the bereaved that such blasphemy is permitted?

JANE: [*After a moment's pause.*] Perhaps I can understand you now. The time we picked for you was not really one for seeing us at our best.

OLUNDE: Don't think it was just the war. Before that even started I had plenty of time to study your people. I saw nothing, finally, that gave you the right to pass judgment on other peoples and their ways. Nothing at all.

JANE: [*Hesitantly.*] Was it the . . . colour thing? I know there is some discrimination.

OLUNDE: Don't make it so simple, Mrs. Pilkings. You make it sound as if when I left, I took nothing at all with me.

JANE: Yes . . . and to tell the truth, only this evening, Simon and I agreed that we never really knew what you left with.

OLUNDE: Neither did I. But I found out over there. I am grateful to your country for that. And I will never give it up.

JANE: Olunde, please . . . promise me something. Whatever you do, don't throw away what you have started to do. You want to be a doctor. My husband and I believe you will make an excellent one, sympathetic and competent. Don't let anything make you throw away your training.

OLUNDE: [*Genuinely surprised.*] Of course not. What a strange idea. I intend to return and complete my training. Once the burial of my father is over.

JANE: Oh, please . . . !

OLUNDE: Listen! Come outside. You can't hear anything against that music.

JANE: What is it?

OLUNDE: The drums. Can you hear the changes? Listen.

[*The drums come over, still distant but more distinct. There is a change of rhythm, it rises to a crescendo and then, suddenly, it is cut off. After a silence, a new beat begins, slow and resonant.*]

There, it's all over.

JANE: You mean he's . . .

OLUNDE: Yes, Mrs. Pilkings, my father is dead. His willpower has always been enormous; I know he is dead.

JANE: [*Screams.*] How can you be so callous! So unfeeling! You announce your father's own death like a surgeon looking down on some strange . . . stranger's body! You're just a savage like all the rest.

6. Short films of news and other events shown in movie houses before the main features. This was common before the age of television, especially during World War II.

AIDE-DE-CAMP: [*Rushing out.*] Mrs. Pilkings. Mrs. Pilkings. [*She breaks down, sobbing.*] Are you all right, Mrs. Pilkings?

OLUNDE: She'll be all right. [*Turns to go.*]

AIDE-DE-CAMP: Who are you? And who the hell asked your opinion?

OLUNDE: You're quite right, nobody. [*Going.*]

AIDE-DE-CAMP: What the hell! Did you hear me ask you who you were?

OLUNDE: I have business to attend to.

AIDE-DE-CAMP: I'll give you business in a moment, you impudent nigger. Answer my question!

OLUNDE: I have a funeral to arrange. Excuse me. [*Going.*]

AIDE-DE-CAMP: I said stop! Orderly!

JANE: No, no, don't do that. I'm alright. And for heaven's sake, don't act so foolishly. He's a family friend.

AIDE-DE-CAMP: Well, he'd better learn to answer civil questions when he's asked them. These natives put a suit on and they get high opinions of themselves.

OLUNDE: Can I go now?

JANE: No no, don't go. I must talk to you. I'm sorry about what I said.

OLUNDE: It's nothing, Mrs. Pilkings. And I'm really anxious to go. I couldn't see my father before, it's forbidden for me, his heir and successor, to set eyes on him from the moment of the king's death. But now . . . I would like to touch his body while it is still warm.

JANE: You will. I promise I shan't keep you long. Only, I couldn't possibly let you go like that. Bob, please excuse us.

AIDE-DE-CAMP: If you're sure . . .

JANE: Of course I'm sure. Something happened to upset me just then, but I'm alright now. Really.

[*The* AIDE-DE-CAMP *goes, somewhat reluctantly.*]

OLUNDE: I mustn't stay long.

JANE: Please, I promise not to keep you. It's just that . . . oh, you saw yourself what happens to one in this place. The Resident's man thought he was being helpful, that's the way we all react. But I can't go in among that crowd just now and if I stay by myself somebody will come looking for me. Please, just say something for a few moments and then you can go. Just so I can recover myself.

OLUNDE: What do you want me to say?

JANE: Your calm acceptance, for instance—can you explain that? It was so unnatural. I don't understand that at all. I feel a need to understand all I can.

OLUNDE: But you explained it yourself. My medical training perhaps. I have seen death too often. And the soldiers who returned from the front, they died on our hands all the time.

JANE: No. It has to be more than that. I feel it has to do with the many things we don't really grasp about your people. At least you can explain.

OLUNDE: All these things are part of it. And anyway, my father has been dead in my mind for nearly a month. Ever since I learnt of the King's death. I've lived with my bereavement so long now that I cannot think of him alive. On that journey on the boat, I kept my mind on my duties as the one who must perform the rites over his body. I went through it all again and again in my mind as he himself had taught me. I didn't want to do anything wrong, something which might jeopardise the welfare of my people.

JANE: But he had disowned you. When you left he swore publicly you were no longer his son.

OLUNDE: I told you, he was a man of tremendous will. Sometimes that's another way of saying stubborn. But among our people, you don't disown a child just like that. Even if I had died before him I would still be buried like his eldest son. But it's time for me to go.

JANE: Thank you. I feel calmer. Don't let me keep you from your duties.

OLUNDE: Goodnight, Mrs. Pilkings.

JANE: Welcome home. [*She holds out her hand. As he takes it footsteps are heard approaching the drive. A short while later a woman's sobbing is also heard.*]

PILKINGS: [*Off.*] Keep them here till I get back. [*He strides into view, reacts at the sight of* OLUNDE *but turns to his wife.*] Thank goodness you're still here.

JANE: Simon, what happened?

PILKINGS: Later, Jane, please. Is Bob still here?

JANE: Yes, I think so. I'm sure he must be.

PILKINGS: Try and get him out here as quickly as you can. Tell him it's urgent.

JANE: Of course. Oh Simon, you remember . . .

PILKINGS: Yes yes. I can see who it is. Get Bob out here. [*She runs off.*] At first I thought I was seeing a ghost.

OLUNDE: Mr. Pilkings, I appreciate what you tried to do. I want you to believe that. I can tell you it would have been a terrible calamity if you'd succeeded.

PILKINGS: [*Opens his mouth several times, shuts it.*] You . . . said what?

OLUNDE: A calamity for us, the entire people.

PILKINGS: [*Sighs.*] I see. Hm.

OLUNDE: And now I must go. I must see him before he turns cold.

PILKINGS: Oh ah . . . em . . . but this is a shock to see you. I mean, er, thinking all this while you were in England and thanking God for that.

OLUNDE: I came on the mail boat. We travelled in the Prince's convoy.

PILKINGS: Ah yes, a-ah, hm . . . er, well . . .

OLUNDE: Goodnight. I can see you are shocked by the whole business. But you must know by now there are things you cannot understand—or help.

PILKINGS: Yes. Just a minute. There are armed policemen that way and they have instructions to let no one pass. I suggest you wait a little. I'll, er . . . give you an escort.

OLUNDE: That's very kind of you. But do you think it could be quickly arranged?

PILKINGS: Of course. In fact, yes, what I'll do is send Bob over with some men to the er . . . place. You can go with them. Here he comes now. Excuse me a minute.

AIDE-DE-CAMP: Anything wrong, sir?

PILKINGS: [*Takes him to one side.*] Listen, Bob, that cellar in the disused annexe of the Residency, you know, where the slaves were stored before being taken down to the coast. . . .

AIDE-DE-CAMP: Oh yes, we use it as a storeroom for broken furniture.

PILKINGS: But it's still got the bars on it?

AIDE-DE-CAMP: Oh yes, they are quite intact.

PILKINGS: Get the keys please. I'll explain later. And I want a strong guard over the Residency tonight.

AIDE-DE-CAMP: We have that already. The detachment from the coast . . .

PILKINGS: No, I don't want them at the gates of the Residency. I want you to deploy them at the bottom of the hill, a long way from the main hall so they can deal with any situation long before the sound carries to the house.

AIDE-DE-CAMP: Yes, of course.

PILKINGS: I don't want His Highness alarmed.

AIDE-DE-CAMP: You think the riot will spread here?

PILKINGS: It's unlikely but I don't want to take a chance. I made them believe I was going to lock the man up in my house, which was what I had planned to do in the first place. They are probably assailing it by now. I took a roundabout route here so I don't think there is any danger at all. At least not before dawn. Nobody is to leave the premises of course—the native employees I mean. They'll soon smell something is up and they can't keep their mouths shut.

AIDE-DE-CAMP: I'll give instructions at once.

PILKINGS: I'll take the prisoner down myself. Two policemen will stay with him throughout the night. Inside the cell.

AIDE-DE-CAMP: Right, sir. [*Salutes and goes off at the double.*]

PILKINGS: Jane. Bob is coming back in a moment with a detachment. Until he gets back please stay with Olunde. [*He makes an extra warning gesture with his eyes.*]

OLUNDE: Please, Mr. Pilkings . . .

PILKINGS: I hate to be stuffy, old son, but we have a crisis on our hands. It has to do with your father's affair, if you must know. And it happens also at a time when we have His Highness here. I am responsible for security so you'll simply have to do as I say. I hope that's understood. [*Marches off quickly, in the direction from which he made his first appearance.*]

OLUNDE: What's going on? All this can't be just because he failed to stop my father killing himself.

JANE: I honestly don't know. Could it have sparked off a riot?

OLUNDE: No. If he'd succeeded that would be more likely to start the riot. Perhaps there were other factors involved. Was there a chieftancy dispute?

JANE: None that I know of.

ELESIN: [*An animal bellow from off.*[7]] Leave me alone! Is it not enough that you have covered me in shame! White man, take your hand from my body!

[OLUNDE *stands frozen to the spot.* JANE, *understanding at last, tries to move him.*]

JANE: Let's go in. It's getting chilly out here.

PILKINGS: [*Off.*] Carry him.

ELESIN: Give me back the name you have taken away from me, you ghost from the land of the nameless!

PILKINGS: Carry him! I can't have a disturbance here. Quickly! stuff up his mouth.

JANE: Oh God! Let's go in. Please, Olunde. [OLUNDE *does not move.*]

ELESIN: Take your albino's hand from me, you . . .

[*Sounds of a struggle. His voice chokes as he is gagged.*]

7. The cries of animals, especially cows, were considered to be a feature of the language of *egungun* and other masked figures.

OLUNDE: [*Quietly.*] That was my father's voice.
JANE: Oh you poor orphan, what have you come home to?

[*There is a sudden explosion of rage from off-stage and powerful steps come running up the drive.*]

PILKINGS: You bloody fools, after him!

[*Immediately* ELESIN, *in handcuffs, comes pounding in the direction of* JANE *and* OLUNDE, *followed some moments afterwards by* PILKINGS *and the* CONSTABLES. ELESIN, *confronted by the seeming statue of his son, stops dead.* OLUNDE *stares above his head into the distance. The* CONSTABLES *try to grab him.* JANE *screams at them.*]

JANE: Leave him alone! Simon, tell them to leave him alone.
PILKINGS: All right, stand aside, you. [*Shrugs.*] Maybe just as well. It might help to calm him down.

[*For several moments they hold the same position.* ELESIN *moves a step forward, almost as if he's still in doubt.*]

ELESIN: Olunde? [*He moves his head, inspecting him from side to side.*] Olunde! [*He collapses slowly at* OLUNDE*'s feet.*] Oh son, don't let the sight of your father turn you blind!
OLUNDE: [*He moves for the first time since he heard his voice, brings his head slowly down to look on him.*] I have no father, eater of leftovers.

[*He walks slowly down the way his father had run. Light fades out on* ELESIN, *sobbing into the ground.*]

Scene 5

A wide iron-barred gate stretches almost the whole width of the cell in which ELESIN *is imprisoned. His wrists are encased in thick iron bracelets, chained together; he stands against the bars, looking out. Seated on the ground to one side on the outside is his recent* BRIDE, *her eyes bent perpetually to the ground. Figures of the two* GUARDS *can be seen deeper inside the cell, alert to every movement* ELESIN *makes.* PILKINGS *now in a police officer's uniform, enters noiselessly, observes him a while. Then he coughs ostentatiously and approaches. Leans against the bars near a corner, his back to* ELESIN. *He is obviously trying to fall in mood with him. Some moments' silence.*

PILKINGS: You seem fascinated by the moon.
ELESIN: [*After a pause.*] Yes, ghostly one. Your twin-brother up there engages my thoughts.
PILKINGS: It is a beautiful night.
ELESIN: Is that so?
PILKINGS: The light on the leaves, the peace of the night . . .
ELESIN: The night is not at peace, District Officer.
PILKINGS: No? I would have said it was. You know, quiet . . .
ELESIN: And does quiet mean peace for you?
PILKINGS: Well, nearly the same thing. Naturally there is a subtle difference . . .
ELESIN: The night is not at peace, ghostly one. The world is not at peace. You have shattered the peace of the world forever. There is no sleep in the world tonight.

PILKINGS: It is still a good bargain if the world should lose one night's sleep as the price of saving a man's life.

ELESIN: You did not save my life, District Officer. You destroyed it.

PILKINGS: Now come on . . .

ELESIN: And not merely my life but the lives of many. The end of the night's work is not over. Neither this year nor the next will see it. If I wished you well, I would pray that you do not stay long enough on our land to see the disaster you have brought upon us.

PILKINGS: Well, I did my duty as I saw it. I have no regrets.

ELESIN: No. The regrets of life always come later.

[*Some moments' pause.*]

You are waiting for dawn, white man. I hear you saying to yourself: Only so many hours until dawn and then the danger is over. All I must do is to keep him alive tonight. You don't quite understand it all but you know that tonight is when what ought to be must be brought about. I shall ease your mind even more, ghostly one. It is not an entire night but a moment of the night, and that moment is past. The moon was my messenger and guide. When it reached a certain gateway in the sky, it touched that moment for which my whole life has been spent in blessings. Even I do not know the gateway. I have stood here and scanned the sky for a glimpse of that door, but I cannot see it. Human eyes are useless for a search of this nature. But in the house of *osugbo*, those who keep watch through the spirit recognised the moment, they sent word to me through the voice of our sacred drums to prepare myself. I heard them and I shed all thoughts of earth. I began to follow the moon to the abode of the gods . . . servant of the white king, that was when you entered my chosen place of departure on feet of desecration.

PILKINGS: I'm sorry, but we all see our duty differently.

ELESIN: I no longer blame you. You stole from me my first-born, sent him to your country so you could turn him into something in your own image. Did you plan it all beforehand? There are moments when it seems part of a larger plan. He who must follow my footsteps is taken from me, sent across the ocean: Then, in my turn, I am stopped from fulfilling my destiny. Did you think it all out before, this plan to push our world from its course and sever the cord that links us to the great origin?

PILKINGS: You don't really believe that. Anyway, if that was my intention with your son, I appear to have failed.

ELESIN: You did not fail in the main thing, ghostly one. We know the roof covers the rafters, the cloth covers blemishes; who would have known that the white skin covered our future, preventing us from seeing the death our enemies had prepared for us? The world is set adrift and its inhabitants are lost. Around them, there is nothing but emptiness.

PILKINGS: Your son does not take so gloomy a view.

ELESIN: Are you dreaming now, white man? Were you not present at the reunion of shame? Did you not see when the world reversed itself and the father fell before his son, asking forgiveness?

PILKINGS: That was in the heat of the moment. I spoke to him and . . . if you want to know, he wishes he could cut out his tongue for uttering the words he did.

ELESIN: No. What he said must never be unsaid. The contempt of my own son rescued something of my shame at your hands. You have stopped me in my duty but I know now that I did give birth to a son. Once I mistrusted him for seeking the companionship of those my spirit knew as enemies of our race. Now I understand. One should seek to obtain the secrets of his enemies. He will avenge my shame, white one. His spirit will destroy you and yours.

PILKINGS: That kind of talk is hardly called for. If you don't want my consolation . . .

ELESIN: No, white man, I do not want your consolation.

PILKINGS: As you wish. Your son, anyway, sends his consolation. He asks your forgiveness. When I asked him not to despise you his reply was: I cannot judge him, and if I cannot judge him, I cannot despise him. He wants to come to you and say goodbye and to receive your blessing.

ELESIN: Goodbye? Is he returning to your land?

PILKINGS: Don't you think that's the most sensible thing for him to do? I advised him to leave at once, before dawn, and he agrees that is the right course of action.

ELESIN: Yes, it is best. And even if I did not think so, I have lost the father's place of honour. My voice is broken.

PILKINGS: Your son honours you. If he didn't he would not ask your blessing.

ELESIN: No. Even a thoroughbred is not without pity for the turf he strikes with his hoof. When is he coming?

PILKINGS: As soon as the town is a little quieter. I advised it.

ELESIN: Yes, white man, I am sure you advised it. You advise all our lives, although on the authority of what gods, I do not know.

PILKINGS: [*Opens his mouth to reply, then appears to change his mind. Turns to go. Hesitates and stops again.*] Before I leave you, may I ask just one thing of you?

ELESIN: I am listening.

PILKINGS: I wish to ask you to search the quiet of your heart and tell me—do you not find great contradictions in the wisdom of your own race?

ELESIN: Make yourself clear, white one.

PILKINGS: I have lived among you long enough to learn a saying or two. One came to my mind tonight when I stepped into the market and saw what was going on. You were surrounded by those who egged you on with song and praises. I thought, are these not the same people who say: "The elder grimly approaches heaven and you ask him to bear your greetings yonder; do you really think he makes the journey willingly?" After that, I did not hesitate.

[*A pause.* ELESIN *sighs. Before he can speak a sound of running feet is heard.*]

JANE: [*Off.*] Simon! Simon!

PILKINGS: What on earth . . . ! [*Runs off.*]

[ELESIN *turns to his new wife, gazes on her for some moments.*]

ELESIN: My young bride, did you hear the ghostly one? You sit and sob in your silent heart but say nothing to all this. First I blamed the white man, then I blamed my gods for deserting me. Now I feel I want to blame you for the mystery of the sapping of my will. But blame is a strange peace offering for a man to bring a world he has deeply wronged, and to its innocent dwellers.

Oh little mother, I have taken countless women in my life but you were more than a desire of the flesh. I needed you as the abyss across which my body must be drawn, I filled it with earth and dropped my seed in it at the moment of preparedness for my crossing. You were the final gift of the living to their emissary to the land of the ancestors, and perhaps your warmth and youth brought new insights of this world to me and turned my feet leaden on this side of the abyss. For I confess to you, daughter, my weakness came not merely from the abomination of the white man who came violently into my fading presence, there was also a weight of longing on my earth-held limbs. I would have shaken it off, already my foot had begun to lift, but then the white ghost entered and all was defiled.

[*Approaching voices of* PILKINGS *and his wife.*]

JANE: Oh Simon, you will let her in, won't you?

PILKINGS: I really wish you'd stop interfering.

[*They come into view.* JANE *is in a dressing-gown.* PILKINGS *is holding a note to which he refers from time to time.*]

JANE: Good gracious, I didn't initiate this. I was sleeping quietly, or trying to anyway, when the servant brought it. It's not my fault if one can't sleep undisturbed even in the Residency.

PILKINGS: He'd have done the same thing if we were sleeping at home, so don't sidetrack the issue. He knows he can get round you or he wouldn't send you the petition in the first place.

JANE: Be fair, Simon. After all, he was thinking of your own interests. He is grateful, you know—you seem to forget that. He feels he owes you something.

PILKINGS: I just wish they'd leave this man alone tonight, that's all.

JANE: Trust him, Simon. He's pledged his word it will all go peacefully.

PILKINGS: Yes, and that's the other thing. I don't like being threatened.

JANE: Threatened? [*Takes the note.*] I didn't spot any threat.

PILKINGS: It's there. Veiled, but it's there. The only way to prevent serious rioting tomorrow—what a cheek!

JANE: I don't think he's threatening you, Simon.

PILKINGS: He's picked up the idiom, alright. Wouldn't surprise me if he's been mixing with commies or anarchists over there. The phrasing sounds too good to be true. Damn! If only the Prince hadn't picked this time for his visit.

JANE: Well, even so, Simon, what have you got to lose? You don't want a riot on your hands, not with the Prince here.

PILKINGS: [*Going up to* ELESIN.] Let's see what he has to say. Chief Elesin, there is yet another person who wants to see you. As she is not a next-of-kin I don't really feel obliged to let her in. But your son sent a note with her, so it's up to you.

ELESIN: I know who that must be. So she found out your hiding-place. Well, it was not difficult. My stench of shame is so strong, it requires no hunter's dog to follow it.

PILKINGS: If you don't want to see her, just say so and I'll send her packing.

ELESIN: Why should I not want to see her? Let her come. I have no more holes in my rag of shame. All is laid bare.

PILKINGS: I'll bring her in. [*Goes off.*]

JANE: [*Hesitates, then goes to* ELESIN.] Please, try and understand. Everything my husband did was for the best.

ELESIN: [*He gives her a long strange stare, as if he is trying to understand who she is.*] You are the wife of the District Officer?

JANE: Yes. My name is Jane.

ELESIN: That is my wife sitting down there. You notice how still and silent she sits? My business is with your husband.

[PILKINGS *returns with* IYALOJA.]

PILKINGS: Here she is. Now first I want your word of honour that you will try nothing foolish.

ELESIN: Honour? White one, did you say you wanted my word of honour?

PILKINGS: I know you to be an honourable man. Give me your word of honour you will receive nothing from her.

ELESIN: But I am sure you have searched her clothing as you would never dare touch your own mother. And there are these two lizards of yours who roll their eyes even when I scratch.

PILKINGS: And I shall be sitting on that tree trunk watching even how you blink. Just the same I want your word that you will not let her pass anything to you.

ELESIN: You have my honour already. It is locked up in that desk in which you will put away your report of this night's events. Even the honour of my people you have taken already; it is tied together with those papers of treachery which make you masters in this land.

PILKINGS: Alright. I am trying to make things easy but if you must bring in politics we'll have to do it the hard way. Madam, I want you to remain along this line and move no nearer to the cell door. Guards! [*They spring to attention.*] If she moves beyond this point, blow your whistle. Come on, Jane. [*They go off.*]

IYALOJA: How boldly the lizard struts before the pigeon when it was the eagle itself he promised us he would confront.

ELESIN: I don't ask you to take pity on me, Iyaloja. You have a message for me or you would not have come. Even if it is the curses of the world, I shall listen.

IYALOJA: You made so bold with the servant of the white king who took your side against death. I must tell your brother chiefs when I return how bravely you waged war against him. Especially with words.

ELESIN: I more than deserve your scorn.

IYALOJA: [*With sudden anger.*] I warned you, if you must leave a seed behind, be sure it is not tainted with the curses of the world. Who are you to open a new life when you dared not open the door to a new existence? I say who are you to make so bold? [*The* BRIDE *sobs and* IYALOJA *notices her. Her contempt noticeably increases as she turns back to* ELESIN.] Oh, you self-vaunted stem of the plantain, how hollow it all proves. The pith is gone in the parent stem, so how will it prove with the new shoot? How will it go with that earth that bears it? Who are you to bring this abomination on us!

ELESIN: My powers deserted me. My charms, my spells, even my voice lacked strength when I made to summon the powers that would lead me over the last measure of earth into the land of the fleshless. You saw it, Iyaloja. You saw me struggle to retrieve my will from the power of the stranger whose shadow fell across the doorway and left me floundering and blundering in a maze I had never before encountered. My senses were numbed when the touch of cold iron came upon my wrists. I could do nothing to save myself.

IYALOJA: You have betrayed us. We fed you sweetmeats[8] such as we hoped awaited you on the other side. But you said, No, I must eat the world's left-overs. We said you were the hunter who brought the quarry down; to you belonged the vital portions of the game. No, you said, I am the hunter's dog and I shall eat the entrails of the game and the faeces of the hunter. We said you were the hunter returning home in triumph, a slain buffalo pressing down on his neck; you said, Wait, I first must turn up this cricket hole with my toes. We said yours was the doorway at which we first spy the tapper when he comes down from the tree, yours was the blessing of the twilight wine,[9] the purl that brings night spirits out of doors to steal their portion before the light of day. We said yours was the body of wine whose burden shakes the tapper like a sudden gust on his perch. You said, No, I am content to lick the dregs from each calabash when the drinkers are done. We said the dew on earth's surface was for you to wash your feet along the slopes of honour. You said, No, I shall step in the vomit of cats and the droppings of mice; I shall fight them for the left-overs of the world.

ELESIN: Enough, Iyaloja, enough.

IYALOJA: We called you leader and oh, how you led us on. What we have no intention of eating should not be held to the nose.

ELESIN: Enough, enough. My shame is heavy enough.

IYALOJA: Wait. I came with a burden.

ELESIN: You have more than discharged it.

IYALOJA: I wish I could pity you.

ELESIN: I need neither your pity nor the pity of the world. I need understanding. Even I need to understand. You were present at my defeat. You were part of the beginnings. You brought about the renewal of my tie to earth, you helped in the binding of the cord.

IYALOJA: I gave you warning. The river which fills up before our eyes does not sweep us away in its flood.

ELESIN: What were warnings beside the moist contact of living earth between my fingers? What were warnings beside the renewal of famished embers lodged eternally in the heart of man? But even that, even if it overwhelmed one with a thousandfold temptations to linger a little while, a man could overcome it. It is when the alien hand pollutes the source of will,[1] when a stranger force of violence shatters the mind's calm resolution, this is when a

8. Delicacies made with sugar or honey; pastries or candies.

9. Palm wine tapped before dawn is considered especially fresh and potent. *Purl:* tonic consisting of alcohol and herbs.

1. In Yoruba cosmology, will is the life source that makes everything happen.

man is made to commit the awful treachery of relief, commit in his thought the unspeakable blasphemy of seeing the hand of the gods in this alien rupture of his world. I know it was this thought that killed me, sapped my powers and turned me into an infant in the hands of unnamable strangers. I made to utter my spells anew but my tongue merely rattled in my mouth. I fingered hidden charms and the contact was damp; there was no spark left to sever the life-strings that should stretch from every fingertip. My will was squelched in the spittle of an alien race, and all because I had committed this blasphemy of thought—that there might be the hand of the gods in a stranger's intervention.

IYALOJA: Explain it how you will, I hope it brings you peace of mind. The bush rat fled his rightful cause, reached the market and set up a lamentation. "Please save me!"—are these fitting words to hear from an ancestral mask? "There's a wild beast at my heels" is not becoming language from a hunter.

ELESIN: May the world forgive me.

IYALOJA: I came with a burden, I said. It approaches the gates which are so well guarded by those jackals whose spittle will from this day be on your food and drink. But first, tell me, you who were once Elesin Oba, tell me, you who know so well the cycle of the plantain: is it the parent shoot which withers to give sap to the younger, or does your wisdom see it running the other way?

ELESIN: I don't see your meaning, Iyaloja.

IYALOJA: Did I ask you for a meaning? I asked a question. Whose trunk withers to give sap to the other? The parent shoot or the younger?

ELESIN: The parent.

IYALOJA: Ah. So you do know that. There are sights in this world which say different, Elesin. There are some who choose to reverse the cycle of our being. Oh, you emptied bark that the world once saluted for a pith-laden being, shall I tell you what the gods have claimed of you?

[*In her agitation she steps beyond the line indicated by* PILKINGS *and the air is rent by piercing whistles. The two* GUARDS *also leap forward and place safe-guarding hands on* ELESIN. IYALOJA *stops, astonished.* PILKINGS *comes racing in, followed by* JANE.]

PILKINGS: What is it? Did they try something?

GUARD: She stepped beyond the line.

ELESIN: [*In a broken voice.*] Let her alone. She meant no harm.

IYALOJA: Oh Elesin, see what you've become. Once you had no need to open your mouth in explanation because evil-smelling goats, itchy of hand and foot, had lost their senses. And it was a brave man indeed who dared lay hands on you because Iyaloja stepped from one side of the earth onto another. Now look at the spectacle of your life. I grieve for you.

PILKINGS: I think you'd better leave. I doubt you have done him much good by coming here. I shall make sure you are not allowed to see him again. In any case we are moving him to a different place before dawn, so don't bother to come back.

IYALOJA: We foresaw that. Hence the burden I trudged here to lay beside your gates.

PILKINGS: What was that you said?

IYALOJA: Didn't our son explain? Ask that one. He knows what it is. At least we hope the man we once knew as Elesin remembers the lesser oaths he need not break.

PILKINGS: Do you know what she is talking about?

ELESIN: Go to the gates, ghostly one. Whatever you find there, bring it to me.

IYALOJA: Not yet. It drags behind me on the slow, weary feet of women. Slow as it is, Elesin, it has long overtaken you. It rides ahead of your laggard will.

PILKINGS: What is she saying now? Christ! Must your people forever speak in riddles?

ELESIN: It will come, white man, it will come. Tell your men at the gates to let it through.

PILKINGS: [*Dubiously.*] I'll have to see what it is.

IYALOJA: You will. [*Passionately.*] But this is one oath he cannot shirk. White one, you have a king here, a visitor from your land. We know of his presence here. Tell me, were he to die would you leave his spirit roaming restlessly on the surface of earth? Would you bury him here among those you consider less than human? In your land have you no ceremonies of the dead?

PILKINGS: Yes. But we don't make our chiefs commit suicide to keep him company.

IYALOJA: Child, I have not come to help your understanding. [*Points to* ELESIN.] This is the man whose weakened understanding holds us in bondage to you. But ask him if you wish. He knows the meaning of a king's passage; he was not born yesterday. He knows the peril to the race when our dead father, who goes as intermediary, waits and waits and knows he is betrayed. He knows when the narrow gate was opened and he knows it will not stay for laggards who drag their feet in dung and vomit, whose lips are reeking of the leftovers of lesser men. He knows he has condemned our King to wander in the void of evil with beings who are enemies of life.

PILKINGS: Yes, er . . . but look here . . .

IYALOJA: What we ask is little enough. Let him release our King so he can ride on homewards alone. The messenger is on his way on the backs of women. Let him send word through the heart that is folded up within the bolt. It is the least of all his oaths, it is the easiest fulfilled.

[*The* AIDE-DE-CAMP *runs in.*]

PILKINGS: Bob?

AIDE-DE-CAMP: Sir, there's a group of women chanting up the hill.

PILKINGS: [*Rounding on* IYALOJA.] If you people want trouble . . .

JANE: Simon, I think that's what Olunde referred to in his letter.

PILKINGS: He knows damned well I can't have a crowd here! Damn it, I explained the delicacy of my position to him. I think it's about time I got him out of town. Bob, send a car and two or three soldiers to bring him in. I think the sooner he takes his leave of his father and gets out the better.

IYALOJA: Save your labour, white one. If it is the father of your prisoner you want, Olunde, he who until this night we knew as Elesin's son, he comes soon himself to take his leave. He has sent the women ahead, so let them in.

[PILKINGS *remains undecided.*]

AIDE-DE-CAMP: What do we do about the invasion? We can still stop them far from here.

PILKINGS: What do they look like?

AIDE-DE-CAMP: They're not many. And they seem quite peaceful.

PILKINGS: No men?

AIDE-DE-CAMP: Mm, two or three at the most.

JANE: Honestly, Simon, I'd trust Olunde. I don't think he'll deceive you about their intentions.

PILKINGS: He'd better not. Alright then, let them in, Bob. Warn them to control themselves. Then hurry Olunde here. Make sure he brings his baggage because I'm not returning him into town.

AIDE-DE-CAMP: Very good, sir. [*Goes.*]

PILKINGS: [*To* IYALOJA.] I hope you understand that if anything goes wrong it will be on your head. My men have orders to shoot at the first sign of trouble.

IYALOJA: To prevent one death you will actually make other deaths? Ah, great is the wisdom of the white race. But have no fear. Your Prince will sleep peacefully. So at long last will ours. We will disturb you no further, servant of the white King. Just let Elesin fulfil his oath and we will retire home and pay homage to our King.

JANE: I believe her, Simon, don't you?

PILKINGS: Maybe.

ELESIN: Have no fear, ghostly one. I have a message to send my King and then you have nothing more to fear.

IYALOJA: Olunde would have done it. The chiefs asked him to speak the words but he said no, not while you lived.

ELESIN: Even from the depths to which my spirit has sunk, I find some joy that this little has been left to me.

[*The* WOMEN *enter, intoning the dirge "Alẹ leẹ leẹ" and swaying from side to side. On their shoulders is borne a longish object roughly like a cylindrical bolt, covered in cloth. They set it down on the spot where* IYALOJA *had stood earlier, and form a semi-circle round it. The* PRAISE-SINGER *and* DRUMMER *stand on the inside of the semi-circle but the drum is not used at all. The* DRUMMER *intones under the* PRAISE-SINGER's *invocations.*]

PILKINGS: [*As they enter.*] What is *that*?

IYALOJA: The burden you have made, white one, but we bring it in peace.

PILKINGS: I said *what* is it?

ELESIN: White man, you must let me out. I have a duty to perform.

PILKINGS: I most certainly will not.

ELESIN: There lies the courier of my King. Let me out so I can perform what is demanded of me.

PILKINGS: You'll do what you need to do from inside there or not at all. I've gone as far as I intend to with this business.

ELESIN: The worshipper who lights a candle in your church to bear a message to his god bows his head and speaks in a whisper to the flame. Have I not seen it, ghostly one? His voice does not ring out to the world. Mine are no words for anyone's ears. They are not words even for the bearers of this load. They are words I must speak secretly, even as my father whispered them in my ears and I in the ears of my first-born. I cannot shout them to the wind and the open night sky.

JANE: Simon . . .

PILKINGS: Don't interfere. Please!

IYALOJA: They have slain the favourite horse of the King and slain his dog. They have borne them from pulse to pulse centre of the land receiving prayers for their King. But the rider has chosen to stay behind. Is it too much to ask that he speak his heart to heart of the waiting courier? [PILKINGS *turns his back on her.*] So be it, Elesin Oba, you see how even the mere leavings are denied you. [*She gestures to the* PRAISE-SINGER.]

PRAISE-SINGER: Elesin Oba! I call you by that name only this last time. Remember when I said, If you cannot come, tell my horse. [*Pause.*] What? I cannot hear you? I said, If you cannot come, whisper in the ears of my horse. Is your tongue severed from the roots, Elesin? I can hear no response. I said, If there are boulders you cannot climb, mount my horse's back, this spotless black stallion, he'll bring you over them. [*Pauses.*] Elesin Oba, once you had a tongue that darted like a drummer's stick. I said, If you get lost my dog will track a path to me. My memory fails me but I think you replied: My feet have found the path, Alafin.

[*The dirge rises and falls.*]

I said at the last, If evil hands hold you back, just tell my horse there is weight on the hem of your smock. I dare not wait too long.

[*The dirge rises and falls.*]

There lies the swiftest ever messenger of a king, so set me free with the errand of your heart. There lie the head and heart of the favourite of the gods, whisper in his ears. Oh my companion, if you had followed when you should, we would not say that the horse preceded its rider. If you had followed when it was time, we would not say the dog has raced beyond and left his master behind. If you had raised your will to cut the thread of life at the summons of the drums, we would not say your mere shadow fell across the gateway and took its owner's place at the banquet. But the hunter, laden with slain buffalo, stayed to root in the cricket's hole with his toes. What now is left? If there is a dearth of bats, the pigeon must serve us for the offering. Speak the words over your shadow which must now serve in your place.

ELESIN: I cannot approach. Take off the cloth. I shall speak my message from heart to heart of silence.

IYALOJA: [*Moves forward and removes the covering.*] Your courier, Elesin, cast your eyes on the favoured companion of the King.

[*Rolled up in the mat, his head and feet showing at either end, is the body of* OLUNDE.]

There lies the honour of your household and of our race. Because he could not bear to let honour fly out of doors, he stopped it with his life. The son has proved the father, Elesin, and there is nothing left in your mouth to gnash but infant gums.

PRAISE-SINGER: Elesin, we placed the reins of the world in your hands yet you watched it plunge over the edge of the bitter precipice. You sat with folded arms while evil strangers tilted the world from its course and crashed it beyond the edge of emptiness—you muttered, There is little that one man can do, you left us floundering in a blind future. Your heir has taken the burden on himself. What the end will be, we are not gods to tell. But this young shoot has poured its sap into the parent stalk, and we know this is not the way of life. Our world is tumbling in the void of strangers, Elesin.

[ELESIN *has stood rock-still, his knuckles taut on the bars, his eyes glued to the body of his son. The stillness seizes and paralyses everyone, including* PILKINGS, *who has turned to look. Suddenly* ELESIN *flings one arm round his neck, once, and with the loop of the chain, strangles himself in a swift, decisive pull. The* GUARDS *rush forward to stop him but they are only in time to let his body down.* PILKINGS *has leapt to the door at the same time and struggles with the lock. He rushes within, fumbles with the handcuffs and unlocks them, raises the body to a sitting position while he tries to give resuscitation. The* WOMEN *continue their dirge, unmoved by the sudden event.*]

IYALOJA: Why do you strain yourself ? Why do you labour at tasks for which no one, not even the man lying there, would give you thanks? He is gone at last into the passage but oh, how late it all is. His son will feast on the meat and throw him bones. The passage is clogged with droppings from the King's stallion; he will arrive all stained in dung.

PILKINGS: [*In a tired voice.*] Was this what you wanted?

IYALOJA: No child, it is what you brought to be, you who play with strangers' lives, who even usurp the vestments of our dead, yet believe that the stain of death will not cling to you. The gods demanded only the old expired plantain but you cut down the sap-laden shoot to feed your pride. There is your board, filled to overflowing. Feast on it. [*She screams at him suddenly, seeing that* PILKINGS *is about to close* ELESIN'S *staring eyes.*] Let him alone! However sunk he was in debt he is no pauper's carrion abandoned on the road. Since when have strangers donned clothes of indigo before the bereaved cries out his loss?

[*She turns to the* BRIDE *who has remained motionless throughout.*]

Child.

[*The girl takes up a little earth, walks calmly into the cell and closes* ELESIN'S *eyes. She then pours some earth over each eyelid and comes out again.*]

IYALOJA: Now forget the dead, forget even the living. Turn your mind only to the unborn.

[*She goes off, accompanied by the* BRIDE. *The dirge rises in volume and the* WOMEN *continue their sway. Lights fade to a black-out.*]

THE END

1975

TENNESSEE WILLIAMS (1911–83)

A Streetcar Named Desire

Born in Columbus, Mississippi, Thomas Lanier Williams moved to St. Louis with his family at the age of seven. Williams's father was a violent alcoholic; his mother was ill; and his sister, Rose, suffered from a variety of mental illnesses: Each family member became a model for the domineering men and sensitive women of his plays. He attended the University of Missouri and Washington University in St. Louis, but earned his BA from the University of Iowa. While there, Williams won prizes for his fiction and began to write plays. His extensive body of work, with its explosive dramatic tension and dazzling dialogue, confronts issues of adultery, homosexuality, incest, and mental illness. In 1944, *The Glass Menagerie* won the New York Drama Critics' Circle Award. In 1948, Williams earned his first Pulitzer Prize, for *A Streetcar Named Desire;* in 1955, he won a second Pulitzer for *Cat on a Hot Tin Roof.* His other dramas include *Suddenly Last Summer* (1958) and *The Night of the Iguana* (1961). Williams also published short fiction, poetry, and a film script.

And so it was I entered the broken world
To trace the visionary company of love, its voice
An instant in the wind (I know not whither hurled)
But not for long to hold each desperate choice.

—"THE BROKEN TOWER" BY HART CRANE[1]

CHARACTERS

BLANCHE	EUNICE	A DOCTOR
STELLA	STEVE	A NURSE (MATRON)
STANLEY	PABLO	A YOUNG COLLECTOR
MITCH	A NEGRO WOMAN	A MEXICAN WOMAN

Scene 1

The exterior of a two-story corner building on a street in New Orleans which is named Elysian Fields and runs between the L & N tracks and the river.[2] *The section is poor but, unlike corresponding sections in other American cities, it has a raffish charm. The houses are mostly white frame, weathered grey, with rickety outside stairs and galleries and quaintly ornamented gables. This building contains two flats, upstairs and down. Faded white stairs ascend to the entrances of both.*

1. American poet (1899–1932).
2. Elysian Fields is in fact a New Orleans street at the northern tip of the French Quarter, between the Louisville & Nashville railroad tracks and the Mississippi River. In Greek mythology, the Elysian Fields are the abode of the blessed in the afterlife; in Paris, the Champs-Élysées ("Elysian Fields") is a grand boulevard.

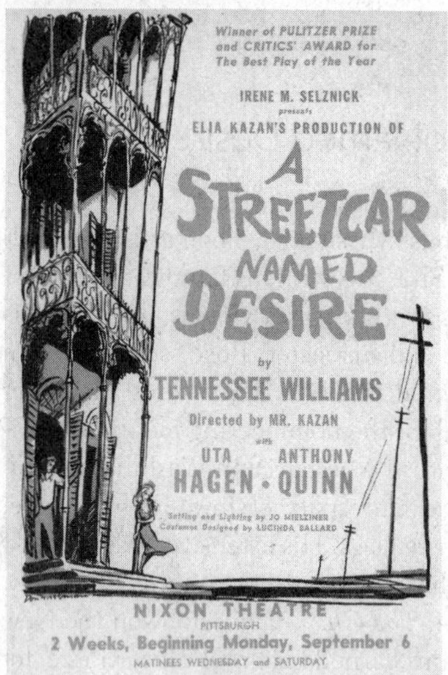

It is first dark of an evening early in May. The sky that shows around the dim white building is a peculiarly tender blue, almost a turquoise, which invests the scene with a kind of lyricism and gracefully attenuates the atmosphere of decay. You can almost feel the warm breath of the brown river beyond the river warehouses with their faint redolences of bananas and coffee. A corresponding air is evoked by the music of Negro entertainers at a barroom around the corner. In this part of New Orleans you are practically always just around the corner, or a few doors down the street, from a tinny piano being played with the infatuated fluency of brown fingers. This "Blue Piano" expresses the spirit of the life which goes on here.

Two women, one white and one colored, are taking the air on the steps of the building. The white woman is EUNICE, *who occupies the upstairs flat; the* NEGRO WOMAN, *a neighbor, for New Orleans is a cosmopolitan city where there is a relatively warm and easy intermingling of races in the old part of town.*

Above the music of the "Blue Piano" the voices of people on the street can be heard overlapping.

[*Two men come around the corner,* STANLEY KOWALSKI *and* MITCH. *They are about twenty-eight, or thirty years old, roughly dressed in blue denim work clothes.* STANLEY *carries his bowling jacket and a red-stained package from a butcher's. They stop at the foot of the steps.*]

STANLEY: [*Bellowing.*] Hey there! Stella, baby!

[STELLA *comes out on the first floor landing, a gentle young woman, about twenty-five, and of a background obviously quite different from her husband's.*]

STELLA: [*Mildly.*] Don't holler at me like that. Hi, Mitch.
STANLEY: Catch!
STELLA: What?
STANLEY: Meat!

[*He heaves the package at her. She cries out in protest but manages to catch it: then she laughs breathlessly. Her husband and his companion have already started back around the corner.*]

STELLA: [*Calling after him.*] Stanley! Where are you going?
STANLEY: Bowling!
STELLA: Can I come watch?
STANLEY: Come on. [*He goes out.*]

STELLA: Be over soon. [*To the* WHITE WOMAN.] Hello, Eunice. How are you?

EUNICE: I'm all right. Tell Steve to get him a poor boy's sandwich[3] 'cause nothing's left here.

[*They all laugh; the* NEGRO WOMAN *does not stop.* STELLA *goes out.*]

NEGRO WOMAN: What was that package he th'ew at 'er? [*She rises from steps, laughing louder.*]

EUNICE: You hush, now!

NEGRO WOMAN: Catch *what*!

[*She continues to laugh.* BLANCHE *comes around the corner, carrying a valise. She looks at a slip of paper, then at the building, then again at the slip and again at the building. Her expression is one of shocked disbelief. Her appearance is incongruous to this setting. She is daintily dressed in a white suit with a fluffy bodice, necklace and earrings of pearl, white gloves and hat, looking as if she were arriving at a summer tea or cocktail party in the garden district.[4] She is about five years older than* STELLA. *Her delicate beauty must avoid a strong light. There is something about her uncertain manner, as well as her white clothes, that suggests a moth.*]

EUNICE: [*Finally.*] What's the matter, honey? Are you lost?

BLANCHE: [*With faintly hysterical humor.*] They told me to take a street-car named Desire, and then transfer to one called Cemeteries[5] and ride six blocks and get off at—Elysian Fields!

EUNICE: That's where you are now.

BLANCHE: At Elysian Fields?

EUNICE: This here is Elysian Fields.

BLANCHE: They mustn't have—understood—what number I wanted. . . .

EUNICE: What number you lookin' for?

[BLANCHE *wearily refers to the slip of paper.*]

BLANCHE: Six thirty-two.

EUNICE: You don't have to look no further.

BLANCHE: [*Uncomprehendingly.*] I'm looking for my sister, Stella DuBois, I mean—Mrs. Stanley Kowalski.

EUNICE: That's the party.—You just did miss her, though.

BLANCHE: This—can this be—her home?

EUNICE: She's got the downstairs here and I got the up.

BLANCHE: Oh. She's—out?

EUNICE: You noticed that bowling alley around the corner?

BLANCHE: I'm—not sure I did.

EUNICE: Well, that's where she's at, watchin' her husband bowl. [*There is a pause.*] You want to leave your suitcase here an' go find her?

3. Usually called just "poor boy" or "po' boy"; similar to a hero or submarine sandwich.

4. Wealthy, fashionable section of New Orleans.

5. End of a streetcar line that stopped at a cemetery. *Desire*: street in New Orleans.

BLANCHE: No.

NEGRO WOMAN: I'll go tell her you come.

BLANCHE: Thanks.

NEGRO WOMAN: You welcome. [*She goes out.*]

EUNICE: She wasn't expecting you?

BLANCHE: No. No, not tonight.

EUNICE: Well, why don't you just go in and make yourself at home till they get back.

BLANCHE: How could I—do that?

EUNICE: We own this place so I can let you in.

[*She gets up and opens the downstairs door. A light goes on behind the blind, turning it light blue.* BLANCHE *slowly follows her into the downstairs flat. The surrounding areas dim out as the interior is lighted. Two rooms can be seen, not too clearly defined. The one first entered is primarily a kitchen but contains a folding bed to be used by* BLANCHE. *The room beyond this is a bedroom. Off this room is a narrow door to a bathroom.*]

EUNICE: [*Defensively, noticing* BLANCHE'*s look.*] It's sort of messed up right now but when it's clean it's real sweet.

BLANCHE: Is it?

EUNICE: Uh-huh, I think so. So you're Stella's sister?

BLANCHE: Yes. [*Wanting to get rid of her.*] Thanks for letting me in.

EUNICE: *Por nada*, as the Mexicans say, *por nada*![6] Stella spoke of you.

BLANCHE: Yes?

EUNICE: I think she said you taught school.

BLANCHE: Yes.

EUNICE: And you're from Mississippi, huh?

BLANCHE: Yes.

EUNICE: She showed me a picture of your home-place, the plantation.

BLANCHE: Belle Reve?[7]

EUNICE: A great big place with white columns.

BLANCHE: Yes . . .

EUNICE: A place like that must be awful hard to keep up.

BLANCHE: If you will excuse me, I'm just about to drop.

EUNICE: Sure, honey. Why don't you set down?

BLANCHE: What I meant was I'd like to be left alone.

EUNICE: [*Offended.*] Aw. I'll make myself scarce, in that case.

BLANCHE: I didn't mean to be rude, but—

EUNICE: I'll drop by the bowling alley an' hustle her up. [*She goes out the door.*]

[BLANCHE *sits in a chair very stiffly with her shoulders slightly hunched and her legs pressed close together and her hands tightly clutching her purse as if she were quite cold. After a while the blind look goes out of her eyes and she begins to look slowly around. A cat screeches. She catches her breath with a startled gesture. Suddenly she notices something in a half opened closet. She springs up and crosses to it, and removes a whiskey bottle. She pours a half tumbler of whiskey and tosses it down. She carefully replaces the bottle and*

6. It's nothing (spanish). 7. Beautiful Dream (French).

washes out the tumbler at the sink. Then she resumes her seat in front of the table.]

BLANCHE: [*Faintly to herself.*] I've got to keep hold of myself!

[STELLA *comes quickly around the corner of the building and runs to the door of the downstairs flat.*]

STELLA: [*Calling out joyfully.*] *Blanche!*

[*For a moment they stare at each other. Then* BLANCHE *springs up and runs to her with a wild cry.*]

BLANCHE: Stella, oh, Stella, Stella! Stella for Star![8] [*She begins to speak with feverish vivacity as if she feared for either of them to stop and think. They catch each other in a spasmodic embrace.*] Now, then, let me look at you. But don't you look at me, Stella, no, no, no, not till later, not till I've bathed and rested! And turn that over-light off! Turn that off! I won't be looked at in this merciless glare! [STELLA *laughs and complies.*] Come back here now! Oh, my baby! Stella! Stella for Star! [*She embraces her again.*] I thought you would never come back to this horrible place! What am I saying? I didn't mean to say that. I meant to be nice about it and say—Oh, what a convenient location and such—Ha-a-ha! Precious lamb! You haven't said a *word* to me.

STELLA: You haven't given me a chance to, honey! [*She laughs, but her glance at* BLANCHE *is a little anxious.*]

BLANCHE: Well, now you talk. Open your pretty mouth and talk while I look around for some liquor! I know you must have some liquor on the place! Where could it be, I wonder? Oh, I spy, I spy! [*She rushes to the closet and removes the bottle; she is shaking all over and panting for breath as she tries to laugh. The bottle nearly slips from her grasp.*]

STELLA: [*Noticing.*] Blanche, you sit down and let me pour the drinks. I don't know what we've got to mix with. Maybe a Coke in the icebox. Look'n see, honey, while I'm—

BLANCHE: No Coke, honey, not with my nerves tonight! Where—where—where is—?

STELLA: Stanley? Bowling! He loves it. They're having a—found some soda!—tournament. . . .

BLANCHE: Just water, baby, to chase it! Now don't get worried, your sister hasn't turned into a drunkard, she's just all shaken up and hot and tired and dirty! You sit down, now, and explain this place to me! What are you doing in a place like this?

STELLA: Now, Blanche—

BLANCHE: Oh, I'm not going to be hypocritical, I'm going to be honestly critical about it! Never, never, never in my worst dreams could I picture—Only Poe! Only Mr. Edgar Allan Poe!—could do it justice! Out there I suppose is the ghoul-haunted woodland of Weir![9] [*She laughs.*]

STELLA: No, honey, those are the L & N tracks.

8. *Stella* is "star" in Latin.
9. From the refrain of Poe's Gothic ballad "Ulalume" (1847).

BLANCHE: No, now seriously, putting joking aside. Why didn't you tell me, why didn't you write me, honey, why didn't you let me know?

STELLA: [*Carefully, pouring herself a drink.*] Tell you what, Blanche?

BLANCHE: Why, that you had to live in these conditions!

STELLA: Aren't you being a little intense about it? It's not that bad at all! New Orleans isn't like other cities.

BLANCHE: This has got nothing to do with New Orleans. You might as well say—forgive me, blessed baby! [*She suddenly stops short.*] The subject is closed!

STELLA: [*A little drily.*] Thanks.

[*During the pause,* BLANCHE *stares at her. She smiles at* BLANCHE.]

BLANCHE: [*Looking down at her glass, which shakes in her hand.*] You're all I've got in the world, and you're not glad to see me!

STELLA: [*Sincerely.*] Why, Blanche, you know that's not true.

BLANCHE: No?—I'd forgotten how quiet you were.

STELLA: You never did give me a chance to say much, Blanche. So I just got in the habit of being quiet around you.

BLANCHE: [*Vaguely.*] A good habit to get into . . . [*Then, abruptly.*] You haven't asked me how I happened to get away from the school before the spring term ended.

STELLA: Well, I thought you'd volunteer that information—if you wanted to tell me.

BLANCHE: You thought I'd been fired?

STELLA: No, I—thought you might have—resigned. . . .

BLANCHE: I was so exhausted by all I'd been through my—nerves broke. [*Nervously tamping cigarette.*] I was on the verge of—lunacy, almost! So Mr. Graves—Mr. Graves is the high school superintendent—he suggested I take a leave of absence. I couldn't put all of those details into the wire.[1] . . . [*She drinks quickly.*] Oh, this buzzes right through me and feels so *good*!

STELLA: Won't you have another?

BLANCHE: No, one's my limit.

STELLA: Sure?

BLANCHE: You haven't said a word about my appearance.

STELLA: You look just fine.

BLANCHE: God love you for a liar! Daylight never exposed so total a ruin! But you—you've put on some weight, yes, you're just as plump as a little partridge! And it's so becoming to you!

STELLA: Now, Blanche—

BLANCHE: Yes, it is, it is or I wouldn't say it! You just have to watch around the hips a little. Stand up.

STELLA: Not now.

BLANCHE: You hear me? I said stand up! [STELLA *complies reluctantly.*] You messy child, you, you've spilt something on that pretty white lace collar! About your hair—you ought to have it cut in a feather bob with your dainty features. Stella, you have a maid, don't you?

1. Telegram.

STELLA: No. With only two rooms it's—

BLANCHE: What? *Two* rooms, did you say?

STELLA: This one and— [*She is embarrassed.*]

BLANCHE: The other one? [*She laughs sharply. There is an embarrassed silence.*] I am going to take just one little tiny nip more, sort of to put the stopper on, so to speak. . . . Then put the bottle away so I won't be tempted. [*She rises.*] I want you to look at *my* figure! [*She turns around.*] You know I haven't put on one ounce in ten years, Stella? I weigh what I weighed the summer you left Belle Reve. The summer Dad died and you left us. . . .

STELLA: [*A little wearily.*] It's just incredible, Blanche, how well you're looking.

BLANCHE: [*They both laugh uncomfortably.*] But, Stella, there's only two rooms, I don't see where you're going to put me!

STELLA: We're going to put you in here.

BLANCHE: What kind of bed's this—one of those collapsible things? [*She sits on it.*]

STELLA: Does it feel all right?

BLANCHE: [*Dubiously.*] Wonderful, honey. I don't like a bed that gives much. But there's no door between the two rooms, and Stanley—will it be decent?

STELLA: Stanley is Polish, you know.

BLANCHE: Oh, yes. They're something like Irish, aren't they?

STELLA: Well—

BLANCHE: Only not so—highbrow? [*They both laugh again in the same way.*] I brought some nice clothes to meet all your lovely friends in.

STELLA: I'm afraid you won't think they are lovely.

BLANCHE: What are they like?

STELLA: They're Stanley's friends.

BLANCHE: Polacks?

STELLA: They're a mixed lot, Blanche.

BLANCHE: Heterogeneous—types?

STELLA: Oh, yes. Yes, types is right!

BLANCHE: Well—anyhow—I brought nice clothes and I'll wear them. I guess you're hoping I'll say I'll put up at a hotel, but I'm not going to put up at a hotel. I want to be *near* you, got to be *with* somebody, I *can't* be *alone*! Because—as you must have noticed—I'm—*not* very *well*. . . . [*Her voice drops and her look is frightened.*]

STELLA: You seem a little bit nervous or overwrought or something.

BLANCHE: Will Stanley like me, or will I be just a visiting in-law, Stella? I couldn't stand that.

STELLA: You'll get along fine together, if you'll just try not to—well—compare him with men that we went out with at home.

BLANCHE: Is he so—different?

STELLA: Yes. A different species.

BLANCHE: In what way; what's he like?

STELLA: Oh, you can't describe someone you're in love with! Here's a picture of him! [*She hands a photograph to* BLANCHE.]

BLANCHE: An officer?

STELLA: A Master Sergeant in the Engineers' Corps. Those are decorations!

BLANCHE: He had those on when you met him?

STELLA: I assure you I wasn't just blinded by all the brass.
BLANCHE: That's not what I—
STELLA: But of course there were things to adjust myself to later on.
BLANCHE: Such as his civilian background! [STELLA *laughs uncertainly.*] How did he take it when you said I was coming?
STELLA: Oh, Stanley doesn't know yet.
BLANCHE: [*Frightened.*] You—haven't told him?
STELLA: He's on the road a good deal.
BLANCHE: Oh. Travels?
STELLA: Yes.
BLANCHE: Good. I mean—isn't it?
STELLA: [*Half to herself.*] I can hardly stand it when he is away for a night . . .
BLANCHE: Why, Stella!
STELLA: When he's away for a week I nearly go wild!
BLANCHE: Gracious!
STELLA: And when he comes back I cry on his lap like a baby. . . . [*She smiles to herself.*]
BLANCHE: I guess that is what is meant by being in love. . . . [STELLA *looks up with a radiant smile.*] Stella—
STELLA: What?
BLANCHE: [*In an uneasy rush.*] I haven't asked you the things you probably thought I was going to ask. And so I'll expect you to be understanding about what *I* have to tell *you.*
STELLA: What, Blanche? [*Her face turns anxious.*]
BLANCHE: Well, Stella—you're going to reproach me, I know that you're bound to reproach me—but before you do—take into consideration—you left! I stayed and struggled! You came to New Orleans and looked out for yourself! *I* stayed at Belle Reve and tried to hold it together! I'm not meaning this in any reproachful way, but *all* the burden descended on *my* shoulders.
STELLA: The best I could do was make my own living, Blanche.

[BLANCHE *begins to shake again with intensity.*]

BLANCHE: I know, I know. But you are the one that abandoned Belle Reve, not I! I stayed and fought for it, bled for it, almost died for it!
STELLA: Stop this hysterical outburst and tell me what's happened? What do you mean fought and bled? What kind of—
BLANCHE: I knew you would, Stella. I knew you would take this attitude about it!
STELLA: About—what?—please!
BLANCHE: [*Slowly.*] The loss—the loss . . .
STELLA: Belle Reve? Lost, is it? No!
BLANCHE: Yes, Stella.

[*They stare at each other across the yellow-checked linoleum of the table.* BLANCHE *slowly nods her head and* STELLA *looks slowly down at her hands folded on the table. The music of the "Blue Piano" grows louder.* BLANCHE *touches her handkerchief to her forehead.*]

STELLA: But how did it go? What happened?

BLANCHE: [*Springing up.*] You're a fine one to ask me how it went!

STELLA: Blanche!

BLANCHE: You're a fine one to sit there *accusing me* of it!

STELLA: *Blanche!*

BLANCHE: I, I, *I* took the blows in my face and my body! All of those deaths! The long parade to the graveyard! Father, Mother! Margaret, that dreadful way! So big with it, it couldn't be put in a coffin! But had to be burned like rubbish! You just came home in time for the funerals, Stella. And funerals are pretty compared to deaths. Funerals are quiet, but deaths—not always. Sometimes their breathing is hoarse, and sometimes it rattles, and sometimes they even cry out to you, "Don't let me go!" Even the old, sometimes, say, "Don't let me go." As if you were able to stop them! But funerals are quiet, with pretty flowers. And, oh, what gorgeous boxes they pack them away in! Unless you were there at the bed when they cried out, "Hold me!" you'd never suspect there was the struggle for breath and bleeding. You didn't dream, but I saw! *Saw! Saw!* And now you sit there telling me with your eyes that I let the place go! How in hell do you think all that sickness and dying was paid for? Death is expensive, Miss Stella! And old Cousin Jessie's right after Margaret's, hers! Why, the Grim Reaper[2] had put up his tent on our doorstep! . . . Stella. Belle Reve was his headquarters! Honey—that's how it slipped through my fingers! Which of them left us a fortune? Which of them left a cent of insurance even? Only poor Jessie—one hundred to pay for her coffin. That was all, Stella! And I with my pitiful salary at the school. Yes, accuse me! Sit there and stare at me, thinking I let the place go! *I* let the place go? Where were *you*! In bed with your—Polack!

STELLA: [*Springing.*] Blanche! You be still! That's enough! [*She starts out.*]

BLANCHE: Where are you going?

STELLA: I'm going into the bathroom to wash my face.

BLANCHE: Oh, Stella, Stella, you're crying!

STELLA: Does that surprise you?

BLANCHE: Forgive me—I didn't mean to—

[*The sound of men's voices is heard.* STELLA *goes into the bathroom, closing the door behind her. When the men appear, and* BLANCHE *realizes it must be* STANLEY *returning, she moves uncertainly from the bathroom door to the dressing table, looking apprehensively toward the front door.* STANLEY *enters, followed by* STEVE *and* MITCH. STANLEY *pauses near his door,* STEVE *by the foot of the spiral stair, and* MITCH *is slightly above and to the right of them, about to go out. As the men enter, we hear some of the following dialogue.*]

STANLEY: Is that how he got it?

STEVE: Sure that's how he got it. He hit the old weather-bird for 300 bucks on a six-number-ticket.[3]

2. Death.

3. That is, he won $300 in a lottery. *Hit the old weather-bird*: in target shooting, to shoot at a barn and hit the ornamental rooster on the weathervane—an extraordinarily lucky shot.

MITCH: Don't tell him those things; he'll believe it. [MITCH *starts out.*]

STANLEY: [*Restraining* MITCH.] Hey, Mitch—come back here.

[BLANCHE, *at the sound of voices, retires in the bedroom. She picks up* STANLEY's *photo from dressing table, looks at it, puts it down. When* STANLEY *enters the apartment, she darts and hides behind the screen at the head of bed.*]

STEVE: [*To* STANLEY *and* MITCH.] Hey, are we playin' poker tomorrow?

STANLEY: Sure—at Mitch's.

MITCH: [*Hearing this, returns quickly to the stair rail.*] No—not at my place. My mother's still sick!

STANLEY: Okay, at my place . . . [MITCH *starts out again.*] But you bring the beer!

[MITCH *pretends not to hear—calls out "Good night, all," and goes out, singing.* EUNICE's *voice is heard, above.*]

EUNICE: Break it up down there! I made the spaghetti dish and ate it myself.

STEVE: [*Going upstairs.*] I told you and phoned you we was playing. [*To the men.*] Jax[4] beer!

EUNICE: You never phoned me once.

STEVE: I told you at breakfast—and phoned you at lunch. . . .

EUNICE: Well, never mind about that. You just get yourself home here once in a while.

STEVE: You want it in the papers?

[*More laughter and shouts of parting come from the men.* STANLEY *throws the screen door of the kitchen open and comes in. He is of medium height, about five feet eight or nine, and strongly, compactly built. Animal joy in his being is implicit in all his movements and attitudes. Since earliest manhood the center of his life has been pleasure with women, the giving and taking of it, not with weak indulgence, dependently, but with the power and pride of a richly feathered male bird among hens. Branching out from this complete and satisfying center are all the auxiliary channels of his life, such as his heartiness with men, his appreciation of rough humor, his love of good drink and food and games, his car, his radio, everything that is his, that bears his emblem of the gaudy seed-bearer. He sizes women up at a glance, with sexual classifications, crude images flashing into his mind and determining the way he smiles at them.*]

BLANCHE: [*Drawing involuntarily back from his stare.*] You must be Stanley. I'm Blanche.

STANLEY: Stella's sister?

BLANCHE: Yes.

STANLEY: H'lo. Where's the little woman?

BLANCHE: In the bathroom.

STANLEY: Oh. Didn't know you were coming in town.

BLANCHE: I—uh—

4. A local brand.

STANLEY: Where you from, Blanche?
BLANCHE: Why, I—live in Laurel.

[*He has crossed to the closet and removed the whiskey bottle.*]

STANLEY: In Laurel, huh? Oh, yeah. Yeah, in Laurel, that's right. Not in my territory. Liquor goes fast in hot weather. [*He holds the bottle to the light to observe its depletion.*] Have a shot?
BLANCHE: No, I—rarely touch it.
STANLEY: Some people rarely touch it, but it touches them often.
BLANCHE: [*Faintly.*] Ha-ha.
STANLEY: My clothes're stickin' to me. Do you mind if I make myself comfortable?

[*He starts to remove his shirt.*]

BLANCHE: Please, please do.
STANLEY: Be comfortable is my motto.
BLANCHE: It's mine, too. It's hard to stay looking fresh. I haven't washed or even powdered my face and—here you are!
STANLEY: You know you can catch cold sitting around in damp things, especially when you been exercising hard like bowling is. You're a teacher, aren't you?
BLANCHE: Yes.
STANLEY: What do you teach, Blanche?
BLANCHE: English.
STANLEY: I never was a very good English student. How long you here for, Blanche?
BLANCHE: I—don't know yet.
STANLEY: You going to shack up here?
BLANCHE: I thought I would if it's not inconvenient for you all.
STANLEY: Good.
BLANCHE: Traveling wears me out.
STANLEY: Well, take it easy.

[*A cat screeches near the window.* BLANCHE *springs up.*]

BLANCHE: What's that?
STANLEY: Cats, . . . Hey, Stella!
STELLA: [*Faintly, from the bathroom.*] Yes, Stanley.
STANLEY: Haven't fallen in, have you? [*He grins at* BLANCHE. *She tries unsuccessfully to smile back. There is a silence.*] I'm afraid I'll strike you as being the unrefined type. Stella's spoke of you a good deal. You were married once, weren't you?

[*The music of the polka rises up, faint in the distance.*]

BLANCHE: Yes. When I was quite young.
STANLEY: What happened?
BLANCHE: The boy—the boy died. [*She sinks back down.*] I'm afraid I'm—going to be sick! [*Her head falls on her arms.*]

Scene 2

It is six o'clock the following evening. BLANCHE *is bathing.* STELLA *is completing her toilette.* BLANCHE'S *dress, a flowered print, is laid out on* STELLA'S *bed.*

STANLEY *enters the kitchen from outside, leaving the door open on the perpetual "Blue Piano" around the corner.*

STANLEY: What's all this monkey doings?

STELLA: Oh, Stan! [*She jumps up and kisses him, which he accepts with lordly composure.*] I'm taking Blanche to Galatoire's[5] for supper and then to a show, because it's your poker night.

STANLEY: How about my supper, huh? I'm not going to no Galatoire's for supper!

STELLA: I put you a cold plate on ice.

STANLEY: Well, isn't that just dandy!

STELLA: I'm going to try to keep Blanche out till the party breaks up because I don't know how she would take it. So we'll go to one of the little places in the Quarter afterward and you'd better give me some money.

STANLEY: Where is she?

STELLA: She's soaking in a hot tub to quiet her nerves. She's terribly upset.

STANLEY: Over what?

STELLA: She's been through such an ordeal.

STANLEY: Yeah?

STELLA: Stan, we've—lost Belle Reve!

STANLEY: The place in the country?

STELLA: Yes.

STANLEY: How?

STELLA: [*Vaguely.*] Oh, it had to be—sacrificed or something. [*There is a pause while* STANLEY *considers.* STELLA *is changing into her dress.*] When she comes in be sure to say something nice about her appearance. And, oh! Don't mention the baby. I haven't said anything yet, I'm waiting until she gets in a quieter condition.

STANLEY: [*Ominously.*] So?

STELLA: And try to understand her and be nice to her, Stan.

BLANCHE: [*Singing in the bathroom.*] "From the land of the sky blue water, They brought a captive maid!"[6]

STELLA: She wasn't expecting to find us in such a small place. You see I'd tried to gloss things over a little in my letters.

STANLEY: So?

STELLA: And admire her dress and tell her she's looking wonderful. That's important with Blanche. Her little weakness!

STANLEY: Yeah. I get the idea. Now let's skip back a little to where you said the country place was disposed of.

STELLA: Oh!—yes . . .

5. Famous old restaurant on Bourbon Street, the principal street in the French Quarter.

6. From the song "From the Land of Sky-Blue Water" (1908), by Nelle Richmond Eberhart (1871–1944) and Charles Wakefield Cadman (1881–1946), popularized by the Andrews Sisters in the late 1930s.

STANLEY: How about that? Let's have a few more details on that subjeck.

STELLA: It's best not to talk much about it until she's calmed down.

STANLEY: So that's the deal, huh? Sister Blanche cannot be annoyed with business details right now!

STELLA: You saw how she was last night.

STANLEY: Uh-hum, I saw how she was. Now let's have a gander at the bill of sale.

STELLA: I haven't seen any.

STANLEY: She didn't show you no papers, no deed of sale or nothing like that, huh?

STELLA: It seems like it wasn't sold.

STANLEY: Well, what in hell was it then, give away? To charity?

STELLA: Shhh! She'll hear you.

STANLEY: I don't care if she hears me. Let's see the papers!

STELLA: There weren't any papers, she didn't show any papers, I don't care about papers.

STANLEY: Have you ever heard of the Napoleonic code?[7]

STELLA: No, Stanley, I haven't heard of the Napoleonic code and if I have, I don't see what it—

STANLEY: Let me enlighten you on a point or two, baby.

STELLA: Yes?

STANLEY: In the state of Louisiana we have the Napoleonic code according to which what belongs to the wife belongs to the husband and vice versa. For instance if I had a piece of property, or you had a piece of property—

STELLA: My head is swimming!

STANLEY: All right. I'll wait till she gets through soaking in a hot tub and then I'll inquire if *she* is acquainted with the Napoleonic code. It looks to me like you have been swindled, baby, and when you're swindled under the Napoleonic code I'm swindled *too*. And I don't like to be *swindled*.

STELLA: There's plenty of time to ask her questions later but if you do now she'll go to pieces again. I don't understand what happened to Belle Reve but you don't know how ridiculous you are being when you suggest that my sister or I or anyone of our family could have perpetrated a swindle on anyone else.

STANLEY: Then where's the money if the place was sold?

STELLA: Not sold—*lost, lost!* [*He stalks into bedroom, and she follows him.*] *Stanley!*

[*He pulls open the wardrobe trunk standing in middle of room and jerks out an armful of dresses.*]

STANLEY: Open your eyes to this stuff! You think she got them out of a teacher's pay?

STELLA: Hush!

STANLEY: Look at these feathers and furs that she come here to preen herself in! What's this here? A solid-gold dress, I believe! And this one! What is these here? Fox-pieces! [*He blows on them.*] Genuine fox fur-pieces, a half a mile

7. This codification of French law (1802), made by Napoleon as emperor, is the basis for Louisiana's civil law.

long! Where are your fox-pieces, Stella? Bushy snowwhite ones, no less! Where are your white fox-pieces?

STELLA: Those are inexpensive summer furs that Blanche has had a long time.

STANLEY: I got an acquaintance who deals in this sort of merchandise. I'll have him in here to appraise it. I'm willing to bet you there's thousands of dollars invested in this stuff here!

STELLA: Don't be such an idiot, Stanley!

[*He hurls the furs to the day bed. Then he jerks open a small drawer in the trunk and pulls up a fistful of costume jewelry.*]

STANLEY: And what have we here? The treasure chest of a pirate!

STELLA: Oh, Stanley!

STANLEY: Pearls! Ropes of them! What is this sister of yours, a deep-sea diver? Bracelets of solid gold, too! Where are your pearls and gold bracelets?

STELLA: Shhh! Be still, Stanley!

STANLEY: And diamonds! A crown for an empress!

STELLA: A rhinestone tiara she wore to a costume ball.

STANLEY: What's rhinestone?

STELLA: Next door to glass.

STANLEY: Are you kidding? I have an acquaintance that works in a jewelry store. I'll have him in here to make an appraisal of this. Here's your plantation, or what was left of it, here!

STELLA: You have no idea how stupid and horrid you're being! Now close that trunk before she comes out of the bathroom!

[*He kicks the trunk partly closed and sits on the kitchen table.*]

STANLEY: The Kowalskis and the DuBoises have different notions.

STELLA: [*Angrily.*] Indeed they have, thank heavens!—*I'm* going outside. [*She snatches up her white hat and gloves and crosses to the outside door.*] You come out with me while Blanche is getting dressed.

STANLEY: Since when do you give me orders?

STELLA: Are you going to stay here and insult her?

STANLEY: You're damn tootin' I'm going to stay here.

[STELLA *goes out to the porch.* BLANCHE *comes out of the bathroom in a red satin robe.*]

BLANCHE: [*Airily.*] Hello, Stanley! Here I am, all freshly bathed and scented, and feeling like a brand new human being!

[*He lights a cigarette.*]

STANLEY: That's good.

BLANCHE: [*Drawing the curtains at the windows.*] Excuse me while I slip on my pretty new dress!

STANLEY: Go right ahead, Blanche.

[*She closes the drapes between the rooms.*]

BLANCHE: I understand there's to be a little card party to which we ladies are cordially *not* invited!

STANLEY: [*Ominously.*] Yeah?

[BLANCHE *throws off her robe and slips into a flowered print dress.*]

BLANCHE: Where's Stella?

STANLEY: Out on the porch.

BLANCHE: I'm going to ask a favor of you in a moment.

STANLEY: What could that be, I wonder?

BLANCHE: Some buttons in back! You may enter! [*He crosses through the drapes with a smoldering look.*] How do I look?

STANLEY: You look all right.

BLANCHE: Many thanks! Now the buttons!

STANLEY: I can't do nothing with them.

BLANCHE: You men with your big clumsy fingers. May I have a drag on your cig?

STANLEY: Have one for yourself.

BLANCHE: Why, thanks! . . . It looks like my trunk has exploded.

STANLEY: Me an' Stella were helping you unpack.

BLANCHE: Well, you certainly did a fast and thorough job of it!

STANLEY: It looks like you raided some stylish shops in Paris.

BLANCHE: Ha-ha! Yes—clothes are my passion!

STANLEY: What does it cost for a string of fur-pieces like that?

BLANCHE: Why, those were a tribute from an admirer of mine!

STANLEY: He must have had a lot of—admiration!

BLANCHE: Oh, in my youth I excited some admiration. But look at me now! [*She smiles at him radiantly.*] Would you think it possible that I was once considered to be—attractive?

STANLEY: Your looks are okay.

BLANCHE: I was fishing for a compliment, Stanley.

STANLEY: I don't go in for that stuff.

BLANCHE: What—stuff?

STANLEY: Compliments to women about their looks. I never met a woman that didn't know if she was good-looking or not without being told, and some of them give themselves credit for more than they've got. I once went out with a doll who said to me, "I am the glamorous type, I am the glamorous type!" I said, "So what?"

BLANCHE: And what did she say then?

STANLEY: She didn't say nothing. That shut her up like a clam.

BLANCHE: Did it end the romance?

STANLEY: It ended the conversation—that was all. Some men are took in by this Hollywood glamor stuff and some men are not.

BLANCHE: I'm sure you belong in the second category.

STANLEY: That's right.

BLANCHE: I cannot imagine any witch of a woman casting a spell over you.

STANLEY: That's—right.

BLANCHE: You're simple, straightforward and honest, a little bit on the primitive side I should think. To interest you a woman would have to— [*She pauses with an indefinite gesture.*]

STANLEY: [*Slowly.*] Lay . . . her cards on the table.

BLANCHE: [*Smiling.*] Well, I never cared for wishy-washy people. That was why, when you walked in here last night, I said to myself—"My sister has married a man!"—Of course that was all that I could tell about you.

STANLEY: [*Booming.*] Now let's cut the re-bop![8]

BLANCHE: [*Pressing hands to her ears.*] Ouuuuu!

STELLA: [*Calling from the steps.*] Stanley! You come out here and let Blanche finish dressing!

BLANCHE: I'm through dressing, honey.

STELLA: Well, you come out, then.

STANLEY: Your sister and I are having a little talk.

BLANCHE: [*Lightly.*] Honey, do me a favor. Run to the drugstore and get me a lemon Coke with plenty of chipped ice in it!—Will you do that for me, sweetie?

STELLA: [*Uncertainly.*] Yes. [*She goes around the corner of the building.*]

BLANCHE: The poor little thing was out there listening to us, and I have an idea she doesn't understand you as well as I do. . . . All right; now, Mr. Kowalski, let us proceed without any more double-talk. I'm ready to answer all questions. I've nothing to hide. What is it?

STANLEY: There is such a thing in this state of Louisiana as the Napoleonic code, according to which whatever belongs to my wife is also mine—and vice versa.

BLANCHE: My, but you have an impressive judicial air!

[*She sprays herself with her atomizer; then playfully sprays him with it. He seizes the atomizer and slams it down on the dresser. She throws back her head and laughs.*]

STANLEY: If I didn't know that you was my wife's sister I'd get ideas about you!

BLANCHE: Such as what!

STANLEY: Don't play so dumb. You know what!

BLANCHE: [*She puts the atomizer on the table.*] All right. Cards on the table. That suits me. [*She turns to* STANLEY.] I know I fib a good deal. After all, a woman's charm is fifty per cent illusion, but when a thing is important I tell the truth, and this is the truth: I haven't cheated my sister or you or anyone else as long as I have lived.

STANLEY: Where's the papers? In the trunk?

BLANCHE: Everything that I own is in that trunk. [STANLEY *crosses to the trunk, shoves it roughly open and begins to open compartments.*] What in the name of heaven are you thinking of! What's in the back of that little boy's mind of yours? That I am absconding with something, attempting some kind of treachery on my sister?—Let me do that! It will be faster and simpler. . . . [*She crosses to the trunk and takes out a box.*] I keep my papers mostly in this tin box. [*She opens it.*]

STANLEY: What's them underneath? [*He indicates another sheaf of paper.*]

BLANCHE: These are love-letters, yellowing with antiquity, all from one boy. [*He snatches them up. She speaks fiercely.*] Give those back to me!

STANLEY: I'll have a look at them first!

BLANCHE: The touch of your hands insults them!

8. Nonsense (from "bop," a form of jazz).

STANLEY: Don't pull that stuff!

[*He rips off the ribbon and starts to examine them.* BLANCHE *snatches them from him, and they cascade to the floor.*]

BLANCHE: Now that you've touched them I'll burn them!

STANLEY: [*Staring, baffled.*] What in hell are they?

BLANCHE: [*On the floor gathering them up.*] Poems a dead boy wrote. I hurt him the way that you would like to hurt me, but you can't! I'm not young and vulnerable any more. But my young husband was and I—never mind about that! Just give them back to me!

STANLEY: What do you mean by saying you'll have to burn them?

BLANCHE: I'm sorry, I must have lost my head for a moment. Everyone has something he won't let others touch because of their—intimate nature. . . . [*She now seems faint with exhaustion and she sits down with the strong box and puts on a pair of glasses and goes methodically through a large stack of papers.*] Ambler & Ambler. Hmmmmm. . . . Crabtree. . . . More Ambler & Ambler.

STANLEY: What is Ambler & Ambler?

BLANCHE: A firm that made loans on the place.

STANLEY: Then it *was* lost on a mortgage?

BLANCHE: [*Touching her forehead.*] That must've been what happened.

STANLEY: I don't want no ifs, ands or buts! What's all the rest of them papers?

[*She hands him the entire box. He carries it to the table and starts to examine the papers.*]

BLANCHE: [*Picking up a large envelope containing more papers.*] There are thousands of papers, stretching back over hundreds of years, affecting Belle Reve as, piece by piece, our improvident grandfathers and father and uncles and brothers exchanged the land for their epic fornications—to put it plainly! [*She removes her glasses with an exhausted laugh.*] The four-letter word deprived us of our plantation, till finally all that was left—and Stella can verify that!—was the house itself and about twenty acres of ground, including a graveyard, to which now all but Stella and I have retreated. [*She pours the contents of the envelope on the table.*] Here all of them are, all papers! I hereby endow you with them! Take them, peruse them—commit them to memory, even! I think it's wonderfully fitting that Belle Reve should finally be this bunch of old papers in your big, capable hands! . . . I wonder if Stella's come back with my lemon Coke. . . . [*She leans back and closes her eyes.*]

STANLEY: I have a lawyer acquaintance who will study these out.

BLANCHE: Present them to him with a box of aspirin tablets.

STANLEY: [*Becoming somewhat sheepish.*] You see, under the Napoleonic code—a man has to take an interest in his wife's affairs—especially now that she's going to have a baby.

[BLANCHE *opens her eyes. The "Blue Piano" sounds louder.*]

BLANCHE: Stella? Stella going to have a baby? [*Dreamily.*] I didn't know she was going to have a baby! [*She gets up and crosses to the outside door.* STELLA *appears around the corner with a carton from the drugstore.* STANLEY *goes into the bedroom with the envelope and the box. The inner rooms fade to darkness and the outside wall of the house is visible.* BLANCHE *meets* STELLA *at the foot of the steps to the sidewalk.*] Stella, Stella for star! How lovely to have a baby! It's all right. Everything's all right.

STELLA: I'm sorry he did that to you.

BLANCHE: Oh, I guess he's just not the type that goes for jasmine perfume, but maybe he's what we need to mix with our blood now that we've lost Belle Reve. We thrashed it out. I feel a bit shaky, but I think I handled it nicely, I laughed and treated it all as a joke. [STEVE *and* PABLO *appear, carrying a case of beer.*] I called him a little boy and laughed and flirted. Yes, I was flirting with your husband! [*As the men approach.*] The guests are gathering for the poker party. [*The two men pass between them, and enter the house.*] Which way do we go now, Stella—this way?

STELLA: No, this way. [*She leads* BLANCHE *away.*]

BLANCHE: [*Laughing.*] The blind are leading the blind!

[*A tamale* VENDOR *is heard calling.*]

VENDOR'S VOICE: Red-hot![9]

Scene 3. The Poker Night

There is a picture of Van Gogh's of a billiard-parlor at night.[1] *The kitchen now suggests that sort of lurid nocturnal brilliance, the raw colors of childhood's spectrum. Over the yellow linoleum of the kitchen table hangs an electric bulb with a vivid green glass shade. The poker players*—STANLEY, STEVE, MITCH *and* PABLO—*wear colored shirts, solid blues, a purple, a red-and-white check, a light green, and they are men at the peak of their physical manhood, as coarse and direct and powerful as the primary colors. There are vivid slices of watermelon on the table, whiskey bottles and glasses. The bedroom is relatively dim with only the light that spills between the portieres and through the wide window on the street.*

For a moment, there is absorbed silence as a hand is dealt.

STEVE: Anything wild this deal?

PABLO: One-eyed jacks are wild.

STEVE: Give me two cards.

PABLO: You, Mitch?

MITCH: I'm out.

PABLO: One.

MITCH: Anyone want a shot?

STANLEY: Yeah. Me.

PABLO: Why don't somebody go to the Chinaman's and bring back a load of chop suey?

STANLEY: When I'm losing you want to eat! Ante up! Openers? Openers! Get y'r ass off the table, Mitch. Nothing belongs on a poker table but cards, chips and whiskey. [*He lurches up and tosses some watermelon rinds to the floor.*]

MITCH: Kind of on your high horse, ain't you?

9. Hot dog! *Blind!*: See Matthew 15.14—"If a blind person leads a blind person, both will fall into a pit."

1. *The Night Café*, by Vincent van Gogh (1853–90), Dutch postimpressionist painter. *The Poker Night* was Williams's first working title for *A Streetcar Named Desire*.

STANLEY: How many?
STEVE: Give me three.
STANLEY: One.
MITCH: I'm out again. I oughta go home pretty soon.
STANLEY: Shut up.
MITCH: I gotta sick mother. She don't go to sleep until I come in at night.
STANLEY: Then why don't you stay home with her?
MITCH: She says to go out, so I go, but I don't enjoy it. All the while I keep wondering how she is.
STANLEY: Aw, for the sake of Jesus, go home, then!
PABLO: What've you got?
STEVE: Spade flush.
MITCH: You all are married. But I'll be alone when she goes.—I'm going to the bathroom.
STANLEY: Hurry back and we'll fix you a sugar-tit.[2]
MITCH: Aw, go rut. [*He crosses through the bedroom into the bathroom.*]
STEVE: [*Dealing a hand.*] Seven card stud. [*Telling his joke as he deals.*] This ole farmer is out in back of his house sittin' down th'owing corn to the chickens when all at once he hears a loud cackle and this young hen comes lickety split around the side of the house with the rooster right behind her and gaining on her fast.
STANLEY: [*Impatient with the story.*] Deal!
STEVE: But when the rooster catches sight of the farmer th'owing the corn he puts on the brakes and lets the hen get away and starts pecking corn. And the old farmer says, "Lord God, I hopes I never gits *that* hongry!"

[STEVE *and* PABLO *laugh. The sisters appear around the corner of the building.*]

STELLA: The game is still going on.
BLANCHE: How do I look?
STELLA: Lovely, Blanche.
BLANCHE: I feel so hot and frazzled. Wait till I powder before you open the door. Do I look done in?
STELLA: Why no. You are as fresh as a daisy.
BLANCHE: One that's been picked a few days.

[STELLA *opens the door and they enter.*]

STELLA: Well, well, well. I see you boys are still at it?
STANLEY: Where you been?
STELLA: Blanche and I took in a show. Blanche, this is Mr. Gonzales and Mr. Hubbell.
BLANCHE: Please don't get up.
STANLEY: Nobody's going to get up, so don't be worried.
STELLA: How much longer is this game going to continue?
STANLEY: Till we get ready to quit.

2. Baby's pacifier dipped in sugar.

BLANCHE: Poker is so fascinating. Could I kibitz?[3]

STANLEY: You could not. Why don't you women go up and sit with Eunice?

STELLA: Because it is nearly two-thirty. [BLANCHE *crosses into the bedroom and partially closes the portieres.*] Couldn't you call it quits after one more hand?

[*A chair scrapes.* STANLEY *gives a loud whack of his hand on her thigh.*]

STELLA: [*Sharply.*] That's not fun, Stanley. [*The men laugh.* STELLA *goes into the bedroom.*] It makes me so mad when he does that in front of people.

BLANCHE: I think I will bathe.

STELLA: Again?

BLANCHE: My nerves are in knots. Is the bathroom occupied?

STELLA: I don't know.

[BLANCHE *knocks.* MITCH *opens the door and comes out, still wiping his hands on a towel.*]

BLANCHE: Oh!—good evening.

MITCH: Hello. [*He stares at her.*]

STELLA: Blanche, this is Harold Mitchell. My sister, Blanche DuBois.

MITCH: [*With awkward courtesy.*] How do you do, Miss DuBois.

STELLA: How is your mother now, Mitch?

MITCH: About the same, thanks. She appreciated your sending over that custard.—Excuse me, please.

[*He crosses slowly back into the kitchen, glancing back at* BLANCHE *and coughing a little shyly. He realizes he still has the towel in his hands and with an embarrassed laugh hands it to* STELLA. BLANCHE *looks after him with a certain interest.*]

BLANCHE: That one seems—superior to the others.

STELLA: Yes, he is.

BLANCHE: I thought he had a sort of sensitive look.

STELLA: His mother is sick.

BLANCHE: Is he married?

STELLA: No.

BLANCHE: Is he a wolf?

STELLA: Why, Blanche! [BLANCHE *laughs.*] I don't think he would be.

BLANCHE: What does—what does he do? [*She is unbuttoning her blouse.*]

STELLA: He's on the precision bench in the spare parts department. At the plant Stanley travels for.

BLANCHE: Is that something much?

STELLA: No. Stanley's the only one of his crowd that's likely to get anywhere.

BLANCHE: What makes you think Stanley will?

STELLA: Look at him.

BLANCHE: I've looked at him.

STELLA: Then you should know.

BLANCHE: I'm sorry, but I haven't noticed the stamp of genius even on Stanley's forehead.

3. That is, watch a card player from behind and offer advice.

[*She takes off the blouse and stands in her pink silk brassiere and white skirt in the light through the portieres. The game has continued in undertones.*]

STELLA: It isn't on his forehead and it isn't genius.
BLANCHE: Oh. Well, what is it, and where? I would like to know.
STELLA: It's a drive that he has. You're standing in the light, Blanche!
BLANCHE: Oh, am I!

[*She moves out of the yellow streak of light.* STELLA *has removed her dress and put on a light blue satin kimona.*][4]

STELLA: [*With girlish laughter.*] You ought to see their wives.
BLANCHE: [*Laughingly.*] I can imagine. Big, beefy things, I suppose.
STELLA: You know that one upstairs? [*More laughter.*] One time [*Laughing.*] the plaster— [*Laughing.*] cracked—
STANLEY: You hens cut out that conversation in there!
STELLA: You can't hear us.
STANLEY: Well, you can hear me and I said to hush up!
STELLA: This is my house and I'll talk as much as I want to!
BLANCHE: Stella, don't start a row.
STELLA: He's half drunk!—I'll be out in a minute.

[*She goes into the bathroom.* BLANCHE *rises and crosses leisurely to a small white radio and turns it on.*]

STANLEY: Awright, Mitch, you in?
MITCH: What? Oh!—No, I'm out!

[BLANCHE *moves back into the streak of light. She raises her arms and stretches, as she moves indolently back to the chair. Rhumba music comes over the radio.* MITCH *rises at the table.*]

STANLEY: Who turned that on in there?
BLANCHE: I did. Do you mind?
STANLEY: Turn it off!
STEVE: Aw, let the girls have their music.
PABLO: Sure, that's good, leave it on!
STEVE: Sounds like Xavier Cugat![5] [STANLEY *jumps up and, crossing to the radio, turns it off. He stops short at the sight of* BLANCHE *in the chair. She returns his look without flinching. Then he sits again at the poker table. Two of the men have started arguing hotly.*] I didn't hear you name it.
PABLO: Didn't I name it, Mitch?
MITCH: I wasn't listenin'.
PABLO: What were you doing, then?
STANLEY: He was looking through them drapes. [*He jumps up and jerks roughly at curtains to close them.*] Now deal the hand over again and let's play cards or quit. Some people get ants when they win.

[MITCH *rises as* STANLEY *returns to his seat.*]

4. Kimono.
5. Spanish-born Cuban bandleader (1900–90), well known for composing and playing rumbas.

STANLEY: [*Yelling.*] Sit down!

MITCH: I'm going to the "head." Deal me out.

PABLO: Sure he's got ants now. Seven five-dollar bills in his pants pocket folded up tight as spitballs.

STEVE: Tomorrow you'll see him at the cashier's window getting them changed into quarters.

STANLEY: And when he goes home he'll deposit them one by one in a piggy bank his mother give him for Christmas. [*Dealing.*] This game is Spit in the Ocean.

[MITCH *laughs uncomfortably and continues through the portieres. He stops just inside.*]

BLANCHE: [*Softly.*] Hello! The Little Boys' Room is busy right now.

MITCH: We've—been drinking beer.

BLANCHE: I hate beer.

MITCH: It's—a hot weather drink.

BLANCHE: Oh, I don't think so; it always makes me warmer. Have you got any cigs?

[*She has slipped on the dark red satin wrapper.*]

MITCH: Sure.

BLANCHE: What kind are they?

MITCH: Luckies.

BLANCHE: Oh, good. What a pretty case. Silver?

MITCH: Yes. Yes; read the inscription.

BLANCHE: Oh, is there an inscription? I can't make it out. [*He strikes a match and moves closer.*] Oh! [*Reading with feigned difficulty.*] "And if God choose,/I shall but love thee better—after—death!" Why, that's from my favorite sonnet by Mrs. Browning![6]

MITCH: You know it?

BLANCHE: Certainly I do!

MITCH: There's a story connected with that inscription.

BLANCHE: It sounds like a romance.

MITCH: A pretty sad one.

BLANCHE: Oh?

MITCH: The girl's dead now.

BLANCHE: [*In a tone of deep sympathy.*] Oh!

MITCH: She knew she was dying when she give me this. A very strange girl, very sweet—very!

BLANCHE: She must have been fond of you. Sick people have such deep, sincere attachments.

MITCH: That's right, they certainly do.

BLANCHE: Sorrow makes for sincerity, I think.

MITCH: It sure brings it out in people.

BLANCHE: The little there is belongs to people who have experienced some sorrow.

MITCH: I believe you are right about that.

6. Elizabeth Barrett Browning (1806–61), British poet, famous for her sequence of love poems, *Sonnets from the Portuguese,* which includes the poem quoted here, "How Do I Love Thee?"

BLANCHE: I'm positive that I am. Show me a person who hasn't known any sorrow and I'll show you a shuperficial—Listen to me! My tongue is a little—thick! You boys are responsible for it. The show let out at eleven and we couldn't come home on account of the poker game so we had to go somewhere and drink. I'm not accustomed to having more than one drink. Two is the limit—and *three*! [*She laughs*.] Tonight I had three.

STANLEY: Mitch!

MITCH: Deal me out. I'm talking to Miss—

BLANCHE: DuBois.

MITCH: Miss DuBois?

BLANCHE: It's a French name. It means woods and Blanche means white, so the two together mean white woods. Like an orchard in spring! You can remember it by that.

MITCH: You're French?

BLANCHE: We are French by extraction. Our first American ancestors were French Huguenots.[7]

MITCH: You are Stella's sister, are you not?

BLANCHE: Yes, Stella is my precious little sister. I call her little in spite of the fact she's somewhat older than I. Just slightly. Less than a year. Will you do something for me?

MITCH: Sure. What?

BLANCHE: I bought this adorable little colored paper lantern at a Chinese shop on Bourbon. Put it over the light bulb! Will you, please?

MITCH: Be glad to.

BLANCHE: I can't stand a naked light bulb, any more than I can a rude remark or a vulgar action.

MITCH: [*Adjusting the lantern*.] I guess we strike you as being a pretty rough bunch.

BLANCHE: I'm very adaptable—to circumstances.

MITCH: Well, that's a good thing to be. You are visiting Stanley and Stella?

BLANCHE: Stella hasn't been so well lately, and I came down to help her for a while. She's very run down.

MITCH: You're not—?

BLANCHE: Married? No, no. I'm an old maid schoolteacher!

MITCH: You may teach school but you're certainly not an old maid.

BLANCHE: Thank you, sir! I appreciate your gallantry!

MITCH: So you are in the teaching profession?

BLANCHE: Yes. Ah, yes . . .

MITCH: Grade school or high school or—

STANLEY: [*Bellowing*.] Mitch!

MITCH: Coming!

BLANCHE: Gracious, what lung-power! . . . I teach high school. In Laurel.

MITCH: What do you teach? What subject?

BLANCHE: Guess!

MITCH: I bet you teach art or music? [BLANCHE *laughs delicately*.] Of course I could be wrong. You might teach arithmetic.

7. Protestants who fled persecution in Catholic France after the Edict of Nantes (1685); many settled in the American South.

BLANCHE: Never arithmetic, sir; never arithmetic! [*With a laugh.*] I don't even know my multiplication tables! No, I have the misfortune of being an English instructor. I attempt to instill a bunch of bobby-soxers and drugstore Romeos with reverence for Hawthorne and Whitman and Poe!

MITCH: I guess that some of them are more interested in other things.

BLANCHE: How very right you are! Their literary heritage is not what most of them treasure above all else! But they're sweet things! And in the spring, it's touching to notice them making their first discovery of love! As if nobody had ever known it before! [*The bathroom door opens and* STELLA *comes out.* BLANCHE *continues talking to* MITCH.] Oh! Have you finished? Wait—I'll turn on the radio.

[*She turns the knobs on the radio and it begins to play "Wien, Wien, nur du allein."*[8] BLANCHE *waltzes to the music with romantic gestures.* MITCH *is delighted and moves in awkward imitation like a dancing bear.* STANLEY *stalks fiercely through the portieres into the bedroom. He crosses to the small white radio and snatches it off the table. With a shouted oath, he tosses the instrument out the window.*]

STELLA: Drunk—drunk—animal thing, you! [*She rushes through to the poker table.*] All of you—please go home! If any of you have one spark of decency in you—

BLANCHE: [*Wildly.*] Stella, watch out, he's—

[STANLEY *charges after* STELLA.]

MEN: [*Feebly.*] Take it easy, Stanley. Easy, fellow.—Let's all—

STELLA: You lay your hands on me and I'll—

[*She backs out of sight. He advances and disappears. There is the sound of a blow,* STELLA *cries out.* BLANCHE *screams and runs into the kitchen. The men rush forward and there is grappling and cursing. Something is overturned with a crash.*]

BLANCHE: [*Shrilly.*] My sister is going to have a baby!

MITCH: This is terrible.

BLANCHE: Lunacy, absolute lunacy!

MITCH: Get him in here, men.

[STANLEY *is forced, pinioned by the two men, into the bedroom. He nearly throws them off. Then all at once he subsides and is limp in their grasp. They speak quietly and lovingly to him and he leans his face on one of their shoulders.*]

STELLA: [*In a high, unnatural voice, out of sight.*] I want to go away, I want to go away!

MITCH: Poker shouldn't be played in a house with women.

[BLANCHE *rushes into the bedroom.*]

BLANCHE: I want my sister's clothes! We'll go to that woman's upstairs!

MITCH: Where is the clothes?

8. "Vienna, Vienna, you are my only" (German), a waltz from an operetta by Franz Lehár (1870–1948).

BLANCHE: [*Opening the closet.*] I've got them! [*She rushes through to* STELLA.] Stella, Stella, precious! Dear, dear little sister, don't be afraid!

[*With her arm around* STELLA, BLANCHE *guides her to the outside door and upstairs.*]

STANLEY: [*Dully.*] What's the matter; what's happened?
MITCH: You just blew your top, Stan.
PABLO: He's okay, now.
STEVE: Sure, my boy's okay!
MITCH: Put him on the bed and get a wet towel.
PABLO: I think coffee would do him a world of good, now.
STANLEY: [*Thickly.*] I want water.
MITCH: Put him under the shower!

[*The men talk quietly as they lead him to the bathroom.*]

STANLEY: Let the rut go of me, you sons of bitches!

[*Sounds of blows are heard. The water goes on full tilt.*]

STEVE: Let's get quick out of here!

[*They rush to the poker table and sweep up their winnings on their way out.*]

MITCH: [*Sadly but firmly.*] Poker should not be played in a house with women.

[*The door closes on them and the place is still. The Negro entertainers in the bar around the corner play "Paper Doll"*[9] *slow and blue. After a moment* STANLEY *comes out of the bathroom dripping water and still in his clinging wet polka dot drawers.*]

STANLEY: Stella! [*There is a pause.*] My baby doll's left me! [*He breaks into sobs. Then he goes to the phone and dials, still shuddering with sobs.*] Eunice? I want my baby! [*He waits a moment; then he hangs up and dials again.*] Eunice! I'll keep on ringin' until I talk with my *baby!* [*An indistinguishable shrill voice is heard. He hurls phone to floor. Dissonant brass and piano sounds as the rooms dim out to darkness and the outer walls appear in the night light. The "Blue Piano" plays for a brief interval. Finally,* STANLEY *stumbles half-dressed out to the porch and down the wooden steps to the pavement before the building. There he throws back his head like a baying hound and bellows his wife's name:* "STELLA! STELLA, *sweetheart!* STELLA!"] Stell-*lahhhhh!*

EUNICE: [*Calling down from the door of her upper apartment.*] Quit that howling out there an' go back to bed!
STANLEY: I want my baby down here. Stella, Stella!
EUNICE: She ain't comin' down so you quit! Or you'll git th' law on you!
STANLEY: Stella!
EUNICE: You can't beat on a woman an' then call 'er back! She won't come! And her goin' t' have a baby! . . . You stinker! You whelp of a Polack, you! I hope they do haul you in and turn the fire hose on you, same as the last time!
STANLEY: [*Humbly.*] Eunice, I want my girl to come down with me!

9. Song by Johnny S. Black (1915), popularized by the Mills Brothers in the early 1940s.

EUNICE: Hah! [*She slams her door.*]
STANLEY: [*With heaven-splitting violence.*] *STELL-LAHHHHH!*

[*The low-tone clarinet moans. The door upstairs opens again.* STELLA *slips down the rickety stairs in her robe. Her eyes are glistening with tears and her hair loose about her throat and shoulders. They stare at each other. Then they come together with low, animal moans. He falls to his knees on the steps and presses his face to her belly, curving a little with maternity. Her eyes go blind with tenderness as she catches his head and raises him level with her. He snatches the screen door open and lifts her off her feet and bears her into the dark flat.* BLANCHE *comes out the upper landing in her robe and slips fearfully down the steps.*]

BLANCHE: Where is my little sister? Stella? Stella?

[*She stops before the dark entrance of her sister's flat. Then catches her breath as if struck. She rushes down to the walk before the house. She looks right and left as if for a sanctuary. The music fades away.* MITCH *appears from around the corner.*]

MITCH: Miss DuBois?
BLANCHE: Oh!
MITCH: All quiet on the Potomac now?[1]
BLANCHE: She ran downstairs and went back in there with him.
MITCH: Sure she did.
BLANCHE: I'm terrified!
MITCH: Ho-ho! There's nothing to be scared of. They're crazy about each other.
BLANCHE: I'm not used to such—
MITCH: Naw, it's a shame this had to happen when you just got here. But don't take it serious.
BLANCHE: Violence! Is so—
MITCH: Set down on the steps and have a cigarette with me.
BLANCHE: I'm not properly dressed.
MITCH: That don't make no difference in the Quarter.
BLANCHE: Such a pretty silver case.
MITCH: I showed you the inscription, didn't I?
BLANCHE: Yes. [*During the pause, she looks up at the sky.*] There's so much—so much confusion in the world. . . . [*He coughs diffidently.*] Thank you for being so kind! I need kindness now.

Scene 4

It is early the following morning. There is a confusion of street cries like a choral chant.

STELLA *is lying down in the bedroom. Her face is serene in the early morning sunlight. One hand rests on her belly, rounding slightly with new maternity. From the other dangles a book of colored comics. Her eyes and lips have that almost narcotized tranquility that is in the faces of Eastern idols.*

1. "All Quiet on the Potomac" was a Civil War catchphrase, attributed to Union general George McClellan, who pushed the Confederate army back over the Potomac River in 1862.

The table is sloppy with remains of breakfast and the debris of the preceding night, and STANLEY'S *gaudy pyjamas lie across the threshold of the bathroom. The outside door is slightly ajar on a sky of summer brilliance.*

BLANCHE *appears at this door. She has spent a sleepless night and her appearance entirely contrasts with* STELLA'S. *She presses her knuckles nervously to her lips as she looks through the door, before entering.*

BLANCHE: Stella?

STELLA: [*Stirring lazily.*] Hmmh?

[BLANCHE *utters a moaning cry and runs into the bedroom, throwing herself down beside* STELLA *in a rush of hysterical tenderness.*]

BLANCHE: Baby, my baby sister!

STELLA: [*Drawing away from her.*] Blanche, what is the matter with you?

[BLANCHE *straightens up slowly and stands beside the bed looking down at her sister with knuckles pressed to her lips.*]

BLANCHE: He's left?

STELLA: Stan? Yes.

BLANCHE: Will he be back?

STELLA: He's gone to get the car greased. Why?

BLANCHE: Why! I've been half crazy, Stella! When I found out you'd been insane enough to come back in here after what happened—I started to rush in after you!

STELLA: I'm glad you didn't.

BLANCHE: What were you thinking of? [STELLA *makes an indefinite gesture.*] Answer me! What? What?

STELLA: Please, Blanche! Sit down and stop yelling.

BLANCHE: All right, Stella. I will repeat the question quietly now. How could you come back in this place last night? Why, you must have slept with him!

[STELLA *gets up in a calm and leisurely way.*]

STELLA: Blanche, I'd forgotten how excitable you are. You're making much too much fuss about this.

BLANCHE: Am I?

STELLA: Yes, you are, Blanche. I know how it must have seemed to you and I'm awful sorry it had to happen, but it wasn't anything as serious as you seem to take it. In the first place, when men are drinking and playing poker anything can happen. It's always a powder-keg. He didn't know what he was doing. . . . He was as good as a lamb when I came back and he's really very, very ashamed of himself.

BLANCHE: And that—that makes it all right?

STELLA: No, it isn't all right for anybody to make such a terrible row, but—people do sometimes. Stanley's always smashed things. Why, on our wedding night—soon as we came in here—he snatched off one of my slippers and rushed about the place smashing light bulbs with it.

BLANCHE: He did—*what*?

STELLA: He smashed all the lightbulbs with the heel of my slipper! [*She laughs.*]

BLANCHE: And you—you *let* him? Didn't *run*, didn't *scream*?
STELLA: I was—sort of—thrilled by it. [*She waits for a moment.*] Eunice and you had breakfast?
BLANCHE: Do you suppose I wanted any breakfast?
STELLA: There's some coffee left on the stove.
BLANCHE: You're so—matter-of-fact about it, Stella.
STELLA: What other can I be? He's taken the radio to get it fixed. It didn't land on the pavement so only one tube was smashed.
BLANCHE: And you are standing there smiling!
STELLA: What do you want me to do?
BLANCHE: Pull yourself together and face the facts.
STELLA: What are they, in your opinion?
BLANCHE: In my opinion? You're married to a madman!
STELLA: No!
BLANCHE: Yes, you are, your fix is worse than mine is! Only you're not being sensible about it. I'm going to *do* something. Get hold of myself and make myself a new life!
STELLA: Yes?
BLANCHE: But you've given in. And that isn't right, you're not old! You can get out.
STELLA: [*Slowly and emphatically.*] I'm not in anything I want to get out of.
BLANCHE: [*Incredulously.*] What—Stella?
STELLA: I said I am not in anything that I have a desire to get out of. Look at the mess in this room! And those empty bottles! They went through two cases last night! He promised this morning that he was going to quit having these poker parties, but you know how long such a promise is going to keep. Oh, well, it's his pleasure, like mine is movies and bridge. People have got to tolerate each other's habits, I guess.
BLANCHE: I don't understand you. [STELLA *turns toward her.*] I don't understand your indifference. Is this a Chinese philosophy you've—cultivated?
STELLA: Is what—what?
BLANCHE: This—shuffling about and mumbling—"One tube smashed—beer bottles—mess in the kitchen!"—as if nothing out of the ordinary has happened! [STELLA *laughs uncertainly and picking up the broom, twirls it in her hands.*] Are you deliberately shaking that thing in my face?
STELLA: No.
BLANCHE: Stop it. Let go of that broom. I won't have you cleaning up for him!
STELLA: Then who's going to do it? Are you?
BLANCHE: I? I!
STELLA: No, I didn't think so.
BLANCHE: Oh, let me think, if only my mind would function! We've got to get hold of some money, that's the way out!
STELLA: I guess that money is always nice to get hold of.
BLANCHE: Listen to me. I have an idea of some kind. [*Shakily she twists a cigarette into her holder.*] Do you remember Shep Huntleigh? [STELLA *shakes her head.*] Of course you remember Shep Huntleigh. I went out with him at college and wore his pin for a while. Well—
STELLA: Well?
BLANCHE: I ran into him last winter. You know I went to Miami during the Christmas holidays?

STELLA: No.

BLANCHE: Well, I did. I took the trip as an investment, thinking I'd meet someone with a million dollars.

STELLA: Did you?

BLANCHE: Yes. I ran into Shep Huntleigh—I ran into him on Biscayne Boulevard, on Christmas Eve, about dusk . . . getting into his car—Cadillac convertible; must have been a block long!

STELLA: I should think it would have been—inconvenient in traffic!

BLANCHE: You've heard of oil wells?

STELLA: Yes—remotely.

BLANCHE: He has them, all over Texas. Texas is literally spouting gold in his pockets.

STELLA: My, my.

BLANCHE: Y'know how indifferent I am to money. I think of money in terms of what it does for you. But he could do it, he could certainly do it!

STELLA: Do what, Blanche?

BLANCHE: Why—set us up in a—shop!

STELLA: What kind of shop?

BLANCHE: Oh, a—shop of some kind! He could do it with half what his wife throws away at the races.

STELLA: He's married?

BLANCHE: Honey, would I be here if the man weren't married? [STELLA *laughs a little.* BLANCHE *suddenly springs up and crosses to phone. She speaks shrilly.*] How do I get Western Union?[2]—Operator! Western Union!

STELLA: That's a dial phone, honey.

BLANCHE: I can't dial, I'm too—

STELLA: Just dial O.

BLANCHE: O?

STELLA: Yes, "O" for Operator!

[BLANCHE *considers a moment; then she puts the phone down.*]

BLANCHE: Give me a pencil. Where is a slip of paper? I've got to write it down first—the message, I mean. . . . [*She goes to the dressing table, and grabs up a sheet of Kleenex and an eyebrow pencil for writing equipment.*] Let me see now. . . . [*She bites the pencil.*] "Darling Shep. Sister and I in desperate situation."

STELLA: I beg your pardon!

BLANCHE: "Sister and I in desperate situation. Will explain details later. Would you be interested in—?" [*She bites the pencil again.*] "Would you be—interested—in . . ." [*She smashes the pencil on the table and springs up.*] You never get anywhere with direct appeals!

STELLA: [*With a laugh.*] Don't be so ridiculous, darling!

BLANCHE: But I'll think of something, I've *got* to think of—*some*thing! Don't laugh at me, Stella! Please, please don't—I—I want you to look at the contents of my purse! Here's what's in it! [*She snatches her purse open.*] Sixty-five measly cents in coin of the realm!

2. America's largest telegraph company throughout most of the twentieth century.

STELLA: [*Crossing to bureau.*] Stanley doesn't give me a regular allowance, he likes to pay bills himself, but—this morning he gave me ten dollars to smooth things over. You take five of it, Blanche, and I'll keep the rest.

BLANCHE: Oh, no. No, Stella.

STELLA: [*Insisting.*] I know how it helps your morale just having a little pocket-money on you.

BLANCHE: No, thank you—I'll take to the streets!

STELLA: Talk sense! How did you happen to get so low on funds?

BLANCHE: Money just goes—it goes places. [*She rubs her forehead.*] Sometime today I've got to get hold of a Bromo![3]

STELLA: I'll fix you one now.

BLANCHE: Not yet—I've got to keep thinking!

STELLA: I wish you'd just let things go, at least for a—while.

BLANCHE: Stella, I can't live with him! You can, he's your husband. But how could I stay here with him, after last night, with just those curtains between us?

STELLA: Blanche, you saw him at his worst last night.

BLANCHE: On the contrary, I saw him at his best! What such a man has to offer is animal force and he gave a wonderful exhibition of that! But the only way to live with such a man is to—go to bed with him! And that's your job—not mine!

STELLA: After you've rested a little, you'll see it's going to work out. You don't have to worry about anything while you're here. I mean—expenses . . .

BLANCHE: I have to plan for us both, to get us both—out!

STELLA: You take it for granted that I am in something that I want to get out of.

BLANCHE: I take it for granted that you still have sufficient memory of Belle Reve to find this place and these poker players impossible to live with.

STELLA: Well, you're taking entirely too much for granted.

BLANCHE: I can't believe you're in earnest.

STELLA: No?

BLANCHE: I understand how it happened—a little. You saw him in uniform, an officer, not here but—

STELLA: I'm not sure it would have made any difference where I saw him.

BLANCHE: Now don't say it was one of those mysterious electric things between people! If you do I'll laugh in your face.

STELLA: I am not going to say anything more at all about it!

BLANCHE: All right, then, don't!

STELLA: But there are things that happen between a man and a woman in the dark—that sort of make everything else seem—unimportant. [*Pause.*]

BLANCHE: What you are talking about is brutal desire—just—Desire!—the name of that rattle-trap streetcar that bangs through the Quarter, up one old narrow street and down another. . . .

STELLA: Haven't you ever ridden on that streetcar?

BLANCHE: It brought me here.—Where I'm not wanted and where I'm ashamed to be. . . .

STELLA: Then don't you think your superior attitude is a bit out of place?

3. Short for "Bromo Seltzer," a headache remedy.

BLANCHE: I am not being or feeling at all superior, Stella. Believe me I'm not! It's just this. This is how I look at it. A man like that is someone to go out with—once—twice—three times when the devil is in you. But live with? Have a child by?

STELLA: I have told you I love him.

BLANCHE: Then I *tremble* for you! I just—*tremble* for you. . . .

STELLA: I can't help your trembling if you insist on trembling!

[*There is a pause.*]

BLANCHE: May I—speak—*plainly*?

STELLA: Yes, do. Go ahead. As plainly as you want to.

[*Outside, a train approaches. They are silent till the noise subsides. They are both in the bedroom. Under cover of the train's noise* STANLEY *enters from outside. He stands unseen by the women, holding some packages in his arms, and overhears their following conversation. He wears an undershirt and grease-stained seersucker pants.*]

BLANCHE: Well—if you'll forgive me—he's *common*!

STELLA: Why, yes, I suppose he is.

BLANCHE: Suppose! You can't have forgotten that much of our bringing up, Stella, that you just *suppose* that any part of a gentleman's in his nature! *Not one particle, no!* Oh, if he was just—*ordinary*! Just *plain*—but good and wholesome, but—*no*. There's something downright—*bestial*—about him! You're hating me saying this, aren't you?

STELLA: [*Coldly.*] Go on and say it all, Blanche.

BLANCHE: He acts like an animal, has an animal's habits! Eats like one, moves like one, talks like one! There's even something—sub-human—something not quite to the stage of humanity yet! Yes, something—ape-like about him, like one of those pictures I've seen in—anthropological studies! Thousands and thousands of years have passed him right by, and there he is—Stanley Kowalski—survivor of the Stone Age! Bearing the raw meat home from the kill in the jungle! And you—*you* here—*waiting* for him! Maybe he'll strike you or maybe grunt and kiss you! That is, if kisses have been discovered yet! Night falls and the other apes gather! There in the front of the cave, all grunting like him, and swilling and gnawing and hulking! His poker night! you call it—this party of apes! Somebody growls—some creature snatches at something—the fight is on! *God!* Maybe we are a long way from being made in God's image, but Stella—my sister—there has been *some* progress since then! Such things as art—as poetry and music—such kinds of new light have come into the world since then! In some kinds of people some tenderer feelings have had some little beginning! That we have got to make *grow*! And *cling* to, and hold as our flag! In this dark march toward whatever it is we're approaching. . . . *Don't—don't hang back with the brutes!*

[*Another train passes outside.* STANLEY *hesitates, licking his lips. Then suddenly he turns stealthily about and withdraws through front door. The women are still unaware of his presence. When the train has passed he calls through the closed front door.*]

STANLEY: Hey! Hey, Stella!
STELLA: [*Who has listened gravely to* BLANCHE.] Stanley!
BLANCHE: Stell, I—

[*But* STELLA *has gone to the front door.* STANLEY *enters casually with his packages.*]

STANLEY: Hiyuh, Stella. Blanche back?
STELLA: Yes, she's back.
STANLEY: Hiyuh, Blanche. [*He grins at her.*]
STELLA: You must've got under the car.
STANLEY: Them darn mechanics at Fritz's don't know their ass fr'm—*Hey!*

[STELLA *has embraced him with both arms, fiercely, and full in the view of* BLANCHE. *He laughs and clasps her head to him. Over her head he grins through the curtains at* BLANCHE. *As the lights fade away, with a lingering brightness on their embrace, the music of the "Blue Piano" and trumpet and drums is heard.*]

Scene 5

BLANCHE *is seated in the bedroom fanning herself with a palm leaf as she reads over a just-completed letter. Suddenly she bursts into a peal of laughter.* STELLA *is dressing in the bedroom.*

STELLA: What are you laughing at, honey?
BLANCHE: Myself, myself, for being such a liar! I'm writing a letter to Shep. [*She picks up the letter.*] "Darling Shep. I am spending the summer on the wing, making flying visits here and there. And who knows, perhaps I shall take a sudden notion to *swoop* down on *Dallas*! How would you feel about that? Ha-ha! [*She laughs nervously and brightly, touching her throat as if actually talking to Shep.*] Forewarned is forearmed, as they say!"—How does that sound?
STELLA: Uh-huh . . .
BLANCHE: [*Going on nervously.*] "Most of my sister's friends go north in the summer but some have homes on the Gulf and there has been a continued round of entertainments, teas, cocktails, and luncheons—"

[*A disturbance is heard upstairs at the Hubbells' apartment.*]

STELLA: Eunice seems to be having some trouble with Steve. [EUNICE'*s voice shouts in terrible wrath.*]
EUNICE: I heard about you and that blonde!
STEVE: That's a damn lie!
EUNICE: You ain't pulling the wool over my eyes! I wouldn't mind if you'd stay down at the Four Deuces, but you always going up.
STEVE: Who ever seen me up?
EUNICE: I seen you chasing her 'round the balcony—I'm gonna call the vice squad!
STEVE: Don't you throw that at me!
EUNICE: [*Shrieking.*] You hit me! I'm gonna call the police!

[*A clatter of aluminum striking a wall is heard, followed by a man's angry roar, shouts, and overturned furniture. There is a crash; then a relative hush.*]

BLANCHE: [*Brightly.*] Did he *kill* her?

[EUNICE *appears on the steps in daemonic disorder.*]

STELLA: No! She's coming downstairs.

EUNICE: Call the police, I'm going to call the police! [*She rushes around the corner.*]

[*They laugh lightly.* STANLEY *comes around the corner in his green and scarlet silk bowling shirt. He trots up the steps and bangs into the kitchen.* BLANCHE *registers his entrance with nervous gestures.*]

STANLEY: What's a matter with Eun-uss?

STELLA: She and Steve had a row. Has she got the police?

STANLEY: Naw. She's gettin' a drink.

STELLA: That's much more practical!

[STEVE *comes down nursing a bruise on his forehead and looks in the door.*]

STEVE: She here?

STANLEY: Naw, naw. At the Four Deuces.

STEVE: That rutting hunk! [*He looks around the corner a bit timidly, then turns with affected boldness and runs after her.*]

BLANCHE: I must jot that down in my notebook. Ha-ha! I'm compiling a notebook of quaint little words and phrases I've picked up here.

STANLEY: You won't pick up nothing here you ain't heard before.

BLANCHE: Can I count on that?

STANLEY: You can count on it up to five hundred.

BLANCHE: That's a mighty high number. [*He jerks open the bureau drawer, slams it shut and throws shoes in a corner. At each noise* BLANCHE *winces slightly. Finally she speaks.*] What sign were you born under?

STANLEY: [*While he is dressing.*] Sign?

BLANCHE: Astrological sign. I bet you were born under Aries. Aries people are forceful and dynamic. They dote on noise! They love to bang things around! You must have had lots of banging around in the army and now that you're out, you make up for it by treating inanimate objects with such a fury!

[STELLA *has been going in and out of closet during this scene. Now she pops her head out of the closet.*]

STELLA: Stanley was born just five minutes after Christmas.

BLANCHE: Capricorn—the Goat!

STANLEY: What sign were *you* born under?

BLANCHE: Oh, my birthday's next month, the fifteenth of September; that's under Virgo.

STANLEY: What's Virgo?

BLANCHE: Virgo is the Virgin.

STANLEY: [*Contemptuously.*] *Hah!* [*He advances a little as he knots his tie.*] Say, do you happen to know somebody named Shaw?

[*Her face expresses a faint shock. She reaches for the cologne bottle and dampens her handkerchief as she answers carefully.*]

BLANCHE: Why, everybody knows somebody named Shaw!

STANLEY: Well, this somebody named Shaw is under the impression he met you in Laurel, but I figure he must have got you mixed up with some other party because this other party is someone he met at a hotel called the Flamingo.

[BLANCHE *laughs breathlessly as she touches the cologne-dampened handkerchief to her temples.*]

BLANCHE: I'm afraid he does have me mixed up with this "other party." The Hotel Flamingo is not the sort of establishment I would dare to be seen in!

STANLEY: You know of it?

BLANCHE: Yes, I've seen it and smelled it.

STANLEY: You must've got pretty close if you could smell it.

BLANCHE: The odor of cheap perfume is penetrating.

STANLEY: That stuff you use is expensive?

BLANCHE: Twenty-five dollars an ounce! I'm nearly out. That's just a hint if you want to remember my birthday! [*She speaks lightly but her voice has a note of fear.*]

STANLEY: Shaw must've got you mixed up. He goes in and out of Laurel all the time so he can check on it and clear up any mistake.

[*He turns away and crosses to the portieres.* BLANCHE *closes her eyes as if faint. Her hand trembles as she lifts the handkerchief again to her forehead.* STEVE *and* EUNICE *come around corner.* STEVE'*s arm is around* EUNICE'*s shoulder and she is sobbing luxuriously and he is cooing love-words. There is a murmur of thunder as they go slowly upstairs in a tight embrace.*]

STANLEY: [*To* STELLA.] I'll wait for you at the Four Deuces!

STELLA: Hey! Don't I rate one kiss?

STANLEY: Not in front of your sister.

[*He goes out.* BLANCHE *rises from her chair. She seems faint; looks about her with an expression of almost panic.*]

BLANCHE: Stella! What have you heard about me?

STELLA: Huh?

BLANCHE: What have people been telling you about me?

STELLA: Telling?

BLANCHE: You haven't heard any—unkind—gossip about me?

STELLA: Why, no, Blanche, of course not!

BLANCHE: Honey, there was—a good deal of talk in Laurel.

STELLA: About *you*, Blanche?

BLANCHE: I wasn't so good the last two years or so, after Belle Reve had started to slip through my fingers.

STELLA: All of us do things we—

BLANCHE: I never was hard or self-sufficient enough. When people are soft—soft people have got to shimmer and glow—they've got to put on soft colors, the colors of butterfly wings, and put a—paper lantern over the light. . . . It isn't enough to be soft *and attractive.* And I—I'm fading now! I don't know how much longer I can turn the trick. [*The afternoon has faded to dusk.* STELLA *goes into the bedroom and turns on the light under the paper lantern. She holds a bottled soft drink in her hand.*] Have you been listening to me?

STELLA: I don't listen to you when you are being morbid! [*She advances with the bottled Coke.*]

BLANCHE: [*With abrupt change to gaiety.*] Is that Coke for me?

STELLA: Not for anyone else!

BLANCHE: Why, you precious thing, you! Is it just Coke?

STELLA: [*Turning.*] You mean you want a shot in it!

BLANCHE: Well, honey, a shot never does a Coke any harm! Let me! You mustn't wait on me!

STELLA: I like to wait on you, Blanche. It makes it seem more like home. [*She goes into the kitchen, finds a glass and pours a shot of whiskey into it.*]

BLANCHE: I have to admit I love to be waited on . . . [*She rushes into the bedroom.* STELLA *goes to her with the glass.* BLANCHE *suddenly clutches* STELLA'S *free hand with a moaning sound and presses the hand to her lips.* STELLA *is embarrassed by her show of emotion.* BLANCHE *speaks in a choked voice.*] You're—you're—so *good* to me! And I—

STELLA: Blanche.

BLANCHE: I know, I won't! You hate me to talk sentimental! But honey, *believe* I feel things more than I *tell* you! I *won't* stay long! I won't, I *promise* I—

STELLA: Blanche!

BLANCHE: [*Hysterically.*] I won't, I promise, *I'll* go! Go *soon*! I will *really*! I *won't* hang around until he—throws me out. . . .

STELLA: Now will you stop talking foolish?

BLANCHE: Yes, honey. Watch how you pour—that fizzy stuff foams over!

[BLANCHE *laughs shrilly and grabs the glass, but her hand shakes so it almost slips from her grasp.* STELLA *pours the Coke into the glass. It foams over and spills.* BLANCHE *gives a piercing cry.*]

STELLA: [*Shocked by the cry.*] Heavens!

BLANCHE: Right on my pretty white skirt!

STELLA: Oh . . . Use my hanky. Blot gently.

BLANCHE: [*Slowly recovering.*] I know—gently—gently . . .

STELLA: Did it stain?

BLANCHE: Not a bit. Ha-ha! Isn't that lucky? [*She sits down shakily, taking a grateful drink. She holds the glass in both hands and continues to laugh a little.*]

STELLA: Why did you scream like that?

BLANCHE: I don't know why I screamed! [*Continuing nervously.*] Mitch—Mitch is coming at seven. I guess I am just feeling nervous about our relations. [*She begins to talk rapidly and breathlessly.*] He hasn't gotten a thing but a goodnight kiss, that's all I have given him, Stella. I want his respect. And men don't want anything they get too easy. But on the other hand men lose interest quickly. Especially when the girl is over—thirty. They think a girl over thirty ought to—the vulgar term is—"put out." . . . And I—I'm not "putting out." Of course he—he doesn't know—I mean I haven't informed him—of my real age!

STELLA: Why are you sensitive about your age?

BLANCHE: Because of hard knocks my vanity's been given. What I mean is—he thinks I'm sort of—prim and proper, you know! [*She laughs out sharply.*] I want to *deceive* him enough to make him—want me . . .

STELLA: Blanche, do you want *him*?

BLANCHE: I want to *rest*! I want to breathe quietly again! Yes—I *want* Mitch . . . *very badly*! Just think! If it happens! I can leave here and not be anyone's problem. . . .

[STANLEY *comes around the corner with a drink under his belt.*]

STANLEY: [*Bawling.*] Hey, Steve! Hey, Eunice! Hey, Stella!

[*There are joyous calls from above. Trumpet and drums are heard from around the corner.*]

STELLA: [*Kissing* BLANCHE *impulsively.*] It *will* happen!

BLANCHE: [*Doubtfully.*] It will?

STELLA: It *will*! [*She goes across into the kitchen, looking back at* BLANCHE.] It will, honey, *it will*. . . . But don't take another drink! [*Her voice catches as she goes out the door to meet her husband.*]

[BLANCHE *sinks faintly back in her chair with her drink.* EUNICE *shrieks with laughter and runs down the steps.* STEVE *bounds after her with goat-like screeches and chases her around corner.* STANLEY *and* STELLA *twine arms as they follow, laughing. Dusk settles deeper. The music from the Four Deuces is slow and blue.*]

BLANCHE: Ah, me, ah, me, ah, me . . . [*Her eyes fall shut and the palm leaf fan drops from her fingers. She slaps her hand on the chair arm a couple of times. There is a little glimmer of lightning about the building. A* YOUNG MAN *comes along the street and rings the bell.*] Come in. [*The* YOUNG MAN *appears through the portieres. She regards him with interest.*] Well, well! What can I do for *you*?

YOUNG MAN: I'm collecting for *The Evening Star*.

BLANCHE: I didn't know that stars took up collections.

YOUNG MAN: It's the paper.

BLANCHE: I know, I was joking—feebly! Will you—have a drink?

YOUNG MAN: No, ma'am. No, thank you. I can't drink on the job.

BLANCHE: Oh, well, now, let's see. . . . No, I don't have a dime! I'm not the lady of the house. I'm her sister from Mississippi. I'm one of those poor relations you've heard about.

YOUNG MAN: That's all right. I'll drop by later. [*He starts to go out. She approaches a little.*]

BLANCHE: Hey! [*He turns back shyly. She puts a cigarette in a long holder.*] Could you give me a light? [*She crosses toward him. They meet at the door between the two rooms.*]

YOUNG MAN: Sure. [*He takes out a lighter.*] This doesn't always work.

BLANCHE: It's temperamental? [*It flares.*] Ah!—thank you. [*He starts away again.*] Hey! [*He turns again, still more uncertainly. She goes close to him.*] Uh—what time is it?

YOUNG MAN: Fifteen of seven, ma'am.

BLANCHE: So late? Don't you just love these long rainy afternoons in New Orleans when an hour isn't just an hour—but a little piece of eternity dropped into your hands—and who knows what to do with it? [*She touches his shoulders.*] You—uh—didn't get wet in the rain?

YOUNG MAN: No, ma'am. I stepped inside.

BLANCHE: In a drugstore? And had a soda?

YOUNG MAN: Uh-huh.

BLANCHE: Chocolate?

YOUNG MAN: No, ma'am. Cherry.

BLANCHE: [*Laughing.*] Cherry!

YOUNG MAN: A cherry soda.

BLANCHE: You make my mouth water. [*She touches his cheek lightly, and smiles. Then she goes to the trunk.*]

YOUNG MAN: Well, I'd better be going—

BLANCHE: [*Stopping him.*] Young man! [*He turns. She takes a large, gossamer scarf from the trunk and drapes it about her shoulders. In the ensuing pause, the "Blue Piano" is heard. It continues through the rest of this scene and the opening of the next. The* YOUNG MAN *clears his throat and looks yearningly at the door.*] Young man! Young, young, young man! Has anyone ever told you that you look like a young Prince out of the Arabian Nights?[4] [*The* YOUNG MAN *laughs uncomfortably and stands like a bashful kid.* BLANCHE *speaks softly to him.*] Well, you do, honey lamb! Come here. I want to kiss you, just once, softly and sweetly on your mouth! [*Without waiting for him to accept, she crosses quickly to him and presses her lips to his.*] Now run along, now, quickly! It would be nice to keep you, but I've got to be good—and keep my hands off children.

[*He stares at her a moment. She opens the door for him and blows a kiss at him as he goes down the steps with a dazed look. She stands there a little dreamily after he has disappeared. Then* MITCH *appears around the corner with a bunch of roses.*]

BLANCHE: [*Gaily.*] Look who's coming! My Rosenkavalier! Bow to me first . . . now present them! *Ahhhh—Merciiii!*[5] [*She looks at him over them, coquettishly pressing them to her lips. He beams at her self-consciously.*]

Scene 6

It is about two a.m. on the same evening. The outer wall of the building is visible. BLANCHE *and* MITCH *come in. The utter exhaustion which only a neurasthenic personality*[6] *can know is evident in* BLANCHE'S *voice and manner.* MITCH *is stolid*

4. *The Arabian Nights* is a collection of Persian, Indian, and Arabic folktales.

5. *Merci*: thank you (French). *Rosenkavalier*: *Knight of the Rose* (German), title of a romantic opera (1911) by Richard Strauss (1864–1949).

6. Nineteenth-century diagnostic term for a psychological disorder characterized by nervous exhaustion and other physical symptoms.

but depressed. They have probably been out to the amusement park on Lake Pontchartrain, for MITCH *is bearing, upside down, a plaster statuette of Mae West,*[7] *the sort of prize won at shooting galleries and carnival games of chance.*

BLANCHE: [*Stopping lifelessly at the steps.*] Well—[MITCH *laughs uneasily.*] Well . . .

MITCH: I guess it must be pretty late—and you're tired.

BLANCHE: Even the hot tamale man has deserted the street, and he hangs on till the end. [MITCH *laughs uneasily again.*] How will you get home?

MITCH: I'll walk over to Bourbon and catch an owl-car.[8]

BLANCHE: [*Laughing grimly.*] Is that street-car named Desire still grinding along the tracks at this hour?

MITCH: [*Heavily.*] I'm afraid you haven't gotten much fun out of this evening, Blanche.

BLANCHE: I spoiled it for *you.*

MITCH: No, you didn't, but I felt all the time that I wasn't giving you much—entertainment.

BLANCHE: I simply couldn't rise to the occasion. That was all. I don't think I've ever tried so hard to be gay and made such a dismal mess of it. I get ten points for trying!—I *did* try.

MITCH: Why did you try if you didn't feel like it, Blanche?

BLANCHE: I was just obeying the law of nature.

MITCH: Which law is that?

BLANCHE: The one that says the lady must entertain the gentleman—or no dice! See if you can locate my door key in this purse. When I'm so tired my fingers are all thumbs!

MITCH: [*Rooting in her purse.*] This it?

BLANCHE: No, honey, that's the key to my trunk which I must soon be packing.

MITCH: You mean you are leaving here soon?

BLANCHE: I've outstayed my welcome.

MITCH: This it?

[*The music fades away.*]

BLANCHE: Eureka! Honey, you open the door while I take a last look at the sky. [*She leans on the porch rail. He opens the door and stands awkwardly behind her.*] I'm looking for the Pleiades,[9] the Seven Sisters, but these girls are not out tonight. Oh, yes they are, there they are! God bless them! All in a bunch going home from their little bridge party. . . . Y' get the door open? Good boy! I guess you—want to go now. . . .

[*He shuffles and coughs a little.*]

MITCH: Can I—uh—kiss you—good night?

BLANCHE: Why do you always ask me if you may?

MITCH: I don't know whether you want me to or not.

7. American star of stage and film (1892–1980). *Lake Pontchartrain*: large coastal inlet in southern Louisiana; New Orleans is located on its south shore. 8. All-night streetcar.

9. Constellation named for the seven daughters of Atlas who were changed into stars.

BLANCHE: Why should you be so doubtful?

MITCH: That night when we parked by the lake and I kissed you, you—

BLANCHE: Honey, it wasn't the kiss I objected to. I liked the kiss very much. It was the other little—familiarity—that I—felt obliged to—discourage. . . . I didn't resent it! Not a bit in the world! In fact, I was somewhat flattered that you—desired me! But, honey, you know as well as I do that a single girl, a girl alone in the world, has got to keep a firm hold on her emotions or she'll be lost!

MITCH: [*Solemnly.*] Lost?

BLANCHE: I guess you are used to girls that like to be lost. The kind that get lost immediately, on the first date!

MITCH: I like you to be exactly the way that you are, because in all my—experience—I have never known anyone like you. [BLANCHE *looks at him gravely; then she bursts into laughter and then claps a hand to her mouth.*] Are you laughing at me?

BLANCHE: No, honey. The lord and lady of the house have not yet returned, so come in. We'll have a nightcap. Let's leave the lights off. Shall we?

MITCH: You just—do what you want to.

[BLANCHE *precedes him into the kitchen. The outer wall of the building disappears and the interiors of the two rooms can be dimly seen.*]

BLANCHE: [*Remaining in the first room.*] The other room's more comfortable—go on in. This crashing around in the dark is my search for some liquor.

MITCH: You want a drink?

BLANCHE: I want *you* to have a drink! You have been so anxious and solemn all evening, and so have I; we have both been anxious and solemn and now for these few last remaining moments of our lives together—I want to create—*joie de vivre*![1] I'm lighting a candle.

MITCH: That's good.

BLANCHE: We are going to be very Bohemian. We are going to pretend that we are sitting in a little artists' cafe on the Left Bank in Paris! [*She lights a candle stub and puts it in a bottle.*] *Je suis la Dame aux Camellias! Vous êtes—Armand!*[2] Understand French?

MITCH: [*Heavily.*] Naw. Naw, I—

BLANCHE: *Voulez-vous couchez avec moi ce soir? Vous ne comprenez pas? Ah, quelle dommage!*[3]—I mean it's a damned good thing. . . . I've found some liquor! Just enough for two shots without any dividends, honey. . . .

MITCH: [*Heavily.*] That's—good.

[*She enters the bedroom with the drinks and the candle.*]

BLANCHE: Sit down! Why don't you take off your coat and loosen your collar?

MITCH: I better leave it on.

BLANCHE: No. I want you to be comfortable.

1. Joy of life (French).

2. I am the Lady of the Camellias! You are—Armand! (French). Both are characters in the popular romantic play *La Dame aux Camélias* (1852) by the French author Alexandre Dumas (1824–95); she is a courtesan who gives up her true love, Armand. *Left Bank*: section of Paris on the westward ("left") bank of the river Seine, long associated with students and artists.

3. Would you like to sleep with me this evening? You don't understand? Ah, what a pity! (French).

MITCH: I am ashamed of the way I perspire. My shirt is sticking to me.

BLANCHE: Perspiration is healthy. If people didn't perspire they would die in five minutes. [*She takes his coat from him.*] This is a nice coat. What kind of material is it?

MITCH: They call that stuff alpaca.

BLANCHE: Oh. Alpaca.

MITCH: It's very light-weight alpaca.

BLANCHE: Oh. Light-weight alpaca.

MITCH: I don't like to wear a wash-coat[4] even in summer because I sweat through it.

BLANCHE: Oh.

MITCH: And it don't look neat on me. A man with a heavy build has got to be careful of what he puts on him so he don't look too clumsy.

BLANCHE: You are not too heavy.

MITCH: You don't think I am?

BLANCHE: You are not the delicate type. You have a massive bone-structure and a very imposing physique.

MITCH: Thank you. Last Christmas I was given a membership to the New Orleans Athletic Club.

BLANCHE: Oh, good.

MITCH: It was the finest present I ever was given. I work out there with the weights and I swim and I keep myself fit. When I started there, I was getting soft in the belly but now my belly is hard. It is so hard now that a man can punch me in the belly and it don't hurt me. Punch me! Go on! See? [*She pokes lightly at him.*]

BLANCHE: Gracious. [*Her hand touches her chest.*]

MITCH: Guess how much I weigh, Blanche?

BLANCHE: Oh, I'd say in the vicinity of—one hundred and eighty?

MITCH: Guess again.

BLANCHE: Not that much?

MITCH: No. More.

BLANCHE: Well, you're a tall man and you can carry a good deal of weight without looking awkward.

MITCH: I weigh two hundred and seven pounds and I'm six feet one and one half inches tall in my bare feet—without shoes on. And that is what I weigh stripped.

BLANCHE: Oh, my goodness, me! It's awe-inspiring.

MITCH: [*Embarrassed.*] My weight is not a very interesting subject to talk about. [*He hesitates for a moment.*] What's yours?

BLANCHE: My weight?

MITCH: Yes.

BLANCHE: Guess!

MITCH: Let me lift you.

BLANCHE: Samson![5] Go on, lift me. [*He comes behind her and puts his hands on her waist and raises her lightly off the ground.*] Well?

MITCH: You are light as a feather.

4. Light washable jacket. 5. Legendary strong man, an Israelite in the Old Testament.

BLANCHE: Ha-ha! [*He lowers her but keeps his hands on her waist.* BLANCHE *speaks with an affectation of demureness.*] You may release me now.

MITCH: Huh?

BLANCHE: [*Gaily.*] I said unhand me, sir. [*He fumblingly embraces her. Her voice sounds gently reproving.*] Now, Mitch. Just because Stanley and Stella aren't at home is no reason why you shouldn't behave like a gentleman.

MITCH: Just give me a slap whenever I step out of bounds.

BLANCHE: That won't be necessary. You're a natural gentleman, one of the very few that are left in the world. I don't want you to think that I am severe and old maid school-teacherish or anything like that. It's just—well—

MITCH: Huh?

BLANCHE: I guess it is just that I have—old-fashioned ideals! [*She rolls her eyes, knowing he cannot see her face.* MITCH *goes to the front door. There is a considerable silence between them.* BLANCHE *sighs and* MITCH *coughs self-consciously.*]

MITCH: [*Finally.*] Where's Stanley and Stella tonight?

BLANCHE: They have gone out. With Mr. and Mrs. Hubbell upstairs.

MITCH: Where did they go?

BLANCHE: I think they were planning to go to a midnight prevue at Loew's State.

MITCH: We should all go out together some night.

BLANCHE: No. That wouldn't be a good plan.

MITCH: Why not?

BLANCHE: You are an old friend of Stanley's?

MITCH: We was together in the Two-forty-first.[6]

BLANCHE: I guess he talks to you frankly?

MITCH: Sure.

BLANCHE: Has he talked to you about me?

MITCH: Oh—not very much.

BLANCHE: The way you say that, I suspect that he has.

MITCH: No, he hasn't said much.

BLANCHE: But what he *has* said. What would you say his attitude toward me was?

MITCH: Why do you want to ask that?

BLANCHE: Well—

MITCH: Don't you get along with him?

BLANCHE: What do you think?

MITCH: I don't think he understands you.

BLANCHE: That is putting it mildly. If it weren't for Stella about to have a baby, I wouldn't be able to endure things here.

MITCH: He isn't—nice to you?

BLANCHE: He is insufferably rude. Goes out of his way to offend me.

MITCH: In what way, Blanche?

BLANCHE: Why, in every conceivable way.

MITCH: I'm surprised to hear that.

6. Battalion of engineers in World War II.

BLANCHE: Are you?

MITCH: Well, I—don't see how anybody could be rude to you.

BLANCHE: It's really a pretty frightful situation. You see, there's no privacy here. There's just these portieres between the two rooms at night. He stalks through the rooms in his underwear at night. And I have to ask him to close the bathroom door. That sort of commonness isn't necessary. You probably wonder why I don't move out. Well, I'll tell you frankly. A teacher's salary is barely sufficient for her living expenses. I didn't save a penny last year and so I had to come here for the summer. That's why I have to put up with my sister's husband. And he has to put up with me, apparently so much against his wishes. . . . Surely he must have told you how much he hates he!

MITCH: I don't think he hates you.

BLANCHE: He hates me. Or why would he insult me? The first time I laid eyes on him I thought to myself, that man is my executioner! That man will destroy me, unless——

MITCH: Blanche—

BLANCHE: Yes, honey?

MITCH: Can I ask you a question?

BLANCHE: Yes. What?

MITCH: How old are you?

[*She makes a nervous gesture.*]

BLANCHE: Why do you want to know?

MITCH: I talked to my mother about you and she said, "How old is Blanche?" And I wasn't able to tell her. [*There is another pause.*]

BLANCHE: You talked to your mother about me?

MITCH: Yes.

BLANCHE: Why?

MITCH: I told my mother how nice you were, and I liked you.

BLANCHE: Were you sincere about that?

MITCH: You know I was.

BLANCHE: Why did your mother want to know my age?

MITCH: Mother is sick.

BLANCHE: I'm sorry to hear it. Badly?

MITCH: She won't live long. Maybe just a few months.

BLANCHE: Oh.

MITCH: She worries because I'm not settled.

BLANCHE: Oh.

MITCH: She wants me to be settled down before she— [*His voice is hoarse and he clears his throat twice, shuffling nervously around with his hands in and out of his pockets.*]

BLANCHE: You love her very much, don't you?

MITCH: Yes.

BLANCHE: I think you have a great capacity for devotion. You will be lonely when she passes on, won't you? [MITCH *clears his throat and nods.*] I understand what that is.

MITCH: To be lonely?

BLANCHE: I loved someone, too, and the person I loved I lost.

MITCH: Dead? [*She crosses to the window and sits on the sill, looking out. She pours herself another drink.*] A man?

BLANCHE: He was a boy, just a boy, when I was a very young girl. When I was sixteen, I made the discovery—love. All at once and much, much too completely. It was like you suddenly turned a blinding light on something that had always been half in shadow, that's how it struck the world for me. But I was unlucky. Deluded. There was something different about the boy, a nervousness, a softness and tenderness which wasn't like a man's, although he wasn't the least bit effeminate looking—still—that thing was there. . . . He came to me for help. I didn't know that. I didn't find out anything till after our marriage when we'd run away and come back and all I knew was I'd failed him in some mysterious way and wasn't able to give the help he needed but couldn't speak of! He was in the quicksands and clutching at me—but I wasn't holding him out, I was slipping in with him! I didn't know that. I didn't know anything except I loved him unendurably but without being able to help him or help myself. Then I found out. In the worst of all possible ways. By coming suddenly into a room that I thought was empty—which wasn't empty, but had two people in it . . . the boy I had married and an older man who had been his friend for years. . . . [*A locomotive is heard approaching outside. She claps her hands to her ears and crouches over. The headlight of the locomotive glares into the room as it thunders past. As the noise recedes she straightens slowly and continues speaking.*] Afterward we pretended that nothing had been discovered. Yes, the three of us drove out to Moon Lake Casino,[7] very drunk and laughing all the way. [*Polka music sounds, in a minor key faint with distance.*] We danced the "Varsouviana!"[8] Suddenly in the middle of the dance the boy I had married broke away from me and ran out of the casino. A few moments later—a shot! [*The polka stops abruptly.* BLANCHE *rises stiffly. Then, the polka resumes in a major key.*] I ran out—all did!—all ran and gathered about the terrible thing at the edge of the lake! I couldn't get near for the crowding. Then somebody caught my arm. "Don't go any closer! Come back! You don't want to see!" See? See what! Then I heard voices say—Allan! Allan! The Grey boy! He'd stuck the revolver into his mouth, and fired—so that the back of his head had been—blown away! [*She sways and covers her face.*] It was because—on the dance floor—unable to stop myself—I'd suddenly said—"I saw! I know! You disgust me. . . ." And then the searchlight which had been turned on the world was turned off again and never for one moment since has there been any light that's stronger than this—kitchen—candle. . . .

[MITCH *gets up awkwardly and moves toward her a little. The polka music increases.* MITCH *stands beside her.*]

MITCH: [*Drawing her slowly into his arms.*] You need somebody. And I need somebody, too. Could it be—you and me, Blanche?

[*She stares at him vacantly for a moment. Then with a soft cry huddles in his embrace. She makes a sobbing effort to speak but the words won't come. He*

7. Casino and nightclub in Dundee, Mississippi, popular during the 1940s.
8. Fast Polish dance, similar to the polka.

kisses her forehead and her eyes and finally her lips. The polka tune fades out. Her breath is drawn and released in long, grateful sobs.]

BLANCHE: Sometimes—there's God—so quickly!

Scene 7

It is late afternoon in mid-September.

The portieres are open and a table is set for a birthday supper, with cake and flowers.

STELLA *is completing the decorations as* STANLEY *comes in.*

STANLEY: What's all this stuff for?
STELLA: Honey, it's Blanche's birthday.
STANLEY: She here?
STELLA: In the bathroom.
STANLEY: [*Mimicking.*] "Washing out some things"?
STELLA: I reckon so.
STANLEY: How long she been in there?
STELLA: All afternoon.
STANLEY: [*Mimicking.*] "Soaking in a hot tub"?
STELLA: Yes.
STANLEY: Temperature 100 on the nose, and she soaks herself in a hot tub.
STELLA: She says it cools her off for the evening.
STANLEY: And you run out an' get her cokes, I suppose? And serve 'em to Her Majesty in the tub? [STELLA *shrugs.*] Set down here a minute.
STELLA: Stanley, I've got things to do.
STANLEY: Set down! I've got th' dope on your big sister, Stella.
STELLA: Stanley, stop picking on Blanche.
STANLEY: That girl calls *me* common!
STELLA: Lately you been doing all you can think of to rub her the wrong way, Stanley, and Blanche is sensitive and you've got to realize that Blanche and I grew up under very different circumstances than you did.
STANLEY: So I been told. And told and told and told! You know she's been feeding us a pack of lies here?
STELLA: No, I don't and—
STANLEY: Well, she has, however. But now the cat's out of the bag! I found out some things!
STELLA: What—things?
STANLEY: Things I already suspected. But now I got proof from the most reliable sources—which I have checked on!

[BLANCHE *is singing in the bathroom a saccharine popular ballad which is used contrapuntally*[9] *with* STANLEY'S *speech.*]

STELLA: [*To* STANLEY.] Lower your voice!
STANLEY: Some canary bird, huh!

9. Musical term meaning "in an alternating or contrasting manner." *Saccharine*: cloyingly sweet; overly sentimental.

STELLA: Now please tell me quietly what you think you've found out about my sister.

STANLEY: Lie Number One: All this squeamishness she puts on! You should just know the line she's been feeding to Mitch. He thought she had never been more than kissed by a fellow! But Sister Blanche is no lily! Ha-ha! Some lily she is!

STELLA: What have you heard and who from?

STANLEY: Our supply-man down at the plant has been going through Laurel for years and he knows all about her and everybody else in the town of Laurel knows all about her. She is as famous in Laurel as if she was the President of the United States, only she is not respected by any party! This supply-man stops at a hotel called the Flamingo.

BLANCHE: [*Singing blithely.*] "Say, it's only a paper moon, Sailing over a cardboard sea /—But it wouldn't be make-believe If you believed in me!"[1]

STELLA: What about the—Flamingo?

STANLEY: She stayed there, too.

STELLA: My sister lived at Belle Reve.

STANLEY: This is after the home-place had slipped through her lily-white fingers! She moved to the Flamingo! A second-class hotel which has the advantage of not interfering in the private social life of the personalities there! The Flamingo is used to all kinds of goings-on. But even the management of the Flamingo was impressed by Dame Blanche! In fact they was so impressed by Dame Blanche that they requested her to turn in her room key—for permanently! This happened a couple of weeks before she showed here.

BLANCHE: [*Singing.*] "It's a Barnum and Bailey[2] world, Just as phony as it can be—/ But it wouldn't be make-believe If you believed in me!"

STELLA: What—contemptible—lies!

STANLEY: Sure, I can see how you would be upset by this. She pulled the wool over your eyes as much as Mitch's!

STELLA: It's pure invention! There's not a word of truth in it and if I were a man and this creature had dared to invent such things in my presence—

BLANCHE: [*Singing.*] "Without your love, / it's a honky-tonk parade! / Without your love, / It's a melody played / In a penny arcade . . ."

STANLEY: Honey, I told you I thoroughly checked on these stories! Now wait till I finish. The trouble with Dame Blanche was that she couldn't put on her act anymore in Laurel! They got wised up after two or three dates with her and then they quit, and she goes on to another, the same old line, same old act, same old hooey! But the town was too small for this to go on forever! And as time went by she became a town character. Regarded as not just different but downright loco—nuts. [STELLA *draws back.*] And for the last year or two she has been washed up like poison. That's why she's here this summer, visiting royalty, putting on all this act—because she's practically told by the mayor to get out of town! Yes, did you know there was an army camp near Laurel and your sister's was one of the places called "Out-of-Bounds"?

1. From "It's Only a Paper Moon" (1933), a popular song by Harold Arlen (1905–86).

2. P. T. Barnum (1810–91) and James Bailey (1847–1906), circus promoters of "The Greatest Show on Earth."

BLANCHE: "It's only a paper moon, / Just as phony as it can be— / But it wouldn't be make-believe / If you believed in me!"

STANLEY: Well, so much for her being such a refined and particular type of girl. Which brings us to Lie Number Two.

STELLA: I don't want to hear any more!

STANLEY: She's not going back to teach school! In fact I am willing to bet you that she never had no idea of returning to Laurel! She didn't resign temporarily from the high school because of her nerves! No, siree, Bob! She didn't. They kicked her out of that high school before the spring term ended—and I hate to tell you the reason that step was taken! A seventeen-year-old boy—she'd gotten mixed up with!

BLANCHE: "It's a Barnum and Bailey world, / Just as phony as it can be—"

[In the bathroom the water goes on loud; little breathless cries and peals of laughter are heard as if a child were frolicking in the tub.]

STELLA: This is making me—sick!

STANLEY: The boy's dad learned about it and got in touch with the high school superintendent. Boy, oh, boy, I'd like to have been in that office when Dame Blanche was called on the carpet! I'd like to have seen her trying to squirm out of that one! But they had her on the hook good and proper that time and she knew that the jig was all up! They told her she better move on to some fresh territory. Yep, it was practickly a town ordinance passed against her!

[The bathroom door is opened and BLANCHE *thrusts her head out, holding a towel about her hair.]*

BLANCHE: Stella!

STELLA: [*Faintly.*] Yes, Blanche?

BLANCHE: Give me another bath-towel to dry my hair with. I've just washed it.

STELLA: Yes, Blanche. [*She crosses in a dazed way from the kitchen to the bathroom door with a towel.*]

BLANCHE: What's the matter, honey?

STELLA: Matter? Why?

BLANCHE: You have such a strange expression on your face!

STELLA: Oh—[*She tries to laugh.*] I guess I'm a little tired!

BLANCHE: Why don't you bathe, too, soon as I get out?

STANLEY: [*Calling from the kitchen.*] How soon is that going to be?

BLANCHE: Not so terribly long! Possess your soul in patience![3]

STANLEY: It's not my soul, it's my kidneys I'm worried about! [BLANCHE *slams the door.* STANLEY *laughs harshly.* STELLA *comes slowly back into the kitchen.*] Well, what do you think of it?

STELLA: I don't believe all of those stories and I think your supply-man was mean and rotten to tell them. It's possible that some of the things he said are partly true. There are things about my sister I don't approve of—things that caused sorrow at home. She was always—flighty!

STANLEY: Flighty!

STELLA: But when she was young, very young, she married a boy who wrote poetry. . . . He was extremely good-looking. I think Blanche didn't just love

3. "In your patience you will possess your souls" (Luke 21.19).

him but worshipped the ground he walked on! Adored him and thought him almost too fine to be human! But then she found out—

STANLEY: What?

STELLA: This beautiful and talented young man was a degenerate. Didn't your supply-man give you that information?

STANLEY: All we discussed was recent history. That must have been a pretty long time ago.

STELLA: Yes, it was—a pretty long time ago. . . .

[STANLEY *comes up and takes her by the shoulders rather gently. She gently withdraws from him. Automatically she starts sticking little pink candles in the birthday cake.*]

STANLEY: How many candles you putting in that cake?

STELLA: I'll stop at twenty-five.

STANLEY: Is company expected?

STELLA: We asked Mitch to come over for cake and ice-cream.

[STANLEY *looks a little uncomfortable. He lights a cigarette from the one he has just finished.*]

STANLEY: I wouldn't be expecting Mitch over tonight.

[STELLA *pauses in her occupation with candles and looks slowly around at* STANLEY.]

STELLA: *Why?*

STANLEY: Mitch is a buddy of mine. We were in the same outfit together—Two-forty-first Engineers. We work in the same plant and now on the same bowling team. You think I could face him if—

STELLA: Stanley Kowalski, did you—did you repeat what that—?

STANLEY: You're goddam right I told him! I'd have that on my conscience the rest of my life if I knew all that stuff and let my best friend get caught!

STELLA: Is Mitch through with her?

STANLEY: Wouldn't you be if—?

STELLA: I said, *Is Mitch through with her?*

[BLANCHE'S *voice is lifted again, serenely as a bell. She sings "But it wouldn't be make-believe / If you believed in me."*]

STANLEY: No, I don't think he's necessarily through with her—just wised up!

STELLA: Stanley, she thought Mitch was—going to—going to marry her. I was hoping so, too.

STANLEY: Well, he's not going to marry her. Maybe he *was*, but he's not going to jump in a tank with a school of sharks—now! [*He rises.*] Blanche! Oh, Blanche! Can I please get in my bathroom? [*There is a pause.*]

BLANCHE: Yes, indeed, sir! Can you wait one second while I dry?

STANLEY: Having waited one hour I guess one second ought to pass in a hurry.

STELLA: And she hasn't got her job? Well, what will she do!

STANLEY: She's not stayin' here after Tuesday. You know that, don't you? Just to make sure I bought her ticket myself. A bus ticket.

STELLA: In the first place, Blanche wouldn't go on a bus.

STANLEY: She'll go on a bus and like it.

STELLA: No, she won't, no, she won't, Stanley!
STANLEY: *She'll go!* Period. P.S. She'll go *Tuesday*!
STELLA: [*Slowly.*] What'll—she—do? What on earth will she—*do*!
STANLEY: Her future is mapped out for her.
STELLA: What do you mean?

[BLANCHE *sings.*]

STANLEY: Hey, canary bird! Toots! Get *OUT* of the *BATHROOM*!

[*The bathroom door flies open and* BLANCHE *emerges with a gay peal of laughter, but as* STANLEY *crosses past her, a frightened look appears in her face, almost a look of panic. He doesn't look at her but slams the bathroom door shut as he goes in.*]

BLANCHE: [*Snatching up a hairbrush.*] Oh, I feel so good after my long, hot bath, I feel so good and cool and—rested!
STELLA: [*Sadly and doubtfully from the kitchen.*] Do you, Blanche?
BLANCHE: [*Snatching up a hairbrush.*] Yes, I do, so refreshed! [*She tinkles her highball glass.*] A hot bath and a long, cold drink always give me a brand new outlook on life! [*She looks through the portieres at* STELLA, *standing between them, and slowly stops brushing.*] Something has happened!—What is it?
STELLA: [*Turning away quickly.*] Why, nothing has happened, Blanche.
BLANCHE: You're lying! Something has! [*She stares fearfully at* STELLA, *who pretends to be busy at the table. The distant piano goes into a hectic breakdown.*]

Scene 8

Three quarters of an hour later.

The view through the big windows is fading gradually into a still-golden dusk. A torch of sunlight blazes on the side of a big water-tank or oil-drum across the empty lot toward the business district which is now pierced by pinpoints of lighted windows or windows reflecting the sunset.

The three people are completing a dismal birthday supper. STANLEY *looks sullen.* STELLA *is embarrassed and sad.*

BLANCHE *has a tight, artificial smile on her drawn face. There is a fourth place at the table which is left vacant.*

BLANCHE: [*Suddenly.*] Stanley, tell us a joke, tell us a funny story to make us all laugh. I don't know what's the matter, we're all so solemn. Is it because I've been stood up by my beau? [STELLA *laughs feebly.*] It's the first time in my entire experience with men, and I've had a good deal of all sorts, that I've actually been stood up by anybody! Ha-ha! I don't know how to take it. . . . Tell us a funny little story, Stanley! Something to help us out.
STANLEY: I didn't think you liked my stories, Blanche.
BLANCHE: I like them when they're amusing but not indecent.
STANLEY: I don't know any refined enough for your taste.
BLANCHE: Then let me tell one.
STELLA: Yes, you tell one, Blanche. You used to know lots of good stories.

[*The music fades.*]

BLANCHE: Let me see, now. . . . I must run through my repertoire! Oh, yes—I love parrot stories! Do you all like parrot stories? Well, this one's about the old maid and the parrot. This old maid, she had a parrot that cursed a blue streak and knew more vulgar expressions than Mr. Kowalski!

STANLEY: Huh.

BLANCHE: And the only way to hush the parrot up was to put the cover back on its cage so it would think it was night and go back to sleep. Well, one morning the old maid had just uncovered the parrot for the day—when who should she see coming up the front walk but the preacher! Well, she rushed back to the parrot and slipped the cover back on the cage and then she let in the preacher. And the parrot was perfectly still, just as quiet as a mouse, but just as she was asking the preacher how much sugar he wanted in his coffee—the parrot broke the silence with a loud— [*She whistles.*] —and said—"God *damn,* but that was a short day!" [*She throws back her head and laughs.* STELLA *also makes an ineffectual effort to seem amused.* STANLEY *pays no attention to the story but reaches way over the table to spear his fork into the remaining chop which he eats with his fingers.*] Apparently Mr. Kowalski was not amused.

STELLA: Mr. Kowalski is too busy making a pig of himself to think of anything else!

STANLEY: That's right, baby.

STELLA: Your face and your fingers are disgustingly greasy. Go and wash up and then help me clear the table.

[*He hurls a plate to the floor.*]

STANLEY: That's how I'll clear the table! [*He seizes her arm.*] Don't ever talk that way to me! "Pig—Polack—disgusting—vulgar—greasy!"—them kind of words have been on your tongue and your sister's too much around here! What do you two think you are? A pair of queens? Remember what Huey Long[4] said—"Every Man is a King!" And I am the king around here, so don't forget it! [*He hurls a cup and saucer to the floor.*] My place is cleared! You want me to clear your places?

[STELLA *begins to cry weakly.* STANLEY *stalks out on the porch and lights a cigarette. The Negro entertainers around the corner are heard.*]

BLANCHE: What happened while I was bathing? What did he tell you, Stella?

STELLA: Nothing, nothing, nothing!

BLANCHE: I think he told you something about Mitch and me! You know why Mitch didn't come but you won't tell me! [STELLA *shakes her head helplessly.*] I'm going to call him!

STELLA: I wouldn't call him, Blanche.

BLANCHE: I am, I'm going to call him on the phone.

STELLA: [*Miserably.*] I wish you wouldn't.

BLANCHE: I intend to be given some explanation from someone!

[*She rushes to the phone in the bedroom.* STELLA *goes out on the porch and stares reproachfully at her husband. He grunts and turns away from her.*]

4. Louisiana political leader, governor, and senator (1893–1935); a fiery and flamboyant populist known as "the Kingfish."

STELLA: I hope you're pleased with your doings. I never had so much trouble swallowing food in my life, looking at that girl's face and the empty chair! [*She cries quietly.*]

BLANCHE: [*At the phone.*] Hello. Mr. Mitchell, please. . . . Oh. . . . I would like to leave a number if I may. Magnolia 9047. And say it's important to call. . . . Yes, very important. . . . Thank you. [*She remains by the phone with a lost, frightened look.*]

[STANLEY *turns slowly back toward his wife and takes her clumsily in his arms.*]

STANLEY: Stell, it's gonna be all right after she goes and after you've had the baby. It's gonna be all right again between you and me the way that it was. You remember the way that it was? Them nights we had together? God, honey, it's gonna be sweet when we can make noise in the night the way that we used to and get the colored lights going with nobody's sister behind the curtains to hear us! [*Their upstairs neighbors are heard in bellowing laughter at something.* STANLEY *chuckles.*] Steve an' Eunice . . .

STELLA: Come on back in. [*She returns to the kitchen and starts lighting the candles on the white cake.*] Blanche?

BLANCHE: Yes. [*She returns from the bedroom to the table in the kitchen.*] Oh, those pretty, pretty little candles! Oh, don't burn them, Stella.

STELLA: I certainly will.

[STANLEY *comes back in.*]

BLANCHE: You ought to save them for baby's birthdays. Oh, I hope candles are going to glow in his life and I hope that his eyes are going to be like candles, like two blue candles lighted in a white cake!

STANLEY: [*Sitting down.*] What poetry!

BLANCHE: [*She pauses reflectively for a moment.*] I shouldn't have called him.

STELLA: There's lots of things could have happened.

BLANCHE: There's no excuse for it, Stella. I don't have to put up with insults. I won't be taken for granted.

STANLEY: Goddamn, it's hot in here with the steam from the bathroom.

BLANCHE: I've said I was sorry three times. [*The piano fades out.*] I take hot baths for my nerves. Hydrotherapy, they call it. You healthy Polack, without a nerve in your body, of course you don't know what anxiety feels like!

STANLEY: I am not a Polack. People from Poland are Poles, not Polacks. But what I am is a one-hundred-per-cent American, born and raised in the greatest country on earth and proud as hell of it, so don't ever call me a Polack.

[*The phone rings.* BLANCHE *rises expectantly.*]

BLANCHE: Oh, that's for me, I'm sure.

STANLEY: *I'm* not sure. Keep your seat. [*He crosses leisurely to phone.*] H'lo. Aw, yeh, hello, Mac.

[*He leans against wall, staring insultingly in at* BLANCHE. *She sinks back in her chair with a frightened look.* STELLA *leans over and touches her shoulder.*]

BLANCHE: Oh, keep your hands off me, Stella. What is the matter with you? Why do you look at me with that pitying look?

STANLEY: [*Bawling.*] QUIET IN THERE!—We've got a noisy woman on the place.—Go on, Mac. At Riley's? No, I don't wanta bowl at Riley's. I had a little trouble with Riley last week. I'm the team captain, ain't I? All right, then, we're not gonna bowl at Riley's, we're gonna bowl at the West Side or the Gala! All right, Mac. See you! [*He hangs up and returns to the table.* BLANCHE *fiercely controls herself, drinking quickly from her tumbler of water. He doesn't look at her but reaches in a pocket. Then he speaks slowly and with false amiability.*] Sister Blanche, I've got a little birthday remembrance for you.

BLANCHE: Oh, have you, Stanley? I wasn't expecting any, I—I don't know why Stella wants to observe my birthday! I'd much rather forget it—when you—reach twenty-seven! Well—age is a subject that you'd prefer to—ignore!

STANLEY: Twenty-seven?

BLANCHE: [*Quickly.*] What is it? Is it for *me*?

[*He is holding a little envelope toward her.*]

STANLEY: Yes, I hope you like it!

BLANCHE: Why, why—Why, it's a—

STANLEY: Ticket! Back to Laurel! On the Greyhound![5] Tuesday! [*The "Varsouviana" music steals in softly and continues playing.* STELLA *rises abruptly and turns her back.* BLANCHE *tries to smile. Then she tries to laugh. Then she gives both up and springs from the table and runs into the next room. She clutches her throat and then runs into the bathroom. Coughing, gagging sounds are heard.*] Well!

STELLA: You didn't need to do that.

STANLEY: Don't forget all that I took off her.

STELLA: You needn't have been so cruel to someone alone as she is.

STANLEY: Delicate piece she is.

STELLA: She is. She was. You didn't know Blanche as a girl. Nobody, nobody, was tender and trusting as she was. But people like you abused her, and forced her to change. [*He crosses into the bedroom, ripping off his shirt, and changes into a brilliant silk bowling shirt. She follows him.*] Do you think you're going bowling now?

STANLEY: Sure.

STELLA: You're not going bowling. [*She catches hold of his shirt.*] Why did you do this to her?

STANLEY: I done nothing to no one. Let go of my shirt. You've torn it.

STELLA: I want to know why. Tell me why.

STANLEY: When we first met, me and you, you thought I was common. How right you was, baby. I was common as dirt. You showed me the snapshot of the place with the columns. I pulled you down off them columns and how you loved it, having them colored lights going! And wasn't we happy together, wasn't it all okay till she showed here? [STELLA *makes a slight movement. Her look goes suddenly inward as if some interior voice had called her name. She begins a slow, shuffling progress from the bedroom to the kitchen, leaning and*

5. Long-distance bus company.

resting on the back of the chair and then on the edge of a table with a blind look and listening expression. STANLEY, *finishing with his shirt, is unaware of her reaction.*] And wasn't we happy together? Wasn't it all okay? Till she showed here. Hoity-Toity, describing me as an ape. [*He suddenly notices the change in* STELLA.] Hey, what is it, Stell? [*He crosses to her.*]

STELLA: [*Quietly.*] Take me to the hospital.

[*He is with her now, supporting her with his arm, murmuring indistinguishably as they go outside.*]

Scene 9

A while later that evening. BLANCHE *is seated in a tense hunched position in a bedroom chair that she has recovered with diagonal green and white stripes. She has on her scarlet satin robe. On the table beside chair is a bottle of liquor and a glass. The rapid, feverish polka tune, the "Varsouviana," is heard. The music is in her mind; she is drinking to escape it and the sense of disaster closing in on her, and she seems to whisper the words of the song. An electric fan is turning back and forth across her.*

MITCH *comes around the corner in work clothes: blue denim shirt and pants. He is unshaven. He climbs the steps to the door and rings.* BLANCHE *is startled.*

BLANCHE: Who is it, please?

MITCH: [*Hoarsely.*] Me. Mitch.

[*The polka tune stops.*]

BLANCHE: Mitch!—Just a minute. [*She rushes about frantically, hiding the bottle in a closet, crouching at the mirror and dabbing her face with cologne and powder. She is so excited that her breath is audible as she dashes about. At last she rushes to the door in the kitchen and lets him in.*] Mitch!—Y'know, I really shouldn't let you in after the treatment I have received from you this evening! So utterly uncavalier! But hello, beautiful! [*She offers him her lips. He ignores it and pushes past her into the flat. She looks fearfully after him as he stalks into the bedroom.*] My, my, what a cold shoulder! And such uncouth apparel! Why, you haven't even shaved! The unforgivable insult to a lady! But I forgive you. I forgive you because it's such a relief to see you. You've stopped that polka tune that I had caught in my head. Have you ever had anything caught in your head? No, of course you haven't, you dumb angel-puss, you'd never get anything awful caught in your head!

[*He stares at her while she follows him while she talks. It is obvious that he has had a few drinks on the way over.*]

MITCH: Do we have to have that fan on?

BLANCHE: No!

MITCH: I don't like fans.

BLANCHE: Then let's turn it off, honey. I'm not partial to them! [*She presses the switch and the fan nods slowly off. She clears her throat uneasily as* MITCH *plumps himself down on the bed in the bedroom and lights a cigarette.*] I don't know what there is to drink. I—haven't investigated.

MITCH: I don't want Stan's liquor.

BLANCHE: It isn't Stan's. Everything here isn't Stan's. Some things on the premises are actually mine! How is your mother? Isn't your mother well?

MITCH: Why?

BLANCHE: Something's the matter tonight, but never mind. I won't cross-examine the witness. I'll just— [*She touches her forehead vaguely. The polka tune starts up again.*]—pretend I don't notice anything different about you! That—music again . . .

MITCH: What music?

BLANCHE: The "Varsouviana"! The polka tune they were playing when Allan—Wait! [*A distant revolver shot is heard.* BLANCHE *seems relieved.*] There now, the shot! It always stops after that. [*The polka music dies out again.*] Yes, now it's stopped.

MITCH: Are you boxed out of your mind?

BLANCHE: I'll go and see what I can find in the way of—[*She crosses into the closet, pretending to search for the bottle.*] Oh, by the way, excuse me for not being dressed. But I'd practically given you up! Had you forgotten your invitation to supper?

MITCH: I wasn't going to see you anymore.

BLANCHE: Wait a minute. I can't hear what you're saying and you talk so little that when you do say something, I don't want to miss a single syllable of it. . . . What am I looking around here for? Oh, yes—liquor! We've had so much excitement around here this evening that I *am* boxed out of my mind! [*She pretends suddenly to find the bottle. He draws his foot up on the bed and stares at her contemptuously.*] Here's something. Southern Comfort![6] What is that, I wonder?

MITCH: If you don't know, it must belong to Stan.

BLANCHE: Take your foot off the bed. It has a light cover on it. Of course you boys don't notice things like that. I've done so much with this place since I've been here.

MITCH: I bet you have.

BLANCHE: You saw it before I came. Well, look at it now! This room is almost—dainty! I want to keep it that way. I wonder if this stuff ought to be mixed with something? Ummm, it's sweet! It's terribly, terribly sweet! Why, it's a *liqueur,* I believe! Yes, that's what it *is,* a liqueur! [MITCH *grunts.*] I'm afraid you won't like it, but try it, and maybe you will.

MITCH: I told you already I don't want none of his liquor and I mean it. You ought to lay off his liquor. He says you been lapping it up all summer like a wild cat!

BLANCHE: What a fantastic statement! Fantastic of him to say it, fantastic of you to repeat it! I won't descend to the level of such cheap accusations to answer them, even!

MITCH: Huh.

BLANCHE: What's in your mind? I see something in your eyes!

MITCH: [*Getting up.*] It's dark in here.

BLANCHE: I like it dark. The dark is comforting to me.

6. Peach-flavored bourbon liqueur.

MITCH: I don't think I ever seen you in the light. [BLANCHE *laughs breathlessly.*] That's a fact!

BLANCHE: Is it?

MITCH: I've never seen you in the afternoon.

BLANCHE: Whose fault is that?

MITCH: You never want to go out in the afternoon.

BLANCHE: Why, Mitch, you're at the plant in the afternoon!

MITCH: Not Sunday afternoon. I've asked you to go out with me sometimes on Sundays but you always make an excuse. You never want to go out till after six and then it's always some place that's not lighted much.

BLANCHE: There is some obscure meaning in this but I fail to catch it.

MITCH: What it means is I've never had a real good look at you, Blanche. Let's turn the light on here.

BLANCHE: [*Fearfully.*] Light? Which light? What for?

MITCH: This one with the paper thing on it.

[*He tears the paper lantern off the light bulb. She utters a frightened gasp.*]

BLANCHE: What did you do that for?

MITCH: So I can take a look at you good and plain!

BLANCHE: Of course you don't really mean to be insulting!

MITCH: No, just realistic.

BLANCHE: I don't want realism. I want magic! [MITCH *laughs.*] Yes, yes, magic! I try to give that to people. I misrepresent things to them. I don't tell truth, I tell what *ought* to be truth. And if that is sinful, then let me be damned for it!—Don't turn the light on!

[MITCH *crosses to the switch. He turns the light on and stares at her. She cries out and covers her face. He turns the lights off again.*]

MITCH: [*Slowly and bitterly.*] I don't mind you being older than what I thought. But all the rest of it—Christ! That pitch about your ideals being so old-fashioned and all the malarkey that you've dished out all summer. Oh, I knew you weren't sixteen anymore. But I was a fool enough to believe you was straight.

BLANCHE: Who told you I wasn't—"straight"? My loving brother-in-law. And you believed him.

MITCH: I called him a liar at first. And then I checked on the story. First I asked our supply-man who travels through Laurel. And then I talked directly over long-distance to this merchant.

BLANCHE: Who is this merchant?

MITCH: Kiefaber.

BLANCHE: The merchant Kiefaber of Laurel! I know the man. He whistled at me. I put him in his place. So now for revenge he makes up stories about me.

MITCH: Three people, Kiefaber, Stanley, and Shaw, swore to them!

BLANCHE: Rub-a-dub-dub, three men in a tub! And such a filthy tub!

MITCH: Didn't you stay at a hotel called The Flamingo?

BLANCHE: Flamingo? No! Tarantula was the name of it! I stayed at a hotel called The Tarantula Arms!

MITCH: [*Stupidly.*] Tarantula?

BLANCHE: Yes, a big spider! That's where I brought my victims. [*She pours herself another drink.*] Yes, I had many intimacies with strangers. After the death of Allan—intimacies with strangers was all I seemed able to fill my empty heart with. . . . I think it was panic, just panic, that drove me from one to another, hunting for some protection—here and there, in the most—unlikely places—even, at last, in a seventeen-year-old boy but—somebody wrote the superintendent about it—"This woman is morally unfit for her position!" [*She throws back her head with convulsive, sobbing laughter. Then she repeats the statement, gasps, and drinks.*] True? Yes, I suppose—unfit somehow—anyway. . . . So I came here. There was nowhere else I could go. I was played out. You know what played out is? My youth was suddenly gone up the water-spout, and—I met you. You said you needed somebody. Well, I needed somebody, too. I thanked God for you, because you seemed to be gentle—a cleft in the rock of the world that I could hide in! But I guess I was asking, hoping—too much! Kiefaber, Stanley, and Shaw have tied an old tin can to the tail of the kite.

[*There is a pause.* MITCH *stares at her dumbly.*]

MITCH: You lied to me, Blanche.

BLANCHE: Don't say I lied to you.

MITCH: Lies, lies, inside and out, all lies.

BLANCHE: Never inside, I didn't lie in my heart. . . .

[*A vendor comes around the corner. She is a blind* MEXICAN WOMAN *in a dark shawl, carrying bunches of those gaudy tin flowers that lower-class Mexicans display at funerals and other festive occasions. She is calling barely audibly. Her figure is only faintly visible outside the building.*]

MEXICAN WOMAN: *Flores. Flores, Flores para los muertos.*[7] *Flores. Flores.*

BLANCHE: What? Oh! Somebody outside . . . [*She goes to the door, opens it and stares at the* MEXICAN WOMAN.]

MEXICAN WOMAN: [*She is at the door and offers* BLANCHE *some of her flowers.*] *Flores? Flores para los muertos?*

BLANCHE: [*Frightened.*] No, no! Not now! Not now! [*She darts back into the apartment, slamming the door.*]

MEXICAN WOMAN: [*She turns away and starts to move down the street.*] *Flores para los muertos.*

[*The polka tune fades in.*]

BLANCHE: [*As if to herself.*] Crumble and fade and—regrets—recriminations . . . "If you'd done this, it wouldn't've cost me that!"

MEXICAN WOMAN: *Corones*[8] *para los muertos. Corones . . .*

BLANCHE: Legacies! Huh. . . . And other things such as bloodstained pillowslips—"Her linen needs changing"—"Yes, Mother. But couldn't we get a colored girl to do it?" No, we couldn't of course. Everything gone but the—

MEXICAN WOMAN: *Flores.*

7. Flowers for the dead (Spanish). 8. Wreaths (Spanish).

BLANCHE: Death—I used to sit here and she used to sit over there and death was as close as you are. . . . We didn't dare even admit we had ever heard of it!

MEXICAN WOMAN: *Flores para los muertos, flores—flores . . .*

BLANCHE: The opposite is desire. So do you wonder? How could you possibly wonder! Not far from Belle Reve, before we had lost Belle Reve, was a camp where they trained young soldiers. On Sunday nights they would go in town to get drunk—

MEXICAN WOMAN: [*Softly.*] *Corones . . .*

BLANCHE: —and on the way back they would stagger onto my lawn and call—"Blanche! Blanche!"—the deaf old lady remaining suspected nothing. But sometimes I slipped outside to answer their calls. . . . Later the paddy-wagon[9] would gather them up like daisies . . . the long way home. . . . [*The* MEXICAN WOMAN *turns slowly and drifts back off with her soft mournful cries.* BLANCHE *goes to the dresser and leans forward on it. After a moment,* MITCH *rises and follows her purposefully. The polka music fades away. He places his hands on her waist and tries to turn her about.*] What do you want?

MITCH: [*Fumbling to embrace her.*] What I been missing all summer.

BLANCHE: Then marry me, Mitch!

MITCH: I don't think I want to marry you anymore.

BLANCHE: No?

MITCH: [*Dropping his hands from her waist.*] You're not clean enough to bring in the house with my mother.

BLANCHE: Go away, then. [*He stares at her.*] Get out of here quick before I start screaming fire! [*Her throat is tightening with hysteria.*] Get out of here quick before I start screaming fire. [*He still remains staring. She suddenly rushes to the big window with its pale blue square of the soft summer light and cries wildly.*] Fire! Fire! Fire!

[*With a startled gasp,* MITCH *turns and goes out the outer door, clatters awkwardly down the steps and around the corner of the building.* BLANCHE *staggers back from the window and falls to her knees. The distant piano is slow and blue.*]

Scene 10

It is a few hours later that night.

BLANCHE *has been drinking fairly steadily since* MITCH *left. She has dragged her wardrobe trunk into the center of the bedroom. It hangs open with flowery dresses thrown across it. As the drinking and packing went on, a mood of hysterical exhilaration came into her and she has decked herself out in a somewhat soiled and crumpled white satin evening gown and a pair of scuffed silver slippers with brilliants*[1] *set in their heels.*

Now she is placing the rhinestone tiara on her head before the mirror of the dressing-table and murmuring excitedly as if to a group of spectral admirers.

BLANCHE: How about taking a swim, a moonlight swim at the old rock-quarry? If anyone's sober enough to drive a car! Ha-ha! Best way in the world to stop

9. Police van. 1. Sparkling gems.

your head buzzing! Only you've got to be careful to dive where the deep pool is—if you hit a rock you don't come up till tomorrow . . . [*Tremblingly she lifts the hand mirror for a closer inspection. She catches her breath and slams the mirror face down with such violence that the glass cracks. She moans a little and attempts to rise.* STANLEY *appears around the corner of the building. He still has on the vivid green silk bowling shirt. As he rounds the corner the honky-tonk music is heard. It continues softly throughout the scene. He enters the kitchen, slamming the door. As he peers in at* BLANCHE, *he gives a low whistle. He has had a few drinks on the way and has brought some quart beer bottles home with him.*] How is my sister?

STANLEY: She is doing okay.

BLANCHE: And how is the baby?

STANLEY: [*Grinning amiably.*] The baby won't come before morning so they told me to go home and get a little shut-eye.

BLANCHE: Does that mean we are to be alone in here?

STANLEY: Yep. Just me and you, Blanche. Unless you got somebody hid under the bed. What've you got on those fine feathers for?

BLANCHE: Oh, that's right. You left before my wire came.

STANLEY: You got a wire?

BLANCHE: I received a telegram from an old admirer of mine.

STANLEY: Anything good?

BLANCHE: I think so. An invitation.

STANLEY: What to? A fireman's ball?

BLANCHE: [*Throwing back her head.*] A cruise of the Caribbean on a yacht!

STANLEY: Well, well. What do you know?

BLANCHE: I have never been so surprised in my life.

STANLEY: I guess not.

BLANCHE: It came like a bolt from the blue!

STANLEY: Who did you say it was from?

BLANCHE: An old beau of mine.

STANLEY: The one that give you the white fox-pieces?

BLANCHE: Mr. Shep Huntleigh. I wore his ATO[2] pin my last year at college. I hadn't seen him again until last Christmas. I ran in to him on Biscayne Boulevard. Then—just now—this wire—inviting me on a cruise of the Caribbean! The problem is clothes. I tore into my trunk to see what I have that's suitable for the tropics!

STANLEY: And come up with that—gorgeous—diamond—tiara?

BLANCHE: This old relic? Ha-ha! It's only rhinestones.

STANLEY: Gosh. I thought it was Tiffany diamonds. [*He unbuttons his shirt.*]

BLANCHE: Well, anyhow, I shall be entertained in style.

STANLEY: Uh-huh. It goes to show, you never know what is coming.

BLANCHE: Just when I thought my luck had begun to fail me—

STANLEY: Into the picture pops this Miami millionaire.

BLANCHE: This man is not from Miami. This man is from Dallas.

STANLEY: This man is from Dallas?

BLANCHE: Yes, this man is from Dallas where gold spouts out of the ground!

2. Probably Alpha Tau Omega, a college fraternity.

STANLEY: Well, just so he's from somewhere! [*He starts removing his shirt.*]

BLANCHE: Close the curtains before you undress any further.

STANLEY: [*Amiably.*] This is all I'm going to undress right now. [*He rips the sack off a quart beer bottle.*] Seen a bottle-opener? [*She moves slowly toward the dresser, where she stands with her hands knotted together.*] I used to have a cousin who could open a beer bottle with his teeth. [*Pounding the bottle cap on the corner of table.*] That was his only accomplishment, all he could do—he was just a human bottle-opener. And then one time, at a wedding party, he broke his front teeth off! After that he was so ashamed of himself he used t' sneak out of the house when company came . . . [*The bottle cap pops off and a geyser of foam shoots up.* STANLEY *laughs happily, holding up the bottle over his head.*] Ha-ha! Rain from heaven! [*He extends the bottle toward her.*] Shall we bury the hatchet and make it a loving-cup? Huh?

BLANCHE: No, thank you.

STANLEY: Well, it's a red-letter night for us both. You having an oil millionaire and me having a baby. [*He goes to the bureau in the bedroom and crouches to remove something from the bottom drawer.*]

BLANCHE: [*Drawing back.*] What are you doing in here?

STANLEY: Here's something I always break out on special occasions like this. The silk pyjamas I wore on my wedding night!

BLANCHE: Oh.

STANLEY: When the telephone rings and they say, "You've got a son!" I'll tear this off and wave it like a flag! [*He shakes out a brilliant pyjama coat.*] I guess we are both entitled to put on the dog. [*He goes back to the kitchen with the coat over his arm.*]

BLANCHE: When I think of how divine it is going to be to have such a thing as privacy once more—I could weep with joy!

STANLEY: This millionaire from Dallas is not going to interfere with your privacy any?

BLANCHE: It won't be the sort of thing you have in mind. This man is a gentleman and he respects me. [*Improvising feverishly.*] What he wants is my companionship. Having great wealth sometimes makes people lonely! A cultivated woman, a woman of intelligence and breeding, can enrich a man's life—immeasurably! I have those things to offer, and this doesn't take them away. Physical beauty is passing. A transitory possession. But beauty of the mind and richness of the spirit and tenderness of the heart—and I have all of those things—aren't taken away, but grow! Increase with the years! How strange that I should be called a destitute woman! When I have all of these treasures locked in my heart. [*A choked sob comes from her.*] I think of myself as a very, very rich woman! But I have been foolish—casting my pearls before swine![3]

STANLEY: Swine, huh?

BLANCHE: Yes, swine! Swine! And I'm thinking not only of you but of your friend, Mr. Mitchell. He came to see me tonight. He dared to come here in his work clothes! And to repeat slander to me, vicious stories that he had gotten from you! I gave him his walking papers . . .

3. See Matthew 7.6: "Do not give what is holy to dogs, or throw your pearls before swine, lest they trample them underfoot, and turn and tear you to pieces."

STANLEY: You did, huh?

BLANCHE: But then he came back. He returned with a box of roses to beg my forgiveness! He implored my forgiveness. But some things are not forgivable. Deliberate cruelty is not forgivable. It is the one unforgivable thing in my opinion and it is the one thing of which I have never, ever been guilty. And so I told him, I said to him, "Thank you," but it was foolish of me to think that we could ever adapt ourselves to each other. Our ways of life are too different. Our attitudes and our backgrounds are incompatible. We have to be realistic about such things. So farewell, my friend! And let there be no hard feelings. . . .

STANLEY: Was this before or after the telegram came from the Texas oil millionaire?

BLANCHE: What telegram? No! No, after! As a matter of fact, the wire came just as—

STANLEY: As a matter of fact there wasn't no wire at all!

BLANCHE: Oh, oh!

STANLEY: There isn't no millionaire! And Mitch didn't come back with roses 'cause I know where he is—

BLANCHE: Oh!

STANLEY: There isn't a goddam thing but imagination!

BLANCHE: Oh!

STANLEY: And lies and conceit and tricks!

BLANCHE: Oh!

STANLEY: And look at yourself! Take a look at yourself in that worn-out Mardi Gras[4] outfit, rented for fifty cents from some ragpicker! And with the crazy crown on! What queen do you think you are?

BLANCHE: Oh—God . . .

STANLEY: I've been on to you from the start! Not once did you pull any wool over this boy's eyes! You come in here and sprinkle the place with powder and spray perfume and cover the light-bulb with a paper lantern, and lo and behold the place has turned into Egypt and you are the Queen of the Nile![5] Sitting on your throne and swilling down my liquor! I say—*Ha!*—*Ha!* Do you hear me? *Ha—ha—ha!* [*He walks into the bedroom.*]

BLANCHE: Don't come in here! [*Lurid reflections appear on the walls around* BLANCHE. *The shadows are of a grotesque and menacing form. She catches her breath, crosses to the phone and jiggles the hook.* STANLEY *goes into the bathroom and closes the door.*] Operator, operator! Give me long-distance, please. . . . I want to get in touch with Mr. Shep Huntleigh of Dallas. He's so well known he doesn't require any address. Just ask anybody who—Wait!!—No, I couldn't find it right now. . . . Please understand, I—No! No, wait! . . . One moment! Someone is—Nothing! Hold on, please! [*She sets the phone down and crosses warily into the kitchen. The night is filled with inhuman voices like cries in a jungle. The shadows and lurid reflections move sinuously as flames along the wall spaces. Through the back wall of the rooms, which have become transparent, can be seen the sidewalk. A prostitute has rolled*[6] *a*

4. Literally, "Fat Tuesday" (French), the carnival before Lent, the period of self-denial, which begins on Ash Wednesday. 5. Cleopatra, Queen of Egypt. 6. Robbed.

drunkard. He pursues her along the walk, overtakes her and there is a struggle. A policeman's whistle breaks it up. The figures disappear. Some moments later the NEGRO WOMAN *appears around the corner with a sequined bag which the prostitute had dropped on the walk. She is rooting excitedly through it.* BLANCHE *presses her knuckles to her lips and returns slowly to the phone. She speaks in a hoarse whisper.*] Operator! Operator! Never mind long-distance. Get Western Union. There isn't time to be—Western—Western Union! [*She waits anxiously.*] Western Union? Yes! I—want to—Take down this message! "In desperate, desperate circumstances! Help me! Caught in a trap. Caught in—" *Oh!*

[*The bathroom door is thrown open and* STANLEY *comes out in the brilliant silk pyjamas. He grins at her as he knots the tassled sash about his waist. She gasps and backs away from the phone. He stares at her for a count of ten. Then a clicking becomes audible from the telephone, steady and rasping.*]

STANLEY: You left th' phone off th' hook.

[*He crosses to it deliberately and sets it back on the hook. After he has replaced it, he stares at her again, his mouth slowly curving into a grin, as he weaves between* BLANCHE *and the outer door. The barely audible "Blue Piano" begins to drum up louder. The sound of it turns into the roar of an approaching locomotive.* BLANCHE *crouches, pressing her fists to her ears until it has gone by.*]

BLANCHE: [*Finally straightening.*] Let me—let me get by you!
STANLEY: Get by me? Sure. Go ahead. [*He moves back a pace in the doorway.*]
BLANCHE: You—you stand over there! [*She indicates a further position.*]
STANLEY: You got plenty of room to walk by me now.
BLANCHE: Not with you there! But I've got to get out somehow!
STANLEY: You think I'll interfere with you? Ha-ha! [*The "Blue Piano" goes softy. She turns confusedly and makes a faint gesture. The inhuman jungle voices rise up. He takes a step toward her, biting his tongue, which protrudes between his lips. Softly.*] Come to think of it—maybe you wouldn't be bad to—interfere with. . . .

[BLANCHE *moves backward through the door into the bedroom.*]

BLANCHE: Stay back! Don't you come toward me another step or I'll—
STANLEY: What?
BLANCHE: Some awful thing will happen! It will!
STANLEY: What are you putting on now?

[*They are now both inside the bedroom.*]

BLANCHE: I warn you, don't, I'm in danger!

[*He takes another step. She smashes a bottle on the table and faces him, clutching the broken top.*]

STANLEY: What did you do that for?
BLANCHE: So I could twist the broken end in your face!
STANLEY: I bet you would do that!
BLANCHE: I would! I will if you—

STANLEY: Oh! So you want some roughhouse! All right, let's have some roughhouse! [*He springs toward her, overturning the table. She cries out and strikes at him with the bottle top but he catches her wrist.*] Tiger—tiger! Drop the bottle-top! Drop it! We've had this date with each other from the beginning!

[*She moans. The bottle-top falls. She sinks to her knees: He picks up her inert figure and carries her to the bed. The hot trumpet and drums from the Four Deuces sound loudly.*]

Scene 11

It is some weeks later. STELLA *is packing* BLANCHE'*s things. Sounds of water can be heard running in the bathroom.*

The portieres are partly open on the poker players—STANLEY, STEVE, MITCH *and* PABLO—*who sit around the table in the kitchen. The atmosphere of the kitchen is now the same raw, lurid one of the disastrous poker night.*

The building is framed by the sky of turquoise. STELLA *has been crying as she arranges the flowery dresses in the open trunk.*

EUNICE *comes down the steps from her flat above and enters the kitchen. There is an outburst from the poker table.*

STANLEY: Drew to an inside straight and made it, by God.
PABLO: *Maldita sea tu suerto!*
STANLEY: Put it in English, greaseball.
PABLO: I am cursing your rutting luck.
STANLEY: [*Prodigiously elated.*] You know what luck is? Luck is believing you're lucky. Take at Salerno.[7] I believed I was lucky. I figured that 4 out of 5 would not come through but I would . . . and I did. I put that down as a rule. To hold front position in this rat-race you've got to believe you are lucky.
MITCH: You . . . you . . . you . . . Brag . . . brag . . . bull . . . bull.

[STELLA *goes into the bedroom and starts folding a dress.*]

STANLEY: What's the matter with him?
EUNICE: [*Walking past the table.*] I always did say that men are callous things with no feelings but this does beat anything. Making pigs of yourselves. [*She comes through the portieres into the bedroom.*]
STANLEY: What's the matter with her?
STELLA: How is my baby?
EUNICE: Sleeping like a little angel. Brought you some grapes. [*She puts them on a stool and lowers her voice.*] Blanche?
STELLA: Bathing.
EUNICE: How is she?
STELLA: She wouldn't eat anything but asked for a drink.
EUNICE: What did you tell her?
STELLA: I—just told her that—we'd made arrangements for her to rest in the country. She's got it mixed in her mind with Shep Huntleigh.

[BLANCHE *opens the bathroom door slightly.*]

7. Important beachhead in the Allied invasion of Italy in World War II (1939–45).

BLANCHE: Stella.

STELLA: Yes.

BLANCHE: That cool yellow silk—the bouclé.[8] See if it's crushed. If it's not too crushed I'll wear it and on the lapel that silver and turquoise pin in the shape of a seahorse. You will find them in the heart-shaped box I keep my accessories in. And Stella . . . Try and locate a bunch of artificial violets in that box, too, to pin with the seahorse on the lapel of the jacket.

[*She closes the door.* STELLA *turns to* EUNICE.]

STELLA: I don't know if I did the right thing.

EUNICE: What else could you do?

STELLA: I couldn't believe her story and go on living with Stanley.

EUNICE: Don't ever believe it. Life has got to go on. No matter what happens, you've got to keep on going.

[*The bathroom door opens a little.*]

BLANCHE: [*Looking out.*] Is the coast clear?

STELLA: Yes, Blanche. [*To* EUNICE.] Tell her how well she's looking.

BLANCHE: Please close the curtains before I come out.

STELLA: They're closed.

STANLEY: —How many for you?

PABLO: Two.

STEVE: Three.

[BLANCHE *appears in the amber light of the door. She has a tragic radiance in her red satin robe following the sculptural lines of her body. The "Varsouviana" rises audibly as* BLANCHE *enters the bedroom.*]

BLANCHE: [*With faintly hysterical vivacity.*] I have just washed my hair.

STELLA: Did you?

BLANCHE: I'm not sure I got the soap out.

EUNICE: Such fine hair!

BLANCHE: [*Accepting the compliment.*] It's a problem. Didn't I get a call?

STELLA: Who from, Blanche?

BLANCHE: Shep Huntleigh . . .

STELLA: Why, not yet, honey!

BLANCHE: How strange! I—

[*At the sound of* BLANCHE'S *voice* MITCH'S *arm supporting his cards has sagged and his gaze is dissolved into space.* STANLEY *slaps him on the shoulder.*]

STANLEY: Hey, Mitch, come to!

[*The sound of this new voice shocks* BLANCHE. *She makes a shocked gesture, forming his name with her lips.* STELLA *nods and looks quickly away.* BLANCHE *stands quite still for some moments—the silver-backed mirror in her hand and a look of sorrowful perplexity as though all human experience shows on her face.* BLANCHE *finally speaks but with sudden hysteria.*]

8. Textile woven with uneven yarn to produce a rough, uneven surface.

BLANCHE: What's going on here? [*She turns from* STELLA *to* EUNICE *and back to* STELLA. *Her rising voice penetrates the concentration of the game.* MITCH *ducks his head lower but* STANLEY *shoves back his chair as if about to rise.* STEVE *places a restraining hand on his arm. Continuing.*] What's happened here? I want an explanation of what's happened here.

STELLA: [*Agonizingly.*] Hush! Hush!

EUNICE: Hush! Hush! Honey.

STELLA: Please, Blanche.

BLANCHE: Why are you looking at me like that? Is something wrong with me?

EUNICE: You look wonderful, Blanche. Don't she look wonderful?

STELLA: Yes.

EUNICE: I understand you are going on a trip.

STELLA: Yes, Blanche *is.* She's going on a vacation.

EUNICE: I'm green with envy.

BLANCHE: Help me, help me get dressed!

STELLA: [*Handing her dress.*] Is this what you—

BLANCHE: Yes, it will do! I'm anxious to get out of here—this place is a trap!

EUNICE: What a pretty blue jacket.

STELLA: It's lilac colored.

BLANCHE: You're both mistaken. It's Della Robbia blue.[9] The blue of the robe in the old Madonna pictures. Are these grapes washed? [*She fingers the bunch of grapes which* EUNICE *had brought in.*]

EUNICE: Huh?

BLANCHE: Washed, I said. Are they washed?

EUNICE: They're from the French Market.

BLANCHE: That doesn't mean they've been washed. [*The cathedral bells chime.*] Those cathedral bells—they're the only clean thing in the Quarter. Well, I'm going now. I'm ready to go.

EUNICE: [*Whispering.*] She's going to walk out before they get here.

STELLA: Wait, Blanche.

BLANCHE: I don't want to pass in front of those men.

EUNICE: Then wait'll the game breaks up.

STELLA: Sit down and . . .

[BLANCHE *turns weakly, hesitantly about. She lets them push her into a chair.*]

BLANCHE: I can smell the sea air. The rest of my time I'm going to spend on the sea. And when I die, I'm going to die on the sea. You know what I shall die of? [*She plucks a grape.*] I shall die of eating an unwashed grape one day out on the ocean. I will die—with my hand in the hand of some nice-looking ship's doctor, a very young one with a small blond mustache and a big silver watch. "Poor lady," they'll say, "the quinine[1] did her no good. That unwashed grape has transported her soul to heaven." [*The cathedral chimes are heard.*] And I'll be buried at sea sewn up in a clean white sack and dropped overboard—at noon—in the blaze of summer—and into an ocean as blue as [*Chimes again.*] my first lover's eyes!

9. Light blue seen in terra-cottas made by the Della Robbia family during the Italian Renaissance.

1. Medicinal salt used to treat malaria.

[A DOCTOR *and a* MATRON[2] *have appeared around the corner of the building and climbed the steps to the porch. The gravity of their profession is exaggerated—the unmistakable aura of the state institution with its cynical detachment. The* DOCTOR *rings the doorbell. The murmur of the game is interrupted.*]

EUNICE: [*Whispering to* STELLA.] That must be them.

[STELLA *presses her fists to her lips.*]

BLANCHE: [*Rising slowly.*] What is it?
EUNICE: [*Affectedly casual.*] Excuse me while I see who's at the door.
STELLA: Yes.

[EUNICE *goes into the kitchen.*]

BLANCHE: [*Tensely.*] I wonder if it's for me.

[*A whispered colloquy takes place at the door.*]

EUNICE: [*Returning, brightly.*] Someone is calling for Blanche.
BLANCHE: It *is* for me, then! [*She looks fearfully from one to the other and then to the portieres. The "Varsouviana" faintly plays.*] Is it the gentleman I was expecting from Dallas?
EUNICE: I think it is, Blanche.
BLANCHE: I'm not quite ready.
STELLA: Ask him to wait outside.
BLANCHE: I . . .

[EUNICE *goes back to the portieres. Drums sound very softly.*]

STELLA: Everything packed?
BLANCHE: My silver toilet articles are still out.
STELLA: Ah!
EUNICE: [*Returning.*] They're waiting in front of the house.
BLANCHE: They! Who's "they"?
EUNICE: There's a lady with him.
BLANCHE: I cannot imagine who this "lady" could be! How is she dressed?
EUNICE: Just—just a sort of a—plain-tailored outfit.
BLANCHE: Possibly she's—[*Her voice dies out nervously.*]
STELLA: Shall we go, Blanche?
BLANCHE: Must we go through that room?
STELLA: I will go with you.
BLANCHE: How do I look?
STELLA: Lovely.
EUNICE: [*Echoing.*] Lovely.

[BLANCHE *moves fearfully to the portieres.* EUNICE *draws them open for her.* BLANCHE *goes into the kitchen.*]

BLANCHE: [*To the men.*] Please don't get up. I'm only passing through.

2. Female supervisor at a hospital or other institution.

[*She crosses quickly to outside door.* STELLA *and* EUNICE *follow. The poker players stand awkwardly at the table—all except* MITCH, *who remains seated, looking down at the table.* BLANCHE *steps out on a small porch at the side of the door. She stops short and catches her breath.*]

DOCTOR: How do you do?

BLANCHE: You are not the gentleman I was expecting. [*She suddenly gasps and starts back up the steps. She stops by* STELLA, *who stands just outside the door, and speaks in a frightening whisper.*] That man isn't Shep Huntleigh.

[*The "Varsouviana" is playing distantly.* STELLA *stares back at* BLANCHE. EUNICE *is holding* STELLA'S *arm. There is a moment of silence—no sound but that of* STANLEY *steadily shuffling the cards.* BLANCHE *catches her breath again and slips back into the flat. She enters the flat with a peculiar smile, her eyes wide and brilliant. As soon as her sister goes past her,* STELLA *closes her eyes and clenches her hands.* EUNICE *throws her arms comfortingly about her. Then she starts up to her flat.* BLANCHE *stops just inside the door.* MITCH *keeps staring down at his hands on the table, but the other men look at her curiously. At last she starts around the table toward the bedroom. As she does,* STANLEY *suddenly pushes back his chair and rises as if to block her way. The* MATRON *follows her into the flat.*]

STANLEY: Did you forget something?

BLANCHE: [*Shrilly.*] Yes! Yes, I forgot something!

[*She rushes past him into the bedroom. Lurid reflections appear on the walls in odd, sinuous shapes. The "Varsouviana" is filtered into a weird distortion, accompanied by the cries and noises of the jungle.* BLANCHE *seizes the back of a chair as if to defend herself.*]

STANLEY: [*Sotto voce.*[3]] Doc, you better go in.

DOCTOR: [*Sotto voce, motioning to the* MATRON.] Nurse, bring her out.

[*The* MATRON *advances on one side,* STANLEY *on the other. Divested of all the softer properties of womanhood, the* MATRON *is a peculiarly sinister figure in her severe dress. Her voice is bold and toneless as a firebell.*]

MATRON: Hello, Blanche.

[*The greeting is echoed and re-echoed by other mysterious voices behind the walls, as if reverberated through a canyon of rock.*]

STANLEY: She says that she forgot something.

[*The echo sounds in threatening whispers.*]

MATRON: That's all right.

STANLEY: What did you forget, Blanche?

BLANCHE: I—I—

MATRON: It don't matter. We can pick it up later.

STANLEY: Sure. We can send it along with the trunk.

3. In an undertone (Italian).

BLANCHE: [*Retreating in panic.*] I don't know you—I don't know you. I want to be—left alone—please!

MATRON: Now, Blanche!

ECHOES: [*Rising and falling.*] Now, Blanche—now, Blanche—now, Blanche!

STANLEY: You left nothing here but spilt talcum and old empty perfume bottles—unless it's the paper lantern you want to take with you. You want the lantern?

[*He crosses to dressing table and seizes the paper lantern, tearing it off the light bulb, and extends it toward her. She cries out as if the lantern was herself. The* MATRON *steps boldly toward her. She screams and tries to break past the* MATRON. *All the men spring to their feet.* STELLA *runs out to the porch, with* EUNICE *following to comfort her, simultaneously with the confused voices of the men in the kitchen.* STELLA *rushes into* EUNICE*'s embrace on the porch.*]

STELLA: Oh, my God, Eunice help me! Don't let them do that to her, don't let them hurt her! Oh, God, oh, please God, don't hurt her! What are they doing to her? What are they doing? [*She tries to break from* EUNICE*'s arms.*]

EUNICE: No, honey, no, no, honey. Stay here. Don't go back in there. Stay with me and don't look.

STELLA: What have I done to my sister? Oh, God, what have I done to my sister?

EUNICE: You done the right thing, the only thing you could do. She couldn't stay here; there wasn't no other place for her to go.

[*While* STELLA *and* EUNICE *are speaking on the porch the voices of the men in the kitchen overlap them.* MITCH *has started toward the bedroom.* STANLEY *crosses to block him.* STANLEY *pushes him aside.* MITCH *lunges and strikes at* STANLEY. STANLEY *pushes* MITCH *back.* MITCH *collapses at the table, sobbing. During the preceding scenes, the* MATRON *catches hold of* BLANCHE*'s arm and prevents her flight.* BLANCHE *turns wildly and scratches at the* MATRON. *The heavy woman pinions her arms.* BLANCHE *cries out hoarsely and slips to her knees.*]

MATRON: These fingernails have to be trimmed. [*The* DOCTOR *comes into the room and she looks at him.*] Jacket,[4] Doctor?

DOCTOR: Not unless necessary. [*He takes off his hat and now he becomes personalized. The unhuman quality goes. His voice is gentle and reassuring as he crosses to* BLANCHE *and crouches in front of her. As he speaks her name, her terror subsides a little. The lurid reflections fade from the walls, the inhuman cries and noises die out and her own hoarse crying is calmed.*] Miss DuBois. [*She turns her face to him and stares at him with desperate pleading. He smiles; then he speaks to the* MATRON.] It won't be necessary.

BLANCHE: [*Faintly.*] Ask her to let go of me.

DOCTOR: [*To the* MATRON.] Let go.

[*The* MATRON *releases her.* BLANCHE *extends her hands toward the* DOCTOR. *He draws her up gently and supports her with his arm and leads her through the portieres.*]

4. That is, straitjacket, used to restrain the mentally ill.

BLANCHE: [*Holding tight to his arm.*] Whoever you are—I have always depended on the kindness of strangers.

[*The poker players stand back as* BLANCHE *and the* DOCTOR *cross the kitchen to the front door. She allows him to lead her as if she were blind. As they go out on the porch,* STELLA *cries out her sister's name from where she is crouched a few steps up on the stairs.*]

STELLA: Blanche! Blanche, Blanche!

[BLANCHE *walks on without turning, followed by the* DOCTOR *and the* MATRON. *They go around the corner of the building.* EUNICE *descends to* STELLA *and places the child in her arms. It is wrapped in a pale blue blanket.* STELLA *accepts the child, sobbingly.* EUNICE *continues downstairs and enters the kitchen where the men, except for* STANLEY, *are returning silently to their places about the table.* STANLEY *has gone out on the porch and stands at the foot of the steps looking at* STELLA.]

STANLEY: [*A bit uncertainly.*] Stella? [*She sobs with inhuman abandon. There is something luxurious in her complete surrender to crying now that her sister is gone. Voluptuously, soothingly.*] Now, honey. Now, love. Now, now, love. [*He kneels beside her and his fingers find the opening of her blouse.*] Now, now, love. Now, love. . . .

[*The luxurious sobbing, the sensual murmur fade away under the swelling music of the "Blue Piano" and the muted trumpet.*]

STEVE: This game is seven-card stud.

CURTAIN

1947

Writing about Literature

When it comes to the study of literature, reading and writing are closely interrelated—even mutually dependent—activities. The quality of whatever we write about literature depends entirely on the quality of our work as readers. Conversely, our reading isn't truly complete until we've tried to capture our sense of the literature in writing so as to make it intelligible, persuasive, and meaningful to other people. We read literature much more actively and attentively when we both integrate informal writing into the reading process—pausing periodically to mark important or confusing passages, to jot down significant facts, to describe the impressions and responses the text provokes—and when we envision our reading of literature as preparation for writing about it in a more sustained and formal way. The actual process of writing, conversely, requires re-reading and rethinking, testing our first impressions and initial hypotheses.

As we've suggested from the beginning of this book, literature itself is a vast conversation in which we participate most fully only when we engage with other readers. Writing allows us the opportunity—and even imposes on us the obligation—to do just that: In writing we respond not only to what other readers have actually said or written about the work but also to how we imagine other readers *might* realistically see it. By considering other readers' points of view and working to persuade them to accept alternative ways of interpreting a literary work, we ourselves learn new ways of seeing.

Writing about literature can take any number of forms, ranging from the very informal and personal to the very formal and public. Your instructor may well ask you to try your hand at more than one form. However, the essay is by far the most common and complex form that writing about literature—or **literary criticism**—takes. As a result, the following chapters will focus primarily on the essay.

Whether they require an essay, a response paper, or something else, however, assignments in literature courses often come equipped with a warning that goes something like this: "DO NOT SIMPLY RESTATE THE FACTS, PARAPHRASE, OR SUMMARIZE." We thus start here with a brief chapter (ch. 31) explaining what paraphrase, summary, and description are and how you can use them to move from response to essay.

Chapter 32, "The Literature Essay," reviews the five basic elements of all literature essays before turning, briefly, to two specific types—the comparative essay and the in-class exam essay. The chapter's goal is to give you a vivid sense of what you want to end up with at the end of the essay-writing process.

Chapter 33, "The Writing Process," focuses on how you get there, providing tips on every stage of essay development, from interpreting an assignment and generating a thesis to editing, proofreading, and manuscript formatting.

Chapter 34, "The Literature Research Essay," introduces the most common types of literature research and the key steps and strategies involved in writing research essays, from identifying and evaluating sources to responsibly and effectively integrating source material into your essay.

Whether they involve research or not, *all* essays about literature require responsible and effective quotation and citation; these are discussed in a separate chapter, "Quotation, Citation, and Documentation" (ch. 35).

Finally, this section concludes with a sample research essay (ch. 36) annotated to point out some of the features and strategies discussed in earlier chapters.

31 BASIC MOVES: PARAPHRASE, SUMMARY, AND DESCRIPTION

In literature courses, writing assignments often come equipped with a warning that goes something like this: "DO NOT SIMPLY RESTATE THE FACTS, PARAPHRASE, OR SUMMARIZE." It's a warning you ignore at your peril: *paraphrase*, *summary*, and *description* are each specific ways of "simply restating the facts," and a paper for a literature course will rarely pass muster if it does only that. Such papers must make arguments *about* facts and their significance, using statements of fact like those that make up paraphrases, summaries, and descriptions in order to substantiate and develop debatable claims about the literary text. (For more on factual statements versus debatable claims, see 32.1.2.)

As this suggests, however, any literature paper will need to include *some* paraphrase, description, and/or summary, since effective arguments must be based on, supported by, and developed with statements of fact. As important, paraphrase, summary, and description can be effective ways to *start* the writing process, helping you to discover potential paper topics and even debatable claims of the sort that drive literature essays.

In later chapters, we'll discuss and demonstrate ways to use paraphrase, summary, and description within literature essays of various types. The rest of this chapter simply defines and models these three basic, nonargumentative forms of writing about literature and discusses how you can use them to move from initial response to more formal, argumentative writing.

31.1 PARAPHRASE

31.1.1 What It Is

To paraphrase a statement is to restate it in your own words. Since the goal of paraphrase is to represent a statement fully and faithfully, a paraphrase tends to be at least as long as the original.

Below are paraphrases of sentences from a work of fiction (Jane Austen's *Pride and Prejudice*), a poem (W. B. Yeats's ALL THINGS CAN TEMPT ME), and a literature essay of the sort that could also be a secondary source in a literature research essay (George L. Dillon's "Styles of Reading").

Three Examples of Paraphrase

ORIGINAL SENTENCE	PARAPHRASE
It is a truth universally acknowledged that a single man in possession of a good fortune must be in want of a wife.	Everyone knows that a wealthy bachelor wants to get married.
All things can tempt me from this craft of verse: One time it was a woman's face, or worse— The seeming needs of my fool-driven land;	Anything can distract me from writing poetry, from a pretty girl to a foolish political cause.
[. . .] making order out of Emily's life is a complicated matter, since the narrator recalls the details through a nonlinear filter.	It's difficult to figure out when things happen to Emily because the narrator doesn't relate events in chronological order.

31.1.2 How to Use It

- Paraphrasing ensures and demonstrates that you understand what you've read. It can be especially helpful when authors' diction and syntax or their logic seems especially difficult, complex, or "foreign" to you. This is why paraphrase can be especially useful when reading and responding to a poem (see "Poetry: Reading, Responding, Writing") and when taking notes on secondary sources (see 34.3.2).
- Paraphrasing can direct your attention to nuances of tone or potentially significant details in any literary text, especially when you pay attention to anything you have difficulty paraphrasing. For example, paraphrasing Austen's sentence (above) might call your attention to the multiple—and thus difficult to paraphrase—meanings of phrases such as *a good fortune* and *in want of.*
- By drawing your attention to such details, paraphrasing can help you begin to generate the kind of interpretive questions an essay might explore. For example, the Austen paraphrase might lead you to ask, *What does* Pride and Prejudice *define as "a good fortune"? Does the novel illustrate different definitions? Does it endorse one definition over another?*

On the use of paraphrase in literature essays, see 32.1.4 (on evidence), 32.2.2 (on in-class exam essays), and 34.4.2 (on incorporating secondary source material into the literature research essay).

31.2 SUMMARY

31.2.1 What It Is

A summary is a fairly succinct restatement or overview—in your own words—of the content of an entire literary text or other source or a significant portion thereof. A summary of a literary work is generally called a *plot summary* because it focuses on the **action** or **plot**. Though a summary should be significantly shorter than the original, it can be any length you need it to be. (For more on plot summary, see ch. 1.)

Different readers—or even the same reader on different occasions and with different purposes in mind—will almost certainly summarize the same text or source in dramatically different ways. Summarizing entails selection and emphasis. As a result, any summary reflects a particular point of view and may even begin to imply a possible interpretation or argument. When writing a summary, you should try to be as objective as possible. Nevertheless, your summary will reflect a particular understanding and attitude, which is actually why it's useful.

Here are three quite different one-sentence summaries of HAMLET.

1. In the process of avenging his uncle's murder of his father, a young prince kills his uncle, himself, and many others.
2. A young Danish prince avenges the murder of his father, the king, by his uncle, who has usurped the throne, but the prince himself is killed, as are others, and a well-led foreign army has no trouble successfully invading the troubled state.
3. When a young prince hears, from the ghost of his murdered father, that his uncle, who has married the prince's mother, is the father's murderer, the prince devotes himself to learning the truth and avenging the wrong, feigning madness, acting erratically, causing the suicide of his beloved and the deaths of numerous others including, ultimately, himself.

31.2.2 How to Use It

Because even the most objective summary implies a point of view, summarizing a literary work may help you begin to figure out just what your particular point of view is or at least what aspects of the work strike you as most important and potentially worthy of analysis, especially if you compare your summary to that of another reader (as in the exercise in ch. 1) or try out different ways of summarizing the same work yourself. The second *Hamlet* summary above, for example, suggests a more political interpretation of the play than either of the other two summaries, by emphasizing the political roles of the various characters, the fact that the crime in the play involves two distinctly political crimes (usurpation and regicide), and the fact that the play ends with a foreign invasion.

On the use of summary in literature essays, see 32.1.4 (on evidence), 32.1.5 (on introductions), 32.2.2 (on in-class exam essays), and 34.4.2 (on incorporating secondary source material into the literature research essay).

31.3 DESCRIPTION

31.3.1 What It Is

Whereas both summary and paraphrase focus on content, a description of a literary text focuses more on its form, style, or structure, or any particular aspect thereof.

Below are two such descriptions, one of the rhyme scheme of Thomas Hardy's THE RUINED MAID, the other of Susan Glaspell's TRIFLES.

"The Ruined Maid"

A dialogue between "the ruined maid," 'Melia, and another woman from her hometown, Hardy's 24-line poem consists of six four-line stanzas. Each stanza consists of two rhyming couplets and ends with the same two words ("said she") and thus with the same (long *e*) rhyme sound. In stanzas 2 through 5, the first couplets each feature different rhymes ("socks/docks," "thou/now," "bleak/cheek," "dream/seem"). But in the first and last stanza they have the same rhyme and even the same final word ("crown/Town," "gown/Town"). As these examples illustrate, most of the end rhymes involve one-syllable words. But in four out of six stanzas, line 3 instead ends with a polysyllabic word (rhyming with "she") in which the rhyming syllable is set off from the first syllables by a dash: "prosperi-ty" (line 3), "compa-ny" (11), "la-dy" (15), "melancho-ly" (19).

Trifles

Trifles is a one-act play featuring only five characters, two women (Mrs. Hale and Mrs. Peters) and three men (the Sheriff, the County Attorney, and Mr. Hale). The play begins with all the characters entering the stage together, and a man (the County Attorney) is the first to speak. The play strictly observes the three classical or dramatic unities—of time, of place, and of action: it all unfolds in one setting (the kitchen of a remote midwestern farmhouse) and over the course of about one hour (on a very cold winter morning), exactly the same amount of time it takes to watch the play. Though the play isn't formally divided into scenes, and its action is continuous, it is broken up into about eight informal segments by the exits and re-entrances of the male characters, who usually (but not always) come and go as a group. The two female characters remain on the stage the entire time. The play ends with all the characters except one (Mr. Hale) onstage and with a woman (Mrs. Hale) speaking the last word.

31.3.2 How to Use It

Responding actively to a text and preparing to write about it require paying close attention to form, style, and structure, as well as content. Describing a text or some aspect of it (its imagery, rhyme scheme, or meter; plotting or point of view; divisions into stanzas, acts and scenes, or chapters; and so on) is a useful way to make sure that you are paying that kind of attention, identifying the sort of details whose significance you might explore in an essay. To move from description to argument begins with asking, "How do these details relate to each other?" "How do they individually and collectively contribute to the text's effect and meaning?"

On the use of description in literature essays, see 32.1.4 (on evidence) and 32.1.5 (on introductions).

32 THE LITERATURE ESSAY

The literature essay is a distinct subgenre of writing with unique elements and conventions. Just as you come to a poem, play, or short story with a specific set of expectations, so will readers approach your essay *about* a poem, play or story. They will be looking for particular elements, anticipating that the work will unfold in a certain way. This chapter explains and explores those elements so as to give you a clear sense of what an effective essay about literature looks like and how it works, along with concrete advice about how to craft your own.

A literature essay has particular elements and a particular form because it serves a specific purpose. Like any essay, it is a relatively short written composition that articulates, supports, and develops one major idea or claim. Like any work of expository prose, it aims to explain something complex—in this case at least one literary work—so that a reader may gain a new and deeper understanding. Explaining in this case entails both *analysis* (breaking the work down into its constituent parts and showing how they work together to form a meaningful whole) and *argument* (working to convince someone that the analysis is valid). Your essay needs to show your readers a particular way to understand the work, to interpret or read it. That interpretation or reading starts with your own personal response. But your essay also needs to persuade its readers that your interpretation is reasonable and enlightening—that though it is distinctive and new, it is more than merely idiosyncratic or subjective.

32.1 ELEMENTS OF THE LITERATURE ESSAY

To achieve its purpose, a literature essay must incorporate five elements: an effective *tone*; a compelling *thesis* and *motive*; ample, appropriate *evidence*; and a coherent *structure*. Though these five elements are essential to essays of any kind, each needs to take a specific shape in literature essays. The goal of this section is to give you a clear sense of that shape.

32.1.1 Tone (and Audience)

Although your reader or audience isn't an element *in* your essay, tone is. And tone and audience are closely interrelated. In everyday life, the tone we adopt has everything to do with whom we're talking to and what situation we're in. We talk very differently to our parents than to our best friends. And in different situations we talk to the same person in different ways, depending in part on what response we want to elicit. What tone do you adopt with your best friend when you need a favor? when you want advice? when you want him to take your advice? In each situation, you act on your knowledge of who your audience is, what information they already have, and what their response is likely to be. But you also try to adopt a tone that will encourage your listener to respond in a specific way. In writing, as in life, your sense of audience shapes your tone, even as you use tone to shape your audience's response.

So who is your audience? When you write an essay for class, the obvious answer is your instructor. But in an important sense, that's the wrong answer. Although your instructor could literally be the only person besides you who will ever read your essay, you write about literature to learn how to write for a general audience of peers—people a lot like you who are sensible and educated and who will appreciate having a literary work explained so that they can understand it more fully. Picture your readers as people with at least the same educational background. Assume they have some experience in reading literature and some familiarity with the basic literary terminology outlined in this book. (You should not feel the need to explain what a stanza is or to define the term ***in medias res***.) But assume, too, that your readers have read the specific literary work(s) only once, have not yet closely analyzed the work(s), and have not been privy to class discussions.

Above all, don't think of yourself as writing for only one reader and especially one reader who already sees the text as you do. Remember that the purpose of your essay is to *persuade* multiple readers with differing outlooks and opinions to see the text your way. That process begins with persuading those readers that you deserve their time, their attention, and their respect. The tone of your paper should be serious and straightforward, respectful toward your readers and the literary work. But its approach and vocabulary, while formal enough for academic writing, should be lively enough to capture and hold the interest of busy, distracted readers. Demonstrate *in* your essay the stance you want readers to take *toward* your essay: Earn careful attention and respect by demonstrating care, attentiveness, and respect; encourage your readers to keep an open mind by doing the same; engage your readers by demonstrating genuine engagement with the text, the topic, and the very enterprise of writing.

WAYS OF SETTING THE RIGHT TONE

- *Write about literature in the present tense.*
  Convincing your readers that you are a knowledgeable student of literature whose ideas they should respect requires not only correctly using—without feeling the need to explain—basic literary terms such as *stanza* and *in medias res* but also following other long-established conventions. Writing in present tense is one such convention, and it has two very practical advantages. One, it helps you avoid confusing tense shifts. Simply put, you can more clearly indicate *when* in a text something happens by simply specifying, "When X first visits Y" or "In the first stanza," and so on than you can by switching tenses. Two, present tense actually makes logical sense if you think about it: Though each time you pick up a story, poem, or play, your interpretation of the work might be different, the work itself isn't. Similarly, though in reading we experience a text as unfolding in time, it actually doesn't: Everything in the text simply, always is. Thus, yesterday, today, and tomorrow, Shakespeare's Ophelia goes mad, "A & P" asks what it means to grow up, John Donne (the implied author) depicts our relationship with God as a lifelong struggle, and so on.

That said, things do get a bit tricky when you write about contexts as well as texts or about *actual* versus *implied authors*. Notice, for example, how the following sentence moves from past to present tense as it moves from a statement about the actual author to one about the text: "In perhaps the same year, Dickinson wrote 'The Bible is an antique Volume,' which shows a mix of skepticism and optimism." Again, this switch (from past to present tense) makes logical sense: The actual author Emily Dickinson *wrote* this poem in the historical past, even as the poem *shows* now what it always has and always will (if we accept this writer's interpretation of it). By the same logic, the same tenses would be appropriate if we revised the sentence so as to make Emily Dickinson, the implied author, rather than her poem the subject of its second half: "In perhaps the same year, Dickinson wrote 'The Bible is an antique Volume,' a poem in which she expresses a mix of skepticism and optimism." (On implied versus actual authors, see ch. 2.)

- *Use the word "I" carefully.*
  On the one hand, many instructors have no problem with your using "I" when context makes that appropriate and effective; and used well, the first person can create a real sense of engagement and of "presence," of a distinctive mind at work. On the other hand, however, you should be aware that many instructors strongly object to any use of the word "I" simply because inexperienced writers so often use it inappropriately and ineffectively. Since the job of a literature essay is to use evidence to persuade readers to accept an interpretation of the work that is generally and objectively, not just personally or subjectively, valid and meaningful, resorting to "I feel" or "I think" can defeat that purpose. Sometimes such phrases can even be a sign that you've gotten way off track, perhaps substituting expressions of feeling for actual argument or dwelling more on your thoughts about an issue the text explores than on your thoughts about the text and the thoughts *it* communicates about that issue (as in the last example in 32.1.2 below). Generally speaking, if everything that follows a phrase like "I feel" or "I think" makes sense and has merit and relevance on its own, cut to the chase by cutting the phrase.

32.1.2 Thesis

A thesis is to an essay what a **theme** is to a short story, play, or poem: the governing idea or claim. Yet where a literary work implies at least one theme and often more, any essay about a literary work needs to have only one thesis that is explicitly stated in about one to three sentences somewhere in the introduction, usually at or near its end. Like a theme, as we have defined that term in earlier chapters, your thesis must be debatable—a claim that all readers won't automatically accept. It's a proposition you *can* prove with evidence from the literary text, yet it's one you *have* to prove, that isn't obviously true or merely factual.

Though it's unlikely that any of that is news to you, even experienced writers sometimes find themselves flummoxed when it comes to figuring out just what makes for a debatable claim or thesis about literature. To clarify, we juxtapose below two sets of sentences. On the left are inarguable statements—ones that are merely factual or descriptive and thus might easily find a home in a paraphrase, summary, or description (see ch. 31). On the right are debatable claims about the same topic or fact of the type that might work very well as the thesis of a literature essay.

FACTUAL STATEMENT	THESIS
"The Story of an Hour" explores the topic of marriage.	"The Story of an Hour" poses a troubling question: Does marriage inevitably encourage people to "impose [their] private will upon a fellow-creature" (par. 14)?
"Cathedral" features a character with a physical handicap.	By depicting an able-bodied protagonist who discovers his own emotional and spiritual shortcomings through an encounter with a physically handicapped person, "Cathedral" invites us to question traditional definitions of "disability."
"London" has three discrete stanzas that each end with a period; two-thirds of the lines are end-stopped.	In "London," William Blake uses various formal devices to suggest the unnatural rigidity of modern urban life.
Creon and Antigone are both similar and different.	Antigone and Creon share the same fatal flaw: Each recognizes only one set of obligations. In the end, however, the play presents Antigone as more admirable.

All of the thesis statements above are arguable because each implicitly answers a compelling interpretive question to which multiple, equally reasonable answers seem possible—for instance, *What is the key similarity between Antigone and Creon? Which character's actions and values does the play as a whole ultimately champion?* or, *What exactly does Blake demonstrate about modern urban life?* But they share other traits as well. All are clear and emphatic. All use *active verbs* to capture what the text and/or its implied author does (*poses, invites, uses, presents* versus *has, is, tries to*). And each entices us to read further by implying further interpretive questions—*What "set of obligations" do Antigone and Creon each "recognize"? Given how alike they are, what makes Antigone more admirable than Creon?* or, *According to Blake, what specifically is "unnatural" and "rigid" about modern urban life?* (Note, by the way, that the arguable claim in the Blake example *isn't* that he "uses various formal devices to suggest" something: *All* authors do that. Instead, the arguable claim has to do with *what* he suggests through formal devices.)

An effective thesis enables the reader to enter the essay with a clear sense that its writer has something to prove and what that is, and it inspires readers with the desire to see the writer prove it. We want to understand how the writer arrived at this view, to test whether it's valid, and to see how the writer will answer the other questions the thesis has generated in our minds. A good thesis captures readers' interest and shapes their expectations. In so doing, it also makes specific promises to readers that the rest of the essay must fulfill.

At the same time, an arguable claim about literature is not one-sided or narrow-minded. A thesis needs to stake out a position, but a position can and should admit complexity. Literature, after all, tends to focus more on exploring problems, conflicts, and questions than on offering easy solutions, resolutions, and answers. Its goal is to complicate and enrich, not to simplify, our way of looking at the world. The best essays about literature and the theses that drive them often do the same. As some of the sample thesis statements above demonstrate, for example, a good thesis can be a claim about just what the key question or conflict explored in a text is rather than about how that question is answered or that conflict resolved. Though an essay with this sort of thesis wouldn't be complete unless it ultimately considered possible answers and resolutions, it doesn't have to *start* there.

INTERPRETATION VERSUS EVALUATION (OR WHY IS A LITERATURE ESSAY *NOT* A REVIEW)

All the sample theses above involve *interpretive* claims—claims about how a literary text works, what it says, how one should understand it. Unless your instructor suggests otherwise, this is the kind of claim you need for a thesis in a literature essay.

Yet it's useful to remember that in reading and writing about literature we often make (and debate) a different type of claim—the *evaluative*. Evaluation entails assessment, and evaluative claims about literature tend to be of two kinds. The first involves aesthetic assessment and/or personal preference—whether a text (or a part or element thereof) succeeds, or seems to you "good," in artistic terms or whether you personally "like" it. This kind of claim features prominently in movie and book reviews, but literature essays are not reviews. Where the thesis of a review of Raymond Carver's CATHEDRAL, for example, might be that "Carver's story fails as a story because of its lack of action and unlikeable narrator" or that " 'Cathedral' does a great job of characterizing its narrator-protagonist," a better thesis for a literature essay might be something like that of Bethany Qualls's "A Narrator's Blindness in Raymond Carver's 'Cathedral' " (see "Fiction: Reading, Responding, Writing"): "Through his words even more than his actions the narrator unwittingly shows us why nothing much happens to him by continually demonstrating his utter inability to connect with others or to understand himself." In other words, where reviewers are mainly concerned with answering the question of *whether* a text "works," literary critics focus primarily on showing *how* it does so and with what effects. Likewise, though personal preferences may well influence your choice of which texts to write about, such preferences shouldn't be the primary focus of your essay—who, after all, can really argue with your personal preferences?

The second kind of evaluative claim involves moral, philosophical, social, or political judgment—whether an idea or action is wise or good, valid or admirable, something you "agree with." Both interpretive and evaluative claims involve informed opinion (which is why they are debatable). But whereas interpretive claims of the kind literary critics tend to privilege aim to elucidate the opinions and values expressed or enacted *in* and *by* a text or its characters, evaluative claims of this second type instead assess the validity *of* those opinions and values, often by comparison with one's own. Our sample thesis statement about ANTIGONE, for example, is a claim about which character *the play presents* as more admirable, not about which character the essay writer herself admires more.

The latter kind of claim is far from irrelevant or unimportant. One major reason why we read and write about literature is because it encourages us to grapple with real moral, social, and political issues of the kind we *should* develop informed opinions about. The question is simply one of emphasis: In a literature essay, the literature itself must be your primary focus, not your personal experience with or opinions about the issues it raises or the situations it explores.

Your main job in a literature essay is to thoughtfully explore *what* the work communicates and *how* it does so. Making an interpretive claim your thesis ensures that you keep your priorities straight. Once you have done that job thoroughly and well in the body of your essay, *then* you can consider evaluative questions in your conclusion (see "End: The Conclusion," in 32.1.5).

The poem "Ulysses" demonstrates that traveling and meeting new people are important parts of life. The speaker argues that staying in one place for too long is equivalent to substituting the simple act of breathing for truly living. I very much agree with the speaker's argument because I also believe that travel is one of life's most valuable experiences. Traveling allows you to experience different cultures, different political systems, and different points of view. It may change your way of thinking or make you realize that people all over the world are more similar than they are different.

This paragraph might be the kernel of a good conclusion to an essay that develops the thesis that "'Ulysses' demonstrates that traveling and meeting new people are important parts of life." Unfortunately, however, this paragraph actually appeared at the beginning of a student paper so full of similar paragraphs that it simply never managed to be *about* ULYSSES at all. Unfortunately, too, then, this paragraph demonstrates one of the reasons why some instructors forbid you to use the word "I" at all in literature essays (see 32.1.1).

32.1.3 Motive ("Although . . . I Think . . .")

One reason inexperienced writers might be tempted to emphasize evaluation over interpretation is that evaluative claims sometimes *seem* more debatable. It isn't always apparent, in other words, why there is anything useful or revelatory, even arguable or debatable, about a claim like "*Antigone* presents Antigone's form of over-simplification as more admirable than Creon's" or "Emily Dickinson questions traditional Christian doctrines." If you read the critical excerpts scattered throughout this book, however, you may notice something important: In the work of professional literary critics, such claims seem compelling because they are never presented in a vacuum but rather as what they truly are—a response to other actual or potential claims about the text. Such a presentation provides a *motive* for the reader of such an essay just as it does its writer.

Boil any good literature essay down to its essence, in other words, and you'll end up with a sentence that goes something like this (even though such a sentence never appears in the essay):

> Although they say / I used to think / someone might reasonably think ________________ about this text, I say / now think ________________ because ________________.

An effective essay doesn't just state a thesis ("I say/now think . . .") and prove it by providing reasons and evidence ("because . . ."); it also interests us in that thesis by framing it as a response to some other actual or potential thesis—something that "they" actually "say" about a text; that you "used to think" about it, perhaps on a first, casual reading; or that some reader *might* reasonably think or say.[1] In a literature research essay, "they" may well be published literary critics. But you don't have to read any published work on a literary text to discover alternative readings to which to respond: If you have discussed a text in class, you have heard plenty of statements made and questions raised about it, all of which are fodder for response. If you've read

1. For a more extensive discussion of this approach to writing, see Gerald Graff and Cathy Birkenstein's *"They Say/I Say": The Moves That Matter in Academic Writing*, 3rd ed., W. W. Norton, 2014.

and re-read a work carefully, your view of it has almost certainly evolved, ensuring that you yourself have a "naive reading" to compare to your more enlightened one. Finally, to write effectively about a text you inevitably have to imagine other possible interpretations, and, again, those *potential* readings are also ones you can "take on" in your essay.

Below, an introduction to one student writer's essay on Emily Dickinson appears first; below that are two different ways of paraphrasing the "Although . . . , I think" statement that introduction implies.

> When cataloguing Christian poets, it might be tempting to place Emily Dickinson between Dante and John Donne. She built many poems around biblical quotations, locations, and characters. She meditated often on the afterlife, prayer, and trust in God. Yet Dickinson was also intensely doubtful of the strand of Christianity that she inherited. In fact, she never became a Christian by the standards of her community in nineteenth-century Amherst, Massachusetts. Rather, like many of her contemporaries in Boston, Dickinson recognized the tension between traditional religious teaching and modern ideas. And these tensions between hope and doubt, between tradition and modernity animate her poetry. In "Some keep the Sabbath going to church—," "The Brain—is wider than the Sky—," "Because I could not stop for Death—," and "The Bible is an antique Volume," the poet uses traditional religious terms and biblical allusions. But she does so in order both to criticize traditional doctrines and practices and to articulate her own unorthodox beliefs.
>
> 1. *Although someone might reasonably think* of Emily Dickinson as a conventionally religious poet, *I think* she only uses traditional religious terms and biblical allusions to criticize traditional doctrines and practices and to articulate her own unorthodox beliefs.
> 2. *Although someone might reasonably think* of Emily Dickinson as either a conventionally religious poet or as an intensely doubtful one, *I think* she is both: Her poetry enacts a tension between traditional religious teaching and the hope it inspires and modern doubt.

The introduction above is an especially useful example because it demonstrates three things you need to keep in mind in articulating motive:

1. *Crafting a strong motive requires giving real substance to the argument you respond to*, taking it seriously enough that your readers do, too. Notice how the introduction above does that by actually listing a few good reasons why it might be entirely reasonable for a reader to think of Emily Dickinson either as a religious poet or as a skeptical one before making the claim that she is both. Simply put, you lose credibility from the get-go rather than generating interest in your thesis if you seem to be building a "straw man" just so you can knock him down.
2. *"Responding" to another point of view doesn't have to mean disagreeing with it.* Instead, you might
   - agree with, but complicate or qualify, the original claim

     > Although my classmates might be right to suggest that Miss Emily is heroic, I think she needs to be seen specifically as a tragic heroine.

   - present your thesis as a middle way between two extreme alternatives (as in the sample introduction above); or

- as in any conversation, change the subject by turning attention to something previously or easily ignored

Though our class discussion about "A Rose for Emily" focused exclusively on Miss Emily, we shouldn't ignore her father, since he makes Miss Emily what she is.

3. *"Although . . . I think . . . because . . ." is a useful sentence to use as you plan or summarize an argument, not a sentence that should actually appear in an essay*, in part because it creates problems with tone (see 32.1.1).

32.1.4 Evidence

Showing readers that your interpretation and argument are valid requires ample, appropriate evidence. And the appropriateness and quality of your evidence will depend on how you prepare and present it. Simply speaking, the term *evidence* refers to facts. But a fact by itself isn't really evidence for anything, or rather—as lawyers well know—any one fact can be evidence for many things. Like lawyers, literary critics turn a fact into evidence by interpreting it, drawing an inference from it, giving the reader a vivid sense of why and how the fact demonstrates a specific claim. You need, then, both to present concrete facts and to actively interpret them. *Show* readers why and how each fact matters.

KINDS OF LITERARY EVIDENCE: QUOTATION, PARAPHRASE, SUMMARY, DESCRIPTION

Quotations are an especially important form of evidence in literature essays. Any essay about literature that contains no quotations is likely to be weak. Readers of such an essay may doubt whether its writer has a thorough knowledge of the literary work or has paid adequate attention to details. And certain kinds of claims—about a character's motivations, a speaker's **tone**, a narrator's attitude toward a character, and so on—just can't be truly substantiated or developed *without* recourse to quotations.

At the same time, inexperienced writers sometimes make the mistake of thinking quotations are the *only* form of evidence in literature essays. They aren't. In fact, because a quotation will lead your reader to expect commentary on, and interpretation of, its language, you should quote directly from the text only when the actual wording is significant. Otherwise, keep attention on the facts that really matter by simply paraphrasing, describing, or summarizing. (For a discussion and examples of paraphrase, summary, and description, see ch. 31.)

In this paragraph, note how the student writer simply summarizes and paraphrases (in bold) when the key facts are what happens (who does what to whom when) and what the "gist" of a

At this point in the novel, Tess is so conflicted about what to do that she can't decide or do anything at all. **Only after asking her to marry him several times and repeatedly wondering aloud why Tess is hesitating does Angel finally get her to say yes or no. Even after agreeing to be his bride, Tess refuses to set a date, and it is Angel who finally, weeks later, suggests December 31.** Once Tess agrees, *the narrator describes this more as a matter of totally letting go than of finally taking charge:* "carried along upon the wings of the hours, without the sense of a will," she simply "drifted into . . . passive responsiveness to all things her lover suggested" (221; ch. 32). *Tess has given up agency and responsibility, letting events take whatever course they will rather than exerting her will,* even though—or maybe because—she is so terrified about the direction they will take.

character's remarks are, but she quotes when the specific wording is the key evidence. Notice, too, how the writer turns quotations into evidence by both introducing and following each with interpretive commentary (in italics) to create what some writing experts call a "quotation sandwich." (For more on effective quotation, see ch. 35.)

Through its form, the poem demonstrates that division can increase instead of lessen meaning, as well as love. On the one hand, just as the poem's content stresses the power of the love among *three people,* so the poem's form also stresses "threeness" as well as "twoness." **It is** after all **divided into *three* distinctly numbered stanzas, and each stanza consists of *three* sentences.** On the other hand, **every *sentence* is "divided equally twixt two" *lines,*** just as the speaker's "passion" is divided equally between two men. Formally, then, the poem mirrors the kinds of division it describes. Sound and especially rhyme reinforce this pattern since **the two lines that make up one sentence usually rhyme with each other to form a couplet. The only lines that don't conform to this pattern come at the beginning of the second stanza where we instead have alternating rhyme—*is* (line 7) rhymes with *miss* (9), *mourn* (8) rhymes with *scorn* (10).** But here, again, form reinforces content since these lines describe how the speaker "miss[es]" one man when the other is "by," a sensation she arguably reproduces in us as we read by ensuring we twice "miss" the rhyme that the rest of the poem leads us to expect.

Description (in bold) provides the evidence in this paragraph from the essay on Aphra Behn's ON HER LOVING TWO EQUALLY that appears earlier in this book ("Poetry: Reading, Responding, Writing").

32.1.5 Structure

Like an effective short story, poem, or play, your essay needs to have a beginning (or introduction), a middle (or body), and an ending (or conclusion). Each of these parts plays its own unique and vital role in creating a coherent, persuasive, and satisfying whole.

BEGINNING: THE INTRODUCTION

Your essay's beginning, or introduction, needs to draw readers in and prepare them for what's to come by not only articulating your thesis and your motive but also providing any basic information—about the author, the topic, the text, or its contexts—readers will need to understand and appreciate your argument. At the very least, you need to specify the title of the work you're writing about and the author's full name. Very short (one-sentence) plot summaries or descriptions of the text can also be useful, but they should be "slanted" so as to emphasize the aspects of the text you'll be most concerned with. (On summary and description, see ch. 31.)

Below are the first few sentences of two different essays on HAMLET. Notice how each uses plot summary to establish motive and build up to a thesis. Though we don't yet know exactly what each thesis will be, each summary is slanted to give readers a pretty clear sense of the essay's general topic and of the kind of thesis it's heading toward.

1. It would be easy to read William Shakespeare's *Hamlet* as a play dealing with exclusively personal issues and questions—"to be or not to be," am I really crazy?, did Mommy really love Daddy?, do I love Mommy too much? What such a reading ignores is the play's political dimension: Hamlet isn't just any person; he's the Prince of Denmark. The crime he investigates isn't just any old murder or even simple fratricide: by killing his brother, who is also Hamlet's father and Denmark's rightful king, Claudius commits regicide only in order to usurp the throne—a throne Hamlet is supposed to inherit. Thanks to their actions, the tragedy ends not only with the decimation of Denmark's entire royal family, including the prince himself, but also with a successful foreign invasion that we—and all of the characters—have been warned about from the beginning.
2. As everyone knows, William Shakespeare's *Hamlet* depicts a young man's efforts to figure out both whether his uncle murdered his father and what to do about it. What everyone may not have thought about is this: does it matter that the young man is a prince? that his uncle is now king? or even that the action takes place in ancient Denmark rather than in modern America? Ultimately, it does not. Though the play's setting and its characters' political roles and responsibilities might add an extra layer of interest, they shouldn't distract us from the universal and deeply personal questions the play explores.

Like the sentences in these partial introductions, each and every sentence in your introduction should *directly* contribute to your effort to spark readers' interest, articulate your thesis and motive, or provide necessary background information. Avoid sentences that are only "filler," especially vapid (hence boring and uninformative) generalizations or "truisms" about literature or life such as "Throughout human history, people have struggled with the question . . ."; "Literature often portrays conflicts"; "This story deals with many relevant issues"; or "In life, joy and sorrow often go together." To offer up one more truism worth keeping in mind in crafting introductions, "you only get one chance to make a first impression," and generalizations, truisms, and clichés seldom make a good one.

MIDDLE: THE BODY

As in any essay, the middle, or body, of your literature essay is where you do the essential work of supporting and developing your thesis by presenting and analyzing evidence. Each body paragraph needs to articulate, support, and develop *one* specific claim—a debatable idea directly related to the thesis, but smaller and more specific. This claim should be stated fairly early in the paragraph in a *topic sentence*. (If your paragraphs open with factual statements, you may have a problem.) And every sentence in the paragraph should help prove and elaborate on that claim. Indeed, each paragraph ideally should build from an initial, general statement of the claim to the more complex form of it that you develop by presenting and analyzing evidence. In this way, each paragraph functions a bit like a miniature essay with its own thesis, body, and conclusion.

Your essay as a whole should develop logically, just as each paragraph does. To ensure that happens, you need to do the following:

- Order your paragraphs so that each builds on the last, with one idea following another in a *logical* sequence. The goal is to lay out a clear path for the reader. Like any path, it should go somewhere. Don't just prove your point; develop it.
- Present each idea/paragraph so that the logic behind the order is clear. Try to start each paragraph with a sentence that functions as a bridge, transporting the reader from one claim to the next. The reader shouldn't have to leap.

The specific sorts of topic and transition sentences you need will depend in part on the kind of literature essay you're writing. Later in this and other chapters, we'll demonstrate what they tend to look like in comparative essays, for example. But your thesis should always be your main guide.

Below are the thesis and topic sentences from the student essay on Raymond Carver's "Cathedral" that appears earlier in this book ("Fiction: Reading, Responding, Writing"). Notice that just as the thesis is a claim about the narrator, so, too, are all the topic sentences and that the writer begins with what she acknowledges to be the most "evident" or obvious claim.

> Thesis: Through his words even more than his actions the narrator unwittingly demonstrates his utter inability to connect with others or to understand himself.
>
> Topic Sentences:
>
> 1. The narrator's isolation is most evident in the distanced way he introduces his own story and the people in it.
> 2. At least three times the narrator himself notices that this habit of not naming or really acknowledging people is significant.
> 3. Also reinforcing the narrator's isolation and dissatisfaction with it are the awkward euphemisms and clichés he uses, which emphasize how disconnected he is from his own feelings and how uncomfortable he is with other people's.
> 4. Once the visit actually begins, the narrator's interactions and conversations with the other characters are even more awkward.
> 5. Despite Robert's best attempt to make a connection with the narrator, the narrator resorts to labels again.
> 6. There is hope for the narrator at the end as he gains some empathy and forges a bond with Robert over the drawing of a cathedral.
> 7. However, even at the very end it isn't clear just whether or how the narrator has really changed.

END: THE CONCLUSION

In terms of their purpose (not their content), conclusions are introductions in reverse. Whereas introductions draw readers away from their world and into your essay, conclusions send them back. Introductions work to convince readers that they should read the essay; conclusions work to show them why and how the experience was worthwhile. You should approach conclusions, then, by thinking about what specific sort of lasting impression you want to create. What can you give readers to take with them as they journey back into the "real world"?

In literature essays, effective conclusions often consider at least one of the following three things:

1. *Implications*—What picture of your author's work or worldview does your argument imply? Alternatively, what might your argument suggest about some real-world issue or situation? Implications don't have to be earth-shattering. It's unlikely that your reading of August Wilson's FENCES will rock your readers' world. But your argument about this play should in some small but worthwhile way change how readers see Wilson's work or provide some new insight into some topic that work explores—how racism works, or how difficult it is for people to adjust to changes in the world around us, or how a parent or spouse might go wrong, and so on. If your essay has not, to this point, dealt with theme, now is a good time to do so. If you have not mentioned the author's name since the introduction, do so now; often, making the implied or actual author the subject of at least some of your sentences is one way to ensure that you are moving from argument to implications.
2. *Evaluation*—Though, as we've stressed, literature essays need to focus primarily on interpretation, conclusions are a good place to move from interpretation to evaluation. In a sense, careful interpretation earns you the right to do some thoughtful evaluation. What might your specific interpretation of the text reveal about its literary quality or effectiveness? Alternatively, to what extent and how exactly do you agree or disagree with the author's conclusions about a particular issue? How, for example, might your own view of how racism works compare to the view implied in *Fences*? (For more on evaluative and/versus interpretive claims, see 32.1.2.)
3. *Areas of ambiguity or unresolved questions*—Are there any remaining puzzles or questions that your argument or the text itself doesn't resolve or answer? Or might your argument suggest a new question or puzzle worth investigating?

Above all, don't merely repeat what you've already said. If your essay has done its job to this point, and especially if your essay is relatively short, your readers may well feel bored or even insulted if they get a mere summary. You should certainly clarify anything that needs clarifying, but you should also go further. The best essays are rounded wholes in which conclusions do, in a sense, circle back to the place where they started. But the best essays remind readers of where they began only in order to give them a more palpable sense of how far they've come and why it matters. Your conclusion is your chance to ensure that readers *don't* leave your essay wondering, "Okay. So what?"

It's possible that not feeling "inside anything" (par. 135) could be a feeling of freedom from his own habits of guardedness and insensitivity, his emotional "blindness." But even with this final hope for connection, for the majority of the story the narrator is a closed, judgmental man who isolates himself and cannot connect with others. The narrator's view of the world is one filled with misconceptions that the visit from Robert starts to slowly change, yet it is not clear what those changes are, how far they will go, or whether they will last. **Living with such a narrator for the length even of a short story and the one night it describes can be a frustrating experience. But in the end that might be Raymond Carver's goal: by making us temporarily see the world through the eyes of its judgmental narrator, "Cathedral" forces us to do what the narrator himself has a hard time doing. The question is, will that change us?**

In its original state, this conclusion to Bethany Qualls's essay on Raymond Carver's "Cathedral" might beg the "So what?" question. Yet notice what happens when we add just three more sentences that try to answer that question. (Qualls's essay appears at the end of "Fiction: Reading, Responding, Writing.")

32.2 COMMON ESSAY TYPES

All literature essays have the same basic purpose and the same five elements. Yet they come in almost infinite varieties, each of which handles those elements somewhat differently and thus also poses somewhat different writing challenges. In the next chapter, for example, we discuss a few literature essay topics so common that they virtually define distinct types or subgenres of the literature essay (32.1.3). The rest of this chapter, however, concentrates exclusively on two especially common and in some ways especially challenging essay types—the comparative essay and the in-class exam essay.

32.2.1 The Comparative Essay

As we have emphasized throughout this book, comparison is a fundamental part of all reading: We develop our expectations about how a poem, play, or story will unfold in part by consciously or unconsciously comparing it to other poems, plays, and stories we've read; we get a sense of just who a character is by comparing her to other characters in the same story or play; and so on. Not surprisingly, then, one of the most common types of essays assigned in literature classes is one that considers similarities and differences within a work, between two works, or among several. One might, for example, write an essay comparing different characters' interpretations of Georgianna's birthmark in Nathaniel Hawthorne's THE BIRTH-MARK or one comparing the use of symbolism in this Hawthorne story to that in Edwidge Danticat's A WALL OF FIRE RISING.

The key challenges involved in writing effective comparison essays are achieving the right balance between comparison and contrast, crafting an appropriate thesis, and effectively structuring the body of the essay.

COMPARISON AND/VERSUS CONTRAST

"Comparison-contrast" is a label commonly applied to comparison essays, but it's a somewhat misleading one: Though some comparative essays give greater stress to similarities, others to differences (or contrast), *all* comparison has to pay at least some attention to both. Contrast is thus *always* part of comparison.

Where the emphasis falls in your essay will depend partly on your assignment, so be sure that you scrutinize it carefully and understand what it requires of you. An assignment that asks you to "explain how and why children feature prominently in Romantic literature" by "analyzing the work of at least two Romantic poets," for example, encourages you to pay more attention to similarities so as to demonstrate understanding of a single "Romantic" outlook. Conversely, an assignment asking you to "contrast Wordsworth and Coleridge" and describe "the major differences in their poetry" obviously emphasizes contrast. Again, however, even an assignment that stresses differences requires you first to establish some similarities as a ground for contrast, even as an assignment that stresses similarities requires you to acknowledge the differences that make the similarities meaningful.

If the assignment gives you leeway, your particular topic and thesis will determine the relative emphasis you give to similarities and differences. In "Out-Sonneting Shakespeare: An Examination of Edna St. Vincent Millay's Use of the Sonnet Form" (ch. 22), for example, student writer Melissa Makolin makes her case for the distinctiveness and even radicalism of Millay's sonnets both by contrasting them to those of Shakespeare and by demonstrating the similarities between two sonnets by Shakespeare, on the one hand, and by Millay, on the other. But one could easily imagine an essay that instead demonstrated Millay's range by emphasizing the differences between her two sonnets, perhaps by building a thesis out of Makolin's claim that one poem is about "impermanent lust," the other "eternal love."

THE COMPARATIVE ESSAY THESIS

Like any essay, a comparative essay needs a thesis—*one* argumentative idea that embraces all the things (texts, characters, etc.) being compared. If you're like most of us, you may well be tempted to fall back on a statement along the lines of "These things are similar but different." Sadly, that won't cut it as a thesis. It isn't arguable (what two or more things *aren't* both similar and different?), nor is it specific enough to give your comparison direction and purpose: What such a thesis promises is less a coherent argument than a series of seemingly random, only loosely related observations about similarities and differences, desperately in search of a point.

At the end of the introduction to his comparative essay, student writer Charles Collins first articulates his main claim about each of the two short stories he will compare and then offers *one* overarching thesis statement.

> In "The Birth-Mark," the main character, Aylmer, views his wife's birthmark as a flaw in her beauty, as well as a symbol of human imperfection, and tries to remove it. In "the Thing in the Forest," the protagonists, Penny and Primrose, react to the Thing both as a real thing and as a symbol. The characters' interpretation of these things is what creates conflict, and the stories are both shaped by the symbolic meanings that the characters ascribe to those things.

(You can find the entire essay at the end of ch. 5.)

COMPARATIVE ESSAY STRUCTURES

In structuring the body of a comparative essay, you have two basic options, though it's also possible to combine these two approaches. Make sure to choose the option that best suits your particular texts, topics, and thesis rather than simply fall back on whichever structure feels most familiar or easy to you. Your structure and your thesis should work together to create a coherent essay that illuminates something about the works that can only be seen through comparison.

The Block Method

The first option tends to work best both for shorter essays and for essays, of any length, in which you want to stress differences at least as much as similarities. As its common label, "the block method," implies, this approach entails dividing your essay into "blocks" or sections that each lay out your entire argument about one of the things you're comparing. Charles Collins's essay comparing two stories, for example, is divided roughly in half: His first three body paragraphs analyze one story (THE BIRTH-MARK), the last four body paragraphs another story (THE THING IN THE FOREST). To knit the two halves of the essay together into one whole, however, Collins begins the second "block" with a paragraph that discusses both stories. Such transitions are crucial to making the "block" method work.

This paragraph of Collins's essay serves as a transition between the two halves or "blocks" of his essay, the first on "The Birth-Mark," the second on "The Thing in the Forest."

> The symbolism in "The Birth-Mark" is fairly straightforward. The characters openly acknowledge the power of the symbol, and the narrator of the story clearly states what meaning Aylmer finds in it. In "The Thing in the Forest" what the thing represents is not as clear. Penny and Primrose, the story's main characters, do not view the Thing as symbolic, as Aylmer does the birthmark. Neither the narrator nor the characters directly say why the Thing is important to Penny and Primrose or even whether the Thing they see in the forest is the monster, the Loathly Worm, that they later read about in the book at the mansion. . . .

In addition to strong, meaty transition paragraphs, effective use of the block method also requires that you

- *make each block or section of your essay match the others* in terms of the issues it takes up or the questions it answers, so as to maintain clear points of comparison. In Collins's symbolism essay (ch. 5), for example, each "block" answers the same questions with regard to each of the two stories and main characters being compared: whether or not the characters in a story see something as a symbol, what it ultimately comes to symbolize to them or to the reader, and how the characters' response to the symbol shapes their behavior.
- *order and present the blocks so that each builds on the last*: Though your blocks should match, their order shouldn't be random; rather, each block should *build* on the one that came before, just as should paragraphs/topic sentences in any essay. In Collins's essay, for example, the discussion of "The Birth-Mark" comes first because his argument is that symbolism here is more "straightforward" or simple than it is in "The Thing in the Forest,"

and the transition homes in on that difference. As in many essays, then, the movement here is from the most to the least obvious and simple points.

The Point-by-Point or Side-by-Side Method

The second method of structuring a comparative essay requires you to integrate your discussions of the things—texts or characters, for example—that you are comparing. Each section of your essay (which might be one paragraph or two) should begin with a topic sentence that refers to all the things you're comparing rather than exclusively to one.

Below is a paragraph from a student essay comparing Samuel Taylor Coleridge's FROST AT MIDNIGHT and Matthew Arnold's DOVER BEACH using the "point-by-point method." Like every other body paragraph in this essay, this one discusses both poems and their speakers.

> Differently but equally disturbed by the thoughts and emotions stirred by the natural scene before them, both speakers turn to the past, without finding much consolation in it. In Coleridge's poem, that past is specific and personal: What the speaker remembers are his schooldays, a time when he was just as bored and lonely and just as trapped inside his own head as he is now. Then, as now, he "gazed upon the" fire and "watch[ed] that fluttering" ash (lines 25–26), feeling no more connection then to his "stern precepto[r]" than he does now to his sleeping baby (37). In Arnold's poem, the past the speaker thinks of is more distant and historical. What he remembers are lines by Sophocles written thousands of years ago and thousands of miles away. But in his case, too, the past just seems to offer more of the same rather than any sort of comfort or relief. Just as he now—standing by a "distant northern sea" (20)—hears in the waves "[t]he eternal note of sadness" (14), so "Sophocles long ago"—"on the Aegean"—"[h]eard" in them "the turbid ebb and flow / Of human misery" (15–16, 18).

Below are the thesis and outline for another point-by-point comparison essay, this one analyzing two short stories—Franz Kafka's A HUNGER ARTIST and Flannery O'Connor's "Everything That Rises Must Converge." In the essay itself, each numbered section consists of two paragraphs, the first (a) discussing O'Connor's protagonist, the second (b) Kafka's.

> Thesis: "A Hunger Artist" and "Everything That Rises Must Converge" depict changing worlds in which the refusal to adapt amounts to a death sentence.
>
> Outline:
>
> 1. Both Julian's mother and the hunger artist live in rapidly changing worlds in which they don't enjoy the status they once did.
>   a) Julian's mother's world: the civil rights movement and economic change > loss of status
>   b) hunger artist's world: declining "interest in professional fasting" > loss of status
> 2. Rather than embracing such changes, both the artist and the mother resist them.
>   a) Julian's mother: verbally expressed nostalgia, refusal to even *see* that things are changing

   b) the hunger artist: nostalgia expressed through behavior, does see that things are changing

3. Both characters take pride in forms of self-sacrifice that they see as essential to upholding "old-world" standards.

   a) Julian's mother: sacrifices for him, upholding family position and honor
   b) hunger artist: sacrifices for himself, upholding traditions of his art

4. Both characters nonetheless die as a result of their unwillingness to adapt.

   a) Julian's mother
   b) hunger artist

5. The endings of both stories create uncertainty about how we are to judge these characters and their attitudes.

   a) Julian's mother: Julian's last words and the story's create more sympathy for the mother
   b) hunger artist: his last words and description of the panther that replaces him make him less sympathetic

32.2.2 The Essay Test

Essays you are required to write for in-class exams do not fundamentally differ from those you write outside of class. Obviously, however, having to generate an essay on the spot presents peculiar challenges. Below, we offer some general tips before discussing the two basic types of in-class essay exams.

GENERAL TIPS

- *Carefully review instructions.*
  Though instructors rarely provide actual exam questions in advance, they usually do give you some indication of how many questions you'll have to answer, what kind of questions they will be, and how much they will each count. Whether you get such instructions before or during the exam, take the time to consider them carefully before you start writing. Make sure you understand exactly what is expected of you, and ask your instructor about anything that seems the least confusing or ambiguous. You don't want to produce a great essay on a Shakespeare sonnet only to discover that your essay was supposed to compare two Shakespeare sonnets. Nor do you want to spend 75 percent of your time on the question worth 25 points and 25 percent on the question worth 75 points.
- *Glean all the information you can from sample questions.*
  In lieu of or in addition to instructions, instructors will sometimes provide sample questions in advance of an exam. Read rightly, such questions can give you a lot of information about what you need to be able to do on the exam. If presented with the sample question "What are three characteristic features of short stories by Flannery O'Connor, and what is their combined effect?," for example, you should come to the exam prepared not only to write an essay addressing this specific question but also or alternatively an essay addressing either a different question about the assigned O'Connor stories (i.e., same texts, different topic) or a similar question about other authors that you read multiple works by (i.e., same topic, different texts).

- *Anticipate questions or topics and strategize about how to use what you know.*
Whether or not an instructor actually gives you sample questions, exam questions rarely, if ever, come entirely out of the blue. Instead they typically emerge directly out of class lectures and discussions. As important, even questions that do ask you to approach a text in what seems like a new way can still be answered effectively by drawing upon the facts and ideas discussed in class. Keeping good notes and reviewing them as you prepare for the exam should thus help you both to anticipate the sorts of topics you'll be asked to address and to master the information and ideas well enough so that you can use what you know in responding even to unanticipated questions.

- *Review and brainstorm with classmates.*
Just as discussing a work in class can broaden and deepen your understanding of it, so reviewing with classmates can help you see different ways of understanding and organizing the material and the information and ideas discussed in class. Compare notes, certainly, but also discuss and brainstorm. What sorts of questions might your classmates anticipate?

- *Read questions carefully and make sure you answer them.*
Once you have the actual exam questions, read them carefully before you start writing. Make sure you understand exactly what the question asks you to do, and—again—ask your instructor to clarify anything confusing or ambiguous.

  Don't ignore any part of a question, but do put your emphasis where the question itself does. Let's suppose your question is, "What does Dickinson seem to mean by 'Telling all the truth but telling it slant'? How might she do just that in her poetry? How might Dickinson's personal experience or historical milieu have encouraged her to approach things this way?" An essay in answer to this question that didn't say anything at all about biographical or historical context or speculate at all about how one or the other shaped Dickinson's notion of truth telling would be less than complete. Yet the question allows you to consider only *one* of these two contexts rather than both. More important, it asks you to devote most of your essay to analyzing *at least two poems* ("poetry") rather than discussing context. A good strategy might thus be to consider context only in your introduction and/or conclusion.

- *Be specific.*
One key difference between good exam essays and so-so or poor ones is the level and kind of detail they provide: One thing an exam is testing is whether you have actually read and really know the material; another is how well you can draw on facts to make an argument rather than simply regurgitating general ideas expressed in class. In response to the question above, for example, noodling on in a general way about Dickinson's use of dashes or metaphor will only take you so far—and not nearly far enough to score well. In answering this question, you should mention the titles of at least two specific poems and carefully explain precisely how each of them tells the truth slantwise or helps us understand what Dickinson means by slantwise truth. For example: "In the poem that actually begins 'Tell all the truth but tell it slant,' Dickinson suggests that to successfully convey the truth, you have to do it in a roundabout way. People need to be eased into the truth; if it comes all at once, it's too much. She even compares that kind of direct truth-telling to being struck by lightning." (See below for further discussion of specificity and how to achieve it in closed- versus open-book exams.)

- *Allow time to review and reconsider your essays.*
  Though you're obviously pressed for time in an exam, leave yourself at least a few minutes to read over your essay before you have to hand it in. In addition to correcting actual mistakes, look for places where you could use more concrete evidence or make tighter, clearer connections between one point or claim and another.

CLOSED- VERSUS OPEN-BOOK EXAMS

How you prepare for exam essays and how those essays will be judged will depend, in part, on whether your exam is "open-book" or "closed-book"—whether, in other words, you are allowed to consult the literary texts and perhaps even your notes about them during the exam itself.

At first glance, open-book exams seem much easier, and in some ways they are. Having the literary text(s) in front of you ensures that you don't have to rely entirely on memory to conjure up factual evidence: You can double-check characters' names, see what a poem's rhyme scheme is, actually quote the text, and so on. The fact that you *can* do all that also means, however, that you need to: Instructors rightly expect more concrete and specific evidence, including quotations, in open-book exam essays. The bar, in short, is higher.

At the same time, there's a danger of spending so much time during the exam looking back through the text that you don't have adequate time to craft your argument about it. Here, good preparation can help. If you know which texts you're likely to be asked about on the exam, make sure that you mark them up in advance, highlighting especially telling passages (including those discussed in class), making notations about **rhyme scheme** and **meter**, and so on, so that you can marshal your evidence faster during the exam. Just make sure that you consult with your instructor in advance about what, if any, notes you are allowed to write in the book you bring with you to the exam.

If the exam is closed-book, your instructor won't be looking for quite the same level of detail when it comes to evidence, but that doesn't mean you don't need any. To prepare for a closed-book exam, you will need to do some memorizing: Knowing a text word-for-word is rarely required or helpful, but it is essential that you master the basic facts about it such as **genre**, title, author, characters' names; have a general sense of its **plot**, structure, and form; and can recall any facts about context that were stressed in class. In your essay, you will need to make good use of paraphrase, summary, and description (see ch. 31).

Below are two versions of a paragraph from an essay written for a closed-book exam. Without consulting the texts, the essayist cannot actually quote them. What the essayist can do is paraphrase an important piece of dialogue and summarize key episodes. What makes the second version better than the first is its much greater specificity about action, timing, characters, and dialogue—who says and does what to whom, when, and in what story.

1. O'Connor's stories often involve moments of extreme violence, like what happens to the old ladies in "Everything That Rises Must Converge" and "A Good Man Is Hard to Find." A character even says it would be a good thing if we were threatened with violence all the time.

2. O'Connor's stories often end with moments of extreme violence. At the end of "Everything That Rises Must Converge," after Julian's mother's

gives a little boy a penny, his mother reacts to what she sees as condescension by whacking Julian's mother in the head with her purse. "A Good Man Is Hard to Find" ends with the Misfit shooting the grandmother point-blank after she has had to watch and listen as each of her family members is dragged off into the woods and shot. Afterward, the Misfit even suggests that the grandmother would have been a better person if she'd been threatened with that kind of violence all the time.

33 THE WRITING PROCESS

Doing anything well requires both knowing what you're trying to achieve and having some strategies for how to go about it. Where "The Literature Essay" chapter (ch. 32) focuses mainly on the *what*, this chapter focuses more on the *how*. In practice, of course, the writing process will vary from writer to writer and from assignment to assignment. No one can give you a recipe. What we instead do here is present you with a menu of strategies to try out and adapt to your particular tendencies as a writer and to the requirements of specific writing occasions and assignments.

As you do so, keep in mind that writing needn't be a solitary enterprise. Ultimately, your essay must be your own work. That is absolutely essential; anything else is plagiarism. But most writers—working in every genre and discipline, at every level—get inspiration, guidance, and feedback from others throughout the writing process, and so can you. Use class discussions to generate and test out topics and theses. Ask your instructor to clarify assignments or to discuss your ideas. Have classmates, friends, or roommates critique your drafts. In writing about literature, as in reading it, we get a much better sense of what our own ideas are and how best to convey them by considering others' impressions.

33.1 GETTING STARTED

33.1.1 Scrutinizing the Assignment

For student essayists, as for most professional ones, the writing process usually begins with an assignment. Though assignments vary, all impose restrictions. These are designed not to hinder your creativity but to direct it into productive channels, ensuring you hone particular skills, try out different approaches, and avoid common pitfalls.

Your first task as a writer is thus to scrutinize your assignment. Make sure that you fully understand what you are being asked to do (and not do), and ask questions about anything unclear or puzzling.

Almost all assignments restrict the length of an essay by imposing word or page limits. Keep those limits in mind as you consider potential topics, making sure to choose a topic you can handle in the space allowed. In three pages, you cannot thoroughly analyze all the characters in August Wilson's FENCES. But you might within that limit say something significant about some specific aspect of a character or of characterization—perhaps how Troy Maxson's approach to parenting relates to the way he was parented or how Wilson's inclusion of the final scene, set after Troy's death, affects our interpretation of his character.

Many assignments impose further restrictions, often indicating the texts and/or topics your essay should explore. As a result, any assignment will shape whether and how you tackle later steps such as "Choosing a Text" or "Identifying Topics."

Below are several representative essay assignments, each of which imposes a particular set of restrictions.

Choose any story in this anthology and write an essay analyzing how and why its protagonist changes.	This assignment dictates your topic and main question. It also provides you with the kernel of a thesis: *In [story title], [protagonist's name] goes from being a _________ to a _________.* OR *By the end of [story title], [protagonist's name] has learned that* _________. Though the assignment lets you choose your story, it limits you to those in which the protagonist changes or learns a lesson of some kind.
Write an essay analyzing one of the following sonnets: "Nuns Fret Not," "In an Artist's Studio," or "In the Park." Be sure to consider how the poem's form contributes to its meaning.	This assignment limits your choice of texts to three. It also requires that your essay address the effects of the poet's choice to use the sonnet form. Notice, though, that the assignment doesn't require that this be the main topic of your essay, but instead leaves you free to pursue any topic related to the poem's meaning.
Write an essay exploring the significance of references to eyes and vision in *A Midsummer Night's Dream.* What, through them, does the play suggest about the power and the limitations of human vision?	This assignment is more restrictive, indicating both text and topic. At the same time, it requires you to narrow the topic and formulate a specific thesis.
Write an essay comparing at least two poems by any one author in your anthology.	This assignment specifies the type of essay you must write (a comparison essay) and limits your choice of texts. Yet it leaves you the choice of which author to focus on, how many and which poems to analyze, what topic to explore, and what relative weight to give to similarities and differences.
Explain how and why children feature prominently in Romantic literature by analyzing the work of at least two Romantic poets.	This assignment is more restrictive, specifying the type of essay (comparison), the topic (depictions of children), and the kinds of texts (Romantic poems), while also encouraging you to focus mainly on similarities so as to define a single Romantic outlook on children and childhood.

33.1.2 Choosing a Text

If your assignment allows you to choose which text to write about, try letting your initial impressions or "gut reactions" guide you. Do that, and your first impulse may be to choose a text that you immediately like or "get." Perhaps its language resembles your own; it depicts speakers, characters, or situations you easily relate to; or it explores issues you care deeply about. Following that first impulse can be a good strategy. Writing an engaging essay requires *being* engaged, and we all find it easier to engage with texts, authors, characters, and so on that we "like" immediately.

Paradoxically, however, writers often discover that they have little interesting or new to say about such a text. Perhaps they're too emotionally invested to analyze it closely or to imagine alternative ways to read it, or maybe its meaning seems so obvious that there's no puzzle or problem to drive an argument. Often, then, it can actually be more productive to choose a work that provokes the opposite reaction—that initially puzzles or even frustrates or angers you, one whose characters seem alien or whom you don't "like," one that investigates an issue you haven't thought much about, or one that articulates a theme you don't agree with. Sometimes such negative first reactions can have surprisingly positive results when it comes to writing. When you have to dig deeper, you sometimes discover more. And your own initial response might also provide you with the kernel of a good motive (see 32.1.3).

So, too, might the responses of your classmates. If you are writing about a text you've discussed in class, in other words, you might also or instead start with your "gut responses" to that discussion. Were you surprised by anything your classmates claimed about the text? Or did you strongly agree or disagree with any of your classmate's interpretations? Especially in hindsight, was anything *not* said or discussed in class that you think should have been?

33.1.3 Generating Topics

When an assignment allows you to create your own topic, you are more likely to build a lively and engaging essay from a particular insight or question that captures your attention and makes you want to say something, solve a problem, or stake out a position. The best essays originate in an individual response to a text and focus on a genuine question about it. Even when an instructor assigns you a topic, your essay's effectiveness will largely depend on whether you have made the topic your own, turning it into a real question to which you discover your own answer.

Often we refer to "finding" a topic, as if there are a bevy of topics "out there" just waiting to be plucked like ripe fruit off the topic tree. In at least two ways, that's true. For one thing, as we read a literary work, certain topics often do jump out and say, "Hey, look at me! I'm a topic!" A title alone may have that effect: *What "lesson" seems to be learned in "The Lesson"? Why is Keats so fixated on that darn nightingale; what does it symbolize for him? Or what the heck is an "ode" anyway, and how might it matter that Keats's poem is an* "Ode to *a Nightingale*"?

For another thing, certain general topics can be adapted to fit many different literary works. In fact, that's just another way of saying that there are certain common types (even subgenres) of literary essays, just as there are of short stories, plays, and poems. Here are a few especially common topics:

- the significance of a seemingly insignificant aspect or element of a work—a word or group of related words, an image or image-cluster, a minor character, a seemingly small incident or action, and so on. (This topic is appealing in part because it practically comes with a built-in motive: "Although a casual reader would likely ignore X . . .")
- the outlook or worldview of a single character or **speaker** (or of a group of characters) and its consequences
- the changes a major character or speaker undergoes over the course of a literary work (What is the change? When, how, and why does it occur?)
- the precise nature and wider significance of an internal or external **conflict** and its ultimate resolution

Especially when you're utterly befuddled about where to begin, it can be very useful to keep in mind such generic topics or essay types and to use them as starting points. But remember that they are just starting points. You always have to adapt and narrow a generic topic such as "imagery" or "character change" in order to produce an effective essay. In practice, then, no writer simply "finds" a topic; she *makes* one.

Here are some other techniques that might help you generate topics. (And generating *topics*, giving yourself a choice, is often a good idea.)

- *Analyze your initial response.*
  If you've chosen a text you feel strongly about, start with those responses. Try to describe your feelings and trace them to their source. Be as specific as possible. What moments, aspects, or elements of the text most affected you? How and why exactly? Try to articulate the question behind your feelings. Often, strong responses result when a work either challenges or affirms an expectation, assumption, or conviction that you bring *to* it. Think about whether and how that's true in your case. Define the specific expectation, assumption, or conviction. How, where, and why does the text challenge it? fulfill or affirm it? Which of your responses and expectations are objectively valid, likely to be shared by other readers?

- *Think through the elements.*
  Start with a list of elements and work your way through them, identifying anything that might be especially unique, interesting, or puzzling about the text in terms of each element. What stands out about the **tone**, the speaker, the **situation**, and so on? Come up with a statement about each. Look for patterns among your statements. Also, think about the questions your statements imply or ignore.

- *Pose motive questions.*
  In articulating a motive in your essay's introduction, your concern is primarily with your readers, your goal to give *them* a substantive reason to find your thesis new and interesting and your essay thus worth reading. But you can also work your way toward a topic and even, eventually, a thesis, by considering motive-related questions. Keep in mind the basic *"Although they say/I used to think/someone might reasonably think . . . , I say/now think . . ."* statement and turn it into questions:
  —What element(s) or aspect(s) of this work might a casual reader misinterpret? Or which might you have misinterpreted on a first reading? Or which did your classmates seem to misinterpret?

—What potentially significant element(s) or aspect(s) of this work were ignored entirely in class discussion? Or which might you have ignored on a first reading? Or which might any reasonable person ignore?
—What aspect(s) or element(s) of this work have your classmates disagreed among themselves about or maybe even taken extreme positions on? Or which have you seen in very different ways as you've read and thought about the work?
—What interesting paradox(es), contradiction(s), or tension(s) do you see in the work?

33.1.4 Formulating a Question and a Thesis

Before you begin writing an essay on any topic, you need to come up with a thesis or hypothesis—an arguable statement about the topic. Quite often, topic and thesis occur to you simultaneously: You might well decide to write about a topic precisely because you've got something specific to say about it. At other times, that's not the case: The topic comes much more easily than the thesis. In this event, it helps to formulate a specific question about the topic and to develop a specific answer. That answer will be your thesis.

Again, remember that your question and thesis should focus on something specific, yet they need to be generally valid, involving more than your personal feelings. One way to move from an initial, subjective response to an arguable thesis is to freewrite, as in the example below. Don't worry what form your writing takes or how good it is: Just write.

> I really admire Bartleby. But why? What in the story encourages me to admire him? Well, he sticks to his guns and insists on doing only what he "prefers" to do. He doesn't just follow orders. That makes him really different from all the other characters in the story, especially the narrator. And also from a lot of people I know, even me. He's a nonconformist. Do I think other readers should feel the same way? Maybe, but maybe not. After all, his refusal to conform does cause problems for everyone around him. And it doesn't do him a lot of good either. Plus, he would be really annoying in real life. I wouldn't want to work in the same office. And even if you admire him, you can't really care about him because he doesn't seem to care much about anybody else. Or even about himself? Maybe that's the point. Through Bartleby, Melville explores both how rare and important and how dangerous nonconformity can be.

However you arrive at your thesis or however strongly you believe in it, you should still think of it for now as a working hypothesis—a claim that's provisional, still open to rethinking and revision.

33.2 PLANNING

Once you've formulated a tentative thesis and, ideally, a motive ("Although . . . , I think . . ."), you need to work on the ". . . because" part of the equation, which means both (1) figuring out how to structure your argument, articulating and ordering your claims or sub-ideas; and (2) identifying the evidence you need to prove and develop each of those claims.

Start by looking closely at your thesis. As in almost every phase of writing, it helps to temporarily fill your readers' shoes: Try to see your thesis and the promises it makes from their point of view. What will they need to be shown, and in what order? If a good thesis shapes readers' expectations, it can also guide you, as a writer.

A good thesis usually implies not only what the essay's claims should be but also how they should be ordered. For instance, a thesis that focuses on the development of a character implies that the first body paragraphs will explain what that character is initially like and that later paragraphs will explore when, how, and why that character changes.

Working wholly from the thesis and this rough sense of structure, generate an outline, either listing each claim (to create a *sentence outline*) or each topic to be covered (to create a *topic outline*). Though a sentence outline is far more helpful, you may find that at this stage you can only identify topics.

Take, for example, the Bartleby thesis developed in the last section (33.1.4)—Through Bartleby, Melville explores both how rare and important, and how dangerous, nonconformity can be. From it, we can generate the following outline, which begins with two clear claims/sentences and then simply describes two other topics that will need to be covered:

1. Claim: Bartleby is a nonconformist.
2. Claim: Bartleby's nonconformity makes him very different from every other character in the story, especially the narrator.
3. Topic: positive aspects or consequences of Bartleby's nonconformity.
4. Topic: negative aspects or consequences of Bartleby's nonconformity—how it's dangerous.

At this stage, in other words, it's clear that our Bartleby essay needs first to show *that* and *how* Bartleby refuses to conform (1) and then to show *that* and *how* such nonconformity differentiates him from other characters (2). Not only are these the most obvious and least debatable claims, but they also lay the essential groundwork for the rest: Questions about why or how Bartleby's nonconformity might be negative or positive (3–4) only make sense once you establish that there is nonconformity and show what it looks like. To further refine the first half of the outline or to draft the first half of the essay, all its hypothetical writer needs to do is review the story and her notes about it to identify appropriate evidence. Her discoveries will also determine whether she can fully develop each of these claims in just one paragraph or whether she might need two.

The shape of the second half of the essay is less clear and will demand more work. In reviewing the story and her notes, the writer would need to come up with claims about what the positive and negative aspects or consequences of Bartleby's nonconformity are. Ultimately she might even need to rethink the order in which she discusses these topics. Since whatever comes last in an essay should usually be not only the most complicated and debatable point but also the one that gets most emphasis as we build toward a conclusion, this writer would need to figure out where she thinks the story puts the most emphasis—the value of nonconformity (3) or its dangers (4).

As this example demonstrates, just as your thesis can guide you to an outline, so an outline can show you exactly what you need to figure out and what evidence you need to look for as you move toward a draft. The more detailed your outline, the easier drafting tends to be. But the truth is that sometimes we can only figure out what our actual claims or ideas are by trying to write them out, which might mean moving straight from a rough outline to a draft rather than further refining the outline before drafting.

As you begin to gather evidence, however, it is important that you let the evidence guide you, as well as your outline. As you look back at the text, you may well discover facts that are relevant to the thesis but that don't seem to relate directly to any of the claims or topics you've articulated. In that case, you may need to insert a new topic into the outline. Additionally, you may find (and should in fact actively look for) facts that challenge your argument. Test and reassess your claims against those facts and adjust them accordingly. Don't ignore inconvenient truths.

33.3 DRAFTING

If you've put time and care into getting started and planning, you may already be quite close to a first draft. If you've instead jumped straight into writing, you may have to move back and forth between composing and some of the steps described in earlier sections of this chapter.

Either way, remember that first drafts are called *rough drafts* for a reason. Think of yourself as a painter "roughing out" a sketch in preparation for the more detailed painting to come. At this stage, try not to worry about grammar, punctuation, and mechanics. Concentrate on the argument—articulating your ideas and proving them.

Sometimes the best way to start is simply to copy your thesis and outline into a new document. Forget about introducing your thesis, and just go right to work on your first body paragraph. Sometimes, however, you'll find that starting with the introduction helps: Having to draw readers in and set up your thesis and motive can give you a clearer sense of where you're going and why.

However you start, you will almost certainly feel frustrated at times. Stick to it. If you become truly stuck, try explaining your point to another person or getting out an actual piece of paper and a pen and *writing* for a few minutes before returning to your computer and your draft. If all else fails, make a note about what needs to go in the spot you can't get through. Then move on and come back to that spot once you've written the next paragraph. Whatever it takes, stay with your draft until you've at least got a middle, or body, that you're relatively satisfied with. Then take a break.

Later or—better yet, tomorrow—come back, look at the draft with a fresh eye, and take another shot, attaching a conclusion and (if necessary) an introduction, filling in any gaps, crafting smooth(er) transitions within and between paragraphs, deleting anything that now seems irrelevant (or, better yet, copying it into a separate "outtakes" document just in case you figure out later how to make it relevant). Do your utmost to create a relatively satisfying whole. Now pat yourself on the back and take another break.

33.4 REVISING

Revision is one of the most important and difficult tasks for any writer. It's a crucial stage in the writing process, yet one that is all too easy to ignore or mismanage. The difference between a so-so essay and a good one, between a good essay and a great one, often depends entirely on effective revision. Give yourself time to revise more than once. As you do so, develop revision strategies that work for you. The investment in time and effort will pay rich dividends on this essay and on future ones.

The essential thing is not to confuse *revising* with *editing and proofreading*. We've devoted separate sections of this chapter to each of these steps because they *are* entirely different processes. Where editing and proofreading focus mainly on sentence-level matters (grammar, punctuation, spelling, and so on), revision is about the whole essay, "the big picture." Revision entails assessing and improving both (1) the essay's working parts or elements and (2) your overall argument. Doing these two things well requires *not* getting distracted by small grammatical errors, spelling mistakes, and so on.

Before considering in depth what it means to assess the elements and enrich the argument, here are a few general tips about how to approach revision:

- *Think like readers.* Effective revision requires you to temporarily play the role of reader, as well as writer, of your essay. Take a step back from your draft, doing your utmost to see it from a more objective, even skeptical standpoint. Revision demands *re-vision*—looking again, seeing anew.
- *Get input from real readers.* This is an especially good time to involve other people in your writing process. Copy the "Assessing the Elements" checklist below and have a friend or classmate use it to critique your draft.
- *Think strengths and weaknesses, not right and wrong.* In critiquing your own draft or someone else's, it helps to think less in absolute terms (right and wrong, good and bad) than in terms of strengths and weaknesses—specific elements and aspects that work well and those that need some work.
- *Work with a hard copy.* Computers are a godsend when it comes to making revisions. But because they only allow us to look at one or two pages of an essay at a time, they actually make it harder to see the essay as a whole and to assess the effects of the changes they make it so easy for us to make. During the revision process, then, move away from the computer sometimes. Print out hard copies so that you can see your essay as a whole and mark it up, identifying problems that you can return to the computer to fix.

33.4.1 Assessing the Elements

The first step in revision is to make sure that all the working parts of your essay are, indeed, working. To help with that process, run through the following checklist to identify the strengths and weaknesses of your draft—or ask someone else to do so. Try to answer each question with ruthless honesty.

Whenever you can't justify a check, remember that you and/or your readers need to identify the specific problems in order to solve them—If information is missing from the introduction, *what information?* If every sentence in the introduction isn't serving a clear purpose, *which sentence* is the problem? And so on.

Thesis and Motive

- ☐ Is there *one* claim that effectively controls the essay?
- ☐ Is the claim debatable?
- ☐ Does the claim demonstrate real thought? Does it truly illuminate the text and topic?
- ☐ Does the writer *show* us that (and why) the thesis is new and worthwhile by suggesting an actual or potential alternative view?

Structure

BEGINNING/INTRODUCTION

- ☐ Does the introduction provide readers all—and only—the information they need about the author, text, context, and topic?
- ☐ Does the introduction imply a clear, substantive, debatable but plausible thesis? Is it clear which claim is the thesis?
- ☐ Does every sentence either help to articulate the thesis and motive or to provide essential information?

MIDDLE/BODY

- ☐ Does each paragraph clearly state one debatable claim? Does everything in the paragraph directly relate to, and help support and develop, that claim?
- ☐ Is each of those claims clearly related to (but different from) the thesis?
- ☐ Are the claims logically ordered?
- ☐ Is that logic clear? Is each claim clearly linked to those that come before and after? Are there any logical "leaps" that readers might have trouble following?
- ☐ Does each claim/paragraph clearly build on the last one? Does the argument move forward, or does it seem more like a list or a tour through a museum of interesting but unrelated observations?
- ☐ Do any key claims or logical steps in the argument seem to be missing?

ENDING/CONCLUSION

- ☐ Does the conclusion give readers the sense that they've gotten somewhere and that the journey has been worthwhile?
- ☐ Does it indicate the implications of the argument, consider relevant evaluative questions, or discuss questions that remain unanswered?

Evidence

- ☐ Is there ample, appropriate evidence for each claim?
- ☐ Are the appropriateness and significance of each fact—its relevance to the claim—perfectly clear?
- ☐ Are there any weak examples or inferences that aren't reasonable? Are there moments when readers might reasonably ask, "But couldn't that fact instead mean this?"
- ☐ Are all the relevant facts considered? What about facts that might complicate or contradict any of the claims? Are there moments when readers might reasonably think, "But what about X?"
- ☐ Is each piece of evidence clearly presented? Do readers have all the contextual information they need to understand a quotation, for example?
- ☐ Is each piece of evidence gracefully presented? Are quotations varied by length and presentation? Are they ever too long? Are there any unnecessary block quotations, or block quotations that require additional analysis? (On responsible and effective quotation, see 35.1–2.)
- ☐ Are there any unnecessary quotations—instances when the writer should instead simply paraphrase, summarize, or describe?

Tone

- ☐ Does the writer establish and maintain an effective tone—do any moments in, or aspects of, the essay make its writer seem anything other than serious, credible, engaged, and engaging? respectful toward the text(s) and a range of readers?
- ☐ Does the writer correctly and consistently use literary terminology?
- ☐ Does the writer ever assume too much or too little readerly knowledge or interest?

COMMON PROBLEMS AND TIPS

Though you want to pay attention to everything on this "assessing the elements" checklist, certain types of problems are common in early drafts. Here are three:

- *mismatch between thesis or argument or between introduction and body*
  Sometimes an early draft ends up being a way to discover what you really want to say. As a result, you may find that the thesis of your draft—or even your entire introduction—no longer truly fits or introduces the argument you've ended up making. If so, you will need to rework the thesis and introduction. Then work your way back through the essay, making sure that each claim or topic sentence fits the new thesis.
- *the list or "museum tour" structure*
  In a draft, writers sometimes present each claim as if it were just an item on a list (*First, second,* and so on) or as a stop on a tour of potentially interesting but unrelated topics (*And this is also important . . .*). But presenting your material in this way fails to help you and your readers make logical connections between ideas. It may also prevent your argument from developing. Sometimes it can even be a sign that you've ceased arguing entirely, falling into mere plot summary or description rather than articulating real *ideas* at all. Check to see if number-like words or phrases appear prominently at the beginning of your paragraphs or if your paragraphs could be put into a different order without fundamentally changing what you're saying. Sometimes solving this problem will require wholesale rethinking and reorganizing—a process that should probably start with crafting a meatier, more specific thesis. But sometimes all that's required is adding or reworking topic sentences. Again, make sure that there is a clearly stated, *debatable* claim at the beginning of each paragraph; that each claim relates to the thesis but does not simply restate it; and that each claim *builds* logically on the one before.
- *missing sub-ideas*
  When you take a step back from your draft, you may discover that you've skipped a logical step in your argument—that the claim you make in, say, body paragraph 3 actually depends on, or makes sense only in light of, a more basic claim that you took for granted. In the second half of an essay about how a character changes, for example, you might suggest that there is something significant about the character being decisive, but decisiveness only counts as change—and thus your point about decisiveness relates to your thesis—if the first part of your essay has demonstrated that the character is initially *indecisive*. Whatever the missing idea is, you'll need to create and insert a new paragraph that articulates, supports, and develops it.

33.4.2 Enriching the Argument

The first step of the revision process is all about ensuring that your essay does the best possible job of making your argument. But revision is also an opportunity to go further—to think about ways in which your overall argument might be made more thorough and complex. In drafting an essay our attention is often and rightly focused on emphatically staking out a particular position and proving its validity. This is the fundamental task of any essay, and you certainly don't want to do anything at this stage to compromise that. At the same time, you do want to make sure that you haven't purchased clarity at the cost of oversimplification by, for example, ignoring facts that might undermine or complicate your claims, alternative interpretations of the evidence you do present, or alternative claims or points of view. Remember, you have a better chance of persuading readers to accept your argument if you show them that it's based on a thorough, open-minded exploration of the text and topic. Don't invent unreasonable or irrelevant complications or counterarguments. Do try to assess your argument objectively and honestly, perhaps testing it against the text one more time. Think like a skeptical reader rather than a writer: Are there moments where such a reader might reasonably disagree with your argument? Are there places where *two* interpretations might be equally plausible? Have you ignored or glossed over any questions that a reasonable reader might expect an essay on this topic to address?

Such questions are ones you should *always* ask in revision. But they are especially crucial if you finish your draft only to discover that it is significantly shorter than the assignment requires. Inexperienced writers of literature essays often run out of things to say too quickly because they simply don't keep asking relevant questions (*How*? *Why*?) or make enough allowance for alternative answers.

33.5 EDITING AND PROOFREADING

Once you've gotten the overall argument in good shape, *then* it's time focus on the small but crucial stuff—words and sentences. Your prose should not only convey your ideas to your readers but also demonstrate how much you care about your essay. Flawless prose can't disguise or make up for a vapid or illogical argument. But faulty, flabby, boring prose can destroy a potentially persuasive and thoughtful one. Don't sabotage all your hard work by failing to correct misspelled words, grammatical problems, misquotations, incorrect citations, and typographical errors. Little oversights make all the difference when it comes to clarity and credibility. Readers care more about careful work. Especially when you are writing about literature, the art of language, *your* language matters.

When it comes to words and sentences, each writer has particular strengths and weaknesses. Likewise every writer tends to be overly fond of certain phrases and sentence structures, which become monotonous and ineffective if overused. With practice, you will learn to watch out for the kinds of mistakes and repetitions to which you are most prone. Then you can develop your own personalized editing checklist. But below is one to start with.

Sentences

☐ Does each one read clearly and crisply?
☐ Are they varied in length, structure, and syntax?
☐ Is the phrasing direct rather than roundabout?
☐ Are tenses appropriate and consistent?

Tips

- Try using the Find function to search for every preposition (especially *of* and *in*) and every *to be* verb. Since these can lead to confusing or roundabout phrasing, weed out as many as you can.
- Try reading your paper aloud or having a friend read it aloud to you. Mark places where you or your friend stumble, and listen for sentences that are hard to get through or understand.

Words

- ☐ Have you used any words whose meaning you're not sure of?
- ☐ Is terminology correct and consistent?
- ☐ Is a "fancy" word or phrase ever used where a simpler one might do?
- ☐ Are there unnecessary words or phrases?
- ☐ Do metaphors and other figures of speech make literal sense?
- ☐ Are verbs active and precise?
- ☐ Are pronoun references always clear and correct?
- ☐ Do subjects and verbs always agree?

Punctuation and Mechanics

- ☐ Are all words spelled correctly? (Double-check your auto-correct and spell-check: these can create new errors in the process of correcting others.)
- ☐ Are all titles formatted correctly? (See the section following this checklist.)
- ☐ Is every quotation accurate and punctuated correctly (See ch. 35.)?

Citation and Documentation (See ch. 35.)

- ☐ Is the source of each quotation, as well as any fact or idea drawn from sources, clearly indicated through parenthetical citation?
- ☐ Do parenthetical citations correctly coordinate with the list of works cited?
- ☐ Are both all parenthetical citations and all entries in the list of works cited formatted correctly?

Titles

Formatting titles correctly in both the body of your essay and your list of works cited is essential to your clarity, as well as to your self-presentation as a knowledgeable and careful writer: Bartleby the Scrivener is a character; "Bartleby, the Scrivener" is a short story. "Interpreter of Maladies" is also a short story, but *Interpreter of Maladies* is a book. To make sure you get this right, here is a quick review:

- *Italicize* the titles of all books and other "stand-alone" works, including
  —novels and novellas (*To Kill a Mockingbird*, *Heart of Darkness*)
  —collections and anthologies of short stories, essays, or poems (*Interpreter of Maladies*, *The Norton Introduction to Literature*)
  —long poems that could be or have been published as books (*The Odyssey*, *Paradise Lost*, *Goblin Market*)
  —plays (*Hamlet*, *A Raisin in the Sun*)
  —periodicals, including newspapers, magazines, and scholarly journals (*USA Today*, *People*, *College English*)
  —Web sites, blogs, and databases (*Google Books*, *Gawker*, *JSTOR*)
  —movies and television programs or series (*The Fault in Our Stars*, *Orange Is the New Black*)

- Put quotation marks around the titles of works that are part of such "stand-alone" works, including
  —short stories ("Interpreter of Maladies," "A Rose for Emily")
  —poems ("Daddy," "Ode to a Nightingale")
  —essays and articles in periodicals ("A Narrator's Blindness in Raymond Carver's 'Cathedral'"; "When We Dead Awaken: Writing as Re-Vision"; "Chicago Fiddles While Trumbull Park Burns")
  —parts of Web sites (e.g., Web pages, blog posts)
  —episodes of a television series

33.6 FINISHING UP

33.6.1 Crafting a Title

Your essay isn't truly complete until you give it a title. A good title both informs and interests. Inform readers by telling them both the work(s) you will analyze ("The Road Not Taken" or "two poems by Robert Frost") and something about your topic ("Symbolism," "Nonconformity"). To interest them, try using one of the following:

- an especially vivid and relevant word or a short phrase from the literary work ("'They Have Eaten Me Alive': Motherhood in 'In the Park' and 'Daystar'")
- a bit of wordplay ("Wordsworth and the Art of Artlessness")
- a bit of both ("'Untrodden Ways': Wordsworth and the Art of Artlessness").

Do not put your own title in quotation marks, but do correctly format any titles that appear in your title.

33.6.2 Formatting Your Essay

Unless your instructor provides specific instructions on how to format your essay, follow these guidelines, adapted from *The MLA Style Center: Writing Resources from the Modern Language Association* (style.mla.org/formatting-papers) and demonstrated in the sample research essay in chapter 36.

- Choose a readable 11- or 12-point font; set your page margins at 1 inch; and double-space throughout. Do not add extra lines between paragraphs or before or after block quotations. Indent the first line of each paragraph ½ inch. An entire block quotation should be indented ½ inch. (For more on formatting quotations, see 35.1.)
- Do not include a title page. Instead, in the top left corner of the first page, type your name, your instructor's name, the course number, and the date, each on a separate line. Then center your title on the next line. (Do not put your own title in quotation marks.)
- Number every page consecutively, and put your last name and the page number in the upper right corner ½ inch below the top of the page and aligned with the right margin. (Do not put any punctuation between your name and the page number.)
- Begin your list of works cited on a new page, *after* the last page of your essay. Center the words *Works Cited* at the top of the page. (Do not put quotation marks around or italicize these words.) Indent the second and subsequent lines of each works cited entry ½ inch. (For more on formatting the list of works cited, see 35.3.2.)

34 THE LITERATURE RESEARCH ESSAY

Whenever we read, discuss, and write about literature, our primary concern is always the text. But literature speaks to and about the real world even when it depicts an entirely unreal one. Both texts and our readings of them are inevitably shaped by, and intervene in, particular contexts. Literary research is simply a way to learn more about those contexts. In a literature research essay we bring what we learn to bear to illuminate the work in a new way.

On the one hand, writing a research essay may at first seem like a daunting task. Research adds a few more steps to the writing process, so you will need to give yourself more time. And those steps require you to draw on and develop skills somewhat different from those involved in crafting essays that focus exclusively on the literary text. Were this not the case, no one would ask you to write a research essay.

On the other hand, however, a literature research essay is still a literature essay. Its core elements are the same, as is its basic purpose—to articulate and develop a debatable, interpretive claim about at least one literary work. As a result, this kind of essay requires many of the same skills and strategies you've already begun to develop. And though you will need to add a few new steps, the process of writing a literature research essay still involves getting started, planning, drafting, revising, editing, and finishing up—exactly the same dance whose rhythms you've already begun to master.

The only distinctive thing about a research essay is that it requires you to draw on sources in addition to the literary text itself. Though that adds to your burden in some ways, it can actually lighten it in others. Think of such sources not as another ball you have to juggle but as another tool you get to add to your tool belt: You're still being asked to build a cabinet, but now you get to use a hammer *and* an electric drill. This chapter will help you make the best use of these powerful tools.

One thing to keep in mind from the beginning is that this anthology includes excerpts from numerous scholarly articles about literature—each one is a published literature research essay. Some of these excerpts may be appropriate sources for your essay. But even if they aren't, they can still be very helpful to you as examples of how professional literary critics go about doing precisely the same things you need to do in your research essay. What do their theses look like? their motives? What kinds of sources do they use, and how do they go about using them? How do they nonetheless manage to stay focused on *their* arguments about the literary text? In this chapter, we'll draw on examples from these and other published essays to show you what we mean.

34.1 TYPES OF ESSAYS AND SOURCES

The three most common types of literature research essay are those suggested by the "Contexts" chapters in this anthology. But though we treat these types separately here for clarity's sake, many literature research essays are in fact hybrids of one sort or another. An essay on Emily Dickinson by student writer Richard Gibson is a case in point: It analyzes three poems by Emily Dickinson by drawing on literary criticism, biographical materials, and studies of Dickinson's historical and cultural context. Should your assignment allow, your essay, too, could combine two or more of these approaches. Either way, it's useful to remember that your secondary sources probably will.

34.1.1 Critical Contexts

Whenever we write a literature essay, we engage in conversation with other readers about the meaning and significance of a literary work. Effective argumentation always depends on anticipating how other readers are likely to respond to, and interpret, that work. As the "Critical Contexts" chapters in this anthology demonstrate, almost all texts and authors are also the subject of actual public conversations, often extending over many years and involving all the numerous scholarly readers who have published their readings of the work. A "critical contexts" research essay is an opportunity both to investigate this conversation and to contribute to it.

For this kind of essay, your secondary sources will be work by literary scholars on the specific text you're writing about; on an author's body of work; or on a relevant genre or body of literature (e.g., *The Development of the Sonnet: An Introduction* or *"Reading the Wind": The Literature of the Vietnam War*). The latter, more general sorts of sources may be especially crucial if you are researching a relatively recent work about which little literary criticism has yet been published. In that case, too, you may want to consult book reviews; just remember that it's reviewers' *interpretive* claims you're most interested in, not their evaluation of the work. (On interpretation versus evaluation, see 32.1.2.) For examples of critical context essays by student writers, see ch. 1 and 30. For examples by professional critics, see the excerpts in ch. 11, 25, and 30.)

34.1.2 Biographical Contexts

If literature *only* reflected, and gave us insight into, its author's psyche, it ultimately wouldn't be that interesting: Good poets, fiction writers, and playwrights write about and for others, not just themselves. Nonetheless, authors are real people whose unique experience and outlook shape both what they write and how. A "biographical contexts" research essay is a chance to learn more about an author's life, work, and ideas and to explore how these might have shaped or be reflected in the text. Sources for this sort of project will likely include biographies (secondary sources) and essays, letters, and other nonfiction prose by the author (primary sources). (For examples of biographical context essays, see the excerpts from Eileen Pollack's FLANNERY O'CONNOR AND THE NEW CRITICISM [ch. 8] and from Steven Gould Axelrod's SYLVIA PLATH: THE WOUND AND THE CURE OF WORDS [ch. 25].)

34.1.3 Historical and Cultural Contexts

Every literary work is both shaped by and speaks to the circumstances, events, and debates peculiar to its historical and cultural context, though some literary works speak of their times by depicting other times. The purpose of a "cultural and historical contexts" essay is to explore the interconnections between a text and the context it was either written in or depicts. Sources useful for this sort of essay might include studies of a relevant historical period or literary movement (secondary sources) or documents dating from that period or written by others involved in that movement (primary sources). (For an example of an historical and cultural context essay by a student writer, see ch. 24. For examples by professional critics, see the excerpts from Steven Kaplan's THE UNDYING UNCERTAINTY OF THE NARRATOR IN TIM O'BRIEN'S *THE THINGS THEY CARRIED* [ch. 11], Steven Gould Axelrod's SYLVIA PLATH: THE WOUND AND THE CURE OF WORDS [ch. 25], and Philip Holt's *POLIS* AND TRAGEDY IN THE *ANTIGONE* [ch. 30].)

34.2 WHAT SOURCES DO

Unless your instructor indicates otherwise, *your* argument about the literary text should be the focus of your essay, and sources should function simply as tools that you use to deepen and enrich your argument about the literary text. They shouldn't substitute for it. Your essay should never simply repeat or report on what other people have already said.

Sources, in other words, are *not* the source of your ideas. Instead, to paraphrase writing expert Gordon Harvey's *Writing with Sources* (Hackett, 1998), they are the source of

- *argument* or *debatable claim*—other readers' views and interpretations of a text, author, topic, literary movement, period, and so on, which "you support, criticize, or develop";
- *information*—facts about an author's life; about the work's composition, publication, or reception; about the era during, or about which, the author wrote; about movements in which the author participated; and so on.
- *concept*—general terms or theoretical frameworks that you borrow and apply to your author or text. (In an essay excerpted in ch. 25, for example, Stephen Gould Axelrod uses concepts drawn from Sigmund Freud's theories of psychological development to interpret Sylvia Plath's poem DADDY; in an essay on Tim O'Brien's *The Things They Carried* excerpted in ch. 11, Steven Kaplan applies those of literary theorist Wolfgang Iser.)

Any one source will in fact likely offer you more than one of these things. In the Axelrod excerpt mentioned above, for example, you will find *argument* about the poem DADDY, as well as potentially useful *information* about its author's life and about the status of the domestic poem in the 1950s. Nonetheless, the distinction between argument or debatable claim, on the one hand, and information or factual statement, on the other, is crucial. As you read a source, you must discriminate between the two.

When drawing on sources in your essay, remember, too, that an argument about the text, no matter how well informed, isn't the same as evidence. Only facts can serve that function. Suppose, for example, you are writing an essay on "Daddy." You claim that the speaker adopts two voices, that of her child self and that of her adult self—a claim Axelrod also makes in his essay. You cannot prove this claim to be true merely by saying that Axelrod makes the same claim. Like any debatable claim, this one must be backed up with evidence from the primary text.

In this situation, however, you must indicate that a source has made the same claim that you do in order to accomplish three things:

- give the source credit for having this idea before you did (to avoid even the appearance of plagiarism; see 34.4.1);
- encourage readers to see you as a knowledgeable, trustworthy writer who has done your research and taken the time to explore, digest, and fairly represent others' views;
- demonstrate that your opinion isn't merely idiosyncratic because another informed, even "expert," reader agrees with you.

Were you to disagree with the source's claim, it would be just as important and helpful to your argument to acknowledge that disagreement in order to demonstrate the originality of your own interpretation, while also, again, encouraging readers to see you as a knowledgeable, careful writer.

You will need to cite sources throughout your essay whenever you make a claim that resembles, complements, or contradicts the claim of another source; rely on information or concepts from a source; or paraphrase, quote, or summarize anything in a source. Especially in a critical contexts essay, you should also at least consider using sources to establish motive (see below).

34.2.1 Source-Related Motives

Not all research essays use sources to articulate motive. However, doing so is one way both to ensure and to demonstrate that your own ideas are the focus of your essay and that your essay contributes to a literary critical conversation rather than just reporting on it or repeating what others have already said. In these essays, in other words, your "Although . . ." statement (as outlined in 32.1.3) may refer to sources—actual "theys" and what they "say." Indeed, whether you ultimately use sources to articulate a motive or not, keeping motive-related questions in mind as you read sources is nonetheless a very good idea, for reasons we'll detail in the next section of this chapter. Here are the three most common source-related motives:

1. Sources offer different opinions about a particular issue in the text, thus suggesting that there is still a problem or puzzle worth investigating. (Your argument might agree with one side or the other or offer a "third way.")

> Almost all interpreters of [*Antigone*] have agreed that the play shows Creon to be morally defective [. . .]. The situation of Antigone is more controversial. Hegel assimilated her defect to Creon's; some more recent writers uncritically hold her up as a blameless heroine. Without entering into an exhaustive study of her role in the tragedy, I should like to claim (with the support of an increasing number of recent critics) that there is at least some justification for the Hegelian assimilation—though the criticism needs to be focused more clearly and specifically than it is in Hegel's brief remarks.

In these sentences from THE FRAGILITY OF GOODNESS (ch. 30), Martha C. Nussbaum summarizes an ongoing debate about *Antigone* and then positions her argument as contributing to that debate by supporting and developing one of the two usual positions.

2. **A source or sources make(s) a faulty claim that needs to be wholly or partly challenged or clarified.**

Modern critics who do not share Sophocles' conviction about the paramount duty of burying the dead and who attach more importance than he did to the claims of political authority have tended to underestimate the way in which he justifies Antigone against Creon.	In this sentence from the introduction to SOPHOCLEAN TRAGEDY (ch. 30), Maurice Bowra makes a generalization about the stance taken by "[m]odern critics" that his essay will challenge. (Subsequent sentences provide more details about that stance.)
While I find Smith's article thoughtful and intriguing, and while I agree with much feminist criticism of Vietnam War literature, this essay proposes that the work of Tim O'Brien, particularly *The Things They Carried*, stands apart from the genre as a whole. O'Brien is much more self-consciously aware of gender issues and critical of traditional gender dichotomies than are the bulk of U.S. writers about the Vietnam War.	In TIM O'BRIEN AND GENDER: A DEFENSE OF *THE THINGS THEY CARRIED* (ch. 11), Susan Farrell does the opposite of what Bowra does. Having first summarized the arguments of one specific critic (Smith), she now (in this sentence) articulates her contrary view.

3. **Sources neglect a significant aspect or element of the text, or a source or sources make(s) a claim that needs to be further developed or applied in a new way (perhaps to a text other than the one the sources actually discuss).**

Tim O'Brien's 1990 book of interlocked stories, *The Things They Carried*, garnered one rave review after another, reinforcing O'Brien's already established position as one of the most important veteran writers of the Vietnam War. The Penguin paperback edition serves up six pages of superlative blurbs like "consummate artistry," "classic," "the best American writer of his generation," "unique," and "master work." [. . .] Yet, O'Brien—and his reviewers—seem curiously unself-conscious about this book's obsession with an ambivalence about representations of masculinity and femininity, particularly in the five stories originally published during the 1980s in *Esquire*.	Here, in "THE THINGS MEN DO": THE GENDERED SUBTEXT IN TIM O'BRIEN'S *ESQUIRE* STORIES (ch. 11), Lorrie Smith suggests not that others' claims are wrong but that they simply miss something that her essay will investigate.

(In ch. 36, you'll find a research essay on Alice Munro's BOYS AND GIRLS that combines versions of the first and third kinds of source-related motives described above.)

34.3 THE RESEARCH PROCESS

34.3.1 Finding Authoritative Secondary Sources

Regardless of your author, text, or topic, you will almost certainly find a wealth of sources to consult. The conversation about literature and its contexts occurs online and in print, in periodicals and in books. Your instructor may well give you specific guidance about which sorts of sources you need to use. If not, it's usually best to consult at least some print sources or sources that appear in both print and digital form (e.g., the scholarly journals housed in databases such as *JSTOR* or *Academic Search Premier*). Citing only one kind of source—books but not articles, online but not print—may cast doubt on the thoroughness of your research; you want your reader to know that you sought out the *best* sources, not just the most easily available ones.

Whatever their form, it is crucial that your secondary sources be authoritative ones, since the credibility and persuasiveness of your research essay will depend on that of your sources: At the very least, you do not want to look like someone who doesn't know the difference or care enough to figure it out. Learning how to identify authoritative sources is one of the rationales for research essay assignments. "Evaluating sources" thus initially means evaluating their credibility and importance. At this stage, concentrate on whether the opinions expressed and information provided in a source are worthy of serious consideration, not on whether you agree with them. Save that question for later.

As a general rule and with the exception of a general dictionary, *you should not rely on or cite any source that is not attributed to a named author.* This includes (but is not limited to) *Wikipedia* and Web sites such as *Schmoop* and *SparkNotes.* Because these will likely be the first things a general *Google* search turns up and because they are almost certainly familiar to you, it's tempting to rely on them. Avoid the temptation. Though much of the information on such sites is correct and useful, much of it isn't. As important, the very virtue of such sites—the fact that they are designed for, and mainly written by, nonexperts—makes them inappropriate as sources for a research essay, since the goal of such an essay is to familiarize yourself with and to enter a conversation among acknowledged experts.

In these terms, the most valuable sources tend to be books published by academic and university presses and articles published in scholarly or professional journals (rather than magazines or newspapers). This isn't mere snobbishness or narcissism: Such work appears in print or online only after a rigorous peer-review process. As a result, you and your readers can trust that these publications have been judged worthwhile by more than one acknowledged expert.

Rather than heading straight to *Google* and searching the entire web, then, try starting instead with your library's Web site. In addition to the catalog, you will here find a wealth of specialized reference works, bibliographies, and databases. Which of these are available to you will depend on your library. But here are two especially common and helpful resources to start with:

- *Oxford Encyclopedia of American Literature* and *Oxford Encyclopedia of British Literature:* Both include signed entries by recognized experts on major authors, texts, and topics. Each entry ends with a short annotated bibliography. In addition to being a source, such an entry will thus lead you to other sources that one expert regards as the most important on the subject. In a sense, this person has already done some of your research for you.
- *MLA International Bibliography*, the "go-to" source for identifying all scholarly work—books, articles, and book chapters—on any author, work, or topic. The virtue and (for your purposes) potential limitation of this bibliography is its inclusiveness: You can generally trust that sources included in the bibliography are, indeed, scholarly, published mainly by academic presses or in scholarly journals. MLA does not, however, discriminate among those sources in terms of quality, importance, and so on.

Once you have identified potentially useful articles and books, you may be able to access some of them online. Many full-text scholarly articles are accessible via subscription databases such as *JSTOR*, *Project Muse*, and *Academic Search Premier*. Your library may have "e-book" versions of some of the books you are interested in, while other, especially older books can be found on the Web: In addition to *Google Books*, try *Hathi Trust* and *Internet Archive*. Again, however, do not neglect any important source simply because you actually have to go to the library to look at it; this includes books only *partly* viewable on *Google*.

Look for the most up-to-date sources but don't automatically discount older ones. You should consult recent sources in order to get the most up-to-date information on your topic and a sense of what scholars today consider the most significant, debatable interpretive questions and claims. But be aware that in literary studies (and the humanities generally), newer work doesn't always entirely supersede older work, as it tends to do in the sciences. As the literary criticism excerpted in chapter 30 demonstrates, twenty-first-century scholars, for example, still cite and debate the arguments about ANTIGONE made well over a hundred years ago by German philosopher Georg Wilhelm Friedrich Hegel (1770–1831).

Once you find an especially good source, its bibliography will lead you to others. Test sources against one another: If multiple reliable sources agree about a given fact, you can probably assume it's accurate; if they all cite a particular article or book, you know it's a key contribution to the conversation.

34.3.2 Reading and Taking Notes

Once you've acquired or accessed your sources, it's a good idea to skim each one. (In the case of a book, concentrate on the introduction and on the chapter that seems most relevant.) Focus at this point on assessing the relevance of each source to your topic. Or, if you're working your way toward a topic, look for things that spark your interest. Either way, try to get a rough sense of the overall conversation—of the issues and topics that come up again and again across the various sources.

Once you've identified the most pertinent sources, it's time to begin reading more carefully and taking notes. For each source, make sure that you note down all the bibliographical information that you will ultimately need to cite the source correctly. (For details, see the guide to citation in ch. 35.) Your notes for each source will likely include four things: summary, paraphrase, quotation, and your own comments and thoughts. To avoid confusion (even plagiarism), it's crucial that you develop your own system for clearly differentiating each of these from the other. Whenever you write down, type out, or paste in two or more consecutive words from a source, you should place these words in quotation marks so that you will later recognize them as direct quotations; make sure to quote with absolute accuracy; and record the page where the quotation is found (if the source is paginated). Keep such quotations to a minimum. In lieu of extensive quotations, try to summarize and paraphrase as much as possible. You can't decide how to use the source or whether you agree with its argument unless you've first understood it, and you can usually best understand and test your understanding through summary and paraphrase. You might, for example, either start or conclude your notes with a one- or two-sentence summary of the author's overall argument, perhaps using the "Although . . . I think . . . because" rubric. Paraphrase especially important points, making sure to note the page on which each appears. (For more on paraphrase, summary, and description, see ch. 31 and 34.4.2 below.)

34.3.3 Synthesizing

It can be very useful to complete the note-taking process by writing a summary that synthesizes all of your secondary sources. Your goal is to show how all the arguments fit together to form one coherent conversation. (Like any conversation, however, a scholarly one usually considers multiple topics.) Doing so will require that you both define the main questions at issue in the conversation and indicate what stance each source takes on each question—where and how their opinions coincide and differ. If you tend to be a visual learner, you might also try diagramming the conversation somehow.

One might say, for example, that the main questions about ANTIGONE that preoccupy all the various scholars represented in chapter 30 are (1) *What is the exact nature of the conflict between Antigone and Creon, or what two conflicting worldviews do they represent?* and (2) *How is that conflict resolved? Which, if either, of the two characters and worldviews does the play ultimately endorse?* A synthetic summary of these sources (i.e., one that combines or "synthesizes" them) would explain how each critic answers each of these questions.

This kind of summary can be especially helpful when you haven't yet identified a specific essay topic or crafted a thesis because it may help you to see gaps in the conversation, places where you can enter and contribute. If you have identified a topic or thesis, a synthetic summary is still useful to identifying points of agreement and disagreement and to articulating motive (34.2). Indeed, students required to write synthetic summaries by their instructors often end up using it as the kernel of their introduction.

34.4 WRITING WITH SOURCES

34.4.1 Using Sources Responsibly and Avoiding Plagiarism

Both the clarity and the credibility of any research essay depend on responsible use of sources. And using sources responsibly entails accurately representing them, clearly discriminating between their ideas and words and your own, giving credit where credit is due. Since ideas, words, information, and concepts not directly and clearly attributed to a source will be taken as your own, any lack of clarity on that score amounts to *plagiarism*. Representing anyone else's ideas or data as your own, even if you state them in your own words, is plagiarism—whether you do so intentionally or unintentionally; whether the ideas or data comes from a published book or article, another student's paper, the Internet, or any other source. Plagiarism is among the most serious of offenses within academe because it amounts both to taking credit for someone else's hard labor and to stealing ideas—the resource most precious to this community and its members. That's why the punishments for plagiarism are severe—including failure, suspension, and expulsion, for students; the loss of a job, for teachers who are also researchers.

To avoid both the offense and its consequences, you must always

- *put quotation marks around any quotation from a source* (a quotation being any two or more consecutive words or any one especially distinctive word, label, or concept) *or indent it to create a "block quotation"*;
- *credit a source whenever you take from it any of the following*:
  —*a quotation* (as described above);

—*a nonfactual or debatable claim* (an idea, opinion, interpretation, evaluation, or conclusion) stated in your own words;
—*a distinctive concept or term;*
—*a fact or piece of data that isn't common knowledge*; or
—*a distinctive way of organizing factual information.*

To clarify, a fact counts as "common knowledge"—and therefore doesn't need to be credited to a source—whenever you can find it in multiple reputable sources, none of which seriously question its validity. It is common knowledge, for instance, that Sherman Alexie is Native American, that he was born in 1966, and that he published a collection of short stories titled *Ten Little Indians*. No source can "own" or get credit for these facts. However, a source can still "own" a particular way of arranging or presenting such facts. If you begin your essay by stating—in your own words—a series of facts about Alexie's life in exactly the same order they appear in a specific source, then you would need to acknowledge that source. When in doubt, cite. (For guidance about *how* to do so, see both 34.4.2 below and ch. 35.)

34.4.2 Integrating Secondary Source Material into Your Essay

The responsible use of sources depends as much on how you integrate ideas, facts, and words from sources into your essay as on how effectively you use a citation and documentation system like that outlined in chapter 35. Indeed, in this (the MLA) system, where a citation belongs and what it looks like depend entirely on what information you provide about the source in your text.

Research essays can refer to secondary sources in a number of ways. You may

- *briefly allude to them:*

    Many critics, including Maurice Bowra and Bernard Knox, see Creon as morally inferior to Antigone.

- *summarize or paraphrase their contents:*

    According to Maurice Bowra, Creon's arrogance is his downfall. However prideful Antigone may occasionally seem, Bowra insists that Creon is genuinely, deeply, and consistently so (1910).

- *quote them directly:*

    Maurice Bowra reads Creon as the prototypical "proud man"; where Antigone's arrogance is only "apparent," says Bowra, Creon's is all too "real" (1910).

Choose whichever strategy suits your purpose in a particular context. But keep the number and length of quotations from secondary sources to a minimum. This is *your* essay. Your ideas about the text are its primary focus. And you should use your own words whenever possible, even when you are describing or articulating what you must clearly acknowledge to be someone else's ideas or facts.

USING SIGNAL PHRASES

Whether you are quoting, summarizing, or paraphrasing a source, always introduce source material with a "signal phrase." Usually, this should include the author's name. You might also include the author's title or any information about the author or source that affects its credibility or clarifies the relationship between the source's argument and your own. Titles can be especially helpful when you cite more than one source by the same author.

Oyin Ogunba, himself a scholar of Yoruban descent, suggests that many of Wole Soyinka's plays attempt to capture the mood and rhythm of traditional Yoruban festivals (8).	Since most of the authors cited in a literature research essay should be scholars, calling them that is usually redundant and unhelpful. Here, however, the phrase "scholar of Yoruban descent" implies that the author is doubly authoritative, since he writes about a culture he knows through experience and study.
As historian R. K. Webb observes, "Britain is a country in miniature" (1).	In a literature research essay, most scholars you cite will be literary critics. If they aren't and it matters, identify their discipline.
In his study of the Frankenstein myth, Chris Baldick claims that "[m]ost myths, in literate societies at least, prolong their lives not by being retold at great length, but by being alluded to" (3)—a claim that definitely applies to the Hamlet myth.	Notice how crucial this signal phrase is to making clear that its author is applying a source's claim about one thing (myths in general and the Frankenstein myth in particular) to another, entirely different thing (the Hamlet myth). Such clarity is key both to accurately representing the source and to establishing the author's own originality.

If your summary goes on for more than a sentence or two, keep using signal phrases to remind readers that you're still summarizing others' ideas rather than stating your own.

The ways of interpreting Emily's decision to murder Homer are numerous. [. . .] For simple clarification, they can be summarized along two lines. One group finds the murder growing out of Emily's demented attempt to forestall the inevitable passage of time—toward her abandonment by Homer, toward her own death, and toward the steady encroachment of the North and the New South on something loosely defined as the "tradition" of the Old South. Another view sees the murder in more psychological terms. It grows out of Emily's complex relationship to her father, who, by elevating her above all of the eligible men of Jefferson, insured that to yield what one commentator called the "normal emotions" associated with desire, his daughter had to "retreat into a marginal world, into fantasy" (O'Connor 416).	In this paragraph from his essay "'We All Said, "She Will Kill Herself"': The Narrator/Detective in William Faulkner's 'A Rose for Emily,'" Lawrence R. Rodgers heads into a general summary of other critics' arguments by announcing that it's coming ("*For simple clarification, they can be summarized . . .*"). Then, as he begins summarizing each view, he reminds us that it is a "view," that he's still articulating others' ideas, not his own. Notice that he only quotes "one commentator" among the many to whom he refers; the others are indicated in a footnote.

For the sake of interest and clarity, vary the content and placement of signal phrases, and always choose the most accurate verb. (*Says*, for example, implies that words are spoken, not written.) Here is a list of verbs you might find useful to describe what sources do.

acknowledges
affirms
argues
asks
asserts
claims
comments
concludes
considers
contends
demonstrates
describes
discusses
draws attention to
emphasizes
explains
explores
finds
identifies
illustrates
implies
indicates
insists
investigates
maintains
notes
observes
points out
remarks
reminds us
reports
sees
shows
speculates
states
stresses
suggests
surmises
writes

35 QUOTATION, CITATION, AND DOCUMENTATION

The bulk of any literature essay you write should consist of your own ideas expressed in your own words. Yet you can develop your ideas and persuade readers to accept them only if you present and analyze evidence. In literature essays of every kind, quotations are an especially privileged kind of evidence, though paraphrase, summary, and description play key roles (see ch. 31 and 32.1.4). Likewise, a literature research essay, which must make use of other primary and secondary sources, typically quotes selectively from these as well (see 34.4.2). In all literature essays, then, your clarity, credibility, and persuasiveness greatly depend on two things: (1) how responsibly, effectively, and gracefully you present, differentiate, and move between others' words and ideas and your own; and (2) how careful you are to let readers know exactly where they can find each quotation and each fact or idea that you paraphrase from a source. This chapter addresses the question of *how* to quote, cite, and document sources of all kinds. (For a discussion of *when* to do so, see 32.1.4 and 34.4.1.)

Rules for quoting, citing, and documenting sources can seem daunting and even, at times, arcane or trivial. Why the heck should it matter whether you put a word in brackets or parentheses, or where in a sentence your parentheses appears? By demonstrating mastery of such conventions, you assert your credibility as a member of the scholarly community. But such conventions also serve an eminently practical purpose: They provide you a system for conveying a wealth of important information clearly, concisely, and unobtrusively, with the least distraction to you and your reader.

As you probably know, there are many such systems. And different disciplines, publications, and even individual instructors prefer or require different ones. In English and other humanities disciplines, however, the preferred system is that developed by the Modern Language Association (MLA) and laid out in the *MLA Handbook* (8th ed., 2016) and *The MLA Style Center: Writing Resources from the Modern Language Association* (style.mla.org). All the rules presented in this chapter accord with, and draw heavily upon, these sources, which we encourage you to consult for more extensive and detailed guidance than we can provide here.

35.1 THE RULES OF RESPONSIBLE QUOTING

When it comes to quoting, there are certain rules that you must follow in order to be responsible both to your sources and to the integrity of your own prose. Additionally, there are certain strategies that, though not required, will do much to make your argument more clear, engaging, and persuasive. The next section of this chapter (35.2) discusses strategies; this one concentrates on the rules, starting with the cardinal principles of responsible quotation before turning first to those rules specific to the genres of prose, poetry, and drama and then to those rules that aren't genre-specific.

35.1.1 Cardinal Principles

Three requirements so crucial to your credibility that you should regard them as cardinal principles rather than simple rules are these:

1. *A quotation means any two or more consecutive words or any one especially distinctive word or label that appears in a source.*

Representation as O'Brien practices it in this book is not a mimetic act but a "game," as Iser also calls it in a more recent essay, "The Play of the Text," a process of acting things out. . . .	In this sentence from THE UNDYING UNCERTAINTY OF THE NARRATOR IN TIM O'BRIEN'S *THE THINGS THEY CARRIED* (ch. 9), Steven Kaplan puts the word game in quotation marks because it is a key concept defined in distinctive ways in his source.

2. *Except in the very few cases and specific ways outlined in the rest of this section, you must reproduce each quotation exactly as it appears in a source, including every word and preserving original spelling, punctuation, capitalization, italics, spacing, and so on.*

ORIGINAL SOURCE	INCORRECT VS. CORRECT QUOTATION
[MRS. PETERS *sits down. The two women sit there not looking at one another, but as if peering into something and at the same time holding back. When they talk now it is in the manner of feeling their way over strange ground, as if afraid of what they are saying, but as if they cannot help saying it.*]	**Incorrect:** After they discover the dead bird and the men leave the room, Mrs. Peters and Mrs. Hale simply "sit there not looking at each other," compelled to speak but also "afraid of what they are saying." **Correct:** After they discover the dead bird and the men leave the room, Mrs. Peters and Mrs. Hale simply "*sit there not looking at one another,*" compelled to speak but also "*afraid of what they are saying.*"

3. *No change to a quotation, however much it accords with the rules outlined below, is acceptable if it in any way distorts the original meaning of the quoted passage.*

35.1.2 Genre-Specific Rules

Because prose, poetry, and drama each work somewhat differently, there are special rules governing how to quote texts in each of these genres. This section spells out the rules specific to prose (both fiction and nonfiction), poetry, and drama; the next section covers rules applicable to all genres.

PROSE (FICTION OR NONFICTION)

- When a quotation from a single paragraph of a prose source takes up no more than four lines of your essay, put it in quotation marks.

  Georgiana's birthmark becomes "a frightful object" only because "Aylmer's somber imagination" turns it into one, "selecting it as the symbol of his wife's liability to sin, sorrow, decay, and death."

- When a prose quotation takes up more than four lines of your essay or includes a paragraph break, indent it ½ inch from the left margin to create a *block quotation.* Do not enclose the quotation in quotation marks, since these are implied by the formatting. On the rare occasions you quote more than one paragraph reproduce any paragraph break that occurs within the quotation by indenting the first line an additional ¼ inch.

Georgiana's birthmark becomes "a frightful object" only because "Aylmer's somber imagination" turns it into a "symbol" of

> the fatal flaw of humanity which Nature, in one shape or another, stamps ineffaceably on all her productions, either to imply that they are temporary and finite, or that their perfection must be wrought by toil and pain. The crimson hand expressed the ineludible gripe in which mortality clutches the highest and purest of earthly mould, degrading them into kindred with the lowest, and even with the very brutes, like whom their visible frames return to dust.

POETRY

- When quoting three or fewer lines of poetry, put the quotation in quotation marks, and use a slash mark (/) with a space on either side to indicate any line break that occurs in the quotation, and a double slash mark (//) to indicate a stanza break.

Before Milton's speaker can question his "Maker" for allowing him to go blind, "Patience" intervenes "to prevent / That murmur."

- When quoting more than three lines, indent the quotation ½ inch from the left margin to create a *block quotation.* Do not enclose the quotation in quotation marks, since these are implied by the formatting, but do reproduce original line and stanza breaks and the spatial arrangement of the original lines, including indentation.

Midway through the poem, the speaker suddenly shifts to second-person, for the first time addressing the drowned girl directly and almost affectionately as he also begins to imagine her as a living person rather than a dead corpse:

> Little adulteress,
> before they punished you
>
> you were flaxen-haired,
> undernourished, and your
> tar-black face was beautiful.

- When a block quotation begins in the middle of a line of verse, indent the partial line as much as you need to in order to approximate its original positioning.

The speaker first demonstrates both his knowledge of persimmons and his understanding of precision by telling us exactly what ripe fruits look and smell like and then, step by careful step,

>   How to eat:
> put the knife away, lay down newspaper.
> Peel the skin tenderly, not to tear the meat.
> Chew the skin, suck it,

and swallow. Now, eat
the meat of the fruit

- **If you omit one or more lines in the middle of a block quotation, indicate the omission with a line of spaced periods approximately the same length as a complete line of the quoted poem.**

About another image on the urn, the speaker has more questions than answers:

> Who are these coming to the sacrifice?
> To what green altar, O mysterious priest,
> Lead'st thou that heifer lowing at the skies,
> And all her silken flanks with garlands dressed?
> What little town by river or sea shore,
> . . . .
> Is emptied of its folk, this pious morn?

DRAMA

- **With one exception (covered in the next rule), a quotation from a play is governed by the same rules as outlined above under "Prose," if the quotation is in prose; under "Poetry," if in verse.**
- **Regardless of its length, if a quotation from a play includes dialogue between two or more characters, indent it ½ inch from the left margin to create a *block quotation*. Begin each character's speech with the character's name in capital letters followed by a period; indent the second and subsequent lines an additional ¼ inch. If a speech is in verse, you must also follow the applicable rules outlined in the "Poetry" section above, by, for example, reproducing original line breaks (as in the second example below).**

1. As soon as the men exit, the women start talking about the men and undoing what the men just did:

> MRS. HALE. I'd hate to have men coming into my kitchen, snooping around and criticizing. [*She arranges the pans under the sink which the* LAWYER *had shoved out of place.*]
>
> MRS. PETERS. Of course it's no more than their duty.

2. Antigone and Ismene's initial exchange climaxes with Antigone declaring her sister an "enemy," even as Ismene declares herself one of Antigone's loving "friends":

> ANTIGONE. If you will talk like this I will loathe you,
> and you will be adjudged an enemy—
> justly—by the dead's decision. Let me alone
> and my folly with me, to endure this terror.
> No suffering of mine will be enough
> to make me die ignobly.
>
> ISMENE. Well, if you will, go on.
> Know this; that though you are wrong to go, your friends
> are right to love you.

35.1.3 General Rules and Strategies

Unlike the rules covered in the last section, the ones laid out here apply regardless of whether you are quoting prose, poetry, or drama.

GRAMMAR, SYNTAX, TENSE, AND THE USE OF BRACKETS

- **Quotations need not be complete sentences and may go anywhere in your sentence.**

1. The narrator says of Mr. Kapasi, "In his youth he'd been a devoted scholar of foreign languages" who "dreamed of being an interpreter for diplomats and dignitaries."
2. "In his youth a devoted scholar of foreign languages," says the narrator, Mr. Kapasi once "dreamed of being an interpreter for diplomats and dignitaries."

- **Every sentence that includes a quotation and every quotation you present as if it is a sentence must—like every other sentence in your essay—observe all the usual rules of grammar, syntax, and consistency of tense. (In terms of these rules, words inside quotation marks don't operate any differently than do words outside of quotation marks.)**

1. The woman in all the portraits is idealized. "Not as she is, but as she fills his dream." 2. The woman in all the portraits is idealized: "Not as she is, but as she fills his dream." 3. The woman in all the paintings is idealized, portrayed by the artist "[n]ot as she is, but as she fills his dream."	Sentence 1 includes a quotation that is treated as a sentence but isn't one. Sentence 2 corrects that problem by using a colon to make the quoted fragment part of the preceding sentence. Yet the fragment still contains a pronoun (*his*) that lacks any clear referent in the sentence, making sentence 3 a better fix.
4. As Joy waits for Manley's arrival, "She looked up and down the empty highway and had the furious feeling that she had been tricked, that he had only meant to make her walk to the gate after the idea of him" rather than the reality. 5. As Joy waits for Manley's arrival, she becomes "furious," convinced that he has "tricked" her and only "meant to make her walk to the gate after the idea of him" rather than the reality.	The fact that fiction typically uses past tense, while we write about it in present tense, often creates confusing tense shifts like that in sentence 4. Usually, partial paraphrase is a good solution: As in sentence 5, quote only the most essential words from the passage, remembering that what those words are will depend on the point you want to make.

- **When necessary to the grammar of your sentence or the intelligibility of your quotation, you may add words to the latter or make minor changes to words within it, but you must enclose your alterations in brackets ([]) to let readers know that they *are* alterations. (In example 3 above, for example, the first letter of the word "not" appears in brackets because a capital "N" has been changed to a lower-case "n.")**

As Joy waits for Manley's arrival, "She look[s] up and down the empty highway and ha[s] the furious feeling that she ha[s] been tricked, that he had only meant to make her walk to the gate after the idea of him."	This sentence demonstrates how changing verb endings and putting the new ones in brackets can be an easy way to solve tense shift problems of the kind found in example 4 above.

(*continued*)

The woman in all the portraits is idealized, represented "[n]ot as she is, but as she fills his [the painter's] dream."	If a pronoun reference in a quotation is unclear, one fix is to put the noun to which the pronoun refers in brackets after the pronoun, as in this sentence. For an alternative fix, see example 3 above.
As Mays explains, a writer "can assume that their reader will recognize the traditional meanings of these ["traditional"] symbols," but "invented symbols" work differently.	In this sentence, the phrase "these symbols" refers to something outside the quoted sentence. The added and thus bracketed word *traditional* appears in quotation marks because it, too, comes directly from the same source.

Tip: Though such alterations are permissible, they are often so much less effective than other techniques that some of them (including changes to verb endings) are not actually mentioned in the *MLA Handbook*. Used too often, this technique can become very distracting and put you at risk of appearing as if you're "fiddling" with sources. As a result, look for other fixes whenever possible.

OMISSIONS AND ELLIPSES

- A quotation that is obviously a sentence fragment need not be preceded or followed by an ellipsis (. . .). But you must use an ellipsis whenever
  —your quotation appears to be a complete sentence but actually isn't one in the source (as in the first and last sentences in the example below),
  —you omit words from the middle of a quoted sentence (as in the second sentence in the example below), or
  —you omit one or more sentences between quoted sentences (as between the second and third sentences in the example below).
- When the ellipsis coincides with the end of your sentence, add a period followed by an ellipsis with a space before and between each ellipsis dot. A space follows the final ellipsis dot only if a new sentence follows (as in the first sentence below).

The narrator says of Mr. Kapasi,

> In his youth he'd been a devoted scholar of foreign languages. . . . He had dreamed of being an interpreter for diplomats and dignitaries, . . . settling disputes of which he alone could understand both sides. . . . Now only a handful of European phrases remained in his memory, scattered words for things like saucers and chairs. . . . Sometimes he feared that his children knew better English than he did, just from watching television.

Note: If you omit the end of a sentence *and* one or more of the sentences that immediately follow it, the four dots are sufficient; you do not need two ellipses.

- If the quoted source uses an ellipsis, put your ellipsis in brackets to distinguish between the two. [NOTE: Throughout this book, we have instead put *every* added ellipsis in brackets.]

As an excited Ruth explains, the prospect of receiving a check is "a whole lot different from having it come and being able to hold it in your hands . . . a piece of paper worth ten thousand dollars." "[. . .] I wish Walter Lee was here!," she exclaims.	The first (unbracketed) ellipsis here occurs in the original source; the second (bracketed) ellipsis doesn't.

OTHER ACCEPTABLE CHANGES TO QUOTATIONS: *SIC* AND *EMPHASIS ADDED*

- **If a quotation includes what is or might seem to your reader an error of fact or of grammar, spelling, and so on, you may signal to the reader that you haven't introduced the error yourself through misquotation by putting the word *sic* (Latin for "thus" or "so") next to the error. Put parentheses around *sic* if it comes *after* the quotation (as in the first example below), brackets if it appears *within* the quotation (as in the second example). Do not use *sic* if context makes it obvious that the error isn't yours or isn't truly an error, as in the case of texts featuring archaic spelling, dialect, and so on.**

1. Shaw admitted, "Nothing can extinguish my interest in Shakespear" (sic). 2. In the preface to *Shakes Versus Shav: A Puppet Play* (1949), Shaw avows, "Nothing can extinguish my interest in Shakespear [sic]. It began when I was a small boy. . . ."	In sentence 1 (from the *MLA Handbook*) parentheses work because nothing has been added *into* the quotation; the second, slightly modified version requires brackets. Either way, the word *sic* appears next to the misspelled word and is not italicized.
3. Charley gets to the heart of the matter when he asks Willy, "when're you gonna realize that them things don't mean anything?"	*Sic* would be inappropriate here, since it's clear this quotation accurately reproduces the character's speech patterns.
4. The Misfit firmly rejects the idea that he should pray, insisting, "I don't want no hep" (sic), "I'm doing all right by myself."	In this case, though use of the word *hep* (for *help*) is entirely characteristic of the character's speech, it could so easily look like a typo, that the word *sic* seems helpful.

- **On the relatively rare occasions when you need to emphasize a specific word or phrase within a quotation, you may put it in italics and indicate this change by putting the words *emphasis added* in parentheses after the quotation, ideally at the end of the clause or sentence.**

Avowing that men "must help them [women] to stay in that beautiful world of their own, *lest ours get worse*" (emphasis added), Marlow acknowledges that men have a selfish interest in preserving women's innocence and idealism.

PUNCTUATING QUOTATIONS

- **Though you must always reproduce original punctuation *within* a quotation, you may *end it* with whatever punctuation your sentence requires, and this is the one change you do not need to indicate with brackets.**

Whether portrayed as "queen," "saint," or "angel," the same "nameless girl" appears in "all his canvases."	In the poem quoted here, no commas appear after the words *queen* and *angel*, but the syntax of the sentence requires they be added. Similarly, the comma that appears after the word *canvases* in the poem is here replaced by a period.
The narrator tells us that Mr. Kapasi's "job was a sign of his failings," for "[i]n his youth he'd been a devoted scholar of foreign languages" who "dreamed of being an interpreter for diplomats and dignitaries."	Here, a comma replaces the original period after *failings*, and a period replaces the original comma after *dignitaries*.

- **Commas and periods belong *inside* the closing quotation mark (as in the above examples). All other punctuation marks belongs *outside* the closing quotation mark if they are your additions, inside if they are not.**

1. Wordsworth calls nature a "homely Nurse"; she has "something of a Mother's Mind."
2. What exactly does Lili mean when she tells Guy, "You are here to protect me if anything happens"?
3. Bobby Lee speaks volumes about the grandmother when he says, "She was a talker, wasn't she?"

- **When your indented, block quotation includes a quotation, put the latter in double quotation marks (" ").**

Written just four years after *A Raisin in the Sun*'s debut, Martin Luther King, Jr.'s "Letter from Birmingham Jail" stresses the urgency of the situation of African Americans like himself and the Youngers by comparing it to those of Africans like Joseph Asagai and white Americans like Karl Lindner:

> We have waited for more than 340 years for our constitutional and God-given rights. The nations of . . . Africa are moving with jetlike speed toward gaining political independence, but we still creep at horse-and-buggy pace toward gaining a cup of coffee at a lunch counter. Perhaps it is easy for those who have never felt the stinging darts of segregation to say, "Wait."

- **When a shorter (non-block) quotation includes a quotation, put the latter in single quotation marks (' ').**

1. As Martin Luther King, Jr., insisted in 1963, "it is easy for those who have never felt the stinging darts of segregation" or the "degenerating sense of 'nobodiness'" it instills, "to say, 'Wait,'" be patient, your time will come.
2. In a poem less about Hard Rock himself than about the way he is perceived by his fellow inmates, it makes sense that many words and lines take the form of unattributed quotations, as in the unforgettable opening, "Hard Rock was 'known not to take no shit / From nobody.' "

- **When your quotation consists *entirely* of words that appear within quotation marks in the source, use double quotation marks, while making sure that you introduce the quotation in a way that makes the special status of these words and their provenance clear.**

1. "[K]nown not to take no shit / From nobody," as his fellow inmates put it, Hard Rock initially appears almost superhuman.
2. The Misfit's response is as shocking as it is simple: "I don't want no hep," "I'm doing all right by myself."
3. In an introductory note quoted by Alvarez, Plath describes the poem's speaker as "a girl with an Electra complex" whose "father died while she thought he was God."

35.2 STRATEGIES FOR EFFECTIVE QUOTING

- **Though it is not a rule that all of your quotations must appear inside one of your sentences, your clarity will be enormously enhanced if you treat it like one, making the connection between quotation and inference as seamless as possible.**

1. Smith is highly critical of O'Brien's portrayal of Martha. "Like other women in the book, she represents all those back home who will never understand the warrior's trauma."
2. Smith is highly critical of O'Brien's portrayal of Martha: "Like other women in the book, she represents all those back home who will never understand the warrior's trauma."
3. Smith is highly critical of O'Brien's portrayal of Martha, claiming that, "[l]ike other women in the book," Martha "represents all those back home who will never understand the warrior's trauma."

Example 1 includes a quotation that isn't part of any sentence. Example 2 corrects that problem with a colon, but the reader still has to pause to figure out that it's Smith who's being quoted here and that the quotation refers to Martha. Sentence 3 thus offers a better solution.

- **Avoid drawing attention to your evidence as evidence with "filler" phrases such as *This statement is proof that . . .* ; *This phrase is significant because . . .* ; *This idea is illustrated by . . .* ; *There is good evidence for this. . . .* Show *why* facts are meaningful or interesting rather than first or only saying *that* they are.**

INEFFECTIVE QUOTATION	EFFECTIVE QUOTATION
Wordsworth calls nature a "homely Nurse" and says that she has "something of a Mother's mind" (lines 81, 79). This diction supports the idea that he sees nature as a healing, maternal force. He is saying that nature heals and cares for us.	Personifying nature as a "homely Nurse" with "something of a Mother's Mind," Wordsworth depicts nature as healing and nurturing the humans it also resembles. OR A "homely Nurse" with "something of a Mother's Mind," nature, implies Wordsworth, both heals and nurtures the humans it also resembles.
Tennyson advocates decisive action, even as he highlights the forces that often prohibited his contemporaries from taking it. This is suggested by the lines "Made weak by time and fate, but strong in will, / To strive, to seek, to find, and not to yield" (lines 69–70).	Tennyson advocates forceful action, encouraging his contemporaries "To strive, to seek to find, and not to yield" (line 70). Yet he recognizes that his generation is more tempted to "yield" than earlier ones because they have been "Made weak by time and fate" (69).

- **On the one hand, make sure that you provide readers the information they need to understand the quotation and to appreciate its relevance to your argument. Quite often, contextual information—for instance, about who's speaking to whom and in what situation—is crucial to a quotation's meaning. On the other hand, keep such contextual information to a minimum and put the emphasis on the words that really matter and on your inferences about why and how they matter.**

1. Strong as Mama is, she and Walter share a similar, traditional vision of gender roles: "I'm telling you to be the head of this family . . . like you supposed to be"; "the colored woman" should be "building their men up and making 'em feel like they somebody."	
2. Strong as Mama is, she shares Walter's traditional vision of gender roles. When she urges him "to be the head of this family from now on like you supposed to be," she affirms that her son is the family's rightful leader—not her daughter, not her daughter-in-law, not even herself, despite her seniority in terms of age. Implicitly, she's also doing what Walter elsewhere says "the colored woman" should do—"building their men up and making 'em feel like they somebody."	Example 2 is more effective because it offers crucial information about who is speaking to whom ("*When Lena tells Walter,*" "*Walter elsewhere says*") and includes inferences ("*she affirms that her son is the family's rightful leader . . .* "; "*Implicitly, she's also doing*"). Purely contextual information is, however, stated briefly and early, in subordinate clauses.
3. Julian expresses disgust for the class distinctions so precious to his mother: "Rolling his eyes upward, he put his tie back on. 'Restored to my class,' he muttered."	

(*continued*)

4. Julian professes disgust for the class distinctions so precious to his mother. At her request, he puts back on his tie, but he can't do so without "[r]olling his eyes" and making fun (at least under his breath) of the idea that he is thereby "[r]estored to [his] class."	Again, example 4 improves on example 3 by providing missing information ("*At her request*") and yet paraphrasing and subordinating what is only information ("*he puts back on his tie*").

- **Lead your readers into long, especially block, quotations with a clear sense of just what in the quotation they should be paying attention to and why. Follow it up with at least a sentence or more of analysis/inferences, perhaps repeating especially key words and phrases from the long quotation.**

Whereas the second stanza individualizes the dead martyrs, the third considers the characteristics they shared with each other and with all those who dedicate themselves utterly to any one cause:

> Hearts with one purpose alone
> Through summer and winter seem
> Enchanted to a stone
> To trouble the living stream. (lines 41–44)

Whereas all other "living" people and things are caught up in the "stream" of change represented by the shift of seasons, those who fill their "hearts with one purpose alone" become as hard, unchanging, and immoveable as stone.

- **Be aware that even though long, especially block quotations can be effective, they should be used sparingly and strategically. All too easily, they can create information overload or confusion for readers, making it hard to see what is most significant and why. When you quote only individual words or short phrases, weaving them into your sentences in the ways demonstrated earlier in this section, you and your readers can more easily stay focused on what's significant and on *why* and *how* it is.**
- **Vary the length of quotations and the way you present them, using a variety of strategies. It can be very tempting to fall into a pattern—always, for example, choosing quotations that are at least a sentence long and attaching them to your sentence with a colon. But overusing *any* one technique can easily render your essay monotonous and might even prompt readers to focus more on the (repetitive) way you present evidence than on the evidence and argument themselves. To demonstrate, here are two sets of sentences that present the very same material in varying ways.**

1. According to Wordsworth, nature is a "homely Nurse" with "something of a Mother's Mind"; it heals and nurtures the humans it also resembles.
2. A "homely Nurse" with "something of a Mother's Mind," nature, suggests Wordsworth, both heals and nurtures the humans it also resembles.
3. Personifying nature as a "homely Nurse" with "something of a Mother's Mind," Wordsworth depicts nature as healing and nurturing the humans it also resembles.
4. Healing and nurturing the humans it also resembles, Wordsworth's nature is a "homely Nurse" with "something of a Mother's Mind."

---

1. Howe insists that the poem's "personal-confessional element . . . is simply too obtrusive," "strident and undisciplined," to allow a reader to interpret "Daddy" "as

a dramatic presentation, a monologue spoken by a disturbed girl not necessarily to be identified with Sylvia Plath," especially given the resemblances between "events" described in the poem and those that actually occurred in Plath's life.

2. "Daddy," argues Howe, cannot be read "as a dramatic presentation, a monologue spoken by a disturbed girl not necessarily to be identified with Sylvia Plath"; its "personal-confessional element . . . is simply too obtrusive," too "strident and undisciplined," he reasons, while the "events of the poem" too closely correspond to "the events of her life."

35.3 CITATION AND DOCUMENTATION

In addition to indicating which words, facts, and ideas in your essay derive from someone else's work, you need to let your readers know where each can be found. You want to enable readers not only to "check up" on you but also to follow in your footsteps and build on your work. After all, you hope that your analysis of a text will entice readers to re-read certain passages from the text in a different way or to consult sources that you've made sound interesting. This is another way your essay contributes to keeping the conversation about literature going. And this is where citation and documentation come into play.

In the MLA system, parenthetical citations embedded in your essay are keyed to an alphabetized list of works cited that follows your essay. By virtue of both their content and placement, parenthetical citations help you to quickly and unobtrusively indicate *what* you have derived from *which* source and *where* in that source your readers can find that material. The list of works cited communicates the information about the source that your readers need both to find it themselves and, in the meantime, to begin evaluating for themselves its relevance, credibility, currency, and so on *without* having to find it.

To demonstrate how this works, here is a typical sentence with parenthetical citation, followed by the coordinating works-cited entry:

In-Text Citation

In one critic's view, "Ode on a Grecian Urn" explores "what great art means" not to the ordinary person, but "to those who create it" (Bowra 148).

Placed at the end of the sentence and beginning with the word *Bowra* (sans quotation marks or italics) and the number 148, this parenthetical citation tells us that the last name of the "critic" the sentence mentions and quotes is *Bowra,* that the source of the quotations is something he authored, and that the quotations come from page 148 of that source. To find out more, we have to turn to the list of works cited and look for an entry, like the following, that begins with the name *Bowra.*

Works Cited Entry

Bowra, C. M. *The Romantic Imagination.* Oxford UP, 1950.

This coordinating works-cited entry gives us Bowra's complete name as it appears in the source and indicates its title, publisher, and date of publication.

That our explanations of this sample parenthetical citation and works-cited entry take up much more space than the citation and entry themselves demonstrates the value of the MLA system. What it also demonstrates is the importance of both the placement and content of each citation and entry: Where the parenthetical citation falls in a sentence is key to clearly indicating what is being "sourced"; what the parenthetical citation and works cited include and in what order are all key to ensuring that the citation leads us seamlessly to *one* source in the works cited and tells us where precisely to look in that source.

The exact content and placement of each parenthetical citation and works-cited entry will thus depend on a host of factors. The next sections explain how this works.

35.3.1 Parenthetical Citation

THE STANDARD PARENTHETICAL CITATION: CONTENT AND PLACEMENT

Because lists of works cited are organized primarily by author, the standard MLA parenthetical citation looks just like, and appears in the same place as, the ones in the sample sentences above and below. It includes an author's name and a page number or numbers with nothing but a space in between. (Do not write *page* or *p.*, for example, or insert a comma.) The citation comes at the end of a sentence—*inside* the period (because it is part of the sentence in which you borrow from a source) and *outside* any quotation marks within the sentence (since it is *not* part of an actual quotation; it is not *in* the source but provides information *about* the source). In keeping with the rules for punctuating quotations laid out earlier in this chapter (35.1.3), you omit any final punctuation mark within your quotation, as in the second example below.

1. Most domestic poems of the 1950s foreground the parent-child relationship (Axelrod 1093).
2. As a character in one of the most famous works of Southern fiction memorably declares of the South, "I dont hate it" (Faulkner 378).

When citing a work from an anthology, refer to the author of the work, not the anthology editor, and make sure to create a corresponding entry in your list of works cited. Below is an example of this kind of citation, as well as the corresponding works-cited entry.

In-Text Citation

By the end of an initiation story, its protagonist may well have to confront "how hard the world" usually is (Updike 167).

Works Cited Entry

Updike, John. "A & P." *The Norton Introduction to Literature*, edited by Kelly J. Mays, 12th ed., W. W. Norton, 2017, pp. 163-67.

The next two sections detail the variations on the standard MLA parenthetical citation format, starting with variations in *where* the citation goes before turning to variations in *what* it includes.

VARIATIONS IN PLACEMENT

- **In the case of a block quotation, the parenthetical citation should immediately *follow* (not precede) the punctuation mark that ends the quotation.**

According to the narrator,

> The job was a sign of his failings. In his youth he'd been a devoted scholar of foreign languages, the owner of an impressive collection of dictionaries. He had dreamed of being an interpreter for diplomats and dignitaries, resolving conflicts between people and nations, settling disputes of which he alone could understand both sides. (Lahiri 451)

- **If a sentence either incorporates material from multiple sources (as in the first example below) or refers both to something from a source and to your own idea (as in the second example), put the appropriate parenthetical citation in midsentence next to the material to which it refers. Ideally, you should insert the citation before a comma or semi-colon, since it will be less obtrusive that way. But your first priority should be clarity about which material comes from which source (see the third example below).**

1. Critics describe Caliban as a creature with an essentially "unalterable natur[e]" (Garner 458), "incapable of comprehending the good or of learning from the past" (Peterson 442), "impervious to genuine moral improvement" (Wright 451).
2. If Caliban is truly "incapable of . . . learning from the past" (Peterson 442), then how do we explain the changed attitude he seems to demonstrate at the play's end?
3. Tanner (7) and Smith (viii) have looked at works from a cultural perspective.

- **If, in a single paragraph, you make several *uninterrupted* references to the same source and especially to the same passage in a source, you may save the parenthetical citation until after the last such reference, as in the following example from Susan Farrell's TIM O'BRIEN AND GENDER: A DEFENSE OF *THE THINGS THEY CARRIED* (ch. 11).**

> Smith connects a 1980s backlash against the feminist movement to the misogyny she reads in Vietnam War literature, a misogyny which she describes as "very visible," as seemingly "natural and expected." In popular presentations, Smith argues, the "Vietnam War is being reconstructed as a site where white American manhood—figuratively as well as literally wounded during the war and assaulted by the women's movement for twenty years—can reassert its dominance in the social hierarchy" ("Back" 115).

VARIATIONS IN CONTENT: IDENTIFYING THE SOURCE

The standard MLA parenthetical citation may contain the author's name and the relevant page number(s). But variations are the rule when it comes to content. In this section, we deal with variations in how a citation indicates *which* source you refer to; the next section instead covers variations in how you indicate *where* in the source borrowed material can be found.

Your parenthetical citation should include something besides or in addition to one author's name whenever you do the following:

- ***Name the author(s) in your text.***

Parenthetical citations should include only information that isn't crucial to the intelligibility and credibility of your argument. Yet in nine cases out of ten, information about *whose* ideas, data, or words you are referring to is crucial. As a result, you should try whenever possible to indicate this in your text, usually via a *signal phrase* (as described in 34.4.2). When you do so, your parenthetical citation usually need only include location information such as page number(s).

1. In Maurice Bowra's view, "Ode on a Grecian Urn" explores "what great art means" not to the ordinary person, but "to those who create it" (148).
2. As Faulkner's Quentin Compson memorably declares of the South, "I dont hate it" (378).

In literature essays, parenthetical citations containing the name of the author whose work you are analyzing should be relatively rare. (Notice that there are none, for example, in any of the critical excerpts on Tim O'Brien's *The Things They Carried* found in chapter 11.)

- *Cite a source with multiple authors.*
  If the source has two authors, and they are not named in your text, the parenthetical citation should include both last names (as in the example below). If the source has three or more authors, include the first author's name followed by the words *et al.* (abbreviated Latin for "and others").

  Surprisingly, "it seems not to have been primarily the coarseness and sexuality of *Jane Eyre* which shocked Victorian reviewers" so much as its "rebellious feminism" (Gilbert and Gubar 338).

- *Cite multiple works by the same author or an anonymous work.*
  In either of these cases, you will need to indicate the title of your source. If possible, do so in your text, putting only location information in the parenthetical citation (as in the first example below). Otherwise, your parenthetical citation must include a shortened version of the title (as in the second example below). If your parenthetical citation also needs to include the author's name(s), this comes first, followed by a comma, the shortened title, and the location information (as in the third example below).

  1. Like Joy, in O'Connor's "Good Country People," the protagonist of her story "Everything that Rises Must Converge" takes enormous pride in his intellect, even believing himself "too intelligent to be a success" (91).
  2. Many of O'Connor's most faulty characters put enormous stock in their intellects, one even secretly believing himself "too intelligent to be a success" ("Everything" 91).
  3. Intellectuals fare poorly in much Southern fiction. When we learn that the protagonist of one short story secretly believes himself "too intelligent to be a success," we can be pretty sure that he's in for a fall (O'Connor, "Everything" 91).

  Be sure to format shortened titles just as you do full titles, either putting them in quotation marks or italicizing them as appropriate (see 33.5).

- *Cite multiple authors with the same last name.*
  In this case, you should ideally indicate the author's full name in the text so that your parenthetical citation need only include location information. Otherwise, the parenthetical citation should begin with the author's first initial followed by a period, followed by his or her last name and the location information

(as in the first example below). If your authors share the same first initial, however, you will need to include a first name instead of initial (as in the second example).

1. As one of Joyce's fellow writers points out, "To be absolutely faithful to what one sees and hears and not to speculate on what may lie behind it . . . is a creed that produces obvious limitations" (F. O'Connor 188).
2. As one of Flannery O'Connor's fellow short story writers points out, "To be absolutely faithful to what one sees and hears and not to speculate on what may lie behind it . . . is a creed that produces obvious limitations" (Frank O'Connor 188).

- *Cite multiple authors simultaneously.*
  In this case, include all the citations within a single set of parentheses, separating them with semicolons.

  Many scholars attribute Caliban's bestiality to a seemingly innate inability to learn or change (Garner 438; Peterson 442; Wright 451).

- *Quote a source quoted in another source.*
  You should quote from an original source whenever possible. But on the rare occasions when you quote something quoted in another source, indicate the original source in your text. Then start your parenthetical citation with the abbreviation *qtd. in* followed by the name of the secondhand source's author and the location information.

  In an introductory note to "Daddy" that Plath wrote for a radio program that never aired, she describes the poem's speaker as "a girl with an Electra complex" whose "father died while she thought he was God" and whose "case is complicated by the fact that her father was also a Nazi and her mother very possibly part Jewish" (qtd. in Alvarez 1080).

VARIATIONS IN CONTENT: INDICATING A LOCATION WITHIN THE SOURCE

Though page numbers are usually the only means we use to identify where in a source a reader can find the ideas, information, or words we cite, there are exceptions. Indeed, exceptions are unusually frequent in literature essays. The most important reason for this is that literary texts tend to be available in different editions, so it's helpful to give readers the information they need to locate material in the text regardless of the edition they use.

When it comes to the question of how to do so, there is frankly a good deal of ambiguity and "wiggle room" in the MLA guidelines. Thus, as we explain below, different instructors may interpret some of these guidelines differently or simply prefer that you use one method rather than another.

Your parenthetical citation will generally need to include location information other than, or in addition to, a page number whenever you cite any of the following:

- *Poetry*
  When citing poetry, it is customary to refer to line (not page) number(s) and to indicate that you are doing so by including the word *line* or *lines,* as appropriate, in your first such parenthetical citation. Though MLA guidelines stipulate that later parenthetical citations include only the line number (as in the

example below), some instructors prefer that the word *line* or *lines* appear in every poem-related parenthetical citation.

In a poem less about Hard Rock himself than about the way he is perceived by his fellow inmates, it makes sense that many words and lines take the form of unattributed quotations, as in the unforgettable opening, "Hard Rock was 'known not to take no shit / From nobody' " (lines 1-2), or "Yeah, remember when he / Smacked the captain with his dinner tray?" (17-18).

- *Play with more than one act or scene*
At least when it comes to canonical plays, MLA guidelines call for omitting page numbers entirely and referring only to act, scene, and/or line numbers as appropriate, always using arabic numerals (*1, 2,* etc.) and separating each with a period (as in the first example below). Some instructors, however, prefer that you use roman numerals (*I, II, i, ii,* etc.) for acts and scenes (as in the second example below).

1. "I know not 'seems,' " Hamlet famously declares (1.2.76).
2. "I know not 'seems,' " Hamlet famously declares (I.ii.76).

- *Commonly studied work of fiction or nonfiction prose*
Parenthetical citations of this kind should always include page numbers unless your instructor indicates otherwise. But you may also need or want to include additional location information. In this case, the page number comes first, followed by a semicolon and the other information. Use common abbreviations to indicate what this information is (e.g., *vol.* for *volume, bk.* for *book, sec.* for *section*), and give it in arabic numerals (*1, 2,* etc.), even if the text uses roman numerals (*I, II,* etc.). (The second example below is quoted directly from the *MLA Handbook.*)

1. "I learned," explains Frankenstein's creature, "that the possessions most esteemed by your fellow-creatures were, high and unsullied descent united with riches" (96; vol. 2, ch. 5).
2. In *A Vindication of the Rights of Woman,* Mary Wollstonecraft recollects many "women who, not led by degrees to proper studies, and not permitted to choose for themselves, have indeed been overgrown children" (185; ch. 13, sec. 2).

When you cite prose works from an anthology like this one, in which paragraphs are numbered, your instructor may allow or even require you to cite paragraph numbers, using the appropriate abbreviation (*par.*). If you include both page and paragraph number, insert a semicolon after the page number (as in the first example below). If your parenthetical citations don't include page, as well as paragraph, numbers, your instructor may also allow you to omit the abbreviation *par.* from the second and subsequent such citations (as in the second example).

1. When they meet years later in the supermarket, Roberta's "lovely and summery and rich" appearance leaves the narrator not only "dying to know" how this transformation came about but also resentful of Roberta and people like her: "Everything is so easy for them," she thinks (216; par. 68).
2. Though "dying to know" just how Roberta came to be so "lovely and summery and rich" since they last met (par. 68), all the narrator initially asks is, "How long you been here?" (69).

◦ *Sacred text*
When citing sacred texts such as the Bible or the Qur'an, indicate either in your text or in your parenthetical citation the title, editor, or translator of the edition you're using on the first occasion you cite it. Then include in your parenthetical citation(s) the book, chapter, and verse (or their equivalent), separated by periods, unless you have indicated these in your text. (Either way, do not include page numbers.) Abbreviate the names of the books of the Bible, but don't put these abbreviations in quotation marks or italicize them. (The second example below is quoted directly from the *MLA Handbook.*)

1. *The New English Bible* version of the verse reads, "In the beginning of creation, when God made heaven and earth, the earth was without form and void, with darkness over the face of the abyss, and a mighty wind that swept over the surface of the waters" (Gen. 1.1-2).
2. In one of the most vivid prophetic visions in the Bible, Ezekiel saw "what seemed to be four living creatures," each with the faces of a man, a lion, an ox, and an eagle (*New Jerusalem Bible,* Ezek. 1.5-10). John of Patmos echoes this passage when describing his vision (Rev. 4.6-8).

◦ *An entire source, a source without page numbers, a source that is only one page long, or an entry in a dictionary or other source organized alphabetically*
When you refer in a blanket way to an entire source rather than to something particular in it, to a source that has no pages or page numbers, to a source that is only one page long or has unnumbered pages, or to an entry in a dictionary or other work organized alphabetically, your parenthetical citation will include no page numbers. If you refer to something specific in a source lacking pages or page numbers but having other numbered divisions such as sections or paragraphs, do include these, using appropriate abbreviations (e.g., *sec., par.*), and make sure to add a comma after the author's name or, if the author is unknown, after the title of the work. Otherwise, if you clearly identify such a source (by author and/or title) in your text, you won't need a parenthetical citation at all (as in the first and second examples below). If you don't clearly identify the source in your text, your citation will include only author's name(s) and/or a shortened title (as in the third and fourth examples).

1. Many critics, including Maurice Bowra, see Creon as morally inferior to Antigone.
2. The entry for *Lord Weary's Castle* in *The Oxford Companion to American Literature,* for example, takes the "[m]ajor works" it includes to be the elegy "The Quaker Graveyard in Nantucket," the Jonathan Edwards-inspired "Mr. Edwards and the Spider," and the war poem "Christmas Eve Under Hooker's Statue."
3. Where some critics see the play as siding unequivocally with Antigone (Bowra), others see it as more ambivalent and/or ambiguous on this score (Nussbaum).
4. According to *The Oxford Companion to American Literature,* the elegy "The Quaker Graveyard in Nantucket" is among the three "[m]ajor works" in Lowell's *Lord Weary's Castle* ("*Lord Weary's Castle*").

OTHER VARIATIONS IN CONTENT: *SIC* AND *EMPHASIS ADDED*

When a parenthetical citation intervenes between the end of a quotation that you need to follow up with the words *sic* or *emphasis added* (for the reasons outlined in

35.1.3), it's usually advisable to put *sic* in brackets within the quotation, next to the error to which it applies (as in the second example below), but to put *emphasis added* at the end of the parenthetical citation, preceding it with a semicolon (as in the second example).

1. Shaw admitted, "Nothing can extinguish my interest in Shakespear [sic]" (1).
2. Avowing that men "must help them [women] to stay in that beautiful world of their own, *lest ours get worse*" (1196; emphasis added), Marlow acknowledges that men have a selfish interest in preserving women's innocence and idealism.

35.3.2 The List of Works Cited

Your list of works cited must include all, and only, the sources that you cite in your essay, providing full publication information about each. This section explains both how to format and organize the list and how to put together each entry in it.

FORMATTING THE LIST

Your list of works cited should begin on a separate page after the conclusion of your essay. Center the heading *Works Cited* (without quotation marks or italics) at the top of the first page, and double space throughout.

The first line of each entry should begin at the left margin; the second and subsequent lines should be indented ½ inch.

Your list should be alphabetized, ignoring articles (such as *A, An, The*) in entries that begin with a title.

If your list includes multiple works by the same author, begin the first entry with the author's name, and each subsequent entry with three hyphens followed by a period. Alphabetize these entries by title, again ignoring articles (*A, An, The*).

Works Cited

Broyles, William. "Why Men Love War." *Esquire,* Nov. 1984, pp. 55-65.

Clarke, Michael Tavel. " 'I Feel Close to Myself': Solipsism and U.S. Imperialism in Tim O'Brien's *The Things They Carried.*" *College Literature*, vol. 40, no. 2, Spring 2013, pp. 130-54. *Project Muse*, doi:10.1353/lit.2013.0018.

O'Brien, Tim. *Going After Cacciato.* Dell Publishing, 1978.

---. *The Things They Carried.* Houghton Mifflin, 1990.

Smith, Lorrie N. " 'The Things Men Do': The Gendered Subtext in Tim O'Brien's *Esquire* Stories." *Critique*, vol. 36, no. 1, Fall 1994, pp. 16-40. *Taylor & Francis Online*, doi:10.1080/00111619.1994.9935239.

FORMATTING INDIVIDUAL ENTRIES—GENERAL GUIDELINES

All information in a works-cited entry should come from the source itself and appear as it does in the source. Many if not most sources cited today are produced or experienced as part of larger wholes—or what MLA calls containers. If you cite a poem from this or any other anthology, for example, the poem is your source, the anthology its container. Works-cited entries may consist of as many as nine "core elements," each of which should be included when it is relevant and available. In general, they must appear in the following order: author, title of source, title of container, other contributors, version, number, publisher, publication date, and location. Some other elements are recommended, but not required: in this book, for instance, dates of access for online sources have been omitted. For further details on required and optional elements, please consult the *MLA Handbook* (8th ed., 2016) and *The MLA Style Center* (style.mla.org).

Below we offer only a few formatting guidelines applicable to all works-cited entries, along with model entries for especially common types of sources.

- *Names*

  Reproduce the names of authors, editors, and so on as they appear *in* the source—on a book's title page; at the beginning or end of a journal, magazine, or newspaper article; and so on. If initials are used, use them. If there are multiple authors or editors, list them in the order the source does, using the following format when they appear at the beginning of your entry:

2 names	Lastname, Firstname, and Firstname Lastname.
3+names	Lastname, Firstname, et al.

If the author is unknown, begin your entry with the title.

- *Publishers*

  Shorten publishers' names by doing the following:
- Omit business words and abbreviations (*Company* or *Co., Inc.*): instead of *W. W. Norton & Co.*, type *W. W. Norton.*
- With university presses, abbreviate *University* to *U* and *Press* to *P*: shorten *University of Chicago Press* to *U of Chicago P, Harvard University Press* to *Harvard UP.*
- *Dates*

  For a book's publication date, use the most recent year on the title or copyright page; for a Web source, use copyright date or the date of the most recent update. Abbreviate the names of all months except May, June, and July.
- *Page numbers*

  If you cite an article from a magazine or newspaper that isn't printed on consecutive pages, include only the first page number and a plus sign (+).

FORMATTING INDIVIDUAL ENTRIES FOR DIFFERENT TYPES OF SOURCES

This section explains how to format works-cited entries for the types of sources most frequently cited in literature essays. For other types of sources, consult the *MLA Handbook.*

1. *Book with an author or authors*

- *Print book*

  Author's Lastname, Firstname. *Book Title.* Publisher, Year of publication.

  O'Brien, Tim. *Going After Cacciato.* Dell Publishing, 1978.

- *Print book on the Web*

  Author's Lastname, Firstname. *Book Title.* Publisher, Year of publication. *Web Site Title*, URL or DOI.

  Melville, Herman. *Moby-Dick: or, The Whale.* Harper and Brothers, 1851. *Google Books*, books.google.com/books/about/Moby_Dick.html?id=J_yoAgAAQBAJ.

- *E-book*

  Author's Lastname, Firstname. *Book Title.* E-book or Kindle ed. [if any], Publisher, Year of Publication.

  Lahiri, Jhumpa. *Interpreter of Maladies.* E-book, Houghton Mifflin Harcourt, 1999.

- *E-book in database*

  Author's Lastname, Firstname. *Book Title.* Publisher, Year of publication. *Database Title,* URL or DOI.

  Boyle, Elizabeth, and Anne-Marie Evans, editors. *Reading America: New Perspectives on the American Novel.* Cambridge Scholars, 2008. *ProQuest Ebrary,* site .ebrary.com.ezproxy.library.unlv.edu/lib/unlv/detail.action?docID=10655216 &p00=reading+America.

2. ***Anthology or other book with editor(s) rather than author(s)***
Format your entry as indicated for a book (1), but after the (last) author's name or the abbreviation *et al.*, insert a comma and the word *editor* or *editors.*

   Kitchen, Judith, and Mary Paumier Jones, editors. *In Short: A Collection of Brief Creative Nonfiction.* W. W. Norton, 1996.

   Rowell, Charles Henry, editor. *Angles of Ascent: A Norton Anthology of Contemporary African American Poetry.* W. W. Norton, 2013.

3. ***Book with author(s) and editor(s) or translator(s)***
If what you cite or emphasize in your essay is the book itself, format your entry as indicated for a book (1), but insert between the book title and publication information the words *edited by* or *translated by*; the first and last names of the editor(s) and/or translator(s); and a period.

   Kafka, Franz. *The Metamorphosis.* Translated by Joyce Crick, edited by Ritchie Robertson, E-book, Oxford UP, 2009.

   Keats, John. *Letters of John Keats to His Family and Friends.* Edited by Sidney Colvin, Macmillan, 1891. *Google Books,* books.google.com/books/about /Letters_of_John_Keats_to_his_family_and.html?id=ULlZnQEACAAJ.

   If what you cite or emphasize in your essay is the work of the editor or translator, your entry should instead start with that person's name, followed by a comma and the word *editor* or *translator* (no capitalization), followed by the title of the book and the author.

   Colvin, Sidney, editor. *Letters of John Keats to His Family and Friends.* By John Keats, Macmillan, 1891. *Google Books,* books.google.com/books/about/Letters_of _John_Keats_to_his_family_and.html?id=ULlZnQEACAAJ.

   Crick, Joyce, translator. *The Metamorphosis.* By Franz Kafka, edited by Ritchie Robertson, E-book, Oxford UP, 2009.

4. ***Graphic narrative or book with author(s) and illustrator(s)***
If the book is written and illustrated by the same person or people, format the entry as you would for any other book (1). Otherwise, your entry will take one of the two forms below, depending upon whether your essay most emphasizes the work of the author(s) or the illustrator(s).

   Crumb, R., illustrator. *American Spendor: Bob and Harv's Comics.* By Harvey Pekar, Four Walls Eight Windows, 1996.

   Pekar, Harvey. *American Splendor: Bob and Harv's Comics.* Illustrated by R. Crumb, Four Walls Eight Windows, 1996.

5. ***Sacred text***

Text Title. Editor's Firstname Lastname, editor [if any]. Publisher, Year of publication.

The New English Bible with the Apocrypha. Oxford UP, 1971.

6. ***Book in an edition other than the first***

Format your entry as indicated for a book (1) or anthology (2), but insert the edition information, followed by a comma, just *before* the publication information. Identify the edition in whatever way the book's title page does, but abbreviate (e.g., *3rd ed.* for *Third edition*, *Rev. ed.* for *Revised edition*).

Drabble, Margaret, editor. *The Oxford Companion to English Literature*. Rev. ed., Oxford UP, 1998.

7. ***Book in a series***

Format your entry as indicated for a book (1) or anthology (2). Then, at the end, add the series title, followed by a period.

Joyce, James. *A Portrait of the Artist as a Young Man*. Oxford UP, 2001. Oxford World's Classics.

Stein, Karen F. *Margaret Atwood Revisited*. Twayne Publishers, 1999. Twayne's World Authors.

8. ***Introduction, preface, foreword, or afterword to a book***

Start your entry with the name of the author of the introduction, preface, and so on. If that author is not the same as the author of the book itself, your entry should look like this:

Part Author's Lastname, Firstname. Introduction, Preface, or Foreword. *Book Title*, by Book Author's Firstname Lastname, Publisher, Year of publication, Page numbers.

O'Prey, Paul. Introduction. *Heart of Darkness*, by Joseph Conrad, Penguin, 1983, pp. 7-24.

Meynell, Viola. Introduction. *Moby-Dick or The Whale*, by Herman Melville, Oxford UP, 1921. *Hathi Trust*, catalog.hathitrust.org/Record/001910361.

If the author of the part of the book you're citing is also the book's editor, and the book has no author, your entry should look like this:

Author's Lastname, Firstname. Introduction, Preface, or Foreword. *Book Title*, edited by Editor's Lastname, Publisher, Year of publication, Page numbers.

Rowell, Charles Henry. Preface. *Angles of Ascent: A Norton Anthology of Contemporary African American Poetry*, edited by Rowell, W. W. Norton, 2013, pp. xxiii–xxvii.

If the introduction, foreword, and so on has a title, format your entry as indicated above, but insert the title (in quotation marks) between its author's name and the word *Introduction*, *Preface*, and so on.

Ozick, Cynthia. "Portrait of the Essay as a Warm Body." Introduction. *The Best American Essays 1998*, edited by Ozick, Houghton Mifflin, 1998, pp. xv–xxi.

9. ***Work(s) in an anthology***

If you cite only one work from an anthology, your entry should look like this:

Author's Lastname, Firstname. "Title of Work" or *Title of Work*. *Title of Anthology*, edited by Editor's Firstname Lastname, Publisher, Year of publication, Page numbers.

Sanchez, Sonia. "A Poem for My Father." *Angles of Ascent: A Norton Anthology of Contemporary African American Poetry*, edited by Charles Henry Rowell, W. W. Norton, 2013, p. 70.

If you cite multiple works from the same anthology, create an entry for the anthology itself, following the guidelines for an anthology (2). Then create shortened entries like the following for each individual work:

Author's Lastname, Firstname. "Title of Work" or *Title of Work*. Anthology Editor's Lastname, Page numbers.

Dove, Rita. "Heroes." Rowell, pp. 215-16.

Jackson, Major. "Some Kind of Crazy." Rowell, pp. 351-52.

Sanchez, Sonia. "A Poem for My Father." Rowell, p. 70.

10. *Entry or article in a well-known general reference work (e.g., encyclopedia, dictionary)*

- *Print*

Author's Lastname, Firstname [if any]. "Title of Article." *Title of Reference Work*, edited by Editor's Firstname Lastname [if any], Edition [if any], Year of publication, Page numbers.

"Histrionics." *Merriam-Webster's Collegiate Dictionary*, 11th ed., 2003, p. 590.

- *Web*

Author's Lastname, Firstname [if any]. "Title of Article." *Title of Reference Work*, edited by Editor's Firstname Lastname [if any], Edition [if any], Publisher, Date published or last updated, URL.

Yoshida, Atsuhiko. "Epic." *Encyclopaedia Britannica*, Encyclopaedia Britannica, 19 Mar. 2014, www.britannica.com/art/epic.

"Fable, n." *OED Online*, Oxford UP, Dec. 2014, www.oed.com/view/Entry67384.

11. *Entry or article in a lesser-known or specialized reference work*

- *Print*

Author's Lastname, Firstname. "Title of Article." *Title of Reference Work*, edited by Editor's Firstname Lastname, Edition number [if other than first], Volume number [if more than one], Publisher, Year of publication, Page numbers.

Sullivan, Erin. "Humours." *The Oxford Companion to Shakespeare*, edited by Michael Dobson and Stanley Wells, 2nd ed., Oxford UP, 2015, p. 170.

- *Database*

Author's Lastname, Firstname. "Title of Article." *Title of Reference Work*, edited by Editor's Firstname Lastname, Edition number [if other than first], Volume number [if more than one], Publisher, Year of publication. *Database Title*, URL.

Carter, Steven R. "Lorraine Hansberry's *A Raisin in the Sun*." *The Oxford Encyclopedia of American Literature*, edited by Jay Parini and Philip W. Leininger, Oxford UP, 2004. *Oxford Reference*, www.oxfordreference.com/view/10.1093/acref/9780195156539.001.0001/acref-9780195156539-e-0106.

- *Web*

Author's Lastname, Firstname. "Title of Article." *Title of Reference Work*, edited by Editor's Firstname Lastname. Publisher or Sponsoring Institution, Date of publication or last update, URL.

Wicks, Robert. "Friedrich Nietzsche." *Stanford Encyclopedia of Philosophy,* edited by Edward N. Zalta. Metaphysics Research Lab, Center for the Study of Language and Information, Stanford U, 29 Apr. 2011, plato.stanford.edu/entries/nietzsche.

12. *Article in a journal*

◦ *Print journal*

Author's Lastname, Firstname. "Title of Article." *Title of Journal,* Volume number, Issue number, Month or Season Year of publication, Page numbers.

Clarke, Michael Tavel. " 'I Feel Close to Myself': Solipsism and U.S. Imperialism in Tim O'Brien's *The Things They Carried.*" *College Literature,* vol. 40, no. 2, Spring 2013, pp. 130-54.

◦ *Journal in database*

Author's Lastname, Firstname. "Title of Article." *Title of Journal,* Volume number, Issue number, Month or Season Year of publication, Page numbers. *Database Title,* URL or DOI.

Clarke, Michael Tavel. " 'I Feel Close to Myself': Solipsism and U.S. Imperialism in Tim O'Brien's *The Things They Carried.*" *College Literature,* vol. 40, no. 2, Spring 2013, pp. 130-54. *Project Muse,* doi:10.1353/lit.2013.0018.

◦ *Web-only journal*

Author's Lastname, Firstname. "Title of Article." *Title of Journal,* Volume number, Issue number, Month or Season Year of publication, Page numbers [if any], URL or DOI.

Joneson, Devan. "Mythic Mentor Figures and Liminal Sacred Spaces in *Doctor Who* and *Battlestar Galactica.*" *Inquire: Journal of Comparative Literature,* vol. 3, no. 1, March 2013, inquire.streetmag.org/articles/113.

13. *Article in a magazine or on a magazine Web site*

For publication date, give day, month, and year of publication if appropriate and available; otherwise, give month and year.

◦ *Print magazine*

Author's Lastname, Firstname. "Title of Article." *Title of Magazine,* Day Month Year of publication, Page numbers.

Alexie, Sherman. "When the Story Stolen Is Your Own." *Time,* 6 Feb. 2006, p. 72.

◦ *Magazine in database*

Author's Lastname, Firstname. "Title of Article." *Title of Magazine,* Day Month Year of Publication, Page numbers. *Database Title,* URL or DOI.

Alexie, Sherman. "When the Story Stolen Is Your Own." *Time,* 6 Feb. 2006, p. 72. *Academic Search Premier,* connection.ebscohost.com/c/essays/19551314/when-story-stolen-your-own.

◦ *Web-only magazine or magazine Web site*

Author's Lastname, Firstname. "Title of Article." *Web Site Title,* Day Month Year of publication, Page numbers [if any], URL.

Alston, Joshua. "Puffy Combs Revives 'Raisin.' " *Newsweek,* 24 Feb. 2008, www.newsweek.com/puffy-combs-revives-raisin-93493.

O'Rourke, Meghan. "Poetry's Lioness: Defending Sylvia Plath from Her Detractors." *Slate*, 28 Oct. 2003, www.slate.com/articles/arts/culturebox/2003/10/poetrys_lioness.html.

14. ***Article in a newspaper or on a newspaper Web site***
If the title doesn't include the city of publication, add that information in brackets after the title (as in the "Database" example below).

- *Print newspaper*

Author's Lastname, Firstname. "Title of Article." *Title of Newspaper*, Day Month Year of publication, Page numbers.

Feeney, Mark. "Gabriel Garcia Marquez, 87; Nobel Winner Popularized Magical Realism." *The Boston Globe*, 18 Apr. 2014, p. B12.

- *Newspaper in database*

Author's Lastname, Firstname. "Title of Article." *Title of Newspaper*, Day Month Year of publication, Page numbers. *Database Title*, URL or DOI.

Malvern, Jack. "Globe Offers Shakespeare on Demand." *The Times* [London], 4 Nov. 2014, p. 3. *EBSCOhost Newspaper Source Plus*, ezproxy.library.unlv.edu/login?url=http://search.ebscohost.com/login.aspx?direct=true&db=n5h&AN=7EH92164329&site=ehost-live.

- *Newspaper Web site*

Author's Lastname, Firstname. "Title of Article." *Title of Newspaper*, Day Month Year of publication, URL.

Wren, Celia. "Family Bonds, Music Play Together in Quiara Alegria Hudes's 'Water by the Spoonful.'" *The Washington Post*, 28 Feb. 2014, www.washingtonpost.com/entertainment/theater_dance/family-bonds-music-play-together-in-quiara-alegria-hudess-water-by-the-spoonful/2014/02/27/941f00de-9b38-11e3-8112-52fdf646027b_story.html.

15. ***Review***
Follow the same guidelines as indicated above for an article in a journal (12), magazine (13), or newspaper (14), but between the title of the review (if any) and the title of the periodical insert the following:

Review of *Title of Work being Reviewed*, by Work Author's Firstname Lastname.

Bunting, Josiah. "Vietnam, Carried On: Tim O'Brien's Intense Collection of Soldiers' Memoirs." Review of *The Things They Carried*, by Tim O'Brien. *The Washington Post*, 23 Apr. 1990, p. B3. *National Newspapers Expanded*, ezproxy.library.unlv.edu/login?url=http://search.proquest.com/docview/408042877?accountid=3611.

Marks, Peter. "'Water by the Spoonful' Dispenses Measured Fury." Review of *Water by the Spoonful*, by Quiara Alegria Hudes. *The Washington Post*, 10 Mar. 2014, www.washingtonpost.com/entertainment/theater_dance/water-by-the-spoonful-dispenses-measured-fury/2014/03/10/840c1a68-a887-11e3-8a7b-c1c684e2671f_story.html.

Review of *The Bluest Eye*, by Toni Morrison. *Kirkus Reviews*, 1 Oct. 1970.

16. ***Interview***
If the interview appears in a book or periodical, your entry will need all of the usual bibliographical information for that kind of source, but it should begin like this:

Interviewee's Lastname, Firstname. "Title of Interview [if any]." Interview by Interviewer's Firstname Lastname [if known but not indicated in title].

Collins, Billy. "Pushing Poetry to Lighten Up—And Brighten Up." Interview. *Newsweek*, 8 July 2001, www.newsweek.com/pushing-poetry-lighten-and-brighten-154859.

Knight, Etheridge. "A MELUS Interview: Etheridge Knight." Interview by Steven C. Tracy. *MELUS*, vol. 12, no. 2, Summer 1985, pp. 7-23. *JSTOR*, www.jstor.org/stable/467427.

For broadcast (television or radio) interviews, format your entry like this:

Interviewee's Lastname, Firstname. Interview. *Title of Program.* Network, Station, Day Month Year.

Gates, Henry Louis, Jr. Interview. *Fresh Air.* NPR, WNYC, 9 Apr. 2002.

17. ***Republished work***

Give the most recent publication information in whatever format is appropriate for that kind of source. Then insert *Originally published in* followed by the original publication information.

Komunyakaa, Yusef. "The Body Is Our First Music: Interview with Tony Barnstone and Michael Garabedian." *Blue Notes: Essays, Interviews, and Commentaries*, edited by Radiclani Clytus, U of Michigan P, 2000, pp. 107-25. Originally published in *Poetry Flash*, no. 227, June-July 1998.

Larkin, Philip. "A Conversation with Ian Hamilton." *Further Requirements: Interviews, Broadcasts, Statements and Book Reviews*, edited by Anthony Thwaite, Faber and Faber, 2001, pp. 19-26. Originally published in *London Magazine*, Nov. 1946.

Stevenson, R. L. "A Gossip on Romance." *A Victorian Art of Fiction: Essays on the Novel in British Periodicals 1870-1900*, Garland, 1979, pp. 187-99. Originally printed in *Longman's Magazine*, Nov. 1882, pp. 69-79.

18. ***Entire Web site***

If the Web site has an author, begin with his or her name. If it instead has an editor, compiler, or director, rather than an author, begin with that person's name, followed by a comma and the appropriate description.

Lastname, Firstname. *Title of Web Site.* Publisher, Date posted or last updated, URL.

Eaves, Morris, et al., editors. *The William Blake Archive.* 1996-2014, www.blakearchive.org/blake/.

19. ***Work from a Web site***

Author's Lastname, Firstname. "Title of Work." *Title of Web Site*, edited by Editor's Firstname Lastname [if any], Publisher. Date posted or last updated, URL.

Viscomi, Joseph. "Illuminated Printing." *The William Blake Archive*, edited by Morris Eaves et al., 1996-2014, www.blakearchive.org/exist/blake/archive/biography.xq?b=illum&targ_div=d1.

20. ***Film***

If your essay emphasizes the whole work, your entry should begin with the title and conclude like this:

Distributor, Date.

In between these, include the names of whatever contributors to the film are most pertinent, preceding each with the appropriate description (e.g., *directed by, performance by, produced by*). You may also or instead indicate the author of the screenplay preceded by the words *Screenplay by.* Elements should be separated by commas.

A Raisin in the Sun. Screenplay by Lorraine Hansberry, directed by Daniel Petrie, performances by Sidney Poitier, Claudia McNeil, and Ruby Dee, Columbia, 1961.

If your essay emphasizes the contribution of a particular individual (e.g., the screenwriter or director), start your entry with that person's name; a comma; his or her title; and a period.

Hansberry, Lorraine, adapter. *A Raisin in the Sun,* by Lorraine Hansberry, directed by Daniel Petrie, performances by Sidney Poitier, Claudia McNeil, and Ruby Dee, Columbia, 1961.

Petrie, Daniel, director. *A Raisin in the Sun.* Screenplay by Lorraine Hansberry, performances by Sidney Poitier, Claudia McNeil, and Ruby Dee, Columbia, 1961.

21. *Videorecording (DVD, etc.)*

Format your entry as indicated above for a film (20), but insert the film's original year of release and a period immediately after the title; end your entry with the year of release of the version consulted.

A Raisin in the Sun. 1961. Screenplay by Lorraine Hansberry, directed by Daniel Petrie, performances by Sidney Poitier, Claudia McNeil, and Ruby Dee, Columbia, 2000.

36 SAMPLE RESEARCH ESSAY

The following research essay analyzes Alice Munro's short story Boys and Girls. As you will see, the essay gives some consideration to the story's biographical and historical contexts, drawing on interviews with Munro and a sociological study of Canadian farm families. Yet the essay is primarily a critical contexts essay, as we define that term in chapter 34. In addition to considering the critical conversation about this specific short story, however, this essay examines another critical conversation, one about the initiation-story genre in general. The essay's literary critical secondary sources thus include three scholarly articles that focus exclusively on "Boys and Girls," as well as two articles that make arguments about the initiation story by instead analyzing a range of other stories. Diverse as are the sources and contexts this essay considers, however, notice that its thesis is an original, debatable interpretive claim about the literary text (Munro's story) and that the body of the essay supports and develops that claim by presenting and analyzing evidence from the text.

Roberts 1

Sarah Roberts
Prof. Jernigan
English 204
15 February 2017

"Only a Girl"? Gendered Initiation in Alice Munro's "Boys and Girls"

In 1960, an article in the *Journal of Aesthetics and Art Criticism* asked a question still worth asking over fifty years later, "What is an initiation story?" That article, by Mordecai Marcus, points out that literary critics frequently "used the term 'initiation' to describe a theme and a type of story" but that they didn't all use or define it exactly the same way. Marcus defines it as a story that "show[s] its young protagonist experiencing a significant change of knowledge about the world or himself, or a change of character, or of both," which "must point or lead him towards an adult world" (222). For him, the only significant difference between initiation stories has to do with their endings. He divides them into three types, depending on how far and "decisively" into that "adult world" their protagonists travel by the end (223). Published fifteen years after Marcus's essay, however, Elaine Ginsberg's "The Female Initiation Theme in American Fiction" (1975) suggests that it matters more what gender the story's protagonist is, at least in American fiction. According to her, "the female initiation story is rare in American literature," the first really "legitimat[e]" ones appearing only in the twentieth century (27, 31). Further, she argues those twentieth-century stories follow a pattern that is distinct in at least five ways: (1) "young girls are always introduced to a heterosexual world, in which relationships between men and women . . . are the most important," "a world in which men are always present, always important, and always more free and independent" (31, 37); (2) they "seem to see their future roles as women almost always in relation to men" (31, 36); (3) their "initiation process" involves both "sexual experience" and (4) "dropping" the attributes like boyish "clothing" or "names" that make them "androgynous creatures" at the beginning of the story; and (5) they never seem "to be aided or guided by an older" person of the same sex, as boys in initiation stories are (31). As a result, according to Ginsberg, the "sense of disillusionment, disappointment, and regret is perhaps the most significant characteristic of the female initiate in American literature" (35).

Roberts establishes a motive for her essay by first presenting two competing scholarly arguments about the initiation story genre, then indicating that she will be both "siding" with the second of these and expanding on it by considering a story the source does not. (Only because her essay will apply and test that source's claims does Roberts need to spell them out in such detail at the end of her opening paragraph.)

Whether Ginsberg is right about all of American literature, her argument does offer a way to think about a story she doesn't consider, Canadian Nobel Prize-winner Alice Munro's "Boys and Girls." Published in 1968, "Boys and Girls" appeared in *Dance of the Happy Shades*, Munro's first book and the event that basically initiated her career as an author. On the one hand, "Boys and Girls" is clearly a female initiation story. Its narrator is a woman remembering events that happened around the time she was eleven, and it ends with her admitting that "[m]aybe" she truly is "only a girl" (par. 65, 64). Her initiation mostly does follow the pattern Ginsberg outlines in a way that draws on Munro's personal experience and reflects that of other Canadian farm families. On the other hand, however, Munro's story does all that even better because it also depicts, as Reingard M. Nischik, Marlene Goldman, and Heliane Ventura show, another character and another initiation—that of the protagonist's younger brother, Laird. As Goldman puts it, the story "highlights the almost invisible societal forces which shape children, in this case, *the narrator and her brother Laird*, into gendered adults" (emphasis added). Rather than being either a male or female initiation story, "Boys and Girls" is both.

Roberts here prepares readers for the consideration of biographical and historical context later in the essay but makes the story and its critical contexts her main focus.

Here, Roberts briefly alludes to the three contributions to the second critical conversation her essay engages with—that about "Boys and Girls" specifically (rather than the initiation story generally).

Roberts 3

Like the heroines in the female initiation stories that Ginsberg discusses, Munro's protagonist starts out as an "androgynous creatur[e]" (31). But in Munro's story, that androgyny doesn't have anything to do with the protagonist's clothes or her name. In "Boys and Girls," clothes and names aren't very important. On the Ontario fox farm where it is set, horses and "foxes all ha[ve] names" (par. 8), but only two human characters in the story do, Laird and "the hired man," Henry Bailey (par. 2). The only pieces of clothing described are a school dress the protagonist wants and her mother makes for her (par. 17), some dresses her mother once wore and describes to her (par. 10), and the aprons both her mother and her father wear when she sees them talking together outside the barn one night (par. 12–13).

Instead of clothes or names, what really makes adult men and women different in the story is, as all the story's critics notice, the kind of work they do, where they do it, and whom they do it with. What makes the outdoor meeting between the parents so "odd" is that the mother does "not often come out of the house" or get much exercise, as the "bumpy" shape and pale color of her legs show. Her workplace is the house and especially the "hot dark kitchen," where she cans and cooks the family's food. The father instead works "out of doors" (par. 13), even if outdoors includes the barn and the fox pens he builds outside it and even if, to the mother's disgust, he has to do the "pelting . . . in the house" in winter (par. 2). Also, the mother performs her work alone and isn't paid for it, but the father gets paid enough for the furs he sells "to the Hudson's Bay Company or the Montreal Fur Traders" to hire Henry Bailey to help him (par. 1).

The narrator's androgyny, then, has to do with two things. One is the way she moves across these male and female places and activities, as Ventura observes, too (83). In the kitchen, she is "given jobs to do" like "peeling peaches . . . or cutting up onions" with her mother (par. 13). Outdoors, her "job" includes getting the foxes water and raking up the grass between their pens after her father cuts it (par. 7, 10). But in terms of her androgyny, the second and just as important thing is how close she is to her brother. The narrator and Laird are so much a unit early on in the story that the narrator slips practically automatically from "I" to "we." After she introduces Laird, Henry Bailey, and her mother in the story's second paragraph, when she says in the next one, "*We* admired him [Henry] for this performance" and "It was . . . always possible that" he "might be [laughing] at *us*," it's not exactly clear who "we" or "us" means until she starts the next paragraph by saying, "After *we* had been sent to bed"

Since Roberts's thesis is a claim about Munro's story, so, too, is the topic sentence of each body paragraph, starting with this one. At the same time, she clearly indicates how that claim relates to that of her source (Ginsberg).

Because Roberts's claim here has to do only with *which* "pieces of clothing" are "described" and *whom* they belong to, not *how* they are described, she simply summarizes rather than quotes. Yet parenthetical citations ensure that her readers can find the specific moments in the text to which she refers.

Roberts can simply refer to "the story's critics" here because her introduction has already indicated who they are.

Roberts is careful to spell out the *inference* that makes the fact (the mother's legs are "bumpy" and "pale") evidence for the claim (she "does not 'often come out of the house' or get much exercise").

Here, Roberts is careful to state her claim in her own words, while indicating that it is one also already made by one of her sources (Ventura).

Roberts doesn't need to include a parenthetical citation here only because the source is unpaginated and its author's name is mentioned in a signal phrase ("As Goldman argues").

Roberts's signal phrase indicates that two sources make the same observation, even though she only quotes one source. To specify which of the two sources she quotes, Roberts repeats its author's name in her parenthetical citation.

Roberts here specifies the basis for the source's claims (a "study of ten," Saskatchewan "farm families") and the author's key credential ("sociologist").

Rather than letting her source get the last word in her paragraph, Roberts summarizes the key point in her own words.

Roberts transitions from one paragraph/claim to another by restating the main idea of the last paragraph in the first part of this sentence and then, in the second part, stating the claim developed in this paragraph.

(emphasis added). And this paragraph is all about the bedroom that she and her brother share, their shared fears about it, and the "rules" they both follow to make themselves feel safe (par. 4). As Goldman argues, this room is the only place in the story that isn't either clearly "male" or "female," its "unfinished state" symbolizing "the undifferentiated consciousness of the children" at this point in the story.

What's strange about this, however, is that even though they share so much, Laird is actually treated differently. He helps out when it comes to outdoor work like watering the foxes, but there's never any hint that he helps out in the house. There is a difference between boy and girl in terms of the work they do from the very beginning, even if it's not a difference the narrator or the story's critics point out. What two critics (Ventura and Nischik) do point out is another difference, that unlike the narrator, Laird gets a name, and his name is Scottish for "landowner": ". . . Laird is a potential laird, the male heir to the family" (Ventura 82).

In these ways, the story seems to accurately reflect the reality of life on Canadian family farms through the 1950s and 1960s. As Munro, who grew up on one, insists in one interview, because "what's going on" on those farms, "chiefly, is [or was] making enough to live on," "everybody has to work and be useful to the family" ("Interview" 183). Based on her study of ten farm families (in Saskatchewan instead of Ontario), sociologist June Corman describes that work as "distinctly gendered." While men had legal "title to the land" and "retained control of the agricultural income-producing work" in which "women . . . were not extensively involved," women "laboured . . . to make home made essentials instead of buying consumer goods so farm income could be used to pay down . . . debt" (70). Furthermore, she argues, "This structured gendered division of labour had implications for their . . . children": "From childhood onward girls learned" both "the skills required of farm wives" and "at least a minimal amount of skills related to grain and livestock production." But boys worked exclusively with their fathers and learned "agricultural skills but . . . not . . . domestic knowledge" (71). Farm families required equal work from all members of the family but not the same work.

At the same time that she reflects this reality about Canadian farm life, Munro's choice to focus specifically on a fox farm like the one she grew up on takes on importance in terms of how female and male worlds are characterized in the story. It's not entirely clear in the story that men are truly any more "free and independent" than women are, as Ginsberg suggests is true in a lot of female initiation stories (37), since both the mother and the father are "enslaved by the farm, harassed by

Roberts 5

[their] work" (Ventura 85). But Goldman does seem right to say that men's work in this story is all about controlling other wild and even dangerous creatures. "Alive, the foxes inhabited a world my father made for them," the narrator explains (par. 7). Here, they "prow[l] up and down" inside "sturdy pens" that are "surrounded by a high guard fence"with a "padlocked" gate that no one but the narrator's father is ever brave enough to go into (par. 9, 7). And, as Goldman points out, the fox pen does sort of resemble "[t]he dark, hot, stifling kitchen [that] imprisons the narrator's mother and threatens to imprison the narrator."

Maybe as a result of his power and bravery, the protagonist—as Nischik, Ventura, and Goldman all notice—clearly sees her father's work and world as superior to her mother's. She "hate[s]" the kitchen, whose "bumpy linoleum" resembles her mother's "lumpy legs," and sees housework as so "endless, dreary and peculiarly depressing" that she runs away as soon as she can (par. 13). But her father's "world," especially the pens he creates, seems to her "tidy and ingenious" (par. 7). And his work seems to her so "tirelessly inventive" (par. 7) and "ritualistically important" (par. 13) that she always helps him "willingly . . . and with a feeling of pride" (par. 10).

Roberts needs quotations in this paragraph because her claim is about how the narrator "sees" things, something she can only prove by showing us how the narrator describes them. Notice, though, how only the most relevant language is quoted.

The adults around her reinforce that feeling. The only time her father praises her, he does it by calling her a "man" (par. 10), even specifically his "new hired man." In saying that, he compares her to Henry Bailey, which is interesting, but more important, he communicates the same message about the jobs of men and women and their unequal worth that the salesman does when he responds to the father by saying, "I thought it was only a girl." Paired with the word *only,* the word *girl*, as the narrator thinks later, becomes a label "always touched . . . with reproach and disappointment" or even "a joke on [her]" that the real hired man, Henry, especially, finds funny (par. 21). The label also gets associated with prohibitions as much as confinement. When the narrator's grandmother (the last of only three female characters total) arrives on the scene, the only thing we hear from her are commands about the things girls shouldn't do—"slam doors," sit with their knees apart, ask questions (par. 22).

The narrator *is* thus, in a way, "aided or guided by an older" person of the same sex, as boys in initiation stories are, according to Ginsberg (31). But that aid isn't positive. In fact, the girl actually sees her mother as her "enemy" because she thinks her mother is the one "plotting" to imprison her in the house and the lesser adult role it implies (par. 17). She sees that her mother is "kinder than [her] father" and "love[s] her" enough to stay up all night making the "difficult" dress she wants for school. But she still sides with her father and even likes his dismissive attitude toward her mother when they talk about

Because Roberts found the quotation from one source (Hallvard Dahlie's biography of Munro) in another (Nischik's article), she puts the essential information about the original source in a signal phrase ("Munro biographer Hallvard Dahlie claims . . ."), then uses the parenthetical citation to tell us which of her sources it was quoted in ("qtd. in Nischik").

Because Roberts doesn't mention the titles of these sources in a signal phrase, she needs parenthetical citations. The latter don't include page numbers only because these sources are unpaginated.

Roberts doesn't cite a source for the fact that Munro's mother had Parkinson's, two daughters, and a son because this is common knowledge.

Roberts 6

her in the yard: "I was pleased by the way he stood listening [to her], politely as he would to a salesman or a stranger, but with an air of wanting to get on with his real work" (par. 15), she says, "I did not expect my father to pay any attention to what she said" (par. 18).

Goldman identifies a parallel between the protagonist's attitudes to her mother and the foxes. As Goldman puts it, just as she earlier in the story "does not comprehend that the hostility she sees in the foxes' 'malevolent faces' . . . is a response to their enforced captivity," so she now interprets "her mother's behaviour . . . not as an expression of frustration and disappointment, or loneliness, but as a manifestation of innate wickedness and petty tyranny. . . ." What Goldman doesn't say is that we learn about these other possible interpretations, however, because the adult narrator *does* see them. When the narrator says, "*It did not occur to me* that she could be lonely, or jealous" (par. 17; emphasis added), it's obvious that it *does* occur to her *now,* as an adult.

In this way, too, the story actually seems to reflect and bend reality, but in this case the reality of Munro's personal life instead of Canadian farm families'. Munro biographer Hallvard Dahlie claims that many Munro stories include "unfulfilled and despairing mothers" like Munro's real mother, a former teacher who "expended her energies during the formative years of the three Laidlaw children in the nurturing of a family under conditions of deprivation and hardship" (qtd. in Nischik). In interviews, Munro often mentions her mother in a way that implies her attitude toward her mother changed in the same way her narrator-protagonist's does. She told *The New Yorker* that her "mother . . . is still a main figure in my life because her life was so sad and unfair and she so brave, but also because she was determined to make me into the Sunday-school-recitation little girl I was, from the age of seven or so, fighting not to be" ("On 'Dear' "). She told *The Paris Review,* "The tenderness I feel now for my mother, I didn't feel for a long time" ("Alice"). At the same time, Munro leaves out of "Boys and Girls" one of the things that made her real-life mother's life particularly "sad and unfair," which was the fact that she had Parkinson's disease. By not giving her fictional mother that kind of illness or even a name, for that matter, Munro makes her more like all women, just as she makes her story about boys versus girls (period) by not giving the protagonist what she had in real life—a sister and a brother.

In the story, the protagonist's full initiation into womanhood doesn't really involve a change in her relationship to her mother. (Late in the story she does think about confiding in her, but she doesn't [par. 51].) Instead, it involves changes in the way she relates to her father, animals, and her brother. That change begins with the scene where she and Laird secretly witness their father and Henry shooting the

Roberts 7

horse, Mack. We can tell that what she sees disturbs her partly because her legs shake and partly because she suddenly mentions a memory of Laird that makes her feel "the sadness of unexorcized guilt" (par. 37). But the question is why, since she and her brother have watched their father killing and skinning other animals and, unlike their mother, weren't bothered by that or the gross smells it produced (par. 2)? Or, as she herself explains,

> I did not have any great feeling of horror and opposition, such as a city child might have had. I was used to seeing the death of animals as a necessity by which we lived. Yet I felt a little ashamed, and there was a new wariness, a sense of holding-off, in my attitude to my father and his work. (par. 43)

There are many possible reasons for her reaction, but one might be that even before this point the girl begins to identify with the horses in a way she never does with the foxes. It is when—in her life and in the story—she is beginning to feel most pressured about being a girl and first expresses a wish to remain "free" that she remembers to mention how the foxes were fed at all and to describe, in detail, the two particular horses, Mack and Flora, and the different ways they respond to their similarly unfree situation (par. 22). (Mack is "slow and easy to handle"; Flora rears and kicks at people and fences [par. 20, 23].) That identification might explain why she might suddenly have a new "wariness" of her father and his work after seeing one of the horses killed (par. 43).

By putting the narrator's characterizations of Mack's and Flora's different reactions to their imprisonment in parentheses, Roberts substantiates her claim about the narrator's detailed descriptions, while staying focused on this paragraph's main topic—the narrator's *feelings about* the horses.

That feeling might be compounded, too, by the way Henry behaves, especially the fact that he laughs about Mack being shot in the same ways he's already laughed at her more than once in the story (par. 2, 21). But her sense of being "ashamed" about the shooting seems to come from seeing how she in a way acted like him long ago when she endangered her little brother's life just "for excitement" (par. 43, 37). As Goldman argues,

> Bailey's laughter [when "the horse kicks its legs in the air"] is particularly unnerving because it fully exposes his delight in power based on sheer inequality.
>
> The narrator recognizes this as an abuse of power . . . as a result of her own experience. She, too, lorded power over an innocent victim. . . .

It doesn't seem surprising, then, that when the narrator has the chance to save Flora ten days later, even just temporarily, she just does it without "mak[ing] any decision" or even "understand[ing] why" (par. 48, 50). By doing that, in Ventura's words, "the girl vicariously achieves her own temporary liberation" (84), and, in Goldman's words, "she radically breaks from her male-identified position." As the

Here, as throughout the essay, Roberts never substitutes the claim of a source for the textual evidence necessary to substantiate and develop it.

narrator points out, she disobeys her father for the very first time in her life and in a way she knows will change their relationship forever (par. 50). Rather than helping him as she's always wanted to do before, she "make[s] more work for" him by letting Flora go (par. 50). Worse, she knows that once he figures out what she's done he won't "trust me any more," but "would know that I was not entirely on his side. I was on Flora's side . . ." (par. 50). Her change of "side[s]," though, isn't complete or recognized by other people until dinner. When the truth about how she let Flora go is revealed, her father responds in a way that "absolved and dismissed [her] for good" by repeating the words the salesman used earlier, "She's only a girl" (par. 64). More important, the narrator doesn't "protest . . . , even in [her] heart" (par. 65). Like Mack and unlike the foxes and Flora, she now silently accepts her fate.

Just as important, though, is the way she separates herself from her brother. At the exact same time that the narrator permanently separates herself from her father, by letting Flora out, she also separates herself from Laird in a way that seems ironic, given that it was in a way sympathy with Laird or guilt about him that started the change in her in the first place. At any rate, when Henry and her father go off to get Flora, Laird goes with them, but the narrator doesn't. When she says, "I shut the gate after they were all gone," it seems like the first time in the story that Henry, the father, and Laird become a "they" that doesn't include her (par. 49). At least it seems like a far cry from the "we" she and Laird are early in the story. Importantly, though, it isn't really true that, as Ventura claims, the narrator "is not allowed aboard the bouncing truck" because she, unlike Laird, never actually asks to go (86). That change in her relationship to Laird is confirmed by the way, in between Flora's escape and the dinner that ends the story, the narrator mentions their bedroom one more time. In addition to decorating her part of the room, she "planned to put up some kind of barricade between [her] bed and Laird's, to keep my section separate from his" (par. 52).

To reinforce her claim about the narrator's development over the course of the story and connect the earlier parts of her essay with the later ones, Roberts briefly alludes to evidence and a point she made earlier.

As Goldman argues, though, Laird's very different initiation and behavior are significant:

> As they lift him into the truck, the little boy becomes a man: he joins the hunting party. Upon his return, he brandishes the streak of blood on his arm. . . . [T]he mark of blood and the domination of the Other continues to function as a crucial element in the rites of manhood. The boy cements his alliance with the father on the basis of their mutual triumph over nature.

In fact, that "alliance" isn't "cemented" until that night, when Laird, "look[ing] across the table at" her "proudly, distinctly" tells her secret

Roberts 9

to everyone (par. 56). In a weird way, he reverses the roles they each play in the memory that sparks her change—now he's the powerful one who leaves her figuratively hanging.

Here, though, is where the male and female initiations in this one story differ in a way that totally accords with Ginsberg's argument. Laird becomes a man in relationship to other men, grown-ups of his own gender, but in a way that has nothing to do with actual sex. Like the protagonists of most female initiation stories, according to Ginsberg, however, the protagonist of this one "seem[s] to see [her] future rol[e] as [a] wom[a]n . . . in relation to men" in a way that involves "sexual experience" (31). We see this in the stories she tells herself at night. Where the stories she makes up at the beginning of the story are all adventure stories in which she does things like shoot animals (just as Laird actually ends up doing by the end of this story), the stories she makes up at the end of the story are more like romances featuring boys she knows from school or one of her male teachers (par. 52).

If we go back to Marcus's question, "What is an initiation story?," then, "Boys and Girls" shows us that Ginsberg is right to say that the answer can depend most on whether the story features boys, girls, or "boys and girls." Or at least it once did, because here is where it might matter that Munro's story was published in 1968 and is set much earlier. In interviews, Munro expresses the idea that things were, in real life, changing even in her generation, which is also, as Nischik points out, her protagonist's. "If I had been a farm girl of a former generation," she says in one interview, "I wouldn't have had a chance" to go to college or be a writer, for example." Instead, her only option would have been to become a farm wife like her own mother or her protagonist's mother. "But in the generation that I was, there were scholarships. Girls were not encouraged to get them, but you could. I could imagine, from an early age, that I would be a writer" ("Interview" 183). Even if her protagonist never explicitly imagines herself some day being a writer, she is writing stories in her head every night. And that doesn't change over the course of the story, even if the kinds of stories she tells do. Even if at the end of the story the protagonist ends up accepting the idea that she is "only a girl" and not saying anything, the fact that she keeps telling herself stories and that she is, in fact, narrating her story to us as an adult suggests that the end of the story *isn't* the end of the story. Girls don't have to grow up to be "only" one thing after all. They can grow up to tell both their stories and their brothers. They can even win Nobel Prizes for it.

Roberts opens her conclusion by referring us back to the "frame" she established in the beginning—the different views of two sources (Marcus and Ginsberg).

Roberts 10

Works Cited

Corman, June. "The 'Good Wife' and Her Farm Husband: Changing Household Practices in Rural Saskatchewan." *Canadian Woman Studies*, vol. 24, no. 4, Summer/Fall 2005, pp. 68-74. *GenderWatch,* ezproxy.library.unlv.edu/login?url=http://search.proquest.com/docview/217447689?accountid=3611.

Ginsberg, Elaine. "The Female Initiation Theme in American Fiction." *Studies in American Fiction*, vol. 3, no. 1, Spring 1975, pp. 27-37. *Periodicals Archive Online,* ezproxy.library.unlv.edu/login?url=http://search.proquest.com/docview/1297894583?accountid=3611.

Goldman, Marlene. "Penning in the Bodies: The Construction of Gendered Subjects in Alice Munro's 'Boys and Girls.'" *Studies in Canadian Literature,* vol. 15, no. 1, 1990, journals.lib.unb.ca/index.php/SCL/article/view/8112.

Marcus, Mordecai. "What Is an Initiation Story?" The *Journal of Aesthetics and Art Criticism,* vol. 19, no. 2, Winter 1960, pp. 221-28. *JSTOR,* doi:10.2307/428289.

Munro, Alice. "Alice Munro, The Art of Fiction No. 137." Interview by Jeanne McCulloch and Mona Simpson. *The Paris Review,* no. 131, Summer 1994, www.theparisreview.org/interviews/1791/the-art-of-fiction-no-137-alice-munro.

---. "Boys and Girls." *The Norton Introduction to Literature,* edited by Kelly J. Mays, 12th ed., W. W. Norton, 2017, pp. 152-62.

---. "An Interview with Alice Munro." Interview by Lisa Dickler Awano. *Virginia Quarterly Review,* vol. 89, no. 2, Spring 2013, pp. 180-84. *Academic Search Main Edition,* ezproxy.library.unlv.edu/login?url=http://search.ebscohost.com/login.aspx?direct=true&db=asm&AN=87119387&site=ehost-live.

---. "On 'Dear Life': An Interview with Alice Munro." Interview by Deborah Treisman. *The New Yorker,* 20 Nov. 2012, www.newyorker.com/books/page-turner/on-dear-life-an-interview-with-alice-munro.

Nischik, Reingard M. "(Un-)Doing Gender: Alice Munro, 'Boys and Girls' (1964)." *Contemporary Literary Criticism*, edited by Lawrence J. Trudeau, vol. 370, Gale, 2015. *Literature Resource Center,* go.galegroup.com/ps/i.do?id=GALE%7CH1100118828&v=2.1&u=unlv_main&it=r&p=LitRC&sw=w&asid=1ec18259fbc8af3aecfc233e918cf0e8. Originally published in *The Canadian Short Story,* edited by Nischik, Camden House, 2007, pp. 203-18.

Ventura, Heliane. "Alice Munro's 'Boys and Girls': Mapping out Boundaries." *Commonwealth*, no. 15, Autumn 1992, pp. 80-87.

Critical Approaches

Few human abilities are more remarkable than the ability to read and interpret literature. A computer program or a database can't perform the complex process of reading and interpreting—not to mention writing about—a literary text, although computers can easily exceed human powers of processing codes and information. Readers follow the sequence of printed words and as if by magic re-create a scene between characters in a novel or play, or they respond to the almost inexpressible emotional effect of a poem's figurative language. Experienced readers can pick up on a multitude of literary signals all at once. With rereading and some research, readers can draw on information such as the author's life or the time period when this work and others like it were first published. Varied and complex as the approaches to literary criticism may be, they are not difficult to learn. For the most part schools of criticism and theory have developed to address questions that any reader can begin to answer.

There are essentially three participants in what could be called the literary exchange or interaction: the *text*, the *source* (the *author* and other factors that produce the text), and the *receiver* (the *reader* and other aspects of *reception*). All the varieties of literary analysis concern themselves with these aspects of the literary exchange in varying degrees and with varying emphases. Although each of these elements has a role in any form of literary analysis, systematic studies of literature and its history have defined approaches or methods that focus on the different elements and circumstances of the literary interaction. The first three sections below—"Emphasis on the Text," "Emphasis on the Source," and "Emphasis on the Receiver"—describe briefly those schools or modes of literary analysis that have concentrated on one of the three participants while de-emphasizing the others. These different emphases, plainly speaking, are habits of asking different kinds of questions. Answers or interpretations will vary according to the questions we ask of a literary work. In practice the range of questions can be—and to some extent *should* be—combined whenever we develop a literary interpretation. Such questions can always generate the thesis or argument of a critical essay.

Although some approaches to literary analysis treat the literary exchange (text, source, receiver) in isolation from the world surrounding that exchange (the world of economics, politics, religion, cultural tradition, and sexuality—in other words, the world in which we live), most contemporary modes of analysis acknowledge the importance of that world to the literary exchange. These days, even if literary scholars want to focus on the text or its source or receiver, they will often incorporate some of the observations and methods developed by theorists and critics who have turned their attention toward the changing world surrounding the formal conventions of literature, the writing process and writer's career, and the reception or response to literature. We describe the work of such theorists and critics in the fourth section below, "Historical and Ideological Criticism."

Before expanding on the kinds of critical approaches within these four categories, let's consider one example in which questions concerning the text, source, and receiver, as well as a consideration of historical and ideological questions, would contribute to a richer interpretation of a text. To begin as usual with preliminary questions about the *text*: *What* is "First Fight. Then Fiddle."? Printed correctly on a separate piece of paper, the text would tell us at once that it is a poem because of its form: rhythm, repeating word sounds, lines that leave very wide margins on the page. Because you are reading this poem in this book, you know even more about its form (in this way, the publication *source* gives clues about the *text*). By putting it in a section with other poetry, we have told you it is a poem worth reading, rereading, and thinking about. (What other ways do you encounter poems, and what does the medium in which a poem is presented tell you about it?)

You should pursue other questions focused on the text. What *kind* of poem is it? Here we have helped you, especially if you are not already familiar with the sonnet form, by grouping this poem with other sonnets (in The Sonnet: An Album). Classifying "First Fight. Then Fiddle." as a sonnet might then prompt you to interpret the ways that this poem is or is not like other sonnets. Well and good: You can check off its fourteen lines of (basically) iambic pentameter and note its somewhat unusual rhyme scheme and meter in relation to the rules of Italian and English sonnets. But *why* does this experiment with the sonnet form matter?

To answer questions about the purpose of form, you need to answer some basic questions about *source*, such as *When* was this sonnet written and published? *Who* wrote it? *What* do you know about Gwendolyn Brooks, about 1949, about African American women and/or poets in the United States at that time? A short historical and biographical essay answering such questions might help put the "sonnetness" of "First Fight. Then Fiddle." in context. But assembling all the available information about the source and original context of the poem, even some sort of documented testimony from Brooks about her intentions or interpretation of it, would still leave room for other questions leading to new interpretations.

What about the *receiver* of "First Fight. Then Fiddle."? Even within the poem a kind of audience exists. This sonnet seems to be a set of instructions addressed to "you." (Although many sonnets are addressed by a speaker, "I," to an auditor, "you," such address rarely sounds like a series of military commands, as it does here.) This internal audience is not of course to be confused with real people responding to the poem, and it is the latter who are its *receivers*. How did readers respond to it when it was first published? Can you find any published reviews, or any criticism of this sonnet published in studies of Gwendolyn Brooks?

Questions about the receiver, like those about the author and other sources, readily connect with questions about historical and cultural context. Would a reader or someone listening to this poem read aloud respond differently in the years after World War II than in an age of global terrorism? Does it make a difference if the audience addressed by the speaker inside the poem is imagined as a group of African American men and women or as a group of European American male commanders? (The latter question could be regarded as an inquiry involving the text and the source as well as the receiver.) Does a reader need to identify with any of the particular groups the poem fictitiously addresses, or would any reader, from any background, respond to it the same way? Even the formal qualities of the text could be examined through historical lenses: The sonnet form has been associated with prestigious European literature, and with themes of love and mortality, since the Renaissance. It is significant that a twentieth-century African American poet chose *this* traditional form to twist "threadwise" into a poem about conflict.

The above are only some of the worthwhile questions that might help illuminate this short, intricate poem. (We will develop a few more thoughts about it in illustrating different approaches to the text and to the source.) Similarly, the complexity of critical approaches far exceeds our four categories. While a great deal of worthwhile scholarship and criticism borrows from a range of theories and methods, below we give necessarily simplified descriptions of various critical approaches that have continuing influence. We cannot trace a history of the issues involved, or the complexity and controversies within these movements. Instead think of what follows as a road map to the terrain of literary analysis. Many available resources describe the entire landscape of literary analysis in more precise detail. If you are interested in learning more about these or any other analytical approaches, consult the works listed in the bibliography at the end of this chapter.

EMPHASIS ON THE TEXT

This broad category encompasses approaches that de-emphasize questions about the author/source or the reader/reception in order to focus on the work itself. In a sense any writing about literature presupposes recognition of form, in that it deems the object of study to *be* a literary work that belongs to a genre or subgenre of literature, as Brooks's poem belongs with sonnets. Moreover, almost all literary criticism notes some details of style or structure, some *intrinsic* features such as the relation between dialogue or narration, or the pattern of rhyme and meter. But *formalist* approaches go further by foregrounding the design of the text itself above all or most other considerations.

Some formalists, reasonably denying the division of content from form (since the form is an aspect of the content or meaning), have more controversially excluded any discussion of *extrinsic* or contextual (versus textual) matters such as the author's biography or questions of psychology, sociology, or history. This has led to accusations that formalism, in avoiding relevance to actual authors and readers or to the world of economic power or social change, also avoids political issues or commitments. Some historical or ideological critics have therefore argued that formalism supports the powers that be, since it precludes protest. Conversely, some formalists charge that any extrinsic—that is, historical, political, ideological, as well as biographical or psychological—interpretations of literature reduce the text to a set of more or less cleverly encoded messages or propaganda. A formalist might maintain that the inventive wonders of art exceed any practical function it serves. In practice, influential formalists have generated modes of *close reading* that balance attention to form, significance, and social context, with some acknowledgment of the political implications of literature. In the early twenty-first century the formalist methods of close reading remain influential, especially in classrooms. Indeed, *The Norton Introduction to Literature* adheres to these methods in its presentation of elements and interpretation of form.

New Criticism

One strain of formalism, loosely identified as the New Criticism, dominated literary studies from approximately the 1920s to the 1970s. New Critics rejected both of the approaches that prevailed then in the relatively new field of English studies:

the dry analysis of the development of the English language, and the misty-eyed appreciation and evaluation of "Great Works." Generally, New Criticism minimizes consideration of both the source and the receiver, emphasizing instead the intrinsic qualities of a unified literary work. Psychological or historical information about the author, the intentions or feelings of authors or readers, and any philosophical or socially relevant "messages" derived from the work all are out of bounds in a New Critical reading. The text in a fundamental way refers to itself: Its medium is its message. Although interested in ambiguity and irony as well as figurative language, a New Critical reader considers the organic unity of the unique work. Like an organism, the work develops in a synergetic relation of parts to whole.

A New Critic might, for example, publish an article titled "A Reading of 'First Fight. Then Fiddle.'" (The method works best with **lyric** or other short forms because it requires painstaking attention to details such as metaphors or alliteration.) Little if anything would be said of Gwendolyn Brooks or the poem's relation to Modernist poetry. The critic's task is to give credit to the poem, not the poet or the period, and if it is a good poem, then—implicitly—it can't be merely "about" World War II or civil rights. New Criticism presumes that a good literary work symbolically embodies universal human themes and may be interpreted objectively on many levels. These levels may be related more by tension and contradiction than harmony, yet that relation demonstrates the coherence of the whole.

Thus the New Critic's essay might include some of the following observations. The title—which reappears as half of the first line—consists of a pair of two-word imperative sentences, and most statements in the poem paraphrase these two sentences, especially the first of them, "First fight." Thus an alliterative two-word command, "Win war" (line 12), follows a longer version of such a command: "But first to arms, to armor" (9). Echoes of this sort of exhortation appear throughout. We, as audience, begin to feel "bewitch[ed], bewilder[ed]" (4) by a buildup of undesirable urgings, whether at the beginning of a line ("Be deaf," 11) or the end of a line ("Be remote," 7; "Carry hate," 9) or in the middle of a line ("Rise bloody," 12). It's hardly what we would want to do. Yet the speaker makes a strong case for the practical view that a society needs to take care of defense before it can "devote" itself to "silks and honey" (6–7), that is, the soft and sweet pleasures of art. But what kind of culture would place "hate / In front of . . . harmony" and try to ignore "music" and "beauty" (9–11)? What kind of people are only "remote / A while from malice and from murdering" (6–7)? A society of warlike heroes would rally to this speech. Yet on rereading, many of the words jar with the tone of heroic battle cry.

The New Critic examines not only the speaker's style and words but also the order of ideas and lines in the poem. Ironically, the poem defies the speaker's command; it fiddles first, and then fights, as the octave (first eight lines) concern art, and the sestet (last six) concern war. The New Critic might be delighted by the irony that the two segments of the poem in fact unite, in that their topics—octave on how to fiddle, sestet on how to fight—mirror each other. The beginning of the poem plays with metaphors for music and art as means of inflicting "hurting love" (line 3) or emotional conquest, that is, ways to "fight." War and art are both, as far as we know, universal in all human societies. The poem, then, is an organic whole that explores timeless concerns.

Later critics have pointed out that New Criticism, despite its avoidance of extrinsic questions, had a political context of its own. The affirmation of unity for the artwork and humanities in general should be regarded as a strategy adapted during the Cold War as a counterbalance to the politicization of art in fascist and communist regimes. New Criticism also provided a program for literary reading that is accessible to beginners regardless of their social background, which was extremely useful at a time when more women, minorities, and members of the working class than ever before were entering college. By the 1970s these same groups had helped generate two sources of opposition to New Criticism's ostensible neutrality and transparency: critical studies that emphasized the politics of social differences (e.g., feminist criticism), and theoretical approaches, based on linguistics, philosophy, and political theory, that effectively distanced nonspecialists once more.

Structuralism

Whereas New Criticism was largely a British and American phenomenon, structuralism and its successor, poststructuralism, derive primarily from French theorists. Strains of structuralism also emerged in the Soviet Union and in Prague. Each of these movements was drawn to scientific objectivity and at the same time wary of political commitment. Politics, after all, had been the rallying cry for censorship of science, art, and inquiry throughout centuries and in recent memory.

Structuralist philosophy, however, was something rather new. Influenced by the French linguist Ferdinand de Saussure (1857–1913), structuralists sought an objective system for studying the principles of language. Saussure distinguished between individual uses of language, such as the sentences you or I might have just spoken or written (*parole*), and the sets of rules of English or any language (*langue*). Just as a structuralist linguist would study the interrelations of signs in the *langue* rather than the variations in specific utterances in *parole*, a structuralist critic of literature or culture would study shared systems of meaning, such as genres or myths that pass from one country or period to another, rather than a certain poem in isolation (the favored subject of New Criticism).

Another structuralist principle derived from Saussure is the emphasis on the arbitrary association between a word and what it is said to signify—that is, between the *signifier* and the *signified*. The word "horse," for example, has no divine, natural, or necessary connection to that four-legged, domesticated mammal, which is named by other combinations of sounds and letters in other languages. Any language is a network of relations among such arbitrary signifiers, just as each word in the dictionary must be defined using other words in that dictionary. Structuralists largely attribute the meanings of words to rules of differentiation from other words. Such differences may be phonetic (as among the words "cat" and "bat" and "hat") or they may belong to conceptual associations (as among the words "dinky," "puny," "tiny," "small," "miniature," "petite," "compact"). Structuralist thought has particularly called attention to the way that opposites or dualisms such as "night" and "day" or "feminine" and "masculine" define each other through their differences from each other rather than in direct reference to objective reality. For example, the earth's motion around the sun produces changing exposure to sunlight daily and seasonally, but by linguistic convention we call it "night" between, let's say, 8 p.m. and 5 a.m., no matter how light it is. (We may differ in opinions about "evening" or "dawn." But our "day" at work may begin or end in the dark.) The point is that arbitrary labels divide what in fact is continuous.

Structuralism's linguistic insights have greatly influenced literary studies. Like New Criticism, structuralism shows little interest in the creative process or in authors, their intentions, or their circumstances. Similarly, structuralism discounts the idiosyncrasies of particular readings; it takes texts to represent interactions of words and ideas that stand apart from individual human identities or sociopolitical commitments. Structuralist approaches have applied less to lyric poetry than to myths, narratives, and cultural practices, such as sports or fashion. Although structuralism tends to affirm a universal humanity just as New Critics do, its work in comparative mythology and anthropology challenged the absolute value that New Criticism tended to grant to time-honored canons of great literature.

The structuralist would regard a text not as a self-sufficient icon but as part of a network of conventions. A structuralist essay on "First Fight. Then Fiddle." might ask why the string is plied with the "feathery sorcery" (line 2) of the "bow" (7). These words suggest the art of a Native American trickster or primitive sorcerer, while at the same time the instrument is a disguised weapon: a stringed bow with feathered arrows (the term "muzzle" is a similar pun, suggesting an animal's snout and the discharging end of a gun). Or is the fiddle—a violin played in musical forms such as bluegrass—a metaphor for popular art or folk resistance to official culture? In many folk tales a hero is taught to play the fiddle by the devil or tricks the devil with a fiddle or similar instrument. Further, a structuralist reading might attach great significance to the sonnet form as a paradigm that has shaped poetic expression for centuries. The classic "turn" or reversal of thought in a sonnet may imitate the form of many narratives of departure and return, separation and reconciliation. Brooks's poem repeats in the numerous short reversing imperatives, as well as in the structure of octave versus sestet, the eternal oscillation between love and death, creation and destruction.

Poststructuralism

By emphasizing the paradoxes of dualisms and the ways that language constructs our awareness, structuralism planted the seeds of its own destruction or, rather, deconstruction. Dualisms (e.g., masculine/feminine, mind/body, culture/nature) cannot be separate-but-equal; rather, they take effect as differences of power in which one dominates the other. Yet as the German philosopher of history Georg Wilhelm Friedrich Hegel (1770–1831) insisted, the relations of the dominant and subordinate, of master and slave readily invert themselves. The master is dominated by his need for the slave's subordination; the possession of subordinates defines his mastery. As Brooks's poem implies, each society reflects its own identity through an opposing "they," in a dualism of civilized/barbaric. The instability of the speaker's position in this poem (is he or she among the conquerors or the conquered?) is a model of the instability of roles throughout the human world. There is no transcendent ground—except on another planet, perhaps—from which to measure the relative positions of the polar opposites on Earth. Roland Barthes (1915–80) and others, influenced by the radical movements of the 1960s and the increasing complexity of culture in an era of mass consumerism and global media, extended structuralism into more profoundly relativist perspectives.

Poststructuralism is the broad term used to designate the philosophical position that attacks the objective, universalizing claims of most fields of knowledge since the eighteenth century. Poststructuralists, distrusting the optimism of a positivist philosophy that suggests the world is knowable and explainable, ultimately doubt the possibility of certainties of any kind, since language signifies only through a chain of other words rather than through any fundamental link to reality. This argument derives from structuralism, yet it also criticizes structuralist universalism and avoidance of political issues. *Ideology* is a key conceptual ingredient in the poststructuralist argument against structuralism. Ideology is a slippery term that can broadly be defined as a socially shared set of ideas that shape behavior; often it refers to the values that legitimate the ruling interests in a society, and in many accounts it is the hidden code that is officially denied. (We discuss kinds of "ideological" criticism later.) Poststructuralist theory has played a part in a number of critical schools introduced below, not all of them focused on the text. But in literary criticism, poststructuralism has marshaled most forces under the banner of deconstruction.

Deconstruction

Deconstruction insists on the logical impossibility of knowledge that is not influenced or biased by the words used to express it. Deconstruction also claims that language is incapable of representing any sort of reality directly. As practiced by its most famous proponent, the French philosopher Jacques Derrida (1930–2004), deconstruction endeavors to trace the way texts imply the contradiction of their explicit meanings. The deconstructionist delights in the sense of dizziness as the grounds of conviction crumble away; *aporia*, or irresolvable doubt, is the desired, if fleeting, end of an encounter with a text. Deconstruction threatens *humanism*, or the worldview that is centered on human values and the self-sufficient individual, because it denies that there is an ultimate, solid reality on which to base truth or the identity of the self. All values and identities are constructed by the competing systems of meaning, or *discourses*. This is a remarkably influential set of ideas that you will meet again as we discuss other approaches.

The traditional concept of the author as creative origin of the text comes under fire in deconstructionist criticism, which emphasizes instead the creative power of language or the text, and the ingenious work of the critic in detecting gaps and contradictions in writing. Thus, like New Criticism, deconstruction disregards the author and concentrates on textual close reading, but unlike New Criticism, it features the role of the reader as well. Moreover, the text need not be respected as a pure and coherent icon. Deconstructionists might "read" many kinds of writing and representation in other media in much the same way that they might read Milton's *Paradise Lost*, that is, irreverently. Indeed, when deconstruction erupted in university departments of literature, traditional critics and scholars feared the breakdown of the distinctions between literature and criticism and between literature and many other kinds of texts. Many attacks on literary theory have particularly lambasted deconstructionists for apparently rejecting all the reasons to care about literature in the first place and for writing in a style so flamboyantly obscure that no one but specialists can understand. Yet in practice Derrida and others have carried harmony before them, to paraphrase Brooks; their readings can delight in the play of figurative language, thereby enhancing rather than debunking the value of literature.

A deconstructionist might read "First Fight. Then Fiddle." in a manner somewhat similar to the New Critic's, but with even more focus on puns and paradoxes and on the poem's resistance to organic unity. For instance, the two alliterative commands, "fight" and "fiddle," might be opposites, twins, or inseparable consequences of each other. The word "fiddle" is tricky. Does it suggest that art is trivial? Does it allude to a dictator who "fiddles while Rome burns," as the saying goes? Someone who "fiddles" is not performing a grand, honest, or even competent act: One fiddles with a hobby, with the books, with car keys in the dark. The artist in this poem defies the orthodoxy of the sonnet form, instead making a kind of harlequin patchwork out of different traditions, breaking the rhythm, intermixing endearments and assaults.

To the deconstructionist the recurring broken antitheses of war and art, art and war cancel each other out. The very metaphors undermine the speaker's summons to war. The command "Be deaf to music and to beauty blind," which takes the form of a *chiasmus*, or X-shaped sequence (adjective, noun; noun, adjective), is a kind of miniature version of this chiasmic poem. (We are supposed to follow a sequence, fight then fiddle, but instead reverse that by imagining ways to do violence with art or to create beauty through destruction.) The poem, a lyric written but imagined as spoken or sung, puts the senses and the arts under erasure; we are somehow not to hear music (by definition audible), not to see beauty (here a visual attribute). "Maybe not too late" comes rather too late: At the end of the poem it will be too late to start over, although "having first to civilize a space / Wherein to play your violin with grace" (lines 12–14) comes across as a kind of beginning. These comforting lines form the only heroic couplet in the poem, the only two lines that run smoothly from end to end. (All the other lines have **caesuras**, **enjambments**, or balanced pairs of concepts, as in "from malice and from murdering" [8].) But the violence behind "civilize," the switch to the high-art term "violin," and the use of the Christian term "grace" suggest that the pagan erotic art promised at the outset, the "sorcery" of "hurting love" that can "bewitch," will be suppressed.

Like other formalisms, deconstruction can appear apolitical or conservative because of its skepticism about the referential connection between literature and the world of economics, politics, and other social forms. Yet poststructuralist linguistics provides a theory of *difference* that clearly pertains to the rankings of status and power in society, as in earlier examples of masculine/feminine, master/slave. The *Other*, the negative of the norm, is always less than an equal counterpart. Deconstruction has been a tool for various poststructuralist thinkers—including the historian Michel Foucault (1926–84), the feminist theorist and psychoanalyst Julia Kristeva (b. 1941), and the psychoanalytic theorist Jacques Lacan (1901–81).

Narrative Theory

Before concluding the discussion of text-centered approaches, we should mention the schools of narratology and narrative theory that have shaped study of the novel and other kinds of narrative. Criticism of fiction has been in a boom period since the 1950s, but the varieties of narrative theory per se have had more limited effect than the approaches we have discussed above. Since the 1960s different analysts of the forms and techniques of narrative, most notably the Chicago formalists and the structuralist narratologists, have developed terminology for the various interactions of author, implied author, narrator, and characters; of plot and the treatment of time in the selection and sequence of scenes; of voice, point of view, or focus and other aspects of fiction. As formalisms, narrative theories tend to exclude the author's biography, individual reader response, and the historical context of the work or its actual reception.

Narratology began by presenting itself as a structuralist science; its branches have grown from psychoanalytic theory or extended to reader-response criticism. In recent decades studies of narrative technique and form have responded to Marxist, feminist, and other ideological criticism that insists on the political contexts of literature. One important influence on this shift has been the revival of the work of the Russian literary theorist Mikhail Bakhtin (1895–1975), which considers the novel as a *dialogic* form that pulls together the many discourses and voices of a culture and its history. Part of the appeal of Bakhtin's work has been the fusion of textual close reading with attention to material factors such as economics and class, and a sense of the open-endedness and contradictoriness of writing (in the spirit of deconstruction more than of New Criticism). Like other Marxist-trained European formalists, Bakhtin sought to place the complex literary modes of communication in the light of politics and history.

EMPHASIS ON THE SOURCE

As the examples above suggest, a great deal can be drawn from a text without any reference to its source or its author. For millennia many anonymous works were shared in oral or manuscript form, and even after printing spread in Europe few thought it necessary to know the author's name or anything about him or her. Yet criticism from its beginnings in ancient Greece has been interested in the designing intention "behind" the text. Even when no evidence remained about the author, a legendary personality has sometimes been invented to satisfy readers' curiosity. From the legend of blind Homer to the latest debates about biographical evidence and portraits of William Shakespeare, literary criticism has been accompanied by interest in the author's life.

Biographical Criticism

This approach reached its height in an era when humanism prevailed in literary studies (roughly the 1750s to the 1960s). At this time there was widely shared confidence in the ideas that art and literature were the direct expressions of the artist's or writer's genius and that criticism of great works supported veneration of the great persons who created them. The lives of some famous writers became the models that aspiring writers emulated. Criticism at times was skewed by social judgments of personalities, as when John Keats was put down as a "Cockney" poet, that is, London-bred and lower-class. Many writers have struggled to get their work taken seriously because of mistaken biographical criticism. Women or minorities have at times used pseudonyms or published anonymously to avoid having their work put down or having it read only through the expectations, negative or positive, of what a woman or person of color might write. Biographical criticism can be diminishing in this respect. Others have objected to reading literature as a reflection of the author's personality. Such critics have supported the idea that the highest literary art is pure form, untouched by gossip or personal emotion. In this spirit some early twentieth-century critics as well as Modernist writers such as T. S. Eliot, James Joyce, and Virginia Woolf tried to dissociate the text from the personality or political commitments of the author. (The theories of these writers and their actual practices did not always coincide.)

In the early twentieth century, psychoanalytic interpretations placed the text in light of the author's emotional conflicts, and other interpretations relied heavily on the author's stated intentions. (Although psychoanalytic criticism entails more than analysis of the author, we will introduce it as an approach that primarily concerns the human source[s] of literature; it usually has less to say about the form and receiver of the text.) Author-based readings can be reductive. All the accessible information about a writer's life cannot definitively explain the writings. As a young man D. H. Lawrence might have hated his father and loved his mother, but all men who hate their fathers and love their mothers do not write fiction as powerful as Lawrence's. Indeed, Lawrence himself cautioned that we should "trust the tale, not the teller."

Any kind of criticism benefits to some extent, however, from being informed by knowledge of the writer's life and career. Certain critical approaches, devoted to recognition of separate literary traditions, make sense only in light of supporting biographical evidence. Studies that concern traditions such as Irish literature, Asian American literature, or literature by Southern women require reliable information about the writers' birth and upbringing and even some judgment of the writers' intentions to write *as* members of such traditions. (We discuss feminist, African American, and other studies of distinct literatures in the "Historical and Ideological Criticism" section that follows, although such studies recognize the biographical "source" as a starting point.)

A reading of "First Fight. Then Fiddle." can become rather different when we know more about Gwendolyn Brooks. An African American, she was raised in Chicago in the 1920s. These facts begin to provide a context for her work. Some of the biographical information has more to do with her time and place than with her race and sex. Brooks began in the 1940s to associate with Harriet Monroe's magazine, *Poetry*, which had been influential in promoting Modernist poetry. Brooks early received acclaim for books of poetry that depict the everyday lives of poor, urban African Americans; in 1950 she was the first African American to win a Pulitzer Prize. In 1967 she became an outspoken advocate for the Black Arts movement, which promoted a separate tradition rather than integration into the aesthetic mainstream. But even before this political commitment, her work never sought to "pass" or to distance itself from the reality of racial difference, nor did it become any less concerned with poetic tradition and form when she published it through small, independent black presses in her "political" phase.

It is reasonable, then, to read "First Fight. Then Fiddle.," published in 1949, in relation to the role of a racial outsider mastering and adapting the forms of a dominant tradition. Perhaps Brooks's speaker addresses an African American audience in the voice of a revolutionary, calling for violence to gain the right to express African American culture. Perhaps the lines "the music that they wrote / Bewitch, bewilder. Qualify to sing / Threadwise" (lines 3–5) suggest the way that the colonized may transform the empire's music rather than the other way around. Ten years before the poem was published, a famous African American singer, Marian Anderson, had more than "qualif[ied] to sing" opera and classical concert music, but had still encountered the color barrier in the United States. Honored throughout Europe as the greatest living contralto, Anderson was barred in 1939 from performing at Constitution Hall in Washington, D.C., because of her race. Instead she performed at the Lincoln Memorial on Easter Sunday to an audience of seventy-five thousand people. It was not easy to find a "space" in which to practice her art. Such a contextual reference, whether or not intended, relates biographically to Brooks's role as an African American woman wisely reweaving classical traditions "threadwise" rather than straining them into "hempen" (5) ropes. Beneath the manifest reference to the recent world war, this poem refers to the segregation of the arts in America. (Questions of source and historical context often interrelate.)

Besides readings that derive from biographical and historical information, there are still other ways to read aspects of the *source* rather than the *text* or the *receiver.* The source of the work extends beyond the life of the person who wrote it to include not only the writer's other works but also the circumstances of contemporary publishing; contemporary literary movements; the history of the composition, editing, and publication of this particular text, with all the variations; and other contributing factors. While entire schools of literary scholarship have been devoted to each of these matters, any analyst of a particular work should bear in mind what is known about the circumstances of writers at that time, the material conditions of the work's first publication, and the means of dissemination ever since. It makes a difference in our interpretation to know that a certain sonnet circulated in manuscript in a small courtly audience or that a particular novel was serialized in a weekly journal cheap enough for the masses to read it.

Psychoanalytic Criticism

With the development of psychology and psychoanalysis toward the end of the nineteenth century, many critics were tempted to apply psychological theories to literary analysis. Symbolism, dreamlike imagery, emotional rather than rational logic, and a pleasure in language all suggested that literature profoundly evoked a mental and emotional landscape, often one of disorder or abnormality. From mad poets to patients speaking in verse, imaginative literature might be regarded as a representation of shared irrational structures within all *psyches* (i.e., souls) or selves. While psychoanalytic approaches have developed along with structuralism and poststructuralist linguistics and philosophy, they rarely focus on textual form. Rather, they attribute latent or hidden meaning to unacknowledged desires in some person, usually the author or source behind the character in a narrative or drama. A psychoanalytic critic can also focus on the response of readers and, in recent decades, usually accepts the influence of changing social history on the structures of sexual desire represented in the work. Nevertheless, psychoanalysis has typically aspired to a universal, unchanging theory of the mind and personality, and criticism that applies it has tended to emphasize the authorial source.

FREUDIAN CRITICISM

For most of the twentieth century, the dominant school of psychoanalytic critics was the Freudian, based on the work of Sigmund Freud (1856–1939). Many of its practitioners assert that the meaning of a literary work exists not on its surface but in the psyche (some would even claim, in the neuroses) of the author. Classic psychoanalytic criticism read works as though they were the recorded dreams of patients; interpreted the life histories of authors as keys to the works; or analyzed characters as though they, like real people, have a set of repressed childhood memories. (In fact, many novels and most plays leave out information about characters' development from infancy through adolescence, the period that psychoanalysis especially strives to reconstruct.)

A well-known Freudian reading of *Hamlet*, for example, insists that Hamlet suffers from an Oedipus complex, a Freudian term for a group of repressed desires and memories that corresponds with the Greek myth that is the basis of Sophocles's play *Oedipus the King.* In this view Hamlet envies his uncle because the son unconsciously wants to sleep with his mother, who was the first object of his desire as a baby. The ghost of Hamlet Sr. may then be a manifestation of Hamlet's unconscious desire or of his guilt for wanting to kill his father, the person who has a right to the desired mother's body. Hamlet's madness is not just acting but the result of this frustrated desire; his cruel mistreatment of Ophelia is a deflection of his disgust at his mother's being "unfaithful" in her love for him. Some Freudian critics stress the author's psyche and so might read *Hamlet* as the expression of Shakespeare's own Oedipus complex. In another mode psychoanalytic critics, reading imaginative literature as symbolic fulfillment of unconscious wishes much as an analyst would interpret a dream, look for objects, spaces, or actions that appear to relate to sexual anatomy or activity. Much as if tracing out the extended metaphors of an erotic poem by John Donne or a blues or Motown lyric, the Freudian reads containers, empty spaces, or bodies of water as female; tools, weapons, towers or trees, trains or planes as male.

JUNGIAN AND MYTH CRITICISM

Just as a Freudian assumes that all human psyches have similar histories and structures, the Jungian critic assumes that we all share a universal or collective unconscious (just as each has a racial and an individual unconscious). According to Carl Gustav Jung (1875–1961) and his followers, the unconscious harbors universal patterns and forms of human experiences, or **archetypes**. We can never know these archetypes directly, but they surface in art in an imperfect, shadowy way, taking the form of archetypes—the snake with its tail in its mouth, rebirth, the mother, the double, the descent into hell. In the classic quest narrative, the hero struggles to free himself (the gender of the pronoun is significant) from the Great Mother to become a separate, self-sufficient being (combating a demonic antagonist), surviving trials to gain the reward of union with his ideal other, the feminine anima. In a related school of *archetypal criticism*, influenced by Northrop Frye (1912–91), the prevailing myth follows a seasonal cycle of death and rebirth. Frye proposed a system for literary criticism that classified all literary forms in all ages according to a cycle of genres associated with the phases of human experience from birth to death and the natural cycle of seasons (e.g., Spring/Romance).

These approaches have been useful in the study of folklore and early literatures as well as in comparative studies of various national literatures. While most myth critics focus on the hero's quest, there have been forays into feminist archetypal criticism. These emphasize variations on the myths of Isis and Demeter, goddesses of fertility or seasonal renewal, who take different forms to restore either the sacrificed woman (Persephone's season in the underworld) or the sacrificed man (Isis's search for Osiris and her rescue of their son, Horus). Many twentieth-century poets were drawn to the heritage of archetypes and myths. Adrienne Rich's "Diving into the Wreck," for example, self-consciously rewrites a number of gendered archetypes, with a female protagonist on a quest into a submerged world.

Most critics today, influenced by poststructuralism, have become wary of universal patterns. Like structuralists, Jungians and archetypal critics strive to compare and unite the ages and peoples of the world and to reveal fundamental truths. Rich, as a feminist poet, suggests that the "book of myths" is an eclectic anthology that needs to be revised. Claims of universality tend to obscure the detailed differences among cultures and often appeal to some idea of *biological determinism*. Such determinism diminishes the power of individuals to design alternative life patterns and even implies that no literature can really surprise us.

LACANIAN CRITICISM

As it has absorbed the indeterminacies of poststructuralism under the influence of thinkers such as Jacques Lacan and Julia Kristeva, psychological criticism has become increasingly complex. Few critics today are direct Freudian analysts of authors or texts, and few maintain that universal archetypes explain the meaning of a tree or water in a text. Yet psychoanalytic theory continues to inform many varieties of criticism, and most new work in this field is affiliated with Lacanian psychoanalysis. Lacan's theory unites poststructuralist linguistics with Freudian theory. The Lacanian critic, like a deconstructionist, focuses on the text that defies conscious authorial control, foregrounding the powerful interpretation of the critic rather than the author or any other reader. Accepting the Oedipal paradigm and the unconscious as the realm of repressed desire, Lacanian theory aligns the development and structure of the individual human *subject* with the development and structure of language. To simplify a purposefully dense theory: The very young infant inhabits the Imaginary, in a preverbal, undifferentiated phase dominated by a sense of union with the Mother. Recognition of identity begins with the Mirror Stage, ironically with a disruption of a sense of oneness. For when one first looks into a mirror, one begins to recognize a split or difference between one's body and the image in the mirror. This splitting prefigures a sense that the *object* of desire is Other and distinct from the subject. With difference or the splitting of subject and object comes language and entry into the Symbolic Order, since we use words to summon the absent object of desire (as a child would cry "Mama" to bring her back). But what language signifies most is the lack of that object. The imaginary, perfectly nurturing Mother would never need to be called.

As in the biblical Genesis, the Lacanian "genesis" of the subject tells of a loss of paradise through knowledge of the difference between subject and object or Man and Woman (eating of the Tree of the Knowledge of Good and Evil leads to the sense of shame that teaches Adam and Eve to hide their nakedness). In Lacanian theory the Father governs language or the Symbolic Order; the Word spells the end of a child's sense of oneness with the Mother. Further, the Father's power claims omnipotence, the possession of male prerogative symbolized by the Phallus, which is not the anatomical difference between men and women but the idea or construction of that difference. Thus it is language or culture rather than nature that generates the difference and inequality between the sexes. Some feminist theorists have adopted aspects of Lacanian psychoanalytic theory, particularly the concept of *the gaze*. This concept notes that the masculine subject is the one who looks, whereas the feminine object is to be looked at.

Another influential concept is *abjection*. The Franco-Bulgarian psychoanalyst Julia Kristeva's theory of abjection most simply reimagines the infant's blissful sense of union with the mother and the darker side of such possible union. To return to the mother's body would be death, as metaphorically we are buried in Mother Earth. Yet according to the theory, people both desire and dread such loss of boundaries. A sense of self or *subjectivity* and hence of independence and power depends on resisting abjection. The association of the maternal body with abjection or with the powerlessness symbolized by the female's Lack of the Phallus can help explain negative cultural images of women. Many narrative genres seem to split the images of women between an angelic and a witchlike type. Lacanian or Kristevan theory has been well adapted to film criticism and to fantasy and other popular forms favored by structuralism or archetypal criticism.

Psychoanalytic literary criticism today—as distinct from specialized discussion of Lacanian theory, for example—treads more lightly than in the past. In James Joyce's "Araby," a young Dublin boy, orphaned and raised by an aunt and uncle, likes to haunt a back room in the house; there the "former tenant, . . . a priest, had died" (par. 2). (Disused rooms at the margins of houses resemble the unconscious, and a dead celibate "father" suggests a kind of failure of the Law, conscience, or in Freudian terms, superego.) The priest had left behind a "rusty bicycle-pump" in the "wild garden" with "a central apple tree" (these echoes of the garden of Eden suggesting the impotence of Catholic religious symbolism). The boy seems to gain consciousness of a separate self—or his subjectivity is constructed—through his gaze upon an idealized female object, Mangan's sister, whose "name was like a summons to all my foolish blood" (par. 4). Though he secretly watches and follows her, she is not so much a sexual fantasy as a beautiful art object (par. 9). He retreats to the back room to think of her in a kind of ecstasy that resembles masturbation. Yet it is not masturbation: It is preadolescent, dispersed through all orifices—the rain feels like "incessant needles . . . playing in the sodden beds"; and it is sublimated, that is, repressed and redirected into artistic or religious forms rather than directly expressed by bodily pleasure: "All my senses seemed to desire to veil themselves" (par. 6).

It is not in the back room but on the street that the girl finally speaks to the hero, charging him to go on a quest to Araby. After several trials the hero carrying the talisman arrives in a darkened hall "girdled at half its height by a gallery," an underworld or maternal space that is also a deserted temple (par. 25). The story ends without his grasping the prize to carry back, the "chalice" or holy grail (symbolic of female sexuality) that he had once thought to bear "safely through a throng of foes" (par. 5).

Such a reading seems likely to raise objections that it is overreading: *You're seeing too much in it; the author didn't mean that.* This has been a popular reaction to psychoanalysis for over a hundred years, but it is only a heightened version of a response to many kinds of criticism. This sample reading pays close attention to the text, but does not really follow a formal approach because its goal is to explain the psychological implications or resonance of the story's details. We have mentioned nothing about the author, though we could have used this reading to forward a psychoanalytic reading of Joyce's biography.

EMPHASIS ON THE RECEIVER

In some sense critical schools develop in reaction to the excesses of other critical schools. By the 1970s, in a time of political upheaval that placed a high value on individual expression, a number of critics felt that the various routes toward objective criticism had proved to be dead ends. New Critics, structuralists, and psychoanalytic or myth critics had sought objective, scientific systems that disregarded changing times, political issues, or the reader's personal response. New Critics and other formalists tended to value a literary canon made up of works that were regarded as complete, unchanging objects to be interpreted according to ostensibly timeless standards.

Reader-Response Criticism

Among critics who challenge New Critical assumptions, reader-response critics regard the work not as what is printed on the page but as what is experienced temporally through each act of reading. According to such critics, the reader effectively performs the text into existence the way a musician performs music from a score. Reader-response critics ask not what a work means but what a work does to and through a reader. Literary texts especially leave gaps that experienced readers fill according to expectations or conventions. Individual readers differ, of course, and gaps in a text provide space for different readings or interpretations. Some of these lacunae are temporary—such as the withholding of the murderer's name until the end of a mystery novel—and are closed by the text sooner or later, though each reader will in the meantime fill them differently. But other lacunae are permanent and can never be filled with certainty; they result in a degree of uncertainty or indeterminacy in the text.

The reader-response critic observes the expectations aroused by a text, how they are satisfied or modified, and how the reader comprehends the work when all of it has been read, and when it is reread in whole or in part. Such criticism attends to the reading habits associated with different genres and to the shared assumptions of a cultural context that seem to furnish what is left unsaid in the text.

Beyond theoretical formulations about reading, there are other approaches to literary study that concern the receiver rather than the text or source. A critic might examine specific documents of a work's reception, from contemporary reviews to critical essays written across the generations since the work was first published. Sometimes we have available diaries or autobiographical evidence about readers' encounters with particular works. Just as there are histories of publishing and of the book, there are histories of literacy and reading practices. Poetry, fiction, and drama often directly represent the theme of reading as well as writing. Many published works over the centuries have debated the benefits and perils of reading works such as sermons or novels. Different genres and particular works construct different classes or kinds of readers in the way they address them or supply what they are supposed to want. Some scholars have found quantitative measures for reading, from sales and library lending rates to questionnaires.

Finally, the role of the reader or receiver in the literary exchange has been portrayed from a political perspective. Literature helps shape social identity, and social status shapes access to different kinds of literature. Feminist critics adapted reader-response criticism, for example, to note that girls often do not identify with many American literary classics as boys do, and thus girls do not simply accept the stereotype of women as angels, temptresses, or scolds who should be abandoned for the sake of all-male adventures. Studies of African American literature and other ethnic literatures have often featured discussion of literacy and of the obstacles for readers who cannot find their counterparts within the texts or who encounter negative stereotypes of their group. Thus, as we will discuss below, most forms of historical and ideological criticism include some consideration of the reader.

HISTORICAL AND IDEOLOGICAL CRITICISM

The approaches to the text, the author, and the reader outlined above may each take some note of historical contexts, including changes in formal conventions, the writer's milieu, or audience expectations. In the nineteenth century, historical criticism took the obvious facts that a work is created in a specific historical and cultural context and that the author is a part of that context as reasons to treat literature as a reflection of society. Twentieth-century formalists rejected the *reflectivist* model of art in the old historical criticism, that is, the assumption that literature and other arts straightforwardly express the collective spirit of the society at a given time. But as we have remarked, formalist rules for isolating the work of art from social and historical context met resistance in the last decades of the twentieth century. In a revival of historical approaches, critics have replaced the reflectivist model with a *constructivist* model, whereby literature and other cultural discourses are seen to help construct social relations and roles rather than merely reflect them. In other words, art is not just the frosting on the cake but an integral part of the recipe's ingredients and instructions. A society's ideology, its system of representations (ideas, myths, images), is inscribed in literature and other cultural forms, which in turn help shape identities and social practices.

Since the 1980s, historical approaches have regained great influence in literary studies. Some critical schools have been insistently *materialist*, that is, seeking causes more in concrete conditions such as technology, production, and distribution of wealth. Such criticism usually owes an acknowledged debt to Marxism. Other historical approaches have been influenced to a degree by Marxist critics and cultural theorists, but work within the realm of ideology, textual production, and interpretation, using some of the methods and concerns of traditional literary history. Still others emerge from the civil rights movement and the struggles for recognition of women and racial, ethnic, and sexual constituencies.

Feminist studies, African American studies, gay and lesbian studies, and studies of the cultures of different immigrant and ethnic populations within and beyond the United States have each developed along similar theoretical lines. These schools, like Marxist criticism, adopt a constructivist position: Literature is not simply a reflection of prejudices and norms; it also helps define social identities, such as what it means to be an African American woman. Each of these schools has moved through stages of first claiming *equality* with the literature dominated by white Anglo American men, then affirming the *difference* of their own separate culture, and then theoretically *questioning the terms and standards* of such comparisons. At a certain point in the thought process, each group rejects *essentialism*, the notion of innate or biological bases for the differences between the sexes, races, or other groups. This rejection of essentialism is usually called the constructivist position, in a somewhat different but related sense to our definition above. Constructivism maintains that identity is socially formed rather than biologically determined. Differences of anatomical sex, skin color, first language, parental ethnicity, and eventual sexual preferences have great impact on how one is classified, brought up, and treated socially, and on one's subjectivity or conception of identity. Constructivists maintain that these differences, however, are more constructed by ideology and the resulting behaviors than by any natural programming.

Marxist Criticism

The most insistent and vigorous historical approach through the twentieth century to the present has been Marxism, based on the work of Karl Marx (1818–83). With roots in nineteenth-century historicism, Marxist criticism was initially reflectivist. Economics, the underlying cause of history, was thus the *base*, and culture, including literature and the other arts, was the *superstructure*, an outcome or reflection of the base. Viewed from the Marxist perspective, the literary works of a period were economically determined; they would *reflect* the state of the struggle between classes in any place and time. History enacted recurrent three-step cycles, a pattern that Hegel had defined as *dialectic* (Hegel was cited above on the interdependence of master and slave). Each socioeconomic phase, or *thesis*, is counteracted by its *antithesis*, and the resulting conflict yields a *synthesis*, which becomes the ensuing *thesis*, and so on. As with early Freudian criticism, early Marxist criticism was often preoccupied with labeling and exposing illusions or deceptions. A novel might be read as a thinly disguised defense of the power of bourgeois industrial capital; its appeal on behalf of the suffering poor might be dismissed as an effort to fend off class rebellion.

As a rationale for state control of the arts, Marxism was abused in the Soviet Union and in other totalitarian states. In the hands of sophisticated critics, however, Marxism has been richly rewarding. Various schools that unite formal close reading and political analysis developed in the early twentieth century under Soviet communism and under fascism in Europe, often in covert resistance. These schools in turn have influenced critical movements in North America; New Criticism, structuralist linguistics, deconstruction, and narrative theory have each borrowed from European Marxist critics.

Most recently, a new mode of Marxist theory has developed, largely guided by the thinking of Walter Benjamin (1892–1940) and Theodor Adorno (1903–69) of the Frankfurt School in Germany, Louis Althusser (1918–90) in France, and Raymond Williams (1921–98) in Britain. This work has generally tended to modify the base/superstructure distinction and to interrelate public and private life, economics and culture. Newer Marxist interpretation assumes that the relation of a literary work to its historical context is *overdetermined*—the relation has multiple determining factors rather than a sole cause or aim. This thinking similarly acknowledges that neither the source nor the receiver of the literary interaction is a mere tool or victim of the ruling powers or state. Representation of all kinds, including literature, always has a political dimension, according to this approach; conversely, political and material conditions such as work, money, or institutions depend on representation.

Showing some influence of psychoanalytic and poststructuralist theories, recent Marxist literary studies examine the effects of ideology by focusing on the works' gaps and silences: Ideology may be conveyed in what is repressed or contradicted. In many ways Marxist criticism has adapted to the conditions of consumer rather than industrial capitalism and to global rather than national economies. The worldwide revolution that was to come when the proletariat or working classes overthrew the capitalists has never taken place; in many countries industrial labor has been swallowed up by the service sector, and workers reject the political Left that would seem their most likely ally. Increasingly, Marxist criticism has acknowledged that the audience of literature may be active rather than passive, just as the text and source may be more than straightforward instructions for toeing a given political line. Marxist criticism has been especially successful with the novel, since that genre more than drama or short fiction is capable of representing numerous people from different classes as they develop over a significant amount of time.

Feminist Criticism

Like Marxist criticism and the schools discussed below, feminist criticism derives from a critique of a history of oppression, in this case the history of women's inequality. Feminist criticism has no single founder like Freud or Marx; it has been practiced to some extent since the 1790s, when praise of women's cultural achievements went hand in hand with arguments that women were rational beings deserving equal rights and education. Contemporary feminist criticism emerged from a "second wave" of feminist activism, in the 1960s and 1970s, associated with the civil rights and antiwar movements. One of the first disciplines in which women's activism took root was literary criticism, but feminist theory and women's studies quickly became recognized methods across the disciplines.

Feminist literary studies began by denouncing the misrepresentation of women in literature and affirming the importance of women's writings, before quickly adopting the insights of poststructuralist theory; yet the early strategies continue to have their use. At first, feminist criticism in the 1970s, like early Marxist criticism, regarded literature as a reflection of patriarchal society's sexist base; the demeaning images of women in literature were symptoms of a system that had to be overthrown. Feminist literary studies soon began, however, to claim the *equal* but distinctive qualities of writings by women and men. Critics such as Elaine Showalter (b. 1941), Sandra M. Gilbert (b. 1936), and Susan Gubar (b. 1944) explored canonical works by women, relying on close reading with some aid from historical and psychoanalytic methods.

Yet by the 1980s it was widely recognized that a New Critical method would leave most of the male-dominated canon intact and most women writers still in obscurity, because many women had written in different genres and styles, on different themes, and for different audiences than had male writers. To affirm the *difference* of female literary traditions, some feminist studies claimed women's innate or universal affinity for fluidity and cycle rather than solidity and linear progress. Others concentrated on the role of the mother in human psychological development. According to this argument, girls, not having to adopt a gender role different from that of their first object of desire, the mother, grow up with less rigid boundaries of self and a relational rather than judgmental ethic.

The dangers of these intriguing generalizations soon became apparent. If the reasons for women's differences from men were biologically based or were due to universal archetypes, there was no solution to women's oppression, which many cultures worldwide had justified in terms of biological reproduction or archetypes of nature. At this point in the debate, feminist literary studies intersected with poststructuralist linguistic theory in *questioning the terms and standards* of comparison. French feminist theory, articulated most prominently by Hélène Cixous (b. 1937) and Luce Irigaray (b. 1932), deconstructed the supposed archetypes of gender written into the founding discourses of Western culture. We have seen that deconstruction helps expose the power imbalance in every dualism. Thus man is to woman as culture is to nature or mind is to body, and in each case the second term is held to be inferior or Other. The language and hence the worldview and social formations of our culture, not nature or eternal archetypes, constructed woman as Other. This insight was helpful in avoiding essentialism or biological determinism.

Having reached a theoretical criticism of the terms on which women might claim equality or difference from men in the field of literature, feminist studies also confronted other issues in the 1980s. Deconstructionist readings of gender difference in texts by men as well as women could lose sight of the real world, in which women are paid less and are more likely to be victims of sexual violence. With this in mind, some feminist critics pursued links with Marxist or African American studies; gender roles, like those of class and race, were interdependent systems for registering the material consequences of people's differences. It no longer seemed so easy to say what the term "women" referred to, when the interests of different kinds of women had been opposed to each other. African American women asked if feminism was really their cause, when white women had so long enjoyed power over both men and women of their race. In a classic Marxist view, women allied with men of their class rather than with women of other classes. It became more difficult to make universal claims about women's literature, as the horizon of the college-educated North American feminists expanded to recognize the range of conditions of women and of literature worldwide. Feminist literary studies have continued to consider famous and obscure women writers; the way women and gender are portrayed in writings by men as well as women; feminist issues concerning the text, source, or receiver in any national literature; theoretical and historical questions about the representation of differences such as gender, race, class, and nationality, and the way these differences shape each other.

Gender Studies and Queer Theory

From the 1970s, feminists sought recognition for lesbian writers and lesbian culture, which they felt had been even less visible than male homosexual writers and gay culture. Concurrently, feminist studies abandoned the simple dualism of male/female, part of the very binary logic of patriarchy that seemed to cause the oppression of women. Thus feminists recognized a zone of inquiry, the study of gender, as distinct from historical studies of women, and increasingly they included masculinity as a subject of investigation. As gender studies turned to interpretation of the text in ideological context regardless of the sex or intention of the author, it incorporated the ideas of Michel Foucault's *History of Sexuality* (1976). Foucault helped show that there was nothing natural, universal, or timeless in the constructions of sexual difference or sexual practices. Foucault also introduced a history of the concept of homosexuality, which had once been regarded in terms of taboo acts and in the later nineteenth century became defined as a disease associated with a personality type. Literary scholars began to study the history of sexuality as a key to the shifts in modern culture that had also shaped literature.

By the 1980s gender had come to be widely regarded as a discourse that imposed binary social norms on human beings' diversity. Theorists such as Donna Haraway (b. 1944) and Judith Butler (b. 1956) insisted further that sex and sexuality have no natural basis; even the anatomical differences are representations from the moment the newborn is put in a pink or blue blanket. Moreover, these theorists claimed that gender and sexuality are *performative* and malleable positions, enacted in many more than two varieties. From cross-dressing to surgical sex changes, the alternatives chosen by real people have influenced critical theory and generated both writings and literary criticism about those writings. Perhaps biographical and feminist studies face new challenges when identity seems subject to radical change and it is less easy to determine the sex of an author.

Gay and lesbian literary studies have included practices that parallel those of feminist criticism. At times critics identify oppressive or positive representations of homosexuality in works by men or women, gay, lesbian, or straight. At other times critics seek to establish the equivalent stature of a work by a gay or lesbian writer or, because these identities tended to be hidden in the past, to reveal that a writer *was* gay or lesbian. Again stages of *equality* and *difference* have yielded to a *questioning of the terms of difference*, in this case what has been called queer theory. The field of queer theory hopes to leave everyone guessing rather than to identify gay or lesbian writers, characters, or themes. One of its founding texts, *Between Men* (1985), by Eve Kosofsky Sedgwick (1950–2009), drew on structuralist insight into desire as well as anthropological models of kinship to show that, in canonical works of English literature, male characters form "homosocial" (versus homosexual) bonds through their rivalry for and exchange of a woman. Queer theory, because it rejects the idea of a fixed identity or innate or essential gender, likes to discover resistance to heterosexuality in unexpected places. Queer theorists value gay writers such as Oscar Wilde, but they also find queer implications regardless of the author's acknowledged identity. This approach emphasizes not the surface signals of the text but the subtler meanings an audience or receiver might detect. It encompasses elaborate close reading of many varieties of literary work; characteristically, a leading queer theorist, D. A. Miller (b. 1948), has written in loving detail about both Jane Austen and Broadway musicals.

African American and Ethnic Literary Studies

Critics sought to define an African American literary tradition as early as the turn of the twentieth century. A period of literary success in the 1920s, known as the Harlem Renaissance, produced some of the first classic essays on writings by African Americans. Criticism and histories of African American literature tended to ignore and dismiss women writers, while feminist literary histories, guided by Virginia Woolf's classic *A Room of One's Own* (1929), neglected women writers of color. Only after feminist critics began to succeed in the academy and African American studies programs were established did the whiteness of feminist studies and the masculinity of African American studies become glaring; both fields have for some time corrected this narrowness of vision, in part by learning from each other. The study of African American literature followed the general pattern that we have noted, first striving to claim equality, on established aesthetic grounds, of works such as Ralph Ellison's magnificent *Invisible Man* (1952). Then in the 1960s the Black Arts or Black Aesthetic emerged. Once launched in the academy, however, African American studies has been devoted less to celebrating an essential racial difference than to tracing the historical construction of a racial Other and a subordinated literature. The field sought to recover neglected genres such as slave narratives and traced common elements in fiction or poetry to the conditions of slavery and segregation. By the 1980s, feminist and poststructuralist theory had an impact in the work of some African American critics such as Henry Louis Gates Jr. (b. 1950), Houston A. Baker Jr. (b. 1943), and Hazel V. Carby (b. 1948), while others objected that the doubts raised by "theory" stood in the way of political commitment. African Americans' cultural contributions to America have gained much more recognition than before. New histories of American culture have been written with the view that racism is not an aberration but inherent to the guiding narratives of national progress. Many critics now regard race as a discourse with only slight basis in genetics but with weighty investments in ideology. This poststructuralist position coexists with scholarship that takes into account the race of the author or reader or that focuses on African American characters or themes.

In recent years a series of fields has arisen in recognition of the literatures of other American ethnic groups, large and small: Asian Americans, Native Americans, Latinos, and Chicanos. Increasingly, such studies avoid romanticizing an original, pure culture or assuming that these literatures by their very nature undermine the values and power of the dominant culture. Instead, critics emphasize the *hybridity* of all cultures in a global economy. The contact and intermixture of cultures across geographical borders and languages (translations, "creole" speech made up of native and acquired languages, dialects) may be read as enriching literature and art, despite being caused by economic exploitation. In method and in aim these fields have much in common with African American studies, though each cultural and historical context is very different. Each field deserves the separate study that we cannot offer here.

Not so very long ago, critics might have been charged with a fundamental misunderstanding of the nature of literature if they pursued matters considered the business of sociologists, matters—such as class, race, and gender—that seemed extrinsic to the text. The rise of the above-noted fields has made it standard practice that a critic will address questions about class, race, and gender to place a text, its source, and its reception in historical and ideological context. One brief example might illustrate the way Marxist, feminist, queer, and African American criticism can contribute to a literary reading.

Tennessee Williams's *A Streetcar Named Desire* was first produced in 1947 and won the Pulitzer Prize in 1948. Part of its acclaim was likely due to its fashionable blend of naturalism and symbolism: The action takes place in a shabby tenement on an otherworldly street, Elysian Fields—in an "atmosphere of decay" laced with "lyricism," as Williams's stage directions put it (1.1). After the Depression and World War II, American audiences welcomed a turn away from world politics into the psychological core of human sexuality. This turn to ostensibly individual conflict was a kind of alibi for at least two sets of issues that Williams and the middle-class theatergoers in New York and elsewhere sought to avoid. First are racial questions that relate to ones of gender and class: What is the play's attitude to race, and what is Williams's attitude? Biography seems relevant, though not the last word on what the play means. Williams's family had included slaveholding cotton growers, and he chose to spend much of his adult life in the South, which he saw as representing a beautiful but dying way of life. He was deeply attached to women in his family who might be models for the brilliant, fragile, cultivated Southern white woman, Blanche DuBois. Blanche ("white" in French), representative of a genteel, feminine past that has gambled, prostituted, dissipated itself, speaks some of the most eloquent lines in the play when she mourns the faded Delta plantation society. Neither the playwright nor his audience wished to deal with segregation in the South, a region that since the Civil War had stagnated as a kind of agricultural working class in relation to the dominant North—which had its racism, too.

The play scarcely notices race. The main characters are white. The cast includes a "Negro Woman" as servant, and a blind Mexican woman who offers artificial flowers to remember the dead, but these figures seem more like props or symbols than fully developed characters. Instead, racial difference is transposed as ethnic and class difference in the story of a working-class Pole intruding into a family clinging to French gentility. Stella warns Blanche that she lives among "heterogeneous types" and that Stanley is "a different species" (1.1). The play thus transfigures contemporary anxieties about miscegenation, as the virile (black) man dominates the ideal white woman and rapes the spirit of the plantation South. A former soldier who works in a factory, Stanley represents as well the defeat of the old, agricultural economy by industrialization.

The second set of issues that neither the playwright nor his audience confronts directly is the disturbance of sexual and gender roles that would in later decades lead to movements for women's and gay rights. It was well known in New Orleans at least that Williams was gay. In the 1940s he lived with his lover, Pancho Rodriguez y Gonzales, in the French Quarter. Like many homosexual writers in other eras, Williams recasts homosexual desire in heterosexual costume. Blanche, performing femininity with a kind of camp excess, might be a fading queen pursuing and failing to capture younger men. Stanley, hypermasculine, might caricature the object of desire of both men and women as well as the anti-intellectual, brute force in postwar America. His conquest of women (he had "the power and pride of a richly feathered male bird among hens" [1.1]) appears to be biologically determined. By the same token it seems natural that Stanley and his buddies go out to work and that their wives become homemakers in the way now seen as typical of the 1950s. In this world, artists, homosexuals, or unmarried working women like Blanche would be both vulnerable and threatening. Blanche after all has secret pleasures—drinking and sex—that Stanley indulges in openly. Blanche is the one who is taken into custody by the medical establishment, which in this period diagnosed homosexuality as a form of insanity.

New Historicism

Three interrelated schools of historical and ideological criticism have been important innovations in the past two decades. These are part of the swing of the pendulum away from formal analysis of the text and toward historical analysis of context. New historicism has less obvious political commitments than Marxism, feminism, or queer theory, but it shares their interest in the power of discourse to shape ideology. Old historicism, in the 1850s–1950s, confidently told a story of civilization's progress from the point of view of a Western nation; a historicist critic would offer a close reading of the plays of Shakespeare and then locate them within the prevailing Elizabethan "worldview." "New Historicism," labeled in 1982 by Stephen Greenblatt (b. 1943), rejected the technique of plugging samples of a culture into a history of ideas. Influenced by poststructuralist anthropology, New Historicism tried to offer a multilayered impression or "thick description" of a culture at one moment in time, including popular as well as elite forms of representation. As a method, New Historicism belongs with those that deny the unity of the text, defy the authority of the source, and license the receiver—much like deconstructionism. Accordingly, New Historicism doubts the accessibility of the past, insisting that all we have is discourse. One model for New Historicism was the historiography of Michel Foucault, who insisted on the power of discourses, that is, not only writing but all structuring myths or ideologies that underlie social relations. The New Historicist, like Foucault, is interested in the transition from the external powers of the state and church in the feudal order to modern forms of power. The rule of the modern state and middle-class ideology is enforced insidiously by systems of surveillance and by each individual's internalization of discipline (not unlike Freud's idea of the superego).

No longer so "new," the New Historicists have had a lasting influence on a more narrative and concrete style of criticism even among those who espouse poststructuralist and Marxist theories. A New Historicist article begins with an anecdote, often a description of a public spectacle, and teases out the many contributing causes that brought disparate social elements together in that way. It usually applies techniques of close reading to forms that would not traditionally have received such attention. Although it often concentrates on events several hundred years ago, in some ways it defies historicity, flouting the idea that a complete objective impression of the entire context could ever be achieved.

Cultural Studies

Popular culture often gets major attention in the work of New Historicists. Yet today most studies of popular culture would acknowledge their debt instead to cultural studies, as filtered through the now-defunct Center for Contemporary Cultural Studies, founded in 1964 by Stuart Hall (1932–2014) and others at the University of Birmingham in England. Method, style, and subject matter may be similar in New Historicism and cultural studies: Both attend to historical context, theoretical method, political commitment, and textual analysis. But whereas the American movement shares Foucault's paranoid view of state domination through discourse, the British school, influenced by Raymond Williams and his concept of "structures of feeling," emphasizes the possibility that ordinary people, the receivers of cultural forms, may resist dominant ideology. The documents examined in a cultural-studies essay may be recent, such as artifacts of tourism at Shakespeare's birthplace, rather than sixteenth-century maps. Cultural studies today influences history, sociology, communications and media, and literature departments; its studies may focus on television, film, romance novels, and advertising, or on museums and the art market, sports and stadiums, New Age religious groups, or other forms and practices.

The questions raised by cultural studies would encourage a critic to place a poem like Marge Piercy's "Barbie Doll" in the context of the history of that toy, a doll whose slender, impossibly long legs, tiptoe feet (not unlike the bound feet of Chinese women of an earlier era), small nose, and torpedo breasts epitomized a 1950s ideal for the female body. A critic influenced by cultural studies might align the poem with other works published around 1973 that express feminist protest concerning cosmetics, body image, consumption, and the objectification of women, while she or he would draw on research into the founding and marketing of Mattel toys. The poem reverses the Sleeping Beauty story: This heroine puts herself into the coffin rather than waking up. The poem omits any hero—Ken?—who would rescue her. "Barbie Doll" protests the pressure a girl feels to fit into a heterosexual plot of romance and marriage; no one will buy her if she is not the right toy or accessory.

Indeed, accessories such as "GE stoves and irons" (line 3) taught girls to plan their lives as domestic consumers, and Barbie's lifestyle is decidedly middle-class and suburban (everyone has a house, car, pool, and lots of handbags). The whiteness of the typical "girlchild" (1) goes without saying. Although Mattel produced Barbie's African American friend, Christie, in 1968, Piercy's title makes the reader imagine Barbie, not Christie. In 1997 Mattel issued Share a Smile Becky, a friend in a wheelchair, as though in answer to the humiliation of the girl in Piercy's poem, who feels so deformed, in spite of her "strong arms and back, / abundant sexual drive and manual dexterity" (8–9), that she finally cripples herself. The icon, in short, responds to changing ideology. Perhaps responding to generations of objections like Piercy's, Barbies over the years have been given feminist career goals, yet women's lives are still plotted according to physical image.

In this manner a popular product might be "read" alongside a literary work. The approach would be influenced by Marxist, feminist, gender, and ethnic studies, but it would not be driven by a desire to destroy Barbie as sinister, misogynist propaganda. Piercy's kind of protest against indoctrination has gone out of style. Girls have found ways to respond to such messages and divert them into stories of empowerment. Such at least is the outlook of cultural studies, which usually affirms popular culture. A researcher could gather data on Barbie sales and could interview girls or videotape their play in order to establish the actual effects of the dolls. Whereas traditional anthropology examined non-European or preindustrial cultures, cultural studies may direct its "field work," or ethnographic research, inward, at home. Nevertheless, many contributions to cultural studies rely on methods of textual close reading or Marxist and Freudian literary criticism developed in the mid-twentieth century.

Postcolonial Criticism and Studies of World Literature

In the middle of the twentieth century, the remaining colonies of the European nations struggled toward independence. French-speaking Frantz Fanon (1925–61) of Martinique was one of the most compelling voices for the point of view of the colonized or exploited countries, which like the feminine Other had been objectified and denied the right to look and talk back. Edward Said (1935–2003), in *Orientalism* (1978), brought a poststructuralist analysis to bear on the history of colonization, illustrating the ways that Western culture feminized and objectified the East. Postcolonial literary studies developed into a distinct field in the 1990s in light of globalization and the replacement of direct colonial power with international corporations and "NGOs" (nongovernmental agencies such as the World Bank). In general this field cannot share the optimism of some cultural studies, given the histories of slavery and economic exploitation of colonies and the violence committed in the name of civilization's progress. Studies by Gayatri Chakravorty Spivak (b. 1942) and Homi K. Bhabha (b. 1949) have further mingled Marxist, feminist, and poststructuralist theory to reread both canonical Western works and the writings of marginalized peoples. Colonial or postcolonial literatures may include works set or published in countries during colonial rule or after independence, or they may feature texts produced in the context of international cultural exchange, such as a novel in English by a woman of Chinese descent writing in Malaysia.

Like feminist studies and studies of African American or other literatures, the field is inspired by recovery of neglected works, redress of a systematic denial of rights and recognition, and increasing realization that the dualisms of opposing groups reveal interdependence. In this field the stage of difference came early, with the celebrations of African heritage known as *Négritude*, but the danger of that essentialist claim was soon apparent: The Dark Continent or wild island might be romanticized and idealized as a source of innate qualities of vitality long repressed in Enlightened Europe. Currently, most critics accept that the context for literature in all countries is hybrid, with immigration and educational intermixing. Close readings of texts are always linked to the author's biography and literary influences and placed within the context of contemporary international politics as well as colonial history. Many fiction writers, from Salman Rushdie to Jhumpa Lahiri, make the theme of cultural mixture or hybridity part of their work, whether in a pastiche of Charles Dickens or a story of an Indian family growing up in New Jersey and returning as tourists to their supposed "native" land. Poststructuralist theories of trauma, and theories of the interrelation of narrative and memory, provide explanatory frames for interpreting writings from Afghanistan to Zambia.

Studies of postcolonial culture retain a clear political mission that feminist and Marxist criticism have found difficult to sustain. Perhaps this is because the scale of the power relations is so vast, between nations rather than the sexes or classes within those nations. Imperialism can be called an absolute evil, and the destruction of local cultures a crime against humanity. Today some of the most exciting literature in English emerges from countries once under the British Empire, and all the techniques of criticism will be brought to bear on it. If history is any guide, in later decades some critical school will attempt to read the diverse literatures of the early twenty-first century in pure isolation from authorship and national origin, as self-enclosed form. The themes of hybridity, indeterminacy, trauma, and memory will be praised as universal. It is even possible that readers' continuing desire to revere authors as creative geniuses in control of their meanings will regain respectability among specialists. The elements of the literary exchange—text, source, and receiver—are always there to provoke questions that generate criticism, which in turn produces articulations of the methods of that criticism. It is an ongoing discussion well worth participating in.

BIBLIOGRAPHY

For good introductions to the issues discussed here, see the following books, from which we have drawn in this overview. Some of these provide bibliographies of the works of critics and schools mentioned above.

Alter, Robert. *The Pleasure of Reading in an Ideological Age.* W. W. Norton, 1996. Originally published as *The Pleasures of Reading: Thinking about Literature in an Ideological Age,* 1989.

Barnet, Sylvan, and William E. Cain. *A Short Guide to Writing about Literature.* 10th ed., Longman, 2005.

Barry, Peter. *Beginning Theory: An Introduction to Literary and Cultural Theory.* 2nd ed., Manchester UP, 2002.

Bressler, Charles E. *Literary Criticism: An Introduction to Theory and Practice.* 3rd ed., Prentice Hall, 2003.

Culler, Jonathan. *Literary Theory: A Very Short Introduction.* Oxford UP, 1997.

Davis, Robert Con, and Ronald Schleifer. *Contemporary Literary Criticism: Literary and Cultural Studies.* 4th ed., Addison Wesley Longman, 1999.

During, Simon. *Cultural Studies: A Critical Introduction.* Routledge, 2005.

---. *The Cultural Studies Reader.* Routledge, 1999.

Eagleton, Mary, editor. *Feminist Literary Theory: A Reader.* 2nd ed., Blackwell, 1996.

Eagleton, Terry. *Literary Theory: An Introduction.* 2nd rev. ed., U of Minnesota P, 1996.

Groden, Michael, and Martin Kreiswirth. *The Johns Hopkins Guide to Literary Theory and Criticism.* Johns Hopkins UP, 1994.

Hawthorn, Jeremy. *A Glossary of Contemporary Literary Theory.* 3rd ed., Arnold, 1998.

Leitch, Vincent B. *American Literary Criticism from the Thirties to the Eighties.* Columbia UP, 1989.

---, et al. *The Norton Anthology of Theory and Criticism.* 2nd ed., W. W. Norton, 2010.

Lentricchia, Frank. *After the New Criticism.* U of Chicago P, 1981.

Macksey, Richard, and Eugenio Donato, editors. *The Structuralist Controversy: The Languages of Criticism and the Sciences of Man.* Johns Hopkins UP, 2007.

Moi, Toril. *Sexual-Textual Politics.* Routledge, 1985.

Murfin, Ross, and Supryia M. Ray. *The Bedford Glossary of Critical and Literary Terms.* Bedford, 1997.

Piaget, Jean. *Structuralism.* Translated and edited by Chaninah Maschler, Basic Books, 1970.

Selden, Raman, and Peter Widdowson. *A Reader's Guide to Contemporary Literary Theory.* 3rd ed., U of Kentucky P, 1993.

Stevens, Anne H. *Literary Theory and Criticism: An Introduction*. Broadview Press, 2015.

Todorov, Tzvetan. *Mikhail Bakhtin: The Dialogic Principle.* Translated by Wlad Godzich, U of Minnesota P, 1984.

Turco, Lewis. *The Book of Literary Terms.* UP of New England, 1999.

Veeser, Harold, editor. *The New Historicism.* Routledge, 1989.

---. *The New Historicism Reader.* Routledge, 1994.

Warhol, Robyn R., and Diane Price Herndl. *Feminisms.* 2nd ed., Rutgers UP, 1997.

Wolfreys, Julian. *Literary Theories: A Reader and Guide.* Edinburgh UP, 1999.

Glossary

Boldface words within definitions are themselves defined in the glossary.

action any event or series of events depicted in a literary work; an event may be verbal as well as physical, so that saying something or telling a story within the story may be an event. *See also* **climax**, **complication**, **falling action**, **inciting incident**, **plot**, *and* **rising action**.

allegory a literary work in which **characters**, **actions**, and even **settings** have two connected levels of meaning. Elements of the literal level signify (or serve as symbols for) a figurative level that often imparts a lesson or moral to the reader. One of the most famous English-language allegories is John Bunyan's *Pilgrim's Progress*, in which a character named Christian has to make his way through obstacles such as the Valley of Humiliation to get to the Celestial City.

alliteration the repetition of usually initial consonant sounds through a sequence of words—for example, "While I *n*odded, *n*early *n*apping" in Edgar Allan Poe's "The Raven."

allusion a brief, often implicit and indirect reference within a literary text to something outside the text, whether another text (e.g., the Bible, a **myth**, another literary work, a painting, or a piece of music) or any imaginary or historical person, place, or thing. Many of the footnotes in this book explain allusions found in literary selections.

amphitheater a theater consisting of a stage area surrounded by a semicircle of tiered seats.

analogy like a **metaphor**, a representation of one thing or idea by something else; in this case, often a simpler explanation that gets at the gist of the more complicated example (e.g., "the brain is like a computer").

anapestic referring to a metrical form in which each **foot** consists of two unstressed syllables followed by a stressed one—for example, "There are mán- | y who sáy | that a dóg | has his dáy" (Dylan Thomas, "The Song of the Mischievous Dog"). A single foot of this type is called an *anapest*.

antagonist a **character** or a nonhuman force that opposes or is in **conflict** with the **protagonist**.

antihero a **protagonist** who is in one way or another the very opposite of a traditional **hero**. Instead of being courageous and determined, for instance, an antihero might be timid, hypersensitive, and indecisive to the point of paralysis. Antiheroes are especially common in modern literary works; examples might include the **speaker** of T. S. Eliot's "The Love Song of J. Alfred Prufrock" or the **protagonist** of Franz Kafka's *The Metamorphosis*.

apostrophe a **figure of speech** in which a **speaker** or **narrator** addresses an abstraction, an object, or a dead or absent person. An example occurs at the end of Melville's "Bartleby, the Scrivener." "Ah, Bartleby! Ah, Humanity!"

archetype a **character**, ritual, **symbol**, or **plot** pattern that recurs in the **myth** and literature of many cultures; examples include the scapegoat or trickster (character type), the rite of passage (ritual), and the quest or descent into the underworld (plot pattern). The term and our contemporary understanding of it derive from the work of psychologist Carl Jung (1875–1961), who argued that archetypes emerge from—and give us a clue to the workings of—the "collective unconscious," a reservoir of memories and impulses that all humans share but aren't consciously aware of.

arena stage a stage design in which the audience is seated all the way around the acting area; actors make their entrances and exits through the auditorium.

assonance the repetition of vowel sounds in a sequence of words with different endings—for example, "The d*ea*th of the po*e*t was k*e*pt from his po*e*ms" in W. H. Auden's "In Memory of W. B. Yeats."

aubade a poem in which the coming of dawn is either celebrated or denounced as a nuisance, as in John Donne's "The Sun Rising."

auditor an imaginary listener within a literary work, as opposed to the actual reader or audience outside the work.

author the *actual* or *real author* of a work is the historical person who actually wrote it and the focus of biographical criticism, which interprets a work by drawing on facts about the author's life and career. The *implied author* is the vision of the author's personality and outlook implied by the work as a whole. Thus when we make a claim about the author that relies solely on evidence from the work rather than from other sources, our subject is the implied author; for example, "In *Dubliners*, James Joyce heavily criticizes the Catholic church."

author time *see* **time**.

autobiography *see* **biography**.

ballad a verse **narrative** that is, or originally was, meant to be sung. Ballads were originally a folk creation, transmitted orally from person to person and age to age and characterized by relatively simple **diction**, **meter**, and **rhyme scheme**; by stock imagery; and by repetition; and often by a refrain (a recurrent phrase or series of phrases). An example is "Sir Patrick Spens."

ballad stanza a common **stanza** form, consisting of a quatrain that alternates four-**foot** and three-foot lines; lines 1 and 3 are unrhymed **iambic tetrameter** (four feet), and lines 2 and 4 are rhymed **iambic trimeter** (three feet), as in "Sir Patrick Spens."

bildungsroman literally, "education novel" (German), a **novel** that depicts the intellectual, emotional, and moral development of its **protagonist** from childhood into adulthood; also sometimes called an *apprenticeship novel*. This type of novel tends to envision character as the product of environment, experience, nurture, and education (in the widest sense) rather than of nature, fate, and so on. Charlotte Brontë's *Jane Eyre* is a famous example.

biography a work of **nonfiction** that recounts the life of a real person. If the person depicted in a biography is also its author, then we instead use the term *autobiography*. An autobiography that focuses only on a specific aspect of, or episode in, its author's life is a *memoir*.

blank verse the metrical verse form most like everyday human speech; blank verse consists of unrhymed lines in **iambic pentameter**. Many of Shakespeare's plays are in blank verse, as is John Milton's *Paradise Lost* and Alfred Tennyson's *Ulysses*.

caesura a short pause within a line of poetry; often but not always signaled by punctuation. Note the two caesuras in this line from Poe's "The Raven": "Once upon a midnight dreary, while I pondered, weak and weary."

canon the range of works that a consensus of scholars, teachers, and readers of a particular time and culture consider "great" or "major."

carpe diem literally, "seize the day" in Latin, a common **theme** of literary works that emphasize the brevity of life and the need to make the most of the present. Andrew Marvell's poem "To His Coy Mistress" is a well-known example.

central consciousness a **character** whose inner thoughts, perceptions, and feelings are revealed by a *third-person limited* **narrator** who does not reveal the thoughts, perceptions, or feelings of other characters.

character an imaginary personage who acts, appears, or is referred to in a literary work. *Major* or *main characters* are those that receive most attention, *minor characters* least. *Flat characters* are relatively simple, have a few dominant traits, and tend to be predictable. Conversely, *round characters* are complex and multifaceted and act in a way that readers might not expect but accept as possible. *Static characters* do not change; *dynamic characters* do. *Stock characters* represent familiar types that recur frequently in literary works, especially of a particular **genre** (e.g., the "mad scientist" of horror fiction and film or the fool in Renaissance, especially Shakespearean, drama).

characterization the presentation of a fictional personage. A term like "a good character" can, then, be ambiguous—it may mean that the personage is virtuous or that he or she is well presented regardless of his or her characteristics or moral qualities. In fiction, *direct characterization* occurs when a narrator explicitly tells us what a character is like. *Indirect characterization* occurs when a character's traits are revealed implicitly, through his or her speech, behavior, thoughts, appearance, and so on.

chorus a group of actors in a drama who comment on and describe the **action**. In classical Greek theater, members of the chorus often wore masks and relied on song, dance, and recitation to make their commentary.

classical unities as derived from Aristotle's *Poetics*, the three principles of structure that require a play to have one **plot** (*unity of action*) that occurs in one place (*unity of place*) and within one day (*unity of time*); also called the *dramatic unities*. Susan Glaspell's *Trifles* and Sophocles's *Antigone* observe the classical unities.

climax the third part of **plot**, the point at which the **action** stops rising and begins falling or reversing; also called *turning point* or (following Aristotle) *peripeteia*. *See also* **crisis**.

closet drama *see* **drama**.

colloquial diction *see* **diction**.

comedy a broad category of literary, especially dramatic, works intended primarily to entertain and amuse an audience. Comedies take many different forms, but they share three basic characteristics: (1) the values that are expressed and that typically cause **conflict**

are determined by the general opinion of society (as opposed to being universal and beyond the control of humankind, as in **tragedy**); (2) **characters** in comedies are often defined primarily in terms of their social identities and roles and tend to be *flat* or *stock characters* rather than highly individualized or *round* ones; (3) comedies conventionally end happily with an act of social reintegration and celebration such as marriage. William Shakespeare's *A Midsummer Night's Dream* is a famous example.

The term *high* or *verbal comedy* may refer either to a particular type of comedy or to a sort of humor found within any literary work that employs subtlety and wit and usually represents high society. Conversely, *low* or *physical comedy* is a type of either comedy or humor that involves burlesque, horseplay, and the representation of unrefined life. *See also* **farce**.

coming-of-age story *see* **initiation story**.

complication in **plot**, an **action** or event that introduces a new **conflict** or intensifies the existing one, especially during the **rising action** phase of plot.

conclusion also called *resolution*, the fifth and last phase or part of **plot**, the point at which the situation that was destabilized at the beginning becomes stable once more and the **conflict** is resolved.

concrete poetry poetry in which the words on the page are arranged to look like an object; also called *shaped verse*. George Herbert's "Easter Wings," for example, is arranged to look like two pairs of wings.

conflict a struggle between opposing forces. A conflict is *external* when it pits a **character** against something or someone outside himself or herself—another character or characters or something in nature or society. A conflict is *internal* when the opposing forces are two drives, impulses, or parts of a single character.

connotation what is suggested by a word, apart from what it literally means or how it is defined in the dictionary. *See also* **denotation**.

consonance the repetition of certain consonant sounds in close proximity, such as mishmash. Especially prominent in Middle English poetry, such as *Beowulf*.

controlling metaphor *see* **metaphor**.

convention in literature, a standard or traditional way of presenting or expressing something, or a traditional or characteristic feature of a particular literary **genre** or subgenre. Division into lines and **stanzas** is a convention of poetry. Conventions of the type of poem known as the **epic** include a **plot** that begins ***in medias res*** and frequent use of **epithets** and extended **similes**.

cosmic irony *see* **irony**.

couplet two consecutive lines of verse linked by **rhyme** and **meter**; the meter of a *heroic couplet* is **iambic pentameter**.

crisis in **plot**, the moment when the **conflict** comes to a head, often requiring the character to make a decision; sometimes the crisis is equated with the **climax** or *turning point* and sometimes it is treated as a distinct moment that precedes and prepares for the climax.

criticism *see* **literary criticism**.

cycle *see* **sequence**.

dactylic referring to the metrical pattern in which each **foot** consists of a stressed syllable followed by two unstressed ones—for example, "Fláshed all their/sábres bare" (Tennyson, "Charge of the Light Brigade"). A single foot of this type is called a *dactyl*.

denotation a word's direct and literal meaning, as opposed to its **connotation**.

dénouement literally, "untying" (as of a knot) in French; a **plot**-related term used in three ways: (1) as a synonym for **falling action**, (2) as a synonym for **conclusion** or resolution, and (3) as the label for a phase following the conclusion in which any loose ends are tied up.

destabilizing event *see* **inciting incident**.

deus ex machina literally, "god out of the machine" (Latin); any improbable, unprepared-for plot contrivance introduced late in a literary work to resolve the **conflict**. The term derives from the ancient Greek theatrical practice of using a mechanical device to lower a god or gods onto the stage to resolve the conflicts of the human characters.

dialogue (1) usually, words spoken by **characters** in a literary work, especially as opposed to words that come directly from the **narrator** in a work of fiction; (2) more rarely, a literary work that consists mainly or entirely of the speech of two or more characters; examples include Thomas Hardy's poem "The Ruined Maid" and Plato's treatise *Republic*.

diction choice of words. Diction is often described as either *informal* or *colloquial* if it resembles everyday speech, or as *formal* if it is instead lofty, impersonal, and dignified. **Tone** is determined largely through diction.

discriminated occasion a specific, discrete moment portrayed in a fictional work, often signaled by phrases such as "At 5:05 in the morning . . . ," "It was about dusk, one evening during the supreme madness of the carnival season . . . ," or "the day before Maggie fell down. . . ."

drama a literary **genre** consisting of works in which **action** is performed and all words are spoken before an audience by an actor or actors impersonating the **characters**. (Drama typically lacks the **narrators** and **narration** found in fiction.) *Closet drama,* however, is a subgenre of drama that has most of these features yet is intended to be read, either silently by a single reader or out loud in a group setting. *Verse drama* is drama written in verse rather than prose.

dramatic irony *see* **irony**.

dramatic monologue a type or subgenre of poetry in which a **speaker** addresses a silent **auditor** or auditors in a specific situation and setting that is revealed entirely through the speaker's words; this kind of poem's primary aim is the revelation of the speaker's personality, views, and values. For example, Alfred Tennyson's "Ulysses" consists of an aged Ulysses's words to the mariners whom he hopes to convince to return to sea with him; most of Robert Browning's best-known poems, such as "My Last Duchess," are dramatic monologues.

dramatic poem a poem structured so as to present a **scene** or series of scenes, as in a work of drama. *See also* **dramatic monologue**.

dramatic unities *see* **classical unities**.

dramatis personae literally, "persons of the drama" (Latin); the list of **characters** that appears either in a play's program or at the top of the first page of the written play.

dynamic character *see* **character**.

elegy (1) since the Renaissance, usually a formal lament on the death of a particular person, but focusing mainly on the speaker's efforts to come to terms with his or her grief; (2) more broadly, any **lyric** in sorrowful mood that takes death as its primary subject. An example is W. H. Auden's "In Memory of W. B. Yeats."

end-stopped line a line of verse that contains or concludes a complete clause and usually ends with a punctuation mark. *See also* **enjambment**.

English sonnet *see* **sonnet**.

enjambment in poetry, the technique of running over from one line to the next without stop, as in the following lines by William Wordsworth: "My heart leaps up when I behold / A rainbow in the sky." The lines themselves would be described as *enjambed*.

epic a long **narrative poem** that celebrates the achievements of mighty **heroes** and **heroines**, usually in founding a nation or developing a culture, and uses elevated language and a grand, high style. Other epic **conventions** include a beginning **in medias res**, an invocation of the muse, a journey to the underworld, battle scenes, and a scene in which the hero arms himself for battle. Examples include *Beowulf* and Homer's *Iliad*. A *mock epic* is a form of **satire** in which epic language and conventions are used to depict **characters**, **actions**, and **settings** utterly unlike those in conventional epics, usually (though not always) with the purpose of ridiculing the social milieu or types of people portrayed in the poem. A famous example is Alexander Pope's *The Rape of the Lock*.

epigram a very short, usually witty verse with a quick turn at the end.

epigraph a quotation appearing at the beginning of a literary work or of one section of such a work; not to be confused with **epigram**.

epilogue (1) in fiction, a short section or chapter that comes after the **conclusion**, tying up loose ends and often describing what happens to the characters after the resolution of the **conflict**; (2) in drama, a short speech, often addressed directly to the audience, delivered by a **character** at the end of a play.

epiphany a sudden revelation of truth, often inspired by a seemingly simple or commonplace event. The term, originally from Christian theology, was first popularized by the Irish fiction writer James Joyce, though Joyce also used the term to describe the individual short stories collected in his book *Dubliners*.

episode a distinct **action** or series of actions within a **plot**.

epistolary novel *see* **novel**.

epithet a characterizing word or phrase that precedes, follows, or substitutes for the name of a person or thing, such as *slain civil rights leader* Martin Luther King Jr., or Zeus, *the god of trophies*; not to be confused with **epitaph**. **Epics** conventionally make frequent use of epithets.

epitaph an inscription on a tombstone or grave marker; not to be confused with **epigram**, **epigraph**, or **epithet**.

eponymous having a name used in the title of a literary work. For example, Lemuel Gulliver is the eponymous **protagonist** of Jonathan Swift's *Gulliver's Travels*.

expectation like **foreshadowing**, a set up for something believed to occur later on in a work of literature.

exposition the first phase or part of **plot**, which sets the scene, introduces and identifies **characters**, and establishes the situation at the beginning of a story or play. Additional exposition is often scattered throughout the work.

extended metaphor *see* **metaphor**.

external conflict *see* **conflict**.

external narration or narrator *see* **narrator**.

fable an ancient type of short **fiction**, in verse or prose, illustrating a **moral** or satirizing human beings. The **characters** in a fable are often animals that talk and act like human beings. The fable is sometimes treated as a specific type of folktale and sometimes as a fictional subgenre in its own right. An example is Aesop's "The Two Crabs."

fairy tale *see* **tale**.

falling action the fourth of the five phases or parts of **plot**, in which the **conflict** or conflicts move toward resolution.

fantasy a genre of literary work featuring strange settings and characters and often involving magic or the supernatural; though closely related to horror and science fiction, fantasy is typically less concerned with the macabre or with science and technology. J. R. R. Tolkien's *The Hobbit* is a well-known example.

farce a literary work, especially drama, characterized by broad humor, wild antics, and often slapstick, pratfalls, or other physical humor. *See also* **comedy**.

fiction any **narrative**, especially in prose, about invented or imagined **characters** and **action**. Today, we tend to divide fiction into three major subgenres based on length—the **short story**, **novella**, and **novel**. Older, originally oral forms of short fiction include the **fable**, **legend**, **parable**, and **tale**. Fictional works may also be categorized not by their length but by their handling of particular elements such as **plot** and **character**. Detective and science fiction, for example, are subgenres that include both novels and novellas such as Frank Herbert's *Dune* and short stories such as Edgar Allan Poe's "The Murders at the Rue Morgue" or Isaac Asimov's "I, Robot." *See also* **gothic fiction**, **historical fiction**, **nonfiction**, and **romance**.

figurative language language that uses **figures of speech**.

figure of speech any word or phrase that creates a "figure" in the mind of the reader by effecting an obvious change in the usual meaning or order of words, by comparing or identifying one thing with another; also called a *trope*. **Metaphor**, **simile**, **metonymy**, **overstatement**, **oxymoron**, **and understatement** are common figures of speech.

first-person narrator *see* **narrator**.

flashback a **plot**-structuring device whereby a scene from the fictional past is inserted into the fictional present or is dramatized out of order.

flashforward a **plot**-structuring device whereby a scene from the fictional future is inserted into the fictional present or is dramatized out of order.

flat character *see* **character**.

focus the visual component of **point of view**, the point from which people, events, and other details in a story are viewed; also called *focalization*. *See also* **voice**.

foil a **character** that serves as a contrast to another.

folktale *see* **tale**.

foot the basic unit of poetic **meter**, consisting of any of various fixed patterns of one to three stressed and unstressed syllables. A foot may contain more than one word or just one syllable of a multisyllabic word. In **scansion**, breaks between feet are usually indicated with a vertical line or slash mark, as in the following example (which contains five feet): "One com- | mon note | on ei- | ther lyre | did strike" (Dryden, "To the Memory of Mr. Oldham"). *For specific examples of metrical feet, see* **anapestic**, **dactylic**, **iambic**, **pyrrhic**, **spondee**, and **trochaic**.

foreshadowing a hint or clue about what will happen at a later moment in the **plot**.

formal diction *see* **diction**.

frame narrative *see* **narrative**.

free verse poetry characterized by varying line lengths, lack of traditional **meter**, and nonrhyming lines.

Freytag's pyramid a diagram of **plot** structure first created by the German novelist and critic Gustav Freytag (1816–95).

general setting *see* **setting**.

genre a type or category of works sharing particular formal or textual features and **conventions**; especially used to refer to the largest categories for classifying literature—**fiction**, **poetry**, **drama**, and **nonfiction**. A smaller division within a genre is usually known as a *subgenre*, such as **gothic fiction** or **epic poetry**.

gothic fiction a subgenre of **fiction** conventionally featuring plots that involve secrets, mystery, and the supernatural (or the seemingly supernatural) and large, gloomy, and usually antiquated (especially medieval) buildings as settings. Examples include Horace Walpole's *The Castle of Otranto* and Edgar Allan Poe's "The Fall of the House of Usher."

haiku a poetic form, Japanese in origin, that consists of seventeen syllables arranged in three unrhymed lines of five, seven, and five syllables, respectively.

hero/heroine a character in a literary work, especially the leading male/female **character**, who is especially virtuous, usually larger than life, sometimes almost godlike. *See also* **antihero**, **protagonist**, and **villain**.

heroic couplet *see* **couplet**.

hexameter a line of poetry with six **feet**: "She comes, | she comes | again, | like ring | dove frayed | and fled" (Keats, *The Eve of St. Agnes*). *See* **alexandrine**.

high (verbal) comedy *see* **comedy**.

historical fiction a subgenre of **fiction**, of whatever length, in which the temporal setting, or plot time, is significantly earlier than the time in which the work was written (typically, a period before the birth of the author). Conventionally, such works describe the atmosphere and mores of the setting in vivid detail and explore the influence of historical factors on the **characters** and **action**; though focusing mainly on invented or imaginary characters and events, historical fiction sometimes includes some characters and action based on actual historical personages and events. The *historical novel* is a type of historical fiction pioneered by nineteenth-century Scottish writer Walter Scott in works such as *Rob Roy* and *Ivanhoe*.

hyperbole *see* **overstatement**. (*See also* **understatement**.)

iambic referring to a metrical form in which each **foot** consists of an unstressed syllable followed by a stressed one; this type of foot is an *iamb*. The most common poetic meter in English is *iambic* **pentameter**—a metrical form in which most lines consist of five iambs: "One cóm- | mon nóte | on éi- | ther lýre | did stríke" (Dryden, "To the Memory of Mr. Oldham").

image/imagery broadly defined, any sensory detail or evocation in a work; more narrowly, the use of **figurative language** to evoke a feeling, to call to mind an idea, or to describe an object. Imagery may be described as *auditory, tactile, visual*, or *olfactory* depending on which sense it primarily appeals to—hearing, touch, vision, or smell. An *image* is a particular instance of imagery.

implied author *see* **author**.

inciting incident an **action** that sets a **plot** in motion by creating **conflict**; also called *destabilizing event*.

informal diction *see* **diction**.

initiation story a kind of **short story** in which a **character**—often a child or young person—first learns a significant, usually life-changing truth about the universe, society, people, or himself or herself; also called a *coming-of-age story*. James Joyce's "Araby" is a notable example.

in medias res "in the midst of things" (Latin); refers to opening a **plot** in the middle of the **action**, and then filling in past details by means of **exposition** and/or **flashback**.

interior monologue *see* **monologue**.

internal conflict *see* **conflict**.

internal narration or **narrator** *see* **narrator**.

intrusive narration or **narrator** *see* **narrator**.

inversion a change in normal **syntax** such as putting a verb before its subject. Common in poetry, the technique is also famously used by *Star Wars'* Yoda, as in "when 900 years old you reach, look as good, you will not."

irony a situation or statement characterized by a significant difference between what is expected or understood and what actually happens or is meant. *Verbal irony* occurs when a word or expression in context means something different from, and usually the opposite of, what it appears to mean; when the intended meaning is harshly critical or satiric, verbal irony becomes *sarcasm*. *Situational irony* occurs when a character holds a position or has an expectation that is reversed or fulfilled in an unexpected way. When there is instead a gap between what an audience knows and what a character believes or expects, we have *dramatic irony*; when this occurs in a **tragedy**, dramatic irony is sometimes called *tragic irony*. Finally, the terms *cosmic irony* and *irony of fate* are sometimes used to refer to situations in which situational irony is the result of fate, chance, the gods, or some other superhuman force or entity.

Italian sonnet *see* **sonnet**.

legend a type of **tale** conventionally set in the real world and in either the present or historical past, based on actual historical people and events and offering an exaggerated or distorted version of the truth about those people and events. American examples might include stories featuring Davy Crockett or Johnny Appleseed or the story about George Washington chopping down the cherry tree. British examples are the legends of King Arthur or Robin Hood.

limerick a light or humorous **poem** or subgenre of poems consisting of mainly **anapestic** lines of which the first, second, and fifth are of three **feet**; the third and fourth lines are of two feet; and the rhyme scheme is *aabba*.

limited narrator *see* **narrator**.

limited point of view *see* **point of view**.

lines in a poem, a discrete organization of words; the length and shape of a line can communicate meaning in a poem, and can be a formal element characterizing a poem, such as the fourteen lines that make up a **sonnet**.

literary criticism the mainly interpretive (versus evaluative) work written by readers of literary texts, especially professional ones (who are thus known as *literary critics*). It is "criticism" not because it is negative or corrective but rather because those who write criticism ask probing, analytical, "critical" questions about the works they read.

litotes a form of **understatement** in which one negates the contrary of what one means. Examples from common speech include "Not bad" (meaning "good") and "a novelist of no small repute" (meaning "a novelist with a big reputation"), and so on.

low (physical) comedy *see* comedy.

lyric originally, a poem meant to be sung to the accompaniment of a lyre; now, any relatively short poem in which the **speaker** expresses his or her thoughts and feelings in the first person rather than recounting a **narrative** or portraying a dramatic situation.

magic realism a type of **fiction** that involves the creation of a fictional world in which the kind of familiar, plausible **action** and **characters** one might find in more straightforwardly realist fiction coexist with utterly fantastic ones straight out of **myths** or dreams. This style of **realism** is associated especially with modern Latin American writers such as Gabriel García Márquez and Jorge Luis Borges. But the label is also sometimes applied to works by other contemporary writers from around the world, including Italo Calvino and Salman Rushdie.

major (main) character *see* **character**.

memoir *see* **biography**.

metafiction a subgenre of works that playfully draw attention to their status as **fiction** in order to explore the nature of fiction and the role of authors and readers.

metaphor a **figure of speech** in which two unlike things are compared implicitly—that is, without the use of a signal such as the word *like* or *as*—as in "Love is a rose, but you better not pick it." *See also* **simile**.

An *extended metaphor* is a detailed and complex metaphor that stretches across a long section of a work. If such a metaphor is so extensive that it dominates or organizes an entire literary work, especially a poem, it is called a *controlling metaphor*. In Linda Pastan's "Marks," for example, the controlling metaphor involves the use of "marks" or grades to talk about the speaker's performance of her familial roles. A *mixed metaphor* occurs when two or more usually incompatible metaphors are entangled together so as to become unclear and often unintentionally humorous, as in "Her blazing words dripped all over him."

meter the more or less regular pattern of stressed and unstressed syllables in a line of poetry. This is determined by the kind of **foot** (**iambic** or **dactylic**, for example) and by the number of feet per line (e.g., five feet = **pentameter**, six feet = **hexameter**).

metonymy a **figure of speech** in which the name of one thing is used to refer to another associated thing. When we say, "The White House has promised to veto the bill," for example, we use the White House as a metonym for the president and his administration. **Synecdoche** is a specific type of metonymy.

minor character *see* character.

mock epic *see* **epic**.

monologue (1) a long speech, usually in a play but also in other **genres**, spoken by one person and uninterrupted by the speech of anyone else, or (2) an entire work consisting of this sort of speech. In fiction, an *interior monologue* takes place entirely within the mind of a character rather than being spoken aloud. A **soliloquy** is a particular type of monologue occurring in drama, while a **dramatic monologue** is a type of poem.

moral a rule of conduct or a maxim for living (that is, a statement about how one should live or behave) communicated in a literary work. Though **fables** often have morals such as "Don't count your chickens before they hatch," more modern literary works instead tend to have **themes**.

motif a recurrent device, formula, or situation within a literary work. For example, the sound of the breaking harp string is a motif of Anton Chekhov's play *The Cherry Orchard*.

motive the animating impulse for an action, the reason why something is done or attempted.

myth (1) originally and narrowly, a **narrative** explaining how the world and humanity developed into their present form and, unlike a folktale, generally considered to be true by the people who develop it. Many, though not all, myths feature supernatural beings and have a religious significance or function within their culture of origin. Two especially common types of myth are the *creation myth*, which explains how the world, human beings, a god or gods, or good and evil came to be (e.g., the myth of Adam and Eve), and the *explanatory myth*, which explains features of the natural landscape or natural processes or events (e.g., "How the Leopard Got His Spots"); (2) more broadly and especially in its adjectival form (*mythic*), any narrative that obviously seeks to work like a myth in the first and more narrow sense, especially by portraying experiences or conveying truths that it implies are universally valid regardless of culture or time.

narration (1) broadly, the act of telling a story or recounting a **narrative**; (2) more narrowly, the portions of a narrative attributable to the **narrator** rather than words spoken by **characters** (that is, **dialogue**).

narrative a **story**, whether fictional or true and in prose or verse, related by a **narrator** or narrators (rather than acted out onstage, as in drama). A *frame narrative* is a narrative that recounts and thus "frames" the telling of another narrative or story. An example is Samuel Taylor Coleridge's "The Rime of the Ancient Mariner," in which an anonymous third-person narrator recounts how an old sailor comes to tell a young wedding guest the story of his adventures at sea.

narrative poem a poem in which a **narrator** tells a story.

narrator someone who recounts a **narrative** or tells a story. Though we usually instead use the term **speaker** when referring to poetry as opposed to prose fiction, *narrative poems* include at least one speaker who functions as a narrator. *See also* **narrative**.

A narrator or narration is said to be *internal* when the narrator is a **character** within the work, telling the story to an equally fictional **auditor** or listener; internal narrators are usually first- or second-person narrators (*see below*). A narrator or narration is instead said to be *external* when the narrator is not a character.

A *first-person narrator* is an internal narrator who consistently refers to himself or herself using the first-person pronouns *I* or *we*. A *second-person narrator* consistently uses the second-person pronoun *you* (a very uncommon technique). A *third-person narrator* uses third-person pronouns such as *she, he, they, it,* and so on; third-person narrators are almost always external narrators. Third-person narrators are said to be *omniscient* (literally, "all-knowing") when they describe the inner thoughts and feelings of multiple characters; they are said to be *limited* when they relate the thoughts, feelings, and perceptions of only one character (the **central consciousness**). If a work encourages us to view a narrator's account of events with suspicion, the narrator (usually first-person) is called *unreliable*. An *intrusive narrator* is a third-person narrator who occasionally disrupts his or her narrative to speak directly to the reader or audience in what is sometimes called *direct address*.

narrator time *see* **time**.

nonfiction a work or **genre** of prose works that describe actual, as opposed to imaginary or fictional, **characters** and events. Subgenres of nonfiction include **biography**, memoir, and the essay. *See also* **fiction**.

novel a long work of **fiction** (approximately 40,000+ words), typically published (or at least publishable) as a stand-alone book; though most novels are written in prose, those written as poetry are called *verse novels*. A novel (as opposed to a **short story**) conventionally has a complex **plot** and, often, at least one **subplot**, as well as a fully realized **setting** and a relatively large number of **characters**. One important novelistic subgenre is the *epistolary novel*—a novel composed entirely of letters written by its characters. Another is the **bildungsroman**.

novella a work of prose **fiction** that falls somewhere in between a **short story** and a **novel** in terms of length, scope, and complexity. Novellas can be, and have been, published either as books in their own right or as parts of books that include other works. Franz Kafka's *The Metamorphosis* is an example.

octameter a line of poetry with eight **feet**: "Once u- | pon a | midnight | dreary | while I | pondered | weak and | weary."

octave eight lines of verse linked by a pattern of end rhymes, especially the first eight lines of an Italian, or Petrarchan, **sonnet**. *See also* **sestet**.

ode a **lyric** poem characterized by a serious topic and formal tone but without a prescribed formal pattern in which the speaker talks about, and often to, an especially revered person or thing. Examples include Keats's odes and Shelley's "Ode to the West Wind."

oeuvre all of the works verifiably written by one author.

omniscient narrator *see* **narrator**.

omniscient point of view *see* **point of view**.

onomatopoeia a word capturing or approximating the sound of what it describes; *buzz* is a good example.

orchestra in classical Greek theater, a semicircular area used mostly for dancing by the **chorus**.

ottava rima literally, "octave (eighth) rhyme" (Italian); a verse form consisting of eight-line **stanzas** with an *abababcc* **rhyme scheme** and **iambic** meter (usually **pentameter**). W. B. Yeats's "Sailing to Byzantium" is written in ottava rima.

overplot especially in Shakespearean drama, a **subplot** that resembles the main plot but stresses the political implications of the depicted action and situation.

overstatement exaggerated language; also called *hyperbole*.

oxymoron a **figure of speech** that combines two apparently contradictory elements, as in *wise fool*.

parable a short work of **fiction** that illustrates an explicit **moral** but that, unlike a **fable**, lacks fantastic or anthropomorphic characters. Especially familiar examples are the stories attributed to Jesus in the Bible—about the prodigal son, the good Samaritan, and so on.

parody any work that imitates or spoofs another work or **genre** for comic effect by exaggerating the style and changing the content of the original; parody is a subgenre of **satire**. Examples include *Scary Movie*, which parodies horror films; *The Colbert Report*, which spoofs conservative talk shows; and Tom Stoppard's *Real Inspector Hound*, a parody of detective fiction and drama.

particular setting *see* **setting**.

pastoral literature a work or category of works—whether fiction, poetry, drama, or nonfiction—describing and idealizing the simple life of country folk, usually shepherds who live a painless life in a world full of beauty, music, and love. An example is Christopher Marlowe's "The Passionate Shepherd to His Love."

pentameter a line of poetry with five **feet**: "Nuns fret | not at | their con- | vent's nar- | row room."

persona the voice or figure of the **author** who tells and structures the work and who may or may not share the values of the actual author. *See also* **author**.

personification a **figure of speech** that involves treating something nonhuman, such as an abstraction, as if it were a person by endowing it with humanlike qualities, as in "Death entered the room."

Petrarchan sonnet *see* **sonnet**.

plot the arrangement of the **action**. The five main parts or phases of plot are **exposition**, rising **action**, **climax** or turning point, **falling action**, and **conclusion** or resolution. *See also* **subplot**, **overplot**.

plot summary a brief recounting of the principal **action** of a work of fiction, drama, or narrative poetry, usually in the same order in which the action is recounted in the original work rather than in chronological order.

plot time *see* **time**.

poetry one of the three major **genres** of imaginative literature, which has its origins in music and oral performance and is characterized by controlled patterns of **rhythm** and **syntax** (often using **meter** and **rhyme**); compression and compactness and an allowance for ambiguity; a particularly concentrated emphasis on the sensual, especially visual and aural, qualities and effects of words and word order; and especially vivid, often **figurative language**.

point of view the perspective from which people, events, and other details in a work of fiction are viewed; also called **focus**, though the term *point of view* usually includes both focus and **voice**. See **narrator**.

prop in drama, an object used on the stage.

proscenium arch an arch over the front of a stage; the proscenium serves as a "frame" for the **action** onstage.

prose the regular form of spoken and written language, measured in sentences rather than lines, as in poetry.

protagonist the most neutral and broadly applicable term for the main **character** in a work, whether male or female, heroic or not heroic. *See also* **antagonist**, **antihero**, and **hero/heroine**.

psychological realism *see* **realism**.

pyrrhic a rarely used metrical **foot** consisting of two unstressed syllables.

quatrain a four-line unit of verse, whether an entire poem, a **stanza**, or a group of four lines linked by a pattern of rhyme (as in an English or Shakespearean **sonnet**).

reader time *see* **time**.

realism (1) generally, the practice in literature, especially fiction and drama, of attempting to describe nature and life as they are without idealization and with attention to detail, especially the everyday life of ordinary people. *See also* **verisimilitude**.

Just as notions of how life and nature differ widely across cultures and time periods, however, so do notions of what is "realistic." Thus, there are many different kinds of realism. *Psychological realism* refers, broadly, to any literary attempt to accurately represent the workings of the human mind and, more specifically, to the practice of a particular group of late-nineteenth- and early-twentieth-century writers including Joseph Conrad, Henry James, James Joyce, and Virginia Woolf, who developed the **stream of consciousness** technique of depicting the flow of thought. *See also* **magic realism**.

(2) more narrowly and especially when capitalized, a mid- to late-nineteenth-century literary and artistic movement, mainly in the U.S. and Europe, that championed realism in the first, more general sense, rejected what its proponents saw as the elitism and idealism of earlier literature and art, and emphasized **settings**, situations, **action**, and (especially middle- and working-class) characters ignored or belittled in earlier literature and art. Writers associated with the movement include Gustave Flaubert and Emile Zola (in France), George Eliot and Thomas Hardy (in Britain), and Theodore Dreiser (in the United States).

resolution *see* **conclusion**.

rhetoric the art and scholarly study of effective communication, whether in writing or speech. Many literary terms, especially those for **figures of speech**, derive from classical and Renaissance rhetoric.

rhyme repetition or correspondence of the terminal sounds of words ("H*ow* n*ow*, br*own* c*ow*?"). The most common type, *end rhyme*, occurs when the last words in two or more lines of a poem rhyme with each other. *Internal rhyme* occurs when a word *within* a line of poetry rhymes with another word in the same or adjacent lines, as in "The D*ew* dr*ew* quivering and chill" (Dickinson). An *eye rhyme* or *sight rhyme* involves words that don't actually rhyme but look like they do because of their similar spelling ("cough" and "bough"). *Off, half, near,* or *slant rhyme* is rhyme that is slightly "off" or only approximate, usually because words' final consonant sounds correspond, but not the vowels that proceed them ("phases" and "houses"). When two syllables rhyme and the last is unstressed or unaccented, they create a *feminine rhyme* ("ocean" and "motion"); *masculine rhyme* involves only a single stressed or accented syllable ("cat" and "hat"). *See also* **rhyme scheme**.

rhyme scheme the pattern of *end* **rhymes** in a poem, often noted by small letters, such as *abab* or *abba*.

rhythm the modulation of weak and strong (or stressed and unstressed) elements in the flow of speech. In most poetry written before the twentieth century, rhythm was often expressed in **meter**; in prose and in **free verse**, rhythm is present but in a much less predictable and regular manner.

rising action the second of the five phases or parts of **plot**, in which events complicate the **situation** that existed at the beginning of a work, intensifying the initial **conflict** or introducing a new one.

romance (1) originally, a long medieval narrative in verse or prose written in one of the Romance languages (French, Spanish, Italian, etc.) and depicting the quests of knights and other chivalric heroes and the vicissitudes of courtly love; also known as *chivalric romance*; (2) later and more broadly, any literary work, especially a long work of prose fiction, characterized by a nonrealistic and idealizing use of the imagination; (3) commonly today, works of prose fiction aimed at a mass, primarily female, audience and focusing on love affairs (as in *Harlequin Romance*).

round character *see* **character**.

sarcasm *see* **irony**.

satire a literary work—whether fiction, poetry, or drama—that holds up human failings to ridicule and censure. Examples include Jonathan Swift's novel *Gulliver's Travels* and Stanley Kubrick's film *Dr. Strangelove*.

scansion the process of analyzing (and sometimes also marking) verse to determine its **meter**, line by line.

scapegoat in a work of literature, the character or characters that take the blame for others' actions; usually an innocent party or only tangentially responsible, their punishment lets others off the hook.

scene a section or subdivision of a play or **narrative** that presents continuous **action** in one specific **setting**.

second-person narrator *see* **narrator**.

sequence (1) the ordering of **action** in a fictional **plot**; (2) a closely linked series or *cycle* of individual literary works, especially short stories or poems, designed to be read or performed together, as in the **sonnet** sequences of William Shakespeare and Edna St. Vincent Millay.

sestet six lines of verse linked by a pattern of **rhyme**, as in the last six lines of the Italian, or Petrarchan, **sonnet**. *See also* **octave**.

sestina an elaborate verse structure written in **blank verse** that consists of six **stanzas** of six lines each followed by a three-line stanza. The final words of each line in the first stanza appear in variable order in the next five stanzas and are repeated in the middle and at the end of the three lines in the final stanza. Elizabeth Bishop's "Sestina" is an example.

set the design, decoration, and scenery of the stage during a play; not to be confused with **setting**.

setting the time and place of the **action** in a work of fiction, poetry, or drama. The *spatial setting* is the place or places in which action unfolds, the *temporal setting* is the time. (Temporal setting is thus the same as *plot* **time**.) It is sometimes also helpful to distinguish between *general setting*—the general time and place in which all the action unfolds—and *particular settings*—the times and places in which individual **episodes** or **scenes** take place. The film version of *Gone with the Wind*, for example, is generally set in Civil War–era Georgia, while its opening scene takes place on the porch of Tara, Scarlett O'Hara's family home, before the war begins.

Shakespearean sonnet *see* **sonnet**.

shaped verse *see* **concrete poetry**.

short short story *see* **short story**.

short story a relatively short work of prose **fiction** (approximately 500 to 10,000 words) that, according to Edgar Allan Poe, can be read in a single sitting of two hours or less and works to create "a single effect." Two types of short story are the **initiation story** and the *short short story*. (Also sometimes called *microfiction*, a short short story is, as its name suggests, a short story that is especially brief; examples include Linda Brewer's "20/20" and Jamaica Kincaid's "Girl.")

simile a **figure of speech** involving a direct, explicit comparison of one thing to another, usually using the words *like* or *as* to draw the connection, as in "My love is like a red, red rose." An *analogy* is an extended simile. *See also* **metaphor**.

situation the basic circumstances depicted in a literary work, especially when the story, play, or poem begins or at a specific later moment in the **action**. In John Keats's "Ode to a Nightingale," for example, the situation involves a man (the **speaker**) sitting under a tree as he listens to a nightingale's song.

situational irony *see* **irony**.

skene a low building in the back of the stage area in classical Greek theaters. It represented the palace or temple in front of which the **action** took place.

soliloquy a **monologue** in which the **character** in a play is alone onstage and thinking out loud, as in the famous Hamlet speech that begins "To be or not to be."

sonnet a fixed verse form consisting of fourteen lines usually in **iambic pentameter**. An *Italian sonnet* consists of eight rhyme-linked lines (an **octave**) plus six rhyme-linked lines (a **sestet**), often with either an *abbaabba cdecde* or *abbacddc defdef* **rhyme scheme**. This type of sonnet is also called the *Petrarchan sonnet* in honor of the Italian poet Petrarch (1304–74). An *English* or *Shakespearean sonnet* instead consists of three **quatrains** (four-line units) and a **couplet** and often rhymes *abab cdcd efef gg*.

spatial setting *see* **setting**.

speaker (1) the person who is the voice of a poem; (2) anyone who speaks **dialogue** in a work of fiction, poetry, or drama.

Spenserian stanza a **stanza** consisting of eight lines of **iambic pentameter** (five **feet**) followed by a ninth line of iambic **hexameter** (six feet). The rhyme scheme is *ababbcbcc*. The stanza form takes its name from Edmund Spenser (ca. 1552–99), who used it in *The Faerie Queene*.

spondee a metrical **foot** consisting of a pair of stressed syllables ("Déad sét").

stage directions the words in the printed text of a play that inform the director, crew, actors, and readers how to stage, perform, or imagine the play. Stage directions are not spoken aloud and may appear at the beginning of a play, before any scene, or attached to a line of dialogue; they are often set in italics. The place and time of the action, the design of the set itself, and at times the characters' actions or tone of voice are given through stage directions and interpreted by the group of people who put on a performance.

stanza a section of a poem, marked by extra line spacing before and after, that often has a single pattern of **meter** and/or **rhyme**. Conventional stanza forms include **ballad stanza**, **Spenserian stanza**, **ottava rima**, and **terza rima**. *See also* **verse paragraph**.

static character *see* **character**.

stock character *see* **character**.

stream of consciousness a type of third-person **narration** that replicates the thought processes of a **character** without much or any intervention by a **narrator**. The term was originally coined by the nineteenth-century American psychologist William James (brother of novelist Henry James) to describe the workings of the human mind and only later adopted to describe the type of narration that seeks to replicate this process. The technique is closely associated with twentieth-century fiction writers of *psychological* **realism** such as Virginia Woolf, James Joyce, and William Faulkner, who were all heavily influenced by early psychologists such as William James and Sigmund Freud.

style a distinctive manner of expression; each author's style is expressed through his or her **diction**, **rhythm**, **imagery**, and so on.

subgenre *see* **genre**.

subplot a secondary **plot** in a work of fiction or drama. *See also* **overplot** and **underplot**.

symbol a person, place, thing, or event that figuratively represents or stands for something else. Often the thing or idea represented is more abstract and general, and the symbol is more concrete and particular. A *traditional symbol* is one that recurs frequently in (and beyond) literature and is thus immediately recognizable to those who belong to a given culture. In Western literature and culture, for example, the rose and snake traditionally symbolize love and evil, respectively. Other symbols such as the scarlet letter in Nathaniel Hawthorne's *The Scarlet Letter* instead accrue their complex meanings only within a particular literary work; these are sometimes called *invented symbols*.

symbolic poem a poem in which the use of symbols is so pervasive and internally consistent that the reference to the outside world being symbolized becomes secondary. William Blake's "The Sick Rose" and W. B. Yeats's "Second Coming" are examples.

synecdoche a type of **metonymy** in which the part is used to name or stand in for the whole, as when we refer to manual laborers as *hands* or say *wheels* to mean a car.

syntax word order; the way words are put together to form phrases, clauses, and sentences.

tale a brief **narrative** with a simple **plot** and **characters**, an ancient and originally oral form of storytelling. Unlike **fables**, tales typically don't convey or state a simple or single **moral**. An especially common type of tale is the *folktale*, the **conventions** of which include a formulaic beginning and ending ("Once upon a time . . . ," ". . . And so they lived happily ever after."); a **setting** that is not highly particularized in terms of time or place; *flat* and often *stock characters*, animal or human; and fairly simple **plots**. Though the term *fairy tale* is often and broadly used as a synonym for *folktale*, it more narrowly and properly designates a specific type of folktale featuring fairies or other fantastic creatures such as pixies or ogres.

temporal setting *see* **setting**.

terza rima literally, "third rhyme" (Italian); a verse form consisting of three-line **stanzas** in which the second line of each stanza rhymes with the first and third of the next. Percy Bysshe Shelley's "Ode to the West Wind" is written in terza rima.

tetrameter a line of poetry with four **feet**: "The Grass | divides | as with | a comb" (Dickinson).

theme (1) broadly and commonly, a topic explored in a literary work (e.g., "the value of all life"); (2) more narrowly and properly, the insight about a topic communicated in a work (e.g., "All living things are equally precious"). Most literary works have multiple themes, though some people reserve the term *theme* for the central or main insight and refer to others as *subthemes*. Usually, a theme is implicitly communicated by the work as a whole rather than explicitly stated in it, though **fables** are an exception. *See also* **moral**.

thesis the central debatable claim articulated, supported, and developed in an essay or other work of expository prose.

third-person narrator *see* **narrator**.

thrust stage a stage design that allows the audience to sit around three sides of the major acting area.

time in literature, at least four potentially quite different time frames are at issue: (1) *author time*, when the author originally created or published a literary text; (2) *narrator time*, when the **narrator** in a work of fiction supposedly narrated the story; (3) *plot time*, when the **action** depicted in the work supposedly took place (in other words, the work's temporal **setting**); and (4) *reader* (or *audience*) *time*, when an actual reader reads the work or an actual audience sees it performed.

In some cases, author, narrator, plot, and reader time will be roughly the same—as when, for example, in 2008 we read Sherman Alexie's "Flight Patterns," a story published in 2003; set some time after September 11, 2001; and presumably narrated not long after the action ends. But in some cases, some or all of these time frames might differ. Walter Scott's novel *Rob Roy*, for example, was written and published in the early nineteenth century (1817); this is its author time. But the novel (a work of **historical fiction**) is set one hundred years earlier (1715); this is its plot time. The novel's narrator is a **character** supposedly writing down the story of his youthful adventures in his old age and long after the deaths of many of the principal characters; this is the narrator time. Were you to read the novel today, reader time would be almost two hundred years later than author time and almost three hundred years later than plot time.

tone the attitude a literary work takes toward its subject, especially the way this attitude is revealed through **diction**.

traditional symbol *see* **symbol**.

tragedy a work, especially of drama, in which a **character** (traditionally a good and noble person of high rank) is brought to a disastrous end in his or her confrontation with a superior force (fortune, the gods, human nature, universal values), but also comes to understand the meaning of his or her deeds and to accept an appropriate punishment. In some cases, the **protagonist**'s downfall can be direct result of a fatal but common character flaw. Examples include Sophocles's *Antigone*, William Shakespeare's *Hamlet*, and Wole Soyinka's *Death and the King's Horseman*.

trimeter a line of poetry with three **feet**: "Little | lamb, who | made thee?" (Blake).

trochaic referring to a metrical form in which the basic **foot** is a *trochee*—a metrical foot consisting of a stressed syllable followed by an unstressed one ("Hómer").

trope *see* **figure of speech**.

turning point *see* **climax**.

underplot a particular type of **subplot**, especially in Shakespeare's plays, that is a parodic or highly romantic version of the main plot. A good example would be the subplot in *A Midsummer Night's Dream* that features the character Bottom. *See also* **overplot**.

understatement language that makes its point by self-consciously downplaying its real emphasis, as in "Final exams aren't exactly a walk in the park"; **litotes** is one form of understatement. *See also* **overstatement**.

unity of action *see* **classical unities**.

unity of place *see* **classical unities**.

unity of time *see* **classical unities**.

unlimited point of view *see* **point of view**.

unreliable narrator *see* **narrator**.

verbal irony *see* **irony**.

verisimilitude from the Latin phrase *veri similes* ("like the truth"); the internal truthfulness, lifelikeness, and consistency of the world created within any literary work when we judge that world on its own terms rather than in terms of its correspondence to the real world. Thus, even a work that contains utterly fantastic or supernatural **characters** or **actions** (and doesn't aim at **realism**) may very well achieve a high degree of verisimilitude.

verse drama *see* **drama**.

verse novel *see* **novel**.

verse paragraph though sometimes used as a synonym for **stanza**, this term technically designates passages of verse, often beginning with an indented line, that are unified by topic (as in a prose paragraph) rather than by **rhyme** or **meter**.

villain a **character** who not only opposes the **hero** or **heroine** (and is thus an **antagonist**) but also is characterized as an especially evil person or "bad guy."

villanelle a verse form consisting of nineteen lines divided into six **stanzas**—five tercets (three-line stanzas) and one quatrain (four-line stanza). The first and third lines of the first tercet rhyme with each other, and this rhyme is repeated through each of the next four tercets and in the last two lines of the concluding **quatrain**. The villanelle is also known for its repetition of select lines. An example is Dylan Thomas's "Do Not Go Gentle into That Good Night."

voice the verbal aspect of **point of view**, the acknowledged or unacknowledged source of a story's words; the **speaker**; the "person" telling the story and that person's particular qualities of insight, attitude, and verbal style. *See also* **focus**.

Permissions Acknowledgments

TEXT CREDITS

Fiction

Sherman Alexie: "Flight Patterns" from TEN LITTLE INDIANS, copyright © 2003 by Sherman Alexie. Used by permission of Grove/Atlantic, Inc. Any third party use of this material, outside of this publication, is prohibited.

Margaret Atwood: "Lusus Naturae" from STONE MATTRESS: NINE TALES, compilation copyright © 2014 by O.W. Toad, Ltd. Used by permission of Nan A. Talese, an imprint of the Knopf Doubleday Publishing Group, a division of Penguin Random House LLC. All rights reserved. Any third party use of this material, outside of this publication, is prohibited. Interested parties must apply directly to Penguin Random House LLC for permission. Rights in Canada by permission of McClelland & Stewart, a division of Penguin Random House Canada Limited, a Penguin Random House Company. "Happy Endings" from GOOD BONES AND SIMPLE MURDERS by Margaret Atwood, copyright © 1983, 1992, 1994 by O.W. Toad Ltd., a Nan Talese Book. Used by permission of Nan A. Talese, an imprint of the Knopf Doubleday Publishing Group, a division of Penguin Random House LLC. All rights reserved. Any third party use of this material, outside of this publication, is prohibited. Interested parties must apply directly to Penguin Random House LLC for permission. Rights in Canada by permission of McClelland & Stewart, a division of Penguin Random House Canada Limited, a Penguin Random House Company.

James Baldwin: "Sonny's Blues" copyright © 1957 by James Baldwin was originally published in *Partisan Review*. Copyright renewed. Collected in GOING TO MEET THE MAN, published by Vintage Books. Reprinted by arrangement with the James Baldwin Estate.

Toni Cade Bambara: "The Lesson" from GORILLA, MY LOVE by Toni Cade Bambara, copyright © 1972 by Toni Cade Bambara. Used by permission of Random House, an imprint and division of Penguin Random House LLC. All rights reserved. Any third party use of this material, outside of this publication, is prohibited. Interested parties must apply directly to Penguin Random House LLC for permission.

Jorge Luis Borges: "The House of Asterion" from COLLECTED FICTIONS, trans. by Andrew Hurley, copyright © 1998 by Maria Kodama. Translation and notes copyright © 1998 by Penguin Random House LLC. Used by permission of Viking Books, an imprint of Penguin Publishing Group, a division of Penguin Random House LLC and Penguin Canada, a division of Penguin Random House Canada Limited.

Ray Bradbury: "The Veldt" by Ray Bradbury, first published in *The Saturday Evening Post*, is reprinted by permission of Don Congdon Associates, Inc. Copyright © 1950 by the Curtis Publishing Company, renewed 1977 by Ray Bradbury.

Linda Brewer: "20/20" from MICRO FICTION: AN ANTHOLOGY OF REALLY SHORT STORIES, ed. by Jerome Stern. Reprinted by permission of the author.

A.S. Byatt: "The Thing in the Forest" from LITTLE BLACK BOOK OF STORIES by A.S. Byatt, copyright © 2003 by A.S. Byatt. Used by permission of the publisher Alfred A. Knopf, an imprint of the Knopf Doubleday Publishing Group, a division of Penguin Random House LLC. All rights reserved. Any third party use of this material, outside of this publication, is prohibited. Interested parties must apply directly to Penguin Random House LLC for permission. Rights in Canada and EU by permission of The Random House Group Limited. Published in Great Britain by Chatto & Windus.

Raymond Carver: "Cathedral" from CATHEDRAL by Raymond Carver, copyright © 1981, 1982, 1983 by Raymond Carver. Used by permission of Alfred A. Knopf, an imprint of the Knopf Doubleday

Publishing Group, a division of Penguin Random House LLC. All rights reserved. Any third party use of this material, outside of this publication, is prohibited. Interested parties must apply directly to Penguin Random House LLC for permission.

Maximus Clarke: excerpt from "Maximus Clarke talks with William Gibson about his 'speculative novels of last Wednesday'" Sept. 22, 2010, online post. Reprinted by permission of Maximus Clarke.

Judith Ortiz Cofer: "Volar" from THE YEAR OF OUR REVOLUTION. Copyright © 1998 by Arte Publico Press-University of Houston. Reprinted with permission of the publisher.

Edwidge Danticat: "A Wall of Fire Rising" from KRIK? KRAK! by Edwidge Danticat, copyright © 1991, 1955 by Edwidge Danticat. Used by permission of Soho Press, Inc. All rights reserved.

Junot Díaz: "Wildwood 1982–1985" from THE BRIEF WONDROUS LIFE OF OSCAR WAO, copyright © 2007 by Junot Díaz. Used by permission of Riverhead, an imprint of Penguin Publishing Group, a division of Penguin Random House LLC.

Jennifer Egan: "Black Box" and "Coming Soon: Jennifer Egan's 'Black Box'" first published in *The New Yorker*. Copyright © 2012 by Jennifer Egan. Used by permission. All rights reserved.

Ralph Ellison: "King of the Bingo Game" by Ralph Ellison, copyright © 1996 by Fanny Ellison, from FLYING HOME AND OTHER STORIES by Ralph Ellison. Used by permission of Random House, an imprint and division of Penguin Random House LLC. All rights reserved. Any third party use of this material, outside of this publication, is prohibited. Interested parties must apply directly to Penguin Random House LLC for permission.

Louise Erdrich: "Love Medicine" from LOVE MEDICINE (new and expanded version) by Louise Erdrich. Copyright © 1984, 1993 by Louise Erdrich. Reprinted by arrangement with Henry Holt and Company, LLC. All rights reserved.

Susan Farrell: "Tim O'Brien and Gender: A Defense of 'The Things They Carried.'" CEA Critic 66:1 (2003), 1–4, 19–20. Copyright © 2003 College English Association. Reprinted with permission of Johns Hopkins University Press.

William Faulkner: "Barn Burning" and "A Rose for Emily" from COLLECTED STORIES OF WILLIAM FAULKNER by William Faulkner. Copyright © 1950 by Random House, Inc., and renewed 1977 by Jill Faulkner Summers. Reprinted by permission of W.W. Norton and Company

Gabriel García Márquez: "A Very Old Man with Enormous Wings" from LEAF STORM AND OTHER STORIES by Gabriel García Márquez, trans. by Gregory Rabassa. Copyright © 1971 by Gabriel García Márquez. Reprinted by permission of HarperCollins Publishers.

William Gibson, "The Gernsback Continuum" from BURNING CHROME (1986) is reprinted by permission of The Martha Millard Literary Agency. Copyright © 1986 by William Gibson.

Mary Gordon: From "Flannery's Kiss" is reprinted by permission of SLL/Sterling Lord Literistic, Inc. Copyright by Mary Gordon.

Ernest Hemingway: "Hills Like White Elephants" is reprinted with the permission of Scribner, a division of Simon & Schuster, Inc., from MEN WITHOUT WOMEN by Ernest Hemingway. Copyright © 1927 by Charles Scribner's Sons. Copyright © renewed 1955 by Ernest Hemingway. All rights reserved.

Robert Jacobs, Dave Truesdale, and Bob Wayne: Excerpts from "Tangent Online Presents: An Interview with Ray Bradbury" originally published in Tangent #5, Summer 1976. Copyright © by Robert Jacobs and Tangent/Tangent Online. Reprinted by permission of Dave Truesdale and Robert Jacobs.

Franz Kafka: "A Hunger Artist" from THE COMPLETE STORIES, copyright © 1946, 1947, 1948, 1949, 1954, 1958, 1971 by Schocken Books, an imprint of the Knopf Doubleday Group, a division of Random House LLC. Used by permission of Schocken Books, an imprint of the Knopf Doubleday Publishing Group, a division of Penguin Random House LLC. All rights reserved. Any third party use of this material, outside of this publication, is prohibited. Interested parties must apply directly to Penguin Random House LLC for permission. "The Metamorphosis" from THE METAMORPHOSIS: A NEW TRANSLATION by Franz Kafka, trans. by Susan Bernofsky. Copyright © 2014 by Susan Bernofsky. Used by permission of W.W. Norton & Company, Inc.

Steve Kaplan: From "The Undying Certainty of the Narrator in Tim O'Brien's 'The Things They Carried'" from *Critique: Studies in Contemporary Fiction* 35.1 (Fall 1993). Reprinted by permission of the publisher, Taylor & Francis Ltd., http://www.tandfonline.com

Yasunari Kawabata: "The Grasshopper and the Bell Cricket" from PALM-OF-THE-HAND STORIES by Yasunari Kawabata. Translated by Lane Dunlop and J. Martin Holman. Translation copyright ©

1988 by Lane Dunlop and J. Martin Holman. Reprinted by permission of North Point Press, a division of Farrar, Straus & Giroux, LLC.

Jamaica Kincaid: "Girl" from AT THE BOTTOM OF THE RIVER by Jamaica Kincaid. Copyright © 1983 by Jamaica Kincaid. Reprinted by permission of Farrar, Straus & Giroux, LLC.

Jhumpa Lahiri: "Interpreter of Maladies" from INTERPRETER OF MALADIES. Copyright © 1999 by Jhumpa Lahiri. Reprinted by permission of Houghton Mifflin Harcourt Publishing Company. All rights reserved.

D. H. Lawrence: "The Rocking-Horse Winner," copyright 1933 by the Estate of D. H. Lawrence, renewed © 1961 by Angelo Ravagli and C.M. Weekley, Executors of the Estate of Frieda Lawrence, from COMPLETE SHORT STORIES OF D.H. LAWRENCE by D. H. Lawrence. Used by permission of Viking Books, an imprint of Penguin Publishing Group, a division of Penguin Random House LLC.

Ursula K. Le Guin: "The Ones Who Walk Away from Omelas." Copyright © 1973 by Ursula K. Le Guin; first appeared in NEW DIMENSIONS, 3 in 1973 and collected in THE WIND'S TWELVE QUARTERS (HarperCollins 1975). Reprinted by permission of Curtis Brown Ltd.

Bobbie Ann Mason: "Shiloh" from SHILOH AND OTHER STORIES by Bobbie Ann Mason. Copyright © 1982 by Bobbie Ann Mason. Reprinted by permission. All rights reserved

Patrick A. McCarthy: From the "Introduction" by Patrick A. McCarthy from REJOYCING: NEW READINGS OF DUBLINERS, ed. by Rosa M. Boliettieri Bosinelli and Harold F. Mosher, Jr. Copyright © 1998 by The University Press of Kentucky. Reprinted by permission of the publisher.

Leonard Michaels: From "Conversation with Grace Paley" by Leonard Michaels from The *Threepenny Review*, 3 (Autumn 1980): 4–6, is reprinted by permission of Katharine Ogden Michaels.

Toni Morrison: "Recitatif," copyright © 2015 by Toni Morrison. Used by permission. All rights reserved.

Bharati Mukherjee: "The Management of Grief" from THE MIDDLEMAN AND OTHER STORIES by Bharati Mukherjee, copyright © 1988 by Bharati Mukherjee. Used by permission of Grove/Atlantic, Inc. Any third party use of this material, outside of this publication, is prohibited.

Alice Munro: "Boys and Girls" from DANCE OF THE HAPPY SHADES: AND OTHER STORIES by Alice Munro is reprinted by permission of the author. Copyright © 1968 by Alice Munro.

Alissa Nutting: "Model's Assistant" from UNCLEAN JOBS FOR WOMEN AND GIRLS (Starcherone Books, 2010) is reprinted by permission of the publisher. Copyright © 2010 by Alissa Nutting.

Joyce Carol Oates: "Where Are You Going, Where Have You Been?" from HIGH LONESOME: NEW AND SELECTED STORIES 1966–2006, pp. 267–283. Copyright © 2006 by Ontario Review, Inc. Reprinted by permission of HarperCollins Publishers. From "Where Are You Going, Where Have You Been? And Smooth Talk: Short Story into Film" from WOMAN WRITER: OCCASIONS AND OPPORTUNITIES. Copyright © 1988 by The Ontario Review, Inc. Used by permission of Dutton, an imprint of Penguin Publishing Group, a division of Random House LLC.

Tim O'Brien: "The Lives of The Dead" and "The Things They Carried" from THE THINGS THEY CARRIED. Copyright © 1990 by Tim O'Brien. Reprinted by permission of Houghton Mifflin Harcourt Publishing Company. All rights reserved.

Flannery O'Connor: Excerpts from THE HABIT OF BEING: LETTERS OF FLANNERY O'CONNOR, edited by Sally Fitzgerald. Copyright © 1979 by Regina O'Connor. Excerpts from MYSTERY AND MANNERS by Flannery O'Connor. Copyright © 1969 by the Estate of Mary Flannery O'Connor. "Everything That Rises Must Converge" from THE COMPLETE STORIES by Flannery O'Connor. Copyright © 1965 by the Estate of Mary Flannery O'Connor. Copyright renewed 1993 by Regina O'Connor. Reprinted by permission of Farrar, Straus & Giroux, LLC. "A Good Man is Hard to Find" and "Good Country People" are reprinted from A GOOD MAN IS HARD TO FIND AND OTHER STORIES by permission of Houghton Mifflin Harcourt Publishing Company. Copyright © 1955 by Flannery O'Connor and renewed 1983 by Regina O'Connor. All rights reserved.

Tillie Olsen: "I Stand Here Ironing" from TELL ME A RIDDLE, reprinted by permission of the University of Nebraska Press. Copyright © 1956 by Tillie Olsen. Rights outside North America by permission of The Frances Goldin Literary Agency. Copyright © 1961 by Tillie Olsen.

Grace Paley: "A Conversation with My Father" from ENORMOUS CHANGES AT THE LAST MINUTE by Grace Paley. Copyright © 1971, 1974 by Grace Paley. Reprinted by permission of Farrar, Straus & Giroux, LLC.

Eileen Pollack: From "Flannery O'Connor and the New Criticism" from *American Literary History* 19:2 (2007) is reprinted by permission of Oxford University Press. Copyright © 2007 by Eileen Pollack.

Annie Proulx: "Job History" is reprinted with the permission of Scribner, a division of Simon & Schuster, Inc., from CLOSE RANGE: WYOMING STORIES by Annie Proulx. Copyright © 1999 by Dead Line Ltd. All rights reserved.

Ann E. Reuman: From "Revolting Fictions" by Ann E. Reuman first published in *Papers on Language and Literature*, vol.29, # 2, Spring 1993. Copyright © 1993 by The Board of Trustees, Southern Illinois University Edwardsville. Reprinted by permission.

Karen Russell: From ST LUCY'S HOME FOR GIRLS RAISED BY WOLVES, copyright © 2006 by Karen Russell. Used by permission of Alfred A. Knopf, an imprint of the Knopf Doubleday Publishing Group, a division of Penguin Random House LLC. All rights reserved. Any third party use of this material, outside of this publication, is prohibited. Interested parties must apply directly to Penguin Random House LLC for permission.

Marjane Satrapi: "The Shabbat" from PERSEPOLIS: THE STORY OF A CHILDHOOD by Marjane Satrapi, trans. by Mattias Ripa & Blake Ferris, translation copyright © 2003 by L'Association, Paris, France. Used by permission of Pantheon Books, an imprint of the Knopf Doubleday Publishing Group, a division of Penguin Random House LLC. All rights reserved. Any third party use of this material, outside of this publication, is prohibited. Interested parties must apply directly to Penguin Random House LLC for permission.

George Saunders: "Puppy" first published in *The New Yorker*, May 28, 2007, is reprinted by permission of the author. Copyright © 2007 by George Saunders.

David Sedaris: "Jesus Shaves" from ME TALK PRETTY ONE DAY by David Sedaris. Copyright © 2000 by David Sedaris. By permission of Little, Brown and Company. All rights reserved.

Lorrie N. Smith, From "The Things Men Do": The Gendered Subtext in Tim O'Brien's Esquire Stories from *Critique: Studies in Contemporary Fiction* 35.1 (Fall 1993). Reprinted by permission of the publisher, Taylor & Francis Ltd., http://www.tandfonline.com

Zadie Smith: "Meet the President," copyright © 2013 by Zadie Smith. First published in The New Yorker, 2013. Reproduced with the permission of the author c/o Rogers, Coleridge & White Ltd., 20 Powis Mews, London W11 1JN.

Amy Tan: "A Pair of Tickets" from THE JOY LUCK CLUB by Amy Tan, copyright © 1989 by Amy Tan. Used by permission of G.P. Putnam's Sons, an imprint of Penguin Publishing Group, a division of Penguin Random House LLC.

John Updike: "A & P" from PIGEON FEATHERS AND OTHER STORIES by John Updike, copyright © 1962 and renewed 1990 by John Updike. Used by permission of Alfred A. Knopf, an imprint of the Knopf Doubleday Publishing Group, a division of Penguin Random House LLC. All rights reserved. Any third party use of this material, outside of this publication, is prohibited. Interested parties must apply directly to Penguin Random House LLC for permission.

Matthew Vollmer: From "Knowable in the Smallest Fragment: An Interview with George Saunders" from *Gutcult*, online, June 14, 2011. Reprinted by permission of Matthew Vollmer.

David Foster Wallace: "Good People" originally published in *The New Yorker*, Feb. 5, 2007. Copyright © 2007 by David Foster Wallace. Used by permission of the David Foster Wallace Literary Trust.

Eudora Welty: "Why I Live at the P.O." from A CURTAIN OF GREEN AND OTHER STORIES, copyright 1941 and renewed 1969 by Eudora Welty, reprinted by permission of Houghton Mifflin Harcourt Publishing Company. All rights reserved.

Edith Wharton: "Roman Fever" is reprinted with permission of Scribner, a Division of Simon & Schuster, Inc. from ROMAN FEVER AND OTHER STORIES by Edith Wharton. Copyright © 1934 by Liberty Magazine. Copyright © renewed 1962 by William R. Tyler. All rights reserved.

Poetry

Kim Addonizio, "First Line is the Deepest" from LUCIFER AT THE STARLIGHT. Copyright © 2009 by Kim Addonizio. Reprinted by permission of W.W. Norton & Company, Inc.

Agha Shahid Ali: "Postcard from Kashmir" from THE HALF-INCH HIMALAYAS by Agha Shahid Ali. Copyright © 1987 by Wesleyan University Press. Reprinted by permission of the publisher. "The Wolf's

Postscript to 'Little Red Riding Hood'" from THE VEILED SUITE: THE COLLECTED POEMS. Copyright © 1987 by Agha Shahid Ali. Reprinted by permission of W.W. Norton & Company, Inc.

Elizabeth Alexander: "Ars Poetica # 100: I Believe" from CRAVE RADIANCE: NEW AND SELECTED POEMS. Copyright © 2005 by Elizabeth Alexander. Reprinted with the permission of The Permissions Company, Inc. on behalf of Graywolf Press, www.graywolfpress.org.

Sherman Alexie: "The Facebook Sonnet" first published in *The New Yorker*, May 16, 2011. Copyright © 2011 by Sherman Alexie. All rights reserved. Reprinted by permission of Nancy Stauffer Associates. "Grief Calls Us to the Things of This World" from FACE, copyright © 2009 by Sherman Alexie. Reprinted by permission of Hanging Loose Press.

Al Alvarez: From "Sylvia Plath" from BEYOND ALL THIS FIDDLE: ESSAYS 1955–1967. Copyright © 1968 by Al Alvarez. Reprinted by permission of the author and Aitken Alexander Associates Ltd.

Julia Alvarez: "Poetry Makes Nothing Happen?" first published in CRY OUT: POETS PROTEST THE WAY (Braziller 2003). Copyright © 2003 by Julia Alvarez. By permission of Susan Bergholz Literary Services, New York, NY and Lamy, NM. All rights reserved.

Yehuda Amichai: Excerpt from "Jerusalem 1967" trans. by Stephen Mitchell from THE SELECTED POETRY OF YEHUDA AMICHAI, trans. by Chana Bloch and Stephen Mitchell. Copyright © 1986, 1996, 2013 by Chana Bloch and Stephen Mitchell. Reprinted by permission of the University of California Press via the Copyright Clearance Center

Maya Angelou: "Africa," copyright © 1975 by Maya Angelou, from OH PRAY MY WINGS ARE GONNA FIT ME WELL by Maya Angelou. Used by permission of Random House, an imprint and division of Penguin Random House LLC. All rights reserved. Any third party use of this material, outside of this publication, is prohibited. Interested parties must apply directly to Penguin Random House LLC for permission.

Pamela J. Annas: From A DISTURBANCE IN MIRRORS: THE POETRY OF SYLVIA PLATH. Copyright © 1988 by Pamela J. Annas. Reproduced with permission of Greenwood Press and ABC-CLIO, LLC via the Copyright Clearance Center.

Margaret Atwood: "Death of a Young Son by Drowning" from THE JOURNALS OF SUSANNA MOODIE and SELECTED POEMS 1966–1984 by Margaret Atwood. Copyright © 1976, 1990 by Oxford University Press. Reprinted by permission of Houghton Mifflin Harcourt Publishing Company and Oxford University Press. All rights reserved.

W. H. Auden: "Stop All the Clocks," "In Memory of W. B. Yeats," and "Musee des Beaux Arts," copyright 1940 & renewed 1968 by W. H. Auden, from COLLECTED POEMS by W. H. Auden. Used by permission of Random House, an imprint and division of Penguin Random House LLC. All rights reserved. Any third party use of this material, outside of this publication, is prohibited. Interested parties must apply directly to Penguin Random House LLC for permission.

Steven Gould Axelrod: From SYLVIA PLATH: THE WOUND AND THE CURE OF WORDS, pp. 51–70. Copyright © 1990 The Johns Hopkins University Press. Reprinted with permission of The Johns Hopkins University Press.

Jimmy Santiago Baca: "Green Chile" from BLACK MESA POEMS, copyright © 1989 by Jimmy Santiago Baca. Reprinted by permission of New Directions Publishing Corp.

William Baer: Excerpt from "Still Negotiating with the Images: An Interview with Yusef Komunyakaa" by William Baer, first published in "Poetry/Flash" June/July 1998. Reprinted by permission of William Baer.

Bashō: "A Village Without Bells" and "This Road" from THE ESSENTIAL HAIKU: VERSIONS OF BASHŌ, BUSON & ISSA, ed. and with an introduction by Robert Hass. Introduction and selection copyright © 1994 by Robert Hass. Unless otherwise noted, all translations copyright © 1994 by Robert Hass. Reprinted by permission of HarperCollins Publishers.

Elizabeth Bishop: "Exchanging Hats" and "Sestina" from THE COMPLETE POEMS 1927–1979 by Elizabeth Bishop. Copyright © 1979, 1983 by Alice Helen Methfessel. Reprinted by permission of Farrar, Straus & Giroux, LLC.

Arna Bontemps: "A Black Man Talks of Reaping" from PERSONALS is reprinted by permission of Harold Ober Associates, Inc. Copyright © 1963 by Arna Bontemps.

Roo Borson: "After a Death" by Roo Borson, reprinted by permission of the author from NIGHT WALK: SELECTED POEMS, Oxford University Press, Toronto, 1994.

Todd Boss: "My Love for You Is So Embarrassingly" from PITCH: POEMS, copyright © 2012 by Todd Boss. Used by permission of W.W. Norton & Company, Inc.

Mary Lynn Broe: From PROTEAN POETIC: THE POETRY OF SYLVIA PLATH by Mary Lynn Broe. Copyright © 1980 by the Curators of the University of Missouri Press. Reprinted by permission of the publisher.

Gwendolyn Brooks: "First Fight, Then Fiddle," and "We Real Cool" are reprinted by consent of Brooks Permissions.

Buson: "Coolness" and "Listening to the Moon" from THE ESSENTIAL HAIKU: VERSIONS OF BASHŌ, BUSON & ISSA, ed. and with an introduction by Robert Hass. Introduction and selection copyright © 1994 by Robert Hass. Unless otherwise noted, all translations copyright © 1994 by Robert Hass. Reprinted by permission of HarperCollins Publishers.

Paul Celan: "Deathfugue" from SELECTED POEMS AND PROSE OF PAUL CELAN, trans. by John Felstiner. Copyright © 2001 by John Felstiner. First published in German as "Todesfuge" from MOHN UND GEDÄCHTNIS. GEDICHTE, © 1952 Deutsche Verlags-Anstalt, Munich, a member of Verlagsgruppe Random House GmbH. Used by permission of W.W. Norton & Company, Inc. and Verlagsgruppe Random House, GmbH.

Helen Chasin: "The Word *Plum*" from COMING CLOSE AND OTHER POEMS by Helen Chasin. Copyright © 1968 by Helen Chasin. Reprinted by permission of Yale University Press.

Kelly Cherry: "Alzheimer's" from DEATH AND TRANSFIGURATION. Copyright © 1997. Reprinted by permission of Louisiana State University Press.

Chiyojo: "Whether astringent I do not know" from ONE HUNDRED FAMOUS HAIKU, selected and trans. by Daniel C. Buchanan, is reprinted by permission of Japan Publications, Inc.

Lucille Clifton: "cream of wheat" from THE COLLECTED POEMS OF LUCILLE CLIFTON, 1965–2019. Copyright © 2008 by Lucille Clifton. Reprinted with the permission of The Permissions Company, Inc., on behalf of BOA Editions Ltd., www.boaeditions.org.

Judith Ortiz Cofer: "The Latin Deli: An Ars Poetica" by Judith Ortiz Cofer is reprinted with permission from the publisher of "The Americas Review." Copyright © 1992 Arte Publico Press-University of Houston. "The Changeling" is reprinted from *Prairie Schooner*, Vol. 66, Issue 3 (Fall 1992) by permission of the University of Nebraska Press. Copyright © 1992 by the University of Nebraska Press

Billy Collins: "Taking off Emily Dickinson's Clothes" from PICNIC, LIGHTNING, copyright © 1998. Reprinted by permission of the University of Pittsburgh Press. "Sonnet," copyright © 2001 by Billy Collins, from SAILING ALONE AROUND THE ROOM. "Divorce" from BALLISTICS, copyright © 2008 by Billy Collins. Used by permission of Random House, an imprint and division of Penguin Random House LLC. All rights reserved. Any third party use of this material, outside of this publication, is prohibited. Interested parties must apply directly to Penguin Random House LLC for permission. "Introduction to Poetry" from THE APPLE THAT ASTONISHED PARIS. Copyright © 1988, 1996 by Billy Collins. Reprinted with the permission of The Permissions Company, Inc. on behalf of the University of Arkansas Press, www.uapress.com

Martha Collins: "Lies" from SOME THINGS WORDS CAN DO (Sheep Meadow Press, 1998). Copyright © 1998 by Martha Collins. Reprinted by permission of the author. "[24]" from WHITE PAPERS, copyright © 2012 by Martha Collins. Reprinted by permission of the University of Pittsburgh Press.

Wendy Cope: "Emily Dickinson" from MAKING COCOA FOR KINGSLEY AMIS, copyright © 1986 Wendy Cope, is reprinted by permission of United Agents (www.unitedagents.co.uk) on behalf of Wendy Cope and Faber & Faber Ltd.

Hart Crane: "To Emily Dickinson," from COMPLETE POEMS OF HART CRANE by Hart Crane, edited by Marc Simon. Copyright © 1933, 1958, 1966 by Liveright Publishing Corporation. Copyright © 1986 by Marc Simon. Used by permission of Liveright Publishing Corporation.

Countee Cullen: "Yet Do I Marvel" and "Saturday's Child" from COLOR. Copyright © 1925 by Harper & Bros., New York. Renewed 1952 by Ida M. Cullen. "From the Dark Tower" from COPPER SUN. Copyright © 1927 by Harper & Bros., New York. Renewed 1954 by Ida M. Cullen. Copyrights held by Amistad Research Center, Tulane University, administered by Thompson and Thompson, Brooklyn, NY.

E. E. Cummings: "next to of course god america I" copyright 1926, 1954, © 1991 by the Trustees for the E.E. Cummings Trust. Copyright © 1985 by George James Firmage. "Buffalo Bill's," copyright

1923, 1951, © 1991 by the Trustees for the E.E. Cummings Trust. Copyright © 1976 by George James Firmage. "in Just-," copyright 1923, 1951, © 1991 by the Trustees for the E.E. Cummings Trust. Copyright © 1976 by George James Firmage. "l(a," copyright © 1958, 1986, 1991 by the Trustees for the E.E. Cummings Trust. From COMPLETE POEMS: 1904–1962 by E.E. Cummings, edited by George J. Firmage. Used by permission of Liveright Publishing Corporation.

Mahmoud Darwish: "Identity Card" translated by John Asfour, first appeared in WHEN THE WORDS BURN: AN ANTHOLOGY OF MODERN ARABIC POETRY, trans. and ed. by John Asfour, published by Cormorant Books, 1988. This translation used by permission of the Estate of John Asfour. Underlying rights granted by Actes Sud. Copyright © Mahmoud Darwish.

Lydia Davis: "Head, Heart" from THE COLLECTED STORIES OF LYDIA DAVIS. Copyright © 2009 by Lydia Davis. Reprinted by permission of Farrar, Straus and Giroux, LLC.

Walter de la Mare: "Slim Cunning Hands" from THE COMPLETE POEMS OF WALTER DE LA MARE. Reprinted by permission of the Literary Trustees of Walter de la Mare and the Society of Authors as their representative.

James Dickey: "The Leap" from POEMS, 1957–1967. Copyright © 1964 and © 1967 by Wesleyan University Press. Reprinted by permission of the publisher.

Emily Dickinson: Poems by Emily Dickinson are reprinted by permission of the publishers and the Trustees of Amherst College from THE POEMS OF EMILY DICKINSON, Thomas H. Johnson, ed., Cambridge, Mass.: The Belknap Press of Harvard University Press. Copyright © 1951, 1955, 1979, 1983 by the President and Fellows of Harvard College and from THE POEMS OF EMILY DICKINSON: READING EDITION, Ralph W. Franklin, ed., Cambridge, Mass.: The Belknap Press of Harvard University Press. Copyright © 1998, 1999 by the President and Fellows of Harvard College. Copyright © 1951, 1955, 1979, 1983 by the President and Fellows of Harvard College. Reprinted by permission of the publishers and the Trustees of Amherst College.

Rita Dove: "Daystar" from THOMAS AND BEULAH (Carnegie-Mellon University Press, 1986). Copyright © 1986 by Rita Dove. Reprinted by permission of the author.

W. E. B. DuBois: W.W. Norton wishes to thank the Crisis Publishing Co., Inc., the publisher of the magazine of the National Association for the Advancement of Colored People, for use of the *Crisis Magazine* material, excerpt from "Two Novels: *Home to Harlem* and *Quicksand*" by W. E. B. DuBois, first published in *Crisis Magazine,* June 1928 issue.

Bob Dylan: Lyrics to "The Times They Are A-Changin'" is reprinted by permission. Copyright © 1963, 1964 by Warner Bros. Inc; renewed 1991, 1992 by Special Rider Music. All rights reserved. International copyright secured.

T. S. Eliot: "The Love Song of J. Alfred Prufrock" from COLLECTED POEMS 1909–1962 by T.S. Eliot is reprinted by permission of the publisher, Faber & Faber Ltd.

David Elliott: From "The Complexity of the Human Heart: A Conversation with Marie Howe" by David Elliot from AGNI online 2004. Copyright © 2004 by David L. Elliott. Reprinted by permission.

Martín Espada: "Litany at the Tomb of Frederick Douglass" from THE TROUBLE BALL by Martin Espada. Copyright © 2011 by Martín Espada. Used by permission of W.W. Norton & Company, Inc. "Of the Threads that Connect the Stars" first published in *Ploughshares,* Spring 2013, is reprinted by permission of the author. Copyright © 2013 by Martín Espada.

U.A. Fanthorpe: "Not My Best Side," from SELECTED POEMS (Enitharmon Press Ltd., 2013). Reprinted by permission of the publisher

Kenneth Fearing: "Dirge" from COMPLETE POEMS by Kenneth Fearing is reprinted by the permission of Russell & Volkening, Inc. as agents for the author. Copyright © 1934 by Kenneth Fearing, renewed in 1972 by the Estate of Kenneth Fearing.

John Felstiner: From "A Fugue after Auschwitz" from PAUL CELAN: POET, SURVIVOR, JEW (1995). Reprinted by permission of the author.

Annie Finch: "Coy Mistress" from SPELLS: NEW AND SELECTED POEMS © 2013 by Annie Finch. Published by Wesleyan University Press and used by permission.

Katie Ford: "Still-Life" from BLOOD LYRICS. Originally in The New Yorker, Sept. 30, 2013. Copyright © 2013, 2014 by Katie Ford. Reprinted with the permission of The Permissions Company, Inc. on behalf of Graywolf Press, www.graywofpress.org.

Laura Frost: From "Every Woman Adores a Fascist: Feminist Visions of Fascism from *Three Guineas* to *Fear of Flying*" from *Women's Studies*. Reprinted by permission of Taylor & Francis Ltd. via the Copyright Clearance Center, http://www.yandfonline.com.

Robert Frost: "Range-Finding," "Stopping by Woods on a Snowy Evening," "The Road Not Taken," "Home Burial," and "Design" from the book THE POETRY OF ROBERT FROST edited by Edward Connery Lathem. Copyright © 1923, 1930, 1939, 1969 by Henry Holt and Company, copyright © 1944, 1951, 1958 by Robert Frost, copyright © 1967 by Lesley Frost Ballantine. Reprinted by permission of Henry Holt and Company, LLC.

Allen Ginsberg: "The Old Pond" and "Looking Over My Shoulder" from COLLECTED POEMS 1947–1980 by Allen Ginsberg. Copyright © 1984 by Allen Ginsberg. "The Velocity of Money" from COSMOPOLITAN GREETINGS: POEMS 1986–1992 by Allen Ginsberg. Copyright © 1994 by Allen Ginsberg. Reprinted by permission of HarperCollins Publishers.

Jose B. Gonzales, "Elvis in the Inner City" first published in *Callaloo* 29.3 (2006), is reprinted by permission of the author.

Angelina Grimke: "Tenebris" and "The Black Finger" from SELECTED WORKS OF ANGELINA GRIMKE, Angelina Grimke Papers, Moorland-Springarn Research Center, Howard University.

Emily Grosholz: "Eden" from REBEL ANGELS (1996). Reprinted by permission of the author and Storyline Press.

Michael Harper: "Dear John, Dear Coltrane" from DEAR JOHN, DEAR COLTRANE by Michael S. Harper. Copyright © 1970 by Michael S. Harper. Reprinted by permission of the author.

Gwen Harwood: "In the Park" from SELECTED POEMS by Gwen Harwood, ed. by Gregory Kratzmann (2001). Reproduced with permission of Penguin Random House Australia.

Robert Hayden: "A Letter from Phillis Wheatley," copyright © 1978 by Robert Hayden. "Those Winter Sundays," "Homage to the Empress of the Blues," "Frederick Douglass." Copyright © 1966 by Robert Hayden. From COLLECTED POEMS OF ROBERT HAYDEN, edited by Frederick Glaysher. Used by permission of Liveright Publishing Corporation.

Terrance Hayes: "Mr. T—" from HIP LOGIC by Terrance Hayes, copyright © 2002 by Terrance Hayes. "Carp Poem" from LIGHTHEAD by Terrance Hayes, copyright © 2010 by Terrance Hayes. Used by permission of Penguin Books, an imprint of Penguin Publishing Group, a division of Penguin Random House LLC.

Seamus Heaney: "Digging," and "Punishment" from OPENED GROUND: SELECTED POEMS 1966–1996 by Seamus Heaney. Copyright © 1998 by Seamus Heaney. Reprinted by permission of Farrar, Straus & Giroux, LLC and Faber & Faber Ltd.

Anthony Hecht: "The Dover Bitch" from COLLECTED EARLIER POEMS by Anthony Hecht, copyright © 1990 by Anthony E. Hecht. Used by permission of Alfred A. Knopf, an imprint of the Knopf Doubleday Publishing Group, a division of Penguin Random House LLC. All rights reserved. Any third party use of this material, outside of this publication, is prohibited. Interested parties must apply directly to Penguin Random House LLC for permission.

Bob Hicok: "O my pa-pa" was first published in *Poetry*, May 2007, copyright © 2006 Bob Hicok and is reprinted by permission of the author.

Edward Hirsch: "An Interview with Derek Walcott" by Edward Hirsch and Derek Walcott was originally published in *Contemporary Literature* 20.3 (Summer 1979): 279–92. Copyright © 1979 by the Board of Regents of the University of Wisconsin System. Reproduced by the permission of the University of Wisconsin Press.

Tony Hoagland: "Dickhead" from DONKEY GOSPEL. Copyright © 1998 by Tony Hoagland. Reprinted with the permission of The Permissions Company, Inc. on behalf of Graywolf Press, www.graywofpress.org.

Margaret Homans: From "A Feminine Tradition" from WOMEN WRITERS AND POETIC IDENTITY by Margaret Homans. Copyright © 1980 by Princeton University Press. Reprinted by permission of Princeton University Press via the Copyright Clearance Center.

Irving Howe: From "The Plath Celebration: A Partial Dissent" from THE CRITICAL POINT OF LITERATURE AND CULTURE by Irving Howe (Horizon Press, 1973). Reprinted by permission of the Literary Estate of Irving Howe.

Marie Howe: "Practicing" from WHAT THE LIVING DO by Marie Howe. Copyright © 1997 by Marie Howe. Used by permission of W.W. Norton & Company, Inc.

Andrew Hudgins: "Begotten" from THE GLASS HAMMER: A SOUTHERN CHILDHOOD. Copyright © 1994 by Andrew Hudgins. Reprinted by permission of Houghton Mifflin Harcourt Publishing Company. All rights reserved.

Langston Hughes: "Ballad of the Landlord," "Harlem (2)," "I, Too," "The Negro Speaks of Rivers," and "The Weary Blues" from THE COLLECTED POEMS OF LANGSTON HUGHES by Langston Hughes, ed. Arnold Rampersad with David Roessel, Associate Editor, copyright © 1994 by the Estate of Langston Hughes. Used by permission of Alfred A. Knopf, an imprint of the Knopf Doubleday Publishing Group, a division of Penguin Random House LLC. All rights reserved. Any third party use of this material, outside of this publication, is prohibited. Interested parties must apply directly to Penguin Random House LLC for permission. "Harlem Literati" from THE BIG SEA by Langston Hughes. Copyright 1940 by Langston Hughes. Copyright renewed 1968 by Arna Bontemps and George Houston Bass. Reprinted by permission of Hill and Wang, a division of Farrar, Straus and Giroux, LLC.

Mark Jarman: "Haiku" from BONE FIRES: NEW AND SELECTED POEMS. Copyright © 2011 by Mark Jarman. Reprinted with the permission of The Permissions Company, Inc. on behalf of Sarabande Books, www.sarabandebooks.org.

Randall Jarrell: "The Death of the Ball Turret Gunner" from THE COMPLETE POEMS by Randall Jarrell. Copyright © 1969 by Randall Jarrell, renewed 1997 by Mary von S. Jarrell. Reprinted by permission of Farrar Straus & Giroux. LLC

Helene Johnson: "Sonnet to a Negro in Harlem" by Helene Johnson is reprinted from THIS WAITING FOR LOVE, copyright © 2000 by Abigail McGrath and published by the University of Massachusetts Press.

June Jordan: "Something Like a Sonnet for Phillis Miracle Wheatley" from DIRECTED BY DESIRE: THE COLLECTED POEMS OF JUNE JORDAN. Copyright © 2005, 2015 by the June M. Jordan Literary Estate. Reprinted with the permission of the June Jordan Literary Estate.

X. J. Kennedy: "In a Prominent Bar in Secaucus One Day" from IN A PROMINENT BAR IN SECAUCUS: NEW AND SELECTED POEMS, 1955–2007, p. 11–12. Copyright © 2007 X. J. Kennedy. Reprinted with permission of The Johns Hopkins University Press.

Galway Kinnell: "Blackberry Eating" from THREE BOOKS by Galway Kinnell. Copyright © 1993 by Galway Kinnell. Reprinted by permission of Houghton Mifflin Harcourt Publishing Company. All Rights Reserved.

Etheridge Knight: "Eastern Guard Tower," "Hard Rock Returns to Prison from the Hospital for the Criminal Insane," "[The falling snow flakes]," and "[Making jazz swing in]" from THE ESSENTIAL ETHERIDGE KNIGHT, copyright © 1986. Reprinted by permission of the University of Pittsburgh Press.

Yusef Komunyakaa: "Tu Do Street" from DIEN CAI DAU by Yusef Komunyakaa. Copyright © 1988 by Yusef Komunyakaa. "Facing It" from PLEASURE DOME. Copyright © 2001 by Yusef Komunyakaa. Reprinted with permission of Wesleyan University Press. Excerpt from commentary by Yusef Komunyakaa on "Facing It" from BLUE NOTES: ESSAYS, INTERVIEWS AND COMMENTARIES by Yusef Komunyakaa, ed. Radiclani Clytus, (U of MI Press, 2000) is reprinted by permission of Yusef Komunyakaa.

Judith Kroll: From "Rituals of Exorcism: 'Daddy'" from CHAPTERS IN A MYTHOLOGY: THE POETRY OF SYLVIA PLATH by Judith Kroll (HarperCollins, 1976). Copyright © 1997 by Judith Kroll.

Maxine Kumin: "Woodchucks" from SELECTED POEMS 1960–1990 by Maxine Kumin. Copyright © 1972, 1997 by Maxine Kumin. Used by permission of W.W. Norton & Company, Inc.

Philip Larkin: "Church Going" and "This Be the Verse" from THE COMPLETE POEMS OF PHILIP LARKIN, ed. Archie Burnett. Copyright © 2012 by the Estate of Philip Larkin. Introduction copyright © 2012 by Archie Burnett. Reprinted by permission of Farrar, Straus and Giroux, LLC and Faber & Faber Ltd. Excerpts from "A Conversation with Ian Hamilton" from "An Interview with John Haffenden" published in FURTHER REQUIREMENTS: INTERVIEWS, BROADCASTS, STATEMENTS AND BOOK REVIEWS, by Philip Larkin, ed. Anthony Thwaite (Faber & Faber 2001) are reprinted by permission of The Society of Authors as the Literary Representative of the Estate of Philip Larkin.

Ann Lauinger: "Marvell Noir" from *Parnassus: Poetry in Review*, 28, nos. 1 & 2 (2005) is reprinted by permission of the author.

Li-Young Lee: "Persimmons" from ROSE. Copyright © 1986 by Li-Young Lee. Reprinted with the permission of The Permissions Company, Inc. on behalf of BOA Editions, Ltd., www.boaeditions.org

Alain Locke: Reprinted with the permission of Scribner, a Division of Simon & Schuster, Inc. from THE NEW NEGRO: VOICES OF THE HARLEM RENAISSANCE by Alain Locke. Copyright © 1925 by Albert & Charles Boni, Inc. Copyright © 1992 by Macmillan Publishing Company. All rights reserved.

Patricia Lockwood: "What Is the Zoo for What?" first published in *The New Yorker*, Oct. 28, 2013 is reprinted by permission of the author.

Archibald MacLeish: "Ars Poetica" from COLLECTED POEMS, 1917–1982 by Archibald MacLeish. Copyright © 1985 by The Estate of Archibald MacLeish. Reprinted by permission of Houghton MIfflin Harcourt Publishing Company. All rights reserved.

Amit Majmudar: "Dothead" originally published in *The New Yorker*, Aug. 1, 2011. Copyright © 2011 by Amit Majmudar. Reprinted by permission of Georges Borchardt, Inc. on behalf of the author.

Edna St. Vincent Millay: "Woman have loved before as I have now," © 1931, 1958 "I, being born a woman and distressed," "What lips my lips have kissed," and "I will put Chaos in fourteen lines" from COLLECTED POEMS. Copyright © 1923, 1928, 1931, 1954, 1955, 1958, 1982 by Edna St. Vincent Millay and Norma Millay Ellis. Reprinted with the permission of The Permissions Company, Inc. on behalf of Holly Peppe, Literary Executor, The Millay Society, www.millay.org

Czeslaw Milosz: "Ars Poetica" (36.1) from NEW AND COLLECTED POEMS: 1931–2001 by Czeslaw Milosz. Copyright © 1988, 1991, 1995, 2001 by Czeslaw Milosz Royalties, Inc. Reprinted by permission of HarperCollins Publishers.

Earl Miner: "The still old pond" from JAPANESE LINKED POETRY by Earl Miner. Copyright © 1979 by Earl Miner. Reprinted by permission of the author.

Marianne Moore: "Poetry" is reprinted with permission of Scribner, a Division of Simon & Schuster, Inc. from THE COLLECTED POEMS OF MARIANNE MOORE. Copyright © 1935, 1963 by Marianne Moore. All rights reserved.

Pat Mora: "Sonrisas" from BORDERS by Pat Mora is reprinted with permission from the publisher (© 1986 Arte Publico Press-Univ. of Houston). "Elena" from CHANTS by Pat Mora is reprinted with permission from the publisher (© 1994 Arte Publico Press-University of Houston). "Gentle Communion" and "Mothers and Daughters" from COMMUNION by Pat Mora Is reprinted with permission from the publisher (© 1991 Arte Publico Press- University of Houston). "La Migra," copyright © 1995 by Pat Mora, and "Ode to Adobe," copyright © 2006 by Pat Mora, are reprinted by permission of Curtis Brown, Ltd.

Mos Def [Dante Smith]: Lyrics to "Hip Hop" words and music by David Axelrod, Michael Axelrod, Dante Smith, Joseph Kirkland and Gabriel Jackson. Copyright © 2000 EMI Blackwood Music Inc., Empire International Music Inc., Medina Sounds Music, Glenwood Music Corp, & Publisher(s) Unknown. All rights on behalf of EMI Blackwood Music Inc., Empire International Music Inc., Medina Sounds Music, & Glenwood Music Corp administered by Sony/ATV Music Publishing LLC., 424 Church Street, Suite 1200, Nashville, TN 37219. All rights reserved. Used by permission. Additional rights licensed by Joseph Kirkland dba Dusty Fingers Music and by Swing Beat Songs (BMI).

Harryette Mullen: "Dim Lady" from SLEEPING WITH THE DICTIONARY by Harryette Mullen, copyright © 2002 by the Regents of the University of California is reprinted by permission of the University of California Press.

Howard Nemerov: "The Vacuum" from THE COLLECTED POEMS OF HOWARD NEMEROV. Copyright © 1977 by Howard Nemerov. Reprinted by permission of the Estate of Howard Nemerov.

Frank O'Hara: "[Lana Turner has collapsed]" from LUNCH POEMS (1964) is reprinted by permission of City Lights Books.

Sharon Olds: "The Victims" and "Sex without Love" from THE DEAD AND THE LIVING by Sharon Olds, copyright © 1987 by Sharon Olds. "Last Night" from THE WELLSPRING by Sharon Olds, copyright © 1996 by Sharon Olds. "Bruise Ghazal" from STAG'S LEAP: POEMS by Sharon Olds, copyright © 2012 by Sharon Olds. Used by permission of Alfred A. Knopf, an imprint of the Knopf

Doubleday Publishing Group, a division of Penguin Random House LLC. All rights reserved. Any third party use of this material, outside of this publication, is prohibited. Interested parties must apply directly to Penguin Random House LLC for permission.

Simon Ortiz: "My Father's Song" is reprinted by permission of the author.

Wilfred Owen: "Disabled" from THE COLLECTED POEMS OF WILFRED OWEN, copyright © 1963 by Chatto & Windus, Ltd. . Reprinted by permission of New Directions Publishing Corp.

Dorothy Parker: "A Certain Lady," copyright 1928, renewed © 1956 by Dorothy Parker "One Perfect Rose," copyright 1926, renewed © 1954 by Dorothy Parker, from THE PORTABLE DOROTHY PARKER, ed. by Marion Meade. Used by permission of Viking Books, an imprint of Penguin Publishing Group, a division of Penguin Random House LLC.

Linda Pastan: "love poem" and "To a Daughter Leaving Home" from THE IMPERFECT PARADISE by Linda Pastan. Copyright © 1988 by Linda Pastan. "Marks" from PM/AM: NEW AND SELECTED POEMS by Linda Pastan. Copyright © 1978 by Linda Pastan. "In the Har-Poen Tea Garden" and "Listening to Bob Dylan, 2005" from TRAVELING LIGHT, copyright © 2011 by Linda Pastan. Used by permission of W.W. Norton & Company, Inc.

Petrarch: Sonnet #90 from CANZONIERE: SELECTED POEMS, trans. Anthony Mortimer (Penguin Classics 2002). Translation copyright © 2002 by Anthony Mortimer. Reproduced by permission of Penguin Books Ltd.

Marge Piercy: "Barbie Doll" from CIRCLES ON THE WATER by Marge Piercy, copyright © 1982 by Middlemarsh, Inc. Used by permission of Alfred A. Knopf, an imprint of the Knopf Doubleday Publishing Group, a division of Penguin Random House LLC. All rights reserved. Any third party use of this material, outside of this publication, is prohibited. Interested parties must apply directly to Penguin Random House LLC for permission.

Sylvia Plath: "Morning Song," copyright © 1961 by Ted Hughes, and "Daddy" from ARIEL by Sylvia Plath. Copyright © 1963 by Ted Hughes. "Lady Lazarus" from ARIEL by Sylvia Plath. Copyright © 1963 by Ted Hughes. Reprinted by permission of HarperCollins Publishers and Faber & Faber Ltd.

Paul Martinez Pompa: "The Abuelita Poem" from MY KILL ADORE HIM (2009). Copyright © 2009 by the University of Notre Dame Press. Used by permission of the publisher.

Ezra Pound: "In a Station of the Metro," and "The River-Merchant's Wife: A Letter" (original by Rihaku) from PERSONAE, copyright © 1926 by Ezra Pound. Reprinted by permission of New Directions Publishing Corp.

Lynn Powell: "Kind of Blue" first appeared in *Poetry*, May 2004. Reprinted by permission of Lynn Powell.

Dudley Randall: "Ballad of Birmingham" from POEM COUNTER POEM by Dudley Randall (Michigan: Broadside Press, 1969). Reprinted by permission of the publisher.

Victoria Redel: This interview, "Marie Howe" was commissioned by and first published in BOMB # 61, Fall 1997. Copyright © Bomb Magazine, New Art Publications, and its Contributors. All rights reserved. The BOMB Digital Archive can be viewed at www.bombsite.com

Adrienne Rich: Excerpt from "A communal poetry" from WHAT IS FOUND THERE: NOTEBOOKS ON POETRY AND POLITICS by Adrienne Rich. Copyright © 1993 by Adrienne Rich. Excerpt from "When We Dead Awaken: Writing as Re-Vision" and excerpts from "Why I Refused the National Medal for the Arts," from ARTS OF THE POSSIBLE: ESSAYS AND CONVERSATIONS by Adrienne Rich. Copyright © 2001 by Adrienne Rich. "Living in Sin," "Planetarium," "Aunt Jennifer's Tigers," "At a Bach Concert," "Storm Warnings," "Snapshots of a Daughter-in-Law," from THE FACT OF A DOORFRAME: SELECTED POEMS 1950–2001 by Adrienne Rich. Copyright © 2002 by Adrienne Rich. Copyright © 2001, 1999, 1995, 1991, 1989, 1986, 1984, 1981, 1967, 1963, 1962, 1961, 1960, 1959, 1958, 1957, 1956, 1955, 1954, 1953, 1952, 1951 by Adrienne Rich. Copyright © 1978, 1975, 1973, 1971, 1969, 1966 by W.W. Norton & Company, Inc. "Tonight No Poetry Will Serve" "Transparencies" "Diving into the Wreck," "For the Record," "Four: history" from "Inscriptions," Poem 3 of "Contradictions: Tracking Poems" from LATER POEMS: SELECTED AND NEW, 1971–2012 by Adrienne rich. Copyright © 2013 by The Adrienne Rich Literary Trust. Copyright © 2011, 2007, 2004, 2001, 1999, 1995, 1991, 1989, 1986, 1981 by Adrienne Rich. Copyright © 1978, 1973 by W.W. Norton & Company, Inc. Excerpts from "Poetry and the Forgotten Future" from A HUMAN EYE: ESSAYS ON ART IN SOCIETY, 1997–2008. Copyright © 2009 by Adrienne Rich. Used by permission of W.W. Norton & Company, Inc.

Theodore Roethke: "My Papa's Waltz," copyright 1942 by Hearst Magazines, Inc., "The Root Cellar," copyright 1943 by Modern Poetry Association, Inc. from COLLECTED POEMS OF THEODORE ROETHKE. Used by permission of Doubleday, an imprint of the Knopf Doubleday Publishing Group, a division of Penguin Random House LLC. All rights reserved. Any third party use of this material, outside of this publication, is prohibited. Interested parties must apply directly to Penguin Random House LLC for permission.

Kay Ryan: "Repulsive Theory" form THE NIAGARA RIVER, copyright © 2005 by Kay Ryan. "Blandeur" from SAY UNCLE, copyright © 1991 by Kay Ryan. Used by permission of Grove/Atlantic, Inc. Any third party use of this material, outside of this publication, is prohibited.

Sonia Sanchez: "Fannie Lou Hamer" and "Rosa Parks" from "9 Haiku" are reproduced from MORNING HAIKU with permission of Beacon Press, Boston. Copyright © 2009 by Sonia Sanchez.

Anne Sexton: "Cinderella" from TRANSFORMATIONS. Copyright © 1971 by Anne Sexton, renewed 1989 by Linda G. Sexton. Reprinted by permission of Houghton Mifflin Harcourt Publishing Company. All rights reserved.

Ciara Shuttleworth: "Sestina" first published in *The New Yorker*, Nov. 29, 2010, is reprinted by permission of the author. Copyright © 2010 by Ciara Shuttleworth.

Charlie Smith: "The Business," copyright © 1995 by Charlie Smith from JUMP SOUL: NEW AND SELECTED POEMS. Used by permission of W.W. Norton & Company, Inc.

W. D. Snodgrass: "Leaving the Motel" is reprinted by permission.

Cathy Song: "Heaven" from FRAMELESS WINDOWS, SQUARES OF LIGHT: POEMS by Cathy Song. Copyright © 1988 by Cathy Song. Used by permission of W.W. Norton & Company, Inc.

Bruce Springsteen: "Nebraska" by Bruce Springsteen. Copyright © 1982 by Bruce Springsteen (ASCAP). Reprinted by permission. International copyright secured. All rights reserved.

A. E. Stallings: "Shoulda, Woulda, Coulda" first published in *The New Yorker*, Sept. 23, 2013. Copyright © 2013 by A. E. Stallings. Reprinted by permission of the author.

Sue Standing: "Diamond Haiku" is reprinted from *Ploughshares*, vol. 37, #4 (Winter 2011–2012) by permission of the author. Copyright © 2011 by Sue Standing.

George Stavros: "An Interview with Gwendolyn Brooks" by George Stavros and Gwendolyn Brooks was originally published in *Contemporary Literature* 11.1 (Winter 1970): 1–20. Copyright © 1970 by the Board of Regents of the University of Wisconsin System. Reproduced by the permission of the University of Wisconsin Press.

George Steiner: From "Dying is an Art" from LANGUAGE AND SILENCE by George Steiner. Copyright © 1958, 1960, 1961, 1962, 1963, 1964, 1965, 1966, 1967 by George Steiner. Reprinted by permission of Georges Borchardt, Inc. on behalf of the author.

Wallace Stevens: "Anecdote of the Jar," "The Emperor of Ice-Cream" from THE COLLECTED POEMS OF WALLACE STEVENS by Wallace Stevens, copyright 1954 by Wallace Stevens and renewed 1982 by Holly Stevens. Used by permission of Alfred A. Knopf, an imprint of the Knopf Doubleday Publishing Group, a division of Penguin Random House LLC. All rights reserved. Any third party use of this material, outside of this publication, is prohibited. Interested parties must apply directly to Penguin Random House LLC for permission.

Adrienne Su: "On Writing" from LIVING QUARTERS, copyright © 2015 by Adrienne Su. "Escape from the Old Country" from SANCTUARY, copyright © 2006 by Adrienne Su. Reprinted by permission of Manic D Press, Inc. Commentary by Adrienne Su from THE BEST AMERICAN POETRY 2013, ed. Denise Duhamel by permission of Adrienne Su.

May Swenson: "Women" is reprinted by permission of The Literary Estate of May Swenson. All rights reserved.

Dylan Thomas: "Do Not Go Gentle into That Good Night" from THE POEMS OF DYLAN THOMAS, copyright © 1952 by Dylan Thomas. Reprinted by permission of New Directions Publishing Corp.

Natasha Trethewey: "Pilgrimage" and "Myth" from NATIVE GUARD: POEMS by Natasha Trethewey. Copyright © 2006 by Natasha Trethewey. Reprinted by permission of Houghton Mifflin Harcourt Publishing Company. All rights reserved.

Brian Turner: "Jundee Ameriki" from PHANTOM NOISE. Copyright © 2010 by Brian Turner. Reprinted with the permission of The Permissions Company, Inc. on behalf of Alice James Books, www.alicejamesbooks.org.

Ellen Bryant Voigt: "My Mother" from HEADWATERS: A POEM, copyright © 2013 by Ellen Bryant Voigt. Used by permission of W.W. Norton & Company, Inc.

David Wagoner: "My Father's Garden" from TRAVELING LIGHT: COLLECTED AND NEW POEMS by David Wagoner. Copyright © 1999 by David Wagoner. Used by permission of the author.

Stacy Waite: "The Kind of Man I Am at the DMV" from BUTCH GEOGRAPHY, published by Tupelo Press. Copyright © 2013 by Stacey Waite. Used with permission of the publisher.

Derek Walcott: "A Far Cry from Africa" from COLLECTED POEMS 1948–1984 by Derek Walcott. Copyright © 1986 by Derek Walcott. Reprinted by permission of Farrar, Straus & Giroux, LLC.

Richard Wilbur: "The Beautiful Changes" from THE BEAUTIFUL CHANGES AND OTHER POEMS, copyright 1947 and renewed 1975 by Richard Wilbur. "Love Calls Us to the Things of This World" from THINGS OF THIS WORLD, copyright © 1956 and renewed 1984 by Richard Wilbur. "Terza Rima" from ANTEROOMS: NEW POEMS AND TRANSLATIONS by Richard Wilbur. Copyright © 2010 by Richard Wilbur. Reprinted by permission of Houghton Mifflin Harcourt Publishing Company. All rights reserved.

C. K. Williams: "The Economy Rescued by My Mother Returning to Shop" from *The New Yorker*, Dec. 9, 2013. Reprinted by permission of the author.

William Carlos Williams: From "Interview with John W. Gerber, Rutherford, NJ, June 1950" and from "Reading and Commentary at Princeton University, March 19, 1952." Reprinted by permission of Daphne Williams Fox, agent for the Estate of Dr. William Carlos Williams and Dr. William Eric Williams. "The Red Wheelbarrow" and "This is Just to Say" from THE COLLECTED POEMS: VOLUME 1, 1909–1939, copyright © 1938 by New Directions Publishing Corp. "The Dance (In Brueghel's)" from THE COLLECTED POEMS: volume 11, 1939–1962, copyright © 1944 by William Carlos Williams. "Landscape with the Fall of Icarus" from THE COLLECTED POEMS: VOLUME 11, 1939–1962, copyright © 1962 by William Carlos Williams. Reprinted by permission of New Directions Publishing Corp.

Richard Wright: "In the Falling Snow" from THE RICHARD WRIGHT READER. Copyright © 1971 by Ellen Wright. Reprinted by permission of John Hawkins & Associates, Inc. and the Estate of Richard Wright.

W. B. Yeats: "Leda and the Swan" and "Sailing to Byzantium" are reprinted with permission of Scribner, a Division of Simon & Schuster, Inc. from THE COLLECTED WORKS OF W. B. YEATS, Vol. 1: THE POEMS, rev., ed. Richard J. Finneran. Copyright © 1928 by The Macmillan Company. Copyright renewed 1956 by Bertha Georgie Yeats. All rights reserved.

Kevin Young: "Ode to Pork" from DEAR DARKNESS: POEMS, copyright © 2008 by Kevin Young. "Greening," "It's death there," "Quickening," "Charity," Breaking Water," "Expecting," "Rue," and "Wintering" from BOOK OF HOURS: POEMS, copyright © 2014 by Kevin Young. Used by permission of Alfred A. Knopf, an imprint of the Knopf Doubleday Publishing Group, a division of Penguin Random House LLC. All rights reserved. Any third party use of this material, outside of this publication, is prohibited. Interested parties must apply directly to Penguin Random House LLC for permission.

Drama

Maurice Bowra: From SOPHOCLEAN TRAGEDY by Maurice Bowra (1945) pp. 65–67. By permission of Oxford University Press.

Wilma Dykeman and James Stokely: From "New Southerner: The Middle-Class Negro" first published in *The New York Times,* magazine, Aug. 9, 1959. Copyright © 2007 by Dykeman C. Stokely and James R. Stokely III. Reprinted by permission of Dykeman C. Stokely and James R. Stokely III.

Phaon Goldman: "The Significance of African Freedom for the Negro Americans" from the *Negro History Bulletin,* Oct. 1960. Property of the Association for the Study of African American Life and History, Inc. Reprinted by permission of the publisher.

Robert Gruenberg: From "Chicago Fiddles While Trumbull Park Burns" from the May 22, 1954 issue of *The Nation,* copyright © 1954 by The Nation Company, LLC. All rights reserved. Used by permission and protected by the Copyright Laws of the United States. The printing, copying, redistribution, or retransmission of this Content without express written permission is prohibited.

Lorraine Hansberry: A RAISIN IN THE SUN [entire play] by Lorraine Hansberry, copyright © 1958 by Robert Nemiroff, as an unpublished work. Copyright © 1959, 1966, 1984 by Robert Nemiroff. Copyright renewed 1986, 1987 by Robert Nemiroff. Used by permission of Random House, Inc. Used by permission of Random House, an imprint and division of Penguin Random House LLC. All rights reserved. Any third party use of this material, outside of this publication, is prohibited. Interested parties must apply directly to Penguin Random House LLC for permission. "Harlem (2)," used as an epigraph, from THE COLLECTED POEMS OF LANGSTON HUGHES, ed. by Arnold Rampersad with David Roessel, Associate Editor, copyright © 1994 by the Estate of Langston Hughes. Used by permission of Alfred A. Knopf, an imprint of the Knopf Doubleday Publishing Group, a division of Penguin Random House LLC. All rights reserved. Any third party use of this material, outside of this publication, is prohibited. Interested parties must apply directly to Penguin Random House LLC for permission. "Willie Loman, Walter Younger, and He Who Must Live" by Lorraine Hansberry, first published in *The Village Voice* (Aug. 12, 1959), copyright © 1959 by Lorraine Hansberry. Reprinted by permission of the Lorraine Hansberry Literary Trust.

Philip Holt: From "Polis and Tragedy in the Antigone." Published in *Mnemosyne*, vol. 52, # 6 (1999), pp. 658–90, is reprinted by permission of Koninklijke Brill NV via the Copyright Clearance Center.

Quiara Alegría Hudes: WATER BY THE SPOONFUL, copyright © 2012 by Quiara Alegría Hudes. Published by Theatre Communications Group. Used by permission of Theatre Communications Group.

Henrik Ibsen: "A Doll House" from THE COMPLETE MAJOR PROSE PLAYS OF HENRIK IBSEN, trans. by Rolf Fjelde, copyright © 1965, 1970, 1978 by Rolf Fjelde. Used by permission of New American Library, an imprint of Penguin Publishing Group, a division of Penguin Random House LLC.

Martin Luther King, Jr.: From "Letter from Birmingham Jail" is reprinted by arrangement with The Heirs to the Estate of Martin Luther King, Jr., c/o Writers House as agent for the proprietor, New York, NY. Copyright © 1963 by Dr. Martin Luther King, Jr; copyright renewed 1991 by Coretta Scott King.

Bernard Knox: From "Introduction" by Bernard Knox, copyright © 1982 by Bernard Knox, from THREE THEBAN PLAYS by Sophocles, trans. by Robert Fagles. Used by permission of Viking Books, an imprint of Penguin Publishing Group, a division of Penguin Random House LLC.

Jane Martin: "Handler" and "French Fries" from TALKING WITH and COLLECTED PLAYS 1980–1995 by Jane Martin are reprinted by permission of Jon Jory.

Arthur Miller: DEATH OF A SALESMAN by Arthur Miller, copyright 1949, renewed © 1977 by Arthur Miller. Used by permission of Penguin Publishing Group, a division of Penguin Random House LLC. Interview with Arthur Miller by William R. Ferris first appeared in the March/April 2001 issue of *Humanities*, the magazine of the National Endowment for the Humanities. Reprinted with the permission of the National Endowment for the Humanities.

Bruce Norris: From CLYBOURNE PARK. Copyright © 2011 by Bruce Norris. Reprinted by permission of Farrar, Straus and Giroux, LLC.

Martha C. Nussbaum: From THE FRAGILITY OF GOODNESS: LUCK AND ETHICS IN GREEK TRAGEDY AND PHILOSOPHY, 2nd ed. Copyright © 1986 by Cambridge University Press. Copyright © 2001 by Martha C. Nussbaum. Reprinted with the permission of Cambridge University Press.

Gertrude Samuels "Even More Crucial Than in the South" from *The New York Times*, June 30, 1963. Copyright © 1963 by The New York Times. All rights reserved. Used by permission and protected by the Copyright Laws of the United States. The printing, copying, redistribution, or retransmission of this Content without express written permission is prohibited.

William Shakespeare: Editor's notes to "A Midsummer Night's Dream" from THE NORTON SHAKESPEARE: BASED ON THE OXFORD EDITION, Third Edition, ed. by Stephen Greenblatt. Copyright © 2015, 2008, 1997 by W.W. Norton & Company, Inc. Used by permission of W.W. Norton & Company, Inc.

Sophocles: OEDIPUS THE KING. and ANTIGONE, trans. by David Grene from COMPLETE GREEK TRAGEDIES, edited by David Grene and Richmond Lattimore. Copyright © 1942 by the University of Chicago. Reprinted by permission of the University of Chicago Press.

Wole Soyinka: DEATH AND THE KING'S HORSEMAN. Copyright ©1975 by Wole Soyinka. Reprinted with permission of W.W. Norton & Company, Inc. Canadian rights administered by Melanie Jackson Agency, LLC. Copyright © 1975, 2003 by Wole Soyinka.

Earl A. Thorpe: "Africa in the Thought of Negro Americans" from *The Negro History Bulletin*, 23.1, Oct. 1959. Property of the Association for the Study of African American Life and History, Inc. Reprinted by permission of the publisher.

Tennessee Williams: A STREETCAR NAMED DESIRE by Tennessee Williams. Copyright © 1947 by Tennessee Williams. CAUTION: Professionals and amateurs are hereby warned that A STREECAR NAMED DESIRE, being fully protected under the copyright laws of the United States of America, the British Empire including the Dominion of Canada, and all other countries of the Copyright Union, is subject to royalty. All rights, including professional, amateur, motion picture, recitation, lecturing, public reading, radio and television broadcasting, and the rights of translation into foreign languages are strictly reserved. Particular emphasis is laid on the question of readings, permission for which must be secured from the author's agent, Luis Sanjurjo, c/o International Creative Management, 40 West 57th Street, New York, NY 10019. Inquiries concerning the amateur acting rights of A STREETCAR NAMED DESIRE should be directed to the Dramatists' Play Service, Inc., 440 Park Avenue South, New York, NY 10016, without whose permission in writing no amateur performance may be given.

August Wilson: FENCES by August Wilson, copyright © 1986 by August Wilson. Used by permission of New American Library, an imprint of Penguin Publishing Group, a division of Penguin Random House LLC.

PHOTO CREDITS

Fiction

Page 2: "Speed Bump," used with the permission of Dave Coverly and the Cartoonist Group. All rights reserved; p. 11: Bettmann/Corbis; p. 20: Sean Gallup/Getty Images; p.32: Sophie Bassouls/Corbis; p. 52, top: Phil Schermeister/Corbis; top center: Gideon Mendel/Corbis; bottom center: Dmitri Baltermants/The Dmitri Baltermants Collection/Corbis; bottom: Corbis Bridge/Alamy; p. 54: Anthony Pidgeon/Redferns/Getty Images; p. 67: Christopher Felver/Corbis; p. 72: Miriam Berkley; p. 87: DOONESBURY ©1985 G. B. Trudeau. Reprinted with permission of UNIVERSAL UCLICK. All rights reserved; p. 93: Sophie Bassouls/Corbis; p. 115: Bettmann/Corbis; p. 125: Christopher Felver/Corbis; p. 144 H. Armstrong Roberts/Corbis; p. 146: Courtesy of Vintage/RandomHouse; p. 152: AP Photo/Paul Hawthorne; p. 163: Francine Fleischer/Corbis; p. 173: Bettmann/Corbis; p. 179: Jeremy Bembaron/Corbis; p. 181: David Shankbone/Wikipedia CC BY-SA 3.0; p. 189: reproduced by courtesy of Charles Dickens Museum, London; p. 196: Everett Collection Inc/Alamy; p. 209: Christopher Felver/Corbis; p. 224: Gary Hannabarger/Corbis; p. 230: © Aaron Mayes/Courtesy of Dzanc Books; p. 238: Bettmann/Corbis; p. 240: Christopher Felver/Corbis; p. 245: Steve Pyke/Contour by Getty Images; p. 257: Charles H. Phillips/The LIFE Picture Collection/Getty Images; p. 266: Bettmann/Corbis; p. 268: The Art Archive at Art Resource, NY; p. 280: Christopher Felver/Corbis; p. 294: © Heinemann (Photo by Melissa Cooperman); p. 302: © J. Paul Getty Trust. Used with permission. Julius Shulman Photography Archive, Research Library at the Getty Research Institute; p. 304: Matthew Mcvay/Corbis; p. 314: Bettmann/Corbis; p. 326: Craig Barritt/Getty Images; p. 335: Cosima Scavolini/Splash News/Corbis; p. 360: Michael Brown/Dreamstime; p. 360 Lftan/Dreamstime; p.360: www.chinesenames.org; p. 360: picerella/iStockphoto; p. 365: Granger Collection; p. 377: Sophie Bassouls/Corbis; p. 392: AP Photo/Gino Domenico; p. 413: Bettmann/Corbis; p. 431 Colita/Corbis; p. 436: Bettmann/Corbis; p. 439: Ulf Andersen/Getty Images; p. 456 top: Hugh Sitton/Corbis; bottom: David Pearson/Alamy; p. 458: Philippe Matsas/Opale/Lebrecht Music & Arts; p. 472: Nancy Kaszerman/Zuma/Corbis; p. 488: Ralph Orlowski/Getty Images; p. 496: Library of Congress; p. 522 Hulton Archive/Getty Images; p. 558: Photograph by Ralph Morrissey. Reprinted by the courtesy of the Morrissey Collection and the Photographic Archives, Vanderbilt University, Nashville, Tennessee; p. 598: Bettmann/Corbis; p. 612: C. P. Curran/Hulton Archive/Getty Images; p. 613: National Library of Ireland; p. 621: Sean Sexton Collection/Corbis; p. 648: Sean Sexton Collection/Corbis; p. 657: Bettmann/Corbis; p. 658: Bettmann/Corbis; p. 668: Berg Collection, New York Public Library; p. 670, top: The Advertising Archives; bottom: Granger Collection; p. 673: Corbis; p. 684: AP Photo; p. 706: History of Medicine, National Institute of Health; p. 746: Christopher

Felver/Corbis; p. 749: Mary Evans Picture Library/Alamy; p. 755: Bettmann/Corbis; p. 762: AP Photo/Eric Miller; p. 784: Rue des Archives/The Granger Collection; p. 795: Hulton Archive/Getty Images; p. 806: Bettmann/Corbis; p. 811: Courtesy of Bobbie Ann Mason/Photo by Pam Spaulding; p. 821: Bettmann/Corbis; p. 827: Christopher Felver/Corbis; p. 833: Marc McAndrews; p. 838: Bettmann/Corbis.

Poetry

Page 849: Time Life Pictures/Pix Inc./The LIFE Picture Collection/Getty Images; p. 878: Tim Hester/Alamy; p. 898: AP Photo: p. 900: Roger Ressmeyer/Corbis; p. 908: Pascal Saez/Sipa/Newscom; p. 921: David Shankbone/Flickr/CC BY 2.0; p. 938: Rosemary Woods/Illustration Works/Corbis; p. 940: Michael Ochs Archives/Getty Images; p. 942: Christopher Felver/Corbis; p. 966, top: Horace Bristol/Corbis; center: H. Armstrong Roberts/Corbis; bottom: Jack Hollingsworth/Getty Images; p. 982: Christopher Felver/Corbis; p. 984: Lisa Larsen/The LIFE Picture Collection/Getty Images; p. 1002, top: Shelly Perry/Vetta/Getty Images; bottom: *St. George and the Dragon*, c. 1470 (oil on canvas), Uccello, Paolo (1397–1475)/National Gallery, London, UK/Bridgeman Images; p. 1031: Alice James Books/MCT/via Getty Images; p. 1053: Instytut Pamieci Narodowej, courtesy of USHMM Photo Archive; p. 1058, top: David Redfern/Getty Images; p. 1058, center: Michael Ochs Archives/Getty Images; p. 1058, bottom: John Cohen/Getty Images; p. 1102: Ink on paper from "Black, Grey and White: A Book of Visual Sonnets" (Veer Books). ©David Miller; p. 1116: Asian Art & Archaeology/Corbis; p. 1120: Judy Ray; p. 1174: Bettmann/Corbis; p.1187: Copyright by Lynda Koolish, PhD; p. 1189: Jason Langer/Glasshouse Images; p. 1192: David Corio/Michael Ochs Archive/Getty Images; p. 1204: Everett Collection Inc/Alamy; p. 1214: E. O. Hoppe/Mansell/Time Life Pictures/Getty Images; p. 1218: Bettmann/Corbis; p. 1226: Corbis; p. 1230: Cheron Banya Ryan; p. 1236: Travel Ink/Getty Images; p. 1248, top: Melanie Dunea/CPi Syndication; bottom: Penguin Random House LLC; p. 1261, top: Underwood & Underwood/Corbis; bottom: Bettmann/Corbis; p. 1264: Bettmann/Corbis; p. 1265, top: Yale Collection of American Literature, Beinecke Rare Book and Manuscript Library; bottom left: Library of Congress; bottom right: National Portrait Gallery, Smithsonian Institution/Art Resource; p. 1266, top: National Portrait Gallery, Smithsonian Institution/Art Resource; bottom: Bettmann/Corbis; p. 1267 top: Library of Congress; bottom: Donna Mussenden VanDerZee; p. 1268: E.O. Hoppe/Corbis; p. 1269: Bettmann/Corbis; p. 1270: Carl Van Vechten/Library of Congress; p. 1272: Moorland-Spingarn Research Center, Howard University; p. 1273: Reproduced by permission of Alfred A. Knopf Publishers, Inc. Yale Collection of American Literature, Beinecke Rare Book and Manuscript Library; p. 1274: The Walter O. Evans Collection: Aaron Douglas, "The Negro Speaks of Rivers (For Langston Hughes)," pen and ink on paper, 5.5"×11", 1941. SCAD Museum of Art Permanent Collection. Gift of Dr. Walter O. Evans and Mrs. Linda J. Evans; p. 1277: Corbis; p. 1288, top: HarperCollins Publishers Inc; bottom: Carl Van Vechten/Library of Congress; p. 1305, left: Courtesy of the Sylvia Plath Collection, Mortimer Rare Book Room, Smith College; right: Courtesy of the Sylvia Plath Collection, Mortimer Rare Book Room, Smith College; p. 1309: The Print Collector/Alamy; p. 1370: (Alexie): Anthony Pidgeon/Redferns/Getty Images; (Auden): Corbis; (Ali): Photo by Michael Paul Thomas; p. 1371: (Bashō): Asian Art & Archaeology/Corbis; (Bishop): Bettmann/Corbis; (Blake): Bettmann/Corbis; (Brooks): AP Photo; (Browning): Bettmann/Corbis; p. 1372: (Coleridge): Bettmann/Corbis; (Billy Collins): AP Photo/Gino Domenico; (Martha Collins): courtesy Martha Collins/photo by Doug Macomber; (Cofer): © Heinemann (Photo by Melissa Cooperman); p. 1373 (Cullen) Bettmann/Corbis; (Dickinson): Everett Collection Inc/Alamy; (Cummings): Bettmann/Corbis; (Donne): Bettmann/Corbis; p. 1374: (Dunbar): Corbis; (Espada) David Shankbone/Flickr/CC BY 2.0; (Frost): E.O. Hoppe/Corbis; (Ginsberg): AP Photo/Susan Ragan; p. 1375 (Grimké): Moorland-Spingarn Research Center, Howard University; (Hardy): GL Archive/Alamy; (Hayden): Pach Brothers/Corbis; p. 1376: (Hayes): AP Photo/Tina Fineberg; (Heaney): Christopher Felver/Corbis; (Hopkins): Granger Collection; (Hughes): National Portrait Gallery, Smithsonian Institution/Art Resource; p. 1377 (Keats): Portrait by Joseph Severn. Reprinted by courtesy of the National Portrait Gallery, London; (Knight): Judy Ray; (Komunyakaa): Chris Felver/Bridgeman Images; (Larkin): TopFoto/The Image Works; p. 1378: (Marvell): Mary Evans Pictures; (McKay): Corbis; (Millay): Underwood & Underwood/Corbis; (Milton): Stefano Bianchetti/Corbis; p. 1379 (Mora): Cheron

Bayna Ryan; (Olds): Christopher Felver/Corbis; (Owen): Hulton-Deutsch Collection/Corbis (Parker): AP Photo; p. 1380: (Pastan): Margaretta K. Mitchell; (Plath): Courtesy of the Sylvia Plath Collection, Mortimer Rare Book Room, Smith College; (Pope): Culture Club/Hulton Archives/Getty Images; (Pound): E.O. Hoppe/Corbis; p. 1381 (Rich): Jason Langer/Glasshouse Images; (Roethke): Bettmann/Corbis; (Rossetti): Popperfoto/Getty Images; p. 1382 (Ryan): Christopher Felver/Corbis; (Shakespeare): Chris Hellier/Corbis; (Shelley): Georgios Kollidas/Alamy; p. 1383: (Stevens): Bettmann/Corbis; (Su): Courtesy Adrienne Su/Photo by Guy Freeman; (Tennyson): Bettmann/Corbis; (Trethewey): AP Photo/Rogelio V. Solis; p. 1384: (Whitman): Library of Congress; (Wilbur): Oscar White/Corbis (Williams): Lisa Larsen/The LIFE Picture Collection/Getty Images; (Wordsworth): Hulton-Deutsch Collection/Corbis; p. 1385: (Yeats): Bettmann/Corbis; (Young): Melanie Dunea/CPi Syndication.

Drama

Page 1387: Sam Falk/The New York Times/Redux; p. 1391: AP Photo; p. 1423: AP Photo/Ted S. Warren; p. 1475: Photo by Joseph Moran; p. 1477: Richard Termine; p. 1526: Greek Art Images/Getty Images; p. 1566: Bettmann/Corbis; p. 1612: Chris Hellier/Corbis; p. 1613: Michael Maslan Historic Photographs/Corbis; p. 1614: Adam Woolfitt/Corbis; p. 1616: Robbie Jack/Corbis; p. 1617: John Springer Collection/Corbis; p. 1772: Bettmann/Corbis; p. 1773: Bettmann/Corbis; p. 1774: Bettmann/Corbis; p. 1776: Library of Congress; p. 1777: Bettmann/Corbis; p. 1778: AP Photo; p. 1781: Bettmann/Corbis; p. 1868: Photo by Craig Schwartz; p. 1874: Bettmann/Corbis; p. 1875: Johan Persson/ArenaPAL; p. 1940: The Art Archive at Art Resource, NY; p. 1978: Bettmann/Corbis; p. 2032: Theatre TCU Laura Saladino (pictured) Directed by Blake Robertson Photo by Amy Peterson; p. 2033: Interfoto/Alamy; p. 2101: Micheline Pelletier/Corbis; p. 2102: Washington Post/Getty Images; p. 2151: Bettmann/Corbis; p. 2152: The Advertising Archives.

Index of Authors

Index of Titles and First Lines

Index of Literary Terms